Webster's New French Dictionary

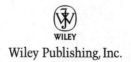

WILEY

Wiley Publishing, Inc.

Trademarks

Words considered to be trademarks have been designated in this diction
by the symbol ®. However, no judgment is implied concerning the legal
tus of any trademark by virtue of the presence of absence of such a symbo

Marques déposées

Les termes considérés comme des marques déposées sont signalés d
ce dictionnaire par le symbole ®. Cependant, la présence ou l'absence de
symbole ne constitue nullement une indication quant à la valeur juridique
ces termes.

This new pocket-sized dictionary is aimed at students at begin and intermediate level. It covers all the essential words and phra needed and packs a wealth of vocabulary into its pages. This completely new edition of the text, which has been reread and c rected. The clear, systematic layout of information makes the d tionary a reliable and user-friendly tool for both finding translati of French items and translating from English into French.

Colloquial and idiomatic language is well represented in this d tionary, as are words from a wide range of technical areas (comp ing, medicine, finance etc). The most up-to-date words from this of the Internet will be found in this book: from **information sup highway** to **cybercafé** and **home page** (**inforoute, cybercafé** an **page d'accueil** in French), as well as the newest terms found in press, such as **BSE, GMOs** and **car-pooling** (**EBS, OGM** and **co oiturage** in French).

In order to be able to include as much information as possible, o the base forms are entered as headwords; derivatives (eg **common** from **common**) are given at the end of the entry in alphabetical ord

The editors would like to acknowledge the contribution made to t dictionary by the editor of the previous edition, Michael Janes.

> **baccalauréat** [bakalɔrea] *nm* = secondary school examination qualifying for entry to university, *Br* ≃ A-levels, *Am* ≃ high school diploma

- The equals sign = introduces an explanation when there is n translation possible.

- The sign ≃ introduces a word that has a roughly equivalent stat but is not identical.

> **forcer** [fɔrse] **1** *vt (obliger)* to force; *(porte)* to force open; *(voix)* to strain; **f. qn à faire qch** to force sb to do sth; **f. la main à qn** to force sb's hand; *Fam* **f. la dose** to overdo it
> **2** *vi (appuyer, tirer)* to force it; *(se surmener)* to overdo it
> **3 se forcer** *vpr* to force oneself (**à faire** to do)

- The different grammatical categories are cleary indicated, in duced by a bold Arabic numeral.

- Usage labels are clearly shown.

> **échoir*** [eʃwar] *vi* **é. à qn** to fall to sb

- The asterisk indicates that the verb is irregular. See the verb tab in the middle of the book for information on how to conjugate it

> **agenda** [ə'dʒendə] *n* ordre *m* du jour
>
> Note that the French noun **agenda** is a false friend and is never a translation for the English noun **agenda**. It means **diary**.

- Usage notes warn users when a word is a false friend.

grand, -e [grã, grãd] **1** *adj* big, large; *(en hauteur)* tall; *(chaleur, découverte, âge, mérite, ami)* great; *(bruit)* loud; *(différence)* big, great; *(adulte, mûr, plus âgé)* grown-up, big; *(âme)* noble; *(illustre)* great; **g. frère** *(plus âgé)* big brother; **le g. air** the open air; **il est g. temps que je parte** it's high time that I left; **il n'y avait pas g. monde** there were not many people

2 *adv* **g. ouvert** *(yeux, fenêtre)* wide open; **ouvrir g.** to open wide; **en g.** on a grand *or* large scale

3 *nmf (à l'école)* senior; *(adulte)* grown-up ●**grandement** *adv (beaucoup)* greatly; *(généreusement)* grandly; **avoir g. de quoi vivre** to have plenty to live on ●**grand-mère** *(pl* **grands-mères)** *nf* grandmother ●**grand-père** *(pl* **grands-pères)** *nm* grandfather ●**grand-route** *(pl* **grand-routes)** *nf* main road ●**grands-parents** *nmpl* grandparents

● Derivatives are placed at the end of each entry in alphabeti order, introduced by ●

différence [diferãs] *nf* difference (**de** in); **à la d. de qn/qch** unlike sb/sth; **faire la d. entre** to make a distinction between

● The most common prepositions used are given after the tra lation.

Ce dictionnaire de poche s'adresse à l'utilisateur débutant ou de veau intermédiaire et au voyageur qui souhaite avoir à portée d main un ouvrage lui permettant de traduire les termes les plus quents de la langue. Reprenant les éditions précédentes, le tex été entièrement revu et corrigé. Ouvrage fiable et de consultat aisée, il permet sans difficulté de sélectionner la traduction cherchée grâce à une présentation claire et systématique.

La langue familière y est bien représentée ainsi que les termes base de divers domaines techniques (informatique, médecine nance etc) et le vocabulaire apparu le plus récemment y fait son trée. A l'heure des internautes, on parle aujourd hui de **l'inforou** des **cybercafés** et des **pages d'accueil** (**information superhighw cybercafé** et **home page** en anglais) tandis que l'**EBS**, les **OGM** le **covoiturage** (**BSE, GMO** et **car-pooling** en anglais) sont termes récurrents dans la presse et les conversations du moment

Par souci de concision, seuls les termes de base apparaissent entrées : leurs dérivés (par exemple **communément** formé à pa de **commun**) sont donnés en fin d'article et présentés par ordre phabétique. La prononciation et l'accent tonique du vocabulaire glais ne sont repris pour les dérivés que s'ils diffèrent de la forme base.

Nous souhaitons remercier le rédacteur de l'édition précéden Michael Janes, pour sa contribution.

> **baccalauréat** [bakalɔrea] *nm* = secondary school examination qualifying for entry to university, *Br* ≃ A-levels, *Am* ≃ high school diploma

● Le signe = introduit une explication quand il n'y a pas de traducti possible.

● Le signe ≃ introduit les équivalents culturels.

> **forcer** [fɔrse] **1** *vt (obliger)* to force; *(porte)* to force open; *(voix)* to strain; **f. qn à faire qch** to force sb to do sth; **f. la main à qn** to force sb's hand; *Fam* **f. la dose** to overdo it
> **2** *vi (appuyer, tirer)* to force it; *(se surmener)* to overdo it
> **3 se forcer** *vpr* to force oneself (**à faire** to do)

● Les différentes catégories grammaticales ressortent clairement elles sont introduites par un chiffre arabe et sont toujours présen tées dans le même ordre.

● Des indicateurs d'usage sont donnés.

> **échoir*** [eʃwar] *vi* **é. à qn** to fall to sb

● * indique que le verbe est irrégulier. Se reporter aux pages c trales.

> **agenda** [aʒɛ̃da] *nm Br* diary, *Am* datebook
> ♪ Il faut noter que le nom anglais **agenda** est un faux ami. Il signifie **ordre du jour**.

● La différence entre les termes anglais et américains est clairem indiquée.

● Une note d'usage avertit le lecteur qu'il a affaire à un faux ami.

grand, -e [grã, grãd] **1** *adj* big, large; *(en hauteur)* tall; *(chaleur, découverte, âge, mérite, ami)* great; *(bruit)* loud; *(différence)* big, great; *(adulte, mûr, plus âgé)* grown-up, big; *(âme)* noble; *(illustre)* great; **g. frère** *(plus âgé)* big brother; **le g. air** the open air; **il est g. temps que je parte** it's high time that I left; **il n'y avait pas g. monde** there were not many people
2 *adv* **g. ouvert** *(yeux, fenêtre)* wide open; **ouvrir g.** to open wide; **en g.** on a grand *or* large scale
3 *nmf (à l'école)* senior; *(adulte)* grown-up
• **grandement** *adv (beaucoup)* greatly; *(généreusement)* grandly; **avoir g. de quoi vivre** to have plenty to live on •**grand-mère** (*pl* **grands-mères**) *nf* grandmother •**grand-père** (*pl* **grands-pères**) *nm* grandfather •**grand-route** (*pl* **grand-routes**) *nf* main road •**grands-parents** *nmpl* grandparents

● Les dérivés sont clairement placés en fin d'article et rangés p ordre alphabétique.

athlète [atlɛt] *nmf* athlete •**athlétique** *adj* athletic •**athlétisme** *nm* athletics *(sing)*

● Indique le nombre lorsqu'une traduction est ambiguë.

différence [diferãs] *nf* difference (**de** in); **à la d. de qn/qch** unlike sb/sth; **faire la d. entre** to make a distinction between

● Les prépositions les plus courantes apparaissent à la suite de l traduction.

[introduces an explanation]		[introduit une explication]
cultural equivalent	≃	équivalent culturel
[introduces a translation		[introduit une traduction
which has a roughly		dont les connotations dan
equivalent status		la langue cible sont
in the target language]		comparables]
abbreviation	*abbr, abrév*	abréviation
adjective	*adj*	adjectif
adverb	*adv*	adverbe
agriculture	*Agr*	agriculture
American English	*Am*	anglais américain
anatomy	*Anat*	anatomie
architecture	*Archit*	architecture
slang	*Arg*	argot
article	*art*	article
astrology	*Astrol*	astrologie
cars	*Aut*	automobile
auxiliary	*aux*	auxiliaire
aviation	*Av*	aviation
Belgian French	*Belg*	belgicisme
biology	*Biol*	biologie
botany	*Bot*	botanique
British English	*Br*	anglais britannique
Canadian French	*Can*	canadianisme
chemistry	*Chem, Chim*	chimie
cinema	*Cin*	cinéma
commerce	*Com*	commerce
computing	*Comput*	informatique
conjunction	*conj*	conjonction
cooking	*Culin*	cuisine
economics	*Econ, Écon*	économie
electricity, electronics	*El, Él*	électricité, électronique
exclamation	*exclam*	exclamation
feminine	*f*	féminin
familiar	*Fam*	familier
figurative	*Fig*	figuré
finance	*Fin*	finance
geography	*Geog, Géog*	géographie
geology	*Geol, Géol*	géologie
history	*Hist*	histoire
humorous	*Hum*	humoristique
industry	*Ind*	industrie
invariable	*inv*	invariable
journalism	*Journ*	journalisme
law	*Jur*	droit
linguistics	*Ling*	linguistique
masculine	*m*	masculin
mathematics	*Math*	mathématique
medicine	*Med, Méd*	médecine
meteorology	*Met, Météo*	météorologie
military	*Mil*	militaire
music	*Mus*	musique
noun	*n*	nom
shipping	*Naut*	nautisme
feminine noun	*nf*	nom féminin
feminine plural noun	*nfpl*	nom féminin pluriel

plural noun	*npl*	nom pluriel
computing	*Ordinat*	ordinateurs, informatique
pejorative	*Pej, Péj*	péjoratif
philosophy	*Phil*	philosophie
photography	*Phot*	photographie
physics	*Phys*	physique
plural	*pl*	pluriel
politics	*Pol*	politique
past participle	*pp*	participe passé
prefix	*pref, préf*	préfixe
preposition	*prep, prép*	préposition
pronoun	*pron*	pronom
past tense	*pt*	prétérit
something	*qch*	quelque chose
registered trademark	®	marque déposée
rail	*Rail*	chemin de fer
religion	*Rel*	religion
somebody	*sb*	quelqu'un
school	*Sch, Scol*	domaine scolaire
Scottish English	*Scot*	anglais d'Écosse
singular	*sing*	singulier
slang	*Sl*	argot
something	*sth*	quelque chose
suffix	*suff*	suffixe
technology	*Tech*	technologie
telecommunications	*Tel, Tél*	télécommunications
textiles	*Tex*	textile
television	*TV*	télévision
typography, printing	*Typ*	typographie, imprimerie
university	*Univ*	domaine universitaire
verb	*v*	verbe
intransitive verb	*vi*	verbe intransitif
reflexive verb	*vpr*	verbe pronominal
transitive verb	*vt*	verbe transitif
inseparable transitive verb	*vt insep*	verbe transitif à particule inséparable [par ex.: **he looks after the children** il s'occupe des enfants]
separable transitive verb	*vt sep*	verbe transitif à particule séparable [par ex.: **she sent the present back** *or* **she se back the present** elle a rendu le cadeau]

Pour indiquer la prononciation anglaise, nous avons utilisé dans
dictionnaire les symboles de l'API (Alphabet phonétique inter
tional). Pour chaque son anglais, vous trouverez dans le tableau
dessous des exemples de mots anglais, suivis de mots français p
sentant un son similaire. Une explication est donnée lorsqu'il n
pas d'équivalent en français.

Caractère API	Exemple en anglais	Exemple en français
Consonnes		
[b]	babble	bébé
[d]	dig	dent
[dʒ]	giant, jig	jean
[f]	fit, physics	face
[g]	grey, big	gag
[h]	happy	h aspiré : à quelques rares exceptions près, il est toujours prononcé en anglais
[j]	yellow	yaourt
[k]	clay, kick	car
[l]	lip, pill	lilas
[m]	mummy	maman
[n]	nip, pin	né
[ŋ]	sing	parking
[p]	pip	papa
[r]	rig, write	Pas d'équivalent français : se prononce en plaçant le bout de la langue au milie du palais
[(r)]		Seulement prononcé en ca de liaison avec la voyelle qu suit comme dans : far away the car is blue
[s]	sick, science	silence
[ʃ]	ship, nation	chèvre
[t]	tip, butt	tartine
[tʃ]	chip, batch	atchoum
[θ]	thick	Son proche du /s/ français, se prononce en plaçant le bout de la langue entre les dents du haut et celles du ba
[ð]	this, with	Son proche du /z/ français, se prononce en plaçant le bout de la langue entre les dents du haut et celles du ba
[v]	vague, give	vie
[w]	wit, why	whisky

[z]	zip, physics	rose
[ʒ]	pleasure	je
[χ]	lo**ch**	Existe seulement dans certains mots écossais. Pa d'équivalent français : se prononce du fond de la gorge, comme Ba**ch** en allemand ou la '**j**ota' espagnole.

Voyelles

[æ]	rag	natte
[ɑː]	**lar**ge, h**al**f	pâte
[e]	set	/e/ moins ouvert que le [ɛ] français
[ɜː]	c**ur**tain, w**ere**	h**eu**re
[ə]	**u**tter	ch**e**val
[ɪ]	b**i**g, w**o**men	/i/ bref, à mi-chemin entre les sons [ɛ] et [i] français (plus proche de 'net' que de 'vite')
[iː]	l**ea**k, w**ee**	/i/ plus long que le [i] français
[ɒ]	l**o**ck	bonne – mais plus ouvert prononcé au fond du pala
[ɔː]	w**a**ll, c**o**rk	baume – mais plus ouvert et prononcé au fond du palais
[ʊ]	p**u**t, l**oo**k	Son à mi-chemin entre un /ou/ bref et un /o/ ouvert
[uː]	m**oo**n	Son /ou/ prolongé
[ʌ]	c**u**p	A mi-chemin entre un /a/ un /e/ ouverts

Diphtongues : Elles sont rares en français et sont la combinaison d deux sons.

[aɪ]	wh**y**, h**igh**, l**ie**	a**ï**e
[aʊ]	h**ow**	mi**a**ou, a**oû**tat – mais se prononce comme un seul son
[eə]	b**ear**, sh**are**, wh**ere**	flair
[eɪ]	d**ay**, m**a**ke, m**ai**n	merv**ei**lle
[əʊ]	sh**ow**, g**o**	Combinaison d'un /o/ fermé et d'un /ou/
[ɪə]	h**ere**, g**ear**	Combinaison d'un /i/ long suivi d'un /e/ ouvert bref
[ɔɪ]	b**oy**, s**oi**l	langue d'**oï**l
[ʊə]	s**ure**	Combinaison d'un son /ou suivi d'un /e/ ouvert bref

French pronunciation is shown in this dictionary using the symb
of the IPA (International Phonetic Alphabet). In the table below,
amples of French words using these sounds are given, followed
English words which have a similar sound. Where there is no equi
lent in English, an explanation is given.

IPA symbol	French example	English example
Consonants		
[b]	bébé	but
[d]	donner	door
[f]	forêt	fire
[g]	gare	get
[ʒ]	jour	pleasure
[k]	carte	kitten
[l]	lire	lonely
[m]	maman	mat
[n]	ni	now
[ŋ]	parking	singing
[ɲ]	campagne	canyon
[p]	patte	pat
[r]	rare	Like an English /r/ but pronounced at the back o the throat
[s]	soir	sit
[ʃ]	chose	sham
[t]	table	tap
[v]	valeur	value
[z]	zéro	zero
Vowels		
[a]	chat	cat
[ɑ]	âge	gasp
[e]	été	bay
[ɛ]	père	bed
[ə]	le	amend
[ø]	deux	Does not exist in English: [e] pronounced with the lips rounded
[œ]	seul	curtain
[i]	vite	bee – not quite as long as the English [i:]
[ɔ]	donner	cot – slightly more open than the English /o/
[o]	chaud	daughter – but higher tha its English equivalent

		English equivalent
[y]	voiture	Does not exist in English: [i] with lips rounded
[ã]	**en**fant	Nasal sound pronounced lower and further back in the mouth than [ɔ̃]
Vowels		
[ɛ̃]	vin	Nasal sound: /a/ sound pronounced letting air pa through the nose
[ɔ̃]	b**on**jour	Nasal sound: closed /o/ sound pronounced letting air pass through the nose
[œ̃]	**un**	Nasal sound: like [ɛ̃] but with lips more rounded
Semi-vowels		
[w]	v**oi**r	week
[j]	**y**o**y**o, pai**ll**e	yard
[ɥ]	n**ui**t	Does not exist in English: the vowel [y] elided with the following vowel

English – French
Anglais – Français

A, a¹ [eɪ] *n* (**a**) A, a *m inv*; **5A** *(in address, street number)* 5 bis; **to go from A to B** aller du point A au point B (**b**) *Mus* A la *m* (**c**) *Sch (grade)* **to get an A in French** = obtenir une très bonne note en français (**d**) *(street atlas)* **an A to Z of London** un plan de Londres

a² [ə, *stressed* eɪ]

> **a** devient **an** [ən, *stressed* æn] devant voyelle ou h muet.

indefinite article (**a**) *(in general)* un, une; **a man** un homme; **an apple** une pomme; **an hour** une heure

(**b**) *(definite article in French)* **60 pence a kilo** 60 pence le kilo; **50 km an hour** 50 km à l'heure; **I have a broken arm** j'ai le bras cassé

(**c**) *(article omitted in French)* **he's a doctor/a father** il est médecin/père; **Caen, a town in Normandy** Caen, ville de Normandie; **what a man!** quel homme!; **a hundred** cent; **a thousand** mille

(**d**) *(a certain)* **a Mr Smith** un certain M. Smith

(**e**) *(time)* **twice a month** deux fois par mois

(**f**) *(some)* **to make a noise/a fuss** faire du bruit/des histoires

aback [əˈbæk] *adv* **taken a. (by)** déconcerté (par)

abandon [əˈbændən] **1** *n (freedom of manner)* abandon *m*

2 *vt* abandonner; **to a. ship** abandonner le navire • **abandonment** *n* abandon *m*

abashed [əˈbæʃt] *adj* honteux, -euse (**at** de)

abate [əˈbeɪt] *vi (of storm, pain)* se calmer; *(of noise)* diminuer; *(of flood)* baisser

abbess [ˈæbes] *n* abbesse *f*

abbey [ˈæbɪ] (*pl* **-eys**) *n* abbaye *f*

abbot [ˈæbət] *n* abbé *m*

abbreviate [əˈbriːvɪeɪt] *vt* abréger • **abbrevi**'**ation** *n* abréviation *f*

abdi'**cate** [ˈæbdɪkeɪt] *vti* abdiquer • **abdi**'**cation** *n* abdication *f*

abdomen [ˈæbdəmən] *n* abdomen *m* • **abdominal** [əbˈdɒmɪnəl] *adj* abdominal

abduct [æbˈdʌkt] *vt (kidnap)* enlever • **abduction** *n* enlèvement *m*, rapt *m*

aberration [æbəˈreɪʃən] *n (folly, lapse)* aberration *f*

abet [əˈbet] (*pt & pp* **-tt-**) *vt Law* **to aid and a. sb** être le complice de qn

abeyance [əˈbeɪəns] *n* **in a.** *(matter)* en suspens; *(law)* en désuétude

abhor [əbˈhɔː(r)] (*pt & pp* **-rr-**) *vt* avoir horreur de, exécrer • **abhorrence** [-ˈhɒrəns] *n* horreur *f* • **abhorrent** [-ˈhɒrənt] *adj* exécrable

abide [əˈbaɪd] **1** *vi* **to a. by** *(promise)* tenir; *(decision)* se plier à

2 *vt* supporter; **I can't a. him** je ne peux pas le supporter

ability [əˈbɪlɪtɪ] (*pl* **-ies**) *n* capacité *f* (**to do** de faire); **a man of great a.** c'est quelqu'un de très compétent; **to the best of my a.** de mon mieux

abject [ˈæbdʒekt] *adj (contemptible)* abject; *(poverty-stricken)* misérable; **a. poverty** la misère noire

ablaze [əˈbleɪz] *adj* en feu; **to set sth a.** *(person)* mettre le feu à qch; *(candle, spark)* embraser qch; **a. with** *(light)* resplendissant de; **his eyes were a. with anger** il avait les yeux brillants de colère

able [ˈeɪbəl] *adj* capable; **to be a. to do sth** être capable de faire qch, pouvoir faire qch; **to be a. to swim/drive** savoir nager/conduire • **able-**'**bodied** *adj* robuste • **ably** *adv* habilement

abnormal [æbˈnɔːməl] *adj* anormal • **abnormality** [-ˈmælɪtɪ] (*pl* **-ies**) *n* anomalie *f*; *(physical)* difformité *f* • **abnormally** *adv (more than usually)* exceptionnellement

aboard [əˈbɔːd] **1** *adv (on ship, plane)* à bord; **all a.** *(on train)* en voiture; **to go a.** monter à bord

2 *prep* **a. the ship/plane** à bord du navire/de l'avion; **a. the train** dans le train

abode [əˈbəʊd] *n Literary* demeure *f*; *Law* domicile *m*; **of no fixed a.** sans domicile fixe

abolish [əˈbɒlɪʃ] *vt* abolir • **abolition** [æbəˈlɪʃən] *n* abolition *f*

abominable [əˈbɒmɪnəbəl] *adj* abominable • **abomination** [-ˈneɪʃən] *n* abomination *f*

Aborigine [æbə'rɪdʒɪnɪ] *n* Aborigène *mf* (d'Australie)

abort [ə'bɔːt] **1** *vt (space flight, computer program)* abandonner; *Med* **the foetus was aborted** la grossesse a été interrompue **2** *vi Med* faire une fausse couche • **abortion** *n* avortement *m*; **to have an a.** se faire avorter • **abortive** *adj (plan, attempt)* manqué, avorté

abound [ə'baʊnd] *vi* abonder (**in** *or* **with** en)

about [ə'baʊt] **1** *adv* (**a**) *(approximately)* à peu près, environ; **at a. two o'clock** vers deux heures; **a. time!** ce n'est pas trop tôt! (**b**) *(here and there)* çà et là, ici et là; *Fig* **there's a lot of flu a. at the moment** il y a beaucoup de cas de grippe en ce moment; **there's a rumour a. (that...)** il y a une rumeur qui circule (selon laquelle...); **to look a.** regarder autour de soi; **to follow someone a.** suivre quelqu'un partout; **there are lots a.** il y en a beaucoup; **(out and) a.** *(after illness)* sur pied; **(up and) a.** *(out of bed)* levé, debout **2** *prep* (**a**) *(around)* **a. the garden** autour du jardin; **a. the streets** par *or* dans les rues (**b**) *(near to)* **a. here** par ici (**c**) *(concerning)* au sujet de; **to talk a. sth** parler de qch; **a book a. sth** un livre sur qch; **what's it (all) a.?** de quoi s'agit-il?; **while you're a. it** pendant que vous y êtes (**d**) *(+ infinitive)* **a. to do** sur le point de faire; **I was a. to say...** j'étais sur le point de dire... • **about-'face, about-'turn** *n Mil* demi-tour *m*; *Fig* volte-face *f inv*

above [ə'bʌv] **1** *adv* au-dessus; *(in book)* ci-dessus; **from a.** d'en haut; **the floor a.** l'étage *m* du dessus **2** *prep* (**a**) au-dessus de; **a. the bridge** *(on river)* en amont du pont; **he's a. me** *(in rank)* c'est mon supérieur; **she's not a. lying** elle n'est pas incapable de mentir; **he's not a. asking** il n'est pas trop fier pour demander; **a. all** surtout (**b**) *(with numbers)* plus de; **the temperature didn't rise above 2°C** la température n'a pas dépassé 2°C • **above-'board 1** *adj* honnête **2** *adv* sans tricherie • **above-mentioned** *adj* susmentionné

abrasion [ə'breɪʒən] **1** *n* frottement *m*; *(wound)* écorchure *f* • **abrasive** [-sɪv] **1** *adj (substance)* abrasif, -ive; *Fig (person, manner)* caustique **2** *n* abrasif *m*

abreast [ə'brest] *adv* côte à côte, de front; **four a.** par rangs de quatre; **to keep a. of** *or* **with** *(events)* se tenir au courant de

abridge [ə'brɪdʒ] *vt (book)* abréger

abroad [ə'brɔːd] *adv* (**a**) *(in or to a foreign country)* à l'étranger; **from a.** de l'étranger (**b**) *(over a wide area)* de tous côtés; **there's a rumour a. that...** il y a un bruit qui court comme quoi...

abrogate ['æbrəgeɪt] *vt* abroger

abrupt [ə'brʌpt] *adj (sudden)* brusque, soudain; *(rude)* brusque, abrupt; *(slope, style)* abrupt • **abruptly** *adv (suddenly)* brusquement; *(rudely)* avec brusquerie

abscess ['æbses] *n* abcès *m*

abscond [əb'skɒnd] *vi Formal* s'enfuir

absence ['æbsəns] *n* absence *f*; **in the a. of** *(person)* en l'absence de; *(thing)* faute de

absent 1 ['æbsənt] *adj* absent (**from** de) **2** [æb'sent] *vt* **to a. oneself (from)** s'absenter (de) • **absent-'minded** *adj* distrait • **absent-'mindedness** *n* distraction *f*

absentee [æbsən'tiː] *n* absent, -ente *mf* • **absenteeism** *n* absentéisme *m*

absolute ['æbsəluːt] *adj* absolu; *(proof)* indiscutable; **he's an a. coward** c'est un vrai lâche; **he's an a. fool!** il est complètement idiot!; **it's an a. disgrace!** c'est une honte! • **absolutely** *adv* absolument; **a. forbidden** formellement interdit; **you're a. right** tu as tout à fait raison

absolve [əb'zɒlv] *vt (sinner, accused)* absoudre; **to a. from** *(vow)* libérer de • **absolution** [æbsə'luːʃən] *n* absolution *f*

absorb [əb'zɔːb] *vt (liquid)* absorber; *(shock)* amortir; **to be absorbed in sth** être plongé dans qch • **absorbing** *adj (work)* absorbant; *(book, film)* passionnant • **absorption** *n* absorption *f*

absorbent [əb'zɔːbənt] *adj* absorbant

abstain [əb'steɪn] *vi Pol* s'abstenir; **to a. from sth/from doing** s'abstenir de qch/ de faire • **abstention** *n Pol* abstention *f*

abstemious [əb'stiːmɪəs] *adj* sobre, frugal

abstinence ['æbstɪnəns] *n* abstinence *f*

abstract ['æbstrækt] **1** *adj* abstrait **2** *n* (**a**) *(notion)* **the a.** l'abstrait *m* (**b**) *(summary)* résumé *m* **3** [əb'strækt] *vt Formal* extraire (**de** from) • **abstraction** *n (idea)* abstraction *f*; *(absent-mindedness)* distraction *f*

abstruse [əb'struːs] *adj* obscur

absurd [əb'sɜːd] *adj* absurde, ridicule • **absurdity** *(pl* **-ies)** *n* absurdité *f* • **absurdly** *adv* absurdement

abundant [ə'bʌndənt] *adj* abondant • **abundance** *n* abondance *f* • **abundantly** *adv* **a. clear** parfaitement clair

abuse 1 [ə'bjuːs] *n (of power)* abus *m* (**of** de); *(of child)* mauvais traitements *mpl*; *(insults)* injures *fpl*

2 [ə'bjuːz] *vt (misuse)* abuser de; *(ill-treat)* maltraiter; *(insult)* injurier • **abusive** [ə'bjuːsɪv] *adj (person, language)* grossier, -ière

abysmal [ə'bɪzməl] *adj Fam (bad)* exécrable

abyss [ə'bɪs] *n* abîme *m*

acacia [ə'keɪʃə] *n (tree)* acacia *m*

academic [ækə'demɪk] **1** *adj* (**a**) *(year, diploma) (of school)* scolaire; *(of university)* universitaire (**b**) *(scholarly)* intellectuel, -uelle (**c**) *(theoretical)* **the issue is of purely a. interest** cette question n'a d'intérêt que d'un point de vue théorique; **this is a. now** cela n'a plus d'importance (**d**) *(style)* académique

2 *n (teacher)* universitaire *mf*

academy [ə'kædəmɪ] *(pl* **-ies**) *n (society)* académie *f*; *(military)* école *f*; **a. of music** conservatoire *m* • **academician** [-'mɪʃən] *n* académicien, -ienne *mf*

accede [ak'siːd] *vi Formal* **to a. to** *(request, throne, position)* accéder à

accelerate [ak'seləreɪt] **1** *vt* accélérer

2 *vi (of pace)* s'accélérer; *(of vehicle, driver)* accélérer • **accele'ration** *f* • **accelerator** *n* accélérateur *m*

accent ['æksənt] *n* accent *m* • **accentuate** [-'sentʃʊeɪt] *vt* accentuer

accept [ak'sept] *vt* accepter • **acceptable** *adj (worth accepting, tolerable)* acceptable; **to be a. to sb** convenir à qn • **acceptance** *n* acceptation *f*; *(approval, favour)* accueil *m* favorable • **accepted** *adj (opinion)* reçu; *(fact)* reconnu

access ['ækses] **1** *n* accès *m* (**to sth** à qch; **to sb** auprès de qn); **a. road** route *f* d'accès; *Comptr* **a. code** code *m* d'accès; *Comptr* **a. provider** fournisseur *m* d'accès

2 *vt Comptr* accéder à • **ac'cessible** *adj* accessible

accessories [ak'sesərɪz] *npl (objects)* accessoires *mpl*

accessory [ak'sesərɪ] *(pl* **-ies**) *n Law (accomplice)* complice *mf* (**to** de)

accident ['æksɪdənt] *n* accident *m*; **by a.** accidentellement; *(by chance)* par hasard • **accident-prone** *adj* prédisposé aux accidents • **accidental** [-'dentəl] *adj* accidentel, -elle • **accidentally** [-'dentəlɪ] *adv* accidentellement; *(by chance)* par hasard

acclaim [ə'kleɪm] **1** *n* **(critical)** **a.** éloges *mpl* **the film enjoys critical a.** ce film est salué par la critique

2 *vt (cheer)* acclamer; *(praise)* faire l'éloge de

acclimatize [ə'klaɪmətaɪz] *(Am* **acclimate** ['ækləmeɪt]) **1** *vt* acclimater

2 *vi* s'acclimater • **acclimatization** *(Am* **acclimation**) acclimatisation *f*

accolade ['ækəleɪd] *n Fig (praise)* louange *f*

accommodate [ə'kɒmədeɪt] *vt* (**a**) *(of house)* loger (**b**) *(reconcile)* concilier (**c**) *(supply)* fournir (**sb with sth** qch à qn) (**d**) *(oblige)* rendre service à • **accommodating** *adj* accommodant, obligeant

> 𝒾 Note that the French verb **accommoder** is a false friend and is rarely a translation for the English verb **to accommodate**. Its most common translations are **to adapt** and **to prepare**.

accommodation [əkɒmə'deɪʃən] *n* (**a**) *(Am* **accommodations**) *(lodging)* logement *m*; *(rented room(s))* chambre(s) *f(pl)* (**b**) *Formal (compromise)* compromis *m*

accompany [ə'kʌmpənɪ] *(pt & pp* **-ied**) *vt* accompagner • **accompaniment** *n* accompagnement *m* • **accompanist** *n (musician)* accompagnateur, -trice *mf*

accomplice [ə'kʌmplɪs] *n* complice *mf*

accomplish [ə'kʌmplɪʃ] *vt (task, duty)* accomplir; *(aim)* atteindre • **accomplished** *adj* accompli • **accomplishment** *n (of task, duty)* accomplissement *m*; *(thing achieved)* réalisation *f*; **writing a novel is a great a.** écrire un roman, c'est vraiment quelque chose; **accomplishments** *(skills)* talents *mpl*

accord [ə'kɔːd] **1** *n* accord *m*; **of my own a.** de mon plein gré

2 *vt (grant)* accorder • **accordance** *n* **in a. with** conformément à

according [ə'kɔːdɪŋ] **according to** *prep* selon, d'après • **accordingly** *adv* en conséquence

accordion [ə'kɔːdɪən] *n* accordéon *m*

accost [ə'kɒst] *vt* accoster, aborder

account [ə'kaʊnt] **1** *n* (**a**) *(with bank or firm)* compte *m*; **accounts department** comptabilité *f* (**b**) *(report)* compte rendu *m*; *(explanation)* explication *f*; **to give a good a. of oneself** s'en tirer à son avantage (**c**) *(expressions)* **by all accounts** au dire de tous; **on a. of** à cause de; **on no a.** en aucun cas; **to take sth into a.** tenir compte de qch

2 *vi* **to a. for** *(explain)* expliquer; *(give reckoning of)* rendre compte de; *(represent)* représenter • **accountable** *adj* responsable (**for** de; **to** devant)

accountant [ə'kaʊntənt] *n* comptable *mf*
• **accountancy** *n* comptabilité *f*
accrue [ə'kru:] *vi Fin (of interest)* s'accumuler; **to a. to sb** *(of advantage)* revenir à qn
accumulate [ə'kju:mjʊleɪt] **1** *vt* accumuler
2 *vi* s'accumuler • **accumulation** [-'leɪʃən] *n* accumulation *f*
accurate ['ækjʊrət] *adj* exact, précis
• **accuracy** *n* exactitude *f*, précision *f*
• **accurately** *adv* avec précision
accuse [ə'kju:z] *vt* **to a. sb (of sth/doing sth)** accuser qn (de qch/faire qch) • **accusation** [ækjʊ'zeɪʃən] *n* accusation *f*; **to make an a. against sb** lancer une accusation contre qn • **accused** *n Law* **the a.** l'accusé, -ée *mf* • **accusing** *adj* accusateur, -trice
accustom [ə'kʌstəm] *vt* habituer, accoutumer • **accustomed** *adj* **to be a. to sth/to doing sth** être habitué à qch/à faire qch; **to get a. to sth/to doing sth** s'habituer à qch/à faire qch
ace [eɪs] *n* (**a**) *(card, person)* as *m* (**b**) *(at tennis)* ace *m*
acetate ['æsɪteɪt] *n* acétate *m*
acetic [ə'si:tɪk] *adj (acid)* acétique
ache [eɪk] **1** *n* douleur *f*
2 *vi* faire mal; **my head aches** j'ai mal à la tête; **I'm aching all over** j'ai mal partout; ur; *Fam* **to be aching to do sth** brûler de faire qch • **aching** *adj* douloureux, -euse
achieve [ə'tʃi:v] *vt (result)* obtenir; *(aim)* atteindre; *(ambition)* réaliser; *(victory)* remporter; **to a. success** réussir; **he'll never a. anything** il n'arrivera jamais à rien • **achievement** *n (success)* réussite *f*; *(of ambition)* réalisation *f*; **writing a novel is quite an a.** écrire un roman, c'est vraiment quelque chose

> 📖 Note that the French words **achever** and **achèvement** are false friends and are never translations for the English words **to achieve** and **achievement**. Their most common meanings are respectively to **complete** and **completion**.

acid ['æsɪd] *adj & n* acide *(m)*; **a. rain** pluies *fpl* acides • **acidity** [ə'sɪdɪtɪ] *n* acidité *f*
acknowledge [ək'nɒlɪdʒ] *vt* reconnaître (**as** pour); *(greeting)* répondre à; **to a. (receipt of)** accuser réception de; **to a. defeat** s'avouer vaincu • **acknowledg(e)ment** *n (of letter)* accusé *m* de réception; *(receipt)* reçu *m*; *(confession)* aveu *m* (**of** de); **in a. of** en reconnaissance de

acme ['ækmɪ] *n* sommet *m*, comble *m*
acne ['æknɪ] *n* acné *f*
acorn ['eɪkɔ:n] *n* gland *m*
acoustic [ə'ku:stɪk] *adj* acoustique
• **acoustics** *npl* acoustique *f*
acquaint [ə'kweɪnt] *vt* **to a. sb with sth** informer qn de qch; **to be acquainted with** *(person)* connaître; *(fact)* savoir; **we are acquainted** on se connaît
• **acquaintance** *n (person, knowledge)* connaissance *f*
acquiesce [ækwɪ'es] *vi* (**a**) *(agree)* acquiescer (**in/to** à) (**b**) *(collude)* **to a. in sth** ne pas s'opposer à qch • **acquiescence** *n* acquiescement *m*
acquire [ə'kwaɪə(r)] *vt* acquérir; *(taste)* prendre (**for** à); *(friends)* se faire; **acquired taste** goût *m* qui s'acquiert • **acquisition** [ækwɪ'zɪʃən] *n* acquisition *f*
• **acquisitive** [ə'kwɪzɪtɪv] *adj* avide, cupide
acquit [ə'kwɪt] *(pt & pp* **-tt-)** *vt* (**a**) *Law* **to a. sb (of a crime)** acquitter qn (**b**) **to a. oneself badly/well** mal/bien s'en tirer
• **acquittal** *n* acquittement *m*
acre ['eɪkə(r)] *n* acre *f* (≃ *0, 4 hectare)*; *Fam* **acres of space** plein de place
• **acreage** *n* superficie *f*
acrid ['ækrɪd] *adj (smell, taste)* âcre
acrimonious [ækrɪ'məʊnɪəs] *adj* acerbe
acrobat ['ækrəbæt] *n* acrobate *mf*
• **acro'batic** *adj* acrobatique; **a. movement** *or* **feat** acrobatie *f* • **acro'batics** *npl* acrobaties *fpl*
acronym ['ækrənɪm] *n* sigle *m*
across [ə'krɒs] **1** *prep (from side to side of)* d'un côté à l'autre de; *(on the other side of)* de l'autre côté de; *(crossways)* en travers de; **a bridge a. the river** un pont sur la rivière; **to walk** *or* **go a.** *(street, lawn)* traverser; **to run/swim a.** traverser en courant/à la nage
2 *adv* **to be a kilometre a.** *(wide)* avoir un kilomètre de large; **to get sth a. to sb** faire comprendre qch à qn
acrylic [ə'krɪlɪk] **1** *adj (paint, fibre)* acrylique; *(garment)* en acrylique
2 *n* acrylique *m*
act [ækt] **1** *n* (**a**) *(deed)* acte *m*; **a. (of parliament)** loi *f*; **caught in the a.** pris sur le fait; **a. of walking** action *f* de marcher; **an a. of folly** une folie (**b**) *Theatre (part of play)* acte *m*; *(in circus, cabaret)* numéro *m*; *Fig* **to get one's a. together** se secouer; *Fam* **to put on an a.** jouer la comédie; *Fam* **in on the a.** dans le coup
2 *vt (part in play or film)* jouer; **to a. the fool** faire l'idiot

3 *vi* (**a**) *(take action, behave)* agir; **it's time to a.** il est temps d'agir; **to a. as secretary**/*etc* faire office de secrétaire/*etc*; **to a. as a warning** servir d'avertissement; **to a. (up)on** *(affect)* agir sur; *(advice)* suivre; **to a. on behalf of sb** représenter qn; *Fam* **to a. up** *(of person, machine)* faire des siennes (**b**) *(in play, film)* jouer; *(pretend)* jouer la comédie • **acting 1** *adj (temporary)* intérimaire **2** *n (of play)* représentation *f*; *(actor's art)* jeu *m*; *(career)* théâtre *m*

action ['ækʃən] *n* action *f*; *(military)* combats *mpl*; *(legal)* procès *m*, action *f*; **to take a.** prendre des mesures; **to put into a.** *(plan)* exécuter; **out of a.** *(machine)* hors service; *(person)* hors de combat; **killed in a.** mort au champ d'honneur

activate ['æktɪveɪt] *vt Chem* activer; *(mechanism)* déclencher

active ['æktɪv] **1** *adj* actif, -ive; *(interest, dislike)* vif *(f* vive); *(volcano)* en activité **2** *n Grammar* actif *m* • **ac'tivity** *(pl* -**ies**) *n* activité *f*; *(in street)* animation *f*

activist ['æktɪvɪst] *n* activiste *mf*

actor ['æktə(r)] *n* acteur *m*

actress ['æktrɪs] *n* actrice *f*

actual ['æktʃʊəl] *adj* réel *(f* réelle); *(example)* concret, -ète; **the a. book** le livre même; **in a. fact** en réalité • **actually** *adv (truly)* réellement; *(in fact)* en réalité, en fait

> 🖉 Note that the French words **actuel** and **actuellement** are false friends and are never translations for the English words **actual** and **actually**. They mean respectively **present** and **at present**.

actuary ['æktʃʊərɪ] *(pl* -**ies**) *n* actuaire *mf*

acumen [*Br* 'ækjʊmən, *Am* ə'kju:mən] *n* perspicacité *f*; **to have business a.** avoir le sens des affaires

acupuncture ['ækjʊpʌŋktʃə(r)] *n* acuponcture *f*

acute [ə'kju:t] *adj (pain, angle)* aigu *(f* aiguë); *(anxiety, emotion)* vif *(f* vive); *(mind, observer)* perspicace; *(shortage)* grave • **acutely** *adv (suffer, feel)* profondément; *(painful)* extrêmement; **he's a. aware that...** il a parfaitement conscience du fait que...

AD [eɪ'di:] *(abbr* **anno Domini)** apr. J.-C.

ad [æd] *n Fam (on radio, TV)* pub *f*; *(private, in newspaper)* annonce *f*; *Br* **small ad,** *Am* **want ad** petite annonce

Adam ['ædəm] *n* **A.'s apple** pomme *f* d'Adam

adamant ['ædəmənt] *adj* catégorique; **to be a. that...** maintenir que...

adapt [ə'dæpt] **1** *vt* adapter (**to** à); **to a. oneself to sth** s'adapter à qch **2** *vi* s'adapter • **adaptable** *adj (person)* souple; *(instrument)* adaptable • **adap'tation** *n* adaptation *f* • **adapter, adaptor** *n (for use abroad)* adaptateur *m*; *(for several plugs)* prise *f* multiple

add [æd] **1** *vt* ajouter (**to** à; **that** que); **to a. (up** *or* **together)** *(numbers)* additionner; **to a. in** inclure **2** *vi* **to a. to** *(increase)* augmenter; **to a. up to** *(total)* s'élever à; *(mean)* signifier; *(represent)* constituer; *Fam* **it all adds up** tout s'explique

adder ['ædə(r)] *n* vipère *f*

addict ['ædɪkt] *n* **drug a.** toxicomane *mf*, drogué, -ée *mf*; **jazz/TV a.** fana(tique) *mf* du jazz/de la télé • **addicted** [ə'dɪktɪd] *adj* **to be a. to drugs** être toxicomane; **to be a. to drink** être alcoolique; **to be a. to cigarettes** ne pas pouvoir se passer de tabac; **to be a. to sport** se passionner pour le sport; **to be a. to work** être un bourreau de travail; **to be a. to doing sth** *(have the habit of)* avoir la manie de faire qch • **addiction** [ə'dɪkʃən] *n (to drugs)* dépendance *f* (**to** à); *(to chocolate)* passion *f* (**to** pour); **drug a.** toxicomanie *f* • **addictive** *adj (drug, TV)* qui crée une dépendance

addition [ə'dɪʃən] *n* addition *f*; *(increase)* augmentation *f*; **in a.** de plus; **in a. to** en plus de • **additional** *adj* supplémentaire

additive ['ædɪtɪv] *n* additif *m*

address [*Br* ə'dres, *Am* 'ædres] **1** *n (on letter, parcel)* adresse *f*; *(speech)* allocution *f* **2** [ə'dres] *vt (person, audience)* s'adresser à; *(words, speech)* adresser (**to** à); *(letter)* mettre l'adresse sur; **I addressed it to you** c'est à vous que je l'ai adressé • **addressee** [ædre'si:] *n* destinataire *mf*

adenoids ['ædɪnɔɪdz] *npl* végétations *fpl*

adept [ə'dept] *adj* expert (**in** *or* **at** à)

adequate ['ædɪkwət] *adj (enough)* suffisant; *(acceptable)* convenable; *(performance)* acceptable • **adequacy** *n (of person)* compétence *f*; **to doubt the a. of sth** douter que qch soit suffisant • **adequately** *adv (sufficiently)* suffisamment; *(acceptably)* convenablement

adhere [əd'hɪə(r)] *vi* **to a. to** adhérer à; *(decision, rule)* s'en tenir à • **adherence** *n (support)* adhésion *f* • **adhesion** [-'hi:ʒən] *n (grip)* adhérence *f* • **adhesive** [-'hi:sɪv] *adj & n* adhésif *(m)*

ad infinitum [ædɪnfɪ'naɪtəm] *adv* à l'infini

adjacent [ə'dʒeɪsənt] *adj (house, angle)* adjacent (**to** à)

adjective ['ædʒɪktɪv] *n* adjectif *m*

adjoin [ə'dʒɔɪn] *vt* être attenant à ●**adjoining** *adj* attenant

adjourn [ə'dʒɜːn] **1** *vt (postpone)* ajourner; *(session)* suspendre
2 *vi* suspendre la séance; **to a. to another room** passer dans une autre pièce ●**adjournment** *n* ajournement *m*; *(of session)* suspension *f* (de séance)

adjudicate [ə'dʒuːdɪkeɪt] *vti* juger ●**adjudication** [-'keɪʃən] *n* jugement *m* ●**adjudicator** *n* juge *m*, arbitre *m*

adjust [ə'dʒʌst] *vt (machine)* régler; *(machine part)* ajuster, régler; *(salaries, prices)* (r)ajuster; *(clothes)* rajuster; **to a. (oneself) to sth** s'adapter à qch ●**adjustable** *adj (seat)* réglable ●**adjustment** *n Tech* réglage *m*; *(of person)* adaptation *f*; *(of salaries, prices)* réajustement *m*

ad-lib [æd'lɪb] **1** *(pt & pp* **-bb-***) vi* improviser
2 *adj (joke)* improvisé
3 *adv* en improvisant

administer [əd'mɪnɪstə(r)] *vt (manage, dispense)* administrer (**to** à) ●**administration** [-'streɪʃən] *n* administration *f*; *(government)* gouvernement *m* ●**administrative** *adj* administratif, -ive ●**administrator** *n* administrateur, -trice *mf*

admirable ['ædmərəbəl] *adj* admirable ●**admiration** [-'reɪʃən] *n* admiration *f*

admiral ['ædmərəl] *n* amiral *m*

admire [əd'maɪə(r)] *vt* admirer (**for sth** pour qch; **for doing** de faire) ●**admirer** *n* admirateur, -trice *mf* ●**admiring** *adj* admiratif, -ive

admit [əd'mɪt] *(pt & pp* **-tt-***)* **1** *vt (let in)* laisser entrer; *(to hospital, college)* admettre; *(acknowledge)* reconnaître, admettre (**that** que)
2 *vi* **to a. to sth** avouer qch; *(mistake)* reconnaître qch ●**admissible** *adj* admissible ●**admission** *n (entry to theatre)* entrée *f* (**to** à ou de); *(to club, school)* admission *f*; *(acknowledgement)* aveu *m*; **a. (charge)** (prix *m* d')entrée *f* ●**admittance** *n* entrée *f*; **'no a.'** 'entrée interdite' ●**admittedly** [-ɪdlɪ] *adv* de l'aveu général; **a., it was dark** je dois convenir qu'il faisait sombre

admonish [əd'mɒnɪʃ] *vt (rebuke)* réprimander; *(warn)* avertir

ado [ə'duː] *n* **without further a.** sans plus de façons

adolescent [ædə'lesənt] *n* adolescent, -ente *mf* ●**adolescence** *n* adolescence *f*

adopt [ə'dɒpt] *vt (child, method, attitude)* adopter; *Pol (candidate)* choisir ●**adopted** *adj (child)* adopté; *(son, daughter)* adoptif, -ive; *(country)* d'adoption ●**adoption** *n* adoption *f* ●**adoptive** *adj (parent)* adoptif, -ive

adore [ə'dɔː(r)] *vt* adorer (**doing** faire); **he adores being flattered** il adore qu'on le flatte ●**adorable** *adj* adorable ●**adoration** [ædə'reɪʃən] *n* adoration *f*

adorn [ə'dɔːn] *vt (room, book)* orner (**with** de); *(person, dress)* parer (**with** de) ●**adornment** *n* ornements *mpl*; *(finery)* parure *f*

adrenalin(e) [ə'drenəlɪn] *n* adrénaline *f*

Adriatic [eɪdrɪ'ætɪk] *n* **the A.** l'Adriatique *f*

adrift [ə'drɪft] *adj & adv (boat)* à la dérive; **to come a.** *(of rope, collar)* se détacher; *Fig* **to turn sb a.** abandonner qn à son sort

adroit [ə'drɔɪt] *adj* habile

adulation [ædjʊ'leɪʃən] *n* adulation *f*

adult ['ædʌlt, ə'dʌlt] **1** *n* adulte *mf*
2 *adj (animal)* adulte; **a. class/film** classe *f*/film *m* pour adultes ●**adulthood** *n* âge *m* adulte

adulterate [ə'dʌltəreɪt] *vt (food)* empoisonner

adultery [ə'dʌltərɪ] *n* adultère *m*; **to commit a.** commettre l'adultère ●**adulterous** *adj* adultère

advance [əd'vɑːns] **1** *n (movement, money)* avance *f*; *(of science)* progrès *mpl*; **advances** *(of love, friendship)* avances *fpl*; **in a.** *(book, inform, apply)* à l'avance; *(pay)* d'avance; *(arrive)* en avance; **in a. of sb** avant qn
2 *adj (payment)* anticipé; **a. booking** réservation *f*; **a. guard** avant-garde *f*
3 *vt* (**a**) *(put forward)* faire avancer; *(chess piece)* avancer (**b**) *(science, one's work)* faire progresser; *(opinion)* avancer
4 *vi (go forward, progress)* avancer; **to a. towards sb** s'avancer *ou* avancer vers qn ●**advanced** *adj* avancé; *(studies, level)* supérieur; *(course)* de niveau supérieur; **a. in years** âgé; **she's very a. for her age** elle est très en avance pour son âge ●**advancement** *n (progress, promotion)* avancement *m*

advantage [əd'vɑːntɪdʒ] *n* avantage *m* (**over** sur); **to take a. of** *(situation)* profiter de; *(person)* exploiter; *(woman)* séduire; **to show sth (off) to a.** mettre qch en valeur; **a. Sampras** *(in tennis)* avantage

Sampras • **advantageous** [ædvən'teɪdʒəs] *adj* avantageux, -euse (**to** pour)

advent ['ædvent] *n* arrivée *f*, avènement *m*; *Rel* **A.** l'Avent *m*

adventure [əd'ventʃə(r)] **1** *n* aventure *f* **2** *adj (film)* d'aventures • **adventurer** *n* aventurier, -ière *mf* • **adventurous** *adj* aventureux, -euse

adverb ['ædvɜːb] *n* adverbe *m*

adversary ['ædvəsərɪ] (*pl* **-ies**) *n* adversaire *mf*

adverse ['ædvɜːs] *adj* défavorable; *(effect)* négatif, -ive • **adversity** [əd'vɜːsɪtɪ] *n* adversité *f*

advert ['ædvɜːt] *n Br* pub *f*; *(private, in newspaper)* annonce *f*

advertise ['ædvətaɪz] **1** *vt (commercially)* faire de la publicité pour; *(privately)* passer une annonce pour vendre; **he didn't want to a. his presence** il ne voulait pas se faire remarquer **2** *vi* faire de la publicité; *(privately)* passer une annonce (**for** pour trouver) • **advertiser** *n* annonceur, -euse *mf* • **advertising** *n* publicité *f*; **a. agency** agence *f* de publicité; **a. campaign** campagne *f* de publicité

> *Note that the French verb* **avertir** *is a false friend and is never a translation for the English verb* **to advertise**. *Its most common meaning is* **to warn**.

advertisement [*Br* əd'vɜːtɪsmənt, *Am* ædvər'taɪzmənt] *n* publicité *f*; *(private or in newspaper)* annonce *f*; *(poster)* affiche *f*; *TV* **the advertisements** la publicité

> *Note that the French noun* **avertissement** *is a false friend and is never a translation for the English noun* **advertisement**. *It means* **warning**.

advice [əd'vaɪs] *n* conseil(s) *m(pl)*; *Com (notification)* avis *m*; **a piece of a.** un conseil; **to ask sb's a.** demander conseil à qn; **to take sb's a.** suivre les conseils de qn

advise [əd'vaɪz] *vt* (**a**) *(counsel)* conseiller; *(recommend)* recommander; **to a. sb to do sth** conseiller à qn de faire qch; **to a. sb against doing sth** déconseiller à qn de faire qch; **he would be well advised to leave** il ferait bien de partir (**b**) *(inform)* **to a. sb that...** aviser qn que... • **advisable** *adj (action)* à conseiller; **it's a. to wait/etc** il est plus prudent d'attendre/*etc* • **advisedly** [-ɪdlɪ] *adv* après réflexion • **adviser, advisor** *n* conseiller, -ère *mf* • **advisory**

adj consultatif, -ive; **in an a. capacity** à titre consultatif

advocate 1 ['ædvəkət] *n (of cause)* défenseur *m*; *(lawyer)* avocat, -ate *mf* **2** ['ædvəkeɪt] *vt* préconiser

aegis ['iːdʒɪs] *n* **under the a. of** sous l'égide de

aeon ['iːɒn] *n* éternité *f*

aerial ['eərɪəl] **1** *n Br* antenne *f* **2** *adj (photo)* aérien, -ienne

aerobatics [eərə'bætɪks] *npl* acrobaties *fpl* aériennes

aerobics [eə'rəʊbɪks] *npl* aérobic *m*

aerodrome ['eərədrəʊm] *n* aérodrome *m*

aerodynamic [eərəʊdaɪ'næmɪk] *adj* aérodynamique

aeronautics [eərə'nɔːtɪks] *n* aéronautique *f*

aeroplane ['eərəpleɪn] *n Br* avion *m*

aerosol ['eərəsɒl] *n* aérosol *m*

aerospace ['eərəspeɪs] *adj (industry)* aérospatial

aesthetic [*Br* iːs'θetɪk, *Am* es'θetɪk] *adj* esthétique

afar [ə'fɑː(r)] *adv Literary* **from a.** de loin

affable ['æfəbəl] *adj* affable

affair [ə'feə(r)] *n (matter, concern)* affaire *f*; **(love) a.** liaison *f*; **state of affairs** situation *f*

affect [ə'fekt] *vt (concern)* concerner; *(move, pretend to have)* affecter; *(harm)* nuire à; *(influence)* influer sur; **to be deeply affected by sth** être très affecté par qch; **to be affected by a disease/ famine** être atteint par une maladie/touché par la famine • **affectation** [æfek-'teɪʃən] *n* affectation *f* • **affected** *adj (manner)* affecté

affection [ə'fekʃən] *n* affection *f* (**for** pour) • **affectionate** *adj* affectueux, -ueuse • **affectionately** *adv* affectueusement

affiliate [ə'fɪlɪeɪt] *vt* affilier; **affiliated company** filiale *f* • **affili'ation** *n* affiliation *f*; **what are his political affiliations?** quels sont ses liens avec les différents partis politiques?

affinity [ə'fɪnɪtɪ] (*pl* **-ies**) *n* affinité *f*

affirm [ə'fɜːm] *vt* affirmer • **affirmation** [æfə'meɪʃən] *n* affirmation *f* • **affirmative 1** *adj* affirmatif, -ive **2** *n* affirmative *f*; **to answer in the a.** répondre par l'affirmative

affix [ə'fɪks] *vt (stamp, signature)* apposer

afflict [ə'flɪkt] *vt* affliger (**with** de) • **affliction** *n (misery)* affliction *f*; *(disability)* infirmité *f*

affluent ['æfluɒnt] *adj* riche; **a. society** société *f* d'abondance • **affluence** *n* richesse *f*

afford [ə'fɔːd] *vt* (**a**) *(pay for)* **to be able to a. sth** avoir les moyens d'acheter qch, pouvoir se payer qch; **he can't a. the time (to read it)** il n'a pas le temps (de le lire); **I can a. to wait** je peux me permettre d'attendre (**b**) *Formal (provide)* fournir, donner; **to a. sb sth** fournir qch à qn • **affordable** *adj (price)* abordable

affray [ə'freɪ] *n Law* rixe *f*

affront [ə'frʌnt] **1** *n* affront *m* **2** *vt* faire un affront à

Afghanistan [æf'gænɪstɑːn] *n* l'Afghanistan *m*

afield [ə'fiːld] *adv* **further a.** plus loin

afloat [ə'fləʊt] *adv (ship, swimmer, business)* à flot; *(awash)* submergé; **to stay a.** *(of ship)* rester à flot; *(of business)* se maintenir à flot

afoot [ə'fʊt] *adv* **there's something a.** il se trame quelque chose; **there's a plan a. to** on prépare un projet pour

aforementioned [ə'fɔːmenʃənd] *adj* susmentionné

afraid [ə'freɪd] *adj* **to be a.** avoir peur (**of sb/sth** de qn/qch); **to be a. to do** *or* **of doing** avoir peur de faire; **to make sb a.** faire peur à qn; **I'm a. (that) he'll fall** j'ai peur qu'il (ne) tombe; **he's a. (that) she may be ill** il a peur qu'elle (ne) soit malade; **I'm a. he's out** *(I regret to say)* je regrette, il est sorti

afresh [ə'freʃ] *adv* de nouveau; **to start a.** recommencer

Africa ['æfrɪkə] *n* l'Afrique *f* • **African 1** *adj* africain **2** *n* Africain, -aine *mf*

after ['ɑːftə(r)] **1** *adv* après; **soon/long a.** peu/longtemps après; **the month a.** le mois d'après; **the day a.** le lendemain **2** *prep* après; **a. three days** au bout de trois jours; **the day a. the battle** le lendemain de la bataille; **a. eating** après avoir mangé; **day a. day** jour après jour; **a. you!** je vous en prie!; **a. all** après tout; **it's a. five** il est cinq heures passées; *Am* **ten a. four** quatre heures dix; **to be a. sb/sth** *(seek)* chercher qn/qch **3** *conj* après que; **a. he saw you** après qu'il t'a vu • **aftercare** *n Med* soins *mpl* postopératoires; *Law* surveillance *f* • **aftereffects** *npl* suites *fpl*, séquelles *fpl* • **afterlife** *n* vie *f* après la mort • **aftermath** *n* suites *fpl* • **aftersales 'service** *n* service *m* après-vente • **aftershave (lotion)** *n* lotion *f* après-rasage, after-shave *m inv* • **aftertaste** *n* arrière-goût *m* • **afterthought** *n*

réflexion *f* après coup; **to add/say sth as an a.** ajouter/dire qch après coup • **afterward(s)** *adv* après, plus tard

afternoon [ɑːftə'nuːn] *n* après-midi *m ou f inv*; **in the a.** l'après-midi; **at three in the a.** à trois heures de l'après-midi; **every Monday a.** tous les lundis après-midi; **good a.!** *(hello)* bonjour!; *(goodbye)* au revoir! • **afternoons** *adv Am* l'après-midi

afters ['ɑːftəz] *npl Br Fam* dessert *m*

again [ə'gen, ə'geɪn] *adv* de nouveau, encore une fois; *(furthermore)* en outre; **to do a.** refaire; **to go down/up a.** redescendre/remonter; **she won't do it a.** elle ne le fera plus; **never a.** plus jamais; **half as much a.** moitié plus; **a. and a.** bien des fois, maintes fois; **what's his name a.?** comment s'appelle-t-il déjà?

against [ə'genst, ə'geɪnst] *prep* contre; **to lean a. sth** s'appuyer contre qch; **to go** *or* **be a. sth** s'opposer à qch; **the law illégal; a law a. drinking** une loi qui interdit de boire; **his age is a. him** son âge lui est défavorable; **a. a background of** sur (un) fond de; **a. the light** à contre-jour; *Br* **a. the rules,** *Am* **a. the rule** interdit, contraire aux règlements; **the pound rose a. the dollar** la livre est en hausse par rapport au dollar

age [eɪdʒ] **1** *n* âge *m*; **(old) a.** vieillesse *f*; **what a. are you?, what's your a.?** quel âge as-tu?; **five years of a.** âgé de cinq ans; **to be of a.** être majeur; **to come of a.** atteindre sa majorité; **under a.** trop jeune, mineur; *Fam* **to wait (for) ages** attendre une éternité; **a. gap** différence *f* d'âge; **a. group** tranche *f* d'âge; **a. limit** limite *f* d'âge **2** *vti (pres p* **ag(e)ing**) vieillir • **aged** *adj* (**a**) [eɪdʒd] **a. ten** âgé de dix ans (**b**) ['eɪdʒɪd] vieux (*f* vieille), âgé; **the a.** les personnes *fpl* âgées • **ageless** *adj* toujours jeune • **age-old** *adj* séculaire

agenda [ə'dʒendə] *n* ordre *m* du jour

> *Note that the French noun* **agenda** *is a false friend and is never a translation for the English noun* **agenda**. *It means* **diary**.

agent ['eɪdʒənt] *n* agent *m*; *(car dealer)* concessionnaire *mf* • **agency** *n* (**a**) *(office)* agence *f* (**b**) **through the a. of sb** par l'intermédiaire de qn

aggravate ['ægrəveɪt] *vt (make worse)* aggraver; *Fam (person)* exaspérer • **aggra'vation** *n* aggravation *f*; *Fam (bother)* embêtements *mpl*

aggregate ['ægrɪgət] **1** *adj* global **2** *n (total)* ensemble *m*; **on a.** au total

aggression [ə'greʃən] *n (act)* agression *f*; *(aggressiveness)* agressivité *f* • **aggressive** *adj* agressif, -ive • **aggressiveness** *n* agressivité *f* • **aggressor** *n* agresseur *m*

aggrieved [ə'griːvd] *adj (offended)* blessé, froissé; *(tone)* peiné

aggro ['ægrəʊ] *n Br Fam (bother)* embêtements *mpl*; *(violence)* bagarre *f*

aghast [ə'gɑːst] *adj* horrifié (**at** par)

agile [*Br* 'ædʒaɪl, *Am* 'ædʒəl] *adj* agile • **agility** [ə'dʒɪlɪtɪ] *n* agilité *f*

agitate ['ædʒɪteɪt] **1** *vt (worry)* agiter; **to be agitated** être agité

2 *vi* **to a. for sth** faire campagne pour qch • **agitation** [-'teɪʃən] *n (anxiety, unrest)* agitation *f* • **agitator** *n (political)* agitateur, -trice *mf*

aglow [ə'gləʊ] *adj (sky)* embrasé; **to be a.** rayonner (**with** de)

agnostic [æg'nɒstɪk] *adj & n* agnostique *(mf)*

ago [ə'gəʊ] *adv* **a year a.** il y a un an; **how long a.?** il y a combien de temps (de cela)?; **long a.** il y a longtemps; **as long a. as 1800** déjà en 1800; **a short time a.** il y a peu de temps

agog [ə'gɒg] *adj (excited)* en émoi; *(eager)* impatient

agonize ['ægənaɪz] *vi* se faire beaucoup de souci • **agonized** *adj (look)* angoissé; *(cry)* de douleur • **agonizing** *adj (pain)* atroce; *(situation)* angoissant

> 📝 Note that the French verb **agoniser** is a false friend and is never a translation for the English verb **to agonize**. It means **to be dying**.

agony ['ægənɪ] *(pl* **-ies***) n (pain)* douleur *f* atroce; *(anguish)* angoisse *f*; **to be in a.** être au supplice; **a. column** *(in newspaper)* courrier *m* du cœur

> 📝 Note that the French noun **agonie** is a false friend and is never a translation for the English noun **agony**. It means **death throes**.

agree [ə'griː] **1** *vi (come to an agreement)* se mettre d'accord; *(be in agreement)* être d'accord (**with** avec); *(of facts, dates)* concorder; *(of verb)* s'accorder; **to a. (up)on** *(decide)* convenir de; **to a. to sth/ to doing** consentir à qch/à faire; **it doesn't a. with me** *(food, climate)* ça ne me réussit pas

2 *vt (plan)* se mettre d'accord sur; *(date, price)* convenir de; *(figures, sums)* faire concorder; *(approve)* approuver; **to a. to do** accepter de faire; **to a. that...** admet-

tre que... • **agreed** *adj (time, place)* convenu; **we are a.** nous sommes d'accord; **a.!** entendu! • **agreement** *n (contract, assent) & Grammar* accord *m* (**with** avec); **to be in a. with sb** être d'accord avec qn; **to be in a. with a decision** approuver une décision; **to come to an a.** se mettre d'accord; **by mutual a.** d'un commun accord

> 📝 Note that the French noun **agrément** is a false friend and is never a translation for the English noun **agreement**. Its most common meaning is **pleasure** or **charm**.

agreeable [ə'griːəbəl] *adj (pleasant)* agréable; **to be a.** *(agree)* être d'accord; **to be a. to sth** consentir à qch

agriculture ['ægrɪkʌltʃə(r)] *n* agriculture *f* • **agri'cultural** *adj* agricole

aground [ə'graʊnd] *adv* **to run a.** *(of ship)* (s')échouer

ah [ɑː] *exclam* ah!

ahead [ə'hed] *adv (in space)* en avant; *(leading)* en tête; *(in the future)* à l'avenir; **a. of** *(space)* devant; *(time)* avant; **one hour/***etc* **a.** une heure/*etc* d'avance (**of** sur); **to be a. of schedule** être en avance; **to go on a.** partir devant; **to go a.** *(advance)* avancer; *(continue)* continuer; *(start)* commencer; **go a.!** allez-y!; **to go a. with** *(task)* mettre à exécution; **to get a.** *(in race)* prendre de l'avance; *(succeed)* réussir; **to think a.** prévoir

aid [eɪd] **1** *n (help)* aide *f*; *(device)* accessoire *m*; **with the a. of sb** avec l'aide de qn; **with the a. of sth** à l'aide de qch; **in a. of** *(charity)* au profit de; *Fam* **what's (all) this in a. of?** ça sert à quoi, tout ça?

2 *vt* aider (**sb to do** qn à faire)

aide [eɪd] *n* collaborateur, -trice *mf*

AIDS [eɪdz] *(abbr* **Acquired Immune Deficiency Syndrome***) n* SIDA *m*; **A. victim/ virus** malade *mf*/virus *m* du SIDA

ail [eɪl] *vt* **what ails you?** de quoi souffrez-vous? • **ailing** *adj (ill)* souffrant; *(company)* en difficulté • **ailment** *n* (petit) ennui *m* de santé

aim [eɪm] **1** *n* but *m*; **to take a. (at)** viser; **with the a. of** dans le but de

2 *vt (gun)* braquer (**at** sur); *(lamp)* diriger (**at** vers); *(stone)* lancer (**at** à *ou* vers); *(blow, remark)* décocher (**at** à); **aimed at children** *(product)* destiné aux enfants

3 *vi* viser; **to a. at sb** viser qn; **to a. to do** *or* **at doing** avoir l'intention de faire • **'aimless** *adj (existence)* sans but • **'aimlessly** *adv* sans but

air [eə(r)] **1** *n* (**a**) *(atmosphère)* air *m*; **in**

the open a. en plein air; **by a.** *(travel)* en ou par avion; *(send letter or goods)* par avion; **to be** *or* **go on the a.** *(of person)* passer à l'antenne; *(of programme)* être diffusé; **to throw (up) in(to) the a.** jeter en l'air; **(up) in the a.** *(plan)* incertain; *Fig* **there's something in the a.** il se prépare quelque chose (**b**) *(appearance, tune)* air *m*; **to put on airs** se donner des airs; **with an a. of sadness** d'un air triste

2 *adj (base)* aérien, -ienne; *Aut* **a. bag** airbag *m*; **a. bed** matelas *m* pneumatique; **a. fare** prix *m* du billet d'avion; **a. force** armée *f* de l'air

3 *vt (room)* aérer; *(views)* exposer; *Br* **airing cupboard** = placard où se trouve le chauffe-eau • **airborne** *adj (troops)* aéroporté; **to become a.** *(of aircraft)* décoller • **air-conditioned** *adj* climatisé • **air-conditioning** *n* climatisation *f* • **aircraft** *n inv* avion *m*; **a. carrier** porte-avions *m inv* • **aircrew** *n* équipage *m* (d'un avion) • **airfield** *n* terrain *m* d'aviation • **air freshener** *n* désodorisant *m (pour la maison)* • **airgun** *n* carabine *f* à air comprimé • **air letter** *n* aérogramme *m* • **airlift 1** *n* pont *m* aérien **2** *vt* transporter par avion • **airline** *n* compagnie *f* aérienne; **a. ticket** billet *m* d'avion • **airliner** *n* avion *m* de ligne • **airlock** *n (in submarine, spacecraft)* sas *m*; *(in pipe)* poche *f* d'air • **airmail** *n* poste *f* aérienne; **by a.** par avion • **airman** *(pl* **-men)** *n* aviateur *m* • **airplane** *n Am* avion *m* • **airpocket** *n* trou *m* d'air • **airport** *n* aéroport *m* • **air-raid shelter** *n* abri *m* antiaérien • **airship** *n* dirigeable *m* • **airsick** *adj* **to be a.** avoir le mal de l'air • **airsickness** *n* mal *m* de l'air • **airstrip** *n* terrain *m* d'atterrissage • **airtight** *adj* hermétique • **air traffic controller** *n* contrôleur *m* aérien, aiguilleur *m* du ciel • **airway** *n (route)* couloir *m* aérien • **airworthy** *adj* en état de voler

airy ['eərɪ] **(-ier, -iest)** *adj (room)* clair et spacieux, -ieuse; *Fig (promise)* vain; *(manner)* désinvolte • **airy-'fairy** *adj Br Fam* farfelu • **airily** *adv (not seriously)* d'un ton léger

aisle [aɪl] *n (in supermarket, cinema)* allée *f*; *(in plane)* couloir *m*; *(in church) (on side)* nef *f* latérale; *(central)* allée centrale

ajar [ə'dʒɑː(r)] *adj & adv (door)* entrouvert

akin [ə'kɪn] *adj* **a. to** apparenté à

alabaster ['æləbɑːstə(r)] *n* albâtre *m*

alacrity [ə'lækrɪtɪ] *n* empressement *m*

à la mode [ælæ'məʊd] *adj Am (dessert)* avec de la crème glacée

alarm [ə'lɑːm] **1** *n (warning, fear, device)* alarme *f*; *(mechanism)* sonnerie *f* (d'alarme); **false a.** fausse alerte *f*; **a. clock** réveil *m*

2 *vt (frighten)* alarmer; *(worry)* inquiéter; **to get alarmed** s'alarmer; **they were alarmed at the news** la nouvelle les a beaucoup inquiétés • **alarmist** *n* alarmiste *mf*

alas [ə'læs] *exclam* hélas!

Albania [æl'beɪnɪə] *n* l'Albanie *f* • **Albanian 1** *adj* albanais **2** *n* Albanais, -aise *mf*

albatross ['ælbətrɒs] *n* albatros *m*

albeit [ɔːl'biːɪt] *conj Literary* quoique (+ subjunctive)

albino [*Br* æl'biːnəʊ, *Am* æl'baɪnəʊ] *(pl -os) n* albinos *mf*

album ['ælbəm] *n (book, record)* album *m*

alchemy ['ælkəmɪ] *n* alchimie *f* • **alchemist** *n* alchimiste *m*

alcohol ['ælkəhɒl] *n* alcool *m* • **alco'holic 1** *adj (person)* alcoolique; **a. drink** boisson *f* alcoolisée **2** *n (person)* alcoolique *mf* • **alcoholism** *n* alcoolisme *m*

alcopop ['ælkəʊpɒp] *n* prémix *m*

alcove ['ælkəʊv] *n* alcôve *f*

ale [eɪl] *n* bière *f*

alert [ə'lɜːt] **1** *adj (watchful)* vigilant; *(lively) (mind, baby)* éveillé

2 *n* alerte *f*; **on the a.** sur le qui-vive

3 *vt* alerter • **alertness** *n* vigilance *f*; *(of mind, baby)* vivacité *f*

A level ['eɪlevəl] *n Br (exam)* ≃ épreuve *f* de baccalauréat

alfalfa [æl'fælfə] *n Am* luzerne *f*

algebra ['ældʒɪbrə] *n* algèbre *f* • **algebraic** [-'breɪk] *adj* algébrique

Algeria [æl'dʒɪərɪə] *n* l'Algérie *f* • **Algerian 1** *adj* algérien, -ienne **2** *n* Algérien, -ienne *mf*

alias ['eɪlɪəs] **1** *adv* alias

2 *(pl* **aliases)** *n* nom *m* d'emprunt

alibi ['ælɪbaɪ] *n* alibi *m*

alien ['eɪlɪən] **1** *adj* étranger, -ère (**to** à)

2 *n Formal (foreigner)* étranger, -ère *mf*; *(from outer space)* extraterrestre *mf* • **alienate** *vt (supporters, readers)* s'aliéner; **to a. sb** *(make unfriendly)* s'aliéner qn; **to feel alienated** se sentir exclu

alight¹ [ə'laɪt] *adj (fire)* allumé; *(building)* en feu; *(face)* éclairé; **to set sth a.** mettre le feu à qch

alight² [ə'laɪt] *(pt & pp* **alighted** *or* **alit)** *vi* (**a**) *Formal (from bus, train)* descendre (**from** de) (**b**) *(of bird)* se poser (**on** sur)

align [əˈlaɪn] *vt* aligner; **to a. oneself with sb** s'aligner sur qn •**alignment** *n* alignement *m*; **in a. (with)** aligné (sur)

alike [əˈlaɪk] **1** *adj (people, things)* semblables, pareils, -eilles; **to look** *or* **be a.** se ressembler

2 *adv* de la même manière; **summer and winter a.** été comme hiver

alimony [*Br* ˈælɪmənɪ, *Am* ˈælɪməʊnɪ] *n Law* pension *f* alimentaire

alit [əˈlɪt] *pt & pp* of **alight²**

alive [əˈlaɪv] *adj* vivant, en vie; **a. to** conscient de; **a. with worms**/etc *(crawling)* grouillant de vers/etc; **to stay a.** survivre; **to keep sb a.** maintenir qn en vie; **to keep a memory/custom a.** entretenir un souvenir/une tradition; **anyone a. will tell you** n'importe qui vous le dira; **a. and well** bien portant; *Fam* **a. and kicking** plein de vie; *Fam* **look a.!** active-toi!

all [ɔːl] **1** *adj* tout, toute, *pl* tous, toutes; **a. day** toute la journée; **a. men** tous les hommes; **a. the girls** toutes les filles; **a. four of them** tous les quatre; **with a. speed** à toute vitesse; **for a. his wealth** malgré toute sa fortune

2 *pron (everyone)* tous *mpl*, toutes *fpl*; *(everything)* tout; **my sisters are a. here** toutes mes sœurs sont ici; **he ate it a., he ate a. of it** il a tout mangé; **take a. of it** prends (le) tout; **a. of us** nous tous; **a. together** tous ensemble; **a. (that) he has** tout ce qu'il a; **a. in a.** à tout prendre; **in a., a. told** en tout; **a. but impossible**/etc *(almost)* presque impossible/etc; **anything at a.** quoi que ce soit; **if he comes at a.** s'il vient effectivement; **if there's any wind at a.** s'il y a le moindre vent; **nothing at a.** rien du tout; **not at a.** pas du tout; *(after 'thank you')* il n'y a pas de quoi

3 *adv* tout; **a. alone** tout seul; **a. bad** entièrement mauvais, -ielle *m*•**all-in** *adj Br* **a. price** prix *m* global •**all-night** *adj (party)* qui dure toute la nuit; *(shop)* ouvert toute la nuit •**all-out** *adj (effort)* acharné; *(war, strike)* tous azimuts •**all-powerful** *adj* tout-puissant *(f* toute-puissante) •**all-purpose** *adj (tool)* universel, -elle •**all-round** *adj (knowledge)* approfondi; *(athlete)* complet, -ète •**all-'rounder** *n* personne *f* qui est forte en tout

•**all-star** *adj* **an a. cast** une distribution prestigieuse •**all-time** *adj (record)* jamais battu; **to reach an a. low/high** arriver à son point le plus bas/le plus haut

allay [əˈleɪ] *vt (fears)* calmer, apaiser; *(doubts)* dissiper

allegation [ælɪˈɡeɪʃən] *n* accusation *f*

allege [əˈledʒ] *vt* prétendre (**that** que) •**alleged** *adj (so-called) (crime, fact)* prétendu; *(author, culprit)* présumé; **he is a. to be...** on prétend qu'il est... •**allegedly** [-ɪdlɪ] *adv* à ce qu'on dit

allegiance [əˈliːdʒəns] *n (to party, cause)* fidélité *f* (**to** à)

allegory [ˈælɪɡərɪ] *(pl* **-ies)** *n* allégorie *f* •**allegorical** [-ˈɡɒrɪkəl] *adj* allégorique

allergy [ˈælədʒɪ] *(pl* **-ies)** *n* allergie *f* (**to** à) •**allergic** [əˈlɜːdʒɪk] *adj* allergique (**to** à)

alleviate [əˈliːvɪeɪt] *vt (pain, suffering)* soulager; *(burden, task)* alléger; *(problem)* remédier à

alley [ˈælɪ] *(pl* **-eys)** *n* ruelle *f*; *(in park)* allée *f*; *Fam* **that's (right) up my a.** c'est mon rayon •**alleyway** *n* ruelle *f*

alliance [əˈlaɪəns] *n* alliance *f*

allied [ˈælaɪd] *adj (country)* allié; *(matters)* lié

alligator [ˈælɪɡeɪtə(r)] *n* alligator *m*

allocate [ˈæləkeɪt] *vt (assign)* affecter (**to** à); *(distribute)* répartir •**allocation** [-ˈkeɪʃən] *n* affectation *f*

allot [əˈlɒt] *(pt & pp* **-tt-)** *vt (assign)* attribuer (**to** à); *(distribute)* répartir; **in the allotted time** dans le temps imparti •**allotment** *n* (**a**) *(action)* attribution *f*; *(share)* part *f* (**b**) *Br (land)* jardin *m* ouvrier

allow [əˈlaʊ] **1** *vt* permettre (**sb sth** qch à qn); *(give, grant)* accorder (**sb sth** qch à qn); *(request)* accéder à; **to a. a discount** accorder une réduction; **to a. sb to do** permettre à qn de faire; **to a. an hour/a metre**/etc *(estimated period or quantity)* prévoir une heure/un mètre/etc; **a. me!** permettez(-moi)!; **it's not allowed** c'est interdit; **you're not allowed to go** on vous interdit de partir

2 *vi* **to a. for sth** tenir compte de qch •**allowable** *adj (acceptable)* admissible; *(expense)* déductible

allowance [əˈlaʊəns] *n* allocation *f*; *(for travel, housing, food)* indemnité *f*; *(for duty-free goods)* tolérance *f*; *(tax-free amount)* abattement *m*; **to make allowances for** *(person)* être indulgent envers; *(thing)* tenir compte de

alloy [ˈælɔɪ] *n* alliage *m*

all right [ɔːl'raɪt] **1** *adj (satisfactory)* bien *inv*; *(unharmed)* sain et sauf; *(undamaged)* intact; *(without worries)* tranquille; **it's a.** ça va; **are you a.?** ça va?; **I'm a.** *(healthy)* je vais bien; *(financially)* je m'en sors; **he's a.** *(trustworthy)* c'est quelqu'un de bien; **to be a. at maths** se débrouiller en maths; **the TV is a. now** *(fixed)* la télé marche maintenant

2 *adv (well)* bien; **a.!** *(agreement)* d'accord!; **I received your letter a.** *(emphatic)* j'ai bien reçu votre lettre; **is it a. if I smoke?** ça ne vous dérange pas si je fume?

allude [ə'luːd] *vi* **to a. to** faire allusion à • **allusion** *n* allusion *f*

alluring [ə'ljʊərɪŋ] *adj* séduisant

ally 1 ['ælaɪ] *(pl* **-ies** *) n* allié, -iée *mf*
2 [ə'laɪ] *(pt & pp* **-ied** *) vt* **to a. oneself with** s'allier à *ou* avec

almanac ['ɔːlmənæk] *n* almanach *m*

almighty [ɔːl'maɪtɪ] **1** *adj* **(a)** *(powerful)* tout-puissant *(f* toute-puissante *)* **(b)** *Fam (enormous)* terrible, formidable
2 *n* **the A.** le Tout-Puissant

almond ['ɑːmənd] *n* amande *f*

almost ['ɔːlməʊst] *adv* presque; **he a. fell** il a failli tomber

alms [ɑːmz] *npl* aumône *f*

aloft [ə'lɒft] *adv Literary* en haut

alone [ə'ləʊn] *adj & adv* seul; **an expert a. can** seul un expert peut; **I did it (all) a.** je l'ai fait (tout) seul; **to leave** *or* **let a.** *(person)* laisser tranquille; *(thing)* ne pas toucher à; **to go it a.** faire cavalier seul; **they can't dance, let a. sing** ils ne savent pas danser, et encore moins chanter

along [ə'lɒŋ] **1** *prep* **(all) a.** (tout) le long de; **to walk a. the shore** marcher le long du rivage; **to go** *or* **walk a. the street** marcher dans la rue; **a. here** par ici; *Fig* **somewhere a. the way** à un moment donné
2 *adv* **to move a.** avancer; **to hobble/ plod a.** avancer en boitant/péniblement; **I'll be** *or* **come a. shortly** je viendrai tout à l'heure; **come a.!** venez donc!; **to bring sth a.** apporter qch; **to bring sb a.** amener qn; **all a.** *(all the time)* dès le début; *(all the way)* d'un bout à l'autre; **a. with** ainsi que

alongside [əlɒŋ'saɪd] *prep & adv* à côté (de); *Naut* **to come a.** *(of ship)* accoster; **a. the kerb** le long du trottoir

aloof [ə'luːf] **1** *adj* distant
2 *adv* à distance; **to keep a. (from sth)** rester à l'écart (de qch) • **aloofness** *n* réserve *f*

aloud [ə'laʊd] *adv* à haute voix

alphabet ['ælfəbet] *n* alphabet *m* • **alpha'betical** *adj* alphabétique

Alps [ælps] *npl* **the A.** les Alpes *fpl* • **Alpine** ['ælpaɪn] *adj (club, range)* alpin; *(scenery)* alpestre

already [ɔːl'redɪ] *adv* déjà

alright [ɔːl'raɪt] *adv Fam* = **all right**

Alsatian [æl'seɪʃən] *n (dog)* berger *m* allemand

also ['ɔːlsəʊ] *adv* aussi, également; *(moreover)* de plus • **also-ran** *n (person)* perdant, -ante *mf*

altar ['ɔːltə(r)] *n* autel *m*

alter ['ɔːltə(r)] **1** *vt* changer; *(clothing)* retoucher
2 *vi* changer • **alteration** [-'reɪʃən] *n* changement *m* (**in** de); *(of clothing)* retouche *f*; **alterations** *(to building)* travaux *mpl*

altercation [ɔːltə'keɪʃən] *n* altercation *f*

alternate 1 ['ɔːltəneɪt] [ɔːl'tɜːnət] *adj* alterné; **on a. days** tous les deux jours
2 *vt* faire alterner
3 *vi* alterner (**with** avec); *El* **alternating current** courant *m* alternatif • **alternately** *adv* alternativement • **alternation** [-'neɪʃən] *n* alternance *f*

alternative [ɔːl'tɜːnətɪv] **1** *adj (other)* de remplacement; **an a. way** une autre façon; **a. answers** d'autres réponses (possibles); **a. energy** énergies *fpl* de substitution; **a. medicine** médecine *f* douce
2 *n (choice)* alternative *f*; **she had no a. but to obey** elle n'a pas pu faire autrement que d'obéir • **alternatively** *adv* **(or) a.** *(or else)* ou alors, ou bien

although [ɔːl'ðəʊ] *adv* bien que (+ *subjunctive)*

altitude ['æltɪtjuːd] *n* altitude *f*

altogether [ɔːltə'geðə(r)] *adv (completely)* tout à fait; *(on the whole)* somme toute; **how much a.?** combien en tout?

aluminium [*Br* æljʊ'mɪnɪəm] *(Am* **aluminum** [ə'luːmɪnəm]*) n* aluminium *m*

alumnus [ə'lʌmnəs] *(pl* **-ni** [-naɪ]*) n Am* ancien(ne) élève *mf*

always ['ɔːlweɪz] *adv* toujours; **he's a. criticizing** il est toujours à critiquer; **as a.** comme toujours

am [æm, *unstressed* əm] *see* **be**

a.m. [eɪ'em] *adv* du matin

amalgam [ə'mælgəm] *n (mix)* amalgame *m*

amalgamate [ə'mælgəmeɪt] *vti* fusionner

amass [ə'mæs] *vt (riches)* amasser

amateur ['æmətə(r)] **1** *n* amateur *m*

2 *adj (interest, sports, performance)* d'amateur; **a. painter/actress** peintre *m/* actrice *f* amateur • **amateurish** *adj Pej (work)* d'amateur • **amateurism** *n* amateurisme *m*

amaze [əˈmeɪz] *vt* stupéfier • **amazed** *adj* stupéfait (**at sth** de qch); *(filled with wonder)* émerveillé; **a. at seeing** stupéfait de voir; **I was a. by his courage** son courage m'a stupéfié • **amazing** *adj (surprising)* stupéfiant; *(incredible)* extraordinaire • **amazingly** *adv* extraordinairement; *(miraculously)* par miracle

amazement [əˈmeɪzmənt] *n* stupéfaction *f*; *(sense of wonder)* émerveillement *m*; **to my a.** à ma grande stupéfaction

ambassador [æmˈbæsədə(r)] *n (man)* ambassadeur *m*; *(woman)* ambassadrice *f*

amber [ˈæmbə(r)] *n* ambre *m*; **a. (light)** *(of traffic signal)* (feu *m*) orange *m*; **the lights are at a.** le feu est à l'orange

ambidextrous [æmbɪˈdekstrəs] *adj* ambidextre

ambiguous [æmˈbɪgjʊəs] *adj* ambigu (*f* ambiguë) • **ambiguously** *adv* de façon ambiguë • **ambiguity** [-ˈgjuːɪtɪ] *n* ambiguïté *f*

ambition [æmˈbɪʃən] *n* ambition *f* • **ambitious** *adj* ambitieux, -ieuse

ambivalent [æmˈbɪvələnt] *adj* ambivalent

amble [ˈæmbəl] *vi* marcher d'un pas tranquille

ambulance [ˈæmbjʊləns] *n* ambulance *f*; **a. driver** ambulancier, -ière *mf*

ambush [ˈæmbʊʃ] **1** *n* embuscade *f* **2** *vt* tendre une embuscade à; **to be ambushed** tomber dans une embuscade

amen [*Br* ɑːˈmen, *Am* eɪˈmen] *exclam* amen

amenable [əˈmiːnəbəl] *adj* docile; **a. to** *(responsive to)* sensible à; **a. to reason** raisonnable

amend [əˈmend] *vt (text)* modifier; *Pol (law)* amender; *(conduct)* corriger • **amendment** *n Pol (to law, rule)* amendement *m*

amends [əˈmendz] *npl* **to make a.** se racheter; **to make a. for sth** réparer qch

amenities [*Br* əˈmiːnɪtɪz, *Am* əˈmenɪtɪz] *npl (pleasant things)* agréments *mpl*; *(of sports club)* équipement *m*; *(of town)* aménagements *mpl*; *(shops)* commerces *mpl*

America [əˈmerɪkə] *n* l'Amérique *f*; **North/South A.** l'Amérique du Nord/du Sud • **American 1** *adj* américain **2** *n* Amé-ricain, -aine *mf* • **Americanism** *n* américanisme *m*

amethyst [ˈæməθɪst] *n* améthyste *f*

amiable [ˈeɪmɪəbəl] *adj* aimable

amicable [ˈæmɪkəbəl] *adj* amical • **amicably** *adv (part)* amicalement; *Law (settle a dispute)* à l'amiable

amid(st) [əˈmɪd(st)] *prep* au milieu de, parmi

amiss [əˈmɪs] *adv & adj* **to take sth a.** mal prendre qch; **something is a.** *(wrong)* quelque chose ne va pas; **that wouldn't come a.** ça ne ferait pas de mal

ammonia [əˈməʊnɪə] *n (gas)* ammoniac *m*; *(liquid)* ammoniaque *f*

ammunition [æmjʊˈnɪʃən] *n* munitions *fpl*

amnesia [æmˈniːzɪə] *n* amnésie *f*

amnesty [ˈæmnəstɪ] (*pl* **-ies**) *n* amnistie *f*

amniocentesis [æmnɪəʊsenˈtiːsɪs] *n* amniocentèse *f*

amok [əˈmɒk] *adv* **to run a.** *(of crowd)* se déchaîner; *(of person, animal)* devenir fou furieux (*f* folle furieuse)

among(st) [əˈmʌŋ(st)] *prep (amidst)* parmi; *(between)* entre; **a. the crowd/ books/others/etc** parmi la foule/les livres/les autres/etc; **a. themselves/ friends** entre eux/amis; **a. other things** entre autres (choses)

amoral [eɪˈmɒrəl] *adj* amoral

amorous [ˈæmərəs] *adj (look, words)* polisson, -onne; *(person)* d'humeur polissonne; *(adventure)* amoureux, -euse

amount [əˈmaʊnt] **1** *n* quantité *f*; *(sum of money)* somme *f*; *(total figure of invoice, debt)* montant *m*; *(scope, size)* importance *f*

2 *vi* **to a. to** *(bill)* s'élever à; *Fig* **it amounts to blackmail** ce n'est rien d'autre que du chantage; **it amounts to the same thing** ça revient au même

amp [æmp] *n (unit of electricity)* ampère *m*; *Br* **3-a. plug** prise *f* avec fusible de 3 ampères

amphibian [æmˈfɪbɪən] *n & adj* amphibie *(m)* • **amphibious** *adj* amphibie

amphitheatre [ˈæmfɪθɪətə(r)] *n (Greek, Roman)* amphithéâtre *m*

ample [ˈæmpəl] *adj* (**a**) *(plentiful)* abondant; **to have a. time to do sth** avoir largement le temps de faire qch; **that's (quite) a.** c'est largement suffisant (**b**) *(large)* (woman, bosom) fort (**c**) *(roomy)* (garment) large • **amply** *adv* largement, amplement

amplify [ˈæmplɪfaɪ] (*pt & pp* **-ied**) *vt*

(essay, remarks) développer; *(sound)* amplifier • **amplifier** *n* amplificateur *m*
amputate [ˈæmpjʊteɪt] *vt* amputer; **to a. sb's hand**/*etc* amputer qn de la main/*etc* • **amputation** [-ˈteɪʃən] *n* amputation *f*
amuck [əˈmʌk] *adv see* amok
amuse [əˈmjuːz] *vt* amuser; **to keep sb amused** distraire qn • **amusement** *n* amusement *m*, divertissement *m*; *(pastime)* distraction *f*; **amusements** *(at fairground)* attractions *fpl*; *(gambling machines)* machines *fpl* à sous; **a. arcade** salle *f* de jeux; **a. park** parc *m* d'attractions • **amusing** *adj* amusant
an [æn, *unstressed* ən] *see* a
anachronism [əˈnækrənɪzəm] *n* anachronisme *m*
an(a)emia [əˈniːmɪə] *n* anémie *f* • **an(a)emic** *adj* anémique; **to become a.** faire de l'anémie
an(a)esthesia [ænɪsˈθiːzɪə] *n* anesthésie *f* • **an(a)esthetic** [ænɪsˈθetɪk] *n* *(process)* anesthésie *f*; *(substance)* anesthésique *m*; **under a.** sous anesthésie; **general**/ **local a.** anesthésie générale/locale • **an(a)esthetize** [əˈniːsθɪtaɪz] *vt* anesthésier
anagram [ˈænəgræm] *n* anagramme *f*
anal [ˈeɪnəl] *adj* anal
analogy [əˈnælədʒɪ] *(pl* **-ies***) n* analogie *f* (**with** avec) • **analogous** *adj* analogue (**to** à)
analyse [ˈænəlaɪz] *vt* analyser • **analysis** [əˈnæləsɪs] *(pl* **-yses** [-əsiːz]*) n* analyse *f*; *Fig* **in the final a.** en fin de compte • **analyst** [-lɪst] *n* analyste *mf* • **analytical** [-ˈlɪtɪkəl] *adj* analytique
anarchy [ˈænəkɪ] *n* anarchie *f* • **anarchic** [æˈnɑːkɪk] *adj* anarchique • **anarchist** *n* anarchiste *mf*
anathema [əˈnæθəmə] *n Rel* anathème *m*; **it is (an) a. to me** j'ai une sainte horreur de cela
anatomy [əˈnætəmɪ] *n* anatomie *f* • **anatomical** [ænəˈtɒmɪkəl] *adj* anatomique
ancestor [ˈænsestə(r)] *n* ancêtre *m* • **ancestral** [-ˈsestrəl] *adj* ancestral; **a. home** demeure *f* ancestrale • **ancestry** *n (lineage)* ascendance *f*; *(ancestors)* ancêtres *mpl*
anchor [ˈæŋkə(r)] **1** *n* ancre *f*; **to drop a.** jeter l'ancre; **to weigh a.** lever l'ancre **2** *vt (ship)* mettre à l'ancre **3** *vi* jeter l'ancre, mouiller • **anchorage** *n* mouillage *m* • **anchored** *adj* ancré, à l'ancre
anchovy [*Br* ˈæntʃəvɪ, *Am* ænˈtʃəʊvɪ] *(pl* **-ies***) n* anchois *m*

ancient [ˈeɪnʃənt] *adj* ancien, -ienne; *(pre-medieval)* antique; *Hum (person)* d'un grand âge; *Fig* **that's a. history!** c'est de l'histoire ancienne!
ancillary [ænˈsɪlərɪ] *adj* auxiliaire
and [ænd, *unstressed* ən(d)] *conj* et; **a knife a. fork** un couteau et une fourchette; **my mother a. father** mon père et ma mère; **two hundred a.** **two** deux cent deux; **four a. three quarters** quatre trois quarts; **nice a. warm** bien chaud; **better a. better** de mieux en mieux; **she can read a. write** elle sait lire et écrire; **go a. see** va voir; **I knocked a.** knocked j'ai frappé pendant un bon moment
anecdote [ˈænɪkdəʊt] *n* anecdote *f*
anemia [əˈniːmɪə] *n* = anaemia
anemic [əˈniːmɪk] *adj* = anaemic
anemone [əˈnemənɪ] *n* anémone *f*
anesthesia [ænɪsˈθiːzɪə] *n* = anaethesia
anesthetic [ænɪsˈθetɪk] *n* = anaesthetic
anesthetize [əˈniːsθɪtaɪz] *vt* = anaesthetize
anew [əˈnjuː] *adv Literary* de nouveau; **to start a.** recommencer
angel [ˈeɪndʒəl] *n* ange *m* • **angelic** [ænˈdʒelɪk] *adj* angélique
anger [ˈæŋgə(r)] **1** *n* colère *f*; **in a., out of a.** sous le coup de la colère **2** *vt* mettre en colère
angina [ænˈdʒaɪnə] *n* angine *f* de poitrine
angle¹ [ˈæŋgəl] *n* angle *m*; **at an a.** en biais; *Fig* **seen from this a.** vu sous cet angle
angle² [ˈæŋgəl] *vi (to fish)* pêcher à la ligne; *Fig* **to a. for** *(compliments)* quêter • **angler** *n* pêcheur, -euse *mf* à la ligne • **angling** *n* pêche *f* à la ligne
Anglican [ˈæŋglɪkən] *adj & n* anglican, -ane *(mf)*
anglicism [ˈæŋglɪsɪzəm] *n* anglicisme *m*
Anglo- [ˈæŋgləʊ] *pref* anglo- • **Anglo-** **'Saxon** *adj & n* anglo-saxon, -onne *(mf)*
angora [æŋˈgɔːrə] *n (wool)* angora *m*; **a.** **sweater**/*etc* pull *m*/*etc* en angora
angry [ˈæŋgrɪ] **(-ier, -iest)** *adj (person)* en colère, fâché; *(look)* furieux, -ieuse; **an a.** **letter** une lettre indignée; **a. words** des paroles indignées; **to get a.** se fâcher (**with** contre) • **angrily** *adv (leave)* en colère; *(speak)* avec colère
anguish [ˈæŋgwɪʃ] *n* angoisse *f* • **anguished** *adj (look, voice)* angoissé; *(cry)* d'angoisse
angular [ˈæŋgjʊlə(r)] *adj (face)* anguleux, -euse

animal ['ænɪməl] **1** adj (kingdom, fat) animal **2** n animal m
animate 1 ['ænɪmeɪt] vt animer **2** ['ænɪmət] adj (alive) animé • **animated** [-meɪtɪd] adj (lively) animé; **to become a.** s'animer • **animation** [-'meɪʃən] n (liveliness) & Cin animation f
animosity [ænɪ'mɒsɪtɪ] n animosité f
aniseed ['ænɪsiːd] n (as flavouring) anis m; **a. drink** boisson f à l'anis
ankle ['æŋkəl] n cheville f; **a. sock** socquette f
annals ['ænəlz] npl annales fpl
annex¹ [ə'neks] vt annexer • **annexation** [ænek'seɪʃən] n annexion f
annex², Br annexe ['æneks] n (building) annexe f
annihilate [ə'naɪəleɪt] vt anéantir • **annihi'lation** n anéantissement m
anniversary [ænɪ'vɜːsərɪ] (pl -ies) n (of event) anniversaire m
annotate ['ænəteɪt] vt annoter • **annotation** [-'teɪʃən] n annotation f
announce [ə'naʊns] vt annoncer; (birth, marriage) faire part de • **announcement** n (statement) annonce f; (notice of birth, marriage, death) avis m; (private letter) faire-part m inv • **announcer** n (on TV) speaker m, speakerine f
annoy [ə'nɔɪ] vt (inconvenience) ennuyer; (irritate) agacer • **annoyance** n contrariété f, ennui m • **annoyed** adj fâché; **to get a.** se fâcher (**with** contre) • **annoying** adj ennuyeux, -euse
annual ['ænjʊəl] **1** adj annuel, -uelle **2** n (yearbook) annuaire m; (children's) album m; (plant) plante f annuelle • **annually** adv (every year) tous les ans; (per year) par an
annuity [ə'njʊətɪ] (pl -ies) n (of retired person) pension f viagère
annul [ə'nʌl] (pt & pp -ll-) vt (contract, marriage) annuler • **annulment** n annulation f
anoint [ə'nɔɪnt] vt oindre (**with** de) • **anointed** adj oint
anomalous [ə'nɒmələs] adj anormal • **anomaly** (pl -ies) n anomalie f
anon [ə'nɒn] adv Literary or Hum tout à l'heure
anonymous [ə'nɒnɪməs] adj anonyme; **to remain a.** garder l'anonymat • **anonymity** [ænə'nɪmɪtɪ] n anonymat m
anorak ['ænəræk] n anorak m
anorexia [ænə'reksɪə] n anorexie f • **anorexic** adj & n anorexique (mf)
another [ə'nʌðə(r)] adj & pron un(e)

autre; **a. man** (different) un autre homme; **a. month** (additional) encore un mois; **a. ten** encore dix; **one a.** l'un(e) l'autre, pl les un(e)s les autres; **they love one a.** ils s'aiment
answer ['ɑːnsə(r)] **1** n réponse f; (to problem, riddle) & Math solution f (**to** de); (reason) explication f; **in a. to your letter** en réponse à votre lettre **2** vt (person, question, letter) répondre à; (prayer, wish) exaucer; **he answered 'yes'** il a répondu 'oui'; **to a. the bell** or **the door** ouvrir la porte; **to a. the phone** répondre au téléphone; **to a. sb back** (be rude to) répondre à qn **3** vi répondre; **to a. back** (rudely) répondre, répliquer; **to a. for sb/sth** (be responsible for) répondre de qn/qch; **to a. (to) a description** (of suspect) correspondre à un signalement • **answering machine** n répondeur m
answerable ['ɑːnsərəbəl] adj responsable (**for sth** de qch; **to sb** devant qn)
ant [ænt] n fourmi f • **anthill** n fourmilière f
antagonism [æn'tægənɪzəm] n (hostility) hostilité f • **antagonist** n adversaire mf • **antago'nistic** adj (hostile) hostile (**to** à) • **antagonize** vt provoquer (l'hostilité de)
Antarctic [æn'tɑːktɪk] **1** adj antarctique **2** n **the A.** l'Antarctique m
antecedent [æntɪ'siːdənt] n antécédent m
antechamber ['æntɪtʃeɪmbə(r)] n antichambre f
antedate ['æntɪdeɪt] vt (letter) antidater
antelope ['æntɪləʊp] n antilope f
antenatal [æntɪ'neɪtəl] Br **1** adj prénatal; **a. classes** préparation f à l'accouchement **2** n examen m prénatal
antenna¹ [æn'tenə] (pl -ae [-iː]) n (of insect) antenne f
**antenna², [æn'tenə] (pl -as) n Am (for TV, radio) antenne f
anteroom ['æntɪrʊm] n antichambre f
anthem ['ænθəm] n **national a.** hymne m national
anthology [æn'θɒlədʒɪ] (pl -ies) n anthologie f
anthropology [ænθrə'pɒlədʒɪ] n anthropologie f
anti- [Br 'æntɪ, Am 'æntaɪ] pref anti-; Fam **to be anti sth** être contre qch • **antiaircraft** adj antiaérien, -ienne • **antibiotic** [-baɪ'ɒtɪk] adj & n antibiotique (m) • **antibody** n anticorps m • **anticlimax** n déception f • **anticlockwise** adv Br dans le

sens inverse des aiguilles d'une montre ● **anticyclone** n anticyclone m ● **antidote** n antidote m ● **antifreeze** n (for vehicle) antigel m ● **antihistamine** n (drug) antihistaminique m ● **antiperspirant** n antisudoral m ● **anti-Semitic** adj antisémite ● **anti-Semitism** n antisémitisme m ● **antiseptic** adj & n antiseptique (m) ● **antisocial** adj (misfit) asocial; (measure, principles) antisocial; (unsociable) peu sociable

anticipate [æn'tɪsɪpeɪt] vt (foresee) anticiper; (expect) s'attendre à, prévoir; (forestall) devancer ● **antici'pation** n (expectation) attente f; (foresight) prévision f; **in a. of** en prévision de; **in a.** (thank, pay) d'avance

antics ['æntɪks] npl singeries fpl; **he's up to his a. again** il a encore fait des siennes

antipathy [æn'tɪpəθɪ] n antipathie f

antipodes [æn'tɪpədiːz] npl antipodes mpl

antiquarian [æntɪ'kweərɪən] adj **a. bookseller** libraire mf spécialisé(e) dans le livre ancien

antiquated ['æntɪkweɪtɪd] adj (expression, custom) vieillot, -otte; (person) vieux jeu inv; (object, machine) antédiluvien, -ienne

antique [æn'tiːk] **1** adj (furniture) ancien, -ienne; (of Greek or Roman antiquity) antique; **a. dealer** antiquaire mf; **a. shop** magasin m d'antiquités **2** n antiquité f, objet m d'époque ● **antiquity** [-'tɪkwɪtɪ] n (period) antiquité f

antithesis [æn'tɪθəsɪs] (pl -eses [-ɪsiːz]) n antithèse f

antlers ['æntləz] npl (of deer) bois mpl

antonym ['æntənɪm] n antonyme m

Antwerp ['æntwɜːp] n Anvers m ou f

anus ['eɪnəs] n anus m

anvil ['ænvɪl] n enclume f

anxiety [æŋ'zaɪətɪ] (pl -ies) n (worry) inquiétude f (**about** au sujet de); (fear) anxiété f; (eagerness) désir m (**to do** de faire; **for sth** de qch)

anxious ['æŋkʃəs] adj (worried) inquiet, -iète (**about/for** pour); (troubled) anxieux, -ieuse; (causing worry) angoissant; (eager) impatient (**to do** de faire); **I'm a. (that) he should leave** je tiens absolument à ce qu'il parte ● **anxiously** adv (worriedly) avec inquiétude; (with impatience) impatiemment

any ['enɪ] **1** adj (a) (in questions) du, de la, des; **have you a. milk/tickets?** avez-vous du lait/des billets?; **is there a. man (at all) who...?** y a-t-il un homme qui...?

(b) (in negatives) de; (not the slightest) aucun; **he hasn't got a. milk/tickets** il n'a pas de lait/de billets; **there isn't a. doubt/problem** il n'y a aucun doute/problème (c) (no matter which) n'importe quel; **ask a. doctor** demande à n'importe quel médecin (d) (every) tout; **at a. moment** à tout moment; **in a. case, at a. rate** de toute façon

2 pron (a) (no matter which one) n'importe lequel; (somebody) quelqu'un; **if a. of you...** si l'un d'entre vous..., si quelqu'un parmi vous...

(b) (quantity) en; **have you got a.?** en as-tu?; **I don't see a.** je n'en vois pas

3 adv not a. **further/happier** pas plus loin/plus heureux, -euse; **I don't see him a. more** je ne le vois plus; **a. more tea?** encore un peu de thé?; **I'm not a. better** je ne vais pas mieux

anybody ['enɪbɒdɪ] pron (a) (somebody) quelqu'un; **do you see a.?** tu vois quelqu'un?; **more than a.** plus que tout autre (b) (in negatives) personne; **he doesn't know a.** il ne connaît personne (c) (no matter who) n'importe qui; **a. would think that** on croirait que

anyhow ['enɪhaʊ] adv (at any rate) de toute façon; Fam (badly) n'importe comment

anyone ['enɪwʌn] pron = **anybody**

anyplace ['enɪpleɪs] adv Am = **anywhere**

anything ['enɪθɪŋ] pron (a) (something) quelque chose; **can you see a.?** tu vois quelque chose? (b) (in negatives) rien; **he doesn't do a.** il ne fait rien; **without a.** sans rien (c) (everything) tout; **a. you like** tout ce que tu veux; Fam **like a.** (work) comme un fou (d) (no matter what) **a. (at all)** n'importe quoi

anyway ['enɪweɪ] adv (at any rate) de toute façon

anywhere ['enɪweə(r)] adv (a) (no matter where) n'importe où (b) (everywhere) partout; **a. you go** où que vous alliez, partout où vous allez; **a. you like** (là) où tu veux (c) (somewhere) quelque part; **is he going a.?** va-t-il quelque part? (d) (in negatives) nulle part; **he doesn't go a.** il ne va nulle part; **without a. to put it** sans un endroit où le/la mettre

apace [ə'peɪs] adv rapidement

apart [ə'pɑːt] adv (a) (separated) **we kept them a.** nous les tenions séparés; **with legs (wide) a.** les jambes écartées; **two years a.** à deux ans d'intervalle; **they are a metre a.** ils se trouvent à un mètre l'un de l'autre; **to come a.** (of two objects) se séparer; **to tell two things/people a.** distinguer deux choses/personnes (l'une de l'autre); **worlds a.** *(very different)* diamétralement opposé

(**b**) *(to pieces)* **to tear a.** mettre en pièces; **to take a.** démonter

(**c**) *(to one side)* à part; **joking a.** sans blague; **a. from** *(except for)* à part

apartheid [ə'pɑːteɪt] *n* apartheid *m*

apartment [ə'pɑːtmənt] *n* appartement *m; Am* **a. building, a. house** immeuble *m* (d'habitation)

apathy ['æpəθɪ] *n* apathie *f* ● **apa'thetic** *adj* apathique

ape [eɪp] **1** *n* grand singe *m*
2 *vt (imitate)* singer

aperitif [əperɪ'tiːf] *n* apéritif *m*

aperture ['æpətʃʊə(r)] *n* ouverture *f*

APEX ['eɪpeks] *adj* **A. ticket** = billet d'avion ou de train à tarif réduit, soumis à certaines restrictions

apex ['eɪpeks] *n (of triangle) & Fig* sommet *m*

aphorism ['æfərɪzəm] *n* aphorisme *m*

aphrodisiac [æfrə'dɪzɪæk] *adj & n* aphrodisiaque *(m)*

apiece [ə'piːs] *adv* chacun; **£1 a.** 1 livre pièce *ou* chacun

apish ['eɪpɪʃ] *adj* simiesque; *(imitative)* imitateur, -trice

apocalypse [ə'pɒkəlɪps] *n* apocalypse *f* ● **apoca'lyptic** *adj* apocalyptique

apocryphal [ə'pɒkrɪfəl] *adj* apocryphe

apologetic [əpɒlə'dʒetɪk] *adj (letter)* plein d'excuses; **a. smile** sourire *m* d'excuse; **to be a. (about)** s'excuser (de) ● **apologetically** *adv* en s'excusant

apology [ə'pɒlədʒɪ] *(pl* **-ies)** *n* excuses *fpl; Fam Pej* **an a. for a dinner** un dîner minable ● **apologize** *vi* s'excuser (**for** de); **he apologized for being late** il s'est excusé de son retard; **to a. to sb** faire ses excuses à qn (**for** pour)

Ɵ Note that the French noun **apologie** is a false friend and is never a translation for the English verb **apology**. It means **defence**.

---

apoplexy ['æpəpleksɪ] *n* apoplexie *f* ● **apo'plectic** *adj & n* apoplectique *(mf)*

apostle [ə'pɒsəl] *n* apôtre *m*

apostrophe [ə'pɒstrəfɪ] *n* apostrophe *f*

appal [ə'pɔːl] *(Am* **appall**) *(pt & pp* **-ll-**) *vt* consterner; **to be appalled (at)** être horrifié (par) ● **appalling** *adj* épouvantable

apparatus [æpə'reɪtəs] *n (equipment, organization)* appareil *m; Br (in gym)* agrès *mpl*

apparent [ə'pærənt] *adj (seeming)* appa-

rent; *(obvious)* évident; **it's a. that...** il est clair que... ● **apparently** *adv* apparemment; **a. she's going to Venice** il paraît qu'elle va à Venise

apparition [æpə'rɪʃən] *n (phantom)* apparition *f*

appeal [ə'piːl] **1** *n (charm)* attrait *m; (interest)* intérêt *m; (call)* appel *m; (pleading)* supplication *f; (to a court)* appel *m*
2 *vt* **to a. to sb** *(attract)* plaire à qn; *(interest)* intéresser qn; *(ask for help)* faire appel à qn; **to a. to sb's generosity** appel à la générosité de qn; **to a. to sb for sth** demander qch à qn; **to a. to sb to do sth** supplier qn de faire
3 *vi (in court)* faire appel; **to a. against a decision** faire appel d'une décision ● **appealing** *adj (attractive) (offer, idea)* séduisant; *(begging) (look)* suppliant

---

Ɵ Note that the French verb **appeler** is a false friend and is never a translation for the English verb **to appeal**. Its most common meaning is **to call**.

---

appear [ə'pɪə(r)] *vi (become visible)* apparaître; *(seem, be published)* paraître; *(on stage, in film)* jouer; *(in court)* comparaître; **it appears that...** *(it seems)* il semble que... *(+ subjunctive or indicative);* *(it is rumoured)* il paraîtrait que... *(+indicative)* ● **appearance** *n (act)* apparition *f; (look)* apparence *f; (of book)* parution *f;* **to put in an a.** faire acte de présence; **to keep up appearances** sauver les apparences

appease [ə'piːz] *vt (soothe)* apaiser; *(curiosity)* satisfaire

append [ə'pend] *vt* joindre, ajouter (**to** à) ● **appendage** *n Anat* appendice *m*

appendix [ə'pendɪks] *(pl* **-ixes** [-ɪksɪz] *or* **-ices** [-ɪsiːz]) *n (in book, body)* appendice *m;* **to have one's a. out** se faire opérer de l'appendicite ● **appendicitis** [-dɪ'saɪtɪs] *n* appendicite *f*

appetite ['æpɪtaɪt] *n* appétit *m;* **to take away sb's a.** couper l'appétit à qn ● **appetizer** *n (drink)* apéritif *m; (food)* amuse-gueule *m inv* ● **appetizing** *adj* appétissant

applaud [ə'plɔːd] **1** *vt (clap)* applaudir; *(approve of)* approuver, applaudir à
2 *vi* applaudir ● **applause** *n* applaudissements *mpl*

apple ['æpəl] *n* pomme *f; Br* **stewed apples,** *Am* **a. sauce** compote *f* de pommes; **cooking a.** pomme *f* à cuire; **eating a.** pomme de dessert; **a. core** trognon *m* de pomme; **a. pie** tarte *f* aux pommes; **a. tree** pommier *m*

appliance [ə'plaɪəns] n appareil m
applicable [ə'plɪkəbəl] adj (rule) applicable (**to** à); (relevant) pertinent
applicant ['æplɪkənt] n candidat, -ate mf (**for** à)
application [æplɪ'keɪʃən] n (**a**) (request) demande f (**for** de); (for job) candidature f (**for** de); (for membership) demande d'inscription; **a. (form)** (for job) formulaire m de candidature; (for club) formulaire d'inscription (**b**) (diligence) application f
apply [ə'plaɪ] (pt & pp **-ied**) **1** vt (put on, carry out) appliquer; (brake of vehicle) appuyer sur; **to a. oneself to** s'appliquer à **2** vi (be relevant) s'appliquer (**to** à); **to a. for** (job) poser sa candidature à; **to a. to sb** (ask) s'adresser à qn (**for** pour) • **applied** adj (math, linguistics) appliqué
appoint [ə'pɔɪnt] vt (person) nommer (**to a post** à un poste; **to do** pour faire); (director, minister) nommer; (secretary, clerk) engager; (time, place) fixer; **at the appointed time** à l'heure dite; **well-appointed** (kitchen) bien équipé • **appointment** n nomination f; (meeting) rendez-vous m inv; (post) situation f; **to make an a. with** prendre rendez-vous avec

> ♬ Note that the French noun **appointements** is a false friend and is never a translation for the English noun **appointment**. It means **salary**.

apportion [ə'pɔːʃən] vt répartir; **to a. blame** dégager les responsabilités de chacun
appraise [ə'preɪz] vt évaluer • **appraisal** n évaluation f
appreciable [ə'priːʃəbəl] adj appréciable, sensible
appreciate [ə'priːʃɪeɪt] **1** vt (enjoy, value, assess) apprécier; (understand) comprendre; (be grateful for) être reconnaissant de **2** vi (of goods) prendre de la valeur • **appreciation** [-'eɪʃən] n (**a**) (gratitude) reconnaissance f; (judgement) appréciation f (**b**) (rise in value) augmentation f (de la valeur) • **appreciative** [-ʃɪətɪv] adj (grateful) reconnaissant (**of** de); (favourable) élogieux, -ieuse; **to be a. of** (enjoy) apprécier
apprehend [æprɪ'hend] vt (seize, arrest) appréhender
apprehension [æprɪ'henʃən] n (fear) appréhension f • **apprehensive** adj inquiet,

-iète (**about** de, au sujet de); **to be a. of** appréhender
apprentice [ə'prentɪs] **1** n apprenti, -ie mf **2** vt **to a. sb to sb** placer qn en apprentissage chez qn • **apprenticeship** n apprentissage m
approach [ə'prəʊtʃ] **1** n (method) façon f de s'y prendre; (path, route) voie f d'accès; (of winter, vehicle) approche f; **at the a. of** à l'approche de; **a. to a question** manière f d'aborder une question; **to make approaches to** faire des démarches auprès de; (sexually) faire des avances à **2** vt (draw near to) s'approcher de; (go up to, tackle) aborder; **to a. sb about sth** parler à qn de qch; **he's approaching forty** il va sur ses quarante ans **3** vi (of person, vehicle) s'approcher; (of date) approcher • **approachable** adj (person) d'un abord facile; (place) accessible (**by road** par la route)
appropriate 1 [ə'prəʊprɪət] adj (place, clothes, means) approprié (**to** à); (remark, time) opportun; **a. to** or **for** qui convient à **2** [ə'prəʊprɪeɪt] vt (steal) s'approprier; (set aside) affecter (**for** à) • **appropriately** adv convenablement
approval [ə'pruːvəl] n approbation f; **on a.** (goods) à l'essai
approve [ə'pruːv] vt approuver; **to a. of** (conduct, decision, idea) approuver; **I don't a. of him** il ne me plaît pas; **I a. of his going** je trouve bon qu'il y aille; **I a. of his accepting** or **having accepted** je l'approuve d'avoir accepté • **approving** adj (look) approbateur, -trice
approximate 1 [ə'prɒksɪmət] adj approximatif, -ive **2** [ə'prɒksɪmeɪt] vi **to a. to sth** se rapprocher de qch • **approximately** adv approximativement • **approxi'mation** n approximation f
apricot ['eɪprɪkɒt] n abricot m
April ['eɪprəl] n avril m; **to make an A. fool of sb** faire un poisson d'avril à qn; **A. fool!** poisson d'avril!
apron ['eɪprən] n (garment) tablier m
apse [æps] n (of church) abside f
apt [æpt] adj (remark, reply, means) qui convient; (word, name) bien choisi; **she/it is a. to fall** /etc (likely) (in general) elle/ça a tendance à tomber/etc; (on a particular occasion) elle/ça pourrait bien tomber/etc; **a. at sth** (manual work) habile à qch; (intellectual) doué pour qch • **aptly** adv (described) justement; (cho-

sen) bien; **a. named** qui porte bien son nom

aptitude ['æptɪtjuːd] *n* aptitude *f* (**for** pour); *(of student)* don *m* (**for** pour)

aqualung ['ækwəlʌŋ] *n* scaphandre *m* autonome

aquarium [ə'kweərɪəm] *n* aquarium *m*

Aquarius [ə'kweərɪəs] *n (sign)* le Verseau; **to be an A.** êtreVerseau

aquatic [ə'kwætɪk] *adj (plant)* aquatique; *(sport)* nautique

aqueduct ['ækwɪdʌkt] *n* aqueduc *m*

aquiline ['ækwɪlaɪn] *adj (nose, profile)* aquilin

Arab ['ærəb] **1** *adj* arabe
   2 *n* Arabe *mf* •**Arabian** [ə'reɪbɪən] *adj* arabe •**Arabic** *adj & n (language)* arabe *(m)*; **A. numerals** chiffres *mpl* arabes

arable ['ærəbəl] *adj (land)* arable

arbiter ['ɑːbɪtə(r)] *n* arbitre *m*

arbitrary ['ɑːbɪtrərɪ] *adj (decision, arrest)* arbitraire

arbitrate ['ɑːbɪtreɪt] *vti* arbitrer •**arbitration** [-'treɪʃən] *n* arbitrage *m*; **to go to a.** avoir recours à l'arbitrage •**arbitrator** *n (in dispute)* médiateur, -trice *mf*

arc [ɑːk] *n (of circle)* arc *m*

arcade [ɑː'keɪd] *n (for shops) (small)* passage *m* couvert; *(large)* galerie *f* marchande

arch [ɑːtʃ] **1** *n (of bridge)* arche *f*; *(of building)* voûte *f*, arc *m*; *(of foot)* cambrure *f*
   2 *vt* **to a. one's back** *(inwards)* se cambrer; *(outwards)* se voûter •**archway** *n* voûte *f*

arch- [ɑːtʃ] *pref (hypocrite)* achevé, fini; **a.-enemy** ennemi *m* juré; **a.-rival** grand rival *m*

arch(a)eology [ɑːkɪ'ɒlədʒɪ] *n* archéologie *f* •**arch(a)eologist** *n* archéologue *mf*

archaic [ɑː'keɪɪk] *adj* archaïque

archangel ['ɑːkeɪndʒəl] *n* archange *m*

archbishop [ɑːtʃ'bɪʃəp] *n* archevêque *m*

archeologist [ɑːkɪ'ɒlədʒɪst] *n* = **archaeologist**

archeology [ɑːkɪ'ɒlədʒɪ] *n* = **archaeology**

archer ['ɑːtʃə(r)] *n* archer *m* •**archery** *n* tir *m* à l'arc

archetype ['ɑːkɪtaɪp] *n* archétype *m*

archipelago [ɑːkɪ'peləgəʊ] *(pl* **-oes** or **-os***) n* archipel *m*

architect ['ɑːkɪtekt] *n* architecte *mf* •**architecture** *n* architecture *f*

archives ['ɑːkaɪvz] *npl* archives *fpl* •**archivist** ['ɑːkɪvɪst] *n* archiviste *mf*

arctic ['ɑːktɪk] **1** *adj* arctique; *(weather)* polaire, glacial
   2 *n* **the A.** l'Arctique *m*

ardent ['ɑːdənt] *adj (supporter)* ardent, chaud •**ardently** *adv* ardemment •**ardour** *n* ardeur *f*

arduous ['ɑːdjʊəs] *adj* pénible, ardu •**arduously** *adv* péniblement, ardument

are [ɑː(r)] *see* **be**

area ['eərɪə] *n (of country)* région *f*; *(of town)* quartier *m*; Mil zone *f*; *(surface)* superficie *f*; Fig *(of knowledge)* domaine *m*; **dining a.** coin-repas *m*; **kitchen a.** coincuisine *m*; **play a.** *(in house)* coin-jeux *m*; *(outdoors)* aire *f* de jeux; Am **a. code** *(in phone number)* indicatif *m*

arena [ə'riːnə] *n (for sports) &* Fig arène *f*

aren't [ɑːnt] = **are not**

Argentina [ɑːdʒən'tiːnə] *n* l'Argentine *f*

Argentine ['ɑːdʒəntaɪn] *n* Old-fashioned **the A.** l'Argentine *f* •**Argentinian** [-'tɪnɪən] **1** *adj* argentin **2** *n* Argentin, -ine *mf*

arguable ['ɑːgjʊəbəl] *adj* discutable •**arguably** *adv* **it is a. the...** on peut dire que c'est le/la...

argue ['ɑːgjuː] **1** *vt (matter)* discuter (de); *(position)* défendre; **to a. that...** soutenir que...
   2 *vi (quarrel)* se disputer (**with** avec); *(about)* au sujet de); *(reason)* raisonner (**with** avec; **about** sur); **to a. in favour of** plaider en faveur de; **don't a.!** ne discute pas!

argument ['ɑːgjʊmənt] *n (quarrel)* dispute *f*; *(debate)* discussion *f*; *(point)* argument *m*; **to have an a. with sb** *(quarrel)* se disputer avec qn •**argumentative** [-'mentətɪv] *adj (person)* querelleur, -euse

aria ['ɑːrɪə] *n* Mus aria *f*

arid ['ærɪd] *adj* aride

Aries ['eəriːz] *n (sign)* le Bélier; **to be A.** être Bélier

arise [ə'raɪz] *(pt* **arose,** *pp* **arisen** [ə'rɪzən]) *vi (of problem, opportunity)* se présenter; *(of cry, objection)* s'élever; *(result)* provenir (**from** de); Literary *(get up)* se lever

aristocracy [ærɪ'stɒkrəsɪ] *n* aristocratie *f* •**aristocrat** [Br 'ærɪstəkræt, Am ə'rɪstəkræt] *n* aristocrate *mf* •**aristocratic** [Br ærɪstə'krætɪk, Am ərɪstə'krætɪk] *adj* aristocratique

arithmetic [ə'rɪθmətɪk] *n* arithmétique *f*

ark [ɑːk] *n* Noah's a. l'arche *f* de Noé

arm[1] [ɑːm] *n* bras *m*; **a. in a.** bras dessus bras dessous; **with open arms** à bras ouverts •**armband** *n* brassard *m* •**arm-**

chair *n* fauteuil *m* •**armful** *n* brassée *f* •**armhole** *n* emmanchure *f* •**armpit** *n* aisselle *f* •**armrest** *n* accoudoir *m*

arm² [ɑːm] *vt (with weapon)* armer (**with** de) •**armaments** *npl* armements *mpl*

armadillo [ɑːməˈdɪləʊ] *(pl* -**os***) n* tatou *m*

armistice [ˈɑːmɪstɪs] *n* armistice *m*

armour [ˈɑːmə(r)] *n (of knight)* armure *f*; *(of tank)* blindage *m* •**armoured, armour-'plated** *adj (car)* blindé •**armoury** *n* arsenal *m*

arms [ɑːmz] *npl (weapons)* armes *fpl*; **the a. race** la course aux armements

army [ˈɑːmɪ] **1** *(pl* -**ies***) n* armée *f*; **to join the a.** s'engager; **the regular a.** l'armée active

2 *adj (uniform)* militaire

A road [ˈeɪrəʊd] *n Br* ≃ route *f* nationale

aroma [əˈrəʊmə] *n* arôme *m* •**aroma-'therapy** *n* aromathérapie *f* •**aromatic** [ærəˈmætɪk] *adj* aromatique

arose [əˈrəʊz] *pp of* **arise**

around [əˈraʊnd] **1** *prep* autour de; *(approximately)* environ; **to travel a. the world** faire le tour du monde

2 *adv* autour; **all a.** tout autour; **a. here** par ici; **to follow sb a.** suivre qn partout; **to rush a.** courir dans tous les sens; **is Jack a.?** est-ce que Jack est dans le coin?; **he's still a.** il est encore là; **there's a lot of flu a.** beaucoup de gens ont la grippe en ce moment

arouse [əˈraʊz] *vt (suspicion, anger, curiosity)* éveiller; *(sexually)* exciter; **to a. sb from sleep** tirer qn du sommeil

arrange [əˈreɪndʒ] *vt* arranger; *(time, meeting)* fixer; **it was arranged that...** il était convenu que...; **to a. to do sth** s'arranger pour faire qch •**arrangement** *n (layout, agreement, for music)* arrangement *m*; **arrangements** *(preparations)* préparatifs *mpl*; *(plans)* projets *mpl*; **to make arrangements to do sth** prendre des dispositions pour faire qch

arrears [əˈrɪəz] *npl (payment)* arriéré *m*; **to be in a.** avoir du retard dans ses paiements; **to be three months in a.** avoir trois mois de retard dans ses paiements; **to be paid monthly in a.** être payé à la fin du mois

arrest [əˈrest] **1** *vt (criminal, progress)* arrêter

2 *n (of criminal)* arrestation *f*; **under a.** en état d'arrestation •**arresting** *adj Fig (striking)* frappant

arrive [əˈraɪv] *vi* arriver; **to a. at** *(conclusion, decision)* arriver à, parvenir à •**arrival** *n* arrivée *f*; **on my a.** à mon arrivée;

new a. nouveau venu *m*, nouvelle venue *f*; *(baby)* nouveau-né, -ée *mf*

arrogant [ˈærəgənt] *adj* arrogant •**arrogance** *n* arrogance *f* •**arrogantly** *adv* avec arrogance

arrow [ˈærəʊ] *n* flèche *f*

arse [ɑːs] *n Br Vulg* cul *m*

arsenal [ˈɑːsənəl] *n* arsenal *m*

arsenic [ˈɑːsnɪk] *n* arsenic *m*

arson [ˈɑːsən] *n* incendie *m* criminel •**arsonist** *n* incendiaire *mf*

art [ɑːt] *n* art *m*; **faculty of arts, arts faculty** faculté *f* des lettres; **arts degree** ≃ licence *f* ès lettres; **a. exhibition** exposition *f* d'œuvres d'art; **a. gallery** *(museum)* musée *m*; *(shop)* galerie *f* d'art; **a. school** école *f* des beaux-arts

artefact [ˈɑːtɪfækt] *n* objet *m*

artery [ˈɑːtərɪ] *(pl* -**ies***) n (in body, main route)* artère *f* •**arterial** [ɑːˈtɪərɪəl] *adj (blood)* artériel, -ielle; *Br* **a. road** route *f* principale

artful [ˈɑːtfəl] *adj* astucieux, -ieuse •**artfully** *adv* astucieusement

arthritis [ɑːˈθraɪtɪs] *n* arthrite *f*

artichoke [ˈɑːtɪtʃəʊk] *n* **(globe) a.** artichaut *m*; **Jerusalem a.** topinambour *m*

article [ˈɑːtɪkəl] *n (object, clause, in newspaper) & Grammar* article *m*; **a. of clothing** vêtement *m*; **articles of value** objets *mpl* de valeur; *Br* **articles** *(of lawyer)* contrat *m* de stage

articulate 1 [ɑːˈtɪkjʊlət] *adj (person)* qui s'exprime clairement; *(speech)* clair

2 [ɑːˈtɪkjʊleɪt] *vti (speak)* articuler •**articulated lorry** *n Br* semi-remorque *m* •**articulation** [-ˈleɪʃən] *n* articulation *f*

artifact [ˈɑːtɪfækt] *n* objet *m*

artifice [ˈɑːtɪfɪs] *n* artifice *m*

artificial [ɑːtɪˈfɪʃəl] *adj* artificiel, -ielle •**artificiality** [-fɪʃɪˈælɪtɪ] *n* caractère *m* artificiel •**artificially** *adv* artificiellement

artillery [ɑːˈtɪlərɪ] *n* artillerie *f*

artisan [ɑːtɪˈzæn] *n* artisan *m*

artist [ˈɑːtɪst] *n* artiste *mf* •**artiste** [ɑːˈtiːst] *n (singer, dancer)* artiste *mf* •**ar'tistic** *adj (pattern, treasure)* artistique; *(person)* artiste •**artistry** *n* art *m*

artless [ˈɑːtləs] *adj* naturel, -elle

arty [ˈɑːtɪ] *adj Pej* du genre artiste

as [æz, *unstressed* əz] **1** *adv* (**a**) *(with manner)* comme; **as promised/planned** comme promis/prévu; **A as in Anne** A comme Anne; **as you like** comme tu veux; **such as** comme, tel que; **as much or as hard as I can** (au)tant que je peux; **as it is** *(this being the case)* les choses étant ainsi; **to leave sth as it is** laisser qch comme ça *ou* tel quel; **it's late as it is** il est déjà tard; **as if, as though** comme si; **you look as if** *or* **as though you're tired** tu as l'air fatigué

(**b**) *(comparison)* **as tall as you** aussi grand que vous; **as white as a sheet** blanc (*f* blanche) comme un linge; **as much** *or* **as hard as you** autant que vous; **as much money as** autant d'argent que; **as many people as** autant de gens que; **twice as big as** deux fois plus grand que; **the same as** le même que

2 *conj* (**a**) *(time)* **as always** comme toujours; **as I was leaving, as I left** comme je partais; **as one grows older** à mesure que l'on vieillit; **as he slept** pendant qu'il dormait; **one day as** un jour que; **as from, as of** *(time)* à partir de

(**b**) *(reason)* puisque, comme; **as it's late...** puisqu'il est tard..., comme il est tard...

(**c**) *(though)* **(as) clever as he is...** si intelligent qu'il soit...

(**d**) *(concerning)* **as for that, as to that** quant à cela

(**e**) (*+ infinitive*) **so as to...** de manière à...; **so stupid as to...** assez bête pour...

3 *prep* (**a**) comme; **she works as a cashier** elle travaille comme caissière, elle travaille comme caissière; **dressed up as a clown** déguisé en clown

(**b**) *(capacity)* **as a teacher** en tant que professeur; **to act as a father** agir en père

asap [eɪeseɪ'piː] *(abbr* **as soon as possible**) dès que possible

asbestos [æs'bestəs] *n* amiante *f*

ascend [ə'send] **1** *vt (throne)* accéder à; *(stairs, mountain)* gravir

2 *vi* monter • **ascent** *n* ascension *f* (**of** de); *(slope)* côte *f*

ascertain [æsə'teɪn] *vt (discover)* établir; *(truth)* découvrir; *(check)* s'assurer de; **to a. that...** s'assurer que...

ascetic [ə'setɪk] **1** *adj* ascétique

2 *n* ascète *mf*

ascribe [ə'skraɪb] *vt* attribuer (**to** à)

ash [æʃ] *n* (**a**) *(of cigarette, fire)* cendre *f*; **A. Wednesday** mercredi *m* des Cendres (**b**) *(tree)* frêne *m* • **ashtray** *n* cendrier *m*

ashamed [ə'ʃeɪmd] *adj* **to be/feel a.** avoir honte (**of sb/sth** de qn/qch); **to be a. of oneself** avoir honte; **to make sb a.** faire honte à qn

ashen ['æʃən] *adj (pale grey)* cendré; *(face)* blême

ashore [ə'ʃɔː(r)] *adv* à terre; **to go a.** débarquer; **to put sb a.** débarquer qn

Asia ['eɪʃə, 'eɪʒə] *n* l'Asie *f* • **Asian 1** *adj*

asiatique; *Br (from India)* indien, -ienne **2** *n* Asiatique *mf*; *Br (Indian)* Indien, -ienne *mf*

aside [ə'saɪd] **1** *adv* de côté; **to draw a.** *(curtain)* écarter; **to take** *or* **draw sb a.** prendre qn à part; **to step a.** s'écarter; *Am* **a. from** en dehors de

2 *n (in play, film)* aparté *m*

asinine ['æsɪnaɪn] *adj* stupide

ask [ɑːsk] **1** *vt (request, inquire about)* demander; *(invite)* inviter (**to sth** à qch); **to a. sb sth** demander qch à qn; **to a. sb about sb/sth** interroger qn sur qn/qch; **to a. (sb) a question** poser une question (à qn); **to a. sb the time/way** demander l'heure/son chemin à qn; **to a. sb for sth** demander qch à qn; **to a. sb to do** *(request)* demander à qn de faire; *(invite)* inviter qn à faire; **to a. to leave/***etc* demander à partir/*etc*

2 *vi (inquire)* se renseigner (**about** sur); *(request)* demander; **to a. for sb/sth** demander qn/qch; **to a. for sth back** redemander qch; **to a. after** *or* **about sb** demander des nouvelles de qn; **the asking price** le prix demandé

askance [ə'skɑːns] *adv* **to look a. at sb** regarder qn de travers

askew [ə'skjuː] *adv* de travers

asleep [ə'sliːp] *adj* endormi; *(arm, leg)* engourdi; **to be a.** dormir; **to fall a.** s'endormir

asparagus [ə'spærəgəs] *n (plant)* asperge *f*; *(for cooking)* asperges *fpl*

aspect ['æspekt] *n* aspect *m*; *(of house)* orientation *f*

aspersions [ə'spɜːʃənz] *npl* **to cast a. on** dénigrer

asphalt ['æsfɔːlt] *n* asphalte *m*

asphyxia [əs'fɪksɪə] *n* asphyxie *f* • **asphyxiate** *vt* asphyxier • **asphyxi'ation** *n* asphyxie *f*

aspire [ə'spaɪə(r)] *vi* **to a. to** aspirer à • **aspiration** [æspə'reɪʃən] *n* aspiration *f*

aspirin ['æsprɪn] *n* aspirine *f*

ass [æs] *n* (**a**) *(animal)* âne *m*; *Fam (person)* imbécile *mf*, âne; **she-a.** ânesse *f* (**b**) *Am Vulg* cul *m*

assail [ə'seɪl] *vt* assaillir (**with** de) • **assailant** *n* agresseur *m*

assassin [ə'sæsɪn] *n* assassin *m* • **assassinate** *vt* assassiner • **assassi'nation** *n* assassinat *m*

assault [ə'sɔːlt] **1** *n (military)* assaut *m*; *(crime)* agression *f*

2 *vt (attack)* agresser; **to be sexually assaulted** être victime d'une agression sexuelle

assemble [ə'sembəl] **1** *vt (objects, ideas)* assembler; *(people)* rassembler; *(machine)* monter
2 *vi* se rassembler • **assembly** *n (meeting)* assemblée *f*; *(of machine)* montage *m*, assemblage *m*; *(in school)* rassemblement *m (avant les cours)*; **a. line** *(in factory)* chaîne *f* de montage

assent [ə'sent] **1** *n* assentiment *m*
2 *vi* consentir (**to** à)

assert [ə'sɜːt] *vt* affirmer (**that** que); *(rights)* faire valoir; **to a. oneself** s'affirmer • **assertion** *n (statement)* affirmation *f*, *(of rights)* revendication *f* • **assertive** *adj (forceful) (tone, person)* affirmatif, -ive; *(authoritarian)* autoritaire

assess [ə'ses] *vt (value, damage)* évaluer; *(situation)* analyser; *(decide amount of)* fixer le montant de; *(person)* juger • **assessment** *n* évaluation *f*, *(of person)* jugement *m* • **assessor** *n (valuer)* expert *m*

asset ['æset] *n (advantage)* atout *m*; **assets** *(of business)* avoir *m*

assiduous [ə'sɪdjʊəs] *adj* assidu • **assiduously** *adv* avec assiduité

assign [ə'saɪn] *vt (give)* attribuer; *(day, time)* fixer; *(appoint)* nommer; *(send, move)* affecter (**to** à); **he was assigned as director** il a été nommé directeur • **assignment** *n (task)* mission *f*; *(for student)* devoir *m*

assimilate [ə'sɪmɪleɪt] **1** *vt (absorb)* assimiler
2 *vi (of immigrants)* s'assimiler • **assimilation** [-'leɪʃən] *n* assimilation *f*

assist [ə'sɪst] *vti* aider (**in doing** *or* **to do** à faire) • **assistance** *n* aide *f*; **to be of a. to sb** aider qn • **assistant 1** *n* assistant, -ante *mf*; *Br (in shop)* vendeur, -euse *mf* **2** *adj* adjoint

assizes [ə'saɪzɪz] *npl Br (court meetings)* assises *fpl*

associate 1 [ə'səʊʃeɪt] **1** *vt* associer (**with** sth à *ou* avec qch; **with sb** à qn)
2 *vi* **to a. with sb** *(mix socially)* fréquenter qn; **to a. (oneself) with sb** *(in business venture)* s'associer à *ou* avec qn
3 [ə'səʊʃɪət] *n & adj* associé, -iée *(mf)* • **association** [-'eɪʃən] *n* association *f*; **associations** *(memories)* souvenirs *mpl*

assorted [ə'sɔːtɪd] *adj (different)* variés; *(foods)* assortis; **a well-a. couple/***etc* un couple/*etc* bien assorti • **assortment** *n (of cheeses)* assortiment *m*; **an a. of people** des gens de toutes sortes

assuage [ə'sweɪdʒ] *vt Literary* apaiser

assume [ə'sjuːm] *vt* (**a**) *(suppose)* supposer (**that** que); **let us a. that…** supposons que… (+ *subjunctive*) (**b**) *(take on)* *(power, control)* prendre; *(responsibility, role)* assumer; *(attitude, name)* adopter • **assumed** *adj (feigned)* faux (*f* fausse); **a. name** nom *m* d'emprunt • **assumption** [ə'sʌmpʃən] *n (supposition)* supposition *f*; **on the a. that…** en supposant que… (+ *subjunctive*)

> **⚠** Note that the French verb **assumer** is a false friend and is never a translation for the English verb **to assume**. It never means **to suppose** or **to adopt**.

assurance [ə'ʃʊərəns] *n* (**a**) *(confidence, promise)* assurance *f* (**b**) *Br (insurance)* assurance *f*

assure [ə'ʃʊə(r)] *vt* assurer (**sb that** à qn que; **sb of sth** qn de qch) • **assuredly** [-ɪdlɪ] *adv* assurément

asterisk ['æstərɪsk] *n* astérisque *m*

astern [ə'stɜːn] *adv (in ship)* à l'arrière

asthma [*Br* 'æsmə, *Am* 'æzmə] *n* asthme *m* • **asthmatic** [-'mætɪk] *adj & n* asthmatique *(mf)*

astonish [ə'stɒnɪʃ] *vt* étonner; **to be astonished (at sth)** s'étonner (de qch) • **astonishing** *adj* étonnant • **astonishingly** *adv* étonnamment • **astonishment** *n* étonnement *m*

astound [ə'staʊnd] *vt* stupéfier • **astounding** *adj* stupéfiant

astray [ə'streɪ] *adv* **to go a.** s'égarer; **to lead a.** détourner du droit chemin

astride [ə'straɪd] **1** *adv* à califourchon
2 *prep* à cheval sur

astringent [ə'strɪndʒənt] *adj* astringent; *Fig (harsh)* sévère

astrology [ə'strɒlədʒɪ] *n* astrologie *f* • **astrologer** *n* astrologue *mf*

astronaut ['æstrənɔːt] *n* astronaute *mf*

astronomy [ə'strɒnəmɪ] *n* astronomie *f* • **astronomer** *n* astronome *mf* • **astronomical** [æstrə'nɒmɪkəl] *adj* astronomique

astute [ə'stjuːt] *adj (crafty)* rusé; *(clever)* astucieux, -ieuse

asunder [ə'sʌndə(r)] *adv Literary* **to tear a.** *(to pieces)* mettre en pièces; **to break a.** *(in two)* casser en deux

asylum [ə'saɪləm] *n* asile *m*; *Pej* **lunatic a.** asile d'aliénés

at [æt, *unstressed* ət] *prep* (**a**) à; **at the end** à la fin; **at school** à l'école; **at work** au travail; **at six (o'clock)** à six heures; **at Easter** à Pâques; **to drive at 10 mph** rouler à ≃ 15 km; **to buy/sell at 10 euros a kilo** acheter/vendre (à) 10 euros le kilo (**b**) chez; **at the doctor's** chez le médecin; **at home** chez soi, à la maison

(**c**) en; **at sea** en mer; **at war** en guerre; **good at maths** fort en maths
(**d**) contre; **angry at** fâché contre
(**e**) sur; **to shoot at** tirer sur; **at my request** sur ma demande
(**f**) de; **to laugh at sb/sth** rire de qn/qch; **surprised at sth** surpris de qch
(**g**) (au)près de; **at the window** près de la fenêtre
(**h**) par; **to come in at the door** entrer par la porte; **six at a time** six par six
(**i**) *(phrases)* **at night** la nuit; **to look at** regarder; **to be (hard) at it** travailler dur; **while you're at it** tant que tu y es; *Br* **he's always (on) at me** *Fam* il est toujours après moi

atchoo [ə'tʃuː] *exclam Am* = atishoo
ate [*Br* et, *Am* eɪt] *pt of* eat
atheism ['eɪθɪɪzəm] *n* athéisme *m* •**atheist** *n* athée *mf*
Athens ['æθənz] *n* Athènes *m ou f*
athlete ['æθliːt] *n* athlète *mf*; **a.'s foot** *(disease)* mycose *f* •**athletic** [-'letɪk] *adj* athlétique; **a. meeting** *Br* réunion *f* d'athlétisme; *Am* réunion *f* sportive •**athletics** [-'letɪks] *npl Br* athlétisme *m*; *Am* sport *m*
atishoo [ə'tɪʃuː] *(Am* **atchoo**) *exclam* atchoum!
Atlantic [ət'læntɪk] **1** *adj (coast, ocean)* atlantique
  2 *n* **the A.** l'Atlantique *m*
atlas ['ætləs] *n* atlas *m*
atmosphere ['ætməsfɪə(r)] *n* atmosphère *f* •**atmospheric** [-'ferɪk] *adj* atmosphérique
atom ['ætəm] *n* atome *m*; **a. bomb** bombe *f* atomique •**atomic** [ə'tɒmɪk] *adj* atomique •**atomizer** *n* atomiseur *m*
atone [ə'təʊn] *vi* **to a. for** *(sin, crime)* expier •**atonement** *n* expiation *f* (**for** de)
atrocious [ə'trəʊʃəs] *adj* atroce •**atrocity** [ə'trɒsɪti] *n (cruel action)* atrocité *f*
atrophy ['ætrəfɪ] *(pt & pp* -**ied**) *vi (of muscle)* s'atrophier
attach [ə'tætʃ] *vt* attacher (**to** à); *(document)* joindre (**to** à); **attached to sb** *(fond of)* attaché à qn •**attachment** *n* (**a**) *(affection)* attachement *m* (**to sb** à qn) (**b**) *(tool)* accessoire *m* (**c**) *(to e-mail)* fichier *m* joint
attaché [ə'tæʃeɪ] *n* (**a**) *(in embassy)* attaché, -ée *mf* (**b**) **a. case** attaché-case *m*
attack [ə'tæk] **1** *n* (**a**) *(military)* attaque *f* (**on** contre); *(on sb's life)* attentat *m*; *(of illness)* crise *f*; *(of fever)* accès *m*; **an a. of migraine** une migraine; **to launch an a. on** attaquer; **to be** *or* **come under a.** être attaqué

  2 *vt* attaquer; *(problem, plan)* s'attaquer à
  3 *vi* attaquer •**attacker** *n* agresseur *m*
attain [ə'teɪn] *vt (aim)* atteindre; *(ambition)* réaliser; *(rank)* parvenir à •**attainable** *adj (aim)* accessible; *(ambition, result)* réalisable •**attainment** *n (of ambition)* réalisation *f* (**of** de); **attainments** *(skills)* talents *mpl*
attempt [ə'tempt] **1** *n* tentative *f*; **to make an a. to do** tenter de faire; **they made no a. to help her** ils n'ont rien fait pour l'aider; **to make an a. on** *(record)* faire une tentative pour battre; **to make an a. on sb's life** attenter à la vie de qn; **at the first a.** du premier coup
  2 *vt* tenter; *(task)* entreprendre; **to a. to do** tenter de faire; **attempted murder** tentative *f* d'assassinat
attend [ə'tend] **1** *vt (meeting)* assister à; *(course)* suivre; *(school, church)* aller à; *(patient)* soigner; *(wait on, serve)* servir; *(escort)* accompagner; **well-attended course** cours *m* très suivi; **the meeting was well attended** il y a eu du monde à la réunion
  2 *vi* assister; **to a. to** *(take care of)* s'occuper de; *Literary (pay attention to)* prêter attention à •**attendance** *n* présence *f* (**at** à); *(people)* assistance *f*; **(school) a.** scolarité *f*; **in a.** de service •**attendant** *n* employé, -ée *mf*; *(in service station)* pompiste *mf*; *Br (in museum)* gardien, -ienne *mf*; **attendants** *(of prince, king)* suite *f*
attention [ə'tenʃən] *n* attention *f*; **to pay a.** faire *ou* prêter attention (**to** à); **for the a. of** à l'attention de; **to stand at a./to a.** *(of soldier)* être/se mettre au garde-à-vous; **a.!** garde-à vous!; **a. to detail** minutie *f*
attentive [ə'tentɪv] *adj (heedful)* attentif, -ive (**to** à); *(thoughtful)* attentionné (**to** pour) •**attentively** *adv* attentivement
attenuate [ə'tenjʊeɪt] *vt* atténuer
attest [ə'test] **1** *vt (certify, confirm)* confirmer
  2 *vi* **to a. to** témoigner de
attic ['ætɪk] *n* grenier *m*
attire [ə'taɪə(r)] *n Literary* vêtements *mpl*
attitude ['ætɪtjuːd] *n* attitude *f*
attorney [ə'tɜːnɪ] *(pl* -**eys**) *n Am (lawyer)* avocat *m*
attract [ə'trækt] *vt* attirer •**attraction** *n (charm, appeal)* attrait *m*; *(place, person)* attraction *f*; *(between people)* attirance *f*; *Phys* attraction terrestre; **attractions** *(at funfair)* attractions *fpl* •**attractive** *adj*

(house, room, person, car) beau *(f* belle); *(price, offer)* intéressant; *(landscape)* attrayant; **do you find her a.?** elle te plaît?
attribute 1 ['ætrɪbjuːt] *n (quality)* attribut *m*
  2 [ə'trɪbjuːt] *vt (ascribe)* attribuer (**to** à) • **attributable** *adj* attribuable (**to** à)
attrition [ə'trɪʃən] *n* **war of a.** guerre *f* d'usure
attuned [ə'tjuːnd] *adj* **a. to** *(of ideas, trends)* en accord avec; *(used to)* habitué à
atypical [eɪ'tɪpɪkəl] *adj* atypique
aubergine ['əʊbəʒiːn] *n Br* aubergine *f*
auburn ['ɔːbən] *adj (hair)* auburn *inv*
auction ['ɔːkʃən] **1** *n* vente *f* aux enchères
  2 *vt* **to a. (off)** vendre aux enchères • **auctioneer** *n* commissaire-priseur *m*
audacious [ɔː'deɪʃəs] *adj* audacieux, -ieuse • **audacity** [ɔː'dæsɪtɪ] *n* audace *f*
audible ['ɔːdɪbəl] *adj (sound, words)* audible • **audibly** *adv* distinctement
audience ['ɔːdɪəns] *n* **(a)** *(of speaker, musician, actor)* public *m*; *(of radio broadcast)* auditeurs *mpl*; **TV a.** téléspectateurs *mpl* **(b)** *(interview)* audience *f* (**with sb** avec qn)
audio ['ɔːdɪəʊ] *adj (cassette, system)* audio *inv*; **a. tape** cassette *f* audio • **audiotypist** *n* audiotypiste *mf* • **audio'visual** *adj* audiovisuel, -uelle
audit ['ɔːdɪt] **1** *n* audit *m*
  2 *vt (accounts)* vérifier • **auditor** *n* commissaire *m* aux comptes
audition [ɔː'dɪʃən] **1** *n* audition *f*
  2 *vti* auditionner
auditorium [ɔːdɪ'tɔːrɪəm] *n* salle *f* de spectacle *or* concert
augment [ɔːg'ment] *vt* augmenter (**with** *or* **by** de)
augur ['ɔːgə(r)] **1** *vi* **to a. well** être de bon augure
  2 *vt* présager
August ['ɔːgəst] *n* août *m*
august [ɔː'gʌst] *adj* auguste
aunt [ɑːnt] *n* tante *f* • **'auntie, 'aunty** *(pl* **aunties**) *n Fam* tata *f*
au pair [əʊ'peə(r)] **1** *n* **a. (girl)** jeune fille *f* au pair **2** *adv* au pair
aura ['ɔːrə] *n (of place)* atmosphère *f*; *(of person)* aura *f*
auspices ['ɔːspɪsɪz] *npl* **under the a. of** sous les auspices de
auspicious [ɔː'spɪʃəs] *adj* prometteur, -euse
austere [ɔː'stɪə(r)] *adj* austère • **austerity** [ɔː'sterɪtɪ] *n* austérité *f*

Australia [ɒ'streɪlɪə] *n* l'Australie *f* • **Australian 1** *adj* australien, -ienne **2** *n* Australien, -ienne *mf*
Austria ['ɒstrɪə] *n* l'Autriche *f* • **Austrian 1** *adj* autrichien, -ienne **2** *n* Autrichien, -ienne *mf*
authentic [ɔː'θentɪk] *adj* authentique • **authenticate** *vt* authentifier • **authenticity** [-'tɪsɪtɪ] *n* authenticité *f*
author ['ɔːθə(r)] *n* auteur *m* • **autho'ress** *n* femme *f* auteur • **authorship** *n (of book)* paternité *f*
authoritarian [ɔːθɒrɪ'teərɪən] *adj & n* autoritaire *(mf)*
authoritative [ɔː'θɒrɪtətɪv] *adj (report, book)* qui fait autorité; *(tone, person)* autoritaire
authority [ɔː'θɒrɪtɪ] *(pl* **-ies**) *n* autorité *f*; *(permission)* autorisation *f* (**to do** de faire); **to be in a.** *(in charge)* être responsable; **to be an a. on** faire autorité en ce qui concerne
authorize ['ɔːθəraɪz] *vt* autoriser (**to do** à faire) • **authori'zation** *n* autorisation *f* (**to do** de faire)
autistic [ɔː'tɪstɪk] *adj* autiste
auto ['ɔːtəʊ] *(pl* **-os**) *n Am* auto *f*
autobiography [ɔːtəʊbaɪ'ɒgrəfɪ] *(pl* **-ies**) *n* autobiographie *f* • **autobiographical** [-baɪə'græfɪkəl] *adj* autobiographique
autocrat ['ɔːtəkræt] *n* autocrate *m* • **auto'cratic** *adj* autocratique
autograph ['ɔːtəgrɑːf] **1** *n* autographe *m*; **a. book** album *m* d'autographes
  2 *vt* dédicacer (**for sb** à qn)
automate ['ɔːtəmeɪt] *vt* automatiser • **auto'mation** *n* automatisation *f*
automatic [ɔːtə'mætɪk] *adj* automatique • **automatically** *adv* automatiquement
automaton [ɔː'tɒmətən] *n* automate *m*
automobile ['ɔːtəməbiːl] *n Am* automobile *f*
autonomous [ɔː'tɒnəməs] *adj* autonome • **autonomy** *n* autonomie *f*
autopsy ['ɔːtɒpsɪ] *(pl* **-ies**) *n* autopsie *f*
autumn ['ɔːtəm] *n* automne *m*; **in a.** en automne • **autumnal** [ɔː'tʌmnəl] *adj (weather, day)* d'automne
auxiliary [ɔːg'zɪljərɪ] *(pl* **-ies**) *adj & n* auxiliaire *(mf)*; **a. (verb)** (verbe *m*) auxiliaire *m*
avail [ə'veɪl] **1** *n* **to no a.** en vain; **of no a.** inutile
  2 *vt* **to a. oneself of** profiter de
available [ə'veɪləbəl] *adj* disponible; **a. to all** *(education, goal)* accessible à tous; **tickets are still a.** il reste des tickets; **this**

model is a. in black or green ce modèle existe en noir et en vert • **availability** [-'bɪlɪtɪ] n (of object) disponibilité f; (of education) accessibilité f

avalanche ['ævəlɑːnʃ] n avalanche f

avarice ['ævərɪs] n avarice f • **avaricious** [-'rɪʃəs] adj avare

Ave abbr = avenue

avenge [ə'vendʒ] vt venger; **to a. oneself** (**on**) se venger (de)

avenue ['ævənjuː] n avenue f; Fig (way to a result) voie f

average ['ævərɪdʒ] **1** n moyenne f; **on a.** en moyenne; **above/below a.** au-dessus/au-dessous de la moyenne
2 adj moyen, -enne
3 vt (do) faire en moyenne; (reach) atteindre la moyenne de; (figures) faire la moyenne de

averse [ə'vɜːs] adj **to be a. to doing** répugner à faire • **aversion** [ə'vɜːʃən] n (dislike) aversion f; **to have an a. to sth/to doing** avoir de la répugnance pour qch/à faire

avert [ə'vɜːt] vt (prevent) éviter; **to a. one's eyes** (turn away) détourner les yeux (**from** de)

aviary ['eɪvɪərɪ] (pl **-ies**) n volière f

aviation [eɪvɪ'eɪʃən] n aviation f • **aviator** n aviateur, -trice mf

avid ['ævɪd] adj avide (**for** de) • **avidly** adv avidement

avocado [ævə'kɑːdəʊ] (pl **-os**) n **a. (pear)** avocat m

avoid [ə'vɔɪd] vt éviter; **to a. doing** éviter de faire; **I can't a. doing it** je ne peux pas ne pas le faire • **avoidable** adj évitable • **avoidance** n **his a. of danger/etc** son désir d'éviter le danger/etc; **tax a.** évasion f fiscale

avowed [ə'vaʊd] adj (enemy) déclaré

await [ə'weɪt] vt attendre

awake [ə'weɪk] **1** adj réveillé, éveillé; (**wide-**) **a.** (not feeling sleepy) éveillé; **he's** (**still**) **a.** il ne dort pas (encore); **to keep sb a.** empêcher qn de dormir, tenir qn éveillé; **to lie a.** être incapable de dormir; **a. to** (conscious of) conscient de
2 (pt **awoke**, pp **awoken**) vi se réveiller
3 vt (person) réveiller; Literary (old memories) éveiller, réveiller • **awaken 1** vti = **awake 2** vt **to a. sb to sth** faire prendre conscience de qch à qn • **awakening** n réveil m; **a rude a.** (shock) un réveil brutal

award [ə'wɔːd] **1** n (prize) prix m, récompense f; (scholarship) bourse f
2 vt (money) attribuer; (prize) décerner;

to a. damages (of judge) accorder des dommages-intérêts

aware [ə'weə(r)] adj **to be a. of** (conscious) être conscient de; (informed) être au courant de; (realize) se rendre compte de; **to become a. of/that** se rendre compte de/que; **to be a. that...** se rendre compte que... • **awareness** n conscience f

awash [ə'wɒʃ] adj inondé (**with** de)

away [ə'weɪ] adv (**a**) (distant) loin; **5 km a.** à 5 km (de distance)
(**b**) (in time) **ten days a.** dans dix jours
(**c**) (absent, gone) absent; **a. with you!** va-t'en!; **to drive a.** partir (en voiture); **to fade/melt a.** disparaître/fondre complètement
(**d**) (to one side) **to look** or **turn a.** détourner les yeux
(**e**) (continuously) **to work/talk a.** travailler/parler sans arrêt
(**f**) Br **to play a.** (of team) jouer à l'extérieur

awe [ɔː] n crainte f (mêlée de respect); **to be in a. of sb** éprouver pour qn une crainte mêlée de respect • **awe-inspiring** adj (impressive) imposant • **awesome** adj (impressive) impressionnant; (frightening) effrayant; Fam (excellent) super inv

awful ['ɔːfəl] adj affreux, -euse; (terrifying) effroyable; (ill) malade; Fam **an a. lot of** un nombre incroyable de; **I feel a.** (about it) j'ai vraiment honte • **awfully** adv (suffer) affreusement; (very) (good, pretty) extrêmement; (bad, late) affreusement; **thanks a.** merci infiniment

awhile [ə'waɪl] adv quelque temps; (stay, wait) un peu

awkward ['ɔːkwəd] adj (**a**) (clumsy) (person, gesture) maladroit (**b**) (difficult) difficile; (cumbersome) gênant; (tool) peu commode; (time) mal choisi; (silence) gêné; **the a. age** l'âge ingrat; Fam **to be an a. customer** ne pas être commode • **awkwardly** adv (walk) maladroitement; (speak) d'un ton gêné; (placed, situated) à un endroit peu pratique • **awkwardness** n maladresse f; (difficulty) difficulté f; (discomfort) gêne f

awl [ɔːl] n poinçon m

awning ['ɔːnɪŋ] n (of tent) auvent m; (over shop, window) store m; (canvas or glass canopy) marquise f

awoke [ə'wəʊk] pt of **awake**

awoken [ə'wəʊkən] pp of **awake**

awry [ə'raɪ] adv **to go a.** (of plan) mal tourner

axe [æks] (Am **ax**) **1** n hache f; Fig (reduc-

tion) coupe *f* sombre; **to get the a.** *(of project)* être abandonné; *(of worker)* être mis à la porte; *Fig* **to have an a. to grind** agir dans un but intéressé

   2 *vt (costs)* réduire; *(job)* supprimer; *(project)* abandonner

axiom ['æksɪəm] *n* axiome *m*

axis ['æksɪs] *(pl* **axes** ['æksiːz]*) n* axe *m*

axle ['æksəl] *n* essieu *m*

ay(e) [aɪ] **1** *adv* oui

   2 *n* **the ayes** *(votes)* les voix *fpl* pour

azalea [ə'zeɪlɪə] *n (plant)* azalée *f*

B

B, b [biː] n B, b m inv; **2B** (number) 2 ter
BA [biːˈeɪ] abbr = Bachelor of Arts
babble [ˈbæbəl] **1** vi (mumble) bredouiller; (of baby, stream) gazouiller
  2 vt **to b. (out)** (words) bredouiller
  3 n inv (of voices) rumeur f; (of baby, stream) gazouillis m
babe [beɪb] n (**a**) Literary bébé m (**b**) Fam (girl) belle nana f
baboon [bəˈbuːn] n babouin m
baby [ˈbeɪbɪ] **1** (pl **-ies**) n bébé m; **b. boy** petit garçon m; **b. girl** petite fille f; **b. tiger/**etc bébé-tigre/etc m; **b. clothes/ toys/**etc vêtements mpl/jouets mpl/etc de bébé; Am **b. carriage** landau m; **b. sling** kangourou m, porte-bébé m; **b. face** visage m poupin
  2 (pt & pp **-ied**) vt Fam dorloter ● **babyminder** n Br nourrice f ● **baby-sit** (pt & pp **-sat,** pres p **-sitting**) vi faire du babysitting; **to b. for sb** garder les enfants de qn ● **baby-sitter** n baby-sitter mf ● **babysnatching** n rapt m d'enfant ● **baby-walker** n trotteur m
babyish [ˈbeɪbɪɪʃ] adj de bébé; (puerile) bébé inv, puéril
bachelor [ˈbætʃələ(r)] n (**a**) (not married) célibataire m; Br **b. flat** garçonnière f (**b**) Univ **B. of Arts/of Science** (person) ≃ licencié, -iée mf ès lettres/ès sciences; (qualification) ≃ licence f de lettres/ sciences
back¹ [bæk] n (of person, animal) dos m; (of chair) dossier m; (of hand) revers m; (of house, vehicle, train, head) arrière m; (of room) fond m; (of page) verso m; (of fabric) envers m; Football arrière m; **at the b. of the book** à la fin du livre; **in** or **at the b. of the car** à l'arrière de la voiture; **at the b. of one's mind** derrière la tête; **b. to front** devant derrière, à l'envers; Fam **to get off sb's b.** ficher la paix à qn; Fam **to get sb's b. up** irriter qn; **at the b. of** derrière ● **backache** n mal m de dos ● **back'bencher** n Br Pol député m de base ● **backbiting** n Fam médisance f ● **backbone** n colonne f vertébrale; (of fish) grande arête f; Fig (main support) pivot m ● **backbreaking** adj éreintant ● **backchat** n Br Fam impertinence f ● **backcloth** n toile f de fond ● **back'date** vt antidater ● **back'handed** adj (compliment) équivoque ● **backhander** n (stroke) revers m; Br Fam (bribe) pot-de-vin m ● **backpack** n sac m à dos ● **backrest** n dossier m ● **back'side** n Fam (buttocks) derrière m ● **back'stage** adv dans les coulisses ● **backstroke** n (in swimming) dos m crawlé ● **backtrack** vi rebrousser chemin ● **backup** n appui m; Am (tailback) embouteillage m; Comptr sauvegarde f ● **backwater** n (place) trou m perdu ● **backwoods** npl forêt(s) f(pl) vierge(s); Fig **to live in the b.** habiter dans le bled ● **back'yard** n Br arrière-cour f; Am jardin m (à l'arrière d'une maison)
back² [bæk] adj (wheel, seat) arrière inv; **b. door** porte f de derrière; **b. end** (of bus) arrière m; **b. number** (of magazine) vieux numéro m; **b. pay** rappel m de salaire; **b. payments** arriéré m; **b. room** pièce f du fond; **b. street** rue f écartée; **b. taxes** arriéré m d'impôts; **b. tooth** molaire f
back³ [bæk] adv (behind) en arrière; **far b., a long way b.** loin derrière; **a long way b. in the past** à une époque reculée; **a month b.** il y a un mois; **to stand b.** (of house) être en retrait (**from the road** par rapport à la route); **to go b. and forth** aller et venir; **to come b.** revenir; **he's b.** il est de retour, il est rentré ou revenu; **the trip there and b.** le voyage aller et retour
back⁴ [bæk] **1** vt (with money) financer; (horse) parier sur; (vehicle) faire reculer; **to be backed with** (of curtain, picture) être renforcé de; **to b. sb (up)** (support) appuyer qn; Comptr **to b. up** sauvegarder
  2 vi (move backwards) reculer; **to b. down** faire marche arrière; **to b. out** (withdraw) se retirer; (of vehicle) sortir en marche arrière; **to b. on to** (of house) donner par derrière sur; **to b. up** (of vehicle) faire marche arrière
backer [ˈbækə(r)] n (supporter) partisan m; (on horses) parieur, -ieuse mf; (financial) commanditaire m
backfire [bækˈfaɪə(r)] vi (**a**) (of vehicle)

pétarader (**b**) *Fig* **to b. on sb** *(of plot)* se retourner contre qn
backgammon ['bækgæmən] *n* backgammon *m*
background ['bækgraʊnd] *n* fond *m*, arrière-plan *m*; *(educational)* formation *f*; *(professional)* expérience *f*; *(environment)* milieu *m*; *(circumstances)* contexte *m*; **to keep sb in the b.** tenir qn à l'écart; **b. music/noise** musique *f*/bruit *m* de fond
backing ['bækɪŋ] *n (aid)* soutien *m*; *(material)* support *m*
backlash ['bæklæʃ] *n* choc *m* en retour, retour *m* de flamme
backlog ['bæklɒg] *n* **b. of work** travail *m* en retard
backward ['bækwəd] **1** *adj (person, country)* arriéré; *(glance)* en arrière
2 *adv* = **backwards** • **backwardness** *n (of person, country)* retard *m* • **backwards** *adv* en arrière; *(to walk)* à reculons; *(to fall)* à la renverse; **to go** *or* **move b.** reculer; **to go b. and forwards** aller et venir
bacon ['beɪkən] *n* lard *m*; *(in rashers)* bacon *m*; **b. and eggs** œufs *mpl* au bacon
bacteria [bæk'tɪərɪə] *npl* bactéries *fpl*
bad [bæd] (**worse, worst**) *adj* mauvais; *(wicked)* méchant; *(sad)* triste; *(accident, wound)* grave; *(tooth)* carié; *(arm, leg)* malade; *(pain)* violent; **b. language** gros mots *mpl*; **b. cheque** chèque *m* sans provision; **it's b. to think that** ce n'est pas bien de penser que; **to feel b.** *(ill)* se sentir mal; **to feel b. about sth** s'en vouloir de qch; **to be b. at maths** être mauvais en maths; **things are b.** ça va mal; **that's not b.!** ce n'est pas mal!; **to go b.** *(of fruit, meat)* se gâter; *(of milk)* tourner; **in a b. way** *(sick)* mal en point; *(in trouble)* dans le pétrin; **too b.!** tant pis! • **bad-'mannered** *adj* mal élevé • **bad-'tempered** *adj* grincheux, -euse
bade [bæd] *pt of* **bid**
badge [bædʒ] *n (of plastic, bearing slogan or joke)* badge *m*; *(of metal, bearing logo)* pin's *m*; *(of postman, policeman)* plaque *f*; *(on school uniform)* insigne *m*
badger ['bædʒə(r)] **1** *n (animal)* blaireau *m*
2 *vt* importuner
badly ['bædlɪ] *adv* mal; *(hurt)* grièvement; **b. affected** très touché; **b. shaken** bouleversé; **to be b. mistaken** se tromper lourdement; **b. off** dans la gêne; **to be b. off for** manquer de; **to want sth b.** avoir grande envie de qch
badminton ['bædmɪntən] *n* badminton *m*

baffle ['bæfəl] *vt (person)* déconcerter
bag¹ [bæg] *n* sac *m*; **bags** *(luggage)* bagages *mpl*; *(under eyes)* poches *fpl*; *Fam* **bags of** *(lots of)* beaucoup de; *Fam Pej* **an old b.** une vieille taupe; *Fam* **in the b.** dans la poche; *Fam* **b. lady** clocharde *f* • **bagful** *n* (plein) sac *m*
bag² [bæg] *(pt & pp* -**gg**-*) vt Fam (take, steal)* piquer; *(hunted animal)* tuer
baggage ['bægɪdʒ] *n* bagages *mpl*; *(of soldier)* équipement *m*; *Am* **b. car** fourgon *m*; **b. handler** *(in airport)* bagagiste *mf*; *Am* **b. room** consigne *f*
baggy ['bægɪ] (**-ier, -iest**) *adj (trousers)* faisant des poches; *(by design)* large
bagpipes ['bægpaɪps] *npl* cornemuse *f*
Bahamas [bə'hɑːməz] *npl* **the B.** les Bahamas *fpl*
bail [beɪl] **1** *n Law* caution *f*; **on b.** sous caution; **to grant sb b.** libérer qn sous caution
2 *vt* **to b. sb out** *Law* se porter garant de qn; *Fig* tirer qn d'affaire; **to b. a company out** renflouer une entreprise
3 *vi* **to b. out** *(from aircraft)* s'éjecter
bailiff ['beɪlɪf] *n (law officer)* huissier *m*; *Br (of landowner)* régisseur *m*
bait [beɪt] **1** *n* appât *m*
2 *vt* (**a**) *(fishing hook)* amorcer (**b**) *(annoy)* tourmenter
baize [beɪz] *n* **green b.** *(on card table)* tapis *m* vert
bake [beɪk] **1** *vt* (faire) cuire au four
2 *vi (of cook)* faire de la pâtisserie/du pain; *(of cake)* cuire (au four); *Fam* **we're** *or* **it's baking (hot)** on crève de chaleur • **baked** *adj (potatoes, apples)* au four; **b. beans** haricots *mpl* blancs à la tomate • **baking** *n* cuisson *f*; **b. powder** levure *f* chimique; **b. tin** moule *m* à pâtisserie
baker ['beɪkə(r)] *n* boulanger, -ère *mf* • **bakery** *n* boulangerie *f*
balaclava [bælə'klɑːvə] *n Br* **b. (helmet)** passe-montagne *m*
balance ['bæləns] **1** *n (equilibrium)* équilibre *m*; *(of account)* solde *m*; *(remainder)* reste *m*; *(in accounting)* bilan *m*; *(for weighing)* balance *f*; **to lose one's b.** perdre l'équilibre; **to strike a b.** trouver le juste milieu; **sense of b.** sens *m* de la mesure; **to be in the b.** être incertain; **on b.** à tout prendre; **b. of payments** balance *f* des paiements; **b. sheet** bilan *m*
2 *vt* maintenir en équilibre (**on** sur); *(budget, account)* équilibrer; *(compare)* mettre en balance; **to b. (out)** *(compensate for)* compenser
3 *vi (of person)* se tenir en équilibre; *(of*

accounts) être en équilibre, s'équilibrer;
to b. (out) *(even out)* s'équilibrer
balcony ['bælkənɪ] *(pl -ies) n* balcon *m*
bald [bɔːld] (**-er, -est**) *adj* chauve; *(statement)* brutal; *(tyre)* lisse; **b. patch** *or* **spot** tonsure *f* • **bald-'headed** *adj* chauve
• **balding** *adj* **to be b.** perdre ses cheveux
• **baldness** *n* calvitie *f*
balderdash ['bɔːldədæʃ] *n Literary* balivernes *fpl*
bale [beɪl] **1** *n (of cotton)* balle *f*
2 *vi* **to b. out** *(from aircraft)* s'éjecter
baleful ['beɪlfəl] *adj Literary* sinistre
balk [bɔːk] *vi* reculer (**at** devant)
Balkans ['bɔːlkənz] *npl* **the B.** les Balkans *fpl*
ball¹ [bɔːl] *n* balle *f*; *(inflated, for football, rugby)* ballon *m*; *Billiards* bille *f*; *(of string, wool)* pelote *f*; *(sphere)* boule *f*; *(of meat, fish)* boulette *f*; *Fam* **to be on the b.** *(alert)* avoir de la présence d'esprit; *(knowledgeable)* connaître son affaire; **b. bearing** roulement *m* à billes; *Am* **b. game** match *m* de base-ball; *Fig* **it's a whole new b. game** c'est une tout autre affaire
ball² [bɔːl] *n (dance)* bal *m (pl* bals*)*
ballad ['bæləd] *n (poem)* ballade *f*; *(song)* romance *f*
ballast ['bæləst] **1** *n* lest *m*
2 *vt* lester
ballcock ['bɔːlkɒk] *n Br* robinet *m* à flotteur
ballerina [bælə'riːnə] *n* ballerine *f*
ballet ['bæleɪ] *n* ballet *m*
ballistic [bə'lɪstɪk] *adj* **b. missile** engin *m* balistique
balloon [bə'luːn] *n (toy, airship)* ballon *m*; *(in cartoon)* bulle *f*; **(weather) b.** ballon-sonde *m*
ballot ['bælət] **1** *n (voting)* scrutin *m*; **b. paper** bulletin *m* de vote; **b. box** urne *f*
2 *vt (members)* consulter (par un scrutin)
ballpoint (pen) ['bɔːlpɔɪnt(pen)] *n* stylo *m* à bille
ballroom ['bɔːlruːm] *n* salle *f* de danse; **b. dancing** danses *fpl* de salon
ballyhoo [bælɪ'huː] *n Fam* battage *m* (publicitaire)
balm [bɑːm] *n (oil, comfort)* baume *m*
• **balmy** (**-ier, -iest**) *adj* (**a**) *(mild)* doux *(f* douce*)*; *Literary (fragrant)* embaumé (**b**) *Br Fam (crazy)* dingue
baloney [bə'ləʊnɪ] *n Fam (nonsense)* âneries *fpl*
Baltic ['bɔːltɪk] *n* **the B.** la Baltique
balustrade ['bæləstreɪd] *n* balustrade *f*
bamboo [bæm'buː] *n* bambou *m*; **b. shoots** pousses *fpl* de bambou

bamboozle [bæm'buːzəl] *vt Fam (cheat)* embobiner
ban [bæn] **1** *n* interdiction *f*; **to impose a b. on sth** interdire qch
2 *(pt & pp* **-nn-***) vt* interdire; **to b. sb from doing sth** interdire à qn de faire qch; **to b. sb from** *(club)* exclure qn de
banal [bə'næl] *adj* banal *(mpl* -als*)*
• **banality** *n* banalité *f*
banana [bə'nɑːnə] *n* banane *f*; **b. skin** peau *f* de banane
band [bænd] **1** *n* (**a**) *(strip)* bande *f*; *(of hat)* ruban *m*; **rubber** *or* **elastic b.** élastique *m* (**b**) *(group of people)* bande *f*; *(of musicians)* (petit) orchestre *m*; *(pop group)* groupe *m*
2 *vi* **to b. together** se (re)grouper
bandage ['bændɪdʒ] **1** *n (strip)* bande *f*; *(dressing)* bandage *m*
2 *vt* **to b. (up)** *(arm, leg)* bander; *(wound)* mettre un bandage sur; **to b. sb's arm** bander le bras à qn
Band-aid® ['bændeɪd] *n* pansement *m* adhésif
B and B [biːənd'biː] *(abbr* **bed and breakfast***) n Br see* **bed**
bandit ['bændɪt] *n* bandit *m*
bandstand ['bændstænd] *n* kiosque *m* à musique
bandwagon ['bændwægən] *n Fig* **to jump on the b.** suivre le mouvement
bandy¹ ['bændɪ] (**-ier, -iest**) *adj* **to have b. legs** avoir les jambes arquées
bandy² ['bændɪ] *(pt & pp* **-ied***) vt* **to b. about** *(story, rumour)* faire circuler
bane [beɪn] *n Literary* fléau *m*
bang¹ [bæŋ] **1** *n (blow, noise)* coup *m* (violent); *(of gun)* détonation *f*; *(of door)* claquement *m*
2 *vt (hit)* cogner, frapper; *(door)* (faire) claquer; **to b. one's head** se cogner la tête; **to b. down** *(lid)* rabattre (violemment)
3 *vi* cogner, frapper; *(of door)* claquer; *(of gun)* détoner; *(of firework)* éclater; **to b. into sb/sth** heurter qn/qch
4 *exclam* vlan!, pan!; **to go b.** éclater
bang² [bæŋ] *adv Br Fam (exactly)* exactement; **b. in the middle** en plein milieu; **b. on six** à six heures tapantes
banger ['bæŋə(r)] *n Br* (**a**) *Fam (sausage)* saucisse *f* (**b**) *(firecracker)* pétard *m* (**c**) *Fam* **old b.** *(car)* vieille guimbarde *f*
Bangladesh [bæŋglə'deʃ] *n* le Bangladesh • **Bangladeshi 1** *adj* bangladeshi **2** *n* Bangladeshi, -e *mf*
bangle ['bæŋgəl] *n* bracelet *m*
bangs [bæŋz] *npl Am (of hair)* frange *f*

banish ['bænɪʃ] *vt* bannir
banister ['bænɪstə(r)] *n* **banister(s)** rampe *f* (d'escalier)
banjo ['bændʒəʊ] (*pl* -os *or* -oes) *n* banjo *m*
bank¹ [bæŋk] **1** *n* (*of river*) bord *m*, rive *f*; (*raised*) berge *f*; (*of earth*) talus *m*; (*of sand*) banc *m*; **the Left B.** (*in Paris*) la Rive gauche
  2 *vt* **to b. (up)** (*earth*) amonceler; (*fire*) couvrir
  3 *vi* (*of aircraft*) virer
bank² [bæŋk] **1** *n* (*for money*) banque *f*; **b. account** compte *m* en banque; **b. card** carte *f* d'identité bancaire; **b. clerk** employé, -ée *mf* de banque; *Br* **b. holiday** jour *m* férié; *Br* **b. note** billet *m* de banque; **b. rate** taux *m* d'escompte
  2 *vt* (*money*) mettre à la banque
  3 *vi* avoir un compte en banque (**with** à)
  • **banker** *n* banquier, -ière *mf*; *Br* **b.'s card** carte *f* d'identité bancaire • **banking 1** *adj* (*transaction*) bancaire **2** *n* (*activity, profession*) la banque
bank³ [bæŋk] *vi* **to b. on sb/sth** (*rely on*) compter sur qn/qch
bankrupt ['bæŋkrʌpt] **1** *adj* **to go b.** faire faillite; *Fig* **morally b.** qui a perdu toute crédibilité
  2 *vt* mettre en faillite • **bankruptcy** *n* faillite *f*
banner ['bænə(r)] *n* banderole *f*; (*military flag*) *& Fig* bannière *f*
banns [bænz] *npl* bans *mpl*; **to put up the b.** publier les bans
banquet ['bæŋkwɪt] *n* banquet *m*
banter ['bæntə(r)] **1** *n* plaisanteries *fpl*
  2 *vi* plaisanter
baptism ['bæptɪzəm] *n* baptême *m* • **Baptist** *n* & *adj* baptiste (*mf*)
baptize [bæp'taɪz] *vt* baptiser
bar [bɑː(r)] **1** *n* (**a**) (*of metal*) barre *f*; (*of gold*) lingot *m*; (*of chocolate*) tablette *f*; (*on window*) barreau *m*; **b. of soap** savonnette *f*; **behind bars** (*criminal*) sous les verrous; **to be a b. to sth** faire obstacle à qch; *Law* **the B.** le barreau; **b. code** (*on product*) code-barres *m* (**b**) (*pub*) bar *m*; (*counter*) bar, comptoir *m* (**c**) (*group of musical notes*) mesure *f*
  2 (*pt & pp* **-rr-**) *vt* (**a**) **to b. sb's way** barrer le passage à qn; **barred window** fenêtre *f* munie de barreaux (**b**) (*prohibit*) interdire (**sb from doing** à qn de faire); (*exclude*) exclure (**from** à)
  3 *prep* (*except*) sauf; **b. none** sans exception • **barmaid** *n* serveuse *f* de bar • **barman** (*pl* -men) *n* barman *m* • **bartender** *n* *Am* barman *m*

Barbados [bɑː'beɪdɒs] *n* la Barbade
barbarian [bɑː'beərɪən] *n* barbare *mf* • **barbaric** [-'bærɪk] *adj* barbare • **barbarity** [-'bærɪtɪ] *n* barbarie *f*
barbecue ['bɑːbɪkjuː] **1** *n* barbecue *m*
  2 *vt* cuire au barbecue
barbed wire [bɑːbd'waɪə(r)] *n* fil *m* de fer barbelé; (*fence*) barbelés *mpl*
barber ['bɑːbə(r)] *n* coiffeur *m* pour hommes
Barbie® ['bɑːbɪ] *n* **B. doll** poupée *f* Barbie®
barbiturate [bɑː'bɪtjʊrət] *n* barbiturique *m*
bare [beə(r)] **1** (**-er, -est**) *adj* nu; (*tree, hill*) dénudé; (*room, cupboard*) vide; (*mere*) simple; **the b. necessities** le strict nécessaire; **with his b. hands** à mains nues
  2 *vt* (*arm, wire*) dénuder; **to b. one's head** se découvrir • **bareback** *adv* **to ride b.** monter à cru • **barefaced** *adj* (*lie*) éhonté • **barefoot 1** *adv* nu-pieds **2** *adj* aux pieds nus • **bare'headed** *adj & adv* nu-tête *inv*
barely ['beəlɪ] *adv* (*scarcely*) à peine; **b. enough** tout juste assez
bargain ['bɑːgɪn] **1** *n* (*deal*) marché *m*, affaire *f*; **a b.** (*cheap buy*) une occasion, une bonne affaire; **a real b.** une véritable occasion *ou* affaire; **it's a b.!** (*agreed*) c'est entendu!; **to make a b.** faire un marché (**with sb** avec qn); **into the b.** (*in addition*) par-dessus le marché; **b. price** prix *m* exceptionnel; **b. counter** rayon *m* des soldes
  2 *vi* (*negotiate*) négocier; (*haggle*) marchander; **to b. for** *or* **on sth** (*expect*) s'attendre à qch; **he got more than he bargained for** il ne s'attendait pas à ça • **bargaining** *n* négociations *fpl*; (*haggling*) marchandage *m*
barge [bɑːdʒ] **1** *n* péniche *f*
  2 *vi* **to b. in** (*enter room*) faire irruption; (*interrupt*) interrompre; **to b. into** (*hit*) se cogner contre
baritone ['bærɪtəʊn] *n* (*voice, singer*) baryton *m*
bark¹ [bɑːk] *n* (*of tree*) écorce *f*
bark² [bɑːk] **1** *n* aboiement *m*
  2 *vi* aboyer; *Fam Fig* **you're barking up the wrong tree** tu fais fausse route • **barking** *n* aboiements *mpl*
barley ['bɑːlɪ] *n* orge *f*; **b. sugar** sucre *m* d'orge
barmy ['bɑːmɪ] (**-ier, -iest**) *adj* *Br Fam* (*crazy*) dingue
barn [bɑːn] *n* (*for crops*) grange *f*; (*for horses*) écurie *f*; (*for cattle*) étable *f* • **barnyard** *n* cour *f* de ferme

barometer [bə'rɒmɪtə(r)] *n* baromètre *m*
baron ['bærən] *n* baron *m*; *Fig (industrialist)* magnat *m*; **press/oil b.** magnat de la presse/du pétrole •**baroness** *n* baronne *f*
baroque [*Br* bə'rɒk, *Am* bə'rəʊk] *adj & n* Archit & Mus baroque *(m)*
barracks ['bærəks] *npl* caserne *f*

⎧ Note that the French word **baraque** is a
⎩ false friend. Its most common translation is **shack**.

barrage [*Br* 'bærɑːʒ, *Am* bə'rɑːʒ] *n* *(across river)* barrage *m*; *Fig* **a b. of questions** un feu roulant de questions
barrel ['bærəl] *n* (**a**) *(cask)* tonneau *m*; *(of oil)* baril *m* (**b**) *(of gun)* canon *m* (**c**) **b. organ** orgue *m* de Barbarie
barren ['bærən] *adj (land, woman, ideas)* stérile; *(style)* aride
barrette [bə'ret] *n* *Am (hair slide)* barrette *f*
barricade ['bærɪkeɪd] **1** *n* barricade *f* **2** *vt* barricader; **to b. oneself (in)** se barricader (dans)
barrier ['bæriə(r)] *n also Fig* barrière *f*; *Br* **(ticket) b.** *(of station)* portillon *m*; **sound b.** mur *m* du son
barring ['bɑːrɪŋ] *prep* sauf
barrister ['bærɪstə(r)] *n Br* ≃ avocat *m*
barrow ['bærəʊ] *n* *(wheelbarrow)* brouette *f*; *(cart)* charrette *f ou* voiture *f* à bras
barter ['bɑːtə(r)] **1** *n* troc *m* **2** *vt* troquer (**for** contre)
base [beɪs] **1** *n* (**a**) *(bottom, main ingredient)* base *f*; *(of tree, lamp)* pied *m*; **b. rate** *(of bank)* taux *m* de base (**b**) *(military)* base *f* **2** *adj* (**a**) *(dishonourable)* bas (*f* basse) (**b**) **b. metal** métal *m* vil **3** *vt* baser, fonder (**on** sur); **based in London** *(person, company)* basé à Londres •**baseless** *adj* sans fondement •**baseness** *n* bassesse *f*
baseball ['beɪsbɔːl] *n* base-ball *m*
baseboard ['beɪsbɔːd] *n Am* plinthe *f*
basement ['beɪsmənt] *n* sous-sol *m*
bash [bæʃ] **1** *n* *(bang)* coup *m*; *Br* **to have a b.** *Fam (try)* essayer un coup **2** *vt* *(hit)* cogner; **to b. (about)** *(ill-treat)* malmener; **to b. sb up** tabasser qn; **to b. in** *or* **down** *(door, fence)* défoncer •**bashing** *n* *Fam (thrashing)* raclée *f*; **to get a b.** prendre une raclée
bashful ['bæʃfəl] *adj* timide
basic ['beɪsɪk] **1** *adj* essentiel, -ielle, de base; *(elementary)* élémentaire; *(pay,*

food) de base; *(room, house, meal)* tout simple **2** *n Fam* **the basics** l'essentiel *m* •**basically** [-klɪ] *adv (on the whole)* en gros; *(in fact)* en fait; *(fundamentally)* au fond
basil [*Br* 'bæzəl, *Am* 'beɪzəl] *n* *(herb)* basilic *m*
basilica [bə'zɪlɪkə] *n* basilique *f*
basin [*Br* 'beɪsən *Am* 'beɪzəl] *n* (**a**) *(made of plastic)* bassine *f*; *(for soup, food)* (grand) bol *m*; *(portable washbasin)* cuvette *f*; *(sink)* lavabo *m* (**b**) *(of river)* bassin *m*
basis ['beɪsɪs] (*pl* **bases** [beɪsiːz]) *n* *(for discussion)* base *f*; *(for opinion, accusation)* fondement *m*; *(of agreement)* bases *fpl*; **on the b. of** d'après; **on that b.** dans ces conditions; **on a weekly b.** chaque semaine
bask [bɑːsk] *vi (in the sun)* se chauffer
basket ['bɑːskɪt] *n* panier *m*; *(for bread, laundry, litter)* corbeille *f* •**basketball** *n* basket(-ball) *m*
Basque [bæsk] **1** *adj* basque **2** *n* Basque *mf*
bass¹ [beɪs] **1** *n Mus* basse *f* **2** *adj (note, voice, instrument)* bas (*f* basse)
bass² [bæs] *n* *(sea fish)* bar *m*; *(freshwater fish)* perche *f*
bassoon [bə'suːn] *n* basson *m*
bastard ['bɑːstəd] **1** *adj (child)* bâtard **2** *n* (**a**) *(child)* bâtard, -arde *mf* (**b**) *Vulg (unpleasant person)* salaud *m*, salope *f*
baste [beɪst] *vt* (**a**) *(fabric)* bâtir (**b**) *(meat)* arroser de son jus
bastion ['bæstɪən] *n also Fig* bastion *m*
bat¹ [bæt] *n (animal)* chauve-souris *f*
bat² [bæt] **1** *n Cricket & Baseball* batte *f*; *(in table-tennis)* raquette *f*; **off my own b.** de ma propre initiative **2** (*pt & pp* **-tt-**) *vt* (**a**) *(ball)* frapper (**b**) **she didn't b. an eyelid** elle n'a pas sourcillé
batch [bætʃ] *n (of people)* groupe *m*; *(of letters)* paquet *m*; *(of books)* lot *m*; *(of loaves)* fournée *f*; *(of papers)* liasse *f*
bated ['beɪtɪd] *adj* **with b. breath** en retenant son souffle
bath [bɑːθ] **1** (*pl* **baths** [bɑːðz]) *n* bain *m*; *(tub)* baignoire *f*; **to have** *or* **take a b.** prendre un bain; **b. towel** drap *m* de bain; *Br* **swimming baths** piscine *f* **2** *vt Br* baigner **3** *vi Br* prendre un bain •**bathrobe** *n Br* peignoir *m* de bain; *Am* robe *f* de chambre •**bathroom** *n* salle *f* de bain(s); *Am (toilet)* toilettes *fpl* •**bathtub** *n* baignoire *f*
bathe [beɪð] **1** *vt* baigner; *(wound)* laver

2 *vi* se baigner; *Am* prendre un bain
3 *n Old-fashioned* bain *m* (de mer), baignade *f*; **to go for a b.** se baigner ● **bathing** *n* baignades *fpl*; **b. suit,** *Br* **b. costume** maillot *m* de bain

baton [*Br* 'bætən, *Am* bə'tɒn] *n* (*of conductor*) baguette *f*; (*of policeman*) matraque *f*; (*of soldier, drum majorette*) bâton *m*; (*in relay race*) témoin *m*

battalion [bə'tæljən] *n* bataillon *m*

batter ['bætə(r)] **1** *n* pâte *f* à frire
2 *vt* (*strike*) cogner sur; (*person*) frapper; (*town*) pilonner; **to b. down** (*door*) défoncer ● **battered** *adj* (*car, hat*) cabossé; (*house*) délabré; (*face*) meurtri; **b. child** enfant *m* martyr; **b. wife** femme *f* battue ● **battering** *n* **to take a b.** souffrir beaucoup

battery ['bætərɪ] (*pl* **-ies**) *n* (*in vehicle, of guns, for hens*) batterie *f*; (*in radio, appliance*) pile *f*; **b. hen** poule *f* de batterie

battle ['bætəl] **1** *n* bataille *f*; (*struggle*) lutte *f*; *Fam* **that's half the b.** la partie est à moitié gagnée
2 *vi* se battre, lutter ● **battlefield** *n* champ *m* de bataille ● **battleship** *n* cuirassé *m*

battlements ['bætəlmənts] *npl* (*indentations*) créneaux *mpl*; (*wall*) remparts *mpl*

batty ['bætɪ] (**-ier, -iest**) *adj Br Fam* toqué

baulk [bɔːk] *vi* reculer (**at** devant)

bawdy ['bɔːdɪ] (**-ier, -iest**) *adj* paillard

bawl [bɔːl] *vti* **to b. (out)** brailler; *Am Fam* **to b. sb out** engueuler qn

bay¹ [beɪ] **1** *n* (**a**) (*part of coastline*) baie *f* (**b**) (*in room*) renfoncement *m*; **b. window** bow-window *m*, oriel *m* (**c**) *Br* (*for loading*) aire *f* de chargement (**d**) **at b.** (*animal, criminal*) aux abois; **to keep** *or* **hold at b.** (*enemy, wild dog*) tenir en respect; (*disease*) juguler
2 *vi* aboyer
3 *adj* (*horse*) bai

bay² [beɪ] *n* (*tree*) laurier *m*; **b. leaf** feuille *f* de laurier

bayonet ['beɪənɪt] *n* baïonnette *f*

bazaar [bə'zɑː(r)] *n* (*market, shop*) bazar *m*; (*charity sale*) vente *f* de charité

bazooka [bə'zuːkə] *n* bazooka *m*

BC [biː'siː] (*abbr* **before Christ**) av. J.-C.

be [biː] (*present tense* **am, are, is;** *past tense* **was, were;** *pp* **been;** *pres p* **being**)

À l'oral et dans un style familier à l'écrit, le verbe **be** peut être contracté: **I am** devient **I'm, he/she/it is** deviennent **he's/she's/it's** et **you/we/they are** deviennent **you're/we're/they're**. Les formes négatives **is not/are not/was not** et **were not** se contractent respectivement en **isn't/aren't/wasn't** et **weren't**.

1 *vi* (**a**) (*gen*) être; **it is green/small**/*etc* c'est vert/petit/*etc*; **he's a doctor** il est médecin; **he's an Englishman** c'est un Anglais; **it's him** c'est lui; **it's them** ce sont eux; **it's three (o'clock)** il est trois heures; **it's the sixth of May,** *Am* **it's May sixth** nous sommes le six mai
(**b**) (*with age, height*) avoir; **to be twenty** (*age*) avoir vingt ans; **to be 2 m high** avoir 2 m de haut; **to be 6 f tall** ≃ mesurer 1,80 m; **to be hot/right/lucky** avoir chaud/raison/de la chance; **my feet are cold** j'ai froid aux pieds
(**c**) (*with health*) aller; **how are you?** comment vas-tu?; **I'm well/not well** je vais bien/mal
(**d**) (*with place, situation*) se trouver, être; **she's in York** elle se trouve *ou* elle est à York (**e**) (*exist*) être; **the best painter there is** le meilleur peintre qui soit; **leave me be** laissez-moi (tranquille); **that may be** cela se peut
(**f**) (*go, come*) **I've been to see her** je suis allé la voir; **he's (already) been** il est (déjà) venu (**g**) (*with weather, calculations*) faire; **it's fine** il fait beau; **it's foggy** il y a du brouillard; **2 and 2 are 4** 2 et 2 font 4 (**h**) (*cost*) coûter, faire; **it's 20 pence** ça coûte 20 pence; **how much is it?** ça fait combien?, c'est combien?

2 *v aux* (**a**) **I am/was doing** je fais/faisais; **I'll be staying** je vais rester; **I'm listening to the radio** je suis en train d'écouter la radio; **what has she been doing?** qu'est-ce qu'elle a fait?; **she's been there some time** elle est là depuis un moment; **he was killed** il a été tué; **I've been waiting (for) two hours** j'attends depuis deux heures; **it is said** on dit; **she's to be pitied** elle est à plaindre
(**b**) (*in questions and answers*) **isn't it?**/**aren't you?**/*etc* n'est-ce pas?, non?; **she's ill, is she?** (*surprise*) alors, comme ça, elle est malade?; **I am!/he is!**/*etc* oui!
(**c**) (**+** *infinitive*) **he is to come at once** (*must*) il doit venir tout de suite; **he's shortly to go** (*intends to*) il va bientôt partir
(**d**) **there is/are** il y a; (*pointing*) voilà; **here is/are** voici; **there she is** la voilà; **here they are** les voici

beach [biːtʃ] *n* plage *f*

beacon ['biːkən] *n* (*for ship, aircraft*) balise *f*; (*lighthouse*) phare *m*

bead [biːd] *n* (*small sphere*) perle *f*; (*of rosary*) grain *m*; (*of sweat*) goutte *f*, gouttelette *f*; (**string of**) **beads** collier *m*

beak [biːk] *n* bec *m*

beaker ['biːkə(r)] *n* gobelet *m*

beam [biːm] **1** *n* (*a*) (*of wood*) poutre *f* (**b**) (*of light, sunlight*) rayon *m*; (*of headlight, flashlight*) faisceau *m* (lumineux)

2 *vi* (*of light*) rayonner; (*of sun, moon*) briller; (*smile broadly*) sourire largement; **to b. with pride/joy** rayonner de fierté/joie

3 *vt* (*signals, programme*) transmettre (**to** à) • **beaming** *adj* (*face, person, smile*) rayonnant

bean [biːn] *n* haricot *m*; (*of coffee*) grain *m*; *Fam* **to be full of beans** être plein d'énergie; **b. curd** pâte *f* de soja • **bean-shoots, beansprouts** *npl* germes *mpl* de soja

bear¹ [beə(r)] *n* (*animal*) ours *m*; **b. cub** ourson *m*

bear² [beə(r)] **1** (*pt* **bore**, *pp* **borne**) *vt* (*carry, show*) porter; (*endure*) supporter; (*resemblance*) offrir; (*comparison*) soutenir; (*responsibility*) assumer; (*child*) donner naissance à; **I can't b. him/it** je ne peux pas le supporter/supporter ça; **to b. sth in mind** (*remember*) se souvenir de qch; (*take into account*) tenir compte de qch; **to b. out** corroborer

2 *vi* **to b. left/right** (*turn*) tourner à gauche/droite; **to b. north/***etc* (*go*) aller en direction du nord/*etc*; **to b. (up)on** (*relate to*) se rapporter à; *Fig* **to b. heavily on sb** (*of burden*) peser sur qn; **to b. with sb** être patient avec qn; **if you could b. with me** si vous voulez bien patienter; **to bring one's energies to b. on a task** consacrer toute son énergie à un travail; **to bring pressure to b. on sb** faire pression sur qn (**to do** pour faire); **to b. up** tenir le coup; **b. up!** courage!

bearable ['beərəbəl] *adj* supportable

beard [bɪəd] *n* barbe *f*; **to have a b.** porter la barbe • **bearded** *adj* barbu

bearer ['beərə(r)] *n* porteur, -euse *mf*

bearing ['beərɪŋ] *n* (*relevance*) rapport *m* (**on** avec); (*posture, conduct*) port *m*; (*of ship, aircraft*) position *f*; **to get one's bearings** s'orienter

beast [biːst] *n* bête *f*; *Fam* (*person*) brute *f*

beastly ['biːstlɪ] *adj Br Fam* (*unpleasant*) horrible

beat [biːt] **1** *n* (*of heart, drum*) battement *m*; (*of policeman*) ronde *f*; (*in music*) rythme *m*

2 (*pt* **beat**, *pp* **beaten** ['biːtən]) *vt* battre; **to b. a drum** battre du tambour; *Fam* **that beats me** ça me dépasse; *Fam* **b. it!** fiche le camp!; **to b. sb to it** devancer qn; **to b. back** *or* **off** repousser; **to b. down** (*price*)

faire baisser; **to b. down** *or* **in** (*door*) défoncer; **to b. out** (*rhythm*) marquer; (*tune*) jouer; **to b. sb up** tabasser qn

3 *vi* battre; (*at door*) frapper (**at** à); *Fam* **to b. about** *or* **around the bush** tourner autour du pot; **to b. down** (*of rain*) tomber à verse; (*of sun*) taper • **beating** *n* (*blows, defeat*) raclée *f*; (*of heart, drums*) battement *m*; **to take a b.** souffrir beaucoup

beater ['biːtə(r)] *n* (*for eggs*) fouet *m*

beautician [bjuː'tɪʃən] *n* esthéticienne *f*

beautiful ['bjuːtɪfəl] *adj* (très) beau (*f* belle); (*superb*) merveilleux, -euse • **beautifully** *adv* (*after verb*) à merveille; (*before adjective*) merveilleusement

beauty ['bjuːtɪ] (*pl* **-ies**) *n* (*quality, woman*) beauté *f*; **it's a b.!** (*car, house*) c'est une merveille!; **the b. of it is (that)** le plus beau, c'est que; **b. parlour** *or* **salon** institut *m* de beauté; **b. spot** (*on skin*) grain *m* de beauté; *Br* (*in countryside*) endroit *m* pittoresque

beaver ['biːvə(r)] **1** *n* castor *m*

2 *vi* **to b. away** travailler dur (**at sth** à qch)

became [bɪ'keɪm] *pt of* **become**

because [bɪ'kɒz] *conj* parce que; **b. of** à cause de

beck [bek] *n* **at sb's b. and call** aux ordres de qn

beckon ['bekən] *vti* **to b. (to) sb** faire signe à qn (**to do** de faire)

become [bɪ'kʌm] **1** (*pt* **became**, *pp* **become**) *vi* devenir; **to b. a painter** devenir peintre; **to b. thin** maigrir; **to b. worried** commencer à s'inquiéter; **what has b. of her?** qu'est-elle devenue?

2 *vt Formal* **that hat becomes her** ce chapeau lui va bien • **becoming** *adj* (*clothes*) seyant; (*modesty*) bienséant

bed [bed] **1** *n* lit *m*; (*flowerbed*) parterre *m*; (*of vegetables*) carré *m*; (*of sea*) fond *m*; (*of river*) lit *m*; (*of rock*) couche *f*; **to go to b.** (aller) se coucher; **to put sb to b.** coucher qn; **in b.** couché; **to get out of b.** se lever; **to make the b.** faire le lit; **b. and breakfast** (*in hotel*) chambre *f* avec petit déjeuner; **to stay in a b. and breakfast** ≃ prendre une chambre d'hôte; *Br* **b. settee** (canapé *m*) convertible *m*

2 *vi* **to b. down** se coucher • **bedbug** *n* punaise *f* • **bedclothes** *npl*, **bedding** *n* couvertures *fpl* et draps *mpl* • **bedpan** *n* bassin *m* (hygiénique) • **bedridden** *adj* alité • **bedroom** *n* chambre *f* à coucher • **bedside** *n* chevet *m*; **b. lamp/book/table** lampe *f*/livre *m*/table *f* de chevet • **bed'sit, bedsitter** *n Br* chambre *f* meu-

blée • **bedspread** n dessus-de-lit m inv
• **bedtime** n heure f du coucher; **b.!** c'est l'heure d'aller se coucher!; **b. story** histoire f (pour endormir les enfants)

bedevil [bɪ'devəl] (Br **-ll-,** Am **-l-**) vt (plague) tourmenter; (confuse) embrouiller; **bedevilled by** (problems) perturbé par

bedlam ['bedləm] n Fam (noise) chahut m

bedraggled [bɪ'drægəld] adj (clothes, person) débraillé et tout trempé

bee [biː] n abeille f • **beehive** n ruche f

beech [biːtʃ] n (tree, wood) hêtre m

beef [biːf] **1** n bœuf m

2 vi Fam (complain) rouspéter (**about** contre) • **beefburger** n hamburger m
• **beefy** (**-ier, -iest**) adj Fam costaud

beekeeper ['biːkiːpə(r)] n apiculteur, -trice mf • **beekeeping** n apiculture f

beeline ['biːlaɪn] n Fam **to make a b. for** aller droit vers

been [biːn] pp of **be**

beer [bɪə(r)] n bière f; **b. garden** = jardin où les clients d'un pub peuvent consommer; **b. glass** chope f

beet [biːt] n betterave f • **beetroot** n betterave f

beetle ['biːtəl] **1** n scarabée m; (any beetle-shaped insect) bestiole f

2 vi Br **to b. off** Fam (run off) se sauver

befall [bɪ'fɔːl] (pt befell [bɪ'fel], pp befallen [bɪ'fɔːlən]) vt Literary arriver à

befit [bɪ'fɪt] (pt & pp **-tt-**) vt Formal convenir à

before [bɪ'fɔː(r)] **1** adv avant; (already) déjà; (in front) devant; **the month b.** le mois d'avant ou précédent; **the day b.** la veille; **I've seen it b.** je l'ai déjà vu; **I've never done it b.** je ne l'ai (encore) jamais fait

2 prep (time) avant; (place) devant; **the year b. last** il y a deux ans; **b. my very eyes** sous mes yeux

3 conj avant que (+ ne) (+ subjunctive), avant de (+ infinitive); **b. he goes** avant qu'il (ne) parte; **b. going** avant de partir
• **beforehand** adv à l'avance; **check b.** vérifiez au préalable

befriend [bɪ'frend] vt **to b. sb** se prendre d'amitié pour qn

befuddled [bɪ'fʌdəld] adj (drunk) ivre

beg [beg] **1** (pt & pp **-gg-**) vt **to b. (for)** (favour, help) demander; (bread, money) mendier; **to b. sb to do sth** supplier qn de faire qch; **I b. to differ** permettez-moi de ne pas être d'accord; **to b. the question** esquiver la question

2 vi (in street) mendier; (ask earnestly)

supplier; **to go begging** (of food, articles) ne pas trouver d'amateurs

began [bɪ'gæn] pt of **begin**

beggar ['begə(r)] n mendiant, -iante mf; Br Fam (person) type m; **lucky b.** veinard, -arde mf

begin [bɪ'gɪn] **1** (pt began, pp begun, pres p **beginning**) vt commencer; (fashion, campaign) lancer; (bottle, sandwich) entamer; (conversation) engager; **to b. doing** ou **to do sth** commencer ou se mettre à faire qch; **he began laughing** il s'est mis à rire

2 vi commencer (**with** par; **by doing** par faire); **to b. on sth** commencer qch; **beginning from** à partir de; **to b. with** (first of all) d'abord

beginner [bɪ'gɪnə(r)] n débutant, -ante mf

beginning [bɪ'gɪnɪŋ] n commencement m, début m; **in** ou **at the b.** au début, au commencement

begrudge [bɪ'grʌdʒ] vt (envy) envier (**sb sth** qch à qn); (reproach) reprocher (**sb sth** qch à qn); (give unwillingly) donner à contrecœur; **to b. doing sth** faire qch à contrecœur

begun [bɪ'gʌn] pt of **begin**

behalf [bɪ'hɑːf] n **on b. of sb, on sb's b.** (representing) au nom de qn, de la part de qn; (in the interests of) en faveur de qn

behave [bɪ'heɪv] vi se conduire; (of machine) fonctionner; **to b. (oneself)** se tenir bien; (of child) être sage

behaviour [bɪ'heɪvjə(r)] (Am **behavior**) n conduite f, comportement m; **to be on one's best b.** se tenir particulièrement bien

behead [bɪ'hed] vt décapiter

behest [bɪ'hest] n Literary **at the b. of** sur l'ordre de

behind [bɪ'haɪnd] **1** prep derrière; (in terms of progress) en retard sur; **what's b. all this?** qu'est-ce que ça cache?

2 adv derrière; (late) en retard; **to be b. with the rent** être en retard pour payer le loyer; **to be b. with one's work** avoir du travail en retard

3 n Fam (buttocks) derrière m • **behindhand** adv en retard (**with** or **in** dans)

beholden [bɪ'həʊldən] adj Formal redevable (**to** à; **for** de)

beige [beɪʒ] adj & n beige (m)

Beijing [beɪ'dʒɪŋ] n Beijing m ou f

being ['biːɪŋ] n (person, soul) être m; **to come into b.** naître; **with all my b.** de tout mon être

belated [bɪ'leɪtɪd] adj tardif, -ive

belch [beltʃ] **1** n renvoi m
2 vi (of person) roter
3 vt **to b. (out)** (smoke) vomir
beleaguered [bɪ'liːgəd] adj (besieged) assiégé
belfry ['belfrɪ] (pl **belfries**) n beffroi m, clocher m
Belgium ['beldʒəm] n la Belgique •**Belgian** [-dʒən] **1** adj belge **2** n Belge mf
belie [bɪ'laɪ] vt (feelings, background) ne pas refléter
belief [bɪ'liːf] n (believing, thing believed) croyance f (**in sb** en qn; **in sth** à ou en qch); (trust) confiance f, foi f (**in** en); (religious faith) foi; **to the best of my b.** pour autant que je sache
believe [bɪ'liːv] **1** vt croire; **I don't b. it** c'est pas possible; **I b. I'm right** je crois avoir raison, je crois que j'ai raison
2 vi croire (**in sth** à qch; **in God/sb** en Dieu/qn); **I b. so/not** je crois que oui/que non; **to b. in doing sth** croire qu'il faut faire qch; **he doesn't b. in smoking** il désapprouve que l'on fume •**believable** adj crédible •**believer** n (religious) croyant, -ante mf; **to be a b. in sth** croire à qch
belittle [bɪ'lɪtəl] vt dénigrer
bell [bel] n (large) (of church) cloche f; (small) clochette f; (in phone, mechanism, alarm) sonnerie f; (on door, bicycle) sonnette f; (on tambourine, dog) grelot m; **b. tower** clocher m •**bellboy, bellhop** n Am groom m
belle [bel] n (woman) beauté f
belligerent [bɪ'lɪdʒərənt] adj & n belligérant, -ante (mf)
bellow ['beləʊ] vi beugler, mugir
bellows ['beləʊz] npl **(pair of) b.** soufflet m
belly ['belɪ] (pl **-ies**) n ventre m; Fam **b. button** nombril m; **b. dancing** danse f du ventre •**bellyache** Fam **1** n mal m au ventre **2** vi (complain) rouspéter (**about sb** après qn; **about sth** au sujet de qch) •**bellyful** n Fam **to have had a b.** en avoir plein le dos
belong [bɪ'lɒŋ] vi appartenir (**to** à); **to b. to a club** être membre d'un club; **that book belongs to me** ce livre m'appartient ou est à moi; **the cup belongs here** cette tasse se range ici; **he doesn't b.** il n'est pas à sa place •**belongings** npl affaires fpl
beloved [bɪ'lʌvɪd] adj & n Literary bien-aimé, -ée (mf)
below [bɪ'ləʊ] **1** prep (lower than) au-dessous de; (under) sous; (with numbers) moins de; Fig (unworthy of) indigne de

2 adv en dessous; (in text) ci-dessous; **on the floor b.** à l'étage du dessous; **it's 10 degrees b.** il fait moins 10
belt [belt] **1** n ceinture f; (in machine) courroie f; (area) zone f, région f
2 vi **to b. up** (fasten seat belt) attacher sa ceinture; Br Fam **to b. (along)** (rush) filer à toute allure; Br Fam **b. up!** (shut up) boucle-la!
3 vt Fam (hit) (ball) cogner dans; (person) flanquer un gnon à
bemoan [bɪ'məʊn] vt déplorer
bemused [bɪ'mjuːzd] adj perplexe
bench [bentʃ] n (seat) banc m; (work table) établi m; Law **the B.** (magistrates) la magistrature (assise); (court) le tribunal; Sport **to be on the b.** être remplaçant(e)
bend [bend] **1** n courbe f; (in river, pipe) coude m; (in road) virage m; (of arm, knee) pli m; Br **double b.** (on road) virage m en S, double virage m; Fam **round the b.** (mad) cinglé
2 (pt & pp **bent**) vt courber; (leg, arm) plier; **to b. one's head** baisser la tête; **to b. the rules** faire une entorse au règlement
3 vi (of branch) plier; (of road) tourner; (of river) faire un coude; **to b. (down)** (stoop) se courber; **to b. (over or forward)** se pencher; Fig **to b. over backwards to do** se mettre en quatre pour faire; **to b. to sb's will/etc** se soumettre à la volonté de qn/etc
bendy ['bendɪ] (**-ier, -iest**) adj Br Fam (road) plein de virages
beneath [bɪ'niːθ] **1** prep sous; (unworthy of) indigne de
2 adv (au-)dessous
benediction [benɪ'dɪkʃən] n bénédiction f
benefactor ['benɪfæktə(r)] n bienfaiteur m •**benefactress** n bienfaitrice f
beneficial [benɪ'fɪʃəl] adj bénéfique
beneficiary [benɪ'fɪʃərɪ] (pl **-ies**) n bénéficiaire mf
benefit ['benɪfɪt] **1** n (advantage) avantage m; (money) allocation f; **benefits** (of science, education) bienfaits mpl; **to sb's b.** dans l'intérêt de qn; **for your (own) b.** pour vous, pour votre bien; **to be of b.** faire du bien (**to sb** à qn); **to give sb the b. of the doubt** accorder à qn le bénéfice du doute; **b. concert** concert m de bienfaisance
2 vt faire du bien à; (be useful to) profiter à
3 vi **you'll b. from the rest** le repos vous fera du bien; **to b. from doing sth** gagner à faire qch

Benelux ['benɪlʌks] n Benelux m
benevolent [bɪ'nevələnt] adj bienveillant ● **benevolence** n bienveillance f
benign [bɪ'naɪn] adj (kind) bienveillant; (climate) doux (f douce); **b. tumour** tumeur f bénigne
bent [bent] **1** adj (nail, mind) tordu; Fam (dishonest) pourri; **b. on doing sth** résolu à faire qch
2 n (talent) aptitude f (**for** pour); (inclination, liking) penchant m, goût m (**for** pour); **to have a musical b.** avoir des dispositions pour la musique
3 pt & pp of bend
bequeath [bɪ'kwiːð] vt Formal léguer (**to** à) ● **bequest** [bɪ'kwest] n Formal legs m
bereaved [bɪ'riːvd] **1** adj endeuillé
2 npl **the b.** la famille du défunt/de la défunte ● **bereavement** n deuil m
bereft [bɪ'reft] adj **b. of** dénué de
beret [Br 'bereɪ, Am bə'reɪ] n béret m
berk [bɜːk] n Br Fam andouille f
Berlin [bɜː'lɪn] n Berlin m ou f; **the B. Wall** le mur de Berlin
Bermuda [bə'mjuːdə] n les Bermudes fpl
berry ['berɪ] (pl -ies) n baie f
berserk [bə'zɜːk] adj **to go b.** devenir fou furieux (f folle furieuse)
berth [bɜːθ] **1** n (**a**) (in ship, train) couchette f (**b**) (anchorage) poste m à quai; Fig **to give sb a wide b.** éviter qn comme la peste
2 vi (of ship) aborder à quai
beseech [bɪ'siːtʃ] (pt & pp besought or beseeched) vt Literary implorer (**to do** de faire)
beset [bɪ'set] (pt & pp beset, pres p besetting) vt assaillir; **b. with obstacles** semé d'obstacles; **b. with difficulties** en proie à toutes sortes de difficultés
beside [bɪ'saɪd] prep à côté de; **that's b. the point** ça n'a rien à voir; **b. oneself** (angry) hors de soi; **to be b. oneself with joy/anger** être fou (f folle) de joie/de colère
besides [bɪ'saɪdz] **1** prep (in addition to) en plus de; (except) excepté; **there are ten of us b. Paul** nous sommes dix sans compter Paul; **what else can you do b. singing?** que savez-vous faire à part chanter?
2 adv (in addition) en plus; (moreover) d'ailleurs; **there are more b.** il y en a d'autres encore
besiege [bɪ'siːdʒ] vt (of soldiers, crowd) assiéger; Fig (annoy) assaillir (**with** de)
besotted [bɪ'sɒtɪd] adj (drunk) abruti; **b. with** (infatuated) entiché de

besought [bɪ'sɔːt] pt & pp of beseech
bespatter [bɪ'spætə(r)] vt éclabousser (**with** de)
bespectacled [bɪ'spektəkəld] adj à lunettes
bespoke [bɪ'spəʊk] adj (tailor) à façon
best [best] **1** adj meilleur; **the b. page in the book** la meilleure page du livre; **my b. dress** ma plus belle robe; **the b. part of** (most) la plus grande partie de; **the b. thing is to accept** le mieux c'est d'accepter; **'b. before...'** (on product) 'à consommer avant...'; **b. man** (at wedding) témoin m
2 n **the b. (one)** le meilleur, la meilleure; **it's for the b.** c'est pour le mieux; **at b.** au mieux; **to do one's b.** faire de son mieux; **to look one's b., to be at one's b.** être à son avantage; **to the b. of my knowledge** autant que je sache; **to make the b. of sth** (accept) s'accommoder de qch; **to get the b. out of sth** tirer le meilleur parti de qch; **to get the b. of it** avoir le dessus; **in one's Sunday b.** endimanché; **all the b.!** (when leaving) prends bien soin de toi!; (good luck) bonne chance!; (in letter) amicalement
3 adv (the) **b.** (play, sing) le mieux; **to like sb/sth (the) b.** aimer qn/qch le plus; **the b. loved** le plus aimé; **I think it b. to wait** je juge prudent d'attendre ● **best-'seller** n (book) best-seller m
bestow [bɪ'stəʊ] vt accorder (**on** à)
bet [bet] **1** n pari m
2 (pt & pp bet or betted, pres p betting) vt parier (**on** sur; **that** que); Fam **you b.!** tu parles!
betray [bɪ'treɪ] vt (person, secret) trahir; **to b. to sb** (give away to) livrer à qn ● **betrayal** n (disloyalty) trahison f; (disclosure) (of secret) révélation f
better ['betə(r)] **1** adj meilleur (**than** que); **I need a b. car** j'ai besoin d'une meilleure voiture; **that's b.** c'est mieux; **she's (much) b.** (in health) elle va (beaucoup) mieux; **to get b.** (recover) se remettre; (improve) s'améliorer; **it's b. to go** il vaut mieux partir; **the b. part of** (most) la plus grande partie de
2 adv mieux (**than** que); **b. dressed/ known/etc** mieux habillé/connu/etc; **to look b.** (of ill person) avoir meilleure mine; **b. and b.** de mieux en mieux; **so much the b., all the b.** tant mieux (**for** pour); **for b. or worse** pour le meilleur et pour le pire; **I had b. go** il vaut mieux que je parte; **to be b. off** (financially) être plus à l'aise
3 n **to get the b. of sb** l'emporter sur qn; **to change for the b.** (of person) changer

en bien; *(of situation)* s'améliorer; **one's betters** ses supérieurs *mpl*
4 *vt (improve)* améliorer; *(do better than)* dépasser; **to b. oneself** améliorer sa condition; **to b. sb's results/***etc (do better than)* dépasser les résultats/*etc* de qn • **betterment** *n* amélioration *f*
betting ['betɪŋ] *n* paris *mpl*; *Br* **b. shop** *or* **office** ≃ PMU *m*
between [bɪ'twiːn] **1** *prep* entre; **we did it b. us** nous l'avons fait à nous deux/trois/ etc; **this is strictly b. you and me** que cela reste entre nous; **in b.** entre
2 *adv* **in b.** *(space)* au milieu; *(time)* dans l'intervalle
bevel ['bevəl] *n (edge)* biseau *m* • **bevelled** (*Am* **beveled**) *adj* **b. edge** biseau *m*
beverage ['bevərɪdʒ] *n* boisson *f*
bevy ['bevɪ] (*pl* **-ies**) *n* **a b. of** *(girls, reporters)* une nuée de
beware [bɪ'weə(r)] *vi* se méfier (**of** de); **b.!** attention!; **b. of falling** prenez garde de ne pas tomber; **'b. of the trains!'** 'attention aux trains!'; **'b. of the dog!'** 'attention, chien méchant!'; **'danger b.!'** 'attention! danger!'
bewilder [bɪ'wɪldə(r)] *vt* dérouter, laisser perplexe • **bewildering** *adj* déroutant • **bewilderment** *n* perplexité *f*
bewitch [bɪ'wɪtʃ] *vt* ensorceler • **bewitching** *adj* enchanteur, -eresse
beyond [bɪ'jɒnd] **1** *prep* (**a**) *(further than)* au-delà de; **b. a year** *(longer than)* plus d'un an; **b. reach/doubt** hors de portée/ de doute; **b. belief** incroyable; **b. my/our/** *etc* **means** au-dessus de mes/nos/*etc* moyens; **due to circumstances b. our control** en raison de circonstances indépendantes de notre volonté; **it's b. me** ça me dépasse (**b**) *(except)* sauf
2 *adv (further)* au-delà
bias ['baɪəs] **1** *n* (**a**) *(inclination)* penchant *m* (**towards** pour); *(prejudice)* préjugé *m*, parti pris *m* (**towards/against** en faveur de/contre) (**b**) **cut on the b.** *(fabric)* coupé dans le biais
2 (*pt & pp* **-ss-** *or* **-s-**) *vt* influencer (**towards/against** en faveur de/contre) • **bias(s)ed** *adj* partial; **to be b. against** avoir des préjugés contre
bib [bɪb] *n (for baby)* bavoir *m*
bible ['baɪbəl] *n* bible *f*; **the B.** la Bible • **biblical** ['bɪblɪkəl] *adj* biblique
bibliography [bɪblɪ'ɒɡrəfɪ] (*pl* **-ies**) *n* bibliographie *f*
bicarbonate [baɪ'kɑːbənət] *n* **b. of soda** bicarbonate *m* de soude
bicentenary [baɪsen'tiːnərɪ], **bicenten-**

nial [baɪsen'tenɪəl] *n* bicentenaire *m*
biceps ['baɪseps] *n inv (muscle)* biceps *m*
bicker ['bɪkə(r)] *vi* se chamailler • **bickering** *n* chamailleries *fpl*
bicycle ['baɪsɪkəl] *n* bicyclette *f*; **by b.** à bicyclette
bid¹ [bɪd] **1** *n* (**a**) *(offer)* offre *f*; *(at auction)* enchère *f* (**for** pour) (**b**) *(attempt)* tentative *f*; **a b. for attention/love** une tentative pour attirer l'attention/se faire aimer; **to make a b. for power** *(legally)* viser le pouvoir; *(illegally)* faire une tentative de coup d'État
2 (*pt & pp* **bid**, *pres p* **bidding**) *vt (sum of money)* offrir; *(at auction)* faire une enchère de
3 *vi* faire une offre (**for** pour); *(at auction)* faire une enchère (**for** sur) • **bidder** *n (at auction)* enchérisseur, -euse *mf*; **to the highest b.** au plus offrant • **bidding** *n (at auction)* enchères *fpl*
bid² [bɪd] (*pt* **bade**, *pp* **bidden** ['bɪdən] *or* **bid**, *pres p* **bidding**) *vt Literary (command)* commander (**sb to do** à qn de faire); *(say, wish)* dire, souhaiter; **to b. sb good day** souhaiter le bonjour à qn • **bidding** *n* **at sb's b.** sur les ordres de qn
bide [baɪd] *vt* **to b. one's time** attendre le bon moment
bier [bɪə(r)] *n (for coffin)* brancards *mpl*
bifocals [baɪ'fəʊkəlz] *npl* verres *mpl* à double foyer
big [bɪɡ] **1** (**bigger, biggest**) *adj (tall, large)* grand; *(fat)* gros *f* grosse; *(drop, increase)* fort; **to get big(ger)** *(taller)* grandir; *(fatter)* grossir; **my b. brother** mon grand frère; *Fam* **b. mouth** grande gueule *f*; **b. toe** gros orteil *m*; *Fam* **the b. time** le succès
2 *adv Fam* **to do things b.** faire les choses en grand; **to think b.** voir grand; **to look b.** faire l'important; **to talk b.** fanfaronner • **bighead** *n Fam* crâneur, -euse *mf* • **big'headed** *adj Fam* crâneur, -euse • **big'hearted** *adj* généreux, -euse • **bigshot, bigwig** *n Fam* gros bonnet *m* • **bigtime** *adj Fam (criminal)* de première
bigamy ['bɪɡəmɪ] *n* bigamie *f* • **bigamist** *n* bigame *mf* • **bigamous** *adj* bigame
bigot ['bɪɡət] *n* sectaire *mf*; *(religious)* bigot, -ote *mf* • **bigoted** *adj* sectaire; *(religious)* bigot • **bigotry** *n* sectarisme *m*; *(religious)* bigoterie *f*

> ℓ Note that the French word **bigot** is a false friend. It is only used to describe an excessively religious person and has no overtones of sectarianism.

bike [baɪk] *n Fam* vélo *m*; *(motorbike)* moto *f*
bikini [bɪ'kiːnɪ] *n* Bikini®*m*; **b. briefs** mini-slip *m*
bilberry ['bɪlbərɪ] *(pl* **-ies**) *n* myrtille *f*
bile [baɪl] *n* bile *f*
bilingual [baɪ'lɪŋgwəl] *adj* bilingue
bill¹ [bɪl] **1** *n* **(a)** *(invoice)* facture *f*; *(in restaurant)* addition *f*; *(in hotel)* note *f* **(b)** *Am (banknote)* billet *m* **(c)** *(bank draft)* effet *m*; **b. of sale** acte *m* de vente **(d)** *(notice)* affiche *f* **(e)** *Pol* projet *m* de loi; **B. of Rights** = les dix premiers amendements de la Constitution américaine **(f)** *(list)* **b. of fare** menu *m*
2 *vt* **(a)** **to b. sb** envoyer la facture à qn **(b)** *(publicize)* annoncer • **billboard** *n Am* panneau *m* d'affichage • **billfold** *n Am* portefeuille *m*
bill² [bɪl] *n (of bird)* bec *m*
billet ['bɪlɪt] *Mil* **1** *n* cantonnement *m*
2 *vt* cantonner
billiards ['bɪljədz] *n* billard *m*
billion ['bɪljən] *n* milliard *m* • **billio'naire** *n* milliardaire *mf*
billow ['bɪləʊ] **1** *n (of smoke)* volute *f*
2 *vi (of smoke)* tourbillonner; *(of sea)* se soulever; *(of sail)* se gonfler; **billowing smoke** des volutes *fpl* de fumée
billy-goat ['bɪlɪgəʊt] *n* bouc *m*
bimbo ['bɪmbəʊ] *(pl* **-os**) *n Fam* minette *f*
bimonthly [baɪ'mʌnθlɪ] *adj (every two weeks)* bimensuel, -uelle; *(every two months)* bimestriel, -ielle
bin [bɪn] **1** *n* boîte *f*; *(for litter)* poubelle *f*
2 *(pt & pp* **-nn-**) *vt Fam* mettre à la poubelle
binary ['baɪnərɪ] *adj* binaire
bind [baɪnd] **1** *(pt & pp* **bound**) *vt (fasten)* attacher; *(book)* relier; *(fabric, hem)* border; *(unite)* lier; **to b. sb hand and foot** ligoter qn; **to b. sb to do sth** obliger qn à faire qch; **to be bound by sth** être lié par qch
2 *n Fam (bore)* plaie *f* • **binding 1** *n (of book)* reliure *f* **2** *adj (contract)* qui lie; **to be b. on sb** *(legally)* lier qn
binder ['baɪndə(r)] *n (for papers)* classeur *m*
binge [bɪndʒ] *n Fam* **to go on a b.** *(drinking)* faire la bringue; *(eating)* se gaver
bingo ['bɪŋgəʊ] *n* ≃ loto *m*
binoculars [bɪ'nɒkjʊləz] *npl* jumelles *fpl*
biochemistry [baɪəʊ'kemɪstrɪ] *n* biochimie *f* • **biochemical** *adj* biochimique
biodegradable [baɪəʊdɪ'greɪdəbəl] *adj* biodégradable
biography ['baɪ'ɒgrəfɪ] *(pl* **-ies**) *n* biogra-

phie *f* • **biographer** *n* biographe *mf*
• **bio'graphical** [baɪə'græfɪkəl] *adj* biographique
biology [baɪ'ɒlədʒɪ] *n* biologie *f* • **biological** [baɪə'lɒdʒɪkəl] *adj* biologique; **b. warfare** guerre *f* bactériologique • **biologist** *n* biologiste *mf*
biped ['baɪped] *n* bipède *m*
birch [bɜːtʃ] **1** *n* **(silver) b.** bouleau *m*; **to give sb the b.** fouetter qn
2 *vt* fouetter
bird [bɜːd] *n* **(a)** *(animal)* oiseau *m*; *(fowl)* volaille *f*; **b. of prey** oiseau de proie; **b. table** mangeoire *f* pour oiseaux; **b.'s-eye view** perspective *f* à vol d'oiseau; *Fig* vue *f* d'ensemble **(b)** *Br Fam (girl)* nana *f*
• **birdseed** *n* graines *fpl* pour oiseaux
Biro® ['baɪrəʊ] *(pl* **-os**) *n Br* stylo *m* à bille
birth [bɜːθ] *n* naissance *f*; **to give b. to** donner naissance à; **from b.** *(blind, deaf)* de naissance; **b. certificate** acte *m* de naissance; **b. control** limitation *f* des naissances; **b. rate** (taux *m* de) natalité *f*
• **birthday** *n* anniversaire *m*; **happy b.!** joyeux anniversaire!; **b. party** fête *f* d'anniversaire; *Fig* **in one's b. suit** *(man)* en costume d'Adam; *(woman)* en costume d'Ève • **birthmark** *n* tache *f* de naissance
• **birthplace** *n* lieu *m* de naissance; *(house)* maison *f* natale
biscuit ['bɪskɪt] *n Br* biscuit *m*, petit gâteau *m*; *Am* petit pain *m* au lait
bishop ['bɪʃəp] *n* évêque *m*; *(in chess)* fou *m*
bison ['baɪsən] *n inv* bison *m*
bit¹ [bɪt] *n* **(a)** *(of string, time)* bout *m*; **a b.** *(a little)* un peu; **a tiny b.** un tout petit peu; **quite a b.** *(very)* très; *(a lot)* beaucoup; **not a b.** pas du tout; **a b. of luck** une chance; **b. by b.** petit à petit; **in bits (and pieces)** en morceaux; **to come to bits** se démonter; **to do one's b.** participer; *Fam* **she's a b. of all right** elle est pas mal **(b)** *(coin)* pièce *f* **(c)** *(of horse)* mors *m* **(d)** *(of drill)* mèche *f* **(e)** *Comptr* bit *m*
bit² [bɪt] *pt of* **bite**
bitch [bɪtʃ] **1** *n* chienne *f*; *very Fam Pej (woman)* garce *f*
2 *vi Fam (complain)* râler **(about** après)
• **bitchy** (**-ier, -iest**) *adj Fam (remark, behaviour)* vache
bite [baɪt] **1** *n* **(a)** *(wound)* morsure *f*; *(from insect)* piqûre *f*; *Fishing* touche *f* **(b)** *(mouthful)* bouchée *f*; **to have a b. to eat** manger un morceau **(c)** *Fig (of style, text)* mordant *m*
2 *(pt* **bit**, *pp* **bitten** ['bɪtən]) *vt* mordre; *(of insect)* piquer; **to b. one's nails** se

ronger les ongles; **to b. sth off** arracher qch d'un coup de dents; **to b. off a piece of apple** mordre dans une pomme

3 *vi (of person, dog)* mordre; *(of insect)* piquer; **to b. into sth** mordre dans qch • **biting** *adj (cold, irony)* mordant; *(wind)* cinglant

bitter ['bɪtə(r)] **1** *n Br (beer)* = bière anglaise brune

2 *adj (person, taste, irony)* amer, -ère; *(cold, wind)* glacial; *(criticism)* acerbe; *(shock, fate)* cruel (f cruelle); *(conflict)* violent; **to feel b. (about sth)** être plein d'amertume (à cause de qch); **to the b. end** jusqu'au bout • **bitterly** *adv* **to cry/ regret b.** pleurer/regretter amèrement; **b. disappointed** cruellement déçu; **it's b. cold** il fait un froid de canard • **bitterness** *n* amertume f; *(of the cold)* âpreté f; *(of conflict)* violence f • **bitter'sweet** *adj* doux-amer (f douce-amère); *Am* **b. chocolate** chocolat m à croquer

bivouac ['bɪvʊæk] **1** *n* bivouac m

2 *(pt & pp* **-ck-***) vi* bivouaquer

bizarre [bɪ'zɑː(r)] *adj* bizarre

blab [blæb] *(pt & pp* **-bb-***) vi* jaser

black [blæk] **1** (**-er, -est**) *adj* noir; **b. eye** œil m au beurre noir; **to give sb a b. eye** pocher l'œil à qn; **b. and blue** *(bruised)* couvert de bleus; *Av* **b. box** boîte f noire; *Br* **b. ice** verglas m; *Br* **b. pudding** boudin m noir; *Fig* **b. sheep** brebis f galeuse

2 *n (colour)* noir m; *(person)* Noir, -e mf; **it says here in b. and white** c'est écrit noir sur blanc

3 *vt* noircir; *(refuse to deal with)* boycotter

4 *vi* **to b. out** *(faint)* s'évanouir • **blackberry** *(pl* **-ies***) n* mûre f • **blackbird** *n* merle m (noir) • **blackboard** *n* tableau m (noir); **on the b.** au tableau • **black'currant** *n* cassis m • **blacken** *vti* noircir • **blackleg** *n Br Fam (strikebreaker)* jaune m • **blacklist 1** *n* liste f noire **2** *vt* mettre sur la liste noire • **blackmail 1** *n* chantage m **2** *vt* faire chanter; **to b. sb into doing sth** faire chanter qn pour qu'il/elle fasse • **blackmailer** *n* maître chanteur m • **blackness** *n* noirceur f; *(of night)* ténèbres fpl • **blackout** *n* panne f d'électricité; *(during war)* blackout m inv; *(fainting fit)* évanouissement m; **(news) b.** black-out m • **blacksmith** *n* forgeron m; *(working with horses)* maréchal-ferrant m

blackguard ['blægɑːd, -gəd] *n Old-fashioned* fripouille f

bladder ['blædə(r)] *n* vessie f

blade [bleɪd] *n* lame f; *(of windscreen*

wiper) caoutchouc m; **b. of grass** brin m d'herbe

blame [bleɪm] **1** *n* responsabilité f; *(criticism)* blâme m; **to lay the b. (for sth) on sb** faire porter à qn la responsabilité (de qch); **to take the b. for sth** endosser la responsabilité de qch

2 *vt* rendre responsable, faire porter la responsabilité à (**for** de); **to b. sb for doing sth** reprocher à qn d'avoir fait qch; **you're to b.** c'est de ta faute; **I b. you for doing that** je considère que c'est toi qui es responsable de cela • **blameless** *adj* irréprochable

blanch [blɑːntʃ] **1** *vt (vegetables)* blanchir **2** *vi (turn pale)* blêmir

blancmange [blə'mɒnʒ] *n Br* blanc-manger m

bland [blænd] (**-er, -est**) *adj (person)* terne; *(food)* insipide; *(remark, joke)* quelconque

blank [blæŋk] **1** *adj (paper, page)* blanc (f blanche), vierge; *(cheque)* en blanc; *(look, mind)* vide; *(puzzled)* ébahi; *(refusal)* absolu; **to leave b.** *(on form)* laisser en blanc; **b. tape** cassette f vierge

2 *n (space)* blanc m; *(cartridge)* cartouche f à blanc; **to fire blanks** tirer à blanc; **my mind's a b.** j'ai un trou • **blankly** *adv* **to look b. at** *(without expression)* regarder, le visage inexpressif; *(without understanding)* regarder sans comprendre

blanket ['blæŋkɪt] **1** *n (on bed)* couverture f; *(of snow, leaves)* couche f

2 *vt Fig (cover)* recouvrir

3 *adj (term, remark)* général

blare [bleə(r)] **1** *n (noise)* beuglements mpl; *(of trumpet)* sonnerie f

2 *vi* **to b. (out)** *(of radio)* beugler; *(of music, car horn)* retentir

blarney ['blɑːnɪ] *n Fam* boniments mpl

blasé ['blɑːzeɪ] *adj* blasé

blaspheme [blæs'fiːm] *vti* blasphémer • **blasphemous** ['blæsfəməs] *adj (text)* blasphématoire; *(person)* blasphémateur, -trice • **blasphemy** ['blæsfəmɪ] *n* blasphème m

blast [blɑːst] **1** *n* explosion f; *(air from explosion)* souffle m; *(of wind)* rafale f; *(of trumpet)* sonnerie f; **(at) full b.** *(loud)* à fond; *(fast)* à toute vitesse; **b. furnace** haut-fourneau m

2 *vt (hole, tunnel)* creuser (en dynamitant); *Fam (criticize)* démolir

3 *exclam Br Fam* zut! **b. you!** tu m'embêtes! • **blasted** *adj Br Fam* fichu • **blast-off** *n (of spacecraft)* mise f à feu

blatant ['bleɪtənt] *adj* *(obvious)* flagrant; *(shameless)* éhonté

blaze [bleɪz] **1** *n* *(fire)* feu *m*; *(large)* incendie *m*; *Fig* *(splendour)* éclat *m*; **a b. of colour** une explosion de couleurs; **b. of light** torrent *m* de lumière
2 *vi* *(of fire, sun)* flamboyer; *(of light, eyes)* être éclatant
3 *vt* *Fig* **to b. a trail** ouvrir la voie • **blazing** *adj* *(burning)* en feu; *(sun)* brûlant; *Fig* *(argument)* violent

blazer ['bleɪzə(r)] *n* blazer *m*

bleach [bliːtʃ] **1** *n* *(household)* (eau *f* de) Javel *f*; *(for hair)* décolorant *m*
2 *vt* *(clothes)* passer à l'eau de Javel; *(hair)* décolorer

bleachers ['bliːtʃərz] *npl Am* *(at stadium)* gradins *mpl*

bleak [bliːk] (**-er, -est**) *adj* *(appearance, countryside, weather)* morne; *(outlook)* lugubre; *(prospect)* peu encourageant

bleary ['blɪərɪ] *adj* *(eyes)* rouge

bleat [bliːt] *vi* bêler

bleed [bliːd] (*pt & pp* **bled** [bled]) **1** *vi* saigner; **to b. to death** saigner à mort; **her nose is bleeding** elle saigne du nez
2 *vt* *(radiator)* purger • **bleeding 1** *adj* (a) *(wound)* qui saigne (b) *Br very Fam* **a b. idiot** espèce de con **2** *n* saignement; **has the b. stopped?** est-ce que ça saigne encore?

bleep [bliːp] **1** *n* bip *m*
2 *vt* appeler au bip
3 *vi* faire bip • **bleeper** *n* *(pager)* bip *m*

blemish ['blemɪʃ] **1** *n* *(fault)* défaut *m*; *(mark)* marque *f*; *Fig* **it left a b. on his reputation** ça a entaché sa réputation
2 *vt* *Fig* *(reputation)* entacher

⟡ Note that the French verb **blêmir** is a false friend and is never a translation for the English verb **to blemish**. It means **to go pale**.

blend [blend] **1** *n* mélange *m*
2 *vt* mélanger (**with** à *ou* avec)
3 *vi* se mélanger; *(of styles, colours)* se marier (**with** avec); **everything blends (in)** *(decor of room)* tout est assorti • **blender** *n* mixer *m*

bless [bles] *vt* bénir; **to be blessed with sth** être doté de qch; **to be blessed with good health** avoir le bonheur d'être en bonne santé; **God b. you!** que Dieu te bénisse!; **b. you!** *(when sneezing)* à vos souhaits! • **blessed** [blesɪd] *adj* (a) *(holy)* béni (b) *Fam* *(blasted)* fichu; **the whole b. day** toute la sainte journée; **I can't see a b. thing** je n'y vois absolument rien • **bles-**sing *n Rel* bénédiction *f*; *(benefit)* bienfait *m*; **it was a b. in disguise** finalement, ça a été une bonne chose

blew [bluː] *pt of* **blow²**

blight [blaɪt] *n* *(on plants)* rouille *f*; *Fig* *(scourge)* fléau *m*; **urban b.** *(area)* quartier *m* délabré; *(condition)* délabrement *m* urbain

blighter ['blaɪtə(r)] *n Br Fam Old-fashioned* gars *m*

blimey ['blaɪmɪ] *exclam Br Fam* zut!

blind¹ [blaɪnd] **1** *adj* aveugle; **b. person** aveugle *mf*; **b. in one eye** borgne; **as b. as a bat** myope comme une taupe; *Fig* **b. with fury** aveuglé par la colère; *Fig* **to be b. to sth** ne pas voir qch; *Fig* **to turn a b. eye to sth** fermer les yeux sur qch; **b. alley** impasse *f*; **b. date** = rencontre arrangée avec quelqu'un qu'on ne connaît pas
2 *npl* **the b.** les aveugles *mpl*
3 *adv* **b. drunk** ivre mort
4 *vt* *(dazzle, make blind)* aveugler • **blindly** *adv Fig* aveuglément • **blindness** *n* cécité *f*

blind² [blaɪnd] *n Br* *(on window)* store *m*

blinders ['blaɪndərz] *npl Am* œillères *fpl*

blindfold ['blaɪndfəʊld] **1** *n* bandeau *m*
2 *vt* bander les yeux à
3 *adv* les yeux bandés

blink [blɪŋk] **1** *n* clignement *m*; *Fam* **on the b.** *(machine)* détraqué
2 *vt* **to b. one's eyes** cligner des yeux
3 *vi* *(of person)* cligner des yeux; *(of eyes)* cligner; *(of light)* clignoter • **blinking** *adj Br Fam* *(for emphasis)* sacré; **you b. idiot!** espèce d'idiot!

blinkers ['blɪŋkəz] *npl Br* *(of horse)* œillères *fpl*; *Fam* *(indicators of vehicle)* clignotants *mpl*

bliss [blɪs] *n* félicité *f* • **blissful** *adj* *(wonderful)* merveilleux, -euse; *(very happy)* *(person)* aux anges • **blissfully** *adv* *(happy)* merveilleusement; **to be b. unaware that...** ne pas se douter le moins du monde que...

blister ['blɪstə(r)] **1** *n* *(on skin)* ampoule *f*
2 *vi* se couvrir d'ampoules

blithe [blaɪð] *adj Literary* joyeux, -euse

blitz [blɪts] **1** *n* *(air attack)* raid *m* éclair; *(bombing)* bombardement *m* aérien; *Fam* *(onslaught)* offensive *f*
2 *vt* bombarder

blizzard ['blɪzəd] *n* tempête *f* de neige

bloated ['bləʊtɪd] *adj* *(swollen)* gonflé

blob [blɒb] *n* *(of water)* grosse goutte *f*; *(of ink, colour)* tache *f*

bloc [blɒk] *n* *(political group)* bloc *m*

block [blɒk] **1** n (of stone) bloc m; (of buildings) pâté m de maisons; (in pipe) obstruction f; **b. of flats** immeuble m; Am **a b. away** une rue plus loin; **school b.** groupe m scolaire; **b. booking** réservation f de groupe; **b. capitals** or **letters** majuscules fpl

2 vt (obstruct) bloquer; (pipe) boucher; (view) cacher; **to b. off** (road) barrer; (light) intercepter; **to b. up** (pipe, hole) boucher • **blockage** n obstruction f

blockade [blɒˈkeɪd] **1** n blocus m
2 vt bloquer

blockbuster [ˈblɒkbʌstə(r)] n (film) film m à grand spectacle

blockhead [ˈblɒkhed] n Fam imbécile mf

bloke [bləʊk] n Br Fam type m

blond [blɒnd] adj & n blond (m) • **blonde** adj & n blonde (f)

blood [blʌd] n sang m; **b. bank** banque f du sang; **b. bath** bain m de sang; **b. donor** donneur, -euse mf de sang; **b. group** groupe m sanguin; **b. poisoning** empoisonnement m du sang; **b. pressure** tension f artérielle; **high b. pressure** hypertension f; **to have high b. pressure** avoir de la tension; Am **b. sausage** boudin m **b. test** prise f de sang; • **bloodcurdling** adj à vous tourner le sang • **bloodhound** n (dog, detective) limier m • **bloodletting** n Med saignée f • **bloodshed** n effusion f de sang • **bloodshot** adj (eye) injecté de sang • **bloodstained** adj taché de sang • **bloodstream** n sang m • **bloodsucker** n (insect, person) sangsue f • **bloodthirsty** adj sanguinaire

bloody [ˈblʌdɪ] **1** (-ier, -iest) adj (a) ensanglanté (b) Br very Fam foutu; **a b. liar** un sale menteur; **b. weather!** sale temps!; **you b. fool!** conard!

2 adv Br Fam (very) vachement; **it's b. hot!** il fait une putain de chaleur! • **bloody-'minded** adj pas commode

bloom [bluːm] **1** n fleur f; **in b.** (tree) en fleur(s); (flower) éclos

2 vi (of tree, flower) fleurir; Fig (of person) s'épanouir • **blooming** adj (a) (in bloom) en fleur(s); (person) resplendissant; (thriving) florissant (b) Br Fam (for emphasis) sacré; **you b. idiot!** espèce d'idiot!

bloomer [ˈbluːmə(r)] n (a) Br Fam (mistake) gaffe f (b) (bread) ≃ bâtard m court

blossom [ˈblɒsəm] **1** n fleurs fpl
2 vi fleurir; **to b. (out)** (of person) s'épanouir

blot [blɒt] **1** n tache f
2 (pt & pp -tt-) vt (stain) tacher; (dry)

sécher; **to b. sth out** (obliterate) effacer qch • **blotter** n buvard m • **blotting paper** n (papier m) buvard m

blotch [blɒtʃ] n tache f • **blotchy** (-ier, -iest) adj couvert de taches; (face, skin) marbré

blouse [blaʊz] n chemisier m

> *ℓ* Note that the French word **blouse** is a false friend. Its most common meaning is **overall**.

blow¹ [bləʊ] n (hit, setback) coup m; **to come to blows** en venir aux mains

blow² [bləʊ] **1** (pt **blew**, pp **blown**) vt (of wind) pousser; (of person) (smoke, glass) souffler; (bubbles) faire; (trumpet) souffler dans; (kiss) envoyer (**to** à); Br Fam (money) claquer (**on sth** pour s'acheter); **to b. a fuse** sauter un plomb; **to b. one's nose** se moucher; **to b. a whistle** donner un coup de sifflet **2** vi (of wind, person) souffler; (of fuse) sauter; (of papers) (in wind) s'éparpiller

• **blowout** n (a) (tyre) éclatement m (**b**) Br Fam (meal) gueuleton m • **blow-up** n (of photo) agrandissement m

▸ **blow away 1** vt sep (of wind) emporter **2** vi (of hat) s'envoler ▸ **blow down 1** vt sep (chimney, fence) faire tomber **2** vi (fall) tomber ▸ **blow off** vt sep (hat) emporter; (arm) arracher ▸ **blow out 1** vt sep (candle) souffler; (cheeks) gonfler **2** vi (of light) s'éteindre ▸ **blow over 1** vti = **blow down 2** vi (of quarrel) se tasser ▸ **blow up 1** vt sep (building) faire sauter; (pump up) gonfler; (photo) agrandir **2** vi (explode) exploser

blow-dry [ˈbləʊdraɪ] **1** n Brushing® m
2 vt **to b. sb's hair** faire un Brushing® à qn

blowlamp [ˈbləʊlæmp] n chalumeau m

blown [bləʊn] pp of **blow**

blowtorch [ˈbləʊtɔːtʃ] n chalumeau m

blowy [ˈbləʊɪ] adj Fam **it's b.** il y a du vent

blowzy [ˈblaʊzɪ] adj Fam négligé

blubber [ˈblʌbə(r)] n graisse f (de baleine)

bludgeon [ˈblʌdʒən] **1** n gourdin m
2 vt matraquer

blue [bluː] **1** (-er, -est) adj bleu; Fam **to feel b.** avoir le cafard; Fam **b. film** film m porno

2 n bleu m; Fam **the blues** (depression) le cafard; (music) le blues; **out of the b.** (unexpectedly) sans crier gare • **bluebell** n jacinthe f des bois • **blueberry** (pl -ies) n airelle f • **bluebottle** n mouche f de la viande • **blueprint** n Fig plan m

bluff [blʌf] **1** *adj (person)* direct
2 *n* bluff *m*
3 *vti* bluffer

blunder ['blʌndə(r)] **1** *n (mistake)* gaffe *f*
2 *vi* faire une gaffe; **to b.** along *(move awkwardly)* avancer maladroitement • **blundering 1** *adj (clumsy)* maladroit **2** *n* maladresse *f*

blunt [blʌnt] **1** (**-er, -est**) *adj (edge)* émoussé; *(pencil)* mal taillé; *(question, statement)* direct; *(person)* brusque
2 *vt (blade)* émousser; *(pencil)* épointer • **bluntly** *adv (say)* franchement • **bluntness** *n (of manner, statement)* rudesse *f*; *(of person)* franchise *f*

blur [blɜː(r)] **1** *n* tache *f* floue
2 (*pt & pp* **-rr-**) *vt (outline)* brouiller • **blurred** *adj (image, outline)* flou

blurb [blɜːb] *n Fam* notice *f* publicitaire

blurt [blɜːt] *vt* **to b. (out)** *(secret)* laisser échapper; *(excuse)* bredouiller

blush [blʌʃ] **1** *n* rougeur *f*; **with a b.** en rougissant; **to spare sb's blushes** éviter un embarras à qn
2 *vi* rougir (**with** de)

bluster ['blʌstə(r)] *vi (of person)* tempêter; *(of wind)* faire rage • **blustery** *adj (weather)* de grand vent; *(wind)* violent

BO [biː'əʊ] *(abbr* body odour) *n Fam* **to have BO** sentir mauvais

boar [bɔː(r)] *n (wild)* **b.** sanglier *m*

board¹ [bɔːd] **1** *n (piece of wood)* planche *f*; *(for notices)* panneau *m*; *(for games)* tableau *m*; *(cardboard)* carton *m*; **on b.** (**a ship/plane**) à bord (d'un navire/avion); **to go on b.** monter à bord; *Fig* **to take sth on b.** tenir compte de qch; **to go by the b.** *(of plan)* être abandonné
2 *vt (ship, plane)* monter à bord de; *(bus, train)* monter dans; **to b. up** *(door)* condamner
3 *vi* **flight Z001 is now boarding** vol Z001, embarquement immédiat • **boarding** *n (of passengers)* embarquement *m*; **b. pass** carte *f* d'embarquement • **boardwalk** *n Am (on beach)* promenade *f*

board² [bɔːd] *n (committee)* conseil *m*; **b. (of directors)** conseil *m* d'administration; **b. (of examiners)** jury *m* (d'examen); *Br Pol* **B. of Trade** ≃ ministère *m* du Commerce; **across the b.** *(pay increase)* global; *(apply)* globalement; **b. room** salle *f* du conseil

board³ [bɔːd] **1** *n (food)* pension *f*; **b. and lodging,** *Br* **full b.** pension *f* complète; *Br* **half b.** demi-pension *f*
2 *vi (lodge)* être en pension (**with** chez); **boarding house** pension *f* de famille;

boarding school pensionnat *m* • **boarder** *n* pensionnaire *mf*

boast [bəʊst] **1** *n* vantardise *f*
2 *vt* se glorifier de; **to b. that one can do sth** se vanter de pouvoir faire qch
3 *vi* se vanter (**about** *or* **of** de) • **boasting** *n* vantardise *f*

boastful ['bəʊstfəl] *adj* vantard

boat [bəʊt] *n* bateau *m*; *(small)* canot *m*; *(liner)* paquebot *m*; **by b.** en bateau; *Fig* **in the same b.** logé à la même enseigne; **b. race** course *f* d'aviron • **boating** *n* canotage *m*; **to go b.** faire du canotage; **b. trip** excursion *f* en bateau

boatswain ['bəʊsən] *n Naut* maître *m* d'équipage

bob [bɒb] *(pt & pp* **-bb-**) *vi* **to b. (up and down)** *(on water)* danser sur l'eau

bobbin ['bɒbɪn] *n* bobine *f*

bobby ['bɒbɪ] *(pl* **-ies**) *n* (**a**) *Br Fam (policeman)* agent *m* (**b**) *Am* **b. pin** pince *f* à cheveux

bode [bəʊd] *vi* **to b. well/ill (for)** être de bon/mauvais augure (pour)

bodice ['bɒdɪs] *n* corsage *m*

bodily ['bɒdɪlɪ] **1** *adj (need)* physique
2 *adv (lift, seize)* à bras-le-corps; *(carry)* dans ses bras

body ['bɒdɪ] *(pl* **-ies**) *n* corps *m*; *(of car)* carrosserie *f*; *(quantity)* masse *f*; *(institution)* organisme *m*; **dead b.** cadavre *m*; **the main b. of the audience** le gros de l'assistance; **b. building** culturisme *m*; **b. piercing** piercing *m*; **b. warmer** gilet *m* matelassé • **bodyguard** *n* garde *m* du corps • **bodywork** *n* carrosserie *f*

boffin ['bɒfɪn] *n Br Fam Hum* scientifique *mf*

bog [bɒg] **1** *n (swamp)* marécage *m*
2 *vt* **to get bogged down in** *(mud, work)* s'enliser (dans); *(details)* se perdre (dans) • **boggy** (**-ier, -iest**) *adj* marécageux, -euse

bogey ['bəʊgɪ] *(pl* **-eys**) *n (of war)* spectre *m* • **bogeyman** *n* croque-mitaine *m*

boggle ['bɒgəl] *vi Fam* **the mind boggles** ça laisse rêveur

bogus ['bəʊgəs] *adj* faux (*f* fausse)

boil¹ [bɔɪl] *n (pimple)* furoncle *m*

boil² [bɔɪl] **1** *n* **to come to the b.** bouillir; **to bring sth to the b.** amener qch à ébullition
2 *vt* **to b. (up)** faire bouillir; **to b. the kettle** mettre de l'eau à chauffer
3 *vi* bouillir; **to b. away** *(until dry)* s'évaporer; *(on and on)* bouillir sans arrêt; *Fig* **to b. down to** *(of situation, question)* revenir à; **to b. over** *(of milk)* déborder;

Fig (of situation) empirer • **boiled** *adj* bouilli; **b. egg** œuf *m* à la coque • **boiling** **1** *n* ébullition *f*; **to be at b. point** *(of liquid)* bouillir **2** *adj* **b. (hot)** bouillant; **it's b. (hot)** *(weather)* il fait une chaleur infernale

boiler ['bɔɪlə(r)] *n* chaudière *f*; *Br* **b. suit** bleus *mpl* de chauffe

boisterous ['bɔɪstərəs] *adj (noisy)* bruyant; *(child)* turbulent; *(meeting)* houleux, -euse

bold [bəʊld] (-**er**, -**est**) *adj* hardi; *Typ* **in b. type** en (caractères) gras • **boldness** *n* hardiesse *f*

Bolivia [bə'lɪvɪə] *n* la Bolivie • **Bolivian** **1** *adj* bolivien, -ienne **2** *n* Bolivien, -ienne *mf*

bollard ['bɒləd, 'bɒlɑːd] *n Br (for traffic)* borne *f*

boloney [bə'ləʊnɪ] *n Fam (nonsense)* âneries *fpl*

bolster ['bəʊlstə(r)] **1** *n (pillow)* traversin *m*
2 *vt (confidence, pride)* renforcer, consolider

bolt [bəʊlt] **1** *n* (**a**) *(on door)* verrou *m*; *(for nut)* boulon *m* (**b**) *(dash)* **to make a b. for the door** se précipiter vers la porte (**c**) **b. of lightning** éclair *m*
2 *adv* **b. upright** tout droit
3 *vt* (**a**) *(door)* verrouiller (**b**) *(food)* engloutir
4 *vi (dash)* se précipiter; *(run away)* détaler; *(of horse)* s'emballer

bomb [bɒm] **1** *n* bombe *f*; **b. scare** alerte *f* à la bombe
2 *vt (from the air)* bombarder; *(of terrorist)* faire sauter une bombe dans *ou* à • **bomber** *n (aircraft)* bombardier *m*; *(terrorist)* poseur *m* de bombe • **bombing** *n* bombardement *m*; *(terrorist)* attentat *m* à la bombe • **bombshell** *n* **to come as a b.** faire l'effet d'une bombe • **bombsite** *n* zone *f* bombardée

bombard [bɒm'bɑːd] *vt (with bombs, questions)* bombarder (**with** de) • **bombardment** *n* bombardement *m*

bona fide [bəʊnə'faɪdɪ] *adj* véritable

bonanza [bə'nænzə] *n* aubaine *f*

bond [bɒnd] **1** *n (link)* lien *m*; *(agreement)* engagement *m*; *Fin* obligation *f*
2 *vt (of glue)* coller (**to** à)
3 *vi (form attachment)* créer des liens affectifs (**with** avec)

bondage ['bɒndɪdʒ] *n* esclavage *m*

bone [bəʊn] **1** *n* os *m*; *(of fish)* arête *f*; **b. of contention** pomme *f* de discorde; **b. china** porcelaine *f* tendre

2 *vt (meat)* désosser; *(fish)* ôter les arêtes de
3 *vi Am Fam* **to b. up on** *(subject)* bûcher • **bone-dry** *adj* complètement sec *(f* sèche) • **bone-'idle** *adj Br* paresseux, -euse • **bony** (-**ier**, -**iest**) *adj (thin)* maigre; *(fish)* plein d'arêtes

bonfire ['bɒnfaɪə(r)] *n (for celebration)* feu *m* de joie; *Br (for dead leaves)* feu *m* (de jardin)

bonkers ['bɒŋkəz] *adj Br Fam* dingue

bonnet ['bɒnɪt] *n (hat)* bonnet *m*; *Br (of vehicle)* capot *m*

bonus ['bəʊnəs] *(pl* -**uses** [-əsɪz]) *n* prime *f*; **no claims b.** *(of car driver)* bonus *m*; **b. number** *(in lottery)* numéro *m* complémentaire

boo [buː] **1** *exclam (to frighten)* hou!
2 *n* boos huées *fpl*
3 *(pt & pp* **booed**) *vti* huer

boob [buːb] *Br Fam* **1** *n* (**a**) *(mistake)* gaffe *f* (**b**) **boobs** *(breasts)* nénés *mpl*
2 *vi* gaffer

booby-trap ['buːbɪtræp] **1** *n* engin *m* piégé
2 *(pt & pp* -**pp**-) *vt* piéger

book¹ [bʊk] *n* livre *m*; *(record)* registre *m*; *(of tickets)* carnet *m*; *(for exercises and notes)* cahier *m*; **books** *(accounts)* comptes *mpl*; **b. club** club *m* du livre • **bookbinding** *n* reliure *f* • **bookcase** *n* bibliothèque *f* • **bookend** *n* serre-livres *m inv* • **bookie** *n Fam* bookmaker *m* • **book-keeping** *n* comptabilité *f* • **booklet** *n* brochure *f* • **book-lover** *n* bibliophile *mf* • **bookmaker** *n* bookmaker *m* • **bookmark** *n* marque-page *m* • **bookseller** *n* libraire *mf* • **bookshelf** *n* étagère *f* • **bookshop** *(Am* **bookstore**) *n* librairie *f* • **bookstall** *n* kiosque *m* à journaux • **bookworm** *n* passionné, -ée *mf* de lecture

book² [bʊk] **1** *vt* **to b. (up)** *(seat)* réserver; *Br* **to b. sb** *(for traffic offence)* dresser une contravention à qn; **fully booked (up)** *(hotel, concert)* complet, -ète; *(person)* pris
2 *vi* **to b. (up)** réserver des places; **to b. in** *(to hotel)* signer le registre; **to b. into a hotel** prendre une chambre dans un hôtel • **bookable** *adj (seat)* qu'on peut réserver • **booking** *n* réservation *f*; **b. clerk** guichetier, -ière *mf*; **b. office** bureau *m* de location

bookish ['bʊkɪʃ] *adj (word, theory)* livresque; *(person)* studieux, -ieuse

boom [buːm] **1** *n* (**a**) *(noise)* grondement *m* (**b**) *(economic)* boom *m*
2 *vi* (**a**) *(of thunder, gun)* gronder (**b**) *(of business, trade)* être florissant

boomerang [ˈbuːməræŋ] *n* boomerang *m*

boor [bʊə(r)] *n* rustre *m* •**boorish** *adj* rustre

boost [buːst] **1** *n* **to give sb a b.** remonter le moral à qn
2 *vt (increase)* augmenter; *(product)* faire de la réclame pour; *(economy)* stimuler; **to b. sb's morale** remonter le moral à qn; **to b. sb (up)** *(push upwards)* soulever qn •**booster** *n* **b. (injection)** rappel *m*

boot¹ [buːt] **1** *n* (**a**) *(shoe)* botte *f*; **(ankle) b.** bottillon *m*; **(knee) b.** bottine *f*; *Fam* **to get the b.** être mis à la porte; **b. polish** cirage *m* (**b**) *Br (of vehicle)* coffre *m* (**c**) **to b.** *(in addition)* en plus
2 *vt Fam (kick)* donner un coup *ou* des coups de pied à; **to b. sb out** mettre qn à la porte •**bootee** *n (of baby)* chausson *m* •**bootlace** *n* lacet *m*

boot² [buːt] *Comptr* **1** *vt* amorcer
2 *vi* s'amorcer

booth [buːθ, buːð] *n (for phone, in language lab)* cabine *f*; *(at fair)* stand *m*; *(for voting)* isoloir *m*

booty [ˈbuːtɪ] *n (loot)* butin *m*

booze [buːz] *Fam* **1** *n* alcool *m*
2 *vi* picoler •**boozer** *n Fam (person)* poivrot, -ote *mf*; *Br (pub)* pub *m* •**booze-up** *n Br Fam* beuverie *f*

border [ˈbɔːdə(r)] **1** *n (of country) & Fig* frontière *f*; *(edge)* bord *m*; *(of garden)* bordure *f*
2 *adj (town)* frontière *inv*; *(incident)* de frontière
3 *vt (street)* border; **to b. (on)** *(country)* avoir une frontière commune avec; **to b. (up)on** *(resemble, verge on)* être voisin de •**borderland** *n* zone *f* frontalière •**borderline** *n* frontière *f*; **b. case** cas *m* limite

bore¹ [bɔː(r)] **1** *vt (weary)* ennuyer; **to be bored** s'ennuyer; **I'm bored with that job** ce travail m'ennuie
2 *n (person)* raseur, -euse *mf*; **it's a b.** c'est ennuyeux *ou* rasoir •**boring** *adj* ennuyeux, -euse

bore² [bɔː(r)] **1** *n (of gun)* calibre *m*
2 *vt (hole)* percer; *(rock, well)* forer, creuser
3 *vi* forer

bore³ [bɔː(r)] *pt of* bear²

boredom [ˈbɔːdəm] *n* ennui *m*

born [bɔːn] *adj* né; **to be b.** naître; **he was b. in Paris/in 1980** il est né à Paris/en 1980

borne [bɔːn] *pp of* bear²

borough [ˈbʌrə] *n* circonscription *f* électorale urbaine

borrow [ˈbɒrəʊ] *vt* emprunter (**from** à) •**borrowing** *n* emprunt *m*

Bosnia [ˈbɒznɪə] *n* la Bosnie

bosom [ˈbʊzəm] *n (chest, breasts)* poitrine *f*; *(breast)* sein *m*; *Fig (heart, soul)* sein; **b. friend** ami, -ie *mf* intime

boss [bɒs] **1** *n* patron, -onne *mf*
2 *vt* **to b. sb around** *or* **about** donner des ordres à qn •**bossy** (**-ier, -iest**) *adj Fam* autoritaire

boss-eyed [ˈbɒsaɪd] *adj* **to be b.** loucher

bosun [ˈbəʊsən] *n Naut* maître *m* d'équipage

botany [ˈbɒtənɪ] *n* botanique *f* •**botanical** [bəˈtænɪkəl] *adj* botanique •**botanist** *n* botaniste *mf*

botch [bɒtʃ] *vt Fam* **to b. (up)** *(spoil)* bâcler; *(repair badly)* rafistoler

both [bəʊθ] **1** *adj* les deux; **b. brothers** les deux frères
2 *pron* tous/toutes (les) deux; **b. of the boys** les deux garçons; **b. of us** tous les deux; **b. of them died** ils sont morts tous les deux
3 *adv (at the same time)* à la fois; **b. in England and in France** en Angleterre comme en France; **b. you and I know that...** vous et moi, nous savons que...

bother [ˈbɒðə(r)] **1** *n (trouble)* ennui *m*; *(effort)* peine *f*; *(inconvenience)* dérangement *m*; *Br* **(oh) b.!** zut alors!
2 *vt (annoy, worry)* ennuyer; *(disturb)* déranger; *(pester)* importuner; *(hurt, itch)* *(of foot, eye)* gêner; **to b. doing** *or* **to do sth** se donner la peine de faire qch; **I can't be bothered!** ça m'embête!
3 *vi* **to b. about** *(worry about)* se préoccuper de; *(deal with)* s'occuper de; **don't b.!** ne prends pas cette peine!

bottle [ˈbɒtəl] **1** *n* bouteille *f*; *(small)* flacon *m*; *(wide-mouthed)* bocal *m*; *(for baby)* biberon *m*; **b. bank** conteneur *m* pour verre usagé; **b. opener** ouvre-bouteilles *m inv*
2 *vt (milk, wine)* mettre en bouteilles; **to b. up** *(feeling)* refouler •**bottle-feed** (*pt & pp* **-fed**) *vt* nourrir au biberon •**bottle-neck** *n (in road)* goulot *m* d'étranglement; *(traffic hold-up)* bouchon *m*

bottom [ˈbɒtəm] **1** *n (of sea, box)* fond *m*; *(of page, hill)* bas *m*; *(of table)* bout *m*; *Fam (buttocks)* derrière *m*; **to be (at the) b. of the class** être le dernier/la dernière de la classe
2 *adj (shelf)* inférieur, du bas; **b. floor** rez-de-chaussée *m*; **b. gear** première vitesse *f*; **b. part** *or* **half** partie *f* inférieure; *Fig* **the b. line is that...** le fait est que...

●**bottomless** *adj (funds)* inépuisable; **b. pit** gouffre *m*

bough [baʊ] *n Literary* rameau *m*

bought [bɔːt] *pt & pp of* **buy**

boulder ['bəʊldə(r)] *n* rocher *m*

boulevard ['buːləvɑːd] *n* boulevard *m*

bounce [baʊns] **1** *n* rebond *m*

2 *vt (ball)* faire rebondir

3 *vi (of ball)* rebondir (**off** contre); *(of person)* faire des bonds; *Fam (of cheque)* être sans provision; **to b. into a hole** *(of ball)* rebondir et atterrir dans un trou

bouncer ['baʊnsə(r)] *n Fam (doorman)* videur *m*

bound¹ [baʊnd] *adj* (**a**) **b. to do** *(obliged)* obligé de faire; *(certain)* sûr de faire; **it's b. to snow** il va sûrement neiger; **to be b. for** *(of person, ship)* être en route pour; *(of train, plane)* être à destination de (**b**) **b. up with** *(connected)* lié à

bound² [baʊnd] **1** *n (leap)* bond *m*

2 *vi* bondir

bound³ [baʊnd] *pt & pp of* **bind**

boundary ['baʊndəri] *(pl -ies) n* limite *f*

bounded ['baʊndɪd] *adj* **b. by** limité par

boundless ['baʊndləs] *adj* sans bornes

bounds [baʊndz] *npl* limites *fpl*; **out of b.** *(place)* interdit

bounty ['baʊntɪ] *(pl -ies) n (reward)* prime *f*

bouquet [bəʊ'keɪ] *n (of flowers, wine)* bouquet *m*

bourbon ['bɜːbən] *n (whisky)* bourbon *m*

bout [baʊt] *n (of fever, coughing, violence)* accès *m*; *(of asthma, malaria)* crise *f*; *(session)* séance *f*; *(period)* période *f*; *Boxing* combat *m*; **a b. of flu** une grippe

boutique [buː'tiːk] *n* boutique *f* (de mode)

bow¹ [bəʊ] *n (weapon)* arc *m*; *(of violin)* archet *m*; *(knot)* nœud *m*; **b. tie** nœud *m* papillon ●**bow-legged** ['bəʊ'legɪd] *adj* aux jambes arquées

bow² [baʊ] **1** *n (with knees bent)* révérence *f*; *(nod)* salut *m*; **to take a b.** *(of actor)* saluer

2 *vt* **to b. one's head** incliner la tête

3 *vi* s'incliner (**to** devant); *(nod)* incliner la tête (**to** devant); **to b. down** *(submit)* s'incliner (**to** devant)

bow³ [baʊ] *n (of ship)* proue *f*

bowels ['baʊəlz] *npl* intestins *mpl*; *Literary* **in the b. of the earth** dans les entrailles de la terre

bowl¹ [bəʊl] *n (small dish)* bol *m*; *(for salad)* saladier *m*; *(for soup)* assiette *f* creuse; *(of toilet)* cuvette *f*

bowl² [bəʊl] **1** *n* **bowls** *(game)* boules *fpl*

2 *vi (in cricket)* lancer la balle ●**bowling** *n* (**tenpin**) **b.** bowling *m*; **b. alley** bowling; **b. ball** boule *f* de bowling; **b. green** terrain *m* de boules

▸**bowl along** *vi (of car, bicycle)* rouler à toute vitesse ▸**bowl over** *vt sep (knock down)* renverser; *Fig (astound)* **to be bowled over by sth** être stupéfié par qch

bowler ['bəʊlə(r)] *n Br* **b.** (**hat**) chapeau *m* melon

box [bɒks] **1** *n* boîte *f*; *(larger)* caisse *f*; *(of cardboard)* carton *m*; *(in theatre)* loge *f*; *(for horse, in stable)* box *m*; *Br Fam (television)* télé *f*; **b. number** *(at post office)* numéro *m* de boîte postale; *(at newspaper)* référence *f* de petite annonce; **b. office** bureau *m* de location; *Br* **b. room** *(lumber room)* débarras *m*; *(bedroom)* petite chambre *f*

2 *vt* (**a**) **to b. (up)** mettre en boîte/ caisse; **to b. in** *(enclose)* enfermer (**b**) **to b. sb's ears** gifler qn

3 *vi* boxer; **to b. against sb** boxer contre qn ●**boxing** *n* (**a**) boxe *f*; **b. gloves/match** gants *mpl*/combat *m* de boxe; **b. ring** ring *m* (**b**) *Br* **B. Day** le lendemain de Noël

boxcar ['bɒkskɑːr] *n Am Rail* wagon *m* couvert

boxer ['bɒksə(r)] *n (fighter)* boxeur *m*; *(dog)* boxer *m*

boy [bɔɪ] *n* garçon *m*; **English b.** jeune Anglais *m*; *Br* **old b.** *(former pupil)* ancien élève *m*; *Br* **yes, old b.!** oui, mon vieux!; *Fam* **the boys** *(pals)* les copains *mpl*; **my dear b.** mon cher ami; **oh b.!** mon Dieu! ●**boyfriend** *n* petit ami *m* ●**boyhood** *n* enfance *f* ●**boyish** *adj* de garçon; *Pej* puéril

boycott ['bɔɪkɒt] **1** *n* boycottage *m*

2 *vt* boycotter

bra [brɑː] *n* soutien-gorge *m*

brace [breɪs] **1** *n (dental)* appareil *m* dentaire; *(on leg, arm)* appareil *m* orthopédique; *(for fastening)* attache *f*; *Br* **braces** *(for trousers)* bretelles *fpl*

2 *vt* **to b. oneself for sth** *(news, shock)* se préparer à qch ●**bracing** *adj (air)* vivifiant

bracelet ['breɪslɪt] *n* bracelet *m*

bracken ['brækən] *n* fougère *f*

bracket ['brækɪt] **1** *n (for shelves)* équerre *f*; *(round sign)* parenthèse *f*; *(square sign)* crochet *m*; *(group)* groupe *m*; *(for tax)* tranche *f*; **in brackets** entre parenthèses/ crochets

2 *vt* mettre entre parenthèses/crochets; **to b. together** mettre dans le même groupe

brag [bræg] *(pt & pp -gg-) vi* se vanter

(**about** *or* **of sth** de qch; **about doing** de faire)

braid [breɪd] **1** *n* (*of hair*) tresse *f*; (*trimming*) galon *m*

2 *vt* (*hair*) tresser; (*trim*) galonner

Braille [breɪl] *n* braille *m*; **in B.** en braille

brain [breɪn] **1** *n* cerveau *m*; (*of animal, bird*) cervelle *f*; *Fam* **to have brains** (*sense*) être intelligent; *Fam* **to have money on the b.** être obsédé par l'argent; *Hum* **use your brain(s)!** réfléchis un peu!; **b. death** mort *f* cérébrale; **b. drain** fuite *f* des cerveaux

2 *vt Fam* (*hit*) assommer • **brainchild** ['breɪntʃaɪld] *n* trouvaille *f* • **brainstorm** *n Am* (*brilliant idea*) idée *f* géniale; *Br* (*mental confusion*) aberration *f* • **brainwash** *vt* faire un lavage de cerveau à • **brainwashing** *n* lavage *m* de cerveau • **brainwave** *n* idée *f* géniale

brainy ['breɪnɪ] (**-ier, -iest**) *adj Fam* intelligent

braise [breɪz] *vt* (*meat*) braiser

brake [breɪk] **1** *n* frein *m*; **b. fluid** liquide *m* de freins; **b. light** (*on vehicle*) stop *m*

2 *vi* freiner • **braking** *n* freinage *m*

bramble ['bræmbəl] *n* ronce *f*

bran [bræn] *n* son *m*

branch [brɑːntʃ] **1** *n* branche *f*; (*of road*) embranchement *m*; (*of river*) bras *m*; (*of store*) succursale *f*; (*of bank*) agence *f*; **b. office** succursale

2 *vi* **to b. off** (*of road*) bifurquer; **to b. out** (*of firm, person*) étendre ses activités; (*of family, tree*) se ramifier

brand [brænd] **1** *n* (*on product, on cattle*) marque *f*; (*type*) type *m*, style *m*; **b. name** marque

2 *vt* (*mark*) marquer; *Fig* **to be branded as a liar/coward** avoir une réputation de menteur/lâche

brandish ['brændɪʃ] *vt* brandir

brand-new [brænd'njuː] *adj* tout neuf (*f* toute neuve)

brandy ['brændɪ] (*pl* **-ies**) *n* cognac *m*; (*made with fruit*) eau-de-vie *f*

brash [bræʃ] *adj* exubérant

brass [brɑːs] *n* cuivre *m*; (*instruments in orchestra*) cuivres *mpl*; *Fam* **the top b.** (*officers, executives*) les huiles *fpl*; **b. band** fanfare *f*

brassiere [*Br* 'bræzɪə(r), *Am* brə'zɪə(r)] *n* soutien-gorge *m*

brat [bræt] *n Pej* (*child*) morveux, -euse *mf*; (*badly behaved*) sale gosse *mf*

bravado [brə'vɑːdəʊ] *n* bravade *f*

brave [breɪv] **1** (**-er, -est**) *adj* courageux, -euse

2 *n* (*native American*) brave *m*

3 *vt* (*danger*) braver • **bravely** *adv* courageusement • **bravery** *n* courage *m*

> ♪ Note that the French word **brave** is a false friend. Its most common meaning is **kind**.

bravo [brɑː'vəʊ] *exclam* bravo!

brawl [brɔːl] **1** *n* (*fight*) bagarre *f*

2 *vi* se bagarrer • **brawling 1** *adj* bagarreur, -euse **2** *n* bagarres *fpl*

brawn [brɔːn] *n Fam* muscles *mpl* • **brawny** (**-ier, -iest**) *adj* musclé

bray [breɪ] *vi* (*of donkey*) braire

brazen ['breɪzən] **1** *adj* (*shameless*) effronté; (*lie*) éhonté

2 *vt* **to b. it out** s'en tirer au culot

Brazil [brə'zɪl] *n* le Brésil • **Brazilian 1** *adj* brésilien, -ienne **2** *n* Brésilien, -ienne *mf*

breach [briːtʃ] **1** *n* (**a**) (*of rule*) violation *f* (**of** de); **b. of contract** rupture *f* de contrat; **b. of trust** abus *m* de confiance (**b**) (*in wall*) brèche *f*

2 *vt* (**a**) (*law, code*) enfreindre à; (*contract*) rompre (**b**) (*wall*) ouvrir une brèche dans

bread [bred] *n* pain *m*; *very Fam* (*money*) blé *m*; **loaf of b.** pain; **brown b.** pain bis; (**slice** *or* **piece of**) **b. and butter** pain beurré; **it's my b. and butter** (*job*) c'est mon gagne-pain; **b. knife** couteau *m* à pain • **breadbin** (*Am* **breadbox**) *n* boîte *f* à pain • **breadboard** *n* planche *f* à pain • **breadcrumb** *n* miette *f* de pain; **breadcrumbs** (*in cooking*) chapelure *f* • **breaded** *adj* pané • **breadline** *n* **on the b.** indigent • **breadwinner** *n* **to be the b.** faire bouillir la marmite

breadth [bretθ] *n* largeur *f*

break [breɪk] **1** *n* cassure *f*; (*in bone*) fracture *f*; (*with person, group*) rupture *f*; (*in journey*) interruption *f*; (*rest*) repos *m*; (*in activity*) pause *f*; (*at school*) récréation *f*; (*holidays*) vacances *fpl*; *Fam* **to have a lucky b.** avoir de la veine; *Fam* **this could be your big b.** ça peut être la chance de ta vie; *Fam* **give him a b.!** laisse-le tranquille!

2 (*pt* **broke**, *pp* **broken**) *vt* casser; (*into pieces, with force*) briser; (*silence, spell, vow*) rompre; (*strike, will, ice*) briser; (*agreement, promise*) manquer à; (*treaty, law*) violer; (*record*) battre; (*journey*) interrompre; (*news*) annoncer (**to** à); (*habit*) se débarrasser de; **to b. one's arm** se casser le bras; **to b. sb's heart** briser le cœur à qn; *Fam* **b. a leg!** bonne chance!; **to b. the sound barrier** franchir le mur du son; **to b. a fall** amortir une chute; **to b. new ground** innover; **to b. open** *(safe)* percer

3 *vi* se casser; *(into pieces, of heart, of voice)* se briser; *(of boy's voice)* muer; *(of spell)* se rompre; *(of weather)* changer; *(of news)* éclater; *(of day)* se lever; *(of wave)* déferler; *(stop work)* faire la pause; **to b. in two** se casser en deux; **to b. free** se libérer; **to b. loose** se détacher; **to b. with sb** rompre avec qn • **breakable** *adj* fragile • **breakage** *n* **were there any breakages?** est-ce qu'il y a eu de la casse? • **breakaway** *adj (group)* dissident • **breakdown** *n (of machine)* panne *f*; *(of argument, figures)* analyse *f*; *(of talks)* échec *m*; *(of person)* dépression *f*; *Br* **b. lorry** *or* **van** dépanneuse *f* • **breaker** *n (wave)* déferlante *f* • **break-in** *n* cambriolage *m* • **breaking-point** *n* **at b.** *(person, patience)* à bout; *(marriage)* au bord de la rupture • **breakthrough** *n (discovery)* découverte *f* fondamentale • **breakup** *n* fin *f*; *(in marriage, friendship)* rupture *f*

▸ **break away 1** *vi* se détacher **2** *vt sep* détacher ▸ **break down 1** *vt sep (door)* enfoncer; *(resistance)* briser; *(argument, figures)* analyser **2** *vi (of machine)* tomber en panne; *(of talks, negotiations)* échouer; *(of person) (collapse)* s'effondrer; *(have nervous breakdown)* craquer; *(start crying)* éclater en sanglots ▸ **break in 1** *vi (of burglar)* entrer par effraction; *(interrupt)* interrompre **2** *vt sep (door)* enfoncer; *(horse)* dresser ▸ **break into** *vt insep (house)* entrer par effraction; *(safe)* forcer; **to b. into song/a run** se mettre à chanter/courir; **to b. into laughter/tears** éclater de rire/en sanglots ▸ **break off 1** *vt sep (detach) (twig, handle)* détacher; *(relations)* rompre **2** *vi (become detached)* se casser; *(stop)* s'arrêter; **to b. off with sb** rompre avec qn ▸ **break out** *vi (of war, fire)* éclater; *(escape)* s'échapper (**of** de); **to b. out in a rash** se couvrir de boutons ▸ **break through 1** *vi (of sun, army)* percer **2** *vt insep (defences)* percer; *(barrier)* forcer; *(wall)* faire une brèche dans ▸ **break up 1** *vt sep (reduce to pieces)* mettre en morceaux; *(marriage)* briser; *(fight)* mettre fin à **2** *vi (end)* prendre fin; *(of group)* se disperser; *(of marriage)* se briser; *(from school)* partir en vacances

breakfast ['brekfəst] *n* petit déjeuner *m*; **to have b.** prendre le petit déjeuner; **b. TV** émissions *fpl* (télévisées) du matin

breakwater ['breɪkwɔːtə(r)] *n* brise-lames *m inv*

breast [brest] *n (of woman)* sein *m*; *(chest)* poitrine *f*; *(of chicken)* blanc *m* • **breastfeed** *(pt & pp* **-fed***) vt* allaiter • **breaststroke** *n (in swimming)* brasse *f*

breath [breθ] *n* souffle *m*; **bad b.** mauvaise haleine *f*; **out of b.** à bout de souffle; **to take a deep b.** respirer profondément; **to hold one's b.** retenir son souffle; **to get a b. of fresh air** prendre l'air; **under one's b.** tout bas; **one's last b.** son dernier soupir • **breathalyser**® *n* Alcotest® *m* • **breathless** *adj* hors d'haleine • **breathtaking** *adj* à couper le souffle

breathe [briːð] **1** *vi (of person, animal)* respirer; **to b. in** inhaler; **to b. out** expirer **2** *vt* respirer; **to b. air into sth** souffler dans qch; **to b. a sigh of relief** pousser un soupir de soulagement; **she didn't b. a word (about it)** elle n'en a pas soufflé mot • **breathing** *n* respiration *f*; *Fig* **b. space** moment *m* de repos

breather ['briːðə(r)] *n Fam* pause *f*; **to have a b.** faire une pause

bred [bred] **1** *pt & pp of* **breed 2** *adj* **well-b.** bien élevé

breed [briːd] **1** *n* race *f* **2** *(pt & pp* **bred***) vt (animals)* élever; *Fig (hatred, violence)* engendrer **3** *vi (of animals)* se reproduire • **breeder** *n* éleveur, -euse *mf* • **breeding** *n (of animals)* élevage *m*; *(procreation)* reproduction *f*; *Fig (manners)* éducation *f*

breeze [briːz] *n* brise *f* • **breezy** (**-ier**, **-iest**) *adj* (**a**) *(weather, day)* frais *(f* fraîche), venteux, -euse (**b**) *(cheerful)* jovial; *(relaxed)* décontracté

breeze-block *n Br* parpaing *m*

brevity ['brevɪtɪ] *n* brièveté *f*

brew [bruː] **1** *n (drink)* breuvage *m*; *(of tea)* infusion *f* **2** *vt (beer)* brasser; *Fig (trouble, plot)* préparer; **to b. some tea** *(make)* préparer du thé **3** *vi (of beer)* fermenter; *(of tea)* infuser; *Fig (of storm)* se préparer; **something is brewing** il se trame quelque chose • **brewer** *n* brasseur *m* • **brewery** *(pl* **-ies***) n* brasserie *f*

bribe [braɪb] **1** *n* pot-de-vin *m* **2** *vt* acheter, soudoyer; **to b. sb into doing sth** soudoyer qn pour qu'il fasse qch • **bribery** *n* corruption *f*

brick [brɪk] **1** *n* brique *f*; *(child's)* cube *m*; **b. wall** mur en briques; *Br Fam* **to drop a b.** faire une gaffe **2** *vt* **to b. up** *(gap, door)* murer • **bricklayer** *n* maçon *m* • **brickwork** *n (bricks)* briques *fpl*; *(construction)* ouvrage *m* en briques

bridal ['braɪdəl] *adj (ceremony, bed)* nuptial; **b. gown** robe *f* de mariée; **b. suite** *(in hotel)* suite *f* nuptiale

bride [braɪd] *n* mariée *f*; **the b. and groom** les mariés *mpl* •**bridegroom** *n* marié *m* •**bridesmaid** *n* demoiselle *f* d'honneur

bridge¹ [brɪdʒ] **1** *n* pont *m*; *(on ship)* passerelle *f*; *(of nose)* arête *f*; *(on teeth)* bridge *m*
2 *vt* **to b. a gap** combler une lacune

bridge² [brɪdʒ] *n (game)* bridge *m*

bridle ['braɪdəl] **1** *n (for horse)* bride *f*; **b. path** allée *f* cavalière
2 *vt (horse)* brider

brief¹ [briːf] (**-er, -est**) *adj* bref (*f* brève); **in b.** en résumé •**briefly** *adv (quickly)* en vitesse; *(say)* brièvement; *(hesitate)* un court instant

brief² [briːf] **1** *n (instructions)* instructions *fpl*; *(legal)* dossier *m*; *Fig (task)* tâche *f*
2 *vt* donner des instructions à; *(inform)* mettre au courant (**on** de) •**briefing** *n (information)* instructions *fpl*; *(meeting)* briefing *m*

briefcase ['briːfkeɪs] *n* serviette *f*

briefs [briːfs] *npl (underwear)* slip *m*

brigade [brɪ'geɪd] *n* brigade *f* •**brigadier** [brɪgə'dɪə(r)] *n* général *m* de brigade

bright [braɪt] **1** (**-er, -est**) *adj (star, eyes, situation)* brillant; *(light, colour)* vif (*f* vive); *(weather, room)* clair; *(clever)* intelligent; *(happy)* joyeux, -euse; *(future)* prometteur, -euse; *(idea)* génial; **b. interval** *(sunny period)* éclaircie *f*
2 *adv* **b. and early** *(to get up)* de bon matin •**brightly** *adv (shine)* avec éclat •**brightness** *n* éclat *m*; *(of person)* intelligence *f*

brighten ['braɪtən] **1** *vt* **to b. (up)** *(room)* égayer
2 *vi* **to b. (up)** *(of weather)* s'éclaircir; *(of face)* s'éclairer; *(of person)* s'égayer

brilliant ['brɪljənt] *adj (light)* éclatant; *(person, idea, career)* brillant; *Br Fam (fantastic)* super *inv* •**brilliance** *n* éclat *m*; *(of person)* intelligence *f*

brim [brɪm] **1** *n (of hat, cup)* bord *m*
2 (*pt & pp* **-mm-**) *vi* **to b. over** déborder (**with** de)

brine [braɪn] *n* saumure *f*

bring [brɪŋ] (*pt & pp* **brought**) *vt (person, animal, car)* amener; *(object)* apporter; *(cause)* provoquer; **it has brought me great happiness** cela m'a procuré un grand bonheur; **to b. tears to sb's eyes** faire venir les larmes aux yeux de qn; **to b. sth to sb's attention** attirer l'attention de qn sur qch; **to b. sth to an end** mettre fin à qch; **to b. sth to mind** rappeler qch; **to b. sth on oneself** s'attirer qch; **I can't b. myself to do it** je ne peux pas me résoudre à le faire
► **bring about** *vt sep* provoquer ► **bring along** *vt sep (object)* apporter; *(person)* amener ► **bring back** *vt sep (person)* ramener; *(object)* rapporter; *(memories)* rappeler ► **bring down** *vt sep (object)* descendre; *(overthrow)* faire tomber; *(reduce)* réduire; *(shoot down) (plane)* abattre ► **bring forward** *vt sep (in time or space)* avancer; *(witness)* produire ► **bring in** *vt sep (object)* rentrer; *(person)* faire entrer/venir; *(introduce)* introduire; *(income)* rapporter ► **bring off** *vt sep (task)* mener à bien ► **bring out** *vt sep (object)* sortir; *(person)* faire sortir; *(meaning)* faire ressortir; *(book)* publier; *(product)* lancer; *(revive)* ► **bring round** *vt sep* ranimer; *(convert)* convaincre; **she brought him round to her point of view** elle a su le convaincre ► **bring to** *vt sep* to **b. sb to** ranimer qn ► **bring together** *vt sep (friends, members)* réunir; *(reconcile)* réconcilier; *(put in touch)* mettre en contact ► **bring up** *vt sep (object)* monter; *(child)* élever; *(question)* soulever; *(subject)* mentionner; *(food)* rendre

brink [brɪŋk] *n* bord *m*; **on the b. of sth** au bord de qch

brisk [brɪsk] (**-er, -est**) *adj (lively)* vif (*f* vive); **at a b. pace** vite; **trading is b.** le marché est actif; **business is b.** les affaires marchent bien •**briskly** *adv* vivement; *(walk)* d'un bon pas •**briskness** *n* vivacité *f*

bristle ['brɪsəl] **1** *n* poil *m*
2 *vi* se hérisser; **bristling with difficulties** hérissé de difficultés

Britain ['brɪtən] *n* la Grande-Bretagne •**British 1** *adj* britannique; **the B. Isles** les îles *fpl* Britanniques; **B. Summer Time** heure *f* d'été *(en Grande-Bretagne)* **2** *npl* **the B.** les Britanniques *mpl* •**Briton** *n* Britannique *mf*

Brittany ['brɪtənɪ] *n* la Bretagne

brittle ['brɪtəl] *adj* cassant

broach [brəʊtʃ] *vt (topic)* aborder

broad¹ [brɔːd] (**-er, -est**) *adj (wide)* large; *(accent)* prononcé; **in b. daylight** en plein jour; **the b. outline of** *(plan)* les grandes lignes de; **b. bean** fève *f*; *Am Sport* **b. jump** saut *m* en longueur • '**broad-'minded** *adj (person)* à l'esprit large; **b.-minded views**

(**on**) des idées *fpl* larges (sur) ●'**broad-**
'**shouldered** *adj* large d'épaules
broad² [brɔːd] *n Am Fam (woman)* gon-
zesse *f*
broadcast ['brɔːdkɑːst] **1** *n* émission *f*
2 (*pt & pp* **broadcast**) *vt* diffuser
3 *vi (of station)* émettre; *(of person)*
parler à la radio/à la télévision ●**broad-**
caster *n* journaliste *mf* de radio/télévi-
sion ●**broadcasting** *n Radio* radiodiffusion *f*; *TV* télévision *f*
broaden ['brɔːdən] **1** *vt* élargir
2 *vi* s'élargir
broadly ['brɔːdlɪ] *adv* b. (**speaking**) en
gros
broccoli ['brɒkəlɪ] *n inv (plant)* brocoli *m*;
(food) brocolis *mpl*
brochure ['brəʊʃə(r)] *n* brochure *f*
brogue [brəʊg] *n (Irish)* accent *m* irlandais
broil [brɔɪl] *vti Am* griller ●**broiler** *n* poulet *m* (à rôtir); *(apparatus)* gril *m*
broke [brəʊk] **1** *pt of* **break**
2 *adj Fam (penniless)* fauché ●**broken 1**
pp of **break 2** *adj (man, voice, line)* brisé;
(ground) accidenté; *(spirit)* abattu; **in b.**
English en mauvais anglais; **b. home** famille *f* désunie ●**broken-**'**down** *adj (ma-*
chine) détraqué
broker ['brəʊkə(r)] *n (for shares, cur-*
rency) agent *m* de change; *(for goods,*
insurance) courtier, -ière *mf*
brolly ['brɒlɪ] (*pl* -**ies**) *n Br Fam (umbrella)*
pépin *m*
bronchitis [brɒŋ'kaɪtɪs] *n* bronchite *f*
bronze [brɒnz] *n* bronze *m*; **b. statue**
statue *f* en bronze
brooch [brəʊtʃ] *n (ornament)* broche *f*
brood [bruːd] **1** *n* couvée *f*
2 *vi (of bird)* couver; *Fig* **to b. over sth** *(of*
person) ruminer qch ●**broody** (-**ier**, -**iest**)
adj (person) (sulky) maussade; *(dreamy)*
rêveur, -euse; *Br Fam (woman)* en mal
d'enfant
brook [brʊk] **1** *n* ruisseau *m*
2 *vt Formal (tolerate)* tolérer
broom [bruːm] **1** *n (for sweeping)* balai *m*
2 *(plant)* genêt *m* ●**broomstick** *n* manche *m* à balai
Bros (*abbr* **Brothers**) *Com* **Richard B.** Richard Frères *mpl*
broth [brɒθ] *n (thin)* bouillon *m*; *(thick)*
potage *m*
brothel ['brɒθəl] *n* maison *f* close
brother ['brʌðə(r)] *n* frère *m* ●**brother-in-**
law (*pl* **brothers-in-law**) *n* beau-frère *m*
●**brotherhood** *n* fraternité *f* ●**brotherly**
adj fraternel, -elle

brought [brɔːt] *pt & pp of* **bring**
brow [braʊ] *n* (**a**) *(forehead)* front *m* (**b**)
(of hill) sommet *m*
browbeat ['braʊbiːt] (*pt* -**beat**, *pp* -**bea-**
ten) *vt* intimider; **to b. sb into doing sth**
faire faire qch à qn à force d'intimidation
brown [braʊn] **1** (-**er**, -**est**) *adj* marron
inv; *(hair)* châtain; *(tanned)* bronzé
2 *n* marron *m*
3 *vt (of sun)* brunir; *(food)* faire dorer; *Br*
Fam **to be browned off** en avoir marre
4 *vi (of food)* dorer
Brownie ['braʊnɪ] *n (girl scout)* ≃ jean-
nette *f*
brownie ['braʊnɪ] *n (cake)* = petit gâteau
au chocolat et aux noix
browse [braʊz] **1** *vt Comptr* **to b. the Web**
naviguer sur le Web
2 *vi* (**a**) *(in bookshop)* feuilleter des
livres; *(in shop, supermarket)* regarder;
to b. through *(book)* feuilleter (**b**) *(of*
animal) brouter
bruise [bruːz] **1** *n* bleu *m*; *(on fruit)* meurtrissure *f*
2 *vt* **to b. one's knee/hand** se faire un
bleu au genou/à la main; **to b. a fruit**
taler un fruit ●**bruised** *adj (covered in*
bruises) couvert de bleus ●**bruising** *n*
(bruises) bleus *mpl*
brunch [brʌntʃ] *n Fam* brunch *m*
brunette [bruː'net] *n* brunette *f*
brunt [brʌnt] *n* **to bear the b. of** *(attack,*
anger) subir le plus gros de; *(expense)*
assumer la plus grosse part de
brush [brʌʃ] **1** *n (tool)* brosse *f*; *(for*
shaving) blaireau *m*; *(for sweeping)* balayette *f*; **to give sth a b.** donner un coup
de brosse à qch
2 *vt (teeth, hair)* brosser; *(clothes)* donner un coup de brosse à; **to b. sb/sth**
aside écarter qn/qch; **to b. sth away** *or*
off enlever qch; **to b. up (on) one's French**
se remettre au français
3 *vi* **to b. against sb/sth** effleurer qn/qch
●**brush-off** *n Fam* **to give sb the b.** envoyer promener qn ●**brush-up** *n* **to have a**
wash and b. faire un brin de toilette
brushwood ['brʌʃwʊd] *n* broussailles
fpl
brusque [bruːsk] *adj* brusque
Brussels ['brʌsəlz] *n* Bruxelles *m ou f*; **B.**
sprouts choux *mpl* de Bruxelles
brutal ['bruːtəl] *adj* brutal; *(attack)* sauvage ●**bru**'**tality** [-'tælɪtɪ] *n* brutalité *f*; *(of*
attack) sauvagerie *f*
brute [bruːt] **1** *n (animal)* bête *f*; *(person)*
brute *f*
2 *adj* **by b. force** par la force

BSc [biːes'siː] (*Am* **BS** [biː'es]) *abbr* = Bachelor of Science

BSE [biːes'iː] (*abbr* **bovine spongiform encephalopathy**) *n* EBS *f*, maladie *f* de la vache folle

bubble ['bʌbəl] 1 *n* (*of air, soap*) bulle *f*; **b. bath** bain *m* moussant; **b. gum** chewinggum *m*
2 *vi* (*of liquid*) bouillonner; **to b. over** (**with**) déborder (de) •**bubbly 1** *adj* (*liquid*) plein de bulles; (*person, personality*) débordant de vitalité 2 *n Fam Hum* champ *m*

buck [bʌk] 1 *n* (**a**) *Am Fam* dollar *m* (**b**) (*of rabbit*) mâle *m* (**c**) *Fam* **to pass the b.** (**to sb**) refiler le bébé (à qn)
2 *vt Fam* **to b. sb up** remonter le moral à qn
3 *vi Fam* **to b. up** (*become livelier*) reprendre du poil de la bête; (*hurry*) se grouiller

bucket ['bʌkɪt] *n* seau *m*

buckle ['bʌkəl] 1 *n* boucle *f*
2 *vt* (**a**) (*fasten*) boucler (**b**) (*deform*) déformer
3 *vi* (*deform*) se déformer; **to b. down to a task** s'atteler à une tâche

buckshot ['bʌkʃɒt] *n inv* chevrotine *f*

buckteeth [bʌk'tiːθ] *npl* dents *fpl* de lapin

bud [bʌd] 1 *n* (*on tree*) bourgeon *m*; (*on flower*) bouton *m*
2 (*pt & pp* **-dd-**) *vi* bourgeonner; (*of flower*) pousser des boutons •**budding** *adj* (*talent*) naissant; (*doctor*) en herbe

Buddhist ['bʊdɪst] *adj & n* bouddhiste (*mf*)

buddy ['bʌdɪ] (*pl* **-ies**) *n Am Fam* pote *m*

budge [bʌdʒ] 1 *vi* bouger
2 *vt* faire bouger

budgerigar ['bʌdʒərɪgɑː(r)] *n Br* perruche *f*

budget ['bʌdʒɪt] 1 *n* budget *m*
2 *vi* dresser un budget; **to b. for sth** inscrire qch au budget •**budgetary** *adj* budgétaire

budgie ['bʌdʒɪ] *n Br Fam* perruche *f*

buff [bʌf] 1 *adj* **b.(-coloured)** chamois *inv*
2 *n Fam* (**a**) **jazz/film b.** fanatique *mf* de jazz/de cinéma (**b**) **in the b.** à poil

buffalo ['bʌfələʊ] (*pl* **-oes** *or* **-o**) *n* buffle *m*; (**American**) **b.** bison *m*

buffer ['bʌfə(r)] *n* (*on train*) tampon *m*; (*at end of track*) butoir *m*; *Fig* (*safeguard*) protection *f* (**against** contre); **b. state** État *m* tampon

buffet¹ ['bʊfeɪ] *n* (*meal, café*) buffet *m*; **cold b.** viandes *fpl* froides; *Br* **b. car** (*on train*) wagon-restaurant *m*

buffet² ['bʌfɪt] *vt* (*of waves*) secouer; (*of wind, rain*) cingler

buffoon [bə'fuːn] *n* bouffon *m*

bug¹ [bʌg] 1 *n* (**a**) (*insect*) bestiole *f*; (*bedbug*) punaise *f*; *Fam* (*germ*) microbe *m*; **the travel/skiing b.** le virus des voyages/du ski (**b**) (*in machine*) défaut *m*; *Comptr* bogue *m* (**c**) (*listening device*) micro *m*
2 (*pt & pp* **-gg-**) *vt* (*room*) installer des micros dans

bug² [bʌg] (*pt & pp* **-gg-**) *vt Fam* (*nag*) embêter

bugbear ['bʌgbeə(r)] *n Fam* cauchemar *m*

buggy ['bʌgɪ] (*pl* **-ies**) *n Br* (**baby**) **b.** (*pushchair*) poussette *f*; *Am* (*pram*) landau *m*

bugle ['bjuːgəl] *n* (*instrument*) clairon *m* •**bugler** *n* (*person*) clairon *m*

build [bɪld] 1 *n* (*of person*) carrure *f*
2 (*pt & pp* **built** [bɪlt]) *vt* construire; **to b. sth up** (*increase*) augmenter qch; (*business*) monter qch; **to b. up speed/one's strength** prendre de la vitesse/des forces
3 *vi* **to b. up** (*of tension, pressure*) augmenter; (*of dust, snow, interest*) s'accumuler; (*of traffic*) devenir dense •**builder** *n* (*skilled*) maçon *m*; (*unskilled*) ouvrier *m*; (*contractor*) entrepreneur *m* •**building** *n* bâtiment *m*; (*flats, offices*) immeuble *m*; (*action*) construction *f*; **b. site** chantier *m*; *Br* **b. society** ≃ société *f* de crédit immobilier •**build-up** *n* (*increase*) augmentation *f*; (*of dust*) accumulation *f*; (*of troops*) concentration *f*; (*for author, book*) publicité *f*; **the b. to Christmas** la période précédant Noël

built-in [bɪlt'ɪn] *adj* (*cupboard*) encastré; (*part of machine*) incorporé; *Fig* (*innate*) inné

built-up ['bɪltʌp] *adj* urbanisé; **b. area** agglomération *f*

bulb [bʌlb] *n* (*of plant*) bulbe *m*; (*of lamp*) ampoule *f*

bulbous ['bʌlbəs] *adj* (*shape, nose*) gros et rond (*f* grosse et ronde); (*table leg*) renflé

Bulgaria [bʌl'geərɪə] *n* la Bulgarie •**Bulgarian 1** *adj* bulgare 2 *n* Bulgare *mf*

bulge [bʌldʒ] 1 *n* renflement *m*; *Fam* (*increase*) augmentation *f*
2 *vi* **to b. (out)** bomber; (*of eyes*) sortir de la tête •**bulging** *adj* bombé; (*eyes*) protubérant; **to be b.** (*of bag, pocket*) être bourré (**with** de)

bulimia [bʊ'lɪmɪə] *n* boulimie *f*

bulk [bʌlk] *n inv* (*of building, parcel*)

volume *m*; *(of person)* grosseur *f*; **the b. of sth** la majeure partie de qch; **in b.** *(buy, sell)* en gros ● **bulky** (**-ier, -iest**) *adj* volumineux, -euse

bull [bʊl] *n* (**a**) *(animal)* taureau *m* (**b**) *very Fam (nonsense)* conneries *fpl* ● **bullfight** *n* corrida *f* ● **bullfighter** *n* torero *m* ● **bullring** *n* arène *f*

bulldog [ˈbʊldɒg] *n* bouledogue *m*; **b. clip** pince *f* (à dessin)

bulldoze [ˈbʊldəʊz] *vt* *(site)* passer au bulldozer; *(building)* démolir au bulldozer ● **bulldozer** *n* bulldozer *m*

bullet [ˈbʊlɪt] *n* balle *f* ● **bulletproof** *adj* *(car)* blindé; **it's b. glass** la vitre est blindée; *Br* **b. jacket**, *Am* **b. vest** gilet *m* pare-balles *inv*

bulletin [ˈbʊlətɪn] *n* bulletin *m*; *Am* **b. board** panneau *m* d'affichage

bullion [ˈbʊljən] *n* **gold b.** lingots *mpl* d'or

bullock [ˈbʊlək] *n* bœuf *m*

bull's-eye [ˈbʊlzaɪ] *n (of target)* centre *m*; **to hit the b.** mettre dans le mille

bully [ˈbʊlɪ] **1** (*pl* **-ies**) *n* terreur *f* **2** (*pt & pp* **-ied**) *vt (ill-treat)* maltraiter; **to b. sb into doing sth** forcer qn à faire qch ● **bullying** *n* brimades *fpl*

bulwark [ˈbʊlwək] *n* rempart *m*

bum [bʌm] *Fam* **1** *n* (**a**) *(loafer)* clochard, -arde *mf*; *(good-for-nothing)* bon *m* à rien, bonne *f* à rien (**b**) *Br (buttocks)* derrière *m*; **b. bag** banane *f* **2** (*pt & pp* **-mm-**) *vi* **to b. (around)** *(be idle)* glander; *(travel)* vadrouiller **3** *vt Am* **to b. sth off sb** *(cigarette)* taxer qch à qn

bumblebee [ˈbʌmbəlbiː] *n* bourdon *m*

bumf [bʌmf] *n Br Fam* paperasse *f*

bump [bʌmp] **1** *n (impact)* choc *m*; *(jerk)* secousse *f*; *(on road, body)* bosse *f* **2** *vt (of car)* heurter; **to b. one's head/knee** se cogner la tête/le genou; **to b. into** *(of person)* se cogner contre; *(of car)* rentrer dans; *(meet)* tomber sur; *Fam* **to b. sb off** liquider qn; *Fam* **to b. up** *(price)* augmenter **3** *vi* **to b. along** *(in car)* cahoter ● **bumper** **1** *n (of car)* pare-chocs *m inv* **2** *adj (crop, year)* exceptionnel, -elle; **b. cars** autos *fpl* tamponneuses

bumpkin [ˈbʌmpkɪn] *n* (**country**) **b.** péquenaud, -aude *mf*

bumptious [ˈbʌmpʃəs] *adj* prétentieux, -ieuse

bumpy [ˈbʌmpɪ] (**-ier, -iest**) *adj (road, ride)* cahoteux, -euse; **we had a b. flight** on a traversé des trous d'air pendant le vol

bun [bʌn] *n* (**a**) *(cake)* petit pain *m* au lait (**b**) *(of hair)* chignon *m*

bunch [bʌntʃ] *n (of flowers)* bouquet *m*; *(of keys)* trousseau *m*; *(of bananas)* régime *m*; *(of grapes)* grappe *f*; *(of people)* bande *f*; *Fam* **a b. of books/ideas** un tas de livres/d'idées

bundle [ˈbʌndəl] **1** *n* paquet *m*; *(of papers)* liasse *f*; *(of firewood)* fagot *m* **2** *vt (put)* fourrer (**into** dans); *(push)* pousser (**into** dans); **to b. up** *(newspapers, letters)* mettre en paquet; **to b. sb off** expédier qn **3** *vi* **to b. (oneself) up** (bien) se couvrir

bung [bʌŋ] **1** *n (stopper)* bonde *f* **2** *vt Br Fam (toss)* balancer; **to b. up** boucher

bungalow [ˈbʌŋgələʊ] *n* pavillon *m* de plain-pied

bungle [ˈbʌŋgəl] **1** *vt* gâcher **2** *vi* se tromper ● **bungler** *n* **to be a b.** faire du mauvais travail ● **bungling 1** *adj (clumsy)* maladroit **2** *n* gâchis *m*

bunion [ˈbʌnjən] *n* oignon *m (au pied)*

bunk [bʌŋk] *n* (**a**) *(in ship, train)* couchette *f*; **b. beds** lits *mpl* superposés (**b**) *Fam* âneries *fpl* ● **bunkum** *n Fam* âneries *fpl*

bunker [ˈbʌŋkə(r)] *n Mil & Golf* bunker *m*; *(for coal)* coffre *m* à charbon

bunny [ˈbʌnɪ] (*pl* **-ies**) *n Fam* **b. (rabbit)** petit lapin *m*

bunting [ˈbʌntɪŋ] *n (flags)* guirlande *f* de drapeaux

buoy [bɔɪ] **1** *n* bouée *f* **2** *vt Fig* **to b. up** *(support)* soutenir

buoyant [ˈbɔɪənt] *adj (in water)* qui flotte; *Fig (economy, prices)* stable; *Fig (person, mood)* plein d'allant

burden [ˈbɜːdən] **1** *n* fardeau *m*; **the tax b.** la pression fiscale; *Law* **b. of proof** charge *f* de la preuve **2** *vt* charger (**with** de); *Fig* accabler (**with** de)

bureau [ˈbjʊərəʊ] (*pl* **-eaux** [-əʊz]) *n (office)* bureau *m*; *Br (desk)* secrétaire *m*; *Am (chest of drawers)* commode *f*

bureaucracy [bjʊəˈrɒkrəsɪ] *n* bureaucratie *f* ● **bureaucrat** [ˈbjʊərəkræt] *n* bureaucrate *mf*

burger [ˈbɜːgə(r)] *n* hamburger *m*

burglar [ˈbɜːglə(r)] *n* cambrioleur, -euse *mf*; **b. alarm** alarme *f* antivol ● **burglarize** *vt Am* cambrioler ● **burglary** (*pl* **-ies**) *n* cambriolage *m* ● **burgle** *vt Br* cambrioler

burial [ˈberɪəl] **1** *n* enterrement *m* **2** *adj (service)* funèbre; **b. ground** cimetière *m*

burly [ˈbɜːlɪ] (**-ier, -iest**) *adj* costaud
Burma [ˈbɜːmə] *n* la Birmanie • **Burmese**
[-ˈmiːz] **1** *adj* birman **2** *n* Birman, -ane *mf*
burn [bɜːn] **1** *n* brûlure *f*
2 (*pt & pp* **burned** *or* **burnt**) *vt* brûler;
burnt alive brûlé vif (*f* brûlée vive); **to b.
sth down** incendier qch; **to b. off** (*paint*)
décaper au chalumeau; **to b. up** (*energy*)
dépenser
3 *vi* brûler; **to b. down** (*of house*) être
détruit par les flammes; **to b. out** (*of fire*)
s'éteindre; (*of fuse*) sauter • **burning 1** *adj*
en feu; (*fire*) allumé; *Fig* (*topic*) brûlant;
(*fever*) dévorant **2** *n* **smell of b.** odeur *f* de
brûlé
burner [ˈbɜːnə(r)] *n* (*on stove*) brûleur *m*;
Fig **to put sth on the back b.** remettre qch
à plus tard
burp [bɜːp] *Fam* **1** *n* rot *m*
2 *vi* roter
burrow [ˈbʌrəʊ] **1** *n* (*hole*) terrier *m*
2 *vti* creuser
bursar [ˈbɜːsə(r)] *n* (*in school*) intendant,
-ante *mf*
bursary [ˈbɜːsərɪ] (*pl* **-ies**) *n* (*scholarship*)
bourse *f*
burst [bɜːst] **1** *n* (*of shell*) éclatement *m*,
explosion *f*; (*of laughter*) éclat *m*; (*of
applause*) salve *f*; (*of thunder*) coup *m*;
(*surge*) élan *m*
2 (*pt & pp* **burst**) *vt* (*bubble, balloon,
boil*) crever; (*tyre*) faire éclater; **to b. a
blood vessel** se rompre une veine; **to b.
open** (*door*) ouvrir brusquement; **the
river b. its banks** le fleuve est sorti de
son lit
3 *vi* (*of bubble, balloon, boil, tyre, cloud*)
crever; (*with force*) (*of shell, boiler, tyre*)
éclater; **to b. into a room** faire irruption
dans une pièce; **to b. into flames** prendre
feu; **to b. into tears** fondre en larmes; **to
b. out laughing** éclater de rire; **to b. open**
(*of door*) s'ouvrir brusquement • **bursting**
adj (*full*) (*pockets*) plein à craquer (**with**
de); **b. with joy** débordant de joie; **to be
b. to do** mourir d'envie de faire
bury [ˈberɪ] (*pt & pp* **-ied**) *vt* (*body*) enterrer; (*hide*) enfouir; (*plunge*) plonger
(**in** dans); **to b. one's face into one's
hands** enfouir son visage dans ses mains;
buried in one's work plongé dans son travail
bus [bʌs] **1** (*pl* **buses** *or* **busses**) *n* autobus
m, bus *m*; (*long-distance*) autocar *m*, car
m; **by b.** en bus/en car; **b. driver/ticket**
chauffeur *m*/ticket *m* de bus/car; **b. lane**
couloir *m* de bus; **b. shelter** Abribus® *m*;
b. station gare *f* routière; **b. stop** arrêt *m*
de bus

2 (*pt & pp* **bused** *or* **bussed**) *vt* (*children*)
transporter en bus • **bus(s)ing** *n* (*of
schoolchildren*) ramassage *m* scolaire
bush [bʊʃ] *n* buisson *m*; **the b.** (*land*) la
brousse; **a b. of hair** une tignasse • **bushy**
(**-ier, -iest**) *adj* (*hair, tail*) touffu
bushed [bʊʃt] *adj Fam* (*tired*) crevé
busily [ˈbɪzɪlɪ] *adv* **to be b. doing sth** être
très occupé à faire qch
business [ˈbɪznɪs] **1** *n* affaires *fpl*,
commerce *m*; (*shop*) commerce; (*company, task, concern, matter*) affaire *f*; **the
textile/construction b.** l'industrie *f* du
textile/de la construction; **the travel b.**
le tourisme; **big b.** les grosses entreprises
fpl; **to travel on b.** partir en voyage d'affaires; **to go out of b.** (*stop trading*)
fermer; **to go about one's b.** vaquer à ses
occupations; **it's quite a b.** c'est toute une
affaire; **it's your b. to** c'est à vous de; **you
have no b. to** vous n'avez pas le droit de;
**that's none of your b.!, mind your own
b.!** ça ne vous regarde pas!; *Fam* **to mean
b.** ne pas plaisanter
2 *adj* commercial; (*meeting, trip, lunch*)
d'affaires; **b. card** carte *f* de visite; **b. hours**
(*office*) heures *fpl* de bureau; (*shop*) heures d'ouverture; **b. school** école *f* de
commerce • **businesslike** *adj* professionnel, -elle • **businessman** (*pl* **-men**) *n*
homme *m* d'affaires • **businesswoman** (*pl*
-women) *n* femme *f* d'affaires
busker [ˈbʌskə(r)] *n Br* musicien, -ienne
mf des rues
bust [bʌst] **1** *n* (*statue*) buste *m*; (*of
woman*) poitrine *f*
2 *adj Fam* (*broken*) fichu; **to go b.**
(*bankrupt*) faire faillite
3 (*pt & pp* **bust** *or* **busted**) *vt Fam* (*break*)
bousiller; (*arrest*) coffrer • **bust-up** *n Fam*
(*quarrel*) engueulade *f*; (*break-up*) rupture *f*
bustle [ˈbʌsəl] **1** *n* animation *f*
2 *vi* **to b. (about)** s'affairer
busy [ˈbɪzɪ] **1** (**-ier, -iest**) *adj* occupé;
(*active*) actif, -ive; (*day*) chargé; (*street*)
animé; *Am* (*phone, line*) occupé; **to be b.
doing** (*in the process of*) être occupé à
faire; **to keep sb b.** occuper qn; **to keep
oneself b.** s'occuper; **the shops were very
b.** il y avait plein de monde dans les
magasins; *Am* **b. signal** sonnerie *f* 'occupé'
2 *vt* **to b. oneself** s'occuper (**with sth** à
qch; **doing** à faire) • **busybody** (*pl* **-ies**) *n
Fam* fouineur, -euse *mf*
but [bʌt, *unstressed* bət] **1** *conj* mais
2 *prep* (*except*) sauf; **b. for that** sans

cela; **b. for him** sans lui; **no one b. you** personne d'autre que toi; **the last b. one** l'avant-dernier, -ière *mf*
  3 *adv Formal (only)* ne...que, seulement; he's **b. a child** ce n'est qu'un enfant; **one can b. try** on peut toujours essayer

butane ['bjuːteɪn] *n* **b. (gas)** butane *m*

butcher ['bʊtʃə(r)] **1** *n* boucher *m*; **b.'s (shop)** boucherie *f*
  2 *vt (people)* massacrer; *(animal)* abattre • **butchery** *n* massacre *m* (**of** de)

butler ['bʌtlə(r)] *n* maître *m* d'hôtel

butt [bʌt] **1** *n (of cigarette)* mégot *m*; *(of gun)* crosse *f*; *Am Fam (buttocks)* derrière *m*; **b. for ridicule** objet *m* de risée
  2 *vt (with head)* donner un coup de tête à
  3 *vi* **to b. in** intervenir

butter ['bʌtə(r)] **1** *n* beurre *m*; *Br* **b. bean** = gros haricot blanc; **b. dish** beurrier *m*
  2 *vt* beurrer; *Fam* **to b. sb up** passer de la pommade à qn • **butterfingers** *n Fam* empoté, -ée *mf* • **buttermilk** *n* babeurre *m* • **butterscotch** *n* caramel *m* dur au beurre

buttercup ['bʌtəkʌp] *n* bouton-d'or *m*

butterfly ['bʌtəflaɪ] *(pl* **-ies)** *n* papillon *m*; *Fam* **to have butterflies** avoir l'estomac noué; **b. stroke** *(in swimming)* brasse *f* papillon

buttock ['bʌtək] *n* fesse *f*

button ['bʌtən] **1** *n* bouton *m*; *(of phone)* touche *f*; *Am (badge)* badge *m*
  2 *vt* **to b. (up)** boutonner
  3 *vi* **to b. (up)** *(of garment)* se boutonner • **buttonhole 1** *n* boutonnière *f* **2** *vt Fam (person)* coincer

buttress ['bʌtrɪs] **1** *n Archit* contrefort *m*; *Fig* soutien *m*
  2 *vt Fig (support)* renforcer

buxom ['bʌksəm] *adj (full-bosomed)* à la poitrine généreuse

buy [baɪ] **1** *n* **a good b.** une bonne affaire
  2 *(pt & pp* **bought)** *vt* **(a)** *(purchase)* acheter (**from sb** à qn; **for sb** à *ou* pour qn); **to b. back** racheter; **to b. over** *(bribe)* corrompre; **to b. up** acheter en bloc (**b)** *Am Fam (believe)* avaler; **I'll b. that!** je veux bien le croire! • **buyer** *n* acheteur, -euse *mf*

buzz [bʌz] **1** *n* **(a)** *(noise)* bourdonnement *m* **(b)** *Fam (phone call)* **to give sb a b.** passer un coup de fil à qn
  2 *vt* **to b. sb** *(using buzzer)* appeler qn
  3 *vi* bourdonner; *Fam* **to b. off** se tirer • **buzzer** *n (internal phone)* Interphone®*m*; *(of bell, clock)* sonnerie *f*

by [baɪ] **1** *prep* **(a)** *(agent)* par; de; **hit / chosen by** frappé/choisi par; **surrounded/followed by** entouré/suivi de; **a book/painting by** un livre/tableau de **(b)** *(manner, means)* par; en; à; de; **by sea** par mer; **by mistake** par erreur; **by car / train** en voiture/train; **by bicycle** à bicyclette; **by moonlight** au clair de lune; **by doing** en faisant; **one by one** un à un; **day by day** de jour en jour; **by sight/day** de vue/jour; **(all) by oneself** tout seul **(c)** *(next to)* à côté de; *(near)* près de; **by the lake/sea** au bord du lac/de la mer; **to go** *or* **pass by the bank/school** passer devant la banque/l'école **(d)** *(before in time)* avant; **by Monday** avant lundi, d'ici lundi; **by now** à cette heure-ci; **by yesterday** (dès) hier **(e)** *(amount, measurement)* à; **by the kilo** au kilo; **taller by a metre** plus grand d'un mètre; **paid by the hour** payé à l'heure **(f)** *(according to)* à, d'après; **by my watch** à ma montre; **it's fine** *or* **OK** *or* **all right by me** je n'y vois pas d'objection
  2 *adv* **close by** tout près; **to go** *or* **pass by** passer; **by and large** en gros • **by-election** *n* élection *f* partielle • **by-law** *n* arrêté *m* (municipal) • **by-product** *n* sous-produit *m* • **by-road** *n* chemin *m* de traverse

bye(-bye) ['baɪ('baɪ)] *exclam Fam* salut!, au revoir!; **b. for now!** à bientôt!

bygone ['baɪgɒn] **1** *adj* **in b. days** jadis
  2 *npl* **let bygones be bygones** oublions le passé

bypass ['baɪpɑːs] **1** *n* rocade *f*; **(heart) b. operation** pontage *m*
  2 *vt (town)* contourner; *Fig (ignore)* court-circuiter

bystander ['baɪstændə(r)] *n* passant, -ante *mf*

byte [baɪt] *n Comptr* octet *m*

byword ['baɪwɜːd] *n* **a b. for** un synonyme de

C

C, c¹ [siː] *n* C, c *m inv*

c² *abbr* = **cent**

cab [kæb] *n* taxi *m*; *(of train, lorry)* cabine *f*; *Hist (horse-drawn)* fiacre *m*

cabaret [ˈkæbəreɪ] cabaret *m*

cabbage [ˈkæbɪdʒ] *n* chou *m* (*pl* choux)

cabbie, cabby [ˈkæbɪ] (*pl* -ies) *n Fam* chauffeur *m* de taxi

cabin [ˈkæbɪn] *n (on ship, plane)* cabine *f*; *(hut)* cabane *f*; *Av* **c. crew** équipage *m*

cabinet¹ [ˈkæbɪnɪt] *n (cupboard)* armoire *f*; *(for display)* vitrine *f*; **(filing) c.** classeur *m (meuble)* • **cabinet-maker** *n* ébéniste *m*

cabinet² [ˈkæbɪnɪt] *n (government ministers)* gouvernement *m*; **c. meeting** ≃ Conseil *m* des ministres; **c. minister** ministre *m*

cable [ˈkeɪbəl] **1** *n* câble *m*; **c. car** *(with overhead cable)* téléphérique *m*; *(on tracks)* funiculaire *m*; **c. television** la télévision par câble; *Fam* **to have c.** avoir le câble

2 *vt (message)* câbler (**to** à)

caboose [kəˈbuːs] *n Am (on train)* fourgon *m* (de queue)

cache [kæʃ] *n (place)* cachette *f*; **an arms c.** une cache d'armes

cachet [ˈkæʃeɪ] *n (mark, character)* cachet *m*

cackle [ˈkækəl] **1** *n (of hen)* caquet *m*; *(laughter)* gloussement *m*

2 *vi (of hen)* caqueter; *Fam (laugh)* glousser

cactus [ˈkæktəs] (*pl* **-ti** [-taɪ] *or* **-tuses** [-təsɪz]) *n* cactus *m*

cad [kæd] *n Old-fashioned & Pej* goujat *m*

cadaverous [kəˈdævərəs] *adj* cadavérique

caddie [ˈkædɪ] *n Golf* caddie *m*

caddy [ˈkædɪ] (*pl* -ies) *n* **(tea) c.** boîte *f* à thé

cadence [ˈkeɪdəns] *n (rhythm)* & *Mus* cadence *f*

cadet [kəˈdet] *n* élève *m* officier

cadge [kædʒ] *vt Fam (meal)* se faire payer (**off sb** par qn); **to c. money from** *or* **off sb** taper qn

Caesarean [sɪˈzeərɪən] *n* **C. (section)** césarienne *f*

café [ˈkæfeɪ] *n* café *m*

cafeteria [kæfɪˈtɪərɪə] *n* cafétéria *f*

caffeine [ˈkæfiːn] *n* caféine *f*

cage [keɪdʒ] **1** *n* cage *f*

2 *vt* **to c. (up)** mettre en cage

cagey [ˈkeɪdʒɪ] *adj (evasive)* évasif, -ive (**about** sur); *(cautious)* prudent

cahoots [kəˈhuːts] *n Fam* **in c.** de mèche (**with sb** avec qn)

Cairo [ˈkaɪərəʊ] *n* Le Caire

cajole [kəˈdʒəʊl] *vt* enjôler

cake¹ [keɪk] *n* gâteau *m*; *(small)* pâtisserie *f*; **c. shop** pâtisserie; **c. of soap** savonnette *f*; **it's a piece of c.** c'est du gâteau

cake² [keɪk] *vt* **caked with blood/mud** couvert de sang/boue

calamity [kəˈlæmɪtɪ] (*pl* -ies) *n* calamité *f* • **calamitous** *adj* désastreux, -euse

calcium [ˈkælsɪəm] *n* calcium *m*

calculate [ˈkælkjʊleɪt] *vti* calculer; **to c. that...** *(estimate)* calculer que... • **calculated** *adj (deliberate)* délibéré; **a c. risk** un risque calculé • **calculating** *adj (shrewd)* calculateur, -trice • **calculation** [-ˈleɪʃən] *n* calcul *m*

calculator [ˈkælkjʊleɪtə(r)] *n* calculatrice *f*

calculus [ˈkælkjʊləs] *n Math & Med* calcul *m*

calendar [ˈkælɪndə(r)] *n* calendrier *m*; *(directory)* annuaire *m*; *Am (for engagements)* agenda *m*; **c. month** mois *m* civil; **c. year** année *f* civile

calf [kɑːf] (*pl* **calves**) *n* **(a)** *(animal)* veau *m* **(b)** *(part of leg)* mollet *m*

calibre [ˈkælɪbə(r)] (*Am* **caliber**) *n* calibre *m* • **calibrate** *vt* calibrer

calico [ˈkælɪkəʊ] *n (fabric)* calicot *m*; *Am (printed)* indienne *f*

call [kɔːl] **1** *n (on phone)* appel *m*; *(shout)* cri *m*; *(vocation)* vocation *f*; *(visit)* visite *f*; **(telephone) c.** appel téléphonique; **to make a c.** téléphoner (**to** à); **to give sb a c.** téléphoner à qn; **to return sb's c.** rappeler qn; **on c.** *(doctor)* de garde; **there's no c. to do that** il n'y a aucune raison de faire cela; **there's no c. for that article** cet article n'est pas très demandé; *Br* **c. box** cabine *f* téléphonique; **c. centre** *n* centre *m* d'appels; **c. girl** call-girl *f*

2 *vt (phone)* appeler; *(shout to)* crier; *(truce)* demander; **he's called David** il s'appelle David; **to c. a meeting** décider d'organiser une réunion; **to c. sb a liar** traiter qn de menteur; **she calls herself an expert** elle se dit expert; **to c. sth into question** mettre qch en question; *Fam* **let's c. it a day** ça suffit pour aujourd'hui **3** *vi* appeler; *(cry out)* crier; *(visit)* passer; **the train will c. at York** le train s'arrêtera à York ●**call-up** *n (of recruits)* appel *m* (sous les drapeaux)
▸**call back 1** *vt sep* rappeler **2** *vi* rappeler
▸**call by** *vi (visit)* passer ▸**call for** *vt insep (require)* demander; *(summon)* appeler; *(collect)* passer prendre ▸**call in 1** *vt sep (into room)* faire entrer; *(police)* appeler; *(product)* rappeler **2** *vi* **to c. in (on sb)** *(visit)* passer (chez qn) ▸**call off** *vt sep (cancel)* annuler; *(strike)* mettre fin à; *(dog)* rappeler ▸**call on** *vt insep (visit)* passer voir; *(invoke)* invoquer; **to c. (up)on sb to do** inviter qn à faire; *(urge)* sommer qn de faire ▸**call out 1** *vt sep (shout)* crier; *(doctor)* appeler; *(workers)* donner une consigne de grève à **2** *vi (shout)* crier; **to c. out to sb** interpeller qn; **to c. out for sth** demander qch à haute voix ▸**call round** *vi (visit)* passer ▸**call up** *vt sep (phone)* appeler; *Mil (recruits)* appeler (sous les drapeaux); *(memories)* évoquer
caller ['kɔːlə(r)] *n* visiteur, -euse *mf*; *(on phone)* correspondant, -ante *mf*
calligraphy [kə'lɪɡrəfɪ] *n* calligraphie *f*
calling ['kɔːlɪŋ] *n* vocation *f*; *Am* **c. card** carte *f* de visite
callous ['kæləs] *adj* **(a)** *(cruel)* insensible **(b)** *(skin)* calleux, -euse
callus ['kæləs] *n* cal *m*
calm [kɑːm] **1** (-**er**, -**est**) *adj* calme, tranquille; **keep c.!** restez calme!
2 *n* calme *m*
3 *vt* **to c. (down)** calmer
4 *vi* **to c. down** se calmer ●**calmly** *adv* calmement ●**calmness** *n* calme *m*
Calor Gas® ['kæləɡæs] *n Br* Butagaz® *m*
calorie ['kælərɪ] *n* calorie *f*
calumny ['kæləmnɪ] *(pl* -**ies**) *n* calomnie *f*
calve [kɑːv] *vi (of cow)* vêler
calves [kɑːvz] *pl of* **calf**
camcorder ['kæmkɔːdə(r)] *n* Caméscope® *m*
came [keɪm] *pt of* **come**
camel ['kæməl] *n* chameau *m*
camellia [kə'miːlɪə] *n* camélia *m*

cameo ['kæmɪəʊ] *(pl* -**os**) *n (gem)* camée *m*; **c. role** *(in film)* brève apparition *f (d'un acteur connu)*
camera ['kæmrə] *n* appareil photo *m*; **(TV** *or* **film) c.** caméra *f* ●**cameraman** *(pl* -**men**) *n* cameraman *m*
camomile ['kæməmaɪl] *n* camomille *f*
camouflage ['kæməflɑːʒ] **1** *n* camouflage *m*
2 *vt also Fig* camoufler
camp¹ [kæmp] **1** *n* camp *m*, campement *m*; **c. bed** lit *m* de camp
2 *vi* **to c. (out)** camper ●**camper** *n (person)* campeur, -euse *mf*; *(vehicle)* camping-car *m* ●**campfire** *n* feu *m* de camp ●**camping** *n* camping; **c. site** (terrain *m* de) camping *m* ●**campsite** *n* camping *m*
camp² [kæmp] *adj (effeminate)* efféminé
campaign [kæm'peɪn] **1** *n (political, military)* campagne *f*; **press/publicity c.** campagne de presse/publicité
2 *vi* faire campagne (**for** pour; **against** contre) ●**campaigner** *n* militant, -ante *mf* (**for** pour)
campus ['kæmpəs] *n (of university)* campus *m*
can¹ [kæn, *unstressed* kən] *(pt* **could**)

Le verbe **can** n'a ni infinitif, ni gérondif, ni participe. Pour exprimer l'infinitif ou le participe, on aura recours à la forme correspondante de **be able to** (he wanted to be able to speak English; she has always been able to swim). La forme négative est **can't**, qui s'écrit **cannot** dans la langue soutenue.

v aux (be able to) pouvoir; *(know how to)* savoir; **he couldn't help me** il ne pouvait pas m'aider; **she c. swim** elle sait nager; **if I could swim** si je savais nager; **he could do it tomorrow** il pourrait le faire demain; **he could have done it** il aurait pu le faire; **you could be wrong** *(possibility)* tu as peut-être tort; **he can't be dead** *(probability)* il ne peut pas être mort; **that can't be right!** ce n'est pas possible!; **c. I come in?** *(permission)* puis-je entrer?; **yes, you c.!** oui!; **I c. see** je vois; **as happy as c. be** aussi heureux, -euse que possible
can² [kæn] **1** *n (for water)* bidon *m*; *(for food)* boîte *f*; *(for beer)* can(n)ette *f*
2 *(pt & pp* -**nn-**) *vt* mettre en boîte ●**canned** *adj* en boîte, en conserve; **c. beer** bière *f* en can(n)ette; **c. food** conserves *fpl* ●**can-opener** *n* ouvre-boîtes *m inv*

Canada ['kænədə] *n* le Canada •**Canadian** [kə'neɪdɪən] **1** *adj* canadien, -ienne **2** *n* Canadien, -ienne *mf*

canal [kə'næl] *n* canal *m*

canary [kə'neərɪ] (*pl* -ies) *n* canari *m*

cancan ['kænkæn] *n* french cancan *m*

cancel ['kænsəl] **1** (*Br* -**ll**-, *Am* -**l**-) *vt* (*flight, appointment*) annuler; (*goods, taxi*) décommander; (*train*) supprimer; (*word, paragraph*) biffer; (*cheque*) faire opposition à; **to c. a ticket** (*punch*) (*with date*) composter un billet; (*with hole*) poinçonner un billet; **to c. each other out** s'annuler

2 *vi* se décommander •**cancellation** [-'leɪʃən] *n* annulation *f*; (*of train*) suppression *f*

Cancer ['kænsə(r)] *n* (*sign*) le Cancer; **to be a C.** être Cancer

cancer ['kænsə(r)] *n* cancer *m*; **stomach/skin c.** cancer de l'estomac/la peau; **c. patient** cancéreux, -euse *mf*; **c. specialist** cancérologue *mf*

candelabra [kændɪ'lɑːbrə] *n* candélabre *m*

candid ['kændɪd] *adj* franc (*f* franche) •**candour** (*Am* **candor**) *n* franchise *f*

> *ℓ* Note that the French words **candide** and **candeur** are false friends and are never translations for the English words **candid** and **candour**. They mean **ingenuous** and **ingenuousness**.

candidate ['kændɪdeɪt] *n* candidat, -ate *mf* (**for** à); **to stand as a c.** être candidat •**candidacy** [-dəsɪ], **candidature** [-dət-ʃə(r)] *n* candidature *f*

candle ['kændəl] *n* (*wax*) bougie *f*; (*tallow*) chandelle *f*; (*in church*) cierge *m*; **c. grease** suif *m* •**candlelight** *n* **by c.** à la (lueur d'une) bougie; **to have dinner by c.** dîner aux chandelles •**candlestick** *n* bougeoir *m*; (*taller*) chandelier *m*

candy ['kændɪ] (*pl* -ies) *n* Am bonbon *m*; (*sweets*) bonbons *mpl*; (**sugar**) **c.** sucre *m* candi; *Am* **c. store** confiserie *f* •**candied** *adj* (*fruit*) confit •**candyfloss** *n* Br barbe *f* à papa

cane [keɪn] **1** *n* (*stick*) canne *f*; (*for basket*) rotin *m*; (*for punishment*) baguette *f*

2 *vt* (*punish*) frapper avec une baguette

canine ['keɪnaɪn] **1** *adj* (*tooth, race*) canin

2 *n* (*tooth*) canine *f*

canister ['kænɪstə(r)] *n* boîte *f* (en métal)

cannabis ['kænəbɪs] *n* (*drug*) cannabis *m*; (*plant*) chanvre *m* indien

cannibal ['kænɪbəl] *n* cannibale *mf*

cannon ['kænən] (*pl* -**s** *or* **cannon**) *n*

canon *m* •**cannonball** *n* boulet *m* de canon

cannot ['kænɒt] = **can not**

canny ['kænɪ] (-**ier**, -**iest**) *adj* rusé

canoe [kə'nuː] **1** *n* canoë *m*; (*dugout*) pirogue *f*

2 *vi* faire du canoë-kayak •**canoeing** *n* **to go c.** faire du canoë-kayak •**canoeist** *n* canoéiste *mf*

canon ['kænən] *n* (*law*) & *Fig* canon *m*; (*priest*) chanoine *m* •**canonize** *vt* Rel canoniser

canopy ['kænəpɪ] (*pl* -ies) *n* (*of baby carriage*) capote *f*; (*awning*) auvent *m*; (*over bed*) baldaquin *m*; (*over altar*) dais *m*; (*made of glass*) marquise *f*; Fig (*of tree branches*) canopée *f*

can't [kɑːnt] = **can not**

cantaloup(e) ['kæntəluːp] *n* (*melon*) cantaloup *m*

cantankerous [kæn'tæŋkərəs] *adj* acariâtre

cantata [kæn'tɑːtə] *n* Mus cantate *f*

canteen [kæn'tiːn] *n* (*in school, factory*) cantine *f*; (*flask*) gourde *f*; Br **c. of cutlery** ménagère *f*

canter ['kæntə(r)] **1** *n* petit galop *m*

2 *vi* aller au petit galop

canvas ['kænvəs] *n* (**a**) (*cloth*) (grosse) toile *f*; (*for embroidery*) canevas *m*; **under c.** (*in a tent*) sous la tente (**b**) Art toile *f*

canvass ['kænvəs] *vt* (*area*) faire du démarchage dans; (*opinions*) sonder; **to c. sb** (*seek votes*) solliciter le suffrage de qn; (*seek orders*) solliciter des commandes de qn •**canvasser** *n* Pol agent *m* électoral; *Com* démarcheur, -euse *mf* •**canvassing** *n* (*for voters*) démarchage *m*; (*for votes*) démarchage électoral

canyon ['kænjən] *n* cañon *m*, canyon *m*

CAP [siːeɪ'piː] (*abbr* **common agricultural policy**) *n* PAC *f*

cap[1] [kæp] *n* (**a**) (*hat*) casquette *f*; (*for shower, of sailor*) bonnet *m*; (*of soldier*) képi *m* (**b**) (*of tube, valve*) bouchon *m*; (*of bottle*) capsule *f*; (*of pen*) capuchon *m* (**c**) (*of child's gun*) amorce *f* (**d**) (**Dutch**) **c.** (*contraceptive*) diaphragme *m*

cap[2] [kæp] (*pt & pp* -**pp**-) *vt* (**a**) (*outdo*) surpasser; **to c. it all...** pour couronner le tout... (**b**) Br (*spending*) limiter (**c**) (*cover*) **capped with** recouvert de; **capped with snow** coiffé de neige

capable ['keɪpəbəl] *adj* (*person*) capable (**of sth** de qch; **of doing** de faire) •**capability** *n* capacité *f* •**capably** *adv* avec compétence

capacity [kə'pæsətɪ] (*pl* -ies) *n* (*of con-*

tainer) capacité *f*; *(ability)* aptitude *f*, capacité *f* (**for sth** pour qch; **for doing à** faire); *(output)* rendement *m*; **in my c. as a doctor** en ma qualité de médecin; **in an advisory c.** à titre consultatif; **filled to c.** *(concert hall)* comble

cape [keɪp] *n* (**a**) *(cloak)* cape *f*; *(of cyclist)* pèlerine *f* (**b**) *(of coast)* cap *m*; **C. Town** Le Cap

caper¹ ['keɪpə(r)] *n Culin* câpre *f*

caper² ['keɪpə(r)] **1** *n (prank)* cabriole *f*
   2 *vi (jump about)* faire des cabrioles

capital ['kæpɪtəl] **1** *adj (letter, importance)* capital; **c. punishment** peine *f* capitale
   2 *n* (**a**) **c. (city)** capitale *f*; **c. (letter)** majuscule *f* (**b**) *(money)* capital *m* • **capitalism** *n* capitalisme *m* • **capitalist** *adj & n* capitaliste *(mf)* • **capitalize** *vi* **to c. on** tirer parti de

capitulate [kə'pɪtʃʊleɪt] *vi* capituler (**to** devant) • **capitu'lation** *n* capitulation *f*

caprice [kə'priːs] *n* caprice *m* • **capricious** [kə'prɪʃəs] *adj* capricieux, -ieuse

Capricorn ['kæprɪkɔːn] *n (sign)* le Capricorne; **to be a C.** être Capricorne

capsicum ['kæpsɪkəm] *n* poivron *m*

capsize [kæp'saɪz] **1** *vt* faire chavirer
   2 *vi* chavirer

capsule [*Br* 'kæpsjuːl, *Am* 'kæpsəl] *n (of medicine)* gélule *f*; **(space) c.** capsule *f* spatiale

captain ['kæptɪn] **1** *n* capitaine *m*
   2 *vt (ship)* commander; *(team)* être le capitaine de

caption ['kæpʃən] *n (of illustration)* légende *f*; *(of film, article)* sous-titre *m*

captivate ['kæptɪveɪt] *vt* captiver • **captivating** *adj* captivant

captive ['kæptɪv] *n* captif, -ive *mf*; **to be taken c.** être fait prisonnier • **cap'tivity** *n* captivité *f*; **in c.** en captivité

capture ['kæptʃə(r)] **1** *n* capture *f*; *(of town)* prise *f*
   2 *vt (person, animal, ship)* capturer; *(escaped prisoner or animal)* reprendre; *(town)* prendre; *(attention)* capter; *Fig (mood)* rendre

car [kɑː(r)] *n* voiture *f*, automobile *f*; *(train carriage)* wagon *m*, voiture; **c. insurance/industry** assurance *f*/industrie *f* automobile; **the c. door** la portière de la voiture; **c. bomb** voiture *f* piégée; *Br* **c. boot sale** = vente à la brocante où les marchandises sont exposées à l'arrière de voitures; **c. chase** poursuite *f* en voiture; **c. crash** accident *m* de voiture; **c. ferry** ferry *m*; *Br* **c. hire** location *f* de voitures; *Br* **c. park**

parking *m*; **c. phone** téléphone *m* de voiture; **c. radio** autoradio *m*; **c. rental** location *f* de voitures; **c. wash** *(machine)* = station de lavage automatique pour voitures; *(sign)* lavage *m* automatique • **carfare** *n Am* frais *mpl* de voyage • **carport** *n* abri *m* pour voiture • **carsick** *adj* **to be c.** être malade en voiture

> ♬ Note that the French word **car** is a false friend and is never a translation for the English word **car**. It means **coach**.

carafe [kə'ræf] *n* carafe *f*

caramel ['kærəməl] *n* caramel *m*

carat ['kærət] *n* carat *m*; **18-c. gold** or *m* (à) 18 carats

caravan ['kærəvæn] *n* caravane *f*; *(horse-drawn)* roulotte *f*; **c. site** camping *m* pour caravanes

caraway ['kærəweɪ] *n (plant)* carvi *m*; **c. seeds** graines *fpl* de carvi

carbohydrates [kɑːbəʊ'haɪdreɪts] *npl* hydrates *mpl* de carbone

carbon ['kɑːbən] *n* carbone *m*; **c. dioxide** dioxyde *m* de carbone, gaz *m* carbonique; **c. fibre** fibre *f* de carbone; **c. paper** (papier *m*) carbone

carbuncle ['kɑːbʌŋkəl] *n Med* furoncle *m*

carburettor [kɑːbjʊ'retə(r)] *(Am* **carburetor** ['kɑːrbəreɪtər]) *n* carburateur *m*

carcass ['kɑːkəs] *n* carcasse *f*

card [kɑːd] *n* carte *f*; *(cardboard)* carton *m*; **(index) c.** fiche *f*; **c. game** jeu *m* de cartes; **c. index** fichier *m*; **c. table** table *f* de jeu; **to play cards** jouer aux cartes; **it is** *Br* **on** *or Am* **in the cards that...** il est bien possible que... • **cardphone** *n* téléphone *m* à carte

cardboard ['kɑːdbɔːd] *n* carton *m*; **c. box** boîte *f* en carton, carton

cardiac ['kɑːdɪæk] *adj* cardiaque; **c. arrest** arrêt *m* du cœur

cardigan ['kɑːdɪgən] *n* cardigan *m*

cardinal ['kɑːdɪnəl] **1** *adj (number, point)* cardinal
   2 *n Rel* cardinal *m*

care [keə(r)] **1** *n (attention)* soin *m*; *(protection)* soins *mpl*; *(worry)* souci *m*; **to take c. to do** veiller à faire; **to take c. not to do** faire attention à ne pas faire; **to take c. of sb/sth** s'occuper de qn/qch; **to take c. of oneself** *(manage)* savoir se débrouiller tout seul; *(keep healthy)* faire bien attention à soi; **that will take c. of itself** ça s'arrangera; **take c.!** *(goodbye)* au revoir!; **'c. of'** *(on envelope)* 'chez'
   2 *vt* **I don't c. what he says** peu m'im-

porte ce qu'il en dit; **would you c. to try?** voulez-vous essayer? **3** *vi* **I don't c.** ça m'est égal; **I couldn't c. less** ça m'est complètement égal; **who cares?** qu'est-ce que ça peut faire?; **to c. about** *(feel concern about)* se soucier de; **I don't c. for it (much)** je n'aime pas tellement ça; **to c. for a drink/a change** avoir envie d'un verre/d'un changement; **to c. about** *or* **for sb** *(be fond of)* avoir de la sympathie pour qn; **to c. for sb** *(look after)* soigner qn

career [kə'rɪə(r)] **1** *n* carrière *f*; **to make a c. in sth** faire carrière dans qch **2** *adj (diplomat)* de carrière; **the job has c. prospects** cet emploi offre des perspectives de carrière; **it's a good c. move** c'est bon pour ma/ta/*etc* carrière **3** *vi* **to c. along** aller à vive allure

carefree ['keəfriː] *adj* insouciant

careful ['keəfəl] *adj (exact, thorough)* soigneux, -euse (**about** de); *(work)* minutieux, -ieuse; *(cautious)* prudent; **c. (about** *or* **with money)** regardant (à la dépense); **to be c. of** *or* **with sth** faire attention à qch; **to be c. to do** veiller à faire; **to be c. not to do** faire attention à ne pas faire; **be c.!** (fais) attention!; **be c. she doesn't see you!** (fais) attention qu'elle ne te voie pas! •**carefully** *adv (thoroughly)* avec soin; *(cautiously)* prudemment

careless ['keələs] *adj* négligent; *(absent-minded)* étourdi; *(work)* peu soigné; **c. about one's work** peu soigneux dans son travail; **c. about one's appearance** négligé; **c. mistake** faute *f* d'étourderie •**carelessness** *n* négligence *f*

carer ['keərə(r)] *n (relative)* = personne s'occupant d'un parent malade ou âgé

caress [kə'res] **1** *n* caresse *f* **2** *vt (stroke)* caresser; *(kiss)* embrasser

caretaker ['keəteɪkə(r)] *n* gardien, -ienne *mf*, concierge *mf*

cargo ['kɑːɡəʊ] *(pl* **-oes** *or* **-os**) *n* cargaison *f*; **c. ship** cargo *m*

> Note that the French word **cargo** is a false friend and is never a translation for the English word **cargo**. It means **cargo ship**.

Caribbean [*Br* kærɪ'biːən, *Am* kə'rɪbɪən] **1** *adj* caraïbe **2** *n* **the C. (islands)** les Antilles *fpl*

caricature ['kærɪkətʃʊə(r)] **1** *n* caricature *f* **2** *vt* caricaturer

caring ['keərɪŋ] **1** *adj (loving)* aimant; *(understanding)* très humain **2** *n* affection *f*

carnage ['kɑːnɪdʒ] *n* carnage *m*

carnal ['kɑːnəl] *adj* charnel, -elle

carnation [kɑː'neɪʃən] *n* œillet *m*

carnival ['kɑːnɪvəl] *n* carnaval *m (pl* -als)

carnivore ['kɑːnɪvɔː(r)] *n* carnivore *m* •**carnivorous** [-'nɪvərəs] *adj* carnivore

carol ['kærəl] *n* chant *m* de Noël

carouse [kə'raʊz] *vi* faire la fête

carp [kɑːp] **1** *n inv (fish)* carpe *f* **2** *vi* se plaindre (**at** de)

carpenter ['kɑːpɪntə(r)] *n (for house building)* charpentier *m*; *(for light woodwork)* menuisier *m* •**carpentry** *n* charpenterie *f*; *(for light woodwork)* menuiserie *f*

carpet ['kɑːpɪt] **1** *n (rug)* & *Fig* tapis *m*; *(fitted)* moquette *f*; **c. sweeper** balai *m* mécanique **2** *vt* recouvrir d'un tapis/d'une moquette; *Fig (of snow)* recouvrir •**carpeting** *n (rugs)* tapis *mpl*; *Am* **(wall-to-wall) c.** moquette *f*

> Note that the French word **carpette** is a false friend and is never a translation for the English word **carpet**. It means **small rug**.

carriage ['kærɪdʒ] *n Br (of train)* voiture *f*; *(horse-drawn)* voiture, équipage *m*; *Br (transport of goods)* transport *m*; *(cost)* frais *mpl*; *(of typewriter)* chariot *m*; *Br* **c. paid** port payé

carriageway ['kærɪdʒweɪ] *n Br* chaussée *f*

carrier ['kærɪə(r)] *n (of illness)* porteur, -euse *mf*; *(company, airline)* transporteur *m*; *Br* **c. (bag)** sac *m* en plastique; **c. pigeon** pigeon *m* voyageur

carrot ['kærət] *n* carotte *f*

carry ['kærɪ] *(pt & pp* **-ied**) **1** *vt* porter; *(goods, passengers)* transporter; *(gun, money)* avoir sur soi; *(by wind)* emporter; *(sound)* conduire; *(disease)* être porteur de; *(sell)* stocker; *Pol (motion)* faire passer, voter; *Math (in calculation)* retenir; **to c. water to** *(of pipe)* amener de l'eau à; **to c. responsibility** *(of job)* comporter des responsabilités; *Fam* **to c. the can** porter le chapeau; **to c. sth too far** pousser qch trop loin; **to c. oneself** se comporter **2** *vi (of sound)* porter •**carryall** ['kærɪɔːl] *n Am (bag)* fourre-tout *m inv* •**carrycot** *n Br* porte-bébé *m inv*

►**carry away** *vt sep* emporter; *Fig (of idea)* transporter; **to be** *or* **get carried away** *(excited)* s'emballer ►**carry back** *vt sep (thing)* rapporter; *(person)* ramener; *(in thought)* reporter ►**carry forward** *vt sep (in bookkeeping)* reporter ►**carry off** *vt sep (take away)* emporter; *(kidnap)* enlever; *(prize)* remporter; **she carried it off** elle s'en est bien sortie ▸ **carry on 1** *vt sep (continue)* continuer (**doing** à faire); *(negotiations)* mener; *(conversation)* poursuivre **2** *vi (continue)* continuer; *Pej (behave badly)* se conduire mal; *(complain)* se plaindre; **to c. on with sth** continuer qch ▸ **carry out** *vt sep (plan, promise)* mettre à exécution; *(order)* exécuter; *(repair, reform)* effectuer; *(duty)* accomplir; *Am (meal)* emporter ▸ **carry through** *vt sep (plan)* mener à bien

cart [kɑːt] **1** *n (horse-drawn)* charrette *f*; *(handcart)* voiture *f* à bras; *Am (in supermarket)* Caddie® *m*

2 *vt (goods, people)* transporter; *Fam* **to c. (around)** trimbaler; **to c. away** emporter • **carthorse** *n* cheval *m* de trait

cartel [kɑːˈtel] *n Econ* cartel *m*

cartilage [ˈkɑːtɪlɪdʒ] *n* cartilage *m*

carton [ˈkɑːtən] *n (box)* carton *m*; *(of milk, fruit juice)* brique *f*; *(of cigarettes)* cartouche *f*; *(of cream)* pot *m*

cartoon [kɑːˈtuːn] *n (in newspaper)* dessin *m* humoristique; *(film)* dessin animé; **c. (strip)** bande *f* dessinée

cartridge [ˈkɑːtrɪdʒ] *n* cartouche *f*; **c. belt** cartouchière *f*

cartwheel [ˈkɑːtwiːl] *n* **to do a c.** faire la roue

carve [kɑːv] *vt (cut)* tailler (**out of** dans); *(name)* graver; *(sculpt)* sculpter; **to c. (up)** *(meat)* découper; **to c. up** *(country)* morceler; **to c. out a career for oneself** faire carrière • **carving 1** *adj* **c. knife** couteau *m* à découper

2 *n* **(wood) c.** sculpture *f* sur bois

cascade [kæsˈkeɪd] **1** *n* cascade *f*

2 *vi* tomber en cascade

case¹ [keɪs] *n (instance, situation)* & *Med* cas *m*; *Law* affaire *f*; *Fig (arguments)* arguments *mpl*; **in any c.** en tout cas; **in c. it rains** au cas où il pleuvrait; **in c. of** en cas de; **(just) in c.** à tout hasard

case² [keɪs] *n (bag)* valise *f*; *(crate)* caisse *f*; *(for pen, glasses, camera, violin, cigarettes)* étui *m*; *(for jewels)* écrin *m*

cash [kæʃ] **1** *n (coins, banknotes)* liquide *m*; *Fam (money)* sous *mpl*; **to pay (in) c.** payer en liquide; **to pay c. (down)** *(not on credit)* payer comptant; **to have c. flow problems** avoir des problèmes d'argent; **c. box** caisse *f*; *Br* **c. desk** caisse; **c. dispenser** *or* **machine** distributeur *m* de billets; **c. price** prix *m* (au) comptant; **c. register** caisse *f* enregistreuse

2 *vt* **to c. a cheque** *or Am* **check** *(of person)* encaisser un chèque; *(of bank)* payer un chèque; *Fam* **to c. in on** *(situation)* profiter de

cashew [ˈkæʃuː] *n* **c. (nut)** noix *f* de cajou

cashier [kæˈʃɪə(r)] *n* caissier, -ière *mf*

cashmere [ˈkæʃmɪə(r)] *n* cachemire *m*

casing [ˈkeɪsɪŋ] *n Tech* boîtier *m*; *(of sausage)* boyau *m*

casino [kəˈsiːnəʊ] *(pl* **-os**) *n* casino *m*

cask [kɑːsk] *n* fût *m*, tonneau *m* • **casket** *n (box)* coffret *m*; *(coffin)* cercueil *m*

casserole [ˈkæsərəʊl] *n (covered dish)* cocotte *f*; *(stew)* ragoût *m*

> *Note that the French word **casserole** is a false friend and is never a translation for the English word **casserole**. It means **saucepan**.*

cassette [kəˈset] *n (audio, video)* cassette *f*; *(for camera)* cartouche *f*; **c. player** lecteur *m* de cassettes; **c. recorder** magnétophone *m* à cassettes

cassock [ˈkæsək] *n* soutane *f*

cast [kɑːst] **1** *n (actors)* acteurs *mpl*; *(list of actors)* distribution *f*; *(mould)* moulage *m*; *(of dice)* coup *m*; *(for broken bone)* plâtre *m*; *Med* **in a c.** dans le plâtre; **to have a c. in one's eye** avoir une coquetterie dans l'œil

2 *(pt & pp* **cast**) *vt (throw)* jeter; *(light, shadow)* projeter; *(blame)* rejeter; *(glance)* jeter (**at** *ou* sur); *(metal)* couler; *(theatrical role)* distribuer; *(actor)* donner un rôle à; **to c. doubt on sth** jeter le doute sur qch; **to c. a spell on sb** jeter un sort à qn; **to c. one's mind back** se reporter en arrière; **to c. a vote** voter; **to c. aside** rejeter; **to c. iron** fonte *f*

3 *vi* **to c. off** *(of ship)* appareiller • **cast-'iron** *adj (pan)* en fonte; *Fig (will)* de fer; *Fig (alibi, excuse)* en béton

castaway [ˈkɑːstəweɪ] *n* naufragé, -ée *mf*

caste [kɑːst] *n* caste *f*

caster [ˈkɑːstə(r)] *n (wheel)* roulette *f*; *Br* **c. sugar** sucre *m* en poudre

castle [ˈkɑːsəl] *n* château *m*; *(in chess)* tour *f*

castoffs [ˈkɑːstɒfs] *npl* vieux vêtements *mpl*

castor [ˈkɑːstə(r)] *n (wheel)* roulette *f*; **c. oil** huile *f* de ricin; *Br* **c. sugar** sucre *m* en poudre

castrate [kæˈstreɪt] *vt* châtrer • **castration** *n* castration *f*

casual [ˈkæʒjʊəl] *adj (offhand) (remark, glance)* en passant; *(relaxed, informal)* décontracté; *(conversation)* à bâtons rompus; *(clothes)* sport *inv*; *(careless)* désinvolte; *(meeting)* fortuit; *(employ-ment, worker)* temporaire • **casually** *adv* *(remark, glance)* en passant; *(informally)* avec décontraction; *(dress)* sport; *(care-lessly)* avec désinvolture; *(meet)* par hasard

casualty ['kæʒjʊəltɪ] *(pl* -**ies**) *n* victime *f*; *Br* **c. (department)** *(in hospital)* (service *m* des) urgences *fpl*

cat [kæt] *n* chat *m*; *(female)* chatte *f*; **c. burglar** monte-en-l'air *m* *inv*; **c.'s eyes**® *Br* Cataphotes® *mpl*; **c. food** pâtée *f*

catalogue ['kætəlɒg] *(Am* **catalog**) 1 *n* catalogue *m* 2 *vt* cataloguer

catalyst ['kætəlɪst] *n* *Chem & Fig* cataly-seur *m*

catapult ['kætəpʌlt] 1 *n* *(toy)* lance-pierres *m* *inv*; *(on aircraft carrier)* cata-pulte *f* 2 *vt* catapulter

cataract ['kætərækt] *n* *Med* cataracte *f*

catarrh [kə'tɑ:(r)] *n* *Br* gros rhume *m*

catastrophe [kə'tæstrəfɪ] *n* catastrophe *f* • **catastrophic** [kætə'strɒfɪk] *adj* catas-trophique

catcall ['kætkɔ:l] *n* sifflet *m*

catch [kætʃ] 1 *n* *(captured animal)* cap-ture *f*, prise *f*; *(in fishing)* prise; *(of a whole day)* pêche *f*; *(difficulty)* piège *m*; *(on door)* loquet *m*; **there's a c.** il y a un piège 2 *(pt & pp* **caught**) *vt* *(ball, thief, illness)* attraper; *(fish, train, bus)* prendre; *(grab)* prendre, saisir; *(surprise)* surprendre; *(understand)* saisir; *(garment)* accrocher (**on** à); **to c. one's fingers in the door** se prendre les doigts dans la porte; **to c. sb's eye** *or* **attention** attirer l'attention de qn; **to c. sight of sb/sth** apercevoir qn/qch; **to c. fire** prendre feu; **to c. the sun** *(of garden, room)* être ensoleillé; *(of person)* prendre des couleurs; *Fam* **to c. sb (in)** trouver qn (chez soi); **to c. one's breath** *(rest a while)* reprendre haleine; *(stop breathing)* retenir son souffle; **to c. sb doing** surprendre qn à faire; **to c. sb out** prendre qn en défaut; **to c. sb up** rattra-per qn 3 *vi* *(of fire)* prendre; **her skirt (got) caught in the door** sa jupe s'est prise dans la porte; **to c. on** *(become popular)* prendre; *Fam (understand)* piger; **to c. up with sb** rattraper qn • **catching** *adj* *(ill-ness)* contagieux, -ieuse • **catchphrase** *n* *(of politician)* slogan *m*; *(of comedian)* formule *f* favorite

catchy ['kætʃɪ] (-**ier**, -**iest**) *adj* *Fam* *(tune, slogan)* facile à retenir

catechism ['kætɪkɪzəm] *n* catéchisme *m*

category ['kætɪgərɪ] *(pl* -**ies**) *n* catégorie *f* • **categorical** [-'gɒrɪkəl] *adj* catégorique • **categorize** *vt* classer (par catégories)

cater ['keɪtə(r)] *vi* *(provide food)* s'occu-per des repas (**for** pour); **to c. to,** *Br* **to c. for** *(need, taste)* satisfaire; *(of book, newspaper)* s'adresser à • **caterer** *n* trai-teur *m* • **catering** *n* restauration *f*; **to do the c.** s'occuper des repas

caterpillar ['kætəpɪlə(r)] *n* chenille *f*; **c. track** chenille

catgut ['kætgʌt] *n* *(cord)* boyau *m*

cathedral [kə'θi:drəl] *n* cathédrale *f*

Catholic ['kæθlɪk] *adj & n* catholique *(mf)* • **Catholicism** [kə'θɒlɪsɪzəm] *n* ca-tholicisme *m*

cattle ['kætəl] *npl* bétail *m*

catty ['kætɪ] (-**ier**, -**iest**) *adj* *Fam* *(spiteful)* vache

catwalk ['kætwɔːk] *n* *Br* *(in fashion show)* podium *m*

caught [kɔːt] *pt & pp of* **catch**

cauldron ['kɔːldrən] *n* chaudron *m*

cauliflower ['kɒlɪflaʊə(r)] *n* chou-fleur *m*; *Br* **c. cheese** chou-fleur au gratin

cause [kɔːz] 1 *n* *(origin, ideal, aim) & Law* cause *f*; *(reason)* raison *f*, motif *m* (**of** de); **c. for complaint/dispute** sujet *m* de plainte/dispute; **to have c. for complaint** avoir des raisons de se plaindre; **to have no c. to worry** n'avoir aucune raison de s'inquiéter 2 *vt* causer, occasionner; **to c. trouble for sb** créer *ou* causer des ennuis à qn; **to c. sb/sth to fall** faire tomber qn/qch

causeway ['kɔːzweɪ] *n* chaussée *f* (*sur un marécage*)

caustic ['kɔːstɪk] *adj* *(substance, remark)* caustique; **c. soda** soude *f* caustique

cauterize ['kɔːtəraɪz] *vt* *(wound)* cautéri-ser

caution ['kɔːʃən] 1 *n* *(care)* prudence *f*; *(warning)* avertissement *m* 2 *vt* *(warn)* avertir; *Sport* donner un avertissement à; **to c. sb against sth** mettre qn en garde contre qch; **to c. sb against doing sth** déconseiller à qn de faire qch

---

⚠ Note that the French word **caution** is a false friend and is never a translation for the English word **caution**. Its most com-mon meanings are **deposit** or **guarantee**.

---

cautionary ['kɔːʃənərɪ] *adj* **c. tale** conte *m* moral

cautious ['kɔːʃəs] *adj* prudent • **cau-tiously** *adv* prudemment

cavalier [kævə'lɪə(r)] **1** *adj* cavalier, -ière **2** *n Hist (horseman, knight)* cavalier *m*
cavalry ['kævəlrɪ] *n* cavalerie *f*
cave [keɪv] **1** *n* grotte *f* **2** *vi* **to c. in** *(of ceiling)* s'effondrer; *(of floor)* s'affaisser • **caveman** *(pl* **-men***) n* homme *m* des cavernes

> *Note that the French word **cave** is a false friend and is never a translation for the English word **cave**. It means **cellar**.*

cavern ['kævən] *n* caverne *f*
caviar(e) ['kævɪɑː(r)] *n* caviar *m*
cavity ['kævɪtɪ] *(pl* **-ies***) n* cavité *f*
cavort [kə'vɔːt] *vi Fam* faire des cabrioles; **to c. naked** se balader tout nu
CD [siː'diː] *(abbr* **compact disc***) n* CD *m*; **CD player** lecteur *m* de CD
CD-ROM [siːdiː'rɒm] *(abbr* **compact disc read-only memory***) n Comptr* CD-ROM *m inv*
cease [siːs] **1** *vt* cesser (**doing** de faire); **to c. fire** cesser le feu **2** *vi* cesser (**from doing** de faire) • **cease-fire** *n* cessez-le-feu *m inv* • **ceaseless** *adj* incessant • **ceaselessly** *adv* sans cesse
cedar ['siːdə(r)] *n (tree, wood)* cèdre *m*
cedilla [sɪ'dɪlə] *n Grammar* cédille *f*
ceiling ['siːlɪŋ] *n (of room) & Fig (limit)* plafond *m*; *Fam* **to hit the c.** piquer une crise
celebrate ['selɪbreɪt] **1** *vt (event)* célébrer, fêter; *(mass)* célébrer **2** *vi* faire la fête; **we should c.!** il faut fêter ça! • **celebrated** *adj* célèbre • **celebration** [-'breɪʃən] *n (event)* fête *f*; **the celebrations** les festivités *fpl*
celebrity [sə'lebrɪtɪ] *(pl* **-ies***) n* célébrité *f*
celery ['selərɪ] *n* céleri *m*; **stick of c.** branche *f* de céleri
celibate ['selɪbət] *adj* **to be c.** ne pas avoir de rapports sexuels; *(by choice)* être chaste • **celibacy** *n* absence *f* de rapports sexuels; *(by choice)* chasteté *f*

> *Note that the French word **célibataire** is a false friend and is never a translation for the English word **celibate**. It means **unmarried**.*

cell [sel] *n* cellule *f*; *El* élément *m*
cellar ['selə(r)] *n* cave *f*

> *Note that the French word **cellier** is a false friend. It means **storeroom**.*

cello ['tʃeləʊ] *(pl* **-os***) n* violoncelle *m* • **cellist** *n* violoncelliste *mf*
cellophane® ['seləfeɪn] *n* Cellophane® *f*
cellular ['seljʊlə(r)] *adj* cellulaire; **c.**

blanket couverture *f* en cellular; **c. phone** téléphone *m* cellulaire
celluloid® ['seljʊlɔɪd] *n* Celluloïd® *m*
cellulose ['seljʊləʊs] *n* cellulose *f*
Celsius ['selsɪəs] *adj* Celsius *inv*
Celt [kelt] *n* Celte *mf* • **Celtic** *adj* celtique, celte
cement [sɪ'ment] **1** *n* ciment *m*; **c. mixer** bétonnière *f* **2** *vt* cimenter
cemetery ['semətrɪ] *(pl* **-ies***) n* cimetière *m*
cenotaph ['senətɑːf] *n* cénotaphe *m*
censor ['sensə(r)] **1** *n* censeur *m* **2** *vt* censurer • **censorship** *n* censure *f*
censure ['senʃə(r)] **1** *n* critique *f*; **c. motion, vote of c.** motion *f* de censure **2** *vt (criticize)* blâmer

> *Note that the French verb **censurer** is a false friend and is never a translation for the English verb **to censure**. It means **to censor**.*

census ['sensəs] *n* recensement *m*
cent [sent] *n (coin)* cent *m*; *Fam* **not a c.** pas un sou
centenary [*Br* sen'tiːnərɪ, *Am* sen'tenərɪ] *(pl* **-ies***) n* centenaire *m*
center ['sentə(r)] *n Am* = **centre**
centigrade ['sentɪɡreɪd] *adj* centigrade
centimetre ['sentɪmiːtə(r)] *n* centimètre *m*
centipede ['sentɪpiːd] *n* mille-pattes *m inv*
central ['sentrəl] *adj* central; **C. London** le centre de Londres; **c. heating** chauffage *m* central; *Br* **c. reservation** *(on motorway)* terre-plein *m* central • **centralize** *vt* centraliser
centre ['sentə(r)] *(Am* **center***)* **1** *n* centre *m*; *Football* **c. forward** avant-centre *m* **2** *vt (attention, interest)* concentrer (**on** sur)
centrifugal [sen'trɪfjʊɡəl] *adj* centrifuge
century ['sentʃərɪ] *(pl* **-ies***) n* siècle *m*; **in the twenty-first c.** au vingt et unième siècle
ceramic [sə'ræmɪk] *adj (tile)* en céramique • **ceramics 1** *npl (objects)* céramiques *fpl* **2** *n (art)* céramique *f*
cereal ['sɪərɪəl] *n* céréale *f*; **(breakfast) c.** céréales *fpl (pour petit déjeuner)*
cerebral [*Br* 'serɪbrəl, *Am* sə'riːbrəl] *adj* cérébral
ceremony ['serɪmənɪ] *(pl* **-ies***) n (event)* cérémonie *f*; **to stand on c.** faire des façons • **ceremonial** [-'məʊnɪəl] **1** *adj* **c. dress** tenue *f* de cérémonie **2** *n* cérémo-

nial *m* • **ceremonious** [-'məʊnɪəs] *adj* cérémonieux, -ieuse

certain ['sɜːtən] *adj* (**a**) *(sure)* certain (that que); **she's c. to come, she'll come for c.** c'est certain qu'elle viendra; **I'm not c. what to do** je ne sais pas très bien quoi faire; **be c. you go!** il faut absolument que tu y ailles!; **to be c. of sth** être certain *ou* sûr de qch; **to make c. of sth** *(find out)* s'assurer de qch; *(be sure to get)* s'assurer qch; **for c.** *(say, know)* avec certitude (**b**) *(particular, some)* certain; **a c. person** une certaine personne; **c. people** certaines personnes • **certainly** *adv* *(undoubtedly)* certainement; *(yes)* bien sûr; *(without fail)* sans faute • **certainty** *(pl* **-ies)** *n* certitude *f*

certificate [sə'tɪfɪkɪt] *n* certificat *m*; *(from university)* diplôme *m*

certify ['sɜːtɪfaɪ] *(pt & pp* **-ied)** **1** *vt (document, signature)* certifier; **to c. sb (insane)** déclarer que l'état de santé de qn nécessite son internement psychiatrique; *Am* **certified letter** ≃ lettre *f* recommandée; *Am* **certified public accountant** expert-comptable *m*

2 *vi* **to c. to sth** attester qch

cervix ['sɜːvɪks] *(pl* **-vices** ['-vɪsiːz]) *n Anat* col *m* de l'utérus

cesspool ['sespuːl] *n* fosse *f* d'aisances; *Fig* cloaque *m*

CFC [siːef'siː] *(abbr* **chlorofluorocarbon)** *n* CFC *m*

chafe [tʃeɪf] *vt (skin)* irriter; *(of shoes)* blesser

chaff [tʃæf] *vt (tease)* taquiner

chaffinch ['tʃæfɪntʃ] *n (bird)* pinson *m*

chain [tʃeɪn] **1** *n (of rings, mountains)* chaîne *f*; *(of ideas)* enchaînement *m*; *(of events)* suite *f*; *(of lavatory)* chasse *f* d'eau; **c. reaction** réaction *f* en chaîne; **c. saw** tronçonneuse *f*; **c. store** magasin *m* à succursales multiples

2 *vt* **to c. (down)** enchaîner; **to c. (up)** *(dog)* mettre à l'attache • **chain-smoker** *n* **to be a c.** fumer cigarette sur cigarette

chair [tʃeə(r)] **1** *n* chaise *f*; *(armchair)* fauteuil *m*; *Univ (of professor)* chaire *f*; **the c.** *(office of chairperson)* la présidence; **c. lift** télésiège *m*

2 *vt (meeting)* présider • **chairman** *(pl* **-men)**, **chairperson** *n* président, -ente *mf* • **chairmanship** *n* présidence *f*

chalet ['ʃæleɪ] *n* chalet *m*

chalk [tʃɔːk] **1** *n* craie *f*; **they are like c. and cheese** c'est le jour et la nuit; *Fam* **not by a long c.** loin de là

2 *vt* marquer à la craie; *Fig* **to c. up**

(success) remporter • **chalky** (**-ier, -iest**) *adj* crayeux, -euse

challenge ['tʃælɪndʒ] **1** *n* défi *m*; *(task)* challenge *m*, gageure *f*; **a c. for sth** *(bid)* une tentative d'obtenir qch

2 *vt* défier (**sb** to do **qn** de faire); *(question, dispute)* contester • **challenger** *n Sport* challenger *m* • **challenging** *adj (book, job)* stimulant

chamber ['tʃeɪmbə(r)] *n (room, assembly, of gun)* chambre *f*; *Br Law* **chambers** *(of judge)* cabinet *m*; **C. of Commerce** Chambre *f* de commerce; **c. music/orchestra** musique *f*/orchestre *m* de chambre; **c. pot** pot *m* de chambre • **chambermaid** *n* femme *f* de chambre

chameleon [kə'miːlɪən] *n* caméléon *m*

chamois ['ʃæmɪ] *n* **c. (leather)** peau *f* de chamois

champagne [ʃæm'peɪn] *n* champagne *m*

champion ['tʃæmpɪən] **1** *n* champion, -ionne *mf*; **c. skier, skiing c.** champion, -ionne de ski

2 *vt (support)* se faire le champion de • **championship** *n* championnat *m*

chance [tʃɑːns] **1** *n (luck)* hasard *m*; *(possibility)* chance *f*; *(opportunity)* occasion *f*; *(risk)* risque *m*; **by c.** par hasard; **by any c.** *(possibly)* par hasard; **to have the c. to do sth** *or* **of doing sth** avoir l'occasion de faire qch; **to give sb a c.** donner une chance à qn; **to take a c.** tenter le coup; **on the off c. (that) you could help me** au cas où tu pourrais m'aider

2 *adj (remark)* fait au hasard; **c. meeting** rencontre *f* fortuite; **c. occurrence** événement *m* fortuit

3 *vt* **to c. doing sth** prendre le risque de faire qch; **to c. to do sth** faire qch par hasard; **to c. it** risquer le coup

chancel ['tʃɑːnsəl] *n (in church)* chœur *m*

chancellor ['tʃɑːnsələ(r)] *n Pol* chancelier *m* • **chancellery** *n* chancellerie *f*

chandelier [ʃændə'lɪə(r)] *n* lustre *m*

> 📖 Note that the French word **chandelier** is a false friend. It means **candlestick**.

change [tʃeɪndʒ] **1** *n* changement *m*; *(money)* monnaie *f*; **for a c.** pour changer; **it makes a c. from...** ça change de...; **to have a c. of heart** changer d'avis; **a c. of clothes** des vêtements de rechange

2 *vt (modify)* changer; *(exchange)* échanger (**for** pour *ou* contre); *(money)* changer (**into** en); *(transform)* changer, transformer (**into** en); **to c. trains/one's skirt** changer de train/de jupe; **to c. gear** *(in vehicle)* changer de vitesse; **to c. col-**

our changer de couleur; **to c. the subject** changer de sujet; **to get changed** *(put on other clothes)* se changer

3 *vi (alter)* changer; *(change clothes)* se changer; **to c. into sth** *(be transformed)* se changer *ou* se transformer en qch; **she changed into a dress** elle a mis une robe; **to c. over** passer (**from** de; **to** à) •**changing** *n Br* **the c. of the guard** la relève de la garde; **c. room** vestiaire *m*; *(in shop)* cabine *f* d'essayage

changeable ['tʃeɪndʒəbəl] *adj (weather, mood)* changeant

changeover ['tʃeɪndʒəʊvə(r)] *n* passage *m* (**from** de; **to** à)

channel ['tʃænəl] **1** *n (on television)* chaîne *f*; *(for boats)* chenal *m*; *(groove)* rainure *f*; *(of communication, distribution)* canal *m*; *Geog* **the C.** la Manche; **the C. Islands** les îles Anglo-Normandes; **the C. Tunnel** le tunnel sous la Manche

2 *(Br* **-ll-,** *Am* **-l-)** *vt (energies, crowd, money)* canaliser (**into** vers)

chant [tʃɑːnt] **1** *n (of demonstrators)* slogan *m*; *(religious)* psalmodie *f*

2 *vt (slogan)* scander

3 *vi (of demonstrators)* scander des slogans; *(of monks)* psalmodier

> Note that the French words **chant** and **chanter** are false friends and are never translations for the English **chant** and **to chant**. They mean **song** and **to sing**.

chaos ['keɪɒs] *n* chaos *m* •**chaotic** [-'ɒtɪk] *adj (situation, scene)* chaotique; *(room)* sens dessus dessous

chap¹ [tʃæp] *n Br Fam (fellow)* type *m*; **old c.!** mon vieux!

chap² [tʃæp] *(pt & pp* **-pp-)** **1** *vt* gercer; **chapped hands/lips** des mains/lèvres gercées

2 *vi* se gercer

chapel ['tʃæpəl] *n* chapelle *f*; *(non-conformist church)* temple *m*

chaperon(e) ['ʃæpərəʊn] **1** *n* chaperon *m*

2 *vt* chaperonner

chaplain ['tʃæplɪn] *n* aumônier *m*

chapter ['tʃæptə(r)] *n* chapitre *m*

character ['kærɪktə(r)] *n* **(a)** *(of person, place)* caractère *m*; *(in book, film)* personnage *m*; *(person)* individu *m*; *(unusual person)* personnage; **he's a bit of a c.** c'est un personnage; **c. reference** *(for job)* références *fpl* **(b)** *(letter)* caractère *m*; **in bold characters** en caractères gras

characteristic ['kærɪktərɪstɪk] *adj & n* caractéristique *(f)* •**characteristically** *adv* typiquement

characterize [kærɪktə'raɪz] *vt* caractériser

charade [*Br* ʃə'rɑːd, *Am* ʃə'reɪd] *n (travesty)* mascarade *f*; **charades** *(game)* charades *fpl* mimées

> Note that the French word **charade** is a false friend. It is a type of word game.

charcoal ['tʃɑːkəʊl] *n* charbon *m* de bois; *Art* fusain *m*; **c. grey** anthracite *inv*

charge¹ [tʃɑːdʒ] **1** *n (in battle)* charge *f*; *Law* chef *m* d'accusation; *(responsibility)* responsabilité *f*, charge; *(care)* garde *f*; **to take c. of sth** prendre qch en charge; **to be in c. of** être responsable de; **who's in c. here?** qui est le chef ici?; **the person in c.** le/la responsable; **the battery is on c.** la batterie est en charge

2 *vt (battery, soldiers)* charger; *Law (accuse)* inculper (**with** de)

3 *vi (rush)* se précipiter; *(soldiers)* charger; **to c. in/out** entrer/sortir en trombe •**charger** *n (for battery)* chargeur *m*

charge² [tʃɑːdʒ] **1** *n (cost)* prix *m*; **charges** *(expenses)* frais *mpl*; **there's a c. (for it)** c'est payant; **to make a c. for sth** faire payer qch; **free of c.** gratuit; **extra c.** supplément *m*; **c. card** carte *f* de paiement *(de magasin)*

2 *vt (amount)* demander (**for** pour); **to c. sb** faire payer qn; **to c. sth (up) to sb** mettre qch sur le compte de qn; **how much do you c.?** combien demandez-vous? •**chargeable** *adj* **c. to sb** aux frais de qn •**charged** *adj Fig* **a highly c. atmosphere** une atmosphère très tendue

chariot ['tʃærɪət] *n* char *m*

charisma [kə'rɪzmə] *n* charisme *m*

charity ['tʃærɪtɪ] *(pl* **-ies)** *n (kindness, alms)* charité *f*; *(society)* œuvre *f* de charité; **to give to c.** faire des dons à des œuvres de charité •**charitable** *adj (person, action)* charitable; *(organization)* caritatif, -ive

charlady ['tʃɑːleɪdɪ] *(pl* **-ies)** *n Br* femme *f* de ménage

charlatan ['ʃɑːlətən] *n* charlatan *m*

charm [tʃɑːm] **1** *n (attractiveness, spell)* charme *m*; *(trinket)* breloque *f*

2 *vt* charmer •**charming** *adj* charmant •**charmingly** *adv* d'une façon charmante

charred [tʃɑːd] *adj (burnt until black)* carbonisé; *(scorched)* brûlé légèrement

chart [tʃɑːt] **1** *n (map)* carte *f*; *(table)* tableau *m*; *(graph)* graphique *m*; **(pop) charts** hit-parade *m*

2 *vt (route)* porter sur une carte; *(make a*

graph of) faire le graphique de; *(of graph)* montrer; *Fig (observe)* suivre

charter ['tʃɑːtə(r)] **1** *n* (**a**) *(aircraft)* charter *m*; **the c. of** *(hiring)* l'affrètement *m* de; **c. flight** vol *m* charter (**b**) *(document)* charte *f*

2 *vt (aircraft)* affréter • **chartered accountant** *n Br* expert-comptable *m*

charwoman ['tʃɑːwʊmən] *(pl* **-women**) *n Br* femme *f* de ménage

chary ['tʃeərɪ] (**-ier, -iest**) *adj (cautious)* prudent; **to be c. of doing sth** hésiter à faire qch

chase [tʃeɪs] **1** *n* poursuite *f*; **to give c. to sb** se lancer à la poursuite de qn

2 *vt* poursuivre; **to c. sb away** *or* **off** chasser qn; *Fam* **to c. sth up** rechercher qch

3 *vi* **to c. after sb/sth** courir après qn/qch

> ℓ Note that the French verb **chasser** is a false friend. It means **to hunt**.

chasm ['kæzəm] *n also Fig* abîme *m*, gouffre *m*

chassis ['ʃæsɪ] *n (of vehicle)* châssis *m*

chaste [tʃeɪst] *adj* chaste • **chastity** ['tʃæstɪtɪ] *n* chasteté *f*

chastening ['tʃeɪsənɪŋ] *adj (experience)* instructif, -ive

chastise [tʃæˈstaɪz] *vt* punir

chat [tʃæt] **1** *n* petite conversation *f*; *Comptr* bavardage *m*; **to have a c.** causer (**with** avec)

2 *(pt & pp* **-tt-**) *vi* causer (**with** avec); *Comptr* bavarder

3 *vt Br Fam* **to c. sb up** draguer qn

chatter ['tʃætə(r)] **1** *n* bavardage *m*; *(of birds)* jacassement *m*

2 *vi (of person)* bavarder; *(of birds, monkeys)* jacasser; **his teeth were chattering** il claquait des dents • **chatterbox** *n* pie *f*

chatty ['tʃætɪ] (**-ier, -iest**) *adj (person)* bavard; *(letter)* plein de détails

chauffeur ['ʃəʊfə(r)] *n* chauffeur *m*

chauvinist ['ʃəʊvɪnɪst] *adj & n* chauvin, -ine *(mf)*; *Pej* **(male) c.** macho *m*, phallocrate *m*

cheap [tʃiːp] **1** (**-er, -est**) *adj* bon marché *inv*, pas cher *(f* pas chère); *(rate, fare)* réduit; *(worthless)* sans valeur; *(vulgar)* de mauvais goût; *(superficial) (emotion, remark)* facile; *(mean, petty)* mesquin; **cheaper** meilleur marché *inv*, moins cher *(f* moins chère); **to feel c.** se sentir minable

2 *adv Fam (buy)* (à) bon marché, au rabais; **it was going c.** c'était bon marché

3 *n* **on the c.** à peu de frais • **cheaply** *adv* (à) bon marché

cheapen ['tʃiːpən] *vt (degrade)* gâcher

cheat [tʃiːt] **1** *n (at games)* tricheur, -euse *mf*; *(crook)* escroc *m*

2 *vt (deceive)* tromper; *(defraud)* frauder; **to c. sb out of sth** escroquer qch à qn; **to c. on sb** tromper qn

3 *vi (at games)* tricher; *(defraud)* frauder • **cheating** *n (at games)* tricherie *f*; *(deceit)* tromperie *f*; **it's c.!** c'est de la triche!

check¹ [tʃek] **1** *adj (pattern)* à carreaux

2 *n* **c. (pattern)** carreaux *mpl* • **checked** *adj (patterned)* à carreaux

check² [tʃek] **1** *n* vérification *f* (**on** de); *(inspection)* contrôle *m*; *(in chess)* échec *m*; *Am (tick)* ≃ croix *f*; *Am (receipt)* reçu *m*; *Am (restaurant bill)* addition *f*; *Am (cheque)* chèque *m*; **to keep a c. on sth** contrôler qch; **to put a c. on sth** mettre un frein à qch; **to keep sb in c.** tenir qn en échec; *Pol* **checks and balances** équilibre *m* des pouvoirs

2 *vt (examine)* vérifier; *(inspect)* contrôler; *(mark off)* cocher; *(inflation)* enrayer; *(emotion, impulse, enemy advance)* contenir; *Am (baggage)* mettre à la consigne

3 *vi* vérifier; **to c. on sth** vérifier qch; **to c. on sb** surveiller qn; **c. with her** pose-lui la question • **checkbook** *n Am* carnet *m* de chèques • **check-in** *n (at airport)* enregistrement *m* (des bagages) • **checking account** *n Am* compte *m* courant • **checklist** *n* liste *f* de contrôle; *Av* check-list *f* • **checkmate** *n (in chess)* échec *m* et mat • **checkout** *n (in supermarket)* caisse *f* • **checkpoint** *n* poste *m* de contrôle • **checkroom** *n Am* vestiaire *m*; *Am (left-luggage office)* consigne *f* • **checkup** *n (medical)* bilan *m* de santé; **to have a c.** faire un bilan de santé

▸ **check in 1** *vt sep (luggage)* enregistrer **2** *vi (arrive)* arriver; *(sign in)* signer le registre; *(at airport)* se présenter à l'enregistrement ▸ **check off** *vt sep (from list)* cocher ▸ **check out 1** *vt sep (confirm)* confirmer **2** *vi (at hotel)* régler sa note ▸ **check up** *vi* vérifier

checkered ['tʃekərd] *adj Am* = **chequered**

checkers ['tʃekərz] *npl Am* jeu *m* de dames • **checkerboard** *n Am* damier *m*

cheddar ['tʃedə(r)] *n* cheddar *m (fromage)*

cheek [tʃiːk] *n* joue *f*; *Br Fam (impudence)* culot *m* • **cheekbone** *n* pommette *f* • **cheeky** (**-ier, -iest**) *adj Br (person, reply)* insolent

cheep [tʃiːp] *vi (of bird)* piailler

cheer [tʃɪə(r)] **1** *n* **cheers** *(shouts)* acclamations *fpl*; *Fam* **cheers!** *(when drinking)* à votre santé!; *(thanks)* merci!

2 *vt (applaud)* acclamer; **to c. sb on** encourager qn; **to c. sb (up)** *(comfort)* remonter le moral à qn; *(amuse)* faire sourire qn

3 *vi* applaudir; **to c. up** reprendre courage; *(be amused)* se dérider; **c. up!** (du) courage! ● **cheering 1** *adj (encouraging)* réjouissant **2** *n (shouts)* acclamations *fpl*

cheerful ['tʃɪəfəl] *adj* gai ● **cheerfully** *adv* gaiement ● **cheerless** *adj* morne

cheerio [tʃɪən'əʊ] *exclam Br* salut!, au revoir!

cheese [tʃiːz] *n* fromage *m*; *Fam* **(say) c.!** *(for photograph)* souriez!; **c. board** plateau *m* de fromages; **c. sandwich** sandwich *m* au fromage ● **cheeseburger** *n* cheeseburger *m* ● **cheesecake** *n* tarte *f* au fromage blanc

cheesed [tʃiːzd] *adj Fam* **to be c. (off)** en avoir marre (**with** de)

cheesy ['tʃiːzɪ] (**-ier, -iest**) *adj Fam* moche

cheetah ['tʃiːtə] *n* guépard *m*

chef [ʃef] *n* chef *m* (cuisinier)

chemical 1 *adj* chimique

2 *n* produit *m* chimique

chemist ['kemɪst] *n Br (pharmacist)* pharmacien, -ienne *mf*; *(scientist)* chimiste *mf*; *Br* **c.'s shop** pharmacie *f* ● **chemistry** *n* chimie *f*

chemotherapy [kiːməʊ'θerəpɪ] *n Med* chimiothérapie *f*; **to have c.** faire de la chimiothérapie

cheque [tʃek] *n Br* chèque *m*; **c. card** carte *f* d'identité bancaire *(sans laquelle un chéquier n'est pas valable)* ● **chequebook** *n Br* carnet *m* de chèques

chequered ['tʃekəd] (*Am* **checkered**) *adj Br (pattern)* à carreaux; *Fig (career)* en dents de scie; *Sport* **c. flag** drapeau *m* à damier

cherish ['tʃerɪʃ] *vt (hope)* nourrir, caresser; *(person, memory)* chérir

cherry ['tʃerɪ] **1** (*pl* **-ies**) *n* cerise *f*; *(tree)* cerisier *m*; **c. brandy** cherry *m*

2 *adj* **c.(-red)** cerise *inv*

chess [tʃes] *n* échecs *mpl* ● **chessboard** *n* échiquier *m*

chest [tʃest] *n* (**a**) *(part of body)* poitrine *f*; *Fig* **to get it off one's c.** dire ce qu'on a sur le cœur (**b**) *(box)* coffre *m*; **c. of drawers** commode *f*

chestnut ['tʃestnʌt] **1** *n (nut)* châtaigne *f*; *(cooked)* châtaigne, marron *m*; **c. (tree)** châtaignier *m*

2 *adj (hair)* châtain

chew [tʃuː] **1** *vt* **to c. (up)** mâcher; **to c. one's nails** se ronger les ongles; *Fam* **to c. over** *(plan, problem)* réfléchir à

2 *vi* mastiquer; **chewing gum** chewing-gum *m*

chewy ['tʃuːɪ] *adj (meat)* caoutchouteux, -euse; *(sweet)* mou (*f* molle)

chick [tʃɪk] *n (chicken)* poussin *m*; *(bird)* oisillon *m*; *Am Fam (girl)* nana *f*

chicken ['tʃɪkɪn] **1** *n* poulet *m*; *Fam* **it's c. feed!** c'est trois fois rien!

2 *adj Fam (cowardly)* froussard

3 *vi Fam* **to c. out** se dégonfler ● **chickenpox** *n* varicelle *f*

chickpea ['tʃɪkpiː] *n* pois *m* chiche

chicory ['tʃɪkərɪ] *n inv (for salad)* endive *f*; *(for coffee)* chicorée *f*

chief [tʃiːf] **1** *n* chef *m*; *Fam (boss)* patron *m*; *Mil* **c. of staff** chef d'état-major

2 *adj (most important)* principal; *Com* **c. executive** directeur *m* général ● **chiefly** *adv* principalement, surtout ● **chieftain** ['tʃiːftən] *n (of clan)* chef *m*

chilblain ['tʃɪlbleɪn] *n* engelure *f*

child [tʃaɪld] (*pl* **children**) *n* enfant *mf*; **it's c. play** c'est un jeu d'enfant; **c. abuse** mauvais traitements *mpl* à enfant, maltraitance *f*; *Br* **c. benefits** ≃ allocations *fpl* familiales; **c. care** *(for working parents)* crèches *fpl* et garderies *fpl*; *Br* **c. minder** assistante *f* maternelle ● **childbearing** *n (motherhood)* maternité *f*; **of c. age** en âge d'avoir des enfants ● **childbirth** *n* accouchement *m* ● **childhood** *n* enfance *f* ● **childish** *adj* puéril ● **childishness** *n* puérilité *f* ● **childlike** *adj* enfantin ● **childproof** *adj (lock, bottle)* que les enfants ne peuvent pas ouvrir

children ['tʃɪldrən] *pl of* **child**

Chile ['tʃɪlɪ] *n* le Chili

chill [tʃɪl] **1** *n* froid *m*; *(in feelings)* froideur *f*; *(illness)* refroidissement *m*; **to catch a c.** prendre froid

2 *vt (wine, melon)* mettre au frais; *(meat)* réfrigérer; **to c. sb** faire frissonner qn; **to be chilled to the bone** être transi; **chilled wine** vin *m* frappé; **chilled dessert** dessert *m* frais ● **chilling** *adj (frightening)* qui fait froid dans le dos

chilli ['tʃɪlɪ] (*pl* **-is** *or* **-ies**) *n (plant)* piment *m* (rouge); *(dish)* chili *m* con carne; **c. powder** ≃ poivre *m* de Cayenne

chilly ['tʃɪlɪ] (**-ier, -iest**) *adj* froid; **it's c.** il fait (un peu) froid

chime [tʃaɪm] **1** *n (of bells)* carillon *m*; *(of clock)* sonnerie *f*
2 *vi (of bell)* carillonner; *(of clock)* sonner; *Fam* **to c. in** *(interrupt)* interrompre
chimney ['tʃɪmnɪ] *(pl* **-eys**) *n* cheminée *f*
• **chimneypot** *n Br* tuyau *m* de cheminée
• **chimneysweep** *n* ramoneur *m*
chimpanzee [tʃɪmpæn'ziː] *n* chimpanzé *m*
chin [tʃɪn] *n* menton *m*; *Fig* **to keep one's c. up** tenir le coup
China ['tʃaɪnə] *n* la Chine • **Chinese** [tʃaɪ'niːz] **1** *adj* chinois; *Br* **C. leaves,** *Am* **C. cabbage** chou *m* chinois **2** *n inv (person)* Chinois, -oise *mf*; *(language)* chinois *m*; *Fam (meal)* repas *m* chinois; *Fam (restaurant)* restaurant *m* chinois
china ['tʃaɪnə] **1** *n inv* porcelaine *f*
2 *adj* en porcelaine • **chinaware** *n (objects)* porcelaine *f*
chink [tʃɪŋk] **1** *n* **(a)** *(slit)* fente *f* **(b)** *(sound)* tintement *m*
2 *vt* faire tinter
3 *vi (of glasses)* tinter
chip [tʃɪp] **1** *n (splinter)* éclat *m*; *(break)* ébréchure *f*; *(counter)* jeton *m*; *Comptr* puce *f*; **chips** *Br (French fries)* frites *fpl*; *Am (crisps)* chips *fpl*; *Br* **c. shop** = boutique où l'on vend du poisson pané et des frites; **to have a c. on one's shoulder** en vouloir à tout le monde
2 *(pt & pp* **-pp-)** *vt (cup, blade)* ébrécher; *(table)* abîmer; *(paint)* écailler; *(cut at) (stone, wood)* tailler
3 *vi Fam* **to c. in** *(contribute)* contribuer; *(interrupt)* mettre son grain de sel • **chipboard** *n* aggloméré *m* • **chippings** *npl* **road** *or* **loose c.** gravillons *mpl*

> *Note that the French word* **chips** *is a false friend for British English speakers. It means* **crisps**.

chiropodist [kɪ'rɒpədɪst] *n Br* pédicure *mf* • **chiropody** *n Br* soins *mpl* du pied
chirp [tʃɜːp] **1** *n* pépiement *m*
2 *vi (of bird)* pépier
chirpy ['tʃɜːpɪ] *(-ier, -iest) adj* d'humeur joyeuse
chisel ['tʃɪzəl] **1** *n* ciseau *m*
2 *(Br* **-ll-,** *Am* **-l-)** *vt* ciseler
chitchat ['tʃɪttʃæt] *n Fam* bavardage *m*
chivalry ['ʃɪvəlrɪ] *n (courtesy)* courtoisie *f*; *(towards women)* galanterie *f*; *Hist (of knights)* chevalerie *f* • **chivalrous** *adj (man)* galant
chives [tʃaɪvz] *npl* ciboulette *f*
chlorine ['klɔːriːn] *n Chem* chlore *m*
chloroform ['klɒrəfɔːm] *n Chem* chloroforme *m*

choc-ice ['tʃɒkaɪs] *n Br* = glace individuelle enrobée de chocolat
chock [tʃɒk] **1** *n (wedge)* cale *f*
2 *vt* caler
chock-a-block [tʃɒkə'blɒk], **chock-full** [tʃɒk'fʊl] *adj Fam* archiplein
chocolate ['tʃɒklɪt] **1** *n* chocolat *m*; **drinking c.** chocolat en poudre; **hot c.** chocolat chaud; **plain c.** chocolat à croquer
2 *adj (made of chocolate)* en chocolat; *(chocolate-flavoured)* au chocolat; *(colour)* chocolat *inv*; **c. egg** œuf *m* en chocolat • **chocolate-coated** *adj* enrobé de chocolat
choice [tʃɔɪs] **1** *n* choix *m*; **to make a c.** choisir; **I had no c.** je n'ai pas eu le choix
2 *adj (goods)* de choix
choir ['kwaɪə(r)] *n* chœur *m* • **choirboy** *n* jeune choriste *m*
choke [tʃəʊk] **1** *n (of car)* starter *m*
2 *vt (strangle)* étrangler; *(clog)* boucher
3 *vi* s'étrangler; **to c. with anger/laughter** s'étrangler de colère/de rire; **she choked on a fishbone** elle a failli s'étouffer avec une arête • **choker** *n (necklace)* collier *m* (de chien)
cholera ['kɒlərə] *n* choléra *m*
cholesterol [kə'lestərɒl] *n* cholestérol *m*
choose [tʃuːz] **1** *(pt* **chose,** *pp* **chosen)** *vt* choisir; **to c. to do sth** choisir de faire qch
2 *vi* choisir; **as I/you/***etc* **c.** comme il me/vous/*etc* plaît
choos(e)y ['tʃuːzɪ] **(choosier, choosiest)** *adj Fam* difficile **(about** sur)
chop [tʃɒp] **1** *n (of lamb, pork)* côtelette *f*; *Br Fam* **to get the c.** être flanqué à la porte
2 *(pt & pp* **-pp-)** *vt (wood)* couper (à la hache); *(food)* couper en morceaux; *(finely)* hacher; **to c. down** *(tree)* abattre; **to c. off** *(branch, finger)* couper; **to c. up** couper en morceaux
3 *vi* **to c. and change** changer sans cesse • **chopper** *n (cleaver)* couperet *m*; *(axe)* hachette *f*; *Fam (helicopter)* hélico *m*
choppy ['tʃɒpɪ] **(-ier, -iest)** *adj (sea, river)* agité
chopsticks ['tʃɒpstɪks] *npl* baguettes *fpl* *(pour manger)*
choral ['kɔːrəl] *adj* choral; **c. society** chorale *f* • **chorister** ['kɒrɪstə(r)] *n* choriste *mf*
chord [kɔːd] *n Mus* accord *m*
chore [tʃɔː(r)] *n* corvée *f*; **(household) chores** travaux *mpl* du ménage; **to do the chores** faire le ménage
chortle ['tʃɔːtəl] **1** *n* gloussement *m* (de joie)
2 *vi (laugh)* glousser (de joie)

chorus ['kɔːrəs] n (of song) refrain m; (singers) chœur m; (dancers) troupe f

chose [tʃəʊz] pt of **choose**

chosen ['tʃəʊzən] pp of **choose**

chowder ['tʃaʊdə(r)] n = soupe de poissons

Christ [kraɪst] n le Christ • **Christian** ['krɪstʃən] adj & n chrétien, -ienne (mf); **C. name** prénom m • **Christianity** [krɪstɪ'ænɪtɪ] n christianisme m

christen ['krɪsən] vt (person, ship) baptiser • **christening** n baptême m

Christmas ['krɪsməs] 1 n Noël m; **at C. (time)** à Noël; **Merry** or **Happy C.!** Joyeux Noël!
2 adj (tree, card, day, party) de Noël; **C. Eve** la veille de Noël

chrome [krəʊm], **chromium** ['krəʊmɪəm] n chrome m

chronic ['krɒnɪk] adj (disease, state) chronique; Fam (bad) atroce

chronicle ['krɒnɪkəl] 1 n chronique f
2 vt faire la chronique de

chronology [krə'nɒlədʒɪ] (pl -ies) n chronologie f • **chronological** [krɒnə-'lɒdʒɪkəl] adj chronologique; **in c. order** par ordre chronologique

chronometer [krə'nɒmɪtə(r)] n chronomètre m

chrysanthemum [krɪ'sænθəməm] n chrysanthème m

chubby ['tʃʌbɪ] (-ier, -iest) adj (person, hands) potelé; (cheeks) rebondi

chuck [tʃʌk] vt Fam (throw) lancer; (boyfriend, girlfriend) plaquer; **to get chucked** se faire plaquer; **to c. away** (old clothes) balancer; (money) gaspiller; (opportunity) ficher en l'air; Br **to c. (in** or **up)** (give up) laisser tomber; **to c. out** (throw away) balancer; (from house, school, club) vider

chuckle ['tʃʌkəl] 1 n petit rire m
2 vi rire tout bas

chuffed [tʃʌft] adj Br Fam super content (about de)

chug [tʃʌg] (pt & pp -gg-) vi **to c. along** (of vehicle) avancer lentement; (of train) haleter

chum [tʃʌm] n Fam copain m, copine f • **chummy** (-ier, -iest) adj Fam **to be c. with sb** être copain (f copine) avec qn

chunk [tʃʌŋk] n (gros) morceau m; (of time) partie f • **chunky** (-ier, -iest) adj Fam (person) trapu; (coat, sweater, material) gros (f grosse)

church [tʃɜːtʃ] n église f; (French Protestant) temple m; **to go to c.** aller à l'église/au temple; **in c.** à l'église; **c. hall** salle f paroissiale • **churchgoer** n pratiquant, -ante mf • **churchyard** n cimetière m

churlish ['tʃɜːlɪʃ] adj (rude) grossier, -ière; (bad-tempered) hargneux, -euse

churn [tʃɜːn] 1 n (for making butter) baratte f; (milk can) bidon m
2 vt Pej **to c. out** (books) pondre (en série); (goods) produire en série

chute [ʃuːt] n Br (in pool, playground) toboggan m; (for rubbish) vide-ordures m inv

chutney ['tʃʌtnɪ] n chutney m, = condiment épicé à base de fruits

CID [siːaɪ'diː] (abbr Criminal Investigation Department) n Br ≃ PJ f

cider ['saɪdə(r)] n cidre m

cigar [sɪ'gɑː(r)] n cigare m

cigarette [sɪgə'ret] n cigarette f; **c. end** mégot m; **c. lighter** briquet m

cinch [sɪntʃ] n Fam **it's a c.** (easy) c'est un jeu d'enfant; (sure) c'est sûr et certain

cinder ['sɪndə(r)] n cendre f; **burnt to a c.** carbonisé; Br **c. track** (for running) cendrée f

Cinderella [sɪndə'relə] n Cendrillon f

cine camera ['sɪnɪkæmrə] n Br caméra f

cinema ['sɪnəmə] n (art) cinéma m; Br (place) cinéma; Br **to go to the c.** aller au cinéma • **cinemagoer** n Br cinéphile mf

cinnamon ['sɪnəmən] n cannelle f

circle ['sɜːkəl] 1 n (shape, group, range) cercle m; (around eyes) cerne m; Theatre balcon m; **to sit in a c.** s'asseoir en cercle; Fig **to go round in circles** tourner en rond; **in political circles** dans les milieux mpl politiques
2 vt (move round) tourner autour de; (surround) entourer (**with** de)
3 vi (of aircraft, bird) décrire des cercles

circuit ['sɜːkɪt] n (electrical path, journey, for motor racing) circuit m; (of entertainers, judge) tournée f; El **c. breaker** disjoncteur m • **circuitous** [sɜː'kjuːɪtəs] adj (route, means) indirect

circular ['sɜːkjʊlə(r)] 1 adj circulaire
2 n (letter) circulaire f; (advertisement) prospectus m

circulate ['sɜːkjʊleɪt] 1 vt faire circuler
2 vi circuler • **circulation** [-'leɪʃən] n (of air, blood, money) circulation f; (of newspaper) tirage m; Fam **to be in c.** (person) être dans le circuit

circumcised ['sɜːkəmsaɪzd] adj circoncis • **circumcision** [-'sɪʒən] n circoncision f

circumference [sɜː'kʌmfərəns] n circonférence f

circumflex ['sɜːkəmfleks] n & adj **c. (accent)** accent m circonflexe

circumspect ['sɜːkəmspekt] adj circonspect

circumstance ['sɜːkəmstæns] *n* circonstance *f*; **circumstances** *(financial)* situation *f* financière; **in** *or* **under the circumstances** étant donné les circonstances; **in** *or* **under no circumstances** en aucun cas ● **circumstantial** [-'stænʃəl] *adj Law* **c. evidence** preuves *fpl* indirectes; **on c. evidence** sur la base de preuves indirectes

circumvent [sɜːkəm'vent] *vt (rule, law, difficulty)* contourner

circus ['sɜːkəs] *n* cirque *m*

cirrhosis [sɪ'rəʊsɪs] *n Med* cirrhose *f*

CIS *(abbr* **Commonwealth of Independent States)** *n* CEI *f*

cistern ['sɪstən] *n* citerne *f*; *(for lavatory)* réservoir *m* de chasse d'eau

citadel ['sɪtədəl] *n* citadelle *f*

cite [saɪt] *vt (quote, commend)* citer ● **ci'tation** *n* citation *f*

citizen ['sɪtɪzən] *n* citoyen, -enne *mf*; *(of city)* habitant, -ante *mf* ● **citizenship** *n* citoyenneté *f*

citrus ['sɪtrəs] *adj* **c. fruit(s)** agrumes *mpl*

city ['sɪtɪ] *(pl* **-ies)** *n* (grande) ville *f*, cité *f*; *Br* **the C.** la City *(quartier des affaires de Londres)*; **c. centre** centre-ville *m*; **c. dweller** citadin, -ine *mf*; *Am* **c. hall** hôtel *m* de ville; *Br* **c. page** *(in newspaper)* rubrique *f* financière

civic ['sɪvɪk] *adj (duty)* civique; **c. centre** salle *f* municipale ● **civics** *n (social science)* instruction *f* civique

civil ['sɪvəl] *adj (a) (rights, war, marriage)* civil; **c. servant** fonctionnaire *mf*; **c. service** fonction *f* publique **(b)** *(polite)* civil ● **civility** [sɪ'vɪlɪtɪ] *n* politesse *f*

civilian [sɪ'vɪljən] *adj & n* civil, -ile *(mf)*

civilize ['sɪvɪlaɪz] *vt* civiliser ● **civilization** [-'zeɪʃən] *n* civilisation *f*

civvies ['sɪvɪz] *npl Fam* **in c.** en civil

clad [klæd] *adj Literary* vêtu *(in* de)

claim [kleɪm] **1** *n (demand) (for damages, compensation)* demande *f* d'indemnisation; *(as a right)* revendication *f*, *(statement)* affirmation *f*; *(right)* droit *m* (**to** à); **(insurance) c.** demande d'indemnité; **to lay c. to sth** revendiquer qch

2 *vt (as a right)* réclamer, revendiquer; *(payment, benefit, reduction)* demander à bénéficier de; **to c. damages (from sb)** réclamer des dommages et intérêts (à qn); **to c. that...** *(assert)* prétendre que... ● **claimant** *n Br (for social benefits, insurance)* demandeur, -euse *mf*

clairvoyant [kleə'vɔɪənt] *n* voyant, -ante *mf*

clam [klæm] **1** *n* palourde *f*

2 *(pt & pp* **-mm-)** *vi Fam* **to c. up** *(stop talking)* se fermer comme une huître

clamber ['klæmbə(r)] *vi* **to c. up** grimper

clammy ['klæmɪ] *(-ier, -iest) adj (hands)* moite (et froid)

clamour ['klæmə(r)] *(Am* **clamor)** **1** *n* clameur *f*

2 *vi* **to c. for sth** demander qch à grands cris

clamp [klæmp] **1** *n (clip-like)* pince *f*; *(in carpentry)* serre-joint *m*; **(wheel) c.** *(for vehicle)* sabot *m* (de Denver)

2 *vt* serrer; *(vehicle)* mettre un sabot à

3 *vi Fam* **to c. down on** sévir contre ● **clampdown** *n Fam* coup *m* d'arrêt (**on** à)

clan [klæn] *n also Fig* clan *m*

clandestine [klæn'destɪn] *adj* clandestin

clang [klæŋ] *n* son *m* métallique

clanger ['klæŋə(r)] *n Br Fam* gaffe *f*; **to drop a c.** faire une gaffe

clap [klæp] **1** *n* battement *m* de mains; *(on back)* tape *f*; *(of thunder)* coup *m*

2 *(pt & pp* **-pp-)** *vti (applaud)* applaudir; **to c. (one's hands)** applaudir; *(once)* frapper dans ses mains ● **'clapped-' out** *adj Br Fam (car, person)* HS *inv* ● **clapping** *n* applaudissements *mpl*

claptrap ['klæptræp] *n Fam* bêtises *fpl*; **to talk c.** dire des bêtises

claret ['klærət] *n (wine)* bordeaux *m* rouge

clarify ['klærɪfaɪ] *(pt & pp* **-ied)** *vt* clarifier ● **clarification** [-ɪ'keɪʃən] *n* clarification *f*

clarinet [klærɪ'net] *n* clarinette *f*

clarity ['klærətɪ] *n (of expression, argument)* clarté *f*; *(of sound)* pureté *f*; *(of water)* transparence *f*

clash [klæʃ] **1** *n (noise)* fracas *m*; *(of interests)* conflit *m*; *(of events)* coïncidence *f*

2 *vi (of objects)* s'entrechoquer; *(of interests, armies)* s'affronter; *(of colours)* jurer (**with** avec); *(coincide)* tomber en même temps (**with** que)

clasp [klɑːsp] **1** *n (fastener)* fermoir *m*; *(of belt)* boucle *f*

2 *vt (hold)* serrer; **to c. one's hands** joindre les mains

class [klɑːs] **1** *n* classe *f*; *(lesson)* cours *m*; *Br (university grade)* mention *f*; *Am* **the c. of 1999** la promotion de 1999; **to have c.** avoir de la classe

2 *vt* classer (**as** comme) ● **classmate** *n* camarade *mf* de classe ● **classroom** *n* (salle *f* de) classe *f*

classic ['klæsɪk] **1** *adj* classique

2 *n (writer, work)* classique *m* ● **classical** *adj* classique

classify ['klæsɪfaɪ] (*pt & pp* **-ied**) *vt* classer • **classification** [-fɪ'keɪʃən] *n* classification *f* • **classified** *adj (information, document)* confidentiel, -ielle; **c. advertisement** petite annonce *f*

classy ['klɑːsɪ] (**-ier, -iest**) *adj Fam* chic *inv*

clatter ['klætə(r)] *n* fracas *m*

clause [klɔːz] *n (in sentence)* proposition *f*; *(in legal document)* clause *f*

claustrophobia [klɔːstrə'fəʊbɪə] *n* claustrophobie *f* • **claustrophobic** *adj (person)* claustrophobe; *(room, atmosphere)* oppressant

claw [klɔː] **1** *n (of lobster)* pince *f*; *(of cat, sparrow)* griffe *f*; *(of eagle)* serre *f*
2 *vt (scratch)* griffer; **to c. back** *(money)* récupérer

clay [kleɪ] *n* argile *f*

clean [kliːn] **1** (**-er, -est**) *adj* propre; *(clear-cut)* net (*f* nette); *(joke)* pour toutes les oreilles; *(game, fight)* dans les règles; **c. living** vie *f* saine; **a c. record** *(of suspect)* un casier judiciaire vierge; **to have a c. driving licence** avoir tous ses points sur son permis de conduire; **to make a c. breast of it, to come c.** tout avouer
2 *adv (utterly)* complètement; **to break c.** (se) casser net; **to cut c.** couper net
3 *n* **to give sth a c.** nettoyer qch
4 *vt* nettoyer; *(wash)* laver; **to c. one's teeth** se brosser *ou* se laver les dents; **to c. out** *(room)* nettoyer à fond; *(empty)* vider; **to c. up** *(room)* nettoyer; *Fig (reform)* épurer
5 *vi* **to c. (up)** faire le nettoyage • **clean-cut** *adj* net (*f* nette) • **cleaner** *n (in home)* femme *f* de ménage; **(dry) c.** teinturier, -ière *mf* • **cleaning** *n* nettoyage *m*; *(housework)* ménage *m*; **c. woman** femme *f* de ménage • '**clean-'living** *adj* honnête • **cleanly** *adv (break, cut)* net • **cleanness** *n* propreté *f* • '**clean-'shaven** *adj (with no beard or moustache)* glabre; *(closely shaven)* rasé de près • **clean-up** *n Fig* purge *f*

cleanliness ['klenlɪnɪs] *n* propreté *f*

cleanse [klenz] *vt* nettoyer; *Fig (soul, person)* purifier (**of** de); **cleansing cream** crème *f* démaquillante • **cleanser** *n (for skin)* démaquillant *m*

clear [klɪə(r)] **1** (**-er, -est**) *adj (sky, water, sound, thought)* clair; *(glass)* transparent; *(outline, photo, skin, majority)* net (*f* nette); *(road)* libre; *(winner)* incontesté; *(obvious)* évident, clair; *(certain)* certain; **on a c. day** par temps clair; **all c.!** la voie est libre!; **to make oneself (completely or abundantly) c.** se faire (bien) compren-

dre; **it is c. that...** il est évident *ou* clair que...; **I wasn't c. what she meant** je n'étais pas sûr de la comprendre; **to have a c. conscience** avoir la conscience tranquille; **two c. weeks** *(complete)* deux semaines entières; **c. profit** bénéfice *m* net
2 *adv* **c. of** *(away from)* à l'écart de; **to keep** *or* **steer c. of** se tenir à l'écart de; **to get c. of** *(away from)* s'éloigner de
3 *vt (table)* débarrasser; *(road, area)* dégager; *(land)* défricher; *(fence)* franchir (sans toucher); *(obstacle)* éviter; *(accused person)* disculper; *(cheque)* compenser; *(debts, goods)* liquider; *(through customs)* dédouaner; *(for security)* autoriser; **to c. one's throat** s'éclaircir la gorge
4 *vi (of weather)* s'éclaircir; *(of fog)* se dissiper • **clearing** *n (in woods)* clairière *f* • **clearly** *adv (explain, write)* clairement; *(see, understand)* bien; *(obviously)* évidemment • **clearness** *n (of sound)* clarté *f*, netteté *f*; *(of mind)* lucidité *f*
▸ **clear away 1** *vt sep (remove)* enlever **2** *vi (of fog)* se dissiper ▸ **clear off** *vi Fam (leave)* filer ▸ **clear out** *vt sep (empty)* vider; *(clean)* nettoyer; *(remove)* enlever ▸ **clear up 1** *vt sep (mystery)* éclaircir; *(room)* ranger **2** *vi (of weather)* s'éclaircir; *(of fog)* se dissiper; *(tidy)* ranger

clearance ['klɪərəns] *n (sale)* liquidation *f*; *(space)* dégagement *m*; *(permission)* autorisation *f*

clear-cut [klɪə'kʌt] *adj* net (*f* nette) • **clear-'headed** *adj* lucide

cleavage ['kliːvɪdʒ] *n (split)* clivage *m*; *(of woman)* décolleté *m*

clef [klef] *n Mus* clef *f*

cleft [kleft] **1** *n* fissure *f*
2 *adj Anat* **c. palate** palais *m* fendu

clement ['klemənt] *adj (person, weather)* clément • **clemency** *n* clémence *f*

clementine ['kleməntaɪn] *n* clémentine *f*

clench [klentʃ] *vt* **to c. one's fist/teeth** serrer le poing/les dents

clergy ['klɜːdʒɪ] *n* clergé *m* • **clergyman** (*pl* **-men**) *n* ecclésiastique *m*

cleric ['klerɪk] *n Rel* ecclésiastique *m* • **clerical** *adj (job)* d'employé; *(work)* de bureau; *(error)* d'écriture; *Rel* clérical

clerk [*Br* klɑːk, *Am* klɜːk] *n* employé, -ée *mf* de bureau; *Am (in store)* vendeur, -euse *mf*; **c. of the court** greffier *m*

clever ['klevə(r)] (**-er, -est**) *adj* intelligent; *(smart, shrewd)* astucieux, -ieuse; *(skilful)* habile (**at sth** à qch; **at doing** à faire); *(ingenious) (machine, plan)* ingénieux, -ieuse; *(gifted)* doué; **c. at English fort** en anglais; **c. with one's hands** adroit de ses mains •**cleverly** *adv* intelligemment; *(ingeniously)* astucieusement; *(skilfully)* habilement •**cleverness** *n* intelligence *f*; *(ingenuity)* astuce *f*; *(skill)* adresse *f*

cliché ['kli:ʃeɪ] *n* cliché *m*

click [klɪk] **1** *n* bruit *m* sec

2 *vt* **to c. one's heels** claquer des talons; **to c. one's tongue** faire claquer sa langue

3 *vi* faire un bruit sec; *Fam (of lovers)* se plaire du premier coup; *Fam* **it suddenly clicked** ça a fait tilt

client ['klaɪənt] *n* client, -iente *mf* •**clientele** [kli:ən'tel] *n* clientèle *f*

cliff [klɪf] *n* falaise *f*

climate ['klaɪmɪt] *n (weather) & Fig (conditions)* climat *m*; **c. of opinion** opinion *f* générale •**climatic** [-'mætɪk] *adj (changes)* climatique

climax ['klaɪmæks] **1** *n* point *m* culminant; *(sexual)* orgasme *m*

2 *vi* atteindre son point culminant; *(sexually)* atteindre l'orgasme

climb [klaɪm] **1** *n* montée *f*

2 *vt* **to c. (up)** *(steps, hill)* gravir; *(mountain)* faire l'ascension de; *(tree, ladder)* grimper à; **to c. (over)** *(wall)* escalader; **to c. down (from)** *(wall, tree)* descendre de; *(hill)* descendre

3 *vi (of plant)* grimper; **to c. (up)** *(steps, tree, hill)* monter; **to c. down** descendre; *Fig (back down)* revenir sur sa décision •**climber** *n* grimpeur, -euse *mf*; *(mountaineer)* alpiniste *mf*; *(on rocks)* varappeur, -euse *mf*; *(plant)* plante *f* grimpante •**climbing** *n* montée *f*; **(mountain) c.** alpinisme *m*; **(rock-)c.** varappe *f*; **c. frame** cage *f* à poule

climb-down ['klaɪmdaʊn] *n* reculade *f*

clinch [klɪntʃ] *vt (deal)* conclure

cling [klɪŋ] *(pt & pp* **clung)** *vi* s'accrocher (**to** à); *(stick)* adhérer (**to** à) •**clinging** *adj (clothes)* collant

clingfilm ['klɪŋfɪlm] *n Br* film *m* alimentaire

clinic ['klɪnɪk] *n Br (private)* clinique *f*; *(part of hospital)* service *m* •**clinical** *adj Med* clinique; *Fig (attitude)* froid

clink [klɪŋk] **1** *n* tintement *m*

2 *vt* faire tinter

3 *vi* tinter

clip [klɪp] **1** *n* (**a**) *(for paper)* trombone *m*; *(fastener)* attache *f*; *(of brooch, of cyclist, for hair)* pince *f* (**b**) *(of film)* extrait *m*; *Br Fam (blow)* taloche *f*

2 *(pt & pp* **-pp-)** *vt (paper)* attacher *(avec*

un trombone); *(cut)* couper; *(hedge)* tailler; *(ticket)* poinçonner; *(sheep)* tondre; **to c. sth out of** *(newspaper)* découper qch dans; **to c. (on)** *(attach)* attacher (**to** à)

3 *vi* **to c. together** s'emboîter •**clippers** *npl (for hair)* tondeuse *f*; *(for fingernails)* coupe-ongles *m inv* •**clipping** *n Am (from newspaper)* coupure *f*

clique [kli:k] *n Pej* clique *f* •**cliquey** *adj Pej* très fermé

cloak [kləʊk] *n* cape *f* •**cloakroom** *n* vestiaire *m*; *Br (lavatory)* toilettes *fpl*

clobber¹ ['klɒbə(r)] *n Br Fam (clothes)* fringues *fpl*; *(belongings)* barda *m*

clobber² ['klɒbə(r)] *vt Fam (hit)* tabasser

clock [klɒk] **1** *n (large)* horloge *f*; *(small)* pendule *f*; *Br Fam (mileometer)* compteur *m*; **a race against the c.** une course contre la montre; **round the c.** vingt-quatre heures sur vingt-quatre; **to put the clocks forward/back** *(in spring, autumn)* avancer/retarder les pendules; *Fig* **to turn the c. back** revenir en arrière; **c. radio** radioréveil *m*; **c. tower** clocher *m*

2 *vt (measure speed of)* chronométrer

3 *vi* **to c. in** *or* **out** *(of worker)* pointer •**clockwise** *adv* dans le sens des aiguilles d'une montre

clockwork ['klɒkwɜ:k] **1** *adj (toy)* mécanique

2 *n* **to go like c.** marcher comme sur des roulettes

clod [klɒd] *n* (**a**) *(of earth)* motte *f* (**b**) *Fam (oaf)* balourd, -ourde *mf*

clog [klɒg] **1** *n (shoe)* sabot *m*

2 *(pt & pp* **-gg-)** *vt* **to c. (up)** *(obstruct)* boucher

cloister ['klɔɪstə(r)] **1** *n* cloître *m*

2 *vt* cloîtrer

close¹ [kləʊs] **1** (**-er, -est)** *adj (in distance, time, relationship)* proche; *(collaboration, resemblance, connection)* étroit; *(friend)* intime; *(contest)* serré; *(study)* rigoureux, -euse; *Ling (vowel)* fermé; *Br* **the weather is c., it's c.** il fait lourd; *Br* **it's c. in this room** cette pièce est mal aérée; **c. to** *(near)* près de, proche de; **c. to tears** au bord des larmes; **I'm very c. to her** *(friendly)* je suis très proche d'elle; **that was a c. shave** *or* **call** il s'en est fallu de peu

2 *adv* **c. (by), c. at hand** tout près; **c. behind** juste derrière; *Fam* **c. on** *(almost)* pas loin de; **we stood/sat c. together** nous étions debout/assis serrés les uns contre les autres; **to follow c. behind** suivre de près; **to hold sb c.** tenir qn contre soi •'**close-'cropped** *adj (hair)* coupé ras • **'close-'fitting** *adj (clothes)* ajusté • **'close-'knit** *adj (group, family)* très uni • **closely** *adv (follow, guard)* de près; *(listen, examine)* attentivement; **c. linked** étroitement lié (**to à**); **c. contested** très disputé • **closeness** *n* proximité *f*; *(of collaboration)* étroitesse *f*; *(of friendship)* intimité *f*; *Br (of weather)* lourdeur *f* • **close-up** *n* gros plan *m*

close² [kləʊz] **1** *n (end)* fin *f*; **to bring to a c.** mettre fin à; **to draw to a c.** tirer à sa fin **2** *vt (door, shop, account, book, eye)* fermer; *(discussion)* clore; *(opening)* boucher; *(road)* barrer; *(gap)* réduire; *(deal)* conclure; **to c. the meeting** lever la séance; **to c. ranks** serrer les rangs **3** *vi (of door)* se fermer; *(of shop)* fermer; *(of wound)* se refermer; *(of meeting, festival)* se terminer • **closed** *adj (door, shop)* fermé; **c.-circuit television** télévision *f* en circuit fermé; **behind c. doors** à huis clos • **close-down** *n* fermeture *f* (définitive); *TV* fin *f* des émissions • **closing 1** *n* fermeture *f*; *(of session)* clôture *f* **2** *adj (words, remarks)* dernier, -ière; **c. date** *(for application)* date *f* limite; **c. speech** discours *m* de clôture; **c. time** heure *f* de fermeture • **closure** ['kləʊʒə(r)] *n* fermeture *f* (définitive)

▸ **close down 1** *vt sep (business, factory)* fermer (définitivement) **2** *vi (of TV station)* terminer les émissions; *(of business, factory)* fermer (définitivement)
▸ **close in** *vt sep (enclose)* enfermer **2** *vi (approach)* approcher; **to c. in on sb** se rapprocher de qn ▸ **close up 1** *vt sep* fermer **2** *vi (of shopkeeper)* fermer; *(of wound)* se refermer; *(of line of people)* se resserrer

closet ['klɒzɪt] *n Am (cupboard)* placard *m*; *(wardrobe)* penderie *f*; *Fig* **to come out of the c.** révéler son homosexualité

clot [klɒt] **1** *n (of blood)* caillot *m*; *Br Fam (person)* andouille *f* **2** *(pt & pp* **-tt-***) vt (blood)* coaguler **3** *vi (of blood)* (se) coaguler

cloth [klɒθ] *n* tissu *m*; *(of linen)* toile *f*; *(for dusting)* chiffon *m*; *(for dishes)* torchon *m*; *(tablecloth)* nappe *f*

clothe [kləʊð] *vt* vêtir (**in** de) • **clothing** *n (clothes)* vêtements *mpl*; **an article of c.** un vêtement

clothes [kləʊðz] *npl* vêtements *mpl*; **to put one's c. on** s'habiller; **to take one's c. off** se déshabiller; **c. brush** brosse *f* à habits; **c. line** corde *f* à linge; *Br* **c. peg,** *Am* **c. pin** pince *f* à linge; **c. shop** magasin *m* de vêtements

cloud [klaʊd] **1** *n* nuage *m*; *Fig (of arrows, insects)* nuée *f* **2** *vt (window, mirror)* embuer; *(mind)* obscurcir; *(judgement)* affecter **3** *vi* **to c. (over)** *(of sky)* se couvrir • **cloudburst** *n* averse *f* • **cloudy (-ier, -iest)** *adj (weather, sky)* nuageux, -euse; *(liquid)* trouble; **it's c., it's a c. day** le temps est couvert

clout [klaʊt] *Fam* **1** *n (blow)* taloche *f*; *(influence)* influence *f*; **to have (plenty of) c.** avoir le bras long **2** *vt (hit)* flanquer une taloche à

clove [kləʊv] *n (spice)* clou *m* de girofle; **c. of garlic** gousse *f* d'ail

clover ['kləʊvə(r)] *n* trèfle *m*

clown [klaʊn] **1** *n* clown *m* **2** *vi* **to c. around** *or* **about** faire le clown

cloying ['klɔɪɪŋ] *adj (smell, sentiments)* écœurant

club [klʌb] **1** *n* **(a)** *(society)* club *m* **(b)** *(nightclub)* boîte *f* de nuit **(c)** *(weapon)* massue *f*; *(in golf)* club *m* **(d)** **clubs** *(in cards)* trèfle *m* **2** *(pt & pp* **-bb-***) vt* frapper avec une massue **3** *vi Br* **to c. together** se cotiser (**to buy sth** pour acheter qch) • **clubhouse** *n* pavillon *m* • **club soda** *n Am* eau *f* gazeuse

cluck [klʌk] *vi (of hen)* glousser

clue [kluː] *n* indice *m*; *(of crossword)* définition *f*; *Fam* **I don't have a c.** je n'en ai pas la moindre idée • **clueless** *adj Br Fam* nul (*f* nulle)

clump [klʌmp] *n (of flowers, trees)* massif *m*

clumsy ['klʌmzɪ] **(-ier, -iest)** *adj* maladroit; *(tool)* peu commode • **clumsily** *adv* maladroitement • **clumsiness** *n* maladresse *f*

clung [klʌŋ] *pt & pp of* **cling**

cluster ['klʌstə(r)] **1** *n* groupe *m*; *(of stars)* amas *m* **2** *vi* se grouper

clutch [klʌtʃ] **1** *n* **(a)** *(in car)* embrayage *m*; *(pedal)* pédale *f* d'embrayage; **to let in/out the c.** embrayer/débrayer **(b)** **to fall into/escape from sb's clutches** tomber dans les griffes/s'échapper des griffes de qn **2** *vt* tenir fermement **3** *vi* **to c. at** essayer de saisir

clutter ['klʌtə(r)] **1** *n (objects)* désordre *m* **2** *vt* **to c. (up)** *(room, table)* encombrer (**with** de)

cm (*abbr* **centimetre(s)**) cm

Co (*abbr* **company**) Cie

co- [kəʊ] *pref* co-

c/o (*abbr* **care of**) (*on envelope*) chez
coach [kəʊtʃ] **1** *n* (**a**) *Br* (*train carriage*) voiture *f*, wagon *m*; *Br* (*bus*) car *m*; (*horse-drawn*) carrosse *m* (**b**) (*for sports*) entraîneur, -euse *mf*
2 *vt* (*sportsman, team*) entraîner; **to c. sb for an exam** préparer qn pour un examen (*en lui donnant des leçons particulières*)
coal [kəʊl] **1** *n* charbon *m*
2 *adj* (*merchant, fire*) de charbon; (*cellar, bucket*) à charbon; **c. industry** industrie *f* houillère • **coalfield** *n* bassin *m* houiller • **coalmine** *n* mine *f* de charbon • **coalminer** *n* mineur *m*
coalition [kəʊə'lɪʃən] *n* coalition *f*
coarse [kɔːs] (**-er, -est**) *adj* (*person, manners*) grossier, -ière, vulgaire; (*accent*) vulgaire; (*surface, fabric*) grossier; **to have c. hair** avoir les cheveux épais; **c. salt** gros sel *m* • **coarsely** *adv* grossièrement
coast [kəʊst] **1** *n* côte *f*; *Fig* **the c. is clear** la voie est libre
2 *vi* **to c.** (**down** *or* **along**) (*of vehicle, bicycle*) descendre en roue libre • **coastal** *adj* côtier, -ière • **coastguard** *n* (*person*) garde-côte *m* • **coastline** *n* littoral *m*
coaster ['kəʊstə(r)] *n* (*for glass*) dessous-de- verre *m inv*
coat [kəʊt] **1** *n* manteau *m*; (*overcoat*) pardessus *m*; (*jacket*) veste *f*; (*of animal*) pelage *m*; (*of paint*) couche *f*; **c. hanger** cintre *m*; **c. of arms** armoiries *fpl*
2 *vt* couvrir (**with** de); (*with chocolate, sugar*) enrober (**with** de) • **coating** *n* couche *f*
coax [kəʊks] *vt* enjôler; **to c. sb to do** *or* **into doing sth** amener qn à faire qch par des cajoleries; **she needed coaxing** elle s'est fait tirer l'oreille • **coaxing** *n* cajoleries *fpl*
cob [kɒb] *n* (*of corn*) épi *m*
cobble ['kɒbəl] **1** *n* pavé *m*
2 *vt Fam* **to c. together** (*text, compromise*) bricoler • **cobbled** *adj* (*street*) pavé • **cobblestone** *n* pavé *m*
cobbler ['kɒblə(r)] *n* cordonnier *m*
cobra ['kəʊbrə] *n* (*snake*) cobra *m*
cobweb ['kɒbweb] *n* toile *f* d'araignée
Coca-Cola® [kəʊkə'kəʊlə] *n* Coca-Cola® *m*
cocaine [kəʊ'keɪn] *n* cocaïne *f*
cock [kɒk] **1** *n* (*rooster*) coq *m*; (*male bird*) mâle *m*
2 *vt* (*gun*) armer; **to c. one's ears** (*listen carefully*) dresser l'oreille • **cock-a-doodle-'doo** *n* & *exclam* cocorico (*m*) • **cock-and-'bull story** *n* histoire *f* à dormir debout

cockatoo [kɒkə'tuː] *n* cacatoès *m*
cocker ['kɒkə(r)] *n* **c.** (**spaniel**) cocker *m*
cockerel ['kɒkərəl] *n* jeune coq *m*
cock-eyed [kɒk'aɪd] *adj Fam* (*plan, idea*) farfelu
cockle ['kɒkəl] *n* (*shellfish*) coque *f*
cockney ['kɒknɪ] *adj & n* cockney (*mf*) (*natif des quartiers est de Londres*)
cockpit ['kɒkpɪt] *n* (*of aircraft*) poste *m* de pilotage
cockroach ['kɒkrəʊtʃ] *n* cafard *m*
cocksure [kɒk'ʃʊə(r)] *adj Fam* présomptueux, -ueuse
cocktail ['kɒkteɪl] *n* cocktail *m*; **fruit c.** macédoine *f* de fruits; **prawn c.** crevettes *fpl* à la mayonnaise; **c. party** cocktail *m*
cocky ['kɒkɪ] (**-ier, -iest**) *adj Fam* culotté
cocoa ['kəʊkəʊ] *n* cacao *m*
coconut ['kəʊkənʌt] *n* noix *f* de coco
cocoon [kə'kuːn] *n* cocon *m*
COD [siːəʊ'diː] (*abbr* **cash on delivery**) *n Br Com* paiement *m* à la livraison
cod [kɒd] *n* morue *f*; (*as food*) cabillaud *m* • **cod-liver 'oil** *n* huile *f* de foie de morue
coddle ['kɒdəl] *vt* dorloter
code [kəʊd] **1** *n* code *m*; **in c.** (*letter, message*) codé; **c. number** numéro *m* de code; **c. word** code
2 *vt* coder • **coding** *n* codage *m*
codeine ['kəʊdiːn] *n* codéine *f*
codify ['kəʊdɪfaɪ] (*pt & pp* **-ied**) *vt* codifier
co-educational [kəʊedjʊ'keɪʃənəl] *adj* (*school, teaching*) mixte
coefficient [kəʊɪ'fɪʃənt] *n Math* coefficient *m*
coerce [kəʊ'ɜːs] *vt* contraindre (**sb into doing** qn à faire) • **coercion** *n* contrainte *f*
coexist [kəʊɪg'zɪst] *vi* coexister • **coexistence** *n* coexistence *f*
coffee ['kɒfɪ] **1** *n* café *m*; **c. with milk**, *Br* **white c.** café au lait; **black c.** café noir; *Br* **c. bar, c. house** café *m*; **c. break** pause-café *f*; **c. cup** tasse *f* à café; **c. pot** cafetière *f*; **c. table** table *f* basse
2 *adj* **c.(-coloured)** café au lait *inv*
coffin ['kɒfɪn] *n* cercueil *m*
cog [kɒg] *n* dent *f*
cogitate ['kɒdʒɪteɪt] *vi Fml* méditer
cognac ['kɒnjæk] *n* cognac *m*
cohabit [kəʊ'hæbɪt] *vi* vivre en concubinage (**with** avec)
coherent [kəʊ'hɪərənt] *adj* (*logical*) cohérent; (*way of speaking*) compréhensible, intelligible • **cohesion** [-'hiːʒən] *n* cohésion *f*
coil [kɔɪl] **1** *n* (*of wire, rope*) rouleau *m*; (*single loop*) (*of hair*) boucle *f*; (*of snake*)

anneau *m*; *(electrical)* bobine *f*; *(contraceptive)* stérilet *m*
2 *vt (rope, hair, hose)* enrouler (**around** autour de)
3 *vi (of snake)* s'enrouler (**around** autour de)
coin [kɔɪn] **1** *n* pièce *f* (de monnaie); *Am* **c. bank** tirelire *f*
2 *vt (money)* frapper; *Fig (word)* inventer; **to c. a phrase...** pour ainsi dire... • **coinage** *n (coins)* monnaie *f*; *Fig* invention *f*; **a recent c.** *(word)* un mot de formation récente • **coin-'operated** *adj (machine)* à pièces
coincide [kəʊɪn'saɪd] *vi* coïncider (**with** avec) • **coincidence** [-'ɪnsɪdəns] *n* coïncidence *f* • **coincidental** [-sɪ'dentəl] *adj (resemblance)* fortuit; **it's c.** c'est une coïncidence
coke [kəʊk] *n (fuel)* coke *m*; *(Coca-Cola®)* Coca® *m inv*
colander ['kʌləndə(r)] *n (for vegetables)* passoire *f*
cold [kəʊld] **1** (**-er, -est**) *adj* froid; **to be** or **feel c.** *(of person)* avoir froid; **to feel the c.** être frileux, -euse; **my hands are c.** j'ai froid aux mains; **it's c.** *(of weather)* il fait froid; **to get c.** *(of weather)* se refroidir; *(of food)* refroidir; **I'm getting c.** je commence à avoir froid; *Fam* **to get c. feet** se dégonfler; **in c. blood** de sang-froid; **c. cream** cold-cream *m*; *Br* **c. meats,** *Am* **c. cuts** viandes *fpl* froides; **c. sore** bouton *m* de fièvre; **c. war** guerre *f* froide
2 *n* (**a**) *(temperature)* froid *m*; **to be out in the c.** être dehors dans le froid; *Fig* **to be left out in the c.** rester sur la touche
(**b**) *(illness)* rhume *m*; **a bad** or **nasty c.** un gros rhume; **to have a c.** être enrhumé; **to catch a c.** attraper un rhume; **to get a c.** s'enrhumer • **coldly** *adv* avec froideur • **coldness** *n* froideur *f*
cold-blooded ['kəʊldblʌdɪd] *adj (person)* insensible; *(murder)* commis de sang-froid
cold-shoulder [kəʊld'ʃəʊldə(r)] *vt* snober
coleslaw ['kəʊlslɔː] *n* = salade de chou cru à la mayonnaise
colic ['kɒlɪk] *n* coliques *fpl*
collaborate [kə'læbəreɪt] *vi* collaborer (**on** à) • **collaboration** [-'reɪʃən] *n* collaboration *f* • **collaborator** *n* collaborateur, -trice *mf*
collage ['kɒlɑːʒ] *n (picture)* collage *m*
collapse [kə'læps] **1** *n* effondrement *m*; *(of government)* chute *f*
2 *vi (of person, building)* s'effondrer;

(faint) se trouver mal; *(of government)* tomber • **collapsible** *adj (chair)* pliant
collar ['kɒlə(r)] *n (on garment)* col *m*; *(of dog)* collier *m*; **to seize sb by the c.** saisir qn au collet • **collarbone** *n* clavicule *f*
collate [kə'leɪt] *vt (documents) (gather)* rassembler; *(compare)* collationner
colleague ['kɒliːg] *n* collègue *mf*
collect [kə'lekt] **1** *vt (pick up)* ramasser; *(gather)* rassembler; *(information)* recueillir; *(taxes)* percevoir; *(rent)* encaisser; *(stamps)* collectionner; **to c. money** *(in street, church)* quêter; **to c. sb** *(pick up)* passer prendre qn
2 *vi (of dust)* s'accumuler; *(of people)* se rassembler; *(in street, church)* quêter (**for** pour)
3 *adv Am* **to call** or **phone sb c.** téléphoner à qn en PCV
collection [kə'lekʃən] *n (of objects, stamps)* collection *f*; *(of poems)* recueil *m*; *(of money for church)* quête *f*; *(of mail, taxes)* levée *f*; *Br (of twigs, rubbish)* ramassage *m*
collective [kə'lektɪv] *adj* collectif, -ive • **collectively** *adv* collectivement
collector [kə'lektə(r)] *n (of stamps)* collectionneur, -euse *mf*
college ['kɒlɪdʒ] *n Br (of further education)* établissement *m* d'enseignement supérieur; *Br (part of university)* = association d'enseignants et d'étudiants d'une même université qui dispose d'une semi-autonomie administrative; *Am (university)* université *f*; *Pol & Rel* collège *m*; **to be at c.** être étudiant; **c. of music** conservatoire *m* de musique
collide [kə'laɪd] *vi* entrer en collision (**with** avec) • **collision** [-'lɪʒən] *n* collision *f*
colliery ['kɒlɪərɪ] *(pl* **-ies**) *n Br* houillère *f*
colloquial [kə'ləʊkwɪəl] *adj* familier, -ière • **colloquialism** *n* expression *f* familière
collywobbles ['kɒlɪwɒbəlz] *npl Fam* **to have the c.** *(feel nervous)* avoir la frousse
cologne [kə'ləʊn] *n* eau *f* de Cologne
colon ['kəʊlən] *n* (**a**) *(punctuation mark)* deux-points *m* (**b**) *Anat* côlon *m*
colonel ['kɜːnəl] *n* colonel *m*
colonial [kə'ləʊnɪəl] *adj* colonial
colonize ['kɒlənaɪz] *vt* coloniser • **colonization** [-'zeɪʃən] *n* colonisation *f*
colony ['kɒlənɪ] *(pl* **-ies**) *n* colonie *f*
colossal [kə'lɒsəl] *adj* colosse
colour ['kʌlə(r)] *(Am* **color**) **1** *n* couleur *f*
2 *adj (photo, television)* en couleurs; *(television set)* couleur *inv*; *(problem)* ra-

cial; **c. supplement** *(of newspaper)* supplément *m* en couleurs; **to be off c.** *(of person)* ne pas être dans son assiette

3 *vt* colorer; **to c. (in)** *(drawing)* colorier • **coloured** *adj (person, pencil)* de couleur; *(glass, water)* coloré • **colouring** *n (in food)* colorant *m*; *(complexion)* teint *m*; *(with crayons)* coloriage *m*; *(shade, effect)* coloris *m*; *(blend of colours)* couleurs *fpl*; **c. book** album *m* de coloriages

colour-blind ['kʌləblaɪnd] *adj* daltonien, -ienne • **colour-blindness** *n* daltonisme *m*

colourfast ['kʌləfɑːst] *adj* grand teint *inv*

colourful ['kʌləfəl] *adj (crowd, story)* coloré; *(person)* pittoresque

colt [kəʊlt] *n (horse)* poulain *m*

column ['kɒləm] *n* colonne *f*; *(newspaper feature)* rubrique *f*

coma ['kəʊmə] *n* coma *m*; **in a c.** dans le coma

comb [kəʊm] **1** *n* peigne *m*
2 *vt (hair)* peigner; *Fig (search)* ratisser, passer au peigne fin; **to c. one's hair** se peigner

combat ['kɒmbæt] **1** *n* combat *m*
2 *vti* combattre (**for** pour)

combine[1] ['kɒmbaɪn] *n* (**a**) *(commercial)* association *f*; *(cartel)* cartel *m* (**b**) **c. harvester** *(machine)* moissonneuse-batteuse *f*

combine[2] [kəm'baɪn] **1** *vt (activities, qualities, features, elements, sounds)* combiner; *(efforts)* joindre, unir; **to c. business with pleasure** joindre l'utile à l'agréable; **our combined efforts have produced a result** en joignant nos efforts, nous avons obtenu un résultat; **combined wealth/etc** *(put together)* richesses/etc *fpl* réunies

2 *vi (of teams, groups)* s'unir; *(of elements)* se combiner; *(of gases)* s'associer • **combination** [kɒmbɪ'neɪʃən] *n* combinaison *f*; *(of qualities)* réunion *f*; **in c. with** en association avec; **c. lock** serrure *f* à combinaison

combustion [kəm'bʌstʃən] *n* combustion *f*

come [kʌm] *(pt* came, *pp* come) *vi* venir (**from** de; **to** à); **I've just c. from Glasgow/Scotland** j'arrive de Glasgow/d'Écosse; **to c. home** rentrer (à la maison); **to c. first** *(in race, exam)* se classer premier; **c. and see me** viens me voir; **coming!** j'arrive!; **it came as a surprise to me** cela m'a surpris; **to c. near *or* close to doing sth** faillir faire qch; **to c. true** se réaliser; **c. next summer** l'été prochain; **in the years to c.** dans les années à venir; **nothing came of it** ça n'a abouti à rien; **c. what may** quoi qu'il

arrive; **c. to think of it...** maintenant que j'y pense...; *Fam* **how c. that...?** comment se fait-il que...? • **comeback** *n* **to make a c.** *(of fashion)* revenir; *(of actor, athlete)* faire un come-back • **comedown** *n Fam* régression *f*

► **come about** *vi (happen)* arriver ► **come across 1** *vi* **to c. across well/badly** bien/mal passer **2** *vt insep (find)* tomber sur ► **come along** *vi* venir (**with** avec); *(progress) (of work)* avancer; *(of student)* progresser; **c. along!** allons, pressons! ► **come at** *vt insep (attack)* attaquer ► **come away** *vi (leave, come off)* partir (**from** de); **to c. away from sb/sth** *(step or move back from)* s'écarter de qn/qch ► **come back** *vi* revenir; *(return home)* rentrer ► **come by** *vt insep (obtain)* obtenir; *(find)* trouver ► **come down 1** *vi* descendre; *(of rain, temperature, price)* tomber; *(of building)* être démoli **2** *vt insep (stairs, hill)* descendre ► **come down with** *vt insep (illness)* attraper ► **come for** *vt insep* venir chercher ► **come forward** *vi (make oneself known, volunteer)* se présenter; **to c. forward with** *(suggestion)* offrir ► **come in** *vi (enter)* entrer; *(of tide)* monter; *(of train, athlete)* arriver; *(of money)* rentrer; **to c. in first** terminer premier; **to c. in useful** être bien utile ► **come in for** *vt insep* **to c. in for criticism** faire l'objet de critiques ► **come into** *vt insep (room)* entrer dans; *(money)* hériter de ► **come off 1** *vi (of button)* se détacher; *(succeed)* réussir; *(happen)* avoir lieu **2** *vt insep (fall from)* tomber de; *(get down from)* descendre de ► **come on** *vi (make progress) (of work)* avancer; *(of student)* progresser; **c. on!** allez! ► **come out** *vi (sortir)*; *(of sun, book)* paraître; *(of stain)* s'enlever, partir; *(of secret)* être révélé; *(of photo)* réussir; **to c. out (on strike)** se mettre en grève ► **come over 1** *vi (visit)* venir (**to** chez); **to c. over to** *(approach)* s'approcher de **2** *vt insep* **I don't know what came over me** je ne sais pas ce qui m'a pris ► **come round** *vi (visit)* passer (**to** chez); *(of date)* revenir; *(regain consciousness)* revenir à soi ► **come through 1** *vi (survive)* s'en tirer **2** *vt insep (crisis)* sortir indemne de ► **come to 1** *vi (regain consciousness)* revenir à soi **2** *vt insep (amount to)* revenir à; **to c. to a conclusion** arriver à une conclusion; **to c. to a decision** se décider; **to c. to an end** toucher à sa fin ► **come under** *vt insep (heading)* être classé sous; **to c. under sb's influence** subir l'influence de qn

▸**come up 1** *vi (rise)* monter; *(of question, job)* se présenter **2** *vt insep (stairs)* monter ▸**come up against** *vt insep (problem)* se heurter à ▸**come upon** *vt insep (book, reference)* tomber sur ▸**come up to** *vt insep (reach)* arriver jusqu'à; *(approach)* s'approcher de; **the film didn't c. up to my expectations** le film n'était pas à la hauteur de mes espérances ▸**come up with** *vt insep (idea, money)* trouver

comedy ['kɒmɪdɪ] *(pl* **-ies)** *n* comédie *f* •**comedian** [kə'miːdɪən] *n* comique *mf*

📖 Note that the French word **comédien** is a false friend. It means **actor**.

comet ['kɒmɪt] *n* comète *f*

comeuppance [kʌm'ʌpəns] *n Fam* **he got his c.** il n'a eu que ce qu'il méritait

comfort ['kʌmfət] **1** *n (ease)* confort *m*; *(consolation)* réconfort *m*, consolation *f*; **to be a c. to sb** être d'un grand réconfort à qn; **too close for c.** trop près à mon/son/ *etc* goût; *Am* **c. station** toilettes *fpl* publiques

2 *vt* consoler; *(cheer)* réconforter •**comfortable** *adj (chair, house)* confortable; *(rich)* aisé; **he's c.** *(in chair)* il est à son aise; *(of patient)* il ne souffre pas; **make yourself c.** mets-toi à ton aise •**comfortably** *adv (sit)* confortablement; *(win)* facilement; **to live c.** avoir une vie aisée; **c. off** *(rich)* à l'aise financièrement •**comforting** *adj (reassuring)* réconfortant

comforter ['kʌmfətər] *n Am (quilt)* édredon *m*; *(for baby)* sucette *f*

comfy ['kʌmfɪ] **(-ier, -iest)** *adj Fam (chair)* confortable; **I'm c.** je suis bien

comic ['kɒmɪk] **1** *adj* comique **2** *n (actor)* comique *mf*; *Br (magazine)* bande *f* dessinée, BD *f*; **c. strip** bande dessinée •**comical** *adj* comique

coming ['kʌmɪŋ] **1** *adj (future)* (years, election, difficulties)* à venir; **the c. month** le mois prochain; **the c. days** les prochains jours

2 *n* **comings and goings** allées *fpl* et venues

comma ['kɒmə] *n* virgule *f*

command [kə'mɑːnd] **1** *n (order)* ordre *m*; *(authority)* commandement *m*; *(mastery)* maîtrise *f* **(of** de); *Comptr* commande *f*; **at one's c.** *(disposal)* à sa disposition; **to be in c. (of)** *(ship, army)* commander; *(situation)* être maître (de); **under the c. of** sous le commandement de

2 *vt (order)* commander **(sb to do** à qn de faire); *(control) (ship, army)* comman-

der; *(dominate) (of building)* dominer; *(be able to use)* disposer de; *(respect)* forcer

3 *vi (of captain)* commander •**commanding** *adj (authoritative)* imposant; *(position)* dominant; **c. officer** commandant *m*

commandant ['kɒməndænt] *n Mil* commandant *m*

commandeer [kɒmən'dɪə(r)] *vt* réquisitionner

commander [kə'mɑːndə(r)] *n Mil* commandant *m*; **c.-in-chief** commandant *m* en chef

commandment [kə'mɑːndmənt] *n Rel* commandement *m*

commando [kə'mɑːndəʊ] *(pl* **-os** *or* **-oes)** *n (soldiers, unit)* commando *m*

commemorate [kə'meməreɪt] *vt* commémorer •**commemoration** [-'reɪʃən] *n* commémoration *f* •**commemorative** [-rətɪv] *adj* commémoratif, -ive

commence [kə'mens] *vti Formal* commencer **(doing** à faire) •**commencement** *n* commencement *m*; *Am (ceremony)* remise *f* des diplômes

commend [kə'mend] *vt (praise)* louer; *(recommend)* recommander •**commendable** *adj* louable •**commendation** [kɒmen'deɪʃən] *n (praise)* éloges *mpl*

comment ['kɒment] **1** *n* commentaire *m* **(on** sur); **no c.!** sans commentaire!

2 *vi* faire des commentaires **(on** sur); **I won't c.** je n'ai rien à dire; **to c. on** *(text, event, news item)* commenter; **to c. that...** remarquer que... •**commentary** [-əntərɪ] *(pl* **-ies)** *n* commentaire *m*; **live c.** *(on TV or radio)* reportage *m* en direct •**commentate** [-əntert] *vi* faire le commentaire; **to c. on sth** commenter qch •**commentator** [-əntertə(r)] *n* commentateur, -trice *mf* **(on** de)

commerce ['kɒmɜːs] *n* commerce *m* •**commercial** [kə'mɜːʃəl] **1** *adj* commercial; **c. break** page *f* de publicité; **c. district** quartier *m* commerçant; *Br* **c. traveller** voyageur *m* de commerce

2 *n (advertisement)* publicité *f*; **the commercials** la publicité

commercialize [kə'mɜːʃəlaɪz] *vt Pej (event)* transformer en une affaire de gros sous •**commercialized** *adj (district)* devenu trop commercial

commiserate [kə'mɪzəreɪt] *vi* **to c. with sb** être désolé pour qn •**commiseration** [-'reɪʃən] *n* commisération *f*

commission [kə'mɪʃən] **1** *n (fee, group)* commission *f*; *(order for work)* commande *f*; **out of c.** *(machine)* hors service; *Mil* **to get one's c.** être nommé officier

2 *vt (artist)* passer une commande à; *(book)* commander; **to c. sb to do sth** charger qn de faire qch; *Mil* **to be commissioned** être nommé officier; **commissioned officer** officier *m* ● **commissioner** *n Pol* commissaire *m*; *Br* **(police) c.** commissaire de police

commissionaire [kəmɪʃə'neə(r)] *n Br (in hotel)* chasseur *m*

commit [kə'mɪt] *(pt & pp* -tt-*) vt (crime)* commettre; *(bind)* engager; *(devote)* consacrer; **to c. suicide** se suicider; **to c. sth to memory** apprendre qch par cœur; **to c. sb to prison** incarcérer qn; **to c. oneself** *(make a promise)* s'engager (**to** à) ● **commitment** *n (duty, responsibility)* obligation *f*; *(promise)* engagement *m*; *(devotion)* dévouement *m* (**to** à)

committee [kə'mɪtɪ] *n* comité *m*; *(parliamentary)* commission *f*

commodity [kə'mɒdɪtɪ] *(pl* -ies*) n Econ* marchandise *f*, produit *m*

common ['kɒmən] **1** (-er, -est) *adj (shared, vulgar)* commun; *(frequent)* courant, commun; **the c. man** l'homme *m* de la rue; **in c.** *(shared)* en commun (**with** avec); **to have nothing in c.** n'avoir rien de commun (**with** avec); **in c. with** *(like)* comme; **c. law** droit *m* coutumier; **c.-law wife** concubine *f*; **C. Market** Marché *m* commun; **c. room** *(for students)* salle *f* commune; *(for teachers)* salle *f* des professeurs; **c. sense** sens *m* commun, bon sens; **c. or garden** ordinaire

2 *n (land)* terrain *m* communal; **the Commons** les Communes *fpl* ● **common-sense** [kɒmən'sens] *adj (sensible)* sensé

commoner ['kɒmənə(r)] *n* roturier, -ière *mf* ● **commonly** *adv* communément ● **commonness** *n (frequency)* fréquence *f*; *(vulgarity)* vulgarité *f*

commonplace ['kɒmənpleɪs] **1** *adj* courant

2 *n* banalité *f*

Commonwealth ['kɒmənwelθ] *n Br* **the C.** le Commonwealth

commotion [kə'məʊʃən] *n (disruption)* agitation *f*

communal [kə'mjuːnəl] *adj (shared)* *(bathroom, kitchen)* commun; *(of the community)* communautaire ● **communally** *adv (own)* en commun; *(live)* en communauté

commune 1 ['kɒmjuːn] *n (district)* commune *f*; *(group)* communauté *f*

2 [kə'mjuːn] *vi* **to c. with nature/God**

être en communion avec la nature/Dieu ● **co'mmunion** *n* communion *f* (**with** avec); **(Holy) C.** communion; **to take C.** communier

communicate [kə'mjuːnɪkeɪt] **1** *vt* communiquer; *(illness)* transmettre (**to** à)

2 *vi (of person, rooms)* communiquer (**with** avec) ● **communication** [-'keɪʃən] *n* communication *f*; *Br* **c. cord** *(on train)* signal *m* d'alarme

communicative [kə'mjuːnɪkətɪv] *adj* communicatif, -ive

communism ['kɒmjʊnɪzəm] *n* communisme *m* ● **communist** *adj & n* communiste *(mf)*

community [kə'mjuːnɪtɪ] **1** *(pl* -ies*) n* communauté *f*; **the student c.** les étudiants *mpl*

2 *adj (rights, life, spirit)* communautaire; **c. centre** centre *m* socioculturel; **c. worker** animateur, -trice *mf* socioculturel(le)

commute [kə'mjuːt] **1** *n (journey)* trajet *m*

2 *vt Law* commuer (**to** en)

3 *vi* **to c. (to work)** faire la navette entre son domicile et son travail ● **commuter** *n* banlieusard, -arde *mf*; **c. train** train *m* de banlieue

compact¹ [kəm'pækt] *adj (car, crowd, substance)* compact; *(style)* condensé; **c. disc** ['kɒmpækt] disque *m* compact

compact² ['kɒmpækt] *n (for face powder)* poudrier *m*

companion [kəm'pænjən] *n (person)* compagnon *m*, compagne *f*; *(handbook)* manuel *m* ● **companionship** *n* camaraderie *f*

company ['kʌmpənɪ] *(pl* -ies*) n (companionship)* compagnie *f*; *(guests)* invités *mpl*, -ées *fpl*; *(people present)* assemblée *f*; *(business)* société *f*, compagnie *f*; **(theatre) c.** compagnie *f* (théâtrale); **to keep sb c.** tenir compagnie à qn; **in sb's c.** en compagnie de qn; **he's good c.** c'est un bon compagnon; **c. car** voiture *f* de société

comparable ['kɒmpərəbəl] *adj* comparable (**with** *or* **to** à)

comparative [kəm'pærətɪv] **1** *adj (method)* comparatif, -ive; *(law, literature)* comparé; *(relative) (costs, comfort)* relatif, -ive

2 *n Grammar* comparatif *m* ● **comparatively** *adv* relativement

compare [kəm'peə(r)] **1** *vt* comparer (**with** *or* **to** à); **compared to** *or* **with** en comparaison de

2 *vi* être comparable (**with** à) • **comparison** [-'pærɪsən] *n* comparaison *f* (**between** entre; **with** avec); **in c. with** en comparaison avec; **by** *or* **in c.** en comparaison; **there is no c.** il n'y a pas de comparaison

compartment [kəm'pɑːtmənt] *n* compartiment *m* • **compartmentalize** [kɒmpɑːt'mentəlaiz] *vt* compartimenter

compass ['kʌmpəs] *n* (**a**) *(for finding direction)* boussole *f*; *(on ship)* compas *m* (**b**) **(pair of) compasses** compas *m*

compassion [kəm'pæʃən] *n* compassion *f* • **compassionate** *adj* compatissant; **on c. grounds** pour raisons personnelles

compatible [kəm'pætɪbəl] *adj* compatible • **compati'bility** *n* compatibilité *f*

compatriot [kəm'pætrɪət, kəm'peɪtrɪət] *n* compatriote *mf*

compel [kəm'pel] (*pt & pp* **-ll-**) *vt* forcer, obliger; *(respect, obedience)* forcer (**from sb** chez qn); **to c. sb to do sth** forcer qn à faire qch • **compelling** *adj* *(film)* captivant; *(argument)* convaincant; *(urge)* irrésistible

compendium [kəm'pendɪəm] *n* abrégé *m*

compensate ['kɒmpənseɪt] **1** *vt* **to c. sb** *(with payment, reward)* dédommager qn (**for** de)

2 *vi* compenser; **to c. for sth** *(make up for)* compenser qch • **compensation** [-'seɪʃən] *n* *(financial)* dédommagement *m*; *(consolation)* compensation *f*; **in c. for** en dédommagement/compensation de

compère ['kɒmpeə(r)] **1** *n* animateur, -trice *mf*

2 *vt* animer

compete [kəm'piːt] *vi* *(take part in race)* concourir (**in** à); **to c. (with sb)** rivaliser (avec qn); *(in business)* faire concurrence (à qn); **to c. for sth** se disputer qch; **to c. in a race/rally** participer à une course/un rallye

competent ['kɒmpɪtənt] *adj* *(capable)* compétent (**to do** pour faire); *(sufficient)* *(knowledge)* suffisant • **competence** *n* compétence *f* • **competently** *adv* avec compétence

competition [kɒmpə'tɪʃən] *n* (**a**) *(rivalry)* rivalité *f*; *(between companies)* concurrence *f*; **to be in c. with sb** être en concurrence avec qn (**b**) *(contest)* concours *m*; *(in sport)* compétition *f*

competitive [kəm'petɪtɪv] *adj* *(price, market)* compétitif, -ive; *(selection)* par concours; *(person)* qui a l'esprit de compétition; **c. examination** concours *m* • **competitor** *n* concurrent, -ente *mf*

compile [kəm'paɪl] *vt* *(list, catalogue)* dresser; *(documents)* compiler

complacent [kəm'pleɪsənt] *adj* content de soi • **complacence, complacency** *n* autosatisfaction *f*; **there is no room for c.** ce n'est pas le moment de faire de l'autosatisfaction

complain [kəm'pleɪn] *vi* se plaindre (**to sb** à qn; **of** *or* **about sb/sth** de qn/qch; **that** que); **to c. of** *or* **about being tired** se plaindre d'être fatigué • **complaint** *n* plainte *f*; *(in shop)* réclamation *f*; *(illness)* maladie *f*

complement 1 ['kɒmplɪmənt] *n* complément *m*

2 ['kɒmplɪment] *vt* compléter • **complementary** [-'mentərɪ] *adj* complémentaire; **c. medicine** médecines *fpl* douces

complete [kəm'pliːt] **1** *adj* *(whole)* complet, -ète; *(utter)* total; *(finished)* achevé; **he's a c. fool** il est complètement idiot

2 *vt* *(finish)* achever; *(form)* compléter • **completely** *adv* complètement • **completion** *n* achèvement *m*; *(of contract, sale)* exécution *f*

complex ['kɒmpleks] **1** *adj* complexe

2 *n* *(feeling, buildings)* complexe *m* • **complexity** [kəm'pleksɪtɪ] (*pl* **-ies**) *n* complexité *f*

complexion [kəm'plekʃən] *n* *(of face)* teint *m*; *Fig* caractère *m* (**of** de)

compliance [kəm'plaɪəns] *n* *(agreement)* conformité *f* (**with** avec)

complicate ['kɒmplɪkeɪt] *vt* compliquer (**with** de) • **complicated** *adj* compliqué • **complication** [-'keɪʃən] *n* complication *f*

compliment 1 ['kɒmplɪmənt] *n* compliment *m*; **compliments** *(of author)* hommages *mpl*; **to pay sb a c.** faire un compliment à qn; **compliments of the season** meilleurs vœux pour Noël et le nouvel an

2 ['kɒmplɪment] *vt* complimenter, faire des compliments à; **to c. sb on sth** *(bravery)* féliciter qn de qch; *(dress, haircut)* faire des compliments à qn sur qch • **complimentary** [-'mentərɪ] *adj* (**a**) *(praising)* élogieux, -ieuse (**b**) *(free)* gratuit; **c. ticket** billet *m* de faveur

comply [kəm'plaɪ] (*pt & pp* **-ied**) *vi* *(obey)* obéir; **to c. with** *(order)* obéir à; *(rule)* se conformer à; *(request)* accéder à

component [kəm'pəʊnənt] **1** *n* *(of structure, self-assembly furniture, problem)* élément *m*; *(of machine)* pièce *f*; *(chemical, electronic)* composant *m*

2 *adj* **c. part** pièce *f* détachée

compose [kəm'pəʊz] *vt* composer; **to c. oneself** se calmer • **composed** *adj* calme • **composer** *n (of music)* compositeur, -trice *mf* • **composition** [kɒmpə'zɪʃən] *n (in music, art, chemistry)* composition *f*; *(school essay)* rédaction *f*

compost [*Br* 'kɒmpɒst, *Am* 'kɑːmpəʊst] *n* compost *m*

composure [kəm'pəʊʒə(r)] *n* sang-froid *m*

compound ['kɒmpaʊnd] **1** *n (word)* & *Chem (substance)* composé *m*; *(area)* enclos *m*
2 *adj (word, substance)* & *Fin (interest)* composé; *(sentence, number)* complexe
3 [kəm'paʊnd] *vt (problem)* aggraver

comprehend [kɒmprɪ'hend] *vt* comprendre • **comprehensible** *adj* compréhensible • **comprehension** *n* compréhension *f*

comprehensive [kɒmprɪ'hensɪv] **1** *adj* complet, -ète; *(study)* exhaustif, -ive; *(knowledge)* étendu; *(view, measure)* d'ensemble; *(insurance)* tous risques *inv*
2 *adj & n Br* **c. (school)** ≃ établissement *m* d'enseignement secondaire *(n'opérant pas de sélection à l'entrée)*

⚠ Note that the French word **compréhensif** is a false friend and is never a translation for the English word **comprehensive**. It means **understanding**.

compress 1 ['kɒmpres] *n Med* compresse *f*
2 [kəm'pres] *vt (gas, air)* comprimer; *Fig (ideas, facts)* condenser • **compression** [-'preʃən] *n* compression *f*

comprise [kəm'praɪz] *vt (consist of)* comprendre; *(make up)* constituer; **to be comprised of** comprendre

compromise ['kɒmprəmaɪz] **1** *n* compromis *m*; **c. solution** solution *f* de compromis
2 *vt (person, security)* compromettre; *(principles)* transiger sur; **to c. oneself** se compromettre
3 *vi* transiger **(on** sur) • **compromising** *adj* compromettant

compulsion [kəm'pʌlʃən] *n (urge)* besoin *m*; *(obligation)* contrainte *f* • **compulsive** *adj (behaviour)* compulsif, -ive; *(smoker, gambler, liar)* invétéré; **c. eater** boulimique *mf*

compulsory [kəm'pʌlsərɪ] *adj* obligatoire; **c. redundancy** licenciement *m* sec

compunction [kəm'pʌŋkʃən] *n* scrupule *m* (**about doing** à faire)

compute [kəm'pjuːt] *vt* calculer • **computing** *n* informatique *f*

computer [kəm'pjuːtə(r)] **1** *n* ordinateur *m*
2 *adj (program, system, network)* informatique; *(course, firm)* d'informatique; **to be c. literate** avoir des connaissances en informatique; **c. game** jeu *m* électronique; **c. language** langage *m* de programmation; **c. operator** opérateur, -trice *mf* sur ordinateur; **c. science** informatique *f*; **c. scientist** informaticien, -ienne *mf* • **computerization** [-raɪ'zeɪʃən] *n* informatisation *f* • **computerized** *adj* informatisé

comrade ['kɒmreɪd] *n* camarade *mf* • **comradeship** *n* camaraderie *f*

con [kɒn] *Fam* **1** *n* arnaque *f*; **c. man** arnaqueur *m*
2 *(pt & pp -nn-)* *vt* arnaquer; **to be conned** se faire arnaquer

concave [kɒn'keɪv] *adj* concave

conceal [kən'siːl] *vt (hide) (object)* dissimuler (**from sb** à qn); *(plan, news)* cacher (**from sb** à qn) • **concealment** *n* dissimulation *f*

concede [kən'siːd] **1** *vt* concéder (**to** à; **that** que); **to c. defeat** s'avouer vaincu
2 *vi* s'incliner

conceit [kən'siːt] *n* vanité *f* • **conceited** *adj* vaniteux, -euse

conceive [kən'siːv] **1** *vt (idea, child)* concevoir
2 *vi (of woman)* concevoir; **to c. of sth** concevoir qch • **conceivable** *adj* concevable; **it's c. that...** il est concevable que... *(+ subjunctive)* • **conceivably** *adv* **yes, c.** oui, c'est concevable

concentrate ['kɒnsəntreɪt] **1** *vt* concentrer (**on** sur)
2 *vi* se concentrer (**on** sur); **to c. on doing sth** s'appliquer à faire qch • **concentration** [-'treɪʃən] *n* concentration *f*; **to have a short c. span** ne pas avoir une grande capacité de concentration; **c. camp** camp *m* de concentration

concentric [kən'sentrɪk] *adj Math* concentrique

concept ['kɒnsept] *n* concept *m* • **conception** [kən'sepʃən] *n (of child, idea)* conception *f*

concern [kən'sɜːn] **1** *n (matter)* affaire *f*; *(worry)* inquiétude *f*; **his c. for** son souci de; **it's no c. of mine** cela ne me regarde pas; **(business) c.** entreprise *f*
2 *vt* concerner; **to c. oneself with sth, to be concerned with sth** *(be busy)* s'occuper de qch; **to be concerned about** *(be worried)* s'inquiéter de; **as far as I'm concerned...** en ce qui me concerne...

• **concerned** adj (anxious) inquiet, -iète (**about/at** au sujet de); **the department c.** (relevant) le service compétent
• **concerning** prep en ce qui concerne
concert ['kɒnsət] n concert m; **in c.** (together) de concert (**with** avec); **c. hall** salle f de concert; **c. pianist** concertiste mf • **concertgoer** n habitué, -uée mf des concerts
concerted [kən'sɜːtɪd] adj (effort) concerté
concertina [kɒnsə'tiːnə] n concertina m; **c. crash** (of vehicles) carambolage m
concerto [kən'tʃɜːtəʊ] (pl -os) n concerto m
concession [kən'seʃən] n concession f (**to** à) • **concessionary** adj (rate, price) réduit
conciliate [kən'sɪlɪeɪt] vt **to c. sb** (win over) se concilier qn; (soothe) apaiser qn • **conciliation** [-'eɪʃən] n conciliation f; (soothing) apaisement m • **conciliatory** [-lɪətərɪ, Am -tɔːrɪ] adj (tone, person) conciliant
concise [kən'saɪs] adj concis • **concisely** adv avec concision • **conciseness, concision** [-'sɪʒən] n concision f
conclude [kən'kluːd] 1 vt (end, settle) conclure; (festival) clore; **to c. that...** (infer) conclure que...
2 vi (of event) se terminer (**with** par); (of speaker) conclure • **concluding** adj (remarks, speech) final (mpl -als) • **conclusion** n conclusion f; **in c.** pour conclure; **to come to the c. that...** arriver à la conclusion que...
conclusive [kən'kluːsɪv] adj concluant • **conclusively** adv de manière concluante
concoct [kən'kɒkt] vt (dish, scheme) concocter • **concoction** n (dish, drink) mixture f
concord ['kɒnkɔːd] n concorde f
concourse ['kɒnkɔːs] n (in airport, train station) hall m
concrete ['kɒnkriːt] 1 n béton m; **c. wall** mur m en béton; **c. mixer** bétonnière f
2 adj (ideas, example) concret, -ète
concur [kən'kɜː(r)] (pt & pp -rr-) vi (a) (agree) être d'accord (**with** avec) (b) (happen together) coïncider; **to c. to** (contribute) concourir à
concurrent [kən'kʌrənt] adj simultané • **concurrently** adv simultanément
concussion [kən'kʌʃən] n (injury) commotion f cérébrale
condemn [kən'dem] vt condamner (**to** à); (building) déclarer inhabitable; **condemned man** condamné m à mort

• **condemnation** [kɒndem'neɪʃən] n condamnation f
condense [kən'dens] 1 vt condenser
2 vi se condenser • **condensation** [kɒndən'seɪʃən] n condensation f (**of** de); (mist) buée f
condescend [kɒndɪ'send] vi condescendre (**to do** à faire) • **condescension** n condescendance f
condiment ['kɒndɪmənt] n condiment m
condition ['kəndɪʃən] 1 n (stipulation, circumstance, rank) condition f; (state) état m, condition f; (disease) maladie f; **on the c. that...** à la condition que... (+ subjunctive); **on c. that I come with you** à condition que je t'accompagne; **in good c.** en bon état; **in/out of c.** en bonne/ mauvaise forme
2 vt (influence) conditionner; (hair) mettre de l'après-shampooing sur; **to c. sb** (train) conditionner qn (**to do** à faire); **to be conditioned by sth** dépendre de qch • **conditional 1** adj conditionnel, -elle; **to be c. upon** dépendre de 2 n Grammar conditionnel m
conditioner [kən'dɪʃənə(r)] n (hair) **c.** après-shampooing m
condo ['kɒndəʊ] (pl -os) n Am = **condominium**
condolences [kən'dəʊlənsɪz] npl condoléances fpl
condom ['kɒndəm, -ɒm] n préservatif m
condominium [kɒndə'mɪnɪəm] n Am (building) immeuble m en copropriété; (apartment) appartement m en copropriété
condone [kən'dəʊn] vt (overlook) fermer les yeux sur; (forgive) excuser
conducive [kən'djuːsɪv] adj **to be c. to** être favorable à; **not to be c. to** ne pas inciter à
conduct 1 ['kɒndʌkt] n (behaviour, directing) conduite f
2 [kən'dʌkt] vt (campaign, inquiry, experiment) mener; (orchestra) diriger; (electricity, heat) conduire; **to c. one's business** diriger ses affaires; **to c. oneself** se conduire; **conducted tour** (of building, region) visite f guidée
conductor [kən'dʌktə(r)] n (of orchestra) chef m d'orchestre; Br (on bus) receveur m; Am (on train) chef m de train; (metal, cable) conducteur m • **conductress** n Br (on bus) receveuse f

> 📝 Note that the French word **conducteur** often is a false friend and is rarely a translation for the English word **conductor**.

cone [kəʊn] *n* cône *m*; *(for ice cream)* cornet *m*; **(paper) c.** cornet (de papier); **pine** *or* **fir c.** pomme *f* de pin; *Br* **traffic c.** cône de chantier

confectioner [kən'fekʃənə(r)] *n (of sweets)* confiseur, -euse *mf*; *(of cakes)* pâtissier, -ière *mf* • **confectionery** *n (sweets)* confiserie *f*; *(cakes)* pâtisserie *f*

confederate [kən'fedərət] **1** *adj Pol* confédéré
2 *n (accomplice)* complice *mf* • **confederacy, confederation** [-'reɪʃən] *n* confédération *f*

confer [kən'fɜː(r)] *(pt & pp* **-rr-)** **1** *vt (grant)* octroyer (**on** à)
2 *vi (talk together)* se consulter (**on** *or* **about** sur); **to c. with sb** consulter qn

conference ['kɒnfərəns] *n* conférence *f*; *(scientific, academic)* congrès *m*; **press** *or* **news c.** conférence de presse; **in c. (with)** en conférence (avec)

confess [kən'fes] **1** *vt* avouer, confesser (**that** que; **to sb** à qn); *Rel* confesser
2 *vi* avouer; *Rel* se confesser; **to c. to sth** *(crime)* avouer *ou* confesser qch; *(feeling)* avouer qch • **confession** *n* aveu *m*, confession *f*; *Rel* confession; **to go to c.** aller à confesse • **confessional** *n Rel* confessionnal *m*

confetti [kən'fetɪ] *n* confettis *mpl*

confidante [kɒnfɪ'dænt] *n* confident, -ente *mf*

confide [kən'faɪd] **1** *vt* confier (**to** à; **that** que)
2 *vi* **to c. in sb** se confier à qn

confidence ['kɒnfɪdəns] *n (trust)* confiance *f* (**in** en); *(secret)* confidence *f*; **(self-)c.** confiance *f* en soi; **in c.** *(adverb)* en confidence; *(adjective)* confidentiel, -ielle; **in strict c.** *(adverb)* tout à fait confidentiellement; *(adjective)* tout à fait confidentiel; **c. trick** escroquerie *f*; **c. trickster** escroc *m* • **confident** *adj (smile, exterior)* confiant; **(self-)c.** sûr de soi • **confidently** *adv* avec confiance

confidential [kɒnfɪ'denʃəl] *adj* confidentiel, -ielle • **confidentially** *adv* en confidence

configuration [kənfɪgjʊ'reɪʃən] *n* configuration *f*

confine [kən'faɪn] *vt* **(a)** *(limit)* limiter (**to** à); **to c. oneself to doing sth** se limiter à faire qch **(b)** *(keep prisoner)* enfermer (**to/in** dans) • **confined** *adj (atmosphere)* confiné; *(space)* réduit; **c. to bed** alité; **c. to the house/one's room** obligé de rester chez soi/de garder la chambre • **confinement** *n (of prisoner)* emprisonnement *m*; *Med Old-fashioned (of pregnant woman)* couches *fpl*

confines ['kɒnfaɪnz] *npl* confins *mpl*; *Fig* limites *fpl*

confirm [kən'fɜːm] *vt* confirmer (**that** que); *Rel* **to be confirmed** recevoir la confirmation • **confirmation** [kɒnfə-'meɪʃən] *n also Rel* confirmation *f*; **it's subject to c.** c'est à confirmer • **confirmed** *adj (bachelor)* endurci; *(smoker, habit)* invétéré

confiscate ['kɒnfɪskeɪt] *vt* confisquer (**from** à) • **confiscation** [-'keɪʃən] *n* confiscation *f*

conflagration [kɒnflə'greɪʃən] *n* incendie *m*

conflict 1 ['kɒnflɪkt] *n* conflit *m*
2 [kən'flɪkt] *vi (of statement)* être en contradiction (**with** avec); *(of dates, events, programmes)* tomber en même temps (**with** que) • **conflicting** *adj (views, theories, evidence)* contradictoire; *(dates)* incompatible

confluence ['kɒnfluəns] *n (of rivers)* confluent *m*

conform [kən'fɔːm] *vi (of person)* se conformer (**to** *or* **with** à); *(of ideas, actions)* être en conformité (**to** with); *(of product)* être conforme (**to** *or* **with** à) • **conformist** *adj & n* conformiste *(mf)* • **conformity** *n* conformité *f*

confound [kən'faʊnd] *vt (surprise, puzzle)* laisser perplexe; **c. him!** que le diable l'emporte!; **c. it!** quelle barbe! • **confounded** *adj Fam (damned)* sacré

confront [kən'frʌnt] *vt (danger)* affronter; *(problem)* faire face à; **to c. sb** *(be face to face with)* se trouver en face de qn; *(oppose)* s'opposer à qn; **to c. sb with sth** mettre qn en face de qch • **confrontation** [kɒnfrən'teɪʃən] *n* confrontation *f*

confuse [kən'fjuːz] *vt (make unsure)* embrouiller; **to c. sb/sth with** *(mistake for)* confondre qn/qch avec; **to c. matters** *or* **the issue** embrouiller la question • **confused** *adj (situation, noises, idea)* confus; **to be c.** *(of person)* s'y perdre; **I'm (all** *or* **quite) c. (about it)** je m'y perds; **to get c.** s'embrouiller • **confusing** *adj* déroutant • **confusion** *n (bewilderment)* perplexité *f*; *(disorder, lack of clarity)* confusion *f*; **in (a state of) c.** en désordre

congeal [kən'dʒiːl] *vi (of blood)* (se) coaguler • **congealed** *adj* **c. blood** sang *m* coagulé

congenial [kən'dʒiːnɪəl] *adj* sympathique

congenital [kən'dʒenɪtəl] *adj* congénital
congested [kən'dʒestɪd] *adj (street, town, lungs)* congestionné; *(nose)* bouché •**congestion** *n (traffic)* encombrements *mpl*; *(overcrowding)* surpeuplement *m*
Congo ['kɒŋgəʊ] *n* (**the**) **C.** le Congo
congratulate [kən'grætʃʊleɪt] *vt* féliciter (**sb on sth** qn de qch; **sb on doing sth** qn d'avoir fait qch) •**congratulations** [-'leɪʃənz] *npl* félicitations *fpl* (**on** pour) •**congratulatory** *adj (telegram)* de félicitations
congregate ['kɒŋgrɪgeɪt] *vi* se rassembler •**congregation** [-'geɪʃən] *n (worshippers)* fidèles *mpl*
congress ['kɒŋgres] *n* congrès *m*; *Am Pol* **C.** le Congrès *(assemblée législative américaine)* •**Congressional** [kən'greʃənəl] *adj Am Pol (committee)* du Congrès •**Congressman** *(pl* -**men)** *n Am Pol* membre *m* du Congrès
conical ['kɒnɪkəl] *adj* conique
conifer ['kɒnɪfə(r)] *n* conifère *m*
conjecture [kən'dʒektʃə(r)] **1** *n* conjecture *f*
2 *vt* supposer
3 *vi* faire des conjectures
conjugal ['kɒndʒʊgəl] *adj* conjugal
conjugate ['kɒndʒʊgeɪt] *Grammar* **1** *vt (verb)* conjuguer
2 *vi* se conjuguer •**conju'gation** *n* conjugaison *f*
conjunction [kən'dʒʌŋkʃən] *n Grammar* conjonction *f*; **in c. with** conjointement avec
conjunctivitis [kəndʒʌŋktɪ'vaɪtɪs] *n* conjonctivite *f*; **to have c.** avoir de la conjonctivite
conjure ['kʌndʒə(r)] *vt* **to c. (up)** *(by magic)* faire apparaître; *Fig* **to c. up** *(memories, images)* évoquer; **conjuring trick** tour *m* de prestidigitation •**conjurer** *n* prestidigitateur, -trice *mf*
conk [kɒŋk] *Fam* **1** *n Br (nose)* pif *m*; *(blow)* gnon *m*
2 *vi* **to c. out** *(break down)* tomber en panne; **the car conked out on me** la voiture m'a claqué entre les doigts
conker ['kɒŋkə(r)] *n Br Fam (chestnut)* marron *m* (d'Inde)
connect [kə'nekt] **1** *vt* relier (**with** *or* **to** à); *(telephone, washing machine)* brancher; **to c. sb with sb** *(on phone)* mettre qn en communication avec qn; **to c. sb/ sth with sb/sth** établir un lien entre qn/ qch et qn/qch
2 *vi (be connected)* être relié; *(of rooms)* communiquer; *(of roads)* se rejoindre; **to c. with** *(of train, bus)* assurer la correspondance avec •**connected** *adj (facts, events)* lié; **to be c. with** *(have to do with, relate to)* avoir un lien avec; *(have dealings with)* être lié à; *(by marriage)* être parent avec; **the two issues are not c.** les deux questions n'ont aucun rapport; **to be well c.** avoir des relations
connection [kə'nekʃən] *n (link)* rapport *m*, lien *m* (**with** avec); *(train, bus)* correspondance *f*; *(phone call)* communication *f*; *(between electrical wires)* contact *m*; *(between pipes)* raccord *m*; **connections** *(contacts)* relations *fpl*; **to have no c. with** n'avoir aucun rapport avec; **in c. with** à propos de; **in this** *or* **that c.** à ce propos; **there's a loose c.** *(in electrical appliance)* il y a un faux contact
connive [kə'naɪv] *vi* **to c. with sb** être de connivence avec qn; **to c. at sth** *(let happen)* laisser faire qch
connoisseur [kɒnə'sɜː(r)] *n* connaisseur *m*
connotation [kɒnə'teɪʃən] *n* connotation *f*
conquer ['kɒŋkə(r)] *vt (country, freedom)* conquérir; *(enemy, habit, difficulty)* vaincre •**conquering** *adj* victorieux, -ieuse •**conqueror** *n* vainqueur *m* •**conquest** ['kɒŋkwest] *n* conquête *f*
cons [kɒnz] *npl* **the pros and (the) c.** le pour et le contre
conscience ['kɒnʃəns] *n* conscience *f*; **to have sth on one's c.** avoir qch sur la conscience
conscientious [kɒnʃɪ'enʃəs] *adj* consciencieux, -ieuse; **c. objector** objecteur *m* de conscience •**conscientiousness** *n* sérieux *m*
conscious ['kɒnʃəs] *adj (awake)* conscient; **to make a c. effort to do sth** faire un effort particulier pour faire qch; **to make a c. decision to do sth** chercher délibérément à faire qch; **c. of sth** *(aware)* conscient de qch; **c. that...** conscient que... •**consciously** *adv (knowingly)* consciemment •**consciousness** *n* conscience *f* (**of** de); **to lose/regain c.** perdre/reprendre connaissance
conscript 1 ['kɒnskrɪpt] *n (soldier)* conscrit *m*
2 [kən'skrɪpt] *vt* enrôler •**conscription** [kən'skrɪpʃən] *n* conscription *f*
consecrate ['kɒnsɪkreɪt] *vt Rel (church, temple, place, bishop)* & *Fig* consacrer •**consecration** [-'kreɪʃən] *n* consécration *f*
consecutive [kən'sekjʊtɪv] *adj* consécu-

tif, -ive •**consecutively** *adv* consécutivement
consensus [kən'sensəs] *n* consensus *m*
consent [kən'sent] **1** *n* consentement *m*;
by common c. de l'aveu de tous; **by mutual c.** d'un commun accord
　2 *vi* consentir (**to** à)
consequence ['kɒnsɪkwəns] *n (result)*
conséquence *f*; *(importance)* importance
f; **of no c.** sans importance •**consequently** *adv* par conséquent
conservative [kən'sɜːvətɪv] **1** *adj (estimate)* modeste; *(view, attitude)* traditionnel, -elle; *(person)* traditionaliste; *Br Pol*
conservateur, -trice; *Br Pol* **the C. Party** le
Parti conservateur
　2 *n Br Pol* conservateur, -trice *mf*
•**conservatism** *n (in behaviour) & Br Pol*
conservatisme *m*
conservatory [kən'sɜːvətrɪ] *(pl* -ies*) n Br*
(room) véranda *f*
conserve [kən'sɜːv] *vt (energy, water,
electricity)* faire des économies de;
(monument, language, tradition) préserver; **to c. one's strength** ménager ses forces
•**conservation** [kɒnsə'veɪʃən] *n (of energy)* économies *fpl*; *(of nature)* protection *f* de l'environnement; **c. area** zone *f*
naturelle protégée •**conservationist**
[kɒnsə'veɪʃənɪst] *n* défenseur *m* de l'environnement
consider [kən'sɪdə(r)] *vt (think over)*
considérer; *(take into account)* tenir
compte de; *(offer)* étudier; **I'll c. it** je vais
y réfléchir; **to c. doing sth** envisager de
faire qch; **to c. that...** considérer que...; **I
c. her as a friend** je la considère comme
une amie; **he's** *or* **she's being considered
for the job** sa candidature est à l'étude
pour ce poste; **all things considered** tout
bien considéré
considerable [kənsɪdərəbəl] *adj (large)*
considérable; *(much)* beaucoup de; **after
c. difficulty** après bien des difficultés
•**considerably** *adv* considérablement
considerate [kən'sɪdərət] *adj* attentionné (**to** à l'égard de)
consideration [kənsɪdə'reɪʃən] *n
(thought, thoughtfulness, reason)* considération *f*; **under c.** à l'étude; **out of c. for
sb** par égard pour qn; **to take sth into c.**
prendre qch en considération
considering [kən'sɪdərɪŋ] **1** *prep* étant
donné
　2 *conj* **c. (that)** étant donné que
　3 *adv Fam* **the result was good, c.** c'est
un bon résultat après tout
consign [kən'saɪn] *vt (send)* expédier;

(give, entrust) confier (**to** à) •**consignment** *n (goods)* envoi *m*; *(sending)* expédition *f*
consist [kən'sɪst] *vi* consister (**of** en; **in**
en; **in doing** à faire)
consistent [kən'sɪstənt] *adj (unchanging) (loyalty, quality, results)* constant;
(coherent) (ideas, argument) cohérent,
logique; **to be c. with** *(of statement)*
concorder avec •**consistency** *n (of
substance, liquid)* consistance *f*; *(of
ideas, arguments)* cohérence *f* •**consis-
tently** *adv (always)* constamment; *(regularly)* régulièrement; *(logically)* avec
logique

🖉 Note that the French word **consistant** is
a false friend and is never a translation for
the English word **consistent**. It means **substantial**.

console¹ [kən'səʊl] *vt* consoler (**for** de)
•**consolation** [kɒnsə'leɪʃən] *n* consolation *f*; **c. prize** lot *m* de consolation
console² ['kɒnsəʊl] *n (control desk)*
console *f*
consolidate [kən'sɒlɪdeɪt] **1** *vt* consolider
　2 *vi* se consolider •**consoli'dation** *n*
consolidation *f*
consonant ['kɒnsənənt] *n* consonne *f*
consort 1 ['kɒnsɔːt] *n* époux *m*, épouse *f*
　2 [kən'sɔːt] *vi* **to c. with** *(criminals, ad-
dicts)* fréquenter
consortium [kən'sɔːtɪəm] *(pl* -iums *or*
-ia*) n Com* consortium *m*
conspicuous [kən'spɪkjʊəs] *adj (noticeable)* bien visible; *(striking)* manifeste;
(showy) voyant; **to look c.** ne pas passer
inaperçu; **to be c. by one's absence** briller
par son absence; **to make oneself c.** se
faire remarquer; **in a c. position** bien en
évidence •**conspicuously** *adv* visiblement
conspire [kən'spaɪə(r)] *vi* conspirer
(**against** contre); **to c. to do sth** comploter de faire qch; **circumstances conspired
against me** les circonstances se sont
liguées contre moi •**conspiracy** [-'spɪrəsɪ]
(pl -ies*) n* conspiration *f*
constable ['kɒnstəbəl] *n Br* **(police) c.**
agent *m* de police; *Br* **chief c.** commissaire *m* de police divisionnaire
constant ['kɒnstənt] **1** *adj (frequent)* incessant; *(unchanging)* constant; *(faithful)* fidèle
　2 *n Math* constante *f* •**constancy** *n* constance *f* •**constantly** *adv* constamment,
sans cesse

constellation [kɒnstə'leɪʃən] *n* constellation *f*

consternation [kɒnstə'neɪʃən] *n* consternation *f*

constipate ['kɒnstɪpeɪt] *vt* constiper • **constipated** *adj* constipé • **consti'pation** *n* constipation *f*

constituent [kən'stɪtjʊənt] **1** *adj (element, part)* constitutif, -ive
2 *n* (**a**) *(part)* élément *m* constitutif (**b**) *Pol (voter)* électeur, -trice *mf* • **constituency** (*pl* **-ies**) *n* circonscription *f* électorale; *(voters)* électeurs *mpl*

constitute ['kɒnstɪtjuːt] *vt* constituer • **consti'tution** *n* constitution *f* • **constitutional** [-'tjuːʃənəl] *adj Pol* constitutionnel, -elle

constrain [kən'streɪn] *vt* (**a**) *(force)* contraindre (**sb to do** qn à faire) (**b**) *(of clothing)* gêner • **constraint** *n* contrainte *f*

constrict [kən'strɪkt] *vt (tighten, narrow)* resserrer; *(movement)* gêner • **constriction** *n (of blood vessel)* constriction *f*; *(of person)* gêne *f*

construct [kən'strʌkt] *vt* construire • **construction** *n (building, structure) & Grammar* construction *f*; **under c.** en construction; **c. site** chantier *m* • **constructive** *adj* constructif, -ive

construe [kən'struː] *vt* interpréter

consul ['kɒnsəl] *n* consul *m* • **consular** [-sjʊlə(r)] *adj* consulaire • **consulate** [-sjʊlət] *n* consulat *m*

consult [kən'sʌlt] **1** *vt* consulter
2 *vi* **to c. with sb** discuter avec qn; *Br* **consulting room** *(of doctor)* cabinet *m* de consultation • **consultation** [kɒnsəl'teɪʃən] *n* consultation *f*; **in c. with** en consultation avec

consultancy [kən'sʌltənsɪ] (*pl* **-ies**) **1** *n* **c. (firm)** cabinet-conseil *m*; **to do c. work** être consultant • **consultant** *n Br (doctor)* spécialiste *mf*; *(adviser)* consultant *m*
2 *adj (engineer)* consultant • **consultative** *adj (committee, role)* consultatif, -ive

consume [kən'sjuːm] *vt (food, supplies)* consommer; *(of fire)* consumer; *(of grief, hate)* dévorer; **to be consumed by** *or* **with jealousy** brûler de jalousie; **consuming ambition/passion** ambition *f*/passion *f* dévorante • **consumer** *n* consommateur, -trice *mf*; **gas/electricity c.** abonné, -ée *mf* au gaz/à l'électricité; **c. goods/society** biens *mpl*/société *f* de consommation; **c. protection** défense *f* du consommateur • **consumerism** *n* consumérisme *m* • **consumption** [-'sʌmpʃən] *n* consommation *f*

consummate 1 [kən'sʌmɪt] *adj (linguist, cook)* de premier ordre; *(snob, hypocrite)* parfait
2 ['kɒnsəmeɪt] *vt (marriage, relationship)* consommer

contact ['kɒntækt] **1** *n (act of touching)* contact *m*; *(person)* relation *f*; **in c. with** en contact avec; **c. lenses** lentilles *fpl* de contact
2 *vt* contacter

contagious [kən'teɪdʒəs] *adj (disease)* contagieux, -ieuse; *(laughter)* communicatif, -ive

contain [kən'teɪn] *vt (enclose, hold back)* contenir; **to c. oneself** se contenir • **container** *n (box, jar)* récipient *m*; *(for transporting goods)* conteneur *m*

contaminate [kən'tæmɪneɪt] *vt* contaminer • **contamination** [-'neɪʃən] *n* contamination *f*

contemplate ['kɒntəmpleɪt] *vt (look at)* contempler; *(consider)* envisager (**doing** de faire) • **contemplation** [-'pleɪʃən] *n* contemplation *f*; **deep in c.** en pleine contemplation

contemporary [kən'tempərərɪ] **1** *adj* contemporain (**with** de); *(pattern, colour, style)* moderne
2 (*pl* **-ies**) *n (person)* contemporain, -aine *mf*

contempt [kən'tempt] *n* mépris *m*; **to hold sb/sth in c.** mépriser qn/qch • **contemptible** *adj* méprisable • **contemptuous** *adj* méprisant (**of** de); **to be c. of sth** mépriser qch

contend [kən'tend] **1** *vi* **to c. with** *(problem)* faire face à; **to c. with sb** *(struggle)* se battre avec qn
2 *vt* **to c. that...** *(claim)* soutenir que... • **contender** *n (in sport)* concurrent, -ente *mf*; *(in election, for job)* candidat, -ate *mf*

content¹ [kən'tent] *adj (happy)* satisfait (**with** de) • **contented** *adj* satisfait • **contentment** *n* contentement *m*

content² ['kɒntent] *n (of book, text, film) (subject matter)* contenu *m*; **contents** contenu *m*; *(of book)* table *f* des matières; **alcoholic/iron c.** teneur *f* en alcool/fer

contention [kən'tenʃən] *n* (**a**) *(claim, belief)* affirmation *f* (**b**) *(disagreement)* désaccord *m*

contentious [kən'tenʃəs] *adj (issue, views)* controversé

contest 1 ['kɒntest] *n (competition)* concours *m*; *(fight)* lutte *f*; *Boxing* combat *m*
2 [kən'test] *vt (dispute)* contester; **to c. a seat** se porter candidat; **a fiercely contested election** une élection très disputée

●**contestant** [kən'testənt] *n* concurrent, -ente *mf*; *(in fight)* adversaire *mf*

context ['kɒntekst] *n* contexte *m*; **in/out of c.** en/hors contexte

continent ['kɒntɪnənt] *n* continent *m*; **the C.** l'Europe *f* continentale; **on the C.** en Europe ●**continental** [-'nentəl] **1** *adj (of Europe)* européen, -enne; *(of other continents)* continental; **c. breakfast** petit déjeuner *m* à la française **2** *n* Européen, -enne *mf* (continental(e))

contingent [kən'tɪndʒənt] *n (group)* contingent *m* ●**contingency** (*pl* -**ies**) *n* éventualité *f*; **c. plan** plan *m* d'urgence

continual [kən'tɪnjʊəl] *adj* continuel, -uelle ●**continually** *adv* continuellement

continue [kən'tɪnjuː] **1** *vt* continuer (**to do** *or* **doing** à *ou* de faire); **to c. (with)** *(work, speech)* poursuivre; *(resume)* reprendre **2** *vi* continuer; *(resume)* reprendre; **to c. in one's job** garder son emploi ●**continuance** [-jʊəns] *n* continuation *f* ●**continuation** [-ʊ'eɪʃən] *n* continuation *f*; *(resumption)* reprise *f*; *(new episode)* suite *f* ●**continued** *adj (interest, attention)* soutenu; *(presence)* continuel, -uelle; **to be c.** *(of story)* à suivre

continuity [kɒntɪ'njuːɪtɪ] *n* continuité *f*

continuous [kən'tɪnjʊəs] *adj* continu; *Sch & Univ* **c. assessment** contrôle *m* continu des connaissances ●**continuously** *adv* sans interruption

contort [kən'tɔːt] **1** *vt (twist)* tordre; **to c. oneself** se contorsionner **2** *vi* se tordre (**with de**) ●**contortion** *n* contorsion *f* ●**contortionist** *n (acrobat)* contorsionniste *mf*

contour ['kɒntʊə(r)] *n* contour *m*; **c. (line)** *(on map)* courbe *f* de niveau

contraband ['kɒntrəbænd] *n* contrebande *f*

contraception [kɒntrə'sepʃən] *n* contraception *f* ●**contraceptive** *n* contraceptif *m*

contract¹ ['kɒntrækt] **1** *n* contrat *m*; **to be under c.** être sous contrat; **c. killer** tueur *m* à gages; **c. work** travail *m* en sous-traitance **2** *vt* **to c. to do sth** s'engager (par un contrat) à faire qch; **to c. work out** sous-traiter du travail **3** *vi* **to c. out** *(of policy, pension plan)* arrêter de souscrire ●**contractor** [kən'træktə(r)] *n* entrepreneur *m*

contract² [kən'trækt] **1** *vt (illness, debt)* contracter **2** *vi (shrink)* se contracter ●**contraction** *n* contraction *f*

contradict [kɒntrə'dɪkt] *vt (person, state-*

ment) contredire; *(deny)* démentir; **to c. oneself** se contredire ●**contradiction** *n* contradiction *f* ●**contradictory** *adj* contradictoire

contralto [kən'træltəʊ] (*pl* -**os**) *n* contralto *mf*

contraption [kən'træpʃən] *n Fam* machin *m*

contrary ['kɒntrərɪ] **1** *adj* (**a**) *(opposite)* contraire (**to** à) (**b**) [kən'treərɪ] *adj (awkward)* contrariant **2** *adv* **c. to** contrairement à **3** *n* contraire *m*; **on the c.** au contraire; **unless you/I/***etc* **hear to the c.** sauf avis contraire

contrast [kən'trɑːst] **1** ['kɒntrɑːst] *n* contraste *m*; **in c. to** par opposition à **2** *vt* mettre en contraste **3** *vi* contraster (**with** avec) ●**contrasting** *adj (opinions)* opposé

contravene [kɒntrə'viːn] *vt (law)* enfreindre ●**contravention** [-'venʃən] *n* **in c. of a treaty** en violation d'un traité

contribute [kən'trɪbjuːt] **1** *vt (time, clothes)* donner (**to** à); *(article)* écrire (**to** pour); **to c. money to** verser de l'argent à **2** *vi* **to c. to** contribuer à; *(publication)* collaborer à; *(discussion)* prendre part à; *(charity)* donner à ●**contribution** [kɒntrɪ'bjuːʃən] *n* contribution *f* ●**contributor** *n (to newspaper)* collaborateur, -trice *mf*; *(of money)* donateur, -trice *mf* ●**contributory** *adj (cause, factor)* concourant; **to be a c. factor in sth** concourir à qch

contrite [kən'traɪt] *adj* contrit ●**contrition** [-'trɪʃən] *n* contrition *f*

contrivance [kən'traɪvəns] *n (device)* dispositif *m*; *(scheme)* système *m*

contrive [kən'traɪv] *vt* **to c. to do sth** trouver moyen de faire qch

contrived [kən'traɪvd] *adj* qui manque de naturel

control [kən'trəʊl] **1** *n* contrôle *m*; *(authority)* autorité *f* (**over** sur); **the controls** *(of plane)* les commandes *fpl*; *(of TV set, radio)* les boutons *mpl*; **(self-)c.** la maîtrise (de soi); **the situation** *or* **everything is under c.** je/il/*etc* contrôle la situation; **to lose c. of** *(situation, vehicle)* perdre le contrôle de; **out of c.** *(situation, crowd)* difficilement maîtrisable; *Comptr* **c. key** touche *f* de contrôle; **c. panel** tableau *m* de bord; **c. tower** *(at airport)* tour *f* de contrôle **2** (*pt & pp* -**ll**-) *vt (business, organization)* diriger; *(prices, quality)* contrôler; *(emotion, reaction)* maîtriser; *(disease)* enrayer; **to c. oneself** se contrôler

controversy [ˈkɒntrəvɜːsɪ] (*pl* **-ies**) *n* controverse *f* •**controversial** [-ˈvɜːʃəl] *adj* controversé

conundrum [kəˈnʌndrəm] *n (riddle)* devinette *f*; *(mystery)* énigme *f*

conurbation [kɒnɜːˈbeɪʃən] *n* conurbation *f*

convalesce [kɒnvəˈles] *vi (rest)* être en convalescence •**convalescence** *n* convalescence *f*

convene [kənˈviːn] **1** *vt (meeting)* convoquer
2 *vi (meet)* se réunir

convenience [kənˈviːnɪəns] *n* commodité *f*; **come at your (own) c.** venez quand vous voudrez; **all modern conveniences** tout le confort moderne; *Br* **(public) conveniences** toilettes *fpl*; **c. food(s)** plats *mpl* tout préparés; **c. store** magasin *m* de proximité

convenient [kənˈviːnɪənt] *adj* commode, pratique; **to be c. (for)** *(suit)* convenir (à) •**conveniently** *adv (arrive, say)* à propos; **c. situated** bien situé

convent [ˈkɒnvənt] *n* couvent *m*; **c. school** école *f* des sœurs

convention [kənˈvenʃən] *n (custom)* usage *m*; *(agreement)* convention *f*; *(conference)* convention, congrès *m* •**conventional** *adj* conventionnel, -elle

converge [kənˈvɜːdʒ] *vi* converger (**on** sur) •**convergence** *n* convergence *f* •**converging** *adj* convergent

conversation [kɒnvəˈseɪʃən] *n* conversation *f* (**with** avec) •**conversational** *adj (tone)* de la conversation; *(person)* loquace •**conversationalist** *n* **to be a good c.** avoir de la conversation

converse 1 [ˈkɒnvɜːs] *adj & n* inverse *(m)*
2 [kənˈvɜːs] *vi* s'entretenir (**with** avec) •**con'versely** [kənˈvɜːslɪ] *adv* inversement

convert [kənˈvɜːt] **1** [ˈkɒnvɜːt] *n* converti, -ie *mf*
2 *vt (change)* convertir (**into** *or* **to** en); *(building)* aménager (**into, to** en); *Rel* **to c. sb** convertir qn (**to** à)
3 *vi (change religion)* se convertir (**to** à) •**conversion** *n* conversion *f*; *(of building)* aménagement *m*; *(in rugby)* transformation *f*

convertible [kənˈvɜːtəbəl] **1** *adj (money, sofa)* convertible
2 *n (car)* décapotable *f*

convex [kɒnˈveks] *adj* convexe

convey [kənˈveɪ] *vt (transport)* transporter; *(communicate)* transmettre •**conveyor belt** *n* tapis *m* roulant

convict 1 [ˈkɒnvɪkt] *n* détenu *m*
2 [kənˈvɪkt] *vt* déclarer coupable (**of** de) •**con'viction** [kənˈvɪkʃən] *n (for crime)* condamnation *f*; *(belief)* conviction *f* (**that** que)

convince [kənˈvɪns] *vt* convaincre (**of sth** de qch; **sb to do sth** qn de faire qch); **I was convinced that I was right** j'étais convaincu d'avoir raison •**convincing** *adj (argument, person)* convaincant •**convincingly** *adv (argue)* de façon convaincante

convivial [kənˈvɪvɪəl] *adj (event)* joyeux, -euse; *(person)* chaleureux, -euse

convoluted [kɒnvəˈluːtɪd] *adj (argument, style)* compliqué

convoy [ˈkɒnvɔɪ] *n* convoi *m*

convulse [kənˈvʌls] *vt (shake)* ébranler; *(face)* convulser; **to be convulsed with pain** se tordre de douleur •**convulsion** *n Med* convulsion *f* •**convulsive** *adj* convulsif, -ive

coo [kuː] (*pt & pp* **cooed**) *vi (of dove)* roucouler

cook [kʊk] **1** *n (person)* cuisinier, -ière *mf*
2 *vt (meal)* préparer; *(food)* (faire) cuire; *Fam* **to c. the accounts** *or* **books** truquer les comptes; *Fam* **to c. up** inventer
3 *vi (of food)* cuire; *(of person)* faire la cuisine; *Fam* **what's cooking?** qu'est-ce qui se passe? •**cookbook** *n* livre *m* de cuisine •**cooker** *n Br (stove)* cuisinière *f* •**cookery** *n* cuisine *f*; *Br* **c. book** livre *m* de cuisine •**cooking** *n (activity, food)* cuisine *f*; *(process)* cuisson *f*; **to do the c.** faire la cuisine; **c. apple** pomme *f* à cuire; **c. utensils** ustensiles *mpl* de cuisine

cookie [ˈkʊkɪ] *n Am* gâteau *m* sec

cool [kuːl] **1** (**-er, -est**) *adj (weather, place, wind)* frais (*f* fraîche); *(tea, soup)* tiède; *(calm)* calme; *(unfriendly)* froid; *Fam (good)* cool *inv*; *Fam (trendy)* branché; **a (nice) c. drink** une boisson (bien) fraîche; **a c. £50** la coquette somme de 50 livres; **the weather is c., it's c.** il fait frais; **to keep sth c.** tenir qch au frais; **to keep a c. head** garder la tête froide
2 *n (of evening)* fraîcheur *f*; **to keep/lose one's c.** garder/perdre son sang-froid
3 *vt* **to c. (down)** refroidir, rafraîchir
4 *vi* **to c. (down** *or* **off)** *(of hot liquid)* refroidir; *(of enthusiasm)* se refroidir; *(of angry person)* se calmer; **to c. off** *(by drinking, swimming)* se rafraîchir •**cooler** *n (for food)* glacière *f* •**cool-'headed** *adj* calme •**coolly** *adv (calmly)* calmement; *(welcome)* froidement; *(boldly)* effrontément •**coolness** *n* fraîcheur *f*; *(unfriendliness)* froideur *f*

coop [kuːp] **1** n *(for chickens)* poulailler m
2 vt **to c. up** *(person, animal)* enfermer;
I've been cooped up je suis resté enfermé
co-op ['kəʊɒp] n coopérative f
cooperate [kəʊ'ɒpəreɪt] vi coopérer (**in**
à; **with** avec) •**coope'ration** n coopération f
cooperative [kəʊ'ɒpərətɪv] **1** adj coopératif, -ive
2 n coopérative f
coopt [kəʊ'ɒpt] vt coopter (**onto** à)
coordinate [kəʊ'ɔːdɪneɪt] vt coordonner
•**coordination** [-'neɪʃən] n coordination f
•**coordinator** n *(of project)* coordinateur,
-trice mf
coordinates [kəʊ'ɔːdɪnəts] npl Math coordonnées fpl; *(clothes)* coordonnés mpl
co-owner [kəʊ'əʊnə(r)] n copropriétaire
mf
cop [kɒp] Fam **1** n *(policeman)* flic m
2 vi **to c. out** se défiler
cope [kəʊp] vi **to c. with** *(problem, de-*
mand) faire face à; **to be able to c.** savoir
se débrouiller; **I (just) can't c.** je n'y arrive
plus
copier ['kɒpɪə(r)] n *(photocopier)* photocopieuse f
copilot ['kəʊpaɪlət] n copilote m
copious ['kəʊpɪəs] adj *(meal)* copieux,
-ieuse; *(sunshine, amount)* abondant
copper ['kɒpə(r)] n (**a**) *(metal)* cuivre m;
Br **coppers** *(coins)* petite monnaie f (**b**) Br
Fam *(policeman)* flic m
coppice ['kɒpɪs], **copse** [kɒps] n taillis m
copulate ['kɒpjʊleɪt] vi copuler
copy ['kɒpɪ] **1** *(pl -ies)* n *(of letter, docu-*
ment) copie f; *(of book, magazine)*
exemplaire m; *(of photo)* épreuve f
2 *(pt & pp -ied)* vt copier; **to c. out** or
down *(text, letter)* copier
3 vi copier •**copyright** n copyright m
coral ['kɒrəl] n corail m
cord [kɔːd] n (**a**) *(of curtain, bell, pyjamas)*
cordon m; *(electrical)* cordon électrique
(**b**) *(corduroy)* velours m côtelé; **cords**
(trousers) pantalon m en velours côtelé
cordial ['kɔːdɪəl] **1** adj *(friendly)* cordial
2 n Br *(fruit)* **c.** sirop m
cordless ['kɔːdləs] adj **c. phone** téléphone m sans fil
cordon ['kɔːdən] **1** n cordon m
2 vt **to c. off** *(road)* barrer; *(area)* boucler
corduroy ['kɔːdərɔɪ] n velours m côtelé
core [kɔː(r)] **1** n *(of apple)* trognon m; *(of*
problem) cœur m; *(group of people)* &
Geol noyau m; **rotten to the c.** corrompu
jusqu'à la moelle; Sch **c. curriculum** tronc

m commun; **c. vocabulary** vocabulaire m
de base
2 vt *(apple)* évider
cork [kɔːk] **1** n *(material)* liège m; *(stop-*
per) bouchon m
2 vt *(bottle)* boucher •**corkscrew** n tire-
bouchon m
corn[1] [kɔːn] n Br *(wheat)* blé m; Am
(maize) maïs m; *(seed)* grain m; **c. on the**
cob maïs en épi, Can blé m en Inde
corn[2] [kɔːn] n *(on foot)* cor m
corned beef [kɔːnd'biːf] n corned-beef m
corner ['kɔːnə(r)] **1** n *(of street, room,*
page, screen) coin m; *(bend in road)* virage m; Football corner m; Fig **in a (tight)**
c. en situation difficile; **it's just round the**
c. c'est juste au coin; Fig **Christmas is just**
round the c. on est tout près de Noël; **c.**
shop épicerie f du coin
2 vt *(person, animal)* acculer; **to c. the**
market monopoliser le marché
3 vi *(of car, driver)* prendre un virage
•**cornerstone** n pierre f angulaire
cornet ['kɔːnɪt] n Br *(of ice cream)* cornet
m; *(instrument)* cornet m à pistons
cornflakes ['kɔːnfleɪks] npl corn flakes
mpl
cornflour ['kɔːnflaʊə(r)] n farine f de
maïs, Maïzena® f
cornflower ['kɔːnflaʊə(r)] n bleuet m
cornstarch ['kɔːnstɑːtʃ] n Am = **cornflour**
Cornwall ['kɔːnwəl] n Cornouailles f
corny ['kɔːnɪ] *(-ier, -iest)* adj Fam *(joke)*
nul *(f* nulle*)*; *(film)* tarte
coronary ['kɒrənərɪ] *(pl -ies)* n infarctus
m
coronation [kɒrə'neɪʃən] n couronnement m
coroner ['kɒrənə(r)] n Law coroner m
corporal ['kɔːpərəl] n *(in army)* caporal-
chef m
corporal ['kɔːpərəl] adj **c. punishment**
châtiment m corporel
corporate ['kɔːpərət] adj *(budget)* de
l'entreprise; *(decision)* collectif, -ive; **c.**
image image f de marque de l'entreprise
corporation [kɔːpə'reɪʃən] n *(business)*
société f; Br *(of town)* conseil m municipal
corps [kɔː(r), pl kɔːz] n inv Mil & Pol corps
m; **the press c.** les journalistes mpl
corpse [kɔːps] n cadavre m
corpuscle ['kɔːpʌsəl] n Anat corpuscule
m; *(blood cell)* globule m
corral [kə'ræl] n Am corral m *(pl -als)*
correct [kə'rekt] **1** adj *(accurate)* exact;
(proper) correct; **he's c.** il a raison; **the c.**
time l'heure exacte

2 *vt* corriger • **correctly** *adv* correctement • **correction** *n* correction *f*; **c. fluid** liquide *m* correcteur

correlate ['kɒrəleɪt] 1 *vt* mettre en corrélation (**with** avec)
2 *vi* être en corrélation (**with** à) • **correlation** [-'leɪʃən] *n* corrélation *f*

correspond [kɒrɪ'spɒnd] *vi* correspondre • **corresponding** *adj* (*matching*) correspondant; (*similar*) semblable

correspondence [kɒrɪ'spɒndəns] *n* correspondance *f*; **c. course** cours *m* par correspondance • **correspondent** *n* correspondant, -ante *mf*

corridor ['kɒrɪdɔː(r)] *n* couloir *m*, corridor *m*

corroborate [kə'rɒbəreɪt] *vt* corroborer

corrode [kə'rəʊd] 1 *vt* (*metal*) corroder
2 *vi* (*of metal*) se corroder • **corroded** *adj* (*rusty*) rouillé • **corrosion** *n* corrosion *f*

corrugated ['kɒrəgeɪtɪd] *adj* ondulé

corrupt [kə'rʌpt] 1 *adj* corrompu
2 *vt* corrompre • **corruption** *n* corruption *f*

Corsica ['kɔːsɪkə] *n* la Corse • **Corsican 1** *adj* corse **2** *n* Corse *mf*

cos [kɒs] *n Br* **c. (lettuce)** romaine *f*

cosh [kɒʃ] *Br* **1** *n* matraque *f*
2 *vt* matraquer

cosiness ['kəʊzɪnəs] *n* confort *m*

cosmetic [kɒz'metɪk] **1** *adj Fig* (*change*) superficiel, -ielle; **c. surgery** chirurgie *f* esthétique
2 *n* produit *m* de beauté

cosmopolitan [kɒzmə'pɒlɪtən] *adj & n* cosmopolite (*mf*)

cost [kɒst] **1** *n* coût *m*; *Econ* **the c. of living** le coût de la vie; **at great c.** à grands frais; **to my c.** à mes dépens; **at any c., at all costs** à tout prix; *Br* **at c. price** au prix coûtant
2 (*pt & pp* **cost**) *vti* coûter; **how much does it c.?** ça coûte combien?; *Fam* **to c. the earth** coûter les yeux de la tête • **cost-effective** *adj* rentable • **costly** (**-ier, -iest**) *adj* (*expensive*) (*car, trip*) coûteux, -euse; (*valuable*) (*jewel, antique*) de (grande) valeur; **it was a c. mistake** c'est une erreur qui a coûté cher

co-star ['kəʊstɑː(r)] *n* (*in film, play*) partenaire *mf*

Costa Rica [kɒstə'riːkə] *n* le Costa Rica

costume ['kɒstjuːm] *n* costume *m*; (*woman's suit*) tailleur *m*; *Br* (**swimming**) **c.** maillot *m* de bain

cosy ['kəʊzɪ] **1** (**-ier, -iest**) *adj Br* (*house*) douillet, -ette; (*atmosphere*) intime; **make yourself (nice and) c.** mets-toi à l'aise; **we're c.** on est bien ici
2 *n* (**tea**) **c.** couvre-théière *m*

cot [kɒt] *n Br* (*for child*) lit *m* d'enfant; *Am* (*camp bed*) lit de camp; *Br* **c. death** mort *f* subite du nourrisson

cottage ['kɒtɪdʒ] *n* petite maison *f* de campagne; (**thatched**) **c.** chaumière *f*; **c. cheese** fromage *m* blanc (maigre); **c. industry** industrie *f* artisanale; (*at home*) industrie familiale; *Br* **c. pie** ≃ hachis *m* Parmentier

cotton ['kɒtən] **1** *n* coton *m*; (*yarn*) fil *m* de coton; *Br* **c. wool,** *Am* **absorbent c.** coton *m* hydrophile, ouate *f*; **c. shirt** chemise *f* en coton; *Am* **c. candy** barbe *f* à papa
2 *vi Fam* **to c. on (to sth)** (*realize*) piger (qch)

couch [kaʊtʃ] **1** *n* (*sofa*) canapé *m*; (*for doctor's patient*) lit *m*
2 *vt* (*express*) formuler

couchette [kuː'ʃet] *n Br* (*on train*) couchette *f*

cough [kɒf] **1** *n* toux *f*; **c. syrup** *or* **medicine,** *Br* **c. mixture** sirop *m* pour la toux
2 *vi* tousser; *Fam* **to c. up** casquer
3 *vt* **to c. up** (*blood*) cracher; *Fam* (*money*) allonger

could [kʊd, *unstressed* kəd] *pt of* **can¹**

couldn't ['kʊdənt] = **could not**

council ['kaʊnsəl] *n* (*assembly*) conseil *m*; (*local government*) municipalité *f*; (**town/city**) **c.** conseil *m* municipal; **C. of Europe** Conseil de l'Europe; *Br* **c. flat/house** ≃ HLM *f*; *Br* **c. tax** = impôt regroupant taxe d'habitation et impôts locaux • **councillor** *n* conseiller, -ère *mf*; (**town**) **c.** conseiller *m* municipal

counsel ['kaʊnsəl] **1** *n* *inv* (*advice*) conseil *m*; *Br* (*lawyer*) avocat, -ate *mf*
2 (*Br* **-ll-,** *Am* **-l-**) *vt* conseiller (**sb to do** à qn de faire) • **counselling** (*Am* **counseling**) *n* assistance *f* psychosociale • **counsellor** (*Am* **counselor**) *n* conseiller, -ère *mf*

count¹ [kaʊnt] **1** *n* (*calculation*) compte *m*; *Law* (*charge*) chef *m* d'accusation; **to keep c. of sth** tenir le compte de qch
2 *vt* (*find number of, include*) compter; (*consider*) considérer; **not counting Paul** sans compter Paul; **to c. in** (*include*) inclure; **c. me in!** j'en suis!; **to c. out** (*exclude*) exclure; (*money*) compter; **c. me out!** ne compte pas sur moi!
3 *vi* compter; **to c. against sb** jouer contre qn; **to c. on sb/sth** (*rely on*) compter sur qn/qch; **to c. on doing sth** compter faire qch • **countdown** *n* compte *m* à rebours

count² [kaʊnt] *n (title)* comte *m*
counter ['kaʊntə(r)] **1** *n* (**a**) *(in shop, bar)* comptoir *m*; *(in bank)* guichet *m*; **the food c.** *(in store)* le rayon alimentation; *Fig* **under the c.** *(buy, sell)* au marché noir; **over the c.** *(medicine)* en vente libre (**b**) *(in games)* jeton *m* (**c**) *(counting device)* compteur *m*
2 *adv* **c. to** contrairement à; **to run c. to** aller à l'encontre de
3 *vt (threat)* répondre à; *(effects)* neutraliser; *(blow)* parer; **to c. that...** riposter que...
4 *vi* riposter (**with** par)
counter- ['kaʊntə(r)] *pref* contre-
counteract [kaʊntə'rækt] *vt (influence)* contrecarrer; *(effects)* neutraliser
counterattack ['kaʊntərətæk] **1** *n* contre-attaque *f*
2 *vti* contre-attaquer
counterbalance ['kaʊntəbæləns] **1** *n* contrepoids *m*
2 *vt* contrebalancer
counterclockwise [kaʊntə'klɒkwaɪz] *adj & adv Am* dans le sens inverse des aiguilles d'une montre
counterfeit ['kaʊntəfɪt] **1** *adj* faux (*f* fausse)
2 *n* faux *m*
3 *vt* contrefaire
counterfoil ['kaʊntəfɔɪl] *n* souche *f*
counterpart ['kaʊntəpɑːt] *n (thing)* équivalent *m*; *(person)* homologue *mf*
counterproductive [kaʊntəprə'dʌktɪv] *adj (action)* contre-productif, -ive
countersign ['kaʊntəsaɪn] *vt* contresigner
countess ['kaʊntɪs] *n* comtesse *f*
countless ['kaʊntlɪs] *adj* innombrable; **on c. occasions** à maintes occasions
country ['kʌntrɪ] (*pl* **-ies**) **1** *n* pays *m*; *(region)* région *f*, pays ; *(opposed to town)* campagne *f*; **in the c.** à la campagne
2 *adj (house, road)* de campagne; **c. and western music** country *f*; **c. dancing** danse *f* folklorique •**countryman** (*pl* **-men**) *n* (**fellow**) **c.** compatriote *m* •**countryside** *n* campagne *f*; **in the c.** à la campagne
county ['kaʊntɪ] (*pl* **-ies**) *n* comté *m*; **c. council** ≃ conseil *m* général; *Br* **c. town,** *Am* **c. seat** chef-lieu *m* de comté
coup [kuː, *pl* kuːz] *n Pol* coup *m* d'État
couple ['kʌpəl] **1** *n (of people)* couple *m*; **a c. of** deux ou trois; *(a few)* quelques
2 *vt (connect)* accoupler
coupon ['kuːpɒn] *n (for discount)* bon *m*; *(form)* coupon *m*

courage ['kʌrɪdʒ] *n* courage *m* •**courageous** [kə'reɪdʒəs] *adj* courageux, -euse
courgette [kʊə'ʒet] *n Br* courgette *f*
courier ['kʊrɪə(r)] *n (for tourists)* guide *mf*; *(messenger)* messager *m*
course [kɔːs] **1** *n* (**a**) *(of river, time, events)* cours *m*; *(of ship)* route *f*; *(means)* moyen *m*; **c. of action** ligne *f* de conduite; **to be on c.** *Naut* suivre le cap; *Fig* être en bonne voie; **your best c. is to** le mieux c'est de; **as a matter of c.** normalement; **in the c. of** au cours de; **in the c. of time** avec le temps; **in due c.** en temps utile (**b**) *(lessons)* cours *m*; **c. of lectures** série *f* de conférences (**c**) *Med* **c. of treatment** traitement *m* (**d**) *(of meal)* plat *m*; **first c.** entrée *f*; **main c.** plat principal (**e**) *(for race)* parcours *m*; *(for horseracing)* champ *m* de courses; *(for golf)* terrain *m*
2 *adv* **of c.!** bien sûr!; **of c. not!** bien sûr que non!
court¹ [kɔːt] *n (of king)* cour *f*; *(for trials)* cour, tribunal *m*; *(for tennis)* court *m*; **c. of law** tribunal *m*; **to go to c.** aller en justice; **to take sb to c.** poursuivre qn en justice; *Br* **c. shoe** escarpin *m* •**courthouse** *n Am* palais *m* de justice •**courtroom** *n Law* salle *f* d'audience •**courtyard** *n* cour *f*
court² [kɔːt] **1** *vt (woman)* faire la cour à; *(danger)* aller au-devant de; *(death)* braver; *(friendship, favour)* rechercher
2 *vi* **to be courting** *(of couple)* se fréquenter •**courtship** *n (of person)* cour *f*; *(of animal)* parade *f* nuptiale
courteous ['kɜːtɪəs] *adj* poli, courtois •**courtesy** [-təsɪ] (*pl* **-ies**) *n* politesse *f*, courtoisie *f*; **c. car** = voiture mise à la disposition d'un client par un hôtel, un garage etc
courtier ['kɔːtɪə(r)] *n Hist* courtisan *m*
court-martial [kɔːt'mɑːʃəl] **1** *n* conseil *m* de guerre
2 *vt* (*Br* **-ll-**, *Am* **-l-**) **to be court-martialled** passer en cour martiale
cousin ['kʌzən] *n* cousin, -ine *mf*
cove [kəʊv] *n* crique *f*
Coventry ['kɒvəntrɪ] *n Br* **to send sb to C.** *(punish)* mettre qn en quarantaine
cover ['kʌvə(r)] **1** *n (lid)* couvercle *m*; *(of book)* couverture *f*; *(for furniture, typewriter)* housse *f*; *(bedspread)* dessus-de-lit *m inv*; **the covers** *(blankets)* les couvertures *fpl*; **to take c.** se mettre à l'abri; **under c.** *(sheltered)* à l'abri; **under separate c.** *(letter)* sous pli séparé; **under c. of darkness** à la faveur de la nuit; **c. charge** *(in restaurant)* couvert *m*; *Br* **c. note** *(insurance)* certificat *m* provisoire d'assurance

2 vt couvrir (**with/in** de); *(include)* englober; *(treat)* traiter; *(distance)* parcourir; *(event)* *(in newspaper, on TV)* couvrir; *(aim gun at)* tenir en joue; *(insure)* assurer (**against** contre); **to c. one's eyes** se couvrir les yeux; **to c. one's costs** couvrir ses frais; **to c. over** *(floor, saucepan)* recouvrir; **to c. up** recouvrir; *(truth, tracks)* dissimuler; *(scandal)* étouffer

3 vi **to c. (oneself) up** *(wrap up)* se couvrir; **to c. up for sb** cacher la vérité pour protéger qn • **cover-up** n **there was a c.** on a étouffé l'affaire

coverage ['kʌvərɪdʒ] n *(on TV, in newspaper)* couverture f médiatique

coveralls' ['kʌvərɔːlz] npl Am bleu m de travail

covering ['kʌvərɪŋ] n *(wrapping)* enveloppe f; *(layer)* couche f; **c. letter** lettre f jointe

covert ['kəʊvɜːt, 'kʌvət] adj secret, -ète; *(look)* furtif, -ive

covet ['kʌvɪt] vt convoiter • **covetous** adj avide

cow¹ [kaʊ] n vache f; very Fam *(nasty woman)* peau f de vache; **c. elephant** éléphante f • **cowboy** n cow-boy m • **cowshed** n étable f

cow² [kaʊ] vt **to be cowed** *(frightened)* être intimidé (**by** par)

coward ['kaʊəd] n lâche mf • **cowardice** n lâcheté f • **cowardly** adj lâche

cower ['kaʊə(r)] vi *(crouch)* se tapir; *(with fear)* trembler; *(move back)* reculer (par peur)

cowslip ['kaʊslɪp] n *(plant)* coucou m

cox [kɒks] **1** n barreur, -euse mf **2** vt *(boat)* barrer

coy [kɔɪ] (**-er, -est**) adj *(shy)* timide; Pej *(affectedly shy)* (faussement) timide

coyote [kaɪ'əʊtɪ] n coyote m

cozy ['kəʊzɪ] adj Am = **cosy**

CPA [siːpiː'eɪ] *(abbr* **certified public accountant)** n Am expert-comptable m

crab [kræb] n (**a**) *(crustacean)* crabe m (**b**) **c. apple** pomme f sauvage

crabby ['kræbɪ] (**-ier, -iest**) adj *(person)* grincheux, -euse

crack¹ [kræk] **1** n *(split)* fente f; *(in glass, china, bone)* fêlure f; *(in skin)* crevasse f; *(noise)* craquement m; *(of whip)* claquement m; *(blow)* coup m; Fam *(joke)* plaisanterie f (**at** aux dépens de); Fam **to have a c. at doing sth** essayer de faire qch; **at the c. of dawn** au point du jour

2 vt *(glass, ice)* fêler; *(nut)* casser; *(ground, skin)* crevasser; *(whip)* faire claquer; *(problem)* résoudre; *(code)* déchif-

frer; *(safe)* percer; Fam *(joke)* raconter; **it's not as hard as it's cracked up to be** ce n'est pas aussi dur qu'on le dit

3 vi se fêler; *(of skin)* se crevasser; *(of branch, wood)* craquer; Fam **to get cracking** *(get to work)* s'y mettre; *(hurry)* se grouiller; **to c. down on** prendre des mesures énergiques en matière de; Fam **to c. up** *(mentally)* craquer

crack² [kræk] adj *(first-rate)* *(driver, skier)* d'élite; **c. shot** fin tireur m

crack³ [kræk] n *(drug)* crack m

cracked [krækt] adj Fam *(crazy)* cinglé

cracker ['krækə(r)] n (**a**) *(biscuit)* biscuit m salé (**b**) *(firework)* pétard m; **Christmas c.** diablotin m (**c**) Br Fam **she's a c.** *(attractive)* elle est canon • **crackers** adj Fam *(mad)* cinglé

crackle ['krækəl] **1** n *(of twigs)* craquement m; *(of fire)* crépitement m; *(of frying)* grésillement m; *(of radio)* crachotement m

2 vi *(of fire)* crépiter; *(of frying)* grésiller; *(of radio)* crachoter

crackpot ['krækpɒt] n Fam cinglé, -ée mf

cradle ['kreɪdəl] **1** n berceau m **2** vt bercer

craft¹ [krɑːft] **1** n *(skill)* art m; *(job)* métier m

2 vt façonner • **craftsman** (pl **-men**) n artisan m • **craftsmanship** n *(skill)* art m; **a fine piece of c.** une belle pièce

craft² [krɑːft] n *(cunning)* ruse f

craft³ [krɑːft] n inv *(boat)* bateau m

crafty ['krɑːftɪ] (**-ier, -iest**) adj astucieux, -ieuse; Pej rusé

crag [kræg] n rocher m à pic • **craggy** adj *(rock)* à pic; *(face)* anguleux, -euse

cram [kræm] *(pt & pp* **-mm-)** **1** vt **to c. sth into** *(force)* fourrer qch dans; **to c. with** *(fill)* bourrer de

2 vi **to c. into** *(of people)* s'entasser dans; **to c. (for an exam)** bûcher

cramp [kræmp] n *(pain)* crampe f (**in** à)

cramped [kræmpt] adj *(surroundings)* exigu *(f* exiguë); **in c. conditions** à l'étroit; **to be c. for space** être à l'étroit

cranberry ['krænbərɪ] (pl **-ies**) n canneberge f

crane [kreɪn] **1** n *(machine, bird)* grue f **2** vt **to c. one's neck** tendre le cou

crank¹ [kræŋk] **1** n *(handle)* manivelle f **2** vt **to c. (up)** *(vehicle)* faire démarrer à la manivelle

crank² [kræŋk] n Fam *(person)* excentrique mf; *(fanatic)* fanatique mf • **cranky** (**-ier, -iest**) adj Fam excentrique; Am *(bad-tempered)* grincheux, -euse

cranny ['krænɪ] (*pl* **-ies**) *n see* **nook**

craps [kræps] *n Am* **to shoot c.** jouer aux dés

crash [kræʃ] **1** *n (accident)* accident *m*; *(collapse of firm)* faillite *f*; *(noise)* fracas *m*; *(of thunder)* coup *m*; **c. course/diet** cours *m*/régime *m* intensif; **c. barrier** *(on road)* glissière *f* de sécurité; **c. helmet** casque *m*; **c. landing** atterrissage *m* en catastrophe

2 *exclam (of fallen object)* patatras!

3 *vt (car)* avoir un accident avec; **to c. one's car into sth** rentrer dans qch (avec sa voiture)

4 *vi (of car, plane)* s'écraser; **to c. into** rentrer dans; **the cars crashed (into each other)** les voitures se sont percutées ● **crash-'land** *vi* atterrir en catastrophe

crass [kræs] *adj* grossier, -ière; **c. stupidity** immense bêtise *f*; **c. ignorance** ignorance *f* crasse

crate [kreɪt] *n (large)* caisse *f*; *(small)* cageot *m*; *(for bottles)* casier *m*

crater ['kreɪtə(r)] *n* cratère *m*; **(bomb) c.** entonnoir *m*

cravat [krə'væt] *n* foulard *m*

crave [kreɪv] *vi* **to c. for** avoir un besoin terrible de ● **craving** *n* envie *f* (**for** de)

craven ['kreɪvən] *adj Literary (cowardly)* lâche

crawl [krɔːl] **1** *n (swimming stroke)* crawl *m*; **to do the c.** nager le crawl; **to move at a c.** *(in vehicle)* avancer au pas

2 *vi (of snake, animal)* ramper; *(of child)* marcher à quatre pattes; *(of vehicle)* avancer au pas; **to be crawling with** grouiller de

crayfish ['kreɪfɪʃ] *n inv (freshwater)* écrevisse *f*

crayon ['kreɪən] *n (wax)* crayon *m* gras

craze [kreɪz] *n* engouement *m* (**for** pour) ● **crazed** *adj* affolé

crazy ['kreɪzɪ] (**-ier, -iest**) *adj* fou (*f* folle); **to go c.** devenir fou; **to drive sb c.** rendre qn fou; **to be c. about sb/sth** être fou de qn/qch; **to run/work like c.** courir/travailler comme un fou; **c. paving** dallage *m* irrégulier ● **craziness** *n* folie *f*

creak [kriːk] *vi (of hinge)* grincer; *(of floor, timber)* craquer ● **creaky** *adj* grinçant; *(floor)* qui craque

cream [kriːm] **1** *n (of milk, lotion)* crème *f*; *Fig* **the c.** *(the best)* la crème de la crème; **c.(-coloured)** crème *inv*; **c. of tomato soup** crème de tomates; **c. cake** gâteau *m* à la crème; **c. cheese** fromage *m* à tartiner; **c. tea** = thé servi avec des scones, de la crème fouettée et de la confiture

2 *vt (milk)* écrémer; *Fig* **they c. off the best students** ils sélectionnent les meilleurs étudiants ● **creamy** (**-ier, -iest**) *adj* crémeux, -euse

crease [kriːs] **1** *n* pli *m*

2 *vt* froisser

3 *vi* se froisser ● **crease-resistant** *adj* infroissable

create [kriː'eɪt] *vt* créer; **to c. a good impression** faire bonne impression ● **creation** *n* création *f* ● **creator** *n* créateur, -trice *mf*

creative [kriː'eɪtɪv] *adj (person, activity)* créatif, -ive ● **creativeness, crea'tivity** *n* créativité *f*

creature ['kriːtʃə(r)] *n (animal)* bête *f*; *(person)* créature *f*; **one's c. comforts** ses aises *fpl*

crèche [kreʃ] *n Br (nursery)* crèche *f*; *Am (nativity scene)* crèche

credence ['kriːdəns] *n* **to give** *or* **lend c. to** ajouter foi à

credentials [krɪ'denʃəlz] *npl (proof of ability)* références *fpl*; *(identity)* pièce *f* d'identité; *(of diplomat)* lettres *fpl* de créance

credible ['kredɪbəl] *adj* crédible; **it is hardly c. that...** on a peine à croire que... ● **credi'bility** *n* crédibilité *f*

credit ['kredɪt] **1** *n (financial)* crédit *m*; *(merit)* mérite *m*; *(from university)* unité *f* de valeur; **credits** *(of film)* générique *m*; **to buy sth on c.** acheter qch à crédit; **to be in c.** *(of account)* être créditeur; *(of person)* avoir un solde positif; **to give c. to sb** *Fin* faire crédit à qn; *Fig* reconnaître le mérite de qn; **to give c. to sth** ajouter foi à qch; **she's a c. to the school** elle fait honneur à l'école; **to her c., she refused** c'est tout à son honneur d'avoir refusé; **c. balance** solde *m* créditeur; **c. card** carte *f* de crédit; **c. facilities** facilités *fpl* de paiement

2 *vt (of bank)* créditer (**sb with sth** qn de qch); *(believe)* croire; **to c. sb/sth with sth** *(qualities)* attribuer qch à qn/qch ● **creditable** *adj* honorable ● **creditor** *n* créancier, -ière *mf* ● **creditworthy** *adj* solvable

credulous ['kredjʊləs] *adj* crédule

creed [kriːd] *n* credo *m*

creek [kriːk] *n (bay)* crique *f*; *Am (stream)* ruisseau *m*; *Br Fam* **to be up the c. (without a paddle)** être dans le pétrin

creep [kriːp] **1** *n Fam (unpleasant man)* type *m* répugnant; *(obsequious person)* lèche-bottes *mf inv*; *Fam* **it gives me the creeps** ça me fait froid dans le dos

2 (*pt & pp* **crept**) *vi* ramper; *(silently)* se glisser (furtivement); *(slowly)* avancer lentement; **it makes my flesh c.** ça me donne la chair de poule • **creepy** (**-ier**, **-iest**) *adj Fam* sinistre • **creepy-'crawly** (*pl* **-ies**) *n Fam* bestiole *f*

cremate [krɪ'meɪt] *vt* incinérer • **cremation** *n* crémation *f*

crematorium [kremə'tɔːrɪəm] (*pl* **-ia** [-ɪə]) (*Am* **crematory** ['kriːmətɔːrɪ]) *n* crématorium *m*

crêpe [kreɪp] *n (fabric)* crêpe *m*; **c.** (**rubber**) **soles** semelles *fpl* de crêpe; **c. bandage** bande *f* Velpeau®; **c. paper** papier *m* crépon

crept [krept] *pt & pp of* **creep**

crescent ['kresənt] *n (shape)* croissant *m*; *Br Fig (street)* rue *f* en demi-lune

cress [kres] *n* cresson *m*

crest [krest] *n (of wave, mountain, bird)* crête *f*; *(of hill)* sommet *m*; *(on seal, letters)* armoiries *fpl*

Crete [kriːt] *n* la Crète

cretin ['kretɪn] *n Fam* crétin, -ine *mf*

crevasse [krɪ'væs] *n (in ice)* crevasse *f*

crevice ['krevɪs] *n (crack)* fente *f*

crew [kruː] *n (of ship, plane)* équipage *m*; *Fam (gang)* équipe *f*; **c. cut** coupe *f* en brosse • **crew-neck(ed) sweater** *n* pull *m* ras du cou

crib [krɪb] **1** *n* (**a**) *Am (cot)* lit *m* d'enfant; *(cradle)* berceau *m*; *(nativity scene)* crèche *f* (**b**) *Br Fam (list of answers)* antisèche *f*
2 (*pt & pp* **-bb-**) *vti Fam* pomper

crick [krɪk] *n* **c. in the neck** torticolis *m*; **c. in the back** tour *m* de reins

cricket¹ ['krɪkɪt] *n (game)* cricket *m*; *Fig* **that's not c.!** ce n'est pas du jeu!

cricket² ['krɪkɪt] *n (insect)* grillon *m*

crikey ['kraɪkɪ] *exclam Br Fam* zut alors!

crime [kraɪm] *n* crime *m*; *Law* délit *m*; *(criminal practice)* criminalité *f*; **c. wave** vague *f* de criminalité

criminal ['krɪmɪnəl] *n* criminel, -elle *mf*
2 *adj* criminel, -elle; **c. offence** *(minor)* délit *m*; *(serious)* crime *m*; **c. record** casier *m* judiciaire

crimson ['krɪmzən] *adj & n* cramoisi *(m)*

cringe [krɪndʒ] *vi (show fear)* avoir un mouvement de recul; *(be embarrassed)* avoir envie de rentrer sous terre

crinkle ['krɪŋkəl] **1** *n (in paper, fabric)* pli *m*
2 *vt (paper, fabric)* froisser

cripple ['krɪpəl] **1** *n (lame)* estropié, -iée *mf*; *(disabled)* infirme *mf*

2 *vt (disable)* rendre infirme; *Fig (nation, system)* paralyser • **crippled** *adj* infirme; *(ship)* désemparé

crisis ['kraɪsɪs] (*pl* **crises** ['kraɪsiːz]) *n* crise *f*

crisp [krɪsp] **1** (**-er**, **-est**) *adj (biscuit)* croustillant; *(apple, vegetables)* croquant; *(snow)* qui crisse sous les pas; *(air, style)* vif (*f* vive)
2 *npl Br* (**potato**) **crisps** chips *fpl*; **packet of crisps** sachet *m* de chips • **crispbread** *n* pain *m* suédois

criss-cross ['krɪskrɒs] **1** *adj (lines)* entre-croisé; *(muddled)* enchevêtré
2 *vi* s'entrecroiser
3 *vt* sillonner (en tous sens)

criterion [kraɪ'tɪərɪən] (*pl* **-ia** [-ɪə]) *n* critère *m*

critic ['krɪtɪk] *n (reviewer)* critique *mf*; *(opponent)* détracteur, -trice *mf* • **critical** *adj* critique • **critically** *adv* (*examine*) en critique; *(harshly)* sévèrement; **to be c. ill** être dans un état critique • **criticism** [-sɪzəm] *n* critique *f* • **criticize** [-saɪz] *vti* critiquer • **critique** [krɪ'tiːk] *n (essay)* critique *f*

croak [krəʊk] **1** *n* croassement *m*
2 *vi (of frog)* croasser; *(of person)* parler d'une voix rauque

Croatia [krəʊ'eɪʃə] *n* la Croatie

crochet ['krəʊʃeɪ] **1** *n* (travail *m* au) crochet *m*; **c. hook** crochet
2 *vt* faire au crochet
3 *vi* faire du crochet

crock [krɒk] *n Fam* **a c., an old c.** *(person)* un croulant; *(car)* un tacot

crockery ['krɒkərɪ] *n* vaisselle *f*

crocodile ['krɒkədaɪl] *n* crocodile *m*

crocus ['krəʊkəs] (*pl* **-uses** [-əsɪz]) *n* crocus *m*

croft [krɒft] *n Br* petite ferme *f*

crony ['krəʊnɪ] (*pl* **-ies**) *n Fam Pej* copain *m*, copine *f*

crook [krʊk] *n* (**a**) *(thief)* escroc *m* (**b**) *(shepherd's stick)* houlette *f*

crooked ['krʊkɪd] *adj (hat, picture)* de travers; *(nose)* tordu; *(smile)* en coin; *(deal, person)* malhonnête

croon [kruːn] *vti* chantonner

crop [krɒp] **1** *n (harvest)* récolte *f*; *(produce)* culture *f*; *Fig (of questions)* série *f*; *(of people)* groupe *m*; **c. of hair** chevelure *f*
2 (*pt & pp* **-pp-**) *vt (hair)* couper ras
3 *vi* **to c. up** *(of issue)* survenir; *(of opportunity)* se présenter; *(of name)* être mentionné • **cropper** *n Br Fam* **to come a c.** se ramasser une pelle

croquet ['krəʊkeɪ] *n (game)* croquet *m*
croquette [krəʊ'ket] *n Culin* croquette *f*
cross¹ [krɒs] **1** *n* croix *f*; **a c. between** *(animal)* un croisement entre; *Fig* **it's a c. between a car and a van** c'est un compromis entre une voiture et une camionnette; **c. street** rue *f* transversale
2 *vt (street, room)* traverser; *(barrier, threshold)* franchir; *(legs, animals)* croiser; *(oppose)* contrecarrer; *(cheque)* barrer; **to c. off** *or* **out** *(word, name)* rayer; **to c. over** *(road)* traverser; **it never crossed my mind that** il ne m'est pas venu à l'esprit que
3 *vi (of paths)* se croiser; **to c. over** traverser ● **crossbow** *n* arbalète *f* ● **'cross-'check** *vt* vérifier (par recoupement) ● **'cross-'country** *adj (walk)* à travers champs; **c. race** cross *m*; **c. runner** coureur, -euse *mf* de fond ● **'cross-exami'na-tion** *n Law* contre-interrogatoire *m* ● **'cross-ex'amine** *vt Law* soumettre à un contre-interrogatoire ● **'cross-'eyed** *adj* qui louche ● **crossfire** *n* feux *mpl* croisés ● **cross-legged** [-'leg(ɪ)d] *adj & adv* **to sit c.** être assis en tailleur ● **'cross-'purposes** *npl* **to be at c.** ne pas parler de la même chose ● **'cross-'reference** *n* renvoi *m* ● **crossroads** *n* carrefour *m* ● **'cross-'section** *n* coupe *f* transversale; *(sample)* échantillon *m* représentatif ● **crosswalk** *n Am* passage *m* clouté ● **crosswind** *n* vent *m* de travers ● **crossword (puzzle)** *n* mots *mpl* croisés
cross² [krɒs] *adj (angry)* fâché (**with** contre); **to get c.** se fâcher (**with** contre)
crossing ['krɒsɪŋ] *n (of sea, river)* traversée *f*; *Br* **(pedestrian) c.** passage *m* clouté
crotch [krɒtʃ] *n (of garment, person)* entrejambe *m*
crotchet ['krɒtʃɪt] *n Mus* noire *f*
crotchety ['krɒtʃɪtɪ] *adj Fam* grognon, -onne
crouch [kraʊtʃ] *vi* **to c. (down)** *(of person)* s'accroupir; *(of animal)* se tapir
crow [krəʊ] **1** *n* corbeau *m*; **as the c. flies** à vol d'oiseau; **c.'s nest** *(on ship)* nid-de-pie *m*
2 *vi (of cock)* chanter; *Fig (boast)* se vanter (**about** de)
crowbar ['krəʊbɑː(r)] *n* levier *m*
crowd [kraʊd] **1** *n* foule *f*; *Fam (group of people)* bande *f*; *Fam (of things)* masse *f*; **there was quite a c.** il y avait beaucoup de monde; *Fig* **to follow the c.** suivre le mouvement
2 *vt (fill)* entasser; *(street)* envahir; **to c. people/objects into** entasser des gens/

des objets dans; *Fam* **don't c. me!** ne me bouscule pas!
3 *vi* **to c. into** *(of people)* s'entasser dans; **to c. round sb/sth** se presser autour de qn/qch; **to c. together** se serrer ● **crowded** *adj* plein (**with** de); *(train, room)* bondé; *(city)* surpeuplé; **it's very c.** il y a beaucoup de monde
crown [kraʊn] **1** *n (of king)* couronne *f*; *(of head, hill)* sommet *m*; **the C.** *(monarchy)* la Couronne; *Br Law* **c. court** ≃ cour *f* d'assises; *Br* **c. jewels** joyaux *mpl* de la Couronne; **c. prince** prince *m* héritier
2 *vt* couronner ● **crowning** *adj (glory)* suprême; **c. achievement** *(of career)* couronnement *m*
crucial ['kruːʃəl] *adj* crucial
crucify ['kruːsɪfaɪ] *(pt & pp -ied)* *vt* crucifier ● **crucifix** [-fɪks] *n* crucifix *m* ● **cruci-fixion** [-'fɪkʃən] *n* crucifixion *f*
crude [kruːd] **(-er, -est)** *adj (manners, person, language)* grossier, -ière; *(painting, work)* rudimentaire; *(fact)* brut; **c. oil** pétrole *m* brut ● **crudely** *adv (say, order)* crûment; *(build, paint)* grossièrement ● **crudeness** *n (of manners)* grossièreté *f*; *(of painting)* état *m* rudimentaire
cruel [krʊəl] **(crueller, cruellest)** *adj* cruel *(f* cruelle*)* ● **cruelty** *n* cruauté *f*; **an act of c.** une cruauté
cruise [kruːz] **1** *n* croisière *f*; **to go on a c.** partir en croisière; *Mil* **c. missile** missile *m* de croisière
2 *vi (of ship)* croiser; *(of vehicle)* rouler; *(of plane)* voler; *(of taxi)* marauder; *(of tourists)* faire une croisière; **cruising speed** *(of ship, plane)* vitesse *f* de croisière ● **cruiser** *n (ship)* croiseur *m*
crumb [krʌm] *n* miette *f*; *Fig (of comfort)* brin *m*
crumble ['krʌmbəl] **1** *n* crumble *m (dessert aux fruits recouvert de pâte sablée)*
2 *vt (bread)* émietter
3 *vi (of bread)* s'émietter; *(collapse) (of resistance)* s'effondrer; **to c. (away)** *(in small pieces)* s'effriter; *(become ruined) (of building)* tomber en ruine ● **crumbly** *adj (pastry)* friable
crummy ['krʌmɪ] **(-ier, -iest)** *adj Fam* minable
crumpet ['krʌmpɪt] *n Br* = petite crêpe grillée servie beurrée
crumple ['krʌmpəl] **1** *vt* froisser
2 *vi* se froisser
crunch [krʌntʃ] **1** *n Fam* **when it comes to the c.** au moment crucial
2 *vt (food)* croquer

3 *vi* *(of snow)* crisser •**crunchy** (**-ier,** **-iest**) *adj* *(apple, vegetables)* croquant; *(bread)* croustillant

crusade [kruːˈseɪd] **1** *n* Hist & Fig croisade f **2** *vi* faire une croisade •**crusader** *n* Hist croisé *m*; Fig militant, -ante *mf*

crush [krʌʃ] **1** *n* *(crowd)* foule f; *(confusion)* bousculade f; Fam **to have a c. on sb** en pincer pour qn **2** *vt* écraser; *(hope)* détruire; *(clothes)* froisser; *(cram)* entasser (**into** dans) •**crushing** *adj* *(defeat)* écrasant

crust [krʌst] *n* croûte f • **crusty** (**-ier, -iest**) *n* *(bread)* croustillant

crutch [krʌtʃ] *n* (**a**) *(of invalid)* béquille f (**b**) *(crotch)* entrejambe *m*

crux [krʌks] *n* **the c. of the matter/problem** le nœud de l'affaire/du problème

cry [kraɪ] **1** (*pl* **cries**) *n* *(shout)* cri *m*; Fam **to have a good c.** pleurer un bon coup **2** (*pt & pp* **cried**) *vt* **to c.** (**out**) *(shout)* crier; **to c. one's eyes out** pleurer toutes les larmes de son corps **3** *vi* *(weep)* pleurer; **to c.** (**out**) pousser un cri; **to c. for help** appeler au secours; **to c. out for sth** *(of person)* demander qch à grands cris; **to be crying out for sth** *(of thing)* avoir grand besoin de qch; **to c. off** *(from invitation)* se décommander; **to c. over sb/sth** pleurer qn/qch •**crying 1** *adj* **a c. need of sth** un besoin urgent de qch; **a c. shame** un scandale **2** *n* *(shouts)* cris *mpl*; *(weeping)* pleurs *mpl*

crypt [krɪpt] *n* crypte f

cryptic [ˈkrɪptɪk] *adj* énigmatique

crystal [ˈkrɪstəl] *n* cristal *m*; **c. ball** boule f de cristal; **c. vase** vase *m* en cristal • **'crystal-'clear** *adj* *(water, sound)* cristallin; *(explanation)* clair comme de l'eau de roche

crystallize [ˈkrɪstəlaɪz] **1** *vt* cristalliser **2** *vi* (se) cristalliser

cub [kʌb] *n* (**a**) *(of animal)* petit *m* (**b**) *(scout)* louveteau *m*

Cuba [ˈkjuːbə] *n* Cuba f •**Cuban 1** *adj* cubain **2** *n* Cubain, -aine *mf*

cubbyhole [ˈkʌbɪhəʊl] *n* cagibi *m*

cube [kjuːb] *n* cube *m*; *(of meat, vegetables)* dé *m*; *(of sugar)* morceau *m* •**cubic** *adj* *(shape)* cubique; **c. capacity** volume *m*; *(of engine)* cylindrée f; **c. metre** mètre *m* cube

cubicle [ˈkjuːbɪkəl] *n* *(for changing clothes)* cabine f; *(in hospital, dormitory)* box *m*

cuckoo [Br ˈkʊkuː, Am ˈkuːkuː] (*pl* **-oos**) **1** *n* *(bird)* coucou *m*; **c. clock** coucou **2** *adj* Fam *(mad)* cinglé

cucumber [ˈkjuːkʌmbə(r)] *n* concombre *m*

cuddle [ˈkʌdəl] **1** *n* câlin *m*; **to give sb a c.** faire un câlin à qn **2** *vt* *(hug)* serrer dans ses bras; *(caress)* câliner **3** *vi* *(of lovers)* se faire des câlins; **to** (**kiss and**) **c.** s'embrasser; **to c. up to sb** *(huddle)* se blottir contre qn •**cuddly** (**-ier, -iest**) *adj* *(person)* mignon, -onne à croquer; **c. toy** peluche f

cudgel [ˈkʌdʒəl] *n* gourdin *m*

cue¹ [kjuː] *n* *(in theatre)* réplique f; *(signal)* signal *m*

cue² [kjuː] *n* *(billiard)* **c.** queue f de billard

cuff [kʌf] **1** *n* *(of shirt)* poignet *m*; Am *(of trousers)* revers *m*; **off the c.** *(remark)* impromptu; **c. link** bouton *m* de manchette **2** *vt* *(strike)* gifler

cul-de-sac [ˈkʌldəsæk] *n* Br impasse f

culinary [ˈkʌlɪnərɪ] *adj* culinaire

cull [kʌl] *vt* choisir (**from** dans); *(animals)* abattre sélectivement

culminate [ˈkʌlmɪneɪt] *vi* **to c. in** aboutir à •**culmination** [-ˈneɪʃən] *n* point *m* culminant

culprit [ˈkʌlprɪt] *n* coupable *mf*

cult [kʌlt] *n* culte *m*; **c. film** film *m* culte

cultivate [ˈkʌltɪveɪt] *vt* *(land, mind)* cultiver •**cultivated** *adj* cultivé •**cultivation** [-ˈveɪʃən] *n* culture f

culture [ˈkʌltʃə(r)] *n* culture f •**cultural** *adj* culturel, -elle •**cultured** *adj* *(person, mind)* cultivé

cumbersome [ˈkʌmbəsəm] *adj* encombrant

cumulative [ˈkjuːmjʊlətɪv] *adj* cumulatif, -ive; **c. effect** *(long-term)* effet *m* à long terme

cunning [ˈkʌnɪŋ] **1** *adj* *(ingenious)* astucieux, -ieuse; *(devious)* rusé **2** *n* astuce f; Pej ruse f •**cunningly** *adv* avec astuce; Pej avec ruse

cup [kʌp] *n* tasse f; *(goblet, prize)* coupe f; Fam **it's not my c. of tea** ce n'est pas mon truc; Football **c. final** finale f de la coupe •**cupful** *n* tasse f

cupboard [ˈkʌbəd] *n* Br armoire f; *(built into wall)* placard *m*

cup-tie [ˈkʌptaɪ] *n* Football match *m* éliminatoire

curate [ˈkjʊərɪt] *n* vicaire *m*

curator [kjʊəˈreɪtə(r)] *n* *(of museum)* conservateur *m*

curb [kɜːb] **1** *n* (**a**) *(limit)* **to put a c. on** mettre un frein à (**b**) Am *(kerb)* bord *m* du trottoir

2 *vt (feelings)* refréner; *(ambitions)* modérer; *(expenses)* réduire

curd [kɜːd] *n* **curd(s)** lait *m* caillé; **c. cheese** fromage *m* blanc battu

curdle [ˈkɜːdəl] **1** *vt* cailler
2 *vi* se cailler

cure [ˈkjʊə(r)] **1** *n* remède *m* (**for** contre)
2 *vt* (**a**) *(person, illness)* guérir; *Fig (poverty)* éliminer; **to c. sb of** guérir qn de (**b**) *(meat, fish) (smoke)* fumer; *(salt)* saler; *(dry)* sécher • **curable** *adj* guérissable

curfew [ˈkɜːfjuː] *n* couvre-feu *m*

curious [ˈkjʊərɪəs] *adj (odd)* curieux, -ieuse; *(inquisitive)* curieux, -ieuse (**about** de); **to be c. to know/see** être curieux de savoir/voir • **curiously** *adv (oddly)* curieusement; *(inquisitively)* avec curiosité

curiosity [kjʊərɪˈɒsɪtɪ] *(pl* **-ies)** *n* curiosité *f* (**about** de)

curl [kɜːl] **1** *n (in hair)* boucle *f*; *Fig (of smoke)* spirale *f*
2 *vti (hair)* boucler; *(with small, tight curls)* friser
3 *vi* **to c. up** *(shrivel)* se racornir; **to c. (oneself) up** *(into a ball)* se pelotonner • **curler** *n* bigoudi *m* • **curly** (**-ier, -iest**) *adj (hair)* bouclé; *(having many tight curls)* frisé

currant [ˈkʌrənt] *n (dried grape)* raisin *m* de Corinthe; *(fruit)* groseille *f*

currency [ˈkʌrənsɪ] *(pl* **-ies)** *n* (**a**) *(money)* monnaie *f*; (**foreign**) **c.** devises *fpl* (étrangères) (**b**) **to gain c.** *(of ideas)* se répandre

current [ˈkʌrənt] **1** *adj (fashion, trend)* actuel, -uelle; *(opinion, use, phrase)* courant; *(year, month)* en cours; **c. account** *(in bank)* compte *m* courant; **c. affairs** questions *fpl* d'actualité; **c. events** actualité *f*; **the c. issue** *(of magazine)* le dernier numéro
2 *n (of river, air, electricity)* courant *m* • **currently** *adv* actuellement

curriculum [kəˈrɪkjʊləm] *(pl* **-la** [-lə]) *n* programme *m* scolaire; *Br* **c. vitae** curriculum vitae *m inv*

curry [ˈkʌrɪ] **1** *(pl* **-ies)** *n (dish)* curry *m*, cari *m*
2 *(pt & pp* **-ied)** *vt* **to c. favour with sb** s'insinuer dans les bonnes grâces de qn

curse [kɜːs] **1** *n* malédiction *f*; *(swearword)* juron *m*; *(scourge)* fléau *m*
2 *vt* maudire; **cursed with sth** affligé de qch
3 *vi (swear)* jurer

cursor [ˈkɜːsə(r)] *n Comptr* curseur *m*

cursory [ˈkɜːsərɪ] *adj* superficiel, -ielle

curt [kɜːt] *adj* brusque • **curtly** *adv* d'un ton brusque • **curtness** *n* brusquerie *f*

curtail [kɜːˈteɪl] *vt (visit)* écourter; *(expenses)* réduire • **curtailment** *n* raccourcissement *m*; *(of expenses)* réduction *f*

curtain [ˈkɜːtən] *n* rideau *m*; **to draw the curtains** *(close)* tirer les rideaux; **c. call** *(in theatre)* rappel *m*

curts(e)y [ˈkɜːtsɪ] **1** *(pl* **-ies** *or* **-eys**) *n* révérence *f*
2 *(pt & pp* **-ied)** *vi* faire une révérence (**to** à)

curve [kɜːv] **1** *n* courbe *f*; *(in road)* virage *m*
2 *vt* courber
3 *vi* se courber; *(of road)* faire une courbe • **curved** *adj (line)* courbe

cushion [ˈkʊʃən] **1** *n* coussin *m*
2 *vt (shock)* amortir • **cushioned** *adj (seat)* rembourré

cushy [ˈkʊʃɪ] (**-ier, -iest**) *adj Fam (job, life)* pépère

custard [ˈkʌstəd] *n* crème *f* anglaise; *(when set)* crème renversée

custodian [kʌˈstəʊdɪən] *n* gardien, -ienne *mf*

custody [ˈkʌstədɪ] *n (of child, important papers)* garde *f*; **in the c. of sb** sous la garde de qn; **to take sb into c.** placer qn en garde à vue • **custodial** [kʌˈstəʊdɪəl] *adj Law* **c. sentence** peine *f* de prison

custom [ˈkʌstəm] *n* coutume *f*; *(of individual)* habitude *f*; *(customers)* clientèle *f* • **'custom-'built, customized** *adj (car)* *(fait)* sur commande • **'custom-'made** *adj (shirt)* *(fait)* sur mesure

customary [ˈkʌstəmərɪ] *adj* habituel, -uelle; **it is c. to...** il est d'usage de...

customer [ˈkʌstəmə(r)] *n* client, -iente *mf*; *Pej (individual)* individu *m*

customs [ˈkʌstəmz] *npl* (**the**) **c.** la douane; **c. duties** droits *mpl* de douane; **c. officer** douanier *m*; **c. union** union *f* douanière

cut [kʌt] **1** *n (mark)* coupure *f*; *(stroke)* coup *m*; *(of clothes, hair)* coupe *f*; *(in salary, prices)* réduction *f*; *(of meat)* morceau *m*
2 *(pt & pp* **cut,** *pres p* **cutting**) *vt* couper; *(meat, chicken)* découper; *(glass, diamond, tree)* tailler; *(hay)* faucher; *(salary, prices, profits)* réduire; **to c. sb's hair** couper les cheveux à qn; **to have one's hair c.** se faire couper les cheveux; **to c. a tooth** *(of child)* faire une dent; **to c. a corner** *(in vehicle)* prendre un virage à la corde; **to c. sth open** ouvrir qch avec un couteau/des ciseaux/*etc*; **to c. sth short**

(visit) écourter qch; **to c. a long story short...** enfin, bref...

3 *vi (of knife, scissors)* couper; **this cloth cuts easily** ce tissu se coupe facilement • **cutback** *n* réduction *f* • **cutout** *n (picture)* découpage *m; (electrical)* coupe-circuit *m inv*

▸ **cut away** *vt sep (remove)* enlever ▸ **cut back** *vt sep & vi* réduire ▸ **cut down 1** *vt sep* (**a**) *(tree)* abattre (**b**) *(reduce)* réduire **2** *vi* réduire ▸ **cut in** *vi (interrupt)* interrompre; *(in vehicle)* faire une queue de poisson (**on sb** à qn) ▸ **cut off** *vt sep (piece, limb, hair)* couper; *(isolate)* isoler ▸ **cut out 1** *vt sep (article)* découper; *(garment)* tailler; *(remove)* enlever; *(eliminate)* supprimer; **to c. out drinking** *(stop)* s'arrêter de boire; *Fam* **c. it out!** ça suffit!; **c. out to be a doctor** fait pour être médecin **2** *vi (of car engine)* caler ▸ **cut up** *vt sep* couper en morceaux; *(meat, chicken)* découper; **to be very c. up about sth** *(upset)* être complètement chamboulé par qch

cute [kjuːt] (**-er, -est**) *adj Fam (pretty)* mignon, -onne; *(shrewd)* astucieux, -ieuse

cuticle ['kjuːtɪkəl] *n* cuticule *f*

cutlery ['kʌtlərɪ] *n* couverts *mpl*

cutlet ['kʌtlɪt] *n* côtelette *f*

cut-price [kʌt'praɪs] *adj* à prix réduit

cutthroat ['kʌtθrəʊt] **1** *n* assassin *m* **2** *adj (competition)* impitoyable

cutting ['kʌtɪŋ] **1** *n* coupe *f; (of glass, diamond)* taille *f; (from newspaper)* coupure *f; (plant)* bouture *f; (for train)* voie *f* en déblai

2 *adj (wind, remark)* cinglant; **c. edge** tranchant *m*

CV [siː'viː] *(abbr* **curriculum vitae**) *n Br* CV *m*

cwt *abbr* = **hundredweight**

cyanide ['saɪənaɪd] *n* cyanure *m*

cybercafé [saɪbə'kæfeɪ] *n* cybercafé *m*

cybernetics [saɪbə'netɪks] *n Comptr* cybernétique *f*

cyberspace ['saɪbəspeɪs] *n Comptr* cyberespace *m*

cycle¹ ['saɪkəl] **1** *n (bicycle)* bicyclette *f;* **c. lane** voie *f* réservée aux vélos; **c. path** piste *f* cyclable; **c. race** course *f* cycliste **2** *vi* aller à bicyclette (**to** à); *(as activity)* faire de la bicyclette • **cycling** *n* cyclisme *m* • **cyclist** *n* cycliste *mf*

cycle² ['saɪkəl] *n (series, period)* cycle *m* • **cyclical** ['sɪklɪkəl] *adj* cyclique

cyclone ['saɪkləʊn] *n* cyclone *m*

cylinder ['sɪlɪndə(r)] *n* cylindre *m* • **cylindrical** [sɪ'lɪndrɪkəl] *adj* cylindrique

cymbal ['sɪmbəl] *n* cymbale *f*

cynic ['sɪnɪk] *n* cynique *mf* • **cynical** *adj* cynique • **cynicism** [-sɪzm] *n* cynisme *m*

cypress ['saɪprəs] *n* cyprès *m*

Cyprus ['saɪprəs] *n* Chypre *f* • **Cypriot** ['sɪprɪət] **1** *adj* cypriote **2** *n* Cypriote *mf*

cyst [sɪst] *n Med* kyste *m*

cystitis [sɪ'staɪtəs] *n Med* cystite *f*

czar [zɑː(r)] *n* tsar *m*

Czech [tʃek] **1** *adj* tchèque; **the C. Republic** la République tchèque **2** *n (person)* Tchèque *mf; (language)* tchèque *m* • **Czechoslovakia** [tʃekəslə'vækɪə] *n Formerly* Tchécoslovaquie *f*

D

D, d [diː] *n* D, d *m inv* • **D.-day** *n* le jour J
dab [dæb] **1** *n* **a**. **of** un petit peu de
2 (*pt & pp* **-bb-**) *vt (wound, brow)* tamponner; **to d. sth on sth** appliquer qch (à petits coups) sur qch
dabble ['dæbəl] *vi* **to d. in politics/journalism** faire vaguement de la politique/du journalisme
dad [dæd] *n Fam* papa *m* • **daddy** (*pl* **-ies**) *n Fam* papa *m*; *Br* **d. longlegs** *(cranefly)* tipule *f*; *Am (spider)* faucheur *m*
daffodil ['dæfədɪl] *n* jonquille *f*
daft [dɑːft] (**-er, -est**) *adj Fam* bête
dagger ['dægə(r)] *n* dague *f*; **at daggers drawn** à couteaux tirés (**with** avec)
dahlia ['deɪlɪə] *n* dahlia *m*
daily ['deɪlɪ] **1** *adj* quotidien, -ienne; *(wage)* journalier, -ière; *Br* **d. help** *(cleaning woman)* femme *f* de ménage; **d. paper** quotidien *m*
2 *adv* chaque jour, quotidiennement; **twice d.** deux fois par jour
3 (*pl* **-ies**) *n* quotidien *m*
dainty ['deɪntɪ] (**-ier, -iest**) *adj* délicat
dairy ['deərɪ] **1** (*pl* **-ies**) *n (factory)* laiterie *f*; *(shop)* crémerie *f*
2 *adj* laitier, -ière; **d. farm/cow** ferme *f*/vache *f* laitière; **d. product** produit *m* laitier; **d. produce** produits *mpl* laitiers
daisy ['deɪzɪ] (*pl* **-ies**) *n* pâquerette *f*; *(bigger)* marguerite *f*; *Fam* **to push up the daisies** manger les pissenlits par la racine
dale [deɪl] *n Literary* vallée *f*
dally ['dælɪ] (*pt & pp* **-ied**) *vi* lambiner
dam [dæm] **1** *n (wall)* barrage *m*
2 (*pt & pp* **-mm-**) *vt (river)* construire un barrage sur
damage ['dæmɪdʒ] **1** *n* dégâts *mpl*; *(harm)* préjudice *m*; **damages** *(in court)* dommages-intérêts *mpl*
2 *vt (object)* endommager, abîmer; *(health)* nuire à; *(eyesight)* abîmer; *(plans, reputation)* compromettre • **damaging** *adj (harmful)* préjudiciable (**to** à)
damn [dæm] **1** *n Fam* **he doesn't care** *or* **give a d.** il s'en fiche pas mal
2 *adj Fam (awful)* fichu; **that d. car** cette fichue bagnole

3 *adv Fam (very)* vachement; *Br* **d. all** que dalle
4 *vt (condemn, doom)* condamner; *(of God)* damner; *(curse)* maudire; *Fam* **d. him!** qu'il aille se faire voir!
5 *exclam Fam* **d. (it)!** mince! • **damned 1** *adj* (**a**) *(soul)* damné (**b**) *Fam (awful)* fichu **2** *adv Fam* vachement • **damning** *adj (evidence)* accablant
damnation [dæm'neɪʃən] **1** *n* damnation *f*
2 *exclam Fam* bon sang!
damp [dæmp] **1** (**-er, -est**) *adj* humide; *(skin)* moite
2 *n* humidité *f* • **damp(en)** *vt* humecter; **to d. (down)** *(enthusiasm, zeal)* refroidir; *(ambition)* freiner; **to d. sb's spirits** décourager qn • **dampness** *n* humidité *f*
damper ['dæmpə(r)] *n* **to put a d. on** jeter un froid sur
damson ['dæmzən] *n* prune *f* de Damas
dance [dɑːns] **1** *n* danse *f*; *(social event)* bal *m* (*pl* bals); **d. floor** piste *f* de danse; **d. hall** dancing *m*
2 *vt (waltz, tango)* danser
3 *vi* danser; **to d. for joy** sauter de joie • **dancer** *n* danseur, -euse *mf* • **dancing** *n* danse *f*; **d. partner** cavalier, -ière *mf*
dandelion ['dændɪlaɪən] *n* pissenlit *m*
dandruff ['dændrʌf] *n* pellicules *fpl*
dandy ['dændɪ] *adj Am Fam* super *inv*
Dane [deɪn] *n* Danois, -oise *mf*
danger ['deɪndʒə(r)] *n* danger *m* (**to** pour); **in d.** en danger; **out of d.** hors de danger; **in d. of** *(threatened by)* menacé de; **to be in d. of doing sth** risquer de faire qch; **on the d. list** *(hospital patient)* dans un état critique; **'d. of fire'** 'risque d'incendie'; **d. zone** zone *f* dangereuse • **dangerous** *adj* dangereux, -euse (**to** pour) • **dangerously** *adv* dangereusement; **d. ill** gravement malade
dangle ['dæŋgəl] **1** *vt* balancer; *Fig* **to d. sth in front of sb** faire miroiter qch à qn
2 *vi (hang)* pendre; *(swing)* se balancer
Danish ['deɪnɪʃ] **1** *adj* danois
2 *n (language)* danois *m*
dank [dæŋk] (**-er, -est**) *adj* humide et froid

dapper ['dæpə(r)] *adj* soigné
dappled ['dæpəld] *adj* tacheté; *(horse)* pommelé
dare [deə(r)] **1** *n* défi *m*; **to do sth for a d.** faire qch par défi
2 *vt* **to d. (to) do sth** oser faire qch; **he doesn't d. (to) go** il n'ose pas y aller; **if you d. (to)** si tu l'oses; **I d. say he tried** il a essayé, c'est bien possible; **to d. sb to do sth** défier qn de faire qch
daredevil ['deədevəl] *n* casse-cou *mf inv*
daring ['deərɪŋ] **1** *adj* audacieux, -ieuse
2 *n* audace *f*
dark [dɑːk] **1** (-er, -est) *adj (room, night)* & *Fig* sombre; *(colour, skin, hair, eyes)* foncé; **it's d.** il fait nuit à six heures; **d. glasses** lunettes *fpl* noires
2 *n* obscurité *f*; **after d.** une fois la nuit tombée; *Fig* **to keep sb in the d.** laisser qn dans l'ignorance (**about** de) •**dark-'haired** *adj* aux cheveux bruns •**dark-'skinned** *adj (person)* à peau brune
darken ['dɑːkən] **1** *vt* assombrir; *(colour)* foncer
2 *vi* s'assombrir; *(of colour)* foncer
darkness ['dɑːknəs] *n* obscurité *f*
darkroom ['dɑːkruːm] *n (for photography)* chambre *f* noire
darling ['dɑːlɪŋ] **1** *adj* chéri; *Fam (delightful)* adorable
2 *n (favourite)* chouchou, -oute *mf*; **(my) d.** (mon) chéri/(ma) chérie; **be a d.!** sois un ange!
darn [dɑːn] **1** *vt (mend)* repriser
2 *exclam* **d. it!** bon sang! •**darning** **1** *n* reprise *f* **2** *adj (needle, wool)* à repriser
dart [dɑːt] **1** *n (in game)* fléchette *f*; **darts** *(game)* fléchettes *fpl*; **to make a d.** se précipiter (**for** vers)
2 *vi (dash)* se précipiter (**for** vers) •**dartboard** *n* cible *f (du jeu de fléchettes)*
dash [dæʃ] **1** *n* (**a**) *(run, rush)* ruée *f*; **to make a d. for sth** se ruer vers qch (**b**) **a d. of sth** un petit peu de qch; **a d. of milk** une goutte de lait (**c**) *(handwritten stroke)* trait *m*; *(punctuation sign)* tiret *m*
2 *vt (throw)* jeter; *Fig (destroy) (hopes)* briser; *Br Fam* **d. (it)!** zut!; **to d. off** *(letter)* écrire en vitesse
3 *vi* se précipiter; *(of waves)* se briser (**against** contre); **to d. in/out** entrer/sortir en vitesse; **to d. off** *or* **away** filer
dashboard ['dæʃbɔːd] *n (of vehicle)* tableau *m* de bord
dashing ['dæʃɪŋ] *adj (person)* fringant
data ['deɪtə] *npl* informations *fpl*; *Comptr* données *fpl*; **d. bank/base** banque *f*/base

f de données; **d. capture** saisie *f* de données; **d. processing** informatique *f*
date¹ [deɪt] **1** *n (day)* date *f*; *Fam (meeting)* rendez-vous *m inv*; *Fam (person)* ami, -ie *mf*; **d. of birth** date de naissance; **up to d.** *(in fashion)* à la mode; *(information)* à jour; *(well-informed)* au courant (**on** de); **out of d.** *(old-fashioned)* démodé; *(expired)* périmé; **to d.** à ce jour; **d. stamp** *(object)* tampon *m* dateur; *(mark)* cachet *m*
2 *vt (letter)* dater; *Fam (girl, boy)* sortir avec
3 *vi (go out of fashion)* dater; **to d. back to, to d. from** dater de
date² [deɪt] *n (fruit)* datte *f*
datebook ['deɪtbʊk] *n Am* agenda *m*
dated ['deɪtɪd] *adj* démodé
daub [dɔːb] *vt* barbouiller (**with** de)
daughter ['dɔːtə(r)] *n* fille *f* •**daughter-in-law** *(pl* **daughters-in-law**) belle-fille *f*
daunt [dɔːnt] *vt* intimider
dawdle ['dɔːdəl] *vi* traînasser
dawn [dɔːn] **1** *n* aube *f*; **at d.** à l'aube
2 *vi (of day)* se lever; *(of new era, idea)* naître; **it dawned upon him that...** il s'est rendu compte que...
day [deɪ] *n (period of daylight, 24 hours)* jour *m*; *(referring to duration)* journée *f*; **all d. (long)** toute la journée; **what d. is it?** quel jour sommes-nous?; **the following** *or* **next d.** le lendemain; **the d. before** la veille; **the d. before yesterday** *or* **before last** avant-hier; **the d. after tomorrow** après-demain; **to the d.** jour pour jour; **in my days** de mon temps; **in those days** en ce temps-là; **these days** de nos jours; *Br* **d. boarder** demi-pensionnaire *mf*; *Br* **d. nursery** crèche *f*; *Br* **d. return** *(on train)* aller et retour *m* (valable une journée); *Br* **d. tripper** excursionniste *mf* •**daybreak** ['deɪbreɪk] *n* point *m* du jour •**daydream 1** *n* rêverie *f* **2** *vi* rêvasser •**daylight** *n* (lumière *f* du) jour *m*; *(dawn)* point *m* du jour; **it's d.** il fait jour •**daytime** *n* journée *f*, jour *m* •**'day-to-'day** *adj* quotidien, -ienne; **on a d. basis** au jour le jour
daze [deɪz] **1** *n* **in a d.** étourdi; *(because of drugs)* hébété; *(astonished)* ahuri
2 *vt (by blow)* étourdir; *(of drug)* hébéter
dazzle ['dæzəl] *vt* éblouir
deacon ['diːkən] *n* diacre *m*
dead [ded] **1** *adj* mort; *(numb) (limb)* engourdi; *(party)* mortel, -elle; **the phone's d.** il n'y a pas de tonalité; **in (the) d. centre** au beau milieu; **d. end** *(street)* & *Fig* impasse *f*; **a d.-end job** un travail sans avenir; *Fam* **to be a d. loss** *(of person)* être

bon (f bonne) à rien; *Fam* **it's a d. loss** ça ne vaut rien; **the D. Sea** la mer Morte; **d. silence** silence *m* de mort; **a d. stop** un arrêt complet

2 *npl* **the d.** les morts *mpl*; **in the d. of night/winter** au cœur de la nuit/l'hiver

3 *adv* *(completely)* totalement; *(very)* très; *Br Fam* **d. beat** éreinté; *Fam* **d. drunk** ivre mort; **'d. slow'** 'roulez au pas'; **to stop d.** s'arrêter net • **deadbeat** *n Am Fam (sponger)* parasite *m* • **deadline** *n* date *f* limite; *(hour)* heure *f* limite • **deadlock** *n Fig* impasse *f* • **deadpan** *adj (face)* figé

deaden ['dedən] *vt (shock)* amortir; *(pain)* calmer; *(feeling)* émousser

deadly ['dedlɪ] **1** (-ier, -iest) *adj (poison, blow, enemy)* mortel, -elle; *(paleness, silence)* de mort; *Fam (boring)* mortel; **d. weapon** arme *f* meurtrière

2 *adv (pale, boring)* mortellement

deaf [def] **1** *adj* sourd; **d. and dumb** sourd-muet (f sourde-muette); **d. in one ear** sourd d'une oreille; **to go d.** devenir sourd; **to be d. to sb's requests** rester sourd aux prières de qn

2 *npl* **the d.** les sourds *mpl* • **deaf-aid** *n Br* appareil *m* acoustique • **deafen** *vt* assourdir • **deafness** *n* surdité *f*

deal¹ [diːl] *n* **a good** *or* **great d. (of)** *(a lot)* beaucoup (de)

deal² [diːl] *n* **1** *(in business)* marché *m*, affaire *f*; *Cards* donne *f*; **to make** *or* **do a d. (with sb)** conclure un marché (avec qn); **to give sb a fair d.** traiter qn équitablement; **to get a fair d. from sb** être traité équitablement par qn; **it's a d.!** d'accord!; *Ironic* **big d.!** la belle affaire!; **it's no big d.** ce n'est pas bien grave

2 (*pt & pp* **dealt**) *vt* **to d. sb a blow** porter un coup à qn; **to d. (out)** *(cards, money)* distribuer

3 *vi (trade)* traiter (**with sb** avec qn); **to d. in** faire le commerce de; **to d. with** *(take care of)* s'occuper de; *(concern) (of book)* traiter de, parler de • **dealer** *n* marchand, -ande *mf* (**in** de); *(agent)* dépositaire *mf*; *(for cars)* concessionnaire *mf*; *(in drugs)* revendeur, -euse *mf*; *Cards* donneur, -euse *mf* • **dealings** *npl* relations *fpl* (**with** avec); *(in business)* transactions *fpl*

deal³ [diːl] *n (wood)* sapin *m*

dealt [delt] *pt & pp of* deal

dean [diːn] *n Br (in church, university)* doyen *m*; *Am (in secondary school)* conseiller, -ère *mf* principal(e) d'éducation

dear [dɪə(r)] **1** (-er, -est) *adj (loved, precious, expensive)* cher (f chère); *(price)* élevé; **D. Sir** *(in letter)* Monsieur; **D. Sirs** Messieurs; **D. Uncle** (mon) cher oncle; **oh d.!** oh là là!

2 *n* **(my) d.** *(darling)* (mon) chéri/(ma) chérie; *(friend)* mon cher/ma chère; **be a d.!** sois un ange!

3 *adv (cost, pay)* cher • **dearly** *adv (love)* tendrement; *(very much)* beaucoup; **to pay d. for sth** payer qch cher

dearth [dɜːθ] *n* pénurie *f*

death [deθ] *n* mort *f*; **to put sb to d.** mettre qn à mort; **to be burnt to d.** mourir carbonisé; **to be bored to d.** s'ennuyer à mourir; **to be scared to d.** être mort de peur; **to be sick to d.** en avoir vraiment marre (**of** de); **there were many deaths** il y a eu de nombreux morts; **d. certificate** acte *m* de décès; *Br* **d. duty** *or* **duties,** *Am* **d. taxes** droits *mpl* de succession; **d. march** marche *f* funèbre; **d. mask** masque *m* mortuaire; **d. penalty** peine *f* de mort; **d. rate** (taux *m* de) mortalité *f*; **d. sentence** condamnation *f* à mort; **d. wish** désir *m* de mort • **deathbed** *n* lit *m* de mort • **deathblow** *n* coup *m* mortel • **deathly** *adj (silence, paleness)* de mort

debar [dɪˈbɑː(r)] (*pt & pp* **-rr-**) *vt* exclure (**from sth** de qch); **to d. sb from doing sth** interdire à qn de faire qch

debase [dɪˈbeɪs] *vt (person)* avilir; *(reputation)* ternir; *(coinage)* altérer

debate [dɪˈbeɪt] **1** *n* débat *m*

2 *vti* discuter; **he debated whether to do it** il se demandait s'il devait le faire • **debatable** *adj* discutable; **it's d. whether she will succeed** il est difficile de dire si elle réussira

debilitate [dɪˈbɪlɪteɪt] *vt* débiliter

debit ['debɪt] **1** *n* débit *m*; **in d.** *(account)* débiteur; **d. balance** solde *m* débiteur

2 *vt* débiter (**sb with sth** qn de qch)

debonair [debəˈneə(r)] *adj* élégant et raffiné

debris ['debriː] *n (of building)* décombres *mpl*; *(of plane, car)* débris *mpl*

debt [det] *n* dette *f*; **to be in d.** avoir des dettes; **to be 50 dollars in d.** devoir 50 dollars; **to run** *or* **get into d.** faire des dettes • **debtor** *n* débiteur, -trice *mf*

debug [diːˈbʌg] (*pt & pp* **-gg-**) *vt Comptr* déboguer

debunk [diːˈbʌŋk] *vt Fam (idea, theory)* discréditer

debut ['debjuː] *n (on stage)* début *m*; **to make one's d.** faire ses débuts

decade ['dekeɪd] *n* décennie *f*

ℓ Note that the French word **décade** is a false friend. It usually refers to a period of ten days.

decadent ['dekədənt] *adj* décadent • **decadence** *n* décadence *f*

decaffeinated [diːˈkæfɪneɪtɪd] *adj* décaféiné

decal ['diːkæl] *n Am* décalcomanie *f*

decant [dɪˈkænt] *vt (wine)* décanter • **decanter** *n* carafe *f*

decapitate [dɪˈkæpɪteɪt] *vt* décapiter

decathlon [dɪˈkæθlɒn] *n Sport* décathlon *m*

decay [dɪˈkeɪ] **1** *n (rot)* pourriture *f; (of building)* délabrement *m; (of tooth)* carie *f; (of nation)* déclin *m;* **to fall into d.** *(of building)* tomber en ruine

2 *vi (go bad)* se gâter; *(rot)* pourrir; *(of tooth)* se carier; *(of building)* tomber en ruine; *Fig (decline) (of nation)* décliner • **decaying** *adj (meat, fruit)* pourrissant; *(nation)* sur le déclin

deceased [dɪˈsiːst] **1** *adj* décédé **2** *n* **the d.** le défunt/la défunte

deceit [dɪˈsiːt] *n* tromperie *f* • **deceitful** *adj (person)* fourbe; *(behaviour)* malhonnête • **deceitfully** *adv* avec duplicité

deceive [dɪˈsiːv] *vti* tromper; **to d. oneself** se faire des illusions

ℓ Note that the French verb **décevoir** is a false friend and is never a translation for the English verb **to deceive**. It means **to disappoint**.

December [dɪˈsembə(r)] *n* décembre *m*

decent ['diːsənt] *adj (respectable)* convenable; *(good)* bon *(f* bonne); *(kind)* gentil, -ille; **that was d. (of you)** c'était chic de ta part • **decency** *n* décence *f; (kindness)* gentillesse *f* • **decently** *adv (respectably)* convenablement

deception [dɪˈsepʃən] *n* tromperie *f* • **deceptive** *adj* trompeur, -euse • **deceptively** *adv* **it looks d. straightforward** ça a l'air simple mais il ne faut pas s'y fier

ℓ Note that the French word **déception** is a false friend and is never a translation for the English word **deception**. It means **disappointment**.

decibel ['desɪbel] *n* décibel *m*

decide [dɪˈsaɪd] **1** *vt (outcome, future)* décider de; *(question, matter)* régler; **to d. to do sth** décider de faire qch; **to d. that...** décider que...; **to d. sb to do sth** décider qn à faire qch

2 *vi (make decisions)* décider; *(make up one's mind)* se décider (**on doing** à faire); **to d. on sth** décider de qch; *(choose)* choisir qch; **the deciding factor** le facteur décisif • **decided** *adj (firm)* décidé; *(clear)* net *(f* nette) • **decidedly** [-ɪdlɪ] *adv (firmly)* résolument; *(clearly)* nettement

ℓ Note that the French word **décidément** is a false friend and is never a translation for the English word **decidedly**.

decimal ['desɪməl] **1** *adj* décimal; **d. point** virgule *f*

2 *n* décimale *f* • **decimalization** [-aɪˈzeɪʃən] *n* décimalisation *f*

decimate ['desɪmeɪt] *vt* décimer

decipher [dɪˈsaɪfə(r)] *vt* déchiffrer

decision [dɪˈsɪʒən] *n* décision *f*

decisive [dɪˈsaɪsɪv] *adj (action, event, tone)* décisif, -ive; *(person)* résolu

deck [dek] **1** *n* (**a**) *(of ship)* pont *m;* **top d.** *(of bus)* impériale *f* (**b**) **d. of cards** jeu *m* de cartes (**c**) *(of record player)* platine *f*

2 *vt* **to d. (out)** *(adorn)* orner • **deckchair** *n* chaise *f* longue

declare [dɪˈkleə(r)] *vt* déclarer (**that** que); *(verdict, result)* proclamer • **declaration** [dekləˈreɪʃən] *n* déclaration *f; (of verdict)* proclamation *f*

decline [dɪˈklaɪn] **1** *n* déclin *m; (fall)* baisse *f*

2 *vt (offer)* décliner; **to d. to do sth** refuser de faire qch

3 *vi (become less) (of popularity, birthrate)* être en baisse; *(deteriorate) (of health, strength)* décliner; *(refuse)* refuser; **to d. in importance** perdre de l'importance; **one's declining years** ses dernières années

decode [diːˈkəʊd] *vt (message)* décoder • **decoder** *n Comptr & TV* décodeur *m*

decompose [diːkəmˈpəʊz] **1** *vt (chemical compound)* décomposer

2 *vi (rot)* se décomposer • **decomposition** [-kɒmpəˈzɪʃən] *n* décomposition *f*

decompression [diːkəmˈpreʃən] *n* décompression *f;* **d. chamber** sas *m* de décompression

decontaminate [diːkənˈtæmɪneɪt] *vt* décontaminer

decor ['deɪkɔː(r)] *n* décor *m*

decorate ['dekəreɪt] *vt (cake, house, soldier)* décorer (**with** de); *(hat, skirt)* orner (**with** de); *(paint)* peindre; *(wallpaper)* tapisser • **decorating** *n* **interior d.** décoration *f* d'intérieurs • **decoration** [-ˈreɪʃən] *n* décoration *f* • **decorative** [-rətɪv] *adj* décoratif, -ive • **decorator** *n Br (house* *painter)* peintre *m* décorateur; **(interior) d.** décorateur, -trice *mf*

decorum [dɪ'kɔːrəm] *n* convenances *fpl*

decoy ['diːkɔɪ] *n (artificial bird)* appeau *m*; *Fig* leurre *m*; **(police) d.** policier *m* en civil

decrease 1 ['diːkriːs] *n* diminution *f* (**in** de)

2 [dɪ'kriːs] *vti* diminuer ● **decreasing** *adj* décroissant ● **decreasingly** *adv* de moins en moins

decree [dɪ'kriː] **1** *n (by king)* décret *m*; *(by court)* jugement *m*; *(municipal)* arrêté *m* **2** *(pt & pp -eed)* *vt* décréter (**that** que)

decrepit [dɪ'krepɪt] *adj (building)* en ruine; *(person)* décrépit

decry [dɪ'kraɪ] *(pt & pp -ied)* *vt* décrier

dedicate ['dedɪkeɪt] *vt (devote)* consacrer (**to** à); *(book)* dédier (**to** à); **to d. oneself to sth** se consacrer à qch ● **dedicated** *adj (teacher)* consciencieux, -ieuse ● **dedi'cation** *n (in book)* dédicace *f*; *(devotion)* dévouement *m*

deduce [dɪ'djuːs] *vt (conclude)* déduire (**from** de; **that** que)

deduct [dɪ'dʌkt] *vt* déduire (**from** de) ● **deductible** *adj (from invoice)* à déduire (**from** de); *(from income) (expenses)* déductible ● **deduction** *n (subtraction, conclusion)* déduction *f*

deed [diːd] *n* action *f*, acte *m*; *(feat)* exploit *m*; *(legal document)* acte *m* notarié

deem [diːm] *vt Formal* juger

deep [diːp] **1** *(-er, -est)* *adj* profond; *(snow)* épais (*f* épaisse); *(voice)* grave; *(musical note)* bas (*f* basse); *(person) (difficult to understand)* insondable; **to be 6 m d.** avoir 6 m de profondeur; **d. in thought** plongé dans ses pensées; **d. end** *(in swimming pool)* le grand bain; **d. red** rouge foncé

2 *adv* profondément; **she went in d.** *(into water)* elle alla (jusqu')où elle n'avait pas pied; **d. into the night** tard dans la nuit

3 *n Literary* **the d.** l'océan *m* ● **deeply** *adv* profondément

deepen ['diːpən] **1** *vt (increase)* augmenter; *(canal, knowledge)* approfondir

2 *vi (of river, silence)* devenir plus profond; *(of mystery)* s'épaissir; *(of voice)* devenir plus grave ● **deepening** *adj (gap)* grandissant; **the d. recession/crisis** l'aggravation *f* de la récession/crise

deep-freeze [diːp'friːz] **1** *n* congélateur *m*

2 *vt* surgeler ● **deep-'fryer** *n* friteuse *f*

● **'deep-'rooted**, **'deep-'seated** *adj* profondément enraciné ● **deep-sea 'diving** *n* plongée *f* sous-marine (en haute mer)

deer [dɪə(r)] *n inv* cerf *m*

deface [dɪ'feɪs] *vt (damage)* dégrader; *(daub)* barbouiller

defamation [defə'meɪʃən] *n* diffamation *f* ● **defamatory** [dɪ'fæmətərɪ] *adj* diffamatoire

default [dɪ'fɔːlt] **1** *n* **by d.** par défaut; **to win by d.** gagner par forfait

2 *vi Law (fail to appear in court)* ne pas comparaître; **to d. on one's payments** être en rupture de paiement

defeat [dɪ'fiːt] **1** *n* défaite *f*

2 *vt (opponent, army)* vaincre; *(plan, effort)* faire échouer; **that defeats the purpose** *or* **object** ça va à l'encontre du but recherché ● **defeatism** *n* défaitisme *m* ● **defeatist** *adj & n* défaitiste (*mf*)

defect¹ ['diːfekt] *n* défaut *m*

defect² [dɪ'fekt] *vi (of party member, soldier)* déserter; **to d. to the enemy** passer à l'ennemi ● **defection** *n* défection *f* ● **defector** *n* transfuge *mf*

defective [dɪ'fektɪv] *adj (machine)* défectueux, -ueuse

defence [dɪ'fens] *(Am* **defense)** *n* défense *f*; *(against* contre); **to speak in d. of sb** prendre la défense de qn; **in his d.** à sa décharge ● **defenceless** *adj* sans défense

defend [dɪ'fend] *vti* défendre ● **defendant** *n (accused)* prévenu, -ue *mf* ● **defender** *n* défenseur *m*; *(of sports title)* tenant, -ante *mf*

defense [dɪ'fens] *n Am* = **defence**

defensible [dɪ'fensəbəl] *adj* défendable

defensive [dɪ'fensɪv] **1** *adj* défensif, -ive; **to be d.** être sur la défensive

2 *n* **on the d.** sur la défensive

defer [dɪ'fɜː(r)] *(pt & pp -rr-)* **1** *vt (postpone)* différer

2 *vi* **to d. to** s'en remettre à ● **deferment** *n (postponement)* report *m*

defiant [dɪ'faɪənt] *adj (tone)* de défi; *(person)* provocant ● **defiance** *n (resistance)* défi *m* (**of** à); **in d. of** *(contempt)* au mépris de ● **defiantly** *adv* d'un air de défi

deficient [dɪ'fɪʃənt] *adj (not adequate)* insuffisant; *(faulty)* défectueux, -ueuse; **to be d. in** manquer de ● **deficiency** *(pl -ies)* *n (shortage)* manque *m*; *(in vitamins, minerals)* carence *f* (**in** de); *(flaw)* défaut *m*

deficit ['defɪsɪt] *n* déficit *m*

defile [dɪ'faɪl] *vt (make dirty)* souiller

define [dɪ'faɪn] *vt* définir

definite ['defɪnɪt] *adj (exact) (date, plan, answer)* précis; *(clear) (improvement, advantage)* net (*f* nette); *(firm) (offer, order)* ferme; *(certain)* certain; **it's d. that...** il est certain que... (+ *indicative*); **I was quite d.** j'ai été tout à fait formel; *Grammar* **d. article** article *m* défini •**definitely** *adv* certainement; *(improved, superior)* nettement; *(say)* catégoriquement

definition [defɪ'nɪʃən] *n* définition *f*

definitive [dɪ'fɪnɪtɪv] *adj* définitif, -ive

deflate [dɪ'fleɪt] *vt (tyre)* dégonfler •**deflation** *n* dégonflement *m*; *Econ* déflation *f*

deflect [dɪ'flekt] **1** *vt (bullet)* faire dévier; **to d. sb from a plan/aim** détourner qn d'un projet/objectif
2 *vi (of bullet)* dévier

deform [dɪ'fɔːm] *vt* déformer •**deformed** *adj (body)* difforme •**deformity** *n* difformité *f*

defraud [dɪ'frɔːd] *vt (customs, State)* frauder; **to d. sb of sth** escroquer qch à qn

defray [dɪ'freɪ] *vt Formal (expenses)* payer

defrost [diː'frɒst] *vt (fridge)* dégivrer; *(food)* décongeler

deft [deft] *adj* adroit (**with** de) •**deftness** *n* adresse *f*

defunct [dɪ'fʌŋkt] *adj* défunt

defuse [diː'fjuːz] *vt (bomb, conflict)* désamorcer

defy [dɪ'faɪ] *(pt & pp* **-ied**) *vt (person, death, logic)* défier; *(efforts)* résister à; **to d. sb to do sth** défier qn de faire qch; **it defies description** cela défie toute description

degenerate 1 [dɪ'dʒenərət] *adj & n* dégénéré, -ée (*mf*)
2 [dɪ'dʒenəreɪt] *vi* dégénérer (**into** en) •**degeneration** [-'reɪʃən] *n* dégénérescence *f*

degrade [dɪ'greɪd] *vt* dégrader •**degrading** *adj* dégradant

degree [dɪ'griː] *n* (**a**) *(angle, temperature, extent)* degré *m*; **it's 20 degrees** il fait 20 degrés; **by degrees** peu à peu; **not in the slightest d.** pas du tout; **to some d., to a certain d.** jusqu'à un certain point; **to such a d.** à tel point (**that** que) (**b**) *(from university)* diplôme *m*; *(Bachelor's)* ≃ licence *f*; *(Master's)* ≃ maîtrise *f*; *(PhD)* ≃ doctorat *m*

dehumanize [diː'hjuːmənaɪz] *vt* déshumaniser

dehydrated [diːhaɪ'dreɪtɪd] *adj* déshydraté; **to get d.** se déshydrater

de-ice [diː'aɪs] *vt (car window)* dégivrer

deign [deɪn] *vt* daigner (**to do** faire)

deity ['diːɪtɪ] *(pl* **-ies**) *n* dieu *m*

dejected [dɪ'dʒektɪd] *adj* abattu •**dejection** *n* abattement *m*

delay [dɪ'leɪ] **1** *n (lateness)* retard *m*; *(waiting period)* délai *m*; **without d.** sans tarder
2 *vt* retarder; *(payment)* différer; **to d. doing sth** tarder à faire qch; **to be delayed** avoir du retard
3 *vi (be slow)* tarder (**in doing** à faire); *(linger)* s'attarder; **don't d.!** faites vite!
•**delayed-'action** *adj (bomb, fuse)* à retardement •**delaying** *adj* **d. tactics** *or* **actions** moyens *mpl* dilatoires

> *Note that the French word* **délai** *is a false friend and is never a translation for the English word* **delay**.

delectable [dɪ'lektəbəl] *adj* délectable

delegate 1 ['delɪgət] *n* délégué, -ée *mf*
2 ['delɪgeɪt] *vt* déléguer (**to** à) •**dele'gation** *n* délégation *f*

delete [dɪ'liːt] *vt* supprimer •**deletion** [-ʃən] *n* suppression *f*

deleterious [delɪ'tɪərɪəs] *adj Formal* délétère

deliberate¹ [dɪ'lɪbərət] *adj (intentional)* délibéré; *(cautious)* réfléchi; *(slow)* mesuré •**deliberately** *adv (intentionally)* délibérément; *(walk)* avec mesure

deliberate² [dɪ'lɪbəreɪt] **1** *vt (discuss)* délibérer
2 *vi* délibérer (**on** sur) •**delibe'ration** *n (discussion)* délibération *f*

delicate ['delɪkət] *adj* délicat •**delicacy** *(pl* **-ies**) *n (quality)* délicatesse *f*; *(food)* mets *m* délicat •**delicately** *adv* délicatement

delicatessen [delɪkə'tesən] *n (shop)* épicerie *f* fine

delicious [dɪ'lɪʃəs] *adj* délicieux, -ieuse

delight [dɪ'laɪt] **1** *n (pleasure)* plaisir *m*, joie *f*; *(food)* délice *m*; **delights** *(pleasures, things)* délices *fpl*; **to my (great) d.** à ma grande joie; **to be the d. of** faire les délices de; **to take d. in sth/in doing sth** se délecter de qch/à faire qch
2 *vt* ravir
3 *vi* **to d. in doing sth** prendre plaisir à faire qch •**delighted** *adj* ravi (**with sth** de qch; **to do** de faire; **that** que)

delightful [dɪ'laɪtfəl] *adj* charmant; *(meal, perfume, sensation)* délicieux, -ieuse •**delightfully** *adv (with charm)* avec beaucoup de charme; *(wonderfully)* merveilleusement

delineate [dɪ'lɪnɪeɪt] *vt (outline)* esquisser; *(plan, proposal)* définir

delinquent [dɪ'lɪŋkwənt] *adj & n* délinquant, -ante *(mf)* •**delinquency** *n* délinquance *f*

delirious [dɪ'lɪrɪəs] *adj* délirant; **to be d.** délirer •**delirium** [-rɪəm] *n (illness)* délire *m*

deliver [dɪ'lɪvə(r)] *vt* (**a**) *(goods)* livrer; *(letters)* distribuer; *(hand over)* remettre (**to** à) (**b**) *(rescue)* délivrer (**from** de) (**c**) *(give birth to)* mettre au monde; **to d. a woman's baby** accoucher une femme (**d**) *(speech)* prononcer; *(warning, ultimatum)* lancer; *(blow)* porter

deliverance [dɪ'lɪvərəns] *n* délivrance *f* (**from** de)

delivery [dɪ'lɪvərɪ] *(pl* -**ies**) *n* (**a**) *(of goods)* livraison *f*; *(of letters)* distribution *f*; *(handing over)* remise *f* (**b**) *(birth)* accouchement *m* (**c**) *(speaking)* débit *m* •**deliveryman** *(pl* -**men**) *n* livreur *m*

delta ['deltə] *n (of river)* delta *m*

delude [dɪ'luːd] *vt* tromper; **to d. oneself** se faire des illusions •**delusion** *n* illusion *f*; *(in mental illness)* aberration *f* mentale

deluge ['deljuːdʒ] **1** *n (rain)* & Fig *(of water, questions)* déluge *m*
2 *vt* inonder (**with** de)

de luxe [dɪ'lʌks] *adj* de luxe

delve [delv] *vi* **to d. into** *(question)* creuser; *(past, books)* fouiller dans

demagogue ['deməɡɒɡ] *n* démagogue *mf*

demand [dɪ'mɑːnd] **1** *n* exigence *f*; *(claim)* revendication *f*; *(for goods)* demande *f* (**for** pour); **to be in (great) d.** être très demandé; **to make demands on sb** exiger beaucoup de qn
2 *vt* exiger (**sth from sb** qch de qn); *(rights, more pay)* revendiquer; **to d. that...** exiger que...; **to d. to know** insister pour savoir •**demanding** *adj* exigeant

demarcation [diːmɑː'keɪʃən] *n* démarcation *f*; **d. line** ligne *f* de démarcation

demean [dɪ'miːn] *vt* **to d. oneself** s'abaisser •**demeaning** *adj* dégradant

demeanour [dɪ'miːnə(r)] *(Am* **demeanor**) *n (behaviour)* comportement *m*

demented [dɪ'mentɪd] *adj* dément

demerara [demə'reərə] *n Br* **d. sugar** cassonade *f*

demise [dɪ'maɪz] *n* disparition *f*

demister [diː'mɪstə(r)] *n Br (for vehicle)* dispositif *m* de désembuage

demo ['deməʊ] *(pl* -**os**) *n Fam (demonstration)* manif *f*

demobilize [diː'məʊbɪlaɪz] *vt* démobiliser

democracy [dɪ'mɒkrəsɪ] *(pl* -**ies**) *n* démocratie *f* •**democrat** ['deməkræt] *n* démocrate *mf* •**democratic** [demə'krætɪk] *adj (institution)* démocratique; *(person)* démocrate •**democratically** [demə'krætɪkəlɪ] *adv* démocratiquement

demography [dɪ'mɒɡrəfɪ] *n* démographie *f*

demolish [dɪ'mɒlɪʃ] *vt* démolir •**demolition** [demə'lɪʃən] *n* démolition *f*

demon ['diːmən] *n* démon *m*

demonstrate ['demənstreɪt] **1** *vt* démontrer; *(machine)* faire une démonstration de; **to d. how to do sth** montrer comment faire qch
2 *vi (protest)* manifester •**demonstration** [-'streɪʃən] *n* démonstration *f*; *(protest)* manifestation *f*; **to hold** *or* **stage a d.** manifester •**demonstrator** *n (protester)* manifestant, -ante *mf*; *(of machine)* démonstrateur, -trice *mf*

demonstrative [dɪ'mɒnstrətɪv] **1** *adj (person, attitude)* démonstratif, -ive
2 *adj & n Grammar* démonstratif *(m)*

demoralize [dɪ'mɒrəlaɪz] *vt* démoraliser

demote [dɪ'məʊt] *vt* rétrograder

demure [dɪ'mjʊə(r)] *adj* réservé

den [den] *n (of lion, person)* antre *m*

denationalize [diː'næʃənəlaɪz] *vt* dénationaliser

denial [dɪ'naɪəl] *n (of rumour, allegation)* démenti *m*; *(psychological)* dénégation *f*; **to issue a d.** publier un démenti

denigrate ['denɪɡreɪt] *vt* dénigrer

denim ['denɪm] *n* denim *m*; **denims** *(jeans)* jean *m*

Denmark ['denmɑːk] *n* le Danemark

denomination [dɪnɒmɪ'neɪʃən] *n (religion)* confession *f*; *(of coin, banknote)* valeur *f*

denominator [dɪ'nɒmɪneɪtə(r)] *n Math & Fig* dénominateur *m*

denote [dɪ'nəʊt] *vt* dénoter

denounce [dɪ'naʊns] *vt (person, injustice)* dénoncer (**to** à); **to d. sb as a spy** accuser qn d'être un espion

dense [dens] (**-er, -est**) *adj* dense; *Fam (stupid)* lourd •**densely** *adv* **d. populated** très peuplé •**density** *n* densité *f*

dent [dent] **1** *n (in car, metal)* bosse *f*; **full of dents** *(car)* cabossé; **to make a d. in sth** cabosser qch; **to make a d. in one's savings** *(of purchase)* faire un trou dans ses économies
2 *vt* cabosser

dental ['dentəl] *adj* dentaire; **d. appointment** rendez-vous *m inv* chez le dentiste; **d. surgeon** chirurgien-dentiste *m*

dentist ['dentɪst] *n* dentiste *mf*; **to go to the d.('s)** aller chez le dentiste • **dentistry** *n* dentisterie *f*; **school of d.** école *f* dentaire
dentures ['dentʃəz] *npl* dentier *m*

> *📖* Note that the French word **denture** is a false friend and is never a translation for the English word **dentures**. It means **a set of teeth.**

denunciation [dɪnʌnsɪ'eɪʃən] *n* dénonciation *f*; *(public)* accusation *f* publique
deny [dɪ'naɪ] *(pt & pp* **-ied)** *vt* nier *(*doing avoir fait; **that** que); *(rumour)* démentir; *(authority)* rejeter; *(disown)* renier; **to d. sb sth** refuser qch à qn
deodorant [diː'əʊdərənt] *n* déodorant *m*
depart [dɪ'pɑːt] **1** *vi* partir; *(deviate)* s'écarter (**from** de)
2 *vt Literary* **to d. this world** quitter ce monde • **departed 1** *adj (dead)* défunt **2** *n* **the d.** le défunt/la défunte
department [dɪ'pɑːtmənt] *n* département *m*; *(in office)* service *m*; *(in shop)* rayon *m*; *(of government)* ministère *m*; *Fig* **that's your d.** c'est ton rayon; **d. store** grand magasin *m* • **departmental** [diːpɑːt'mentəl] *adj* **d. manager** *(in office)* chef de service; *(in shop)* chef *m* de rayon
departure [dɪ'pɑːtʃə(r)] *n* départ *m*; *Fig* **a d. from the rule** une entorse au règlement; **to be a new d. for** constituer une nouvelle voie pour; **d. lounge** *(in airport)* salle *f* d'embarquement
depend [dɪ'pend] *vi* dépendre (**on** *or* **upon** de); **to d. (up)on** *(rely on)* compter sur (**for sth** pour qch); **you can d. on it!** tu peux compter là-dessus! • **dependable** *adj (person, information)* sûr; *(machine)* fiable • **dependant** *n* personne *f* à charge • **dependence** *n* dépendance *f* (**on** de) • **dependency** *(pl* **-ies)** *n (country)* dépendance *f* • **dependent** *adj* dépendant (**on** *or* **upon** de); *(relative, child)* à charge; **to be d. (up)on** dépendre de; **to be d. on sb** *(financially)* être à la charge de qn
depict [dɪ'pɪkt] *vt (describe)* décrire; *(in pictures)* représenter • **depiction** *n (description)* peinture *f*; *(in picture form)* représentation *f*
deplete [dɪ'pliːt] *vt (use up)* épuiser; *(reduce)* réduire • **depletion** *n* épuisement *m*; *(reduction)* réduction *f*
deplore [dɪ'plɔː(r)] *vt* déplorer • **deplorable** *adj* déplorable • **deplorably** *adv* déplorablement
deploy [dɪ'plɔɪ] *vt (troops)* déployer
depopulate [diː'pɒpjʊleɪt] *vt* dépeupler

• **depopulation** [-'leɪʃən] *n* dépeuplement *m*
deport [dɪ'pɔːt] *vt (foreigner, criminal)* expulser; *Hist (to concentration camp)* déporter • **deportation** [diːpɔː'teɪʃən] *n* expulsion *f*; *Hist* déportation *f*
deportment [dɪ'pɔːtmənt] *n* maintien *m*
depose [dɪ'pəʊz] *vt (ruler)* déposer
deposit [dɪ'pɒzɪt] **1** *n* (**a**) *(in bank)* dépôt *m*; *(part payment)* acompte *m*; *(returnable)* caution *f*; **d. account** compte *m* de dépôt (**b**) *(sediment)* dépôt *m*; *(of gold, oil)* gisement *m*
2 *vt (object, money)* déposer
depot [*Br* 'depəʊ, *Am* 'diːpəʊ] *n (for goods)* dépôt *m*; *Am (railroad station)* gare *f*; *Am (bus)* **d.** gare *f* routière
deprave [dɪ'preɪv] *vt* dépraver • **depraved** *adj* dépravé • **depravity** [dɪ'prævɪtɪ] *n* dépravation *f*
depreciate [dɪ'priːʃɪeɪt] **1** *vt (reduce in value)* déprécier
2 *vi (fall in value)* se déprécier • **depreciation** [-'eɪʃən] *n* dépréciation *f*
depress [dɪ'pres] *vt (discourage)* déprimer; *(push down)* appuyer sur • **depressed** *adj (person, market)* déprimé; *(industry) (in decline)* en déclin; *(in crisis)* en crise; **to get d.** se décourager • **depression** *n* dépression *f*
deprive [dɪ'praɪv] *vt* priver (**of** de) • **deprivation** [deprə'veɪʃən] *n (hardship)* privations *fpl*; *(loss)* perte *f* • **deprived** *adj (child)* défavorisé
depth [depθ] *n* profondeur *f*; *(of snow)* épaisseur *f*; *(of interest)* intensité *f*; **in the depths of** *(forest, despair)* au plus profond de; *(winter)* au cœur de; *Fig* **to get out of one's d.** *(be unable to cope)* ne pas être à la hauteur; **in d.** en profondeur
deputation [depjʊ'teɪʃən] *n* députation *f*
deputize ['depjʊtaɪz] **1** *vt* députer (**sb to do** qn pour faire)
2 *vi* assurer l'intérim (**for sb** de qn)
deputy ['depjʊtɪ] *(pl* **-ies)** *n (replacement)* remplaçant, -ante *mf*; *(assistant)* adjoint, -ointe *mf*; *Am* **d. (sheriff)** shérif *m* adjoint; **d. chairman** vice-président, -ente *mf*
derailed [dɪ'reɪld] *adj* **to be d.** *(of train)* dérailler • **derailment** *n* déraillement *m*
deranged [dɪ'reɪndʒd] *adj* **he's (mentally) d., his mind is d.** il a le cerveau dérangé
derby [*Br* 'dɑːbɪ, *Am* 'dɜːrbɪ] *(pl* **-ies)** *n* (**a**) *Am (hat)* chapeau *m* melon (**b**) *Sport* derby *m*
derelict ['derɪlɪkt] *adj (building)* abandonné

deride [dɪ'raɪd] *vt* tourner en dérision • **derision** [-rɪʒən] *n* dérision *f* • **derisive** *adj (laughter)* moqueur, -euse; *(amount)* dérisoire • **derisory** *adj (amount)* dérisoire

ℓ Note that the French word **dérider** is a false friend and is never a translation for the English word **to deride**.

derive [dɪ'raɪv] **1** *vt* provenir (**from** de); **to d. pleasure from sth** prendre plaisir à qch; **to be derived from** provenir de **2** *vi* **to d. from** provenir de • **derivation** [derɪ'veɪʃən] *n Ling* dérivation *f* • **derivative** [dɪ'rɪvətɪv] **1** *adj* banal **2** *n Ling & Chem* dérivé *(m)*

dermatitis [dɜːmə'taɪtəs] *n Med* dermatite *f*

derogatory [dɪ'rɒgətərɪ] *adj (word)* péjoratif, -ive; *(remark)* désobligeant (**to** pour)

derrick ['derɪk] *n (of oil well)* derrick *m*

derv [dɜːv] *n Br* gazole *m*, gas-oil *m*

descend [dɪ'send] **1** *vt (stairs, hill)* descendre; **to be descended from** descendre de **2** *vi* descendre (**from** de); *(of darkness, rain)* tomber; **to d. upon** *(of tourists)* envahir; *(attack)* faire une descente sur; **in descending order** en ordre décroissant

descendant [dɪ'sendənt] *n* descendant, -ante *mf*

descent [dɪ'sent] *n* (**a**) *(of aircraft)* descente *f* (**b**) *(ancestry)* origine *f*; **to be of Norman d.** être d'origine normande

describe [dɪ'skraɪb] *vt* décrire • **description** [dɪ'skrɪpʃən] *n* description *f*; *(on passport)* signalement *m*; **of every d.** de toutes sortes • **descriptive** [dɪ'skrɪptɪv] *adj* descriptif, -ive

desecrate ['desɪkreɪt] *vt* profaner • **dese'cration** *n* profanation *f*

desegregate [diː'segrɪgeɪt] *vt (school)* supprimer la ségrégation raciale dans • **desegre'gation** *n* déségrégation *f*

desert¹ ['dezət] *n* désert *m*; **d. climate** climat *m* désertique; **d. animal/plant** animal *m*/plante *f* du désert; **d. island** île *f* déserte

desert² [dɪ'zɜːt] **1** *vt (person)* abandonner; *(place, cause)* déserter **2** *vi (of soldier)* déserter • **deserted** *adj* désert • **deserter** *n* déserteur *m*

desertion [dɪ'zɜːʃən] *n (by soldier)* désertion *f*; *(by spouse)* abandon *m* du domicile conjugal

deserts [dɪ'zɜːts] *npl* **to get one's just d.** avoir ce qu'on mérite

deserve [dɪ'zɜːv] *vt* mériter (**to do** de faire) • **deservedly** [-ɪdlɪ] *adv* à juste titre • **deserving** *adj (person)* méritant; *(action, cause)* méritoire; **to be d. of** *(praise, love)* être digne de

desiccated ['desɪkeɪtɪd] *adj* desséché

design [dɪ'zaɪn] **1** *n* (**a**) *(pattern)* motif *m*; *(sketch)* plan *m*; *(of dress, car, furniture)* modèle *m*; *(planning)* conception *f*; **industrial d.** dessin *m* industriel; **to study d.** étudier le design (**b**) *(aim)* dessein *m*; **by d.** intentionnellement; **to have designs on** avoir des vues sur **2** *vt (car, building)* concevoir; *(dress)* créer; **designed to do sth/for sth** conçu pour faire qch/pour qch; **well designed** bien conçu • **designer** *n (artistic)* dessinateur, -trice *mf*; *(industrial)* concepteur-dessinateur *m*; *(of clothes)* styliste *mf*; *(well-known)* couturier *m*; **d. clothes** vêtements *mpl* de marque

designate ['dezɪgneɪt] *vt* désigner • **designation** [-'neɪʃən] *n* désignation *f*

desire [dɪ'zaɪə(r)] **1** *n* désir *m*; **I've got no d. to do that** je n'ai aucune envie de faire cela **2** *vt* désirer (**to do** faire) • **desirable** *adj* désirable; **d. property** *(in advertising)* (très) belle propriété

desk [desk] *n (in school)* table *f*; *(in office)* bureau *m*; *Br (in shop)* caisse *f*; **(reception) d.** *(in hotel)* réception *f*; **the news d.** le service des informations; *Am* **d. clerk** *(in hotel)* réceptionniste *mf;* **d. job** travail *m* de bureau

desktop ['desktɒp] *n* **d. computer** ordinateur *m* de bureau; **d. publishing** publication *f* assistée par ordinateur

desolate ['desələt] *adj (deserted)* désolé; *(in ruins)* dévasté; *(dreary, bleak)* morne, triste; *(person)* abattu • **desolation** [-'leɪʃən] *n (ruin)* dévastation *f*; *(emptiness)* solitude *f*; *(of person)* affliction *f*

despair [dɪ'speə(r)] **1** *n* désespoir *m*; **to drive sb to d.** désespérer qn; **to be in d.** être au désespoir **2** *vi* désespérer (**of sb** de qn; **of doing** de faire) • **despairing** *adj* désespéré

despatch [dɪ'spætʃ] *n & vt* = **dispatch**

desperate ['despərət] *adj* désespéré; **to be d. for** *(money, love)* avoir désespérément besoin de; *(cigarette, baby)* mourir d'envie d'avoir • **desperately** *adv (ill)* gravement; *(in love)* éperdument

desperation [despə'reɪʃən] *n* désespoir *m*; **in d.** en désespoir de cause

despicable [dɪ'spɪkəbəl] *adj* méprisable

despise [dɪ'spaɪz] *vt* mépriser

despite [dɪ'spaɪt] *prep* malgré
despondent [dɪ'spɒndənt] *adj* abattu • **despondency** *n* abattement *m*
dessert [dɪ'zɜːt] *n* dessert *m* • **dessertspoon** *n Br* cuillère *f* à dessert
destabilize [diː'steɪbəlaɪz] *vt* déstabiliser
destination [destɪ'neɪʃən] *n* destination *f*
destine ['destɪn] *vt* destiner (**for** à; **to do** à faire); **it was destined to happen** ça devait arriver
destiny ['destɪnɪ] (*pl* **-ies**) *n* destin *m*, destinée *f*
destitute ['destɪtjuːt] *adj (poor)* indigent; **d. of** *(lacking in)* dénué de • **desti'tution** *n* dénuement *m*
destroy [dɪ'strɔɪ] *vt* détruire; *(horse, monkey)* abattre; *(cat, dog)* faire piquer • **destroyer** *n (ship)* contre-torpilleur *m*; *(person)* destructeur, -trice *mf*
destruction [dɪ'strʌkʃən] *n* destruction *f* • **destructive** *adj (person, war)* destructeur, -trice; *(power)* destructif, -ive
detach [dɪ'tætʃ] *vt* détacher (**from** de) • **detached** *adj (indifferent) (person, manner)* détaché; *(without bias) (view)* désintéressé; *Br* **d. house** maison *f* individuelle
detachable [dɪ'tætʃəbəl] *adj* amovible
detachment [dɪ'tætʃmənt] *n (attitude, group of soldiers)* détachement *m*; **the d. of** *(action)* la séparation de
detail ['diːteɪl] **1** *n* (**a**) *(item of information)* détail *m*; **in d.** en détail; **to go into d.** entrer dans les détails (**b**) *Mil* détachement *m*
2 *vt* (**a**) *(describe)* détailler (**b**) *Mil* **to d. sb to do sth** donner l'ordre à qn de faire qch • **detailed** *adj (account)* détaillé
detain [dɪ'teɪn] *vt (delay)* retenir; *(prisoner)* placer en détention; *(in hospital)* garder • **detainee** [diːteɪ'niː] *n Pol & Law* détenu, -ue *mf* • **detention** [dɪ'tenʃən] *n (at school)* retenue *f*; *(in prison)* détention *f*
detect [dɪ'tekt] *vt* détecter • **detection** *n* découverte *f*; *(identification)* identification *f*; *(of mine)* détection *f*
detective [dɪ'tektɪv] *n (police officer)* ≃ inspecteur *m* de police; *(private)* détective *m* privé; **d. film/novel** film *m*/roman *m* policier
detector [dɪ'tektə(r)] *n* détecteur *m*
deter [dɪ'tɜː(r)] (*pt & pp* **-rr-**) *vt* **to d. sb** dissuader qn (**from doing** de faire; **from sth** de qch)
detergent [dɪ'tɜːdʒənt] *n* détergent *m*
deteriorate [dɪ'tɪərɪəreɪt] *vi* se détériorer • **deterioration** [-'reɪʃən] *n* détérioration *f*

determine [dɪ'tɜːmɪn] *vt (cause, date)* déterminer; *(price)* fixer; **to d. to do sth** décider de faire qch; **to d. sb to do sth** décider qn à faire qch; **to d. that...** décider que... • **determined** *adj (look, person, quantity)* déterminé; **to be d. to do** *or* **on doing sth** être décidé à faire qch; **I'm d. she'll succeed** je suis bien décidé à ce qu'elle réussisse
deterrent [dɪ'terənt] *n (military)* force *f* de dissuasion; *Fig* **to be a d., to act as a d.** être dissuasif, -ive
detest [dɪ'test] *vt* détester (**doing** faire) • **detestable** *adj* détestable
detonate ['detəneɪt] **1** *vt* faire exploser **2** *vi* exploser • **detonation** [-'neɪʃən] *n* détonation *f* • **detonator** *n* détonateur *m*
detour ['diːtʊə(r)] *n* détour *m*; **to make a d.** faire un détour
detract [dɪ'trækt] *vi* **to d. from** *(make less)* diminuer • **detractor** *n* détracteur, -trice *mf*
detriment ['detrɪmənt] *n* **to the d. of** au détriment de • **detrimental** [-'mentəl] *adj* préjudiciable (**to** à)
devalue [diː'væljuː] *vt (money)* dévaluer; *(person, achievement)* dévaloriser • **devalu'ation** *n (of money)* dévaluation *f*
devastate ['devəsteɪt] *vt (crop, village)* dévaster; *(person)* anéantir • **devastating** *adj (storm)* dévastateur, -trice; *(news, results)* accablant; *(shock)* terrible; *(charm)* irrésistible
develop [dɪ'veləp] **1** *vt (theory, argument)* développer; *(area, land)* mettre en valeur; *(habit, illness)* contracter; *(talent)* manifester; *(photo)* développer; **to d. a liking for sth** prendre goût à qch **2** *vi (grow)* se développer; *(of event, argument, crisis)* se produire; *(of talent, illness)* se manifester; **to d. into** devenir • **developing 1** *adj* **d. country** pays *m* en voie de développement **2** *n (of photos)* développement *m*
developer [dɪ'veləpə(r)] *n (property)* **d.** promoteur *m*
development [dɪ'veləpmənt] *n (growth, progress)* développement *m*; *(of land)* mise *f* en valeur; **(housing) d.** lotissement *m*; *(large)* grand ensemble *m*; **a (new) d.** *(in situation)* un fait nouveau
deviate ['diːvɪeɪt] *vi* dévier (**from** de); **to d. from the norm** s'écarter de la norme • **deviant** [-ənt] *adj (behaviour)* anormal • **deviation** [-'eɪʃən] *n* déviation *f*
device [dɪ'vaɪs] *n (instrument, gadget)* dispositif *m*; *(scheme)* procédé *m*; **explosive/nuclear d.** engin *m* explosif/nu-

cléaire; **safety d.** dispositif de sécurité; **left to one's own devices** livré à soi-même

devil ['devəl] *n* diable *m*; *Fam* **a** *or* **the d. of a problem** un problème épouvantable; *Fam* **a** *or* **the d. of a noise** un bruit infernal; *Fam* **I had a** *or* **the d. of a job doing it** j'ai eu un mal fou à le faire; *Fam* **what/where/why the d....?** que/où/pourquoi diable...?; **to run like the d.** courir comme un fou (*f* une folle) •**devilish** *adj* diabolique

devious ['diːvɪəs] *adj (mind, behaviour)* tortueux, -ueuse; **he's d.** il a l'esprit tortueux

devise [dɪ'vaɪz] *vt* imaginer; *(plot)* ourdir

devitalize [diː'vaɪtəlaɪz] *vt* rendre exsangue

devoid [dɪ'vɔɪd] *adj* **d. of** dénué *ou* dépourvu de; *(guilt)* exempt de

devolution [diːvə'luːʃən] *n Pol* décentralisation *f*; **the d. of** *(power)* la délégation de

devolve [dɪ'vɒlv] *vi* **to d. upon** incomber à

devote [dɪ'vəʊt] *vt* consacrer (**to** à) •**devoted** *adj* dévoué; *(admirer)* fervent

devotee [dɪvəʊ'tiː] *n (of music, sport)* passionné, -ée *mf* (**of** de)

devotion [dɪ'vəʊʃən] *n (to friend, family, cause)* dévouement *m* (**to sb** à qn); *(religious)* dévotion *f*; **devotions** *(prayers)* prières *fpl*

devour [dɪ'vaʊə(r)] *vt (eat, engulf, read)* dévorer

devout [dɪ'vaʊt] *adj* dévot; *(supporter, prayer)* fervent

dew [djuː] *n* rosée *f*

dext(e)rous ['dekstərəs] *adj* adroit •**dexterity** [-'sterɪtɪ] *n* dextérité *f*

diabetes [daɪə'biːtiːz] *n* diabète *m* •**diabetic** [-'betɪk] **1** *adj* diabétique; **d. jam** confiture *f* pour diabétiques **2** *n* diabétique *mf*

diabolical [daɪə'bɒlɪkəl] *adj* diabolique; *Fam (very bad)* épouvantable

diadem ['daɪədem] *n* diadème *m*

diagnose [daɪəg'nəʊz] *vt* diagnostiquer •**diagnosis** [-'nəʊsɪs] *(pl* -**oses** [-əʊsiːz]) *n* diagnostic *m*

diagonal [daɪ'æɡənəl] **1** *adj* diagonal **2** *n* diagonale *f* •**diagonally** *adv* en diagonale

diagram ['daɪəɡræm] *n* schéma *m*; *(geometrical)* figure *f*

dial ['daɪəl] **1** *n* cadran *m* **2** *(Br* -**ll**-, *Am* -**l**-) *vt (phone number)* composer; *(person)* appeler •**dialling**

code *n Br* indicatif *m* •**dialling tone** *n Br* tonalité *f* •**dial tone** *n Am* tonalité *f*

dialect ['daɪəlekt] *n* dialecte *m*

dialogue ['daɪəlɒɡ] *(Am* **dialog**) *n* dialogue *m*

dialysis [daɪ'ælɪsɪs] *n Med* dialyse *f*; **to be in d.** être sous dialyse

diameter [daɪ'æmɪtə(r)] *n* diamètre *m* •**diametrically** [daɪə'metrɪklɪ] *adv* **d. opposed** *(opinion)* diamétralement opposé

diamond ['daɪəmənd] *n* (**a**) *(stone)* diamant *m*; *(shape)* losange *m*; *Am* (**base-ball**) **d.** terrain *m* de baseball; **d. necklace** rivière *f* de diamants (**b**) *Cards* **diamond(s)** carreau *m*

diaper ['daɪpər] *n Am* couche *f*

diaphragm ['daɪəfræm] *n* diaphragme *m*

diarrh(o)ea [daɪə'riːə] *n* diarrhée *f*; **to have d.** avoir la diarrhée

diary ['daɪərɪ] *(pl* -**ies**) *n Br (calendar)* agenda *m*; *(private)* journal *m* (intime)

dice [daɪs] **1** *n inv* dé *m* **2** *vt (food)* couper en dés

dicey ['daɪsɪ] *(*-**ier**, -**iest**) *adj Fam* risqué

dichotomy [daɪ'kɒtəmɪ] *(pl* -**ies**) *n* dichotomie *f*

dickens ['dɪkɪnz] *n Br Fam* **where/why/what the d.?** où/pourquoi/que diable?

Dictaphone® ['dɪktəfəʊn] *n* Dictaphone® *m*

dictate [dɪk'teɪt] **1** *vt (letter, conditions)* dicter (**to** à) **2** *vi* dicter; **to d. to sb** *(order around)* donner des ordres à qn •**dictation** *n* dictée *f*

dictates ['dɪkteɪts] *npl* préceptes *mpl*; **the d. of conscience** la voix de la conscience

dictator [dɪk'teɪtə(r)] *n* dictateur *m* •**dicta-'torial** [-tə'tɔːrɪəl] *adj* dictatorial •**dictatorship** *n* dictature *f*

dictionary ['dɪkʃənərɪ] *(pl* -**ies**) *n* dictionnaire *m*; **English d.** dictionnaire *m* d'anglais

did [dɪd] *pt of* **do**

diddle ['dɪdəl] *vt Br Fam (cheat)* rouler; **to d. sb out of sth** carotter qch à qn; **to get diddled out of sth** se faire refaire de qch

die¹ [daɪ] *(pt & pp* **died**, *pres p* **dying**) *vi* mourir (**of** *or* **from** de); *Fig* **to be dying to do sth** mourir d'envie de faire qch; **to be dying for sth** avoir une envie folle de qch; **to d. away** *(of noise)* mourir; **to d. down** *(of fire)* mourir; *(of storm)* se calmer; **to d. off** mourir (les uns après les autres); **to d. out** *(of custom)* mourir; *(of family)* s'éteindre

die² [daɪ] *n* (**a**) *(pl* **dice** [daɪs]) *(in games)* dé *m*; **the d. is cast** les dés sont jetés (**b**) *(mould)* matrice *f*

die-hard ['daɪhɑːd] *n* réactionnaire *mf*

diesel ['diːzəl] *adj & n* **d. (engine)** (moteur *m*) diesel *m*; **d. (oil)** gazole *m*

diet ['daɪət] **1** *n (usual food)* alimentation *f*; *(restricted food)* régime *m*; **to go on a d.** faire un régime

2 *vi* être au régime • **dietary** *adj* alimentaire; **d. fibre** fibres *fpl* alimentaires • **dietician** [-'tɪʃən] *n* diététicien, -ienne *mf*

differ ['dɪfə(r)] *vi* différer (**from** de); *(disagree)* ne pas être d'accord (**from** avec)

difference ['dɪfərəns] *n* différence *f* (**in** de); **d. of opinion** différend *m*; **it makes no d.** ça n'a pas d'importance; **it makes no d. to me** ça m'est égal; **that will make a big d.** ça va changer pas mal de choses

different ['dɪfərənt] *adj* différent (**from** de); *(another)* autre; *(various)* divers • **differently** *adv* différemment (**from** de)

differentiate [dɪfə'renʃɪeɪt] **1** *vt* différencier (**from** de)

2 *vi* faire la différence (**between** entre)

difficult ['dɪfɪkəlt] *adj* difficile (**to do** à faire); **it's d. for us to** il nous est difficile de; **the d. thing is** to le plus difficile est de

difficulty ['dɪfɪkəltɪ] *(pl* **-ies**) *n* difficulté *f*; **to have d. doing sth** avoir du mal à faire qch; **to be in d.** avoir des difficultés; **to have d.** *or* **difficulties with sb/sth** *(problems)* avoir des ennuis avec qn/qch

diffident ['dɪfɪdənt] *adj (person)* qui manque d'assurance; *(smile, tone)* mal assuré • **diffidence** *n* manque *m* d'assurance

diffuse 1 [dɪ'fjuːs] *adj (spread out, wordy)* diffus

2 [dɪ'fjuːz] *vt (spread)* diffuser • **diffusion** *n* diffusion *f*

dig [dɪg] **1** *n (in archaeology)* fouilles *fpl*; *(with spade)* coup *m* de bêche; *(with elbow)* coup de coude; *(with fist)* coup de poing; *Fam (remark)* pique *f*

2 *(pt & pp* **dug**, *pres p* **digging**) *vt (ground, garden)* bêcher; *(hole, grave)* creuser; *very Fam (understand)* piger; *very Fam (appreciate)* aimer; **to d. sth into sth** *(push)* planter qch dans qch; **to d. out** *(animal, object)* déterrer; *(accident victim)* dégager; *Fam (find)* dénicher; **to d. up** *(from ground)* déterrer; *(weed)* arracher; *(road)* excaver

3 *vi (dig a hole)* creuser; *(of pig)* fouiller; **to d. (oneself) in** *(of soldier)* se retrancher; *Fam* **to d. in** *(eat)* attaquer; **to d. into** *(past)* fouiller dans

digest 1 ['daɪdʒest] *n (summary)* condensé *m*

2 [daɪ'dʒest] *vti* digérer • **digestible** [-'dʒestəbəl] *adj* digeste • **di'gestion** *n* digestion *f* • **digestive** [-'dʒestɪv] *adj* digestif, -ive

digger ['dɪgə(r)] *n (machine)* pelleteuse *f*

digit ['dɪdʒɪt] *n (number)* chiffre *m* • **digital** *adj* numérique; *(tape, recording)* audionumérique

dignified ['dɪgnɪfaɪd] *adj* digne • **dignitary** *(pl* **-ies**) *n* dignitaire *m* • **dignity** *n* dignité *f*

digress [daɪ'gres] *vi* faire une digression; **to d. from** s'écarter de • **digression** *n* digression *f*

digs [dɪgz] *npl Br* chambre *f* meublée

dike [daɪk] *n* = **dyke**

dilapidated [dɪ'læpɪdeɪtɪd] *adj (house)* délabré

dilate [daɪ'leɪt] **1** *vt* dilater

2 *vi* se dilater • **dilation** *n* dilatation *f*

dilemma [daɪ'lemə] *n* dilemme *m*

diligent ['dɪlɪdʒənt] *adj* appliqué; **to be d. in doing sth** faire qch avec zèle • **diligence** *n* zèle *m*

dilly-dally ['dɪlɪ'dælɪ] *(pt & pp* **-ied**) *vi Fam (dawdle)* lambiner; *(hesitate)* tergiverser

dilute [daɪ'luːt] **1** *vt* diluer

2 *adj* dilué

dim [dɪm] **1** (**dimmer, dimmest**) *adj (light)* faible; *(colour)* terne; *(room)* sombre; *(memory, outline)* vague; *(person)* stupide

2 *(pt & pp* **-mm-**) *vt (light)* baisser; *(glory)* ternir; *(memory)* estomper; *Am* **to d. one's headlights** se mettre en code • **dimly** *adv (shine)* faiblement; *(vaguely)* vaguement; **d. lit** mal éclairé • **dimness** *n* faiblesse *f*; *(of memory)* flou *m*; *(of room)* pénombre *f*

dime [daɪm] *n Am* (pièce *f* de) dix cents *mpl*; **it's not worth a d.** ça ne vaut pas un clou; **a d. store** ≃ un Prisunic®, ≃ un Monoprix®

dimension [daɪ'menʃən] *n* dimension *f*

diminish [dɪ'mɪnɪʃ] *vti* diminuer • **diminishing** *adj* décroissant

diminutive [dɪ'mɪnjʊtɪv] **1** *adj (tiny)* minuscule

2 *adj & n Grammar* diminutif *(m)*

dimmer ['dɪmə(r)] *n* **d. (switch)** variateur *m*

dimmers ['dɪməz] *npl Am Aut* codes *mpl*

dimple ['dɪmpəl] *n* fossette *f* • **dimpled** *adj (chin, cheek)* à fossettes

dimwit ['dɪmwɪt] *n Fam* andouille *f* • **'dim'witted** *adj Fam* tarte

din [dɪn] **1** *n (noise)* vacarme *m*
2 *(pt & pp* **-nn-)** *vt* **to d. into sb that...**
rabâcher à qn que...

dine [daɪn] *vi* dîner (**on** *or* **off** de); **to d.
out** dîner dehors •**diner** *n (person)* dî-
neur, -euse *mf*; *Am (restaurant)* petit restaurant *m* •**dining car** *n (on train)* wagon-
restaurant *m* •**dining room** *n* salle *f* à
manger

dinghy ['dɪŋgɪ] *(pl* **-ies)** *n* petit canot *m*;
(rubber) d. canot pneumatique

dingy ['dɪndʒɪ] (**-ier, -iest**) *adj (room)*
minable; *(colour)* terne

dinner ['dɪnə(r)] *n (evening meal)* dîner
m; *(lunch)* déjeuner *m*; *(for dog, cat)*
pâtée *f*; **to have d.** dîner; **to have sb to d.**
avoir qn à dîner; **it's d. time** c'est l'heure
de dîner; *(lunch)* c'est l'heure de déjeuner; **d. dance** dîner-dansant *m*; **d. jacket**
smoking *m*; **d. party** dîner *m*; **d. plate**
grande assiette *f*; **d. service, d. set** service
m de table

dinosaur ['daɪnəsɔː(r)] *n* dinosaure *m*

dint [dɪnt] *n Formal* **by d. of sth/of doing**
à force de qch/de faire

diocese ['daɪəsɪs] *n Rel* diocèse *m*

dip [dɪp] **1** *n (in road)* petit creux *m*; **to go
for a d.** *(swim)* faire trempette
2 *(pt & pp* **-pp-)** *vt* plonger; *Br* **to d. one's
headlights** se mettre en code
3 *vi (of road)* plonger; *(of sun)* descendre; **to d. into** *(pocket, savings)* puiser
dans; *(book)* feuilleter

diphtheria [dɪf'θɪərɪə] *n Med* diphtérie *f*

diphthong ['dɪfθɒŋ] *n Ling* diphtongue
f

diploma [dɪ'pləʊmə] *n* diplôme *m*

diplomacy [dɪ'pləʊməsɪ] *n* diplomatie *f*

diplomat ['dɪpləmæt] *n* diplomate *mf*
•**diplo'matic** *adj* diplomatique; **to be d.**
(tactful) être diplomate

dipper ['dɪpə(r)] *n Br* **the big d.** *(at fairground)* les montagnes russes *fpl*

dipstick ['dɪpstɪk] *n* jauge *f* de niveau
d'huile

dire ['daɪə(r)] *adj (situation)* affreux,
-euse; *(consequences)* tragique; *(poverty,
need)* extrême; **to be in d. straits** être
dans une mauvaise passe

direct¹ [daɪ'rekt] **1** *adj (result, flight, person)* direct; *(danger)* immédiat; *Br* **d.
debit** prélèvement *m* automatique
2 *adv* directement •**directness** *n (of person, reply)* franchise *f*

direct² [daɪ'rekt] *vt (gaze, light, company,
attention)* diriger (**at** sur); *(traffic)* régler;
(letter, remark) adresser (**to** à); *(efforts)*
consacrer (**towards** à); *(film)* réaliser;

(play) mettre en scène; **to d. sb** *(place)*
indiquer à qn le chemin de; **to d. sb to do
sth** charger qn de faire qch

direction [daɪ'rekʃən] *n* direction *f*, sens
m; *(management)* direction; *(of film)* réalisation *f*; *(of play)* mise *f* en scène; **directions** *(orders)* indications *fpl*; **directions
(for use)** mode *m* d'emploi; **in the opposite d.** en sens inverse

directive [dɪ'rektɪv] *n* directive *f*

directly [daɪ'rektlɪ] **1** *adv (without detour)* directement; *(exactly)* juste; *(at
once)* tout de suite; *(speak)* franchement;
d. in front/behind juste devant/derrière
2 *conj Br Fam (as soon as)* aussitôt que
(*+ indicative*)

director [daɪ'rektə(r)] *n* directeur, -trice
mf; *(board member)* administrateur, -trice
mf; *(of film)* réalisateur, -trice *mf*; *(of play)*
metteur *m* en scène •**directorship** *n*
poste *m* de directeur; *(as board member)*
poste d'administrateur

directory [daɪ'rektərɪ] *(pl* **-ies)** *n (phone
book)* annuaire *m*; *(of streets)* guide *m*; *(of
addresses)* & *Comptr* répertoire *m*; **telephone d.** annuaire *m* du téléphone; *Br* **d.
enquiries** renseignements *mpl* téléphoniques

dirt [dɜːt] *n* saleté *f*; *(mud)* boue *f*; *(earth)*
terre *f*; *Fig (talk)* obscénité(s) *f(pl)*; *Fam* **d.
cheap** très bon marché; **d. road** chemin *m*
de terre; *Sport* **d. track** cendrée *f*

dirty ['dɜːtɪ] **1** (**-ier, -iest**) *adj* sale; *(job)*
salissant; *(word)* grossier, -ière; **to get d.**
se salir; **to get sth d.** salir qch; **a d. joke**
une histoire cochonne; **a d. trick** un sale
tour; **a d. old man** un vieux cochon
2 *adv (fight)* déloyalement
3 *vt* salir; *(machine)* encrasser

disability [dɪsə'bɪlɪtɪ] *(pl* **-ies)** *n (injury)*
infirmité *f*; *(condition)* invalidité *f*; *Fig*
désavantage *m*

disable [dɪs'eɪbəl] *vt* rendre infirme •**disabled 1** *adj* handicapé **2** *npl* **the d.** les
handicapés *mpl*

disadvantage [dɪsəd'vɑːntɪdʒ] **1** *n* désavantage *m*
2 *vt* désavantager

disaffected [dɪsə'fektɪd] *adj* mécontent
•**disaffection** *n* désaffection *f*

disagree [dɪsə'griː] *vi* ne pas être d'accord (**with** avec); *(of figures, reports)* ne
pas concorder; **to d. with sb** *(of food,
climate, medicine)* ne pas réussir à qn
•**disagreement** *n* désaccord *m*; *(quarrel)*
différend *m*

disagreeable [dɪsə'griːəbəl] *adj* désagréable

disallow [dɪsə'laʊ] *vt Formal* rejeter
disappear [dɪsə'pɪə(r)] *vi* disparaître
• **disappearance** *n* disparition *f*
disappoint [dɪsə'pɔɪnt] *vt* décevoir; **I'm disappointed with it** ça m'a déçu • **disappointing** *adj* décevant • **disappointment** *n* déception *f*
disapproval [dɪsə'pruːvəl] *n* désapprobation *f*
disapprove [dɪsə'pruːv] *vi* **to d. of sb/sth** désapprouver qn/qch; **I d.** je suis contre • **disapproving** *adj (look, tone)* désapprobateur, -trice
disarm [dɪs'ɑːm] *vti* désarmer • **disarmament** *n* désarmement *m*
disarray [dɪsə'reɪ] *n (distress)* désarroi *m; (disorder)* désordre *m;* **in d.** *(army, political party)* en plein désarroi; *(clothes, hair)* en désordre
disaster [dɪ'zɑːstə(r)] *n* désastre *m*, catastrophe *f;* **d. area** région *f* sinistrée • **disastrous** *adj* désastreux, -euse
disband [dɪs'bænd] **1** *vt* dissoudre **2** *vi* se dissoudre
disbelief [dɪsbə'liːf] *n* incrédulité *f*
disc [dɪsk] *(Am* **disk***) n* disque *m;* **d. jockey** disc-jockey *m*
discard [dɪs'kɑːd] *vt (get rid of)* se débarrasser de; *(plan)* abandonner
discern [dɪ'sɜːn] *vt* discerner • **discerning** *adj (person)* averti
discernible [dɪ'sɜːnəbəl] *adj* perceptible
discernment [dɪ'sɜːnmənt] *n* discernement *m*
discharge 1 ['dɪstʃɑːdʒ] *n (of gun, electricity)* décharge *f; (of pus, liquid)* écoulement *m; (dismissal)* renvoi *m; (freeing)* libération *f; (of unfit soldier)* réforme *f* **2** [dɪs'tʃɑːdʒ] *vt (patient)* laisser sortir; *(employee)* renvoyer; *(soldier, prisoner)* libérer; *(unfit soldier)* réformer; *(gun)* décharger; *(liquid)* déverser
disciple [dɪ'saɪpəl] *n* disciple *m*
disciplinary [dɪsɪ'plɪnərɪ] *adj (measure)* disciplinaire
discipline ['dɪsɪplɪn] **1** *n (behaviour, subject)* discipline *f* **2** *vt (control)* discipliner; *(punish)* punir
disclaim [dɪs'kleɪm] *vt (renounce)* renoncer à; *(deny)* démentir
disclose [dɪs'kləʊz] *vt* révéler • **disclosure** [-ʒə(r)] *n* révélation *f*
disco ['dɪskəʊ] *(pl* **-os***) n* discothèque *f*
discolour [dɪs'kʌlə(r)] *(Am* **discolor***)* **1** *vt* décolorer; *(teeth)* jaunir **2** *vi* se décolorer; *(of teeth)* jaunir
discomfort [dɪs'kʌmfət] *n (physical)* petite douleur *f; (mental)* malaise *m*

disconcerting [dɪskən'sɜːtɪŋ] *adj* déconcertant
disconnect [dɪskə'nekt] *vt (unfasten)* détacher; *(unplug)* débrancher; *(gas, telephone, electricity)* couper
discontent [dɪskən'tent] *n* mécontentement *m* • **discontented** *adj* mécontent *(* **with** de)
discontinue [dɪskən'tɪnjuː] *vt* interrompre
discord ['dɪskɔːd] *n (disagreement)* discorde *f; Mus* dissonance *f*
discotheque ['dɪskətek] *n (club)* discothèque *f*
discount 1 ['dɪskaʊnt] *n (on article)* réduction *f; (on account paid early)* escompte *m;* **at a d.** *(buy, sell)* au rabais; **d. store** solderie *f* **2** [dɪs'kaʊnt] *vt (story)* ne pas tenir compte de
discourage [dɪs'kʌrɪdʒ] *vt* décourager *(* **sb from doing** qn de faire); **to get discouraged** se décourager • **discouragement** *n* découragement *m*
discourse ['dɪskɔːs] *n* discours *m*
discourteous [dɪs'kɜːtɪəs] *adj* discourtois *(* **towards** envers)
discover [dɪs'kʌvə(r)] *vt* découvrir *(* **that** que) • **discovery** *(pl* **-ies***) n* découverte *f*
discredit [dɪs'kredɪt] **1** *n* discrédit *m* **2** *vt (cast slur on)* discréditer; *(refuse to believe)* ne pas croire • **discreditable** *adj* indigne
discreet [dɪ'skriːt] *adj* discret, -ète
discrepancy [dɪ'skrepənsɪ] *(pl* **-ies***) n* décalage *m (* **between** entre)
discretion [dɪ'skreʃən] *n (tact)* discrétion *f;* **I'll use my own d.** je jugerai par moi-même
discriminate [dɪ'skrɪmɪneɪt] *vi* **to d. against** faire de la discrimination envers; **to be discriminated against** être victime de discrimination; **to d. between** distinguer entre • **discriminating** *adj* perspicace • **discrimination** [-'neɪʃən] *n (bias)* discrimination *f; (judgement)* discernement *m; (distinction)* distinction *f* • **discriminatory** [-nətərɪ] *adj* discriminatoire
discus ['dɪskəs] *n Sport* disque *m*
discuss [dɪ'skʌs] *vt* discuter de • **discussion** *n* discussion *f;* **under d.** en discussion
disdain [dɪs'deɪn] **1** *n* dédain *m* **2** *vt* dédaigner *(* **to do** de faire) • **disdainful** *adj* dédaigneux, -euse; **to be d. of** dédaigner
disease [dɪ'ziːz] *n* maladie *f* • **diseased** *adj* malade

disembark [dɪsɪm'bɑːk] *vti* débarquer • **disembarkation** [-embɑː'keɪʃən] *n* débarquement *m*

disembodied [dɪsɪm'bɒdɪd] *adj* désincarné

disembowel [dɪsɪm'baʊəl] (*Br* -ll-, *Am* -l-) *vt* éviscérer

disenchanted [dɪsɪn'tʃɑːntɪd] *adj* désenchanté

disengage [dɪsɪn'geɪdʒ] *vt* (*object*) dégager (**from** de); (*troops*) désengager; *Br* **to d. the clutch** débrayer

disentangle [dɪsɪn'tæŋgəl] *vt* (*string*) démêler; **to d. oneself from** se dégager de

disfavour [dɪs'feɪvə(r)] (*Am* **disfavor**) *n* défaveur *f*

disfigure [dɪs'fɪgə(r)] *vt* défigurer • **disfigured** *adj* défiguré • **disfigurement** *n* défigurement *m*

disgorge [dɪs'gɔːdʒ] *vt* *Fig* (*water, passengers*) dégorger; (*food*) vomir

disgrace [dɪs'greɪs] **1** *n* (*shame*) honte *f* (**to** à); (*disfavour*) disgrâce *f*
2 *vt* déshonorer • **disgraced** *adj* disgracié

disgraceful [dɪs'greɪsfəl] *adj* honteux, -euse • **disgracefully** *adv* honteusement

> *Note that the French word **disgracieux** is a false friend and is never a translation for the English word **disgraceful**. It means **ungainly**.*

disgruntled [dɪs'grʌntəld] *adj* mécontent

disguise [dɪs'gaɪz] **1** *n* déguisement *m*; **in d.** déguisé
2 *vt* déguiser (**as** en)

disgust [dɪs'gʌst] **1** *n* dégoût *m* (**for** *or* **at** *or* **with** de); **in d.** dégoûté
2 *vt* dégoûter • **disgusted** *adj* dégoûté (**at** *or* **by** *or* **with** de); **to be d. with sb** (*annoyed*) être fâché contre qn; **I was d. to hear that** j'ai été indigné d'apprendre que • **disgusting** *adj* dégoûtant

dish [dɪʃ] **1** *n* (*container, food*) plat *m*; **the dishes** la vaisselle; **to do the dishes** faire la vaisselle
2 *vt* *Fam* **to d. out** (*money, advice*) distribuer; **to d. out** *or* **up** (*food*) servir • **dishpan** *n* *Am* bassine *f* (*pour la vaisselle*) • **dishtowel** *n* torchon *m* (à vaisselle) • **dishwasher** *n* lave-vaisselle *m inv*

disharmony [dɪs'hɑːmənɪ] *n* désaccord *m*; (*in music*) dissonance *f*

dishcloth ['dɪʃklɒθ] *n* (*for washing*) lavette *f*; (*for drying*) torchon *m*

dishevelled [dɪ'ʃevəld] (*Am* **disheveled**) *adj* (*person, hair*) ébouriffé

dishonest [dɪs'ɒnɪst] *adj* malhonnête • **dishonesty** *n* malhonnêteté *f*

dishonour [dɪs'ɒnə(r)] (*Am* **dishonor**) **1** *n* déshonneur *m*
2 *vt* déshonorer; (*cheque*) refuser d'honorer • **dishonourable** (*Am* **dishonorable**) *adj* déshonorant • **dishonourably** (*Am* **dishonorably**) *adv* avec déshonneur

dishy ['dɪʃɪ] (-**ier**, -**iest**) *adj* *Br* *Fam* mignon, -onne

disillusion [dɪsɪ'luːʒən] **1** *n* désillusion *f*
2 *vt* décevoir; **to be disillusioned (with)** être déçu (de) • **disillusionment** *n* désillusion *f*

disinclined [dɪsɪn'klaɪnd] *adj* peu disposé (**to do** à faire) • **disinclination** [-klɪ'neɪʃən] *n* répugnance *f* (**to do** à faire)

disinfect [dɪsɪn'fekt] *vt* désinfecter • **disinfectant** *adj* & *n* désinfectant (*m*) • **disinfection** *n* désinfection *f*

disinherit [dɪsɪn'herɪt] *vt* déshériter

disintegrate [dɪs'ɪntɪgreɪt] **1** *vt* désintégrer
2 *vi* se désintégrer • **disintegration** [-'greɪʃən] *n* désintégration *f*

disinterested [dɪs'ɪntrɪstɪd] *adj* (*impartial*) désintéressé; *Fam* (*uninterested*) indifférent (**in** à)

disjointed [dɪs'dʒɔɪntɪd] *adj* (*words, style*) décousu

disk [dɪsk] *n* (**a**) *Am* = **disc** (**b**) *Comptr* disque *m*; (*floppy*) disquette *f*; **on d.** sur disque; **hard d.** disque *m* dur; **d. drive** unité *f* de disques • **diskette** [dɪs'ket] *n* *Comptr* disquette *f*

dislike [dɪs'laɪk] **1** *n* aversion *f* (**for** *or* **of** pour); **to take a d. to sb/sth** prendre qn/qch en grippe; **our likes and dislikes** nos goûts *mpl*
2 *vt* ne pas aimer (**doing** faire); **he doesn't d. it** ça ne lui déplaît pas

dislocate ['dɪsləkeɪt] *vt* (*limb*) démettre; *Fig* (*disrupt*) désorganiser; **to d. one's shoulder** se démettre l'épaule • **dislo'cation** *n* dislocation *f*

dislodge [dɪs'lɒdʒ] *vt* faire bouger, déplacer; (*enemy*) déloger

disloyal [dɪs'lɔɪəl] *adj* déloyal • **disloyally** *adv* (*act*) déloyalement • **disloyalty** *n* déloyauté *f*

dismal ['dɪzməl] *adj* lugubre • **dismally** *adv* (*fail, behave*) lamentablement

dismantle [dɪs'mæntəl] *vt* (*machine*) démonter; (*organization*) démanteler

dismay [dɪs'meɪ] **1** *n* consternation *f*
2 *vt* consterner

dismiss [dɪs'mɪs] *vt* (*from job*) renvoyer

(**from** de); *(official)* destituer; *(thought, suggestion)* écarter; **to d. an appeal** *(in court)* rejeter un appel; **to d. a case** *(of judge)* classer une affaire; **d.!** *(to soldiers)* rompez!; *(to class)* vous pouvez partir •**dismissal** *n* renvoi *m*; *(of official)* destitution *f*

dismount [dɪs'maʊnt] **1** *vi (of person)* descendre (**from** de)
2 *vt (of horse)* désarçonner

disobedience [dɪsə'biːdɪəns] *n* désobéissance *f* •**disobedient** *adj* désobéissant

disobey [dɪsə'beɪ] **1** *vt* désobéir à
2 *vi* désobéir

disorder [dɪs'ɔːdə(r)] *n (confusion)* désordre *m*; *(illness, riots)* troubles *mpl* •**disorderly** *adj (behaviour, person, room)* désordonné; *(meeting, crowd)* houleux, -euse

disorganize [dɪs'ɔːgənaɪz] *vt* désorganiser; **to be disorganized** être désorganisé

disorientate [dɪs'ɔːrɪənteɪt] *(Am* **disorient** [dɪs'ɔːrɪənt]*) vt* désorienter

disown [dɪs'əʊn] *vt* renier

disparage [dɪs'pærɪdʒ] *vt* dénigrer •**disparaging** *adj (remark)* désobligeant

disparate ['dɪspərət] *adj* disparate •**disparity** [-'pærɪtɪ] *(pl* **-ies**) *n* disparité *f* (**between** entre)

dispassionate [dɪs'pæʃənət] *adj (unemotional)* calme; *(not biased)* impartial

dispatch [dɪ'spætʃ] **1** *n (sending)* expédition *f* (**of** de); *(message)* dépêche *f*
2 *vt (send, finish off)* expédier; *(troops, messenger)* envoyer

dispel [dɪ'spel] *(pt & pp* **-ll-***) vt* dissiper

dispensary [dɪ'spensərɪ] *(pl* **-ies**) *n (in hospital)* pharmacie *f*; *(in chemist's shop)* officine *f*

dispense [dɪ'spens] **1** *vt (give out)* distribuer; *(justice)* administrer; *(medicine)* préparer; *Br* **dispensing chemist** pharmacien, -ienne *mf*; *(shop)* pharmacie *f*
2 *vi* **to d. with** *(do without)* se passer de; **that dispenses with the need for** cela rend superflu •**dispensation** [-'seɪʃən] *n* distribution *f*; **special d.** *(exemption)* dérogation *f* •**dispenser** *n (device)* distributeur *m*

disperse [dɪ'spɜːs] **1** *vt* disperser
2 *vi* se disperser •**dispersal, dispersion** *n* dispersion *f*

dispirited [dɪ'spɪrɪtɪd] *adj* découragé

displace [dɪs'pleɪs] *vt (shift)* déplacer; *(replace)* supplanter; **displaced person** personne *f* déplacée

display [dɪ'spleɪ] **1** *n (in shop)* étalage *m*;

(of paintings, handicrafts) exposition *f*; *(of force)* déploiement *m*; *(of anger)* manifestation *f*; **d. (unit)** *(of computer)* moniteur *m*; **on d.** exposé
2 *vt (goods)* exposer; *(sign, notice)* afficher; *(emotion)* manifester; *(talent, concern, ignorance)* faire preuve de

displease [dɪs'pliːz] *vt* mécontenter •**displeased** *adj* mécontent (**with** de)

displeasure [dɪs'pleʒə(r)] *n* mécontentement *m*

disposable [dɪ'spəʊzəbəl] *adj Br (plate, nappy)* jetable; *(income)* disponible

disposal [dɪ'spəʊzəl] *n (sale)* vente *f*; *(of waste)* évacuation *f*; **at the d. of** à la disposition de

dispose¹ [dɪ'spəʊz] *vi* **to d. of** *(get rid of)* se débarrasser de; *(throw away)* jeter; *(matter, problem)* régler; *Fam (kill)* liquider

dispose² [dɪ'spəʊz] *vt* **to d. sb to do** *(make willing)* disposer qn à faire; **to be disposed to do** être disposé à faire; **well-disposed towards** bien disposé envers

disposition [dɪspə'zɪʃən] *n (placing)* disposition *f*; *(character)* tempérament *m*; *(readiness)* inclination *f*

dispossess [dɪspə'zes] *vt* déposséder (**of** de)

disproportion [dɪsprə'pɔːʃən] *n* disproportion *f* •**disproportionate** *adj* disproportionné

disprove [dɪs'pruːv] *(pp* **disproved,** *Law* **disproven** [-'prəʊvən]*) vt* réfuter

dispute [dɪ'spjuːt] **1** *n (quarrel)* dispute *f*; *(debate)* controverse *f*; *(legal)* litige *m*; **beyond d.** incontestable; **in d.** *(matter)* débattu; *(facts, territory)* contesté; *(competence)* en question; **(industrial) d.** conflit *m* social
2 *vt (claim, will)* contester

disqualify [dɪs'kwɒlɪfaɪ] *(pt & pp* **-ied**) *vt (make unfit)* rendre inapte (**from** à); *Sport* disqualifier; **to d. sb from driving** retirer son permis à qn •**disqualification** [-fɪ'keɪʃən] *n Sport* disqualification *f*; **his d. from driving** le retrait de son permis de conduire

disquiet [dɪs'kwaɪət] **1** *n* inquiétude *f*
2 *vt* inquiéter •**disquieting** *adj* inquiétant

disregard [dɪsrɪ'gɑːd] **1** *n* mépris *m* (**for** de)
2 *vt* ne tenir aucun compte de

disrepair [dɪsrɪ'peə(r)] *n* **in (a state of) d.** délabré

disreputable [dɪs'repjʊtəbəl] *adj* peu

recommandable; *(behaviour)* honteux, -euse

disrepute [dɪsrɪ'pjuːt] *n* discrédit *m*; **to bring sb/sth into d.** discréditer qn/qch

disrespect [dɪsrɪ'spekt] *n* irrespect *m* • **disrespectful** *adj* irrespectueux, -ueuse (**to** envers)

disrupt [dɪs'rʌpt] *vt (traffic, class)* perturber; *(communications)* interrompre; *(plan)* déranger • **disruption** *n* perturbation *f*; *(of communications)* interruption *f*; *(of plan)* dérangement *m*

disruptive [dɪs'rʌptɪv] *adj* perturbateur, -trice

dissatisfied [dɪ'sætɪsfaɪd] *adj* mécontent (**with** de) • **dissatisfaction** [-'fækʃən] *n* mécontentement *m* (**with** devant)

dissect [daɪ'sekt] *vt* disséquer • **dissection** *n* dissection *f*

disseminate [dɪ'semɪneɪt] *vt* disséminer

dissension [dɪ'senʃən] *n* dissension *f*

dissent [dɪ'sent] **1** *n* désaccord *m* **2** *vi* être en désaccord (**from** avec) • **dissenting** *adj (voice)* dissident

dissertation [dɪsə'teɪʃən] *n* mémoire *m*

disservice [dɪ'sɜːvɪs] *n* **to do sb a d.** rendre un mauvais service à qn

dissident ['dɪsɪdənt] *adj & n* dissident, -ente *(mf)* • **dissidence** *n* dissidence *f*

dissimilar [dɪ'sɪmɪlə(r)] *adj* différent (**to** de)

dissipate ['dɪsɪpeɪt] *vt (clouds, fog, fears)* dissiper; *(energy, fortune)* gaspiller

dissociate [dɪ'səʊʃɪeɪt] *vt* dissocier (**from** de)

dissolute ['dɪsəluːt] *adj* dissolu

dissolve [dɪ'zɒlv] **1** *vt* dissoudre **2** *vi* se dissoudre • **dissolution** [dɪsə'luːʃən] *n* dissolution *f*

dissuade [dɪ'sweɪd] *vt* dissuader (**from doing** de faire); **to d. sb from sth** détourner qn de qch • **dissuasion** [-ʒən] *n* dissuasion *f*

distance ['dɪstəns] *n* distance *f*; **in the d.** au loin; **from a d.** de loin; **at a d.** assez loin; **it's within walking d.** on peut y aller à pied; **to keep one's d.** garder ses distances

distant ['dɪstənt] *adj* lointain; *(relative)* éloigné; *(reserved)* distant; **5 km d. from** à (une distance de) 5 km de • **distantly** *adv* **we're d. related** nous sommes parents éloignés

distaste [dɪs'teɪst] *n* aversion *f* (**for** pour) • **distasteful** *adj* déplaisant

distemper¹ [dɪ'stempə(r)] *n (paint)* détrempe *f*

distemper² [dɪ'stempə(r)] *n (disease)* maladie *f* de Carré

distil [dɪ'stɪl] *(pt & pp -ll-) vt* distiller; **distilled water** *(for battery, iron)* eau *f* déminéralisée • **distillation** [-'leɪʃən] *n* distillation *f* • **distillery** *(pl -ies) n* distillerie *f*

distinct [dɪ'stɪŋkt] *adj* (**a**) *(clear)* clair; *(preference, improvement, difference)* net *(f* nette) (**b**) *(different)* distinct (**from** de) • **distinctly** *adv (see, hear)* distinctement; *(remember)* très bien; *(better, easier)* nettement; *(stupid, ill-mannered)* vraiment; **d. possible** tout à fait possible

distinction [dɪ'stɪŋkʃən] *n* distinction *f*; *(in exam)* mention *f* bien; **singer/writer of d.** chanteur, -euse *mf*/écrivain *m* réputé(e)

distinctive [dɪ'stɪŋktɪv] *adj* distinctif, -ive

distinguish [dɪ'stɪŋgwɪʃ] *vti* distinguer (**from** de; **between** entre); **to d. oneself** se distinguer (**as** en tant que) • **distinguished** *adj* distingué

distort [dɪ'stɔːt] *vt* déformer • **distorted** *adj* déformé; *(false) (idea)* faux *(f* fausse) • **distortion** *n (of features, sound)* distorsion *f*; *(of truth)* déformation *f*

distract [dɪ'strækt] *vt* distraire (**from** de) • **distracted** *adj* préoccupé • **distracting** *adj (noise)* gênant

> ✎ Note that the French word **distrait** is a false friend. It means **absent-minded**.

distraction [dɪ'strækʃən] *n (lack of attention, amusement)* distraction *f*; **to drive sb to d.** rendre qn fou/folle

distraught [dɪ'strɔːt] *adj* éperdu

distress [dɪ'stres] **1** *n (mental)* détresse *f*; *(physical)* douleur *f*; **in d.** *(ship, soul)* en détresse; **in (great) d.** *(poverty)* dans la détresse **2** *vt* bouleverser • **distressing** *adj* bouleversant

distribute [dɪ'strɪbjuːt] *vt (give out) & Com (supply)* distribuer; *(spread evenly)* répartir • **distribution** [-'bjuːʃən] *n* distribution *f*; *(even spread)* répartition *f* • **distributor** *n (in car, of films)* distributeur *m*; *(of cars)* concessionnaire *mf*

district ['dɪstrɪkt] *n* région *f*; *(of town)* quartier *m*; *(administrative)* district *m*; *Am* **d. attorney** ≃ procureur *m* de la République; *Br* **d. nurse** infirmière *f* visiteuse

distrust [dɪs'trʌst] **1** *n* méfiance *f* (**of** à l'égard de) **2** *vt* se méfier de • **distrustful** *adj* méfiant; **to be d. of** se méfier de

disturb [dɪ'stɜːb] *vt (sleep, water)* troubler; *(papers, belongings)* déranger; **to d. sb** *(bother)* déranger qn; *(worry, alarm)* troubler qn •**disturbed** *adj (person) (worried, mentally unbalanced)* perturbé; *(sleep)* agité •**disturbing** *adj (worrying)* inquiétant; *(annoying, irksome)* gênant

disturbance [dɪ'stɜːbəns] *n (noise)* tapage *m*; **disturbances** *(riots)* troubles *mpl*

disunity [dɪs'juːnɪtɪ] *n* désunion *f*

disuse [dɪs'juːs] *n* **to fall into d.** tomber en désuétude •**disused** [-'juːzd] *adj (building)* désaffecté

ditch [dɪtʃ] **1** *n* fossé *m*
2 *vt Fam (get rid of)* se débarrasser de; *(plan)* laisser tomber

dither ['dɪðə(r)] *vi Fam* tergiverser; **to d. (around)** *(waste time)* tourner en rond

ditto ['dɪtəʊ] *adv* idem

divan [dɪ'væn] *n* divan *m*

dive [daɪv] **1** *n* (**a**) *(of swimmer, goalkeeper)* plongeon *m*; *(of submarine)* plongée *f*; *(of aircraft)* piqué *m* (**b**) *Fam Pej (bar)* boui-boui *m*
2 *(pt* **dived,** *Am* **dove)** *vi* plonger; *(of plane)* piquer; **to d. for pearls** pêcher des perles; **to d. for the exit/into the pub** se précipiter vers la sortie/dans le pub •**diver** *n* plongeur, -euse *mf*; *(deepsea)* scaphandrier *m* •**diving** *n (underwater)* plongée *f* sous-marine; **d. suit** scaphandre *m*; **d. board** plongeoir *m*

diverge [daɪ'vɜːdʒ] *vi* diverger (**from** de) •**divergence** *n* divergence *f* •**divergent** *adj* divergent

diverse [daɪ'vɜːs] *adj* divers •**diversify** *(pt & pp* **-ied) 1** *vt* diversifier
2 *vi (of firm)* se diversifier •**diversity** *n* diversité *f*

diversion [daɪ'vɜːʃən] *n Br (on road)* déviation *f*; *(amusement)* distraction *f*; **to create a d.** faire diversion

divert [daɪ'vɜːt] *vt (attention, suspicions, river, plane)* détourner; *Br (traffic)* dévier; *(amuse)* divertir; **to d. sb from** détourner qn de

divest [daɪ'vest] *vt Formal* **to d. of** *(power, rights)* priver de

divide [dɪ'vaɪd] **1** *vt Math* diviser (**into** en; **by** par); *(food, money, time)* partager (**between** *or* **among** entre); **to d. sth (off) (from sth)** séparer qch (de qch); **to d. sth up** *(share out)* partager qch
2 *vi (of group, road)* se diviser (**into** en); **dividing line** ligne *f* de démarcation •**divided** *adj* divisé

dividend ['dɪvɪdend] *n* dividende *m*

divine [dɪ'vaɪn] *adj* divin •**divinity**

[-'vɪnɪtɪ] *(pl* **-ies**) *n (quality, god)* divinité *f*; *(study)* théologie *f*

division [dɪ'vɪʒən] *n* division *f*; *(distribution)* partage *m*; *(dividing object)* séparation *f*; *Sport* **first d.** première division •**divisible** [-'vɪzɪbəl] *adj* divisible •**divisive** [-'vaɪsɪv] *adj* qui cause des dissensions

divorce [dɪ'vɔːs] **1** *n* divorce *m*
2 *vt (husband, wife)* divorcer de; *Fig (idea)* séparer (**from** de)
3 *vi* divorcer •**divorced** *adj* divorcé (**from** de); **to get d.** divorcer •**divorcee** [*Br* dɪvɔː'siː, *Am* dɪvɔːr'seɪ] *n* divorcé, -ée *mf*

divulge [dɪ'vʌldʒ] *vt* divulguer

DIY [diːaɪ'waɪ] *(abbr* **do-it-yourself**) *n Br* bricolage *m*

dizzy ['dɪzɪ] **(-ier, -iest)** *adj* **to be** *or* **feel d.** avoir le vertige; **to make sb (feel) d.** donner le vertige à qn

DJ ['diːdʒeɪ] *abbr* = **disc jockey**

do [duː]

> Les formes négatives sont **don't / doesn't** et **didn't,** qui deviennent **do not / does not** et **did not** à l'écrit, dans un style plus soutenu.

1 *(3rd person sing present tense* **does**; *pt* **did**; *pp* **done**; *pres p* **doing)** *v aux* **do you know?** savez-vous?, est-ce que vous savez?; **I do not** *or* **don't see** je ne vois pas; **he DID say so** *(emphasis)* il l'a bien dit; **do stay** reste donc; **you know him, don't you?** tu le connais, n'est-ce pas?; **better than I do** mieux que je ne le fais; **neither do I** moi non plus; **so do I** moi aussi; **oh, does he?** *(surprise)* ah oui?; **don't!** non!
2 *vt* faire; **to do nothing but sleep** ne faire que dormir; **what does she do?** *(in general)*, **what is she doing?** *(now)* qu'est-ce qu'elle fait?, que fait-elle?; **what have you done (with...)?** qu'as-tu fait (de...)?; **well done** *(congratulations)* bravo!; *(steak)* bien cuit; **that'll do me** *(suit)* ça m'ira; *Br Fam* **I've been done** *(cheated)* je me suis fait avoir; *Fam* **I'll do you!** je t'aurai!; **to do sb out of sth** escroquer qch à qn; **he's hard done by** on le traite durement; *Fam* **I'm done (in)** *(tired)* je suis claqué; *Fam* **he's done for** il est fichu; *Fam* **to do in** *(kill)* zigouiller; **to do out** *(clean)* nettoyer; **to do over** *(redecorate)* refaire; **to do up** *(coat, buttons)* boutonner; *(zip)* fermer; *(house)* refaire; *(goods)* emballer; **do yourself up (well)!** *(wrap up)* couvre-toi (bien)!

3 *vi* **to do well/badly** bien/mal se débrouiller; **do as you're told** fais ce qu'on te dit; **that will do** *(be OK)* ça ira; *(be enough)* ça suffit; **have you done?** vous avez fini?; **business is doing well** les affaires marchent bien; **how are you doing?** (comment) ça va?; **how do you do** *(introduction)* enchanté; *(greeting)* bonjour; **he did well** *or* **right to leave** il a bien fait de partir; **do as I do** fais comme moi; **to make do** se débrouiller; **to do away with sb/sth** supprimer qn/qch; **I could do with a coffee** *(need, want)* je prendrais bien un café; **to do without sb/sth** se passer de qn/qch; **it has to do with** *(relates to)* cela a à voir avec; *(concerns)* cela concerne; *Fam* **anything doing?** est-ce qu'il se passe quelque chose?

4 *n* (**a**) *(pl* **dos**) *Br Fam (party)* fête *f* (**b**) **the do's and don'ts** les choses à faire et à ne pas faire

docile ['dəʊsaɪl] *adj* docile

dock¹ [dɒk] **1** *n* (**a**) *(for ship)* dock *m* (**b**) *(in court)* banc *m* des accusés
2 *vi (of ship) (at quayside)* accoster; *(in port)* relâcher; *(of spacecraft)* s'arrimer • **docker** *n* docker *m* • **dockyard** *n* chantier *m* naval

dock² [dɒk] *vt* (**a**) *(wages)* rogner; **to d. sth from** *(wages)* retenir qch sur (**b**) *(animal's tail)* couper

doctor ['dɒktə(r)] **1** *n (medical)* médecin *m*, docteur *m*; *(having doctor's degree)* docteur
2 *vt (text, food)* altérer; *(cat)* châtrer • **doctorate** *n* doctorat *m* (**in** ès/en)

doctrine ['dɒktrɪn] *n* doctrine *f*

document 1 ['dɒkjʊmənt] *n* document *m*
2 ['dɒkjʊment] *vt (inform)* documenter; *(report in detail) (of film, author)* rendre compte de; *(support)* étayer; **well-documented** *(person)* bien renseigné; *(book)* bien documenté • **documentary** [-'mentərɪ] **1** *adj* documentaire **2** *(pl* **-ies**) *n (film)* documentaire *m*

doddering ['dɒdərɪŋ] *adj (senile)* gâteux, -euse; *(shaky)* branlant

doddle ['dɒdəl] *n Br Fam* **it's a d.** c'est simple comme bonjour

dodge [dɒdʒ] **1** *n (to one side)* mouvement *m* de côté; *Fig (trick)* truc *m*
2 *vt (question)* esquiver; *(person)* éviter; *(pursuer)* échapper à; *(tax)* éviter de payer
3 *vi (to one side)* faire un saut de côté; **to d. out of sight** s'esquiver; **to d. through** *(crowd)* se faufiler dans

Dodgems® ['dɒdʒəmz] *npl* autos *fpl* tamponneuses

dodgy ['dɒdʒɪ] (**-ier, -iest**) *adj Fam (suspect)* louche; *(not working properly)* en mauvais état; *(risky)* risqué

doe [dəʊ] *n (deer)* biche *f*

does [dʌz] *see* **do** • **doesn't** ['dʌzənt] = **does not**

dog¹ [dɒg] *n* chien *m*; *(female)* chienne *f*; **d. biscuit** biscuit *m* pour chien; **d. collar** collier *m* de chien; *Fam (of clergyman)* col *m* de pasteur; **d. days** canicule *f*; **d. food** nourriture *f* pour chien • **dog-eared** *adj (page)* corné • **dog-'tired** *adj Fam* claqué

dog² [dɒg] *(pt & pp* **-gg-**) *vt (follow)* suivre de près

dogged ['dɒgɪd] *adj* obstiné • **doggedly** *adv* obstinément

doggy ['dɒgɪ] *(pl* **-ies**) *n Fam* toutou *m*; **d. bag** *(in restaurant)* = petit sac fourni par certains restaurants pour que les clients puissent emporter les restes

doghouse ['dɒghaʊs] *n Am (kennel)* niche *f*; *Fam* **to be in the d.** ne pas être en odeur de sainteté

dogsbody ['dɒgzbɒdɪ] *(pl* **-ies**) *n Br Fam Pej* factotum *m*

doily ['dɔɪlɪ] *(pl* **-ies**) *n* napperon *m*

doing ['duːɪŋ] *n* **that's your d.** c'est toi qui as fait ça; *Fam* **doings** *(activities)* activités *fpl*

do-it-yourself [duːɪtjə'self] *n Br* bricolage *m*; **d. store/book** magasin *m*/livre *m* de bricolage

doldrums ['dɒldrəmz] *npl* **to be in the d.** *(of person)* avoir le cafard; *(of business)* être en plein marasme

dole [dəʊl] **1** *n Br* **d. (money)** allocation *f* de chômage; **to go on the d.** s'inscrire au chômage
2 *vt Fam* **to d. out** distribuer au compte-gouttes

doleful ['dəʊlfəl] *adj* triste

doll [dɒl] **1** *n* poupée *f*; *Br* **doll's house,** *Am* **dollhouse** maison *f* de poupée
2 *vt Fam* **to d. oneself up** se bichonner

dollar ['dɒlə(r)] *n* dollar *m*

dollop ['dɒləp] *n (of cream, purée)* grosse cuillerée *f*

dolly ['dɒlɪ] *(pl* **-ies**) *n Fam (doll)* poupée *f*

dolphin ['dɒlfɪn] *n* dauphin *m*

domain [dəʊ'meɪn] *n (land, sphere)* domaine *m*

dome [dəʊm] *n* dôme *m*

domestic [də'mestɪk] *adj (appliance, use, tasks)* ménager, -ère; *(animal)* domestique; *(policy, flight, affairs)* intérieur; *(economy, currency)* national; *Br Sch* **d.**

science cours *mpl* de couture et de cuisine • **domesticated** *adj* **to be d.** *(of person)* se débrouiller plutôt bien avec les travaux ménagers; *(of animal)* être domestiqué

domicile [ˈdɒmɪsaɪl] *n Law* domicile *m*

dominant [ˈdɒmɪnənt] *adj* dominant; *(person)* dominateur, -trice • **dominance** *n* prédominance *f*

dominate [ˈdɒmɪneɪt] *vti* dominer • **domination** [-ˈneɪʃən] *n* domination *f*

domineering [dɒmɪˈnɪərɪŋ] *adj (person, character)* dominateur, -trice

domino [ˈdɒmɪnəʊ] *(pl* **-oes***) n* domino *m*; **dominoes** *(game)* dominos *mpl*

don [dɒn] **1** *n Br Univ* professeur *m*
2 *(pt & pp* **-nn-***) vt Literary (clothing)* revêtir

donate [dəʊˈneɪt] **1** *vt* faire don de; *(blood)* donner
2 *vi* donner • **donation** *n* don *m*

done [dʌn] *pp of* **do**

donkey [ˈdɒŋkɪ] *(pl* **-eys***) n* âne *m*; *Br Fam* **I haven't seen him for d.'s years** je ne l'ai pas vu depuis belle lurette; **d. work** travail *m* pénible

donor [ˈdəʊnə(r)] *n* donneur, -euse *mf*

don't [dəʊnt] = **do not**

donut [ˈdəʊnʌt] *n Am* beignet *m*

doodle [ˈduːdəl] *vi* griffonner

doom [duːm] **1** *n (fate)* destin *m*; **to be all d. and gloom** voir tout en noir
2 *vt* condamner (**to** à); **to be doomed** *(unlucky)* être marqué par le destin; *(about to die)* être perdu; **to be doomed (to failure)** *(of project)* être voué à l'échec

door [dɔː(r)] *n* porte *f*; *(of vehicle, train)* portière *f*; **out of doors** dehors; **d.-to-d. salesman** démarcheur *m* • **doorbell** *n* sonnette *f* • **door handle** *n* poignée *f* de porte • **doorknob** *n* bouton *m* de porte • **doorknocker** *n* marteau *m* • **doorman** *(pl* **-men***) n (of hotel)* portier *m*; *(in block of flats)* concierge *m* • **doormat** *n* paillasson *m* • **doorstep** *n* seuil *m* • **doorstop-(per)** *n* butoir *m* • **doorway** *n* **in the d.** dans l'embrasure de la porte

dope [dəʊp] **1** *n Fam* (**a**) *(drugs)* drogue *f*; *(for horse, athlete)* dopant *m* (**b**) *(information)* tuyaux *mpl* (**c**) *(idiot)* andouille *f*
2 *vt* doper

dopey [ˈdəʊpɪ] *(*-**ier**, -**iest***) adj Fam (stupid)* abruti; *(sleepy)* endormi

dorm [dɔːm] *n Fam* = **dormitory**

dormant [ˈdɔːmənt] *adj (volcano)* en sommeil

dormer [ˈdɔːmə(r)] *n* **d. (window)** lucarne *f*

dormitory [*Br* ˈdɔːmɪtrɪ, *Am* ˈdɔːrmɪtɔːrɪ] *(pl* **-ies***) n* dortoir *m*; *Am (university residence)* résidence *f* universitaire

dormouse [ˈdɔːmaʊs] *(pl* **-mice** [-maɪs]*) n* loir *m*

dose [dəʊs] **1** *n* dose *f*; *(of illness)* attaque *f*; **a d. of flu** une grippe
2 *vt* **to d. oneself (up)** se bourrer de médicaments • **dosage** [ˈdəʊsɪdʒ] *n (amount)* dose *f*

doss [dɒs] *vi Br Fam* **to d. down** crécher

dosshouse [ˈdɒshaʊs] *n Br Fam* asile *m* de nuit

dossier [ˈdɒsɪeɪ] *n (papers)* dossier *m*

dot [dɒt] **1** *n* point *m*; *Fam* **on the d.** à l'heure pile
2 *(pt & pp* **-tt-***) vt (letter)* mettre un point sur; **dotted with** parsemé de; **dotted line** pointillé *m* • **dot-matrix printer** *n Comptr* imprimante *f* matricielle

dote [dəʊt] *vt* **to d. on** adorer

dotty [ˈdɒtɪ] *(*-**ier**, -**iest***) adj Br Fam* cinglé

double [ˈdʌbəl] **1** *adj* double; **a d. bed** un grand lit; **a d. room** une chambre pour deux personnes; **d. 's** deux 's'; **d. six** deux fois six; **d. three four two** *(phone number)* trente-trois quarante-deux
2 *adv (twice)* deux fois; *(fold)* en deux; **he earns d. what I earn** il gagne le double de moi; **to see d.** voir double
3 *n* double *m*; *(person)* double, sosie *m*; *(stand-in in film)* doublure *f*; **on** *or* **at the d.** au pas de course
4 *vt* doubler; **to d. sth back** *or* **over** *(fold)* replier qch; **to be doubled over in pain** être plié (en deux) de douleur
5 *vi* doubler; **to d. back** *(of person)* revenir en arrière; **to d. up with pain/laughter** être plié (en deux) de douleur/rire • **double-barrelled** [dʌbəlˈbærəld] *adj (gun)* à deux canons; *(name)* à rallonges • **double-bass** [dʌbəlˈbeɪs] *n Br (instrument)* contrebasse *f* • **'double-'breasted** *adj (jacket)* croisé • **'double-'check** *vti* revérifier • **'double-'cross** *vt* doubler • **'double-'dealing** *n* double jeu *m* • **'double-'decker (bus)** *n* autobus *m* à impériale • **double-'door(s)** *n* porte *f* à deux battants • **double-'Dutch** *n Fam* baragouin *m* • **double-'glazing** *n (window)* double vitrage *m* • **double-'jointed** *adj* désarticulé • **double-'parking** *n* stationnement *m* en double file • **double-'quick** *adv* en vitesse

doubly [ˈdʌblɪ] *adv* doublement

doubt [daʊt] **1** *n* doute *m*; **to be in d. about sth** avoir des doutes sur qch; **I have no d. about it** je n'en doute pas; **no d.**

(probably) sans doute; **in d.** *(result, career)* dans la balance; **when in d.** dans le doute **2** *vt* douter de; **to d. whether** *or* **that** *or* **if...** douter que... *(+ subjunctive)*

doubtful ['daʊtfəl] *adj (person, future, success)* incertain; *(dubious) (quality)* douteux, -euse; **to d. (about sth)** avoir des doutes (sur qch); **it's d. whether** *or* **that** *or* **if...** il n'est pas certain que... *(+ subjunctive)* •**doubtless** *adv* sans doute

dough [dəʊ] *n* pâte *f*; *Fam (money)* blé *m*

doughnut ['dəʊnʌt] *n* beignet *m*

dour ['dʊə(r)] *adj* austère

douse [daʊs] *vt* arroser; *Fam (light)* éteindre

dove¹ [dʌv] *n* colombe *f* •**dovecote** ['dʌvkɒt] *n* colombier *m*

dove² [dəʊv] *Am pt of* **dive**

Dover ['dəʊvə(r)] *n* Douvres *m ou f*

dovetail ['dʌvteɪl] **1** *n (wood joint)* queue-d'aronde *f*
2 *vi Fig (fit)* concorder (**with** avec)

dowdy ['daʊdɪ] (**-ier, -iest**) *adj* peu élégant

down¹ [daʊn] **1** *adv* en bas; *(to the ground)* à terre; **d. (in writing)** inscrit; **(lie) d.!** *(to dog)* couché!; **to come** *or* **go d.** descendre; **to come d. from** *(place)* arriver de; **to fall d.** tomber (par terre); **d. there** *or* **here** en bas; **d. with traitors!** à bas les traîtres!; **d. with (the) flu** grippé; *Fam* **to feel d.** *(depressed)* avoir le cafard; **d. to** *(in series, numbers, dates)* jusqu'à; **d. payment** acompte *m*; **d. under** aux antipodes, en Australie; *Br* **d. at heel**, *Am* **d. at the heels** miteux, -euse
2 *prep (at bottom of)* en bas de; *(from top to bottom of)* du haut en bas de; *(along)* le long de; **to go d.** *(hill, street, stairs)* descendre; **to live d. the street** habiter plus loin dans la rue
3 *vt (shoot down)* abattre; *(knock down)* terrasser; **to d. a drink** vider un verre •**down-and-out** ['daʊnən'aʊt] **1** *adj* sur le pavé **2** *n* clochard, -arde *mf* •**downbeat** *adj Fam (gloomy)* pessimiste •**downcast** *adj* découragé •**downfall** *n* chute *f* •**downgrade** *vt (job)* déclasser; *(person)* rétrograder •**down'hearted** *adj* découragé •**down'hill** *adv* en pente; **to go d.** descendre; *(of sick person, business)* aller de plus en plus mal •**down'market** *adj Br (car, furniture)* bas de gamme *inv*; *(neighbourhood, accent)* populaire; *(person, crowd)* ordinaire •**downpour** *n* averse *f* •**downright 1** *adj (rogue)* véritable; *(refusal)* catégorique; *Br* **d. nerve**

or **cheek** un sacré culot **2** *adv (rude, disagreeable)* franchement •**down'scale** *adj Am* = **downmarket** •**downstairs 1** ['daʊnsteəz] *adj (room, neighbours) (below)* d'en bas; *(on the ground floor)* du rez-de-chaussée **2** [daʊn'steəz] *adv* en bas/au rez-de-chaussée; **to come** *or* **go d.** descendre l'escalier •**down'stream** *adv* en aval •**'down-to-'earth** *adj* terre-à-terre *inv* •**'down'town** *adv* en ville; **d. Chicago** le centre de Chicago •**'down-trodden** *adj* opprimé •**downward** *adj* vers le bas; *(path)* qui descend; *(trend)* à la baisse •**downward(s)** *adv* vers le bas

down² [daʊn] *n (on bird, person)* duvet *m* •**downy** (**-ier, -iest**) *adj (skin)* duveté

Down's [daʊnz] *adj* **D. syndrome** trisomie *f* 21; **a D. baby** un bébé trisomique *ou* mongolien

downs [daʊnz] *npl Br (hills)* collines *fpl*

dowry ['daʊərɪ] *(pl* **-ies)** *n* dot *f*

doz *abbr* = **dozen**

doze [dəʊz] **1** *n* petit somme *m*
2 *vi* sommeiller; **to d. off** s'assoupir •**dozy** (**-ier, -iest**) *adj* somnolent; *Br Fam (silly)* gourde

dozen ['dʌzən] *n* douzaine *f*; **a d. books/ eggs** une douzaine de livres/d'œufs; *Fig* **dozens of** des dizaines de

Dr *(abbr* **Doctor)** Docteur

drab [dræb] *adj* terne; *(weather)* gris

draft¹ [drɑːft] **1** *n* (**a**) *(outline)* ébauche *f*; *(of letter)* brouillon *m*; *(commercial document)* traite *f* (**b**) *Am (military)* conscription *f*; *(men)* contingent *m*; **d. dodger** insoumis *m*
2 *vt* (**a**) **to d. (out)** *(sketch out)* faire le brouillon de; *(write out)* rédiger (**b**) *(conscript)* appeler sous les drapeaux

draft² [drɑːft] *n Am* = **draught**

draftsman ['drɑːftsmən] *(pl* **-men)** *n Am* = **draughtsman**

drafty ['drɑːftɪ] (**-ier, -iest**) *adj Am* = **draughty**

drag [dræg] **1** *n Fam (boring task)* corvée *f*; *(boring person)* raseur, -euse *mf*; *(on cigarette)* taffe *f* (**on** de); **it's a d.!** c'est la barbe!; **to be in d.** être travesti; *Am* **the main d.** la rue principale
2 *(pt & pp* **-gg-)** *vt* traîner; *(river)* draguer; *Fig* **to d. sth from sb** *(confession, promise)* arracher qch à qn; **to d. sb/sth along** (en)traîner qn/qch; **to d. sb away from** arracher qn à; **to d. sb into** entraîner qn dans
3 *vi* traîner; **to d. on** *or* **out** *(of film, day)* traîner en longueur

dragon ['drægən] *n* dragon *m*

dragonfly ['drægənflaɪ] (*pl* **-ies**) *n* libellule *f*

drain [dreɪn] **1** *n* (*sewer*) égout *m*; (*in street*) bouche *f* d'égout; **that's one year's work down the d.** voilà une année de travail perdue; **that's my holiday down the d.** mes vacances tombent à l'eau; **to be a d. on** (*resources, patience*) épuiser
2 *vt* (*glass, tank*) vider; (*vegetables*) égoutter; (*land*) drainer; (*resources*) épuiser; **to d. (off)** (*liquid*) faire écouler; **to d. sb/sth of** (*deprive of*) priver qn/qch de; **to feel drained** être épuisé
3 *vi* **to d. (off)** (*of liquid*) s'écouler; **to d. away** (*of strength*) s'épuiser; **draining board** paillasse *f* • **drainage** *n* drainage *m* • **drainer** *n* (*board*) paillasse *f*; (*rack, basket*) égouttoir *m*

drainboard ['dreɪnbɔːd] *n Am* paillasse *f*
drainpipe ['dreɪnpaɪp] *n* tuyau *m* d'évacuation

drake [dreɪk] *n* canard *m* (mâle)

dram [dræm] *n Fam* (*of whisky*) goutte *f*

drama ['drɑːmə] *n* (*event*) drame *m*; (*dramatic art*) théâtre *m*; **d. critic** critique *m* dramatique

dramatic [drə'mætɪk] *adj* dramatique; (*very great, striking*) spectaculaire • **dramatics** *n* théâtre *m*

dramatist ['dræmətɪst] *n* dramaturge *m*

dramatize ['dræmətaɪz] *vt* (*exaggerate*) dramatiser; (*novel*) adapter pour la scène/l'écran

drank [dræŋk] *pt of* **drink**

drape [dreɪp] *vt* (*person, shoulders*) draper (**with** de); (*wall*) tapisser (de tentures) • **drapes** *npl Br* (*hangings*) tentures *fpl*; *Am* (*curtains*) rideaux *mpl*

drastic ['dræstɪk] *adj* (*change, measure*) radical; (*remedy*) puissant; **d. reductions** (*in shop*) soldes *mpl* • **drastically** *adv* radicalement; **d. reduced prices** prix *mpl* cassés

draught [drɑːft] (*Am* **draft**) *n* (**a**) (*wind*) courant *m* d'air; (*for fire*) tirage *m*; **d. excluder** bourrelet *m* (**b**) *Br* **draughts** (*game*) dames *fpl* • **draught 'beer** *n* bière *f* (à la) pression • **draughtboard** *n Br* damier *m* • **draught-horse** *n* cheval *m* de trait

draughtsman ['drɑːftsmən] (*Am* **draftsman**) (*pl* **-men**) *n* dessinateur, -trice *mf* (industriel(le))

draughty ['drɑːftɪ] (*Am* **drafty**) (**-ier, -iest**) *adj* (*room*) plein de courants d'air

draw¹ [drɔː] **1** *n Sport* match *m* nul; (*of lottery*) tirage *m* au sort; (*attraction*) attraction *f*

2 (*pt* **drew,** *pp* **drawn**) *vt* (**a**) (*pull*) tirer; (*pass, move*) passer (**over** sur; **into** dans); **to d. in** (*claws*) rentrer; **to d. out** (*meeting*) faire traîner en longueur; **to d. up** (*chair*) approcher; (*contract, list, plan*) dresser, rédiger
(**b**) (*extract*) retirer; (*pistol, sword*) dégainer; (*water, wine*) tirer; *Fig* (*strength, comfort*) retirer, puiser (**from** de); (*applause*) provoquer
(**c**) (*attract*) attirer; **to d. a smile** faire sourire (**from sb** qn)
(**d**) *Sport* **to d. a match** faire match nul
3 *vi Sport* faire match nul; **to d. near (to)** s'approcher (de); (*of time*) approcher (de); **to d. to a close** tirer à sa fin; **to d. aside** (*step aside*) s'écarter; **to d. away** (*go away*) s'éloigner; **to d. back** (*go backwards*) reculer; **to d. in** (*of days*) diminuer; (*of train*) arriver (en gare); **to d. into the station** (*of train*) entrer en gare; **to d. on** (*of time*) s'avancer; **to d. up** (*of vehicle*) s'arrêter

draw² [drɔː] **1** (*pt* **drew,** *pp* **drawn**) *vt* (*picture*) dessiner; (*circle*) tracer; *Fig* (*parallel, distinction*) faire (**between** entre)
2 *vi* (*as artist*) dessiner

drawback ['drɔːbæk] *n* inconvénient *m*

drawbridge ['drɔːbrɪdʒ] *n* pont-levis *m*

drawer [drɔː(r)] *n* (*in furniture*) tiroir *m*

drawing ['drɔːɪŋ] *n* dessin *m*; **d. board** planche *f* à dessin; *Br* **d. pin** punaise *f*; **d. room** salon *m*

drawl [drɔːl] **1** *n* voix *f* traînante
2 *vi* parler d'une voix traînante

drawn [drɔːn] **1** *pp of* **draw¹,²**
2 *adj* (*face*) tiré, crispé; **d. match** *or* **game** match *m* nul

dread [dred] **1** *n* terreur *f*
2 *vt* (*exam*) appréhender; **to d. doing sth** appréhender de faire qch

dreadful ['dredfəl] *adj* épouvantable; (*child*) insupportable; **I feel d.** (*ill*) je ne me sens vraiment pas bien; **I feel d. about it** j'ai vraiment honte • **dreadfully** *adv* terriblement; **to be** *or* **feel d. sorry** regretter infiniment

dream [driːm] **1** *n* rêve *m*; *Fam* (*wonderful thing or person*) merveille *f*; **to have a d.** faire un rêve (**about** de); **to have dreams of** rêver de; **a d. house** une maison de rêve; **a d. world** un monde imaginaire
2 (*pt & pp* **dreamed** *or* **dreamt** [dremt]) *vt* rêver (**that** que); **I never dreamt that...** (*imagined*) je n'aurais jamais songé que...; **to d. sth up** imaginer qch
3 *vi* rêver (**of** *or* **about sb/sth** de qn/qch; **of** *or* **about doing** de faire); **I wouldn't d.**

of it! je n'y songerais même pas!
•**dreamer** *n* rêveur,-euse *mf* •**dreamy**
(**-ier, -iest**) *adj* rêveur, -euse
dreary ['drɪərɪ] (**-ier, -iest**) *adj* morne
dredge [dredʒ] **1** *n* drague *f*
2 *vt (river)* draguer
dregs [dregz] *npl (of wine)* lie *f; Fig* **the d.**
of society les bas-fonds *mpl* de la société
drench [drentʃ] *vt* tremper; **to get**
drenched se faire tremper (jusqu'aux os)
dress [dres] **1** *n (garment)* robe *f; (style of*
dressing) tenue *f; Br* **d. circle** *(in theatre)*
premier balcon *m;* **d. designer** styliste *mf;*
(well-known) couturier *m;* **d. rehearsal** *(in*
theatre) (répétition *f*) générale *f;* **d. shirt**
chemise *f* de soirée
2 *vt (person)* habiller; *(wound)* panser;
(salad) assaisonner; *(chicken)* préparer;
to get dressed s'habiller; **dressed for**
tennis en tenue de tennis
3 *vi* s'habiller; **to d. up** *(smartly)* bien
s'habiller; *(in disguise)* se déguiser (**as**
en)
dresser ['dresə(r)] *n* (**a**) *Br (furniture)*
vaisselier *m; Am (dressing table)* coiffeuse *f* (**b**) **she's a good d.** elle s'habille
toujours bien
dressing ['dresɪŋ] *n (for wound)* pansement *m; (seasoning)* assaisonnement *m;*
Fam **to give sb a d.-down** passer un
savon à qn; *Br* **d. gown** robe *f* de chambre; *(of boxer)* peignoir *m;* **d. room** *(in*
theatre) loge *f; (in store)* cabine *f* d'essayage; **d. table** coiffeuse *f*
dressmaker ['dresmeɪkə(r)] *n* couturière
f •**dressmaking** *n* couture *f*
dressy ['dresɪ] (**-ier, -iest**) *adj (smart)*
chic *inv;* **(too) d.** trop habillé
drew [druː] *pt of* **draw**¹,²
dribble ['drɪbəl] *vi* (**a**) *(of baby)* baver; *(of*
liquid) tomber goutte à goutte (**b**) *Foot-*
ball dribbler
dribs [drɪbz] *npl* **in d. and drabs** par
petites quantités; *(arrive)* par petits
groupes
dried [draɪd] *adj (fruit)* sec (*f* sèche);
(milk, eggs) en poudre; *(flowers)* séché
drier ['draɪə(r)] *n* = **dryer**
drift [drɪft] **1** *n (movement)* mouvement
m; (direction) sens *m; (of events)* cours *m;*
(of snow) congère *f; (meaning)* sens général
2 *vi (through air)* être emporté par le
vent; *(on water)* être emporté par le courant; *(of ship)* dériver; *Fig (of person,*
nation) aller à la dérive; *(of snow)* s'amonceler; **to d. about (aimlessly)** *(walk*
around) se promener sans but; **to d.**

apart *(of husband and wife)* devenir des
étrangers l'un pour l'autre •**driftwood** *n*
bois *m* flotté
drill [drɪl] **1** *n* (**a**) *(tool)* perceuse *f; (bit)*
mèche *f; (pneumatic)* marteau *m* pi-
queur; *(dentist's)* roulette *f; (for rock)* fo-
reuse *f* (**b**) *(exercise)* exercice *m; (correct*
procedure) marche *f* à suivre
2 *vt* (**a**) *(wood)* percer; *(tooth)* fraiser;
(oil well) forer (**b**) *(of troops)* faire faire
l'exercice à
3 *vi* (**a**) **to d. for oil** faire de la recherche
pétrolière (**b**) faire l'exercice
drily ['draɪlɪ] *adv (remark)* sèchement,
d'un ton sec
drink [drɪŋk] **1** *n* boisson *f;* **to give sb a d.**
donner (quelque chose) à boire à qn; **to**
have a d. boire quelque chose; *(alcoholic)*
prendre un verre
2 (*pt* **drank**, *pp* **drunk**) *vt* boire; **he drank**
himself to death c'est l'alcool qui l'a tué;
to d. sth up finir (de boire) qch
3 *vi* boire (**out of** dans); **to d. like a fish**
boire comme un trou; **to d. up** finir son
verre; **to d. to sb** boire à la santé de qn;
drinking chocolate chocolat *m* en poudre; **drinking fountain** fontaine *f* publique; **drinking trough** abreuvoir *m;*
drinking water eau *f* potable
drinkable ['drɪŋkəbəl] *adj (fit for drink-*
ing) potable; *(not unpleasant)* buvable
drip [drɪp] **1** *n (drop)* goutte *f; (sound)*
bruit *m* de l'eau qui goutte; *(in hospital)*
goutte-à-goutte *m inv; Fam (weak person)*
mou *m,* molle *f;* **to be on a d.** être sous
perfusion
2 (*pt & pp* **-pp-**) *vt (paint)* laisser tomber
goutte à goutte; **you're dripping water**
everywhere! tu mets de l'eau partout!
3 *vi (of water, rain)* goutter; *(of washing,*
vegetables) s'égoutter; *(of tap)* fuir •**'drip-**
'dry *adj (shirt)* qui ne nécessite pas de
repassage
dripping ['drɪpɪŋ] **1** *adj & adv* **d. (wet)**
trempé
2 *n (fat)* graisse *f* de rôti
drive [draɪv] **1** *n (in car)* promenade *f* en
voiture; *(road to private house)* allée *f;*
(energy) énergie *f; (campaign)* campagne
f; Comptr lecteur *m;* **an hour's d.** une
heure de voiture; **left-hand d.** *(vehicle)*
conduite *f* à gauche; **front-wheel d.**
(vehicle) traction *f* avant; **the sex d.** la
pulsion sexuelle
2 (*pt* **drove**, *pp* **driven**) *vt (vehicle, train,*
passenger) conduire (**to** à); *(machine)*
actionner; *(chase away)* chasser; **to d. sb**
to do sth pousser qn à faire qch; **to d. sb**

to despair réduire qn au désespoir; **to d. sb mad** or **crazy** rendre qn fou/folle; **to d. the rain/smoke against** (of wind) rabattre la pluie/fumée contre; **to d. sb hard** surmener qn; **he drives a Ford** il a une Ford
3 vi (drive a car) conduire; (go by car) rouler; **to d. on the left** rouler à gauche; **to d. to Paris** aller en voiture à Paris; **to d. to work** aller au travail en voiture; Fig **what are you driving at?** où veux-tu en venir?
▸ **drive along** vi (in car) rouler ▸ **drive away 1** vt sep (chase away) chasser **2** vi (in car) partir en voiture ▸ **drive back 1** vt sep (passenger) ramener (en voiture); (enemy) repousser **2** vi (in car) revenir (en voiture) ▸ **drive in** vt sep (nail, knife) enfoncer ▸ **drive off** vi (in car) partir (en voiture) ▸ **drive on** vi (in car) continuer sa route ▸ **drive out** vt sep (chase away) chasser ▸ **drive over** vt insep (crush) écraser ▸ **drive up** vi (in car) arriver (en voiture)
drive-in ['draɪvɪn] adj Am accessible en voiture; **d. (movie theater)** drive-in m inv; **d. (restaurant)** = restaurant où l'on est servi dans sa voiture
drivel ['drɪvəl] n idioties fpl
driven ['drɪvən] pp of **drive**
driver ['draɪvə(r)] n (of car) conducteur, -trice mf; (of taxi, truck) chauffeur m; **(train** or **engine) d.** mécanicien m; **she's a good d.** elle conduit bien; Am **d.'s license** permis m de conduire
driveway ['draɪvweɪ] n (road to house) allée f
driving ['draɪvɪŋ] **1** n (in car) conduite f; **d. conditions** état m des routes; **d. lesson** leçon f de conduite; Br **d. licence** permis m de conduire; **d. school** auto-école f; **d. test** examen m du permis de conduire
2 adj (forceful) **d. force** moteur m; **d. rain** pluie f battante
drizzle ['drɪzəl] **1** n bruine f
2 vi bruiner • **drizzly** adj **it's d.** il bruine
droll [drəʊl] adj drôle, comique
dromedary ['drɒmədərɪ] (pl **-ies**) n dromadaire m
drone [drəʊn] **1** n (**a**) (bee) faux-bourdon m (**b**) (hum) bourdonnement m; (purr) ronronnement m; Fig (of person) débit m monotone
2 vi (of engine) ronronner; (of bee) bourdonner; Fig **to d. (on)** (of person) parler d'une voix monotone
drool [druːl] vi (slaver) baver; Fig (talk nonsense) radoter; Fig **to d. over sb/sth** baver d'admiration devant qn/qch

droop [druːp] vi (of flower) se faner; (of head) pencher; (of eyelids, shoulders) tomber
drop [drɒp] **1** n (**a**) (of liquid) goutte f; **eye/nose drops** gouttes fpl pour les yeux/le nez (**b**) (fall) baisse f, chute f (**in** de); (distance of fall) hauteur f de chute; (slope) descente f; (of supplies from aircraft) parachutage m
2 (pt & pp **-pp-**) vt laisser tomber; (price, voice) baisser; (bomb) larguer; (passenger, goods from vehicle) déposer; (from boat) débarquer; (leave out) faire sauter, omettre; (remark) laisser échapper; (get rid of) supprimer; (habit) abandonner; (team member) écarter; **to d. sb off** (from vehicle) déposer qn; **to d. a line/postcard to sb** écrire un petit mot/une carte postale à qn; **to d. a hint** faire une allusion; **to d. a hint that...** laisser entendre que...; **to d. one's h's** ne pas prononcer les h; **to d. a word in sb's ear** glisser un mot à l'oreille de qn
3 vi (fall) tomber; (of person) se laisser tomber; (of price) baisser; Fam **he's ready to d.** il tombe de fatigue; Fam **let it d.!** laisse tomber!; **to d. away** (diminish) diminuer; **to d. back** or **behind** rester en arrière; **to d. by** or **in** (visit sb) passer; **to d. off** (fall asleep) s'endormir; (fall off) tomber; (of interest, sales) diminuer; **to d. out** (fall out) tomber; (withdraw) se retirer; (socially) se mettre en marge de la société; (of student) laisser tomber ses études; **to d. over** or **round** (visit sb) passer
dropout ['drɒpaʊt] n marginal, -ale mf; (student) étudiant, -iante mf qui abandonne ses études
dropper ['drɒpə(r)] n (for medicine) compte-gouttes m inv
droppings ['drɒpɪŋz] npl (of animal) crottes fpl; (of bird) fiente f
dross [drɒs] n Fam rebut m
drought [draʊt] n sécheresse f
drove [drəʊv] pt of **drive**
droves [drəʊvz] npl (of people) foules fpl; **in d.** en foule
drown [draʊn] **1** vt noyer; **to d. oneself, to be drowned** se noyer
2 vi se noyer • **drowning 1** adj (person) qui se noie **2** n (death) noyade f
drowse [draʊz] vi somnoler
drowsy ['draʊzɪ] (**-ier, -iest**) adj somnolent; **to be** or **feel d.** avoir sommeil; **to make sb (feel) d.** assoupir qn • **drowsiness** n somnolence f
drudge [drʌdʒ] **1** n (man) homme m de

peine; *(woman)* bonne *f* à tout faire
2 *vi* trimer • **drudgery** *n* corvée *f*

drug [drʌg] **1** *n (against illness)* médicament *m*; *(narcotic)* drogue *f*; *Fig (activity, hobby)* drogue; **drugs** *(narcotics in general)* la drogue; **hard/soft drugs** drogues dures/douces; **to be on drugs, to take drugs** se droguer; **d. addict** drogué, -ée *mf*; **d. addiction** toxicomanie *f*; **d. dealer** *(large-scale)* trafiquant *m* de drogue; *(small-scale)* petit trafiquant de drogue, dealer *m*; **d. taking** usage *m* de la drogue
2 *(pt & pp* **-gg-***) vt* droguer; *(drink)* mettre un médicament dans

druggist [ˈdrʌgɪst] *n Am* pharmacien, -ienne *mf*

drugstore [ˈdrʌgstɔːr] *n Am* drugstore *m*

drum [drʌm] **1** *n Mus* tambour *m*; *(for oil)* bidon *m*; *Mus* **the big** *or* **bass d.** la grosse caisse; **the drums** *(of rock group)* la batterie
2 *(pt & pp* **-mm-***) vt* **to d. one's fingers** tambouriner avec ses doigts; **to d. sth into sb** enfoncer qch dans la tête de qn; **to d. up** *(support, interest)* rechercher; **to d. up business** *or* **custom** attirer les clients
3 *vi (with fingers)* tambouriner • **drummer** *n* tambour *m*; *(in pop or jazz group)* batteur *m* • **drumstick** *n (for drum)* baguette *f* de tambour; *(of chicken)* pilon *m*

drunk [drʌŋk] **1** *pp of* **drink**
2 *adj* ivre; **to get d.** s'enivrer; *Fig* **d. with power/success** grisé par le pouvoir/le succès
3 *n* ivrogne *mf* • **drunkard** *n* ivrogne *mf* • **drunken** *adj (person) (regularly)* ivrogne; *(driver)* ivre; *(quarrel, brawl)* d'ivrogne; **d. driving** conduite *f* en état d'ivresse • **drunkenness** *n (state)* ivresse *f*; *(habit)* ivrognerie *f*

dry [draɪ] **1** (**drier, driest**) *adj* sec *(f* sèche); *(well, river)* à sec; *(day)* sans pluie; *(toast)* sans beurre; *(wit)* caustique; *(subject, book)* aride; **on d. land** sur la terre ferme; **to keep sth d.** tenir qch au sec; **to wipe sth d.** essuyer qch; **to run d.** se tarir; **to feel** *or* **be d.** *(thirsty)* avoir soif; *Am* **d. goods store** cale *f* sèche; *Am* **d. goods store** épicerie *f*
2 *vt* sécher; *(by wiping)* essuyer; *(clothes)* faire sécher; **to d. the dishes** essuyer la vaisselle; **to d. sth off** *or* **up** sécher qch
3 *vi* sécher; **to d. off** sécher; **to d. up** sécher; *(dry the dishes)* essuyer la vaisselle; *(of stream)* se tarir • **dryer** *n (for hair, clothes)* séchoir *m*; *(helmet-style for hair)* casque *m* • **dryness** *n* sécheresse *f*; *(of wit)* causticité *f*; *(of book)* aridité *f*

dry-clean [draɪˈkliːn] *vt* nettoyer à sec • **dry-cleaner** *n* teinturier, -ière *mf*; **the d.'s** *(shop)* le pressing, la teinturerie

DSS [diːesˈes] *(abbr* **Department of Social Security)** *n Br* ≃ Sécurité *f* sociale

dual [ˈdjuːəl] *adj* double; **d. carriageway** route *f* à deux voies • **duality** [-ˈælɪtɪ] *n* dualité *f*

dub [dʌb] *(pt & pp* **-bb-***) vt* **(a)** *(film)* doubler **(into** en) **(b)** *(nickname)* surnommer • **dubbing** *n (of film)* doublage *m*

dubious [ˈdjuːbɪəs] *adj (offer, person)* douteux, -euse; **I'm d. about going** *or* **about whether to go** je me demande si je dois y aller

duchess [ˈdʌtʃɪs] *n* duchesse *f*

duck [dʌk] **1** *n* canard *m*
2 *vt (head)* baisser subitement; **to d. sb** plonger qn dans l'eau; *Fig* **to d. the issue** se dérober
3 *vi* se baisser • **ducking** *n* bain *m* forcé • **duckling** *n* caneton *m*

duct [dʌkt] *n (tube in body, pipe)* conduit *m*

dud [dʌd] *Fam* **1** *adj (coin)* faux *(f* fausse); *(cheque)* en bois; *(watch)* qui ne marche pas; *(bomb)* qui n'a pas éclaté
2 *n (person)* type *m* nul

dude [duːd] *n Am Fam* type *m*; **d. ranch** ranch(-hôtel) *m*

due[1] [djuː] **1** *adj (money, sum)* dû *(f* due) **(to** à); *(rent, bill)* à payer; *(fitting, proper)* qui convient; **to fall d.** échoir; **she's d. for a salary increase** elle mérite une augmentation de salaire; **he's d. (to arrive)** il doit arriver d'un moment à l'autre; **I'm d. there** il faut que j'y sois; **when is the baby d.?** pour quand la naissance est-elle prévue?; **with all d. respect...** avec tout le respect que je vous dois...; **in d. course** *(when appropriate)* en temps voulu; *(eventually)* le moment venu; **d. to** par suite de, en raison de; *Fin* **d. date** échéance *f*
2 *n* dû *m*; **dues** *(of club)* cotisation *f*; *(official charges)* droits *mpl*; **to give him his d....** pour lui rendre justice...

due[2] [djuː] *adv* **d. north/south** plein nord/sud

duel [ˈdjuːəl] **1** *n* duel *m*
2 *(Br* **-ll-**, *Am* **-l-***) vi* se battre en duel

duet [djuːˈet] *n* duo *m*

duffel, duffle [ˈdʌfəl] *adj* **d. bag** sac *m* de marin; **d. coat** duffel-coat *m*

dug [dʌg] *pt & pp of* **dig** • **dugout** *n* **(a)** *(canoe)* pirogue *f* **(b)** *Mil* tranchée-abri *f*; *Sport* banc *m* de touche

duke [djuːk] *n* duc *m*

dull [dʌl] **1** (-er, -est) adj (boring) ennuyeux, -euse; (colour, character) terne; (weather) maussade; (sound, ache) sourd; (mind) lent; (edge, blade) émoussé; (hearing, sight) faible **2** vt (sound) amortir; (pain) endormir; (senses) émousser; (mind) engourdir; (colour) ternir • **dullness** n (of life, town) monotonie f; (of colour) manque m d'éclat; (of mind) lourdeur f

duly ['dju:lɪ] adv (properly) dûment; (as expected) comme prévu

dumb [dʌm] (-er, -est) adj muet (f muette); Fam (stupid) bête; **d. animals** les bêtes fpl

dumbbell ['dʌmbel] n haltère m

dumbfound [dʌm'faʊnd] vt sidérer

dumbwaiter [dʌm'weɪtə(r)] n (lift for food) monte-plats m inv

dummy ['dʌmɪ] **1** (pl -ies) n Br (of baby) tétine f; (for displaying clothes) mannequin m; (of ventriloquist) pantin m; Fam (fool) idiot, -iote mf **2** adj factice

dump [dʌmp] **1** n (for refuse) décharge f; (for ammunition) dépôt m; Fam Pej (town) trou m; Fam Pej (house) baraque f; Fam **to be (down) in the dumps** avoir le cafard; **d. truck** tombereau m **2** vt (rubbish) déposer; (waste) déverser; (bricks) décharger; Comptr (memory) vider; **to d. (down)** déposer; Fam **to d. sb** plaquer qn • **dumper** n Br **d. (truck)** tombereau m

dumpling ['dʌmplɪŋ] n (in stew) boulette f de pâte; (in Scotland) = sorte de plumpudding

Dumpster® ['dʌmpstə(r)] n Am benne f à ordures

dumpy ['dʌmpɪ] (-ier, -iest) adj Fam (person) boulot, -otte

dunce [dʌns] n cancre m

dune [dju:n] n (sand) **d.** dune f

dung [dʌŋ] n (of horse) crottin m; (of cattle) bouse f; (manure) fumier m

dungarees [dʌŋgə'ri:z] npl (of child, workman) salopette f; Am (jeans) jean m

dungeon ['dʌndʒən] n cachot m

dunk [dʌŋk] vt tremper

dupe [dju:p] **1** n dupe f **2** vt duper

duplex ['du:pleks] n Am (apartment) duplex m

duplicate 1 ['dju:plɪkət] n double m; **in d.** en deux exemplaires; **a d. copy** un duplicata; **a d. key** un double **2** ['dju:plɪkeɪt] vt (key, map) faire un double de; (on machine) photocopier

• **duplication** [-'keɪʃən] n (on machine) reproduction f; (of effort) répétition f

durable ['djʊərəbəl] adj (material, shoes) résistant; (friendship, love) durable • **durability** n résistance f; (of friendship) durabilité f

duration [djʊə'reɪʃən] n durée f

duress [djʊ'res] n **under d.** sous la contrainte

during ['djʊərɪŋ] prep pendant, durant

dusk [dʌsk] n (twilight) crépuscule m

dusky ['dʌskɪ] (-ier, -iest) adj (complexion) basané

dust [dʌst] **1** n poussière f; Am **d. cloth** chiffon m; **d. cover** or **sheet** (for furniture) housse f; **d. cover** or **jacket** (for book) jaquette f **2** vt (**a**) (furniture) dépoussiérer (**b**) (sprinkle) saupoudrer (**with** de) **3** vi faire la poussière • **dustbin** n Br poubelle f • **dustcart** n Br benne f à ordures • **dustman** (pl -men) n Br éboueur m • **dustpan** n pelle f (à poussière)

duster ['dʌstə(r)] n Br chiffon m

dusty ['dʌstɪ] (-ier, -iest) adj poussiéreux, -euse

Dutch [dʌtʃ] **1** adj hollandais; Fam **to go D.** partager les frais (**with** avec) **2** n (**a**) **the D.** (people) les Hollandais mpl (**b**) (language) hollandais m • **Dutchman** (pl -men) n Hollandais m • **Dutchwoman** (pl -women) n Hollandaise f

dutiful ['dju:tɪfəl] adj (son, child) obéissant

duty ['dju:tɪ] (pl -ies) n devoir m; (tax) droit m; **duties** (responsibilities) fonctions fpl; **to be on/off d.** être/ne pas être de service • **duty-'free** adj (goods, shop) hors taxe inv

duvet ['du:veɪ] n Br couette f

DVD [di:vi:'di:] (abbr Digital Versatile Disk, Digital Video Disk) n Comptr DVD m inv, disque m vidéo numérique

dwarf [dwɔ:f] **1** n nain m, naine f **2** vt (of building, trees) écraser; (of person) éclipser

dwell [dwel] (pt & pp dwelt [dwelt]) vi demeurer; **to d. (up)on** (think about) penser sans cesse à; (speak about) parler sans cesse de; (insist on) appuyer sur

dwindle ['dwɪndəl] vi diminuer (peu à peu) • **dwindling** adj (interest, resources) décroissant; (supplies) qui s'épuisent

dye [daɪ] **1** n teinture f **2** vt teindre; **to d. sth green** teindre qch en vert • **dyeing** n teinture f; (industry) teinturerie f • **dyer** n teinturier, -ière mf

dying ['daɪɪŋ] **1** pres p of **die**¹

2 *adj (person, animal)* mourant; *(custom)* qui se perd; *(wish, words)* dernier, -ière; **to my d. day** jusqu'à ma mort
3 *n (death)* mort *f*
dyke [daɪk] *n (wall)* digue *f*; *(ditch)* fossé *m*
dynamic [daɪ'næmɪk] *adj* dynamique ● **dynamism** ['daɪnəmɪzəm] *n* dynamisme *m*

dynamite ['daɪnəmaɪt] **1** *n* dynamite *f*
2 *vt* dynamiter
dynamo ['daɪnəməʊ] *(pl* **-os***) n* dynamo *f*
dynasty [*Br* 'dɪnəstɪ, *Am* 'daɪnəstɪ] *(pl* **-ies***) n* dynastie *f*
dysentery ['dɪsəntrɪ] *n (illness)* dysenterie *f*
dyslexia [dɪs'leksɪə] *n* dyslexie *f* ● **dyslexic** [-'leksɪk] *adj & n* dyslexique *(mf)*

E, e [iː] *n* (**a**) *(letter)* E, e *m inv* (**b**) *Mus* mi *m* (**c**) *Fam (ecstasy)* ecsta *f*, X *f*

each [iːtʃ] **1** *adj* chaque; **e. one** chacun, -une; **e. one of us** chacun d'entre nous **2** *pron* chacun, -une; **e. other** l'un(e) l'autre, *pl* les un(e)s les autres; **to see/ greet e. other** se voir/se saluer; **separated from e. other** séparés l'un de l'autre; **e. of us** chacun, -une d'entre nous

eager ['iːgə(r)] *adj* impatient (**to do** de faire); *(enthusiastic)* plein d'enthousiasme; **to be e. for sth** désirer qch vivement; **e. for money** avide d'argent; **to be e. to do** *(want)* tenir (beaucoup) à faire; **e. to help** empressé (à aider) •**eagerly** *adv (work)* avec enthousiasme; *(await)* avec impatience •**eagerness** *n* impatience *f* (**to do** de faire); *(zeal)* enthousiasme *m* (**for sth** pour qch)

eagle ['iːgəl] *n* aigle *m* • **'eagle-'eyed** *adj* au regard d'aigle

ear¹ [ɪə(r)] *n* oreille *f*; **to be all ears** être tout ouïe; **up to one's ears in work** débordé de travail; **to play it by e.** improviser; **to give sb a thick e.** donner une gifle à qn •**earache** *n* mal *m* d'oreille •**eardrum** *n* tympan *m* •**earmuffs** *npl* protège-oreilles *m inv* •**earphones** *npl* écouteurs *mpl* •**earpiece** *n* écouteur *m* •**earplug** *n* boule *f* Quiès® •**earring** *n* boucle *f* d'oreille •**earshot** *n* **within e.** à portée de voix •**ear-splitting** *adj* assourdissant

ear² [ɪə(r)] *n (of corn)* épi *m*

earl [3ːl] *n* comte *m*

early ['3ːlɪ] **1** (**-ier, -iest**) *adj (first)* premier, -ière; *(fruit, season)* précoce; *(death)* prématuré; *(age)* jeune; *(painting, work)* de jeunesse; *(reply)* rapide; *(return, retirement)* anticipé; *(ancient)* ancien, -ienne; **it's e.** *(on clock)* il est tôt; *(referring to meeting, appointment)* c'est tôt; **it's too e. to get up** il est trop tôt pour se lever; **to be e.** *(ahead of time)* être en avance; *(in getting up)* être matinal; **to have an e. meal/night** manger/se coucher de bonne heure; **in e. times** jadis; **in e. summer** au début de l'été; **in the e. nineties** au début des années 90; **to be in one's e. fifties** avoir à peine plus de cinquante ans; **one's e. life** sa jeunesse

2 *adv* tôt, de bonne heure; *(ahead of time)* en avance; *(die)* prématurément; **as e. as possible** le plus tôt possible; **earlier (on)** plus tôt; **at the earliest** au plus tôt; **as e. as yesterday** déjà hier •**early-'warning system** *n Mil* système *m* radar de préalerte

earmark ['ɪəmɑːk] *vt (funds)* assigner (**for** à)

earn [3ːn] *vt* gagner; *(interest)* rapporter; **to e. one's living** gagner sa vie •**earnings** *npl (wages)* salaire *m*; *(profits)* bénéfices *mpl*

earnest ['3ːnɪst] **1** *adj (serious)* sérieux, -ieuse; *(sincere)* sincère **2** *n* **in e.** sérieusement; **it's raining in e.** il pleut pour de bon; **he's in e.** il est sérieux •**earnestness** *n* sérieux *m*; *(sincerity)* sincérité *f*

earth [3ːθ] *n (ground)* sol *m*; *(soil)* terre *f*; *Br (electrical wire)* terre, masse *f*; **the E.** *(planet)* la Terre; **to fall to e.** tomber à *ou* par terre; **nothing/nobody on e.** rien/personne au monde; **where/what on e....?** où/que diable...? •**earthquake** *n* tremblement *m* de terre •**earthworks** *npl (excavations)* terrassements *mpl* •**earthworm** *n* ver *m* de terre

earthenware ['3ːθənweə(r)] *n* terre *f* cuite

earthly ['3ːθlɪ] *adj (existence, possessions)* terrestre; *Fam* **not an e. chance** pas la moindre chance; *Fam* **for no e. reason** sans la moindre raison

earthy ['3ːθɪ] (**-ier, -iest**) *adj (taste, smell)* terreux, -euse; *Fig (person)* terre-à-terre *inv*

earwig ['ɪəwɪg] *n (insect)* perce-oreille *m*

ease [iːz] **1** *n (facility)* facilité *f*; *(physical)* bien-être *m*; *(mental)* tranquillité *f*; **with e.** facilement; **to be at e.** être à l'aise; **to be ill at e.** être mal à l'aise; **my mind is at e.** j'ai l'esprit tranquille; *Mil* **(stand) at e.!** repos!

2 *vt (pain)* soulager; *(mind)* calmer; *(tension)* réduire; *(restrictions)* assouplir; **to e. sth off/along** enlever/déplacer qch doucement; **to e. oneself through** se glisser par

3 *vi* **to e.** **(off** *or* **up)** *(become less)* *(of pressure)* diminuer; *(of demand)* baisser; *(of pain)* se calmer; *(not work so hard)* se relâcher; **the situation is easing** la situation se détend

easel [ˈiːzəl] *n* chevalet *m*

easily [ˈiːzɪlɪ] *adv* facilement; **e. the best** de loin le meilleur/la meilleure; **that could e. be the case** ça pourrait bien être le cas ● **easiness** *n* aisance *f*

east [iːst] **1** *n* est *m*; **(to the) e.** of à l'est de; **the E.** *(Eastern Europe)* l'Est *m*; *(the Orient)* l'Orient *m*

2 *adj* *(coast)* est *inv*; *(wind)* d'est; **E. Africa** l'Afrique *f* orientale; *Formerly* **E. Germany** l'Allemagne *f* de l'Est

3 *adv* à l'est; *(travel)* vers l'est ● **eastbound** *adj* *(traffic)* en direction de l'est; *Br* *(carriageway)* est *inv* ● **easterly** *adj* *(point)* est *inv*; *(direction)* de l'est; *(wind)* d'est ● **eastern** *adj* *(coast)* est *inv*; **E. France** l'est *m* de la France; **E. Europe** l'Europe *f* de l'est ● **easterner** *n* habitant, -ante *mf* de l'est ● **eastward(s)** *adj & adv* vers l'est

Easter [ˈiːstə(r)] *n* Pâques *fpl*; **Happy E.!** joyeuses Pâques!; **E. egg** œuf *m* de Pâques; **E. week** semaine *f* de Pâques

easy [ˈiːzɪ] **1** (**-ier, -iest**) *adj* *(not difficult)* facile; *(solution)* simple; *(pace)* modéré; *(manners)* naturel, -elle; *(style)* aisé; **an e. life** une vie tranquille; **it's e. to do** c'est facile à faire; **it's e. for them to do it** il leur est facile de faire ça; **to feel e. in one's mind** être tranquille; **to be an e. first** *(in race)* être bon premier; *Br Fam* **I'm e.** ça m'est égal; **e. chair** fauteuil *m*

2 *adv* doucement; **go e. on the salt** vas-y mollo avec le sel; **go e. on him** ne sois pas trop dur avec lui; **take it e.** *(rest)* repose-toi; *(work less)* ne te fatigue pas; *(calm down)* calme-toi; *(go slow)* ne te presse pas ● **'easy-'going** *adj* *(carefree)* insouciant; *(easy to get along with)* facile à vivre

eat [iːt] (*pt* **ate** [*Br* et, eɪt, *Am* eɪt], *pp* **eaten** [ˈiːtən]) **1** *vt* manger; *(meal)* prendre; **to e. breakfast** prendre le petit déjeuner; *Fig* **to e. one's words** se rétracter; *Fam* **what's eating you?** qu'est-ce qui te tracasse?; **to e. sth up** *(finish)* finir qch; **eaten up with jealousy** dévoré de jalousie

2 *vi* manger; **to e. into sth** *(of acid)* ronger qch; **to e. into one's savings** entamer ses économies; **to e. out** manger

dehors; **eating place** restaurant *m* ● **eatable** *adj* mangeable ● **eater** *n* **big e.** gros mangeur *m*, grosse mangeuse *f*

eau de Cologne [əʊdəkəˈləʊn] *n* eau *f* de Cologne

eaves [iːvz] *npl* avant-toit *m* ● **eavesdrop** (*pt & pp* **-pp-**) *vti* **to e. (on)** écouter avec indiscrétion

ebb [eb] **1** *n* reflux *m*; **the e. and flow** le flux et le reflux; **e. tide** marée *f* descendante; *Fig* **to be at a low e.** *(of patient, spirits)* être déprimé

2 *vi* refluer; *Fig* **to e. (away)** *(of strength)* décliner

ebony [ˈebənɪ] *n* ébène *f*

ebullient [ɪˈbʌlɪənt] *adj* exubérant

EC [iːˈsiː] (*abbr* **European Community**) *n* CE *f*

eccentric [ɪkˈsentrɪk] *adj & n* excentrique *(mf)* ● **eccentricity** [eksenˈtrɪsɪtɪ] *n* excentricité *f*

ecclesiastic [ɪkliːzɪˈæstɪk] *adj & n* ecclésiastique *(m)* ● **ecclesiastical** *adj* ecclésiastique

echelon [ˈeʃəlɒn] *n* échelon *m*

echo [ˈekəʊ] **1** (*pl* **-oes**) *n* écho *m*

2 (*pt & pp* **echoed**) *vt* *(sound)* répercuter; *Fig* *(repeat)* répéter

3 *vi* résonner (**with** de); **the explosion echoed** le bruit de l'explosion se répercuta; **the room echoes** il y a de l'écho dans cette pièce

éclair [eɪˈkleə(r)] *n* *(cake)* éclair *m*

eclectic [ɪˈklektɪk] *adj* éclectique

eclipse [ɪˈklɪps] **1** *n* *(of sun, moon)* & *Fig* *(loss of fame)* éclipse *f*

2 *vt also Fig* éclipser

ecology [ɪˈkɒlədʒɪ] *n* écologie *f* ● **ecological** [iːkəˈlɒdʒɪkəl] *adj* écologique

e-commerce [iːˈkɒmɜːs] *n* *Comptr* commerce *m* électronique

economic [iːkəˈnɒmɪk] *adj* économique; *(profitable)* rentable ● **economical** *adj* économique; *(thrifty)* économe ● **economically** *adv* économiquement ● **economics 1** *n* économie *f* **2** *npl* *(profitability)* aspect *m* financier

economist [ɪˈkɒnəmɪst] *n* économiste *mf*

economize [ɪˈkɒnəmaɪz] *vti* économiser (**on** sur)

economy [ɪˈkɒnəmɪ] (*pl* **-ies**) *n* *(saving, system, thrift)* économie *f*; *Av* **e. class** classe *f* économique

ecstasy [ˈekstəsɪ] (*pl* **-ies**) *n* *(state)* extase *f*; *(drug)* ecstasy *f* ● **ecstatic** [ɪkˈstætɪk] *adj* fou *(f* folle) de joie; **to be e. about** s'extasier sur

Ecuador [ˈekwədɔː(r)] *n* l'Équateur *m*

ecumenical [iːkjʊ'menɪkəl] *adj* œcuménique

eczema ['eksɪmə] *n Med* eczéma *m*; **to have e.** avoir de l'eczéma

eddy ['edɪ] (*pl* **-ies**) *n* tourbillon *m*

edge [edʒ] **1** *n* bord *m*; (*of forest*) lisière *f*; (*of town*) abords *mpl*; (*of page*) marge *f*; (*of knife, blade*) tranchant *m*; **to be on e.** (*of person*) être énervé; **to set sb's teeth on e.** crisper qn; *Fig* **to have the e.** *or a* **slight e.** être légèrement supérieur (**over** à) **2** *vt* (*clothing*) border (**with** de) **3** *vi* **to e. into** (*move*) se glisser dans; **to e. forward** avancer doucement • **edging** *n* (*border*) bordure *f*

edgeways ['edʒweɪz] (*Am* **edgewise** ['edʒwaɪz]) *adv* de côté; *Fam* **I can't get a word in e.** je ne peux pas en placer une

edgy ['edʒɪ] (**-ier, -iest**) *adj* énervé • **edginess** *n* nervosité *f*

edible ['edɪbəl] *adj* (*safe to eat*) comestible; (*fit to eat*) mangeable

edict ['iːdɪkt] *n Formal* édit *m*

edifice ['edɪfɪs] *n* (*building, organization*) édifice *m*

edify ['edɪfaɪ] (*pt & pp* **-ied**) *vt* édifier

Edinburgh ['edɪnbərə] *n* Édimbourg *m ou f*

edit ['edɪt] *vt* (*newspaper*) diriger; (*article*) corriger; (*prepare for publication*) préparer pour la publication; (*film*) monter; *Comptr* éditer; **to e. (out)** (*cut out*) couper

edition [ɪ'dɪʃən] *n* édition *f*

editor ['edɪtə(r)] *n* (*in charge of newspaper*) rédacteur, -trice *mf* en chef; (*in charge of magazine*) directeur, -trice *mf*; (*of section*) rédacteur, -trice *mf*; (*proofreader*) correcteur, -trice *mf*; (*of film*) monteur, -euse *mf*; *Comptr* (*software*) éditeur *m*; **sports e.** (*in newspaper*) rédacteur *m* sportif, rédactrice *f* sportive; **the e. in chief** (*of newspaper*) le rédacteur/la rédactrice en chef • **editorial** [-'tɔːrɪəl] **1** *adj* de la rédaction; **e. staff** rédaction *f* **2** *n* éditorial *m*

educate ['edʊkeɪt] *vt* (*bring up*) éduquer; (*in school*) instruire; (*mind*) former; **to be educated at** faire ses études à • **educated** *adj* (*voice*) cultivé; (**well-)e.** (*person*) instruit

education [edʊ'keɪʃən] *n* éducation *f*; (*teaching*) enseignement *m*; (*training*) formation *f*; (*university subject*) pédagogie *f*; **the e. system** le système éducatif • **educational** *adj* (*qualification*) d'enseignement; (*method, theory, content*) pédagogique; (*game, film, system*) éducatif,

-ive; (*establishment*) scolaire; (*experience*) instructif, -ive; **e. qualifications** diplômes *mpl*

educator ['edʊkeɪtə(r)] *n* éducateur, -trice *mf*

EEC [iːiː'siː] (*abbr* **European Economic Community**) *n* CEE *f*

eel [iːl] *n* anguille *f*

eerie ['ɪərɪ] (**-ier, -iest**) *adj* sinistre

efface [ɪ'feɪs] *vt* effacer

effect [ɪ'fekt] **1** *n* (*result, impression*) effet *m* (**on** sur); **to no e.** en vain; **in e.** en fait; **to put sth into e.** mettre qch en application; **to come into e., to take e.** (*of law*) entrer en vigueur; **to take e.** (*of medicine*) agir; **to have an e.** (*of medicine*) faire de l'effet; **to write a letter to the e. that...** écrire une lettre comme quoi...; **or words to that e.** ou quelque chose d'approchant; *Formal* **personal effects** effets *mpl* personnels **2** *vt* (*change, rescue*) effectuer; (*saving, wish*) réaliser

effective [ɪ'fektɪv] *adj* (*efficient*) efficace; (*actual*) réel (*f* réelle); **to become e.** (*of law*) prendre effet • **effectively** *adv* (*efficiently*) efficacement; (*in fact*) effectivement • **effectiveness** *n* efficacité *f*

> 🖉 Note that the French word **effectivement** is a false friend and is never a translation for the English word **effectively**. It means **actually**.

effeminate [ɪ'femɪnɪt] *adj* efféminé

effervescent [efə'vesənt] *adj* (*drink*) gazeux, -euse; (*mixture, liquid, youth*) effervescent • **effervescence** *n* (*excitement, bubbling*) effervescence *f*; (*of drink*) pétillement *m*

effete [ɪ'fiːt] *adj* (*person*) veule; (*gesture*) efféminé

efficient [ɪ'fɪʃənt] *adj* efficace; (*productive*) performant • **efficiency** *n* efficacité *f*; (*of machine*) performances *fpl* • **efficiently** *adv* efficacement; **to work e.** (*of machine*) bien fonctionner

effigy ['efɪdʒɪ] (*pl* **-ies**) *n* effigie *f*

effort ['efət] *n* effort *m*; **to make an e.** faire un effort (**to** pour); **it isn't worth the e.** ça n'en vaut pas la peine; *Fam* **his/her latest e.** sa dernière tentative • **effortless** *adj* (*victory, progress*) facile; (*skill, grace*) naturel, -elle; **with e. ease** sans effort • **effortlessly** *adv* sans effort

effrontery [ɪ'frʌntərɪ] *n* effronterie *f*

effusive [ɪ'fjuːsɪv] *adj* (*person*) expansif, -ive; (*thanks, excuses*) sans fin • **effusively** *adv* avec effusion

e.g. [iːˈdʒiː] (*abbr* **exempli gratia**) p. ex.
egalitarian [ɪɡælɪˈteərɪən] *adj (society)* égalitaire
egg¹ [eg] *n* œuf *m*; **e. timer** sablier *m* • **eggcup** *n* coquetier *m* • **egghead** *n Pej or Hum* intello *mf* • **eggplant** *n Am* aubergine *f* • **eggshell** *n* coquille *f* d'œuf • **eggwhisk** *n* fouet *m*
egg² [eg] *vt* **to e. sb on** encourager qn (**to do** à faire)
ego [ˈiːɡəʊ] (*pl* **-os**) *n* the e. l'ego *m*; **to have an enormous e.** avoir très haute opinion de soi-même • **ego'centric** *adj* égocentrique
egoism [ˈiːɡəʊɪzəm] *n* égoïsme *m* • **egoist** *n* égoïste *mf* • **ego'istic(al)** *adj* égoïste
egotism [ˈiːɡətɪzəm] *n* égotisme *m* • **egotist** *n* égotiste *mf*
Egypt [ˈiːdʒɪpt] *n* l'Égypte *f* • **Egyptian** [ɪˈdʒɪpʃən] **1** *adj* égyptien, -ienne **2** *n* Égyptien, -ienne *mf*
eiderdown [ˈaɪdədaʊn] *n* édredon *m*
eight [eɪt] *adj & n* huit (*m*) • **eighth** *adj & n* huitième (*mf*); **an e.** un huitième
eighteen [eɪˈtiːn] *adj & n* dix-huit (*m*) • **eighteenth** *adj & n* dix-huitième (*mf*)
eighty [ˈeɪtɪ] *adj & n* quatre-vingts (*m*); **e.-one** quatre-vingt-un; **in the eighties** dans les années 80 • **eightieth** *adj & n* quatre-vingtième (*mf*)
Eire [ˈeərə] *n* l'Eire *f*
either [ˈaɪðə(r)] **1** *adj & pron (one or other)* l'un(e) ou l'autre; *(with negative)* ni l'un(e) ni l'autre; *(each)* chaque; **on e. side** des deux côtés; **I don't know e. man** *or* **e. of the men** je ne connais ni l'un ni l'autre de ces hommes
2 *adv* **she can't swim e.** elle ne sait pas nager non plus; **I don't e.** (ni) moi non plus; **and it's not so far off e.** et ce n'est pas si loin d'ailleurs
3 *conj* **e.... or** ou... ou, soit... soit; *(with negative)* ni... ni; **it isn't e. green or red** ce n'est ni vert ni rouge
eject [ɪˈdʒekt] **1** *vt (troublemaker)* expulser (**from** de); *(from aircraft, machine)* éjecter
2 *vi (of pilot)* s'éjecter • **ejector** *adj* **e. seat** siège *m* éjectable
eke [iːk] ▸ **eke out** *vt sep (money)* dépenser avec parcimonie; **to e. out a living** gagner péniblement sa vie
elaborate¹ [ɪˈlæbərət] *adj (meal)* élaboré; *(scheme)* compliqué; *(description)* détaillé; *(preparation)* minutieux, -ieuse; *(style)* recherché; *(meal)* raffiné • **elaborately** *adv (plan)* minutieusement; *(decorate)* avec recherche

elaborate² [ɪˈlæbəreɪt] **1** *vt (theory)* élaborer
2 *vi* entrer dans les détails (**on** de) • **elaboration** [-ˈreɪʃən] *n* élaboration *f*
elapse [ɪˈlæps] *vi* s'écouler
elastic [ɪˈlæstɪk] **1** *adj also Fig* élastique; *Br* **e. band** élastique *m*
2 *n (fabric)* élastique *m* • **elasticity** [iːlæsˈtɪsɪtɪ] *n* élasticité *f*
elated [ɪˈleɪtɪd] *adj* transporté de joie • **elation** *n* exaltation *f*
elbow [ˈelbəʊ] **1** *n* coude *m*; *Fam* **e. grease** huile *f* de coude
2 *vt* **to e. one's way** se frayer un chemin en jouant des coudes (**through** à travers) • **elbowroom** *n Fam* **to have enough e.** avoir assez de liberté
elder¹ [ˈeldə(r)] *adj & n (of two people)* aîné, -ée (*mf*) • **eldest** *adj & n* aîné, -ée (*mf*); **his/her e. brother** l'aîné de ses frères
elder² [ˈeldə(r)] *n (tree)* sureau *m*
elderly [ˈeldəlɪ] **1** *adj* âgé
2 *npl* **the e.** les personnes *fpl* âgées
elect [ɪˈlekt] **1** *vt (by voting)* élire (**to** à); *Formal* **to e. to do sth** choisir de faire qch
2 *adj* **the president e.** le président élu
election [ɪˈlekʃən] **1** *n* élection *f*; **general e.** élections *fpl* législatives
2 *adj (campaign)* électoral; *(day, results)* des élections • **electio'neering** *n* propagande *f* électorale
elective [ɪˈlektɪv] *adj Am (course)* optionnel, -elle
electoral [ɪˈlektərəl] *adj* électoral • **electorate** *n* électorat *m*
electric [ɪˈlektrɪk] *adj* électrique; **e. blanket** couverture *f* chauffante; *Br* **e. fire** radiateur *m* électrique; **e. shock** décharge *f* électrique; **e. shock treatment** électrochoc *m* • **electrical** *adj* électrique; **e. engineer** ingénieur *m* électricien
electrician [ɪlekˈtrɪʃən] *n* électricien *m*
electricity [ɪlekˈtrɪsɪtɪ] *n* électricité *f*
electrify [ɪˈlektrɪfaɪ] (*pt & pp* **-ied**) *vt* électrifier; *Fig (excite)* électriser
electrocute [ɪˈlektrəkjuːt] *vt* électrocuter
electrode [ɪˈlektrəʊd] *n* électrode *f*
electron [ɪˈlektrɒn] *n* électron *m*
electronic [ɪlekˈtrɒnɪk] *adj* électronique • **electronics** *(subject) n* électronique *f*
elegant [ˈelɪɡənt] *adj* élégant • **elegance** *n* élégance *f* • **elegantly** *adv* avec élégance
elegy [ˈelədʒɪ] (*pl* **-ies**) *n* élégie *f*
element [ˈeləmənt] *n (component, chemical, person)* élément *m*; *(of heater,*

kettle) résistance *f*; **an e. of truth** une part de vérité; **the human/chance e.** le facteur humain/chance; **the elements** *(bad weather)* les éléments *mpl*; **to be in one's e.** être dans son élément

elementary [elɪ'mentərɪ] *adj* élémentaire; *Am (school)* primaire

elephant ['elɪfənt] *n* éléphant *m* • **elephantine** [-'fæntaɪn] *adj (large)* éléphantesque; *(clumsy)* gauche

elevate ['elɪveɪt] *vt* élever (**to** à) • **elevation** [-'veɪʃən] *n* élévation *f* (**of** de); *(height)* altitude *f*

elevator ['elɪveɪtə(r)] *n Am* ascenseur *m*

eleven [ɪ'levən] *adj & n* onze *(m)* • **elevenses** [ɪ'levənzɪz] *n Br Fam* pause-café *f (vers onze heures du matin)* • **eleventh** *adj & n* onzième *(mf)*

elf [elf] *(pl* **elves***) n* lutin *m*

elicit [ɪ'lɪsɪt] *vt* tirer (**from** de)

eligible ['elɪdʒəbəl] *adj (for post)* admissible (**for** à); *(for political office)* éligible (**for** à); **to be e. for sth** avoir droit à qch; **an e. young man** un beau parti • **eligi-'bility** *n* admissibilité *f*; *Pol* éligibilité *f*

eliminate [ɪ'lɪmɪneɪt] *vt* éliminer • **elimination** [-'neɪʃən] *n* élimination *f*

elite [eɪ'liːt] *n* élite *f* (**of** de)

elk [elk] *n* élan *m*

ellipse [ɪ'lɪps] *n Math* ellipse *f* • **elliptical** *adj* elliptique

elm [elm] *n* orme *m*

elocution [elə'kjuːʃən] *n* élocution *f*

elongate ['iːlɒŋgeɪt] *vt* allonger • **elongated** *adj* allongé

elope [ɪ'ləʊp] *vi (of lovers)* s'enfuir (**with** avec)

eloquent ['eləkwənt] *adj* éloquent • **eloquence** *n* éloquence *f* • **eloquently** *adv* avec éloquence

El Salvador [el'sælvədɔː(r)] *n* El Salvador *m*

else [els] *adv* d'autre; **somebody/anybody e.** quelqu'un/n'importe qui d'autre; **everybody e.** tous les autres; **nobody/nothing e.** personne/rien d'autre; **something e.** autre chose; **anything e.?** *(in shop)* est-ce qu'il vous faut autre chose?; **anything e. to add?** avez-vous quelque chose d'autre à ajouter?; **somewhere e.,** *Am* **someplace e.** ailleurs, autre part; **anywhere/nowhere e.** n'importe où/nulle part ailleurs; **who e.?** qui d'autre?; **how e.?** de quelle autre façon?; **or e.** ou bien, sinon • **else'where** *adv* ailleurs; **e. in the town** dans une autre partie de la ville

elucidate [ɪ'luːsɪdeɪt] *vt* élucider

elude [ɪ'luːd] *vt* échapper à • **elusive** *adj*

(person) insaisissable; *(reply)* évasif, -ive

elves [elvz] *pl of* **elf**

emaciated [ɪ'meɪsɪeɪtɪd] *adj* émacié

e-mail ['iːmeɪl] **1** *n* courrier *m* électronique, mél *m*; **e. address** adresse *f* électronique
  2 *vt* envoyer un courrier électronique *ou* mél à

emanate ['eməneɪt] *vi* émaner (**from** de)

emancipate [ɪ'mænsɪpeɪt] *vt* émanciper • **emancipation** [-'peɪʃən] *n* émancipation *f*

embalm [ɪm'bɑːm] *vt* embaumer

embankment [ɪm'bæŋkmənt] *n (of path)* talus *m*; *(of river)* berge *f*

embargo [ɪm'bɑːgəʊ] *(pl* **-oes***) n* embargo *m*; **to impose an e. on** mettre l'embargo sur

embark [ɪm'bɑːk] **1** *vt (passengers, goods)* embarquer
  2 *vi* (s')embarquer; **to e. on sth** s'embarquer dans qch • **embarkation** [embɑː'keɪʃən] *n* embarquement *m*

embarrass [ɪm'bærəs] *vt* embarrasser • **embarrassing** *adj* embarrassant • **embarrassment** *n* embarras *m*

embassy ['embəsɪ] *(pl* **-ies***) n* ambassade *f*

embattled [ɪm'bætəld] *adj* assiégé de toutes parts

embedded [ɪm'bedɪd] *adj (stick, bullet)* enfoncé (**in** dans); *(jewel)* enchâssé; *(in memory)* gravé; *(in stone)* scellé

embellish [ɪm'belɪʃ] *vt* embellir • **embellishment** *n* embellissement *m*

embers ['embəz] *npl* braises *fpl*

embezzle [ɪm'bezəl] *vt (money)* détourner • **embezzlement** *n* détournement *m* de fonds • **embezzler** *n* escroc *m*

embitter [ɪm'bɪtə(r)] *vt (person)* aigrir; *(relations, situation)* envenimer • **embittered** *adj (person)* aigri

emblem ['embləm] *n* emblème *m*

embody [ɪm'bɒdɪ] *(pt & pp* **-ied***) vt (express)* exprimer; *(represent)* incarner • **embodiment** *n* incarnation *f* (**of** de)

emboss [ɪm'bɒs] *vt (paper)* gaufrer; *(metal)* bosseler • **embossed** *adj (pattern, characters)* en relief; **e. paper** papier *m* gaufré

embrace [ɪm'breɪs] **1** *n* étreinte *f*
  2 *vt (person)* étreindre; *Fig (belief)* embrasser
  3 *vi* s'étreindre

embroider [ɪm'brɔɪdə(r)] *vt (cloth)* broder; *Fig (story, facts)* enjoliver • **embroidery** *n* broderie *f*

embroil [ɪm'brɔɪl] *vt* **to e. sb in sth** mêler qn à qch

embryo ['embrɪəʊ] (*pl* **-os**) *n* embryon *m* • **embryonic** [-ɪ'ɒnɪk] *adj (plan, state)* à l'état embryonnaire

emcee [em'siː] *n Am* présentateur, -trice *mf*

emend [ɪ'mend] *vt* corriger

emerald ['emərəld] *n* émeraude *f*

emerge [ɪ'mɜːdʒ] *vi* apparaître (**from** de); *(from hole)* sortir; *(from water)* émerger; *(of nation)* naître; **it emerges that...** il apparaît que... • **emergence** *n* apparition *f*; *(of state, leader)* émergence *f*

emergency [ɪ'mɜːdʒənsɪ] **1** (*pl* **-ies**) *n (situation, case)* urgence *f*; **in an e.** en cas d'urgence; **this is an e.** *(speaking on telephone)* j'appelle pour une urgence
2 *adj (measure, operation)* d'urgence; **e. exit/brake** sortie *f*/frein *m* de secours; **e. landing** atterrissage *m* forcé; **e. powers** *(of government)* pouvoirs *mpl* extraordinaires; **e. services** services *mpl* d'urgence; **e. stop** arrêt *m* d'urgence; *Br* **e. ward**, *Am* **e. room** salle *f* des urgences

emery ['emərɪ] *adj* **e. board** lime *f* à ongles *(en carton)*; **e. cloth** toile *f* (d')émeri

emigrant ['emɪgrənt] *n* émigrant, -ante *mf* • **emigrate** [-greɪt] *vi* émigrer • **emigration** [-'greɪʃən] *n* émigration *f*

eminent ['emɪnənt] *adj* éminent • **eminence** *n* distinction *f*; **Your E.** *(to cardinal)* Votre Éminence • **eminently** *adv* éminemment

emir [e'mɪə(r)] *n* émir *m* • **emirate** ['emɪrət] *n* émirat *m*

emissary ['emɪsərɪ] (*pl* **-ies**) *n* émissaire *m*

emission [ɪ'mɪʃən] *n (of gas, light)* émission *f*

emit [ɪ'mɪt] (*pt & pp* **-tt-**) *vt (light, heat)* émettre; *(smell)* dégager

emotion [ɪ'məʊʃən] *n (strength of feeling)* émotion *f*; *(individual feeling)* sentiment *m*

emotional [ɪ'məʊʃənəl] *adj (person, reaction)* émotif, -ive; *(story, speech, plea)* émouvant; *(moment)* d'intense émotion; **an e. state** un état émotionnel • **emotionally** *adv (to say)* avec émotion; **to be e. unstable** avoir des troubles émotifs

emotive [ɪ'məʊtɪv] *adj (word)* affectif, -ive; *(person)* émotif, -ive; **an e. issue** une question sensible

empathy ['empəθɪ] *n* compassion *f*

emperor ['empərə(r)] *n* empereur *m*

emphasis ['emfəsɪs] (*pl* **-ases** [-əsiːz]) *n (in word or phrase)* accent *m*; *(insistence)* insistance *f*; **to lay** *or* **put e. on sth** mettre l'accent sur qch

emphasize ['emfəsaɪz] *vt (importance)* souligner; *(word, fact)* insister sur, souligner; *(syllable)* appuyer sur; **to e. that...** souligner que...

emphatic [em'fætɪk] *adj (denial, refusal) (clear)* catégorique; *(forceful)* énergique; **to be e. about sth** insister sur qch; **she was e.** elle a été catégorique • **emphatically** *adv (refuse)* catégoriquement; *(forcefully)* énergiquement; **e. no!** absolument pas!

empire ['empaɪə(r)] *n* empire *m*

empirical [em'pɪrɪkəl] *adj* empirique • **empiricism** *n* empirisme *m*

employ [ɪm'plɔɪ] **1** *vt (person, means)* employer
2 *n Formal* **in the e. of** employé par • **employee** [ɪm'plɔɪiː, emplɔɪ'iː] *n* employé, -ée *mf* • **employer** *n* patron, -onne *mf* • **employment** *n* emploi *m*; **place of e.** lieu *m* de travail; **to be in the e. of** être employé par; **e. agency** bureau *m* de placement

empower [ɪm'paʊə(r)] *vt* autoriser (**to do** à faire)

empress ['emprɪs] *n* impératrice *f*

empty ['emptɪ] **1** (**-ier, -iest**) *adj* vide; *(threat, promise)* vain; **on an e. stomach** à jeun; **to return e.-handed** revenir les mains vides
2 *npl* **empties** *(bottles)* bouteilles *fpl* vides
3 (*pt & pp* **-ied**) *vt* **to e. (out)** *(box, pocket, liquid)* vider; *(vehicle)* décharger; *(objects from box)* sortir (**from** *or* **out of** de)
4 *vi (of building, tank)* se vider; **to e. into** *(of river)* se jeter dans • **emptiness** *n* vide *m*; **I was surprised by the e. of the theatre** j'ai été surpris de trouver le théâtre vide

EMU [iːem'juː] (*abbr* **Economic and Monetary Union**) *n* UME *f*

emulate ['emjʊleɪt] *vt* imiter • **emulation** *n* émulation *f*

emulsion [ɪ'mʌlʃən] *n (paint)* peinture *f* acrylique (mate); *Phot* émulsion *f*

enable [ɪ'neɪbəl] *vt* **to e. sb to do sth** permettre à qn de faire qch

enact [ɪ'nækt] *vt (law)* promulguer; *(play, part in play)* jouer

enamel [ɪ'næməl] **1** *n* émail *m* (*pl* émaux)
2 *adj* en émail
3 (*Br* **-ll-**, *Am* **-l-**) *vt* émailler

enamoured [ɪ'næməd] *adj* **e. of** *(thing)* séduit par; *(person)* amoureux, -euse de

encamp [ɪnˈkæmp] *vi* camper • **encampment** *n* campement *m*

encapsulate [ɪnˈkæpsjʊleɪt] *vt (ideas, views)* résumer

encase [ɪnˈkeɪs] *vt (cover)* envelopper (**in** dans)

enchant [ɪnˈtʃɑːnt] *vt* enchanter • **enchanting** *adj* enchanteur, -eresse • **enchantment** *n* enchantement *m*

encircle [ɪnˈsɜːkəl] *vt* entourer; *(of army, police)* encercler

encl (*abbr* **enclosure(s)**) PJ

enclave [ˈenkleɪv] *n* enclave *f*

enclose [ɪnˈkləʊz] *vt (send with letter)* joindre (**in** *or* **with** à); *(fence off)* clôturer; **to e. sth with a wall** entourer qch d'un mur • **enclosed** *adj (receipt, document)* ci-joint; *(market)* couvert; **e. space** espace *m* clos; **please find e....** veuillez trouver ci-joint...

enclosure [ɪnˈkləʊʒə(r)] *n (in letter)* pièce *f* jointe; *(place, fence)* enceinte *f*

encompass [ɪnˈkʌmpəs] *vt (include)* inclure; *(surround)* entourer

encore [ˈɒŋkɔː(r)] **1** *exclam & n* bis *(m)*　**2** *vt* bisser

encounter [ɪnˈkaʊntə(r)] **1** *n* rencontre *f*　**2** *vt (person, resistance)* rencontrer

encourage [ɪnˈkʌrɪdʒ] *vt* encourager (**to do** à faire) • **encouragement** *n* encouragement *m*

encroach [ɪnˈkrəʊtʃ] *vi* empiéter (**on** *or* **upon** sur)

encumber [ɪnˈkʌmbə(r)] *vt* encombrer (**with** de) • **encumbrance** *n* embarras *m*

encyclical [ɪnˈsɪklɪkəl] *n Rel* encyclique *f*

encyclop(a)edia [ɪnsaɪkləˈpiːdɪə] *n* encyclopédie *f* • **encyclop(a)edic** *adj* encyclopédique

end [end] **1** *n (extremity)* bout *m*, extrémité *f*; *(of month, meeting, book)* fin *f*; *(purpose)* but *m*; **at an e.** *(discussion, war)* fini; *(period of time)* écoulé; **my patience is at an e.** ma patience est à bout; **in the e.** à la fin; **to come to an e.** prendre fin; **to put an e. to sth**, **to bring sth to an e.** mettre fin à qch; **there's no e. to it** ça n'en finit plus; *Fam* **no e. of** énormément de; **six days on e.** six jours d'affilée; **for days on e.** pendant des jours et des jours; **to stand sth on e.** mettre qch debout

2 *adj (row, house)* dernier, -ière; **e. product** *(industrial)* produit *m* fini; *Fig* résultat *m*

3 *vt* finir, terminer (**with** par); *(rumour, speculation)* mettre fin à

4 *vi* finir, se terminer; **to e. in failure** se

solder par un échec; **to e. in a point** finir en pointe; **to e. up doing sth** finir par faire qch; **to e. up in London** se retrouver à Londres; **he ended up in prison/a doctor** il a fini en prison/médecin

endanger [ɪnˈdeɪndʒə(r)] *vt* mettre en danger; **endangered species** espèce *f* menacée

endear [ɪnˈdɪə(r)] *vt* faire aimer (**to** de); **that's what endears him to me** c'est cela qui me plaît en lui • **endearing** *adj (person)* attachant; *(quality)* qui inspire la sympathie • **endearment** *n* mot *m* tendre; **term of e.** terme *m* d'affection

endeavour [ɪnˈdevə(r)] (*Am* **endeavor**) **1** *n* effort *m* (**to do** pour faire)
2 *vi* s'efforcer (**to do** de faire)

ending [ˈendɪŋ] *n* fin *f*; *(of word)* terminaison *f*; **a happy e.** *(in story)* un heureux dénouement

endive [ˈendaɪv] *n (curly)* chicorée *f*; *(smooth)* endive *f*

endless [ˈendləs] *adj (speech, series, list)* interminable; *(patience)* infini; *(countless)* innombrable • **endlessly** *adv* interminablement

endorse [ɪnˈdɔːs] *vt (cheque)* endosser; *(action, plan)* approuver; *(claim, application)* appuyer • **endorsement** *n Br (on driving licence)* ≃ point(s) enlevé(s) sur le permis de conduire

endow [ɪnˈdaʊ] *vt (institution)* doter (**with** de); **to be endowed with** *(of person)* être doté de • **endowment** *n* dotation *f*

endurance [ɪnˈdjʊərəns] *n* endurance *f*; **e. test** épreuve *f* d'endurance

endure [ɪnˈdjʊə(r)] **1** *vt (violence)* endurer; *(person, insult)* supporter
2 *vi (last)* survivre • **enduring** *adj* durable

enemy [ˈenəmɪ] **1** (*pl* **-ies**) *n* ennemi, -ie *mf*
2 *adj (army, tank)* ennemi

energetic [enəˈdʒetɪk] *adj* énergique; **to feel e.** se sentir plein d'énergie • **energetically** *adv* énergiquement

energy [ˈenədʒɪ] **1** (*pl* **-ies**) *n* énergie *f*
2 *adj (resources)* énergétique; **e. crisis** crise *f* de l'énergie

enforce [ɪnˈfɔːs] *vt (law)* faire respecter; *(discipline)* imposer (**on** à) • **enforced** *adj (rest, silence)* forcé

engage [ɪnˈgeɪdʒ] **1** *vt (take on)* engager; **to e. sb in conversation** engager la conversation avec qn; *Br* **to e. the clutch** embrayer

2 *vi* **to e. in** *(launch into)* se lancer dans; *(be involved in)* être mêlé à

engaged [ɪnˈgeɪdʒd] *adj* (**a**) *(occupied)* *(person, toilet, phone)* occupé; **e. in doing sth** occupé à faire qch; **to be e. in business** être dans les affaires (**b**) **e. (to be married)** fiancé; **to get e.** se fiancer

engagement [ɪnˈgeɪdʒmənt] *n (to marry)* fiançailles *fpl*; *(meeting)* rendez-vous *m inv*; *(undertaking)* engagement *m*; **to have a prior e.** être déjà pris; **e. ring** bague *f* de fiançailles

engaging [ɪnˈgeɪdʒɪŋ] *adj* engageant

engender [ɪnˈdʒendə(r)] *vt* engendrer

engine [ˈendʒɪn] *n (of vehicle, aircraft)* moteur *m*; *(of train)* locomotive *f*; *(of ship)* machine *f*; *Br* **e. driver** *(of train)* mécanicien *m*

> ⚠ Note that the French word **engin** is a false friend and is rarely a translation for the English word **engine**. Its most common meaning is **machine**.

engineer [endʒɪˈnɪə(r)] **1** *n* ingénieur *m*; *Br (repairer)* dépanneur *m*; *(on ship, train)* mécanicien *m*; **civil e.** ingénieur des travaux publics; **mechanical e.** ingénieur mécanicien
2 *vt (arrange secretly)* manigancer • **engineering** *n* ingénierie *f*; **(civil) e.** génie *m* civil; **(mechanical) e.** mécanique *f*; **e. factory** atelier *m* de construction mécanique

England [ˈɪŋglənd] *n* l'Angleterre *f*

English [ˈɪŋglɪʃ] **1** *adj* anglais; **E. teacher** professeur *m* d'anglais; **the E. Channel** la Manche
2 *n (language)* anglais *m*; **the E.** *(people)* les Anglais *mpl* • **Englishman** *(pl* **-men)** *n* Anglais *m* • **English-speaking** *adj* anglophone • **Englishwoman** *(pl* **-women)** *n* Anglaise *f*

engrave [ɪnˈgreɪv] *vt* graver • **engraver** *n* graveur *m* • **engraving** *n* gravure *f*

engrossed [ɪnˈgrəʊst] *adj* **e. in one's work** absorbé par son travail; **e. in one's book** absorbé dans sa lecture

engulf [ɪnˈgʌlf] *vt* engloutir

enhance [ɪnˈhɑːns] *vt (beauty, prestige)* rehausser; *(value)* augmenter

enigma [ɪˈnɪgmə] *n* énigme *f* • **enigmatic** enɪgˈmætɪk] *adj* énigmatique

enjoy [ɪnˈdʒɔɪ] *vt (like)* aimer (**doing** faire); *(meal)* savourer; *(benefit from)* jouir de; **to e. the evening** passer une bonne soirée; **to e. oneself** s'amuser; **to e. being in London** se plaire à Londres • **enjoyable** *adj* agréable; *(meal)* excellent • **enjoyably** *adv* agréablement • **enjoyment** *n* plaisir *m*

enlarge [ɪnˈlɑːdʒ] **1** *vt* agrandir
2 *vi* s'agrandir; **to e. (up)on sth** s'étendre sur qch • **enlargement** *n (increase)* & *Phot* agrandissement *m*

enlighten [ɪnˈlaɪtən] *vt* éclairer (**sb on** *or* **about sth** qn sur qch) • **enlightening** *adj* instructif, -ive • **enlightenment** *n (explanations)* éclaircissements *mpl*; **an age of e.** une époque éclairée

enlist [ɪnˈlɪst] **1** *vt (recruit)* engager; *(supporter)* recruter; *(support)* s'assurer
2 *vi (in the army)* s'engager

enliven [ɪnˈlaɪvən] *vt (meeting)* animer; *(people)* égayer

enmeshed [ɪnˈmeʃt] *adj* empêtré (**in** dans)

enmity [ˈenmɪtɪ] *n* inimitié *f* (**between** entre)

enormous [ɪˈnɔːməs] *adj* énorme; *(explosion, blow)* terrible; *(patience, gratitude)* immense; **an e. success** un immense succès • **enormity** *n (vastness, extent)* énormité *f*; *(atrocity)* atrocité *f* • **enormously** *adv (very much)* énormément; *(very)* extrêmement

enough [ɪˈnʌf] **1** *adj* assez de; **e. time/cups** assez de temps/de tasses
2 *pron* assez; **to have e. to live on** avoir de quoi vivre; **to have e. to drink** avoir assez à boire; **to have e. of sb/sth** en avoir assez de qn/qch; **it's e. for me to see that** il me suffit de voir que; **that's e.** ça suffit
3 *adv (work, sleep)* assez; **big/good e.** assez grand/bon (**to** pour); **strangely e., he left** chose curieuse, il est parti

enquire [ɪnˈkwaɪə(r)] *vti* = **inquire**

enquiry [ɪnˈkwaɪərɪ] *n* = **inquiry**

enrage [ɪnˈreɪdʒ] *vt* mettre en rage

enrapture [ɪnˈræptʃə(r)] *vt* ravir

enrich [ɪnˈrɪtʃ] *vt* enrichir; *(soil)* fertiliser • **enrichment** *n* enrichissement *m*

enrol [ɪnˈrəʊl] *(Am* **enroll)** *(pt & pp* **-ll-)** **1** *vt* inscrire
2 *vi* s'inscrire (**in/for** à) • **enrolment** *(Am* **enrollment)** *n* inscription *f*; *(people enrolled)* effectif *m*

ensconced [ɪnˈskɒnst] *adj* bien installé (**in** dans)

ensemble [ɒnˈsɒmbəl] *n (musicians, clothes)* ensemble *m*

ensign [ˈensən, ˈensaɪn] *n (flag)* pavillon *m*; *Am (naval rank)* enseigne *m* de vaisseau *(de deuxième classe)*

enslave [ɪnˈsleɪv] *vt* asservir

ensue [ɪnˈsjuː] *vi* s'ensuivre • **ensuing** *adj (in the past)* qui a suivi; *(in the future)* qui suivra

ensure [ɪnˈʃʊə(r)] *vt* assurer; **to e. that...** s'assurer que...

entail [ɪnˈteɪl] *vt (involve)* occasionner; *(difficulties)* comporter; **what does the job e.?** en quoi le travail consiste-t-il?

entangle [ɪnˈtæŋɡəl] *vt* enchevêtrer; **to get entangled in sth** *(of person, animal)* s'empêtrer dans qch

enter [ˈentə(r)] **1** *vt (room, vehicle, army)* entrer dans; *(road)* s'engager dans; *(university)* entrer à; *(race, competition)* participer à; *(write down) (on list)* inscrire (**in** dans; **on** sur); *(in accounts book)* porter (**in** sur); *Comptr (data)* entrer; **to e. sb for an exam** inscrire qn à un examen; **to e. a painting in a competition** présenter un tableau à un concours; **it didn't e. my head** *or* **mind** ça ne m'est pas venu à l'esprit (**that** que)

2 *vi* entrer; **to e. for** *(exam)* se présenter à; *(race)* se faire inscrire à; **to e. into** *(relations)* entrer en; *(explanation)* entamer; *(contract)* passer (**with** avec); **to e. into a conversation with sb** engager une conversation avec qn; **you don't e. into it** tu n'y es pour rien; **to e. into** *or* **upon** *(career)* entrer dans; *(negotiations)* entamer; *(agreement)* conclure

enterprise [ˈentəpraɪz] *n (undertaking, firm)* entreprise *f*; *(spirit, initiative)* initiative *f* • **enterprising** *adj (person)* entreprenant

entertain [entəˈteɪn] **1** *vt* amuser, distraire; *(guest)* recevoir; *(idea, possibility)* envisager; *(doubt, hope)* nourrir; **to e. sb to a meal** recevoir qn à dîner

2 *vi (receive guests)* recevoir • **entertainer** *n* comique *mf* • **entertaining** *adj* amusant • **entertainment** *n* amusement *m*; *(show)* spectacle *m*

> *Note that the French verb* **entretenir** *is a false friend and is never a translation for the English verb* **to entertain.** *Its most common meaning is* **to maintain.**

enthral(l) [ɪnˈθrɔːl] *(pt & pp* -ll-*) vt (delight)* captiver

enthuse [ɪnˈθjuːz] *vi* **to e. over** s'enthousiasmer pour

enthusiasm [ɪnˈθjuːzɪæzəm] *n* enthousiasme *m* • **enthusiast** *n* enthousiaste *mf*; **jazz e.** passionné, -ée *mf* de jazz

enthusiastic [ɪnθjuːzɪˈæstɪk] *adj* enthousiaste; *(golfer, photographer)* passionné; **to get e.** s'emballer (**about** pour) • **enthusiastically** *adv* avec enthousiasme

entice [ɪnˈtaɪs] *vt* attirer (**into** dans); **to e. sb to do sth** inciter qn à faire qch • **en-**

ticement *n (bait)* attrait *m* • **enticing** *adj* séduisant

entire [ɪnˈtaɪə(r)] *adj* entier, -ière • **entirely** *adv* entièrement

entirety [ɪnˈtaɪərətɪ] *n* intégralité *f*; **in its e.** dans son intégralité

entitle [ɪnˈtaɪtəl] *vt* **to e. sb to do sth** donner à qn le droit de faire qch; **to e. sb to sth** donner à qn le droit à qch; **that entitles me to believe that** ça m'autorise à croire que • **entitled** *adj* (**a**) **to be e. to do sth** avoir le droit de faire qch; **to be e. to sth** avoir droit à qch (**b**) **a book e.** un livre intitulé • **entitlement** *n* **one's e.** son dû

entity [ˈentɪtɪ] *(pl* -ies*) n* entité *f*

entourage [ˈɒntʊrɑːʒ] *n* entourage *m*

entrails [ˈentreɪlz] *npl* entrailles *fpl*

entrance¹ [ˈentrəns] *n* entrée *f* (**to** de); *(to university, school)* admission *f* (**to** à); **e. examination** examen *m* d'entrée; **e. fee** droit *m* d'entrée

entrance² [ɪnˈtrɑːns] *vt (charm)* transporter

entrant [ˈentrənt] *n (in race)* concurrent, -ente *mf*; *(for exam)* candidat, -ate *mf*

entreat [ɪnˈtriːt] *vt* implorer (**to do** de faire) • **entreaty** *(pl* -ies*) n* supplication *f*

entrée [ˈɒntreɪ] *n Br Culin* entrée *f*; *Am (main dish)* plat *m* principal

entrench [ɪnˈtrentʃ] *vt* **to e. oneself** *(of soldier) & Fig* se retrancher

entrepreneur [ɒntrəprəˈnɜː(r)] *n* entrepreneur *m*

entrust [ɪnˈtrʌst] *vt* confier (**to** à); **to e. sb with sth** confier qch à qn

entry [ˈentrɪ] *n* entrée *f*; *(in race)* concurrent, -ente *mf*; *(to be judged in competition)* objet *m*/œuvre *f*/projet *m* soumis au jury; **to gain e. to** pénétrer dans; **e. form** feuille *f* d'inscription; **'no e.'** *(on door)* 'entrée interdite'; *(road sign)* 'sens interdit'

entwine [ɪnˈtwaɪn] *vt* entrelacer

enumerate [ɪˈnjuːməreɪt] *vt* énumérer • **enumeration** [-ˈreɪʃən] *n* énumération *f*

enunciate [ɪˈnʌnsɪeɪt] *vt (word)* articuler; *(theory)* énoncer • **enunciation** [-ˈeɪʃən] *n* articulation *f*; *(of theory)* énonciation *f*

envelop [ɪnˈveləp] *vt* envelopper (**in** dans); **enveloped in mystery** entouré de mystère

envelope [ˈenvələʊp] *n* enveloppe *f*

enviable [ˈenvɪəbəl] *adj* enviable

envious [ˈenvɪəs] *adj* envieux, -ieuse (**of** de); **to be e. of sb** envier qn • **enviously** *adv* avec envie

environment [ɪn'vaɪərənmənt] *n (social, moral)* milieu *m*; **the e.** *(natural)* l'environnement *m*; **e.-friendly product** produit *m* qui ne nuit pas à l'environnement • **environmental** [-'mentəl] *adj (policy)* de l'environnement; **e. disaster** catastrophe *f* écologique • **environmentalist** [-'mentəlɪst] *n* écologiste *mf*

envisage [ɪn'vɪzɪdʒ] *(Am* **envision** [ɪn'vɪʒən]) *vt (imagine)* envisager; *(foresee)* prévoir; **to e. doing sth** envisager de faire qch

envoy ['envɔɪ] *n (messenger)* envoyé, -ée *mf*; *(diplomat)* ministre *m* plénipotentiaire

envy ['envɪ] **1** *n* envie *f*
2 *(pt & pp* **-ied**) *vt* envier; **to e. sb sth** envier qch à qn

ephemeral [ɪ'femərəl] *adj* éphémère

epic ['epɪk] **1** *adj* épique
2 *n (poem, novel)* épopée *f*; *(film)* film *m* à grand spectacle

epidemic [epɪ'demɪk] *n* épidémie *f*

epidural [epɪ'djʊərəl] *n Med* péridurale *f*

epilepsy ['epɪlepsɪ] *n* épilepsie *f* • **epi-'leptic** *adj & n* épileptique *(mf)*

epilogue ['epɪlɒg] *n* épilogue *m*

episode ['epɪsəʊd] *n (part of story)* épisode *m*; *(incident)* incident *m* • **episodic** [-'sɒdɪk] *adj* épisodique

epistle [ɪ'pɪsəl] *n* épître *f*

epitaph ['epɪtɑːf] *n* épitaphe *f*

epithet ['epɪθet] *n* épithète *f*

epitome [ɪ'pɪtəmɪ] *n* **to be the e. of sth** être l'exemple même de qch • **epitomize** *vt* incarner

epoch ['iːpɒk] *n* époque *f* • **epoch-making** *adj (event)* qui fait date

equal ['iːkwəl] **1** *adj* égal **(to** à); **with e. hostility/respect** avec la même hostilité/ le même respect; **to be e. to sth** *(in quantity)* égaler qch; *(good enough)* être à la hauteur de qch
2 *n (person)* égal, -ale *mf*; **to treat sb as an e.** traiter qn d'égal à égal; **he doesn't have his e.** il n'a pas son pareil
3 *(Br* **-ll-,** *Am* **-l-)** *vt* égaler **(in** en) • **equals sign** *n* signe *m* d'égalité

equality [ɪ'kwɒlɪtɪ] *n* égalité *f*

equalize ['iːkwəlaɪz] **1** *vt* égaliser; *(chances)* équilibrer
2 *vi (in sport)* égaliser

equalizer ['iːkwəlaɪzə(r)] *n (goal)* but *m* égalisateur

equally ['iːkwəlɪ] *adv (to an equal degree, also)* également; *(divide)* en parts égales; **he's e. stupid** il est tout aussi bête

equanimity [ekwə'nɪmɪtɪ] *n* égalité *f* d'humeur

equate [ɪ'kweɪt] *vt* assimiler **(with** à)

equation [ɪ'kweɪʒən] *n Math* équation *f*

equator [ɪ'kweɪtə(r)] *n* équateur *m*; **at** *or* **on the e.** sous l'équateur • **equatorial** [ekwə'tɔːrɪəl] *adj* équatorial

equestrian [ɪ'kwestrɪən] *adj* équestre

equilibrium [iːkwɪ'lɪbrɪəm] *n* équilibre *m*

equinox ['iːkwɪnɒks, 'ekwɪnɒks] *n* équinoxe *m*

equip [ɪ'kwɪp] *(pt & pp* **-pp-**) *vt (provide with equipment)* équiper **(with** de); *(prepare)* préparer **(for** pour); **(well-) equipped with** pourvu de; **to be (well-)equipped to do** être compétent pour faire • **equipment** *n* équipement *m*; *(in factory)* matériel *m*

equity ['ekwɪtɪ] *(pl* **-ies**) *n* **(a)** *(fairness)* équité *f* **(b)** *Fin (of shareholders)* fonds *mpl* propres; *(of company)* capital *m* actions; **equities** *(shares)* actions *fpl* ordinaires • **equitable** *adj* équitable

equivalent [ɪ'kwɪvələnt] *adj & n* équivalent *(m)* • **equivalence** *n* équivalence *f*

equivocal [ɪ'kwɪvəkəl] *adj* équivoque

era [*Br* 'ɪərə, *Am* 'erə] *n* époque *f*; *(historical, geological)* ère *f*

eradicate [ɪ'rædɪkeɪt] *vt* éradiquer

erase [*Br* ɪ'reɪz, *Am* ɪ'reɪs] *vt* effacer; *(with eraser)* gommer • **eraser** *n* gomme *f*

erect [ɪ'rekt] **1** *adj (upright)* droit
2 *vt (building)* construire; *(statue, monument)* ériger; *(scaffolding)* monter; *(tent)* dresser • **erection** *n* construction *f*; *(of statue)* érection *f*

ERM [iːɑː'rem] *n (abbr* **Exchange Rate Mechanism)** *n* = mécanisme de change

ermine ['ɜːmɪn] *n* hermine *f*

erode [ɪ'rəʊd] *vt (of sea)* éroder; *Fig (confidence)* miner • **erosion** [-ʒən] *n* érosion *f*

erotic [ɪ'rɒtɪk] *adj* érotique • **eroticism** *n* érotisme *m*

err [ɜː(r)] *vi (be wrong)* faire erreur; *(sin)* pécher; **to e. on the side of caution** pécher par excès de prudence

errand ['erənd] *n* commission *f*, course *f*; **to run errands for sb** faire des courses pour qn; **e. boy** garçon *m* de courses

erratic [ɪ'rætɪk] *adj (unpredictable) (behaviour)* imprévisible; *(service, machine)* fantaisiste; *(person)* lunatique; *(irregular) (performance, results)* irrégulier, -ière

erroneous [ɪ'rəʊnɪəs] *adj* erroné

error ['erə(r)] *n (mistake)* erreur *f*; **to do sth in e.** faire qch par erreur; **typing/ printing e.** faute *f* de frappe/d'impression

erudite ['erʊdaɪt] *adj* érudit • **erudition** [-'dɪʃən] *n* érudition *f*

erupt [ɪˈrʌpt] *vi (of volcano)* entrer en éruption; *(of pimples)* apparaître; *(of war, violence)* éclater • **eruption** *n (of volcano, pimples)* éruption *f* (**of** de); *(of violence, anger)* flambée *f*

escalate [ˈeskəleɪt] **1** *vt* intensifier

2 *vi (of war, violence)* s'intensifier; *(of prices)* monter en flèche • **esca'lation** *n* escalade *f*; *(of prices)* montée *f* en flèche

escalator [ˈeskəleɪtə(r)] *n* escalier *m* roulant

escapade [ˈeskəpeɪd] *n* frasque *f*

escape [ɪˈskeɪp] **1** *n (of gas, liquid)* fuite *f*; *(of person)* évasion *f*; **he had a lucky** *or* **narrow e.** il l'a échappé belle

2 *vt (death, punishment)* échapper à; **her name escapes me** son nom m'échappe; **to e. notice** passer inaperçu

3 *vi (of gas, animal)* s'échapper (**from** de); *(of prisoner)* s'évader (**from** de); **to e. unhurt** s'en tirer indemne; **escaped prisoner** évadé, -ée *mf*

escapism [ɪˈskeɪpɪzəm] *n* évasion *f* (hors de la réalité) • **escapist** *adj (film, novel)* d'évasion

escort 1 [ˈeskɔːt] *n (for convoy)* escorte *f*; *(for tourist)* guide *m*; *(of woman)* cavalier *m*; **under e.** sous escorte; **it's dangerous – she needs an e.** c'est dangereux – il faut que quelqu'un l'accompagne

2 [ɪˈskɔːt] *vt* escorter; *(prisoner)* conduire sous escorte

Eskimo [ˈeskɪməʊ] **1** *adj* esquimau, -aude

2 *(pl* **-os)** *n* Esquimau, -aude *mf*

esoteric [esəʊˈterɪk] *adj* ésotérique

especial [ɪˈspeʃəl] *adj* (tout) spécial • **especially** *adv (in particular)* surtout; *(more than normally)* particulièrement; *(for purpose)* (tout) spécialement; **e. as** d'autant plus que

espionage [ˈespɪɒnɑːʒ] *n* espionnage *m*

esplanade [ˈespləneɪd] *n* esplanade *f*

espouse [ɪˈspaʊz] *vt (cause)* épouser

espresso [eˈspresəʊ] *(pl* **-os)** *n* express *m*

Esq *(abbr* **Esquire)** *Br* **J. Smith Esq** = Monsieur J. Smith

essay [ˈeseɪ] *n (in school)* rédaction *f*; *(in university)* dissertation *f* (**on** sur)

essence [ˈesəns] *n (distinctive quality)* essence *f*; *Culin (extract)* extrait *m*; **the e. of sth** *(main point)* l'essentiel *m* de qch; **in e.** essentiellement

essential [ɪˈsenʃəl] **1** *adj (principal)* essentiel, -ielle; *(necessary)* indispensable, essentiel; **it's e. that...** il est indispensable que... (+ *subjunctive)*

2 *npl* **the essentials** l'essentiel *m* (**of** de); *(basic foodstuffs)* les produits *mpl* de

première nécessité; *(of grammar)* les éléments *mpl* • **essentially** *adv* essentiellement

establish [ɪˈstæblɪʃ] *vt* établir; *(state, society, company)* fonder; *(post)* créer • **established** *adj* **(well-)e.** *(company)* solide; *(fact)* reconnu; *(reputation)* établi; **she's (well-)e.** *(well-known)* elle a une réputation établie • **establishment** *n (institution, company)* établissement *m*; **the e. of** *(action)* l'établissement de; *(state)* la fondation de; *(post)* la création de; **the E.** *(dominant group)* les classes *fpl* dirigeantes

estate [ɪˈsteɪt] *n (land)* terres *fpl*, propriété *f*; *(possessions)* biens *mpl*; *(property after death)* succession *f*; *Br* **e. agency** agence *f* immobilière; *Br* **e. agent** agent *m* immobilier; *Br* **e. car** break *m*; *Br* **e. duty**, *Am* **e. tax** droits *mpl* de succession

esteem [ɪˈstiːm] **1** *n* estime *f*; **to hold sb in high e.** avoir qn en haute estime

2 *vt* estimer; **highly esteemed** très estimé

esthetic [esˈθetɪk] *adj Am* esthétique

estimate 1 [ˈestɪmət] *n* évaluation *f*; *Com* devis *m*; **rough e.** chiffre *m* approximatif

2 [ˈestɪmeɪt] *vt (value)* estimer, évaluer; *(consider)* estimer (**that** que) • **estimation** [-ˈmeɪʃən] *n* jugement *m*; *(esteem)* estime *f*; *(calculation)* estimation *f*; **in my e.** à mon avis

estranged [ɪˈstreɪndʒd] *adj* **her e. husband** son mari, dont elle vit séparée

estuary [ˈestjʊərɪ] *(pl* **-ies)** *n* estuaire *m*

etc [etˈsetərə] *(abbr* **et cetera)** *adv* etc

etch [etʃ] *vti* graver à l'eau forte • **etching** *n (picture)* eau-forte *f*

eternal [ɪˈtɜːnəl] *adj* éternel, -elle • **eternally** *adv* éternellement • **eternity** *n* éternité *f*

ether [ˈiːθə(r)] *n* éther *m*

ethic [ˈeθɪk] *n* éthique *f* • **ethical** *adj* moral, éthique • **ethics** *n* éthique *f*, morale *f*; *(of profession)* déontologie *f*

Ethiopia [iːθɪˈəʊpɪə] *n* l'Éthiopie *f* • **Ethiopian 1** *adj* éthiopien, -ienne **2** *n* Éthiopien, -ienne *mf*

ethnic [ˈeθnɪk] *adj* ethnique; **e. cleansing** purification *f* ethnique; **e. minority** minorité *f* ethnique; **e. dancing** danses *fpl* traditionnelles; **e. music** musique *f* traditionnelle

ethos [ˈiːθɒs] *n* génie *m*

etiquette [ˈetɪket] *n* étiquette *f*

etymology [etɪˈmɒlədʒɪ] *n* étymologie *f*

EU [iːˈjuː] *(abbr* **European Union**) *n* UE *f*

eucalyptus [juːkəˈlɪptəs] *n* eucalyptus *m*

eulogy ['juːlədʒɪ] (*pl* **-ies**) *n* éloge *m*

euphemism ['juːfəmɪzəm] *n* euphémisme *m*

euphoria [juːˈfɔːrɪə] *n* euphorie *f* • **euphoric** [-ˈfɒrɪk] *adj* euphorique

Euro ['jʊərəʊ] (*pl* **-os**) *n* (*currency*) euro *m*

Euro- ['jʊərəʊ] *pref* euro-; **E.-MP** député *m* européen

Eurocheque ['jʊərəʊtʃek] *n* eurochèque *m*

Europe ['jʊərəp] *n* l'Europe *f* • **European** [-ˈpiːən] **1** *adj* européen, -éenne; **E. Commission** Commission *f* européenne; **E. Union** Union *f* européenne **2** *n* Européen, -éenne *mf*

euthanasia [juːθəˈneɪzɪə] *n* euthanasie *f*

evacuate [ɪˈvækjʊeɪt] *vt* évacuer • **evacuation** [-ˈeɪʃən] *n* évacuation *f*

evade [ɪˈveɪd] *vt* éviter, esquiver; (*pursuer*) échapper à; (*law, question*) éluder; **to e. tax** frauder le fisc

> *Note that the French verb **s'évader** is a false friend and is never a translation for the English verb **to evade**. It means **to escape.***

evaluate [ɪˈvæljʊeɪt] *vt* évaluer (**at** à) • **evalu'ation** *n* évaluation *f*

evangelical [iːvænˈdʒelɪkəl] *adj* évangélique • **evangelist** [ɪˈvændʒəlɪst] *n* évangéliste *m*

evaporate [ɪˈvæpəreɪt] *vi* (*of liquid*) s'évaporer; (*of hopes*) s'évanouir; **evaporated milk** lait *m* condensé • **evapo'ration** *n* évaporation *f*

evasion [ɪˈveɪʒən] *n* (*escape*) fuite *f*; (*of pursuer, responsibilities, question*) dérobade *f*; (**tax**) **e.** évasion *f* fiscale

> *Note that the French word **évasion** is a false friend and is rarely a translation for the English word **evasion**. Its most common meaning is **escape.***

evasive [ɪˈveɪsɪv] *adj* évasif, -ive

eve [iːv] *n* **on the e. of** à la veille de

even ['iːvən] **1** *adj* (*equal, flat*) égal; (*smooth*) uni; (*regular*) régulier, -ière; (*temperature*) constant; (*number*) pair; *Fig* **to get e. with sb** prendre sa revanche sur qn; **I'll get e. with him (for that)** je lui revaudrai ça; **we're e.** (*morally*) nous sommes quittes; (*in score*) nous sommes à égalité; **to break e.** (*financially*) s'y retrouver

2 *adv* même; **e. better/more** encore mieux/plus; **e. if** *or* **though...** bien que... (*+ subjunctive*); **e. so** quand même

3 *vt* **to e. sth (out** *or* **up)** égaliser qch

• **evenly** *adv* (*equally*) de manière égale; (*uniformly*) uniformément; (*regularly*) régulièrement • **evenness** *n* (*of surface, temper*) égalité *f* • **even-'tempered** *adj* d'humeur égale

evening ['iːvnɪŋ] *n* soir *m*; (*referring to duration, event*) soirée *f*; **tomorrow/yesterday e.** demain/hier soir; **in the e.,** *Am* **evenings** le soir; **at seven in the e.** à sept heures du soir; **every Tuesday e.** tous les mardis soir; **all e. (long)** toute la soirée; **good e.!** bonsoir!; **e. meal/paper** repas *m*/journal *m* du soir; **e. class** cours *m* du soir; **e. dress** (*of man*) tenue *f* de soirée; (*of woman*) robe *f* du soir; **e. performance** (*in theatre*) soirée

event [ɪˈvent] *n* événement *m*; *Sport* épreuve *f*; **in the e. of fire** en cas d'incendie; **in any e.** en tout cas; **after the e.** après coup

eventful [ɪˈventfəl] *adj* (*day, journey, life*) mouvementé; (*occasion*) mémorable

eventual [ɪˈventʃʊəl] *adj* (*final*) final, définitif, -ive • **eventuality** [-tʃʊˈælɪtɪ] (*pl* **-ies**) *n* éventualité *f* • **eventually** *adv* finalement; (*some day*) par la suite; **he'll do it e.** il le fera un jour ou l'autre

> *Note that the French words **éventuel** and **éventuellement** are false friends and are never translations for the English words **eventual** and **eventually**. They mean **possible** and **possibly**.*

ever ['evə(r)] *adv* jamais; **have you e. been to Spain?** es-tu déjà allé en Espagne?; **has he e. seen it?** l'a-t-il jamais vu?; **more than e.** plus que jamais; **nothing e.** jamais rien; **hardly e.** presque jamais; **e. ready** toujours prêt; **the first e.** le tout premier; **e. since (1990)** depuis (1990); **e. since then** depuis lors; **for e.** pour toujours; **the best son e.** le meilleur fils du monde; **e. so sorry** vraiment désolé; *Br* **thank you e. so much** merci mille fois; *Br* **it's e. such a pity** c'est vraiment dommage; **she's e. so nice** elle est tellement gentille; **all she e. does is criticize** elle ne fait que critiquer; **why e. not?** mais pourquoi pas?

evergreen ['evəɡriːn] *n* arbre *m* à feuilles persistantes

everlasting [evəˈlɑːstɪŋ] *adj* éternel, -elle

evermore [evəˈmɔː(r)] *adv* *Formal* **for e.** à (tout) jamais

every ['evrɪ] *adj* chaque; **e. child** chaque enfant; **e. time** chaque fois (**that** que); **e.**

one chacun; **e. single one** tous/toutes (sans exception); **e. second** *or* **other day** tous les deux jours; **her e.** gesture ses moindres gestes; **e. bit as big** tout aussi grand (**as** que); **e. so often, e. now and then** de temps en temps; **to have e. confidence in sb** avoir pleine confiance en qn
everybody ['evrɪbɒdɪ] *pron* tout le monde; **e. in turn** chacun à son tour • **everyday** *adj (happening, life)* de tous les jours; *(ordinary)* banal (*mpl* -als); **in e. use** d'usage courant • **everyone** *pron* = **everybody** • **everyplace** *adv Am* = **everywhere** • **everything** *pron* tout; **e. I have** tout ce que j'ai • **everywhere** *adv* partout; **e. she goes** où qu'elle aille
evict [ɪ'vɪkt] *vt* expulser (**from** de) • **eviction** *n* expulsion *f*
evidence ['evɪdəns] *n (proof)* preuve(s) *f(pl)*; *(testimony)* témoignage *m*; **to give e.** témoigner (**against** contre); **to accept the e.** se rendre à l'évidence; **to show e. of** donner des signes de; **in e.** *(noticeable)* (bien) en vue

> ♪ Note that the French word **évidence** is a false friend and is never a translation for the English word **evidence**. It means **obviousness**.

evident ['evɪdənt] *adj* évident (**that** que); **it is e. from** il apparaît de (**that** que) • **evidently** *adv (clearly)* manifestement; *(apparently)* apparemment

> ♪ Note that the French word **évidemment** is a false friend and is never a translation for the English word **evidently**. It means **of course**.

evil ['iːvəl] **1** *adj (spell, influence, person)* malfaisant; *(deed, advice, system)* mauvais; *(consequence)* funeste
2 *n* mal *m*; **to speak e.** dire du mal (**about** *or* **of** de)
evince [ɪ'vɪns] *vt Formal* manifester

> ♪ Note that the French verb **évincer** is a false friend and is never a translation for the English verb **to evince**. It means **to oust**.

evocative [ɪ'vɒkətɪv] *adj* évocateur, -trice (**of** de)
evoke [ɪ'vəʊk] *vt (conjure up)* évoquer; *(provoke)* susciter
evolution [iːvə'luːʃən] *n* évolution *f*
evolve [ɪ'vɒlv] **1** *vt (system)* mettre au point
2 *vi (of society, idea)* évoluer; *(of plan)* se développer

ewe [juː] *n* brebis *f*
ex [eks] *n Fam (former spouse)* ex *mf*
ex- [eks] *pref* ex-; **ex-wife** ex-femme *f*; **ex-minister** ancien ministre *m*
exacerbate [ɪk'sæsəbeɪt] *vt* aggraver; *(pain)* exacerber
exact [ɪg'zækt] **1** *adj* exact; **to be (more) e. about sth** préciser qch
2 *vt (demand)* exiger (**from** de); *(money, promise)* extorquer (**from** à) • **exactly** *adv* exactement
exacting [ɪg'zæktɪŋ] *adj* exigeant
exaggerate [ɪg'zædʒəreɪt] *vti* exagérer • **exaggeration** [-'reɪʃən] *n* exagération *f*
exalt [ɪg'zɔːlt] *vt Formal* exalter • **exaltation** [-'teɪʃən] *n* exaltation *f* • **exalted** *adj (position, rank)* élevé
exam [ɪg'zæm] *(abbr* **examination**) *n* examen *m*
examine [ɪg'zæmɪn] *vt (evidence, patient, question)* examiner; *(accounts, luggage)* vérifier; *(passport)* contrôler; *(student)* interroger • **examination** *n* examen *m*; *(of accounts)* vérification *f*; *(of passport)* contrôle *m*; **to take** *or* **sit an e.** passer un examen; **class e.** devoir *m* sur table • **examiner** *n (for school exam)* examinateur, -trice *mf*
example [ɪg'zɑːmpəl] *n* exemple *m*; **for e.** par exemple; **to set an e.** *or* **a good e.** donner l'exemple (**to** à); **to set a bad e.** donner le mauvais exemple (**to** à); **to make an e. of sb** punir qn pour l'exemple
exasperate [ɪg'zɑːspəreɪt] *vt* exaspérer; **to get exasperated** s'irriter (**at** de) • **exasperation** [-'reɪʃən] *n* exaspération *f*
excavate ['ekskəveɪt] *vt (dig)* creuser; *(uncover)* déterrer; *(site)* faire des fouilles dans • **excavation** [-'veɪʃən] *n (digging)* creusement *m*; *(archaeological)* fouilles *fpl*
exceed [ɪk'siːd] *vt* dépasser; *(one's powers)* excéder
exceedingly [ɪk'siːdɪŋlɪ] *adv* extrêmement
excel [ɪk'sel] *(pt & pp* **-ll-**) **1** *vt (be better than)* surpasser
2 *vi* **to e. in** *or* **at sth** exceller en qch; **to e. at** *or* **in doing sth** exceller à faire qch
Excellency ['eksələnsɪ] *(pl* **-ies**) *n* **Your E.** Votre Excellence *f*
excellent ['eksələnt] *adj* excellent • **excellence** *n* excellence *f* • **excellently** *adv* parfaitement, admirablement
except [ɪk'sept] **1** *prep* sauf, excepté; **e. for** à part; **e. that...** sauf que...; **e. if...** sauf si...; **to do nothing e. wait** ne rien faire sinon attendre
2 *vt* excepter (**de** from)

exception [ɪkˈsepʃən] *n* exception *f*; **with the e. of...** à l'exception de...; **to take e. to sth** *(object to)* trouver à redire de qch; *(be hurt by)* s'offenser de qch

exceptional [ɪkˈsepʃənəl] *adj* exceptionnel, -elle • **exceptionally** *adv* exceptionnellement

excerpt [ˈeksɜːpt] *n (from film, book)* extrait *m*

excess [ˈekses] *n* excès *m*; *(surplus)* excédent *m*; **to eat/drink to e.** manger/boire à l'excès; **a sum in e. of** une somme qui dépasse; **e. calories** des calories *fpl* en trop; **e. fare** supplément *m*; **e. luggage** excédent *m* de bagages

excessive [ɪkˈsesɪv] *adj* excessif, -ive • **excessively** *adv (too much)* excessivement; *(very)* extrêmement; *(drink, eat)* à l'excès

exchange [ɪksˈtʃeɪndʒ] **1** *n* échange *m*; *Fin (of currency)* change *m*; **(telephone) e.** central *m* téléphonique; **in e.** en échange (**for** de); **e. rate** taux *m* de change
2 *vt* échanger (**for** contre)

Exchequer [ɪksˈtʃekə(r)] *n Br* Chancellor **of the E.** ≃ Ministre *m* des Finances

excise [ˈeksaɪz] *n* taxe *f* (**on** sur)

excitable [ɪkˈsaɪtəbəl] *adj* nerveux, -euse

excite [ɪkˈsaɪt] *vt (get worked up)* surexciter; *(enthuse)* passionner; *(provoke, stimulate)* exciter • **excited** *adj (happy)* surexcité; *(nervous)* énervé; *(enthusiastic)* enthousiaste; **to get e. (about)** s'exciter (pour); *(angry)* s'énerver (contre) • **excitedly** [-ɪdlɪ] *adv* avec agitation; *(wait)* avec une impatience fébrile • **exciting** *adj (book, adventure)* passionnant

excitement [ɪkˈsaɪtmənt] *n* agitation *f*; *(enthusiasm)* enthousiasme *m*; **to cause great e.** faire sensation

exclaim [ɪkˈskleɪm] *vti* s'écrier (**that** que) • **exclamation** [ekskləˈmeɪʃən] *n* exclamation *f*; *Br* **e. mark,** *Am* **e. point** point *m* d'exclamation

exclude [ɪkˈskluːd] *vt* exclure (**from** de); *(doubt, suspicion)* écarter; **excluding...** à l'exclusion de... • **exclusion** [-ʒən] *n* exclusion *f* (**from** de)

exclusive [ɪkˈskluːsɪv] *adj (right, interest, interview, design)* exclusif, -ive; *(club, group)* fermé; **e. of wine** vin non compris • **exclusively** *adv* exclusivement

excommunicate [ekskəˈmjuːnɪkeɪt] *vt* excommunier • **excommunication** [-ˈkeɪʃən] *n* excommunication *f*

excrement [ˈekskrəmənt] *n* excrément *m*

excruciating [ɪkˈskruːʃɪeɪtɪŋ] *adj* atroce

excursion [ɪkˈskɜːʃən] *n* excursion *f*

excuse 1 [ɪkˈskjuːs] *n* excuse *f*; **to make an e., to make excuses** se trouver une excuse
2 [ɪkˈskjuːz] *vt (forgive, justify)* excuser; *(exempt)* dispenser (**from** de); **e. me for asking** permettez-moi de demander; **e. me!** excusez-moi!, pardon!; **you're excused** *(you may go)* tu peux sortir

ex-directory [eksdaɪˈrektərɪ] *adj Br* **to be e.** être sur la liste rouge

execute [ˈeksɪkjuːt] *vt (prisoner, order)* exécuter; *(plan)* mettre à exécution • **exe'cution** *n* exécution *f* • **exe'cutioner** *n* bourreau *m*

executive [ɪgˈzekjʊtɪv] **1** *adj (job)* de cadre; *(car)* de luxe; *Br* **e. director** directeur *m* administratif
2 *n (person)* cadre *m*; *(committee)* bureau *m*; **the e.** *(part of government)* l'exécutif *m*; **senior e.** cadre *m* supérieur; **sales e.** cadre commercial

exemplary [ɪgˈzemplərɪ] *adj* exemplaire

exemplify [ɪgˈzemplɪfaɪ] *(pt & pp* -**ied**) *vt* illustrer

exempt [ɪgˈzempt] **1** *adj (person)* dispensé (**from** de)
2 *vt* dispenser (**from** de; **from doing** de faire) • **exemption** *n* dispense *f* (**from** de)

exercise [ˈeksəsaɪz] **1** *n* exercice *m*; **e. bike** vélo *m* d'appartement; **e. book** cahier *m*
2 *vt* exercer; *(dog, horse)* promener; *(caution, restraint)* user de
3 *vi* faire de l'exercice

exert [ɪgˈzɜːt] *vt* exercer; *(force)* employer; **to e. oneself** se donner du mal • **exertion** *n* effort *m*; *(of force)* emploi *m*

exhale [eksˈheɪl] *vi* expirer

exhaust [ɪgˈzɔːst] **1** *n* **e. (fumes)** gaz *mpl* d'échappement; **e. (pipe)** tuyau *m* d'échappement
2 *vt (person, resources)* épuiser • **exhausted** *adj (person, resources)* épuisé • **exhausting** *adj* épuisant

exhaustion [ɪgˈzɔːstʃən] *n* épuisement *m*

exhaustive [ɪgˈzɔːstɪv] *adj (list)* exhaustif, -ive; *(analysis)* détaillé; *(inquiry)* approfondi

exhibit [ɪgˈzɪbɪt] **1** *n* objet *m* exposé; *(in court)* pièce *f* à conviction
2 *vt (put on display)* exposer; *(ticket, courage)* montrer • **exhibition** [eksɪˈbɪʃən] *n* exposition *f*; *Fam* **to make an e. of oneself** se donner en spectacle • **exhibitionist** [eksɪˈbɪʃənɪst] *n* exhibitionniste *mf*

_♪_ Note that the French word **exhibition** is a false friend and is never a translation for the English word **exhibition**.

exhibitor [ɪgˈzɪbɪtə(r)] _n_ exposant, -ante _mf_

exhilarate [ɪgˈzɪləreɪt] _vt_ stimuler; _(of air)_ vivifier; _(make happy)_ rendre fou (_f_ folle) de joie •**exhilarating** _adj (experience)_ grisant; _(air)_ vivifiant •**exhila'ration** _n_ joie _f_

exhort [ɪgˈzɔːt] _vt_ exhorter (**to do sth** à faire qch)

exhume [eksˈhjuːm] _vt_ exhumer

exile [ˈegzaɪl] **1** _n (banishment)_ exil _m_; _(person)_ exilé, -ée _mf_
  2 _vt_ exiler

exist [ɪgˈzɪst] _vi_ exister; _(live)_ survivre (**on** avec) •**existing** _adj (situation, circumstances)_ actuel, -uelle; _(law)_ existant

existence [ɪgˈzɪstəns] _n_ existence _f_; **to come into e.** être créé; **to be in e.** exister

exit [ˈeksɪt, ˈegzɪt] **1** _n_ sortie _f_
  2 _vi (leave) & Comptr_ sortir

exodus [ˈeksədəs] _n inv_ exode _m_

exonerate [ɪgˈzɒnəreɪt] _vt (from blame)_ disculper (**from** de)

exorbitant [ɪgˈzɔːbɪtənt] _adj_ exorbitant

exorcize [ˈeksɔːsaɪz] _vt_ exorciser •**exorcism** [-sɪzəm] _n_ exorcisme _m_

exotic [ɪgˈzɒtɪk] _adj_ exotique

expand [ɪkˈspænd] **1** _vt (production, influence)_ accroître; _(knowledge)_ étendre; _(trade, range, idea)_ développer; _(mind)_ élargir
  2 _vi (of knowledge)_ s'étendre; _(of trade)_ se développer; _(of production)_ augmenter; _(of gas)_ se dilater; **to e. on** développer; **(fast** _or_ **rapidly) expanding sector** secteur _m_ en (pleine) expansion

expanse [ɪkˈspæns] _n_ étendue _f_

expansion [ɪkˈspænʃən] _n (economic, colonial)_ expansion _f_; _(of trade)_ développement _m_; _(of production)_ augmentation _f_; _(of gas)_ dilatation _f_ •**expansionism** _n_ expansionnisme _m_

expansive [ɪkˈspænsɪv] _adj (person)_ expansif, -ive

expatriate [_Br_ eksˈpætrɪət, _Am_ eksˈpeɪtrɪət] _adj & n_ expatrié, -iée _(mf)_

expect [ɪkˈspekt] _vt (anticipate)_ s'attendre à; _(think)_ penser (**that** que); _(await)_ attendre; **to e. sth from sb/sth** attendre qch de qn/qch; **to e. to do sth** compter faire qch; **to e. that...** _(anticipate)_ s'attendre à ce que... (+ _subjunctive_); **to e. sb to do sth** _(anticipate)_ s'attendre à ce que qn fasse qch; _(require)_ attendre de qn qu'il/

elle fasse qch; **to be expecting a baby** attendre un enfant; **as expected** comme prévu

expectancy [ɪkˈspektənsɪ] _n_ attente _f_

expectant [ɪkˈspektənt] _adj_ impatient; **e. mother** future mère _f_

expectation [ekspekˈteɪʃən] _n_ espérance _f_; **in the e.** dans l'attente de qch; **contrary to all expectations** contre toute attente; **to come up to expectations** se montrer à la hauteur

expedient [eksˈpiːdɪənt] **1** _adj_ opportun
  2 _n_ expédient _m_

expedite [ˈekspədaɪt] _vt Formal (hasten)_ accélérer; _(task)_ expédier

expedition [ekspɪˈdɪʃən] _n_ expédition _f_

expel [ɪkˈspel] _(pt & pp_ **-ll-**) _vt_ expulser (**from** de); _(from school)_ renvoyer

expend [ɪkˈspend] _vt (energy, money)_ dépenser •**expendable** _adj (person)_ qui n'est pas irremplaçable; _(troops)_ que l'on peut sacrifier

expenditure [ɪkˈspendɪtʃə(r)] _n (of money, energy)_ dépense _f_

expense [ɪkˈspens] _n_ frais _mpl_, dépense _f_; _Com_ **expenses** frais; **to go to some e.** faire des frais; **at the e. of sb/sth** aux dépens de qn/qch; **to laugh at sb's e.** rire aux dépens de qn; **e. account** note _f_ de frais

expensive [ɪkˈspensɪv] _adj (goods, hotel, shop)_ cher (_f_ chère); _(tastes)_ de luxe; **to be e.** coûter cher; **an e. mistake** une faute qui coûte cher •**expensively** _adv_ **e. dressed/furnished** habillé/meublé luxueusement; **to do sth e.** faire qch à grands frais

experience [ɪkˈspɪərɪəns] **1** _n_ expérience _f_; **to have e. of** _or_ **by e.** par expérience; **I've had e. of driving** j'ai déjà conduit
  2 _vt (emotion)_ ressentir; _(hunger, success)_ connaître; _(difficulty, remorse)_ éprouver •**experienced** _adj (person)_ expérimenté; _(eye, ear)_ exercé; **to be e. in sth** s'y connaître en qch

experiment 1 [ɪkˈsperɪmənt] _n_ expérience _f_
  2 [ɪkˈsperɪment] _vi_ expérimenter (**on** sur); **to e. with sth** _(technique, drugs)_ essayer qch •**experimental** [-ˈmentəl] _adj_ expérimental

expert [ˈekspɜːt] **1** _n_ expert _m_ (**on** _or_ **in** en)
  2 _adj_ expert (**in** en qch; **in** _or_ **at doing** à faire); **e. advice** le conseil d'un expert; **an e. eye** l'œil d'un connaisseur •**expertise** [-ˈtiːz] _n_ compétence _f_ (**in** en) •**expertly** _adv_ habilement

expiration [ekspə'reɪʃən] *n Am* = **expiry**
expire [ɪk'spaɪə(r)] *vi* expirer • **expired** *adj (ticket, passport)* périmé
expiry [ɪk'spaɪərɪ] *(Am* **expiration** [ekspə'reɪʃən]*) n* expiration *f*; **e. date** *(on ticket)* date *f* d'expiration; *(on product)* date limite d'utilisation
explain [ɪk'spleɪn] *vt* expliquer (**to** à; **that** que); *(reasons)* exposer; *(mystery)* éclaircir; **e. yourself!** explique-toi!; **to e. sth away** justifier qch • **explainable** *adj* explicable
explanation [eksplə'neɪʃən] *n* explication *f*
explanatory [ɪk'splænətərɪ] *adj* explicatif, -ive
expletive [ɪk'spliːtɪv] *n* juron *m*
explicit [ɪk'splɪsɪt] *adj* explicite • **explicitly** *adv* explicitement
explode [ɪk'spləʊd] **1** *vt (bomb)* faire exploser; *Fig (theory)* discréditer
2 *vi (of bomb)* exploser; *Fig* **to e. with laughter** éclater de rire
exploit 1 ['eksplɔɪt] *n* exploit *m*
2 [ɪk'splɔɪt] *vt (person, land)* exploiter • **exploitation** [eksplɔɪ'teɪʃən] *n* exploitation *f*
exploratory [ɪk'splɒrətərɪ] *adj (trip)* d'exploration; *(talks, step, surgery)* exploratoire
explore [ɪk'splɔː(r)] *vt* explorer; *(causes, possibilities)* examiner • **exploration** [eksplə'reɪʃən] *n* exploration *f*
explorer [ɪk'splɔːrə(r)] *n* explorateur, -trice *mf*
explosion [ɪk'spləʊʒən] *n* explosion *f*
explosive [ɪk'spləʊsɪv] **1** *adj (weapon, situation, question)* explosif, -ive
2 *n* explosif *m*
exponent [ɪk'spəʊnənt] *n (of theory)* avocat, -ate *mf*; *(of music)* interprète *m*
export 1 ['ekspɔːt] *n (activity)* exportation *f*; **e. goods/permit** marchandises *fpl*/permis *m* d'exportation
2 [ɪk'spɔːt] *vt* exporter (**to** vers; **from** de) • **exporter** *n* exportateur, -trice *mf*; *(country)* pays *m* exportateur
expose [ɪk'spəʊz] *vt (to air, cold, danger)* & *Phot* exposer (**to** à); *(wire)* dénuder; *(plot, scandal)* révéler; *(criminal)* démasquer; **to e. oneself** *(in public place)* s'exhiber • **exposition** [ekspə'zɪʃən] *n* exposition *f*
exposure [ɪk'spəʊʒə(r)] *n* exposition *f* (**to** à); *(of plot)* révélation *f*; *Phot* pose *f*; **to die of e.** mourir de froid; **to get a lot of e.** *(in the media)* faire l'objet

d'une importante couverture médiatique
expound [ɪk'spaʊnd] *vt Formal* exposer
express¹ [ɪk'spres] *vt* exprimer; **to e. oneself** s'exprimer
express² [ɪk'spres] **1** *adj (letter, delivery)* exprès *inv*; *(train)* rapide, express *inv*; *(order)* exprès; **with the e. purpose of doing sth** dans le seul but de faire qch
2 *adv (send)* en exprès
3 *n (train)* rapide *m*, express *m inv* • **expressly** *adv (forbid)* expressément
expression [ɪk'spreʃən] *n* expression *f*; **an e. of gratitude** un témoignage de gratitude
expressive [ɪk'spresɪv] *adj* expressif, -ive
expressway [ɪk'spresweɪ] *n Am* autoroute *f*
expulsion [ɪk'spʌlʃən] *n* expulsion *f*; *(from school)* renvoi *m*
expurgate ['ekspəgeɪt] *vt* expurger
exquisite [ɪk'skwɪzɪt] *adj* exquis • **exquisitely** *adv* d'une façon exquise
ex-serviceman [eks'sɜːvɪsmən] *(pl* **-men**) *n Br* ancien combattant *m*
extant ['ekstənt, ek'stænt] *adj* qui existe encore
extend [ɪk'stend] **1** *vt (in space)* étendre; *(in time)* prolonger (**by** de); *(hand)* tendre (**to sb** à qn); *(house)* agrandir; *(knowledge)* accroître; *(help, thanks)* offrir (**to** à); **to e. an invitation to** faire une invitation à
2 *vi (in space)* s'étendre (**to** jusqu'à); *(in time)* se prolonger
extension [ɪk'stenʃən] *n (for table)* rallonge *f*; *(to building)* annexe *f*; *(for telephone)* poste *m*; *(in time)* prolongation *f*; *(for essay)* délai *m* supplémentaire; *(in space)* prolongement *m*; *(of meaning, powers, strike)* extension *f*
extensive [ɪk'stensɪv] *adj (powers, forests)* vaste; *(repairs, damage)* important; **to make e. use of sth** faire un usage considérable de qch • **extensively** *adv (very much)* énormément; **to use sth e.** se servir beaucoup de qch
extent [ɪk'stent] *n (scope)* étendue *f*; *(size)* importance *f*; **to a large** *or* **great e.** dans une large mesure; **to some e.** *or* **a certain e.** dans une certaine mesure; **to such an e. that...** à tel point que...
extenuating [ɪk'stenjʊeɪtɪŋ] *adj* **e. circumstances** circonstances *fpl* atténuantes
exterior [ɪk'stɪərɪə(r)] *adj* & *n* extérieur (*m*)
exterminate [ɪk'stɜːmɪneɪt] *vt* extermi-

ner; *(disease)* éradiquer •**extermi'nation** *n* extermination *f*; *(of disease)* éradication *f*

external [ɪk'stɜːnəl] *adj (trade, debt, event)* extérieur; *(wall)* externe; **for e. use** *(on medicine)* à usage externe; *Pol* **e. affairs** affaires *fpl* étrangères

extinct [ɪk'stɪŋkt] *adj (volcano)* éteint; *(species, animal)* disparu •**extinction** *n* extinction *f*

extinguish [ɪk'stɪŋgwɪʃ] *vt* éteindre •**extinguisher** *n* **(fire) e.** extincteur *m*

extol [ɪk'stəʊl] *(pt & pp* -**ll**-) *vt (virtues)* exalter; *(beauty)* chanter

extort [ɪk'stɔːt] *vt (money)* extorquer (**from** à); *(consent)* arracher (**from** à) •**extortion** *n (crime)* extorsion *f* de fonds

extortionate [ɪk'stɔːʃənət] *adj* exorbitant; **that's e.!** c'est du vol!

extra ['ekstrə] **1** *adj (additional)* supplémentaire; **to be e.** *(spare)* être en trop; *(cost more)* être en supplément; **postage is e.** les frais d'envoi sont en sus; **e. care** un soin tout particulier; **e. charge** supplément *m*; *Sport* **e. time** prolongation *f*

  2 *adv (more than usual)* extrêmement; **to pay e.** payer un supplément; **wine costs** *or* **is 10 euros e.** il y a un supplément de 10 euros pour le vin

  3 *n (perk)* à-côté *m*; *(actor in film)* figurant, -ante *mf*; *(on bill)* supplément *m*; **an optional e.** *(for car)* un accessoire en option

extra- ['ekstrə] *pref* extra- •**extra-dry** *adj (champagne)* brut •**extra-fine** *adj* extra-fin •**extra-strong** *adj* extra-fort

extract 1 ['ekstrækt] *n* extrait *m*

  2 [ɪk'strækt] *vt* extraire (**from** de); *(promise)* arracher (**from** à); *(information, money)* soutirer (**from** à) •**extraction** [ɪk'strækʃən] *n* (**a**) *(removal)* extraction *f* (**b**) *(descent)* origine *f*

extra-curricular [ekstrəkə'rɪkjʊlə(r)] *adj Sch* extrascolaire

extradite ['ekstrədaɪt] *vt* extrader •**extradition** [-'dɪʃən] *n* extradition *f*

extramarital [ekstrə'mærɪtəl] *adj* extra-conjugal

extramural [ekstrə'mjʊərəl] *adj Br Univ* de formation continue

extraneous [ɪk'streɪnɪəs] *adj Formal* accessoire

extraordinary [ɪk'strɔːdənərɪ] *adj* extraordinaire •**extraordinarily** *adv* extraordinairement

extra-special [ekstrə'speʃəl] *adj (occa-

sion)* très spécial; *(care)* tout particulier (*f* toute particulière)

extraterrestrial [ekstrətə'restrɪəl] *adj & n* extraterrestre *(mf)*

extravagant [ɪk'strævəgənt] *adj (behaviour, idea)* extravagant; *(wasteful)* dépensier, -ière; *(tastes)* dispendieux, -ieuse •**extravagance** *n (of behaviour)* extravagance *f*; *(wastefulness)* gaspillage *m*; *(thing bought)* folie *f*

extravaganza [ɪkstrævə'gænzə] *n* spectacle *m* somptueux

extreme [ɪk'striːm] **1** *adj* extrême; **at the e. end** à l'extrémité; **of e. importance** de première importance

  2 *n* extrême *m*; **to carry** *or* **take sth to extremes** pousser qch à l'extrême; **extremes of temperature** températures *fpl* extrêmes •**extremely** *adv* extrêmement

extremist [ɪk'striːmɪst] *adj & n* extrémiste *(mf)* •**extremism** *n* extrémisme *m*

extremity [ɪk'stremɪtɪ] *(pl* -**ies**) *n* extrémité *f*

extricate ['ekstrɪkeɪt] *vt (free)* dégager (**from** de); **to e. oneself from a difficulty** se tirer d'une situation difficile

extrovert ['ekstrəvɜːt] *n* extraverti, -ie *mf*

exuberant [ɪg'zjuːbərənt] *adj* exubérant •**exuberance** *n* exubérance *f*

exude [ɪg'zjuːd] *vt (health, honesty)* respirer

eye [aɪ] **1** *n* œil *m (pl* yeux); **before my very eyes** sous mes yeux; **as far as the e. can see** à perte de vue; **up to one's eyes in debt** endetté jusqu'au cou; **up to one's eyes in work** débordé de travail; **to have one's e. on sth** avoir qch en vue; **to keep an e. on sb/sth** surveiller qn/qch; **to lay** *or* **set eyes on sth** poser les yeux sur qch; **to take one's eyes off sb/sth** quitter qn/qch des yeux; **to catch sb's e.** attirer l'attention de qn; **to make e. contact with sb** regarder qn dans les yeux; *Fam* **to make eyes at sb** faire de l'œil à qn; **keep your eyes open!, keep an e. out!** ouvre l'œil!; **we don't see e. to e.** nous ne voyons pas les choses du même œil

  2 *vt* regarder •**eyeball** *n* globe *m* oculaire •**eyebrow** *n* sourcil *m* •**eye-catching** *adj (title)* accrocheur, -euse •**eye doctor** *n Am* opticien, -ienne *mf* •**eye drops** *npl* gouttes *fpl* (pour les yeux) •**eyeglass** *n* monocle *m* •**eyeglasses** *npl Am (spectacles)* lunettes *fpl* •**eyelash** *n* cil *m* •**eyelid** *n* paupière *f* •**eyeliner** *n* eye-liner *m* •**eye-opener** *n* **to be an e. for sb** être une révélation pour qn • **eyepiece** *n (of tele-scope)* oculaire *m* • **eyeshadow** *n* fard *m* à paupières • **eyesight** *n* vue *f* • **eyesore** *n* horreur *f* • **eyestrain** *n* fatigue *f* oculaire

• **eye-wash** *n* collyre *m*; *Fam (nonsense)* sottises *fpl* • **eye-witness** *n* témoin *m* oculaire

▸ **eye up** *vt sep* reluquer

F, f [ef] *n* (**a**) *(letter)* F, f *m inv* (**b**) *Mus* fa *m*

fab [fæb] *adj Br Fam* sensass *inv*

fable [ˈfeɪbəl] *n* fable *f*

fabric [ˈfæbrɪk] *n (cloth)* tissu *m*, étoffe *f*; *(of building)* structure *f*; *Fig* **the f. of society** le tissu social

> 🖉 Note that the French word **fabrique** is a false friend and is never a translation for the English word **fabric**. Its most common meaning is **factory**.

fabricate [ˈfæbrɪkeɪt] *vt* fabriquer • **fabriˈcation** *n* fabrication *f*

fabulous [ˈfæbjʊləs] *adj (legendary, incredible)* fabuleux, -euse

façade [fəˈsɑːd] *n (of building)* & *Fig (appearance)* façade *f*

face [feɪs] **1** *n (of person)* visage *m*, figure *f*; *(expression)* mine *f*; *(of clock)* cadran *m*; *(of building)* façade *f*; *(of cube, mountain)* face *f*; *(of cliff)* paroi *f*; **the f. of the earth** la surface de la terre; **she laughed in my f.** elle m'a ri au nez; **to show one's f.** se montrer; **f. down(wards)** *(person)* face contre terre; *(thing)* à l'envers; **f. to f.** face à face; **in the f. of** devant; *(despite)* en dépit de; **to save/lose f.** sauver/perdre la face; **to make** *or* **pull faces** faire des grimaces; **to tell sb sth to his/her f.** dire qch à qn en face; **f. powder** poudre *f*; **f. value** *(of stamp, coin)* valeur *f*; *Fig* **to take sth at f. value** prendre qch au pied de la lettre; *Br* **f. cloth** gant *m* de toilette

2 *vt (danger, enemy, problem)* faire face à; **to f., to be facing** *(be opposite)* être en face de; *(of window, door, room)* donner sur; **faced with** *(prospect, problem)* confronté à; *(defeat)* menacé par; *(bill)* contraint à payer; **he can't f. leaving** il n'a pas le courage de partir; **let's f. it** soyons réalistes

3 *vi* **to f. north** *(of building)* être orienté au nord; **to f. towards** *(of person)* se tourner vers; **to f. up to** *(danger, problem)* faire face à; *(fact)* accepter

faceless [ˈfeɪsləs] *adj* anonyme

face-lift [ˈfeɪslɪft] *n (by surgeon)* lifting *m*; *(of building)* ravalement *m*

facet [ˈfæsɪt] *n* facette *f*

facetious [fəˈsiːʃəs] *adj (person)* facétieux, -ieuse; **don't be f.!** ne plaisante pas!

facial [ˈfeɪʃəl] **1** *adj (expression)* du visage **2** *n* soin *m* du visage

facile [*Br* ˈfæsaɪl, *Am* ˈfæsəl] *adj Pej* facile

facilitate [fəˈsɪlɪteɪt] *vt* faciliter

facility [fəˈsɪlɪtɪ] *(pl* **-ies**) *n (ease)* facilité *f*; *Comptr* option *f* • **facilities** *npl (for sports, cooking)* équipements *mpl*; *(in harbour, airport)* installations *fpl*; **shopping f.** magasins *mpl*; **transport f.** moyens *mpl* de transports; **special f.** conditions *fpl* spéciales (**for** pour)

fact [fækt] *n* fait *m*; **as a matter of f., in f.** en fait; **it's a f.** c'est une réalité; **is that a f.?** c'est vrai?; **to distinguish f. from fiction** distinguer la fiction de la réalité

faction [ˈfækʃən] *n* faction *f*

factor [ˈfæktə(r)] *n* facteur *m*

factory [ˈfæktərɪ] *(pl* **-ies**) *n (large)* usine *f*; *(small)* fabrique *f*; **arms/porcelain f.** manufacture *f* d'armes/de porcelaine; **f. farming** élevage *m* industriel

factual [ˈfæktʃʊəl] *adj* basé sur les faits

faculty [ˈfækəltɪ] *(pl* **-ies**) *n (of mind, in university)* faculté *f*

fad [fæd] *n (fashion)* mode *f* (**for** de); *(personal habit)* marotte *f*

fade [feɪd] **1** *vt* faner **2** *vi (of flower, material, colour)* se faner; *(of light)* baisser; **to f. (away)** *(of memory, smile)* s'effacer; *(of sound)* s'affaiblir; *(of person)* dépérir

fag [fæg] *n* (**a**) *Br Fam (cigarette)* clope *m ou f*; **f. end** mégot *m* (**b**) *Am very Fam Pej (homosexual)* pédé *m*

faggot [ˈfægət] *n* (**a**) *Br (meatball)* boulette *f* de viande (**b**) *Am very Fam Pej (homosexual)* pédé *m*

fail [feɪl] **1** *n* **without f.** sans faute **2** *vt (exam)* échouer à; *(candidate)* recaler; **to f. sb** *(let down)* laisser tomber qn, décevoir qn; **words f. me** les mots me manquent; **to f. to do** *(forget)* manquer de faire; *(not be able)* ne pas arriver à faire; **I f. to see the reason** je n'en vois pas la raison

3 *vi (of person, plan)* échouer; *(of business)* faire faillite; *(of health, sight, light)* baisser; *(of memory, strength)* défaillir; *(of brakes)* lâcher; *(of engine)* tomber en panne; *(run short) (of supplies)* manquer; *(of gas, electricity)* être coupé; **to f. in an exam** échouer à un examen; **to f. in one's duty** manquer à son devoir • **failed** *adj (attempt, poet)* raté • **failing 1** *n (fault)* défaut *m* **2** *prep* à défaut de; **f. this, f. that** à défaut

failure ['feɪljə(r)] *n* échec *m*; *(of business)* faillite *f*; *(of engine, machine)* panne *f*; *(of gas)* coupure *f*; *(person)* raté, -ée *mf*; **her f. to leave** le fait qu'elle ne soit pas partie; **to end in f.** se solder par un échec

faint [feɪnt] **1** (**-er, -est**) *adj (weak) (voice, trace, breeze, hope)* faible; *(colour)* pâle; *(idea)* vague; **I haven't got the faintest idea** je n'en ai pas la moindre idée; **to feel f.** se sentir mal
2 *vi* s'évanouir (**with** *or* **from** de); **she fainted with hunger** elle s'est évanouie tellement elle avait faim • **faintly** *adv (weakly)* faiblement; *(slightly)* légèrement

faint-hearted [feɪnt'hɑːtɪd] *adj* timoré

fair¹ [feə(r)] *n (trade fair)* foire *f*; *Br (funfair)* fête *f* foraine • **fairground** *n* parc *m* d'attractions

fair² [feə(r)] **1** (**-er, -est**) *adj* (**a**) *(just)* juste; *(game, fight)* loyal; **she's f. to him** elle est juste envers lui; **to beat sb f. and square** battre qn à plates coutures; **f. play** fair-play *m inv*; **that's not f. play!** ce n'est pas du jeu!; **f. enough!** *(OK)* d'accord!; *(rightly so)* ça se comprend!
(**b**) *(rather good)* assez bon (*f* bonne); *(price)* raisonnable; **a f. amount (of)** *(a lot)* pas mal (de); **f. copy** copie *f* au propre (**c**) *(wind)* favorable; *(weather)* beau (*f* belle)
2 *adv (fight)* loyalement; **to play f.** jouer franc jeu • **fairly** *adv* (**a**) *(treat)* équitablement; *(act, fight, get)* loyalement
(**b**) *(rather)* assez; **f. sure** presque sûr • 'fair-'minded *adj* équitable • **fairness¹** *n* justice *f*; *(of person, decision)* impartialité *f*; **in all f.** en toute justice • 'fair-'sized *adj* assez grand

fair³ [feə(r)] *adj (hair, person)* blond; *(complexion, skin)* clair • 'fair-'haired *adj* blond • **fairness²** *n (of hair)* blondeur *f*; *(of skin)* pâleur *f* • 'fair-'skinned *adj* à la peau claire

fairy ['feərɪ] *(pl* **-ies**) *n* fée *f*; *Br* **f. lights** guirlande *f* lumineuse *(de sapin de Noël)* • **fairytale** *n* conte *m* de fées

faith [feɪθ] *n* foi *f*; **to be of the Catholic/** *etc* **f.** être de religion catholique/*etc*; **to have f. in sb** avoir foi en qn; **to put one's f. in** *(justice, medicine)* avoir foi en; **in good/bad f.** *(act)* de bonne/mauvaise foi; **f. healer** guérisseur, -euse *mf*

faithful ['feɪθfəl] *adj* fidèle • **faithfully** *adv* fidèlement; *Br* **yours f.** *(in letter)* veuillez agréer l'expression de mes sentiments distingués • **faithfulness** *n* fidélité *f*

fake [feɪk] **1** *adj* faux (*f* fausse); *(elections)* truqué
2 *n (object)* faux *m*; *(person)* imposteur *m*
3 *vt (signature)* contrefaire
4 *vi (pretend)* faire semblant

falcon ['fɔːlkən] *n* faucon *m*

fall [fɔːl] **1** *n (of person, snow, city)* chute *f*; *(in price, demand)* baisse *f*; **falls** *(waterfall)* chutes *fpl*; *Am* **the f.** *(season)* l'automne *m*
2 (*pt* **fell**, *pp* **fallen**) *vi* tomber; *(of price, temperature)* baisser; **the dollar is falling** le dollar est en baisse; **her face fell** son visage se rembrunit; **to f. into** *(hole, trap)* tomber dans; *(habit)* prendre; **to f. into several categories** se diviser en plusieurs catégories; **to f. off a bicycle** tomber d'une bicyclette; **to f. off** *or* **down a ladder** tomber d'une échelle; **to f. out of a window** tomber d'une fenêtre; **to f. over sth** tomber en butant contre qch; **to f. on a Monday** tomber un lundi; **the responsibility falls on you** c'est à vous qu'en incombe la responsabilité; **to f. short of sb's expectations** ne pas répondre à l'attente de qn; **to f. short of being** être loin d'être; **to f. victim** devenir victime (**to** de); **to f. asleep** s'endormir; **to f. ill** tomber malade; **to f. due** échoir
► **fall apart** *vi (of book, machine)* tomber en morceaux; *(of group)* se désagréger; *(of person)* s'effondrer ► **fall away** *vi (come off)* tomber; *(of numbers)* diminuer ► **fall back on** *vt insep (resort to)* se rabattre sur ► **fall behind** *vi (stay behind)* rester en arrière; *(in work, payments)* prendre du retard ► **fall down** *vi* tomber; *(of building)* s'effondrer ► **fall for** *vt insep (person)* tomber amoureux, -euse de; *(trick)* se laisser prendre à ► **fall in** *vi (collapse)* s'écrouler ► **fall in with** *vt insep (tally with)* cadrer avec; *(agree to)* accepter ► **fall off** *vi (come off)* tomber; *(of numbers)* diminuer ► **fall out** *vi (quarrel)* se brouiller (**with** avec) ► **fall over** *vi* tomber; *(of table, vase)* se renverser ► **fall**

through *vi (of plan)* tomber à l'eau, échouer

fallacious [fə'leɪʃəs] *adj* faux (*f* fausse) • **fallacy** ['fæləsɪ] (*pl* **-ies**) *n* erreur *f*

fallen ['fɔːlən] **1** *pp of* **fall**
2 *adj* tombé; *(angel)* déchu; *(woman)* perdu; **f. leaf** feuille *f* morte

fallible ['fæləbəl] *adj* faillible

fallout ['fɔːlaʊt] *n (radioactive)* retombées *fpl*; **f. shelter** abri *m* antiatomique

fallow ['fæləʊ] *adj (land, fields)* en jachère

false [fɔːls] *adj* faux (*f* fausse); **f. alarm** fausse alerte *f*; **f. bottom** double fond *m*; **f. teeth** dentier *m* • **falsehood** *n* mensonge *m* • **falseness** *n* fausseté *f*

falsify ['fɔːlsɪfaɪ] (*pt & pp* **-ied**) *vt (forge)* falsifier

falter ['fɔːltə(r)] *vi (of step, courage)* vaciller; *(of voice, speaker)* hésiter

fame [feɪm] *n* renommée *f* • **famed** *adj* renommé (**for** pour)

familiar [fə'mɪljə(r)] *adj (well-known)* familier, -ière (**to** à); **to be f. with sb/sth** bien connaître qn/qch; **I'm f. with her voice** sa voix m'est familière; **to make oneself f. with** se familiariser avec; **he looks f. (to me)** je l'ai déjà vu (quelque part)

familiarity [fəmɪlɪ'ærətɪ] *n* familiarité *f* (**with** avec); *(of event, sight)* caractère *m* familier

familiarize [fə'mɪljəraɪz] *vt* familiariser (**with** avec); **to f. oneself with sth** se familiariser avec qch

family ['fæmɪlɪ] **1** (*pl* **-ies**) *n* famille *f*; **to start a f.** fonder une famille
2 *adj (name, doctor, jewels)* de famille; *(planning, problems, business)* familial; **f. friend** ami *m*/amie *f* de la famille; **f. man** homme *m* attaché à sa famille; **f. tree** arbre *m* généalogique

famine ['fæmɪn] *n* famine *f*

famished ['fæmɪʃt] *adj* affamé

famous ['feɪməs] **1** *adj* célèbre (**for** pour)
2 *npl* **the f.** les célébrités *fpl* • **famously** *adv Fam (very well)* rudement bien

fan¹ [fæn] **1** *n (held in hand)* éventail *m* (*pl* **-ails**); *(mechanical)* ventilateur *m*; **f. belt** *(of vehicle)* courroie *f* de ventilateur; **f. heater** radiateur *m* soufflant
2 (*pt & pp* **-nn-**) *vt (person)* éventer; *(fire, quarrel)* attiser
3 *vi* **to f. out** se déployer (en éventail)

fan² [fæn] *n (of person)* fan *mf*; *(of team)* supporter *m*; **to be a jazz/sports f.** être passionné de jazz/de sport; **f. mail** courrier *m* des admirateurs

fanatic [fə'nætɪk] *n* fanatique *mf* • **fanatical** *adj* fanatique • **fanaticism** *n* fanatisme *m*

fanciful ['fænsɪfəl] *adj* fantaisiste

fancy ['fænsɪ] **1** (*pl* **-ies**) *n (imagination)* imagination *f*; *(whim)* fantaisie *f*; **to take a f. to sb** se prendre d'affection pour qn; **I took a f. to it, it took my f.** j'en ai eu envie; **when the f. takes me** quand ça me chante
2 *adj (jewels, hat, button)* fantaisie *inv*; *(car)* de luxe; *(house, restaurant)* chic *inv*; *(idea)* fantaisiste; *Br* **f. dress** déguisement *m*; *Br* **f. dress party** soirée *f* déguisée
3 (*pt & pp* **-ied**) *vt* (**a**) *Br Fam (want)* avoir envie de; *(like)* aimer; **he fancies her** elle lui plaît; **to f. oneself as a writer** se prendre pour un écrivain; *Pej* **she fancies herself!** elle ne se prend pas pour n'importe qui!
(**b**) **to f. that...** *(imagine)* se figurer que...; *(think)* croire que...; **f. that!** tiens (donc)!; **f. meeting you here!** si je m'attendais à vous rencontrer ici!

fanfare ['fænfeə(r)] *n* fanfare *f*

fang [fæŋ] *n (of dog, wolf)* croc *m*; *(of snake)* crochet *m*

fanny ['fænɪ] (*pl* **-ies**) *n Am Fam (buttocks)* derrière *m*; **f. pack** banane *f*

fantastic [fæn'tæstɪk] *adj* fantastique; *(price)* astronomique; *(wealth, size)* prodigieux, -ieuse; *(unbelievable)* absurde; *Fam (excellent)* formidable

fantasy ['fæntəsɪ] (*pl* **-ies**) *n (imagination)* fantaisie *f*; *(dream)* chimère *f*; *(fanciful, sexual)* fantasme *m* • **fantasize** *vi* fantasmer (**about** sur)

⌐ Note that the French word **fantaisie** is a false friend and is never a translation for the English word **fantasy**.

far [fɑː(r)] **1** (**farther** *or* **further**, **farthest** *or* **furthest**) *adj* **the f. side/end** l'autre côté/bout; **it's a f. cry from...** ça n'a rien à voir avec...; **the F. East** l'Extrême-Orient *m*; *Pol* **the f. left/right** l'extrême gauche *f*/droite *f*
2 *adv* (**a**) *(in distance)* loin (**from** de); **how f. is it to Toulouse?** combien y a-t-il d'ici à Toulouse?; **is it f. to...?** sommes-nous/suis-je/*etc* loin de...?; **how f. are you going?** jusqu'où vas-tu?; **how f. has he got with his work?** où en est-il dans son travail?; **as f. as** jusqu'à; **as f.** *or* **so f. as I know** autant que je sache; **as f.** *or* **so f. as I'm concerned** en ce qui me concerne; **f. from doing sth** loin de faire qch; **f. from**

it! loin de là!; **f. away** or **off** au loin; **to be f. away** être loin (**from** de); **f. and wide** partout (**b**) (in time) **as f. back as 1820** dès 1820; **so f.** jusqu'ici; **so f. so good** jusqu'ici, tout va bien; **by f.** de loin; **f. into the night** jusqu'à une heure très avancée de la nuit (**c**) (much) **f. bigger/more expensive** beaucoup plus grand/plus cher (f chère) (**than** que); **f. more/better** beaucoup plus/mieux (**than** que); **f. advanced** très avancé • **far-away** adj (country) lointain; (look) perdu dans le vague • 'far-'fetched adj tiré par les cheveux • 'far-'flung, 'far-'off adj (country) lointain • 'far-'reaching adj de grande portée • 'far-'sighted adj clairvoyant

farce [fɑːs] n farce f • **farcical** adj grotesque

fare [feə(r)] **1** n (**a**) (for journey) (in train, bus) prix m du billet; (in taxi) prix de la course; (taxi passenger) client, -iente mf (**b**) Formal (food) chère f
2 vi (manage) se débrouiller

farewell [feə'wel] **1** n & exclam adieu (m)
2 adj (party, speech) d'adieu

farm [fɑːm] **1** n ferme f; **to work on a f.** travailler dans une ferme
2 adj (worker, produce) agricole; **f. land** terres fpl cultivées
3 vt cultiver
4 vi être agriculteur, -trice • **farmer** n fermier, -ière mf, agriculteur, -trice mf • **farmhand** n ouvrier, -ière mf agricole • **farmhouse** n ferme f • **farming** n agriculture f; (breeding) élevage m • **farm worker** n ouvrier, -ière mf agricole • **farmyard** n cour f de ferme

fart [fɑːt] Fam **1** n pet m
2 vi péter

farther ['fɑːðə(r)] **1** comparative of **far**
2 adj **at the f. end of** à l'autre bout de
3 adv plus loin; **nothing is f. from the truth** rien n'est plus éloigné de la vérité; **f. forward** plus avancé; **to get f. away** s'éloigner • **farthest 1** superlative of **far 2** adj le plus éloigné **3** adv le plus loin

fascinate ['fæsɪneɪt] vt fasciner • **fascinating** adj fascinant • **fasci'nation** n fascination f

fascism ['fæʃɪzəm] n fascisme m • **fascist** adj & n fasciste (mf)

fashion ['fæʃən] **1** n (**a**) (in clothes) mode f; **in f.** à la mode; **out of f.** démodé; **f. designer** styliste mf; (famous) couturier m; **f. house** maison f de couture; **f. show** défilé m de mode (**b**) (manner) façon f; **after a f.** tant bien que mal

2 vt (form) façonner; (make) confectionner • **fashionable** adj à la mode • **fashionably** adv (dressed) à la mode

fast¹ [fɑːst] **1** (-**er**, -**est**) adj rapide; **to be f.** (of clock) avancer (**by** de); **f. colour** couleur f grand teint inv; **f. food** restauration f rapide; **f. food restaurant** fastfood m
2 adv (**a**) (quickly) vite; **how f.?** à quelle vitesse? (**b**) **f. asleep** profondément endormi (**c**) **to hold f.** (of person) tenir bon

fast² [fɑːst] **1** n jeûne m
2 vi jeûner

fasten ['fɑːsən] **1** vt attacher (**to** à); (door, window) fermer; **to f. sth down** attacher qch
2 vi (of dress) s'attacher; (of door, window) se fermer • **fastener, fastening** n (clip) attache f; (hook) agrafe f; (press stud) bouton-pression m; (of bag) fermoir m

fastidious [fæ'stɪdɪəs] adj difficile

> 🖉 Note that the French word **fastidieux** is a false friend and is never a translation for the English word **fastidious**. It means **tedious**.

fat [fæt] **1** (**fatter, fattest**) adj gras (f grasse); (cheeks, salary, book) gros (f grosse); **to get f.** grossir; Fam Ironic **a f. lot of good that will do you!** ça te fera une belle jambe!; Fam **f. cat** (person) gros salaire m
2 n graisse f; (on meat) gras m • **fathead** n imbécile mf

fatal ['feɪtəl] adj mortel, -elle • **fatally** adv **f. wounded** mortellement blessé

> 🖉 Note that the French word **fatalement** is a false friend and is never a translation for the English word **fatally**. It means **inevitably**.

fatality [fə'tælɪtɪ] (pl -**ies**) n (**a**) (person) victime f (**b**) (fate) fatalité f

fate [feɪt] n destin m, sort m • **fated** adj **to be f. to do sth** être destiné à faire qch • **fateful** adj (words, day) fatidique

father ['fɑːðə(r)] **1** n père m; **F. Christmas** le père Noël; **F. Martin** (priest) le Père Martin; **yes, F.** (to priest) oui, mon père
2 vt (child) engendrer • **father-in-law** (pl **fathers-in-law**) n beau-père m

fatherhood ['fɑːðəhʊd] n paternité f

fatherland ['fɑːðəlænd] n patrie f

fatherly ['fɑːðəlɪ] adj paternel, -elle

fathom ['fæðəm] **1** n (nautical measurement) brasse f (= 1,8 m)
2 vt **to f. (out)** (understand) comprendre

fatigue [fə'tiːg] **1** n (**a**) (tiredness) fatigue f (**b**) Mil f. (duty) corvée f
2 vt fatiguer
fatten ['fætən] vt **to f. (up)** engraisser • **fattening** adj (food) qui fait grossir
fatty ['fætɪ] **1** (-ier, -iest) adj (food) gras (f grasse); (tissue) adipeux, -euse
2 n Fam (person) gros m, grosse f
fatuous ['fætʃʊəs] adj stupide
faucet ['fɔːsɪt] n Am (tap) robinet m
fault [fɔːlt] **1** n (blame) faute f; (defect, failing) défaut m; Geol faille f; **to find f. (with)** trouver à redire (à); **to be at f.** être en faute; **it's your f.** c'est (de) ta faute
2 vt **to f. sb/sth** trouver des défauts chez qn/à qch
faultless ['fɔːltləs] adj irréprochable
faulty ['fɔːltɪ] (-ier, -iest) adj défectueux, -ueuse
fauna ['fɔːnə] n faune f
faux pas [fəʊ'pɑː] n inv gaffe f
favour ['feɪvə(r)] (Am **favor**) **1** n (act of kindness) service m; (approval) faveur f; **to do sb a f.** rendre service à qn; **in f.** (fashion) en vogue; **in f. (with sb)** bien vu (de qn); **it's in her f. to do that** elle a intérêt à faire cela; **in f. of** en faveur de; **to be in f. of sth** être partisan de qch
2 vt (encourage) favoriser; (support) être partisan de; **he favoured me with a visit** il a eu la gentillesse de me rendre visite • **favourable** (Am **favorable**) adj favorable (**to** à)
favourite ['feɪvərɪt] (Am **favorite**) **1** adj favori, -ite, préféré
2 n favori, -ite mf • **favouritism** (Am **favoritism**) n favoritisme m
fawn¹ [fɔːn] **1** n (deer) faon m
2 adj & n (colour) fauve (m)
fawn² [fɔːn] vi **to f. (up)on sb** ramper devant qn
fax [fæks] **1** n (message) télécopie f, fax m; **f. (machine)** télécopieur m, fax m; **f. number** numéro m de fax
2 vt (message) faxer; **to f. sb** envoyer un fax à qn
fear [fɪə(r)] **1** n peur f; (worry) crainte f; **for f. of doing sth** de peur de faire qch; **for f. that...** de peur que... (+ ne + subjunctive); **there's no f. of his going** il ne risque pas d'y aller; **there are fears (that) he might leave** on craint qu'il ne parte
2 vt craindre; **I f. that he might leave** je crains qu'il ne parte
3 vi **to f. for one's life/career** craindre pour sa vie/carrière • **fearful** adj (person) apeuré; (noise, pain, consequence) épouvantable • **fearless** adj intrépide • **fear**-

lessness n intrépidité f • **fearsome** adj effrayant
feasible ['fiːzəbəl] adj faisable • **feasibility** n possibilité f (**of doing** de faire); (of plan) faisabilité f; **f. study** étude f de faisabilité
feast [fiːst] **1** n festin m; (religious) fête f
2 vi **to f. on sth** se régaler de qch
feat [fiːt] n exploit m; **f. of skill** tour m de force
feather ['feðə(r)] **1** n plume f; **f. duster** plumeau m
2 vt Fig **to f. one's nest** faire son beurre
feature ['fiːtʃə(r)] **1** n (of face, person) trait m; (of thing, place, machine) caractéristique f; **f. (article)** article m de fond; **f. (film)** long métrage m; **to be a regular f.** (in newspaper) paraître régulièrement
2 vt (of newspaper, exhibition, film) (present) présenter; (portray) représenter; **a film featuring...** un film ayant pour vedette...
3 vi (appear) figurer (**in** dans)
February ['febrʊərɪ] n février m
fed [fed] **1** pt & pp of **feed**
2 adj Fam **to be f. up** en avoir marre ou ras le bol (**with** de)
federal ['fedərəl] adj fédéral • **federate** [-reɪt] vt fédérer • **federation** [-'reɪʃən] n fédération f
fee [fiː] n **fee(s)** (of doctor, lawyer) honoraires mpl; (of artist) cachet m; (for registration, examination) droits mpl; (for membership) cotisation f; **to charge a f. (for a job)** se faire payer (pour un travail); **for a small f.** pour une petite somme; **school** or **tuition fees** frais mpl d'inscription; **f.-paying school** école f privée
feeble ['fiːbəl] (-er, -est) adj faible; (excuse, smile) pauvre; (attempt) peu convaincant • **'feeble-'minded** adj faible d'esprit
feed [fiːd] **1** n (animal food) nourriture f; (for baby) (from breast) tétée f; (from bottle) biberon m
2 (pt & pp **fed**) vt donner à manger à; (baby) (from breast) donner la tétée à; (from bottle) donner son biberon à; Fig (machine) alimenter; **to f. sb sth** faire manger qch à qn; **to f. sth into a machine** introduire qch dans une machine
3 vi (eat) manger; **to f. on sth** se nourrir de qch • **feeding** n alimentation f
feedback ['fiːdbæk] n (response) réactions fpl
feel [fiːl] **1** n (touch) toucher m; (feeling) sensation f
2 (pt & pp **felt**) vt (be aware of) sentir;

(experience) éprouver, ressentir; *(touch)* tâter; **to f. that...** penser que...; **to f. one's way** avancer à tâtons

3 *vi* **to f. (about)** *(grope)* tâtonner; *(in pocket)* fouiller (**for sth** pour trouver qch); **it feels hard** c'est dur au toucher; **to f. tired/old** se sentir fatigué/vieux *(f vieille)*; **I f. hot/sleepy/hungry** j'ai chaud/ sommeil/faim; **she feels better** elle va mieux; **he doesn't f. well** il ne se sent pas bien; **how are you feeling?** comment te sens-tu?; **to f. like sth** avoir envie de qch; **it feels like cotton** on dirait du coton; **to f. as if...** avoir l'impression que...; **what do you f. about...?** que pensez-vous de...?; **I f. bad about it** ça m'ennuie; **what does it f. like?** quelle impression ça (te) fait?; **to f. for sb** plaindre qn; **to f. up to doing sth** *(well enough)* être assez bien pour faire qch; *(competent enough)* se sentir de taille à faire qch

feeler ['fiːlə(r)] *n (of insect)* antenne *f; Fig* **to put out feelers** tâter le terrain

feeling ['fiːlɪŋ] *n (emotion, impression)* sentiment *m; (physical)* sensation *f;* **(sense of) f.** toucher *m;* **to have a f. for** *(person)* avoir de la sympathie pour; *(music, painting)* être sensible à; **to hurt sb's feelings** blesser qn; **no hard feelings!** sans rancune!

feet [fiːt] *pl of* **foot¹**

feign [feɪn] *vt* feindre

feint [feɪnt] *n (in combat sports)* feinte *f*

feisty ['faɪstɪ] **(-ier, -iest)** *adj Am Fam (lively)* plein d'entrain

feline ['fiːlaɪn] *adj & n* félin *(m)*

fell [fel] **1** *pt of* **fall**

2 *vt (tree)* abattre; *(opponent)* terrasser

fellow ['feləʊ] *n* (**a**) *(man, boy)* gars *m* (**b**) *(companion)* camarade *mf;* **f. being** semblable *mf;* **f. citizen** concitoyen, -enne *mf;* **f. countryman/f. countrywoman** compatriote *mf;* **f. passenger** compagnon *m* de voyage, compagne *f* de voyage; **f. worker** collègue *mf* (**c**) *(of society)* membre *m; (teacher)* professeur *m; (student)* boursier, -ière *mf*

fellowship ['feləʊʃɪp] *n (friendship)* camaraderie *f; (group)* association *f; (scholarship)* bourse *f* de recherche

felony ['felənɪ] *(pl* **-ies**) *n Law* crime *m*

felt¹ [felt] *pt & pp of* **feel**

felt² [felt] *n* feutre *m* • **'felt-'tip, 'felt-tip 'pen** *n* crayon-feutre *m*

female ['fiːmeɪl] **1** *adj (person, name, voice)* féminin; *(animal)* femelle; **the f. vote** le vote des femmes; **f. student** étudiante *f*

2 *n (woman)* femme *f; (girl)* fille *f; (animal, plant)* femelle *f*

feminine ['femɪnɪn] **1** *adj* féminin

2 *n Grammar* féminin *m* • **femi'ninity** *n* féminité *f* • **feminist** *adj & n* féministe *(mf)*

fence [fens] **1** *n* (**a**) *(barrier)* clôture *f; (more solid)* barrière *f; (in race)* obstacle *m* (**b**) *Fam (person)* receleur, -euse *mf*

2 *vt* **to f. (in)** *(land)* clôturer

3 *vi (as sport)* faire de l'escrime • **fencing** *n Sport* escrime *f*

fend [fend] **1** *vi* **to f. for oneself** se débrouiller

2 *vt* **to f. off** *(blow)* parer

fender ['fendə(r)] *n* (**a**) *Am (of car)* aile *f* (**b**) *(for fire)* garde-feu *m inv*

fennel ['fenəl] *n* fenouil *m*

ferment 1 ['fɜːment] *n (substance)* ferment *m; Fig (excitement)* effervescence *f*

2 [fə'ment] *vi* fermenter • **fermentation** [fɜːmen'teɪʃən] *n* fermentation *f*

fern [fɜːn] *n* fougère *f*

ferocious [fə'rəʊʃəs] *adj* féroce • **ferocity** [fə'rɒsɪtɪ] *n* férocité *f*

ferret ['ferɪt] **1** *n (animal)* furet *m*

2 *vt* **to f. out** *(object, information)* dénicher

3 *vi* **to f. about for sth** fouiller pour trouver qch

ferris wheel ['ferɪswiːl] *n* grande roue *f*

ferry ['ferɪ] **1** *(pl* **-ies**) *n* ferry-boat *m; (small, for river)* bac *m*

2 *(pt & pp* **-ied**) *vt* transporter

fertile [*Br* 'fɜːtaɪl, *Am* 'fɜːrtəl] *adj (land, imagination)* fertile; *(person, animal)* fécond • **fertility** [-'tɪlɪtɪ] *n* fertilité *f;* **f. treatment** traitement *m* de la stérilité

fertilize ['fɜːtɪlaɪz] *vt (land)* fertiliser; *(egg, animal)* féconder • **fertilizer** *n* engrais *m*

fervent ['fɜːvənt] *adj* fervent • **fervour** (*Am* **fervor**) *n* ferveur *f*

fester ['festə(r)] *vi (of wound)* s'infecter; *Fig (of situation)* s'envenimer

festival ['festɪvəl] *n (of music, film)* festival *m (pl* -als); *(religious)* fête *f*

festive ['festɪv] *adj* de fête; *(mood)* festif, -ive; **the f. season** les fêtes *fpl* de fin d'année • **fe'stivities** *npl* festivités *fpl*

festoon [fe'stuːn] *vt* orner (**with** de)

fetch [fetʃ] *vt* (**a**) *(bring)* aller chercher; **to f. sth in** rentrer qch (**b**) *(be sold for)* rapporter; **it fetched a high price** cela a atteint un prix élevé • **fetching** *adj (smile)* charmant

fête [feɪt] **1** *n Br* fête *f*

2 *vt* fêter

fetid ['fetɪd] *adj* fétide
fetish ['fetɪʃ] *n (object)* fétiche *m*
fetter ['fetə(r)] *vt (hinder)* entraver
fettle ['fetəl] *n* **in fine f.** en pleine forme
fetus ['fiːtəs] *n Am* = **foetus**
feud [fjuːd] *n* querelle *f*
fever ['fiːvə(r)] *n* fièvre *f*; **to have a f.** *(temperature)* avoir de la fièvre; **a high f.** une forte fièvre • **feverish** *adj (person, activity)* fiévreux, -euse
few [fjuː] **1** *adj* (**a**) *(not many)* peu de; **f. towns** peu de villes; **f. of them** un petit nombre d'entre eux; **every f. days** tous les trois ou quatre jours; **one of the f. books** l'un des rares livres; **f. and far between** rarissime (**b**) *(some)* **a f.** quelques-un(e)s (**of** de); **a f. towns** quelques villes; **a f. of us** quelques-uns d'entre nous; **a f. more books** encore quelques livres; **quite a f., a good f.** bon nombre de
2 *pron* peu; **f. came** peu sont venus; **the examples are f.** les exemples sont peu nombreux
fewer ['fjuːə(r)] **1** *adj* moins de (**than** que); **f. houses** moins de maisons (**than** que); **no f. than thirty** pas moins de trente; **to be f. (than)** être moins nombreux (que)
2 *pron* moins • **fewest** ['fjuːɪst] **1** *adj* le moins de **2** *pron* le moins
fiancé [fɪ'ɒnseɪ] *n* fiancé *m*
fiancée [fɪ'ɒnseɪ] *n* fiancée *f*
fiasco [fɪ'æskəʊ] *(pl* **-os,** *Am* **-oes)** *n* fiasco *m*
fib [fɪb] *Fam* **1** *n* bobard *m*
2 *(pt & pp* **-bb-)** *vi* raconter des bobards • **fibber** *n Fam* menteur, -euse *mf*
fibre ['faɪbə(r)] *(Am* **fiber)** *n* fibre *f*; *(in diet)* fibres *fpl*; **high-f. diet** alimentation *f* riche en fibres; **f. optics** technologie *f* des fibres optiques • **fibreglass** *(Am* **fiberglass)** *n* fibre *f* de verre
fickle ['fɪkəl] *adj* inconstant
fiction ['fɪkʃən] *n (imagination)* fiction *f*; **(works of) f.** livres *mpl* de fiction; **that's pure f.** ce sont des histoires • **fictional** *adj (character)* fictif, -ive
fictitious [fɪk'tɪʃəs] *adj* fictif, -ive
fiddle ['fɪdəl] **1** *n* (**a**) *(violin)* violon *m* (**b**) *Br Fam (dishonest act)* combine *f*; **to be on the f.** traficoter
2 *vt Br Fam (accounts)* truquer
3 *vi* (**a**) *(play violin)* jouer du violon (**b**) **to f. about** *(waste time)* traînailler; **to f. (about) with sth** tripoter qch • **fiddler** *n* (**a**) *(violin player)* violoniste *mf* (**b**) *Br Fam (swindler)* combinard, -arde *mf*
fiddly ['fɪdlɪ] **(-ier, -iest)** *adj Fam* minutieux, -ieuse

fidelity [fɪ'delɪtɪ] *n* fidélité *f* (**to** à)
fidget ['fɪdʒɪt] **1** *n* **to be a f.** ne pas tenir en place
2 *vi* **to f. (about)** gigoter; **to f. (about) with sth** tripoter qch • **fidgety** *adj* agité
field [fiːld] *n* champ *m*; *(for sports)* terrain *m*; *(sphere)* domaine *m*; **to have a f. day** *(a good day)* s'en donner à cœur joie; **f. glasses** jumelles *fpl*; *Am* **f. hockey** hockey *m* (sur gazon); **f. marshal** ≃ maréchal *m* de France
fiend [fiːnd] *n* démon *m*; *Fam* **a jazz f.** un(e) fana de jazz; *Fam* **(sex) f.** obsédé *m* sexuel; **fresh-air f.** maniaque *mf* du grand air • **fiendish** *adj (cruel)* diabolique; *(difficult, awful)* abominable
fierce [fɪəs] **(-er, -est)** *adj (animal, warrior, tone)* féroce; *(attack, wind)* violent • **fierceness** *n* férocité *f*; *(of attack)* violence *f*
fiery ['faɪərɪ] **(-ier, -iest)** *adj (person, speech)* fougueux, -ueuse; *(sun, eyes)* ardent; *(taste)* très épicé
fifteen [fɪf'tiːn] *adj & n* quinze *(m)* • **fifteenth** *adj & n* quinzième *(mf)*
fifth [fɪfθ] *adj & n* cinquième *(mf)*; **a f.** un cinquième
fifty ['fɪftɪ] *adj & n* cinquante *(m)*; **a f.-f. chance** une chance sur deux; **to split the profits f.-f.** partager les bénéfices moitié-moitié • **fiftieth** *adj & n* cinquantième *(mf)*
fig [fɪg] *n* figue *f*; **f. tree** figuier *m*
fight [faɪt] **1** *n (between people)* bagarre *f*; *(between boxers, soldiers)* combat *m*; *(struggle)* lutte *f* (**against/for** contre/pour); *(quarrel)* dispute *f*; **to put up a good f.** bien se défendre
2 *(pt & pp* **fought)** *vt (person)* se battre contre; *(decision, enemy)* combattre; *(fire, temptation)* lutter contre; **to f. a battle** livrer bataille; *Pol* **to f. an election** se présenter à une élection; **to f. back** *(tears)* retenir; **to f. off** *(attacker, attack)* repousser; *(illness)* lutter contre; **to f. it out** se bagarrer
3 *vi* se battre (**against** contre); *(of soldiers)* combattre; *(struggle)* lutter; *(quarrel)* se disputer; **to f. back** *(retaliate)* se défendre; **to f. over sth** se disputer qch; **to f. against an illness/for a cause** lutter contre une maladie/pour une cause
fighter ['faɪtə(r)] *n (determined person)* battant, -ante *mf*; *(in brawl, battle)* combattant, -ante *mf*; *(boxer)* boxeur *m*; *(aircraft)* avion *m* de chasse
fighting ['faɪtɪŋ] *n (brawling)* bagarres *fpl*; *Mil* combat *m*; **f. spirit** combativité *f*; **f. troops** troupes *fpl* de combat

figment ['fɪgmənt] *n* **it's a f. of your imagination** c'est le fruit de ton imagination

figurative ['fɪgjʊrətɪv] *adj (meaning)* figuré; *(art)* figuratif, -ive

figure¹ [*Br* 'fɪgə(r), *Am* 'fɪgjə(r)] *n* (**a**) *(numeral)* chiffre *m*; **figures** *(arithmetic)* calcul *m* (**b**) *(shape)* forme *f*; *(outline)* silhouette *f*; **she has a nice f.** elle est bien faite (**c**) *(diagram)* figure *f*; *Br* **f. of eight,** *Am* **f. eight** huit *m*; **f. skating** patinage *m* artistique (**d**) *(expression, word)* **a f. of speech** une figure de rhétorique; *Fig* **it's just a f. of speech** c'est une façon de parler (**e**) *(important person)* personnage *m*

figure² [*Br* 'fɪgə(r), *Am* 'fɪgjə(r)] **1** *vt* **to f. that...** *(think)* penser que...; *(estimate)* supposer que...; **to f. out** *(person, motive)* arriver à comprendre; *(answer)* trouver; *(amount)* calculer

2 *vi* (**a**) *(appear)* figurer (**on** sur); **to f. on doing sth** compter faire qch (**b**) *Fam* **that figures!** *(makes sense)* ça se tient!

figurehead ['fɪgəhed] *n (of ship)* figure *f* de proue; *Fig & Pej (of organization)* homme *m* de paille

filament ['fɪləmənt] *n* filament *m*

filch [fɪltʃ] *vt Fam* faucher (**from** à)

file¹ [faɪl] **1** *n (tool)* lime *f*

2 *vt* **to f. (down)** limer

file² [faɪl] **1** *n (folder)* chemise *f*; *(documents)* dossier *m* (**on** sur); *(loose-leaf)* classeur *m*; *Comptr* fichier *m*; **to be on f.** figurer au dossier; *Comptr* **f. manager** gestionnaire *m* de fichiers

2 *vt (document)* classer; *(complaint, claim)* déposer

3 *vi* **to f. for divorce** demander le divorce • **filing** *adj* **f. clerk** documentaliste *mf*; **f. cabinet** classeur *m (meuble)*

file³ [faɪl] **1** *n (line)* file *f*; **in single f.** en file indienne

2 *vi* **to f. in/out** entrer/sortir à la queue leu leu; **to f. past sb/sth** défiler devant qn/qch

Filipino [fɪlɪ'piːnəʊ] *(pl -os) n* Philippin, -ine *mf*

fill [fɪl] **1** *n* **to eat one's f.** manger à sa faim; **to have had one's f. of sb/sth** en avoir assez de qn/qch

2 *vt* remplir (**with** de); *(tooth)* plomber; *(time)* occuper; **to f. a need** répondre à un besoin; **to f. a vacancy** pourvoir à un poste vacant; **to be filled with hope** être plein d'espoir; **to f. in** *(form)* remplir; *(hole)* combler; *(door, window)* condamner; **to f. sb in on sth** mettre qn au

courant de qch; **to f. out** *(form)* remplir; **to f. up** *(container, form)* remplir

3 *vi* **f. (up)** se remplir (**with** de); **to f. in for sb** remplacer qn; **to f. out** *(get fatter)* grossir; **to f. up** *(with petrol)* faire le plein

fillet [*Br* 'fɪlɪt, *Am* fɪ'leɪ] **1** *n (of fish, meat)* filet *m*

2 (*Am pt & pp* [fɪ'leɪd]) *vt (fish)* découper en filets; *(meat)* désosser

filling ['fɪlɪŋ] **1** *adj (meal)* nourrissant

2 *n (in tooth)* plombage *m*; *(in food)* garniture *f*; **f. station** station-service *f*

fillip ['fɪlɪp] *n (stimulus)* coup *m* de fouet

filly ['fɪlɪ] *(pl -ies) n (horse)* pouliche *f*

film [fɪlm] **1** *n* film *m*; *(for camera, layer)* pellicule *f*; *(for food)* film *m* plastique

2 *adj (studio, technician, critic)* de cinéma; **f. club** ciné-club *m*; **f. fan** *or* **buff** cinéphile *mf*; **f. festival** festival *m* du film; **f. library** cinémathèque *f*; **f. maker** cinéaste *mf*; **f. star** vedette *f* de cinéma

3 *vt* filmer

4 *vi (of film maker, actor)* tourner

Filofax® ['faɪləfæks] *n* organiseur *m*

filter ['fɪltə(r)] **1** *n* filtre *m*; *Br (traffic sign)* flèche *f* de dégagement; **f. coffee** café *m* filtre; *Br Aut* **f. lane** = voie réservée aux véhicules qui tournent; **f. tip** bout *m* filtre

2 *vt* filtrer

3 *vi* **to f. through** filtrer

filth [fɪlθ] *n* saleté *f*; *Fig (obscenities)* saletés *fpl* • **filthy 1** (**-ier, -iest**) *adj (hands, shoes)* sale; *(language)* obscène; *(habit)* dégoûtant; *Br Fam* **f. weather** un sale temps **2** *adv Fam* **f. riche** pourri de fric

fin [fɪn] *n (of fish, seal)* nageoire *f*; *(of shark)* aileron *m*; *Am (of swimmer)* palme *f*

final ['faɪnəl] **1** *adj (last)* dernier, -ière; *(definite)* définitif, -ive

2 *n Sport* finale *f*; *Univ* **finals** examens *mpl* de dernière année • **finalist** *n* finaliste *mf* • **finalize** *vt (plan)* mettre au point; *(date)* fixer définitivement; *(deal)* conclure • **finally** *adv (lastly)* enfin; *(eventually)* finalement; *(irrevocably)* définitivement

finale [fɪ'nɑːlɪ] *n (musical)* finale *m*

finance ['faɪnæns] **1** *n* finance *f*; **finances** *(of person)* finances *fpl*; *(of company)* situation *f* financière; **f. company** société *f* financière

2 *vt* financer

financial [faɪ'nænʃəl] *adj* financier, -ière; **it was a f. success** ça a rapporté beaucoup d'argent; *Br* **f. year** exercice *m* comptable • **financially** *adv* financièrement

financier [faɪ'nænsɪə(r)] *n* financier *m*

find [faɪnd] **1** n (discovery) découverte f
2 (pt & pp **found**) vt trouver; **I f. that...** je
trouve que...; **I found him waiting in the
hall** je l'ai trouvé qui attendait dans le
vestibule; **she was nowhere to be found**
elle était introuvable; **he found it impossible to understand her** il avait beaucoup de mal à la comprendre; **£20 all
found** 20 livres logé et nourri; **to f. difficulty doing sth** éprouver de la difficulté à
faire qch; **to f. one's feet** (settle in) s'adapter; **to f. oneself** (spiritually) se trouver
▸**find out 1** vt (secret, information) découvrir; (person) prendre en défaut **2** vi
(inquire) se renseigner (**about** sur); **to f.
out about sth** (discover) apprendre qch
findings ['faɪndɪŋz] npl conclusions fpl
fine¹ [faɪn] **1** n (money) amende f; (for
driving offence) contravention f
2 vt **to f. sb £10** infliger une amende de
10 livres à qn
fine² [faɪn] **1** (-er, -est) adj (**a**) (thin, not
coarse) (hair, needle) fin; (gold, metal)
pur; (feeling) délicat; (distinction) subtil
(**b**) (very good) excellent; (beautiful)
(weather, statue) beau (f belle); **it's f.**
(weather) il fait beau; **he's f.** (healthy) il
va bien; **f. arts** beaux-arts mpl
2 adv (**a**) (very well) très bien; **f.!** très
bien! (**b**) (cut, write) menu ▸**finely** adv
(dressed) magnifiquement; (embroi-
dered, ground) finement; (painted, ex-
pressed) délicatement; **f. chopped** haché
menu
finery ['faɪnərɪ] n (clothes) parure f
finesse [fɪ'nes] n finesse f
finger ['fɪŋgə(r)] **1** n doigt m; **to keep
one's fingers crossed** croiser les doigts;
little f. petit doigt m, auriculaire m;
middle f. majeur m; **f. mark** trace f de
doigt
2 vt tâter ▸**fingernail** n ongle m ▸**fingerprint** n empreinte f digitale ▸**fingertip** n
bout m du doigt; **to have sth at one's
fingertips** savoir qch sur le bout des
doigts
finicky ['fɪnɪkɪ] adj (precise) tatillon,
-onne; (difficult) difficile (**about** sur)
finish ['fɪnɪʃ] **1** n (end) fin f; (of race)
arrivée f; (of article, car) finition f; **paint
with a matt f.** peinture f mate
2 vt **to f. sth** (off or up) finir qch; **to f.
doing sth** finir de faire qch; **to f. sb off**
(kill) achever qn
3 vi (of meeting, event) finir, se terminer;
(of person) finir, terminer; **to f. first** terminer premier; **to have finished with**
(object) ne plus avoir besoin de; (situ-

ation, person) en avoir fini avec; **to f. off**
or **up** (of person) finir, terminer; **to f. up in**
(end up in) se retrouver à; **to f. up doing
sth** finir par faire qch; **finishing line** (of
race) ligne f d'arrivée; **to put the finishing
touches to sth** mettre la dernière main à
qch ▸**finished** adj (ended, complete,
ruined) fini
finite ['faɪnaɪt] adj fini
Finland ['fɪnlənd] n la Finlande ▸**Finn** n
Finlandais, -aise mf, Finnois, -oise mf
▸**Finnish 1** adj finlandais, finnois **2** n
(language) finnois m
fir [fɜː(r)] n sapin m
fire ['faɪə(r)] **1** n feu m; (accidental) incendie m; Br (electric heater) radiateur m;
to light or **make a f.** faire du feu; **to set f.
to sb/sth** mettre le feu à qn/qch; **to catch
f.** prendre feu; **on f.** en feu; **f.!** (alarm) au
feu!; (to soldiers) feu!; **to open f.** ouvrir le
feu; **f. alarm** sirène f d'incendie; Br **f.
brigade,** Am **f. department** pompiers
mpl; **f. engine** voiture f des pompiers; **f.
escape** escalier m de secours; **f. exit**
sortie f de secours; **f. station** caserne f
des pompiers
2 vt (cannon) tirer; (pottery) cuire; Fig
(imagination) enflammer; **to f. a gun** tirer
un coup de fusil/de pistolet; **to f. questions at sb** bombarder de questions;
to f. sb (dismiss) renvoyer qn
3 vi tirer (**at** sur); Fam **f. away!** (start
speaking) vas-y!; Fig Br **in** or Am **on the
firing line** en butte aux attaques; **firing
squad** peloton m d'exécution ▸**firearm** n
arme f à feu ▸**firecracker** n pétard m
▸**fireguard** n garde-feu m inv ▸**fireman**
(pl **-men**) n sapeur-pompier m ▸**fireplace**
n cheminée f ▸**fireproof** adj (door) ignifugé ▸**fireside** n **by the f.** au coin du feu;
▸**firewood** n bois m de chauffage ▸**firework** n fusée f; (firecracker) pétard m; Br
f. display feu m d'artifice
firm¹ [fɜːm] n (company) entreprise f,
firme f
firm² [fɜːm] **1** (-er, -est) adj (earth, decision) ferme; (foundations, faith) solide;
(character) résolu; **to be f. with sb** être
ferme avec qn
2 adv **to stand f.** tenir bon ou ferme
▸**firmly** adv (believe) fermement; (speak)
d'une voix ferme; (shut) bien ▸**firmness** n
fermeté f
first [fɜːst] **1** adj premier, -ière; **I'll do it f.
thing in the morning** je le ferai dès le
matin; **f. aid** premiers secours mpl; **f.
cousin** cousin, -ine mf germain(e)
2 adv d'abord; (for the first time) pour la

première fois; **f. of all, f. and foremost**
tout d'abord; **at f.** d'abord; **to come f.** *(in
race)* arriver premier; *(in exam)* être reçu
premier

3 *n (person, thing)* premier, -ière *mf*;
(British university degree) ≃ licence *f*
avec mention très bien; **from the f.** dès
le début; **f. (gear)** *(of vehicle)* première *f*
• **'first-'class 1** *adj* excellent; *(ticket)* de
première classe; *(mail)* ordinaire **2** *adv
(travel)* en première • **'first-'hand 1** *adj
(news)* de première main; **to have (had)
f. experience of sth** avoir fait l'expérience
personnelle de qch **2** *adv (hear news)* de
première main • **'first-'rate** *adj* excellent

firstly ['fɜːstlɪ] *adv* premièrement

fiscal ['fɪskəl] *adj* fiscal

fish [fɪʃ] **1** *(pl inv or -es* [-ɪz]*)* *n* poisson *m*;
f. bone arête *f*; **f. bowl** bocal *m*; **f. cake**
croquette *f* de poisson; *Br* **f. fingers,** *Am* **f.
sticks** bâtonnets *mpl* de poisson; **f. market** marché *m* aux poissons; **f. shop** poissonnerie *f*; **f. tank** aquarium *m*; *Br* **f.-and-
chip shop** = magasin où on vend du
poisson frit et des frites

2 *vt* **to f. sth out** *(from water)* repêcher
qch; **to f. sb/sth from somewhere**
(remove) sortir qn/qch de quelque part

3 *vi* pêcher; **to f. for salmon** pêcher le
saumon; *Fig* **to f. for compliments** rechercher les compliments • **fishing** *n* pêche *f*; **to go f.** aller à la pêche; **f. boat**
bateau *m* de pêche; **f. line** ligne *f*; **f. net** *(of
fisherman)* filet *m* (de pêche); *(of angler)*
épuisette *f*; *Am* **f. pole** canne *f* à pêche; **f.
rod** canne à pêche

fisherman ['fɪʃəmən] *(pl -men)* *n* pêcheur *m*

fishmonger ['fɪʃmʌŋgə(r)] *n* poissonnier, -ière *mf*

fishy ['fɪʃɪ] *(-ier, -iest)* *adj (smell, taste)*
de poisson; *Fig (suspicious)* louche

fission ['fɪʃən] *n* **nuclear f.** fission *f* nucléaire

fissure ['fɪʃə(r)] *n (in rock)* fissure *f*

fist [fɪst] *n* poing *m* • **fistful** *n* poignée *f*
(**of** de)

fit¹ [fɪt] **1** *(fitter, fittest)* *adj* (**a**) *(healthy)*
en forme; **to keep f.** se maintenir en
forme

(**b**) *(suitable)* propre (**for** à; **to do** à faire);
(worthy) digne (**for** de; **to do** de faire);
(able) apte (**for** à; **to do** à faire); **f. to eat**
or **for eating** mangeable; **to see f. to do
sth** juger bon de faire qch; **as you see f.**
comme bon vous semblera; *Fam* **I was f.
to drop** je ne tenais plus debout

2 *n* **a good f.** *(clothes)* à la bonne taille; **a**

close *or* **tight f.** *(clothes)* ajusté

3 *(pt & pp -tt-)* *vt (be the right size for)*
aller bien à; *(match)* correspondre à; *(put
in)* poser; *(go in)* aller dans; *(go on)* aller
sur; **to f. sth on sb** *(garment)* ajuster qch à
qn; **to f. sth (on) to sth** *(put)* poser qch
sur qch; *(adjust)* adapter qch à qch; *(fix)*
fixer qch à qch; **to f. sth (out** *or* **up) with
sth** équiper qch de qch; **to f. sth in**
(install) poser qch; *(insert)* faire entrer
qch; **to f. in a customer** *(find time to see)*
prendre un client

4 *vi (of clothes, lid, key, plug)* aller; **this
shirt fits** cette chemise me/te/*etc* va; **to f.
(in)** *(go in)* aller; *(of facts, plans)* cadrer
(**with** avec); **he doesn't f. in** il n'est pas à
sa place

fit² [fɪt] *n (seizure)* attaque *f*; **to have a f.**
avoir une attaque; *Fam (get angry)* piquer
une crise; **a f. of coughing** une quinte de
toux; **a f. of crying** une crise de larmes; **a
f. of enthusiasm** un accès d'enthousiasme; **in fits and starts** par à-coups

fitful ['fɪtfəl] *adj (sleep)* agité

fitness ['fɪtnɪs] *n (health)* santé *f*; *(of
remark)* à-propos *m*; *(for job)* aptitude *f*
(**for** à)

fitted ['fɪtɪd] *adj Br (cupboard)* encastré;
(garment) ajusté; **f. carpet** moquette *f*; **f.
kitchen** cuisine *f* intégrée; **f. (kitchen)
units** éléments *mpl* de cuisine

fitter ['fɪtə(r)] *n Br (of machinery)* monteur, -euse *mf*

fitting ['fɪtɪŋ] **1** *adj (suitable)* approprié
(**to** à)

2 *n (of clothes)* essayage *m*; **f. room**
cabine *f* d'essayage • **fittings** *npl (in
house)* installations *fpl*

five [faɪv] *adj & n* cinq (*m*) • **fiver** *n Br Fam*
billet *m* de 5 livres

fix [fɪks] **1** *vt (make firm, decide)* fixer (**to**
à); *(mend)* réparer; *(deal with)* arranger;
(prepare) préparer; *Fam (election)* truquer; **to f. one's attention on sb/sth** fixer
son attention sur qn/qch; **to f. one's
hopes on sb/sth** mettre ses espoirs en
qn/qch; **to f. the blame on sb** rejeter la
responsabilité sur qn; *Fam* **to f. sb
(punish) régler son compte à qn; **it's fixed
in my mind** c'est gravé dans mon esprit;
to f. sth (on) *(lid)* mettre qch en place; **to
f. sth up** *(trip)* arranger qch; **to f. sb up
with a job** procurer un travail à qn

2 *n Fam (of drug)* dose *f*; *Fam* **in a f.** dans
le pétrin

fixation [fɪk'seɪʃən] *n* fixation *f*

fixed [fɪkst] *adj (price)* fixe; *(resolution)*
inébranlable; *(idea)* bien arrêté; *Fam*

how's he f. for cash? a-t-il de l'argent?; *Fam* **how are you f. for tomorrow?** qu'est-ce que tu fais demain?

fixer ['fɪksə(r)] *n Fam* combinard, -arde *mf*

fixture ['fɪkstʃə(r)] *n* (a) *Sport* rencontre *f* (b) **fixtures** *(in house)* installations *fpl*

fizz [fɪz] *vi (of champagne)* pétiller ▪ **fizzy** (**-ier, -iest**) *adj* gazeux, -euse

fizzle ['fɪzəl] ▸ **fizzle out** *vi (of firework)* rater; *Fam (of plan)* tomber à l'eau; *Fam (of enthusiasm)* retomber; *Fam (of custom)* disparaître   ▪

flabbergasted ['flæbəgɑːstɪd] *adj Fam* sidéré

flabby ['flæbɪ] (**-ier, -iest**) *adj (person)* bouffi; *(skin, character)* mou (*f* molle)

flag [flæg] **1** *n* drapeau *m*; *Naut* pavillon *m*; *(for charity)* insigne *m*
2 (*pt & pp* **-gg-**) *vt* marquer; **to f. (down) a taxi** héler un taxi
3 *vi (of person, conversation)* faiblir; *(of plant)* dépérir ▪ **flagpole** *n* mât *m*

flagrant ['fleɪgrənt] *adj* flagrant

flagstone ['flægstəʊn] *n* dalle *f*

flair [fleə(r)] *n (intuition)* don *m* (**for** pour); **to have a f. for business** avoir le sens des affaires

flak [flæk] *n Fam* **to get a lot of f.** *(be criticized)* se faire rentrer dedans

flake [fleɪk] **1** *n (of snow)* flocon *m*; *(of paint)* écaille *f*; *(of soap, metal)* paillette *f*
2 *vi* **to f. (off)** *(of paint)* s'écailler ▪ **flaky** *adj Br* **f. pastry** pâte *f* feuilletée

flamboyant [flæm'bɔɪənt] *adj (person)* extraverti

flame [fleɪm] **1** *n* flamme *f*; **to go up in flames** prendre feu; **to burst into flames** s'enflammer; **to be in flames** être en flammes
2 *vi* **to f. (up)** *(of fire, house)* flamber ▪ **flaming 1** *adj* (a) *(sun)* flamboyant (b) *Br Fam (damn)* sacré **2** *n Comptr* = échange d'insultes sur l'Internet

flamingo [flə'mɪŋgəʊ] *(pl* **-os** *or* **-oes**) *n* flamant *m*

flammable ['flæməbəl] *adj* inflammable

flan [flæn] *n* tarte *f*

flank [flæŋk] **1** *n* flanc *m*
2 *vt* flanquer (**with** *or* **by** de)

flannel ['flænəl] *n (cloth)* flanelle *f*; *Br (face cloth)* gant *m* de toilette; *Br* **flannels** *(trousers)* pantalon *m* de flanelle ▪ **flanne'lette** *n* pilou *m*, finette *f*; **f. sheet** drap *m* en flanelle

flap [flæp] **1** *n (noise)* battement *m*; *(of pocket, envelope)* rabat *m*; *(of table)* abattant *m*; *(of door)* battant *m*

2 (*pt & pp* **-pp-**) *vt* **to f. its wings** *(of bird)* battre des ailes
3 *vi (of wings, sail, shutter)* battre

flare [fleə(r)] **1** *n* (a) *(signal)* signal *m* lumineux; *(rocket)* fusée *f* éclairante (b) **(pair of) flares** pantalon *m* pattes d'éléphant
2 *vi (of fire)* flamboyer; **to f. up** *(of fire)* s'embraser; *(of violence, anger, trouble)* éclater ▪ **flare-up** *n (of violence, fire)* flambée *f*; *(of region)* embrasement *m*

flared [fleəd] *adj (skirt)* évasé; *(trousers)* (à) pattes d'éléphant

flash [flæʃ] **1** *n (of light, genius)* éclair *m*; *(for camera)* flash *m*; **f. of lightning** éclair; **in a f.** en un clin d'œil
2 *vt (light)* projeter; *(aim)* diriger (**on/at** sur); *(smile, look)* jeter (**at** à); **to f. sth (around)** montrer qch rapidement; **to f. one's headlights** faire un appel de phares
3 *vi (shine)* briller; *(on and off)* clignoter; **to f. past** *or* **by** *(rush)* passer comme un éclair; **flashing lights** clignotants *mpl* ▪ **flashback** *n* retour *m* en arrière ▪ **flashlight** *n Br (torch)* lampe *f* électrique; *(for camera)* flash *m*

flashy ['flæʃɪ] (**-ier, -iest**) *adj* tape-à-l'œil *inv*

flask [flɑːsk] *n* Thermos® *m ou f inv*; *(for alcohol)* flasque *f*; *(phial)* fiole *f*

flat¹ [flæt] **1** (**flatter, flattest**) *adj* plat; *(tyre, battery)* à plat; *(drink)* éventé; *(refusal)* net (*f* nette); **f. nose** nez *m* aplati; **f. fee** prix *m* unique; **f. rate** tarif *m* unique; **to put sth (down) flat** mettre qch à plat; **to be f.-footed** avoir les pieds plats
2 *n (puncture)* crevaison *f*; *(of hand)* plat *m*; *(in music)* bémol *m*
3 *adv* **to sing f.** chanter trop bas; **to fall f. on one's face** tomber à plat ventre; **to fall f.** *(of joke, play)* tomber à plat; **to fold f.** *(of ironing board)* se (re)plier; **I told him f.** je le lui ai dit carrément; *Fam* **f. broke** complètement fauché; **in two minutes f.** en deux minutes pile; **f. out** *(work)* d'arrache-pied; *(run)* à toute vitesse; **to be lying f. out** être étendu de tout son long ▪ **flatly** *adv (deny, refuse)* catégoriquement

flat² [flæt] *n Br (in building)* appartement *m*

flatmate ['flætmeɪt] *n Br* colocataire *mf*

flatten ['flætən] *vt* aplatir; *(crops)* coucher; *(town, buildings)* raser

flatter ['flætə(r)] *vt* flatter; *(of clothes)* avantager ▪ **flatterer** *n* flatteur, -euse *mf* ▪ **flattering** *adj (remark, words)* flatteur, -euse; *(clothes, colour)* qui avantage

flattery [ˈflætərɪ] n flatterie f
flatulence [ˈflætjʊləns] n **to have f.** avoir des gaz
flaunt [flɔːnt] vt (show off) faire étalage de
flautist [ˈflɔːtɪst] n Br flûtiste mf
flavour [ˈfleɪvə(r)] (Am **flavor**) 1 n (taste) goût m; (of ice cream) parfum m
  2 vt (food) relever (**with** de); (ice cream) parfumer (**with** à); **lemon-flavoured** (parfumé) au citron • **flavouring** (Am **flavoring**) n (seasoning) assaisonnement m; (in cake, ice cream) parfum m
flaw [flɔː] n défaut m • **flawed** adj qui a un défaut/des défauts • **flawless** adj parfait
flax [flæks] n lin m • **flaxen** adj de lin
flay [fleɪ] vt (flog) fouetter; Fig (criticize) éreinter
flea [fliː] n puce f; **f. market** marché m aux puces
fleck [flek] n (mark) petite tache f
fled [fled] pt & pp of **flee**
fledgling [ˈfledʒlɪŋ] n (bird) oisillon m
flee [fliː] 1 (pt & pp **fled**) vt (place) s'enfuir de; (danger) fuir
  2 vi s'enfuir, fuir
fleece [fliːs] 1 n (of sheep) toison f; (garment) fourrure f polaire
  2 vt Fam (overcharge) écorcher; (cheat) arnaquer • **fleecy** (**-ier, -iest**) adj (gloves) molletonné
fleet [fliːt] n (of ships) flotte f; (of taxis, buses) parc m
fleeting [ˈfliːtɪŋ] adj (visit, moment) bref (f brève); (beauty) éphémère • **fleetingly** adv fugitivement, un bref instant
Flemish [ˈflemɪʃ] 1 adj flamand
  2 n (language) flamand m; **the F.** (people) les Flamands mpl
flesh [fleʃ] n chair f; **in the f.** en chair et en os; **he's your (own) f. and blood** (child) c'est la chair de ta chair; (brother, cousin) il est de ton sang; **f. wound** blessure f superficielle • **fleshy** (**-ier, -iest**) adj charnu
flew [fluː] pt of **fly²**
flex [fleks] 1 n (wire) fil m; (for telephone) cordon m
  2 vt (limb) fléchir; (muscle) faire jouer
flexible [ˈfleksɪbəl] adj flexible • **flexi-'bility** n flexibilité f
flexitime [ˈfleksɪtaɪm] n horaires mpl flexibles ou à la carte
flick [flɪk] 1 n (with finger) chiquenaude f; (with whip) petit coup m; Br **f. knife** couteau m à cran d'arrêt
  2 vt (with whip) donner un petit coup à;

(with finger) donner une chiquenaude à; **to f. sth off** (remove) enlever qch d'une chiquenaude; **to f. a switch** pousser un bouton; **to f. on/off the light** allumer/éteindre
  3 vi **to f. over** or **through** (pages) feuilleter
flicker [ˈflɪkə(r)] 1 n vacillement m; **f. of light** lueur f vacillante
  2 vi (of flame, light) vaciller
flier [ˈflaɪə(r)] n (a) (leaflet) prospectus m (b) (person) = personne qui voyage en avion
flies [flaɪz] npl (of trousers) braguette f
flight [flaɪt] n (a) (of bird, aircraft) vol m; **f. to/from** vol à destination de/en provenance de; **to have a good f.** faire bon voyage; **f. attendant** (man) steward m; (woman) hôtesse f de l'air; **f. deck** cabine f de pilotage; **f. path** trajectoire f de vol (b) (floor) étage m; **f. of stairs** escalier m (c) (escape) fuite f (**from** de); **to take f.** prendre la fuite
flighty [ˈflaɪtɪ] (**-ier, -iest**) adj volage
flimsy [ˈflɪmzɪ] (**-ier, -iest**) adj (cloth, structure) (light) (trop) léger, -ère; (thin) (trop) mince; (excuse) piètre
flinch [flɪntʃ] vi (with pain) tressaillir; **without flinching** (complaining) sans broncher
fling [flɪŋ] 1 n (affair) aventure f; **to have one's** or **a f.** (indulge oneself) s'en donner à cœur joie
  2 (pt & pp **flung**) vt jeter; (ball) lancer; **to f. a door open** ouvrir brutalement une porte
flint [flɪnt] n (stone) silex m; (of lighter) pierre f
flip [flɪp] 1 n chiquenaude f; **the f. side** (of record) la face B; **f. chart** tableau m à feuilles
  2 (pt & pp **-pp-**) vt (with finger) donner une chiquenaude à; **to f. a switch** pousser un bouton; **to f. a coin** jouer à pile ou face; **to f. sth over** retourner qch
  3 vi **to f. through a book** feuilleter un livre
  4 adj Am Fam (impudent) effronté
flip-flops [ˈflɪpflɒps] npl tongs fpl
flippant [ˈflɪpənt] adj désinvolte
flipper [ˈflɪpə(r)] n (of swimmer) palme f; (of animal) nageoire f
flipping [ˈflɪpɪŋ] Br Fam 1 adj (idiot, rain) sacré
  2 adv sacrément, bougrement
flirt [flɜːt] 1 n charmeur, -euse mf
  2 vi flirter (**with** avec) • **flir'tation** n flirt m
flit [flɪt] (pt & pp **-tt-**) vi (fly) voltiger; Fig

to **f. in and out** *(of person)* entrer et sortir rapidement

float [fləʊt] **1** *n* Fishing bouchon *m*; *(for swimming)* flotteur *m*; *(in procession)* char *m*

2 *vt (ship)* mettre à flot; *(wood)* faire flotter; *(idea, rumour)* lancer; *(company)* introduire en Bourse

3 *vi* flotter (**on** sur); **to f. down the river** descendre la rivière • **floating** *adj (wood, debt)* flottant; *(population)* fluctuant; **f. voters** électeurs *mpl* indécis

flock [flɒk] **1** *n (of sheep)* troupeau *m*; *(of birds)* volée *f*; *(of people)* foule *f*; *(religious congregation)* ouailles *fpl*

2 *vi* **to f. round sb** s'attrouper autour de qn; **people are flocking to the exhibition** les gens vont en foule voir l'exposition

flog [flɒg] *(pt & pp* **-gg-**) *vt (beat)* flageller; *Br Fam (sell)* vendre

flood [flʌd] **1** *n* inondation *f*; *Fig (of light)* flot *m*; **to be in floods of tears** verser des torrents de larmes; **the F.** *(in the Bible)* le Déluge

2 *vt (land, bathroom, market)* inonder (**with** de); **the river flooded its banks** la rivière est sortie de son lit; **to f. (out)** *(house)* inonder

3 *vi (of river)* déborder; **to f. in** *(of people, money)* affluer; **to f. into** *(of tourists)* envahir • **flooding** *n* inondation(s) *f(pl)*

floodgate ['flʌdgeɪt] *n (in water)* vanne *f*

floodlight ['flʌdlaɪt] **1** *n* projecteur *m*

2 *(pt & pp* **-lit**) *vt* illuminer

floor [flɔː(r)] **1** *n (of room, forest)* sol *m*; *(wooden)* plancher *m*; *(storey)* étage *m*; **on the f.** par terre; *Br* **on the first f.** au premier étage; *Am (ground floor)* au rez-de-chaussée; **f. polish** cire *f*; **f. show** spectacle *m* de cabaret

2 *vt (knock down)* envoyer au tapis; *(puzzle)* stupéfier

floorboard ['flɔːbɔːd] *n* latte *f* *(de plancher)*

flop [flɒp] **1** *n Fam* fiasco *m*; *(play)* four *m*

2 *(pt & pp* **-pp-**) *vi (fail) (of business, efforts)* échouer; *(of play, film)* faire un four; **to f. down** s'effondrer; **to f. about** s'agiter mollement

floppy ['flɒpɪ] (**-ier, -iest**) *adj (soft)* mou *(f* molle); *(clothes)* (trop) large; *(ears)* pendant; *Comptr* **f. disk** disquette *f*

flora ['flɔːrə] *n (plant life)* flore *f* • **floral** *adj (material, pattern)* à fleurs

florid ['flɒrɪd] *adj (style)* fleuri; *(complexion)* rubicond

florist ['flɒrɪst] *n* fleuriste *mf*

floss [flɒs] *n* **(dental) f.** fil *m* dentaire

flotilla [flə'tɪlə] *n (of ships)* flottille *f*

flounce [flaʊns] *n (on dress, tablecloth)* volant *m*

flounder ['flaʊndə(r)] **1** *n (fish)* carrelet *m*

2 *vi (in water)* patauger; *Fig (in speech)* perdre pied

flour ['flaʊə(r)] *n* farine *f*

flourish ['flʌrɪʃ] **1** *n (gesture)* grand geste *m*; *(decoration)* fioriture *f*

2 *vt (wave)* brandir

3 *vi (of person, plant)* prospérer; *(of arts, business)* être florissant • **flourishing** *adj (plant)* qui prospère; *(business)* florissant

flout [flaʊt] *vt* défier

flow [fləʊ] **1** *n (of river)* courant *m*; *(of tide)* flux *m*; *(of current, information, blood)* circulation *f*; *(of liquid)* écoulement *m*; **f. of traffic** circulation *f*; **a f. of visitors/words** un flot de visiteurs/paroles; *Fig* **to go with the f.** suivre le mouvement; **f. chart** organigramme *m*

2 *vi* couler; *(of electric current, information)* circuler; *(of hair, clothes)* flotter; *(of traffic)* s'écouler; **to f. back** *(of liquid)* refluer; **to f. in** *(of people, money)* affluer; **to f. into the sea** *(of river)* se jeter dans la mer • **flowing** *adj (movement, style)* fluide; *(hair, beard)* flottant

flower ['flaʊə(r)] **1** *n* fleur *f*; **in f.** en fleur(s); **f. bed** parterre *m*; **f. pot** pot *m* de fleurs; **f. shop** fleuriste *mf*; **f. show** floralies *fpl*

2 *vi* fleurir • **flowered** *adj (dress)* à fleurs • **flowering 1** *n* floraison *f* **2** *adj (in bloom)* en fleurs; *(producing flowers) (shrub)* à fleurs

flowery ['flaʊərɪ] *adj (style)* fleuri; *(material)* à fleurs

flown [fləʊn] *pp of* **fly²**

flu [fluː] *n (influenza)* grippe *f*

fluctuate ['flʌktʃʊeɪt] *vi* varier • **fluctuation** [-'eɪʃən] *n* variation *f* (**in** de)

flue [fluː] *n (of chimney)* tuyau *m*

fluent ['fluːənt] *adj (style)* fluide; **he's f. in Russian, his Russian is f.** il parle couramment le russe; **to be a f. speaker** s'exprimer avec facilité • **fluency** *n* facilité *f* • **fluently** *adv (write, express oneself)* avec facilité; *(speak language)* couramment

fluff [flʌf] **1** *n* peluche *f*

2 *vt Fam (bungle)* rater • **fluffy** (**-ier, -iest**) *adj (bird)* duveteux, -euse; *(toy)* en peluche

fluid ['fluːɪd] **1** *adj* fluide; *(plans)* mal défini; **f. ounce** = 0,03 l

2 *n* fluide *m*, liquide *m*

fluke [fluːk] *n Fam* coup *m* de chance; **by a f.** par hasard

flummox ['flʌməks] *vt Br Fam* scier

flung [flʌŋ] *pt & pp of* **fling**

flunk [flʌŋk] *Am Fam* **1** *vt (exam)* être collé à; *(pupil)* coller
2 *vi (in exam)* être collé

flunkey, flunky ['flʌŋkɪ] (*pl* **flunkeys** *or* **flunkies**) *n Fam Pej* larbin *m*

fluorescent [flʊə'resənt] *adj* fluorescent

fluoride ['flʊəraɪd] *n* fluorure *m*; **f. toothpaste** dentifrice *m* au fluor

flurry ['flʌrɪ] (*pl* **-ies**) *n (of snow)* bourrasque *f*; **a f. of activity** une soudaine activité

flush [flʌʃ] **1** *adj (level)* de niveau (**with** de); *Fam (rich)* plein aux as
2 *n* (**a**) *(blush)* rougeur *f*; *(of youth, beauty)* éclat *m*; **hot flushes** bouffées *fpl* de chaleur (**b**) *(in cards)* flush *m* (**c**) *(in toilet)* chasse *f* d'eau
3 *vt* **to f. sth (out)** *(clean)* nettoyer qch à grande eau; **to f. the toilet** tirer la chasse d'eau
4 *vi (blush)* rougir (**with** de) • **flushed** *adj (cheeks)* rouge; **f. with success** ivre de succès

fluster ['flʌstə(r)] *vt* démonter; **to get flustered** se démonter

flute [fluːt] *n* flûte *f* • **flutist** *n Am* flûtiste *mf*

flutter ['flʌtə(r)] **1** *n Br Fam* **to have a f.** *(bet)* jouer une petite somme (**on** sur)
2 *vt* **to f. its wings** *(of bird)* battre des ailes
3 *vi (of bird, butterfly)* voleter; *(of heart)* battre; *(of flag)* flotter

flux [flʌks] *n* **in a state of f.** en changement constant

fly¹ [flaɪ] (*pl* **-ies**) *n (insect)* mouche *f*

fly² [flaɪ] **1** (*pt* **flew**, *pp* **flown**) *vt (aircraft)* piloter; *(passengers)* transporter; *(airline)* voyager par; *(flag)* arborer; *(kite)* faire voler; **to f. the French flag** battre pavillon français; **to f. the Atlantic** traverser l'Atlantique en avion
2 *vi (of bird, aircraft)* voler; *(of passenger)* aller en avion; *(of time)* passer vite; *(of flag)* flotter; **to f. away** *or* **off** s'envoler; **to f. out** *(of passenger)* partir en avion; **to f. out of a room** sortir d'une pièce à toute vitesse; **to f. at sb** *(attack)* sauter sur qn; **to f. across** *or* **over** *(country, city)* survoler; **the door flew open** la porte s'ouvrit brusquement; **I must f.!** il faut que je file!
• **flyby** *n (by plane)* défilé *m* aérien • **fly-by-night** *adj (firm)* véreux, -euse • **flyer** *n* = **flier** • **flying 1** *n (as pilot)* pilotage *m*; *(as passenger)* voyage *m* en avion **2** *adj (doctor, personnel)* volant; **to succeed with f. colours** réussir haut la main; **to get off to a f. start** prendre un très bon départ; **f. saucer** soucoupe *f* volante; **f. visit** visite *f* éclair *inv*; **f. time** heures *fpl* de vol • **flyover** *n Br (bridge)* Toboggan® *m* • **flypast** *n (by plane)* défilé *m* aérien

fly³ [flaɪ] *n Br (on trousers)* braguette *f*

FM [ef'em] (*abbr* **frequency modulation**) *n* FM *f*

foal [fəʊl] *n* poulain *m*

foam [fəʊm] **1** *n (on sea, mouth)* écume *f*; *(on beer)* mousse *f*; **f. bath** bain *m* moussant; **f. rubber** caoutchouc *m* Mousse®
2 *vi (of sea, mouth)* écumer; *(of beer, soap)* mousser

fob [fɒb] (*pt & pp* **-bb-**) *vt Fam* **to f. sb off with an excuse** se débarrasser de qn en lui racontant des salades; **to f. sth off (to) sb** refiler qch à qn

focal ['fəʊkəl] *adj* focal

focus ['fəʊkəs] **1** (*pl* **focuses** ['fəʊkəsəz] *or* **foci** ['fəʊkaɪ]) *n (of attention, interest)* centre *m*; *(optical, geometrical)* foyer *m*; **the photo is in f./out of f.** la photo est nette/floue; **f. group** groupe-témoin *m*
2 *vt (image, camera)* mettre au point; *(attention, efforts)* concentrer (**on** sur)
3 *vi (converge) (of light)* converger (**on** sur); **to f. on sb/sth** *(with camera)* faire la mise au point sur qn/qch
4 *vti* **to f. (one's eyes) on sb/sth** fixer les yeux sur qn/qch; **to f. (one's attention) on sb/sth** se tourner vers qn/qch

fodder ['fɒdə(r)] *n* fourrage *m*

foe [fəʊ] *n* ennemi, -ie *mf*

foetus ['fiːtəs] (*Am* **fetus**) *n* fœtus *m*

fog [fɒg] **1** *n* brouillard *m*
2 (*pt & pp* **-gg-**) *vt* **to f. the issue** embrouiller la question • **fogbound** *adj* bloqué en raison du brouillard • **foghorn** *n* corne *f* de brume • **foglamp, foglight** *n (on vehicle)* phare *m* anti-brouillard *inv*

fogey ['fəʊgɪ] *n* = **fogy**

foggy ['fɒgɪ] (**-ier, -iest**) *adj* brumeux, -euse; **it's f.** il y a du brouillard; **on a f. day** par un jour de brouillard; *Fam* **I haven't got the foggiest (idea)** je n'en ai pas la moindre idée

fogy ['fəʊgɪ] *n* **old f.** vieux schnock *m*

foible ['fɔɪbəl] *n (habit)* petite manie *f*; *(weakness)* point *m* faible

foil [fɔɪl] **1** *n* (**a**) *(for cooking)* papier *m* alu; *(metal sheet)* feuille *f* de métal (**b**) *(person)* repoussoir *m* (**c**) *(sword)* fleuret *m*
2 *vt (plans)* contrecarrer

foist [fɔɪst] *vt* **to f. sth (off) on sb** refiler qch à qn; **to f. oneself on sb** s'imposer à qn

fold¹ [fəʊld] **1** *n (in paper, cloth)* pli *m*
2 *vt* plier; **to f. away** *or* **down** *or* **up** *(chair)* plier; **to f. back** *or* **over** *(blanket)* replier; **to f. one's arms** croiser les bras
3 *vi (of chair)* se plier; *Fam (of business)* fermer ses portes; **to f. away** *or* **down** *or* **up** *(of chair)* se plier; **to f. back** *or* **over** *(of blanket)* se replier • **folding** *adj (chair, bed)* pliant

fold² [fəʊld] *n (for sheep)* parc *m* à moutons; *Fig* **to return to the f.** rentrer au bercail

-fold [fəʊld] *suff* **1** *adj* **tenfold** par dix
2 *adv* **tenfold** dix fois

folder ['fəʊldə(r)] *n (file holder)* chemise *f*; *(for drawings)* carton *m* à dessins; *Comptr* répertoire *m*

foliage ['fəʊlɪɪdʒ] *n* feuillage *m*

folk [fəʊk] **1** *(Am* **folks**) *npl* gens *mpl*; *Fam* **my folks** *(parents)* mes parents *mpl*; *Fam* **hello, folks!** salut tout le monde!; *Br* **old f.** les vieux *mpl*
2 *adj (dance, costume)* folklorique; **f. music** *(contemporary)* folk *m*

folklore ['fəʊklɔː(r)] *n* folklore *m*

follow ['fɒləʊ] **1** *vt* suivre; *(career)* poursuivre; **followed by** suivi de; **to f. suit** *(do the same)* faire de même; **to f. sb around** suivre qn partout; **to f. through** *(plan, idea)* mener à son terme; **to f. up** *(idea, story)* creuser; *(clue, case)* suivre; *(letter)* donner suite à; *(remark)* faire suivre (**with** de); *(advantage)* exploiter
2 *vi (of person, event)* suivre; **it follows that...** il s'ensuit que...; **that doesn't f.** ce n'est pas logique; **to f. on** *(come after)* suivre • **follow-up** *n Com (of orders)* suivi *m* (**to** de); *(letter)* rappel *m*; **f. visit** *(by doctor)* visite *f* de contrôle; **f. treatment** traitement *m* complémentaire

follower ['fɒləʊə(r)] *n (of ideas, politician)* partisan *m*

following ['fɒləʊɪŋ] **1** *adj* suivant
2 *n (of ideas, politician)* partisans *mpl*; **to have a large f.** avoir de nombreux partisans; *(of programme)* être très suivi
3 *prep* à la suite de

folly ['fɒlɪ] *(pl* **-ies***) n* folie *f*

foment [fəʊ'ment] *vt Literary* fomenter

fond [fɒnd] *(-er, -est) adj (loving)* affectueux, -ueuse; *(memory, thought)* doux *(f* douce); **to be (very) f. of sb/sth** aimer beaucoup qn/qch; **with f. regards** *(in letter)* bien amicalement • **fondly** *adv* tendrement • **fondness** *n* penchant *m*

(for sth pour qch); *(affection)* affection *f* *(for sb* pour qn)

fondle ['fɒndəl] *vt* caresser

font [fɒnt] *n* **(a)** *Rel* fonts *mpl* baptismaux **(b)** *Typ & Comptr* police *f* de caractères

food [fuːd] **1** *n* nourriture *f*; *(particular substance)* aliment *m*; *(cooking)* cuisine *f*; *(for cats, dogs, pigs)* pâtée *f*; *(for plants)* engrais *m*; **foods** *(foodstuffs)* aliments *mpl*
2 *adj (needs, industry)* alimentaire; **f. poisoning** intoxication *f* alimentaire; **f. value** valeur *f* nutritive

foodstuffs ['fuːdstʌfs] *npl* denrées *fpl* alimentaires

fool [fuːl] **1** *n* imbécile *mf*; **(you) silly f.!** espèce d'imbécile!; **to make a f. of sb** *(ridicule)* ridiculiser qn; *(trick)* rouler qn; **to make a f. of oneself** se couvrir de ridicule; **to be f. enough to do sth** être assez stupide pour faire qch; **to play the f.** faire l'imbécile
2 *vt (trick)* duper
3 *vi* **to f. about** *or* **around** faire l'imbécile; *(waste time)* perdre son temps; *Fam* **to f. around** *(have affairs)* avoir des aventures

foolhardy ['fuːlhɑːdɪ] *adj (rash)* téméraire • **foolhardiness** *n* témérité *f*

foolish ['fuːlɪʃ] *adj* bête • **foolishly** *adv* bêtement • **foolishness** *n* bêtise *f*

foolproof ['fuːlpruːf] *adj (scheme)* infaillible

foot¹ [fʊt] *(pl* **feet**) *n* pied *m*; *(of animal)* patte *f*; *(unit of measurement)* = 30,48 cm, pied *m*; **at the f. of** *(page, stairs)* au bas de; *(table)* au bout de; **on f.** à pied; **to be on one's feet** *(standing)* être debout; *(recovered from illness)* être sur pied; **f. brake** *(of vehicle)* frein *m* au plancher; **f.-and-mouth disease** fièvre *f* aphteuse • **football** *n (soccer)* football *m*; *(American game)* football américain; *(ball)* ballon *m* • **footballer** *n Br* joueur, -euse *mf* de football • **footbridge** *n* passerelle *f* • **foothills** *npl* contreforts *mpl* • **foothold** *n* prise *f* (de pied); *Fig* position *f*; **to gain a f.** *(of person)* prendre pied (**in** dans) • **footlights** *npl (in theatre)* rampe *f* • **footloose** *adj* libre de toute attache • **footman** *(pl* **-men**) *n* valet *m* de pied • **footmark** *n* empreinte *f* de pied • **footnote** *n* note *f* de bas de page; *Fig (extra comment)* postscriptum *m inv* • **footpath** *n* sentier *m* • **footstep** *n* pas *m*; **to follow in sb's footsteps** suivre les traces de qn • **footstool** *n* petit tabouret *m* • **footwear** *n* chaussures *fpl*

foot² [fʊt] vt (bill) payer

footage ['fʊtɪdʒ] n Cin séquences fpl

footing ['fʊtɪŋ] n (a) (balance) **to lose one's f.** perdre l'équilibre (b) (level) **to be on an equal f.** être sur un pied d'égalité (**with** avec)

for [fɔ:(r), unstressed fə(r)] **1** prep pour; (for a distance or period of) pendant; (in spite of) malgré; **f. you/me** pour toi/moi; **it's f. tomorrow/f. eating** c'est pour demain/pour manger; **what's it f.?** ça sert à quoi?; **I did it f. love/pleasure** je l'ai fait par amour/par plaisir; **to swim/rush f.** (towards) nager/se précipiter vers; **a train f.** un train à destination de; **the road f. London** la route de Londres; **it's time f. breakfast** c'est l'heure du petit déjeuner; **to come f. dinner** venir dîner; **to sell sth f. 7 dollars** vendre qch 7 dollars; **what's the French f. 'book'?** comment dit-on 'book' en français?; **A f. Alice** A comme Alice; **she walked f. a kilometre** elle a marché pendant un kilomètre; **he was away f. a month** il a été absent pendant un mois; **he won't be back f. a month** il ne sera pas de retour avant un mois; **he's been here f. a month** il est ici depuis un mois; **I haven't seen him f. ten years** voilà dix ans que je ne l'ai vu, je ne l'ai pas vu depuis dix ans; **it's easy f. her to do it** il lui est facile de le faire; **it's f. you to say** c'est à toi de dire; **f. that to be done** pour que ça soit fait

2 conj (because) car

forage ['fɒrɪdʒ] vi fouiller (**for** pour trouver)

foray ['fɒreɪ] n incursion f (**into** dans)

forbad [fə'bæd] pt of **forbid**

forbade [fə'bæd, fə'beɪd] pt of **forbid**

forbearance [fɔ:'beərəns] n Formal patience f

forbid [fə'bɪd] (pt **forbad(e)**, pp **forbidden** [fə'bɪdən], pres p **forbidding**) vt interdire, défendre (**sb to do** à qn de faire); **to f. sb sth** interdire qch à qn; **God f.!** Dieu nous en préserve! • **forbidden** adj (fruit, region, palace) défendu; **she is f. to leave** il lui est interdit de partir • **forbidding** adj (look, landscape) sinistre

force [fɔ:s] **1** n force f; **the (armed) forces** les forces armées; **by f.** de force; **by sheer f.** par la force; **in f.** (rule) en vigueur; (in great numbers) en force

2 vt forcer (**to do** à faire); (impose) imposer (**on** à); (door, lock) forcer; (confession) arracher (**from** à); **to f. one's way into** entrer de force dans; **to f. back** (enemy, demonstrators) faire reculer; (tears) refouler; **to f. down** (aircraft) for-

cer à atterrir; **to f. sth into sth** faire entrer qch de force dans qch; **to f. sth out** faire sortir qch de force • **forced** adj **f. to do** obligé ou forcé de faire; **a f. smile** un sourire forcé • **force-feed** (pt & pp **-fed**) vt nourrir de force

forceful ['fɔ:sfəl] adj énergique

forceps ['fɔ:seps] npl forceps m

forcible ['fɔ:sɪbəl] adj (powerful) puissant; Law **f. entry** entrée f par effraction • **forcibly** adv (by force) de force; (argue, express) avec force

ford [fɔ:d] **1** n gué m

2 vt (river) passer à gué

fore [fɔ:(r)] n **to come to the f.** (of issue) passer au premier plan

forearm ['fɔ:rɑ:m] n avant-bras m inv

forebode [fɔ:'bəʊd] vt (warn) présager • **foreboding** n (feeling) pressentiment m

forecast ['fɔ:kɑ:st] **1** n (of weather) prévisions fpl; (in racing) pronostic m

2 (pt & pp **forecast(ed)**) vt prévoir; (in racing) pronostiquer

forecourt ['fɔ:kɔ:t] n (of hotel) avant-cour f; (of petrol station) devant m

forefathers ['fɔ:fɑ:ðəz] npl aïeux mpl

forefinger ['fɔ:fɪŋgə(r)] n index m

forefront ['fɔ:frʌnt] n **in the f. of** au premier plan de

forego [fɔ:'gəʊ] (pp **-gone**) vt renoncer à; **it's a foregone conclusion** c'est couru d'avance

foreground ['fɔ:graʊnd] n premier plan m

forehead ['fɒrɪd, 'fɔ:hed] n front m

foreign ['fɒrɪn] adj (language, person, country) étranger, -ère; (trade) extérieur; (travel, correspondent) à l'étranger; Med **f. body** corps m étranger; **F. Minister, Br F. Secretary** ministre m des Affaires étrangères; Br **F. Office** ministère m des Affaires étrangères • **foreigner** n étranger, -ère mf

foreman ['fɔ:mən] (pl **-men**) n (worker) contremaître m; (of jury) président m

foremost ['fɔ:məʊst] adj principal

forensic [fə'rensɪk] adj **f. medicine** médecine f légale

forerunner ['fɔ:rʌnə(r)] n (person) précurseur m

foresee [fɔ:'si:] (pt **-saw**, pp **-seen**) vt prévoir • **foreseeable** adj prévisible

foreshadow [fɔ:'ʃædəʊ] vt annoncer

foresight ['fɔ:saɪt] n prévoyance f

forest ['fɒrɪst] n forêt f • **forester** n garde m forestier

forestall [fɔ:'stɔ:l] vt devancer

foretaste ['fɔ:teɪst] n avant-goût m (**of** de)

foretell [fɔːˈtel] (*pt & pp* **-told**) *vt* prédire
forethought [ˈfɔːθɔːt] *n* prévoyance *f*
forever [fəˈrevə(r)] *adv (for always)* pour toujours; *(continually)* sans cesse
forewarn [fɔːˈwɔːn] *vt* avertir
foreword [ˈfɔːwɜːd] *n* avant-propos *m inv*
forfeit [ˈfɔːfɪt] **1** *n (in game)* gage *m*; *Law* amende *f*
   2 *vt (lose)* perdre
forge [fɔːdʒ] **1** *n* forge *f*
   2 *vt* (**a**) *(metal, alliance)* forger (**b**) *(signature, money)* contrefaire; **to f. a passport** faire un faux passeport
   3 *vi* **to f. ahead** *(progress)* aller de l'avant •**forged** *adj* faux (*f* fausse); **f. money** fausse monnaie *f* •**forger** *n (of documents, money)* faussaire *m*
forgery [ˈfɔːdʒərɪ] (*pl* **-ies**) *n* contrefaçon *f*
forget [fəˈget] **1** (*pt* **forgot**, *pp* **forgotten**, *pres p* **forgetting**) *vt* oublier (**to do** de faire); *Fam* **f. it!** *(when thanked)* pas de quoi!; *(it doesn't matter)* laisse tomber!; **to f. oneself** s'oublier
   2 *vi* oublier; **to f. about sb/sth** oublier qn/qch •**forget-me-not** *n* myosotis *m*
forgetful [fəˈgetfəl] *adj* **to be f.** avoir une mauvaise mémoire •**forgetfulness** *n* manque *m* de mémoire; *(carelessness)* négligence *f*; **in a moment of f.** dans un moment d'oubli
forgive [fəˈgɪv] (*pt* **-gave**, *pp* **-given**) *vt* pardonner (**sb sth** qch à qn) •**forgiveness** *n* pardon *m* •**forgiving** *adj* indulgent
forgo [fɔːˈgəʊ] (*pp* **-gone**) *vt* renoncer à
forgot [fəˈgɒt] *pt of* **forget**
forgotten [fəˈgɒtən] *pp of* **forget**
fork [fɔːk] **1** *n (for eating)* fourchette *f*; *(for gardening, in road)* fourche *f*
   2 *vt Fam* **to f. out** *(money)* allonger
   3 *vi (of road)* bifurquer; *Fam* **to f. out** *(pay)* casquer (**on** pour) •**forked** *adj (branch, tongue)* fourchu •**forklift truck** *n* chariot *m* élévateur
forlorn [fəˈlɔːn] *adj (forsaken)* abandonné; *(unhappy)* triste
form [fɔːm] **1** *n (shape, type, style)* forme *f*; *(document)* formulaire *m*; *Br Sch* classe *f*; **it's good f.** c'est ce qui se fait; **in the f. of** sous forme de; **a f. of speech** une façon de parler; **on f., in good** or **top f.** en (pleine) forme
   2 *vt (group, basis, character)* former; *(clay)* façonner; *(habit)* contracter; *(obstacle)* constituer; **to f. part of sth** faire partie de qch; **to f. an opinion** se faire une opinion (**of** de)
   3 *vi (appear)* se former

formal [ˈfɔːməl] *adj (person, tone)* cérémonieux, -ieuse; *(announcement, dinner, invitation)* officiel, -ielle; *(agreement)* en bonne et due forme; *(denial, logic)* formel, -elle; *(language)* soutenu; **f. dress** tenue *f* de soirée; **f. education** éducation *f* scolaire •**formality** [-ˈmælɪtɪ] (*pl* **-ies**) *n (procedure)* formalité *f* •**formally** *adv (declare)* officiellement; **f. dressed** en tenue de soirée

> ⚠ Note that the French word **formellement** is a false friend. Its most common meaning is **strictly**.

format [ˈfɔːmæt] **1** *n* format *m*
   2 (*pt & pp* **-tt-**) *vt Comptr* formater
formation [fɔːˈmeɪʃən] *n* formation *f*
formative [ˈfɔːmətɪv] *adj* formateur, -trice
former [ˈfɔːmə(r)] **1** *adj (previous) (president, teacher, job, house)* ancien, -ienne *(before noun)*; *(situation, life)* antérieur; **her f. husband** son ex-mari; **in f. days** autrefois
   2 *pron* **the f.** celui-là, celle-là •**formerly** *adv* autrefois
formidable [ˈfɔːmɪdəbəl] *adj* effroyable
formula [ˈfɔːmjʊlə] *n* (**a**) (*pl* **-as** or **-ae** [-iː]) *(rule, symbols)* formule *f*; *Aut* **f. 1** formule 1 (**b**) (*pl* **-as**) *(baby food)* lait *m* en poudre •**formulate** [-leɪt] *vt* formuler •**formulation** [-ˈleɪʃən] *n* formulation *f*
forsake [fəˈseɪk] (*pt* **-sook** [-ˈsʊk], *pp* **-saken** [-ˈseɪkən]) *vt Literary* abandonner
fort [fɔːt] *n Mil* fort *m*; *Fam* **to hold the f.** monter la garde
forte [*Br* ˈfɔːteɪ, *Am* fɔːt] *n* fort *m*
forth [fɔːθ] *adv* en avant; **from this day f.** désormais; **and so f.** et ainsi de suite; **to go back and f.** aller et venir
forthcoming [fɔːθˈkʌmɪŋ] *adj* (**a**) *(event)* à venir; *(book, film)* qui va sortir; **my f. book** mon prochain livre (**b**) *(available)* disponible (**c**) *(informative)* expansif, -ive (**about** sur)
forthright [ˈfɔːθraɪt] *adj* franc (*f* franche)
forthwith [fɔːθˈwɪð] *adv Formal* sur-le-champ
fortieth [ˈfɔːtɪəθ] *adj & n* quarantième (*mf*)
fortify [ˈfɔːtɪfaɪ] (*pt & pp* **-ied**) *vt (strengthen)* fortifier; **to f. sb** *(of food, drink)* réconforter qn, remonter qn •**fortification** [-fɪˈkeɪʃən] *n* fortification *f*
fortitude [ˈfɔːtɪtjuːd] *n* force *f* morale
fortnight [ˈfɔːtnaɪt] *n Br* quinzaine *f* de jours •**fortnightly 1** *adj Br* bimensuel, -uelle **2** *adv* tous les quinze jours

fortress ['fɔːtrɪs] *n* forteresse *f*
fortuitous [fɔː'tjuːɪtəs] *adj* fortuit
fortunate ['fɔːtʃənət] *adj* heureux,
-euse; **to be f.** *(of person)* avoir de la
chance; **to be f. enough to** avoir la
chance de; **it's f. (for her) that...** c'est
heureux (pour elle) que... *(+ subjunctive)*
• **fortunately** *adv* heureusement
fortune ['fɔːtʃuːn] *n (wealth)* fortune *f*;
(luck) chance *f*; **to have the good f. to do**
sth avoir la chance de faire qch; **to tell**
sb's f. dire la bonne aventure à qn; **to**
make one's f. faire fortune; **to cost a f.**
coûter une (petite) fortune • **fortune-**
teller *n* diseur, -euse *mf* de bonne aventure
forty ['fɔːtɪ] *adj & n* quarante *(m)*
forum ['fɔːrəm] *n* forum *m*; *Comptr*
groupe *m* de discussions
forward ['fɔːwəd] **1** *adj (position)* avant
inv; *(movement)* en avant; *Fig (impudent)*
effronté
2 *n Sport* avant *m*
3 *adv* en avant; **to go f.** avancer; **to put**
the clocks f. avancer les pendules; **from**
this day f. à partir d'aujourd'hui
4 *vt (letter)* faire suivre; *(goods)* expédier • **forward-looking** *adj* progressiste
forwards ['fɔːwədz] *adv* = **forward**
fossil ['fɒsəl] *n* fossile *m*
foster ['fɒstə(r)] **1** *vt* (**a**) *(music, art)*
encourager (**b**) *(child)* élever en famille
d'accueil
2 *adj* **f. child** = enfant placé dans une
famille d'accueil; **f. home** *or* **family** famille *f* d'accueil; **f. parents** parents *mpl*
nourriciers
fought [fɔːt] *pt & pp of* **fight**
foul [faʊl] **1** (**-er, -est**) *adj* (**a**) *(smell,*
taste, weather, person) infect; *(air)* vicié;
(breath) fétide; *(language)* grossier, -ière;
(place) immonde; **to be in a f. mood** être
d'une humeur massacrante; **to be f.-**
mouthed avoir un langage grossier (**b**)
Sport **f. play** jeu *m* irrégulier; *Law* acte *m*
criminel
2 *n Sport* faute *f*
3 *vt* **to f. (up)** *(get dirty)* salir; *(air)* vicier;
Fam **to f. up** *(ruin)* gâcher
found¹ [faʊnd] *pt & pp of* **find**
found² [faʊnd] *vt (town, party)* fonder;
(opinion, suspicions) fonder, baser (**on**
sur) • **founder** *n* fondateur, -trice *mf*
foundation [faʊn'deɪʃən] *n (of city, or-*
ganization) fondation *f*; *(basis)* fondement *m*; **the foundations** *(of building)*
les fondations *fpl*; **without f.** sans fondement; **f. (cream)** fond *m* de teint

founder ['faʊndə(r)] *vi (of ship)*
s'échouer
foundry ['faʊndrɪ] *(pl* -**ies**) *n* fonderie *f*
fountain ['faʊntɪn] *n* fontaine *f*; **f. pen**
stylo-plume *m*
four [fɔː(r)] *adj & n* quatre *(m)*; **on all**
fours à quatre pattes; **f.-letter word** gros
mot *m* • **fourth** *adj & n* quatrième *(mf)*
fourfold ['fɔːfəʊld] **1** *adj* **a f. increase** une
augmentation au quadruple
2 *adv* **to increase f.** quadrupler
foursome ['fɔːsəm] *n* groupe *m* de quatre personnes
fourteen [fɔː'tiːn] *adj & n* quatorze *(m)*
• **fourteenth** *adj & n* quatorzième *(mf)*
fowl [faʊl] *n inv* volaille *f*
fox [fɒks] **1** *n* renard *m*
2 *vt (puzzle)* laisser perplexe; *(deceive)*
duper • **foxy** *adj Fam (sly)* rusé
foxglove ['fɒksglʌv] *n* digitale *f*
foyer ['fɔɪeɪ] *n (in theatre)* foyer *m*; *(in*
hotel) hall *m*
fraction ['frækʃən] *n* fraction *f* • **fraction-**
ally *adv* un tout petit peu
fractious ['frækʃəs] *adj* grincheux,
-euse
fracture ['fræktʃə(r)] **1** *n* fracture *f*
2 *vt* fracturer; **to f. one's leg** se fracturer
la jambe
3 *vi* se fracturer
fragile [*Br* 'frædʒaɪl, *Am* 'frædʒəl] *adj*
fragile • **fragility** [frə'dʒɪlətɪ] *n* fragilité *f*
fragment ['frægmənt] *n* fragment *m*
• **fragmented** [-'mentɪd], **fragmentary**
[-'mentərɪ] *adj* fragmentaire
fragrant ['freɪgrənt] *adj* parfumé • **fra-**
grance *n* parfum *m*
frail [freɪl] (**-er, -est**) *adj (person)* frêle;
(hope, health) fragile • **frailty** *n* fragilité *f*
frame [freɪm] **1** *n (of building)* charpente
f; *(of person)* ossature *f*; *(of picture, bicy-*
cle) cadre *m*; *(of door, window)* encadrement *m*; *(of car)* châssis *m*; *(of spectacles)*
monture *f*; **f. of mind** état *m* d'esprit
2 *vt (picture)* encadrer; *Fig (proposals,*
ideas) formuler; *Fam* **to f. sb** monter un
coup contre qn • **framework** *n* structure *f*;
(with)in the f. of *(context)* dans le cadre de
franc [fræŋk] *n* franc *m*
France [frɑːns] *n* la France
franchise ['fræntʃaɪz] *n (right to vote)*
droit *m* de vote; *(right to sell product)*
franchise *f*
Franco- ['fræŋkəʊ] *pref* franco-
frank¹ [fræŋk] (**-er, -est**) *adj (honest)*
franc (*f* franche) • **frankly** *adv* franchement • **frankness** *n* franchise *f*
frank² [fræŋk] *vt (letter)* affranchir

frankfurter [ˈfræŋkfɜːtə(r)] *n* saucisse *f* de Francfort

frantic [ˈfræntɪk] *adj (activity, shouts, pace)* frénétique; *(attempt, efforts)* désespéré; **f. with joy** fou (*f* folle) de joie • **frantically** *adv* frénétiquement; *(run, search)* comme un fou/une folle; *(work)* avec frénésie

fraternal [frəˈtɜːnəl] *adj* fraternel, -elle • **fraternity** (*pl* **-ies**) *n (brotherliness)* fraternité *f*; *(in American university)* = association d'étudiants; **the banking/medical f.** la confrérie des banquiers/médecins • **fraternize** [ˈfrætənaɪz] *vi* fraterniser (**with** avec)

fraud [frɔːd] *n* (**a**) *(crime)* fraude *f*; **to obtain sth by f.** obtenir qch frauduleusement (**b**) *(person)* imposteur *m* • **fraudulent** [ˈfrɔːdjʊlənt] *adj* frauduleux, -euse

fraught [frɔːt] *adj (situation)* tendu; **f. with** plein de

fray [freɪ] **1** *n (fight)* bagarre *f*
2 *vt (garment)* effilocher; *(rope)* user; **my nerves are frayed** j'ai les nerfs à vif; **tempers were frayed** on s'énervait
3 *vi (of garment)* s'effilocher; *(of rope)* s'user

freak [friːk] **1** *n (person)* monstre *m*; *Fam* **jazz f.** fana *f* de jazz
2 *adj (result, weather)* anormal; **f. accident** accident imprévisible
▸ **freak out** *Fam* **1** *vt sep (shock, scare)* faire flipper **2** *vi (panic)* paniquer; *(get angry)* piquer une crise

freckle [ˈfrekəl] *n* tache *f* de rousseur • **freckled** *adj* couvert de taches de rousseur

free [friː] **1** (**freer, freest**) *adj (at liberty, not occupied)* libre; *(without cost)* gratuit; *(lavish)* généreux, -euse (**with** de); **to get f.** se libérer; **to be f. to do sth** être libre de faire qch; **to let sb go f.** relâcher qn; **to be f. of sb** être débarrassé de qn; **f. of charge** gratuit; *Fig* **to have a f. hand** avoir carte blanche (**to do** pour faire); **f. and easy** décontracté; **f. gift** cadeau *m*; *Football* **f. kick** coup *m* franc; *Br* **f.-range egg** œuf *m* de ferme; **f. speech** liberté *f* d'expression; **f. trade** libre-échange *m*
2 *adv* **f. (of charge)** gratuitement
3 (*pt & pp* **freed**) *vt (prisoner, country)* libérer; *(trapped person)* dégager; *(untie)* détacher • **Freefone**® *n Br (phone number)* ≃ numéro *m* vert • **free-for-'all** *n* bagarre *f* • **freehold** *n Law* propriété *f* foncière perpétuelle et libre • **freelance** **1** *adj* indépendant **2** *n* travailleur, -euse *mf* indépendant(e) **3** *adv* **to work f.** tra-

vailler en indépendant • **freeloader** *n Fam* parasite *m* • **Freemason** *n* francmaçon *m* • **Freepost**® *n Br* ≃ correspondance-réponse *f* • **freestyle** *n (in swimming)* nage *f* libre • **free'thinker** *n* libre penseur, -euse *mf* • **freeway** *n Am* autoroute *f* • **freewheel** *vi (on bicycle)* être en roue libre

freebie [ˈfriːbiː] *n Fam* petit cadeau *m*

freedom [ˈfriːdəm] *n* liberté *f*; **f. of information** libre accès *m* à l'information; **f. of speech** liberté *f* d'expression; **f. from worry/responsibility** absence *f* de souci/de responsabilité; **f. fighter** guérillero *m*

freely [ˈfriːlɪ] *adv (speak, act, circulate)* librement; *(give)* sans compter

freeze [friːz] **1** *n (in weather)* gel *m*; *(of prices, salaries)* blocage *m*
2 (*pt* **froze**, *pp* **frozen**) *vt (food)* congeler; *(credits, river)* geler; *(prices, wages)* bloquer; **frozen food** surgelés *mpl*
3 *vi* geler; *(of person)* s'arrêter net; **f.!** ne bougez plus!; **to f. to death** mourir de froid; **to f. up** *or* **over** *(of lake)* geler • **freeze-dry** *vt* lyophiliser • **freezer** *n (deep-freeze)* congélateur *m*; *(ice-box)* freezer *m* • **freezing 1** *adj (weather)* glacial; *(hands, feet)* gelé; **it's f.** il gèle; *Fam* **I'm f.!** je gèle! **2** *n* **it's 5 degrees below f.** il fait 5 degrés au-dessous de zéro **3** *adv* **f. cold** très froid; **it's f. cold in here!** on meurt de froid ici!

freight [freɪt] *Com* **1** *n (transport)* fret *m*; *(goods)* cargaison *f*; **f. train** train *m* de marchandises
2 *vt (goods)* transporter • **freighter** *n (ship)* cargo *m*

French [frentʃ] **1** *adj* français; *(teacher)* de français; *(embassy)* de France; **F. fries** frites *fpl*; **F. loaf** baguette *f*
2 *n (language)* français *m*; **the F.** *(people)* les Français *mpl* • **Frenchman** (*pl* **-men**) *n* Français *m* • **French-speaking** *adj* francophone • **Frenchwoman** (*pl* **-women**) *n* Française *f*

frenzy [ˈfrenzɪ] (*pl* **-ies**) *n* frénésie *f* • **frenzied** *adj (activity)* frénétique; *(person)* affolé; *(attack)* violent

frequency [ˈfriːkwənsɪ] (*pl* **-ies**) *n* fréquence *f*

frequent 1 [ˈfriːkwənt] *adj* fréquent; **f. visitor** habitué, -uée *mf* (**to** de)
2 [frɪˈkwent] *vt* fréquenter • **frequently** *adv* fréquemment

fresco [ˈfreskəʊ] (*pl* **-oes** *or* **-os**) *n* fresque *f*

fresh [freʃ] **1** (**-er, -est**) *adj* frais (*f* fraî-

che); *(new)* nouveau *(f* nouvelle); *Am Fam
(cheeky)* insolent; **to get some f. air** prendre l'air; **f.-water fish** poisson *m* d'eau
douce
2 *adv* **to be f. from** *(city, country)* arriver
tout juste de; *(school, university)* sortir
tout juste de ● **freshly** *adv (arrived,
picked)* fraîchement ● **freshness** *n* fraîcheur *f*
freshen ['freʃən] **1** *vi (of wind)* fraîchir;
to f. up *(have a wash)* faire un brin de
toilette
2 *vt* **to f. up** *(house)* retaper; **to f. sb up**
(of bath, shower) rafraîchir qn
fresher ['freʃə(r)] *n Br Univ* étudiant,
-iante *mf* de première année
freshman ['freʃmən] *(pl* **-men**) *n Am
Univ* étudiant, -iante *mf* de première année
fret [fret] *(pt & pp* **-tt-**) *vi (worry)* se faire
du souci ● **fretful** *adj* inquiet, -iète
friar ['fraɪə(r)] *n* moine *m*
friction ['frɪkʃən] *n* friction *f*
Friday ['fraɪdeɪ] *n* vendredi *m*; **Good F.** le
Vendredi saint
fridge [frɪdʒ] *n* frigo *m*
fried [fraɪd] **1** *pt & pp* of **fry¹**
2 *adj* frit; **f. egg** œuf *m* sur le plat
friend [frend] *n* ami, -ie *mf*; **to be friends
with sb** être ami avec qn; **to make friends
with sb** devenir ami avec qn ● **friendly 1**
(-ier, -iest) *adj* amical; **f. advice** conseils
mpl d'ami; **to be f. with sb** être ami avec
qn; **to be on f. terms with sb** être en bons
termes avec qn **2** *n Sport* match *m* amical
● **friendship** *n* amitié *f*
frieze [friːz] *n (on building)* frise *f*
frigate ['frɪgət] *n* frégate *f*
fright [fraɪt] *n* peur *f*; **to take f.** prendre
peur; **to give sb a f.** faire peur à qn; *Fam*
you look a f.! tu es à faire peur!
frighten ['fraɪtən] *vt* effrayer, faire peur
à; **to f. sb away** *or* **off** faire fuir qn
● **frightened** *adj* effrayé; **to be f.** avoir
peur (**of** de) ● **frightening** *adj* effrayant
frightful ['fraɪtfəl] *adj* affreux, -euse
● **frightfully** *adv* terriblement
frigid ['frɪdʒɪd] *adj (greeting, manner)*
glacial; *(woman)* frigide
frill [frɪl] *n* volant *m*; **no frills** *(machine,
holiday)* rudimentaire; *(ceremony)* sans
chichis
fringe [frɪndʒ] *n* (**a**) *(of hair, on clothes)*
frange *f* (**b**) *(of forest)* lisière *f*; *(of town)*
abords *mpl*; **on the fringes of society** en
marge de la société; **f. benefits** avantages *mpl* divers; **f. group** groupuscule *m*;
Br **f. theatre** théâtre *m* expérimental

Frisbee® ['frɪzbiː] *n* Frisbee® *m*
frisk [frɪsk] **1** *vt (search)* fouiller
2 *vi* **to f. (about)** gambader
frisky ['frɪskɪ] *(-ier, -iest)* *adj (lively)* vif *(f*
vive)
fritter ['frɪtə(r)] **1** *n Culin* beignet *m*
2 *vt* **to f. away** gaspiller
frivolous ['frɪvələs] *adj* frivole ● **frivolity**
[-'vɒlɪtɪ] *(pl* **-ies**) *n* frivolité *f*
frizzy ['frɪzɪ] *adj* crépu
fro [frəʊ] *adv* **to go to and f.** aller et venir
frock [frɒk] *n (dress)* robe *f*; *(of monk)*
froc *m*
Frog [frɒg] *n Br Fam (French person)* =
terme injurieux désignant un Français
frog [frɒg] *n* grenouille *f*; **f.'s legs** cuisses
fpl de grenouille; *Fam* **to have a f. in one's
throat** avoir un chat dans la gorge
● **'frogman** *(pl* **-men**) *n* homme-
grenouille *m*
frolic ['frɒlɪk] *(pt & pp* **-ck-**) *vi* **to f.
(about)** gambader ● **frolics** *npl (playing)*
gambades *fpl*; *(pranks)* gamineries *fpl*
from [frɒm, *unstressed* frəm] *prep* (**a**)
(expressing origin) de; **a letter f. sb** une
lettre de qn; **to suffer f. sth** souffrir de
qch; **where are you f.?** d'où êtes-vous?; **I
come f. Portugal** je viens du Portugal; **a
train f. Paris** un train en provenance de
Paris; **to be 10 m (away) f. the house** être
à 10 m de la maison; **f. York to London** de
York à Londres
(**b**) *(expressing time)* à partir de; **f. today
(on), as f. today** à partir d'aujourd'hui; **f.
then on** depuis ce jour-là; **f. the beginning** dès le début
(**c**) *(expressing range)* **f.... to...** de... à...; **f.
six to seven o'clock** de six à sept heures; **f.
morning till night** du matin au soir; **they
take children f. the age of five** ils acceptent les enfants à partir de cinq ans
(**d**) *(expressing source)* de; **to take/bor-
row sth f. sb** prendre/emprunter qch à
qn; **to drink f. a cup** boire dans une tasse
(**e**) *(expressing removal)* de; **to take sth f.
sb** prendre qch à qn; **to take sth f. a box**
prendre qch dans une boîte; **to take sth f.
the table** prendre qch sur la table (**f**)
(according to) d'après; **f. what I saw...**
d'après ce que j'ai vu...
(**g**) *(on behalf of)* de la part de; **tell her f.
me** dis-lui de ma part
front [frʌnt] **1** *n* devant *m*; *(of boat, car)*
avant *m*; *(of building)* façade *f*; *(of crowd)*
premier rang *m*; *Mil & Pol* front *m*; *Br* **on
the sea f.** sur le front de mer; **in f. of sb/
sth** devant qn/qch; **in f.** devant; *(further
ahead)* en avant; *(in race)* en tête; **I sat in**

the **f.** *(of car)* j'étais assis à l'avant; *Fig* **it's just a f.** *(appearance)* ce n'est qu'une façade; *Met* **cold/warm f.** front froid/chaud

2 *adj (tooth, garden)* de devant; *(car seat)* avant *inv*; *(row, page)* premier, -ière; **f. door** porte *f* d'entrée; *Mil* **f. line** front *m*; *Br* **f. room** *(lounge)* salon *m*; **f. view** vue *f* de face; *Aut* **f.-wheel drive** traction *f* avant

3 *vt (organization)* être à la tête de; *(government)* diriger; *(TV programme)* présenter

4 *vi* **to f. on to** *(of windows)* donner sur • **frontrunner** *n Fig* favori, -ite *mf*

frontage ['frʌntɪdʒ] *n* façade *f*

frontal ['frʌntəl] *adj Anat & (attack)* frontal

frontier ['frʌntɪə(r)] *n* frontière *f*; **f. town** ville *f* frontalière

frost [frɒst] **1** *n* gel *m*

2 *vi* **to f. up** *(of window)* se couvrir de givre

frostbite ['frɒstbaɪt] *n* gelure *f* • **frostbitten** *adj* gelé

frosted ['frɒstɪd] *adj* (**a**) *(glass)* dépoli (**b**) *Am (cake)* glacé

frosting ['frɒstɪŋ] *n Am (icing on cake)* glaçage *m*

frosty ['frɒstɪ] *adj (air, night)* glacé; *(window)* givré; *Fig (welcome)* glacial; **it's f.** il gèle

froth [frɒθ] **1** *n (on beer)* mousse *f*; *(on waves)* écume *f*

2 *vi (liquid)* mousser • **frothy** (-ier, -iest) *adj (beer)* mousseux, -euse

frown [fraʊn] **1** *n* froncement *m* de sourcils

2 *vi* froncer les sourcils; *Fig* **to f. (up)on** désapprouver

froze [frəʊz] *pt of* **freeze**

frozen ['frəʊzən] *pp of* **freeze**

frugal ['fruːɡəl] *adj* frugal • **frugally** *adv* frugalement

fruit [fruːt] *n* fruit *m*; **some f.** *(one item)* un fruit; *(more than one)* des fruits; **to like f.** aimer les fruits; **f. basket/bowl** corbeille *f*/coupe *f* à fruits; **f. drink** boisson *f* aux fruits; **f. juice** jus *m* de fruit; **f. salad** salade *f* de fruits; **f. tree** arbre *m* fruitier; *Br* **f. machine** *(for gambling)* machine *f* à sous • **fruitcake** *n* cake *m*

fruitful ['fruːtfəl] *adj (meeting, discussion)* fructueux, -ueuse • **fruitless** *adj (attempt, search)* infructueux, -ueuse

fruition [fruː'ɪʃən] *n* **to come to f.** *(of plan)* porter ses fruits

fruity ['fruːtɪ] (-ier, -iest) *adj (taste)* de fruit

frumpish ['frʌmpɪʃ], **frumpy** ['frʌmpɪ] *adj Fam* **to be f.** faire mémère

frustrate [frʌ'streɪt] *vt (person)* frustrer; *(plans)* contrarier • **frustrated** *adj (person)* frustré; • **frustrating** *adj* frustrant • **frustration** *n* frustration *f*

fry¹ [fraɪ] **1** *(pt & pp* **fried)** *vt* faire frire

2 *vi* frire • **frying** *n* friture *f*; **f. pan** poêle *f* (à frire) • **fry-up** *n Br Fam* = pommes de terre, bacon, saucisses etc frits ensemble

fry² [fraɪ] *n* **small f.** *(people)* menu fretin *m*

ft *abbr (unit of measurement)* = **foot, feet**

fuddy-duddy ['fʌdɪdʌdɪ] *n Fam* **he's an old f.** c'est un vieux schnock

fudge [fʌdʒ] **1** *n (sweet)* caramel *m* mou

2 *vt* **to f. the issue** éluder une question

fuel [fjʊəl] **1** *n* combustible *m*; *(for engine)* carburant *m*; **f. oil** mazout *m*; **f. tank** *(in vehicle)* réservoir *m*

2 *(Br* **-ll-,** *Am* **-l-)** *vt (stove)* alimenter; *(vehicle, plane, ship)* ravitailler (en combustible); *Fig (anger, hatred)* attiser; **to be fuelled by diesel** *(of engine)* marcher au gazole

fugitive ['fjuːdʒɪtɪv] *n* fugitif, -ive *mf*

fugue [fjuːɡ] *n Mus* fugue *f*

fulfil [fʊl'fɪl] *(Am* **fulfill**) *(pt & pp* **-ll-)** *vt (ambition, dream)* réaliser; *(condition, duty)* remplir; *(desire, need)* satisfaire; **to f. oneself** s'épanouir • **fulfilling** *adj* satisfaisant • **fulfilment** *(Am* **fulfillment**) *n (of ambition)* réalisation *f* (**of** de); *(satisfaction)* épanouissement *m*

full [fʊl] **1** *(-er, -est)* *adj* plein (**of** de); *(bus, theatre, hotel, examination)* complet, -ète; *(amount)* intégral; *(day, programme)* chargé; *(skirt)* bouffant; **to be f. (up)** *(of person)* n'avoir plus faim; *(of hotel)* être complet; **to wait a f. hour** attendre une heure entière; **to pay (the) f. fare** *or* **price** payer plein tarif; **to lead a f. life** mener une vie bien remplie; **at f. speed** à toute vitesse; **f. house** *(in theatre)* salle *f* comble; **f. member** membre à part entière; **f. name** nom et prénom; *Br* **f. stop** point *m*

2 *n* **in f.** *(pay)* intégralement; *(read, publish)* en entier; *(write)* en toutes lettres; **the text in f.** le texte intégral; **to live life to the f.** vivre pleinement

3 *adv* **to know f. well** savoir fort bien; **f. in the face** *(hit)* en pleine figure • **fullback** *n Sport* arrière • **'full-'blown** *adj (row)* vrai; **to have f. AIDS** avoir le SIDA • **'full-'grown** *adj* adulte • **'full-'length** *adj (portrait)* en pied; *(dress)* long (*f* longue); **f. film** long métrage *m* • **'full-'scale** *adj* *(model)* grandeur nature *inv*; *(operation)* de grande envergure ● 'full-'sized *adj (model)* grandeur nature *inv* ● 'full-'time *adj & adv (work)* à plein temps

fullness ['fʊlnɪs] *n (of details)* abondance *f*; *(of dress)* ampleur *f*; **in the f. of time** avec le temps

fully ['fʊlɪ] *adv (completely)* entièrement; *(understand)* parfaitement; *(at least)* au moins ● 'fully-'fledged *(Am* 'full-'fledged) *adj (engineer, teacher)* diplômé; *(member)* à part entière ● 'fully-'grown *adj* adulte

fulsome ['fʊlsəm] *adj (praise)* excessif, -ive; **a f. apology** de plates excuses

fumble ['fʌmbəl] *vi* **to f. (about)** *(grope)* tâtonner; *(search)* fouiller (**for** pour trouver); **to f. (about) with sth** tripoter qch

fume [fjuːm] *vi* (**a**) *(give off fumes)* fumer (**b**) **to be fuming** *(of person)* rager ● **fumes** *npl* émanations *fpl*; *(from car)* gaz *mpl* d'échappement

---

⚡ Note that the French verb **fumer** is a false friend and is never a translation for the English verb **to fume**. It means **to smoke**.

---

fumigate ['fjuːmɪgeɪt] *vt* désinfecter (par fumigation)

fun [fʌn] *n* plaisir *m*; **for f., for the f. of it** pour le plaisir; **to be (good** *or* **great) f.** être (très) amusant; **to have (some) f.** s'amuser; **to make f. of sb/sth** se moquer de qn/qch; **to spoil sb's f.** empêcher qn de s'amuser

function ['fʌŋkʃən] **1** *n (role, duty) & Comptr* fonction *f*; *(party)* réception *f*; *(ceremony)* cérémonie *f* **2** *vi* fonctionner; **to f. as** faire fonction de ● **functional** *adj* fonctionnel, -elle

fund [fʌnd] **1** *n (of money)* fonds *m*; *Fig (of information)* mine *f*; **funds** fonds *mpl*; **f. manager** gestionnaire *mf* de fonds **2** *vt* financer

fundamental [fʌndə'mentəl] *adj* fondamental **2** *npl* **fundamentals** principes *mpl*

funeral ['fjuːnərəl] *n* enterrement *m*; *(grandiose)* funérailles *fpl*; **f. service/march** service *m*/marche *f* funèbre; *Br* **f. parlour,** *Am* **f. home** entreprise *f* de pompes funèbres

funfair ['fʌnfeə(r)] *n Br* fête *f* foraine

fungus ['fʌŋgəs] *(pl* **-gi** [-gaɪ]*) n (plant)* champignon *m*; *(on walls)* moisissure *f*

funicular [fjʊ'nɪkjʊlə(r)] *n* funiculaire *m*

funky ['fʌŋkɪ] *adj Fam* cool *inv*

funnel ['fʌnəl] *n* (**a**) *(of ship)* cheminée *f* (**b**) *(for filling)* entonnoir *m*

funny ['fʌnɪ] (**-ier, -iest**) *adj (amusing)* drôle; *(strange)* bizarre; **a f. idea** une drôle d'idée; **there's some f. business going on** il y a quelque chose de louche; **to feel f.** ne pas se sentir très bien ● **funnily** *adv (amusingly)* drôlement; *(strangely)* bizarrement; **f. enough, I was just about to** bizarrement, j'étais sur le point de

fur [fɜː(r)] **1** *n* (**a**) *(of animal, for wearing)* fourrure *f*; *(of dog, cat)* poil *m*; **f. coat** manteau *m* de fourrure (**b**) *Br (in kettle, boiler)* tartre *m* **2** *(pt & pp* **-rr-***) vi Br* **to f. (up)** *(of kettle)* s'entartrer

furious ['fjʊərɪəs] *adj (violent, angry)* furieux, -ieuse (**with** *or* **at** contre); *(efforts, struggle)* violent; **at a f. speed** à une allure folle ● **furiously** *adv* furieusement; *(struggle)* avec acharnement; *(drive, rush)* à une allure folle

furlong ['fɜːlɒŋ] *n (measurement)* = 201 m

furnace ['fɜːnɪs] *n (forge)* fourneau *m*; *Fig (hot room)* fournaise *f*

furnish ['fɜːnɪʃ] *vt* (**a**) *(room, house)* meubler (**b**) *Formal (supply)* fournir (**sb with sth** qch à qn) ● **furnishings** *npl* ameublement *m*

furniture ['fɜːnɪtʃə(r)] *n* meubles *mpl*; **a piece of f.** un meuble; **f. shop** magasin *m* d'ameublement

furrow ['fʌrəʊ] *n (in earth, on brow)* sillon *m*

furry ['fɜːrɪ] *adj (animal)* à poil; *(toy)* en peluche

further ['fɜːðə(r)] **1** *adv & adj* = **farther** **2** *adj (additional)* supplémentaire; **a f. case** *(another)* un autre cas; **without f. delay** sans plus attendre; **until f. notice** jusqu'à nouvel ordre; **for f. information...** pour de plus amples renseignements...; *Br* **f. education** = enseignement supérieur dispensé par un établissement autre qu'une université **3** *adv (more)* davantage; *Formal (besides)* en outre; **f. to my letter...** suite à ma lettre...; **he did not question us any f.** il ne nous a pas interrogés davantage **4** *vt (cause, research, career)* promouvoir ● **further'more** *adv Formal* en outre ● **furthest** *adj & adv* = **farthest**

furtive ['fɜːtɪv] *adj* sournois

fury ['fjʊərɪ] *n (violence, anger)* fureur *f*

fuse [fjuːz] **1** *n (wire)* fusible *m*; *(of bomb)* amorce *f* **2** *vt (melt)* fondre; *(join)* fusionner; *Br* **to**

f. the lights faire sauter les plombs
3 *vi (of metals)* fondre; *(of organizations)* fusionner; *Br* **the lights have fused** les plombs ont sauté

fused [fjuːzd] *adj Br* **f. plug** fiche *f* avec fusible incorporé

fuselage ['fjuːzəlɑːʒ] *n* fuselage *m*

fusion ['fjuːʒən] *n* fusion *f*

fuss [fʌs] **1** *n* histoires *fpl*; **what a (lot of) f.!** quelle histoire!; **to kick up** *or* **make a f.** faire des histoires; **to make a f. of sb** être aux petits soins pour qn
2 *vi* faire des histoires; **to f. about** s'activer; **to f. over sb** être aux petits soins pour qn • **fusspot** (*Am* **fussbudget**) *n Fam* chichiteux, -euse *mf* • **fussy** (**-ier**, **-iest**) *adj* exigeant (**about** sur); **I'm not f.** (*I don't mind*) ça m'est égal

fusty ['fʌstɪ] (**-ier**, **-iest**) *adj (smell)* de renfermé

futile [*Br* 'fjuːtaɪl, *Am* 'fjuːtəl] *adj (remark)* futile; *(attempt)* vain • **fu'tility** *n* futilité *f*

futon ['fuːtɒn] *n* futon *m*

future ['fjuːtʃə(r)] **1** *n* avenir *m*; *Grammar* futur *m*; **in (the) f.** à l'avenir
2 *adj* futur; **my f. wife** ma future épouse; **the f. tense** le futur; **at a** *or* **some f. date** à une date ultérieure

fuze [fjuːz] *n & vti Am* = **fuse**

fuzz [fʌz] *n (on face, legs)* duvet *m*; *Am (of fabric)* peluches *fpl*

fuzzy ['fʌzɪ] (**-ier**, **-iest**) *adj* (**a**) *(unclear)* *(picture, idea)* flou (**b**) *Am (material, coat)* pelucheux, -euse (**c**) *(hair)* crépu

G, g [dʒiː] *n* (**a**) *(letter)* G, g *m inv* (**b**) *Mus*
sol *m* • **G-string** *n* string *m*
gab [gæb] *n Fam* **to have the gift of the g.**
(be talkative) avoir la langue bien pendue; *(speak persuasively)* avoir du bagout
gabardine [gæbə'diːn] *n (material, coat)*
gabardine *f*
gabble ['gæbəl] **1** *n* **a g. of conversation**
un bruit de conversation
2 *vi (chatter)* jacasser; *(indistinctly)* bredouiller
gable ['geɪbəl] *n* pignon *m*
gad [gæd] *(pt & pp* -**dd-**) *vi* **to g. about** *or*
around vadrouiller
gadget ['gædʒɪt] *n* gadget *m*
Gaelic ['geɪlɪk, 'gælɪk] *adj & n* gaélique
(m)
gaffe [gæf] *n (blunder)* gaffe *f*
gag [gæg] **1** *n* (**a**) *(on mouth)* bâillon *m*
(**b**) *Fam (joke)* blague *f*
2 *(pt & pp* -**gg-**) *vt (person)* bâillonner;
Fig (press) museler
3 *vi (choke)* s'étouffer (**on** avec); *(retch)*
avoir des haut-le-cœur
gaggle ['gægəl] *n* troupeau *m*
gaiety ['geɪtɪ] *n* gaieté *f* • **gaily** *adv* gaiement
gain [geɪn] **1** *n (increase)* augmentation
f (**in** de); *(profit)* gain *m*; *Fig* avantage
m
2 *vt (obtain, win)* gagner; *(experience,
reputation)* acquérir; **to g. speed/weight**
prendre de la vitesse/du poids; **to g.
support** *(of person, idea)* recueillir de
plus en plus d'opinions favorables
3 *vi (of clock)* avancer; **to g. in popularity** devenir populaire; **to g. on sb** gagner
du terrain sur qn; **to g. by sth** bénéficier
de qch
gainful ['geɪnfəl] *adj* **g. employment** emploi *m* rémunéré
gainsay [geɪn'seɪ] *(pt & pp* -**said** [-sed]) *vt
Formal (person)* contredire; *(facts)* nier
gait [geɪt] *n* démarche *f*
gala [*Br* 'gɑːlə, *Am* 'geɪlə] *n* gala *m*; *Br*
swimming g. concours *m* de natation
galaxy ['gæləksɪ] *(pl* -**ies**) *n* galaxie *f*
gale [geɪl] *n* grand vent *m*
gall [gɔːl] **1** *n (bitterness)* fiel *m*; *(impu-*

dence) culot *m*; **g. bladder** vésicule *f*
biliaire
2 *vt (annoy)* irriter
gallant ['gælənt] *adj (brave)* brave; *(polite)* galant • **gallantry** *n (bravery)* bravoure *f*; *(politeness)* galanterie *f*
galleon ['gælɪən] *n Hist (ship)* galion *m*
gallery ['gælərɪ] *(pl* -**ies**) *n (room, shop,
in theatre)* galerie *f*; *(museum)* musée *m*;
(for public, press) tribune *f*
galley ['gælɪ] *(pl* -**eys**) *n Hist (ship)* galère
f; *(kitchen)* cuisine *f*
Gallic ['gælɪk] *adj (French)* français
galling ['gɔːlɪŋ] *adj* humiliant
gallivant ['gælɪvænt] *vi Fam* **to g.
(about)** vadrouiller
gallon ['gælən] *n* gallon *m (Br = 4,5 l, Am
= 3,8 l)*
gallop ['gæləp] **1** *n* galop *m*
2 *vi* galoper; **to g. away** *(rush off)* partir
en vitesse; **galloping inflation** inflation *f*
galopante
gallows ['gæləʊz] *n* potence *f*
gallstone ['gɔːlstəʊn] *n Med* calcul *m*
biliaire
galore [gə'lɔː(r)] *adv Fam* à gogo
galvanize ['gælvənaɪz] *vt (metal, person)*
galvaniser
Gambia ['gæmbɪə] *n* **The G.** la Gambie
gambit ['gæmbɪt] *n* **opening g.** *(ploy)*
manœuvre *f* d'approche
gamble ['gæmbəl] **1** *n (risk)* coup *m*
risqué; **to take a g.** prendre un risque
2 *vt (bet)* parier, jouer; **to g. sth away**
(lose) perdre qch au jeu
3 *vi* jouer (**on** sur; **with** avec); **to g. on
the horses** jouer aux courses; **to g. on sth**
(count on) miser sur qch • **gambler** *n*
joueur, -euse *mf* • **gambling** *n* jeu *m*
game¹ [geɪm] *n* (**a**) *(activity)* jeu *m*; *(of
football, cricket)* match *m*; *(of tennis,
chess, cards)* partie *f*; **to have a g. of
football/tennis** faire un match de foot-
ball/une partie de tennis; *Br* **games** *(in
school)* le sport; *Br* **games teacher** professeur *m* d'éducation physique; **g. show**
jeu *m* télévisé (**b**) *(animals, birds)* gibier
m; *Fig* **to be fair g. for sb** être une proie
idéale pour qn

game² [geɪm] *adj (brave)* courageux, -euse; **to be g. (to do sth)** être partant (pour faire qch)
gamekeeper ['geɪmkiːpə(r)] *n* garde-chasse *m*
gammon ['gæmən] *n Br* jambon *m*
gammy ['gæmɪ] *adj Fam* **a g. leg** une patte folle
gamut ['gæmət] *n Mus & Fig* gamme *f*
gang [gæŋ] **1** *n (of children, friends)* bande *f; (of workers)* équipe *f; (of criminals)* gang *m*
   2 *vi* **to g. up on** *or* **against** se mettre à plusieurs contre
Ganges ['gændʒiːz] *n* **the G.** le Gange *m*
gangling ['gæŋglɪŋ] *adj* dégingandé
gangrene ['gæŋgriːn] *n* gangrène *f*
gangster ['gæŋstə(r)] *n* gangster *m*
gangway ['gæŋweɪ] *n Br* passage *m; (in train, plane)* couloir *m; (on ship)* passe-relle *f; (in bus, cinema, theatre)* allée *f;* **g.!** dégagez!
gaol [dʒeɪl] *n & vt Br* = **jail**
gap [gæp] *n (space)* espace *m* (**between** entre); *(in wall, fence)* trou *m; (in time)* intervalle *m; (in knowledge)* lacune *f;* **the g. between** *(difference)* l'écart *m* entre
gape [geɪp] *vi (stare)* rester bouche bée; **to g. at sb/sth** regarder qn/qch bouche bée • **gaping** *adj* béant
garage [*Br* 'gærɑː(d)ʒ, 'gærɪdʒ, *Am* gə'rɑːʒ] *n* garage *m*
garbage ['gɑːbɪdʒ] *n Am* ordures *fpl;* **g. can** poubelle *f;* **g. man** *or* **collector** éboueur *m*
garbled ['gɑːbəld] *adj* confus
garden ['gɑːdən] **1** *n* jardin *m;* **gardens** *(park)* parc *m;* **g. centre** jardinerie *f;* **g. party** garden-party *f;* **g. produce** produits *mpl* maraîchers
   2 *vi* jardiner, faire du jardinage • **gardener** *n* jardinier, -ière *mf* • **gardening** *n* jardinage *m*
gargle ['gɑːgəl] *vi* se gargariser
gargoyle ['gɑːgɔɪl] *n Archit* gargouille *f*
garish [*Br* 'geərɪʃ, *Am* 'gærɪʃ] *adj (clothes)* voyant; *(colour)* criard; *(light)* cru
garland ['gɑːlənd] *n* guirlande *f*
garlic ['gɑːlɪk] *n* ail *m;* **g. bread** = pain chaud à l'ail; **g. sausage** saucisson *m* à l'ail
garment ['gɑːmənt] *n* vêtement *m*
garnish ['gɑːnɪʃ] **1** *n* garniture *f*
   2 *vt* garnir (**with** de)
garret ['gærət] *n* mansarde *f*
garrison ['gærɪsən] *n* garnison *f*
garrulous ['gærələs] *adj (talkative)* loquace

garter ['gɑːtə(r)] *n (round leg)* jarretière *f; Am (attached to belt)* jarretelle *f; (for men)* fixe-chaussette *m*
gas [gæs] **1** *n* gaz *m inv; Am (gasoline)* essence *f; Med (for operation)* anesthé-sique *m; Am Fam* for **a g.** pour rire; **g. chamber** chambre *f* à gaz; *Br* **g. cooker** cuisinière *f* à gaz; *Br* **g. heater, g. fire** radiateur *m* à gaz; **g. heating** chauffage *m* au gaz; **g. mask** masque *m* à gaz; **g. pipe** tuyau *m* de gaz; **g. ring** *(burner)* brûleur *m; Am* **g. station** station-service *f;* **g. stove** *(large)* cuisinière à gaz; *(portable)* réchaud *m* à gaz; *Am* **g. tank** réservoir *m* à essence
   2 *(pt & pp* **-ss-)** *vt (person)* asphyxier; *(deliberately)* gazer
   3 *vi Fam (talk)* bavarder • **gasman** *(pl* **-men)** *n* employé *m* du gaz • **gasworks** *n Br* usine *f* à gaz
gasbag ['gæsbæg] *n Fam (chatterbox)* bavard, -arde *mf*
gash [gæʃ] **1** *n* entaille *f*
   2 *vt (skin)* entailler; **to g. one's knee** se faire une blessure profonde au genou
gasket ['gæskɪt] *n (in engine)* joint *m* de culasse
gasoline ['gæsəliːn] *n Am* essence *f*
gasp [gɑːsp] **1** *n* halètement *m; (of surprise)* sursaut *m*
   2 *vt* dire d'une voix pantelante
   3 *vi* avoir le souffle coupé (**with** *or* **in** de); **to g. for breath** haleter
gassy ['gæsɪ] **(-ier, -iest)** *adj* gazeux, -euse
gastric ['gæstrɪk] *adj* gastrique; **g. flu** grippe *f* gastro-intestinale
gastronomy [gæ'strɒnəmɪ] *n* gastrono-mie *f*
gate [geɪt] *n (in garden, field)* barrière *f; (made of metal)* grille *f; (of castle, city, airport)* porte *f; (at stadium)* entrée *f;* **gate(s)** *(of park)* grilles *fpl*
gâteau ['gætəʊ] *(pl* **-eaux** [-əʊz]) *n Br (cake)* gros gâteau *m* à la crème
gatecrash ['geɪtkræʃ] *vt* **to g. a party** s'inviter à une réception
gateway ['geɪtweɪ] *n* entrée *f;* **the g. to success** le chemin du succès
gather ['gæðə(r)] **1** *vt* **(a)** *(people, objects)* rassembler; *(pick up)* ramasser; *(flowers, fruit)* cueillir; *(information)* re-cueillir; **to g. speed** prendre de la vitesse; **to g. in** *(crops, harvest)* rentrer; *(exam papers)* ramasser; **to g. (up) one's strength** rassembler ses forces; **to g. up papers** ramasser des papiers
   (b) *(understand)* **I g. that** je crois

comprendre que (**c**) *(sew pleats in)* froncer
  2 *vi (of people)* se rassembler; *(of clouds)* se former; *(of dust)* s'accumuler; **to g. round** *(come closer)* s'approcher; **to g. round sb** entourer qn
gathering ['gæðərɪŋ] *n (group)* rassemblement *m*
gaudy ['gɔːdɪ] (**-ier, -iest**) *adj* voyant
gauge [geɪdʒ] **1** *n (instrument)* jauge *f*; *(of railway track)* écartement *m*; *Fig* **to be a g. of sth** permettre de jauger qch
  2 *vt* évaluer
gaunt [gɔːnt] *adj* décharné
gauntlet ['gɔːntlɪt] *n* gant *m*; **to run the g. of sth** s'exposer à qch
gauze [gɔːz] *n* gaze *f*
gave [geɪv] *pt of* **give**
gawk [gɔːk], **gawp** [gɔːp] *vi* **to g. at sb/ sth** regarder qn/qch bouche bée
gay [geɪ] (**-er, -est**) **1** *adj* (**a**) *Old-fashioned (cheerful)* gai (**b**) *(homosexual)* homosexuel, -uelle
  2 *n* homosexuel *m*
gaze [geɪz] **1** *n* regard *m*
  2 *vi* **to g. at sb/sth** regarder fixement qn/qch
gazelle [gə'zel] *n* gazelle *f*
gazette [gə'zet] *n* journal *m* officiel
gazetteer [gæzə'tɪə(r)] *n* index *m* géographique
gazump [gə'zʌmp] *vt Br* = revenir sur une promesse de vente pour accepter l'offre plus élevée d'une tierce personne
GB [dʒiː'biː] *(abbr* **Great Britain**) *n* GB
GCSE [dʒiːsiːes'iː] *(abbr* **General Certificate of Secondary Education**) *n Br* = diplôme de fin de premier cycle de l'enseignement secondaire, sanctionnant une matière déterminée
GDP [dʒiːdiː'piː] *(abbr* **gross domestic product**) *n Econ* PIB *m*
gear [gɪə(r)] **1** *n* (**a**) *Fam (equipment)* attirail *m*; *(belongings)* affaires *fpl*; *(clothes)* fringues *fpl* (**b**) *(on car, bicycle)* vitesse *f*; **in g.** *(vehicle)* en prise; **not in g.** au point mort; *Br* **g. lever**, *Am* **g. shift** levier *m* de (changement de) vitesse
  2 *vt* **to g. sth to sth** adapter qch à qch; **to be geared (up) to do sth** être prêt à faire qch; **to g. oneself up for sth** se préparer pour qch • **gearbox** *n* boîte *f* de vitesses
gee [dʒiː] *exclam Am Fam* ça alors!
geese [giːs] *pl of* **goose**
geezer ['giːzə(r)] *n Br Fam* type *m*
Geiger counter ['gaɪgəkaʊntə(r)] *n* compteur *m* Geiger
gel [dʒel] *n* gel *m*

gelatin(e) [*Br* 'dʒelətiːn, *Am* -tən] *n* gélatine *f*
gelignite ['dʒelɪgnaɪt] *n* gélignite *f*
gem [dʒem] *n (stone)* pierre *f* précieuse; *Fig (person)* perle *f*; *Fig (thing)* bijou *m (pl* -oux); *Ironic (error)* perle *f*
Gemini ['dʒemɪnaɪ] *n (sign)* les Gémeaux *mpl*; **to be a G.** être Gémeaux
gen [dʒen] *Br Fam* **1** *n (information)* tuyaux *mpl*
  2 *(pt & pp* **-nn-**) *vi* **to g. up on sb/sth** se rancarder sur qn/qch
gender ['dʒendə(r)] *n Grammar* genre *m*; *(of person)* sexe *m*
gene [dʒiːn] *n Biol* gène *m*
genealogy [dʒiːnɪ'ælədʒɪ] *n* généalogie *f*
general ['dʒenərəl] **1** *adj* général; **in g.** en général; **the g. public** le grand public; **for g. use** à l'usage du public; *Am* **g. delivery** poste *f* restante; **g.-purpose tool** outil *m* universel
  2 *n Mil* général *m*
generality [dʒenə'rælətɪ] *(pl* **-ies**) *n* généralité *f*
generalize ['dʒenərəlaɪz] *vti* généraliser; **to become generalized** se généraliser • **generalization** [-'zeɪʃən] *n* généralisation *f*
generally ['dʒenərəlɪ] *adv* généralement; **g. speaking** de manière générale
generate ['dʒenəreɪt] *vt (fear, hope, unemployment) & Ling* engendrer; *(heat, electricity)* produire; *(interest, ideas)* faire naître; *(income, jobs)* créer
generation [dʒenə'reɪʃən] *n (of people, products)* génération *f*; *(of electricity)* production *f*; **from g. to g.** de génération en génération; **g. gap** conflit *m* des générations
generator ['dʒenəreɪtə(r)] *n* générateur *m*
generous ['dʒenərəs] *adj* généreux, -euse (**with** de); *(helping, meal)* copieux, -ieuse • **generosity** [-'rɒsɪtɪ] *n* générosité *f* • **generously** *adv* généreusement; *(serve with food)* copieusement
genesis ['dʒenəsɪs] *n* genèse *f*
genetic [dʒɪ'netɪk] *adj* génétique; **g. code** code *m* génétique; **g. engineering** génie *m* génétique • **genetically** *adv* **g. modified** génétiquement modifié • **genetics** *n* génétique *f*
Geneva [dʒɪ'niːvə] *n* Genève *m ou f*
genial ['dʒiːnɪəl] *adj* cordial

> 🖉 *Note that the French word* **génial** *is a false friend and is never a translation for the English word* **genial**. *It means* **brilliant**.

genie ['dʒiːnɪ] *n (goblin)* génie *m*
genital ['dʒenɪtəl] *adj* génital •**genitals**
npl organes *mpl* génitaux
genius ['dʒiːnɪəs] *n (ability, person)* génie
m; *Ironic* **to have a g. for sth/for doing
sth** avoir le génie de qch/de faire qch
genocide ['dʒenəsaɪd] *n* génocide *m*
gent [dʒent] *n Br Fam* monsieur *m*; **gents'
shoes** chaussures *fpl* pour hommes; **the
gents** les toilettes *fpl* des hommes
genteel [dʒen'tiːl] *adj* distingué

> ⚠ Note that the French word **gentil** is a
> false friend and is never a translation for
> the English word **genteel**. It means **kind**.

gentle ['dʒentəl] (**-er, -est**) *adj (person,
sound, slope)* doux (*f* douce); *(hint)* discret, -ète; *(exercise, speed, progress)* modéré; **g. breeze** légère brise *f*; **to be g. to
sb** traiter qn avec douceur; **be g. with
your sister!** ne sois pas brutal avec ta
sœur!; **to be g. with sth** faire attention à
qch; **of g. birth** bien né •**gentleness** *n*
douceur *f* •**gently** *adv* doucement; *(remind)* gentiment; *(land)* en douceur

> ⚠ Note that the French word **gentil** is a
> false friend and is never a translation for
> the English word **gentle**. It means **kind**.

gentleman ['dʒentəlmən] (*pl* **-men**) *n*
monsieur *m*; *(well-bred)* gentleman *m*
genuine ['dʒenjʊɪn] *adj (leather, diamond)* véritable; *(signature, work of art)*
authentique; *(sincere)* sincère •**genu-
inely** *adv (sincerely)* sincèrement; *(surprised)* véritablement
geography [dʒɪ'ɒɡrəfɪ] *n* géographie *f*
•**geographical** [dʒɪə'ɡræfɪkəl] *adj* géographique
geology [dʒɪ'ɒlədʒɪ] *n* géologie *f* •**geological** [dʒɪə'lɒdʒɪkəl] *adj* géologique
•**geologist** *n* géologue *mf*
geometry [dʒɪ'ɒmɪtrɪ] *n* géométrie *f*
•**geometric(al)** [dʒɪə'metrɪk(əl)] *adj* géométrique
geostationary [dʒɪəʊ'steɪʃənərɪ] *adj*
géostationnaire
geranium [dʒɪ'reɪnɪəm] *n* géranium *m*
geriatric [dʒerɪ'ætrɪk] *adj (hospital)* gé-
riatrique; **g. ward** service *m* de gériatrie
germ [dʒɜːm] *n (causing disease)* microbe *m*; *(seed of plant, idea)* germe *m*; **g.
warfare** guerre *f* bactériologique
German ['dʒɜːmən] **1** *adj* allemand; **G.
teacher** professeur *m* d'allemand; **G.
measles** rubéole *f*; **G. shepherd** berger *m*
allemand
2 *n (person)* Allemand, -ande *mf*; *(lan-*

guage) allemand *m* • **Germanic** [-'mænɪk]
adj germanique
Germany ['dʒɜːmənɪ] *n* l'Allemagne *f*
germinate ['dʒɜːmɪneɪt] *vi (of seed, idea)*
germer
gerund ['dʒerənd] *n Grammar* gérondif
m
gestation [dʒe'steɪʃən] *n* gestation *f*
gesticulate [dʒe'stɪkjʊleɪt] *vi* gesticuler
gesture ['dʒestʃə(r)] **1** *n* geste *m*
2 *vi* **to g. to sb to do sth** faire signe à qn
de faire qch
get [get] (*pt & Br pp* **got,** *Am pp* **gotten,**
pres p **getting**) **1** *vt (obtain)* obtenir, avoir;
(find) trouver; *(buy)* acheter; *(receive)*
recevoir; *(catch)* attraper; *(bus, train)*
prendre; *(seize)* prendre, saisir; *(fetch)*
aller chercher; *(put)* mettre; *(derive)* tirer
(**from** de); *(prepare)* préparer; *(lead)* mener; *(hit with fist, stick)* atteindre; *(reputation)* se faire; *Fam (understand)* piger;
Fam (annoy) énerver; **to g. sb to do sth**
faire faire qch à qn; **to g. sth done** faire
faire qch; **to g. sth built** faire construire
qch; **to g. things started** faire démarrer
les choses; **to g. sth clean/dirty** nettoyer/
salir qch; **to g. sth to sb** *(send)* faire
parvenir qch à qn; **to g. sb to the station**
amener qn à la gare; **can I g. you anything?** je te rapporte quelque chose?;
what's that got to do with it? qu'est-ce
que ça a à voir?
2 *vi (go)* aller (**to** à); *(arrive)* arriver (**to**
à); *(become)* devenir; **to g. old** vieillir; **to
g. better** s'améliorer; **to g. caught/run
over** se faire prendre/écraser; **to g. married** se marier; **to g. dressed/washed**
s'habiller/se laver; **to g. paid** être payé;
to g. killed se faire tuer; **where have you
got** *or Am* **gotten to?** où en es-tu?; **you've
got to stay** *(must)* tu dois rester; **to g. to
do sth** *(succeed in doing)* parvenir à faire
qch; **I'm getting to understand** *(starting)*
je commence à comprendre; **to g. going**
(leave) se mettre en route; *(start)* se mettre au travail • **getaway** *n (escape)* fuite *f*
•**get-together** *n Fam* réunion *f* •**get-up** *n
Fam (clothes)* accoutrement *m*
▸**get about, get around** *vi* se déplacer;
(of news) circuler ▸**get across 1** *vt sep
(message)* faire passer; **to g. sb across**
faire traverser qn **2** *vi (cross)* traverser; *(of speaker)* se faire comprendre (**to** de); **to g.
across to sb that...** faire comprendre à qn
que... ▸**get along** *vi (manage)* se débrouiller; *(progress)* avancer; *(be on good
terms)* s'entendre (**with** avec); *(leave)* s'en
aller ▸**get at** *vt insep (reach)* atteindre;

Fam (taunt) s'en prendre à; **what is he getting at?** où veut-il en venir? ▸ **get away** *vi (leave)* s'en aller; *(escape)* se sauver; **to g. away with a fine** s'en tirer avec une amende; **he got away with that crime** il n'a pas été inquiété pour ce crime; **there's no getting away from it** c'est comme ça ▸ **get back 1** *vt sep (recover)* récupérer **2** *vi (return)* revenir; **to g. back at sb, to g. one's own back on sb** *(punish)* se venger de qn ▸ **get by** *vi (manage)* se débrouiller ▸ **get down 1** *vi (go down)* descendre (**from** de); **to g. down to** *(work)* se mettre à **2** *vt sep (bring down)* descendre (**from** de); *Fam* **to g. sb down** *(depress)* déprimer qn **3** *vt insep* **to g. down the stairs/a ladder** descendre l'escalier/d'une échelle ▸ **get in 1** *vt sep (stock up with)* faire provision de; **to g. sb in** *(call for)* faire venir qn **2** *vi (enter)* entrer; *(come home)* rentrer; *(enter vehicle or train)* monter; *(arrive)* arriver; *(be elected)* être élu ▸ **get into** *vt insep* entrer dans; *(vehicle, train)* monter dans; *(habit)* prendre; **to g. into bed/a rage** se mettre au lit/en colère ▸ **get off 1** *vt sep (remove)* enlever; *(send)* expédier; *(in court)* faire acquitter; *Fam* **to g. off doing sth** se dispenser de faire qch **2** *vt insep* **to g. off a chair** se lever d'une chaise; **to g. off a bus** descendre d'un bus **3** *vi (leave)* partir; *(from vehicle or train)* descendre (**from** de); *(escape)* s'en tirer ▸ **get on 1** *vt sep (shoes, clothes)* mettre **2** *vt insep (bus, train)* monter dans **3** *vi (enter bus or train)* monter; *(manage)* se débrouiller; *(succeed)* réussir; *(be on good terms)* s'entendre (**with** avec); **how are you getting on?** comment ça va?; **how did you g.** *(in exam)* comment ça s'est passé?; **to be getting on (in years)** se faire vieux (*f* vieille); **to g. onto sb** *(on phone)* contacter qn; **to g. on with** *(task)* continuer ▸ **get out 1** *vt sep (remove)* enlever; *(bring out)* sortir **2** *vi* sortir; *(from vehicle or train)* descendre (**of** *or* **from** de); **to g. out of** *(obligation)* échapper à; *(danger)* se tirer de; *(habit)* perdre ▸ **get over 1** *vt sep (ideas)* faire passer; **let's g. it over with** finissons-en **2** *vt insep (illness)* se remettre de; *(shock)* revenir de ▸ **get round 1** *vt insep (obstacle)* contourner **2** *vi (visit)* passer; **to g. round to doing sth** trouver le temps de faire qch ▸ **get through 1** *vt sep (communicate)* **to g. sth through to sb** faire comprendre qch à qn **2** *vt insep (hole)* passer par; *(task)* venir à bout de; *(exam, interview)* survivre à; *(food)*

consommer **3** *vi (pass)* passer; *(finish)* finir; *(pass exam)* être reçu; **to g. through to sb** *(communicate with)* se faire comprendre de qn; *(on the phone)* obtenir la communication avec qn ▸ **get together** *vi (of people)* se réunir ▸ **get up 1** *vt sep* **to g. sb up** *(out of bed)* faire lever qn; **to g. sth up** *(bring up)* monter qch **2** *vt insep (ladder, stairs)* monter **3** *vi (rise, stand up)* se lever (**from** de); **to g. up to something** *or* **to mischief** faire des bêtises; **where have you got up to?** *(in book)* où en es-tu?

geyser ['gi:zə(r)] *n* (**a**) *Br (water heater)* chauffe-eau *m inv* (**b**) *(spring)* geyser *m*

Ghana ['gɑːnə] *n* le Ghana

ghastly ['gɑːstlɪ] (**-ier, -iest**) *adj (horrible)* épouvantable; *(pale)* blême

gherkin ['gɜːkɪn] *n* cornichon *m*

ghetto ['getəʊ] *(pl* **-oes** *or* **-os***) n* ghetto *m*; *Fam* **g. blaster** radiocassette *m*

ghost [gəʊst] *n* fantôme *m*; **not the g. of a chance** pas la moindre chance; **g. story** histoire *f* de fantômes; **g. ship** vaisseau *m* fantôme; **g. town** ville *f* fantôme ●**ghostly** *adj* spectral

giant ['dʒaɪənt] **1** *adj (tree, packet)* géant; *(struggle, efforts)* gigantesque; **with g. steps** à pas de géant
2 *n* géant *m*

gibberish ['dʒɪbərɪʃ] *n* baragouin *m*; **to talk g.** dire n'importe quoi

gibe [dʒaɪb] **1** *n* moquerie *f*
2 *vi* **to g. at sb** se moquer de qn

giblets ['dʒɪblɪts] *npl* abats *mpl*

giddy ['gɪdɪ] (**-ier, -iest**) *adj* **to be** *or* **feel g.** avoir le vertige; **to make sb g.** donner le vertige à qn ●**giddiness** *n* vertige *m*

gift [gɪft] *n* cadeau *m*; *(talent, donation)* don *m*; *Br* **g. voucher** *or* **token** chèque-cadeau *m* ●**gifted** *adj* doué (**with** de; **for** pour)

gift-wrapped ['gɪftræpt] *adj* sous paquet-cadeau

gig [gɪg] *n Fam (pop concert)* concert *m*

gigabyte ['dʒɪgəbaɪt] *n Comptr* gigaoctet *m*

gigantic [dʒaɪˈgæntɪk] *adj* gigantesque

giggle ['gɪgəl] **1** *n* petit rire *m* bête; **to have the giggles** avoir le fou rire
2 *vi* rire (bêtement)

gild [gɪld] *vt* dorer ●**gilt 1** *adj* doré **2** *n* dorure *f*

gills [gɪlz] *npl (of fish)* ouïes *fpl*

gimmick ['gɪmɪk] *n (trick, object)* truc *m*

gin [dʒɪn] *n (drink)* gin *m*

ginger ['dʒɪndʒə(r)] **1** *adj (hair)* roux (*f* rousse)

2 *n (plant, spice)* gingembre *m*; **g. beer** limonade *f* au gingembre • **gingerbread** *n* pain *m* d'épice

gingerly ['dʒɪndʒəlɪ] *adv* avec précaution

gipsy ['dʒɪpsɪ] (*pl* **-ies**) *n* bohémien, -ienne *mf*; *(Eastern European)* Tsigane *mf*; *(Spanish)* gitan, -ane *mf*

giraffe [dʒɪ'ræf, *Br* dʒɪ'rɑːf] *n* girafe *f*

girder ['ɡɜːdə(r)] *n (metal beam)* poutre *f*

girdle ['ɡɜːdəl] *n (corset)* gaine *f*

girl [ɡɜːl] *n (child)* (petite) fille *f*, fillette *f*; *(young woman)* jeune fille *f*; **English g.** jeune Anglaise *f*; **G. Guide** éclaireuse *f* • **girlfriend** *n (of girl)* amie *f*; *(of boy)* petite amie *f* • **girlish** *adj* de (jeune) fille

giro ['dʒaɪrəʊ] (*pl* **-os**) *n Br* **bank g.** virement *m* bancaire; **g. account** compte *m* courant postal, CCP *m*

girth [ɡɜːθ] *n (of tree)* circonférence *f*; *(of person)* corpulence *f*

gist [dʒɪst] *n* **to get the g. of sth** saisir l'essentiel de qch

give [ɡɪv] **1** *n (of fabric)* élasticité *f*

2 (*pt* **gave,** *pp* **given**) *vt* donner; *(as present)* offrir; *(support)* apporter; *(smile, gesture, pleasure)* faire; *(sigh)* pousser; *(look)* jeter; *(blow)* porter; **to g. sth to sb, to g. sb sth** donner/offrir qch à qn; *Fam* **she doesn't g. a damn** elle s'en fiche pas mal; **to g. way** *(of branch, person)* céder; *(of roof)* s'effondrer; *(in vehicle)* céder la priorité (**to** à)

3 *vi* (**a**) *(donate)* donner

(**b**) *(of shoes)* se faire; *(of support)* céder

▸ **give away** *vt sep (prize)* distribuer; *(money)* donner; *(betray)* trahir ▸ **give back** *vt sep (return)* rendre ▸ **give in 1** *vt sep (hand in)* remettre **2** *vi (surrender)* céder (**to** à) ▸ **give off** *vt sep (smell, heat)* dégager ▸ **give onto** *vt insep* donner sur ▸ **give out** *vt sep (hand out)* distribuer; *(make known)* annoncer ▸ **give over 1** *vt sep (devote)* consacrer (**to** à); **to g. one-self over to** *(despair, bad habit)* s'abandonner à **2** *vi Br Fam* **g. over!** arrête! ▸ **give up 1** *vt sep (possessions)* abandonner; *(activity)* renoncer à; *(seat)* céder (**to** à); **to g. up smoking** cesser de fumer **2** *vi* abandonner

given ['ɡɪvən] **1** *pp of* **give**

2 *adj (fixed)* donné; **at a g. time** à un moment donné; **to be g. to doing sth** avoir tendance à faire qch

3 *conj (considering)* étant donné; **g. that...** étant donné que...

glacier [*Br* 'ɡlæsɪə(r), *Am* 'ɡleɪʃər] *n* glacier *m*

glad [ɡlæd] *adj (person)* content (**of/ about** de; **that** que + *subjunctive*); **I'm g. to know/hear that...** je suis content de savoir/d'apprendre que...; **I would be g. to help you** je serais ravi de vous aider • **gladden** *vt* réjouir • **gladly** *adv* volontiers

glade [ɡleɪd] *n Literary* clairière *f*

gladiolus [ɡlædɪ'əʊləs] (*pl* **-li** [-laɪ]) *n* glaïeul *m*

glamour ['ɡlæmə(r)] (*Am* **glamor**) *n (of person)* séduction *f*; *(of career)* prestige *m* • **glamorize** *vt* rendre séduisant • **glamorous** *adj (person, dress)* élégant; *(job)* prestigieux, -ieuse

glance [ɡlɑːns] **1** *n* coup *m* d'œil

2 *vi* **to g. at sb/sth** jeter un coup d'œil à qn/qch; **to g. off sth** *(of bullet)* ricocher sur qch

gland [ɡlænd] *n* glande *f* • **glandular** 'fever *n Br* mononucléose *f* infectieuse

glare [ɡleə(r)] **1** *n (of sun)* éclat *m* aveuglant; *(look)* regard *m* furieux

2 *vi (of sun)* briller d'un éclat aveuglant; **to g. at sb** foudroyer qn (du regard) • **glaring** *adj (light)* éblouissant; *(sun)* aveuglant; *(eyes)* furieux, -ieuse; **a g. mistake** une faute grossière

glass [ɡlɑːs] **1** *n* verre *m*

2 *adj (bottle)* de verre; **g. door** porte *f* vitrée; **g. wool** laine *f* de verre • **glassful** *n* (plein) verre *m* • **glassware** *n* verrerie *f*

glasses ['ɡlɑːsɪz] *npl (spectacles)* lunettes *fpl*

glaze [ɡleɪz] **1** *n (on pottery)* vernis *m*

2 *vt (window)* vitrer; *(pottery)* vernisser • **glazier** *n* vitrier *m*

gleam [ɡliːm] **1** *n* lueur *f*

2 *vi* luire

glean [ɡliːn] *vt (information, grain)* glaner

glee [ɡliː] *n* joie *f* • **gleeful** *adj* joyeux, -euse

glen [ɡlen] *n Scot* vallon *m*

glib [ɡlɪb] *adj (person, excuse)* désinvolte; *(reply)* spécieux, -ieuse

glide [ɡlaɪd] *vi* glisser; *(of aircraft, bird)* planer • **glider** *n (aircraft)* planeur *m* • **gliding** *n (sport)* vol *m* à voile

glimmer ['ɡlɪmə(r)] **1** *n (light, of hope)* faible lueur *f*

2 *vi* luire (faiblement)

glimpse [ɡlɪmps] **1** *n* aperçu *m*; **to catch** *or* **get a g. of sth** entrevoir qch

2 *vt* entrevoir

glint [ɡlɪnt] **1** *n* éclat *m*; *(in eye)* étincelle *f*

2 *vi (of light, eye)* briller

glisten ['ɡlɪsən] *vi (of wet surface)* briller; *(of water)* miroiter

glitch [glɪtʃ] *n Fam* problème *m* (technique)

glitter ['glɪtə(r)] **1** *n* scintillement *m*

2 *vi* scintiller • **glittering** *adj* scintillant; *(prize, career)* extraordinaire

gloat [gləʊt] *vi* jubiler (**over** à l'idée de)

global ['gləʊbəl] *adj (universal)* mondial; *(comprehensive)* global; **g. village** village *m* planétaire; **g. warming** réchauffement *m* de la planète

globe [gləʊb] *n* globe *m*

gloom [gluːm] *n (sadness)* morosité *f*; *(darkness)* obscurité *f* • **gloomy** (**-ier, -iest**) *adj (sad)* morose; *(dark, dismal)* sombre

glorify ['glɔːrɪfaɪ] (*pt & pp* **-ied**) *vt (praise)* glorifier; *Br* **it's a glorified barn** ce n'est guère plus qu'une grange

glorious ['glɔːrɪəs] *adj (splendid)* magnifique; *(full of glory)* glorieux, -ieuse

glory ['glɔːrɪ] **1** *n* gloire *f*; *(great beauty)* splendeur *f*

2 *vi* **to g. in sth** se glorifier de qch

gloss [glɒs] **1** *n (shine)* lustre *m*; **g. paint** peinture *f* brillante; **g. finish** brillant *m*

2 *vt* **to g. over sth** glisser sur qch • **glossy** (**-ier, -iest**) *adj* brillant; *(photo)* glacé; *(magazine)* de luxe

glossary ['glɒsərɪ] (*pl* **-ies**) *n* glossaire *m*

glove [glʌv] *n* gant *m*; **g. compartment** *(in car)* boîte *f* à gants

glow [gləʊ] **1** *n (light)* lueur *f*; *(on cheeks)* couleurs *fpl*

2 *vi (of sky, fire, embers)* rougeoyer; *Fig (of eyes, person)* rayonner (**with** de) • **glowing** *adj (account, terms, reference)* enthousiaste • **glow-worm** *n* ver *m* luisant

glucose ['gluːkəʊs] *n* glucose *m*

glue [gluː] **1** *n* colle *f*

2 *vt* coller (**to/on** à); *Fam* **to be glued to the television** être cloué devant la télévision • **glue-sniffing** *n* inhalation *f* de colle

glum [glʌm] (**glummer, glummest**) *adj* triste

glut [glʌt] **1** *n (of goods)* surplus *m* (**of** de)

2 *vt* **the market is glutted** le marché est saturé (**with** de)

glutton ['glʌtən] *n* goinfre *mf*; **g. for punishment** masochiste *mf* • **gluttony** *n* goinfrerie *f*

glycerin ['glɪsərɪn], **glycerine** ['glɪsəriːn] *n* glycérine *f*

GM [dʒiː'em] *abbr* = **genetically modified**

GMO [dʒiːem'əʊ] (*abbr* **genetically modified organism**) *n* OGM *m*

GMT [dʒiːem'tiː] (*abbr* **Greenwich Mean Time**) *n* GMT *m*

gnarled [nɑːld] *adj* noueux, -euse

gnash [næʃ] *vt* **to g. one's teeth** grincer des dents

gnat [næt] *n* moucheron *m*

gnaw [nɔː] *vti* **to g. (at) sth** ronger qch

gnome [nəʊm] *n* gnome *m*

GNP [dʒiːen'piː] (*abbr* **gross national product**) *n Econ* PNB *m*

go [gəʊ] **1** (*pl* **goes**) *n (turn)* tour *m*; **to have a go at (doing) sth** essayer (de faire) qch; **at one go** d'un seul coup; **on the go** en mouvement; **to make a go of sth** réussir qch

2 (*3rd person sing present tense* **goes**; *pt* **went**; *pp* **gone**; *pres p* **going**) *vt (make sound)* faire; **cows go moo** les vaches font meuh; **to go it alone** se lancer en solo

3 *vi* aller (**to** à; **from** de); *(depart)* partir, s'en aller; *(disappear)* disparaître; *(be sold)* se vendre; *(function)* marcher; *(progress)* aller; *(become)* devenir; *(of time)* passer; *(of hearing, strength)* baisser; *(of fuse)* sauter; *(of light bulb)* griller; *(of material)* s'user; *(of rope)* céder; **to go well/badly** *(of event)* se passer bien/ mal; **she's going to do sth** *(is about to, intends to)* elle va faire qch; **it's going to rain** il va pleuvoir; **it's all gone** *(finished)* il n'y en a plus; **to go and get sb/sth** *(fetch)* aller chercher qn/qch; **to go and see** aller voir; **to go riding/on a trip** faire du cheval/un voyage; **to let go of sth** lâcher qch; **to go to a doctor/lawyer** aller voir un médecin/un avocat; **to get things going** faire démarrer les choses; **let's get going** allons-y; **is there any beer going?** y a-t-il de la bière?; **it goes to show that** ça montre que; **two hours to go** encore deux heures

▸ **go about, go around** *vi (of person)* se promener; *(of rumour)* circuler ▸ **go about** *vt insep (task)* vaquer à; **to go about doing sth** s'y prendre pour faire qch ▸ **go across 1** *vt insep* traverser **2** *vi (cross)* traverser; *(go)* aller (**to** à); **to go across to sb('s)** faire un saut chez qn ▸ **go after** *vt insep (chase)* poursuivre; *(seek)* rechercher; *(job)* essayer d'obtenir ▸ **go against** *vt insep (contradict)* aller à l'encontre de; *(be unfavourable to)* être défavorable à ▸ **go ahead** *vi (take place)* avoir lieu; *(go in front)* passer devant; **to go ahead of sb** devancer qn; **to go ahead with sth** entreprendre qch; **go ahead!** allez-y! ▸ **go along** *vi (proceed)* se dérouler; **to go along with sb/sth** être d'accord avec qn/qch; **we'll see as we go along** nous verrons au fur et à mesure; ▸**go away** *vi* partir, s'en aller ▸**go back** *vi* (*return*) revenir; (*step back, retreat*) reculer; **to go back to sleep** se rendormir; **to go back to doing sth** se remettre à faire qch; **to go back to** (*in time*) remonter à; **to go back on one's promise** *or* **word** revenir sur sa promesse ▸**go by 1** *vt insep* (*act according to*) se fonder sur; (*judge from*) juger d'après; **to go by the rules** respecter les règles; **to go by the name of...** être connu sous le nom de... **2** *vi* passer ▸**go down 1** *vt insep* (*stairs, street*) descendre **2** *vi* descendre; (*fall down*) tomber; (*of ship*) sombrer; (*of sun*) se coucher; (*of temperature, price*) baisser; (*of tyre, balloon*) se dégonfler; **to go down well/ badly** être bien/mal reçu; **he has gone down in history as a tyrant** l'histoire a retenu de lui l'image d'un tyran ▸**go for** *vt insep* (*fetch*) aller chercher; (*attack*) attaquer; *Fam* (*like*) avoir un faible pour; **the same goes for you** ça vaut aussi pour toi ▸**go forward(s)** *vi* avancer ▸**go in** *vi* (r)entrer; (*of sun*) se cacher; *Br* **to go in for** (*exam*) s'inscrire à; **she doesn't go in for cooking** elle n'est pas très portée sur la cuisine ▸**go into** *vt insep* (*enter*) entrer dans; (*examine*) examiner ▸**go off 1** *vt insep* (*lose liking for*) se lasser de **2** *vi* (*leave*) partir; (*go bad*) se gâter; (*of alarm*) se déclencher; (*of bomb*) exploser; **the gun went off** le coup est parti; **the light went off** la lumière s'est éteinte ▸**go on** *vi* continuer (**doing** à faire); (*travel*) poursuivre sa route; (*happen*) se passer; (*last*) durer; **as time went on** avec le temps; **to go on to sth** passer à qch; *Fam* **to go on at sb** (*nag*) s'en prendre à qn; *Fam* **to go on about sb/sth** parler sans cesse de qn/qch ▸**go out** *vi* sortir; (*of light, fire*) s'éteindre; (*of tide*) descendre; (*depart*) partir; (*date*) sortir ensemble; **to go out for a meal** aller au restaurant; **to go out with sb** sortir avec qn; **to go out to work** travailler (hors de chez soi) ▸**go over** *vt insep* (**a**) (*cross over*) traverser; **the ball went over the wall** la balle est passée par-dessus le mur (**b**) (*examine*) passer en revue; (*speech*) revoir; **to go over sth in one's mind** repasser qch dans son esprit **2** *vi* (*go*) aller (**to** à); (*to enemy*) passer (**to** à); **to go over to sb** aller vers qn; (*visit*) faire un saut chez qn ▸**go round 1** *vt insep* **to go round a corner** tourner au coin; **to go round the shops** faire les magasins; **to go round the world** faire le tour du monde **2** *vi* (*turn*) tourner; (*make a detour*) faire le tour; (*of rumour*) circuler; **to go round to sb's** faire un saut chez qn; **there is enough to go round** il y en a assez pour tout le monde ▸**go through 1** *vt insep* (*suffer, undergo*) subir; (*examine*) passer en revue; (*search*) fouiller; (*spend*) dépenser; (*wear out*) user; (*perform*) accomplir; **we've gone through six bottles of wine** nous avons bu six bouteilles de vin; **to go through with sth** aller jusqu'au bout de qch **2** *vi* passer; (*of deal*) être conclu ▸**go under** *vi* (*of ship*) couler; *Fig* (*of firm*) faire faillite ▸**go up 1** *vt insep* monter **2** *vi* monter; (*explode*) sauter; **to go up in sb's estimation** monter dans l'estime de qn; **to go up to sth** (*approach*) se diriger vers qch; (*reach*) aller jusqu'à qch ▸**go with** *vt insep* aller de pair avec; **the company car goes with the job** le poste donne droit à une voiture de fonction ▸**go without** *vt insep* se passer de

goad [gəʊd] *vt* **to g. sb (on)** aiguillonner

go-ahead ['gəʊəhed] **1** *adj* dynamique **2** *n* **to get the g.** avoir le feu vert; **to give sb the g.** donner le feu vert à qn

goal [gəʊl] *n* but *m*; **to score a g.** marquer un but •**goalie** *n* *Br* *Fam* *Sport* goal *m* •**goalkeeper** *n* *Sport* gardien *m* de but, goal *m* •**goalpost** *n* poteau *m* de but

goat [gəʊt] *n* chèvre *f*; *Fam* **to get sb's g.** énerver qn

goatee [gəʊ'tiː] *n* barbiche *f*

gobble ['gɒbəl] *vt* **to g. (up** *or* **down)** (*food*) engloutir

go-between ['gəʊbɪtwiːn] *n* intermédiaire *mf*

goblet ['gɒblɪt] *n* verre *m* à pied

goblin ['gɒblɪn] *n* lutin *m*

god [gɒd] *n* dieu *m*; **G.** Dieu; *Fam* **oh G.!, my G.!** mon Dieu!; *Fam* **thank G.!** heureusement!; *Fam* **for G.'s sake!** pour l'amour de Dieu!; *Fam* **the gods** (*in theatre*) le poulailler •**godchild** (*pl* -**children**) *n* filleul, -eule *mf* •**goddaughter** *n* filleule *f* •**godfather** *n* parrain *m* •**godfearing** *adj* croyant •**godforsaken** *adj* (*place*) perdu •**godmother** *n* marraine *f* •**godson** *n* filleul *m*

goddam(n) ['gɒdæm] *adj* *Am* *Fam* foutu

goddess ['gɒdɪs] *n* déesse *f*

godsend ['gɒdsend] *n* **to be a g.** être un don du ciel

goes [gəʊz] *3rd person sing present tense & npl of* **go**

goggle ['gɒgəl] *vi* **to g. at sb/sth** regarder qn/qch avec des yeux ronds •**gog-**

gles *npl* lunettes *fpl (de protection, de plongée)* •**'goggle-'eyed** *adj Fam* **to be g.** avoir les yeux ronds

going ['gəʊɪŋ] **1** *n (condition of ground)* terrain *m*; **it's hard** *or* **heavy g.** c'est difficile; **it's slow g.** *(at work)* ça n'avance pas vite
2 *adj* **the g. price** le prix pratiqué (**for** pour); **the g. rate** le tarif en vigueur; **the g. salary** le salaire habituel; **a g. concern** une affaire qui tourne •**goings-'on** *npl Pej* activités *fpl*

go-kart ['gəʊkɑːt] *n (for racing)* kart *m*

gold [gəʊld] **1** *n or m*
2 *adj (watch)* en or; *(coin, dust)* d'or; *Sport* **g. medal** médaille *f* d'or •**golden** *adj (of gold colour)* doré; **g. rule** règle *f* d'or; **it's a g. opportunity** c'est une occasion en or •**goldmine** *n* mine *f* d'or •**'gold-'plated** *adj* plaqué or •**goldsmith** *n* orfèvre *m*

goldfinch ['gəʊldfɪntʃ] *n* chardonneret *m*

goldfish ['gəʊldfɪʃ] *n* poisson *m* rouge

golf [gɒlf] *n* golf *m*; **g. club** *(stick, association)* club *m* de golf; **g. course** parcours *m* de golf •**golfer** *n* golfeur, -euse *mf* •**golfing** *n* **to go g.** faire du golf

gondola ['gɒndələ] *n (boat)* gondole *f* •**gondolier** [-'lɪə(r)] *n* gondolier *m*

gone [gɒn] **1** *pp of* **go**
2 *adj Br Fam* **it's g. two** il est plus de deux heures •**goner** *n Fam* **to be a g.** être fichu

gong [gɒŋ] *n* gong *m*

goo [guː] *n Fam* truc *m* visqueux

good [gʊd] **1** (**better, best**) *adj* bon *(f* bonne); *(kind)* gentil, -ille; *(well-behaved)* sage; **my g. friend** mon cher ami; **a g. fellow** un brave type; **g.!** bon!, bien!; **very g.!** *(all right)* très bien!; **that isn't g. enough** *(bad)* ça ne va pas; *(not sufficient)* ça ne suffit pas; **would you be g. enough to...?** auriez-vous la gentillesse de...?; **that's g. of you** c'est gentil de ta part; **it's g. for us** ça nous fait du bien; **to taste g.** avoir bon goût; **to feel g.** se sentir bien; **to have g. weather** avoir beau temps; **to be g. at French** être bon en français; **to be g. at swimming/telling jokes** savoir bien nager/raconter des blagues; **to be g. with children** savoir s'y prendre avec les enfants; **it's a g. thing (that)** heureusement que; **a g. many, a g. deal (of)** beaucoup (de); **as g. as** *(almost)* pratiquement; **g. afternoon, g. morning** bonjour; *(on leaving someone)* au revoir; **g. evening** bonsoir; **g. night** bonsoir; *(before going to bed)* bonne nuit

2 *n (advantage, virtue)* bien *m*; **for her (own) g.** pour son bien; **for the g. of your family/career** pour ta famille/carrière; **it will do you (some) g.** ça te fera du bien; **it's no g. crying/shouting** ça ne sert à rien de pleurer/crier; **that's no g.** *(worthless)* ça ne vaut rien; *(bad)* ça ne va pas; **what's the g. of crying?** à quoi bon pleurer?; **for g.** *(leave, give up)* pour de bon •**good-for-'nothing** *n* propre-à-rien *mf* •**'good-'humoured** *(Am* **-humored**) *adj* détendu •**'good-'looking** *adj* beau *(f* belle) •**'good-'natured** *adj (person)* d'un caractère agréable

goodbye [gʊd'baɪ] *exclam & n* au revoir *(m inv)*

goodness ['gʊdnɪs] *n* bonté *f*; **my g.!** mon Dieu!

goods [gʊdz] *npl* marchandises *fpl*; **g. train** train *m* de marchandises

goodwill [gʊd'wɪl] *n (willingness)* bonne volonté *f*; *(benevolence)* bienveillance *f*

gooey ['guːɪ] *adj Fam* gluant

goof [guːf] *vi Am Fam* **to g. (up)** faire une gaffe

goon [guːn] *n Br Fam* idiot, -iote *mf*

goose [guːs] *(pl* **geese**) *n* oie *f*; **g.** *Br* **pimples** *or Am* **bumps** chair *f* de poule •**gooseflesh** *n* chair *f* de poule

gooseberry ['gʊzbərɪ] *(pl* **-ies**) *n* groseille *f* à maquereau

gorge [gɔːdʒ] **1** *n (ravine)* gorge *f*
2 *vt* **to g. oneself** se gaver (**on** de)

gorgeous ['gɔːdʒəs] *adj* magnifique

gorilla [gə'rɪlə] *n* gorille *m*

gormless ['gɔːmləs] *adj Br Fam* balourd

gorse [gɔːs] *n inv* ajoncs *mpl*

gory ['gɔːrɪ] (**-ier, -iest**) *adj (bloody)* sanglant; *Fig (details)* horrible

gosh [gɒʃ] *exclam Fam* mince (alors)!

gosling ['gɒzlɪŋ] *n* oison *m*

go-slow [gəʊ'sləʊ] *n Br (strike)* grève *f* du zèle

gospel ['gɒspəl] *n* évangile *m*

gossip ['gɒsɪp] **1** *n (talk)* bavardages *mpl*; *(malicious)* cancans *mpl*; *(person)* commère *f*; **g. column** *(in newspaper)* échos *mpl*
2 *vi* bavarder; *(maliciously)* colporter des commérages •**gossiping, gossipy** *adj* bavard; *(maliciously)* cancanier, -ière

got [gɒt] *pt & Br pp of* **get**

Gothic ['gɒθɪk] *adj & n* gothique *(m)*

gotten ['gɒtən] *Am pp of* **get**

gouge [gaʊdʒ] *vt* **to g. sb's eye out** arracher l'œil à qn

goulash ['guːlæʃ] *n* goulache *m*

gourmet ['gʊəmeɪ] *n* gourmet *m*; **g. restaurant** restaurant *m* gastronomique

gout [gaʊt] *n (illness)* goutte *f*

govern ['gʌvən] **1** *vt (rule)* gouverner; *(city, province)* administrer; *(emotion)* maîtriser; *(influence)* déterminer
2 *vi (rule)* gouverner; **governing body** conseil *m* d'administration

governess ['gʌvənɪs] *n* gouvernante *f*

government ['gʌvənmənt] **1** *n* gouvernement *m*; **local g.** administration *f* locale
2 *adj (decision, policy)* gouvernemental; **g. loan** emprunt *m* d'État • **governmental** [-'mentəl] *adj* gouvernemental

governor ['gʌvənə(r)] *n* gouverneur *m*; *(of school)* administrateur, -trice *mf*; *(of prison)* directeur, -trice *mf*

gown [gaʊn] *n (of woman)* robe *f*; *Br (of judge, lecturer)* toge *f*

GP [dʒiː'piː] *(abbr* **general practitioner***) n* généraliste *mf*

grab [græb] *(pt & pp* **-bb-***) vt* **to g. (hold of) sb/sth** saisir qn/qch; **to g. sth from sb** arracher qch à qn; **I'll g. a sandwich later** j'avalerai un sandwich plus tard

grace [greɪs] **1** *n (charm, goodwill, religious mercy)* grâce *f*; *Rel* **to say g.** dire le bénédicité; **to be in sb's good graces** être dans les bonnes grâces de qn; **g. (period)** *(extension)* délai *m* de grâce; **ten days' g.** dix jours de grâce
2 *vt (adorn)* orner; *(honour)* honorer (**with** de) • **graceful** *adj (movement, person)* gracieux, -ieuse • **gracefully** *adv* avec grâce

gracious ['greɪʃəs] *adj (kind)* aimable (**to** envers); *(elegant)* élégant; *Fam* **good g.!** bonté divine! • **graciously** *adv (accept)* de bonne grâce

gradation [*Br* grə'deɪʃən, *Am* greɪ-'deɪʃən] *n* gradation *f*

grade [greɪd] **1** *n* (**a**) *(rank)* grade *m*; *(in profession)* échelon *m*; *(quality)* qualité *f*; *(of eggs, fruit)* calibre *m*; *Am* **g. crossing** passage *m* à niveau (**b**) *Am Sch (mark)* note *f*; *(year)* classe *f*; *Am* **g. school** école *f* primaire
2 *vt (classify)* classer; *Am (exam)* noter

gradient ['greɪdɪənt] *n (slope)* dénivellation *f*

gradual ['grædʒʊəl] *adj* progressif, -ive; *(slope)* doux (*f* douce) • **gradually** *adv* progressivement

graduate¹ 1 ['grædʒʊət] *n Br (from university)* ≃ licencié, -iée *mf*; *Am (from high school)* ≃ bachelier, -ière *mf*; *Am Univ* **g. studies** études *fpl* de troisième cycle

2 ['grædʒʊeɪt] *vi Br (from university)* ≃ obtenir sa licence; *Am (from high school)* ≃ obtenir son baccalauréat; **to g. from sth to sth** passer de qch à qch • **graduation** [-'eɪʃən] *n Univ* remise *f* des diplômes

graduate² ['grædʒʊeɪt] *vt (mark with degrees)* graduer • **graduated** *adj (tube, thermometer)* gradué

graffiti [grə'fiːtɪ] *npl* graffiti *mpl*

graft¹ [grɑːft] **1** *n (technique)* greffe *f*; *(thing grafted)* greffon *m*
2 *vt* greffer (**on to** à)

graft² [grɑːft] *n* (**a**) *Am Fam (bribe)* pot-de-vin *m* (**b**) *Br Fam* **hard g.** boulot *m*

grain [greɪn] *n* (**a**) *(seed, particle)* grain *m*; *(cereals)* céréales *fpl*; *Fig* **a g. of truth** une once de vérité (**b**) *(in wood, leather, paper)* grain *m*; *(in cloth)* fil *m*

gram [græm] *n* gramme *m*

grammar ['græmə(r)] *n* grammaire *f*; **g. (book)** grammaire *f*; **g. school** *Br* ≃ lycée *m*, *Am* ≃ école *f* primaire • **grammatical** [grə'mætɪkəl] *adj* grammatical

gramme [græm] *n* gramme *m*

gramophone ['græməfəʊn] *n* phonographe *m*

gran [græn] *n Fam* mamie *f*

granary ['grænərɪ] *(pl* **-ies***) n* grenier *m*; *Br* **g. bread** = pain complet

grand [grænd] **1** (**-er, -est***) adj (splendid)* grandiose; *Fam (excellent)* excellent; **with a g. gesture** d'un geste majestueux; **she went on a g. tour of Italy** elle a visité toute l'Italie; **g. duke** grand-duc *m*; **g. piano** piano *m* à queue; **g. total** somme *f* totale
2 *n inv Br Fam* mille livres *fpl*; *Am Fam* mille dollars *mpl* • **grandchild** *(pl* **-children***) n* petit-fils *m*, petite-fille *f*; **grandchildren** petits-enfants *mpl* • **grand(d)ad** *n Fam* papi *m* • **granddaughter** *n* petite-fille *f* • **grandfather** *n* grand-père *m* • **grandma** [-mɑː] *n Fam* mamie *f* • **grandmother** *n* grand-mère *f* • **grandpa** [-pɑː] *n Fam* papi *m* • **grandparents** *npl* grands-parents *mpl* • **grandson** *n* petit-fils *m*

grandeur ['grændʒə(r)] *n* grandeur *f*; *(of person, country)* magnificence *f*

grandstand ['grændstænd] *n* tribune *f*

granite ['grænɪt] *n* granit *m*

granny ['grænɪ] *(pl* **-ies***) n Fam* mamie *f*

grant [grɑːnt] **1** *n* subvention *f*; *(for student)* bourse *f*
2 *vt* accorder (**to** à); *(request)* accéder à; *(prayer, wish)* exaucer; *(admit)* admettre (**that** que); **to take sth for granted** considérer qch comme allant de soi; **to take sb**

for granted considérer qn comme faisant partie du décor; **I take it for granted that** je présume que

granule ['grænju:l] *n* granule *m* •**granulated sugar** [grænjʊleɪtɪd'ʃʊɡə(r)] *n* sucre *m* semoule

grape [greɪp] *n* grain *m* de raisin; **some grapes** du raisin; **to eat (some) grapes** manger du raisin; **g. harvest** vendange *f*; **g. juice** jus *m* de raisin

> *Note that the French word **grappe** is a false friend. It means **bunch** or **cluster**.*

grapefruit ['greɪpfru:t] *n* pamplemousse *m*
grapevine ['greɪpvaɪn] *n* *Fig* **on** or **through the g.** par le téléphone arabe
graph [græf, grɑ:f] *n* graphique *m*; **g. paper** papier *m* millimétré
graphic ['græfɪk] *adj* (*description*) très détaillé; (*language*) cru; **in g. detail** de façon très détaillée; **g. artist** graphiste *mf*; **g. arts** arts *mpl* graphiques •**graphically** *adv* (*describe*) de façon très détaillée •**graphics** *npl* (*computer*) **g.** graphiques *mpl*
grapple ['græpəl] *vi* (*with problem*) se débattre (**with** avec)
grasp [grɑ:sp] **1** *n* (*hold*) prise *f*; (*understanding*) compréhension *f*; **within sb's g.** à la portée de qn
    2 *vt* (*seize, understand*) saisir •**grasping** *adj* (*mean*) avide
grass [grɑ:s] **1** *n* herbe *f*; (*lawn*) gazon *m*; *Fig* **the g. roots** (*of organization*) la base
    2 *vt Fam* **to g. on sb** balancer qn •**grasshopper** *n* sauterelle *f* •**grassland** *n* prairie *f* •**grassy** *adj* herbeux, -euse
grate [greɪt] **1** *n* (*for fireplace*) grille *f*
    2 *vt* (*cheese, carrot*) râper
    3 *vi* (*of sound*) grincer; **to g. on the ears** écorcher les oreilles; **to g. on sb's nerves** taper sur les nerfs de qn •**grater** *n* râpe *f* •**grating 1** *adj* (*sound*) grinçant; (*voice*) éraillé **2** *n* (*bars*) grille *f*
grateful ['greɪtfəl] *adj* reconnaissant (**to** à; **for** de); (*words, letter*) de remerciement; **I would be g. if you could let me know** je vous serais reconnaissant de m'en informer •**gratefully** *adv* avec reconnaissance
gratify ['grætɪfaɪ] (*pt & pp* **-ied**) *vt* (*whim*) satisfaire; **to g. sb** faire plaisir à qn •**grati'fication** *n* satisfaction *f* •**gratified** *adj* (*pleased*) satisfait (**by** or **with** de; **to do** de faire) •**gratifying** *adj* très satisfaisant
gratis ['grætɪs, 'greɪtɪs] *adv* gratis
gratitude ['grætɪtju:d] *n* gratitude *f* (**for** de)

gratuitous [grə'tju:ɪtəs] *adj* (*act*) gratuit
gratuity [grə'tju:ɪtɪ] (*pl* **-ies**) *n Formal* (*tip*) pourboire *m*

> *Note that the French word **gratuité** is a false friend and is never a translation for the English word **gratuity**. It indicates something that is free of charge.*

grave¹ [greɪv] *n* tombe *f* •**gravedigger** *n* fossoyeur *m* •**gravestone** *n* pierre *f* tombale •**graveyard** *n* cimetière *m*
grave² [greɪv] (**-er, -est**) *adj* (*serious*) grave; (*manner, voice*) solennel, -elle; **to make a g. mistake** se tromper lourdement •**gravely** *adv* gravement; **g. concerned** extrêmement inquiet, -iète
gravel ['grævəl] *n* gravier *m*; **g. path** allée *f* de gravier
gravitate ['grævɪteɪt] *vi* **to g. towards sth** (*be drawn to*) être attiré par qch; (*move towards*) se diriger vers qch •**gravitation** [-'teɪʃən] *n* gravitation *f*
gravity ['grævɪtɪ] *n* (**a**) *Phys* (*force*) pesanteur *f* (**b**) (*seriousness*) gravité *f*
gravy ['greɪvɪ] *n* = sauce à base de jus de viande
gray [greɪ] *adj, n & vi Am* = **grey**
graze¹ [greɪz] **1** *n* (*wound*) écorchure *f*
    2 *vt* (*scrape*) écorcher
graze² [greɪz] *vi* (*of cattle*) paître
grease [gri:s] **1** *n* graisse *f*
    2 *vt* graisser •**greaseproof 'paper** *n Br* papier *m* sulfurisé •**greasy** (**-ier, -iest**) *adj* graisseux, -euse; (*hair, skin, food*) gras (*f* grasse)
great [greɪt] (**-er, -est**) *adj* grand; (*effort, heat, parcel*) gros (*f* grosse); grand; *Fam* (*very good*) génial; **to reach a g. age** parvenir à un âge avancé; **to be g. at tennis** être très doué pour le tennis; **a g. deal** or **number (of), a g. many** beaucoup (de); **the greatest team** (*best*) la meilleure équipe; **Great Britain** la Grande-Bretagne; **Greater London** le grand Londres •**great-'grandfather** *n* arrière-grand-père *m* •**great-'grandmother** *n* arrière-grand-mère *f*
greatly ['greɪtlɪ] *adv* très; **you'll be g. missed** vous nous manquerez beaucoup
greatness ['greɪtnɪs] *n* (*in size, importance*) grandeur *f*; (*in degree*) intensité *f*
Greece [gri:s] *n* la Grèce
greed [gri:d] *n* avidité *f* (**for** de); (*for food*) gourmandise *f*
greedy ['gri:dɪ] (**-ier, -iest**) *adj* avide (**for** de); (*for food*) gourmand •**greedily** *adv* avidement; (*eat*) goulûment •**greediness** *n* = **greed**

Greek [griːk] **1** *adj* grec (*f* grecque)
2 *n* (*person*) Grec *m*, Grecque *f*; (*language*) grec *m*

green [griːn] **1** (**-er, -est**) *adj* vert; (*pale*) blême; *Fig* (*immature*) inexpérimenté; *Pol* écologiste; **to turn** *or* **go g.** (*of traffic lights*) passer au vert; (*of person, garden, tree*) verdir; *Fig* **to get the g. light** avoir le feu vert; *Fig* **to have g. fingers** *or Am* **a g. thumb** avoir la main verte; *Fig* **g. with envy** vert de jalousie; *Br* **the g. belt** la zone verte; *Am* **g. card** ≃ permis *m* de travail
2 *n* (*colour*) vert *m*; (*grassy area*) pelouse *f*; **greens** (*vegetables*) légumes *mpl* verts; *Pol* **the Greens** les Verts *mpl* •**greenery** *n* verdure *f* •**greenfly** (*pl* **-ies**) *n* puceron *m* •**greengage** *n* reine-claude *f* •**greengrocer** *n Br* marchand, -ande *mf* de fruits et légumes •**greenhouse** *n* serre *f*; **the g. effect** l'effet *m* de serre •**greenish** *adj* verdâtre

Greenland ['griːnlənd] *n* le Groenland

greet [griːt] *vt* (*say hello to*) saluer; (*welcome*) accueillir •**greeting** *n* accueil *m*; (*more formal*) salutation *f*; **greetings** (*for birthday, festival*) vœux *mpl*; **greetings card** carte *f* de vœux

gregarious [grɪˈɡeərɪəs] *adj* sociable; (*instinct, animal*) grégaire

gremlin ['ɡremlɪn] *n Fam* diablotin *m*

grenade [grəˈneɪd] *n* (*bomb*) grenade *f*

grew [gruː] *pt of* **grow**

grey [ɡreɪ] **1** *adj* (**-er, -est**) gris; *Fig* (*pale*) morne; **to be going g.** grisonner; **g. matter** matière *f* grise
2 *n* gris *m*
3 *vi* (*of hair*) grisonner •'**grey-**'**haired** *adj* aux cheveux gris •**greyhound** *n* lévrier *m* •**greyish** *adj* grisâtre

grid [ɡrɪd] *n* (*bars*) grille *f*; (*on map*) quadrillage *m*; *Br* **the** (**national**) **g.** le réseau électrique national

griddle ['ɡrɪdəl] *n* (*for cooking*) tôle *f*

gridlock ['ɡrɪdlɒk] *n* (*traffic jam*) embouteillage *m*

grief [griːf] *n* chagrin *m*; **to come to g.** échouer; *Fam* **good g.!** mon Dieu!

🖉 Note that the French word **grief** is a false friend and is never a translation for the English word **grief**. It means **grievance**.

---

grievance ['griːvəns] *n* grief *m*; **grievances** (*complaints*) doléances *fpl*; **to have a g. against sb** avoir à se plaindre de qn

grieve [griːv] **1** *vt* affliger
2 *vi* **to g. for sb/over sth** pleurer qn/qch

grievous ['griːvəs] *adj Formal* grave; *Br Law* **g. bodily harm** coups *mpl* et blessures *fpl*

grill [ɡrɪl] **1** *n* (*utensil*) gril *m*; (*dish*) grillade *f*
2 *vt* griller; *Fam* (*question*) cuisiner

grille [ɡrɪl] *n* (*bars*) grille *f*; (**radiator**) **g.** (*of vehicle*) calandre *f*

grim [ɡrɪm] (**grimmer, grimmest**) *adj* (*stern*) sinistre; *Fam* (*bad*) lamentable; **a g. determination** une volonté inflexible; **the g. truth** la triste vérité •**grimly** *adv* (*fight*) avec acharnement

grimace ['ɡrɪməs] **1** *n* grimace *f*
2 *vi* grimacer

grime [ɡraɪm] *n* crasse *f* •**grimy** (**-ier, -iest**) *adj* crasseux, -euse

grin [ɡrɪn] **1** *n* large sourire *m*
2 (*pt & pp* **-nn-**) *vi* avoir un large sourire

grind [ɡraɪnd] **1** *n Fam* (*work*) corvée *f*; **the daily g.** le train-train quotidien
2 (*pt & pp* **ground**) *vt* (*coffee, pepper*) moudre; *Am* (*meat*) hacher; (*blade, tool*) aiguiser; **to g. one's teeth** grincer des dents
3 *vi* **to g. to a halt** s'immobiliser; **grinding poverty** la misère noire •**grinder** *n* **coffee g.** moulin *m* à café

grip [ɡrɪp] **1** *n* (*hold*) prise *f*; (*handle*) poignée *f*; *Fam* (*of subject*) connaissance *f*; **to have a firm g. on the situation** avoir la situation bien en main; **to get a g. on oneself** se ressaisir; *Fig* **to lose one's g.** ne plus être à la hauteur; *Fig* **to get to grips with sth** s'attaquer à qch; **in the g. of a disease** en proie à une maladie
2 (*pt & pp* **-pp-**) *vt* (*seize*) saisir; (*hold*) empoigner; (*of tyre*) adhérer à; **the audience was gripped by the play** la pièce a captivé les spectateurs
3 *vi* (*of tyre*) adhérer •**gripping** *adj* passionnant

gripe [ɡraɪp] *vi Fam* (*complain*) rouspéter

grisly ['ɡrɪzlɪ] *adj* (*gruesome*) horrible

gristle ['ɡrɪsəl] *n* (*in meat*) nerfs *mpl*

grit [ɡrɪt] **1** *n* (**a**) (*sand*) sable *m*; (*gravel*) gravillons *mpl* (**b**) *Fam* (*courage*) cran *m*
2 (*pt & pp* **-tt-**) *vt* (**a**) (*road*) sabler (**b**) **to g. one's teeth** serrer les dents

grizzly ['ɡrɪzlɪ] (*pl* **-ies**) *n* **g.** (**bear**) grizzli *m*

groan [ɡrəʊn] **1** *n* (*of pain*) gémissement *m*; (*of dissatisfaction*) grognement *m*
2 *vi* (*with pain*) gémir; (*complain*) grogner

grocer ['ɡrəʊsə(r)] *n* épicier, -ière *mf*; **g.'s shop** épicerie *f* •**groceries** *npl* (*food*) provisions *fpl* •**grocery** (*pl* **-ies**) *n Am* (*shop*) épicerie *f*

groggy [ˈgrɒgɪ] (**-ier, -iest**) *adj Fam* groggy *inv*

groin [grɔɪn] *n* aine *f*

groom [gruːm] **1** *n* (**a**) *(bridegroom)* marié *m* (**b**) *(for horses)* lad *m*
2 *vt (horse)* panser; **to g. sb for sth** préparer qn pour qch; **well-groomed** *(person)* très soigné

groove [gruːv] *n (in wood, metal)* rainure *f*; *(in record)* sillon *m*

grope [grəʊp] *vi* **to g. (about) for sth** chercher qch à tâtons

gross [grəʊs] **1** *adj* (**a**) *(total) (weight, income, profit)* brut; *Econ* **g. domestic product** produit *m* intérieur brut; *Econ* **g. national product** produit national brut (**b**) (**-er, -est**) *(coarse)* grossier, -ière; *(injustice)* flagrant; **g. error** erreur *f* grossière
2 *n inv* grosse *f*
3 *vt* gagner brut • **grossly** *adv (negligent)* extrêmement; *(exaggerated)* grossièrement; *(unfair)* vraiment; **g. overweight** obèse

grotesque [grəʊˈtesk] *adj* grotesque

grotto [ˈgrɒtəʊ] *(pl* **-oes** *or* **-os***) n* grotte *f*

grotty [ˈgrɒtɪ] (**-ier, -iest**) *adj Br Fam* minable

ground¹ [graʊnd] **1** *n (earth)* terre *f*, sol *m*; *(land)* terrain *m*; *(estate)* terres *fpl*; **grounds** *(gardens)* parc *m*; *Fig (reasons)* motifs *mpl*; **on the g.** *(lying, sitting)* par terre; **to gain/lose g.** gagner/perdre du terrain; *Fig* **to hold one's g.** tenir bon; **g. crew** *(at airport)* personnel *m* au sol; *Br* **g. floor** rez-de-chaussée *m inv*; **g. frost** gelée *f* blanche; **g. rules** règles *fpl* de base
2 *vt (aircraft)* interdire de vol • **grounding** *n (basis)* fondement *m*; *(basic knowledge)* bases *fpl* (**in** de) • **groundless** *adj* sans fondement • **groundnut** *n* arachide *f* • **groundsheet** *n* tapis *m* de sol • **groundswell** *n* lame *f* de fond • **groundwork** *n* travail *m* préparatoire

ground² [graʊnd] **1** *pt & pp of* **grind**
2 *adj (coffee)* moulu; *Am* **g. meat** viande *f* hachée
3 *npl* (**coffee**) **grounds** marc *m* (de café)

group [gruːp] **1** *n* groupe *m*; **g. decision** décision *f* collective
2 *vt* **to g. (together)** grouper
3 *vi* se grouper • **grouping** *n (group)* groupe *m*

grouse¹ [graʊs] *n inv (bird)* tétras *m*

grouse² [graʊs] *vi Fam (complain)* rouspéter

grove [grəʊv] *n* bosquet *m*

grovel [ˈgrɒvəl] (*Br* **-ll-,** *Am* **-l-**) *vi (be humble)* ramper, s'aplatir (**to** devant)

grow [grəʊ] **1** *(pt* **grew**, *pp* **grown***) vt (vegetables)* cultiver; **to g. a beard** se laisser pousser la barbe
2 *vi (of person)* grandir; *(of plant, hair)* pousser; *(of economy, feeling)* croître; *(of firm, town)* se développer; *(of gap, family)* s'agrandir; **to g. fat(ter)** grossir; **to g. old** vieillir; **to g. to like sth** finir par aimer qch; **to g. into a man** devenir un homme; **to g. up** grandir; **when I g. up** quand je serai grand; **he's grown out of his shoes** ses chaussures sont maintenant trop petites pour lui; **it'll g. on you** *(of music, book)* tu finiras par t'y intéresser • **grower** *n (person)* cultivateur, -trice *mf* (**of** de) • **growing** *adj (child)* en pleine croissance; *(number, discontent)* grandissant • **grown** *adj (man, woman)* adulte • **grown-up 1** [ˈgrəʊnʌp] *n* grande personne *f* **2** [ˈgrəʊnˈʌp] *adj (ideas, behaviour)* d'adulte

growl [graʊl] **1** *n* grognement *m*
2 *vi* grogner (**at** contre)

grown [grəʊn] *pp of* **grow**

growth [grəʊθ] *n* croissance *f*; *(increase)* augmentation *f* (**in** de); *(lump)* grosseur *f* (**on** à); **a week's g. of beard** une barbe de huit jours

grub [grʌb] *n* (**a**) *Fam (food)* bouffe *f* (**b**) *(insect)* larve *f*

grubby [ˈgrʌbɪ] (**-ier, -iest**) *adj* sale

grudge [grʌdʒ] **1** *n* rancune *f*; **to have a g. against sb** garder rancune à qn
2 *vt* **to g. sb sth** donner qch à qn à contrecœur; **to g. doing sth** faire qch à contrecœur; **he grudges her her success** il lui en veut parce qu'elle a réussi • **grudging** *adj* accordé à contrecœur • **grudgingly** *adv* à contrecœur

gruelling [ˈgrʊəlɪŋ] (*Am* **grueling**) *adj (journey, experience)* épuisant

gruesome [ˈgruːsəm] *adj* horrible

gruff [grʌf] (**-er, -est**) *adj* bourru

grumble [ˈgrʌmbəl] *vi (complain)* grommeler; **to g. about sth** rouspéter contre qch

grumpy [ˈgrʌmpɪ] (**-ier, -iest**) *adj* grincheux, -euse

grunt [grʌnt] **1** *n* grognement *m*
2 *vti* grogner

guarantee [gærənˈtiː] **1** *n* garantie *f*
2 *vt* garantir (**against** contre); *(vouch for)* se porter garant de; **to g. sb that...** garantir à qn que... • **guarantor** [-tɔː(r)] *n* garant, -ante *mf*

guard [gɑːd] **1** *n (supervision)* garde *f*;

(sentry) garde *m*; *(on train)* chef *m* de train; **under g.** sous surveillance; **on one's g.** sur ses gardes; **on g. (duty)** de garde; **to stand g.** monter la garde; **to catch sb off his g.** prendre qn au dépourvu

2 *vt (protect)* garder; **to g. sb from danger** protéger qn d'un danger

3 *vt insep* **to g. against** *(protect oneself)* se prémunir contre; *(prevent)* empêcher; **to g. against doing sth** se garder de faire qch
• **guarded** *adj (cautious)* prudent

guardian ['gɑːdɪən] *n Law (of child)* tuteur, -trice *mf*; *(protector)* gardien, -ienne *mf*; **g. angel** ange *m* gardien

Guatemala [gwætɪ'mɑːlə] *n* le Guatemala

Guernsey ['gɜːnzɪ] *n* Guernesey *m* ou *f*

guerrilla [gə'rɪlə] *n (person)* guérillero *m*; **g. warfare** guérilla *f*

> ℓ Note that the French word **guérilla** is a false friend and is never a translation for the English word **guerrilla**. It means **guerrilla warfare**.

guess [ges] **1** *n (estimate)* estimation *f*; **to make** *or* **take a g.** deviner; **at a g.** à vue de nez

2 *vt* deviner (**that** que); *(suppose)* supposer, croire

3 *vi* deviner; **to g. right** deviner juste; **to g. wrong** se tromper; *Am* **I g. (so)** je crois
• **guesswork** *n* conjecture *f*; **by g.** au jugé

guest [gest] *n* invité, -ée *mf*; *(in hotel)* client, -iente *mf*; *(at meal)* convive *mf*; **be my g.!** je t'en prie!; **g. room** chambre *mf* d'amis; **g. speaker** conférencier, -ière *mf*
• **guesthouse** *n* pension *f* de famille

guffaw [gə'fɔː] *vi* rire bruyamment

guidance ['gaɪdəns] *n (advice)* conseils *mpl*

guide [gaɪd] **1** *n (person)* guide *m*; *(indication)* indication *f*; **g. (book)** guide *m*; *Br* **G.** éclaireuse *f*; **g. dog** chien *m* d'aveugle

2 *vt (lead)* guider; **guiding principle** principe *m* directeur • **guided** *adj (missile, rocket)* guidé; **g. tour** visite *f* guidée
• **guidelines** *npl* directives *fpl*

guild [gɪld] *n* association *f*; *Hist* corporation *f*

guile [gaɪl] *n* ruse *f*

guillotine ['gɪlətiːn] *n (for execution)* guillotine *f*; *Br (for paper)* massicot *m*

guilt [gɪlt] *n* culpabilité *f* • **guilty** (-**ier**, -**iest**) *adj* coupable; **to find sb g./not g.** déclarer qn coupable/non coupable

guinea pig ['gɪnɪpɪg] *n (animal)* & *Fig* cobaye *m*

guise [gaɪz] *n* **under the g. of** sous l'apparence de

guitar [gɪ'tɑː(r)] *n* guitare *f* • **guitarist** *n* guitariste *mf*

gulf [gʌlf] *n (in sea)* golfe *m*; *(chasm)* gouffre *m* (**between** entre); **the G.** le golfe Persique; **the G. War** la guerre du Golfe

gull [gʌl] *n* mouette *f*

gullet ['gʌlɪt] *n* gosier *m*

gullible ['gʌlɪbəl] *adj* crédule

gully ['gʌlɪ] *(pl* -**ies**) *n* petit ravin *m*

gulp [gʌlp] **1** *n* (**a**) *(of drink)* gorgée *f*; **in** *or* **at one g.** d'un coup (**b**) *(of surprise)* serrement *m* de gorge

2 *vt* **to g. (down)** engloutir

3 *vi (with surprise)* avoir la gorge serrée

gum¹ [gʌm] *n (in mouth)* gencive *f*

gum² [gʌm] **1** *n* (**a**) *(glue)* colle *f*; *(from tree)* gomme *f* (**b**) *(for chewing)* chewing-gum *m*

2 *(pt & pp* -**mm-**) *vt* coller

gumption ['gʌmpʃən] *n Fam (courage)* cran *m*; *(common sense)* jugeote *f*

gun [gʌn] **1** *n* pistolet *m*; *(rifle)* fusil *m*; *(firing shells)* canon *m*

2 *(pt & pp* -**nn-**) *vt sep* **to g. down** abattre
• **gunfight** *n* fusillade *f* • **gunfire** *n* coups *mpl* de feu; *(in battle)* tir *m* d'artillerie
• **gunman** *(pl* -**men**) *n* homme *m* armé
• **gunner** *n* artilleur *m* • **gunpoint** *n* **to hold sb at g.** tenir qn sous la menace d'une arme • **gunpowder** *n* poudre *f* à canon • **gunshot** *n* coup *m* de feu; **g. wound** blessure *f* par balle

gung-ho [gʌŋ'həʊ] *adj* **g. about sth** très enthousiaste à l'idée de qch

gurgle ['gɜːgəl] **1** *n* gargouillement *m*; *(of baby)* gazouillis *m*

2 *vi (of water)* gargouiller; *(of baby)* gazouiller

guru ['gʊruː] *n* gourou *m*

gush [gʌʃ] **1** *n* jaillissement *m*

2 *vi* **to g. (out)** jaillir (**of** de)

gust [gʌst] **1** *n (of wind)* rafale *f*; *(of hot air)* bouffée *f*

2 *vi (of wind)* souffler par rafales • **gusty** (-**ier**, -**iest**) *adj (weather)* venteux, -euse; *(day)* de grand vent

gusto ['gʌstəʊ] *n* **with g.** avec entrain

gut [gʌt] **1** *n (inside body)* intestin *m*; *Fam* **guts** *(insides)* entrailles *fpl*; *(courage)* cran *m*; *Fam* **he hates your guts** il ne peut pas te sentir

2 *(pt & pp* -**tt-**) *vt (of fire)* ravager

gutter ['gʌtə(r)] *n (on roof)* gouttière *f*; *(in street)* caniveau *m* • **guttering** *n* gouttières *fpl*

guttural ['gʌtərəl] *adj* guttural

guy [gaɪ] *n Fam (man)* type *m*

guzzle ['gʌzəl] *vt (eat)* engloutir; *(drink)* siffler

gym [dʒɪm] *n* gym *f*; *(gymnasium)* gymnase *m*; **g. shoes** chaussures *fpl* de gym • **gymnasium** [-'neɪzɪəm] *n* gymnase *m* • **gymnast** *n* gymnaste *mf* • **gym'nastics** *n* gymnastique *f*

gynaecology [gaɪnɪ'kɒlədʒɪ] (*Am* **gynecology**) *n* gynécologie *f* • **gynaecologist** (*Am* **gynecologist**) *n* gynécologue *mf*

gypsy ['dʒɪpsɪ] *n* = gipsy

gyrate [dʒaɪ'reɪt] *vi* tournoyer

H

H, h [eɪtʃ] *n (letter)* H, h *m inv*; **H bomb** bombe *f* H

haberdasher ['hæbədæʃə(r)] *n Br (selling sewing items)* mercier, -ière *mf*; *Am (men's outfitter)* chemisier *m* •**haberdashery** (*pl* **-ies**) *n* mercerie *f*; *Am* chemiserie *f*

habit ['hæbɪt] *n* (**a**) *(custom, practice)* habitude *f*; **to be in/get into the h. of doing sth** avoir/prendre l'habitude de faire qch; **to make a h. of doing sth** avoir pour habitude de faire qch (**b**) *Fam (addiction)* accoutumance *f*; **a h.-forming drug** une drogue qui crée une accoutumance (**c**) *(of monk, nun)* habit *m*

habitable ['hæbɪtəbəl] *adj* habitable •**habitat** [-tæt] *n (of animal, plant)* habitat *m* •**habi'tation** *n* habitation *f*; **fit for (human) h.** habitable

habitual [hə'bɪtʃʊəl] *adj* habituel, -uelle; *(smoker, drunk)* invétéré •**habitually** *adv* habituellement

hack¹ [hæk] *vt (cut)* tailler

hack² [hæk] *n Pej* **h. (writer)** écrivaillon *m*

hacker ['hækə(r)] *n Comptr* pirate *m* informatique

hackneyed ['hæknɪd] *adj (saying)* rebattu

had [hæd] *pt & pp of* **have**

haddock ['hædək] *n* aiglefin *m*; **smoked h.** haddock *m*

haemorrhage ['hemərɪdʒ] (*Am* **hemorrhage**) *n* hémorragie *f*

haemorrhoids ['hemərɔɪdz] (*Am* **hemorrhoids**) *npl Med* hémorroïdes *fpl*

hag [hæg] *n Pej (old)* **h.** vieille taupe *f*

haggard ['hægəd] *adj* hâve

haggle ['hægəl] *vi* marchander; **to h. over sth** marchander qch; **to h. over the price of sth** chicaner sur le prix de qch •**haggling** *n* marchandage *m*

Hague [heɪg] *n* **The H.** La Haye

hail¹ [heɪl] *n* grêle *f*; *Fig* **a h. of bullets** une pluie de balles

2 *vi* **it's hailing** il grêle •**hailstone** *n* grêlon *m*

hail² [heɪl] **1** *vt (greet)* saluer (**as** comme); *(taxi)* héler

2 *vt insep* **to h. from** *(of person)* être

originaire de; *(of ship, train)* être en provenance de

hair [heə(r)] *n (on head)* cheveux *mpl*; *(on body, of animal)* poils *mpl*; **a h.** *(on head)* un cheveu; *(on body, of animal)* un poil; **by a h.'s breadth** de justesse •**hairbrush** *n* brosse *f* à cheveux •**haircut** *n* coupe *f* de cheveux; **to have a h.** se faire couper les cheveux •**hairdo** (*pl* **-dos**) *n Fam* coiffure *f* •**hairdresser** *n* coiffeur, -euse *mf* •**hairdryer** *n* sèche-cheveux *m inv* •**hairgrip** *n* pince *f* à cheveux •**hairnet** *n* résille *f* •**hairpiece** *n* postiche *m* •**hairpin** *n* épingle *f* à cheveux; **h. bend** *(in road)* virage *m* en épingle à cheveux •**hair-raising** *adj* à faire dresser les cheveux sur la tête •**hair-splitting** *n* ergotage *m* •**hairspray** *n* laque *f* •**hairstyle** *n* coiffure *f*

-haired [heəd] *suff* **long-/red-h.** aux cheveux longs/roux

hairy ['heərɪ] (**-ier, -iest**) *adj (person, animal, body)* poilu; *Fam (frightening)* effrayant

hake [heɪk] *n* colin *m*

hale [heɪl] *adj* **h. and hearty** vigoureux, -euse

half [hɑːf] **1** (*pl* **halves**) *n* moitié *f*; *(part of match)* mi-temps *f*; *Br (half fare)* demi-tarif *m*; *Br (beer)* demi *m*; **h. (of) the apple** la moitié de la pomme; **h. past one** une heure et demie; **ten and a h.** dix et demi; **ten and a h. weeks** dix semaines et demie; **h. a day** une demi-journée; **h. a dozen** une demi-douzaine; **to cut in h.** couper en deux; **to go halves with sb** partager avec qn

2 *adj* demi; **h. board** demi-pension *f*; **a h.-day** une demi-journée; **a h.-dozen** une demi-douzaine; **h. fare** demi-tarif *m*; **at h. price** à moitié prix; **h. man h. beast** mi-homme mi-bête

3 *adv (dressed, full)* à moitié; **h.-asleep** à moitié endormi; *Br Fam* **he isn't h. lazy** il est rudement paresseux; **h. as much as** moitié moins que; **h. as much again** moitié plus •**halfback** *n Sport* demi *m* •**'half-'baked** *adj Fam (idea)* à la manque •**half-caste** *n* métis, -isse *mf* •**half-'dozen** *n* demi-douzaine *f* •**'half-'hearted** *adj (per-*

son, manner) peu enthousiaste; *(effort)* timide • **half-'hour** *n* demi-heure *f* • **half- light** *n* demi-jour *m* • **half-'mast** *n* **at h.** *(flag)* en berne • **'half-'open** *adj* entrouvert • **'half-'price** *adj & adv* à moitié prix • **half-'term** *n Br Sch* congé *m* de milieu de trimestre • **half-'time** *n (in game)* mi-temps *f* • **'half'way** *adv (between places)* à mi-chemin (**between** entre); **to fill sth h.** remplir qch à moitié; **to be h. through a book** être à la moitié d'un livre • **halfwit** *n* imbécile *mf* • **halfwitted** *adj* imbécile

halibut ['hælɪbət] *n (fish)* flétan *m*

hall [hɔːl] *n (room)* salle *f*; *(entrance room)* entrée *f*; *(of hotel)* hall *m*; *(mansion)* manoir *m*; *(for meals, in British university)* réfectoire *m*; *Br Univ* **h. of residence** résidence *f* universitaire

hallelujah [hælɪ'luːjə] *n & exclam* alléluia *(m)*

hallmark ['hɔːlmɑːk] *n (on metal)* poinçon *m*; *Fig (typical quality)* signe *m*

hallo [hə'ləʊ] *exclam* = **hello**

Hallowe'en [hæləʊ'iːn] *n* = veille de la Toussaint durant laquelle les enfants se déguisent en fantôme ou en sorcière

hallucination [həluːsɪ'neɪʃən] *n* hallucination *f*

hallway ['hɔːlweɪ] *n* entrée *f*

halo ['heɪləʊ] *(pl* **-oes** *or* **-os)** *n* auréole *f*

halogen ['hælədʒən] *n* **h. lamp** lampe *f* halogène

halt [hɔːlt] **1** *n* halte *f*; **to call a h. to sth** mettre fin à qch; **to come to a h.** s'arrêter
2 *exclam* halte!
3 *vt* arrêter
4 *vi (of soldiers)* faire halte; *(of production)* s'arrêter • **halting** *adj (voice)* hésitant

halve [hɑːv] *vt (reduce by half)* réduire de moitié; *(divide in two)* diviser en deux

ham [hæm] *n* (**a**) *(meat)* jambon *m*; **h. and eggs** œufs *mpl* au jambon; **h. sandwich** sandwich *m* au jambon (**b**) *Pej (actor)* cabotin, -ine *mf*

hamburger ['hæmbɜːgə(r)] *n* hamburger *m*

ham-fisted [hæm'fɪstɪd] *adj Fam* maladroit

hamlet ['hæmlɪt] *n* hameau *m*

hammer ['hæmə(r)] **1** *n* marteau *m*
2 *vt (nail)* enfoncer (**into** dans); *(metal)* marteler; *Fam (defeat)* écraser; *Fam (criticize)* démolir; **to h. sth out** *(agreement, plan)* mettre au point qch
3 *vi (with a marteau)* frapper; **to h. on the door** frapper à la porte à coups redoublés • **hammering** *n Fam (defeat)* raclée *f*

hammock ['hæmək] *n* hamac *m*

hamper ['hæmpə(r)] **1** *n Br (for food)* panier *m*; *Am (laundry basket)* panier *m* à linge
2 *vt (hinder)* gêner

hamster ['hæmstə(r)] *n* hamster *m*

hand¹ [hænd] **1** *n* (**a**) *(part of the body)* main *f*; **to hold sth in one's h.** tenir qch à la main; **to hold hands** se tenir par la main; **by h.** *(make, sew)* à la main; **to deliver sth by h.** remettre qch en mains propres; **at** *or* **to h.** *(within reach)* à portée de la main; **(close) at h.** *(person)* tout près; **the situation is in h.** la situation est bien en main; **the matter in h.** l'affaire *f* en question; **to have money in h.** avoir de l'argent disponible; **work in h.** travail *m* en cours; **on h.** *(ready for use)* disponible; *Fig* **to have sb on one's hands** avoir qn sur les bras; **on the right h.** du côté droit (**of** de); **on the one h.** d'une part; **on the other h.** d'autre part; **hands up!** *(in attack)* haut les mains!; *(to schoolchildren)* levez la main!; **hands off!** bas les pattes!; *Fig* **my hands are full** je suis très occupé; **to lend sb a (helping) h.** donner un coup de main à qn; **to get out of h.** *(of child)* devenir impossible; *(of situation)* devenir incontrôlable; **h. in h.** la main dans la main; *Fig* **it goes h. in h. with...** *(together with)* cela va de pair avec...; **at first h.** de première main; **to win hands down** gagner haut la main

(**b**) *(worker)* ouvrier, -ière *mf*; *(of clock)* aiguille *f*; *Cards* jeu *m*; *(style of writing)* écriture *f*

2 *adj (luggage, grenade)* à main; *(cream, lotion)* pour les mains • **handbag** *n* sac *m* à main • **handball** *n* handball *m* • **handbook** *n (manual)* manuel *m*; *(guide)* guide *m* • **handbrake** *n* frein *m* à main • **handcuff** *vt* passer les menottes à; **to be handcuffed** avoir les menottes aux poignets • **handcuffs** *npl* menottes *fpl* • **'hand'made** *adj* fait à la main • **'hand-'picked** *adj (team member)* trié sur le volet • **handrail** *n* rampe *f* • **handshake** *n* poignée *f* de main • **hands-on** *adj (experience)* pratique • **handwriting** *n* écriture *f* • **'hand'written** *adj* écrit à la main

hand² [hænd] *vt (give)* donner (**to** à); **to h. sth down** *(give)* passer qch; **to be handed down from generation to generation** se transmettre de génération en génération; **to h. sth in** remettre qch; **to h. sth out** distribuer qch; **to h. sth over** remettre qch; **to h. sth round** faire circuler qch

handful ['hændfʊl] *n (bunch, group)* poignée *f*; *Fig* she's **(quite) a h.** elle n'est pas facile

handicap ['hændɪkæp] **1** *n (disadvantage) & Sport* handicap *m* **2** *(pt & pp* **-pp-)** *vt* handicaper ● **handicapped** *adj (disabled)* handicapé

handicraft ['hændɪkrɑːft] *n (skill)* artisanat *m*; *(object)* objet *m* artisanal ● **handiwork** *n* travail *m* manuel; *(result)* ouvrage *m*

handkerchief ['hæŋkətʃɪf] *(pl* **-chiefs**) *n* mouchoir *m*

handle ['hændəl] **1** *n (of door)* poignée *f*; *(of knife)* manche *m*; *(of cup)* anse *f*; *(of saucepan)* queue *f*; *(of pump)* bras *m* **2** *vt (manipulate)* manier; *(touch)* toucher à; *(deal with)* s'occuper de; *(vehicle, ship)* manœuvrer; *(difficult child)* s'y prendre avec **3** *vi* **to h. well** *(of machine)* être maniable

handlebars ['hændəlbɑːz] *npl* guidon *m*

handout ['hændaʊt] *n (leaflet)* prospectus *m*; *(money)* aumône *f*

handsome ['hænsəm] *adj (person, building)* beau *(f* belle); *(profit, sum)* considérable; *(gift)* généreux, -euse ● **handsomely** *adv (generously)* généreusement

handy ['hændɪ] **(-ier, -iest)** *adj (convenient)* commode; *(useful)* pratique; *(within reach)* à portée de la main; *(skilful)* habile **(at doing** à faire); **to come in h.** être utile; **to keep sth h.** avoir qch sous la main; **the flat is h. for the shops** l'appartement est près des commerces ● **handyman** *(pl* **-men**) *n* homme *m* à tout faire

hang¹ [hæŋ] **1** *n Fam* **to get the h. of sth** piger qch **2** *(pt & pp* **hung**) *vt* suspendre **(on/from** à); *(on hook)* accrocher **(on** *or* **from** à); *(wallpaper)* poser; **to h. sth with sth** *(decorate with)* orner qch de qch **3** *vi (dangle)* pendre; *(of threat)* planer; *(of fog, smoke)* flotter ● **hanging** *adj* suspendu **(from** à); **h. on the wall** accroché au mur ● **hang-up** *n Fam* complexe *m* ▸ **hang about, hang around** *vi (loiter)* traîner; *Fam (wait)* poireauter ▸ **hang down** *vi (dangle)* pendre; *(of hair)* tomber ▸ **hang on 1** *vi (hold out)* tenir le coup; *Fam (wait)* patienter; **to h. on to sth** garder qch **2** *(vi insep (depend on)* dépendre de ▸ **hang out 1** *vt sep (washing)* étendre **2** *vi (from pocket, box)* dépasser; *Fam (spend time)* traîner ▸ **hang together** *vi (of facts)* se tenir; *(of plan)* tenir debout ▸ **hang up 1** *vt sep (picture)* accrocher **2** *vi (on phone)* raccrocher

hang² [hæŋ] *(pt & pp* **hanged**) **1** *vt (criminal)* pendre **(for** pour) **2** *vi (of criminal)* être pendu ● **hanging** *n (execution)* pendaison *f* ● **hangman** *(pl* **-men**) *n* bourreau *m*

hangar ['hæŋə(r)] *n* hangar *m*

hanger ['hæŋə(r)] *n* **(coat) h.** cintre *m* ● **hanger-on** *(pl* **hangers-on**) *n* parasite *m*

hang-glider ['hæŋglaɪdə(r)] *n* deltaplane *m* ● **hang-gliding** *n* vol *m* libre

hangnail ['hæŋneɪl] *n* envie *f*

hangover ['hæŋəʊvə(r)] *n Fam (after drinking)* gueule *f* de bois

hanker ['hæŋkə(r)] *vi* **to h. after** *or* **for** sth avoir envie de qch ● **hankering** *n* forte envie *f*

hankie, hanky ['hæŋkɪ] *(pl* **-ies**) *n Fam* mouchoir *m*

hanky-panky [hæŋkɪ'pæŋkɪ] *n inv Fam (sexual behaviour)* galipettes *fpl*; *(underhand behaviour)* entourloupettes *fpl*

haphazard [hæp'hæzəd] *adj (choice, decision)* pris au hasard; *(attempt)* mal organisé ● **haphazardly** *adv* n'importe comment

hapless ['hæplɪs] *adj Literary* infortuné

happen ['hæpən] *vi* arriver, se produire; **to h. to sb** arriver à qn; **I h. to know, it (so)** happens that I know il se trouve que je le sais; **do you h. to have...?** est-ce que par hasard vous avez...?; **what happened?** que s'est-il passé?; **whatever happens** quoi qu'il arrive ● **happening** *n* événement *m*

happily ['hæpɪlɪ] *adv* joyeusement; *(contentedly)* tranquillement; *(fortunately)* heureusement; **h. married couple** couple *m* heureux

happiness ['hæpɪnəs] *n* bonheur *m*

happy ['hæpɪ] **(-ier, -iest)** *adj* heureux, -euse **(to do** de faire; **about** de); **I'm not h. about it** ça ne me plaît pas; **H. New Year!** bonne année!; **h. birthday/Christmas!** joyeux anniversaire/Noël! ● **'happy-go-'lucky** *adj* insouciant

harass [*Br* 'hærəs, *Am* hə'ræs] *vt* harceler ● **harassment** *n* harcèlement *m*; **sexual h.** harcèlement *m* sexuel

> *Note that the French verb* **harasser** *is a false friend and is never a translation for the English verb* **to harass.** *It means* **to exhaust.**

harbour ['hɑːbə(r)] *(Am* **harbor**) **1** *n* port *m* **2** *vt (fugitive)* cacher; *(hope, suspicion)* nourrir; **to h. a grudge against sb** garder rancune contre qn

hard [hɑːd] (**-er, -est**) **1** adj (not soft, severe) dur; (difficult) difficile, dur; (water) calcaire; **to be h. on sb** être dur avec qn; **to find it h. to sleep** avoir du mal à dormir; **to be h. of hearing** être dur d'oreille; **it was h. work persuading him** ça n'a pas été facile de le convaincre; Fam **h. up** (broke) fauché; **to be h. up for sth** manquer de qch; **no h. feelings!** sans rancune!; **h. cash** espèces fpl; Comptr **h. copy** copie f sur papier; **h. core** (of group) noyau m dur; Comptr **h. disk** disque m dur; **h. drugs** drogues fpl dures; **h. evidence** preuves fpl tangibles; **h. frost** forte gelée f; **h. labour** travaux mpl forcés; **h. shoulder** (on motorway) bande f d'arrêt d'urgence; **h. worker** gros travailleur m
2 adv (work) dur; (pull, push, hit) fort; (study) assidûment; (rain) à verse; **to look h. at sb/sth** regarder fixement qn/qch; **to look h.** (seek) chercher bien; **to think h.** réfléchir bien; **to try h.** faire de son mieux; **to be h. at work** en plein travail; **h. by** tout près de; **to be h. done by** se sentir brimé • **'hard-and-'fast** adj (rule) strict • **'hardback** n livre m relié • **'hardboard** n aggloméré m • **'hard-'boiled** adj (egg) dur • **'hard-core** adj (supporter) inconditionnel, -elle • **'hard-'earned** adj (money) durement gagné; (rest) bien mérité • **'hard-'headed** adj réaliste • **'hard'wearing** adj résistant • **'hard-'working** adj travailleur, -euse

harden ['hɑːdən] **1** vt endurcir; **to become hardened to sth** s'endurcir à qch
2 vi (of substance, attitude) durcir • **hardened** adj (criminal) endurci

hardly ['hɑːdlɪ] adv à peine; **h. had I arrived when...** j'étais à peine arrivé que...; **h. anyone/anything** presque personne/rien; **h. ever** presque jamais

hardness ['hɑːdnɪs] n dureté f

hardship ['hɑːdʃɪp] n (ordeal) épreuve f; **to live in h.** vivre dans la misère

hardware ['hɑːdweə(r)] n inv quincaillerie f; Comptr & Mil matériel m; **h. shop** quincaillerie

hardy ['hɑːdɪ] (**-ier, -iest**) adj résistant

hare [heə(r)] n lièvre m • **harebrained** adj (person) écervelé; (scheme) insensé

harem [hɑː'riːm] n harem m

hark [hɑːk] vi Literary écouter; Fam **to h. back to sth** évoquer qch

harm [hɑːm] **1** n (hurt) mal m; (wrong) tort m; **to do sb h.** faire du mal à qn; **he means no h.** il ne veut pas faire de mal; **she'll come to no h.** il ne lui arrivera rien; **out of h.'s way** en lieu sûr

2 vt (physically) faire du mal à; (health, interests, cause) nuire à; (object) abîmer • **harmful** adj (influence) néfaste; (substance) nocif, -ive • **harmless** adj (person, treatment) inoffensif, -ive; (hobby, joke) innocent

harmonica [hɑː'mɒnɪkə] n harmonica m

harmonious [hɑː'məʊnɪəs] adj harmonieux, -ieuse

harmonium [hɑː'məʊnɪəm] n harmonium m

harmonize ['hɑːmənaɪz] **1** vt harmoniser
2 vi s'harmoniser

harmony ['hɑːmənɪ] (pl **-ies**) n harmonie f

harness ['hɑːnɪs] **1** n (for horse, baby) harnais m
2 vt (horse) harnacher; Fig (resources) exploiter

harp [hɑːp] **1** n harpe f
2 vi Fam **to h. on about sth** revenir sans arrêt sur qch • **harpist** n harpiste mf

harpoon [hɑː'puːn] **1** n harpon m
2 vt harponner

harpsichord ['hɑːpsɪkɔːd] n clavecin m

harrowing ['hærəʊɪŋ] adj (story, memory) poignant; (experience) très éprouvant; (account, cry, sight) déchirant

harsh [hɑːʃ] (**-er, -est**) adj (person, treatment) dur; (winter, climate) rude; (sound, voice) strident; (light) cru; **to be h. with sb** être dur envers qn • **harshly** adv durement • **harshness** n dureté f; (of winter, climate) rigueur f; (of sound) discordance f

harvest ['hɑːvɪst] **1** n moisson f; (of fruit) récolte f
2 vt moissonner; (fruit) récolter

has [hæz] see **have** • **has-been** n Fam Pej has been mf inv

hash [hæʃ] **1** n (**a**) (food) hachis m; Fam **to make a h. of sth** faire un beau gâchis de qch (**b**) Fam (hashish) hasch m
2 vt **to h. (up)** hacher

hashish ['hæʃiːʃ] n haschisch m

hassle ['hæsəl] Fam **1** n embêtements mpl; **it's too much h.** c'est trop compliqué
2 vt embêter

haste [heɪst] n hâte f; **in h.** à la hâte; **to make h.** se hâter

hasten ['heɪsən] **1** vt hâter
2 vi se hâter (**to do** de faire)

hasty ['heɪstɪ] (**-ier, -iest**) adj (departure, removal) précipité; (visit) rapide; (decision, work) hâtif, -ive • **hastily** adv (write, prepare) hâtivement; (say, eat) précipitamment

hat [hæt] n chapeau m; (of child) bonnet m; Fam **that's old h.** c'est vieux; Sport **to**

score *or* **get a h. trick** *(of goals)* marquer trois buts au cours d'un match; **h. stand** portemanteau *m*

hatch [hætʃ] **1** *n Br (in kitchen)* passe-plat *m*; *(on ship)* écoutille *f*
2 *vt* faire éclore; *Fig (plot)* tramer
3 *vi (of chick, egg)* éclore

hatchback ['hætʃbæk] *n (car) (three-door)* trois-portes *f inv*; *(five-door)* cinq-portes *f inv*; *(door)* hayon *m*

hatchet ['hætʃɪt] *n* hachette *f*

hate [heɪt] **1** *n* haine *f*
2 *vt* haïr, détester; **to h. doing** *or* **to do sth** détester faire qch; **I h. to say it but...** ça m'ennuie de le dire mais... ● **hateful** *adj* odieux, -ieuse ● **hatred** ['heɪtrɪd] *n* haine *f*

haughty ['hɔːtɪ] (**-ier, -iest**) *adj* hautain ● **haughtily** *adv* avec hauteur

haul [hɔːl] **1** *n (fish caught)* prise *f*; *(of thief)* butin *m*; **a long h.** *(trip)* un long voyage
2 *vt* (**a**) *(pull)* tirer (**b**) *(goods)* transporter par camion ● **haulage** ['hɔːlɪdʒ] *n* transport *m* routier; *(cost)* frais *mpl* de transport ● **haulier** (*Am* **hauler**) *n* transporteur *m* routier

haunt [hɔːnt] **1** *n (place)* lieu *m* de rendez-vous; *(of criminal)* repaire *m*
2 *vt* hanter ● **haunted** *adj (house)* hanté ● **haunting** *adj* obsédant

have [hæv] **1** *npl* **the haves and (the) have-nots** les riches *mpl* et les pauvres *mpl*
2 (*3rd person sing present tense* **has**; *pt & pp* **had**; *pres p* **having**) *vt* avoir; *(meal, bath, lesson)* prendre; **he has (got) a big house** il a une grande maison; **she doesn't h.** *or* **hasn't got a car** elle n'a pas de voiture; **to h. a drink** prendre un verre; **to h. a walk/dream** faire une promenade/un rêve; **to h. a wash** se laver; **to h. a swim** se baigner; **to h. a pleasant holiday** passer d'agréables vacances; **to h. a party** faire une soirée; **to h. a cold** être enrhumé; **to h. flu** avoir la grippe; **will you h. some tea?** est-ce que tu veux du thé?; **to h. sth to do** avoir qch à faire; **to let sb h. sth** donner qch à qn; **he had me by the hair** il me tenait par les cheveux; **I won't h. this** *(allow)* je ne tolérerai pas ça; **to h. it from sb that...** tenir de qn que...; *Fam* **had it with sb/sth** en avoir assez de qn/qch; *Fam* **you've had it!** tu es fichu!; *Fam* **I've been had** *(cheated)* je me suis fait avoir; **to h. gloves/a dress on** porter des gants/une robe; **to h. a lot on** avoir beaucoup à faire; **to h. sb over** *or* **round** inviter qn chez soi

3 *v aux* avoir; *(with* **entrer, monter, sortir** *etc & pronominal verbs)* être; **to h. decided** avoir décidé; **to h. gone** être allé; **to h. cut oneself** s'être coupé; **she has been punished** elle a été punie, on l'a punie; **I've just done it** je viens de le faire; **I haven't seen it yet**, *Formal* **I h. not seen it yet** je ne l'ai pas encore vu; **to h. to do sth** *(must)* devoir faire qch; **I've got to go, I h. to go** je dois partir, il faut que je parte; **I don't h. to go** je ne suis pas obligé de partir; **to h. sb do sth** faire faire qch à qn; **to h. sth done** faire faire qch; **to h. one's hair cut** se faire couper les cheveux; **he's had his suitcase brought up** il a fait monter sa valise; **I've had my car stolen** on m'a volé mon auto; **I've been doing it for months** je le fais depuis des mois; **you h. told him, haven't you?** tu le lui as dit, n'est-ce pas?; **you've seen this film before – no I haven't!** tu as déjà vu ce film – mais non!; **you haven't done the dishes – yes I h.!** tu n'as pas fait la vaisselle – mais si, je l'ai faite!; **after he had eaten** *or* **after having eaten, he left** après avoir mangé, il partit

▸ **have on** *vt sep* (**a**) *(be wearing)* porter (**b**) *Fam (fool)* **to h. sb on** faire marcher qn (**c**) *(have arranged)* **to h. a lot on** avoir beaucoup à faire; **to h. nothing on** n'avoir rien de prévu ▸ **have out** *vt sep* (**a**) *(have removed)* **to h. a tooth out** se faire arracher une dent (**b**) *(resolve)* **to h. it out with sb** s'expliquer avec qn

haven ['heɪvən] *n* refuge *m*

haven't ['hævənt] = **have not**

haversack ['hævəsæk] *n* sac *m* à dos

havoc ['hævək] *n* ravages *mpl*; **to wreak** *or* **cause h.** faire des ravages; **to play h. with sth** *(plans)* chambouler qch

hawk¹ [hɔːk] *n (bird) & Pol* faucon *m*

hawk² [hɔːk] *vt* **to h. one's wares** *(from door to door)* faire du porte-à-porte ● **hawker** *n* colporteur, -euse *mf*

hawthorn ['hɔːθɔːn] *n* aubépine *f*

hay [heɪ] *n* foin *m* ● **hayfever** *n* rhume *m* des foins ● **haystack** *n* meule *f* de foin

haywire ['heɪwaɪə(r)] *adj* **to go h.** *(of machine)* se détraquer; *(of plan)* mal tourner

hazard ['hæzəd] **1** *n* risque *m*; **to be a health h.** présenter un risque pour la santé; **it's a fire h.** ça risque de provoquer un incendie; *Br Aut* **h. (warning) lights** feux *mpl* de détresse
2 *vt (fortune, remark)* risquer ● **hazardous** *adj* dangereux, -euse

⌀ Note that the French word **hasard** is a false friend and is never a translation for the English word **hazard**. It means **chance**.

haze [heɪz] **1** *n* brume *f*; *Fig* **in a h.** *(confused)* dans le brouillard
2 *vt Am (student)* bizuter • **hazing** *n Am* bizutage *m*

hazel ['heɪzəl] **1** *n (tree)* noisetier *m*
2 *adj* **to have h. eyes** avoir les yeux noisette • **hazelnut** *n* noisette *f*

hazy ['heɪzɪ] **(-ier, -iest)** *adj (weather)* brumeux, -euse; *(photo, idea)* flou; **h. sunshine** soleil *m* voilé; **to be h. about sth** *(remember vaguely)* n'avoir qu'un vague souvenir de qch

he [hiː] **1** *pron* il; *(stressed)* lui; **he wants** il veut; **he's a happy man** c'est un homme heureux; **if I were he** si j'étais lui; **he and I** lui et moi
2 *n* **he** *(male)* mâle *m*; **he-bear** ours *m* mâle; *Fam* **it's a he** *(baby)* c'est un garçon

head [hed] **1** *n (of person, hammer)* tête *f*; *(leader)* chef *m*; *Br (headmaster)* directeur *m*; *Br (headmistress)* directrice *f*; *(of bed)* chevet *m*, tête *f*; *(of arrow)* pointe *f*; *(subject heading)* rubrique; **(tape) h.** *(of tape recorder, VCR)* tête magnétique; **h. of hair** chevelure *f*; **h. of state** chef *m* d'État; **h. first** la tête la première; **at the h. of** *(in charge of)* à la tête de; **at the h. of the table** en bout de table; **at the h. of the list** en tête de liste; **at the h. of the page** en haut de la page; **it didn't enter my h.** ça ne m'est pas venu à l'esprit **(that** que); **to take it into one's h. to do sth** se mettre en tête de faire qch; **to have a good h. for business** avoir le sens des affaires; *Fam* **to shout one's h. off** crier à tue-tête; **it's above my h.** ça me dépasse; **to keep one's h.** garder son sang-froid; **to lose one's h.** perdre la tête; **to go off one's h.** devenir fou *(f* folle); **it's coming to a h.** *(of situation)* ça devient critique; **heads or tails?** pile ou face?; **per h., a h.** *(each)* par personne; **h. cold** rhume *m* de cerveau
2 *adj* **h. gardener** jardinier *m* en chef; **h. office** siège *m* social; **h. waiter** maître *m* d'hôtel; **to have a h. start over** avoir beaucoup d'avance sur
3 *vt (group, firm)* être à la tête de; *(list, poll)* en tête de; *(vehicle)* diriger **(towards** vers); *Football* **to h. the ball** faire une tête; **to h. sb off** détourner qn de son chemin; **to h. sth off** éviter qch; *Am* **to be headed for** se diriger vers
4 *vi* **to h. for, to be heading for** *(place)* se diriger vers • **headache** *n* mal *m* de tête;

Fig (problem) casse-tête *m inv*; **to have a h.** avoir mal à la tête • **headdress** *n (ornamental)* coiffe *f* • **headlamp, headlight** *n (of vehicle)* phare *m* • **headline** *n (of newspaper, TV news)* titre *m*; **to hit the headlines** faire la une des journaux • **headlong** *adv (fall)* la tête la première; *(rush)* tête baissée • **head'master** *n Br (of school)* directeur *m*; *(of lycée)* proviseur *m* • **head'mistress** *n Br (of school)* directrice *f*; *(of lycée)* proviseur *m* • **'head-'on** *adv & adj* de front • **headphones** *npl* écouteurs *mpl* • **headquarters** *npl (of company, political party)* siège *m* (social); *(of army, police)* quartier *m* général, QG *m* • **headrest** *n* appuie-tête *m inv* • **headscarf** *(pl* **-scarves**) *n* foulard *m* • **headstrong** *adj* têtu • **headway** *n* **to make h.** faire des progrès

headed ['hedɪd] *adj Br* **h. (note)paper** papier *m* à en-tête

-headed ['hedɪd] *suff* **two-h.** *(monster)* à deux têtes; **curly-h.** aux cheveux frisés

header ['hedə(r)] *n Football* (coup *m* de) tête *f*

headhunter ['hedhʌntə(r)] *n Com* chasseur *m* de têtes

heading ['hedɪŋ] *n (of chapter, page)* titre *m*; *(of subject)* rubrique *f*; *(printed on letter)* en-tête *m*

heady ['hedɪ] **(-ier, -iest)** *adj (wine, perfume)* capiteux, -euse; *(atmosphere)* enivrant

heal [hiːl] **1** *vt (wound)* cicatriser; *Fig (person, sorrow)* guérir
2 *vi* **to h. (up)** *(of wound)* cicatriser • **healer** *n* guérisseur, -euse *mf*

health [helθ] *n* santé *f*; **in good/bad h.** en bonne/mauvaise santé; **h. care** soins *mpl* médicaux; *Br* **h. centre** dispensaire *m*; **h. food** produit *m* de culture biologique; **h. food shop** *or Am* **store** magasin *m* de produits biologiques; **h. resort** station *f* climatique; *Br* **the (National) H. Service** ≃ la Sécurité Sociale

healthy ['helθɪ] **(-ier, -iest)** *adj (person)* en bonne santé; *(food, attitude)* sain; *(appetite)* robuste

heap [hiːp] **1** *n* tas *m*; *Fam* **heaps of** *(money, people)* des tas de; *Fam* **to have heaps of time** avoir largement le temps
2 *vt* entasser; **to h. sth on sb** *(praise, gifts)* couvrir qn de qch; *(insults, work)* accabler qn de qch; **a heaped spoonful** une cuillerée bien pleine

hear [hɪə(r)] *(pt & pp* **heard** [hɜːd]) **1** *vt* entendre; *(listen to)* écouter; *(learn)* apprendre (that que); **I heard him come** or **coming** je l'ai entendu venir; **have you heard the news?** connais-tu la nouvelle?; **to h. it said that...** entendre dire que...; **I h. you're not well** j'ai appris que vous n'alliez pas bien; **to h. sb out** écouter qn jusqu'au bout; **h., h.!** bravo!

2 *vi* entendre; **to h. from sb** avoir des nouvelles de qn; **I've heard of** or **about him** j'ai entendu parler de lui; **she wouldn't h. of it** elle ne voulait pas en entendre parler; **I won't h. of it!** pas question! • **hearing** *n* (**a**) *(sense)* ouïe *f*; **hard of h.** dur d'oreille; **h. aid** audiophone *m* (**b**) *(of committee)* séance *f*; *Law (inquiry)* audition *f*; **to give sb a fair h.** laisser qn s'expliquer

hearsay ['hɪəseɪ] *n* **by h.** par ouï-dire; **it's only h.** ce ne sont que des on-dit

hearse [hɜːs] *n* corbillard *m*

heart [hɑːt] *n* cœur *m*; *Cards* **hearts** cœur *m*; **(off) by h.** *(know)* par cœur; **at h.** au fond; **the h. of the matter** le fond du problème; **to lose h.** perdre courage; **to one's h.'s content** tout son soûl; **his h. is set on it** il y tient; **his h. is set on doing it** il tient à le faire; **h. attack** crise *f* cardiaque; **h. disease** maladie *f* de cœur; **h. failure** arrêt *m* cardiaque • **heartache** *n* chagrin *m* • **heartbeat** *n* battement *m* de cœur; *(rhythm)* pouls *m* • **heartbreaking** *adj* navrant • **heartbroken** *adj* inconsolable • **heartburn** *n (indigestion)* brûlures *fpl* d'estomac • **heartfelt** *adj* sincère • **heartlands** *npl (of country)* cœur *m*, centre *m* • **heartthrob** *n Fam* idole *f*

hearten ['hɑːtən] *vt* encourager • **heartening** *adj* encourageant

hearth [hɑːθ] *n* foyer *m*

hearty ['hɑːtɪ] (**-ier, -iest**) *adj (appetite, meal)* gros (*f* grosse) • **heartily** *adv (eat)* avec appétit; *(laugh, detest)* de tout son cœur; *(approve, agree)* absolument

heat [hiːt] **1** *n* (**a**) chaleur *f*; *(heating)* chauffage *m*; *(of oven)* température *f*; **in the h. of the argument** dans le feu de la discussion; **at low h., on a low h.** *(cook)* à feu doux; **h. wave** vague *f* de chaleur (**b**) *(in competition)* éliminatoire *f*; **it was a dead h.** ils sont arrivés ex aequo

2 *vti* **to h. (up)** chauffer • **heated** *adj (swimming pool)* chauffé; *(argument)* animé; **the house is centrally h.** la maison a le chauffage central • **heatedly** *adv* avec passion • **heating** *n* chauffage *m*; **central h.** chauffage *m* central

heater ['hiːtə(r)] *n* radiateur *m*

heath [hiːθ] *n (land)* lande *f*

heathen ['hiːðən] *adj & n Rel* païen, païenne *(mf)*

heather ['heðə(r)] *n* bruyère *f*

heave [hiːv] **1** *n (effort)* effort *m*

2 *vt (lift)* soulever avec effort; *(pull)* tirer fort; *(push)* pousser fortement; *Fam (throw)* balancer; **to h. a sigh** pousser un soupir

3 *vi (of stomach, chest)* se soulever; *Fam (feel sick)* avoir des haut-le-cœur

heaven ['hevən] *n* paradis *m*, ciel *m*; **in h.** au paradis; *Fig (overjoyed)* aux anges; *Fam* **h. knows why...** Dieu sait pourquoi...; *Fam* **good heavens!** mon Dieu!; *Fam* **it was h.** c'était divin • **heavenly** *adj Fam (pleasing)* divin; **h. body** corps *m* céleste

heavily ['hevɪlɪ] *adv (walk, tax)* lourdement; *(breathe)* bruyamment; *(smoke, drink)* beaucoup; **h. in debt** lourdement endetté; **to rain h.** pleuvoir à verse; **to snow h.** neiger beaucoup; **to depend h. on** dépendre beaucoup de; **to be h. defeated** subir une lourde défaite; **to be h. involved in sth** être lourdement impliqué dans qch

heavy ['hevɪ] (**-ier, -iest**) *adj* lourd; *(work, cold)* gros (*f* grosse); *(blow)* violent; *(rain, concentration)* fort; *(traffic)* dense; *(film, text)* difficile; *(timetable, schedule)* chargé; **how h. are you?** combien pesez-vous?; **h. snow** d'abondantes chutes de neige; **to be a h. drinker/smoker** boire/ fumer beaucoup; **to be h. on** *Br* **petrol** or *Am* **gas** *(of vehicle)* consommer beaucoup; **it's h. going** c'est difficile; *Br* **h. goods vehicle** poids *m* lourd • **heaviness** *n* pesanteur *f*, lourdeur *f* • **heavyweight** *n Boxing* poids *m* lourd; *Fig* personnage *m* important

Hebrew ['hiːbruː] **1** *adj* hébraïque

2 *n (language)* hébreu *m*

Hebrides ['hebrɪdiːz] *n* **the H.** les Hébrides *fpl*

heck [hek] *n Fam* zut!; **what the h.!** et puis zut!; **a h. of a lot** des masses

heckle ['hekəl] *vt* interpeller • **heckler** *n* chahuteur, -euse *mf* • **heckling** *n* chahut *m*

hectic ['hektɪk] *adj (busy)* agité; *(eventful)* mouvementé; **h. life** vie *f* trépidante

he'd [hiːd] **= he had, he would**

hedge [hedʒ] **1** *n (in garden, field)* haie *f*

2 *vi (answer evasively)* ne pas se mouiller

hedgehog ['hedʒhɒg] *n* hérisson *m*

hedgerow ['hedʒrəʊ] *n Br* haie *f*

heed [hiːd] **1** n **to pay h. to sth, to take h. of sth** tenir compte de qch
2 vt tenir compte de • **heedless** adj **to be h. of sth** ne pas tenir compte de qch

heel [hiːl] n (**a**) (of foot, shoe) talon m; **down at h.,** Am **down at the heels** (shabby) miteux, -euse; **h. bar** cordonnerie f express (**b**) Am Fam (person) salaud m

hefty ['heftɪ] (**-ier, -iest**) adj (large, heavy) gros (f grosse); (person) costaud

heifer ['hefə(r)] n génisse f

height [haɪt] n hauteur f; (of person) taille f; (of mountain, aircraft) altitude f; **to be afraid of heights** avoir le vertige; **the h. of** (success, fame, glory) l'apogée m de; (folly, pain) le comble de; **at the h. of** (summer, storm) au cœur de; **it's the h. of fashion** c'est la dernière mode

heighten ['haɪtən] vt (tension, interest) augmenter

heinous ['heɪnəs] adj Formal (crime) atroce

> ✏ Note that the French word **haineux** is a false friend and is never a translation for the English word **heinous**. It means **full of hatred**.

heir [eə(r)] n héritier m; **to be h. to sth** être l'héritier de qch • **heiress** n héritière f • **heirloom** n **a family h.** un objet de famille

held [held] pt & pp of **hold**

helicopter ['helɪkɒptə(r)] n hélicoptère m • **heliport** n héliport m

hell [hel] n enfer m; Fam **a h. of a lot (of sth)** énormément (de qch); Fam **a h. of a nice guy** un type super; Fam **what the h. are you doing?** qu'est-ce que tu fous?; Fam **to h. with him!** qu'il aille se faire voir!; Fam **h.!** zut! • **hellbent** adj Br Fam **to be h. on doing** or **to do sth** vouloir à tout prix faire qch • **hellish** adj Fam infernal

he'll [hiːl] = **he will**

hello [hə'ləʊ] exclam bonjour!; (answering phone) allô!

helm [helm] n (of ship) barre f

helmet ['helmɪt] n casque m

help [help] **1** n aide f; Br (cleaning woman) femme f de ménage; (office or shop workers) employés, -ées mfpl; **with the h. of sth** à l'aide de qch; **to be of h. to sb** aider qn; **to cry** or **shout for h.** appeler à l'aide; **h.!** au secours!
2 vt aider; **to h. sb do** or **to do sth** aider qn à faire qch; **to h. oneself (to sth)** se servir (de qch); **to h. sb out** aider qn; **to h. sb up** aider qn à monter; **I can't h. laugh-**ing je ne peux pas m'empêcher de rire; **he can't h. being bald** ce n'est pas sa faute s'il est chauve; **it can't be helped** on n'y peut rien
3 vi aider; **to h. out** donner un coup de main • **helper** n assistant, -ante mf • **helping** n (serving) portion f

helpful ['helpfəl] adj (person) serviable; (useful) utile

helpless ['helpləs] adj (powerless) impuissant; (disabled) impotent • **helplessly** adv (struggle) en vain

helpline ['helplaɪn] n service m d'assistance téléphonique

helter-skelter [heltə'skeltə(r)] **1** n (slide) toboggan m
2 adv **to run h.** courir comme un fou/une folle

hem [hem] **1** n ourlet m
2 (pt & pp **-mm-**) vt (garment) ourler; **to be hemmed in** (surrounded) être cerné (**by** de)

he-man ['hiːmæn] n Fam mâle m

hemisphere ['hemɪsfɪə(r)] n hémisphère m

hemorrhage ['hemərɪdʒ] n Am = **haemorrhage**

hemorrhoids ['hemərɔɪdz] npl Am = **haemorrhoids**

hemp [hemp] n chanvre m

hen [hen] n poule f; **h. bird** oiseau m femelle; **to have a h. night** or **h. party** enterrer sa vie de célibataire

hence [hens] adv (**a**) (thus) d'où (**b**) (from now) **ten years h.** d'ici dix ans • **hence-'forth** adv Formal désormais

henchman ['hentʃmən] (pl **-men**) n Pej acolyte m

henpecked ['henpekt] adj (husband) mené par le bout du nez

hepatitis [hepə'taɪtɪs] n Med hépatite f

her [hɜː(r)] **1** pron la, l'; (after prep, 'than', 'it is') elle; (**to**) **h.** (indirect) lui; **I see h.** je la vois; **I saw h.** je l'ai vue; **I gave it to h.** je le lui ai donné; **with h.** avec elle
2 possessive adj son, sa, pl ses; **h. husband** son mari; **h. sister** sa sœur; **h. parents** ses parents

herald ['herəld] vt annoncer

heraldry ['herəldrɪ] n héraldique f

herb [Br hɜːb, Am ɜːb] n herbe f aromatique; Br **h. tea** tisane f • **herbal** adj **h. tea** tisane f

herd [hɜːd] **1** n troupeau m
2 vt (cattle, people) rassembler

here [hɪə(r)] **1** adv ici; **h. it/he is** le voici; **h. she comes!** la voilà!; **h. comes the teacher** voici le professeur qui arrive; **h.**

is a good example voici un bon exemple; **h. are my friends** voici mes amis; **I won't be h. tomorrow** je ne serai pas là demain; **summer is h.** c'est l'été; **h. and there** çà et là; **h. you are!** *(take this)* tenez!; **h.'s to you!** *(toast)* à la tienne!

  2 *exclam* **h.!** *(giving sb sth)* tenez! • **here-abouts** *adv* par ici • **here'after** *adv Formal (below)* ci-après; *(in the future)* dorénavant • **hereby** *adv Formal (declare)* par le présent acte; *(in writing)* par la présente • **here'with** *adv Formal (with letter)* ci-joint

heredity [hɪ'redɪtɪ] *n* hérédité *f* • **hereditary** *adj* héréditaire

heresy ['herəsɪ] *(pl* -ies) *n* hérésie *f* • **heretic** *n* hérétique *mf*

heritage ['herɪtɪdʒ] *n* patrimoine *m*

hermetic [hɜ:'metɪk] *adj* hermétique • **hermetically** *adv* hermétiquement

hermit ['hɜ:mɪt] *n* ermite *m*

hernia ['hɜ:nɪə] *n Med* hernie *f*

hero ['hɪərəʊ] *(pl* -oes) *n* héros *m* • **heroic** [hɪ'rəʊɪk] *adj* héroïque • **heroics** [hɪ'rəʊɪks] *npl (action)* coup *m* d'éclat • **heroine** ['herəʊɪn] *n* héroïne *f* • **heroism** ['herəʊɪzəm] *n* héroïsme *m*

heroin ['herəʊɪn] *n (drug)* héroïne *f*

heron ['herən] *n* héron *m*

herring ['herɪŋ] *n* hareng *m*; *Fig* **a red h.** une diversion

hers [hɜ:z] *possessive pron* le sien, la sienne, *pl* les sien(ne)s; **this hat is h.** ce chapeau est à elle *ou* est le sien; **a friend of h.** un ami à elle

herself [hɜ:'self] *pron* elle-même; *(reflexive)* se, s'; *(after prep)* elle; **she did it h.** elle l'a fait elle-même; **she cut h.** elle s'est coupée; **she thinks of h.** elle pense à elle

hesitant ['hezɪtənt] *adj* hésitant • **hesitantly** *adv* avec hésitation

hesitate ['hezɪteɪt] **1** *vt* **to h. to do sth** hésiter à faire qch

  2 *vi* hésiter (**over** *or* **about** sur) • **hesi'tation** *n* hésitation *f*

heterogeneous [hetərəʊ'dʒi:nɪəs] *adj* hétérogène

heterosexual [hetərəʊ'seksjʊəl] *adj & n* hétérosexuel, -uelle *(mf)*

het up [het'ʌp] *adj Fam* énervé

hew [hju:] *(pp* **hewn** [hju:n] *or* **hewed)** *vt* tailler

hexagon ['heksəgən] *n* hexagone *m* • **hexagonal** [-'sægənəl] *adj* hexagonal

hey [heɪ] *exclam (calling sb)* hé!, ohé!; *(expressing surprise, annoyance)* ho!

heyday ['heɪdeɪ] *n* apogée *m*; **in its h.** à son apogée; **in his h.** au sommet de sa gloire

hi [haɪ] *exclam Fam* salut!

hiatus [haɪ'eɪtəs] *n (interruption)* interruption *f*; *(in conversation)* silence *m*

hibernate ['haɪbəneɪt] *vi* hiberner • **hibernation** [-'neɪʃən] *n* hibernation *f*

hiccup, hiccough ['hɪkʌp] **1** *n* hoquet *m*; *Fig (in plan)* accroc *m*; **to have (the) hiccups** *or* **(the) hiccoughs** avoir le hoquet

  2 *vi* hoqueter

hick [hɪk] *n Am Fam Pej (peasant)* plouc *mf*

hide¹ [haɪd] *(pt* **hid** [hɪd], *pp* **hidden** [hɪdən]) **1** *vt* cacher (**from** à)

  2 *vi* **to h. (away** *or* **out)** se cacher (**from** de) • **hide-and-'seek** *n* cache-cache *m inv*; **to play h.** jouer à cache-cache

hide² [haɪd] *n (skin)* peau *f*

hideaway ['haɪdəweɪ] *n* cachette *f*

hideous ['hɪdɪəs] *adj (ugly)* hideux, -euse; *(horrific)* horrible • **hideously** *adv* horriblement

hide-out ['haɪdaʊt] *n* cachette *f*

hiding¹ ['haɪdɪŋ] *n* **to go into h.** se cacher; **h. place** cachette *f*

hiding² ['haɪdɪŋ] *n Fam* **a good h.** *(thrashing)* une bonne raclée

hierarchy ['haɪərɑ:kɪ] *(pl* -ies) *n* hiérarchie *f*

hi-fi ['haɪfaɪ] **1** *n (system, equipment)* chaîne *f* hi-fi; *(sound reproduction)* hi-fi *f inv*

  2 *adj* hi-fi *inv*

high [haɪ] **1** (-er, -est) *adj* haut; *(speed)* grand; *(price, standards)* élevé; *(number, ideal)* grand, élevé; *(voice, tone)* aigu (*f* aiguë); *(wind)* violent; *(meat, game)* faisandé; *Fam (on drugs)* défoncé; **to be 5 m h.** avoir 5 m de haut; **h. and mighty** arrogant; **to be in h. spirits** être plein d'entrain; **it is h. time that you went** il est grand temps que tu y ailles; *Fam* **to leave sb h. and dry** laisser qn en plan; **h. fever** forte fièvre *f*; *Sport* **h. jump** saut *m* en hauteur; **h. noon** plein midi *m*; **h. priest** grand prêtre *m*; **h. school** ≃ lycée *m*; *Am* **h. school diploma** diplôme *m* de fin d'études secondaires; **h. spot** *(of visit, day)* point *m* culminant; *(of show)* clou *m*; *Br* **h. street** grand-rue *f*; **h. summer** plein été *m*; **h. table** table *f* d'honneur; **h. tea** = dîner pris tôt dans la soirée; **h. tide** marée *f* haute

  2 *adv* **h. (up)** *(fly, throw, aim)* haut; **feelings were running h.** la tension montait

  3 *n* sommet *m*; **a new h., an all-time h.** *(peak)* un nouveau record; **to be on a h.** *(from drugs)* planer; *(from success)* être sur un petit nuage •**highchair** *n* chaise *f* haute •'**high-'class** *adj (service)* de premier ordre; *(building)* de luxe; *(person)* raffiné •**high-'five** *n Fam* = tape amicale donnée dans la paume de quelqu'un, bras levé, en signe de victoire •**high-'flier, high'flyer** *n* jeune loup *m* •'**high-'handed** *adj* tyrannique •'**high-'minded** *adj* noble •'**high-'pitched** *adj (sound)* aigu (*f* aiguë) •'**high-'powered** *adj (engine, car)* très puissant; *(job)* à hautes responsabilités •'**high-'profile** *adj (person)* très en vue; *(campaign)* de grande envergure •'**high-'rise** *adj Br* **h. building** tour *f* •'**high-'speed** *adj* ultrarapide; **h. train** train *m* à grande vitesse •'**high-'strung** *adj Am* nerveux, -euse •'**high-'tech** *adj (appliance)* perfectionné; *(industry)* de pointe •**high-'up** *adj Fam (important)* haut placé

highbrow ['haɪbraʊ] *adj & n* intellectuel, -uelle *(mf)*

higher ['haɪə(r)] **1** *adj (number, speed, quality)* supérieur (**than** à); **h. education** enseignement *m* supérieur

2 *adv (fly, aim)* plus haut (**than** que)

3 *n Scot* **H.** = diplôme de fin d'études secondaires sanctionnant une matière déterminée

highlands ['haɪləndz] *npl* régions *fpl* montagneuses

highlight ['haɪlaɪt] **1** *n (of visit, day)* point *m* culminant; *(of show)* clou *m*; *(in hair)* reflet *m*

2 *vt* souligner; *(with marker)* surligner •**highlighter** *n (pen)* surligneur *m*

highly ['haɪlɪ] *adv (very)* très; *(recommend)* chaudement; **h. paid** très bien payé; **to speak h. of sb** dire beaucoup de bien de qn; *Br* **h. strung** hypersensible

Highness ['haɪnɪs] *n* **His/Her Royal H.** Son Altesse *f*

highroad ['haɪrəʊd] *n Br Old-fashioned* grand-route *f*; *Fig* **the h. to success** la voie du succès

highway ['haɪweɪ] *n Am (main road)* nationale *f*; *(motorway)* autoroute *f*; *Br* **public h.** voie *f* publique; *Br* **H. Code** code *m* de la route

hijack ['haɪdʒæk] **1** *n* détournement *m*

2 *vt (plane)* détourner •**hijacker** *n (of plane)* pirate *m* de l'air •**hijacking** *n (air piracy)* piraterie *f* aérienne; *(hijack)* détournement *m*

hike [haɪk] **1** *n* (**a**) *(walk)* randonnée *f* (**b**) *Fam (increase)* hausse *f*

2 *vt Fam (price)* augmenter

3 *vi* faire de la randonnée •**hiker** *n*

randonneur, -euse *mf* •**hiking** *n* randonnée *f*; **to go h.** faire de la randonnée

hilarious [hɪ'leərɪəs] *adj* hilarant

hill [hɪl] *n* colline *f*; *(slope)* pente *f* •**hillbilly** (*pl* **-ies**) *n Am Fam* péquenaud, -aude *mf* •**hillside** *n* **on the h.** à flanc de coteau •**hilly** (**-ier, -iest**) *adj* vallonné

hilt [hɪlt] *n (of sword)* poignée *f*; *Fig* **to the h.** au maximum

him [hɪm] *pron* le, l'; *(after prep, 'than', 'it is')* lui; **I see h.** je le vois; **I saw h.** je l'ai vu; **I gave it to h.** je lui ai donné; **with h.** avec lui

himself [hɪm'self] *pron* lui-même; *(reflexive)* se, s'; *(after prep)* lui; **he did it h.** il l'a fait lui-même; **he cut h.** il s'est coupé; **he thinks of h.** il pense à lui

hind [haɪnd] *adj* **h. legs** pattes *fpl* de derrière •**hindquarters** *npl* arrière-train *m*

hinder ['hɪndə(r)] *vt (obstruct)* gêner; *(delay)* retarder; **to h. sb from doing sth** empêcher qn de faire qch •**hindrance** *n* obstacle *m*

hindsight ['haɪndsaɪt] *n* **with h.** avec le recul

Hindu ['hɪnduː] **1** *adj* hindou

2 *n* Hindou, -oue *mf*

hinge [hɪndʒ] **1** *n* gond *m*, charnière *f*

2 *vt insep* **to h. on** *(depend on)* dépendre de •**hinged** *adj* à charnière(s)

hint [hɪnt] **1** *n (insinuation)* allusion *f*; *(sign)* signe *m*; *(clue)* indice *m*; **hints** *(advice)* conseils *mpl*; **to drop sb a h.** faire une allusion à l'intention de qn

2 *vt* laisser entendre (**that** que)

3 *vt insep* **to h. at sb/sth** faire allusion à qn/qch

hip [hɪp] *n* hanche *f*

hippie ['hɪpɪ] *n* hippie *mf*

hippopotamus [hɪpə'pɒtəməs] *n* hippopotame *m*

hire ['haɪə(r)] **1** *n* location *f*; **for h.** à louer; *Br (sign on taxi)* 'libre'; **on h.** en location; *Br* **h. purchase** achat *m* à crédit; *Br* **on h. purchase** à crédit

2 *vt (vehicle)* louer; *(worker)* engager; **to h. sth out** louer qch

his [hɪz] **1** *possessive pron* le sien, la sienne, *pl* les sien(ne)s; **this hat is h.** ce chapeau est à lui *ou* est le sien; **a friend of h.** un ami à lui

2 *possessive adj* son, sa, *pl* ses

Hispanic [hɪ'spænɪk] *Am* **1** *adj* hispano-américain

2 *n* Hispano-Américain, -aine *mf*

hiss [hɪs] **1** *n* sifflement *m*; **hisses** *(booing)* sifflets *mpl*

2 *vti* siffler •**hissing** *n* sifflement *m*

history ['hɪstərɪ] (*pl* **-ies**) *n* (*study, events*) histoire *f*; **to make h., to go down in h.** (*of event*) faire date; (*of person*) entrer dans l'histoire; **medical h.** antécédents *mpl* médicaux • **historian** [hɪ'stɔːrɪən] *n* historien, -ienne *mf* • **historic(al)** [hɪ'stɒrɪk(əl)] *adj* historique

histrionic [hɪstrɪ'ɒnɪk] *adj Pej* théâtral • **histrionics** *npl Pej* scène *f*

hit [hɪt] **1** *n* (*blow*) coup *m*; (*in shooting*) tir *m* réussi; (*success*) succès *m*; *Comptr* (*visit to website*) hit *m*, contact *m*; **to score a direct h.** taper dans le mille; **h. man** tueur *m* à gages; **h. list** liste *f* noire; **h. (song)** hit *m*

2 (*pt & pp* **hit**, *pres p* **hitting**) *vt* (*beat*) frapper; (*bump into*) heurter; (*reach*) atteindre; (*affect*) toucher; (*problem, difficulty*) rencontrer; *Fam* **to h. it off** s'entendre bien (**with sb** avec qn)

3 *vi* frapper; **to h. back** riposter (**at** à); *Fam* **to h. out at sb** (*physically*) frapper qn; (*verbally*) s'en prendre à qn; **to h. (up)on sth** (*solution, idea*) trouver qch • **'hit-and-'run driver** *n* chauffard *m* (qui prend la fuite) • **'hit-or-'miss** *adj* (*chancy, random*) aléatoire

hitch [hɪtʃ] **1** *n* (*difficulty*) problème *m*

2 *vt* (*fasten*) accrocher (**to** à)

3 *vti* **to h. (a ride)**, *Br* **to h. a lift** faire du stop (**to** jusqu'à) • **hitchhike** *vi* faire du stop (**to** jusqu'à) • **hitchhiker** *n* autostoppeur, -euse *mf* • **hitchhiking** *n* autostop *m*

hitherto [hɪðə'tuː] *adv* jusqu'ici

HIV [eɪtʃaɪ'viː] (*abbr* **human immunodeficiency virus**) *n* (*virus*) VIH *m*; **HIV positive/negative** séropositif, -ive/séronégatif, -ive

hive [haɪv] **1** *n* ruche *f*

2 *vt* **to h. off** (*separate*) séparer

HMS ['eɪtʃemes] (*abbr* **Her/His Majesty's Ship**) *n Br* = abréviation précédant le nom des navires de la marine britannique

hoard [hɔːd] **1** *n* réserve *f*; (*of money*) trésor *m*

2 *vt* amasser

hoarding ['hɔːdɪŋ] *n Br* (*for advertising*) panneau *m* d'affichage

hoarfrost ['hɔːfrɒst] *n* givre *m*

hoarse [hɔːs] (**-er, -est**) *adj* enroué

hoax [həʊks] **1** *n* canular *m*

2 *vt* faire un canular à

hob [hɒb] *n* (*on stove*) plaque *f* chauffante

hobble ['hɒbəl] *vi* boitiller

hobby ['hɒbɪ] (*pl* **-ies**) *n* passe-temps *m*

inv • **hobbyhorse** *n* (*favourite subject*) dada *m*

hobnob ['hɒbnɒb] (*pt & pp* **-bb-**) *vi Fam* **to h. with sb** frayer avec qn

hobo ['həʊbəʊ] (*pl* **-oes** *or* **-os**) *n Am* vagabond, -onde *mf*

hock [hɒk] *Fam* **1** *n* **in h.** (*object*) au clou

2 *vt* mettre au clou

hockey ['hɒkɪ] *n* hockey *m*; *Br* (*field hockey*) hockey sur gazon; *Am* (*ice hockey*) hockey sur glace; **h. stick** crosse *f* de hockey

hocus-pocus [həʊkəs'pəʊkəs] *n* (*deception*) tromperie *f*; (*talk*) paroles *fpl* trompeuses

hoe [həʊ] **1** *n* binette *f*, houe *f*

2 (*pt & pp* **hoed**) *vt* biner

hog [hɒg] **1** *n* (*pig*) porc *m* châtré; *Fam* **to go the whole h.** aller jusqu'au bout

2 (*pt & pp* **-gg-**) *vt Fam* monopoliser

Hogmanay [hɒgmə'neɪ] *n Scot* la Saint-Sylvestre

hoist [hɔɪst] **1** *n* (*machine*) palan *m*

2 *vt* hisser

hold [həʊld] **1** *n* (*grip*) prise *f*; (*of ship*) cale *f*; (*of plane*) soute *f*; **to get h. of** (*grab*) saisir; (*contact*) joindre; (*find*) trouver; *Fam* **to get a h. of oneself** se maîtriser; **to be on h.** (*of project*) être en suspens; **to put sb on h.** (*on phone*) mettre qn en attente

2 (*pt & pp* **held**) *vt* tenir; (*heat, attention*) retenir; (*post*) occuper; (*record*) détenir; (*title, opinion*) avoir; (*party, exhibition*) organiser; (*ceremony, mass*) célébrer; (*contain*) contenir; (*keep*) garder; **to h. sb prisoner** retenir qn prisonnier; **to h. one's breath** retenir son souffle; **I h. that** (*believe*) je maintiens que; **to h. one's own** se défendre; **h. the line!** (*on phone*) ne quittez pas!; **h. it!** (*stay still*) ne bouge pas!; **to be held** (*of event*) avoir lieu

3 *vi* (*of nail, rope*) tenir; (*of weather*) se maintenir; **the same holds for you** cela vaut aussi pour toi • **hold-up** *n* (*attack*) hold-up *m inv*; *Br* (*traffic jam*) ralentissement *m*; (*delay*) retard *m*

▸ **hold back** *vt sep* (*restrain*) retenir; (*hide*) cacher (**from sb** à qn) ▸ **hold down** *vt sep* (*price*) bloquer; (*person on ground*) maintenir au sol; **to h. down a job** (*keep*) garder un emploi; (*occupy*) avoir un emploi ▸ **hold forth** *vi Pej* (*talk*) disserter ▸ **hold in** *vt sep* **to h. one's stomach in** rentrer son ventre ▸ **hold off 1** *vt sep* (*enemy*) tenir à distance **2** *vi* **if the rain holds off** s'il ne pleut pas ▸ **hold on1** *vt sep* (*keep in place*) tenir en place **2** *vi* (*wait*) patienter; *(stand firm)* tenir bon; **h. on!** *(on phone)* ne quittez pas!; **h. on (tight)!** tenez bon! ▸ **hold on to** *vt insep (cling to)* tenir bien; *(keep)* garder ▸ **hold out 1** *vt sep (offer)* offrir; *(hand)* tendre **2** *vi (resist)* résister; *(last)* durer ▸ **hold over** *vt sep (postpone)* remettre ▸ **hold together** *vt sep (nation, group)* assurer l'union de ▸ **hold up** *vt sep (raise)* lever; *(support)* soutenir; *(delay)* retarder; *(rob)* attaquer

holdall ['hǝʊldɔːl] *n Br* fourre-tout *m inv*

holder ['hǝʊldǝ(r)] *n* (**a**) *(of passport, degree, post)* titulaire *mf*; *(of record, card, ticket)* détenteur, -trice *mf* (**b**) *(container)* support *m*

hole [hǝʊl] **1** *n* trou *m*; *Fam (town, village)* bled *m*, trou; *Fam (room)* baraque *f* **2** *vt (ship)* faire une brèche dans **3** *vi Fam* **to h. up** *(hide)* se terrer

holiday ['hɒlɪdeɪ] **1** *n Br* **holiday(s)** *(from work, school)* vacances *fpl*; **a h.** *(day off)* un congé; **a (public** *or* **bank) h.,** *Am* **a legal h.** un jour férié; **a religious h.** une fête; **a month's h.** un mois de vacances; **on h.** en vacances; **to be/go on h.** être/ partir en vacances; **holidays with pay** congés *mpl* payés **2** *adj (camp, clothes)* de vacances; **h. home** résidence *f* secondaire; **h. season** saison *f* touristique • **holidaymaker** *n Br* vacancier, -ière *mf*

holiness ['hǝʊlɪnǝs] *n* sainteté *f*

Holland ['hɒlǝnd] *n* la Hollande

hollow ['hɒlǝʊ] **1** *adj* creux *(f* creuse); *(victory)* faux *(f* fausse); *(promise)* vain **2** *n* creux *m* **3** *adv* **to sound h.** sonner creux **4** *vt* **to h. sth out** évider qch

holly ['hɒlɪ] *n* houx *m*

holocaust ['hɒlǝkɔːst] *n* holocauste *m*

hologram ['hɒlǝgræm] *n* hologramme *m*

holster ['hǝʊlstǝ(r)] *n* étui *m* de revolver

holy ['hǝʊlɪ] (**-ier, -iest**) *adj* saint; *(bread, water)* bénit; *(ground)* sacré; **the H. Bible** la Sainte Bible

homage ['hɒmɪdʒ] *n* hommage *m*; **to pay h. to sb** rendre hommage à qn

home¹ [hǝʊm] **1** *n* maison *f*; *(country)* patrie *f*; *(for old soldiers, sailors)* foyer *m*; **old people's h.** maison *f* de retraite; **at h.** à la maison, chez soi; **to feel at h.** se sentir chez soi; **make yourself at h.** faites comme chez vous; **to play at h.** *(of football team)* jouer à domicile; **at h. and abroad** dans notre pays et à l'étranger; **far from h.** loin de chez soi; **a broken h.** un foyer désuni; **a good h.** une bonne famille; **to make one's h. in France** s'ins-

taller en France; **my h. is here** j'habite ici **2** *adv* à la maison, chez soi; **to go** *or* **come (back) h.** rentrer chez soi; **to be h.** être rentré; **to drive sb h.** ramener qn; **to drive a nail h.** enfoncer complètement un clou; *Fig* **to bring sth h. to sb** faire voir qch à qn **3** *adj (pleasures, atmosphere, cooking)* familial; *(visit, match)* à domicile; *(product, market)* national; **h. address** adresse *f* personnelle; **h. banking** banque *f* à domicile; **h. computer** ordinateur *m* domestique; **h. economics** économie *f* domestique; *Br* **h. help** aide *f* ménagère; **h. life** vie *f* de famille; **h. loan** prêt *m* immobilier; *Br* **H. Office** ≃ ministère *m* de l'Intérieur; **h. owner** propriétaire *mf*; *Comptr* **h. page** page *f* d'accueil; **h. rule** autonomie *f*; *Br* **H. Secretary** ≃ ministre *m* de l'Intérieur; **h. team** équipe *f* qui reçoit; **h. town** ville *f* natale • **homecoming** *n* retour *m* (au foyer) • **'home-'grown** *adj (fruit, vegetables)* du jardin; *(not grown abroad)* du pays • **homeland** *n* patrie *f* • **homeloving** *adj* casanier, -ière • **'home'made** *adj* (fait) maison *inv*
• **homesick** *adj* **to be h.** avoir le mal du pays • **homesickness** *n* mal *m* du pays

home² [hǝʊm] *vi* **to h. in on sth** se diriger automatiquement sur qch

homeless ['hǝʊmlɪs] **1** *adj* sans abri **2** *npl* **the h.** les sans-abri *mpl*

homely ['hǝʊmlɪ] (**-ier, -iest**) *adj (comfortable)* agréable et sans prétention; *Am (ugly)* sans charme

homeopathic [hǝʊmɪǝʊ'pæθɪk] *adj* homéopathique

homeward ['hǝʊmwǝd] **1** *adj (trip)* de retour **2** *adv* **h.-bound** sur le chemin de retour

homework ['hǝʊmwɜːk] *n Sch* devoirs *mpl*

homey ['hǝʊmɪ] (**-ier, -iest**) *adj Am Fam* accueillant

homicide ['hɒmɪsaɪd] *n* homicide *m*

homogeneous [hǝʊmǝ'dʒiːnɪǝs] *adj* homogène

homosexual [hǝʊmǝ'sekʃʊǝl] *adj & n* homosexuel, -uelle *(mf)* • **homosexuality** [-ʊ'ælɪtɪ] *n* homosexualité *f*

Honduras [hɒn'djʊǝrǝs] *n* le Honduras

honest ['ɒnɪst] *adj* honnête (**with** avec); *(profit, money)* honnêtement gagné; **the h. truth** la vérité vraie; **to earn an h. living** gagner honnêtement sa vie; **to be h., I don't know** franchement, je ne sais pas • **honestly** *adv* honnêtement; **h.!** *(show-*

ing annoyance) vraiment! • **honesty** *n* honnêteté *f*

honey ['hʌnɪ] *n* miel *m*; *Fam (person)* chéri, -ie *mf* • **honeycomb** [-kəʊm] *n* rayon *m* de miel • **honeymoon** *n* voyage *m* de noces • **honeysuckle** *n* chèvrefeuille *m*

Hong Kong [hɒŋˈkɒŋ] *n* Hongkong *m ou f*

honk [hɒŋk] **1** *n* coup *m* de Klaxon®
2 *vi (of driver)* klaxonner

honorary ['ɒnərərɪ] *adj (member)* honoraire; *(title)* honorifique

honour ['ɒnə(r)] *(Am* **honor***)* **1** *n* honneur *m*; **in h. of** en l'honneur de; **to have the h. of doing sth** avoir l'honneur de faire qch; *Br Univ* **honours degree** diplôme *m* universitaire
2 *vt* honorer (**with** de)

honourable ['ɒnərəbəl] *(Am* **honorable***) adj* honorable

hood [hʊd] *n* (**a**) *(of coat)* capuche *f*; *(with eye-holes)* cagoule *f*; *Br (of car, pram)* capote *f*; *Am (car bonnet)* capot *m*; *(above stove)* hotte *f* (**b**) *Am Fam (gangster)* truand *m* • **hooded** *adj (person)* encapuchonné; *(coat)* à capuchon

hoodlum ['huːdləm] *n Fam* voyou *m* (*pl* -ous)

hoodwink ['hʊdwɪŋk] *vt Fam* embobiner

hoof [huːf] *(pl* **hoofs** [huːfs] *or* **hooves** [huːvz]) *n* sabot *m*

hoo-ha ['huːhɑː] *n Fam* tintouin *m*

hook [hʊk] **1** *n* crochet *m*; *(on clothes)* agrafe *f*; *Fishing* hameçon *m*; **off the h.** *(phone)* décroché; *Fam* **to let** *or* **get sb off the h.** tirer qn d'affaire
2 *vt* **to h. (on** *or* **up)** accrocher (**to** à); **to h. a computer up** connecter un ordinateur • **hooked** *adj (nose, beak)* crochu; *(end, object)* recourbé; *Fam* **to be h. on sth** être accro à qch; *Fam* **to be h. on sb** *(infatuated with)* être entiché de qn; *Fam* **to be h. on drugs** être accro

hooker ['hʊkə(r)] *n Am Fam* prostituée *f*

hook(e)y ['hʊkɪ] *n Am Fam* **to play h.** sécher (les cours)

hooligan ['huːlɪɡən] *n* hooligan *m* • **hooliganism** *n* hooliganisme *m*

hoop [huːp] *n* cerceau *m*

hoot [huːt] **1** *n* huée *f*; *Br (of vehicle)* coup *m* de Klaxon®
2 *vti (jeer)* huer
3 *vi Br (of vehicle)* klaxonner; *(of train)* siffler; *(of owl)* hululer • **hooter** *n Br (of vehicle)* Klaxon® *m*; *(of factory)* sirène *f*; *Fam (nose)* pif *m*

hoover® ['huːvə(r)] **1** *n Br* aspirateur *m*
2 *vt Br (room)* passer l'aspirateur dans;

(carpet) passer l'aspirateur sur; **to h. sth up** *(dust, crumbs)* enlever qch à l'aspirateur

hop [hɒp] **1** *n (leap)* saut *m*
2 *(pt & pp* **-pp-***) vi (jump)* sautiller; *(on one leg)* sauter à cloche-pied; **h. in!** *(to car)* allez! grimpe!; **he hopped onto the first train** il a sauté dans le premier train
3 *vt Fam* **h. it!** fiche le camp!

hope [həʊp] **1** *n* espoir *m*
2 *vt* **to h. to do sth** espérer faire qch; **to h. that...** espérer que...
3 *vi* espérer; **to h. for sth** espérer qch; **I h. so/not** j'espère que oui/non • **hopeful** ['həʊpfʊl] **1** *adj (person)* optimiste; *(situation)* encourageant; **to be h. that...** avoir bon espoir que... **2** *n* **a young h.** un jeune espoir • **hopefully** *adv* avec un peu de chance; **to do sth h.** faire qch plein d'espoir • **hopeless** ['həʊpləs] *adj* désespéré; *Fam (useless, bad)* nul (*f* nulle) • **hopelessly** *adv (lost, out-of-date)* complètement; *(in love)* éperdument; *(live, act)* sans espoir

hops [hɒps] *npl (for beer)* houblon *m*

hopscotch ['hɒpskɒtʃ] *n* marelle *f*

horde [hɔːd] *n* horde *f*

horizon [həˈraɪzən] *n* horizon *m*; **on the h.** à l'horizon • **horizontal** [hɒrɪˈzɒntəl] *adj* horizontal • **horizontally** [hɒrɪˈzɒntəlɪ] *adv* horizontalement

hormone ['hɔːməʊn] *n* hormone *f*; **h. replacement therapy** hormonothérapie *f* de substitution

horn [hɔːn] **1** *n (of animal)* corne *f*; *(on vehicle)* Klaxon® *m*; *(musical instrument)* cor *m*
2 *vi Am Fam* **to h. in** mêler son grain de sel (**on** à); *(interrupt)* interrompre

hornet ['hɔːnɪt] *n* frelon *m*

horny ['hɔːnɪ] *(-ier, -iest) adj very Fam (aroused)* excité

horoscope ['hɒrəskəʊp] *n* horoscope *m*

horrendous [hɒˈrendəs] *adj* horrible

horrible ['hɒrəbəl] *adj* horrible • **horribly** *adv* horriblement

horrid ['hɒrɪd] *adj (unpleasant)* affreux, -euse; *(unkind)* méchant

horrific [həˈrɪfɪk] *adj* horrible

horrify ['hɒrɪfaɪ] *(pt & pp* **-ied***) vt* horrifier

horror ['hɒrə(r)] *n* horreur *f*; *Fam (little)* **h.** *(child)* petit monstre *m*; **h. film** film *m* d'horreur; **h. story** histoire *f* épouvantable

hors d'œuvre [ɔːˈdɜːv] *(pl inv or* **hors d'œuvres***) n* hors-d'œuvre *m inv*

horse [hɔːs] *n* (**a**) *(animal)* cheval *m*; **to**

go h. riding faire du cheval; **h. racing** courses *fpl*; **h. show** concours *m* hippique (**b**) **h. chestnut** *(fruit)* marron *m* • **horseback** *n* **on h.** à cheval; *Am* **to go h. riding** faire du cheval • **horseman** (*pl* **-men**) *n* cavalier *m* • **horseplay** *n* chahut *m* • **horsepower** *n (unit)* cheval-vapeur *m* • **horseradish** *n* raifort *m* • **horseshoe** *n* fer *m* à cheval • **horsewoman** (*pl* **-women**) *n* cavalière *f*

horticulture ['hɔːtɪkʌltʃə(r)] *n* horticulture *f* • **horti'cultural** *adj* horticole

hose [həʊz] **1** *n (pipe)* tuyau *m*; **garden h.** tuyau d'arrosage
2 *vt* arroser (au jet d'eau); **to h. sth down** *(car)* laver qch au jet • **hosepipe** *n Br* tuyau *m* d'arrosage

hosiery [*Br* 'həʊzɪərɪ, *Am* 'həʊʒərɪ] *n* bonneterie *f*

hospice ['hɒspɪs] *n (hospital)* = établissement pour malades en phase terminale

hospitable [hɒ'spɪtəbəl] *adj* hospitalier, -ière (**to** envers) • **hospitably** *adv* avec hospitalité • **hospitality** [-'tælɪtɪ] *n* hospitalité *f*

hospital ['hɒspɪtəl] *n* hôpital *m*; **in h.,** *Am* **in the h.** à l'hôpital; **h. bed** lit *m* d'hôpital; **h. staff/services** personnel *m*/services *mpl* hospitalier(s) • **hospitalize** *vt* hospitaliser

host¹ [həʊst] **1** *n (of guests)* hôte *m*; *(on TV or radio show)* présentateur, -trice *mf*; **h. country** pays *m* d'accueil
2 *vt (programme)* présenter

host² [həʊst] *n* **a h. of** *(many)* une foule de

host³ [həʊst] *n Rel* hostie *f*

hostage ['hɒstɪdʒ] *n* otage *m*; **to take sb h.** prendre qn en otage; **to be held h.** être retenu en otage

hostel ['hɒstəl] *n* foyer *m*; **(youth) h.** auberge *f* de jeunesse

hostess ['həʊstɪs] *n (in house, nightclub)* hôtesse *f*; **(air) h.** hôtesse *f* (de l'air)

hostile [*Br* 'hɒstaɪl, *Am* 'hɒstəl] *adj* hostile (**to** or **towards** à) • **hos'tility** *n* hostilité *f* (**to** or **towards** envers); **hostilities** *(in battle)* hostilités *fpl*

hot¹ [hɒt] (**hotter, hottest**) *adj* chaud; *(spice)* fort; *(temperament)* passionné; *Fam (news)* dernier, -ière; **to be** or **feel h.** avoir chaud; **it's h.** il fait chaud; *Fam* **to be h. on sth** *(knowledgeable)* être calé en qch; *Fam* **not so h.** *(bad)* pas fameux, -euse; *Sport* **h. favourite** grand(e) favori(te) *mf* • **hotbed** *n Pej* foyer *m* (**of** de) • **'hot-'blooded** *adj* passionné • **hotcake** *n Am (pancake)* crêpe *f* • **hotdog** *n* hot dog

m • **hothead** *n* tête *f* brûlée • **'hot'headed** *adj* exalté • **hothouse** *n* serre *f* (chaude) • **hotly** *adv* passionnément • **hotplate** *n* chauffe-plat *m*; *(on stove)* plaque *f* chauffante • **'hot-'tempered** *adj* emporté • **hot-'water bottle** *n* bouillotte *f*

hot² [hɒt] *(pt & pp* **-tt-**) *vi Fam* **to h. up** *(increase)* s'intensifier; *(become dangerous or excited)* s'envenimer

hotchpotch ['hɒtʃpɒtʃ] *n Fam* fatras *m*

hotel [həʊ'tel] *n* hôtel *m*; **h. room/bed** chambre *f*/lit *m* d'hôtel; **the h. trade** l'industrie *f* hôtelière • **hotelier** [həʊ'telɪeɪ] *n* hôtelier, -ière *mf*

hound [haʊnd] **1** *n (dog)* chien *m* de chasse
2 *vt (pursue)* traquer; *(bother, worry)* harceler

hour ['aʊə(r)] *n* heure *f*; **half an h.** une demi-heure; **a quarter of an h.** un quart d'heure; **paid 20 euros an h.** payé 20 euros (de) l'heure; **10 miles an h.** 10 miles à l'heure; **open all hours** ouvert à toute heure; **h. hand** *(of watch, clock)* petite aiguille *f*

hourly ['aʊəlɪ] **1** *adj (rate, pay)* horaire; **an h. bus/train** un bus/train toutes les heures
2 *adv* toutes les heures; **h. paid, paid h.** payé à l'heure

house 1 [haʊs] (*pl* **-ses** [-zɪz]) *n* maison *f*; *(audience in theatre)* salle *f*, auditoire *m*; *Pol* **the H. of Commons** la Chambre des communes; *Pol* **the H. of Lords** la Chambre des lords; **the Houses of Parliament** le Parlement; **the H. of Representatives** la Chambre des représentants; **at/to my h.** chez moi; **on the h.** *(free of charge)* aux frais de la maison; *Br* **h. doctor** interne *mf*; **h. guest** invité, -ée *mf*; **h. plant** plante *f* d'intérieur; **h. prices** prix *mpl* de l'immobilier; **h. wine** vin *m* de la maison
2 [haʊz] *vt* loger; *(of building)* abriter • **houseboat** *n* péniche *f* aménagée • **housebound** *adj* confiné chez soi • **housebreaking** *n (crime)* cambriolage *m* • **housebroken** *adj Am (dog)* propre • **housecoat** *n* robe *f* d'intérieur • **housefly** (*pl* **-flies**) *n* mouche *f* (domestique) • **household** *n* ménage *m*; **h. chores** tâches *fpl* ménagères; **a h. name** un nom très connu • **householder** *n (owner)* propriétaire *mf*; • **househusband** *n* homme *m* au foyer • **housekeeper** *n (employee)* gouvernante *f* • **housekeeping** *n* ménage *m* • **houseman** (*pl* **-men**) *n Br Med* interne *m* • **houseproud** *adj* qui s'occupe méticuleusement de sa maison • **housetrained** *adj Br (dog)* propre • **housewarming** *n &*

adj **to have a h. (party)** pendre la crémaillère • **housewife** (*pl* **-wives**) *n* ménagère *f* • **housework** *n* ménage *m*

housing ['haʊzɪŋ] *n* logement *m*; (*houses*) logements *mpl*; **h. crisis** crise *f* du logement; *Br* **h. estate** lotissement *m*; (*council-owned*) cité *f*

hovel ['hɒvəl] *n* taudis *m*

hover ['hɒvə(r)] *vi* (*of bird, aircraft, danger*) planer; **to h. (around)** (*of person*) rôder

hovercraft ['hɒvəkrɑːft] *n* aéroglisseur *m*

how [haʊ] *adv* comment; **h. kind!** comme c'est gentil!; **h. long/high is...?** quelle est la longueur/hauteur de...?; **h. much?, h. many?** combien?; **h. much time?** combien de temps?; **h. many apples?** combien de pommes?; **h. about a walk?** si on faisait une promenade?; **h. about some coffee?** (si on prenait) du café?; **h. about me?** et moi?; **h. do you do** (*greeting*) bonjour; *Fam* **h.'s that?, h. so?, h. come?** comment ça?

howdy ['haʊdɪ] *exclam Am Fam* salut!

however [haʊ'evə(r)] **1** *adv* **h. big he may be** si grand soit-il; **h. she may do it, h. she does it** de quelque manière qu'elle le fasse; **h. that may be** quoi qu'il en soit; **h. did she find out?** comment a-t-elle bien pu l'apprendre?
2 *conj* cependant

howl [haʊl] **1** *n* hurlement *m*; (*of baby*) braillement *m*; (*of wind*) mugissement *m*; **h. of laughter** éclat *m* de rire
2 *vi* hurler; (*of baby*) brailler; (*of wind*) mugir

howler ['haʊlə(r)] *n Fam* (*mistake*) gaffe *f*

HP [eɪtʃ'piː] *Br abbr* = **hire purchase**

hp (*abbr* **horsepower**) CV

HQ [eɪtʃ'kjuː] (*abbr* **headquarters**) *n* QG *m*

hub [hʌb] *n* (*of wheel*) moyeu *m*; *Fig* centre *m* • **hubcap** *n* (*of wheel*) enjoliveur *m*

hubbub ['hʌbʌb] *n* brouhaha *m*

huckleberry ['hʌkəlbərɪ] (*pl* **-ies**) *n Am* myrtille *f*

huddle ['hʌdəl] *vi* **to h. (together)** se blottir (les uns contre les autres)

hue [hjuː] *n* (**a**) (*colour*) teinte *f* (**b**) **h. and cry** tollé *m*

huff [hʌf] *n Fam* **in a h.** (*offended*) fâché

hug [hʌg] **1** *n* **to give sb a h.** serrer qn (dans ses bras)
2 (*pt & pp* **-gg-**) *vt* (*person*) serrer dans ses bras; **to h. the kerb/coast** serrer le trottoir/la côte

huge [hjuːdʒ] *adj* énorme • **hugely** *adv* énormément

hulk [hʌlk] *n* (*person*) mastodonte *m*

hull [hʌl] *n* (*of ship*) coque *f*

hullabaloo [hʌləbə'luː] (*pl* **-oos**) *n Fam* (*noise*) raffut *m*

hullo [hʌ'ləʊ] *exclam Br* bonjour!; (*answering phone*) allô!; (*surprise*) tiens!

hum [hʌm] **1** *n* (*of insect*) bourdonnement *m*
2 (*pt & pp* **-mm-**) *vt* (*tune*) fredonner
3 *vi* (*of insect*) bourdonner; (*of person*) fredonner; (*of engine*) ronronner

human ['hjuːmən] **1** *adj* humain; **h. being** être *m* humain; **h. rights** droits *mpl* de l'homme
2 *n* être *m* humain • **humanly** *adv* humainement

humane [hjuː'meɪn] *adj* (*kind*) humain • **humanely** *adv* humainement

humanitarian [hjuːmænɪ'teərɪən] *adj & n* humanitaire (*mf*)

humanity [hjuː'mænətɪ] *n* (*human beings, kindness*) humanité *f*

humble ['hʌmbəl] **1** *adj* humble
2 *vt* humilier • **humbly** *adv* humblement

humdrum ['hʌmdrʌm] *adj* monotone

humid ['hjuːmɪd] *adj* humide • **hu'midify** (*pt & pp* **-ied**) *vt* humidifier • **hu'midity** *n* humidité *f*

humiliate [hjuː'mɪlɪeɪt] *vt* humilier • **humiliation** [-'eɪʃən] *n* humiliation *f*

humility [hjuː'mɪlətɪ] *n* humilité *f*

humorist ['hjuːmərɪst] *n* humoriste *mf*

humorous ['hjuːmərəs] *adj* (*book, writer*) humoristique; (*person, situation*) drôle • **humorously** *adv* avec humour

humour ['hjuːmə(r)] (*Am* **humor**) **1** *n* (*fun*) humour *m*; *Formal* (*temper*) humeur *f*; **to have a sense of h.** avoir le sens de l'humour; **in a good h.** de bonne humeur
2 *vt* **to h. sb** faire plaisir à qn

hump [hʌmp] **1** *n* (*lump, mound in road*) bosse *f*; *Br Fam* **to have the h.** (*be depressed*) avoir le cafard; (*be angry*) être en rogne
2 *vt Fam* (*carry*) trimbaler • **'humpback(ed) 'bridge** *n Br* pont *m* en dos d'âne

hunch [hʌntʃ] **1** *n Fam* (*intuition*) intuition *f*
2 *vt* **to h. one's shoulders** rentrer les épaules • **hunchback** *n* bossu, -ue *mf*

hundred ['hʌndrəd] *adj & n* cent (*m*); **a h. pages** cent pages; **two h. pages** deux cents pages; **hundreds of** des centaines de • **hundredfold 1** *adj* centuple **2** *adv* au centuple • **hundredth** *adj & n* centième *(mf)* • **hundredweight** *n Br* = 50,8 kg, 112 livres; *Am* = 45,3 kg, 100 livres

hung [hʌŋ] *pt & pp of* **hang**¹

Hungary [ˈhʌŋgərɪ] *n* la Hongrie • **Hungarian** [-ˈgeərɪən] **1** *adj* hongrois **2** *n (person)* Hongrois, -oise *mf; (language)* hongrois *m*

hunger [ˈhʌŋgə(r)] *n* faim *f;* **h. strike** grève *f* de la faim • **hungrily** *adv* avidement • **hungry** (**-ier, -iest**) *adj* **to be** *or* **feel h.** avoir faim; **to go h.** souffrir de la faim; **to make sb h.** donner faim à qn; **h. for sth** avide de qch

hunk [hʌŋk] *n* gros morceau *m*

hunt [hʌnt] **1** *n (search)* recherche *f* (**for** de); *(for animals)* chasse *f*
2 *vt (animals)* chasser; *(pursue)* poursuivre; **to h. down** *(animal, fugitive)* traquer; **to h. out** *(information)* dénicher
3 *vi (kill animals)* chasser; **to h. for sth** • **hunter** *n* chasseur *m* • **hunting** *n* chasse *f*

hurdle [ˈhɜːdəl] *n (fence in race)* haie *f; Fig (problem)* obstacle *m*

hurl [hɜːl] *vt (throw)* jeter, lancer (**at** à); **to h. oneself at sb** se ruer sur qn; **to h. insults** *or* **abuse at sb** lancer des insultes à qn

hurly-burly [ˈhɜːlɪbɜːlɪ] *n Fam* tohu-bohu *m inv*

hurray [hʊˈreɪ] *exclam* hourra!

hurricane [*Br* ˈhʌrɪkən, *Am* ˈhʌrɪkeɪn] *n* ouragan *m*

hurry [ˈhʌrɪ] **1** *n* hâte *f;* **in a h.** à la hâte; **to be in a h.** être pressé; **to be in a h. to do sth** avoir hâte de faire qch; **there's no h.** rien ne presse
2 (*pt & pp* **-ied**) *vt (person)* presser; *(work)* hâter; **to h. one's meal** manger à toute vitesse; **to h. sb out** faire sortir qn à la hâte; **he was hurried to hospital** on l'a transporté d'urgence à l'hôpital
3 *vi* se dépêcher, se presser (**to do** de faire); **to h. up** se dépêcher; **to h. back** se dépêcher de revenir; **to h. out** sortir à la hâte; **to h. towards sb/sth** se précipiter vers qn/qch • **hurried** *adj (steps, decision)* précipité; *(work)* fait à la hâte; *(visit)* éclair *inv;* **to be h.** *(in a hurry)* être pressé

hurt [hɜːt] **1** *adj (wounded, offended)* blessé
2 *n (emotional)* blessure *f*
3 (*pt & pp* **hurt**) *vt (physically)* faire du mal à; *(causing a wound)* blesser; *(emotionally)* faire de la peine à; *(reputation, chances)* nuire à; **to h. sb's feelings** blesser qn
4 *vi* faire mal; **where does it h.?** où avez-

vous mal?; **his arm hurts (him)** son bras lui fait mal • **hurtful** *adj (remark)* blessant

hurtle [ˈhɜːtəl] *vi* **to h. along** aller à toute vitesse; **to h. down the street** dévaler la rue

husband [ˈhʌzbənd] *n* mari *m*

hush [hʌʃ] **1** *n* silence *m*
2 *exclam* chut!
3 *vt (person)* faire taire; *(baby)* calmer; **to h. up** *(scandal)* étouffer • **hushed** *adj (voice)* étouffé; *(silence)* profond • **'hush-'hush** *adj Fam* top secret *inv*

husk [hʌsk] *n (of rice, grain)* enveloppe *f*

husky [ˈhʌskɪ] (**-ier, -iest**) *adj (voice)* rauque

hussy [ˈhʌsɪ] (*pl* **-ies**) *n Old-fashioned or Hum* gourgandine *f*

hustings [ˈhʌstɪŋz] *npl Br* campagne *f* électorale

hustle [ˈhʌsəl] **1** **h. and bustle** effervescence *f*
2 *vt (shove, push)* **to h. sb away** emmener qn de force
3 *vi Am (work busily)* se démener (**to get sth** pour avoir qch)

hut [hʌt] *n* cabane *f; (dwelling)* hutte *f*

hutch [hʌtʃ] *n (for rabbit)* clapier *m*

hyacinth [ˈhaɪəsɪnθ] *n* jacinthe *f*

hybrid [ˈhaɪbrɪd] *adj & n* hybride *(m)*

hydrangea [haɪˈdreɪndʒə] *n* hortensia *m*

hydrant [ˈhaɪdrənt] *n* (**fire**) **h.** bouche *f* d'incendie

hydraulic [haɪˈdrɔːlɪk] *adj* hydraulique

hydrocarbon [haɪdrəʊˈkɑːbən] *n* hydrocarbure *m*

hydroelectric [haɪdrəʊɪˈlektrɪk] *adj* hydroélectrique

hydrogen [ˈhaɪdrədʒən] *n Chem* hydrogène *m*

hyena [haɪˈiːnə] *n (animal)* hyène *f*

hygiene [ˈhaɪdʒiːn] *n* hygiène *f* • **hygienic** *adj* hygiénique • **hygienist** *n* (**dental**) **h.** spécialiste *mf* de l'hygiène dentaire

hymn [hɪm] *n* cantique *m*

hype [haɪp] *n Fam (publicity)* battage *m* publicitaire

hyper- [ˈhaɪpə(r)] *pref* hyper-

hypermarket [ˈhaɪpəmɑːkɪt] *n* hypermarché *m*

hyphen [ˈhaɪfən] *n* trait *m* d'union • **hyphenate** *vt* mettre un trait d'union à • **hyphenated** *adj (word)* à trait d'union

hypnosis [hɪpˈnəʊsɪs] *n* hypnose *f* • **hypnotism** [ˈhɪpnətɪzəm] *n* hypnotisme *m* • **hypnotist** [ˈhɪpnətɪst] *n* hypnotiseur *m* • **hypnotize** [ˈhɪpnətaɪz] *vt* hypnotiser

hypoallergenic [haɪpəʊælə'dʒenɪk] *adj* hypoallergénique

hypochondriac [haɪpə'kɒndrɪæk] *n* hypocondriaque *mf*

hypocrisy [hɪ'pɒkrɪsɪ] *n* hypocrisie *f* • **hypocrite** ['hɪpəkrɪt] *n* hypocrite *mf* • **hypocritical** [hɪpə'krɪtɪkəl] *adj* hypocrite

hypodermic [haɪpə'dɜːmɪk] *adj* hypodermique

hypothermia [haɪpə'θɜːmɪə] *n Med* hypothermie *f*

hypothesis [haɪ'pɒθɪsɪs] (*pl* **-theses** [-θɪsiːz]) *n* hypothèse *f* • **hypothetical** [haɪpə'θetɪkəl] *adj* hypothétique

hysteria [hɪ'stɪərɪə] *n* hystérie *f* • **hysterical** [hɪ'sterɪkəl] *adj (very upset)* qui a une crise de nerfs; *Fam (funny)* tordant; **to become h.** avoir une crise de nerfs • **hysterically** [hɪ'sterɪkəlɪ] *adv (cry)* sans pouvoir s'arrêter; **to laugh h.** rire aux larmes • **hysterics** [hɪ'sterɪks] *npl (tears)* crise *f* de nerfs; *(laughter)* fou rire *m*; **to be in h.** avoir une crise de nerfs; *(with laughter)* être écroulé de rire; **he had us in h.** il nous a fait tordre de rire

I¹, i [aɪ] *n (letter)* I, i *m inv*

I² [aɪ] *pron* je, j'; *(stressed)* moi; **I want** je veux; **she and I** elle et moi

ice¹ [aɪs] **1** *n* glace *f*; *(on road)* verglas *m*; *Br* **black i.** *(on road)* verglas

 2 *vi* **to i. (over** *or* **up)** *(of lake)* geler; *(of window)* se givrer ●**iceberg** *n* iceberg *m* ●**icebox** *n Am (fridge)* réfrigérateur *m*; *Br (in fridge)* freezer *m* ●**ice-'cold** *adj* glacial; *(drink)* glacé ●**ice 'cream** *n* glace *f* ●**ice cube** *n* glaçon *m* ●**iced** *adj (tea, coffee)* glacé ●**ice hockey** *n* hockey *m* sur glace ●**ice-skating** *n* patinage *m* (sur glace)

ice² [aɪs] *vt Br (cake)* glacer ●**icing** *n Br (on cake)* glaçage *m*

Iceland ['aɪslənd] *n* l'Islande *f* ●**Icelandic** [-'lændɪk] *adj* islandais

icicle ['aɪsɪkəl] *n* glaçon *m (de gouttière etc)*

icon ['aɪkɒn] *n* icône *f*

icy ['aɪsɪ] (**-ier, -iest**) *adj (road)* verglacé; *(ground)* gelé; *(water, hands)* glacé

ID [aɪ'diː] *n* pièce *f* d'identité

I'd [aɪd] = **I had, I would**

idea [aɪ'dɪə] *n* idée *f*; **I have an i. that** j'ai l'impression que; **that's my i. of rest** c'est ce que j'appelle du repos; *Fam* **that's the i.!** c'est ça!; **not the slightest** *or* **foggiest i.** pas la moindre idée

ideal [aɪ'dɪəl] *adj & n* idéal *(m)*

idealism [aɪ'dɪəlɪzəm] *n* idéalisme *m* ●**idealist** *n* idéaliste *mf* ●**idea'listic** *adj* idéaliste ●**idealize** *vt* idéaliser

ideally [aɪ'dɪəlɪ] *adv* idéalement; **i., we should stay** l'idéal, ce serait que nous restions

identical [aɪ'dentɪkəl] *adj* identique (**to** *or* **with** à)

identify [aɪ'dentɪfaɪ] (*pt & pp* **-ied**) *vt* identifier; **to i. (oneself) with** s'identifier avec ●**identification** [-fɪ'keɪʃən] *n* identification *f*; **to have (some) i.** *(document)* avoir une pièce d'identité

identikit [aɪ'dentɪkɪt] *n* portrait-robot *m*

identity [aɪ'dentɪtɪ] (*pl* **-ies**) *n* identité *f*; **i. card** carte *f* d'identité; **i. disc** plaque *f* d'identité

ideology [aɪdɪ'ɒlədʒɪ] (*pl* **-ies**) *n* idéolo-gie *f* ●**ideological** [aɪdɪə'lɒdʒɪkəl] *adj* idéologique

idiocy ['ɪdɪəsɪ] *n* idiotie *f*

idiom ['ɪdɪəm] *n (phrase)* expression *f* idiomatique; *(language)* idiome *m* ●**idio-'matic** *adj* idiomatique

idiosyncrasy [ɪdɪə'sɪŋkrəsɪ] (*pl* **-ies**) *n* particularité *f*

idiot ['ɪdɪət] *n* idiot, -iote *mf* ●**idiotic** [-'ɒtɪk] *adj* idiot, bête ●**idiotically** [-'ɒtɪkəlɪ] *adv* idiotement

idle ['aɪdəl] **1** *adj (unoccupied)* désœuvré; *(lazy)* oisif, -ive; *(promise)* vain; *(pleasure, question)* futile, vain; *(rumour)* sans fondement; **to lie i.** *(of machine)* être au repos; **an i. moment** un moment de loisir

 2 *vt* **to i. away** the *or* one's **time** passer son temps à ne rien faire

 3 *vi (of engine, machine)* tourner au ralenti ●**idleness** *n (inaction)* inactivité *f*; *(laziness)* oisiveté *f* ●**idler** *n* paresseux, -euse *mf* ●**idly** *adv (lazily)* paresseusement; *(suggest, say)* négligemment

idol ['aɪdəl] *n* idole *f* ●**idolize** *vt (adore)* idolâtrer

idyllic [aɪ'dɪlɪk] *adj* idyllique

i.e. [aɪ'iː] (*abbr* **id est**) c'est-à-dire

if [ɪf] *conj* si; **if he comes** s'il vient; **even if** même si; **if so** si c'est le cas; **if not** sinon; **if only I were rich** si seulement j'étais riche; **if only to look** ne serait-ce que pour regarder; **as if** comme si; **as if nothing had happened** comme si de rien n'était; **as if to say** comme pour dire; **if necessary** s'il le faut

igloo ['ɪgluː] (*pl* **-oos**) *n* igloo *m*

ignite [ɪg'naɪt] **1** *vt* mettre le feu à

 2 *vi* prendre feu ●**ignition** [-'nɪʃən] *n (in vehicle)* allumage *m*; **to switch on/off the i.** mettre/couper le contact; **i. key** clef *f* de contact

ignominious [ɪgnə'mɪnɪəs] *adj* ignominieux, -ieuse

ignoramus [ɪgnə'reɪməs] *n* ignare *mf*

ignorance ['ɪgnərəns] *n* ignorance *f* (**of** de) ●**ignorant** *adj* ignorant (**of** de) ●**ignorantly** *adv* par ignorance

ignore [ɪg'nɔː(r)] *vt* ignorer; **just i. him!** ne fais pas attention à lui!

iguana [ɪgˈwɑːnə] n iguane m
ilk [ɪlk] n of that i. de cet acabit
ill [ɪl] **1** adj (sick) malade; (bad) mauvais;
i. will malveillance f
   2 npl **ills** maux mpl
   3 adv mal; **to speak i. of sb** dire du mal
de qn • **ˈill-adˈvised** adj (person) malavisé; (decision) peu judicieux, -ieuse
• **ˈill-ˈfated** adj (day) fatal; (enterprise)
malheureux, -euse • **ill-gotten** adj **i.
gains** biens mpl mal acquis • **ˈill-inˈ-
ˈformed** adj mal renseigné • **ˈill-ˈman-
nered** adj mal élevé • **ˈill-ˈnatured** adj
(mean, unkind) désagréable • **ˈill-ˈtimed**
adj inopportun • **ill-ˈtreat** vt maltraiter
I'll [aɪl] = I will, I shall
illegal [ɪˈliːgəl] adj illégal • **illegality**
[ɪlɪˈgæl-ɪtɪ] n illégalité f
illegible [ɪˈledʒəbəl] adj illisible
illegitimate [ɪlɪˈdʒɪtɪmət] adj illégitime
• **illegitimacy** n illégitimité f
illicit [ɪˈlɪsɪt] adj illicite
illiterate [ɪˈlɪtərət] adj & n analphabète
(mf) • **illiteracy** n analphabétisme m
illness [ˈɪlnɪs] n maladie f
illogical [ɪˈlɒdʒɪkəl] adj illogique
illuminate [ɪˈluːmɪneɪt] vt (monument)
illuminer; (street, question) éclairer • **illu-
miˈnation** n (lighting) éclairage m; Br **the
illuminations** (decorative lights) les illuminations fpl
illusion [ɪˈluːʒən] n illusion f (**about** sur);
to have the i. that... avoir l'illusion que...;
I'm not under any i. about... je ne me fais
aucune illusion sur... • **illusive, illusory**
adj illusoire
illustrate [ˈɪləstreɪt] vt (with pictures, examples) illustrer (**with** de) • **illuˈstration** n
illustration f
illustrious [ɪˈlʌstrɪəs] adj illustre
image [ˈɪmɪdʒ] n image f; (public) **i.** (of
company) image f de marque; **he's the
(living** or **spitting** or **very) i. of his brother**
c'est tout le portrait de son frère • **imagery** n imagerie f
imaginable [ɪˈmædʒɪnəbəl] adj imaginable; **the worst thing i.** le pire que l'on
puisse imaginer
imaginary [ɪˈmædʒɪnərɪ] adj imaginaire
imagination [ɪmædʒɪˈneɪʃən] n imagination f
imaginative [ɪˈmædʒɪnətɪv] adj (plan,
novel) original; (person) imaginatif, -ive
imagine [ɪˈmædʒɪn] vt imaginer (**that**
que); **to i. sb doing sth** imaginer qn
faisant qch; **you're imagining things!** tu
te fais des idées!
imbalance [ɪmˈbæləns] n déséquilibre m

imbecile [Br ˈɪmbəsiːl, Am ˈɪmbəsəl] adj
& n imbécile (mf) • **imbecility** [-ˈsɪlɪtɪ] n
imbécillité f
imbibe [ɪmˈbaɪb] vt Formal absorber
imbued [ɪmˈbjuːd] adj Formal **i. with**
(ideas) imprégné de; (feelings) empreint
de
IMF [aɪemˈef] (abbr **International Monetary Fund**) n FMI m
imitate [ˈɪmɪteɪt] vt imiter • **imiˈtation** n
imitation f; Br **i. jewellery**, Am **i. jewelry**
faux bijoux mpl; **i. leather** similicuir m
imitative [ˈɪmɪtətɪv] adj (sound) imitatif,
-ive; (person) imitateur, -trice
imitator [ˈɪmɪteɪtə(r)] n imitateur, -trice
mf
immaculate [ɪˈmækjʊlət] adj impeccable
immaterial [ɪməˈtɪərɪəl] adj sans importance (**to** pour)
immature [ɪməˈtʃʊə(r)] adj (person) immature; (fruit) vert
immeasurable [ɪˈmeʒərəbəl] adj incommensurable
immediate [ɪˈmiːdɪət] adj immédiat
• **immediacy** n immédiateté f • **immediately 1** adv (at once) tout de suite, immédiatement; (concern, affect) directement;
it's i. above/below c'est juste au-dessus/
en dessous **2** conj Br (as soon as) dès que
immense [ɪˈmens] adj immense • **immensely** adv (rich) immensément; (painful) extrêmement; **to enjoy oneself i.**
s'amuser énormément • **immensity** n immensité f
immerse [ɪˈmɜːs] vt (in liquid) plonger;
Fig **to i. oneself in sth** se plonger dans
qch • **immersion** n immersion f; Br **i.
heater** chauffe-eau m inv électrique
immigrate [ˈɪmɪgreɪt] vi immigrer • **immigrant** adj & n immigré, -ée (mf) • **im-
miˈgration** n immigration f; **i. control**
contrôle m de l'immigration
imminent [ˈɪmɪnənt] adj imminent • **imminence** n imminence f
immobile [Br ɪˈməʊbaɪl, Am ɪˈməʊbəl]
adj immobile • **immoˈbility** n immobilité f
• **immobilize** [-bɪlaɪz] vt immobiliser
immoderate [ɪˈmɒdərət] adj immodéré
immodest [ɪˈmɒdɪst] adj impudique
immoral [ɪˈmɒrəl] adj immoral • **immorality** [ɪməˈrælɪtɪ] n immoralité f
immortal [ɪˈmɔːtəl] adj immortel, -elle
• **immortality** [-ˈtælɪtɪ] n immortalité f
• **immortalize** vt immortaliser
immune [ɪˈmjuːn] adj Med (to disease)
immunisé (**to** contre); **i. system** système
m immunitaire; Fig **i. to criticism** imper-

méable à la critique • **immunity** *n* immunité *f* • **immunize** ['ɪmjʊnaɪz] *vt* immuniser (**against** contre)

immutable [ɪ'mjuːtəbəl] *adj* immuable

imp [ɪmp] *n* lutin *m*; (**you**) **little i.!** *(to child)* petit coquin!

impact 1 ['ɪmpækt] *n* impact *m*; **on i.** au moment de l'impact; **to make an i. on sb/ sth** avoir un impact sur qn/qch
  2 [ɪm'pækt] *vt (collide with)* heurter; *(influence)* avoir un impact sur

impair [ɪm'peə(r)] *vt (sight, hearing)* diminuer, affaiblir; *(relations, chances)* compromettre

impale [ɪm'peɪl] *vt* empaler (**on** sur)

impart [ɪm'pɑːt] *vt Formal (heat, light)* donner; *(knowledge, news)* transmettre (**to** à)

impartial [ɪm'pɑːʃəl] *adj* impartial • **impartiality** [-ʃɪ'ælɪtɪ] *n* impartialité *f*

impassable [ɪm'pɑːsəbəl] *adj (road)* impraticable; *(river)* infranchissable

impasse [*Br* æm'pɑːs, *Am* 'ɪmpæs] *n (situation)* impasse *f*

impassioned [ɪm'pæʃənd] *adj (speech, request)* passionné

impassive [ɪm'pæsɪv] *adj* impassible • **impassively** *adv* impassiblement • **impassiveness** *n* impassibilité *f*

impatient [ɪm'peɪʃənt] *adj* impatient (**to do** de faire); **to get i.** (**with sb**) s'impatienter (contre qn) • **impatience** *n* impatience *f* • **impatiently** *adv* avec impatience, impatiemment

impeccable [ɪm'pekəbəl] *adj (manners, person)* impeccable • **impeccably** *adv* impeccablement

impede [ɪm'piːd] *vt* gêner; **to i. sb from doing** *(prevent)* empêcher qn de faire

impediment [ɪm'pedɪmənt] *n* obstacle *m*; **speech i.** défaut *m* d'élocution

impel [ɪm'pel] (**-ll-**) *vt (drive)* pousser; *(force)* obliger (**to do** à faire)

impending [ɪm'pendɪŋ] *adj* imminent

impenetrable [ɪm'penɪtrəbəl] *adj (forest, mystery)* impénétrable

imperative [ɪm'perətɪv] **1** *adj (need, tone)* impérieux, -ieuse; **it is i. that he should come** il faut impérativement qu'il vienne
  2 *n Grammar* impératif *m*

imperceptible [ɪmpə'septəbəl] *adj* imperceptible (**to** à)

imperfect [ɪm'pɜːfɪkt] **1** *adj* imparfait; *(goods)* défectueux, -ueuse
  2 *adj & n Grammar* **i.** (**tense**) imparfait *(m)* • **imperfection** [-pə'fekʃən] *n* imperfection *f*

imperial [ɪm'pɪərɪəl] *adj* impérial; *Br* **i. measure** = système de mesure anglo-saxon utilisant les miles, les pints etc • **imperialism** *n* impérialisme *m*

imperil [ɪm'perɪl] *(Br* **-ll-**, *Am* **-l-**) *vt* mettre en péril

imperious [ɪm'pɪərɪəs] *adj* impérieux, -ieuse

impersonal [ɪm'pɜːsənəl] *adj* impersonnel, -elle

impersonate [ɪm'pɜːsəneɪt] *vt (pretend to be)* se faire passer pour; *(imitate)* imiter • **imperso'nation** *n* imitation *f* • **impersonator** *n (mimic)* imitateur, -trice *mf*

impertinent [ɪm'pɜːtɪnənt] *adj* impertinent (**to** envers) • **impertinence** *n* impertinence *f* • **impertinently** *adv* avec impertinence

impervious [ɪm'pɜːvɪəs] *adj also Fig* imperméable (**to** à)

impetuous [ɪm'petjʊəs] *adj* impétueux, -ueuse • **impetuosity** [-ʊ'ɒsɪtɪ] *n* impétuosité *f*

impetus ['ɪmpɪtəs] *n* impulsion *f*

impinge [ɪm'pɪndʒ] *vi* **to i. on sth** *(affect)* affecter qch; *(encroach on)* empiéter sur qch

impish ['ɪmpɪʃ] *adj* espiègle

implacable [ɪm'plækəbəl] *adj* implacable

implant 1 ['ɪmplɑːnt] *n Med* implant *m*
  2 [ɪm'plɑːnt] *vt Med* implanter (**in** dans); *(ideas)* inculquer (**in** à)

implement¹ ['ɪmplɪmənt] *n (tool)* instrument *m*; *(utensil)* ustensile *m*; **farm implements** matériel *m* agricole

implement² ['ɪmplɪment] *vt (carry out)* mettre en œuvre • **implemen'tation** *n* mise *f* en œuvre

implicate ['ɪmplɪkeɪt] *vt* impliquer (**in** dans) • **impli'cation** *n (consequence)* conséquence *f*; *(involvement)* implication *f*; *(innuendo)* insinuation *f*; *(impact)* portée *f*; **by i.** implicitement

implicit [ɪm'plɪsɪt] *adj (implied)* implicite; *(absolute)* absolu • **implicitly** *adv* implicitement

implore [ɪm'plɔː(r)] *vt* implorer (**sb to do** qn de faire)

imply [ɪm'plaɪ] *(pt & pp* **-ied**) *vt (insinuate)* insinuer (**that** que); *(presuppose)* supposer (**that** que); *(involve)* impliquer (**that** que) • **implied** *adj* implicite

impolite [ɪmpə'laɪt] *adj* impoli • **impoliteness** *n* impolitesse *f*

import 1 ['ɪmpɔːt] *n* (**a**) *(item, activity)* importation *f* (**b**) *Formal (importance)* importance *f*

2 [ɪm'pɔːt] *vt (goods) & Comptr* importer (**from** de) •**importer** *n* importateur, -trice *mf*

importance [ɪm'pɔːtəns] *n* importance *f*; **to be of i.** avoir de l'importance; **of no i.** sans importance

important [ɪm'pɔːtənt] *adj* important (**to/for** pour); **it's i. that...** il est important que... (+ *subjunctive*); **to become more i.** prendre de l'importance •**importantly** *adv (speak)* d'un air important; **but, more i....** mais, plus important...

impose [ɪm'pəʊz] **1** *vt (conditions, silence)* imposer (**on** à); *(fine, punishment)* infliger (**on sb** à qn); **to i. a tax on sth** taxer qch

2 *vi (take advantage)* s'imposer; **to i. on sb** abuser de la gentillesse de qn •**imposition** [-pə'zɪʃən] *n* imposition *f* (**of** de); *(inconvenience)* dérangement *m*

imposing [ɪm'pəʊzɪŋ] *adj* imposant

impossible [ɪm'pɒsəbəl] **1** *adj* impossible (**to do** à faire); **it is i. (for us) to do it** il (nous) est impossible de le faire; **it is i. that...** il est impossible que... (+ *subjunctive*); **to make it i. for sb to do sth** mettre qn dans l'impossibilité de faire qch

2 *n* **to do the i.** faire l'impossible •**impossi'bility** (*pl* **-ies**) *n* impossibilité *f* •**impossibly** *adv (extremely)* incroyablement

impostor [ɪm'pɒstə(r)] *n* imposteur *m*

impotent ['ɪmpətənt] *adj* impuissant •**impotence** *n* impuissance *f*

impound [ɪm'paʊnd] *vt (of police)* saisir; *(vehicle)* mettre à la fourrière

impoverish [ɪm'pɒvərɪʃ] *vt* appauvrir •**impoverished** *adj* appauvri

impracticable [ɪm'præktɪkəbəl] *adj* impraticable, irréalisable

impractical [ɪm'præktɪkəl] *adj* peu réaliste

imprecise [ɪmprɪ'saɪs] *adj* imprécis

impregnable [ɪm'pregnəbəl] *adj (fortress)* imprenable; *Fig (argument)* inattaquable

impregnate ['ɪmpregneɪt] *vt (soak)* imprégner (**with** de); *(fertilize)* féconder

impresario [ɪmprɪ'sɑːrɪəʊ] (*pl* **-os**) *n* impresario *m*

impress [ɪm'pres] *vt (person)* impressionner; **to i. sth on sb** faire comprendre qch à qn; **to i. sth on sth** imprimer qch sur qch; **to be impressed with** *or* **by sb/sth** être impressionné par qn/qch

impression [ɪm'preʃən] *n* impression *f*; **to be under** *or* **have the i. that...** avoir l'impression que...; **to make a good/bad**

i. on sb faire une bonne/mauvaise impression à qn •**impressionable** *adj (person)* impressionnable; *(age)* où l'on est impressionnable

impressionist [ɪm'preʃənɪst] *n (mimic)* imitateur, -trice *mf*; *(artist)* impressionniste *mf*

impressive [ɪm'presɪv] *adj* impressionnant

imprint 1 ['ɪmprɪnt] *n* empreinte *f*

2 [ɪm'prɪnt] *vt* imprimer; **the words are imprinted on my memory** ces mots restent gravés dans ma mémoire

imprison [ɪm'prɪzən] *vt* emprisonner •**imprisonment** *n* emprisonnement *m*; **life i.** la prison à vie

improbable [ɪm'prɒbəbəl] *adj (unlikely)* improbable; *(unbelievable)* invraisemblable •**improba'bility** (*pl* **-ies**) *n* improbabilité *f*; *(of story)* invraisemblance *f*

impromptu [ɪm'prɒmptjuː] **1** *adj (speech, party)* improvisé

2 *adv (unexpectedly)* à l'improviste; *(ad lib)* au pied levé

improper [ɪm'prɒpə(r)] *adj* (**a**) *(indecent)* indécent (**b**) *(use, purpose)* mauvais; *(behaviour)* déplacé; *Law* **i. practices** pratiques *fpl* malhonnêtes •**impropriety** [-prə'praɪətɪ] *n (of behaviour)* inconvenance *f*; *(of language)* impropriété *f*

improve [ɪm'pruːv] **1** *vt* améliorer; *(technique, invention)* perfectionner; **to i. sb's looks** embellir qn; **to i. one's chances** augmenter ses chances; **to i. one's English** se perfectionner en anglais; **to i. one's mind** se cultiver

2 *vi* s'améliorer; *(of business)* reprendre; **to i. on sth** *(do better than)* faire mieux que qch •**improvement** *n* amélioration *f* (**in** de); *(progress)* progrès *mpl*; **there has been some** *or* **an i.** il y a du mieux; **to be an i. on sth** *(be better than)* être meilleur que qch

improvise ['ɪmprəvaɪz] *vti* improviser •**improvi'sation** *n* improvisation *f*

impudent ['ɪmpjʊdənt] *adj* impudent •**impudence** *n* impudence *f*

impulse ['ɪmpʌls] *n* impulsion *f*; **on i.** sur un coup de tête •**im'pulsive** *adj (person)* impulsif, -ive; *(remark)* irréfléchi •**im'pulsively** *adv (act)* de manière impulsive

impunity [ɪm'pjuːnɪtɪ] *n* impunité *f*; **with i.** impunément

impure [ɪm'pjʊə(r)] *adj* impur •**impurity** (*pl* **-ies**) *n* impureté *f*

in [ɪn] **1** *prep* (**a**) dans; **in the box/the school** dans la boîte/l'école; **in an hour('s**

time) dans une heure; **in the garden** dans le jardin, au jardin; **in luxury** dans le luxe; **in so far as** dans la mesure où

(**b**) à; **in school** à l'école; **in Paris** à Paris; **in the USA** aux USA; **in Portugal** au Portugal; **in fashion** à la mode; **in pencil** au crayon; **in ink** à l'encre; **in my opinion** à mon avis; **in spring** au printemps; **the woman in the red dress** la femme à la robe rouge

(**c**) en; **in summer/secret/French** en été/secret/français; **in Spain** en Espagne; **in May** en mai; **in 1999** en 1999; **in season** *(fruit)* de saison; **in an hour** *(during an hour)* en une heure; **in doing sth** en faisant qch; **dressed in black** habillé en noir; **in all** en tout

(**d**) de; **in a soft voice** d'une voix douce; **the best in the class** le meilleur/la meilleure de la classe; **an increase in salary** une augmentation de salaire; **at six in the evening** à six heures du soir

(**e**) chez; **in children/adults/animals** chez les enfants/les adultes/les animaux; **in Shakespeare** chez Shakespeare

(**f**) **in the rain** sous la pluie; **in the morning** le matin; **he hasn't done it in months/years** ça fait des mois/années qu'il ne l'a pas fait; **in an hour** *(at the end of an hour)* au bout d'une heure; **one in ten** un sur dix; **in tens** dix par dix; **in hundreds/thousands** par centaines/milliers; **in here** ici; **in there** là-dedans

2 *adv* **to be in** *(home)* être là; *(of train)* être arrivé; *(in fashion)* être en vogue; *(in power)* être au pouvoir; **day in, day out** jour après jour; **in on a secret** au courant d'un secret; **we're in for some rain/trouble** on va avoir de la pluie/des ennuis; *Fam* **it's the in thing** c'est à la mode

3 *npl* **the ins and outs of** les moindres détails de

in- [ɪn] *pref* in-

inability [ɪnəˈbɪlɪtɪ] *(pl* **-ies***) n* incapacité *f* (**to do** de faire)

inaccessible [ɪnəkˈsesəbəl] *adj* inaccessible

inaccurate [ɪnˈækjʊrət] *adj* inexact ● **inaccuracy** *(pl* **-ies***) n* inexactitude *f*

inaction [ɪnˈækʃən] *n* inaction *f*

inactive [ɪnˈæktɪv] *adj* inactif, -ive ● **inac'tivity** *n* inactivité *f*

inadequate [ɪnˈædɪkwət] *adj (quantity)* insuffisant; *(person)* pas à la hauteur; *(work)* médiocre ● **inadequacy** *(pl* **-ies***) n* insuffisance *f* ● **inadequately** *adv* insuffisamment

inadmissible [ɪnədˈmɪsəbəl] *adj* inadmissible

inadvertently [ɪnədˈvɜːtəntlɪ] *adv* par inadvertance

inadvisable [ɪnədˈvaɪzəbəl] *adj (action)* à déconseiller; **it is i. to go out alone** il est déconseillé de sortir seul

inane [ɪˈneɪn] *adj* inepte

inanimate [ɪnˈænɪmət] *adj* inanimé

inappropriate [ɪnəˈprəʊprɪət] *adj (unsuitable) (place, clothes)* peu approprié; *(remark, moment)* inopportun

inarticulate [ɪnɑːˈtɪkjʊlət] *adj (person)* incapable de s'exprimer; *(sound)* inarticulé

inasmuch as [ɪnəzˈmʌtʃəz] *conj Formal (because)* dans la mesure où; *(to the extent that)* en ce sens que

inattentive [ɪnəˈtentɪv] *adj* inattentif, -ive (**to** à)

inaudible [ɪnˈɔːdɪbəl] *adj* inaudible

inaugural [ɪˈnɔːɡjʊrəl] *adj (speech, meeting)* inaugural

inaugurate [ɪˈnɔːɡjʊreɪt] *vt (building, policy)* inaugurer; *(official)* installer (dans ses fonctions) ● **inaugu'ration** *n* inauguration *f*; *(of official)* investiture *f*

inauspicious [ɪnɔːˈspɪʃəs] *adj* peu propice

inborn [ɪnˈbɔːn] *adj* inné

inbred [ɪnˈbred] *adj (quality)* inné; *(person)* de parents consanguins

Inc *(abbr* **Incorporated***) Am Com* ≃ SARL

incalculable [ɪnˈkælkjʊləbəl] *adj* incalculable

incandescent [ɪnkænˈdesənt] *adj* incandescent

incapable [ɪnˈkeɪpəbəl] *adj* incapable (**of doing** de faire); **i. of pity** inaccessible à la pitié

incapacitate [ɪnkəˈpæsɪteɪt] *vt* rendre infirme ● **incapacity** *(pl* **-ies***) n (inability)* incapacité *f*

incarcerate [ɪnˈkɑːsəreɪt] *vt* incarcérer ● **incarce'ration** *n* incarcération *f*

incarnate 1 [ɪnˈkɑːnət] *adj* incarné

2 [ɪnˈkɑːneɪt] *vt* incarner ● **incar'nation** *n* incarnation *f*

incendiary [ɪnˈsendɪərɪ] *adj* **i. device** *or* **bomb** bombe *f* incendiaire

incense¹ [ˈɪnsens] *n (substance)* encens *m*

incense² [ɪnˈsens] *vt* rendre furieux, -ieuse

ℓ Note that the French verb **encenser** is a false friend and is never a translation for the English word **to incense**. It means **to praise lavishly**.

incentive [ɪn'sentɪv] *n* motivation *f*; *(payment)* prime *f*; **to give sb an i. to work** encourager qn à travailler

incessant [ɪn'sesənt] *adj* incessant • **incessantly** *adv* sans cesse

> *Note that the French word **incessamment** is a false friend. It means **very shortly.***

incest ['ɪnsest] *n* inceste *m* • **in'cestuous** *adj* incestueux, -ueuse

inch [ɪntʃ] **1** *n* pouce *m (2,54 cm)*; **a few inches from the edge** à quelques centimètres du bord; **within an i. of death** à deux doigts de la mort; **i. by i.** petit à petit **2** *vti* **to i. (one's way) forward** avancer tout doucement

incidence ['ɪnsɪdəns] *n (frequency)* taux *m*; *(of disease)* incidence *f*

incident ['ɪnsɪdənt] *n* incident *m*; *(in book, film)* épisode *m*

incidental [ɪnsɪ'dentəl] *adj (additional)* accessoire; **it's i. to the main plot** c'est secondaire par rapport à l'intrigue principale; **i. expenses** faux frais *mpl*; **i. music** *(in film)* musique *f* • **incidentally** *adv (by the way)* au fait; *(additionally)* accessoirement

incinerate [ɪn'sɪnəreɪt] *vt (refuse, leaves)* incinérer • **incinerator** *n* incinérateur *m*

incision [ɪn'sɪʒən] *n* incision *f*

incisive [ɪn'saɪsɪv] *adj* incisif, -ive

incisor [ɪn'saɪzə(r)] *n (tooth)* incisive *f*

incite [ɪn'saɪt] *vt* inciter (**to do** à faire) • **incitement** *n* incitation *f* (**to do** à faire)

inclination [ɪnklɪ'neɪʃən] *n (liking)* inclination *f*; *(desire)* envie *f* (**to do** de faire); **to have no i. to do sth** n'avoir aucune envie de faire qch

incline 1 ['ɪnklaɪn] *n (slope)* pente *f* **2** [ɪn'klaɪn] *vt (bend, tilt)* incliner; **to be inclined to do sth** *(feel a wish to)* avoir bien envie de faire qch; *(tend to)* avoir tendance à faire qch; **to be inclined towards** *(indulgence)* incliner à; *(opinion)* pencher pour; **to i. sb to do sth** inciter qn à faire qch **3** *vi* **to i. to** *or* **towards sth** pencher pour qch

include [ɪn'kluːd] *vt (contain)* comprendre, inclure; *(in letter)* joindre; **my invitation includes you** mon invitation s'adresse aussi à vous; **to be included** être compris; *(on list)* être inclus • **including** *prep* y compris; **not i.** sans compter; **i. service** service *m* compris

inclusion [ɪn'kluːʒən] *n* inclusion *f*

inclusive [ɪn'kluːsɪv] *adj* inclus; **from the fourth to the tenth of May i.** du quatre au dix mai inclus; **to be i. of** comprendre; **i. of tax** toutes taxes comprises; **i. charge** *or* **price** prix *m* global

incognito [ɪnkɒg'niːtəʊ] *adv* incognito

incoherent [ɪnkəʊ'hɪərənt] *adj* incohérent • **incoherently** *adv (speak, act)* de façon incohérente

income ['ɪŋkʌm] *n* revenu *m* (**from** de); **private i.** rentes *fpl*; **i. support** ≃ RMI *m*; **i. tax** impôt *m* sur le revenu

incoming ['ɪnkʌmɪŋ] *adj (tenant, president)* nouveau (*f* nouvelle); **i. calls** *(on telephone)* appels *mpl* de l'extérieur; **i. mail** courrier *m* à l'arrivée; **i. tide** marée *f* montante

incommunicado [ɪnkəmjuːnɪ'kɑːdəʊ] *adj* injoignable

incomparable [ɪn'kɒmpərəbəl] *adj* incomparable

incompatible [ɪnkəm'pætəbəl] *adj* incompatible (**with** avec) • **incompati'bility** *n* incompatibilité *f*

incompetent [ɪn'kɒmpɪtənt] *adj* incompétent • **incompetence** *n* incompétence *f*

incomplete [ɪnkəm'pliːt] *adj* incomplet, -ète

incomprehensible [ɪnkɒmprɪ'hensəbəl] *adj* incompréhensible

inconceivable [ɪnkən'siːvəbəl] *adj* inconcevable

inconclusive [ɪnkən'kluːsɪv] *adj* peu concluant

incongruous [ɪn'kɒŋgrʊəs] *adj (building, colours)* qui jure(nt) (**with** avec); *(remark, attitude)* incongru

inconsequential [ɪnkɒnsɪ'kwenʃəl] *adj* sans importance

inconsiderate [ɪnkən'sɪdərət] *adj (action, remark)* inconsidéré; *(person)* sans égards pour les autres

inconsistent [ɪnkən'sɪstənt] *adj (person)* incohérent; *(uneven)* irrégulier, -ière; **to be i. with sth** ne pas concorder avec qch • **inconsistency** *(pl* -**ies**) *n (in argument)* incohérence *f*; *(between reports)* contradiction *f*; *(uneven quality)* irrégularité *f*

> *Note that the French word **inconsistant** is a false friend. It means **thin** or **runny.***

inconsolable [ɪnkən'səʊləbəl] *adj* inconsolable

inconspicuous [ɪnkən'spɪkjʊəs] *adj* qui passe inaperçu • **inconspicuously** *adv* discrètement

incontinent [ɪn'kɒntɪnənt] *adj* incontinent

inconvenience [ɪnkən'viːnɪəns] **1** *n*

(bother) dérangement *m*; *(disadvantage)* inconvénient *m*
2 *vt* déranger

inconvenient [ɪnkən'viːnɪənt] *adj (moment)* mauvais; *(arrangement)* peu commode; *(building)* mal situé; **it's i. (for me) to** ça me dérange de; **that's very i.** c'est très gênant ●**inconveniently** *adv (arrive, happen)* à un moment gênant; **i. situated** mal situé

incorporate [ɪn'kɔːpəreɪt] *vt (contain)* contenir; *(introduce)* incorporer (**into** dans); *Am* **incorporated society** société *f* anonyme, société à responsabilité limitée

incorrect [ɪnkə'rekt] *adj* incorrect; **you're i.** vous avez tort

incorrigible [ɪn'kɒrɪdʒəbəl] *adj* incorrigible

incorruptible [ɪnkə'rʌptəbəl] *adj* incorruptible

increase 1 [ɪn'kriːs] [ˈɪnkriːs] *n* augmentation *f* (**in** *or* **of** de); **on the i.** en hausse
2 *vt* augmenter; **to i. one's efforts** redoubler d'efforts
3 *vi* augmenter; **to i. in weight** prendre du poids; **to i. in price** augmenter ●**increasing** *adj* croissant ●**increasingly** *adv* de plus en plus

incredible [ɪn'kredəbəl] *adj* incroyable ●**incredibly** *adv* incroyablement

incredulous [ɪn'kredjʊləs] *adj* incrédule ●**incredulity** [-krɪ'djuːlɪtɪ] *n* incrédulité *f*

increment [ˈɪŋkrəmənt] *n* augmentation *f*

incriminate [ɪn'krɪmɪneɪt] *vt* incriminer ●**incriminating** *adj* compromettant

incubate [ˈɪŋkjʊbeɪt] **1** *vt (eggs)* couver
2 *vi (of illness)* être en période d'incubation ●**incu'bation** *n* incubation *f* ●**incubator** *n (for baby)* couveuse *f*

inculcate [ˈɪnkʌlkeɪt] *vt Formal* inculquer (**in** à)

incumbent [ɪn'kʌmbənt] *adj* **it is i. upon him/her to...** il lui incombe de...

incur [ɪn'kɜː(r)] *(pt & pp* **-rr-***) vt (expenses)* encourir; *(loss)* subir; *(debt)* contracter; *(criticism, anger)* s'attirer

incurable [ɪn'kjʊərəbəl] *adj* incurable

incursion [ɪn'kɜːʃən] *n* incursion *f* (**into** dans)

indebted [ɪn'detɪd] *adj (financially)* endetté; **i. to sb for sth/for doing sth** redevable à qn de qch/d'avoir fait qch

indecent [ɪn'diːsənt] *adj (obscene)* indécent; *Br* **i. assault** attentat *m* à la pudeur ●**indecency** *(pl* **-ies***) n* indécence *f*; *Br Law* outrage *m* à la pudeur ●**indecently** *adv* indécemment

indecisive [ɪndɪ'saɪsɪv] *adj (person, answer)* indécis ●**inde'cision** *n* ●**indecisiveness** *n* indécision *f*

indeed [ɪn'diːd] *adv* en effet; **very good i.** vraiment très bon; **yes i.!** bien sûr!; **thank you very much i.!** merci infiniment!

indefensible [ɪndɪ'fensəbəl] *adj* indéfendable

indefinable [ɪndɪ'faɪnəbəl] *adj* indéfinissable

indefinite [ɪn'defɪnət] *adj (duration, number)* indéterminé; *(plan)* mal défini ●**indefinitely** *adv* indéfiniment

indelible [ɪn'deləbəl] *adj (ink, memory)* indélébile; **i. pen** stylo *m* à encre indélébile

indelicate [ɪn'delɪkət] *adj* indélicat

indemnify [ɪn'demnɪfaɪ] *(pt & pp* **-ied***) vt* indemniser (**for** de) ●**indemnity** *(pl* **-ies***) n (compensation)* indemnité *f*; **an i. against** *(protection)* une garantie contre

indented [ɪn'dentɪd] *adj (edge, coastline)* découpé ●**inden'tation** *n* dentelure *f*, découpure *f*; *Typ* alinéa *m*

independence [ɪndɪ'pendəns] *n* indépendance *f*

independent [ɪndɪ'pendənt] *adj* indépendant (**of** de); *(opinions, reports)* de sources différentes ●**independently** *adv* de façon indépendante; **i. of** indépendamment de

indescribable [ɪndɪ'skraɪbəbəl] *adj* indescriptible

indestructible [ɪndɪ'strʌktəbəl] *adj* indestructible

indeterminate [ɪndɪ'tɜːmɪnət] *adj* indéterminé

index [ˈɪndeks] **1** *n (in book)* index *m*; *(in library)* fichier *m*; *(number, sign)* indice *m*; **i. card** fiche *f*; **i. finger** index
2 *vt (classify)* classer ●**'index-'linked** *adj (wages)* indexé (**to** sur)

India [ˈɪndɪə] *n* l'Inde *f* ●**Indian 1** *adj* indien, -ienne **2** *n* Indien, -ienne *mf*

indicate [ˈɪndɪkeɪt] *vt* indiquer (**that** que); **I was indicating right** *(in vehicle)* j'avais mis mon clignotant droit ●**indi'cation** *n (sign)* signe *m*; *(information)* indication *f*; **there is every i. that...** tout porte à croire que...

indicative [ɪn'dɪkətɪv] **1** *adj* **to be i. of** *(symptomatic)* être symptomatique de **2** *n Grammar* indicatif *m*

indicator [ˈɪndɪkeɪtə(r)] *n (sign)* indication *f* (**of** de); *Br (in vehicle)* clignotant *m*

indict [ɪn'daɪt] *vt Law* inculper (**for** de) ●**indictment** *n* inculpation *f*

Indies ['ɪndɪz] *npl* **the West I.** les Antilles *fpl*
indifferent [ɪn'dɪfərənt] *adj* indifférent (**to** à); *(mediocre)* médiocre • **indifference** *n* indifférence *f* (**to** à) • **indifferently** *adv* indifféremment
indigenous [ɪn'dɪdʒɪnəs] *adj* indigène
indigestion [ɪndɪ'dʒestʃən] *n* troubles *mpl* digestifs; **(an attack of) i.** une indigestion • **indigestible** *adj* indigeste
indignant [ɪn'dɪgnənt] *adj* indigné (**at** *or* **about** de); **to become i.** s'indigner • **indignantly** *adv* avec indignation • **indig'nation** *n* indignation *f*
indignity [ɪn'dɪgnɪtɪ] *n* indignité *f*
indigo ['ɪndɪgəʊ] *n & adj (colour)* indigo *(m) inv*
indirect [ɪndaɪ'rekt] *adj* indirect • **indirectly** *adv* indirectement
indiscreet [ɪndɪ'skriːt] *adj* indiscret, -ète • **indiscretion** [-'skreʃən] *n* indiscrétion *f*
indiscriminate [ɪndɪ'skrɪmɪnət] *adj (person)* qui manque de discernement; **to be i. in one's praise** distribuer les compliments à tort et à travers • **indiscriminately** *adv (at random)* au hasard; *(without discrimination)* sans discernement
indispensable [ɪndɪ'spensəbəl] *adj* indispensable (**to** à)
indisposed [ɪndɪ'spəʊzd] *adj (unwell)* indisposé
indisputable [ɪndɪ'spjuːtəbəl] *adj* incontestable
indistinct [ɪndɪ'stɪŋkt] *adj* indistinct
indistinguishable [ɪndɪ'stɪŋgwɪʃəbəl] *adj* indifférenciable (**from** de)
individual [ɪndɪ'vɪdʒʊəl] **1** *adj (separate, personal)* individuel, -uelle; *(specific)* particulier, -ière
2 *n (person)* individu *m* • **individuality** [-ʊ'ælɪtɪ] *n (distinctiveness)* individualité *f* • **individually** *adv (separately)* individuellement; *(unusually)* de façon (très) personnelle
individualist [ɪndɪ'vɪdʒʊəlɪst] *n* individualiste *mf* • **individua'listic** *adj* individualiste
indivisible [ɪndɪ'vɪzəbəl] *adj* indivisible
Indo-China [ɪndəʊ'tʃaɪnə] *n* l'Indochine *f*
indoctrinate [ɪn'dɒktrɪneɪt] *vt* endoctriner • **indoctri'nation** *n* endoctrinement *m*
indolent ['ɪndələnt] *adj* indolent • **indolence** *n* indolence *f*
indomitable [ɪn'dɒmɪtəbəl] *adj (will, energy)* indomptable
Indonesia [ɪndəʊ'niːzɪə] *n* l'Indonésie *f*
indoor ['ɪndɔː(r)] *adj (games, shoes)* d'in-

térieur; *(swimming pool)* couvert • **in-'doors** *adv* à l'intérieur; **to go/come i.** rentrer
induce [ɪn'djuːs] *vt (persuade)* persuader (**to do** de faire); *(cause)* provoquer; **to i. labour** *(in pregnant woman)* déclencher l'accouchement • **inducement** *n* encouragement *m* (**to do** à faire)
indulge [ɪn'dʌldʒ] **1** *vt (sb's wishes)* satisfaire; *(child)* gâter; **to i. oneself** se faire plaisir
2 *vi* **to i. in sth** *(ice cream, cigar)* s'offrir qch; *(hobby, vice)* s'adonner à qch • **indulgence** *n* indulgence *f* • **indulgent** *adj* indulgent (**to** envers)
industrial [ɪn'dʌstrɪəl] *adj* industriel, -ielle; *(legislation)* du travail; *Br* **i. action** grève *f*; *Br* **to take i. action** se mettre en grève; *Br* **i. estate,** *Am* **i. park** zone *f* industrielle; **i. relations** relations *fpl* patronat-salariés; **i. tribunal** ≃ conseil *m* de prud'hommes • **industrialist** *n* industriel *m* • **industrialized** *adj* industrialisé
industrious [ɪn'dʌstrɪəs] *adj* travailleur, -euse
industry ['ɪndəstrɪ] *(pl* **-ies)** *n (economic sector)* industrie *f*; *(hard work)* application *f*
inebriated [ɪn'iːbrɪeɪtɪd] *adj* ivre
inedible [ɪn'edəbəl] *adj* immangeable
ineffective [ɪnɪ'fektɪv] *adj (measure)* inefficace; *(person)* incapable • **ineffectiveness** *n* inefficacité *f*
ineffectual [ɪnɪ'fektʃʊəl] *adj (measure)* inefficace; *(person)* incompétent
inefficient [ɪnɪ'fɪʃənt] *adj (person, measure)* inefficace; *(machine)* peu performant • **inefficiency** *n* inefficacité *f*
ineligible [ɪn'elɪdʒəbəl] *adj (candidate)* inéligible; **to be i. for sth** *(scholarship)* ne pas avoir droit à qch
inept [ɪ'nept] *adj (incompetent)* incompétent; *(foolish)* inepte • **ineptitude** *n (incapacity)* incompétence *f*
inequality [ɪnɪ'kwɒlɪtɪ] *(pl* **-ies)** *n* inégalité *f*
inert [ɪ'nɜːt] *adj* inerte • **inertia** [-ʃə] *n* inertie *f*
inescapable [ɪnɪ'skeɪpəbəl] *adj (outcome)* inéluctable; *(conclusion)* incontournable
inevitable [ɪn'evɪtəbəl] *adj* inévitable • **inevitably** *adv* inévitablement
inexcusable [ɪnɪk'skjuːzəbəl] *adj* inexcusable
inexhaustible [ɪnɪg'zɔːstəbəl] *adj* inépuisable

inexorable [ɪn'eksərəbəl] *adj* inexorable

inexpensive [ɪnɪk'spensɪv] *adj* bon marché *inv*

inexperience [ɪnɪk'spɪərɪəns] *n* inexpérience *f* • **inexperienced** *adj* inexpérimenté

inexplicable [ɪnɪk'splɪkəbəl] *adj* inexplicable

inexpressible [ɪnɪk'spresəbəl] *adj* inexprimable

inextricable [ɪnɪk'strɪkəbəl] *adj* inextricable

infallible [ɪn'fæləbəl] *adj* infaillible • **infalli'bility** *n* infaillibilité *f*

infamous ['ɪnfəməs] *adj (well-known)* tristement célèbre; *(crime, rumour)* infâme • **infamy** *n* infamie *f*

infancy ['ɪnfənsɪ] *n* petite enfance *f*; **to be in its i.** *(of art, technique)* en être à ses premiers balbutiements

infant ['ɪnfənt] *n* bébé *m*; *Br* **i. school** = école primaire pour enfants de cinq à sept ans

infantile ['ɪnfəntaɪl] *adj Pej* infantile

infantry ['ɪnfəntrɪ] *n* infanterie *f*

infatuated [ɪn'fætʃʊeɪtɪd] *adj* entiché (**with** de) • **infatu'ation** *n (with person)* tocade *f* (**for** *or* **with** pour)

infect [ɪn'fekt] *vt (wound, person)* infecter; *(water, food)* contaminer; **to get** *or* **become infected** s'infecter; **to i. sb with sth** transmettre qch à qn • **infection** *n* infection *f*

infectious [ɪn'fekʃəs] *adj (disease)* infectieux, -ieuse; *(person)* contagieux, -ieuse; *(laughter)* communicatif, -ive

infer [ɪn'fɜː(r)] *(pt & pp* **-rr-**) *vt* déduire (**from** de; **that** que) • **inference** ['ɪnfərəns] *n* déduction *f*; **by i.** par déduction; **to draw an i. from sth** tirer une conclusion de qch

inferior [ɪn'fɪərɪə(r)] **1** *adj* inférieur (**to** à); *(goods, work)* de qualité inférieure
2 *n (person)* inférieur, -ieure *mf* • **inferiority** [-rɪ'ɒrɪtɪ] *n* infériorité *f*; **i. complex** complexe *m* d'infériorité

infernal [ɪn'fɜːnəl] *adj* infernal

inferno [ɪn'fɜːnəʊ] *(pl* **-os**) *n (blaze)* brasier *m*; *(hell)* enfer *m*

infertile [*Br* ɪn'fɜːtaɪl, *Am* ɪn'fɜːrtəl] *adj (person, land)* stérile • **infertility** [-'tɪlɪtɪ] *n* stérilité *f*

infest [ɪn'fest] *vt* infester (**with** de); **rat-/shark-infested** infesté de rats/requins

infidelity [ɪnfɪ'delɪtɪ] *(pl* **-ies**) *n* infidélité *f*

infighting ['ɪnfaɪtɪŋ] *n* luttes *fpl* intestines

infiltrate ['ɪnfɪltreɪt] **1** *vt* infiltrer
2 *vi* s'infiltrer (**into** dans) • **infil'tration** *n* infiltration *f*; *Pol* noyautage *m*

infinite ['ɪnfɪnɪt] *adj & n* infini *(m)* • **infinitely** *adv* infiniment • **in'finity** *n Math & Phot* infini *m*; *Math* **to i.** à l'infini

infinitive [ɪn'fɪnɪtɪv] *n Grammar* infinitif *m*

infirm [ɪn'fɜːm] *adj* infirme

infirmary [ɪn'fɜːmərɪ] *(pl* **-ies**) *n (hospital)* hôpital *m*; *(sickbay)* infirmerie *f*

infirmity [ɪn'fɜːmətɪ] *(pl* **-ies**) *n (disability)* infirmité *f*

inflame [ɪn'fleɪm] *vt* enflammer • **inflamed** *adj (throat, wound)* enflammé; **to become i.** s'enflammer

inflammable [ɪn'flæməbəl] *adj* inflammable • **inflammation** [-flə'meɪʃən] *n* inflammation *f* • **inflammatory** *adj (remark, speech)* incendiaire

inflate [ɪn'fleɪt] *vt (balloon, prices)* gonfler • **inflatable** *adj* gonflable

inflation [ɪn'fleɪʃən] *n Econ* inflation *f* • **inflationary** *adj Econ* inflationniste

inflection [ɪn'flekʃən] *n Grammar* flexion *f*; *(of voice)* inflexion *f*

inflexible [ɪn'fleksəbəl] *adj* inflexible

inflexion [ɪn'flekʃən] *n Br* = **inflection**

inflict [ɪn'flɪkt] *vt (punishment, defeat)* infliger (**on** à); *(wound, damage)* occasionner (**on** à); **to i. pain on sb** faire souffrir qn

influence ['ɪnflʊəns] **1** *n* influence *f* (**on** sur); **to have i. over sb** avoir de l'influence sur qn; **under the i. of drink/anger** sous l'empire de la boisson/de la colère
2 *vt* influencer • **influential** [-'enʃəl] *adj* influent

influenza [ɪnflʊ'enzə] *n* grippe *f*

influx ['ɪnflʌks] *n* afflux *m* (**of** de)

info ['ɪnfəʊ] *n Fam* renseignements *mpl* (**on** sur)

inform [ɪn'fɔːm] **1** *vt* informer (**of** *or* **about** de; **that** que)
2 *vi* **to i. on sb** dénoncer qn • **informed** *adj (person, public)* informé; **to keep sb i. of sth** tenir qn au courant de qch

informal [ɪn'fɔːməl] *adj (unaffected)* simple; *(casual)* décontracté; *(tone, language)* familier, -ière; *(unofficial)* officieux, -ieuse • **informality** [-'mælɪtɪ] *n (unaffectedness)* simplicité *f*; *(casualness)* décontraction *f*; *(of talks)* caractère *m* officieux • **informally** *adv (unaffectedly)* avec simplicité; *(casually)* avec décontraction; *(meet, discuss)* officieusement

informant [ɪn'fɔːmənt] *n* informateur, -trice *mf*

information [ɪnfə'meɪʃən] n (facts, news) renseignements mpl (about or on sur); Comptr information f; **a piece of i.** un renseignement, une information; **to get some i.** se renseigner; **the i. superhighway** l'autoroute f de l'information; **i. technology** informatique f
informative [ɪn'fɔːmətɪv] adj instructif, -ive
informer [ɪn'fɔːmə(r)] n (police) i. indicateur, -trice mf
infrared [ɪnfrə'red] adj infrarouge
infrequent [ɪn'friːkwənt] adj peu fréquent • **infrequently** adv rarement
infringe [ɪn'frɪndʒ] 1 vt (rule, law) enfreindre à
2 vt insep **to i. upon sth** empiéter sur qch • **infringement** n (of rule, law) infraction f (of à)
infuriate [ɪn'fjʊərieɪt] vt exaspérer • **infuriating** adj exaspérant
infuse [ɪn'fjuːz] vt (tea) (faire) infuser • **infusion** n (drink) infusion f
ingenious [ɪn'dʒiːnɪəs] adj ingénieux, -ieuse • **ingenuity** [ɪndʒɪ'nuːɪtɪ] n ingéniosité f
ingot ['ɪŋgət] n lingot m
ingrained [ɪn'greɪnd] adj (prejudice, attitude) enraciné; **i. dirt** crasse f
ingratiate [ɪn'greɪʃɪeɪt] vt **to i. oneself with sb** s'insinuer dans les bonnes grâces de qn • **ingratiating** adj (person, smile) doucereux, -euse
ingratitude [ɪn'grætɪtjuːd] n ingratitude f
ingredient [ɪn'griːdɪənt] n ingrédient m
ingrowing ['ɪngrəʊɪŋ] (Am **ingrown** ['ɪngrəʊn]) adj (toenail) incarné
inhabit [ɪn'hæbɪt] vt habiter • **inhabitable** adj habitable • **inhabitant** n habitant, -ante mf

⎧ Note that the French words **inhabitable** and **inhabité** are false friends and are never translations for the English words **inhabitable** and **inhabited**. They mean respectively **uninhabitable** and **uninhabited**.

inhale [ɪn'heɪl] vt (gas, fumes) inhaler; (cigarette smoke) avaler • **inhalation** [ɪnhə'leɪʃən] n inhalation f • **inhaler** n (for medication) inhalateur m
inherent [ɪn'hɪərənt] adj inhérent (in à) • **inherently** adv intrinsèquement
inherit [ɪn'herɪt] vt hériter (from de); (title) accéder à • **inheritance** n héritage m; (legal process) succession f; **cultural i.** patrimoine m
inhibit [ɪn'hɪbɪt] vt (progress, growth) entraver; (of person) inhiber; **to i. sb from**

doing sth empêcher qn de faire qch • **inhibited** adj (person) inhibé • **inhi'bition** n inhibition f
inhospitable [ɪnhɒ'spɪtəbəl] adj inhospitalier, -ière
inhuman [ɪn'hjuːmən] adj inhumain • **inhumane** [-'meɪn] adj inhumain • **inhumanity** [-'mænɪtɪ] n inhumanité f, cruauté f
inimitable [ɪ'nɪmɪtəbəl] adj inimitable
iniquitous [ɪ'nɪkwɪtəs] adj inique • **iniquity** (pl -ies) n iniquité f
initial [ɪ'nɪʃəl] **1** adj initial
2 npl **initials** (letters) initiales fpl; (signature) paraphe m
3 (Br -ll-, Am -l-) vt parapher • **initially** adv au début, initialement
initiate [ɪ'nɪʃɪeɪt] vt (reform, negotiations) amorcer; (attack, rumour, project) lancer; (policy, period) inaugurer; **to i. sb into a gang** faire subir à qn les épreuves initiatiques d'un gang; Law **to i. proceedings against sb** entamer des poursuites contre qn • **initi'ation** n (beginning) amorce f; (induction) initiation f; **i. ceremony** rite m d'initiation • **initiator** n initiateur, -trice mf
initiative [ɪ'nɪʃətɪv] n initiative f
inject [ɪn'dʒekt] vt injecter (into dans); Fig (enthusiasm) communiquer (into à); **to i. sth into sb, to i. sb with sth** faire une piqûre de qch à qn; Fig **to i. new life into sth** donner un nouvel essor à qch • **injection** n injection f, piqûre f; **to give sb an i.** faire une piqûre à qn
injunction [ɪn'dʒʌŋkʃən] n Law arrêt m
injure ['ɪndʒə(r)] vt (physically) blesser; (reputation, interest) nuire à; **to i. one's foot** se blesser au pied; **to i. sb's feelings** blesser qn • **injured 1** adj blessé **2** npl **the i.** les blessés mpl

⎧ Note that the French verb **injurier** is a false friend and is never a translation for the English verb **to injure**. It means **to insult**.

injurious [ɪn'dʒʊərɪəs] adj préjudiciable (to à)
injury ['ɪndʒərɪ] (pl -ies) n (physical) blessure f; Fig (wrong) préjudice m; Sport **i. time** arrêts mpl de jeu

⎧ Note that the French word **injure** is a false friend. It means **insult**.

injustice [ɪn'dʒʌstɪs] n injustice f
ink [ɪŋk] n encre f • **inkpot, inkwell** n encrier m • **inky** adj couvert d'encre
inkling ['ɪŋklɪŋ] n petite idée f; **to have an**

i. of sth avoir une petite idée de qch; **I had no i.** je ne m'en doutais pas du tout
inlaid [ɪn'leɪd] *adj (with jewels)* incrusté (**with** de); *(with wood)* marqueté
inland 1 ['ɪnlənd, 'ɪnlænd] *adj* intérieur; *Br* **the I. Revenue** ≃ le fisc
2 [ɪn'lænd] *adv (travel)* vers l'intérieur; *(live)* dans les terres
in-laws ['ɪnlɔːz] *npl* belle-famille *f*
inlet ['ɪnlet] *n (of sea)* crique *f*; **i. pipe** tuyau *m* d'arrivée
in-line skates [ɪnlaɪn'skeɪts] *npl* patins *mpl* in-line
inmate ['ɪnmeɪt] *n (of prison)* détenu, -ue *mf*; *(of asylum)* interné, -ée *mf*
inmost ['ɪnməʊst] *adj* le plus profond (*f* la plus profonde)
inn [ɪn] *n* auberge *f*
innards ['ɪnədz] *npl Fam* entrailles *fpl*
innate [ɪ'neɪt] *adj* inné
inner ['ɪnə(r)] *adj* intérieur; *(feelings)* intime; *(ear)* interne; **i. circle** *(of society)* initiés *mpl*; **i. city** quartiers *mpl* déshérités du centre-ville; **i. tube** chambre *f* à air
• **innermost** *adj* le plus profond (*f* la plus profonde); *(thoughts)* le plus secret (*f* la plus secrète)
inning ['ɪnɪŋ] *n Baseball* tour *m* de batte
• **innings** *n inv Cricket* tour *m* de batte; *Fig* **a good i.** une longue vie
innkeeper ['ɪnkiːpə(r)] *n* aubergiste *mf*
innocent ['ɪnəsənt] *adj* innocent • **innocence** *n* innocence *f* • **innocently** *adv* innocemment
innocuous [ɪ'nɒkjʊəs] *adj* inoffensif, -ive
innovate ['ɪnəveɪt] *vi* innover • **inno'vation** *n* innovation *f* • **innovator** *n* innovateur, -trice *mf*
innuendo [ɪnjʊ'endəʊ] *(pl* -**oes** *or* -**os***) n* insinuation *f*
innumerable [ɪ'njuːmərəbəl] *adj* innombrable
inoculate [ɪ'nɒkjʊleɪt] *vt* vacciner (**against** contre) • **inocu'lation** *n* inoculation *f*
inoffensive [ɪnə'fensɪv] *adj* inoffensif, -ive
inoperative [ɪn'ɒpərətɪv] *adj (machine)* arrêté; *(rule)* inopérant
inopportune [ɪn'ɒpətjuːn] *adj* inopportun
inordinate [ɪ'nɔːdɪnət] *adj* excessif, -ive • **inordinately** *adv* excessivement
in-patient ['ɪnpeɪʃənt] *n Br* malade *mf* hospitalisé(e)
input ['ɪnpʊt] **1** *n (contribution)* contribution *f*; *Comptr* entrée *f*; *(data)* données *fpl*; *El* puissance *f* d'alimentation
2 *(pt & pp* -**put***) vt Comptr (data)* entrer

inquest ['ɪnkwest] *n Law* enquête *f*
inquire [ɪn'kwaɪə(r)] **1** *vt* demander; **to i. how to get to...** demander le chemin de...
2 *vi* se renseigner (**about** sur); **to i. after sb** demander des nouvelles de qn; **to i. into sth** faire des recherches sur qch
• **inquiring** *adj (mind, look)* curieux, -ieuse
inquiry [ɪn'kwaɪərɪ] *(pl* -**ies***) n (request for information)* demande *f* de renseignements; *(official investigation)* enquête *f*; **'inquiries'** *(sign)* 'renseignements'; **to make inquiries** demander des renseignements; *(of police)* enquêter
inquisitive [ɪn'kwɪzɪtɪv] *adj* curieux, -ieuse • **inqui'sition** *n (inquiry) & Rel* inquisition *f* • **inquisitively** *adv* avec curiosité
inroads ['ɪnrəʊdz] *npl (attacks)* incursions *fpl* (**into** dans); **to make i. into** *(savings, capital)* entamer; *(market)* pénétrer
insane [ɪn'seɪn] *adj* dément, fou (*f* folle); **to go i.** perdre la raison; **to be i. with grief** être fou de chagrin • **insanely** *adv* comme un fou (*f* une folle) • **insanity** [-'sænɪtɪ] *n* démence *f*
insanitary [ɪn'sænɪtərɪ] *adj* insalubre
insatiable [ɪn'seɪʃəbəl] *adj* insatiable
inscribe [ɪn'skraɪb] *vt* inscrire; *(book)* dédicacer (**to** à) • **inscription** [-'skrɪpʃən] *n* inscription *f*; *(in book)* dédicace *f*
inscrutable [ɪn'skruːtəbəl] *adj* impénétrable
insect ['ɪnsekt] *n* insecte *m*; **i. powder/spray** poudre *f*/bombe *f* insecticide; **i. repellent** anti-moustiques *m inv* • **in'secticide** *n* insecticide *m*
insecure [ɪnsɪ'kjʊə(r)] *adj (unsafe)* peu sûr; *(job, future)* précaire; *(person)* angoissé; **to be financially i.** être dans une situation financièrement précaire • **insecurity** *n (of job, future)* précarité *f*; *(of person)* angoisse *f*
insemination [ɪnsemɪ'neɪʃən] *n* **artificial i.** insémination artificielle
insensible [ɪn'sensəbəl] *adj (unaware, unconscious)* inconscient (**to** de)
insensitive [ɪn'sensɪtɪv] *adj (person)* insensible (**to** à); *(remark)* indélicat • **insensi'tivity** *n* insensibilité *f*
inseparable [ɪn'sepərəbəl] *adj* inséparable (**from** de)
insert [ɪn'sɜːt] *vt* insérer (**in** *or* **into** dans) • **insertion** *n* insertion *f*
inshore 1 ['ɪnʃɔː(r)] *adj* côtier, -ière
2 [ɪn'ʃɔː(r)] *adv (fish)* près des côtes

inside 1 ['ɪnsaɪd] *adj* intérieur; *(information)* obtenu à la source; **the i. lane** *Br* la voie de gauche, *Am* la voie de droite

2 ['ɪn'saɪd] *n* intérieur *m*; *Fam* **insides** *(stomach)* entrailles *fpl*; **on the i.** à l'intérieur (**of** de); **i. out** *(clothes)* à l'envers; *(know, study)* à fond; *Fig* **to turn everything i. out** tout chambouler

3 [ɪn'saɪd] *adv* à l'intérieur; *Fam (in prison)* en taule; **come i.!** entrez!

4 [ɪn'saɪd] *prep* à l'intérieur de, dans; *(time)* en moins de

insider [ɪn'saɪdə(r)] *n* initié, -iée *mf*; *Fin* **i. dealing** *or* **trading** délit *m* d'initié

insidious [ɪn'sɪdɪəs] *adj* insidieux, -ieuse

insight ['ɪnsaɪt] *n* perspicacité *f*; *(into question)* aperçu *m*; **to give sb an i. into** *(sb's character)* permettre à qn de comprendre; *(question)* donner à qn un aperçu de

insignia [ɪn'sɪgnɪə] *n* insignes *mpl*

insignificant [ɪnsɪg'nɪfɪkənt] *adj* insignifiant • **insignificance** *n* insignifiance *f*

insincere [ɪnsɪn'sɪə(r)] *adj* peu sincère • **insincerity** [-'serɪtɪ] *n* manque *m* de sincérité

insinuate [ɪn'sɪnjʊeɪt] *vt (suggest)* insinuer (**that** que); **to i. oneself into sb's good favours** s'insinuer dans les bonnes grâces de qn • **insinu'ation** *n* insinuation *f*

insipid [ɪn'sɪpɪd] *adj* insipide

insist [ɪn'sɪst] **1** *vt (maintain)* soutenir (**that** que); **I i. that you come** *or* **on your coming** *(I demand it)* j'insiste pour que tu viennes

2 *vi* insister; **to i. on sth** *(demand)* exiger qch; *(assert)* affirmer qch; **to i. on doing sth** tenir à faire qch

insistence [ɪn'sɪstəns] *n* insistance *f*; **her i. on seeing me** l'insistance qu'elle met à vouloir me voir

insistent [ɪn'sɪstənt] *adj (person, request)* pressant; **to be i. (that)** insister (pour que + *subjunctive*); **I was i. about it** j'ai insisté • **insistently** *adv* avec insistance

insolent ['ɪnsələnt] *adj* insolent • **insolence** *n* insolence *f* • **insolently** *adv* insolemment

insoluble [ɪn'sɒljʊbəl] *adj* insoluble

insolvent [ɪn'sɒlvənt] *adj (financially)* insolvable

insomnia [ɪn'sɒmnɪə] *n* insomnie *f* • **insomniac** [-nɪæk] *n* insomniaque *mf*

insomuch as [ɪnsəʊ'mʌtʃəz] *adv* = **inasmuch as**

inspect [ɪn'spekt] *vt* inspecter; *(tickets)* contrôler; *(troops)* passer en revue • **inspection** *n* inspection *f*; *(of tickets)*

contrôle *m*; *(of troops)* revue *f* • **inspector** *n* inspecteur, -trice *mf*; *(on train)* contrôleur, -euse *mf*

inspire [ɪn'spaɪə(r)] *vt* inspirer; **to i. sb to do sth** pousser qn à faire qch; **to i. sb with sth** inspirer qch à qn • **inspiration** [-spə'reɪʃən] *n* inspiration *f*; *(person)* source *f* d'inspiration • **inspired** *adj* inspiré • **inspiring** *adj* exaltant

instability [ɪnstə'bɪlɪtɪ] *n* instabilité *f*

install [ɪn'stɔːl] *(Am* **instal**) *vt* installer • **installation** [-stə'leɪʃən] *n* installation *f*

instalment [ɪn'stɔːlmənt] *(Am* **installment**) *n (part payment)* versement *m*; *(of serial, story)* épisode *m*; *(of publication)* fascicule *m*; **to pay by instalments** payer par versements échelonnés; *Am* **to buy on the i. plan** acheter à crédit

instance ['ɪnstəns] *n (example)* exemple *m*; *(case)* cas *m*; **for i.** par exemple; **in this i.** dans le cas présent; **in the first i.** en premier lieu

instant ['ɪnstənt] **1** *adj* immédiat; **i. camera** appareil photo *m* à développement instantané; **i. coffee** café *m* instantané

2 *n (moment)* instant *m*; **this (very) i.** *(at once)* à l'instant; **the i. that I saw her** dès que je l'ai vue • **instantly** *adv* immédiatement

instantaneous [ɪnstən'teɪnɪəs] *adj* instantané

instead [ɪn'sted] *adv (in place of sth)* à la place; *(in place of sb)* à ma/ta/*etc* place; **i. of sth** au lieu de qch; **i. of doing sth** au lieu de faire qch; **i. of sb** à la place de qn; **i. of him/her** à sa place

instep ['ɪnstep] *n (of foot)* cou-de-pied *m*; *(of shoe)* cambrure *f*

instigate ['ɪnstɪgeɪt] *vt* provoquer • **insti'gation** *n* instigation *f* • **instigator** *n* instigateur, -trice *mf*

instil [ɪn'stɪl] *(Am* **instill**) *(pt & pp* **-ll-**) *vt (idea)* inculquer (**into** à); *(courage)* insuffler (**into** à); *(doubt)* instiller (**in** à)

instinct ['ɪnstɪŋkt] *n* instinct *m*; **by i.** d'instinct • **in'stinctive** *adj* instinctif, -ive • **in'stinctively** *adv* instinctivement

institute ['ɪnstɪtjuːt] **1** *n* institut *m*

2 *vt (rule, practice)* instituer; *Law (inquiry)* ordonner; *Law* **to i. proceedings against sb** entamer des poursuites contre qn

institution [ɪnstɪ'tjuːʃən] *n (organization, custom)* institution *f*; *(public, financial, religious, psychiatric)* établissement *m* • **institutional** *adj* institutionnel, -elle

instruct [ɪn'strʌkt] *vt (teach)* enseigner (**sb in sth** qch à qn); **to i. sb about sth**

(inform) instruire qn de qch; **to i. sb to do** *(order)* charger qn de faire

instruction [ɪn'strʌkʃən] *n (teaching)* instruction *f*; **instructions** *(orders)* instructions *fpl*; **instructions (for use)** mode *m* d'emploi

instructive [ɪn'strʌktɪv] *adj* instructif, -ive

instructor [ɪn'strʌktə(r)] *n (for judo, dance)* professeur *m*; *(for skiing, swimming)* moniteur, -trice *mf*; *(military)* instructeur *m*; *(in American university)* maître-assistant, -ante *mf*; **driving i.** moniteur, -trice *mf* d'auto-école

instrument ['ɪnstrəmənt] *n* instrument *m*

instrumental [ɪnstrə'mentəl] *adj (music)* instrumental; **to be i. in sth/in doing sth** contribuer à qch/à faire qch • **instrumentalist** *n* instrumentiste *mf*

instrumentation [ɪnstrəmən'teɪʃən] *n* *Mus* orchestration *f*

insubordinate [ɪnsə'bɔːdɪnət] *adj* insubordonné • **insubordi'nation** *n* insubordination *f*

insubstantial [ɪnsəb'stænʃəl] *adj (argument, evidence)* peu solide

insufferable [ɪn'sʌfərəbəl] *adj* intolérable

insufficient [ɪnsə'fɪʃənt] *adj* insuffisant • **insufficiently** *adv* insuffisamment

insular ['ɪnsjʊlə(r)] *adj (climate)* insulaire; *(views)* étroit, borné

insulate ['ɪnsjʊleɪt] *vt (against cold) & El* isoler; *(against sound)* insonoriser; *Fig* **to i. sb from sth** protéger qn de qch; **insulating tape** chatterton *m* • **insu'lation** *n* isolation *f*; *(against sound)* insonorisation *f*; *(material)* isolant *m*

insulin ['ɪnsjʊlɪn] *n* insuline *f*

insult 1 ['ɪnsʌlt] *n* insulte *f* (**to** à); **to add i. to injury** pour aggraver les choses

2 [ɪn'sʌlt] *vt* insulter • **in'sulting** *adj (words, offer)* insultant

insuperable [ɪn'suːpərəbəl] *adj* insurmontable

insure [ɪn'ʃʊə(r)] *vt* (**a**) *(house, car, goods)* assurer (**against** contre) (**b**) *Am* = **ensure** • **insurance** *n* assurance *f*; **i. company** compagnie *f* d'assurances; **i. policy** police *f* d'assurance

insurgent [ɪn'sɜːdʒənt] *n* insurgé, -ée *mf*

insurmountable [ɪnsə'maʊntəbəl] *adj* insurmontable

insurrection [ɪnsə'rekʃən] *n* insurrection *f*

intact [ɪn'tækt] *adj* intact

intake ['ɪnteɪk] *n (of food)* consommation *f*; *(of students, schoolchildren)* admissions *fpl*; *(of recruits)* contingent *m*; *Tech (of gas, air)* admission *f*

intangible [ɪn'tændʒəbəl] *adj* intangible

integral ['ɪntɪgrəl] *adj* intégral; **to be an i. part of sth** faire partie intégrante de qch

integrate ['ɪntɪgreɪt] **1** *vt* intégrer (**into** dans); **integrated school** école *f* où se pratique la déségrégation raciale

2 *vi* s'intégrer (**into** dans) • **inte'gration** *n* intégration *f*; **(racial) i.** déségrégation *f* raciale

integrity [ɪn'tegrɪtɪ] *n* intégrité *f*

intellect ['ɪntɪlekt] *n* intelligence *f*, intellect *m* • **inte'llectual** *adj & n* intellectuel, -uelle *(mf)*

intelligence [ɪn'telɪdʒəns] *n* intelligence *f*; *(information)* renseignements *mpl*; **i. service** services *mpl* secrets

intelligent [ɪn'telɪdʒənt] *adj* intelligent • **intelligently** *adv* intelligemment

intelligentsia [ɪntelɪ'dʒentsɪə] *n* intelligentsia *f*

intelligible [ɪn'telɪdʒəbəl] *adj* intelligible • **intelligi'bility** *n* intelligibilité *f*

intemperance [ɪn'tempərəns] *n* intempérance *f*

intend [ɪn'tend] *vt (gift, remark)* destiner (**for** à); **to be intended for sb** être destiné à qn; **to be intended to do sth** être destiné à faire qch; **to i. to do sth** avoir l'intention de faire qch; **I i. you to stay** mon intention est que vous restiez • **intended** *adj (deliberate)* voulu; *(planned)* prévu; *(effect)* escompté; **was that i.?** était-ce intentionnel?

intense [ɪn'tens] *adj* intense; *(interest)* vif *(f* vive); *(person)* passionné • **intensely** *adv (look at)* intensément; *Fig (very)* extrêmement

intensify [ɪn'tensɪfaɪ] *(pt & pp* -**ied**) **1** *vt* intensifier

2 *vi* s'intensifier • **intensification** [-fɪ'keɪʃən] *n* intensification *f*

intensity [ɪn'tensətɪ] *n* intensité *f*

intensive [ɪn'tensɪv] *adj* intensif, -ive; **in i. care** en réanimation; **i. care unit** service *m* de réanimation

intent [ɪn'tent] **1** *adj (look)* intense; **to be i. on doing** être résolu à faire; **i. on one's task** absorbé par son travail

2 *n* intention *f*; **to all intents and purposes** quasiment

intention [ɪn'tenʃən] *n* intention *f* (**of doing** de faire); **to have every i. of doing sth** avoir la ferme intention de faire qch

intentional [ɪn'tenʃənəl] *adj* intentionnel, -elle; **it wasn't i.** ce n'était pas fait exprès ● **intentionally** adv intentionnellement, exprès

inter [ɪnˈtɜː(r)] (pt & pp **-rr-**) vt enterrer

inter- [ˈɪntə(r)] pref inter-

interact [ɪntərˈækt] vi (of person) communiquer (**with** avec); (of several people) communiquer entre eux/elles; (of ideas) être interdépendant(e)s; (of chemicals) réagir (**with** avec) ● **interaction** n interaction f ● **interactive** adj Comptr interactif, -ive

intercede [ɪntəˈsiːd] vi intercéder (**with** auprès de)

intercept [ɪntəˈsept] vt intercepter ● **interception** n interception f

interchange [ˈɪntətʃeɪndʒ] n Br (on road) échangeur m

interchangeable [ɪntəˈtʃeɪndʒəbəl] adj interchangeable

inter-city [ɪntəˈsɪtɪ] adj Br **i. service** grandes lignes fpl; Br **i. train** train m de grandes lignes

intercom [ˈɪntəkɒm] n Interphone® m

interconnected [ɪntəkəˈnektɪd] adj (facts) lié(e)s ● **interconnecting** adj **i. rooms** pièces fpl communicantes

intercontinental [ɪntəkɒntɪˈnentəl] adj intercontinental

intercourse [ˈɪntəkɔːs] n (sexual) rapports mpl sexuels

interdependent [ɪntədɪˈpendənt] adj interdépendant; (parts of machine) solidaire

interest [ˈɪntərest, ˈɪntrɪst] **1** n intérêt m; (hobby) centre m d'intérêt; (money) intérêts mpl; **to take an i. in** sb/sth s'intéresser à qn/qch; **to lose i. in** sb/sth se désintéresser de qn/qch; **to have a financial i. in** sth avoir investi financièrement dans qch; **to act in** sb's **i.** agir dans l'intérêt de qn; **it's in my i. to do it** j'ai tout intérêt à le faire; **to be of i.** être intéressant; **to be of i. to** sb intéresser qn

2 vt intéresser ● **interested** adj intéressé; **to seem i.** sembler intéressé (**in** par); **to be i. in** sb/sth s'intéresser à qn/qch; **I'm i. in doing that** ça m'intéresse de faire ça; **are you i.?** ça vous intéresse? ● **interest-free** adj (loan) sans intérêts; (credit) gratuit ● **interesting** adj intéressant ● **interestingly** adv **i. (enough), she...** curieusement, elle...

interface [ˈɪntəfeɪs] n Comptr interface f

interfere [ɪntəˈfɪə(r)] vi (meddle) se mêler (**in** de); **to i. with** sth (hinder) gêner qch; (touch) toucher à qch; **don't i.!** ne te mêle pas de ce qui ne te regarde pas!

● **interfering** adj (person) qui se mêle de tout

interference [ɪntəˈfɪərəns] n ingérence f; TV & Radio parasites mpl

interim [ˈɪntərɪm] **1** n **in the i.** entretemps

2 adj (measure) provisoire; (post) intérimaire

interior [ɪnˈtɪərɪə(r)] **1** adj intérieur

2 n intérieur m; Am **Department of the I.** ministère m de l'Intérieur

interjection [ɪntəˈdʒekʃən] n interjection f

interlock [ɪntəˈlɒk] vi (of machine parts) s'emboîter

interloper [ˈɪntələʊpə(r)] n intrus, -use mf

interlude [ˈɪntəluːd] n (on TV) interlude m; (in theatre) intermède m; (period of time) intervalle m

intermarry [ɪntəˈmærɪ] (pt & pp **-ied**) vi se marier (au sein d'une même famille) ● **intermarriage** n (within a family) mariage m consanguin; (with member of another group) mariage

intermediary [ɪntəˈmiːdɪərɪ] (pl **-ies**) adj & n intermédiaire (mf)

intermediate [ɪntəˈmiːdɪət] adj intermédiaire; (course, student) de niveau moyen

interminable [ɪnˈtɜːmɪnəbəl] adj interminable

intermingle [ɪntəˈmɪŋgəl] vi se mélanger

intermission [ɪntəˈmɪʃən] n entracte m

intermittent [ɪntəˈmɪtənt] adj intermittent ● **intermittently** adv par intermittence

intern 1 [ˈɪntɜːn] n Am Med interne mf

2 [ɪnˈtɜːn] vt (imprison) interner ● **internment** n Pol internement m

internal [ɪnˈtɜːnəl] adj interne; (flight, policy) intérieur; **i. combustion engine** moteur m à combustion interne; Am **the I. Revenue Service** ≃ le fisc ● **internally** adv intérieurement; **'not to be taken i.'** (medicine) 'à usage externe'

international [ɪntəˈnæʃənəl] **1** adj international

2 n (match) rencontre f internationale; (player) international m ● **internationally** adv **i. famous** mondialement connu; **i. recognized** reconnu dans le monde entier

Internet [ˈɪntənet] n Comptr **the I.** l'Internet m; **I. access** accès m (à l')Internet; **I. service provider** fournisseur m d'accès Internet

interplanetary [ɪntəˈplænɪtərɪ] adj interplanétaire

interplay ['ɪntəpleɪ] *n* interaction *f* (**of** *or* **between** de)

interpret [ɪn'tɜːprɪt] *vt* interpréter
2 *vi (translate for people)* faire l'interprète •**interpre'tation** *n* interprétation *f* •**interpreter** *n* interprète *mf*

interrelated [ɪntərɪ'leɪtɪd] *adj* lié •**interrelation** *n* corrélation *f*

interrogate [ɪn'terəgeɪt] *vt* interroger •**interro'gation** *n* interrogation *f*; *(by police)* interrogatoire *m* •**interrogator** *n* interrogateur, -trice *mf*

interrogative [ɪntə'rɒgətɪv] *adj & n Grammar* interrogatif, -ive *(m)*

interrupt [ɪntə'rʌpt] **1** *vt* interrompre
2 *vi* **I'm sorry to i.** je suis désolé de vous interrompre •**interruption** *n* interruption *f*

intersect [ɪntə'sekt] **1** *vt* couper
2 *vi* se couper •**intersection** *n* intersection *f*; *(of roads)* croisement *m*

interspersed [ɪntə'spɜːst] *adj* **i. with sth** parsemé de qch; **weeks of work i. with visits to the theatre** des semaines de travail entrecoupées de sorties au théâtre

intertwine [ɪntə'twaɪn] **1** *vt* entrelacer
2 *vi* s'entrelacer

interval ['ɪntəvəl] *n* intervalle *m*; *Br (in theatre, cinema)* entracte *m*; *(time)* de temps à autre; *(space)* par intervalles; **at five-minute intervals** toutes les cinq minutes; **bright** *or* **sunny intervals** éclaircies *fpl*

intervene [ɪntə'viːn] *vi (of person)* intervenir (**in** dans); *(of event)* survenir; **ten years intervened** dix années s'écoulèrent; **if nothing intervenes** s'il n'arrive rien entre-temps •**intervention** [-'venʃən] *n* intervention *f*

interview ['ɪntəvjuː] **1** *n* entretien *m* (**with** avec); *TV & Journ* interview *m ou f*; **to call sb for** *or* **to an i.** convoquer qn
2 *vt (for job)* faire passer un entretien à; *TV & Journ* interviewer •**interviewer** *n TV* intervieweur, -euse *mf*; *(for research, in canvassing)* enquêteur, -euse *mf*

intestine [ɪn'testɪn] *n* intestin *m*

intimate¹ ['ɪntɪmət] *adj* intime; *(friendship)* profond; *(knowledge)* approfondi •**intimacy** *n* intimité *f* •**intimately** *adv* intimement

intimate² ['ɪntɪmeɪt] *vt (hint at)* faire comprendre; *(make known)* signifier •**inti'mation** *n (announcement)* annonce *f*; *(hint)* suggestion *f*; *(sign)* indication *f*

intimidate [ɪn'tɪmɪdeɪt] *vt* intimider •**intimi'dation** *n* intimidation *f*

into ['ɪntuː, *unstressed* 'ɪntə] *prep* (**a**) dans; **to put sth i.** sth mettre qch dans qch; **to go i. a room** entrer dans une pièce; **to go i. detail** entrer dans les détails (**b**) en; **to translate i. French** traduire en français; **to change sb i.** sth changer qn en qch; **to break sth i. pieces** briser qch en morceaux; **to go i. town** aller en ville (**c**) *Math* **three i. six goes two** six divisé par trois fait deux (**d**) *Fam* **to be i. jazz** être branché jazz

intolerable [ɪn'tɒlərəbəl] *adj* intolérable (**that** que + *subjunctive*)

intolerance [ɪn'tɒlərəns] *n* intolérance *f* •**intolerant** *adj* intolérant; **to be i. of sb** être intolérant à l'égard de qn; **to be i. of sth** ne pas tolérer qch

intonation [ɪntə'neɪʃən] *n* intonation *f*

intoxicate [ɪn'tɒksɪkeɪt] *vt* enivrer •**intoxicated** *adj* ivre; *Fig* **to be i. with fame** être ivre de gloire •**intoxi'cation** *n* ivresse *f*

intractable [ɪn'træktəbəl] *adj (person)* intraitable; *(problem)* épineux, -euse

intransigent [ɪn'trænsɪdʒənt] *adj* intransigeant •**intransigence** *n* intransigeance *f*

intransitive [ɪn'trænsɪtɪv] *adj Grammar* intransitif, -ive

intravenous [ɪntrə'viːnəs] *adj Med* intraveineux, -euse

in-tray ['ɪntreɪ] *n (in office)* bac *m* du courrier à traiter

intrepid [ɪn'trepɪd] *adj* intrépide

intricate ['ɪntrɪkət] *adj* compliqué •**intricacy** *(pl -ies)* *n* complexité *f*

intrigue 1 ['ɪntriːg] *n (plot)* intrigue *f*
2 [ɪn'triːg] *vt (interest)* intriguer; **I'm intrigued to know** je suis curieux de savoir •**intriguing** *adj (news, attitude)* curieux, -ieuse

intrinsic [ɪn'trɪnsɪk] *adj* intrinsèque •**intrinsically** *adv* intrinsèquement

introduce [ɪntrə'djuːs] *vt (bring in, insert)* introduire (**into** dans); *(programme, subject)* présenter; **to i. sb (to sb)** présenter qn (à qn); **to i. oneself (to sb)** se présenter (à qn); **to i. sb to Dickens/geography** faire découvrir Dickens/la géographie à qn

introduction [ɪntrə'dʌkʃən] *n* introduction *f*; *(of person to person)* présentation *f*; **i. to computing** initiation *f* à l'informatique; **her i. to life abroad** son premier contact avec la vie à l'étranger

introductory [ɪntrə'dʌktərɪ] *adj (words, speech)* d'introduction; *(course)* d'initiation; **i. price** prix *m* de lancement

introspective [ɪntrə'spektɪv] *adj* introspectif, -ive •**introspection** n introspection f

introvert ['ɪntrəvɜːt] n introverti, -ie mf

intrude [ɪn'truːd] vi (of person) déranger (**on** sb qn); **to i. on sb's time** abuser du temps de qn; **to i. on sb's privacy** s'immiscer dans la vie privée de qn •**intruder** n intrus, -use mf •**intrusion** n (bother) dérangement m; (interference) intrusion f (**into** dans); **forgive my i.** pardonnez-moi de vous avoir dérangé

intuition [ɪntjuː'ɪʃən] n intuition f •**in-'tuitive** adj intuitif, -ive

Inuit ['ɪnjuːɪt] **1** adj inuit inv
  2 n Inuit mf inv

inundate ['ɪnʌndeɪt] vt inonder (**with** de); **inundated with work/letters** submergé de travail/lettres •**inun'dation** n inondation f

invade [ɪn'veɪd] vt envahir; **to i. sb's privacy** s'immiscer dans la vie privée de qn •**invader** n envahisseur, -euse mf

invalid¹ ['ɪnvəlɪd] adj & n malade (mf); (disabled person) infirme (mf)

invalid² [ɪn'vælɪd] adj (ticket) non valable •**invalidate** vt (ticket) annuler; (election, law) invalider; (theory) infirmer

invaluable [ɪn'væljʊəbəl] adj inestimable

invariable [ɪn'veərɪəbəl] adj invariable •**invariably** adv invariablement

invasion [ɪn'veɪʒən] n invasion f; **i. of sb's privacy** atteinte f à la vie privée de qn

invective [ɪn'vektɪv] n invectives fpl

inveigh [ɪn'veɪ] vi Formal **to i. against sb/sth** invectiver contre qn/qch

inveigle [ɪn'veɪgəl] vt **to i. sb into doing sth** entortiller qn pour qu'il fasse qch

invent [ɪn'vent] vt inventer •**invention** n invention f; (creativity) inventivité f •**inventive** adj inventif, -ive •**inventiveness** n inventivité f •**inventor** n inventeur, -trice mf

inventory ['ɪnvəntərɪ] (pl **-ies**) n inventaire m

inverse [ɪn'vɜːs] adj inverse; **in i. proportion to sth** inversement proportionnel, -elle à qch

invert [ɪn'vɜːt] vt (order) intervertir; (turn upside down) renverser; Br **inverted commas** guillemets mpl •**inversion** n interversion f; Grammar & Anat inversion f

invest [ɪn'vest] **1** vt (money) investir (**in** dans); (time, effort) consacrer (**in** à); **to i. sb with** (right, power) investir qn de
  2 vi **to i. in** (company) investir dans; Fig (car) se payer •**investment** n investissement m •**investor** n (in shares) investisseur m

investigate [ɪn'vestɪgeɪt] **1** vt (examine) examiner; (crime) enquêter sur
  2 vi Fam **to go and i.** aller voir ce qui se passe •**investi'gation** n examen m, étude f; (inquiry by journalist, police) enquête f (**of** or **into** sur) •**investigator** n (detective) enquêteur, -euse mf; (private) détective m

investiture [ɪn'vestɪtʃə(r)] n investiture f

inveterate [ɪn'vetərət] adj invétéré

invidious [ɪn'vɪdɪəs] adj (unfair) injuste; (unpleasant) ingrat, pénible

invigilate [ɪn'vɪdʒɪleɪt] vi Br (in school) être de surveillance à un examen •**invigilator** n Br surveillant, -ante mf (à un examen)

invigorate [ɪn'vɪgəreɪt] vt revigorer •**invigorating** adj vivifiant

invincible [ɪn'vɪnsəbəl] adj invincible

invisible [ɪn'vɪzəbəl] adj invisible; **i. ink** encre f sympathique

invite 1 [ɪn'vaɪt] vt inviter (**to do** à faire); (ask for) demander; (criticism) attirer au devant de; **you're inviting trouble** tu cherches les ennuis; **to i. sb out** inviter qn (à sortir); **to i. sb over** inviter qn (à venir)
  2 ['ɪnvaɪt] n Fam invit' f •**invitation** [-və'teɪʃən] n invitation f •**in'viting** adj (prospect) engageant; (food) appétissant

invoice ['ɪnvɔɪs] **1** n facture f
  2 vt (goods) facturer; (person) envoyer la facture à

invoke [ɪn'vəʊk] vt invoquer

involuntary [ɪn'vɒləntərɪ] adj involontaire •**involuntarily** adv involontairement

involve [ɪn'vɒlv] vt (entail) entraîner; **to i. sb in sth** impliquer qn dans qch; (in project) associer qn à qch; **the job involves going abroad** le poste nécessite des déplacements à l'étranger; **what does the job i.?** en quoi consiste le travail?

involved [ɪn'vɒlvd] adj (**a**) **to be i. in sth** (crime, affair) être impliqué dans qch; **to be i. in an accident** avoir un accident; **to be i. in teaching** être dans l'enseignement; **fifty people were i. in the project** cinquante personnes ont pris part au projet; **the police became i.** la police est intervenue; **to get i. in a book** s'absorber dans un livre; **to be i. with sb** (emotionally) avoir une liaison avec qn; **I don't want to get i.** (be a part of it) je ne veux pas m'en mêler; (emotionally) je ne veux pas m'engager; **the factors i.** (at stake) les facteurs en jeu; **the person i.** (concerned) la personne en question; **to be directly i.** être directement concerné
  (**b**) (complicated) compliqué

involvement [ɪn'vɒlvmənt] *n* participation *f* (**in** à); *(commitment)* engagement *m* (**in** dans); **emotional i.** liaison *f*

invulnerable [ɪn'vʌlnərəbəl] *adj* invulnérable

inward ['ɪnwəd] **1** *adj & adv (movement, move)* vers l'intérieur
2 *adj (inner) (happiness)* intérieur; *(thoughts)* intime • **inward-looking** *adj* replié sur soi-même • **inwardly** *adv (laugh, curse)* intérieurement • **inwards** *adv* vers l'intérieur

in-your-face [ɪnjə'feɪs] *adj (documentary, film)* sans fard; *(attitude)* agressif, -ive

iodine [*Br* 'aɪədiːn, *Am* 'aɪədaɪn] *n Chem* iode *m*; *(antiseptic)* teinture *f* d'iode

iota [aɪ'əʊtə] *n (of truth, guilt)* once *f*

IOU [aɪəʊ'juː] *(abbr* **I owe you**) *n* reconnaissance *f* de dette

IQ [aɪ'kjuː] *(abbr* **intelligence quotient**) *n* QI *m inv*

Iran [ɪ'rɑːn, ɪ'ræn] *n* l'Iran *m* • **Iranian** [ɪ'reɪnɪən, *Am* ɪ'rɑːnɪən] **1** *adj* iranien, -ienne **2** *n* Iranien, -ienne *mf*

Iraq [ɪ'rɑːk] *n* l'Irak *m* • **Iraqi 1** *adj* irakien, -ienne **2** *n* Irakien, -ienne *mf*

irascible [ɪ'ræsəbəl] *adj* irascible

ire ['aɪə(r)] *n Literary* courroux *m* • **irate** [aɪ'reɪt] *adj* furieux, -ieuse

Ireland ['aɪələnd] *n* l'Irlande *f* • **Irish** ['aɪrɪʃ] **1** *adj* irlandais **2** *n (language)* irlandais *m*; **the I.** *(people)* les Irlandais *mpl* • **Irishman** *(pl* **-men**) *n* Irlandais *m* • **Irishwoman** *(pl* **-women**) *n* Irlandaise *f*

iris ['aɪərɪs] *n (plant, of eye)* iris *m*

irk [ɜːk] *vt* agacer • **irksome** *adj* agaçant

iron ['aɪən] **1** *n* fer *m*; *(for clothes)* fer à repasser; **i. and steel industry** sidérurgie *f*; **an i. will** une volonté de fer; **the I. Curtain** le rideau de fer; *Br* **old i., scrap i.** ferraille *f*
2 *vt (clothes)* repasser; *Fig* **to i. out difficulties** aplanir les difficultés • **ironing** *n* repassage *m*; **i. board** planche *f* à repasser

ironmonger ['aɪənmʌŋgə(r)] *n* quincaillier, -ière *mf*; **i.'s shop** quincaillerie *f* • **ironmongery** *n* quincaillerie *f*

ironwork ['aɪənwɜːk] *n* ferronnerie *f*

irony ['aɪərənɪ] *n* ironie *f* • **ironic(al)** [aɪ'rɒnɪk(əl)] *adj* ironique

irradiate [ɪ'reɪdɪeɪt] *vt (subject to radiation)* irradier; **irradiated food** aliments *mpl* irradiés

irrational [ɪ'ræʃənəl] *adj* irrationnel, -elle

irreconcilable [ɪrekən'saɪləbəl] *adj (people)* irréconciliable; *(views, laws)* inconciliable

irrefutable [ɪrɪ'fjuːtəbəl] *adj (evidence)* irréfutable

irregular [ɪ'regjʊlə(r)] *adj* irrégulier, -ière • **irregularity** [-'lærɪtɪ] *(pl* **-ies**) *n* irrégularité *f*

irrelevant [ɪ'reləvənt] *adj* sans rapport (**to** avec); *(remark)* hors de propos; **that's i.** ça n'a rien à voir (avec la question) • **irrelevance** *n* manque *m* de rapport

irreparable [ɪ'repərəbəl] *adj (harm, loss)* irréparable

irreplaceable [ɪrɪ'pleɪsəbəl] *adj* irremplaçable

irrepressible [ɪrɪ'presəbəl] *adj (laughter, urge)* irrépressible

irreproachable [ɪrɪ'prəʊtʃəbəl] *adj* irréprochable

irresistible [ɪrɪ'zɪstəbəl] *adj (person, charm)* irrésistible

irresolute [ɪ'rezəluːt] *adj* irrésolu, indécis

irrespective [ɪrɪ'spektɪv] *prep* **i. of** indépendamment de

irresponsible [ɪrɪ'spɒnsəbəl] *adj (act)* irréfléchi; *(person)* irresponsable • **irresponsibly** *adv (behave)* de façon irresponsable

irretrievable [ɪrɪ'triːvəbəl] *adj (loss, mistake, situation)* irréparable

irreverent [ɪ'revərənt] *adj* irrévérencieux, -ieuse

irreversible [ɪrɪ'vɜːsəbəl] *adj (process)* irréversible; *(decision)* irrévocable

irrevocable [ɪ'revəkəbəl] *adj* irrévocable

irrigate ['ɪrɪgeɪt] *vt* irriguer • **irri'gation** *n* irrigation *f*

irritable ['ɪrɪtəbəl] *adj (easily annoyed)* irritable

irritant ['ɪrɪtənt] *n (to eyes, skin)* irritant *m*

irritate ['ɪrɪteɪt] *vt (annoy, inflame)* irriter • **irritating** *adj* irritant

irritation [ɪrɪ'teɪʃən] *n (anger, inflammation)* irritation *f*

IRS [aɪɑː'res] *abbr Am* = **Internal Revenue Service**

is [ɪz] *see* **be**

Islam ['ɪzlɑːm] *n* l'Islam *m* • **Islamic** ['ɪzlæmɪk] *adj* islamique

island ['aɪlənd] *n* île *f*; **(traffic) i.** refuge *m* (pour piétons) • **islander** *n* insulaire *mf*

isle [aɪl] *n* île *f*; **the British Isles** les îles Britanniques

isn't ['ɪzənt] = **is not**

isolate ['aɪsəleɪt] *vt* isoler (**from** de) • **isolated** *adj (remote, unique)* isolé • **iso'lation** *n* isolement *m*; **in i.** isolément

ISP [aɪes'piː] *(abbr* **Internet Service Provi-**

der) *n Comptr* fournisseur *m* d'accès Internet

Israel ['ɪzreɪl] *n* Israël *m* • **Is'raeli 1** *adj* israélien, -ienne **2** *n* Israélien, -ienne *mf*

issue ['ɪʃuː] **1** *n (of newspaper, magazine)* numéro *m; (matter)* question *f; (of stamps, banknotes)* émission *f;* **at i.** *(at stake)* en cause; **to make an i.** *or* **a big i. of sth** faire toute une affaire de qch; **to take i. with sb** exprimer son désaccord à qn
  2 *vt (book)* publier; *(tickets)* distribuer; *(passport)* délivrer; *(order)* donner; *(warning)* lancer; *(stamps, banknotes)* émettre; *(supply)* fournir (**with** de; **to** à); **to i. a statement** faire une déclaration
  3 *vi Formal* **to i. from** *(of smell, water)* se dégager de; *(of noise)* provenir de

🖉 Note that the French word **issue** is a false friend and is never a translation for the English word **issue**. It means **exit**.

isthmus ['ɪsməs] *n Geog* isthme *m*

it [ɪt] *pron* (**a**) *(subject)* il, elle; *(object)* le, la, l'; **(to) it** *(indirect object)* lui; **it bites** *(dog)* il mord; **I've done it** je l'ai fait
  (**b**) *(impersonal)* il; **it's snowing** il neige; **it's hot** il fait chaud
  (**c**) *(non-specific)* ce, cela, ça; **it's good** c'est bon; **it was pleasant** c'était agréable; **who is it?** qui est-ce?; **that's it!** *(I agree)* c'est ça!; *(it's done)* ça y est!; **to consider it wise to do sth** juger prudent de faire qch; **it was Paul who…** c'est Paul qui… **she's got it in her to succeed** elle est capable de réussir; **to have it in for sb** en vouloir à qn
  (**d**) **of it, from it, about it** en; **in it, to it, at it** y; **on it** dessus; **under it** dessous

italic [ɪ'tælɪk] *adj* italique • **italics** *npl* italique *m;* **in i.** en italique

Italy ['ɪtəlɪ] *n* l'Italie *f* • **Italian 1** [ɪ'tælɪən] *adj* italien, -ienne **2** *n (person)* Italien, -ienne *mf; (language)* italien *m*

itch [ɪtʃ] **1** *n* démangeaison *f;* **to have an i. to do sth** brûler d'envie de faire qch
  2 *vi (of person)* avoir des démangeaisons; **his arm itches** son bras le *ou* lui démange; *Fig* **to be itching to do sth** brûler d'envie de faire qch • **itching** *n* démangeaisons *fpl* • **itchy** *adj* **I have an i. hand** j'ai la main qui me démange; **I'm (all) i.** j'ai des démangeaisons

item ['aɪtəm] *n (in collection, on list, in newspaper)* article *m; (matter)* question *f; (on entertainment programme)* numéro *m;* **i. of clothing** vêtement *m;* **news i.** information *f* • **itemize** *vt (invoice)* détailler

itinerant [aɪ'tɪnərənt] *adj (musician, actor)* ambulant; *(judge, preacher)* itinérant

itinerary [aɪ'tɪnərərɪ] *(pl* -**ies**) *n* itinéraire *m*

its [ɪts] *possessive adj* son, sa, *pl* ses • **it-'self** *pron* lui-même, elle-même; *(reflexive)* se, s'; **goodness i.** la bonté même; **by i.** tout seul

IUD [aɪjuː'diː] *(abbr* **intrauterine device**) *n Med* stérilet *m*

I've [aɪv] = **I have**

IVF [aɪviː'ef] *(abbr* **in vitro fertilization**) *n* FIV *f*

ivory ['aɪvərɪ] *n* ivoire *m;* **i. statuette** statuette *f* en ivoire

ivy ['aɪvɪ] *n* lierre *m*

J, j [dʒeɪ] *n (letter)* J, j *m inv*
jab [dʒæb] **1** *n* coup *m*; *Br Fam (injection)* piqûre *f*
2 (*pt & pp* **-bb-**) *vt (knife, stick)* enfoncer (**into** dans); *(prick)* piquer (**with** du bout de)
jabber ['dʒæbə(r)] *Fam* **1** *vt* **to j. out** *(excuse)* marmonner
2 *vi* marmonner • **jabbering** *n* bavardage *m*
jack [dʒæk] **1** *n* (**a**) *(for vehicle)* cric *m* (**b**) *Cards* valet *m* (**c**) **j. of all trades** homme *m* à tout faire
2 *vt* **to j. up** *(vehicle)* soulever *(avec un cric)*; *Fig (price)* augmenter; *Br Fam* **to j. in** *(job)* plaquer • **jack-in-the-box** *n* diable *m* (à ressort)
jackal ['dʒækəl] *n* chacal *m* (*pl* -als)
jackass ['dʒækæs] *n (animal, person)* âne *m*
jackdaw ['dʒækdɔː] *n* choucas *m*
jacket ['dʒækɪt] *n (coat)* veste *f*; *(of book)* jaquette *f*; *Br* **j. potato** pomme *f* de terre en robe des champs
jackknife ['dʒæknaɪf] **1** (*pl* **-knives**) *n* couteau *m* de poche
2 *vi Br (of truck)* se mettre en travers de la route
jackpot ['dʒækpɒt] *n* gros lot *m*
Jacuzzi® [dʒə'kuːzɪ] *n* Jacuzzi® *m*
jade [dʒeɪd] *n (stone)* jade *m*
jaded ['dʒeɪdɪd] *adj* blasé
jagged ['dʒægɪd] *adj* déchiqueté
jaguar [*Br* 'dʒægjʊə(r), *Am* 'dʒægwɑːr] *n* jaguar *m*
jail [dʒeɪl] **1** *n* prison *f*
2 *vt* emprisonner (**for** pour); **to j. sb for ten years** condamner qn à dix ans de prison; **to j. sb for life** condamner qn à perpétuité • **jailer** *n* gardien, -ienne *mf* de prison
jalopy [dʒə'lɒpɪ] (*pl* -**ies**) *n Fam (car)* vieux tacot *m*
jam¹ [dʒæm] *n (preserve)* confiture *f*; **strawberry j.** confiture de fraises • **jamjar** *n* pot *m* à confiture
jam² [dʒæm] **1** *n* (**traffic**) **j.** embouteillage *m*; *Fam* **in a j.** *(trouble)* dans le pétrin
2 (*pt & pp* **-mm-**) *vt (squeeze, make stuck)*

coincer; *(gun)* enrayer; *(street, corridor)* encombrer; *(broadcast, radio station)* brouiller; **to j. sth into sth** entasser qch dans qch; **to j. people into a room** entasser des gens dans une pièce; **to j. a stick into sth** enfoncer un bâton dans qch; **to j. on the brakes** écraser la pédale de frein
3 *vi* (**a**) *(get stuck)* se coincer; *(of gun)* s'enrayer; *(of crowd)* s'entasser (**into** dans) (**b**) *(of musicians)* improviser • **jammed** *adj (machine)* coincé; *(street)* encombré • '**jam-'packed** *adj (hall, train)* bourré
Jamaica [dʒə'meɪkə] *n* la Jamaïque
jangle ['dʒæŋgəl] **1** *n* cliquetis *m*
2 *vi* cliqueter
janitor ['dʒænɪtə(r)] *n Am & Scot (caretaker)* concierge *m*
January ['dʒænjʊərɪ] *n* janvier *m*
Japan [dʒə'pæn] *n* le Japon • **Japanese** [dʒæpə'niːz] **1** *adj* japonais **2** *n (person)* Japonais, -aise *mf*; *(language)* japonais *m*
jar¹ [dʒɑː(r)] *n (container)* pot *m*; *(large, glass)* bocal *m*
jar² [dʒɑː(r)] **1** *n (jolt)* choc *m*
2 (*pt & pp* **-rr-**) *vt (shake)* ébranler
3 *vi (of noise)* grincer; *(of musical note)* détonner; *(of colours, words)* jurer (**with** avec); **it jars on my nerves** ça me tape sur les nerfs; **it jars on my ears** cela m'écorche les oreilles • **jarring** *adj (noise, voice)* discordant
jargon ['dʒɑːgən] *n* jargon *m*
jasmine ['dʒæzmɪn] *n* jasmin *m*
jaundice ['dʒɔːndɪs] *n (illness)* jaunisse *f* • **jaundiced** *adj (bitter)* aigri; **to take a j. view of sth** voir qch d'un mauvais œil
jaunt [dʒɔːnt] *n (journey)* balade *f*
jaunty ['dʒɔːntɪ] (**-ier, -iest**) *adj (carefree)* insouciant; *(cheerful, lively)* allègre; *(hat)* coquet, -ette • **jauntily** *adv* avec insouciance; *(cheerfully)* allègrement
javelin ['dʒævlɪn] *n* javelot *m*
jaw [dʒɔː] **1** *n Anat* mâchoire *f*; *Fam* **to have a j.** tailler une bavette
2 *vi Fam (talk)* papoter
jay [dʒeɪ] *n* geai *m*
jaywalker ['dʒeɪwɔːkə(r)] *n* = piéton qui traverse en dehors des passages cloutés

jazz [dʒæz] **1** n jazz m
  2 vt Fam **to j. sth up** (clothes, room, style)
égayer qch; (music) jazzifier qch
JCB® [dʒeɪsiːˈbiː] n Br tractopelle m ou f
jealous [ˈdʒeləs] adj jaloux, -ouse (**of**
de) • **jealousy** n jalousie f
jeans [dʒiːnz] npl **(pair of) j.** jean m
Jeep® [dʒiːp] n Jeep® f
jeer [dʒɪə(r)] **1** n raillerie f; **jeers** (boos)
huées fpl
  2 vt (boo) huer; (mock) se moquer de
  3 vi **to j. at sb/sth** (boo) huer qn/qch;
(mock) se moquer de qn/qch • **jeering 1**
adj railleur, -euse **2** n (mocking) railleries
fpl; (of crowd) huées fpl
jell [dʒel] vi Fam (of ideas) prendre tournure
jello® [ˈdʒeləʊ] n Am (dessert) gelée f
jelly [ˈdʒelɪ] (pl **-ies**) n (preserve, dessert)
gelée f; **j. baby** = bonbon à base de
gélatine, en forme de bébé • **jellybean** n
= bonbon recouvert de sucre, en forme
de haricot • **jellyfish** n méduse f
jeopardy [ˈdʒepədɪ] n danger m, péril m
  • **jeopardize** vt mettre en danger
jerk¹ [dʒɜːk] **1** n secousse f
  2 vt (pull) tirer brusquement; (in order to
move) déplacer par à-coups
  3 vi **to j. forward** (of car) faire un bond
en avant
jerk² [dʒɜːk] n Fam (person) abruti, -ie mf
jerky [ˈdʒɜːkɪ] (**-ier, -iest**) adj (**a**) (movement, voice) saccadé (**b**) Am Fam (stupid)
stupide, bête • **jerkily** adv par saccades
Jersey [ˈdʒɜːzɪ] n Jersey m ou f
jersey [ˈdʒɜːzɪ] (pl **-eys**) n (garment) tricot m; Football maillot m; (cloth) jersey m
jest [dʒest] **1** n plaisanterie f; **in j.** pour rire
  2 vi plaisanter • **jester** n Hist (court) **j.** fou
m (du roi)
Jesus [ˈdʒiːzəs] n Jésus m; **J. Christ** Jésus-
Christ m
jet [dʒet] **1** n (**a**) (plane) avion m à réaction; **j. engine** réacteur m, moteur m à
réaction; **j. lag** fatigue f due au décalage
horaire; **j. ski** scooter m des mers, jet-ski
m (**b**) (steam, liquid) jet m
  2 vi Fam **to j. off** s'envoler (**to** pour)
jet-black [ˈdʒetˈblæk] adj (noir) de jais
jetfoil [ˈdʒetfɔɪl] n hydroglisseur m
jet-lagged [ˈdʒetlægd] adj Fam qui souffre du décalage horaire
jettison [ˈdʒetɪsən] vt (cargo from ship)
jeter à la mer; (fuel from plane) larguer;
Fig (plan, tradition) abandonner
jetty [ˈdʒetɪ] (pl **-ies**) n jetée f; (landing
place) embarcadère m
Jew [dʒuː] n (man) Juif m; (woman) Juive f

• **Jewess** n Juive f • **Jewish** adj juif (f
juive)
jewel [ˈdʒuːəl] n bijou m (pl **-oux**); (in
watch) rubis m • **jewelled** (Am **jeweled**)
adj orné de bijoux • **jeweller** (Am **jeweler**) n bijoutier, -ière mf • **jewellery** (Am
jewelry) n bijoux mpl
jib [dʒɪb] (pt & pp **-bb-**) vi rechigner (**at**
devant); **to j. at doing sth** rechigner à
faire qch
jibe [dʒaɪb] n & vi = **gibe**
jiffy [ˈdʒɪfɪ] n Fam instant m
Jiffy bag® [ˈdʒɪfɪbæg] n enveloppe f ma-
telassée
jig [dʒɪg] n (dance, music) gigue f
jigsaw [ˈdʒɪgsɔː] n **j. (puzzle)** puzzle m
jilt [dʒɪlt] vt (lover) laisser tomber
jingle [ˈdʒɪŋgəl] **1** n tintement m; (in
advertisement) jingle m
  2 vt faire tinter
  3 vi (of keys, bell) tinter
jinx [dʒɪŋks] n (person, object) porte-
malheur m inv; (spell, curse) mauvais sort m
jitters [ˈdʒɪtəz] npl Fam **to have the j.** être
à cran • **jittery** adj Fam **to be j.** être à cran
job [dʒɒb] n (employment, post) travail m,
emploi m; (task) tâche f; Fam (crime) coup
m; Fam **to have a (hard) j. doing** or **to do
sth** avoir du mal à faire qch; **to have the j.
of doing sth** (unpleasant task) être obligé
de faire qch; (for a living) être chargé de
faire qch; Br Fam **it's a good j. (that)...**
heureusement que... (+ indicative); Fam
that's just the j. c'est juste ce qu'il faut;
out of a j. au chômage; **j. losses** suppres-
sions fpl d'emplois; **j. offer** offre f d'emploi
jobcentre [ˈdʒɒbsentə(r)] n Br ≃ agence
f nationale pour l'emploi
jobless [ˈdʒɒbləs] adj au chômage
jock [dʒɒk] n Am Fam (sportsman) sportif
m
jockey [ˈdʒɒkɪ] **1** (pl **-eys**) n jockey m
  2 vi **to j. for position** jouer des coudes
jockstrap [ˈdʒɒkstræp] n slip m à coquille
jocular [ˈdʒɒkjʊlə(r)] adj jovial
jog [dʒɒg] **1** n (shake, jolt) secousse f;
(nudge) coup m de coude
  2 (pt & pp **-gg-**) vt (shake) secouer;
(push) pousser; Fig (memory) rafraîchir
  3 vi Sport faire du jogging; **to go jogging**
aller faire un jogging; **to j. along** (of
vehicle) cahoter; (of work) aller tant bien
que mal; (of person) faire son petit bonhomme de chemin • **jogging** n Sport jogging m
john [dʒɒn] n Am Fam **the j.** (lavatory) le
petit coin

join [dʒɔɪn] **1** n raccord m
2 vt (**a**) (put together) joindre; (wires, pipes) raccorder; (words, towns) relier; **to j. sth to sth** joindre qch à qch; (link) relier qch à qch; **to j. two things together** relier une chose à une autre; **to j. sb** (catch up with, meet) rejoindre qn; (associate oneself with, go with) se joindre à qn (**in doing** pour faire); **to j. the sea** (of river) rejoindre la mer; **to j. hands** se donner la main; **to j. forces** s'unir (**b**) (become a member of) s'inscrire à; (army, police, company) entrer dans; **to j. the queue** or Am **line** prendre la queue
3 vi (**a**) (of roads, rivers) se rejoindre; **to j. (together** or **up)** (of objects) se joindre (**with** à); **to j. in sth** prendre part à qch (**b**) (become a member) devenir membre; Mil **to j. up** s'engager
joiner ['dʒɔɪnə(r)] n Br menuisier m
joint [dʒɔɪnt] **1** n (**a**) (in body) articulation f; Br (meat) rôti m; Tech joint m; (in carpentry) assemblage m; **out of j.** (shoulder) déboîté (**b**) Fam (nightclub) boîte f (**c**) Fam (cannabis cigarette) joint m
2 adj (decision) commun; **j. account** compte m joint; **j. author** coauteur m; **j. efforts** efforts mpl conjugués • **jointly** adv conjointement
joist [dʒɔɪst] n solive f
joke [dʒəʊk] **1** n plaisanterie f; (trick) tour m; **it's no j.** (it's unpleasant) ce n'est pas drôle (**doing** de faire)
2 vi plaisanter (**about** sur) • **joker** n plaisantin m; Fam (fellow) type m; Cards joker m • **jokingly** adv (say) en plaisantant
jolly¹ ['dʒɒlɪ] (**-ier, -iest**) adj (happy) gai; Fam (drunk) éméché
jolly² ['dʒɒlɪ] adv Br Fam (very) rudement; **j. good!** très bien!

⟋ Note that the French word **joli** is a false friend and is never a translation for the English word **jolly**. It means **pretty**.

jolt [dʒɒlt] **1** n secousse f
2 vt (shake) secouer; **to j. sb into action** secouer les puces à qn
3 vi **to j. (along)** (of vehicle) cahoter
Jordan ['dʒɔːdən] n la Jordanie
jostle ['dʒɒsəl] **1** vt (push) bousculer; **don't j.!** ne bousculez pas!
2 vi (push each other) se bousculer (**for** sth pour obtenir qch)
jot [dʒɒt] (pt & pp **-tt-**) vt **to j. sth down** noter qch • **jotter** n (notepad) bloc-notes m
journal ['dʒɜːnəl] n (periodical) revue f

• **journa'lese** n Pej jargon m journalistique
journalism ['dʒɜːnəlɪzəm] n journalisme m • **journalist** n journaliste mf
journey ['dʒɜːnɪ] **1** (pl **-eys**) n (trip) voyage m; (distance) trajet m; **to go on a j.** partir en voyage
2 vi voyager

⟋ Note that the French word **journée** is a false friend and is never a translation for the English word **journey**. It means **day**.

jovial ['dʒəʊvɪəl] adj jovial
joy [dʒɔɪ] n joie f; **the joys of** (countryside, motherhood) les plaisirs mpl de • **joyful, joyous** adj joyeux, -euse
joyride ['dʒɔɪraɪd] n = virée dans une voiture volée • **joyrider** n = chauffard qui conduit une voiture volée
joystick ['dʒɔɪstɪk] n (of aircraft, computer) manche m à balai
JP [dʒeɪ'piː] abbr Br = **Justice of the Peace**
jubilant ['dʒuːbɪlənt] adj **to be j.** jubiler • **jubi'lation** n jubilation f
jubilee ['dʒuːbɪliː] n (**golden**) **j.** jubilé m
Judaism ['dʒuːdeɪɪzəm] n judaïsme m
judder ['dʒʌdə(r)] **1** n vibration f
2 vi (shake) vibrer
judge [dʒʌdʒ] **1** n juge m
2 vti juger; **to j. sb by** or **on sth** juger qn sur ou d'après qch; **judging by...** à en juger par... • **judg(e)ment** n jugement m
judg(e)mental [dʒʌdʒ'mentəl] adj critique
judicial [dʒuː'dɪʃəl] adj judiciaire
judiciary [dʒuː'dɪʃərɪ] n magistrature f
judicious [dʒuː'dɪʃəs] adj judicieux, -ieuse
judo ['dʒuːdəʊ] n judo m
jug [dʒʌɡ] n cruche f; (for milk) pot m
juggernaut ['dʒʌɡənɔːt] n Br (truck) poids m lourd
juggle ['dʒʌɡəl] **1** vt jongler avec
2 vi jongler (**with** avec) • **juggler** n jongleur, -euse mf
juice [dʒuːs] n jus m; (in stomach) suc m • **juicy** (**-ier, -iest**) adj (fruit) juteux, -euse; (meat) succulent; Fig (story) savoureux, -euse
jukebox ['dʒuːkbɒks] n juke-box m
July [dʒuː'laɪ] n juillet m
jumble ['dʒʌmbəl] **1** n (disorder) fouillis m; Br (unwanted articles) bric-à-brac m inv; Br **j. sale** (used clothes) vente f de charité
2 vt **to j. (up)** (objects, facts) mélanger

jumbo ['dʒʌmbəʊ] **1** *adj (packet)* géant
2 *(pl -os) adj & n* **j. (jet)** jumbo-jet *(m)*
jump [dʒʌmp] **1** *n (leap)* saut *m; (start)*
sursaut *m; (increase)* hausse *f* soudaine;
Br **j. leads** câbles *mpl* de démarrage; *Am* **j.
rope** corde *f* à sauter
2 *vt (ditch)* sauter; **to j. the lights** *(in car)*
griller un feu rouge; **to j. the rails** *(of train)*
dérailler; *Br* **to j. the queue** passer avant
son tour, resquiller; *Am* **to j. rope** sauter à
la corde
3 *vi* sauter **(at** sur); *(start)* sursauter; *(of
price, heart)* faire un bond; **to j. about**
sautiller; **to j. across sth** traverser qch
d'un bond; **to j. to conclusions** tirer des
conclusions hâtives; **to j. in** *or* **on** *(train,
vehicle, bus)* sauter dans; **j. in** *or* **on!**
montez!; **to j. off** *or* **out** sauter; *(from
bus)* descendre; **to j. off sth, to j. out of
sth** sauter de qch; **to j. out of the window**
sauter par la fenêtre; **to j. up** se lever d'un
bond •**jumpy** ['dʒʌmpɪ] (**-ier, -iest**) *adj*
nerveux, -euse
jumper ['dʒʌmpə(r)] *n Br* pull(-over) *m;
Am (dress)* robe *f* chasuble; *Am* **j. cables**
câbles *mpl* de démarrage
junction ['dʒʌŋkʃən] *n (crossroads)* carrefour *m; (joining)* jonction *f;* **j. 23** *Br (on
motorway) (exit)* la sortie 23; *(entrance)*
l'entrée *f* 23
juncture ['dʒʌŋktʃə(r)] *n Formal* **at this j.**
à ce moment-là
June [dʒuːn] *n* juin *m*
jungle ['dʒʌŋgəl] *n* jungle *f*
junior ['dʒuːnɪə(r)] **1** *adj (younger)* plus
jeune; *(in rank, status)* subalterne; *(teacher, doctor)* jeune; **to be sb's j., to be j. to
sb** être plus jeune que qn; *(in rank, status)*
être au-dessous de qn; **Smith j.** Smith fils;
Br **j. school** école *f* primaire *(entre 7 et 11
ans); Am* **j. high school** ≃ collège *m*
d'enseignement secondaire
2 *n* cadet, -ette *mf; (in school)* petit, -ite
mf; Sport junior *mf,* cadet, -ette *mf;* **he's
three years my j.** il a trois ans de moins
que moi
junk [dʒʌŋk] **1** *n (unwanted objects)* bric-
à-brac *m inv; (inferior goods)* camelote *f;
(bad film, book)* navet *m; (nonsense)* idioties *fpl;* **j. food** cochonneries *fpl;* **j. mail**
prospectus *mpl;* **j. shop** boutique *f* de
brocanteur

2 *vt Fam (get rid of)* balancer •**junkyard**
n dépôt *m* de ferrailleur
junkie ['dʒʌŋkɪ] *n Fam* drogué, -ée *mf*
jurisdiction [dʒʊərɪs'dɪkʃən] *n* juridiction *f;* **to be within the j. of** être sous la
juridiction de
jury ['dʒʊərɪ] *(pl -ies) n (in competition,
court)* jury *m* •**juror** *n (in court)* juré *m*
just [dʒʌst] **1** *adv (exactly, slightly)* juste;
(only) juste, seulement; *(simply)* (tout)
simplement; **j. before/after** juste avant/
après; **it's j. as I thought** c'est bien ce que
je pensais; **j. at that time** à cet instant
même; **she has/had j. left** elle vient/
venait de partir; **I've j. come from...** j'arrive de...; **I'm j. coming!** j'arrive!; **he'll
(only) j. catch the bus** il aura son bus de
justesse; **he j. missed it** il l'a manqué de
peu; **j. as big/light** tout aussi grand/léger
(**as** que); **j. listen!** écoute donc!; **j. a
moment!** un instant!; **j. over ten** un peu
plus de dix; **j. one** un(e) seul(e) (**of** de); **j.
about** *(approximately)* à peu près; *(almost)* presque; **to be j. about to do sth**
être sur le point de faire qch
2 *adj (fair)* juste (**to** envers) •**justly** *adv
(fairly)* avec justice; *(deservedly)* à juste
titre
justice ['dʒʌstɪs] *n* justice *f; (judge)* juge
m; **to do j. to a meal** faire honneur à un
repas; **it doesn't do you j.** *(hat, photo)*
cela ne vous avantage pas; *(attitude)* cela
ne vous fait pas honneur; **J. of the Peace**
juge *m* de paix
justify ['dʒʌstɪfaɪ] *(pt & pp -ied) vt* justifier; **to be justified in doing sth** *(have
right)* être en droit de faire qch; *(have
reason)* être fondé à faire qch •**justifiable**
adj justifiable •**justifiably** *adv* à juste titre
•**justification** [-fɪ'keɪʃən] *n* justification *f*
jut [dʒʌt] *(pt & pp -tt-) vi* **to j. out** faire
saillie; **to j. out over sth** *(overhang)* surplomber qch
jute [dʒuːt] *n* jute *m*
juvenile ['dʒuːvənaɪl, *Am* -ənəl] **1** *n Law*
mineur, -eure *mf*
2 *adj (court, book)* pour enfants; *Pej
(behaviour)* puéril; **j. delinquent** jeune
délinquant, -ante *mf*
juxtapose [dʒʌkstə'pəʊz] *vt* juxtaposer
•**juxtaposition** [-pə'zɪʃən] *n* juxtaposition *f*

K

K, k [keɪ] *n (letter)* K, k *m inv*
kaleidoscope [kə'laɪdəskəʊp] *n* kaléidoscope *m*
kangaroo [kæŋgə'ruː] *n* kangourou *m*
kaput [kə'pʊt] *adj Fam* kaput *inv*
karate [kə'rɑːtɪ] *n Sport* karaté *m*
kebab [kə'bæb] *n* brochette *f*
keel [kiːl] **1** *n (of boat)* quille *f*
2 *vi* **to k. over** *(of boat)* chavirer
keen [kiːn] *adj* (**a**) *Br (eager, enthusiastic)* plein d'enthousiasme; **he's a k. sportsman** c'est un passionné de sport; **to be k. on sth** *(music, sport)* être passionné de qch; **he is k. on her/the idea** elle/l'idée lui plaît beaucoup; **to be k. on doing sth** *(habitually)* adorer faire qch; *(want to do)* avoir très envie de faire qch; **to be k. to do sth** avoir très envie de faire qch (**b**) *(edge, appetite)* aiguisé; *(interest, feeling)* vif (*f* vive); *(mind)* pénétrant; *(wind)* glacial; **to have k. eyesight** avoir la vue perçante • **keenly** *adv Br (work)* avec enthousiasme; *(feel, interest)* vivement
keep¹ [kiːp] **1** *(pt & pp* **kept**) *vt* garder; *(shop, car)* avoir; *(diary, promise)* tenir; *(family)* entretenir; *(rule)* respecter; *(feast day)* célébrer; *(birthday)* fêter; *(delay, detain)* retenir; *(put)* mettre; **to k. doing sth** continuer à faire qch; **to k. sth clean** garder qch propre; **to k. sth from sb** dissimuler qch à qn; **to k. sb from doing sth** empêcher qn de faire qch; **to k. sb waiting/working** faire attendre/travailler qn; **to k. sth going** *(engine, machine)* laisser qch en marche; **to k. sb in whisky** fournir qn en whisky; **to k. an appointment** se rendre à un rendez-vous
2 *vi (remain)* rester; *(continue)* continuer; *(of food)* se conserver; **how is he keeping?** comment va-t-il?; **to k. still** rester immobile; **to k. quiet** se tenir tranquille; **to k. left** tenir sa gauche; **to k. from doing sth** s'abstenir de faire qch; **to k. going** continuer; **to k. at it** *(keep doing it)* persévérer
3 *n (food)* subsistance *f*; **to have one's k.** être logé et nourri; *Fam* **for keeps** pour toujours
▸ **keep away 1** *vt (person)* éloigner (**from**

de) **2** *vi* ne pas s'approcher (**from** de)
▸ **keep back 1** *vt sep (crowd)* contenir; *(delay, withhold)* retarder; *(hide)* cacher (**from** à) **2** *vi* ne pas s'approcher (**from** de) ▸ **keep down** *vt sep (restrict)* limiter; *(control)* maîtriser; *(price, costs)* maintenir bas ▸ **keep in** *vt sep* empêcher de sortir; *(as punishment in school)* garder en retenue ▸ **keep off 1** *vt sep (person)* éloigner; **k. your hands off!** n'y touche pas! **2** *vt insep* **'k. off the grass'** 'défense de marcher sur les pelouses' **3** *vi (not go near)* ne pas s'approcher; **if the rain keeps off** s'il ne pleut pas ▸ **keep on** *vt sep (hat, employee)* garder; **to k. on doing sth** continuer à faire qch **2** *vi* **to k. on at sb** harceler qn ▸ **keep out** *vt sep* empêcher d'entrer **2** *vi* rester en dehors (**of** de) ▸ **keep to 1** *vt insep (subject, path)* ne pas s'écarter de; *(room)* garder **2** *vi* **to k. to the left** tenir la gauche; **to k. to oneself** rester à l'écart ▸ **keep up** *vt sep (continue, maintain)* continuer (**doing** à faire); *(keep awake)* empêcher de dormir; **to k. up appearances** sauver les apparences **2** *vi (continue)* continuer; *(follow)* suivre; **to k. up with sb** *(follow)* aller à la même allure que qn; *(in quality of work)* se maintenir à la hauteur de qn
keep² [kiːp] *n Hist (tower)* donjon *m*
keeper ['kiːpə(r)] *n (in park, zoo)* & *Football* gardien, -ienne *mf*
keeping ['kiːpɪŋ] *n* **in k. with** conformément à; **to have sth in one's k.** avoir qch sous sa garde
keepsake ['kiːpseɪk] *n* souvenir *m*
keg [keg] *n* baril *m*
kennel ['kenəl] *n Br* niche *f*; *(for boarding dogs)* chenil *m*; *Br* **kennels** chenil
Kenya ['kiːnjə, 'kenjə] *n* le Kenya
kept [kept] **1** *pt & pp of* **keep¹**
2 *adj* **well** *or* **nicely k.** *(house)* bien tenu
kerb [kɜːb] *n Br* bord *m* du trottoir
kernel ['kɜːnəl] *n (of nut)* amande *f*
kerosene ['kerəsiːn] *n Am (paraffin)* pétrole *m* (lampant); *(aviation fuel)* kérosène *m*
ketchup ['ketʃəp] *n* ketchup *m*
kettle ['ketəl] *n* bouilloire *f*; **the k. is**

boiling l'eau bout; **to put the k. on** mettre l'eau à chauffer

key [ki:] **1** *n* clef *f*, clé *f*; *(of piano, typewriter, computer)* touche *f*
2 *adj (industry, post)* clef *(f inv)*, clé *(f inv)*; **k. person** pivot *m*; *Br Sch* **k. stage** ≃ cycle *m* de l'enseignement
3 *vt* **to k. in** *(data)* saisir • **keyboard 1** *n* *(of piano, computer)* clavier *m*; **k. operator** opérateur, -trice *mf* de saisie **2** *vt* *(data)* faire la saisie de • **keyhole** *n* trou *m* de serrure • **keynote** *n (of speech)* point *m* essentiel • **keyring** *n* porte-clefs *m inv* • **keystone** *n* *(of policy)* & *Archit* clef *f* de voûte

keyed [ki:d] *adj* **to be k. up** être surexcité
khaki ['kɑːki] *adj* & *n* kaki *(m) inv*
kibbutz [kɪ'bʊts] *(pl* **kibbutzim** [kɪbʊt-'siːm] *n* kibboutz *m*
kick [kɪk] **1** *n* coup *m* de pied; *(of horse)* ruade *f*; *Fam* **to get a k. out of doing sth** prendre son pied à faire qch; *Fam* **for kicks** pour le plaisir
2 *vt* donner un coup de pied/des coups de pied à; *(of horse)* lancer une ruade à
3 *vi* donner des coups de pied; *(of horse)* ruer • **kickback** *n Fam (bribe)* pot-de-vin *m* • **kickoff** *n Football* coup *m* d'envoi
▸ **kick back** *vt sep (ball)* renvoyer (du pied) ▸ **kick down, kick in** *vt sep (door)* démolir à coups de pied ▸ **kick off** *vi Football* donner le coup d'envoi; *Fam (start)* démarrer ▸ **kick out** *vt sep Fam (throw out)* flanquer dehors ▸ **kick up** *vt sep Br Fam* **to k. up a fuss/row** faire des histoires/du vacarme
kid [kɪd] **1** *n* (**a**) *Fam (child)* gosse *mf*; *Am Fam* **my k. brother** mon petit frère (**b**) *(goat)* chevreau *m*
2 *(pt & pp* **-dd-**) *vti Fam (joke, tease)* faire marcher; **to k. oneself** se faire des illusions; **to be kidding** plaisanter; **no kidding!** sans blague!
kidnap ['kɪdnæp] *(pt & pp* **-pp-**) *vt* kidnapper • **kidnapper** *n* ravisseur, -euse *mf* • **kidnapping** *n* enlèvement *m*
kidney ['kɪdnɪ] *(pl* **-eys**) *n* rein *m*; *(as food)* rognon *m*; **on a k. machine** sous rein artificiel; **k. bean** haricot *m* rouge
kill [kɪl] **1** *n* mise *f* à mort; *(prey)* tableau *m* de chasse
2 *vt (person, animal, plant)* tuer; *Fig (rumour)* étouffer; *Fam (engine)* arrêter; **to k. oneself** se tuer; *Fam* **my feet are killing me** j'ai les pieds en compote; *Journ* **to k. a story** retirer une information; **to k. time** tuer le temps; **to k. off** *(bacteria)* & *Fig* détruire

3 *vi* tuer • **killer** *n* tueur *m*, tueuse *f* • **killing 1** *n (of person)* meurtre *m*; *(of group)* massacre *m*; *(of animal)* mise *f* à mort; **to make a k.** *(financially)* faire un bénéfice énorme **2** *adj Fam (tiring)* tuant; *(amusing)* tordant
killjoy ['kɪldʒɔɪ] *n* rabat-joie *m inv*
kiln [kɪln] *n* four *m*
kilo ['kiːləʊ] *(pl* **-os**) *n* kilo *m* • **kilogram(me)** ['kɪləʊgræm] *n* kilogramme *m*
kilobyte ['kɪləbaɪt] *n Comptr* kilo-octet *m*
kilometre [kɪ'lɒmɪtə(r)] *(Am* **kilometer**) *n* kilomètre *m*
kilowatt ['kɪləʊwɒt] *n* kilowatt *m*
kilt [kɪlt] *n* kilt *m*
kimono [kɪ'məʊnəʊ] *(pl* **-os**) *n* kimono *m*
kin [kɪn] *n Formal (relatives)* parents *mpl*; **one's next of k.** son plus proche parent
kind¹ [kaɪnd] *n (sort, type)* genre *m*, espèce *f* (**of** de); **to pay in k.** payer en nature; **what k. of drink is it?** qu'est-ce que c'est comme boisson?; **that's the k. of man he is** il est comme ça; **nothing of the k.!** absolument pas!; *Fam* **k. of worried/sad** plutôt inquiet, -iète/triste; **in a k. of way** d'une certaine façon; **it's the only one of its k., it's one of a k.** c'est unique en son genre; **we are two of a k.** nous nous ressemblons
kind² [kaɪnd] *(-er, -est) adj (helpful, pleasant)* gentil, -ille (**to** avec); **that's k. of you** c'est gentil de votre part; **would you be so k. as to...?** auriez-vous la bonté de...? • **'kind-'hearted** *adj* qui a bon cœur
kindergarten ['kɪndəgɑːtən] *n* jardin *m* d'enfants
kindle ['kɪndəl] **1** *vt* allumer
2 *vi* s'allumer
kindly ['kaɪndlɪ] **1** *adv* gentiment; **k. wait** ayez la bonté d'attendre; **not to take k. to sth** ne pas apprécier qch
2 *adj (person)* bienveillant
kindness ['kaɪndnɪs] *n* gentillesse *f*
kindred ['kɪndrɪd] *adj* du même genre, de la même nature; **k. spirits** âmes *fpl* sœurs
king [kɪŋ] *n* roi *m* • **king-size(d)** *adj* géant; *(cigarette)* long *(f* longue*)*
kingdom ['kɪŋdəm] *n* royaume *m*; **animal/plant k.** règne *m* animal/végétal
kingfisher ['kɪŋfɪʃə(r)] *n* martin-pêcheur *m*
kingly ['kɪŋlɪ] *(-ier, -iest) adj* royal
kink [kɪŋk] *n (in rope)* boucle *f*
kinky ['kɪŋkɪ] *(-ier, -iest) adj (person)* qui a des goûts bizarres; *(clothes, tastes)* bizarre
kinship ['kɪnʃɪp] *n* parenté *f*

kiosk [ˈkiːɒsk] *n* kiosque *m*; *Br* **(telephone) k.** cabine *f* téléphonique

kip [kɪp] (*pt & pp* **-pp-**) *vi Br Fam (sleep)* roupiller

kipper [ˈkɪpə(r)] *n* hareng *m* salé et fumé

kiss [kɪs] **1** *n* baiser *m*; **the k. of life** *(in first aid)* le bouche-à-bouche
2 *vt (person)* embrasser; **to k. sb's hand** baiser la main de qn; **to k. sb goodbye** dire au revoir à qn en l'embrassant
3 *vi* s'embrasser

kit [kɪt] **1** *n* équipement *m*, matériel *m*; *(set of articles)* trousse *f*; *Br (belongings)* affaires *fpl*; *Br (sports clothes)* tenue *f*; **first-aid k.** trousse de pharmacie; **tool k.** trousse à outils; **(do-it-yourself) k.** kit *m*; **model aircraft k.** maquette *f* d'avion; **in k. form** en kit
2 (*pt & pp* **-tt-**) *vt Br* **to k. sb out** équiper qn (**with** de) • **kitbag** *n* sac *m* de marin; *Mil* sac à paquetage

kitchen [ˈkɪtʃɪn] *n* cuisine *f*; **k. cabinet** buffet *m* de cuisine; **k. garden** jardin *m* potager; **k. sink** évier *m*; **k. units** éléments *mpl* de cuisine • **kitcheˈnette** *n* coin-cuisine *m* • **kitchenware** *n* ustensiles *mpl* de cuisine; *(dishes)* vaisselle *f* de cuisine

kite [kaɪt] *n (toy)* cerf-volant *m*

kith [kɪθ] *n* **k. and kin** parents *mpl* et amis *mpl*

kitten [ˈkɪtən] *n* chaton *m*

kitty [ˈkɪtɪ] (*pl* **-ies**) *n* (**a**) *Fam (cat)* minou *m* (**b**) *(fund)* cagnotte *f*

kiwi [ˈkiːwiː] *n (bird, fruit)* kiwi *m*

km *(abbr* **kilometre**) km

knack [næk] *n (skill)* talent *m*; **to have the k. of doing sth** avoir le don de faire qch

knackered [ˈnækəd] *adj Br Fam (tired)* vanné

knapsack [ˈnæpsæk] *n* sac *m* à dos

knead [niːd] *vt (dough)* pétrir

knee [niː] *n* genou *m*; **to go down on one's knees** s'agenouiller; **k. pad** genouillère *f* • **kneecap** *n* rotule *f* • ˈ**knee-**ˈ**deep** *adj (in water, snow)* jusqu'aux genoux • ˈ**knee-**ˈ**high** *adj* jusqu'aux genoux • **knees-up** *n Br Fam (party)* soirée *f*

kneel [niːl] (*pt & pp* **knelt** *or* **kneeled**) *vi* **to k. (down)** s'agenouiller (**before** devant); **to be kneeling (down)** être à genoux

knell [nel] *n Literary* glas *m*

knelt [nelt] *pt & pp of* **kneel**

knew [n(j)uː] *pt of* **know**

knickers [ˈnɪkəz] *npl Br (underwear)* culotte *f*

knick-knack [ˈnɪknæk] *n Fam* babiole *f*

knife [naɪf] **1** (*pl* **knives**) *n* couteau *m*; *(pen-knife)* canif *m*
2 *vt* poignarder

knight [naɪt] **1** *n* chevalier *m*; *Chess* cavalier *m*
2 *vt Br* **to be knighted** être fait chevalier • **knighthood** *n* titre *m* de chevalier

knit [nɪt] (*pt & pp* **-tt-**) **1** *vt* tricoter; **to k. one's brow** froncer les sourcils
2 *vi* tricoter; **to k. (together)** *(of bones)* se ressouder • **knitting** *n (activity, material)* tricot *m*; **k. needle** aiguille *f* à tricoter • **knitwear** *n* lainages *mpl*

knob [nɒb] *n (on door)* poignée *f*; *(on cane)* pommeau *m*; *(on radio)* bouton *m*; **k. of butter** noix *f* de beurre

knock [nɒk] **1** *n (blow)* coup *m*; **there's a k. at the door** on frappe à la porte; **I heard a k.** j'ai entendu frapper
2 *vt (strike)* frapper; *(collide with)* heurter; *Fam (criticize)* critiquer; **to k. one's head on sth** se cogner la tête contre qch; **to k. sb senseless** assommer qn; **to k. sb to the ground** faire tomber qn en le frappant
3 *vi (strike)* frapper; **to k. against** *or* **into sth** heurter qch • **knockdown** *adj Br* **k. price** prix *m* imbattable • ˈ**knock-**ˈ**kneed** *adj* cagneux, -euse • **knockout** *n Boxing* knock-out *m inv*; *Fam* **to be a k.** *(of person, film)* être formidable
▸ **knock about 1** *vt sep (ill-treat)* malmener **2** *vi Fam (travel)* bourlinguer; *Fam (lie around, stand around)* traîner ▸ **knock back** *vt sep Br Fam (drink, glass)* s'envoyer (derrière la cravate) ▸ **knock down** *vt sep (object, pedestrian)* renverser; *(house, tree, wall)* abattre; *(price)* baisser ▸ **knock in** *vt sep (nail)* enfoncer ▸ **knock off 1** *vt sep (person, object)* faire tomber (**from** de); *Fam (do quickly)* expédier; *Br Fam (steal)* piquer; **to k. £5 off (the price)** baisser le prix de 5 livres **2** *vi Fam (stop work)* s'arrêter de travailler ▸ **knock out** *vt sep (make unconscious)* assommer; *Boxing* mettre K.-O.; *(beat in competition)* éliminer; *Fam* **to k. oneself out** s'esquinter (**doing** à faire) ▸ **knock over** *vt sep (pedestrian, object)* renverser ▸ **knock up** *vt sep Br Fam (meal)* préparer en vitesse

knocker [ˈnɒkə(r)] *n (for door)* marteau *m*

knot [nɒt] **1** *n* (**a**) *(in rope)* nœud *m*; **to tie a k.** faire un nœud; *Fig* **to tie the k.** se marier (**b**) *Naut (unit of speed)* nœud *m*
2 (*pt & pp* **-tt-**) *vt* nouer • **knotty** (**-ier, -iest**) *adj (wood)* noueux, -euse; *Fig (problem)* épineux, -euse

know [nəʊ] **1** *n Fam* **to be in the k.** être au courant

2 (*pt* **knew**, *pp* **known**) *vt (facts, language)* savoir; *(person, place)* connaître; *(recognize)* reconnaître (**by** à); **to k. that...** savoir que...; **to k. how to do sth** savoir faire qch; **for all I k.** que je sache; **I'll let you k.** je vous le ferai savoir; **I'll have you k. that** sachez que; **to k. (a lot) about** *(person, event)* en savoir long sur; **to k. (a lot) about cars/sewing** s'y connaître en voitures/couture; **I've never known him to complain** je ne l'ai jamais vu se plaindre; **to get to k. (about) sth** apprendre qch; **to get to k. sb** apprendre à connaître qn

3 *vi* savoir; **I k.** je (le) sais; **I wouldn't k., I k. nothing about it** je n'en sais rien; **to k. about sth** être au courant de qch; **to k. of** *(have heard of)* avoir entendu parler de; **do you k. of a good dentist?** connais-tu un bon dentiste?; **you (should) k. better than to do that** tu es trop intelligent pour faire ça; **you should have known better** tu aurais dû réfléchir • **know-all** *n Fam Pej* je-sais-tout *mf inv* • **know-how** *n Fam* savoir-faire *m inv* • **knowing** *adj (smile, look)* entendu • **knowingly** *adv (consciously)* sciemment **know-it-all** *n Fam*
Pej je-sais-tout *mf inv* • **known** *adj* connu; **a k. expert** un expert reconnu; **she is k. to be** on sait qu'elle est

knowledge ['nɒlɪdʒ] *n (of fact)* connaissance *f; (learning)* connaissances *fpl*, savoir *m*; **to (the best of) my k.** à ma connaissance; **without sb's k.** à l'insu de qn; **to have no k. of sth** ignorer qch; **general k.** culture *f* générale • **knowledgeable** *adj* savant; **to be k. about sth** bien s'y connaître en qch

known [nəʊn] *pp of* **know**

knuckle ['nʌkəl] *n* articulation *f* (du doigt)

▸ **knuckle down** *vi Fam* se mettre au boulot; **to k. down to sth** se mettre à qch

Koran [kə'rɑːn] *n* **the K.** le Coran

Korea [kə'rɪə] *n* la Corée • **Korean 1** *adj* coréen, -éenne **2** *n (person)* Coréen, -éenne *mf; (language)* coréen *m*

kosher ['kəʊʃə(r)] *adj Rel (food)* kasher *inv*

kowtow [kaʊ'taʊ] *vi* **to k. to sb** faire des courbettes devant qn

kudos ['kjuːdɒs] *n (glory)* gloire *f; (prestige)* prestige *m*

Kuwait [kʊ'weɪt] *n* le Koweït • **Kuwaiti 1** *adj* koweïtien, -ienne **2** *n* Koweïtien, -ienne *mf*

L, l [el] *n (letter)* L, l *m inv*; *Br* **L-plate** = plaque apposée sur une voiture pour signaler que le conducteur est en conduite accompagnée

lab [læb] *n Fam* labo *m* • **laboratory** [*Br* lə'bɒrətərɪ, *Am* 'læbrətɔːrɪ] *n* laboratoire *m*; **l. assistant** laborantin, -ine *mf*

label ['leɪbəl] **1** *n* étiquette *f*; *(of record company)* label *m*
2 (*Br* **-ll-**, *Am* **-l-**) *vt* étiqueter; *Fig (person)* cataloguer; *Fig* **to l. sb as a liar** qualifier qn de menteur

laborious [lə'bɔːrɪəs] *adj* laborieux, -ieuse

labour ['leɪbə(r)] (*Am* **labor**) **1** *n (work)* travail *m*; *(workers)* main-d'œuvre *f*; *Br* **L. (political party)** le parti travailliste; **in l.** *(woman)* en train d'accoucher
2 *adj (market)* du travail; *(relations)* ouvriers-patronat *inv*; **l. dispute** conflit *m* social; **l. force** effectifs *mpl*; *Am* **l. union** syndicat *m*; **l. unrest** agitation *f* ouvrière
3 *vt* **to l. a point** insister sur un point
4 *vi (toil)* peiner (**over** sur) • **laboured** (*Am* **labored**) *adj (style)* laborieux, -ieuse • **labourer** (*Am* **laborer**) *n (on roads)* manœuvre *m*; *(on farm)* ouvrier *m* agricole

labyrinth ['læbərɪnθ] *n* labyrinthe *m*

lace [leɪs] **1** *n* (**a**) *(cloth)* dentelle *f* (**b**) *(of shoe)* lacet *m*
2 *vt* (**a**) **to l. (up)** *(tie up)* lacer (**b**) *(drink)* additionner (**with** de)

lacerate ['læsəreɪt] *vt* lacérer • **lace'ration** *n* lacération *f*

lack [læk] **1** *n* manque *m* (**of** de); **for l. of sth** à défaut de qch
2 *vt* manquer de
3 *vi* **to be lacking** manquer (**in** de); **they l. for nothing** ils ne manquent de rien

lackey ['lækɪ] (*pl* **-eys**) *n Pej* laquais *m*

lacklustre ['læklʌstə(r)] (*Am* **lack-luster**) *adj* terne

laconic [lə'kɒnɪk] *adj* laconique

lacquer ['lækə(r)] **1** *n* laque *f*
2 *vt* laquer

lad [læd] *n Fam (young man)* jeune gars *m*; *(child)* garçon *m*; **when I was a l.** quand j'étais gamin; **come on lads!** allez les mecs!

ladder ['lædə(r)] **1** *n* échelle *f*; *Br (in tights)* maille *f* filée
2 *vti Br* filer

laden ['leɪdən] *adj* chargé (**with** de)

ladle ['leɪdəl] *n* louche *f*

lady ['leɪdɪ] (*pl* **-ies**) *n* dame *f*; **a young l.** une jeune fille; *(married)* une jeune dame; **the l. of the house** la maîtresse de maison; **Ladies and Gentlemen!** Mesdames, Mesdemoiselles, Messieurs!; **l. doctor** femme *f* médecin; **l. friend** amie *f*; **the ladies' room,** *Br* **the ladies** les toilettes *fpl* pour dames • **lady-in-'waiting** (*pl* **ladies-in-waiting**) *n* dame *f* d'honneur

ladybird ['leɪdɪbɜːd] (*Am* **ladybug** ['leɪdɪ-bʌg]) *n* coccinelle *f*

ladylike ['leɪdɪlaɪk] *adj (manner)* distingué; **she's (very) l.** elle fait très grande dame

lag [læg] **1** *n* **time l.** *(between events)* décalage *m*; *(between countries)* décalage horaire
2 (*pt & pp* **-gg-**) *vt (pipe)* isoler
3 *vi* **to l. behind** *(in progress, work)* avoir du retard; *(dawdle)* être à la traîne; **to l. behind sb** être à la traîne derrière qn

lager ['lɑːgə(r)] *n Br* bière *f* blonde

lagoon [lə'guːn] *n* lagune *f*; *(of atoll)* lagon *m*

laid [leɪd] *pt & pp of* **lay³** • **'laid-'back** *adj Fam* cool *inv*

lain [leɪn] *pp of* **lie²**

lair [leə(r)] *n* tanière *f*

laity ['leɪtɪ] *n* **the l.** les laïcs *mpl*

lake [leɪk] *n* lac *m*

lamb [læm] *n* agneau *m* • **lambswool** *n* lambswool *m*; **l. sweater** pull *m* en lambswool

lame [leɪm] (**-er, -est**) *adj (person, argument)* boiteux, -euse; *(excuse)* piètre; **to be l.** boiter • **lameness** *n Med* claudication *f*; *Fig (of excuse)* faiblesse *f*

lament [lə'ment] **1** *n* lamentation *f*
2 *vt* **to l. (over)** se lamenter sur • **lamentable** *adj* lamentable • **lamentation** [læmen'teɪʃən] *n* lamentation *f*

laminated ['læmɪneɪtɪd] *adj (glass)* feuilleté; *(wood, plastic)* stratifié

lamp [læmp] *n* lampe *f* • **lamppost** *n*

réverbère m • **lampshade** n abat-jour m inv
lance [lɑːns] 1 n (weapon) lance f
   2 vt (abscess) inciser
land [lænd] 1 n terre f; (country) pays m;
(plot of) l. terrain m; **on dry l.** sur la terre
ferme; **to travel by l.** voyager par voie de
terre
   2 adj (transport, flora) terrestre; (reform,
law) agraire; (tax) foncier, -ière
   3 vt (passengers, cargo) débarquer; (aircraft) poser; (blow) flanquer (**on** à); Fam
(job, prize) décrocher; Fam **to l. sb in
trouble** mettre qn dans le pétrin; Fam **to
be landed with** (person) avoir sur les
bras; (fine) écoper de; Fam **to l. sb one**
(hit) en coller une à qn
   4 vi (of aircraft) atterrir; (of ship) mouiller; (of passengers) débarquer; (of bomb,
missile) tomber; **to l. up in a ditch/in jail**
se retrouver dans un fossé/en prison
• **landing** n (**a**) (of aircraft) atterrissage
m; (of cargo, troops) débarquement m;
forced l. atterrissage m forcé; **l. stage**
débarcadère m (**b**) (of staircase) palier
m • **landlady** (pl **-ies**) n propriétaire f; (of
pub) patronne f • **landlocked** adj sans
accès à la mer • **landlord** n propriétaire
m; (of pub) patron m • **landmark** n point m
de repère • **landowner** n propriétaire m
foncier • **landslide** n (falling rocks) glissement m de terrain; (election victory) raz
de marée m inv électoral
landed ['lændɪd] adj (owning land) terrien, -ienne
landscape ['lændskeɪp] n paysage m
lane [leɪn] n (in country) chemin m; (in
town) ruelle f; (division of road) voie f;
(line of traffic) file f; (for aircraft, shipping,
swimming) couloir m; **'get in l.'** (traffic
sign) 'prenez votre file'
language ['læŋgwɪdʒ] 1 n (of a people)
langue f; (faculty, style) langage m
   2 adj (laboratory) de langues; (teacher,
studies) de langue(s)
languid ['læŋgwɪd] adj languissant
• **languish** vi languir (**for** or **after** après)
lank [læŋk] adj (hair) plat et terne
lanky ['læŋkɪ] (**-ier, -iest**) adj dégingandé
lantern ['læntən] n lanterne f; **Chinese l.**
lampion m
lap [læp] 1 n (**a**) (of person) genoux mpl;
in the l. of luxury dans le luxe (**b**) (in
race) tour m de piste
   2 (pt & pp **-pp-**) vt **to l. up** (drink) laper;
Fam (like very much) se délecter de; Fam
(believe) gober
   3 vi (of waves) clapoter; **to l. over** (overlap) se chevaucher

lapdog ['læpdɒg] n chien m d'appartement; Fig toutou m
lapel [lə'pel] n revers m
lapse [læps] 1 n (**a**) (in concentration,
standards) baisse f; **a l. of memory** un
trou de mémoire; **a l. in behaviour** un
écart de conduite (**b**) (interval) laps m de
temps; **a l. of time** un intervalle (**between** entre)
   2 vi (**a**) (of concentration, standards)
baisser; (of person) retomber dans un
travers; **to l. into silence** se taire; **to l. into
bad habits** reprendre de mauvaises habitudes (**b**) (expire) (of ticket, passport,
subscription) expirer
laptop ['læptɒp] adj & n **l. (computer)**
ordinateur m portable
larceny ['lɑːsənɪ] n Law vol m
lard [lɑːd] n saindoux m

> 🖉 Note that the French word **lard** is a false
> friend. Its most common meaning is **bacon**.

larder ['lɑːdə(r)] n garde-manger m
inv
large [lɑːdʒ] (**-er, -est**) adj (big) grand;
(fat, bulky) gros (f grosse); (quantity)
grand, important; **to become** or **grow** or
get l. s'agrandir; (of person) grossir; **to a l.
extent** en grande partie; **l.** (of prisoner,
animal) en liberté; (as a whole) en général; **by and l.** dans l'ensemble • **'large-
'scale** adj (operation, reform) de grande
envergure
largely ['lɑːdʒlɪ] adv en grande partie

> 🖉 Note that the French word **largement** is
> a false friend. It means **widely** or **gener-
> ously** depending on the context.

largesse [lɑː'ʒes] n largesse f
lark[1] [lɑːk] n (bird) alouette f
lark[2] [lɑːk] Fam 1 n (joke) rigolade f
   2 vi Br **to l. about** faire le fou/la folle
larva ['lɑːvə] (pl **-vae** [-viː]) n larve f
larynx ['lærɪŋks] n larynx m • **laryngitis**
[-rɪn'dʒaɪtəs] n Med laryngite f
lasagne [lə'zænjə] n lasagnes fpl
lascivious [lə'sɪvɪəs] adj lascif, -ive
laser ['leɪzə(r)] n laser m; **l. beam/printer**
rayon m/imprimante f laser
lash[1] [læʃ] 1 n (with whip) coup m de fouet
   2 vt (strike) fouetter; (tie) attacher (**to**
à); **the dog lashed its tail** le chien donna
un coup de queue
   3 vi Fam **to l. out** (spend wildly) claquer
son argent; **to l. out at sb** (hit) donner des
coups à qn; (insult) s'en prendre violemment à qn; (criticize) fustiger qn
lash[2] [læʃ] n (eyelash) cil m

lashings ['læʃɪŋz] *npl Br Fam* **l. of cream/ jam** une tonne de crème/confiture

lass [læs] *n Br* jeune fille *f*

lassitude ['læsɪtjuːd] *n* lassitude *f*

lasso [læ'suː] **1** (*pl* **-oes** *or* **-os**) *n* lasso *m*
2 (*pt & pp* **-oed**) *vt* attraper au lasso

last¹ [lɑːst] **1** *adj* dernier, -ière; **the l. ten lines** les dix dernières lignes; **l. night** (*evening*) hier soir; (*night*) la nuit dernière; **l. name** nom *m* de famille
2 *adv* (*lastly*) en dernier lieu; (*on the last occasion*) (pour) la dernière fois; **to leave l.** sortir le dernier; **when I saw him l.** la dernière fois que je l'ai vu
3 *n* (*person, object*) dernier, -ière *mf*; **l. but one** avant-dernier *m* (*f* avant-dernière); **that's the l. of the beer** on a fini la bière; **the day before l.** avant-hier; **at (long) l.** enfin • **'last-'ditch** *adj* ultime • **'last-'minute** *adj* (*decision*) de dernière minute

last² [lɑːst] *vi* durer; **to l. (out)** (*endure, resist*) tenir (le coup); (*of money, supplies*) suffire; **it lasted me ten years** ça m'a fait dix ans • **lasting** *adj* (*impression, peace*) durable

lastly ['lɑːstlɪ] *adv* en dernier lieu

latch [lætʃ] **1** *n* loquet *m*; **the door is on the l.** la porte n'est pas fermée à clef
2 *vt insep Fam* **to l. onto** (*understand*) piger; (*grab*) s'accrocher à; (*adopt*) adopter • **latchkey** (*pl* **-eys**) *n* clef *f* de la porte d'entrée

late¹ [leɪt] **1** (**-er, -est**) *adj* (*not on time*) en retard (**for** à); (*meal, fruit, season, hour*) tardif, -ive; (*stage*) avancé; (*edition*) dernier, -ière; **to be l. (for sth)** être en retard (pour qch); **to be l. (in) coming** arriver en retard; **to make sb l.** mettre qn en retard; **he's an hour l.** il a une heure de retard; **it's l.** il est tard; **in l. June** fin juin; **in the l. nineties** à la fin des années 90; **to be in one's l. forties** approcher de la cinquantaine; **a later edition** (*more recent*) une édition plus récente; **the latest edition** (*last*) la dernière édition; **to take a later train** prendre un train plus tard; **in later life** plus tard (dans la vie); **at a later date** à une date ultérieure; **at the latest** au plus tard
2 *adv* (*in the day, season*) tard; (*not on time*) en retard; **it's getting l.** il se fait tard; **l. into the night** jusqu'à une heure avancée de la nuit; **l. in the year** vers la fin de l'année; **later (on)** plus tard; **of l.** récemment; **not** *or* **no later than** pas plus tard que

late² [leɪt] *adj* **the l. Mr Smith** feu Monsieur Smith; **our l. friend** notre regretté ami

latecomer ['leɪtkʌmə(r)] *n* retardataire *mf*

lately ['leɪtlɪ] *adv* dernièrement

lateness ['leɪtnəs] *n* (*of person, train*) retard *m*; **the l. of the hour** l'heure *f* tardive

latent ['leɪtənt] *adj* (*disease, tendency*) latent

lateral ['lætərəl] *adj* latéral

lathe [leɪð] *n* (*machine*) tour *m*

lather ['lɑːðə(r)] **1** *n* mousse *f*
2 *vt* savonner
3 *vi* mousser

Latin ['lætɪn] **1** *adj* latin; **L. America** l'Amérique *f* latine
2 *n* (*person*) Latin, -ine *mf*; (*language*) latin *m* • **Latin American 1** *adj* d'Amérique latine **2** *n* Latino-Américain, -aine *mf*

latitude ['lætɪtjuːd] *n* (*on map, freedom*) latitude *f*

latrines [lə'triːnz] *npl* latrines *fpl*

latter ['lætə(r)] **1** *adj* (*later, last-named*) dernier, -ière; (*second*) deuxième; **the l. part of June** la deuxième moitié du mois de juin
2 *n* **the l.** le dernier (*f* la dernière); (*of two*) le second (*f* la seconde) • **latterly** *adv* (*recently*) récemment, dernièrement

lattice ['lætɪs] *n* treillis *m*

laudable ['lɔːdəbəl] *adj* louable

laugh [lɑːf] **1** *n* rire *m*; **to have a good l.** bien rire
2 *vt* **to l. sth off** tourner qch en plaisanterie; *Fam* **to l. one's head off** être mort de rire
3 *vi* rire (**at/about** de); **to l. to oneself** rire en soi-même • **laughing** *adj* riant; **it's no l. matter** il n'y a pas de quoi rire; **to be the l. stock of** être la risée de

laughable ['lɑːfəbəl] *adj* ridicule

laughter ['lɑːftə(r)] *n* rire(s) *m(pl)*; **to roar with l.** rire aux éclats

launch [lɔːntʃ] **1** *n* (**a**) (*motorboat*) vedette *f*; (*pleasure boat*) bateau *m* de plaisance (**b**) (*of ship, rocket, product*) lancement *m*; **l. pad** aire *f* de lancement
2 *vt* (*ship, rocket, product*) lancer
3 *vi* **to l. (out) into** (*begin*) se lancer dans • **launching** *n* (*of ship, rocket, product*) lancement *m*; **l. pad** aire *f* de lancement

launder ['lɔːndə(r)] *vt* (*clothes, money*) blanchir • **laundering** *n* blanchiment *m*

launderette [lɔːndə'ret] (*Am* **Laundromat**®) ['lɔːndrəmæt]) *n* laverie *f* automatique

laundry ['lɔːndrɪ] *n* (*place*) blanchisserie

f; (clothes) linge *m;* **to do the l.** faire la lessive

laurel ['lɒrəl] *n* laurier *m; Fig* **to rest on one's laurels** se reposer sur ses lauriers

lava ['lɑːvə] *n* lave *f*

lavatory ['lævətərɪ] *(pl* **-ies**) *n* toilettes *fpl*

lavender ['lævɪndə(r)] *n* lavande *f*

lavish ['lævɪʃ] **1** *adj* prodigue (**with** de); *(meal, décor, gift)* somptueux, -ueuse; *(expenditure)* excessif, -ive

2 *vt* **to l. sth on sb** couvrir qn de qch • **lavishly** *adv (furnish)* somptueusement; **to spend l.** dépenser sans compter

law [lɔː] *n (rule, rules)* loi *f; (study, profession, system)* droit *m;* **against the l.** illégal; **to break the l.** enfreindre la loi; **to be above the l.** être au-dessus des lois; **court of l., l. court** cour *f* de justice; **l. and order** l'ordre *m* public; **l. firm** cabinet *m* d'avocat; *Am* **l. school** faculté *f* de droit; **l. student** étudiant, -iante *mf* en droit • **law-abiding** *adj* respectueux, -ueuse des lois

lawful ['lɔːfəl] *adj (action, age)* légal; *(wife, claim)* légitime • **lawfully** *adv* légalement

lawless ['lɔːləs] *adj (country)* anarchique • **lawlessness** *n* anarchie *f*

lawn [lɔːn] *n* pelouse *f,* gazon *m;* **l. mower** tondeuse *f* à gazon; **l. tennis** tennis *m*

lawsuit ['lɔːsuːt] *n* procès *m*

lawyer ['lɔːjə(r)] *n (in court)* avocat, -ate *mf; (for wills, sales)* notaire *m; (legal expert, author)* juriste *m*

lax [læks] *adj (person)* laxiste; *(discipline, behaviour)* relâché; **to be l. in doing sth** négliger de faire qch • **laxity, laxness** *n* laxisme *m; (of discipline)* relâchement *m*

laxative ['læksətɪv] **1** *adj* laxatif, -ive **2** *n* laxatif *m*

lay¹ [leɪ] *pt of* **lie²**

lay² [leɪ] *adj (non-religious)* laïque; *(non-specialized) (opinion)* d'un profane; **l. person** profane *mf* • **layman** *(pl* **-men**) *n (non-specialist)* profane *mf*

lay³ [leɪ] *(pt & pp* **laid**) **1** *vt (put down, place)* poser; *(blanket)* étendre (**over** sur); *(trap)* tendre; *(money)* miser (**on** sur); *(accusation)* porter; *(ghost)* exorciser; *(egg)* pondre; **to l. sth flat** poser qch à plat; *Br* **to l. the table** mettre la table; **to l. a bet** parier; **to l. sth bare** mettre qch à nu; **to l. oneself open to criticism** s'exposer aux critiques; **to l. one's hands on sth** mettre la main sur qch; **to l. a hand** *or* **a finger on sb** lever la main sur qn

2 *vi (of bird)* pondre • **layabout** *n Fam*

fainéant, -éante *mf* • **lay-by** *(pl* **-bys**) *n Br (for vehicles)* aire *f* de stationnement • **layout** *n* disposition *f; (of text)* mise *f* en page • **lay-over** *n Am* halte *f*

▸ **lay down** *vt sep (put down)* poser; *(arms)* déposer; *(principle, condition)* établir; **to l. down one's life** sacrifier sa vie (**for** pour); **to l. down the law** dicter sa loi (**to** à) ▸ **lay into** *vt insep Fam (physically)* 'osser; *(verbally)* voler dans les plumes à ▸ **lay off 1** *vt sep* **to l. sb off** *(worker)* licencier qn **2** *vt insep Fam (stop)* arrêter; *Fam* **to l. off sb** *(leave alone)* ficher la paix à **3** *vi Fam (desist)* arrêter; **l. off!** *(don't touch)* pas touche! ▸ **lay on** *vt sep Br (install)* installer; *(supply)* fournir; *Fam* **to l. it on (thick)** y aller un peu fort ▸ **lay out** *vt sep (garden)* dessiner; *(house)* concevoir; *(prepare)* préparer; *(display)* disposer; *Fam (money)* mettre (**on** dans)

layer ['leɪə(r)] *n* couche *f*

laze [leɪz] *vi* **to l. (about** *or* **around)** paresser

lazy ['leɪzɪ] *(-ier, -iest) adj (person)* paresseux, -euse; *(afternoon)* passé à ne rien faire • **lazybones** *n Fam* flemmard, -arde *mf*

lb *(abbr* **libra**) livre *f (unité de poids)*

lead¹ [led] *n (metal)* plomb *m; (of pencil)* mine *f;* **l. pencil** crayon *m* à papier • **leaded** *adj (petrol)* au plomb • **leaden** *adj* **l. sky** ciel *m* de plomb • **'lead-'free** *adj (petrol, paint)* sans plomb

lead² [liːd] **1** *n (distance or time ahead)* avance *f* (**over** sur); *(example)* exemple *m; (clue)* indice *m; (in film)* rôle *m* principal; *Br (for dog)* laisse *f; (electric wire)* fil *m* électrique; **to take the l.** *(in race)* prendre la tête; **to be in the l.** *(in race)* être en tête; *(in match)* mener (à la marque); **l. singer** *(in pop group)* chanteur, -euse *mf* vedette

2 *(pt & pp* **led**) *vt (guide, conduct, take)* mener, conduire (**to** à); *(team, government)* diriger; *(expedition, attack)* commander; *(procession)* être en tête de; **to l. a happy life** mener une vie heureuse; **to l. sb in/out** faire entrer/ sortir qn; **to l. sb to do sth** *(cause, induce)* amener qn à faire qch; **to l. the way** montrer le chemin; **to l. the world** tenir le premier rang mondial; **easily led** influençable

3 *vi (of street, door)* mener, conduire (**to** à); *(in race)* être en tête; *(in match)* mener (à la marque); *(go ahead)* aller devant; **to l. to sth** *(result in)* aboutir à qch; *(cause)* mener à qch; **to l. up to** *(of street)*

conduire à, mener à; *(precede)* précéder; *(approach gradually)* en venir à

▸ **lead away** *vt sep* emmener ▸ **lead back** *vt sep* ramener ▸ **lead off** *vt sep* emmener ▸ **lead on** *vt sep (deceive)* tromper, duper

leader ['liːdə(r)] *n* (**a**) chef *m*; *(of country, party)* dirigeant, -ante *mf*; *(of strike, riot)* meneur, -euse *mf*; *(guide)* guide *m*; **to be the l.** *(in race)* être en tête (**b**) *Br (newspaper article)* éditorial *m* • **leadership** *n* direction *f*; *(qualities)* qualités *fpl* de chef; *(leaders) (of country, party)* dirigeants *mpl*

leading ['liːdɪŋ] *adj (best, most important)* principal; **the l. car** la voiture de tête; **a l. figure, a l. light** un personnage marquant; **the l. lady** *(in film)* le premier rôle féminin; *Br* **l. article** *(in newspaper)* éditorial *m*

leaf [liːf] **1** (*pl* **leaves**) *n* feuille *f*; *(of book)* feuillet *m*; *(of table)* rallonge *f*

2 *vi* **to l. through** *(book)* feuilleter • **leafy** (**-ier, -iest**) *adj (tree)* feuillu

leaflet ['liːflɪt] *n* prospectus *m*; *(containing instructions)* notice *f*

league [liːg] *n* (**a**) *(alliance)* ligue *f*; *Sport* championnat *m*; *Pej* **in l. with** de connivence avec (**b**) *Hist (measure)* lieue *f*

leak [liːk] **1** *n (in pipe, information)* fuite *f*; *(in boat)* voie *f* d'eau

2 *vt Fig (information)* divulguer; **the pipe was leaking gaz** du gaz fuyait du tuyau

3 *vi (of liquid, pipe, tap)* fuir; *(of ship)* faire eau; *Fig* **to l. out** *(of information)* être divulgué • **leakage** [-ɪdʒ] *n* fuite *f*; *(amount lost)* perte *f* • **leaky** (**-ier, -iest**) *adj (kettle, pipe, tap)* qui fuit; *(roof)* qui a une fuite

lean¹ [liːn] (**-er, -est**) *adj (meat)* maigre; *(person)* mince; *(year)* difficile

lean² [liːn] (*pt & pp* **leaned** *or* **leant** [lent]) **1** *vt* **to l. sth on/against sth** appuyer qch sur/contre qch

2 *vi (of object)* pencher; *(of person)* se pencher; **to l. against/on sth** *(of person)* s'appuyer contre/sur qch; **to l. back against** s'adosser à; *Fam* **to l. on sb** *(influence)* faire pression sur qn (**to do** pour faire); **to l. forward** *(of person)* se pencher (en avant); **to l. over** *(of person)* se pencher; *(of object)* pencher • **leaning** *adj* penché; **l. against** *(resting)* appuyé contre • **leanings** *npl* tendances *fpl* (**towards** à) • **lean-to** (*pl* **-tos**) *n Br (building)* appentis *m*

leap [liːp] **1** *n (jump)* bond *m*, saut *m*; *Fig (change, increase)* bond *m*; **l. year** année *f*

bissextile; **in leaps and bounds** à pas de géant

2 (*pt & pp* **leaped** *or* **leapt**) *vi* bondir, sauter; *(of flames)* jaillir; *(of profits)* faire un bond; **to l. for joy** sauter de joie; **to l. to one's feet, to l. up** se lever d'un bond

leapfrog ['liːpfrɒg] *n* saute-mouton *m*; **to play l.** jouer à saute-mouton

leapt [lept] *pt & pp of* **leap**

learn [lɜːn] (*pt & pp* **learned** *or* **learnt** [lɜːnt]) **1** *vt* apprendre (**that** que); **to l. (how) to do sth** apprendre à faire qch

2 *vi* apprendre; **to l. about sth** *(study)* étudier qch; *(hear about)* apprendre qch • **learned** [-ɪd] *adj* savant • **learner** *n (beginner)* débutant, -ante *mf*; *(student)* étudiant, -iante *mf*; **to be a quick/slow l.** apprendre vite/lentement • **learning** *n (of language)* apprentissage *m* (**of** de); *(knowledge)* savoir *m*; **l. curve** courbe *f* d'assimilation

lease [liːs] **1** *n* bail *m* (*pl* baux); *Fig* **to give sb a new l. of life** *or Am* **on life** redonner à qn goût à la vie

2 *vt (house)* louer à bail (**from/to** à) • **leasehold** *n (property)* location *f* à bail

leash [liːʃ] *n (of dog)* laisse *f*; **on a l.** en laisse

least [liːst] **1** *adj* **the l.** *(smallest amount of)* le moins de; **he has (the) l. talent** il a le moins de talent (**of all** de tous); **the l. effort/noise** le moindre effort/bruit

2 *n* **the l.** le moins; **at l.** du moins; *(with quantity)* au moins; **at l. that's what she says** du moins, c'est ce qu'elle dit; **not in the l.** pas du tout

3 *adv (work, eat)* le moins; **the l. difficult** le/la moins difficile; **l. of all** *(especially not)* surtout pas

leather ['leðə(r)] *n* cuir *m*; **(wash) l.** peau *f* de chamois • **leathe'rette®** *n* Skaï® *m*

leave [liːv] **1** *n (holiday)* congé *m*; *(of soldier, permission)* permission *f*; **to be on l.** être en congé; *(of soldier)* être en permission; **l. of absence** congé exceptionnel; **to take (one's) l. of sb** prendre congé de qn

2 (*pt & pp* **left**) *vt (allow to remain, forget)* laisser; *(depart from)* quitter; **to l. the table** sortir de table; **to l. sb in charge of sb/sth** laisser à qn la garde de qn/qch; **to l. sth with sb** *(entrust, give)* laisser qch à qn; **to be left (over)** rester; **there's no hope/bread left** il ne reste plus d'espoir/de pain; **l. it to me!** laisse-moi faire!; **I'll l. it (up) to you** je m'en remets à toi

3 *vi (go away)* partir (**from** de; **for** pour) ▸ **leave behind** *vt sep* **to l. sth behind** *(on*

purpose) laisser qch; *(accidentally)* oublier qch; **to l. sb behind** *(not take)* partir sans qn; *(surpass)* dépasser qn; *(in race, at school)* distancer qn ▸ **leave off 1** *vt sep (lid)* ne pas remettre; *Fam* **to l. off doing sth** *(stop)* arrêter de faire qch **2** *vi Fam (stop)* s'arrêter ▸ **leave on** *vt sep (clothes)* garder ▸ **leave out** *vt sep (forget to put)* oublier de mettre; *(word, line)* sauter; *(exclude)* exclure

Lebanon ['lebənən] *n* le Liban ● **Leba'nese 1** *adj* libanais **2** *n* Libanais, -aise *mf*

lecher ['let∫ə(r)] *n* débauché *m* ● **lecherous** *adj* lubrique

lectern ['lektən] *n (for giving speeches)* pupitre *m*; *(in church)* lutrin *m*

lecture ['lekt∫ə(r)] **1** *n (public speech)* conférence *f*; *(as part of series at university)* cours *m* magistral; *Fam (scolding)* sermon *m*; **l. hall** amphithéâtre *m* **2** *vt Fam (scold)* faire la morale à **3** *vi* faire une conférence/un cours; **she lectures in chemistry** elle est professeur de chimie ● **lecturer** *n* conférencier, -ière *mf*; *(at university)* enseignant, -ante *mf*

> Note that the French word **lecture** is a false friend and is never a translation for the English word **lecture**. It means **reading**.

led [led] *pt & pp of* **lead²**

ledge [ledʒ] *n (on wall, window)* rebord *m*; *(on mountain)* saillie *f*

ledger ['ledʒə(r)] *n* grand livre *m*

leech [li:t∫] *n (worm, person)* sangsue *f*

leek [li:k] *n* poireau *m*

leer [lɪə(r)] **1** *n (lustful)* regard *m* lubrique; *(cruel)* regard sadique **2** *vi* **to l. at sb** *(lustfully)* regarder qn d'un air lubrique; *(cruelly)* regarder qn d'un air sadique

leeway ['li:weɪ] *n* marge *f* (de manœuvre)

left¹ [left] *pt & pp of* **leave** ● **left-'luggage office** *n Br* consigne *f*

left² [left] **1** *adj (side, hand)* gauche **2** *n* gauche *f*; **on** *or* **to the l.** à gauche (**of** de) **3** *adv* à gauche ● **left-'hand** *adj* de gauche; **on the l. side** à gauche (**of** de); **l. drive** conduite *f* à gauche ● **left-'handed** *adj (person)* gaucher, -ère ● **'left-'wing** *adj (views, government)* de gauche

leftist ['leftɪst] *n & adj Pol* gauchiste *(mf)*

leftovers ['leftəʊvəz] *npl* restes *mpl*

leg [leg] *n* jambe *f*; *(of dog, bird)* patte *f*; *(of table)* pied *m*; *(of journey)* étape *f*; **l. of chicken** cuisse *f* de poulet; **l. of lamb** gigot *m* d'agneau; **to pull sb's l.** *(make fun of)*

mettre qn en boîte; *Fam* **on its last legs** *(machine, car)* prêt à claquer; *Fam* **to be on one's last legs** avoir un pied dans la tombe

legacy ['legəsɪ] *(pl* **-ies)** *n Law & Fig* legs *m*

legal ['li:gəl] *adj (lawful)* légal; *(affairs, adviser, mind)* juridique; *(error)* judiciaire; *Br* **l. aid** aide *f* judiciaire; **l. expert** juriste *mf*; **l. proceedings** procès *m* ● **legality** [lɪ'gælɪtɪ] *n* légalité *f* ● **legalize** *vt* légaliser ● **legally** *adv* légalement

legation [lɪ'geɪ∫ən] *n Pol* légation *f*

legend ['ledʒənd] *n (story, inscription)* légende *f* ● **legendary** *adj* légendaire

leggings ['legɪŋz] *npl (of woman)* caleçon *m*; *(of cowboy)* jambières *fpl*

leggy ['legɪ] **(-ier, -iest)** *adj (person)* tout en jambes

legible ['ledʒɪbəl] *adj* lisible ● **legi'bility** *n* lisibilité *f* ● **legibly** *adv* lisiblement

legion ['li:dʒən] *n* légion *f*

legislate ['ledʒɪsleɪt] *vi* légiférer ● **legis-'lation** *n (laws)* législation *f*; *(action)* élaboration *f* des lois; **(piece of) l.** loi *f*

legislative ['ledʒɪslətɪv] *adj* législatif, -ive

legitimate [lɪ'dʒɪtɪmət] *adj* légitime ● **legitimacy** *n* légitimité *f*

legless ['legləs] *adj Br Fam (drunk)* complètement bourré

legroom ['legru:m] *n* place *f* pour les jambes

leisure [*Br* 'leʒə(r), *Am* 'li:ʒər] *n* **l. (time)** loisirs *mpl*; **l. activities** loisirs; **l. centre** *or* **complex** centre *m* de loisirs; **moment of l.** moment *m* de loisir; **at (one's) l.** à tête reposée ● **leisurely** *adj (walk, occupation)* peu fatigant; *(meal, life)* tranquille; **at a l. pace, in a l. way** sans se presser

lemon ['lemən] *n* citron *m*; *Br* **l. drink, l. squash** citronnade *f*; **l. tea** thé *m* au citron ● **lemo'nade** *n Br (fizzy)* limonade *f*; *Am (still)* citronnade *f*

lend [lend] *(pt & pp* **lent)** *vt* prêter (**to** à); *(support)* apporter (**to** à); *Fig (charm, colour)* donner (**to** à); **to l. an ear to sth** prêter l'oreille à qch; **to l. credibility to sth** rendre qch crédible ● **lender** *n* prêteur, -euse *mf* ● **lending** *n* prêt *m*; **l. library** bibliothèque *f* de prêt

length [leŋθ] *n (in space)* longueur *f*; *(of road, string)* tronçon *m*; *(of cloth)* métrage *m*; *(duration)* durée *f*; **a great l. of time** longtemps; **at l.** *(at last)* enfin; **at (great) l.** *(in detail)* dans le détail; *(for a long time)* longuement; **to go to great lengths** se donner beaucoup de mal (**to do** pour faire)

lengthen ['leŋθən] **1** vt (garment) allonger; (holiday, visit) prolonger

2 vi (of days) allonger • **lengthwise** adv dans le sens de la longueur • **lengthy** (-ier, -iest) adj long (f longue)

lenient ['li:nɪənt] adj indulgent (**to** envers) • **leniency** n indulgence f • **leniently** adv avec indulgence

lens [lenz] (pl **lenses** [-zəz]) n lentille f; (in spectacles) verre m; (of camera) objectif m

Lent [lent] n Rel carême m

lent [lent] pt & pp of **lend**

lentil ['lentəl] n (seed, plant) lentille f

Leo ['li:əʊ] (pl **Leos**) n (sign) le Lion; **to be a L.** être Lion

leopard ['lepəd] n léopard m

leotard ['li:əta:d] n justaucorps m

leper ['lepə(r)] n lépreux, -euse mf • **leprosy** ['leprəsɪ] n lèpre f

lesbian ['lezbɪən] **1** adj lesbien, -ienne

2 n lesbienne f

lesion ['li:ʒən] n Med lésion f

less [les] **1** adj & pron moins (de) (**than** que); **l. time** moins de temps; **she has l.** (**than you**) elle en a moins (que toi); **l. than a kilo/ten** moins d'un kilo/de dix

2 adv moins (**than** que); **l.** (**often**) moins souvent; **l. and l.** de moins en moins; **one l.** un(e) de moins

3 prep moins; **l. 6 euros** moins 6 euros

-less [ləs] suff sans; **childless** sans enfants

lessen ['lesən] vti diminuer • **lessening** n diminution f

lesser ['lesə(r)] **1** adj moindre

2 n **the l. of** le/la moindre de

lesson ['lesən] n leçon f; **an English l.** une leçon d'anglais; **I have lessons now** j'ai cours maintenant; Fig **he has learnt his l.** ça lui a servi de leçon

lest [lest] conj Literary de peur que... (+ ne + subjunctive)

let¹ [let] **1** (pt & pp **let**, pres p **letting**) vt (allow) **to l. sb do sth** laisser qn faire qch; **to l. sb have sth** donner qch à qn

2 v aux **l. us eat/go**, **l.'s eat/go** mangeons/partons; **l.'s go for a stroll** allons nous promener; **l. him come** qu'il vienne • **letdown** n déception f • **letup** n répit m

▸ **let away** vt sep (allow to leave) laisser partir ▸ **let down** vt sep (lower) baisser; (hair) dénouer; (dress) rallonger; (tyre) dégonfler; **to l. sb down** (disappoint) décevoir qn; **don't l. me down** je compte sur toi; **the car l. me down** la voiture est tombée en panne ▸ **let in** vt sep (person, dog) faire entrer; (noise, light) laisser entrer; Br **to l. in the clutch** (in vehicle) embrayer; **to l. sb in on sth** mettre qn au courant de qch; **to l. oneself in for a lot of expense** se laisser entraîner à des dépenses; **to l. oneself in for trouble** s'attirer des ennuis; **what are you letting yourself in for?** sais-tu à quoi tu t'exposes? ▸ **let off** vt sep (firework) tirer; (bomb) faire exploser; (gun) faire partir; **to l. sb off** (allow to leave) laisser partir qn; (not punish) ne pas punir qn; (clear of crime) disculper qn; **to be l. off with a fine** s'en tirer avec une amende; **to l. sb off doing sth** dispenser qn de faire qch ▸ **let on** vi Fam **not to l. on** ne rien dire; Fam **to l. on that...** (admit) avouer que...; (reveal) dire que... ▸ **let out** vt sep (allow to leave) laisser sortir; (prisoner) relâcher; (cry, secret) laisser échapper; (skirt) élargir; **my secretary will l. you out** ma secrétaire va vous reconduire; Br **to l. out the clutch** (in vehicle) débrayer ▸ **let up** vi (of rain, person) s'arrêter

let² [let] (pt & pp **let**, pres p **letting**) vt **to l.** (**off** or **out**) (house, room) louer • **letting** n (renting) location f

lethal ['li:θəl] adj (blow, dose) mortel, -elle; (weapon) meurtrier, -ière

lethargy ['leθədʒɪ] n léthargie f • **lethargic** [lɪ'θa:dʒɪk] adj léthargique

letter ['letə(r)] n (message, part of word) lettre f; **man of letters** homme m de lettres; **l. of introduction** lettre de recommandation; **l. bomb** lettre piégée; **l. opener** coupe-papier m inv • **letterbox** n Br boîte f aux lettres • **letterhead** n en-tête m • **letterheaded** adj **l. paper** papier m à en-tête • **lettering** n (letters) lettres fpl; (on tomb) inscription f

lettuce ['letɪs] n laitue f

leukaemia [lu:'ki:mɪə] (Am **leukemia**) n leucémie f

level ['levəl] **1** n niveau m; **at international l.** à l'échelon international; **at eye l.** à hauteur des yeux; Fam **on the l.** (honest) régulier, -ière; (honestly) franchement

2 adj (surface) plat; (equal in score) à égalité (**with** avec); (in height) à la même hauteur (**with** que); **l. spoonful** cuillerée f rase; Br **l. crossing** (for train) passage m à niveau

3 (Br -ll-, Am -l-) vt (surface, differences) aplanir; (plane down) raboter; (building) raser; (gun) braquer (**at** sur); (accusation) lancer (**at** contre)

4 vi **to l. off** or **out** (of prices) se stabiliser; Fam **to l. with sb** être franc (f franche) avec qn • '**level-'headed** adj équilibré

lever [Br 'li:və(r), Am 'levər] n levier m • **leverage** n (power) influence f

levity ['levɪtɪ] n légèreté f
levy ['levɪ] **1** (pl **-ies**) n (tax) impôt m (**on**
sur)
  2 (pt & pp **-ied**) vt (tax, troops) lever
lewd [luːd] (**-er, -est**) adj obscène
liability [laɪə'bɪlɪtɪ] n Law responsabilité
f (**for** de); (disadvantage) handicap m;
Fin **liabilities** (debts) passif m
liable ['laɪəbəl] adj **l. to** (dizziness) sujet,
-ette à; (fine, tax) passible de; **to be l. to
do sth** risquer de faire qch; **l. for sth**
(responsible) responsable de qch
liaise [liː'eɪz] vi travailler en liaison (**with**
avec) • **liaison** [liː'eɪzɒn] n (contact, love
affair) & Mil liaison f
liar ['laɪə(r)] n menteur, -euse mf
libel ['laɪbəl] Law **1** n diffamation f; **l.
action** procès m en diffamation
  2 (Br **-ll-**, Am **-l-**) vt diffamer (par écrit)
liberal ['lɪbərəl] **1** adj (open-minded) &
Pol libéral; (generous) généreux, -euse
(**with** de)
  2 n Pol libéral, -ale mf • **liberalism** n
libéralisme m
liberate ['lɪbəreɪt] vt libérer • **libe'ration**
n libération f • **liberator** n libérateur,
-trice mf
liberty ['lɪbətɪ] (pl **-ies**) n liberté f; **to be
at l. to do sth** être libre de faire qch; **to
take liberties with sb/sth** prendre des
libertés avec qn/qch; Fam **what a l.!**
(impudence) quel culot!
Libra ['liːbrə] n (sign) la Balance; **to be a
L.** être Balance
library ['laɪbrərɪ] (pl **-ies**) n bibliothèque
f; **l. card** carte f de bibliothèque • **librarian**
[-'breərɪən] n bibliothécaire mf

> 🖉 Note that the French words **libraire** and
> **librairie** are false friends and are never
> translations for the English words **librarian**
> and **library**. They mean **bookseller** and
> **bookshop**.

libretto [lɪ'bretəʊ] (pl **-os**) n Mus livret m
Libya ['lɪbɪə] n la Libye • **Libyan 1** adj
libyen, -enne **2** n Libyen, -enne mf
lice [laɪs] pl of **louse**
licence ['laɪsəns] (Am **license**) n (**a**)
(permit) permis m; (for trading) licence f;
(for flying) brevet m; (**TV**) **l.** redevance f; **l.
plate/number** (of vehicle) plaque f/nu-
méro m d'immatriculation (**b**) (excessive
freedom) licence f
license ['laɪsəns] **1** n Am = **licence**
  2 vt accorder un permis/une licence/un
brevet à; **to be licensed to carry a gun**
avoir un permis de port d'armes; Br **licensed premises** débit m de boissons;

licensing laws lois fpl relatives aux débits
de boissons
licit ['lɪsɪt] adj licite
lick [lɪk] **1** n coup m de langue; **a l. of
paint** un coup de peinture
  2 vt lécher; Fam (defeat) écraser; **to l.
one's lips** s'en lécher les babines • **licking**
n Fam (defeat) déculottée f
licorice ['lɪkərɪʃ, 'lɪkərɪs] n réglisse f
lid [lɪd] n (**a**) (of box) couvercle m (**b**) (of
eye) paupière f
lie¹ [laɪ] **1** n mensonge m; **to tell a l.** dire
un mensonge; **to give the l. to sth** (show
as untrue) démentir qch; **l. detector** détecteur m de mensonges
  2 (pt & pp **lied**, pres p **lying**) vi (tell lies)
mentir; **to l. through one's teeth** mentir
effrontément
lie² [laɪ] (pt **lay**, pp **lain**, pres p **lying**) vi (**a**)
(of person, animal) (be in a flat position)
être allongé; (get down) s'allonger; **to be
lying on the grass** être allongé sur
l'herbe; **to l. in bed** rester au lit; **he lay
asleep** il dormait; **I lay awake all night** je
n'ai pas dormi de la nuit; **she lay dead at
my feet** elle était étendue morte à mes
pieds; Fig **to l. low** garder un profil bas;
here lies... (on tomb) ci-gît... (
b) (of object) être, se trouver; **snow lay
on the hills** il y avait de la neige sur les
collines; **to l. in ruins** (of building) être en
ruines; (of career) être détruit; **the problem lies in that...** le problème réside
dans le fait que...; **a brilliant future lies
before her** un brillant avenir s'ouvre devant elle; **it's lying heavy on my stomach**
(of meal) cela me pèse sur l'estomac • **'lie-
'down** n Br **to have a l.** faire une sieste
• **'lie-'in** n Br **to have a l.** faire la grasse
matinée
  ▸ **lie about, lie around** vi (of objects,
person) traîner ▸ **lie down** vi s'allonger;
to be lying down être allongé ▸ **lie in** vi Br
Fam faire la grasse matinée
lieu [luː] n **in l.** à la place; **in l. of sth** au
lieu de qch
lieutenant [Br lef'tenənt, Am luː'tenənt]
n lieutenant m
life [laɪf] (pl **lives**) n vie f; (of battery,
machine) durée f de vie; **to come to l.** (of
party, street) s'animer; **at your time of l.** à
ton âge; **loss of l.** perte f en vies humaines; **true to l.** conforme à la réalité; **to
take one's (own) l.** se donner la mort; **bird
l.** les oiseaux mpl; **l. annuity** rente f viagère; **l. expectancy** espérance f de vie; **l.
force** force f vitale; **l. insurance** assu-
rance-vie f; **l. jacket** gilet m de sauvetage;

Br **l. peer** pair *m* à vie; *Am* **l. preserver** ceinture *f* de sauvetage; **l. raft** radeau *m* de sauvetage; **l. span** durée *f* de vie • **life-belt** *n* ceinture *f* de sauvetage • **lifeblood** *n (of person)* souffle *m* vital; *(of economy)* moteur *m* • **lifeboat** *n* canot *m* de sauvetage • **lifebuoy** *n* bouée *f* de sauvetage • **lifeguard** *n* maître nageur *m* • **lifeless** *adj* sans vie • **lifelike** *adj* très ressemblant • **life-line** *n* **to be sb's l.** être essentiel, -ielle à la survie de qn • **lifelong** *adj* de toute sa vie; *(friend)* de toujours • **lifesaving** *n* sauvetage *m* • **lifesize(d)** *adj* grandeur nature *inv* • **life-style** *n* style *m* de vie • **life-sup'port system** *n* respirateur *m* artificiel • **lifetime** *n* vie *f*; *Fig* éternité *f*; **in my l.** de mon vivant; **it's the chance of a l.** une telle chance ne se présente qu'une fois dans une vie; **the holidays of a l.** des vacances exceptionnelles; **a once-in-a-l. experience** une expérience inoubliable

lift [lɪft] **1** *n Br (elevator)* ascenseur *m*; **to give sb a l.** emmener qn en voiture (**to** à) **2** *vt* lever; *(heavy object)* soulever; *Fig (ban, siege)* lever; *Fig (steal)* piquer (**from** à) **3** *vi (of fog)* se lever • **lift-off** *n (of space vehicle)* décollage *m*
▸ **lift down** *vt sep (take down)* descendre (**from** de) ▸ **lift off 1** *vt sep (take down)* descendre (**from** de) **2** *vi (of spacecraft)* décoller ▸ **lift out** *vt sep (take out)* sortir ▸ **lift up** *vt sep (arm, object, eyes)* lever; *(heavy object)* soulever

ligament ['lɪɡəmənt] *n* ligament *m*

light¹ [laɪt] **1** *n* lumière *f*; *(on vehicle)* feu *m*; *(vehicle headlight)* phare *m*; **by the l. of sth** à la clarté de qch; **in the l. of...** *(considering)* à la lumière de...; *Fig* **in that l.** sous cet éclairage; **against the l.** à contre-jour; **to bring sth to l.** mettre qch en lumière; **to come to l.** être découvert; **to throw l. on sth** *(matter)* éclaircir qch; **do you have a l.?** *(for cigarette)* est-ce que vous avez du feu?; **to set l. to sth** mettre le feu à qch; **turn right at the lights** tournez à droite après les feux; **l. bulb** ampoule *f*; **l. switch** interrupteur *m* **2** *adj* **it will soon be l.** il fera bientôt jour **3** *(pt & pp* **lit** *or* **lighted)** *vt (fire, candle, gas)* allumer; *(match)* allumer, gratter; **to l. (up)** *(room)* éclairer; *(cigarette)* allumer **4** *vi* **to l. up** *(of window)* s'allumer • **lighting** *n (act, system)* éclairage *m* • **light-year** *n* année-lumière *f*

light² [laɪt] *adj (bright, not dark)* clair; **a l. green jacket** une veste vert clair • **lightness** *n (brightness)* clarté *f*

light³ [laɪt] *adj (in weight, quantity, strength)* léger, -ère; *(task, exercise)* facile; *(low-fat)* allégé; *(low-calorie)* pauvre en calories; **l. rain** pluie *f* fine; **to travel l.** voyager avec peu de bagages • **light-'fingered** *adj* chapardeur, -euse • **light-'headed** *adj (giddy, foolish)* étourdi • **'light-'hearted** *adj* enjoué • **lightness** *n (in weight)* légèreté *f*

light⁴ [laɪt] *(pt & pp* **lit** *or* **lighted)** *vi Literary* **to l. upon** trouver par hasard

lighten ['laɪtən] **1** *vt* (**a**) *(make less dark)* éclaircir (**b**) *(make less heavy)* alléger; *Fig* **to l. sb's load** soulager qn **2** *vi (of sky)* s'éclaircir; *Fam* **to l. up** se détendre

lighter ['laɪtə(r)] *n* briquet *m*; *(for cooker)* allume-gaz *m inv*

lighthouse ['laɪthaʊs] *n* phare *m*

lightly ['laɪtlɪ] *adv* légèrement; **l. boiled egg** œuf *m* à la coque; **to get off l.** s'en tirer à bon compte

lightning ['laɪtnɪŋ] **1** *n (flashes of light)* éclairs *mpl*; *(charge)* foudre *f*; **(flash of) l.** éclair *m* **2** *adj (speed)* foudroyant; *(visit)* éclair *inv*; *Br* **l. conductor,** *Am* **l. rod** paratonnerre *m*

lightweight ['laɪtweɪt] **1** *adj (shoes, fabric)* léger, -ère; *Fig & Pej (person)* pas sérieux, -ieuse **2** *n Boxing* poids *m* léger

like¹ [laɪk] **1** *prep* comme; **l. this** comme ça; **what's he l.?** comment est-il?; **to be** *or* **look l. sb/sth** ressembler à qn/qch; **what was the book l.?** comment as-tu trouvé le livre?; **what does it smell l.?** cela sent quoi?; **I have one l. it** j'en ai un pareil **2** *adv* **nothing l. as big** loin d'être aussi grand **3** *conj Fam (as)* comme; **it's l. I say** c'est comme je te le dis; **do l. I do** fais comme moi **4** *n* **and the l.** et ainsi de suite; **the l. of which we shall never see again** comme on n'en reverra plus; **the likes of you** des gens de ton acabit

like² [laɪk] **1** *vt* aimer (bien) (**to do** *or* **doing** faire); **I l. him** je l'aime bien; **she likes it here** elle se plaît ici; **to l. sb/sth best** aimer mieux qn/qch; **I'd l. to come** *(want)* j'aimerais bien venir; **I'd l. a kilo of apples** je voudrais un kilo de pommes; **would you l. an apple?** voulez-vous une pomme?; **if you l.** si vous voulez; **how would you l. to come?** ça te dirait de venir?

2 *npl* **one's likes and dislikes** nos préférences *fpl* • **liking** *n* **a l. for** *(person)* de la sympathie pour; *(thing)* du goût pour; **to my l.** à mon goût

likeable ['laɪkəbəl] *adj* sympathique

likely ['laɪklɪ] **1** (**-ier, -iest**) *adj (result, event)* probable; *(excuse)* vraisemblable; *(place)* propice; *(candidate)* prometteur, -euse; *Ironic* **a l. excuse!** la belle excuse!; **it's l. (that) she'll come** il est probable qu'elle viendra; **he's l. to come** il viendra probablement; **he's not l. to come** il ne risque pas de venir

2 *adv* **very l.** très probablement; **not l.!** pas question! • **likelihood** *n* probabilité *f*; **there isn't much l. that...** il y a peu de chances que... (+ *subjunctive*)

liken ['laɪkən] *vt* comparer (**to** à)

likeness ['laɪknɪs] *n* (**a**) *(similarity)* ressemblance *f*; **a family l.** un air de famille; **it's a good l.** c'est très ressemblant (**b**) *(portrait)* portrait *m*

likewise ['laɪkwaɪz] *adv (similarly)* de même

lilac ['laɪlək] **1** *n* lilas *m*
2 *adj (colour)* lilas *inv*

Lilo® ['laɪləʊ] (*pl* **-os**) *n Br* matelas *m* pneumatique

lilt [lɪlt] *n (in song, voice)* modulation *f*

lily ['lɪlɪ] (*pl* **-ies**) *n* lis *m*; **l. of the valley** muguet *m*

limb [lɪm] *n (of body)* membre *m*; *Fig* **to be out on a l.** *(in dangerous position)* être sur la corde raide

limber ['lɪmbə(r)] *vi* **to l. up** s'échauffer

limbo ['lɪmbəʊ] *adv* **in l.** *(uncertain, waiting)* dans l'incertitude

lime¹ [laɪm] *n* (**a**) *(fruit)* citron *m* vert; **l. juice** jus *m* de citron vert (**b**) *(tree)* tilleul *m*

lime² [laɪm] *n Chem* chaux *f*

limelight ['laɪmlaɪt] *n* **to be in the l.** occuper le devant de la scène

limerick ['lɪmərɪk] *n* = poème humoristique de cinq vers

limit ['lɪmɪt] **1** *n* limite *f*; *(restriction)* limitation *f* (**on** de); *Fam* **that's the l.!** c'est le comble!; **within limits** jusqu'à un certain point

2 *vt* limiter (**to** à); **to l. oneself to sth/doing sth** se borner à qch/faire qch • **limi'tation** *n* limitation *f* • **limited** *adj (restricted)* limité; *(edition)* à tirage limité; *(mind)* borné; *Br* **l. company** société *f* à responsabilité limitée; *Br* (**public**) **l. company** *(with shareholders)* société *f* anonyme; **to a l. degree** jusqu'à un certain point • **limitless** *adj* illimité

limousine [lɪmə'ziːn] *n (car)* limousine *f*

limp¹ [lɪmp] **1** *n* **to have a l.** boiter

2 *vi (of person)* boiter; *Fig* **to l. along** *(of vehicle, ship)* avancer tant bien que mal

limp² [lɪmp] (**-er, -est**) *adj (soft)* mou (*f* molle); *(flabby) (skin)* flasque; *(person, hat)* avachi

limpid ['lɪmpɪd] *adj* limpide

linchpin ['lɪntʃpɪn] *n (person)* pivot *m*

linctus ['lɪŋktəs] *n Br (cough medicine)* sirop *m* (pour la toux)

line¹ [laɪn] **1** *n* ligne *f*; *(stroke)* trait *m*; *(of poem)* vers *m*; *(wrinkle)* ride *f*; *(track)* voie *f*; *(rope)* corde *f*; *(row)* rangée *f*; *(of vehicles)* file *f*; *(queue of people)* file, queue *f*; *(family)* lignée *f*; *(of goods)* ligne (de produits); **to learn one's lines** *(of actor)* apprendre son texte; **to be on the l.** *(at other end of phone line)* être au bout du fil; *(at risk) (of job)* être menacé; **hold the l.!** *(remain on phone)* ne quittez pas!; **the hot l.** le téléphone rouge; *Am* **to stand in l.** faire la queue; *Fig* **to step** *or* **get out of l.** refuser de se conformer; *(misbehave)* faire une incartade; **out of l. with** *(sb's ideas)* en désaccord avec; **in l. with sth** conforme à qch; **to be in l. for promotion** être sur la liste des promotions; **to take a hard l.** adopter une attitude ferme; **along the same lines** *(work, think, act)* de la même façon; **something along those lines** quelque chose dans ce genre-là; *Fam* **to drop a l.** *(send a letter)* envoyer un mot (**to** à); **where do we draw the l.?** où fixer les limites?; **what l. of business are you in?** vous travaillez dans quelle branche?; **l. dancing** = danse de style country effectuée en rangs

2 *vt* **to l. the street** *(of trees)* border la rue; *(of people)* s'aligner le long du trottoir; **to l. up** *(children, objects)* aligner; *(arrange)* organiser; **to have something lined up** *(in mind)* avoir quelque chose en vue; **lined face** visage *m* ridé; **lined paper** papier *m* réglé

3 *vi* **to l. up** s'aligner; *Am (queue up)* faire la queue; **to l. up in twos** se mettre en rangs par deux • **line-up** *n (row of people)* file *f*; *Pol (of countries)* front *m*; *TV (of programmes)* programme *m*; *TV (of guests)* plateau *m*; *Am (identity parade)* séance *f* d'identification

line² [laɪn] *vt (clothes)* doubler; *Fig* **to l. one's pockets** se remplir les poches • **lining** *n (of clothes)* doublure *f*; **brake l.** garniture *f* de frein

lineage ['lɪnɪɪdʒ] *n* lignée *f*

linear ['lɪnɪə(r)] *adj* linéaire

linen ['lɪnɪn] *n (sheets)* linge *m*; *(material)* (toile *f* de) lin *m*; *Br* **l. basket** panier *m* à linge; *Br* **l. cupboard,** *Am* **l. closet** armoire *f* à linge; **l. sheet** drap *m* de lin

liner ['laɪnə(r)] *n* (**a**) (**ocean**) **l.** paquebot *m* (**b**) *Br* (**dust**)**bin l.,** *Am* **garbage can l.** sac *m* poubelle

linesman ['laɪnzmən] (*pl* **-men**) *n Football* juge *m* de touche

linger ['lɪŋɡə(r)] *vi* **to l. (on)** *(of person)* s'attarder; *(of smell, memory)* persister; *(of doubt)* subsister; **a lingering death** une mort lente

lingo ['lɪŋɡəʊ] (*pl* **-oes**) *n Fam* jargon *m*

linguist ['lɪŋɡwɪst] *n (specialist)* linguiste *mf*; **to be a good l.** être doué pour les langues • **lin'guistic** *adj* linguistique • **lin'guistics** *n* linguistique *f*

liniment ['lɪnɪmənt] *n* pommade *f*

link [lɪŋk] **1** *n (connection)* & *Comptr* lien *m*; *(of chain)* maillon *m*; *(by road, rail)* liaison *f*

2 *vt (connect)* relier (**to** à); *(relate, associate)* lier (**to** à); **to l. up** relier; *(computer)* connecter

3 *vi* **to l. up** *(of companies, countries)* s'associer; *(of computers)* se connecter; *(of roads)* se rejoindre • **linkup** *n (of spacecraft)* jonction *f*; *(between TV stations)* liaison *f*

lino ['laɪnəʊ] (*pl* **-os**) *n Br* lino *m* • **linoleum** [lɪ'nəʊlɪəm] *n* linoléum *m*

linseed ['lɪnsiːd] *n* **l. oil** huile *f* de lin

lint [lɪnt] *n (bandage)* tissu *m* ouaté; *(fluff)* peluches *fpl*

lion ['laɪən] *n* lion *m*; **l. cub** lionceau *m*; **l. tamer** dompteur, -euse *mf* de lions • **lioness** *n* lionne *f*

lip [lɪp] *n (of person, wound)* lèvre *f*; *(of cup)* bord *m*; *Fam (impudence)* culot *m*; **to pay l. service to sth** faire semblant de s'intéresser à qch • **lip-read** (*pt & pp* **-read** [-red]) *vi* lire sur les lèvres • **lipstick** *n* rouge *m* à lèvres

liquefy ['lɪkwɪfaɪ] (*pt & pp* **-ied**) **1** *vt* liquéfier

2 *vi* se liquéfier

liqueur [*Br* lɪ'kjʊə(r), *Am* lɪ'kɜːr] *n* liqueur *f*

liquid ['lɪkwɪd] *n & adj* liquide (*m*)

liquidate ['lɪkwɪdeɪt] *vt (debt, firm)* & *Fam (kill)* liquider • **liqui'dation** *n* liquidation *f*

liquidizer ['lɪkwɪdaɪzə(r)] *n Br (for fruit juices, purées)* mixeur *m* • **liquidize** *vt Br* passer au mixeur

liquor ['lɪkə(r)] *n Am* alcool *m*; **l. store** magasin *m* de vins et de spiritueux

liquorice ['lɪkərɪʃ, 'lɪkərɪs] *n Br* réglisse *f*

lira ['lɪərə] (*pl* **lire** ['lɪəreɪ]) *n* lire *f*

lisp [lɪsp] **1** *n* **to have a l.** zézayer

2 *vi* zézayer

list¹ [lɪst] **1** *n* liste *f*

1 *vt (things)* faire la liste de; *(names)* mettre sur la liste; *(name one by one)* énumérer; *Br* **listed building** monument *m* classé

list² [lɪst] *vi (of ship)* gîter

listen ['lɪsən] *vi* écouter; **to l. to sb/sth** écouter qn/qch; **to l. (out) for** *(telephone, person)* guetter; **to l. in (to)** *(on radio)* écouter • **listener** *n (to radio)* auditeur, -trice *mf*; **to be a good l.** *(pay attention)* savoir écouter • **listening** *n* écoute *f* (**to** de)

listless ['lɪstləs] *adj* apathique • **listlessness** *n* apathie *f*

lit [lɪt] *pt & pp of* **light**[1,4]

litany ['lɪtənɪ] (*pl* **-ies**) *n* litanie *f*

liter ['liːtə(r)] *n Am* litre *m*

literal ['lɪtərəl] *adj* littéral; *(not exaggerated)* réel (*f* réelle) • **literally** *adv* littéralement; *(really)* réellement; **he took it l.** il l'a pris au pied de la lettre

literary ['lɪtərərɪ] *adj* littéraire

literate ['lɪtərət] *adj* qui sait lire et écrire; **highly l.** *(person)* très instruit • **literacy** *n (of country)* degré *m* d'alphabétisation; *(of person)* capacité *f* de lire et d'écrire

literature ['lɪtərətʃə(r)] *n* littérature *f*; *(pamphlets)* documentation *f*

lithe [laɪð] *adj* agile

litigation [lɪtɪ'geɪʃən] *n Law* litige *m*

litre ['liːtə(r)] (*Am* **liter**) *n* litre *m*

litter ['lɪtə(r)] **1** *n (rubbish)* détritus *mpl*; *(papers)* papiers *mpl*; *(young animals)* portée *f*; *(for cat)* litière *f*; *Fig (jumble, confusion)* fouillis *m*; *Br* **l. basket** *or* **bin** boîte *f* à ordures

2 *vt Br* **to be littered with sth** être jonché de qch • **litterbug** *n Fam* = personne qui jette des détritus n'importe où

little ['lɪtəl] **1** *n* peu *m*; **I've l. left** il m'en reste peu; **she eats l.** elle mange peu; **to have l. to say** avoir peu de choses à dire; **I have a l.** j'en ai un peu; **the l. that I have** le peu que j'ai

2 *adj* (**a**) *(small)* petit; **the l. ones** les petits; **a l. bit** un (petit) peu

(**b**) *(not much)* peu de; **l. time/money** peu de temps/d'argent; **a l. time/money** un peu de temps/d'argent

2 *adv (somewhat, rather)* peu; **l. by l.** peu à peu; **as l. as possible** le moins possible; **a l. heavy** un peu lourd; **to work a l.**

travailler un peu; **it's a l. better** c'est un peu mieux; **it's l. better** *(not much)* ce n'est guère mieux

liturgy ['lɪtədʒɪ] *(pl* **-ies)** *n* liturgie *f*

live¹ [laɪv] **1** *adj* (**a**) *(electric wire)* sous tension; *(switch)* mal isolé; *(plugged in) (appliance)* branché; *(ammunition)* réel *(f* réelle), de combat; *(bomb)* non explosé; *(coal)* ardent (**b**) *(alive) (animal)* vivant; **a real l. king** un roi en chair et en os

2 *adj & adv* Radio & TV en direct; **a l. broadcast** une émission en direct; **l. audience** public *m*; **a l. recording** un enregistrement public

live² [lɪv] **1** *vt (life)* mener, vivre; *(one's faith)* vivre pleinement; *Fam* **to l. it up** mener la grande vie

2 *vi* vivre; **where do you l.?** où habitez-vous?; **to l. in Paris** habiter (à) Paris

▸ **live down** *vt sep* faire oublier ▸ **live off, live on** *vt insep (eat)* vivre de; *(sponge off)* vivre aux crochets de ▸ **live on** *vi (of memory)* survivre ▸ **live through** *vt insep (experience)* vivre; **to l. through the winter** passer l'hiver ▸ **live up to** *vt insep (one's principles)* vivre selon; *(sb's expectations)* se montrer à la hauteur de

livelihood ['laɪvlɪhʊd] *n* moyens *mpl* de subsistance; **my l.** mon gagne-pain; **to earn one's** *or* **a l.** gagner sa vie

lively ['laɪvlɪ] (**-ier, -iest**) *adj (person, style)* plein de vie; *(street, story)* vivant; *(mind, colour)* vif *(f* vive); *(discussion, conversation)* animé; *(protest, campaign)* vigoureux, -euse • **liveliness** *n* vivacité *f*

liven ['laɪvən] **1** *vt* **to l. up** *(person)* égayer; *(party)* animer

2 *vi* **to l. up** *(of person, party)* s'animer

liver ['lɪvə(r)] *n* foie *m*

livery ['lɪvərɪ] *n (uniform)* livrée *f*; **in l.** en livrée

livestock ['laɪvstɒk] *n* bétail *m*

livid ['lɪvɪd] *adj (angry)* furieux, -ieuse; *(blue-grey)* livide; **l. with cold** blême de froid

living ['lɪvɪŋ] **1** *adj (alive)* vivant; **not a l. soul** *(nobody)* pas âme qui vive; **within l. memory** de mémoire d'homme; **l. or dead** mort ou vif *(f* morte ou vive); **the l.** les vivants *mpl*

2 *n (livelihood)* vie *f*; **to make** *or* **earn a** *or* **one's l.** gagner sa vie; **to work for a l.** travailler pour vivre; **l. conditions** conditions *fpl* de vie; **a l. wage** un salaire qui permet de vivre • **living room** *n* salle *f* de séjour

lizard ['lɪzəd] *n* lézard *m*

llama ['lɑːmə] *n* lama *m*

load [ləʊd] **1** *n (object carried, burden)* charge *f*; *(freight)* chargement *m*; *(strain, weight)* poids *m*; *Fam* **a l. of, loads of** *(people, money)* un tas de; **to take a l. off sb's mind** ôter un grand poids à qn

2 *vt (truck, gun)* charger (**with** de); **to l. sb down with** *(presents)* charger qn de; **to l. up** *(car, ship)* charger (**with** de)

3 *vi* **to l. (up)** prendre un chargement

loaded ['ləʊdɪd] *adj (gun, vehicle)* chargé; *Fam (rich)* plein aux as; **a l. question** une question piège; **the dice are l.** les dés sont pipés; **l. (down) with** *(debts)* accablé de

loaf [ləʊf] **1** *(pl* **loaves)** *n* pain *m*

2 *vi* **to l. (about)** fainéanter • **loafer** *n* (**a**) *(person)* fainéant, -éante *mf* (**b**) *(shoes)* mocassin *m*

loam [ləʊm] *n* terreau *m*

loan [ləʊn] **1** *n (money lent)* prêt *m*; *(money borrowed)* emprunt *m*; **on l. from** prêté par; **(out) on l.** *(book)* sorti; **may I have the l. of...?** puis-je emprunter...?

2 *vt (lend)* prêter (**to** à)

loath [ləʊθ] *adj* **to be l. to do sth** répugner à faire qch

loathe [ləʊð] *vt* détester (**doing** faire) • **loathing** *n* dégoût *m* • **loathsome** *adj* répugnant

lobby ['lɒbɪ] **1** *(pl* **-ies)** *n* (**a**) *(of hotel)* hall *m*; *(of theatre)* foyer *m* (**b**) *(in politics)* groupe *m* de pression

2 *(pt & pp* **-ied)** *vt* faire pression sur

3 *vi* **to l. for sth** faire pression pour obtenir qch

lobe [ləʊb] *n* lobe *m*

lobster ['lɒbstə(r)] *n* homard *m*; *(spiny)* langouste *f*

local ['ləʊkəl] **1** *adj* local; *(regional)* régional; *(of the neighbourhood)* du quartier; **are you l.?** êtes-vous du coin?; **the doctor is l.** le médecin est tout près d'ici; **a l. phone call** *(within town)* une communication urbaine

2 *n Br Fam (pub)* bistrot *m* du coin; **she's a l.** elle est du coin; **the locals** *(people)* les gens *mpl* du coin

locality [ləʊ'kælətɪ] *(pl* **-ies)** *n (neighbourhood)* environs *mpl*

localize ['ləʊkəlaɪz] *vt (confine)* localiser

locally ['ləʊkəlɪ] *adv* dans le quartier

locate [ləʊ'keɪt] *vt (find)* repérer; *(pain, noise, leak)* localiser; *(situate)* situer; **to be located in Paris** être situé à Paris • **location** *n (site)* emplacement *m*; *(act)* repérage *m*; *(of pain)* localisation *f*; **on l.** *(shoot a film)* en extérieur

⌀ Note that the French word **location** is a false friend and is never a translation for the English word **location**. It means **renting** or **rented accommodation** depending on the context.

lock¹ [lɒk] n (of hair) mèche f

lock² [lɒk] **1** n (**a**) (on door, chest) serrure f; (of gun) cran m de sûreté; (**anti-theft**) **l.** (on vehicle) antivol m; **under l. and key** (object) sous clef (**b**) (on canal) écluse f **2** vt (door, car) fermer à clef; **to l. the wheels** (of vehicle) bloquer les roues **3** vi fermer à clef ▸ **lock away** vt sep (prisoner) enfermer; (jewels) mettre sous clef ▸ **lock in** vt sep (person) enfermer; **to l. sb in sth** enfermer qn dans qch ▸ **lock out** vt sep (person) enfermer dehors ▸ **lock up 1** vt sep (house, car) fermer à clef; (prisoner) enfermer; (jewels) mettre sous clef, enfermer **2** vi fermer à clef

locker ['lɒkə(r)] n (in school) casier m; (for luggage) (at station, airport) casier m de consigne automatique; (for clothes) vestiaire m (métallique); Am Sport **l. room** vestiaire

locket ['lɒkɪt] n médaillon m

lock-out ['lɒkaʊt] n (industrial) lock-out m inv

locksmith ['lɒksmɪθ] n serrurier m

lockup ['lɒkʌp] n Br (garage) garage m

loco ['ləʊkəʊ] adj Am Fam (crazy) cinglé

locomotion [ləʊkə'məʊʃən] n locomotion f

locomotive [ləʊkə'məʊtɪv] n locomotive f

locum ['ləʊkəm] n Br (doctor) remplaçant, -ante mf

locust ['ləʊkəst] n sauterelle f

lodge [lɒdʒ] **1** n (house) pavillon m; (of porter) loge f **2** vt (person) loger; **to l. a complaint** porter plainte **3** vi (of bullet) se loger (**in** dans); **to be lodging** (accommodated) être logé (**with** chez)

lodger ['lɒdʒə(r)] n (room and meals) pensionnaire mf; (room only) locataire mf

lodging ['lɒdʒɪŋ] n (accommodation) logement m; **lodgings** (flat) logement m; (room) chambre f; **in lodgings** en meublé

loft [lɒft] n grenier m

lofty ['lɒftɪ] (**-ier, -iest**) adj (high, noble) élevé; (haughty, superior) hautain ● **loftiness** n hauteur f

log [lɒg] **1** n (tree trunk) tronc m d'arbre; (for fire) bûche f; **l. cabin** hutte f en rondin; **l. fire** feu m de bois

2 (pt & pp **-gg-**) vt (facts) noter; **to l. (up)** (distance) couvrir **3** vi Comptr **to l. in/out** entrer/sortir ● **logbook** n (on ship) journal m de bord; (on plane) carnet m de vol; Br (of vehicle) ≃ carte f grise

loggerheads ['lɒgəhedz] n **at l.** en désaccord (**with** avec)

logic ['lɒdʒɪk] n logique f ● **logical** adj logique ● **logically** adv logiquement

logistics [lə'dʒɪstɪks] n logistique f

logo ['ləʊgəʊ] (pl **-os**) n logo m

loin [lɔɪn] n (meat) filet m; **l. chop** côtes fpl premières

loincloth ['lɔɪnklɒθ] n pagne m

loins [lɔɪnz] npl (of person) reins mpl

loiter ['lɔɪtə(r)] vi traîner

loll [lɒl] vi (in armchair) se prélasser

lollipop ['lɒlɪpɒp] n sucette f; Br **l. man/ lady** = contractuel qui aide les écoliers à traverser la rue ● **lolly** (pl **-ies**) n (**a**) Fam sucette f; (ice) **l.** glace f à l'eau (**b**) Fam (money) fric m

London ['lʌndən] **1** n Londres m ou f **2** adj (taxi) londonien, -ienne ● **Londoner** n Londonien, -ienne mf

lone [ləʊn] adj solitaire; Fig **l. wolf** solitaire mf

loneliness ['ləʊnlɪnəs] n solitude f ● **lonely** (**-ier, -iest**) adj (road, house, life) solitaire; (person) seul

loner ['ləʊnə(r)] n solitaire mf

lonesome ['ləʊnsəm] adj solitaire

long¹ [lɒŋ] **1** (**-er, -est**) adj long (f longue); **to be 10 m l.** avoir 10 m de long; **to be six weeks l.** durer six semaines; **how l. is...?** quelle est la longueur de...?; (time) quelle est la durée de...?; **a l. time** longtemps; **in the l. run** à la longue; **a l. face** une grimace; **a l. memory** une bonne mémoire; Sport **l. jump** saut m en longueur

2 adv (a long time) longtemps; **l. before/ after** longtemps avant/après; **has he been here l.?** il y a longtemps qu'il est ici?; **how l.?** (in time) combien de temps?; **how l. ago?** il y a combien de temps?; **not l.** peu de temps; **before l.** sous peu; **no longer** ne plus; **she no longer swims** elle ne nage plus; **a bit longer** (wait) encore un peu; **I won't be l.** je n'en ai pas pour longtemps; **don't be l.** dépêche-toi; **at the longest** (tout) au plus; **all summer/ winter l.** tout l'été/l'hiver; **l. live the queen!** vive la reine!; **as l. as, so l. as** (provided that) pourvu que (+ subjunctive); **as l. as I live** tant que je vivrai ● **long-awaited** adj tant attendu ● **'long-'distance**

adj (race) de fond; *(phone call)* interurbain; *(flight)* long-courrier • **long-drawn-out** *adj* interminable • **'long'haired** *adj* aux cheveux longs • **'long-'life** *adj (battery)* longue durée *inv*; *(milk)* longue conservation • **long-playing** *adj* **l. record** 33 tours *m inv* • **'long-'range** *adj (forecast)* à long terme • **long'sighted** *adj (person)* presbyte • **'long'standing** *adj* de longue date • **'long'suffering** *adj* très patient • **long-term** *adj* à long terme • **'long'winded** *adj (speech, speaker)* verbeux, -euse

long² [lɒŋ] *vi* **to l. for sth** avoir très envie de qch; **to l. for sb** languir après qn; **to l. to do sth** avoir très envie de faire qch • **longing** *n* désir *m*

longevity [lɒn'dʒevɪtɪ] *n* longévité *f*

longitude ['lɒndʒɪtjuːd] *n* longitude *f*

longways ['lɒŋweɪz] *adv* en longueur

loo [luː] *(pl* **loos***)* *n Br Fam* **the l.** le petit coin

look [lʊk] **1** *n (glance)* regard *m*; *(appearance)* air *m*, allure *f*; **good looks** beauté *f*; **to have a l. (at sth)** jeter un coup d'œil (à qch); **to have a l. (for sth)** chercher (qch); **to have a l. (a)round** regarder; *(walk)* faire un tour; **let me have a l.** fais voir; **I like the l. of him** il me plaît

2 *vt* **to l. sb in the face** regarder qn dans les yeux; **to l. sb up and down** toiser qn

3 *vi* regarder; **to l. tired/happy** *(seem)* avoir l'air fatigué/heureux; **to l. pretty/ugly** *(be)* être joli/laid; **to l. one's age** faire son âge; **l. here!** dites donc!; **you l. like** *or* **as if** *or* **as though you're tired** tu as l'air fatigué; **it looks like** *or* **as if** *or* **as though she won't leave** on dirait qu'elle n'a pas l'air de vouloir partir; **it looks like it** c'est probable; **to l. like a child** avoir l'air d'un enfant; **to l. like an apple** avoir l'air d'être une pomme; **you l. like my brother** *(resemble)* tu ressembles à mon frère; **it looks like rain (to me)** on dirait qu'il va pleuvoir; **what does he l. like?** *(describe him)* comment est-il?; **to l. well** *or* **good** *(of person)* avoir bonne mine; **you l. good in that hat** ce chapeau te va très bien; **that looks bad** *(action)* ça fait mauvais effet

▸ **look after** *vt insep (take care of)* s'occuper de; *(keep safely)* garder (**for sb** pour qn); **to l. after oneself** *(keep healthy)* faire bien attention à soi; *(manage, cope)* se débrouiller ▸ **look around 1** *vt insep (town, shops)* faire un tour dans **2** *vi (have a look)* regarder; *(walk round)* faire un tour ▸ **look at** *vt insep* regarder; *(consider)* considérer; *(check)* vérifier ▸ **look away**

vi détourner les yeux ▸ **look back** *vi* regarder derrière soi; *(in time)* regarder en arrière ▸ **look down** *vi* baisser les yeux; *(from a height)* regarder en bas; **to l. down on** *(consider scornfully)* regarder de haut ▸ **look for** *vt insep (seek)* chercher ▸ **look forward to** *vt insep (event)* attendre avec impatience; **to l. forward to doing sth** avoir hâte de faire qch ▸ **look in** *vi* regarder à l'intérieur; **to l. in on sb** passer voir qn ▸ **look into** *vt insep (examine)* examiner; *(find out about)* se renseigner sur ▸ **look on 1** *vt insep (consider)* considérer (**as** comme) **2** *vi (watch)* regarder ▸ **look out** *vi (be careful)* faire attention; **to l. out for sb/sth** *(seek)* chercher qn/qch; *(watch)* guetter qn/qch; **to l. (out) on to** *(of window, house)* donner sur ▸ **look over** *vt insep (examine fully)* examiner; *(briefly)* parcourir; *(region, town)* parcourir, visiter ▸ **look round 1** *vt insep (visit)* visiter **2** *vi (have a look)* regarder; *(walk round)* faire un tour; *(look back)* se retourner; **to l. round for sb/sth** *(seek)* chercher qn/qch ▸ **look through** *vt insep (inspect)* passer en revue; **to l. straight through sb** *(not see)* regarder qn sans le voir; *(deliberately)* ignorer qn ▸ **look up 1** *vt sep (word)* chercher; **to l. sb up** *(visit)* passer voir qn **2** *vi (of person)* lever les yeux; *(into the air or sky)* regarder en l'air; *(improve)* *(of situation)* s'améliorer; *Fig* **to l. up to sb** respecter qn

-looking ['lʊkɪŋ] *suff* **pleasant-/tired-l.** à l'air agréable/fatigué

looking-glass ['lʊkɪŋglɑːs] *n* miroir *m*

lookout ['lʊkaʊt] *n (soldier)* guetteur *m*; *(sailor)* vigie *f*; **l. (post)** observatoire *m*; *(on ship)* vigie *f*; **to be on the l.** faire le guet; **to be on the l. for sb/sth** guetter qn/qch; *Fam* **that's your l.!** c'est ton problème!

loom [luːm] **1** *n (weaving machine)* métier *m* à tisser

2 *vi* **to l. (up)** *(of mountain)* apparaître indistinctement; *(of event)* paraître imminent

loony ['luːnɪ] *(pl* **-ies***)* *n & adj Fam* dingue *(mf)*

loop [luːp] **1** *n* boucle *f*

2 *vt* **to l. the loop** *(in plane)* faire un looping

loophole ['luːphəʊl] *n (in law)* vide *m* juridique

loose [luːs] **1** *(***-er, -est***)* *adj (screw, belt, knot)* desserré; *(tooth, stone)* qui bouge; *(page)* détaché; *(clothes)* flottant; *(hair)* dénoué; *(flesh)* flasque; *(wording, trans-*

lation, link) vague; *(discipline)* relâché; *(articles for sale)* en vrac; *Br (cheese, tea)* au poids; *Pej (woman)* facile; **there's an animal/prisoner l.** *(having escaped)* il y a un animal échappé/un prisonnier évadé; **l. change** petite monnaie *f*; **l. connection** *(in appliance)* mauvais contact *m*; *Br* **l. covers** housses *fpl*; **l. living** vie *f* dissolue; **to come** *or* **get l.** *(of knot, screw)* se desserrer; *(of page)* se détacher; *(of tooth)* se mettre à bouger; **to get l.** *(of dog)* se détacher; **to set** *or* **turn l.** *(dog)* lâcher; *Br* **he's at a l. end** il ne sait pas trop quoi faire

2 *n* **on the l.** *(prisoner)* en cavale; *(animal)* en liberté

loosely ['luːslɪ] *adv (hang)* lâchement; *(hold, tie)* sans serrer; *(translate)* de façon approximative; *(link)* vaguement

loosen ['luːsən] **1** *vt (knot, belt, screw)* desserrer; *(rope)* détendre; **to l. one's grip** relâcher son étreinte

2 *vi Sport* **to l. up** faire des exercices d'assouplissement

loot [luːt] **1** *n* butin *m*; *Fam (money)* fric *m*
2 *vt* piller •**looter** *n* pillard, -arde *mf* •**looting** *n* pillage *m*

lop [lɒp] *(pt & pp -pp-) vt* **to l. (off)** couper

lop-sided [lɒp'saɪdɪd] *adj (crooked)* de travers; **to walk l.** *(limp)* se déhancher

loquacious [ləʊ'kweɪʃəs] *adj* loquace

lord [lɔːd] **1** *n* seigneur *m*; *(British title)* lord *m*; **the L.** *(God)* le Seigneur; **L. knows if** Dieu sait si; *Fam* **good L.!** bon sang!; *Fam* **oh L.!** mince!; *Br* **my l.** *(to judge)* Monsieur le juge

2 *vt Fam* **to l. it over sb** traiter qn de haut

lordly ['lɔːdlɪ] *adj* digne d'un grand seigneur; *(arrogant)* hautain

lordship ['lɔːdʃɪp] *n Br* **Your L.** *(to judge)* Monsieur le juge

lore [lɔː(r)] *n* traditions *fpl*

lorry ['lɒrɪ] *(pl -ies)* *n Br* camion *m*; *(heavy)* poids *m* lourd; **l. driver** camionneur *m*; **(long-distance) l. driver** routier *m*

lose [luːz] *(pt & pp lost)* **1** *vt* perdre; **to l. interest in sth** se désintéresser de qch; **to l. one's life** trouver la mort (**in** dans); **to have nothing to l.** n'avoir rien à perdre; **to be lost at sea** périr en mer; **to l. one's way, to get lost** *(of person)* se perdre; **the ticket got lost** on a perdu le billet; *Fam* **get lost!** fous le camp!; **that lost us the war/our jobs** cela nous a coûté la guerre/ notre travail; **I've lost my bearings** je suis désorienté; **you've lost me** je ne vous suis plus; **the clock loses six minutes a day** la pendule retarde de six minutes par jour

2 *vi* perdre; **to l. out** être perdant; **to l. to sb** *(in contest)* être battu par qn •**loser** *n* *(in contest)* perdant, -ante *mf*; *Fam (failure in life)* minable *mf*; **to be a good l.** être beau joueur •**losing** *adj (number, team, horse)* perdant; **to fight a l. battle** être battu d'avance

loss [lɒs] *n* perte *f*; **at a l.** *(confused)* perplexe; **to sell sth at a l.** vendre qch à perte; **at a l. to do sth** *(unable)* incapable de faire qch; **to be at a l. (to know) what to say** ne savoir que dire; **to make a l.** *(financially)* perdre de l'argent

lost [lɒst] **1** *pt & pp of* **lose**

2 *adj* perdu; *Br* **l. property,** *Am* **l. and found** objets *mpl* trouvés

lot¹ [lɒt] *n (destiny)* sort *m*; *(batch)* lot *m*; *(plot of land)* terrain *m*; **to draw lots** tirer au sort

lot² [lɒt] *n* **the l.** *(everything)* (le) tout; **the l. of you** vous tous; **a l. of, lots of** beaucoup de; **a l.** beaucoup; **quite a l.** pas mal (**of** de); **such a l.** tellement (**of** de); **what a l. of flowers/water!** regarde toutes ces fleurs/toute cette eau!; **what a l. of flowers you have!** que vous avez de fleurs!; *Br Fam* **a bad l.** *(person)* un sale type; *Fam* **listen, you l.!** écoutez, vous tous!

lotion ['ləʊʃən] *n* lotion *f*

lottery ['lɒtərɪ] *(pl -ies)* *n* loterie *f*; **l. ticket** billet *m* de loterie

lotto ['lɒtəʊ] *n* loto *m*

loud [laʊd] **1** (**-er, -est**) *adj (voice, music)* fort; *(noise, cry)* grand; *(laugh)* gros (*f* grosse); *(gaudy)* voyant; **the radio is too l.** la radio est trop forte

2 *adv (shout)* fort; **out l.** tout haut •**loud-'hailer** *n Br* mégaphone *m* •**loudly** *adv (speak, laugh, shout)* fort •**loudmouth** *n Fam (person)* grande gueule *f* •**loudness** *n (of noise, music, voice)* volume *m* •**loud'speaker** *n* haut-parleur *m*; *(for speaking to crowd)* porte-voix *m inv*; *(of stereo system)* enceinte *f*

lounge [laʊndʒ] **1** *n (in house, hotel)* salon *m*; **airport l.** salle *f* d'aéroport; *Br* **l. suit** complet-veston *m*

2 *vi (loll in armchair)* se prélasser; **to l. about** *(idle)* paresser; *(stroll)* flâner

louse [laʊs] **1** *n* (**a**) *(pl* **lice**) *(insect)* pou *m* (**b**) *(pl* **louses**) *Fam (person)* salaud *m*

2 *vt Fam* **to l. sth up** *(spoil)* foutre qch en l'air

lousy ['laʊzɪ] (**-ier, -iest**) *adj Fam (bad)* nul (*f* nulle); *(food, weather)* dégueulasse; **to feel l.** être mal fichu; **l. with** *(crammed, loaded)* bourré de

lout [laʊt] *n* voyou *m* (*pl* -ous) • **loutish** *adj* (*attitude*) de voyou

lovable ['lʌvəbəl] *adj* attachant

love [lʌv] **1** *n* (**a**) (*feeling*) amour *m*; **in l.** amoureux, -euse (**with** de); **they're in l.** ils s'aiment; **art is their l.** l'art est leur passion; **yes, my l.** oui mon amour; *Fam* **yes, l.!** oui monsieur/madame!; **give him/her my l.** (*greeting*) dis-lui bien des choses de ma part; **l. affair** liaison *f*; **l. life** vie *f* sentimentale (**b**) *Tennis* rien *m*; **15 l.** 15 à rien

2 *vt* (*person*) aimer; (*thing, activity*) adorer (**to do** *or* **doing** faire) • **loving** *adj* affectueux, -ueuse

lovely ['lʌvlɪ] (**-ier, -iest**) *adj* (*idea, smell*) très bon (*f* bonne); (*weather*) beau (*f* belle); (*pretty*) joli; (*charming*) charmant; (*kind*) gentil, -ille; **the weather's l.** il fait beau; **l. to see you!** je suis ravi de te voir!; **l. and warm/dry** bien chaud/sec (*f* sèche)

lover ['lʌvə(r)] *n* (*man*) amant *m*; (*woman*) maîtresse *f*; **a l. of music/art** un amateur de musique/d'art; **a nature l.** un amoureux de la nature

lovesick ['lʌvsɪk] *adj* amoureux, -euse

low¹ [ləʊ] **1** (**-er, -est**) *adj* bas (*f* basse); (*speed, income, intelligence*) faible; (*opinion, quality*) mauvais; **she's l. on** (*money*) elle n'a plus beaucoup de; **to feel l.** (*depressed*) être déprimé; **in a l. voice** à voix basse; **lower** inférieur; **the lower middle class** la petite bourgeoisie

2 (**-er, -est**) *adv* bas; **to turn (down) l.** mettre plus bas; **to run l.** (*of supplies*) s'épuiser

3 *n Met* dépression *f*; *Fig* **to reach a new l.** *or* **an all-time l.** (*of prices*) atteindre leur niveau le plus bas • **low 'beams** *npl Am* (*of vehicle*) codes *mpl* • **'low-'calorie** *adj* (*diet*) (à) basses calories • **'low-'cost** *adj* bon marché *inv* • **'low-'cut** *adj* décolleté • **lowdown** *n Fam* (*facts*) tuyaux *mpl* • **low-down** *adj* méprisable • **'low-'fat** *adj* (*milk*) écrémé; (*cheese*) allégé • **low-'key** *adj* (*discreet*) discret, -ète • **lowland(s)** *n* basses terres *fpl* • **'low-'level** *adj* bas (*f* basse) • **'low-'lying** *adj* (*region*) bas (*f* basse) • **'low-'paid** *adj* mal payé • **'low-'salt** *adj* (*food*) à faible teneur en sel

low² [ləʊ] *vi* (*of cattle*) meugler

lower ['ləʊə(r)] *vt* baisser; **to l. sb/sth** (*by rope*) descendre qn/qch; *Fig* **to l. oneself** s'abaisser • **lowering** *n* (*drop*) baisse *f*

lowly ['ləʊlɪ] (**-ier, -iest**) *adj* humble

lox [lɒks] *n Am* saumon *m* fumé

loyal ['lɔɪəl] *adj* loyal (**to** envers) • **loyalty** *n* loyauté *f*

lozenge ['lɒzɪndʒ] *n* (*tablet*) pastille *f*; (*shape*) losange *m*

LP [el'piː] (*abbr* **long-playing record**) *n* 33 tours *m inv*

Ltd (*abbr* **Limited**) *Br Com* ≃ SARL

lubricate ['luːbrɪkeɪt] *vt* lubrifier; (*machine, car wheels*) graisser • **lubricant** *n* lubrifiant *m* • **lubri'cation** *n* (*of machine*) graissage *m*

lucid ['luːsɪd] *adj* lucide

luck [lʌk] *n* (*chance*) chance *f*; (*good fortune*) (bonne) chance, bonheur *m*; **to be in l.** avoir de la chance; **to be out of l.** ne pas avoir de chance; **to wish sb l.** souhaiter bonne chance à qn; **to try one's l.** tenter sa chance; **bad l.** malchance *f*; **hard l.!, tough l.!** pas de chance!; **just my l.!** c'est bien ma chance!; **worse l.** (*unfortunately*) malheureusement

luckily ['lʌkɪlɪ] *adv* heureusement

lucky ['lʌkɪ] (**-ier, -iest**) *adj* (*person*) chanceux, -euse; **to be l.** (*of person*) avoir de la chance; **to make a l. guess** tomber juste; **to strike it l.** décrocher le gros lot; **it's l. that...** c'est une chance que... (+ *subjunctive*); **I've had a l. day** j'ai eu de la chance aujourd'hui; **l. charm** porte-bonheur *m inv*; **l. number** chiffre *m* porte-bonheur; *Fam* **l. devil** veinard, -arde *mf*; **how l.!** quelle chance!

lucrative ['luːkrətɪv] *adj* lucratif, -ive

ludicrous ['luːdɪkrəs] *adj* ridicule

lug [lʌg] (*pt & pp* **-gg-**) *vt Fam* **to l. sth (around)** trimbaler qch

luggage ['lʌgɪdʒ] *n* bagages *mpl*; **a piece of l.** un bagage; **hand l.** bagages à main; **l. compartment** compartiment *m* à bagages; *Br* **l. van** (*on train*) fourgon *m*

lugubrious [luːˈguːbrɪəs] *adj* lugubre

lukewarm ['luːkwɔːm] *adj* tiède

lull [lʌl] **1** *n* arrêt *m*; (*in storm*) accalmie *f*

2 *vt* apaiser; **to l. sb to sleep** endormir qn en le/la berçant; **to l. sb into a false sense of security** endormir la méfiance de qn

lullaby ['lʌləbaɪ] (*pl* **-ies**) *n* berceuse *f*

lumbago [lʌmˈbeɪgəʊ] *n* lumbago *m*

lumber¹ ['lʌmbə(r)] *n* (*timber*) bois *m* de charpente; *Br* (*junk*) bric-à-brac *m inv* • **lumberjack** *n* bûcheron *m* • **lumberroom** *n Br* débarras *m*

lumber² ['lʌmbə(r)] *vt Br Fam* **to l. sb with sb/sth** coller qn/qch à qn; **he got lumbered with the job** il s'est appuyé la corvée

luminous ['luːmɪnəs] *adj (colour, paper, ink)* fluorescent; *(dial, clock)* lumineux, -euse

lump [lʌmp] **1** *n* morceau *m*; *(in soup)* grumeau *m*; *(bump)* bosse *f*; *(swelling)* grosseur *f*; **l. sum** somme *f* forfaitaire
   2 *vt* **to l. together** réunir; *Fig & Pej* mettre dans le même sac ● **lumpy** (**-ier, -iest**) *adj (soup)* grumeleux, -euse; *(surface)* bosselé

lunacy ['luːnəsɪ] *n* folie *f*; **it's (sheer) l.** c'est de la folie

lunar ['luːnə(r)] *adj* lunaire; **l. eclipse** éclipse *f* de lune; **l. module** module *m* lunaire

lunatic ['luːnətɪk] **1** *adj* fou (*f* folle)
   2 *n* fou *m*, folle *f*

> *Note that the French word* **lunatique** *is a false friend and is never a translation for the English word* **lunatic**. *It means* **moody**.

lunch [lʌntʃ] **1** *n* déjeuner *m*; **to have l.** déjeuner; **l. break, l. hour, l. time** heure *f* du déjeuner
   2 *vi* déjeuner (**on** *or* **off** de) ● **lunchbox** *n* = boîte dans laquelle on transporte son déjeuner

luncheon ['lʌnʃən] *n* déjeuner *m*; **l. meat** = tranches de viande à base de porc; *Br* **l. voucher** chèque-restaurant *m*

lung [lʌŋ] *n* poumon *m*; **l. cancer** cancer *m* du poumon

lunge [lʌndʒ] **1** *n* mouvement *m* brusque en avant
   2 *vi* **to l. at sb** se ruer sur qn

lurch [lɜːtʃ] **1** *n Fam* **to leave sb in the l.** laisser qn dans le pétrin
   2 *vi (of person)* tituber; *(of ship, car)* faire une embardée

lure [lʊə(r)] **1** *n (attraction)* attrait *m*
   2 *vt* attirer (par la ruse) (**into** dans)

lurid ['lʊərɪd] *adj (story, description)* cru; *(gaudy)* voyant

lurk [lɜːk] *vi (hide)* être tapi (**in** dans); *(prowl)* rôder; *(of suspicion, fear)* subsister

luscious ['lʌʃəs] *adj (food)* appétissant

lush [lʌʃ] **1** *adj (vegetation)* luxuriant; *(wealthy) (surroundings)* luxueux, -ueuse
   2 *n Fam (drunkard)* poivrot, -ote *mf*

lust [lʌst] **1** *n (for person)* désir *m*; *(for object)* convoitise *f* (**for** de); *(for power, knowledge)* soif *f* (**for** de)
   2 *vi* **to l. after** *(object, person)* convoiter; *(power, knowledge)* avoir soif de

lustre ['lʌstə(r)] (*Am* **luster**) *n (gloss)* lustre *m*

lusty ['lʌstɪ] (**-ier, -iest**) *adj* vigoureux, -euse

lute [luːt] *n* luth *m*

Luxembourg ['lʌksəmbɜːg] *n* le Luxembourg

luxuriant [lʌgˈʒʊərɪənt] *adj* luxuriant

luxuriate [lʌgˈʒʊərɪeɪt] *vi (laze about)* paresser

luxury ['lʌkʃərɪ] **1** *n* luxe *m*
   2 *adj (goods, car, home)* de luxe ● **luxurious** [lʌgˈʒʊərɪəs] *adj* luxueux, -ueuse

> *Note that the French word* **luxure** *is a false friend and is never a translation for the English word* **luxury**. *It means* **lust**.

lychee ['laɪtʃiː] *n* litchi *m*

lying ['laɪɪŋ] **1** *pres p of* **lie**[1,2]
   2 *n* mensonges *mpl*
   3 *adj (person)* menteur, -euse

lynch [lɪntʃ] *vt* lyncher ● **lynching** *n* lynchage *m*

lynx [lɪŋks] *n* lynx *m*

lyre ['laɪə(r)] *n* lyre *f*

lyric ['lɪrɪk] *adj* lyrique ● **lyrical** *adj (person) (effusive)* lyrique ● **lyricism** *n* lyrisme *m* ● **lyrics** *npl (of song)* paroles *fpl*

M

M, m [em] *n (letter)* M, m *m inv*
m (**a**) (*abbr* **metre**) mètre *m* (**b**) (*abbr* **mile**) mile *m*
MA (*abbr* **Master of Arts**) *n Univ* **to have an MA in French** ≃ avoir une maîtrise de français; **John Smith MA** John Smith, titulaire d'une maîtrise (*en lettres, anglais, droit etc*)
ma'am [mæm] *n* madame *f*
mac [mæk] *n Br Fam (raincoat)* imper *m*
macabre [mə'kɑːbrə] *adj* macabre
macaroni [mækə'rəʊnɪ] *n* macaronis *mpl*; *Br* **m. cheese** macaronis au gratin
macaroon [mækə'ruːn] *n* macaron *m*
mace [meɪs] *n (staff, rod)* masse *f*
machinations [mækɪ'neɪʃənz] *npl* machinations *fpl*
machine [mə'ʃiːn] *n (apparatus, car, system)* machine *f*; **change/cash m.** distributeur *m* de monnaie/billets; *Comptr* **m. code** code *m* machine; **m. gun** mitrailleuse *f*
machine-gun [mə'ʃiːngʌn] (*pt & pp* **-nn-**) *vt* mitrailler
machinery [mə'ʃiːnərɪ] *n (machines)* machines *fpl*; *(works)* mécanisme *m*; *Fig (of organization)* rouages *mpl*
machinist [mə'ʃiːnɪst] *n Br (on sewing machine)* piqueur, -euse *mf*
macho ['mætʃəʊ] (*pl* **-os**) *adj & n* macho *(m) inv*
mackerel ['mækrəl] *n* maquereau *m*
mackintosh ['mækɪntɒʃ] *n Br* imperméable *m*
macro ['mækrəʊ] (*pl* **-os**) *n Comptr* macrocommande *f*
mad [mæd] (**madder, maddest**) *adj* fou (*f* folle); **to go m.** devenir fou; **to be m. at sb** être furieux, -ieuse contre qn; *Fam* **to be m. about** *or* **m. keen on sb/sth** être fou de qn/qch; **to drive sb m.** rendre qn fou; *Fam* **to run/work like m.** courir/travailler comme un fou; *Med* **m. cow disease** maladie *f* de la vache folle; **m. dog** chien *m* enragé •**madhouse** *n Fam* maison *f* de fous •**madly** *adv (insanely, desperately)* comme un fou/une folle; *Fam (exciting, interested, jealous)* follement •**madman** (*pl* **-men**) *n* fou *m* •**madness** *n* folie *f* •**madwoman** (*pl* **-women**) *n* folle *f*

Madagascar [mædə'gæskə(r)] *n* Madagascar *f*
madam ['mædəm] *n (married)* madame *f*; *(unmarried)* mademoiselle *f*
maddening ['mædənɪŋ] *adj* exaspérant
made [meɪd] *pt & pp of* **make** •**made-to-'measure** *adj Br (garment)* (fait) sur mesure
Madeira [mə'dɪərə] *n (island)* Madère *f*; *(wine)* madère *m*
madonna [mə'dɒnə] *n Rel* madone *f*
maestro ['maɪstrəʊ] (*pl* **-os**) *n* maestro *m*
Mafia ['mæfɪə] *n* **the M.** la Mafia
magazine [mægə'ziːn] *n* (**a**) *(periodical, TV/radio broadcast)* magazine *m* (**b**) *(of gun, slide projector)* magasin *m*
maggot ['mægət] *n* asticot *m*
magic ['mædʒɪk] **1** *adj* magique; **m. spell** sort *m*; **the m. word** la formule magique **2** *n* magie *f*; **as if by m.** comme par enchantement •**magical** *adj* magique •**magician** [mə'dʒɪʃən] *n* magicien, -ienne *mf*
magistrate ['mædʒɪstreɪt] *n* magistrat *m*
magnanimous [mæg'nænɪməs] *adj* magnanime
magnate ['mægneɪt] *n* magnat *m*
magnesium [mæg'niːzɪəm] *n Chem* magnésium *m*
magnet ['mægnɪt] *n* aimant *m* •**magnetic** [-'netɪk] *adj* magnétique; **m. tape** bande *f* magnétique •**magnetism** *n* magnétisme *m* •**magnetize** *vt* magnétiser
magnificent [mæg'nɪfɪsənt] *adj* magnifique •**magnificence** *n* magnificence *f* •**magnificently** *adv* magnifiquement
magnify ['mægnɪfaɪ] (*pt & pp* **-ied**) *vt (image)* grossir; *(sound)* amplifier; *Fig (exaggerate)* exagérer; **magnifying glass** loupe *f* •**magnification** [-fɪ'keɪʃən] *n* grossissement *m*; *(of sound)* amplification *f*
magnitude ['mægnɪtjuːd] *n* ampleur *f*
magnolia [mæg'nəʊlɪə] *n (tree)* magnolia *m*
magpie ['mægpaɪ] *n* pie *f*
mahogany [mə'hɒgənɪ] *n (wood, colour)* acajou *m*
maid [meɪd] *n (servant)* bonne *f*; *Am* **m. of**

honor *(at wedding)* première demoiselle
f d'honneur

maiden ['meɪdən] **1** *n Old-fashioned*
jeune fille f

2 *adj (flight, voyage)* inaugural; **m. name**
nom *m* de jeune fille; **m. speech** *(of MP)*
premier discours *m*

mail [meɪl] **1** *n (system)* poste f; *(letters)*
courrier *m*; *(e-mails)* méls *mpl*, courrier *m*
électronique

2 *adj (bag, train)* postal; **m. order** vente f
par correspondance; *Br* **m. van** *(vehicle)*
camion *m* des postes; *(in train)* fourgon *m*
postal

3 *vt* poster; **mailing list** liste f d'adresses
• **mailbox** *n Am & Comptr* boîte f aux
lettres • **mailman** *(pl* **-men)** *n Am* facteur
m

maim [meɪm] *vt* mutiler

main¹ [meɪn] *adj* principal; **the m. thing
is to** l'essentiel est de; **in the m.** *(generally)* en gros; **m. course** plat *m* de résistance; *Rail* **m. line** grande ligne f; **m. road**
grande route f; *Fam* **m. squeeze** petit ami
m, petite amie f • **mainframe** *n* **m. (computer)** ordinateur *m* central • **mainland** *n*
continent *m* • **mainly** *adv* principalement; **they were m. Spanish** la plupart
étaient espagnols • **mainstream** *n* tendance f dominante

main² [meɪn] *n* **water/gas m.** conduite f
d'eau/de gaz; **the mains** *(electricity)* le
secteur

mainstay ['meɪnsteɪ] *n (of family)* soutien
m; *(of organization, policy)* pilier *m*

maintain [meɪn'teɪn] *vt (continue)* maintenir; *(machine, road)* entretenir; *(family)*
subvenir aux besoins de; *(silence)* garder;
to m. law and order faire respecter l'ordre
public; **to m. that...** affirmer que...
• **maintenance** ['meɪntənəns] *n (of vehicle, road)* entretien *m*; *(of tradition,
prices, position)* maintien *m*; *Law (alimony)* pension f alimentaire

maisonette [meɪzə'net] *n Br* duplex *m*

maître d' [metrə'diː] *n Am (in restaurant)*
maître *m* d'hôtel

maize [meɪz] *n Br* maïs *m*

majesty ['mædʒəstɪ] *n* majesté f; **Your M.**
Votre Majesté • **majestic** [mə'dʒestɪk] *adj*
majestueux, -ueuse

major ['meɪdʒə(r)] **1** *adj (main, great) &
Mus* majeur; *(accident)* très grave; **a m.
road** une grande route

2 *n* **(a)** *(officer)* commandant *m* **(b)** *Am
Univ (subject of study)* dominante f

3 *vi Am Univ* **to m. in** se spécialiser en

Majorca [mə'jɔːkə] *n* Majorque f

majorette [meɪdʒə'ret] *n* **(drum) m.** majorette f

majority [mə'dʒɒrɪtɪ] **1** *(pl* **-ies)** *n* majorité f **(of** de); **to be in the** *or* **a m.** être
majoritaire; **the m. of people** la plupart
des gens

2 *adj (vote)* majoritaire

make [meɪk] **1** *(pt & pp* **made)** *vt* faire;
(tool, vehicle) fabriquer; **to m. a decision**
prendre une décision; **to m. sb happy/
sad** rendre qn heureux/triste; **to m. sb
tired** fatiguer qn; **to m. sth ready** préparer qch; **to m. sth yellow** jaunir qch; **to m.
sb do sth** faire faire qch à qn; **to m.
oneself heard** se faire entendre; **she
made him her husband** elle en a fait son
mari; **he'll m. a good doctor** il fera un bon
médecin; *Fam* **to m. it** *(succeed)* réussir;
sorry I can't m. it to the meeting désolé,
je ne pourrai pas assister à la réunion;
what time do you m. it? quelle heure
avez-vous?; **I m. it five o'clock** j'ai cinq
heures; **what do you m. of it?** qu'en
penses-tu?; **I can't m. anything of it** je
n'y comprends rien; **m. my day!** fais-moi
plaisir!; *Fam* **she made the train** *(did not
miss)* elle a eu le train; **he made 10 euros
on it** ça lui a rapporté 10 euros; **to m.
good** réussir; **to m. good a loss** compenser une perte; **to m. good the damage**
réparer les dégâts; **to m. light of sth**
prendre qch à la légère; **to be made of
wood** être en bois; **made in France** fa-
briqué en France

2 *vi* **to m. sure** *or* **certain of sth** s'assurer
de qch; **to m. do** *(manage)* se débrouiller
(**with** avec); **to m. do with sb/sth** *(be
satisfied with)* se contenter de qn/qch;
to m. as if to do sth *(appear to)* faire mine
de faire qch; **to m. believe** *(pretend)* faire
semblant; **to m. believe that one is** faire
semblant d'être

3 *n (brand)* marque f; **of French m.** de
fabrication française • **make-believe** *n* **it's
m.** *(story)* c'est pure invention; **to live in a
world of m.** se bercer d'illusions • **make-up**
n (for face) maquillage *m*; *(of team, group)*
constitution f; *(of person)* caractère *m*; **to
wear m.** se maquiller; **m. artist** maquilleur,
-euse *mf*; **m. bag** trousse f de maquillage

▸ **make for** *vt insep (go towards)* aller vers

▸ **make off** *vi Fam (leave)* filer ▸ **make out 1**
vt sep (see, hear) distinguer; *(understand)*
comprendre; *(decipher)* déchiffrer;
(cheque, list) faire; *Fam* **to m. out that...**
(claim) prétendre que...; **you made me
out to be stupid** tu m'as fait passer pour

un idiot 2 *vi Fam (manage)* se débrouiller
▸**make over** *vt sep (transfer)* céder (**to** à);
(change, convert) transformer (**into** en)
▸**make up 1** *vt sep (story)* inventer; *(put together) (list, collection, bed)* faire; *(prepare) (form)* préparer; *(form)* former, composer; *(loss)* compenser; *(quantity)* compléter; *(quarrel)* régler; **to m. oneself up** se maquiller **2** *vi (of friends)* se réconcilier; **to m. up for** *(loss, damage, fault)* compenser; *(lost time, mistake)* rattraper

maker ['meɪkə(r)] *n (of product)* fabricant, -ante *mf*

makeshift ['meɪkʃɪft] *adj (arrangement, building)* de fortune

making ['meɪkɪŋ] *n (manufacture)* fabrication *f*; *(of dress)* confection *f*; **history in the m.** l'histoire en train de se faire; **the film was three years in the m.** le tournage du film a duré trois ans; **she has the makings of a pianist** elle a tout ce qu'il faut pour devenir pianiste

maladjusted [mælə'dʒʌstɪd] *adj* inadapté

malaise [mæ'leɪz] *n* malaise *m*

malaria [mə'leərɪə] *n Med* malaria *f*

Malaysia [mə'leɪzɪə] *n* la Malaisie

male [meɪl] **1** *adj (child, animal, hormone)* mâle; *(clothes, sex)* masculin; **m. nurse** infirmier *m*
2 *n (person)* homme *m*; *(animal)* mâle *m*

malevolent [mə'levələnt] *adj* malveillant ● **malevolence** *n* malveillance *f*

malfunction [mæl'fʌŋkʃən] **1** *n* mauvais fonctionnement *m*
2 *vi* fonctionner mal

malice ['mælɪs] *n* méchanceté *f*; **to bear sb m.** vouloir du mal à qn ● **malicious** [mə'lɪʃəs] *adj* malveillant; *Law* **m. damage** dommage *m* causé avec intention de nuire ● **maliciously** [mə'lɪʃəslɪ] *adv* avec malveillance

> *𝒍* Note that the French words **malice** and **malicieux** are false friends and are never translations for the English words **malice** and **malicious**. They mean respectively **mischief** and **mischievous**.

malign [mə'laɪn] *vt* calomnier; **much maligned** très dénigré

malignant [mə'lɪgnənt] *adj (person)* malveillant; **m. tumour** *or* **growth** tumeur *f* maligne

malingerer [mə'lɪŋgərə(r)] *n* simulateur, -trice *mf*

mall [mɔːl] *n Am* **(shopping) m.** centre *m* commercial

malleable ['mælɪəbəl] *adj* malléable

mallet ['mælɪt] *n* maillet *m*

malnutrition [mælnjuː'trɪʃən] *n* malnutrition *f*

malpractice [mæl'præktɪs] *n* faute *f* professionnelle

malt [mɔːlt] *n* malt *m*; **m. vinegar** vinaigre *m* de malt

Malta ['mɔːltə] *n* Malte *f* ● **Mal'tese 1** *adj* maltais **2** *n* Maltais, -aise *mf*

mammal ['mæməl] *n* mammifère *m*

mammoth ['mæməθ] **1** *adj (huge)* gigantesque
2 *n (animal)* mammouth *m*

man [mæn] **1** *(pl* **men)** *n (adult male)* homme *m*; *(player in sports team)* joueur *m*; *(humanity)* l'homme; *Chess* pièce *f*; **the m. in the street** l'homme de la rue; **a m.'s jacket** une veste d'homme; **a m. of God** un homme d'église; **a m. of the world** un homme d'expérience; **he's a Bristol m.** *(by birth)* il est de Bristol; **to be m. and wife** être mari et femme; **he took it like a m.** il a pris ça courageusement; *Fam* **my old m.** *(father)* mon père; *(husband)* mon homme
2 *(pt & pp* **-nn-)** *vt (be on duty at)* être de service à; *(machine)* assurer le fonctionnement de; *(plane, ship)* être membre de l'équipage de; *(guns)* servir; **manned spacecraft** engin *m* spatial habité ● **manfully** *adv* vaillamment ● **manhood** *n (period)* âge *m* d'homme ● **manhunt** *n* chasse *f* à l'homme ● **manly** **(-ier, -iest)** *adj* viril ● **'man-'made** *adj (lake, beach)* artificiel, -ielle; *(fibre)* synthétique ● **manservant** *(pl* **menservants)** *n* domestique *m* ● **'man-to-'man** *adj & adv (discussion, discuss)* d'homme à homme

manacles ['mænɪkəlz] *npl* menottes *fpl*

manage ['mænɪdʒ] **1** *vt (company, project)* diriger; *(shop, hotel)* être le gérant de; *(economy, money, time, situation)* gérer; **to m. to do sth** *(succeed)* réussir *ou* arriver à faire qch; *(by being smart)* se débrouiller pour faire qch; **I'll m. it** j'y arriverai; **I can't m. three suitcases** je ne peux pas porter trois valises
2 *vi (succeed)* y arriver; *(make do)* se débrouiller (**with** avec); **to m. without sb/sth** se passer de qn/qch; **managing director** directeur *m* général ● **manageable** *adj (parcel, car)* maniable; *(hair)* facile à coiffer; *(task)* faisable ● **management** *n (running, managers)* direction *f*; *(of property, economy)* gestion *f*; *(executive staff)* cadres *mpl*

manager ['mænɪdʒə(r)] *n (of shop, company)* directeur, -trice *mf*; *(of shop, café)* gérant *m*; (**business**) **m.** *(of singer, boxer)* manager *m* • **manage'ress** *n* directrice *f*; *(of shop, café)* gérante *f*

managerial [mænə'dʒɪərɪəl] *adj* directorial; **m. job** poste *m* de direction; **the m. staff** les cadres *mpl*

mandarin ['mændərɪn] **1** *adj & n* **m.** (**orange**) mandarine *(f)*
2 *n Br (official)* mandarin *m*

mandate ['mændeɪt] *n* mandat *m*

mandatory ['mændətərɪ] *adj* obligatoire

mane [meɪn] *n* crinière *f*

maneuver [mə'nuːvər] *n & vti Am* = manoeuvre

mangle ['mæŋgəl] **1** *n (for clothes)* essoreuse *f*
2 *vt (body)* mutiler

mango ['mæŋgəʊ] *(pl* -oes *or* -os*) n* mangue *f*

mangy ['meɪndʒɪ] *adj (animal)* galeux, -euse

manhandle [mæn'hændəl] *vt (person)* malmener

manhole ['mænhəʊl] *n* bouche *f* d'égout; **m. cover** plaque *f* d'égout

mania ['meɪnɪə] *n (liking)* passion *f*; *(psychological)* manie *f*

maniac ['meɪnɪæk] *n* fou *m*, folle *f*

manic ['mænɪk] *adj Fig (person)* stressé; *(activity)* frénétique

manicure ['mænɪkjʊə(r)] **1** *n* manucure *f*
2 *vt* **to m. one's nails** se faire les ongles

manifest ['mænɪfest] **1** *adj (plain)* manifeste
2 *vt (show)* manifester

manifesto [mænɪ'festəʊ] *(pl* -os *or* -oes*) n Pol* manifeste *m*

manifold ['mænɪfəʊld] *adj Literary* multiple

manipulate [mə'nɪpjʊleɪt] *vt* manipuler • **manipu'lation** *n* manipulation *f*

mankind [mæn'kaɪnd] *n* l'humanité *f*

manner ['mænə(r)] *n (way)* manière *f*; *(behaviour)* comportement *m*; **manners** *(social habits)* manières *fpl*; **it's bad manners to stare** il est mal élevé de dévisager les gens; **in this m.** *(like this)* de cette manière; **all m. of people/things** toutes sortes de gens/choses; **to have good/ bad manners** être bien/mal élevé

mannered ['mænəd] *adj* maniéré

mannerism ['mænərɪzəm] *n Pej* tic *m*

manoeuvre [mə'nuːvə(r)] *(Am* **maneuver**) **1** *n* manœuvre *f*
2 *vti* manœuvrer • **manoeuvra'bility** *n (of vehicle)* maniabilité *f*

manor ['mænə(r)] *n Br* **m.** (**house**) manoir *m*

manpower ['mænpaʊə(r)] *n (labour)* main-d'œuvre *f*

mansion ['mænʃən] *n (in town)* hôtel *m* particulier; *(in country)* manoir *m*

manslaughter ['mænslɔːtə(r)] *n Law* homicide *m* involontaire

mantelpiece ['mæntəlpiːs] *n* dessus *m* de cheminée; **on the m.** sur la cheminée

manual ['mænjʊəl] **1** *adj (work, worker)* manuel, -uelle
2 *n (book)* manuel *m*

manufacture [mænjʊ'fæktʃə(r)] **1** *n* fabrication *f*; *(of cars)* construction *f*
2 *vt* fabriquer; *(cars)* construire • **manufacturer** *n* fabricant, -ante *mf*; *(of cars)* constructeur *m*

manure [mə'njʊə(r)] *n* fumier *m*

manuscript ['mænjʊskrɪpt] *n* manuscrit *m*

many ['menɪ] **1** *adj* beaucoup de; **m. people/things** beaucoup de gens/choses; **very m., a good** *or* **great m.** un très grand nombre de; (**a good** *or* **great**) **m. of,** (**very**) **m. of** un (très) grand nombre de; **m. times** bien des fois; **m. kinds** toutes sortes (**of** de); **how m.?** combien (de)?; **too m.** trop de; **there were so m. people that...** il y avait tant de monde que...; **as m. books as you like** autant de livres que tu veux
2 *pron* beaucoup; **m. came** beaucoup sont venus; **not m.** pas beaucoup; **too m.** trop; *Fam* **he's had one too m.** il a bu un coup de trop; **m. of them** beaucoup d'entre eux; **there are too m. of them** ils sont trop nombreux; **m. a time** bien des fois; **as m. as fifty** *(up to)* jusqu'à cinquante

map [mæp] **1** *n* carte *f*; *(plan of town, underground)* plan *m*
2 *(pt & pp* -pp-*) vt (country, town)* dresser une carte de; **to m. out** *(road)* tracer; *Fig (plan, programme)* élaborer

maple ['meɪpəl] *n (tree, wood)* érable *m*; **m. syrup** sirop *m* d'érable

mar [mɑː(r)] *(pt & pp* -rr-*) vt* gâcher

marathon ['mærəθən] *n* marathon *m*

maraud [mə'rɔːd] *vi* piller • **marauder** *n* maraudeur, -euse *mf* • **marauding** *adj* en maraude

marble ['mɑːbəl] *n (substance)* marbre *m*; *(toy ball)* bille *f*

March [mɑːtʃ] *n* mars *m*

march [mɑːtʃ] **1** *n* marche *f*
2 *vt* **to m. sb off to prison** emmener qn en prison
3 *vi (of soldiers, demonstrators)* défiler; *(walk in step)* marcher au pas; **to m. past** (**sb/sth**) défiler (devant qn/qch); *Fig* **to**

m. in/out entrer/sortir d'un pas décidé • **march past** n Br défilé m

marchioness ['mɑːʃənes] n (title) marquise f

mare [meə(r)] n jument f

margarine [mɑːdʒə'riːn] n margarine f

marge [mɑːdʒ] n Br Fam margarine f

margin ['mɑːdʒɪn] n (on page) marge f; Com marge bénéficiaire; **to win by a narrow m.** gagner de justesse; **m. of error** marge d'erreur • **marginal** adj marginal; (unimportant) négligeable; Br Pol **m. seat** siège m à majorité précaire • **marginally** adv très légèrement

marigold ['mærɪgəʊld] n souci m

marijuana [mærɪ'wɑːnə] n marijuana f

marina [mə'riːnə] n marina f

marinate ['mærɪneɪt] vti Culin (faire) mariner

marine [mə'riːn] **1** adj (life, flora) marin
2 n (soldier) fusilier m marin; Am marine m

marionette [mærɪə'net] n marionnette f

marital ['mærɪtəl] adj conjugal; **m. status** situation f de famille

maritime ['mærɪtaɪm] adj maritime

marjoram ['mɑːdʒərəm] n marjolaine f

mark¹ [mɑːk] **1** n (symbol) marque f; (stain, trace) tache f, marque; (token, sign) signe m; (in test, exam) note f; (target) but m; (model of machine, aircraft) série f; **as a m. of respect** en signe de respect; Fig **to make one's m.** (succeed) faire ses preuves; **she isn't up to the m.** elle n'est pas à la hauteur; **on your marks! get set! go!** à vos marques! prêts! partez!
2 vt marquer; (exam) noter; **to m. time** (of soldier) marquer le pas; Fig (wait) piétiner; Br **m. you...!** remarquez que...!; **m. my words** notez bien ce que je vais dire; **to m. a price down** baisser un prix; **to m. sth off** (separate qch); (on list) cocher qch; **to m. sb out** distinguer qn; **to m. sb out for promotion** désigner qn pour obtenir une promotion; **to m. a price up** augmenter un prix

mark² [mɑːk] n (currency) mark m

marked [mɑːkt] adj (noticeable) marqué • **markedly** [-ɪdlɪ] adv visiblement

marker ['mɑːkə(r)] n (pen) marqueur m; (flag) balise f; (bookmark) signet m; (person) correcteur, -trice mf

market ['mɑːkɪt] **1** n marché m; **to put sth on the m.** mettre qch en vente; **on the open m.** en vente libre; **on the black m.** au marché noir; **(free) m. economy** économie f de marché; Br **m. garden** jardin m maraîcher; Br **m. gardener** maraîcher,

-ère mf; **m. price** prix m courant; **m. share** part f de marché; **m. survey** étude f de marché; **m. value** valeur f marchande
2 vt commercialiser • **marketable** adj commercialisable • **marketing** n marketing m, mercatique f • **marketplace** n (in village, town) place f du marché; Econ marché m; **in the m.** sur le marché

markings ['mɑːkɪŋz] npl (on animal) taches fpl; (on road) signalisation f horizontale

marksman ['mɑːksmən] (pl **-men**) n tireur m d'élite

marmalade ['mɑːməleɪd] n confiture f d'oranges

maroon [mə'ruːn] adj (colour) bordeaux inv

marooned [mə'ruːnd] adj abandonné; (in snowstorm) bloqué (**by** par)

marquee [mɑː'kiː] n grande f tente; (at circus) chapiteau m; Am (awning) marquise f

marquis ['mɑːkwɪs] n marquis m

marriage ['mærɪdʒ] n mariage m; **to be related by m. to sb** être parent par alliance de qn; **m. bureau** agence f matrimoniale; **m. certificate** extrait m d'acte de mariage • **marriageable** adj en état de se marier

marrow ['mærəʊ] n (**a**) (of bone) moelle f (**b**) Br (vegetable) courge f

marry ['mærɪ] **1** (pt & pp **-ied**) vt épouser, se marier avec; **to m. sb (off)** (of priest) marier qn
2 vi se marier • **married** adj marié; **m. life** vie f maritale; **m. name** nom m de femme mariée; **to get m.** se marier

marsh [mɑːʃ] n marais m, marécage m • **marshland** n marécages mpl

marshal ['mɑːʃəl] **1** n (army officer) maréchal m; Br (at public event) membre m du service d'ordre
2 (Br **-ll-**, Am **-l-**) vt (troops, vehicles) rassembler; (crowd) canaliser

marshmallow [mɑːʃ'mæləʊ] n guimauve f

martial ['mɑːʃəl] adj martial; **m. arts** arts mpl martiaux; **m. law** loi f martiale

Martian ['mɑːʃən] n & adj martien, -ienne (mf)

martyr ['mɑːtə(r)] **1** n martyr, -yre mf
2 vt martyriser • **martyrdom** n martyre m

marvel ['mɑːvəl] **1** n (wonder) merveille f; **it's a m. they survived** c'est un miracle qu'ils aient survécu
2 (Br **-ll-**, Am **-l-**) vi s'émerveiller (**at** de)

marvellous ['mɑːvələs] (Am **marvelous**) adj merveilleux, -euse

Marxism ['mɑːksɪzəm] *n* marxisme *m*
• **Marxist** *adj & n* marxiste *(mf)*
marzipan ['mɑːzɪpæn] *n* pâte *f* d'amandes
mascara [mæ'skɑːrə] *n* mascara *m*
mascot ['mæskɒt] *n* mascotte *f*
masculine ['mæskjʊlɪn] *adj* masculin
• **mascu'linity** *n* masculinité *f*
mash [mæʃ] **1** *n Br (potatoes)* purée *f* (de pommes de terre); *(for poultry, pigs)* pâtée *f*
   2 *vt* **to m. (up)** *(vegetables)* écraser (en purée); **mashed potatoes** purée *f* de pommes de terre
mask [mɑːsk] **1** *n* masque *m*
   2 *vt (cover, hide)* masquer (**from** à)
masochism ['mæsəkɪzəm] *n* masochisme *m* • **masochist** *n* masochiste *mf*
• **maso'chistic** *adj* masochiste
mason ['meɪsən] *n (stonemason, Freemason)* maçon *m* • **masonry** *n* maçonnerie *f*
masquerade [mɑːskə'reɪd] **1** *n (gathering, disguise)* mascarade *f*
   2 *vi* **to m. as sb** se faire passer pour qn
mass¹ [mæs] **1** *n Phys & (shapeless substance)* masse *f*; **a m. of** *(many)* une multitude de; *Fam* **I've got masses of things to do** j'ai des tas de choses à faire; *Fam* **there's masses of room** il y a plein de place; *Pol* **the masses** le peuple
   2 *adj (demonstration, culture)* de masse; *(protests, departure)* en masse; *(unemployment, destruction)* massif, -ive; **m. grave** charnier *m*; **m. hysteria** hystérie *f* collective; **m. media** mass media *mpl*; **m. murderer** tueur *m* fou; **m. production** production *f* en série
   3 *vi (of troops, people)* se masser • **mass-pro'duce** *vt* fabriquer en série
mass² [mæs] *n (church service)* messe *f*
massacre ['mæsəkə(r)] **1** *n* massacre *m*
   2 *vt* massacrer
massage ['mæsɑːʒ] **1** *n* massage *m*
   2 *vt* masser; *Fig* **to m. the figures** manipuler les chiffres • **masseur** *n* masseur [-'sɜː(r)] *m* • **masseuse** [-'sɜːz] *n* masseuse *f*
massive ['mæsɪv] *adj (increase, dose, vote)* massif, -ive; *(amount, building)* énorme; *(heart attack)* foudroyant • **massively** *adv (increase, reduce)* considérablement
mast [mɑːst] *n (of ship)* mât *m*; *(for TV, radio)* pylône *m*
master ['mɑːstə(r)] **1** *n* maître *m*; *Br (teacher)* professeur *m*; **old m.** *(painting)* tableau *m* de maître; **I'm my own m.** je ne

dépends que de moi; *Univ* **m.'s degree** maîtrise *f* (**in** de); **M. of Arts/Science** *(qualification)* ≃ maîtrise ès lettres/ sciences; *(person)* ≃ maître *mf* ès lettres/sciences; *Am* **m. of ceremonies** *(presenter)* animateur, -trice *mf*; **m. card** carte *f* maîtresse; **m. copy** original *m*; **m. key** passe-partout *m inv*; **m. plan** plan *m* d'action
   2 *vt* maîtriser; *(subject, situation)* dominer • **masterstroke** *n* coup *m* de maître
masterly ['mɑːstəlɪ] *adj* magistral
mastermind ['mɑːstəmaɪnd] **1** *n (person)* cerveau *m*
   2 *vt* organiser
masterpiece ['mɑːstəpiːs] *n* chef-d'œuvre *m*
mastery ['mɑːstərɪ] *n* maîtrise *f* (**of** de)
mastic ['mæstɪk] *n (filler, seal)* mastic *m*
masturbate ['mæstəbeɪt] *vi* se masturber • **mastur'bation** *n* masturbation *f*
mat [mæt] *n* tapis *m*; *(of straw)* natte *f*; *(at door)* paillasson *m*; **(table) m.** *(for plates)* set *m* de table; *(for dishes)* dessous-de-plat *m inv*
match¹ [mætʃ] *n (for lighting fire, cigarette)* allumette *f* • **matchbox** *n* boîte *f* d'allumettes • **matchstick** *n* allumette *f*
match² [mætʃ] *n (in sport)* match *m*; **m. point** *(in tennis)* balle *f* de match
match³ [mætʃ] **1** *n (equal)* égal, -ale *mf*; *(marriage)* mariage *m*; **to be a good m.** *(of colours, people)* aller bien ensemble; **he's a good m.** *(man to marry)* c'est un bon parti; **to meet one's m.** trouver son maître
   2 *vt (of clothes, colour)* être assorti à; *(coordinate)* assortir; *(equal)* égaler; **to m. up** *(colours, clothes, plates)* assortir; **to m. (up to)** *(equal)* égaler; **to m. up to sb's expectations** répondre à l'attente de qn
   3 *vi (of colours, clothes)* être assortis, -ies • **matching** *adj* assorti
mate¹ [meɪt] **1** *n (of animal)* mâle *m*/ femelle *f*; *Br (friend)* copain *m*, copine *f*; *Br* **builder's/electrician's m.** aide-maçon/-électricien *m*
   2 *vi (of animals)* s'accoupler (**with** avec)
mate² [meɪt] *Chess* **1** *n* mat *m*
   2 *vt* mettre mat
material [mə'tɪərɪəl] **1** *adj (needs, world)* matériel, -ielle; *(important)* essentiel, -ielle
   2 *n (substance)* matière *f*; *(cloth)* tissu *m*; *(for book)* matériaux *mpl*; **material(s)** *(equipment)* matériel *m*; **building materials** matériaux de construction; **reading m.** de quoi lire • **materialism** *n* matéria-

lisme *m* • **materialist** *n* matérialiste *mf*
• **materia'listic** *adj* matérialiste • **materially** *adv* matériellement
materialize [mə'tɪərɪəlaɪz] *vi* se matérialiser; *(of hope, threat)* se réaliser; *(of
event)* avoir lieu
maternal [mə'tɜːnəl] *adj* maternel, -elle
maternity [mə'tɜːnətɪ] *n* maternité *f*; *Br*
m. allowance *or* **benefit** allocation *f* de
maternité; **m. dress** robe *f* de grossesse;
m. hospital, m. unit maternité; **m. leave**
congé *m* de maternité
mathematical [mæθə'mætɪkəl] *adj* mathématique
mathematician [mæθəmə'tɪʃən] *n* mathématicien, -ienne *mf*
mathematics [mæθə'mætɪks] *n (subject)*
mathématiques *fpl*; *(calculations)* calculs
mpl • **maths** (*Am* **math**) *n Fam* maths *fpl*
matinée ['mætɪneɪ] *n (of play, film)* matinée *f*
matriculation [mətrɪkjʊ'leɪʃən] *n Univ*
inscription *f*
matrimony ['mætrɪmənɪ] *n* mariage *m*
• **matrimonial** [-'məʊnɪəl] *adj* matrimonial
matrix ['meɪtrɪks] (*pl* **-ices** [-ɪsiːz]) *n Math
& Tech* matrice *f*
matron ['meɪtrən] *n Br (nurse)* infirmière
f en chef; *Br (in boarding school)* infirmière *f*; *(older woman)* matrone *f* • **mat-
ronly** *adj (air)* de mère de famille; *(stout)*
corpulent
matt [mæt] *adj (paint, paper)* mat
matted ['mætɪd] *adj (hair)* emmêlé
matter¹ ['mætə(r)] **1** *n (substance)* matière *f*; *(issue, affair)* question *f*; **that's a
m. of taste** c'est une question de goût;
and to make matters worse... et pour
aggraver les choses...; **as a m. of fact** en
fait; **no m.!** peu importe!; **no m. what she
does** quoi qu'elle fasse; **no m. where you
go** où que tu ailles; **no m. who you are** qui
que vous soyez; **no m. when** quel que soit
le moment; **what's the m.?** qu'est-ce qu'il
y a?; **what's the m. with you?** qu'est-ce
que tu as?; **there's something the m.** il y a
quelque chose qui ne va pas; **there's
something the m. with my leg** j'ai
quelque chose à la jambe; **there's nothing the m. with him** il n'a rien
2 *vi (be important)* importer (**to** à); **it
doesn't m. if/when/who...** peu importe
si/quand/qui...; **it doesn't m.** ça ne fait
rien; **it doesn't m. to me** ça m'est égal
matter² ['mætə(r)] *n Med* pus *m*
matter-of-fact [mætərəv'fækt] *adj (person, manner)* terre à terre *inv*; *(voice)*
neutre

matting ['mætɪŋ] *n (material)* nattage *m*;
a piece of m., some m. une natte
mattress ['mætrəs] *n* matelas *m*
mature [mə'tʃʊə(r)] **1** *adj (person, fruit)*
mûr; *(cheese)* fort; *Univ* **m. student** =
adulte qui reprend des études
2 *vi (person, fruit)* mûrir; *(of cheese)* se
faire; *Fin (of interest)* arriver à échéance
• **maturity** *n* maturité *f*
maul [mɔːl] *vt (of animal)* mutiler; *Fig (of
person)* malmener
Mauritius [mə'rɪʃəs] *n* l'île *f* Maurice
mausoleum [mɔːsə'lɪəm] *n* mausolée *m*
mauve [məʊv] *adj & n (colour)* mauve *(m)*
maverick ['mævərɪk] *n* non-conformiste
mf
mawkish ['mɔːkɪʃ] *adj Pej* mièvre
maxim ['mæksɪm] *n* maxime *f*
maximize ['mæksɪmaɪz] *vt* maximaliser
maximum ['mæksɪməm] **1** (*pl* **-ima**
[-ɪmə] *or* **-imums**) *n* maximum *m*
2 *adj* maximal
May [meɪ] *n* mai *m*; **M. Day** le Premier Mai
may [meɪ] (*pt* **might** [maɪt]) *v aux*

May et might peuvent s'utiliser indifféremment ou presque dans les expressions de la catégorie (**a**).

(**a**) *(expressing possibility)* **he m. come** il
se peut qu'il vienne; **I m.** *or* **might be
wrong** je me trompe peut-être; **he m.** *or*
might have lost it il se peut qu'il l'ait perdu; **I m.** *or* **might have forgotten it** je l'ai
peut-être oublié; **we m.** *or* **might as well
go** autant y aller; **she's afraid I m.** *or* **might
get lost** elle a peur que je ne me perde
(**b**) *Formal (for asking permission)* **m. I
stay?** puis-je rester?; **m. I?** vous permettez?; **you m. go** tu peux partir
(**c**) *Formal (expressing wish)* **m. you be
happy** sois heureux; **m. the best man
win!** que le meilleur gagne!
maybe ['meɪbiː] *adv* peut-être
mayday ['meɪdeɪ] *n (distress signal)* mayday *m*, SOS *m*
mayhem ['meɪhem] *n (chaos)* pagaille *f*
mayonnaise [meɪə'neɪz] *n* mayonnaise *f*
mayor [meə(r)] *n* maire *m* • **mayoress**
['meərɪs] *n* mairesse *f*; *(mayor's wife)*
femme *f* du maire
maze [meɪz] *n* labyrinthe *m*
MB [em'biː] (*abbr* **megabyte**) *Comptr* Mo
MC [em'siː] *abbr* = **master of ceremonies**
MD [em'diː] *n* (**a**) *Br* (*abbr* **managing
director**) directeur *m* général (**b**) (*abbr*
Doctor of Medicine) docteur *m* en médecine
me [miː] *pron* me, m'; *(after prep, 'than', 'it*

is') moi; **(to) me** *(indirect)* me, m'; **she knows me** elle me connaît; **he helps me** il m'aide; **he gave it to me** il me l'a donné; **with me** avec moi

meadow ['medəʊ] *n* pré *m*, prairie *f*

meagre ['miːgə(r)] (*Am* **meager**) *adj* maigre

meal¹ [miːl] *n (food)* repas *m*

meal² [miːl] *n (flour)* farine *f*

mealy-mouthed [miːlɪ'maʊ ð d] *adj Pej* mielleux, -euse

mean¹ [miːn] (*pt & pp* meant) *vt (of word, event)* signifier; *(of person)* vouloir dire; *(result in)* entraîner; *(represent)* représenter; **to m. to do sth** avoir l'intention de faire qch; **I know what you m.** je comprends; **I m. it, I m. what I say** je parle sérieusement; **it means a lot to me** c'est très important pour moi; **it means something to me** *(name, face)* ça me dit quelque chose; **I didn't m. to!** je ne l'ai pas fait exprès!; **you were meant to come** vous étiez censé venir; **it's meant to be a good film** il paraît que c'est un bon film; **it was meant for you** ça t'était destiné; **it was meant as a joke** c'était une plaisanterie

mean² [miːn] (**-er, -est**) *adj (miserly)* avare; *(petty)* mesquin; *(nasty)* méchant; *(shabby)* misérable; **she's no m. dancer** c'est une excellente danseuse ● **meanness** *n (greed)* avarice *f*; *(nastiness)* méchanceté *f*

mean³ [miːn] **1** *adj (average)* moyen, -enne **2** *n (middle position)* milieu *m*; *Math (average, mid-point)* moyenne *f*; **the happy m.** le juste milieu

meander [mɪ'ændə(r)] *vi (of river)* faire des méandres

meaning ['miːnɪŋ] *n* sens *m*, signification *f* ● **meaningful** *adj* significatif, -ive ● **meaningless** *adj* vide de sens; *Fig (absurd)* insensé

means [miːnz] **1** *n (method)* moyen *m* (**to do** *or* **of doing** de faire); **by m. of...** au moyen de...; **by m. of hard work** à force de travail; **by all m.!** *(certainly)* je vous en prie!; **by no m.** nullement; **m. of communication/transport** moyen de communication/transport **2** *npl (wealth)* moyens *mpl*; **to have independent** *or* **private m.** avoir une fortune personnelle; **to live beyond one's m.** vivre au-dessus de ses moyens

meant [ment] *pt & pp of* **mean¹**

meantime ['miːntaɪm] *adv & n* **(in the) m.** *(at the same time)* pendant ce temps; *(between two events)* entre-temps

meanwhile ['miːnwaɪl] *adv* entre-temps

measles ['miːzəlz] *n Med* rougeole *f*

measly ['miːzlɪ] *adj Fam* minable

measure ['meʒə(r)] **1** *n* mesure *f*; *(ruler)* règle *f*; *Br* **made to m.** fait sur mesure **2** *vt* mesurer; **to m. sth out** *(ingredient)* mesurer qch; **to m. sth up** *(plank)* mesurer qch **3** *vi* **to m. up to** *(task)* être à la hauteur de ● **measured** *adj (careful)* mesuré ● **measuring** *adj* **m. jug** verre *m* gradué; **m. tape** mètre *m* ruban

measurement ['meʒəmənt] *n* mesure *f*; **hip/waist measurement(s)** tour *m* de hanches/de taille

meat [miːt] *n* viande *f*; *(of crab, lobster)* chair *f*; *Fig* substance *f*; **m. diet** régime *m* carné; **m. pie** pâté *m* en croûte ● **meatball** *n* boulette *f* de viande ● **meaty** (**-ier, -iest**) *adj (fleshy)* charnu; *(flavour)* de viande; *Fig (book, film)* substantiel, -ielle

Mecca ['mekə] *n* La Mecque

mechanic [mɪ'kænɪk] *n* mécanicien, -ienne *mf* ● **mechanical** *adj* mécanique; *Fig (reply, gesture)* machinal ● **mechanics** *n (science)* mécanique *f*; **the m.** *(working parts)* le mécanisme

> 🖉 Note that the French word **mécanique** is a false friend and is never a translation for the English word **mechanic**. It means **mechanics**.

mechanism ['mekənɪzəm] *n* mécanisme *m*

mechanize ['mekənaɪz] *vt* mécaniser

medal ['medəl] *n* médaille *f*

medallion [mə'dæljən] *n* médaillon *m*

medallist ['medəlɪst] (*Am* **medalist**) *n* médaillé, -ée *mf*; **to be a gold/silver m.** être médaille d'or/d'argent

meddle ['medəl] *vi (interfere)* se mêler (**in** de); *(tamper)* toucher (**with** à) ● **meddlesome** *adj* qui se mêle de tout

media ['miːdɪə] *npl* **1 the m.** les médias *mpl*; **m. event** événement *m* médiatique **2** *pl of* **medium**

mediaeval [medɪ'iːvəl] *adj* médiéval

median ['miːdɪən] *adj & n Am* **m. (strip)** *(on highway)* bande *f* médiane

mediate ['miːdɪeɪt] *vi* servir d'intermédiaire (**between** entre) ● **medi'ation** *n* médiation *f* ● **mediator** *n* médiateur, -trice *mf*

Medicaid ['medɪkeɪd] *n Am* = assistance médicale aux défavorisés

medical ['medɪkəl] **1** *adj* médical; *(school, studies)* de médecine; *(student)* en médecine; **to seek m. advice** demander conseil à un médecin; **m. examina-tion** examen *m* médical; **m. insurance** assurance *f* maladie

2 *n* (*in school, army*) visite *f* médicale; (*private*) examen *m* médical

Medicare ['medɪkeə(r)] *n Am* ≃ assistance *f* médicale aux personnes âgées

medicated ['medɪkeɪtɪd] *adj* **m. sham-poo** shampooing *m* traitant

medication [medɪ'keɪʃən] *n* médica-ments *mpl*; **to be on m.** être en traitement

medicine ['medəsən] *n* (*substance*) médicament *m*; (*science*) médecine *f*; **m. cabinet, m. chest** (armoire *f* à) pharmacie *f* • **medicinal** [mə'dɪsənəl] *adj* médicinal

medieval [medɪ'iːvəl] *adj* médiéval

mediocre [miːdɪ'əʊkə(r)] *adj* médiocre • **mediocrity** [-'ɒkrɪtɪ] *n* médiocrité *f*

meditate ['medɪteɪt] *vi* méditer (**on** sur) • **medi'tation** *n* méditation *f*

Mediterranean [medɪtə'reɪnɪən] **1** *adj* méditerranéen, -éenne

2 *n* **the M.** la Méditerranée

medium ['miːdɪəm] **1** *adj* (*average, middle*) moyen, -enne

2 *n* (**a**) (*pl* **media** ['miːdɪə]) (*of thought*) véhicule *m*; *Biol* milieu *m*; (*for conveying data or publicity*) support *m*; **through the m. of sb/sth** par l'intermédiaire de qn/qch; **to find a happy m.** trouver le juste milieu (**b**) (*pl* **mediums**) (*person*) médium *m* • '**medium-sized** *adj* de taille moyenne

medley ['medlɪ] (*pl* **-eys**) *n* mélange *m*; (*of songs, tunes*) pot-pourri *m*

meek [miːk] (**-er, -est**) *adj* docile

meet [miːt] **1** *vt* (*pt & pp* **met**) (*person, team*) rencontrer; (*by arrangement*) retrouver; (*pass in street, road*) croiser; (*fetch*) aller chercher; (*wait for*) attendre; (*debt, enemy, danger*) faire face à; (*need*) combler; **to arrange to m. sb** donner rendez-vous à qn; **have you met my husband?** connaissez-vous mon mari?

2 *vi* (*of people, teams, looks*) se rencontrer; (*by arrangement*) se retrouver; (*of club, society*) se réunir; (*of rivers*) se rejoindre; (*of trains, vehicles*) se croiser; **we've never met** nous ne nous connaissons pas

3 *n Am Sport* réunion *f*

▸ **meet up** *vi* (*of people*) se rencontrer; (*by arrangement*) se retrouver; **to m. up with sb** rencontrer qn; (*by arrangement*) retrouver qn ▸ **meet with** *vt insep* (*problem, refusal*) se heurter à; (*loss*) essuyer; (*danger*) affronter; (*accident*) avoir; *Am* **to m.**

with sb rencontrer qn; (*as arranged*) retrouver qn

meeting ['miːtɪŋ] *n* (*for business*) réunion *f*; (*large*) assemblée *f*; (*by accident*) rencontre *f*; (*by arrangement*) rendez-vous *m inv*; **to be in a m.** être en réunion; **m. place** lieu *m* de rendez-vous

megabyte ['megəbaɪt] *n Comptr* méga-octet *m*

megalomania [megələʊ'meɪnɪə] *n* mégalomanie *f* • **megalomaniac** *n* mégalomane *mf*

megaphone ['megəfəʊn] *n* porte-voix *m inv*

melancholy ['melənkəlɪ] **1** *adj* mélancolique

2 *n* mélancolie *f*

mellow ['meləʊ] **1** (**-er, -est**) *adj* (*fruit*) mûr; (*wine*) moelleux, -euse; (*flavour*) suave; (*colour, voice*) chaud; (*person*) détendu, serein

2 *vi* (*of person*) s'adoucir

melodrama ['melədrɑːmə] *n* mélodrame *m* • **melodramatic** [-drə'mætɪk] *adj* mélodramatique

melody ['melədɪ] (*pl* **-ies**) *n* mélodie *f* • **melodic** [mə'lɒdɪk] *adj* mélodique • **melodious** [mə'ləʊdɪəs] *adj* mélodieux, -ieuse

melon ['melən] *n* melon *m*

melt [melt] **1** *vt* faire fondre; **to m. down** (*metal object*) fondre; **melting point** point *m* de fusion; *Fig* **melting pot** creuset *m*

2 *vi* fondre; **to m. away** (*of snow*) fondre complètement; **the green melts into the blue** le vert se fond dans le bleu • **melt-down** *n Phys* fusion *f*

member ['membə(r)] *n* membre *m*; *Br* **M. of Parliament,** *Am* **M. of Congress** ≃ député *m*; **she's a m. of the family** elle fait partie de la famille; **m. state** État *m* membre • **membership** *n* (*state*) adhésion *f* (**of** à); (*members*) membres *mpl*; (*number*) nombre *m* de membres; **m. card** carte *f* de membre; **m. fee** cotisation *f*

membrane ['membreɪn] *n* membrane *f*

memento [mə'mentəʊ] (*pl* **-os** *or* **-oes**) *n* souvenir *m*

memo ['meməʊ] (*pl* **-os**) *n* note *f* de service; **m. pad** bloc-notes *m* • **memoran-dum** [memə'rændəm] *n* (*in office*) note *f* de service; *Pol & Com* mémorandum *m*

memoir ['memwɑː(r)] *n* (*essay*) mémoire *m* • **memoirs** *npl* (*autobiography*) mémoires *mpl*

memorable ['memərəbəl] *adj* mémorable

memorial [mə'mɔːrɪəl] **1** *adj* commémo-

ratif, -ive; **m. service** commémoration f
2 n mémorial m
memorize ['meməraɪz] vt mémoriser
memory ['meməri] (pl -ies) n (faculty) &
Comptr mémoire f; (recollection) souvenir
m; **from m.** de mémoire; **to the** or **in m.
of...** à la mémoire de...
men [men] npl see man; **the men's room**
les toilettes fpl pour hommes • **menfolk** n
Old-fashioned hommes mpl
menace ['menɪs] **1** n (danger) danger m;
(threat) menace f; Fam (nuisance) plaie f
2 vt menacer • **menacing** adj menaçant
• **menacingly** adv (say) d'un ton menaçant; (do) d'une manière menaçante
menagerie [mɪ'nædʒərɪ] n ménagerie f
mend [mend] **1** n (in clothes) raccommodage m; **to be on the m.** (of patient) aller
mieux
2 vt (repair) réparer; (clothes) raccommoder; **to m. one's ways** s'amender
menial ['miːnɪəl] adj (work) subalterne
meningitis [menɪn'dʒaɪtɪs] n Med méningite f
menopause ['menəpɔːz] n ménopause
f
menstruate ['menstrʊeɪt] vi avoir ses
règles • **menstru'ation** n menstruation f
menswear ['menzweə(r)] n vêtements
mpl pour hommes
mental ['mentəl] adj mental; Br Fam
(mad) dingue; **m. block** blocage m; **m.
breakdown** dépression f nerveuse; **m.
hospital** hôpital m psychiatrique • **mentally** adv mentalement; **he's m. handicapped** c'est un handicapé mental; **she's
m. ill** c'est une malade mentale
mentality [men'tælətɪ] (pl -ies) n mentalité f
mention ['menʃən] **1** n mention f
2 vt mentionner; **not to m.** sans parler
de; **don't m. it!** il n'y a pas de quoi!; **she
has no savings worth mentioning** elle n'a
pratiquement pas d'économies
mentor ['mentɔː(r)] n mentor m
menu ['menjuː] n (in restaurant) (for set
meal) menu m; (list) carte f; Comptr menu
MEP [emiː'piː] (abbr Member of the European Parliament) n député m du Parlement européen
mercantile ['mɜːkəntaɪl] adj (activity,
law) commercial; (nation) commerçant
mercenary ['mɜːsɪnərɪ] **1** adj intéressé
2 (pl -ies) n mercenaire m
merchandise ['mɜːtʃəndaɪz] n marchandises fpl
merchant ['mɜːtʃənt] **1** n (trader) négociant, -iante mf; (retailer) commerçant,

-ante mf; **wine m.** négociant, -iante en
vins; (retail) marchand m de vins
2 adj (navy) marchand; (seaman) de la
marine marchande; Br **m. bank** banque f
d'affaires; **m. vessel** navire m marchand
merciful ['mɜːsɪfəl] adj miséricordieux,
-ieuse (**to** pour) • **mercifully** adv (fortunately) heureusement
merciless ['mɜːsɪləs] adj impitoyable
mercury ['mɜːkjʊrɪ] n (metal) mercure m
mercy ['mɜːsɪ] (pl -ies) n pitié f; (of God)
miséricorde f; **to beg for m.** demander
grâce; **at the m. of** à la merci de; **it's a m.
that** (stroke of luck) c'est une chance que;
m. killing acte m d'euthanasie
mere [mɪə(r)] adj simple; **she's a m. child**
ce n'est qu'une enfant; **it's a m. kilometre**
ça ne fait qu'un kilomètre; **by m. chance**
par pur hasard; **the m. sight of them...**
leur seule vue... • **merely** adv simplement
merge [mɜːdʒ] **1** vt (companies) & Comptr
fusionner
2 vi (blend) se mêler (**with** à); (of roads)
se rejoindre; (of companies, banks) fusionner • **merger** n Com fusion f
meridian [mə'rɪdɪən] n méridien m
meringue [mə'ræŋ] n meringue f
merit ['merɪt] **1** n mérite m; **to judge sth
on its merits** juger qch objectivement
2 vt mériter
mermaid ['mɜːmeɪd] n sirène f
merrily ['merɪlɪ] adv gaiement • **merri-
ment** n gaieté f
merry ['merɪ] (-ier, -iest) adj (happy,
drunk) gai; **M. Christmas!** Joyeux Noël!
• **merry-go-round** n manège m • **merry-
making** n réjouissances fpl
mesh [meʃ] n (of net, sieve) mailles fpl;
(fabric) tissu m à mailles
mesmerize ['mezməraɪz] vt hypnotiser
mess¹ [mes] **1** n (confusion) désordre m;
(muddle) gâchis m; (dirt) saletés fpl; **in a
m.** en désordre; (in trouble) dans le pétrin; (in a sorry state) dans un triste état;
my life's a m. ma vie est un désastre; **to
make a m. of sth** (do sth badly, get sth
dirty) saloper qch
2 vt Br Fam **to m. sb about** (bother, treat
badly) embêter qn; **to m. sth up** (plans)
ficher qch en l'air; (hair, room, papers)
mettre qch en désordre
3 vi **to m. about** or **around** (waste time)
traîner; (play the fool) faire l'imbécile; **to
m. about** or **around with sth** (fiddle with)
tripoter avec qch • **mess-up** n Br Fam
(disorder) gâchis m
mess² [mes] n Mil (room) mess m
message ['mesɪdʒ] n message m

messenger ['mesɪndʒə(r)] *n* messager, -ère *mf*; *(in office, hotel)* coursier, -ière *mf*
Messiah [mɪ'saɪə] *n Rel* Messie *m*
Messrs ['mesəz] *(abbr* **Messieurs**) MM
messy ['mesɪ] **(-ier, -iest)** *adj (untidy)* en désordre; *(dirty)* sale; *(job)* salissant; *(handwriting)* peu soigné; *Fig (situation, solution)* confus
met [met] *pt & pp of* **meet**
metal ['metəl] *n* métal *m*; **m. detector** détecteur *m* de métaux; **m. ladder** échelle *f* métallique • **metallic** [mə'tælɪk] *adj (sound)* métallique; *(paint)* métallisé; **a m. green car** une voiture vert métallisé • **metalwork** *n (study, craft)* travail *m* des métaux; *(objects)* ferronnerie *f*
metamorphosis [metə'mɔːfəsɪs] *(pl* **-oses** [-əsiːz]) *n* métamorphose *f*
metaphor ['metəfə(r)] *n* métaphore *f* • **metaphorical** [-'fɒrɪkəl] *adj* métaphorique
metaphysical [metə'fɪzɪkəl] *adj* métaphysique
mete [miːt] *vt* **to m. out** *(punishment)* infliger **(to à)**; **to m. out justice** rendre la justice
meteor ['miːtɪə(r)] *n* météore *m* • **meteoric** [-tɪ'ɒrɪk] *adj* **m. rise** *(of politician, film star)* ascension *f* fulgurante • **meteorite** *n* météorite *f*
meteorology [miːtɪə'rɒlədʒɪ] *n* météorologie *f* • **meteorological** [-rə'lɒdʒɪkəl] *adj* météorologique
meter¹ ['miːtə(r)] *n (device)* compteur *m*; **(parking) m.** parcmètre *m*; *Am* **m. maid** *(for traffic)* contractuelle *f*; *Am* **m. man** contractuel *m*
meter² ['miːtə(r)] *n Am (measurement)* mètre *m*
method ['meθəd] *n* méthode *f* • **methodical** [mɪ'θɒdɪkəl] *adj* méthodique
Methodist ['meθədɪst] *adj & n Rel* méthodiste *(mf)*
methylated ['meθɪleɪtɪd] *adj Br* **m. spirit(s)** alcool *m* à brûler • **meths** *n Br Fam* alcool *m* à brûler
meticulous [mɪ'tɪkjʊləs] *adj* méticuleux, -euse • **meticulousness** *n* minutie *f*
Met Office ['metɒfɪs] *n Br* ≃ Météo France
metre ['miːtə(r)] *(Am* **meter**) *n* mètre *m* • **metric** ['metrɪk] *adj* métrique
metropolis [mə'trɒpəlɪs] *n (chief city)* métropole *f* • **metropolitan** [metrə-'pɒlɪtən] *adj* métropolitain; **the M. Police** la police de Londres
mettle ['metəl] *n* courage *m*
mew [mjuː] *vi (of cat)* miauler

mews [mjuːz] *n Br (street)* ruelle *f*; *Br* **m. flat** appartement *m* chic *(aménagé dans une ancienne écurie)*
Mexico ['meksɪkəʊ] *n* le Mexique • **Mexican 1** *adj* mexicain **2** *n* Mexicain, -aine *mf*
mezzanine ['mezəniːn] *n* **m. (floor)** mezzanine *f*
miaow [miː'aʊ] **1** *n* miaulement *m* **2** *exclam* miaou ! **3** *vi* miauler
mice [maɪs] *pl of* **mouse**
mickey ['mɪkɪ] *n Br Fam* **to take the m. out of sb** charrier qn
microbe ['maɪkrəʊb] *n* microbe *m*
microchip ['maɪkrəʊtʃɪp] *n Comptr* microprocesseur *m*
microcosm ['maɪkrəʊkɒzəm] *n* microcosme *m*
microfilm ['maɪkrəʊfɪlm] *n* microfilm *m*
microlight ['maɪkrəʊlaɪt] *n (plane)* ULM *m*
microphone ['maɪkrəfəʊn] *n* micro *m*
microprocessor [maɪkrəʊ'prəʊsesə(r)] *n* microprocesseur *m*
microscope ['maɪkrəskəʊp] *n* microscope *m* • **microscopic** [-'skɒpɪk] *adj* microscopique
microwave ['maɪkrəʊweɪv] *n* microonde *f*; **m. (oven)** (four *m* à) micro-ondes *m inv*
mid [mɪd] *adj* **(in) m. June** (à) la mi-juin; **in m. air** en plein ciel; **to be in one's m.-twenties** avoir environ vingt-cinq ans • **mid-'morning** *n* milieu *m* de matinée • **Mid-'West** *n Am* **the M.** le Midwest
midday [mɪd'deɪ] **1** *n* midi *m*; **at m.** à midi **2** *adj (sun, meal)* de midi
middle ['mɪdəl] **1** *n* milieu *m*; *Fam (waist)* taille *f*; **(right) in the m. of sth** au (beau) milieu de qch; **I was in the m. of saying...** j'étais en train de dire... **2** *adj (central)* du milieu; **the M. Ages** le Moyen Âge; **the Middle E.** le Moyen-Orient; **in m. age** vers la cinquantaine; **the m. class(es)** les classes moyennes; **the m. ear** l'oreille moyenne; **m. name** deuxième prénom *m* • **'middle-'aged** *adj* d'âge mûr • **'middle-'class** *adj* bourgeois • **'middleman** *n* intermédiaire *mf* • **'middle-of-the-'road** *adj (politics, views)* modéré; *(music)* grand public *inv*
middling ['mɪdlɪŋ] *adj (fairly good)* moyen, -enne; *(mediocre)* médiocre
midge [mɪdʒ] *n* moucheron *m*
midget ['mɪdʒɪt] **1** *adj (tiny)* minuscule **2** *n (small person)* nain *m*, naine *f*
Midlands ['mɪdləndz] *npl* **the M.** les Midlands *fpl*

midnight ['mɪdnaɪt] *n* minuit *m*
midpoint ['mɪdpɔɪnt] *n* milieu *m*
midriff ['mɪdrɪf] *n (belly)* ventre *m*
midst [mɪdst] *n* **in the m. of** *(middle)* au milieu de; **in our/their m.** parmi nous/eux
midsummer [mɪd'sʌmə(r)] *n* milieu *m* de l'été; *(solstice)* solstice *m* d'été; **M.'s Day** la Saint-Jean
midterm ['mɪdtɜːm] *adj Br Sch & Univ* **m. holidays** vacances *fpl* de milieu de trimestre
midway [mɪd'weɪ] *adj & adv* à mi-chemin
midweek [mɪd'wiːk] *adv* en milieu de semaine
midwife ['mɪdwaɪf] *(pl* **-wives)** *n* sage-femme *f*
midwinter [mɪd'wɪntə(r)] *n* milieu *m* de l'hiver; *(solstice)* solstice *m* d'hiver
miffed [mɪft] *adj Fam (offended)* vexé (**at de)**
might¹ [maɪt] *v aux see* **may**

> La forme négative **mightn't** s'écrit **might not** dans un style plus soutenu.

might² [maɪt] *n (strength)* force *f* • **mighty** (**-ier, -iest)** **1** *adj* puissant; *(ocean)* vaste; *Fam (very great)* sacré **2** *adv Am Fam (very)* rudement
migraine ['miːgreɪn, 'maɪgreɪn] *n* migraine *f*
migrate [maɪ'greɪt] *vi (of people)* émigrer; *(of birds)* migrer • **migrant** ['maɪgrənt] *adj & n.* **(worker)** (travailleur *m)* immigré *m*, (travailleuse *f)* immigrée *f* • **migration** *n (of birds)* migration *f*; *(of people)* immigration *f*
mike [maɪk] *(abbr* **microphone***) n Fam* micro *m*
mild [maɪld] (**-er, -est)** *adj (weather, cheese, soap, person)* doux (*f* douce); *(punishment)* léger, -ère; *(curry)* peu épicé • **mildly** *adv (say)* doucement; *(moderately)* légèrement; **to put it m.** pour ne pas dire plus • **mildness** *n (of weather)* douceur *f*
mildew ['mɪldjuː] *n* moisissure *f*
mile [maɪl] *n* mile *m (= 1,6 km);* **to see for miles** voir à des kilomètres; **to walk for miles** marcher pendant des kilomètres; **he lives miles away** il habite très loin d'ici; *Fam* **miles better** cent fois mieux • **mileage** *n (distance)* ≃ kilométrage *m*; *(rate of fuel consumption)* consommation *f* • **mileometer** [maɪ'lɒmɪtə(r)] *n Br* ≃ compteur *m* kilométrique • **milestone** *n* ≃ borne *f* kilométrique; *Fig (in history, career)* étape *f* importante

militant ['mɪlɪtənt] *adj & n* militant, -ante *(mf)*
military ['mɪlɪtərɪ] **1** *adj* militaire; **m. service** service *m* militaire **2** *n* **the m.** les militaires *mpl*
militate ['mɪlɪteɪt] *vi* **to m. against/in favour of** *(of facts, arguments)* militer contre/pour
militia [mə'lɪʃə] *n* milice *f* • **militiaman** *(pl* **-men)** *n* milicien *m*
milk [mɪlk] **1** *n* lait *m*; **m. bottle** bouteille *f* de lait; **m. chocolate** chocolat *m* au lait; **m. diet** régime *m* lacté; *Br* **m. float** camionnette *f* de laitier; *Br* **m. round** tournée *f* du laitier; **m. shake** milk-shake *m* **2** *vt (cow)* traire; *Fig (exploit)* exploiter; *Fig* **to m. sb of sth** soutirer qch à qn • **milking** *n* traite *f* • **milkman** *(pl* **-men)** *n* laitier *m* • **milky** (**-ier, -iest)** *adj (diet)* lacté; *(coffee, tea)* au lait; *(colour)* laiteux, -euse; **the M. Way** la Voie lactée
mill [mɪl] **1** *n (for flour)* moulin *m*; *(textile factory)* filature *f* **2** *vt (grind)* moudre **3** *vi* **to m. around** *(of crowd)* grouiller • **miller** *n* meunier, -ière *mf*
millennium [mɪ'lenɪəm] *(pl* **-nia** [-nɪə]) *n* millénaire *m*
millet ['mɪlɪt] *n* millet *m*
milligram(me) ['mɪlɪgræm] *n* milligramme *m*
millimetre ['mɪlɪmiːtə(r)] (*Am* **millimeter***) n* millimètre *m*
million ['mɪljən] *n* million *m*; **a m. men** un million d'hommes; **two m.** deux millions; *Fam* **she's one in a m.** elle est unique • **millio'naire** *n* millionnaire *mf* • **millionth** *adj & n* millionième *(mf)*
millstone ['mɪlstəʊn] *n* meule *f*; *Fig* **it's a m. around my neck** c'est un boulet que je traîne
milometer [maɪ'lɒmɪtə(r)] *n Br* ≃ compteur *m* kilométrique
mime [maɪm] **1** *n (actor)* mime *mf*; *(art)* mime *m* **2** *vti* mimer; *(of singer)* chanter en play-back
mimeograph® ['mɪmɪəgræf] *vt* ronéotyper
mimic ['mɪmɪk] **1** *n* imitateur, -trice *mf* **2** *(pt & pp* **-ck-***) vt* imiter • **mimicry** [-krɪ] *n* imitation *f*
minaret [mɪnə'ret] *n* minaret *m*
mince [mɪns] **1** *n (meat)* viande *f* hachée; **m. pie** *Br (containing meat)* tourte *f* à la viande; *(containing fruit)* = tartelette fourrée aux fruits secs et aux épices **2** *vt* hacher; **not to m. matters** *or* **one's**

words ne pas mâcher ses mots •**mince-meat** n (dried fruit) = mélange de fruits secs et d'épices utilisé en pâtisserie; Br (meat) viande f hachée •**mincer** n (machine) hachoir m

mind¹ [maɪnd] n esprit m; (sanity) raison f; Br **to my m.** à mon avis; **to change one's m.** changer d'avis; **to speak one's m.** dire ce que l'on pense; Br **to be in two minds** (undecided) hésiter; **to bear** or **keep sth in m.** garder qch à l'esprit; **to have sb/sth in m.** avoir qn/qch en vue; **to make up one's m.** se décider; Fam **to be out of one's m.** avoir perdu la tête; **to be bored out of one's m.** s'ennuyer à mourir; **to bring sth to m.** rappeler qch; **I couldn't get it off my m.** je ne pouvais pas m'empêcher d'y penser; **it's on my m.** cela me préoccupe; **my m. isn't on the job** je n'ai pas la tête à ce que je fais; **her m. is going** elle perd la raison; Br **to have a good m. to do sth** avoir bien envie de faire qch

mind² [maɪnd] **1** vt Br (pay attention to) faire attention à; (look after) garder; **to m. one's language** surveiller son langage; Fam **to m. one's p's and q's** bien se tenir; Br **m. you don't fall** fais attention à ne pas tomber; Br **m. you do it** n'oublie pas de le faire; **I don't m. the cold/noise** le froid/bruit ne me gêne pas; **I don't m. trying** je veux bien essayer; **I wouldn't m. a cup of tea** je prendrais bien une tasse de thé; **I m. that** ça me gêne que; **if you don't m. my asking…** si je peux me permettre…; **never m. the car** peu importe la voiture; Br **m. you** remarquez; **m. your own business!** occupe-toi de tes affaires!

2 vi **I don't m.** ça m'est égal; **do you m. if I smoke?** ça vous gêne si je fume?; **never m.!** ça ne fait rien!, tant pis!; Br **m. (out)!** (watch out) attention!

mind-boggling [ˈmaɪndbɒɡlɪŋ] adj stupéfiant

-minded [ˈmaɪndɪd] suff **fair-m.** impartial; **like-m.** de même opinion

minder [ˈmaɪndə(r)] n Fam (bodyguard) gorille m

mindful [ˈmaɪndfəl] adj **m. of sth/doing** attentif, -ive à qch/à faire

mindless [ˈmaɪndləs] adj (job, destruction) stupide

mine¹ [maɪn] possessive pron le mien, la mienne, pl les mien(ne)s; **this hat is m.** ce chapeau est à moi ou est le mien; **a friend of m.** un ami à moi, un de mes amis

mine² [maɪn] **1** n (**a**) (for coal, gold) & Fig mine f (**b**) (explosive) mine f

2 vt (**a**) (coal, gold) extraire (**b**) (beach, bridge) miner

3 vi **to m. for coal** extraire du charbon •**miner** n mineur m •**mining 1** n exploitation f minière **2** adj (industry, region) minier, -ière

mineral [ˈmɪnərəl] adj & n minéral (m); **m. water** eau f minérale

minestrone [mɪnɪˈstrəʊnɪ] n minestrone m

mingle [ˈmɪŋɡəl] vi (of things) se mêler (**with** à); (of people) parler un peu à tout le monde; **to m. with the crowd** se mêler à la foule

mingy [ˈmɪndʒɪ] (**-ier, -iest**) adj Br Fam radin

miniature [ˈmɪnɪtʃə(r)] **1** adj (tiny) minuscule; (train, model) miniature inv **2** n miniature f; **in m.** en miniature

minibus [ˈmɪnɪbʌs] n minibus m •**minicab** n Br radio-taxi m

minim [ˈmɪnɪm] n Br Mus blanche f

minima [ˈmɪnɪmə] pl of **minimum**

minimal [ˈmɪnɪməl] adj minimal

minimize [ˈmɪnɪmaɪz] vt minimiser

minimum [ˈmɪnɪməm] **1** (pl **-ima** or **-imums**) n minimum m

2 adj minimal; **m. wage** salaire m minimum

mining [ˈmaɪnɪŋ] n see **mine²**

miniskirt [ˈmɪnɪskɜːt] n minijupe f

minister¹ [ˈmɪnɪstə(r)] n Br (politician) ministre m; (of religion) pasteur m •**ministerial** [-ˈstɪərɪəl] adj Br Pol ministériel, -ielle •**ministry** (pl **-ies**) n Br Pol ministère m; Rel **to enter** or **join the m.** devenir pasteur

minister² [ˈmɪnɪstə(r)] vi **to m. to sb's needs** subvenir aux besoins de qn

mink [mɪŋk] n vison m

minor [ˈmaɪnə(r)] **1** adj (unimportant) & Mus mineur; (operation) bénin, -igne; (road) secondaire

2 n Law (child) mineur, -eure mf; **to be a m.** être mineur(e)

Minorca [mɪˈnɔːkə] n Minorque f

minority [maɪˈnɒrɪtɪ] (pl **-ies**) n minorité f; **to be in the** or **a m.** être minoritaire **2** adj minoritaire

mint¹ [mɪnt] **1** n **the (Royal) M.** ≃ l'hôtel m de la Monnaie; Fig **to make a m. (of money)** faire une petite fortune

2 adj **m. stamp** timbre m neuf; **in m. condition** à l'état neuf

3 vt (coins) frapper

mint² [mɪnt] n (herb) menthe f; (sweet) bonbon m à la menthe; **m. sauce** sauce f à la menthe; **m. tea** infusion f de menthe

minus ['maɪnəs] **1** *adj & n* **m. (sign)** (signe *m*) moins *m*

2 *prep (with numbers)* moins; *Fam (without)* sans; **it's m. 10 (degrees)** il fait moins 10

minute¹ ['mɪnɪt] *n (of time)* minute *f*; **this (very) m.** *(now)* tout de suite; **any m. (now)** d'une minute à l'autre; **m. hand** *(of clock)* grande aiguille *f* • **minutes** *npl (of meeting)* procès-verbal *m*

minute² [maɪ'njuːt] *adj (tiny)* minuscule; *(detailed)* minutieux, -ieuse

miracle ['mɪrəkəl] *n* miracle *m*; **to work miracles** faire des miracles; **by some m.** par miracle • **miraculous** [mɪ'rækjʊləs] *adj* miraculeux, -euse

mirage ['mɪrɑːʒ] *n* mirage *m*

mire [maɪə(r)] *n Literary* fange *f*; *Fig (difficult situation)* bourbier *m*

mirror ['mɪrə(r)] **1** *n* miroir *m*, glace *f*; *Fig (representation)* miroir; **(rear view) m.** *(of vehicle)* rétroviseur *m*

2 *vt (reflect)* refléter

mirth [mɜːθ] *n Literary* gaieté *f*

misadventure [mɪsəd'ventʃə(r)] *n* mésaventure *f*; *Law* **death by m.** mort *f* accidentelle

misanthropist [mɪ'zænθrəpɪst] *n* misanthrope *mf*

misapprehension [mɪsæprɪ'henʃən] *n* malentendu *m*; **to be under a m.** se méprendre

misappropriate [mɪsə'prəʊprɪeɪt] *vt (money)* détourner

misbehave [mɪsbɪ'heɪv] *vi* se conduire mal

miscalculate [mɪs'kælkjʊleɪt] **1** *vt* mal calculer

2 *vi* faire une erreur de calcul; *Fig* faire un mauvais calcul • **miscalcu'lation** *n* erreur *f* de calcul

miscarriage [mɪs'kærɪdʒ] *n Med* fausse couche *f*; **to have a m.** faire une fausse couche; *Law* **m. of justice** erreur *f* judiciaire • **miscarry** *(pt & pp* **-ied)** *vi (of woman)* faire une fausse couche; *Fig (of plan)* avorter

miscellaneous [mɪsə'leɪnɪəs] *adj* divers

mischief ['mɪstʃɪf] *n* espièglerie *f*; **to get into m.** faire des bêtises; **to make m. for sb** créer des ennuis à qn; **to do oneself a m.** *(harm oneself)* se faire mal

mischievous ['mɪstʃɪvəs] *adj (naughty)* espiègle; *(malicious)* méchant

misconception [mɪskən'sepʃən] *n* idée *f* fausse

misconduct [mɪs'kɒndʌkt] *n (bad behaviour)* inconduite *f*; *Com (bad manage-* *ment)* mauvaise gestion *f*; **(professional) m.** faute *f* professionnelle

misconstrue [mɪskən'struː] *vt* mal interpréter

misdemeanour [mɪsdɪ'miːnə(r)] *(Am* **misdemeanor**) *n* écart *m* de conduite; *Am Law* délit *m*

miser ['maɪzə(r)] *n* avare *mf* • **miserly** *adj* avare

miserable ['mɪzərəbəl] *adj (wretched)* misérable; *(unhappy)* malheureux, -euse; *(awful)* affreux, -euse; *(derisory) (salary)* dérisoire • **miserably** *adv (wretchedly)* misérablement; *(fail)* lamentablement

misery ['mɪzərɪ] *(pl* **-ies)** *n (suffering)* malheur *m*; *(sadness)* détresse *f*; *Fam (sad person)* grincheux, -euse *mf*; **his life is a m.** il est malheureux; **to put an animal out of its m.** achever un animal

> 🖉 Note that the French word **misère** is a false friend and is never a translation for the English word **misery**. It means **extreme poverty**.

misfire [mɪs'faɪə(r)] *vi (of gun)* faire long feu; *(of engine)* avoir des ratés; *Fig (of plan)* rater

misfit ['mɪsfɪt] *n Pej* inadapté, -ée *mf*

misfortune [mɪs'fɔːtʃuːn] *n* malheur *m*

misgivings [mɪs'gɪvɪŋz] *npl (doubts)* doutes *mpl* (**about** sur); *(fears)* craintes *fpl* (**about** à propos de)

misguided [mɪs'gaɪdɪd] *adj (attempt)* malencontreux, -euse; *(decision)* peu judicieux, -ieuse; **to be m.** *(of person)* se tromper

mishandle [mɪs'hændəl] *vt (device)* mal utiliser; *(situation)* mal gérer; *(person)* malmener

mishap ['mɪshæp] *n* incident *m*; **without m.** sans encombre

misinform [mɪsɪn'fɔːm] *vt* mal renseigner

misinterpret [mɪsɪn'tɜːprɪt] *vt* mal interpréter

misjudge [mɪs'dʒʌdʒ] *vt (person, distance)* mal juger

mislay [mɪs'leɪ] *(pt & pp* **-laid)** *vt* égarer

mislead [mɪs'liːd] *(pt & pp* **-led)** tromper • **misleading** *adj* trompeur, -euse

mismanage [mɪs'mænɪdʒ] *vt* mal gérer • **mismanagement** *n* mauvaise gestion *f*

misnomer [mɪs'nəʊmə(r)] *n* terme *m* impropre

misogynist [mɪ'sɒdʒɪnɪst] *n* misogyne *mf*

misplace [mɪs'pleɪs] *vt (lose)* égarer; *(trust)* mal placer • **misplaced** *adj (re-*

mark) déplacé; **m. accent** accent *m* mal placé

misprint ['mɪsprɪnt] *n* faute *f* d'impression, coquille *f*

mispronounce [mɪsprə'naʊns] *vt* mal prononcer

misquote [mɪs'kwəʊt] *vt* citer incorrectement

misrepresent [mɪsreprɪ'zent] *vt (theory)* dénaturer; *(person)* présenter sous un faux jour

Miss [mɪs] *n* Mademoiselle *f*; **M. World** Miss Monde

miss [mɪs] **1** *n* coup *m* raté; **that was** *or* **we had a near m.** on l'a échappé belle; *Fam* **I'll give it a m.** *(not go)* je n'y irai pas; *(not take or drink or eat)* je n'en prendrai pas

2 *vt (train, target, opportunity)* manquer, rater; *(not see)* ne pas voir; *(not understand)* ne pas comprendre; *(feel the lack of)* regretter; **he misses Paris** Paris lui manque; **I m. you** tu me manques; **we'll be missed** on nous regrettera; **I'm missing my wallet!** je n'ai plus mon portefeuille!; **the table is missing a leg** il manque un pied à la table; **don't m. seeing this play** il faut absolument que tu voies cette pièce; **to m. sth out** *(accidentally)* oublier qch; *(intentionally)* omettre qch

3 *vi* manquer *ou* rater son coup; **to m. out** *(lose a chance)* rater l'occasion; **to m. out on sth** rater qch

misshapen [mɪs'ʃeɪpən] *adj* difforme

missile [*Br* 'mɪsaɪl, *Am* 'mɪsəl] *n (rocket)* missile *m*; *(object thrown)* projectile *m*

missing ['mɪsɪŋ] *adj (absent)* absent; *(in war, after disaster)* disparu; *(object)* manquant; **there are two cups/students m.** il manque deux tasses/deux étudiants; **nothing is m.** il ne manque rien; **to go m.** disparaître; *Mil* **m. in action** porté disparu

mission ['mɪʃən] *n* mission *f*

missionary ['mɪʃənərɪ] *(pl* **-ies**) *n Rel* missionnaire *m*

missive ['mɪsɪv] *n Formal* missive *f*

misspell [mɪs'spel] *(pt & pp* **-ed** *or* **-spelt**) *vt* mal écrire

mist [mɪst] **1** *n (fog)* brume *f*; *(on glass)* buée *f*

2 *vi* **to m. over** *or* **up** s'embuer

mistake [mɪ'steɪk] **1** *n* erreur *f*, faute *f*; **to make a m.** faire une erreur; **by m.** par erreur

2 *(pt* **-took***, pp* **-taken**) *vt (meaning, intention)* se tromper sur; **to m. the date/place** se tromper de date/de lieu; **there's no mistaking his face** il est impos-

sible de ne pas reconnaître son visage; **to m. sb for** prendre qn pour • **mistaken** *adj (belief, impression)* erroné; **to be m.** *(of person)* se tromper *(about* sur) • **mistakenly** *adv* par erreur

Mister ['mɪstə(r)] *n* Monsieur *m*

mistletoe ['mɪsəltəʊ] *n* gui *m*

mistreat [mɪs'triːt] *vt* maltraiter

mistress ['mɪstrɪs] *n* maîtresse *f*; *Br (in secondary school)* professeur *m*

mistrust [mɪs'trʌst] **1** *n* méfiance *f*

2 *vt* se méfier de • **mistrustful** *adj* méfiant

misty ['mɪstɪ] *(-ier, -iest) adj (foggy)* brumeux, -euse; *(outline)* flou

misunderstand [mɪsʌndə'stænd] *(pt & pp* **-stood**) *vti* mal comprendre • **misunderstanding** *n (disagreement)* mésentente *f*; *(misconception)* malentendu *m* • **misunderstood** *adj (person)* incompris

misuse 1 [mɪs'juːs] *n (of equipment, resources)* mauvais emploi *m*; *(of funds)* détournement *m*; *(of power)* abus *m*

2 [mɪs'juːz] *vt (equipment, resources)* mal employer; *(funds)* détourner; *(power)* abuser de

mite [maɪt] *n* **(a)** *(bug)* acarien *m* **(b)** *Fam* **(poor) little m.** *(child)* pauvre petit, -ite *mf* **(c)** *Fam* **a m. tired** un tantinet fatigué

mitigate ['mɪtɪgeɪt] *vt* atténuer; *Law* **mitigating circumstances** circonstances *fpl* atténuantes

mitt(en) [mɪt, 'mɪtən] *n (glove)* moufle *f*

mix [mɪks] **1** *n (mixture)* mélange *m*

2 *vt* mélanger; *(cement, drink, cake)* préparer; *(salad)* remuer; **to m. up** *(drinks, papers)* mélanger; *(mistake)* confondre (**with** avec); **to be mixed up in sth** être mêlé à qch; **to get mixed up with sb** se mettre à fréquenter qn

3 *vi (blend)* se mélanger; *(of colours)* aller ensemble; **to m. with sb** *(socially)* fréquenter qn; **she doesn't m.** elle n'est pas sociable

mixed [mɪkst] *adj (school, marriage)* mixte; *(results)* divers; *(nuts, chocolates)* assortis; **m. grill** assortiment *m* de grillades; **m. feelings** sentiments *mpl* mitigés; **to be (all) m. up** *(of person)* être désorienté; *(of facts, account)* être confus; **in m. company** en présence de personnes des deux sexes

mixer ['mɪksə(r)] *n* **(a)** *(for cooking)* mixeur *m*; *Br* **m. tap** *(robinet m)* mélangeur *m* **(b)** **to be a good m.** *(of person)* être sociable

mixture ['mɪkstʃə(r)] *n* mélange *m*

mix-up ['mɪksʌp] *n* confusion *f*

mm (*abbr* **millimetre**) mm

moan [məʊn] **1** *n (sound)* gémissement *m*; *(complaint)* plainte *f*
2 *vi (make sound)* gémir; *(complain)* se plaindre (**to** à; **about** de; **that** que)

moat [məʊt] *n* douve *f*

mob [mɒb] **1** *n (crowd)* foule *f*; *Am Fam* **the M.** la Mafia
2 (*pt & pp* **-bb-**) *vt* prendre d'assaut • **mobster** *n Am Fam* gangster *m*

mobile [*Br* ˈməʊbaɪl, *Am* ˈməʊbəl] **1** *adj* mobile; *Fam* **to be m.** être motorisé; **m. home** mobile home *m*; **m. library** bibliobus *m*; **m. phone** téléphone *m* portable
2 *n* (**a**) (*Am* [ˈməʊbiːl]) *(ornament)* mobile *m* (**b**) *(phone)* portable *m* • **mobility** *n* mobilité *f*

mobilize [ˈməʊbɪlaɪz] *vti* mobiliser • **mobiliˈzation** *n* mobilisation *f*

moccasin [ˈmɒkəsɪn] *n* mocassin *m*

mocha [*Br* ˈmɒkə, *Am* ˈməʊkə] *n* moka *m*

mock [mɒk] **1** *adj (false)* simulé; *Br Sch* **m. exam** examen *m* blanc
2 *vt* se moquer de; *(mimic)* singer • **mocking** *n* moquerie *f*

mockery [ˈmɒkərɪ] *n (act)* moqueries *fpl*; *(farce, parody)* parodie *f*; **to make a m. of sth** tourner qch en ridicule

mock-up [ˈmɒkʌp] *n* maquette *f*

mod cons [mɒdˈkɒnz] *npl Fam* **with all m.** *(house)* tout confort *inv*

mode [məʊd] *n (manner, way)* & *Comptr* mode *m*

model [ˈmɒdəl] **1** *n (example, person)* modèle *m*; *(small version)* maquette *f*; **(fashion) m.** mannequin *m*; **(scale) m.** modèle réduit
2 *adj (behaviour, factory, student)* modèle; *(car, plane)* modèle réduit *inv*
3 (*Br* **-ll-**, *Am* **-l-**) *vt (clay)* modeler; *(hats, dresses)* présenter; *Comptr* modéliser; **to m. sth on** modeler qch sur; **to m. oneself on sb** prendre exemple sur qn
4 *vi (for fashion)* être mannequin; *(pose for artist)* poser • **modelling** (*Am* **modeling**) *n (of statues, in clay)* modelage *m*; **to make a career in m.** faire une carrière de mannequin

modem [ˈməʊdəm] *n Comptr* modem *m*

moderate¹ [ˈmɒdərət] **1** *adj* modéré
2 *n Pol* modéré, -ée *mf* • **moderately** *adv (in moderation)* modérément; *(averagely)* moyennement

moderate² [ˈmɒdəreɪt] **1** *vt (diminish, tone down)* modérer
2 *vi (of wind)* se calmer • **moderˈation** *n* modération *f*; **in m.** avec modération

modern [ˈmɒdən] *adj* moderne; **m. lan-**

guages langues *fpl* vivantes • **modernism** *n* modernisme *m*

modernize [ˈmɒdənaɪz] **1** *vt* moderniser
2 *vi* se moderniser • **moderniˈzation** *n* modernisation *f*

modest [ˈmɒdɪst] *adj (unassuming, moderate)* modeste; *(chaste)* pudique • **modesty** *n (of person)* modestie *f*

modicum [ˈmɒdɪkəm] *n* **a m. of** un minimum de

modify [ˈmɒdɪfaɪ] (*pt & pp* **-ied**) *vt* modifier • **modification** [-fɪˈkeɪʃən] *n* modification *f* (**to** à)

modulate [ˈmɒdjʊleɪt] *vt* moduler • **moduˈlation** *n* modulation *f*

module [ˈmɒdjuːl] *n* module *m*

mogul [ˈməʊgəl] *n Fig* magnat *m*

mohair [ˈməʊheə(r)] *n* mohair *m*; **m. sweater** pull *m* en mohair

moist [mɔɪst] (**-er, -est**) *adj* humide; *(skin, hand)* moite • **moisten** [ˈmɔɪsən] *vt* humecter

moisture [ˈmɔɪstʃə(r)] *n* humidité *f*; *(on glass)* buée *f*

moisturize [ˈmɔɪstʃəraɪz] *vt* hydrater • **moisturizer** *n* crème *f* hydratante

molar [ˈməʊlə(r)] *n* molaire *f*

molasses [məˈlæsɪz] *n Am (treacle)* mélasse *f*

mold [məʊld] *n & vt Am* = **mould**

mole [məʊl] *n* (**a**) *(on skin)* grain *m* de beauté (**b**) *(animal, spy)* taupe *f*

molecule [ˈmɒlɪkjuːl] *n* molécule *f*

molest [məˈlest] *vt (annoy)* importuner; *Law (child, woman)* agresser (sexuellement)

mollusc [ˈmɒləsk] *n* mollusque *m*

molt [məʊlt] *vi Am* = **moult**

molten [ˈməʊltən] *adj (metal, rock)* en fusion

mom [mɒm] *n Am Fam* maman *f*

moment [ˈməʊmənt] *n* moment *m*, instant *m*; **at the m.** en ce moment; **for the m.** pour le moment; **in a m.** dans un instant; **the m. she leaves** dès qu'elle partira; **any m. (now)** d'un instant à l'autre

momentary [ˈməʊməntərɪ] *adj* momentané • **momentarily** [-ˈterɪlɪ] *adv (temporarily)* momentanément; *Am (soon)* tout de suite

momentous [məʊˈmentəs] *adj* capital

momentum [məʊˈmentəm] *n (speed)* élan *m*; **to gather** *or* **gain m.** *(of ideas)* gagner du terrain; *(of campaign)* prendre de l'ampleur

mommy [ˈmɒmɪ] *n Am Fam* maman *f*

Monaco [ˈmɒnəkəʊ] *n* Monaco *m*

monarch ['mɒnək] *n* monarque *m* • **monarchy** (*pl* **-ies**) *n* monarchie *f*

monastery ['mɒnəstərɪ] (*pl* **-ies**) *n* monastère *m*

Monday ['mʌndeɪ] *n* lundi *m*

monetary ['mʌnɪtərɪ] *adj* monétaire

money ['mʌnɪ] *n* argent *m*; **to make m.** (*of person*) gagner de l'argent; (*of business*) rapporter de l'argent; **to get one's m.'s worth** en avoir pour son argent; **he gets** *or* **earns good m.** il gagne bien sa vie; *Fam* **to be in the m.** rouler sur l'or; **m. order** mandat *m* • **moneybags** *n Fam Pej* richard, -arde *mf* • **moneybox** *n* tirelire *f* • **moneychanger** *n* changeur *m* de monnaie • **moneylender** *n* prêteur, -euse *mf* • **moneymaking** *adj* lucratif, -ive • **moneyspinner** *n Fam* (*project*) mine *f* d'or

> *ℓ* Note that the French word **monnaie** is a false friend and is rarely a translation for the English word **money**. It means **change** or **currency** depending on the context.

mongol ['mɒŋgəl] *n & adj Old-fashioned Med* mongolien, -ienne (*mf*), = terme injurieux désignant un trisomique

mongrel ['mʌŋgrəl] *n* bâtard *m*

monitor ['mɒnɪtə(r)] **1** *n Comptr, TV & Tech* (*screen, device*) moniteur *m*
2 *vt* (*broadcast, conversation*) écouter; (*check*) surveiller

monk [mʌŋk] *n* moine *m*

monkey ['mʌŋkɪ] **1** (*pl* **-eys**) *n* singe *m*; *Fam* **little m.** (*child*) polisson, -onne *mf*; *Fam* **m. business** (*mischief*) singeries *fpl*; (*dishonest behaviour*) magouilles *fpl*; *Br* **m. nut** cacah(o)uète *f*; **m. wrench** clef *f* anglaise
2 *vi Fam* **to m. about** *or* **around** faire l'imbécile

mono ['mɒnəʊ] **1** *adj* (*record*) mono *inv*
2 *n* **in m.** en monophonie

monocle ['mɒnəkəl] *n* monocle *m*

monogram ['mɒnəgræm] *n* monogramme *m*

monologue ['mɒnəlɒg] *n* monologue *m*

mononucleosis [mɒnəʊnjuːklɪ'əʊsɪs] *n Am Med* mononucléose *f* infectieuse

monopoly [mə'nɒpəlɪ] *n* monopole *m* • **monopolize** *vt* monopoliser

monosyllable ['mɒnəsɪləbəl] *n* monosyllabe *m* • **monosyllabic** [-'læbɪk] *adj* monosyllabique

monotone ['mɒnətəʊn] *n* **in a m.** sur un ton monocorde

monotony [mə'nɒtənɪ] *n* monotonie *f* • **monotonous** *adj* monotone

monsoon [mɒn'suːn] *n* mousson *f*

monster ['mɒnstə(r)] *n* monstre *m*

monstrosity [mɒn'strɒsətɪ] (*pl* **-ies**) *n* monstruosité *f*

monstrous ['mɒnstrəs] *adj* monstrueux, -ueuse

month [mʌnθ] *n* mois *m*

monthly ['mʌnθlɪ] **1** *adj* mensuel, -uelle; **m. payment** mensualité *f*
2 (*pl* **-ies**) *n* (*periodical*) mensuel *m*
3 *adv* tous les mois

Montreal [mɒntrɪ'ɔːl] *n* Montréal *m ou f*

monument ['mɒnjʊmənt] *n* monument *m*

monumental [mɒnjʊ'mentəl] *adj* monumental

moo [muː] **1** (*pl* **moos**) *n* meuglement *m*
2 *exclam* meuh!
3 (*pt & pp* **mooed**) *vi* meugler

mooch [muːtʃ] *Fam* **1** *vi* **to m. around** flâner
2 *vt Am* **to m. sth off sb** (*cadge*) taper qch à qn

mood [muːd] *n* (*of person*) humeur *f*; (*of country*) état *m* d'esprit; *Grammar* mode *m*; **in a good/bad m.** de bonne/mauvaise humeur; **to be in the m. to do** *or* **for doing sth** être d'humeur à faire qch

moody ['muːdɪ] (**-ier, -iest**) *adj* (*bad-tempered*) maussade; (*changeable*) lunatique

moon [muːn] *n* lune *f*; **full m.** pleine lune; **once in a blue m.** (*rarely*) tous les trente-six du mois; *Br Fam* **over the m.** aux anges (**about** de) • **moonlight 1** *n* clair *m* de lune; **by m.** au clair de lune **2** *vi Fam* travailler au noir • **moonlit** *adj* (*landscape*) éclairé par la lune

moonshine ['muːnʃaɪn] *n Fam* (*nonsense*) balivernes *fpl*

moor [mʊə(r)] **1** *n* (*heath*) lande *f*
2 *vt* (*ship*) amarrer
3 *vi* (*of ship*) mouiller • **moorings** *npl Naut* (*ropes*) amarres *fpl*; (*place*) mouillage *m*

moose [muːs] *n inv* (*animal*) élan *m*; (*Canadian*) orignal *m*

moot [muːt] *adj* **it's a m. point** c'est discutable

mop [mɒp] **1** *n* (*for floor*) balai *m* à franges; (*with sponge*) balai-éponge *m*; **dish m.** lavette *f*; *Fam* **m. of hair** tignasse *f*
2 (*pt & pp* **-pp-**) *vt* **to m. one's brow** s'essuyer le front; **to m. (up) the floor** laver par terre; **to m. sth up** (*liquid*) éponger qch

mope [məʊp] *vi* **to m. about** broyer du noir

moped ['məʊped] *n* Mobylette® *f*

moral ['mɒrəl] **1** *adj* moral

2 *n (of story)* morale *f*; **morals** *(principles)* moralité *f* • **morale** [mə'ræl, *Br* mɒ'rɑːl] *n* moral *m* • **moralist** *n* moraliste *mf* • **morality** [mə'rælɪtɪ] *n* moralité *f* • **moralize** *vi* moraliser • **morally** *adv* moralement; **m. wrong** immoral

morass [mə'ræs] *n (land)* marais *m*; *Fig (mess, situation)* bourbier *m*

moratorium [mɒrə'tɔːrɪəm] *n* moratoire *m* (**on** sur)

morbid ['mɔːbɪd] *adj* morbide • **morbidly** *adv* de façon morbide

more [mɔː(r)] **1** *adj* plus de; **m. cars** plus de voitures; **m. water** plus d'eau; **he has m. books than you** il a plus de livres que toi; **a few m. months** quelques mois de plus; **(some) m. tea** encore du thé; **(some) m. details** d'autres détails; **m. than a kilo/ten** plus d'un kilo/de dix

2 *adv (to form comparative of adjectives and adverbs)* plus (**than** que); **m. interesting** plus intéressant; **m. easily** plus facilement; **m. and m.** de plus en plus; **m. or less** plus ou moins

3 *pron* plus; **have some m.** reprenez-en; **she knows m. than you** elle en sait plus que toi; **she doesn't have any m.** elle n'en a plus; **the m. he shouts, the m. hoarse he gets** plus il crie, plus il s'enroue; **what's m.** qui plus est

moreish ['mɔːrɪʃ] *adj Br Fam* qui a un goût de revenez-y

moreover [mɔː'rəʊvə(r)] *adv* de plus

mores ['mɔːreɪz] *npl Formal* mœurs *fpl*

morgue [mɔːg] *n* morgue *f*

moribund ['mɒrɪbʌnd] *adj* moribond

morning ['mɔːnɪŋ] **1** *n* matin *m*; *(referring to duration)* matinée *f*; **in the m.** le matin; *(during the course of the morning)* pendant la matinée; *(tomorrow)* demain matin; **tomorrow/yesterday m.** demain/hier matin; **at seven in the m.** à sept heures du matin; **every Tuesday m.** tous les mardis matin; **in the early m.** au petit matin

2 *adj (newspaper)* du matin; **m. sickness** *(of pregnant woman)* nausées *fpl* matinales • **mornings** *adv Am* le matin

Morocco [mə'rɒkəʊ] *n* le Maroc • **Moroccan 1** *adj* marocain **2** *n* Marocain, -aine *mf*

moron ['mɔːrɒn] *n* crétin, -ine *mf*

morose [mə'rəʊs] *adj* morose

morphine ['mɔːfiːn] *n* morphine *f*

Morse [mɔːs] *n & adj* **M. (code)** morse *m*

morsel ['mɔːsəl] *n* morceau *m*

mortal ['mɔːtəl] *adj & n* mortel, -elle *(mf)* • **mortality** [-'tælɪtɪ] *n* mortalité *f*

mortar ['mɔːtə(r)] *n* mortier *m*

mortgage ['mɔːgɪdʒ] **1** *n (from lender's viewpoint)* prêt *m* immobilier; *(from borrower's viewpoint)* emprunt *m* immobilier; **m. rate** taux *m* de crédit immobilier

2 *vt (house, one's future)* hypothéquer

mortician [mɔː'tɪʃən] *n Am* entrepreneur *m* de pompes funèbres

mortify ['mɔːtɪfaɪ] *(pt & pp* **-ied**) *vt* mortifier; **I was mortified!** j'étais vexé!

mortuary ['mɔːtʃʊərɪ] *(pl* **-ies**) *n* morgue *f*

mosaic [məʊ'zeɪɪk] *n* mosaïque *f*

Moscow [*Br* 'mɒskəʊ, *Am* 'mɒskaʊ] *n* Moscou *m ou f*

Moses ['məʊzɪz] *adj* **M. basket** couffin *m*

Moslem ['mɒzlɪm] *adj & n* musulman, -ane *(mf)*

mosque [mɒsk] *n* mosquée *f*

mosquito [mɒ'skiːtəʊ] *(pl* **-oes** *or* **-os**) *n* moustique *m*; **m. net** moustiquaire *f*

moss [mɒs] *n* mousse *f* • **mossy** *adj* moussu

most [məʊst] **1** *adj* (a) *(the majority of)* la plupart de; **m. women** la plupart des femmes (b) *(greatest amount of)* **the m.** le plus de; **I have the m. books** j'ai le plus de livres

2 *adv* (a) *(to form superlative of adjectives and adverbs)* plus; **the m. beautiful** le plus beau *(f* la plus belle) (**in/of** de); **to talk (the) m.** parler le plus; **what I want m.** ce que je veux par-dessus tout; **m. of all** *(especially)* surtout

(b) *(very)* extrêmement; **it was m. interesting** c'était extrêmement intéressant

3 *pron* (a) *(the majority)* la plupart; **m. of the people** la plupart des gens; **m. of the time** la plupart du temps; **m. of the cake** la plus grande partie du gâteau; **m. of them** la plupart d'entre eux

(b) *(greatest amount)* le plus; **he earns the m.** c'est lui qui gagne le plus; **to make the m. of sth** *(situation, talent)* tirer le meilleur parti de qch; *(holiday)* profiter au maximum de qch; **at (the very) m.** tout au plus • **mostly** *adv (in the main)* surtout; *(most often)* le plus souvent

MOT [eməʊ'tiː] *(abbr* **Ministry of Transport**) *n Br* = contrôle obligatoire des véhicules de plus de trois ans

motel [məʊ'tel] *n* motel *m*

moth [mɒθ] *n* papillon *m* de nuit; **(clothes) m.** mite *f* • **mothball** *n* boule *f* de naphtaline • **moth-eaten** *adj* mité

mother ['mʌðə(r)] **1** *n* mère *f*; **M.'s Day** la fête des Mères; **m. tongue** langue *f* maternelle

2 *vt* materner • **motherhood** *n* maternité *f* • **mother-in-law** *(pl* **mothers-in-law**) *n*

belle-mère f • **motherly** adj maternel, -elle • **mother-of-'pearl** n nacre f • **mother-to-'be** (pl mothers-to-be) n future mère f
motion ['məʊʃən] **1** n (of arm) mouvement m; (in meeting) motion f; **to set sth in m.** mettre qch en mouvement; **m. picture** film m
2 vti **to m. (to) sb to do sth** faire signe à qn de faire qch • **motionless** adj immobile
motivate ['məʊtɪveɪt] vt (person, decision) motiver • **motivated** adj motivé • **moti'vation** n motivation f
motive ['məʊtɪv] n motif m (for de); Law mobile m (for de)
motley ['mɒtlɪ] adj (collection) hétéroclite; (coloured) bigarré
motor ['məʊtə(r)] **1** n (engine) moteur m; Br Fam (car) auto f
2 adj (industry, vehicle, insurance) automobile; (accident) d'auto; Br **m. mechanic** mécanicien-auto m; **m. racing** courses fpl automobiles; **m. show** salon m de l'automobile
3 vi Br (drive) voyager en auto • **motorbike** n moto f • **motorboat** n canot m à moteur • **motorcade** n cortège m de voitures • **motorcar** n Br automobile f • **motorcycle** n moto f, motocyclette f • **motorcyclist** n motocycliste mf • **motoring** n Br conduite f; **school of m.** auto-école f • **motorist** n Br automobiliste mf • **motorized** adj motorisé • **motorway** n Br autoroute f
mottled ['mɒtəld] adj tacheté
motto ['mɒtəʊ] (pl -oes or -os) n devise f
mould¹ [məʊld] (Am **mold**) **1** n (shape) moule m
2 vt (clay, person's character) modeler
mould² [məʊld] (Am **mold**) n (fungus) moisissure f • **mouldy** (Am **moldy**) (-ier, -iest) adj moisi; **to go m.** moisir
moult [məʊlt] (Am **molt**) vi muer • **moulting** (Am **molting**) n mue f
mound [maʊnd] n (of earth) tertre m; Fig (untidy pile) tas m
Mount [maʊnt] n M. Vesuvius le Vésuve
mount [maʊnt] **1** n (frame for photo or slide) cadre m; (horse) monture f
2 vt (horse, hill, jewel, photo, demonstration) monter; (ladder, tree) monter à
3 vi (a) **to m. (up)** (on horse) se mettre en selle (b) (increase, rise) monter; **to m. up** (add up) chiffrer (**to** à); (accumulate) (of debts, bills) s'accumuler
mountain ['maʊntɪn] **1** n montagne f
2 adj (plant, shoes) de montagne; **m. bike** vélo m tout terrain; **m. range** chaîne f de montagnes; **m. rescue team** équipe f

de secours en montagne • **mountai'neer** n alpiniste mf • **mountaineering** n alpinisme m • **mountainous** adj montagneux, -euse
mourn [mɔːn] vti **to m. (for) sb, to m. the loss of sb** pleurer qn; **she's mourning** elle est en deuil • **mourner** n = personne assistant aux obsèques • **mournful** adj triste • **mourning** n deuil m; **in m.** en deuil
mouse [maʊs] (pl **mice** [maɪs]) n (animal) & Comptr souris f • **mousetrap** n souricière f
mousse [muːs] n mousse f; **chocolate m.** mousse au chocolat
moustache [Br məˈstɑːʃ, Am ˈmʌstæʃ] n moustache f
mousy ['maʊsɪ] (-ier, -iest) adj Br Pej (hair) châtain terne; Fig (shy) timide
mouth 1 [maʊθ] (pl **-s** [maʊðz]) n (of person, horse) bouche f; (of other animals) gueule f; (of river) embouchure f; (of cave, harbour) entrée f
2 [maʊð] vt Pej débiter • **mouthful** ['maʊθfʊl] n (of food) bouchée f; (of liquid) gorgée f • **mouthorgan** n harmonica m • **mouthpiece** n (of musical instrument) embouchure f; (spokesperson) porte-parole m inv • **mouthwash** n bain m de bouche • **mouth-watering** adj appétissant
movable ['muːvəbəl] adj mobile
move [muːv] **1** n mouvement m; (change of house) déménagement m; (change of job) changement m d'emploi; (transfer of employee) mutation f; (in game) coup m; (step) pas m; **to make a m.** (leave) se préparer à partir; (act) passer à l'action; **to make a m. towards sb/sth** se diriger vers qn/qch; **to make the first m.** faire le premier pas; **it's your m.** (turn) c'est à toi de jouer; Fam **to get a m. on** se grouiller; **on the m.** en marche
2 vt déplacer; (arm, leg) remuer; (employee) muter; (piece in game) jouer; (propose in debate) proposer (**that** que); **to m. sb** (emotionally) émouvoir qn; (transfer in job) muter qn; **to m. sb to tears** émouvoir qn jusqu'aux larmes; **to m. house** déménager
3 vi bouger; (change position) se déplacer (**to** à); (leave) partir; (act) agir; (play) jouer; (change house) déménager; **to m. to Paris** aller habiter Paris; **to m. into a house** emménager dans une maison; **to get things moving** faire avancer les choses
▸ **move about** or **around** vi se déplacer; (fidget) remuer ▸ **move along** vi avancer

▸**move away** *vi (go away)* s'éloigner; *(move house)* déménager ▸**move back 1** *vt sep (chair)* reculer; *(to its original position)* remettre en place **2** *vi (withdraw)* reculer; *(return)* retourner (**to** à) ▸**move down 1** *vt sep (take down)* descendre **2** *vi (come down)* descendre ▸**move forward** *vt sep & vi* avancer ▸**move in** *vi (into house)* emménager ▸**move off** *vi (go away)* s'éloigner; *(of vehicle)* démarrer ▸**move out** *vi (out of house)* déménager ▸**move over 1** *vt sep* pousser **2** *vi (make room)* se pousser ▸**move up** *vi (on seats)* se pousser

moveable ['muːvəbəl] *adj* mobile

movement ['muːvmənt] *n* mouvement *m*

movie ['muːvɪ] *n* film *m*; **the movies** *(cinema)* le cinéma; **m. camera** caméra *f*; **m. star** vedette *f* de cinéma; *Am* **m. theater** cinéma • **moviegoer** *n* cinéphile *mf*

moving ['muːvɪŋ] *adj* en mouvement; *(vehicle)* en marche; *(touching)* émouvant; **m. part** *(of machine)* pièce *f* mobile; **m. stairs** escalier *m* mécanique

mow [məʊ] *(pp* **mown** [məʊn] *or* **mowed**) *vt (field, wheat)* faucher; **to m. the lawn** tondre le gazon; *Fig* **to m. down** *(kill)* • **mower** *n* **(lawn) m.** tondeuse *f* (à gazon)

Mozambique [məʊzæm'biːk] *n* le Mozambique

MP [em'piː] *(abbr* **Member of Parliament**) *n* député *m*

mph [empiː'eɪtʃ] *(abbr* **miles per hour**) ≈ km/h

Mr ['mɪstə(r)] *n* **Mr Brown** M. Brown

Mrs ['mɪsɪz] *n* **Mrs Brown** Mme Brown

Ms [mɪz] *n* **Ms Brown** ≈ Mme Brown *(ne renseigne pas sur le statut de famille)*

MS [em'es] (**a**) *(abbr* **multiple sclerosis**) *Med* sclérose *f* en plaques (**b**) *(abbr* **Master of Science**) *Am Univ see* **MSc**

MSc [emes'siː] *(abbr* **Master of Science**) *n* *Univ* **to have an M. in chemistry** avoir une maîtrise de chimie; **John Smith M.** John Smith, titulaire d'une maîtrise *(en sciences, chimie etc)*

MSP [emes'piː] *(abbr* **Member of the Scottish Parliament**) *n* député *m* du parlement écossais

much [mʌtʃ] **1** *adj*

> Hormis dans la langue soutenue et dans certaines expressions, ne s'utilise que dans des structures négatives ou interrogatives.

beaucoup de; **not m. time/money** pas beaucoup de temps/d'argent; **how m. sugar do you want?** combien de sucre voulez-vous?; **as m. wine as** autant de vin que; **twice as m. traffic** deux fois plus de circulation; **too m. work** trop de travail; **so m. time** tant *ou* tellement de temps; **this m. wine** ça de vin

2 *adv* beaucoup; **very m.** beaucoup; **not (very) m.** pas beaucoup; **m. better** bien meilleur; **m. more difficult** beaucoup plus difficile; **I love him so m.** je l'aime tellement; **she doesn't say very m.** elle ne dit pas grand-chose; **everything had stayed m. the same** rien n'avait vraiment changé

3 *pron* beaucoup; **not m.** pas beaucoup; **there isn't m. left** il n'en reste pas beaucoup; **it's not m. of a garden** ce n'est pas terrible comme jardin; **twice as m.** deux fois plus; **as m. as possible** autant que possible; **as m. as you like** autant que tu veux; **he knows as m. as you do** il en sait autant que toi; **so m. so that...** à tel point que...; **he had drunk so m. that...** il avait tellement bu que...; *Fam* **that's a bit m.!** c'est un peu fort!

muck [mʌk] **1** *n (manure)* fumier *m*; *Fig (filth)* saleté *f*

2 *vt Br Fam* **to m. sb about** faire perdre son temps à qn; *Br Fam* **to m. sth up** *(task)* bâcler qch; *(plans)* chambouler qch

3 *vi Br Fam* **to m. about** *or* **around** *(waste time)* traîner; *(play the fool)* faire l'imbécile; *Br Fam* **to m. about** *or* **around with sth** *(fiddle with)* tripoter qch; *Br Fam* **to m. in** *(help)* s'y mettre • **mucky** (**-ier, -iest**) *adj Fam* sale

mucus ['mjuːkəs] *n* mucosités *fpl*

mud [mʌd] *n* boue *f* • **muddy** (**-ier, -iest**) *adj (water, road)* boueux (*f* boueuse); *(hands)* couvert de boue • **mudguard** *n* garde-boue *m inv*

muddle ['mʌdəl] **1** *n* confusion *f*; **to be in a m.** *(person)* ne plus s'y retrouver; *(of things)* être en désordre

2 *vt (person, facts)* mélanger; **to get muddled** s'embrouiller

3 *vi Fam* **to m. through** se débrouiller

muff [mʌf] *n (for hands)* manchon *m*

muffin ['mʌfɪn] *n (cake)* ≈ sorte de madeleine; *Br (teacake)* muffin *m*

muffle ['mʌfəl] *vt (noise)* assourdir • **muffled** *adj (noise)* sourd • **muffler** *n* *Am (on vehicle)* silencieux *m*

mug¹ [mʌg] *n* (**a**) *(for tea, coffee)* grande tasse *f*; **(beer) m.** chope *f* (**b**) *Fam (face)* gueule *f*; **m. shot** photo *f* d'identité judiciaire (**c**) *Br Fam (fool)* poire *f*

mug² [mʌg] *(pt & pp* **-gg-**) *vt (attack in*

street) agresser • **mugger** *n* agresseur *m*
• **mugging** *n* agression *f*
muggy ['mʌgɪ] (**-ier, -iest**) *adj (weather)*
lourd
mulberry ['mʌlbərɪ] (*pl* **-ies**) *n (fruit)*
mûre *f*
mule [mjuːl] *n (male)* mulet *m*; *(female)*
mule *f*
▶ **mull over** [mʌl'əʊvə(r)] *vt sep (think over)* ruminer
mulled wine ['mʌld'waɪn] *n* vin *m*
chaud épicé
mullet ['mʌlɪt] *n (fish)* mulet *m*; **red m.**
rouget *m*
multicoloured ['mʌltɪkʌləd] *adj* multicolore
multifarious [mʌltɪ'feərɪəs] *adj* divers
multimedia [mʌltɪ'miːdɪə] *adj* multimédia
multimillionaire [mʌltɪmɪljə'neə(r)] *n* multimillionnaire *mf*
multinational [mʌltɪ'naeʃənəl] *n & adj*
m. (company) multinationale *(f)*
multiple ['mʌltɪpəl] **1** *adj* multiple; *Med*
m. sclerosis sclérose *f* en plaques
2 *n Math* multiple *m*
multiple-choice ['mʌltɪpəl'tʃɔɪs] *adj* à
choix multiple
multiplicity [mʌltɪ'plɪsɪtɪ] *n* multiplicité *f*
multiply ['mʌltɪplaɪ] (*pt & pp* **-ied**) **1** *vt*
multiplier
2 *vi (of animals, insects)* se multiplier
• **multiplication** [-plɪ'keɪʃən] *n* multiplication *f*
multiracial [mʌltɪ'reɪʃəl] *adj* multiracial
multistorey [mʌltɪ'stɔːrɪ] (*Am* **multistoried**) *adj (car park)* à plusieurs niveaux
multitude ['mʌltɪtjuːd] *n* multitude *f*
mum [mʌm] *Fam* **1** *n Br* maman *f*
2 *adj* **to keep m. (about sth)** ne pas
souffler mot (de qch)
mumble ['mʌmbəl] *vti* marmotter
mumbo jumbo ['mʌmbəʊ'dʒʌmbəʊ] *n*
(nonsense) âneries *fpl*
mummy¹ ['mʌmɪ] (*pl* **-ies**) *n Br Fam*
(mother) maman *f*
mummy² ['mʌmɪ] (*pl* **-ies**) *n (embalmed body)* momie *f*
mumps [mʌmps] *n Med* oreillons *mpl*
munch [mʌntʃ] *vti (chew)* mâcher
mundane [mʌn'deɪn] *adj* banal (*mpl* -als)

ℓ Note that the French word **mondain** is a
false friend and is never a translation for the
English word **mundane**. It refers to people
and events in high society.

---

municipal [mjuː'nɪsɪpəl] *adj* municipal
• **municipality** [-'pælɪtɪ] (*pl* **-ies**) *n* municipalité *f*
munitions [mjuː'nɪʃənz] *npl* munitions *fpl*
mural ['mjʊərəl] **1** *adj* mural
2 *n* peinture *f* murale
murder ['mɜːdə(r)] **1** *n* meurtre *m*; *Fam*
it's m. *(dreadful)* c'est affreux
2 *vt (kill)* assassiner; *Fig (spoil)* massacrer • **murderer** *n* meurtrier, -ière *mf*, assassin *m* • **murderous** *adj* meurtrier, -ière
murky ['mɜːkɪ] (**-ier, -iest**) *adj (water, business, past)* trouble; *(weather)* nuageux, -euse
murmur ['mɜːmə(r)] **1** *n* murmure *m*; *(of traffic, conversation)* bourdonnement *m*;
(heart) m. souffle *m* au cœur
2 *vti* murmurer
muscle ['mʌsəl] **1** *n* muscle *m*
2 *vi* **to m. in** intervenir (**on** dans) • **muscular** ['mʌskjʊlə(r)] *adj (person, arm)*
musclé; *(tissue, pain)* musculaire
muse [mjuːz] *vi* songer (**on** à)
museum [mjuː'zɪəm] *n* musée *m*
mush [mʌʃ] *n (pulp)* bouillie *f*; *Fig (sentimentality)* mièvrerie *f* • **mushy** (**-ier, -iest**)
adj (food) en bouillie; *Fig (sentimental)*
mièvre
mushroom ['mʌʃrʊm] **1** *n* champignon
m
2 *vi (of buildings, towns)* pousser
comme des champignons; *(of problems)*
se multiplier
music ['mjuːzɪk] *n* musique *f*; **m. centre**
chaîne *f* stéréo compacte; **m. critic** critique *m* musical; **m. hall** music-hall *m*; **m. lover** mélomane *mf*; **canned** *or* **piped m.**
musique *f* (de fond) enregistrée • **musical**
1 *adj* musical; **m. instrument** instrument
m de musique; **to be (very) m.** être (très)
musicien **2** *n (film, play)* comédie *f* musicale • **musician** [-'zɪʃən] *n* musicien,
-ienne *mf*
musk [mʌsk] *n* musc *m*
Muslim ['mʊzlɪm] *adj & n* musulman,
-ane *(mf)*
muslin ['mʌzlɪn] *n* mousseline *f*
mussel ['mʌsəl] *n* moule *f*
must [mʌst] **1** *n* **this is a m.** c'est indispensable; **this film is a m.** il faut absolument voir ce film
2 *v aux* (**a**) *(expressing necessity)* **you m. obey** tu dois obéir, il faut que tu obéisses
(**b**) *(expressing probability)* **she m. be clever** elle doit être intelligente; **I m. have seen it** j'ai dû le voir; **you m. be joking!** tu
veux rire!; **m. you be so silly?** qu'est-ce
que tu peux être bête!

mustache [ˈmʌstæʃ] *n Am* moustache *f*
mustard [ˈmʌstəd] *n* moutarde *f*
muster [ˈmʌstə(r)] **1** *vt (gather)* rassembler; *(sum)* réunir
 2 *vi* se rassembler
mustn't [ˈmʌsənt] = must not
musty [ˈmʌstɪ] (**-ier, -iest**) *adj (smell, taste)* de moisi; **it smells m., it's m.** ça sent le moisi
mutant [ˈmjuːtənt] *n Biol* mutant *m*
 • **mu'tation** *n Biol* mutation *f*
mute [mjuːt] **1** *adj (silent) & Ling* muet (*f* muette)
 2 *vt (sound)* assourdir • **muted** *adj (criticism)* voilé; *(colour)* sourd
mutilate [ˈmjuːtɪleɪt] *vt* mutiler • **muti'lation** *n* mutilation *f*
mutiny [ˈmjuːtɪnɪ] **1** (*pl* **-ies**) *n* mutinerie *f*
 2 (*pt & pp* **-ied**) *vi* se mutiner • **mutinous** *adj (troops)* rebelle
mutter [ˈmʌtə(r)] *vti* marmonner
mutton [ˈmʌtən] *n (meat)* mouton *m*; **leg of m.** gigot *m*
mutual [ˈmjuːtʃʊəl] *adj (help, love)* mutuel, -uelle; *(friend)* commun; *Am Fin* **m. fund** fonds *m* commun de placement
 • **mutually** *adv* mutuellement

muzzle [ˈmʌzəl] **1** *n (device for dog)* muselière *f*; *(snout)* museau *m*; *(of gun)* gueule *f*
 2 *vt (animal, the press)* museler
muzzy [ˈmʌzɪ] (**-ier, -iest**) *adj (confused) (person)* aux idées confuses; *(ideas)* confus; *(blurred) (outline)* flou
my [maɪ] *possessive adj* mon, ma, *pl* mes
myself [maɪˈself] *pron* moi-même; *(reflexive)* me, m'; *(after prep)* moi; **I did it m.** je l'ai fait moi-même; **I wash m.** je me lave; **I think of m.** je pense à moi
mystery [ˈmɪstərɪ] (*pl* **-ies**) *n* mystère *m*
 • **mysterious** [mɪˈstɪərɪəs] *adj* mystérieux, -ieuse
mystic [ˈmɪstɪk] *adj & n* mystique (*mf*)
 • **mystical** *adj* mystique • **mysticism** [-tɪsɪzəm] *n* mysticisme *m* • **mystique** [mɪˈstiːk] *n (mystery, power)* mystique *f* (**of** de)
mystify [ˈmɪstɪfaɪ] (*pt & pp* **-ied**) *vt (bewilder)* déconcerter; *(fool)* mystifier
myth [mɪθ] *n* mythe *m* • **mythical** *adj* mythique • **mytho'logical** *adj* mythologique • **my'thology** (*pl* **-ies**) *n* mythologie *f*

N, n [en] *n (letter)* N, n *m inv*; **the nth time** la énième fois

nab [næb] *(pt & pp* **-bb-**) *vt Fam (catch, arrest)* coffrer

naff [næf] *adj Br Fam (poor-quality)* nul (*f* nulle); *(unfashionable)* ringard

nag [næg] *(pt & pp* **-gg-**) *vti* **to n. (at) sb** *(of person)* être sur le dos de qn ● **nagging** **1** *adj (doubt, headache)* tenace **2** *n* plaintes *fpl* continuelles

nail [neɪl] **1** *n* (**a**) *(of finger, toe)* ongle *m*; **n. brush** brosse *f* à ongles; **n. file** lime *f* à ongles; **n. polish,** *Br* **n. varnish** vernis *m* à ongles (**b**) *(metal)* clou *m* **2** *vt* clouer; *Fam* **to n. sb** épingler qn; **to n. sth down** *(lid)* clouer qch

naïve [naɪˈiːv] *adj* naïf (*f* naïve) ● **naïveté** [naɪˈiːvtɪ] *n* naïveté *f*

naked [ˈneɪkɪd] *adj (person)* nu; **to see sth with the n. eye** voir qch à l'œil nu; **n. flame** flamme *f* nue ● **nakedness** *n* nudité *f*

name [neɪm] **1** *n* nom *m*; *(reputation)* réputation *f*; **my n. is** je m'appelle; **in the n. of** au nom de; **to put one's n. down for** *(school, course)* s'inscrire à; **to call sb names** insulter qn; **first n., given n.** prénom *m*; *Fig* **to have a good/bad n.** avoir une bonne/mauvaise réputation **2** *vt* nommer; *(ship, street)* baptiser; *(date, price)* fixer; **to n. sb to do sth** nommer qn pour faire qch; **he was named** *Br* **after** *or Am* **for** on lui a donné le nom de ● **nameless** *adj* anonyme ● **nameplate** *n* plaque *f*

namely [ˈneɪmlɪ] *adv* à savoir

namesake [ˈneɪmseɪk] *n* homonyme *mf*

nanny [ˈnænɪ] *(pl* **-ies**) *n* nurse *f*; *Fam (grandmother)* mamie *f*

nanny goat [ˈnænɪɡəʊt] *n* chèvre *f*

nap [næp] **1** *n (sleep)* petit somme *m*; **to have** *or* **take a n.** faire un petit somme **2** *(pt & pp* **-pp-**) *vi* faire un somme; *Fig* **to catch sb napping** prendre qn au dépourvu

nape [neɪp] *n* **n. (of the neck)** nuque *f*

napkin [ˈnæpkɪn] *n (at table)* serviette *f* ● **nappy** *(pl* **-ies**) *n Br (for baby)* couche *f*; **n. rash** érythème *m* fessier ● **nappy-liner** *n Br* protège-couche *m*

narcotic [nɑːˈkɒtɪk] *adj & n* narcotique *(m)*

narrate [nəˈreɪt] *vt* raconter ● **narrative** [ˈnærətɪv] *n* récit *m* ● **narrator** *n* narrateur, -trice *mf*

narrow [ˈnærəʊ] **1** (**-er, -est**) *adj* étroit; *(majority)* faible
2 *vt* **to n. (down)** *(choice, meaning)* limiter
3 *vi (of path)* se rétrécir ● **narrowly** *adv (only just)* de peu; *(strictly)* strictement; **he n. escaped** *or* **missed being killed** il a bien failli être tué ● **narrowness** *n* étroitesse *f*

narrow-minded [nærəʊˈmaɪndɪd] *adj* borné ● **narrow-mindedness** *n* étroitesse *f* d'esprit

nasal [ˈneɪzəl] *adj* nasal; *(voice)* nasillard

nasty [ˈnɑːstɪ] (**-ier, -iest**) *adj (bad)* mauvais; *(spiteful)* méchant (**to** *or* **towards** avec) ● **nastily** *adv (behave)* méchamment ● **nastiness** *n (malice)* méchanceté *f*

nation [ˈneɪʃən] *n* nation *f*

national [ˈnæʃənəl] **1** *adj* national; **n. anthem** hymne *m* national; *Br* **N. Health Service** ≃ Sécurité *f* sociale; *Br* **n. insurance** contributions *fpl* sociales
2 *n (citizen)* ressortissant, -ante *mf*

nationalist [ˈnæʃənəlɪst] *n* nationaliste *mf* ● **nationalistic** *adj Pej* nationaliste

nationality [næʃəˈnælətɪ] *(pl* **-ies**) *n* nationalité *f*

nationalize [ˈnæʃənəlaɪz] *vt* nationaliser

nationally [ˈnæʃənəlɪ] *adv* dans tout le pays

nationwide [ˈneɪʃənˈwaɪd] *adj & adv* dans tout le pays

native [ˈneɪtɪv] **1** *adj (country)* natal *(mpl* -als); *(tribe, plant)* indigène; **n. language** langue *f* maternelle; **to be an English n. speaker** avoir l'anglais comme langue maternelle
2 *n (person)* indigène *mf*; **to be a n. of** être originaire de

Nativity [nəˈtɪvɪtɪ] *n Rel* **the N.** la Nativité

NATO [ˈneɪtəʊ] *(abbr* **North Atlantic Treaty Organization**) *n Mil* OTAN *f*

natter [ˈnætə(r)] *Br Fam* **1** *n* **to have a n.** bavarder
2 *vi* bavarder

natural ['nætʃərəl] **1** *adj* naturel, -elle; *(talent)* inné
2 *n Fam* **to be a n. for sth** être fait pour qch; **he's a n.** *(as actor)* c'est un acteur né •**naturalist** *n* naturaliste *mf* •**naturally** *adv (unaffectedly, of course)* naturellement; *(by nature)* de nature

naturalize ['nætʃərəlaɪz] *vt (person)* naturaliser; **to become naturalized** se faire naturaliser •**naturali'zation** *n* naturalisation *f*

nature ['neɪtʃə(r)] *n (world, character)* nature *f*; **by n.** de nature; **problems of this n.** des problèmes de cette nature; **n. reserve** réserve *f* naturelle; **n. study** sciences *fpl* naturelles

naturist ['neɪtʃərɪst] *n* naturiste *mf*

naught [nɔːt] *n* (a) *Br Math* zéro *m* (b) *Literary (nothing)* néant *m*

naughty ['nɔːtɪ] (-ier, -iest) *adj (child)* vilain; *(joke, story)* coquin •**naughtily** *adv (behave)* mal; *(say)* avec malice

nausea ['nɔːzɪə] *n* nausée *f* •**nauseate** [-zɪeɪt] *vt* écœurer •**nauseating** [-zɪeɪtɪŋ] *adj* écœurant *[Br* 'nɔːzɪəs, *Am* 'nɔːʃəs] *adj (smell)* nauséabond; *Am* **to feel n.** *(sick)* avoir envie de vomir

nautical ['nɔːtɪkəl] *adj* nautique

naval ['neɪvəl] *adj* naval *(mpl* -als); *(hospital, power)* maritime; *(officer)* de marine

nave [neɪv] *n (of church)* nef *f*

navel ['neɪvəl] *n* nombril *m*

navigate ['nævɪgeɪt] **1** *vt (boat)* piloter; *(river)* naviguer sur; *Comptr* naviguer sur; **to n. the Net** naviguer sur l'Internet
2 *vi* naviguer •**navigable** *adj (river)* navigable; *(boat)* en état de naviguer •**navi'gation** *n* navigation *f* •**navigator** *n (on aircraft, boat)* navigateur *m*

navvy ['nævɪ] *(pl* **-ies**) *n Br (labourer)* terrassier *m*

navy ['neɪvɪ] **1** *(pl* **-ies**) *n* marine *f*
2 *adj* **n. (blue)** bleu marine *inv*

Nazi ['nɑːtsɪ] *adj & n Pol & Hist* nazi, -ie *(mf)*

NB [en'biː] *(abbr* **nota bene**) NB

near [nɪə(r)] **1** (-er, -est) *prep* **n. (to)** près de; **n. the bed** près du lit; **to be n. (to) victory/death** frôler la victoire/la mort; **n. (to) the end** vers la fin; **to come n. sb** s'approcher de qn
2 (-er, -est) *adv* près; **quite n., n. at hand** tout près; **n. to sth** près de qch; **to come n. to being killed** manquer d'être tué; **n. enough** *(more or less)* plus ou moins
3 (-er, -est) *adj* proche; **the nearest hospital** l'hôpital le plus proche; **the nearest way** la route la plus directe; **in the n. future** dans un avenir proche; **to the nearest euro** *(calculate)* à un euro près; *Aut* **n. side** côté *m* gauche, *Am* côté *m* droit; **the N. East** le Proche-Orient
4 *vt (approach)* approcher de; **nearing completion** presque terminé

nearby 1 [nɪə'baɪ] *adv* tout près
2 ['nɪəbaɪ] *adj* proche

nearly ['nɪəlɪ] *adv* presque; **she (very) n. fell** elle a failli tomber; **not n. as clever as** loin d'être aussi intelligent que

near-sighted [nɪə'saɪtɪd] *adj* myope

neat [niːt] (-er, -est) *adj (clothes, work)* soigné; *(room)* bien rangé; *(style)* élégant; *Am Fam (good)* super *inv*; **to drink one's whisky n.** boire son whisky sec •**neatly** *adv (carefully)* avec soin; *(skilfully)* habilement

nebulous ['nebjʊləs] *adj (vague)* flou

necessary ['nesɪsərɪ] **1** *adj* nécessaire; **it's n. to do it** il faut le faire; **to make it n. for sb to do sth** mettre qn dans la nécessité de faire qch; **to do what's n.** faire le nécessaire *(for* pour)
2 *n Fam* **to do the n.** faire le nécessaire •**necessarily** [-'serɪlɪ] *adv* **not n.** pas forcément

necessitate [nɪ'sesɪteɪt] *vt* nécessiter

necessity [nɪ'sesɪtɪ] *(pl* **-ies**) *n (obligation, need)* nécessité *f*; **out of n.** par nécessité; **to be a n.** être indispensable; **the necessities** *(things needed)* le nécessaire

neck¹ [nek] *n* cou *m*; *(of dress)* encolure *f*; *(of bottle)* goulot *m*; **low n.** *(of dress)* décolleté *m*; **to finish n. and n.** *(in race)* finir au coude à coude •**necklace** *n* collier *m* •**neckline** *n* encolure *f* •**necktie** *n* cravate *f*

neck² [nek] *vi Fam (kiss)* se peloter

nectarine ['nektəriːn] *n (fruit)* nectarine *f*, brugnon *m*

née [neɪ] *adv* **n. Dupont** née Dupont

need [niːd] **1** *n* besoin *m*; **in n.** dans le besoin; **to be in n. of sth** avoir besoin de qch; **there's no n. (for you) to do that** tu n'as pas besoin de faire cela; **if n. be** si besoin est
2 *vt* avoir besoin de; **you n. it** tu en as besoin; **it needs an army** *or* **an army is needed to do that** il faut une armée pour faire cela; **this sport needs patience** ce sport demande de la patience; **her hair needs cutting** il faut qu'elle se fasse couper les cheveux
3 *v aux*

La forme modale de **need** est la même à toutes les personnes, et s'utilise sans **do/does**. (**he need only worry about himself**; **need she go?**; **it needn't matter**).

n. I say more? ai-je besoin d'en dire plus?; **I needn't have rushed** ce n'était pas la peine de me presser; **you needn't worry** inutile de t'inquiéter • **needy** (**-ier, -iest**) *adj* nécessiteux, -euse

needle ['niːdəl] **1** *n* aiguille *f*; *(of record player)* saphir *m*

2 *vt Fam (irritate)* agacer • **needlework** *n* couture *f*; *(object)* ouvrage *m*

needless ['niːdləs] *adj* inutile • **needlessly** *adv* inutilement

negate [nɪ'geɪt] *vt (nullify)* annuler; *(deny)* nier • **ne'gation** *n (denial) & Grammar* négation *f*

negative ['negətɪv] **1** *adj* négatif, -ive

2 *n (of photo)* négatif *m*; *(word, word group)* négation *f*; *(grammatical form)* forme *f* négative; **to answer in the n.** répondre par la négative

neglect [nɪ'glekt] **1** *n (of person)* négligence *f*; *(of duty)* manquement *m* (**of** à); **in a state of n.** *(garden, house)* mal tenu

2 *vt (person, health, work)* négliger; *(garden, car)* ne pas s'occuper de; *(duty)* manquer à; **to n. to do sth** négliger de faire qch • **neglected** *adj (appearance, person)* négligé; *(garden, house)* mal tenu; **to feel n.** se sentir abandonné • **neglectful** *adj* négligent; **to be n. of sb/sth** négliger qn/qch

negligent ['neglɪdʒənt] *adj* négligent • **negligence** *n* négligence *f* • **negligently** *adv* négligemment

negligible ['neglɪdʒəbəl] *adj* négligeable

negotiate [nɪ'gəʊʃɪeɪt] **1** *vti (discuss)* négocier

2 *vt (fence, obstacle)* franchir; *(bend) (in vehicle)* négocier • **negotiable** *adj* négociable • **negoti'ation** *n* négociation *f*; **in n. with** en pourparlers avec • **negotiator** *n* négociateur, -trice *mf*

Negro ['niːgrəʊ] **1** (*pl* **-oes**) *n Old-fashioned (man)* Noir *m*; *(woman)* Noire *f*

2 *adj* noir; *(art, sculpture)* nègre

neigh [neɪ] **1** *n* hennissement *m*

2 *vi* hennir

neighbour ['neɪbə(r)] (*Am* **neighbor**) *n* voisin, -ine *mf* • **neighbourhood** (*Am* **neighborhood**) *n (district)* quartier *m*, voisinage *m*; *(neighbours)* voisinage *m*; **in the n. of $10/kilos** dans les 10 dollars/kilos • **neighbouring** (*Am* **neighboring**)

adj voisin • **neighbourly** (*Am* **neighborly**) *adj (feeling)* de bon voisinage; **they're n. (people)** ils sont bons voisins

neither [*Br* 'naɪðə(r), *Am* 'niːðə(r)] **1** *conj* **n.... nor...** ni... ni...; **n. you nor me** ni toi ni moi; **he n. sings nor dances** il ne chante ni ne danse

2 *adv* **n. will I go** je n'y irai pas non plus; **n. do I/n. can I** (ni) moi non plus

3 *adj* **n. boy came** aucun des deux garçons n'est venu; **on n. side** ni d'un côté ni de l'autre

4 *pron* **n. (of them)** aucun(e) (des deux)

neon ['niːɒn] *n* néon *m*; **n. lighting/sign** éclairage *m*/enseigne *f* au néon

nephew ['nevjuː, 'nefjuː] *n* neveu *m*

nepotism ['nepətɪzəm] *n* népotisme *m*

nerd [nɜːd] *n Fam (stupid person)* nullard, -arde *mf*

nerve [nɜːv] *n* nerf *m*; *(courage)* courage *m*; *Fam (impudence)* culot *m*; *Fam* **he gets on my nerves** il me tape sur les nerfs; **to have an attack of nerves** *(fear, anxiety)* avoir le trac; *Fam* **she's a bundle** *or* **mass** *or* **bag of nerves** c'est un paquet de nerfs; **n. centre** centre *m* nerveux • **nerve-racking** *adj* éprouvant

nervous ['nɜːvəs] *adj (apprehensive)* nerveux, -euse; **to be n. about sth/doing sth** être nerveux à l'idée de qch/de faire qch; **to have a n. breakdown** faire une dépression nerveuse • **nervously** *adv* nerveusement • **nervousness** *n* nervosité *f*

nervy ['nɜːvɪ] (**-ier, -iest**) *adj Fam (anxious)* nerveux, -euse; *Am (brash)* culotté

nest [nest] **1** *n* nid *m*; *Fig* **n. egg** pécule *m*; **n. of tables** tables *fpl* gigognes

2 *vi (of bird)* nicher

nestle ['nesəl] *vi* se pelotonner (**up to** contre); **a village nestling in** *(forest, valley)* un village niché dans

Net [net] *n Comptr* **the N.** le Net

net¹ [net] **1** *n* filet *m*; **n. curtain** voilage *m*

2 (*pt & pp* **-tt-**) *vt (fish)* prendre au filet • **netting** *n (nets)* filets *mpl*; *(mesh)* mailles *fpl*

net² [net] **1** *adj (profit, weight, value)* net (*f* nette)

2 (*pt & pp* **-tt-**) *vt (of person, company)* gagner net; **this venture netted them** cette entreprise leur a rapporté

Netherlands ['neðələndz] *npl* **the N.** les Pays-Bas *mpl*

nettle ['netəl] *n* ortie *f*

network ['netwɜːk] **1** *n* réseau *m*

2 *vi (make contacts)* établir un réseau de contacts

neurosis [njʊ'rəʊsɪs] (*pl* **-oses** [-əʊsiːz]) *n*

névrose f •**neurotic** [-'rɒtɪk] adj & n névrosé, -ée (mf)

neuter ['nju:tə(r)] **1** adj & n Grammar neutre (m)

2 vt (cat) châtrer

neutral ['nju:trəl] **1** adj neutre; (policy) de neutralité

2 n (electrical wire) neutre m; **in n. (gear)** (vehicle) au point mort •**neutrality** [-'trælɪtɪ] n neutralité f •**neutralize** vt neutraliser

never ['nevə(r)] adv (not ever) (ne) jamais; **she n. lies** elle ne ment jamais; **n. in (all) my life** jamais de ma vie; **n. again** plus jamais; Fam **I n. did it** je ne l'ai pas fait; Fam **I n. expected this** je ne m'attendais vraiment pas à ça; Fam **well I n.!** ça alors! •'**never-'ending** adj interminable

nevertheless [nevəðə'les] adv néanmoins

new [nju:] adj (a) (-er, -est) nouveau (f nouvelle); (brand-new) neuf (f neuve); **to be n. to** (job) être nouveau dans; (city) être un nouveau-venu (f nouvelle-venue) dans; **a n. boy** (in school) un nouveau; **a n. girl** une nouvelle; **to look** (of person) nouveau look m; (of company) nouvelle image f; **it's as good as n.** c'est comme neuf; Fam **what's n.?** quoi de neuf?

(b) (different) **a n. glass/pen** un autre verre/stylo •**newborn** adj **a n. baby** un nouveau-né, une nouveau-née •**newcomer** [-kʌmə(r)] n nouveau-venu m, nouvelle-venue f (**to** dans) •**new-found** adj nouveau (f nouvelle) •**newly** adv nouvellement •**newlyweds** n jeunes mariés mpl

news [nju:z] n nouvelles fpl; (in the media) informations fpl; **a piece of n.** une nouvelle; **sports n.** (newspaper column) rubrique f sportive; **n. agency** agence f de presse; **n. stand** kiosque m à journaux •**newsagent** n Br marchand, -ande mf de journaux •**newscaster** n présentateur, -trice mf de journal •**newsdealer** n Am marchand, -ande mf de journaux •**newsflash** n flash m d'informations •**newsletter** n (of club, group) bulletin m •**newspaper** n journal m •**newspaperman** (pl -men) n journaliste m •**newsprint** n papier m journal •**newsreader** n Br présentateur, -trice mf de journal •**newsreel** n actualités fpl •**newsworthy** adj d'intérêt médiatique

newt [nju:t] n triton m

New Zealand [nju:'zi:lənd] **1** n la Nouvelle-Zélande

2 adj néo-zélandais •**New Zealander** n Néo-Zélandais, -aise mf

next [nekst] **1** adj prochain; (room, house) d'à côté; (following) suivant; **n. month** (in the future) le mois prochain; **he returned the n. month** il revint le mois suivant; **the n. day** le lendemain; **the n. morning** le lendemain matin; **within the n. ten days** d'ici dix jours; **who's n.?** c'est à qui?; **you're n.** c'est ton tour; **n. (please)!** au suivant!; **the n. size up** la taille au-dessus; **to live n. door** habiter à côté (**to** de); **n.-door neighbour/room** voisin m/ pièce f d'à côté

2 n (in series) suivant, -ante mf; **from one year to the n.** d'une année sur l'autre

3 adv (afterwards) ensuite, après; (now) maintenant; **when you come n.** la prochaine fois que tu viendras; **the n. best solution is...** à défaut, il y a une autre solution qui est...; **n. to** (beside) à côté de; **n. to nothing** presque rien

NHS [eneɪtʃ'es] (abbr National Health Service) n Br ≃ Sécurité f sociale

nib [nɪb] n plume f

nibble ['nɪbəl] vti grignoter

Nicaragua [nɪkə'ræɡjʊə] n le Nicaragua

nice [naɪs] (-er, -est) adj (pleasant) agréable; (tasty) bon (f bonne); (physically attractive) beau (f belle); (kind) gentil, -ille (**to** avec); **n. and warm** bien chaud; **n. and easy** très facile; **have a n. day!** bonne journée! •**nice-looking** adj beau (f belle) •**nicely** adv (kindly) gentiment; (well) bien

niceties ['naɪsətɪz] npl subtilités fpl

niche [ni:ʃ, nɪtʃ] n (recess) niche f; **to make a n. for oneself** faire son trou; (market) **n.** créneau m

nick [nɪk] **1** n (a) (on skin, wood) entaille f; (in blade, crockery) brèche f; **in the n. of time** juste à temps; Br Fam **in good n.** en bon état (b) Br Fam (prison) taule f

2 vt Br Fam (steal) piquer; (arrest) pincer

nickel ['nɪkəl] n (metal) nickel m; Am (coin) pièce f de 5 cents

nickname ['nɪkneɪm] **1** n (informal) surnom m; (short form) diminutif m

2 vt surnommer

nicotine ['nɪkəti:n] n nicotine f

niece [ni:s] n nièce f

nifty ['nɪftɪ] (-ier, -iest) adj Fam (idea, device) génial; (agile) vif (f vive)

Nigeria [naɪ'dʒɪərɪə] n le Nigeria •**Nigerian 1** adj nigérian **2** n Nigérian, -iane mf

niggardly ['nɪɡədlɪ] adj (person) avare; (amount) maigre

niggling ['nɪglɪŋ] *adj (trifling)* insignifiant; *(irksome)* irritant; *(doubt)* persistant

night [naɪt] **1** *n* nuit *f*; *(evening)* soir *m*; **at n.** la nuit; **by n.** de nuit; **last n.** *(evening)* hier soir; *(night)* cette nuit; **to have an early/a late n.** se coucher tôt/tard; **to have a good n.'s sleep** bien dormir; **first n.** *(of play)* première *f*; **the last n.** *(of play)* la dernière
2 *adj (work, flight)* de nuit; **n. school** cours *mpl* du soir; **n. shift** *(job)* poste *m* de nuit; *(workers)* équipe *f* de nuit; **n. watchman** veilleur *m* de nuit • **nightcap** *n (drink)* = boisson alcoolisée ou chaude prise avant de se coucher • **nightclub** *n* boîte *f* de nuit • **nightdress, nightgown,** *Fam* **nightie** *n* chemise *f* de nuit • **nightfall** *n* **at n.** à la tombée de la nuit • **nightlife** *n* vie *f* nocturne • **nightlight** *n* veilleuse *f* • **night-time** *n* nuit *f*

nightingale ['naɪtɪŋgeɪl] *n* rossignol *m*
nightly ['naɪtlɪ] **1** *adv* chaque nuit/soir
2 *adj* de chaque nuit/soir

nightmare ['naɪtmeə(r)] *n* cauchemar *m*
nil [nɪl] *n (nothing)* & *Br Sport* zéro *m*; **two n.** deux à zéro; **the risk is n.** le risque est nul

Nile [naɪl] *n* **the N.** le Nil
nimble ['nɪmbəl] (**-er, -est**) *adj (person)* souple

nincompoop ['nɪŋkəmpuːp] *n Fam* nigaud, -aude *mf*

nine [naɪn] *adj & n* neuf *(m)*
nineteen [naɪn'tiːn] *adj & n* dix-neuf *(m)* • **nineteenth** *adj & n* dix-neuvième *(mf)*
ninety ['naɪntɪ] *adj & n* quatre-vingt-dix *(m)* • **ninetieth** *adj & n* quatre-vingt-dixième *(mf)*
ninth ['naɪnθ] *adj & n* neuvième *(mf)*; **a n.** un neuvième

nip [nɪp] **1** *n* pinçon *m*; **there's a n. in the air** il fait frisquet
2 (*pt & pp* **-pp-**) *vt (pinch)* pincer; **to n. sth in the bud** étouffer qch dans l'œuf
3 *vi Br Fam* **to n. round to sb's house** faire un saut chez qn; **to n. out** sortir un instant

nipper ['nɪpə(r)] *n Br Fam (child)* gosse *mf*

nipple ['nɪpəl] *n* mamelon *m*; *Am (on baby's bottle)* tétine *f*

nippy ['nɪpɪ] (**-ier, -iest**) *adj Fam* (**a**) *(chilly)* frais *(f* fraîche); **it's n.** ça pince (**b**) *Br* **to be n. (about it)** faire vite
nit [nɪt] *n* (**a**) *Br Fam (fool)* idiot, -iote *mf* (**b**) *(of louse)* lente *f*
nitrogen ['naɪtrədʒən] *n* azote *m*

nitty-gritty ['nɪtɪ'grɪtɪ] *n Fam* **to get down to the n.** entrer dans le vif du sujet
nitwit ['nɪtwɪt] *n Fam* idiot, -iote *mf*
no [nəʊ] **1** (*pl* **noes** *or* **nos**) *n* non *m inv*; **she won't take no for an answer** elle n'accepte pas qu'on lui dise non; **the noes** *(in voting)* les non
2 *adj (not any)* pas de; **there's no bread** il n'y a pas de pain; **I have no idea** je n'ai aucune idée; **I have no time to play** je n'ai pas le temps de jouer; **no child came** aucun enfant n'est venu; **of no importance** sans importance; **with no gloves/hat on** sans gants/chapeau; **there's no knowing** impossible de savoir; **'no smoking'** 'défense de fumer'; *Fam* **no way!** pas question!
3 *adv (interjection)* non; **no more time** plus de temps; **no more/less than ten** pas plus/moins de dix; **no more/less than you** pas plus/moins que vous; **you can do no better** tu ne peux pas faire mieux
noble ['nəʊbəl] (**-er, -est**) *adj* noble; *(building)* majestueux, -ueuse • **nobility** *n* noblesse *f* • **nobleman** (*pl* **-men**) *n* noble *m* • **noblewoman** (*pl* **-women**) *n* noble *f*
nobody ['nəʊbɒdɪ] **1** *pron* (ne) personne; **n. came** personne n'est venu; **he knows n.** il ne connaît personne; **n.!** personne!
2 *n* **a n.** une nullité
nocturnal [nɒk'tɜːnəl] *adj* nocturne
nod [nɒd] **1** *n* signe *m* de tête
2 (*pt & pp* **-dd-**) *vti* **to n. (one's head)** faire un signe de tête
3 *vi Fam* **to n. off** s'assoupir
noise [nɔɪz] *n* bruit *m*; **to make a n.** faire du bruit • **noiselessly** *adv* sans bruit
noisy ['nɔɪzɪ] (**-ier, -iest**) *adj (person, street)* bruyant • **noisily** *adv* bruyamment
nomad ['nəʊmæd] *n* nomade *mf* • **nomadic** *adj* nomade
nominal ['nɒmɪnəl] *adj* nominal; *(rent, salary)* symbolique
nominate ['nɒmɪneɪt] *vt (appoint)* nommer; *(propose)* proposer (**for** comme candidat à) • **nomination** *n (appointment)* nomination *f*; *(proposal)* candidature *f* • **nominee** *n (candidate)* candidat *m*
non-aligned [nɒnə'laɪnd] *adj (country)* non-aligné
nonchalant ['nɒnʃələnt] *adj* désinvolte
noncommissioned [nɒnkə'mɪʃənd] *adj Mil* **n. officer** sous-officier *m*
non-committal [nɒnkə'mɪtəl] *adj (answer)* de Normand; **to be n.** ne pas s'engager
nonconformist [nɒnkən'fɔːmɪst] *adj & n* non-conformiste *(mf)*

nondescript [ˈnɒndɪskrɪpt] *adj* très ordinaire

none [nʌn] **1** *pron* aucun(e) *mf*; *(in filling out a form)* néant; **n. of them** aucun d'eux; **she has n. (at all)** elle n'en a pas (du tout); **n. came** pas un(e) seul(e) n'est venu(e); **n. can tell** personne ne peut le dire; **n. of it** *or* **this** rien (de ceci)

2 *adv* **n. too hot** pas très chaud; **he's n. the wiser (for it)** il n'est pas plus avancé • **nonethe'less** *adv* néanmoins

nonentity [nɒˈnentɪtɪ] *(pl -ies)* *n (person)* nullité *f*

nonexistent [nɒnɪgˈzɪstənt] *adj* inexistant

non-fiction [nɒnˈfɪkʃən] *n* ouvrages *mpl* généraux

nonflammable [nɒnˈflæməbəl] *adj* ininflammable

non-iron [nɒnˈaɪən] *adj* qui ne se repasse pas

no-nonsense [nəʊˈnɒnsəns] *adj* direct

nonplus [nɒnˈplʌs] *(pt & pp -ss-)* *vt* dérouter

non-profit-making [nɒnˈprɒfɪtmeɪkɪŋ] *(Am **non-profit** [nɒnˈprɒfɪt])* *adj* à but non lucratif

nonsense [ˈnɒnsəns] *n* bêtises *fpl*; **that's n.** c'est absurde • **nonsensical** [-ˈsensɪkəl] *adj* absurde

non-smoker [nɒnˈsməʊkə(r)] *n (person)* non-fumeur, -euse *mf*; *(compartment on train)* compartiment *m* non-fumeurs

nonstick [ˈnɒnˈstɪk] *adj (pan)* qui n'attache pas

non-stop [nɒnˈstɒp] **1** *adj* sans arrêt; *(train, flight)* sans escale

2 *adv (work)* sans arrêt; *(fly)* sans escale

noodles [ˈnuːdəlz] *npl* nouilles *fpl*; *(in soup)* vermicelles *mpl*

nook [nʊk] *n* coin *m*; **in every n. and cranny** dans le moindre recoin

noon [nuːn] **1** *n* midi *m*; **at n.** à midi

2 *adj (sun)* de midi

no-one [ˈnəʊwʌn] *pron* = **nobody**

noose [nuːs] *n* nœud *m* coulant

nor [nɔː(r)] *conj* ni; **neither you n. me** ni toi ni moi; **she neither drinks n. smokes** elle ne fume ni ne boit; **n. do I/n. can I/**etc (ni) moi non plus; **n. will I (go)** je n'y irai pas non plus

norm [nɔːm] *n* norme *f*

normal [ˈnɔːməl] **1** *adj* normal

2 *n* **above/below n.** au-dessus/au-dessous de la normale • **normality** [-ˈmælɪtɪ] *n* normalité *f* • **normalize** *vt* normaliser • **normally** *adv* normalement

Norman [ˈnɔːmən] *adj* normand • **Normandy** *n* la Normandie

north [nɔːθ] **1** *n* nord *m*; **(to the) n. of** au nord de

2 *adj (coast)* nord *inv*; *(wind)* du nord; **N. America/Africa** Amérique *f*/Afrique *f* du Nord; **N. American** *adj* nord-américain; *n* Nord-Américain, -aine *mf*

3 *adv* au nord; *(travel)* vers le nord • **northbound** *adj (traffic)* en direction du nord; *Br (carriageway)* nord *inv* • **'north-'east** *n & adj* nord-est *(m)* • **northerly** [ˈnɔːðəlɪ] *adj (point)* nord *inv*; *(direction, wind)* du nord • **northern** [ˈnɔːðən] *adj (coast)* nord *inv*; *(town)* du nord; **n. France** le nord de la France; **n. Europe** l'Europe *f* du Nord; **N. Ireland** l'Irlande *f* du Nord • **northerner** [ˈnɔːðənə(r)] *n* habitant, -ante *mf* du Nord • **northward(s)** *adj & adv* vers le nord • **north-'west** *n & adj* nord-ouest *(m)*

Norway [ˈnɔːweɪ] *n* la Norvège • **Norwegian** [-ˈwiːdʒən] **1** *adj* norvégien, -ienne **2** *n (person)* Norvégien, -ienne *mf*; *(language)* norvégien *m*

nose [nəʊz] **1** *n* nez *m*; **her n. is bleeding** elle saigne du nez; *Fig* **to turn one's n. up** faire le dégoûté (**at** devant)

2 *vi Fam* **to n. about** fouiner • **nosebleed** *n* saignement *m* de nez • **nose-dive** *n (of aircraft)* piqué *m*; *(in prices)* chute *f*

nosey [ˈnəʊzɪ] *(-ier, -iest)* *adj Fam* indiscret, -ète; *Br* **n. parker** fouineur, -euse *mf*

nosh [nɒʃ] *Fam* **1** *n (light meal)* en-cas *m*; *Br (food)* bouffe *f*

2 *vi (have a light meal)* grignoter; *Br (eat)* bouffer

no-smoking [nəʊˈsməʊkɪŋ] *adj (carriage, area)* non-fumeurs; *(person)* non-fumeur (*f* non-fumeuse)

nostalgia [nɒˈstældʒɪə] *n* nostalgie *f* • **nostalgic** *adj* nostalgique

nostril [ˈnɒstrəl] *n (of person)* narine *f*; *(of horse)* naseau *m*

nosy [ˈnəʊzɪ] *adj* = **nosey**

not [nɒt] *adv*

À l'oral, et à l'écrit dans un style familier, on utilise généralement **not** à la forme contractée lorsqu'il suit un modal ou un auxiliaire. (**don't go!**; **she wasn't there**; **he couldn't see me**).

(**a**) (ne) pas; **he's n. there, he isn't there** il n'est pas là; **n. yet** pas encore; **why n.?** pourquoi pas?; **n. one reply** pas une seule réponse; **n. at all** pas du tout; *(after 'thank you')* je vous en prie (**b**) non; **I think/hope n.** je pense/j'espère que non; **n. guilty** non coupable; **isn't she?/ don't you?**/etc non?

notable [ˈnəʊtəbəl] *adj & n* notable *(m)* •**notably** *adv (noticeably)* notablement; *(particularly)* notamment

notary [ˈnəʊtərɪ] *(pl* -**ies***) n* notaire *m*

notation [nəʊˈteɪʃən] *n* notation *f*

notch [nɒtʃ] **1** *n (in wood)* encoche *f; (in belt, wheel)* cran *m*
2 *vt* **to n. up** *(points)* marquer; *(victory)* remporter

note [nəʊt] **1** *n (information, reminder) & Mus* note *f; Br (banknote)* billet *m; (letter)* mot *m;* **to take (a) n. of sth, to make a n. of sth** prendre note de qch; **actor of n.** acteur *m* remarquable
2 *vt (notice)* remarquer, noter; **to n. sth down** *(word, remark)* noter qch •**notebook** *n* carnet *m; (for school)* cahier *m; (pad)* bloc-notes *m* •**notepad** *n* bloc-notes *m* •**notepaper** *n* papier *m* à lettres

noted [ˈnəʊtɪd] *adj* éminent; **to be n. for one's beauty** être connu pour sa beauté

noteworthy [ˈnəʊtwɜːðɪ] *adj* remarquable

nothing [ˈnʌθɪŋ] **1** *pron* (ne) rien; **he knows n.** il ne sait rien; **n. happened** il ne s'est rien passé; **n. at all** rien du tout; **n. big** rien de grand; **n. much** pas grand-chose; **n. but problems** rien que des problèmes; **to have n. to do** n'avoir rien à faire; **I've got n. to do with it** je n'y suis pour rien; **I can do n. about it** je n'y peux rien; **there's n. like it** il n'y a rien de tel; **for n.** *(in vain, free of charge)* pour rien; **to have n. on** être tout nu
2 *adv* **to look n. like sb** ne ressembler nullement à qn; **n. like as large** loin d'être aussi grand
3 *n* **a (mere) n.** *(person)* une nullité; *(thing)* un rien; **to come to n.** être anéanti

notice [ˈnəʊtɪs] **1** *n (notification)* avis *m; (in newspaper)* annonce *f; (sign)* pancarte *f,* écriteau *m; (poster)* affiche *f; (review of film)* critique *f;* **(advance) n.** préavis *m;* **to give sb (advance) n.** *(inform)* avertir qn (**of** de); **n. (to quit), n. (of dismissal)** congé *m;* **to give (in) one's n.** *(resign)* donner sa démission; **to take n.** faire attention (**of** à); **to bring sth to sb's n.** porter qch à la connaissance de qn; **until further n.** jusqu'à nouvel ordre; **at short n.** au dernier moment
2 *vt* remarquer (**that** que); **to get noticed** se faire remarquer
3 *vi* remarquer •**noticeboard** *n Br* tableau *m* d'affichage

📝 Note that the French word **notice** is a false friend and is never a translation for the English word **notice**. Its most common meaning is **directions for use.**

noticeable [ˈnəʊtɪsəbəl] *adj* perceptible

notify [ˈnəʊtɪfaɪ] *(pt & pp* -**ied***) vt (inform)* avertir (**sb of sth** qn de qch); *(announce)* notifier (**to** à) •**notification** [-fɪˈkeɪʃən] *n* avis *m*

notion [ˈnəʊʃən] *n* notion *f;* **to have some n. of sth** avoir quelques notions de qch; **to have a n. that...** avoir dans l'idée que... •**notions** *npl Am (sewing articles)* mercerie *f*

notorious [nəʊˈtɔːrɪəs] *adj* tristement célèbre; *(stupidity, criminal)* notoire •**notoriety** [-təˈraɪətɪ] *n* triste notoriété *f*

notwithstanding [nɒtwɪðˈstændɪŋ] *Formal* **1** *prep* en dépit de
2 *adv* néanmoins

nougat [*Br* ˈnuːgɑː, ˈnʌgət] *n* nougat *m*

nought [nɔːt] *n Br Math* zéro *m; Br* **noughts and crosses** *(game)* ≃ morpion *m*

noun [naʊn] *n Grammar* nom *m*

nourish [ˈnʌrɪʃ] *vt* nourrir •**nourishing** *adj* nourrissant •**nourishment** *n* nourriture *f*

novel [ˈnɒvəl] **1** *n* roman *m*
2 *adj (new)* nouveau *(f* nouvelle), original •**novelist** *n* romancier, -ière *mf* •**novelty** *n* nouveauté *f*

November [nəʊˈvembə(r)] *n* novembre *m*

novice [ˈnɒvɪs] *n (beginner)* débutant, -ante *mf* (**at** en)

now [naʊ] **1** *adv* maintenant; **right n.** en ce moment; **for n.** pour le moment; **even n.** encore maintenant; **from n. on** désormais; **until n., up to n.** jusqu'ici, jusqu'à maintenant; **before n.** avant; **n. and then** de temps à autre; **n. hot, n. cold** tantôt chaud, tantôt froid; **she ought to be here by n.** elle devrait déjà être ici; **n. n.!** allons, allons!
2 *conj* **n. (that)...** maintenant que...

nowadays [ˈnaʊədeɪz] *adv* de nos jours

nowhere [ˈnəʊweə(r)] *adv* nulle part; **n. else** nulle part ailleurs; **it's n. I know** ce n'est pas un endroit que je connais; **n. near the house** loin de la maison; **n. near enough** loin d'être assez

nozzle [ˈnɒzəl] *n* embout *m; (of hose)* jet *m; (of petrol pump)* pistolet *m*

nth [enθ] *adj* nième

nuance [ˈnjuːɑːns] *n* nuance *f*

nub [nʌb] *n (of problem)* cœur *m*

nuclear ['njuːklɪə(r)] *adj* nucléaire; **n. scientist** chercheur, -euse *mf* en physique nucléaire
nucleus ['njuːklɪəs] (*pl* **-clei** [-klɪaɪ]) *n* noyau *m* (*pl* -aux)
nude [njuːd] **1** *adj* nu
2 *n* nu *m*; **in the n.** tout nu (*f* toute nue)
nudge [nʌdʒ] **1** *n* coup *m* de coude
2 *vt* pousser du coude
nudism ['njuːdɪzəm] *n* nudisme *m* • **nudist 1** *n* nudiste *mf* **2** *adj* (*camp*) de nudistes
nudity ['njuːdɪtɪ] *n* nudité *f*
nugget ['nʌgɪt] *n* (*of gold*) pépite *f*
nuisance ['njuːsəns] *n* **to be a n.** être embêtant; **to make a n. of oneself** embêter le monde
null [nʌl] *adj* **n. (and void)** nul (et non avenu) (*f* nulle (et non avenue)) • **nullify** (*pt & pp* **-ied**) *vt* infirmer
numb [nʌm] **1** *adj* (*stiff*) (*hand*) engourdi; *Fig* (*with fear*) paralysé; (*with shock, horror*) hébété; **n. with cold** engourdi par le froid
2 *vt* engourdir; *Fig* (*of fear*) paralyser; (*of shock*) hébéter • **numbness** *n* (*of hand*) engourdissement *m*
number ['nʌmbə(r)] **1** *n* nombre *m*; (*of page, house, telephone*) numéro *m*; (*song*) chanson *f*; **a/any n. of** un certain/grand nombre de
2 *vt* (*assign number to*) numéroter; (*count*) compter; **they n. eight** ils sont au nombre de huit • **numbering** *n* numérotage *m* • **numberplate** *n* *Br* plaque *f* d'immatriculation
numeral ['njuːmərəl] **1** *n* chiffre *m*
2 *adj* numéral
numerate ['njuːmərət] *adj* **to be n.** savoir compter

numerical [njuːˈmerɪkəl] *adj* numérique
numerous ['njuːmərəs] *adj* nombreux, -euse
nun [nʌn] *n* religieuse *f*
nurse [nɜːs] **1** *n* infirmière *f*; (*for children*) nurse *f*
2 *vt* (*look after*) soigner; (*suckle*) allaiter; (*cradle*) bercer; *Fig* (*feeling*) nourrir • **nursing 1** *adj* **the n. staff** le personnel soignant **2** *n* (*care*) soins *mpl*; (*job*) profession *f* d'infirmière; *Br* **n. home** (*for old people*) maison *f* de retraite
nursery ['nɜːsərɪ] (*pl* **-ies**) *n* (*children's room*) chambre *f* d'enfants; (*for plants, trees*) pépinière *f*; **(day) n.** (*school*) garderie *f*; *Br* **n. education** enseignement *m* en maternelle; *Br* **n. nurse** puéricultrice *f*; **n. rhyme** comptine *f*; **n. school** école *f* maternelle
nurture ['nɜːtʃə(r)] *vt* (*educate*) éduquer
nut¹ [nʌt] *n* (*fruit*) = noix, noisette ou autre fruit sec de cette nature; **Brazil n.** noix *f* du Brésil • **nutcrackers** *npl* casse-noix *m inv* • **nutshell** *n* coquille *f* de noix; *Fig* **in a n.** en un mot
nut² [nʌt] *n* (*for bolt*) écrou *m*; *Fam* (*head*) caboche *f*
nut³ [nʌt] *n* *Fam* (*crazy person*) cinglé, -ée *mf* • **nutcase** *n* *Fam* cinglé, -ée *mf* • **nuts** *adj* *Fam* (*crazy*) cinglé
nutmeg ['nʌtmeg] *n* muscade *f*
nutrient ['njuːtrɪənt] *n* élément *m* nutritif
nutrition [njuːˈtrɪʃən] *n* nutrition *f* • **nutritional** *adj* nutritionnel, -elle
nutritious [njuːˈtrɪʃəs] *adj* nutritif, -ive
nylon ['naɪlɒn] *n* Nylon® *m*; **nylons** (*stockings*) bas *mpl* Nylon®; **n. shirt** chemise *f* en Nylon®
nymph [nɪmf] *n* nymphe *f* • **nymphomaniac** [nɪmfəˈmeɪnɪæk] *n* nymphomane *f*

O

O, o [əʊ] *n (letter)* O, o *m inv*; *Br Sch Formerly* **O-level** = diplôme de fin de premier cycle de l'enseignement secondaire sanctionnant une matière particulière

oaf [əʊf] *n* balourd *m* • **oafish** *adj* lourdaud

oak [əʊk] *n (tree, wood)* chêne *m*; **o. table** table *f* en chêne

OAP [əʊeɪˈpiː] *(abbr* **old age pensioner**) *n Br* retraité, -ée *mf*

oar [ɔː(r)] *n* aviron *m*, rame *f*

oasis [əʊˈeɪsɪs] *(pl* **oases** [əʊˈeɪsiːz]) *n* oasis *f*

oath [əʊθ] *(pl* **-s** [əʊðz]) *n (promise)* serment *m*; *(profanity)* juron *m*; **to take an o. to do sth** faire le serment de faire qch

oatmeal [ˈəʊtmiːl] *n* farine *f* d'avoine

oats [əʊts] *npl* avoine *f*; **(porridge) o.** flocons *mpl* d'avoine

obedient [əˈbiːdɪənt] *adj* obéissant • **obedience** *n* obéissance *f* (**to** à) • **obediently** *adv* docilement

obelisk [ˈɒbəlɪsk] *n* obélisque *m*

obese [əʊˈbiːs] *adj* obèse • **obesity** *n* obésité *f*

obey [əˈbeɪ] **1** *vt* obéir à; **to be obeyed** être obéi
2 *vi* obéir

obituary [əˈbɪtʃʊərɪ] *(pl* **-ies**) *n* nécrologie *f*

object¹ [ˈɒbdʒɪkt] *n (thing)* objet *m*; *(aim)* but *m*, objet; *Grammar* complément *m* d'objet; **money is no o.** le prix importe peu

object² [əbˈdʒekt] **1** *vt* **to o. that...** objecter que...
2 *vi* émettre une objection; **to o. to sth/ to doing sth** ne pas être d'accord avec qch/pour faire qch; **I o.!** je proteste!; **she didn't o. when** elle n'a fait aucune objection quand

objection [əbˈdʒekʃən] *n* objection *f*; **I've got no o.** je n'y vois pas d'objection

objectionable [əbˈdʒekʃənəbəl] *adj* déplaisant

objective [əbˈdʒektɪv] **1** *adj (impartial)* objectif, -ive

2 *n (aim, target)* objectif *m* • **objectively** *adv* objectivement • **objectivity** [ɒbdʒekˈtɪvɪtɪ] *n* objectivité *f*

objector [əbˈdʒektə(r)] *n* opposant, -ante *mf* (**to** à)

obligate [ˈɒblɪgeɪt] *vt* contraindre (**to do** à faire) • **obli'gation** *n* obligation *f*; **to be under an o. to do sth** être dans l'obligation de faire qch; **to be under an o. to sb** avoir une dette envers qn

obligatory [əˈblɪgətərɪ] *adj* obligatoire

oblige [əˈblaɪdʒ] *vt* **(a)** *(compel)* obliger; **to o. sb to do sth** obliger qn à faire qch **(b)** *(help)* rendre service à; **to be obliged to sb** être reconnaissant à qn (**for** de); **much obliged!** merci infiniment! • **obliging** *adj* serviable • **obligingly** *adv* obligeamment

oblique [əˈbliːk] *adj (line, angle, look)* oblique; *(reference, route)* indirect

obliterate [əˈblɪtəreɪt] *vt* effacer

oblivion [əˈblɪvɪən] *n* oubli *m*

oblivious [əˈblɪvɪəs] *adj* inconscient (**to** *or* **of** de)

oblong [ˈɒblɒŋ] **1** *adj (elongated)* oblong *(f* oblongue); *(rectangular)* rectangulaire
2 *n* rectangle *m*

obnoxious [əbˈnɒkʃəs] *adj (person, behaviour)* odieux, -ieuse; *(smell)* nauséabond

oboe [ˈəʊbəʊ] *n* hautbois *m*

obscene [əbˈsiːn] *adj* obscène • **obscenity** [əbˈsenətɪ] *(pl* **-ies**) *n* obscénité *f*

obscure [əbˈskjʊə(r)] **1** *adj* obscur
2 *vt (hide)* cacher; *(confuse)* obscurcir • **obscurely** *adv* obscurément • **obscurity** *n* obscurité *f*

obsequious [əbˈsiːkwɪəs] *adj* obséquieux, -ieuse

observance [əbˈzɜːvəns] *n (of rule, custom)* observation *f*

observant [əbˈzɜːvənt] *adj* observateur, -trice

observation [ɒbzəˈveɪʃən] *n (observing, remark)* observation *f*; *(by police)* surveillance *f*; **under o.** *(hospital patient)* en observation

observatory [əbˈzɜːvətərɪ] *(pl* **-ies**) *n* observatoire *m*

observe [əb'zɜːv] *vt* observer; **to o. the speed limit** respecter la limitation de vitesse • **observer** *n* observateur, -trice *mf*

obsess [əb'ses] *vt* obséder • **obsession** *n* obsession *f*; **to have an o. with** *or* **about sth** avoir l'obsession de qch; **to have an o. with sb** être obsédé par qn • **obsessive** *adj (memory, idea)* obsédant; *(person)* obsessionnel, -elle; **to be o. about sth** être obsédé par qch

obsolescent [ɒbsə'lesənt] *adj* un peu désuet, -uète • **obsolescence** *n* built-in o. *(of car, appliance)* obsolescence *f* programmée

obsolete ['ɒbsəliːt] *adj* obsolète; *(design, model)* dépassé

obstacle ['ɒbstəkəl] *n* obstacle *m*

obstetrician [ɒbstə'trɪʃən] *n* obstétricien, -ienne *mf*

obstetrics [əb'stetrɪks] *n* *Med* obstétrique *f*

obstinate ['ɒbstɪnət] *adj* obstiné; **to be o. about doing sth** s'obstiner à vouloir faire qch • **obstinacy** *n* obstination *f* • **obstinately** *adv* obstinément

obstreperous [əb'strepərəs] *adj* tapageur, -euse

obstruct [əb'strʌkt] *vt (block) (road, pipe)* obstruer; *(view)* cacher; *(hinder)* gêner • **obstruction** *n (action) & Med, Pol & Sport* obstruction *f*; *(obstacle)* obstacle *m*; *(in pipe)* bouchon *m*; *(traffic jam)* encombrement *m* • **obstructive** *adj* **to be o.** faire de l'obstruction

obtain [əb'teɪn] **1** *vt* obtenir
2 *vi Formal (of practice)* avoir cours • **obtainable** *adj (available)* disponible; *(on sale)* en vente

obtrusive [əb'truːsɪv] *adj (person)* importun; *(building)* trop en voyant

obtuse [əb'tjuːs] *adj (angle, mind)* obtus

obviate ['ɒbvɪeɪt] *vt Formal (difficulty, danger)* parer à

obvious ['ɒbvɪəs] *adj* évident (**that** que); **the o. thing to do is...** la seule chose à faire, c'est de... • **obviously** *adv (of course)* évidemment; *(conspicuously)* manifestement

occasion [ə'keɪʒən] **1** *n* (**a**) *(time, opportunity)* occasion *f*; *(event)* événement *m*; **on the o. of...** à l'occasion de...; **on o.** parfois; **on one o.** une fois; **on several occasions** à plusieurs reprises (**b**) *Formal (cause)* raison *f*
2 *vt Formal* occasionner

occasional [ə'keɪʒənəl] *adj* occasionnel, -elle; *(showers)* intermittent; **she drinks the o. whisky** elle boit un whisky de temps en temps • **occasionally** *adv* de temps en temps; **very o.** de temps en temps

occult [ə'kʌlt] **1** *adj* occulte
2 *n* **the o.** l'occulte *m*

occupant ['ɒkjʊpənt] *n (of house, car)* occupant, -ante *mf*; *(of bus, plane)* passager, -ère *mf*

occupation [ɒkjʊ'peɪʃən] *n* (**a**) *(pastime)* occupation *f*; *(profession)* métier *m* (**b**) *(of house, land)* occupation *f*; **fit for o.** habitable • **occupational** *adj* **o. hazard** risque *m* du métier; **o. disease** maladie *f* professionnelle; **o. therapy** ergothérapie *f*

occupier ['ɒkjʊpaɪə(r)] *n (of house)* occupant, -ante *mf*; *(of country)* occupant *m*

occupy ['ɒkjʊpaɪ] *(pt & pp -ied)* *vt (space, time, attention)* occuper; **to keep oneself occupied** s'occuper *(doing* à faire)

occur [ə'kɜː(r)] *(pt & pp -rr-)* *vi (happen)* avoir lieu; *(of opportunity)* se présenter; *(be found)* se trouver; **it occurs to me that** il me vient à l'esprit que; **the idea occurred to her to** l'idée lui est venue de

occurrence [ə'kʌrəns] *n* (**a**) *(event)* événement *m* (**b**) *(of disease)* incidence *f*; *Ling (of word)* occurrence *f*

ocean ['əʊʃən] *n* océan *m* • **oceanic** [əʊʃɪ'ænɪk] *adj* océanique

o'clock [ə'klɒk] *adv* (**it's**) **three o.** (il est) trois heures

octagon ['ɒktəgən] *n* octogone *m* • **octagonal** [ɒk'tægənəl] *adj* octogonal

octave ['ɒktɪv, 'ɒkteɪv] *n Mus* octave *f*

October [ɒk'təʊbə(r)] *n* octobre *m*

octogenarian [ɒktəʊdʒɪ'neərɪən] *n* octogénaire *mf*

octopus ['ɒktəpəs] *n* pieuvre *f*

OD [əʊ'diː] *vi Fam* faire une overdose (**on** de)

odd [ɒd] *adj* (**a**) *(strange)* bizarre, curieux, -ieuse
(**b**) *(number)* impair
(**c**) *(left over)* **I have an o. penny** il me reste un penny; **sixty o.** soixante et quelques; **to be the o. man out** être à part; **an o. glove/sock** un gant/une chaussette dépareillé(e)
(**d**) *(occasional)* **to find the o. mistake** trouver de temps en temps une erreur; **I smoke the o. cigarette** je fume une cigarette de temps en temps; **at o. moments** de temps en temps; **o. jobs** petits travaux *mpl*; *Br* **o. job man** homme *m* à tout faire • **oddly** *adv* bizarrement; **o. enough, he was elected** chose curieuse, il a été élu

oddity ['ɒdɪtɪ] (*pl* **-ies**) *n* (*person*) excentrique *mf*; (*object*) curiosité *f*; **oddities** (*of language, situation*) bizarreries *fpl*

oddment ['ɒdmənt] *n Br Com* fin *f* de série

odds [ɒdz] *npl* (**a**) (*in betting*) cote *f*; (*chances*) chances *fpl*; **we have heavy o. against us** nous avons très peu de chances de réussir; *Fam* **it makes no o.** ça n'a pas d'importance (**b**) (*expressions*) **to be at o. (with sb)** être en désaccord (avec qn); *Fam* **o. and ends** des bricoles *fpl*

ode [əʊd] *n* ode *f*

odious ['əʊdɪəs] *adj* odieux, -ieuse

odometer [əʊ'dɒmɪtə(r)] *n Am* compteur *m* kilométrique

odour ['əʊdə(r)] (*Am* **odor**) *n* odeur *f* • **odourless** (*Am* **odorless**) *adj* inodore

of [əv, *stressed* ɒv] *prep* de, d'; **of the table** de la table; **of the boy** du garçon; **of the boys** des garçons; **of a book** d'un livre; **of wood/paper** de *ou* en bois/papier; **she has a lot of it/of them** elle en a beaucoup; **I have ten of them** j'en ai dix; **there are ten of us** nous sommes dix; **a friend of his** un ami à lui, un de ses amis; **that's nice of you** c'est gentil de ta part; **of no value/interest** sans valeur/intérêt; **a man of fifty** un homme de cinquante ans; *Br* **the fifth of June** le cinq juin

off [ɒf] **1** *adj* (*light, gas, radio*) éteint; (*tap*) fermé; (*switched off at mains*) coupé; (*gone away*) parti; (*removed*) enlevé; (*cancelled*) annulé; (*not fit to eat or drink*) mauvais; (*milk, meat*) tourné; **the strike's o.** la grève est annulée; **I'm o. today** j'ai congé aujourd'hui **2** *adv* **to be o.** (*leave*) partir; **where are you o. to?** où vas-tu?; **with my/his/***etc* **gloves o.** sans gants; **a day o.** (*holiday*) un jour de congé; **time o.** du temps libre; **I have today o.** j'ai congé aujourd'hui; **5 percent o.** une réduction de 5 pour cent; **hands o.!** pas touche!; **on and o., o. and on** (*sometimes*) de temps à autre **3** *prep* (*from*) de; (*distant*) éloigné de; **to fall o. the wall/ladder** tomber du mur/de l'échelle; **to get o. the bus** descendre du bus; **to take sth o. the table** prendre qch sur la table; **to eat o. a plate** manger dans une assiette; **to keep** *or* **stay o. the grass** ne pas marcher sur la pelouse; **she's o. her food** elle ne mange plus rien; **o. Dover** (*ship*) au large de Douvres; **it's o. limits** c'est interdit • **offbeat** *adj Fam* original • **offchance** *n* **on the o.** à tout hasard • **off-'colour** (*Am* **off-color**) *adj Br* (*ill*) patraque; (*indecent*) d'un goût dou-teux • **'off-'duty** *adj* qui n'est pas de service • **'off'hand 1** *adj* désinvolte **2** *adv* (*immediately*) au pied levé • **off-licence** *n Br* ≃ magasin *m* de vins et de spiritueux • **'off-'line** *adj Comptr* (*computer*) autonome; (*printer*) déconnecté • **off-'load** *vt* (*vehicle*) décharger; **to o. sth onto sb** (*task*) se décharger de qch sur qn • **'off-'peak** *adj* (*traffic*) aux heures creuses; (*rate, price*) heures creuses *inv*; **o. hours** heures *fpl* creuses • **'off-'putting** *adj Br Fam* peu engageant • **offshore** *adj* (*waters*) proche de la côte • **off'side** *adj Football* **to be o.** être hors jeu • **offspring** *n* progéniture *f* • **'off'stage** *adj & adv* dans les coulisses • **'off-the-'cuff 1** *adj* impromptu **2** *adv* au pied levé • **'off-the-'peg** (*Am* **off-the-'rack**) *adj* (*clothes*) de confection • **'off-the-'record** *adj* officieux, -ieuse • **'off-the-'wall** *adj Fam* loufoque • **'off-'white** *adj* blanc cassé *inv*

offal ['ɒfəl] *n* abats *mpl*

offence [ə'fens] (*Am* **offense**) *n Law* infraction *f*; (*more serious*) délit *m*; **to take o.** s'offenser (**at** de); **to give o. (to sb)** offenser (qn)

offend [ə'fend] *vt* offenser; **to o. the eye/ear** choquer la vue/l'oreille; **to be offended (at sth)** s'offenser (de qch) • **offender** *n Law* (*criminal*) délinquant, -ante *mf* • **offending** *adj* (*object, remark*) incriminé

offense [ə'fens] *n Am* = **offence**

offensive [ə'fensɪv] **1** *adj* choquant; (*smell*) repoussant; **to be o. to sb** se montrer blessant envers qn; *Law* **o. weapon** arme *f* offensive **2** *n* offensive *f*; **to be on the o.** être passé à l'offensive

offer ['ɒfə(r)] **1** *n* offre *f*; **to make sb an o.** faire une offre à qn; **on (special) o.** en promotion; **o. of marriage** demande *f* en mariage **2** *vt* offrir; (*explanation*) donner; (*apologies*) présenter; **to o. sb sth, to o. sth to sb** offrir qch à qn; **to o. to do sth** proposer *ou* offrir de faire qch • **offering** *n* (*gift*) offrande *f*; (*act*) offre *f*

office ['ɒfɪs] *n* (**a**) (*room*) bureau *m*; *Am* (*of doctor*) cabinet *m*; (*of lawyer*) étude *f*; **o. block** *or* **building** immeuble *m* de bureaux; **o. boy** garçon *m* de bureau; **o. hours** heures *fpl* de bureau; **o. worker** employé, -ée *mf* de bureau (**b**) (*position*) fonctions *fpl*; **to be in o.** être au pouvoir

officer ['ɒfɪsə(r)] *n* (*in the army, navy*) officier *m*; (**police**) **o.** agent *m* de police

official [ə'fɪʃəl] **1** *adj* officiel, -ielle **2** *n* responsable *mf*; (*civil servant*) fonc-

tionnaire *mf* • **officialdom** *n Pej* bureau-cratie *f* • **officially** *adv* officiellement
officiate [əˈfɪʃɪeɪt] *vi (preside)* présider; *(of priest)* officier; **to o. at a wedding** célébrer un mariage
officious [əˈfɪʃəs] *adj Pej* trop zélé
offing [ˈɒfɪŋ] *n* **in the o.** en perspective
offset [ˈɒfset, ɒfˈset] (*pt & pp* offset, *pres p* **offsetting**) *vt (compensate for)* compenser
offshoot [ˈɒfʃuːt] *n (of organization)* ramification *f*; *(of family)* branche *f*
often [ˈɒf(t)ən] *adv* souvent; **how o.?** combien de fois?; **how o. do they run?** *(trains, buses)* il y en a tous les combien?; **every so o.** de temps en temps
ogle [ˈəʊgəl] *vt Pej* reluquer
ogre [ˈəʊgə(r)] *n* ogre *m*
oh [əʊ] *exclam* oh!, ah!; *(in pain)* aïe!; **oh yes!** mais oui!; **oh yes?** ah oui?, ah bon?
OHP [əʊeɪtʃˈpiː] (*abbr* overhead projector) *n* rétroprojecteur *m*
oil [ɔɪl] **1** *n (for machine, cooking)* huile *f*; *(petroleum)* pétrole *m*; *(fuel)* mazout *m*; **to paint in oils** faire de la peinture à l'huile
2 *adj (industry, product)* pétrolier, -ière; *(painting, paint)* à l'huile; **o. change** *(in vehicle)* vidange *f*; **o. lamp** lampe *f* à pétrole; **o. refinery** raffinerie *f* de pétrole; **o. slick** nappe *f* de pétrole
3 *vt (machine)* huiler • **oilcan** *n* burette *f* • **oilfield** *n* gisement *m* de pétrole • **oil-fired** *adj (central heating)* au mazout • **oil-producing** *adj* producteur, -trice de pétrole • **oilskins** *npl (garment)* ciré *m* • **oily** (**-ier**, **-iest**) *adj (hands, rag)* graisseux, -euse; *(skin, hair)* gras (*f* grasse); *(food)* huileux, -euse
ointment [ˈɔɪntmənt] *n* pommade *f*
OK, okay [əʊˈkeɪ] **1** *adj & adv see* **all right**
2 (*pt & pp* OKed, okayed, *pres p* OKing, okaying) *vt* donner le feu vert à
old [əʊld] **1** (**-er**, **-est**) *adj* vieux (*f* vieille); *(former)* ancien, -ienne; **how o. is he?** quel âge a-t-il?; **he's ten years o.** il a dix ans; **he's older than me** il est plus âgé que moi; **an older son** un fils aîné; **the oldest son** le fils aîné; **o. enough to do sth** assez grand pour faire qch; **o. enough to marry/vote** en âge de se marier/de voter; **to get** *or* **grow old(er)** vieillir; **o. age** vieillesse *f*; *Pej* **o. maid** vieille fille *f*; **o. man** vieillard *m*, vieil homme *m*; **o. people** les personnes *fpl* âgées; **o. people's home** maison *f* de retraite; **o. woman** vieille femme *f*; **the O. World** l'Ancien

Monde; *Fam* **any o. how** n'importe comment
2 *npl* **the o.** les personnes *fpl* âgées
olden [ˈəʊldən] *adj* **in o. days** jadis
old-fashioned [əʊldˈfæʃənd] *adj (out-of-date)* démodé; *(person)* vieux jeu *inv*; *(traditional)* d'autrefois
old-timer [əʊldˈtaɪmə(r)] *n Fam (old man)* ancien *m*
olive [ˈɒlɪv] **1** *n (fruit)* olive *f*
2 *adj* **o. (green)** vert olive *inv*; **o. oil** huile *f* d'olive; **o. tree** olivier *m*
Olympic [əˈlɪmpɪk] *adj* **the O. Games** les jeux *mpl* Olympiques
ombudsman [ˈɒmbʊdzmən] (*pl* **-men**) *n* ≃ médiateur *m* de la République
omelet(te) [ˈɒmlɪt] *n* omelette *f*; **cheese o.** omelette au fromage
omen [ˈəʊmən] *n* augure *m*
ominous [ˈɒmɪnəs] *adj* inquiétant; *(event)* de mauvais augure; *(tone, sky)* menaçant; *(noise)* sinistre
omit [əʊˈmɪt] (*pt & pp* **-tt-**) *vt* omettre (**to do** de faire) • **omission** *n* omission *f*
omnipotent [ɒmˈnɪpətənt] *adj* omnipotent
on [ɒn] **1** *prep* (**a**) *(expressing position)* sur; **on the chair** sur la chaise; **on page 4** à la page 4; **on the right/left** à droite/gauche; **to put on (to) sth** mettre sur qch; **to look out on to sth** donner sur qch (**b**) *(about)* sur; **an article on sth** un article sur qch
(**c**) *(expressing manner or means)* **on foot** à pied; **on the blackboard** au tableau; **on the radio** à la radio; **on the train/plane** dans le train/l'avion; **to be on** *(course)* suivre; *(project)* travailler à; *(salary)* toucher; *(team, committee)* faire partie de; **to keep** *or* **stay on** *(road, path)* suivre; *Fam* **it's on me!** *(I'll pay)* c'est moi pour moi!
(**d**) *(with time)* **on Monday** lundi; **on Mondays** le lundi; **on May 3rd** le 3 mai; **on the evening of May 3rd** le 3 mai au soir; **on my arrival** à mon arrivée
(**e**) (+ *present participle*) en; **on learning that** en apprenant que; **on seeing this** en voyant ceci
2 *adv (ahead)* en avant; *(in progress)* en cours; *(lid, brake)* mis; *(light, radio)* allumé; *(gas, tap)* ouvert; *(machine)* en marche; **she has her hat on** elle a mis son chapeau; **he has something/nothing on** il est habillé/tout nu; **I've got something on** *(I'm busy)* je suis pris; **the strike is on** la grève aura lieu; **what's on?** *(on TV)* qu'est-ce qu'il y a à la télé?; *(in theatre, cinema)* qu'est-ce qu'on joue?; **is**

the meeting still on? la réunion doit-elle toujours avoir lieu?; **to play on** continuer à jouer; **he went on and on about it** il n'en finissait pas; *Fam* **that's just not on!** c'est inadmissible!; **I've been on to him** *(on phone)* je l'ai eu au bout du fil; **to be on to sb** *(of police)* être sur la piste de qn • **on-coming** *adj (vehicle)* qui vient en sens inverse • **'on'going** *adj (project, discussion)* en cours • **'on-'line** *adj (computer)* en ligne

once [wʌns] **1** *adv (on one occasion)* une fois; *(formerly)* autrefois; **o. a month** une fois par mois; **o. again, o. more** encore une fois; **o. and for all** une fois pour toutes; **o. upon a time** il était une fois; **at o.** *(immediately)* tout de suite; **all at o.** *(suddenly)* tout à coup; *(at the same time)* à la fois

2 *conj* une fois que; **o. he reached home, he collapsed** une fois arrivé chez lui, il s'effondra • **once-over** *n Fam* **to give sth the o.** jeter un coup d'œil à qch

one [wʌn] **1** *adj* (**a**) un, une; **o. man** un homme; **o. woman** une femme; **page o.** la page un; **twenty-o.** vingt et un (**b**) *(only)* seul; **my o. (and only) aim** mon seul (et unique) but (**c**) *(same)* le même (*f* la même); **in the o. bus** dans le même bus

2 *pron* (**a**) un, une; **do you want o.?** en veux-tu (un)?; **he's o. of us** il est des nôtres; **o. of them** l'un d'eux, l'une d'elles; **a big/small o.** un grand/petit; **this book is o. that I've read** ce livre est parmi ceux que j'ai lus; **I'm a teacher and she's o.** too je suis professeur et elle aussi; **this o.** celui-ci, celle-ci; **that o.** celui-là, celle-là; **the o. who/which...** celui/celle qui...; *Br Fam* **it's Paul's o.** c'est celui de Paul; *Br Fam* **it's my o.** c'est le mien/la mienne; **another o.** un(e) autre; **I for o.** pour ma part (**b**) *(impersonal)* on; **o. knows** on sait; **it helps o.** ça vous aide; **o.'s family** sa famille • **'one-'armed** *adj (person)* manchot • **'one-'eyed** *adj* borgne • **one-legged** ['wʌn'legɪd] *adj* unijambiste • **one-man** *adj (business, office)* pour un seul homme; **o. show** one-man-show *m inv* • **'one-'off** (*Am* **'one-of-a-'kind**) *adj Fam* unique • **one-parent 'family** *n* famille *f* monoparentale • **'one-'sided** *adj (biased)* partial; *(contest)* inégal; *(decision)* unilatéral • **one-time** *adj (former)* ancien, -ienne • **'one-to-'one** *adj (discussion)* en tête-à-tête • **one-track 'mind** *n* **to have a o.** avoir une idée fixe • **one-'upmanship** *n Fam* = tendance à s'affirmer supérieur

aux autres • **one-way** *adj (street)* à sens unique; *(traffic)* en sens unique; **o. ticket** billet *m* simple

onerous ['əʊnərəs] *adj (task)* difficile; *(taxes)* lourd

> ⚠ Note that the French word **onéreux** is a false friend and is never a translation for the English word **onerous**. It means **expensive**.

oneself [wʌn'self] *pron* soi-même; *(reflexive)* se, s'; **to cut o.** se couper; **to do sth all by o.** faire qch tout seul

onion ['ʌnjən] *n* oignon *m*

onlooker ['ɒnlʊkə(r)] *n* spectateur, -trice *mf*

only ['əʊnlɪ] **1** *adj* seul; **the o. house** la seule maison; **the o. one** le seul, la seule; **an o. son** un fils unique

2 *adv* seulement, ne... que; **I o. have ten, I have ten o.** je n'en ai que dix, j'en ai dix seulement; **if o.** si seulement; **not o.** non seulement; **I have o. just seen it** je viens tout juste de le voir; **o. he knows** lui seul le sait

3 *conj Fam (but)* mais

onset ['ɒnset] *n (of disease, winter)* début *m*; *(of old age)* approche *f*

onslaught ['ɒnslɔːt] *n* attaque *f* (**on** contre)

onto ['ɒntuː, *unstressed* 'ɒntə] *prep* = **on to**

onus ['əʊnəs] *n inv* **the o. is on you to...** c'est à vous qu'il incombe de...

onward(s) ['ɒnwəd(z)] *adv* en avant; **from that day o.** à partir de ce jour-là

onyx ['ɒnɪks] *n* onyx *m*

ooze [uːz] **1** *vt* laisser suinter

2 *vi* **to o. (out)** suinter

opal ['əʊpəl] *n* opale *f*

opaque [əʊ'peɪk] *adj* opaque; *Fig (unclear)* obscur

open ['əʊpən] **1** *adj* ouvert; *(site, view, road)* dégagé; *(meeting)* public, -ique; *(competition)* ouvert à tous; *(post, job)* vacant; *(attempt, envy)* manifeste; *(airline ticket)* open *inv*; **in the o. air** au grand air; **in (the) o. country** en rase campagne; **o. spaces** *(parks)* espaces *mpl* verts; **it's o. to doubt** c'est douteux; **to be o. to** *(criticism, attack)* exposé à; *(ideas, suggestions)* ouvert à; **I've got an o. mind on it** je n'ai pas d'opinion arrêtée là-dessus; **to leave sth o.** *(date)* ne pas préciser qch

2 *n* **(out) in the o.** *(outside)* dehors; **to sleep (out) in the o.** dormir à la belle étoile; **to bring sth (out) into the o.** *(reveal)* divulguer qch

3 *vt* ouvrir; *(conversation)* entamer; *(arms, legs)* écarter; **to o. sth out** *(paper, map)* ouvrir qch; **to o. sth up** *(door, shop)* ouvrir qch
4 *vi (of flower, door, eyes)* s'ouvrir; *(of shop, office, person)* ouvrir; *(of play)* débuter; *(of film)* sortir; **to o. on to sth** *(of window)* donner sur qch; **to o. out** *(of flower)* s'ouvrir; *(widen)* s'élargir; **to o. up** *(of flower, person)* s'ouvrir; *(of shopkeeper, shop)* ouvrir • **'open-'air** *adj (pool)* en plein air • **'open-'heart** *adj (operation)* à cœur ouvert • **'open-'minded** *adj* à l'esprit ouvert • **'open-'necked** *adj (shirt)* sans cravate • **'open-'plan** *adj (office)* paysager, -ère

opening ['əʊpənɪŋ] **1** *n* ouverture *f*; *(of flower)* éclosion *f*; *(job, trade outlet)* débouché *m*; *(opportunity)* occasion *f* favorable; **late-night o.** *(of shops)* nocturne *f*
2 *adj (time, hours, speech)* d'ouverture; **o. night** *(of play, musical)* première *f*

openly ['əʊpənlɪ] *adv* ouvertement • **openness** *n (frankness)* franchise *f*

opera ['ɒprə] *n* opéra *m*; **o. glasses** jumelles *fpl* de théâtre

operate ['ɒpəreɪt] **1** *vt (machine)* faire fonctionner; *(service)* assurer
2 *vi* (**a**) **to o. on sb (for sth)** *(of surgeon)* opérer qn (de qch); **to be operated on** se faire opérer (**b**) *(of machine)* fonctionner; *(of company)* opérer • **operating** *adj* **o. costs** frais *mpl* d'exploitation; *Br* **o. theatre,** *Am* **o. room** salle *f* d'opération; *Comptr* **o. system** système *m* d'exploitation

operation [ɒpə'reɪʃən] *n Med, Mil & Math* opération *f*; *(of machine)* fonctionnement *m*; **in o.** *(machine)* en service; *(plan)* en vigueur; **to have an o.** se faire opérer • **operational** *adj* opérationnel, -elle

operative ['ɒpərətɪv] **1** *adj (scheme, measure, law)* en vigueur; *Med* opératoire
2 *n (worker)* ouvrier, -ière *mf*

operator ['ɒpəreɪtə(r)] *n (on phone, machine)* opérateur, -trice *mf*

opinion [ə'pɪnjən] *n* opinion *f*; **to form an o.** se faire une opinion; **in my o.** à mon avis • **opinionated** *adj* dogmatique

opium ['əʊpɪəm] *n* opium *m*

opponent [ə'pəʊnənt] *n* adversaire *mf*

opportune ['ɒpətjuːn] *adj* opportun

opportunism ['ɒpətjuːnɪzəm, -'tjuːnɪzəm] *n* opportunisme *m*

opportunity [ɒpə'tjuːnɪtɪ] *(pl* **-ies***) n* occasion *f* (**to do** *or* **of doing** de faire); **opportunities** *(prospects)* perspectives

fpl; **equal opportunities** égalité *f* des chances; **to take the o. to do sth** profiter de l'occasion pour faire qch

oppose [ə'pəʊz] *vt* s'opposer à • **opposed** *adj* opposé (**to** à); **as o. to...** par opposition à... • **opposing** *adj (characters, viewpoints)* opposé; *(team)* adverse

opposite ['ɒpəzɪt] **1** *adj (side)* opposé; *(house, page)* d'en face; **in the o. direction** en sens inverse; **o. number** homologue *mf*
2 *adv* en face; **the house o.** la maison d'en face
3 *prep* **o. (to)** en face de
4 *n* **the o.** le contraire

opposition [ɒpə'zɪʃən] *n* opposition *f* (**to** à); **the o.** *(rival camp)* l'adversaire *m*; *(in business)* la concurrence; **he put up no/considerable o.** il n'a opposé aucune résistance/a fait preuve d'une résistance acharnée

oppress [ə'pres] *vt (treat cruelly)* opprimer; *(of heat, anguish)* oppresser • **oppressed** *npl* **the o.** les opprimés *mpl* • **oppression** *n* oppression *f* • **oppressive** *adj (heat)* accablant, étouffant; *(weather)* étouffant; *(ruler, regime)* oppressif, -ive • **oppressor** *n* oppresseur *m*

opt [ɒpt] *vi* **to o. for sth** opter pour qch; **to o. to do sth** choisir de faire qch; **to o. out** se désengager (**of** de)

optical ['ɒptɪkəl] *adj* optique; *(instrument, illusion)* d'optique; *Comptr* **o. character reader** lecteur *m* optique de caractères

optician [ɒp'tɪʃən] *n (dispensing)* opticien, -ienne *mf*

optimism ['ɒptɪmɪzəm] *n* optimisme *m* • **optimist** *n* optimiste *mf* • **opti'mistic** *adj* optimiste (**about** quant à) • **opti'mistically** *adv* avec optimisme

optimum ['ɒptɪməm] *adj & n* optimum *(m)* • **optimal** *adj* optimal

option ['ɒpʃən] *n (choice)* choix *m*; *(school subject)* matière *f* à option; **she has no o.** elle n'a pas le choix • **optional** *adj* facultatif, -ive; **o. extra** *(on car)* option *f*

opulent ['ɒpjʊlənt] *adj* opulent • **opulence** *n* opulence *f*

or [ɔː(r)] *conj* ou; **one or two** un ou deux; **he doesn't drink or smoke** il ne boit ni ne fume; **ten or so** environ dix

oracle ['ɒrəkəl] *n* oracle *m*

oral ['ɔːrəl] **1** *adj* oral
2 *n (exam)* oral *m* • **orally** *adv* oralement; *Med* par voie orale

orange ['ɒrɪndʒ] **1** *n (fruit)* orange *f*; **o.**

drink boisson *f* à l'orange; **o. juice** jus *m* d'orange; **o. tree** oranger *m*
2 *adj & n (colour)* orange *(m) inv* • **orange'ade** *n* orangeade *f*
orang-outang [ɔːræŋuːˈtæŋ], **orang-utan** [ɔːræŋuːˈtæn] *n* orang-outan(g) *m*
oration [ɔːˈreɪʃən] *n* funeral o. oraison *f* funèbre
orator [ˈɒrətə(r)] *n* orateur *m* • **oratory** *(pl* **-ies)** *n* art *m* oratoire
orbit [ˈɔːbɪt] **1** *n (of planet, sphere of influence)* orbite *f*
2 *vt* être en orbite autour de
orchard [ˈɔːtʃəd] *n* verger *m*
orchestra [ˈɔːkɪstrə] *n* orchestre *m*; *Am* **the o.** *(in theatre)* l'orchestre *m* • **orchestral** [ɔːˈkestrəl] *adj (music)* orchestral; *(concert)* symphonique • **orchestrate** *vt (organize) & Mus* orchestrer
orchid [ˈɔːkɪd] *n* orchidée *f*
ordain [ɔːˈdeɪn] *vt (priest)* ordonner; *Formal* **to o. that...** décréter que...
ordeal [ɔːˈdiːl] *n* épreuve *f*
order [ˈɔːdə(r)] **1** *n (instruction, arrangement) & Rel* ordre *m*; *(purchase)* commande *f*; **in o.** *(passport)* en règle; *(drawer, room)* en ordre; **in numerical o.** en ordre numérique; **in working o.** en état de marche; **in o. of age** par ordre d'âge; **in o. to do sth** afin de faire qch; **in o. that...** afin que... *(+ subjunctive)*; **out of o.** *(machine)* en panne; *(telephone)* en dérangement; *Com* **to make** *or* **place an o. (with sb)** passer une commande (à qn); **on o.** *(goods)* commandé; **o. form** bon *m* de commande
2 *vt (meal, goods)* commander; *(taxi)* appeler; **to o. sb to do sth** ordonner à qn de faire qch; **to o. sb around** commander qn
3 *vi (in café)* commander; **are you ready to o.?** avez-vous choisi?
orderly [ˈɔːdəlɪ] **1** *adj (tidy) (room, life)* ordonné; *(mind)* méthodique; *(crowd)* discipliné; **in an o. fashion** calmement
2 *(pl* **-ies)** *n (soldier)* planton *m*; *(in hospital)* aide-soignant, -ante *mf*
ordinal [ˈɔːdɪnəl] *adj* ordinal
ordinary [ˈɔːdənrɪ] *adj* ordinaire; **in o. use** d'usage courant; **in the o. course of events** en temps normal; **in the o. way** normalement; **it's out of the o.** ça sort de l'ordinaire; **she was just an o. tourist** c'était une touriste comme une autre
ordination [ɔːdɪˈneɪʃən] *n Rel* ordination *f*
ordnance [ˈɔːdnəns] *n Mil (guns)* artillerie *f*; *Br* **O. Survey** ≃ Institut *m* géographique national

ore [ɔː(r)] *n* minerai *m*
oregano [ɒrɪˈgɑːnəʊ] *n* origan *m*
organ [ˈɔːgən] *n* **(a)** *(part of body, newspaper)* organe *m* **(b)** *(musical instrument)* orgue *m* • **organist** *n* organiste *mf*
organic [ɔːˈgænɪk] *adj* organique; *(vegetables, farming)* biologique
organism [ˈɔːgənɪzəm] *n* organisme *m*
organization [ɔːgənaɪˈzeɪʃən] *n* organisation *f*
organize [ˈɔːgənaɪz] *vt* organiser • **organizer** *n (person)* organisateur, -trice *mf*; **(personal) o.** *(diary)* agenda *m*
orgasm [ˈɔːgæzəm] *n* orgasme *m*
orgy [ˈɔːdʒɪ] *(pl* **-ies)** *n* orgie *f*
Orient [ˈɔːrɪənt] *n* **the O.** l'Orient *m* • **oriental** [ɔːrɪˈentəl] **1** *adj* oriental **2** *n* Oriental, -ale *mf*
orientate [ˈɔːrɪənteɪt] *(Am* **orient** [ˈɔːrɪənt])* vt* orienter
orifice [ˈɒrɪfɪs] *n* orifice *m*
origin [ˈɒrɪdʒɪn] *n* origine *f*
original [əˈrɪdʒɪnəl] **1** *adj (novel, innovative)* original; *(first)* d'origine; *Rel* **o. sin** péché *m* originel
2 *n (document, painting)* original *m* • **originality** [-ˈnælɪtɪ] *n* originalité *f* • **originally** *adv (at first)* à l'origine; *(in an innovative way)* de façon originale; **where do you come from o.?** d'où êtes-vous originaire?
originate [əˈrɪdʒɪneɪt] **1** *vt* être à l'origine de
2 *vi (begin)* prendre naissance (**in** dans); **to o. from** *(of idea)* émaner de; *(of person)* être originaire de
Orkneys [ˈɔːknɪz] *npl* **the O.** les Orcades *fpl*
ornament [ˈɔːnəmənt] *n* ornement *m* • **ornamental** [-ˈmentəl] *adj* ornemental • **ornamentation** [-menˈteɪʃən] *n* ornementation *f*
ornate [ɔːˈneɪt] *adj* très orné • **ornately** *adv* de façon très orné; **o. decorated** richement décoré
orphan [ˈɔːfən] **1** *adj* **an o. child** un orphelin, une orpheline
2 *n* orphelin, -ine *mf* • **orphanage** *n* orphelinat *m* • **orphaned** *adj* **to be o.** devenir orphelin
orthodox [ˈɔːθədɒks] *adj* orthodoxe • **orthodoxy** *n* orthodoxie *f*
orthop(a)edic [ɔːθəˈpiːdɪk] *adj* orthopédique • **orthop(a)edics** *n* orthopédie *f*
Oscar [ˈɒskə(r)] *n Cin* oscar *m*
oscillate [ˈɒsɪleɪt] *vi* osciller
ostensibly [ɒˈstensɪblɪ] *adv* soi-disant
ostentation [ɒstenˈteɪʃən] *n* ostentation *f* • **ostentatious** *adj* prétentieux, -ieuse

osteopath ['ɒstɪəpæθ] *n* ostéopathe *mf*

ostracism ['ɒstrəsɪzəm] *n* ostracisme *m* • **ostracize** *vt* frapper d'ostracisme

ostrich ['ɒstrɪtʃ] *n* autruche *f*

other ['ʌðə(r)] **1** *adj* autre; **o. doctors** d'autres médecins; **the o. one** l'autre *mf*; **I have no o. gloves than these** je n'ai pas d'autres gants que ceux-ci

2 *pron* **the o.** l'autre *mf*; **(some) others** d'autres; **some do, others don't** les uns le font, les autres ne le font pas; **none o. than, no o. than** nul autre que

3 *adv* **o. than** autrement que; **the colour's odd, but o. than that, it's fine** la couleur est bizarre, mais à part ça, ça va • **otherwise 1** *adv & conj* autrement **2** *adj (different)* autre

OTT [əʊtiː'tiː] *(abbr* **over the top)** *adj Br Fam* trop *inv*

otter ['ɒtə(r)] *n* loutre *f*

ouch [aʊtʃ] *exclam* aïe!

ought [ɔːt] *v aux*

La forme négative **ought not** s'écrit **oughtn't** en forme contractée.

(**a**) *(expressing obligation, desirability)* **you o. to leave** tu devrais partir; **I o. to have done it** j'aurais dû le faire; **he said he o. to stay** il a dit qu'il devait rester (**b**) *(expressing probability)* **it o. to be ready** ça devrait être prêt

ounce [aʊns] *n (unit of weight)* = 28,35 g, once *f*; *Fig (bit)* once *f* (**of** de)

our [aʊə(r)] *possessive adj* notre, *pl* nos

ours [aʊəz] *possessive pron* le nôtre, la nôtre, *pl* les nôtres; **this book is o.** ce livre est à nous *ou* est le nôtre; **a friend of o.** un de nos amis

ourselves [aʊə'selvz] *pron* nous-mêmes; *(reflexive and after prep)* nous; **we wash o.** nous nous lavons; **we told you o.** nous vous l'avons dit nous-mêmes

oust [aʊst] *vt* évincer (**from** de)

out [aʊt] **1** *adv (outside)* dehors; *(not at home)* sorti; *(light, fire)* éteint; *(flower)* ouvert; *(book)* publié; *(not in fashion)* passé de mode; **to go o. a lot** sortir beaucoup; **to have a day o.** sortir pour la journée; **5 km o.** *(from the shore)* à 5 km du rivage; **the sun's o.** il fait soleil; **the tide's o.** la marée est basse; **the secret is o.** on a révélé le secret; **you're o.** *(wrong)* tu t'es trompé; *(in game)* tu es éliminé (**of** de); **I was £10 o.** *(over)* j'avais 10 livres de trop; *(under)* il me manquait 10 livres; **before the week is o.** avant la fin de la semaine; **to be o. to do sth** chercher à

faire qch; **the journey o.** l'aller *m*; **o. here** ici; **o. there** là-bas; *Tennis* **o.!** faute!

2 *prep* **o. of** *(outside)* hors de; **5 km o. of** *(away from)* à 5 km de; **to be o. of the country** être à l'étranger; **she's o. of town** elle n'est pas en ville; **to look/jump o. of the window** regarder/sauter par la fenêtre; **to drink/take/copy o. of sth** boire/prendre/copier dans qch; **to feel o. of place** ne pas se sentir à sa place; *Fam* **to feel o. of it** se sentir hors du coup; **made o. of wood** fait en bois; **to make sth o. of a box/rag** faire qch avec une boîte/un chiffon; **o. of danger** hors de danger; **o. of pity/love** par pitié/amour; **four o. of five** quatre sur cinq • **'out-and-'out** *adj (cheat, liar)* achevé; *(failure)* total • **out-of-date** *adj (expired)* périmé; *(old-fashioned)* démodé • **out-of-'doors** *adv* dehors • **'out-of-the-'way** *adj (place)* isolé

outbid [aʊt'bɪd] *(pt & pp* **-bid,** *pres p* **outbidding)** *vt* **to o. sb** enchérir avec succès sur qn

outboard ['aʊtbɔːd] *adj* **o. motor** moteur *m* hors-bord *inv*

outbreak ['aʊtbreɪk] *n (of war, epidemic)* début *m*; *(of violence)* flambée *f*; *(of hostilities)* déclenchement *m*; *(of fever)* accès *m*

outbuilding ['aʊtbɪldɪŋ] *n* dépendance *f*

outburst ['aʊtbɜːst] *n (of anger, joy)* explosion *f*; *(of violence)* flambée *f*; *(of laughter)* éclat *m*

outcast ['aʊtkɑːst] *n* **(social) o.** paria *m*

outcome ['aʊtkʌm] *n* résultat *m*, issue *f*

outcry ['aʊtkraɪ] *(pl* **-ies)** *n* tollé *m*

outdated [aʊt'deɪtɪd] *adj* démodé

outdistance [aʊt'dɪstəns] *vt* distancer

outdo [aʊt'duː] *(pt* **-did,** *pp* **-done)** *vt* surpasser (**in** en)

outdoor ['aʊtdɔː(r)] *adj (life)* au grand air; *(game)* de plein air; *(pool, market)* découvert • **out'doors 1** *adv* dehors **2** *n* **the great o.** les grands espaces *mpl*

outer ['aʊtə(r)] *adj* extérieur; **O. London** la grande banlieue de Londres; **o. space** l'espace *m* intersidéral

outfit ['aʊtfɪt] *n (clothes)* ensemble *m*; *Fam (group, gang)* bande *f*; *Fam (company)* boîte *f*; **sports/ski o.** tenue *f* de sport/de ski • **outfitter** *n Br* chemisier *m*

outgoing ['aʊtgəʊɪŋ] *adj* (**a**) *(minister)* sortant; *(mail, ship)* en partance; **o. calls** *(on phone)* appels *mpl* vers l'extérieur (**b**) *(sociable)* liant • **outgoings** *npl (expenses)* dépenses *fpl*

outgrow [aʊt'grəʊ] *(pt* **-grew,** *pp*

-grown) *vt (habit)* passer l'âge de; **to o. sb** grandir plus vite que qn; **she's outgrown her jacket** sa veste est devenue trop petite pour elle

outhouse ['aʊthaʊs] *n Br (of mansion, farm)* dépendance *f; Am (lavatory)* cabinets *mpl* extérieurs

outing ['aʊtɪŋ] *n (excursion)* sortie *f*

outlandish [aʊt'lændɪʃ] *adj (weird)* bizarre; *(barbaric)* barbare

outlast [aʊt'lɑːst] *vt (object)* durer plus longtemps que; *(person)* survivre à

outlaw ['aʊtlɔː] **1** *n* hors-la-loi *m inv* **2** *vt (ban)* proscrire; *(person)* mettre hors la loi

outlay ['aʊtleɪ] *n (expense)* dépenses *fpl*

outlet ['aʊtlet] *n (shop)* point *m* de vente; *(market for goods)* débouché *m; (for liquid, of tunnel)* sortie *f; (electrical)* prise *f* de courant; *(for feelings, energy)* exutoire *m;* **retail o.** point de vente, magasin *m;* **factory o.** magasin d'usine

outline ['aʊtlaɪn] **1** *n (shape)* contour *m; (of play, novel)* résumé *m;* **rough o.** *(of article, plan)* esquisse *f;* **the broad** *or* **general** *or* **main o.** *(of plan, policy)* les grandes lignes **2** *vt (plan, situation)* esquisser; *(book, speech)* résumer; **to be outlined against sth** se profiler sur qch

outlive [aʊt'lɪv] *vt* survivre à

outlook ['aʊtlʊk] *n inv (for future)* perspectives *fpl; (point of view)* façon *f* de voir les choses; *(of weather)* prévisions *fpl*

outlying ['aʊtlaɪɪŋ] *adj (remote)* isolé

outmoded [aʊt'məʊdɪd] *adj* démodé

outnumber [aʊt'nʌmbə(r)] *vt* l'emporter en nombre sur

outpatient ['aʊtpeɪʃənt] *n Br* malade *mf* en consultation externe

outpost ['aʊtpəʊst] *n Mil* avant-poste *m*

output ['aʊtpʊt] **1** *n (of goods)* production *f; (computer data)* données *fpl* de sortie; *(computer process)* sortie *f* **2** *(pt & pp* **-put)** *vt* produire; *(data, information)* sortir

outrage ['aʊtreɪdʒ] **1** *n (scandal)* scandale *m; (anger)* indignation *f* (**at** face à); *(crime)* atrocité *f* **2** *vt (make indignant)* scandaliser

outrageous [aʊt'reɪdʒəs] *adj (shocking)* scandaleux, -euse; *(atrocious)* atroce; *(dress, hat)* grotesque

outright 1 [aʊt'raɪt] *adv (say, tell)* franchement; *(refuse)* catégoriquement; *(be killed)* sur le coup; **to buy sth o.** acheter qch au comptant **2** ['aʊtraɪt] *adj (failure)* total; *(refusal)*

catégorique; *(folly)* pur; *(winner)* incontesté

outset ['aʊtset] *n* **at the o.** au début; **from the o.** dès le départ

outside [aʊt'saɪd] **1** *adv* dehors, à l'extérieur; **to go o.** sortir **2** *prep* à l'extérieur de, en dehors de; *(in front of)* devant; *(apart from)* en dehors de; **o. my room** *or* **door** à la porte de ma chambre; **o. office hours** en dehors des heures de bureau **3** *n* extérieur *m* **4** ['aʊtsaɪd] *adj* extérieur; *(bus or train seat)* côté couloir *inv; Br* **the o. lane** *(on road)* la voie de droite, *Am* la voie de gauche; **an o. chance** une petite chance

outsider [aʊt'saɪdə(r)] *n (stranger)* étranger, -ère *mf; (horse in race)* outsider *m*

outskirts ['aʊtskɜːts] *npl* banlieue *f*

outsmart [aʊt'smɑːt] *vt* être plus malin, -igne que

outspoken [aʊt'spəʊkən] *adj (frank)* franc *(f* franche)

outstanding [aʊt'stændɪŋ] *adj* exceptionnel, -elle; *(problem, business)* en suspens; *(debt)* impayé

outstay [aʊt'steɪ] *vt* **to o. one's welcome** abuser de l'hospitalité de son hôte

outstretched [aʊt'stretʃt] *adj (arm)* tendu; *(wings)* déployé

outstrip [aʊt'strɪp] *(pt & pp* **-pp-)** *vt* dépasser

out-tray ['aʊttreɪ] *n (in office)* corbeille *f* (du courrier) 'départ'

outward ['aʊtwəd] *adj (sign, appearance)* extérieur; *(movement, look)* vers l'extérieur; **o. journey** *or* **trip** aller *m* • **outward(s)** *adv* vers l'extérieur

outweigh [aʊt'weɪ] *vt (be more important than)* l'emporter sur

outwit [aʊt'wɪt] *(pt & pp* **-tt-)** *vt* être plus malin, -igne que

oval ['əʊvəl] *adj & n* ovale *(m)*

ovary ['əʊvərɪ] *(pl* **-ies)** *n Anat* ovaire *m*

ovation [əʊ'veɪʃən] *n* ovation *f;* **to give sb a standing o.** se lever pour applaudir qn

oven ['ʌvən] *n* four *m; Fig (hot place)* fournaise *f;* **o. glove** gant *m* isolant

over ['əʊvə(r)] **1** *prep (on)* sur; *(above)* au-dessus de; *(on the other side of)* par-dessus; **the bridge o. the river** le pont qui traverse le fleuve; **to jump/look o. sth** sauter/regarder par-dessus qch; **to fall o. the balcony** tomber du balcon; **o. it** *(on)* dessus; *(above)* au-dessus; **to jump o. it** sauter par-dessus; **to fight o. sth** se battre pour qch; **o. the phone** au télé-

phone; *Br* **o. the holidays** pendant les vacances; **o. ten days** *(more than)* plus de dix jours; **men o. sixty** les hommes de plus de soixante ans; **o. and above** en plus de; **he's o. his flu** il est remis de sa grippe
2 *adv (above)* par-dessus; **jump o.!** sautez par-dessus!; **o. here** ici; **o. there** là-bas; **he's o. in Italy** il est en Italie; **she's o. from Paris** elle est venue de Paris; **to ask sb o.** inviter qn; **to be (all) o.** être terminé; **to start all o. (again)** recommencer à zéro; **a kilo or o.** *(more)* un kilo ou plus; **I have ten o.** *(left)* il m'en reste dix; **there's some bread o.** il reste du pain; **o. and o. (again)** *(often)* à plusieurs reprises; **to do sth all o. again** refaire qch; **three times o.** trois fois; **famous the world o.** célèbre dans le monde entier; **children of five and o.** les enfants de cinq ans et plus • **overa'bundant** *adj* surabondant • **over-de'veloped** *adj* trop développé • **over-fa'miliar** *adj* trop familier, -ière • **overin'dulge** *vt (desires, whims)* céder trop facilement à; *(person)* trop gâter • **oversub'scribed** *adj (course)* ayant trop d'inscrits

overall ['əʊvərɔːl] **1** *adj (measurement, length)* total; *(result, effort)* global
2 [əʊvər'ɔːl] *adv* dans l'ensemble
3 *n (protective coat)* blouse *f*; *Am (boiler suit)* bleu *m* de travail • **overalls** *npl Br (boiler suit)* bleu *m* de travail; *Am (dungarees)* salopette *f*

overawe [əʊvər'ɔː] *vt* intimider

overbalance [əʊvə'bæləns] *vi (of person)* perdre l'équilibre; *(of pile, load)* se renverser

overbearing ['əʊvə'beərɪŋ] *adj* autoritaire

overboard ['əʊvəbɔːd] *adv* par-dessus bord; **man o.!** un homme à la mer!

overbook [əʊvə'bʊk] *vt* faire du surbooking sur

overburden [əʊvə'bɜːdən] *vt* surcharger

overcast [əʊvə'kɑːst] *adj* nuageux, -euse

overcharge [əʊvə'tʃɑːdʒ] *vt* **to o. sb for sth** faire payer qch trop cher à qn

overcoat ['əʊvəkəʊt] *n* pardessus *m*

overcome [əʊvə'kʌm] *(pt* -**came,** *pp* -**come)** *vt (problem, disgust)* surmonter; *(shyness, fear, enemy)* vaincre; **to be o. by grief** être accablé de chagrin; **he was o. by emotion** l'émotion eut raison de lui

overcook [əʊvə'kʊk] *vt* faire cuire trop

overcrowded [əʊvə'kraʊdɪd] *adj (house, country)* surpeuplé; *(bus, train)* bondé • **overcrowding** *n* surpeuplement *m*

overdo [əʊvə'duː] *(pt* -**did,** *pp* -**done)** *vt* exagérer; *(overcook)* faire cuire trop; **to o. it** se surmener

overdose ['əʊvədəʊs] **1** *n* overdose *f*
2 *vi* faire une overdose (**on** de); *Fam* **to o. on chocolate** exagérer avec le chocolat

overdraft ['əʊvədrɑːft] *n Fin* découvert *m* • **over'drawn** *adj (account)* à découvert

overdress [əʊvə'dres] *vi* s'habiller avec trop de recherche

overdue [əʊvə'djuː] *adj (train, bus)* en retard; *(bill)* impayé; *(book)* qui n'a pas été rendu

overeat [əʊvər'iːt] *(pt* -**ate,** *pp* -**eaten)** *vi* manger trop

overestimate [əʊvər'estɪmeɪt] *vt* surestimer

overexcited [əʊvərɪk'saɪtɪd] *adj* surexcité

overfeed [əʊvə'fiːd] *(pt & pp* -**fed)** *vt* suralimenter

overflow 1 ['əʊvəfləʊ] *n (outlet)* trop-plein *m*; *Fig (of people, objects)* excédent *m*
2 [əʊvə'fləʊ] *vi (of river, bath)* déborder; **to be overflowing with sth** *(of town, shop, house)* regorger de qch

overgrown [əʊvə'grəʊn] *adj* envahi par la végétation; **o. with weeds** envahi par les mauvaises herbes; *Fig & Pej* **you're an o. schoolgirl** tu as la mentalité d'une écolière

overhang [əʊvə'hæŋ] *(pt & pp* -**hung)** **1** *vt* surplomber
2 *vi* faire saillie

overhaul 1 ['əʊvəhɔːl] *n* révision *f*
2 [əʊvə'hɔːl] *vt (vehicle, schedule, text)* réviser

overhead ['əʊvəhed] **1** [əʊvə'hed] *adv* au-dessus
2 *adj (cable)* aérien, -ienne
3 *n Am* = **overheads** • **overheads** *npl Br (expenses)* frais *mpl* généraux

overhear [əʊvə'hɪə(r)] *(pt & pp* -**heard)** *vt (conversation)* surprendre; *(person)* entendre

overheat [əʊvə'hiːt] **1** *vt* surchauffer
2 *vi (of engine)* chauffer

overjoyed [əʊvə'dʒɔɪd] *adj* fou *(f* folle) de joie

overland ['əʊvəlænd] *adj & adv* par voie de terre

overlap [əʊvə'læp] **1** ['əʊvəlæp] *n* chevauchement *m*
2 *(pt & pp* -**pp-)** *vt* chevaucher
3 *vi* se chevaucher

overleaf [əʊvə'liːf] *adv* au verso

overload [əʊvə'ləʊd] *vt* surcharger

overlook [əʊvə'lʊk] *vt* (**a**) *(not notice)* ne pas remarquer; *(forget)* oublier; *(disregard)* fermer les yeux sur (**b**) *(of window, house)* donner sur; *(of tower, fort)* dominer

overly ['əʊvəlɪ] *adv* excessivement

overmanning [əʊvə'mænɪŋ] *n* sureffectifs *mpl*

overmuch [əʊvə'mʌtʃ] *adv* trop

overnight 1 [əʊvə'naɪt] *adv (during the night)* pendant la nuit; *Fig (suddenly)* du jour au lendemain; **to stay o.** passer la nuit
2 ['əʊvənaɪt] *adj (train, flight)* de nuit; *(stay)* d'une nuit; *(clothes)* pour une nuit; **o. bag** (petit) sac *m* de voyage

overpass ['əʊvəpɑːs] *n Am (bridge)* Toboggan® *m*

overpopulated [əʊvə'pɒpjʊleɪtɪd] *adj* surpeuplé

overpower [əʊvə'paʊə(r)] *vt* maîtriser • **overpowering** *adj (heat, smell)* suffocant; *(charm, desire)* irrésistible

overpriced [əʊvə'praɪst] *adj* trop cher (*f* trop chère)

overrated [əʊvə'reɪtɪd] *adj* surfait

overreach [əʊvə'riːtʃ] *vt* **to o. oneself** trop présumer de ses forces

overreact [əʊvərɪ'ækt] *vi* réagir excessivement

override [əʊvə'raɪd] *(pt* **-rode,** *pp* **-ridden)** *vt (be more important than)* l'emporter sur; *(invalidate)* annuler; *(take no notice of)* passer outre à • **over'riding** *adj (importance)* capital; *(factor)* prédominant

overrule [əʊvə'ruːl] *vt (decision)* annuler; *(argument, objection)* rejeter

overrun [əʊvə'rʌn] *(pt* **-ran,** *pp* **-run,** *pres p* **-running)** *vt (invade)* envahir; *(go beyond)* dépasser

overseas 1 ['əʊvəsiːz] *adj* d'outre-mer; *(trade, debt)* extérieur
2 [əʊvə'siːz] *adv* à l'étranger

oversee [əʊvə'siː] *(pt* **-saw,** *pp* **-seen)** *vt (work)* superviser • **overseer** ['əʊvəsɪə(r)] *n (foreman)* contremaître *m*

overshadow [əʊvə'ʃædəʊ] *vt (make less important)* éclipser; *(make gloomy)* assombrir

overshoot [əʊvə'ʃuːt] *(pt & pp* **-shot)** *vt* dépasser

oversight ['əʊvəsaɪt] *n* oubli *m*, omission *f*

oversimplify [əʊvə'sɪmplɪfaɪ] *(pt & pp* **-ied)** *vti* trop simplifier

oversize(d) ['əʊvəsaɪz(d)] *adj* trop grand

oversleep [əʊvə'sliːp] *(pt & pp* **-slept)** *vi* ne pas se réveiller à temps

overspend [əʊvə'spend] *(pt & pp* **-spent)** *vi* dépenser trop

overstaffing [əʊvə'stɑːfɪŋ] *n* sureffectifs *mpl*

overstate [əʊvə'steɪt] *vt* exagérer

overstay [əʊvə'steɪ] *vt* **to o. one's welcome** abuser de l'hospitalité de son hôte

overstep [əʊvə'step] *(pt & pp* **-pp-)** *vt* outrepasser; *Fig* **to o. the mark** dépasser les bornes

overt ['əʊvɜːt] *adj* manifeste

overtake [əʊvə'teɪk] *(pt* **-took,** *pp* **-taken)** *vt* dépasser; **overtaken by nightfall** surpris par la nuit
2 *vi (in vehicle)* doubler, dépasser

overtax [əʊvə'tæks] *vt* (**a**) **to o. one's brain** se fatiguer la cervelle; **to o. one's strength** abuser de ses forces (**b**) *(person)* surimposer; *(goods)* surtaxer

overthrow 1 ['əʊvəθrəʊ] *n* renversement *m*
2 [əʊvə'θrəʊ] *(pt* **-threw,** *pp* **-thrown)** *vt* renverser

overtime ['əʊvətaɪm] **1** *n* heures *fpl* supplémentaires
2 *adv* **to work o.** faire des heures supplémentaires

overtones ['əʊvətəʊnz] *npl* nuance *f* (**of** de)

overture ['əʊvətjʊə(r)] *n Mus* ouverture *f*; *Fig* **to make overtures to sb** faire des avances à qn

overturn 1 [əʊvə'tɜːn] **1** *vt (chair, table, car)* renverser; *(boat)* faire chavirer; *Fig (decision)* annuler
2 *vi (of car)* capoter; *(of boat)* chavirer

overweight [əʊvə'weɪt] *adj* trop gros (*f* trop grosse)

overwhelm [əʊvə'welm] *vt (of feelings, heat)* accabler; *(enemy, opponent)* écraser; *(amaze)* bouleverser • **overwhelmed** *adj (overjoyed)* ravi (**by** or **with** de); **o. with** *(work, offers)* submergé de; **o. with grief** accablé par le chagrin; **o. by** *(kindness, gift)* vivement touché par • **overwhelming** *adj (heat, grief)* accablant; *(majority, defeat)* écrasant; *(desire)* irrésistible; *(impression)* dominant; **the o. majority of people** l'écrasante majorité des gens • **overwhelmingly** *adv (vote, reject)* en masse; *(utterly)* carrément

overwork [əʊvə'wɜːk] **1** *n* surmenage *m*
2 *vt (person)* surcharger de travail
3 *vi* se surmener

overwrite [əʊvə'raɪt] *(pt* **-wrote,** *pp* **-written)** *vt Comptr (file)* écraser

overwrought [əʊvə'rɔːt] *adj (tense)* à bout

owe [əʊ] *vt* devoir; **to o. sb sth, to o. sth to sb** devoir qch à qn; **I'll o. it to you** je te le devrai; **to o. it to oneself to do sth** se devoir de faire qch • **owing 1** *adj* **the money o. to me** l'argent que l'on me doit **2** *prep* **o. to** à cause de

owl [aʊl] *n* hibou *m* (*pl* -oux)

own [əʊn] **1** *adj* propre; **my o. house** ma propre maison

2 *pron* **my o.** le mien, la mienne; **a house of his o.** sa propre maison, sa maison à lui; **it's my (very) o.** c'est à moi (tout seul); **to do sth on one's o.** faire qch tout seul; **to be (all) on one's o.** être tout seul; **to get one's o. back (on sb)** se venger (de qn); **to come into one's o.** montrer ce dont on est capable

3 *vt* (*possess*) posséder; **who owns this ball?** à qui appartient cette balle?

4 *vi* **to o. up** (*confess*) avouer; **to o. up to sth** avouer qch

own-brand ['əʊnbrænd] *adj* *Com* vendu sous la marque du distributeur

owner ['əʊnə(r)] *n* propriétaire *mf* • **ownership** *n* possession *f*; **to encourage home o.** encourager l'accession à la propriété; *Econ* **to be in public o.** appartenir au secteur public

ox [ɒks] (*pl* **oxen** ['ɒksən]) *n* bœuf *m*

oxide ['ɒksaɪd] *n* *Chem* oxyde *m* • **oxidize** ['ɒksɪdaɪz] *Chem* **1** *vt* oxyder **2** *vi* s'oxyder

oxygen ['ɒksɪdʒən] *n* oxygène *m*; **o. mask/tent** masque *m*/tente *f* à oxygène

oyster ['ɔɪstə(r)] *n* huître *f*

oz (*abbr* **ounce**) once *f*

ozone ['əʊzəʊn] *n* *Chem* ozone *m*; **o. friendly** (*product*) qui préserve la couche d'ozone; **o. layer** couche *f* d'ozone

P

P, p¹ [piː] *n (letter)* P, p *m inv*

p² [piː] *(abbr* **penny, pence)** *Br* penny *m/* pence *mpl*

PA [piːˈeɪ] *(abbr* **personal assistant)** *n* secrétaire *mf* de direction

pa [pɑː] *n Fam (father)* papa *m*

pace [peɪs] **1** *n (speed)* allure *f; (step, measure)* pas *m;* **to set the p.** donner l'allure; **to keep p. with sb** *(follow)* suivre qn; *(in quality of work)* se maintenir à la hauteur de qn

2 *vi* **to p. up and down** faire les cent pas **3** *vt (room)* arpenter

pacemaker [ˈpeɪsmeɪkə(r)] *n (for heart)* stimulateur *m* cardiaque

Pacific [pəˈsɪfɪk] *adj (coast)* pacifique; **the P. (Ocean)** le Pacifique, l'océan *m* Pacifique

pacifier [ˈpæsɪfaɪə(r)] *n Am (of baby)* tétine *f*

pacifist [ˈpæsɪfɪst] *n & adj* pacifiste *(mf)*

pacify [ˈpæsɪfaɪ] *(pt & pp* -ied) *vt (country)* pacifier; *(crowd, person)* calmer

pack [pæk] **1** *n* (a) *(of cigarettes, washing powder)* paquet *m; (of beer) & Rugby* pack *m; (of cards)* jeu *m; (of hounds, wolves)* meute *f; (of runners, cyclists)* peloton *m; (of thieves)* bande *f;* **a p. of lies** un tissu de mensonges; **p. animal** animal *m* de bât; **p. ice** banquise *f*

(b) *(rucksack)* sac *m* à dos; *(of soldier)* paquetage *m*

2 *vt (fill)* remplir (**with** de); *(excessively)* bourrer; *(object into box, suitcase)* mettre; *(make into package)* empaqueter; *(crush, compress)* tasser; **to p. one's bags** faire ses valises

3 *vi (fill one's bags)* faire sa valise/ses valises

▸ **pack away** *vt sep (tidy away)* ranger ▸ **pack down** *vt sep (crush, compress)* tasser ▸ **pack in** *vt sep Br Fam (stop)* arrêter; *(give up)* laisser tomber; **p. it in!** laisse tomber! ▸ **pack into 1** *vt sep (cram)* entasser dans; *(put)* mettre dans **2** *vt insep (crowd into)* s'entasser dans ▸ **pack off** *vt sep Fam (person)* expédier ▸ **pack up 1** *vt sep (put into box)* emballer; *(put into suitcase)* mettre dans sa valise; *Fam*

(give up) laisser tomber **2** *vi* faire sa valise/ses valises; *Fam (stop)* s'arrêter; *(of machine, vehicle)* tomber en panne

package [ˈpækɪdʒ] **1** *n* paquet *m; (contract)* contrat *m* global; *Br* **p. deal** *or* **holiday** forfait *m (comprenant au moins transport et logement)*

2 *vt* emballer • **packaging** *n (material, action)* emballage *m*

packed [pækt] *adj (bus, room)* bondé; *Br* **p. lunch** = déjeuner que l'on emporte à l'école ou au bureau; *Br Fam* **p. out** *(crowded)* bourré

packet [ˈpækɪt] *n* paquet *m; Fam* **to cost a p.** coûter les yeux de la tête; *Fam* **to make a p.** se faire un fric fou

packing [ˈpækɪŋ] *n (material, action)* emballage *m;* **to do one's p.** faire sa valise/ses valises

pact [pækt] *n* pacte *m*

pad [pæd] **1** *n (of cotton wool)* tampon *m; (for writing)* bloc *m; Fam (home)* piaule *f;* **ink(ing) p.** tampon encreur

2 *(pt & pp* -dd-) *vt (furniture)* capitonner (**with** avec); *(clothes)* matelasser; **to p. out** *(speech, essay)* étoffer • **padded** *adj (armchair)* capitonné; *(jacket)* matelassé • **padding** *n (material)* rembourrage *m; (in speech, essay)* remplissage *m*

paddle [ˈpædəl] **1** *n (for canoe)* pagaie *f;* **p. boat** bateau *m* à aubes; **to have a p.** patauger

2 *vt* **to p. a canoe** pagayer

3 *vi (in canoe)* pagayer; *(walk in water)* patauger • **paddling pool** *n Br (inflatable)* piscine *f* gonflable; *(in park)* pataugeoire *f*

paddock [ˈpædək] *n* enclos *m; (at race-course)* paddock *m*

paddy [ˈpædɪ] *(pl* -ies) *n* **p. (field)** rizière *f*

padlock [ˈpædlɒk] **1** *n* cadenas *m*

2 *vt* cadenasser

paediatrician [piːdɪəˈtrɪʃən] *(Am* **pediatrician)** *n* pédiatre *mf* • **paediatrics** [-dɪˈætrɪks] *(Am* **pediatrics)** *n* pédiatrie *f*

pagan [ˈpeɪɡən] *adj & n* païen, -enne *(mf)* • **paganism** *n* paganisme *m*

page¹ [peɪdʒ] *n (of book)* page *f;* **on p. 6** à la page 6

page² [peɪdʒ] **1** n Hist (at court) page m; **p. (boy)** (in hotel) groom m; (at wedding) garçon m d'honneur

2 vt **to p. sb** faire appeler qn; (by electronic device) biper qn •**pager** n récepteur m d'appel

pageant ['pædʒənt] n grand spectacle m •**pageantry** n pompe f

pagoda [pə'gəʊdə] n pagode f

paid [peɪd] **1** pt & pp of **pay**

2 adj (person, work) rémunéré; Br **to put p. to sb's hopes** anéantir les espoirs de qn; Br **to put p. to sb** (ruin) couler qn

pail [peɪl] n seau m

pain [peɪn] **1** n (physical) douleur f; (emotional) peine f; **to have a p. in one's arm** avoir une douleur au bras; **to be in p.** souffrir; **to go to** or **take (great) pains to do sth** se donner du mal pour faire qch; **to go to** or **take (great) pains not to do sth** prendre bien soin de ne pas faire qch; Fam **to be a p. (in the neck)** être casse-pieds

2 vt peiner •**painful** adj (physically) douloureux, -euse; (emotionally) pénible; Fam (bad) nul (f nulle) •**painfully** adv (walk) avec difficulté; Fig **p. shy** d'une timidité maladive; Fig **p. boring** ennuyeux, -euse à mourir •**painless** adj (not painful) indolore; Fam (easy) facile •**painlessly** adv sans douleur; (easily) sans effort

painkiller ['peɪnkɪlə(r)] n calmant m; **on painkillers** sous calmants

painstaking ['peɪnzteɪkɪŋ] adj minutieux, -ieuse •**painstakingly** adv avec un soin minutieux

paint [peɪnt] **1** n peinture f; **'wet p.'** 'peinture fraîche'; **p. stripper** décapant m

2 vt peindre; **to p. sth blue** peindre qch en bleu

3 vi peindre •**painter** n peintre m; Br **p. and decorator,** Am **(house) p.** peintretapissier m •**painting** n (activity) la peinture; (picture) tableau m, peinture f

paintbrush ['peɪntbrʌʃ] n pinceau m

paintwork ['peɪntwɜːk] n (of building, vehicle) peinture f

pair [peə(r)] **1** n paire f; **a p. of shorts** un short

2 vt **to p. sb with sb** mettre qn avec qn

3 vi **to p. off** (of people) se mettre deux par deux

pajama(s) [pə'dʒɑːmə(z)] adj & npl Am = **pyjama(s)**

Pakistan [pɑːkɪ'stɑːn] n le Pakistan •**Pakistani 1** adj pakistanais **2** n Pakistanais, -aise mf

pal [pæl] n Fam copain m, copine f

palace ['pælɪs] n palais m •**palatial** [pə'leɪʃəl] adj grandiose

> ⓘ Note that the French word **palace** is a false friend and is never a translation for the English word **palace**. It means **luxury hotel**.

palatable ['pælətəbəl] adj (food) agréable au palais; Fig (idea, fact) acceptable

palate ['pælɪt] n (in mouth) palais m

palaver [pə'lɑːvə(r)] n Br Fam (fuss) histoire f

pale [peɪl] **1** (-er, -est) adj pâle; Br **p. ale** = bière blonde

2 vi pâlir •**paleness** n pâleur f

Palestine ['pæləstaɪn] n la Palestine •**Palestinian** [-'stɪnɪən] **1** adj palestinien, -ienne **2** n Palestinien, -ienne mf

palette ['pælɪt] n (of artist) palette f

palings ['peɪlɪŋz] n (fence) palissade f

pall¹ [pɔːl] n (of smoke) voile m

pall² [pɔːl] vi (become uninteresting) perdre son attrait

pallbearer ['pɔːlbeərə(r)] n = personne qui aide à porter un cercueil

pallid ['pælɪd] adj pâle •**pallor** n pâleur f

pally ['pælɪ] (-ier, -iest) adj Fam **to be p. with sb** être copain (f copine) avec qn

palm¹ [pɑːm] **1** n (of hand) paume f

2 vt Fam **to p. sth off on sb** refiler qch à qn

palm² [pɑːm] n (symbol) palme f; **p. (tree)** palmier m; **p. (leaf)** palme; **P. Sunday** le Dimanche des Rameaux

palmist ['pɑːmɪst] n chiromancien, -ienne mf •**palmistry** n chiromancie f

palpable ['pælpəbəl] adj (obvious) manifeste

palpitate ['pælpɪteɪt] vi palpiter •**palpitation** n palpitation f; **to have** or **get palpitations** avoir des palpitations

paltry ['pɔːltrɪ] (-ier, -iest) adj (sum) dérisoire; (excuse) piètre

pamper ['pæmpə(r)] vt dorloter; **to p. oneself** se dorloter

pamphlet ['pæmflɪt] n brochure f; (political) pamphlet m

pan [pæn] **1** n (saucepan) casserole f; (for frying) poêle f; Br (of lavatory) cuvette f

2 (pt & pp **-nn-**) vt Fam (criticize) descendre en flammes

3 vi Fam **to p. out** (turn out) marcher

panacea [pænə'sɪə] n panacée f

panache [pə'næʃ] n panache m

Panama ['pænəmɑː] n le Panama; **the P. Canal** le canal de Panama

pancake ['pænkeɪk] n crêpe f; **P. Day** mardi m gras
pancreas ['pæŋkrɪəs] n Anat pancréas m
panda ['pændə] n panda m
pandemonium [pændɪ'məʊnɪəm] n (confusion) chaos m; (uproar) vacarme m
pander ['pændə(r)] vi **to p. to sb/sth** flatter qn/qch
pane [peɪn] n vitre f
panel ['pænəl] n (a) (of door) panneau m; (instrument) p. (in aircraft, vehicle) tableau m de bord (b) (of judges) jury m; (of experts) comité m; (of TV or radio guests) invités mpl; **p. game** (on TV) jeu m télévisé; (on radio) jeu radiodiffusé
panelled ['pænəld] (Am **paneled**) adj (room) lambrissé • **panelling** (Am **paneling**) n lambris m
panellist ['pænəlɪst] (Am **panelist**) n (on radio, TV) invité, -ée mf
pangs [pæŋz] npl **p. of conscience** remords mpl; **p. of hunger** tiraillements mpl d'estomac; **p. of death/jealousy** affres fpl de la mort/de la jalousie
panic ['pænɪk] **1** n panique f; **to get into a p.** paniquer
2 (pt & pp -ck-) vi paniquer • **panicky** adj Fam **to get p.** paniquer • **panic-stricken** adj pris de panique
panorama [pænə'rɑːmə] n panorama m • **panoramic** [-'ræmɪk] adj panoramique
pansy ['pænzɪ] (pl -ies) n (a) (flower) pensée f (b) (effeminate man) tante f
pant [pænt] vi haleter
panther ['pænθə(r)] n panthère f
panties ['pæntɪz] npl petite culotte f
pantomime ['pæntəmaɪm] n Br (show) = spectacle de Noël

> Note that the French word **pantomime** is a false friend and is never a translation for the English word **pantomime**. It means **mime**.

pantry ['pæntrɪ] (pl -ies) n (larder) garde-manger m inv; (storeroom in hotel, ship) office m
pants [pænts] npl (underwear) slip m; Am (trousers) pantalon m
pantyhose ['pæntɪhəʊz] n Am (tights) collant m
papacy ['peɪpəsɪ] n papauté f • **papal** adj papal
paper ['peɪpə(r)] **1** n papier m; (newspaper) journal m; (wallpaper) papier peint; (exam) épreuve f écrite; (student's exercise) copie f; (scholarly study, report) article m; **a piece of p.** un bout de papier; **to put sth down on p.** mettre qch par écrit;

brown p. papier d'emballage; **papers** (documents) papiers
2 adj (bag) en papier; (cup, plate) en carton; **p. mill** papeterie f; **p. money** papier-monnaie m; **p. round** tournée f de distribution des journaux; Br **p. shop** marchand m de journaux; **p. towel** essuie-tout m inv; Comptr **p. tray** chariot m d'alimentation en papier
3 vt (room, wall) tapisser • **paperback** n livre m de poche • **paperboy** n (delivering papers) livreur m de journaux • **paperclip** n trombone m • **paperknife** (pl **-knives**) n coupe-papier m • **paperweight** n presse-papiers m inv • **paperwork** n (in office) écritures fpl; Pej (red tape) paperasserie f
paprika ['pæprɪkə] n paprika m
par [pɑː(r)] n Golf par m; **on a p.** au même niveau (**with** que); Fam **to feel below p.** ne pas être dans son assiette
parable ['pærəbəl] n (story) parabole f
paracetamol [pærə'siːtəmɒl] n paracétamol m
parachute ['pærəʃuːt] **1** n parachute m; **p. jump** saut m en parachute
2 vt parachuter
3 vi sauter en parachute • **parachutist** n parachutiste mf
parade [pə'reɪd] **1** n (a) (procession) défilé m; **to make a p. of sth** faire étalage de qch; Mil **p. ground** terrain m de manœuvres (b) Br (street) avenue f; **a p. of shops** une rangée de magasins
2 vt (troops) faire défiler; Fig (wealth, knowledge) faire étalage de
3 vi (of troops) défiler; **to p. about** (of person) se pavaner
paradise ['pærədaɪs] n paradis m
paradox ['pærədɒks] n paradoxe m • **para'doxically** adv paradoxalement
paraffin ['pærəfɪn] n Br pétrole m lampant; Am (wax) paraffine f; Br **p. lamp** lampe f à pétrole
paragliding ['pærəglaɪdɪŋ] n parapente m; **to go p.** faire du parapente
paragon ['pærəgən] n **p. of virtue** modèle m de vertu
paragraph ['pærəgrɑːf] n paragraphe m; **'new p.'** 'à la ligne'
Paraguay ['pærəgwaɪ] n le Paraguay
parakeet ['pærəkiːt] n perruche f
parallel ['pærəlel] **1** adj Math parallèle (**with** or **to** à); Fig (comparable) semblable (**with** or **to** à); **to run p. to** or **with sth** être parallèle à qch
2 n Math (line) parallèle f; Fig (comparison) & Geog parallèle m
3 vt être semblable à

paralysis [pə'ræləsɪs] (*pl* **-yses** [-əsiːz]) *n* paralysie *f* • **paralyse** ['pærəlaɪz] (*Am* **paralyze**) *vt* paralyser • **paralytic** [pærə'lɪtɪk] *adj & n* paralytique (*mf*)

paramedic [pærə'medɪk] *n* auxiliaire *mf* médical(e)

parameter [pə'ræmɪtə(r)] *n* paramètre *m*

paramount ['pærəmaʊnt] *adj* **of p. importance** de la plus haute importance

paranoia [pærə'nɔɪə] *n* paranoïa *f* • '**paranoid** *adj & n* paranoïaque (*mf*)

parapet ['pærəpɪt] *n* parapet *m*

paraphernalia [pærəfə'neɪlɪə] *n* attirail *m*

paraphrase ['pærəfreɪz] **1** *n* paraphrase *f* **2** *vt* paraphraser

paraplegic [pærə'pliːdʒɪk] *n* paraplégique *mf*

parascending ['pærəsendɪŋ] *n* parachute *m* ascensionnel

parasite ['pærəsaɪt] *n* (*person, organism*) parasite *m*

parasol ['pærəsɒl] *n* (*over table, on beach*) parasol *m*; (*lady's*) ombrelle *f*

paratrooper ['pærətruːpə(r)] *n* parachutiste *m*

parboil [paː'bɔɪl] *vt* faire cuire à demi

parcel ['paːsəl] **1** *n* colis *m*, paquet *m*; **to be part and p. of sth** faire partie intégrante de qch; **p. bomb** colis piégé **2** (*Br* **-ll-**, *Am* **-l-**) *vt* **to p. sth out** répartir; **to p. sth up** empaqueter

parch [paːtʃ] *vt* dessécher; **to be parched** (*of person*) être assoiffé; **to make sb parched** donner très soif à qn

parchment ['paːtʃmənt] *n* parchemin *m*

pardon ['paːdən] **1** *n* (*forgiveness*) pardon *m*; *Law* grâce *f*; **I beg your p.** (*apologizing*) je vous prie de m'excuser; **I beg your p.?** (*not hearing*) pardon? **2** *vt Law* grâcier; **to p. sb (for sth)** pardonner (qch) à qn; **p. (me)!** (*sorry*) pardon!

pare [peə(r)] *vt* (*trim*) rogner; (*peel*) éplucher; *Fig* **to p. sth down** réduire qch

parent ['peərənt] *n* père *m*/mère *f*; **parents** parents *mpl*; **p. company,** *Br* **p. firm** maison *f* mère • **parentage** *n* origine *f* • **parental** [pə'rentəl] *adj* parental • **parenthood** *n* paternité *f*/maternité *f*

parenthesis [pə'renθəsɪs] (*pl* **-eses** [-əsiːz]) *n* parenthèse *f*

Paris ['pærɪs] *n* Paris *m ou f* • **Parisian** [*Br* pə'rɪzɪən, *Am* pə'riːʒən] **1** *adj* parisien, -ienne **2** *n* Parisien, -ienne *mf*

parish ['pærɪʃ] **1** *n* (*religious*) paroisse *f*; (*civil*) ≃ commune *f* **2** *adj* (*church, register, hall*) paroissial; **p. council** conseil *m* municipal • **parishioner** [pə'rɪʃənə(r)] *n* paroissien, -ienne *mf*

parity ['pærɪtɪ] *n* égalité *f* (**with** avec; **between** entre)

park¹ [paːk] *n* (*garden*) parc *m*; **p. keeper** gardien, -ienne *mf* de parc

park² [paːk] **1** *vt* (*vehicle*) garer; *Fam* (*put*) mettre **2** *vi* (*of vehicle*) se garer; (*remain parked*) stationner • **parking** *n* stationnement *m*; **'no p.'** 'défense de stationner'; **p. bay** place *f* de parking; *Br* **p. lights** (*on car*) feux *mpl* de position; *Am* **p. lot** parking *m*; **p. meter** parcmètre *m*; **p. place** *or* **space** place de parking; **p. ticket** contravention *f*

parka ['paːkə] *n* parka *f ou m*

parkland ['paːklænd] *n* espace *m* vert

parkway ['paːkweɪ] *n Am* avenue *f*

parliament ['paːləmənt] *n* parlement *m*; • **parliamen'tarian** *n* parlementaire *mf* • **parliamentary** [-'mentərɪ] *adj* parlementaire

parlour ['paːlə(r)] (*Am* **parlor**) *n* (*in mansion*) salon *m*; **p. game** jeu *m* de société

parochial [pə'rəʊkɪəl] *adj Rel* paroissial; *Pej* (*mentality, quarrel*) de clocher; *Pej* (*person*) provincial; *Am* **p. school** école *f* catholique

parody ['pærədɪ] **1** (*pl* **-ies**) *n* parodie *f* **2** (*pt & pp* **-ied**) *vt* parodier

parole [pə'rəʊl] *n Law* **to be (out) on p.** être en liberté conditionnelle

parquet ['paːkeɪ] *n* **p. (floor)** parquet *m*

parrot ['pærət] *n* perroquet *m*; *Pej* **p. fashion** comme un perroquet

parry ['pærɪ] **1** (*pl* **-ies**) *n* (*in fencing, boxing*) parade *f* **2** (*pt & pp* **-ied**) *vt* (*blow*) parer; (*question*) éluder

parsimonious [paːsɪ'məʊnɪəs] *adj* parcimonieux, -ieuse • **parsimoniously** *adv* avec parcimonie

parsley ['paːslɪ] *n* persil *m*

parsnip ['paːsnɪp] *n* panais *m*

parson ['paːsən] *n* pasteur *m*

part¹ [paːt] **1** *n* partie *f*; (*quantity in mixture*) mesure *f*; (*of machine*) pièce *f*; (*of serial*) épisode *m*; (*role in play, film*) rôle *m*; *Am* (*in hair*) raie *f*; **to take p.** participer (**in** à); **to take sb's p.** (*side*) prendre parti pour qn; **to be a p. of sth** faire partie de qch; **in p.** en partie; **for the most p.** dans l'ensemble; **on the p. of...** de la part de...; **for my p.** pour ma part; **in these parts** dans ces parages; **p. exchange** reprise *f*; **to take sth in p. exchange** reprendre qch;

p. owner copropriétaire *mf*; **p. payment** paiement *m* partiel
2 *adv (partly)* en partie; **p. silk, p. cotton** soie et coton
part² [pɑːt] **1** *vt (separate)* séparer; *(crowd)* écarter; **to p. one's hair** se faire une raie; **to p. company with sb** *(leave sb)* quitter qn
2 *vi (of friends)* se quitter; *(of married couple)* se séparer; **to p. with sth** se défaire de qch
partake [pɑːˈteɪk] *(pt* -**took**, *pp* -**taken**) *vi Formal* **to p. in sth** prendre part à qch; **to p. of a meal** prendre un repas
partial [ˈpɑːʃəl] *adj (not total)* partiel, -ielle; *(biased)* partial *(*towards* envers)*; **to be p. to sth** avoir un faible pour qch
• **partiality** [-ʃɪˈælɪtɪ] *(pl* -**ies**) *n (bias)* partialité *f*; *(liking)* faible *m*
participate [pɑːˈtɪsɪpeɪt] *vi* participer *(*in* à)* • **participant** *n* participant, -ante *mf*
• **partici'pation** *n* participation *f*
participle [ˈpɑːtɪsɪpəl] *n Grammar* participe *m*
particle [ˈpɑːtɪkəl] *n (of atom, dust, name)* particule *f*; *(of truth)* grain *m*
particular [pəˈtɪkjʊlə(r)] **1** *adj (specific, special)* particulier, -ière; *(exacting)* méticuleux, -euse; **this p. book** ce livre en particulier; **to be p. about sth** faire très attention à qch
2 *n* **in p.** en particulier • **particularly** *adv* particulièrement • **particulars** *npl (details)* détails *mpl*; **to go into p.** entrer dans les détails; **to take down sb's p.** noter les coordonnées de qn
parting [ˈpɑːtɪŋ] **1** *n (separation)* séparation *f*; *Br (in hair)* raie *f*
2 *adj (gift, words)* d'adieu
partisan [*Br* pɑːtɪˈzæn, *Am* ˈpɑːtɪzən] *n* partisan *m*
partition [pɑːˈtɪʃən] **1** *n (of room)* cloison *f*; *Pol (of country)* partition *f*
2 *vt (country)* partager; **to p. sth off** cloisonner qch
partly [ˈpɑːtlɪ] *adv* en partie; **p. English, p. French** moitié anglais, moitié français
partner [ˈpɑːtnə(r)] *n (in game)* partenaire *mf*; *(in business)* associé, -iée *mf*; *(of racing driver)* coéquipier, -ière *mf*; *(in relationship)* compagnon *m*, compagne *f*; **(dancing) p.** cavalier, -ière *mf* • **partnership** *n* association *f*; **to take sb into p.** prendre qn comme associé(e); **in p. with** en association avec
partridge [ˈpɑːtrɪdʒ] *n* perdrix *f*
part-time [ˈpɑːtˈtaɪm] *adj & adv* à temps partiel

party [ˈpɑːtɪ] *(pl* -**ies**) *n* **(a)** *(gathering)* fête *f*; **to have** *or* **throw a p.** donner une fête **(b)** *(group)* groupe *m*; *(political)* parti *m*; *Law (in contract, lawsuit)* partie *f*; **to be (a) p. to sth** être complice de qch; **p. line** *(telephone line)* ligne *f* commune *(à plusieurs abonnés)*; *Pol* ligne du parti; *Br* **p. ticket** billet *m* collectif
pass¹ [pɑːs] *n (over mountains)* col *m*
pass² [pɑːs] *n (entry permit)* laissez-passer *m inv*; *(for travel)* carte *f* d'abonnement; *(in sport)* passe *f*; *Fam* **to make a p. at sb** faire des avances à qn; *Br* **to get a p.** *(in exam)* avoir la moyenne; **p. mark** *(in exam)* moyenne • **passkey** *n* passe-partout *m inv*
pass³ [pɑːs] **1** *vt (move, give)* passer *(*to* à)*; *(go past)* passer devant; *(vehicle, runner)* dépasser; *(exam)* être reçu à; *(bill, law)* voter; **to p. sb** *(in street)* croiser qn; **to p. the time** passer le temps; **to p. judgement on sb** porter un jugement sur qn; *Law* **to p. sentence** prononcer le verdict
2 *vi (go past, go away)* passer *(*to* à; *through* par)*; *(overtake in vehicle)* dépasser; *(in exam)* avoir la moyenne; *(of time)* passer; **he can p. for thirty** on lui donnerait trente ans
▸ **pass along** *vi* passer ▸ **pass away** *vi* décéder ▸ **pass by 1** *vt insep (building)* passer devant; **to p. by sb** *(in street)* croiser qn **2** *vi* passer à côté ▸ **pass off** *vt sep* **to p. oneself off as sb** se faire passer pour qn ▸ **pass on 1** *vt sep (message, illness, title)* transmettre *(*to* à)* **2** *vi* **to p. on to sth** *(move on to)* passer à qch ▸ **pass out 1** *vt sep (hand out)* distribuer **2** *vi (faint)* s'évanouir ▸ **pass over** *vt insep (ignore)* passer sur ▸ **pass round** *vt sep (cakes, document)* faire passer; *(hand out)* distribuer ▸ **pass through** *vi* passer ▸ **pass up** *vt sep (opportunity)* laisser passer
passable [ˈpɑːsəbəl] *adj (not bad)* passable; *(road)* praticable; *(river)* franchissable
passage [ˈpæsɪdʒ] *n* **(a)** *(act of passing, way through)* passage *m*; *(corridor)* couloir *m*; *(by boat)* traversée *f*; **with the p. of time** avec le temps **(b)** *(of text)* passage *m* • **passageway** *n (corridor)* couloir *m*; *(alleyway, way through)* passage *m*
passbook [ˈpɑːsbʊk] *n* livret *m* de caisse d'épargne
passenger [ˈpæsɪndʒə(r)] *n* passager, -ère *mf*; *(on train)* voyageur, -euse *mf*
passer-by [pɑːsəˈbaɪ] *(pl* **passers-by**) *n* passant, -ante *mf*

passing [ˈpɑːsɪŋ] **1** *adj (vehicle)* qui passe; *(beauty)* passager, -ère; **p. place** *(on road)* aire *f* de croisement
 2 *n (of vehicle, visitor)* passage *m; (of time)* écoulement *m; (death)* disparition *f*; **in p.** en passant

passion [ˈpæʃən] *n* passion *f*; **to have a p. for sth** adorer qch; **p. fruit** fruit *m* de la passion • **passionate** *adj* passionné • **passionately** *adv* passionnément

passive [ˈpæsɪv] **1** *adj* passif, -ive; **p. smoking** tabagisme *m* passif
 2 *n Grammar* passif *m*; **in the p.** au passif • **passiveness** *n* passivité *f*

Passover [ˈpɑːsəʊvə(r)] *n Rel* la Pâque juive

passport [ˈpɑːspɔːt] *n* passeport *m*; **p. photo** photo *f* d'identité

password [ˈpɑːswɜːd] *n* mot *m* de passe

past [pɑːst] **1** *n* passé *m*; **in the p.** autre-fois; **it's a thing of the p.** ça n'existe plus
 2 *adj (gone by)* passé; *(former)* ancien, -ienne; **these p. months** ces derniers mois; **that's all p.** c'est du passé; **to be p. master at sth** être passé maître dans l'art de qch; *Grammar* **in the p. tense** au passé
 3 *prep (in front of)* devant; *(after)* après; *(beyond)* au-delà de; **it's p. four o'clock** il est quatre heures passées; **to be p. fifty** avoir cinquante ans passés; *Fam* **to be p. it** avoir fait son temps; *Fam* **I wouldn't put it p. him** il en est bien capable
 4 *adv* devant; **to go p.** passer; **to run p.** passer en courant

pasta [ˈpæstə] *n* pâtes *fpl*

paste [peɪst] **1** *n* (**a**) *(mixture)* pâte *f; (of meat)* pâté *m* (**b**) *(glue)* colle *f*
 2 *vt* coller; **to p. sth up** coller qch

pastel [*Br* ˈpæstəl, *Am* pæˈstel] **1** *n* pastel *m*
 2 *adj (drawing)* au pastel; **p. shade** ton *m* pastel *inv*

pasteurized [ˈpæstʃəraɪzd] *adj* **p. milk** lait *m* pasteurisé

pastiche [pæˈstiːʃ] *n* pastiche *m*

pastille [*Br* ˈpæstɪl, *Am* pæˈstiːl] *n* pastille *f*

pastime [ˈpɑːstaɪm] *n* passe-temps *m inv*

pastor [ˈpɑːstə(r)] *n Rel* pasteur *m* • **pastoral** *adj* pastoral

pastry [ˈpeɪstrɪ] *(pl* **-ies)** *n (dough)* pâte *f; (cake)* pâtisserie *f* • **pastrycook** *n* pâtis-sier, -ière *mf*

pasture [ˈpɑːstʃə(r)] *n* pré *m*, pâture *f*

pasty¹ [ˈpæstɪ] *(pl* **-ies)** *n (pie)* feuilleté *m*

pasty² [ˈpeɪstɪ] **(-ier, -iest)** *adj (complex-ion)* terreux, -euse

pat [pæt] **1** *n (tap)* petite tape *f; (of animal)* caresse *f*

 2 *adv* **to answer p.** avoir la réponse toute prête; **to know sth off p.** savoir qch sur le bout du doigt
 3 *(pt & pp* **-tt-)** *vt (tap)* tapoter; *(animal)* caresser

patch [pætʃ] **1** *n (for clothes)* pièce *f; (over eye)* bandeau *m; (tyre)* Rustine® *f; (of colour)* tache *f; (of fog)* nappe *f; (of ice)* plaque *f;* **a cabbage p.** un carré de choux; **a p. of blue sky** un coin de ciel bleu; *Fig* **to be going through a bad p.** traverser une mauvaise passe; *Fam* **not to be a p. on** *(not as good as) (of person)* ne pas arriver à la cheville de; *(of thing)* n'être rien à côté de
 2 *vt* **to p. (up)** *(clothing)* rapiécer; **to p. sth up** *(marriage, friendship)* raccommo-der; **to p. things up** *(after argument)* se raccommoder

patchwork [ˈpætʃwɜːk] *n* patchwork *m*

patchy [ˈpætʃɪ] **(-ier, -iest)** *adj* inégal

patent 1 [ˈpeɪtənt] *adj* manifeste; **p. leather** cuir *m* verni
 2 [ˈpeɪtənt, ˈpætənt] *n* brevet *m* d'inven-tion
 3 *vt* (faire) breveter • **patently** *adv* ma-nifestement; **it's p. obvious** c'est absolu-ment évident

paternal [pəˈtɜːnəl] *adj* paternel, -elle • **paternity** *n* paternité *f*

path [pɑːθ] *(pl* **-s** [pɑːðz]*) n* chemin *m; (narrow)* sentier *m; (in park)* allée *f; (of river)* cours *m; (of bullet, rocket, planet)* trajectoire *f;* **the storm destroyed every-thing in its p.** la tempête a tout détruit sur son passage

pathetic [pəˈθetɪk] *adj* pitoyable

pathology [pəˈθɒlədʒɪ] *n* pathologie *f* • **pathological** [pæθəˈlɒdʒɪkəl] *adj* pa-thologique

pathos [ˈpeɪθɒs] *n* pathétique *m*

pathway [ˈpɑːθweɪ] *n* sentier *m*

patience [ˈpeɪʃəns] *n* (**a**) *(quality)* pa-tience *f;* **to lose p.** perdre patience (**with sb** avec qn); **I have no p. with him** il m'énerve (**b**) *Br (card game)* réussite *f;* **to play p.** faire une réussite

patient [ˈpeɪʃənt] **1** *adj* patient
 2 *n* patient, -iente *mf* • **patiently** *adv* patiemment

patio [ˈpætɪəʊ] *(pl* **-os)** *n* patio *m; Br* **p. doors** portes *f* vitrées *(donnant sur un patio)*

patriarch [ˈpeɪtrɪɑːk] *n* patriarche *m*

patriot [ˈpætrɪət, ˈpeɪtrɪət] *n* patriote *mf* • **patriotic** [-rɪˈɒtɪk] *adj (views, speech)* patriotique; *(person)* patriote • **patriot-ism** *n* patriotisme *m*

patrol [pə'trəʊl] **1** *n* patrouille *f*; **to be on p.** être de patrouille; **p. boat** patrouilleur *m*; **p. car** voiture *f* de police
2 (*pt & pp* -**ll**-) *vt* patrouiller dans
3 *vi* patrouiller • **patrolman** (*pl* -**men**) *n* Am (*policeman*) agent *m* de police

patron ['peɪtrən] *n* (*of arts*) protecteur, -trice *mf*; (*of charity*) patron, -onne *mf*; (*customer*) client, -iente *mf*; (*of theatre*) spectateur, -trice *mf*; *Rel* **p. saint** patron, -onne *mf* • **patronage** ['pætrənɪdʒ] *n* (*of arts, charity*) patronage *m*

> *ℓ* Note that the French word **patron** is a false friend and is never a translation for the English word **patron**. It means **boss**.

patronize [*Br* 'pætrənaɪz, *Am* 'peɪtrənaɪz] *vt* (**a**) (*be condescending towards*) traiter avec condescendance (**b**) (*store, hotel*) fréquenter; (*arts*) protéger • **patronizing** *adj* condescendant

patter¹ ['pætə(r)] **1** *n* (*of footsteps*) petit bruit *m*; (*of rain, hail*) crépitement *m*
2 *vi* (*of rain, hail*) crépiter

patter² ['pætə(r)] *n Fam* (*talk*) baratin *m*

pattern ['pætən] *n* (*design*) dessin *m*, motif *m*; (*in sewing*) patron *m*; (*in knitting*) & *Fig* (*norm*) modèle *m*; (*tendency*) tendance *f*; *Fig* **to set a p.** créer un modèle; **p. book** catalogue *m* d'échantillons • **patterned** *adj* (*fabric*) à motifs

paunch [pɔːntʃ] *n* ventre *m* • **paunchy** (-**ier**, -**iest**) *adj* bedonnant

pauper ['pɔːpə(r)] *n* indigent, -ente *mf*

pause [pɔːz] **1** *n* pause *f*; (*in conversation*) silence *m*
2 *vi* (*stop*) faire une pause; (*hesitate*) hésiter

pave [peɪv] *vt* (*road*) paver (**with** de); *Fig* **to p. the way for sth** ouvrir la voie à qch • **paved** *adj* pavé • **paving** *n* (*with tiles*) carrelage *m*; (*with slabs*) dallage *m*; **p. stone** pavé *m*

pavement ['peɪvmənt] *n Br* (*beside road*) trottoir *m*; *Am* (*roadway*) chaussée *f*

pavilion [pə'vɪljən] *n* pavillon *m*

paw [pɔː] **1** *n* patte *f*
2 *vt* (*of animal*) donner un coup/des coups de patte à; *Fam* (*of person*) tripoter

pawn¹ [pɔːn] *n Chess* pion *m*

pawn² [pɔːn] **1** *n* **in p.** en gage
2 *vt* mettre en gage • **pawnbroker** *n* prêteur, -euse *mf* sur gages • **pawnshop** *n* mont-de-piété *m*

pay [peɪ] **1** *n* paie *f*, salaire *m*; (*of soldier*) solde *f*; *Br* **p. cheque** chèque *m* de paie; **p. packet** enveloppe *f* de paie; **p. rise** aug-

mentation *f* de salaire; *Br* **p. slip,** *Am* **p. stub** fiche *f* de paie
2 (*pt & pp* **paid**) *vt* (*person, money, bill*) payer; (*sum, deposit*) verser; (*yield*) (*of investment*) rapporter; **I paid £5 for it** je l'ai payé 5 livres; **to p. sb to do sth** *or* **for doing sth** payer qn pour qu'il fasse qch; **to p. sb for sth** payer qch à qn; **to p. money into one's account** *or* **the bank** verser de l'argent sur son compte; **to p. attention** faire attention (**to** à); **to p. sb a visit** rendre visite à qn; **to p. sb a compliment** faire un compliment à qn; **to p. homage** *or* **tribute to sb** rendre hommage à qn
3 *vi* payer; **to p. a lot** payer cher; **it pays to be cautious** on a intérêt à être prudent • **payable** *adj* (*due*) payable; **to make a cheque p. to sb** libeller un chèque à l'ordre de qn • **paycheck** *n Am* chèque *m* de paie • **payday** *n* jour *m* de paie • **paying** *adj* (*guest*) payant; (*profitable*) rentable • **payment** *n* paiement *m*; (*of deposit*) versement *m*; (*reward*) récompense *f*; **on p. of 20 euros** moyennant 20 euros • **payoff** *n Fam* (*reward*) récompense *f*; (*bribe*) pot-de-vin *m* • **pay-per-'view** *adj* TV à péage • **payphone** *n* téléphone *m* public • **payroll** *n* **to be on the p.** faire partie du personnel; **to have twenty workers on the p.** employer vingt ouvriers
▸ **pay back** *vt sep* (*person, loan*) rembourser; *Fig* **I'll p. you back for this!** tu me le paieras! ▸ **pay for** *vt insep* payer ▸ **pay in** *vt sep* (*cheque, money*) verser sur un compte ▸ **pay off 1** *vt sep* (*debt, person*) rembourser; (*in instalments*) rembourser par acomptes; (*staff, worker*) licencier **2** *vi* (*of work, effort*) porter ses fruits ▸ **pay out** *vt sep* (*spend*) dépenser ▸ **pay up** *vi* payer

PC [piː'siː] (**a**) (*abbr* **personal computer**) PC *m*, micro *m* (**b**) (*abbr* **politically correct**) politiquement correct

PE [piː'iː] (*abbr* **physical education**) *n* EPS *f*

pea [piː] *n* pois *m*; **peas,** *Br* **garden** *or* **green peas** petits pois *mpl*

peace [piːs] *n* paix *f*; **p. of mind** tranquillité *f* d'esprit; **in p.** en paix; **at p.** en paix (**with** avec); **to hold one's p.** garder le silence; *Law* **to disturb the p.** troubler l'ordre public; **I'd like to have some p. and quiet** j'aimerais un peu de silence; **p. talks** pourparlers *mpl* de paix; **p. treaty** traité *m* de paix • **peacekeeping** *adj* (*force*) de maintien de la paix;

(measure) de pacification • **peace-loving** *adj* pacifique • **peacetime** *n* temps *m* de paix

peaceable ['piːsəbəl] *adj* pacifique

peaceful ['piːsfəl] *adj (calm)* paisible; *(non-violent)* pacifique • **peacefully** *adv* paisiblement • **peacefulness** *n* paix *f*

peach [piːtʃ] **1** *n (fruit)* pêche *f*; **p. (tree)** pêcher *m*
2 *adj (colour)* pêche *inv*

peacock ['piːkɒk] *n* paon *m*

peak [piːk] **1** *n (mountain top)* sommet *m*; *(mountain)* pic *m*; *(of cap)* visière *f*; *Fig (of fame, success)* apogée *m*; **the traffic has reached** *or* **is at its p.** la circulation est à son maximum
2 *adj (hours, period)* de pointe; *(demand, production)* maximum
3 *vi* culminer à

peaked [piːkt] *adj* **p. cap** casquette *f*

peaky ['piːkɪ] (**-ier, -iest**) *adj Br Fam (ill)* patraque

peal [piːl] **1** *n (of bells)* sonnerie *f*; *(of thunder)* coup *m*; **peals of laughter** éclats *mpl* de rire
2 *vi* **to p. (out)** *(of bells)* sonner à toute volée

peanut ['piːnʌt] *n* cacah(o)uète *f*; *Fam* **to earn peanuts** gagner des clopinettes; **p. butter** beurre *m* de cacah(o)uètes; **p. oil** huile *f* d'arachide

pear [peə(r)] *n* poire *f*; **p. tree** poirier *m*

pearl [pɜːl] *n* perle *f*; **p. necklace** collier *m* de perles • **pearly** (**-ier, -iest**) *adj (colour)* nacré

peasant ['pezənt] *n & adj* paysan, -anne *(mf)*

peashooter ['piːʃuːtə(r)] *n* sarbacane *f*

peat [piːt] *n* tourbe *f*; **p. bog** tourbière *f*

pebble ['pebəl] *n (stone)* caillou *m* (*pl* -oux); *(on beach)* galet *m* • **pebbly** *adj (beach)* de galets

pecan ['piːkən] *n (nut)* noix *f* de pécan

peck [pek] **1** *n* coup *m* de bec; *(kiss)* bise *f*
2 *vti* **to p. (at)** *(grain)* picorer; *(person)* donner un coup de bec à; **to p. at one's food** *(of person)* manger du bout des dents; *Fig* **the pecking order** la hiérarchie

peckish ['pekɪʃ] *adj Br* **to be p.** avoir un petit creux

peculiar [pɪ'kjuːlɪə(r)] *adj (strange)* bizarre; *(special, characteristic)* particulier, -ière (**to** à) • **peculiarity** [-lɪ'ærɪtɪ] (*pl* **-ies**) *n (feature)* particularité *f*; *(oddity)* bizarrerie *f* • **peculiarly** *adv* bizarrement; *(specially)* particulièrement

pedal ['pedəl] **1** *n* pédale *f*; **p. bin** pou-

belle *f* à pédale; **p. boat** Pédalo® *m*
2 *(Br* **-ll-***, Am* **-l-***) vt* **to p. a bicycle** être à bicyclette
3 *vi* pédaler

pedant ['pedənt] *n* pédant, -ante *mf* • **pedantic** [pɪ'dæntɪk] *adj* pédant • **pedantry** *n* pédantisme *m*

peddle ['pedəl] *vt (goods, ideas, theories)* colporter; *(drugs)* faire du trafic de • **peddler** *n (door-to-door)* colporteur, -euse *mf*; *(in street)* camelot *m*; **(drug) p.** trafiquant, -ante *mf* de drogue

pedestal ['pedɪstəl] *n* piédestal *m*; *Fig* **to put sb on a p.** mettre qn sur un piédestal

pedestrian [pə'destrɪən] **1** *n* piéton *m*; *Br* **p. crossing** passage *m* pour piétons; *Br* **p. precinct** zone *f* piétonnière
2 *adj (speech, style)* prosaïque • **pedestrianize** *vt (street)* rendre piétonnier; **pedestrianized street** rue *f* piétonne *ou* piétonnière

pediatrician [piːdɪə'trɪʃən] *n Am* pédiatre *mf* • **pediatrics** [-dɪ'ætrɪks] *n Am* pédiatrie *f*

pedigree ['pedɪgriː] **1** *n (of animal)* pedigree *m*; *(of person)* ascendance *f*
2 *adj (animal)* de race

pedlar ['pedlə(r)] *n (door-to-door)* colporteur, -euse *mf*; *(in street)* camelot *m*

pee [piː] *Fam* **1** *n* **to go for a p.** faire pipi
2 *vi* faire pipi

peek [piːk] **1** *n* **to have a p. (at)** jeter un coup d'œil furtif (à)
2 *vi* jeter un coup d'œil furtif (**at** à)

peel [piːl] **1** *n (of vegetable, fruit)* peau *f*; *(of orange, lemon)* écorce *f*
2 *vt (vegetable)* éplucher; *(fruit)* peler; **to keep one's eyes peeled** ouvrir l'œil; **to p. sth off** *(label)* décoller qch
3 *vi (of skin, person)* peler; *(of paint)* s'écailler; **to p. easily** *(of fruit)* se peler facilement • **peeler** *n* **(potato) p.** épluche-légumes *m inv* • **peelings** *npl* épluchures *fpl*

peep [piːp] **1** *n* **to have a p. (at)** jeter un coup d'œil furtif à
2 *vi* jeter un coup d'œil furtif (**at** à); **to p. out** se montrer
3 *vi (of bird)* pépier • **peephole** *n* judas *m* • **Peeping 'Tom** *n Fam* voyeur *m*

peer [pɪə(r)] **1** *n (equal) & Br (nobleman)* pair *m*; **p. pressure** influence *f* du groupe
2 *vi* **to p. at sb/sth** scruter qn/qch du regard; **to p. into the darkness** scruter l'obscurité • **peerage** ['pɪərɪdʒ] *n Br (rank)* pairie *f*

peeved [piːvd] *adj* en rogne

peevish ['piːvɪʃ] *adj* irritable

peg [peg] **1** *n (for coat, hat)* patère *f*; *(for clothes)* pince *f* à linge; *(for tent)* piquet *m*; *(wooden)* cheville *f*; *(metal)* fiche *f*; *Br* **to buy sth off the p.** acheter qch en prêt-à-porter
2 *(pt & pp* **-gg-***) vt (prices)* stabiliser
pejorative [pɪˈdʒɒrətɪv] *adj* péjoratif, -ive
pekinese [piːkɪˈniːz] *n (dog)* pékinois *m*
Peking [piːˈkɪŋ] *n* Pékin *m ou f*
pekingese [piːkɪˈniːz] *n (dog)* pékinois *m*
pelican [ˈpelɪkən] *n* pélican *m*; *Br* **p. crossing** feux *mpl* à commande manuelle
pellet [ˈpelɪt] *n (of paper, bread)* boulette *f*; *(for gun)* plomb *m*
pelmet [ˈpelmɪt] *n (fabric, wood)* cantonnière *f*
pelt [pelt] **1** *n (skin)* peau *f*; *(fur)* fourrure *f*
2 *vt* bombarder (**with** de)
3 *vi Fam* **(a)** **it's pelting down** il pleut à verse (**b**) *(go fast)* aller à toute allure
pelvis [ˈpelvɪs] *n Anat* pelvis *m*
pen¹ [pen] **1** *n (for writing)* stylo *m*; **to live by one's p.** vivre de sa plume; **p. friend** *or* **pal** correspondant, -ante *mf*; **p. name** nom *m* de plume; *Pej* **p. pusher** gratte-papier *m inv*
2 *(pt & pp* **-nn-***) vt* écrire
pen² [pen] *n (for sheep, cattle)* parc *m*
penal [ˈpiːnəl] *adj (code, law)* pénal; *(colony)* pénitentiaire • **penalize** *vt* pénaliser
penalty [ˈpenəltɪ] *(pl* **-ies***) n (prison sentence)* peine *f*; *(fine)* amende *f*; *Football* penalty *m*; *Rugby* pénalité *f*; *Fig* **to pay the p. for sth** subir les conséquences de qch
penance [ˈpenəns] *n* pénitence *f*
pence [pens] *pl of* **penny**
pencil [ˈpensəl] **1** *n* crayon *m*; **in p.** au crayon; **p. case** trousse *f*; **p. sharpener** taille-crayon *m*
2 *(Br* **-ll-***, Am* **-l-***) vt (draw)* dessiner au crayon; *(write)* écrire au crayon; *Fig* **to p. sth in** fixer qch provisoirement
pendant [ˈpendənt] *n (around neck)* pendentif *m*
pending [ˈpendɪŋ] **1** *adj (matter, business)* en attente; *(trial)* en instance
2 *prep (until)* en attendant
pendulum [ˈpendjʊləm] *n* pendule *m*
penetrate [ˈpenɪtreɪt] **1** *vt (substance)* pénétrer; *(secret, plan)* découvrir; *(mystery)* percer
2 *vti* **to p. (into)** *(forest)* pénétrer dans; *(group)* s'infiltrer dans • **penetrating** *adj (mind, cold)* pénétrant • **pene'tration** *n* pénétration *f*
penguin [ˈpeŋgwɪn] *n* manchot *m*

penicillin [penɪˈsɪlɪn] *n* pénicilline *f*; **to be on p.** prendre de la pénicilline
peninsula [pəˈnɪnsjʊlə] *n* presqu'île *f*; *(larger)* péninsule *f* • **peninsular** *adj* péninsulaire
penis [ˈpiːnɪs] *n* pénis *m*
penitent [ˈpenɪtənt] *adj* pénitent • **penitence** *n* pénitence *f*
penitentiary [penɪˈtenʃərɪ] *(pl* **-ies***) n Am* prison *f* centrale
penknife [ˈpennaɪf] *(pl* **-knives***) n* canif *m*
pennant [ˈpenənt] *n* flamme *f*
penniless [ˈpenɪləs] *adj* sans le sou
penny [ˈpenɪ] *n* **(a)** *(pl* **-ies***) Br (coin)* penny *m*; *Am & Can (cent)* cent *m*; **I don't have a p.** je n'ai pas un sou; **you won't get a p.** tu n'auras pas un sou; **it was worth every p.** ça valait vraiment le coup **(b)** *(pl* **pence***) Br (value, currency)* penny *m*
pension [ˈpenʃən] **1** *n* pension *f*; **(retirement) p.** retraite *f*; *Br* **old age p.** pension de vieillesse; **to retire on a p.** toucher une retraite; **p. fund** fonds *m* de retraite; *Br* **p. scheme** plan *m* de retraite
2 *vt* **to p. sb off** mettre qn à la retraite • **pensionable** *adj (age)* de la retraite; *(job)* qui donne droit à une retraite • **pensioner** *n* retraité, -ée *mf*; *Br* **old age p.** retraité, -ée *mf*
pensive [ˈpensɪv] *adj* pensif, -ive
Pentagon [ˈpentəgən] *n Am Pol* **the P.** le Pentagone
pentathlon [penˈtæθlən] *n Sport* pentathlon *m*
penthouse [ˈpenthaʊs] *n* = appartement de luxe au dernier étage d'un immeuble
pent-up [ˈpentˈʌp] *adj (feelings)* refoulé
penultimate [pɪˈnʌltɪmət] *adj* avant-dernier, -ière
peony [ˈpiːənɪ] *(pl* **-ies***) n (plant)* pivoine *f*
people [ˈpiːpəl] **1** *n (nation)* peuple *m*
2 *npl (as group)* gens *mpl*; *(as individuals)* personnes *fpl*; **the p.** *(citizens)* le peuple; **two p.** deux personnes; **English p.** les Anglais *mpl*; **a lot of p.** beaucoup de gens; **p. think that** les gens pensent que
3 *vt* peupler (**with** de)
pep [pep] *Fam* **1** *n* entrain *m*; **p. talk** petit discours *m* d'encouragement
2 *(pt & pp* **-pp-***) vt* **to p. sb up** ragaillardir qn
pepper [ˈpepə(r)] **1** *n* poivre *m*; *(vegetable)* poivron *m*; **p. mill** moulin *m* à poivre; **p. pot** poivrière *f*
2 *vt* poivrer • **peppercorn** *n* grain *m* de poivre • **peppery** *adj* poivré

peppermint ['pepəmɪnt] *n (flavour)* menthe *f*; *(sweet)* bonbon *m* à la menthe
per [pɜː(r)] *prep* par; **p. annum** par an; **p. head, p. person** par personne; **50 pence p. kilo** 50 pence le kilo; **40 km p. hour** 40 km à l'heure; *Formal* **as p. your instructions** conformément à vos instructions
perceive [pə'siːv] *vt (see, hear)* percevoir; *(notice)* remarquer (**that** que)
percentage [pə'sentɪdʒ] *n* pourcentage *m* • **percent** *adv* pour cent
perceptible [pə'septəbəl] *adj* perceptible • **perception** *n* perception *f* (**of** de) • **perceptive** *adj (person)* perspicace; *(study, remark)* pertinent
perch¹ [pɜːtʃ] **1** *n (for bird)* perchoir *m*
2 *vi* se percher
perch² [pɜːtʃ] *n (fish)* perche *f*
percolate ['pɜːkəleɪt] **1** *vt (coffee)* passer; **percolated coffee** = café préparé dans une cafetière à pression
2 *vi (of liquid)* passer (**through** par) • **percolator** *n* cafetière *f* à pression; *(in café, restaurant)* percolateur *m*
percussion [pə'kʌʃən] *n Mus* percussion *f*
peremptory [pə'remptərɪ] *adj* péremptoire; *(refusal)* absolu
perennial [pə'renɪəl] **1** *adj (plant)* vivace; *(worry)* perpétuel, -uelle; *(beauty)* éternel, -elle
2 *n* plante *f* vivace
perfect ['pɜːfɪkt] **1** *adj* parfait
2 *adj & n Grammar* **p. (tense)** parfait *m*
3 [pə'fekt] *vt* parfaire; *(one's French)* parfaire ses connaissances en • **perfectly** *adv* parfaitement
perfection [pə'fekʃən] *n (quality)* perfection *f*; *(of technique)* mise *f* au point (**of** de); **to p.** à la perfection • **perfectionist** *n* perfectionniste *mf*
perfidious [pə'fɪdɪəs] *adj Literary* perfide
perforate ['pɜːfəreɪt] *vt* perforer • **perfo'ration** *n* perforation *f*
perform [pə'fɔːm] **1** *vt (task, miracle)* accomplir; *(duty, function)* remplir; *(play, piece of music)* jouer; **to p. an operation on sb** opérer qn
2 *vi (act, play)* jouer; *(sing)* chanter; *(dance)* danser; *(of machine, vehicle)* marcher; **to p. well/badly** *(in job)* bien/mal s'en tirer; **how does she p. under pressure?** comment réagit-elle lorsqu'elle est sous pression? • **performing** *adj (dog, seal)* savant
performance [pə'fɔːməns] *n* (**a**) *(of play)* représentation *f* (**b**) *(of actor, musician)* interprétation *f*; *(of athlete)* performance *f*; *(of machine)* performances *fpl*; *(of company)* résultats *mpl*; *Fam* **to make a p.** faire toute une histoire
performer [pə'fɔːmə(r)] *n (entertainer)* artiste *mf*; *(in play, of music)* interprète *mf* (**of** de)
perfume **1** ['pɜːfjuːm] *n* parfum *m*
2 [pə'fjuːm] *vt* parfumer
perfunctory [pə'fʌŋktərɪ] *adj (examination, glance)* rapide; *(smile)* mécanique; *(letter)* sommaire
perhaps [pə'hæps] *adv* peut-être; **p. not/so** peut-être que non/que oui; **p. she'll come** peut-être qu'elle viendra, elle viendra peut-être
peril ['perɪl] *n* péril *m*, danger *m*; **at your p.** à vos risques et périls • **perilous** *adj* périlleux, -euse
perimeter [pə'rɪmɪtə(r)] *n* périmètre *m*
period ['pɪərɪəd] **1** *n* (**a**) *(stretch of time)* période *f*; *(historical)* époque *f*; *(school lesson)* heure *f* de cours; **in the p. of a month** en l'espace d'un mois; *(monthly)* **period(s)** *(of woman)* règles *fpl* (**b**) *Am (full stop)* point *m*; **I refuse, p.!** je refuse, un point c'est tout!
2 *adj (furniture, costume)* d'époque; *TV* **p. drama** drame *m* historique • **periodic** [-rɪ'ɒdɪk] *adj* périodique • **periodical** [-rɪ'ɒdɪkəl] *n (magazine)* périodique *m* • **periodically** [-rɪ'ɒdɪkəlɪ] *adv* périodiquement
periphery [pə'rɪfərɪ] *(pl -***ies***) n* périphérie *f* • **peripheral** *adj (area, vision) & Comptr* périphérique; *(question)* sans rapport direct (**to** avec); *(issue, importance)* accessoire • **peripherals** *npl Comptr* périphériques *mpl*
periscope ['perɪskəʊp] *n* périscope *m*
perish ['perɪʃ] *vi (of person)* périr; *(of rubber, leather)* se détériorer; *(of food)* s'avarier; **p. the thought!** loin de moi cette pensée! • **perishing** *adj Fam (cold, weather)* glacial
perishable ['perɪʃəbəl] *adj (food)* périssable • **perishables** *npl* denrées *fpl* périssables
perjure ['pɜːdʒə(r)] *vt Law* **to p. oneself** faire un faux témoignage • **perjurer** *n Law* faux témoin *m* • **perjury** *n Law* faux témoignage *m*; **to commit p.** faire un faux témoignage
perk [pɜːk] **1** *n Br Fam (in job)* avantage *m*
2 *vt* **to p. sb up** *(revive)* ragaillardir qn; *(cheer up)* remonter le moral à qn
3 *vi* **to p. up** reprendre du poil de la bête

• **perky** (**-ier, -iest**) *adj Fam (lively)* plein d'entrain; *(cheerful)* guilleret, -ette
perm [pɜːm] **1** *n* permanente *f*
2 *vt* **to have one's hair permed** se faire faire une permanente
permanent ['pɜːmənənt] *adj* permanent; *(address)* fixe; *(ink)* indélébile; **she's p. here** *(of worker)* elle est ici à titre permanent • **permanence** *n* permanence *f* • **permanently** *adv* à titre permanent
permeable ['pɜːmɪəbəl] *adj* perméable
permeate ['pɜːmɪeɪt] *vt (of ideas)* se répandre dans; **to p. (through) sth** *(of liquid)* pénétrer qch
permissible [pə'mɪsəbəl] *adj* permis
permission [pə'mɪʃən] *n* permission *f*, autorisation *f* (**to do** de faire); **to ask for p. (to do sth)** demander la permission (de faire qch); **to give sb p. (to do sth)** donner la permission à qn (de faire qch)
permissive [pə'mɪsɪv] *adj* permissif, -ive • **permissiveness** *n* permissivité *f*
permit 1 [pə'mɪt] ['pɜːmɪt] *n* permis *m*
2 *(pt & pp* **-tt-**) *vt* permettre (**sb to do** à qn de faire)
3 *vi* **weather permitting** si le temps le permet
permutation [pɜːmjʊ'teɪʃən] *n* permutation *f*
pernicious [pə'nɪʃəs] *adj* pernicieux, -ieuse
pernickety [pə'nɪkətɪ] *adj Br Fam (person)* pointilleux, -euse; *(task)* délicat
peroxide [pə'rɒksaɪd] **1** *n Chem* peroxyde *m*
2 *adj (hair)* oxygéné; **p. blonde** blonde *f* décolorée
perpendicular [pɜːpən'dɪkjʊlə(r)] *adj & n* perpendiculaire *(f)*
perpetrate ['pɜːpɪtreɪt] *vt (crime)* perpétrer • **perpetrator** *n* auteur *m*
perpetual [pə'petʃʊəl] *adj* perpétuel, -uelle • **perpetually** *adv* perpétuellement • **perpetuate** [-veɪt] *vt* perpétuer • **perpetuity** [pɜːpɪ'tjuːɪtɪ] *n* perpétuité *f*
perplex [pə'pleks] *vt* rendre perplexe • **perplexed** *adj* perplexe • **perplexing** *adj* déroutant
persecute ['pɜːsɪkjuːt] *vt* persécuter • **perse'cution** *n* persécution *f*
persevere [pɜːsɪ'vɪə(r)] *vi* persévérer (**with** dans) • **perseverance** *n* persévérance *f* • **persevering** *adj* persévérant
Persian ['pɜːʃən, 'pɜːʒən] **1** *adj (language, cat)* persan; **P. carpet** tapis *m* persan; **the P. Gulf** le golfe Persique
2 *n (language)* persan *m*
persist [pə'sɪst] *vi* persister (**in doing à** faire; **in sth** dans qch); **to p. in one's belief that...** persister à croire que... • **persistence** *n (of person)* ténacité *f*; *(of fog, belief)* persistance *f* • **persistent** *adj (person)* tenace; *(fever, smell, rumours)* persistant; *(noise, attempts)* continuel, -uelle; *Law* **p. offender** récidiviste *mf* • **persistently** *adv (stubbornly)* obstinément; *(continually)* continuellement
person ['pɜːsən] *n* personne *f*; **in p.** en personne; **a p. to p. call** *(on telephone)* une communication avec préavis
personable [pɜːsənəbəl] *adj* charmant
personal ['pɜːsənəl] *adj* personnel, -elle; *(friend)* intime; *(life)* privé; *(indiscreet)* indiscret, -ète; **to make a p. appearance** venir en personne; **p. ad** petite annonce *f*; **p. assistant, p. secretary** secrétaire *m* particulier, secrétaire *f* particulière; **the p. column** les petites annonces *fpl*; **p. computer** ordinateur *m* individuel; **p. hygiene** hygiène *f*; **p. organizer** agenda *m*; **p. stereo** baladeur *m*; **p. test** test *m* de personnalité
personality [pɜːsə'nælətɪ] *(pl* **-ies**) *n (character, famous person)* personnalité *f*; **a television p.** une vedette de la télévision; **p. disorder** trouble *m* de la personnalité
personalize ['pɜːsənəlaɪz] *vt* personnaliser
personally ['pɜːsənəlɪ] *adv* personnellement; *(in person)* en personne; **don't take it p.** n'en faites pas une affaire personnelle
personify [pə'sɒnɪfaɪ] *(pt & pp* **-ied**) *vt* personnifier • **personification** [-fɪ'keɪʃən] *n* personnification *f*
personnel [pɜːsə'nel] *n (staff)* personnel *m*; **p. department** service *m* du personnel
perspective [pə'spektɪv] *n* perspective *f*; *Fig* **in (its true) p.** sous son vrai jour
Perspex® ['pɜːspeks] *n Br* Plexiglas® *m*
perspire [pə'spaɪə(r)] *vi* transpirer • **perspiration** [pɜːspə'reɪʃən] *n* transpiration *f*
persuade [pə'sweɪd] *vt* persuader (**sb to do** qn de faire) • **persuasion** *n* persuasion *f*; *(creed)* religion *f* • **persuasive** *adj (person, argument)* persuasif, -ive • **persuasively** *adv* de façon persuasive
pert [pɜːt] *adj (cheeky)* espiègle; *(hat)* coquet, -ette • **pertly** *adv* avec impertinence
pertain [pə'teɪn] *vi Formal* **to p. to** *(relate)* se rapporter à; *(belong)* appartenir à
pertinent ['pɜːtɪnənt] *adj* pertinent • **pertinently** *adv* pertinemment
perturb [pə'tɜːb] *vt* troubler

Peru [pə'ruː] *n* le Pérou •**Peruvian 1** *adj* péruvien, -ienne **2** *n* Péruvien, -ienne *mf*

peruse [pə'ruːz] *vt Formal (read carefully)* lire attentivement; *(skim through)* parcourir •**perusal** *n Formal* lecture *f*

pervade [pə'veɪd] *vt* imprégner •**pervasive** *adj (feeling)* général; *(smell)* envahissant; *(influence)* omniprésent

perverse [pə'vɜːs] *adj (awkward)* contrariant; *(sexually deviant)* pervers •**perversion** [*Br* -ʃən, *Am* -ʒən] *n (sexual)* perversion *f*; *(of justice, truth)* travestissement *m* •**perversity** (*pl* -**ies**) *n* esprit *m* de contradiction; *(sexual deviance)* perversité *f*

pervert 1 ['pɜːvɜːt] *n (sexual deviant)* pervers, -erse *mf*
2 [pə'vɜːt] *vt* pervertir; *(mind)* corrompre; *Law* **to p. the course of justice** entraver le bon fonctionnement de la justice

pesky ['peskɪ] (-**ier**, -**iest**) *adj Am Fam (troublesome)* embêtant

pessimism ['pesɪmɪzəm] *n* pessimisme *m* •**pessimist** *n* pessimiste *mf* •**pessi'mistic** *adj* pessimiste •**pessi'mistically** *adv* avec pessimisme

pest [pest] *n (animal)* animal *m* nuisible; *(insect)* insecte *m* nuisible; *Fam (person)* plaie *f*

pester ['pestə(r)] *vt* tourmenter; **to p. sb to do sth** harceler qn pour qu'il fasse qch; **to p. sb for sth** harceler qn jusqu'à ce qu'il donne qch

pesticide ['pestɪsaɪd] *n* pesticide *m*

pet [pet] **1** *n* animal *m* domestique; *(favourite person)* chouchou, -oute *mf*; *(term of address)* petit chou *m*; **to have** *or* **keep a p.** avoir un animal chez soi
2 *adj (dog, cat)* domestique; *(tiger)* apprivoisé; *(favourite)* favori, -ite; *Br* **p. hate** bête *f* noire; **p. name** petit nom *m*; **p. shop** animalerie *f*; **p. subject** dada *m*
3 (*pt & pp* -**tt**-) *vt (fondle)* caresser
4 *vi Fam* se peloter

petal ['petəl] *n* pétale *m*

peter ['piːtə(r)] *vi* **to p. out** *(of conversation, enthusiasm)* tarir; *(of scheme)* n'aboutir à rien; *(of path, stream)* disparaître

petite [pə'tiːt] *adj (woman)* menu

petition [pə'tɪʃən] **1** *n (signatures)* pétition *f*; *(request to court of law)* requête *f*; *Law* **p. for divorce** demande *f* en divorce
2 *vt* adresser une pétition/une requête à (**for sth** pour demander qch)
3 *vi* **to p. for sth** faire une pétition pour qch; *Law* **to p. for divorce** faire une demande de divorce

petrify ['petrɪfaɪ] (*pt & pp* -**ied**) *vt* pétrifier

petrol ['petrəl] *n Br* essence *f*; **I've run out of p.** je suis tombé en panne d'essence; **p. can** bidon *m* d'essence; **p. station** station-service *f*; **p. tank** réservoir *m* d'essence

> ⚠ Note that the French word **pétrole** is a false friend and is never a translation for the English word **petrol**. It means **oil**.

petroleum [pə'trəʊlɪəm] *n* pétrole *m*; **p. jelly** vaseline *f*

petticoat ['petɪkəʊt] *n* jupon *m*

petty ['petɪ] (-**ier**, -**iest**) *adj (trivial)* insignifiant; *(mean)* mesquin; **p. cash** petite caisse *f*; **p. criminal** petit délinquant *m*; **p. officer** *(on ship)* second maître *m* •**pettiness** *n (triviality)* insignifiance *f*; *(meanness)* mesquinerie *f*

petulant ['petjʊlənt] *adj* irritable •**petulance** *n* irritabilité *f*

> ⚠ Note that the French word **pétulant** is a false friend and is never a translation for the English word **petulant**. It means **exuberant**.

petunia [pɪ'tjuːnɪə] *n* pétunia *m*

pew [pjuː] *n* banc *m* d'église; *Hum* **take a p.!** assieds-toi!

pewter ['pjuːtə(r)] *n* étain *m*

phallic ['fælɪk] *adj* phallique

phantom ['fæntəm] *n* fantôme *m*

pharmacy ['fɑːməsɪ] (*pl* -**ies**) *n* pharmacie *f* •**pharmaceutical** [-'sjuːtɪkəl] *adj* pharmaceutique •**pharmacist** *n* pharmacien, -ienne *mf*

pharynx ['færɪŋks] *n Anat* pharynx *m*

phase [feɪz] **1** *n* phase *f*; **it's just a p.** ça lui passera
2 *vt* **to p. sth in/out** introduire/supprimer qch progressivement •**phased** *adj* progressif, -ive

PhD [piːeɪtʃ'diː] *n (abbr* **Doctor of Philosophy**) *(degree)* doctorat *m* (**in** de); *(person)* docteur *m*

pheasant ['fezənt] *n* faisan *m*

phenomenon [fɪ'nɒmɪnən] (*pl* -**ena** [-ɪnə]) *n* phénomène *m* •**phenomenal** *adj* phénoménal

phew [fjuː] *exclam (in relief)* ouf!; *(when hot)* pfff!

philanderer [fɪ'lændərə(r)] *n Pej* coureur *m* de jupons

philanthropist [fɪ'lænθrəpɪst] *n* philanthrope *mf* •**philanthropic** [fɪlən'θrɒpɪk] *adj* philanthropique

philately [fɪ'lætəlɪ] *n* philatélie *f* •**philatelist** *n* philatéliste *mf*

philharmonic [fɪləˈmɒnɪk] *adj & n* philharmonique *(m)*
Philippines [ˈfɪlɪpiːnz] *npl* **the P.** les Philippines *fpl*
philistine [ˈfɪlɪstaɪn] *n* béotien, -ienne *mf*, philistin *m*
philosophy [fɪˈlɒsəfɪ] *(pl* -ies) *n* philosophie *f* ●**philosopher** *n* philosophe *mf* ●**philosophical** [fɪləˈsɒfɪkəl] *adj* philosophique; *Fig (stoical, resigned)* philosophe ●**philosophically** [fɪləˈsɒfɪklɪ] *adv (say)* avec philosophie ●**philosophize** *vi* philosopher (**on** sur)
phlegm [flem] *n (in throat)* glaires *fpl*; *Fig (calmness)* flegme *m* ●**phlegmatic** [flegˈmætɪk] *adj* flegmatique
phobia [ˈfəʊbɪə] *n* phobie *f*
phone [fəʊn] **1** *n* téléphone *m*; **to be on the p.** *(be talking)* être au téléphone; *(have a telephone)* avoir le téléphone; **p. call** coup *m* de téléphone; **to make a p. call** téléphoner (**to** à); **p. book** annuaire *m*; **p. box,** *Br* **p. booth** cabine *f* téléphonique; **p. number** numéro *m* de téléphone
2 *vt* téléphoner (**to** à); **to p. sb (up)** téléphoner à qn; **to p. sb back** rappeler qn
3 *vi* **to p. (up)** téléphoner; **to p. back** rappeler ●**phonecard** *n Br* carte *f* de téléphone ●**phone-in** *n* = émission au cours de laquelle les auditeurs ou les téléspectateurs peuvent intervenir par téléphone
phonetic [fəˈnetɪk] *adj* phonétique ●**phonetics 1** *n (science)* phonétique *f* **2** *npl (words)* transcription *f* phonétique
phoney [ˈfəʊnɪ] *Fam* **1** (-ier, -iest) *adj (jewels, writer)* faux (*f* fausse); *(company, excuse)* bidon *inv*; *(attitude)* de faux jeton
2 *n (impostor)* imposteur *m*; *(insincere person)* faux jeton *m*; **it's a p.** *(jewel, coin)* c'est du faux
phonograph [ˈfəʊnəgræf] *n Am* électrophone *m*
phosphate [ˈfɒsfeɪt] *n Chem* phosphate *m*
phosphorus [ˈfɒsfərəs] *n Chem* phosphore *m*
photo [ˈfəʊtəʊ] *(pl* -os) *n* photo *f*; **to take sb's p.** prendre qn en photo; **to have one's p. taken** se faire prendre en photo; **p. album** album *m* de photos
photocopy [ˈfəʊtəʊkɒpɪ] **1** *(pl* -ies) *n* photocopie *f*
2 *(pt & pp* -ied) *vt* photocopier ●**photocopier** *n* photocopieuse *f*
photogenic [fəʊtəʊˈdʒenɪk] *adj* photogénique

photograph [ˈfəʊtəgrɑːf] **1** *n* photographie *f*
2 *vt* photographier
3 *vi* **to p. well** être photogénique ●**photographer** [fəˈtɒgrəfə(r)] *n* photographe *mf* ●**photographic** [-ˈgræfɪk] *adj* photographique ●**photography** [fəˈtɒgrəfɪ] *n (activity)* photographie *f*

⚠ Note that the French word **photographe** is a false friend and is never a translation for the English word **photograph**. It means **photographer**.

Photostat® [ˈfəʊtəʊstæt] *n* photostat *m*
phrase [freɪz] **1** *n (saying)* expression *f*; *(idiom)* & *Grammar* locution *f*; **p. book** manuel *m* de conversation
2 *vt (verbally)* exprimer; *(in writing)* rédiger
Phys Ed [fɪzˈed] *(abbr* **physical education**) *n Am* EPS *f*
physical [ˈfɪzɪkəl] **1** *adj* physique; **p. education** éducation *f* physique; **p. examination** visite *f* médicale
2 *n (examination)* visite *f* médicale ●**physically** *adv* physiquement; **it's p. impossible** c'est matériellement impossible
physician [fɪˈzɪʃən] *n* médecin *m*

⚠ Note that the French word **physicien** is a false friend and is never a translation for the English word **physician**. It means **physicist**.

physics [ˈfɪzɪks] *n (science)* physique *f* ●**physicist** [ˈfɪzɪsɪst] *n* physicien, -ienne *mf*
physiology [fɪzɪˈɒlədʒɪ] *n* physiologie *f* ●**physiological** [fɪzɪəˈlɒdʒɪkəl] *adj* physiologique
physiotherapy [fɪzɪəʊˈθerəpɪ] *n* kinésithérapie *f* ●**physiotherapist** *n* kinésithérapeute *mf*
physique [fɪˈziːk] *n* physique *m*
piano [pɪˈænəʊ] *(pl* -os) *n* piano *m* ●**pianist** [ˈpɪənɪst] *n* pianiste *mf*
piazza [pɪˈætsə] *n (square)* place *f*
picayune [pɪkəˈjuːn] *adj Am Fam (petty)* mesquin
pick¹ [pɪk] **1** *n (choice)* choix *m*; **to take one's p.** choisir; **the p. of the bunch** le meilleur/la meilleure du lot
2 *vt (choose)* choisir; *(flower, fruit)* cueillir; *(hole)* faire (**in** dans); *(pimple)* tripoter; *(lock)* crocheter; **to p. one's nose** se mettre les doigts dans le nez; **to p. one's teeth** se curer les dents; **to p. a fight** chercher la bagarre (**with** avec); *Fig* **to p. holes in sth** relever les failles dans qch
3 *vi* **to p. and choose** se permettre de choisir

▸**pick at** *vt insep* **to p. at one's food** picorer ▸ **pick off** *vt sep (remove)* enlever ▸ **pick on** *vt insep (nag, blame)* s'en prendre à ▸ **pick out** *vt sep (choose)* choisir; *(identify)* repérer ▸ **pick up 1** *vt sep (lift up)* ramasser; *(to upright position)* relever; *(person into air, weight)* soulever; *(baby)* prendre dans ses bras; *(cold)* attraper; *(habit, accent, speed)* prendre; *(fetch, collect)* passer prendre; *(radio programme)* capter; *(survivor)* recueillir; *(arrest)* arrêter; *(learn)* apprendre; **to p. up the phone** décrocher le téléphone **2** *vi (improve)* s'améliorer; *(of business)* reprendre; *(of patient)* se remettre; **let's p. up where we left off** reprenons (là où nous en étions restés)

pick² [pɪk] *n (tool)* pic *m*; **ice p.** pic à glace

pickaxe ['pɪkæks] *(Am* **pickax)** *n* pioche *f*

picket ['pɪkɪt] **1** *n* (**a**) *(stake)* piquet *m* (**b**) *(in strike)* **p. (line)** piquet *m* de grève
2 *vt (factory)* installer un piquet de grève aux portes de

pickings ['pɪkɪŋz] *npl (leftovers)* restes *mpl*; *(profits)* bénéfices *mpl*; **rich p.** gros bénéfices

pickle ['pɪkəl] **1** *n* = condiment à base de légumes conservés dans du vinaigre; **pickles** *(vegetables)* Br conserves *fpl* (au vinaigre); *Am* concombres *mpl*, cornichons *mpl*; *Fam* **to be in a p.** être dans le pétrin
2 *vt* conserver dans du vinaigre; **pickled onion** oignon *m* au vinaigre

pick-me-up ['pɪkmiːʌp] *n Fam* remontant *m*

pickpocket ['pɪkpɒkɪt] *n* pickpocket *m*

pick-up ['pɪkʌp] *n* **p. (truck)** pick-up *m inv (petite camionnette à plateau)*; **p. point** *(for goods, passengers)* point *m* de ramassage

picky ['pɪkɪ] (**-ier, -iest**) *adj Am Fam (choosy)* difficile (**about** sur)

picnic ['pɪknɪk] **1** *n* pique-nique *m*; *Br* **p. basket, p. hamper** panier *m* à pique-nique
2 (*pt & pp* **-ck-**) *vi* pique-niquer

pictorial [pɪk'tɔːrɪəl] *adj (representation)* en images; *(periodical)* illustré

picture ['pɪktʃə(r)] **1** *n* image *f*; *(painting)* tableau *m*; *(drawing)* dessin *m*; *(photo)* photo *f*; *Fig (situation)* situation *f*; *Br Fam (film)* film *m*; *Br Fam* **the pictures** le cinéma; **to be the p. of health** respirer la santé; *Fig* **to put sb in the p.** mettre qn au courant; **p. frame** cadre *m*
2 *vt (in painting, photo)* représenter; *Fig*

(in words) décrire; **to p. sth (to oneself)** s'imaginer qch; **to p. sb doing sth** s'imaginer qn en train de faire qch

picturesque [pɪktʃə'resk] *adj* pittoresque

piddling ['pɪdlɪŋ] *adj Pej* dérisoire

pidgin ['pɪdʒɪn] *n* pidgin *m*; **p. English/French** ≃ petit nègre *m*

pie [paɪ] *n (open)* tarte *f*; *(with pastry on top)* tourte *f*; **p. chart** camembert *m*

piebald ['paɪbɔːld] *adj* pie *inv*

piece [piːs] **1** *n* morceau *m*; *(smaller)* bout *m*; *(in chess, puzzle)* pièce *f*; **in pieces** en morceaux; **to smash sth to pieces** briser qch en morceaux; **to take sth to pieces** démonter qch; **to come to pieces** se démonter; *Fig* **to go to pieces** *(of person)* s'effondrer (complètement); **a p. of news/advice/luck** une nouvelle/un conseil/une chance; **in one p.** *(object)* intact; *(person)* indemne
2 *vt* **to p. together** *(facts)* reconstituer; *(one's life)* refaire

piecemeal ['piːsmiːl] **1** *adv* petit à petit
2 *adj (unsystematic)* peu méthodique

piecework ['piːswɜːk] *n* travail *m* à la tâche *ou* à la pièce

pier [pɪə(r)] *n (for walking, with entertainments)* jetée *f*; *(for landing)* embarcadère *m*

pierce [pɪəs] *vt* percer; *(of cold, bullet, sword)* transpercer; **to have one's ears pierced** se faire percer les oreilles ● **piercing** *adj (voice, look)* perçant; *(wind)* vif *(f* vive)

piety ['paɪətɪ] *n* piété *f*

pig [pɪg] **1** *n (animal)* cochon *m*, porc *m*; *Fam (greedy person)* goinfre *m*; *Fam (unpleasant man)* salaud *m*
2 (*pt & pp* **-gg-**) *vi Am Fam* **to p. out** *(overeat)* se goinfrer (**on** de) ● **piggish** *adj (dirty)* sale; *(greedy)* goinfre ● **piggy** *adj Fam (greedy)* goinfre; **p. eyes** des yeux de cochon ● **piggy bank** *n* tirelire *f (en forme de cochon)*

pigeon ['pɪdʒɪn] *n* pigeon *m*

pigeonhole ['pɪdʒɪnhəʊl] **1** *n* casier *m*
2 *vt (classify, label)* classer; *(person)* étiqueter; *(shelve)* mettre en suspens

piggyback ['pɪgɪbæk] *n* **to give sb a p.** porter qn sur son dos

pig-headed [pɪg'hedɪd] *adj* têtu

pigment ['pɪgmənt] *n* pigment *m* ● **pigmen'tation** *n* pigmentation *f*

pigsty ['pɪgstaɪ] *(pl* **-ies**) *n* porcherie *f*

pigtail ['pɪgteɪl] *n (hair)* natte *f*

pike [paɪk] *n* (**a**) *(fish)* brochet *m* (**b**) *Hist (weapon)* pique *f*

pilchard ['pɪltʃəd] *n* pilchard *m*
pile¹ [paɪl] **1** *n (heap)* tas *m; (stack)* pile *f; Fam* **to have piles of** *or* **a p. of things to do** avoir un tas de choses à faire; *Fam* **to have piles** *or* **a p. of work to do** avoir des tonnes de travail à faire; *Fam* **to make one's p.** faire fortune
2 *vt* entasser; *(stack)* empiler
3 *vi Fam* **to p. into a car** s'entasser dans une voiture
▸ **pile up 1** *vt sep* entasser; *(stack)* empiler
2 *vi (accumulate)* s'accumuler
pile² [paɪl] *n (of carpet)* poils *mpl*
piles [paɪlz] *npl (illness)* hémorroïdes *fpl*
pile-up ['paɪlʌp] *n Fam (on road)* carambolage *m*
pilfer ['pɪlfə(r)] *vti* chaparder • **pilfering, pilferage** *n* chapardage *m*
pilgrim ['pɪlgrɪm] *n* pèlerin *m* • **pilgrimage** *n* pèlerinage *m*
pill [pɪl] *n* pilule *f;* **to be on the p.** *(of woman)* prendre la pilule; **to go off the p.** arrêter la pilule
pillage ['pɪlɪdʒ] **1** *n* pillage *m*
2 *vti* piller
pillar ['pɪlə(r)] *n* pilier *m; Br* **p. box** boîte *f* aux lettres
pillion ['pɪljən] *adv* **to ride p.** *(on motorbike)* monter derrière
pillory ['pɪlərɪ] *(pt & pp* **-ied)** *vt* mettre au pilori
pillow ['pɪləʊ] *n* oreiller *m* • **pillowcase, pillowslip** *n* taie *f* d'oreiller
pilot ['paɪlət] **1** *n (of plane, ship)* pilote *m*
2 *adj* **p. light** veilleuse *f;* **p. scheme** projet-pilote *m*
3 *vt (plane, ship)* piloter
pimento [pɪ'mentəʊ] *(pl* **-os)** *n* piment *m*
pimp [pɪmp] *n* souteneur *m*
pimple ['pɪmpəl] *n* bouton *m* • **pimply** (**-ier, -iest)** *adj* boutonneux, -euse
PIN [pɪn] *(abbr* **personal identification number)** *n Br* **P. (number)** code *m* confidentiel
pin [pɪn] **1** *n* épingle *f; (for surgery)* broche *f; Br (drawing pin)* punaise *f; (in machine, grenade)* goupille *f;* **to have pins and needles** avoir des fourmis (**in** dans); **p. money** argent *m* de poche
2 *(pt & pp* **-nn-)** *vt (attach)* épingler (**to** à); *(to wall)* punaiser (**to** *or* **on** à); **to p. one's hopes on sb/sth** mettre tous ses espoirs en qn/qch; **to p. the blame on sb** rejeter la responsabilité sur qn; **to p. down** *(immobilize)* immobiliser; *(fix)* fixer; *(trap)* coincer; *Fig* **to p. sb down** forcer qn à s'engager; **to p. sth up** *(notice)* fixer qch au mur

pinafore ['pɪnəfɔː(r)] *n Br (apron)* tablier *m; (dress)* robe *f* chasuble
pinball ['pɪnbɔːl] *n* flipper *m;* **p. machine** flipper
pincers ['pɪnsəz] *npl (tool)* tenailles *fpl*
pinch [pɪntʃ] **1** *n (action)* pincement *m; (of salt)* pincée *f;* **to give sb a p.** pincer qn; *Br* **at a p.,** *Am* **in a p.** à la rigueur; *Fig* **to feel the p.** être gêné
2 *vt* pincer; *Br Fam (steal)* piquer (**from** à); *Fam (arrest)* pincer
3 *vi (of shoes)* serrer
pincushion ['pɪnkʊʃən] *n* pelote *f* à épingles
pine [paɪn] **1** *n (tree, wood)* pin *m;* **p. forest** pinède *f;* **p. nut** pignon *m*
2 *vi* **to p. for sb/sth** se languir de qn/qch; **to p. away** languir
pineapple ['paɪnæpəl] *n* ananas *m*
ping [pɪŋ] *n* tintement *m*
ping-pong ['pɪŋpɒŋ] *n* ping-pong *m*
pink [pɪŋk] *adj & n (colour)* rose *(m)*
pinkie ['pɪŋkɪ] *n Am & Scot* petit doigt *m*
pinnacle ['pɪnəkəl] *n Fig (of fame, career)* apogée *m*
pinpoint ['pɪnpɔɪnt] *vt (locate)* repérer; *(identify)* identifier
pinstripe ['pɪnstraɪp] *adj (suit)* rayé
pint [paɪnt] *n* pinte *f (Br* = 0,57 *l, Am* = 0,47 l); **a p. of beer** ≃ un demi
pin-up ['pɪnʌp] *n Fam (girl)* pin-up *f inv*
pioneer [paɪə'nɪə(r)] **1** *n* pionnier, -ière *mf*
2 *vt* **to p. sth** être le premier/la première à mettre au point qch
pious ['paɪəs] *adj (person, deed)* pieux (*f* pieuse)
pip [pɪp] *n Br (of fruit)* pépin *m; Br* **the pips** *(on radio)* les bips *mpl* sonores
pipe [paɪp] **1** *n* tuyau *m; (for smoking)* pipe *f; (musical instrument)* pipeau *m;* **the pipes** *(bagpipes)* la cornemuse; **to smoke a p.** fumer la pipe; **p. cleaner** cure-pipes *m inv;* **p. dream** chimère *f*
2 *vt (water, oil)* transporter par canalisation; **piped music** musiquette *f*
3 *vi Fam* **to p. down** *(shut up)* se taire • **piping 1** *n (pipes)* canalisations *fpl;* **length of p.** tuyau *m* **2** *adv* **p. hot** très chaud
pipeline ['paɪplaɪn] *n (for oil)* pipeline *m; Fig* **to be in the p.** être en préparation
pique [piːk] *n* dépit *m*
pirate ['paɪərət] **1** *n* pirate *m*
2 *adj (radio, ship)* pirate • **piracy** *n (of ships)* piraterie *f; (of videos, software)* piratage *m* • **pirated** *adj (book, record, CD)* pirate

Pisces ['paɪsiːz] n (sign) les Poissons mpl; **to be a P.** être Poissons

pissed [pɪst] adj very Fam (drunk) bourré; Am (angry) en rogne

pistachio [pɪ'stæʃɪəʊ] (pl **-os**) n (nut, flavour) pistache f

pistol ['pɪstəl] n pistolet m

piston ['pɪstən] n (of engine) piston m

pit¹ [pɪt] n (hole) fosse f; (mine) mine f; (of stomach) creux m; Br (in theatre) parterre m; **the pits** (in motor racing) les stands mpl de ravitaillement; Fam **it's the pits** c'est complètement nul

pit² [pɪt] n Am (stone of fruit) noyau m (pl -aux); (smaller) pépin m

pit³ [pɪt] (pt & pp **-tt-**) vt **to p. oneself against sb** se mesurer à qn

pitch¹ [pɪtʃ] 1 n (a) Football terrain m; (in market) place f (b) (degree) degré m; (of voice) hauteur f; (musical) ton m

2 vt (tent) dresser; (camp) établir; (ball) lancer; **a pitched battle** (between armies) une bataille rangée; Fig une belle bagarre

3 vi (of ship) tanguer

4 vi Fam **to p. in** (cooperate) mettre du sien; **to p. into sb** attaquer qn

pitch² [pɪtʃ] n (tar) poix f • **pitch-'black, pitch-'dark** adj noir comme dans un four

pitcher ['pɪtʃə(r)] n cruche f

pitchfork ['pɪtʃfɔːk] n fourche f

pitfall ['pɪtfɔːl] n (trap) piège m

pith [pɪθ] n (of orange) peau f blanche; Fig (essence) moelle f • **pithy** (**-ier, -iest**) adj concis

pitiful ['pɪtɪfəl] adj pitoyable • **pitiless** adj impitoyable

pitta ['pɪtə] adj & n **p. bread** pita m

pittance ['pɪtəns] n (income) salaire m de misère; (sum) somme f dérisoire

> ♪ Note that the French word **pitance** is a false friend and is never a translation for the English word **pittance**. It means **sustenance.**

pitted ['pɪtɪd] adj (a) (face) grêlé; **p. with rust** piqué de rouille (b) Am (fruit) dénoyauté

pitter-patter ['pɪtəpætə(r)] n = patter¹

pity ['pɪtɪ] 1 n pitié f; **to take** or **have p. on sb** avoir pitié de qn; **what a p.!** quel dommage!; **it's a p. that...** c'est dommage que... (+ subjunctive)

2 (pt & pp **-ied**) vt plaindre

pivot ['pɪvət] 1 n pivot m

2 vi pivoter (**on** sur)

pixie ['pɪksɪ] n (fairy) lutin m

pizza ['piːtsə] n pizza f; **p. parlour** pizzeria f • **pizzeria** [piːtsə'riːə] n pizzeria f

placard ['plækɑːd] n (on wall) affiche f; (hand-held) pancarte f

> ♪ Note that the French word **placard** is a false friend and is never a translation for the English word **placard**. Its most common meaning is **cupboard**.

placate [Br plə'keɪt, Am 'pleɪkeɪt] vt calmer

place [pleɪs] 1 n endroit m, lieu m; (in street name) rue f; (seat, position, rank) place f; Fam **my p.** chez moi; Fam **my parents' p.** chez mes parents; **to lose one's p.** (in queue) perdre sa place; (in book) perdre sa page; **to change** or **swap** or **trade places** changer de place; **to take the p. of sb/sth** remplacer qn/qch; **to take p.** (happen) avoir lieu; Br **to set** or **lay three places** (at the table) mettre trois couverts; Am **some p.** (somewhere) quelque part; Am **no p.** (nowhere) nulle part; **all over the p.** un peu partout; **in the first p.** (firstly) en premier lieu; **in p. of** à la place de; **out of p.** (remark) déplacé; (object) pas à sa place; **p. of work** lieu m de travail; **p. mat** set m de table; **p. setting** couvert m

2 vt (put, situate, invest) & Sport placer; **to be placed third** se classer troisième; **to p. an order with sb** passer une commande à qn; **to p. sb** (remember, identify) remettre qn

placement ['pleɪsmənt] n stage m

placid ['plæsɪd] adj placide

plagiarize ['pleɪdʒəraɪz] vt plagier • **plagiarism** n plagiat m

plague [pleɪg] 1 n (disease) peste f; (of insects) invasion f; **to avoid sb/sth like the p.** éviter qn/qch comme la peste

2 vt (of person) harceler (**with** de)

plaice [pleɪs] n (fish) carrelet m

plaid [plæd] n (fabric) tissu m écossais

plain¹ [pleɪn] 1 (**-er, -est**) adj (clear, obvious) clair; (simple) simple; (without a pattern) uni; (not beautiful) quelconque; **in p. English** clairement; **in p. clothes** en civil; **to make it p. to sb that...** faire comprendre à qn que...; **I'll be quite p. with you** je vais être franc/franche avec vous; Fam **that's p. madness** c'est de la pure folie; **p. chocolate** chocolat m noir; **p. flour** farine f (sans levure); **p. speaking** franc-parler m

2 adv Fam (utterly) complètement • **plainly** adv (clearly) clairement; (frankly) franchement

plain² [pleɪn] n (land) plaine f

plaintiff ['pleɪntɪf] n Law plaignant, -ante mf

plaintive ['pleɪntɪv] *adj* plaintif, -ive
plait [plæt] **1** *n* tresse *f*, natte *f*
2 *vt* tresser, natter
plan [plæn] **1** *n (proposal, intention)* projet *m*; *(of building, town, essay)* plan *m*; **the best p. would be to** le mieux serait de; **to go according to p.** se passer comme prévu; **to have no plans** *(be free)* n'avoir rien de prévu; **to change one's plans** *(decide differently)* changer d'idée
2 (*pt & pp* **-nn-**) *vt (arrange)* projeter; *(crime)* comploter; *(building, town)* faire le plan de; *(economy)* planifier; **to p. to do** *or* **on doing sth** *(intend)* projeter de faire qch; **as planned** comme prévu
3 *vi* faire des projets; **to p. for the future** faire des projets d'avenir
plane¹ [pleɪn] *n (aircraft)* avion *m*
plane² [pleɪn] **1** *n (tool)* rabot *m*
2 *vt* raboter
plane³ [pleɪn] *n* **p. (tree)** platane *m*
plane⁴ [pleɪn] *n (level, surface) & Fig* plan *m*
planet ['plænɪt] *n* planète *f* • **planetarium** [-'teərɪəm] *n* planétarium *m* • **planetary** [-tərɪ] *adj* planétaire
plank [plæŋk] *n* planche *f*
planner ['plænə(r)] *n* planificateur, -trice *mf*; **(town) p.** urbaniste *mf*
planning ['plænɪŋ] *n* conception *f*; **family p.** planning *m* familial; **p. permission** permis *m* de construire
plant [plɑːnt] **1** (**a**) *(living thing)* plante *f* (**b**) *(factory)* usine *f*; *(machinery)* matériel *m*
2 *vt (tree, flower)* planter; *(crops, field)* semer (**with** en); *Fig (bomb)* poser; **to p. sth on sb** *(hide)* cacher qch dans les affaires de qn *(pour le compromettre)* • **plan'tation** *n (trees, land)* plantation *f*
plaque [plæk] *n (sign)* plaque *f*; *(on teeth)* plaque *f* dentaire
plasma ['plæzmə] *n* plasma *m*
plaster ['plɑːstə(r)] **1** *n* (**a**) *(on wall)* plâtre *m*; **p. of Paris** plâtre de Paris; **to put sb's leg in p.** mettre la jambe de qn dans le plâtre; **p. cast** *(for broken bone)* plâtre (**b**) *Br* **(sticking) p.** pansement *m* adhésif
2 *vt (wall)* plâtrer; **to p. sth with** *(cover)* couvrir qch de • **plastered** *adj Fam (drunk)* bourré • **plasterer** *n* plâtrier *m*
plastic ['plæstɪk] **1** *adj (object)* en plastique; *(bullet)* de plastique; **p. bag** sac *m* en plastique; **p. explosive** plastic *m*; **p. surgery** *(cosmetic)* chirurgie *f* esthétique
2 *n* plastique *m*; *Fam* **do they take p.?** est-ce qu'ils acceptent les cartes de crédit?

Plasticine® ['plæstɪsiːn] *n Br* pâte *f* à modeler
plate [pleɪt] **1** *n (dish)* assiette *f*; *(metal sheet)* plaque *f*; *(book illustration)* gravure *f*; *Fam* **to have a lot on one's p.** avoir du pain sur la planche; **p. glass** vitrage *m* très épais
2 *vt (with gold)* plaquer en or; *(with silver)* plaquer en argent • **plateful** *n* assiettée *f*
plateau ['plætəʊ] (*pl* **-eaus** [-əʊz] *or* **-eaux**) *n (flat land)* plateau *m*
platform ['plætfɔːm] *n (raised surface)* plate-forme *f*; *(in train station)* quai *m*; *(for speaker)* estrade *f*; *(political programme)* programme *m*; **p. shoes** = chaussures à grosses semelles et à talons hauts, typiques des années 70
platinum ['plætɪnəm] **1** *n (metal)* platine *m*
2 *adj* **p.** *or* **p.-blond(e) hair** cheveux *mpl* blond platine
platitude ['plætɪtjuːd] *n* platitude *f*
platonic [plə'tɒnɪk] *adj* platonique
platoon [plə'tuːn] *n Mil* section *f*
platter ['plætə(r)] *n (dish)* plat *m*
plaudits ['plɔːdɪts] *npl Literary (commendation)* applaudissements *mpl*
plausible ['plɔːzəbəl] *adj (argument, excuse)* plausible; *(person)* convaincant
play [pleɪ] **1** *n (drama)* pièce *f* (de théâtre); *(amusement, looseness)* jeu *m*; **to come into p.** entrer en jeu; **a p. on words** un jeu de mots
2 *vt (part, tune, card)* jouer; *(game)* jouer à; *(instrument)* jouer de; *(match)* disputer (**with** avec); *(team, opponent)* jouer contre; *(record, compact disc)* passer; *(radio, tape recorder)* faire marcher; *Fig* **to p. the fool** faire l'idiot; *Fig* **to p. a part in doing/in sth** contribuer à faire/à qch; *Fig* **to p. ball with** coopérer avec; *Fam* **to p. it cool** garder son sang-froid
3 *vi* jouer (**with** avec; **at** à); *(of record player, tape recorder)* marcher; *Fam* **what are you playing at?** à quoi tu joues? • **play-act** *vi* jouer la comédie • **playboy** *n* play-boy *m* • **playground** *n Br (in school)* cour *f* de récréation; *(in park)* terrain *m* de jeux • **playgroup** *n* garderie *f* • **playmate** *n* camarade *mf* de jeu • **playpen** *n* parc *m* *(pour bébé)* • **playroom** *n (in house)* salle *f* de jeux • **playschool** *n* garderie *f* • **plaything** *n (toy, person)* jouet *m* • **playtime** *n (in school)* récréation *f* • **playwright** *n* dramaturge *mf*
▸**play about, play around** *vi* jouer, s'amuser ▸ **play back** *vt sep (tape)* réécou-

ter ▸ **play down** *vt sep* minimiser ▸ **play on** *vt insep (feelings, fears)* jouer sur ▸ **play out** *vt sep (scene, fantasy)* jouer; *Fam* **to be played out** *(of idea, method)* être périmé *ou* vieux jeu *inv* ▸ **play up** *Fam* **1** *vi (of child, machine)* faire des siennes; **to p. up to sb** faire de la lèche à qn **2** *vt sep* **to p. sb up** *(of child)* faire enrager qn

player ['pleɪə(r)] *n (in game, of instrument)* joueur *m*, joueuse *f*; *(in theatre)* acteur *m*, actrice *f*; **clarinet p.** joueur/ joueuse *f* de clarinette

playful ['pleɪfəl] *adj (mood, tone)* enjoué; *(child, animal)* joueur *(f* joueuse*)* • **playfully** *adv (say)* en badinant • **playfulness** *n* enjouement *m*

playing ['pleɪɪŋ] *n* jeu *m*; **p. card** carte *f* à jouer; **p. field** terrain *m* de jeux

plc [piːel'siː] *(abbr* **public limited company***) n Br Com* ≃ SARL *f*

plea [pliː] *n (request)* appel *m*; *(excuse)* excuse *f*; *Law* **to enter a p. of guilty** plaider coupable

plead [pliːd] **1** *vt (argue)* plaider; *(as excuse)* alléguer; *Law* **to p. sb's case** plaider la cause de qn **2** *vi (in court)* plaider; **to p. with sb (to do sth)** implorer qn (de faire qch); *Law* **to p. guilty** plaider coupable

pleasant ['plezənt] *adj* agréable *(* **to** avec*)* • **pleasantly** *adv (smile, behave)* aimablement; *(surprised)* agréablement

pleasantries ['plezəntrɪz] *npl (jokes)* plaisanteries *fpl*; **to exchange p.** *(polite remarks)* échanger des politesses

please [pliːz] **1** *adv* s'il te/vous plaît; **p. sit down** asseyez-vous, je vous prie; **p. do!** bien sûr!, je vous en prie!; **'no smoking p.'** 'prière de ne pas fumer' **2** *vt* **to p. sb** faire plaisir à qn; *(satisfy)* contenter qn; **easy/hard to p.** facile/difficile (à contenter); **p. yourself!** comme tu veux! **3** *vi* plaire; **to be eager to p.** vouloir plaire; **do as you p.** fais comme tu veux; **as much/as many as you p.** autant qu'il vous plaira • **pleased** *adj* content *(* **with** de*)*; **to be p. to do sth** faire qch avec plaisir; **p. to meet you!** enchanté!; **I'd be p. to!** avec plaisir!; **I'm p. to say that...** je suis heureux/heureuse de vous dire que... • **pleasing** *adj* agréable, plaisant

pleasure ['pleʒə(r)] *n* plaisir *m*; **p. boat** bateau *m* de plaisance • **pleasurable** *adj* très agréable

pleat [pliːt] **1** *n* pli *m* **2** *vt* plisser • **pleated** *adj* plissé

plebiscite ['plebɪsaɪt] *n* plébiscite *m*

pledge [pledʒ] **1** *n (promise)* promesse *f* *(* **to do** de faire*)*; *(object)* gage *m* **2** *vt* promettre *(* **to do** de faire*)*; *(as security, pawn)* engager

plenty ['plentɪ] *n* abondance *f*; **p. of** beaucoup de; **that's p.** *(of food)* merci, j'en ai assez • **plentiful** *adj* abondant

plethora ['pleθərə] *n* pléthore *f*

pliable ['plaɪəbəl] *adj* souple

pliers ['plaɪəz] *npl* pince *f*

plight [plaɪt] *n (crisis)* situation *f* critique; **to be in a sorry p.** être dans une situation désespérée

plimsolls ['plɪmsəʊlz] *npl Br* tennis *mpl*

plinth [plɪnθ] *n* socle *m*

plod [plɒd] *(pt & pp* -dd-*) vi* **to p. (along)** *(walk)* avancer laborieusement; *(work)* travailler laborieusement; **to p. through a book** se forcer à lire un livre • **plodding** *adj (slow)* lent; *(step)* pesant

plonk¹ [plɒŋk] **1** *exclam (thud)* vlan!; *(splash)* plouf! **2** *vt Fam* **to p. sth (down)** *(drop)* poser qch

plonk² [plɒŋk] *n Br Fam (wine)* pinard *m*

plot [plɒt] **1** *n (conspiracy)* complot *m*; *(of novel, film)* intrigue *f*; **p. (of land)** parcelle *f* de terrain; **(vegetable) p.** potager *m* **2** *(pt & pp* -tt-*) vti* comploter *(* **to do** de faire*)* **3** *vt* **to p. (out)** *(route)* déterminer; *(diagram, graph)* tracer; *(one's position)* relever

plough [plaʊ] *(Am* **plow***)* **1** *n* charrue *f*; **the P.** *(constellation)* le Grand Chariot **2** *vt (field)* labourer; *Fig (money)* réinvestir; **to p. money back into sth** réinvestir de l'argent dans qch **3** *vi* labourer; *Fig* **to p. into sth** *(crash into)* percuter qch; *Fig* **to p. through sth** *(snow, work)* avancer péniblement dans qch • **ploughman** *(pl* **-men***) n* laboureur *m*; *Br* **p.'s lunch** = assiette de fromage ou jambon avec de la salade et des condiments

ploy [plɔɪ] *n* stratagème *m*

pluck [plʌk] **1** *n* courage *m* **2** *vt (hair, feathers)* arracher; *(flower)* cueillir; *(fowl)* plumer; *(eyebrows)* épiler; *(string of guitar)* pincer; **to p. up the courage to do sth** trouver le courage de faire qch • **plucky** *(* -ier, -iest*) adj* courageux, -euse

plug [plʌg] **1** *n* **(a)** *(of cotton wool, wood)* tampon *m*; *(for sink, bath)* bonde *f*; **(wall) p.** *(for screw)* cheville *f* **(b)** *(electrical) (on device)* fiche *f*; *(socket)* prise *f* (de cou-

rant); *Aut* **(spark) p.** bougie *f* (**c**) *Fam (publicity)* pub *f*
2 (*pt & pp* **-gg-**) *vt* (**a**) **to p. (up)** *(gap, hole)* boucher; **to p. sth in** *(appliance)* brancher qch (**b**) *Fam (promote)* faire de la pub pour; **to p. away** s'acharner (**at** sur) • **plughole** *n* trou *m* d'écoulement
plum [plʌm] *n* prune *f*; *Fam* **a p. job** un boulot en or
plumage ['pluːmɪdʒ] *n* plumage *m*
plumb [plʌm] **1** *vt Fig* **to p. the depths** toucher le fond
2 *adv Am Fam (crazy)* complètement; **p. in the middle** en plein centre
▸ **plumb in** *vt sep (washing machine)* brancher
plumber ['plʌmə(r)] *n* plombier *m* • **plumbing** *n (job, system)* plomberie *f*
plume [pluːm] *n (feather)* plume *f*; *(on hat)* aigrette *f*; **a p. of smoke** une volute de fumée
plummet ['plʌmɪt] *vi (of prices)* s'effondrer; *(of aircraft)* plonger
plump [plʌmp] **1** (**-er, -est**) *adj (person, arm)* potelé; *(chicken)* dodu; *(cushion, cheek)* rebondi
2 *vi Fam* **to p. for sth** se décider pour qch
plunder ['plʌndə(r)] **1** *n (act)* pillage *m*; *(goods)* butin *m*
2 *vt* piller
plunge [plʌndʒ] **1** *n (dive)* plongeon *m*; *Fig (decrease)* chute *f*; *Fam* **to take the p.** *(take on difficult task)* se jeter à l'eau; *Fam (get married)* se marier
2 *vt (thrust)* plonger (**into** dans)
3 *vi (dive)* plonger (**into** dans); *Fig (decrease)* chuter • **plunger** *n (for clearing sink)* ventouse *f*
plural ['plʊərəl] **1** *adj (form)* pluriel, -ielle; *(noun)* au pluriel
2 *n* pluriel *m*; **in the p.** au pluriel
plus [plʌs] **1** *prep* plus; *(as well as)* en plus de; **two p. two** deux plus deux
2 *adj (factor, quantity) & El* positif, -ive; **twenty p.** plus de vingt
3 (*pl* **plusses** ['plʌsɪz]) *n* **p. (sign)** (signe *m*) plus *m*; **that's a p.** c'est un plus
plush [plʌʃ] (**-er, -est**) *adj Fam* luxueux, -ueuse
plutonium [pluːˈtəʊnɪəm] *n Chem* plutonium *m*
ply [plaɪ] (*pt & pp* **plied**) **1** *vt (trade)* exercer; **to p. sb with drink** ne pas arrêter de verser à boire à qn; **to p. sb with questions** bombarder qn de questions
2 *vi* **to p. between** *(travel)* faire la navette entre
plywood ['plaɪwʊd] *n* contreplaqué *m*

PM [piːˈem] (*abbr* **Prime Minister**) *n* Premier ministre *m*
p.m. [piːˈem] *adv (afternoon)* de l'après-midi; *(evening)* du soir
pneumatic [njuːˈmætɪk] *adj* **p. drill** marteau-piqueur *m*
pneumonia [njuːˈməʊnɪə] *n* pneumonie *f*
poach [pəʊtʃ] **1** *vt (egg)* pocher; *(employee)* débaucher
2 *vi (hunt)* braconner • **poacher** *n (person)* braconnier *m* • **poaching** *n* braconnage *m*
PO Box [piːˈəʊbɒks] (*abbr* **Post Office Box**) *n* boîte *f* postale, BP *f*
pocket ['pɒkɪt] **1** *n* poche *f*; **to be out of p.** en être de sa poche; **p. calculator** calculette *f*; **p. money** argent *m* de poche
2 *vt (put in pocket)* empocher; *Fam (steal)* rafler • **pocketbook** *n (notebook)* carnet *m*; *Am (handbag)* sac *m* à main • **pocketful** *n* **a p. of** une pleine poche de
pockmarked ['pɒkmɑːkt] *adj* grêlé
pod [pɒd] *n* gousse *f*
podgy ['pɒdʒɪ] (**-ier, -iest**) *adj* grassouillet, -ette
podiatrist [pəˈdaɪətrɪst] *n Am* pédicure *mf*
podium ['pəʊdɪəm] *n* podium *m*
poem ['pəʊɪm] *n* poème *m* • **poet** *n* poète *m* • **poetic** [pəʊˈetɪk] *adj* poétique • **poetry** *n* poésie *f*
po-faced ['pəʊˈfeɪst] *adj Pej (expression, person)* pincé
poignant ['pɔɪnjənt] *adj* poignant
point [pɔɪnt] **1** (**a**) *n (of knife, needle)* pointe *f*; *Br* **points** *(for train)* aiguillage *m*; *Br* **(power) p.** prise *f* (de courant)
(**b**) *(dot, score, degree, argument)* point *m*; *(location)* endroit *m*; *(importance)* intérêt *m*; **the highest p.** le point le plus haut; **to make a p.** faire une remarque; **to make a p. of doing sth** mettre un point d'honneur à faire qch; **I take your p.** je comprends ce que tu veux dire; **you have a p.** tu as raison; **what's the p.?** à quoi bon?; **there's no p. (in) staying** ça ne sert à rien de rester; **that's not the p.** il ne s'agit pas de ça; **that's beside the p.** ça n'a rien à voir; **to the p.** *(relevant)* pertinent; **to get to the p.** en arriver au fait; **at this p. in time** en ce moment; **at this p., the phone rang** à ce moment-là, le téléphone sonna; **to be on the p. of doing sth** être sur le point de faire qch; **his good points** ses qualités *fpl*; **his bad points** ses défauts *mpl*; **p. of sale** point de vente; **p. of view** point de vue

(**c**) *Math* **three p. five** trois virgule cinq
2 *vt (aim)* diriger; *(camera, gun)* braquer
(**at** sur); **to p. the way** montrer le chemin
(**to** à); *Fig* montrer la voie (**to** à); **to p.
one's finger at sb** montrer qn du doigt; **to
p. sth out** *(show)* montrer qch; *(error,
fact)* signaler qch
3 *vi* **to p. at** *or* **to sb/sth** *(with finger)*
montrer qn/qch du doigt; **to p. north** *(of
arrow, compass)* indiquer le nord; **to be
pointing at sb/sth** *(of gun)* être braqué
sur qn/qch; **to be pointing towards sth**
(of car, chair) être face à qch; **everything
points to suicide** tout laisse penser à un
suicide

point-blank [pɔɪnt'blæŋk] **1** *adj (refusal)*
catégorique; **at p. range** à bout portant
2 *adv (fire)* à bout portant; *(refuse)* (tout)
net; *(request)* de but en blanc

pointed ['pɔɪntɪd] *adj* pointu; *(beard)* en
pointe; *Fig (remark, criticism)* pertinent;
(incisive) mordant • **pointedly** *adv (mean-
ingfully)* de façon insistante; *(markedly)*
de façon marquée *ou* prononcée

pointer ['pɔɪntə(r)] *n (on dial)* aiguille *f*;
(stick) baguette *f*; *(clue)* indice *m*; *Fam
(advice)* tuyau *m*

pointless ['pɔɪntləs] *adj* inutile • **point-
lessly** *adv* inutilement

poise [pɔɪz] **1** *n (composure)* assurance *f*;
(grace) grâce *f*; *(balance)* équilibre *m*
2 *vt (balance)* tenir en équilibre • **poised**
adj (composed) calme; *(hanging)* suspendu; *(balanced)* en équilibre; **to be p.
to do sth** *(ready)* être prêt à faire qch

poison ['pɔɪzən] **1** *n* poison *m*; *(of snake)*
venin *m*; **p. gas** gaz *m* toxique
2 *vt* empoisonner; **to p. sb's mind** corrompre qn • **poisoning** *n* empoisonnement *m* • **poisonous** *adj (fumes,
substance)* toxique; *(snake)* venimeux,
-euse; *(plant)* vénéneux, -euse

poke [pəʊk] **1** *n* petit coup *m*
2 *vt (person)* donner un coup à; *(object)*
tâter; *(fire)* attiser; **to p. sth into sth**
enfoncer qch dans qch; **to p. sb in the
eye** mettre le doigt dans l'œil à qn; **to p.
one's finger at sb** pointer son doigt vers
qn; *Fig* **to p. one's nose into sth** mettre
son nez dans qch; **to p. a hole in sth** faire
un trou dans qch; **to p. one's head out of
the window** passer la tête par la fenêtre;
to p. sb's eye out crever l'œil à qn
3 *vi* **to p. at sth** *(with finger, stick)* tâter
qch; **to p. about** *or* **around in sth** fouiner
dans qch

poker¹ ['pəʊkə(r)] *n (for fire)* tisonnier *m*
poker² ['pəʊkə(r)] *n Cards* poker *m*

poky ['pəʊkɪ] (**-ier, -iest**) *adj Br (small)
(house, room)* riquiqui *inv;Am (slow)* lent

Poland ['pəʊlənd] *n* la Pologne • **Pole** *n*
Polonais, -aise *mf* • **Polish** ['pəʊlɪʃ] **1** *adj*
polonais **2** *n (language)* polonais *m*

polarize ['pəʊləraɪz] *vt (opinion, country)*
diviser

Polaroid® ['pəʊlərɔɪd] *n (camera, photo)*
Polaroid® *m*

pole¹ [pəʊl] *n (rod)* perche *f*; *(fixed)* poteau *m*; *(for flag)* hampe *f*; *Sport* **p. vault-
(ing)** saut *m* à la perche

pole² [pəʊl] *n Geog* pôle *m*; **North/South
P.** pôle Nord/Sud • **polar** *adj* polaire; **p.
bear** ours *m* blanc; **the P. Star** l'étoile *f*
polaire

polemic [pə'lemɪk] *n* polémique *f* • **polemical** *adj* polémique

police [pə'liːs] **1** *n* police *f*; **a hundred p.**
cent policiers *mpl*
2 *adj (inquiry, dog, State)* policier, -ière;
(protection, intervention) de la police; *Br*
p. cadet agent *m* de police stagiaire; **p.
car** voiture *f* de police; *Am* **p. chief, chief
of p.** commissaire *m* de police; *Am* **the p.
department** service *m* de police; **p. force**
police; **p. station** poste *m* de police; *Br* **p.
van** fourgon *m* cellulaire
3 *vt (city, area)* maintenir l'ordre dans;
(frontier) contrôler • **policeman** (*pl* **-men**)
n agent *m* de police • **policewoman** (*pl*
-women) *n* femme *f* agent de police

policy ['pɒlɪsɪ] (*pl* **-ies**) *n* (**a**) *(of government, organization)* politique *f*; **it's a matter of p.** c'est une question de principe
(**b**) **(insurance) p.** police *f* (d'assurance);
p. holder assuré, -ée *mf*

polio ['pəʊlɪəʊ] *n* polio *f*; **p. victim** polio
mf

polish ['pɒlɪʃ] **1** *n (for shoes)* cirage *m*;
(for floor, furniture) cire *f*; *(for nails)* vernis
m; *Fig* raffinement *m*; **to give sth a p.** faire
briller qch
2 *vt (floor, table, shoes)* cirer; *(metal)*
astiquer; *(rough surface)* polir; *Fig (manners)* raffiner; *(style)* polir; *Fam* **to p.
off** *(food)* avaler; *(drink)* descendre;
(work) expédier; **to p. up one's French**
travailler son français

polite [pə'laɪt] (**-er, -est**) *adj* poli (**to** *or*
with avec); **in p. society** chez les gens
bien • **politely** *adv* poliment • **politeness**
n politesse *f*

politic ['pɒlɪtɪk] *adj Formal (wise)* sage

political [pə'lɪtɪkəl] *adj* politique; **p. asylum** asile *m* politique • **politically** *adv*
politiquement; **p. correct** politiquement
correct • **politicize** *vt* politiser

politician [pɒlɪ'tɪʃən] *n* homme *m*/femme *f* politique
politics ['pɒlɪtɪks] *n* politique *f*; **office p.** intrigues *fpl* de bureau
polka [*Br* 'pɒlkə, *Am* 'pəʊlkə] *n* polka *f*; **p. dot** pois *m*
poll [pəʊl] **1** *n* (*voting*) scrutin *m*; **to go to the polls** aller aux urnes; (*opinion*) **p.** sondage *m* (d'opinion)
　2 *vt* (*votes*) obtenir; (*people*) sonder
● **polling** *n* (*election*) élections *fpl*; **p. booth** isoloir *m*; *Br* **p. station**, *Am* **p. place** bureau *m* de vote
pollen ['pɒlən] *n* pollen *m*
pollute [pə'luːt] *vt* polluer ● **pollutant** *n* polluant *m* ● **pollution** *n* pollution *f*; **noise p.** pollution sonore
polo ['pəʊləʊ] *n Sport* polo *m*; **p. neck** (*sweater, neckline*) col *m* roulé
polyester [pɒlɪ'estə(r)] *n* polyester *m*; **p. shirt** chemise *f* en polyester
Polynesia [pɒlɪ'niːʒə] *n* la Polynésie
polyp ['pɒlɪp] *n Med* polype *m*
polystyrene [pɒlɪ'staɪriːn] *n* polystyrène *m*
polytechnic [pɒlɪ'teknɪk] *n Br* établissement *m* d'enseignement supérieur

> ⏣ Note that the French word **Polytechnique** is a false friend and is never a translation for the English word **polytechnic**. It is the name of one of the *grandes écoles*.

polythene ['pɒlɪθiːn] *n Br* polyéthylène *m*; **p. bag** sac *m* en plastique
polyunsaturated [pɒlɪʌn'sætʃʊreɪtɪd] *adj* polyinsaturé
pomegranate ['pɒmɪgrænɪt] *n* (*fruit*) grenade *f*
pomp [pɒmp] *n* pompe *f*
pompom ['pɒmpɒm] *n* pompon *m*
pompous ['pɒmpəs] *adj* pompeux, -euse ● **pomposity** [-'pɒsɪtɪ] *n* suffisance *f*
poncho ['pɒntʃəʊ] (*pl* -**os**) *n* poncho *m*
pond [pɒnd] *n* étang *m*; (*smaller*) mare *f*; (*artificial*) bassin *m*
ponder ['pɒndə(r)] **1** *vt* réfléchir à
　2 *vi* **to p.** (**over sth**) réfléchir (à qch)
ponderous ['pɒndərəs] *adj* (*movement, person*) lourd; (*progress*) laborieux, -ieuse
pong [pɒŋ] *Br Fam* **1** *n* (*smell*) puanteur *f*
　2 *vi* puer
pontificate [pɒn'tɪfɪkeɪt] *vi* pontifier (**about** sur)
pony ['pəʊnɪ] (*pl* -**ies**) *n* poney *m* ● **ponytail** *n* queue *f* de cheval
poo [puː] *n Fam* caca *m*
poodle ['puːdəl] *n* caniche *m*

poof [pʊf] *n Br very Fam Pej* pédé *m*, = terme injurieux désignant un homosexuel
pooh [puː] *exclam* bah!
pooh-pooh ['puː'puː] *vt* dédaigner
pool¹ [puːl] *n* (*puddle*) flaque *f*; (*of blood*) mare *f*; (*pond*) étang *m*; (*for swimming*) piscine *f*
pool² [puːl] **1** *n* (*of money, helpers*) réserve *f*; (*of typists*) pool *m*; *Br* **the (football) pools** = concours de pronostics des matchs de football
　2 *vt* (*share*) mettre en commun
pool³ [puːl] *n* (*game*) billard *m* américain
pooped [puːpt] *adj Am Fam* vanné
poor [pʊə(r)] **1** (-**er**, -**est**) *adj* (*not rich*) pauvre; (*bad*) mauvais; (*chances*) maigre; (*harvest, reward*) faible; **to be in p. health** ne pas bien se porter; **p. thing!** le/la pauvre!
　2 *npl* **the p.** les pauvres *mpl* ● **poorly 1** *adv* mal; (*clothed, furnished*) pauvrement
　2 *adj Br Fam* malade
pop¹ [pɒp] **1** *exclam* pan!
　2 *n* (*noise*) bruit *m* sec; **to go p.** faire pan
　3 (*pt & pp* -**pp**-) *vt* (**a**) (*balloon*) crever; (*cork, button*) faire sauter (**b**) *Fam* (*put*) mettre
　4 *vi* (**a**) (*burst*) éclater; (*of cork*) sauter; (*of ears*) se déboucher (**b**) *Br Fam* **to p. in** passer; **to p. off** partir; **to p. out** sortir (un instant); **to p. over** *or* **round** (**to sb's house**) faire un saut (chez qn); **to p. up** surgir
pop² [pɒp] **1** *n* (*music*) pop *f*
　2 *adj* (*concert, singer, group*) pop *inv*; **p. art** pop art *m*
pop³ [pɒp] *n Am Fam* (*father*) papa *m*
pop⁴ [pɒp] *n Am* (**soda**) **p.** (*drink*) soda *m*
popcorn ['pɒpkɔːn] *n* pop-corn *m*
pope [pəʊp] *n* pape *m*
pop-eyed [pɒp'aɪd] *adj* aux yeux écarquillés
poplar ['pɒplə(r)] *n* (*tree, wood*) peuplier *m*
popper ['pɒpə(r)] *n Br* (*fastener*) pression *f*
poppy ['pɒpɪ] (*pl* -**ies**) *n* (*red, wild*) coquelicot *m*; (*cultivated*) pavot *m*
Popsicle® ['pɒpsɪkəl] *n Am* (*ice lolly*) ≃ Esquimau® *m*
popular ['pɒpjʊlə(r)] *adj* populaire; (*fashionable*) à la mode; (*restaurant*) qui a beaucoup de succès; **to be p. with** plaire beaucoup à ● **popularity** [-'lærɪtɪ] *n* popularité *f* (**with** auprès de) ● **popularize** *vt* populariser; (*science, knowledge*) vulgariser ● **popularly** *adv* communément

populate ['pɒpjʊleɪt] *vt* peupler; **highly/ sparsely populated** très/peu peuplé; **populated by** *or* **with** peuplé de

population [pɒpjʊ'leɪʃən] *n* population *f*

populous ['pɒpjʊləs] *adj* populeux, -euse

pop-up book ['pɒpʌpbʊk] *n* livre *m* en relief

porcelain ['pɔːsəlɪn] *n* porcelaine *f*

porch [pɔːtʃ] *n* porche *m*; *Am (veranda)* véranda *f*

porcupine ['pɔːkjʊpaɪn] *n* porc-épic *m*

pore [pɔː(r)] **1** *n (of skin)* pore *m*
2 *vi* **to p. over sth** *(book, question)* étudier qch de près • **porous** *adj* poreux, -euse

pork [pɔːk] *n (meat)* porc *m*; **p. pie** ≃ pâté *m* en croûte

pornography [pɔː'nɒgrəfɪ] *n* pornographie *f* • **pornographic** [-nə'græfɪk] *adj* pornographique

porpoise ['pɔːpəs] *n* marsouin *m*

porridge ['pɒrɪdʒ] *n* porridge *m*; **p. oats** flocons *mpl* d'avoine

port¹ [pɔːt] **1** *n (harbour)* port *m*; **p. of call** escale *f*
2 *adj (authorities, installations)* portuaire

port² [pɔːt] *n Naut (left-hand side)* bâbord *m*

port³ [pɔːt] *n (wine)* porto *m*

portable ['pɔːtəbəl] *adj* portable

portal ['pɔːtəl] *n Literary & Comptr* portail *m*

porter ['pɔːtə(r)] *n (for luggage)* porteur *m*; *(door attendant)* chasseur *m*; *(in hospital)* brancardier *m*

portfolio [pɔːt'fəʊlɪəʊ] *(pl* -os*) n (for documents)* porte-documents *m inv*; *(of shares, government minister)* portefeuille *m*

porthole ['pɔːthəʊl] *n* hublot *m*

portion ['pɔːʃən] **1** *n* partie *f*; *(share, helping)* portion *f*
2 *vt* **to p. sth out** partager qch

portly ['pɔːtlɪ] *(-ier, -iest) adj* corpulent

portrait ['pɔːtreɪt, 'pɔːtrɪt] *n* portrait *m*; **p. painter** portraitiste *mf*

portray [pɔː'treɪ] *vt (describe)* dépeindre; *(of actor)* interpréter • **portrayal** *n (description)* tableau *m*; *(by actor)* interprétation *f*

Portugal ['pɔːtjʊgəl] *n* le Portugal • **Portuguese** [-'giːz] **1** *adj* portugais **2** *n (person)* Portugais, -aise *mf*; *(language)* portugais *m*; **the P.** *(people)* les Portugais

pose [pəʊz] **1** *n (position)* pose *f*
2 *vt (question)* poser; *(threat)* représenter

3 *vi* poser (**for** pour); **to p. as a lawyer** se faire passer pour un avocat • **poser** *n Fam (person)* poseur, -euse *mf*; *(question)* colle *f* • **poseur** [-'zɜː(r)] *n (show-off)* poseur, -euse *mf*

posh [pɒʃ] *adj Fam (smart)* chic *inv*; *(snobbish)* snob *(f inv)*

position [pə'zɪʃən] **1** *n (place, posture, opinion)* position *f*; *(of building, town)* emplacement *m*; *(job, circumstances)* situation *f*; *(window in bank)* guichet *m*; **in a p. to do sth** en mesure de faire qch; **in a good p. to do sth** bien placé pour faire qch; **in p.** en place
2 *vt (put)* placer; *(troops)* poster

positive ['pɒzɪtɪv] *adj (person, answer, test)* positif, -ive; *(progress, change)* réel *(f* réelle); *(evidence)* formel, -elle; *(tone)* assuré; *(certain)* sûr, certain (**of** de; **that** que); *Fam* **a p. genius** un véritable génie • **positively** *adv (identify)* formellement; *(think, react)* de façon positive; *(for emphasis)* véritablement; **to reply p.** *(saying yes)* répondre par l'affirmative

possess [pə'zes] *vt* posséder • **possession** *n (ownership)* possession *f*; *(thing possessed)* bien *m*; **to be in p. of sth** être en possession de qch; **to take p. of sth** prendre possession de qch • **possessor** *n* possesseur *m*

possessive [pə'zesɪv] **1** *adj* possessif, -ive
2 *adj & n Grammar* possessif *(m)*

possibility [pɒsɪ'bɪlɪtɪ] *(pl* -ies*) n* possibilité *f*; **there is some p. of...** il y a quelques chances de...; **it's a distinct p.** c'est bien possible

possible ['pɒsəbəl] **1** *adj* possible; **it is p. (for us) to do it** il (nous) est possible de le faire; **it is p. that...** il est possible que... *(+ subjunctive)*; **as soon as p.** dès que possible; **as much/as many as p.** autant que possible; **if p.** si possible
2 *n Fam (person)* candidat *m* possible; *(thing)* option *f*

possibly ['pɒsɪblɪ] *adv* **(a)** *(perhaps)* peut-être **(b)** *(for emphasis)* **to do all one p. can** faire tout son possible (**to do** pour faire); **if you p. can** si cela t'est possible; **he cannot p. stay** il ne peut absolument pas rester

post¹ [pəʊst] **1** *n Br (postal system)* poste *f*; *(letters)* courrier *m*; **by p.** par la poste; **to catch/miss the p.** avoir/manquer la levée; **p. office** (bureau *m* de) poste; **the P. Office** *(government department)* ≃ la Poste
2 *vt (letter)* poster; **to keep sb posted**

tenir qn au courant •**postbag** *n Br* sac *m* postal •**postbox** *n Br* boîte *f* aux lettres •**postcard** *n* carte *f* postale •**postcode** *n Br* code *m* postal •**postman** (*pl* **-men**) *n Br* facteur *m* •**postmark 1** *n* cachet *m* de la poste **2** *vt* oblitérer •**postmaster** *n Br* receveur *m* des postes •**postmistress** *n Br* receveuse *f* des postes

post² [pəʊst] **1** *n (job, place)* poste *m* **2** *vt (sentry, guard)* poster; *Br (employee)* affecter (**to** à)

post³ [pəʊst] **1** *n (pole)* poteau *m*; *(of door, bed)* montant *m*; **finishing** *or* **winning p.** *(in race)* poteau *m* d'arrivée
 2 *vt* to **p. (up)** *(notice)* afficher

post- [pəʊst] *pref* post-; **post-1800** après 1800

postage ['pəʊstɪdʒ] *n* affranchissement *m* (**to** pour); **p. paid** port *m* payé; **p. stamp** timbre-poste *m*

postal ['pəʊstəl] *adj (services)* postal; *(inquiries)* par la poste; *(vote)* par correspondance; **p. district** secteur *m* postal; *Br* **p. order** mandat *m* postal; **p. worker** employé, -ée *mf* des postes

postdate [pəʊst'deɪt] *vt* postdater

poster ['pəʊstə(r)] *n* affiche *f*; *(for decoration)* poster *m*

posterior [pɒ'stɪərɪə(r)] *n Hum (buttocks)* postérieur *m*

posterity [pɒ'sterɪtɪ] *n* postérité *f*

postgraduate [pəʊst'grædjʊət] **1** *adj* de troisième cycle
 2 *n* étudiant, -iante *mf* de troisième cycle

posthumous ['pɒstjʊməs] *adj* posthume; **to receive a p. award** recevoir un prix à titre posthume •**posthumously** *adv* à titre posthume

postmortem [pəʊst'mɔːtəm] *adj & n* **p. (examination)** autopsie *f* (**on** de)

postnatal ['pəʊstneɪtəl] *adj* postnatal (*mpl* -als)

postpone [pəʊs'pəʊn] *vt* reporter •**postponement** *n* report *m*

postscript ['pəʊstskrɪpt] *n* post-scriptum *m inv*

postulate ['pɒstjʊleɪt] *vt* poser comme hypothèse

posture ['pɒstʃə(r)] **1** *n (of body)* posture *f*; *Fig* attitude *f*
 2 *vi Pej* prendre des poses

postwar ['pəʊstwɔː(r)] *adj* d'après-guerre

posy ['pəʊzɪ] (*pl* **-ies**) *n* petit bouquet *m*

pot¹ [pɒt] **1** *n (for tea)* théière *f*; *(for cooking)* casserole *f*; **pots and pans** casseroles *fpl*; **jam p.** pot à confiture; *Fam* **to go to p.** aller à la ruine; *Fam* **gone to p.** *(person, plans)* fichu
 2 (*pt & pp* **-tt-**) *vt* mettre en pot •**pothole** *n (in road)* nid-de-poule *m*; *(cave)* caverne *f* •**potholer** *n Br* spéléologue *mf* •**potholing** *n Br* spéléologie *f* •**pot'luck** *n* **to take p.** prendre ce que l'on trouve

pot² [pɒt] *n Fam (drug)* hasch *m*

potassium [pə'tæsɪəm] *n* potassium *m*

potato [pə'teɪtəʊ] (*pl* **-oes**) *n* pomme *f* de terre; *Br* **p. crisps**, *Am* **p. chips** chips *fpl*

potbelly ['pɒtbelɪ] (*pl* **-ies**) *n* bedaine *f* •'pot'bellied *adj* bedonnant

potent ['pəʊtənt] *adj* puissant; *(drink)* fort •**potency** *n* puissance *f*; *(of man)* virilité *f*

potential [pə'tenʃəl] **1** *adj* potentiel, -ielle
 2 *n* potentiel *m*; **to have p.** avoir du potentiel •**potentiality** [-ʃɪ'ælɪtɪ] (*pl* **-ies**) *n* potentialité *f*; **to have potentialities** offrir de nombreuses possibilités •**potentially** *adv* potentiellement

potion ['pəʊʃən] *n* potion *f*

potted ['pɒtɪd] *adj* (**a**) *(plant)* en pot; *(food)* en terrine (**b**) *Br (version)* abrégé

potter ['pɒtə(r)] **1** *n (person)* potier, -ière *mf*
 2 *vi Br* to **p. about** *(do odd jobs)* bricoler •**pottery** *n (art)* poterie *f*; *(objects)* poteries *fpl*; **a piece of p.** une poterie

potty¹ ['pɒtɪ] *n (for baby)* pot *m*

potty² ['pɒtɪ] (**-ier, -iest**) *adj Br Fam (mad)* dingue

pouch [paʊtʃ] *n* bourse *f*; *(for tobacco)* blague *f*; *(of kangaroo)* poche *f*

pouf(fe) [puːf] *n* pouf *m*

poultice ['pəʊltɪs] *n* cataplasme *m*

poultry ['pəʊltrɪ] *n* volaille *f* •**poulterer** *n* volailler *m*

pounce [paʊns] *vi (of animal)* bondir (**on** sur); *(of person)* se précipiter (**on** sur)

pound¹ [paʊnd] *n* (**a**) *(weight)* livre *f* (= 453,6 g) (**b**) **p. (sterling)** livre *f* (sterling)

pound² [paʊnd] *n (for cars, dogs)* fourrière *f*

pound³ [paʊnd] **1** *vt (spices, nuts)* piler; *(meat)* attendrir; *(town)* pilonner
 2 *vi (of heart)* battre à tout rompre; **to p. on the door** cogner à la porte

pour [pɔː(r)] **1** *vt* verser; **to p. sb a drink** verser à boire à qn; **to p. money into sth** investir beaucoup d'argent dans qch
 2 *vi* **it's pouring** il pleut à verse
 ▸ **pour down** *vi* **it's pouring down** il pleut à verse ▸ **pour in 1** *vt sep (liquid)* verser **2** *vi (of water, rain, sunshine)* entrer à flots; *Fig (of people, money)* affluer ▸ **pour off**

vt sep (liquid) vider ▶**pour out 1** *vt sep (liquid)* verser; *Fig (anger, grief)* déverser **2** *vi (of liquid)* se déverser; *Fig (of people)* sortir en masse (**from** de); *(of smoke)* s'échapper (**from** de)
pout [paʊt] **1** *n* moue *f*
2 *vi* faire la moue
poverty ['pɒvətɪ] *n* pauvreté *f*; **extreme p.** la misère; **p. line** seuil *m* de pauvreté ●**poverty-stricken** *adj (person)* indigent; *(neighbourhood, conditions)* misérable
powder ['paʊdə(r)] **1** *n* poudre *f*; *Fig* **p. keg** *(dangerous place)* poudrière *f*; **p. puff** houppette *f*; **p. room** toilettes *fpl* pour dames
2 *vt (body, skin)* poudrer; **to p. one's face** *or* **nose** se poudrer ●**powdered** *adj (milk, eggs)* en poudre ●**powdery** *adj (snow)* poudreux, -euse; *(face)* couvert de poudre
power ['paʊə(r)] **1** *n (ability, authority)* pouvoir *m*; *(strength, nation)* puissance *f*; *(energy)* énergie *f*; *(electric current)* courant *m*; **to be in p.** être au pouvoir; **to have sb in one's p.** tenir qn à sa merci; *Math* **three to the p. of ten** trois puissance dix; *Law* **p. of attorney** procuration *f*; **p. of speech** usage *m* de la parole; *Br* **p. failure** *or* **cut** coupure *f* de courant; **p. point** prise *f* de courant; *Br* **p. station,** *Am* **p. plant** centrale *f* électrique; *Aut* **p. steering** direction *f* assistée
2 *vt (provide with power)* actionner; **to be powered by two engines** être propulsé par deux moteurs
powerful ['paʊəfəl] *adj* puissant; *(drug)* fort ●**powerfully** *adv* puissamment ●**powerless** *adj* impuissant (**to do** à faire)
PR [piː'ɑː(r)] *(abbr* **public relations***) n* RP
practicable ['præktɪkəbəl] *adj* réalisable
practical ['præktɪkəl] *adj (tool, knowledge, solution)* pratique; **to be p.** *(of person)* avoir l'esprit pratique; **p. joke** farce *f* ●**practicality** [-'kælɪtɪ] *n (of person)* sens *m* pratique; **practicalities** *(of situation, scheme)* détails *mpl* pratiques
practically ['præktɪkəlɪ] *adv (almost)* pratiquement
practice ['præktɪs] **1** *n (action, exercise, custom)* pratique *f*; *(in sport)* entraînement *m*; *(of profession)* exercice *m* (**of** de); *(surgery)* centre *m* médical; **in p.** *(in reality)* dans la *ou* en pratique; **to put sth into p.** mettre qch en pratique; **to be out of p.** avoir perdu l'habitude; **to make a p. of doing sth** se faire une règle de faire qch; **to be good/bad p.** être conseillé/déconseillé
2 *vti Am* = **practise**

practise ['præktɪs] *(Am* **practice***)* **1** *vt (sport, language, art, religion)* pratiquer; *(medicine, law)* exercer; *(musical instrument)* travailler
2 *vi (of musician)* s'exercer; *(of sportsperson)* s'entraîner; *(of doctor, lawyer)* exercer ●**practised** *adj (experienced)* expérimenté; *(ear, eye)* exercé ●**practising** *adj (doctor, lawyer)* en exercice; *Rel* pratiquant
practitioner [præk'tɪʃənə(r)] *n* praticien, -ienne *mf*; **general p.** (médecin *m*) généraliste *m*
pragmatic [præg'mætɪk] *adj* pragmatique
Prairie ['preərɪ] *n* **the P.** *(in USA)* la Grande Prairie; *(in Canada)* les Prairies *fpl*
praise [preɪz] **1** *n* éloges *mpl*
2 *vt* faire l'éloge de; *(God)* louer; **to p. sb for doing** *or* **having done sth** louer qn d'avoir fait qch ●**praiseworthy** *adj* digne d'éloges
pram [præm] *n Br* landau *m (pl* -aus)
prance [prɑːns] *vi (of horse)* caracoler; *(of person)* sautiller; **to p. in/out** entrer/sortir en sautillant
prank [præŋk] *n* farce *f*
prat [præt] *n Br Fam* andouille *f*
prattle ['prætəl] *vi* papoter (**about** de)
prawn [prɔːn] *n* crevette *f* rose; **p. cracker** beignet *m* de crevette
pray [preɪ] **1** *vt* **to p. that...** prier pour que... *(+ subjunctive)*
2 *vi* prier; **to p. to God** prier Dieu; *Fig* **to p. for good weather** prier pour qu'il fasse beau
prayer [preə(r)] *n* prière *f*
pre- [priː] *pref* **pre-1800** avant 1800
preach [priːtʃ] *vti* prêcher; **to p. to sb** prêcher qn; *Fig* faire la morale à qn; **to p. a sermon** faire un sermon ●**preacher** *n* prédicateur, -trice *mf* ●**preaching** *n* prédication *f*
preamble [priː'æmbəl] *n* préambule *m*
prearrange [priːə'reɪndʒ] *vt* arranger à l'avance
precarious [prɪ'keərɪəs] *adj* précaire
precaution [prɪ'kɔːʃən] *n* précaution *f*; **as a p.** par précaution
precede [prɪ'siːd] *vti* précéder ●**preceding** *adj* précédent
precedence ['presɪdəns] *n (priority)* priorité *f*; *(in rank)* préséance *f*; **to take p. over sb** avoir la préséance sur qn; **to take p. over sth** passer avant qch
precedent ['presɪdənt] *n* précédent *m*; **to create** *or* **set a p.** créer un précédent

precept ['priːsept] *n* précept *m*
precinct ['priːsɪŋkt] *n (of convent, palace)* enceinte *f; (boundary)* limite *f; Br (for shopping)* zone *f* commerçante piétonnière; *Am (electoral district)* circonscription *f; Am (police district)* secteur *m; Am* **p. station** *(police station)* commissariat *m* de quartier
precious ['preʃəs] **1** *adj* précieux, -ieuse; *Ironic* **her p. little bike** son cher petit vélo **2** *adv* **p. little** très peu (de)
precipice ['presɪpɪs] *n* précipice *m*
precipitate [prɪ'sɪpɪteɪt] *vt (hasten, throw) & Chem* précipiter ● **precipi'tation** *n (haste) & Chem* précipitation *f; (rainfall)* précipitations *fpl*
précis ['preɪsiː, *pl* -iːz] *n inv* précis *m*
precise [prɪ'saɪs] *adj (exact)* précis; *(meticulous)* méticuleux, -euse ● **precisely** *adv* précisément; **at three o'clock p.** à trois heures précises ● **precision** [-'sɪʒən] *n* précision *f*
preclude [prɪ'kluːd] *vt (prevent)* empêcher (**from doing** de faire); *(possibility)* exclure
precocious [prɪ'kəʊʃəs] *adj* précoce ● **precociousness** *n* précocité *f*
preconceived [priːkən'siːvd] *adj* préconçu ● **preconception** *n* idée *f* préconçue
precondition [priːkən'dɪʃən] *n* condition *f* préalable
precursor [priː'kɜːsə(r)] *n* précurseur *m*
predate [priː'deɪt] *vt (precede)* précéder; *(put earlier date on)* antidater
predator ['predətə(r)] *n* prédateur *m* ● **predatory** *adj* prédateur, -trice
predecessor ['priːdɪsesə(r)] *n* prédécesseur *m*
predicament [prɪ'dɪkəmənt] *n* situation *f* difficile
predicate ['predɪkət] *n Grammar* prédicat *m*
predict [prɪ'dɪkt] *vt* prédire ● **predictable** *adj* prévisible ● **prediction** *n* prédiction *f*
predispose [priːdɪs'pəʊz] *vt* prédisposer (**to do** à faire) ● **predisposition** [-pə'zɪʃən] *n* prédisposition *f*
predominant [prɪ'dɒmɪnənt] *adj* prédominant ● **predominance** *n* prédominance *f* ● **predominantly** *adv* en majorité
predominate [prɪ'dɒmɪneɪt] *vi* prédominer (**over** sur)
pre-eminent [priː'emɪnənt] *adj* prééminent
pre-empt [priː'empt] *vt* devancer
preen [priːn] *vt* **to p. itself** *(of bird)* se lisser les plumes; **to p. oneself** *(of person)* se faire beau *(f* belle)

prefab ['priːfæb] *n Br Fam* maison *f* préfabriquée ● **pre'fabricate** *vt* préfabriquer
preface ['prefɪs] **1** *n (of book)* préface *f* **2** *vt* commencer (**with** par)
prefect ['priːfekt] *n Br Sch* = élève chargé de la surveillance
prefer [prɪ'fɜː(r)] *(pt & pp* **-rr-**) *vt* préférer (**to** à); **to p. to do sth** préférer faire qch; *Law* **to p. charges** porter plainte
preferable ['prefərəbəl] *adj* préférable (**to** à) ● **preferably** *adv* de préférence
preference ['prefərəns] *n* préférence *f* (**for** pour); **in p. to** plutôt que ● **preferential** [-'renʃəl] *adj (terms, price)* préférentiel, -ielle; **p. treatment** traitement *m* de faveur
prefix ['priːfɪks] *n Grammar* préfixe *m*
pregnant ['pregnənt] *adj (woman)* enceinte; *(animal)* pleine; **five months p.** enceinte de cinq mois ● **pregnancy** *(pl* **-ies)** *n* grossesse *f;* **p. test** test *m* de grossesse
prehistoric [priːhɪ'stɒrɪk] *adj* préhistorique
prejudge [priː'dʒʌdʒ] *vt (question)* préjuger de; *(person)* juger sans connaître
prejudice ['predʒədɪs] **1** *n (bias)* préjugé *m; Law* **without p. to** sans préjudice de **2** *vt (bias)* prévenir (**against/in favour of** contre/en faveur de); *(harm)* nuire à ● **prejudiced** *adj (idea)* partial; **to be p.** avoir des préjugés (**against/in favour of** contre/en faveur de) ● **preju'dicial** *adj Law* préjudiciable (**to** à)
preliminary [prɪ'lɪmɪnərɪ] *adj* préliminaire ● **preliminaries** *npl* préliminaires *mpl*
prelude ['preljuːd] *n* prélude *m* (**to** à)
premarital [priː'mærɪtəl] *adj* avant le mariage
premature [*Br* 'premətʃʊə(r), *Am* priːmə-'tʃʊər] *adj* prématuré ● **prematurely** *adv* prématurément
premeditate [priː'medɪteɪt] *vt* préméditer ● **premedi'tation** *n* préméditation *f*
premier [*Br* 'premɪə(r), *Am* prɪ'mɪər] **1** *adj* premier, -ière **2** *n* Premier ministre *m*
première [*Br* 'premɪeə(r), *Am* prɪ'mɪər] *n (of play, film)* première *f*
premise ['premɪs] *n Phil* prémisse *f*
premises ['premɪsɪz] *npl* locaux *mpl;* **on the p.** sur place; **off the p.** en dehors de l'établissement
premium ['priːmɪəm] *n Fin (for insurance)* prime *f; (additional sum)* supplément *m;* **at a p.** au prix fort; *Br* **p. bonds** ≈ obligations *fpl* à lots

premonition [*Br* premə'nɪʃən, *Am* priːmə'nɪʃən] *n* prémonition *f*

prenatal [priː'neɪtəl] *adj Am* prénatal

preoccupy [priː'ɒkjʊpaɪ] (*pt & pp* **-ied**) *vt* préoccuper au plus haut point; **to be preoccupied** être préoccupé (**with** par) • **preoccu'pation** *n* préoccupation *f* (**with** pour); **to have a p. with sth** être préoccupé par qch

prep [prep] **1** *adj* **p. school** *Br* école *f* primaire privée; *Am* école secondaire privée

2 *n* (*homework*) devoirs *mpl*

pre-packed [priː'pækt] *adj* (*meat, vegetables*) préemballé

prepaid [priː'peɪd] *adj* prépayé

preparation [prepə'reɪʃən] *n* préparation *f*; **preparations** préparatifs *mpl* (**for** de)

preparatory [prə'pærətərɪ] *adj* préparatoire; **p. school** *Br* école *f* primaire privée; *Am* école secondaire privée

prepare [prɪ'peə(r)] **1** *vt* préparer (**sth for** qch pour; **sb for** qn à)

2 *vi* se préparer pour; **to p. to do sth** se préparer à faire qch • **prepared** *adj* (*made in advance*) préparé à l'avance; (*ready*) prêt (**to do** à faire); **to be p. for sth** s'attendre à qch

preposition [prepə'zɪʃən] *n* préposition *f*

prepossessing [priːpə'zesɪŋ] *adj* avenant

preposterous [prɪ'pɒstərəs] *adj* ridicule

prerecorded [priːrɪ'kɔːdɪd] *adj* préenregistré

prerequisite [priː'rekwɪzɪt] *n* (condition *f*) préalable *m*

prerogative [prɪ'rɒgətɪv] *n* prérogative *f*

Presbyterian [prezbɪ'tɪərɪən] *adj & n Rel* presbytérien, -ienne (*mf*)

preschool ['priːskuːl] *adj* préscolaire

prescribe [prɪ'skraɪb] *vt* (*of doctor*) prescrire • **prescribed** *adj* (*textbook*) (inscrit) au programme • **prescription** *n* (*for medicine*) ordonnance *f*; (*order*) prescription *f*; **on p.** sur ordonnance; **p. charge** = prix payé sur un médicament prescrit sur ordonnance

presence ['prezəns] *n* présence *f*; **in the p. of** en présence de; **p. of mind** présence d'esprit

present¹ ['prezənt] **1** *adj* (**a**) (*in attendance*) présent (**at** à; **in** dans); **those p.** les personnes présentes (**b**) (*current*) actuel, -uelle; *Grammar* **the p. tense** le présent

2 *n* **the p.** (*time, tense*) le présent; **for the p.** pour l'instant; **at p.** en ce moment • '**present-**'**day** *adj* actuel, -uelle • **presently** *adv* (*soon*) bientôt; *Am* (*now*) actuellement

present² **1** ['prezənt] *n* (*gift*) cadeau *m*

2 [prɪ'zent] *vt* (*show, introduce*) présenter (**to** à); (*concert, film*) donner; (*proof*) fournir; **to p. sb with** (*gift*) offrir à qn; (*prize*) remettre à qn • **presentable** [prɪ'zentəbəl] *adj* (*person, appearance*) présentable • **presenter** [prɪ'zentə(r)] *n* présentateur, -trice *mf*

presentation [prezən'teɪʃən] *n* présentation *f*; (*of prize*) remise *f*

preservation [prezə'veɪʃən] *n* (*of building*) conservation *f*; (*of species*) protection *f*

preservative [prɪ'zɜːvətɪv] *n* conservateur *m*

---

*Note that the French word **préservatif** is a false friend and is never a translation for the English word **preservative**. It means **condom**.*

---

preserve [prɪ'zɜːv] **1** *n* (*jam*) confiture *f*; (*sphere*) domaine *m*

2 *vt* (*keep, maintain*) conserver; (*fruit*) mettre en conserve; **to p. from** (*protect*) préserver de

preside [prɪ'zaɪd] *vi* présider; **to p. over** *or* **at a meeting** présider une réunion

presidency ['prezɪdənsɪ] (*pl* **-ies**) *n* présidence *f*

president ['prezɪdənt] *n* (*of country*) président, -ente *mf* • **presidential** [-'denʃəl] *adj* présidentiel, -ielle

press¹ [pres] *n* (**a**) **the p.** la presse; **p. agency** agence *f* de presse; **p. campaign** campagne *f* de presse; **p. conference** conférence *f* de presse; **p. release** communiqué *m* de presse (**b**) (*machine*) presse *f*; (*for making wine*) pressoir *m*; (*printing*) **p.** presse; **to go to p.** (*of newspaper*) partir à l'impression

press² [pres] **1** *n* pression *f*; **to give sth a p.** repasser qch; **p. stud** bouton-pression *m*

2 *vt* (*button, doorbell*) appuyer sur; (*tube, lemon*) presser; (*hand*) serrer; (*clothes*) repasser; (*pressurize*) faire pression sur; **to p. sb to do sth** presser qn de faire qch; *Law* **to p. charges** engager des poursuites (**against** contre)

3 *vi* (*push*) appuyer (**on** sur); (*of weight*) faire pression (**on** sur) • **pressgang** *vt* **to p. sb into doing sth** forcer qn à faire qch • **press-up** *n* (*exercise*) pompe *f*

▶**press down** *vt insep (button)* appuyer sur ▶**press for** *vt sep (demand)* exiger ▶**press on** *vi (carry on)* continuer; **to p. on with one's work** continuer de travailler

pressed [prest] *adj* **to be hard p.** *(in difficulties)* être en difficultés; *(busy)* être débordé; **to be p. for time** être pressé par le temps

pressing ['presɪŋ] *adj (urgent)* pressant

pressure ['preʃə(r)] **1** *n* pression *f*; **the p. of work** le stress lié au travail; **to be under p.** être stressé; **to put p. on sb (to do sth)** faire pression sur qn (pour qu'il fasse qch); **p. cooker** Cocotte-Minute® *f*; **p. gauge** manomètre *m*; **p. group** groupe *m* de pression

2 *vt* **to p. sb to do sth** *or* **into doing sth** faire pression sur qn pour qu'il fasse qch

pressurize ['preʃəraɪz] *vt (aircraft)* pressuriser; **pressurized cabin** cabine *f* pressurisée; **to p. sb (into doing sth)** faire pression sur qn (pour qu'il fasse qch)

prestige [pre'stiːʒ] *n* prestige *m* •**prestigious** [*Br* pre'stɪdʒəs, *Am* -'stiːdʒəs] *adj* prestigieux, -ieuse

presume [prɪ'zjuːm] *vt (suppose)* présumer (that que); **to p. to do sth** se permettre de faire qch •**presumably** *adv* sans doute; **p. she'll come** je suppose qu'elle viendra •**presumption** [-'zʌmp-ʃən] *n* présomption *f*

presumptuous [prɪ'zʌmptʃʊəs] *adj* présomptueux, -ueuse

presuppose [priːsə'pəʊz] *vt* présupposer (that que)

pretence (*Am* **pretense**) [prɪ'tens] *n (sham)* simulation *f*; *(claim, affectation)* prétention *f*; **to make a p. of sth/of doing sth** feindre qch/de faire qch; **on** *or* **under false pretences** sous des prétextes fallacieux

pretend [prɪ'tend] **1** *vt (make believe)* faire semblant (**to do** de faire); *(claim, maintain)* prétendre (**to do** faire; **that** que)

2 *vi* faire semblant; **to p. to sth** prétendre à qch

pretense [prɪ'tens] *n Am* = **pretence**

pretension [prɪ'tenʃən] *n* prétention *f*

pretentious [prɪ'tenʃəs] *adj* prétentieux, -euse

pretext ['priːtekst] *n* prétexte *m*; **on the p. of/that** sous prétexte de/que

pretty ['prɪtɪ] **1** (-ier, -iest) *adj* joli

2 *adv Fam (rather, quite)* assez; **p. well, p. much, p. nearly** *(almost)* pratiquement

prevail [prɪ'veɪl] *vi (predominate)* prédo-

miner; *(be successful)* l'emporter (**over** sur); **to p. (up)on sb to do sth** persuader qn de faire qch •**prevailing** *adj* prédominant; *(wind)* dominant

prevalent ['prevələnt] *adj* très répandu •**prevalence** *n (predominance)* prédominance *f*; *(frequency)* fréquence *f*

prevaricate [prɪ'værɪkeɪt] *vi* tergiverser

prevent [prɪ'vent] *vt* empêcher (**from doing** de faire) •**preventable** *adj* évitable •**prevention** *n* prévention *f* •**preventive** *adj* préventif, -ive

preview ['priːvjuː] *n (of film, painting)* avant-première *f*; *Fig (overall view)* aperçu *m*

previous ['priːvɪəs] **1** *adj* précédent; **to have p. experience** avoir une expérience préalable; **to have a p. engagement** être déjà pris

2 *adv* **p. to** avant •**previously** *adv* auparavant

prewar ['priː'wɔː(r)] *adj* d'avant-guerre

prey [preɪ] **1** *n* proie *f*; *Fig* **to be (a) p. to** être en proie à

2 *vi* **to p. on** *(person)* prendre pour cible; *(fears, doubts)* exploiter; **to p. on sb's mind** tourmenter qn

price [praɪs] **1** *n* prix *m*; **to pay a high p. for sth** payer cher qch; *Fig* payer chèrement qch; **he wouldn't do it at any p.** il ne le ferait à aucun prix

2 *adj (control, war, rise)* des prix; **p. list** tarif *m*

3 *vt* mettre un prix à; **it's priced at £5** ça coûte 5 livres

priceless ['praɪsləs] *adj (invaluable)* qui n'a pas de prix; *Fam (funny)* impayable

pricey ['praɪsɪ] (-ier, -iest) *adj Fam* cher (*f* chère)

prick [prɪk] **1** *n (of needle)* piqûre *f*

2 *vt (jab)* piquer (**with** avec); *(burst)* crever; **to p. up one's ears** *(of animal)* dresser les oreilles; *(of person)* tendre l'oreille

prickle ['prɪkəl] *n (of animal)* piquant *m*; *(of plant)* épine *f* •**prickly** (-ier, -iest) *adj (plant)* à épines; *(animal)* couvert de piquants; *(beard)* piquant; *Fig (subject)* épineux, -euse; *Fig (person)* susceptible

pride [praɪd] **1** *n (satisfaction)* fierté *f*; *(self-esteem)* amour-propre *m*; *Pej (vanity)* orgueil *m*; **to take p. in sth** mettre toute sa fierté dans qch; **to take p. in doing sth** mettre toute sa fierté à faire qch; **to be sb's p. and joy** faire le bonheur de qn; **to have p. of place** trôner

2 *vt* **to p. oneself on sth/on doing sth** s'enorgueillir de qch/de faire qch

priest [priːst] *n* prêtre *m* • **priesthood** *n* prêtrise *f*; **to enter the p.** entrer dans les ordres • **priestly** *adj* sacerdotal

prig [prɪg] *n* prêcheur, -euse *mf* • **priggish** *adj* prêcheur, -euse

prim [prɪm] (**primmer, primmest**) *adj* **p. (and proper)** *(person, expression)* collet monté *inv*; *(manner)* guindé

primacy ['praɪməsɪ] *n* primauté *f*

primarily [*Br* 'praɪmərəlɪ, *Am* praɪ'merəlɪ] *adv* essentiellement

primary ['praɪmərɪ] **1** *adj (main)* principal; *(initial)* primaire; **of p. importance** de première importance; **p. education** enseignement *m* primaire; *Br* **p. school** école *f* primaire
2 (*pl* **-ies**) *n Am (election)* primaire *f*

primate ['praɪmeɪt] *n (animal)* primate *m*

prime [praɪm] **1** *adj (principal)* principal; *(importance)* capital; *(excellent)* excellent; **P. Minister** Premier ministre *m*; *Math* **p. number** nombre *m* premier; **p. quality** de premier choix
2 *n* **in the p. of life** dans la fleur de l'âge
3 *vt (gun, pump)* amorcer; *(surface)* apprêter • **primer** *n* (**a**) *(book)* manuel *m* élémentaire (**b**) *(paint)* apprêt *m*

primeval [praɪ'miːvəl] *adj* primitif, -ive

primitive ['prɪmɪtɪv] *adj (original)* primitif, -ive; *(basic)* de base

primrose ['prɪmrəʊz] *n (plant)* primevère *f*

prince [prɪns] *n* prince *m*; **the P. of Wales** le prince de Galles • **princely** *adj* princier, -ière • **prin'cess** *n* princesse *f*

principal ['prɪnsɪpəl] **1** *adj (main)* principal
2 *n (of school)* proviseur *m*; *(of university)* ≃ président, -ente *mf* • **principally** *adv* principalement

principality [prɪnsɪ'pælətɪ] (*pl* **-ies**) *n* principauté *f*

principle ['prɪnsɪpəl] *n* principe *m*; **in p.** en principe; **on p.** par principe

print [prɪnt] **1** *n (of finger, foot)* empreinte *f*; *(letters)* caractères *mpl*; *(engraving)* estampe *f*; *(photo)* épreuve *f*; *(fabric)* imprimé *m*; **in p.** *(book)* disponible en librairie; **out of p.** *(book)* épuisé
2 *vt (book, newspaper)* imprimer; *(photo)* tirer; *(write)* écrire en script; **to p. 100 copies of a book** tirer un livre à 100 exemplaires; **to have a book printed** publier un livre; *Comptr* **to p. out** imprimer • **printed** *adj* imprimé; **p. matter** imprimés *mpl* • **printing** *n (technique, industry)* imprimerie *f*; *(action)* tirage *m*; **p. error** faute *f* d'impression • **printout** *n Comptr* sortie *f* papier

printer ['prɪntə(r)] *n (person)* imprimeur *m*; *(machine)* imprimante *f*

prior ['praɪə(r)] **1** *adj* antérieur; *(experience)* préalable
2 *adv* **p. to sth** avant qch; **p. to doing sth** avant de faire qch

priority [praɪ'ɒrɪtɪ] (*pl* **-ies**) *n* priorité *f* (**over** sur)

priory ['praɪərɪ] (*pl* **-ies**) *n Rel* prieuré *m*

prise [praɪz] *vt Br* **to p. sth off/open** retirer/ouvrir qch en forçant

prism ['prɪzəm] *n* prisme *m*

prison ['prɪzən] **1** *n* prison *f*; **in p.** en prison
2 *adj (life, system)* pénitentiaire; *(camp)* de prisonniers; **p. officer** gardien, -ienne *mf* de prison • **prisoner** *n* prisonnier, -ière *mf*; **to take sb p.** faire qn prisonnier; **p. of war** prisonnier de guerre

prissy ['prɪsɪ] (**-ier, -iest**) *adj Fam* collet monté *inv*

pristine ['prɪstiːn] *adj (immaculate)* impeccable; **in p. condition** en parfait état

privacy ['praɪvəsɪ, *Br* 'prɪvəsɪ] *n* intimité *f*; **to give sb some p.** laisser qn seul

private ['praɪvɪt] **1** *adj* privé; *(lesson, car)* particulier, -ière; *(report, letter)* confidentiel, -ielle; *(personal)* personnel, -elle; *(dinner, wedding)* intime; **a p. citizen** un simple particulier; **p. detective, p. investigator, p. eye** détective *m* privé; *Fam* **p. parts** parties *fpl* (génitales); **p. property** propriété *f* privée; **p. secretary** secrétaire *m* particulier, secrétaire *f* particulière; **p. tutor** professeur *m* particulier; **to be a very p. person** aimer la solitude
2 *n* (**a**) **in p.** *(not publicly)* en privé; *(have dinner, get married)* dans l'intimité (**b**) *(soldier)* simple soldat *m*

privately ['praɪvɪtlɪ] *adv (in private)* en privé; *(in one's heart of hearts)* en son for intérieur; *(personally)* à titre personnel; **p. owned** *(company)* privé; *(hotel)* familial; **to be p. educated** faire sa scolarité dans le privé; **to be treated p.** ≃ se faire soigner par un médecin non conventionné

privatize ['praɪvətaɪz] *vt* privatiser • **privati'zation** *n* privatisation *f*

privet ['prɪvɪt] *n* troène *m*

privilege ['prɪvɪlɪdʒ] *n* privilège *m* • **privileged** *adj* privilégié; **to be p. to do sth** avoir le privilège de faire qch

privy ['prɪvɪ] *adj Formal* **to be p. to sth** avoir connaissance de qch

prize[1] [praɪz] *n* prix *m*; *(in lottery)* lot *m*; **the first p.** *(in lottery)* le gros lot • **prize-giving** *n* distribution *f* des prix • **prize-**

winner *n (in contest)* lauréat, -éate *mf*; *(in lottery)* gagnant, -ante *mf* • **prizewinning** *adj (essay, animal)* primé; *(ticket)* gagnant

prize² [praɪz] *vt (value)* attacher de la valeur à; **my most prized possession** mon bien le plus précieux

prize³ [praɪz] *vt Br* = **prise**

pro [prəʊ] *(pl* **pros***) n Fam (professional)* pro *mf*

proactive [prəʊ'æktɪv] *adj* qui fait preuve d'initiative

probable ['prɒbəbəl] *adj* probable (**that** que) • **proba'bility** *(pl* **-ies***) n* probabilité *f*; **in all p.** selon toute probabilité • **probably** *adv* probablement

probation [prə'beɪʃən] *n* **on p.** *(criminal)* en liberté surveillée; *(in job)* en période d'essai; **p. officer** agent *m* de probation • **probationary** *adj (in job)* d'essai; *(of criminal)* de liberté surveillée

probe [prəʊb] **1** *n (device)* sonde *f*; *(inquiry)* enquête *f* (**into** dans)
2 *vt (prod)* sonder; *(inquire into)* enquêter sur
3 *vi* **to p. into sth** *(past, private life)* fouiller dans qch • **probing** *adj (question)* perspicace

problem ['prɒbləm] *n* problème *m*; **he's got a drug/a drink p.** c'est un drogué/un alcoolique; *Fam* **no p.!** pas de problème!; **p. child** enfant *mf* à problèmes; **p. page** courrier *m* du cœur • **proble'matic** *adj* problématique

procedure [prə'siːdʒə(r)] *n* procédure *f*

proceed [prə'siːd] *vi (go on)* se poursuivre; **to p. to sth** passer à qch; **to p. with sth** poursuivre qch; **to p. to do sth** se mettre à faire qch

proceedings [prə'siːdɪŋz] *npl (events)* opérations *fpl*; *(minutes of meeting)* actes *mpl*; **to take (legal) p.** intenter un procès (**against** contre)

proceeds ['prəʊsiːdz] *npl* recette *f*

process ['prəʊses] **1** *n* processus *m*; *(method)* procédé *m*; **by a p. of elimination** par élimination; **in p.** *(work)* en cours; **in the p. of doing sth** en train de faire qch
2 *vt (food, data)* traiter; *(film)* développer; **processed food** aliments *mpl* conditionnés • **processing** *n* traitement *m*; *(of photo)* développement *m*

procession [prə'seʃən] *n* défilé *m*

processor ['prəʊsesə(r)] *n Comptr* processeur *m*; **food p.** robot *m* de cuisine

proclaim [prə'kleɪm] *vt* proclamer (**that** que); **to p. sb king** proclamer qn roi • **proclamation** [prɒklə'meɪʃən] *n* proclamation *f*

procrastinate [prə'kræstɪneɪt] *vi* atermoyer • **procrasti'nation** *n* atermoiements *mpl*

procreate ['prəʊkrɪeɪt] *vt* procréer • **procre'ation** *n* procréation *f*

procure [prə'kjʊə(r)] *vt* **to p. sth (for oneself)** se procurer qch; **to p. sth for sb** procurer qch à qn

prod [prɒd] **1** *n* petit coup *m*
2 *(pt & pp* **-dd-***) vti (poke)* donner un petit coup (dans); *Fig* **to p. sb into doing sth** pousser qn à faire qch

prodigal ['prɒdɪgəl] *adj* prodigue

prodigious [prə'dɪdʒəs] *adj* prodigieux, -ieuse

prodigy ['prɒdɪdʒɪ] *(pl* **-ies***) n* prodige *m*; **child p.** enfant *mf* prodige

produce¹ [prə'djuːs] *vt (create)* produire; *(machine)* fabriquer; *(passport, ticket)* présenter; *(documents, alibi)* fournir; *(from bag, pocket)* sortir; *(film, play, programme)* produire; *(reaction)* entraîner • **producer** *n* producteur, -trice *mf*

produce² ['prɒdjuːs] *n (products)* produits *mpl*

product ['prɒdʌkt] *n (article, creation) & Math* produit *m*

production [prə'dʌkʃən] *n* production *f*; *(of play)* mise *f* en scène; *Radio* réalisation *f*; **to work on the p. line** travailler à la chaîne

productive [prə'dʌktɪv] *adj* productif, -ive • **productivity** [prɒdʌk'tɪvɪtɪ] *n* productivité *f*

profane [prə'feɪn] **1** *adj (secular)* profane; *(language)* grossier, -ière
2 *vt* profaner

profess [prə'fes] *vt (declare)* professer; **to p. to be** prétendre être • **professed** *adj (self-declared)* avoué

profession [prə'feʃən] *n* profession *f*; **the medical p.** le corps médical; **by p.** de profession • **professional 1** *adj* professionnel, -elle; *(man, woman)* qui exerce une profession libérale; *(army)* de métier; *(diplomat)* de carrière; *(piece of work)* de professionnel **2** *n* professionnel, -elle *mf* • **professionalism** *n* professionnalisme *m* • **professionally** *adv* professionnellement; *(perform, play)* en professionnel

professor [prə'fesə(r)] *n Br* ≃ professeur *m* d'université; *Am* = enseignant d'université

proffer ['prɒfə(r)] *vt Formal (advice)* offrir

proficient [prə'fɪʃənt] *adj* compétent (**in** en) • **proficiency** *n* compétence *f* (**in** en)

profile ['prəʊfaɪl] *n (of person, object)* profil *m; (description)* portrait *m;* **in p.** de profil; *Fig* **to keep a low p.** garder un profil bas • **profiled** *adj* **to be p. against** se profiler sur

profit ['prɒfɪt] **1** *n* profit *m,* bénéfice *m;* **to sell at a p.** vendre à profit; **p. margin** marge *f* bénéficiaire

2 *vi* **to p. by** *or* **from sth** tirer profit de qch • **profit-making** *adj (aiming to make profit)* à but lucratif; *(profitable)* rentable; **non** *or* **not p.** à but non lucratif

profitable ['prɒfɪtəbəl] *adj (commercially)* rentable; *Fig (worthwhile)* profitable • **profita'bility** *n* rentabilité *f* • **profitably** *adv* à profit

profiteer [prɒfɪ'tɪə(r)] *Pej* **1** *n* profiteur, -euse *mf*

2 *vi* profiter d'une situation pour faire des bénéfices

profound [prə'faʊnd] *adj* profond • **profoundly** *adv* profondément • **profundity** [-'fʌndɪtɪ] *(pl* **-ies)** *n* profondeur *f*

profuse [prə'fjuːs] *adj* abondant • **profusely** *adv (bleed)* abondamment; *(flow)* à profusion; *(thank)* avec effusion; **to apologize p.** se confondre en excuses • **profusion** *n* profusion *f;* **in p.** à profusion

progeny ['prɒdʒɪnɪ] *(pl* **-ies)** *n Formal* progéniture *f*

programme ['prəʊɡræm] *(Am* **program**) **1** *n (for play, political party, computer)* programme *m; (on TV, radio)* émission *f*

2 *(pt & pp* **-mm-)** *vt (machine)* programmer • **programmer** *n* **(computer) p.** programmeur, -euse *mf* • **programming** *n* **(computer) p.** programmation *f*

progress 1 ['prəʊɡres] *n* progrès *m;* **to make (good) p.** faire des progrès; **to make p. in sth** progresser dans qch; **in p.** en cours

2 [prə'ɡres] *vi (advance, improve)* progresser; *(of story, meeting)* se dérouler

progression [prə'ɡreʃən] *n* progression *f*

progressive [prə'ɡresɪv] *adj (gradual)* progressif, -ive; *(company, ideas, political party)* progressiste • **progressively** *adv* progressivement

prohibit [prə'hɪbɪt] *vt* interdire (**sb from doing** à qn de faire); **we're prohibited from leaving** il nous est interdit de partir • **prohibition** [prəʊhɪ'bɪʃən] *n* interdiction *f*

prohibitive [prə'hɪbɪtɪv] *adj* prohibitif, -ive

project [prə'dʒekt] **1** ['prɒdʒekt] *n (plan, undertaking)* projet *m; (at school)* dossier *m; Am* **(housing) p.** cité *f* HLM

2 *vt (plan)* prévoir; *(propel, show)* projeter

3 *vi (protrude)* dépasser • **projected** *adj (planned, forecast)* prévu

projection [prə'dʒekʃən] *n* projection *f; (protruding part)* saillie *f* • **projectionist** *n* projectionniste *mf* • **projector** *n* projecteur *m*

proletarian [prəʊlə'teərɪən] **1** *adj (class)* prolétarien, -ienne; *(outlook)* de prolétaire

2 *n* prolétaire *mf* • **proletariat** *n* prolétariat *m*

proliferate [prə'lɪfəreɪt] *vi* proliférer • **prolife'ration** *n* prolifération *f*

prolific [prə'lɪfɪk] *adj* prolifique

prologue ['prəʊlɒɡ] *n* prologue *m* (**to** de)

prolong [prə'lɒŋ] *vt* prolonger

prom [prɒm] *(abbr* **promenade**) *n* (**a**) *Br (at seaside)* promenade *f* (**b**) *Am (dance)* bal *m* d'étudiants • **proms** *npl Br Fam* **the p.** = festival de concerts-promenades

promenade [prɒmə'nɑːd] *n Br (at seaside)* front *m* de mer

prominent ['prɒmɪnənt] *adj (important)* important; *(nose, chin)* proéminent; *(tooth)* en avant; *(peak, landscape)* en saillie; **in a p. position** en évidence • **prominence** *n (importance)* importance *f* • **prominently** *adv* bien en vue

promiscuous [prə'mɪskjʊəs] *adj* qui a de multiples partenaires • **promiscuity** [prɒmɪs'kjuːətɪ] *n* promiscuité *f* sexuelle

promise ['prɒmɪs] **1** *n* promesse *f;* **to show p., to be full of p.** promettre

2 *vt* promettre (**to do** de faire); **to p. sth to sb, to p. sb sth** promettre qch à qn

3 *vi* **I p.!** je te le promets!; **p.?** promis? • **promising** *adj* prometteur, -euse; **that looks p.** ça s'annonce bien

promote [prə'məʊt] *vt (raise in rank, encourage)* promouvoir; *(advertise)* faire la promotion de • **promoter** *n (of theory)* défenseur, -euse *mf; (of boxing match, show)* organisateur, -trice *mf; Com* promoteur *m* • **promotion** *n* promotion *f*

prompt¹ [prɒmpt] **1** *adj (speedy)* rapide; *(punctual)* ponctuel, -uelle; **p. to act** prompt à agir

2 *adv* **at eight o'clock p.** à huit heures précises • **promptly** *adv (rapidly)* rapidement; *(punctually)* ponctuellement; *(immediately)* immédiatement • **promptness** *n* rapidité *f; (readiness to act)* promptitude *f; (punctuality)* ponctualité *f*

prompt² [prɒmpt] **1** *vt* (**a**) *(cause)* provoquer; **to p. sb to do sth** pousser qn à faire qch (**b**) *(actor)* souffler à

2 *n Comptr* invite *f* • **prompter** *n Theatre* souffleur, -euse *mf*

prone [prəʊn] *adj* (**a**) **to be p. to sth** être sujet, -ette à qch; **to be p. to do sth** avoir tendance à faire qch (**b**) *Formal (lying flat)* sur le ventre

prong [prɒŋ] *n (of fork)* dent *f*

pronoun ['prəʊnaʊn] *n Grammar* pronom *m* • **pro'nominal** *adj* pronominal

pronounce [prə'naʊns] **1** *vt (say, articulate)* prononcer; **to p. that...** déclarer que...; **he was pronounced dead** on l'a déclaré mort

2 *vi (articulate)* prononcer; *(give judgement)* se prononcer (**on** sur) • **pronouncement** *n Formal* déclaration *f* • **pronunciation** [-nʌnsɪ'eɪʃən] *n* prononciation *f*

pronto ['prɒntəʊ] *adv Fam* illico

proof [pru:f] **1** *n (evidence)* preuve *f*; *(of book, photo)* épreuve *f*; *(of drink)* teneur *f* en alcool; **to give p. of sth** prouver qch; **p. of identity** pièce *f* d'identité

2 *adj* **to be p. against sth** être résistant à qch • **proofreader** *n* correcteur, -trice *mf*

prop [prɒp] **1** *n (physical support)* support *m*; *Fig (emotional support)* soutien *m*; *Theatre* accessoire *m*

2 *(pt & pp* **-pp-***) vt* **to p. sth (up) against sth** appuyer qch contre qch; **to p. sth up** *(building, tunnel)* étayer qch; *Fig (economy, regime)* soutenir qch

propaganda [prɒpə'gændə] *n* propagande *f*

propagate ['prɒpəgeɪt] **1** *vt* propager **2** *vi* se propager

propel [prə'pel] *(pt & pp* **-ll-***) vt* propulser • **propeller** *n* hélice *f*

propensity [prə'pensɪtɪ] *(pl* **-ies***) n* propension *f* (**for** à)

proper ['prɒpə(r)] *adj* (**a**) *(correct)* vrai; *(word)* correct; **the village p.** le village proprement dit; *Grammar* **p. noun** nom *m* propre (**b**) *(appropriate)* bon (*f* bonne); *(equipment)* adéquat; *(behaviour)* convenable; **in the p. way** comme il faut (**c**) **p. to sb/sth** *(characteristic of)* propre à qn/qch (**d**) *Br (downright)* véritable • **properly** *adv (suitably)* convenablement; *(correctly)* correctement

property ['prɒpətɪ] **1** *(pl* **-ies***) n* (**a**) *(land, house)* propriété *f*; *(possessions)* biens *mpl* (**b**) *(quality)* propriété *f*

2 *adj (market, speculator)* immobilier, -ière; *(tax)* foncier, -ière; **p. developer** promoteur *m* immobilier; **p. owner** propriétaire *m* foncier

prophecy ['prɒfɪsɪ] *(pl* **-ies***) n* prophétie *f*

• **prophesy** [-ɪsaɪ] *(pt & pp* **-ied***) vt* prédire

prophet ['prɒfɪt] *n* prophète *m* • **prophetic** [prə'fetɪk] *adj* prophétique

proportion [prə'pɔ:ʃən] **1** *n (ratio, part)* proportion *f*; **proportions** *(size)* proportions *fpl*; **in p.** proportionné (**to** avec); **out of p.** disproportionné (**to** par rapport à)

2 *vt* proportionner (**to** à); **well** *or* **nicely proportioned** bien proportionné • **proportional, proportionate** *adj* proportionnel, -elle (**to** à); *Pol* **proportional representation** proportionnelle *f*

proposal [prə'pəʊzəl] *n* proposition *f*; *(plan)* projet *m*; *(for marriage)* demande *f* en mariage • **proposition** [prɒpə'zɪʃən] *n* proposition *f*

propose [prə'pəʊz] **1** *vt* proposer; **to p. to do sth, to p. doing sth** *(suggest)* proposer de faire qch; *(intend)* se proposer de faire qch

2 *vi* **to p. to sb** demander qn en mariage

proprietor [prə'praɪətə(r)] *n* propriétaire *mf* • **proprietary** *adj (article, goods)* de marque déposée; **p. name** marque *f* déposée

propriety [prə'praɪətɪ] *n (behaviour)* bienséance *f*; *(of conduct, remark)* justesse *f*; **to observe the proprieties** observer les convenances

> *ℓ* Note that the French word **propriété** is a false friend and is never a translation for the English word **propriety**. It means **property**.

propulsion [prə'pʌlʃən] *n* propulsion *f*

pros [prəʊz] *npl* **the p. and cons** le pour et le contre

prosaic [prəʊ'zeɪɪk] *adj* prosaïque

proscribe [prəʊ'skraɪb] *vt* proscrire

prose [prəʊz] *n* prose *f*; *Br (translation)* thème *m*; **French p. (translation)** thème *m* français

prosecute ['prɒsɪkju:t] *vt Law* poursuivre (en justice) • **prose'cution** *n Law* poursuites *fpl* judiciaires; **the p.** *(lawyers)* ≃ le ministère public • **prosecutor** *n Law* **(public) p.** procureur *m*

prospect¹ ['prɒspekt] *n (expectation, thought)* perspective *f*; *(chance, likelihood)* perspectives *fpl*; *(view)* vue *f*; **(future) prospects** perspectives d'avenir • **prospective** [prə'spektɪv] *adj (potential)* potentiel, -ielle; *(future)* futur

prospect² [prə'spekt] **1** *vt (land)* prospecter

2 *vi* **to p. for gold** chercher de l'or • **prospector** *n* prospecteur, -trice *mf*

prospectus [prə'spektəs] *n (publicity leaflet)* prospectus *m*; *Br (for university)* guide *m* (de l'étudiant)
prosper ['prɒspə(r)] *vi* prospérer ●**prosperity** [-'sperɪtɪ] *n* prospérité *f* ●**prosperous** *adj* prospère
prostate ['prɒsteɪt] *n Anat* **p. (gland)** prostate *f*
prostitute ['prɒstɪtjuːt] **1** *n (woman)* prostituée *f*; **male p.** prostitué *m*
2 *vt* **to p. oneself** se prostituer ●**prostitution** *n* prostitution *f*
prostrate 1 ['prɒstreɪt] *adj (prone)* sur le ventre
2 [prɒ'streɪt] *vt* **to p. oneself** se prosterner (**before** devant)
protagonist [prəʊ'tægənɪst] *n* protagoniste *mf*
protect [prə'tekt] *vt* protéger (**from** *or* **against** de) ●**protection** *n* protection *f* ●**protective** *adj (clothes, screen)* de protection; *(person, attitude)* protecteur, -trice (**to** *or* **towards** envers); *Econ (barrier)* protecteur; **to be too** *or* **over p. towards** *(child)* surprotéger ●**protector** *n* protecteur, -trice *mf*
protein ['prəʊtiːn] *n* protéine *f*
protest 1 ['prəʊtest] *n* protestation *f* (**against** contre); **in p.** en signe de protestation (**at** contre); **under p.** contre son gré; **p. vote** vote *m* de protestation
2 *vt* protester contre; *(one's innocence)* protester de; **to p. that...** protester en disant que...
3 *vi* protester (**against** contre) ●**protester** [prə'testə(r)] *n* contestataire *mf*
Protestant ['prɒtɪstənt] *adj & n* protestant, -ante *(mf)* ●**Protestantism** *n* protestantisme *m*
protocol ['prəʊtəkɒl] *n* protocole *m*
proton ['prəʊtɒn] *n Phys* proton *m*
prototype ['prəʊtəʊtaɪp] *n* prototype *m*
protracted [prə'træktɪd] *adj* prolongé
protractor [prə'træktə(r)] *n* rapporteur *m*
protrude [prə'truːd] *vi* dépasser (**from** de); *(of tooth)* avancer; *(of balcony, cliff)* faire saillie ●**protruding** *adj (chin, veins, eyes)* saillant; *(tooth)* qui avance
proud [praʊd] (**-er, -est**) **1** *adj (person)* fier *(f* fière) (**of** de)
2 *adv* **to do sb p.** faire honneur à qn ●**proudly** *adv* fièrement
prove [pruːv] **1** *vt* prouver (**that** que); **to p. sb wrong** prouver que qn a tort; **to p. oneself** faire ses preuves
2 *vi* **to p. (to be) difficult** s'avérer difficile ●**proven** *adj (method)* éprouvé

proverb ['prɒvɜːb] *n* proverbe *m* ●**proverbial** [prə'vɜːbɪəl] *adj* proverbial
provide [prə'vaɪd] **1** *vt* (**a**) *(supply)* fournir; *(service)* offrir (**to** à); **to p. sb with sth** fournir qch à qn (**b**) *(stipulate)* stipuler
2 *vi* **to p. for sb** *(sb's needs)* pourvoir aux besoins de qn; *(sb's future)* assurer l'avenir de qn; **to p. for sth** *(make allowance for)* prévoir qch ●**provided** *conj* **p. (that)...** pourvu que... (*+ subjunctive*) ●**providing** *conj* **p. (that)...** pourvu que... (*+ subjunctive*)
providence ['prɒvɪdəns] *n* providence *f*
province ['prɒvɪns] *n* province *f*; *Fig (field of knowledge)* domaine *m*; **in the provinces** en province ●**provincial** [prə'vɪnʃəl] *adj & n* provincial, -iale *(mf)*
provision [prə'vɪʒən] *n (clause)* disposition *f*; **the p. of sth** *(supplying)* l'approvisionnement *m* en qch; **the provisions** *(supplies)* les provisions *fpl*; **to make p. for sth** prévoir qch
provisional [prə'vɪʒənəl] *adj* provisoire ●**provisionally** *adv* provisoirement
proviso [prə'vaɪzəʊ] (*pl* **-os**) *n* condition *f*
provocation [prɒvə'keɪʃən] *n* provocation *f*
provocative [prə'vɒkətɪv] *adj* provocateur, -trice
provoke [prə'vəʊk] *vt* provoquer; **to p. sb into doing sth** pousser qn à faire qch ●**provoking** *adj (annoying)* agaçant
prow [praʊ] *n (of ship)* proue *f*
prowess ['praʊes] *n (bravery)* vaillance *f*; *(skill)* talent *m*
prowl [praʊl] **1** *n* **to be on the p.** rôder
2 *vi* **to p. (around)** rôder ●**prowler** *n* rôdeur, -euse *mf*
proximity [prɒk'sɪmɪtɪ] *n* proximité *f*
proxy ['prɒksɪ] (*pl* **-ies**) *n* procuration *f*; **by p.** par procuration
prude [pruːd] *n* prude *f* ●**prudish** *adj* pudibond
prudent ['pruːdənt] *adj* prudent ●**prudence** *n* prudence *f* ●**prudently** *adv* prudemment
prune¹ [pruːn] *n (dried plum)* pruneau *m*
prune² [pruːn] *vt (tree, bush)* tailler; *Fig (article, speech)* élaguer ●**pruning** *n (of tree)* taille *f*; **p. shears** sécateur *m*
pry [praɪ] **1** (*pt & pp* **pried**) *vt Am* **to p. open** forcer (avec un levier)
2 *vi* être indiscret, -ète; **to p. into sth** *(meddle)* mettre son nez dans qch; *(sb's reasons)* chercher à découvrir qch ●**prying** *adj* indiscret, -ète
PS [piː'es] *(abbr* **postscript***) n* PS *m*

psalm [sɑːm] *n* psaume *m*
pseud [sjuːd] *n Br Fam* bêcheur, -euse *mf*
pseudonym ['sjuːdənɪm] *n* pseudonyme *m*
psyche ['saɪkɪ] *n* psychisme *m*
psychiatry [saɪ'kaɪətrɪ] *n* psychiatrie *f* • **psychiatric** [-kɪ'ætrɪk] *adj* psychiatrique • **psychiatrist** *n* psychiatre *mf*
psychic ['saɪkɪk] **1** *adj (paranormal)* paranormal; *Fam* **I'm not p.** je ne suis pas devin
  2 *n* médium *m*
psycho- ['saɪkəʊ] *pref* psycho- • **psychoanalysis** [-ə'næli sɪs] *n* psychanalyse *f* • **psychoanalyst** [-'ænəlɪst] *n* psychanalyste *mf*
psychology [saɪ'kɒlədʒɪ] *n* psychologie *f* • **psychological** [-kə'lɒdʒɪkəl] *adj* psychologique • **psychologist** *n* psychologue *mf*
psychopath ['saɪkəʊpæθ] *n* psychopathe *mf*
psychosis [saɪ'kəʊsɪs] (*pl* -oses [-əʊsiːz]) *n Med* psychose *f*
psychosomatic [saɪkəʊsə'mætɪk] *adj* psychosomatique
psychotherapy [saɪkəʊ'θerəpɪ] *n* psychothérapie *f* • **psychotherapist** *n* psychothérapeute *mf*
psychotic [saɪ'kɒtɪk] *n & adj* psychotique *(mf)*
PTO (*abbr* **please turn over**) TSVP
pub [pʌb] *n Br* pub *m*
puberty ['pjuːbətɪ] *n* puberté *f*
pubic ['pjuːbɪk] *adj* du pubis
public ['pʌblɪk] **1** *adj* public, -ique; *(library, swimming pool)* municipal; **to make sth p.** rendre qch public; **to go p. with sth** prévéler qch *(à la presse)*; **the company is going p.** la compagnie va être cotée en Bourse; **in the p. eye** très en vue; **p. building** édifice *m* public; **p. figure** personnalité *f* en vue; **p. holiday** jour *m* férié; *Br* **p. house** pub *m*; **p. opinion** l'opinion *f* publique; **p. relations** relations *fpl* publiques; *Br* **p. school** école *f* privée; *Am* école scolaire; *Am* **p. television** la télévision éducative; **p. transport** transports *mpl* en commun
  2 *n* public *m*; **in p.** en public; **the sporting p.** les amateurs *mpl* de sport
publican ['pʌblɪkən] *n Br* patron, -onne *mf* d'un pub
publication [pʌblɪ'keɪʃən] *n* publication *f*
publicity [pʌ'blɪsɪtɪ] *n* publicité *f*
publicize ['pʌblɪsaɪz] *vt* faire connaître au public

publicly ['pʌblɪklɪ] *adv* publiquement; **p. owned** à capitaux publics
public-spirited [pʌblɪk'spɪrɪtɪd] *adj* **to be p.** avoir le sens civique
publish ['pʌblɪʃ] *vt* publier; **'published weekly'** 'paraît toutes les semaines' • **publisher** *n* éditeur, -trice *mf* • **publishing** *n* édition *f*; **the p. of** la publication de; **p. house** maison *f* d'édition
pucker ['pʌkə(r)] **1** *vt* **to p. (up)** *(brow)* froncer; *(lips)* pincer
  2 *vi* **to p. (up)** *(face)* se rider; *(lips)* se plisser
pudding ['pʊdɪŋ] *n (dish)* pudding *m*; *Br (dessert)* dessert *m*
puddle ['pʌdəl] *n* flaque *f* (d'eau)
pudgy ['pʌdʒɪ] (-ier, -iest) *adj* rondelet, -ette
puerile [*Br* 'pjʊəraɪl, *Am* 'pjʊərəl] *adj* puérile
Puerto Rico [pwɜːtəʊ'riːkəʊ] *n* Porto Rico *f*
puff [pʌf] **1** *n (of smoke)* bouffée *f*; *(of wind, air)* souffle *m*; *Fam* **to be out of p.** être essoufflé; **p. pastry,** *Am* **p. paste** pâte *f* feuilletée
  2 *vt (smoke)* souffler (**into** dans); **to p. sth out** *(cheeks, chest)* gonfler qch
  3 *vi (of person)* souffler; *(of steam engine)* lancer des bouffées de vapeur; **to p. at a cigar** tirer sur un cigare • **puffy** (-ier, -iest) *adj* gonflé
puke [pjuːk] *vi Fam* dégueuler
pukka ['pʌkə] *adj Br Fam* authentique
pull [pʊl] **1** *n (attraction)* attraction *f*; *(of water current)* force *f*; *Fam (influence)* influence *f*; **to give sth a p.** tirer qch
  2 *vt (draw, tug)* tirer; *(tooth)* arracher; *(stopper)* enlever; *(trigger)* appuyer sur; *(muscle)* se froisser; **to p. sth apart** *or* **to bits** *or* **to pieces** démolir qch; **to p. a face** faire la grimace; *Fig* **to (get sb to) p. strings** se faire pistonner (par qn)
  3 *vi (tug)* tirer (**on** sur); **to p. into the station** *(of train)* entrer en gare; **to p. clear of sth** s'éloigner de qch • **pull-up** *n (exercise on bars or rings)* traction *f*
  ▸ **pull along** *vt sep (drag)* traîner (**to** jusqu'à) ▸ **pull away 1** *vt sep (move)* éloigner; *(snatch)* arracher (**from** à) **2** *vi (in vehicle)* démarrer; **to p. away from** s'éloigner de • **pull back 1** *vt sep* retirer; *(curtains)* ouvrir **2** *vi (withdraw)* se retirer ▸ **pull down** *vt sep (lower)* baisser; *(knock down)* faire tomber; *(demolish)* démolir ▸ **pull in 1** *vt sep (drag into room)* faire entrer (de force); *(rope)* ramener; *(stomach)* rentrer; *(crowd)* attirer **2** *vi*

(arrive) arriver; *(stop in vehicle)* s'arrêter ▸ **pull off** *vt sep (remove)* enlever; *Fig (plan, deal)* réaliser; **to p. it off** réussir son coup ▸ **pull on** *vt sep (boots, clothes)* mettre ▸ **pull out 1** *vt sep (tooth, hair)* arracher; *(cork, pin)* enlever (**from** de); *(from pocket, bag)* sortir (**from** de); *(troops)* retirer **2** *vi (of car)* déboîter; *(of train)* partir; *(withdraw)* se retirer (**from** de) ▸ **pull over 1** *vt sep (drag)* traîner (**to** jusqu'à); *(knock down)* faire tomber **2** *vi (in vehicle)* s'arrêter ▸ **pull round** *vi (recover)* se remettre ▸ **pull through** *vi (recover)* s'en tirer ▸ **pull together** *vt sep* **to p. oneself together** se ressaisir ▸ **pull up 1** *vt sep (socks, blinds)* remonter; *(haul up)* hisser; *(plant, tree)* arracher; *(stop)* arrêter; *Fig* **to p. one's socks up** se ressaisir **2** *vi (of car)* s'arrêter

pulley ['pʊlɪ] *(pl* **-eys)** *n* poulie *f*

pull-out ['pʊlaʊt] *n (in newspaper)* supplément *m* détachable

pullover ['pʊləʊvə(r)] *n* pull-over *m*

pulp [pʌlp] *n (of fruit)* pulpe *f*; **to reduce sth to a p.** écraser qch; **p. fiction** romans *mpl* de gare

pulpit ['pʊlpɪt] *n* chaire *f*

pulsate [pʌl'seɪt] *vi (beat)* palpiter; *(vibrate)* vibrer • **pulsation** *n* pulsation *f*

pulse [pʌls] *n Med* pouls *m*; *(of light, sound)* vibration *f* • **pulses** *npl (seeds)* légumineuses *fpl*

pulverize ['pʌlvəraɪz] *vt* pulvériser

pumice ['pʌmɪs] *n* **p. (stone)** pierre *f* ponce

pump¹ [pʌmp] **1** *n (machine)* pompe *f*; *Br* petrol p., *Am* gas p. pompe *f* à essence; *Br* **(petrol) p. attendant** pompiste *mf* **2** *vt* pomper; *Fig (money, resources)* injecter (**into** dans); *Fam* **to p. sb for information** tirer les vers du nez à qn; *Fam* **to p. iron** faire de la gonflette; **to p. sth in** *(liquid)* refouler qch; **to p. sth out** *(liquid)* pomper qch (**of** de); **to p. air into sth, to p. sth up** *(mattress)* gonfler qch **3** *vi* pomper; *(of heart)* battre

pump² [pʌmp] *n (flat shoe)* escarpin *m*; *(for sports)* tennis *m* ou *f*

pumpkin ['pʌmpkɪn] *n* potiron *m*; *Am* **p. pie** tarte *f* au potiron

pun [pʌn] *n* jeu *m* de mots

Punch [pʌntʃ] *n* **P. and Judy show** ≃ guignol *m*

punch¹ [pʌntʃ] **1** *n (blow)* coup *m* de poing; *Fig (energy)* punch *m*; *Boxing & Fig* **to pack a p.** avoir du punch; **p. line** *(of joke, story)* chute *f* **2** *vt (person)* donner un coup de poing à;

(sb's nose) donner un coup de poing sur; *(ball)* frapper d'un coup de poing • **punch-up** *n Br Fam* bagarre *f*

punch² [pʌntʃ] **1** *n (for paper)* perforeuse *f*; *(tool)* poinçon *m*; *(for tickets)* poinçonneuse *f*; *Comptr* **p. card** carte *f* perforée **2** *vt (ticket)* poinçonner; *(with date)* composter; *(paper, card)* perforer; **to p. a hole in sth** faire un trou dans qch

punch³ [pʌntʃ] *n (drink)* punch *m*

punctilious [pʌŋk'tɪlɪəs] *adj* pointilleux, -euse

punctual ['pʌŋktʃʊəl] *adj* ponctuel, -elle • **punctuality** [-tʃʊ'ælɪtɪ] *n* ponctualité *f* • **punctually** *adv* à l'heure

punctuate ['pʌŋktʃʊeɪt] *vt* ponctuer (**with** de) • **punctu'ation** *n* ponctuation *f*; **p. mark** signe *m* de ponctuation

puncture ['pʌŋktʃə(r)] **1** *n (in tyre)* crevaison *f*; **to have a p.** crever **2** *vt (tyre)* crever; *(metal)* perforer; *(blister)* percer **3** *vi (of tyre)* crever

pundit ['pʌndɪt] *n* expert *m*

pungent ['pʌndʒənt] *adj* âcre • **pungency** *n* âcreté *f*

punish ['pʌnɪʃ] *vt* punir (**for** de); **to p. sb for doing sth** punir qn pour avoir fait qch • **punishing** *adj (tiring)* éreintant

punishable ['pʌnɪʃəbəl] *adj* punissable (**by** de)

punishment ['pʌnɪʃmənt] *n* punition *f*; *Law* peine *f*; **as (a) p. for** en punition de; *Fig* **to take a lot of p.** être mis à rude épreuve

punitive ['pjuːnɪtɪv] *adj* punitif, -ive

punk [pʌŋk] **1** *n* (a) punk *mf*; **p. (rock)** le punk (b) *Am Fam (hoodlum)* voyou *m (pl* -ous) **2** *adj* punk *inv*

punnet ['pʌnɪt] *n Br* barquette *f*

punt¹ [pʌnt] **1** *n* barque *f* à fond plat **2** *vi* **to go punting** faire de la barque • **punter** *n Br (gambler)* parieur, -ieuse *mf*; *Fam (customer)* client *m*, cliente *f* • **punting** *n* canotage *m*

punt² [pʌnt] *n (currency)* livre *f* irlandaise

puny ['pjuːnɪ] *(* **-ier, -iest)** *adj* chétif, -ive

pup [pʌp] *n (dog)* chiot *m*

pupil¹ ['pjuːpəl] *n (student)* élève *mf*

pupil² ['pjuːpəl] *n (of eye)* pupille *f*

puppet ['pʌpɪt] **1** *n* marionnette *f*; **p. show** spectacle *m* de marionnettes **2** *adj (government, leader)* fantoche

puppy ['pʌpɪ] *(pl* **-ies)** *n (dog)* chiot *m*

purchase ['pɜːtʃɪs] **1** *n (action, thing bought)* achat *m* **2** *vt* acheter (**from** à qn); **purchasing**

power pouvoir *m* d'achat •**purchaser** *n* acheteur, -euse *mf*

Note that the French word **pourchasser** is a false friend and is never a translation for the English word **purchase**. It means **to chase**.

pure [pjʊə(r)] (**-er, -est**) *adj* pur
purée ['pjʊəreɪ] *n* purée *f*
purely ['pjʊəlɪ] *adv* purement; **p. and simply** purement et simplement
purgatory ['pɜːɡətrɪ] *n Rel* purgatoire *m*
purge [pɜːdʒ] **1** *n* purge *f*
2 *vt* purger (**of** de)
purify ['pjʊərɪfaɪ] (*pt & pp* **-ied**) *vt* purifier •**purification** [-fɪ'keɪʃən] *n* purification *f* •**purifier** *n* (*for water*) épurateur *m*; (*for air*) purificateur *m*
purist ['pjʊərɪst] *n* puriste *mf*
puritan ['pjʊərɪtən] *n & adj* puritain, -aine *(mf)* •**puritanical** [-'tænɪkəl] *adj* puritain
purity ['pjʊərɪtɪ] *n* pureté *f*
purl [pɜːl] *n* maille *f* à l'envers
purple ['pɜːpəl] **1** *adj* violet, -ette; **to go** *or* **turn p.** (*of person*) devenir cramoisi
2 *n* violet *m*
purport [pɜː'pɔːt] *vt Formal* **to p. to be sth** prétendre être qch
purpose ['pɜːpəs] *n* (**a**) (*aim*) but *m*; **on p.** exprès; **to no p.** inutilement; **to serve no p.** ne servir à rien; **for the purposes of** pour les besoins de (**b**) (*determination*) résolution *f*; **to have a sense of p.** savoir ce que l'on veut •'**purpose-'built** *adj* construit spécialement
purposeful ['pɜːpəsfəl] *adj* résolu •**purposefully** *adv* (*for a reason*) dans un but précis; (*resolutely*) résolument
purposely ['pɜːpəslɪ] *adv* exprès
purr [pɜː(r)] **1** *n* ronron *m*
2 *vi* ronronner
purse [pɜːs] **1** *n* (*for coins*) porte-monnaie *m inv*; *Am* (*handbag*) sac *m* à main
2 *vt* **to p. one's lips** pincer les lèvres
pursue [pə'sjuː] *vt* poursuivre; (*fame, pleasure*) rechercher; (*profession*) exercer •**pursuer** *n* poursuivant, -ante *mf* •**pursuit** *n* (*of person*) poursuite *f*; (*of pleasure, glory*) quête *f*; (*activity*) occupation *f*; **to go in p. of sb/sth** se lancer à la poursuite de qn/qch
purveyor [pə'veɪə(r)] *n Formal* fournisseur *m*
pus [pʌs] *n* pus *m*
push [pʊʃ] **1** *n* (*act of pushing, attack*) poussée *f*; **to give sb/sth a p.** pousser qn/qch; *Br Fam* **to give sb the p.** (*of employer*) virer qn; **at a p.** à la rigueur
2 *vt* pousser (**to** *ou* **as far as** jusqu'à); (*button*) appuyer sur; (*lever*) abaisser; (*product*) faire la promotion de; (*theory*) promouvoir; *Fam* (*drugs*) vendre; **to p. sth into/between** enfoncer qch dans/entre; *Fig* **to p. sb into doing sth** pousser qn à faire qch; **to p. sth off the table** faire tomber qch de la table (en le poussant); **to p. sb off a cliff** pousser qn du haut d'une falaise; **to p. one's way through the crowd** se frayer un chemin à travers la foule; **to p. a door open** ouvrir une porte (en poussant); **to p. one's luck** y aller un peu fort; *Fam* **to be pushing forty** friser la quarantaine
3 *vi* pousser; (*on button*) appuyer (**on** sur) •**push-bike** ['pʊʃbaɪk] *n Br Fam* vélo *m* •**push-button** *n* bouton *m*; (*of phone*) touche *f*; **p. phone** téléphone *m* à touches; **p. controls** commandes *fpl* automatiques •**pushchair** *n Br* poussette *f* •**pushover** *n Fam* **to be a p.** être un jeu d'enfant •**push-up** *n Am* (*exercise*) pompe *f*
▸**push about, push around** *vt sep Fam* **to p. sb about** faire de qn ce que l'on veut
▸**push aside** *vt sep* écarter ▸**push away, push back** *vt sep* repousser ▸**push down** *vt sep* (*button*) appuyer sur; (*lever*) abaisser
▸**push for** *vt insep* faire pression pour obtenir ▸**push in** *vi Br* (*in queue*) resquiller ▸**push off** *vi Fam* ficher le camp ▸**push on** *vi* (*go on*) continuer; **to p. on with sth** continuer qch ▸**push over** *vt sep* faire tomber ▸**push through** *vt sep* (*law*) faire adopter ▸**push up** *vt sep* (*lever, collar*) relever; (*sleeves*) remonter; (*increase*) augmenter
pushed [pʊʃt] *adj* **to be p. for time** être très pressé
pusher ['pʊʃə(r)] *n Fam* (*of drugs*) dealer *m*
pushy ['pʊʃɪ] (**-ier, -iest**) *adj Fam* batailleur, -euse
puss, pussy ['pʊs, 'pʊsɪ] (*pl* **-ies**) *n Fam* (*cat*) minou *m*
put [pʊt] (*pt & pp* **put**, *pres p* **putting**) **1** *vt* mettre; (*on flat surface*) poser; (*problem, argument*) présenter (**to** à); (*question*) poser (**to** à); (*say*) dire; (*estimate*) évaluer (**at** à); **to p. pressure on sb/sth** faire pression sur qn/qch; **to p. a mark on sth** faire une marque sur qch; **to p. money on a horse** parier sur un cheval; **to p. a lot of work into sth** beaucoup travailler à qch; **to p. sth well** bien tourner qch; **to p. it bluntly** pour parler franc
2 *vi* **to p. to sea** prendre la mer •**put-up**

job *n Fam* coup *m* monté
▸ **put across** *vt sep (message, idea)* faire comprendre (**to** à) ▸ **put aside** *vt sep (money, object)* mettre de côté ▸ **put away** *vt sep (tidy away)* ranger; **to p. sb away** *(criminal)* mettre qn en prison; *(insane person)* enfermer qn ▸ **put back** *vt sep (replace, postpone)* remettre; *(telephone receiver)* raccrocher; *(clock, schedule)* retarder ▸ **put by** *vt sep (money)* mettre de côté ▸ **put down** *vt sep (on floor, table)* poser; *(deposit)* verser; *(revolt)* réprimer; *(write down)* inscrire; *(attribute)* attribuer (**to** à); *(kill)* faire piquer; **to p. oneself down** se rabaisser ▸ **put forward** *vt sep (clock, meeting, argument)* avancer; *(opinion)* exprimer; *(candidate)* proposer (**for** à) ▸ **put in 1** *vt sep (into box)* mettre dedans; *(insert)* introduire; *(add)* ajouter; *(install)* installer; *(claim, application)* soumettre; *(time)* passer (**doing** à faire) **2** *vi* **to p. in for sth** *(new job, transfer)* faire une demande de qch; **to p. in (at)** *(of ship)* faire escale (à) ▸ **put off** *vt sep (postpone)* remettre (à plus tard); *(dismay)* déconcerter; *(make wait)* faire attendre; **to p. off doing sth** retarder le moment de faire qch; **to p. sb off sth** dégoûter qn de qch; **to p. sb off doing sth** ôter à qn l'envie de faire qch ▸ **put on** *vt sep (clothes, shoe, record)* mettre; *(accent)* prendre; *(play, show)* monter; *(gas, radio)* allumer; *(clock)* avancer; **to p. on weight** prendre du poids; *Am* **to p. sb on** *(tease)* faire marcher qn; **she p. me on to you** elle m'a donné votre adresse; **p. me on to him!** *(on phone)* passez-le-moi! ▸ **put out** *vt sep (take outside)* sortir; *(arm, leg, hand)* tendre; *(gas, light)* éteindre; *(inconvenience)* déranger; *(upset)* vexer; *(report, statement)* publier; **to p. one's shoulder out** se démettre l'épaule ▸ **put through** *vt*

sep **to p. sb through (to sb)** *(on phone)* passer qn (à qn) ▸ **put together** *vt sep (assemble)* assembler; *(meal, team)* composer; *(file, report)* préparer; *(collection)* rassembler; *Fig* **to p. two and two together** tirer ses conclusions ▸ **put up** *vt sep (lift)* lever; *(tent, fence)* monter; *(statue, ladder)* dresser; *(flag)* hisser; *(building)* construire; *(umbrella)* ouvrir; *(picture, poster)* mettre; *(price, sales, numbers)* augmenter; *(resistance, plea, suggestion)* offrir; *(candidate)* présenter (**for** à); *(guest)* loger; **to p. sth up for sale** mettre qch en vente ▸ **put up with** *vt insep* supporter

putrid [ˈpjuːtrɪd] *adj* putride ● **putrefy** [-trɪfaɪ] *(pt & pp* **-ied***) vi* se putréfier

putt [pʌt] *n Golf* putt *m* ● **putting** *n Golf* putting *m*; **p. green** green *m*

putty [ˈpʌtɪ] *n* mastic *m*

puzzle [ˈpʌzəl] **1** *n (jigsaw)* puzzle *m*; *(game)* casse-tête *m inv*; *(mystery)* mystère *m*
2 *vt* laisser perplexe; **to p. out why/when...** essayer de comprendre pourquoi/quand...
3 *vi* **to p. over sth** essayer de comprendre qch ● **puzzled** *adj* perplexe ● **puzzling** *adj* bizarre

PVC [piːviːˈsiː] *n* PVC *m*; **P. belt** ceinture *f* en PVC

pygmy [ˈpɪɡmɪ] *(pl* **-ies***) n* pygmée *m*

pyjama [pɪˈdʒɑːmə] *adj Br (jacket)* de pyjama ● **pyjamas** *npl Br* pyjama *m*; **a pair of p.** un pyjama; **to be in (one's) p.** être en pyjama

pylon [ˈpaɪlən] *n* pylône *m*

pyramid [ˈpɪrəmɪd] *n* pyramide *f*

Pyrenees [pɪrəˈniːz] *npl* **the P.** les Pyrénées *fpl*

Pyrex® [ˈpaɪreks] *n* Pyrex® *m*; **P. dish** plat *m* en Pyrex®

python [ˈpaɪθən] *n* python *m*

Q, q [kjuː] *n (letter)* Q, q *m inv*
QC [kjuːˈsiː] *(abbr* **Queen's Counsel***) n Br Law* = membre haut placé du barreau
quack¹ [kwæk] *n (of duck)* coin-coin *m inv*
quack² [kwæk] *n Pej (doctor)* charlatan *m*
quadrangle [ˈkwɒdræŋgəl] *n Br (of college, school)* cour *f*
quadruple [kwɒˈdruːpəl] *vti* quadrupler
quadruplets [kwɒˈdruːplɪts] *(Fam* **quads** [kwɒdz]) *npl* quadruplés, -ées *mfpl*
quagmire [ˈkwægmaɪə(r)] *n* bourbier *m*
quail [kweɪl] *n inv (bird)* caille *f*
quaint [kweɪnt] *(-er, -est) adj (picturesque)* pittoresque; *(old-fashioned)* vieillot, -otte; *(odd)* bizarre
quake [kweɪk] **1** *n Fam* tremblement *m* de terre
2 *vi* trembler (**with** de)
Quaker [ˈkweɪkə(r)] *n Rel* quaker, -eresse *mf*
qualification [kwɒlɪfɪˈkeɪʃən] *n (diploma)* diplôme *m*; *(skill)* compétence *f*; *(modification)* précision *f*; *(for competition)* qualification *f*; **on q.** une fois le diplôme obtenu
qualify [ˈkwɒlɪfaɪ] *(pt & pp* **-ied) 1** *vt* (**a**) *(make competent) & Sport* qualifier (**for** sth pour qch); **to q. sb to do sth** donner à qn les compétences nécessaires pour faire qch
(**b**) *(modify)* nuancer; *Grammar* qualifier
2 *vi Sport* se qualifier (**for** pour); **to q. as a doctor** obtenir son diplôme de médecin; **to q. for sth** *(be eligible)* avoir droit à qch • **qualified** *adj (competent)* compétent; *(having diploma)* diplômé; *(opinion)* nuancé; *(support)* mitigé; **to be q. to do sth** *(be competent)* avoir les compétences requises pour faire qch; *(have diploma)* avoir les diplômes requis pour faire qch; **a q. success** un demi-succès • **qualifying** *adj* **q. exam** examen *m* d'entrée; *Sport* **q. round** épreuve *f* éliminatoire
quality [ˈkwɒlɪtɪ] *(pl* **-ies**) *n* qualité *f*; **q. product** produit *m* de qualité • **qualitative** [-tətɪv] *adj* qualitatif, -ive
qualms [kwɑːmz] *npl* **to have no q. about**

doing sth *(scruples)* n'avoir aucun scrupule à faire qch; *(doubts)* ne pas hésiter une seconde avant de faire qch
quandary [ˈkwɒndərɪ] *(pl* **-ies**) *n* dilemme *m*; **to be in a q.** être bien embarrassé
quantify [ˈkwɒntɪfaɪ] *(pt & pp* **-ied**) *vt* évaluer
quantity [ˈkwɒntɪtɪ] *(pl* **-ies**) *n* quantité *f*; **in q.** *(purchase)* en grande(s) quantité(s); **q. surveyor** métreur *m* vérificateur • **quantitative** [-tətɪv] *adj* quantitatif, -ive
quarantine [ˈkwɒrəntiːn] **1** *n* quarantaine *f*
2 *vt* mettre en quarantaine
quarrel [ˈkwɒrəl] **1** *n* dispute *f*, querelle *f*; **to pick a q. with sb** chercher querelle à qn
2 *(Br* **-ll-,** *Am* **-l-**) *vi* se disputer (**with** avec); **to q. with sth** ne pas être d'accord avec qch • **quarrelling** *(Am* **quarreling**) *n* disputes *fpl* • **quarrelsome** *adj* querelleur, -euse
quarry¹ [ˈkwɒrɪ] *(pl* **-ies**) *n (for stone)* carrière *f*
quarry² [ˈkwɒrɪ] *(pl* **-ies**) *n (prey)* proie *f*
quart [kwɔːt] *n (liquid measurement) Br* = 1,14 l, *Am* = 0,95 l
quarter¹ [ˈkwɔːtə(r)] **1** *n* quart *m*; *(of fruit, moon)* quartier *m*; *(division of year)* trimestre *m*; *Am & Can (money)* pièce *f* de 25 cents; **to divide sth into quarters** diviser qch en quatre; **q. (of a) pound** quart de livre; *Br* **a q. past nine,** *Am* **a q. after nine** neuf heures et quart; **a q. to nine** neuf heures moins le quart
2 *vt* partager en quatre
quarter² [ˈkwɔːtə(r)] **1** *n (district)* quartier *m*; **quarters** *(circles)* milieux *mpl*; **(living) quarters** logements *mpl*; *(of soldier)* quartiers *mpl*; **from all quarters** de toutes parts
2 *vt (troops)* loger
quarterfinal [kwɔːtəˈfaɪnəl] *n Sport* quart *m* de finale
quarterly [ˈkwɔːtəlɪ] **1** *adj (magazine, payment)* trimestriel, -ielle
2 *adv* tous les trimestres
3 *(pl* **-ies**) *n* publication *f* trimestrielle

quartet(te) [kwɔː'tet] *n (music, players)* quatuor *m*; **(jazz) q.** quartette *m*
quartz [kwɔːts] **1** *n* quartz *m*
2 *adj (watch)* à quartz
quash [kwɒʃ] *vt (rebellion)* réprimer; *Law (sentence)* annuler
quasi- ['kweɪzaɪ] *pref* quasi-
quaver ['kweɪvə(r)] **1** *n* (**a**) *Br (musical note)* croche *f* (**b**) *(in voice)* tremblement *m*
2 *vi (of voice)* trembler
quay [kiː] *n* quai *m* • **quayside** *n* **on the q.** sur les quais
queasy ['kwiːzɪ] (**-ier, -iest**) *adj* **to feel** *or* **be q.** avoir mal au cœur • **queasiness** *n* mal *m* au cœur
Quebec [kwɪ'bek] *n* le Québec
queen [kwiːn] *n* reine *f*; **the Q. Mother** la reine mère
queer ['kwɪə(r)] **1** (**-er, -est**) *adj (strange)* bizarre
2 *n very Fam (homosexual)* pédé *m*, = terme injurieux désignant un homosexuel
quell [kwel] *vt (revolt)* réprimer
quench [kwentʃ] *vt (fire)* éteindre; *(thirst)* étancher
querulous ['kwerʊləs] *adj (complaining)* grognon, -onne
query ['kwɪərɪ] **1** (*pl* **-ies**) *n* question *f*
2 (*pt & pp* **-ied**) *vt* mettre en question
quest [kwest] *n* quête *f* (**for** de); **in q. of sth** en quête de qch
question ['kwestʃən] **1** *n* question *f*; **there is some q. of it** il en est question; **there's no q. of it, it's out of the q.** c'est hors de question; **without q.** incontestablement; **the matter/person in q.** l'affaire/la personne en question; **q. mark** point *m* d'interrogation; **q. master** *(on television, radio)* animateur, -trice *mf*
2 *vt* interroger (**about** sur); *(doubt)* mettre en question; **to q. whether...** douter que... (*+ subjunctive*) • **questioning 1** *adj (look)* interrogateur, -trice **2** *n* interrogation *f*
questionable ['kwestʃənəbəl] *adj* discutable
questionnaire [kwestʃə'neə(r)] *n* questionnaire *m*
queue [kjuː] *Br* **1** *n (of people)* queue *f*; *(of cars)* file *f*; **to form a q., to stand in a q.** faire la queue
2 *vi* **to q. (up)** faire la queue
quibble ['kwɪbəl] *vi* chipoter (**over** à propos de) • **quibbling** *n* chipotage *m*
quiche [kiːʃ] *n* quiche *f*

quick [kwɪk] **1** (**-er, -est**) *adj (rapid)* rapide; *(clever)* vif (*f* vive); **q. to react** prompt à réagir; **be q.!** fais vite!; **to have a q. shower/meal** se doucher/ manger en vitesse; **to be a q. worker** travailler vite; **as q. as a flash** rapide comme l'éclair
2 (**-er, -est**) *adv Fam* vite
3 *n Fig* **to cut sb to the q.** piquer qn au vif • **'quick-'tempered** *adj* emporté • **'quick-'witted** *adj* vif (*f* vive)
quicken ['kwɪkən] **1** *vt* accélérer
2 *vi* s'accélérer
quickie ['kwɪkɪ] *n Fam* **to have a q.** *(drink)* prendre un pot en vitesse
quickly ['kwɪklɪ] *adv* vite
quicksands ['kwɪksændz] *npl* sables *mpl* mouvants
quid [kwɪd] *n inv Br Fam (pound)* livre *f*
quiet ['kwaɪət] **1** (**-er, -est**) *adj (silent, still, peaceful)* tranquille, calme; *(machine, vehicle)* silencieux, -ieuse; *(person, voice, music)* doux (*f* douce); **to be** *or* **keep q.** *(say nothing)* se taire; *(make no noise)* ne pas faire de bruit; **to keep q. about sth, to keep sth q.** ne rien dire au sujet de qch; **q.!** silence!; **a q. wedding** un mariage célébré dans l'intimité
2 *n Fam* **on the q.** *(secretly)* en cachette
quieten ['kwaɪətən] *Br* **1** *vt* **to q. (down)** calmer
2 *vi* **to q. down** se calmer
quietly ['kwaɪətlɪ] *adv* tranquillement; *(gently, not loudly)* doucement; *(silently)* silencieusement; *(secretly)* en cachette; *(discreetly)* discrètement • **quietness** *n (of person, place)* tranquillité *f*
quill [kwɪl] *n (pen)* plume *f* d'oie
quilt [kwɪlt] *n* édredon *m*; *Br* (**continental**) **q.** *(duvet)* couette *f*
quintessence [kwɪn'tesəns] *n* quintessence *f*
quintet [kwɪn'tet] *n* quintette *m*
quintuplets [*Br* kwɪn'tjuːplɪts, *Am* -'tʌplɪts] *npl* quintuplés, -ées *mfpl*
quip [kwɪp] **1** *n* boutade *f*
2 (*pt & pp* **-pp-**) *vti* plaisanter
quirk [kwɜːk] *n (of character)* particularité *f*; *(of fate)* caprice *m* • **quirky** (**-ier, -iest**) *adj* bizarre
quit [kwɪt] (*pt & pp* **quit** *or* **quitted**, *pres p* **quitting**) **1** *vt (leave)* quitter; *Comptr* sortir de; **to q. doing sth** arrêter de faire qch
2 *vi (give up)* abandonner; *(resign)* démissionner; *Comptr* sortir
quite [kwaɪt] *adv (entirely)* tout à fait; *(really)* vraiment; *(fairly)* assez; **I q. un-**

derstand je comprends parfaitement; **q. enough** bien assez; **q. another matter** une tout autre affaire; **q. a genius** un véritable génie; **q. good** *(not bad)* pas mal du tout; **q. (so)!** exactement!; **q. a lot** pas mal (**of** de); **q. a long time ago** il y a pas mal de temps

quits [kwɪts] *adj* quitte (**with** envers); **to call it q.** en rester là

quiver [ˈkwɪvə(r)] *vi (of person)* frémir (**with** de); *(of voice)* trembler; *(of flame)* vaciller

quiz [kwɪz] **1** *(pl* **-zz-***) n (on radio)* jeu *m* radiophonique; *(on TV)* jeu télévisé; *(in magazine)* questionnaire *m*
 2 *(pt & pp* **-zz-***) vt* interroger • **quizmaster** *n TV & Radio* animateur, -trice *mf*

quizzical [ˈkwɪzɪkəl] *adj (look, air)* interrogateur, -trice

quorum [ˈkwɔːrəm] *n* quorum *m*

quota [ˈkwəʊtə] *n* quota *m*

quotation [kwəʊˈteɪʃən] *n (from author)* citation *f*; *(estimate)* devis *m*; *(on Stock Exchange)* cote *f*; **q. marks** guillemets *mpl*; **in q. marks** entre guillemets

quote [kwəʊt] **1** *n (from author)* citation *f*; *(estimate)* devis *m*; **in quotes** entre guillemets
 2 *vt (author, passage)* citer; *(reference number)* rappeler; *(price)* indiquer; *Fin* **quoted company** société *f* cotée en Bourse
 3 *vi* **to q. from** *(author, book)* citer

quotient [ˈkwəʊʃənt] *n Math* quotient *m*

R

R, r [ɑː(r)] *n (lettre)* R, r *m inv*
rabbi ['ræbaɪ] *n* rabbin *m*; **chief r.** grand rabbin
rabbit ['ræbɪt] *n* lapin *m*
rabble ['ræbəl] *n* foule *f* bruyante
rabies ['reɪbiːz] *n* rage *f* • **rabid** ['ræbɪd] *adj (animal)* enragé; *Fig (communist)* fanatique
raccoon [rə'kuːn] *n* raton *m* laveur
race¹ [reɪs] **1** *n (contest)* course *f*
2 *vt (horse)* faire courir; **to r. (against *or* with) sb** faire une course avec qn
3 *vi (run)* courir; *(of engine)* s'emballer; *(of pulse)* battre la chamade • **racecar** *n Am* voiture *f* de course • **racecourse** *n* champ *m* de courses • **racegoer** *n* turfiste *mf* • **racehorse** *n* cheval *m* de course • **racetrack** *n Am (for horses)* champ *m* de courses; *Br (for cars, bicycles)* piste *f* • **racing** *n* courses *fpl*; **r. car/bicycle** voiture *f*/vélo *m* de course; **r. driver** coureur *m* automobile
race² [reɪs] **1** *n (group)* race *f*
2 *adj (prejudice)* racial; **r. relations** relations *fpl* interraciales • **racial** ['reɪʃəl] *adj* racial • **racialism** ['reɪʃəlɪzəm] *n* racisme *m* • **racism** *n* racisme *m* • **racist** *adj & n* raciste *(mf)*
rack [ræk] **1** **(a)** *n (for bottles, letters, records)* casier *m*; *(for plates)* égouttoir *m*; *(set of shelves)* étagère *f*; **(luggage) r.** porte-bagages *m inv*; **(roof) r.** *(of car)* galerie *f*; **(drying) r.** séchoir *m* à linge **(b)** *(expression)* **to go to r. and ruin** aller de mal en pis
2 *vt* **to r. one's brains** se creuser la cervelle
racket¹ ['rækɪt] *n (for tennis)* raquette *f*
racket² ['rækɪt] *n Fam* **(a)** *(din)* vacarme *m* **(b)** *(criminal activity)* racket *m* • **racke'teer** *n* racketteur *m* • **racke'teering** *n* racket *m*
racoon [rə'kuːn] *n* raton *m* laveur
racy ['reɪsɪ] (-**ier**, -**iest**) *adj (lively)* savoureux, -euse; *(risqué)* osé
radar ['reɪdɑː(r)] *n* radar *m*; **r. control** contrôle *m* radar *inv*; **r. operator** radariste *mf*
radiant ['reɪdɪənt] *adj (person, face)* res-

plendissant (**with** de); *(sun)* éclatant • **radiance** *n* éclat *m* • **radiantly** *adv (shine)* avec éclat; **r. happy** rayonnant de joie
radiate ['reɪdɪeɪt] **1** *vt (heat, light)* dégager; *Fig (joy, health)* être rayonnant de
2 *vi* rayonner (**from** de) • **radi'ation** *n (of heat)* rayonnement *m* (**of** de); *(radioactivity)* radiation *f*; **r. sickness** mal *m* des rayons
radiator ['reɪdɪeɪtə(r)] *n (heater)* radiateur *m*
radical ['rædɪkəl] *adj & n* radical, -ale *(mf)*
radii ['reɪdɪaɪ] *pl of* radius
radio ['reɪdɪəʊ] **1** *(pl* -**os***)* radio *f*; **on** *or* **over the r.** à la radio; **r. cassette (player)** radiocassette *m*; **r. operator** radio *m*; **r. wave** onde *f* hertzienne
2 *(pt & pp* -**oed***) vt (message)* transmettre par radio (**to** à); **to r. sb** contacter qn par radio • **'radio-con'trolled** *adj* radioguidé • **radiographer** [-'ɒgrəfə(r)] *n* radiologue *mf* • **radiography** [-'ɒgrəfɪ] *n* radiographie *f* • **radiologist** [-'ɒlədʒɪst] *n* radiologue *mf* • **radiology** [-'ɒlədʒɪ] *n* radiologie *f*
radioactive [reɪdɪəʊ'æktɪv] *adj* radioactif, -ive • **radioac'tivity** *n* radioactivité *f*
radish ['rædɪʃ] *n* radis *m*
radius ['reɪdɪəs] *(pl* -**dii***) n* rayon *m*; **within a r. of 10 km** dans un rayon de 10 km
RAF [ɑːreɪ'ef] *(abbr* **Royal Air Force***) n* = armée de l'air britannique
raffia ['ræfɪə] *n* raphia *m*
raffle ['ræfəl] *n* tombola *f*
raft [rɑːft] *n* radeau *m*
rafter ['rɑːftə(r)] *n* chevron *m*
rag [ræg] *n* **(a)** *(piece of old clothing)* chiffon *m*; **in rags** *(clothes)* en loques; *(person)* en haillons **(b)** *Fam Pej (newspaper)* torchon *m* **(c)** *Br Univ* **r. week** = semaine de divertissements organisés par les étudiants au profit d'œuvres de charité
ragamuffin ['rægəmʌfɪn] *n* polisson, -onne *mf*
rage [reɪdʒ] **1** *n (of person)* rage *f*; *(of sea)*

furie *f*; **to fly into a r.** entrer dans une rage folle; *Fam* **to be all the r.** *(of fashion)* faire fureur

2 *vi (be angry)* être furieux, -ieuse; *(of storm, battle)* faire rage • **raging** *adj (storm, fever, fire)* violent; **in a r. temper** furieux, -ieuse

ragged ['rægɪd] *adj (clothes)* en loques; *(person)* en haillons; *(edge)* irrégulier, -ière

raid [reɪd] **1** *n (military)* raid *m*; *(by police)* descente *f*; *(by thieves)* hold-up *m inv*; **air r.** raid *m* aérien

2 *vt* faire un raid/une descente/un hold-up dans; *Hum* **to r. the fridge** faire la razzia dans le frigo • **raider** *n (criminal)* malfaiteur *m*; **raiders** *(soldiers)* commando *m*

rail [reɪl] **1** *n* (**a**) *(for train)* rail *m*; **by r.** par le train; **to go off the rails** *(of train)* dérailler (**b**) *(rod on balcony)* balustrade *f*; *(on stairs, for spotlight)* rampe *f*; *(curtain rod)* tringle *f*

2 *adj (ticket)* de chemin de fer; *(network)* ferroviaire; *(strike)* des cheminots • **railcard** *n* carte *f* d'abonnement de train

railings ['reɪlɪŋz] *npl* grille *f*

railroad ['reɪlrəʊd] *n Am (system)* chemin *m* de fer; *(track)* voie *f* ferrée

railway ['reɪlweɪ] *Br* **1** *n (system)* chemin *m* de fer; *(track)* voie *f* ferrée

2 *adj (ticket)* de chemin de fer; *(time-table, employee)* des chemins de fer; *(network, company)* ferroviaire; **r. carriage** voiture *f*; **r. line** ligne *f* de chemin de fer; **r. station** gare *f* • **railwayman** *(pl* **-men**) *n Br* cheminot *m*

rain [reɪn] **1** *n* pluie *f*; **in the r.** sous la pluie

2 *vi* pleuvoir; **to r. (down)** *(of blows, bullets)* pleuvoir; **it's raining** il pleut • **rainbow** ['-bəʊ] *n* arc-en-ciel *m* • **raincheck** *n Am Fam* **I'll give you a r.** *(for invitation)* j'accepterai volontiers à une date ultérieure • **raincoat** *n* imperméable *m* • **raindrop** *n* goutte *f* de pluie • **rainfall** *n (amount)* précipitations *fpl* • **rainforest** *n* forêt *f* tropicale humide • **rainproof** *adj* imperméable • **rainstorm** *n* pluie *f* torrentielle • **rainwater** *n* eau *f* de pluie • **rainy** (**-ier, -iest**) *adj* pluvieux, -ieuse; *(day)* de pluie; **the r. season** la saison des pluies

raise [reɪz] **1** *vt (lift)* lever; *(child, family, voice, statue)* élever; *(crops)* cultiver; *(salary, price)* augmenter; *(temperature)* faire monter; *(question, protest)* soulever; *(taxes, blockade)* lever; **to r. a smile/a laugh** *(in others)* faire sourire/rire; **to r. sb's hopes** donner trop d'espoir à qn; **to r.**

money réunir des fonds; **to r. the alarm** donner l'alarme

2 *n Am (pay rise)* augmentation *f* (de salaire)

raisin ['reɪzən] *n* raisin *m* sec

> ⚠ Note that the French word **raisin** is a false friend and is never a translation for the English word **raisin**. It means **grapes**.

rake [reɪk] **1** *n* râteau *m*

2 *vt (garden)* ratisser; **to r. (up)** *(leaves)* ratisser; *Fam* **to r. money in** ramasser l'argent à la pelle; **to r. through** *(drawers, papers)* fouiller dans; **to r. up sb's past** fouiller dans le passé de qn

rally ['rælɪ] **1** *(pl* **-ies**) *n (political)* rassemblement *m*; *(car race)* rallye *m*; *(in tennis)* échange *m*

2 *(pt & pp* **-ied**) *vt (unite, win over)* rallier (**to** à); **to r. support** rallier des partisans (**for** autour de); *Fig* **to r. one's strength** reprendre ses forces

3 *vi* se rallier (**to** à); *(recover)* reprendre ses forces; *(of share prices)* se redresser; **to r. round sb** venir en aide à qn; **rallying point** point *m* de ralliement

RAM [ræm] *(abbr* **random access memory**) *n Comptr* mémoire *f* vive

ram [ræm] **1** *n (animal)* bélier *m*

2 *(pt & pp* **-mm-**) *vt (vehicle)* emboutir; *(ship)* aborder; **to r. sth into sth** enfoncer qch dans qch

ramble ['ræmbəl] **1** *n (hike)* randonnée *f*

2 *vi* faire une randonnée; **to r. on** divaguer • **rambler** *n* randonneur, -euse *mf* • **ramblings** *npl* divagations *fpl*

rambling ['ræmblɪŋ] *adj* (**a**) *(house)* plein de coins et de recoins; *(spread out)* vaste; *(rose)* grimpant (**b**) *(speech)* décousu

ramification [ræmɪfɪ'keɪʃən] *n* ramification *f*

ramp [ræmp] *n (for wheelchair)* rampe *f* d'accès; *(in garage)* pont *m* (de graissage); *(to plane)* passerelle *f*; *(on road)* petit dos *m* d'âne

rampage ['ræmpeɪdʒ] *n* **to go on the r.** *(lose control)* se déchaîner; *(loot)* tout saccager

rampant ['ræmpənt] *adj* endémique

rampart ['ræmpɑːt] *n* rempart *m*

ramshackle ['ræmʃækəl] *adj* délabré

ran [ræn] *pt of* **run**

ranch [rɑːntʃ] *n* ranch *m*

rancid ['rænsɪd] *adj* rance

rancour ['ræŋkə(r)] *(Am* **rancor**) *n* rancœur *f*

random ['rændəm] **1** *n* **at r.** au hasard

2 *adj (choice)* (fait) au hasard; *(sample)* prélevé au hasard; *(pattern)* irrégulier, -ière; *Comptr* **r. access memory** mémoire *f* vive; **r. check** *(by police)* contrôle-surprise *m*

randy ['rændɪ] (**-ier, -iest**) *adj Br Fam* excité

rang [ræŋ] *pt of* **ring²**

range [reɪndʒ] **1** *n* (**a**) *(of gun, voice)* portée *f*; *(of singer's voice)* registre *m*; *(of aircraft, ship)* rayon *m* d'action; *(of colours, prices, products)* gamme *f*; *(of sizes)* choix *m*; *(of temperature)* variations *fpl*; *Fig (sphere)* champ *m* (**b**) *(of mountains)* chaîne *f* (**c**) *(stove)* fourneau *m* (**d**) *(shooting)* **r.** champ *m* de tir
2 *vi (vary)* varier (**from** de; **to** à); *(extend)* s'étendre

ranger ['reɪndʒə(r)] *n* (**forest**) **r.** garde *m* forestier

rank¹ [ræŋk] **1** *n (position, class)* rang *m*; *(military grade)* grade *m*; *(row)* rangée *f*; *(for taxis)* station *f*; *Mil* **the ranks** les hommes *mpl* du rang
2 *vt* placer (**among** parmi)
3 *vi* compter (**among** parmi) • **rank-and-'file** *n* **the r.** *(in army)* les hommes *mpl* du rang; *(in political party)* la base

rank² [ræŋk] (**-er, -est**) *adj* (**a**) *(smell)* fétide (**b**) *(absolute)* total

rankle ['ræŋkəl] *vi* **it rankles with me** ça m'est resté sur l'estomac

ransack ['rænsæk] *vt (house)* mettre sens dessus dessous; *(shop, town)* piller

ransom ['rænsəm] **1** *n* rançon *f*; **to hold sb to r.** rançonner qn
2 *vt* rançonner

rant [rænt] *vi Fam* **to r. and rave** tempêter (**at** contre)

rap [ræp] **1** *n* (**a**) *(blow)* coup *m* sec (**b**) **r.** *(music)* rap *m*
2 *(pt & pp* -pp-*)* *vt (window, door)* frapper à; *Fig* **to r. sb over the knuckles** taper sur les doigts de qn
3 *vi (hit)* frapper (**on** à)

rapacious [rə'peɪʃəs] *adj* rapace

rape [reɪp] **1** *n* viol *m*
2 *vt* violer • **rapist** *n* violeur *m*

rapid ['ræpɪd] *adj* rapide • **rapidity** [rə'pɪdɪtɪ] *n* rapidité *f* • **rapidly** *adv* rapidement

rapids ['ræpɪdz] *npl (of river)* rapides *mpl*

rapport [ræ'pɔː(r)] *n* **to have a good r. with sb** avoir de bons rapports avec qn

rapt [ræpt] *adj (attention)* profond

rapture ['ræptʃə(r)] *n* extase *f*; **to go into raptures** s'extasier (**about** sur) • **rapturous** *adj (welcome, applause)* enthousiaste

rare [reə(r)] *adj* (**a**) (**-er, -est**) rare; **it's r. for her to do it** il est rare qu'elle le fasse (**b**) *(meat)* bleu; **(medium) r.** saignant • **rarely** *adv* rarement • **rarity** (*pl* -ies) *n (quality, object)* rareté *f*

rarebit ['reəbɪt] *n Br* **Welsh r.** = toast au fromage

rarefied ['reərɪfaɪd] *adj* raréfié

raring ['reərɪŋ] *adj* **r. to do sth** impatient de faire qch

rascal ['rɑːskəl] *n* coquin, -ine *mf*

rash¹ [ræʃ] *n (on skin) (red patches)* rougeurs *fpl*; *(spots)* (éruption *f* de) boutons *mpl*; **to come out in a r.** faire une éruption de boutons

rash² [ræʃ] (**-er, -est**) *adj (imprudent)* irréfléchi • **rashly** *adv* sans réfléchir

rasher ['ræʃə(r)] *n Br* tranche *f (de bacon)*

rasp [rɑːsp] *n (tool)* râpe *f*

raspberry ['rɑːzbərɪ] (*pl* -ies) *n (fruit)* framboise *f*; **r. (bush)** framboisier *m*

rasping ['rɑːspɪŋ] *adj (voice)* âpre; *(sound)* grinçant

Rastafarian [ræstə'feərɪən] *n & adj* rastafari *(mf) inv*

rat [ræt] *n* rat *m*; **r. poison** mort-aux-rats *f*; *Fig* **r. race** foire *f* d'empoigne
2 *(pt & pp* -tt-*)* *vi Fam* **to r. on sb** *(denounce)* dénoncer qn

rate [reɪt] **1** *n (level, percentage)* taux *m*; *(speed)* rythme *m*; *(price)* tarif *m*; **exchange/interest r.** taux de change/d'intérêt; **at the r. of** au rythme de; *(amount)* à raison de; **at this r.** *(slow speed)* à ce train-là; **at any r.** en tout cas
2 *vt (regard)* considérer (**as** comme); *(deserve)* mériter; **to r. sb/sth highly** tenir qn/qch en haute estime

rather ['rɑːðə(r)] *adv (preferably, quite)* plutôt; **I'd r. stay** j'aimerais mieux rester (**than** que); **I'd r. you came** j'aimerais mieux que vous veniez; **r. than leave** plutôt que de partir; **r. more tired** un peu plus fatigué (**than** que); **I r. liked it** j'ai bien aimé; **it's r. nice** c'est bien

ratify ['rætɪfaɪ] *(pt & pp* -ied*)* *vt* ratifier • **ratification** [-fɪ'keɪʃən] *n* ratification *f*

rating ['reɪtɪŋ] *n (classification)* classement *m*; **the ratings** *(for TV, radio)* l'indice *m* d'écoute

ratio ['reɪʃɪəʊ] (*pl* -os) *n* rapport *m*

ration ['ræʃən] **1** *n* ration *f*; **rations** *(food)* vivres *mpl*
2 *vt* rationner • **rationing** *n* rationnement *m*

rational ['ræʃənəl] *adj (sensible)* raisonnable; *(sane)* rationnel, -elle • **rationalize**

vt (organize) rationaliser; *(explain)* justifier • **rationally** *adv (behave)* raisonnablement

rattle ['rætəl] **1** *n* (**a**) *(for baby)* hochet *m* (**b**) *(noise)* cliquetis *m*; *(of gunfire)* crépitement *m*

2 *vt (window)* faire vibrer; *(keys, chains)* faire cliqueter; *Fam* **to r. sb** *(make nervous)* démonter qn; *Fam* **to r. sth off** débiter qch

3 *vi (of window)* vibrer; *(of chains, keys)* cliqueter; *(of gunfire)* crépiter

rattlesnake ['rætəlsneɪk] *n* serpent *m* à sonnette

ratty ['rætɪ] (-ier, -iest) *adj Fam* (**a**) *Am (shabby)* minable (**b**) *Br* **to get r.** *(annoyed)* prendre la mouche

raucous ['rɔːkəs] *adj (noisy, rowdy)* bruyant

raunchy ['rɔːntʃɪ] (-ier, -iest) *adj Fam (lewd)* cochon, -onne; *(sexy)* sexy *inv*

ravage ['rævɪdʒ] *vt* ravager • **ravages** *npl (of old age, time)* ravages *mpl*

rave [reɪv] **1** *adj (review)* dithyrambique

2 *n* rave *f*

3 *vi (talk nonsense)* délirer; **to r. about sb/sth** *(enthuse)* ne pas tarir d'éloges sur qn/qch • **raving** *adj* **to be r. mad** être complètement fou *(f* folle)

raven ['reɪvən] *n* corbeau *m*

ravenous ['rævənəs] *adj (appetite)* vorace; **I'm r.** j'ai une faim de loup

ravine [rə'viːn] *n* ravin *m*

ravioli [rævɪ'əʊlɪ] *n* ravioli(s) *mpl*

ravishing ['rævɪʃɪŋ] *adj (beautiful)* ravissant • **ravishingly** *adv* **r. beautiful** d'une beauté ravissante

raw [rɔː] (-er, -est) *adj (vegetable)* cru; *(sugar, data)* brut; *(skin)* écorché; *(wound)* à vif; *(immature)* inexpérimenté; *(weather)* rigoureux, -euse; **r. material** matière *f* première; *Fam* **to get a r. deal** être mal traité

Rawlplug® ['rɔːlplʌg] *n Br* cheville *f*

ray¹ [reɪ] *n (of light, sun)* rayon *m*; *Fig (of hope)* lueur *f*

ray² [reɪ] *n (fish)* raie *f*

rayon ['reɪɒn] **1** *n* rayonne *f*

2 *adj* en rayonne

raze [reɪz] *vt* **to r. sth to the ground** raser qch

razor ['reɪzə(r)] *n* rasoir *m*; **r. blade** lame *f* de rasoir

Rd *(abbr* **road***)* rue

re [riː] *prep Com* en référence à; **re your letter** suite à votre lettre

reach [riːtʃ] **1** *n* portée *f*; **within r. of** à portée de; *(near)* à proximité de; **within**

(easy) r. *(object)* à portée de main; *(shops)* tout proche

2 *vt (place, aim, distant object)* atteindre, arriver à; *(decision)* prendre; *(agreement)* aboutir à; *(contact)* joindre; **to r. a conclusion** arriver à une conclusion; **to r. out one's arm** tendre le bras

3 *vi (extend)* s'étendre (**to** jusqu'à); *(of voice)* porter; **to r. for sth** tendre le bras pour prendre qch; **to r. out** tendre le bras (**for** pour prendre)

react [rɪ'ækt] *vi* réagir (**against** contre; **to** à) • **reaction** *n* réaction *f*

reactionary [rɪ'ækʃənərɪ] *(pl* -ies) *adj & n* réactionnaire *(mf)*

reactor [rɪ'æktə(r)] *n* réacteur *m*

read [riːd] **1** *(pt & pp* **read** [red]*) vt* lire; *(meter)* relever; *(of instrument)* indiquer; *Br Univ (study)* étudier; **the sign reads...** sur le panneau, on peut lire...

2 *vi (of person)* lire (**about** sur); **to r. well** *(of text)* se lire bien; **to r. to sb** faire la lecture à qn

3 *n Fam* **to have a r.** lire; **to be a good r.** être agréable à lire • **readable** *adj (handwriting)* lisible; *(book)* facile à lire

▸ **read back** *vt sep* relire ▸ **read for** *vt insep Br (university degree)* préparer ▸ **read out** *vt sep* lire (à haute voix) ▸ **read over** *vt sep* relire ▸ **read through** *vt sep (skim)* parcourir ▸ **read up (on)** *vt insep (study)* étudier

readdress [riːə'dres] *vt (letter)* faire suivre

reader ['riːdə(r)] *n* lecteur, -trice *mf*; *(book)* livre *m* de lecture • **readership** *n* nombre *m* de lecteurs

readily ['redɪlɪ] *adv (willingly)* volontiers; *(easily)* facilement • **readiness** *n* empressement *m* (**to do** à faire)

reading ['riːdɪŋ] *n* lecture *f*; *(of meter)* relevé *m*; **it's light/heavy r.** c'est facile/difficile à lire; **r. book/room** livre *m*/salle *f* de lecture; **r. glasses** lunettes *fpl* de lecture; **r. lamp** *(on desk)* lampe *f* de bureau; *(at bedside)* lampe *f* de chevet; **r. matter** de quoi lire

readjust [riːə'dʒʌst] **1** *vt (instrument)* régler; *(salary)* réajuster

2 *vi (of person)* se réadapter (**to** à) • **readjustment** *n* réglage *m*; *(of salary)* réajustement *m*; *(of person)* réadaptation *f*

read-only [riːd'əʊnlɪ] *adj Comptr* **r. memory** mémoire *f* morte

ready ['redɪ] **1** (-ier, -iest) *adj* prêt (**to do** à faire; **for sth** pour qch); **to get sb/sth r.** préparer qn/qch; **to get r.** se préparer

(**for sth** pour qch; **to do** à faire); **r.!
steady! go!** à vos marques, prêts, partez!; **r. cash, r. money** argent *m* liquide
　2 *n* **to be at the r.** être tout prêt (*f* toute
prête) ● **'ready-'cooked** *adj* cuisiné
● **'ready-'made** *adj* (*food*) tout prêt (*f*
toute prête); (*excuse*) tout fait (*f* toute
faite); **r. clothes** le prêt-à-porter ● **'ready-
to-'wear** *adj* **r. clothes** le prêt-à-porter

real [rɪəl] **1** *adj* vrai; (*leather*) véritable;
(*world, fact, danger*) réel (*f* réelle); **in r.
life** dans la réalité; **in r. terms** en termes
réels; *Fam* **it's the r. thing** c'est du vrai de
vrai; *Am* **r. estate** immobilier *m*
　2 *adv Fam* vraiment; **r. stupid** vraiment
bête
　3 *n Fam* **for r.** pour de vrai

realism ['rɪəlɪzəm] *n* réalisme *m* ● **realist**
n réaliste *mf* ● **rea'listic** *adj* réaliste ● **rea'l-
istically** *adv* avec réalisme

reality [rɪ'ælɪtɪ] (*pl* **-ies**) *n* réalité *f*; **in r.**
en réalité

realize ['rɪəlaɪz] *vt* (**a**) (*become aware of*)
se rendre compte de; **to r. that...** se
rendre compte que... (**b**) (*carry out,
convert into cash*) réaliser ● **reali'zation** *n*
(**a**) (*awareness*) prise *f* de conscience *f*
(**b**) (*of dream, plan, assets*) réalisation *f*

really ['rɪəlɪ] *adv* vraiment; **is it r. true?**
est-ce bien vrai?

realm [relm] *n* (*kingdom*) royaume *m*; *Fig*
(*field*) domaine *m*

realtor ['rɪəltə(r)] *n Am* agent *m* immobilier

ream [riːm] *n* (*of paper*) rame *f*

reap [riːp] *vt* (*field, crop*) moissonner; *Fig*
(*profits*) récolter

reappear [riːə'pɪə(r)] *vi* réapparaître

reappraise [riːə'preɪz] *vt* réévaluer

rear¹ [rɪə(r)] **1** *n* (*back part*) arrière *m*; (*of
military column*) queue *f*; **in** *or* **at the r.** à
l'arrière (**of** de); **from the r.** par derrière
　2 *adj* (*entrance, legs*) de derrière; (*lights,
window*) arrière *inv* ● **rearguard** *n Mil*
arrière-garde *f* ● **rearview 'mirror** *n* rétroviseur *m*

rear² [rɪə(r)] **1** *vt* (*child, animals*) élever;
(*one's head*) relever
　2 *vi* **to r. (up)** (*of horse*) se cabrer

rearrange [riːə'reɪndʒ] *vt* (*hair, room*)
réarranger; (*plans*) changer

reason ['riːzən] **1** *n* (*cause, sense*) raison *f*;
the r. for/why la raison de/pour laquelle;
the r. that... la raison pour laquelle...; **for
no r.** sans raison; **it stands to r.** cela va de
soi; **within r.** dans des limites raisonna-
bles; **to have every r. to believe that...**
avoir tout lieu de croire que...

2 *vt* **to r. that...** estimer que...
　3 *vi* raisonner (**about** sur); **to r. with sb**
raisonner qn ● **reasoning** *n* raisonnement *m*

reasonable ['riːzənəbəl] *adj* (*fair*) raisonnable; (*quite good*) passable ● **reasonably** *adv* (*behave, act*) raisonnablement; (*quite*) plutôt; **r. fit** en assez
bonne forme

reassess [riːə'ses] *vt* reconsidérer

reassure [riːə'ʃʊə(r)] *vt* rassurer ● **re-
assurance** *n* réconfort *m* ● **reassuring** *adj*
rassurant

reawaken [riːə'weɪkən] **1** *vt* (*interest,
feeling*) faire renaître
　2 *vi* (*of person*) se réveiller de nouveau
● **reawakening** *n* réveil *m*

rebate ['riːbeɪt] *n* (*discount*) rabais *m*;
(*refund*) remboursement *m*

rebel ['rebəl] **1** *n* rebelle *mf*
　2 *adj* (*camp, chief, attack*) des rebelles
　3 [rɪ'bel] (*pt & pp* **-ll-**) *vi* se rebeller
(**against** contre) ● **rebellion** [rɪ'beljən] *n*
rébellion *f* ● **rebellious** [rɪ'beljəs] *adj* rebelle

rebirth ['riːbɜːθ] *n* renaissance *f*

rebound 1 ['riːbaʊnd] *n* (*of ball*) rebond
m; *Fig* **to marry sb on the r.** épouser qn à
la suite d'une déception sentimentale
　2 [rɪ'baʊnd] *vi* (*of ball*) rebondir; *Fig* (*of
lies, action*) se retourner (**on** contre)

rebuff [rɪ'bʌf] **1** *n* rebuffade *f*
　2 *vt* repousser

rebuild [riː'bɪld] (*pt & pp* **-built**) *vt* reconstruire

rebuke [rɪ'bjuːk] **1** *n* réprimande *f*
　2 *vt* réprimander

rebut [rɪ'bʌt] (*pt & pp* **-tt-**) *vt* réfuter

recalcitrant [rɪ'kælsɪtrənt] *adj* récalcitrant

recall [rɪ'kɔːl] **1** *n* (*calling back*) rappel *m*;
my powers of r. (*memory*) ma mémoire
　2 *vt* (*remember*) se rappeler (**that** que;
doing avoir fait); (*call back*) rappeler; **to r.
sth to sb** rappeler qch à qn

recant [rɪ'kænt] *vi* se rétracter

recap ['riːkæp] **1** *n* récapitulation *f*
　2 (*pt & pp* **-pp-**) *vi* récapituler ● **recapitulate** [-kə'pɪtʃʊleɪt] *vti* récapituler ● **recapitulation** [-kəpɪtʃʊ'leɪʃən] *n* récapitulation *f*

recapture [riː'kæptʃə(r)] **1** *n* (*of prisoner*)
capture *f*
　2 *vt* (*prisoner*) capturer; (*town*) reprendre; (*recreate*) recréer

recede [rɪ'siːd] *vi* (*into the distance*)
s'éloigner; (*of floods*) baisser ● **receding**
adj (*forehead, chin*) fuyant; **his hairline is
r.** son front se dégarnit

receipt [rɪ'siːt] *n (for payment, object)* reçu *m* (**for** de); *(for letter, parcel)* récépissé *m*; **receipts** *(at box office)* recette *f*; **on r. of sth** dès réception de qch

receive [rɪ'siːv] *vt* recevoir; *(stolen goods)* receler • **receiving** *n (of stolen goods)* recel *m*

receiver [rɪ'siːvə(r)] *n* (**a**) *(of phone)* combiné *m*; *(radio)* récepteur *m*; **to pick up** *or* **lift the r.** *(of phone)* décrocher (**b**) *(of stolen goods)* receleur, -euse *mf; Br Fin (in bankruptcy)* administrateur *m* judiciaire • **receivership** *n Fin* **to go into r.** être placé sous règlement judiciaire

recent ['riːsənt] *adj* récent; *(development)* dernier, -ière; **in r. months** au cours des derniers mois • **recently** *adv* récemment; **as r. as yesterday** pas plus tard qu'hier

receptacle [rɪ'septəkəl] *n* récipient *m*

reception [rɪ'sepʃən] *n (party, of radio)* réception *f*; *(welcome)* accueil *m*; **r. (desk)** réception • **receptionist** *n* réceptionniste *mf*

receptive [rɪ'septɪv] *adj* réceptif, -ive (**to** à)

recess [*Br* rɪ'ses, *Am* 'riːses] *n* (**a**) *(holiday)* vacances *fpl*; *Am (between classes)* récréation *f* (**b**) *(in wall)* renfoncement *m*; *(smaller) & Fig* recoin *m*

recession [rɪ'seʃən] *n* récession *f*

recharge [riː'tʃɑːdʒ] *vt (battery)* recharger • **rechargeable** *adj (battery)* rechargeable

recipe ['resɪpɪ] *n (for food) & Fig* recette *f* (**for sth** de qch; **for doing** pour faire)

recipient [rɪ'sɪpɪənt] *n (of gift, letter)* destinataire *mf; (of award)* lauréat, -éate *mf*

> *Note that the French word* **récipient** *is a false friend and is never a translation for the English word* **recipient**. *It means* **container**.

reciprocal [rɪ'sɪprəkəl] *adj* réciproque

reciprocate [rɪ'sɪprəkeɪt] **1** *vt* retourner **2** *vi* rendre la pareille

recital [rɪ'saɪtəl] *n (of music)* récital *m (pl -als)*

recite [rɪ'saɪt] *vt (poem)* réciter; *(list)* énumérer • **recitation** [resɪ'teɪʃən] *n* récitation *f*

reckless ['rekləs] *adj (rash)* imprudent; **r. driver** chauffard *m* • **recklessly** *adv* imprudemment

reckon ['rekən] **1** *vt (calculate)* calculer; *(consider)* considérer; *Fam (think)* penser (**that** que) **2** *vi* calculer; compter; **to r. with** *(take into account)* compter avec; *(deal with)* avoir affaire à; **to r. on/without sb/sth** compter sur/sans qn/qch; **to r. on doing sth** compter faire qch • **reckoning** *n* calcul *m*

reclaim [rɪ'kleɪm] **1** *vt (lost property, waste material, luggage)* récupérer; *(expenses)* se faire rembourser; **to r. land from the sea** gagner du terrain sur la mer **2** *n* **'baggage r.'** *(in airport)* 'retrait des bagages'

> *Note that the French word* **réclamer** *is a false friend and is never a translation for the English verb* **to reclaim**. *It means* **to claim** *or* **to demand**.

recline [rɪ'klaɪn] **1** *vt (head)* appuyer (**on** sur) **2** *vi (of person)* être allongé • **reclining** **'seat** *n* siège *m* à dossier inclinable

recluse [rɪ'kluːs] *n* reclus, -use *mf*

recognition [rekəg'nɪʃən] *n* reconnaissance *f*; **to change beyond** *or* **out of all r.** devenir méconnaissable; **to gain r.** être reconnu

recognize ['rekəgnaɪz] *vt* reconnaître • **recognizable** *adj* reconnaissable

recoil [rɪ'kɔɪl] *vi (of gun)* reculer; *(of person)* avoir un mouvement de recul

recollect [rekə'lekt] *vt* se souvenir de • **recollection** *n* souvenir *m*

recommend [rekə'mend] *vt (praise, support, advise)* recommander (**to** à; **for** pour); **to r. sb to do sth** recommander à qn de faire qch • **recommen'dation** *n* recommandation *f*

recompense ['rekəmpens] **1** *n* récompense *f* **2** *vt (reward)* récompenser

reconcile ['rekənsaɪl] *vt (person)* réconcilier (**with** *or* **to** avec); *(opinions, facts)* concilier; **to r. oneself to sth** se résigner à qch • **reconciliation** [-sɪlɪ'eɪʃən] *n* réconciliation *f*

reconditioned [riːkən'dɪʃənd] *adj (engine, machine)* remis à neuf

reconnaissance [rɪ'kɒnɪsəns] *n Mil* reconnaissance *f* • **reconnoitre** [rekə'nɔɪtə(r)] *(Am* **reconnoiter** [riːkə'nɔɪtər]) *vt (land, enemy troops)* reconnaître

reconsider [riːkən'sɪdə(r)] **1** *vt* réexaminer **2** *vi* réfléchir

reconstruct [riːkən'strʌkt] *vt* reconstruire; *(crime)* reconstituer

record ['rekɔːd] **1** *n* (**a**) *(disc)* disque *m*; **r. company** maison *f* de disques; **r. library** discothèque *f*; **r. player** électrophone *m*

(**b**) *Sport (best performance)* record *m*
(**c**) *(report)* rapport *m*; *(background)* antécédents *mpl*; *(file)* dossier *m*; **to make** *or* **keep a r. of sth** garder une trace écrite de qch; **to have a good safety r.** avoir une bonne réputation en matière de sécurité; **on r.** *(fact, event)* attesté; **the highest figures on r.** les chiffres les plus élevés jamais enregistrés; **(police) r.** casier *m* judiciaire; **(public) records** archives *fpl*
2 *adj* record *inv*; **in r. time** en un temps record; **to be at a r. high/low** être à son taux le plus haut/bas
3 [rɪ'kɔːd] *vt (on tape, in register)* enregistrer; *(in diary)* noter; *(relate)* rapporter (**that** que)
4 *vi (on tape, of tape recorder)* enregistrer ●**record-holder** *n* détenteur, -trice *mf* du record

recorded [rɪ'kɔːdɪd] *adj* enregistré; *(fact)* attesté; *(TV broadcast)* en différé; *Br* **to send sth (by) r. delivery** ≃ envoyer qch en recommandé avec accusé de réception

recorder [rɪ'kɔːdə(r)] *n (musical instrument)* flûte *f* à bec

recording [rɪ'kɔːdɪŋ] *n* enregistrement *m*; **r. studio** studio *m* d'enregistrement

recount [rɪ'kaʊnt] *vt (relate)* raconter

re-count ['riːkaʊnt] *n (of votes)* deuxième décompte *m*

recoup [rɪ'kuːp] *vt* récupérer

recourse ['riːkɔːs] *n* recours *m*; **to have r. to** avoir recours à

recover [rɪ'kʌvə(r)] **1** *vt (get back)* récupérer; *(one's appetite, balance)* retrouver
2 *vi (from illness, shock, surprise)* se remettre (**from** de); *(of economy, country, Stock Market)* se redresser; *(of currency)* remonter; *(of sales)* reprendre ●**recovery** (*pl* **-ies**) *n* (**a**) *(from illness)* rétablissement *m*; *(of economy, Stock Market)* redressement *m*; **to make a r.** se rétablir (**b**) *(of goods)* récupération *f*; *Br* **r. vehicle** dépanneuse *f*

re-create [riːkrɪ'eɪt] *vt* recréer

recreation [rekrɪ'eɪʃən] *n Sch (break)* récréation *f*; **r. ground** terrain *m* de jeux ●**recreational** *adj (activity)* de loisir

recrimination [rɪkrɪmɪ'neɪʃən] *n* récrimination *f*

recruit [rɪ'kruːt] **1** *n* recrue *f*
2 *vt* recruter ●**recruitment** *n* recrutement *m*

rectangle ['rektæŋgəl] *n* rectangle *m* ●**rectangular** [-'tæŋgʊlə(r)] *adj* rectangulaire

rectify ['rektɪfaɪ] *(pt & pp* **-ied**) *vt* rectifier

●**rectification** [-fɪ'keɪʃən] *n* rectification *f*

rector ['rektə(r)] *n (priest)* pasteur *m* anglican; *(of Scottish school)* ≃ proviseur *m*

rectum ['rektəm] *n* rectum *m*

recuperate [rɪ'kuːpəreɪt] *vi (from illness)* récupérer ●**recupe'ration** *n (after illness)* rétablissement *m*

recur [rɪ'kɜː(r)] *(pt & pp* **-rr-**) *vi (of event, problem)* se reproduire; *(of illness)* réapparaître; *(of theme)* revenir ●**recurrence** [-'kʌrəns] *n* récurrence *f* ●**recurrent** [-'kʌrənt] *adj* récurrent

recycle [riː'saɪkəl] *vt* recycler

red [red] **1** (**redder, reddest**) *adj* rouge; *(hair)* roux (*f* rousse); **to turn** *or* **go r.** rougir; **the R. Cross** la Croix-Rouge; **R. Indian** Peau-Rouge *mf*; **r. light** *(traffic light)* feu *m* rouge; **the r. light district** le quartier chaud; *Fig* **r. tape** paperasserie *f*; **the R. Sea** la mer Rouge
2 *n (colour)* rouge *m*; **in the r.** *(in debt)* dans le rouge ●**redden** ['redən] *vti* rougir ●**reddish** *adj* rougeâtre; *(hair)* légèrement roux (*f* rousse) ●**'red-'faced** *adj* rougeaud; *Fig (with confusion)* rouge ●**'red-'handed** *adv* **to be caught r.** être pris la main dans le sac ●**redhead** *n* roux *m*, rousse *f* ●**'red-'hot** *adj* brûlant ●**redness** *n* rougeur *f*; *(of hair)* rousseur *f*

redcurrant [red'kʌrənt] *n* groseille *f*

redecorate [riː'dekəreɪt] *vt (repaint)* refaire la peinture de

redeem [rɪ'diːm] *vt (restore to favour, buy back, free)* racheter; *(debt, loan)* rembourser; *(gift token, coupon)* échanger; **his one redeeming feature is...** la seule chose qui le rachète, c'est... ●**redemption** [-'dempʃən] *n* rachat *m*; *(of debt, loan)* remboursement *m*; *Rel* rédemption *f*

redeploy [riːdɪ'plɔɪ] *vt (staff)* réorganiser; *(troops)* redéployer

redial [riː'daɪəl] *(Br* **-ll-,** *Am* **-l-**) *vt* recomposer

redirect [riːdaɪ'rekt] *vt (mail)* faire suivre; *(plane, traffic)* dévier

redo [riː'duː] *(pt* **-did**, *pp* **-done**) *vt* refaire

redolent ['redələnt] *adj* **to be r. of** *(smell of)* sentir; *(suggest)* avoir un parfum de

redress [rɪ'dres] *n* **to seek r.** demander réparation (**for** de)

reduce [rɪ'djuːs] *vt* réduire (**to** à; **by** de); *(temperature, price)* baisser; **at a reduced price** à prix réduit; **to r. speed** ralentir; **to r. sb to silence** réduire qn au silence; **to r. sb to tears** faire pleurer qn; **to be reduced to doing sth** en être réduit à faire qch ●**reduction** [-'dʌkʃən] *n (of temperature,* *price)* baisse *f*; *(discount)* réduction *f* (**in/on** de/sur)

redundant [rɪ'dʌndənt] *adj (not needed)* superflu; *Br* **to make sb r.** licencier qn; **to be made r.** être licencié • **redundancy** (*pl* **-ies**) *n Br (of worker)* licenciement *m*; **r. pay(ment)** *or* **money** prime *f* de licenciement

reed [riːd] *n* (**a**) *(plant)* roseau *m* (**b**) *(of musical instrument)* anche *f*

re-educate [riː'edjʊkeɪt] *vt (criminal, limb)* rééduquer

reef [riːf] *n* récif *m*

reek [riːk] **1** *n* relent *m*
2 *vi* **to r. (of sth)** puer (qch)

reel [riːl] **1** *n (of thread, film)* bobine *f*; *(for fishing line)* moulinet *m*
2 *vt sep* **to r. off** *(names, statistics)* débiter
3 *vi (stagger)* chanceler; *Fig* **my head is reeling** la tête me tourne

re-elect [riːɪ'lekt] *vt* réélire

re-enact [riːɪ'nækt] *vt* reconstituer

re-entry [riː'entrɪ] *n (of spacecraft)* rentrée *f*

re-establish [riːɪ'stæblɪʃ] *vt* rétablir

re-examine [riːɪg'zæmɪn] *vt* réexaminer

ref [ref] *(abbr* **referee)** *n Fam Sport* arbitre *m*

refectory [rɪ'fektərɪ] *(pl* **-ies**) *n* réfectoire *m*

refer [rɪ'fɜː(r)] *(pt & pp* **-rr-**) **1** *vt* **to r. sth to sb** *(submit)* soumettre qch à qn; **to r. sb to a specialist** envoyer qn voir un spécialiste
2 *vt insep* **to r. to** *(allude to)* faire allusion à; *(mention)* parler de; *(apply to)* s'appliquer à; *(consult)* consulter

referee [refə'riː] **1** *n Sport* arbitre *m*; **to give the names of two referees** *(for job)* fournir deux références
2 *vti* arbitrer

reference ['refərəns] *n (source, consultation)* référence *f*; *(allusion)* allusion *f* (**to** à); *(mention)* mention *f* (**to** de); *(for employer)* lettre *f* de référence; **with** *or* **in r. to** concernant; *Com* **with** *or* **in r. to your letter** suite à votre lettre; **for future r.** à titre d'information; **r. book** ouvrage *m* de référence; **r. point** point *m* de repère

referendum [refə'rendəm] *n* référendum *m*

refill 1 ['riːfɪl] *n (for notebook)* feuillets *mpl* de rechange; *(for pen)* cartouche *f*; *(for lighter)* recharge *f*; **would you like a r.?** *(of drink)* je te ressers?
2 [riː'fɪl] *vt (glass)* remplir à nouveau; *(lighter, pen)* recharger

refine [rɪ'faɪn] **1** *vt (oil, sugar, manners)* raffiner; *(technique, machine)* perfectionner
2 *vi* **to r. upon sth** parfaire qch • **refined** *adj (person, manners)* raffiné • **refinement** *n (of person, manners)* raffinement *m*; *(of sugar, oil)* raffinage *m*; *(of technique)* perfectionnement *m*; **refinements** *(technical improvements)* améliorations *fpl* • **refinery** *(pl* **-ies**) *n* raffinerie *f*

refit 1 ['riːfɪt] *n (of ship)* remise *f* en état
2 [riː'fɪt] *(pt & pp* **-tt-**) *vt (ship)* remettre en état

reflate [riː'fleɪt] *vt (economy)* relancer

reflect [rɪ'flekt] **1** *vt* (**a**) *(light, image)* refléter, réfléchir; *Fig (portray)* refléter; **to be reflected (in)** *(of light)* se refléter (dans) (**b**) **to r. that...** se dire que...
2 *vi* (**a**) **to r. on sb, to be reflected on sb** *(of prestige, honour)* rejaillir sur qn; **to r. badly on sb** faire du tort à qn; **to r. well on sb** faire honneur à qn (**b**) *(think)* réfléchir (**on** à)

reflection [rɪ'flekʃən] *n* (**a**) *(image)* & *Fig* reflet *m*; *Fig* **it is no r. on your own capabilities** cela ne remet pas en cause vos compétences (**b**) *(thought, criticism)* réflexion (**on** sur); **on r.** tout bien réfléchi

reflector [rɪ'flektə(r)] *n (on bicycle, vehicle)* catadioptre *m*

reflex ['riːfleks] *n & adj* réflexe *(m)*; **r. action** réflexe *m*

reflexion [rɪ'flekʃən] *n Br =* **reflection**

reflexive [rɪ'fleksɪv] *adj Grammar* réfléchi

reflexology [riːflek'sɒlədʒɪ] *n* réflexologie *f*

refloat [riː'fləʊt] *vt (ship, company)* renflouer

reform [rɪ'fɔːm] **1** *n* réforme *f*; *Am* **r. school** centre *m* d'éducation surveillée
2 *vt* réformer; *(person, conduct)* corriger
3 *vi (of person)* se réformer • **reformer** *n* réformateur, -trice *mf*

reformatory [rɪ'fɔːmətərɪ] *(pl* **-ies**) *n Am* centre *m* d'éducation surveillée

refrain [rɪ'freɪn] **1** *n (of song)* & *Fig* refrain *m*
2 *vi* s'abstenir (**from sth** de qch; **from doing** de faire)

refresh [rɪ'freʃ] *vt (of drink)* rafraîchir; *(of bath)* revigorer; *(of sleep, rest)* reposer; **to r. oneself** *(drink)* se rafraîchir; **to r. one's memory** se rafraîchir la mémoire • **refreshing** *adj (drink)* rafraîchissant; *(bath)* revigorant; *(sleep)* reposant; *(original)* nouveau *(f* nouvelle)

refresher course [rɪ'freʃəkɔːs] *n* cours *m* de recyclage

refreshments [rɪ'freʃmənts] npl rafraîchissements mpl

refrigerate [rɪ'frɪdʒəreɪt] vt réfrigérer • **refrigerator** n (domestic) réfrigérateur m

refuel [riː'fjʊəl] **1** (Br -ll-, Am -l-) vt (aircraft) ravitailler en carburant **2** vi (of aircraft) se ravitailler en carburant

refuge ['refjuːdʒ] n refuge m; **to take r.** se réfugier (**in** dans)

refugee [refjʊ'dʒiː] n réfugié, -iée mf

refund 1 ['riːfʌnd] n remboursement m **2** [rɪ'fʌnd] vt rembourser

refurbish [riː'fɜːbɪʃ] vt rénover

refusal [rɪ'fjuːzəl] n refus m

refuse¹ [rɪ'fjuːz] **1** vt refuser; **to r. to do sth** refuser de faire qch; **to r. sb sth** refuser qch à qn **2** vi refuser

refuse² ['refjuːs] n Br (rubbish) ordures fpl; (industrial waste materials) déchets mpl; **r. collection** ramassage m des ordures; **r. dump** dépôt m d'ordures

refute [rɪ'fjuːt] vt réfuter

regain [rɪ'geɪn] vt (lost ground, favour) regagner; (health, sight) retrouver; (power) reconquérir; **to r. one's strength** reprendre des forces; **to r. consciousness** reprendre connaissance; **to r. possession of sth** reprendre possession de qch

regal ['riːɡəl] adj royal

regalia [rɪ'ɡeɪlɪə] npl insignes mpl

regard [rɪ'ɡɑːd] **1** n (admiration) respect m; (consideration) égard m; **to hold sb in high r.** tenir qn en haute estime; **with r. to** en ce qui concerne; **without r. to** sans tenir compte de; **to give** or **send one's regards to sb** transmettre son meilleur souvenir à qn **2** vt (admire, respect) estimer; **to r. sb/sth as...** considérer qn/qch comme...; **as regards...** en ce qui concerne... • **regarding** prep en ce qui concerne

> ℓ Note that the French words **regard** and **regarder** are false friends and are never translations for the English words **regard** and **to regard**. They mean **look** and **to look at**.

regardless [rɪ'ɡɑːdləs] **1** adj **r. of...** (without considering) sans tenir compte de... **2** adv (all the same) quand même

regatta [rɪ'ɡætə] n régate f

regency ['riːdʒənsɪ] (pl **-ies**) n régence f • **regent** n régent, -ente mf

regenerate [rɪ'dʒenəreɪt] **1** vt régénérer **2** vi se régénérer

reggae ['reɡeɪ] **1** n (music) reggae m **2** adj (group, musician) reggae inv

régime [reɪ'ʒiːm] n régime m

regiment 1 ['redʒɪmənt] n régiment m **2** ['redʒɪment] vt régimenter • **regimental** [-'mentəl] adj du régiment • **regimentation** [-men'teɪʃən] n discipline f draconienne

region ['riːdʒən] n région f; Fig **in the r. of** (about) environ • **regional** adj régional

register ['redʒɪstə(r)] **1** n registre m; (in school) cahier m d'appel; **electoral r.** liste f électorale; **to take the r.** (of teacher) faire l'appel **2** vt (birth, death) déclarer; (record, note, speed) enregistrer; (vehicle) immatriculer; (complaint) déposer; (astonishment, displeasure) manifester; Fam (realize) réaliser **3** vi (enrol) s'inscrire (**for a course** à un cours); (at hotel) signer le registre; (of voter) s'inscrire sur les listes électorales; Fam **I told him but it didn't r.** je lui ai dit mais il n'a pas enregistré • **registered** adj (member) inscrit; (letter, package) recommandé; (charity) agréé; **to send sth by r. post** or Am **mail** envoyer qch en recommandé; **r. trademark** marque f déposée; Br **r. unemployed** inscrit au chômage

registrar [redʒɪ'strɑː(r)] n Br (record keeper) officier m de l'état civil; (in university) responsable m des inscriptions; (in hospital) chef m de clinique

registration [redʒɪ'streɪʃən] n (enrolment) inscription f; (of complaint) enregistrement m; Br **r. (number)** (of vehicle) numéro m d'immatriculation; Br **r. document** (of vehicle) ≃ carte f grise

registry ['redʒɪstrɪ] adj & n Br **r. (office)** bureau m de l'état civil; **to get married in a r. office** se marier à la mairie

regress [rɪ'ɡres] vi régresser • **regression** n régression f

regret [rɪ'ɡret] **1** n regret m **2** (pt & pp **-tt-**) vt regretter (**to do** de faire; **that** que (+ subjunctive); **I r. to hear that** j'ai le regret d'apprendre que; **to r. doing sth** regretter d'avoir fait qch • **regretfully** adv **r., I...** à mon grand regret, je...

regrettable [rɪ'ɡretəbəl] adj regrettable (**that** que + subjunctive) • **regrettably** adv malheureusement; (poor, ill) fâcheusement

regroup [riː'ɡruːp] **1** vt regrouper **2** vi se regrouper

regular ['reɡjʊlə(r)] **1** adj (a) (steady, even) & Grammar régulier, -ière; (usual)

habituel, -uelle; *(price)* normal; *(size)* moyen, -enne; *(listener, reader)* fidèle; *(staff)* permanent; *Fam (for emphasis)* vrai; **on a r. basis** régulièrement; *Am Fam* **a r. guy** un chic type (**b**) *(army, soldier)* régulier, -ière
2 *n (in bar)* habitué, -uée *mf* ● **regularity** [-'lærɪtɪ] *n* régularité *f* ● **regularly** *adv* régulièrement

regulate ['regjʊleɪt] *vt (adjust)* régler; *(control)* réglementer ● **regu'lation 1** *n* (**a**) **regulations** *(rules)* règlement *m* (**b**) *(regulating)* réglage *m* **2** *adj (statutory)* réglementaire

rehabilitate [riːhə'bɪlɪteɪt] *vt* réhabiliter ● **rehabili'tation** *n* réadaptation *f*

rehash 1 ['riːhæʃ] *n* resucée *f*
2 [riː'hæʃ] *vt (text, film)* remanier

rehearse [rɪ'hɜːs] *vt* répéter ● **rehearsal** *n* répétition *f*

reign [reɪn] **1** *n* règne *m*; **in** *or* **during the r. of** sous le règne de
2 *vi* régner (**over** sur)

reimburse [riːɪm'bɜːs] *vt* rembourser (**for** de) ● **reimbursement** *n* remboursement *m*

rein [reɪn] *n* **to give sb free r. to do sth** donner carte blanche à qn pour qu'il fasse qch

reincarnation [riːɪnkɑː'neɪʃən] *n* réincarnation *f*

reindeer ['reɪndɪə(r)] *n inv* renne *m*

reinforce [riːɪn'fɔːs] *vt* renforcer (**with** de); **reinforced concrete** béton *m* armé ● **reinforcement** *n* renforcement *m* (**of** de); **reinforcements** *(troops)* renforts *mpl*

reins [reɪnz] *npl (for horse)* rênes *fpl*; *(for baby)* bretelles *fpl* de sécurité

reinstate [riːɪn'steɪt] *vt* réintégrer ● **reinstatement** *n* réintégration *f*

reissue [riː'ɪʃjuː] *vt (book)* rééditer

reiterate [riː'ɪtəreɪt] *vt* réitérer

reject 1 ['riːdʒekt] *n (object)* rebus *m*; *Fam (person)* inadapté, -ée *mf*; **r. article** article *m* de deuxième choix; *Br* **r. shop** solderie *f*
2 [rɪ'dʒekt] *vt* rejeter; *(candidate, goods, offer)* refuser ● **rejection** [rɪ'dʒekʃən] *n* rejet *m*; *(of candidate, goods, offer)* refus *m*

rejoice [rɪ'dʒɔɪs] *vi* se réjouir (**over** *or* **at** de) ● **rejoicing** *n* réjouissance *f*

rejoin¹ [rɪ'dʒɔɪn] *vt* (**a**) *(join up with)* rejoindre (**b**) *(join again)* réintégrer

rejoin² [rɪ'dʒɔɪn] *vi (retort)* répliquer

rejuvenate [rɪ'dʒuːvəneɪt] *vt* rajeunir

rekindle [riː'kɪndəl] *vt* raviver

relapse 1 ['riːlæps] *n* rechute *f*

2 [rɪ'læps] *vi* rechuter; *Fig* **to r. into** retomber dans

relate [rɪ'leɪt] **1** *vt* (**a**) *(narrate)* raconter (**that** que); *(report)* rapporter (**that** que) (**b**) *(connect)* mettre en rapport (**to** avec)
2 *vi* **to r. to** *(apply to)* avoir rapport à; *(person)* avoir des affinités avec ● **related** *adj (linked)* lié (**to** à); *(languages, styles)* apparenté; **to be r. to sb** *(by family)* être parent de qn

relation [rɪ'leɪʃən] *n* (**a**) *(relative)* parent, -ente *mf*; **what r. are you to him?** quel est ton lien de parenté avec lui? (**b**) *(relationship)* rapport *m*; **international relations** relations *fpl* internationales; **sexual relations** rapports *mpl* sexuels

relationship [rɪ'leɪʃənʃɪp] *n (within family)* lien *m* de parenté; *(between people)* relation *f*; *(between countries)* relations *fpl*; *(connection)* rapport *m*; **to have a good r. with sb** bien s'entendre avec qn

relative ['relətɪv] **1** *n* parent, -ente *mf*
2 *adj (comparative)* relatif, -ive; *(respective)* respectif, -ive; **r. to** relativement à; **to be r. to** *(depend on)* être fonction de ● **relatively** *adv* relativement

relax [rɪ'læks] **1** *vt (person, mind)* détendre; *(grip, pressure)* relâcher; *(law, control)* assouplir
2 *vi (of person)* se détendre; *(of muscle)* se relâcher; **r.!** *(calm down)* du calme! ● **relaxed** *adj* détendu ● **relaxing** *adj* délassant

relaxation [riːlæk'seɪʃən] *n* (**a**) *(of person)* détente *f*; *(of discipline)* relâchement *m*; *(of law, control)* assouplissement *m* (**b**) *(as therapy)* relaxation *f*

relay 1 ['riːleɪ] *n (of workers)* équipe *f* de relais; **to work in relays** se relayer; **r. (race)** *(course f* de) relais *m*
2 [riː'leɪ] *vt* retransmettre; *(information)* transmettre (**to** à)

release [rɪ'liːs] **1** *n (of prisoner)* libération *f*; *(of film, book)* sortie *f* (**of** de); *(film)* nouveau film *m*; *(record)* nouveau disque *m*; *(emotional)* soulagement *m*; *Br* **to be on general r.** *(of film)* passer dans toutes les grandes salles
2 *vt (person)* libérer (**from** de); *(bomb)* lâcher; *(brake)* desserrer; *(smoke, funds)* dégager; *(film, record)* sortir; *(news, facts)* communiquer; **to r. sb's hand** lâcher la main de qn

relegate ['relɪgeɪt] *vt* reléguer (**to** à); *Br* **to be relegated** *(of team)* descendre en division inférieure

relent [rɪ'lent] *vi (of storm, wind)* se calmer; *(of person)* céder

relentless [rɪ'lentləs] *adj* implacable
relevant ['reləvənt] *adj* (**a**) *(apt)* pertinent; **to be r.** *to sth* avoir rapport à qch; **that's not r.** ça n'a rien à voir (**b**) *(appropriate) (chapter)* correspondant; *(authorities)* compétent; *(qualifications)* requis (**c**) *(topical)* d'actualité • **relevance** *n* pertinence *f* (**to** à); *(connection)* rapport *m* (**to** avec)
reliable [rɪ'laɪəbəl] *adj (person, machine)* fiable; *(information)* sûr • **relia'bility** *n (of person)* sérieux *m*; *(of machine)* fiabilité *f* • **reliably** *adv* **to be r. informed that...** tenir de source sûre que...
reliance [rɪ'laɪəns] *n (dependence)* dépendance *f* (**on** vis-à-vis de); *(trust)* confiance *f* (**on** en) • **reliant** *adj* **to be r. on** *(dependent)* dépendre de; *(trusting)* avoir confiance en
relic ['relɪk] *n* relique *f*; *Fig* **relics** vestiges *mpl*
relief [rɪ'liːf] **1** *n (comfort)* soulagement *m*; *(help)* secours *m*; *(in art)* relief *m*
  2 *adj (train, bus)* supplémentaire; *(work, troops)* de secours; **r. map** carte *f* en relief; *Br* **r. road** route *f* de délestage
relieve [rɪ'liːv] *vt (alleviate)* soulager; *(boredom)* tromper; *(replace)* remplacer; *(free)* libérer; **to r. sb of sth** débarrasser qn de qch; **to r. sb of his duties** relever qn de ses fonctions; **to r. congestion in** *(street)* décongestionner; *Hum* **to r. oneself** se soulager
religion [rɪ'lɪdʒən] *n* religion *f* • **religious** *adj* religieux, -ieuse; *(war)* de religion • **religiously** *adv* religieusement
relinquish [rɪ'lɪŋkwɪʃ] *vt (hope, habit, thought)* abandonner; *(share, claim)* renoncer à
relish ['relɪʃ] **1** *n (pickle)* condiments *mpl*; *(pleasure)* goût *m* (**for** pour); *(pleasure)* plaisir *m*; **to do sth with r.** faire qch avec délectation
  2 *vt* savourer
reload [riː'ləʊd] *vt (gun, camera)* recharger
relocate [*Br* riːləʊ'keɪt, *Am* riː'ləʊkeɪt] *vi (of company)* être transféré; *(of person)* se déplacer
reluctant [rɪ'lʌktənt] *adj (greeting, gift, promise)* accordé à contrecœur; **to be r. (to do sth)** être réticent (à faire qch) • **reluctance** *n* réticence *f* (**to do** à faire) • **reluctantly** *adv* à contrecœur
rely [rɪ'laɪ] *(pt & pp* **-ied)** *vi* **to r. (up)on** *(count on)* compter sur; *(be dependent on)* dépendre de
remain [rɪ'meɪn] *vi (stay behind, continue*

to be) rester; *(be left)* subsister • **remaining** *adj* restant • **remains** *npl* restes *mpl*; *mortal* **r.** dépouille *f* mortelle
remainder [rɪ'meɪndə(r)] **1** *n* reste *m*; *(book)* invendu *m* soldé
  2 *vt (book)* solder
remand [rɪ'mɑːnd] *Law* **1** *n* **on r.** en détention préventive; *Br* **r. centre** centre *m* de détention préventive
  2 *vt* **to r. sb (in custody)** placer qn en détention préventive
remark [rɪ'mɑːk] **1** *n* remarque *f*
  2 *vt* faire remarquer
  3 *vi* **to r. on sth** *(comment)* faire un commentaire sur qch; *(criticize)* faire des remarques sur qch • **remarkable** *adj* remarquable • **remarkably** *adv* remarquablement

⚠ Note that the French verb **remarquer** is a false friend and is never a translation for the English verb **to remark**. It means **to notice**.

remarry [riː'mærɪ] *(pt & pp* **-ied)** *vi* se remarier
remedial [rɪ'miːdɪəl] *adj* **to take r. measures** prendre des mesures; **r. class** cours *m* de rattrapage
remedy ['remɪdɪ] **1** *(pl* **-ies)** *n* remède *m*
  2 *(pt & pp* **-ied)** *vt* remédier à
remember [rɪ'membə(r)] **1** *vt* se souvenir de, se rappeler; *(commemorate)* commémorer; **to r. that/doing** se rappeler que/d'avoir fait; **to r. to do sth** penser à faire qch; **to r. sb to sb** rappeler qn au bon souvenir de qn
  2 *vi* se souvenir, se rappeler • **remembrance** *n Formal (memory)* souvenir *m*; **in r. of** en souvenir de; *Br & Can* **R. Day** *or* **Sunday** ≃ le 11 novembre *(commémoration de la fin des deux guerres mondiales)*
remind [rɪ'maɪnd] *vt* **to r. sb of sth** rappeler qch à qn; **to r. sb to do sth** rappeler à qn de faire; **that** *or* **which reminds me...** à propos... • **reminder** *n (of event, letter)* rappel *m*; **it's a r. (for him/her) that...** c'est pour lui rappeler que...
reminisce [remɪ'nɪs] *vi* évoquer des souvenirs; **to r. about sth** évoquer qch • **reminiscence** *n* souvenir *m*
reminiscent [remɪ'nɪsənt] *adj* **r. of** qui rappelle
remiss [rɪ'mɪs] *adj* négligent
remission [rɪ'mɪʃən] *n Law* remise *f* de peine; *Med* **to be in r.** être en rémission
remit [rɪ'mɪt] *(pt & pp* **-tt-)** *vt (money)* envoyer • **remittance** *n (sum)* paiement *m*

remnant ['remnənt] *n (remaining part)* reste *m*; *(of civilization, building)* vestige *m*; *(of fabric)* coupon *m*; *(oddment)* fin *f* de série
remodel [ri:'mɒdəl] (*Br* **-ll-**, *Am* **-l-**) *vt* remodeler (**on** sur)
remonstrate ['remənstreɪt] *vi* **to r. with sb** faire des remontrances à qn
remorse [rɪ'mɔːs] *n* remords *m*; **to feel r.** avoir du *ou* des remords • **remorseless** *adj* impitoyable • **remorselessly** *adv* impitoyablement
remote [rɪ'məʊt] (**-er, -est**) *adj* (**a**) *(far-off) (in space)* éloigné (**from** de); *(in time)* lointain (**from** de); *Fig (aloof)* distant; **r. control** télécommande *f* (**b**) *(slight)* vague; **not the remotest idea** pas la moindre idée • **remotely** *adv (slightly)* vaguement; **r. situated** isolé; **not r. aware** nullement conscient • **remoteness** *n* éloignement *m*; *(isolation)* isolement *m*; *Fig (aloofness)* attitude *f* distante
remould ['ri:məʊld] *n Br* pneu *m* rechapé
removable [rɪ'muːvəbəl] *adj (lining)* amovible
removal [rɪ'muːvəl] *n* (**a**) *(of control, threat)* suppression *f*; *(of politician)* renvoi *m* (**b**) *Br (moving house)* déménagement *m*; *Br* **r. man** déménageur *m*; *Br* **r. van** camion *m* de déménagement
remove [rɪ'muːv] *vt (clothes, stain, object)* enlever (**from sb** à qn; **from sth** de qch); *Br (furniture)* déménager; *(obstacle, threat, word)* supprimer; *(fear, doubt)* dissiper; *(politician)* renvoyer; (**far) removed from** loin de
remover [rɪ'muːvə(r)] *n (for nail polish)* dissolvant *m*; *(for paint)* décapant *m*; *(for stains)* détachant *m*
remunerate [rɪ'mjuːnəreɪt] *vt* rémunérer • **remune'ration** *n* rémunération *f*
renaissance [rə'neɪsəns] *n* renouveau *m*
rename [riː'neɪm] *vt* rebaptiser; *Comptr (file)* renommer
render ['rendə(r)] *vt Formal (give, make)* rendre; *(piece of music)* interpréter; **to r. assistance to sb** prêter main-forte à qn • **rendering** *n (musical)* interprétation *f*; *(translation)* traduction *f*
rendezvous ['rɒndɪvuː, *pl* -vuːz] *n inv* rendez-vous *m inv*
renegade ['renɪgeɪd] *n* renégat, -ate *mf*
renege [rɪ'niːg, *Br* rɪ'neɪg] *vi* **to r. on sth** revenir sur qch
renew [rɪ'njuː] *vt* renouveler; *(resume)* reprendre; *(library book)* renouveler le prêt de • **renewed** *adj (efforts)* renouvelé;

(attempt) nouveau (*f* nouvelle); **with r. vigour** avec un regain de vigueur
renewable [rɪ'njuːəbəl] *adj* renouvelable
renewal [rɪ'njuːəl] *n* renouvellement *m*; *(of activity, negotiations)* reprise *f*; *(of optimism, strength)* regain *m*
renounce [rɪ'naʊns] *vt (give up)* renoncer à; *(disown)* renier
renovate ['renəveɪt] *vt (house)* rénover; *(painting)* restaurer • **reno'vation** *n* rénovation *f*; *(of painting)* restauration *f*
renown [rɪ'naʊn] *n* renommée *f* • **renowned** *adj* renommé (**for** pour)
rent [rent] **1** *n (for house, flat)* loyer *m*; **for r.** à louer
2 *vt* louer; **to r. out** louer; **rented car** voiture *f* de location • **'rent-'free 1** *adv* sans payer de loyer **2** *adj* exempt de loyer
rental ['rentəl] *n (of television, car)* location *f*; *(of telephone)* abonnement *m*
reopen [riː'əʊpən] *vti* rouvrir • **reopening** *n* réouverture *f*
reorder [riː'ɔːdə(r)] *vt (goods)* passer une nouvelle commande de
reorganize [riː'ɔːgənaɪz] *vt* réorganiser
rep [rep] *n Fam* VRP *m*
repair [rɪ'peə(r)] **1** *n* réparation *f*; **beyond r.** irréparable; **under r.** en travaux; **in good/bad r.** en bon/mauvais état
2 *vt* réparer • **repairman** (*pl* **-men**) *n* réparateur *m*
reparation [repə'reɪʃən] *n Formal* réparation *f* (**for** de); **reparations** *(after war)* réparations *fpl*
repartee [repɑː'tiː] *n* repartie *f*
repatriate [riː'pætrɪeɪt] *vt* rapatrier (**to** vers)
repay [riː'peɪ] (*pt & pp* **-paid**) *vt (pay back)* rembourser; *(kindness)* payer de retour; *(reward)* remercier (**for** de) • **repayment** *n* remboursement *m*
repeal [rɪ'piːl] **1** *n* abrogation *f*
2 *vt* abroger
repeat [rɪ'piːt] **1** *n (of event)* répétition *f*; *(on TV, radio)* rediffusion *f*; **r. performance** *(of play)* deuxième représentation *f*
2 *vt* répéter (**that** que); *(promise, threat)* réitérer; *(class)* redoubler; *(TV programme)* rediffuser; **to r. oneself** se répéter
3 *vi* répéter; **r. after me** répétez après moi; **I r., you're wrong** je le répète, vous avez tort; • **repeated** *adj (attempts)* répété; *(efforts)* renouvelé • **repeatedly** *adv* à maintes reprises
repel [rɪ'pel] (*pt & pp* **-ll-**) *vt* repousser • **repellent 1** *adj (disgusting)* repoussant **2** *n* **insect r.** crème *f* anti-insecte

repent [rɪ'pent] *vi* se repentir (**of** de) • **repentance** *n* repentir *m* • **repentant** *adj* repentant

repercussions [ri:pə'kʌʃənz] *npl* répercussions *fpl* (**on** sur)

repertoire ['repətwɑ:(r)] *n Theatre & Fig* répertoire *m* • **repertory** [-tərɪ] (*pl* **-ies**) (*in Theatre & Fig* répertoire *m*; **r. (theatre)** théâtre *m* de répertoire

repetition [repɪ'tɪʃən] *n* répétition *f* • **repetitious, repetitive** [rɪ'petɪtɪv] *adj* répétitif, -ive

rephrase [ri:'freɪz] *vt* reformuler

replace [rɪ'pleɪs] *vt (take the place of)* remplacer (**by** *or* **with** par); *(put back)* remettre (à sa place); **to r. the receiver** *(on phone)* raccrocher • **replacement** *n (substitution)* remplacement *m* (**of** de); *(person)* remplaçant, -ante *mf*; *(machine part)* pièce *f* de rechange

replay **1** ['ri:pleɪ] *n Sport* nouvelle rencontre *f*; **(instant** *or* **action) r.** *(on TV)* = répétition d'une séquence précédente

2 [ri:'pleɪ] *vt (match)* rejouer

replenish [rɪ'plenɪʃ] *vt (refill)* remplir (de nouveau) (**with** de); **to r. one's supplies** se réapprovisionner

replete [rɪ'pli:t] *adj Formal* **r. with** rempli de; **r. (with food)** rassasié

replica ['replɪkə] *n* réplique *f*

reply [rɪ'plaɪ] **1** (*pl* **-ies**) *n* réponse *f*; **in r.** en réponse (**to** à)

2 (*pt & pp* **-ied**) *vti* répondre (**to** à; **that** que)

report [rɪ'pɔ:t] **1** *n* (**a**) *(analysis)* rapport *m*; *(account)* compte rendu *m*; *(in media)* reportage *m*; *Br* **(school) r.,** *Am* **r. card** bulletin *m* scolaire

(**b**) *(of gun)* détonation *f*

2 *vt (information)* rapporter; *(accident, theft)* signaler (**to** à); **to r. sb missing** signaler la disparition de qn; **to r. sb to the police** dénoncer qn à la police; **to r. one's findings (to sb)** faire un rapport (à qn)

3 *vi (give account)* faire un rapport (**on** sur); *(of journalist)* faire un reportage (**on** sur); *(go)* se présenter (**to** à); **to r. to sb** *(be accountable)* rendre compte à qn • **reported** *adj Grammar* **r. speech** discours *m* indirect; **it is r. that...** on dit que...; **to be r. missing** être porté disparu • **reportedly** *adv* à ce qu'on dit • **reporter** *n* reporter *m*

ℓ Note that the French words **report** and **reporter** are false friends and are never translations for the English words **report** and **to report**. Their most common meanings are **postponement** and **to postpone**.

repose [rɪ'pəʊz] *n Literary* repos *m*

repository [rɪ'pɒzɪtərɪ] (*pl* **-ies**) *n* dépôt *m*

repossess [ri:pə'zes] *vt* saisir

reprehensible [reprɪ'hensəbəl] *adj* répréhensible

represent [reprɪ'zent] *vt* représenter • **represen'tation** *n* représentation *f*

representative [reprɪ'zentətɪv] **1** *adj* représentatif, -ive (**of** de)

2 *n* représentant, -ante *mf*; *Am Pol* ≃ député *m*

repress [rɪ'pres] *vt* réprimer; *(memory, feeling)* refouler; **to be repressed** *(of person)* être un(e) refoulé(e) • **repression** *n* répression *f* • **repressive** *adj (régime)* répressif, -ive; *(measures)* de répression

reprieve [rɪ'pri:v] *Law* **1** *n (cancellation)* commutation *f* de la peine capitale; *(temporary) & Fig* sursis *m*

2 *vt* **to r. sb** *(cancel punishment of)* commuer la peine capitale de qn en réclusion à perpétuité; *(postpone punishment of)* accorder un sursis à qn

reprimand ['reprɪmɑ:nd] **1** *n* réprimande *f*

2 *vt* réprimander

reprint **1** ['ri:prɪnt] *n* réimpression *f*

2 [ri:'prɪnt] *vt* réimprimer

reprisal [rɪ'praɪzəl] *n* représailles *fpl*; **as a r. for, in r. for** en représailles de

reproach [rɪ'prəʊtʃ] **1** *n (blame)* reproche *m*; **beyond r.** irréprochable

2 *vt* faire des reproches à; **to r. sb with sth** reprocher qch à qn • **reproachful** *adj* réprobateur, -trice • **reproachfully** *adv* d'un ton/air réprobateur

reprocess [ri:'prəʊses] *vt* retraiter; **reprocessing plant** usine *f* de retraitement

reproduce [ri:prə'dju:s] **1** *vt* reproduire

2 *vi* se reproduire • **reproduction** [-'dʌkʃən] *n* reproduction *f* • **reproductive** [-'dʌktɪv] *adj* reproducteur, -trice

reproof [rɪ'pru:f] *n Literary* réprobation *f*

reptile ['reptaɪl] *n* reptile *m*

republic [rɪ'pʌblɪk] *n* république *f* • **republican** *adj & n* républicain, -aine *(mf)*

repudiate [rɪ'pju:dɪeɪt] *vt Formal (behaviour, violence)* condamner; *(offer, accusation)* rejeter; *(idea)* renier; *(spouse)* répudier

repugnant [rɪ'pʌgnənt] *adj* répugnant; **he's r. to me** il me répugne • **repugnance** *n* répugnance *f* (**for** pour)

repulse [rɪ'pʌls] *vt* repousser • **repulsion** *n* répulsion *f* • **repulsive** *adj* repoussant

reputable ['repjʊtəbəl] *adj* de bonne réputation • **repute** [rɪ'pju:t] *n* réputation

f; **of r.** réputé ●**reputed** [rɪ'pju:tɪd] *adj*
she's r. to be wealthy on la dit riche ●**re-**
putedly [rɪ'pju:tɪdlɪ] *adv* à ce qu'on dit
reputation [repjʊ'teɪʃən] *n* réputation *f*;
to have a r. for being frank *or* **for frank-**
ness avoir la réputation d'être franc
request [rɪ'kwest] **1** *n* demande *f* (**for**
de); **on r.** sur demande; **at sb's r.** à la
demande de qn; **by popular r.** à la demande générale; *Br* **r. stop** *(for bus)* arrêt
m facultatif
   2 *vt* demander; **to r. sb to do sth** prier qn
de faire qch
requiem ['rekwɪəm] *n* requiem *m inv*
require [rɪ'kwaɪə(r)] *vt (of task, problem,*
situation) requérir; *(of person)* avoir besoin de; **to be required to do sth** être tenu
de faire qch; **if required** si besoin est/
était; **the required qualities** les qualités
fpl requises ●**requirement** *n (need)* exigence *f*; *(condition)* condition *f* (requise)
requisite ['rekwɪzɪt] **1** *adj* requis
   2 *n* élément *m* essentiel
requisition [rekwɪ'zɪʃən] **1** *n* réquisition
f
   2 *vt* réquisitionner
reroute [ri:'ru:t] *vt* dérouter
rerun ['ri:rʌn] *n (of film)* reprise *f*; *(of TV*
programme) rediffusion *f*
resale ['ri:seɪl] *n* revente *f*
reschedule [*Br* ri:'ʃedju:l, *Am* ri:'sked-
ʒʊəl] *vt* changer la date/l'heure de
rescind [rɪ'sɪnd] *vt Law* annuler; *(law)*
abroger
rescue ['reskju:] **1** *n (action)* sauvetage *m*
(**of** de); *(help, troops)* secours *mpl*; **to go/**
come to sb's r. aller/venir au secours de
qn; **to the r.** à la rescousse
   2 *adj (team, operation, attempt)* de sauvetage
   3 *vt (save)* sauver; *(set free)* délivrer
(**from** de) ●**rescuer** *n* sauveteur *m*
research [rɪ'sɜːtʃ] **1** *n* recherches *fpl* (**on**
or **into** sur); **some r.** des recherches; **to do**
r. faire de la recherche; **to do r. into sth**
faire des recherches sur qch
   2 *vi* faire des recherches (**on** *or* **into** sur)
●**researcher** *n* chercheur, -euse *mf*
resemble [rɪ'zembəl] *vt* ressembler à
●**resemblance** *n* ressemblance *f* (**to** avec)
resent [rɪ'zent] *vt* ne pas aimer ●**resent-**
ful *adj* **to be r.** éprouver du ressentiment
●**resentment** *n* ressentiment *m*
reservation [rezə'veɪʃən] *n* (**a**) *(book-*
ing) réservation *f*; **to make a r.** réserver;
do you have a r.? avez-vous réservé? (**b**)
(doubt) réserve *f* (**c**) *(land for Indians,*
animals) réserve *f*

reserve [rɪ'zɜːv] **1** *n* (**a**) *(reticence)* réserve *f* (**b**) *(land, stock)* réserve *f*; **r.**
(player) *(in team)* remplaçant, -ante *mf*;
Mil **the reserves** les réservistes *mpl*; **in r.**
en réserve; **r. tank** *(of vehicle, aircraft)*
réservoir *m* de secours
   2 *vt (room, decision)* réserver; *(right)* se
réserver; **to r. one's strength** ménager
ses forces ●**reserved** *adj (person, room)*
réservé
reservoir ['rezəvwɑː(r)] *n (of water)* réservoir *m*; *Fig* réserve *f*
reset [ri:'set] *vt (clock, watch)* mettre à
l'heure; *(counter)* remettre à zéro
reshape [ri:'ʃeɪp] *vt* réorganiser
reshuffle [ri:'ʃʌfəl] *n* réorganisation *f*;
(cabinet) r. remaniement *m* (ministériel)
reside [rɪ'zaɪd] *vi* résider
residence ['rezɪdəns] *n (home)* résidence *f*; *(of students)* foyer *m*; **to take up**
r. s'installer; **in r.** *(doctor)* sur place; *Br*
(students on campus) sur le campus; *Br (in*
halls of residence) rentrés; *Br* **r. permit**
permis *m* de séjour
resident ['rezɪdənt] **1** *n (of country, street)*
habitant, -ante *mf*; *(of hotel)* pensionnaire *mf*; *(foreigner)* résident, -ente *mf*;
Am (doctor) interne *mf*
   2 *adj* résidant, qui habite sur place;
(doctor, nurse) à demeure; **to be r. in**
London résider à Londres
residential [rezɪ'denʃəl] *adj (neighbour-*
hood) résidentiel, -ielle
residue ['rezɪdju:] *n Chem* résidu *m* ;
(remainder) reste *m* ●**residual** [rɪ'zɪdjʊəl]
adj résiduel, -uelle; *(pain, doubt)* qui per-
siste
resign [rɪ'zaɪn] **1** *vt (job)* démissionner
de; **to r. oneself to sth/to doing sth** se
résigner à qch/à faire qch
   2 *vi* démissionner (**from** de) ●**resigned**
adj résigné
resignation [rezɪg'neɪʃən] *n (from job)*
démission *f*; *(attitude)* résignation *f*
resilient [rɪ'zɪlɪənt] *adj* élastique; *Fig*
(person) résistant ●**resilience** *n* élasticité
f; *Fig* résistance *f*
resin ['rezɪn] *n* résine *f*
resist [rɪ'zɪst] **1** *vt* résister à; **to r. doing**
sth s'empêcher de faire qch; **she can't r.**
cakes elle ne peut pas résister devant des
gâteaux
   2 *vi* résister ●**resistance** *n* résistance *f*
(**to** à); **r. fighter** résistant, -ante *mf*
●**resistant** *adj* résistant (**to** à); **to be r. to**
sth résister à qch
resit [ri:'sɪt] *(pt & pp* **-sat**, *pres p* **-sitting**)
vt Br (exam) repasser

resolute ['rezəluːt] *adj* résolu •**resolutely** *adv* résolument •**reso'lution** *n* résolution *f*

resolve [rɪ'zɒlv] **1** *n* résolution *f*

2 *vt (problem)* résoudre; **to r. to do sth** *(of person)* se résoudre de faire qch; *(of committee)* décider de faire qch

resonant ['rezənənt] *adj* qui résonne; **to be r. with** résonner de •**resonance** *n* résonance *f*

resonate ['rezəneɪt] *vi* résonner

resort [rɪ'zɔːt] **1** *n* (**a**) *(holiday place)* lieu *m* de villégiature; *Br* **seaside r.**, *Am* **beach r.** station *f* balnéaire; **ski r.** station de ski (**b**) *(recourse)* recours *m* (**to** à); **as a last r., in the last r.** en dernier ressort; **without r. to** sans avoir recours à

2 *vi* **to r. to sth** avoir recours à qch; **to r. to doing sth** finir par faire qch

resound [rɪ'zaʊnd] *vi* résonner (**with** de); *Fig Literary* avoir du retentissement •**resounding** *adj (noise, failure)* retentissant; *(success)* éclatant

resource [rɪ'sɔːs, rɪ'zɔːs] *n* ressource *f* •**resourceful** *adj* ingénieux, -ieuse •**resourcefulness** *n* ingéniosité *f*

respect [rɪ'spekt] **1** *n* respect *m* (**for** pour); *(aspect)* égard *m*; **in many respects** à bien des égards; **with r. to, in r. of** en ce qui concerne; **with all due r.** sans vouloir vous/te vexer

2 *vt* respecter •**respecta'bility** *n* respectabilité *f*

respectable [rɪ'spektəbəl] *adj (decent, fairly large)* respectable; *(fairly good)* honorable •**respectably** *adv (decently)* de manière respectable; *(dressed)* convenablement; *(fairly well)* honorablement

respectful [rɪ'spektfəl] *adj* respectueux, -ueuse (**to** envers; **of** de) •**respectfully** *adv* respectueusement

respective [rɪ'spektɪv] *adj* respectif, -ive •**respectively** *adv* respectivement

respiration [respɪ'reɪʃən] *n* respiration *f*

respite ['respɪt, *Br* 'respaɪt] *n* répit *m*

resplendent [rɪ'splendənt] *adj Literary* resplendissant

respond [rɪ'spɒnd] *vi (answer)* répondre (**to** à); *(react)* réagir (**to** à); **to r. to treatment** bien réagir (au traitement) •**response** *n (answer)* réponse *f*; *(reaction)* réaction *f*; **in r. to** en réponse à

responsible [rɪ'spɒnsəbəl] *adj* responsable (**for** de); *(job)* à responsabilités •**responsi'bility** *(pl* **-ies**) *n* responsabilité *f* (**for** de) •**responsibly** *adv* de façon responsable

responsive [rɪ'spɒnsɪv] *adj (reacting)* qui réagit bien; *(alert)* éveillé; **r. to** *(kindness)* sensible à; *(suggestion)* réceptif, -ive à •**responsiveness** *n* (bonne) réaction *f*

respray [riː'spreɪ] *vt (vehicle)* repeindre

rest¹ [rest] **1** *n (relaxation)* repos *m*; *(support)* support *m*; *Mus (pause)* silence *m*; **to have** *or* **take a r.** se reposer; **to set** *or* **put sb's mind at r.** tranquilliser qn; **to come to r.** *(of ball, car)* s'immobiliser; **r. home** maison *f* de repos; *Am* **r. room** toilettes *fpl*

2 *vt (lean)* poser (**on** sur); *(base)* fonder (**on** sur); *(horse)* laisser reposer; **to r. one's eyes** se reposer les yeux

3 *vi (relax)* se reposer; *(be buried)* reposer; *(lean)* être posé (**on** sur); **to r. on** *(of argument, roof)* reposer sur; **I won't r. till...** je n'aurai de cesse que... *(+ subjunctive)*; **a resting place** un lieu de repos

rest² [rest] **1** *n (remainder)* reste *m* (**of** de); **the r.** *(others)* les autres *mfpl*; **the r. of the men** le reste des hommes

2 *vi (remain)* **r. assured** soyez assuré (**that** que); **to r. with sb** *(of decision, responsibility)* incomber à qn

restaurant ['restərɒnt] *n* restaurant *m*; *Br* **r. car** *(on train)* wagon-restaurant *m*

restful ['restfəl] *adj* reposant

restitution [restɪ'tjuːʃən] *n (compensation for damage)* réparation *f*

restive ['restɪv] *adj* agité

restless ['restləs] *adj* agité •**restlessly** *adv* avec agitation •**restlessness** *n* agitation *f*

restore [rɪ'stɔː(r)] *vt (give back)* rendre (**to** à); *(order, peace, rights)* rétablir; *(building, painting, monarchy)* restaurer; **to r. sb to health** redonner la santé à qn •**restoration** [restə'reɪʃən] *n (of order, peace)* rétablissement *m*; *(of building, painting, monarchy)* restauration *f*

restrain [rɪ'streɪn] *vt (person, dog)* maîtriser; *(crowd, anger)* contenir; *(passions)* refréner; **to r. sb from doing sth** retenir qn pour qu'il ne fasse pas qch; **to r. oneself (from doing sth)** se retenir (de faire qch) •**restrained** *adj (feelings)* contenu; *(tone)* mesuré; *(manner)* réservé •**restraint** *n (moderation)* mesure *f*; *(restriction)* restriction *f*

restrict [rɪ'strɪkt] *vt* restreindre; **to r. oneself to sth/doing sth** se limiter à qch/à faire qch •**restricted** *adj* restreint; **r. area** *Mil* zone *f* interdite; *(for parking)* zone bleue •**restriction** *n* restriction *f* (**on** à) •**restrictive** *adj* restrictif, -ive

result [rɪ'zʌlt] **1** n (outcome, success) résultat m; **as a r.** en conséquence; **as a r. of** à la suite de

2 vi résulter (**from** de); **to r. in sth** aboutir à qch

resume [rɪ'zjuːm] vti reprendre; **to r. doing sth** se remettre à faire qch • **resumption** [-'zʌmpʃən] n reprise f

résumé ['rezjʊmeɪ] n (summary) résumé m; Am curriculum vitae m inv

resurface [riː'sɜːfɪs] **1** vt (road) refaire le revêtement de

2 vi refaire surface

resurgence [rɪ'sɜːdʒəns] n réapparition f

resurrect [rezə'rekt] vt Rel ressusciter; Fig (fashion) remettre au goût du jour • **resurrection** n Rel résurrection f

resuscitate [rɪ'sʌsɪteɪt] vt Med ranimer • **resusci'tation** n réanimation f

> ⚠ Note that the French word **ressusciter** is a false friend and is never a translation for the English verb **to resuscitate**. It means **to resurrect**.

retail ['riːteɪl] **1** n (vente f au) détail m

2 adj (price, shop) de détail

3 vt vendre au détail

4 vi se vendre (au détail) (**at** à) • **retailer** n détaillant m

retain [rɪ'teɪn] vt (keep) conserver; (hold in place) retenir; (remember) maintenir • **retainer** n (fee) acompte m, avance f

retaliate [rɪ'tælɪeɪt] vi riposter • **retali-'ation** n représailles fpl; **in r. for** en représailles à

retarded [rɪ'tɑːdɪd] adj (mentally) **r.** arriéré

retch [retʃ] vi avoir des haut-le-cœur

rethink [riː'θɪŋk] (pt & pp **-thought**) vt repenser

reticent ['retɪsənt] adj peu communicatif, -ive • **reticence** n réticence f

> ⚠ Note that the French word **réticent** is a false friend and is never a translation for the English word **reticent**. It means **hesitant**.

retina ['retɪnə] n Anat rétine f

retire [rɪ'taɪə(r)] **1** vt mettre à la retraite

2 vi (**a**) (from work) prendre sa retraite (**b**) (withdraw) se retirer (**from** de; **to** à); (go to bed) aller se coucher • **retired** adj (no longer working) retraité • **retiring** adj (**a**) (official, president) sortant; **r. age** l'âge m de la retraite (**b**) (reserved) réservé

retirement [rɪ'taɪəmənt] n retraite f; **to take early r.** partir en retraite anticipée; **r. age** l'âge m de la retraite

retort [rɪ'tɔːt] **1** n réplique f

2 vti rétorquer

retrace [riː'treɪs] vt (past event) se remémorer; **to r. one's steps** revenir sur ses pas

retract [rɪ'trækt] **1** vt (**a**) (statement) revenir sur (**b**) (claws, undercarriage) rentrer

2 vi (of person) se rétracter • **retraction** n (of statement) rétractation f

retrain [riː'treɪn] **1** vt recycler

2 vi se recycler • **retraining** n recyclage m

retread ['riːtred] n pneu m rechapé

retreat [rɪ'triːt] **1** n (withdrawal) retraite f; (place) refuge m

2 vi se réfugier; (of troops) battre en retraite

retrial [riː'traɪəl] n Law nouveau procès m

retribution [retrɪ'bjuːʃən] n châtiment m

> ⚠ Note that the French word **rétribution** is a false friend and is never a translation for the English word **retribution**. It means **reward**.

retrieve [rɪ'triːv] vt (recover) récupérer; Comptr (file) ouvrir • **retrieval** n récupération f (**of** de) • **retriever** n (dog) retriever m

retroactive [retrəʊ'æktɪv] adj (pay increase) avec effet rétroactif

retrograde ['retrəgreɪd] adj rétrograde

retrospect ['retrəspekt] n **in r.** rétrospectivement

retrospective [retrə'spektɪv] **1** adj rétrospectif, -ive; (law, effect) à effet rétroactif

2 n (exhibition) rétrospective f

retune [riː'tjuːn] vi **to r. to** (radio station, wavelength) régler la radio sur

return [rɪ'tɜːn] **1** n retour m; (of goods) renvoi m; Fin (on investment) rapport m; **returns** (profits) bénéfices mpl; Br **r. (ticket)** (billet m) aller et retour m; **many happy returns!** bon anniversaire!; **on my r.** à mon retour; **in r.** en échange (**for** de); **by r. of post** par retour du courrier

2 adj (trip, flight) (de) retour; **r. match** match m retour

3 vt (give back) rendre; (put back) remettre; (bring back) rapporter; (send back) renvoyer; (greeting) répondre à; Fin (profit) rapporter; **'r. to sender'** 'retour à l'envoyeur'; **to r. sb's call** (on phone) rappeler qn; Law **to r. a verdict of guilty** déclarer l'accusé coupable

4 vi (come back) revenir; (go back) retourner; (go back home) rentrer; **to r. to**

(subject) revenir à •**returnable** *adj (bottle)* consigné

reunion [riː'juːnɪən] *n* réunion *f* • **reu'nite** *vt* réconcilier; **to be reunited with sb** retrouver qn; **they reunited him with his family** ils lui ont fait retrouver sa famille

reuse [riː'juːz] *vt* réutiliser

Rev [rev] *(abbr* **Reverend)** **R. Gray** le révérend Gray

rev [rev] *Fam* **1** *n (of car engine)* tour *m*; **r. counter** compte-tours *m inv* **2** *(pt & pp* **-vv-)** *vt* **to r. the engine (up)** faire monter le régime

revamp [riː'væmp] *vt Fam (image)* rajeunir; *(company)* restructurer

reveal [rɪ'viːl] *vt (make known)* révéler *(that* que); *(make visible)* laisser voir •**revealing** *adj (sign, comment)* révélateur, -trice

revel ['revəl] *(Br* **-ll-,** *Am* **-l-)** *vi* faire la fête; **to r. in sth** savourer qch •**reveller** *(Am* **reveler)** *n* noceur, -euse *mf* •**revelling** *(Am* **reveling), revelry** *n* festivités *fpl*

revelation [revə'leɪʃən] *n* révélation *f*

revenge [rɪ'vendʒ] **1** *n* vengeance *f*; *Sport* revanche *f*; **to have** *or* **get one's r. (on sb)** se venger (de qn); **in r.** pour se venger **2** *vt* venger

revenue ['revənjuː] *n (income)* revenu *m*; *(from sales)* recettes *fpl*

reverberate [rɪ'vɜːbəreɪt] *vi (of sound)* se répercuter; *(of news)* se propager

revere [rɪ'vɪə(r)] *vt* révérer

reverence ['revərəns] *n* révérence *f*

reverend ['revərənd] **1** *adj Rel* **r. father** révérend père *m* **2** *n* **R. Smith** *(Anglican)* le révérend Smith; *(Catholic)* l'abbé *m* Smith; *(Jewish)* le rabbin Smith

reverent ['revərənt] *adj* respectueux, -ueuse

reversal [rɪ'vɜːsəl] *n (of situation, roles)* renversement *m*; *(of policy, opinion)* revirement *m*; **r. (of fortune)** revers *m* (de fortune)

reverse [rɪ'vɜːs] **1** *adj (opposite)* contraire; *(image)* inverse; **in r. order** dans l'ordre inverse; **r. side** *(of coin)* revers *m*; *(of paper)* verso *m* **2** *n* contraire *m*; *(of coin)* revers *m*; *(of fabric)* envers *m*; *(paper)* verso *m*; *Fig (setback)* revers; **in r. (gear)** *(when driving)* en marche arrière **3** *vt (situation)* renverser; *(order, policy)* inverser; *(decision)* revenir sur; **to r. the car** faire marche arrière; *Br* **to r. the charges** *(when phoning)* téléphoner en PCV

4 *vi Br (in car)* faire marche arrière; **to r. in/out** rentrer/sortir en marche arrière; **to r. into a tree** rentrer dans un arbre en faisant marche arrière

reversible [rɪ'vɜːsəbəl] *adj (fabric)* réversible

revert [rɪ'vɜːt] *vi* **to r. to** revenir à

review [rɪ'vjuː] **1** *n* **(a)** *(of book, film)* critique *f*; *(of troops)* revue *f*; *(of salary, opinion)* révision *f*; **to be under r.** faire l'objet d'une révision **(b)** *(magazine)* revue *f* **2** *vt (book, film)* faire la critique de; *(troops)* passer en revue; *(situation)* faire le point sur; *(salary, opinion)* réviser •**reviewer** *n* critique *m*

revile [rɪ'vaɪl] *vt Formal* vilipender

revise [rɪ'vaɪz] **1** *vt (opinion, notes, text)* réviser **2** *vi (for exam)* réviser (**for** pour) •**revision** [-'vɪʒən] *n* révision *f*

revitalize [riː'vaɪtəlaɪz] *vt (person)* revigorer

revival [rɪ'vaɪvəl] *n (of custom, business, play)* reprise *f*; *(of hopes)* renaissance *f*; *(of faith, fashion, arts)* renouveau *m*

revive [rɪ'vaɪv] **1** *vt (person, memory, conversation)* ranimer; *(custom, industry)* faire renaître; *(fashion)* relancer **2** *vi (of person)* reprendre connaissance; *(of industry)* connaître un renouveau; *(of hope, interest)* renaître

revoke [rɪ'vəʊk] *vt (law)* abroger; *(decision)* revenir sur; *(contract)* résilier

revolt [rɪ'vəʊlt] **1** *n* révolte *f* **2** *vt (disgust)* révolter **3** *vi (rebel)* se révolter (**against** contre) •**revolting** *adj* dégoûtant; *(injustice)* révoltant

revolution [revə'luːʃən] *n* révolution *f* •**revolutionary** *(pl* **-ies)** *adj & n* révolutionnaire *(mf)* •**revolutionize** *vt* révolutionner

revolve [rɪ'vɒlv] *vi* tourner (**around** autour de) •**revolving** *adj* **r. chair** fauteuil *m* pivotant; **r. door(s)** porte *f* à tambour

revolver [rɪ'vɒlvə(r)] *n* revolver *m*

revue [rɪ'vjuː] *n (theatrical)* revue *f*

revulsion [rɪ'vʌlʃən] *n (disgust)* dégoût *m*

reward [rɪ'wɔːd] **1** *n* récompense *f* (**for** de) **2** *vt* récompenser (**for** de *ou* pour) •**rewarding** *adj* intéressant

rewind [riː'waɪnd] *(pt & pp* **-wound)** **1** *vt (tape, film)* rembobiner **2** *vi (of tape)* se rembobiner

rewire [riː'waɪə(r)] *vt (house)* refaire l'installation électrique de

rewrite [riːˈraɪt] (*pt* **-wrote,** *pp* **-written**) *vt* réécrire

rhapsody [ˈræpsədɪ] (*pl* **-ies**) *n* rhapsodie *f*

rhesus [ˈriːsəs] *n* rhésus *m*; **r. positive/ negative** rhésus positif/négatif

rhetoric [ˈretərɪk] *n* rhétorique *f* • **rhetorical** [rɪˈtɒrɪkəl] *adj* **r. question** question *f* de pure forme

rheumatism [ˈruːmətɪzəm] *n* rhumatisme *m*; **to have r.** avoir des rhumatismes • **rheumatic** [-ˈmætɪk] *adj (pain)* rhumatismal; *(person)* rhumatisant

Rhine [raɪn] *n* **the R.** le Rhin

rhinoceros [raɪˈnɒsərəs] *n* rhinocéros *m*

rhododendron [rəʊdəˈdendrən] *n* rhododendron *m*

Rhône [rəʊn] *n* **the R.** le Rhône

rhubarb [ˈruːbɑːb] *n* rhubarbe *f*

rhyme [raɪm] **1** *n* rime *f*; *(poem)* vers *mpl* **2** *vi* rimer (**with** avec)

rhythm [ˈrɪðəm] *n* rythme *m* • **rhythmic(al)** [ˈrɪðmɪkəl] *adj* rythmé

rib [rɪb] *n (bone)* côte *f*; **to have a broken r.** avoir une côte cassée • **ribbed** *adj (fabric, jumper)* à côtes

ribald [ˈrɪbəld] *adj Literary* grivois

ribbon [ˈrɪbən] *n* ruban *m*; **to tear sth to ribbons** déchiqueter qch

rice [raɪs] *n* riz *m*; **brown r.** riz complet; **r. pudding** riz au lait • **ricefield** *n* rizière *f*

rich [rɪtʃ] **1** (**-er, -est**) *adj (person, food)* riche; **to be r. in sth** être riche en qch **2** *npl* **the r.** les riches *mpl* • **riches** *npl* richesses *fpl* • **richly** *adv (illustrated, dressed)* richement; **r. deserved** bien mérité • **richness** *n* richesse *f*

rick [rɪk] *vt* **to r. one's back** se donner un tour de rein

rickets [ˈrɪkɪts] *n Med* rachitisme *m*

rickety [ˈrɪkɪtɪ] *adj (furniture)* branlant

rickshaw [ˈrɪkʃɔː] *n* pousse-pousse *m inv*

ricochet [ˈrɪkəʃeɪ] **1** *n* ricochet *m* **2** (*pt & pp* **-tt-**) *vi* ricocher (**off** sur)

rid [rɪd] (*pt & pp* **rid,** *pres p* **ridding**) *vt* débarrasser (**of** de); **to get r. of, to r. oneself of** se débarrasser de • **riddance** [ˈrɪdəns] *n Fam* **good r.!** bon débarras!

ridden [ˈrɪdən] *pp of* **ride**

-ridden [ˈrɪdən] *suff* debt-**r.** criblé de dettes; **disease-r.** en proie à la maladie

riddle [ˈrɪdəl] **1** *n (puzzle)* devinette *f*; *(mystery)* énigme *f* **2** *vt* cribler (**with** de); **riddled with mistakes** truffé de fautes

ride [raɪd] **1** *n (on horse)* promenade *f*; *(on bicycle, in car)* tour *m*; *(in taxi)* course *f*; *(on merry-go-round)* tour; **to go for a r.**

aller faire un tour; **to give sb a r.** *(in car)* emmener qn en voiture; **to have a r. on** *(bicycle)* monter sur; **it's only a short r. away** ce n'est pas très loin; *Fam* **to take sb for a r.** mener qn en bateau **2** (*pt* **rode,** *pp* **ridden**) *vt (horse, bicycle)* monter à; *(a particular horse)* monter; *(bus, train)* prendre; **to know how to r. a bicycle** savoir faire de la bicyclette; **to r. a bicycle to...** aller à bicyclette à...; *Am Fam* **to r. sb** *(annoy)* harceler qn **3** *vi (on horse)* faire du cheval; *(on bicycle)* faire de la bicyclette; **to go riding** *(on horse)* faire du cheval; **to be riding in a car** être en voiture; **to r. up** *(of skirt)* remonter

rider [ˈraɪdə(r)] *n* **(a)** *(on horse)* cavalier, -ière *mf*; *(cyclist)* cycliste *mf* **(b)** *Law (to document)* annexe *f*; *(to bill)* clause *f* additionnelle

ridge [rɪdʒ] *n (of mountain)* crête *f*

ridicule [ˈrɪdɪkjuːl] **1** *n* ridicule *m*; **to hold sb/sth up to r.** tourner qn/qch en ridicule; **object of r.** objet *m* de risée **2** *vt* tourner en ridicule, ridiculiser

ridiculous [rɪˈdɪkjʊləs] *adj* ridicule

riding [ˈraɪdɪŋ] *n* **(horse) r.** équitation *f*; **r. boots** bottes *fpl* de cheval; **r. school** école *f* d'équitation

rife [raɪf] *adj (widespread)* répandu

riffraff [ˈrɪfræf] *n* racaille *f*

rifle [ˈraɪfəl] **1** *n* fusil *m* **2** *vt* **to r. (through) sth** fouiller dans qch

rift [rɪft] *n (in political party)* scission *f*; *(disagreement)* désaccord *m*; *(crack in rock)* fissure *f*

rig [rɪg] **1** *n* **(oil) r.** derrick *m*; *(at sea)* plateforme *f* pétrolière **2** (*pt & pp* **-gg-**) *vt Fam (result, election)* truquer; **to r. up** *(equipment)* installer; *Fam (meeting)* arranger; *Br Fam* **to be rigged out in** être attifé de

rigging [ˈrɪgɪŋ] *n (on ship)* gréement *m*

right[1] [raɪt] **1** *adj* **(a)** *(correct)* bon *(f* bonne*)*, exact; *(word)* juste; **to be r.** *(of person)* avoir raison (**to do** de faire); **it's the r. time** c'est l'heure exacte; **that's r.** c'est ça; **r.!** bon! **(b)** *(appropriate)* bon *(f* bonne*)*; **the r. thing to do** la meilleure chose à faire; **he's the r. man** c'est l'homme qu'il faut **(c)** *(morally good)* bien *inv*; **to do the r. thing** faire ce qu'il faut **(d)** *(mentally, physically well)* **it doesn't look r.** il y a quelque chose qui ne va pas **(e)** *Fam (for emphasis)* véritable; **I felt a r. fool** je me suis vraiment senti stupide **(f)** *Math* **r. angle** angle *m* droit

2 *adv (straight)* (tout) droit; *(completely)* tout à fait; *(correctly)* correctement; **to put sth r.** *(rectify)* corriger qch; *(fix)* arranger qch; **to put things r.** arranger les choses; **to put sb r.** détromper qn; **to remember r.** bien se souvenir; **r. round** tout autour (**sth** de qch); **r. behind** juste derrière; **r. here** ici même; **r. away, r. now** tout de suite; **I'll be r. back** je reviens tout de suite; *Br* **the R. Honourable** *(to Member of Parliament)* le Très Honorable

3 *n* **to be in the r.** avoir raison; **r. and wrong** le bien et le mal

4 *vt (error, wrong, boat, car)* redresser

right² [raɪt] **1** *adj (not left)* *(hand, side)* droit

2 *adv* à droite

3 *n* droite *f*; **on** *or* **to the r.** à droite (**of** de) • **'right-'hand** *adj* de droite; **on the r. side** à droite (**of** de); **to be sb's r. man** être le bras droit de qn • **'right-'handed** *adj (person)* droitier, -ière • **'right-'wing** *adj Pol* de droite

right³ [raɪt] *n (entitlement)* droit *m* (**to do** de faire); **to have a r. to sth** avoir droit à qch; **he's famous in his own r.** il est lui-même célèbre; **to have the r. of way** *(on road)* avoir la priorité

righteous ['raɪtʃəs] *adj (person)* vertueux, -ueuse; *(cause, indignation)* juste

rightful ['raɪtfəl] *adj* légitime • **rightfully** *adv* légitimement

rightly ['raɪtlɪ] *adv (correctly)* bien; *(justifiably)* à juste titre; **r. or wrongly** à tort ou à raison

rigid ['rɪdʒɪd] *adj* rigide • **ri'gidity** *n* rigidité *f*

rigmarole ['rɪgmərəʊl] *n (process)* procédure *f* compliquée

rigour ['rɪgə(r)] *(Am* **rigor***)* *n* rigueur *f* • **rigorous** *adj* rigoureux, -euse

rile [raɪl] *vt (annoy)* agacer

rim [rɪm] *n (of cup)* bord *m*; *(of wheel)* jante *f*; *(of spectacles)* monture *f*

rind [raɪnd] *n (of cheese)* croûte *f*; *(of bacon)* couenne *f*; *(of melon, lemon)* écorce *f*

ring¹ [rɪŋ] **1** *n (for finger, curtain)* anneau *m*; *(for finger, with stone)* bague *f*; *(for napkin)* rond *m*; *(on stove)* brûleur *m*; *(of people, chairs)* cercle *m*; *(of criminals)* bande *f*; *(at circus)* piste *f*; *Boxing* ring *m*; **to have rings under one's eyes** avoir les yeux cernés; *Gym* **the rings** les anneaux; *Br* **r. road** périphérique *m*

2 *vt* **to r. (round)** *(surround)* entourer (**with** de)

ring² [rɪŋ] **1** *n (sound)* sonnerie *f*; **there's a**

r. at the door on sonne à la porte; *Fam* **to give sb a r.** passer un coup de fil à qn; **it has a r. of truth (about it)** cela a l'air vrai

2 *(pt* **rang,** *pp* **rung)** *vt (bell)* sonner; *(alarm)* déclencher; **to r. sb** *(on phone)* téléphoner à qn; **to r. the bell** sonner; **to r. the doorbell** sonner à la porte; *Fam* **that rings a bell** ça me dit quelque chose

3 *vi (of bell, phone, person)* sonner; *(of sound, words)* retentir; *(of ears)* bourdonner; *(make a phone call)* téléphoner; **to r. for sb** sonner qn • **ringing 1** *adj Br* **r. tone** *(on phone)* sonnerie *f* **2** *n (of bell)* sonnerie *f*; **a r. in one's ears** un bourdonnement dans les oreilles

▸ **ring back 1** *vt sep* **to r. sb back** rappeler qn **2** *vi* rappeler ▸ **ring off** *vi (on phone)* raccrocher ▸ **ring out** *vi (of bell)* sonner; *(of voice, shout)* retentir ▸ **ring up 1** *vt sep* **to r. sb up** téléphoner à qn **2** *vi* téléphoner

ringleader ['rɪŋliːdə(r)] *n Pej (of gang)* chef *m* de bande; *(of rebellion, strike)* meneur, -euse *mf*

ringlet ['rɪŋlɪt] *n* anglaise *f*

rink [rɪŋk] *n (for ice-skating)* patinoire *f*; *(for roller-skating)* piste *f*

rinse [rɪns] **1** *n* rinçage *m*; **to give sth a r.** rincer qch

2 *vt* rincer; **to r. one's hands** se rincer les mains; **to r. out** rincer

riot ['raɪət] **1** *n (uprising)* émeute *f*; *Fig* **a r. of colour** une explosion de couleurs; **to run r.** se déchaîner; **the r. police** ≃ les CRS *mpl*

2 *vi (rise up)* faire une émeute; *(of prisoners)* se mutiner • **rioter** *n* émeutier, -ière *mf*; *(vandal)* casseur *m* • **rioting** *n* émeutes *fpl*

riotous ['raɪətəs] *adj (crowd, party)* tapageur, -euse; **r. living** vie *f* dissolue

rip [rɪp] **1** *n* déchirure *f*

2 *(pt & pp* **-pp-***)* *vt* déchirer; **to r. sth off** arracher qch (**from** de); *Fam (steal)* faucher qch; *Fam* **to r. sb off** *(deceive)* rouler qn; **to r. sth up** déchirer qch

3 *vi (of fabric)* se déchirer; **the explosion ripped through the building** l'explosion souffla dans tout le bâtiment • **rip-off** *n* *Fam* arnaque *f*

ripe [raɪp] *(-er, -est)* *adj (fruit)* mûr; *(cheese)* fait • **ripen** *vti* mûrir

ripple ['rɪpəl] **1** *n (on water)* ride *f*; *Fig (of laughter)* cascade *f*

2 *vi (of water)* se rider

rise [raɪz] **1** *n (in price, pressure)* hausse *f* (**in** de); *(in river)* crue *f*; *(slope in ground)* montée *f*; *(hill)* éminence *f*; *(of leader,* *party)* ascension *f; (of technology, industry)* essor *m;* **his r. to power** son accession au pouvoir; *Br* **(pay) r.** augmentation *f* (de salaire); **to give r. to sth** donner lieu à qch

2 (*pt* **rose,** *pp* **risen** [ˈrɪzən]) *vi (of temperature, balloon, price)* monter; *(in society)* s'élever; *(of hope)* grandir; *(of sun, theatre curtain, wind)* se lever; *(of dough)* lever; *(get up from chair or bed)* se lever; **to r. to the surface** remonter à la surface; **the river rises in** le fleuve prend sa source dans; **to r. (up)** *(rebel)* se soulever (**against** contre); **to r. to power** accéder au pouvoir; **to r. from the dead** ressusciter; **to r. to the occasion** se montrer à la hauteur de la situation

riser [ˈraɪzə(r)] *n* **early r.** lève-tôt *mf inv;* **late r.** lève-tard *mf inv*

rising [ˈraɪzɪŋ] **1** *n (of curtain in theatre)* lever *m; (revolt)* soulèvement *m; (of river)* crue *f*

2 *adj (sun)* levant; *(tide)* montant; *(number)* croissant; *(prices)* en hausse; *(artist, politician)* qui monte

risk [rɪsk] **1** *n* risque *m;* **at r.** *(person)* en danger; *(job)* menacé; **at your own r.** à tes risques et périls; **to run the r. of doing sth** courir le risque de faire qch

2 *vt (life, reputation)* risquer; **I can't r. going** je ne peux pas prendre le risque d'y aller; **we can't r. it** nous ne pouvons pas prendre ce risque • **risky** (**-ier, -iest**) *adj* risqué

rissole [ˈrɪsəʊl] *n Br Culin* croquette *f*

rite [raɪt] *n* rite *m; Rel* **the last rites** les derniers sacrements *mpl* • **ritual** [ˈrɪtʃʊəl] **1** *adj* rituel, -uelle **2** *n* rituel *m*

rival [ˈraɪvəl] **1** *adj* rival

2 *n* rival, -ale *mf*

3 (*Br* **-ll-,** *Am* **-l-**) *vt (compete with)* rivaliser avec (**in** de); *(equal)* égaler (**in** en) • **rivalry** (*pl* **-ies**) *n* rivalité *f* (**between** entre)

river [ˈrɪvə(r)] **1** *n (small)* rivière *f; (flowing into sea)* fleuve *m; Fig (of lava, tears)* flot *m;* **the R. Thames** la Tamise

2 *adj (port, navigation)* fluvial; **r. bank** rive *f;* **r. bed** lit *m* de rivière/de fleuve • **riverside 1** *n* bord *m* de l'eau **2** *adj* au bord de l'eau

rivet [ˈrɪvɪt] **1** *n* rivet *m*

2 *vt* riveter; *Fig (eyes)* fixer (**on** sur); **to be riveted to the TV set** être cloué devant la télé • **riveting** *adj Fig* fascinant

Riviera [rɪvɪˈeərə] *n* **the (French) R.** la Côte d'Azur

roach [rəʊtʃ] *n Am (cockroach)* cafard *m*

road [rəʊd] **1** *n* route *f; (small)* chemin *m; (in town)* rue *f; (roadway)* chaussée *f;* **the Paris r.** la route de Paris; **by r.** par la route; **down/up the r.** un peu plus loin dans la rue; **to live across** *or* **over the r.** habiter en face; **to be on the r. to recovery** être en voie de la guérison

2 *adj (map, safety)* routier, -ière; *(accident)* de la route; *Fam* **r. hog** chauffard *m;* **r. sign** panneau *m* de signalisation; *Br* **r. works,** *Am* **r. work** travaux *mpl* de voirie • **roadblock** *n* barrage *m* routier • **roadside 1** *n* bord *m* de la route **2** *adj* **r. bar** bar *m* situé en bord de route • **roadway** *n* chaussée *f* • **roadworthy** *adj (vehicle)* en état de rouler

roam [rəʊm] **1** *vt* parcourir

2 *vi* errer; **to r. (about) the streets** traîner dans les rues

roar [rɔː(r)] **1** *n (of lion)* rugissement *m; (of person)* hurlement *m; (of thunder)* grondement *m*

2 *vt* **to r. sth (out)** hurler qch

3 *vi (of lion, wind, engine)* rugir; *(of person, crowd)* hurler; *(of thunder)* gronder; **to r. with laughter** hurler de rire; **to r. past** *(of truck)* passer dans un bruit de tonnerre • **roaring** *adj* **a r. fire** une belle flambée; **a r. success** un succès fou; **to do a r. trade** faire des affaires en or

roast [rəʊst] **1** *n (meat)* rôti *m*

2 *adj* rôti; **r. beef** rosbif *m*

3 *vt (meat, potatoes)* faire rôtir; *(coffee)* faire griller

4 *vi (of meat)* rôtir; *Fam* **it's roasting in here** on cuit ici

rob [rɒb] (*pt & pp* **-bb-**) *vt (person)* voler; *(shop, bank)* dévaliser; *(house)* cambrioler; **to r. sb of sth** voler qch à qn; *Fig (deprive)* priver qn de qch • **robber** *n* voleur, -euse *mf* • **robbery** (*pl* **-ies**) *n* vol *m;* **it's daylight r.!** c'est du vol pur et simple!; **armed r.** vol à main armée

robe [rəʊb] *n (dressing gown)* robe *f* de chambre; *(of priest, judge)* robe

robin [ˈrɒbɪn] *n (bird)* rouge-gorge *m*

robot [ˈrəʊbɒt] *n* robot *m* • **ro'botics** *n* robotique *f*

robust [rəʊˈbʌst] *adj* robuste

rock¹ [rɒk] **1** *n (music)* rock *m*

2 *vt (boat)* balancer; *(building)* secouer; **to r. a baby to sleep** bercer un bébé pour qu'il s'endorme

3 *vi (sway)* se balancer; *(of building, ground)* trembler • **rocking chair** *n* fauteuil *m* à bascule • **rocking horse** *n* cheval *m* à bascule

rock² [rɒk] **1** *n (substance)* roche *f*; *(boulder, rock face)* rocher *m*; *Am (stone)* pierre *f*; *Br (sweet)* = sucrerie en forme de bâton parfumée à la menthe; **on the rocks** *(whisky)* avec des glaçons; *(marriage)* en pleine débâcle; **r. climbing** varappe *f*; **r. face** paroi *f* rocheuse • **'rock-'bottom 1** *n* point le plus bas; **he has reached r.** il a touché le fond **2** *adj (prices)* les plus bas (*f* basses)

rockery ['rɒkərɪ] *(pl -ies) n* rocaille *f*

rocket ['rɒkɪt] **1** *n* fusée *f*
  2 *vi (of prices, unemployment)* monter en flèche

rocky ['rɒkɪ] (**-ier, -iest**) *adj (road)* rocailleux, -euse; *(hill)* rocheux, -euse; *Fig (relationship)* instable

rod [rɒd] *n (wooden)* baguette *f*; *(metal)* tige *f*; *(of curtain)* tringle *f*; *(for fishing)* canne *f* à pêche

rode [rəʊd] *pt of* ride

rodent ['rəʊdənt] *n* rongeur *m*

rodeo [*Br* 'rəʊdɪəʊ, *Am* rəʊ'deɪəʊ] *(pl -os) n Am* rodéo *m*

roe [rəʊ] *n* (**a**) *(eggs)* œufs *mpl* de poisson (**b**) **r. (deer)** chevreuil *m*

rogue [rəʊg] *n (dishonest)* crapule *f*; *(mischievous)* coquin, -ine *mf* • **roguish** *adj (smile)* coquin

role [rəʊl] *n* rôle *m*; **r. model** modèle *m*

roll [rəʊl] **1** *n (of paper)* rouleau *m*; *(of fat, flesh)* bourrelet *m*; *(of drum, thunder)* roulement *m*; *(of ship)* roulis *m*; *(bread)* petit pain *m*; *(list)* liste *f*; **r. of film** pellicule *f*; **to have a r. call** faire l'appel; **r. neck** col *m* roulé
  2 *vt (cigarette)* rouler; *(ball)* faire rouler
  3 *vi (of ball, ship)* rouler; *(of camera)* tourner; *(of thunder)* gronder; **to r. into a ball** *(of animal)* se rouler en boule; *Fam* **to be rolling in money, to be rolling in it** rouler sur l'or • **rolling** *adj (hills)* ondulant; *(sea)* gros (*f* grosse
  ▸ **roll down** *vt sep (car window)* baisser; *(sleeves)* redescendre ▸ **roll in** *vi Fam (flow in)* affluer; *(of person)* s'amener ▸ **roll on 1** *vt sep (paint)* appliquer au rouleau **2** *vi Fam* **r. on tonight!** vivement ce soir! ▸ **roll out** *vt sep (dough)* étaler ▸ **roll over 1** *vt sep* retourner **2** *vi (many times)* se rouler; *(once)* se retourner ▸ **roll up 1** *vt sep (map, cloth)* rouler; *(sleeve)* retrousser **2** *vi Fam (arrive)* s'amener

roller ['rəʊlə(r)] **1** *n (for hair, painting)* rouleau *m*; **r. coaster** montagnes *fpl* russes; **r. skate** patin *m* à roulettes • **rollerskate** *vi* faire du patin à roulettes

rollerblades ['rəʊləbleɪdz] *npl* patins *mpl* en ligne

rollicking ['rɒlɪkɪŋ] **1** *adj* joyeux, -euse (et bruyant)
  2 *n Br Fam* **to give sb a r.** engueuler qn

rolling pin ['rəʊlɪŋpɪn] *n* rouleau *m* à pâtisserie

ROM [rɒm] (*abbr* **read only memory**) *n Comptr* mémoire *f* morte

Roman ['rəʊmən] **1** *adj* romain
  2 *n* Romain, -aine *mf*
  3 *adj & n* **R. Catholic** catholique *(mf)*

romance [rəʊ'mæns] **1** *n (love)* amour *m*; *(affair)* aventure *f* amoureuse; *(story)* histoire *f* d'amour; *(charm)* poésie *f*
  2 *adj* **R. language** langue *f* romane

Romania [rəʊ'meɪnɪə] *n* la Roumanie • **Romanian 1** *adj* roumain **2** *n (person)* Roumain, -aine *mf*; *(language)* roumain *m*

romantic [rəʊ'mæntɪk] **1** *adj (of love, tenderness)* romantique; *(fanciful, imaginary)* romanesque
  2 *n* romantique *mf* • **romantically** *adv* de façon romantique • **romanticism** *n* romantisme *m*

romp [rɒmp] **1** *n* **to have a r.** chahuter
  2 *vi* s'ébattre; **to r. through an exam** avoir un examen les doigts dans le nez

rompers ['rɒmpəz] *npl (for baby)* barboteuse *f*

roof [ruːf] *n (of building, vehicle)* toit *m*; *(of tunnel, cave)* plafond *m*; **r. of the mouth** voûte *f* du palais; **r. rack** *(of car)* galerie *f* • **roofing** *n* toiture *f* • **rooftop** *n* toit *m*

rook [rʊk] *n (bird)* freux *m*; *Chess* tour *f*

rookie ['rʊkɪ] *n Am Fam (new recruit)* bleu *m*

room [ruːm, rʊm] *n* (**a**) *(in house)* pièce *f*; *(bedroom)* chambre *f*; *(large, public)* salle *f*; *Am* **men's r., ladies' r.** toilettes *fpl* (**b**) *(space)* place *f*; **to make r.** faire de la place (**for** pour); **there's r. for doubt** le doute est permis; **no r. for doubt** aucun doute possible • **rooming house** *n Am* maison *f* de rapport • **roommate** *n* camarade *mf* de chambre • **roomy** (**-ier, -iest**) *adj* spacieux, -ieuse; *(clothes)* ample

roost [ruːst] **1** *n* perchoir *m*
  2 *vi* se percher

rooster ['ruːstə(r)] *n* coq *m*

root [ruːt] **1** *n (of plant, tooth, hair) & Math* racine *f*; *Fig (origin)* origine *f*; *(cause)* cause *f*; **to pull sth up by the root(s)** déraciner qch; **to take r.** *(of plant, person)* prendre racine; *Fig* **to find one's roots** retrouver ses racines; *Fig* **to put down**

(new) roots *(of person)* s'intégrer; **r. beer** = boisson gazeuse aux extraits végétaux; **r. cause** cause *f* première
2 *vt* **to r. sth out** supprimer qch
3 *vi (of plant cutting)* s'enraciner; **to r. about** *or* **around for sth** fouiller pour trouver qch; **Fam to r. for sb** appuyer qn • **rooted** *adj* **deeply r.** bien enraciné (**in** dans); **r. to the spot** *(immobile)* cloué sur place • **rootless** *adj* sans racines
rope [rəʊp] **1** *n* corde *f*; *(on ship)* cordage *m*; *Fam* **to know the ropes** connaître son affaire
2 *vt (tie)* lier; *Fam* **to r. sb in** recruter qn; **to r. sth off** *(of police)* interdire l'accès de qch
rop(e)y ['rəʊpɪ] (**-ier, -iest**) *adj Br Fam (thing)* minable; *(person)* patraque
rosary ['rəʊzərɪ] (*pl* **-ies**) *n Rel* chapelet *m*
rose¹ [rəʊz] *n* (**a**) *(flower)* rose *f*; **r. bush** rosier *m* (**b**) *(of watering can)* pomme *f* • **rosebud** *n* bouton *m* de rose
rose² [rəʊz] *pt of* **rise**
rosé ['rəʊzeɪ] *n* rosé *m*
rosemary ['rəʊzmərɪ] *n (plant, herb)* romarin *m*
rosette [rəʊ'zet] *n* rosette *f*
roster ['rɒstə(r)] *n* (**duty**) **r.** liste *f* de service
rostrum ['rɒstrəm] *n* tribune *f*; *(for prize-winner)* podium *m*
rosy ['rəʊzɪ] (**-ier, -iest**) *adj (pink)* rose; *Fig (future)* prometteur, -euse
rot [rɒt] **1** *n* pourriture *f*; *Br Fam (nonsense)* inepties *fpl*
2 (*pt & pp* **-tt-**) *vti* pourrir
rota ['rəʊtə] *n* roulement *m*
rotary ['rəʊtərɪ] **1** *adj* rotatif, -ive
2 (*pl* **-ies**) *n Am (for traffic)* rond-point *m* • **ro'tation** *n* rotation *f*; **in r.** à tour de rôle
rotate [rəʊ'teɪt] **1** *vt* faire tourner; *(crops)* alterner
2 *vi* tourner
rote [rəʊt] *n* **by r.** machinalement
rotten ['rɒtən] *adj (fruit, egg, wood)* pourri; *Fam (bad)* nul (*f* nulle); *Fam (weather)* pourri; *Fam* **to feel r.** *(ill)* être mal fichu • **rotting** *adj (meat, fruit)* qui pourrit
rouble ['ruːbəl] (*Am* **ruble**) *n (currency)* rouble *m*
rouge [ruːʒ] *n Old-fashioned* rouge *m* (à joues)
rough¹ [rʌf] **1** (**-er, -est**) *adj (surface)* rugueux, -ueuse; *(ground)* accidenté; *(manners)* fruste; *(climate, life, voice)* rude; *(wine)* âpre; *(neighbourhood)* dur; *(sea)* agité; *(diamond)* brut; *(brutal)* bru-

tal; *Br (justice)* sommaire; *Fig* **to feel r.** *(ill)* être mal fichu
2 *adv Br* **to sleep/live r.** coucher/vivre à la dure; **to play r.** jouer avec brutalité
3 *vt Fam* **to r. it** vivre à la dure; *Fam* **to r. sb up** tabasser qn; **to r. up sb's hair** ébouriffer les cheveux de qn • **rough-and-'ready** *adj (solution)* rudimentaire; *(meal, accommodation)* sommaire • **rough-and-'tumble** *n* bousculade *f* • **roughen** *vt* rendre rugueux, -ueuse • **roughly¹** *adv (brutally)* brutalement; *(crudely)* grossièrement • **roughness** *n (of surface)* rugosité *f*; *(of behaviour)* rudesse *f*
rough² [rʌf] **1** (**-er, -est**) *adj (approximate)* approximatif, -ive; **I have a r. idea of what he wants** j'ai une petite idée de ce qu'il veut; **r. guess, r. estimate** approximation *f*; *Br* **r. book** cahier *m* de brouillon; **r. copy, r. draft** brouillon *m*; **r. paper** papier *m* brouillon
2 *vt* **to r. sth out** *(plan)* ébaucher • **roughly²** *adv (approximately)* à peu près; **r. speaking** en gros
roughage ['rʌfɪdʒ] *n* fibres *fpl* (alimentaires)
roulette [ruː'let] *n* roulette *f*
round [raʊnd] **1** (**-er, -est**) *adj* rond; *Am* **r. trip** aller (et) retour *m*
2 *adv* autour; **all r., right r.** tout autour; **all year r.** toute l'année; **the long way r.** le chemin le plus long; **the wrong way r.** à l'envers; **the other way r.** dans l'autre sens; **to go r. to sb's** passer chez qn; **to ask sb r.** inviter qn chez soi
3 *prep* autour de; **r. here** par ici; **r. about** *(approximately)* environ; **r. (about) midday** vers midi; **to go r. the corner** tourner le coin; **it's just r. the corner** c'est juste au coin; **to go r. the world** parcourir le monde
4 *n Br (slice)* tranche *f*; *Br (sandwich)* sandwich *m*; *(in competition)* manche *f*; *(of golf)* partie *f*; *Boxing* round *m*; *(of talks)* série *f*; *(of drinks, visits)* tournée *f*; **to be on one's round(s), to do one's round(s)** *(of milkman)* faire sa tournée; *(of doctor)* faire ses visites; *(of policeman)* faire sa ronde; **r. of applause** salve *f* d'applaudissements; **r. of ammunition** cartouche *f*
5 *vt* **to r. a corner** *(in car)* prendre un virage; **to r. sth off** *(meal, speech)* terminer qch (**with** par); **to r. up** *(gather)* rassembler; *(price)* arrondir au chiffre supérieur • **round-'shouldered** *adj* voûté

roundabout [ˈraʊndəbaʊt] **1** *adj (method, route)* indirect
2 *n Br (at funfair)* manège *m*; *(road junction)* rond-point *m*
rounded [ˈraʊndɪd] *adj* arrondi • **roundness** *n* rondeur *f*
rounders [ˈraʊndəz] *npl* = jeu similaire au base-ball
roundup [ˈraʊndʌp] *n (of criminals)* rafle *f*
rouse [raʊz] *vt (awaken)* éveiller; **roused** *(to anger)* en colère; **to r. sb to action** inciter qn à agir • **rousing** *adj (welcome)* enthousiaste; *(speech)* vibrant; *(music)* allègre
rout [raʊt] **1** *n* déroute *f*
2 *vt* mettre en déroute
route¹ [ruːt] **1** *n* itinéraire *m*; *(of aircraft, ship)* route *f*; **bus r.** ligne *f* d'autobus
2 *vt (train)* fixer l'itinéraire de
route² [raʊt] *n Am (delivery round)* tournée *f*
routine [ruːˈtiːn] **1** *n (habit)* routine *f*; *(on stage)* numéro *m*; *Comptr* sous-programme *m*; **the daily r.** le train-train quotidien; **as a matter of r.** de façon systématique
2 *adj (inquiry, work)* de routine; *Pej* routinier, -ière
rove [raʊv] **1** *vt* parcourir
2 *vi* rôder • **roving** *adj (life)* nomade; *(ambassador)* itinérant
row¹ [raʊ] *n (line)* rangée *f*; **two days in a r.** deux jours d'affilée
row² [raʊ] **1** *n* **to go for a r.** canoter; *Am* **r. boat** bateau *m* à rames
2 *vt (boat)* faire aller à la rame; *(person)* transporter en canot
3 *vi (in boat)* ramer • **rowing** *n* canotage *m*; *(as sport)* aviron *m*; *Br* **r. boat** bateau *m* à rames
row³ [raʊ] **1** *n (noise)* vacarme *m*; *(quarrel)* dispute *f*
2 *vi* se disputer (**with** avec)
rowdy [ˈraʊdɪ] **1** (**-ier, -iest**) *adj* chahuteur, -euse
2 (*pl* **-ies**) *n* chahuteur, -euse *mf*
royal [ˈrɔɪəl] **1** *adj* royal; **the R. Air Force** = l'armée de l'air britannique
2 *npl Fam* **the royals** la famille royale • **royalist** *adj & n* royaliste *(mf)* • **royally** *adv (treat)* royalement • **royalty 1** *n (rank, position)* royauté *f*; *(person)* membre *m* de la famille royale **2** *npl* **royalties** *(from book)* droits *mpl* d'auteur; *(from invention, on oil)* royalties *fpl*
rpm [ɑːpiːˈem] *(abbr* **revolutions per minute***) Aut* tours/minute

Rt Hon *(abbr* **Right Honourable***) see* **right¹**
rub [rʌb] **1** *n (massage)* friction *f*; **to give sth a r.** frotter qch
2 *(pt & pp* **-bb-***) vt* frotter; *Fig* **to r. shoulders with** côtoyer; *Fam* **to r. sb up the wrong way** prendre qn à rebrousse-poil
3 *vi* frotter
▸ **rub away** *vt sep (mark)* effacer; *(tears)* essuyer ▸ **rub down** *vt sep (person)* frictionner; *(wood, with sandpaper)* poncer ▸ **rub in** *vt sep (cream)* faire pénétrer (en massant); *Fam* **to r. it in** retourner le couteau dans la plaie ▸ **rub off 1** *vt sep (mark)* effacer **2** *vi (of mark)* partir; *Fig (of manners)* déteindre (**on** sur) ▸ **rub out** *vt sep (mark)* effacer
rubber [ˈrʌbə(r)] *n (substance)* caoutchouc *m*; *Br (eraser)* gomme *f*; *Am Fam (contraceptive)* capote *f*; **r. band** élastique *m*; **r. stamp** tampon *m* • **rubber-ˈstamp** *vt Pej* approuver (sans discuter) • **rubbery** *adj* caoutchouteux, -euse
rubbing alcohol [ˈrʌbɪŋælkəhɒl] *n Am* alcool *m* à 90°
rubbish [ˈrʌbɪʃ] **1** *n Br (waste)* ordures *fpl*; *(industrial)* déchets *mpl*; *(junk)* cochonneries *fpl*; *Fig (nonsense)* idioties *fpl*; *Fam* **that's r.** *(absurd)* c'est absurde; *(worthless)* ça ne vaut rien; **r. bin** poubelle *f*; **r. dump** décharge *f* publique
2 *vt Fam* **to r. sb/sth** *(criticize)* dénigrer qn/qch
rubbishy [ˈrʌbɪʃɪ] *adj (book, film)* nul *(f* nulle*)*; *(goods)* de mauvaise qualité
rubble [ˈrʌbəl] *n* décombres *mpl*
rubella [ruːˈbelə] *n Med* rubéole *f*
ruble [ˈruːbəl] *n Am (currency)* rouble *m*
ruby [ˈruːbɪ] *(pl* **-ies***) n (gem)* rubis *m*
rucksack [ˈrʌksæk] *n* sac *m* à dos
rudder [ˈrʌdə(r)] *n* gouvernail *m*
ruddy [ˈrʌdɪ] (**-ier, -iest**) *adj (complexion)* rose; *Br Fam (bloody)* fichu
rude [ruːd] (**-er, -est**) *adj (impolite)* impoli (**to** envers); *(coarse, insolent)* grossier, -ière (**to** envers); *(indecent)* obscène; *(shock)* violent • **rudely** *adv (impolitely)* impoliment; *(coarsely)* grossièrement • **rudeness** *n (impoliteness)* impolitesse *f*; *(coarseness)* grossièreté *f*

Note that the French word **rude** *is a false friend and is never a translation for the English word* **rude**. *It means* **harsh** *or* **rough**.

rudiments [ˈruːdɪmənts] *npl* rudiments *mpl* • **rudimentary** [-ˈmentərɪ] *adj* rudimentaire

rueful ['ruːfəl] *adj Literary (voice, smile)* de regret

ruffian ['rʌfiən] *n* voyou *m* (*pl* -ous)

ruffle ['rʌfəl] **1** *vt (hair)* ébouriffer; *(water)* troubler; **to r. sb** *(offend)* froisser qn **2** *n (frill)* ruche *f*

rug [rʌg] *n* tapis *m*; *(over knees)* plaid *m*; **(bedside) r.** descente *f* de lit

rugby ['rʌgbɪ] *n* **r. (football)** rugby *m*

rugged ['rʌgɪd] *adj (surface)* rugueux, -ueuse; *(terrain, coast)* accidenté; *(features, manners)* rude; *Fig (determination)* farouche

rugger ['rʌgə(r)] *n Br Fam* rugby *m*

ruin ['ruːɪn] **1** *n (destruction, rubble, building)* ruine *f*; **in ruins** *(building)* en ruine **2** *vt (health, country, person)* ruiner; *(clothes)* abîmer; *(effect, meal, party)* gâcher • **ruined** *adj (person, country)* ruiné; *(building)* en ruine • **ruinous** *adj* ruineux, -euse

rule [ruːl] **1** *n* (a) *(principle)* règle *f*; *(regulation)* règlement *m*; *(government)* autorité *f*; *Br* **against the rules** *or Am* **r.** contraire au règlement; **as a r.** en règle générale; **it's the** *or* **a r. that...** il est de règle que... (+ *subjunctive*) (b) *(for measuring)* règle *f* **2** *vt (country)* gouverner; *(decide) (of judge, referee)* décider (**that** que); **to r. sth out** *(exclude)* exclure qch **3** *vi (of king)* régner (**over** sur); *(of judge)* statuer (**against** contre; **on** sur) • **ruled** *adj (paper)* réglé • **ruling 1** *adj (passion, fear)* dominant; **the r. class** la classe dirigeante; *Pol* **the r. party** le parti au pouvoir **2** *n (of judge, referee)* décision *f*

ruler ['ruːlə(r)] *n* (a) *(for measuring)* règle *f* (b) *(king, queen)* souverain, -aine *mf*; *(political leader)* dirigeant, -ante *mf*

rum [rʌm] *n* rhum *m*

Rumania [ruːˈmeɪnɪə] *see* **Romania**

rumble ['rʌmbəl] **1** *n* grondement *m*; *(of stomach)* gargouillement *m* **2** *vi (of train, thunder, gun)* gronder; *(of stomach)* gargouiller

ruminate ['ruːmɪneɪt] *vi Formal* **to r. over sth** *(scheme)* ruminer qch

rummage ['rʌmɪdʒ] *vi* **to r. (about)** farfouiller • **rummage sale** *n Am (used clothes)* vente *f* de charité

rumour ['ruːmə(r)] (*Am* **rumor**) *n* rumeur *f* • **rumoured** (*Am* **rumored**) *adj* **it is r. that...** on dit que...

rump [rʌmp] *n (of horse)* croupe *f*; *(of fowl)* croupion *m*; **r. steak** romsteck *m*

rumple ['rʌmpəl] *vt (clothes)* chiffonner

rumpus ['rʌmpəs] *n Fam (noise)* chahut *m*

run [rʌn] **1** *n (series)* série *f*; *(period)* période *f*; *(running)* course *f*; *(outing)* tour *m*; *(journey)* trajet *m*; *(rush)* ruée *f* (**on** sur); *(for skiing)* piste *f*; *(in cricket, baseball)* point *m*; *Cards* suite *f*; *(in stocking)* maille *f* filée; **to go for a r.** aller courir; **on the r.** *(prisoner)* en fuite; **to have the r. of** *(house)* avoir à sa disposition; **in the long/short r.** à long/court terme; *Fam* **to have the runs** avoir la courante

2 (*pt* **ran**, *pp* **run**, *pres p* **running**) *vt (distance, race)* courir; *(machine)* faire fonctionner; *(test)* effectuer; *(business, country)* diriger; *(courses, events)* organiser; *Comptr (program)* exécuter; *(newspaper article)* publier (**on** sur); *(bath)* faire couler; **to r. a temperature** avoir de la fièvre; **to r. one's hand over** passer la main sur; **to r. one's eye over sth** jeter un coup d'œil à qch; **to r. its course** *(of illness)* suivre son cours; **to r. sb to the airport** conduire qn à l'aéroport; **to r. a car** avoir une voiture

3 *vi* courir; *(flee)* fuir; *(of river, nose, pen, tap)* couler; *(of colour in washing)* déteindre; *(of ink)* baver; *(melt)* fondre; *(function) (of machine)* marcher; *(idle) (of engine)* tourner; *(of stocking, tights)* filer; **to r. down/in/out** descendre/entrer/sortir en courant; **to go running** faire du jogging; **to r. for president** être candidat à la présidence; **to r. with blood** ruisseler de sang; **to r. between** *(of bus)* faire le service entre; **the road runs to...** la route va à...; **the river runs into the sea** le fleuve se jette dans la mer; **it runs into £100** ça va a chercher dans les 100 livres; **it runs in the family** ça tient de famille

▸ **run about, run around** *vi* courir çà et là ▸ **run across** *vt insep (meet)* tomber sur ▸ **run along** *vi* **r. along!** filez! ▸ **run away** *vi (flee)* s'enfuir (**from** de) ▸ **run back** *vt sep (person in vehicle)* ramener (**to** à) ▸ **run down** *vt sep (pedestrian)* renverser; *(knock over and kill)* écraser; *Fig (belittle)* dénigrer; *(restrict)* limiter peu à peu ▸ **run in** *vt sep Br (engine)* roder ▸ **run into** *vt insep (meet)* tomber sur; *(crash into) (of vehicle, train)* percuter; **to r. into debt** s'endetter ▸ **run off** *vt sep (print)* tirer **2** *vi (flee)* s'enfuir (**with** avec) ▸ **run out 1** *vt sep* **to r. sb out of** *(chase)* chasser qn de **2** *vi (of stocks)* s'épuiser; *(of lease)* expirer; *(of time)* manquer; **to r. out of time/money** manquer de temps/d'argent; **we've r. out of coffee** on n'a plus de café; **I ran out of petrol** *or Am* **gas** je suis tombé en panne d'essence ▸**run over 1** *vt sep* *(kill)* écraser; *(knock down)* renverser **2** *vt insep (notes, text)* revoir **3** *vi (of liquid)* déborder ▸**run round** *vt insep (surround)* entourer ▸**run through** *vt insep (recap)* revoir ▸**run up** *vt sep (debts, bill)* laisser s'accumuler

runaway ['rʌnəweɪ] **1** *n* fugitif, -ive *mf* **2** *adj (car, horse)* fou *(f* folle*); (inflation)* galopant; *(victory)* remporté haut la main

run-down [rʌn'daʊn] *adj (weak, tired)* fatigué; *(district)* délabré

rung¹ [rʌŋ] *n (of ladder)* barreau *m*

rung² [rʌŋ] *pp of* **ring²**

runner ['rʌnə(r)] *n (athlete)* coureur *m; Br* **r. bean** haricot *m* d'Espagne

runner-up [rʌnər'ʌp] *n (in race)* second, -onde *mf*

running ['rʌnɪŋ] **1** *n* course *f; (of machine)* fonctionnement *m; (of business, country)* gestion *f;* **to be in/out of the r.** être/ne plus être dans la course **2** *adj* **six days r.** six jours de suite; **r. water** eau *f* courante; **a r. battle with** *(cancer, landlord)* une lutte de tous les instants avec; **to give a r. commentary (on)** *(on TV)* faire un commentaire en direct (de); **r. costs** *(of factory)* frais *mpl* d'exploitation; *(of car)* dépenses *fpl* courantes

runny ['rʌnɪ] (-ier, -iest) *adj (cream, sauce)* liquide; *(nose)* qui coule; **r. om-elet(te)** omelette *f* baveuse

run-of-the-mill [rʌnəvðə'mɪl] *adj* ordinaire

run-up ['rʌnʌp] *n* **in the r. to** *(elections, Christmas)* dans la période qui précède

runway ['rʌnweɪ] *n (for aircraft)* piste *f* (d'envol); *Am (for fashion parade)* podium *m*

rupture ['rʌptʃə(r)] **1** *n (hernia)* hernie *f;* **the r. of** *(breaking)* la rupture de **2** *vt* rompre; **to r. oneself** se faire une hernie

rural ['rʊərəl] *adj* rural

ruse [ruːz] *n* ruse *f*

rush¹ [rʌʃ] **1** *n (demand)* ruée *f (* **for** vers; **on** sur*); (confusion)* bousculade *f;* **to be in a r.** être pressé (**to do** de faire); **to leave in a r.** partir en vitesse; **the gold r.** la ruée vers l'or; **r. hour** heures *fpl* de pointe; **a r. job** un travail urgent **2** *vt Mil (attack)* prendre d'assaut; **to r. sb** *(hurry)* bousculer qn; **to r. sb to hospital** *or Am* **the hospital** transporter qn d'urgence à l'hôpital; **to r. (through) sth** *(job)* faire qch en vitesse; *(decision)* prendre qch à la hâte; **to be rushed into a decision** être forcé à prendre une décision à la hâte **3** *vi (move fast, throw oneself)* se ruer (**at** sur; **towards** vers); *(of blood)* affluer (**to** à); *(hurry)* se dépêcher (**to do** de faire); *(of vehicle)* foncer; **to r. out** sortir précipitamment

rush² [rʌʃ] *n (plant)* jonc *m*

rusk [rʌsk] *n Br* biscotte *f*

russet ['rʌsɪt] *adj* brun roux *inv*

Russia ['rʌʃə] *n* la Russie •**Russian 1** *adj* russe **2** *n (person)* Russe *mf; (language)* russe *m*

rust [rʌst] **1** *n* rouille *f* **2** *vi* rouiller •**rust-proof** *adj* inoxydable •**rusty** (-ier, -iest) *adj* rouillé

rustic ['rʌstɪk] *adj* rustique

rustle¹ ['rʌsəl] **1** *n* bruissement *m* **2** *vt Fam* **to r. sth up** *(meal, snack)* improviser qch; **to r. up support** rassembler des partisans **3** *vi (of leaves)* bruire

rustle² ['rʌsəl] *vt Am (steal)* voler •**rustler** *n Am (thief)* voleur *m* de bétail

rut [rʌt] *n* ornière *f; Fig* **to be in a r.** être encroûté

rutabaga [ruːtə'beɪgə] *n Am (swede)* rutabaga *m*

ruthless ['ruːθləs] *adj* impitoyable •**ruthlessly** *adv* impitoyablement •**ruthlessness** *n* cruauté *f*

rye [raɪ] *n* seigle *m;* **r. bread** pain *m* de seigle

S, s [es] *n (letter)* S, s *m inv*
Sabbath ['sæbəθ] *n (Jewish)* sabbat *m*; *(Christian)* jour *m* du seigneur
sabbatical [sə'bætɪkəl] **1** *adj (university year, term)* sabbatique
  2 *n* **to be on s.** être en congé sabbatique
sabotage ['sæbətɑːʒ] **1** *n* sabotage *m*
  2 *vt* saboter • **saboteur** [-'tɜː(r)] *n* saboteur, -euse *mf*
sabre ['seɪbə(r)] *(Am* **saber)** *n* sabre *m*
saccharin ['sækərɪn] *n* saccharine *f*
sachet ['sæʃeɪ] *n* sachet *m*
sack [sæk] **1** *n (bag)* sac *m*; *Fam* **to get the s.** se faire virer; *Fam* **to give sb the s.** virer qn; *Fam* **to hit the s.** se pieuter
  2 *vt (town)* mettre à sac; *Fam (dismiss)* virer • **sacking** *n (cloth)* toile *f* à sac; *Fam (dismissal)* renvoi *m*
sacrament ['sækrəmənt] *n Rel* sacrement *m*
sacred ['seɪkrɪd] *adj* sacré
sacrifice ['sækrɪfaɪs] **1** *n* sacrifice *m*
  2 *vt* sacrifier (**to** à)
sacrilege ['sækrɪlɪdʒ] *n* sacrilège *m* • **sacrilegious** [-'lɪdʒəs] *adj* sacrilège
sacrosanct ['sækrəʊsæŋkt] *adj Ironic* sacro-saint
sad [sæd] **(sadder, saddest)** *adj* triste • **sadden** *vt* attrister • **sadly** *adv (unhappily)* tristement; *(unfortunately)* malheureusement; **to be s. mistaken** se tromper lourdement • **sadness** *n* tristesse *f*
saddle ['sædəl] **1** *n* selle *f*; *Fig* **to be in the s.** *(in control)* être aux commandes
  2 *vt (horse)* seller; *Fam* **to s. sb with sb/ sth** refiler qn/qch à qn • **saddlebag** *n* sacoche *f*
sadism ['seɪdɪzəm] *n* sadisme *m* • **sadist** *n* sadique *mf* • **sadistic** [sə'dɪstɪk] *adj* sadique
sae [eseɪ'iː] *(abbr Br =* **stamped addressed envelope,** *Am =* **self-addressed envelope)** *n* enveloppe *f* timbrée
safari [sə'fɑːrɪ] *n* safari *m*; **to go on s.** faire un safari; **s. park** réserve *f* d'animaux sauvages
safe [seɪf] **1 (-er, -est)** *adj (person)* en sécurité; *(equipment, animal)* sans danger; *(place, investment, method)* sûr;

(winner) assuré; **s. (and sound)** sain et sauf (*f* saine et sauve); **in s. hands** entre de bonnes mains; **to be s. from** être à l'abri de; **... to be on the s. side** ... pour plus de sûreté; **to wish sb a s. journey** souhaiter bon voyage à qn; **it's s. to go out** on peut sortir sans danger; **the safest thing to do is** le plus sûr est de; **s. sex** rapports *mpl* sexuels protégés
  2 *n (for money)* coffre-fort *m* • **safe-'conduct** *n* sauf-conduit *m* • **safe-de'posit box** *n (in bank)* coffre *m* • **safeguard 1** *n* garantie *f* (**against** contre) **2** *vt* sauvegarder **3** *vi* **to s. against sth** se protéger contre qch • **safe-'keeping** *n* **to give sb sth for s.** donner qch à la garde de qn
safely ['seɪflɪ] *adv (without risk)* en toute sécurité; *(drive)* prudemment; *(with certainty)* avec certitude; **to arrive s.** bien arriver
safety ['seɪftɪ] **1** *n* sécurité *f*
  2 *adj (belt, device, screen, margin)* de sécurité; *(pin, chain, valve)* de sûreté; **s. curtain** *(in theatre)* rideau *m* de fer; **s. net** *(in circus)* filet *m*; *Fig (safeguard)* mesure *f* de sécurité
saffron ['sæfrən] *n* safran *m*
sag [sæg] *(pt & pp* **-gg-)** *vi (of roof, ground, bed)* s'affaisser; *(of breasts)* tomber; *(of flesh)* être flasque; *(of prices)* baisser
saga ['sɑːgə] *n* saga *f*
sage¹ [seɪdʒ] *n (plant, herb)* sauge *f*
sage² [seɪdʒ] *n (wise man)* sage *m*
Sagittarius [sædʒɪ'teərɪəs] *n (sign)* le Sagittaire; **to be a S.** être Sagittaire
Sahara [sə'hɑːrə] *n* **the S. (desert)** le Sahara
said [sed] *pt & pp of* **say**
sail [seɪl] **1** *n (on boat)* voile *f*; *(of mill)* aile *f*; **to set s.** prendre la mer
  2 *vt (boat)* commander; *(seas)* parcourir
  3 *vi (of person, ship)* naviguer; *(leave)* prendre la mer; *(do as sport)* faire de la voile; **to s. into port** entrer au port; **to s. round the world** faire le tour du monde en bateau; *Fam* **to s. through an exam** réussir un examen haut la main; **the clouds sailed by** les nuages passaient

dans le ciel • **sailboard** n planche f à voile • **sailboat** n Am voilier m • **sailing** n (sport) voile f; (departure) appareillage m; **to go s.** faire de la voile; Br **s. boat** voilier m

sailor ['seɪlə(r)] n marin m

saint [seɪnt] n saint m, sainte f; **S. John** saint Jean; **All Saints' Day** la Toussaint • **saintly** (**-ier, -iest**) adj (life) de saint

sake [seɪk] n **for my/your/his s.** pour moi/toi/lui; **for heaven's** or **God's s.**! pour l'amour de Dieu!; **for your own s.** pour ton bien; **(just) for the s. of eating** simplement pour manger

salable [seɪləbəl] adj Am vendable

salacious [sə'leɪʃəs] adj salace

salad ['sæləd] n salade f; **s. bowl** saladier m; Br **s. cream** = sorte de mayonnaise; **s. dressing** = sauce pour salade

salamander ['sæləmændə(r)] n salamandre f

salami [sə'lɑːmɪ] n salami m

salary ['sælərɪ] (pl **-ies**) n salaire m • **salaried** adj salarié

sale [seɪl] n (action, event) vente f; (at reduced price) solde m; **the sales** les soldes; **on s.** en vente; **in the sales** en solde; **(up) for s.** à vendre; **to put sth up for s.** mettre qch en vente; **s. price** prix m de vente; **sales department** service m commercial; **sales pitch** arguments mpl de vente; Am **sales check** or **slip** reçu m • **saleable** (Am **salable**) adj vendable • **salesclerk** n Am vendeur, -euse mf • **salesman** (pl **-men**) n (in shop) vendeur m; (for company) représentant m • **saleswoman** (pl **-women**) n (in shop) vendeuse f; (for company) représentante f

salient ['seɪlɪənt] adj (feature, fact) marquant

saliva [sə'laɪvə] n salive f • **salivate** ['sælɪveɪt] vi saliver

sallow ['sæləʊ] (**-er, -est**) adj jaunâtre

sally ['sælɪ] (pt & pp **-ied**) vi Literary **to s. forth** partir

salmon ['sæmən] n inv saumon m; **s. trout** truite f saumonée

salmonella [sælmə'nelə] n salmonelle f

salon ['sælɒn] n **beauty s.** institut m de beauté; **hairdressing s.** salon m de coiffure

saloon [sə'luːn] n (room) salle f; Am (bar) bar m; Br **s. car** berline f

salt [sɔːlt] **1** n sel m; **s. beef** bœuf m salé; **s. mine** mine f de sel; **s. water** eau f salée
2 vt saler • **saltcellar** n Br salière f • **'salt-'free** adj sans sel • **saltshaker** n Am salière f • **saltwater** adj (lake) salé; (fish) de mer • **salty** (**-ier, -iest**) adj salé

salubrious [sə'luːbrɪəs] adj Formal salubre

salutary [Br 'sæljʊtərɪ, Am -erɪ] adj salutaire

salute [sə'luːt] **1** n salut m
2 vt (greet) & Mil saluer
3 vi faire un salut

salvage ['sælvɪdʒ] **1** n (of ship) sauvetage m; (of waste material) récupération f; **s. operation** opération f de sauvetage
2 vt (ship) sauver; (waste material) récupérer

salvation [sæl'veɪʃən] n salut m; **the S. Army** l'Armée f du salut

same [seɪm] **1** adj même; **the (very) s. house as...** (exactement) la même maison que...
2 pron **the s.** le même, la même, pl les mêmes; **I would have done the s.** j'aurais fait la même chose; **it's all the s. to me** ça m'est égal
3 adv **to look the s.** (of two things) sembler pareils; **to taste the s.** avoir le même goût; **all the s.** (nevertheless) tout de même • **sameness** n monotonie f

sample ['sɑːmpəl] **1** n échantillon m; (of blood) prélèvement m
2 vt (wine, cheese) goûter; (public opinion) sonder; (piece of music) sampler

sanatorium [sænə'tɔːrɪəm] (pl **-ria** [-rɪə]) n Br sanatorium m

sanctify ['sæŋktɪfaɪ] (pt & pp **-ied**) vt sanctifier

sanctimonious [sæŋktɪ'məʊnɪəs] adj moralisateur, -trice

sanction ['sæŋkʃən] **1** n (penalty) sanction f; Formal (consent) consentement m
2 vt Formal (approve) sanctionner

sanctity ['sæŋktətɪ] n sainteté f; (of marriage) caractère m sacré

sanctuary [Br 'sæŋktʃʊərɪ, Am -erɪ] (pl **-ies**) n Rel sanctuaire m; (for fugitive, refugee) refuge m; (for wildlife) réserve f

sand [sænd] **1** n sable m; **s. castle** château m de sable; **s. dune** dune f
2 vt (road) sabler; **to s. (down)** (wood) poncer • **sandbag** n sac m de sable • **sandbank** n banc m de sable • **sandbox** n Am bac m à sable • **sander** n (machine) ponceuse f • **sandpaper 1** n papier m de verre **2** vt (wood) poncer • **sandpit** n Br bac m à sable • **sandstone** n (rock) grès m • **sandstorm** n tempête f de sable

sandal ['sændəl] n sandale f

sandwich ['sænwɪdʒ] **1** n sandwich m; **cheese s.** sandwich au fromage; Br **s. bar** snack m (qui ne vend que des sandwichs); Br **s. course** formation f professionnelle en alternance

2 *vt* **to be sandwiched between** *(of layer)* être intercalé entre; *(of person, building)* être coincé entre

sandy ['sændɪ] (**-ier, -iest**) *adj* (**a**) *(beach)* de sable; *(road, ground)* sablonneux, -euse; *(water)* sableux, -euse (**b**) *(hair)* blond roux *inv*

sane [seɪn] (**-er, -est**) *adj (person)* sain d'esprit; *(action, remark)* sensé

sang [sæŋ] *pt of* **sing**

sanguine ['sæŋgwɪn] *adj* optimiste

sanitarium [sænɪ'teərɪəm] *n Am* sanatorium *m*

sanitary [*Br* 'sænɪtərɪ, *Am* -erɪ] *adj (fittings, conditions)* sanitaire; *(clean)* hygiénique; *Br* **s. towel,** *Am* **s. napkin** serviette *f* hygiénique

sanitation [sænɪ'teɪʃən] *n* hygiène *f* publique; *(plumbing)* installations *fpl* sanitaires; *Am* **s. department** service *m* de collecte des ordures ménagères

sanity ['sænɪtɪ] *n* santé *f* mentale

sank [sæŋk] *pt of* **sink²**

Santa Claus ['sæntəklɔːz] *n* le père Noël

sap [sæp] **1** *n (of tree, plant)* sève *f*

2 (*pt & pp* **-pp-**) *vt (weaken)* saper

sapphire ['sæfaɪə(r)] *n (jewel, needle)* saphir *m*

sarcasm ['sɑːkæzəm] *n* sarcasme *m* • **sar'castic** *adj* sarcastique

sardine [sɑː'diːn] *n* sardine *f*

Sardinia [sɑː'dɪnɪə] *n* la Sardaigne

sardonic [sɑː'dɒnɪk] *adj* sardonique

sash [sæʃ] *n (on dress)* ceinture *f*; *(of mayor)* écharpe *f*; **s. window** fenêtre *f* à guillotine

sat [sæt] *pt & pp of* **sit**

Satan ['seɪtən] *n* Satan *m* • **satanic** [sə'tænɪk] *adj* satanique

satchel ['sætʃəl] *n* cartable *m*

satellite ['sætəlaɪt] *n* satellite *m*; **s. (country)** pays *m* satellite; **s. dish** antenne *f* parabolique; **s. television** télévision *f* par satellite; **s. picture** *(for weather)* animation *f* satellite

satiate ['seɪʃɪeɪt] *vt Formal* assouvir

satin ['sætɪn] *n* satin *m*; **s. dress** robe *f* de *ou* en satin

satire ['sætaɪə(r)] *n* satire *f* (**on** contre) • **satirical** [sə'tɪrɪkəl] *adj* satirique • **satirist** ['sætɪrɪst] *n* écrivain *m* satirique • **satirize** ['sætɪraɪz] *vt* faire la satire de

satisfaction [sætɪs'fækʃən] *n* satisfaction *f* • **satisfactory** *adj* satisfaisant

satisfy ['sætɪsfaɪ] *(pt & pp* **-ied**) *vt* satisfaire; *(convince)* persuader (**that** que); *(condition)* remplir; **to s. oneself that...** s'assurer que...; **to be satisfied (with)**

être satisfait (de) • **satisfying** *adj* satisfaisant; *(meal, food)* substantiel, -ielle

satsuma [sæt'suːmə] *n Br* mandarine *f*

saturate ['sætʃəreɪt] *vt* saturer (**with** de) • **satu'ration** *n* saturation *f*; **to reach s. point** arriver à saturation

Saturday ['sætədeɪ] *n* samedi *m*

sauce [sɔːs] *n* (**a**) sauce *f*; **mint s.** sauce à la menthe; **s. boat** saucière *f* (**b**) *Fam (impudence)* toupet *m* • **saucy** (**-ier, -iest**) *adj Fam (impudent)* insolent; *(risqué)* coquin

saucepan ['sɔːspən] *n* casserole *f*

saucer ['sɔːsə(r)] *n* soucoupe *f*

Saudi Arabia [saʊdɪə'reɪbɪə] *n* l'Arabie *f* Saoudite

sauerkraut ['saʊəkraʊt] *n* choucroute *f*

sauna ['sɔːnə] *n* sauna *m*

saunter ['sɔːntə(r)] *vi* flâner

sausage ['sɒsɪdʒ] *n* saucisse *f*; *Br* **s. roll** feuilleté *m* à la viande

sauté ['saʊteɪ] **1** *adj* sauté

2 *(pt & pp* **-éed**) *vt* faire sauter

savage ['sævɪdʒ] **1** *adj (animal, person)* féroce; *(attack, criticism)* violent

2 *n* Old-fashioned sauvage *mf*

3 *vt (physically)* attaquer • **savagery** *n (cruelty)* sauvagerie *f*

save¹ [seɪv] **1** *vt (rescue)* sauver (**from** de); *(keep)* garder; *(money)* économiser; *(time)* gagner; *Comptr* sauvegarder; **to s. energy** faire des économies d'énergie; **to s. sb's life** sauver la vie de qn; **to s. sb from doing sth** empêcher qn de faire qch; **to s. sb sth** éviter qch à qn; **to s. up** mettre de l'argent de côté (**for** pour); **God s. the Queen!** vive la reine!

2 *vi* **to s. (up)** faire des économies (**for/on** pour/sur)

3 *n Football* arrêt *m* • **saving** *n (of time, money)* économie *f*; **savings** *(money saved)* économies *fpl*; **savings account** compte *m* d'épargne; **savings bank** caisse *f* d'épargne

save² [seɪv] *prep Formal (except)* hormis

saviour ['seɪvjə(r)] (*Am* **savior**) *n* sauveur *m*

savour ['seɪvə(r)] (*Am* **savor**) **1** *n* saveur *f*

2 *vt* savourer • **savoury** (*Am* **savory**) *adj (not sweet)* salé; *Fig (conduct)* honorable

saw¹ [sɔː] **1** *n* scie *f*

2 (*pt* **sawed,** *pp* **sawn** *or* **sawed**) *vt* scier; **to s. sth off** scier qch; **a** *Br* **sawn-off** *or Am* **sawed-off shotgun** un fusil à canon scié • **sawdust** *n* sciure *f* • **sawmill** *n* scierie *f*

saw² [sɔː] *pt of* **see¹**

sawn [sɔːn] *pp of* **saw¹**

saxophone ['sæksəfəʊn] *n* saxophone *m*

say [seɪ] **1** (*pt & pp* **said**) *vt* dire (**to** à; **that** que); (*of dial, watch*) indiquer; **to s. again** répéter; **it is said that** on dit que; **what do you s. to a walk?** que dirais-tu d'une promenade?; **let's s. tomorrow** disons demain; **to s. the least** c'est le moins que l'on puisse dire; **to s. nothing of** sans parler de; **that is to s.** c'est-à-dire

2 *vi* dire; *Fam* **you don't s.!** sans blague!; *Br Old-fashioned* **I s.!** dites donc!; *Am Fam* **s.!** dis donc!; **that goes without saying** ça va sans dire

3 *n* **to have one's s.** avoir son mot à dire; **to have no s.** ne pas avoir voix au chapitre (**in** concernant)

saying ['seɪɪŋ] *n* maxime *f*

scab [skæb] *n* (*of wound*) croûte *f*; *Fam* (*strikebreaker*) jaune *mf*

scaffold ['skæfəld] *n* (*gallows*) échafaud *m*; (*for construction work*) échafaudage *m* • **scaffolding** *n* échafaudage *m*

scald [skɔːld] **1** *n* brûlure *f*
2 *vt* ébouillanter

scale¹ [skeɪl] **1** *n* (*of instrument, map*) échelle *f*; (*of salaries*) barème *m*; *Fig* (*of problem*) étendue *f*; **on a small/large s.** sur une petite/grande échelle; **s. model** modèle *m* réduit
2 *vt* **to s. sth down** revoir qch à la baisse

scale² [skeɪl] **1** *n* (*on fish*) écaille *f*; (*in kettle*) dépôt *m* calcaire
2 *vt* (*fish*) écailler

scale³ [skeɪl] *vt* (*climb*) escalader

scales [skeɪlz] *npl* (*for weighing*) balance *f*; (**bathroom**) **s.** pèse-personne *m*; (**baby**) **s.** pèse-bébé *m*

scallion ['skæljən] *n Am* (*onion*) oignon *m* blanc

scallop ['skɒləp] *n* coquille *f* Saint-Jacques

scalp [skælp] *n* cuir *m* chevelu

scalpel ['skælpəl] *n* scalpel *m*

scam [skæm] *n Fam* arnaque *f*

scamp [skæmp] *n* coquin, -ine *mf*

scamper ['skæmpə(r)] *vi* **to s. off** *or* **away** détaler

scampi ['skæmpɪ] *n* scampi *mpl*

scan [skæn] **1** *n* **to have a s.** (*of pregnant woman*) passer une échographie
2 (*pt & pp* **-nn-**) *vt* (*look at briefly*) parcourir; (*scrutinize*) scruter; *Comptr* passer au scanner

scandal ['skændəl] *n* (*outrage*) scandale *m*; (*gossip*) ragots *mpl*; **to cause a s.** faire scandale • **scandalize** *vt* scandaliser • **scandalous** *adj* scandaleux, -euse

Scandinavia [skændɪ'neɪvɪə] *n* la Scan-

dinavie • **Scandinavian 1** *adj* scandinave
2 *n* Scandinave *mf*

scanner ['skænə(r)] *n Med & Comptr* scanner *m*

scant [skænt] *adj* insuffisant • **scantily** *adv* insuffisamment; **s. dressed** légèrement vêtu • **scanty** (**-ier, -iest**) *adj* insuffisant; (*bikini*) minuscule

scapegoat ['skeɪpgəʊt] *n* bouc *m* émissaire

scar [skɑː(r)] **1** *n* cicatrice *f*
2 (*pt & pp* **-rr-**) *vt* marquer d'une cicatrice; *Fig* (*of experience*) marquer; *Fig* **to be scarred for life** être marqué à vie

scarce [skeəs] (**-er, -est**) *adj* rare; **to make oneself s.** filer • **scarceness, scarcity** *n* pénurie *f*

scarcely ['skeəslɪ] *adv* à peine; **he could s. talk** il pouvait à peine parler; **s. anything** presque rien; **s. ever** presque jamais

scare [skeə(r)] **1** *n* frayeur *f*; **to give sb a s.** faire peur à qn
2 *vt* faire peur à; **to s. sb off** faire fuir qn • **scared** *adj* effrayé; **to be s. of sb/sth** avoir peur de qn/qch; **to be s. stiff** être mort de peur

scarecrow ['skeəkrəʊ] *n* épouvantail *m*

scaremonger ['skeəmʌŋgə(r)] *n* alarmiste *mf*

scarf [skɑːf] (*pl* **scarves**) *n* (*long*) écharpe *f*; (*square*) foulard *m*

scarlet ['skɑːlət] *adj* écarlate; **s. fever** scarlatine *f*

scary ['skeərɪ] (**-ier, -iest**) *adj Fam* effrayant; **it's s.** ça fait peur

scathing ['skeɪðɪŋ] *adj* (*remark*) acerbe; **to be s. about sb/sth** faire des remarques acerbes sur qn/qch

scatter ['skætə(r)] **1** *vt* (*clouds, demonstrators*) disperser; (*corn, seed*) jeter à la volée; (*papers*) laisser traîner
2 *vi* (*of crowd*) se disperser

scatterbrain ['skætəbreɪn] *n* écervelé, -ée *mf*

scatty ['skætɪ] (**-ier, -iest**) *adj Br Fam* écervelé

scavenge ['skævɪndʒ] *vi* **to s. for sth** fouiller pour trouver qch • **scavenger** *n* (*animal*) charognard *m*

scenario [sɪ'nɑːrɪəʊ] (*pl* **-os**) *n* (*of film*) scénario *m*

scene [siːn] *n* (*in book, film, play*) scène *f*; (*of event, crime, accident*) lieu *m*; (*fuss*) scandale *m*; *also Fig* **behind the scenes** dans les coulisses; **on the s.** sur les lieux; **a s. of devastation** un spectacle de dévastation; **to make a s.** faire un scandale

scenery ['siːnərɪ] (*pl* **-ies**) *n* (*landscape*)

paysage *m*; *(in play, film)* décors *mpl*; *Fam* **I need a change of s.** j'ai besoin de changer d'air

scenic ['si:nɪk] *adj* pittoresque; **s. route** route *f* touristique

scent [sent] **1** *n (smell)* odeur *f*; *(perfume)* parfum *m*; *(in hunting)* fumet *m*; **she threw her pursuers off the s.** elle sema ses poursuivants
2 *vt (perfume)* parfumer (**with** de); *(smell)* flairer

scepter ['septər] *n Am* sceptre *m*

sceptic ['skeptɪk] *(Am* **skeptic***) adj & n* sceptique *(mf)* • **sceptical** *(Am* **skeptical***) adj* sceptique • **scepticism** *(Am* **skepticism***) n* scepticisme *m*

sceptre ['septə(r)] *(Am* **scepter***) n* sceptre *m*

schedule [*Br* 'ʃedju:l, *Am* 'skedʒʊl] **1** *n (plan)* programme *m*; *(for trains, buses)* horaire *m*; *(list)* liste *f*; **to be on s.** *(train, bus)* être à l'heure; *(person)* être dans les temps; **to be ahead of s.** être en avance sur le programme; **to be behind s.** être en retard sur le programme; **according to s.** comme prévu
2 *vt* prévoir; *(event)* fixer la date/l'heure de • **scheduled** *adj (planned)* prévu; *(service, flight, train)* régulier, -ière; **she's s. to leave at eight** son départ est prévu pour huit heures

scheme [ski:m] **1** *n (plan)* plan *m* (**to do** pour faire); *(plot)* complot *m*; *(arrangement)* arrangement *m*; **(housing) s.** lotissement *m*
2 *vi Pej* comploter • **scheming** *Pej* **1** *adj* intrigant **2** *n* machinations *fpl*

schizophrenia [skɪtsəʊ'fri:nɪə] *n* schizophrénie *f* • **schizophrenic** [-'frenɪk] *adj & n* schizophrène *(mf)*

scholar ['skɒlə(r)] *n* érudit, -ite *mf* • **scholarly** *adj* érudit • **scholarship** *n (learning)* érudition *f*; *(grant)* bourse *f* d'études • **scholastic** [skə'læstɪk] *adj* scolaire

school [sku:l] **1** *n* école *f*; *(within university)* département *m*; *Am Fam (college)* université *f*; **in** *or* **at s.** à l'école; *Br* **secondary s.**, *Am* **high s.** établissement *m* d'enseignement secondaire
2 *adj (year, book, equipment)* scolaire; **s. bag** cartable *m*; **s. bus** car *m* de ramassage scolaire; **s. fees** frais *mpl* de scolarité; **s. hours** les heures *fpl* de cours; **s. leaver** = jeune qui vient de terminer ses études secondaires; *Am* **s. yard** cour *f* de récréation • **schoolboy** *n* écolier *m* • **schoolchildren** *npl* écoliers *mpl* • **school-friend** *n* camarade *mf* de classe • **schoolgirl** *n* écolière *f* • **schooling** *n* scolarité *f* • **schoolmaster** *n Br (primary)* instituteur *m*; *(secondary)* professeur *m* • **schoolmate** *n* camarade *mf* de classe • **schoolmistress** *n Br (primary)* institutrice *f*; *(secondary)* professeur *m* • **schoolroom** *n* salle *f* de classe • **schoolteacher** *n (primary)* instituteur, -trice *mf*; *(secondary)* professeur *m*

schooner ['sku:nə(r)] *n (ship)* goélette *f*

sciatica [saɪ'ætɪkə] *n* sciatique *f*

science ['saɪəns] *n* science *f*; **to study s.** étudier les sciences; **s. teacher** professeur *m* de sciences; **s. fiction** science-fiction *f* • **scien'tific** *adj* scientifique • **scientist** *n* scientifique *mf*

sci-fi ['saɪfaɪ] *n Fam* SF *f*

Scilly Isles ['sɪlɪaɪlz] *npl* **the S.** les Sorlingues *fpl*

scintillating ['sɪntɪleɪtɪŋ] *adj* brillant

scissors ['sɪzəz] *npl* ciseaux *mpl*; **a pair of s.** une paire de ciseaux

sclerosis [sklɪ'rəʊsɪs] *n Med* sclérose *f*

scoff [skɒf] **1** *vt* **to s. at sb/sth** se moquer de qn/qch
2 *vti Br Fam (eat)* bouffer

scold [skəʊld] *vt* gronder (**for doing** pour avoir fait) • **scolding** *n* **to get a s.** se faire gronder

scone [skəʊn, skɒn] *n Br* scone *m*

scoop [sku:p] **1** *n (for flour, sugar)* pelle *f*; *(for ice cream)* cuillère *f*; *Fam (in newspaper)* scoop *m*; **at one s.** d'un seul coup
2 *vt* **to s. sth out** évider qch; **to s. sth up** ramasser qch

scoot [sku:t] *vi Fam* filer

scooter ['sku:tə(r)] *n (for child)* trottinette *f*; *(motorcycle)* scooter *m*

scope [skəʊp] *n (range)* étendue *f*; *(of action)* possibilité *f*; **to give s. for...** *(interpretation)* laisser le champ libre à...

scorch [skɔ:tʃ] **1** *n* **s. (mark)** brûlure *f*
2 *vt* roussir • **scorcher** *n Fam* jour *m* de canicule • **scorching** *adj (day)* torride; *(sun, sand)* brûlant

score[1] [skɔ:(r)] **1** *n (in sport)* score *m*; *(in music)* partition *f*; *(of film)* musique *f*
2 *vt (point, goal)* marquer; *(exam mark)* avoir; *(piece of music)* adapter (**for** pour)
3 *vi (score a goal)* marquer; *(count points)* marquer les points • **scoreboard** *n* tableau *m* d'affichage • **scorer** *n* marqueur *m*

score[2] [skɔ:(r)] *n* **a s.** *(twenty)* vingt; *Fam* **scores of** des tas de

score[3] [skɔ:(r)] *vt (cut line in)* entailler; **to s. sth off** *or* **out** *(delete)* biffer

scorn [skɔːn] **1** *n* mépris *m*
2 *vt* mépriser • **scornful** *adj* méprisant;
to be s. of sb/sth considérer qn/qch avec
mépris • **scornfully** *adv* avec mépris

Scorpio [ˈskɔːpɪəʊ] *n (sign)* le Scorpion;
to be a S. être Scorpion

scorpion [ˈskɔːpɪən] *n* scorpion *m*

Scot [skɒt] *n* Écossais, -aise *mf* • **Scotland**
n l'Écosse *f* • **Scotsman** (*pl* **-men**) *n* Écossais *m* • **Scotswoman** (*pl* **-women**) *n*
Écossaise *f* • **Scottish** *adj* écossais

Scotch [skɒtʃ] *n (whisky)* scotch *m*

scotch¹ [skɒtʃ] *adj Am* **S. tape**® Scotch®
m

scotch² [skɒtʃ] *vt (rumour)* étouffer

scot-free [ˈskɒtˈfriː] *adv* sans être puni

scoundrel [ˈskaʊndrəl] *n* crapule *f*

scour [ˈskaʊə(r)] *vt (pan)* récurer; *Fig
(streets, house)* ratisser (**for** à la recherche de) • **scourer** *n* tampon *m* à récurer

scourge [skɜːdʒ] *n* fléau *m*

scout [skaʊt] **1** *n (soldier)* éclaireur *m*;
(boy) s. scout *m*, éclaireur; *Am* **(girl) s.**
éclaireuse *f*
2 *vi* **to s. round for sth** chercher qch; **to
s. for talent** dénicher les talents

scowl [skaʊl] *vi* lancer des regards noirs
(**at** à)

scrabble [ˈskræbəl] *vi* **to s. around for
sth** chercher qch à tâtons

scraggy [ˈskrægɪ] (**-ier, -iest**) *adj (bony)*
maigre

scram [skræm] (*pt & pp* **-mm-**) *vi Fam* se
tirer

scramble [ˈskræmbəl] **1** *n (rush)* ruée *f*
(**for** vers); *(struggle)* bousculade *f* (**for**
pour)
2 *vt (signal)* brouiller; **scrambled eggs**
œufs *mpl* brouillés
3 *vi* **to s. for sth** se ruer vers qch; **to s. up
a hill** gravir une colline en s'aidant des
mains

scrap¹ [skræp] **1** *n* (**a**) *(piece)* bout *m* (**of**
de); *(of information)* bribe *f*; **scraps** *(food)*
restes *mpl*; **not a s. of** *(truth, good sense)*
pas une once de; **s. paper** papier *m*
brouillon (**b**) **s. (metal)** ferraille *f*; **to sell
sth for s.** vendre qch à la ferraille; **s. heap**
tas *m* de ferraille; **s. dealer, s. merchant**
ferrailleur *m*; **s. yard** casse *f*
2 (*pt & pp* **-pp-**) *vt (get rid of)* se débarrasser de; *(car)* envoyer à la casse; *Fig
(plan, idea)* abandonner

scrap² [skræp] *n Fam (fight)* bagarre *f*; **to
get into a s. with sb** en venir aux mains
avec qn

scrapbook [ˈskræpbʊk] *n* album *m (de
coupures de presse etc)*

scrape [skreɪp] **1** *n (on skin)* éraflure *f*;
(sound) raclement *m*; *Fam* **to get into a s.**
se mettre dans le pétrin
2 *vt* gratter; *(skin)* érafler; **to s. a living**
arriver tout juste à vivre
3 *vi* **to s.** against sth frotter contre qch
• **scraper** *n* racloir *m* • **scraping** *n (of butter)* mince couche *f*
▶ **scrape along** *vi (financially)* se débrouiller ▶ **scrape away, scrape off** *vt
sep* racler ▶ **scrape through** *vt insep & vi*
to s. through (an exam) passer de justesse (à un examen) ▶ **scrape together** *vt
sep (money, people)* parvenir à rassembler

scratch [skrætʃ] **1** *n (mark, injury)* éraflure *f*; *(on glass, wood)* rayure *f*; *Fam* **to
start from s.** repartir de zéro; **it isn't up to
s.** ce n'est pas au niveau; **he isn't up to s.** il
n'est pas à la hauteur
2 *vt (to relieve itching)* gratter; *(by accident)* érafler; *(glass)* rayer; *(with claw)*
griffer; *(write, draw)* griffonner (**on** sur)
3 *vi (of person)* se gratter; *(of pen, new
clothes)* gratter • **scratchcard** *n (lottery
card)* carte *f* à gratter

scrawl [skrɔːl] **1** *n* gribouillis *m*
2 *vt* gribouiller

scrawny [ˈskrɔːnɪ] (**-ier, -iest**) *adj* maigrichon, -onne

scream [skriːm] **1** *n* hurlement *m*
2 *vt* hurler
3 *vi* hurler; **to s. at sb** crier après qn; **to s.
with pain** hurler de douleur

screech [skriːtʃ] **1** *n* cri *m* strident
2 *vti* hurler

screen [skriːn] **1** *n (of TV set, computer)*
écran *m*; **(folding) s.** paravent *m*; *Comptr*
on s. à l'écran; *Comptr* **s. saver** économi-
seur *m* d'écran; *Cin* **s. test** bout *m* d'essai
2 *vt (hide)* cacher (**from sb** à qn); *(protect)* protéger (**from** de); *(film)* projeter;
(visitors, calls) filtrer; *(for disease)* faire
subir un test de dépistage à; **to s. off**
(hide) cacher • **screening** *n (of film)* projection *f*; *(selection)* tri *m*; *(for disease)*
dépistage *m* • **screenplay** *n (of film)* scénario *m*

screw [skruː] **1** *n* vis *f*; *Fam* **to have a s.
loose** avoir une case de moins; *Vulg* **to
have a s.** *(sex)* s'envoyer en l'air
2 *vt* visser (**to** à); **to s. sth down** *or* **on**
visser qch; **to s. sth off** dévisser qch; **to s.
sth up** *(paper)* chiffonner qch; *very Fam
(spoil)* foutre qch en l'air; **to s. up one's
eyes** plisser les yeux; **to s. one's face up**
faire la grimace • **screwball** *n & adj Am
Fam* cinglé, -ée (*mf*) • **screwdriver** *n* tour-

nevis *m* • **screwy** (**-ier, -iest**) *adj (person)* timbré; *(idea)* de timbré

scribble ['skrɪbəl] **1** *n* griffonnage *m*
2 *vti* griffonner

scribe [skraɪb] *n* scribe *m*

script [skrɪpt] *n* (**a**) *(of film)* script *m*; *(of play)* texte *m*; *(in exam)* copie *f* (**b**) *(handwriting)* script *m* • **scriptwriter** *n (for films)* scénariste *mf*; *(for TV or radio)* dialoguiste *mf*

Scripture(s) ['skrɪptʃə(z)] *n(pl) Rel* les saintes Écritures *fpl*

scroll [skrəʊl] **1** *n* rouleau *m*; *(book)* manuscrit *m*
2 *vi Comptr* défiler; **to s. down/up** défiler vers le bas/haut

scrooge [skruːdʒ] *n* avare *m*

scrounge [skraʊndʒ] **1** *vt (meal)* se faire payer (**off** *or* **from sb** par qn); *(steal)* taper (**off** *or* **from sb** à qn); **to s. money off** *or* **from sb** taper qn
2 *vi* vivre en parasite; *Pej* **to s. around for sth** essayer de mettre la main sur qch • **scrounger** *n Fam* parasite *m*

scrub [skrʌb] **1** *n* (**a**) **to give sth a s.** bien frotter qch; *Am* **s. brush** brosse *f* dure (**b**) *(land)* broussailles *fpl*
2 *(pt & pp -bb-) vt (surface)* frotter; *(pan)* récurer; *Fig (cancel)* annuler; **to s. sth off** *(remove)* enlever qch (à la brosse *ou* en frottant); *Fig* **to s. sth out** *(erase)* effacer qch • **scrubbing brush** *n* brosse *f* dure

scruff [skrʌf] *n Fam (person)* individu *m* peu soigné; **by the s. of the neck** par la peau du cou • **scruffy** (**-ier, -iest**) *adj (person)* peu soigné

scrum [skrʌm] *n Rugby* mêlée *f*

scrumptious ['skrʌmpʃəs] *adj Fam* fameux, -euse

scruple ['skruːpəl] *n* scrupule *m* • **scrupulous** [-pjʊləs] *adj* scrupuleux, -euse • **scrupulously** [-pjʊləslɪ] *adv* scrupuleusement

scrutinize ['skruːtɪnaɪz] *vt (document)* éplucher; *(votes)* vérifier • **scrutiny** *n* examen *m* minutieux; **to come under s.** être examiné

scuba ['skuːbə] *n* **s. diver** plongeur, -euse *mf*; **s. diving** la plongée sous-marine

scuff [skʌf] *vt* **to s. sth (up)** *(shoe)* érafler

scuffle ['skʌfəl] *n* bagarre *f*

scullery ['skʌlərɪ] *n Br* arrière-cuisine *f*

sculpt [skʌlpt] *vti* sculpter • **sculptor** *n* sculpteur *m* • **sculptress** *n* femme *f* sculpteur • **sculpture 1** *n (art, object)* sculpture *f*
2 *vti* sculpter

scum [skʌm] *n* (**a**) *(of dirt)* crasse *f*; *(froth)* écume *f* (**b**) *very Fam Pej (people)*

racaille *f*; *(person)* ordure *f*; **the s. of the earth** le rebut de la société

scupper ['skʌpə(r)] *vt Br (ship, project)* couler

scurrilous ['skʌrɪləs] *adj* calomnieux, -ieuse

scurry ['skʌrɪ] *vi (rush)* courir; **to s. off** se sauver

scurvy ['skɜːvɪ] *n Med* scorbut *m*

scuttle ['skʌtəl] **1** *vt (ship)* saborder
2 *vi* **to s. off** filer

scuzzy ['skʌzɪ] (**-ier, -iest**) *adj Am Fam (dirty)* cradingue, cracra *inv*

scythe [saɪð] *n* faux *f*

sea [siː] **1** *n* mer *f*; **(out) at s.** en mer; **by s.** par mer; **by** *or* **beside the s.** au bord de la mer; *Fig* **to be all at s.** nager complètement
2 *adj (level, breeze)* de la mer; *(water, fish, salt)* de mer; *(air)* marin; *(battle)* naval *(mpl* -als**)**; *(route)* maritime; **s. bed, s. floor** fond *m* de la mer; **s. change** changement *m* radical; **s. horse** hippocampe *m*; **s. lion** otarie *f*; **s. urchin** oursin *m*; **s. voyage** voyage *m* en mer • **seaboard** *n* littoral *m* • **seafarer** *n* marin *m* • **seafood** *n* fruits *mpl* de mer • **seafront** *n Br* front *m* de mer • **seagull** *n* mouette *f* • **seaman** *(pl* -men**)** *n* marin *m* • **seaport** *n* port *m* maritime • **seashell** *n* coquillage *m* • **seashore** *n* rivage *m* • **seasick** *adj* **to be s.** avoir le mal de mer • **seasickness** *n* mal *m* de mer • **seaside** *n Br* bord *m* de la mer; **s. resort** station *f* balnéaire; **s. town** ville *f* au bord de la mer • **seaway** *n* route *f* maritime • **seaweed** *n* algues *fpl* • **seaworthy** *adj* en état de naviguer

seal¹ [siːl] *n (animal)* phoque *m*

seal² [siːl] **1** *n (stamp)* sceau *m*; *(device for sealing)* joint *m* d'étanchéité; *(on medicine bottle, food container)* = fermeture garantissant la fraîcheur d'un produit; **to give one's s. of approval to sth** donner son approbation à qch
2 *vt (document, container)* sceller; *(stick down)* cacheter; *(make airtight)* fermer hermétiquement; **to s. sb's fate** décider du sort de qn; **to s. off an area** boucler un quartier

seam [siːm] *n (in cloth)* couture *f*; *(of coal, quartz)* veine *f*

seamy ['siːmɪ] (**-ier, -iest**) *adj* **the s. side** le côté sordide (**of** de)

séance ['seɪɒns] *n* séance *f* de spiritisme

search [sɜːtʃ] **1** *n* recherches *fpl* (**for** de); *(of place)* fouille *f*; **in s. of** à la recherche de; *Comptr* **to do a s. for sth** rechercher qch; *Comptr* **s. engine** moteur *m* de recherche; **s. party** équipe *f* de secours; *Law* **s. warrant** mandat *m* de perquisition **2** *vt (person, place)* fouiller (**for** pour trouver); **to s. (through) one's papers for sth** chercher qch dans ses papiers; *Comptr* **to s. a file** rechercher dans un fichier; *Comptr* **to s. a file for sth** rechercher qch dans un fichier **3** *vi* chercher; **to s. for sth** chercher qch; *Comptr* **s. and replace** rechercher et remplacer ● **searching** *adj (look)* pénétrant; *(examination)* minutieux, -ieuse ● **searchlight** *n* projecteur *m*

season¹ ['si:zən] *n* saison *f*; *(of films)* cycle *m*; **in the peak s.,** **in (the) high s.** en haute saison; **in the low** *or* **off s.** en basse saison; **'season's greetings'** 'meilleurs vœux de fin d'année'; **s. ticket** abonnement *m*

season² ['si:zən] *vt (food)* assaisonner; *(with spice)* épicer ● **seasoning** *n Culin* assaisonnement *m*

seasonable ['si:zənəbəl] *adj (weather)* de saison

seasonal ['si:zənəl] *adj (work, change)* saisonnier, -ière

seasoned ['si:zənd] *adj* (**a**) **a highly s. dish** un plat très relevé (**b**) *(person)* expérimenté; *(soldier)* aguerri

seat [si:t] **1** *n* siège *m*; *(of trousers)* fond *m*; **to take** *or* **have a s.** s'asseoir; *Fig* **to be in the hot s.** être sur la sellette; **s. belt** ceinture *f* de sécurité **2** *vt (at table)* placer; *(on one's lap)* asseoir; **the bus seats 50** il y a 50 places assises dans ce bus; **be seated!** asseyez-vous! ● **seated** *adj (sitting)* assis ● **seating** *n (seats)* places *fpl* assises; *(positioning)* placement *m*; **s. capacity** nombre *m* de places assises; **s. plan** plan *m* de table

-seater ['si:tə(r)] *suff* **two-seater (car)** voiture *f* à deux places

secateurs [sekə'tɜ:z] *npl Br* sécateur *m*

secede [sɪ'si:d] *vi* faire sécession ● **secession** [-'seʃən] *n* sécession *f*

secluded [sɪ'klu:dɪd] *adj (remote)* isolé ● **seclusion** *n* solitude *f*

second¹ ['sekənd] **1** *adj* deuxième, second; **every s. week** une semaine sur deux; *Aut* **in s. (gear)** en seconde; **s. to none** sans égal; **to be s. in command** commander en second **2** *adv (say)* deuxièmement; **to come s.** *(in competition)* se classer deuxième; **the s. biggest** le deuxième en ordre de grandeur; **my s. best (choice)** mon deuxième choix **3** *n (in series)* deuxième *mf*, second,

-onde *mf*; *(in month)* deux *m*; **Louis the S.** Louis Deux; **seconds** *(goods)* articles *mpl* défectueux; **anyone for seconds?** *(at meal)* est-ce que quelqu'un veut du rab? **4** *vt (motion, proposal)* appuyer ● **'second-'class** *adj (ticket on train)* de seconde (classe); *(mail)* non urgent; *(product)* de qualité inférieure ● **secondly** *adv* deuxièmement ● **'second-'rate** *adj* médiocre

second² ['sekənd] *n (part of minute)* seconde *f*; **s. hand** *(of clock, watch)* trotteuse *f*

second³ [sɪ'kɒnd] *vt Br (employee)* détacher (**to** à) ● **secondment** *n Br* détachement *m*; **on s.** en détachement (**to** à)

secondary ['sekəndərɪ] *adj* secondaire; *Br* **s. school** établissement *m* secondaire

second-hand ['sekənd'hænd] **1** *adj & adv (not new)* d'occasion **2** *adj (report, news)* de seconde main

secrecy ['si:krəsɪ] *n (discretion, silence)* secret *m*; **in s.** en secret; **to swear sb to s.** faire jurer le silence à qn

secret ['si:krɪt] **1** *adj* secret, -ète; **s. agent** agent *m* secret; **s. service** services *mpl* secrets **2** *n* secret *m*; **in s.** en secret; **it's no s.** tout le monde le sait ● **secretly** *adv* secrètement

secretary [*Br* 'sekrətərɪ, *Am* -erɪ] *(pl* **-ies**) *n* secrétaire *mf*; *Br* **Foreign S.,** *Am* **S. of State** ≃ ministre *m* des Affaires étrangères ● **secretarial** [-'teərɪəl] *adj (work)* administratif, -ive; *(job, course)* de secrétariat ● **secretariat** [-'teərɪət] *n* secrétariat *m*

secrete [sɪ'kri:t] *vt (discharge)* sécréter ● **secretion** *n* sécrétion *f*

secretive ['si:krətɪv] *adj (person)* secret, -ète; **to be s. about sth** faire des cachotteries à propos de qch

sect [sekt] *n* secte *f* ● **sectarian** [-'teərɪən] *adj & n* sectaire *(mf)*

section ['sekʃən] **1** *n* partie *f*; *(of road)* tronçon *m*; *(of machine)* élément *m*; *(of organization)* département *m*; *(of soldiers)* section *f*; **the sports s.** *(of newspaper)* la page des sports **2** *vt* sectionner

sector ['sektə(r)] *n* secteur *m*

secular ['sekjʊlə(r)] *adj (teaching)* laïque; *(music, art)* profane

secure [sɪ'kjʊə(r)] **1** *adj (person)* en sécurité; *(investment, place)* sûr; *(foothold)* solide; *(door, window)* bien fermé; *(nomination)* assuré; **I feel s. knowing that...** je suis tranquille car je sais que...

2 *vt (fasten)* attacher; *(window, door)* bien fermer; *(position, future)* assurer; *(support, promise)* procurer; **to s. sth against sth** protéger qch de qch; **to s. sth (for oneself)** se procurer qch • **securely** *adv (firmly)* solidement; *(safely)* en sûreté

security [sɪ'kjʊərətɪ] *(pl* **-ies)** *n* sécurité *f*; *Fin (for loan, bail)* garantie *f*; **job s.** sécurité de l'emploi; **to tighten s.** renforcer les mesures de sécurité; **to be a s. risk** être un danger pour la sécurité; **S. Council** Conseil *m* de sécurité; **s. guard** garde *m*; **securities** *(stocks, bonds)* titres *mpl*

sedan [sɪ'dæn] *n Am (saloon)* berline *f*

sedate [sɪ'deɪt] **1** *adj* calme
2 *vt* mettre sous calmants • **sedation** *n* **under s.** sous calmants

sedative ['sedətɪv] *n* calmant *m*

sedentary ['sedəntərɪ] *adj* sédentaire

sediment ['sedɪmənt] *n* sédiment *m*

sedition [sɪ'dɪʃən] *n* sédition *f* • **seditious** *adj* séditieux, -ieuse

seduce [sɪ'djuːs] *vt* séduire • **seducer** *n* séducteur, -trice *mf* • **seduction** [-'dʌkʃən] *n* séduction *f* • **seductive** [-'dʌktɪv] *adj (person, offer)* séduisant

see¹ [siː] *(pt* **saw**, *pp* **seen)** *vti* voir; **we'll s.** on verra; **I s. what you mean** je vois ce que tu veux dire; **I can s. a hill** je vois une colline; **I don't s. the point** je ne vois pas l'intérêt; **I'll go and s.** je vais voir; **I saw him run(ning)** je l'ai vu courir; **to s. reason** entendre raison; **to s. the joke** comprendre la plaisanterie; **s. you (later)!** à tout à l'heure!; **s. you (soon)!** à bientôt!; **to s. that...** *(make sure that)* faire en sorte que... *(+ subjunctive)*; *(check)* s'assurer que... *(+ indicative)*; **to s. sb to the door** accompagner qn jusqu'à la porte ▸ **see about** *vt insep (deal with)* s'occuper de; *(consider)* songer à ▸ **see in** *vt sep* **to s. in the New Year** fêter le Nouvel An ▸ **see off** *vt sep (say goodbye to)* dire au revoir à ▸ **see out** *vt sep* accompagner jusqu'à la porte ▸ **see through 1** *vt sep (task)* mener à bien **2** *vt insep* **to s. through sb** percer qn à jour ▸ **see to** *vt insep (deal with)* s'occuper de; *(mend)* réparer; **to s. to it that...** *(make sure that)* faire en sorte que... *(+ subjunctive)*; *(check)* s'assurer que... *(+ indicative)*

see² [siː] *n Rel* évêché *m*

seed [siːd] *n* graine *f*; *(of fruit)* pépin *m*; *Fig (source)* germe *m*; *Tennis* tête *f* de série; **to go to s.** *(of plant)* monter en graine • **seeded** *adj Tennis* **s. players** têtes *fpl* de série • **seedling** *n* plant *m*

seedy ['siːdɪ] *(-ier, -iest) adj* miteux, -euse

seeing ['siːɪŋ] *conj* **s. (that)** vu que

seek [siːk] *(pt & pp* **sought)** *vt* chercher *(to do* à faire); *(ask for)* demander *(from* à); **to s. (after)** rechercher; **to s. sb out** dénicher qn

seem [siːm] *vi* sembler *(to do* faire); **it seems that** *(impression)* il semble que *(+ subjunctive)*; **it seems to me that** il me semble que *(+ indicative)*; **we s. to know each other** il me semble qu'on se connaît; **I can't s. to do it** je n'arrive pas à le faire

seeming ['siːmɪŋ] *adj* apparent • **seemingly** *adv* apparemment

seemly ['siːmlɪ] *adj Formal* bienséant

seen [siːn] *pp of* **see¹**

seep [siːp] *vi* suinter; **to s. into sth** s'infiltrer dans qch • **seepage** [-ɪdʒ] *n (oozing)* suintement *m*; *(infiltration)* infiltration *f* *(into* dans)

seesaw ['siːsɔː] *n* balançoire *f* à bascule

seethe [siːð] *vi* **to s. with anger** bouillir de colère; **to s. with people** *(of street)* grouiller de monde

see-through ['siːθruː] *adj* transparent

segment ['segmənt] *n* segment *m*; *(of orange)* quartier *m*

segregate ['segrɪgeɪt] *vt* séparer *(from* de) • **segre'gation** *n* ségrégation *f*

Seine [seɪn] *n* **the S.** la Seine

seize [siːz] **1** *vt* saisir; *(power, land)* s'emparer de
2 *vi* **to s. (up)on** *(offer)* sauter sur; **to s. up** *(of engine)* se bloquer

seizure ['siːʒə(r)] *n (of goods, property)* saisie *f*; *Med* crise *f*; **s. of power** prise *f* de pouvoir

seldom ['seldəm] *adv* rarement

select [sɪ'lekt] **1** *vt* sélectionner
2 *adj (exclusive)* sélect • **selection** *n* sélection *f*; **a wide s.** un grand choix

selective [sɪ'lektɪv] *adj* sélectif, -ive

self [self] *(pl* **selves** [selvz]) *n* **the s.** le moi; *Fam* **he's back to his old s.** il est redevenu comme avant • **'self-addressed 'envelope** *n* enveloppe *f* libellée à ses nom et adresse • **'self-as'surance** *n* assurance *f* • **'self-as'sured** *adj* sûr de soi • **'self-'catering** *adj Br (holiday)* en appartement meublé; *(accommodation)* meublé • **'self-'centred** *(Am* **-centered)** *adj* égocentrique • **'self-'cleaning** *adj (oven)* autonettoyant • **'self-con'fessed** *adj (liar)* de son propre aveu • **'self-'confidence** *n* confiance *f* en soi • **'self-'confident** *adj* sûr de soi • **'self-'conscious** *adj* gêné • **'self-con'tained** *adj (flat)* indépendant • **'self-con'trol** *n* maîtrise *f* de soi

• **'self-de'feating** adj qui va à l'encontre du but recherché • **'self-de'fence** (Am -defense) n Law légitime défense f; **in s.** en état de légitime défense • **self-de'nial** n abnégation f • **'self-determi'nation** n autodétermination f • **'self-'discipline** n autodiscipline f • **'self-em'ployed** adj indépendant • **'self-es'teem** n confiance f en soi • **'self-'evident** adj évident • **'self-ex'planatory** adj qui se passe d'explications • **'self-'governing** adj autonome • **'self-im'portant** adj suffisant • **'self-in'dulgent** adj complaisant • **'self-'interest** n intérêt m personnel • **'self-made 'man** n self-made-man m • **'self-o'pinionated** adj entêté • **'self-'pity** n to be full of s. s'apitoyer sur son propre sort • **'self-'portrait** n autoportrait m • **'self-pos'sessed** adj qui a une grande maîtrise de soi • **self-'raising flour** (Am **self-'rising flour**) n = farine contenant de la levure chimique • **'self-re'liant** adj indépendant • **'self-re'spect** n amour-propre m • **'self-re'specting** adj qui se respecte • **'self-'righteous** adj suffisant • **'self-'sacrifice** n abnégation f • **'self-'satisfied** adj content de soi • **'self-'service** n & adj libre-service (m inv) • **'self-'starter** n (person) personne f très motivée • **'self-'styled** adj soi-disant inv • **'self-suf'ficient** adj indépendant • **'self-sup'porting** adj (business, person) financièrement indépendant • **'self-'taught** adj autodidacte

selfish ['selfɪʃ] adj égoïste; (motive) intéressé • **selfishness** n égoïsme m • **selfless** adj désintéressé

selfsame ['selfseɪm] adj même

sell [sel] **1** (pt & pp **sold**) vt vendre; Fig (idea) faire accepter; **to s. sb sth, to s. sth to sb** vendre qch à qn; **she sold it to me for £20** elle me l'a vendu 20 livres
2 vi (of product) se vendre; (of person) vendre • **sell-by date** n date f limite de vente • **seller** n vendeur, -euse mf • **selling price** n prix m de vente • **sellout** n (a) **it was a s.** (of play, film) tous les billets ont été vendus (b) (betrayal) trahison f
▸ **sell back** vt sep revendre ▸ **sell off** vt sep liquider ▸ **sell out** vt insep **to have** or **be sold out of sth** n'avoir plus de qch; **to be sold out** (of book, item) être épuisé; (of show, concert) afficher complet ▸ **sell up** vi (sell home, business) tout vendre

Sellotape® ['seləteɪp] n Br Scotch® m

semantic [sɪ'mæntɪk] adj sémantique • **semantics** n sémantique f

semaphore ['seməfɔː(r)] n signaux mpl à bras

semblance ['sembləns] n semblant m

semen ['siːmən] n sperme m

semester [sɪ'mestə(r)] n semestre m

semi- ['semɪ] pref semi-, demi- • **'semi-auto'matic** adj semi-automatique • **'semi-breve** [-briːv] n Br (musical note) ronde f • **'semicircle** n demi-cercle m • **'semi'circular** adj semi-circulaire • **semi'colon** n point-virgule m • **'semi-'conscious** adj à demi conscient • **'semide'tached** adj Br s. house maison f jumelée • **'semi'final** n demi-finale f • **'semi-'skilled** adj s. worker ouvrier m spécialisé • **'semi-'skimmed** adj (milk) demi-écrémé • **'semi('trailer)** n Am (truck) semi-remorque f

seminar ['semɪnɑː(r)] n séminaire m

semolina [semə'liːnə] n semoule f

senate ['senɪt] n the S. le Sénat • **senator** [-nətə(r)] n sénateur m

send [send] (pt & pp **sent**) vt envoyer (**to** à); **to s. sth to sb, to s. sb sth** envoyer qch à qn; **to s. sb home** renvoyer qn chez soi; Fam **to s. sb packing** envoyer promener qn • **sender** n expéditeur, -trice mf • **sendoff** n Fam **to give sb a good s.** faire des adieux en règle à qn • **send-up** n Br Fam parodie f
▸ **send away 1** vt sep (person) renvoyer **2** vi **to s. away for sth** se faire envoyer qch ▸ **send back** vt sep renvoyer ▸ **send for** vt insep envoyer chercher; (doctor) faire venir ▸ **send in** vt sep (form, invoice, troops) envoyer; (person) faire entrer ▸ **send off** vt sep (letter) envoyer (**to** à); (player) expulser **2** vi **to s. off for sth** se faire envoyer qch ▸ **send on** vt sep (letter) faire suivre ▸ **send out 1** vt sep envoyer **2** vi **to s. out for sth** envoyer chercher qch ▸ **send up** vt sep Br Fam (parody) se moquer de

senile ['siːnaɪl] adj sénile • **senility** [sɪ'nɪlɪtɪ] n sénilité f

senior ['siːnɪə(r)] **1** adj (in age) aîné; (in position, rank) supérieur; **to be sb's s., to be s. to sb** être l'aîné de qn; (in rank, status) être le supérieur de qn; **Brown s.** Brown père; **s. citizen** personne f âgée; **s. partner** associé m principal; Am **s. year** (in school, college) dernière année f
2 n aîné, -ée mf; Am (in last year of school or college) étudiant, -iante mf de dernière année; Sport senior mf • **seniority** [-nɪ'ɒrɪtɪ] n (in service) ancienneté f; (in rank) supériorité f

sensation [sen'seɪʃən] n sensation f • **sensational** adj sensationnel, -elle

sense [sens] **1** n (faculty, awareness, meaning) sens m; **s. of smell** l'odorat m;

s. of hearing l'ouïe *f*; **a s. of shame** un sentiment de honte; **a s. of warmth/ pleasure** une sensation de chaleur/plaisir; **s. of direction** sens de l'orientation; **a s. of time** la notion de l'heure; **to have a s. of humour** avoir le sens de l'humour; **to have (good) s.** avoir du bon sens; **to have the s. to do sth** avoir l'intelligence de faire qch; **to bring sb to his senses** ramener qn à la raison; **to make s.** être logique; **to make s. of sth** comprendre qch
  2 *vt* sentir (**that** que); *(have a foreboding of)* pressentir
senseless ['sensləs] *adj (pointless)* absurde; *(unconscious)* sans connaissance
sensibility [sensɪ'bɪlətɪ] *n* sensibilité *f*; **sensibilities** *(touchiness)* susceptibilité *f*
sensible ['sensəbəl] *adj (wise)* sensé; *(clothes, shoes)* pratique

> *Note that the French word **sensible** is a false friend and is almost never a translation for the English word **sensible**. It means **sensitive**.*

sensitive ['sensɪtɪv] *adj (person)* sensible (**to** à); *(skin, question)* délicat; *(information)* confidentiel, -ielle • **sensi'tivity** *n* sensibilité *f*; *(touchiness)* susceptibilité *f*
sensor ['sensə(r)] *n* détecteur *m*
sensory ['sensərɪ] *adj* sensoriel, -ielle
sensual ['senʃʊəl] *adj* sensuel, -uelle • **sensuality** [-ʃʊ'ælɪtɪ] *n* sensualité *f* • **sensuous** *adj* sensuel, -uelle • **sensuousness** *n* sensualité *f*
sent [sent] *pt & pp of* **send**
sentence ['sentəns] **1** *n* (**a**) *(words)* phrase *f* (**b**) *(in prison)* peine *f*; **to pass s.** prononcer la sentence; **to serve a s.** purger une peine
  2 *vt (criminal)* condamner; **to s. sb to three years (in prison)/to death** condamner qn à trois ans de prison/à mort
sentiment ['sentɪmənt] *n* sentiment *m* • **sentimental** [-'mentəl] *adj* sentimental • **sentimentality** [-men'tælɪtɪ] *n* sentimentalité *f*
sentry ['sentrɪ] *(pl* -**ies**) *n* sentinelle *f*; **to be on s. duty** être de garde; **s. box** guérite *f*
separate ['sepəreɪt] **1** ['sepərət] *adj (distinct)* séparé; *(organization)* indépendant; *(occasion, entrance)* différent; *(room)* à part; **they went their s. ways** ils sont partis chacun de leur côté
  2 *vt* séparer (**from** de)
  3 *vi* se séparer (**from** de) • **separately** ['sepərətlɪ] *adv* séparément • **sepa'ration** *n* séparation *f*

separates ['sepərəts] *npl (clothes)* coordonnés *mpl*
separatist ['sepərətɪst] *n* séparatiste *mf*
September [sep'tembə(r)] *n* septembre *m*
septic ['septɪk] *adj* septique; *(wound)* infecté; **to go s.** s'infecter; **s. tank** fosse *f* septique
sequel ['si:kwəl] *n (book, film)* suite *f*
sequence ['si:kwəns] *n (order)* ordre *m*; *(series)* succession *f*; *(in film)* & *Comptr, Mus & Cards* séquence *f*; **in s.** dans l'ordre
sequin ['si:kwɪn] *n* paillette *f*
Serb [sɜ:b] **1** *adj* serbe
  2 *n* Serbe *mf* • **Serbia** *n* la Serbie
serenade [serə'neɪd] **1** *n* sérénade *f*
  2 *vt* chanter la sérénade à
serene [sə'ri:n] *adj* serein • **serenity** [-'renɪtɪ] *n* sérénité *f*
sergeant ['sɑ:dʒənt] *n Mil* sergent *m*; *(in police)* brigadier *m*
serial ['sɪərɪəl] *n (story, film)* feuilleton *m*; **s. killer** tueur *m* en série; **s. number** numéro *m* de série • **serialize** *vt (in newspaper)* publier en feuilleton; *(on television or radio)* adapter en feuilleton
series ['sɪəri:z] *n inv* série *f*
serious ['sɪərɪəs] *adj (person)* sérieux, -ieuse; *(illness, mistake, tone)* grave; *(damage)* important; **to be s. about doing sth** envisager sérieusement de faire qch; *Fam* **s. money** un bon paquet d'argent • **seriously** *adv* sérieusement; *(ill, damaged)* gravement; **to take sb/sth s.** prendre qn/qch au sérieux • **seriousness** *n* sérieux *m*; *(of illness, situation)* gravité *f*; *(of damage)* importance *f*; **in all s.** sérieusement
sermon ['sɜ:mən] *n* sermon *m*
serrated [sə'reɪtɪd] *adj* en dents de scie
serum ['sɪərəm] *n* sérum *m*
servant ['sɜ:vənt] *n* domestique *mf*
serve [sɜ:v] **1** *n Tennis* service *m*
  2 *vt (country, cause, meal, customer)* servir; *(be useful to)* servir à; *(prison sentence)* purger; *(apprenticeship)* faire; **to s. a purpose** avoir une utilité; *Law* **to s. a summons on sb** remettre une assignation à qn; **it has served me well** ça m'a fait de l'usage; *Fam* **(it) serves you right!** ça t'apprendra!; **to s. up** *or* **out a meal** servir un repas
  3 *vi* servir (**as** de); **to s. on** *(committee, jury)* être membre de • **server** *n Tennis* serveur, -euse *mf*; *Comptr* serveur *m*
service ['sɜ:vɪs] **1** *n (with army, firm, in restaurant)* & *Rel & Tennis* service *m*; *(of machine)* entretien *m*; *(of car)* révision *f*;

to be at sb's s. être au service de qn; **to be of s. to sb** être utile à qn; **the (armed) services** les forces *fpl* armées; **s. charge** service; *Br* **s. area** *(on motorway)* aire *f* de service; **s. station** station-service *f*
2 *vt (machine)* entretenir; *(car)* réviser
serviceable ['sɜːvɪsəbəl] *adj (usable)* en état de marche; *(durable)* résistant
serviceman ['sɜːvɪsmən] *(pl* **-men**) *n* militaire *m*
serviette [sɜːvɪ'et] *n Br* serviette *f* de table
servile ['sɜːvaɪl] *adj* servile
serving ['sɜːvɪŋ] *n (of food)* portion *f*; **s. dish** plat *m*
session ['seʃən] *n (meeting, period)* séance *f*; *(university term)* trimestre *m*; *(university year)* année *f* universitaire; **to be in s.** siéger; **the parliamentary s.** la session parlementaire
set [set] **1** *n (of keys, needles, tools)* jeu *m*; *(of stamps, numbers)* série *f*; *(of people)* groupe *m*; *(of facts, laws)* & *Math* ensemble *m*; *(of books)* collection *f*; *(of dishes)* service *m*; *(of tyres)* train *m*; *(kit)* trousse *f*; *(in theatre)* décor *m*; *(for film)* plateau *m*; *Tennis* set *m*; **s. of teeth** dentition *f*; **chess s.** jeu d'échecs; **construction s.** jeu de construction; **film s.** plateau de tournage; **radio s.** poste *m* de radio; **tea s.** service à thé; **television s., TV s.** téléviseur *m*
2 *adj (time, price)* fixe; *(lunch)* à prix fixe; *(school book)* au programme; *(ideas, purpose)* déterminé; **to be s. on doing sth** être résolu à faire qch; **to be s. on sth** avoir fixé son choix sur qch; **to be s. in one's ways** tenir à ses habitudes; **to be dead s. against sth** être formellement opposé à qch; **to be all s.** être prêt (**to do** pour faire); **to be s. back from the road** *(of house)* être en retrait de la route; **s. menu** menu *m*; **s. phrase** expression *f* figée
3 *(pt & pp* **set,** *pres p* **setting)** *vt (put)* mettre, poser; *(date, limit, task)* fixer; *(homework)* donner (**for sb** à qn); *(jewel)* sertir; *(watch)* régler; *(alarm clock)* mettre (**for** pour); *(bone fracture)* réduire; *(trap)* tendre (**for** à); **to s. a record** établir un record; **to s. a precedent** créer un précédent; **to have one's hair s.** se faire faire une mise en plis; **to s. sb thinking** faire réfléchir qn; **to s. sb free** libérer qn; **to s. sth on fire** mettre le feu à qch
4 *vi (of sun)* se coucher; *(of jelly)* prendre; *(of bone)* se ressouder
▸ **set about** *vt insep (begin)* se mettre à;

to s. about doing sth se mettre à faire qch
▸ **set back** *vt sep (in time)* retarder; *Fam (cost)* coûter ▸ **set down** *vt sep (object)* poser ▸ **set in** *vi (of winter)* s'installer; *(of fog)* tomber ▸ **set off 1** *vt sep (bomb)* faire exploser; *(mechanism)* déclencher; *Fig (beauty, complexion)* rehausser; **to s. sb off crying** faire pleurer qn **2** *vi (leave)* partir ▸ **set out 1** *vt sep (display, explain)* exposer; *(arrange)* disposer **2** *vi (leave)* partir; **to s. out to do sth** avoir l'intention de faire qch ▸ **set up 1** *vt sep (tent, statue)* dresser; *(roadblock)* mettre en place; *(company)* créer; *(meeting)* organiser; *(inquiry)* ouvrir; **to s. sb up in business (as)** installer qn (comme) **2** *vi* **to s. up in business (as)** s'installer (comme) ▸ **set upon** *vt insep (attack)* attaquer
setback ['setbæk] *n* revers *m*
set-square ['setskweə(r)] *n Br* équerre *f* (à dessin)
settee [se'tiː] *n* canapé *m*
setter ['setə(r)] *n* setter *m*
setting ['setɪŋ] *n (surroundings)* cadre *m*; *(of sun)* coucher *m*; *(on machine)* réglage *m*
settle ['setəl] **1** *vt (put in place)* installer; *(decide, arrange, pay)* régler; *(date, venue)* fixer; *(nerves)* calmer; *(land)* coloniser; **to s. a matter out of court** régler une affaire à l'amiable; **that settles it!** c'est décidé!
2 *vi (of person, family)* s'installer; *(of dust)* se déposer; *(of bird)* se poser; **to s. into an armchair** s'installer confortablement dans un fauteuil; **to s. into one's job** s'habituer à son travail ● **settled** *adj (weather, period)* stable; *(life)* rangé
▸ **settle down** *vi (in chair, house)* s'installer; *(become quieter)* s'assagir; *(of situation)* se calmer; **to s. down in one's job** s'habituer à son travail; **to s. down with sb** mener une vie stable avec qn; **to s. down to work** se mettre au travail ▸ **settle for** *vt insep* se contenter de ▸ **settle in** *vi (in new home)* s'installer; *(in new school)* s'adapter ▸ **settle up** *vi (pay)* régler; **to s. up with sb** régler qn
settlement ['setəlmənt] *n (agreement)* accord *m*; *(payment)* règlement *m*; *(colony)* colonie *f*
settler ['setlə(r)] *n* colon *m*
set-to [set'tuː] *(pl* **-os**) *n Br Fam (quarrel)* prise *f* de bec
setup ['setʌp] *n Fam (arrangement)* système *m*
seven ['sevən] *adj & n* sept *(m)* ● **seventh** *adj & n* septième *(mf)*

seventeen ['sevənti:n] *adj & n* dix-sept
(*m*) • **seventeenth** *adj & n* dix-septième (*mf*)
seventy ['sevəntɪ] *adj & n* soixante-dix
(*m*); **s.-one** soixante et onze • **seventieth**
adj & n soixante-dixième (*mf*)
sever ['sevə(r)] *vt* couper; *Fig (relations)*
rompre • **severance** *n (of relations)* rupture *f*; **s. pay** indemnité *f* de licenciement
several ['sevrəl] *adj & pron* plusieurs
(**of** d'entre)
severe [sə'vɪə(r)] *adj (person, punishment, tone)* sévère; *(winter, training)* rigoureux, -euse; *(illness, injury)* grave;
(blow, pain) violent; *(cold, frost)* intense;
(weather) très mauvais; **to have a s. cold**
avoir un gros rhume • **severely** *adv (criticize, punish)* sévèrement; *(damaged,
wounded)* gravement; **to be s. handicapped** *or* **disabled** être gravement
handicapé • **severity** [-'verɪtɪ] *n* sévérité
f; *(of winter)* rigueur *f*; *(of injury)* gravité *f*;
(of blow) violence *f*
sew [səʊ] (*pt* **sewed**, *pp* **sewn** *or* **sewed**)
vt coudre; **to s. a button on a shirt** coudre
un bouton à une chemise; **to s. sth up**
recoudre qch • **sewing** *n* couture *f*; **s.
machine** machine *f* à coudre
sewage ['su:ɪdʒ] *n* eaux *fpl* d'égout
• **sewer** ['su:ə(r)] *n* égout *m*
sewn [səʊn] *pp of* **sew**
sex [seks] **1** *n* sexe *m*; **to have s. with sb**
coucher avec qn
2 *adj (education, life, act)* sexuel, -uelle;
s. appeal sex-appeal *m*; **s. maniac** obsédé
m sexuel, obsédée *f* sexuelle; **s. symbol**
sex-symbol *m* • **sexist** *adj & n* sexiste (*mf*)
sextet [sek'stet] *n* sextuor *m*
sexual ['sekʃʊəl] *adj* sexuel, -uelle
• **sexuality** [-ʃʊ'ælɪtɪ] *n* sexualité *f* • **sexy**
['seksɪ] (**-ier, -iest**) *adj Fam* sexy *inv*; *Fig
(car)* branché
Seychelles [seɪ'ʃelz] *npl* **the S.** les Seychelles *fpl*
sh [ʃ] *exclam* chut!
shabby ['ʃæbɪ] (**-ier, -iest**) *adj* miteux,
-euse; *(behaviour, treatment)* mesquin
• **shabbily** *adv (dressed)* pauvrement
• **shabbiness** *n* aspect *m* miteux; *Fig
(meanness)* mesquinerie *f*
shack [ʃæk] **1** *n* cabane *f*
2 *vi Fam* **to s. up with sb** vivre à la colle
avec qn
shackles ['ʃækəlz] *npl* chaînes *fpl*
shade [ʃeɪd] **1** *n* ombre *f*; *(of colour,
meaning, opinion)* nuance *f*; **in the s.** à
l'ombre; **a s. faster/taller** un rien plus
vite/plus grand; *Fam* **shades** *(glasses)* lunettes *fpl* de soleil

2 *vt (of tree)* ombrager; *(protect)* abriter
(**from** de) • **shady** (**-ier, -iest**) *adj (place)*
ombragé; *Fig (person, business)* louche
shadow ['ʃædəʊ] **1** *n* ombre *f*; **to cast a s.**
projeter une ombre; *Fig* **to cast a s. over**
sth jeter une ombre sur qch
2 *adj Br Pol* **s. cabinet** cabinet *m* fantôme; **the S. Education Secretary** le
porte-parole de l'opposition sur les
questions de l'éducation
3 *vt* **to s. sb** *(follow)* filer qn • **shadowy**
(**-ier, -iest**) *adj (form)* vague
shaft [ʃɑ:ft] *n* (**a**) *(of tool)* manche *m*; **s.
of light** rayon *m* de lumière (**b**) *(of mine)*
puits *m*; *(of lift)* cage *f*
shaggy ['ʃægɪ] (**-ier, -iest**) *adj (hairy)*
hirsute
shake[1] [ʃeɪk] **1** *n* secousse *f*; **to give sth a
s.** secouer qch; **with a s. of his head** en
secouant la tête; *Fam* **in two shakes** en un
rien de temps
2 (*pt* **shook**, *pp* **shaken**) *vt (move up and
down)* secouer; *(bottle, fist)* agiter;
(building) faire trembler; *Fig (belief, resolution)* ébranler; **to s. one's head** faire non
de la tête; **to s. hands with sb** serrer la
main à qn; **we shook hands** nous nous
sommes serré la main; **to s. off** *(dust)*
secouer; *Fig (illness, pursuer)* se débarrasser de; **to s. up** *(reorganize)* réorganiser de fond en comble; **to s. sb up** secouer
qn; **to s. sth out of sth** faire tomber qch
de qch (en secouant)
3 *vi (of person, windows, voice)* trembler
(**with** de) • **shake-up** *n Fam (reorganization)* chambardement *m*
shake[2] [ʃeɪk] *n (milk shake)* milk-shake *m*
shaken ['ʃeɪkən] *pp of* **shake**[1]
shaky [ʃeɪkɪ] (**-ier, -iest**) *adj (voice)* trem-
blant; *(table, chair)* branlant; *(handwriting)* tremblé; *(health)* précaire
shall [ʃæl, *unstressed* ʃəl]

On trouve généralement **I/you/he**/*etc*
shall sous leurs formes contractées **I'll/
you'll/he'll**/*etc*. La forme négative correspondante est **shan't**, que l'on écrira
shall not dans des contextes formels.

v aux (**a**) *(expressing future tense)* **I s.
come, I'll come** je viendrai; **we s. not
come, we shan't come** nous ne viendrons
pas (**b**) *(making suggestion)* **s. I leave?**
veux-tu que je parte?; **let's go in, s. we?**
entrons, tu veux bien? (**c**) *Formal (expressing order)* **he s. do it if I order it** il le fera
si je l'ordonne
shallot [ʃə'lɒt] *n Br* échalote *f*
shallow ['ʃæləʊ] (**-er, -est**) **1** *adj (water,*

river) peu profond; *Fig & Pej (argument, person)* superficiel, -ielle

2 *npl* **the shallows** *(of river)* le bas-fond

sham [ʃæm] **1** *n (pretence)* comédie *f; (person)* imposteur *m;* **to be a s.** *(of jewel)* être faux *(f* fausse); **it's a s.!** *(election promises)* c'est du bidon!

2 *adj (false)* faux *(f* fausse); *(illness, emotion)* feint

3 *(pt & pp* **-mm-**) *vt* feindre

4 *vi* faire semblant

shambles ['ʃæmbəlz] *n* pagaille *f;* **this place is a s.!** quelle pagaille!

shame [ʃeɪm] **1** *n (guilt, disgrace)* honte *f;* **it's a s.** c'est dommage (**to do** de faire); **it's a s. (that)...** c'est dommage que... *(+ subjunctive);* **s. on you!** tu devrais avoir honte!; **what a s.!** quel dommage!; **to put sb to s.** faire honte à qn

2 *vt (make ashamed)* faire honte à ● '**shame**'**faced** *adj (embarrassed)* honteux, -euse

shameful ['ʃeɪmfəl] *adj* honteux, -euse ● **shamefully** *adv* honteusement

shameless ['ʃeɪmləs] *adj* impudique; **to be s. about doing sth** n'avoir aucun scrupule à faire qch ● **shamelessly** *adv* sans la moindre honte

shammy ['ʃæmɪ] *n Fam* **s. (leather)** peau *f* de chamois

shampoo [ʃæm'puː] **1** *n* shampooing *m*

2 *vt (carpet)* shampouiner; **to s. sb's hair** faire un shampooing à qn

shandy ['ʃændɪ] *n Br* panaché *m*

shan't [ʃɑːnt] = **shall not**

shanty¹ ['ʃæntɪ] *n (hut)* baraque *f;* **s. town** bidonville *m*

shanty² ['ʃæntɪ] *n* **sea s.** chanson *f* de marins

shape [ʃeɪp] **1** *n* forme *f;* **what s. is it?** quelle forme cela a-t-il?; **in the s. of a pear/bell** en forme de poire/cloche; *Fig* **in any s. or form** quel qu'il soit *(f* quelle qu'elle soit); **to take s.** *(of plan)* prendre forme; **to be in good/bad s.** *(of person)* être en bonne/mauvaise forme; *(of business)* marcher bien/mal; **to keep in s.** garder la forme

2 *vt (clay)* modeler; *(wood)* façonner (**into** en); *Fig (events, future)* influencer

3 *vi* **to s. up** *(of person)* progresser; *(of teams, plans)* prendre forme ● **-shaped** *suff* **pear-shaped** en forme de poire ● **shapeless** *adj* informe ● **shapely** (**-ier, -iest**) *adj* bien fait

share [ʃeə(r)] **1** *n* part *f* (**of** or **in** de); *Fin (in company)* action *f;* **to have one's (fair)**

s. of sth avoir sa part de qch; **to do one's (fair) s.** mettre la main à la pâte

2 *vt* partager; *(characteristic)* avoir en commun; **to s. sth out** partager qch

3 *vi* partager; **to s. in sth** avoir sa part de qch ● **shareholder** *n Fin* actionnaire *mf*

shark [ʃɑːk] *n (fish, crook)* requin *m*

sharp [ʃɑːp] **1** (**-er, -est**) *adj (knife)* bien aiguisé; *(pencil)* bien taillé; *(razor)* qui coupe bien; *(point)* aigu *(f* aiguë); *(claws)* acéré; *(rise, fall)* brusque; *(focus)* net *(f* nette); *(contrast)* marqué; *(eyesight, sound)* perçant; *(taste)* acide; *(intelligent)* vif *(f* vive)

2 *adv* **to stop s.** s'arrêter net; **five o'clock s.** cinq heures pile; **to turn s. right/left** tourner tout de suite à droite/à gauche; *Fam* **look s.!** grouille-toi!

3 *n Mus* dièse *m* ● '**sharp**-'**eyed** *adj* observateur, -trice

sharpen ['ʃɑːpən] *vt (knife)* aiguiser; *(pencil)* tailler ● **sharpener** *n (for pencils)* taille-crayon *m; (for blades)* aiguisoir *m*

sharply ['ʃɑːplɪ] *adv (rise, fall)* brusquement; *(contrast)* nettement ● **sharpness** *n (of blade)* tranchant *m; (of picture)* netteté *f*

sharpshooter ['ʃɑːpʃuːtə(r)] *n* tireur *m* d'élite

shatter ['ʃætə(r)] **1** *vt (glass)* faire voler en éclats; *(career, health, hopes)* briser

2 *vi (of glass)* voler en éclats ● **shattered** *adj Fam (exhausted)* crevé ● **shattering** *adj (defeat)* accablant; *(news, experience)* bouleversant

shave [ʃeɪv] **1** *n* **to have a s.** se raser; *Fig* **that was a close s.** c'était moins une

2 *vt (person, head)* raser; **to s. one's legs** se raser les jambes; **to s. off one's beard** se raser la barbe

3 *vi* se raser ● **shaven** *adj* rasé (de près) ● **shaver** *n* rasoir *m* électrique ● **shaving** *n (strip of wood)* copeau *m;* **s. brush** blaireau *m;* **s. cream, s. foam** mousse *f* à raser

shawl [ʃɔːl] *n* châle *m*

she [ʃiː] **1** *pron* elle; **s. wants** elle veut; **she's a happy woman** c'est une femme heureuse; **ifI were s.** si j'étais elle; **s. and I** elle et moi

2 *n Fam (female)* femelle *f;* **s.-bear** ourse *f;* **it's a s.** *(of baby)* c'est une fille

sheaf [ʃiːf] *(pl* **sheaves** [ʃiːvz]) *n (of corn)* gerbe *f; (of paper)* liasse *f*

shear [ʃɪə(r)] **1** *vt* tondre

2 *npl* **shears** cisaille *f*

sheath [ʃiːθ] *(pl* **-s** [shiːðz]) *n (for sword)* fourreau *m; (for electric cable)* gaine *f; (contraceptive)* préservatif *m*

shed¹ [ʃed] n (in garden) abri m; (in factory) atelier m

shed² [ʃed] (pt & pp shed, pres p shedding) vt (leaves) perdre; (tears, blood) verser; **to s. its skin** (of snake) muer; Fig **to s. light on sth** éclairer qch

she'd [ʃiːd] = she had, she would

sheen [ʃiːn] n lustre m

sheep [ʃiːp] n inv mouton m • **sheepdog** n chien m de berger • **sheepskin** n peau f de mouton; **s. jacket** veste f en peau de mouton

sheepish [ˈʃiːpɪʃ] adj penaud • **sheepishly** adv d'un air penaud

sheer [ʃɪə(r)] adj (pure) pur; (stockings) très fin; (cliff) à pic; **by s. chance** tout à fait par hasard

sheet [ʃiːt] n (on bed) drap m; (of paper) feuille f; (of glass, ice) plaque f; **s. metal** tôle f

sheikh [ʃeɪk] n cheik m

shelf [ʃelf] (pl **shelves** [ʃelvz]) n étagère f; (in shop) rayon m; (on cliff) rebord m; **set of shelves** étagères fpl; Com **s. life** durée f de conservation avant vente

shell [ʃel] 1 n (**a**) (of egg, snail, nut) coquille f; (of tortoise, lobster) carapace f; (on beach) coquillage m; (of peas) cosse f; (of building) carcasse f (**b**) (explosive) obus m
2 vt (**a**) (peas) écosser; (nut, shrimp) décortiquer (**b**) (town) bombarder (**c**) Fam **to s. out a lot of money** sortir pas mal d'argent • **shelling** n bombardement m • **shell suit** n survêtement m (en synthétique brillant)

she'll [ʃiːl] = she will, she shall

shellfish [ˈʃelfɪʃ] 1 n inv (crustacean) crustacé m; (mollusc) coquillage m
2 npl Culin (as food) fruits mpl de mer

shelter [ˈʃeltə(r)] 1 n (place, protection) abri m; **to take s.** se mettre à l'abri (**from** de); **to seek s.** chercher un abri
2 vt abriter (**from** de); (criminal) accueillir
3 vi s'abriter (**from** de) • **sheltered** adj (place) abrité; **she's had a s. life** elle a eu une enfance très protégée

shelve [ʃelv] vt (postpone) mettre au placard

shelving [ˈʃelvɪŋ] n rayonnages mpl

shepherd [ˈʃepəd] 1 n berger m; Br **s.'s pie** ≃ hachis m Parmentier
2 vt **to s. sb in** faire entrer qn; **to s. sb around** piloter qn • **shepherdess** n bergère f

sherbet [ˈʃɜːbət] n Br (powder) poudre f acidulée; Am (sorbet) sorbet m

sheriff [ˈʃerɪf] n Am shérif m

sherry [ˈʃerɪ] n sherry m, xérès m

Shetlands [ˈʃetləndz] npl **the S.** les Shetland fpl

shield [ʃiːld] 1 n bouclier m; (police badge) badge m
2 vt protéger (**from** de)

shift [ʃɪft] 1 n (change) changement m (**of** or **in** de); (period of work) poste m; (workers) équipe f; **s. key** (on computer, typewriter) touche f des majuscules
2 vt (move) déplacer; (stain) enlever; (employee) muter (**to** à); **to s. places** changer de place; **to s. the blame on to sb** rejeter la responsabilité sur qn; Am **to s. gear(s)** (in vehicle) changer de vitesse
3 vi bouger; (of stain) partir • **shiftwork** n travail m posté

shiftless [ˈʃɪftləs] adj fainéant

shifty [ˈʃɪftɪ] (-ier, -iest) adj (person) louche; (look) fuyant

shilly-shally [ˈʃɪlɪʃælɪ] (pt & pt -ied) vi hésiter

shimmer [ˈʃɪmə(r)] 1 n (of silk) chatoiement m; (of water) miroitement m
2 vi (of silk) chatoyer; (of water) miroiter

shin [ʃɪn] n tibia m; **s. pad** (of hockey player) jambière f

shindig [ˈʃɪndɪg] n Fam nouba f

shine [ʃaɪn] 1 n brillant m; (on metal) éclat m
2 (pt & pp shone) vt (polish) faire briller; (light, torch) braquer
3 vi briller; **to s. with joy** (of face) rayonner de joie; (of eyes) briller de joie • **shining** adj brillant; **a s. example of** un parfait exemple de

shingle [ˈʃɪŋgəl] n (on beach) galets mpl; (on roof) bardeau m

shingles [ˈʃɪŋgəlz] n Med zona m

shiny [ˈʃaɪnɪ] (-ier, -iest) adj brillant

ship [ʃɪp] 1 n navire m
2 (pt & pp -pp-) vt (send) expédier; (transport) transporter; (take on board) embarquer (**on to** sur) • **shipbuilding** n construction f navale • **shipmate** n camarade m de bord • **shipment** n cargaison f • **shipowner** n armateur m • **shipping** n (traffic) navigation f; (ships) navires mpl; **s. agent** agent m maritime; **s. line** compagnie f de navigation • **shipshape** adj & adv en ordre • **shipwreck** n naufrage m • **shipwrecked** adj naufragé; **to be s.** faire naufrage • **shipyard** n chantier m naval

shire [ˈʃaɪə(r)] n Br comté m

shirk [ʃɜːk] 1 vt (duty) se dérober à; (work) éviter de faire
2 vi tirer au flanc • **shirker** n tire-au-flanc m inv

shirt [ʃɜːt] *n* chemise *f*; *(of woman)* chemisier *m*; *(of sportsman)* maillot *m* • **shirtsleeves** *npl* **in (one's) s.** en bras de chemise

shiver [ˈʃɪvə(r)] **1** *n* frisson *m*; **to send shivers down sb's spine** donner le frisson à qn

2 *vi* frissonner (**with** de) • **shivery** *adj* **to be s.** frissonner

shoal [ʃəʊl] *n (of fish)* banc *m*

shock [ʃɒk] **1** *n (impact, emotional blow)* choc *m*; *(of earthquake)* secousse *f*; **(electric) s.** décharge *f* (électrique); **to be in s.** être en état de choc; **the news came as a s. to me** la nouvelle m'a stupéfié

2 *adj (wave, tactics, troops)* de choc; **s. absorber** amortisseur *m*; **s. therapy** électrochocs *mpl*

3 *vt (offend)* choquer; *(surprise)* stupéfier • **shocking** *adj (outrageous)* choquant; *(very bad)* atroce • **shockingly** *adv (extremely, badly)* atrocement • **shockproof** *adj* antichoc *inv*

shod [ʃɒd] *pt & pp of* **shoe**

shoddy [ˈʃɒdɪ] (-**ier**, -**iest**) *adj (goods)* de mauvaise qualité • **shoddily** *adv (made, done)* mal

shoe [ʃuː] **1** *n* chaussure *f*; *(for horse)* fer *m* à cheval; **(brake) s.** *(in vehicle)* sabot *m* (de frein); *Fig* **I wouldn't like to be in your shoes** je n'aimerais pas être à ta place; **s. polish** cirage *m*; **s. repair shop** cordonnerie *f*; **s. shop** magasin *m* de chaussures

2 *(pt & pp* **shod**) *vt (horse)* ferrer • **shoehorn** *n* chausse-pied *m* • **shoelace** *n* lacet *m* • **shoemaker** *n* fabricant *m* de chaussures; *(cobbler)* cordonnier *m* • **shoestring** *n Fam* **on a s.** avec trois fois rien

shone [*Br* ʃɒn, *Am* ʃəʊn] *pt & pp of* **shine**

shoo [ʃuː] **1** *(pt & pp* **shooed**) *vt* **to s. (away)** chasser

2 *exclam* ouste!

shook [ʃʊk] *pt of* **shake**¹

shoot [ʃuːt] **1** *n (of plant)* pousse *f*

2 *(pt & pp* **shot**) *vt (bullet)* tirer; *(arrow)* lancer; *(film, scene)* tourner; **to s. sb** *(kill)* tuer qn par balle; *(wound)* blesser qn par balle; *(execute)* fusiller qn

3 *vi (with gun)* tirer (**at** sur); *Football* shooter • **shooting 1** *n (shots)* coups *mpl* de feu; *(incident)* fusillade *f*; *(of film, scene)* tournage *m* **2** *adj* **s. star** étoile *f* filante • **shoot-out** *n Fam* fusillade *f*

▸ **shoot away** *vi (of vehicle, person)* partir à toute vitesse ▸ **shoot back** *vi (return fire)* riposter ▸ **shoot down** *vt sep (plane)* abattre ▸ **shoot off** *vi (leave quickly)* filer ▸ **shoot out** *vi (spurt out)* jaillir ▸ **shoot up**

vi (of price) monter en flèche; *(of plant, child)* pousser vite; *(spurt)* jaillir; *(of rocket)* s'élever

shop [ʃɒp] **1** *n* magasin *m*; *(small)* boutique *f*; *(workshop)* atelier *m*; **at the baker's s.** à la boulangerie, chez le boulanger; *Br* **s. assistant** vendeur, -euse *mf*; *Br* **s. floor** *(workers)* ouvriers *mpl*; *Br* **s. front** devanture *f*; *Br* **s. steward** délégué, -ée *mf* syndical(e); **s. window** vitrine *f*

2 *(pt & pp* -**pp**-) *vt Br Fam* **to s. sb** balancer qn

3 *vi* faire ses courses (**at** chez); **to s. around** comparer les prix • **shopkeeper** *n* commerçant, -ante *mf* • **shoplifter** *n* voleur, -euse *mf* à l'étalage • **shoplifting** *n* vol *m* à l'étalage • **shopper** *n (customer)* client *m*, cliente *f*; *Br (bag)* sac *m* à provisions • **shopping 1** *n (goods)* achats *mpl*; **to go s.** faire les courses; **to do one's s.** faire ses courses **2** *adj (street, district)* commerçant; **s. bag/basket** sac *m*/panier *m* à provisions; **s. centre** centre *m* commercial; **s. list** liste *f* des commissions • **'shop'soiled** (*Am* **'shop'worn**) *adj* défraîchi

shore [ʃɔː(r)] **1** *n (of sea)* rivage *m*; *(of lake)* bord *m*; **on s.** à terre

2 *vt* **to s. up** *(wall)* étayer; *Fig (company, economy)* consolider

shorn [ʃɔːn] *adj (head)* tondu; *Literary* **s. of** *(stripped of)* dénué de

short [ʃɔːt] **1** (-**er**, -**est**) *adj* court; *(person, distance)* petit; *(syllable)* bref (*f* brève); *(impatient, curt)* brusque; **to be s. of sth** être à court de qch; **we're s. of ten men** il nous manque dix hommes; **s. of a miracle, we won't...** à moins d'un miracle, nous ne...; **money/time is s.** l'argent/le temps manque; **in a s. time** *or* **while** dans un petit moment; **a s. time** *or* **while ago** il y a peu de temps; **I'll stay for a s. time** *or* **while** je resterai un petit moment; **Tony is s. for Anthony** Tony est le diminutif d'Anthony; **he's not far s. of forty** il n'est pas loin de la quarantaine; **in s.** bref; *Br* **s. list** liste *f* de candidats retenus; **s. story** nouvelle *f*

2 *adv* **to cut s.** *(hair)* couper court; *(visit)* abréger; *(person)* couper la parole à; **to stop s. of doing sth** se retenir tout juste de faire qch; **to be running s. of sth** n'avoir presque plus de qch; **to fall s. of sth** ne pas atteindre qch

3 *n Fam El* court-circuit *m* • **shortbread** *n* sablé *m* • **'short-'change** *vt (buyer)* ne pas rendre assez de monnaie à • **'short-'circuit 1** *n* court-circuit *m* **2** *vt* court-

circuiter **3** *vi* se mettre en court-circuit
●**shortcoming** *n* défaut *m* ●**short cut** *n*
raccourci *m* ●**shortfall** *n* manque *m*
●**shorthand** *n* sténo *f*; **in s.** en sténo; **s.
typist** sténodactylo *f* ● **short-'handed** *adj*
à court de personnel ● **short-'lived** *adj* de
courte durée ●**short'sighted** *adj* myope;
Fig (in one's judgements) imprévoyant
●**short'sightedness** *n* myopie *f*; *Fig* imprévoyance *f* ● 'short-'sleeved *adj* à manches courtes ●**short-'staffed** *adj* à court
de personnel ●**short-'tempered** *adj* irascible ● 'short-'term *adj* à court terme
●**short-time** 'working *n* *Br* chômage *m*
partiel
shortage ['ʃɔːtɪdʒ] *n* pénurie *f*; **to have
no s. of sth** ne pas manquer de qch
shorten ['ʃɔːtən] *vt* raccourcir
shortening ['ʃɔːtənɪŋ] *n* *Br Culin* matière
f grasse
shortly ['ʃɔːtlɪ] *adv (soon)* bientôt; **s.
before/after** peu avant/après
shorts [ʃɔːts] *npl* **(a pair of) s.** un short; **
boxer s.** caleçon *m*
shot [ʃɒt] **1** *pt & pp of* **shoot**
2 *n (from gun)* coup *m*; *(with camera)*
prise *f* de vues; *Football* coup de pied;
Fam (injection) piqûre *f*; **to fire a s.** tirer;
to be a good s. être bon tireur;
to have a s. at sth/doing sth essayer qch/
de faire qch; **it's a long s.** c'est un coup
à tenter; *Fig* **like a s.** sans hésiter; *Fam*
to get s. of sb/sth *(get rid of)* se débarrasser de qn/qch ●**shotgun** *n* fusil *m* de
chasse
should [ʃʊd, *unstressed* ʃəd]

La forme négative **should not** s'écrit
shouldn't en forme contractée.

v aux (**a**) *(expressing obligation)* **you s. do
it** vous devriez le faire; **I s. have stayed**
j'aurais dû rester
(**b**) *(expressing possibility)* **the weather s.
improve** le temps devrait s'améliorer; **she
s. have arrived by now** elle devrait être
arrivée à l'heure qu'il est
(**c**) *(expressing preferences)* **I s. like to stay**
j'aimerais bien rester; **I s. like to** j'aimerais
bien; **I s. hope so** j'espère bien
(**d**) *(in subordinate clauses)* **it's strange
(that) she s. say no** il est étrange qu'elle
dise non; **he insisted that she s. meet
her parents** il a insisté pour qu'elle rencontre ses parents
(**e**) *(in conditional clauses)* **if he s. come,
s. he come** s'il vient
(**f**) *(in rhetorical questions)* **why s. you
suspect me?** pourquoi me soupçonnez-

vous?; **who s. I meet but Martin!** et qui
a-t-il fallu que je rencontre? Martin!
shoulder ['ʃəʊldə(r)] **1** *n* épaule *f*; **to
have round shoulders** être voûté; *Fig* **to
be looking over one's s.** être constamment sur ses gardes; **s.-length hair** cheveux *mpl* mi-longs; **s. bag** sac *m* besace;
s. blade omoplate *f*; **s. pad** épaulette *f*; **s.
strap** *(of garment)* bretelle *f*
2 *vt (responsibility)* endosser
shout [ʃaʊt] **1** *n* cri *m*; **to give sb a s.**
appeler qn
2 *vt* **to s. sth (out)** crier qch; **to s. sb
down** empêcher qn de parler
3 *vi* **to s. (out)** crier; **to s. to sb to do sth**
crier à qn de faire qch; **to s. at sb** crier
après qn ●**shouting** *n (shouts)* cris *mpl*
shove [ʃʌv] **1** *n* poussée *f*; **to give sb/sth
a s.** pousser qn/qch
2 *vt* pousser; *Fam* **to s. sth into sth**
fourrer qch dans qch; *Fam* **to s. sb around**
chahuter qn
3 *vi* pousser; *Fam* **to s. off** *(leave)* dégager; *Fam* **to s. over** *(move over)* se pousser
shovel ['ʃʌvəl] **1** *n* pelle *f*
2 *(Br* -ll-*, Am* -l-*) vt* pelleter; **to s. snow up**
or **away** enlever la neige à la pelle; **to s.
leaves up** ramasser des feuilles à la pelle;
Fam **to s. sth into sth** fourrer qch dans
qch
show [ʃəʊ] **1** *n (concert, play)* spectacle
m; (on TV) émission *f*; *Cin* séance *f*;
(exhibition) exposition *f*; *(of force,
friendship)* démonstration *f*; *(pretence)*
semblant *m* (**of** de); **to be on s.** être
exposé; **to put sth on s.** exposer qch; *Br*
to give a good s. *(of sportsman, musician,
actor)* jouer bien; **good s.!** bravo!; **it's
(just) for s.** c'est pour épater la galerie;
to make a s. of one's wealth faire étalage
de ses richesses; **to make a s. of being
angry** faire semblant d'être en colère; **s.
business** le monde du spectacle; *Br* **s. flat**
appartement *m* témoin; **s. girl** girl *f*; **s.
jumping** jumping *m*
2 *(pt* **showed***, pp* **shown***) vt* montrer (**to**
à; **that** que); *(in exhibition)* exposer;
(film) passer; *(indicate)* indiquer; **to s. sb
sth, to s. sth to sb** montrer qch à qn; **to s.
sb to the door** reconduire qn; **to s. sb
how to do sth** montrer à qn comment
faire qch; **it (just) goes to s. that** ça
montre bien que; *Fam* **I'll s. him!** je vais
lui apprendre!
3 *vi (be visible)* se voir; *(of film)* passer;
'now showing' *(film)* 'à l'affiche' ●**show-
case** *n* vitrine *f* ●**showdown** *n* confrontation *f* ●**showmanship** *n* sens *m* du

spectacle • **show-off** n Pej crâneur, -euse mf • **showpiece** n joyau m • **showroom** n magasin m

▸ **show around** vt sep **to s. sb around the town** faire visiter la ville à qn; **she was shown around the house** on lui a fait visiter la maison ▸ **show in** vt sep (visitor) faire entrer ▸ **show off 1** vt sep Pej (display) étaler; (highlight) faire valoir **2** vi Pej crâner ▸ **show out** vt sep (visitor) reconduire ▸ **show round** vt sep = **show around** ▸ **show up 1** vt sep (embarrass) faire honte à; (reveal) faire ressortir **2** vi (stand out) ressortir (**against** contre); (of error) être visible; Fam (of person) se présenter

shower [ˈʃaʊə(r)] **1** n (bathing, device) douche f; (of rain) averse f; (of blows) déluge m; Am (party) réception f (avec remise de cadeaux); **to have** or **take a s.** prendre une douche; **s. curtain** rideau m de douche; **s. gel** gel m de douche; **s. head** pomme f de douche

2 vt **to s. sb with** (gifts, abuse) couvrir qn de • **showery** adj pluvieux, -ieuse

showing [ˈʃəʊɪŋ] n (film show) séance f; (of team, player) performance f

shown [ʃəʊn] pp of **show**

showy [ˈʃəʊɪ] (**-ier, -iest**) adj voyant

shrank [ʃræŋk] pt of **shrink**

shrapnel [ˈʃræpnəl] n éclats mpl d'obus

shred [ʃred] **1** n lambeau m; **to tear sth to shreds** mettre qch en lambeaux; Fig **not a s. of truth** pas une once de vérité; Fig **not a s. of evidence** pas la moindre preuve

2 (pt & pp **-dd-**) vt mettre en lambeaux; (documents) déchiqueter; (food) couper grossièrement • **shredder** n (for paper) déchiqueteuse f

shrew [ʃruː] n Pej (woman) mégère f

shrewd [ʃruːd] (**-er, -est**) adj (person, plan) astucieux, -ieuse • **shrewdly** adv astucieusement • **shrewdness** n astuce f

shriek [ʃriːk] **1** n cri m strident

2 vi pousser un cri strident; **to s. with pain/laughter** hurler de douleur/de rire

shrift [ʃrɪft] n **to get short s.** être traité sans ménagement

shrill [ʃrɪl] (**-er, -est**) adj aigu (f aiguë)

shrimp [ʃrɪmp] n crevette f; Pej (small person) nabot, -ote mf

shrine [ʃraɪn] n (place of worship) lieu m saint; (tomb) tombeau m

shrink [ʃrɪŋk] **1** n Am Fam (psychiatrist) psy mf

2 (pt **shrank** or Am **shrunk,** pp **shrunk** or **shrunken**) vt (of clothes) faire rétrécir

3 vi rétrécir; **to s. from doing sth** répugner à faire qch; **to s. from an obligation** se dérober devant une obligation • **shrinkage** [-ɪdʒ] n (of material) rétrécissement m; (in sales, profits) diminution f • **'shrink-'wrapped** adj emballé sous film plastique

shrivel [ˈʃrɪvəl] (Br **-ll-**, Am **-l-**) **1** vt **to s. (up)** dessécher

2 vi **to s. (up)** se dessécher

shroud [ʃraʊd] **1** n linceul m; Fig **a s. of mystery** un voile de mystère

2 vt **to be shrouded in sth** être enveloppé de qch

Shrove Tuesday [Br ʃrəʊvˈtjuːzdɪ] n Mardi m gras

shrub [ʃrʌb] n arbuste m • **shrubbery** (pl **-ies**) n massif m d'arbustes

shrug [ʃrʌg] **1** n haussement m d'épaules

2 (pt & pp **-gg-**) vt **to s. one's shoulders** hausser les épaules; **to s. sth off** dédaigner qch

shrunk(en) [ˈʃrʌŋk(ən)] pp of **shrink**

shudder [ˈʃʌdə(r)] **1** n frémissement m; (of machine) vibration f

2 vi (of person) frémir (**with** de); (of machine) vibrer; **I s. to think of it** j'ai des frissons quand j'y pense

shuffle [ˈʃʌfəl] **1** vt (cards) battre

2 vti **to s. (one's feet)** traîner les pieds

shun [ʃʌn] (pt & pp **-nn-**) vt fuir, éviter

shunt [ʃʌnt] vt (train, conversation) aiguiller (**on to** sur); Fam **we were shunted (to and fro)** on nous a baladés

shush [ʃʊʃ] exclam chut!

shut [ʃʌt] **1** (pt & pp **shut,** pp **shutting**) vt fermer; **to s. one's finger in a door** se prendre le doigt dans une porte

2 vi (of door) se fermer; (of shop, museum) fermer; **the door doesn't s.** la porte ne ferme pas • **shutdown** n (of factory) fermeture f

▸ **shut away** vt sep (lock away) enfermer ▸ **shut down 1** vt sep fermer (définitivement) **2** vi fermer (définitivement) ▸ **shut in** vt sep (lock in) enfermer ▸ **shut off** vt sep (gas, electricity) couper; (engine) arrêter; (road) fermer; (isolate) isoler ▸ **shut out** vt sep (keep outside) empêcher d'entrer; (exclude) exclure (**of** or **from** de); (view) boucher; **to s. sb out** enfermer qn dehors • **shut up 1** vt sep (close) fermer; (confine) enfermer; Fam (silence) faire taire **2** vi Fam (be quiet) se taire

shutter [ˈʃʌtə(r)] n (on window) volet m; (of shop) store m; (of camera) obturateur m

shuttle [ˈʃʌtəl] **1** *n (bus, train, plane)* navette *f*; **s. service** navette
2 *vt* transporter
3 *vi* faire la navette
shuttlecock [ˈʃʌtəlkɒk] *n* volant *m*
shy [ʃaɪ] **1** (**-er, -est**) *adj* timide; **to be s. of doing sth** éviter de faire qch à tout prix
2 *vi* **to s. away from sb/from doing sth** éviter qch/de faire qch • **shyness** *n* timidité *f*
Siamese [saɪəˈmiːz] *adj* **S. cat** chat *m* siamois; **S. twins** *(boys)* frères *mpl* siamois; *(girls)* sœurs *fpl* siamoises
sibling [ˈsɪblɪŋ] *n (brother)* frère *m*; *(sister)* sœur *f*
Sicily [ˈsɪsɪlɪ] *n* la Sicile • **Si'cilian 1** *adj* sicilien, -ienne **2** *n* Sicilien, -ienne *mf*
sick [sɪk] **1** (**-er, -est**) *adj (ill)* malade; *(humour)* de mauvais goût; **to be s.** *(be ill)* être malade; *(vomit)* vomir; **to feel s.** avoir mal au cœur; **to be off** *or* **away s., to be on s. leave** être en congé de maladie; **to be s. of sb/sth** en avoir assez de qn/qch; **to be s. and tired of sb/sth** en avoir ras le bol de qn/qch; **to have a s. mind** avoir l'esprit dérangé; *Fig* **he makes me s.** il m'écœure
2 *n Br Fam (vomit)* vomi *m*
3 *npl* **the s.** *(sick people)* les malades *mpl*
• **sickbay** *n* infirmerie *f* • **sickbed** *n* lit *m* de malade
sicken [ˈsɪkən] **1** *vt* écœurer
2 *vi Br* **to be sickening for something** couver quelque chose • **sickening** *adj* écœurant
sickly [ˈsɪklɪ] (**-ier, -iest**) *adj* maladif, -ive; *(pale, faint)* pâle; *(taste)* écœurant
sickness [ˈsɪknɪs] *n (illness)* maladie *f*; *(vomiting)* vomissements *mpl*; *Br* **s. benefit** indemnité *f* journalière
side [saɪd] **1** *n* côté *m*; *(of hill, animal)* flanc *m*; *(of road, river)* bord *m*; *(of beef)* quartier *m*; *(of question, character)* aspect *m*; *(team)* équipe *f*; **the right s.** *(of fabric)* l'endroit *m*; **the wrong s.** *(of fabric)* l'envers *m*; **at** *or* **by the s. of** *(nearby)* à côté de; **at** *or* **by my s.** à côté de moi, à mes côtés; **s. by s.** l'un à côté de l'autre; **to move to one s.** s'écarter; **on this s.** de ce côté; **on the other s.** de l'autre côté; *Fam* **it's a bit on the big s.** c'est un peu grand; **to take sides with sb** se ranger du côté de qn; **she's on our s.** elle est de notre côté; **to change sides** changer de camp; **to do sth on the s.** *(as extra job)* faire qch pour arrondir ses fins de mois
2 *adj (lateral)* latéral; *(view, glance)* de côté; *(street)* transversal; *(effect, issue)* secondaire

3 *vi* **to s. with sb** se ranger du côté de qn
• **sideboard** *n* buffet *m* • **sideboards** *npl Br (hair)* pattes *fpl* • **sideburns** *npl (hair)* pattes *fpl* • **sidecar** *n* side-car *m* • **-sided** *suff* **ten-sided** à dix côtés • **sidekick** *n Fam* acolyte *m* • **sidelight** *n Br (on vehicle)* feu *m* de position • **sideline** *n (activity)* activité *f* secondaire; *(around playing field)* ligne *f* de touche • **side-saddle** *adv* **to ride s.** monter en amazone • **sidestep** *(pt & pp* **-pp-)** *vt* éviter • **sidetrack** *vt* distraire; **to get sidetracked** s'écarter du sujet • **sidewalk** *n Am* trottoir *m* • **sideways 1** *adv (look, walk)* de côté **2** *adj* **a s. look/move** un regard/mouvement de côté
siding [ˈsaɪdɪŋ] *n Rail* voie *f* de garage
sidle [ˈsaɪdəl] *vi* **to s. up to sb** se glisser vers sb
siege [siːdʒ] *n (by soldiers, police)* siège *m*; **to lay s. to a town** assiéger une ville; **under s.** assiégé
siesta [sɪˈestə] *n* sieste *f*; **to take** *or* **have a s.** faire la sieste
sieve [sɪv] **1** *n* tamis *m*; *(for liquids)* passoire *f*, *(for gravel, ore)* crible *m*
2 *vt* tamiser • **sift 1** *vt (flour)* tamiser; *(stones)* cribler; *Fig* **to s. out the truth** dégager la vérité **2** *vi* **to s. through** *(papers)* examiner (à la loupe)
sigh [saɪ] **1** *n* soupir *m*
2 *vi* soupirer; **to s. with relief** pousser un soupir de soulagement
3 *vt* **'yes', she sighed** 'oui', soupira-t-elle
sight [saɪt] **1** *n (faculty)* vue *f*; *(thing seen)* spectacle *m*; *(on gun)* viseur *m*; **to lose s. of sb/sth** perdre qn/qch de vue; **to catch s. of sb/sth** apercevoir qn/qch; **to come into s.** apparaître; **at first s.** à première vue; **by s.** de vue; **on** *or* **at s.** à vue; **in s.** *(target, end, date)* en vue; **out of s.** *(hidden)* caché; *(no longer visible)* disparu; **to disappear out of s.** disparaître; **keep out of s.!** ne te montre pas!; **he hates the s. of me** il ne peut pas me voir; **it's a lovely s.** c'est beau à voir; **the (tourist) sights** les attractions *fpl* touristiques; **to set one's sights on** *(job)* viser; *Fam* **a s. longer** bien plus long
2 *vt (land)* apercevoir • **sighted** *adj* voyant • **sighting** *n* **to make a s. of sb** apercevoir qn
sightly [ˈsaɪtlɪ] *adj* **not very s.** pas très beau *(f* belle*)* à voir
sightseer [ˈsaɪtsiːə(r)] *n* touriste *mf* • **sightseeing** *n* **to go s., to do some s.** faire du tourisme
sign [saɪn] **1** *n* signe *m*; *(notice)* panneau *m*; *(over shop, inn)* enseigne *f*; **no s. of**

aucune trace de; **s. language** langage *m* des sourds-muets

2 *vt (put signature to)* signer; *(in sign language)* dire en langage des sourds-muets; **to s. sth away** *(rights)* renoncer à qch; **to s. on** *or* **up** *(worker, soldier)* engager

3 *vi* signer; **to s. for** *(letter)* signer le reçu de; **to s. in** *(in hotel)* signer le registre; **to s. off** *(say goodbye)* dire au revoir; *Br* **to s. on** *(on the dole)* s'inscrire au chômage; **to s. on** *or* **up** *(of soldier, worker)* s'engager; *(for course)* s'inscrire

signal ['sɪɡnəl] **1** *n* signal *m*; *Rail Br* **s. box**, *Am* **s. tower** poste *m* d'aiguillage

2 *(Br* **-ll-**, *Am* **-l-)** *vt (be a sign of)* indiquer; *(make gesture to)* faire signe à

3 *vi (make gesture)* faire signe (**to** à); *(of driver)* mettre son clignotant; **to s. (to) sb to do sth** faire signe à qn de faire qch • **signalman** *(pl* **-men**) *n Rail* aiguilleur *m*

signature ['sɪɡnətʃə(r)] *n* signature *f*; **s. tune** indicatif *m* • **signatory** [-tərɪ] *(pl* **-ies**) *n* signataire *mf*

signet ring ['sɪɡnɪtrɪŋ] *n* chevalière *f*

significant [sɪɡ'nɪfɪkənt] *adj (important, large)* important; *(meaningful)* significatif, -ive • **significance** *n (meaning)* signification *f*; *(importance)* importance *f* • **significantly** *adv (appreciably)* sensiblement; **s., he…** fait significatif, il…

signify ['sɪɡnɪfaɪ] *(pt & pp* **-ied**) *vt (mean)* signifier (**that** que); *(make known)* signifier (**to** à)

signpost ['saɪnpəʊst] **1** *n* poteau *m* indicateur

2 *vt* signaliser

Sikh [siːk] *adj & n* sikh *(mf)*

silence ['saɪləns] **1** *n* silence *m*; **in s.** en silence

2 *vt* faire taire • **silencer** *n (on car, gun)* silencieux *m*

silent ['saɪlənt] *adj* silencieux, -ieuse; *(film, anger)* muet *(f* muette); **to keep** *or* **be s.** garder le silence (**about** sur) • **silently** *adv* silencieusement

silhouette [sɪluːˈet] *n* silhouette *f* • **silhouetted** *adj* **to be s. against** se profiler contre

silicon ['sɪlɪkən] *n* silicium *m*; **s. chip** puce *f* électronique

silicone ['sɪlɪkəʊn] *n* silicone *f*

silk [sɪlk] *n* soie *f*; **s. dress** robe *f* de *ou* en soie • **silky** *(-ier, -iest)* *adj* soyeux, -euse

sill [sɪl] *n (of window)* rebord *m*

silly ['sɪlɪ] **1** *(-ier, -iest)* *adj* bête, idiot; **to do something s.** faire une bêtise; **to look**

s. avoir l'air ridicule; **to laugh oneself s.** mourir de rire

2 *adv (act, behave)* bêtement • **silliness** *n* bêtise *f*

silo ['saɪləʊ] *(pl* **-os**) *n* silo *m*

silt [sɪlt] *n* vase *f*

silver ['sɪlvə(r)] **1** *n* argent *m*; *(plates)* argenterie *f*; *Br* **£5 in s.** 5 livres en pièces d'argent

2 *adj (spoon)* en argent, d'argent; *(hair, colour)* argenté; **s. jubilee** vingt-cinquième anniversaire *m*; *Br* **s. paper** papier *m* d'argent; **s. plate** *(articles)* argenterie *f* • **'silver-'plated** *adj* plaqué argent • **silversmith** *n* orfèvre *m* • **silverware** *n* argenterie *f* • **silvery** *adj (colour)* argenté

similar ['sɪmɪlə(r)] *adj* semblable (**to** à) • **similarity** [-'lærɪtɪ] *(pl* **-ies**) *n* ressemblance *f* (**between** entre; **to** avec) • **similarly** *adv* de la même façon; *(likewise)* de même

simile ['sɪmɪlɪ] *n* comparaison *f*

simmer ['sɪmə(r)] **1** *vt (vegetables)* mijoter; *(water)* laisser frémir

2 *vi (of vegetables)* mijoter; *(of water)* frémir; *Fig (of revolt, hatred)* couver; **to s. with rage** bouillir de rage; *Fam* **to s. down** se calmer

simper ['sɪmpə(r)] *vi* minauder

simple ['sɪmpəl] *(-er, -est)* *adj (easy)* simple; *(unintelligent)* simplet, -ette • **'simple-'minded** *adj* simple d'esprit • **'simple-'mindedness** *n* simplicité *f* d'esprit • **simpleton** *n* simple *mf* d'esprit • **sim'plicity** *n* simplicité *f*

simplify ['sɪmplɪfaɪ] *(pt & pp* **-ied**) *vt* simplifier • **simplification** [-fɪˈkeɪʃən] *n* simplification *f*

simplistic [sɪmˈplɪstɪk] *adj* simpliste

simply ['sɪmplɪ] *adv (plainly, merely)* simplement; *(absolutely)* absolument

simulate ['sɪmjʊleɪt] *vt* simuler

simultaneous [*Br* sɪməlˈteɪnɪəs, *Am* saɪməl-'teɪnɪəs] *adj* simultané • **simultaneously** *adv* simultanément

sin [sɪn] **1** *n* péché *m*

2 *(pt & pp* **-nn-**) *vi* pécher

since [sɪns] **1** *prep (in time)* depuis; **s. 1999/my departure** depuis 1999/mon départ; **s. then** depuis

2 *conj (in time)* depuis que; *(because)* puisque; **s. she's been here** depuis qu'elle est ici; **it's a year s. I saw him** ça fait un an que je ne l'ai pas vu

3 *adv (ever)* **s.** depuis

sincere [sɪnˈsɪə(r)] *adj* sincère • **sincerely** *adv* sincèrement; *Br* **yours s.**, *Am* **s.** *(in* *letter)* veuillez agréer, Madame/Monsieur, l'expression de mes salutations distinguées • **sincerity** [-'serɪtɪ] *n* sincérité *f*

sinew ['sɪnjuː] *n Anat* tendon *m*

sinful ['sɪnfəl] *adj (act)* coupable; *(waste)* scandaleux, -euse; **he's s.** c'est un pécheur; **that's s.** c'est un péché

sing [sɪŋ] *(pt* **sang,** *pp* **sung)** *vti* chanter; **to s. up** chanter plus fort • **singer** *n* chanteur, -euse *mf* • **singing 1** *(of bird, musical technique)* chant *m*; *(way of singing)* façon *f* de chanter **2** *adj* **s. lesson/teacher** leçon *f*/professeur *m* de chant

Singapore [sɪŋɡə'pɔː(r)] *n* Singapour *m* ou *f*

singe [sɪndʒ] *vt (cloth)* roussir; *(hair)* brûler

single ['sɪŋɡəl] **1** *adj (only one)* seul; *(room, bed)* pour une personne; *(unmarried)* célibataire; **not a s.** book pas un seul livre; **every s. day** tous les jours sans exception; *Br* **s. ticket** aller *m* simple; **s. parent** père *m*/mère *f* célibataire; **s. parent family** famille *f* monoparentale; *Pol* **s. party** parti *m* unique; **s. European market** marché *m* unique européen

2 *n Br (ticket)* aller *m* simple; *(record)* single *m*; *Tennis* **singles** simples *mpl*; **singles bar** bar *m* pour célibataires

3 *vt* **to s. sb out** sélectionner qn • **'single-'breasted** [-'brestɪd] *adj (jacket)* droit • **single-'decker** *n* = autobus sans impériale • **'single-'handedly** *adv* tout seul (*f* toute seule) • **'single-'minded** *adj (person)* résolu; *(determination)* farouche • **'single-'mindedly** *adv* résolument • **single-sex 'school** *n Br* école *f* non mixte

singlet ['sɪŋɡlɪt] *n Br* maillot *m* de corps

singly ['sɪŋɡlɪ] *adv (one by one)* un à un

singsong ['sɪŋsɒŋ] *n* **to get together for a s.** se réunir pour chanter

singular ['sɪŋɡjʊlə(r)] **1** *adj Grammar* singulier, -ière; *(remarkable)* remarquable

2 *n* singulier *m*; **in the s.** au singulier

sinister ['sɪnɪstə(r)] *adj* sinistre

sink¹ [sɪŋk] *n (in kitchen)* évier *m*; *(in bathroom)* lavabo *m*

sink² [sɪŋk] *(pt* **sank,** *pp* **sunk) 1** *vt (ship)* couler; *(well)* creuser; **to s. a knife into sth** enfoncer un couteau dans qch; **to s. money into a company** investir de l'argent dans une société; **a sinking feeling** un serrement de cœur

2 *vi (of ship, person)* couler; *(of water level, sun, price)* baisser; *(collapse)* s'affaisser; **my heart sank** j'ai eu un pince-

ment de cœur; **to s. (down) into** *(mud)* s'enfoncer dans; *(armchair)* s'affaler dans; **to s. in** *(of ink, water)* pénétrer; *Fam (of fact, idea)* être assimilé; *Fam* **it hasn't sunk in yet** je n'ai/il n'a/etc pas encore digéré la nouvelle

sinner ['sɪnə(r)] *n* pécheur *m*, pécheresse *f*

sinuous ['sɪnjʊəs] *adj* sinueux, -ueuse

sinus [saɪnəs] *n Anat* sinus *m* • **sinusitis** [-'saɪtəs] *n Med* sinusite *f*; **to have s.** avoir une sinusite

sip [sɪp] **1** *n* petite gorgée *f*

2 *(pt & pp* **-pp-)** *vt* siroter

siphon ['saɪfən] **1** *n* siphon *m*

2 *vt* **to s. sth off** *(liquid)* siphonner qch; *(money)* détourner qch

sir [sɜː(r)] *n* monsieur *m*; **S.Walter Raleigh** *(title)* sir Walter Raleigh

siren ['saɪərən] *n* sirène *f*

sirloin ['sɜːlɔɪn] *n (beef)* aloyau *m*

sissy ['sɪsɪ] *n Fam (boy, man)* femmelette *f*

sister ['sɪstə(r)] *n* sœur *f*; *(nurse)* infirmière-chef *f* • **sister-in-law** *(pl* **sisters-in-law)** *n* belle-sœur *f* • **sisterly** *adj* fraternel, -elle

sit [sɪt] *(pt & pp* **sat,** *pres p* **sitting) 1** *vt (child on chair)* asseoir; *Br (exam)* se présenter à

2 *vi (of person)* s'asseoir; *(for artist)* poser (**for** pour); *(of assembly)* siéger; **to s. at home** rester chez soi; **to be sitting** *(of person, cat)* être assis; **to be sitting on its perch** *(of bird)* être sur son perchoir; **she was sitting reading, she sat reading** elle était assise à lire

▸ **sit around** *vi* rester assis à ne rien faire

▸ **sit back** *vi (in chair)* se caler; *(rest)* se détendre; *(do nothing)* ne rien faire ▸ **sit down 1** *vt* **to s. sb down** asseoir qn **2** *vi* s'asseoir; **to be sitting down** être assis

▸ **sit for** *vt insep Br (exam)* se présenter à

▸ **sit in on** *vt insep (lecture)* assister à ▸ **sit on** *vt insep (jury)* être membre de; *Fam (fact)* garder pour soi ▸ **sit out** *vt sep (event, dance)* ne pas prendre part à; *(film)* rester jusqu'au bout de ▸ **sit through** *vt insep (film)* rester jusqu'au bout de ▸ **sit up** *vi* **to s. up (straight)** s'asseoir (bien droit); *(straighten one's back)* se redresser; **to s. up waiting for sb** veiller jusqu'au retour de qn

sitcom ['sɪtkɒm] *n* sitcom *m*

sit-down ['sɪtdaʊn] *adj* **s. meal** repas *m* servi à table; **s. strike** grève *f* sur le tas

site [saɪt] **1** *n (position)* emplacement *m*;

(*archaeological*) site *m*; **(building) s.** chantier *m* (de construction)
  2 *vt* (*building*) placer
sit-in ['sɪtɪn] *n* (*protest*) sit-in *m inv*
sitter ['sɪtə(r)] *n* (*for child*) baby-sitter *mf*
sitting ['sɪtɪŋ] **1** *n* séance *f*; (*in restaurant*) service *m*
  2 *adj* (*committee*) en séance; *Fam* **s. duck** cible *f* facile; **s. tenant** locataire *mf* dans les lieux ● **sitting room** *n* salon *m*
situate ['sɪtʃʊeɪt] *vt* situer; **to be situated** être situé ● **situ'ation** *n* situation *f*
six [sɪks] *adj & n* six (*m*) ● **sixth** *adj & n* sixième (*mf*); *Br Sch* (*lower*) **s. form** ≃ classe *f* de première; *Br Sch* (*upper*) **s. form** ≃ classe *f* terminale; **a s.** (*fraction*) un sixième
sixteen [sɪk'stiːn] *adj & n* seize (*m*) ● **sixteenth** *adj & n* seizième (*mf*)
sixty ['sɪkstɪ] *adj & n* soixante (*m*) ● **sixtieth** *adj & n* soixantième (*mf*)
size [saɪz] **1** *n* (*of person, animal, clothes*) taille *f*; (*of shoes, gloves*) pointure *f*; (*of shirt*) encolure *f*; (*measurements*) dimensions *fpl*; (*of egg, fruit, packet*) grosseur *f*; (*of book*) grandeur *f*; (*of town, damage, problem*) étendue *f*; (*of sum*) montant *m*; **hip/chest s.** tour *m* de hanches/de poitrine; **it's the s. of** c'est grand comme
  2 *vt* **to s. up** (*person*) jauger; (*situation*) évaluer
sizeable ['saɪzəbəl] *adj* non négligeable
sizzle ['sɪzəl] *vi* grésiller ● **sizzling** *adj* **s. (hot)** brûlant
skate¹ [skeɪt] **1** *n* patin *m*; *Fam* **to get one's skates on** se dépêcher
  2 *vi* (*on ice-skates*) faire du patin à glace; (*on roller skates*) faire du roller ● **skateboard** *n* planche *f* à roulettes ● **skater** *n* patineur, -euse *mf* ● **skating** *n* patinage *m*; **to go s.** faire du patinage; **s. rink** (*for ice-skating*) patinoire *f*; (*for roller-skating*) piste *f*
skate² [skeɪt] *n* (*fish*) raie *f*
skeleton ['skelɪtən] *n* squelette *m*; *Fig* **to have a s. in the closet** avoir un secret honteux; **s. key** passe-partout *m inv*; **s. staff** personnel *m* minimum
skeptic ['skeptɪk] *adj & n Am* sceptique (*mf*)
skeptical ['skeptɪkəl] *adj Am* sceptique
skepticism ['skeptɪsɪzəm] *n Am* scepticisme *m*
sketch [sketʃ] **1** *n* (*drawing*) croquis *m*; (*comic play*) sketch *m*; **a rough s. of the situation** un résumé rapide de la situation
  2 *vt* **to s. (out)** (*idea, view*) exposer brièvement; *Fig* **to s. in** esquisser

3 *vi* faire un/des croquis ● **sketchbook** *n* carnet *m* de croquis ● **sketchy** (-ier, -iest) *adj* vague
skew [skjuː] *n* **on the s.** de travers
skewer ['skjuːə(r)] *n* (*for meat*) broche *f*; (*for kebab*) brochette *f*
ski [skiː] **1** (*pl* **skis**) *n* ski *m*; **s. boot** chaussure *f* de ski; **s. jump** (*slope*) tremplin *m*; (*jump*) saut *m* à skis; **s. lift** remonte-pente *m*; **s. mask** cagoule *f*, passe-montagne *m*; **s. pants** fuseau *m*; **s. resort** station *f* de ski; **s. run** *or* **slope** piste *f* de ski; **s. tow** téléski *m*; **s. wax** fart *m*
  2 (*pt* **skied** [skiːd], *pres p* **skiing**) *vi* skier, faire du ski ● **skier** *n* skieur, -ieuse *mf* ● **skiing 1** *n* (*sport*) ski *m* **2** *adj* (*school, clothes*) de ski; *Br* **s. holiday,** *Am* **s. vacation** vacances *fpl* de neige
skid [skɪd] **1** *n* dérapage *m*
  2 *adj Am Fam* **to be on s. row** être à la rue
  3 (*pt & pp* -**dd**-) *vi* déraper; **to s. into sth** déraper et heurter qch
skill [skɪl] *n* (*ability*) qualités *fpl*; (*technique*) compétence *f* ● **skilful** (*Am* **skillful**) *adj* habile (**at doing** à faire; **at sth** en qch) ● **skilled** *adj* habile (**at doing** à faire; **at sth** en qch); (*worker*) qualifié; (*work*) de spécialiste
skillet ['skɪlɪt] *n Am* poêle *f* (à frire)
skim [skɪm] (*pt & pp* -**mm**-) **1** *vt* (*milk*) écrémer; (*soup*) écumer; **to s. (over) sth** (*surface*) effleurer qch; **skimmed milk** lait *m* écrémé
  2 *vt insep* **to s. through** (*book*) parcourir
skimp [skɪmp] *vi* (*on food, fabric*) lésiner (**on** sur) ● **skimpy** (-ier, -iest) *adj* (*clothes*) étriqué; (*meal*) maigre
skin [skɪn] **1** *n* peau *f*; *Fig* **he has thick s.** c'est un dur; **s. cancer** cancer *m* de la peau; **s. diving** plongée *f* sous-marine; **s. test** cuti(-réaction) *f*
  2 (*pt & pp* -**nn**-) *vt* (*fruit*) peler; (*animal*) écorcher ● **'skin-'deep** *adj* superficiel, -ielle ● **'skin-'tight** *adj* moulant
skinflint ['skɪnflɪnt] *n* avare *mf*
skinhead ['skɪnhed] *n Br* skinhead *mf*
skinny ['skɪnɪ] (-ier, -iest) *adj* maigre
skint [skɪnt] *adj Br Fam* (*penniless*) fauché
skip¹ [skɪp] **1** *n* petit saut *m*
  2 (*pt & pp* -**pp**-) *vt* (*miss, omit*) sauter; **to s. classes** sécher les cours
  3 *vi* (*hop about*) sautiller; *Br* (*with rope*) sauter à la corde; *Fam* **to s. off** filer; *Br* **skipping rope** corde *f* à sauter
skip² [skɪp] *n Br* (*for rubbish*) benne *f*
skipper ['skɪpə(r)] *n* (*of ship, team*) capitaine *m*

skirmish ['skɜːmɪʃ] *n* accrochage *m*
skirt [skɜːt] **1** *n* jupe *f*
 2 *vt* **to s. round sth** *(bypass, go round)* contourner qch • **skirting board** *n Br* plinthe *f*
skittish ['skɪtɪʃ] *adj* espiègle
skittle ['skɪtəl] *n Br* quille *f*; **skittles** *(game)* jeu *m* de quilles; **to play skittles** jouer aux quilles
skive [skaɪv] *vi Br Fam* tirer au flanc; **to s. off** *(slip away)* se défiler • **skiver** *n Br Fam* tire-au-flanc *m inv*
skivvy ['skɪvɪ] *(pl* **-ies)** *n Br Fam Pej* bonne *f* à tout faire
skulk [skʌlk] *vi* rôder
skull [skʌl] *n* crâne *m* • **skullcap** *n* calotte *f*
skunk [skʌŋk] *n (animal)* moufette *f*; *Pej (person)* mufle *m*
sky [skaɪ] *n* ciel *m* • **'sky-'blue** *adj* bleu ciel *inv* • **skydiving** *n* parachutisme *m* en chute libre • **'sky-'high** *adj (prices)* exorbitant • **skylark** *n* alouette *f* • **skylight** *n* lucarne *f* • **skyline** *n (horizon)* horizon *m* • **skyrocket** *vi Fam (of prices)* monter en flèche • **skyscraper** *n* gratte-ciel *m inv*
slab [slæb] *n (of concrete)* bloc *m*; *(thin, flat)* plaque *f*; *(of chocolate)* tablette *f*; *(of meat)* tranche *f* épaisse; *(paving stone)* dalle *f*
slack [slæk] **1** **(-er, -est)** *adj (not tight)* mou *(f* molle); *(careless)* négligent; **to be s.** *(of rope)* avoir du mou; **trade is s.** le commerce va mal; **in s. periods** en périodes creuses
 2 *vi* **to s. off** *(in effort)* se relâcher • **slackness** *n (negligence)* négligence *f*; *(laziness)* fainéantise *f*; *(of rope)* mou *m*; *(of trade)* stagnation *f*
slacken ['slækən] **1** *vt* **to s. (off)** *(rope)* relâcher; *(pace, effort)* ralentir
 2 *vi* **to s. (off)** *(in effort)* se relâcher; *(of production, demand, speed, enthusiasm)* diminuer
slacker ['slækə(r)] *n Fam (person)* flemmard, -arde *mf*
slacks [slæks] *npl* pantalon *m*
slag [slæg] *Br very Fam* **1** *n (woman)* salope *f*
 2 *vt* **to s. sb off** *(criticize)* débiner qn
slag heap ['slæghiːp] *n (near mine)* terril *m*; *(near steelworks)* crassier *m*
slain [sleɪn] *pp of* **slay**
slake [sleɪk] *vt Literary (thirst)* étancher
slalom ['slɑːləm] *n (ski race)* slalom *m*
slam [slæm] **1** *n* claquement *m*
 2 *(pt & pp* **-mm-)** *vt (door, lid)* claquer; *(hit)* frapper violemment; *Fam (criticize)* éreinter; **to s. the door in sb's face** cla-

quer la porte au nez de qn; **to s. sth (down)** *(put down)* poser qch violemment
 3 *vi (of door)* claquer; **to s. on the brakes** écraser la pédale de frein
slander ['slɑːndə(r)] **1** *n* calomnie *f*
 2 *vt* calomnier
slang [slæŋ] **1** *n* argot *m*
 2 *adj (word)* d'argot, argotique; **s. expression** expression *f* argotique • **slanging match** *n Br Fam* échange *m* d'insultes
slant [slɑːnt] **1** *n* pente *f*; *Fig (point of view)* perspective *f*; *Fig (bias)* parti *m* pris; **on a s.** penché; *(roof)* en pente
 2 *vt (writing)* incliner; *Fig (news)* présenter de façon partiale
 3 *vi (of roof, handwriting)* être incliné • **slanted, slanting** *adj* penché; *(roof)* en pente
slap [slæp] **1** *n (with hand)* claque *f*; **a s. in the face** une gifle
 2 *(pt & pp* **-pp-)** *vt (person)* donner une claque à; **to s. sb's face** gifler qn; **to s. sb's bottom** donner une fessée à qn; **to s. some paint on sth** passer un coup de peinture sur qch; *Fig* **to s. sb down** remettre qn à sa place
 3 *adv Fam* **s. in the middle** en plein milieu
slapdash ['slæpdæʃ] **1** *adj (person)* négligent; *(task)* fait à la va-vite
 2 *adv (carelessly)* à la va-vite
slapstick ['slæpstɪk] *adj & n* **s. (comedy)** grosse farce *f*
slap-up ['slæpʌp] *adj Br Fam* **s. meal** gueuleton *m*
slash [slæʃ] **1** *n* entaille *f*
 2 *vt (cut)* taillader; *(reduce)* réduire considérablement; **prices slashed** prix *mpl* sacrifiés
slat [slæt] *n* latte *f*
slate [sleɪt] **1** *n* ardoise *f*
 2 *vt Br Fam (book)* démolir
slaughter ['slɔːtə(r)] **1** *n (of people)* massacre *m*; *(of animal)* abattage *m*
 2 *vt (people)* massacrer; *(animal)* abattre; *Fam (defeat)* massacrer • **slaughterhouse** *n* abattoir *m*
Slav [slɑːv] **1** *adj* slave
 2 *n* Slave *mf* • **Slavonic** [slə'vɒnɪk] *adj (language)* slave
slave [sleɪv] **1** *n* esclave *mf*; *Hist* **the s. trade** la traite des Noirs; *Fig & Pej* **s. driver** négrier *m*
 2 *vi* **to s. (away)** trimer; **to s. away doing sth** s'escrimer à faire qch • **slavery** *n* esclavage *m* • **slavish** *adj* servile
slaver ['slævə(r)] *vi (dribble)* baver (**over** sur)

slay [sleɪ] (*pt* **slew,** *pp* **slain**) *vt Literary* tuer

sleazy ['sliːzɪ] (**-ier, -iest**) *adj Fam* sordide

sledge [sledʒ] (*Am* **sled** [sled]) *n Br* luge *f; (horse-drawn)* traîneau *m*

sledgehammer ['sledʒhæmə(r)] *n* masse *f*

sleek [sliːk] (**-er, -est**) *adj (smooth)* lisse et brillant; *Pej (manner)* mielleux, -euse

sleep [sliːp] **1** *n* sommeil *m*; **to have a s., to get some s.** dormir; **to go to s.** *(of person)* s'endormir; *Fam (of arm, foot, hand)* s'engourdir; **to put sb to s.** endormir qn; **to put an animal to s.** *(kill)* faire piquer un animal; *Fig* **to send sb to s.** *(bore)* endormir qn

2 (*pt & pp* **slept**) *vi* dormir; **to s. rough** dormir à la dure; *Euph* **to s. with sb** coucher avec qn; **s. tight** *or* **well!** dors bien!; *Fig* **I'll s. on it** la nuit portera conseil

3 *vt* **this flat sleeps six** on peut dormir à six dans cet appartement; **I haven't slept a wink all night** je n'ai pas fermé l'œil de la nuit; *Fam* **to s. it off, to s. off a hangover** cuver son vin • **sleeping** *adj (asleep)* endormi; **s. bag** sac *m* de couchage; **s. car** wagon-lit *m*; **s. pill** somnifère *m*; **s. quarters** chambres *fpl*

sleeper ['sliːpə(r)] *n* (**a**) **to be a light/ sound s.** avoir le sommeil léger/lourd (**b**) *Br Rail (on track)* traverse *f; (bed in train)* couchette *f; (train)* train-couchettes *m* • **sleepless** *adj (night)* d'insomnie; *(hours)* sans sommeil

sleepwalker ['sliːpwɔːkə(r)] *n* somnambule *mf* • **sleepwalking** *n* somnambulisme *m*

sleepy ['sliːpɪ] (**-ier, -iest**) *adj (town, voice)* endormi; **to be s.** *(of person)* avoir sommeil • **sleepiness** *n* torpeur *f*

sleet [sliːt] **1** *n* neige *f* fondue; *Am (sheet of ice)* verglas *m*

2 *vi* **it's sleeting** il tombe de la neige fondue

sleeve [sliːv] *n (of shirt, jacket)* manche *f; (of record)* pochette *f*; **long-/short-sleeved** à manches longues/courtes; *Fig* **he still has something up his s.** il n'a pas dit son dernier mot

sleigh [sleɪ] *n* traîneau *m*

sleight [slaɪt] *n* **s. of hand** tour *m* de passe-passe

slender ['slendə(r)] *adj (person)* svelte; *(neck, hand, waist)* fin; *Fig (small, feeble)* faible

slept [slept] *pt & pp of* **sleep**

sleuth [sluːθ] *n Hum (detective)* limier *m*

slew [sluː] **1** *n Am Fam* **a s. of** un tas de

2 *pt of* **slay**

slice [slaɪs] **1** *n* tranche *f; Fig (portion)* part *f*

2 *vt* **to s. sth (up)** couper qch en tranches; **to s. sth off** couper qch • **sliced 'bread** *n* pain *m* en tranches

slick [slɪk] **1** (**-er, -est**) *adj (campaign)* bien mené; *(reply, person)* habile; *(surface, tyre)* lisse

2 *n (on beach)* marée *f* noire

slide [slaɪd] **1** *n (in playground)* toboggan *m; (for hair)* barrette *f; Phot* diapositive *f; (of microscope)* lamelle *f; (in prices, popularity)* baisse *f*

2 (*pt & pp* **slid** [slɪd]) *vt* glisser (**into** dans); *(table, chair)* faire glisser; **s. the lid off** faites glisser le couvercle

3 *vi* glisser; **to s. into a room** se glisser dans une pièce • **sliding** *adj (door, panel)* coulissant; **s. roof** toit *m* ouvrant; **s. scale** échelle *f* mobile

slight [slaɪt] **1** (**-er, -est**) *adj (small, unimportant)* léger, -ère; *(chance)* faible; *(person)* menu; **the slightest thing** la moindre chose; **not in the slightest** pas le moins du monde

2 *n* affront *m* (**on** à)

3 *vt (offend)* offenser; *(ignore)* bouder • **slighting** *adj (remark)* désobligeant

slightly ['slaɪtlɪ] *adv* légèrement; **to know sb s.** connaître qn un peu; **s. built** fluet (*f* fluette)

slim [slɪm] **1** (**slimmer, slimmest**) *adj* mince

2 (*pt & pp* **-mm-**) *vi Br* suivre un régime • **slimmer** *n Br* personne *f* qui suit un régime amaigrissant • **slimming** *adj Br* **s. diet** régime *m* amaigrissant; **s. food** aliment *m* qui ne fait pas grossir • **slimness** *n* minceur *f*

slime [slaɪm] *n* vase *f; (of snail)* bave *f* • **slimy** (**-ier, -iest**) *adj (muddy)* boueux (*f* boueuse); *Fig (sticky, smarmy)* visqueux, -euse

sling [slɪŋ] **1** *n (weapon)* fronde *f; (for injured arm)* écharpe *f*; **in a s.** en écharpe

2 (*pt & pp* **slung**) *vt (throw)* lancer; **to s. sth over one's shoulder** mettre qch sur son épaule; *Fam* **to s. away** *or* **out** *(throw out)* balancer • **slingshot** *n Am* lance-pierres *m inv*

slip [slɪp] **1** *n (mistake)* erreur *f; (garment)* combinaison *f; (fall)* chute *f*; **a s. of paper** un bout de papier; *(printed)* un bordereau; **a s. of the tongue** un lapsus; **a s. of a girl** un petit bout de femme; **to give sb the s.** fausser compagnie à qn; *Br* **s. road** bretelle *f*

2 (*pt & pp* **-pp-**) *vt* (*slide*) glisser (**to** à; **into** dans); **it slipped her notice** ça lui a échappé; **it slipped my mind** ça m'est sorti de l'esprit; **to have a slipped disc** avoir une hernie discale
3 *vi* glisser; *Fam* (*of popularity, ratings*) baisser; **to let sth s.** (*chance, oath, secret*) laisser échapper qch

Note that the French noun **slip** *is a false friend and is never a translation for the English noun* **slip**. *It means* **underpants**.

▸ **slip away** *vi* (*escape*) s'éclipser ▸ **slip back** *vi* retourner furtivement ▸ **slip in** *vi* (*enter*) entrer furtivement ▸ **slip into** *vt insep* (*room*) se glisser dans; (*bathrobe*) passer; (*habit*) prendre ▸ **slip off** *vt sep* (*coat*) enlever ▸ **slip on** *vt sep* (*coat*) mettre ▸ **slip out** *vi* (*leave*) sortir furtivement; (*for a moment*) sortir (un instant); (*of secret*) s'éventer ▸ **slip past** *vt insep* (*guard*) passer sans être vu de ▸ **slip through 1** *vt insep* **to s. through the crowd** se faufiler parmi la foule **2** *vi* (*of error*) échapper à l'attention de ▸ **slip up** *vi Fam* se planter
slipcover ['slɪpkʌvə(r)] *n Am* housse *f*
slipper ['slɪpə(r)] *n* pantoufle *f*
slippery ['slɪpərɪ] *adj* glissant
slipshod ['slɪpʃɒd] *adj* (*negligent*) négligent; (*slovenly*) négligé
slip-up ['slɪpʌp] *n Fam* gaffe *f*
slipway ['slɪpweɪ] *n Naut* cale *f* de lancement
slit [slɪt] **1** *n* fente *f*
2 (*pt & pp* **slit**, *pres p* **slitting**) *vt* (*cut*) couper; (*tear*) déchirer; **to s. open** (*sack*) éventrer
slither ['slɪðə(r)] *vi* glisser; (*of snake*) se couler
sliver ['slɪvə(r)] *n* (*of wood*) éclat *m*; (*of cheese*) fine tranche *f*
slob [slɒb] *n Fam* (*lazy person*) gros fainéant *m*; (*dirty person*) porc *m*
slobber ['slɒbə(r)] **1** *n* bave *f*
2 *vi* (*of dog, baby*) baver
sloe [sləʊ] *n* (*fruit*) prunelle *f*
slog [slɒg] *Br Fam* **1** *n* **a (hard) s.** (*effort*) un gros effort; **it was a bit of a s.** ça a été dur
2 (*pt & pp* **-gg-**) *vt* (*ball, person*) donner un grand coup à
3 *vi* **to s. (away)** trimer
slogan ['sləʊgən] *n* slogan *m*
slop [slɒp] **1** (*pt & pp* **-pp-**) *vt* renverser
2 *vi* **to s. (over)** se renverser
slope [sləʊp] **1** *n* pente *f*; (*of mountain*) versant *m*; (*for skiing*) piste *f*; (*slant of handwriting, pipe*) inclinaison *f*

2 *vi* (*of ground, roof*) être en pente; (*of handwriting*) pencher; **to s. down** (*of path*) descendre en pente ▪ **sloping** *adj* (*roof*) en pente; (*handwriting*) penché
sloppy ['slɒpɪ] (**-ier, -iest**) *adj* (*work, appearance*) négligé; (*person*) négligent; (*sentimental*) sentimental
slosh [slɒʃ] *Fam* **1** *vt* (*pour, spill*) renverser, répandre
2 *vi* (*of liquid*) clapoter; (*spill*) se renverser; **to s. about** (*walk in water, mud*) patauger; (*splash in bath*) barboter ▪ **sloshed** *adj Br Fam* (*drunk*) bourré
slot [slɒt] **1** *n* (*slit*) fente *f*; (*in schedule, list*) créneau *m*; **s. machine** (*for vending*) distributeur *m* automatique; (*for gambling*) machine *f* à sous
2 (*pt & pp* **-tt-**) *vt* (*insert*) insérer (**into** dans)
3 *vi* s'insérer (**into** dans)
sloth [sləʊθ] *n Literary* paresse *f*
slouch [slaʊtʃ] **1** *n* **to have a s.** avoir le dos voûté; *Fam* **he's no s.** il n'est pas empoté
2 *vi* ne pas se tenir droit; (*have a stoop*) avoir le dos voûté; (*in chair*) être avachi; **he slouched out of the room** il est sorti de la pièce en traînant les pieds
Slovakia [sləʊ'vækɪə] *n* la Slovaquie
Slovenia [sləʊ'viːnɪə] *n* la Slovénie
slovenly ['slʌvənlɪ] *adj* négligé
slow [sləʊ] **1** (**-er, -est**) *adj* lent; **at (a) s. speed** à vitesse réduite; **in s. motion** au ralenti; **to be a s. walker** marcher lentement; **to be s.** (*of clock, watch*) retarder; **to be five minutes s.** retarder de cinq minutes; **to be s. to do sth** être lent à faire qch; **business is s.** les affaires tournent au ralenti
2 *adv* lentement
3 *vt* **to s. sth down** *or* **up** ralentir qch; (*delay*) retarder qch
4 *vi* **to s. down** *or* **up** ralentir ▪ **slowcoach** *n Br Fam* lambin, -ine *mf* ▪ **slow-down** *n* ralentissement *m*; *Am* **s. (strike)** grève *f* perlée ▪ **slowly** *adv* lentement; (*bit by bit*) peu à peu ▪ **'slow-'moving** *adj* (*vehicle*) lent ▪ **slowness** *n* lenteur *f* ▪ **slowpoke** *n Am Fam* lambin, -ine *mf*
sludge [slʌdʒ] *n* gadoue *f*
slue [sluː] *n Am Fam* = **slew**
slug [slʌg] **1** *n* **(a)** (*mollusc*) limace *f* **(b)** *Am Fam* (*bullet*) pruneau *m*
2 (*pt & pp* **-gg-**) *vt Am Fam* (*hit*) frapper
sluggish ['slʌgɪʃ] *adj* (*person*) amorphe; (*business*) au ralenti
sluice [sluːs] *n* **s. (gate)** vanne *f*
slum [slʌm] **1** *n* (*house*) taudis *m*; **the**

slums les quartiers *mpl* délabrés; **s. dwelling** taudis *m*

2 (*pt & pp* **-mm-**) *vt Fam* **to s. it** s'encanailler • **slummy** (**-ier, -iest**) *adj* sordide

slumber [ˈslʌmbə(r)] *n Literary* sommeil *m*

slump [slʌmp] **1** *n* baisse *f* soudaine (**in** de); (*in prices*) effondrement *m*; (*economic depression*) crise *f*

2 *vi* (*of person, prices*) s'effondrer

slung [slʌŋ] *pt & pp of* **sling**

slur [slɜː(r)] **1** *n* (*insult*) insulte *f*; **to cast a s. on sb's reputation** entacher la réputation de qn; **to speak with a s.** manger ses mots

2 (*pt & pp* **-rr-**) *vt* mal articuler; **to s. one's words** manger ses mots • **slurred** *adj* (*speech*) indistinct

slush [slʌʃ] *n* (*snow*) neige *f* fondue; (*mud*) gadoue *f*; *Fam Pol* **s. fund** caisse *f* noire • **slushy** (**-ier, -iest**) *adj* (*road*) couvert de neige fondue

slut [slʌt] *n Pej* (*immoral woman*) salope *f*; (*untidy woman*) souillon *f*

sly [slaɪ] **1** (**-er, -est**) *adj* (*deceitful*) sournois; (*cunning, crafty*) rusé

2 *n* **on the s.** en douce

smack [smæk] **1** *n* (*blow*) claque *f*; (*on bottom*) fessée *f*

2 *vt* (*person*) donner une claque à; **to s. sb's face** gifler qn; **to s. sb('s bottom)** donner une fessée à qn

3 *vi* **to s. of** (*be suggestive of*) avoir des relents de

4 *adv Fam* **s. in the middle** en plein milieu • **smacking** *n* fessée *f*

small [smɔːl] **1** (**-er, -est**) *adj* petit; **in the s. hours** au petit matin; **s. change** petite monnaie *f*; **s. talk** banalités *fpl*

2 *adv* (*cut, chop*) menu; (*write*) petit

3 *n* **the s. of the back** la chute des reins • ˈsmall-ˈminded *adj* à l'esprit étroit • ˈsmall-ˈmindedness *n* étroitesse *f* d'esprit • **smallness** *n* petitesse *f* • **small-scale** *adj* (*model*) réduit; (*research*) à petite échelle • **small-time** *adj Fam* (*crook, dealer*) petit

smallholding [ˈsmɔːlhəʊldɪŋ] *n Br* petite ferme *f*

smallpox [ˈsmɔːlpɒks] *n* variole *f*

smarmy [ˈsmɑːmɪ] (**-ier, -iest**) *adj Fam Pej* obséquieux, -ieuse

smart¹ [smɑːt] (**-er, -est**) *adj* (*in appearance*) élégant; (*clever*) intelligent; (*astute*) astucieux, -ieuse; (*quick*) rapide; *Fam* **s. aleck** je-sais-tout *mf inv*; **s. card** carte *f* à puce

smart² [smɑːt] *vi* (*sting*) brûler

smarten [ˈsmɑːtən] **1** *vt* **to s. sth up** égayer qch

2 *vti* **to s. (oneself) up** se faire beau (*f* belle)

smartly [ˈsmɑːtlɪ] *adv* (*dressed*) avec élégance; (*quickly*) en vitesse; (*cleverly*) avec intelligence; (*astutely*) astucieusement

smash [smæʃ] **1** *n* (*accident*) collision *f*; (*noise*) fracas *m*; (*blow*) coup *m*; *Tennis* smash *m*; *Fam* **s. hit** gros succès *m*

2 *vt* (*break*) briser; (*shatter*) fracasser; (*record*) pulvériser; (*enemy*) écraser; **to s. sth to pieces** fracasser qch; *Fam* **to s. sb's face (in)** casser la gueule à qn

3 *vi* **to s. into sth** s'écraser contre qch; **to s. into pieces** éclater en mille morceaux • **smash-and-ˈgrab raid** *n Br* pillage *m* de vitrines • **smash-up** *n* collision *f* ▸ **smash down, smash in** *vt sep* (*door*) enfoncer ▸ **smash into** *vt insep* (*of vehicle*) entrer dans ▸ **smash up** *vt sep* (*vehicle*) esquinter; (*room*) saccager

smashing [ˈsmæʃɪŋ] *adj* (*blow*) violent; *Br Fam* (*wonderful*) génial • **smasher** *n Br* **to be a (real) s.** *Fam* être génial

smattering [ˈsmætərɪŋ] *n* **a s. of French** quelques notions *fpl* de français

smear [smɪə(r)] **1** *n* (*mark*) trace *f*; (*stain*) tache *f*; *Med* **s. (test)** frottis *m* vaginal; **a s. on sb's reputation** une atteinte à la réputation de qn; **s. campaign** campagne *f* de diffamation; **to use s. tactics** avoir recours à la diffamation

2 *vt* (*coat*) enduire (**with** de); (*stain*) tacher (**with** de); (*smudge*) faire une trace sur; **to s. sb** calomnier qn

smell [smel] **1** *n* odeur *f*; (**sense of) s.** odorat *m*

2 (*pt & pp* **smelled** *or* **smelt**) *vt* sentir; (*of animal*) flairer

3 *vi* (*stink*) sentir mauvais; (*have a smell*) sentir; **to s. of smoke** sentir la fumée; **smelling salts** sels *mpl* • **smelly** (**-ier, -iest**) *adj* **to be s.** sentir mauvais

smelt¹ [smelt] *pt & pp of* **smell**

smelt² [smelt] *vt* (*ore*) fondre; **smelting works** fonderie *f*

smidgen [ˈsmɪdʒən] *n Fam* **a s.** (*a little*) un brin (**of** de)

smile [smaɪl] **1** *n* sourire *m*

2 *vi* sourire (**at sb** à qn; **at sth** de qch) • **smiling** *adj* souriant

smirk [smɜːk] *n* (*smug*) sourire *m* suffisant; (*scornful*) sourire goguenard

smith [smɪθ] *n* forgeron *m*

smithereens [smɪðəˈriːnz] *npl* **to smash sth to s.** briser qch en mille morceaux

smitten [ˈsmɪtən] *adj Literary* **to be s.**

with **terror** être terrorisé; **to be s. with remorse** être pris de remords

smock [smɒk] *n* blouse *f*

smog [smɒg] *n* smog *m*

smoke [sməʊk] **1** *n* fumée *f*; **to have a s.** fumer une cigarette; **s. detector** *or* **alarm** détecteur *m* de fumée; *Fig* **s. screen** rideau *m* de fumée

2 *vt (cigarette)* fumer; **to s. a room out** enfumer une pièce; **smoked salmon** saumon *m* fumé

3 *vi* fumer; **to s. like a chimney** *(of person)* fumer comme un pompier; **'no smoking'** 'défense de fumer'; **smoking compartment** *(on train)* compartiment *m* fumeurs • **smokeless** *adj* **s. fuel** combustible *m* non polluant • **smoker** *n* fumeur, -euse *mf*; *(train compartment)* compartiment *m* fumeurs • **smokestack** *n* cheminée *f* d'usine • **smoky** (**-ier, -iest**) *adj (room, air)* enfumé; *(ceiling, wall)* noirci par la fumée; **it's s. here** il y a de la fumée ici

smooth [smuːð] **1** (**-er, -est**) *adj (surface, skin)* lisse; *(cream, sauce)* onctueux, -ueuse; *(sea, flight)* calme; *Pej (person, manners)* doucereux, -euse; **the s. running of** *(machine, service, business)* la bonne marche de; **to be a s. talker** être beau parleur; **to be a s. operator** savoir y faire

2 *vt* **to s. sth down** *(hair, sheet, paper)* lisser qch; **to s. sth out** *(paper, sheet, dress)* lisser qch; *(crease)* faire disparaître qch; *Fig* **to s. difficulties out** *or* **over** aplanir des difficultés • **smoothly** *adv* sans problèmes • **smoothness** *n* aspect *m* lisse; *(of road)* surface *f* égale

smother ['smʌðə(r)] *vt (stifle)* étouffer; **to s. sth in sth** recouvrir qch de qch; *Fig* **to s. sb with kisses** couvrir qn de baisers

smoulder ['sməʊldə(r)] *(Am* **smolder**) *vi Fig (of fire, passion)* couver

smudge [smʌdʒ] **1** *n* tache *f*

2 *vt (paper)* faire des taches sur; *(ink)* étaler

smug [smʌg] (**smugger, smuggest**) *adj (smile)* béat; *(person)* content de soi

smuggle ['smʌgəl] *vt* passer en fraude; **smuggled goods** contrebande *f* • **smuggler** *n* contrebandier, -ière *mf*; *(of drugs)* trafiquant *m* • **smuggling** *n* contrebande *f*

smut [smʌt] *n inv (obscenity)* cochonneries *fpl* • **smutty** (**-ier, -iest**) *adj (joke)* cochon, -onne

snack [snæk] *n (meal)* casse-croûte *m inv*; **to eat a s.** *or* **snacks** grignoter quelque chose; **s. bar** snack-bar *m*

snag [snæg] *n (hitch)* problème *m*; *(in cloth)* accroc *m*

snail [sneɪl] *n* escargot *m*; **at a s.'s pace** comme un escargot

snake [sneɪk] **1** *n* serpent *m*; **snakes and ladders** ≃ jeu *m* de l'oie

2 *vi (of river)* serpenter • **snakebite** *n* morsure *f* de serpent

snap [snæp] **1** *n (sound)* craquement *m*; *Fam (photo)* photo *f*; **s. (fastener)** pression *f*; **cold s.** coup *m* de froid

2 *adj (judgement, decision)* hâtif, -ive

3 *(pt & pp* **-pp-**) *vt (break)* casser net; *(fingers, whip)* faire claquer; **to s. up a bargain** sauter sur une occasion

4 *vi* se casser net; *(of whip)* claquer; *Fig (of person)* parler sèchement (**at** à); **to s. at sb** *(of dog)* essayer de mordre qn; **to s. off** se casser net; *Fam* **s. out of it!** secoue-toi!

snapdragon ['snæpdrægən] *n* gueule-de-loup *f*

snappy ['snæpɪ] (**-ier, -iest**) *adj (pace)* vif *(f* vive); *Fam* **make it s.!** dépêche-toi!

snapshot ['snæpʃɒt] *n Fam* photo *f*

snare [sneə(r)] *n* piège *m*

snarl [snɑːl] **1** *n* grognement *m*

2 *vi* grogner (en montrant les dents) • **snarl-up** *n Fam (traffic jam)* bouchon *m*; *(confusion)* pagaille *f*

snatch [snætʃ] *vt (grab)* saisir; *(steal)* arracher; **to s. sth from sb** arracher qch à qn; **to s. some sleep** dormir un peu

snatches ['snætʃɪz] *npl (bits)* fragments *mpl* (**of** de)

snazzy ['snæzɪ] (**-ier, -iest**) *adj Fam (smart)* chic; **she's a s. dresser** elle s'habille avec chic

sneak [sniːk] **1** *n Br Fam (telltale)* mouchard, -arde *mf*; **to get a s. preview of sth** voir qch en avant-première

2 *(pt & pp* **sneaked** *or Am* **snuck**) *vi Br Fam (tell tales)* rapporter; **to s. in/out** entrer/sortir furtivement; **to s. off** s'esquiver • **sneaky** (**-ier, -iest**) *adj Fam* sournois

sneaker ['sniːkə(r)] *n Am (shoe)* chaussure *f* de sport

sneer [snɪə(r)] **1** *n* ricanement *m*

2 *vi* ricaner; **to s. at sb/sth** se moquer de qn/qch

sneeze [sniːz] **1** *n* éternuement *m*

2 *vi* éternuer

snicker ['snɪkə(r)] *n & vi Am* = **snigger**

snide [snaɪd] *adj* méprisant

sniff [snɪf] **1** *n* **to give sth a s.** renifler qch; **to take a s. at sth** renifler qch

2 *vt* renifler; **to s. glue** sniffer de la colle;

Fam **it's not to be sniffed at** il ne faut pas cracher dessus

3 *vi* renifler

sniffle ['snɪfəl] **1** *n Fam* **to have a s.** *or the* **sniffles** avoir un petit rhume

2 *vi* renifler

snigger ['snɪgə(r)] **1** *n* (petit) ricanement *m*

2 *vi* ricaner • **sniggering** *n* ricanements *mpl*

snip [snɪp] **1** *n* (*cut*) petite entaille *f*; (*piece*) bout *m*; *Br Fam* (*bargain*) bonne affaire *f*

2 (*pt & pp* **-pp-**) *vt* **to s. sth (off)** couper qch

sniper ['snaɪpə(r)] *n Mil* tireur *m* embusqué

snippet ['snɪpɪt] *n* (*of conversation*) bribe *f*

snivel ['snɪvəl] (*Br* **-ll-,** *Am* **-l-**) *vi* pleurnicher • **snivelling** (*Am* **sniveling**) *adj* pleurnicheur, -euse

snob [snɒb] *n* snob *mf* • **snobbery** *n* snobisme *m* • **snobbish** *adj* snob *inv*

snog [snɒg] *Br Fam* **1** *n* **to have a s.** se bécoter

2 *vi* se bécoter

snooker ['snuːkə(r)] *n* (*game*) = billard qui se joue avec vingt-deux billes

snoop [snuːp] *vi* fouiner; **to s. on sb** espionner qn

snooty ['snuːtɪ] (**-ier, -iest**) *adj Fam* prétentieux, -ieuse

snooze [snuːz] **1** *n* petit somme *m*; **to have a s.** faire un petit somme

2 *vi* faire un petit somme

snore [snɔː(r)] **1** *n* ronflement *m*

2 *vi* ronfler • **snoring** *n* ronflements *mpl*

snorkel ['snɔːkəl] **1** *n* tuba *m*

2 (*Br* **-ll-,** *Am* **-l-**) *vi* nager sous l'eau avec un tuba

snort [snɔːt] **1** *n* (*of person*) grognement *m*; (*of horse*) ébrouement *m*

2 *vi* (*of person*) grogner; (*of horse*) s'ébrouer

snot [snɒt] *n Fam* morve *f* • **snotty** (**-ier, -iest**) *adj Fam* (*nose*) qui coule; (*handkerchief*) plein de morve; (*child*) morveux, -euse; (*arrogant*) arrogant • **snotty-nosed** *adj Fam* morveux, -euse

snout [snaʊt] *n* museau *m*

snow [snəʊ] **1** *n* neige *f*

2 *vi* neiger; **it's snowing** il neige

3 *vt* **to be snowed in** être bloqué par la neige; *Fig* **to be snowed under with work** être submergé de travail • **snowball 1** *n* boule *f* de neige **2** *vi* (*increase*) faire boule de neige • **snowbound** *adj* bloqué par la

neige • **snow-capped** *adj* couronné de neige • **snowdrift** *n* congère *f* • **snowdrop** *n* (*flower*) perce-neige *m ou f inv* • **snowfall** *n* chute *f* de neige • **snowflake** *n* flocon *m* de neige • **snowman** (*pl* **-men**) *n* bonhomme *m* de neige • **snowmobile** ['snəʊməʊbiːl] *n* motoneige *f* • **snowplough** (*Am* **snowplow**) *n* chasse-neige *m inv* • **snowshoe** *n* raquette *f* • **snowstorm** *n* tempête *f* de neige • **'Snow 'White** *n* Blanche-Neige *f* • **snowy** (**-ier, -iest**) *adj* (*weather, hills*) neigeux, -euse; (*day*) de neige

snub [snʌb] **1** *n* rebuffade *f*

2 (*pt & pp* **-bb-**) *vt* (*offer*) rejeter; **to s. sb** snober qn • **snub 'nose** *n* nez *m* retroussé

snuck [snʌk] *Am pt & pp of* **sneak**

snuff [snʌf] **1** *n* tabac *m* à priser

2 *vt* **to s. (out)** (*candle*) moucher • **snuff-box** *n* tabatière *f*

snuffle ['snʌfəl] *n & vi* = **sniffle**

snug [snʌg] (**snugger, snuggest**) *adj* (*house*) douillet, -ette; (*garment*) bien ajusté; **s. in bed** bien au chaud dans son lit

snuggle ['snʌgəl] *vi* **to s. up to sb** se blottir contre qn

so [səʊ] **1** *adv* (*to such a degree*) si, tellement (**that** que); (*thus*) ainsi, comme ça; **to work/drink so much that...** travailler/boire tellement que...; **so much courage** tellement de courage (**that** que); **so many books** tant de livres (**that** que); **so very fast** tellement vite; **ten or so** environ dix; **and so on** et ainsi de suite; **I think so** je crois que oui; **do so!** faites-le!; **is that so?** c'est vrai?; **so am I** moi aussi; **you're late – so I am** tu es en retard – ah oui! tu as raison; **I told you so** je vous l'avais bien dit; *Fam* **so long!** au revoir!

2 *conj* (*therefore*) donc; (*in that case*) alors; **so what?** et alors?; **so that...** pour que... (+ *subjunctive*); **so as to do sth** pour faire qch • **So-and-so** *n* **Mr S.** Monsieur Untel • **so-called** *adj* soi-disant *inv* • **so-so** *adj & adv Fam* comme ci comme ça

soak [səʊk] **1** *n* **to give sth a s.** faire tremper qch

2 *vt* (*drench*) tremper; (*washing, food*) faire tremper; **to be soaked through** *or* **to the skin** être trempé jusqu'aux os; **to s. sth up** absorber qch

3 *vi* (*of washing*) tremper; **to s. in** (*of liquid*) s'infiltrer • **soaked** *adj* trempé • **soaking 1** *adj & adv* **s. (wet)** trempé **2** *n* **to get a s.** se faire tremper; **to give sth a s.** faire tremper qch

soap [səʊp] **1** *n* savon *m*; **s. opera** feuille-

ton *m* populaire; **s. powder** lessive *f*
　2 *vt* **to s. sth (down)** savonner qch
● **soapflakes** *npl* savon *m* en paillettes
● **soapsuds** *npl* mousse *f* de savon ● **soapy**
(**-ier, -iest**) *adj* savonneux, -euse

soar [sɔː(r)] *vi (of bird)* s'élever; *(of price)*
monter en flèche

sob [sɒb] **1** *n* sanglot *m*
　2 (*pt & pp* **-bb-**) *vi* sangloter ● **sobbing** *n*
(*sobs*) sanglots *mpl*

sober ['səʊbə(r)] **1** *adj (sensible)* sobre;
he's s. *(not drunk)* il n'est pas ivre
　2 *vti* **to s. up** dessoûler

soccer ['sɒkə(r)] *n* football *m*

sociable ['səʊʃəbəl] *adj (person)* sociable; *(evening)* amical ● **sociably** *adv*
(act, reply) aimablement

social ['səʊʃəl] **1** *adj* social; **to have a
good s. life** sortir beaucoup; **s. class**
classe *f* sociale; **s. evening** soirée *f*; **s.
gathering** réunion *f* mondaine; **s. sci-
ence(s)** sciences *fpl* humaines; **S. Security** ≃ la Sécurité sociale; **s. security** *(aid)*
aide *f* sociale; *Am (retirement pension)*
pension *f* de retraite; **the s. services** les
services *mpl* sociaux; **s. worker** assistant, -ante *mf* social(e)
　2 *n (party)* fête *f*

socialism ['səʊʃəlɪzəm] *n* socialisme *m*
● **socialist** *adj & n* socialiste *(mf)*

socialite ['səʊʃəlaɪt] *n* mondain, -aine *mf*

socialize ['səʊʃəlaɪz] *vi* fréquenter des
gens; **to s. with sb** fréquenter qn

socially ['səʊʃəlɪ] *adv* socialement;
(meet, behave) en société; **to see sb s.**
fréquenter qn

society [sə'saɪətɪ] **1** (*pl* **-ies**) *n (community, club, companionship)* société *f*;
(school/university club) club *m*; **(high) s.**
haute société *f*
　2 *adj (wedding, news)* mondain

sociology [səʊsɪ'ɒlədʒɪ] *n* sociologie *f*
● **sociological** [-sɪə'lɒdʒɪkəl] *adj* sociologique ● **sociologist** *n* sociologue *mf*

sock [sɒk] **1** *n* chaussette *f*
　2 *vt Fam (hit)* donner un coup de poing à

socket ['sɒkɪt] *n Br (of electric plug)* prise
f de courant; *Br (of lamp)* douille *f*; *(of eye)*
orbite *f*

soda ['səʊdə] *n Chem* soude *f*; **baking s.**
bicarbonate *m* de soude; *Am* **s. (pop)**
boisson *f* gazeuse; **s. (water)** eau *f* de
Seltz

sodden ['sɒdən] *adj (ground)* détrempé

sodium ['səʊdɪəm] *n Chem* sodium *m*

sofa ['səʊfə] *n* canapé *m*; **s. bed** canapé-
lit *m*

soft [sɒft] (**-er, -est**) *adj (gentle, not stiff)*

doux *(f* douce); *(butter, ground, paste,
snow)* mou *(f* molle); *(wood, heart, colour)* tendre; *(easy)* facile; *(indulgent)* indulgent; *Fam (cowardly)* poltron, -onne;
Fam (stupid) ramolli; **to have a s. spot for
sb** avoir un faible pour qn; **s. cheese**
fromage *m* frais; **s. drink** boisson *f* non
alcoolisée; **s. drugs** drogues *fpl* douces; **s.
toy** peluche *f*; **s. water** eau *f* douce ● **'soft-
'boiled** *adj (egg)* à la coque ● **'soft-
'hearted** *adj* qui se laisse facilement
attendrir ● **'soft-'spoken** *adj* qui a une
voix douce

soften ['sɒfən] **1** *vt (object)* ramollir; *(colour, light, voice, skin)* adoucir
　2 *vi* ramollir; *(of colour)* s'adoucir
● **softener** *n* adoucissant *m*

softie ['sɒftɪ] *n Fam (gentle person)*
bonne pâte *f*; *(weakling)* mauviette *f*

softly ['sɒftlɪ] *adv* doucement ● **softness**
n douceur *f*; *(of butter, ground, paste)*
mollesse *f*

software ['sɒftweə(r)] *n inv Comptr* logiciel *m*; **s. package** progiciel *m*

soggy ['sɒgɪ] (**-ier, -iest**) *adj* trempé

soil [sɔɪl] **1** *n (earth)* terre *f*
　2 *vt (dirty)* salir
　3 *vi (of fabric)* se salir

solar ['səʊlə(r)] *adj* solaire; **s. power**
énergie *f* solaire

sold [səʊld] *pt & pp of* **sell**

solder ['sɒldə(r)] **1** *n* soudure *f*
　2 *vt* souder

soldier ['səʊldʒə(r)] **1** *n* soldat *m*
　2 *vi* **to s. on** persévérer

sole¹ [səʊl] **1** *n (of shoe)* semelle *f*; *(of foot)*
plante *f*
　2 *vt (shoe)* ressemeler

sole² [səʊl] *adj (only)* unique; *(rights,
representative, responsibility)* exclusif,
-ive ● **solely** *adv* uniquement; **you're s.
to blame** tu es seul coupable

sole³ [səʊl] *n (fish)* sole *f*; **lemon s.** limande *f*

solemn ['sɒləm] *adj* solennel, -elle ● **solemnity** [sə'lemnɪtɪ] *n* solennité *f* ● **solemnly** *adv (promise)* solennellement;
(say) gravement

solicit [sə'lɪsɪt] **1** *vt (seek)* solliciter
　2 *vi (of prostitute)* racoler

solicitor [sə'lɪsɪtə(r)] *n Br (for wills)* notaire *m*

solid ['sɒlɪd] **1** *adj (not liquid)* solide; *(not
hollow)* plein; *(gold, silver)* massif, -ive; **s.
line** ligne *f* continue
　2 *adv* **frozen s.** complètement gelé; **ten
days s.** dix jours d'affilée
　3 *n* solide *m*; **solids** *(food)* aliments *mpl*

solides • **solidify** [səˈlɪdɪfaɪ] (*pt & pp* **-ied**) *vi* se solidifier • **solidity** [səˈlɪdɪtɪ] *n* solidité *f* • **solidly** *adv (built)* solidement; *(support, vote)* en masse; *(work)* sans interruption

solidarity [sɒlɪˈdærətɪ] *n* solidarité *f* (**with** avec)

soliloquy [səˈlɪləkwɪ] (*pl* **-ies**) *n* monologue *m*

solitary [ˈsɒlɪtərɪ] *adj (lonely, alone)* solitaire; *(only)* seul; **s. confinement** isolement *m* cellulaire • **solitude** *n* solitude *f*

solo [ˈsəʊləʊ] **1** (*pl* **-os**) *n Mus* solo *m* **2** *adj (guitar, violin)* solo *inv* **3** *adv (play, sing)* en solo; *(fly)* en solitaire • **soloist** *n Mus* soliste *mf*

solstice [ˈsɒlstɪs] *n* solstice *m*

soluble [ˈsɒljʊbəl] *adj (substance, problem)* soluble

solution [səˈluːʃən] *n* (**a**) *(to problem)* solution *f* (**to** de) (**b**) *(liquid)* solution *f*

solve [sɒlv] *vt (problem)* résoudre

solvent [ˈsɒlvənt] **1** *adj (financially)* solvable **2** *n Chem* solvant *m*; **s. abuse** = usage de solvants comme stupéfiants • **solvency** *n (of company)* solvabilité *f*

Somalia [səˈmɑːlɪə] *n* la Somalie

sombre [ˈsɒmbə(r)] (*Am* **somber**) *adj* sombre

some [sʌm] **1** *adj* (**a**) *(a certain quantity of)* du, de la, des; **s. wine** du vin; **s. glue** de la colle; **s. water** de l'eau; **s. dogs** des chiens; **s. pretty flowers** de jolies fleurs (**b**) *(unspecified)* un, une; **s. man (or other)** un homme (quelconque); **s. other way** un autre moyen; **for s. reason or other** pour une raison ou pour une autre; **I have been waiting s. time** ça fait un moment que j'attends; *Fam* **that's s. book!** ça, c'est un livre! (**c**) *(a few)* quelques; *(in contrast to others)* certains; **s. days ago** il y a quelques jours; **s. people think that** certains pensent que **2** *pron* (**a**) *(a certain quantity)* en; **I want s.** j'en veux; **do you have s.?** en as-tu?; **s. of my wine** un peu de mon vin; **s. of the time** une partie du temps (**b**) *(as opposed to others)* certain(e)s; **some say...** certains disent...; **s. of the guests** certains invités **3** *adv (about)* environ; **s. ten years** environ dix ans • **somebody** *pron* = someone • **someday** *adv* un jour • **somehow** *adv (in some way)* d'une manière ou d'une autre; *(for some reason)* on ne sait pourquoi • **someone** *pron* quelqu'un; **s. small** quel-

qu'un de petit • **someplace** *adv Am* quelque part • **something 1** *pron* quelque chose; **s. awful** quelque chose d'affreux; **he's s. of a liar** il est plutôt menteur **2** *adv* **she plays s. like...** elle joue un peu comme...; **it was s. awful** c'était vraiment affreux • **sometime 1** *adv* un jour; **s. in May** au mois de mai **2** *adj (former)* ancien, -ienne • **sometimes** *adv* quelquefois, parfois • **somewhat** *adv* quelque peu, assez • **somewhere** *adv* quelque part; **s. about fifteen** *(approximately)* environ quinze

somersault [ˈsʌməsɔːlt] **1** *n (on ground)* roulade *f*; *(in air)* saut *m* périlleux **2** *vi* faire une roulade; *(in air)* faire un saut périlleux

son [sʌn] *n* fils *m* • **son-in-law** (*pl* **sons-in-law**) *n* gendre *m*

sonar [ˈsəʊnɑː(r)] *n* sonar *m*

sonata [səˈnɑːtə] *n* sonate *f*

song [sɒŋ] *n* chanson *f*; *(of bird)* chant *m* • **songbook** *n* recueil *m* de chansons

sonic [ˈsɒnɪk] *adj* **s. boom** bang *m*

sonnet [ˈsɒnɪt] *n* sonnet *m*

soon [suːn] (**-er, -est**) *adv (in a short time)* bientôt; *(quickly)* vite; *(early)* tôt; **he s. forgot about it** il l'oublia vite; **s. after** peu après; **as s. as...** aussitôt que...; **no sooner had he spoken than** à peine avait-il parlé que; **I'd sooner leave** je préférerais partir; **I'd just as s. leave** j'aimerais autant partir; **sooner or later** tôt ou tard

soot [sʊt] *n* suie *f* • **sooty** (**-ier, -iest**) *adj* couvert de suie

soothe [suːð] *vt* calmer • **soothing** *adj* calmant

sophisticated [səˈfɪstɪkeɪtɪd] *adj (person, taste)* raffiné; *(machine, method, technology)* sophistiqué

sophomore [ˈsɒfəmɔː(r)] *n Am* étudiant, -iante *mf* de deuxième année

soporific [sɒpəˈrɪfɪk] *adj* soporifique

sopping [ˈsɒpɪŋ] *adj & adv* **s. (wet)** trempé

soppy [ˈsɒpɪ] (**-ier, -iest**) *adj Br Fam (sentimental)* sentimental

soprano [səˈprɑːnəʊ] (*pl* **-os**) *n (singer)* soprano *mf*; *(voice)* soprano *m*

sorbet [ˈsɔːbeɪ] *n* sorbet *m*

sorcerer [ˈsɔːsərə(r)] *n* sorcier *m*

sordid [ˈsɔːdɪd] *adj* sordide

sore [sɔː(r)] **1** (**-er, -est**) *adj (painful)* douloureux, -euse; *Am (angry)* fâché (**at** contre); **to have a s. throat** avoir mal à la gorge; **he's still s.** *(in pain)* il a encore mal; *Fig* **it's a s. point** c'est un sujet délicat

2 *n (wound)* plaie *f* •**sorely** *adv (tempted)* très; *(regretted)* amèrement; **it's s. needed** on en a grand besoin •**soreness** *n (pain)* douleur *f*

sorrow ['sɒrəʊ] *n* chagrin *m* •**sorrowful** *adj* triste

sorry ['sɒrɪ] (-**ier**, -**iest**) *adj (sight, state)* triste; **to be s. (about sth)** *(regret)* être désolé (de qch); **to feel** *or* **be s. for sb** plaindre qn; **I'm s. she can't come** je regrette qu'elle ne puisse pas venir; **s.!** pardon!; **s. to keep you waiting** désolé de vous faire attendre; **to say s.** demander pardon (**to** à)

sort¹ [sɔ:t] *n* sorte *f*; **a s. of** une sorte de; **all sorts of** toutes sortes de; **what s. of drink is it?** qu'est-ce que c'est comme boisson?; *Br Fam* **he's a good s.** c'est un brave type; **s. of sad** *(somewhat)* plutôt triste

sort² [sɔ:t] **1** *vt (papers)* trier; **to s. out** *(classify, select)* trier; *(separate)* séparer (**from** de); *(organize)* ranger; *(problem)* régler; *Br Fam* **to s. sb out** régler son compte à qn

2 *vi* **to s. through letters/magazines** trier des lettres/magazines; *Br* **sorting office** *(for mail)* centre *m* de tri

SOS [esəʊ'es] *(abbr* **save our souls**) *n* SOS *m*

soufflé ['su:fleɪ] *n Culin* soufflé *m*

sought [sɔ:t] *pt & pp of* **seek**

soul [səʊl] *n* âme *f*; **not a living s.** pas âme qui vive; *Fig* **a good s.** un brave type; **s. mate** âme *f* sœur •**soul-destroying** *adj* abrutissant •**soul-searching** *n* examen *m* de conscience

sound¹ [saʊnd] **1** *n* son *m*; *(noise)* bruit *m*; **I don't like the s. of it** ça ne me plaît pas du tout; **s. archives** phonothèque *f*; **s. barrier** mur *m* du son; **s. bite** petite phrase *f*; **s. effects** bruitage *m*; **s. engineer** ingénieur *m* du son; **s. recording** enregistrement *m* sonore; **s. wave** onde *f* sonore

2 *vt (bell, alarm)* sonner; *(bugle, horn)* sonner de; *(letter, syllable)* prononcer; **to s. one's horn** *(in vehicle)* klaxonner

3 *vi (of trumpet, bugle)* sonner; *(seem)* sembler; **to s. like** sembler être; *(resemble)* ressembler à; **it sounds like** *or* **as if...** il semble que... (*+ subjunctive or indicative)*; **(it) sounds good!** bonne idée!; *Pej* **to s. off (about sth)** *(boast)* se vanter (de qch); *(complain)* se plaindre (de qch)

sound² [saʊnd] **1** (-**er**, -**est**) *adj (healthy)* sain; *(in good condition)* en bon état;

(basis) solide; *(argument)* valable; *(advice)* bon (*f* bonne); *(investment)* sûr; **a s. beating** une bonne correction

2 *adv* **s. asleep** profondément endormi •**soundly** *adv (asleep, sleep)* profondément; *(reasoned)* solidement; *(beaten)* complètement •**soundness** *n (of mind)* santé *f*; *(of argument)* solidité *f*

sound³ [saʊnd] *vt (test, measure)* sonder; **to s. sb out** sonder qn (**about** sur)

soundproof ['saʊndpru:f] **1** *adj* insonorisé **2** *vt* insonoriser

soundtrack ['saʊndtræk] *n (of film)* bande *f* sonore

soup [su:p] *n* soupe *f*; **s. dish** *or* **plate** assiette *f* creuse; *Fam* **to be in the s.** *(in trouble)* être dans le pétrin

sour ['saʊə(r)] **1** (-**er**, -**est**) *adj* aigre; *(milk)* tourné; **to turn s.** *(of wine)* s'aigrir; *(of milk)* tourner; *(of friendship)* se détériorer; *(of conversation)* tourner au vinaigre

2 *vi (of temper)* s'aigrir

source [sɔ:s] *n (origin)* source *f*; **s. of energy** source d'énergie

south [saʊθ] **1** *n* sud *m*; **(to the) s. of** au sud de

2 *adj (coast)* sud *inv*; *(wind)* du sud; **S. America/Africa** l'Amérique *f*/l'Afrique *f* du Sud; **S. American** *adj* sud-américain; *n* Sud-Américain, -aine *mf*; **S. African** *adj* sud-africain; *n* Sud-Africain, -aine *mf*

3 *adv* au sud; *(travel)* vers le sud •**southbound** *adj (traffic)* en direction du sud; *Br (carriageway)* sud *inv* • 'south-'east *n & adj* sud-est *(m)* •**southerly** ['sʌðəlɪ] *adj (point)* sud *inv*; *(direction, wind)* du sud •**southern** ['sʌðən] *adj (town)* du sud; *(coast)* sud *inv*; **s. Italy** le sud de l'Italie; **S. Africa** l'Afrique *f* australe •**southerner** ['sʌðənə(r)] *n* habitant, -ante *mf* du sud •**southward(s)** *adj & adv* vers le sud • 'south-'west *n & adj* sud-ouest *(m)*

souvenir [su:və'nɪə(r)] *n* souvenir *m*

sovereign ['sɒvrɪn] **1** *n* souverain, -aine *mf*

2 *adj (State, authority)* souverain; *(rights)* de souveraineté •**sovereignty** [-rəntɪ] *n* souveraineté *f*

Soviet ['səʊvɪət] *adj* soviétique; *Formerly* **the S. Union** l'Union *f* soviétique

sow¹ [saʊ] *n (pig)* truie *f*

sow² [səʊ] *(pt* **sowed**, *pp* **sowed** *or* **sown** [səʊn]) *vt (seeds, doubt)* semer; *(land)* ensemencer (**with** de)

soya ['sɔɪə] *n Br* soja *m* •**soybean** *n Am* graine *f* de soja

sozzled ['sɒzəld] *adj Fam (drunk)* bourré
spa [spɑː] *n (town)* station f thermale; *(spring)* source f thermale
space [speɪs] **1** *n (gap, emptiness, atmosphere)* espace *m*; *(for parking)* place f; **in the s. of two hours** en l'espace de deux heures; **to take up s.** prendre de la place; **blank s.** espace, blanc *m*; **s. bar** *(on keyboard)* barre f d'espacement; **s. heater** *(electric)* radiateur *m*
2 *adj (voyage, capsule)* spatial; **s. shuttle** navette f spatiale
3 *vt* **to s. out** espacer • **spacecraft** *n inv* vaisseau *m* spatial • **spaceman** *(pl* **-men)** *n* astronaute *m* • **spaceship** *n* vaisseau *m* spatial • **spacesuit** *n* combinaison f spatiale • **spacewoman** *(pl* **-women)** *n* astronaute f • **spacing** *n Typ* **in double/single s.** à double/simple interligne
spacious ['speɪʃəs] *adj* spacieux, -ieuse • **spaciousness** *n* grandeur f
spade [speɪd] *n* (**a**) *(for garden)* bêche f; *(of child)* pelle f (**b**) *Cards* **spade(s)** pique *m*
spaghetti [spə'getɪ] *n* spaghettis *mpl*
Spain [speɪn] *n* l'Espagne f
span [spæn] **1** *n (of arch)* portée f; *(of wings)* envergure f; *Fig (of life)* durée f
2 *(pt & pp* **-nn-)** *vt (of bridge)* enjamber; *Fig (in time)* couvrir
Spaniard ['spænjəd] *n* Espagnol, -ole *mf* • **Spanish 1** *adj* espagnol **2** *n (language)* espagnol *m* • **Spanish-A'merican 1** *adj* hispano-américain **2** *n* Hispano-Américain, -aine *mf*
spaniel ['spænjəl] *n* épagneul *m*
spank [spæŋk] **1** *n* **to give sb a s.** donner une tape sur les fesses à qn
2 *vt* donner une tape sur les fesses à • **spanking** *n* fessée f
spanner ['spænə(r)] *n Br (tool)* clef f; **adjustable s.** clef f à molette
spar [spɑː(r)] *(pt & pp* **-rr-)** *vi (of boxer)* s'entraîner (**with** avec)
spare¹ [speə(r)] **1** *adj (extra, surplus)* de ou en trop; *(reserve)* de rechange; *(wheel)* de secours; *(available)* disponible; **s. room** chambre f d'ami; **s. time** loisirs *mpl*
2 *n* **s. (part)** *(for vehicle, machine)* pièce f détachée
3 *vt (do without)* se passer de; *(efforts, sb's feelings)* ménager; **to s. sb** *(not kill)* épargner qn; **to s. sb's life** épargner la vie de qn; **to s. sb sth** *(grief, details)* épargner qch à qn; *(time)* accorder qch à qn; **I can't s. the time** je n'ai pas le temps; **to s. no expense** ne pas regarder à la dépense; **five to s.** *(extra)* cinq de trop; **with five minutes to s.** avec cinq minutes d'avance

spare² [speə(r)] *adj (lean)* maigre
sparing ['speərɪŋ] *adj* **her s. use of** l'usage modéré qu'elle fait de; **to be s. with the butter** utiliser le beurre avec modération • **sparingly** *adv* en petite quantité
spark [spɑːk] **1** *n* étincelle f
2 *vt* **to s. off** *(cause)* provoquer • **spark(ing) plug** *n (for vehicle)* bougie f
sparkle ['spɑːkəl] **1** *n* éclat *m*
2 *vi* briller; *(of diamond, star)* scintiller • **sparkling** *adj (wine, water)* pétillant
sparrow ['spærəʊ] *n* moineau *m*
sparse [spɑːs] *adj* clairsemé • **sparsely** *adv (populated, wooded)* peu; **s. furnished** à peine meublé
spartan ['spɑːtən] *adj* spartiate
spasm ['spæzəm] *n (of muscle)* spasme *m*; *Fig (of coughing, jealousy)* accès *m* • **spas'modic** *adj (pain)* spasmodique; *Fig* intermittent
spastic ['spæstɪk] *n Med* handicapé, -ée *mf* moteur
spat [spæt] *pt & pp of* **spit**
spate [speɪt] *n* **a s. of sth** *(of letters, calls)* une avalanche de qch; *(of crimes)* une vague de qch
spatter ['spætə(r)] **1** *vt (clothes, person)* éclabousser (**with** de)
2 *vi* **to s. over sb** *(of mud)* éclabousser qn
spatula ['spætjʊlə] *n* spatule f
spawn [spɔːn] **1** *n (of fish)* frai *m*
2 *vt Fig (bring about)* engendrer
3 *vi* frayer
speak [spiːk] **1** *(pt* **spoke,** *pp* **spoken)** *vt (language)* parler; *(say)* dire; **to s. one's mind** dire ce que l'on pense
2 *vi* parler (**about** *or* **of** de); *(formally, in assembly)* prendre la parole; **so to s.** pour ainsi dire; **that speaks for itself** c'est évident; **to s. well of sb/sth** dire du bien de qn/qch; **Bob speaking!** *(on the telephone)* Bob à l'appareil!; **that's spoken for** c'est déjà pris; **to s. out** *or* **up** *(boldly)* parler (franchement); **to s. up** *(more loudly)* parler plus fort • **speaking 1** *n* **public s.** l'art *m* oratoire **2** *adj (toy, robot)* parlant; **they're not on s. terms** ils ne se parlent plus; **English-/French-s.** anglophone/francophone
speaker ['spiːkə(r)] *n (at meeting)* intervenant, -ante *mf*; *(at conference)* conférencier, -ière *mf*; *(loudspeaker)* enceinte f; **to be a Spanish s.** parler espagnol
spear [spɪə(r)] *n* lance f • **spearhead** *vt (attack, campaign)* être le fer de lance de

spearmint ['spɪəmɪnt] **1** n (plant) menthe f verte

2 adj (sweet) à la menthe; (flavour) de menthe; (chewing gum) mentholé

spec [spek] n Br Fam **on s.** à tout hasard

special ['speʃəl] **1** adj spécial; (care, attention) particulier, -ière; (favourite) préféré; Pol (measures) extraordinaire; Br **by s. delivery** en exprès; **s. effects** effets mpl spéciaux; **s. offer** offre f spéciale

2 n **today's s.** (in restaurant) le plat du jour

specialist ['speʃəlɪst] **1** n spécialiste mf (**in** de)

2 adj (dictionary, knowledge) spécialisé; (equipment) de spécialiste • **speciality** [-ʃɪ'ælɪtɪ] (pl -**ies**) n Br spécialité f

specialize ['speʃəlaɪz] vi se spécialiser (**in** dans) • **specialized** adj spécialisé

specially ['speʃəlɪ] adv (specifically) spécialement; (particularly) particulièrement

specialty ['speʃəltɪ] (pl -**ies**) n Am spécialité f

species ['spiːʃiːz] n inv espèce f

specific [spə'sɪfɪk] adj précis • **specifically** adv (explicitly) expressément; (exactly) précisément; (specially) spécialement

specify ['spesɪfaɪ] (pt & pp -**ied**) vt (state exactly) préciser; (stipulate) stipuler • **specification** [-fɪ'keɪʃən] n spécification f

specimen ['spesɪmɪn] n (individual example) spécimen m; (of urine, blood) échantillon m; **s. signature** spécimen de signature; **s. copy** (of book) spécimen

specious ['spiːʃəs] adj spécieux, -ieuse

speck [spek] n (stain) petite tache f; (of dust) grain m; (dot) point m

speckled ['spekəld] adj tacheté

specs [speks] npl Fam lunettes fpl

spectacle ['spektəkəl] n (sight) spectacle m • **spectacles** npl (glasses) lunettes fpl

spectacular [spek'tækjʊlə(r)] adj spectaculaire • **spectacularly** adv de façon spectaculaire

spectator [spek'teɪtə(r)] n spectateur, -trice mf

spectre ['spektə(r)] n spectre m (**of** de)

spectrum ['spektrəm] (pl -**tra** [-trə]) n spectre m; Fig (range) gamme f

speculate ['spekjʊleɪt] **1** vt **to s. that...** (guess) conjecturer que...

2 vi Fin & Phil spéculer; **to s. about** (make guesses) faire des suppositions sur • **specu'lation** n suppositions fpl; Fin & Phil spéculation f • **speculative** [-lətɪv] adj Fin & Phil spéculatif, -ive • **speculator** n Fin spéculateur, -trice mf

sped [sped] pt & pp of **speed**

speech [spiːtʃ] n (talk, lecture) discours m (**on** or **about** sur); (faculty) parole f; (diction) élocution f; (spoken language of group) langue f; **to make a s.** faire un discours; **part of s.** partie f du discours; Grammar **direct/indirect s.** discours m direct/indirect • **speechless** adj muet (f muette) (**with** de)

speed [spiːd] **1** n (rapidity, gear) vitesse f; **at top** or **full s.** à toute vitesse; **s. limit** (on road) limitation f de vitesse

2 (pt & pp **sped**) vt **to s. sth up** accélérer qch

3 vi (**a**) **to s. up** (of person) aller plus vite; (of pace) s'accélérer; **to s. past sth** passer à toute vitesse devant qch (**b**) (pt & pp **speeded**) (exceed speed limit) faire un excès de vitesse • **speedboat** n vedette f • **speeding** n (in vehicle) excès m de vitesse • **speedometer** [spɪ'dɒmɪtə(r)] n Br (in vehicle) compteur m de vitesse • **speedway** n Sport speedway m

speedy ['spiːdɪ] (-**ier**, -**iest**) adj rapide • **speedily** adv rapidement

spell¹ [spel] n (magic words) formule f magique; **to cast a s. on sb** jeter un sort à qn; **to be under a s.** être envoûté • **spellbound** adj fasciné

spell² [spel] n (period) période f; **cold s.** vague f de froid

spell³ [spel] (pt & pp **spelled** or **spelt** [spelt]) vt (write) écrire; (say aloud) épeler; (of letters) former; Fig (mean) signifier; **to be able to s.** savoir l'orthographe; **how do you s. it?** comment ça s'écrit?; **to s. sth out** (word) épeler qch; Fig (explain) expliquer clairement qch • **spell-checker** n Comptr correcteur m d'orthographe • **spelling** n orthographe f; **s. mistake** faute f d'orthographe

spend [spend] (pt & pp **spent**) vt (money) dépenser (**on** pour/en); (time) passer (**on sth** sur qch; **doing** à faire); (energy) consacrer (**on sth** à qch; **doing** à faire) • **spender** n **to be a big s.** dépenser beaucoup • **spending** n dépenses fpl; **s. money** argent m de poche • **spendthrift** n **to be a s.** être dépensier, -ière

spent [spent] **1** pt & pp of **spend**

2 adj (used) utilisé; **to be a s. force** ne plus avoir d'influence

sperm [spɜːm] n sperme m

spew [spjuː] vt vomir

sphere [sfɪə(r)] n (of influence, action) & Math & Pol sphère f; **it's outside my s.** ça n'est pas dans mes compétences; **s. of influence** sphère d'influence • **spherical** ['sferɪkəl] adj sphérique

sphinx [sfɪŋks] *n* sphinx *m*

spice [spaɪs] **1** *n* épice *f; Fig (interest)* piquant *m*

2 *vt (food)* épicer; **to s. sth (up)** *(add interest to)* ajouter du piquant à qch • **spicy** (**-ier, -iest**) *adj* épicé

spick-and-span [spɪkən'spæn] *adj (clean)* impeccable

spider ['spaɪdə(r)] *n* araignée *f;* **s.'s web** toile *f* d'araignée

spiel [ʃpiːl] *n Fam* baratin *m*

spike [spaɪk] **1** *n (of metal)* pointe *f*

2 *vt (pierce)* transpercer • **spiky** (**-ier, -iest**) *adj (stem, stick)* garni de piquants; *(hair)* tout hérissé

spill [spɪl] *(pt & pp* **spilled** *or* **spilt** [spɪlt]) **1** *vt (liquid)* renverser; *Fam* **to s. the beans** vendre la mèche

2 *vi* se répandre

▸ **spill out** *vt sep (empty)* vider ▸ **spill over** *vi (of liquid)* déborder

spin [spɪn] **1** *n (motion)* tournoiement *m; (on ball)* effet *m; Fam* **to go for a s.** *(in car)* aller faire un tour; **s. doctor** = spécialiste de la communication chargé de présenter l'information de façon à mettre en valeur un parti politique

2 *(pt & pp* **spun,** *pres p* **spinning)** *vt (wool, cotton)* filer; *(wheel, top)* faire tourner; *(spin-dry)* essorer; **to s. sth out** *(speech)* faire durer qch

3 *vi* tourner; **to s. round** *(of dancer, wheel, top, planet)* tourner; **my head's spinning** j'ai la tête qui tourne • **spinning** *n (by hand)* filage *m; Tech (process)* filature *f;* **s. top** toupie *f;* **s. wheel** rouet *m*

spinach ['spɪnɪdʒ] *n* épinards *mpl*

spindle ['spɪndəl] *n* fuseau *m*

spindly ['spɪndlɪ] (**-ier, -iest**) *adj (legs, arms)* grêle

spin-dry ['spɪn'draɪ] *vt* essorer • **spindryer** *n* essoreuse *f*

spine [spaɪn] *n (backbone)* colonne *f* vertébrale; *(of book)* dos *m; (of plant)* épine *f* • **spinal** *adj* **s. column** colonne *f* vertébrale; **s. cord** moelle *f* épinière; **s. injury** blessure *f* à la colonne vertébrale • **spineless** *adj Fig* mou *(f* molle)

spin-off ['spɪnɒf] *n (result)* retombée *f; (TV programme)* = feuilleton tiré d'un film ou d'un autre feuilleton

spinster ['spɪnstə(r)] *n* vieille fille *f*

spiral ['spaɪərəl] **1** *n* spirale *f*

2 *adj* en spirale; *(staircase)* en colimaçon

3 *(Br* **-ll-,** *Am* **-l-)** *vi (of prices)* s'envoler

spire ['spaɪə(r)] *n (of church)* flèche *f*

spirit ['spɪrɪt] **1** *n (soul, ghost, mood)* esprit *m; Fig (determination)* courage *m;*

spirits *(drink)* spiritueux *mpl;* **in good spirits** de bonne humeur; **to break sb's s.** entamer le courage de qn; *Fam* **that's the right s.!** à la bonne heure!

2 *adj (lamp)* à alcool; **s. level** niveau *m* (à bulle)

3 *vt* **to s. away** *(person)* faire disparaître (mystérieusement); *Hum (steal)* subtiliser • **spirited** *adj (campaign, attack)* vigoureux, -euse; *(person, remark)* énergique

spiritual ['spɪrɪtʃʊəl] **1** *adj* spirituel, -uelle

2 *n* **(Negro) s.** negro spiritual *m* • **spiritualism** [-ʊlɪzəm] *n* spiritisme *m* • **spiritualist** [-ʊlɪst] *n* spirite *mf*

spit¹ [spɪt] **1** *n (on ground)* crachat *m; (in mouth)* salive *f*

2 *(pt & pp* **spat** *or* **spit,** *pres p* **spitting)** *vt* cracher; **to s. sth out** cracher qch; **to be the spitting image of sb** être le portrait (tout craché) de qn

3 *vi* cracher; *(splutter) (of fat, fire)* crépiter

spit² [spɪt] *n (for meat)* broche *f*

spite [spaɪt] **1** *n (dislike)* dépit *m;* **in s. of sb/sth** malgré qn/qch; **in s. of the fact that...** bien que... (+ *subjunctive)*

2 *vt* vexer • **spiteful** *adj* vexant

spittle ['spɪtəl] *n* crachat *m; (in mouth)* salive *f*

splash [splæʃ] **1** *n (of liquid)* éclaboussure *f; (sound)* plouf *m; Fig (of colour)* tache *f; Fam* **to make a s.** faire sensation

2 *vt (spatter)* éclabousser **(with** de); **to s. one's face with water** se passer le visage à l'eau

3 *vi (of mud, ink)* faire des éclaboussures; *(of waves)* clapoter; **to s. over sb/sth** éclabousser qn/qch; **to s. (about)** *(in river, mud)* patauger; *(in bath)* barboter; *Fam* **to s. out** *(spend money)* claquer des ronds

spleen [spliːn] *n Anat* rate *f*

splendid ['splendɪd] *adj* splendide • **splendour** *(Am* **splendor)** *n* splendeur *f*

splint [splɪnt] *n* attelle *f*

splinter ['splɪntə(r)] *n (of wood, glass)* éclat *m; (in finger)* écharde *f; Pol* **s. group** groupe *m* dissident

split [splɪt] **1** *n* fente *f; (tear)* déchirure *f; (of couple)* rupture *f; (in political party)* scission *f;* **to do the splits** faire le grand écart; *Fam* **one's s.** *(share)* sa part

2 *adj* **in a s. second** en une fraction de seconde; **s. ends** *(in hair)* fourches *fpl;* **s.-level house** maison *f* à deux niveaux; **s.-level apartment** duplex *m;* **s. personality**

dédoublement *m* de la personnalité

3 (*pt & pp* split, *pres p* **splitting**) *vt* (*break apart*) fendre; (*tear*) déchirer; **to s. (up)** (*group*) diviser; (*money, work*) partager (**between** entre); **to s. one's head open** s'ouvrir la tête; *Fam* **to s. one's sides (laughing)** se tordre (de rire); **to s. hairs** (*make trivial distinctions*) couper les cheveux en quatre

4 *vi* se fendre; (*tear*) se déchirer; **to s. (up)** (*of group*) se diviser (**into** en); **to s. off** (*become loose*) se détacher (**from** de); **to s. up** (*because of disagreement*) (*of couple, friends*) se séparer; (*of crowd*) se disperser; **to s. up with sb** rompre avec qn

splitting ['splɪtɪŋ] *adj* **to have a s. headache** avoir un mal de tête épouvantable

splodge [splɒdʒ], **splotch** [splɒtʃ] *n* (*mark*) tache *f*

splurge [splɜːdʒ] *vi Fam* (*spend money*) claquer de l'argent

splutter ['splʌtə(r)] *vi* (*spit*) (*of person*) crachoter; (*of sparks, fat*) crépiter; (*stammer*) bredouiller

spoil [spɔɪl] (*pt & pp* spoilt *or* spoiled) *vt* (*ruin*) gâcher; (*indulge*) gâter; **to s. sb's appetite** couper l'appétit à qn; **to be spoilt for choice** avoir l'embarras du choix • **spoilsport** *n* rabat-joie *m inv*

spoils [spɔɪlz] *npl* (*rewards*) butin *m*

spoilt [spɔɪlt] *pt & pp of* spoil

spoke¹ [spəʊk] *n* (*of wheel*) rayon *m*

spoke² [spəʊk] *pt of* speak • **spoken 1** *pp of* speak **2** *adj* (*language*) parlé; **to be softly s.** avoir la voix douce • **spokesman** (*pl* -men), **spokesperson, spokeswoman** (*pl* -women) *n* porte-parole *m inv* (**for** *or* **of** de)

sponge [spʌndʒ] **1** *n* éponge *f*; *Br* **s. bag** trousse *f* de toilette; **s. cake** génoise *f*

2 *vt* **to s. sth down/off** laver/enlever qch avec une éponge; *Fam* **to s. sth off sb** taper qn de qch

3 *vi Fam* **to s. off** *or* **on sb** vivre aux crochets de qn • **sponger** *n Fam* parasite *m* • **spongy** (-ier, -iest) *adj* spongieux, -ieuse

sponsor ['spɒnsə(r)] **1** *n* sponsor *m*; (*for membership*) parrain *m*/marraine *f*

2 *vt* sponsoriser; (*student*) financer les études de; (*member*) parrainer • **sponsorship** *n* sponsoring *m*; (*of member*) parrainage *m*

spontaneous [spɒn'teɪnɪəs] *adj* spontané • **spontaneity** [-tə'neɪɪtɪ] *n* spontanéité *f* • **spontaneously** *adv* spontanément

spoof [spuːf] *n Fam* (*parody*) parodie *f* (**on** de)

spooky ['spuːkɪ] (-ier, -iest) *adj Fam* qui donne le frisson

spool [spuːl] *n* bobine *f*

spoon [spuːn] *n* cuillère *f* • **spoonfeed** (*pt & pp* -fed) *vt* faire manger à la cuillère; *Fig* (*help*) mâcher le travail à • **spoonful** *n* cuillerée *f*

sporadic [spə'rædɪk] *adj* sporadique • **sporadically** *adv* sporadiquement

sport¹ [spɔːt] *n* sport *m*; *Fam* **a (good) s.** (*man*) un chic type; (*woman*) une chic fille; **to play** *Br* **s.** *or Am* **sports** faire du sport; **sports club** club *m* de sport; **sports car/ground** voiture *f*/terrain *m* de sport; **sports jacket** veste *f* sport • **sporting** *adj* (*attitude, conduct, person*) sportif, -ive; *Fig* **that's s. of you** c'est chic de ta part • **sportsman** (*pl* -men) *n* sportif *m* • **sportsmanlike** *adj* sportif, -ive • **sportsmanship** *n* sportivité *f* • **sportswear** *n* vêtements *mpl* de sport • **sportswoman** (*pl* -women) *n* sportive *f* • **sporty** (-ier, -iest) *adj* sportif, -ive

sport² [spɔːt] *vt* (*wear*) arborer

spot¹ [spɒt] *n* (*stain, mark*) tache *f*; (*dot*) point *m*; (*polka dot*) pois *m*; (*drop*) goutte *f*; (*pimple*) bouton *m*; (*place*) endroit *m*; (*advertising*) spot *m* publicitaire; *Fam* **a s. of bother** de petits problèmes; **to have a soft s. for sb** avoir un faible pour qn; **on the s.** sur place; (*at once*) sur le coup; **to be in a tight s.** (*difficulty*) être dans le pétrin; *Br* (**accident**) **black s.** (*on road*) point *m* noir; **blind s.** (*in vehicle*) angle *m* mort; *Fig* **bright s.** point *m* positif; **s. check** contrôle *m* surprise

spot² [spɒt] (*pt & pp* -tt-) *vt* (*notice*) apercevoir; **well spotted!** bien vu!

spotless ['spɒtləs] *adj* (*clean*) impeccable • **spotlessly** *adv* **s. clean** impeccable

spotlight ['spɒtlaɪt] *n* projecteur *m*; (*for photography*) spot *m*; **to be in the s.** être sous le feu des projecteurs

spot-on ['spɒt'ɒn] *adj Br Fam* tout à fait exact

spotted ['spɒtɪd] *adj* (*fur*) tacheté; (*dress*) à pois; (*stained*) taché

spotty ['spɒtɪ] (-ier, -iest) *adj* (*face, person*) boutonneux, -euse; *Am* (*patchy*) inégal

spouse [spaʊs, spaʊz] *n* époux *m*, épouse *f*

spout [spaʊt] **1** *n* (*of teapot, jug*) bec *m*; *Br Fam* **to be up the s.** être fichu

2 *vt Pej* (*say*) débiter

3 *vi* **to s. (out)** (*of liquid*) jaillir

sprain [spreɪn] *n* entorse *f*; **to s. one's ankle/wrist** se fouler la cheville/le poignet

sprang [spræŋ] *pt of* **spring¹**

sprawl [sprɔːl] **1** *n* **the urban s.** les banlieues *fpl* tentaculaires
2 *vi (of town, person)* s'étaler • **sprawling** *adj (city)* tentaculaire; *(person)* affalé

spray [spreɪ] **1** *n* (**a**) *(can, device)* vaporisateur *m*; *(water drops)* gouttelettes *fpl*; *(from sea)* embruns *mpl* (**b**) *(of flowers)* petit bouquet *m*
2 *vt (liquid, surface)* vaporiser; *(plant, crops)* pulvériser; *(car)* peindre à la bombe

spread [spred] **1** *n (of idea, religion, language)* diffusion *f*; *(of disease)* propagation *f*; *Fam (meal)* festin *m*; **cheese s.** fromage *m* à tartiner; **full-page s.** *(in newspaper)* double page *f*
2 *(pt & pp* **spread***) vt (stretch, open out)* étendre; *(legs, fingers)* écarter; *(paint, payment, visits, cards)* étaler; *(sand, fear, knowledge)* répandre; *(news, germ, illness)* propager; **to s. out** *(map, payments, visits)* étaler; *(fingers)* écarter; **to be s. out** *(of city)* s'étendre
3 *vi (of town, fog)* s'étendre; *(of fire, epidemic, fear)* se propager; *(of news, fear)* se répandre; **to s. out** *(of people)* se disperser • **spread-'eagled** *adj* bras et jambes écartés • **spreadsheet** *n Comptr* tableur *m*

spree [spriː] *n* **to go on a spending s.** faire des folies dans les magasins

sprig [sprɪg] *n (of parsley)* brin *m*; *(of holly)* branche *f*

sprightly ['spraɪtlɪ] (**-ier, -iest**) *adj* alerte

spring¹ [sprɪŋ] **1** *n (device)* ressort *m*; *(leap)* bond *m*
2 *(pt* **sprang,** *pp* **sprung***) vt (news)* annoncer brusquement (**on** à); *(surprise)* faire (**on** à); **to s. a leak** *(of boat)* commencer à prendre l'eau
3 *vi (leap)* bondir; **to s. to mind** venir à l'esprit; **to s. into action** passer rapidement à l'action; **to s. from** *(stem from)* provenir de; **to s. up** *(appear)* surgir • **springboard** *n* tremplin *m* • **springy** (**-ier, -iest**) *adj* souple

spring² [sprɪŋ] *n (season)* printemps *m*; **in (the) s.** au printemps; *Br* **s. onion** oignon *m* nouveau • **spring-cleaning** *n* nettoyage *m* de printemps • **springlike** *adj* printanier, -ière • **springtime** *n* printemps *m*

spring³ [sprɪŋ] *n (of water)* source *f*; **s. water** eau *f* de source

sprinkle ['sprɪŋkəl] *vt (sand)* répandre (**on** *or* **over** sur); **to s. sth with water, to s. water on sth** arroser qch; **to s. sth with sth** *(sugar, salt, flour)* saupoudrer qch de qch • **sprinkler** *n (in garden)* arroseur *m* • **sprinkling** *n* **a s. of customers** *(a few)* quelques rares clients

sprint [sprɪnt] **1** *n (race)* sprint *m*
2 *vi (run)* sprinter • **sprinter** *n* sprinter *m*, sprinteuse *f*

sprout [spraʊt] **1** *n* (**Brussels) s.** chou *m* de Bruxelles
2 *vt (leaves)* pousser; *Fig (beard, whiskers)* se laisser pousser
3 *vi (of seed, bulb)* pousser; **to s. up** *(grow)* pousser vite; *(appear)* surgir

spruce¹ [spruːs] **1** (**-er, -est**) *adj (neat)* impeccable
2 *vt* **to s. oneself up** se faire beau *(f* belle)

spruce² [spruːs] *n (tree)* épicéa *m*

sprung [sprʌŋ] **1** *pp of* **spring¹**
2 *adj (mattress, seat)* à ressorts

spry [spraɪ] (**spryer, spryest**) *adj* alerte

spud [spʌd] *n Fam (potato)* patate *f*

spun [spʌn] *pt & pp of* **spin**

spur [spɜː(r)] **1** *n (of horse rider)* éperon *m*; *Fig (stimulus)* aiguillon *m*; **to do sth on the s. of the moment** faire qch sur un coup de tête
2 *(pt & pp* **-rr-***) vt* **to s. sb on** *(urge on)* aiguillonner qn

spurious ['spjʊərɪəs] *adj* faux *(f* fausse)

spurn [spɜːn] *vt* rejeter

spurt [spɜːt] **1** *n (of liquid)* giclée *f*; *(of energy)* regain *m*; **to put on a s.** foncer
2 *vi (of liquid)* gicler; *(of person)* foncer; **to s. out** *(of liquid)* gicler

spy [spaɪ] **1** *(pl* **-ies***) n* espion, -ionne *mf*
2 *adj (story, film)* d'espionnage; **s. hole** judas *m*; **s. ring** réseau *m* d'espionnage
3 *(pt & pp* **-ied***) vt (notice)* repérer
4 *vi* espionner; **to s. on sb** espionner qn • **spying** *n* espionnage *m*

sq *(abbr* **square***)* carré

squabble ['skwɒbəl] **1** *n* querelle *f*
2 *vi* se quereller (**over** à propos de) • **squabbling** *n* querelles *fpl*

squad [skwɒd] *n (of workmen, footballers)* équipe *f*; *(of soldiers)* section *f*; *(of police)* brigade *f*; *Br* **s. car** voiture *f* de police

squadron ['skwɒdrən] *n Mil* escadron *m*; *Naut & Av* escadrille *f*

squalid ['skwɒlɪd] *adj* sordide • **squalor** *n (poverty)* misère *f*

squall [skwɔːl] *n (of wind)* rafale *f*

squander ['skwɒndə(r)] *vt (money, resources)* gaspiller; *(time)* perdre

square ['skweə(r)] **1** n carré m; (on chessboard, map) case f; (in town) place f; Br (drawing implement) équerre f; Fig **to be back to s. one** être de retour à la case départ; Fam **to be a s.** être ringard, -arde **2** adj carré; Fam Old-fashioned (unfashionable) vieux jeu inv; **to be s. with sb** être honnête avec qn; Fam **we're (all) s.** nous sommes quittes; **s. corner** angle m droit; **s. deal** arrangement m équitable; **s. meal** bon repas m; Math **s. root** racine f carrée
3 vt (settle) régler; Math (number) élever au carré; **to s. sth with sb** arranger qch avec qn
4 vi (tally) cadrer (**with** avec); **to s. up to sb/sth** faire face à qn/qch •**squarely** adv (honestly) honnêtement; **to hit sb s. in the face** frapper qn en pleine figure

squash [skwɒʃ] **1** n (game) squash m; Am (vegetable) courge f; Br **lemon/orange s.** ≃ sirop m de citron/d'orange
2 vt écraser •**squashy** (**-ier, -iest**) adj (fruit) mou (f molle)

squat [skwɒt] **1** n (dwelling) squat m
2 adj (person, object, building) trapu
3 (pt & pp **-tt-**) vi squatter; **to s. (down)** s'accroupir; **to be squatting (down)** être accroupi •**squatter** n squatter m

squawk [skwɔːk] **1** n cri m rauque
2 vi pousser un cri rauque

squeak [skwiːk] **1** n (of animal, person) cri m aigu; (of door) grincement m
2 vi (of person) pousser un cri aigu; (of door) grincer •**squeaky** (**-ier, -iest**) adj (door) grinçant; (shoe) qui craque; **s. clean** impeccable

squeal [skwiːl] **1** n cri m perçant
2 vi pousser un cri perçant; (of tyres) crisser; Fam **to s. on sb** balancer qn

squeamish ['skwiːmɪʃ] adj de nature délicate

squeeze [skwiːz] **1** n **to give sth a s.** presser qch; **to give sb's hand/arm a s.** serrer la main/le bras à qn; **to give sb a s.** serrer qn dans ses bras; Fam **it's a tight s.** il n'y a pas beaucoup de place
2 vt (press) presser; **to s. sb's hand** serrer la main à qn; **to s. sth into sth** faire rentrer qch dans qch; **to s. the juice (out)** faire sortir le jus (**of** de); **to s. sth out of sb** (information, secret) arracher qch à qn
3 vi **to s. through/into sth** (force oneself) se glisser par/dans qch; **to s. in** trouver de la place; **to s. up** se serrer (**against** contre) •**squeezer** n **lemon s.** presse-citron m inv

squelch [skweltʃ] vi patauger

squid [skwɪd] n inv calmar m

squiggle ['skwɪɡəl] n gribouillis m

squint [skwɪnt] **1** n (eye defect) strabisme m; **to have a s.** loucher
2 vi loucher; (in the sunlight) plisser les yeux

squire ['skwaɪə(r)] n Br châtelain m

squirm [skwɜːm] vi (wriggle) se tortiller; **to s. in pain** se tordre de douleur

squirrel [Br 'skwɪrəl, Am 'skwɜːrəl] n écureuil m

squirt [skwɜːt] **1** n giclée f; Fam **little s.** (person) petit(e) morveux, -euse mf
2 vt (liquid) faire gicler
3 vi (of liquid) gicler

Sri Lanka [sriː'læŋkə] n le Sri Lanka

St abbr (**a**) = **Street** (**b**) = **Saint**

stab [stæb] **1** n **s. (wound)** coup m de couteau
2 (pt & pp **-bb-**) vt (with knife) poignarder; **to s. sb to death** tuer qn d'un coup de couteau •**stabbing** n **there has been a s.** quelqu'un a été poignardé; **a s. pain** une douleur lancinante

stability [stə'bɪlɪtɪ] n stabilité f

stabilize ['steɪbəlaɪz] **1** vt stabiliser
2 vi se stabiliser •**stabilizer** n (on bicycle) stabilisateur m

stable¹ ['steɪbəl] (**-er, -est**) adj stable

stable² ['steɪbəl] n écurie f; **s. boy** lad m

> 🖉 Note that the French word **étable** is a false friend and is never a translation for the English word **stable**. It means **cowshed**.

stack [stæk] **1** n (**a**) (heap) tas m; Fam **stacks of** (lots of) des tas de (**b**) **chimney s.** (of factory) tuyau m de cheminée
2 npl **the stacks** (in library) la réserve
3 vt **to s. (up)** entasser

stadium ['steɪdɪəm] n stade m

staff [stɑːf] **1** n personnel m; (of school, university) professeurs mpl; (of army) état-major m; Literary (stick) bâton m; **to be on the s.** faire partie du personnel; **member of (the) s., s. member** (in office) employé, -ée mf; (in school) professeur m; Br **s. meeting** (in school, university) conseil m des professeurs; Br **s. room** (in school) salle f des professeurs
2 vt pourvoir en personnel; **the desk is staffed at all times** il y a toujours quelqu'un au bureau

stag [stæg] n cerf m; **s. party** enterrement m de la vie de garçon

stage¹ [steɪdʒ] **1** n (platform) scène f; **the s.** (profession) le théâtre; **on s.** sur scène;

s. door entrée *f* des artistes; **s. fright** trac *m*

2 *vt (play)* monter; *Fig* organiser; **it was staged** *(not real)* c'était un coup monté •**stagehand** *n* machiniste *m* •**stage-manager** *n* régisseur *m*

stage² [steɪdʒ] *n (phase)* stade *m*; **to do sth in (easy) stages** faire qch par étapes; **at an early s.** au début (**of** de); **at this s. in the work** à ce stade des travaux; **at this s.** *(at this moment)* à l'heure qu'il est

> ✐ Note that the French word **stage** is a false friend and is never a translation for the English word **stage**. It means **training course.**

stagecoach [ˈsteɪdʒkəʊtʃ] *n Hist* diligence *f*

stagger [ˈstægə(r)] **1** *vt (holidays)* échelonner; *(astound)* stupéfier

2 *vi (reel)* chanceler •**staggering** *adj* stupéfiant

stagnant [ˈstægnənt] *adj* stagnant •**stag-'nate** *vi* stagner •**stag'nation** *n* stagnation *f*

staid [steɪd] *adj* collet monté *inv*

stain [steɪn] **1** *n (mark)* tache *f*; *(dye)* teinture *f*; **s. remover** détachant *m*

2 *vt (mark)* tacher (**with** de); *(dye)* teinter; **stained-glass window** vitrail *m (pl* vitraux) •**stainless 'steel** *n* acier *m* inoxydable, Inox® *m*; **s. knife** couteau *m* en Inox®

stair [steə(r)] *n* **a s.** *(step)* une marche; **the stairs** *(staircase)* l'escalier *m* •**staircase, stairway** *n* escalier *m*

stake [steɪk] **1** *n* (**a**) *(post)* pieu *m*; *(for plant)* tuteur *m*; *Hist* **to be burned at the s.** périr sur le bûcher (**b**) *(betting)* enjeu *m*; **to have a s. in sth** *(share)* avoir des intérêts dans qch; **at s.** en jeu; **there's a lot at s.** l'enjeu est considérable

2 *vt* (**a**) **to s. (out)** *(land)* délimiter; **to s. a claim to sth** revendiquer qch (**b**) *(bet)* jouer (**on** sur)

stale [steɪl] (**-er, -est**) *adj (bread)* rassis; *(beer)* éventé; *(air)* vicié; *(smell)* âcre; *(news)* vieux (*f* vieille); *(joke)* éculé; *(person)* blasé

stalemate [ˈsteɪlmeɪt] *n Chess* pat *m*; *Fig* impasse *f*

stalk [stɔːk] **1** *n (of plant)* tige *f*; *(of fruit)* queue *f*

2 *vt (animal, criminal)* traquer; *(celebrity)* harceler

3 *vi* **to s. out** *(walk angrily)* sortir d'un air furieux mais digne •**stalker** *n* = admira-

teur obsessionnel qui harcèle une célébrité

stall [stɔːl] **1** *n (in market)* étal *m*; *Br (for newspapers, flowers)* kiosque *m*; *(in stable)* stalle *f*; *Br* **the stalls** *(in cinema, theatre)* l'orchestre *m*

2 *vt (engine, car)* caler

3 *vi (of car)* caler; **to s. (for time)** chercher à gagner du temps

stallion [ˈstæljən] *n* étalon *m*

stalwart [ˈstɔːlwət] **1** *adj* résolu

2 *n* fidèle *mf*

stamina [ˈstæmɪnə] *n* résistance *f* physique

stammer [ˈstæmə(r)] **1** *n* bégaiement *m*; **to have a s.** être bègue

2 *vi* bégayer

3 *vt* **to s. out an apology** balbutier des excuses

stamp [stæmp] **1** *n (for letter)* timbre *m*; *(mark)* cachet *m*; *(device)* tampon *m*; *Fig* **to bear the s. of sth** porter l'empreinte de qch; **to be given the s. of approval** être approuvé; **s. album** album *m* de timbres; **s. collector** philatéliste *mf*

2 *vt (document)* tamponner; *(letter)* timbrer; *(metal)* estamper; **to s. one's foot** taper du pied; *Fig* **to s. sth out** *(rebellion, evil)* écraser qch; *(disease)* éradiquer qch; *Br* **stamped addressed envelope,** *Am* **stamped self-addressed envelope** enveloppe *f* timbrée libellée à ses noms et adresse

3 *vi* **to s. on sth** écraser qch; *Fam* **stamping ground** lieu *m* favori

stampede [stæmˈpiːd] **1** *n* débandade *f*

2 *vi* se ruer

stance [stɑːns] *n* position *f*

stand [stænd] **1** *n (opinion)* position *f*; *(support)* support *m*; *(stall)* étal *m*; *(at exhibition)* stand *m*; *(at sports ground)* tribune *f*; **to take a s.** prendre position

2 *(pt & pp stood)* *vt (pain, journey)* supporter; *(put straight)* mettre debout; **to s. a chance** avoir des chances; **to s. one's ground** tenir bon; **I can't s. him** je ne peux pas le supporter; **I can't s. it** je ne supporte pas ça; *Br* **to s. sb sth** *(pay for)* payer qch à qn

3 *vi (be upright)* se tenir debout; *(get up)* se mettre debout; *(remain)* rester debout; *(of building)* se trouver; *(of object)* être; **to s. still** se tenir immobile; **to leave sth to s.** *(liquid)* laisser qch reposer; **to s. to do sth** risquer de faire qch; **inflation stands at...** l'inflation s'élève à...; **the offer still stands** l'offre tient toujours

▸ **stand about, stand around** *vi (in street)*

traîner ▸**stand aside** *vi* s'écarter ▸**stand back** *vi* reculer ▸**stand by 1** *vt insep (opinion)* s'en tenir à; *(person)* soutenir **2** *vi (do nothing)* rester sans rien faire; *(be ready)* être prêt ▸**stand down** *vi (withdraw)* se retirer ▸**stand for** *vt insep (mean)* signifier; *(represent)* représenter; *Br (be candidate for)* être candidat à; *(tolerate)* supporter ▸**stand in for** *vt insep (replace)* remplacer ▸**stand out** *vi (be visible)* ressortir (**against** sur) ▸**stand over** *vt insep (watch closely)* surveiller ▸**stand up 1** *vt sep* mettre debout; *Fam* **to s. sb up** poser un lapin à qn **2** *vi (get up)* se lever ▸**stand up for** *vt insep (defend)* défendre ▸**stand up to** *vt insep (resist)* résister à; *(defend oneself against)* tenir tête à

standard¹ ['stændəd] **1** *n (norm)* norme *f*; *(level)* niveau *m*; *(of weight, gold)* étalon *m*; **standards** principes *mpl* moraux; **to be** *or* **come up to s.** *(of person)* être à la hauteur; *(of work)* être au niveau; **s. of living, living standards** niveau de vie

2 *adj (average)* ordinaire; *(model, size)* standard *inv*; *(weight)* étalon *inv*; *(dictionary, book)* classique; **it's s. practice** c'est une pratique courante; *Br* **s. lamp** lampadaire *m* •**standardize** *vt* standardiser

standard² ['stændəd] *n (flag)* étendard *m*

stand-by ['stændbaɪ] **1** *(pl* -**bys**) *n* **on s.** *(troops, emergency services)* prêt à intervenir **2** *adj (battery)* de réserve; *(plane ticket)* en stand-by

stand-in ['stændɪn] *n* remplaçant, -ante *mf* (**for** de); *(actor)* doublure *f* (**for** de)

standing ['stændɪŋ] **1** *adj (upright)* debout; *(permanent)* permanent; **I have a s. invitation** je peux y aller quand je veux; **s. joke** plaisanterie *f* classique; *Br* **s. order** virement *m* automatique

2 *n (reputation)* réputation *f*; *(social, professional)* rang *m*; **a friendship of six years' s.** une amitié de six ans; **of long s.** de longue date

stand-offish [stænd'ɒfɪʃ] *adj* distant

standpoint ['stændpɔɪnt] *n* point *m* de vue

standstill ['stændstɪl] *n* **to bring sth to a s.** immobiliser qch; **to come to a s.** s'immobiliser; **at a s.** immobile; *(negotiations, industry)* paralysé

stand-up ['stændʌp] *adj* **s. comic** *or* **comedian** comique *m* de scène

stank [stæŋk] *pt of* **stink**

stanza ['stænzə] *n* strophe *f*

staple¹ ['steɪpəl] *adj (basic)* de base; **s. food** *or* **diet** nourriture *f* de base

staple² ['steɪpəl] **1** *n (for paper)* agrafe *f* **2** *vt* agrafer •**stapler** *n (for paper)* agrafeuse *f*

star [stɑː(r)] **1** *n* étoile *f*; *(famous person)* star *f*; **the Stars and Stripes, the S.-Spangled Banner** la bannière étoilée; *Br* **four-s. (petrol)** du super; **s. player** vedette *f*; **s. sign** signe *m* du zodiaque

2 *(pt & pp* -**rr-**) *vt (of film)* avoir pour vedette

3 *vi (of actor, actress)* être la vedette (**in** de)

starboard ['stɑːbəd] *n Naut* tribord *m*

starch [stɑːtʃ] **1** *n* amidon *m* **2** *vt* amidonner •**starchy** (-**ier**, -**iest**) *adj Fam (manner, person)* guindé; **s. food(s)** féculents *mpl*

stardom ['stɑːdəm] *n* célébrité *f*

stare [steə(r)] **1** *n* regard *m* fixe **2** *vt* **to be staring sb in the face** *(be obvious)* crever les yeux à qn **3** *vi* **to s. at sb/sth** fixer qn/qch (du regard)

starfish ['stɑːfɪʃ] *n* étoile *f* de mer

stark [stɑːk] **1** (-**er**, -**est**) *adj (place)* désolé; *(fact, reality)* brutal; **to be in s. contrast to** contraster nettement avec; **the s. truth** la vérité toute nue

2 *adv* **s. naked** complètement nu •**starkers** *adj Br Fam* à poil

starling ['stɑːlɪŋ] *n* étourneau *m*

starlit ['stɑːlɪt] *adj* étoilé

starry ['stɑːrɪ] (-**ier**, -**iest**) *adj* étoilé •**starry-'eyed** *adj* naïf (*f* naïve)

start¹ [stɑːt] **1** *n* début *m*; *(of race)* départ *m*; **for a s.** pour commencer; **from the s.** dès le début; **to make a s.** commencer; **to give sb a 10 m s.** donner 10 m d'avance à qn

2 *vt* commencer; *(packet, conversation)* entamer; *(fashion, campaign, offensive)* lancer; *(engine, vehicle)* mettre en marche; *(business)* fonder; **to s. a war** provoquer une guerre; **to s. a fire** *(deliberately)* *(in grate)* allumer un feu; *(accidentally)* provoquer un incendie; **to s. doing** *or* **to do sth** commencer à faire qch

3 *vi* commencer (**with sth** par qch; **by doing** par faire); *(of vehicle)* démarrer; *(leave)* partir (**for** pour); *(in job)* débuter; **to s. with** *(firstly)* pour commencer; **starting from now/10 euros** à partir de maintenant/10 euros •**starting** *adj (point, line, salary)* de départ; **s. post** *(in race)* ligne *f* de départ; **s. place** point *m* de départ

▸**start off 1** *vt sep* **to s. sb off** *(in business)*

aider qn à démarrer 2 *vi (leave)* partir (**for** pour); *(in job)* débuter ▸ **start out** *vi (begin)* débuter; *(on journey)* se mettre en route ▸ **start up 1** *vt sep (engine, vehicle)* mettre en marche; *(business)* fonder **2** *vi (of engine, vehicle)* démarrer

start² [stɑːt] **1** *n (movement)* sursaut *m*; **to give sb a s.** faire sursauter qn **2** *vi* sursauter

starter ['stɑːtə(r)] *n (in vehicle)* démarreur *m*; *(in meal)* entrée *f*; *(runner)* partant, -ante *mf*; *(official in race)* starter *m*; *Fam* **for starters** *(firstly)* pour commencer

startle ['stɑːtəl] *vt* faire sursauter

starvation [stɑːˈveɪʃən] **1** *n* faim *f* **2** *adj (wage, ration)* de misère; **to be on a s. diet** *(to lose weight)* suivre un régime draconien

starve [stɑːv] **1** *vt (make suffer)* faire souffrir de la faim; *Fig (deprive)* priver (**of** de); **to s. sb to death** laisser qn mourir de faim **2** *vi (suffer)* souffrir de la faim; **to s. to death** mourir de faim; *Fam* **I'm starving!** je meurs de faim!

stash [stæʃ] *vt Fam* **to s. away** *(hide)* cacher; *(save up)* mettre de côté

state¹ [steɪt] **1** *n* (**a**) *(condition)* état *m*; *(situation)* situation *f*; **not in a (fit) s. to, in no (fit) s. to** hors d'état de; **in (quite) a s.** *(bad shape)* dans un drôle d'état; **to lie in s.** *(of body)* être exposé (**b**) **S.** *(nation)* État *m*; *Fam* **the States** les États-Unis *mpl* **2** *adj (secret, document)* d'État; *(security)* de l'État; *Br (school, education)* public, -ique; **s. visit** voyage *m* officiel; *Am* **S. Department** ≃ ministère *m* des Affaires étrangères ▸ **stateless** *adj* apatride; **s. person** apatride *mf* ▸ **'state-'owned** *adj* étatisé

state² [steɪt] *vt* déclarer (**that** que); *(opinion)* formuler; *(problem)* exposer; *(time, date)* fixer

stately ['steɪtlɪ] (**-ier, -iest**) *adj* imposant; *Br* **s. home** château *m*

statement ['steɪtmənt] *n* déclaration *f*; *(in court)* déposition *f*; (**bank) s., s. of account** relevé *m* de compte

state-of-the-art ['steɪtəvðiːˈɑːt] *adj (technology)* de pointe; *(computer, television)* ultramoderne

statesman ['steɪtsmən] (*pl* **-men**) *n* homme *m* d'État ▸ **statesmanship** *n* diplomatie *f*

static ['stætɪk] **1** *adj* statique **2** *n* électricité *f* statique

station ['steɪʃən] **1** *n (for trains)* gare *f*;

(underground) station *f*; *(position)* & *Mil* poste *m*; *(social)* rang *m*; **coach s.** gare *f* routière; **police s.** poste *m* de police; **space/radio s.** station *f* spatiale/de radio; *Am* **s. wagon** break *m* **2** *vt (position)* placer; **to be stationed at/in** *(of troops)* être en garnison à/en ▸ **station master** *n Rail* chef *m* de gare

stationary ['steɪʃənərɪ] *adj (vehicle)* à l'arrêt; *(person)* immobile

stationer ['steɪʃənə(r)] *n* papetier, -ière *mf*; **s.'s (shop)** papeterie *f* ▸ **stationery** *n (articles)* articles *mpl* de bureau; *(paper)* papier *m*

statistic [stəˈtɪstɪk] *n (fact)* statistique *f*; **statistics** *(science)* la statistique ▸ **statistical** *adj* statistique

statue ['stætjuː] *n* statue *f* ▸ **statuesque** [-tʃʊˈesk] *adj* sculptural

stature ['stætʃə(r)] *n (height)* stature *f*; *Fig (importance)* envergure *f*

status ['steɪtəs] *n (position)* situation *f*; *(legal, official)* statut *m*; *(prestige)* prestige *m*; **s. symbol** marque *f* de prestige; **s. quo** statu quo *m inv*

statute ['stætʃuːt] *n (law)* loi *f*; **statutes** *(of institution, club)* statuts *mpl* ▸ **statutory** [-tʃʊtərɪ] *adj (right, duty)* statutaire; *Br* **s. holiday** fête *f* légale

staunch [stɔːntʃ] (**-er, -est**) *adj (resolute)* convaincu; *(supporter)* ardent ▸ **staunchly** *adv* résolument

stave [steɪv] *n Mus* portée *f* **2** *vt* **to s. sth off** *(disaster, danger)* conjurer qch; **to s. off hunger** tromper la faim

stay [steɪ] **1** *n (visit)* séjour *m* **2** *vi (remain)* rester; *(reside)* loger; *(visit)* séjourner; **to s. put** ne pas bouger ▸ **staying power** *n* endurance *f* ▸ **stay away** *vi* ne pas s'approcher (**from** de); **to s. away from school** ne pas aller à l'école ▸ **stay behind** *vi* rester en arrière ▸ **stay in** *vi (at home)* rester à la maison; *(of nail, screw, tooth)* tenir ▸ **stay out** *vi (outside)* rester dehors; *(not come home)* ne pas rentrer; **to s. out of sth** *(not interfere in)* ne pas se mêler de qch; *(avoid)* éviter qch ▸ **stay up** *vi (at night)* ne pas se coucher; *(of fence)* tenir; **to s. up late** se coucher tard ▸ **stay with** *vt insep (plan, idea)* ne pas lâcher

St Bernard [*Br* səntˈbɜːnəd, *Am* seɪntbərˈnɑːrd] *n (dog)* saint-bernard *m inv*

stead [sted] *n* **to stand sb in good s.** être bien utile à qn; **in sb's s.** à la place de qn

steadfast ['stedfɑːst] *adj* dévoué; *(opponent)* constant

steady ['stedɪ] **1** (**-ier, -iest**) *adj (firm,*

stable) stable; *(hand, voice)* assuré; *(progress, speed, demand)* constant; *(relationship)* durable; **to have a s. boyfriend** avoir un copain; **a s. flood** *or* **stream of insults** un flot ininterrompu d'insultes; **to be s. on one's feet** être solide sur ses jambes
   2 *adv Fam* **to go s. with sb** sortir avec qn
   3 *vt* faire tenir; **to s. one's nerves** se calmer; **to s. oneself** retrouver son équilibre ● **steadily** *adv (gradually)* progressivement; *(regularly)* régulièrement; *(continuously)* sans arrêt; *(walk)* d'un pas assuré

steak [steɪk] *n (beef)* steak *m*; *Br* **s. and kidney pie** = tourte aux rognons et à la viande de bœuf ● **steakhouse** *n* grill *m*

steal¹ [stiːl] *(pt* **stole,** *pp* **stolen)** *vti* voler (**from sb** à qn)

steal² [stiːl] *(pt* **stole,** *pp* **stolen)** *vi* **to s. in/out** entrer/sortir furtivement ● **stealth** [stelθ] *n* **by s.** furtivement ● **stealthy** ['stelθɪ] *(-ier, -iest) adj* furtif, -ive

steam [stiːm] **1** *n* vapeur *f*; *(on glass)* buée *f*; *Fam* **to let off s.** se défouler; **s. engine/iron** locomotive *f*/fer *m* à vapeur
   2 *vt (food)* cuire à la vapeur; **to get steamed up** *(of glass)* se couvrir de buée; *Fam (of person)* s'énerver
   3 *vi (give off steam)* fumer; **to s. up** *(of glass)* s'embuer ● **steamer** *n* bateau *m* à vapeur; *(for food)* panier *m* pour cuisson à la vapeur

steamroller ['stiːmrəʊlə(r)] *n* rouleau *m* compresseur

steamship ['stiːmʃɪp] *n* bateau *m* à vapeur

steamy ['stiːmɪ] *(-ier, -iest) adj* plein de vapeur; *(window)* embué; *Fam (love affair, relationship)* torride

steel [stiːl] **1** *n* acier *m*; **s. industry** sidérurgie *f*; **s. mill** aciérie *f*
   2 *vt* **to s. oneself** s'armer de courage; **to s. oneself against failure** s'endurcir contre l'échec ● **steelworks** *n* aciérie *f*

steep [stiːp] **1** *(-er, -est) adj (stairs, slope)* raide; *(hill, path)* escarpé; *Fig (price)* excessif, -ive
   2 *vt (soak)* tremper (**in** dans); *Fig* **steeped in** *(history, prejudice)* imprégné de ● **steeply** *adv (rise)* en pente raide; *Fig (of prices)* excessivement

steeple ['stiːpəl] *n* clocher *m*

steeplechase ['stiːpəltʃeɪs] *n* steeplechase *m*

steer [stɪə(r)] **1** *vt* diriger
   2 *vi (of person)* conduire; *(of ship)* se diriger (**for** vers); **to s. towards** faire

route vers; **to s. clear of sb/sth** éviter qn/qch ● **steering** *n (in vehicle)* direction *f*; **s. wheel** volant *m*

stem [stem] **1** *n (of plant)* tige *f*; *(of glass)* pied *m*
   2 *(pt & pp* **-mm-)** *vt (stop)* arrêter; **to s. the flow** *or* **tide of sth** endiguer le flot de qch
   3 *vi* **to s. from sth** provenir de qch

stench [stentʃ] *n* puanteur *f*

stencil ['stensəl] **1** *n (metal, plastic)* pochoir *m*; *(paper, for typing)* stencil *m*
   2 *(Br* **-ll-,** *Am* **-l-)** *vt (notes)* polycopier

stenographer [stə'nɒɡrəfə(r)] *n Am* sténodactylo *f*

step [step] **1** *n (movement, sound)* pas *m*; *(of stairs)* marche *f*; *(on train, bus)* marchepied *m*; *(doorstep)* pas de la porte; *Fig (action)* mesure *f*; **(flight of) steps** *(indoors)* escalier *m*; *(outdoors)* perron *m*; *Br* **(pair of) steps** *(ladder)* escabeau *m*; **s. by s.** pas à pas; **to keep in s.** marcher au pas; *Fig* **to be in s. with** *(of opinions)* être en accord avec
   2 *(pt & pp* **-pp-)** *vi (walk)* marcher (**on** sur); **s. this way!** (venez) par ici! ● **stepbrother** *n* demi-frère *m* ● **stepdaughter** *n* belle-fille *f* ● **stepfather** *n* beau-père *m* ● **stepmother** *n* belle-mère *f* ● **stepsister** *n* demi-sœur *f* ● **stepson** *n* beau-fils *m*
▸ **step aside** *vi* s'écarter ▸ **step back** *vi* reculer ▸ **step down** *vi* descendre (**from** de); *Fig (withdraw)* se retirer ▸ **step forward** *vi* faire un pas en avant ▸ **step in** *vi (enter)* entrer; *(into car)* monter; *Fig (intervene)* intervenir ▸ **step into** *vt insep (car)* monter dans ▸ **step off** *vt insep (chair)* descendre de ▸ **step out** *vi (of car)* descendre (**of** de) ▸ **step over** *vt insep (obstacle)* enjamber ▸ **step up** *vt sep (increase)* augmenter; *(speed up)* accélérer

stepladder ['steplædə(r)] *n* escabeau *m*

stepping-stone ['stepɪŋstəʊn] *n (in career)* tremplin *m*

stereo ['sterɪəʊ] **1** *(pl* **-os)** *n (hi-fi, record player)* chaîne *f* stéréo; *(sound)* stéréo *f*; **in s.** en stéréo
   2 *adj (record)* stéréo *inv*; *(broadcast)* en stéréo ● **stereophonic** [-rɪə'fɒnɪk] *adj* stéréophonique

stereotype ['sterɪətaɪp] *n* stéréotype *m* ● **stereotyped** *adj* stéréotypé

sterile [*Br* 'steraɪl, *Am* 'sterəl] *adj* stérile ● **sterility** [stə'rɪlɪtɪ] *n* stérilité *f*

sterilize ['sterəlaɪz] *vt* stériliser ● **sterili'zation** *n* stérilisation *f*

sterling ['stɜːlɪŋ] **1** *n Br (currency)* livre *f* sterling

2 adj (silver) fin; Fig (quality, person) sûr

stern¹ [stɜːn] (-er, -est) adj sévère

stern² [stɜːn] n (of ship) arrière m

steroid ['stɪərɔɪd] n stéroïde m

stethoscope ['steθəskəʊp] n stéthoscope m

Stetson ['stetsən] n chapeau m à larges bords

stevedore ['stiːvədɔː(r)] n docker m

stew [stjuː] **1** n ragoût m; Fig **to be in a s.** être dans le pétrin
2 vt (meat) faire cuire en ragoût; (fruit) faire de la compote de; **stewed fruit** compote f
3 vi cuire • **stewing** adj (pears, apples) à cuire; **s. steak** bœuf m à braiser

steward ['stjuːəd] n (on plane, ship) steward m • **stewardess** n (on plane) hôtesse f

stick¹ [stɪk] n (piece of wood, chalk, dynamite) bâton m; (for walking) canne f; Fam Pej **in the sticks** (countryside) à la cambrousse; Br Fam **to give sb some s.** (scold) engueuler qn

stick² [stɪk] **1** (pt & pp **stuck**) vt (glue) coller; Fam (put) fourrer; Fam (tolerate) supporter; **to s. sth into sth** fourrer qch dans qch; Fig **to s. to one's guns** ne pas en démordre
2 vi coller (**to** à); (of food in pan) attacher (**to** dans); (of drawer) se coincer; **to s. to the facts** s'en tenir aux faits; **to s. to one's principles** rester fidèle à ses principes • **sticking plaster** n Br sparadrap m
▸ **stick around** vi Fam (hang around) rester dans les parages ▸ **stick by** vt insep rester fidèle à ▸ **stick down** vt sep (envelope, stamp) coller; Fam (put down) poser ▸ **stick on** vt sep (stamp, label) coller ▸ **stick out 1** vt sep (tongue) tirer; Fam (head or arm from window) sortir; Fam **to s. it out** (resist) tenir bon **2** vi (of shirt) dépasser; (of tooth) avancer ▸ **stick up** vt sep (notice) coller; Fam (hand) lever ▸ **stick up for** vt insep défendre

sticker ['stɪkə(r)] n autocollant m

stickler ['stɪklə(r)] n **to be a s. for sth** être à cheval sur qch

stick-on ['stɪkɒn] adj autocollant

stick-up ['stɪkʌp] n Fam braquage m

sticky ['stɪkɪ] (-ier, -iest) adj collant; (label) adhésif, -ive; Fig (problem, matter) délicat

stiff [stɪf] (-er, -est) adj raide; (joint) ankylosé; (brush, paste) dur; Fig (person) guindé; (difficult) difficile; (price) élevé;

(whisky) bien tassé; **to have a s. neck** avoir un torticolis; **to feel s.** être courbaturé; Fam **to be bored s.** s'ennuyer à mourir; Fam **frozen s.** complètement gelé

stiffen ['stɪfən] **1** vt raidir
2 vi se raidir

stiffly ['stɪflɪ] adv Fig (coldly) froidement • **stiffness** n raideur f; (hardness) dureté f

stifle ['staɪfəl] **1** vt (feeling, person) étouffer
2 vi **it's stifling** on étouffe

stigma ['stɪgmə] n (moral stain) flétrissure f; **there's no s. attached to** il n'y a aucune honte à • **stigmatize** vt stigmatiser

stile [staɪl] n échalier m

stiletto [stɪ'letəʊ] adj Br **s. heels** talons mpl aiguille

still¹ [stɪl] adv encore, toujours; (even) encore; (nevertheless) tout de même; **better s., s. better** encore mieux

still² [stɪl] **1** (-er, -est) adj (not moving) immobile; (calm) calme; Br (drink) non gazeux, -euse; **to stand s.** rester tranquille; **s. life** nature f morte
2 n (photo of film) photo f (tirée d'un film); **in the s. of the night** dans le silence de la nuit • **stillborn** (baby) adj mort-né (f mort-née) • **stillness** n immobilité f; (calm) calme m

still³ [stɪl] n (distilling equipment) alambic m

stilt [stɪlt] n (for walking) échasse f

stilted ['stɪltɪd] adj (speech, person) guindé

stimulate ['stɪmjʊleɪt] vt stimuler • **stimulant** n stimulant m • **stimu'lation** n stimulation f • **stimulus** (pl **-li** [-laɪ]) n (encouragement) stimulant m; (physiological) stimulus m inv

sting [stɪŋ] **1** n piqûre f; (insect's organ) dard m
2 (pt & pp **stung**) vt (of insect, ointment, wind) piquer; Fig (of remark) blesser
3 vi piquer • **stinging** adj (pain) cuisant; (remark) cinglant

stingy ['stɪndʒɪ] (-ier, -iest) adj avare; **to be s. with** (money, praise) être avare de; (food, wine) lésiner sur • **stinginess** n avarice f

stink [stɪŋk] **1** n puanteur f; Fam **to cause or make a s.** (trouble) faire tout un foin
2 (pt & pp **stank** or **stunk**, pp **stunk**) vi puer; Fam (of book, film) être infect; **to s. of smoke** empester la fumée
3 vt **to s. out** (room) empester • **stinker** n Fam (person) peau f de vache; (question, task) vacherie f • **stinking** adj Fam puant

stint [stɪnt] **1** *n (period)* période *f* de travail; *(share)* part *f* de travail
2 *vi* **to s. on sth** lésiner sur qch
stipend ['staɪpend] *n* traitement *m*
stipulate ['stɪpjʊleɪt] *vt* stipuler (**that** que) • **stipu'lation** *n* stipulation *f*
stir [stɜː(r)] **1** *n* agitation *f*; **to give sth a s.** remuer qch; *Fig* **to cause a s.** faire du bruit
2 *(pt & pp* **-rr-)** *vt (coffee, leaves)* remuer; *Fig (excite)* exciter; *(incite)* inciter (**sb to do** qn à faire); **to s. oneself** se secouer; **to s. sth up** *(leaves)* remuer qch; *(rebellion)* attiser qch; **to s. up trouble** semer la zizanie; **to s. up trouble for sb** attirer des ennuis à qn; **to s. things up** envenimer les choses
3 *vi (move)* remuer, bouger • **stirring** *adj (speech)* émouvant
stirrup ['stɪrəp] *n* étrier *m*
stitch [stɪtʃ] **1** *n* point *m*; *(in knitting)* maille *f*; *(in wound)* point de suture; *(sharp pain)* point de côté; *Fam* **to be in stitches** être plié (de rire)
2 *vt* **to s. (up)** *(sew up)* coudre; *Med* recoudre; *Fam* **to s. sb up** *(incriminate)* faire porter le chapeau à qn
stoat [stəʊt] *n* hermine *f*
stock [stɒk] **1** *n (supply)* provisions *fpl*; *Com* stock *m*; *Fin* valeurs *fpl*; *(soup)* bouillon *m*; *(cattle)* bétail *m*; *Fin* **stocks and shares** valeurs mobilières; *Hist* **the stocks** le pilori; **in s.** *(goods)* en stock; **out of s.** *(goods)* épuisé; **to be of German s.** être de souche allemande; *Fig* **to take s.** faire le point (**of** de); **s. reply/size** réponse *f*/taille *f* classique; **s. phrase** expression *f* toute faite; **the S. Exchange** *or* **Market** la Bourse
2 *vt (sell)* vendre; *(keep in store)* stocker; **to s. (up)** *(shop)* approvisionner; *(fridge, cupboard)* remplir; **well-stocked** *(shop)* bien approvisionné; *(fridge)* bien rempli
3 *vi* **to s. up** s'approvisionner (**with** en) • **stockbroker** ['stɒkbrəʊkə(r)] *n* agent *m* de change • **stockcar** *n* stock-car *m* • **stockholder** *n Fin* actionnaire *mf* • **stockist** *n* stockiste *m* • **stockpile** *vt* faire des réserves de • **stockroom** *n* réserve *f*, magasin *m* • **stocktaking** *n Br Com* inventaire *m*
stockade [stɒ'keɪd] *n* palissade *f*
stocking ['stɒkɪŋ] *n (garment)* bas *m*
stocky ['stɒkɪ] (**-ier, -iest**) *adj* trapu
stodge [stɒdʒ] *n Fam (food)* étouffe-chrétien *m inv* • **stodgy** (**-ier, -iest**) *adj Fam (food)* bourratif, -ive; *Fig (book)* indigeste

stoic ['stəʊɪk] *adj & n* stoïque *(mf)* • **stoical** *adj* stoïque • **stoicism** [-ɪsɪzəm] *n* stoïcisme *m*
stoke [stəʊk] *vt (fire)* entretenir; *(furnace)* alimenter; *(engine)* chauffer • **stoker** *n (of boiler, engine)* chauffeur *m*
stole¹ [stəʊl] *n (shawl)* étole *f*
stole² [stəʊl] *pt of* **steal**
stolen ['stəʊlən] *pp of* **steal**
stolid ['stɒlɪd] *adj* impassible
stomach ['stʌmək] **1** *n* ventre *m*; *(organ)* estomac *m*
2 *vt (put up with)* supporter • **stomachache** *n* mal *m* de ventre; **to have a s.** avoir mal au ventre
stone [stəʊn] **1** *n* pierre *f*; *(pebble)* caillou *m*; *(in fruit)* noyau *m*; *(in kidney)* calcul *m*; *Br (unit of weight)* = 6,348 kg; *Fig* **it's a stone's throw away** c'est à deux pas d'ici
2 *vt (person)* lapider; *(fruit)* dénoyauter • **stonemason** *n* maçon *m*
stone- [stəʊn] *pref* complètement • **'stone-'broke** *adj Am Fam* fauché • **'stone-'cold** *adj* glacé • **'stone-'dead** *adj* raide mort • **'stone-'deaf** *adj* sourd comme un pot
stoned [stəʊnd] *adj Fam (on drugs)* défoncé (**on** à)
stony ['stəʊnɪ] (**-ier, -iest**) *adj (path)* cailouteux, -euse; *Br Fam* **s. broke** *(penniless)* fauché
stood [stʊd] *pt & pp of* **stand**
stooge [stuːdʒ] *n (actor)* comparse *mf*; *Pej (flunkey)* larbin *m*; *Pej (dupe)* pigeon *m*
stool [stuːl] *n* tabouret *m*
stoop¹ [stuːp] *n Am (in front of house)* perron *m*; **to have a s.** être voûté
stoop² [stuːp] *vi* se baisser; *Fig* **to s. to doing/to sth** s'abaisser à faire/à qch
stop [stɒp] **1** *n (place, halt)* arrêt *m*; *(for plane, ship)* escale *f*; **to put a s. to sth** mettre fin à qch; **to make a s.** *(of vehicle)* s'arrêter; *(of plane)* faire escale; **to bring a car to a s.** arrêter une voiture; **to come to a s.** s'arrêter; **without a s.** sans arrêt; *Br* **s. light** *(on vehicle)* stop *m*; **s. sign** *(on road)* stop
2 *(pt & pp* **-pp-)** *vt* arrêter; *(end)* mettre fin à; *(cheque)* faire opposition à; **to s. sb/sth from doing sth** empêcher qn/qch de faire qch
3 *vi* s'arrêter; *(of pain, bleeding)* cesser; *(stay)* rester; **to s. eating** s'arrêter de manger; **to s. snowing** cesser de neiger • **stopcock** *n Br* robinet *m* d'arrêt • **stopgap 1** *n* bouche-trou *m* **2** *adj (solution)* intérimaire • **stopoff** *n* halte *f*; *(in plane*

journey) escale *f* • **stopover** *n* arrêt *m*; *(in plane journey)* escale *f*; **to make a s.** faire halte; *(of plane)* faire escale • **stop-press** *adj* de dernière minute • **stopwatch** *n* chronomètre *m*
▸ **stop by** *vi (visit)* passer (**sb's** chez qn)
▸ **stop off, stop over** *vi (on journey)* s'arrêter ▸ **stop up** *vt sep (sink, pipe, leak)* boucher

stoppage ['stɒpɪdʒ] *n (of flow, traffic)* arrêt *m*; *(strike)* débrayage *m*; *Br (in pay)* retenue *f*; *(blockage)* obstruction *f*; *Sport* **s. time** arrêts *mpl* de jeu

stopper ['stɒpə(r)] *n* bouchon *m*

store [stɔː(r)] **1** *n (supply)* provision *f*; *Fig (of knowledge)* fonds *m*; *(warehouse)* entrepôt *m*; *Br (shop)* grand magasin *m*, *Am* magasin *m*; **to have sth in s. for sb** réserver qch à qn; **to keep sth in s.** garder qch en réserve; **to set great s. by sth** faire grand cas de qch
2 *vt (in warehouse)* stocker; *(furniture)* entreposer; *(food)* ranger; *(heat)* emmagasiner; *Comptr (in memory)* mettre en mémoire • **storage** [-rɪdʒ] *n* emmagasinage *m*; **s. space** espace *m* de rangement; *Comptr* **s. capacity** capacité *f* de mémoire
▸ **store away** *vt sep (put away, file away)* ranger; *(furniture)* entreposer ▸ **store up** *vt sep* accumuler

storekeeper ['stɔːkiːpə(r)] *n Am (shopkeeper)* commerçant, -ante *mf*; *Br (warehouseman)* magasinier *m*

storeroom ['stɔːruːm] *n (in house)* débarras *m*; *(in office, shop)* réserve *f*

storey ['stɔːrɪ] *(pl* -**eys**) *n Br (of building)* étage *m*

stork [stɔːk] *n* cigogne *f*

storm [stɔːm] **1** *n (bad weather)* tempête *f*; *(thunderstorm)* orage *m*; **s. cloud** nuée *f* d'orage; *Fig* **a s. of protest** une tempête de protestations; *Mil* **to take sth by s.** prendre qch d'assaut; *Fig* **she took London by s.** elle a eu un succès foudroyant à Londres
2 *vt (of soldiers, police)* prendre d'assaut
3 *vi* **to s. out** *(angrily)* sortir comme une furie • **stormy** (-**ier,** -**iest**) *adj (weather, meeting)* orageux, -euse; *(wind)* d'orage

story¹ ['stɔːrɪ] *(pl* -**ies**) *n* histoire *f*; *(newspaper article)* article *m*; **s. line** *(plot)* intrigue *f* • **storybook** *n* livre *m* d'histoires • **storyteller** *n* conteur, -euse *mf*

story² ['stɔːrɪ] *(pl* -**ies**) *n Am (of building)* étage *m*

stout [staʊt] **1** (-**er,** -**est**) *adj (person)* corpulent; *(resistance)* acharné; *(shoes)* solide

2 *n Br (beer)* bière *f* brune • **stoutness** *n* corpulence *f*

stove [stəʊv] *n (for cooking)* cuisinière *f*; *(for heating)* poêle *m*

stow [stəʊ] **1** *vt (cargo)* arrimer; **to s. sth away** *(put away)* ranger qch
2 *vi* **to s. away** *(on ship)* voyager clandestinement • **stowaway** *n (on ship)* passager, -ère *mf* clandestin(e)

straddle ['strædəl] *vt (chair, fence)* se mettre à califourchon sur; *(step over, span)* enjamber

straggle ['strægəl] *vi* (**a**) *(of hair)* pendouiller (**b**) *(lag behind)* être à la traîne; **to s. in** entrer par petits groupes • **straggler** *n* retardataire *mf*

straight [streɪt] **1** (-**er,** -**est**) *adj* droit; *(hair)* raide; *(honest)* honnête; *(answer)* clair; *(consecutive)* consécutif, -ive; *(conventional)* conformiste; *Fam (heterosexual)* hétéro; **let's get this s.** comprenons-nous bien; **to keep a s. face** garder son sérieux; **to be s. with sb** jouer franc jeu avec qn
2 *n* **the s.** *(on racetrack)* la ligne droite
3 *adv (in straight line)* droit; *(directly)* directement; *(immediately)* tout de suite; **s. away** *(at once)* tout de suite; **s. out, s. off** sans hésiter; **s. opposite** juste en face; *Br* **s. ahead** *or* **on** *(walk)* tout droit; **to look s. ahead** regarder droit devant soi; **to drink whisky s.** boire son whisky sec

straightaway [streɪtə'weɪ] *adv* tout de suite

straighten ['streɪtən] *vt* **to s. (out)** *(wire)* redresser; **to s. (up)** *(tie, hair, room)* arranger; **to s. things out** arranger les choses

straight-faced ['streɪt'feɪst] *adj* impassible

straightforward [streɪt'fɔːwəd] *adj (easy, clear)* simple; *(frank)* franc (*f* franche)

strain¹ [streɪn] **1** *n* tension *f*; *(mental stress)* stress *m*; *(on ankle)* foulure *f*
2 *vt* (**a**) *(rope, wire)* tendre excessivement; *(muscle)* se froisser; *(ankle, wrist)* se fouler; *(eyes)* fatiguer; *(voice)* forcer; *Fig (patience, friendship)* mettre à l'épreuve; **to s. one's ears** tendre l'oreille; **to s. one's back** se faire mal au dos; **to s. oneself** *(hurt oneself)* se faire mal; *(tire oneself)* se fatiguer (**b**) *(soup)* passer; *(vegetables)* égoutter
3 *vi* faire un effort (**to do** pour faire); **to s. at a rope** tirer sur une corde

strain² [streɪn] *n (of plant)* variété *f*; *(of virus)* souche *f*; *(streak)* tendance *f*

strained [streɪnd] *adj (muscle)* froissé; *(ankle, wrist)* foulé; *(relations)* tendu; *(laugh)* forcé

strainer ['streɪnə(r)] *n* passoire *f*

strait [streɪt] *n Geog* **strait(s)** détroit *m*; **in financial straits** dans l'embarras

straitjacket ['streɪtdʒækɪt] *n* camisole *f* de force

straitlaced ['streɪt'leɪst] *adj* collet monté *inv*

strand [strænd] *n (of wool)* brin *m*; *(of hair)* mèche *f*; *Fig (of story)* fil *m*

stranded ['strændɪd] *adj (person, vehicle)* en rade

strange [streɪndʒ] (**-er, -est**) *adj (odd)* bizarre; *(unknown)* inconnu ● **strangely** *adv* étrangement; **s. (enough), she...** chose étrange, elle... ● **strangeness** *n* étrangeté *f*

stranger ['streɪndʒə(r)] *n (unknown)* inconnu, -ue *mf*; *(outsider)* étranger, -ère *mf*; **he's a s. here** il n'est pas d'ici; **she's a s. to me** elle m'est inconnue

strangle ['stræŋɡəl] *vt* étrangler ● **strangler** *n* étrangleur, -euse *mf*

stranglehold ['stræŋɡəlhəʊld] *n* **to have a s. on sth** avoir la mainmise sur qch

strap [stræp] **1** *n* sangle *f*; *(on dress)* bretelle *f*; *(on watch)* bracelet *m*; *(on sandal)* lanière *f*
2 *(pt & pp* **-pp-**) *vt* **to s. (down** *or* **in)** attacher *(avec une sangle)*; **to s. sb in** attacher qn avec une ceinture de sécurité

strapping ['stræpɪŋ] *adj* robuste

stratagem ['strætədʒəm] *n* stratagème *m*

strategy ['strætədʒɪ] *(pl* **-ies**) *n* stratégie *f* ● **strategic** [strə'tiːdʒɪk] *adj* stratégique

stratum ['strɑːtəm] *(pl* **-ta** [-tə]) *n* couche *f*

straw [strɔː] *n (from wheat, for drinking)* paille *f*; **that's the last s.!** c'est le comble!

strawberry ['strɔːbərɪ] **1** *(pl* **-ies**) *n* fraise *f*
2 *adj (flavour, ice cream)* à la fraise; *(jam)* de fraises; *(tart)* aux fraises

stray [streɪ] **1** *adj (animal, bullet)* perdu; **a few s. cars** quelques rares voitures; **s. dog** chien *m* errant
2 *n (dog)* chien *m* errant; *(cat)* chat *m* égaré
3 *vi* s'égarer; **to s. from** *(subject, path)* s'écarter de; **don't s. too far** ne t'éloigne pas

streak [striːk] *n (of paint, dirt)* traînée *f*; *(of light)* rai *m*; *(in hair)* mèche *f*; **to have a mad s.** avoir une tendance à la folie; **to be**

on **a winning s.** être dans une période de chance; **s. of lightning** éclair *m* ● **streaked** *adj (marked)* strié; *(stained)* taché *(*with de*)* ● **streaky** (**-ier, -iest**) *adj* strié; *Br* **s. bacon** bacon *m* entrelardé

stream [striːm] **1** *n (brook)* ruisseau *m*; *(current)* courant *m*; *(of light, blood)* jet *m*; *(of tears)* torrent *m*; *(of people)* flot *m*
2 *vt* **to s. blood** ruisseler de sang; *Br Sch* **to s. pupils** répartir des élèves par niveaux
3 *vi* ruisseler *(*with de*)*; **to s. in** *(of sunlight, people)* entrer à flots

streamer ['striːmə(r)] *n (banner)* banderole *f*

streamline ['striːmlaɪn] *vt (work, method)* rationaliser ● **streamlined** *adj (shape)* aérodynamique; *(industry, production)* rationalisé

street [striːt] *n* rue *f*; **s. door** porte *f* d'entrée; **s. lamp, s. light** lampadaire *m*; **s. map** plan *m* des rues; *Fam* **s. cred** look *m* branché; *Br Fam* **that's (right) up my s.** c'est mon rayon; *Br Fam* **to be streets ahead** dépasser tout le monde ● **streetcar** *n Am (tram)* tramway *m* ● **streetwise** *adj Fam* dégourdi

strength [streŋθ] *n* force *f*; *(of wood, fabric)* solidité *f*; *Fig* **on the s. of** sur la base de; **in** *or* **at full s.** *(of troops)* au (grand) complet ● **strengthen** *vt (building, position)* renforcer; *(body, soul, limb)* fortifier

strenuous ['strenjʊəs] *adj (effort)* vigoureux, -euse; *(work)* fatigant; *(denial)* énergique ● **strenuously** *adv* énergiquement

strep [strep] *adj Am* **s. throat** forte angine *f*

stress [stres] **1** *n (physical)* tension *f*; *(mental)* stress *m*; *(emphasis)* & *Grammar* accent *m*; **under s.** *(person)* stressé, sous pression; *(relationship)* tendu
2 *vt* insister sur; *(word)* accentuer; **to s. that...** souligner que... ● **stressful** *adj* stressant ● **stress-related** *adj* **to be s.** être dû *(*f due*)* au stress

stretch [stretʃ] **1** *n (area, duration)* étendue *f*; *(period of time)* période *f*; *(of road)* tronçon *m*; **ten hours at a s.** dix heures d'affilée; **for a long s. of time** *(pendant)* longtemps; *Fam* **to do a three-year s.** *(in prison)* faire trois ans de prison
2 *vt (rope, neck)* tendre; *(shoe, rubber)* étirer; *Fig (meaning)* forcer; *(income, supplies)* faire durer; **to s. (out)** *(arm, leg)* tendre; *Fig* **to s. one's legs** se dégourdir les jambes; *Fig* **to s. sb** pousser qn à son

maximum; **we're fully stretched at the moment** nous sommes au maximum de nos capacités en ce moment

3 *vi (of person, elastic)* s'étirer; *(of influence)* s'étendre; **to s. (out)** *(of rope, plain)* s'étendre • **stretch marks** *npl* vergetures *fpl*

stretcher ['stretʃə(r)] *n* brancard *m*

strew [struː] *(pt* strewed, *pp* strewed *or* strewn [struːn]) *vt (scatter)* éparpiller; **strewn with** *(covered)* jonché de

stricken ['strɪkən] *adj (town, region)* sinistré; **s. with grief** accablé par le chagrin; **s. with illness** atteint de maladie

strict [strɪkt] (**-er, -est**) *adj (severe, absolute)* strict • **strictly** *adv* strictement; **s. forbidden** formellement interdit • **strictness** *n* sévérité *f*

stride [straɪd] **1** *n* pas *m*; *Fig* **to make great strides** faire de grands progrès

2 *(pt* strode) *vi* **to s. across** *or* **over** enjamber; **to s. along/out** avancer/sortir à grands pas; **to s. up and down a room** arpenter une pièce

strident ['straɪdənt] *adj* strident

strife [straɪf] *n inv* conflits *mpl*

strike [straɪk] **1** *n (of workers)* grève *f; (of ore, oil)* découverte *f; Mil* raid *m;* **to go (out) on s.** se mettre en grève

2 *(pt & pp* struck) *vt (hit, impress)* frapper; *(collide with)* heurter; *(gold, oil)* trouver; *(coin)* frapper; *(match)* craquer; **to s. the time** *(of clock)* sonner l'heure; **to s. a blow** donner un coup; **to s. a balance** trouver un équilibre; **to s. oil** trouver du pétrole; *Fam* **to s. it rich** faire fortune; **it strikes me that...** il me semble que... *(+ indicative)*; **how did it s. you?** quelle impression ça t'a fait?

3 *vi (of workers)* faire grève; *(attack)* attaquer; *Fig* **to s. home** faire mouche

▸ **strike at** *vt insep (attack)* attaquer

▸ **strike back** *vi (retaliate)* riposter

▸ **strike down** *vt sep (of illness)* terrasser; *(of bullet)* abattre ▸ **strike off** *vt sep (from list)* rayer **(from** de); **to be struck off** *(of doctor)* être radié ▸ **strike out** *vi* **to s. out at sb** essayer de frapper qn ▸ **strike up** *vt sep* **to s. up a friendship** se lier amitié **(with** avec qn)

striker ['straɪkə(r)] *n (worker)* gréviste *mf; Football* buteur *m*

striking ['straɪkɪŋ] *adj (impressive)* frappant • **strikingly** *adv (beautiful, intelligent)* extraordinairement

string [strɪŋ] **1** *n* ficelle *f; (of apron)* cordon *m; (of violin, racket)* corde *f; (of onions)* chapelet *m; (of questions)* série *f;*

s. of pearls collier *m* de perles; **s. of beads** collier; *(for praying)* chapelet; *Fig* **to pull strings** faire jouer ses relations; *Fig* **to pull strings for sb** pistonner qn

2 *adj (instrument, quartet)* à cordes; **s. bean** haricot *m* vert

3 *(pt & pp* strung) *vt (beads)* enfiler

4 *vi Fam* **to s. along** *(follow)* suivre • **stringed** *adj (musical instrument)* à cordes

stringent ['strɪndʒənt] *adj* rigoureux, -euse • **stringency** *n* rigueur *f*

stringy ['strɪŋɪ] (**-ier, -iest**) *adj* filandreux, -euse

strip [strɪp] **1** *n (piece)* bande *f; (of metal)* lame *f; (of sports team)* tenue *f;* **landing s.** piste *f* d'atterrissage; **s. cartoon** bande dessinée; *Br* **s. lighting** éclairage *m* au néon

2 *(pt & pp* **-pp-**) *vt (undress)* déshabiller; *(bed)* défaire; *(deprive)* dépouiller **(of** de); **stripped to the waist** torse nu; **to s. (down)** *(machine)* démonter; **to s. off** *(remove)* enlever

3 *vi* **to s. (off)** *(get undressed)* se déshabiller • **stripper** *n (woman)* strip-teaseuse *f;* **(paint) s.** décapant *m* • **striptease** *n* strip-tease *m*

stripe [straɪp] *n* rayure *f; (indicating rank)* galon *m* • **striped** *adj* rayé **(with** de) • **stripy** *adj (fabric, pattern)* rayé

strive [straɪv] *(pt* strove, *pp* striven ['strɪvən]) *vi* s'efforcer **(to do** de faire; **for** d'obtenir)

strobe [strəʊb] *adj* **s. lighting** éclairage *m* stroboscopique

strode [strəʊd] *pt of* stride

stroke [strəʊk] **1** *n (movement)* coup *m; (of pen)* trait *m; (of brush)* touche *f; (caress)* caresse *f; Med (illness)* attaque *f;* **(swimming) s.** nage *f;* **at a s.** d'un coup; **on the s. of nine** à neuf heures sonnantes; **s. of luck** coup de chance; **s. of genius** coup de génie; **you haven't done a s. of work** tu n'as rien fait; **four-s. engine** moteur *m* à quatre temps

2 *vt (caress)* caresser

stroll [strəʊl] **1** *n* promenade *f*

2 *vi* se promener; **to s. in** entrer sans se presser • **strolling** *adj (musician)* ambulant

stroller ['strəʊlə(r)] *n Am (for baby)* poussette *f*

strong [strɒŋ] **1** (**-er, -est**) *adj* fort; *(shoes, chair, nerves)* solide; *(interest)* vif *(f* vive); *(measures)* énergique; *(supporter)* ardent; **they were sixty s.** ils étaient au nombre de soixante

2 *adv* **to be going s.** aller toujours bien ● **strong-arm** *adj* **s. tactics** la manière forte ● **strong-box** *n* coffre-fort *m* ● **stronghold** *n* bastion *m* ● **strongly** *adv* (*protest, defend*) énergiquement; (*advise, remind, desire*) fortement; **s. built** solide; **to feel s. about sth** être convaincu de qch ● **strongroom** *n* chambre *f* forte ● ˈstrong-ˈwilled *adj* résolu

strove [strəʊv] *pt of* **strive**

struck [strʌk] *pt & pp of* **strike**

structure [ˈstrʌktʃə(r)] *n* structure *f*; (*building*) édifice *m* ● **structural** *adj* structural; (*building defect*) de construction; **s. damage** (*to building*) dégâts *mpl* de structure

struggle [ˈstrʌɡəl] **1** *n* (*fight*) lutte *f* (**to do** pour faire); **to put up a s.** résister; **to have a s. doing** *or* **to do sth** avoir du mal à faire qch
2 *vi* (*fight*) lutter (**with** avec); **to be struggling** (*financially*) avoir du mal; **to s. to do sth** s'efforcer de faire qch; **to s. out of** sortir péniblement de; **to s. into** entrer péniblement dans; **to s. along** *or* **on** se débrouiller

strum [strʌm] (*pt & pp* **-mm-**) *vt* (*guitar*) gratter

strung [strʌŋ] *pt & pp of* **string**

strut¹ [strʌt] (*pt & pp* **-tt-**) *vi* **to s.** (**about** *or* **around**) se pavaner

strut² [strʌt] *n* (*for frame*) étai *m*

stub [stʌb] **1** *n* (*of pencil, cigarette*) bout *m*; (*of cheque*) talon *m*
2 (*pt & pp* **-bb-**) *vt* **to s. one's toe** se cogner l'orteil (**on** *or* **against** contre); **to s. out** (*cigarette*) écraser

stubble [ˈstʌbəl] *n* (*on face*) barbe *f* de plusieurs jours

stubborn [ˈstʌbən] *adj* (*person*) têtu; (*determination*) farouche; (*stain*) rebelle ● **stubbornness** *n* (*of person*) entêtement *m*; (*of determination*) inflexibilité *f*

stubby [ˈstʌbɪ] (**-ier, -iest**) *adj* (*finger*) court et boudiné; (*person*) trapu

stucco [ˈstʌkəʊ] (*pl* **-os** *or* **-oes**) *n* stuc *m*

stuck [stʌk] **1** *pt & pp of* **stick²**
2 *adj* (*caught, jammed*) coincé; **s. in bed/indoors** cloué au lit/chez soi; **to get s.** être coincé; **I'm s. for an answer** je ne sais que répondre; **to be s. with sb/sth** se farcir qn/qch

stuck-up [stʌˈkʌp] *adj Fam* snob *inv*

stud¹ [stʌd] *n* (*on football boot*) crampon *m*; (*earring*) clou *m* d'oreille; (**collar**) **s.** bouton *m* de col ● **studded** *adj* (*boots, tyres*) clouté; *Fig* **s. with** (*covered*) constellé de

stud² [stʌd] *n* (*farm*) haras *m*; (*stallion*) étalon *m*; *Fam* (*virile man*) mâle *m*

student [ˈstjuːdənt] **1** *n* (*at university*) étudiant, -iante *mf*; (*at school*) élève *mf*; **music s.** étudiant, -iante en musique
2 *adj* (*life, protest*) étudiant; (*restaurant, residence, grant*) universitaire

studied [ˈstʌdɪd] *adj* (*deliberate*) étudié

studio [ˈstjuːdɪəʊ] (*pl* **-os**) *n* studio *m*; (*of artist*) atelier *m*; **s. audience** public *m* présent lors de l'enregistrement; *Br* **s. flat,** *Am* **s. apartment** studio

studious [ˈstjuːdɪəs] *adj* (*person*) studieux, -ieuse ● **studiously** *adv* (*carefully*) avec soin

study [ˈstʌdɪ] **1** (*pl* **-ies**) *n* étude *f*; (*office*) bureau *m*
2 (*pp & pp* **-ied**) *vt* (*learn, observe*) étudier
3 *vi* étudier; **to s. to be a doctor** faire des études de médecine; **to s. for an exam** préparer un examen

stuff [stʌf] **1** *n* (*possessions*) affaires *fpl*; (*cloth*) étoffe *f*; *Fam* **some s.** (*substance*) un truc; *Fam* **he knows his s.** il connaît son affaire; *Fam* **this s.'s good, it's good s.** c'est bien
2 *vt* (*pocket*) remplir (**with** de); (*cushion*) rembourrer (**with** avec); (*animal*) empailler; (*chicken, tomatoes*) farcir; **to s. sth into sth** fourrer qch dans qch; **to s. (up)** (*hole*) colmater; **my nose is stuffed (up)** j'ai le nez bouché ● **stuffing** *n* (*padding*) bourre *f*; (*for chicken, tomatoes*) farce *f*

stuffy [ˈstʌfɪ] (**-ier, -iest**) *adj* (*room*) qui sent le renfermé; (*person*) vieux jeu *inv*

stumble [ˈstʌmbəl] *vi* trébucher; **to s. across** *or* **on** (*find*) tomber sur; **stumbling block** pierre *f* d'achoppement

stump [stʌmp] *n* (*of tree*) souche *f*; (*of limb*) moignon *m*; (*of pencil*) bout *m*; *Cricket* piquet *m*

stumped [ˈstʌmpt] *adj* **to be s. by sth** (*baffled*) ne savoir que penser de qch

stun [stʌn] (*pt & pp* **-nn-**) *vt* (*make unconscious*) assommer; *Fig* (*amaze*) stupéfier ● **stunned** *adj* (*amazed*) stupéfait (**by** par) ● **stunning** *adj* (*news*) stupéfiant; *Fam* (*excellent*) excellent; *Fam* (*beautiful*) superbe

stung [stʌŋ] *pt & pp of* **sting**

stunk [stʌŋk] *pt & pp of* **stink**

stunt¹ [stʌnt] *n* (*in film*) cascade *f*; (*for publicity*) coup *m* de pub; **s. man** cascadeur *m*; **s. woman** cascadeuse *f*

stunt² [stʌnt] *vt* (*growth*) retarder ● **stunted** *adj* (*person*) rabougri

stupefy ['stjuːpɪfaɪ] (*pt & pp* **-ied**) *vt (of drink)* abrutir; *Fig (amaze)* stupéfier
stupendous [stjuːˈpendəs] *adj* fantastique
stupid ['stjuːpɪd] *adj* stupide; **to do/say a s. thing** faire/dire une stupidité • **stu'pidity** *n* stupidité *f* • **stupidly** *adv* bêtement
stupor ['stjuːpə(r)] *n (daze)* stupeur *f*
sturdy ['stɜːdɪ] (**-ier, -iest**) *adj (person, shoe)* robuste • **sturdiness** *n* robustesse *f*
sturgeon ['stɜːdʒən] *n* esturgeon *m*
stutter ['stʌtə(r)] **1** *n* bégaiement *m*; **to have a s.** être bègue
  2 *vi* bégayer
sty¹ [staɪ] *n (for pigs)* porcherie *f*
sty², stye [staɪ] *n (on eye)* orgelet *m*
style [staɪl] **1** *n* style *m*; *(sophistication)* classe *f*; **to have s.** avoir de la classe; **to live in s.** mener grand train
  2 *vt (design)* créer; **to s. sb's hair** coiffer qn • **styling** *n (of hair)* coupe *f*
stylish ['staɪlɪʃ] *adj* chic *inv* • **stylishly** *adv* élégamment
stylist ['staɪlɪst] *n* **(hair) s.** coiffeur, -euse *mf*
stylistic [staɪ'lɪstɪk] *adj* stylistique
stylized ['staɪlaɪzd] *adj* stylisé
stylus ['staɪləs] *n (of record player)* pointe *f* de lecture
suave [swɑːv] (**-er, -est**) *adj* courtois; *Pej* doucereux, -euse

> ⟋ Note that the French word **suave** is a false friend and is almost never a translation for the English word **suave**. It means **sweet**.

sub- [sʌb] *pref* sous-, sub-
subconscious [sʌb'kɒnʃəs] *adj & n* subconscient *(m)* • **subconsciously** *adv* inconsciemment
subcontract [sʌbkən'trækt] *vt* sous-traiter • **subcontractor** *n* sous-traitant *m*
subdivide [sʌbdɪ'vaɪd] *vt* subdiviser (**into** en) • **subdivision** [-'vɪʒən] *n* subdivision *f*
subdue [səb'djuː] *vt (country, people)* soumettre; *(feelings)* maîtriser • **subdued** *adj (light)* tamisé; *(voice, tone)* bas *(f* basse); *(person)* inhabituellement calme
subheading ['sʌbhedɪŋ] *n* sous-titre *m*
subject¹ ['sʌbdʒɪkt] *n* (**a**) *(matter) & Grammar* sujet *m*; *(at school, university)* matière *f*; **s. matter** *(topic)* sujet; *(content)* contenu *m* (**b**) *(of monarch)* sujet, -ette *mf*; *(in experiment)* sujet *m*
subject² ['sʌbdʒekt] *adj* **to be s. to depression/jealousy** avoir tendance à la dépression/à la jalousie; **it's s. to my**

agreement c'est sous réserve de mon accord; **prices are s. to change** les prix peuvent être modifiés
  2 [səb'dʒekt] *vt* soumettre (**to** à) • **subjection** [səb'dʒekʃən] *n* soumission *f* (**to** à)
subjective [səb'dʒektɪv] *adj* subjectif, -ive • **subjectively** *adv* subjectivement • **subjectivity** [sʌbdʒek'tɪvɪtɪ] *n* subjectivité *f*
subjugate ['sʌbdʒʊgeɪt] *vt* subjuguer
subjunctive [səb'dʒʌŋktɪv] *n Grammar* subjonctif *m*
sublet [sʌb'let] (*pt & pp* **-let, **pres p* -letting) *vt* sous-louer
sublimate ['sʌblɪmeɪt] *vt* sublimer
sublime [sə'blaɪm] **1** *adj* sublime; *(utter)* suprême
  2 *n* sublime *m*; **to go from the s. to the ridiculous** passer du sublime au grotesque
sub-machine gun [sʌbmə'ʃiːngʌn] *n* mitraillette *f*
submarine ['sʌbməriːn] *n* sous-marin *m*
submerge [səb'mɜːdʒ] **1** *vt (flood, overwhelm)* submerger; *(immerse)* immerger (**in** dans)
  2 *vi (of submarine)* s'immerger
submit [səb'mɪt] **1** (*pt & pp* **-tt-**) *vt* soumettre (**to** à)
  2 *vi* se soumettre (**to** à) • **submission** *n* soumission *f* (**to** à) • **submissive** *adj (person)* soumis; *(attitude)* de soumission • **submissively** *adv* avec soumission
subnormal [sʌb'nɔːməl] *adj (temperature)* au-dessous de la normale; *Old-fashioned & Pej* **educationally s.** arriéré
subordinate [sə'bɔːdɪnət] **1** *adj* subalterne; **s. to** subordonné à; *Grammar* **s. clause** proposition *f* subordonnée
  2 *n* subordonné, -ée *mf*
  3 [sə'bɔːdɪneɪt] *vt* subordonner (**to** à) • **subordi'nation** *n* subordination *f* (**to** à)
subpoena [səb'piːnə] *Law* **1** *n (summons)* citation *f* à comparaître
  2 (*pt & pp* **-aed**) *vt (witness)* citer à comparaître
subscribe [səb'skraɪb] **1** *vt (money)* donner (**to** à)
  2 *vi (pay money)* cotiser (**to** à); **to s. to a newspaper** s'abonner à un journal; **to s. to an opinion** souscrire à une opinion • **subscriber** *n (to newspaper, telephone)* abonné, -ée *mf* • **subscription** [-'skrɪpʃən] *n (to newspaper)* abonnement *m*; *(to club)* cotisation *f*
subsequent ['sʌbsɪkwənt] *adj* ultérieur (**to** à); **our s. problems** les problèmes que

nous avons eus par la suite; **s. to** *(as a result of)* consécutif, -ive à • **subsequently** *adv* par la suite
subservient [səb'sɜːvɪənt] *adj* servile
subside [səb'saɪd] *vi (of ground, building)* s'affaisser; *(of wind, flood, fever)* baisser; *(of threat, danger)* se dissiper • **subsidence** *n (of ground)* affaissement *m*
subsidiary [Br səb'sɪdɪərɪ, Am -dɪerɪ] **1** *adj* subsidiaire
2 *(pl -ies) n (company)* filiale *f*
subsidize ['sʌbsɪdaɪz] *vt* subventionner • **subsidy** *(pl -ies) n* subvention *f*
subsist [səb'sɪst] *vi (of doubts)* subsister; **to s. on** sth vivre de qch • **subsistence** *n* subsistance *f*
substance ['sʌbstəns] *n* substance *f*; *(solidity, worth)* fondement *m*; **s. abuse** usage *m* de stupéfiants
substandard [sʌb'stændəd] *adj* de qualité inférieure
substantial [səb'stænʃəl] *adj* important; *(meal)* substantiel, -ielle • **substantially** *adv* considérablement; **s. true** *(to a great extent)* en grande partie vrai; **s. different** très différent
substantiate [səb'stænʃɪeɪt] *vt (statement)* corroborer; *(claim)* justifier
substitute ['sʌbstɪtjuːt] **1** *n (thing)* produit *m* de remplacement; *(person)* remplaçant, -ante *mf* (**for** de); **s. teacher** suppléant, -éante *mf*; **there's no s. for** rien ne peut remplacer
2 *vt* **to s. sb/sth for** substituer qn/qch à
3 *vi* **to s. for sb** remplacer qn • **substitution** *n* substitution *f*
subterranean [sʌbtə'reɪnɪən] *adj* souterrain
subtitle ['sʌbtaɪtəl] **1** *n (of film)* sous-titre *m*
2 *vt (film)* sous-titrer
subtle ['sʌtəl] (**-er, -est**) *adj* subtil • **subtlety** *n* subtilité *f* • **subtly** *adv* subtilement
subtotal [sʌb'təʊtəl] *n* sous-total *m*
subtract [səb'trækt] *vt* soustraire (**from** de) • **subtraction** *n* soustraction *f*
subtropical [sʌb'trɒpɪkəl] *adj* subtropical
suburb ['sʌbɜːb] *n* banlieue *f*; **the suburbs** la banlieue; **in the suburbs** en banlieue • **suburban** [sə'bɜːbən] *adj (train, house)* de banlieue; *(accent)* de la banlieue • **suburbia** [sə'bɜːbɪə] *n* la banlieue; **in s.** en banlieue
subversive [səb'vɜːsɪv] *adj* subversif, -ive • **subversion** [Br -ʃən, Am -ʒən] *n* subversion *f* • **subvert** *vt (system)* bouleverser; *(person)* corrompre

subway ['sʌbweɪ] *n Br (under road)* passage *m* souterrain; *Am (railroad)* métro *m*
succeed [sək'siːd] **1** *vt* **to s. sb** succéder à qn
2 *vi* réussir (**in doing** à faire; **in sth** dans qch); **to s. to the throne** monter sur le trône • **succeeding** *adj (in past)* suivant; *(in future)* futur; *(consecutive)* consécutif, -ive
success [sək'ses] *n* succès *m*, réussite *f*; **to make a s. of sth** mener qch à bien; **he was a s.** il a eu du succès; **it was a s.** c'était réussi; **her s. in the exam** sa réussite à l'examen; **s. story** réussite *f*
successful [sək'sesfəl] *adj (effort, venture)* couronné de succès; *(outcome)* heureux, -euse; *(company, businessman)* prospère; *(candidate in exam)* admis, reçu; *(candidate in election)* élu; *(writer, film)* à succès; **to be s.** réussir; **to be s. in doing sth** réussir à faire qch • **successfully** *adv* avec succès
succession [sək'seʃən] *n* succession *f*; **in s.** successivement; **ten days in s.** dix jours consécutifs; **in rapid s.** coup sur coup • **successive** *adj* successif, -ive; **ten s. days** dix jours consécutifs • **successor** *n* successeur *m* (**to** de)
succinct [sək'sɪŋkt] *adj* succinct
succulent ['sʌkjʊlənt] *adj* succulent
succumb [sə'kʌm] *vi* succomber (**to** à)
such [sʌtʃ] **1** *adj (of this or that kind)* tel (*f* telle); **s. a car** une telle voiture; **s. happiness/noise** tant de bonheur/bruit; **there's no s. thing** ça n'existe pas; **I said no s. thing** je n'ai rien dit de tel; **s. as** comme, tel que; **s. and s. a/an** tel ou tel
2 *adv (so very)* si; *(in comparisons)* aussi; **s. long trips** de si longs voyages; **s. a large helping** une si grosse portion; **s. a kind woman as you** une femme aussi gentille que vous
3 *pron* **happiness as s.** le bonheur en tant que tel; **s. was my idea** telle était mon idée • **suchlike** *pron & adj* **and s.** et autres
suck [sʌk] **1** *vt* sucer; *(of baby)* téter; **to s. (up)** *(with straw, pump)* aspirer; **to s. up** *or* **in** *(absorb)* absorber
2 *vi (of baby)* téter; **to s. at** *(pencil)* sucer; **to s. at its mother's breast** *(of baby)* téter sa mère
sucker ['sʌkə(r)] *n (rubber pad)* ventouse *f*; *Fam (fool)* pigeon *m*, dupe *f*
suckle ['sʌkəl] **1** *vt (of woman)* allaiter
2 *vi (of baby)* téter
suction ['sʌkʃən] *n* succion *f*
Sudan [suː'dɑːn, -'dæn] *n* le Soudan
sudden ['sʌdən] *adj* soudain; **all of a s.**

tout à coup • **suddenly** *adv* tout à coup, soudain; *(die)* subitement • **suddenness** *n* soudaineté *f*

suds [sʌdz] *npl* mousse *f* de savon

sue [suː] **1** *vt* poursuivre (en justice) **2** *vi* engager des poursuites judiciaires

suede [sweɪd] *n* daim *m*; **s. coat/shoes** manteau *m*/chaussures *fpl* de daim

suet ['suːt] *n* graisse *f* de rognon

suffer ['sʌfə(r)] **1** *vt (loss, damage, defeat)* subir; *(pain)* ressentir; *(tolerate)* supporter **2** *vi* souffrir (**from** de); **your work will s.** ton travail s'en ressentira • **sufferer** *n (from misfortune)* victime *f*; **AIDS s.** malade *mf* du SIDA; **asthma s.** asthmatique *mf* • **suffering** *n* souffrance *f*

suffice [sə'faɪs] *vi* suffire

sufficient [sə'fɪʃənt] *adj* suffisant; **s. money** *(enough)* suffisamment d'argent; **to be s.** suffire • **sufficiently** *adv* suffisamment

suffix ['sʌfɪks] *n Grammar* suffixe *m*

suffocate ['sʌfəkeɪt] **1** *vt* étouffer **2** *vi* suffoquer • **suffo'cation** *n* étouffement *m*; **to die of s.** mourir asphyxié

suffrage ['sʌfrɪdʒ] *n* droit *m* de vote; **universal s.** le suffrage universel

suffused [sə'fjuːzd] *adj* **s. with light/tears** baigné de lumière/larmes

sugar ['ʃʊgə(r)] **1** *n* sucre *m*; **s. beet/cane/tongs** betterave *f*/canne *f*/pince *f* à sucre; **s. bowl** sucrier *m*; **s. lump** morceau *m* de sucre **2** *vt (tea)* sucrer • **sugar-free** *adj* sans sucre • **sugary** *adj (taste, tone)* sucré

suggest [sə'dʒest] *vt (propose)* suggérer; *(imply)* indiquer • **suggestion** *n* suggestion *f* • **suggestive** *adj* suggestif, -ive; **to be s. of** évoquer

suicide ['suːɪsaɪd] *n* suicide *m*; **to commit s.** se suicider • **sui'cidal** *adj* suicidaire

suit¹ [suːt] *n* (**a**) *(man's)* costume *m*; *(woman's)* tailleur *m*; **flying/diving/ski s.** combinaison *f* de vol/plongée/ski (**b**) *Cards* couleur *f*; *Fig* **to follow s.** faire de même (**c**) *(lawsuit)* procès *m*

suit² [suːt] *vt (please, be acceptable to)* convenir à; *(of dress, colour)* aller (bien) à; *(adapt)* adapter (**to** à); **it suits me to stay** ça m'arrange de rester; **s. yourself!** comme tu voudras!; **suited to** *(job, activity)* fait pour; *(appropriate to)* qui convient à; **to be well suited** *(of couple)* être bien assorti

suitability [suːtə'bɪlətɪ] *n (of remark)* à-propos *m*; *(of person)* aptitude *f* (**for** pour)

suitable ['suːtəbəl] *adj* convenable (**for** à); *(candidate, date)* adéquat; *(example)* approprié; **this film is not s. for children** ce film n'est pas pour les enfants • **suitably** *adv (dress, behave)* convenablement

suitcase ['suːtkeɪs] *n* valise *f*

suite [swiːt] *n (rooms)* suite *f*; **bedroom s.** *(furniture)* chambre *f* à coucher

suitor ['suːtə(r)] *n* soupirant *m*

sulfur ['sʌlfə(r)] *n Am Chem* soufre *m*

sulk [sʌlk] *vi* bouder • **sulky** (**-ier, -iest**) *adj* boudeur, -euse

sullen ['sʌlən] *adj* maussade • **sullenly** *adv* d'un air maussade

sully ['sʌlɪ] *(pt & pp -ied) vt Literary* souiller

sulphur ['sʌlfə(r)] (*Am* **sulfur**) *n Chem* soufre *m*

sultan ['sʌltən] *n* sultan *m*

sultana [sʌl'tɑːnə] *n* raisin *m* de Smyrne

sultry ['sʌltrɪ] (**-ier, -iest**) *adj (heat)* étouffant; *Fig* sensuel, -uelle

sum [sʌm] **1** *n (amount of money)* somme *f*; *(mathematical problem)* problème *m*; **to do sums** *(arithmetic)* faire du calcul; **s. total** somme totale **2** (*pt & pp* **-mm-**) *vt* **to s. up** *(summarize)* résumer; *(assess)* évaluer **3** *vi* **to s. up** résumer • **summing-'up** *(pl* **summings-up**) *n* résumé *m*

summarize ['sʌməraɪz] *vt* résumer • **summary 1** *(pl* **-ies**) *n* résumé *m* **2** *adj (brief)* sommaire

summer ['sʌmə(r)] **1** *n* été *m*; **in (the) s.** en été; **Indian s.** été indien **2** *adj* d'été; *Am* **s. camp** colonie *f* de vacances; **s. school** cours *mpl* d'été; *Br* **s. holidays,** *Am* **s. vacation** grandes vacances *fpl* • **summerhouse** *n* pavillon *m* • **summertime** *n* été *m*; **in (the) s.** en été • **summery** *adj (weather, temperature)* estival; *(dress, day)* d'été

summit ['sʌmɪt] *n* sommet *m*

summon ['sʌmən] *vt (call)* appeler; *(meeting, person)* convoquer (**to** à); **to s. sb to do sth** sommer qn de faire qch; **to s. up courage/strength** rassembler son courage/ses forces

summons ['sʌmənz] *Law* **1** *n* assignation *f* à comparaître **2** *vt* assigner à comparaître

sump [sʌmp] *n Br (in engine)* carter *m* à huile

sumptuous ['sʌmptʃʊəs] *adj* somptueux, -ueuse • **sumptuousness** *n* somptuosité *f*

sun [sʌn] **1** *n* soleil *m*; **in the s.** au soleil; **the s. is shining** il fait soleil **2** (*pt & pp* **-nn-**) *vt* **to s. oneself** prendre le soleil • **sunbaked** *adj* brûlé par le soleil • **sunbathe** *vi* prendre un bain de soleil • **sunbeam** *n* rayon *m* de soleil • **sunbed** *n* lit *m* à ultraviolets • **sunblock** *n* (*cream*) écran *m* total • **sunburn** *n* coup *m* de soleil • **sunburnt** *adj* brûlé par le soleil • **sundial** *n* cadran *m* solaire • **sundown** *n* coucher *m* du soleil • **sundrenched** *adj* (*beach*) brûlé par le soleil • **sunflower** *n* tournesol *m* • **sunglasses** *npl* lunettes *fpl* de soleil • **sunhat** *n* chapeau *m* de soleil • **sunlamp** *n* lampe *f* à bronzer • **sunlight** *n* lumière *f* du soleil • **sunlit** *adj* ensoleillé • **sun lounge** *n* (*in house*) véranda *f* • **sunrise** *n* lever *m* du soleil • **sunroof** *n* (*in car*) toit *m* ouvrant • **sunset** *n* coucher *m* du soleil • **sunshade** *n* (*on table*) parasol *m*; (*portable*) ombrelle *f* • **sunshine** *n* soleil *m* • **sunspot** *n Br* (*resort*) lieu *m* de vacances au soleil • **sunstroke** *n* insolation *f* • **suntan** *n* bronzage *m*; **s. lotion/oil** crème *f*/huile *f* solaire • **suntanned** *adj* bronzé • **sunup** *n Am* lever *m* du soleil

sundae ['sʌndeɪ] *n* coupe *f* glacée

Sunday ['sʌndeɪ] *n* dimanche *m*; **S. school** ≃ catéchisme *m*; **in one's S. best** dans ses habits du dimanche

sundry ['sʌndrɪ] **1** *adj* divers
2 *n* **all and s.** tout le monde • **sundries** *npl Com* articles *mpl* divers

sung [sʌŋ] *pp of* sing

sunk [sʌŋk] **1** *pp of* sink²
2 *adj Fam* **I'm s.** je suis fichu • **sunken** *adj* (*rock, treasure*) submergé; (*eyes*) cave

sunny ['sʌnɪ] (**-ier, -iest**) *adj* (*day*) ensoleillé; **it's s.** il fait soleil; **s. periods** *or* **intervals** éclaircies *fpl*

super ['suːpə(r)] *adj Fam* super *inv*

super- ['suːpə(r)] *pref* super-

superannuation [supərænjʊ'eɪʃən] *n Br* (*money*) cotisations *fpl* (pour la) retraite

superb [suː'pɜːb] *adj* superbe

supercilious [suːpə'sɪlɪəs] *adj* hautain

superficial [suːpə'fɪʃəl] *adj* superficiel, -ielle • **superficially** *adv* superficiellement

superfluous [suː'pɜːfluəs] *adj* superflu

superglue ['suːpəgluː] *n* colle *f* extra-forte

superhuman [suːpə'hjuːmən] *adj* surhumain

superimpose [suːpərɪm'pəʊz] *vt* superposer (**on** à)

superintendent [suːpərɪn'tendənt] *n* (*in police force*) commissaire *m*; (*manager*) directeur, -trice *mf*

superior [suː'pɪərɪə(r)] **1** *adj* supérieur (**to** à); (*goods*) de qualité supérieure

2 *n* (*person*) supérieur, -ieure *mf* • **superiority** [-rɪ'ɒrɪtɪ] *n* supériorité *f*

superlative [suː'pɜːlətɪv] **1** *adj* sans pareil
2 *adj & n Grammar* superlatif (*m*)

superman ['suːpəmæn] (*pl* **-men**) *n* surhomme *m*

supermarket ['suːpəmɑːkɪt] *n* supermarché *m*

supermodel ['suːpəmɒdəl] *n* supermodel *m*

supernatural [suːpə'nætʃərəl] *adj & n* surnaturel, -elle (*m*)

superpower ['suːpəpaʊə(r)] *n Pol* super-puissance *f*

supersede [suːpə'siːd] *vt* supplanter

supersonic [suːpə'sɒnɪk] *adj* supersonique

superstar ['suːpəstɑː(r)] *n* (*in films*) superstar *f*

superstition [suːpə'stɪʃən] *n* superstition *f* • **superstitious** *adj* superstitieux, -ieuse

superstore ['suːpəstɔːr] *n* hypermarché *m*

supertanker ['suːpətæŋkə(r)] *n* pétrolier *m* géant

supervise ['suːpəvaɪz] *vt* (*person, work*) surveiller; (*office, research*) superviser • **supervision** [-'vɪʒən] *n* (*of person*) surveillance *f*; (*of office*) supervision *f* • **supervisor** *n* surveillant, -ante *mf*; (*in office*) chef *m* de service; (*in store*) chef de rayon; *Br* (*in university*) directeur, -trice *mf* de thèse • **supervisory** *adj* (*post*) de supervision

supine [suː'paɪn] *adj Literary* étendu sur le dos

supper ['sʌpə(r)] *n* (*meal*) dîner *m*; (*snack*) ≃ casse-croûte pris avant d'aller se coucher

supple ['sʌpəl] *adj* souple • **suppleness** *n* souplesse *f*

supplement 1 ['sʌplɪmənt] *n* supplément *m* (**to** à)
2 ['sʌplɪment] *vt* compléter; **to s. one's income** arrondir ses fins de mois • **supplementary** [-'mentərɪ] *adj* supplémentaire

supplier [sə'plaɪə(r)] *n Com* fournisseur *m*; 'obtainable from your usual s.' 'disponible chez votre fournisseur habituel'

ℓ Note that the French word **supplier** is a false friend and is never a translation for the English word **supplier**. It means **to beg**.

supply [sə'plaɪ] **1** (*pl* **-ies**) *n* (*stock*) provision *f*; **the s. of** (*act*) la fourniture de; **the**

s. of gas/electricity/water to... l'alimentation *f* en gaz/électricité/eau de...; **to be in short s.** manquer; **(food) supplies** vivres *mpl*; **(office) supplies** fournitures *fpl* de bureau; **s. and demand** l'offre *f* et la demande; **s. ship/train** navire *m*/train *m* ravitailleur; *Br* **s. teacher** suppléant, -éante *mf*

2 (*pt & pp* **-ied**) *vt* (*provide*) fournir; (*with gas, electricity, water*) alimenter (**with** en); (*equip*) équiper (**with** de); **to s. a need** subvenir à un besoin; **to s. sb with sth, to s. sth to sb** fournir qch à qn

support [sə'pɔːt] **1** *n* (*backing, person supporting*) soutien *m*; (*thing supporting*) support *m*; **in s. of** (*person*) en faveur de; (*evidence, theory*) à l'appui de; **s. tights** bas *mpl* de contention

2 *vt* (*bear weight of*) supporter; (*help, encourage*) soutenir; (*theory, idea*) appuyer; (*family, wife, husband*) subvenir aux besoins de • **supporting** *adj* (*film*) qui passe en première partie; **s. cast** seconds rôles *mpl*

supporter [sə'pɔːtə(r)] *n* partisan *m*; *Football* supporter *m*

supportive [sə'pɔːtɪv] *adj* **to be s. of sb** être d'un grand soutien à qn

suppose [sə'pəʊz] *vti* supposer (**that** que); **I'm supposed to be working** je suis censé travailler; **he's supposed to be rich** on le dit riche; **I s. (so)** je pense; **I don't s. so, I s. not** je ne pense pas; **you're tired, I s.** vous êtes fatigué, je suppose; **s. or supposing we go** (*suggestion*) et si nous partions; **s. or supposing (that) you're right** supposons que tu aies raison • **supposed** *adj* prétendu • **supposedly** [-ɪdlɪ] *adv* soi-disant; **he went away, s. to get help** il est parti, soi-disant pour chercher de l'aide • **supposition** [sʌpə'zɪʃən] *n* supposition *f*

suppository [*Br* sə'pɒzɪtərɪ, *Am* -ɔːrɪ] (*pl* **-ies**) *n Med* suppositoire *m*

suppress [sə'pres] *vt* (*revolt, feelings, smile*) réprimer; (*fact, evidence*) faire disparaître • **suppression** *n* (*of revolt, feelings*) répression *f*; (*of fact*) dissimulation *f*

> ⚠ Note that the French verb **supprimer** is a false friend and is almost never a translation for the English verb **to suppress**. Its most common meaning is **to cancel**.

supreme [suː'priːm] *adj* suprême • **supremacy** [sə'preməsɪ] *n* suprématie *f* (**over** sur)

supremo [suː'priːməʊ] (*pl* **-os**) *n Br Fam* grand chef *m*

surcharge ['sɜːtʃɑːdʒ] *n* (*extra charge*) supplément *m*; (*on stamp*) surcharge *f*; (*tax*) surtaxe *f*

sure [ʃʊə(r)] (**-er, -est**) *adj* sûr (**of** de; **that** que); **she's s. to accept** c'est sûr qu'elle acceptera; **it's s. to snow** il va sûrement neiger; **to make s. of sth** s'assurer de qch; **for s.** à coup sûr; *Fam* **s.!, s. thing!** bien sûr!; **s. enough** (*in effect*) en effet; *Am* **it s. is cold** il fait vraiment froid; **be s. to do it!** ne manquez pas de le faire! • **surely** *adv* (*certainly*) sûrement; **s. he didn't refuse?** il n'a quand même pas refusé?

surety ['ʃʊərətɪ] *n Law* caution *f*

surf [sɜːf] **1** *n* (*waves*) ressac *m*

2 *vt Comptr* **to s. the Net** naviguer sur l'Internet • **surfboard** *n* planche *f* de surf • **surfing** *n Sport* surf *m*; **to go s.** faire du surf

surface ['sɜːfɪs] **1** *n* surface *f*; **s. area** superficie *f*; **s. mail** courrier *m* par voie(s) de terre; **on the s.** (*of water*) à la surface; *Fig* (*to all appearances*) en apparence

2 *vt* (*road*) revêtir

3 *vi* (*of swimmer*) remonter à la surface; *Fam* (*of person, thing*) réapparaître

surfeit ['sɜːfɪt] *n* (*excess*) excès *m* (**of** de)

surge [sɜːdʒ] **1** *n* (*of enthusiasm*) vague *f*; (*of anger, pride*) bouffée *f*; (*rise*) (*of prices*) montée *f*; (*in electrical current*) surtension *f*

2 *vi* (*of crowd, hatred*) déferler; (*of prices*) monter (*soudainement*); **to s. forward** (*of person*) se lancer en avant

surgeon ['sɜːdʒən] *n* chirurgien *m* • **surgery** [-dʒərɪ] *n Br* (*doctor's office*) cabinet *m*; (*period, sitting*) consultation *f*; (*science*) chirurgie *f*; **to have heart s.** se faire opérer du cœur • **surgical** *adj* chirurgical; **s. appliance** appareil *m* orthopédique; *Br* **s. spirit** alcool *m* à 90°

surly ['sɜːlɪ] (**-ier, -iest**) *adj* revêche

surmise [sə'maɪz] *vt* conjecturer (**that** que)

surmount [sə'maʊnt] *vt* surmonter

surname ['sɜːneɪm] *n* nom *m* de famille

> ⚠ Note that the French word **surnom** is a false friend and is never a translation for the English word **surname**. It means **nickname**.

surpass [sə'pɑːs] *vt* surpasser (**in** en)

surplus ['sɜːpləs] **1** *n* surplus *m*

2 *adj* (*goods*) en surplus; **some s. material** (*left over*) un surplus de tissu; **s. stock** surplus *mpl*

surprise [sə'praɪz] **1** *n* surprise *f*; **to give sb a s.** faire une surprise à qn; **to take sb**

by s. prendre qn au dépourvu; **s. visit/ result** visite *f*/résultat *m* inattendu(e)
 2 *vt* étonner, surprendre • **surprised** *adj* surpris (**that** que + *subjunctive*, **at sth** de qch; **at seeing** de voir); **I'm s. at his stupidity** sa bêtise m'étonne; **I'm s. to see you** je suis surpris de te voir • **surprising** *adj* surprenant • **surprisingly** *adv* étonnamment; **s. (enough), he…** chose étonnante, il…

surreal [sə'rɪəl] *adj (surrealist)* surréaliste; *Fam (strange)* délirant

surrender [sə'rendə(r)] **1** *n (of soldiers)* reddition *f*
 2 *vt (town)* livrer; *(right, claim)* renoncer à
 3 *vi (give oneself up)* se rendre (**to** à)

surreptitious [sʌrəp'tɪʃəs] *adj* furtif, -ive

surrogate ['sʌrəgət] *n* substitut *m*; **s. mother** mère *f* porteuse

surround [sə'raʊnd] *vt* entourer (**with** de); *(of army, police)* cerner; **surrounded by** entouré de • **surrounding** *adj* environnant • **surroundings** *npl (of town)* environs *mpl*; *(setting)* cadre *m*

surveillance [sɜː'veɪləns] *n* surveillance *f*

survey 1 ['sɜːveɪ] *n (investigation)* enquête *f*; *(of opinion)* sondage *m*; *(of house)* inspection *f*; **a (general) s. of** une étude générale de
 2 [sə'veɪ] *vt (look at)* regarder; *(review)* passer en revue; *(house)* inspecter; *(land)* faire un relevé de • **surveying** [sə'veɪɪŋ] *n (of land)* relevé *m* • **surveyor** [sə'veɪə(r)] *n (of land)* géomètre *m*; *(of house)* expert *m*

> ℓ Note that the French verb **surveiller** is a false friend and is never a translation for the English verb **to survey**. Its most common meaning is **to supervise**.

survive [sə'vaɪv] **1** *vt* survivre à
 2 *vi* survivre • **survival** *n (act)* survie *f*; *(relic)* vestige *m* • **survivor** *n* survivant, -ante *mf*

susceptible [sə'septəbəl] *adj (sensitive)* sensible (**to** à); **s. to colds** prédisposé aux rhumes • **suscepti'bility** *n* sensibilité *f*; *(to colds)* prédisposition *f*; **susceptibilities** susceptibilité

suspect 1 ['sʌspekt] *n & adj* suspect, -ecte *(mf)*
 2 [sə'spekt] *vt* soupçonner (**sb of sth** qn de qch; **sb of doing** qn d'avoir fait); *(have intuition of)* se douter de; **I suspected as much** je m'en doutais

suspend [sə'spend] *vt* **(a)** *(hang)* sus-

pendre (**from** à) (**b**) *(service, employee, player)* suspendre; *(pupil)* renvoyer temporairement; *Law* **suspended sentence** condamnation *f* avec sursis

suspender [sə'spendə(r)] *n Br (for stocking)* jarretelle *f*; **suspenders** *(for trousers)* bretelles *fpl*; *Br* **s. belt** porte-jarretelles *m inv*

suspense [sə'spens] *n (uncertainty)* incertitude *f*; *(in film, book)* suspense *m*; **to keep sb in s.** tenir qn en haleine

suspension [sə'spenʃən] *n* **(a)** *(of car)* suspension *f*; **s. bridge** pont *m* suspendu (**b**) *(of service, employee, player)* suspension *f*; *(of pupil)* renvoi *m*

suspicion [sə'spɪʃən] *n* soupçon *m*; **to arouse s.** éveiller les soupçons; **to be under s.** être soupçonné

suspicious [sə'spɪʃəs] *adj (person)* soupçonneux, -euse; *(behaviour)* suspect; **s.-looking** suspect; **to be s. of** *or* **about sth** se méfier de qch • **suspiciously** *adv (behave)* de manière suspecte; *(consider)* avec méfiance

suss [sʌs] *vt Br Fam* **to s. out** piger

sustain [sə'steɪn] *vt (effort, theory)* soutenir; *(weight)* supporter; *(life)* maintenir; *(damage, loss, attack)* subir; **to s. an injury** être blessé; **a proper breakfast will s. you until lunchtime** un bon petit déjeuner vous permettra de tenir jusqu'à midi • **sustainable** *adj (growth)* durable

sustenance ['sʌstənəns] *n (means)* subsistance *f*; *(nourishment)* valeur *f* nutritive

swab [swɒb] *n (pad)* tampon *m*; *(specimen)* prélèvement *m*

swagger ['swægə(r)] **1** *n* démarche *f* de fanfaron
 2 *vi (walk)* se pavaner

swallow¹ ['swɒləʊ] **1** *vt* avaler; **to s. sth down** *or* **up** avaler qch; *Fig* **to s. a country up** engloutir un pays
 2 *vi* avaler

swallow² ['swɒləʊ] *n (bird)* hirondelle *f*

swam [swæm] *pt of* **swim**

swamp [swɒmp] **1** *n* marais *m*
 2 *vt (flood, overwhelm)* submerger (**with** de) • **swampy** (**-ier, -iest**) *adj* marécageux, -euse

swan [swɒn] *n* cygne *m*

swank [swæŋk] *vi Fam (show off)* frimer

swap [swɒp] **1** *n* échange *m*
 2 *(pt & pp* **-pp-***) vt* échanger (**for** contre); **to s. seats** *or* **places** changer de place
 3 *vi* échanger

swarm [swɔːm] **1** *n (of bees, people)* essaim *m*

2 *vi (of streets, insects, people)* fourmiller (**with** de); **to s. in** *(of people)* accourir en masse

swarthy ['swɔːðɪ] (**-ier, -iest**) *adj* basané

swastika ['swɒstɪkə] *n* croix *f* gammée

swat [swɒt] *(pt & pp* **-tt-***) vt* écraser

sway [sweɪ] **1** *n* balancement *m*; *Fig* influence *f*

2 *vt* balancer; *Fig (person, public opinion)* influencer

3 *vi* se balancer

swear [sweə(r)] **1** *(pt* **swore,** *pp* **sworn***) vt (promise)* jurer (**to do** de faire; **that** que); **to s. an oath** prêter serment; **to s. sb to secrecy** faire jurer le silence à qn; **sworn enemies** ennemis *mpl* jurés

2 *vi (take an oath)* jurer (**to sth** de qch); **to s. at sb** injurier qn; **she swears by this lotion** elle ne jure que par cette lotion
• **swearword** *n* juron *m*

▶ **swear in** *vt sep Law* **to s. sb in** *(jury, witness)* faire prêter serment à qn

sweat [swet] **1** *n* sueur *f*; *Fam* **no s.!** pas de problème!

2 *vi* suer

3 *vt* **to s. out a cold** se débarrasser d'un rhume *(en transpirant)* • **sweatshirt** *n* sweat-shirt *m*

sweater ['swetə(r)] *n* pull *m*

sweatshop ['swetʃɒp] *n* = atelier de confection où les ouvriers sont exploités

sweaty ['swetɪ] (**-ier, -iest**) *adj (shirt)* plein de sueur; *(hand)* moite; *(person)* en sueur

Swede [swiːd] *n* Suédois, -oise *mf* • **Sweden** *n* la Suède • **Swedish 1** *adj* suédois **2** *n (language)* suédois *m*

swede [swiːd] *n Br (vegetable)* rutabaga *m*

sweep [swiːp] **1** *n (with broom)* coup *m* de balai; *(movement)* geste *m* large; *(of road, river)* courbe *f*; *Fig* **at one s.** d'un seul coup; **to make a clean s.** *(win everything)* tout gagner

2 *(pt & pp* **swept***) vt (with broom)* balayer; *(chimney)* ramoner; *(river)* draguer

3 *vi* balayer

▶ **sweep along** *vt sep (carry off)* emporter

▶ **sweep aside** *vt sep (opposition, criticism)* écarter ▶ **sweep away** *vt sep (leaves)* balayer; *(carry off)* emporter

▶ **sweep off** *vt sep* **to s. sb off** *(take away)* emmener qn (**to** à); **to s. sb off their feet** faire perdre la tête à qn ▶ **sweep out** *vt sep (room)* balayer ▶ **sweep through** *vt insep (of fear)* saisir; *(of disease)* ravager

▶ **sweep up** *vt sep & vi* balayer

sweeping ['swiːpɪŋ] *adj (gesture)* large; *(change)* radical; *(statement)* trop général

sweepstake ['swiːpsteɪk] *n* sweepstake *m*

sweet [swiːt] **1** (**-er, -est**) *adj* doux *(f* douce); *(tea, coffee, cake)* sucré; *(smell)* agréable; *(pretty, kind)* adorable; **to have a s. tooth** aimer les sucreries; **s. pea** pois *m* de senteur; **s. potato** patate *f* douce; *Fam* **s. talk** cajoleries *fpl*, douceurs *fpl*

2 *n Br (piece of confectionery)* bonbon *m*; *Br (dessert)* dessert *m*; **my s.!** *(darling)* mon ange!; *Br* **s. shop** confiserie *f* • 'sweet-and-'sour *adj* aigre-doux, -douce • **sweetcorn** *n Br* maïs *m* • 'sweet-'smelling *adj* **to be s.** sentir bon

sweetbreads ['swiːtbredz] *npl* ris *m (de veau, d'agneau)*

sweeten ['swiːtən] *vt (food)* sucrer; *Fig (offer, task)* rendre plus alléchant; *(person)* amadouer • **sweetener** *n (in food)* édulcorant *m*

sweetheart ['swiːthɑːt] *n* petit(e) ami(e) *mf*; **my s.!** *(darling)* mon chéri!

sweetie ['swiːtɪ] *n Fam (darling)* chou *m*

sweetly ['swiːtlɪ] *adv (smile, answer)* gentiment; *(sing)* d'une voix douce • **sweetness** *n* douceur *f*

swell¹ [swel] **1** *(pt* **swelled,** *pp* **swollen** *or* **swelled***) vt (river, numbers)* grossir

2 *vi (of hand, leg)* enfler; *(of wood)* gonfler; *(of sails)* se gonfler; *(of river, numbers)* grossir; **to s. up** *(of body part)* enfler • **swelling** *n (on body)* enflure *f*

swell² [swel] *n (of sea)* houle *f*

2 *adj Am Fam (excellent)* super *inv*

swelter ['sweltə(r)] *vi* étouffer • **sweltering** *adj* étouffant; **it's s.** on étouffe

swept [swept] *pt & pp of* **sweep**

swerve [swɜːv] *vi (of vehicle)* faire une embardée; *(of player)* faire un écart

swift [swɪft] **1** (**-er, -est**) *adj* rapide; **to be s. to act** être prompt à agir

2 *n (bird)* martinet *m* • **swiftly** *adv* rapidement • **swiftness** *n* rapidité *f*

swig [swɪg] *n Fam* lampée *f*; **to take a s.** avaler une lampée

swill [swɪl] *vt Fam (drink)* écluser; **to s.** **(out** *or* **down)** rincer à grande eau

swim [swɪm] **1** *n* **to go for a s.** aller nager

2 *(pt* **swam,** *pp* **swum,** *pres p* **swimming***) vt (river)* traverser à la nage; *(length, crawl)* nager

3 *vi (of person)* nager; *(as sport)* faire de la natation; **to go swimming** aller nager; **to s. away** s'éloigner à la nage • **swimmer** *n* nageur, -euse *mf* • **swimming** *n* natation *f*; **s. cap** bonnet *m* de bain; *Br* **s. costume** maillot *m* de bain; *Br* **s. pool** piscine *f*; **s. trunks** slip *m* de bain • **swimsuit** *n* maillot *m* de bain

swindle ['swɪndəl] **1** n escroquerie f
2 vt escroquer; **to s. sb out of money** escroquer de l'argent à qn • **swindler** n escroc m
swine [swaɪn] n inv Pej (person) salaud m
swing [swɪŋ] **1** n (in playground) balançoire f; (movement) balancement m; (of pendulum) oscillation f; (in opinion) revirement m; Golf swing m; **to be in full s.** (of party) battre son plein; Fam **to get into the s. of things** se mettre dans le bain; Br **s. door** porte f battante
2 (pt & pp swung) vt (arms, legs) balancer; (axe) brandir; Fam (influence) influencer; **to s. round** (car) faire tourner
3 vi (sway) se balancer; (of pendulum) osciller; (turn) virer; **to s. round** (turn suddenly) se retourner; **to s. into action** passer à l'action
swingeing ['swɪndʒɪŋ] adj Br énorme
swipe [swaɪp] **1** n grand coup m
2 vt (card) passer dans un lecteur de cartes; Fam **to s. sth** (steal) faucher qch (**from sb** à qn)
3 vi **to s. at sth** essayer de frapper qch
swirl [swɜːl] **1** n tourbillon m
2 vi tourbillonner
swish [swɪʃ] **1** n (of whip) sifflement m; (of fabric) froufrou m
2 adj Fam (posh) chic inv
3 vi (of whip) siffler; (of fabric) froufrouter
Swiss [swɪs] **1** adj suisse; Br **S. roll** roulé m
2 n inv Suisse m, Suissesse f; **the S.** les Suisses mpl
switch [swɪtʃ] **1** n (electrical) interrupteur m; (change) changement m (**in** de); (reversal) revirement m (**in** de)
2 vt (money, employee) transférer (**to** à); (support, affection) reporter (**to** sur); (exchange) échanger (**for** contre); **to s. buses** changer de bus; **to s. places** or **seats** changer de place
3 vi **to s. to** (change to) passer à • **switchback** n route f en lacets • **switchblade** n Am couteau m à cran d'arrêt • **switchboard** n Tel standard m; **s. operator** standardiste mf
▸ **switch off 1** vt sep (lamp, gas, radio) éteindre; (engine) arrêter; (electricity) couper; **to s. itself off** (of heating) s'éteindre tout seul **2** vi (of appliance) s'éteindre
▸ **switch on 1** vt sep (lamp, gas, radio) allumer; (engine) mettre en marche **2** vi (of appliance) s'allumer ▸ **switch over** vi (change TV channels) changer de chaîne; **to s. over to** (change to) passer à
Switzerland ['swɪtsələnd] n la Suisse

swivel ['swɪvəl] **1** (Br -ll-, Am -l-) vi **to s. (round)** (of chair) pivoter
2 adj **s. chair** chaise f pivotante
swollen ['swəʊlən] **1** pp of swell¹
2 adj (leg) enflé; (stomach) gonflé
swoon [swuːn] vi Literary se pâmer
swoop [swuːp] **1** n (of police) descente f
2 vi faire une descente (**on** dans); **to s. (down) on** (of bird) fondre sur
swop [swɒp] n & vti = swap
sword [sɔːd] n épée f • **swordfish** n espadon m
swore [swɔː(r)] pt of swear
sworn [swɔːn] pp of swear
swot [swɒt] Br Fam Pej **1** n bûcheur, -euse mf
2 (pt & pp -tt-) vti **to s. (up)** bûcher; **to s. (up) for an exam** bûcher un examen; **to s. up on sth** bûcher qch
swum [swʌm] pp of swim
swung [swʌŋ] pt & pp of swing
sycamore ['sɪkəmɔː(r)] n (maple) sycomore m; Am (plane tree) platane m
sycophant ['sɪkəfænt] n Literary flagorneur, -euse mf
syllable ['sɪləbəl] n syllabe f
syllabus ['sɪləbəs] n programme m
symbol ['sɪmbəl] n symbole m • **symbolic** [-'bɒlɪk] adj symbolique • **symbolism** n symbolisme m • **symbolize** vt symboliser
symmetry ['sɪmətrɪ] n symétrie f • **symmetrical** [-'metrɪkəl] adj symétrique
sympathetic [sɪmpə'θetɪk] adj (showing pity) compatissant; (understanding) compréhensif, -ive; **s. to sb/sth** (favourable) bien disposé à l'égard de qn/qch

ℓ° Note that the French adjective **sympathique** is a false friend and is never a translation for the English adjective **sympathetic**. It means **friendly**.

sympathize ['sɪmpəθaɪz] vi **I s. with you** (pity) je suis désolé (pour vous); (understanding) je vous comprends • **sympathizer** n Pol sympathisant, -ante mf

ℓ° Note that the French verb **sympathiser avec** is a false friend and is almost never a translation for the English verb **to sympathize with**. It means **to be friendly with**.

sympathy ['sɪmpəθɪ] n (pity) compassion f; (understanding) compréhension f; **to have s. for sb** éprouver de la compassion pour qn; **to be in s. with sb's opinion** être en accord avec les opinions de qn

---

_Ω_ Note that the French noun **sympathie** is a false friend and is rarely a translation for the English noun **sympathy**. It is usually used to convey the idea of liking somebody.

symphony ['sɪmfənɪ] **1** (*pl* **-ies**) *n* symphonie *f*

2 *adj (orchestra, concert)* symphonique • **symphonic** [-'fɒnɪk] *adj* symphonique

symposium [sɪm'pəʊzɪəm] (*pl* **-sia** [-zɪə]) *n* symposium *m*

symptom ['sɪmptəm] *n Med & Fig* symptôme *m* • **sympto'matic** *adj* symptomatique (**of** de)

synagogue ['sɪnəgɒg] *n* synagogue *f*

synchronize ['sɪŋkrənaɪz] *vt* synchroniser

syndicate ['sɪndɪkət] *n* syndicat *m*

syndrome ['sɪndrəʊm] *n Med & Fig* syndrome *m*

synod ['sɪnəd] *n Rel* synode *m*

synonym ['sɪnənɪm] *n* synonyme *m* • **synonymous** [-'nɒnɪməs] *adj* synonyme (**with** de)

synopsis [sɪ'nɒpsɪs] (*pl* **-opses** [-ɒpsiːz]) *n* résumé *m*; *(of film)* synopsis *m*

syntax ['sɪntæks] *n* syntaxe *f*

synthesis ['sɪnθəsɪs] (*pl* **-theses** [-θəsiːz]) *n* synthèse *f*

synthesizer ['sɪnθəsaɪzə(r)] *n* synthétiseur *m*

synthetic [sɪn'θetɪk] *adj* synthétique

syphilis ['sɪfɪlɪs] *n Med* syphilis *f*

syphon ['saɪfən] *n & vt* = **siphon**

Syria ['sɪrɪə] *n* la Syrie • **Syrian 1** *adj* syrien, -ienne **2** *n* Syrien, -ienne *mf*

syringe [sə'rɪndʒ] *n* seringue *f*

syrup ['sɪrəp] *n* sirop *m*; *Br* **(golden) s.** mélasse *f* raffinée • **syrupy** *adj* sirupeux, -euse

system ['sɪstəm] *n (structure) & Comptr* système *m*; *(human body)* organisme *m*; *(method)* méthode *f*; *Fam* **to get sth out of one's s.** se sortir qch de la tête; **the digestive s.** l'appareil *m* digestif; *Comptr* **s. disk** disque *m* système; *Comptr* **s. software** logiciel *m* système *ou* d'exploitation; **systems analyst** analyste *m* programmeur

systematic [sɪstə'mætɪk] *adj* systématique • **systematically** *adv* systématiquement

T, t [tiː] *n (letter)* T, t *m inv*
ta [tɑː] *exclam Br Fam* merci!
tab [tæb] *n* (**a**) *(label)* étiquette *f; Fam* **to keep tabs on sb** avoir qn à l'œil (**b**) *Am Fam (bill)* addition *f;* **to pick up the t.** payer l'addition (**c**) *(on computer, type-writer)* tabulateur *m;* **t. key** touche *f* de tabulation
tabby ['tæbɪ] *adj* **t. cat** chat *m* tigré
table¹ ['teɪbəl] *n* (**a**) *(furniture)* table *f;* **card/operating t.** table de jeu/d'opération; *Br* **to set** *or* **lay/clear the t.** mettre/débarrasser la table; (**sitting**) **at the t.** à table; **t. tennis** tennis *m* de table; **t. top** dessus *m* de table; **t. wine** vin *m* de table (**b**) *(list)* table *f;* **t. of contents** table des matières • **tablecloth** *n* nappe *f* • **table mat** *n* set *m* de table • **tablespoon** *n* ≃ cuillère *f* à soupe • **tablespoonful** *n* ≃ cuillerée *f* à soupe
table² ['teɪbəl] *vt Br (motion)* présenter; *Am (postpone)* ajourner
tablet ['tæblɪt] *n* (**a**) *(pill)* comprimé *m* (**b**) *(inscribed stone)* tablette *f*
tabloid ['tæblɔɪd] *n (newspaper)* tabloïd *m*
taboo [tə'buː] *(pl* **-oos**) *adj & n* tabou *(m)*
tabulate ['tæbjʊleɪt] *vt* présenter sous forme de tableau
tacit ['tæsɪt] *adj* tacite • **tacitly** *adv* tacitement
taciturn ['tæsɪtɜːn] *adj* taciturne
tack [tæk] **1** *n (nail)* clou *m; Am (thumb-tack)* punaise *f; Naut (course)* bordée *f; Fig* **to change t.** changer de tactique; *Fig* **to get down to brass tacks** en venir aux faits
2 *vt* **to t. (down)** clouer; *Fig* **to t. sth on** rajouter qch
3 *vi Naut* louvoyer
tackle ['tækəl] **1** *n (gear)* matériel *m; Rugby* placage *m; Football* tacle *m*
2 *vt (task, problem)* s'attaquer à; *(subject)* aborder; *Rugby* plaquer; *Football* tacler
tacky ['tækɪ] (**-ier, -iest**) *adj (sticky)* collant; *Fam (person)* vulgaire; *(remark)* de mauvais goût
taco ['tækəʊ] *(pl* **-os**) *n* crêpe *f* de maïs farcie

tact [tækt] *n* tact *m* • **tactful** *adj (remark)* diplomatique; **to be t.** *(of person)* avoir du tact • **tactfully** *adv* avec tact • **tactless** *adj (person, remark)* qui manque de tact • **tactlessly** *adv* sans tact
tactic ['tæktɪk] *n* **a t.** une tactique; **tactics** la tactique • **tactical** *adj* tactique
tactile ['tæktaɪl] *adj* tactile
tadpole ['tædpəʊl] *n* têtard *m*
tag [tæg] **1** *n (label)* étiquette *f*
2 *(pt & pp* **-gg-**) *vt (label)* étiqueter; *Fam* **to t. sth on** *(add)* rajouter qch (**to** à)
3 *vi* **to t. along with sb** venir avec qn
Tahiti [tə'hiːtɪ] *n* Tahiti *f*
tail [teɪl] **1** *n (of animal)* queue *f; (of shirt)* pan *m;* **tails, t. coat** queue-de-pie *f;* **the t. end** *(of film)* la fin (**of** de); *(of cloth, string)* le bout (**of** de)
2 *vt Fam (follow)* filer
3 *vi* **to t. off** *(lessen)* diminuer; *Br* **the traffic is tailing back (for miles)** ça bouchonne (sur des kilomètres) • **tailback** *n Br (of traffic)* bouchon *m* • **tailgate 1** *n Br (of car)* hayon *m* **2** *vt Am* **to t. sb** *(in vehicle)* coller au pare-chocs de qn • **tail-light** *n Am (of vehicle)* feu *m* arrière *inv*
tailor ['teɪlə(r)] **1** *n (person)* tailleur *m*
2 *vt (garment)* faire; *Fig (adjust)* adapter (**to** à) • **tailored** *adj* ajusté • **'tailor-'made** *adj* fait sur mesure
tainted ['teɪntɪd] *adj (air)* pollué; *(food)* gâté; *Fig (reputation, system)* souillé
Taiwan [taɪ'wɑːn] *n* Taïwan *m* ou *f*
take [teɪk] **1** *n (recording of film)* prise *f*
2 *(pt* **took,** *pp* **taken**) *vt* prendre; *(bring)* amener (**to** à); *(by car)* conduire (**to** à); *(escort)* accompagner (**to** à); *(lead away)* emmener (**to** à); *(of road)* mener (**to** à); *(prize)* remporter; *(exam)* passer; *(credit card)* accepter; *(contain)* avoir une capacité de; *(tolerate)* supporter; *Math (sub-tract)* soustraire (**from** de); **to t. sth to sb** apporter qch à qn; **to t. sb (out) to the theatre** emmener qn au théâtre; **to t. sth with one** emporter qch; **to t. sb home** ramener qn; **it takes an army/courage** il faut une armée/du courage (**to do** pour faire); **I took an hour to do it** *or* **over it** j'ai mis une heure à le faire; **I t.**

it that... je présume que...

3 *vi* *(of vaccination, fire)* prendre • **takeaway** *Br* **1** *adj (meal)* à emporter **2** *n (shop)* restaurant *m* qui fait des plats à emporter; *(meal)* plat *m* à emporter • **takeoff** *n (of plane)* décollage *m* • **takeout** *adj & n Am* = **takeaway** • **takeover** *n (of company)* rachat *m*; *(of government, country)* prise *f* de pouvoir
▸ **take after** *vt insep* **to t. after sb** ressembler à qn ▸ **take along** *vt sep (object)* emporter; *(person)* emmener ▸ **take apart** *vt sep (machine)* démonter ▸ **take away** *vt sep (thing)* emporter; *(person)* emmener; *(remove)* enlever (**from** à); *Math (subtract)* soustraire (**from** de) ▸ **take back** *vt sep* reprendre; *(return)* rapporter; *(statement)* retirer; *(accompany)* ramener (**to** à) ▸ **take down** *vt sep (object)* descendre; *(notes)* prendre ▸ **take in** *vt sep (chair, car)* rentrer; *(orphan)* recueillir; *(skirt)* reprendre; *(distance)* couvrir; *(include)* inclure; *(understand)* saisir; *Fam (deceive)* rouler ▸ **take off 1** *vt sep (remove)* enlever; *(train, bus)* supprimer; *(lead away)* emmener; *(mimic)* imiter; *Math (deduct)* déduire (**from** de) **2** *vi (of aircraft)* décoller ▸ **take on** *vt sep (work, staff, passenger, shape)* prendre ▸ **take out** *vt sep (from pocket)* sortir; *(stain)* enlever; *(tooth)* arracher; *(insurance policy, patent)* prendre; **to t. sb out to the theatre** emmener qn au théâtre; *Fam* **to t. it out on sb** passer sa colère sur qn ▸ **take over 1** *vt sep (become responsible for)* reprendre; *(buy out)* racheter; *(overrun)* envahir; **to t. over sb's job** remplacer qn **2** *vi (relieve)* prendre la relève (**from** de); *(succeed)* prendre la succession (**from** de); *(of dictator, general)* prendre le pouvoir ▸ **take round** *vt sep (bring)* apporter (**to** à); *(distribute)* distribuer; *(visitor)* faire visiter ▸ **take to** *vt insep* **to t. to doing sth** se mettre à faire qch; **I didn't t. to him/it** il/ça ne m'a pas plu ▸ **take up 1** *vt sep (carry up)* monter; *(continue)* reprendre; *(space, time)* prendre; *(offer)* accepter; *(hobby)* se mettre à; *(hem)* raccourcir **2** *vi* **to t. up with sb** se lier avec qn

taken ['teɪkən] *adj (seat)* pris; *(impressed)* impressionné (**with** or **by** par); **to be t. ill** tomber malade

taking ['teɪkɪŋ] *n (capture of town)* prise *f*; **takings** *(money)* recette *f*; **it's yours for the t.** tu n'as plus qu'à accepter

talc [tælk], **talcum powder** ['tælkəmpaʊdə(r)] *n* talc *m*

tale [teɪl] *n (story)* histoire *f*; *(legend)* conte *m*; *(lie)* salades *fpl*; **to tell tales** rapporter (**on sb** sur qn)

talent ['tælənt] *n* talent *m*; **to have a t. for** avoir du talent pour • **talented** *adj* talentueux, -ueuse

talisman ['tælɪzmən] *(pl* **-mans**) *n* talisman *m*

talk [tɔːk] **1** *n (conversation)* conversation *f* (**about** à propos de); *(lecture)* exposé *m* (**on** sur); **talks** *(negotiations)* pourparlers *mpl*; **to have a t. with sb** parler avec qn; **to do the talking** parler; **there's t. of** on parle de; **t. show** talk-show *m*
2 *vt (nonsense)* dire; **to t. politics** parler politique; **to t. sb into doing/out of doing sth** persuader qn de faire/de ne pas faire qch; **to t. sth over** discuter (de) qch; **to t. sb round** persuader qn
3 *vi* parler (**to/about** à/de); *(gossip)* jaser; **to t. down to sb** parler à qn sur un ton de supériorité • **talking** *adj* **t. film** film *m* parlant • **talking-to** *n* **to give sb a t.** passer un savon à qn

talkative ['tɔːkətɪv] *adj* bavard

talker ['tɔːkə(r)] *n* causeur, -euse *mf*; **she's a good t.** elle parle bien

tall [tɔːl] **(-er, -est)** *adj (person)* grand; *(tree, house)* haut; **how t. are you?** combien mesures-tu?; *Fig* **a t. story** une histoire invraisemblable • **tallness** *n (of person)* grande taille *f*; *(of building)* hauteur *f*

tallboy ['tɔːlbɔɪ] *n Br* grande commode *f*

tally ['tælɪ] *(pt & pp* **-ied**) *vi* correspondre (**with** à)

talon ['tælən] *n* serre *f*

tambourine [tæmbə'riːn] *n* tambourin *m*

tame [teɪm] **1** **(-er, -est)** *adj (animal)* apprivoisé; *Fig (person)* docile; *(book, play)* fade
2 *vt (animal)* apprivoiser; *Fig (emotions)* maîtriser

tamper ['tæmpə(r)] *vt insep* **to t. with** *(lock, car)* essayer de forcer; *(machine)* toucher à; *(documents)* trafiquer • **tamper-proof** *adj (lock)* inviolable; *(jar)* à fermeture de sécurité; **t. seal** fermeture *f* de sécurité

tampon ['tæmpɒn] *n* tampon *m* (hygiénique)

tan [tæn] **1** *n (suntan)* bronzage *m*
2 *adj (colour)* marron clair *inv*
3 *(pt & pp* **-nn-**) *vt (skin)* hâler; *(leather)* tanner
4 *vi (of person, skin)* bronzer

tandem ['tændəm] *n (bicycle)* tandem *m*;

in t. en tandem; **in t. with sth** parallèlement à qch

tang [tæŋ] *n (taste)* saveur *f* acidulée; *(smell)* odeur *f* acidulée • **tangy** (**-ier, -iest**) *adj* acidulé

tangent ['tændʒənt] *n Math* tangente *f*; **to go off at a t.** changer de sujet

tangerine [tændʒə'riːn] *n* mandarine *f*

tangible ['tændʒəbəl] *adj* tangible

tangle ['tæŋɡəl] *n* enchevêtrement *m*; **to get into a t.** *(of rope)* s'enchevêtrer; *(of hair)* s'emmêler; *Fig (of person)* s'embrouiller • **tangled** *adj* enchevêtré; *(hair)* emmêlé

tango ['tæŋɡəʊ] *(pl* **-os**) *n* tango *m*

tank [tæŋk] *n (container)* réservoir *m*; *(military vehicle)* tank *m*

tankard ['tæŋkəd] *n Br* chope *f*

tanker ['tæŋkə(r)] *n (lorry)* camion-citerne *m*; **(oil) t.** *(ship)* pétrolier *m*

Tannoy® ['tænɔɪ] *n Br* **over the T.** au haut-parleur

tantalizing ['tæntəlaɪzɪŋ] *adj* alléchant

tantamount ['tæntəmaʊnt] *adj* **it's t. to...** cela équivaut à...

tantrum ['tæntrəm] *n* caprice *m*; **to have a t.** faire un caprice

Tanzania [tænzə'nɪə] *n* la Tanzanie

tap¹ [tæp] **1** *n Br (for water)* robinet *m*; *Fig* **on t.** disponible; **t. water** eau *f* du robinet
2 *(pt & pp* **-pp-**) *vt (resources)* puiser dans; *(phone)* placer sur écoute

tap² [tæp] **1** *n (blow)* petit coup *m*; **t. dancing** claquettes *fpl*
2 *(pt & pp* **-pp-**) *vt (hit)* tapoter

tape [teɪp] **1** *n* (**a**) *(ribbon)* ruban *m*; **(sticky** *or* **adhesive) t.** ruban adhésif; **t. measure** mètre *m* (**à**) ruban (**b**) *(for recording)* bande *f*; *(cassette)* cassette *f*; **t. deck** platine *f* cassette; **t. recorder** magnétophone *m*
2 *vt* (**a**) *(stick)* scotcher (**b**) *(record)* enregistrer

taper ['teɪpə(r)] **1** *n (candle)* bougie *f* filée
2 *vi* s'effiler; *Fig* **to t. off** diminuer • **tapered** *adj (trousers)* en fuseau

tapestry ['tæpəstrɪ] *n* tapisserie *f*

tapeworm ['teɪpwɜːm] *n* ver *m* solitaire

tapioca [tæpɪ'əʊkə] *n* tapioca *m*

tar [tɑː(r)] **1** *n* goudron *m*
2 *(pt & pp* **-rr-**) *vt* goudronner

tarantula [tə'ræntjʊlə] *(pl* **-as**) *n* tarentule *f*

tardy ['tɑːdɪ] (**-ier, -iest**) *adj (belated)* tardif, -ive; *(slow)* lent

target ['tɑːɡɪt] **1** *n* cible *f*; *(objective)* objectif *m*; **t. market** marché *m* ciblé
2 *vt (campaign, product)* destiner (**at** à); *(age group)* viser

tariff ['tærɪf] *n (tax)* tarif *m* douanier; *Br (price list)* tarif

tarmac ['tɑːmæk] *n Br (on road)* macadam *m*; *(runway)* piste *f*

tarnish ['tɑːnɪʃ] *vt* ternir

tarpaulin [tɑː'pɔːlɪn] *n* bâche *f*

tarragon ['tærəgən] *n* estragon *m*

tart [tɑːt] **1** (**-er, -est**) *adj (sour)* aigre
2 *n* (**a**) *(pie) (large)* tarte *f*; *(small)* tartelette *f* (**b**) *Br Fam Pej (prostitute)* pute *f*
3 *vt Br Fam Pej* **t. up** *(decorate)* retaper

tartan ['tɑːtən] **1** *n* tartan *m*
2 *adj (skirt, tie)* écossais

tartar¹ ['tɑːtə(r)] *adj* **t. sauce** sauce *f* tartare

tartar² ['tɑːtə(r)] *n (on teeth)* tartre *m*

task [tɑːsk] *n* tâche *f*; **to take sb to t. for sth** reprocher qch à qn • **taskforce** *n Mil* corps *m* expéditionnaire; *Pol* commission *f* spéciale

tassel ['tæsəl] *n* gland *m*

taste [teɪst] **1** *n* goût *m*; **in good/bad t.** de bon/mauvais goût; **to have a t. of sth** goûter à qch; **to get a t. for sth** prendre goût à qch
2 *vt (detect flavour of)* sentir; *(sample)* goûter; *Fig (experience)* goûter à
3 *vi* **to t. of** *or* **like sth** avoir un goût de qch; **to t. good** être bon (*f* bonne) • **taste bud** *n* papille *f* gustative

tasteful ['teɪstfəl] *adj* de bon goût • **tastefully** *adv* avec goût • **tasteless** *adj (food)* insipide; *Fig (joke)* de mauvais goût • **tasty** (**-ier, -iest**) *adj* savoureux, -euse

tat [tæt] *see* **tit¹**

ta-ta [tæ'tɑː] *exclam Br Fam* au revoir!

tattered ['tætəd] *adj (clothes)* en lambeaux; *(person)* déguenillé • **tatters** *npl* **in t.** *(clothes)* en lambeaux

tattoo¹ [tæ'tuː] **1** *(pl* **-oos**) *n (design)* tatouage *m*; **to get a t.** se faire tatouer
2 *(pt & pp* **-ooed**) *vt* tatouer

tattoo² [tæ'tuː] *(pl* **-oos**) *n Mil* spectacle *m* militaire

tatty ['tætɪ] (**-ier, -iest**) *adj Br Fam* minable

taught [tɔːt] *pt & pp of* **teach**

taunt [tɔːnt] **1** *n* raillerie *f*
2 *vt* railler

Taurus ['tɔːrəs] *n (sign)* le Taureau; **to be a T.** être Taureau

taut [tɔːt] *adj* tendu

tavern ['tævən] *n* taverne *f*

tawdry ['tɔːdrɪ] (**-ier, -iest**) *adj Pej* tape-à-l'œil *inv*

tawny ['tɔːnɪ] *adj (colour)* fauve; **t. owl** (chouette *f*) hulotte *f*

tax¹ [tæks] **1** n (on goods) taxe f, impôt m; Br **road t.** ≃ vignette f automobile **2** adj fiscal; **t. collector** percepteur m; **t. relief** dégrèvement m fiscal; **t. return** déclaration f d'impôt; Br **(road) t. disc** ≃ vignette f automobile **3** vt (person) imposer; (goods) taxer • **taxable** adj imposable • **tax'ation** n (taxes) impôts mpl; (act) imposition f; **the burden of t.** le poids de l'impôt • **'tax-'free** adj exempt d'impôts • **taxman** (pl -men) n Br Fam percepteur m • **taxpayer** n contribuable mf

tax² [tæks] vt (put under strain) mettre à l'épreuve • **taxing** adj (journey) éprouvant

taxi ['tæksɪ] **1** n taxi m; **t. cab** taxi; Br **t. rank,** Am **t. stand** station f de taxis **2** vi (of aircraft) rouler

TB [tiː'biː] n tuberculose f

tea [tiː] n (plant, drink) thé m; Br (snack) goûter m; Br (evening meal) repas m du soir; Br **high t.** dîner m (pris tôt dans la soirée); **to have t.** prendre le thé; Br **t. break** ≃ pause-café f; **t. cloth** torchon m; **t. party** thé m; **t. set** service m à thé; **t. strainer** passoire f à thé; Br **t. towel** torchon m • **teabag** n sachet m de thé • **teacup** n tasse f à thé • **tea leaves** npl feuilles fpl de thé • **teapot** n théière f • **tearoom** n salon m de thé • **teashop** n Br salon m de thé • **teaspoon** n petite cuillère f • **teaspoonful** n cuillerée f à café • **teatime** n l'heure f du thé

teach [tiːtʃ] **1** (pt & pp taught) vt apprendre (**sb sth** qch à qn; **that** que); (in school, at university) enseigner (**sb sth** qch à qn); **to t. sb (how) to do sth** apprendre à qn à faire qch; **to t. oneself sth** apprendre qch tout seul; Am **to t. school** enseigner **2** vi enseigner • **teaching 1** n enseignement m **2** adj (staff) enseignant; (method, material) pédagogique; Br **t. hospital** centre m hospitalo-universitaire; **the t. profession** l'enseignement m; (teachers) le corps enseignant; **t. qualification** diplôme m permettant d'enseigner; **the t. staff** le personnel enseignant

teacher ['tiːtʃə(r)] n professeur m; (in primary school) instituteur, -trice mf; Br **teachers' training college** ≃ IUFM m

teak [tiːk] n teck m; **a t. sideboard** un buffet en teck

team [tiːm] **1** n équipe f; (of horses, oxen) attelage m; **t. mate** coéquipier, -ière mf **2** vi **to t. up** faire équipe (**with sb** avec qn) • **teamster** n Am routier m • **teamwork** n travail m d'équipe

tear¹ [teə(r)] **1** n déchirure f **2** (pt **tore,** pp **torn**) vt (rip) déchirer; (snatch) arracher (**from** à); Fig **torn between** tiraillé entre; **to t. sb away from sth** arracher qn à qch; **to t. down** (house) démolir; **to t. off** or **out** arracher; **to t. up** déchirer **3** vi (of cloth) se déchirer; **to t. along/past/away** aller/passer/partir à toute vitesse

tear² [tɪə(r)] n larme f; **in tears** en larmes; **close to** or **near (to) tears** au bord des larmes • **tearful** adj (eyes) larmoyant; (person) en larmes; **in a t. voice** avec des larmes dans la voix • **tearfully** adv en pleurant • **tear gas** n gaz m lacrymogène

tearaway ['teərəweɪ] n Br Fam casse-cou m inv

tease [tiːz] **1** n (person) taquin, -ine mf **2** vt taquiner • **teaser** n (person) taquin, -ine mf; Fam (question) colle f • **teasing** adj (remark) taquin

teat [tiːt] n Br (of animal) trayon m; (of baby's bottle) tétine f

technical ['teknɪkəl] adj technique; Br **t. college** ≃ institut m universitaire; **t. drawing** dessin m industriel • **technicality** [-'kælɪtɪ] n (detail) détail m technique • **technically** adv techniquement

technician ['teknɪʃən] n technicien, -ienne mf

technique [tek'niːk] n technique f

technocrat ['teknəkræt] n technocrate m

technology [tek'nɒlədʒɪ] (pl -ies) n technologie f • **technological** [-nə'lɒdʒɪkəl] adj technologique

teddy ['tedɪ] n **t. (bear)** ours m en peluche

tedious ['tiːdɪəs] adj fastidieux, -ieuse • **tediousness, tedium** n ennui m

teem [tiːm] vi (swarm) grouiller (**with** de); **to t. (with rain)** pleuvoir à torrents • **teeming** adj grouillant; **t. rain** pluie f torrentielle

teenage ['tiːneɪdʒ] adj (boy, girl, behaviour) adolescent; (fashion, magazine) pour adolescents • **teenager** n adolescent, -ente mf • **teens** npl **to be in one's t.** être adolescent

teeny(-weeny) ['tiːnɪ('wiːnɪ)] adj Fam (tiny) minuscule

tee-shirt ['tiːʃɜːt] n tee-shirt m

teeter ['tiːtə(r)] vi (be unsteady) chanceler; Fig **to t. on the brink of sth** être au bord de qch

teeth [tiːθ] pl of **tooth**

teethe [tiːð] vi faire ses dents • **teething** n

poussée f dentaire; *Fig* **t. troubles** difficultés *fpl* de mise en route

teetotal [tiː'təʊtəl] *adj* **to be t.** ne jamais boire d'alcool • **teetotaller** (*Am* **teetotaler**) *n* personne f qui ne boit jamais d'alcool

TEFL ['tefəl] (*abbr* **Teaching of English as a Foreign Language**) *n* enseignement *m* de l'anglais langue étrangère

telecommunications [telɪkəmjuːnɪ'keɪʃənz] *npl* télécommunications *fpl*

telegram ['telɪɡræm] *n* télégramme *m*

telegraph ['telɪɡrɑːf] *adj* **t. pole/wire** poteau *m*/fil *m* télégraphique

Telemessage® ['telɪmesɪdʒ] *n* (*in UK*) ≃ télégramme *m* (téléphoné)

telepathy [tə'lepəθɪ] *n* télépathie f

telephone ['telɪfəʊn] **1** *n* téléphone *m*; **to be on the t.** (*speaking*) être au téléphone **2** *adj* (*call, line, message*) téléphonique; *Br* **t. booth, t. box** cabine f téléphonique; **t. directory** annuaire *m* du téléphone; **t. number** numéro *m* de téléphone **3** *vt* (*message*) téléphoner (**to** à); **to t. sb** téléphoner à qn **4** *vi* téléphoner • **telephonist** [tɪ'lefənɪst] *n Br* téléphoniste *mf*

telephoto ['telɪfəʊtəʊ] *adj* **t. lens** téléobjectif *m*

teleprinter ['telɪprɪntə(r)] *n Br* téléimprimeur *m*

telescope ['telɪskəʊp] *n* télescope *m* • **telescopic** [-'skɒpɪk] *adj* télescopique

teletext ['telɪtekst] *n* télétexte *m*

teletypewriter [telɪ'taɪpraɪtə(r)] *n Am* téléscripteur *m*

televise ['telɪvaɪz] *vt* téléviser

television [telɪ'vɪʒən] **1** *n* télévision f; **on (the) t.** à la télévision; **to watch (the) t.** regarder la télévision **2** *adj* (*programme, screen*) de télévision; (*interview, report*) télévisé; **t. set** téléviseur *m*

teleworking ['telɪwɜːkɪŋ] *n* télétravail *m*

telex ['teleks] **1** *n* (*service, message*) télex *m* **2** *vt* (*message*) télexer

tell [tel] **1** (*pt & pp* **told**) *vt* dire (**sb sth** à qn; **that** que); (*story*) raconter; (*distinguish*) distinguer (**from** de); **to t. sb to do sth** dire à qn de faire qch; **to know how to t. the time** savoir lire l'heure; **to t. the difference** voir la différence (**between** entre); **I could t. she was lying** je savais qu'elle mentait; *Fam* **to t. sb off** disputer qn **2** *vi* dire; (*have an effect*) se faire sentir; **to t. of** *or* **about sb/sth** parler de qn/qch;

it's hard to t. c'est difficile à dire; **you can never t.** on ne sait jamais; *Fam* **to t. on sb** dénoncer qn

teller ['telə(r)] *n* (*in bank*) guichetier, -ière *mf*

telling ['telɪŋ] *adj* (*revealing*) révélateur, -trice; (*decisive*) qui porte

telltale ['telteɪl] **1** *adj* révélateur, -trice **2** *n* rapporteur, -euse *mf*

telly ['telɪ] *n Br Fam* télé f; **on the t.** à la télé

temerity [tə'merɪtɪ] *n* témérité f

temp [temp] *Br Fam* **1** *n* intérimaire *mf* **2** *vi* faire de l'intérim

temper ['tempə(r)] **1** *n* (*mood, nature*) humeur f; (*bad mood*) mauvaise humeur; **in a bad t.** de mauvaise humeur; **to have a (bad) t.** avoir un caractère de cochon; **to lose one's t.** se mettre en colère **2** *vt* (*moderate*) tempérer; (*steel*) tremper

temperament ['tempərəmənt] *n* tempérament *m* • **temperamental** [-'mentəl] *adj* (*person, machine*) capricieux, -ieuse; (*inborn*) inné

temperance ['tempərəns] *n* (*in drink*) tempérance f

temperate ['tempərət] *adj* (*climate*) tempéré

temperature ['tempərət∫ə(r)] *n* température f; **to have a t.** avoir de la température

tempest ['tempɪst] *n Literary* tempête f • **tempestuous** [-'pestjʊəs] *adj* (*meeting*) orageux, -euse

template ['templət, -pleɪt] *n* gabarit *m*; *Comptr* modèle *m*

temple¹ ['tempəl] *n* (*religious building*) temple *m*

temple² ['tempəl] *n Anat* tempe f

tempo ['tempəʊ] (*pl* **-os**) *n* (*of life, work*) rythme *m*; *Mus* tempo *m*

temporal ['tempərəl] *adj* temporel, -elle

temporary [*Br* 'tempərərɪ, *Am* -erɪ] *adj* temporaire; (*secretary*) intérimaire • **temporarily** [*Br* 'tempərərɪlɪ, *Am* tempə'reərɪlɪ] *adv* temporairement

tempt [tempt] *vt* tenter; **tempted to do sth** tenté de faire qch; **to t. sb to do sth** inciter qn à faire qch • **temp'tation** *n* tentation f • **tempting** *adj* tentant

ten [ten] *adj & n* dix (*m*)

tenable ['tenəbəl] *adj* défendable; **the post is t. for three years** ce poste peut être occupé pendant trois ans

tenacious [tə'neɪ∫əs] *adj* tenace • **tenacity** [-'næsɪtɪ] *n* ténacité f

tenant ['tenənt] *n* locataire *mf* • **tenancy** *n (lease)* location *f; (period)* occupation *f*

tend¹ [tend] *vi* **to t. to do sth** avoir tendance à faire qch; **to t. towards** incliner vers • **tendency** (*pl* **-ies**) *n* tendance *f* (**to do** à faire)

tend² [tend] *vt (look after)* s'occuper de

tendentious [ten'denʃəs] *adj Pej* tendancieux, -ieuse

tender¹ ['tendə(r)] *adj (soft, delicate, loving)* tendre; *(painful)* sensible • **tenderly** *adv* tendrement • **tenderness** *n* tendresse *f; (pain)* (petite) douleur *f; (of meat)* tendreté *f*

tender² ['tendə(r)] **1** *n Com (bid)* soumission *f* (**for** pour); **to be legal t.** *(of money)* avoir cours
2 *vt (offer)* offrir; **to t. one's resignation** donner sa démission

tendon ['tendən] *n Anat* tendon *m*

tenement ['tenəmənt] *n* immeuble *m*

tenet ['tenɪt] *n* principe *m*

tenfold ['tenfəʊld] **1** *adj* décuple
2 *adv* **to increase t.** être multiplié par dix

tenner ['tenə(r)] *n Br Fam* billet *m* de 10 livres

tennis ['tenɪs] *n* tennis *m*; **t. court** court *m* de tennis

tenor ['tenə(r)] *n* (**a**) *Formal (sense, course)* teneur *f* (**b**) *Mus* ténor *m*

tenpin ['tenpɪn] *adj Br* **t. bowling** bowling *m*

tense¹ [tens] **1** (**-er, -est**) *adj (person, muscle, situation)* tendu
2 *vt* tendre; *(muscle)* contracter
3 *vi* **to t. (up)** *(of person, face)* se crisper • **tension** *n* tension *f*

tense² [tens] *n Grammar* temps *m*; **in the future t.** au futur

tent [tent] *n* tente *f; Br* **t. peg** piquet *m* de tente; *Br* **t. pole,** *Am* **t. stake** mât *m* de tente

tentacle ['tentəkəl] *n* tentacule *m*

tentative ['tentətɪv] *adj (not definite)* provisoire; *(hesitant)* timide • **tentatively** *adv* provisoirement; *(hesitantly)* timidement

tenterhooks ['tentəhʊks] *npl* **to be on t.** être sur des charbons ardents

tenth [tenθ] *adj & n* dixième *(mf);* **a t.** un dixième

tenuous ['tenjʊəs] *adj (link, suspicion)* ténu

tepid ['tepɪd] *adj (liquid) & Fig* tiède

term [tɜːm] **1** *n (word)* terme *m; (period)* période *f; Br (of school or university year)* trimestre *m; Am (semester)* semestre *m; Pol* **t. (of office)** mandat *m*; **terms** *(conditions)* conditions *fpl; (of contract)* termes *mpl*; **terms of reference** *(of commission)* attributions *fpl*; **to be on good/bad terms** être en bons/mauvais termes (**with sb** avec qn); **to buy sth on easy terms** acheter qch avec facilités de paiement; **in terms of** *(speaking of)* sur le plan de; **in real terms** dans la pratique; **to come to terms with sth** se résigner à qch; **in the long/short/medium t.** à long/court/moyen terme; **at (full) t.** *(baby)* à terme
2 *vt* appeler

terminal ['tɜːmɪnəl] **1** *n (electronic) & Comptr* terminal *m; (of battery)* borne *f;* **(air) t.** aérogare *f;* **(oil) t.** terminal pétrolier
2 *adj (patient, illness)* en phase terminale; **in its t. stage** *(illness)* en phase terminale • **terminally** *adv* **t. ill** *(patient)* en phase terminale

terminate ['tɜːmɪneɪt] **1** *vt* mettre fin à; *(contract)* résilier; *(pregnancy)* interrompre
2 *vi* se terminer • **termi'nation** *n* fin *f; (of contract)* résiliation *f; (of pregnancy)* interruption *f*

terminology [tɜːmɪ'nɒlədʒɪ] (*pl* **-ies**) *n* terminologie *f*

terminus ['tɜːmɪnəs] *n* terminus *m*

termite ['tɜːmaɪt] *n (insect)* termite *m*

terrace ['terɪs] *n (next to house, on hill)* terrasse *f; Br (houses)* = rangée de maisons attenantes; *Br* **the terraces** *(at football ground)* les gradins *mpl* • **terrace house, terraced house** *n Br* = maison située dans une rangée d'habitations attenantes

terracotta [terə'kɒtə] *n* terre *f* cuite

terrain [tə'reɪn] *n Mil & Geol* terrain *m*

terrestrial [tə'restrɪəl] *adj* terrestre

terrible ['terəbəl] *adj* terrible • **terribly** *adv (badly)* affreusement mal; *(injured)* très gravement

terrier ['terɪə(r)] *n (dog)* terrier *m*

terrific [tə'rɪfɪk] *adj Fam (excellent)* super *inv* • **terrifically** *adv Fam (extremely)* terriblement; *(extremely well)* terriblement bien

terrify ['terɪfaɪ] *(pt & pp* **-ied**) *vt* terrifier; **to be terrified of sb/sth** avoir une peur bleue de qn/qch • **terrifying** *adj* terrifiant

territory ['terɪtərɪ] *(pl* **-ies**) *n* territoire *m* • **territorial** [-'tɔːrɪəl] *adj* territorial; *Br* **the T. Army** = armée de réserve, constituée de volontaires

terror ['terə(r)] *n* terreur *f; Fam* **that child is a t.** cet enfant est une vraie terreur • **terrorism** *n* terrorisme *m* • **terrorist** *n & adj* terroriste *(mf)* • **terrorize** *vt* terroriser

terse [tɜːs] *adj* laconique
tertiary ['tɜːʃərɪ] *adj* tertiaire; **t. education** enseignement *m* supérieur
test [test] **1** *n* (*trial*) essai *m*; (*of product*) test *m*; *Sch & Univ* interrogation *f*; (*by doctor*) examen *m*; (*of blood*) analyse *f*; **to put sb to the t.** mettre qn à l'épreuve; **eye t.** examen de la vue; **driving t.** examen du permis de conduire
2 *adj* **t. pilot/flight** pilote *m*/vol *m* d'essai; **t. drive** *or* **run** essai *m* sur route; *Law* **t. case** précédent *m*; *Cricket* **t. match** match *m* international; **t. tube** éprouvette *f*; **t. tube baby** bébé-éprouvette *m*
3 *vt* (*try*) essayer; (*product, machine*) tester; (*pupil*) interroger; (*of doctor*) examiner; (*blood*) analyser; *Fig* (*try out*) mettre à l'épreuve; **to t. sb for AIDS** faire subir à qn un test de dépistage du SIDA
4 *vi* **to t. positive** (*for drugs*) être positif, -ive
testament ['testəmənt] *n* (*will*) testament *m*; (*tribute*) preuve *f*; *Rel* **the Old/ New T.** l'Ancien/le Nouveau Testament
testicle ['testɪkəl] *n* *Anat* testicule *m*
testify ['testɪfaɪ] (*pt & pp* **-ied**) *Law* **1** *vt* **to t. that...** témoigner que...
2 *vi* témoigner (**against** contre); **to t. to sth** (*be proof of*) témoigner de qch • **testimonial** [-'məʊnɪəl] *n* références *fpl* • **testimony** ['testɪmənɪ] (*pl* **-ies**) *n* témoignage *m*
testy ['testɪ] (**-ier, -iest**) *adj* irritable
tetanus ['tetənəs] *n* *Med* tétanos *m*
tetchy ['tetʃɪ] (**-ier, -iest**) *adj* irritable
tête-à-tête [teɪtɑː'teɪt] *n* tête-à-tête *m inv*
tether ['teðə(r)] **1** *n* **at the end of one's t.** à bout
2 *vt* (*animal*) attacher
text [tekst] *n* texte *m* • **textbook** *n* manuel *m*
textile ['tekstaɪl] *adj & n* textile (*m*)
texture ['tekstʃə(r)] *n* (*of fabric, cake*) texture *f*; (*of paper, wood*) grain *m*
Thai [taɪ] **1** *adj* thaïlandais
2 *n* Thaïlandais, -aise *mf* • **Thailand** *n* la Thaïlande
Thames [temz] *n* **the T.** la Tamise
than [ðən, *stressed* ðæn] *conj* que; **happier t. me** plus heureux que moi; **less happy t. you** moins heureux que toi; **he has more/less t. you** il en a plus/moins que toi; **she has fewer oranges t. plums** elle a moins d'oranges que de prunes; **more t. six** plus de six
thank [θæŋk] *vt* remercier (**for sth** de qch; **for doing** d'avoir fait); **t. you** merci; **no, t. you** (non) merci; **t. God!, t.**

heavens!, t. goodness! Dieu merci! • **thanks** *npl* remerciements *mpl*; (**many**) **t.!** merci (beaucoup)!; **t. to** (*because of*) grâce à
thankful ['θæŋkfəl] *adj* reconnaissant (**for** de); **to be t. that...** être heureux, -euse que... (+ *subjunctive*) • **thankfully** *adv* (*gratefully*) avec reconnaissance; (*fortunately*) heureusement • **thankless** *adj* ingrat
thanksgiving [θæŋks'gɪvɪŋ] *n* action *f* de grâce; *Am* **T. (Day)** = 4ème jeudi de novembre, commémorant la première action de grâce des colons anglais
that [ðət, *stressed* ðæt] **1** *conj* (*souvent omise*) que; **she said (t.) she would come** elle a dit qu'elle viendrait
2 *relative pron*

> On peut omettre le pronom relatif **that** sauf s'il est en position sujet.

(*subject*) qui; (*object*) que; (*with preposition*) lequel, laquelle, *pl* lesquel(le)s; **the boy t. left** le garçon qui est parti; **the book (t.) I read** le livre que j'ai lu; **the carpet (t.) I put it on** le tapis sur lequel je l'ai mis; **the house (t.) she told me about** la maison dont elle m'a parlé; **the day/ morning (t.) she arrived** le jour/matin où elle est arrivée
3 (*pl* **those**) *demonstrative adj* ce, cet (*before vowel or mute h*), cette; (*opposed to 'this'*) ce...-là (*f* cette...-là); **t. woman** cette femme(-là); **t. day** ce jour-là; **t. one** celui-là *m*, celle-là *f*
4 (*pl* **those**) *demonstrative pron* cela, *Fam* ça; **give me t.** donne-moi ça; **before t.** avant cela; **t.'s right** c'est exact; **who's t.?** qui est-ce?; **t.'s the house** voilà la maison; **what do you mean by t.?** qu'entends-tu par là?; **t. is (to say)** c'est-à-dire
5 *adv Fam* (*so*) si; **not t. good** pas si bon que ça; **t. high** (*pointing*) haut comme ça; **it cost t. much** ça a coûté tant que ça
thatch [θætʃ] *n* chaume *m* • **thatched** *adj* (*roof*) de chaume; **t. cottage** chaumière *f*
thaw [θɔː] **1** *n* dégel *m*
2 *vt* (*snow, ice*) faire fondre; **to t. (out)** (*food*) se décongeler
3 *vi* dégeler; (*of snow, ice*) fondre; (*of food*) décongeler; *Fig* **to t. (out)** (*of person*) se dérider
the [ðə, *before vowel* ðɪ, *stressed* ðiː] *definite article* le, l', la, *pl* les; **t. roof** le toit; **t. man** l'homme; **t. moon** la lune; **t. orange** l'orange; **t. boxes** les boîtes; **t. smallest** le plus petit (*f* la plus petite); **of t., from t.** du, de l', de la, *pl* des; **to t., at t.**

au, à l', à la, *pl* aux; **Elizabeth t. Second** Élisabeth Deux

theatre ['θɪətə(r)] (*Am* **theater**) *n* (*place, art*) théâtre *m*; *Br* (**operating**) **t.** (*in hospital*) salle *f* d'opération; *Mil* **t. of operations** théâtre des opérations • **theatregoer** *n* amateur *m* de théâtre • **theatrical** [θɪ'ætrɪkəl] *adj* théâtral; **t. company** troupe *f* de théâtre

theft [θeft] *n* vol *m*

their [ðeə(r)] *possessive adj* leur, *pl* leurs; **t. house** leur maison *f* • **theirs** *possessive pron* le leur, la leur, *pl* les leurs; **this book is t.** ce livre est à eux *ou* est le leur; **a friend of t.** un ami à eux

them [ðəm, *stressed* ðem] *pron* les; (*after prep, 'than', 'it is'*) eux *mpl*, elles *fpl*; **(to) t.** (*indirect*) leur; **I see t.** je les vois; **I gave it to t.** je le leur ai donné; **with t.** avec eux/elles; **ten of t.** dix d'entre eux/elles; **all of t. came** tous sont venus, toutes sont venues; **I like all of t.** je les aime tous/toutes

theme [θiːm] *n* thème *m*; **t. song** or **tune** chanson *f* de générique; **t. park** parc *m* à thème

themselves [ðəm'selvz, *stressed* ðem'-selvz] *pron* eux-mêmes *mpl*, elles-mêmes *fpl*; (*reflexive*) se, s'; (*after prep*) eux *mpl*, elles *fpl*; **they did it t.** ils/elles l'ont fait eux-mêmes/elles-mêmes; **they cut t.** ils/elles se sont coupé(e)s; **they wash t.** ils/elles se lavent; **they think of t.** ils pensent à eux/elles pensent à elles

then [ðen] **1** *adv* (*at that time*) à cette époque-là, alors; (*just a moment ago*) à ce moment-là; (*next*) ensuite, puis; (*therefore*) donc, alors; **from t. on** dès lors; **before t.** avant cela; **until t.** jusque-là, jusqu'alors

2 *adj* **the t. mayor** le maire d'alors

theology [θɪ'ɒlədʒɪ] *n* théologie *f* • **theologian** [θɪə'ləʊdʒən] *n* théologien *m* • **theological** [θɪə'lɒdʒɪkəl] *adj* théologique

theorem ['θɪərəm] *n* théorème *m*

theory ['θɪərɪ] (*pl* -**ies**) *n* théorie *f*; **in t.** en théorie • **theo'retical** *adj* théorique • **theo'retically** *adv* théoriquement • **theorist** *n* théoricien, -ienne *mf* • **theorize** *vi* théoriser (**about** sur)

therapy ['θerəpɪ] (*pl* -**ies**) *n* thérapeutique *f* • **therapeutic** [-'pjuːtɪk] *adj* thérapeutique • **therapist** *n* thérapeute *mf*

there [ðeə(r)] *adv* là; (**down** *or* **over**) **t.** là-bas; **on t.** là-dessus; **she'll be t.** elle y sera; **t. is, t. are** il y a; (*pointing*) voilà; **t. he is** le voilà; **t. she is** la voilà; **t. they are** les

voilà; **that man t.** cet homme-là; **t. (you are)!** (*take this*) tenez!; **t., (t.,) don't cry!** allons, allons, ne pleure pas! • **there-a'bouts** *adv* dans les environs; (*in amount*) à peu près • **there'after** *adv* *Formal* après cela • **thereby** *adv* *Formal* ainsi • **therefore** *adv* donc • **thereu'pon** *adv* *Formal* sur ce

thermal ['θɜːməl] *adj* (*underwear*) en Thermolactyl®; (*energy, unit*) thermique

thermometer [θə'mɒmɪtə(r)] *n* thermomètre *m*

thermonuclear [θɜːməʊ'njuːklɪə(r)] *adj* thermonucléaire

Thermos® ['θɜːməs] (*pl* -**moses** [-mə-səz]) *n* **T.** (**flask**) Thermos® *m ou f*

thermostat ['θɜːməstæt] *n* thermostat *m*

thesaurus [θɪ'sɔːrəs] *n* dictionnaire *m* de synonymes

these [ðiːz] (*sing* **this**) **1** *demonstrative adj* ces; (*opposed to 'those'*) ces...-ci; **t. men** ces hommes(-ci); **t. ones** ceux-ci *mpl*, celles-ci *fpl*

2 *demonstrative pron* ceux-ci *mpl*, celles-ci *fpl*; **t. are my friends** ce sont mes amis

thesis ['θiːsɪs] (*pl* **theses** ['θiːsiːz]) *n* thèse *f*

they [ðeɪ] *pron* (**a**) (*subject*) ils *mpl*, elles *fpl*; (*stressed*) eux *mpl*, elles *fpl*; **t. go** ils/elles vont; **t. are doctors** ce sont des médecins (**b**) (*people in general*) on; **t. say** on dit • **they'd** = **they had, they would** • **they'll** = **they will**

thick [θɪk] **1** (-**er**, -**est**) *adj* épais (*f* épaisse); *Fam* (*stupid*) lourd

2 *adv* (*spread*) en couche épaisse; (*grow*) dru

3 *n* **in the t. of battle** au cœur de la bataille • **thickly** *adv* (*spread*) en couche épaisse; (*grow*) dru; **t. populated/wooded** très peuplé/boisé

thicken ['θɪkən] **1** *vt* épaissir

2 *vi* (*of fog*) s'épaissir; (*of cream, sauce*) épaissir • **thickness** *n* épaisseur *f*

thicket ['θɪkɪt] *n* fourré *m*

thickset [θɪk'set] *adj* (*person*) trapu • '**thick-'skinned** *adj* (*person*) peu susceptible

thief [θiːf] (*pl* **thieves**) *n* voleur, -euse *mf*; **stop t.!** au voleur! • **thieve** *vti* voler • **thieving 1** *adj* voleur, -euse **2** *n* vol *m*

thigh [θaɪ] *n* cuisse *f* • **thighbone** *n* fémur *m*

thimble ['θɪmbəl] *n* dé *m* à coudre

thin [θɪn] **1** (**thinner, thinnest**) *adj* (*person, slice, paper*) mince; (*soup*) peu épais (*f* peu épaisse); (*crowd, hair*) clairsemé;

(powder) fin; *Fig (excuse, profit)* maigre **2** *adv (spread)* en couche mince; *(cut)* en tranches minces **3** *(pt & pp* **-nn-)** *vt* **to t. (down)** *(paint)* diluer **4** *vi* **to t. out** *(of crowd, mist)* s'éclaircir • **thinly** *adv (spread)* en couche mince; *(cut)* en tranches minces; **t. disguised** à peine déguisé; **t. populated/wooded** peu peuplé/boisé • **thinness** *n* minceur *f*

thing [θɪŋ] *n* chose *f*; **one's things** *(belongings, clothes)* ses affaires *fpl*; **it's a funny t.** c'est drôle; **poor little t.!** pauvre petit!; **that's just the t.** voilà exactement ce qu'il faut; **how are things?, how's things?** *Fam* comment ça va?; **I'll think things over** j'y réfléchirai; **for one t.... and for another t....** d'abord... et ensuite ...; *Br* **the tea things** *(set)* le service à thé; *(dishes)* la vaisselle • **thingamabob** ['θɪŋəməbɒb] *(Br* **thingummy** ['θɪŋəmɪ]) *n Fam* truc *m*, machin *m*

think [θɪŋk] **1** *(pt & pp* **thought)** *vt* penser *(* that que*)*; **I t. so** je pense *ou* crois que oui; **what do you t. of him?** que penses-tu de lui?; **I thought it difficult** j'ai trouvé ça difficile; **to t. out** *(plan, method)* élaborer; *(reply)* réfléchir sérieusement à; **to t. sth over** réfléchir à qch; **to t. sth through** réfléchir à qch sous tous les angles; **to t. sth up** *(invent)* inventer qch **2** *vi* penser *(* about/of à*)*; **to t. (carefully)** réfléchir *(* about/of à*)*; **to t. of doing sth** penser à faire qch; **to t. highly of sb** penser beaucoup de bien de qn; **she doesn't t. much of it** ça ne lui dit pas grand-chose; **to t. better of it** se raviser; **I can't t. of it** je n'arrive pas à m'en souvenir **3** *n Fam* **to have a t.** réfléchir *(* about à*)*; **t.-tank** comité *m* d'experts • **thinker** *n* penseur, -euse *mf* • **thinking 1** *adj* **t. person** personne *f* intelligente **2** *n (opinion)* opinion *f*; **to my t.** à mon avis

thinner ['θɪnə(r)] *n* diluant *m*

thin-skinned [θɪn'skɪnd] *adj Fig* susceptible

third [θɜːd] **1** *adj* troisième; **t. person** *or* **party** tiers *m*; **t.-party insurance** assurance *f* au tiers; **the T. World** le tiers-monde **2** *n* troisième *mf*; **a t.** *(fraction)* un tiers **3** *adv* **to come t.** *(in race)* se classer troisième • **thirdly** *adv* troisièmement

third-class ['θɜːd'klɑːs] *adj* de troisième classe; *Br* **t. degree** ≃ licence *f* avec mention passable • 'third-'rate *adj* très inférieur

thirst [θɜːst] *n* soif *f* *(* for de*)* • **thirsty**

(-ier, -iest) *adj* **to be** *or* **feel t.** avoir soif; **to make sb t.** donner soif à qn; *Fig* **to be t. for power** être assoiffé de pouvoir

thirteen [θɜː'tiːn] *adj & n* treize *(m)* • **thirteenth** *adj & n* treizième *(mf)*

thirty ['θɜːtɪ] *adj & n* trente *(m)* • **thirtieth** *adj & n* trentième *(mf)*

this [ðɪs] **1** *(pl* **these)** *demonstrative adj* ce, cet *(before vowel or mute h)*, cette; *(opposed to 'that')* ce...-ci; **t. book** ce livre(-ci); **t. man** cet homme(-ci); **t. photo** cette photo(-ci); **t. one** celui-ci *m*, celle-ci *f*

2 *(pl* **these)** *demonstrative pron (subject)* ce, ceci; *(object)* ceci; **give me t.** donne-moi ceci; **I prefer t.** je préfère celui-ci; **before t.** avant ceci; **who's t.?** qui est-ce?; **t. is Paul** c'est Paul; *(pointing)* voici Paul

3 *adv (so)* **t. high** *(pointing)* haut comme ceci; **t. far** *(until now)* jusqu'ici

thistle ['θɪsəl] *n* chardon *m*

thorax ['θɔːræks] *n Anat* thorax *m*

thorn [θɔːn] *n* épine *f* • **thorny** *(-ier, -iest)* *adj (bush, problem)* épineux, -euse

thorough ['θʌrə] *adj (search, cleaning, preparation)* minutieux, -ieuse; *(knowledge, examination)* approfondi; **to give sth a t. washing** laver qch à fond • **thoroughly** *adv (completely)* tout à fait; *(carefully)* avec minutie; *(know, clean, wash)* à fond • **thoroughness** *n* minutie *f*

thoroughbred ['θʌrəbred] *n* pur-sang *m inv*

thoroughfare ['θʌrəfeə(r)] *n* voie *f* de communication; *Br* **'no t.'** 'passage interdit'

those [ðəʊz] **1** *(sing* **that)** *demonstrative adj* ces; *(opposed to 'these')* ces...-là; **t. men** ces hommes(-là); **t. ones** ceux-là *mpl*, celles-là *fpl*

2 *(sing* **that)** *demonstrative pron* ceux-là *mpl*, celles-là *fpl*; **t. are my friends** ce sont mes amis

though [ðəʊ] **1** *conj* bien que *(+ subjunctive)*; **(even) t.** même si; **as t.** comme si; **strange t. it may seem** si étrange que cela puisse paraître

2 *adv (however)* pourtant

thought [θɔːt] **1** *pt & pp of* **think**

2 *n* pensée *f*; **(careful) t.** réflexion *f*; **to have second thoughts** changer d'avis; *Br* **on second thoughts,** *Am* **on second t.** à la réflexion; **I didn't give it another t.** je n'y ai plus pensé

thoughtful ['θɔːtfəl] *adj (considerate, kind)* attentionné; *(pensive)* pensif, -ive; *(serious)* sérieux, -ieuse • **thoughtfully**

adv (considerately) gentiment •**thought-fulness** *n* gentillesse *f*

thoughtless ['θɔːtləs] *adj* irréfléchi

thousand ['θaʊzənd] *adj & n* mille *(m)* *inv*; **a t. pages** mille pages; **two t. pages** deux mille pages; **thousands of** des milliers de; **they came in their thousands** ils sont venus par milliers

thrash [θræʃ] **1** *vt* **to t. sb** donner une correction à qn; *(defeat)* écraser qn; **to t. out** *(plan)* discuter de
2 *vi* **to t. around** *or* **about** *(struggle)* se débattre •**thrashing** *n (beating)* correction *f*

thread [θred] **1** *n (yarn) & Fig* fil *m*; *(of screw)* filetage *m*
2 *vt (needle, beads)* enfiler; **to t. one's way between...** se faufiler entre... •**threadbare** *adj* élimé

threat [θret] *n* menace *f* •**threaten 1** *vt* menacer (**to do** de faire; **with sth** de qch) **2** *vi* menacer •**threatening** *adj* menaçant •**threateningly** *adv (say)* d'un ton menaçant

three [θriː] *adj & n* trois *(m)*; *Br* **t.-piece suite** canapé *m* et deux fauteuils assortis •**three-'D** *adj (film)* en 3-D •**three-di-'mensional** *adj* à trois dimensions •**three-fold 1** *adj* triple **2** *adv* **to increase t.** tripler •**three-point** '**turn** *n Aut* demi-tour *m* en trois manœuvres •'**three-'quarters 1** *n* **t. (of)** les trois quarts *mpl* (de) **2** *adv* **it's t. full** c'est aux trois quarts plein •**three-some** *n* groupe *m* de trois personnes •**three-way** *adj (division)* en trois; *(conversation)* à trois •**three-'wheeler** *n (tricycle)* tricycle *m*; *(car)* voiture *f* à trois roues

thresh [θreʃ] *vt* battre

threshold ['θreʃhəʊld] *n* seuil *m*; **pain t.** seuil de résistance à la douleur

threw [θruː] *pt of* **throw**

thrift [θrɪft] *n* économie *f* •**thrifty** (**-ier**, **-iest**) *adj* économe

thrill [θrɪl] **1** *n* frisson *m*; **to get a t. out of doing sth** prendre plaisir à faire qch
2 *vt (delight)* réjouir; *(excite)* faire frissonner •**thrilled** *adj* ravi (**with sth** de qch; **to do** de faire) •**thriller** *n* thriller *m* •**thrilling** *adj* passionnant

thrive [θraɪv] *vi (of business, person, plant)* prospérer; **to t. on sth** avoir besoin de qch pour s'épanouir •**thriving** *adj (business)* prospère

throat [θrəʊt] *n* gorge *f*; **to clear one's t.** se racler la gorge •**throaty** *adj (voice)* rauque; *(person)* à la voix rauque

throb [θrɒb] **1** *n (of heart)* battement *m*; *(of engine)* vibration *f*; *(of pain)* élancement *m*
2 *(pt & pp* **-bb-)** *vi (of heart)* palpiter; *(of engine)* vibrer; **my head is throbbing** j'ai une douleur lancinante dans la tête

throes [θrəʊz] *npl* **the t. of death** les affres *fpl* de la mort; **in the t. of** au milieu de; *(illness, crisis)* en proie à; **in the t. of doing sth** en train de faire qch

thrombosis [θrɒm'bəʊsɪs] *n Med* thrombose *f*

throne [θrəʊn] *n* trône *m*

throng [θrɒŋ] **1** *n Literary* foule *f*
2 *vt (station, street)* se presser dans; **it was thronged with people** c'était noir de monde
3 *vi (rush)* affluer

throttle ['θrɒtəl] **1** *n (valve)* papillon *m* des gaz; *(accelerator)* manette *f* des gaz
2 *vt (strangle)* étrangler

through [θruː] **1** *prep (place)* à travers; *(by means of)* par; *(because of)* à cause de; **t. the window/door** par la fenêtre/ porte; **t. ignorance** par ignorance; **all t. his life** toute sa vie; **halfway t. the book** à la moitié du livre; **to go** *or* **get t.** *(forest)* traverser; *(hole)* passer par; *(wall)* passer à travers; **to speak t. one's nose** parler du nez; *Am* **Tuesday t. Saturday** de mardi à samedi
2 *adv* à travers; **to go t.** *(of bullet, nail)* traverser; **to let sb t.** laisser passer qn; *Am* **to be t. with sb/sth** *(finished)* en avoir fini avec qn/qch; *Am* **I'm t. with the book** je n'ai plus besoin du livre; **to sleep all night t.** dormir toute la nuit; **t. to** *or* **till** jusqu'à; **French t. and t.** français jusqu'au bout des ongles; **I'll put you t. (to him)** *(on telephone)* je vous le passe
3 *adj (train, ticket)* direct; *Br* **'no t. road'** *(no exit)* 'voie sans issue'

throughout [θruː'aʊt] **1** *prep* **t. the neighbourhood** dans tout le quartier; **t. the day** pendant toute la journée
2 *adv (everywhere)* partout; *(all the time)* tout le temps

throw [θrəʊ] **1** *n (of stone)* jet *m*; *Sport* lancer *m*; *(of dice)* coup *m*
2 *(pt* **threw**, *pp* **thrown**) *vt* jeter (**to/at** à); *(javelin, discus)* lancer; *(image, shadow)* projeter; *(of horse)* désarçonner; *(party)* donner; *Fam (baffle)* déconcerter ▶ **throw away** *vt sep (discard)* jeter; *Fig (life, chance)* gâcher ▶ **throw back** *vt sep (ball)* renvoyer (**to** à); *(one's head)* rejeter en arrière ▶ **throw in** *vt sep Fam (include as extra)* donner en prime ▶ **throw off** *vt*

sep (get rid of) se débarrasser de ▸ **throw out** *vt sep (unwanted object)* jeter; *(suggestion)* repousser; *(expel)* mettre à la porte ▸ **throw over** *vt sep (abandon)* abandonner ▸ **throw up** *vi Fam (vomit)* vomir

throwaway ['θrəʊəweɪ] *adj (disposable)* jetable

thrown [θrəʊn] *pp of* **throw**

thrush¹ [θrʌʃ] *n (bird)* grive *f*

thrush² [θrʌʃ] *n Med* muguet *m*

thrust [θrʌst] **1** *n (movement)* mouvement *m* en avant; *(of argument)* idée *f* principale; *(of engine)* poussée *f*

  2 (*pt & pp* **thrust**) *vt* **to t. sth into sth** enfoncer qch dans qch; **to t. sb/sth aside** écarter qn/qch; *Fig* **to t. sth (up)on sb** imposer qch à qn

thruway ['θruːweɪ] *n Am* autoroute *f*

thud [θʌd] *n* bruit *m* sourd

thug [θʌg] *n* voyou *m (pl* -ous)

thumb [θʌm] **1** *n* pouce *m*; **with a t. index** *(book)* à onglets

  2 *vt Fam* **to t. a lift** *or* **a ride** faire du stop

  3 *vi* **to t. through a book** feuilleter un livre ● **thumbtack** *n Am* punaise *f*

thump [θʌmp] **1** *n (blow)* coup *m*; *(noise)* bruit *m* sourd

  2 *vt (hit)* frapper; *(put down heavily)* poser lourdement; **to t. one's head** se cogner la tête (**on** contre)

  3 *vi* frapper, cogner (**on** sur); *(of heart)* battre la chamade ● **thumping** *adj Fam (huge, great)* énorme

thunder ['θʌndə(r)] **1** *n* tonnerre *m*

  2 *vi* tonner; **to t. past** *(of train, truck)* passer dans un bruit de tonnerre ● **thunderbolt** *n* éclair *m* suivi d'un coup de tonnerre ● **thunderclap** *n* coup de tonnerre ● **thunderstorm** *n* orage *m* ● **thunderstruck** *adj* abasourdi

Thursday ['θɜːzdeɪ] *n* jeudi *m*

thus [ðʌs] *adv* ainsi

thwart [θwɔːt] *vt* contrecarrer

thyme [taɪm] *n* thym *m*

thyroid ['θaɪrɔɪd] *adj & n Anat* thyroïde *(f)*

tiara [tɪ'ɑːrə] *n (jewellery)* diadème *m*

Tibet [tɪ'bet] *n* le Tibet

tic [tɪk] *n* tic *m*

tick¹ [tɪk] **1** *n (of clock)* tic-tac *m inv*; *(mark)* ≃ croix *f*; *Fam (moment)* instant *m*

  2 *vt* **to t. sth (off)** *(on list)* cocher qch; *Fam* **to t. sb off** passer un savon à qn

  3 *vi* faire tic-tac; *Br* **to t. over** *(of engine, factory)* tourner au ralenti ● **ticking** *n (of clock)* tic-tac *m inv*; *Br Fam* **to give sb a t.-off** passer un savon à qn

tick² [tɪk] *n (insect)* tique *f*

tick³ [tɪk] *adv Br Fam* **on t.** à crédit

ticket ['tɪkɪt] *n* billet *m*; *(for bus, metro)* ticket *m*; *Fam (for parking, speeding)* contravention *f*; *Am Pol (list of candidates)* liste *f* électorale; **(price) t.** étiquette *f*; **t. collector** contrôleur, -euse *mf*; **t. holder** personne *f* munie d'un billet; **t. office** guichet *m*; *Am* **t. scalper,** *Br* **t. tout** revendeur, -euse *mf* (en fraude)

tickle ['tɪkəl] **1** *n* chatouillement *m*

  2 *vt* chatouiller; *Fig (amuse)* amuser ● **ticklish** *adj (person)* chatouilleux, -euse; *Fig (problem)* délicat

tick-tack-toe [tɪktæk'təʊ] *n Am* morpion *m*

tidal ['taɪdəl] *adj (river)* régi par les marées; **t. wave** raz de marée *m inv*

tidbit ['tɪdbɪt] *n Am (food)* bon morceau *m*

tiddlywinks ['tɪdlɪwɪŋks] *n* jeu *m* de puce

tide [taɪd] **1** *n* marée *f*; *Fig* **against the t.** à contre-courant; **the rising t. of discontent** le mécontentement grandissant

  2 *vt* **to t. sb over** dépanner qn ● **tidemark** *n Br Fig & Hum (on neck, in bath)* ligne *f* de crasse

tidings ['taɪdɪŋz] *npl Literary* nouvelles *fpl*

tidy ['taɪdɪ] **1** (**-ier, -iest**) *adj (place, toys)* bien rangé; *(clothes, hair)* soigné; *(person) (methodical)* ordonné; *(in appearance)* soigné; *Fam* **a t. sum** *or* **amount** une jolie somme; **to make sth t.** ranger qch

  2 *vt* **to t. sth (up** *or* **away)** ranger qch; **to t. sth out** mettre de l'ordre dans qch; **to t. oneself up** s'arranger

  3 *vi* **to t. up** ranger ● **tidily** *adv (put away)* soigneusement, avec soin ● **tidiness** *n (of drawer, desk)* ordre *m*; *(of appearance)* soin *m*

tie [taɪ] **1** *n (garment)* cravate *f*; *(link)* lien *m*; *Am (on railroad track)* traverse *f*; *Sport* égalité *f*; *(drawn match)* match *m* nul

  2 *vt (fasten)* attacher (**to** à); *(knot)* faire (**in** à); *(shoe)* lacer

  3 *vi Sport* être à égalité; *Football* faire match nul; *(in race)* être ex aequo

  ▸ **tie down** *vt sep* attacher; **to t. sb down to a date** obliger qn à accepter une date ▸ **tie in** *vi (of facts)* concorder ▸ **tie up** *vt sep (animal)* attacher; *(parcel)* ficeler; *(deal)* conclure; *(money)* immobiliser; *Fig* **to be tied up** *(busy)* être occupé

tier [tɪə(r)] *n (of seats)* gradin *m*; *(of cake)* étage *m*

tiff [tɪf] *n Fam* querelle *f*

tiger [ˈtaɪɡə(r)] *n* tigre *m* • **tigress** [-ɡrɪs] *n* tigresse *f*

tight [taɪt] **1** (**-er, -est**) *adj (clothes, knot, race, bend)* serré; *(control)* strict; *Fam (mean)* radin; *Fam (drunk)* bourré; *Fam* **a t. spot** *or* **corner** une mauvaise passe; **it's a t. squeeze** il y a juste la place **2** *adv (hold, shut)* bien; *(squeeze)* fort; **to sit t.** ne pas bouger; **sleep t.!** dors bien! • **'tight-'fisted** *adj Fam* radin • **'tight-'fitting** *adj (garment)* ajusté • **'tight'knit** *adj (community)* uni • **tightly** *adv (hold)* bien; *(squeeze)* fort • **tightness** *n (of garment)* étroitesse *f*; *(of control)* rigueur *f*; *(of rope)* tension *f* • **tightrope** *n* corde *f* raide • **tightwad** *n Am Fam (miser)* grippe-sou *m*

tighten [ˈtaɪtən] **1** *vt* **to t. (up)** *(bolt)* serrer; *(rope)* tendre; *Fig (security)* renforcer **2** *vi* **to t. up on sth** se montrer plus strict à l'égard de qch

tights [taɪts] *npl Br (garment)* collant *m*

tile [taɪl] **1** *n (on roof)* tuile *f*; *(on wall, floor)* carreau *m* **2** *vt (wall, floor)* carreler • **tiled** *adj (roof)* de tuiles; *(wall, floor)* carrelé • **tiler** *n* carreleur *m*

till¹ [tɪl] *prep & conj* = **until**

till² [tɪl] *n Br (for money)* caisse *f* enregistreuse

till³ [tɪl] *vt (land)* labourer

tiller [ˈtɪlə(r)] *n (of boat)* barre *f*

tilt [tɪlt] **1** *n* inclinaison *f*; **(at) full t.** à toute vitesse **2** *vti* pencher

timber [ˈtɪmbə(r)] **1** *n Br (wood)* bois *m* (de construction) **2** *adj Br (house)* de bois • **timberyard** *n Br* entrepôt *m* de bois

time [taɪm] **1** *n* temps *m*; *(period, moment)* moment *m*; *(age)* époque *f*; *(on clock)* heure *f*; *(occasion)* fois *f*; *Mus* mesure *f*; **in t., with t.** avec le temps; **it's t. to do sth** il est temps de faire qch; **I have no t. to play** je n'ai pas le temps de jouer; **I have no t. to waste** je n'ai pas de temps à perdre; **some of the t.** *(not always)* une partie du temps; **most of the t.** la plupart du temps; **all (of) the t.** tout le temps; **in a year's t.** dans un an; **a long t.** longtemps; **a short t.** peu de temps; **to have a good** *or* **a nice t.** s'amuser (bien); **to have a hard t. doing sth** avoir du mal à faire qch; **to have t. off** avoir du temps libre; **in no t. (at all)** en un rien de temps; **(just) in t.** *(arrive)* à temps **(for sth** pour qch; **to do** pour faire); **in my t.** *(formerly)* de mon temps; **from t. to t.** de temps en temps; **what t. is it?** quelle heure est-il?; **the right** *or* **exact t.** l'heure *f* exacte; **on t.** à l'heure; **at the same t.** en même temps **(as** que); *(simultaneously)* à la fois; **for the t. being** pour le moment; **at the** *or* **that t.** à ce moment-là; **at the present t.** à l'heure actuelle; **at times** parfois; **at one t.** à un moment donné; **this t. tomorrow** demain à cette heure-ci; **(the) next t. you come** la prochaine fois que tu viendras; **(the) last t.** la dernière fois; **one at a t.** un à un; **t. and (t.) again, t. after t.** encore et encore; **ten times ten** dix fois dix; **t. bomb** bombe *f* à retardement; **t. difference** décalage *m* horaire; **t. lag** *(between events)* décalage; **t. limit** délai *m*; **t. switch** minuterie *f*; **t. zone** fuseau *m* horaire **2** *vt (sportsman, worker)* chronométrer; *(activity, programme)* minuter; *(choose the time of)* choisir le moment de; *(plan)* prévoir • **time-consuming** *adj* qui prend du temps • **time-honoured** *adj* consacré (par l'usage) • **time-share** *n* multipropriété *f*

timeless [ˈtaɪmləs] *adj* intemporel, -elle

timely [ˈtaɪmlɪ] *adj* à propos • **timeliness** *n* à-propos *m*

timer [ˈtaɪmə(r)] *n (device)* minuteur *m*; *(sand-filled)* sablier *m*; *(built into appliance)* programmateur *m*; *(plugged into socket)* prise *f* programmable

timescale [ˈtaɪmskeɪl] *n* période *f*

timetable [ˈtaɪmteɪbəl] *n* horaire *m*; *(in school)* emploi *m* du temps

timid [ˈtɪmɪd] *adj* timide • **timidly** *adv* timidement

timing [ˈtaɪmɪŋ] *n (of sportsman)* chronométrage *m*; *(of election)* moment *m* choisi; *(of musician)* sens *m* du rythme; **what (good) t.!** quelle synchronisation!

tin [tɪn] *n (metal)* étain *m*; *Br (can)* boîte *f*; **cake t.** moule *m* à gâteaux; **t. opener** ouvre-boîtes *m inv*; **t. plate** fer-blanc *m*; **t. soldier** soldat *m* de plomb • **tinfoil** *n* papier *m* aluminium

tinge [tɪndʒ] *n* pointe *f* • **tinged** *adj* **t. with sth** teinté de qch

tingle [ˈtɪŋɡəl] *vi* picoter; **it's tingling** ça me picote • **tingly** *adj* **t. feeling** sensation *f* de picotement

tinker [ˈtɪŋkə(r)] *vi* **to t. (about** *or* **around) with sth** bricoler qch

tinkle [ˈtɪŋkəl] **1** *n* tintement *m*; *Br Fam* **to give sb a t.** *(phone sb)* passer un coup de fil à qn **2** *vi* tinter

tinned [tɪnd] *adj Br* **t. pears/salmon** poires *fpl*/saumon *m* en boîte; **t. food** conserves *fpl*

tinny ['tɪnɪ] (**-ier, -iest**) *adj (sound)* métallique

tinsel ['tɪnsəl] *n* guirlandes *fpl* de Noël

tint [tɪnt] *n* teinte *f*; *(for hair)* rinçage *m* • **tinted** *adj (paper, glass)* teinté

tiny ['taɪnɪ] (**-ier, -iest**) *adj* minuscule

tip¹ [tɪp] *n (end)* bout *m*; *(pointed)* pointe *f*; *Fig* **the t. of the iceberg** la partie visible de l'iceberg

tip² [tɪp] **1** *n Br (rubbish dump)* décharge *f*; *Fam* **this room is a real t.** cette pièce est un vrai dépotoir
  2 *(pt & pp -pp-)* *vt (pour)* déverser; **to t. sth up** *or* **over** renverser qch; **to t. sth out** *(liquid, load)* déverser qch (**into** dans)
  3 *vi* **to t. (up** *or* **over)** *(tilt)* se renverser; *(overturn)* basculer

tip³ [tɪp] **1** *n (money)* pourboire *m*; *(advice)* conseil *m*; *(information)* tuyau *m*
  2 *(pt & pp -pp-)* *vt (waiter)* donner un pourboire à; **to t. a horse** donner un cheval gagnant; **to t. off** *(police)* prévenir

tip-off ['tɪpɒf] *n* **to get a t.** se faire tuyauter

tipple ['tɪpəl] *vi Fam (drink)* picoler

tipsy ['tɪpsɪ] (**-ier, -iest**) *adj (drunk)* éméché, gai

tiptoe ['tɪptəʊ] **1** *n* **on t.** sur la pointe des pieds
  2 *vi* marcher sur la pointe des pieds; **to t. into/out of a room** entrer dans une pièce/sortir d'une pièce sur la pointe des pieds

tiptop ['tɪptɒp] *adj Fam* excellent

tirade [taɪ'reɪd] *n* diatribe *f*

tire¹ ['taɪə(r)] **1** *vt* fatiguer; **to t. sb out** épuiser qn
  2 *vi* se fatiguer • **tired** *adj* fatigué; **to be t. of sth/doing** avoir assez de qch/de faire; **to get t. of doing sth** se lasser de faire qch • **tiredness** *n* fatigue *f* • **tireless** *adj* infatigable • **tiresome** *adj* ennuyeux, -euse • **tiring** *adj* fatigant

tire² ['taɪə(r)] *n Am* pneu *m (pl* pneus)

tissue ['tɪʃuː] *n (handkerchief)* mouchoir *m* en papier; *Biol* tissu *m*; **t. paper** papier *m* de soie

tit¹ [tɪt] *n* **to give t. for tat** rendre coup pour coup

tit² [tɪt] *n (bird)* mésange *f*

titbit ['tɪtbɪt] *n Br (food)* bon morceau *m*

titillate ['tɪtɪleɪt] *vt* exciter

title ['taɪtəl] **1** *n (name, claim)* & *Sport* titre *m*; **t. deeds** titres *mpl* de propriété; **t. role** *(in film, play)* rôle-titre *m*
  2 *vt* intituler • **titled** *adj (person)* titré • **titleholder** *n Sport* tenant, -ante *mf* du titre

titter ['tɪtə(r)] *vi* rire bêtement

tittle-tattle ['tɪtəltætəl] *n Fam* cancans *mpl*

T-junction ['tiːdʒʌŋkʃən] *n Br (of roads)* intersection *f* en T

to [tə, *stressed* tuː] **1** *prep* **(a)** *(towards)* à; *(until)* jusqu'à; **give it to him/her** donne-le-lui; **to go to town** aller en ville; **to go to France/Portugal** aller au Portugal/en France; **to go to the butcher's** aller chez le boucher; **the road to London** la route de Londres; **the train to Paris** le train pour Paris; **kind/cruel to sb** gentil/cruel envers qn; **to my surprise** à ma grande surprise; **from bad to worse** de mal en pis; **it's ten (minutes) to one** il est une heure moins dix; **ten to one** *(proportion)* dix contre un; **one person to a room** une personne par chambre
  (b) *(with infinitive)* **to say/jump** dire/sauter; **(in order) to do sth** pour faire qch; **she tried to** elle a essayé; **wife-to-be** future femme *f* **(c)** *(with adjective)* **I'd be happy to do it** je serais heureux de le faire; **it's easy to do** c'est facile à faire
  2 *adv* **to push the door to** fermer la porte; **to go** *or* **walk to and fro** aller et venir

toad [təʊd] *n* crapaud *m*

toadstool ['təʊdstuːl] *n* champignon *m* vénéneux

toast¹ [təʊst] **1** *n (bread)* pain *m* grillé; **piece** *or* **slice of t.** tranche *f* de pain grillé
  2 *vt (bread)* faire griller • **toaster** *n* grille-pain *m inv*

toast² [təʊst] **1** *n (drink)* toast *m*
  2 *vt (person)* porter un toast à; *(success, event)* arroser

tobacco [tə'bækəʊ] *(pl* **-os**) *n* tabac *m*; *Am* **t. store** (bureau *m* de) tabac • **tobacconist** [-kənɪst] *n* buraliste *mf*; *Br* **t.'s (shop)** (bureau *m* de) tabac *m*

toboggan [tə'bɒgən] *n* luge *f*

> 𝒍 Note that the French word **toboggan** is a false friend. Its most common meaning is **slide** (in a playground).

today [tə'deɪ] *adv* aujourd'hui; **t.'s date** la date d'aujourd'hui

toddle ['tɒdəl] *vi Br Fam* **to t. off** ficher le camp

toddler ['tɒdlə(r)] *n* enfant *mf* (en bas âge)

toddy ['tɒdɪ] *n* **(hot) t.** grog *m*

to-do [tə'duː] *n Fam (fuss)* histoire *f*

toe [təʊ] **1** *n* orteil *m*; *Fig* **on one's toes** vigilant
2 *vt* **to t. the line** bien se tenir; **to t. the party line** respecter la ligne du parti • **toenail** *n* ongle *m* de pied
toffee ['tɒfɪ] *n Br* caramel *m* (dur); **t. apple** pomme *f* d'amour
together [tə'geθə(r)] *adv* ensemble; *(at the same time)* en même temps; **t. with** ainsi que • **togetherness** *n* harmonie *f*
togs [tɒgz] *npl Fam (clothes)* fringues *fpl*
toil [tɔɪl] **1** *n* labeur *m*
2 *vi* travailler dur
toilet ['tɔɪlɪt] *n Br (room)* toilettes *fpl*; *(bowl, seat)* cuvette *f* des toilettes; *Br* **to go to the t.** aller aux toilettes; **t. flush** chasse *f* d'eau; **t. paper** papier *m* hygiénique; **t. roll** rouleau *m* de papier hygiénique; **t. soap** savon *m* de toilette • **toiletries** *npl* articles *mpl* de toilette • **toilet-trained** *adj (child)* propre
token ['təʊkən] **1** *n (for vending machine)* jeton *m*; *(symbol)* signe *m*; **as a t. of respect** en signe de respect; **by the same t.** de même; *Br* **book t.** chèque-livre *m*
2 *adj* symbolique
told [təʊld] **1** *pt & pp of* **tell**
2 *adv* **all t.** *(taken together)* en tout
tolerable ['tɒlərəbəl] *adj (bearable)* tolérable; *(fairly good)* acceptable • **tolerably** *adv (fairly, fairly well)* passablement
tolerant ['tɒlərənt] *adj* tolérant (**of** à l'égard de) • **tolerance** *n* tolérance *f* • **tolerantly** *adv* avec tolérance
tolerate ['tɒləreɪt] *vt* tolérer
toll [təʊl] **1** *n* (**a**) *(fee)* péage *m*; **t. road/bridge** route *f*/pont *m* à péage (**b**) **the death t.** le nombre de morts; *Fig* **to take its t.** faire des dégâts
2 *vi (of bell)* sonner • '**toll-'free** *Am* **1** *adj* **t. number** ≃ numéro *m* vert **2** *adv (call)* gratuitement
tomato [*Br* tə'mɑːtəʊ, *Am* tə'meɪtəʊ] (*pl* **-oes**) *n* tomate *f*; **t. sauce** sauce *f* tomate
tomb [tuːm] *n* tombeau *m* • **tombstone** *n* pierre *f* tombale
tomboy ['tɒmbɔɪ] *n* garçon *m* manqué
tomcat ['tɒmkæt] *n* matou *m*
tome [təʊm] *n Formal* gros volume *m*
tomfoolery [tɒm'fuːlərɪ] *n* bêtises *fpl*
tomorrow [tə'mɒrəʊ] *adv & n* demain (*m*); **t. morning/evening** demain matin/soir; **the day after t.** après-demain; **a week from t,** *Br* **a week t.** demain en huit
ton [tʌn] *n* tonne *f*; **metric t.** tonne; *Fam* **tons of** *(lots of)* des tonnes de
tone [təʊn] **1** *n* ton *m*; *(of telephone, radio)* tonalité *f*; *(of answering machine)* signal

m sonore; *Br* **the engaged t.** *(on telephone)* la sonnerie 'occupé'; **to set the t.** donner le ton; **she's t.-deaf** elle n'a pas d'oreille
2 *vt* **to t. sth down** atténuer qch; **to t. up** *(muscles, skin)* tonifier
3 *vi* **to t. in** *(blend in)* s'harmoniser (**with** avec)
tongs [tɒŋz] *npl* pinces *fpl*; **sugar t.** pince *f* à sucre; **curling t.** fer *m* à friser
tongue [tʌŋ] *n (in mouth, language)* langue *f*; **to say sth t. in cheek** dire qch en plaisantant • **tongue-tied** *adj* muet (*f* muette)
tonic ['tɒnɪk] *n (medicine)* fortifiant *m*; **t. (water)** Schweppes® *m*; **gin and t.** gin-tonic *m*
tonight [tə'naɪt] *adv & n (this evening)* ce soir (*m*); *(during the night)* cette nuit (*f*)
tonne [tʌn] *n (metric)* tonne *f* • **tonnage** ['tʌnɪdʒ] *n* tonnage *m*
tonsil ['tɒnsəl] *n* amygdale *f* • **tonsillitis** [-'laɪtəs] *n* **to have t.** avoir une angine
too [tuː] *adv* (**a**) *(excessively)* trop; **t. tired to play** trop fatigué pour jouer; **t. much, t. many** trop; **t. much salt** trop de sel; **t. many people** trop de gens; **one t. many** un de trop; *Fam* **t. right!** et comment! (**b**) *(also)* aussi; *(moreover)* en plus
took [tʊk] *pt of* **take**
tool [tuːl] *n* outil *m*; **t. bag, t. kit** trousse *f* à outils; **t. shed** remise *f*
toot [tuːt] *vti Aut* **to t. (the horn)** klaxonner
tooth [tuːθ] (*pl* **teeth**) *n* dent *f*; **front t.** dent de devant; **back t.** molaire *f*; **milk/wisdom t.** dent de lait/de sagesse; **t. decay** carie *f* dentaire; **to have a sweet t.** aimer les sucreries; *Hum* **long in the t.** *(old)* chenu, vieux (*f* vieille) • **toothache** *n* mal *m* de dents; **to have t.** avoir mal aux dents • **toothbrush** *n* brosse *f* à dents • **toothpaste** *n* dentifrice *m* • **toothpick** *n* cure-dents *m inv*
top[1] [tɒp] **1** *n (of mountain, tower, tree)* sommet *m*; *(of wall, ladder, page)* haut *m*; *(of table, box, surface)* dessus *m*; *(of list)* tête *f*; *(of bottle, tube)* bouchon *m*; *(bottle cap)* capsule *f*; *(of pen)* capuchon *m*; **pyjama t.** veste *f* de pyjama; **(at the) t. of the class** le premier/la première de la classe; **on t.** dessus; *(in bus)* en haut; **on t. of** sur; *Fig (in addition to)* en plus de; **from t. to bottom** de fond en comble; *Fam* **over the t.** *(excessive)* exagéré
2 *adj (drawer, layer)* du haut; *(step, layer)* dernier, -ière; *(upper)* supérieur; *(in rank, exam)* premier, -ière; *(chief)* principal;

(best) meilleur; **on the t. floor** au dernier étage; **in t. gear** *(vehicle)* en quatrième vitesse; **at t. speed** à toute vitesse; **t. hat** haut-de-forme *m* • 'top-'heavy *adj* trop lourd du haut • 'top-'level *adj (talks)* au sommet • 'top-'notch *adj Fam* excellent • 'top-'ranking *adj (official)* haut placé • 'top-'secret *adj* top secret *inv*

top² [tɒp] *(pt & pp* **-pp-)** *vt (exceed)* dépasser; *Br* **to t. up** *(glass)* remplir (de nouveau); **and to t. it all** et pour comble; **topped with cream** nappé de crème; **topped with cherries** décoré de cerises • **topping** *n (of pizza)* garniture *f*; **with a t. of cream** nappé de crème

top³ [tɒp] *n* **(spinning) t.** toupie *f*

topaz ['təʊpæz] *n* topaze *f*

topic ['tɒpɪk] *n* sujet *m* • **topical** *adj* d'actualité • **topicality** [-'kælɪtɪ] *n* actualité *f*

topless ['tɒpləs] *adj (woman)* aux seins nus

topography [tə'pɒgrəfɪ] *n* topographie *f*

topple ['tɒpəl] **1** *vt* **to t. sth (over)** faire tomber qch
2 *vi* **to t. (over)** tomber

topside ['tɒpsaɪd] *n Br (of beef)* gîte *m*

topsy-turvy [tɒpsɪ'tɜːvɪ] *adj & adv* sens dessus dessous [sɑ̃dsydsu]

torch [tɔːtʃ] *n Br (electric)* lampe *f* de poche; *(flame)* torche *f* • **torchlight 1** *n* **by t.** à la lumière d'une lampe de poche **2** *adj* **t. procession** retraite *f* aux flambeaux

tore [tɔː(r)] *pt of* **tear¹**

torment 1 ['tɔːment] *n* supplice *m*
2 [tɔː'ment] *vt* tourmenter

torn [tɔːn] *pp of* **tear¹**

tornado [tɔː'neɪdəʊ] *(pl* **-oes)** *n* tornade *f*

torpedo [tɔː'piːdəʊ] **1** *(pl* **-oes)** *n* torpille *f*; **t. boat** torpilleur *m*
2 *vt* torpiller

torrent ['tɒrənt] *n* torrent *m* • **torrential** [tə'renʃəl] *adj* **t. rain** pluie *f* torrentielle

torrid ['tɒrɪd] *adj (weather, love affair)* torride

torso ['tɔːsəʊ] *(pl* **-os)** *n* torse *m*

tortoise ['tɔːtəs] *n* tortue *f* • **tortoiseshell** *adj (comb)* en écaille; *(spectacles)* à monture d'écaille

tortuous ['tɔːtʃʊəs] *adj* tortueux, -ueuse

torture ['tɔːtʃə(r)] **1** *n* torture *f*; *Fig* **it's (sheer) t.!** quel supplice!
2 *vt* torturer • **torturer** *n* tortionnaire *mf*

Tory ['tɔːrɪ] *Pol* **1** *n* tory *m*
2 *adj* tory *inv*

toss [tɒs] **1** *n* **with a t. of the head** d'un mouvement brusque de la tête
2 *vt (throw)* lancer (**to** à); *(pancake)* faire sauter; **to t. sb (about)** *(of boat,*

vehicle) ballotter qn; **to t. a coin** jouer à pile ou face; **to t. back one's head** rejeter la tête en arrière
3 *vi* **to t. (about), to t. and turn** *(in bed)* se tourner et se retourner; **let's t. up, let's t. (up) for it** jouons-le à pile ou face • **toss-up** *n Fam* **it's a t. whether she leaves or stays** on ne sait vraiment pas si elle va partir

tot [tɒt] **1** *n* **(tiny) t.** tout-petit *m*; *Br* **a t. of whisky** une goutte de whisky
2 *(pt & pp* **-tt-)** *vt Fam* **to t. up** *(total)* additionner

total ['təʊtəl] **1** *adj* total; **the t. sales** le total des ventes
2 *n* total *m*; **in t.** au total
3 *(Br* **-ll-,** *Am* **-l-)** *vt (of sum)* s'élever à; *Am Fam (car)* bousiller; **to t. (up)** *(find the total of)* totaliser; **that totals \$9** ça fait 9 dollars en tout • **totally** *adv* totalement

totalitarian [təʊtælɪ'teərɪən] *adj Pol* totalitaire

tote [təʊt] **1** *n Br Fam Sport* pari *m* mutuel
2 *vt Fam (carry)* trimballer • **tote bag** *n Am* fourre-tout *m inv*

totter ['tɒtə(r)] *vi* chanceler

touch [tʌtʃ] **1** *n (contact)* contact *m*; *(sense)* toucher *m*; *(of painter)* & *Football & Rugby* touche *f*; **a t. of** *(small amount)* une pointe de; **to have a t. of flu** être un peu grippé; **to be/get in t. with sb** être/ se mettre en contact avec qn; **to stay in/ lose t. with sb** rester en/perdre contact avec qn; **it's t. and go whether he'll live** on n'est pas sûr du tout qu'il survivra
2 *vt* toucher; *(interfere with, eat)* toucher à; **I don't t. the stuff** *(I hate it)* je n'en bois/ mange jamais; *Fig* **there's nothing to t. it** c'est sans égal
3 *vi (of lines, hands, ends)* se toucher; **don't t.!** ne touche pas! • **touchdown** *n (of aircraft)* atterrissage *m*; *American Football* but *m* • **touched** *adj (emotionally)* touché (**by** de); *Fam (crazy)* cinglé • **touching** *adj (moving)* touchant • **touchline** *n* ligne *f* de touche
▸ **touch down** *vi (of plane)* atterrir
▸ **touch on** *vt insep* aborder ▸ **touch up** *vt sep (photo)* retoucher

touchy ['tʌtʃɪ] *(***-ier, -iest)** *adj (sensitive)* susceptible (**about** à propos de)

tough [tʌf] **1** *(***-er, -est)** *adj (strict, hard)* dur; *(sturdy)* solide; **t. guy** dur *m* à cuire; *Fam* **t. luck!** pas de chance!
2 *n* dur *m* • **toughen** *vt (body, person)* endurcir; *(conditions)* durcir • **toughness** *n (hardness)* dureté *f*; *(sturdiness)* solidité *f*; *(strength)* force *f*

toupee ['tuːpeɪ] *n* postiche *m*

tour [tʊə(r)] **1** *n (journey)* voyage *m; (visit)* visite *f; (by artist)* tournée *f; (on bicycle, on foot)* randonnée *f;* **to be on a t.** *(of tourist)* faire un voyage organisé; **to go on t.** *(of artist)* être en tournée; **(package) t.** voyage organisé; **t. guide** guide *mf;* **t. operator** voyagiste *m*
2 *vt* visiter; *(of artist)* être en tournée en/dans

tourism ['tʊərɪzəm] *n* tourisme *m* •**tourist 1** *n* touriste *mf* **2** *adj (region)* touristique; *Av* **t. class** classe *f* touriste; **t. office** syndicat *m* d'initiative • **touristy** *adj Fam Pej* trop touristique

tournament ['tʊənəmənt] *n Sport & Hist* tournoi *m*

tousled ['taʊzəld] *adj (hair)* ébouriffé

tout [taʊt] **1** *n* racoleur, -euse *mf*
2 *vi* **to t. for trade** racoler des clients

tow [təʊ] **1** *n Br* **'on t.'**, *Am* **'in t.'** 'en remorque'; *Am* **t. truck** dépanneuse *f*
2 *vt* remorquer; **to t. a car away** *(of police)* mettre une voiture à la fourrière • **towpath** *n* chemin *m* de halage • **towrope** *n* câble *m* de remorque

toward(s) [tə'wɔːd(z)] *prep* vers; *(of feelings)* envers; **cruel t. sb** cruel envers qn; **the money is going t. a new car** l'argent servira à l'achat d'une nouvelle voiture

towel ['taʊəl] *n* serviette *f* (de toilette); *Br* **t. rail,** *Am* **t. rack** porte-serviettes *m inv* • **towelling** (*Am* **toweling**) *n* tissu-éponge *m; Am* **(kitchen) t.** essuie-tout *m inv*

tower ['taʊə(r)] **1** *n* tour *f; Br* **t. block** tour; *Fig* **ivory t.** tour d'ivoire
2 *vi* **to t. over sb/sth** dominer qn/qch • **towering** *adj* immense

town [taʊn] *n* ville *f;* **to go into t.** aller en ville; **country t.** bourg *m;* **t. centre** centre-ville *m; Br* **t. clerk** secrétaire *mf* de mairie; *Br* **t. council** conseil *m* municipal; *Br* **t. hall** mairie *f; Br* **t. planner** urbaniste *mf; Br* **t. planning** urbanisme *m* • **township** *n (in South Africa)* township *f*

toxic ['tɒksɪk] *adj* toxique • **toxin** *n* toxine *f*

toy [tɔɪ] **1** *n* jouet *m*
2 *adj (gun)* d'enfant; *(house, car, train)* miniature
3 *vi* **to t. with an idea** caresser une idée • **toy shop** *n* magasin *m* de jouets

trace [treɪs] **1** *n* trace *f; without t.* sans laisser de traces; *Chem* **t. element** oligoélément *m*
2 *vt (diagram, picture)* tracer; *(person)* retrouver la trace de; *(history)* retracer;

to t. sth back to... faire remonter qch à...
• **tracing** *n (drawing)* calque *m;* **t. paper** papier-calque *m*

track [træk] **1** *n (mark)* trace *f; (trail)* piste *f; (path)* chemin *m,* piste; *(for trains)* voie *f; (of rocket)* trajectoire *f; (of record)* morceau *m; Am Sch* classe *f* (de niveau); *Am (racetrack)* champ *m* de courses; **to keep t. of sth** surveiller qch; **to lose t. of** *(friend)* perdre de vue; *(argument)* perdre le fil de; **to be on the right t.** être sur la bonne voie; **off the beaten t.** *(remote)* loin des sentiers battus; *Fam* **to make tracks** filer; *Sport* **t. event** épreuve *f* sur piste; *Fig* **t. record** passé *m*
2 *vt* **to t. (down)** *(find)* retrouver • **tracker dog** *n* chien *m* policier • **tracking shot** *n Cin* **to do a t.** faire un travelling • **track shoes** *npl Am* chaussures *fpl* d'athlétisme • **tracksuit** *n* survêtement *m*

tract [trækt] *n (stretch of land)* étendue *f*

traction ['trækʃən] *n Tech* traction *f*

tractor ['træktə(r)] *n* tracteur *m*

trade [treɪd] **1** *n* commerce *m; (job)* métier *m; (exchange)* échange *m*
2 *adj (fair, balance, route)* commercial; *(price)* de (demi-)gros; *(secret)* de fabrication; *(barrier)* douanier, -ière; *Br* **t. union** syndicat *m; Br* **t. unionist** syndicaliste *mf*
3 *vt (exchange)* échanger (**for** contre); **to t. sth in** *(old article)* faire reprendre qch
4 *vi* faire du commerce (**with** avec); **to t. in** *(sugar)* faire le commerce de • **trade-in** *n Com* reprise *f* • **trademark** *n* marque *f* de fabrique • **trade-off** *n (compromise)* compromis *m* • **trader** *n Br (shopkeeper)* commerçant, -ante *mf; (on Stock Exchange)* opérateur, -trice *mf; Br* **street t.** vendeur, -euse *mf* de rue • **tradesman** (*pl* -**men**) *n Br* commerçant *m*

trading ['treɪdɪŋ] **1** *n* commerce *m*
2 *adj (port, debts, activity)* commercial; *(nation)* commerçant; *Br* **t. estate** zone *f* industrielle

tradition [trə'dɪʃən] *n* tradition *f* • **traditional** *adj* traditionnel, -elle • **traditionalist** *n* traditionaliste *mf* • **traditionally** *adv* traditionnellement

traffic ['træfɪk] **1** *n* (**a**) *(on road)* circulation *f; (air, sea, rail)* trafic *m; Am* **t. circle** rond-point *m; Br* **t. cone** cône *m* de signalisation; **t. island** refuge *m* (pour piétons); **t. jam** embouteillage *m;* **t. lights** feux *mpl* (de signalisation); **t. warden** contractuel, -uelle *mf* (**b**) *Pej (trade)* trafic *m* (**in** de); **the drug t.** le trafic de la drogue
2 (*pt & pp* -**ck**-) *vi* trafiquer (**in** de) • **trafficker** *n Pej* trafiquant, -ante *mf*

tragedy ['trædʒədɪ] (*pl* **-ies**) *n* tragédie *f* • **tragic** *adj* tragique • **tragically** *adv* tragiquement

trail [treɪl] **1** *n* (*of smoke, blood, powder*) traînée *f*; (*path*) piste *f*, sentier *m*; **in its t.** (*wake*) dans son sillage

2 *vt* (*drag*) traîner; (*caravan*) tracter; (*follow*) suivre

3 *vi* (*drag*) traîner; (*of plant*) ramper; (*move slowly*) se traîner; *Sport* **to be trailing** (**behind**) être mené • **trailer** *n* (**a**) (*for car*) remorque *f*; *Am* (*caravan*) caravane *f*; *Am* (*camper*) camping-car *m* (**b**) (*advertisement for film*) bande *f* annonce

train [treɪn] **1** *n* (**a**) (*engine, transport*) train *m*; (*underground*) rame *f*; **t. set** (*toy*) petit train *m* (**b**) (*procession*) file *f*; (*of events*) suite *f*; (*of dress*) traîne *f*; **my t. of thought** le fil de ma pensée

2 *vt* (*person*) former (**to do** à faire); *Sport* entraîner; (*animal*) dresser (**to do** à faire); (*ear*) exercer; **to t. oneself to do sth** s'entraîner à faire qch; **to t. sth on sb/sth** braquer qch sur qn/qch

3 *vi Sport* s'entraîner; **to t. as a nurse** faire une formation d'infirmière • **trained** *adj* (*skilled*) qualifié; (*nurse, engineer*) diplômé; (*animal*) dressé; (*ear*) exercé • **training** *n* formation *f*; *Sport* entraînement *m*; (*of animal*) dressage *m*; *Sport* **to be in t.** s'entraîner

trainee [treɪ'niː] *n & adj* stagiaire (*mf*)

trainer ['treɪnə(r)] *n* (*of athlete, racehorse*) entraîneur *m*; (*of animals*) dresseur *m*; *Br* **trainers** (*shoes*) chaussures *fpl* de sport

traipse [treɪps] *vi Fam* **to t. around** (*tiredly*) traîner les pieds; (*wander*) se balader; **to t. in** se pointer, se ramener

trait [treɪt] *n* trait *m* (de caractère)

traitor ['treɪtə(r)] *n* traître *m*, traîtresse *f*

trajectory [trə'dʒektərɪ] (*pl* **-ies**) *n* trajectoire *f*

tram [træm] *n* tram(way) *m*

tramp [træmp] **1** *n Br* (*vagrant*) clochard, -arde *mf*; *Fam Pej* (*woman*) traînée *f*; (*sound*) pas *mpl* lourds; **to go for a t.** faire une randonnée

2 *vt* (*country*) parcourir

3 *vi* marcher d'un pas lourd

trample ['træmpəl] *vti* **to t. sth** (**underfoot**)**, to t. on sth** piétiner qch

trampoline [træmpə'liːn] *n* trampoline *m*

trance [trɑːns] *n* **to be in a t.** être en transe; **to go into a t.** entrer en transe

tranquil ['træŋkwɪl] *adj* tranquille • **tran-'quillity** (*Am* **tran'quility**) *n* tranquillité *f*

• **tranquillizer** (*Am* **tranquilizer**) *n* tranquillisant *m*

transaction [træn'zækʃən] *n* opération *f*, transaction *f*

transatlantic [trænzət'læntɪk] *adj* transatlantique

transcend [træn'send] *vt* transcender • **transcen'dental** *adj* transcendantal

transcribe [træn'skraɪb] *vt* transcrire • **'transcript** *n* transcription *f* • **tran'scription** *n* transcription *f*

transept ['trænsept] *n* transept *m*

transfer 1 [træns'fɜː(r)] **1** ['trænsfɜː(r)] *n* transfert *m* (**to** à); (*of political power*) passation *f*; *Br* (*picture, design*) décalcomanie *f*; **credit t.** virement *m* bancaire

2 (*pt & pp* **-rr-**) *vt* transférer (**to** à); (*political power*) faire passer (**to** à); *Br* **to t. the charges** téléphoner en PCV

3 *vi* être transféré (**to** à) • **trans'ferable** *adj* **'not t.'** (*on ticket*) 'titre de transport nominal'

transform [træns'fɔːm] *vt* transformer (**into** en) • **transformation** [-fə'meɪʃən] *n* transformation *f* • **transformer** *n El* transformateur *m*

transfusion [træns'fjuːʒən] *n* (**blood**) **t.** transfusion *f* (sanguine)

transgenic [trænz'dʒenɪk] *adj* transgénique

transgress [trænz'gres] *vt Formal* (*law*) transgresser • **transgression** *n* transgression *f*

transient ['trænzɪənt] *adj* éphémère

transistor [træn'zɪstə(r)] *n* (*device*) transistor *m*; **t.** (**radio**) transistor

transit ['trænzɪt] *n* transit *m*; **in t.** en transit; *Br* **t. lounge** (*in airport*) salle *f* de transit

transition [træn'zɪʃən] *n* transition *f* • **transitional** *adj* de transition

transitive ['trænsɪtɪv] *adj Grammar* transitif

transitory ['trænzɪtərɪ] *adj* transitoire

translate [træns'leɪt] *vt* traduire (**from** de; **into** en) • **translation** *n* traduction *f* • **translator** *n* traducteur, -trice *mf*

transmit [trænz'mɪt] **1** (*pt & pp* **-tt-**) *vt* transmettre

2 *vti* (*broadcast*) émettre • **transmission** *n* transmission *f*; (*broadcast*) émission *f* • **transmitter** *n Radio & TV* émetteur *m*

transparent [træn'spærənt] *adj* transparent • **transparency** *n* transparence *f*; *Br* (*photographic slide*) diapositive *f*

transpire [træn'spaɪə(r)] *vi* (*of secret*) s'ébruiter; *Fam* (*happen*) arriver; **it transpired that…** il s'est avéré que…

ℓ Note that the French word **transpirer** is a false friend. Its most common meaning is **to sweat**.

---

transplant 1 ['trænsplɑːnt] *n (surgical)* greffe *f*, transplantation *f*
2 [træns'plɑːnt] *vt* transplanter
transport 1 ['trænspɔːt] *n* transport *m* (**of** de); **do you have t.?** es-tu motorisé?; *Br* **t. café** routier *m (restaurant)*
2 [træn'spɔːt] *vt* transporter ● **transpor-'tation** *n* transport *m*
transpose [træn'spəʊz] *vt* transposer ● **transposition** [-pə'zɪʃən] *n* transposition *f*
transvestite [trænz'vestaɪt] *n* travesti *m*
trap [træp] **1** *n* piège *m*; *Fam (mouth)* gueule *f*
2 (*pt & pp* **-pp-**) *vt* prendre au piège; **to t. one's finger** se coincer le doigt (**in** dans); **to t. sb into doing sth** faire faire qch à qn en usant de ruse ● **trapdoor** *n* trappe *f* ● **trapper** *n (hunter)* trappeur *m*
trapeze [trə'piːz] *n* trapèze *m*; **t. artist** trapéziste *mf*
trappings ['træpɪŋz] *npl* signes *mpl* extérieurs
trash [træʃ] *n (nonsense)* bêtises *fpl*; *(junk)* bric-à-brac *m inv*; *Am (waste)* ordures *fpl*; *Am (riffraff)* racaille *f* ● **trash can** *n Am* poubelle *f* ● **trashy** (**-ier**, **-iest**) *adj Fam* à la noix
trauma ['trɔːmə, 'traʊmə] *n* traumatisme *m* ● **traumatic** [-'mætɪk] *adj* traumatisant ● **traumatize** *vt* traumatiser
travel ['trævəl] **1** *n* voyage *m*; **on my travels** au cours de mes voyages; **t. agency/agent** agence *f*/agent *m* de voyages; **t. book** récit *m* de voyages; **t. documents** titre *m* de transport; **t. insurance** assurance *f* voyage
2 (*Br* **-ll-**, *Am* **-l-**) *vt (country, distance, road)* parcourir
3 *vi (of person)* voyager; *(of vehicle, light, sound)* se déplacer ● **travelled** (*Am* **traveled**) *adj* **to be well** *or* **widely t.** avoir beaucoup voyagé ● **travelling** (*Am* **traveling**) **1** *n* voyages *mpl* **2** *adj (bag, clothes)* de voyage; *(expenses)* de déplacement; *(musician, circus)* ambulant
traveller ['trævələ(r)] (*Am* **traveler**) *n* voyageur, -euse *mf*; **t.'s cheque** chèque *m* de voyage
travelogue ['trævəlɒg] (*Am* **travelog**) *n (book)* récit *m* de voyages
travel sickness ['trævəlsɪknɪs] *n (in car)* mal *m* de la route; *(in aircraft)* mal de l'air
travesty ['trævəstɪ] (*pl* **-ies**) *n* parodie *f*; **a t. of justice** un simulacre de justice

trawler ['trɔːlə(r)] *n (ship)* chalutier *m*
tray [treɪ] *n* plateau *m*; *(in office)* corbeille *f*; **baking t.** plaque *f* de four
treacherous ['tretʃərəs] *adj (road, conditions)* très dangereux, -euse; *(journey)* parsemé d'embûches; *(person, action)* traître ● **treacherously** *adv (act)* traîtreusement; *(dangerously)* dangereusement ● **treachery** (*pl* **-ies**) *n* traîtrise *f*
treacle ['triːkəl] *n Br* mélasse *f*
tread [tred] **1** *n (footstep)* pas *m*; *(step of stairs)* marche *f*; *(of tyre)* chape *f*
2 (*pt* **trod**, *pp* **trodden**) *vt* marcher sur; **to t. sth into a carpet** étaler qch sur un tapis (avec ses chaussures); **to t. sth underfoot** fouler qch au pied
3 *vi (walk)* marcher (**on** sur)
treadmill ['tredmɪl] *n* tapis *m* roulant de jogging; *Pej & Fig* routine *f*
treason ['triːzən] *n* trahison *f*
treasure ['treʒə(r)] **1** *n* trésor *m*; **t. hunt** chasse *f* au trésor
2 *vt (value)* tenir beaucoup à ● **treasurer** *n* trésorier, -ière *mf* ● **Treasury** *n Br Pol* **the T.** ≃ le ministère des Finances
treat [triːt] **1** *n (pleasure)* plaisir *m*; *(gift)* cadeau *m*; **to give sb a t.** faire plaisir à qn; **it's my t.** c'est moi qui régale; *Fam* **to work a t.** marcher à merveille
2 *vt (person, illness, product)* traiter; **to t. sb/sth with care** prendre soin de qn/qch; **to t. sb like a child** traiter qn comme un enfant; **to t. sb to sth** offrir qch à qn
treatise ['triːtɪz] *n* traité *m* (**on** de)
treatment ['triːtmənt] *n* traitement *m*; **his t. of her** la façon dont il la traite/traitait
treaty ['triːtɪ] (*pl* **-ies**) *n (international)* traité *m*
treble ['trebəl] **1** *adj* triple; *Mus* **t. clef** clef *f* de sol; *Mus* **t. voice** voix *f* de soprano
2 *n* le triple; **it's t. the price** c'est le triple du prix
3 *vti* tripler
tree [triː] *n* arbre *m* ● **tree-lined** *adj* bordé d'arbres ● **treetop** *n* cime *f* (d'un arbre) ● **tree trunk** *n* tronc *m* d'arbre
trek [trek] **1** *n (long walk)* randonnée *f*; *Fig* **it's quite a t. to the shops** ça fait loin à pied jusqu'aux magasins
2 (*pt & pp* **-kk-**) *vi* faire de la randonnée; *Fig* **to t. to the shops** se taper le chemin à pied jusqu'aux magasins
trellis ['trelɪs] *n* treillage *m*, treillis *m*
tremble ['trembəl] *vi* trembler (**with** de) ● **tremor** *n* tremblement *m*
tremendous [trə'mendəs] *adj (huge)* énorme; *(dreadful)* terrible; *(wonderful)*

formidable • **tremendously** adv (very) extrêmement

trench [trentʃ] n Mil tranchée f • **trench coat** n trench-coat m

trend [trend] n tendance f (**towards** à); (fashion) mode f; **to set a** or **the t.** lancer une mode • **trendy** (**-ier, -iest**) adj Br Fam branché

trepidation [trepɪ'deɪʃən] n Formal inquiétude f

trespass ['trespəs] vi s'introduire illégalement dans une propriété privée; **'no trespassing'** 'entrée interdite'

> ⚠ Note that the French verb **trépasser** is a false friend and is never a translation for the English verb **to trespass**. It means **to die**.

tresses ['tresɪz] npl Literary chevelure f

trestle ['tresəl] n tréteau m

trial ['traɪəl] 1 n Law procès m; (test) essai m; (ordeal) épreuve f; **to go** or **be on t., to stand t.** passer en jugement; **to put sb on t.** juger qn; **to be on t.** (of product) être à l'essai; **by t. and error** par tâtonnements 2 adj (period, flight, offer) d'essai; **t. run** essai m

triangle ['traɪæŋgəl] n triangle m; Am (set-square) équerre f • **triangular** [-'æŋgjʊlə(r)] adj triangulaire

tribe [traɪb] n tribu f • **tribal** adj tribal • **tribesman** (pl **-men**) n membre d'une tribu

tribulations [trɪbjʊ'leɪʃənz] npl **trials and t.** tribulations fpl

tribunal [traɪ'bjuːnəl] n tribunal m

tributary [Br 'trɪbjʊtərɪ, Am -erɪ] (pl **-ies**) n affluent m

tribute ['trɪbjuːt] n hommage m; **to pay t. to** rendre hommage à

trick [trɪk] 1 n (joke, deception, of conjurer) tour m; (clever method) astuce f; (in card game) pli m; **card t.** tour de cartes; **the tricks of the trade** les ficelles fpl du métier; **to play a t. on sb** jouer un tour à qn; Fam **to do the t.** marcher; **t. photo** photo f truquée; **t. question** question f piège

2 vt (deceive) duper; **to t. sb into doing sth** amener qn à faire qch par la ruse • **trickery** n ruse f

trickle ['trɪkəl] 1 n (of liquid) filet m; Fig **a t. of** (letters, people) un petit nombre de

2 vi (of liquid) couler goutte à goutte; Fig **to t. in** (of letters, people) arriver en petit nombre

tricky ['trɪkɪ] (**-ier, -iest**) adj (problem) délicat

tricycle ['traɪsɪkəl] n tricycle m

trier ['traɪə(r)] n Fam **to be a t.** être persévérant

trifle ['traɪfəl] 1 n (insignificant thing) bagatelle f; Br (dessert) = dessert où alternent génoise, fruits en gelée et crème anglaise

2 adv **a t. wide** un tantinet trop large

3 vi **to t. with** plaisanter avec • **trifling** adj insignifiant

trigger ['trɪgə(r)] 1 n (of gun) détente f

2 vt **to t. sth (off)** déclencher qch • **trigger-happy** adj (person) qui a la gâchette facile

trilby ['trɪlbɪ] n Br **t. (hat)** chapeau m en feutre

trilingual [traɪ'lɪŋgwəl] adj trilingue

trilogy ['trɪlədʒɪ] (pl **-ies**) n trilogie f

trim [trɪm] 1 (**trimmer, trimmest**) adj (neat) soigné; (slim) svelte

2 n **to give sb's hair a t.** faire une coupe d'entretien à qn; **to keep in t.** garder la forme

3 (pt & pp **-mm-**) vt couper (un peu); **to t. sth with sth** orner qch de qch • **trimmings** npl (on clothes) garniture f; (of meal) accompagnements mpl traditionnels

Trinity ['trɪnɪtɪ] n Rel **the T.** la Trinité

trinket ['trɪŋkɪt] n babiole f

trio ['triːəʊ] (pl **-os**) n trio m

trip [trɪp] 1 n (journey) voyage m; (outing) excursion f; (stumble) faux pas m; **to take a t. to the shops** aller dans les magasins

2 (pt & pp **-pp-**) vt **to t. sb up** faire trébucher qn

3 vi (walk gently) marcher d'un pas léger; **to t. (over** or **up)** trébucher; **to t. over sth** trébucher sur qch

tripe [traɪp] n (food) tripes fpl; Fam (nonsense) bêtises fpl

triple ['trɪpəl] 1 adj triple

2 vti tripler • **triplets** npl (children) triplés, -ées mfpl

triplicate ['trɪplɪkət] n **in t.** en trois exemplaires

tripod ['traɪpɒd] n trépied m

tripper ['trɪpə(r)] n Br **day t.** excursionniste mf

trite [traɪt] adj banal (mpl **-als**) • **triteness** n banalité f

triumph ['traɪəmf] 1 n triomphe m (**over** sur)

2 vi triompher (**over** de) • **triumphal** [traɪ'ʌmfəl] adj triomphal • **triumphant** [traɪ'ʌmfənt] adj triomphant; (success, welcome, return) triomphal • **triumphantly** [traɪ'ʌmfəntlɪ] adv triomphalement

trivia ['trɪvɪə] *npl* vétilles *fpl* • **trivial** *adj* (*unimportant*) insignifiant; (*trite*) banal (*mpl* -als) • **triviality** [-vɪ'ælɪtɪ] *n* insignifiance *f*; (*triteness*) banalité *f* • **trivialize** *vt* banaliser

> Note that the French word **trivial** is a false friend. It means **vulgar**.

trod [trɒd] *pt of* tread
trodden ['trɒdən] *pp of* tread
trolley ['trɒlɪ] (*pl* -**eys**) *n Br* chariot *m*; *Br* (**tea**) **t.** table *f* roulante; *Am* **t.** (**car**) tramway *m* • **trolleybus** *n* trolley *m*
trombone [trɒm'bəʊn] *n* trombone *m*
troop [truːp] **1** *n* bande *f*; (*of soldiers*) troupe *f*; **the troops** (*soldiers*) les troupes *fpl*
2 *vi* **to t. in/out** entrer/sortir en groupe • **trooper** *n Am* (**state**) **t.** membre *m* de la police montée • **trooping** *n Br* **t. the colour** salut *m* au drapeau
trophy ['trəʊfɪ] (*pl* -**ies**) *n* trophée *m*
tropic ['trɒpɪk] *n* tropique *m*; **in the tropics** sous les tropiques • **tropical** *adj* tropical
trot [trɒt] **1** *n* trot *m*; *Fam* **on the t.** (*consecutively*) de suite
2 (*pt & pp* -**tt**-) *vt Fam* **to t. sth out** débiter qch
3 *vi* trotter; *Br Fam Hum* **to t. off** *or* **along** (*leave*) se sauver
trouble ['trʌbəl] **1** *n* (*difficulty*) ennui *m*; (*inconvenience*) problème *m*; (*social unrest, illness*) trouble *m*; **to be in t.** avoir des ennuis; **to get into t.** s'attirer des ennuis; **to have t. with sb/sth** avoir des problèmes avec qn/qch; **to have t. doing sth** avoir du mal à faire qch; **to go to the t. of doing sth** se donner la peine de faire qch; **the t. with you is** l'ennui avec toi, c'est que; **it's no t.** pas de problème; *Br* **a spot of t.** un petit problème; **t. spot** point *m* chaud
2 *vt* (*inconvenience*) déranger; (*worry*) inquiéter; **to t. to do sth** se donner la peine de faire qch; **to t. oneself** se déranger • **troubled** *adj* (*person*) inquiet, -iète; (*period, region*) agité • '**trouble-'free** *adj* sans souci
troublemaker ['trʌbəlmeɪkə(r)] *n* (*in school*) élément *m* perturbateur; (*political*) fauteur *m* de troubles
troubleshooter ['trʌbəlʃuːtə(r)] *n Tech* dépanneur *m*; *Pol* conciliateur, -trice *mf*; (*for firm*) expert *m*
troublesome ['trʌbəlsəm] *adj* pénible
trough [trɒf] *n* (*for drinking*) abreuvoir *m*; (*for feeding*) auge *f*; **t. of low pressure** (*in weather front*) dépression *f*

trounce [traʊns] *vt* (*defeat*) écraser
troupe [truːp] *n* (*of actors*) troupe *f*
trousers ['traʊzəz] *npl Br* pantalon *m*; **a pair of t., some t.** un pantalon; **short t.** culottes *fpl* courtes • **trouser suit** *n* tailleur-pantalon *m*
trousseau ['truːsəʊ] (*pl* -**eaux** *or* -**eaus** [-əʊz]) *n* trousseau *m*
trout [traʊt] *n inv* truite *f*
trowel ['traʊəl] *n* (*for cement or plaster*) truelle *f*; (*for plants*) déplantoir *m*
truant ['truːənt] *n* (*pupil*) élève *mf* qui fait l'école buissonnière; **to play t.** faire l'école buissonnière • **truancy** *n* absentéisme *m* scolaire

> Note that the French word **truand** is a false friend. It means **crook**.

truce [truːs] *n Mil* trêve *f*
truck [trʌk] *n* (*lorry*) camion *m*; *Br Rail* wagon *m*; **t. driver** camionneur *m*; *Am* **t. farmer** maraîcher, -ère *mf*; *Am* **t. stop** (*restaurant*) routier *m* • **trucker** *n Am* camionneur *m*
truculent ['trʌkjʊlənt] *adj* agressif, -ive

> Note that the French word **truculent** is a false friend. It means **colourful** or **vivid**.

trudge [trʌdʒ] *vi* marcher péniblement
true [truː] (-**er**, -**est**) *adj* vrai; (*genuine*) véritable; (*accurate*) exact; (*faithful*) fidèle (**to** à); **t. to life** conforme à la réalité; **to come t.** se réaliser; **to hold t.** être vrai (**for** de); *Fam* **too t.!** ah, ça oui!; **t. love** grand amour *m* • **truly** *adv* vraiment; **well and t.** bel et bien; **yours t.** (*in letter*) je vous prie, Madame/Monsieur, d'agréer l'expression de mes sentiments distingués; *Fam Hum* mézigue
truffle ['trʌfəl] *n* truffe *f*
truism ['truːɪzəm] *n* truisme *m*
trump [trʌmp] **1** *n* atout *m*; **spades are t.** atout pique
2 *vt* **to t. sth up** inventer qch de toutes pièces
trumpet ['trʌmpɪt] *n* trompette *f*; **t. player** trompettiste *mf*
truncate [trʌŋ'keɪt] *vt* tronquer
truncheon ['trʌntʃən] *n Br* matraque *f*
trundle ['trʌndəl] *vti* **to t. along** rouler bruyamment
trunk [trʌŋk] *n* (*of tree, body*) tronc *m*; (*of elephant*) trompe *f*; (*case*) malle *f*; *Am* (*of vehicle*) coffre *m*; **trunks** (*for swimming*) slip *m* de bain; *Br* **t. call** communication *f* interurbaine; *Br* **t. road** route *f* nationale

truss [trʌs] **1** *n (belt, bandage)* bandage *m* herniaire
2 *vt* **to t. sb (up)** ligoter qn

trust [trʌst] **1** *n (faith)* confiance *f* (**in** en); *Fin* trust *m*; *Law* fidéicommis *m*; **to take sth on t.** accepter qch de confiance
2 *vt (believe in)* faire confiance à; **to t. sb with sth, to t. sth to sb** confier qch à qn; **to t. sb to do sth** laisser à qn le soin de faire qch; **I t. that...** j'espère que...; *Fam* **t. him to say that!** c'est bien de lui!
3 *vi* **to t. in sb** faire confiance à qn; **to t. to luck** s'en remettre au hasard • **trusted** *adj (method)* éprouvé; **he is a t. friend** c'est un ami en qui j'ai une confiance totale • **trusting** *adj* qui fait confiance aux gens

trustee [trʌs'tiː] *n (of school, charity)* administrateur -trice *mf*; *Law* fidéicommissaire *m*

trustworthy ['trʌstwɜːðɪ] *adj* digne de confiance

truth [truːθ] *(pl* **-s** [truːðz]*) n* vérité *f*; **to tell the t.** dire la vérité; **there's some t. in** il y a du vrai dans • **truthful** *adj (story)* véridique; *(person)* sincère • **truthfully** *adv* sincèrement

try [traɪ] **1** *(pl* **-ies**) *n (attempt)* & *Rugby* essai *m*; **to have a t. at sth/doing sth** essayer qch/de faire qch; **at (the) first t.** du premier coup; **it's worth a t.** ça vaut la peine d'essayer
2 *(pt & pp* **-ied**) *vt (attempt, sample)* essayer; *(food, drink)* goûter à; *Law (person)* juger (**for** pour); **to t. doing** *or* **to do sth** essayer de faire qch; **to t. one's hand at** s'essayer à; **to t. sb's patience** mettre à l'épreuve la patience de qn
3 *vi* essayer; **to t. hard** faire un gros effort; **t. and come!** essaie de venir! • **trying** *adj* difficile
▶ **try on** *vt sep (clothes, shoes)* essayer
▶ **try out** *vt sep (car, method, recipe)* essayer; *(person)* mettre à l'essai

tsar [zɑː(r)] *n* tsar *m*

T-shirt ['tiːʃɜːt] *n* tee-shirt *m*

tub [tʌb] *n (basin)* baquet *m*; *(bath)* baignoire *f*; *Br (for ice cream)* pot *m*; *Br (for flower, bush)* bac *m*

tuba ['tjuːbə] *n* tuba *m*

tubby ['tʌbɪ] *(* **-ier, -iest**) *adj Fam* grassouillet, -ette

tube [tjuːb] *n* tube *m*; *(of tyre)* chambre *f* à air; *Br Fam* **the t.** *(underground railway)* le métro; **to go down the tubes** *(of money)* être foutu en l'air • **tubing** *n* tuyaux *mpl* • **tubular** *adj* tubulaire

tuberculosis [tjuːbɜːkjʊ'ləʊsɪs] *n Med* tuberculose *f*

TUC [tiːjuːˈsiː] *(abbr* **Trades Union Congress**) *n Br* = confédération des syndicats britanniques

tuck [tʌk] **1** *n (in garment)* pli *m*; *Br* **t. shop** *(in school)* boutique *f* de friandises
2 *vt (put)* mettre; **to t. sth away** *(put)* ranger qch; *(hide)* cacher qch; **to t. in** *(shirt, blanket)* rentrer; *(child)* border; **to t. one's sleeves up** remonter ses manches
3 *vi Br Fam* **to t. in** *(start eating)* attaquer; **to t. into a meal** attaquer un repas

Tuesday ['tjuːzdeɪ] *n* mardi *m*

tuft [tʌft] *n* touffe *f*

tug [tʌg] **1** *n* **to give sth a t.** tirer sur qch
2 *(pt & pp* **-gg-**) *vt (pull)* tirer sur
3 *vi* tirer (**at** *or* **on** sur) • **tug(boat)** *n* remorqueur *m*

tuition [tjuːˈɪʃən] *n (lessons)* cours *mpl*; *(fee)* frais *mpl* de scolarité

tulip ['tjuːlɪp] *n* tulipe *f*

tumble ['tʌmbəl] **1** *n (fall)* chute *f*; **to take a t.** faire une chute; *Fig (of prices)* chuter
2 *vi (of person)* faire une chute; *Fig (of prices)* chuter; **to t. down** s'écrouler • **tumble 'dryer, tumble 'drier** *n Br* sèche-linge *m inv*

tumbledown ['tʌmbəldaʊn] *adj* délabré

tumbler ['tʌmblə(r)] *n* verre *m* droit

tummy ['tʌmɪ] *n Fam* ventre *m*; **to have a t. ache** avoir mal au ventre

tumour ['tjuːmə(r)] *(Am* **tumor**) *n* tumeur *f*

tumult ['tjuːmʌlt] *n* tumulte *m* • **tumultuous** [-'mʌltjʊəs] *adj* tumultueux, -ueuse

tuna ['tjuːnə] *n* **t. (fish)** thon *m*

tune [tjuːn] **1** *n (melody)* air *m*; **in t.** *(instrument)* accordé; **out of t.** *(instrument)* désaccordé; **to be** *or* **sing in t./out of t.** chanter juste/faux; *Fig* **to be in t. with sb/sth** être en harmonie avec qn/qch; **to the t. of £50** d'un montant de 50 livres
2 *vt* **to t. (up)** *(instrument)* accorder; *(engine)* régler
3 *vi* **to t. in** brancher son poste (**to** sur) • **tuning** *n (of engine)* réglage *m*; *Mus* **t. fork** diapason *m*

tuneful ['tjuːnfəl] *adj* mélodieux, -ieuse

tuner ['tjuːnə(r)] *n (on TV, radio)* tuner *m*

tunic ['tjuːnɪk] *n* tunique *f*

Tunisia [tjuːˈnɪzɪə] *n* la Tunisie • **Tunisian 1** *adj* tunisien, -ienne **2** *n* Tunisien, -ienne *mf*

tunnel ['tʌnəl] **1** *n* tunnel *m*; *(in mine)* galerie *f*
2 *(Br* **-ll-,** *Am* **-l-**) *vi* creuser un tunnel (**into** dans)

turban ['tɜːbən] *n* turban *m*

turbine [*Br* 'tɜːbaɪn, *Am* 'tɜːrbɪn] *n* turbine *f*

turbulence ['tɜːbjʊləns] *n* turbulence *f*

turbulent ['tɜːbjʊlənt] *adj* agité

tureen [*Br* tjʊ'riːn, *Am* tə'riːn] *n* (soup) t. soupière *f*

turf [tɜːf] **1** *n* (grass) gazon *m*; **the t.** (horseracing) le turf; *Br* **t. accountant** bookmaker *m*

2 *vt Br Fam* **to t. sb out** (get rid of) jeter qn dehors

turgid ['tɜːdʒɪd] *adj* (style) ampoulé

Turkey ['tɜːkɪ] *n* laTurquie • **Turk** *n* Turc *m*, Turque *f* • **Turkish 1** *adj* turc (*f* turque); **T. bath/coffee** bain *m*/café *m* turc; **T. delight** loukoum *m* **2** *n* (language) turc *m*

turkey ['tɜːkɪ] (*pl* -**eys**) *n* (bird) dinde *f*

turmoil ['tɜːmɔɪl] *n* (of person) émoi *m*; (of country) agitation *f*; **to be in t.** (of person) être dans tous ses états; (of country) être en ébullition

turn [tɜːn] **1** *n* (of wheel, in game, queue) tour *m*; (in road) tournant *m*; (of events, mind) tournure *f*; (performance) numéro *m*; *Br Fam* (fit) crise *f*; **to take turns** se relayer; **to take it in turns to do sth** se relayer pour faire qch; **in t.** à tour de rôle; **in one's t.** à son tour; **by turns** tour à tour; **it's your t. (to play)** c'est à toi (de jouer); **to do sb a good t.** rendre service à qn; **the t. of the century** le tournant du siècle; **t. of phrase** tournure de phrase

2 *vt* tourner; (mechanically) faire tourner; (mattress, pancake) retourner; **to t. sb/sth into sb/sth** changer qn/qch en qn/qch; **to t. sth red/black** rougir/noircir qch; **to t. sth on sb** (aim) braquer qch sur qn; **she has turned twenty** elle a vingt ans passés; **it has turned seven** il est sept heures passées; **it turns my stomach** cela me soulève le cœur

3 *vi* (of wheel, driver) tourner; (of person) se retourner; **to t. red/black** rougir/noircir; **to t. nasty** (of person) devenir méchant; (of situation) mal tourner; **to t. to sb** se tourner vers qn; **to t. into sb/sth** devenir qn/qch; **to t. against sb** se retourner contre qn • **turn-off** *n* (on road) sortie *f*; *Fam* **to be a t.** être rébarbatif, -ive • **turnout** *n* (people) assistance *f*; (at polls) participation *f* • **turnover** *n Com* (sales) chiffre *m* d'affaires; (of stock) rotation *f*; (of staff) renouvellement *m*; *Br* **apple t.** chausson *m* aux pommes • **turnup** *n Br* (on trousers) revers *m*

▸ **turn around** *vi* (of person) se retourner

▸ **turn away 1** *vt sep* (eyes) détourner (**from** de); (person) refuser **2** *vi* se détourner ▸ **turn back 1** *vt sep* (sheets) rabattre; (person) refouler; (clock) retarder **2** *vi* (return) faire demi-tour ▸ **turn down** *vt sep* (gas, radio) baisser; (fold down) rabattre; (refuse) rejeter ▸ **turn in 1** *vt sep* (lost property) rapporter à la police; (person) livrer à la police **2** *vi Fam* (go to bed) aller au pieu ▸ **turn off 1** *vt sep* (light, radio) éteindre; (tap) fermer; (machine) arrêter; *Fam* **to t. sb off** dégoûter qn **2** *vi* (leave road) sortir ▸ **turn on 1** *vt sep* (light, radio) allumer; (tap) ouvrir; (machine) mettre en marche; *Fam* **to t. sb on** (sexually) exciter qn **2** *vi* **to t. on sb** (attack) attaquer qn ▸ **turn out 1** *vt sep* (light) éteindre; (pocket, box) vider; (produce) produire **2** *vi* (appear, attend) se déplacer; **it turns out that...** il s'avère que...; **she turned out to be** elle s'est révélée être ▸ **turn over 1** *vt sep* (page) tourner **2** *vi* (of vehicle, person) se retourner; (of car) faire un tonneau ▸ **turn round 1** *vt sep* (head) tourner; (object) retourner; (situation) renverser **2** *vi* (of person) se retourner; (in vehicle) faire demi-tour ▸ **turn up 1** *vt sep* (radio, heat) mettre plus fort; (collar) remonter **2** *vi* (arrive) arriver; (be found) être retrouvé

turncoat ['tɜːnkəʊt] *n* renégat, -ate *mf*

turning ['tɜːnɪŋ] *n Br* (street) petite rue *f*; (bend in road) tournant *m*; *Br Aut* **t. circle** rayon *m* de braquage; *Fig* **t. point** tournant *m*

turnip ['tɜːnɪp] *n* navet *m*

turnpike ['tɜːnpaɪk] *n Am* autoroute *f* à péage

turnstile ['tɜːnstaɪl] *n* tourniquet *m*

turntable ['tɜːnteɪbəl] *n* platine *f*

turpentine ['tɜːpəntaɪn] (*Br Fam* **turps** [tɜːps]) *n* térébenthine *f*

turquoise ['tɜːkwɔɪz] *adj* turquoise *inv*

turret ['tʌrɪt] *n* tourelle *f*

turtle ['tɜːtəl] *n Br* tortue *f* de mer; *Am* tortue *f* • **turtle dove** *n* tourterelle *f* • **turtleneck 1** *adj* (sweater) à col montant **2** *n* col *m* montant

tusk [tʌsk] *n* défense *f*

tussle ['tʌsəl] *n* bagarre *f*

tutor ['tjuːtə(r)] **1** *n* professeur *m* particulier; (in British university) directeur, -trice *mf* d'études; (in American university) assistant, -ante *mf*

2 *vt* donner des cours particuliers à • **tutorial** [-'tɔːrɪəl] *n Univ* ≃ travaux *mpl* dirigés

tuxedo [tʌk'siːdəʊ] (*pl* -**os**) *n Am* smoking *m*

TV [tiː'viː] *n* télé *f*; **on TV** à la télé

twaddle ['twɒdəl] *n Fam* fadaises *fpl*

twang [twæŋ] **1** *n (sound)* vibration *f*; *(nasal voice)* ton *m* nasillard

2 *vi (of wire)* vibrer

twee [twiː] *adj Br Fam Pej* cucul (la praline) *inv*

tweed [twiːd] *n* tweed *m*; **t. jacket** veste *f* en tweed

tweezers ['twiːzəz] *npl* pince *f* à épiler

twelve [twelv] *adj & n* douze *(m)* •**twelfth** *adj & n* douzième *(mf)*

twenty ['twentɪ] *adj & n* vingt *(m)* •**twentieth** *adj & n* vingtième *(mf)*

twerp [twɜːp] *n Br Fam* crétin, -ine *mf*

twice [twaɪs] *adv* deux fois; **t. as heavy (as...)** deux fois plus lourd (que...); **t. a month, t. monthly** deux fois par mois

twiddle ['twɪdəl] *vti* **to t. (with) sth** tripoter qch; **to t. one's thumbs** se tourner les pouces

twig¹ [twɪg] *n (of branch)* brindille *f*

twig² [twɪg] *(pt & pp* **-gg-)** *vti Br Fam* piger

twilight ['twaɪlaɪt] *n* crépuscule *m*

twin [twɪn] **1** *n* jumeau *m*, jumelle *f*; **identical t.** vrai jumeau, vraie jumelle; **t. brother** frère *m* jumeau; **t. sister** sœur *f* jumelle; **t. beds** lits *mpl* jumeaux; **t. town** ville *f* jumelée

2 *(pt & pp* **-nn-)** *vt (town)* jumeler

twine [twaɪn] **1** *n (string)* ficelle *f*

2 *vi (twist)* s'enrouler (**round** autour de)

twinge [twɪndʒ] *n* **a t. (of pain)** un élancement; **a t. of remorse** un peu de remords

twinkle ['twɪŋkəl] **1** *n* scintillement *m*; *(in eye)* pétillement *m*

2 *vi (of star)* scintiller; *(of eye)* pétiller

twirl [twɜːl] **1** *vt* faire tournoyer; *(moustache)* tortiller

2 *vi* tournoyer

twist [twɪst] **1** *n (action)* tour *m*; *(bend)* tortillement *m*; *(in road)* tournant *m*; *Fig (in story)* tour inattendu; **t. of lemon** rondelle *f* de citron; **twists and turns** *(of road)* tours et détours *mpl*; *(of events)* rebondissements *mpl*

2 *vt (wire, arm)* tordre; *(roll)* enrouler (**round** autour de); *(weave together)* entortiller; **to t. one's ankle** se tordre la cheville; *Fig* **to t. sb's arm** forcer la main à qn; **to t. sth off** *(lid)* dévisser qch

3 *vi (wind)* s'entortiller (**round sth** autour de qch); *(of road, river)* serpenter •**twisted** *adj (person, mind, logic)* tordu

•**twister** *n* **tongue t.** = mot ou phrase imprononçable

twit [twɪt] *n Br Fam* andouille *f*

twitch [twɪtʃ] **1** *n (jerk)* secousse *f*; *(nervous)* tic *m*

2 *vi (of person)* avoir un tic; *(of muscle)* se contracter nerveusement

twitter ['twɪtə(r)] **1** *n (of bird)* pépiement *m*

2 *vi* pépier

two [tuː] *adj & n* deux *(m)* •**two-cycle** *adj Am (engine)* à deux temps • '**two-di'men-sional** *adj* à deux dimensions • '**two-'faced** *adj Fig* hypocrite • '**two-'legged** [-legɪd] *adj* bipède •**two-piece** *adj (suit, swimsuit)* deux pièces •**two-'seater** *n (car)* voiture *f* à deux places •**two-stroke** *adj Br (engine)* à deux temps •**two-way** *adj* **t. mirror** miroir *m* sans tain; **t. radio** émetteur-récepteur *m*; **t. traffic** circulation *f* dans les deux sens

twofold ['tuːfəʊld] **1** *adj* double

2 *adv* **to increase t.** doubler

twosome ['tuːsəm] *n* couple *m*

tycoon [taɪ'kuːn] *n* magnat *m*

type¹ [taɪp] *n* (**a**) *(sort)* genre *m*, type *m*; **blood t.** groupe *m* sanguin (**b**) *(print)* caractères *mpl*; **in large t.** en gros caractères •**typeface** *n* police *f* de caractères •**typeset** *(pt & pp* **-set,** *pres p* **-setting**) *vt* composer •**typesetter** *n* compositeur, -trice *mf*

type² [taɪp] **1** *vti (write)* taper (à la machine)

2 *vt* **to t. sth in** *(on computer)* entrer qch au clavier; **to t. sth out** *(letter)* taper qch •**typewriter** *n* machine *f* à écrire •**type-written** *adj* dactylographié •**typing** *n* dactylographie *f*; **a page of t.** une page dactylographiée; **t. error** faute *f* de frappe •**typist** *n* dactylo *f*

typhoid ['taɪfɔɪd] *n Med* **t. (fever)** typhoïde *f*

typhoon [taɪ'fuːn] *n* typhon *m*

typical ['tɪpɪkəl] *adj* typique (**of** de); **that's t. (of him)!** c'est bien lui! •**typically** *adv* typiquement •**typify** *(pt & pp* **-ied**) *vt* caractériser

typo ['taɪpəʊ] *(pl* **-os**) *n Fam (misprint)* coquille *f*

tyranny ['tɪrənɪ] *n* tyrannie *f* •**tyrannical** [-'rænɪkəl] *adj* tyrannique •**tyrant** ['taɪərənt] *n* tyran *m*

tyre ['taɪə(r)] *n Br* pneu *m (pl* pneus); **t. pressure** pression *f* des pneus

U, u [juː] *n (letter)* U, u *m inv*
ubiquitous [juːˈbɪkwɪtəs] *adj* omniprésent
udder [ˈʌdə(r)] *n* pis *m*
UFO [juːefˈəʊ, ˈjuːfəʊ] *(pl* **UFOs)** *(abbr*
unidentified flying object) *n* OVNI *m*
Uganda [juːˈgændə] *n* l'Ouganda *m*
ugh [ʌχ] *exclam* berk!
ugly [ˈʌglɪ] *(-ier, -iest) adj* laid • **ugliness**
n laideur *f*
UK [juːˈkeɪ] *abbr* = **United Kingdom**
Ukraine [juːˈkreɪn] *n* **the U.** l'Ukraine *f*
ulcer [ˈʌlsə(r)] *n* ulcère *m* • **ulcerated** *adj*
ulcéré
ulterior [ʌlˈtɪərɪə(r)] *adj* ultérieur; **u.**
motive arrière-pensée *f*
ultimate [ˈʌltɪmət] *adj (last)* final; *(su-*
preme, best) absolu; **the u. holidays** les
vacances *fpl* idéales • **ultimately** *adv*
(finally) finalement; *(basically)* en fin de
compte
ultimatum [ʌltɪˈmeɪtəm] *n* ultimatum *m*;
to give sb an u. lancer un ultimatum à qn
ultra- [ˈʌltrə] *pref* ultra-
ultramodern [ʌltrəˈmɒdən] *adj* ultramoderne
ultrasound [ˈʌltrəsaʊnd] *n* ultrason *m*;
Fam **to have an u.** passer une échographie
ultraviolet [ʌltrəˈvaɪələt] *adj* ultraviolet,
-ette
umbilical [ʌmˈbɪlɪkəl] *adj* **u. cord** cordon
m ombilical
umbrage [ˈʌmbrɪdʒ] *n Literary* **to take u.**
prendre ombrage (**at** de)
umbrella [ʌmˈbrelə] *n* parapluie *m*; **u.**
stand porte-parapluies *m inv*

> *Note that the French word* **ombrelle** *is a*
> *false friend. It means* **sunshade.**

umpire [ˈʌmpaɪə(r)] **1** *n* arbitre *m*
2 *vt* arbitrer
umpteen [ʌmpˈtiːn] *adj Fam* **u. times** je
ne sais combien de fois • **umpteenth** *adj*
Fam énième
UN [juːˈen] *abbr* = **United Nations**
unabashed [ʌnəˈbæʃt] *adj* imperturbable
unabated [ʌnəˈbeɪtɪd] *adj* **to continue u.**
continuer avec la même intensité

unable [ʌnˈeɪbəl] *adj* **to be u. to do sth**
être incapable de faire qch; **he's u. to**
swim il ne sait pas nager
unabridged [ʌnəˈbrɪdʒd] *adj* intégral
unacceptable [ʌnəkˈseptəbəl] *adj* inacceptable; **it's u. that...** il est inacceptable
que... *(+ subjunctive)*
unaccompanied [ʌnəˈkʌmpənɪd] *adj*
(person) non accompagné; *(singing)*
sans accompagnement
unaccountable [ʌnəˈkaʊntəbəl] *adj*
inexplicable • **unaccountably** *adv* inex-
plicablement
unaccounted [ʌnəˈkaʊntɪd] *adj* **to be u.**
for rester introuvable
unaccustomed [ʌnəˈkʌstəmd] *adj* inac-
coutumé; **to be u. to sth/to doing sth** ne
pas être habitué à qch/à faire qch
unadulterated [ʌnəˈdʌltəreɪtɪd] *adj* pur;
(food) naturel, -elle
unaided [ʌnˈeɪdɪd] *adv* sans aide
unanimity [juːnəˈnɪmɪtɪ] *n* unanimité *f*
• **unanimous** [-ˈnænɪməs] *adj* unanime
• **unanimously** *adv* à l'unanimité
unannounced [ʌnəˈnaʊnst] **1** *adj* non
annoncé
2 *adv* sans prévenir
unappetizing [ʌnˈæpɪtaɪzɪŋ] *adj* peu appétissant
unapproachable [ʌnəˈprəʊtʃəbəl] *adj*
inaccessible
unarmed [ʌnˈɑːmd] *adj* non armé; **u.**
combat combat *m* à mains nues
unashamed [ʌnəˈʃeɪmd] *adj (person)*
sans honte; *(look, curiosity)* non dissi-
mulé; **she's u. about it** elle n'en a pas
honte • **unashamedly** [-ɪdlɪ] *adv* sans aucune honte
unassailable [ʌnəˈseɪləbəl] *adj (castle)*
imprenable; *(argument, reputation)* inattaquable
unassuming [ʌnəˈsjuːmɪŋ] *adj* sans prétention
unattached [ʌnəˈtætʃt] *adj (not con-*
nected) détaché; *(without partner)* sans
attaches
unattainable [ʌnəˈteɪnəbəl] *adj* inac-
·cessible
unattended [ʌnəˈtendɪd] *adv* **to leave**

sb/sth u. laisser qn/qch sans surveillance
unattractive [ʌnə'træktɪv] *adj* peu attrayant
unauthorized [ʌn'ɔːθəraɪzd] *adj* non autorisé
unavailable [ʌnə'veɪləbəl] *adj* non disponible; **to be u.** ne pas être disponible
unavoidable [ʌnə'vɔɪdəbəl] *adj* inévitable • **unavoidably** *adv* inévitablement; **to be u. detained** être retardé pour des raisons indépendantes de sa volonté
unaware [ʌnə'weə(r)] *adj* **to be u. of sth** ignorer qch; **to be u. that...** ignorer que... • **unawares** *adv* **to catch sb u.** prendre qn au dépourvu
unbalanced [ʌn'bælənst] *adj (mind, person)* instable
unbearable [ʌn'beərəbəl] *adj* insupportable • **unbearably** *adv* insupportablement
unbeatable [ʌn'biːtəbəl] *adj* imbattable • **unbeaten** *adj (player)* invaincu; *(record)* jamais battu
unbeknown(st) [ʌnbɪ'nəʊn(st)] *adj* **u. to sb** à l'insu de qn
unbelievable [ʌnbɪ'liːvəbəl] *adj* incroyable • **unbelieving** *adj* incrédule
unbias(s)ed [ʌn'baɪəst] *adj* impartial
unblock [ʌn'blɒk] *vt (sink, pipe)* déboucher
unbolt [ʌn'bəʊlt] *vt (door)* déverrouiller
unborn ['ʌn'bɔːn] *adj* **u. child** enfant *mf* à naître
unbounded [ʌn'baʊndɪd] *adj* sans borne(s)
unbreakable [ʌn'breɪkəbəl] *adj* incassable • **unbroken** *adj (intact)* intact; *(continuous)* continu; *(record)* jamais battu
unbridled [ʌn'braɪdəld] *adj* débridé
unburden [ʌn'bɜːdən] *vt* **to u. oneself** se confier (**to** à)
unbutton [ʌn'bʌtən] *vt* déboutonner
uncalled-for [ʌn'kɔːldfɔː(r)] *adj* déplacé
uncanny [ʌn'kænɪ] (**-ier, -iest**) *adj* étrange
unceasing [ʌn'siːsɪŋ] *adj* incessant • **unceasingly** *adv* sans cesse
unceremoniously [ʌnserɪ'məʊnɪəslɪ] *adv (to treat sb)* sans ménagement; *(show sb out)* brusquement
uncertain [ʌn'sɜːtən] *adj* incertain; **to be u. about sth** ne pas être certain de qch; **it's u. whether** *or* **that...** il n'est pas certain que... (*+ subjunctive*); **I'm u. whether to stay (or not)** je ne sais pas très bien si je dois rester (ou pas) • **uncertainty** (*pl* **-ies**) *n* incertitude *f*

unchanged [ʌn'tʃeɪndʒd] *adj* inchangé • **unchanging** *adj* immuable
uncharitable [ʌn'tʃærɪtəbəl] *adj* peu charitable
unchecked [ʌn'tʃekt] *adv* sans que rien ne soit fait
uncivil [ʌn'sɪvəl] *adj* impoli
uncivilized [ʌn'sɪvɪlaɪzd] *adj* non civilisé
unclaimed [ʌn'kleɪmd] *adj (luggage)* non réclamé
uncle ['ʌŋkəl] *n* oncle *m*
unclear [ʌn'klɪə(r)] *adj* vague; *(result)* incertain; **it's u. whether** on ne sait pas très bien si
uncomfortable [ʌn'kʌmftəbəl] *adj* inconfortable; *(heat, experience)* désagréable; *(silence)* gêné; **to feel u.** *(physically)* ne pas être à l'aise; *(ill at ease)* être mal à l'aise
uncommitted [ʌnkə'mɪtɪd] *adj* indécis
uncommon [ʌn'kɒmən] *adj* peu commun • **uncommonly** *adv (very)* extraordinairement; **not u.** *(fairly often)* assez souvent
uncommunicative [ʌnkə'mjuːnɪkətɪv] *adj* peu communicatif, -ive
uncomplicated [ʌn'kɒmplɪkeɪtɪd] *adj* simple
uncompromising [ʌn'kɒmprəmaɪzɪŋ] *adj* intransigeant
unconcerned [ʌnkən'sɜːnd] *adj* indifférent
unconditional [ʌnkən'dɪʃənəl] *adj* sans condition
unconfirmed [ʌnkən'fɜːmd] *adj* non confirmé
unconnected [ʌnkə'nektɪd] *adj* sans lien
unconscious [ʌn'kɒnʃəs] **1** *adj (person)* sans connaissance; *(desire)* inconscient; **to be u. of sth** ne pas avoir conscience de qch
 2 *n* **the u.** l'inconscient *m* • **unconsciously** *adv* inconsciemment
uncontrollable [ʌnkən'trəʊləbəl] *adj* incontrôlable • **uncontrollably** *adv (laugh, sob)* sans pouvoir s'arrêter
unconventional [ʌnkən'venʃənəl] *adj* non conformiste
unconvinced [ʌnkən'vɪnst] *adj* **to be** *or* **remain u.** ne pas être convaincu (**of** de) • **unconvincing** *adj* peu convaincant
uncooked [ʌn'kʊkt] *adj* cru
uncooperative [ʌnkəʊ'ɒpərətɪv] *adj* peu coopératif, -ive
uncork [ʌn'kɔːk] *vt* déboucher
uncouth [ʌn'kuːθ] *adj* fruste
uncover [ʌn'kʌvə(r)] *vt* découvrir

unctuous [ˈʌŋktʃʊəs] *adj (insincere)* onctueux, -ueuse

uncut [ʌnˈkʌt] *adj (film, play, version)* intégral; *(diamond)* brut

undamaged [ʌnˈdæmɪdʒd] *adj* intact

undated [ʌnˈdeɪtɪd] *adj* non daté

undaunted [ʌnˈdɔːntɪd] *adj* nullement impressionné

undecided [ʌndɪˈsaɪdɪd] *adj (person)* indécis (about sur); **I'm u. whether to do it or not** je n'ai pas décidé si je le ferai ou non

undefeated [ʌndɪˈfiːtɪd] *adj* invaincu

undeniable [ʌndɪˈnaɪəbəl] *adj* indéniable

under [ˈʌndə(r)] **1** *prep* sous; *(less than)* moins de; **children u. nine** les enfants de moins de neuf ans; **u. there** là-dessous; **u. it** dessous; **u. (the command of) sb** sous les ordres de qn; **u. the terms of the agreement** selon l'accord; **u. the circumstances** dans ces circonstances; **to be u. age** être mineur; **to be u. discussion/repair** être en discussion/réparation; **to be u. way** *(in progress)* être en cours; *(on the way)* être en route; **to get u. way** *(of campaign)* démarrer; **to be u. the impression that...** avoir l'impression que...
2 *adv* au-dessous

undercarriage [ˈʌndəkærɪdʒ] *n* train *m* d'atterrissage

undercharge [ʌndəˈtʃɑːdʒ] *vt* se tromper dans l'addition de *(à l'avantage du client)*; **I undercharged him (for it)** je ne (le) lui aipas fait payer assez

underclothes [ˈʌndəkləʊðz] *npl* sous-vêtements *mpl*

undercoat [ˈʌndəkəʊt] *n* sous-couche *f*

undercooked [ʌndəˈkʊkt] *adj* pas assez cuit

undercover [ˈʌndəkʌvə(r)] *adj* secret, -ète

undercurrent [ˈʌndəkʌrənt] *n (in sea)* courant *m* sous-marin; **an u. of discontent** un mécontentement sous-jacent

undercut [ʌndəˈkʌt] *(pt & pp* -**cut**, *pres p* -**cutting**) *vt* vendre moins cher que

underdeveloped [ʌndədɪˈveləpt] *adj (country, region)* sous-développé

underdog [ˈʌndədɒg] *n (politically, socially)* opprimé, -ée *mf*; *(likely loser)* outsider *m*

underdone [ʌndəˈdʌn] *adj (food)* pas assez cuit; *(steak)* saignant

underestimate [ʌndərˈestɪmeɪt] *vt* sous-estimer

underfed [ʌndəˈfed] *adj* sous-alimenté

underfoot [ʌndəˈfʊt] *adv* sous les pieds; **to trample sth u.** piétiner qch

undergo [ʌndəˈgəʊ] *(pt* -**went**, *pp* -**gone**) *vt* subir; **to u. surgery** être opéré

undergraduate [ʌndəˈgrædʒʊət] *n* étudiant, -iante *mf* de licence

underground [ˈʌndəgraʊnd] **1** *adj* souterrain; *Fig (secret)* clandestin
2 *n Br (railway)* métro *m*; *Pol (organization)* résistance *f*
3 [ʌndəˈgraʊnd] *adv* sous terre; *Fig* **to go u.** *(of fugitive)* passer dans la clandestinité

undergrowth [ˈʌndəgrəʊθ] *n* broussailles *fpl*

underhand [ʌndəˈhænd] *adj* sournois

underlie [ʌndəˈlaɪ] *(pt* -**lay**, *pp* -**lain**, *pres p* -**lying**) *vt* sous-tendre ● **underlying** *adj* sous-jacent

underline [ʌndəˈlaɪn] *vt* souligner

underling [ˈʌndəlɪŋ] *n Pej* subalterne *mf*

undermanned [ʌndəˈmænd] *adj (office)* à court de personnel

undermine [ʌndəˈmaɪn] *vt (weaken)* saper

underneath [ʌndəˈniːθ] **1** *prep* sous
2 *adv* (en) dessous; **the book u.** le livre d'en dessous
3 *n* the u. (of) le dessous (de)

undernourished [ʌndəˈnʌrɪʃt] *adj* sous-alimenté

underpants [ˈʌndəpænts] *npl (male underwear)* slip *m*

underpass [ˈʌndəpɑːs] *n (for pedestrians)* passage *m* souterrain; *(for vehicles)* passage inférieur

underpay [ʌndəˈpeɪ] *vt* sous-payer ● **underpaid** *adj* sous-payé

underprice [ʌndəˈpraɪs] *vt* vendre au-dessous de sa valeur

underprivileged [ʌndəˈprɪvɪlɪdʒd] *adj* défavorisé

underrate [ʌndəˈreɪt] *vt* sous-estimer

underscore [ʌndəˈskɔː(r)] *vt* souligner

undersecretary [ʌndəˈsekrətərɪ] *n Pol* sous-secrétaire *mf*

undershirt [ˈʌndəʃɜːt] *n Am* maillot *m* de corps

underside [ˈʌndəsaɪd] *n* the u. (of) le dessous (de)

undersigned [ˈʌndəsaɪnd] *adj* **I, the u.** je soussigné(e)

undersized [ʌndəˈsaɪzd] *adj* trop petit

underskirt [ˈʌndəskɜːt] *n* jupon *m*

understaffed [ʌndəˈstɑːft] *adj* **to be u.** manquer de personnel

understand [ʌndəˈstænd] *(pt & pp* -**stood**) *vti* comprendre; **I u. that...** je crois comprendre que...; **I've been given to u. that...** on m'a fait comprendre que...;

to **make** oneself **understood** se faire comprendre ● **understanding 1** n *(act, faculty)* compréhension f; *(agreement)* accord m, entente f; *(sympathy)* entente; **on the u. that...** à condition que... *(+ subjunctive)* **2** adj *(person)* compréhensif, -ive ● **understood** adj *(agreed)* entendu; *(implied)* sous-entendu

understandable [ʌndə'stændəbəl] adj compréhensible ● **understandably** adv naturellement

understatement ['ʌndəsteɪtmənt] n euphémisme m

understudy ['ʌndəstʌdɪ] *(pl -ies)* n doublure f

undertake [ʌndə'teɪk] *(pt -took, pp -taken)* vt *(task)* entreprendre; *(responsibility)* assumer; **to u. to do sth** entreprendre de faire qch ● **undertaking** n *(task)* entreprise f; *(promise)* promesse f

undertaker ['ʌndəteɪkə(r)] n entrepreneur m de pompes funèbres

undertone ['ʌndətəʊn] n **in an u.** à mi-voix; *Fig* **an u. of** *(criticism, sadness)* une nuance de

undervalue [ʌndə'væljuː] vt sous-évaluer; **it's undervalued at £10** ça vaut plus que 10 livres

underwater 1 ['ʌndəwɔːtə(r)] adj de plongée **2** [ʌndə'wɔːtə(r)] adv sous l'eau

underwear ['ʌndəweə(r)] n sous-vêtements mpl

underweight [ʌndə'weɪt] adj *(person)* trop maigre

underworld ['ʌndəwɜːld] n **the u.** *(criminals)* la pègre

undeserved [ʌndɪ'zɜːvd] adj immérité

undesirable [ʌndɪ'zaɪərəbəl] adj & n indésirable *(mf)*

undetected [ʌndɪ'tektɪd] adj *(crime)* non découvert; **to go u.** *(of crime)* ne pas être découvert; *(of person)* passer inaperçu

undies ['ʌndɪz] npl Fam dessous mpl

undignified [ʌn'dɪgnɪfaɪd] adj indigne

undisciplined [ʌn'dɪsɪplɪnd] adj indiscipliné

undiscovered [ʌndɪ'skʌvəd] adj **to remain u.** *(of crime, body)* ne pas être découvert

undisputed [ʌndɪ'spjuːtɪd] adj incontesté

undistinguished [ʌndɪ'stɪŋgwɪʃt] adj médiocre

undisturbed [ʌndɪ'stɜːbd] adj **to leave sb u.** ne pas déranger qn

undivided [ʌndɪ'vaɪdɪd] adj **my u. attention** toute mon attention

undo [ʌn'duː] *(pt -did, pp -done)* vt défaire; *(bound person)* détacher; *(parcel)* ouvrir; *(mistake, damage)* réparer; *Comptr (command)* annuler ● **undoing** n ruine f ● **undone** [ʌn'dʌn] adj **to come u.** *(of knot)* se défaire; **to leave sth u.** *(work)* ne pas faire qch

undoubted [ʌn'daʊtɪd] adj indubitable ● **undoubtedly** adv indubitablement

undreamt-of [ʌn'dremtɒv] adj inimaginable

undress [ʌn'dres] **1** vt déshabiller; **to get undressed** se déshabiller **2** vi se déshabiller

undrinkable [ʌn'drɪnkəbəl] adj imbuvable

undue [ʌn'djuː] adj excessif, -ive ● **unduly** adv excessivement

undulating ['ʌndjʊleɪtɪŋ] adj *(movement)* onduleux, -euse; *(countryside)* vallonné

undying [ʌn'daɪɪŋ] adj *(love)* éternel, -elle

unearned [ʌn'ɜːnd] adj **u. income** rentes fpl

unearth [ʌn'ɜːθ] vt *(from ground)* déterrer; *Fig (discover)* mettre à jour

unearthly [ʌn'ɜːθlɪ] adj mystérieux, -ieuse; *Fam* **at an u. hour** à une heure impossible

uneasy [ʌn'iːzɪ] adj *(person)* mal à l'aise; *(sleep)* agité; *(silence)* gêné

uneatable [ʌn'iːtəbəl] adj *(bad)* immangeable; *(poisonous)* non comestible

uneconomic(al) [ʌniːkə'nɒmɪk(əl)] adj peu économique

uneducated [ʌn'edjʊkeɪtɪd] adj *(person)* sans éducation; *(accent)* populaire

unemotional [ʌnɪ'məʊʃənəl] adj impassible; *(speech)* sans passion

unemployed [ʌnɪm'plɔɪd] **1** adj au chômage **2** npl **the u.** les chômeurs mpl ● **unemployment** n chômage m; Br **u. benefit** allocation f chômage

unending [ʌn'endɪŋ] adj interminable

unenthusiastic [ʌnɪnθjuːzɪ'æstɪk] adj peu enthousiaste

unenviable [ʌn'envɪəbəl] adj peu enviable

unequal [ʌn'iːkwəl] adj inégal; **to be u. to the task** ne pas être à la hauteur de la tâche ● **unequalled** *(Am* **unequaled)** adj *(incomparable)* inégalé

unequivocal [ʌnɪ'kwɪvəkəl] adj sans équivoque ● **unequivocally** adv sans équivoque

unerring [ʌn'ɜːrɪŋ] adj infaillible

unethical [ʌn'eθɪkəl] *adj* contraire à l'éthique

uneven [ʌn'iːvən] *adj* inégal

uneventful [ʌnɪ'ventfəl] *adj* sans histoires

unexceptionable [ʌnɪk'sepʃənəbəl] *adj* irréprochable

unexpected [ʌnɪk'spektɪd] *adj* inattendu • **unexpectedly** *adv (arrive)* à l'improviste; *(fail, succeed)* contre toute attente

unexplained [ʌnɪk'spleɪnd] *adj* inexpliqué

unfailing [ʌn'feɪlɪŋ] *adj (optimism, courage)* à toute épreuve; *(supply)* inépuisable

unfair [ʌn'feə(r)] *adj* injuste (**to** sb envers qn); *(competition)* déloyal • **unfairly** *adv* injustement • **unfairness** *n* injustice *f*

unfaithful [ʌn'feɪθfəl] *adj* infidèle (**to** à)

unfamiliar [ʌnfə'mɪlɪə(r)] *adj* inconnu; **to be u. with** sth ne pas connaître qch

unfashionable [ʌn'fæʃənəbəl] *adj* démodé

unfasten [ʌn'fɑːsən] *vt* défaire

unfavourable [ʌn'feɪvərəbəl] *(Am* **unfavorable**) *adj* défavorable

unfeeling [ʌn'fiːlɪŋ] *adj* insensible

unfinished [ʌn'fɪnɪʃt] *adj* inachevé; **to have some u. business** avoir une affaire à régler

unfit [ʌn'fɪt] *adj (unsuitable)* inapte; *(in bad shape)* pas en forme; **to be u. to do sth** être incapable de faire qch; **u. for human consumption** impropre à la consommation; **u. mother** mère *f* indigne

unflagging [ʌn'flægɪŋ] *adj (optimism, zeal)* inépuisable; *(interest, attention)* sans faille

unflappable [ʌn'flæpəbəl] *adj Br Fam* imperturbable

unflattering [ʌn'flætərɪŋ] *adj* peu flatteur, -euse

unflinching [ʌn'flɪntʃɪŋ] *adj (courage)* inépuisable; *(resolve, loyalty, support)* à toute épreuve

unfold [ʌn'fəʊld] **1** *vt* déplier; *(wings)* déployer; *Fig (intentions, plan)* dévoiler **2** *vi (of story, view)* se dérouler

unforeseeable [ʌnfɔː'siːəbəl] *adj* imprévisible • **unforeseen** *adj* imprévu

unforgettable [ʌnfə'getəbəl] *adj* inoubliable

unforgivable [ʌnfə'gɪvəbəl] *adj* impardonnable

unforgiving [ʌnfə'gɪvɪŋ] *adj* implacable, impitoyable

unfortunate [ʌn'fɔːtʃənət] *adj* mal-

chanceux, -euse; *(event)* fâcheux, -euse; **you were u.** tu n'as pas eu de chance • **unfortunately** *adv* malheureusement

unfounded [ʌn'faʊndɪd] *adj (rumour, argument)* sans fondement

unfreeze [ʌn'friːz] *(pt* -**froze,** *pp* -**frozen**) *vt (funds)* dégeler

unfriendly [ʌn'frendlɪ] *adj* peu aimable (**to** avec) • **unfriendliness** *n* froideur *f*

unfulfilled [ʌnfʊl'fɪld] *adj (desire)* insatisfait; *(plan, dream)* non réalisé; *(condition)* non rempli

unfurl [ʌn'fɜːl] *vt* déployer

unfurnished [ʌn'fɜːnɪʃt] *adj* non meublé

ungainly [ʌn'geɪnlɪ] *adj (clumsy)* gauche

unglued [ʌn'gluːd] *adj Am Fam* **to come u.** *(confused)* perdre les pédales, s'affoler

ungodly [ʌn'gɒdlɪ] *adj (sinful)* impie; *Fam* **at an u. hour** à une heure impossible

ungracious [ʌn'greɪʃəs] *adj* peu aimable

ungrammatical [ʌngrə'mætɪkəl] *adj* non grammatical

ungrateful [ʌn'greɪtfəl] *adj* ingrat

unguarded [ʌn'gɑːdɪd] *adj (place)* sans surveillance; **in an u. moment** dans un moment d'inattention

unhappy [ʌn'hæpɪ] (-**ier,** -**iest**) *adj (sad, unfortunate)* malheureux, -euse; *(not pleased)* mécontent; **to be u. about doing sth** ne pas vouloir faire qch • **unhappily** *adv (unfortunately)* malheureusement • **unhappiness** *n* tristesse *f*

unharmed [ʌn'hɑːmd] *adj* indemne

unhealthy [ʌn'helθɪ] (-**ier,** -**iest**) *adj (person)* maladif, -ive; *(climate, place, job)* malsain; *(lungs)* malade

unheard-of [ʌn'hɜːdɒv] *adj (unprecedented)* inouï

unheeded [ʌn'hiːdɪd] *adj* **it went u.** on n'en a pas tenu compte

unhelpful [ʌn'helpfəl] *adj (person)* peu serviable; *(advice)* peu utile

unhinged [ʌn'hɪndʒd] *adj (person, mind)* déséquilibré

unholy [ʌn'həʊlɪ] (-**ier,** -**iest**) *adj* impie; *Fam (noise)* de tous les diables

unhook [ʌn'hʊk] *vt (picture, curtain)* décrocher; *(dress)* dégrafer

unhoped-for [ʌn'həʊptfɔː(r)] *adj* inespéré

unhurried [ʌn'hʌrɪd] *adj (movement)* lent; *(stroll, journey)* fait sans hâte

unhurt [ʌn'hɜːt] *adj* indemne

unhygienic [ʌnhaɪ'dʒiːnɪk] *adj* contraire à l'hygiène

unicorn ['juːnɪkɔːn] *n* licorne *f*

unidentified [ʌnaɪ'dentɪfaɪd] *adj* **u. flying object** objet *m* volant non identifié

uniform ['juːnɪfɔːm] **1** *n* uniforme *m*
2 *adj (regular)* uniforme; *(temperature)* constant • **uniformed** *adj (police officer)* en uniforme • **uni'formity** *n* uniformité *f* • **uniformly** *adv* uniformément
unify ['juːnɪfaɪ] *(pt & pp* **-ied)** *vt* unifier • **unification** [-fɪ'keɪʃən] *n* unification *f*
unilateral [juːnɪ'lætərəl] *adj* unilatéral
unimaginable [ʌnɪ'mædʒɪnəbəl] *adj* inimaginable • **unimaginative** *adj (person, plan)* qui manque d'imagination
unimpaired [ʌnɪm'peəd] *adj* intact
unimportant [ʌnɪm'pɔːtənt] *adj* sans importance
uninformative [ʌnɪn'fɔːmətɪv] *adj* peu instructif, -ive
uninhabitable [ʌnɪn'hæbɪtəbəl] *adj* inhabitable • **uninhabited** *adj* inhabité
uninhibited [ʌnɪn'hɪbɪtɪd] *adj (person)* sans complexes
uninitiated [ʌnɪ'nɪʃɪeɪtɪd] *npl* **the u.** les non-initiés *mpl*
uninjured [ʌn'ɪndʒəd] *adj* indemne
uninspiring [ʌnɪn'spaɪərɪŋ] *adj (subject)* pas très inspirant
unintelligible [ʌnɪn'telɪdʒəbəl] *adj* inintelligible
unintended [ʌnɪn'tendɪd] *adj* involontaire
unintentional [ʌnɪn'tenʃənəl] *adj* involontaire
uninterested [ʌn'ɪntrɪstɪd] *adj* indifférent (**in** à) • **uninteresting** *adj* inintéressant
uninterrupted [ʌnɪntə'rʌptɪd] *adj* ininterrompu
uninvited [ʌnɪn'vaɪtɪd] *adv (arrive)* sans invitation • **uninviting** *adj* peu attrayant
union ['juːnɪən] **1** *n* union *f*; *(trade union)* syndicat *m*
2 *adj* syndical; **u. member** syndicaliste *mf*; **the U. Jack** = le drapeau britannique • **unionist** *n Br* **trade u.,** *Am* **labor u.** syndicaliste *mf* • **unionize** *vt* syndiquer
unique [juː'niːk] *adj* unique • **uniquely** *adv (remarkably)* exceptionnellement
unisex ['juːnɪseks] *adj (clothes)* unisexe
unison ['juːnɪsən] *n* **in u.** à l'unisson (**with** de)
unit ['juːnɪt] *n* unité *f*; *(of furniture)* élément *m*; *(system)* bloc *m*; *(group, team)* groupe *m*; **psychiatric/heart u.** *(of hospital)* service *m* de psychiatrie/cardiologie; **research u.** centre *m* de recherche; *Br Fin* **u. trust** fonds *m* commun de placement
unite [juː'naɪt] **1** *vt* unir; *(country, party)* unifier; **the United Kingdom** le Royaume-Uni; **the United Nations** les Nations *fpl*

unies; **the United States of America** les États-Unis *mpl* d'Amérique
2 *vi* s'unir
unity ['juːnətɪ] *n (cohesion)* unité *f*; *Fig (harmony)* harmonie *f*
universal [juːnɪ'vɜːsəl] *adj* universel, -elle • **universally** *adv* universellement
universe ['juːnɪvɜːs] *n* univers *m*
university [juːnɪ'vɜːsɪtɪ] **1** *(pl* **-ies)** *n* université *f*; **to go to u.** aller à l'université; *Br* **at u.** à l'université
2 *adj (teaching, town, restaurant)* universitaire; *(student, teacher)* d'université
unjust [ʌn'dʒʌst] *adj* injuste
unjustified [ʌn'dʒʌstɪfaɪd] *adj* injustifié
unkempt [ʌn'kempt] *adj* négligé
unkind [ʌn'kaɪnd] *adj* pas gentil (*f* pas gentille) (**to sb** avec qn) • **unkindly** *adv* méchamment
unknowingly [ʌn'nəʊɪŋlɪ] *adv* inconsciemment
unknown [ʌn'nəʊn] **1** *adj* inconnu; **u. to me, he had left** il était parti, ce que j'ignorais
2 *n (person)* inconnu, -ue *mf*; *Phil* **the u.** l'inconnu *m*; *Math & Fig* **u. (quantity)** inconnue *f*
unlawful [ʌn'lɔːfəl] *adj* illégal
unleaded [ʌn'ledɪd] *adj* sans plomb
unleash [ʌn'liːʃ] *vt (dog)* détacher; *Fig (emotion)* susciter
unless [ʌn'les] *conj* à moins que (*+ subjunctive)*; **u. she comes** à moins qu'elle ne vienne; **u. you work harder, you'll fail** à moins de travailler plus dur, vous échouerez
unlicensed [ʌn'laɪsənst] *adj Br* **u. premises** = établissement qui n'a pas de licence de débit de boissons
unlike [ʌn'laɪk] *prep* **to be u. sb/sth** ne pas être comme qn/qch; **u. her brother, she** à la différence de son frère, elle; **it's very u. him to...** ça ne lui ressemble pas du tout de...
unlikely [ʌn'laɪklɪ] *adj* improbable; *(unbelievable)* invraisemblable; **she's u. to win** il est peu probable qu'elle gagne; **in the u. event of an accident...** dans le cas fort peu probable d'un accident...
unlimited [ʌn'lɪmɪtɪd] *adj* illimité
unlisted [ʌn'lɪstɪd] *adj Am (phone number)* sur liste rouge
unload [ʌn'ləʊd] *vti* décharger
unlock [ʌn'lɒk] *vt* ouvrir
unlucky [ʌn'lʌkɪ] **(-ier, -iest)** *adj (person)* malchanceux, -euse; *(number, colour)* qui porte malheur; **you're u.** tu n'as pas

de chance • **unluckily** *adv* malheureusement

unmade [ʌn'meɪd] *adj (bed)* défait

unmanageable [ʌn'mænɪdʒəbəl] *adj
(child)* difficile; *(hair)* difficile à coiffer;
(package, large book, size) peu maniable

unmanned [ʌn'mænd] *adj (spacecraft)*
inhabité

unmarked [ʌn'mɑːkt] *adj (grave)* sans
inscription; *Br* **u. police car** voiture *f*
banalisée

unmarried [ʌn'mærɪd] *adj* non marié

unmask [ʌn'mɑːsk] *vt* démasquer

unmentionable [ʌn'menʃənəbəl] *adj*
dont il ne faut pas parler

unmistakable [ʌnmɪ'steɪkəbəl] *adj (obvious)* indubitable; *(face, voice)* caractéristique

unmitigated [ʌn'mɪtɪgeɪtɪd] *adj (disaster)* absolu; *(folly)* pur

unmoved [ʌn'muːvd] *adj* **to be u. by sth**
rester insensible à qch

unnamed [ʌn'neɪmd] *adj (person)* anonyme; *(thing)* sans nom

unnatural [ʌn'nætʃərəl] *adj (abnormal)*
anormal; *(love)* contre nature; *(affected)*
affecté • **unnaturally** *adv* **not u.** naturellement

unnecessary [ʌn'nesəsərɪ] *adj* inutile;
(superfluous) superflu

unnerve [ʌn'nɜːv] *vt* troubler

> 𝄢 Note that the French verb **énerver** is a
> false friend. It means **to irritate** or **to make
> nervous** depending on the context.

unnoticed [ʌn'nəʊtɪst] *adv* **to go u.** passer inaperçu

unobstructed [ʌnəb'strʌktɪd] *adj (road,
view)* dégagé

unobtainable [ʌnəb'teɪnəbəl] *adj* impossible à obtenir

unobtrusive [ʌnəb'truːsɪv] *adj* discret, -ète

unoccupied [ʌn'ɒkjʊpaɪd] *adj (house,
person)* inoccupé; *(seat)* libre

unofficial [ʌnə'fɪʃəl] *adj* officieux,
-ieuse; *(visit)* privé; *(strike)* sauvage
• **unofficially** *adv* officieusement

unorthodox [ʌn'ɔːθədɒks] *adj* peu orthodoxe

unpack [ʌn'pæk] **1** *vt (suitcase)* défaire;
(contents) déballer; *(box)* ouvrir
2 *vi* défaire sa valise

unpaid [ʌn'peɪd] *adj (bill, sum)* impayé;
(work, worker) bénévole; *(leave)* non
payé

unpalatable [ʌn'pælətəbəl] *adj (food)*
qui n'est pas bon *(f* bonne) à manger; *Fig
(truth)* désagréable à entendre

unparalleled [ʌn'pærəleld] *adj* sans
égal

unperturbed [ʌnpə'tɜːbd] *adj* nullement déconcerté

unplanned [ʌn'plænd] *adj* imprévu

unpleasant [ʌn'plezənt] *adj* désagréable (**to sb** avec qn)

unplug [ʌn'plʌg] *(pt & pp* **-gg-**) *vt (appliance)* débrancher; *(unblock)* déboucher

unpopular [ʌn'pɒpjʊlə(r)] *adj* impopulaire; **to be u. with sb** ne pas plaire à qn

unprecedented [ʌn'presɪdentɪd] *adj*
sans précédent

unpredictable [ʌnprɪ'dɪktəbəl] *adj* imprévisible; *(weather)* indécis

unprepared [ʌnprɪ'peəd] *adj (meal,
room)* non préparé; *(speech)* improvisé;
to be u. for sth *(not expect)* ne pas s'attendre à qch

unprepossessing [ʌnpriːpə'zesɪŋ] *adj*
peu avenant

unpretentious [ʌnprɪ'tenʃəs] *adj* sans
prétentions

unprincipled [ʌn'prɪnsɪpəld] *adj* sans
scrupules

unprofessional [ʌnprə'feʃənəl] *adj
(person, behaviour)* pas très professionnel, -elle

unprovoked [ʌnprə'vəʊkt] *adj* gratuit

unpublished [ʌn'pʌblɪʃt] *adj (text,
writer)* inédit

unpunished [ʌn'pʌnɪʃt] *adv* **to go u.**
rester impuni

unqualified [ʌn'kwɒlɪfaɪd] *adj (teacher)*
non diplômé; *(support)* sans réserve;
(success, liar) parfait; **to be u. to do sth**
ne pas être qualifié pour faire qch

unquestionable [ʌn'kwestʃənəbəl] *adj*
incontestable • **unquestionably** *adv* incontestablement

unravel [ʌn'rævəl] *(Br* **-ll-,** *Am* **-l-)** *vt
(threads)* démêler; *Fig (mystery)* éclaircir

unreal [ʌn'rɪəl] *adj* irréel, -éelle

unrealistic [ʌn'rɪəlɪstɪk] *adj* irréaliste

unreasonable [ʌn'riːzənəbəl] *adj (person, attitude)* déraisonnable; *(price)* excessif, -ive

unrecognizable [ʌn'rekəgnaɪzəbəl] *adj*
méconnaissable

unrelated [ʌnrɪ'leɪtɪd] *adj (facts)* sans
rapport (**to** avec); **we're u.** il n'y a aucun
lien de parenté entre nous

unrelenting [ʌnrɪ'lentɪŋ] *adj* incessant;
(person) tenace

unreliable [ʌnrɪ'laɪəbəl] *adj* peu fiable

unremarkable [ʌnrɪ'mɑːkəbəl] *adj* quelconque

unrepentant [ʌnrɪ'pentənt] *adj* impénitent; **the murderer was u.** le meurtrier n'a manifesté aucun remords

unreservedly [ˌʌnrɪˈzɜːvɪdlɪ] *adv* sans réserve

unrest [ʌnˈrest] *n* agitation *f*, troubles *mpl*

unrestricted [ˌʌnrɪˈstrɪktɪd] *adj* illimité; **u. access** libre accès *m* (**to** à)

unrewarding [ˌʌnrɪˈwɔːdɪŋ] *adj* ingrat; *(financially)* peu rémunérateur, -trice

unripe [ʌnˈraɪp] *adj (fruit)* qui n'est pas mûr

unrivalled [ʌnˈraɪvəld] (*Am* **unrivaled**) *adj* hors pair *inv*

unroll [ʌnˈrəʊl] **1** *vt* dérouler
2 *vi* se dérouler

unruffled [ʌnˈrʌfəld] *adj* imperturbable

unruly [ʌnˈruːlɪ] (**-ier, -iest**) *adj* indiscipliné

unsafe [ʌnˈseɪf] *adj (place, machine)* dangereux, -euse; *(person)* en danger; **u. sex** rapports *mpl* sexuels non protégés

unsaid [ʌnˈsed] *adj* **to leave sth u.** passer qch sous silence

unsaleable [ʌnˈseɪləbəl] *adj* invendable

unsatisfactory [ˌʌnsætɪsˈfæktərɪ] *adj* peu satisfaisant • **un'satisfied** *adj* insatisfait; **u. with sb/sth** peu satisfait de qn/qch

unsavoury [ʌnˈseɪvərɪ] (*Am* **unsavory**) *adj (person, place)* peu ragoûtant

unscathed [ʌnˈskeɪðd] *adj* indemne

unscheduled [*Br* ʌnˈʃedjuːld, *Am* ʌnˈskedjʊld] *adj* imprévu

unscrew [ʌnˈskruː] *vt* dévisser

unscrupulous [ʌnˈskruːpjʊləs] *adj (person)* peu scrupuleux, -euse; *(action)* malhonnête

unseemly [ʌnˈsiːmlɪ] *adj* inconvenant

unseen [ʌnˈsiːn] **1** *adj* invisible
2 *n Br Sch & Univ* traduction *f* à vue
3 *adv* **to do sth u.** faire qch sans qu'on vous voie

unselfish [ʌnˈselfɪʃ] *adj (person, motive)* désintéressé

unsettle [ʌnˈsetəl] *vt (person)* troubler • **unsettled** *adj (weather, situation)* instable; *(person)* troublé; *(in a job)* mal à l'aise

unshak(e)able [ʌnˈʃeɪkəbəl] *adj* inébranlable

unshaven [ʌnˈʃeɪvən] *adj* pas rasé

unsightly [ʌnˈsaɪtlɪ] *adj* laid

unskilled [ʌnˈskɪld] *adj* non qualifié

unsociable [ʌnˈsəʊʃəbəl] *adj* peu sociable

unsocial [ʌnˈsəʊʃəl] *adj* **to work u. hours** travailler en dehors des heures de bureau

unsolved [ʌnˈsɒlvd] *adj (mystery)* inexpliqué; *(crime)* dont l'auteur n'est pas connu

unsophisticated [ˌʌnsəˈfɪstɪkeɪtɪd] *adj* simple

unsound [ʌnˈsaʊnd] *adj (construction)* peu solide; *(method)* peu sûr; *(decision)* peu judicieux, -ieuse; *Law* **to be of u. mind** ne pas jouir de toutes ses facultés mentales

unspeakable [ʌnˈspiːkəbəl] *adj* indescriptible

unspecified [ʌnˈspesɪfaɪd] *adj* non spécifié

unsporting [ʌnˈspɔːtɪŋ] *adj* qui n'est pas fair-play

unstable [ʌnˈsteɪbəl] *adj* instable

unsteady [ʌnˈstedɪ] *adj (hand, voice, step)* mal assuré; *(table, ladder)* bancal (*mpl* -als) • **unsteadily** *adv (walk)* d'un pas mal assuré

unstinting [ʌnˈstɪntɪŋ] *adj (generosity)* sans bornes; *(praise)* sans réserve

unstoppable [ʌnˈstɒpəbəl] *adj* qu'on ne peut arrêter

unstuck [ʌnˈstʌk] *adj* **to come u.** *(of stamp)* se décoller; *Br Fam (of person, plan)* se casser la figure

unsuccessful [ˌʌnsəkˈsesfəl] *adj (attempt)* infructueux, -ueuse; *(outcome, candidate)* malheureux, -euse; *(application)* non retenu; **to be u.** ne pas réussir (**in doing** à faire); *(of book, film, artist)* ne pas avoir de succès • **unsuccessfully** *adv* en vain, sans succès

unsuitable [ʌnˈsuːtəbəl] *adj* qui ne convient pas (**for** à); *(example)* peu approprié; *(manners, clothes)* peu convenable; **to be u. for sth** ne pas convenir à qch • **unsuited** *adj* **to be u. to sth** ne pas être fait pour qch; **they're u. to each other** ils ne sont pas compatibles

unsupervised [ʌnˈsuːpəvaɪzd] *adv (play)* sans surveillance

unsure [ʌnˈʃʊə(r)] *adj* incertain (**of** *or* **about** de)

unsuspecting [ˌʌnsəˈspektɪŋ] *adj* qui ne se doute de rien

unswerving [ʌnˈswɜːvɪŋ] *adj* à toute épreuve

unsympathetic [ˌʌnsɪmpəˈθetɪk] *adj* peu compatissant (**to** à); **u. to a cause/request** insensible à une cause/requête

untangle [ʌnˈtæŋgəl] *vt (rope, hair)* démêler

untapped [ʌnˈtæpt] *adj (resources)* inexploité

untenable [ʌnˈtenəbəl] *adj (position, argument)* indéfendable

unthinkable [ʌnˈθɪŋkəbəl] *adj* impensable, inconcevable

untidy [ʌn'taɪdɪ] (**-ier, -iest**) *adj (clothes, hair)* peu soigné; *(room)* en désordre; *(person)* désordonné • **untidily** *adv* sans soin

untie [ʌn'taɪ] *vt (person, hands)* détacher; *(knot, parcel)* défaire

until [ʌn'tɪl] **1** *prep* jusqu'à; **u. now** jusqu'à présent; **u. then** jusque-là; **not u. tomorrow** pas avant demain; **I didn't see her u. Monday** c'est seulement lundi que je l'ai vue

2 *conj* jusqu'à ce que (+ *subjunctive)*; **u. she comes** jusqu'à ce qu'elle vienne; **do nothing u. I come** ne fais rien avant que j'arrive

untimely [ʌn'taɪmlɪ] *adj (remark, question)* inopportun; *(death)* prématuré

untiring [ʌn'taɪərɪŋ] *adj* infatigable

untold [ʌn'təʊld] *adj (wealth, quantity)* incalculable; *(beauty)* immense

untoward [ʌntə'wɔːd] *adj* fâcheux, -euse

untranslatable [ʌntræns'leɪtəbəl] *adj* intraduisible

untroubled [ʌn'trʌbəld] *adj (calm)* calme

untrue [ʌn'truː] *adj* faux *(f* fausse) • '**untruth** *n* mensonge *m* • **un'truthful** *adj (person)* menteur, -euse; *(statement)* mensonger, -ère

unusable [ʌn'juːzəbəl] *adj* inutilisable

unused¹ [ʌn'juːzd] *adj (new)* neuf *(f* neuve); *(not in use)* inutilisé

unused² [ʌn'juːst] *adj* **u. to sth/to doing** peu habitué à qch/à faire

unusual [ʌn'juːʒʊəl] *adj (not common)* inhabituel, -uelle; *(strange)* étrange • **unusually** *adv* exceptionnellement

unveil [ʌn'veɪl] *vt* dévoiler • **unveiling** *n (ceremony)* inauguration *f*

unwanted [ʌn'wɒntɪd] *adj* non désiré

unwarranted [ʌn'wɒrəntɪd] *adj* injustifié

unwavering [ʌn'weɪvərɪŋ] *adj* inébranlable

unwelcome [ʌn'welkəm] *adj (news)* fâcheux, -euse; *(gift, visit)* inopportun; *(person)* importun

unwell [ʌn'wel] *adj* souffrant

unwieldy [ʌn'wiːldɪ] *adj (package)* encombrant; *(system)* lourd

unwilling [ʌn'wɪlɪŋ] *adj* **to be u. to do sth** être réticent à faire qch • **unwillingly** *adv* à contrecœur

unwind [ʌn'waɪnd] (*pt & pp* **-wound-) 1** *vt (thread)* dérouler

2 *vi* se dérouler; *Fam (relax)* décompresser

unwise [ʌn'waɪz] *adj* imprudent • **unwisely** *adv* imprudemment

unwitting [ʌn'wɪtɪŋ] *adj* involontaire • **unwittingly** *adv* involontairement

unworkable [ʌn'wɜːkəbəl] *adj (idea)* impraticable

unworthy [ʌn'wɜːðɪ] *adj* indigne *(* **of** de)

unwrap [ʌn'ræp] (*pt & pp* **-pp-)** *vt* déballer

unwritten [ʌn'rɪtən] *adj (agreement)* verbal

unyielding [ʌn'jiːldɪŋ] *adj* inflexible

unzip [ʌn'zɪp] (*pt & pp* **-pp-)** *vt* ouvrir (la fermeture Éclair® de)

up [ʌp] **1** *adv* en haut; **to come/go up** monter; **to walk up and down** marcher de long en large; **up there** là-haut; **up above** au-dessus; **up on the roof** sur le toit; **further** *or* **higher up** plus haut; **up to** *(as far as)* jusqu'à; **to be up to doing sth** *(capable of)* être de taille à faire qch; *(in a position to)* être à même de faire qch; **to be a goal up** avoir un but d'avance; **it's up to you to do it** c'est à toi de le faire; **it's up to you** *(you decide)* c'est à toi de décider; **where are you up to?** *(in book)* où en es-tu?; *Fam* **what are you up to?** que faistu?; *Fam* **to be well up in** *(versed in)* s'y connaître en; *Fam* **up (with) the workers!** vive(nt) les travailleurs!

2 *prep* **up a hill** en haut d'une colline; **up a tree** dans un arbre; **up a ladder** sur une échelle; **to go up the stairs** monter les escaliers; **to live up the street** habiter plus loin dans la rue; *Fig* **to be up against sth** avoir affaire à qch

3 *adj (out of bed)* levé; **we were up all night** nous sommes restés debout toute la nuit; **the two weeks were up** les deux semaines étaient terminées; **your time's up** c'est terminé; *Fam* **what's up?** qu'est-ce qu'il y a?; **to be up and running** être opérationnel, -elle

4 *npl* **ups and downs** des hauts et des bas *mpl*

5 (*pt & pp* **-pp-)** *vt Fam (price, offer)* augmenter • '**up-and-**'**coming** *adj* qui monte • '**up-**'**beat** *adj Fam* optimiste • **up-bringing** *n* éducation *f* • **upcoming** *adj Am* imminent • **up**'**date** *vt* mettre à jour • **up-**'**grade** *vt (job)* revaloriser; *(person)* promouvoir; *Comptr (hardware)* augmenter la puissance de • **uphill 1** [ʌp'hɪl] *adv* **to go u.** monter **2** ['ʌphɪl] *adj Fig (struggle, task)* pénible • **up**'**hold** (*pt & pp* **-held**) *vt (decision)* maintenir • **upkeep** *n* entretien *m* • **uplift 1** ['ʌplɪft] *n* élévation *f* spirituelle **2** [ʌp'lɪft] *vt* élever • **up**'**lifting** *adj* édifiant • **'up-'market** *adj Br (car, product)* haut de gamme *inv; (area, place)* chic *inv* • **upright 1** *adv (straight)* droit **2** *adj (vertical, honest)* droit **3** *n (post)* montant *m* • **uprising** *n* insurrection *f* • **up'root** *vt (plant, person)* déraciner • **upside 'down** *adv* à l'envers; **to turn sth u.** retourner qch; *Fig* mettre qch sens dessus dessous • **upstairs 1** [ʌpˈsteəz] *adv* en haut; **to go u.** monter **2** [ˈʌpsteəz] *adj (people, room)* du dessus • **up'stream** *adv* en amont • **upsurge** *n (of interest)* recrudescence *f; (of anger)* accès *m* • **uptake** *n Fam* **to be quick on the u.** piger vite • **'up'tight** *adj Fam (tense)* crispé; *(inhibited)* coincé • **'up-to-'date** *adj* moderne; *(information)* à jour; *(well-informed)* au courant (**on** de) • **'up-to-the-'minute** *adj (news, information)* de dernière minute; *(style, fashion)* dernier cri *inv* • **upturn** *n (improvement)* amélioration *f* (**in** de) • **upturned** *adj (nose)* retroussé • **upward** *adj (movement)* ascendant; *(path)* qui monte; *(trend)* à la hausse • **upwards** *adv* vers le haut; **from 5 euros u.** à partir de 5 euros; **u. of fifty** cinquante et plus

upheaval [ʌpˈhiːvəl] *n* bouleversement *m*

upholster [ʌpˈhəʊlstə(r)] *vt (pad)* rembourrer; *(cover)* recouvrir • **upholsterer** *n* tapissier *m* • **upholstery** *n (padding)* rembourrage *m; (covering)* revêtement *m; (in car)* sièges *mpl*

upon [əˈpɒn] *prep* sur

upper [ˈʌpə(r)] **1** *adj* supérieur; **u. class** aristocratie *f;* **to have/get the u. hand** avoir/prendre le dessus; *Br Theatre* **u. circle** deuxième balcon *m*
2 *n (of shoe)* empeigne *f* • **'upper-'class** *adj* aristocratique • **uppermost** *adj* le plus haut (*f* la plus haute); **it was u. in my mind** c'était la première de mes préoccupations

uppity [ˈʌpɪtɪ] *adj Fam* crâneur, -euse

uproar [ˈʌprɔː(r)] *n* tumulte *m*

upset [ʌpˈset] **1** *(pt & pp* **-set,** *pres p* **-setting)** *vt (knock over, spill)* renverser; *(person, plans, schedule)* bouleverser
2 *adj (unhappy)* bouleversé (**about** par); **to have an u. stomach** avoir l'estomac dérangé
3 [ˈʌpset] *n (disturbance)* bouleversement *m; (surprise)* défaite *f;* **to have a stomach u.** avoir l'estomac dérangé • **upsetting** *adj* bouleversant

upshot [ˈʌpʃɒt] *n* résultat *m*

upstart [ˈʌpstɑːt] *n Pej* parvenu, -ue *mf*

upstate [ʌpˈsteɪt] *Am* **1** *adj* du nord *(d'un*

État); u. **New York** le nord de l'État de New York
2 *adv* **to go u.** aller vers le nord *(d'un État)*

uranium [jʊˈreɪnɪəm] *n* uranium *m*

urban [ˈɜːbən] *adj* urbain

urbane [ɜːˈbeɪn] *adj* courtois

urchin [ˈɜːtʃɪn] *n* polisson, -onne *mf*

urge [ɜːdʒ] **1** *n* forte envie *f;* **to have an u. to do sth** avoir très envie de faire qch
2 *vt* **to u. sb to do sth** presser qn de faire qch; **to u. sb on to do sth** encourager qn à faire qch

urgency [ˈɜːdʒənsɪ] *n* urgence *f; (of tone, request)* insistance *f;* **it's a matter of u.** il y a urgence • **urgent** *adj* urgent; **to be in u. need of sth** avoir un besoin urgent de qch • **urgently** *adv* d'urgence

urinal [jʊˈraɪnəl] *n* urinoir *m*

urine [ˈjʊərɪn] *n* urine *f* • **urinate** *vi* uriner

URL [juːɑːrˈel] *(abbr* **uniform resource locator)** *n Comptr* (adresse *f)* URL *m*

urn [ɜːn] *n* urne *f; (for coffee or tea)* fontaine *f*

Uruguay [ˈjʊərəgwaɪ] *n* l'Uruguay *m*

US [juːˈes] *(abbr* **United States)** *n* **the US** les USA *mpl*

us [əs, *stressed* ʌs] *pron* nous; **(to) us** *(indirect)* nous; **she sees us** elle nous voit; **she saw us** elle nous a vus; **he gave it to us** il nous l'a donné; **with us** avec nous; **all of us** nous tous; **let's** *or* **let us eat!** mangeons!

USA [juːesˈeɪ] *(abbr* **United States of America)** *n* **the U.** les USA *mpl*

usage [ˈjuːsɪdʒ] *n* usage *m*

use 1 [juːs] *n (utilization)* emploi *m,* usage *m; (ability, permission to use)* emploi; **to have the u. of sth** avoir l'usage de qch; **to make (good) u. of sth** faire (bon) usage de qch; **to be of u. to sb** être utile à qn; **in u.** en usage; **not in u., out of u.** hors d'usage; **ready for u.** prêt à l'emploi; **it's no u. crying** ça ne sert à rien de pleurer; **what's the u. of worrying?** à quoi bon s'inquiéter?; **I have no u. for it** je n'en ai pas l'usage; *Fam* **he's no u.** il est nul
2 [juːz] *vt (utilize)* utiliser, se servir de; *(force, diplomacy)* avoir recours à; *(electricity)* consommer; **it's used to do** *or* **for doing sth** ça sert à faire qch; **it's used as...** ça sert de...; **to u. sth up** *(food, fuel)* finir; *(money)* dépenser
3 *v aux* • **used to** [juːstə] **I used to sing** avant, je chantais; **she u. to jog every Sunday** elle faisait du jogging tous les dimanches • **use-by date** [ˈjuːz-] *n* date *f* limite de consommation

used 1 [juːzd] *adj (second-hand)* d'occasion; *(stamp)* oblitéré

2 [juːst] *adj* **to be u. to sth/to doing sth** être habitué à qch/à faire qch; **to get u. to sb/sth** s'habituer à qn/qch

useful ['juːsfəl] *adj* utile (**to** à); **to come in u.** être utile; **to make oneself u.** se rendre utile •**usefulness** *n* utilité *f* •**useless** *adj* inutile; *(unusable)* inutilisable; *(person)* nul (*f* nulle) (**at** en)

user ['juːzə(r)] *n (of train, telephone)* usager *m; (of road, machine, dictionary)* utilisateur, -trice *mf* •'**user-'friendly** *adj* convivial

> ⌀ Note that the French verb **user** is a false friend. Its most common meaning is **to wear out**.

usher ['ʌʃə(r)] **1** *n (in church, theatre)* ouvreur *m; (in court)* huissier *m*

2 *vt* **to u. sb in** faire entrer qn •**ushe'rette** *n* ouvreuse *f*

USSR [juːeses'ɑː(r)] (*abbr* **Union of Soviet Socialist Republics**) *n Formerly* URSS *f*

usual ['juːʒʊəl] **1***adj* habituel, -uelle; **as u.** comme d'habitude; **you're not your u. self today** tu n'es pas aussi gai que d'habitude aujourd'hui

2 *n Fam* **the u.** *(food, excuse)* la même chose que d'habitude •**usually** *adv* d'habitude

usurer ['juːʒərə(r)] *n* usurier, -ière *mf*

usurp [juː'zɜːp] *vt* usurper

utensil [juː'tensəl] *n* ustensile *m;* **kitchen u.** ustensile de cuisine

uterus ['juːtərəs] *n Anat* utérus *m*

utilitarian [juːtɪlɪ'teərɪən] *adj* utilitaire

utility [juː'tɪlɪtɪ] *n (usefulness)* utilité *f;* **(public) utilities** services *mpl* publics; *Am* **utilities** *(service charges)* charges *fpl; Comptr* **u. program** utilitaire *m;* **u. room** pièce *f* de rangement

utilize ['juːtɪlaɪz] *vt* utiliser •**utili'zation** *n* utilisation *f*

utmost ['ʌtməʊst] **1** *adj* **the u. ease** *(greatest)* la plus grande facilité; **the u. danger/limit** *(extreme)* un danger/une limite extrême; **it is of the u. importance that...** il est de la plus haute importance que... (+ *subjunctive*)

2 *n* **to do one's u.** faire de son mieux (**to do** pour faire)

utopia [juː'təʊpɪə] *n* utopie *f* •**utopian** *adj* utopique

utter¹ ['ʌtə(r)] *adj* total; *(folly, lie)* pur; **it's u. nonsense** c'est complètement absurde •**utterly** *adv* complètement

utter² ['ʌtə(r)] *vt (cry, sigh)* pousser; *(word)* prononcer; *(threat)* proférer •**utterance** *n (act)* énonciation *f; (words spoken)* déclaration *f; Ling* énoncé *m*

U-turn ['juːtɜːn] *n (in vehicle)* demi-tour *m; Fig (change of policy)* virage *m* à 180°

V, v [viː] *n (letter)* V, v *m inv*

vacant ['veɪkənt] *adj (room, seat)* libre; *(post)* vacant; *(look)* absent; *Br* **'situations v.'** *(in newspaper)* 'offres d'emploi' • **vacancy** *(pl -ies)* *n (post)* poste *m* vacant; *(room)* chambre *f* libre; **'no vacancies'** *(in hotel)* 'complet' • **vacantly** *adv* d'un air absent

> ⚠ Note that the French word **vacances** is a false friend. It means **holiday**.

vacate [*Br* və'keɪt, *Am* 'veɪkeɪt] *vt* quitter

vacation [veɪ'keɪʃən] *n Am* vacances *fpl*; **to take a v.** prendre des vacances • **vacationer** *n Am* vacancier, -ière *mf*

vaccinate ['væksɪneɪt] *vt* vacciner • **vaccination** *n* vaccination *f* • **vaccine** [-'siːn] *n* vaccin *m*

vacillate ['væsɪleɪt] *vi* hésiter

vacuum ['vækjʊəm] **1** *n* vide *m*; **v. cleaner** aspirateur *m*; *Br* **v. flask** Thermos® *m ou f* **2** *vt (room)* passer l'aspirateur dans; *(carpet)* passer l'aspirateur sur • **vacuum-packed** *adj* emballé sous vide

vagabond ['vægəbɒnd] *n* vagabond, -onde *mf*

vagary ['veɪɡərɪ] *(pl -ies)* *n* caprice *m*

vagina [və'dʒaɪnə] *n Anat* vagin *m*

vagrant ['veɪɡrənt] *n Law* vagabond, -onde *mf* • **vagrancy** *n Law* vagabondage *m*

vague [veɪɡ] **(-er, -est)** *adj* vague; *(outline, photo)* flou; **I haven't got the vaguest idea** je n'en ai pas la moindre idée; **he was v. (about it)** il est resté vague • **vaguely** *adv* vaguement

vain [veɪn] **(-er, -est)** *adj* **(a)** *(attempt, hope)* vain; **in v.** en vain; **her efforts were in v.** ses efforts ont été inutiles **(b)** *(conceited)* vaniteux, -euse

valentine ['væləntaɪn] *n (card)* carte *f* de la Saint-Valentin; **(Saint) V.'s Day** la Saint-Valentin

valet ['vælɪt, 'væleɪ] *n* valet *m* de chambre

valiant ['væljənt] *adj* vaillant • **valour** *(Am* **valor)** *n* bravoure *f*

valid ['vælɪd] *adj* valable • **validate** *vt* valider • **validity** [və'lɪdɪtɪ] *n* validité *f*

valley ['vælɪ] *(pl -eys)* *n* vallée *f*

valuable ['væljʊəbəl] **1** *adj (object)* de valeur; *Fig (help, time)* précieux, -ieuse **2** *npl* **valuables** objets *mpl* de valeur

value ['væljuː] **1** *n* valeur *f*; **to be of v.** avoir de la valeur; **to be good v. (for money)** être d'un bon rapport qualité-prix; *Br* **v.-added tax** taxe *f* sur la valeur ajoutée **2** *vt (appreciate)* apprécier; *(assess)* évaluer • **valuation** [-jʊ'eɪʃən] *n (assessment)* évaluation *f*; *(by expert)* expertise *f*

valve [vælv] *n (of machine, car)* soupape *f*; *(of pipe, tube)* valve *f*; *(of heart)* valvule *f*

vampire ['væmpaɪə(r)] *n* vampire *m*

van [væn] *n (vehicle)* camionnette *f*, fourgonnette *f*; *Br Rail* fourgon *m*

vandal ['vændəl] *n* vandale *mf* • **vandalism** *n* vandalisme *m* • **vandalize** *vt* saccager

vanguard ['vænɡɑːd] *n* **in the v. of** à l'avant-garde de

vanilla [və'nɪlə] **1** *n* vanille *f* **2** *adj (ice cream)* à la vanille; **v. flavour** parfum *m* vanille

vanish ['vænɪʃ] *vi* disparaître; **to v. into thin air** se volatiliser

vanity ['vænɪtɪ] *n* vanité *f*; **v. case** vanity-case *m*

vanquish ['væŋkwɪʃ] *vt Literary* vaincre

vantage point ['vɑːntɪdʒpɔɪnt] *n* point *m* de vue; *Fig* position *f* objective

vapour ['veɪpə(r)] *(Am* **vapor)** *n* vapeur *f*

variable ['veərɪəbəl] *adj & n* variable *(f)*

variance ['veərɪəns] *n* **at v.** en désaccord (**with** avec)

variant ['veərɪənt] **1** *adj* différent **2** *n* variante *f*

variation [veərɪ'eɪʃən] *n* variation *f*

varicose ['værɪkəʊs] *adj* **v. veins** varices *fpl*

variety [və'raɪətɪ] *n* **(a)** *(diversity)* variété *f*; **a v. of** toutes sortes de; **a v. of articles/products** toute une gamme d'articles/de produits **(b)** *(entertainment)* variétés *fpl*; **v. show** spectacle *m* de variétés

various ['veərɪəs] *adj* divers • **variously** *adv* diversement

varnish ['vɑːnɪʃ] **1** n vernis m
  2 vt vernir
vary ['veərɪ] (pt & pp -ied) vti varier (in/
  with en/selon) •**varied** adj varié •**vary-**
  ing adj variable
vase [Br vɑːz, Am veɪs] n vase m
vasectomy [və'sektəmɪ] n vasectomie f
Vaseline® ['væsəliːn] n vaseline f
vast [vɑːst] adj immense •**vastly** adv à
  l'extrême; (superior) infiniment •**vast-**
  ness n immensité f
VAT [viːeɪ'tiː, væt] (abbr value added tax)
  n BrTVA f
vat [væt] n cuve f
Vatican ['vætɪkən] n the V. le Vatican
vault¹ [vɔːlt] n (roof) voûte f; (tomb) caveau m; (cellar) cave f; (in bank) salle f des
  coffres
vault² [vɔːlt] vti (jump) sauter
VCR [viːsiːˈɑː(r)] (abbr video cassette re-
  corder) n magnétoscope m
VD [viːˈdiː] (abbr venereal disease) n
  maladie f vénérienne
VDU [viːdiːˈjuː] (abbr visual display unit)
  n Comptr moniteur m
veal [viːl] n veau m
veer [vɪə(r)] vi (of car) virer; (of wind)
  tourner; (of road) décrire un virage; to v.
  off the road quitter la route
veg [vedʒ] npl Br Fam légumes mpl
vegan ['viːgən] n végétalien, -ienne
  mf
vegeburger ['vedʒɪbɜːgə(r)] n hamburger m végétarien
vegetable ['vedʒtəbəl] n légume m; **v.**
  fat graisse f végétale; **v. garden** potager
  m; **v. kingdom** règne m végétal; **v. oil**
  huile f végétale •**vegetarian** [vedʒɪ-
  teərɪən] adj & n végétarien, -ienne (mf)
  •**vegetation** [vedʒɪˈteɪʃən] n végétation f
vegetate ['vedʒɪteɪt] vi Pej (of person)
  végéter
veggie ['vedʒɪ] (abbr vegetarian) n Br
  Fam végétarien, -ienne mf
vehement ['viːəmənt] adj véhément
  •**vehemently** adv avec véhémence
vehicle ['viːɪkəl] n véhicule m
veil [veɪl] **1** n (covering) & Fig voile m
  2 vt voiler •**veiled** adj voilé
vein [veɪn] n (in body, rock) veine f; (in
  leaf) nervure f; Fig in a similar v. de la
  même veine
Velcro® ['velkrəʊ] n Velcro® m
vellum ['veləm] n vélin m
velocity [vəˈlɒsɪtɪ] n vélocité f
velvet ['velvɪt] **1** n velours m
  2 adj de velours •**velvety** adj velouté
vendetta [venˈdetə] n vendetta f

vending machine ['vendɪŋməʃiːn] n
  distributeur m automatique
vendor ['vendə(r)] n vendeur, -euse mf
veneer [vəˈnɪə(r)] n (wood) placage m;
  Fig (appearance) vernis m
venerable ['venərəbəl] adj vénérable
  •**venerate** vt vénérer
venereal [vəˈnɪərɪəl] adj vénérien,
  -ienne
venetian [vəˈniːʃən] adj **v. blind** store m
  vénitien
Venezuela [venɪˈzweɪlə] n le Venezuela
vengeance ['vendʒəns] n vengeance f;
  to take v. on sb se venger de qn; Fig with
  a v. de plus belle
venison ['venɪsən] n venaison f
venom ['venəm] n (poison) & Fig venin m
  •**venomous** adj (snake, speech) venimeux, -euse
vent [vent] **1** n conduit m; Fig to give v. to
  sth donner libre cours à qch
  2 vt to v. one's anger on sb décharger sa
  colère sur qn
ventilate ['ventɪleɪt] vt ventiler, aérer
  •**ventiˈlation** n ventilation f, aération f
  •**ventilator** n ventilateur m; Med respirateur m; Med to be on a v. être branché sur
  un respirateur
ventriloquist [venˈtrɪləkwɪst] n ventriloque mf
venture ['ventʃə(r)] **1** n entreprise f
  (hasardeuse); Fin v. capital capital-
  risque m
  2 vt risquer; to v. to do sth se risquer à
  faire qch
  3 vi s'aventurer (into dans)
venue ['venjuː] n (for meeting, concert)
  salle f; (for football match) stade m

> **⚠** Note that the French word **venue** is a
> false friend and is never a translation for
> the English word **venue**. It means **arrival**.

veranda(h) [vəˈrændə] n véranda f
verb [vɜːb] n verbe m •**verbal** adj verbal
verbatim [vɜːˈbeɪtɪm] adj & adv mot pour
  mot
verbose [vɜːˈbəʊs] adj verbeux, -euse
verdict ['vɜːdɪkt] n verdict m
verdigris ['vɜːdɪgriːs] n vert-de-gris m inv
verge [vɜːdʒ] **1** n Br (of road) bord m; on
  the v. of ruin/tears au bord de la ruine/
  des larmes; on the v. of a discovery à la
  veille d'une découverte; to be on the v. of
  doing sth être sur le point de faire qch
  2 vi to v. on friser; (of colour) tirer sur
verger ['vɜːdʒə(r)] n (church official) bedeau m
verify ['verɪfaɪ] (pt & pp -ied) vt vérifier

• **verification** [-fɪ'keɪʃən] n vérification f

veritable ['verɪtəbəl] adj Formal véritable

vermin ['vɜːmɪn] n (animals) animaux mpl nuisibles; (insects, people) vermine f

vermouth ['vɜːməθ] n vermouth m

vernacular [və'nækjʊlə(r)] n langue f vernaculaire

versatile [Br 'vɜːsətaɪl, Am 'vɜːrsətəl] adj polyvalent • **versatility** [-'tɪlɪtɪ] n polyvalence f

> ⌀ Note that the French word **versatile** is a false friend and is never a translation for the English word **versatile**. It means **changeable**.

verse [vɜːs] n (poetry) vers mpl; (stanza) strophe f; (of Bible) verset m

versed [vɜːst] adj (well) v. in sth versé dans qch

version [Br 'vɜːʃən, Am 'vɜːʒən] n version f

versus ['vɜːsəs] prep (in sport, law) contre; (compared to) comparé à

vertebra ['vɜːtɪbrə] (pl -ae [-iː]) n vertèbre f

vertical ['vɜːtɪkəl] 1 adj vertical
2 n verticale f • **vertically** adv verticalement

vertigo ['vɜːtɪɡəʊ] n vertige m

verve [vɜːv] n verve f

very ['verɪ] 1 adv très; v. little très peu; v. much beaucoup; I'm v. hot j'ai très chaud; the v. first le tout premier (f la toute première); the v. next day le lendemain même; at the v. least/most tout au moins/plus; at the v. latest au plus tard
2 adj (emphatic use) this v. house cette maison même; at the v. end tout à la fin; to the v. end jusqu'au bout; those were her v. words c'est ce qu'elle a dit mot pour mot

vespers ['vespəz] npl (church service) vêpres fpl

vessel ['vesəl] n (ship) vaisseau m; (container) récipient m

vest [vest] n maillot m de corps; Am (waistcoat) gilet m

> ⌀ Note that the French word **veste** is a false friend and is never a translation for the English word **vest**. It means **jacket**.

vested ['vestɪd] adj to have a v. interest in sth avoir un intérêt personnel dans qch

vestige ['vestɪdʒ] n vestige m; not a v. of truth pas une once de vérité

vestry ['vestrɪ] (pl -ies) n (in church) sacristie f

vet¹ [vet] n vétérinaire mf • **veterinarian** [vetərɪ'neərɪən] n Am vétérinaire mf • **veterinary** ['vetərɪnərɪ] adj vétérinaire; Br v. surgeon vétérinaire mf

vet² [vet] (pt & pp -tt-) vt Br faire une enquête sur

vet³ [vet] n Am Fam Mil ancien combattant m

veteran ['vetərən] 1 n Mil ancien combattant m; Fig vétéran m
2 adj de longue date; v. golfer golfeur expérimenté

veto ['viːtəʊ] 1 (pl -oes) n veto m inv; right or power of v. droit m de veto
2 (pt & pp -oed) vt mettre son veto à

VHF [viːeɪtʃ'ef] (abbr very high frequency) n on V. en VHF f

VHS [viːeɪtʃ'es] (abbr video home system) n VHS m

via [Br 'vaɪə, Am 'vɪə] prep via, par

viable ['vaɪəbəl] adj viable • **via'bility** n viabilité f

viaduct ['vaɪədʌkt] n viaduc m

vibrant ['vaɪbrənt] adj (person) plein de vie; (speech) vibrant; (colour) vif (f vive)

vibrate [vaɪ'breɪt] vi vibrer • **vibration** n vibration f • **vibrator** n vibromasseur m

vicar ['vɪkə(r)] n (in Church of England) pasteur m • **vicarage** [-rɪdʒ] n presbytère m

vicarious [vɪ'keərɪəs] adj indirect • **vicariously** adv indirectement

vice [vaɪs] n (depravity, fault) vice m; Br (tool) étau m; the v. squad ≃ la brigade des mœurs

vice- [vaɪs] pref vice- • **vice-'chancellor** n (of British university) président m • **vice-'president** n vice-président, -ente mf

vice versa [vaɪs(ɪ)'vɜːsə] adv vice versa

vicinity [və'sɪnɪtɪ] n environs mpl; in the v. of aux environs de

vicious ['vɪʃəs] adj (malicious) méchant; (violent) brutal; v. circle cercle m vicieux • **viciously** adv (spitefully) méchamment; (violently) brutalement • **viciousness** n (spite) méchanceté f; (violence) brutalité f

> ⌀ Note that the French word **vicieux** is a false friend. It means **depraved** or **underhand** depending on the context.

vicissitudes [vɪ'sɪsɪtjuːdz] npl vicissitudes fpl

victim ['vɪktɪm] n victime f; to be the v. of être victime de; to fall v. to a disease contracter une maladie

victimize ['vɪktɪmaɪz] vt persécuter • **victimi'zation** n persécution f

victor [ˈvɪktə(r)] *n Old-fashioned* vainqueur *m*

Victorian [vɪkˈtɔːrɪən] **1** *adj* victorien, -ienne **2** *n* Victorien, -ienne *mf*

victory [ˈvɪktərɪ] (*pl* -**ies**) *n* victoire *f* • **victorious** [-ˈtɔːrɪəs] *adj* victorieux, -ieuse

video [ˈvɪdɪəʊ] **1** (*pl* -**os**) *n* (*medium*) vidéo *f*; (*cassette*) cassette *f* vidéo; (*recorder*) magnétoscope *m*; **on v.** sur cassette vidéo; **to make a v. of** faire une cassette vidéo de **2** *adj* (*camera*) vidéo *inv*; **v. cassette** cassette *f* vidéo; **v. game** jeu *m* vidéo; **v. recorder** magnétoscope *m* **3** (*pt & pp* -**oed**) *vt* (*on camcorder*) filmer en vidéo; (*on video recorder*) enregistrer (sur magnétoscope) • **videodisc** *n* vidéodisque *m* • **videotape** *n* bande *f* vidéo

vie [vaɪ] (*pres p* **vying**) *vi* **to v. with sb (for sth/to do sth)** rivaliser avec qn (pour qch/pour faire qch)

Vienna [vɪˈenə] *n* Vienne *m ou f*

Vietnam [*Br* vjetˈnæm, *Am* -ˈnɑːm] *n* le Viêt Nam • **Vietnamese** [-nəˈmiːz] **1** *adj* vietnamien, -ienne **2** *n* Vietnamien, -ienne *mf*

view [vjuː] **1** *n* vue *f*; (*opinion*) opinion *f*; **to come into v.** apparaître; **in full v. of everyone** à la vue de tous; **in my v.** (*opinion*) à mon avis; **in v. of** (*considering*) étant donné; **on v.** (*exhibit*) exposé; **with a v. to doing sth** dans l'intention de faire qch **2** *vt* (*regard*) considérer; (*look at*) voir; (*house*) visiter • **viewer** *n* (**a**) *TV* téléspectateur, -trice *mf* (**b**) (*for slides*) visionneuse *f* • **viewfinder** *n* (*in camera*) viseur *m* • **viewpoint** *n* point *m* de vue

vigil [ˈvɪdʒɪl] *n* veillée *f*

> Note that the French word **vigile** is a false friend. Its most common meaning is **security guard**.

vigilant [ˈvɪdʒɪlənt] *adj* vigilant • **vigilance** *n* vigilance *f*

vigilante [vɪdʒɪˈlæntɪ] *n Pej* = membre d'une milice privée

vigour [ˈvɪɡə(r)] (*Am* **vigor**) *n* vigueur *f* • **vigorous** *adj* vigoureux, -euse

vile [vaɪl] (-**er**, -**est**) *adj* (*unpleasant*) abominable; (*food, drink*) infect

vilify [ˈvɪlɪfaɪ] (*pt & pp* -**ied**) *vt* calomnier

villa [ˈvɪlə] *n* villa *f*

village [ˈvɪlɪdʒ] *n* village *m* • **villager** *n* villageois, -oise *mf*

villain [ˈvɪlən] *n* (*scoundrel*) scélérat *m*;

(*in story, play*) méchant *m* • **villainous** *adj* diabolique • **villainy** *n* infamie *f*

vindicate [ˈvɪndɪkeɪt] *vt* justifier • **vindi-ˈcation** *n* justification *f*

vindictive [vɪnˈdɪktɪv] *adj* vindicatif, -ive

vine [vaɪn] *n* vigne *f*; **v. grower** viticulteur, -trice *mf* • **vineyard** [ˈvɪnjəd] *n* vigne *f*

vinegar [ˈvɪnɪɡə(r)] *n* vinaigre *m*

vintage [ˈvɪntɪdʒ] **1** *n* (*year*) année *f*; (*wine*) cru *m* **2** *adj* (*wine*) de cru; (*car*) de collection (*datant généralement des années 1920*)

vinyl [ˈvaɪnəl] *n* vinyle *m*; **v. seats** sièges *mpl* en vinyle

viola [vɪˈəʊlə] *n* alto *m*

violate [ˈvaɪəleɪt] *vt* (*agreement*) violer • **vioˈlation** *n* violation *f*

violence [ˈvaɪələns] *n* violence *f* • **violent** *adj* violent; **to take a v. dislike to sb/sth** se prendre d'une aversion violente pour qn/qch • **violently** *adv* violemment; *Br* **to be v. sick** être pris de violents vomissements

violet [ˈvaɪələt] **1** *adj* (*colour*) violet, -ette **2** *n* (*colour*) violet *m*; (*plant*) violette *f*

violin [vaɪəˈlɪn] *n* violon *m*; **v. concerto** concerto *m* pour violon • **violinist** *n* violoniste *mf*

VIP [viːaɪˈpiː] (*abbr* **very important person**) *n* VIP *mf*

viper [ˈvaɪpə(r)] *n* vipère *f*

viral [ˈvaɪrəl] *adj* viral

virgin [ˈvɜːdʒɪn] **1** *n* vierge *f*; **to be a v.** être vierge **2** *adj* (*territory, forest*) vierge; **v. snow** neige *f* d'une blancheur virginale • **virˈginity** *n* virginité *f*; **to lose one's v.** perdre sa virginité

Virgo [ˈvɜːɡəʊ] *n* (*sign*) la Vierge; **to be a V.** être Vierge

virile [*Br* ˈvɪraɪl, *Am* ˈvɪrəl] *adj* viril • **virility** [-ˈrɪlɪtɪ] *n* virilité *f*

virtual [ˈvɜːtʃʊəl] *adj* quasi; *Comptr* virtuel, -uelle; **v. reality** réalité *f* virtuelle • **virtually** *adv* (*in fact*) en fait; (*almost*) quasiment

virtue [ˈvɜːtʃuː] *n* (*goodness, chastity*) vertu *f*; (*advantage*) mérite *m*; **by v. of** en vertu de • **virtuous** [-tʃʊəs] *adj* vertueux, -ueuse

virtuoso [vɜːtʃʊˈəʊsəʊ] (*pl* -**si** [-siː]) *n* virtuose *mf* • **virtuosity** [-tʃʊˈɒsɪtɪ] *n* virtuosité *f*

virulent [ˈvɪrʊlənt] *adj* virulent • **virulence** *n* virulence *f*

virus [ˈvaɪərəs] *n Med & Comptr* virus *m*

Visa® [ˈviːzə] *n* **V. (card)** carte *f* Visa®

visa ['viːzə] *n* visa *m*
vis-à-vis [viːzə'viː] *prep* vis-à-vis de
viscount ['vaɪkaʊnt] *n* vicomte *m* •**viscountess** *n* vicomtesse *f*
viscous ['vɪskəs] *adj* visqueux, -euse
vise [vaɪs] *n Am (tool)* étau *m*
visible ['vɪzəbəl] *adj* visible •**visi'bility** *n* visibilité *f* • **visibly** *adv* visiblement
vision ['vɪʒən] *n (eyesight)* vue *f; (foresight)* clairvoyance *f; (apparition)* vision *f; Fig* a man of v. un homme clairvoyant •**visionary** *(pl* -ies) *adj & n* visionnaire *(mf)*
visit ['vɪzɪt] **1** *n* visite *f;* to pay sb a v. rendre visite à qn
2 *vt (place)* visiter; *(person)* rendre visite à
3 *vi* to be visiting être de passage; to go visiting aller en visites; *Br* v. hours/card heures *fpl*/carte *f* de visite •**visitor** *n* visiteur, -euse *mf; (guest)* invité, -ée *mf*
visor ['vaɪzə(r)] *n* visière *f*
vista ['vɪstə] *n* vue *f; Fig (of future)* perspective *f*
visual ['vɪʒʊəl] *adj* visuel, -uelle; v. aid support *m* visuel; v. arts arts *mpl* plastiques; *Comptr* v. display unit console *f* de visualisation •**visualize** *vt (imagine)* visualiser; *(foresee)* envisager
vital ['vaɪtəl] *adj* vital; it's v. that... il est vital que... *(+ subjunctive);* of v. importance d'une importance vitale; *Hum* v. statistics *(of woman)* mensurations *fpl* •**vitally** *adv* v. important d'une importance vitale
vitality [vaɪ'tælɪtɪ] *n* vitalité *f*
vitamin [*Br* 'vɪtəmɪn, *Am* 'vaɪtəmɪn] *n* vitamine *f;* with added vitamins vitaminé *m*
vitriol ['vɪtrɪəl] *n (acid, bitter speech)* vitriol *m* •**vitriolic** [-ɪ'ɒlɪk] *adj* au vitriol
viva ['vaɪvə] *n Br Univ* oral *m*
vivacious [vɪ'veɪʃəs] *adj* enjoué
vivid ['vɪvɪd] *adj* vif *(f* vive); *(description)* vivant; *(memory)* clair •**vividly** *adv (describe)* de façon vivante; to remember sth v. se souvenir clairement de qch
vivisection [vɪvɪ'sekʃən] *n* vivisection *f*
vixen ['vɪksən] *n* renarde *f*
V-neck [viː'nek] **1** *adj* à col en V
2 *n* col *m* en V
vocabulary [*Br* və'kæbjʊlərɪ, *Am* -erɪ] *n* vocabulaire *m*
vocal ['vəʊkəl] **1** *adj (cords, music)* vocal; *(outspoken)* franc *(f* franche); *(noisy, critical)* qui se fait entendre
2 *n* on vocals au chant •**vocalist** *n* chanteur, -euse *mf*
vocation [vəʊ'keɪʃən] *n* vocation *f* •**vo-**

cational *adj* professionnel, -elle; v. course *(short)* stage *m* de formation professionnelle; *(longer)* enseignement *m* professionnel; v. school établissement *m* d'enseignement professionnel; v. training formation *f* professionnelle
vociferous [və'sɪfərəs] *adj* bruyant
vodka ['vɒdkə] *n* vodka *f*
vogue [vəʊg] *n* vogue *f;* in v. en vogue
voice [vɔɪs] **1** *n* voix *f;* at the top of one's v. à tue-tête; I've lost my v. je n'ai plus de voix
2 *vt (opinion, feelings)* exprimer •**voiceless** *adj Med* aphone
void [vɔɪd] **1** *n* vide *m*
2 *adj Law (deed, contract)* nul *(f* nulle); *Literary* v. of dépourvu de
volatile [*Br* 'vɒlətaɪl, *Am* 'vɒlətəl] *adj (person)* inconstant; *(situation)* explosif, -ive
volcano [vɒl'keɪnəʊ] *(pl* -oes) *n* volcan *m* •**volcanic** [-'kænɪk] *adj* volcanique
volition [və'lɪʃən] *n Formal* of one's own v. de son propre gré
volley ['vɒlɪ] *n (of gunfire)* salve *f; (of blows)* volée *f; Fig (of insults)* bordée *f; Tennis* volée •**volleyball** *n Sport* volley(-ball) *m*
volt [vəʊlt] *n* volt *m* •**voltage** [-tɪdʒ] *n* voltage *m*
volume ['vɒljuːm] *n (book, capacity, loudness)* volume *m;* v. control *(on TV, radio)* bouton *m* de réglage du volume •**voluminous** [və'luːmɪnəs] *adj* volumineux, -euse
voluntary [*Br* 'vɒləntərɪ, *Am* -erɪ] *adj* volontaire; *(unpaid)* bénévole; v. redundancy départ *m* volontaire •**voluntarily** *adv* volontairement; *(on an unpaid basis)* bénévolement
volunteer [vɒlən'tɪə(r)] **1** *n* volontaire *mf; (for charity)* bénévole *mf*
2 *vt (information)* donner spontanément
3 *vi* se porter volontaire (for sth pour qch; to do pour faire); *(for the army)* s'engager (for dans)
voluptuous [və'lʌptʃʊəs] *adj* voluptueux, -ueuse
vomit ['vɒmɪt] **1** *n* vomi *m*
2 *vti* vomir
voracious [və'reɪʃəs] *adj* vorace
vote [vəʊt] **1** *n (choice)* vote *m; (election)* scrutin *m; (paper)* voix *f;* to put sth to the v. soumettre qch au vote; to take a v. on sth voter sur qch; to have the v. avoir le droit de vote; they got 12 percent of the v. ils ont obtenu 12 pour cent des voix; v. of no confidence motion *f* de censure; v. of thanks discours *m* de remerciement

2 *vt (funds, bill)* voter; *(person)* élire; **to v. sb in** élire qn; **to be voted president** être élu président

3 *vi* voter; **to v. Labour/Democrat** voter travailliste/démocrate •**voter** *n (elector)* électeur, -trice *mf* •**voting** *n (of funds)* vote *m* (**of** de); *(polling)* scrutin *m*

vouch [vaʊtʃ] *vi* **to v. for sb/sth** répondre de qn/qch

voucher [ˈvaʊtʃə(r)] *n* coupon *m*, bon *m*; **(gift-)v.** chèque-cadeau *m*

vow [vaʊ] **1** *n* vœu *m*

2 *vt* jurer (**to** à); **to v. to do sth** jurer de faire qch

vowel [ˈvaʊəl] *n* voyelle *f*

voyage [ˈvɔɪdʒ] *n* voyage *m*

vulgar [ˈvʌlgə(r)] *adj* vulgaire •**vulgarity** [-ˈgærɪtɪ] *n* vulgarité *f*

vulnerable [ˈvʌlnərəbəl] *adj* vulnérable •**vulneraˈbility** *n* vulnérabilité *f*

vulture [ˈvʌltʃə(r)] *n* vautour *m*

W, w [ˈdʌbəljuː] *n (letter)* W, w *m inv*
wacky [ˈwækɪ] (**-ier, -iest**) *adj Fam* far-felu
wad [wɒd] *n (of papers, banknotes)* liasse *f*; *(of cotton wool)* morceau *m*
waddle [ˈwɒdəl] *vi Fig (of duck, person)* se dandiner
wade [weɪd] *vi* **to w. through** *(mud, water)* patauger dans; *Fig (book)* venir péniblement à bout de • **wading pool** *n Am (inflatable)* piscine *f* gonflable; *(purpose-built)* pataugeoire *f*
wafer [ˈweɪfə(r)] *n (biscuit)* gaufrette *f*; *Rel* hostie *f*
waffle¹ [ˈwɒfəl] *n (cake)* gaufre *f*
waffle² [ˈwɒfəl] *Br Fam* **1** *n* remplissage *m* **2** *vi* faire du remplissage
waft [wɒft] *vi (of smell, sound)* parvenir
wag¹ [wæg] (*pt & pp* **-gg-**) **1** *vt* remuer, agiter; **to w. one's finger at sb** menacer qn du doigt
2 *vi* remuer; **its tail was wagging** *(of dog)* il remuait la queue; *Fam* **tongues are wagging** les langues vont bon train
wag² [wæg] *n Fam (joker)* farceur, -euse *mf*
wage [weɪdʒ] **1** *n* **wage(s)** salaire *m*, paie *f*; **a living w.** un salaire qui permet de vivre; **w. claim** revendication *f* salariale; **w. earner** salarié, -iée *mf*; **w. freeze** gel *m* des salaires; **w. increase** augmentation *f* de salaire; *Br* **w. packet** *(envelope)* enveloppe *f* de paie; *(money)* paie
2 *vt* **to w. war** faire la guerre (**on** à); **to w. a campaign against smoking** mener une campagne antitabac
wager [ˈweɪdʒə(r)] **1** *n* pari *m*
2 *vt* parier (**that** que)
waggle [ˈwægəl] *vti* remuer
wag(g)on [ˈwægən] *n Br (of train)* wagon *m* (découvert); *(horse-drawn)* charrette *f*; *Fam* **to be on the w.** *(no longer drinking)* être au régime sec
waif [weɪf] *n (child)* enfant *mf* abandonné(e); *(very thin girl)* fille *f* excessivement maigre
wail [weɪl] **1** *n (of person)* gémissement *m*; *(of siren)* hurlement *m*
2 *vi (of person)* gémir; *(of siren)* hurler

waist [weɪst] *n* taille *f* • **waistband** *n* ceinture *f* • **waistcoat** *n Br* gilet *m* • **waist-line** *n* taille *f*
wait [weɪt] **1** *n* attente *f*; **to lie in w. for sb** guetter qn
2 *vt* attendre; **to w. one's turn** attendre son tour
3 *vi* (**a**) attendre; **to w. for sb/sth** attendre qn/qch; **to keep sb waiting** faire attendre qn; **w. till** *or* **until I've gone, w. for me to go** attends que je sois parti; **w. and see!** tu verras bien!; **I can't w. to see her** j'ai vraiment hâte de la voir
(**b**) **to w. at table** servir à table; **to w. on sb** servir qn • **waiting** *n* attente *f*; *Br* **'no w.'** 'arrêt interdit' **2** *adj* **w. list/room** liste *f*/salle *f* d'attente
▸ **wait about, wait around** *vi* attendre; **to w. about** *or* **around for sb/sth** attendre qn/qch ▸ **wait behind** *vi* rester ▸ **wait up** *vi* veiller; **to w. up for sb** attendre le retour de qn pour aller se coucher
waiter [ˈweɪtə(r)] *n* serveur *m* • **waitress** *n* serveuse *f*
waive [weɪv] *vt (renounce)* renoncer à; **to w. a requirement for sb** dispenser qn d'une condition requise
wake¹ [weɪk] (*pt* **woke**, *pp* **woken**) **1** *vt* **to w. sb (up)** réveiller qn
2 *vi* **to w. (up)** se réveiller; **to w. up to sth** prendre conscience de qch • **waking** *adj* **to spend one's w. hours working** passer ses journées à travailler
wake² [weɪk] *n (of ship)* sillage *m*; *Fig* **in the w. of sth** à la suite de qch
wake³ [weɪk] *n (before funeral)* veillée *f* mortuaire
waken [ˈweɪkən] *vt* réveiller
Wales [weɪlz] *n* le pays de Galles
walk [wɔːk] **1** *n (short)* promenade *f*; *(long)* marche *f*; *(gait)* démarche *f*; *(pace)* pas *m*; *(path)* avenue *f*; **to go for a w., to take a w.** aller se promener; **to take sb for a w.** emmener qn se promener; **to take the dog for a w.** promener le chien; **five minutes' w. (away)** à cinq minutes à pied; *Fig* **from all walks of life** de tous les milieux
2 *vt* **to w. the dog** promener le chien; **to**

w. sb home raccompagner qn; **to w. sb to** *(place)* accompagner qn à; **to w. the streets** battre le pavé; **I walked 3 miles** j'ai fait presque 5 km à pied

3 *vi* marcher; *(as opposed to cycling, driving)* aller à pied; *(for exercise, pleasure)* se promener; **to w. home** rentrer à pied; **w.!** *(don't run)* ne cours pas! • **walker** *n* marcheur, -euse *mf*; *(for pleasure)* promeneur, -euse *mf* • **walking 1** *n* marche *f* (à pied) **2** *adj Fig* **a w. corpse/dictionary** *(person)* un cadavre/dictionnaire ambulant; **w. shoes** chaussures *fpl* de marche; **w. stick** canne *f*; **at a w. pace** au pas • **walkout** *n* *(strike)* grève *f* surprise; *(from meeting)* départ *m* en signe de protestation • **walkover** *n Fam* **it was a w.** c'était du gâteau • **walkway** *n* passage *m* couvert; **moving w.** trottoir *m* roulant
▸ **walk away** *vi* s'en aller (**from** de); *Fig* **to w. away with a prize** remporter un prix
▸ **walk in** *vi* entrer; **to w. into a tree** rentrer dans un arbre; **to w. into a trap** tomber dans un piège ▸ **walk off** *vi* s'en aller; **to w. off with sth** *(steal)* partir avec qch; *(win easily)* remporter qch ▸ **walk out** *vi* *(leave)* sortir; *Br (of workers)* se mettre en grève; **to w. out on sb** quitter qn ▸ **walk over** *vi* **to w. over to** *(go up to)* s'approcher de; *Fam* **to w. over sb** marcher sur les pieds de qn

walkie-talkie [wɔːkɪ'tɔːkɪ] *n* talkie-walkie *m*

Walkman® ['wɔːkmən] *(pl* **-mans)** *n* baladeur *m*

wall [wɔːl] **1** *n* mur *m*; *(of cabin, tunnel, stomach)* paroi *f*; *Fig* **a. w. of smoke** un rideau de fumée; *Fig* **to go to the w.** faire faillite; *Fam* **I might as well talk to the w.** c'est comme si je parlais à un mur

2 *adj (map, hanging)* mural

3 *vt* **to w. a door up** murer une porte • **walled** *adj* **w. city** ville *f* fortifiée • **wallflower** *n* *(plant)* giroflée *f*; *Fig* **to be a w.** *(of person)* faire tapisserie • **wallpaper 1** *n* papier *m* peint **2** *vt* tapisser • '**wall-to-wall** 'carpet(ing) *n* moquette *f*

wallet ['wɒlɪt] *n* portefeuille *m*

wallop ['wɒləp] *Fam* **1** *n* beigne *f*
2 *vt* filer une beigne à

wallow ['wɒləʊ] *vi* se vautrer; *Fig* **to w. in self-pity** s'apitoyer sur son sort

wally ['wɒlɪ] *(pl* **-ies)** *n Br Fam (idiot)* andouille *f*

walnut ['wɔːlnʌt] *n* *(nut)* noix *f*; *(tree, wood)* noyer *m*

walrus ['wɔːlrəs] *(pl* **-ruses** [-rəsəz]) *n* morse *m*

waltz [*Br* wɔːls, *Am* wɒlts] **1** *n* valse *f*
2 *vi* valser

wan [wɒn] *adj* blême

wand [wɒnd] *n* **(magic) w.** baguette *f* magique

wander ['wɒndə(r)] **1** *vt* **to w. the streets** errer dans les rues

2 *vi* *(of thoughts)* vagabonder; *(of person)* errer, vagabonder; **to w. from** *(path, subject)* s'écarter de; **to w. around town** se promener dans la ville; **to w. in/out** entrer/sortir tranquillement; **my mind's wandering** je suis distrait • **wanderer** *n* vagabond, -onde *mf* • **wandering** *adj (life)* vagabond; *(tribe)* nomade
▸ **wander about, wander around** *vi* *(roam)* errer, vagabonder; *(stroll)* flâner
▸ **wander off** *vi* *(go away)* s'éloigner; **to w. off the path/the subject** s'écarter du chemin/du sujet

wane [weɪn] **1** *n* **to be on the w.** *(of moon)* décroître; *(of fame, enthusiasm, power)* décliner

2 *vi* *(of moon)* décroître; *(of fame, strength)* décliner

wangle ['wæŋgəl] *vt Br Fam (obtain)* se débrouiller pour avoir; *(through devious means)* carotter (**from** à)

want [wɒnt] **1** *n (lack)* manque *m* (**of** de); *(poverty)* besoin *m*; **for w. of** par manque de; **for w. of money/time** faute d'argent/de temps; **for w. of anything better** faute de mieux

2 *vt* vouloir (**to do** faire); *Fam (need)* avoir besoin de; **I w. him to go** je veux qu'il parte; **the lawn wants cutting** la pelouse a besoin d'être tondue; *Br* **you w. to try** *(should)* tu devrais essayer; **you're wanted on the phone** on vous demande au téléphone; *Br* '**situations wanted**' *(in newspaper)* 'demandes d'emploi'

3 *vi* **to w. for nothing** ne manquer de rien • **wanted** *adj (criminal, man)* recherché par la police; **to feel w.** sentir qu'on vous aime • **wanting** *adj* **to be w. in sth** manquer de qch; **to be found w.** *(of person)* se révéler incapable; *(of thing)* laisser à désirer

wanton ['wɒntən] *adj (gratuitous)* gratuit; *Old-fashioned (immoral)* impudique

war [wɔː(r)] **1** *n* guerre *f*; **at w.** en guerre (**with** avec); **to go to w.** entrer en guerre (**with** avec); **to declare w.** déclarer la guerre (**on** à); **the First/Second World W.** la Première/Deuxième Guerre mondiale

2 *adj (wound, crime, criminal, corres-*

pondent) de guerre; **w. memorial** monument *m* aux morts

warble ['wɔːbəl] *vi* gazouiller

ward¹ [wɔːd] *n (in hospital)* salle *f; Br (electoral division)* circonscription *f* électorale; *Law* **w. of court** pupille *mf* sous tutelle judiciaire

ward² [wɔːd] *vt* **to w. off** *(blow, anger)* éviter; *(danger)* chasser

warden ['wɔːdən] *n (of institution, hostel)* directeur, -trice *mf; Br (of park)* gardien, -ienne *mf*

warder ['wɔːdə(r)] *n Br* gardien *m* (de prison)

wardrobe ['wɔːdrəʊb] *n (cupboard)* penderie *f; (clothes)* garde-robe *f*

warehouse ['weəhaʊs] *(pl* **-ses** [-zɪz]*) n* entrepôt *m*

wares [weəz] *npl* marchandises *fpl*

warfare ['wɔːfeə(r)] *n* guerre *f •* **warhead** *n* ogive *f*

warily ['weərɪlɪ] *adv* avec précaution

warlike ['wɔːlaɪk] *adj* guerrier, -ière

warm [wɔːm] **1** (**-er, -est**) *adj* chaud; *Fig (welcome, thanks)* chaleureux, -euse; **to be** *or* **feel w.** avoir chaud; **to get w.** *(of person, room)* se réchauffer; *(of food, water)* chauffer; **it's w.** *(of weather)* il fait chaud

2 *vt* **to w. (up)** *(person, food)* réchauffer; *(engine)* faire chauffer

3 *vi* **to w. up** *(of person, room, engine)* se réchauffer; *(of athlete)* s'échauffer; *(of food, water)* chauffer; *Fig* **to w. to sb** se prendre de sympathie pour qn **•** **'warm-'hearted** *adj* chaleureux, -euse **•** **warmly** *adv (dress)* chaudement; *Fig (welcome, thank)* chaleureusement **•** **warmth** *n* chaleur *f •* **warm-up** *n (of athlete)* échauffement *m*

warmonger ['wɔːmʌŋɡə(r)] *n* belliciste *mf*

warn [wɔːn] *vt* avertir, prévenir (**that** que); **to w. sb against** *or* **of sth** mettre qn en garde contre qch; **to w. sb against doing sth** déconseiller à qn de faire qch **•** **warning** *n (caution)* avertissement *m; (advance notice)* avis *m; (without w.** sans prévenir; **gale/storm w.** avis de coup de vent/de tempête; **a word** *or* **note of w.** une mise en garde; **w. light** *(on appliance)* voyant *m* lumineux; *Br* **w. lights** feux *mpl* de détresse; **w. triangle** triangle *m* de présignalisation

warp [wɔːp] **1** *vt (wood)* gauchir; *Fig (judgement, person)* pervertir; **a warped mind** un esprit tordu

2 *vi (of door)* gauchir

warpath ['wɔːpɑːθ] *n Fam* **to be on the w.** en vouloir à tout le monde

warrant ['wɒrənt] **1** *n Law* mandat *m;* **I have a w. for your arrest** j'ai un mandat d'arrêt contre vous; **search w.** mandat de perquisition

2 *vt (justify)* justifier; **I w. you that** je vous assure que **•** **warranty** *(pl* **-ies**) *n Com* garantie *f;* **under w.** sous garantie

warren ['wɒrən] *n* **(rabbit) w.** garenne *f*

warring ['wɔːrɪŋ] *adj (countries)* en guerre

warrior ['wɒrɪə(r)] *n* guerrier, -ière *mf*

Warsaw ['wɔːsɔː] *n* Varsovie *m ou f*

warship ['wɔːʃɪp] *n* navire *m* de guerre

wart [wɔːt] *n* verrue *f*

wartime ['wɔːtaɪm] *n* **in w.** en temps de guerre

wary ['weərɪ] (**-ier, -iest**) *adj* prudent; **to be w. of sb/sth** se méfier de qn/qch; **to be w. of doing sth** hésiter beaucoup à faire qch

was [wəz, *stressed* wɒz] *pt of* **be**

wash [wɒʃ] **1** *n (action)* lavage *m; (of ship)* remous *m;* **to have a w.** se laver; **to give sth a w.** laver qch; **to be in the w.** être au lavage

2 *vt* laver; *(of sea)* baigner; **to w. one's hands** se laver les mains (**of sth** de qch); **to w. sb/sth ashore** rejeter qn/qch sur le rivage

3 *vi (have a wash)* se laver; *Fam* **that won't w.!** ça ne marche pas! **•** **washbasin** *n Br* lavabo *m •* **washcloth** *n Am* gant *m* de toilette **•** **washed-'out** *adj Fam (tired)* lessivé **•** **washed-'up** *adj Fam* **(all) w.** *(person, plan)* fichu **•** **washroom** *n Am* toilettes *fpl*

▸ **wash away 1** *vt sep (stain)* faire partir (en lavant); **to w. sb/sth away** *(of sea)* emporter qn/qch **2** *vi (of stain)* partir (au lavage) ▸ **wash down** *vt sep (car, deck)* laver à grande eau; *(food)* arroser (**with** de) ▸ **wash off 1** *vt sep* enlever **2** *vi* partir ▸ **wash out 1** *vt sep (bowl, cup)* rincer; *(stain)* faire partir (en lavant) **2** *vi (of stain)* partir (au lavage) ▸ **wash up 1** *vt sep Br (dishes, forks)* laver **2** *vi Br (do the dishes)* faire la vaisselle; *Am (have a wash)* se débarbouiller

washable ['wɒʃəbəl] *adj* lavable

washer ['wɒʃə(r)] *n (ring)* joint *m*

washing ['wɒʃɪŋ] *n (action)* lavage *m; (clothes)* linge *m;* **to do the w.** faire la lessive; **w. line** corde *f* à linge; **w. machine** machine *f* à laver; *Br* **w. powder** lessive *f* **•** **washing-'up** *n Br* vaisselle *f;* **to do the w.** faire la vaisselle; **w. liquid** liquide *m* vaisselle

washout ['wɒʃaʊt] *n Fam (event)* bide *m*
wasp [wɒsp] *n* guêpe *f*
wastage ['weɪstɪdʒ] *n* gaspillage *m*;
(losses) pertes *fpl*; **some w.** *(of goods,
staff)* du déchet

waste [weɪst] **1** *n* gaspillage *m*; *(of time)*
perte *f*; *(rubbish)* déchets *mpl*; **wastes**
(land) étendues *fpl* désertiques; *Br* **w.**
disposal unit broyeur *m* d'ordures; **w.**
material *or* **products** déchets; **w.**
ground *(in town)* terrain *m* vague; **w. land**
(uncultivated) terres *fpl* incultes; *(in
town)* terrain vague; **w. pipe** tuyau *m*
d'évacuation
2 *vt (money, food)* gaspiller; *(time)* perdre; *(opportunity)* gâcher; **to w. no time
doing sth** ne pas perdre de temps pour
faire qch; **to w. one's life** gâcher sa vie
3 *vi* **to w. away** dépérir • **wasted** *adj*
(effort) inutile; *(body)* émacié
wastebin ['weɪstbɪn] *n (in kitchen)* poubelle *f*
wasteful ['weɪstfəl] *adj (person)* gaspil-
leur, -euse; *(process)* peu économique
wastepaper [weɪst'peɪpə(r)] *n* vieux papiers *mpl*; **w. basket** corbeille *f* à papier
watch [wɒtʃ] **1** *n* (**a**) *(clock)* montre *f*
(**b**) *(over suspect, baby)* garde *f*; *(guard)*
sentinelle *f*; *(on ship)* quart *m*; **to keep a
close w. on sb/sth** surveiller qn/qch de
près; **to keep w.** faire le guet; **to be on w.**
monter la garde
2 *vt* regarder; *(observe)* observer; *(suspect, baby, luggage)* surveiller; *(be careful
of)* faire attention à; **w. it!** attention!
3 *vi* regarder; **to w. out for sb/sth** guetter qn/qch; **to w. out** *(take care)* faire
attention (**for** à); **w. out!** attention!; **to
w. over** surveiller • **watchdog** *n* chien *m*
de garde • **watchmaker** *n* horloger, -ère
mf • **watchman** *(pl* **-men**) *n* gardien *m*
• **watchstrap** *n* bracelet *m* de montre
• **watchtower** *n* tour *f* de guet
watchful ['wɒtʃfəl] *adj* vigilant
water ['wɔːtə(r)] **1** *n* eau *f*; **under w.**
(road, field) inondé; *(swim)* sous l'eau;
Fig **it doesn't hold w.** *(of theory)* ça ne
tient pas debout; *Fig* **in hot w.** dans le
pétrin; **w. cannon** canon *m* à eau; **w.
chestnut** macre *f*; **w. heater** chauffe-eau
m inv; *Br* **w. ice** sorbet *m*; **w. lily** nénuphar
m; **w. main** conduite *f* d'eau; **w. pistol**
pistolet *m* à eau; *Sport* **w. polo** water-
polo *m*; **w. power** énergie *f* hydraulique;
Br **w. rates** taxes *fpl* sur l'eau; **w. skiing** ski
m nautique; **w. tank** réservoir *m* d'eau; **w.
tower** château *m* d'eau; **w. wings** bras-
sards *mpl* de natation

2 *vt (plant)* arroser; **to w. sth down**
(wine) diluer qch; *(text)* édulcorer qch
3 *vi (of eyes)* larmoyer; **it makes my
mouth w.** ça me met l'eau à la bouche
• **watercolour** *(Am* **-color**) *n* aquarelle *f*
• **watercress** *n* cresson *m* (de fontaine)
• **waterfall** *n* cascade *f* • **waterfront** *n (by
sea)* front *m* de mer; *(by river)* bord *m* de
l'eau • **watering** *n (of plant)* arrosage *m*
• **watering can** *n* arrosoir *m* • **waterline** *n*
(on ship) ligne *f* de flottaison • **waterlogged** *adj (clothes)* trempé; *(land)*
détrempé • **watermark** *n* filigrane *m*
• **watermelon** *n* pastèque *f* • **waterproof**
adj imperméable; *(watch)* étanche
• **water-repellent** *adj* imperméable • **water-
shed** *n Fig (turning point)* tournant *m*
• **watertight** *adj (container)* étanche
• **waterway** *n* voie *f* navigable • **water-
works** *n* station *f* hydraulique
watery ['wɔːtərɪ] *adj (soup)* trop liquide;
(coffee, tea) insipide; *(colour)* délavé;
(eyes) larmoyant
watt [wɒt] *n* watt *m*
wave [weɪv] **1** *n (of water, crime)* vague *f*;
(in hair) ondulation *f*; *(sign)* signe *m* (de la
main); *Radio & Phys* onde *f*, *Fig* **to make
waves** faire des vagues
2 *vt (arm, flag)* agiter; *(stick)* brandir; **to
w. goodbye to sb** faire au revoir de la
main à qn; **to w. sb on** faire signe à qn
d'avancer; **to w. sth aside** *(objection)*
écarter qch
3 *vi (of person)* faire signe (de la main);
(of flag) flotter; **to w. to sb** *(signal)* faire
signe de la main à qn; *(greet)* saluer qn de
la main • **waveband** *n Radio* bande *f* de
fréquences • **wavelength** *n Radio* longueur *f* d'onde; *Fig* **on the same w.** sur la
même longueur d'onde
waver ['weɪvə(r)] *vi (of person, flame)*
vaciller
wavy ['weɪvɪ] (**-ier, -iest**) *adj (line)* qui
ondule; *(hair)* ondulé
wax¹ [wæks] **1** *n* cire *f*; *(for ski)* fart *m*
2 *adj (candle, doll)* de cire; *Am* **w. paper**
(for wrapping) papier *m* paraffiné
3 *vt* cirer; *(ski)* farter; *(car)* lustrer • **wax-
work** *n (dummy)* moulage *m* de cire;
waxworks musée *m* de cire
wax² [wæks] *vi (of moon)* croître; *Literary*
to w. lyrical devenir lyrique
way [weɪ] **1** *n* (**a**) *(path, road)* chemin *m*
(**to** de); *(direction)* sens *m*, direction *f*;
(street) rue *f*; **the w. in** l'entrée *f*; **the w.
out** la sortie; **the w. to the station** le
chemin pour aller à la gare; **to ask sb
the w.** demander son chemin à qn; **to**

show sb the w. montrer le chemin à qn; **to lose one's w.** se perdre; **I'm on my w.** *(coming)* j'arrive; *(going)* je pars; **to stand in sb's w.** barrer le passage à qn; **to make one's w. towards** se diriger vers; **to make w. for sb** faire de la place à qn; **out of the w.** *(isolated)* isolé; **to get out of the w.** s'écarter; *Fig* **to go out of one's w. to help sb** se mettre en quatre pour aider qn; *Fig* **to find a w. out of a problem** trouver une solution à un problème; **to go part of the w.** faire un bout de chemin; **to go all the w.** aller jusqu'au bout; **we talked all the w.** nous avons parlé pendant tout le chemin; **to give w.** céder; *Br (in vehicle)* céder le passage (**to** à); **it's a long w. away** *or* **off** c'est très loin; **it's the wrong w. up** c'est dans le mauvais sens; **do it the other w. round** fais le contraire; **this w.** par ici; **that w.** par là; **which w.?** par où? (**b**) *(manner)* manière *f*; **in this w.** de cette manière; **in a w.** d'une certaine manière; **by w. of** *(via)* par; *Fig (as)* comme; *Fig* **by the w.** à propos; **to find a w. of doing sth** trouver une manière de faire qch; **to get one's w.** arriver à ses fins; **to be in a good/bad w.** aller bien/mal; *Fam* **no w.!** *(certainly not)* pas question!; *Am Fam* **w. to go!** c'est géant!; **w. of life** mode *m* de vie
  2 *adv Fam* **w. behind** très en arrière; **w. ahead** très en avance (**of** sur)
wayfarer ['weɪfeərə(r)] *n* voyageur, -euse *mf*
waylay [weɪ'leɪ] *(pt & pp* -laid*) vt (attack)* agresser; *Fig (stop)* arrêter au passage
way-out [weɪ'aʊt] *adj Fam* excentrique
wayside ['weɪsaɪd] *n* **by the w.** au bord de la route
wayward ['weɪwəd] *adj* difficile
WC [dʌbəljuː'siː] *n* W.-C. *mpl*
we [wiː] *pron* nous; *(indefinite)* on; **we go** nous allons; **we teachers** nous autres professeurs; **WE are right, not you** *(stressed)* nous, nous avons raison, pas vous; **we all make mistakes** tout le monde peut se tromper
weak [wiːk] (-**er**, -**est**) *adj* faible; *(tea, coffee)* léger, -ère; **to have a w. heart** avoir le cœur fragile; **to be w. at sth** *(school subject)* être faible en qch •**weakly** *adv* faiblement •**weakness** *n* faiblesse *f*; *(of heart)* fragilité *f*; *(fault)* point *m* faible; **to have a w. for sb/sth** avoir un faible pour qn/qch
weaken ['wiːkən] **1** *vt* affaiblir
  2 *vi* s'affaiblir
weakling ['wiːklɪŋ] *n (in body)* mauviette *f*; *(in character)* faible *mf*

weak-willed ['wiːk'wɪld] *adj* sans volonté
weal [wiːl] *n* trace *f* de coup
wealth [welθ] *n* richesse *f*; *Fig* **a w. of sth** une abondance de qch •**wealthy 1** (-**ier**, -**iest**) *adj* riche **2** *npl* **the w.** les riches *mpl*
wean [wiːn] *vt (baby)* sevrer
weapon ['wepən] *n* arme *f* •**weaponry** *n* armes *fpl*
wear [weə(r)] **1** *n* (**a**) **men's w.** vêtements *mpl* pour hommes; **evening w.** tenue *f* de soirée (**b**) *(use)* usure *f*; **to get a lot of w. out of sth** porter qch longtemps; **w. and tear** usure naturelle
  2 *(pt* wore, *pp* worn*) vt (garment, glasses)* porter; *Fig (patience)* user; **to w. black** porter du noir; **to have nothing to w.** n'avoir rien à se mettre
  3 *vi (of clothing)* s'user; **to w. thin** s'user; *Fig* **that excuse is wearing thin** cette excuse ne prend plus; **to w. well** *(of clothing, film)* bien vieillir •**wearing** *adj* lassant
  ▸ **wear away 1** *vt sep (clothes, patience)* user **2** *vi (of material)* s'user; *(of colours, ink)* s'effacer ▸ **wear down 1** *vt sep* user; *Fig* **to w. sb down** avoir qn à l'usure **2** *vi* s'user ▸ **wear off** *vi (of colour, pain)* disparaître ▸ **wear on** *vi (of time)* s'écouler ▸ **wear out 1** *vt sep (clothes, patience)* user; **to w. sb out** épuiser qn **2** *vi (of clothes)* s'user; *Fig (of patience)* s'épuiser
weary ['wɪərɪ] **1** (-**ier**, -**iest**) *adj* las (*f* lasse) (**of doing** de faire)
  2 *vi* se lasser (**of** de) •**wearily** *adv* avec lassitude •**weariness** *n* lassitude *f*
weasel ['wiːzəl] *n* belette *f*
weather ['weðə(r)] **1** *n* temps *m*; **what's the w. like?** quel temps fait-il?; **in (the) hot w.** par temps chaud; **under the w.** *(ill)* patraque
  2 *adj* **w. chart/conditions/station** carte *f*/conditions *fpl*/station *f* météorologique(s); **w. forecast** prévisions *fpl* météorologiques; **w. report** (bulletin *m*) météo *f*; **w. vane** girouette *f*
  3 *vt (storm, hurricane)* essuyer; *Fig (crisis)* surmonter •**weatherbeaten** *adj (face, person)* hâlé •**weathercock** *n* girouette *f* •**weatherman** *(pl* -**men***) n (on TV, radio)* présentateur *m* météo
weave [wiːv] **1** *n (style)* tissage *m*
  2 *(pt* wove, *pp* woven*) vt (cloth, plot)* tisser; *(basket, garland)* tresser
  3 *vi* tisser; *Fig* **to w. in and out of** *(crowd, cars)* se faufiler entre •**weaver** *n* tisserand, -ande *mf* •**weaving** *n* tissage *m*
web [web] *n (of spider)* toile *f*; *Fig (of lies)*

tissu *m*; *Comptr* **the W.** le Web; **w. page** page *f* Web; **w. site** site *m* Web •**webbed** *adj (foot)* palmé •**webbing** *n (in chair)* sangles *fpl*

wed [wed] *(pt & pp* **-dd-)** **1** *vt (marry)* épouser; *Fig (qualities)* allier (**to** à)

2 *vi* se marier •**wedded** *adj (bliss, life)* conjugal

we'd [wiːd] = we had, we would

wedding ['wedɪŋ] **1** *n* mariage *m*; **golden/silver w.** noces *fpl* d'or/d'argent

2 *adj (anniversary, present, cake)* de mariage; *(dress)* de mariée; *(night)* de noces; **his/her w. day** le jour de son mariage; *Br* **w. ring,** *Am* **w. band** alliance *f*

wedge [wedʒ] **1** *n (of wheel, table)* cale *f*; *(for splitting)* coin *m*; *(of cake)* part *f*; **w. heel** *(of shoe)* semelle *f* compensée

2 *vt (wheel, table)* caler; *(push)* enfoncer (**into** dans); **to w. a door open** maintenir une porte ouverte avec une cale; **wedged (in) between** coincé entre

wedlock ['wedlɒk] *n* **born out of w.** illégitime

Wednesday ['wenzdeɪ] *n* mercredi *m*

wee¹ [wiː] *adj Scot Fam (tiny)* tout petit *(f* toute petite)

wee² [wiː] *vi Br Fam* faire pipi

weed [wiːd] **1** *n (plant)* mauvaise herbe *f*; *Fam (weak person)* mauviette *f*

2 *vti* désherber; *Fig* **to w. sth out** éliminer qch (**from** de) •**weedkiller** *n* désherbant *m* •**weedy** *(-ier, -iest) adj Fam (person)* malingre

week [wiːk] *n* semaine *f*; **the w. before last** pas la semaine dernière, celle d'avant; **the w. after next** pas la semaine prochaine, celle d'après; **tomorrow w.** demain en huit •**weekday** *n* jour *m* de semaine

weekend [wiːk'end] *n* week-end *m*; **at** *or* **on** *or* **over the w.** ce week-end; *(every weekend)* le week-end

weekly ['wiːklɪ] **1** *adj* hebdomadaire

2 *adv* toutes les semaines

3 *n (magazine)* hebdomadaire *m*

weep [wiːp] *(pt & pp* **wept)** *vti* pleurer; **to w. for sb** pleurer qn •**weeping 'willow** *n* saule *m* pleureur

weewee ['wiːwiː] *n Fam* pipi *m*; **to do a w.** faire pipi

weft [weft] *n* trame *f*

weigh [weɪ] **1** *vt* peser; **to w. sb/sth down** *(with load)* surcharger qn/qch (**with** de); **to w. down a branch** *(of fruit)* faire plier une branche; **to be weighed down by** *(of branch)* plier sous le poids de; *Fig* **weighed down with worry** accablé de

soucis; **to w. up** *(goods, chances)* peser

2 *vi* peser; **how much do you w.?** combien pèses-tu?; **it's weighing on my mind** ça me tracasse; **to w. down on sb** *(of worries)* accabler qn •**weighing-machine** *n* balance *f*

weight [weɪt] **1** *n* poids *m*; **by w.** au poids; **to put on w.** grossir; **to lose w.** maigrir; *Fig* **to carry w.** *(of argument)* avoir du poids; *Fig* **to pull one's w.** faire sa part du travail

2 *vt* **to w. sth (down)** *(hold down)* faire tenir qch avec un poids; **to w. sb/sth down with sth** *(overload)* surcharger qn/qch de qch •**weightlifter** *n* haltérophile *mf* •**weightlifting** *n* haltérophilie *f*

weighting ['weɪtɪŋ] *n Fin* pondération *f*; **London w.** = indemnité de résidence à Londres

weightless ['weɪtləs] *adj (in space)* en apesanteur •**weightlessness** *n* apesanteur *f*

weighty ['weɪtɪ] *(-ier, -iest) adj (heavy)* lourd; *Fig (serious, important)* grave

weir [wɪə(r)] *n* barrage *m*

weird [wɪəd] *(-er, -est) adj* bizarre •**weirdo** ['wɪədəʊ] *(pl* **-os)** *n Fam* type *m* bizarre

welcome ['welkəm] **1** *adj (person, news, change)* bienvenu; **to make sb w.** faire un bon accueil à qn; **to feel w.** se sentir le/la bienvenu(e); **w.!** bienvenue!; **w. home!** ça fait plaisir de te revoir!; **you're always w.** vous êtes toujours le/la bienvenu(e); **you're w.!** *(after 'thank you')* il n'y a pas de quoi!; **you're w. to use my bike** mon vélo est à ta disposition

2 *n* accueil *m*; **to give sb a warm w.** faire un accueil chaleureux à qn

3 *vt (person)* souhaiter la bienvenue à; *(news, change)* accueillir favorablement •**welcoming** *adj* accueillant; *(speech, words)* de bienvenue

weld [weld] **1** *n* soudure *f*

2 *vt* souder •**welder** *n* soudeur, -euse *mf* •**welding** *n* soudure *f*

welfare ['welfeə(r)] *n (wellbeing)* bien-être *m*; *Am Fam* **to be on w.** recevoir l'aide sociale; *Br* **the W. State** l'État *m* providence; **w. work** assistance *f* sociale

well¹ [wel] **1** *n (for water, oil)* puits *m*; *(of stairs, lift)* cage *f*

2 *vi* **to w. up** *(tears)* monter

well² [wel] **1** *(better, best) adj* bien; **to be w.** aller bien; **to get w.** se remettre; **it's just as w....** heureusement que...; **all's w.** tout va bien; **that's all very w. but...** tout ça c'est très bien mais...

2 *adv* bien; **w. before/after** bien avant/
après; **to speak w. of sb** dire du bien de
qn; **you'd do w. to refuse** tu ferais bien de
refuser; **she might (just) as w.** have left
elle aurait mieux fait de partir; **to be w.
aware of sth** avoir parfaitement conscience de qch; **it's w. worth the effort**
ça vaut vraiment la peine; **w. done!** bravo!; **as w.** *(also)* aussi; **as w. as** aussi bien
que; **as w. as two cats, he has…** en plus
de deux chats, il a…

3 *exclam* eh bien!; **w., w.!** *(surprise)*
tiens, tiens!; **huge, w. quite big** énorme,
enfin, assez grand • **well-be'haved** *adj*
sage • **well-'being** *n* bien-être *m* • **'well-
'built** *adj (person, car)* solide • **'well-
'dressed** *adj* bien habillé • **'well-'fed** *adj*
bien nourri • **'well-'founded** *adj* fondé
• **'well-'heeled** *adj Fam* cossu • **'well-in-
'formed** *adj* bien informé • **'well-'known**
adj (bien) connu • **'well-'mannered** *adj*
bien élevé • **'well-'matched** *adj* assorti
• **'well-'meaning** *adj* bien intentionné
• **'well-'nigh** *adv* presque • **'well-'off** *adj*
riche • **'well-'paid** *adj* bien payé • **'well-
'read** *adj* instruit • **'well-'spoken** *adj* qui
parle bien • **'well-'thought-of** *adj* bien
considéré • **'well-thought-'out** *adj* bien
conçu • **'well-'timed** *adj* opportun
• **'well-to-'do** *adj* aisé • **'well-'tried** *adj
(method)* éprouvé • **'well-'trodden** *adj
(path)* battu • **wellwisher** *n* sympathisant, -ante *mf* • **well-'woman clinic** *n Br*
centre *m* de dépistage gynécologique
• **'well-'worn** *adj (clothes, carpet)* très usé
we'll [wiːl] = **we will, we shall**
wellington ['welɪŋtən] *(Fam* **welly**
[welɪ], *pl* **-ies)** *n Br* **w. (boot)** botte *f* de
caoutchouc
Welsh [welʃ] **1** *adj* gallois; *Br* **W. rabbit** *or*
rarebit = toast au fromage
  2 *n (language)* gallois *m*; **the W.** *(people)*
les Gallois *mpl* • **Welshman** *(pl* **-men)** *n*
Gallois *m* • **Welshwoman** *(pl* **-women)** *n*
Galloise *f*
welsh [welʃ] *vi* **to w. on** *(debt, promise)*
ne pas honorer
wench [wentʃ] *n Old-fashioned & Hum*
jeune fille *f*
wend [wend] *vt Literary* **to w. one's way**
s'acheminer (**to** vers)
went [went] *pt of* **go**
wept [wept] *pt & pp of* **weep**
were [wə(r), *stressed* wɜː(r)] *pt of* **be**
we're [wɪə(r)] = **we are**
werewolf ['weəwʊlf] *(pl* **-wolves)** *n*
loup-garou *m*
west [west] **1** *n* ouest *m*; **(to the) w. of** à

l'ouest de; *Pol* **the W.** l'Occident *m*
  2 *adj (coast)* ouest *inv*; *(wind)* d'ouest;
W. Africa l'Afrique *f* occidentale; *Formerly*
W. Germany l'Allemagne *f* de l'Ouest; **W.
Indian** *adj* antillais; *n* Antillais, -aise *mf*;
the W. Indies les Antilles *fpl*; *Br* **the W.
Country** le sud-ouest de l'Angleterre
  3 *adv* à l'ouest; *(travel)* vers l'ouest
• **westbound** *adj (traffic)* en direction de
l'ouest; *Br (carriageway)* ouest *inv* • **west-
erly** *adj (point)* ouest *inv*; *(direction)* de
l'ouest; *(wind)* d'ouest • **western 1** *adj
(coast)* ouest *inv*; *Pol (culture)* occidental;
W. Europe l'Europe *f* de l'Ouest **2** *n (film)*
western *m* • **westerner** *n* habitant, -ante
mf de l'Ouest; *Pol* occidental, -ale *mf*
• **westernize** *vt* occidentaliser • **west-
ward** *adj & adv* vers l'ouest • **westwards**
adv vers l'ouest

wet [wet] **1** (**wetter, wettest**) *adj*
mouillé; *(weather)* pluvieux, -ieuse;
(day) de pluie; *Fam (feeble)* minable; **to
get w.** se mouiller; **to be w. through** être
trempé; **it's w.** *(raining)* il pleut; **'w. paint'**
'peinture fraîche'; **the ink is w.** l'encre est
fraîche; *Fig* **w. blanket** rabat-joie *m inv*;
w. nurse nourrice *f*; **w. suit** combinaison *f*
de plongée
  2 *n* **the w.** *(rain)* la pluie; *(damp)* l'humidité *f*
  3 *(pt & pp* **-tt-)** *vt* mouiller
we've [wiːv] = **we have**
whack [wæk] *Fam* **1** *n (blow)* grand coup
m
  2 *vt* donner un grand coup à • **whacked**
adj Br Fam **w. (out)** *(tired)* nase • **whack-
ing** *adj Br Fam (big)* énorme
whale [weɪl] *n* baleine *f* • **whaling** *n* pêche *f* à la baleine
wham [wæm] *exclam* vlan!
wharf [wɔːf] *(pl* **wharfs** *or* **wharves)** *n
(for ships)* quai *m*
what [wɒt] **1** *adj* quel, quelle, *pl* quel(le)s;
w. book? quel livre?; **w. a fool!** quel
idiot!; **I know w. book it is** je sais quel
livre c'est; **w. little she has** le peu qu'elle a
  2 *pron* **(a)** *(in questions) (subject)* qu'est-
ce qui; *(object)* (qu'est-ce) que; *(after
prep)* quoi; **w.'s happening?** qu'est-ce qui
se passe?; **w. does he do?** qu'est-ce qu'il
fait?, que fait-il?; **w. is it?** qu'est-ce que
c'est?; **w.'s that book?** c'est quoi, ce livre?;
w.! *(surprise)* quoi!, comment!; **w.'s it
called?** comment ça s'appelle?; **w. for?**
pourquoi?; **w. about me?** et moi?; **w.
about going out for lunch?** si on allait
déjeuner?
  (b) *(in relative construction) (subject)* ce

qui; *(object)* ce que; **I know w. will happen/w. she'll do** je sais ce qui arrivera/ce qu'elle fera; **w. happens is** ce qui arrive, c'est que; **w. I need...** ce dont j'ai besoin...

whatever [wɒt'evə(r)] **1** *adj* **w. (the) mistake** quelle que soit l'erreur; **of w. size** de n'importe quelle taille; **no chance w.** pas la moindre chance; **nothing w.** rien du tout

2 *pron (no matter what)* quoi que *(+ subjunctive)*; **w. you do** quoi que tu fasses; **w. happens** quoi qu'il arrive; **do w. is important** fais tout ce qui est important; **do w. you want** fais tout ce que tu veux

whatsit ['wɒtsɪt] *n Fam* machin *m*

whatsoever [wɒtsəʊ'evə(r)] *adj* **for no reason w.** sans aucune raison; **none w.** aucun

wheat [wiːt] *n* blé *m* • **wheatgerm** *n* germe *m* de blé

wheedle ['wiːdəl] *vt* **to w. sb** enjôler qn (**into doing** pour qu'il/elle fasse); **to w. sth out of sb** obtenir qch de qn par la flatterie

wheel [wiːl] **1** *n* roue *f*; **to be at the w.** être au volant

2 *vt (push)* pousser

3 *vi (turn)* tourner; *(of person)* se retourner brusquement; *Fam* **to w. and deal** faire des combines • **wheelbarrow** *n* brouette *f* • **wheelchair** *n* fauteuil *m* roulant • **wheelclamp** *n* sabot *m* de Denver

wheeze [wiːz] **1** *n (noise)* respiration *f* sifflante; *Br Fam (trick)* combine *f*

2 *vi* respirer bruyamment • **wheezy** (**-ier, -iest**) *adj* poussif, -ive

whelk [welk] *n* bulot *m*

when [wen] **1** *adv* quand

2 *conj (with time)* quand, lorsque; *(whereas)* alors que; **w. I came into the room** quand *ou* lorsque je suis entré dans la pièce; **w. I finish, w. I've finished** quand j'aurai fini; **the day/moment w.** le jour/moment où; *Fam* **say w.!** *(when pouring drink)* dis-moi stop!

whenever [wen'evə(r)] **1** *adv* n'importe quand

2 *conj (at whatever time)* quand; *(each time that)* chaque fois que

where [weə(r)] **1** *adv* où; **w. are you from?** d'où êtes-vous?

2 *conj* où; *(whereas)* alors que; **I found it w. she'd left it** je l'ai trouvé là où elle l'avait laissé; **the place/house w. I live** l'endroit/la maison où j'habite; **I went to w. he was** je suis allé à l'endroit où il était; **that's w. you'll find it** c'est là que tu le trouveras • **whereabouts 1** [weərə'baʊts]

adv où **2** ['weərəbaʊts] *n* **his w.** l'endroit *m* où il est • **where'as** *conj* alors que • **where'by** *adv Formal* par quoi • **where-u'pon** *adv Literary* sur quoi • **where-withal** ['weəwɪðɔːl] *n* **to have the w. to do sth** avoir les moyens de faire qch

wherever [weər'evə(r)] **1** *adv* n'importe où

2 *conj* **w. you go** *(everywhere)* partout où tu iras, où que tu ailles; **I'll go w. you like** j'irai (là) où vous voudrez

whet [wet] *(pt & pp* **-tt-**) *vt (appetite, desire)* aiguiser

whether ['weðə(r)] *conj* si; **I don't know w. to leave** je ne sais pas si je dois partir; **w. she does it or not** qu'elle le fasse ou non; **w. now or tomorrow** que ce soit maintenant ou demain; **it's doubtful w....** il est douteux que... *(+ subjunctive)*

which [wɪtʃ] **1** *adj (in questions)* quel, quelle, *pl* quel(le)s; **w. hat?** quel chapeau?; **w. one?** lequel/laquelle?; **in w. case** auquel cas

2 *relative pron (subject)* qui; *(object)* que; *(after prep)* lequel, laquelle, *pl* lesquel(le)s; *(referring to a whole clause) (subject)* ce qui; *(object)* ce que; **the house w. is old...** la maison qui est vieille...; **the book w. I like...** le livre que j'aime...; **the table w. I put it on...** la table sur laquelle je l'ai mis...; **the film of w. she was speaking** le film dont *ou* duquel elle parlait; **she's ill, w. is sad** elle est malade, ce qui est triste; **he lies, w. I don't like** il ment, ce que je n'aime pas; **after w.** *(whereupon)* après quoi

3 *interrogative pron (in questions)* lequel, laquelle, *pl* lesquel(le)s; **w. of us?** lequel/laquelle d'entre nous?; **w. are the best of the books?** quels sont les meilleurs de ces livres?

4 *pron* **w. (one)** *(the one that) (subject)* celui qui, celle qui, *pl* ceux qui, celles qui; *(object)* celui que; **I know w. (ones) you want** je sais ceux/celles que vous désirez

whichever [wɪtʃ'evə(r)] **1** *adj (no matter which)* **take w. books interest you** prenez les livres qui vous intéressent; **take w. one you like** prends celui/celle que tu veux

2 *pron (no matter which)* quel que soit celui qui (*f* quelle que soit celle qui); **w. you choose...** quel que soit celui que tu choisiras...; **take w. you want** prends celui/celle que tu veux

whiff [wɪf] *n* odeur *f*

while [waɪl] **1** *conj (when)* pendant que; *(although)* bien que *(+ subjunctive)*; *(as*

long as) tant que; *(whereas)* tandis que;
w. eating en mangeant

2 *n* **a w.** un moment; **all the w.** tout le
temps; **it's not worth my w.** ça n'en vaut
pas la peine

3 *vt* **to w. away the time** passer le temps
(**doing** à faire) • **whilst** [waɪlst] *conj Br* =
while

whim [wɪm] *n* caprice *m*; **on a w.** sur un
coup de tête

whimper ['wɪmpə(r)] **1** *n* gémissement
m; **without a w.** sans broncher

2 *vi* gémir

whimsical ['wɪmzɪkəl] *adj (look, idea)*
bizarre; *(person)* fantasque

whine [waɪn] **1** *n* gémissement *m*

2 *vi* gémir

whip [wɪp] **1** *n* fouet *m*; *Br Pol* chef *m* de
file

2 (*pt & pp* **-pp-**) *vt* fouetter; *Fam (defeat)*
battre à plates coutures; **whipped cream**
crème *f* fouettée • **whipround** *n Br Fam*
collecte *f*

▸ **whip off** *vt sep Fam (clothes)* enlever
rapidement ▸ **whip out** *vt sep Fam* sortir
brusquement (**from** de) ▸ **whip round** *vi*
Fam (turn quickly) se retourner brusquement ▸ **whip up** *vt sep (interest)* susciter;
(eggs) fouetter; *Fam (meal)* préparer rapidement

whirl [wɜːl] **1** *n* tourbillon *m*

2 *vt* **to w. sb/sth (round)** faire tourbillonner qn/qch

3 *vi* **to w. (round)** tourbillonner • **whirlpool** *n* tourbillon *m* • **whirlwind** *n* tourbillon *m*

whirr [wɜː(r)] **1** *n* ronflement *m*

2 *vi* ronfler

whisk [wɪsk] **1** *n (for eggs)* fouet *m*

2 *vt* battre; **to w. away** *or* **off** *(object)*
enlever rapidement; *(person)* emmener
rapidement

whiskers ['wɪskəz] *npl (of cat)* mousta-
ches *fpl*; *(of man)* favoris *mpl*

whisky ['wɪskɪ] *(Am* **whiskey***) n* whisky
m

whisper ['wɪspə(r)] **1** *n* chuchotement *m*

2 *vti* chuchoter; **to w. sth to sb** chuchoter qch à l'oreille de qn; **w. to me!** chu-
chote à mon oreille!

whist [wɪst] *n Br (card game)* whist *m*

whistle ['wɪsəl] **1** *n* sifflement *m*; *(object)*
sifflet *m*; **to blow the** *or* **one's w.** siffler,
donner un coup de sifflet; **to give a w.**
siffler

2 *vti* siffler; **to w. for** *(dog, taxi)* siffler

Whit [wɪt] *adj Br* **W. Sunday** la Pentecôte

white [waɪt] **1** (**-er, -est**) *adj* blanc (*f*

blanche); **to go** *or* **turn w.** blanchir; *Br*
w. coffee café *m* au lait; *Fig* **w. elephant** =
chose coûteuse et peu rentable; **w. lie**
pieux mensonge *m*; **w. man** Blanc *m*; **w.
woman** Blanche *f*; **w. spirit** white-spirit *m*

2 *n (colour, of egg, eye)* blanc *m*; *(person)*
Blanc *m*, Blanche *f* • **white-'collar worker**
n col *m* blanc • **whiten** *vti* blanchir
• **whiteness** *n* blancheur *f* • **whitewash 1** *n*
(paint) badigeon *m* à la chaux **2** *vt (paint)*
badigeonner à la chaux; *Fig (person)*
blanchir; *Fig (events, faults)* camoufler

whiting ['waɪtɪŋ] *n inv (fish)* merlan *m*

Whitsun ['wɪtsən] *n Br* la Pentecôte

whittle ['wɪtəl] *vt* **to w. down** *(wood)*
tailler (au couteau); *Fig (price)* réduire

whizz [wɪz] **1** *vi (rush)* aller à toute vitesse; **to w. past** *or* **by** passer à toute
vitesse; **to w. through the air** *(of bullet,
spear)* fendre l'air

2 *adj Fam* **w. kid** petit prodige *m*

who [huː] *pron* qui; **w. did it?** qui (est-ce
qui) a fait ça?; **the woman w. came** la
femme qui est venue; **w. did you see?** qui
as-tu vu?; **w. were you talking to?** à qui
est-ce que tu parlais?

whodunit [huːˈdʌnɪt] *n Fam* polar *m*

whoever [huːˈevə(r)] *pron (no matter
who) (subject)* qui que ce soit qui; *(object)*
qui que ce soit que; **w. has seen this**
(anyone who) quiconque a vu cela; **w.
you are** qui que vous soyez; **this man, w.
he is** cet homme, quel qu'il soit; **w. did
that?** qui donc a fait ça?

whole [həʊl] **1** *adj* entier, -ière; **the w.
time** tout le temps; **the w. apple** toute la
pomme, la pomme tout entière; **the w.
truth** toute la vérité; **the w. world** le
monde entier; **the w. lot** le tout; **to swallow sth w.** avaler qch sans le mâcher

2 *n* totalité *f*; **the w. of the village** le
village tout entier, tout le village; **the w.
of the night** toute la nuit; **on the w., as a
w.** dans l'ensemble • **wholefood** *n* aliment *m* complet • 'whole-'hearted *adj*
sans réserve • **wholemeal** *(Am* **whole-
wheat***) adj (bread)* complet, -ète • **wholesome** *adj (food, climate)* sain

wholesale ['həʊlseɪl] **1** *n* **to deal in w.**
faire de la vente en gros

2 *adj (price)* de gros; *Fig (destruction)* en
masse; **w. business** *or* **trade** commerce *m*
de gros

3 *adv (buy or sell one article)* au prix de
gros; *(in bulk)* en gros; *Fig (destroy)* en
masse • **wholesaler** *n* grossiste *mf*

wholly ['həʊlɪ] *adv* entièrement

whom [huːm] *pron Formal (object)* que;

(in questions and after prep) qui; **w. did she see?** qui a-t-elle vu?; **the man w. you know** l'homme que tu connais; **with w.** avec qui; **the man of w. we were speaking** l'homme dont nous parlions

whooping cough ['huːpɪŋkɒf] *n* coqueluche *f*

whoops [wʊps] *exclam* houp-là!

whopping ['wɒpɪŋ] *adj Fam (big)* énorme • **whopper** *n Fam* chose *f* énorme

whore [hɔː(r)] *n Fam* putain *f*

whose [huːz] *possessive pron & adj* à qui, de qui; **w. book is this?, w. is this book?** à qui est ce livre?; **w. daughter are you?** de qui es-tu la fille?; **the woman w. book I have** la femme dont j'ai le livre; **the man w. mother I spoke to** l'homme à la mère de qui j'ai parlé

why [waɪ] **1** *adv* pourquoi; **w. not?** pourquoi pas?

2 *conj* **the reason w. they…** la raison pour laquelle ils…

3 *npl* **the whys and wherefores** le pourquoi et le comment

4 *exclam (surprise)* tiens!

wick [wɪk] *n (of candle, lighter, oil lamp)* mèche *f*

wicked ['wɪkɪd] *adj (evil)* méchant; *Fig (dreadful)* affreux, -euse; *Fam (excellent)* génial • **wickedness** *n* méchanceté *f*

wicker ['wɪkə(r)] *n* osier *m*; **w. basket** panier *m* d'osier; **w. chair** fauteuil *m* en osier • **wickerwork** *n (objects)* vannerie *f*

wicket ['wɪkɪt] *n (cricket stumps)* guichet *m*

wide [waɪd] **1** (*-er, -est*) *adj* large; *(ocean, desert)* vaste; *(choice, variety, knowledge)* grand; **to be 3 m w.** avoir 3 m de large

2 *adv (fall, shoot)* loin du but; **w. open** *(eyes, mouth, door)* grand ouvert; **w. awake** complètement réveillé • **widely** *adv (travel)* beaucoup; *(broadcast, spread)* largement; **w. different** très différent; **it's w. thought that** on pense généralement que • **widen 1** *vt* élargir **2** *vi* s'élargir

widespread ['waɪdspred] *adj* répandu

widow ['wɪdəʊ] *n* veuve *f* • **widowed** *adj* **to be w.** *(of man)* devenir veuf; *(of woman)* devenir veuve; **her w. uncle** son oncle qui est veuf • **widower** *n* veuf *m*

width [wɪdθ] *n* largeur *f*

wield [wiːld] *vt (brandish)* brandir; *(handle)* manier; *Fig* **to w. power** exercer le pouvoir

wife [waɪf] (*pl* **wives**) *n* femme *f*, épouse *f* • **wife-to-'be** *n* future femme *f*

wig [wɪg] *n* perruque *f*

wiggle ['wɪgəl] **1** *vt* remuer

2 *vi (of worm)* se tortiller; *(of tail)* remuer

wild [waɪld] **1** (*-er, -est*) *adj (animal, flower, region)* sauvage; *(sea)* déchaîné; *(idea)* fou (*f* folle); *(enthusiasm)* délirant; **w. with joy/anger** fou de joie/colère; **to be w.** *(of person)* mener une vie agitée; **to be w. about sb** *(very fond of)* être dingue de qn; *Fam* **I'm not w. about it** ça ne m'emballe pas; *Am* **the W. West** le Far West

2 *adv* **to grow w.** *(of plant)* pousser à l'état sauvage; **to run w.** *(of animals)* courir en liberté; *(of crowd)* se déchaîner

3 *n* **in the w.** à l'état sauvage; **in the wilds** en pleine brousse • **wildcard character** *n Comptr* caractère *m* joker • **wildcat 'strike** *n* grève *f* sauvage • **wild-'goose chase** *n* fausse piste *f* • **wildlife** *n* nature *f*

wilderness ['wɪldənəs] *n* région *f* sauvage; *(overgrown garden)* jungle *f*

wildly ['waɪldlɪ] *adv (cheer)* frénétiquement; *(guess)* au hasard; *(for emphasis)* extrêmement

wilful ['wɪlfəl] (*Am* **willful**) *adj (intentional, obstinate)* volontaire • **wilfully** *adv* volontairement

will¹ [wɪl]

> On trouve généralement **I/you/he**/etc **will** sous leurs formes contractées **I'll/you'll/he'll**/etc. La forme négative correspondante est **won't**, que l'on écrira **will not** dans des contextes formels.

v aux (expressing future tense) **he w. come, he'll come** il viendra; **you w. not come, you won't come** tu ne viendras pas; **w. you have some tea?** veux-tu du thé?; **w. you be quiet!** veux-tu te taire!; **yes I w.!** oui!; **it won't open** ça ne s'ouvre pas

will² [wɪl] **1** *n (resolve, determination)* volonté *f*; *(legal document)* testament *m*; **ill w.** mauvaise volonté; **free w.** libre arbitre *m*; **of one's own free w.** de son plein gré; **against one's w.** à contrecœur; **at w.** à volonté; *(cry)* à la demande

2 *vt Old-fashioned (intend, wish)* vouloir (**that** que + *subjunctive*); **to w. oneself to do sth** faire un effort de volonté pour faire qch

willing ['wɪlɪŋ] *adj (helper, worker)* plein de bonne volonté; *(help, advice)* spontané; **to be w. to do sth** bien vouloir faire qch; **to show w.** faire preuve de bonne volonté • **willingly** *adv (with pleasure)* volontiers; *(voluntarily)* de son plein gré • **willingness** *n* bonne volonté *f*; **her w. to do sth** *(enthusiasm)* son empressement *m* à faire qch

willow ['wɪləʊ] *n (tree, wood)* saule *m*

willowy ['wɪləʊɪ] *adj (person)* svelte
willpower ['wɪlpaʊə(r)] *n* volonté *f*
willy-nilly [wɪlɪ'nɪlɪ] *adv* bon gré mal gré
wilt [wɪlt] *vi (of plant)* dépérir; *Fig (of enthusiasm)* décliner
wily [waɪlɪ] (-ier, -iest) *adj* rusé
wimp [wɪmp] *n Fam (weakling)* mauviette *f*
win [wɪn] **1** *n (victory)* victoire *f*
2 *(pt & pp* **won,** *pres p* **winning)** *vt (money, race, prize)* gagner; *(victory)* remporter; *(fame)* acquérir; *(friends)* se faire; *Br* **to w. sb over** *or* **round** gagner qn (**to à**)
3 *vi* gagner **•winning 1** *adj (number, horse)* gagnant; *(team)* victorieux, -ieuse; *(goal)* décisif, -ive; *(smile)* engageant **2** *npl* **winnings** gains *mpl*
wince [wɪns] *vi* faire une grimace; **without wincing** sans sourciller
winch [wɪntʃ] **1** *n* treuil *m*
2 *vt* **to w. (up)** hisser
wind¹ [wɪnd] **1** *n* vent *m*; *(breath)* souffle *m*; **to have w.** *(in stomach)* avoir des gaz; **to get w. of sth** avoir vent de qch; *Mus* **w. instrument** instrument *m* à vent
2 *vt* **to w. sb** *(of blow)* couper le souffle à qn **•windbreak** *n* brise-vent *m inv* **•windcheater** (*Am* **windbreaker**) *n* coupe-vent *m inv* **•windfall** *n (piece of fruit)* fruit *m* abattu par le vent; *Fig (unexpected money)* aubaine *f* **•windmill** *n* moulin *m* à vent **•windpipe** *n Anat* trachée *f* **•windscreen** (*Am* **windshield**) *n (of vehicle)* pare-brise *m inv*; **w. wiper** essuie-glace *m* **•windsurfer** *n (person)* véliplanchiste *mf*; *(board)* planche *f* à voile **•windsurfing** *n* **to go w.** faire de la planche à voile **•windswept** *adj (street)* balayé par le vent **•windy** (-ier, -iest) *adj* **it's w.** *(of weather)* il y a du vent; **w. day** jour *m* de grand vent; **w. place** endroit *m* plein de vent
wind² [waɪnd] **1** *(pt & pp* **wound**) *vt (roll)* enrouler (**round** autour de); *(clock)* remonter; **to w. a cassette back** rembobiner une cassette
2 *vi (of river, road)* serpenter **•winder** *n (of watch)* remontoir *m* **•winding** *adj (road)* sinueux, -ueuse; *(staircase)* en colimaçon
►wind down 1 *vt sep (car window)* baisser **2** *vi Fam (relax)* se détendre **►wind up 1** *vt sep (clock)* remonter; *(meeting, speech)* terminer; *Br Fam* **to w. sb up** faire marcher qn **2** *vi (end up)* finir (**doing** par faire); **to w. up with sb/sth** se retrouver avec qn/qch
window ['wɪndəʊ] *n* fenêtre *f*; *(pane)*

vitre *f*; *(of shop)* vitrine *f*; *(counter)* guichet *m*; **to go w.-shopping** faire du lèche-vitrines; **w. of opportunity** ouverture *f*; *Br* **French w.** porte-fenêtre *f*; **w. box** jardinière *f*; *Br* **w. cleaner,** *Am* **w. washer** laveur, -euse *mf* de vitres; **w. dresser** étalagiste *mf*; *Br* **w. ledge** rebord *m* de fenêtre; *Am* **w. shade** store *m* **•windowpane** *n* vitre *f*, carreau *m* **•windowsill** *n* rebord *m* de fenêtre
windy ['wɪndɪ] *adj see* **wind¹**
wine [waɪn] **1** *n* vin *m*; **w. bar/bottle** bar *m*/bouteille *f* à vin; **w. cellar** cave *f* à vin; **w. grower** viticulteur, -trice *mf*; **w. list** carte *f* des vins; **w. taster** dégustateur, -trice *mf*; **w. tasting** dégustation *f*; **w. waiter** sommelier *m*
2 *vt* **to w. and dine sb** inviter qn dans de bons restaurants **•wineglass** *n* verre *m* à vin **•wine-growing** *adj* viticole
wing [wɪŋ] *n* aile *f*; **the wings** *(in theatre)* les coulisses *fpl*; *Fig* **to take sb under one's w.** prendre qn sous son aile **•winged** *adj* ailé **•winger** *n Football* ailier *m* **•wingspan** *n* envergure *f*
wink [wɪŋk] **1** *n* clin *m* d'œil
2 *vi* faire un clin d'œil (**at** à); *(of light)* clignoter
winkle ['wɪŋkəl] *n* bigorneau *m*
winner ['wɪnə(r)] *n* gagnant, -ante *mf*; *Fam* **that book is a w.** ce livre est assuré d'avoir du succès
winter ['wɪntə(r)] **1** *n* hiver *m*; **in (the) w.** en hiver; **a w.'s day** un jour d'hiver
2 *adj* d'hiver **•wintertime** *n* hiver *m* **•wintry** *adj* hivernal; **w. day** jour *m* d'hiver
wipe [waɪp] **1** *n* lingette *f*; **to give sth a w.** essuyer qch
2 *vt* essuyer; **to w. one's feet/hands** s'essuyer les pieds/les mains; **to w. sth away** *or* **off** *or* **up** *(liquid)* essuyer qch; **to w. sth out** *(clean)* essuyer qch; *(destroy)* anéantir qch; *(erase)* effacer qch
3 *vi* **to w. up** *(dry the dishes)* essuyer la vaisselle **•wiper** *n* essuie-glace *m*
wire ['waɪə(r)] **1** *n* fil *m*; **w. mesh** *or* **netting** toile *f* métallique
2 *vt* **to w. (up)** *(house)* faire l'installation électrique de; **to w. sth (up) to sth** *(connect electrically)* relier qch à qch; **to w. a hall (up) for sound** sonoriser une salle **•wiring** *n (system)* installation *f* électrique; *(wires)* fils *mpl* électriques
wirecutters ['waɪəkʌtəz] *npl* pince *f* coupante
wireless ['waɪələs] *n Br Old-fashioned (set)* TSF *f*

wiry ['waɪərɪ] (**-ier, -iest**) *adj (person)* petit et musclé

wisdom ['wɪzdəm] *n* sagesse *f*; **w. tooth** dent *f* de sagesse

wise [waɪz] (**-er, -est**) *adj (in knowledge)* sage; *(advisable)* prudent; *(learned)* savant; **to be none the wiser** ne pas être plus avancé; *Fam* **to be w.** to être au courant de; *Fam* **w. guy** gros malin *m* • **wisecrack** *n Fam (joke)* vanne *f* • **wisely** *adv* sagement

-wise [waɪz] *suff (with regard to)* **money-wise** question argent

wish [wɪʃ] **1** *n (specific)* souhait *m*, vœu *m*; *(general)* désir *m*; **to make a w.** faire un vœu; **to do sth against sb's wishes** faire qch contre le souhait de qn; **best wishes, all good wishes** *(on greetings card)* meilleurs vœux; *(in letter)* amitiés *fpl*; **send him my best wishes** fais-lui mes amitiés

2 *vt* souhaiter (**to do** faire); **to w. sb well** souhaiter à qn que tout se passe bien; **I w. (that) you could help me** je voudrais que vous m'aidiez; **I w. she could come** j'aurais bien aimé qu'elle vienne; **I w. I hadn't done that** je regrette d'avoir fait ça; **if you w.** si tu veux; **I w. you (a) happy birthday/(good) luck** je vous souhaite bon anniversaire/bonne chance; **I w. I could** si seulement je pouvais

3 *vi* **to w. for sth** souhaiter qch; **I wished for him to recover quickly** j'ai souhaité qu'il se rétablisse vite; **as you w.** comme vous voudrez • **wishbone** *n* bréchet *m* • **wishful** *adj* **it's w. thinking** tu prends tes désirs pour des réalités

wishy-washy ['wɪʃɪwɒʃɪ] *adj (taste, colour)* délavé

wisp [wɪsp] *n (of smoke)* traînée *f*; *(of hair)* mèche *f*; *(of straw)* brin *m*; *Hum* **a (mere) w. of a girl** une fillette toute menue

wisteria [wɪ'stɪərɪə] *n* glycine *f*

wistful ['wɪstfəl] *adj* nostalgique • **wistfully** *adv* avec nostalgie

wit [wɪt] *n (humour)* esprit *m*; *(person)* homme *m*/femme *f* d'esprit; **wits** *(intelligence)* intelligence *f*; **he didn't have the w. to do it** il n'a pas eu l'intelligence de le faire; **to be at one's wits' or w.'s end** ne plus savoir que faire

witch [wɪtʃ] *n* sorcière *f* • **witchcraft** *n* sorcellerie *f* • **witch-hunt** *n Pol* chasse *f* aux sorcières

with [wɪð] *prep* (**a**) *(expressing accompaniment)* avec; **come w. me** viens avec moi; **w. no hat/gloves** sans chapeau/gants; **I'll be right w. you** je suis à vous

dans une seconde; *Fam* **I'm w. you** *(I understand)* je te suis; *Fam* **to be w. it** *(up-to-date)* être dans le vent

(**b**) *(at the house, flat of)* chez; **she's staying w. me** elle loge chez moi; *Fig* **it's a habit w. me** c'est une habitude chez moi

(**c**) *(expressing cause)* de; **to tremble w. fear** trembler de peur; **to be ill w. measles** être malade de la rougeole

(**d**) *(expressing instrument, means)* **to write w. a pen** écrire avec un stylo; **to walk w. a stick** marcher avec une canne; **to fill w. sth** remplir de qch; **satisfied w. sb/sth** satisfait de qn/qch; **w. my own eyes** de mes propres yeux; **w. two hands** à deux mains

(**e**) *(in description)* à; **a woman w. blue eyes** une femme aux yeux bleus

(**f**) *(despite)* malgré; **w. all his faults** malgré tous ses défauts

withdraw [wɪð'drɔː] **1** (*pt* **-drew**, *pp* **-drawn**) *vt* retirer (**from** de)

2 *vi* se retirer (**from** de) • **withdrawal** *n* retrait *m*; **to suffer from w. symptoms** *(of drug addict)* être en manque • **withdrawn** *adj (person)* renfermé

wither ['wɪðə(r)] *vi (of plant)* se flétrir • **withered** *adj (plant)* flétri; *(limb)* atrophié; *(old man)* desséché • **withering** *adj (look)* foudroyant; *(remark)* cinglant

withhold [wɪð'həʊld] (*pt & pp* **-held**) *vt (permission, help)* refuser (**from** à); *(decision)* différer; *(money)* retenir (**from** de); *(information)* cacher (**from** à)

within [wɪð'ɪn] **1** *prep (inside)* à l'intérieur de; **w. 10 km (of)** *(less than)* à moins de 10 km (de); *(inside an area of)* dans un rayon de 10 km (de); **w. a month** *(return)* avant un mois; *(finish)* en moins d'un mois; **it's w. my means** c'est dans mes moyens; **to live w. one's means** vivre selon ses moyens; **w. sight** en vue

2 *adv* à l'intérieur

without [wɪð'aʊt] **1** *prep* sans; **w. a tie** sans cravate; **w. doing sth** sans faire qch; **to do w. sth** se passer de qch

2 *adv* **to do w.** se priver

withstand [wɪð'stænd] (*pt & pp* **-stood**) *vt* résister à

witness ['wɪtnɪs] **1** *n (person)* témoin *m*; **to bear w. to sth** témoigner de qch; *Br* **w. box**, *Am* **w. stand** barre *f* des témoins

2 *vt (accident)* être témoin de; *(document)* signer (pour attester l'authenticité de)

witty ['wɪtɪ] (**-ier, -iest**) *adj* spirituel, -uelle • **witticism** *n* mot *m* d'esprit

wives [waɪvz] *pl of* **wife**

wizard ['wɪzəd] *n* magicien *m*; *Fig (genius)* as *m* • **wizardry** *n Fig* génie *m*

wizened ['wɪzənd] *adj* ratatiné

wobble ['wɒbəl] *vi (of chair)* branler; *(of jelly, leg)* trembler; *(of wheel)* tourner de façon irrégulière; *(of person)* chanceler • **wobbly** *adj (table, chair)* branlant; *(person)* chancelant

woe [wəʊ] *n* malheur *m* • **woeful** *adj* affligé

wok [wɒk] *n* poêle *f* chinoise

woke [wəʊk] *pt of* **wake**[1]

woken ['wəʊkən] *pp of* **wake**[1]

wolf [wʊlf] **1** *(pl* **wolves**) *n* loup *m*; **w. whistle** = sifflement admiratif au passage de quelqu'un

2 *vt* **to w. (down)** *(food)* engloutir

woman ['wʊmən] *(pl* **women**) *n* femme *f*; **young w.** jeune femme; **she's a London w.** c'est une Londonienne; **w. friend** amie *f*; **women's** *(clothes, attitudes, magazine)* féminin; **women's rights** droits *mpl* des femmes • **womanhood** *n (quality)* féminité *f*; **to reach w.** devenir une femme • **womanizer** *n Pej* coureur *m* de jupons • **womanly** *adj* féminin

womb [wuːm] *n Anat* utérus *m*

women ['wɪmɪn] *pl of* **woman**

won [wʌn] *pt & pp of* **win**

wonder ['wʌndə(r)] **1** *n (marvel)* merveille *f*, *(feeling)* émerveillement *m*; **to work wonders** *(of medicine)* faire merveille; **in w.** avec émerveillement; **it's no w.** ce n'est pas étonnant (**that** que + *subjunctive*); **it's a w. she wasn't killed** c'est un miracle qu'elle n'ait pas été tuée

2 *vt (ask oneself)* se demander (**if** si; **why** pourquoi); **I w. that...** je m'étonne que... (*+ subjunctive*)

3 *vi* (**a**) *(ask oneself questions)* s'interroger (**about** au sujet de *ou* sur); **I was just wondering** je réfléchissais (**b**) *Literary (be amazed)* s'étonner (**at** de)

wonderful ['wʌndəfəl] *adj* merveilleux, -euse • **wonderfully** *adv (+ adj)* merveilleusement; *(+ verb)* à merveille

wonky ['wɒŋkɪ] (**-ier, -iest**) *adj Br Fam (table)* déglingué; *(hat, picture)* de travers

won't [wəʊnt] = **will not**

woo [wuː] *(pt & pp* **wooed**) *vt (woman)* courtiser; *(voters)* chercher à plaire à

wood [wʊd] *n (material, forest)* bois *m*; *Fig* **we're not out of the woods yet** nous ne sommes pas encore tirés d'affaire • **woodcut** *n* gravure *f* sur bois • **wooded** *adj* boisé • **wooden** *adj* en bois; *Fig (manner, dancer, actor)* raide • **woodland** *n*

région *f* boisée • **woodlouse** *(pl* **-lice**) *n* cloporte *m* • **woodpecker** *n* pic *m* • **wood pigeon** *n* (pigeon *m*) ramier *m* • **woodwind** *n* **the w.** *(musical instruments)* les bois *mpl* • **woodwork** *n (school subject)* menuiserie *f* • **woodworm** *n (larvae)* ver *m* du bois; **it has w.** c'est vermoulu • **woody** (**-ier, -iest**) *adj (hill)* boisé; *(stem)* ligneux, -euse

wool [wʊl] *n* laine *f*; **w. cloth/garment** tissu *m*/vêtement *m* de laine • **woollen** *(Am* **woolen**) **1** *adj (dress)* en laine **2** *npl* **woollens** *(Am* **woolens**) *(garments)* lainages *mpl* • **woolly** (**-ier, -iest**) **1** *adj* en laine; *Fig (unclear)* nébuleux, -euse **2** *n Br Fam (garment)* lainage *m*

word [wɜːd] **1** *n* mot *m*; *(promise)* parole *f*; **words** *(of song)* paroles *fpl*; **to have a w. with sb** parler à qn; **to keep one's w.** tenir sa promesse; **in other words** autrement dit; **w. for w.** *(report)* mot pour mot; *(translate)* mot à mot; **by w. of mouth** de bouche à oreille; **to receive w. from sb** avoir des nouvelles de qn; **to send w. that** faire savoir que; **to leave w. that** faire dire que; **the last w. in** *(latest development)* le dernier cri en matière de; **w. processing** traitement *m* de texte; **w. processor** machine *f* à traitement de texte

2 *vt (express)* formuler • **wording** *n* termes *mpl* • **wordy** (**-ier, -iest**) *adj* prolixe

wore [wɔː(r)] *pt of* **wear**

work [wɜːk] **1** *n* travail *m*; *(literary, artistic)* œuvre *f*; **works** *(construction)* travaux *mpl*; **to be at w.** travailler; **it's hard w. (doing that)** ça demande beaucoup de travail (de faire ça); **to be out of w.** être sans travail; **a day off w.** un jour de congé; **he's off w. today** il n'est pas allé travailler aujourd'hui; **'w. in progress'** *(sign)* 'travaux'; **the works** *(of clock)* le mécanisme; **w. permit** permis *m* de travail; **w. station** poste *m* de travail; **w. of art** œuvre *f* d'art

2 *vt (person)* faire travailler; *(machine)* faire marcher; *(mine)* exploiter; *(metal, wood)* travailler

3 *vi (of person)* travailler; *(of machine)* marcher, fonctionner; *(of drug)* agir; **to w. loose** *(of knot, screw)* se desserrer; **to w. towards** *(result, agreement, aim)* travailler à • **workable** *adj* possible • **workaholic** [-ə'hɒlɪk] *n Fam* bourreau *m* de travail • **workbench** *n* établi *m* • **workday** *n Am* jour *m* ouvrable • **workforce** *n* main-d'œuvre *f* • **workload** *n* charge *f* de travail • **workman** *(pl* **-men**) *n* ouvrier *m* • **workmanship** *n* travail *m* • **workmate** *n Br*

camarade *mf* de travail • **workout** *n Sport* séance *f* d'entraînement • **workshop** *n* *(place, study course)* atelier *m* • **workshy** [-ʃaɪ] *adj Br* peu enclin au travail • **'work-to-'rule** *n Br* grève *f* du zèle
▸ **work at** *vt insep (improve)* travailler
▸ **work off** *vt sep (debt)* payer en travaillant; *(excess fat)* se débarrasser de (par l'exercice); *(anger)* passer ▸ **work on 1** *vt insep (book, problem)* travailler à; *(French)* travailler **2** *vi* continuer à travailler ▸ **work out 1** *vt sep (calculate)* calculer; *(problem)* résoudre; *(plan)* préparer; *(understand)* comprendre **2** *vi (succeed)* marcher; *(do exercises)* s'entraîner; **it works out at 50 euros** ça fait 50 euros ▸ **work up** *vt sep* **to w. up enthusiasm** s'enthousiasmer (**for** pour); **I worked up an appetite** ça m'a ouvert l'appétit; **to w. one's way up** *(rise socially)* faire du chemin; **to get worked up** s'énerver **2** *vi* **to w. up to sth** se préparer à qch

worker ['wɜːkə(r)] *n* travailleur, -euse *mf*; *(manual)* ouvrier, -ière *mf*; **(office) w.** employé, -ée *mf* (de bureau); **blue-collar w.** col *m* bleu

working ['wɜːkɪŋ] **1** *adj (day, clothes)* de travail; *Br* **Monday is a w. day** on travaille le lundi; **in w. order** en état de marche; **a w. wife** une femme qui travaille; **w. class** classe *f* ouvrière; **w. conditions** conditions *fpl* de travail; **w. population** population *f* active
2 *npl* **the workings of** *(clock)* le mécanisme de • **'working-'class** *adj* ouvrier, -ière

world [wɜːld] **1** *n* monde *m*; **all over the w.** dans le monde entier; **the richest in the w.** le/la plus riche du monde; **to think the w. of sb** admirer énormément qn; **it did me the** *or* **a w. of good** ça m'a beaucoup fait du bien; **why in the w....?** pourquoi diable...?; *Fam* **out of this w.** *(wonderful)* extra *inv*
2 *adj (war, production)* mondial; *(champion, record)* du monde; *Football* **the W. Cup** la Coupe du Monde • **'world-'famous** *adj* de renommée mondiale • **worldly** *adj (pleasures)* de ce monde; *(person)* qui a l'expérience du monde • **world'wide 1** *adj* mondial; **the W. Web** le Worldwide Web **2** *adv* dans le monde entier

worm [wɜːm] **1** *n* ver *m*
2 *vt* **to w. one's way into** s'insinuer dans; **to w. sth out of sb** soutirer qch à qn • **wormeaten** *adj (wood)* vermoulu; *(fruit)* véreux, -euse

worn [wɔːn] **1** *pp of* **wear**

2 *adj (clothes, tyre)* usé • **'worn-'out** *adj (object)* complètement usé; *(person)* épuisé

worry ['wʌrɪ] **1** *(pl -ies)* *n* souci *m*; **it's a w.** ça me cause du souci
2 *(pt & pp -ied)* *vt* inquiéter; **to w. oneself sick** se ronger les sangs
3 *vi* s'inquiéter (**about sth** de qch; **about sb** pour qn) • **worried** *adj* inquiet, -iète (**about** au sujet de); **to be w. sick** se ronger les sangs • **worrier** *n* anxieux, -ieuse *mf* • **worryguts** *(Am* **worrywart** [-wɔːt]*)* *n Fam* anxieux, -ieuse *mf* • **worrying** *adj* inquiétant

worse [wɜːs] **1** *adj* pire (**than** que); **to get w.** se détériorer; **he's getting w.** *(in health)* il va de plus en plus mal; *(in behaviour)* il se conduit de plus en plus mal
2 *adv* plus mal (**than** que); **to go from bad to w.** aller de mal en pis; **I could do w.** j'aurais pu tomber plus mal; **she's w. off (than before)** sa situation est pire (qu'avant); *(financially)* elle est encore plus pauvre (qu'avant)
3 *n* **there's w. to come** le pire reste à venir; **a change for the w.** une détérioration

worsen ['wɜːsən] **1** *vt* aggraver
2 *vi* empirer

worship ['wɜːʃɪp] **1** *n* culte *m*; *Br* **his W. the Mayor** Monsieur le Maire
2 *(pt & pp -pp-)* *vt (person, god)* adorer; *Pej (money)* avoir le culte de
3 *vi (pray)* faire ses dévotions (**at** à) • **worshipper** *n (in church)* fidèle *mf*; *(of person)* adorateur, -trice *mf*

worst [wɜːst] **1** *adj* pire; **the w. book I've ever read** le plus mauvais livre que j'aie jamais lu
2 *adv* **(the) w.** le plus mal; **to come off w.** *(in struggle)* avoir le dessous
3 *n* **the w. (one)** *(object, person)* le/la pire, le/la plus mauvais(e); **the w. (thing) is that** le pire, c'est que; **at (the) w.** au pire; **to be at its w.** *(of crisis)* avoir atteint son paroxysme; **the situation is at its w.** la situation est on ne peut plus mauvaise; **to get the w. of it** *(in struggle)* avoir le dessous; **the w. is yet to come** on n'a pas encore vu le pire

worsted ['wʊstɪd] *n* laine *f* peignée

worth [wɜːθ] **1** *adj* **to be w. sth** valoir qch; **how much** *or* **what is it w.?** ça vaut combien?; **it's w. a great deal** *or* **a lot** avoir beaucoup de valeur; **the film's (well) w. seeing** le film vaut la peine d'être vu

2 *n* valeur *f*; **to buy 50 pence w. of chocolates** acheter pour 50 pence de chocolats; **to get one's money's w.** en avoir pour son argent • **worthless** *adj* qui ne vaut rien

worthwhile ['wɜːθ'waɪl] *adj (book, film)* qui vaut la peine d'être lu/vu ; *(activity)* qui vaut la peine; *(plan, contribution)* valable; *(cause)* louable; *(satisfying)* qui donne des satisfactions

worthy ['wɜːðɪ] **1** (**-ier, -iest**) *adj (person)* digne; *(cause, act)* louable; **to be w. of sb/sth** être digne de qn/qch
2 *n (person)* notable *m*

would [wʊd, *unstressed* wəd]

> On trouve généralement **I/you/he**/etc **would** sous leurs formes contractées **I'd/you'd/he'd**/etc. La forme négative correspondante est **wouldn't**, que l'on écrira **would not** dans des contextes formels.

v aux (**a**) *(expressing conditional tense)* **I w. stay if I could** je resterais si je le pouvais; **he w. have done it** il l'aurait fait; **I said she'd come** j'ai dit qu'elle viendrait (**b**) *(willingness, ability)* **w. you help me, please?** veux-tu bien m'aider?; **she wouldn't help me** elle n'a pas voulu m'aider; **w. you like some tea?** prendrez-vous du thé?; **the car wouldn't start** la voiture ne démarrait pas (**c**) *(expressing past habit)* **I w. see her every day** je la voyais chaque jour • **would-be** *adj (musician, actor)* en puissance

wound¹ [wuːnd] **1** *n* blessure *f*
2 *vt (hurt)* blesser; **the wounded** les blessés *mpl*

wound² [waʊnd] *pt & pp of* **wind²**

wove [wəʊv] *pt of* **weave**

woven ['wəʊvən] *pp of* **weave**

wow [waʊ] *exclam Fam* oh là là!

WP [dʌbəljuː'piː] *abbr* = **word processor**

wrangle ['ræŋgəl] **1** *n* dispute *f*
2 *vi* se disputer

wrap [ræp] **1** *n (shawl)* châle *m*; *Am* **plastic w.** film *m* plastique
2 (*pt & pp* **-pp-**) *vt* **to w. (up)** envelopper; *(parcel)* emballer; *Fig* **wrapped up in** *(engrossed)* absorbé par
3 *vti* **to w. (oneself) up** *(dress warmly)* s'emmitoufler • **wrapper** *n (of sweet)* papier *m* • **wrapping** *n (action, material)* emballage *m*; **w. paper** papier *m* d'emballage

wrath [rɒθ] *n Literary* courroux *m*

wreak [riːk] *vt* **to w. vengeance on** se venger de; **to w. havoc** faire des ravages

wreath [riːθ] (*pl* **-s** [riːðz]) *n* couronne *f*

wreck [rek] **1** *n (ship)* épave *f*; *(sinking)* naufrage *m*; *(train)* train *m* accidenté; *(person)* épave *f* (humaine); **to be a nervous w.** être à bout de nerfs
2 *vt (break, destroy)* détruire; *(ship)* provoquer le naufrage de; *Fig (spoil)* gâcher; *Fig (career, hopes)* briser • **wreckage** [-ɪdʒ] *n (of plane, train)* débris *mpl* • **wrecker** *n Am (truck)* dépanneuse *f*

wren [ren] *n (bird)* roitelet *m*

wrench [rentʃ] **1** *n* faux mouvement *m*; *Fig (emotional)* déchirement *m*; *Am (tool)* clef *f* (à écrous); **(adjustable) w.** clef à molette
2 *vt (tug at)* tirer sur; **to w. sth from sb** arracher qch à qn; **to w. one's ankle** se tordre la cheville

wrest [rest] *vt* **to w. sth from sb** arracher qch à qn

wrestle ['resəl] *vi* lutter (**with sb** avec qn); *Fig* **to w. with a problem** se débattre avec un problème • **wrestler** *n* lutteur, -euse *mf*; *(in all-in wrestling)* catcheur, -euse *mf* • **wrestling** *n* lutte *f*; **(all-in) w.** *(with relaxed rules)* catch *m*

wretch [retʃ] *n (unfortunate person)* malheureux, -euse *mf*; *(rascal)* misérable *mf* • **wretched** [-ɪd] *adj (poor, pitiful)* misérable; *(dreadful)* affreux, -euse; *Fam (annoying)* maudit

wriggle ['rɪgəl] **1** *vt (toes, fingers)* tortiller; **to w. one's way out of a situation** se sortir d'une situation
2 *vi* **to w. (about)** se tortiller; *(of fish)* frétiller; **to w. out of sth** couper à qch

wring [rɪŋ] (*pt & pp* **wrung**) *vt* **to w. (out)** *(clothes)* essorer; **to w. one's hands** tordre les mains; *Fam* **I'll w. your neck** je vais te tordre le cou; *Fig* **to w. sth out of sb** arracher qch à qn; **to be wringing wet** être trempé

wrinkle ['rɪŋkəl] **1** *n (on skin)* ride *f*; *(in cloth, paper)* pli *m*
2 *vt (skin)* rider; *(cloth, paper)* plisser
3 *vi (of skin)* se rider; *(of cloth)* faire des plis • **wrinkled** *adj (skin)* ridé; *(cloth)* froissé

wrist [rɪst] *n* poignet *m* • **wristwatch** *n* montre-bracelet *f*

writ [rɪt] *n* ordre *m*; **to issue a w. against sb** assigner qn en justice

write [raɪt] (*pt* **wrote,** *pp* **written**) *vti* écrire; **to w. to sb** écrire à qn • **write-off** *n Br* **to be a (complete) w.** *(of vehicle)* être bon pour la casse • **'write-pro'tected** *adj Comptr* protégé en écriture • **write-up** *n (of play)* critique *f*

▸**write away for** *vt insep (details)* écrire pour demander ▸**write back** *vi* répondre ▸**write down** *vt sep* noter ▸**write in 1** *vt sep (insert)* inscrire **2** *vi (send letter)* écrire ▸**write off** *vt sep (debt)* annuler ▸**write out** *vt sep (list, recipe)* noter; *(cheque)* faire ▸**write up** *vt sep (notes)* rédiger; *(diary)* tenir

writer ['raɪtə(r)] *n* auteur *m* (**of** de); *(literary)* écrivain *m*

writhe [raɪð] *vi (in pain)* se tordre (**in** de)

writing ['raɪtɪŋ] *n (handwriting, action, profession)* écriture *f*; **writings** *(of author)* écrits *mpl*; **to put sth (down) in w.** mettre qch par écrit; **w. desk** secrétaire *m*; **w. pad** bloc-notes *m*; **w. paper** papier *m* à lettres

written ['rɪtən] *pp of* write

wrong [rɒŋ] **1** *adj (sum, idea)* faux (*f* fausse); *(direction, time)* mauvais; *(unfair)* injuste; **to be w.** *(of person)* avoir tort (**to do** de faire); **it's w. to swear** *(morally)* c'est mal de jurer; **it's the w. road** ce n'est pas la bonne route; **you're the w. man for the job** tu n'es pas l'homme qu'il faut pour ce travail; **the clock's w.** la pendule n'est pas à l'heure; **something's w.** quelque chose ne va pas; **something's w. with the phone** le téléphone ne marche pas bien; **something's w. with her leg** elle a quelque chose à la jambe; **nothing's w.** tout va bien; **what's w. with you?** qu'est-ce que tu as?; **the w. way round** *or* **up** à l'envers; **the w. way round** *or* **up** à l'envers; **to rub sb up the w. way** prendre qn à rebrousse-poil

2 *adv* mal; **to go w.** *(of plan)* mal tourner; *(of vehicle, machine)* tomber en panne; *(of clock, watch, camera)* se détraquer; *(of person)* se tromper; **to get the date w.** se tromper de date; **to get the w. number** *(on phone)* se tromper de numéro

3 *n (injustice)* injustice *f*; *(evil)* mal *m*; **to be in the w.** être dans son tort; **right and w.** le bien et le mal

4 *vt* faire du tort à •**wrongdoer** *n (criminal)* malfaiteur *m* •**wrongful** *adj (accusation)* injustifié; **w. arrest** arrestation *f* arbitraire •**wrongfully** *adv* à tort •**wrongly** *adv (inform, translate)* mal; *(accuse, condemn, claim)* à tort

wrote [rəʊt] *pt of* write

wrought [rɔːt] *adj* **w. iron** fer *m* forgé • **'wrought-'iron** *adj* en fer forgé

wrung [rʌŋ] *pt & pp of* wring

wry [raɪ] (**wryer, wryest**) *adj* ironique; **to pull a w. face** grimacer •**wryly** *adv* d'un air ironique

X, x [eks] *n (letter)* X, x *m inv*
xenophobia [*Br* zenəˈfəʊbɪə, *Am* ziːnəʊ-] *n* xénophobie *f*
Xerox® [ˈzɪərɒks] **1** *n (copy)* photocopie *f*
  2 *vt* photocopier
Xmas [ˈkrɪsməs] *n Fam* Noël *m*

X-ray [ˈeksreɪ] **1** *n (picture)* radio *f*; *(radiation)* rayon *m* X; **to have an X.** passer une radio
  2 *vt* radiographier
xylophone [ˈzaɪləfəʊn] *n* xylophone *m*

Y, y [waɪ] *n (letter)* Y, y *m inv* • **Y-fronts** slip *m* ouvert

yacht [jɒt] *n (sailing boat)* voilier *m*; *(large private boat)* yacht *m* • **yachting** *n* voile *f*

Yank [jæŋk], **Yankee** ['jæŋkɪ] *n Fam* Ricain, -aine *mf*

yank [jæŋk] *Fam* **1** *n* coup *m* sec
2 *vt* tirer d'un coup sec; **to y. sth off** *or* **out** arracher qch

yap [jæp] *(pt & pp -pp-)* *vi (of dog)* japper; *Fam (of person)* jacasser

yard¹ [jɑːd] *n (of house, farm, school, prison)* cour *f*; *(for working)* chantier *m*; *(for storage)* dépôt *m* de marchandises; *Am (garden)* jardin *m*; *Br* **(builder's) y.** chantier de construction

yard² [jɑːd] *n (measure)* yard *m* (= 91,44 *cm*) • **yardstick** *n (criterion)* critère *m*

yarn [jɑːn] *n (thread)* fil *m*; *Fam (tale)* histoire *f* à dormir debout

yawn [jɔːn] **1** *n* bâillement *m*
2 *vi* bâiller • **yawning** *adj (gap)* béant

yeah [jeə] *adv Fam* ouais

year [jɪə(r)] *n* an *m*, année *f*; *(of wine)* année *f*; **school/tax y.** année scolaire/fiscale; **this y.** cette année; **in the y. 2001** en (l'an) 2001; **y. in y. out** chaque année; **over the years** au fil des ans; **years ago** il y a des années; **he's ten years old** il a dix ans; **New Y.** Nouvel An; **New Y.'s Day** le jour de l'An; **New Y.'s Eve** la Saint-Sylvestre • **yearbook** *n* almanach *m* • **yearly 1** *adj* annuel, -uelle **2** *adv* annuellement; **twice y.** deux fois par an

yearn [jɜːn] *vi* **to y. for sb** languir après qn; **to y. for sth** désirer ardemment qch; **to y. to do sth** brûler de faire qch • **yearning** *n (desire)* désir *m* ardent; *(nostalgia)* nostalgie *f*

yeast [jiːst] *n* levure *f*

yell [jel] **1** *n* hurlement *m*
2 *vti* **to y. (out)** hurler; **to y. at sb** *(scold)* crier après qn

yellow ['jeləʊ] **1** *adj (in colour)* jaune; *Fam (cowardly)* trouillard; *Football* **y. card** carton jaune; **Med y. fever** fièvre *f* jaune; **the Y. Pages**® les pages *fpl* jaunes
2 *n* jaune *m*

3 *vi* jaunir • **yellowish** *adj* jaunâtre

yelp [jelp] **1** *n* jappement *m*
2 *vi* japper

Yemen ['jemən] *n* le Yémen

yen¹ [jen] *n* **to have a y. for sth/to do sth** avoir envie de qch/de faire qch

yen² [jen] *n (currency)* yen *m*

yes [jes] **1** *adv* oui; *(after negative question)* si; **aren't you coming? – y.(, I am)!** tu ne viens pas? – mais si!
2 *n* oui *m inv*

yesterday ['jestədeɪ] **1** *adv* hier
2 *n* hier *m*; **y. morning/evening** hier matin/soir; **the day before y.** avant-hier

yet [jet] **1** *adv* **(a)** *(still)* encore; *(already)* déjà; **she hasn't arrived (as) y.** elle n'est pas encore arrivée; **the best y.** le meilleur jusqu'ici; **y. more complicated** *(even more)* encore plus compliqué; **y. another mistake** encore une erreur; **not (just) y.**, *Br* **not y. awhile** pas pour l'instant **(b)** *(in questions)* **has he come y.?** est-il arrivé?
2 *conj (nevertheless)* pourtant

yew [juː] *n (tree, wood)* if *m*

Yiddish ['jɪdɪʃ] *n & adj* yiddish *(m) inv*

yield [jiːld] **1** *n (of field, shares)* rendement *m*; *(of mine)* production *f*
2 *vt (result)* donner; *(interest)* rapporter; *(territory, right)* céder; **to y. a profit** rapporter
3 *vi (surrender)* se rendre; **to y. to force** céder devant la force; **to y. to temptation** céder à la tentation; *Am* **'y.'** *(road sign)* 'cédez le passage'

yippee [jɪ'piː] *exclam* youpi!

YMCA [waɪemsiː'eɪ] *(abbr* **Young Men's Christian Association***)* *n* = association chrétienne proposant hébergement et activités sportives

yob [jɒb], **yobbo** ['jɒbəʊ] *(pl* **yob(bo)s***)* *n Br Fam* loubard *m*

yoga ['jəʊgə] *n* yoga *m*

yog(h)urt [*Br* 'jɒgət, *Am* 'jəʊgərt] *n* yaourt *m*

yoke [jəʊk] *n (for oxen) & Fig* joug *m*

yokel ['jəʊkəl] *n Pej* plouc *m*

yolk [jəʊk] *n* jaune *m* (d'œuf)

yonder ['jɒndə(r)] *adv Literary* là-bas

you [juː] *pron* **(a)** *(subject)* (*pl, polite form*

sing) vous; *(familiar form sing)* tu; *(object)* vous; te, t'; *pl* vous; *(after prep, 'than', 'it is')* vous; toi; *pl* vous; **(to) y.** *(indirect)* vous; te, t'; *pl vous*; **y. are** vous êtes/tu es; **I see y.** je vous/te vois; **I gave it to y.** je vous/te l'ai donné; **with y.** avec vous/toi; **y. teachers** vous autres professeurs; **y. idiot!** espèce d'imbécile!

(**b**) *(indefinite)* on; *(object)* vous; te, t'; *pl* vous; **y. never know** on ne sait jamais; **it surprises y.** cela surprend •**you'd** = **you had, you would** •**you'll** = **you will**

young [jʌŋ] **1** (**-er, -est**) *adj* jeune; **she's two years younger than me** elle a deux ans de moins que moi; **my young(er) brother** mon (frère) cadet; **my young(er) sister** ma (sœur) cadette; **her youngest brother** le cadet de ses frères; **my young-est sister** la cadette de mes sœurs; **the youngest son/daughter** le cadet/la ca-dette; **to be y. at heart** être jeune d'esprit; **y. people** les jeunes *mpl*

2 *n (of animals)* petits *mpl*; **the y.** *(people)* les jeunes *mpl*; **she's my youngest (daughter)** c'est ma petite dernière •**young-looking** *adj* qui a l'air jeune •**youngster** *n* jeune *mf*

your [jɔː(r)] *possessive adj (polite form sing, polite and familiar form pl)* votre, *pl* vos; *(familiar form sing)* ton, ta, *pl* tes; *(one's)* son, sa, *pl* ses

yours [jɔːz] *possessive pron* le vôtre, la vôtre, *pl* les vôtres; *(familiar form sing)* le tien, la tienne, *pl* les tien(ne)s; **this book is y.** ce livre est à vous *ou* est le vôtre/ce livre est à toi *ou* est le tien; **a friend of y.** un ami à vous/toi

yourself [jɔː'self] *pron (polite form)* vous-même; *(familiar form)* toi-même; *(reflex-ive)* vous; te, t'; *(after prep)* vous; toi; **you wash y.** vous vous lavez/tu te laves •**yourselves** *pron pl* vous-mêmes; *(reflex-ive and after prep)* vous; **did you cut y.?** est-ce que vous vous êtes coupés?

youth [juːθ] *(pl* **-s** [juːðz]) *n (age)* jeu-nesse *f*; *(young man)* jeune *m*; **y. club** centre *m* de loisirs pour les jeunes; **y. hostel** auberge *f* de jeunesse •**youthful** *adj (person)* jeune; *(quality, smile)* juvé-nile •**youthfulness** *n* jeunesse *f*

you've [juːv] = **you have**

yo-yo ['jəʊjəʊ] *(pl* **yo-yos**) *n* Yo-Yo® *m inv*

yucky ['jʌkɪ] *adj Fam* dégueulasse

yummy ['jʌmɪ] (**-ier, -iest**) *adj Fam* super bon *(f* super bonne)

yuppie ['jʌpɪ] *n* yuppie *mf*; **y. area** quar-tier *m* riche et branché

Z, z [*Br* zed, *Am* ziː] *n (letter)* Z, z *m inv*
zany [ˈzeɪnɪ] (**-ier, -iest**) *adj* loufoque
zap [zæp] (*pt & pp* **-pp-**) *vt Fam Comptr* effacer ● **zapper** *n Fam (for TV channels)* télécommande *f*
zeal [ziːl] *n* zèle *m* ● **zealous** [ˈzeləs] *adj* zélé; *(supporter)* ardent
zebra [ˈziːbrə, *Br* ˈzebrə] *n* zèbre *m*; *Br* **z. crossing** passage *m* pour piétons
zenith [ˈzenɪθ] *n* zénith *m*
zero [ˈzɪərəʊ] (*pl* **-os**) *n* zéro *m*; *Fig* **z. hour** *(for military operation)* l'heure *f* H
zest [zest] *n (enthusiasm)* enthousiasme *m*; *(of lemon, orange)* zeste *m*
zigzag [ˈzɪgzæg] **1** *n* zigzag *m*
2 *adj & adv* en zigzag
3 (*pt & pp* **-gg-**) *vi* zigzaguer
Zimbabwe [zɪmˈbɑːbweɪ] *n* le Zimbabwe
zinc [zɪŋk] *n* zinc *m*
zip [zɪp] **1** *n* (**a**) *Br* **z. (fastener)** fermeture *f* Éclair®; **z. pocket** poche *f* à fermeture Éclair® (**b**) *Fam (vigour)* punch *m*
2 *adj Am* **z. code** code *m* postal
3 (*pt & pp* **-pp-**) *vt* **to z. sth (up)** remonter la fermeture Éclair® de qch
4 *vi* **to z. past** *(of car)* passer en trombe; *(of bullet)* passer en sifflant; **to z. through a book** lire un livre à toute vitesse ● **zipper** *n Am* fermeture *f* Éclair® ● **zippy** *adj* plein de punch
zit [zɪt] *n Fam (pimple)* bouton *m*
zither [ˈzɪðə(r)] *n* cithare *f*
zodiac [ˈzəʊdɪæk] *n* zodiaque *m*
zombie [ˈzɒmbɪ] *n Fam* zombi *m*
zone [zəʊn] *n* zone *f*
zonked [zɒŋkt] *adj Fam* **z. (out)** *(exhausted)* cassé; *(drugged)* défoncé
zoo [zuː] (*pl* **zoos**) *n* zoo *m* ● **zoological** [zuːəˈlɒdʒɪkəl] *adj* zoologique ● **zoology** [zuːˈɒlədʒɪ] *n* zoologie *f*
zoom [zuːm] **1** *n* **z. lens** zoom *m*
2 *vi* **to z. in** *(of camera)* faire un zoom avant (**on** sur); *Fam* **to z. past** passer comme une flèche
zucchini [zuːˈkiːnɪ] (*pl* **-ni** *or* **-nis**) *n Am* courgette *f*
zwieback [ˈzwiːbæk] *n Am (rusk)* biscotte *f*

FRENCH VERB CONJUGATIONS

Regular Verbs

	-ER verbs	**-IR verbs**	**-RE verbs**
Infinitive	*donn/er*	*fin/ir*	*vend/re*
1 Present	je donne	je finis	je vends
	tu donnes	tu finis	tu vends
	il donne	il finit	il vend
	nous donnons	nous finissons	nous vendons
	vous donnez	vous finissez	vous vendez
	ils donnent	ils finissent	ils vendent
2 Imperfect	je donnais	je finissais	je vendais
	tu donnais	tu finissais	tu vendais
	il donnait	il finissait	il vendait
	nous donnions	nous finissions	nous vendions
	vous donniez	vous finissiez	vous vendiez
	ils donnaient	ils finissaient	ils vendaient
3 Past historic	je donnai	je finis	je vendis
	tu donnas	tu finis	tu vendis
	il donna	il finit	il vendit
	nous donnâmes	nous finîmes	nous vendîmes
	vous donnâtes	vous finîtes	vous vendîtes
	ils donnèrent	ils finirent	ils vendirent
4 Future	je donnerai	je finirai	je vendrai
	tu donneras	tu finiras	tu vendras
	il donnera	il finira	il vendra
	nous donnerons	nous finirons	nous vendrons
	vous donnerez	vous finirez	vous vendrez
	ils donneront	ils finiront	ils vendront
5 Subjunctive	je donne	je finisse	je vende
	tu donnes	tu finisses	tu vendes
	il donne	il finisse	il vende
	nous donnions	nous finissions	nous vendions
	vous donniez	vous finissiez	vous vendiez
	ils donnent	ils finissent	ils vendent
6 Imperative	donne	finis	vends
	donnons	finissons	vendons
	donnez	finissez	vendez
7 Present participle	donnant	finissant	vendant
8 Past participle	donné	fini	vendu

Note The conditional is formed by adding the following endings to the infinitive: **-ais**, **-ais**, **-ait**, **-ions**, **-iez**, **-aient**. The final **e** is dropped in infinitives ending **-re**.

IRREGULAR FRENCH VERBS

Listed below are those verbs considered to be the most useful. Forms and tenses not given are fully derivable, such as the third person singular of the present tense which is normally formed by substituting 't' for the final 's' of the first person singular, eg 'crois' becomes 'croit', 'dis' becomes 'dit'. Note that the endings of the past historic fall into three categories, the 'a' and 'i' categories shown at *donner*, and at *finir* and *vendre*, and the 'u' category which has the following endings: -us, -ut, -ûmes, -ûtes,-urent. Most of the verbs listed below form their past historic with 'u'.

The imperfect may usually be formed by adding -ais, -ait, -ions, -iez, -aient to the stem of the first person plural of the present tense, eg 'je buvais' etc may be derived from 'nous buvons' (stem 'buv-' and ending '-ons'); similarly, the present participle may generally be formed by substituting -ant for -ons (eg buvant). The future may usually be formed by adding -ai, -as, -a, -ons, -ez, -ont to the infinitive or to an infinitive without final 'e' where the ending is -re (eg conduire). The imperative usually has the same forms as the second persons singular and plural and first person plural of the present tense.

1 = Present	2 = Imperfect	3 = Past historic	4 = Future
5 = Subjunctive	6 = Imperative	7 = Present participle	
8 = Past participle	n = nous	v = vous	† verbs conjugated with **être** only

abattre	*like*	**battre**
absoudre	1 j'absous, n absolvons 2 j'absolvais 3 j'absolus *(rarely used)* 5 j'absolve 7 absolvant 8 absous, absoute	
†s'abstenir	*like*	**tenir**
abstraire	1 j'abstrais, n abstrayons 2 j'abstrayais 3 none 5 j'abstraie 7 abstrayant 8 abstrait	
accourir	*like*	**courir**
accroître	*like*	**croître** *except* 8 accru
accueillir	*like*	**cueillir**
acquérir	1 j'acquiers, n acquérons 2 j'acquérais 3 j'acquis 4 j'acquerrai 5 j'acquière 7 acquérant 8 acquis	
adjoindre	*like*	**joindre**
admettre	*like*	**mettre**
advenir	*like*	**venir** *(third person only)*
†aller	1 je vais, tu vas, il va, n allons, v allez, ils vont 4 j'irai 5 j'aille, n allions, ils aillent 6 va, allons, allez *(but note* vas-y)	
apercevoir	*like*	**recevoir**
apparaître	*like*	**connaître**
appartenir	*like*	**tenir**
apprendre	*like*	**prendre**
asseoir	1 j'assieds, il assied, n asseyons, ils asseyent 2 j'asseyais 3 j'assis 4 j'assiérai 5 j'asseye 7 asseyant 8 assis	
astreindre	*like*	**atteindre**
atteindre	1 j'atteins, n atteignons, ils atteignent 2 j'atteignais 3 j'atteignis 4 j'atteindrai 5 j'atteigne 7 atteignant 8 atteint	
avoir	1 j'ai, tu as, il a, n avons, v avez, ils ont 2 j'avais 3 j'eus 4 j'aurai 5 j'aie, il ait, n ayons, ils aient 6 aie, ayons, ayez 7 ayant 8 eu	
battre	1 je bats, il bat, n battons 5 je batte	
boire	1 je bois, n buvons, ils boivent 2 je buvais 3 je bus 5 je boive, n buvions 7 buvant 8 bu	

(ii)

bouillir		1 je bous, n bouillons, ils bouillent 2 je bouillais
		3 je bouillis 5 je bouille 7 bouillant
braire		(*defective*) 1 il brait, ils braient 4 il braira, ils brairont
circonscrire	*like*	**écrire**
circonvenir	*like*	**tenir**
clore	*like*	**éclore**
combattre	*like*	**battre**
commettre	*like*	**mettre**
comparaître	*like*	**connaître**
complaire	*like*	**plaire**
comprendre	*like*	**prendre**
compromettre	*like*	**mettre**
concevoir	*like*	**recevoir**
conclure		1 je conclus, n concluons, ils concluent 5 je conclue
concourir	*like*	**courir**
conduire		1 je conduis, n conduisons 3 je conduisis 5 je conduise
		8 conduit
confire	*like*	**suffire**
connaître		1 je connais, il connaît, n connaissons 3 je connus
		5 je connaisse 7 connaissant 8 connu
conquérir	*like*	**acquérir**
consentir	*like*	**mentir**
construire	*like*	**conduire**
contenir	*like*	**tenir**
contraindre	*like*	**craindre**
contredire	*like*	**dire** *except* 1 v contredisez
convaincre	*like*	**vaincre**
convenir	*like*	**tenir**
corrompre	*like*	**rompre**
coudre		1 je couds, ils coud, n cousons, ils cousent 3 je cousis
		5 je couse 7 cousant 8 cousu
courir		1 je cours, n courons 3 je courus 4 je courrai 5 je coure
		8 couru
couvrir		1 je couvre, n couvrons 2 je couvrais 5 je couvre 8 couvert
craindre		1 je crains, n craignons, ils craignent 2 je craignais
		3 je craignis 4 je craindrai 5 je craigne 7 craignant
		8 craint
croire		1 je crois, n croyons, ils croient 2 je croyais 3 je crus
		5 je croie, n croyions 7 croyant 8 cru
croître		1 je croîs, il croît, n croissons 2 je croissais 3 je crûs
		5 je croisse 7 croissant 8 crû, crue
cueillir		1 je cueille, n cueillons 2 je cueillais 4 je cueillerai
		5 je cueille 7 cueillant
cuire		1 je cuis, n cuisons 2 je cuisais 3 je cuisis 5 je cuise
		7 cuisant 8 cuit
débattre	*like*	**battre**
décevoir	*like*	**recevoir**
déchoir		(*defective*) 1 je déchois 2 *none* 3 je déchus 4 je déchoirai
		6 *none* 7 *none* 8 déchu
découdre	*like*	**coudre**
découvrir	*like*	**couvrir**
décrire	*like*	**écrire**
décroître	*like*	**croître** *except* 8 décru
†**se dédire**	*like*	**dire**
déduire	*like*	**conduire**
défaillir		1 je défaille, n défaillons 2 je défaillais 3 je défaillis
		5 je défaille 7 défaillant 8 défailli
défaire	*like*	**faire**
démentir	*like*	**mentir**

démettre	*like*	**mettre**
†se départir	*like*	**mentir**
dépeindre	*like*	**atteindre**
déplaire	*like*	**plaire**
déteindre	*like*	**atteindre**
détenir	*like*	**tenir**
détruire	*like*	**conduire**
†devenir	*like*	**tenir**
†se dévêtir	*like*	**vêtir**
devoir		1 je dois, n devons, ils doivent 2 je devais 3 je dus
		4 je devrai 5 je doive, n devions 6 *not used* 7 devant
		8 dû, due, *pl* dus, dues
dire		1 je dis, n disons, v dites 2 je disais 3 je dis 5 je dise
		7 disant 8 dit
disconvenir	*like*	**tenir**
disjoindre	*like*	**joindre**
disparaître	*like*	**connaître**
dissoudre	*like*	**absoudre**
distraire	*like*	**abstraire**
dormir	*like*	**mentir**
†échoir		(*defective*) 1 il échoit 2 *none* 3 il échut, ils échurent
		4 il échoira 6 *none* 7 échéant 8 échu
éclore		1 il éclôt, ils éclosent 8 éclos
éconduire	*like*	**conduire**
écrire		1 j'écris, n écrivons 2 j'écrivais 3 j'écrivis 5 j'écrive
		7 écrivant 8 écrit
élire	*like*	**lire**
émettre	*like*	**mettre**
émouvoir	*like*	**mouvoir** *except* 8 ému
enclore	*like*	**éclore**
encourir	*like*	**courir**
endormir	*like*	**mentir**
enduire	*like*	**conduire**
enfreindre	*like*	**atteindre**
†s'enfuir	*like*	**fuir**
enjoindre	*like*	**joindre**
†s'enquérir	*like*	**acquérir**
†s'ensuivre	*like*	**suivre** (*third person only*)
entreprendre	*like*	**prendre**
entretenir	*like*	**tenir**
entrevoir	*like*	**voir**
entrouvrir	*like*	**couvrir**
envoyer		4 j'enverrai
†s'éprendre	*like*	**prendre**
équivaloir	*like*	**valoir**
éteindre	*like*	**atteindre**
être		1 je suis, tu es, il est, n sommes, v êtes, ils sont 2 j'étais
		3 je fus 4 je serai 5 je sois, n soyons, ils soient
		6 sois, soyons, soyez 7 étant 8 été
étreindre	*like*	**atteindre**
exclure	*like*	**conclure**
extraire	*like*	**abstraire**
faillir		(*defective*) 3 je faillis 4 je faillirai 8 failli
faire		1 je fais, n faisons, v faites, ils font 2 je faisais 3 je fis
		4 je ferai 5 je fasse 7 faisant 8 fait
falloir		(*impersonal*) 1 il faut 2 il fallait 3 il fallut 4 il faudra
		5 il faille 6 *none* 7 *none* 8 fallu
feindre	*like*	**atteindre**

foutre	1 je fous, n foutons 2 je foutais 3 *none* 5 je foute
	7 foutant 8 foutu
frire	(*defective*) 1 je fris, tu fris, il frit 4 je frirai 6 fris
	8 frit (*for other persons and tenses use* faire frire)
fuir	1 je fuis, n fuyons, ils fuient 2 je fuyais 3 je fuis 5 je fuie
	7 fuyant 8 fui
geindre	*like* **atteindre**
haïr	1 je hais, il hait, n haïssons
inclure	*like* **conclure**
induire	*like* **conduire**
inscrire	*like* **écrire**
instruire	*like* **conduire**
interdire	*like* **dire** *except* 1 v interdisez
interrompre	*like* **rompre**
intervenir	*like* **tenir**
introduire	*like* **conduire**
joindre	1 je joins, n joignons, ils joignent 2 je joignais 3 je joignis
	4 je joindrai 5 je joigne 7 joignant 8 joint
lire	1 je lis, n lisons 2 je lisais 3 je lus 5 je lise 7 lisant 8 lu
luire	*like* **nuire**
maintenir	*like* **tenir**
maudire	1 je maudis, n maudissons 2 je maudissais 3 je maudis
	4 je maudirai 5 je maudisse 7 maudissant 8 maudit
méconnaître	*like* **connaître**
médire	*like* **dire** *except* 1 v médisez
mentir	1 je mens, n mentons 2 je mentais 5 je mente 7 mentant
mettre	1 je mets, n mettons 2 je mettais 3 je mis 5 je mette
	7 mettant 8 mis
moudre	1 je mouds, il moud, n moulons 2 je moulais 3 je moulus
	5 je moule 7 moulant 8 moulu
†mourir	1 je meurs, n mourons, ils meurent 2 je mourais 3 je mourus
	4 je mourrai 5 je meure, n mourions 7 mourant 8 mort
mouvoir	1 je meus, n mouvons, ils meuvent 2 je mouvais 3 je mus
	4 je mouvrai 5 je meuve, n mouvions
	8 mû, mue, *pl* mus, mues
†naître	1 je nais, il naît, n naissons 2 je naissais 3 je naquis
	4 je naîtrai 5 je naisse 7 naissant 8 né
nuire	1 je nuis, n nuisons 2 je nuisais 3 je nuisis 5 je nuise
	7 nuisant 8 nui
obtenir	*like* **tenir**
offrir	*like* **couvrir**
omettre	*like* **mettre**
ouvrir	*like* **couvrir**
paître	(*defective*) 1 il paît 2 ils paissait 3 *none* 4 il paîtra
	5 il paisse 7 paissant 8 *none*
paraître	*like* **connaître**
parcourir	*like* **courir**
parfaire	*like* **faire** (*present tense, infinitive and past participle only*)
†partir	*like* **mentir**
†parvenir	*like* **tenir**
peindre	*like* **atteindre**
percevoir	*like* **recevoir**
permettre	*like* **mettre**
plaindre	*like* **craindre**
plaire	1 je plais, il plaît, n plaisons 2 je plaisais 3 je plus 5 je plaise
	7 plaisant 8 plu
pleuvoir	(*impersonal*) 1 il pleut 2 il pleuvait 3 il plut 4 il pleuvra
	5 il pleuve 6 *none* 7 pleuvant 8 plu
poindre	(*defective*) 1 il point 4 il poindra 8 point

poursuivre	*like*	**suivre**
pourvoir	*like*	**voir** *except* 3 je pourvus *and* 4 je pourvoirai
pouvoir		1 je peux *or* je puis, tu peux, il peut, n pouvons, ils peuvent
		2 je pouvais 3 je pus 4 je pourrai 5 je puisse 6 *not used*
		7 pouvant 8 pu
prédire	*like*	**dire** *except* v prédisez
prendre		1 je prends, il prend, n prenons, ils prennent 2 je prenais 3 je pris
		5 je prenne 7 prenant 8 pris
prescrire	*like*	**écrire**
pressentir	*like*	**mentir**
prévaloir	*like*	**valoir** *except* 5 je prévale
prévenir	*like*	**tenir**
prévoir	*like*	**voir** *except* 4 je prévoirai
produire	*like*	**conduire**
promettre	*like*	**mettre**
promouvoir	*like*	**mouvoir** *except* 8 promu
proscrire	*like*	**écrire**
†provenir	*like*	**tenir**
rabattre	*like*	**battre**
rasseoir	*like*	**asseoir**
réapparaître	*like*	**connaître**
recevoir		1 je reçois, n recevons, ils reçoivent 2 je recevais 3 je reçus
		4 je recevrai 5 je reçoive, n recevions, ils reçoivent 7 recevant
		8 reçu
reconduire	*like*	**conduire**
reconnaître	*like*	**connaître**
reconquérir	*like*	**acquérir**
reconstruire	*like*	**conduire**
recoudre	*like*	**coudre**
recourir	*like*	**courir**
recouvrir	*like*	**couvrir**
récrire	*like*	**écrire**
recueillir	*like*	**cueillir**
†redevenir	*like*	**tenir**
redire	*like*	**dire**
réduire	*like*	**conduire**
réécrire	*like*	**écrire**
réélire	*like*	**lire**
refaire	*like*	**faire**
rejoindre	*like*	**joindre**
relire	*like*	**lire**
reluire	*like*	**nuire**
remettre	*like*	**mettre**
†renaître	*like*	**naître**
rendormir	*like*	**mentir**
renvoyer	*like*	**envoyer**
†se repaître	*like*	**paître**
reparaître	*like*	**connaître**
†repartir	*like*	**mentir**
repeindre	*like*	**atteindre**
repentir	*like*	**mentir**
reprendre	*like*	**prendre**
reproduire	*like*	**conduire**
résoudre		1 je résous, n résolvons 2 je résolvais 3 je résolus
		5 je résolve 7 résolvant 8 résolu
ressentir	*like*	**mentir**
resservir	*like*	**mentir**
ressortir	*like*	**mentir**
restreindre	*like*	**atteindre**

retenir	*like*	**tenir**
retransmettre	*like*	**mettre**
†revenir	*like*	**tenir**
revêtir	*like*	**vêtir**
revivre	*like*	**vivre**
revoir	*like*	**voir**

rire 1 je ris, n rions 2 je riais 3 je ris 5 je rie, n riions 7 riant 8 ri

rompre *regular except* 1 il rompt

rouvrir	*like*	**couvrir**
satisfaire	*like*	**faire**

savoir 1 je sais, n savons, il savent 2 je savais 3 je sus 4 je saurai 5 je sache 6 sache, sachons, sachez 7 sachant 8 su

séduire	*like*	**conduire**
sentir	*like*	**mentir**
servir	*like*	**mentir**
sortir	*like*	**mentir**
souffrir	*like*	**couvrir**
soumettre	*like*	**mettre**
sourire	*like*	**rire**
souscrire	*like*	**écrire**
soustraire	*like*	**abstraire**
soutenir	*like*	**tenir**
†se souvenir	*like*	**tenir**
subvenir	*like*	**tenir**

suffire 1 je suffis, n suffisons 2 je suffisais 3 je suffis 5 je suffise 7 suffisant 8 suffi

suivre 1 je suis, n suivons 2 je suivais 3 je suivis 5 je suive 7 suivant 8 suivi

surprendre	*like*	**prendre**
†survenir	*like*	**tenir**
survivre	*like*	**vivre**

taire 1 je tais, n taisons 2 je taisais 3 je tus 5 je taise 7 taisant 8 tu

teindre *like* **atteindre**

tenir 1 je tiens, ne tenons, ils tiennent 2 je tenais 3 je tins, tu tins, il tint, n tînmes, v tîntes, ils tinrent 4 je tiendrai 5 je tienne 7 tenant 8 tenu

traduire	*like*	**conduire**
traire	*like*	**abstraire**
transcrire	*like*	**écrire**
transmettre	*like*	**mettre**
transparaître	*like*	**connaître**
tressaillir	*like*	**défaillir**

vaincre 1 je vaincs, il vainc, n vainquons 2 je vainquais 3 je vainquis 5 je vainque 7 vainquant 8 vaincu

valoir 1 je vaux, il vaut, n valons 2 je valais 3 je valus 4 je vaudrai 5 je vaille 6 *not used* 7 valant 8 valu

†venir *like* **tenir**

vêtir 1 je vêts, n vêtons 2 je vêtais 5 je vête 7 vêtant 8 vêtu

vivre 1 je vis, n vivons 2 je vivais 3 je vécus 5 je vive 7 vivant 8 vécu

voir 1 je vois, n voyons 2 je voyais 3 je vis 4 je verrai 5 je voie, n voyions 7 voyant 8 vu

vouloir 1 je veux, il veut, n voulons, ils veulent 2 je voulais 3 je voulus 4 je voudrai 5 je veuille 6 veuille, veuillons, veuillez 7 voulant 8 voulu

VERBES ANGLAIS IRRÉGULIERS

Infinitif	Prétérit	Participe passé
arise	arose	arisen
awake	awoke	awoken
awaken	awoke, awakened	awakened, awoken
be	were/was	been
bear	bore	borne
beat	beat	beaten
become	became	become
begin	began	begun
bend	bent	bent
beseech	besought, beseeched	besought, beseeched
bet	bet, betted	bet, betted
bid	bade, bid	bidden, bid
bind	bound	bound
bite	bit	bitten
bleed	bled	bled
blow	blew	blown
break	broke	broken
breed	bred	bred
bring	brought	brought
build	built	built
burn	burnt, burned	burnt, burned
burst	burst	burst
bust	bust, busted	bust, busted
buy	bought	bought
cast	cast	cast
catch	caught	caught
chide	chided, chid	chided, chidden
choose	chose	chosen
cleave	cleaved, cleft, clove	cleaved, cleft, cloven
cling	clung	clung
clothe	clad, clothed	clad, clothed
come	came	come
cost	cost	cost
creep	crept	crept
crow	crowed, crew	crowed
cut	cut	cut
deal	dealt	dealt
dig	dug	dug
dive	dived, *Am* dove	dived
do	did	done
draw	drew	drawn
dream	dreamt, dreamed	dreamt, dreamed
drink	drank	drunk
drive	drove	driven
dwell	dwelt	dwelt
eat	ate	eaten
fall	fell	fallen
feed	fed	fed
feel	felt	felt
fight	fought	fought
find	found	found
flee	fled	fled

Irregular French Verbs

Infinitif	Prétérit	Participe passé
fling	flung	flung
fly	flew	flown
forget	forgot	forgotten
forgive	forgave	forgiven
forsake	forsook	forsaken
freeze	froze	frozen
get	got	got, *Am* gotten
gild	gilded, gilt	gilded, gilt
gird	girded, girt	girded, girt
give	gave	given
go	went	gone
grind	ground	ground
grow	grew	grown
hang	hung/hanged	hung/hanged
have	had	had
hear	heard	heard
hew	hewed	hewn, hewed
hide	hid	hidden
hit	hit	hit
hold	held	held
hurt	hurt	hurt
keep	kept	kept
kneel	knelt	knelt
knit	knitted, knit	knitted, knit
know	knew	known
lay	laid	laid
lead	led	led
lean	leant, leaned	leant, leaned
leap	leapt, leaped	leapt, leaped
learn	learnt, learned	learnt, learned
leave	left	left
lend	lent	lent
let	let	let
lie	lay	lain
light	lit	lit
lose	lost	lost
make	made	made
mean	meant	meant
meet	met	met
mow	mowed	mown
pay	paid	paid
plead	pleaded, *Am* pled	pleaded, *Am* pled
prove	proved	proved, proven
put	put	put
quit	quit	quit
read	read	read
rend	rent	rent
rid	rid	rid
ride	rode	ridden
ring	rang	rung
rise	rose	risen
run	ran	run
saw	sawed	sawn, sawed
say	said	said
see	saw	seen
seek	sought	sought
sell	sold	sold
send	sent	sent

Infinitif	**Prétérit**	**Participe passé**
set	set	set
sew	sewed	sewn
shake	shook	shaken
shear	sheared	shorn, sheared
shed	shed	shed
shine	shone	shone
shit	shitted, shat	shitted, shat
shoe	shod	shod
shoot	shot	shot
show	showed	shown
shrink	shrank	shrunk
shut	shut	shut
sing	sang	sung
sink	sank	sunk
sit	sat	sat
slay	slew	slain
sleep	slept	slept
slide	slid	slid
sling	slung	slung
slink	slunk	slunk
slit	slit	slit
smell	smelled, smelt	smelled, smelt
smite	smote	smitten
sow	sowed	sown, sowed
speak	spoke	spoken
speed	sped, speeded	sped, speeded
spell	spelt, spelled	spelt, spelled
spend	spent	spent
spill	spilt, spilled	spilt, spilled
spin	span	spun
spit	spat, *Am* spit	spat, *Am* spit
split	split	split
spoil	spoilt, spoiled	spoilt, spoiled
spread	spread	spread
spring	sprang	sprung
stand	stood	stood
stave in	staved in, stove in	staved in, stove in
steal	stole	stolen
stick	stuck	stuck
sting	stung	stung
stink	stank, stunk	stunk
strew	strewed	strewed, strewn
stride	strode	stridden
strike	struck	struck
string	strung	strung
strive	strove	striven
swear	swore	sworn
sweep	swept	swept
swell	swelled	swollen, swelled
swim	swam	swum
swing	swung	swung
take	took	taken
teach	taught	taught
tear	tore	torn
tell	told	told
think	thought	thought
thrive	thrived, throve	thrived
throw	threw	thrown

Irregular French Verbs

Infinitif	Prétérit	Participe passé
thrust	thrust	thrust
tread	trod	trodden
wake	woke	woken
wear	wore	worn
weave	wove, weaved	woven, weaved
weep	wept	wept
wet	wet, wetted	wet, wetted
win	won	won
wind	wound	wound
wring	wrung	wrung
write	wrote	written

Français – Anglais
French – English

A, a [ɑ] *nm inv* A, a; **connaître un sujet de A à Z** to know a subject inside out; **A1** *(autoroute) Br* ≃ M1, *Am* ≃ I1
a [a] *voir* **avoir**
à [a] *prép*

à + le = **au** [o], à + les = **aux** [o]

(**a**) *(indique la direction)* to; **aller à Paris** to go to Paris; **partir au Venezuela** to leave for Venezuela; **au lit!** off to bed!
(**b**) *(indique la position)* at; **être au bureau/à la ferme/à Paris** to be at *or* in the office/on *or* at the farm/in Paris; **à la maison** at home; **à l'horizon** on the horizon
(**c**) *(dans l'expression du temps)* **à 8 heures** at 8 o'clock; **au vingt-et-unième siècle** in the twenty-first century; **à mon arrivée** on (my) arrival; **à lundi!** see you (on) Monday!
(**d**) *(dans les descriptions)* **l'homme à la barbe** the man with the beard; **verre à liqueur** liqueur glass
(**e**) *(introduit le complément d'objet indirect)* **donner qch à qn** to give sth to sb, to give sth sb; **penser à qn/qch** to think about *or* of sb/sth
(**f**) *(devant infinitif)* **apprendre à lire** to learn to read; **avoir du travail à faire** to have work to do; **maison à vendre** house for sale; **'à louer'** *Br* 'to let', *Am* 'to rent'; **prêt à partir** ready to leave
(**g**) *(indique l'appartenance)* **un ami à moi** a friend of mine; **c'est (son livre) à lui** it's his (book); **c'est à vous de...** *(il vous incombe de)* it's up to you to...; *(c'est votre tour)* it's your turn to...; **à toi!** your turn!
(**h**) *(indique le moyen, la manière)* **à bicyclette** by bicycle; **à la main** by hand; **à pied** on foot; **au crayon** in pencil; **au galop** at a gallop; **à la française** in the French style; **deux à deux** two by two
(**i**) *(indique la conséquence)* **laid à faire peur** hideously ugly; **c'était à mourir de rire** it was hilarious
(**j**) *(prix)* **pain à 2 euros** loaf for 2 euros
(**k**) *(poids)* **vendre au kilo** to sell by the kilo
(**l**) *(vitesse)* **100 km à l'heure** 100 km an *or* per hour

(**m**) *(pour appeler)* **au voleur!** (stop) thief!; **au feu!** (there's a) fire! (**n**) *(avec de)* to; **de Paris à Lyon** from Paris to Lyons; **du lundi au vendredi** from Monday to Friday, *Am* Monday through Friday
abaisser [abese] **1** *vt (levier, pont-levis)* to lower; *(store)* to pull down; **a. qn** to humiliate sb
2 s'abaisser *vpr* (**a**) *(barrière)* to lower; **s'a. à faire qch** to stoop to doing sth (**b**) *(être en pente)* to slope down
abandon [abɑ̃dɔ̃] *nm (d'un enfant, d'un projet)* abandonment; *(d'un lieu)* neglect; *(de sportif)* withdrawal; *(nonchalance)* abandon; *Ordinat* abort; **à l'a.** in a neglected state; **a. de poste** desertion of one's post
abandonner [abɑ̃dɔne] **1** *vt (personne, animal, lieu)* to desert, to abandon; *(pouvoir, combat)* to give up; *(projet)* to abandon; *(cours)* to withdraw from; **a. ses études** to drop out (of school); **a. le navire** to abandon ship; **a. qch à qn** to give sb sth
2 *vi (renoncer)* to give up; *(sportif)* to withdraw
3 s'abandonner *vpr (se détendre)* to let oneself go; **s'a. au sommeil** to drift off to sleep
abasourdi, -ie [abazurdi] *adj* stunned
abat-jour [abaʒur] *nm inv* lampshade
abats [aba] *nmpl* offal; *(de volaille)* giblets
abattant [abatɑ̃] *nm (de table)* flap; *(des toilettes)* lid
abattis [abati] *nmpl* giblets
abattoir [abatwar] *nm* slaughterhouse
abattre* [abatr] **1** *vt (mur)* to knock down; *(arbre)* to cut down; *(personne, gros gibier)* to kill; *(animal de boucherie)* to slaughter; *(animal blessé ou malade)* to destroy; *(avion)* to shoot down; *Fig (déprimer)* to demoralize; *Fig (épuiser)* to exhaust
2 s'abattre *vpr (tomber)* to crash down (**sur** on); *(pluie)* to pour down (**sur** on); *(oiseau)* to swoop down (**sur** on) •**abattage** *nm (d'arbre)* felling; *(de vache)* slaughter(ing) •**abattement** *nm (faiblesse)* exhaustion; *(désespoir)* dejection; **a. fiscal** tax allowance

ℓ Il faut noter que le nom anglais **abatement** est un faux ami. Il signifie **apaisement**.

abattu, -ue [abaty] *adj (triste)* dejected; *(faible)* exhausted
abbaye [abei] *nf* abbey
abbé [abe] *nm (d'abbaye)* abbot; *(prêtre)* priest • **abbesse** *nf* abbess
abcès [apsɛ] *nm* abscess
abdiquer [abdike] *vti* to abdicate • **abdication** *nf* abdication
abdomen [abdɔmɛn] *nm* abdomen • **abdominal, -e, -aux, ales** *adj* abdominal • **abdominaux** *nmpl* abdominal muscles; **faire des a.** to do exercises for the stomach muscles
abeille [abɛj] *nf* bee
aberrant, -ante [aberɑ̃, -ɑ̃t] *adj* absurd • **aberration** *nf (égarement)* aberration; *(idée)* ludicrous idea; **dire des aberrations** to talk sheer nonsense
abhorrer [abɔre] *vt Littéraire* to abhor
abîme [abim] *nm* abyss; *Fig* **être au bord de l'a.** to be on the brink of disaster
abîmer [abime] **1** *vt* to spoil, to damage **2 s'abîmer** *vpr (object)* to get spoilt; *(fruit)* to go bad; **s'a. les yeux** to ruin one's eyesight; *Littéraire* **s'a. en mer** to be engulfed by the sea
abject, -e [abʒɛkt] *adj* despicable
abjurer [abʒyre] *vti* to abjure
ablation [ablasjɔ̃] *nf* removal
ablutions [ablysjɔ̃] *nfpl Littéraire ou Hum* **faires ses a.** to perform one's ablutions
abnégation [abnegasjɔ̃] *nf* self-sacrifice, abnegation
abois [abwa] **aux abois** *adv (animal)* at bay
abolir [abɔlir] *vt* to abolish • **abolition** *nf* abolition
abominable [abɔminabl] *adj* appalling • **abominablement** [-əmɑ̃] *adv* appallingly; *(laid)* hideously
abondant, -ante [abɔ̃dɑ̃, -ɑ̃t] *adj* plentiful, abundant • **abondamment** *adv* abundantly; *(parler)* at length • **abondance** *nf* abundance (**de** of); **en a.** in abundance; **des années d'a.** years of plenty • **abonder** *vi* to be plentiful; **a. en qch** to abound in sth; **a. dans le sens de qn** to agree entirely with sb
abonné, -ée [abɔne] *nmf (d'un journal, du téléphone)* subscriber; *(de train, d'un théâtre) & Sport* season-ticket holder; *(du gaz)* consumer • **abonnement** *nm (de journal)* subscription; *(de téléphone)* line

rental; *(de train, de théâtre)* season ticket • **s'abonner** *vpr (à un journal)* to subscribe (**à** to); *Rail & Théâtre* to buy a season ticket
abord [abɔr] *nm* (**a**) *(accès)* **d'un a. facile** easy to approach; **abords** *(d'un bâtiment)* surroundings; *(d'une ville)* outskirts; **aux abords de la ville** on the outskirts of the town (**b**) *(vue)* **au premier a., de prime a.** at first sight; **d'a., tout d'a.** *(pour commencer)* at first, to begin with; *(premièrement)* first (and foremost) • **abordable** *adj (prix, marchandises)* affordable; *(personne)* approachable
aborder [abɔrde] **1** *vt (personne, lieu, virage)* to approach; *(problème)* to tackle; *(navire) (attaquer)* to board; *(se mettre le long de)* to come alongside **2** *vi* to land • **abordage** *nm (d'un bateau) (assaut)* boarding; *(pour s'amarrer)* coming alongside
aborigène [abɔriʒɛn] *nm (d'un pays)* native; **les Aborigènes d'Australie** the (Australian) Aborigines
abortif, -ive [abɔrtif, -iv] *adj voir* **pilule**
aboutir [abutir] *vi* (**a**) *(réussir)* to be successful; **nos efforts n'ont abouti à rien** our efforts came to nothing (**b**) **a. à qch** *(avoir pour résultat)* to result in sth; **a. à un endroit** to lead to a place • **aboutissants** *nmpl voir* **tenants** • **aboutissement** *nm (résultat)* outcome; *(succès)* success
aboyer [abwaje] *vi* to bark • **aboiement** *nm* bark; **aboiements** barking
abrasif, -ive [abrazif, -iv] *adj & nm* abrasive
abréger [abreʒe] *vt (récit)* to shorten; *(visite)* to cut short; *(mot)* to abbreviate • **abrégé** *nm (d'un texte)* summary; *(livre)* abstract; **en a.** *(mot)* in abbreviated form
abreuver [abrœve] **1** *vt (cheval)* to water **2 s'abreuver** *vpr* to drink • **abreuvoir** *nm (lieu)* watering place; *(récipient)* drinking trough
abréviation [abrevjasjɔ̃] *nf* abbreviation
abri [abri] *nm* shelter; **mettre qn/qch à l'a.** to shelter sb/sth; **se mettre à l'a.** to take shelter; **être à l'a. de qch** to be sheltered from sth; **être à l'a. du besoin** to have no financial worries; **sans a.** homeless; **a. de jardin** garden shed
Abribus® [abribys] *nm* bus shelter
abricot [abriko] *nm* apricot • **abricotier** *nm* apricot tree
abriter [abrite] **1** *vt (protéger)* to shelter (**de** from); *(loger)* to house **2 s'abriter** *vpr* to (take) shelter (**de**

from); **s'a. du soleil** to shade oneself from the sun

abroger [abrɔʒe] *vt* to repeal ● **abrogation** *n* repeal

abrupt, -e [abrypt] *adj (pente, rocher)* steep; *Fig (personne)* abrupt

abrutir [abrytir] *vt (hébéter)* to daze; **a. qn de travail** to work sb to the point of exhaustion ● **abruti, -ie 1** *adj Fam (bête)* idiotic; **a. par l'alcool** stupefied with drink **2** *nmf* idiot ● **abrutissant, -ante** *adj* mind-numbing

absence [apsɑ̃s] *nf (d'une personne)* absence; *(manque)* lack ● **absent, -ente 1** *adj (personne)* absent (**de** from); *(chose)* missing; **avoir un air a.** to be miles away **2** *nmf* absentee ● **absentéisme** *nm* absenteeism ● **s'absenter** *vpr* to go away

abside [apsid] *nf* apse

absolu, -ue [apsɔly] *adj* absolute ● **absolument** *adv* absolutely; **il faut a. y aller** you simply MUST go!

absolution [apsɔlysjɔ̃] *nf Rel* absolution

absorber [apsɔrbe] *vt (liquid)* to absorb; *(nourriture)* to eat; *(boisson)* to drink; *(médicament)* to take; **son travail l'absorbe** she is engrossed in her work ● **absorbant, -ante** *adj (papier)* absorbent; *(travail, lecture)* absorbing ● **absorption** *nf (de liquide)* absorption; *(de nourriture)* eating; *(de boisson)* drinking; *(de médicament)* taking

absoudre* [apsudr] *vt Rel ou Littéraire* **a. qn de qch** to forgive sb sth

abstenir* [apstənir] **s'abstenir** *vpr (ne pas voter)* to abstain; **s'a. de qch/de faire qch** to refrain from sth/from doing sth ● **abstention** *nf Pol* abstention

abstinence [apstinɑ̃s] *nf* abstinence

abstrait, -aite [apstrɛ, -ɛt] *adj* abstract ● **abstraction** *nf* abstraction; **faire a. de qch** to disregard sth

absurde [apsyrd] **1** *adj* absurd **2** *nm* **l'a. de cette situation** the absurdity of this situation ● **absurdité** *nf* absurdity; **dire des absurdités** to talk nonsense

abus [aby] *nm (excès)* overindulgence (**de** in); *(pratique)* abuse (**de** of); **a. de pouvoir** abuse of power; **a. d'alcool** alcohol abuse; **a. de tabac** excessive smoking; **a. de confiance** breach of trust; *Fam* **il y a de l'a.** that's going too far! ● **abuser 1** *vi* to go too far; **a. de** *(situation, personne)* to take unfair advantage of; *(autorité)* to abuse; *(nourriture)* to overindulge in; **a. du tabac** to smoke too much **2** **s'abuser** *vpr* **si je ne m'abuse** if I am not mistaken

abusif, -ive [abyzif, -iv] *adj* excessive; *(mère)* possessive; **emploi a.** *(d'un mot)* improper use

acabit [akabi] *nm Péj* **de cet a.** of that type

acacia [akasja] *nm* acacia

académie [akademi] *nf* academy; *(administration scolaire)* ≃ local education authority; **a. de musique** school of music; **l'A. française** = learned society responsible for promoting the French language and imposing standards ● **académicien, -ienne** *nmf* = member of the 'Académie française' ● **académique** *adj Péj (style)* conventional

acajou [akaʒu] *nm* mahogany

acariâtre [akarjɑtr] *adj* cantankerous

acarien [akarjɛ̃] *nm* dust mite

accablement [akɑbləmɑ̃] *nm* dejection

accabler [akɑble] *vt* to overwhelm (**de** with); **a. qn de travail** to overload sb with work; **a. qn de reproches** to heap criticism on sb; **accablé de dettes** (over)burdened with debt; **accablé de chaleur** overcome by heat ● **accablant, -ante** *adj (chaleur)* oppressive; *(témoignage)* damning

accalmie [akalmi] *nf* lull

accaparer [akapare] *vt (personne, conversation)* to monopolize

accéder [aksede] *vi* **a. à** *(lieu)* to reach; *(responsabilité, rang)* to gain; *(requête)* to comply with; *Ordinat (programme)* to access; **a. au trône** to accede to the throne

accélérer [akselere] **1** *vt (travaux)* to speed up; *(allure, pas)* to quicken; *Fig* **a. le mouvement** to get a move on **2** *vi (en voiture)* to accelerate **3** **s'accélérer** *vpr* to speed up ● **accélérateur** *nm (de voiture, d'ordinateur)* accelerator ● **accélération** *nf* acceleration; *(de travaux)* speeding up

accent [aksɑ̃] *nm* accent; *(sur une syllabe)* stress; *Fig* **mettre l'a. sur qch** to stress sth; **a. aigu/circonflexe/grave** acute/circumflex/grave (accent); **a. tonique** stress ● **accentuation** *nf (sur lettre)* accentuation; *(de phénomène)* intensification ● **accentuer 1** *vt (syllabe)* to stress; *Fig (renforcer)* to emphasize **2** **s'accentuer** *vpr* to become more pronounced

accepter [aksɛpte] *vt* to accept; **a. de faire qch** to agree to do sth ● **acceptable** *adj (recevable)* acceptable ● **acceptation** *nf* acceptance

acception [aksɛpsjɔ̃] *nf (de mot)* meaning; **sans a. de race** irrespective of race

accès [aksɛ] nm (**a**) (approche) & Ordinat access (**à** to); **être facile d'a.** to be easy to reach; **avoir a. à qch** to have access to sth; **'a. interdit'** 'no entry'; **'a. aux quais'** to the trains (**b**) (de folie, colère) fit; (de fièvre) bout; **a. de toux** coughing fit • **accessible** adj (lieu, livre) accessible; (personne) approachable • **accession** nf accession (**à** to); **a. à la propriété** home ownership

accessoire [akseswar] adj minor • **accessoires** nmpl (de théâtre) props; (de mode, de voiture) accessories; **a. de toilette** toilet requisites • **accessoirement** adv if necessary; (en plus) also

accident [aksidã] nm accident; **a. d'avion** plane crash; **a. de chemin de fer** train crash; **a. de la route** road accident; **a. du travail** industrial accident; **a. de parcours** hitch; **par a.** by accident, by chance • **accidenté, -ée 1** adj (terrain) uneven; (voiture) damaged **2** nmf accident victim • **accidentel, -elle** adj accidental • **accidentellement** adv (par hasard) accidentally

acclamer [aklame] vt to cheer • **acclamations** nfpl cheers

acclimater [aklimate] **1** vt to acclimatize, Am to acclimate (**à** to)
2 s'acclimater vpr to become acclimatized or Am acclimated (**à** to) • **acclimatation** nf Br acclimatization, Am acclimation (**à** to)

accointances [akwɛ̃tãs] nfpl contacts

accolade [akɔlad] nf (embrassade) embrace; (signe) curly bracket

accoler [akɔle] vt (mettre ensemble) to put side by side

accommoder [akɔmɔde] **1** vt (nourriture) to prepare; (restes) to use up
2 vi (œil) to focus
3 s'accommoder vpr **s'a. de qch** to put up with sth • **accommodant, -ante** adj accommodating

> Il faut noter que le verbe anglais **to accommodate** est un faux ami. Il ne signifie jamais **accommoder**.

accompagner [akɔ̃paɲe] vt (personne) to accompany; **a. qn à la gare** (en voiture) to take sb to the station; **a. qn au piano** to accompany sb on the piano • **accompagnateur, -trice** nmf (musical) accompanist; (de touristes) guide • **accompagnement** [-əmã] nm Mus accompaniment

accomplir [akɔ̃plir] vt (tache) to carry out; (exploit) to accomplish; (terminer) to complete • **accompli, -ie** adj accomplished

accord [akɔr] nm (traité, entente) & Grammaire agreement; (autorisation) consent; (musical) chord; **arriver à un a.** to reach an agreement; **être d'a.** to agree (**avec** with); **d'a.!** all right!

accordéon [akɔrdeɔ̃] nm accordion; Fig **en a.** (chaussette) at half-mast

accorder [akɔrde] **1** vt (instrument) to tune; **a. qch à qn** (faveur) to grant sb sth; (augmentation) to award sb sth; (prêt) to authorize sth to sb; Grammaire **a. qch avec qch** to make sth agree with sth; **a. la plus grande importance à qch** to attach the utmost importance to sth; Formel **il est timide, je vous l'accorde** he is shy, I must admit
2 s'accorder vpr (se mettre d'accord) to agree (**avec** with, **sur** on); Grammaire (mots) to agree (**avec** with); **s'a. qch** to allow oneself sth; **on s'accorde à penser que...** there is a general belief that...

accoster [akɔste] **1** vt (personne) to approach
2 vi Naut to dock

accotement [akɔtmã] nm (de route) verge; (de voie ferrée) shoulder

accoucher [akuʃe] **1** vt **a. qn** to deliver sb's baby
2 vi to give birth (**de** to); Fam **accouche!** spit it out! • **accouchement** nm delivery • **accoucheur** nm (**médecin**) **a.** obstetrician

accouder [akude] **s'accouder** vpr **s'a. à** ou **sur qch** to lean one's elbows on sth • **accoudoir** nm armrest

accoupler [akuple] **s'accoupler** vpr (animaux) to mate • **accouplement** [-əmã] nm (d'animaux) mating

accourir* [akurir] vi to run up

accoutrement [akutrəmã] nm Péj rig-out

accoutumer [akutyme] **1** vt **a. qn à qch** to accustom sb to sth
2 s'accoutumer vpr to get accustomed (**à** to) • **accoutumance** nf (adaptation) familiarization (**à** with); Méd (dépendance) addiction • **accoutumé, -ée** adj usual; **comme à l'accoutumée** as usual

accréditer [akredite] vt (ambassadeur) to accredit; (rumeur) to lend credence to

accro [akro] adj Fam (drogué) addicted (**à** to)

accroc [akro] nm (déchirure) tear; (difficulté) hitch; **sans a.** without a hitch

accrocher [akrɔʃe] **1** vt (déchirer) to catch; (fixer) to hook (**à** onto); (suspendre) to hang up (**à** on); (pare-chocs) to clip
2 vi (achopper) to hit a stumbling block; (se remarquer) to grab one's attention

3 s'accrocher *vpr (se fixer)* to fasten; *Fam (persévérer)* to stick at it; *Fam (se disputer)* to clash; **s'a. à qn/qch** *(s'agripper)* to cling to sb/sth; *Fam* **accroche-toi, tu n'as pas tout entendu!** brace yourself, you haven't heard everything yet! • **accrochage** *nm (de véhicules)* minor accident; *Fam (dispute)* clash • **accrocheur, -euse** *adj (personne)* tenacious; *(titre, slogan)* catchy

accroître* [akrwatr] **1** *vt* to increase

2 s'accroître *vpr* to increase • **accroissement** *nm* increase (**de** in)

accroupir [akrupir] **s'accroupir** *vpr* to squat (down) • **accroupi, -ie** *adj* squatting

accueil [akœj] *nm* reception • **accueillant, -ante** *adj* welcoming • **accueillir*** *vt (personne, proposition)* to greet; *(sujet: hôtel)* to accommodate

acculer [akyle] *vt* **a. qn à qch** to drive sb to sth; **acculé à la faillite** forced into bankruptcy

accumuler [akymyle] *vt*, **s'accumuler** *vpr* to accumulate • **accumulateur** *nm* battery • **accumulation** *nf* accumulation

accuser [akyze] **1** *vt (dénoncer)* to accuse; *(tendance, baisse)* to show; *(faire ressortir)* to bring out; **a. qn de qch/de faire qch** to accuse sb of sth/of doing sth; **a. réception** to acknowledge receipt (**de** of); *Fig* **a. le coup** to be obviously shaken

2 s'accuser *vpr (se déclarer coupable)* to confess (**de** to) • **accusateur, -trice 1** *adj (regard)* accusing **2** *nmf* accuser • **accusation** *nf* accusation; **porter une a. contre qn** to make an accusation against sb • **accusé, -ée 1** *adj (trait)* prominent **2** *nmf* **l'a.** the accused; *(au tribunal)* the defendant

acerbe [asɛrb] *adj* acerbic; **d'un ton a.** sharply

acéré, -ée [asere] *adj (lame)* sharp

acétone [asetɔn] *nf* acetone

achalandé, -ée [aʃalãde] *adj* **bien a.** *(magasin)* well-stocked

acharner [aʃarne] **s'acharner** *vpr* **s'a. sur** *ou* **contre qn** *(persécuter)* to be always after sb; **s'a. sur qn** *(sujet: meurtrier)* to savage sb; *(sujet: examinateur)* to give sb a hard time; **s'a. à faire qch** to try very hard to do sth • **acharné, -ée** *adj (effort, travail)* relentless; *(combat)* fierce • **acharnement** [-əmã] *nm* relentlessness; *(dans un combat)* fury; **avec a.** relentlessly

achat [aʃa] *nm* purchase; **faire l'a. de qch** to buy sth; **achats** *(provisions, paquets)* shopping; **aller faire ses achats** to go shopping

acheminer [aʃəmine] **1** *vt (marchandises)* to ship (**vers** to); *(courrier)* to handle

2 s'acheminer *vpr* **s'a. vers qch** to make one's way towards sth

acheter [aʃte] **1** *vti* to buy; **a. qch à qn** *(faire une transaction)* to buy sth from sb; *(faire un cadeau)* to buy sth for sb

2 s'acheter *vpr* **je vais m'acheter une glace** I'm going to buy (myself) an ice cream • **acheteur, -euse** *nmf* buyer; *(dans un magasin)* shopper

achever [aʃve] *vt* (**a**) *(finir)* to end; *(travail)* to complete; **a. de faire qch** to finish doing sth (**b**) *(tuer) (animal blessé ou malade)* to put out of its misery; **a. qn** to finish sb off

2 s'achever *vpr* to end • **achèvement** [-ɛvmã] *nm* completion

> ✏ Il faut noter que les termes anglais **achievement** et **to achieve** sont des faux amis. Le premier signifie **réussite** et le second ne se traduit jamais par **achever**.

achoppement [aʃɔpmã] *nm* *voir* **pierre**

acide [asid] **1** *adj* acid(ic); *(au goût)* sour

2 *nm* acid • **acidité** *nf* acidity; *(au goût)* sourness

acier [asje] *nm* steel; **a. inoxydable** stainless steel • **aciérie** *nf* steelworks

acné [akne] *nf* acne

acolyte [akɔlit] *nm Péj* accomplice

acompte [akɔ̃t] *nm* down payment; **verser un a.** to make a down payment

à-côté [akote] *(pl* **à-côtés***) nm (d'une question)* side issue; **à-côtés** *(gains)* little extras

à-coup [aku] *(pl* **à-coups***) nm* jolt; **sans à-coups** smoothly; **par à-coups** *(avancer, travailler)* in fits and starts

acoustique [akustik] **1** *adj* acoustic

2 *nf (qualité)* acoustics *(pluriel)*

acquérir* [akerir] *vt (acheter)* to purchase; *(obtenir, prendre)* to acquire; **a. de la valeur** to increase in value; **tenir qch pour acquis** to take sth for granted • **acquéreur** *nm* purchaser • **acquis** *nm* experience; **les a. sociaux** social benefits • **acquisition** *nf (action)* acquisition; *(bien acheté)* purchase

acquiescer [akjese] *vi* to acquiesce (**à** to)

acquit [aki] *nm* receipt; **'pour a.'** 'paid'; **par a. de conscience** to ease one's conscience

acquitter [akite] **1** *vt (accusé)* to acquit; *(dette)* to pay

2 s'acquitter *vpr* **s'a. d'un devoir** to fulfil a duty; **s'a. envers qn** to repay sb • **acquit-**

tement *nm (d'un accusé)* acquittal; *(d'une dette)* payment

âcre [akr] *adj (goût)* bitter; *(odeur)* acrid

acrobate [akrɔbat] *nmf* acrobat • **acrobatie** [-basi] *nf* acrobatics *(sing)*; **acrobaties aériennes** acrobatics *(sing)* • **acrobatique** *adj* acrobatic

acrylique [akrilik] *adj & nm* acrylic

acte [akt] *nm (action) & Théâtre* act; *Jur* deed; **faire a. de candidature à un emploi** to apply for a job; **prendre a. de qch** to take note of sth; **a. terroriste** terrorist act; **a. unique européen** Single European Act; **actes** *(de procès)* proceedings; *Jur* **a. d'accusation** bill of indictment; **a. de mariage** marriage certificate; **a. de naissance** birth certificate; **a. de vente** bill of sale

acteur [aktœr] *nm* actor

actif, -ive [aktif, -iv] **1** *adj* active
2 *nm Grammaire* active; *Com (d'une entreprise)* assets; **avoir qch à son a.** to have sth to one's name

action [aksjɔ̃] *nf* action; *(en Bourse)* share; **bonne a.** good deed; **passer à l'a.** to take action • **actionnaire** *nmf Fin* shareholder

actionner [aksjɔne] *vt (mettre en marche)* to start up; *(faire fonctionner)* to operate

activer [aktive] **1** *vt (accélérer)* to speed up; *(feu)* to stoke; *Ordinat (option)* to select
2 s'activer *vpr (être actif)* to be busy; *Fam (se dépêcher)* to get a move on

activiste [aktivist] *nmf* activist

activité [aktivite] *nf* activity; **en a.** *(personne)* working; *(volcan)* active

actrice [aktris] *nf* actress

actuaire [aktɥer] *nmf* actuary

actualisation [aktɥalizasjɔ̃] *nf (de texte)* updating

actualité [aktɥalite] *nf (d'un problème)* topicality; **l'a.** current affairs; **les actualités** *(à la radio, à la télévision)* the news; **d'a.** topical

actuel, -elle [aktɥel] *adj (présent)* present; *(d'actualité)* topical; **l'a. président** the President in office • **actuellement** *adv* at present

   ⚠ Il faut noter que les termes anglais **actual** et **actually** sont des faux amis. Le premier ne signifie jamais **actuel** et le second se traduit par **en fait**.

acuité [akɥite] *nf (de douleur)* acuteness; **a. visuelle** keenness of vision

acupuncture [akypɔ̃ktyr] *nf* acupuncture • **acupuncteur, -trice** *nmf* acupuncturist

adage [adaʒ] *nm* adage

adapter [adapte] **1** *vt* to adapt (à to)
2 s'adapter *vpr (s'acclimater)* to adapt (à to); **s'a. à qn/qch** to get used to sb/sth • **adaptable** *adj* adaptable • **adaptateur, -trice** *nmf* adapter • **adaptation** *nf* adaptation; **faculté d'a.** adaptability

additif [aditif] *nm (substance)* additive

addition [adisjɔ̃] *nf* addition (à to); *(au restaurant) Br* bill, *Am* check • **additionner 1** *vt* to add (up) (à to) **2 s'additionner** *vpr* to add up

adepte [adept] *nmf* follower; **faire des adeptes** to attract a following

adéquat, -ate [adekwa, -wat] *adj* appropriate; *(quantité)* adequate

adhérer [adere] *vi* **a. à qch** *(coller)* to stick to sth; *(s'inscrire)* to join sth; **a. à la route** *(pneus)* to grip the road • **adhérence** *nf (de pneu)* grip • **adhérent, -ente** *nmf* member

adhésif, -ive [adezif, -iv] **1** *adj* adhesive
2 *nm* adhesive • **adhésion** *nf (inscription)* joining (à of); *(accord)* support (à for)

adieu, -x [adjø] *exclam & nm* farewell; **faire ses adieux** to say one's goodbyes

adipeux, -euse [adipø, -øz] *adj (tissu)* adipose; *(visage)* fat

adjacent, -ente [adʒasɑ̃, -ɑ̃t] *adj* adjacent (à to)

adjectif [adʒɛktif] *nm* adjective

adjoint, -ointe [adʒwɛ̃, -ɛ̃t] *adj & nmf* assistant; **a. au maire** deputy mayor

adjonction [adʒɔ̃ksjɔ̃] *n* **sans a. de sucre** no sugar added

adjudant [adʒydɑ̃] *nm* warrant officer

adjuger [adʒyʒe] **1** *vt* **a. qch à qn** *(prix, contrat)* to award sth to sb; *(aux enchères)* to knock sth down to sb
2 s'adjuger *vpr* **s'a. qch** to appropriate sth

adjurer [adʒyre] *vt Formel* to entreat

admettre* [admɛtr] *vt (accueillir, reconnaître)* to admit; *(autoriser)* to allow; **être admis à un examen** to pass an examination

administrer [administre] *vt (gérer)* to administer; *(pays)* to govern; *(justice)* to dispense • **administrateur, -trice** *nmf (de société)* director • **administratif, -ive** *adj* administrative • **administration** *nf* administration; **l'A.** *(service public)* ≃ the Civil Service; *(fonctionnaires)* civil servants

admirer [admire] *vt* to admire • **admirable** *adj* admirable • **admirateur, -trice** *nmf* admirer • **admiratif, -ive** *adj* admiring • **admiration** *nf* admiration; **être en a. devant qn/qch** to be filled with admiration for sb/sth

admissible [admisibl] *adj (tolérable)* acceptable, admissible; *Scol & Univ* **candidats admissibles** = candidates who have qualified for the oral examination • **admission** *nf* admission (**à/dans** to)

ADN [adeɛn] (*abrév* **acide désoxyribonucléique**) *nm* DNA

adolescent, -ente [adɔlesã, -ãt] **1** *adj* teenage

2 *nmf* adolescent, teenager • **adolescence** *nf* adolescence

adonner [adɔne] **s'adonner** *vpr* **s'a. à qch** to devote oneself to sth; **s'a. à la boisson** to be an alcoholic

adopter [adɔpte] *vt* to adopt • **adoptif, -ive** *adj (enfant, patrie)* adopted; *(parents)* adoptive • **adoption** *nf* adoption; **pays d'a.** adopted country

adorer [adɔre] **1** *vt (dieu)* to worship; *(chose, personne)* to adore; **a. faire qch** to adore doing sth

2 **s'adorer** *vpr* **ils s'adorent** they adore each other • **adorable** *adj* adorable • **adoration** *nf* adoration; **être en a. devant qn** to worship sb

adosser [adose] **1** *vt* **a. qch à qch** to lean sth against sth

2 **s'adosser** *vpr* **s'a. à qch** to lean (back) against sth

adoucir [adusir] **1** *vt (voix, traits, peau)* to soften; *(chagrin)* to ease

2 **s'adoucir** *vpr (temps)* to turn milder; *(voix)* to soften; *(caractère)* to mellow • **adoucissement** *nm* **a. de la température** rise in temperature

adrénaline [adrenalin] *nf* adrenalin(e)

adresse [adrɛs] *nf* (**a**) *(domicile)* address; **a. électronique** e-mail address (**b**) *(habileté)* skill

adresser [adrese] **1** *vt (lettre, remarque)* to address (**à** to); **a. qch à qn** *(lettre)* to send sb sth; *(compliment)* to present sb with sth; **a. la parole à qn** to speak to sb; **on m'a adressé à vous** I have been referred to you

2 **s'adresser** *vpr* **s'a. à qn** *(parler)* to speak to sb; *(aller trouver)* to go and see sb; *(être destiné à)* to be aimed at sb

Adriatique [adriatik] *nf* **l'A.** the Adriatic

adroit, -oite [adrwa, -wat] *adj (habile)* skilful; *(réponse)* clever

adulation [adylasjɔ̃] *nf* adulation

adulte [adylt] **1** *adj (personne, animal, attitude)* adult

2 *nmf* adult, grown-up

adultère [adyltɛr] *nm* adultery

advenir* [advǝnir] *(aux* **être** *) v* impersonnel to happen; **a. de qn** *(devenir)* to become of sb; **advienne que pourra** come what may

adverbe [advɛrb] *nm* adverb • **adverbial, -e, -aux, -ales** *adj* adverbial

adversaire [advɛrsɛr] *nmf* opponent • **adverse** *adj* opposing

adversité [advɛrsite] *nf* adversity

aérer [aere] **1** *vt (pièce, lit, linge)* to air

2 **s'aérer** *vpr* to get some fresh air • **aération** *nf* ventilation • **aéré, -ée** *adj (pièce)* airy; *(texte)* nicely spaced

aérien, -ienne [aerjɛ̃, -jɛn] *adj (transport, attaque, défense)* air; *(photo)* aerial; *(câble)* overhead; *(léger)* airy

aérobic [aerɔbik] *nf* aerobics *(sing)* • **aéro-club** *(pl* **aéro-clubs** *) nm* flying club • **aérodrome** *nm* aerodrome • **aérodynamique** *adj* streamlined • **aérogare** *nf* air terminal • **aéroglisseur** *nm* hovercraft • **aérogramme** *nm* airmail letter • **aéromodélisme** *nm* model aircraft building and flying • **aéronautique** *nf* aeronautics *(sing)* • **Aéronavale** *nf Br* ≃ Fleet Air Arm, *Am* ≃ Naval Air Service • **aéroport** *nm* airport • **aéroporté, -ée** *adj* airborne • **aérosol** *nm* aerosol

affable [afabl] *adj* affable

affaiblir [afeblir] *vt,* **s'affaiblir** *vpr* to weaken • **affaiblissement** *nm* weakening

affaire [afɛr] *nf (question)* matter, affair; *(marché)* deal; *(firme)* concern, business; *(histoire, scandale)* affair; *(procès)* case; **affaires** *(commerce)* business *(sing)*; *(effets personnels)* belongings; **les Affaires étrangères** *Br* ≃ the Foreign Office, *Am* ≃ the State Department; **avoir a. à qn/qch** to have to deal with sb/sth; **faire une bonne a.** to get a bargain; **tirer qn d'affaire** to get sb out of trouble; **c'est mon a.** that's my business; **ça fera l'a.** that will do nicely; **c'est toute une a.!** it's quite a business!; **a. de cœur** love affair

affairer [afere] **s'affairer** *vpr* to busy oneself; **s'a. autour de qn** to fuss around sb • **affairé, -ée** *adj* busy

affaisser [afese] **s'affaisser** *vpr (personne, bâtiment)* to collapse; *(sol)* to subside • **affaissement** [-ɛsmã] *nm (du sol)* subsidence

affaler [afale] **s'affaler** *vpr* to collapse; **affalé dans un fauteuil** slumped in an armchair

affamé, -ée [afame] *adj* starving

affecter [afɛkte] *vt* (**a**) *(employé)* to appoint (**à** to); *(soldat)* to post (**à** to); *(fonds, crédits, locaux)* to assign (**à** to) (**b**) *(feindre, émouvoir, frapper)* to affect; **a. de faire qch** to pretend to do sth • **affecta-**

tion nf (d'employé) appointment (à to); (de soldat) posting (à to); (de fonds) assignment (à to); Péj (pose, simulacre) affectation • **affecté, -ée** adj Péj (manières, personne) affected

affectif, -ive [afɛktif, -iv] adj emotional

affection [afɛksjɔ̃] nf (attachement) affection; (maladie) ailment; **avoir de l'a. pour qn** to be fond of sb • **affectionner** vt to be fond of

affectueux, -ueuse [afɛktɥø, -ɥøz] adj affectionate

affermir [afɛrmir] vt (autorité) to strengthen; (muscles) to tone up; (voix) to steady

affiche [afiʃ] nf notice; (publicitaire) poster; **être à l'a.** (spectacle) to be on • **affichage** nm bill-posting; Ordinat display; **'a. interdit'** 'stick no bills' • **afficher** vt (avis, affiche) to put up; (prix, horaire, résultat) & Ordinat (message) to display; Péj (sentiment) to show; **a. complet** (spectacle) to be sold out

affilée [afile] **d'affilée** adv in a row

affiler [afile] vt to sharpen

affilier [afilje] **s'affilier** vpr **s'a. à qch** to join sth • **affiliation** nf affiliation

affiner [afine] **1** vt (métal, goût) to refine **2 s'affiner** vpr (goût) to become more refined; (visage) to get thinner

affinité [afinite] nf affinity

affirmatif, -ive [afirmatif, -iv] **1** adj (réponse) & Grammaire affirmative; **il a été a. à ce sujet** he was quite positive about it **2** nf **répondre par l'affirmative** to answer yes

affirmer [afirme] **1** vt (manifester) to assert; (soutenir) to maintain **2 s'affirmer** vpr (personne) to assert oneself; (tendance) to be confirmed • **affirmation** nf assertion

affleurer [aflœre] vi to appear on the surface

affliger [afliʒe] vt (peiner) to distress; (atteindre) to afflict (**de** with)

affluence [aflyɑ̃s] nf (de personnes) crowd; (de marchandises) abundance

affluent [aflyɑ̃] nm tributary

affluer [aflye] vi (sang) to rush (à to); (gens) to flock (**vers** to)

afflux [afly] nm (de sang) rush; (de visiteurs) flood; (de capitaux) influx

affoler [afɔle] **1** vt to throw into a panic **2 s'affoler** vpr to panic • **affolant, -ante** adj terrifying • **affolement** nm panic

affranchir [afrɑ̃ʃir] vt (timbrer) to put a stamp on; (émanciper) to free • **affranchissement** nm (tarif) postage

affréter [afrete] vt to charter

affreux, -euse [afrø, -øz] adj (laid) hideous; (atroce) dreadful; Fam (épouvantable) awful • **affreusement** adv horribly; (en intensif) awfully

affriolant, -ante [afriɔlɑ̃, -ɑ̃t] adj alluring

affront [afrɔ̃] nm insult; **faire un a. à qn** to insult sb

affronter [afrɔ̃te] **1** vt to confront; (mauvais temps) to brave; **a. la colère de qn** to brave the wrath of sb **2 s'affronter** vpr (ennemis, équipes) to clash • **affrontement** nm confrontation

affubler [afyble] vt Péj **a. qn de qch** to set sb up in sth

affût [afy] nm Fig **à l'a. de** on the lookout for

affûter [afyte] vt to sharpen

Afghanistan [afganistɑ̃] nm **l'A.** Afghanistan

afin [afɛ̃] **1** prép **a. de faire qch** in order to do sth **2** conj **a. que...** (+ subjunctive) so that...

Afrique [afrik] nf **l'A.** Africa • **africain, -aine 1** adj African **2** nmf **A., Africaine** African

agacer [agase] vt (personne) to irritate • **agaçant, -ante** adj irritating

âge [ɑʒ] nm age; **quel â. as-tu?** how old are you?; **avant l'â.** before one's time; **d'un certain â.** middle-aged; **d'un â. avancé** elderly; **l'â. adulte** adulthood • **âgé, -ée** adj old; **être â. de six ans** to be six years old; **un enfant â. de six ans** a six-year-old child

agence [aʒɑ̃s] nf agency; (de banque) branch; **a. de voyage** travel agent's; **a. immobilière** Br estate agent's, Am real estate office; **a. matrimoniale** marriage bureau

agencer [aʒɑ̃se] vt to arrange; **bien agencé** (maison, pièce) well laid-out; (phrase) well put-together • **agencement** nm (de maison) layout

agenda [aʒɛ̃da] nm Br diary, Am datebook

> 📖 Il faut noter que le nom anglais **agenda** est un faux ami. Il signifie **ordre du jour**.

agenouiller [aʒnuje] **s'agenouiller** vpr to kneel (down); **être agenouillé** to be kneeling (down)

agent [aʒɑ̃] nm (employé, espion) agent; **a. (de police)** police officer; **a. de change** stockbroker; **a. immobilier** Br estate agent, Am real estate agent; **a. secret** secret agent

aggloméré [aglɔmere] *nm* chipboard
agglomérer [aglɔmere] **s'agglomérer**
vpr to bind together • **agglomération** *nf*
(ville) built-up area, town; **l'a. parisienne**
Paris and its suburbs
agglutiner [aglytine] **s'agglutiner** *vpr*
(personnes) to congregate
aggraver [agrave] **1** *vt (situation, mala-die)* to make worse; *(difficultés)* to in-crease
  2 s'aggraver *vpr (situation, maladie)* to
get worse; *(état de santé)* to deteriorate;
(difficultés) to increase • **aggravation** *nf*
(de maladie) aggravation; *(de conflit)*
worsening
agile [aʒil] *adj* agile, nimble • **agilité** *nf*
agility, nimbleness
agir [aʒir] **1** *vi* to act; *Jur* **a. au nom de qn**
to act on behalf of sb
  2 s'agir *v impersonnel* **de quoi s'agit-il?**
what is it about?; **il s'agit d'argent** it's a
question of money; **il s'agit de se dépêcher** we have to hurry • **agissements** *nmpl*
Péj dealings
agitation [aʒitɑsjɔ̃] *nf (inquiétude)* agitation; *(bougeotte)* restlessness; *(troubles)* unrest
agiter [aʒite] **1** *vt (remuer)* to stir; *(secouer)* to shake; *(brandir)* to wave; *(troubler)* to agitate
  2 s'agiter *vpr (enfant)* to fidget; **s'a. dans
son sommeil** to toss and turn in one's
sleep • **agitateur, -trice** *nmf* agitator
• **agité, -ée** *adj (mer)* rough; *(personne)*
restless; *(enfant)* fidgety; *(period)* unsettled
agneau, -x [aɲo] *nm* lamb
agonie [agɔni] *nf* death throes; **être à l'a.**
to be at death's door • **agoniser** *vi* to be
dying

┌─────────────────────────────────────┐
│ 🖉 Il faut noter que les termes anglais │
│ **agony** et **to agonize** sont des faux amis. │
│ Le premier signifie **douleur atroce** ou **an-** │
│ **goisse** selon le contexte, et le second se │
│ traduit par **se faire beaucoup de souci**. │
└─────────────────────────────────────┘

agrafe [agraf] *nf (pour vêtement)* hook;
(pour papiers) staple • **agrafer** *vt (vêtement)* to fasten; *(papiers)* to staple • **agrafeuse** *nf* stapler
agrandir [agrɑ̃dir] **1** *vt (rendre plus
grand)* to enlarge; *(grossir)* to magnify;
ça agrandit la pièce it makes the room
look bigger
  2 s'agrandir *vpr (entreprise)* to expand;
(ville) to grow • **agrandissement** *nm (d'entreprise)* expansion; *(de ville)* growth; *(de
maison)* extension; *(de photo)* enlargement

agréable [agreabl] *adj* pleasant • **agréablement** [-əmɑ̃] *adv* pleasantly
agréer [agree] *vt (fournisseur)* to approve; **veuillez a. l'expression de mes
salutations distinguées** *(dans une lettre)*
Br yours faithfully, *Am* sincerely • **agréé,
-ée** *adj (fournisseur, centre)* approved
agrégation [agregɑsjɔ̃] *nf* = competitive
examination for recruitment of lycée and
university teachers • **agrégé, -ée** *nmf* =
teacher who has passed the *agrégation*.
agrément [agremɑ̃] *nm (attrait)* charm;
(accord) assent; **voyage d'a.** pleasure trip
• **agrémenter** *vt* to adorn (**de** with); **a. un
récit d'anecdotes** to pepper a story with
anecdotes

┌─────────────────────────────────────┐
│ 🖉 Il faut noter que le nom anglais **agree-** │
│ **ment** est un faux ami. Il signifie **accord**. │
└─────────────────────────────────────┘

agrès [agrɛ] *nmpl (de voilier)* tackle; *(de
gymnastique) Br* apparatus, *Am* equipment
agresser [agrese] *vt* to attack; *(peau)* to
damage; **se faire a.** to be attacked; *(pour
son argent)* to be mugged • **agresseur** *nm*
attacker; *(dans un conflit)* aggressor
• **agression** *nf* attack; *(pour de l'argent)*
mugging; *(d'un État)* aggression; **être victime d'une a.** to be attacked; *(pour son
argent)* to be mugged
agressif, -ive [agresif, -iv] *adj* aggressive • **agressivité** *nf* aggressiveness
agricole [agrikɔl] *adj* agricultural; *(ouvrier, machine)* farm; *(peuple)* farming;
travaux agricoles farm work
agriculteur [agrikyltœr] *nm* farmer
• **agriculture** *nf* farming, agriculture
agripper [agripe] **1** *vt* to clutch
  2 s'agripper *vpr* **s'a. à qn/qch** to cling on
to sb/sth
agronomie [agrɔnɔmi] *nf* agronomics
(sing)
agrume [agrym] *nm* citrus fruit
aguerri, -ie [ageri] *adj* seasoned, hardened
aguets [agɛ] **aux aguets** *adv* on the
lookout
aguicher [agiʃe] *vt* to seduce • **agui-
chant, -ante** *adj* seductive
ahurir [ayrir] *vt (étonner)* to astound;
avoir l'air ahuri to look astounded • **ahuri, -ie** *nmf* numbskull
ai [e] *voir* **avoir**
aide [ɛd] **1** *nf* help, assistance; **à l'a. de
qch** with the aid of sth; **appeler à l'a.** to
call for help; **venir en a. à qn** to help sb; **a.
humanitaire** aid
  2 *nmf (personne)* assistant; **a. familiale**
Br home help, *Am* mother's helper; **a. de**

camp aide-de-camp • **aide-mémoire** *nm inv* notes • **aide-soignante** (*mpl* **aides-soignants,** *fpl* **aides-soignantes**) *nf Br* nursing auxiliary, *Am* nurse's aid

aider [ede] **1** *vt* to help; **a. qn à faire qch** to help sb to do sth **2 s'aider** *vpr* **s'a. de qch** to use sth

aïe [aj] *exclam* ouch!

aie(s), aient [ɛ] *voir* **avoir**

aïeul, -e [ajœl] *nmf Littéraire* grandfather, *f* grandmother

aïeux [ajø] *nmpl Littéraire* forefathers

aigle [ɛgl] *nm* eagle

aiglefin [ɛgləfɛ̃] *nm* haddock

aigre [ɛgr] *adj (acide)* sour; (*parole*) cutting; **d'un ton a.** sharply • **aigre-doux, -douce** (*mpl* **aigres-doux,** *fpl* **aigres-douces**) *adj (sauce)* bitter-sweet • **aigreur** *nf (de goût)* sourness; (*de ton*) sharpness; **aigreurs d'estomac** heartburn

aigrette [ɛgrɛt] *nf (d'oiseau)* crest; (*panache*) plume

aigrir [ɛgrir] **s'aigrir** *vpr (vin)* to turn sour; (*caractère*) to sour • **aigri, -ie** *adj (personne)* embittered

aigu, -uë [egy] *adj (douleur, crise, accent)* acute; (*son*) high-pitched

aiguille [egɥij] *nf (à coudre)* needle; (*de montre*) hand; (*de balance*) pointer; **a. (rocheuse)** peak; **a. de pin** pine needle

aiguiller [egɥije] *vt (train) Br* to shunt, *Am* to switch; *Fig (personne)* to steer (**vers** towards) • **aiguillage** *nm (appareil) Br* points, *Am* switches • **aiguilleur** *nm (de trains)* signalman; **a. du ciel** air-traffic controller

aiguillon [egɥijɔ̃] *nm (dard)* sting; (*stimulant*) spur • **aiguillonner** *vt (stimuler)* to spur on; (*curiosité*) to arouse

aiguiser [egize] *vt (outil)* to sharpen; *Fig (appétit)* to whet

ail [aj] *nm* garlic

aile [ɛl] *nf (de) wing; (de moulin)* sail; (*de voiture*) *Br* wing, *Am* fender; *Fig* **battre de l'a.** to be struggling • **ailé, -ée** [ele] *adj* winged • **aileron** *nm (de requin)* fin; (*d'avion*) aileron; (*d'oiseau*) pinion • **ailier** [elje] *nm Football* winger; *Rugby* wing

aille(s), aillent [aj] *voir* **aller¹**

ailleurs [ajœr] *adv* somewhere else, elsewhere; **partout a.** everywhere else; **d'a.** (*du reste*) besides, anyway; **par a.** (*en outre*) moreover; (*par d'autres côtés*) in other respects

ailloli [ajɔli] *nm* garlic mayonnaise

aimable [ɛmabl] *adj (gentil)* kind; **vous êtes bien a.** it's very kind of you • **aimablement** [-əmã] *adv* kindly

aimant¹ [ɛmã] *nm* magnet • **aimanter** *vt* to magnetize

aimant², -ante [ɛmã, -ãt] *adj* loving

aimer [eme] **1** *vt* to love; **a. bien qn/qch** to like sb/sth; **a. faire qch** to like doing sth; **j'aimerais qu'il vienne** I would like him to come; **a. mieux** to prefer; **j'aimerais mieux qu'elle reste** I'd rather she stayed **2 s'aimer** *vpr* **ils s'aiment** they're in love

aine [ɛn] *nf* groin

aîné, -ée 1 [ene] *adj (de deux enfants)* elder; (*de plus de deux*) eldest **2** *nmf (de deux enfants)* elder; (*de plus de deux*) eldest; **c'est mon a.** he's older than me

ainsi [ɛ̃si] *adv (de cette façon)* in this way; (*alors*) so; **a. que...** as well as...; **et a. de suite** and so on; **pour a. dire** so to speak; *Rel* **a. soit-il!** amen!

air [ɛr] *nm* (**a**) (*gaz, ciel*) air; **prendre l'a.** to get some fresh air; **au grand a.** in the fresh air; **en plein a.** outside; **en l'a.** (*jeter*) (up) in the air; (*paroles, menaces*) empty; **regarder en l'a.** to look up; *Fam* **ficher qch en l'a.** to mess sth up; **dans l'a.** (*grippe, idées*) about, around (**b**) (*expression*) look, appearance; **avoir l'a. fatigué/content** to look tired/happy; **avoir l'a. de s'ennuyer** to look bored; **avoir l'a. de dire la vérité** to look as if one is telling the truth; **a. de famille** family likeness (**c**) (*mélodie*) tune; **a. d'opéra** aria

aire [ɛr] *nf (surface) & Math* area; (*d'oiseau*) eyrie; **a. d'atterrissage** landing strip; **a de jeux** (*children's*) play area; **a. de lancement** launch pad; **a. de repos** (*sur autoroute*) rest area; **a. de stationnement** lay-by

airelle [ɛrɛl] *nf (rouge)* cranberry

aisance [ɛzãs] *nf (facilité)* ease; (*prospérité*) affluence

aise [ɛz] *nf* **à l'a.** (*dans un vêtement*) comfortable; (*dans une situation*) at ease; (*fortuné*) comfortably off; **aimer ses aises** to like one's comforts; **mal à l'a.** uncomfortable, ill at ease • **aisé, -ée** [eze] *adj (fortuné)* comfortably off; (*facile*) easy • **aisément** *adv* easily

aisselle [ɛsɛl] *nf* armpit

ait [ɛ] *voir* **avoir**

ajonc [aʒɔ̃] *nm* gorse

ajouré, -ée [aʒure] *adj (dentelle, architecture)* openwork

ajourner [aʒurne] *vt* to postpone; (*après le début de la séance*) to adjourn • **ajournement** [-əmã] *nm* postponement

ajout [aʒu] *nm* addition (**à** to) • **ajouter 1** *vti* to add (**à** to) **2 s'ajouter** *vpr* **s'a. à qch** to add to sth

ajuster [aʒyste] *vt (appareil, outil)* to adjust; *(coiffure)* to arrange; *(coup)* to aim; *(adapter)* to fit (**à** to); *(vêtement)* to alter • **ajusté, -ée** *adj (veste)* fitting • **ajusteur** *nm (ouvrier)* fitter

alaise [alɛz] *nf* (waterproof) undersheet

alambic [alɑ̃bik] *nm* still

alambiqué, -ée [alɑ̃bike] *adj* convoluted

alangui [alɑ̃gi] *adj* languid

alarme [alarm] *nf* alarm; **sonner l'a.** to sound the alarm; **a. antivol/d'incendie** burglar/fire alarm • **alarmer 1** *vt* to alarm **2 s'alarmer** *vpr* **s'a. de qch** to become alarmed at sth

Albanie [albani] *nf* **l'A.** Albania • **albanais, -aise 1** *adj* Albanian **2** *nmf* **A., Albanaise** Albanian

albâtre [albɑtr] *nm* alabaster

albatros [albatros] *nm* albatross

albinos [albinos] *nmf & adj inv* albino

album [albɔm] *nm* album; **a. de photos** photo album

alcalin, -ine [alkalɛ̃, -in] *adj Chim* alkaline

alchimie [alʃimi] *nf* alchemy

alcool [alkɔl] *nm Chim* alcohol; *(spiritueux)* spirits; **a. à 90°** *Br* surgical spirit, *Am* rubbing alcohol; **a. à brûler** *Br* methylated spirits, *Am* wood alcohol; **a. de poire** pear brandy • **alcoolique** *adj & nmf* alcoholic • **alcoolisée** *adj f* **boisson a.** alcoholic drink; **boisson non a.** soft drink • **alcoolisme** *nm* alcoholism • **Alcootest®** *nm* breath test; *(appareil)* Breathalyzer ®

alcôve [alkov] *nf* alcove

aléas [alea] *nmpl* hazards • **aléatoire** *adj (résultat)* uncertain; *(sélection, nombre)* & *Ordinat* random

alentour [alɑ̃tur] *adv* round about, around; **les villages a.** the surrounding villages • **alentours** *nmpl* surroundings; **aux a. de la ville** in the vicinity of the town; **aux a. de midi** around midday

alerte [alert] **1** *adj (leste)* sprightly; *(éveillé)* alert **2** *nf* alarm; **en état d'a.** on the alert; **donner l'a.** to give the alarm; **a. à la bombe** bomb scare; **fausse a.** false alarm • **alerter** *vt* to alert (**sur** to)

alezan, -ane [alzɑ̃, -an] *adj & nmf (cheval)* chestnut

algèbre [alʒɛbr] *nf* algebra • **algébrique** *adj* algebraic

Alger [alʒe] *nm ou f* Algiers

Algérie [alʒeri] *nf* **l'A.** Algeria • **algérien, -ienne 1** *adj* Algerian **2** *nmf* **A., Algérienne** Algerian

algues [alg] *nfpl* seaweed

alias [aljɑs] *adv* alias

alibi [alibi] *nm* alibi

aliéner [aljene] **1** *vt* to alienate **2 s'aliéner** *vpr* **s'a. qn** to alienate sb • **aliéné, -ée** *nmf* insane person

aligner [aliɲe] **1** *vt* to line up; *(politique)* to align (**sur** with) **2 s'aligner** *vpr (personnes)* to line up; *(pays)* to align oneself (**sur** with) • **alignement** [-əmɑ̃] *nm* alignment; **être dans l'a. de qch** to be in line with sth

aliment [alimɑ̃] *nm* food • **alimentaire** *adj (ration, industrie)* food; **produits alimentaires** foods • **alimentation** *nf (action)* feeding; *(en eau, électricité)* supply(ing); *(régime)* diet; *(nourriture)* food; **magasin d'a.** grocer's, grocery store; **a. papier** *(d'imprimante)* paper feed • **alimenter** *vt (nourrir)* to feed; *(fournir)* to supply (**en** with); *(débat, feu)* to fuel

alinéa [alinea] *nm (texte)* paragraph

alité, -ée [alite] *adj* bedridden

allaiter [alete] *vt (femme)* to breast-feed; *(sujet: animal)* to suckle

allant [alɑ̃] *nm* energy

allécher [aleʃe] *vt* to tempt

allée [ale] *nf (de parc)* path; *(de ville)* avenue; *(de cinéma, de supermarché)* aisle; *(devant une maison)* driveway; **allées et venues** comings and goings

allégation [alegasjɔ̃] *nf* allegation

alléger [aleʒe] *vt (impôt)* to reduce; *(fardeau)* to lighten • **allégé, -ée** *adj (fromage)* low-fat

allégorie [alegɔri] *nf* allegory

allègre [alɛgr] *adj* lively, cheerful • **allégresse** *nf* joy

alléguer [alege] *vt (excuse)* to put forward

alléluia [aleluja] *nm* hallelujah

Allemagne [almaɲ] *nf* **l'A.** Germany • **allemand, -ande 1** *adj* German **2** *nmf* **A., Allemande** German **3** *nm (langue)* German

aller¹* [ale] **1** *(aux être)* *vi* to go; **a. à Paris** to go to Paris; **a. à la pêche** to go fishing; **a. faire qch** to go and do sth; **va voir!** go and see!; **a. bien/mieux** *(personne)* to be well/better; **comment vas-tu?, (comment) ça va?** how are you?; **ça va!** all right!, fine!; **allez-y** go ahead; **j'y vais** I'm coming; **allons (donc)!** come on!, come off it!; **allez! au lit!** go to bed!; **ça va de soi** that's obvious

2 *v aux (futur proche)* **a. faire qch** to be going to do sth; **il va venir** he'll come; **il va partir** he's about to leave

3 s'en aller [sɑ̃nale] *vpr (personne)* to go away; *(tache)* to come out
aller² [ale] *nm* outward journey; **a. (simple)** *Br* single (ticket), *Am* one-way (ticket); **a. (et) retour** *Br* return (ticket), *Am* round-trip (ticket)
allergie [alɛrʒi] *nf* allergy • **allergique** *adj* allergic (**à** to).
alliage [aljaʒ] *nm* alloy
alliance [aljɑ̃s] *nf (anneau)* wedding ring; *(mariage)* marriage; *(de pays)* alliance
allier [alje] **1** *vt (associer)* to combine (**à** with); *(pays)* to ally (**à** with); *(famille)* to unite by marriage; **a. l'intelligence à la beauté** to combine intelligence and beauty
2 s'allier *vpr (couleurs)* to combine; *(pays)* to become allied (**à** with); **s'a. à contre qn/qch** to unite against sb/sth • **allié, -ée** *nmf* ally
alligator [aligatɔr] *nm* alligator
allô [alo] *exclam* hello!
allocation [alɔkasjɔ̃] *nf (somme)* allowance; **a. (de) chômage** unemployment benefit; **a. (de) logement** housing benefit; **allocations familiales** child benefit
allocution [alɔkysjɔ̃] *nf* address
allonger [alɔ̃ʒe] **1** *vt (bras)* to stretch out; *(jupe)* to lengthen; *(sauce)* to thin; **a. le pas** to quicken one's pace
2 *vi (jours)* to get longer
3 s'allonger *vpr (jours)* to get longer; *(personne)* to lie down • **allongé, -ée** *adj (étiré)* elongated; **être a.** to be lying down
allouer [alwe] *vt* **a. qch à qn** *(ration)* to allocate sb sth; *(indemnité)* to grant sb sth
allumer [alyme] **1** *vt (feu, pipe)* to light; *(électricité, radio)* to switch on; *(incendie)* to start; *Fig (passion)* to arouse; **laisser la cuisine allumée** to leave the light on in the kitchen
2 s'allumer *vpr (lumière, lampe)* to come on; **où est-ce que ça s'allume?** where does it switch? • **allumage** *nm (de feu)* lighting; *(de moteur)* ignition • **allume-gaz** *nm inv* gas lighter • **allumeuse** *nf Fam (femme)* teaser
allumette [alymɛt] *nf* match
allure [alyr] *nf (vitesse)* speed; *(démarche)* gait, walk; *(maintien)* bearing; **à toute a.** at top speed; **avoir de l'a.** to look stylish; **avoir des allures de malfrat** to look like a crook
allusion [alyzjɔ̃] *nf* allusion (**à** to); *(voilée)* hint; **faire a. à qch** to allude to sth; *(en termes voilés)* to hint at sth
almanach [almana] *nm* almanac

aloi [alwa] *nm* **de bon a.** *(succès)* deserved; *(plaisanterie)* in good taste
alors [alɔr] *adv (donc)* so; *(à ce moment-là)* then; *(dans ce cas)* in that case; **a. que...** *(lorsque)* when...; *(tandis que)* whereas...; **et a.?** so what?; **a., tu viens?** are you coming then?
alouette [alwɛt] *nf* (sky)lark
alourdir [alurdir] **1** *vt (chose)* to make heavier; *Fig (phrase)* to make cumbersome; *(charges)* to increase
2 s'alourdir *vpr* to get heavy
aloyau [alwajo] *nm* sirloin
alpage [alpaʒ] *nm* mountain pasture • **Alpes** *nfpl* **les A.** the Alps • **alpestre, alpin, -ine** *adj* alpine
alphabet [alfabɛ] *nm* alphabet • **alphabétique** *adj* alphabetical • **alphabétisation** *nf* teaching of literacy
alphanumérique [alfanymerik] *adj* alphanumeric
alpinisme [alpinism] *nm* mountaineering; **faire de l'a.** to go mountaineering • **alpiniste** *nmf* mountaineer
altercation [altɛrkasjɔ̃] *nf* altercation
altérer [altere] **1** *vt* (**a**) *(viande, vin)* to spoil; *(santé)* to damage (**b**) *(changer)* to affect
2 s'altérer *vpr (santé, relations)* to deteriorate
alternatif, -ive [altɛrnatif, -iv] *adj (successif)* alternating; *(de remplacement)* alternative • **alternative** *nf* alternative • **alternativement** *adv* alternately
alterner [altɛrne] **1** *vt (crops)* to rotate
2 *vi (se succéder)* to alternate (**avec** with); *(personnes)* to take turns (**avec** with) • **alternance** *nf* alternation; **en a.** alternately
Altesse [altɛs] *nf* **son A. royale** His/Her Royal Highness
altier, -ière [altje, -jɛr] *adj* haughty
altitude [altityd] *nf* altitude; **en a.** at altitude; **prendre de l'a.** to climb
alto [alto] *nm (instrument)* viola
altruisme [altrɥism] *nm* altruism • **altruiste** *adj* altruistic
aluminium [alyminjɔm] *nm Br* aluminium, *Am* aluminum; **papier (d')a.** tinfoil
alunir [alynir] *vi* to land on the moon
alvéole [alveɔl] *nf (de ruche)* cell; *(dentaire)* socket • **alvéolé, -ée** *adj* honeycombed
amabilité [amabilite] *nf* kindness; **auriez-vous l'a. de...?** would you be so kind as to...?
amadouer [amadwe] *vt* to coax
amaigrir [amɛgrir] *vt* to make thin(ner);

régime **amaigrissant** *Br* slimming diet, *Am* weight reduction diet •**amaigri, -ie** *adj* thin(-ner) •**amaigrissement** *nm (involontaire)* weight loss; *(volontaire)* dieting, *Br* slimming

amalgame [amalgam] *nm (mélange)* combination •**amalgamer** *vt (confondre)* to lump together

amande [amɑ̃d] *nf* almond

amant [amɑ̃] *nm* lover

amarre [amar] *nf (mooring)* rope; **amarres** moorings •**amarrer** *vt (bateau)* to moor

amas [amɑ] *nm* heap, pile •**amasser 1** *vt* to amass **2 s'amasser** *vpr (preuves, foule)* to build up; *(neige)* to pile up

amateur [amatœr] **1** *nm (non professionnel)* amateur; **a. de tennis** tennis enthusiast; **a. d'art** art lover; **faire de la photo en a.** to be an amateur photographer; *Péj* **c'est du travail d'a.** it's amateurish work

  2 *adj* **une équipe a.** an amateur team; •**amateurisme** *nm Sport* amateurism

amazone [amazɔn] *nf* horsewoman; **monter en a.** to ride sidesaddle

ambages [ɑ̃baʒ] **sans ambages** *adv* without beating about the bush

ambassade [ɑ̃basad] *nf* embassy •**ambassadeur, -drice** *nmf* ambassador; **l'a. de France au Japon** the French ambassador to Japan

ambiance [ɑ̃bjɑ̃s] *nf* atmosphere; *Fam* **mettre de l'a.** to liven things up •**ambiant, -ante** *adj* surrounding; *(gaieté, enthousiasme)* pervading; **température a.** room temperature

ambidextre [ɑ̃bidɛkstr] *adj* ambidextrous

ambigu, -uë [ɑ̃bigy] *adj* ambiguous •**ambiguïté** [-gɥite] *nf* ambiguity

ambitieux, -ieuse [ɑ̃bisjø, -jøz] *adj* ambitious •**ambition** *nf* ambition •**ambitionner** *vt* to aspire to; **il ambitionne de faire qch** his ambition is to do sth

ambre [ɑ̃br] *nm (résine)* amber

ambulance [ɑ̃bylɑ̃s] *nf* ambulance •**ambulancier, -ière** *nmf* ambulance driver

ambulant, -ante [ɑ̃bylɑ̃, -ɑ̃t] *adj* travelling, itinerant; **marchand a.** (street) hawker

âme [ɑm] *nf* soul; **de toute mon â.** with all my heart; **en mon â. et conscience** to the best of my knowledge and belief; **rendre l'â.** to give up the ghost; **avoir charge d'âmes** to be responsible for human life; **je n'ai rencontré â. qui vive** I didn't meet a (living) soul; **â. sœur** soul mate

améliorer [ameljɔre] *vt*, **s'améliorer** *vpr* to improve •**amélioration** *nf* improvement

amen [amɛn] *adv* amen

aménager [amenaʒe] *vt (changer)* to adjust, *(maison)* to convert (**en** into) •**aménagement** *nm (changement)* adjustment; *(de pièce)* conversion (**en** into); **a. du temps de travail** flexibility of working hours; **a. du territoire** regional development

amende [amɑ̃d] *nf* fine; **infliger une a. à qn** to impose a fine on sb; **faire a. honorable** to apologize

amender [amɑ̃de] **1** *vt (texte de loi)* to amend

  2 s'amender *vpr* to mend one's ways

amener [amne] **1** *vt (apporter)* to bring; *(causer)* to bring about; *(tirer à soi)* to pull in; **a. qn à faire qch** *(sujet: personne)* to get sb to do sth; **ce qui nous amène à parler de...** which brings us to the issue of...

  2 s'amener *vpr Fam* to turn up

amenuiser [amənɥize] **s'amenuiser** *vpr* to dwindle; *(écart)* to get smaller

amer, -ère [amɛr] *adj* bitter •**amèrement** *adv* bitterly

Amerindien, -ienne [amerɑ̃djɛ̃, -jɛn] *nmf* American Indian

Amérique [amerik] *nf* **l'A.** America; **l'A. du Nord/du Sud** North/South America; **l'A. latine** Latin America •**américain, -aine 1** *adj* American **2** *nmf* **A., Américaine** American

amerrir [amerir] *vi* to make a sea landing; *(cabine spatiale)* to splash down

amertume [amɛrtym] *nf* bitterness

améthyste [ametist] *nf* amethyst

ameublement [amœbləmɑ̃] *nm (meubles)* furniture

ameuter [amøte] *vt (personnes)* to bring out; **elle va a. tout le quartier si elle continue à hurler comme ça!** she'll have the whole neighbourhood out if she carries on shouting like that!

ami, -ie [ami] **1** *nmf* friend; **petit a.** boyfriend; **petite amie** girlfriend

  2 *adj* friendly; **être a. avec qn** to be friends with sb

amiable [amjabl] **à l'amiable 1** *adj* amicable **2** *adv* amicably

amiante [amjɑ̃t] *nm* asbestos

amical, -e, -aux, -ales [amikal, -o] *adj* friendly •**amicale** *nf* association •**amicalement** *adv* in a friendly manner

amidon [amidɔ̃] *nm* starch •**amidonner** *vt* to starch

amincir [amɛ̃sir] **1** *vt* to make thin(ner); **cette robe t'amincit** that dress makes you look thinner
2 s'amincir *vpr* to become thinner
amiral, -aux [amiral, -o] *nm* admiral • **amirauté** *nf* admiralty
amitié [amitje] *nf* friendship; **prendre qn en a.** to befriend sb; **faites-moi l'a.** **de le lui dire** would you be so kind as to tell him?; **mes amitiés à votre mère** best wishes to your mother
ammoniaque [amɔnjak] *nf (liquide)* ammonia
amnésie [amnezi] *nf* amnesia • **amnésique** *adj* amnesic
amniocentèse [amnjosɛ̃tɛz] *nf Méd* amniocentesis
amnistie [amnisti] *nf* amnesty
amocher [amɔʃe] *vt Fam (personne)* to beat up; **se faire a.** to get beaten up
amoindrir [amwɛ̃drir] *vt*, **s'amoindrir** *vpr* to diminish
amollir [amɔlir] *vt*, **s'amollir** *vpr* to soften
amonceler [amɔ̃sle] *vt*, **s'amonceler** *vpr* to pile up; *(preuves)* to accumulate • **amoncellement** [-sɛlmɑ̃] *nm* heap, pile
amont [amɔ̃] **en amont** *adv* upstream (**de** from)
amoral, -e, -aux, -ales [amɔral, -o] *adj* amoral
amorce [amɔrs] *nf (début)* start; *(de pêcheur)* bait; *(détonateur)* detonator; *(de pistolet d'enfant)* cap • **amorcer 1** *vt (commencer)* to start; *(hameçon)* to bait; *(bombe)* to arm; *Ordinat* to boot up **2 s'amorcer** *vpr* to start
amorphe [amɔrf] *adj* listless, apathetic
amortir [amɔrtir] *vt (coup)* to absorb; *(bruit)* to deaden; *(chute)* to break; *(achat)* to recoup the costs of; *Fin (dette)* to pay off; *Football* to trap • **amortissement** *nm (d'un emprunt)* redemption • **amortisseur** *nm (de véhicule)* shock absorber
amour [amur] *nm (sentiment, liaison)* love; **avec a.** lovingly; **faire qch par a. pour qn** to do sth out of love for sb; **faire l'a. avec qn** to make love with sb; **pour l'a. du ciel!** for heaven's sake; **mon a.** my darling, my love; **tu es un a.!** you're an angel!; **à tes amours!** *(quand on éternue)* bless you! • **s'amouracher** *vpr Péj* to become infatuated (**de** with) • **amoureux, -euse 1** *adj* **être a. de qn** in love with sb; **tomber a. de qn** to fall in love with sb; **vie amoureuse** love life **2** *nm* boyfriend; **un couple d'a.** a pair of lovers • **amour-propre** *nm* self-respect

amovible [amɔvibl] *adj* removable, detachable
ampère [ɑ̃pɛr] *nm Él* ampere
amphétamine [ɑ̃fetamin] *nf* amphetamine
amphi [ɑ̃fi] *nm Fam (à l'université)* lecture hall
amphibie [ɑ̃fibi] *adj* amphibious
amphithéâtre [ɑ̃fiteatr] *nm (romain)* amphitheatre; *(à l'université)* lecture hall
ample [ɑ̃pl] *adj (vêtement)* full; *(geste)* sweeping; **de plus amples renseignements** more detailed information; **jusqu'à plus a. informé** until further information is available • **amplement** [-əmɑ̃] *adv* amply, fully; **c'est a. suffisant** it is more than enough • **ampleur** *nf (de vêtement)* fullness; *(importance)* scale, extent; **prendre de l'a.** to grow in size
amplifier [ɑ̃plifje] **1** *vt (son)* to amplify; *(phénomène)* to intensify
2 s'amplifier *vpr (son)* to increase; *(phénomène)* to intensify • **amplificateur** *nm* amplifier • **amplification** *nf (de son)* amplification; *(de phénomène)* intensification
amplitude [ɑ̃plityd] *nf (de désastre)* magnitude; *(variation)* range
ampoule [ɑ̃pul] *nf (électrique)* (light) bulb; *(sur la peau)* blister; *(de médicament)* phial
ampoulé, -ée [ɑ̃pule] *adj (style)* bombastic
amputer [ɑ̃pyte] *vt (membre)* to amputate; *Fig* to slash; **a. qn de la jambe** to amputate sb's leg • **amputation** *nf (de membre)* amputation
amuse-gueule [amyzgœl] *nm inv* appetizer
amuser [amyze] **1** *vt* to amuse; **cette histoire l'a beaucoup amusé** he found the story very amusing
2 s'amuser *vpr* to amuse oneself; **s'a. avec qn/qch** to play with sb/sth; **s'a. à faire qch** to amuse oneself doing sth; **bien s'a.** to have a good time • **amusant, -ante** *adj* amusing • **amusement** *nm* amusement
amygdales [amidal] *nfpl* tonsils
an [ɑ̃] *nm* year; **il a dix ans** he's ten (years old); **par a.** per year; **en l'an 2000** in the year 2000; **bon a., mal a.** on average over the years
anabolisant [anabɔlizɑ̃] *nm* anabolic steroid
anachronisme [anakrɔnism] *nm* anachronism • **anachronique** *adj* anachronistic

anagramme [anagram] *nf* anagram

analogie [analɔʒi] *nf* analogy • **analogue** *adj* similar (**à** to)

analphabète [analfabɛt] *adj & nmf* illiterate • **analphabétisme** *nm* illiteracy

analyse [analiz] *nf* analysis; **a. grammaticale** parsing; **a. du sang/d'urine** blood/urine test; **être en a.** *(en traitement)* to be in analysis • **analyser** *vt* to analyse; *(phrase)* to parse • **analytique** *adj* analytical

ananas [anana(s)] *nm* pineapple

anarchie [anarʃi] *nf* anarchy • **anarchique** *adj* anarchic • **anarchiste 1** *adj* anarchistic **2** *nmf* anarchist

anathème [anatɛm] *nm (condamnation) & Rel* anathema

anatomie [anatɔmi] *nf* anatomy • **anatomique** *adj* anatomical

ancestral, -e, -aux, -ales [ɑ̃sɛstral, -o] *adj* ancestral

ancêtre [ɑ̃sɛtr] *nm* ancestor

anche [ɑ̃ʃ] *nf Mus* reed

anchois [ɑ̃ʃwa] *nm* anchovy

ancien, -ienne [ɑ̃sjɛ̃, -jɛn] **1** *adj (vieux)* old; *(meuble)* antique; *(qui n'est plus)* former, old; *(dans une fonction)* senior; **dans l'a. temps** in the old days; **a. élève** *Br* former pupil, *Am* alumnus; **a. combattant** *Br* ex-serviceman, *Am* veteran

2 *nmf (par l'âge)* elder; **c'est un a. de la maison** he's been in the firm for a long time • **anciennement** *adv* formerly • **ancienneté** *nf (âge)* age; *(expérience)* seniority

ancre [ɑ̃kr] *nf* anchor; **jeter l'a.** to (cast) anchor; **lever l'a.** to weigh anchor • **ancrer** *vt* (**a**) *(navire)* to anchor; **être ancré** to be at anchor (**b**) *Fig (idée, sentiment)* to become rooted; **ancré dans** rooted in

Andorre [ɑ̃dɔr] *nf* Andorra

andouille [ɑ̃duj] *nf* (**a**) *(charcuterie)* = sausage made from pigs' intestines (**b**) *Fam (idiot)* twit

âne [ɑn] *nm (animal)* donkey; *Péj (personne)* ass

aneantir [aneɑ̃tir] *vt (ville)* to destroy; *(armée)* to crush; *(espoirs)* to shatter • **anéanti, -ie** *adj (épuisé)* exhausted; *(accablé)* overwhelmed; **a. par le chagrin** overcome by grief • **anéantissement** *nm (de ville)* destruction; *(d'espoir)* shattering; **dans un état d'a. total** utterly crushed

anecdote [anɛkdɔt] *nf* anecdote • **anecdotique** *adj* anecdotal

anémie [anemi] *nf* an(a)emia • **anémique** *adj* an(a)emic

anémone [anemɔn] *nf* anemone

ânerie [ɑnri] *nf (parole)* stupid remark; *(action)* stupid act

ânesse [ɑnɛs] *nf* she-ass

anesthésie [anɛstezi] *nf* an(a)esthesia; **être sous a.** to be under ana(e)sthetic; **a. générale/locale** general/local an(a)esthetic • **anesthésier** *vt* to an(a)esthetize • **anesthésiste** *nmf Br* an(a)esthetist, *Am* anesthesiologist

aneth [anɛt] *nm* dill

ange [ɑ̃ʒ] *nm* angel; **être aux anges** to be in seventh heaven; **a. gardien** guardian angel • **angélique 1** *adj* angelic **2** *nf Culin* angelica

angine [ɑ̃ʒin] *nf* sore throat; **a. de poitrine** angina (pectoris)

anglais, -aise [ɑ̃glɛ, -ez] **1** *adj* English **2** *nmf* **A., Anglaise** Englishman, Englishwoman; **les A.** the English **3** *nm (langue)* English **4** *nf Fam* **filer à l'anglaise** to slip away

angle [ɑ̃gl] *nm (point de vue) & Math* angle; *(coin de rue)* corner; **la maison qui fait l'a.** the house on the corner; *Aut* **a. mort** blind spot

Angleterre [ɑ̃glətɛr] *nf* **l'A.** England

anglican, -ane [ɑ̃glikɑ̃, -an] *adj & nmf* Anglican

anglicisme [ɑ̃glisism] *nm* Anglicism

anglo- [ɑ̃glɔ] *préf* Anglo- • **anglo-normand, -ande** *adj* **les îles anglo-normandes** the Channel Islands • **anglophile** *adj & nmf* anglophile • **anglophone 1** *adj* English-speaking **2** *nmf* English speaker • **anglo-saxon, -onne** *(mpl* **anglo-saxons,** *fpl* **anglo-saxonnes)** *adj & nmf* Anglo-Saxon

angoisse [ɑ̃gwas] *nf* anguish; **une crise d'a.** an anxiety attack; *Fam* **c'est l'a.!** what a drag! • **angoissant, -ante** *adj (nouvelle)* distressing; *(attente)* agonizing; *(livre)* frightening • **angoissé, -ée** *adj (personne)* anxious; *(cri, regard)* anguished • **angoisser 1** *vt* **a. qn** to make sb anxious **2** *vi Fam* to get worked up **3 s'angoisser** *vpr* to get anxious

angora [ɑ̃gɔra] *nm (laine)* angora; **pull en a.** angora sweater

anguille [ɑ̃gij] *nf* eel

angulaire [ɑ̃gylɛr] *adj* **pierre a.** cornerstone • **anguleux, -euse** *adj (visage)* angular

anicroche [anikrɔʃ] *nf* hitch, snag

animal, -aux [animal, -o] **1** *nm* animal; **a. domestique** pet **2** *adj (règne, graisse)* animal

animateur, -trice [animatœr, -tris] *nmf*

(de télévision, de radio) presenter; *(de club)* leader

animer [anime] **1** *vt (débat, groupe)* to lead; *(jeu télévisé)* to present; *(désir, ambition)* to drive; **la joie qui animait son visage** the joy which made his/her face light up

2 s'animer *vpr (rue)* to come to life; *(visage)* to light up; *(conversation)* to get more lively • **animation** *nf (vie)* life; *(divertissement)* event; *Cin* animation; **parler avec a.** to speak animatedly; **mettre de l'a. dans une soirée** to liven up a party • **animé, -ée** *adj (personne, réunion, conversation)* lively; *(rue, quartier)* busy

animosité [animozite] *nf* animosity

anis [ani(s)] *nm (boisson, parfum)* aniseed; **boisson à l'a.** aniseed drink • **anisette** *nf* anisette

ankylose [ɑ̃kiloz] *nf* stiffness • **ankylosé, -ée** *adj* stiff • **s'ankyloser** *vpr* to stiffen up

annales [anal] *nfpl* annals; *Fig* **rester dans les a.** to go down in history

anneau, -x [ano] *nm (bague)* ring; *(de chaîne)* link; *Gym* **les anneaux** the rings

année [ane] *nf* year; **les années 90** the nineties; **bonne a.!** Happy New Year!

annexe [anɛks] **1** *nf (bâtiment)* annexe; *(de lettre)* enclosure; *(de livre)* appendix; **document en a.** enclosed document

2 *adj (pièces)* enclosed; *(revenus)* supplementary; **bâtiment a.** annex(e) • **annexer** *vt (pays)* to annex; *(document)* to append • **annexion** *nf* annexation

annihiler [aniile] *vt (ville, armée)* to annihilate

anniversaire [anivɛrsɛr] **1** *nm (d'événement)* anniversary; *(de naissance)* birthday; **gâteau d'a.** birthday cake

2 *adj* **date a.** anniversary

annonce [anɔ̃s] *nf (déclaration)* announcement; *(publicitaire)* advertisement; *(indice)* sign; **passer une a. dans un journal** to put an advert in a newspaper; **petites annonces** classified advertisements; *Br* small ads • **annoncer 1** *vt (déclarer)* to announce; *(dans la presse)* *(soldes, exposition)* to advertise; *(indiquer)* to herald; **a. qn** *(visiteur)* to show sb in **2 s'annoncer** *vpr* **ça s'annonce bien/mal** things aren't looking too bad/good • **annonceur** *nm (publicitaire)* advertiser • **annonciateur, -trice** *adj* **signes annonciateurs de crise** signs that a crisis is on the way

Annonciation [anɔ̃sjasjɔ̃] *nf* **l'A.** Annunciation

annoter [anɔte] *vt* to annotate • **annotation** *nf* annotation

annuaire [anɥɛr] *nm (d'organisme)* yearbook; *(liste d'adresses)* directory; **a. téléphonique** telephone directory; **a. électronique** electronic phone directory

annualiser [anɥalize] *vt* to annualize

annuel, -elle [anɥɛl] *adj* annual, yearly • **annuellement** *adv* annually • **annuité** *nf (d'emprunt)* annual repayment

annulaire [anɥlɛr] *nm* ring finger

annuler [anyle] *vt (commande, rendez-vous)* to cancel; *(dette)* to write off; *(mariage)* to annul; *(jugement)* to quash

2 s'annuler *vpr* to cancel each other out • **annulation** *nf (de commande, de rendez-vous)* cancellation; *(de dette)* writing off; *(de mariage)* annulment; *(de jugement)* quashing; *Ordinat* deletion

anoblir [anɔblir] *vt* to ennoble

anodin, -ine [anɔdɛ̃, -in] *adj (remarque)* harmless; *(personne)* insignificant; *(blessure)* slight

anomalie [anɔmali] *nf (bizarrerie)* anomaly; *(difformité)* abnormality

ânon [ɑnɔ̃] *nm* little donkey

ânonner [ɑnɔne] *vt* to stumble through

anonymat [anɔnima] *nm* anonymity; **garder l'a.** to remain anonymous • **anonyme** *adj & nmf* anonymous

anorak [anɔrak] *nm* anorak

anorexie [anɔrɛksi] *nf Méd* anorexia • **anorexique** *adj & nmf* anorexic

anormal, -e, -aux, -ales [anɔrmal, -o] *adj (non conforme)* abnormal; *(mentalement)* educationally subnormal; *(injuste)* unfair

ANPE [aɛnpeø] *(abrév* **agence nationale pour l'emploi)** *nf* = French State employment agency

anse [ɑ̃s] *nf* **(a)** *(de tasse, de panier)* handle **(b)** *(baie)* cove

antagonisme [ɑ̃tagɔnism] *nm* antagonism • **antagoniste 1** *adj* antagonistic **2** *nmf* antagonist

antan [ɑ̃tɑ̃] **d'antan** *adj Littéraire* of yesteryear

antarctique [ɑ̃tarktik] **1** *adj* Antarctic **2** *nm* **l'A.** the Antarctic, Antarctica

antécédent [ɑ̃tesedɑ̃] *nm Grammaire* antecedent; **antécédents** *(de personne)* past record; **antécédents médicaux** medical history

antenne [ɑ̃tɛn] *nf (de radio, de satellite)* aerial, antenna; *(d'insecte)* antenna, feeler; *(société)* branch; **être à l'a.** to be on the air; **rendre l'a.** to hand over; **hors a.** off the air; *Mil* **a. chirurgicale** field hospital; **a. parabolique** satellite dish

antérieur, -e [ɑ̃terjœr] *adj (période)* former; *(année)* previous; *(date)* earlier; *(placé devant)* front; **membre a.** forelimb; **a. à qch** prior to sth • **antérieurement** *adv* previously • **antériorité** *nf* precedence

anthologie [ɑ̃tɔlɔʒi] *nf* anthology

anthropologie [ɑ̃trɔpɔlɔʒi] *nf* anthropology

anthropophage [ɑ̃trɔpɔfaʒ] *nm* cannibal • **anthropophagie** *nf* cannibalism

antiaérien, -ienne [ɑ̃tiaerjɛ̃, -jɛn] *adj* **canon a.** anti-aircraft gun; **abri a.** air-raid shelter

antiatomique [ɑ̃tiatɔmik] *adj* **abri a.** fallout shelter

antibiotique [ɑ̃tibjɔtik] *nm* antibiotic; **sous antibiotiques** on antibiotics

antibrouillard [ɑ̃tibrujar] *adj & nm* **(phare) a.** fog lamp

anticancéreux, -euse [ɑ̃tikɑ̃serø, -øz] *adj* **centre a.** cancer hospital

antichambre [ɑ̃tiʃɑ̃br] *nf* antechamber

antichoc [ɑ̃tiʃɔk] *adj inv* shock-proof

anticiper [ɑ̃tisipe] *vti* **a. (sur)** to anticipate • **anticipation** *nf* anticipation; **par a.** in advance; **d'a.** *(roman, film)* science-fiction • **anticipé, -ée** *adj (retraite, retour)* early; *(paiement)* advance; **avec mes remerciements anticipés** thanking you in advance

anticlérical, -e, -aux, -ales [ɑ̃tiklerikal, -o] *adj* anticlerical

anticommuniste [ɑ̃tikɔmynist] *adj* anti-communist

anticonformiste [ɑ̃tikɔ̃fɔrmist] *adj & nmf* nonconformist

anticonstitutionnel, -elle [ɑ̃tikɔ̃stitysjɔnɛl] *adj* unconstitutional

anticorps [ɑ̃tikɔr] *nm* antibody

anticyclone [ɑ̃tisiklon] *nm* anticyclone

antidémocratique [ɑ̃tidemɔkratik] *adj* undemocratic

antidépresseur [ɑ̃tidepresœr] *nm* antidepressant

antidérapant, -ante [ɑ̃tiderapɑ̃, -ɑ̃t] *adj (surface, pneu)* non-skid; *(semelle)* non-slip

antidopage [ɑ̃tidɔpaʒ] *adj* **contrôle a.** drug detection test

antidote [ɑ̃tidɔt] *nm* antidote

antigel [ɑ̃tiʒɛl] *nm* antifreeze

antihistaminique [ɑ̃tiistaminik] *adj* *Méd* antihistamine

anti-inflamatoire [ɑ̃tiɛ̃flamatwar] *adj* *Méd* anti-inflamatory

Antilles [ɑ̃tij] *nfpl* **les A.** the West Indies • **antillais, -aise 1** *adj* West Indian **2** *nmf* **A., Antillaise** West Indian

antilope [ɑ̃tilɔp] *nf* antelope

antimilitariste [ɑ̃timilitarist] *adj* antimilitarist

antimite [ɑ̃timit] *nm* **de l'a.** mothballs

antinomie [ɑ̃tinɔmi] *nf* antinomy

antinucléaire [ɑ̃tinykleɛr] *adj* antinuclear

Antiope [ɑ̃tjɔp] *n =* French Teletex system providing subtitles for the deaf

antioxydant, -ante [ɑ̃tiɔksidɑ̃, -ɑ̃t] *adj & nm* antioxydant

antipathie [ɑ̃tipati] *nf* antipathy • **antipathique** *adj* unpleasant; **elle m'est a.** I find her unpleasant

antipelliculaire [ɑ̃tipelikylɛr] *adj* **shampooing a.** dandruff shampoo

antipodes [ɑ̃tipɔd] *nmpl* antipodes; **être aux a. de** to be on the other side of the world from; *Fig* to be the exact opposite of

antipoison [ɑ̃tipwazɔ̃] *adj inv* *Méd* **centre a.** poisons unit

antique [ɑ̃tik] *adj (de l'Antiquité)* ancient • **antiquaire** *nmf* antique dealer • **antiquité** *nf (objet ancien)* antique; **l'a. grecque/romaine** ancient Greece/Rome; **antiquités** *(dans un musée)* antiquities

antirabique [ɑ̃tirabik] *adj* *Méd* antirabies

antireflet [ɑ̃tirəflɛ] *adj inv* non-reflecting

antirides [ɑ̃tirid] *adj inv* anti-wrinkle

antirouille [ɑ̃tiruj] *adj inv* antirust

antisèche [ɑ̃tisɛʃ] *nf* *Fam* crib sheet

antisémite [ɑ̃tisemit] *adj* anti-Semitic • **antisémitisme** *nm* anti-Semitism

antiseptique [ɑ̃tisɛptik] *adj & nm* antiseptic

antisocial, -e, -aux, -ales [ɑtisɔsjal, -o] *adj* antisocial

antitabac [ɑ̃titaba] *adj inv* **lutte a.** anti-smoking campaign

antiterroriste [ɑ̃titerɔrist] *adj* anti-terrorist

antithèse [ɑ̃titɛz] *nf* antithesis

antivariolique [ɑ̃tivarjɔlik] *adj* *Méd* **vaccin a.** smallpox vaccine

antivol [ɑ̃tivɔl] *nm* anti-theft device

antre [ɑ̃tr] *nm (de lion)* den

anus [anys] *nm* anus

Anvers [ɑ̃ver(s)] *nm ou f* Antwerp

anxiété [ɑ̃ksjete] *nf* anxiety • **anxieux, -ieuse 1** *adj* anxious **2** *nmf* worrier

août [u(t)] *nm* August • **aoûtien, -ienne** [ausjɛ̃, -jen] *nmf* August *Br* holidaymaker *or Am* vacationer

apaiser [apeze] **1** *vt (personne)* to calm (down); *(douleur)* to soothe; *(craintes)* to allay

2 s'apaiser *vpr (personne, colère)* to calm down; *(tempête, douleur)* to subside • **apaisant, -ante** *adj* soothing

apanage [apanaʒ] *nm* prerogative

aparté [aparte] *nm Théâtre* aside; *(dans une réunion)* private exchange; **en a.** in private

apartheid [aparted] *nm* apartheid

apathie [apati] *nf* apathy • **apathique** *adj* apathetic

apatride [apatrid] *nmf* stateless person

apercevoir* [apɛrsəvwar] **1** *vt* to see; *(brièvement)* to catch a glimpse of

2 s'apercevoir *vpr* **s'a. de qch** to realize sth; **s'a. que...** to realize that... • **aperçu** *nm (idea)* general idea; **donner à qn un a. de la situation** to give sb a general idea of the situation

apéritif [aperitif] *nm* aperitif; **prendre un a.** to have a drink before the meal • **apéro** *nm Fam* aperitif

apesanteur [apəzɑ̃tœr] *nf* weightlessness

à-peu-près [apøprɛ] *nm inv* vague approximation

apeuré, -ée [apœre] *adj* frightened, scared

aphone [afɔn] *adj* voiceless; **je suis a. aujourd'hui** I've lost my voice today

aphorisme [afɔrism] *nm* aphorism

aphrodisiaque [afrɔdizjak] *nm & adj* aphrodisiac

aphte [aft] *nm* mouth ulcer • **aphteuse** *adj f* **fièvre a.** foot-and-mouth disease

apiculture [apikyltyr] *nf* beekeeping • **apiculteur, -trice** *nmf* beekeeper

apitoyer [apitwaje] **1** *vt* **a. qn** to move sb to pity

2 s'apitoyer *vpr* **s'a. sur qn** to feel sorry for sb; **s'a. sur son sort** to feel sorry for oneself • **apitoiement** *nm* pity

aplanir [aplanir] *vt (terrain, route)* to level; *(difficulté)* to iron out

aplatir [aplatir] **1** *vt* to flatten

2 s'aplatir *vpr (être plat)* to be flat; *(devenir plat)* to go flat; **s'a. contre qch** to flatten oneself against sth; *Fam* **s'a. devant qn** to grovel to sb • **aplati, -ie** *adj* flat

aplomb [aplɔ̃] *nm (assurance)* self-confidence; *Péj* cheek; **mettre qch d'a.** to stand sth up straight; **je ne me sens pas d'a. aujourd'hui** I'm feeling out of sorts today

apnée [apne] *nf* **plonger en a.** to dive without breathing apparatus

apocalypse [apɔkalips] *nf* apocalypse; **d'a.** *(vision)* apocalyptic • **apocalyptique** *adj* apocalyptic

apogée [apɔʒe] *nm (d'orbite)* apogee; *Fig* **être à l'a. de sa carrière** to be at the height of one's career

apolitique [apɔlitik] *adj* apolitical

apollon [apɔlɔ̃] *nm (bel homme)* Adonis

apologie [apɔlɔʒi] *nf (défense)* apologia (**de** for); *(éloge)* eulogy; **faire l'a. de qch** to eulogize sth

> *⚠* Il faut noter que le nom anglais **apology** est un faux ami. Il signifie **excuses**.

apoplexie [apɔplɛksi] *nf* apoplexy

apostolat [apɔstɔla] *nm (mission)* vocation

apostrophe [apɔstrɔf] *nf* (**a**) *(signe)* apostrophe (**b**) *(interpellation)* rude remark • **apostropher** *vt (pour attirer l'attention)* to shout at

apothéose [apɔteoz] *nf (consécration)* crowning glory; **finir en a.** to end spectacularly

apôtre [apotr] *nm* apostle

apparaître* [aparɛtr] *(aux être)* *vi (se montrer, sembler)* to appear; **il m'est apparu en rêve** he appeared to me in a dream; **il m'apparaît comme le seul capable d'y parvenir** he seems to me to be the only person capable of doing it

apparat [apara] *nm* pomp; **tenue d'a.** ceremonial dress

appareil [aparɛj] *nm (instrument, machine)* apparatus; *(téléphone)* telephone; *(avion)* aircraft; **l'a. de la justice** the legal system; *Hum* **dans le plus simple a.** in one's birthday suit; **qui est à l'a.?** *(au téléphone)* who's speaking?; **a. (dentaire)** *(correctif)* brace; *Anat* **a. digestif** digestive system; **a. photo** camera; **appareils ménagers** household appliances

appareiller [apareje] *vi (navire)* to get under way

apparence [aparɑ̃s] *nf* appearance; **en a.** outwardly; **sous l'a. de** under the guise of; **sauver les apparences** to keep up appearances • **apparemment** [-amɑ̃] *adv* apparently • **apparent, -ente** *adj* apparent

apparenter [aparɑ̃te] **s'apparenter** *vpr (ressembler)* to be akin (**à** to) • **apparenté, -ée** *adj (allié)* related; *(semblable)* similar

appariteur [aparitœr] *nm Univ Br* porter, *Am ≃* janitor

apparition [aparisjɔ̃] *nf (manifestation)* appearance; *(fantôme)* apparition; **faire son a.** *(personne)* to make one's appearance

appartement [apartəmɑ̃] *nm Br* flat, *Am* apartment

appartenir* [apartənir] **1** *vi* to belong (**à** to)

2 *v impersonnel* **il vous appartient de prendre la décision** it's up to you to decide ● **appartenance** *nf (de groupe)* belonging (**à** to); *(de parti)* membership (**à** of)

appât [apɑ] *nm (amorce)* bait; *Fig (attrait)* lure; **l'a. du gain** the lure of money ● **appâter** *vt (hameçon)* to bait; *(animal)* to lure; *Fig (personne)* to entice

appauvrir [apovrir] **1** *vt* to impoverish

2 s'appauvrir *upr* to become impoverished ● **appauvrissement** *nm* impoverishment

appel [apεl] *nm (cri, attrait)* call; *(invitation)* & *Jur* appeal; *Mil (recrutement)* call-up; *(pour sauter)* take-off; **faire l'a.** *(à l'école)* to take the register; *Mil* to have a roll call; **faire a. à qn** to appeal to sb; *(plombier, médecin)* to send for sb; *Jur* **faire a. d'une décision** to appeal against a decision; *Fig* **la décision est sans a.** the decision is final; *Com* **lancer un a. d'offre** to invite bids; **a. au secours** call for help; **a. d'air** draught; **a. gratuit** *Br* freefone call, *Am* toll-free call; **a. téléphonique** telephone call

appeler [aple] **1** *vt (personne, nom)* to call; *(en criant)* to call out to; *Mil (recruter)* to call up; *(nécessiter)* to call for; **a. qn à l'aide** to call to sb for help; **a. qn au téléphone** to call sb; **a. un taxi** to call for a taxi; **a. qn à faire qch** *(inviter)* to call on sb to do sth; **être appelé à témoigner** to be called upon to give evidence; **il est appelé à de hautes fonctions** he is marked out for high office; **en a.** à to appeal to

2 s'appeler *upr* to be called; **comment vous appelez-vous?** what's your name?; **je m'appelle David** my name is David ● **appellation** [apεlasjɔ̃] *nf (nom)* term; **a. contrôlée** *(de vin)* guaranteed vintage ● **appelé** *nm Mil* conscript

⟋ Il faut noter que le verbe anglais **to appeal** est un faux ami. Il ne signifie jamais **appeler**.

appendice [apɛ̃dis] *nm (du corps, de livre)* appendix; *(d'animal)* appendage ● **appendicite** *nf* appendicitis

appesantir [apəzɑ̃tir] **s'appesantir** *upr* to become heavier; **s'a. sur** *(sujet)* to dwell upon

appétit [apeti] *nm* appetite (**de** for); **mettre qn en a.** to whet sb's appetite; **couper l'a. à qn** to spoil sb's appetite; **manger de**

bon a. to tuck in; **bon a.!** enjoy your meal! ● **appétissant, -ante** *adj* appetizing

applaudir [aplodir] *vti* to applaud; **a. à qch** *(approuver)* to applaud sth ● **applaudimètre** *mn* clapometer ● **applaudissements** *nmpl* applause

applicable [aplikabl] *adj* applicable (**à** to) ● **application** *nf (action, soin)* application; *(de loi)* enforcement; **mettre une théorie en a.** to put a theory into practice; **mettre une loi en a.** to enforce a law; **entrer en a.** to come into force

applique [aplik] *nf* wall light

appliquer [aplike] **1** *vt* to apply (**à/sur** to); *(loi, décision)* to enforce

2 s'appliquer *upr (se concentrer)* to apply oneself (**à** to); **s'a. à faire qch** to take pains to do sth; **cette décision s'applique à** *(concerne)* this decision applies to ● **appliqué, -ée** *adj (personne)* hard-working; *(écriture)* careful; *(sciences)* applied

appoint [apwɛ̃] *nm* (**a**) **faire l'a.** to give the exact money (**b**) **radiateur d'a.** extra radiator; **salaire d'a.** extra income

appointements [apwɛ̃tmɑ̃] *nmpl* salary

⟋ Il faut noter que le nom anglais **appointment** est un faux ami. Il signifie **rendez-vous** ou **nomination** selon le contexte.

apport [apɔr] *nm* contribution (**à** to)

apporter [apɔrte] *vt* to bring (**à** to); *(preuve)* to provide; *(modification)* to bring about; **je te l'ai apporté** I brought it to you

apposer [apoze] *vt (sceau, signature)* to affix (**à** to); *(affiche)* to put up ● **apposition** *nf Grammaire* apposition

apprécier [apresje] *vt (aimer, percevoir)* to appreciate; *(évaluer)* to estimate; *Fam* **je n'ai pas apprécié** I wasn't too pleased ● **appréciable** *adj* appreciable ● **appréciation** *nf (opinion de professeur)* comment (**sur** on); *(évaluation)* valuation; *(augmentation de valeur)* appreciation; **laisser qch à l'a. de qn** to leave sth to sb's discretion

appréhender [apreɑ̃de] *vt (craindre)* to dread (**de faire** doing); *(arrêter)* to arrest; *(comprendre)* to grasp ● **appréhension** *nf (crainte)* apprehension (**de** about)

apprendre* [aprɑ̃dr] *vti (étudier)* to learn; *(nouvelle)* to hear; *(mariage, mort)* to hear of; **a. à faire qch** to learn to do sth; **a. qch à qn** *(enseigner)* to teach sb sth; *(informer)* to tell sb sth; **a. à qn à faire qch** to teach sb to do sth; **a. que...** to learn that...; *(être informé)* to hear that...

apprenti, -ie [aprɑ̃ti] *nmf* apprentice

•**apprentissage** *nm (professionnel)* training; *(chez un artisan)* apprenticeship; *(d'une langue)* learning (**de** of); *Fig* **faire l'a. de qch** to learn about sth

apprêter [aprete] **s'apprêter** *vpr* to get ready (**à faire** to do)

apprivoiser [aprivwaze] **1** *vt* to tame **2 s'apprivoiser** *vpr* to become tame •**apprivoisé, -ée** *adj* tame

approbation [aprɔbasjɔ̃] *nf* approval •**approbateur, -trice** *adj* approving

approche [aprɔʃ] *nf* approach; **approches** *(de ville)* outskirts; **à l'a. de la vieillesse** as old age draws/drew nearer

approcher [aprɔʃe] **1** *vt (objet)* to bring up; *(personne)* to approach, to get close to; **a. qch de qn** to bring sth near to sb **2** *vi* to approach, to get closer; **a. de qn/qch** to approach sb/sth; **la nuit approchait** it was beginning to get dark; **approche, je vais te montrer** come here, I'll show you **3 s'approcher** *vpr* to approach, to get closer; **s'a. de qn/qch** to approach sb/sth; **il s'est approché de moi** he came up to me •**approchant, -ante** *adj* similar

approfondir [aprɔfɔ̃dir] *vt (trou, puits)* to dig deeper; *(question, idée)* to go thoroughly into •**approfondi, -ie** *adj (étude, examen)* thorough

approprié, -ée [aprɔprije] *adj* appropriate (**à** for)

approprier [aprɔprije] **s'approprier** *vpr* **s'a. qch** to appropriate sth

approuver [apruve] *vt (facture, contrat)* to approve; *(décision, choix)* to approve of

approvisionner [aprɔvizjɔne] **1** *vt (ville, armée)* to supply (**en** with); *(magasin)* to stock (**en** with); *(compte bancaire)* to pay mony into; **le compte n'est plus approvisionné** the account is no longer in credit **2 s'approvisionner** *vpr* to get supplies (**en** of) •**approvisionnement** *nm (d'une ville, d'une armée)* supplying (**en** with); *(d'un magasin)* stocking (**en** with)

approximatif, -ive [aprɔksimatif, -iv] *adj* approximate •**approximation** *nf* approximation •**approximativement** *adv* approximately

appui [apɥi] *nm* support; **prendre a. sur qch** to lean on sth; **à l'a. de qch** in support of sth; **preuves à l'a.** with supporting evidence; **a. de fenêtre** window sill •**appui-tête** *(pl* appuis-tête*) nm* headrest

appuyer [apɥije] **1** *vt (poser)* to lean, to rest; *Fig (candidat)* to support, to back; *Fig (proposition)* to second; **a. qch sur qch** *(poser)* to rest sth on sth; *(presser)* to press sth on sth **2** *vi (presser)* to press; **a. sur un bouton** to press a button; **a. sur la pédale de frein** to put one's foot on the brake, to apply the brake **3 s'appuyer** *vpr* **s'a. sur qch** to lean on sth, to rest on sth; *Fig (compter)* to rely on sth; *Fig (être basé sur)* to be based on sth; *Fam* **s'a. qch** *(corvée)* to be lumbered with sth •**appuyé, -ée** *adj (plaisanterie)* laboured; **lancer à qn des regards appuyés** to stare intently at sb

âpre [ɑpr] *adj* sour; *Fig (concurrence, lutte)* fierce; **être â. au gain** to be money-grabbing •**âpreté** [-əte] *nf* sourness; *Fig (concurrence, lutte)* fierceness

après [aprɛ] **1** *prép (dans le temps)* after; *(dans l'espace)* beyond; **a. un an** after a year; **a. le pont** beyond the bridge; **a. coup** after the event; **a. tout** after all; **a. quoi** after which; **a. avoir mangé** after eating; **a. qu'il t'a vu** after he saw you; **jour a. jour** day after day; **d'a.** *(selon)* according to **2** *adv* after(wards); **l'année d'a.** the following year; **et a.?** *(et ensuite)* and then what?; *(et alors)* so what? •**après-demain** *adv* the day after tomorrow •**après-guerre** *nm* post-war period; **d'a.** post-war •**après-midi** *nm ou f inv* afternoon; **trois heures de l'a.** three o'clock in the afternoon •**après-rasage** *(pl* après-rasages*) nm* aftershave •**après-shampooing** *nm inv* conditioner •**après-ski** *(pl* après-skis*) nm* snowboot •**après-vente** *adj inv Com* **service a.** aftersales service

> Il faut noter que le mot anglais **après-ski** est un faux ami. Il désigne les activités récréatives auxquelles on se livre après une séance de ski.

a priori [aprijɔri] *adv* in principle

à-propos [aprɔpo] *nm* aptness; **avoir l'esprit d'a.** to have presence of mind

apte [apt] *adj* **a. à qch/à faire qch** fit to sth/for doing sth; *Mil* **a. au service** fit for military service •**aptitude** *nf* aptitude (**à** *ou* **pour** for); **avoir des aptitudes pour qch** to have an aptitude for sth

aquarelle [akwarɛl] *nf* watercolour

aquarium [akwarjɔm] *nm* aquarium

aquatique [akwatik] *adj* aquatic

aqueduc [akədyk] *nm* aqueduct

aquilin [akilɛ̃] *adj m* **nez a.** aquiline nose

arabe [arab] **1** *adj (peuple, monde, littérature)* Arab; *(langue)* Arabic; **chiffres arabes** Arabic numerals

2 *nmf* **A.** Arab
3 *nm (langue)* Arabic ● **Arabie** *nf* **l'A.**
Arabia; **l'A. Saoudite** Saudi Arabia
arabesque [arabɛsk] *nf* arabesque
arable [arabl] *adj* arable
arachide [araʃid] *nf* peanut, groundnut
araignée [arɛɲe] *nf* spider
arbalète [arbalɛt] *nf* crossbow
arbitraire [arbitrɛr] *adj* arbitrary
arbitre [arbitr] *nm Football* referee; *Tennis* umpire; *(d'un litige)* arbitrator; *(maître absolu)* arbiter; *Phil* **libre a.** free will ● **arbitrage** *nm Football* refereeing; *Tennis* umpiring; *(de litige)* arbitration ● **arbitrer** *vt (match de football)* to referee; *(partie de tennis)* to umpire; *(litige)* to arbitrate
arborer [arbɔre] *vt (insigne, vêtement)* to sport
arbre [arbr] *nm (végétal)* tree; *Tech* shaft; **a. fruitier** fruit tree; **a. à cames** camshaft; **a. de transmission** transmission shaft ● **arbrisseau, -x** *nm* shrub ● **arbuste** *nm* shrub
arc [ark] *nm (arme)* bow; *(voûte)* arch; *(de cercle)* arc ● **arcade** *nf* archway; **arcades** *(de place)* arcade; **l'a. sourcilière** the arch of the eyebrows
arc-boutant [arkbutã] *(pl* **arcs-boutants***)* *nm* flying buttress ● **s'arc-bouter** *vpr* **s'a. contre qch** to brace oneself against sth
arceau, -x [arso] *nm (de voûte)* arch
arc-en-ciel [arkãsjɛl] *(pl* **arcs-en-ciel***)* *nm* rainbow
archaïque [arkaik] *adj* archaic
archange [arkãʒ] *nm* archangel
arche [arʃ] *nf (voûte)* arch; **l'a. de Noé** Noah's ark
archéologie [arkeɔlɔʒi] *nf* archaeology ● **archéologique** *adj* archaeological ● **archéologue** *nmf* archaeologist
archer [arʃe] *nm* archer
archet [arʃɛ] *nm (de violon)* bow
archétype [arketip] *nm* archetype
archevêque [arʃəvɛk] *nm* archbishop
archicomble [arʃikɔbl] *adj* jam-packed
archi-connu [arʃikɔny] *adj Fam* very well-known
archiduc [arʃidyk] *nm* archduke ● **archiduchesse** *nf* archduchess
archipel [arʃipɛl] *nm* archipelago
archiplein, -pleine [arʃiplɛ̃, -plɛn] *adj* chock-full, *Br* chock-a-block
architecte [arʃitɛkt] *nm* architect ● **architecture** *nf* architecture
archives [arʃiv] *nfpl* archives, records ● **archiviste** *nmf* archivist
arctique [arktik] **1** *adj* arctic
2 *nm* **l'A.** the Arctic

ardent, -ente [ardã, -ãt] *adj (tempérament)* fiery; *(désir)* burning; *(soleil)* scorching ● **ardemment** [-amã] *adv* fervently; **désirer a. qch** to yearn for sth ● **ardeur** *nf (énergie)* fervour, ardour; *(du soleil)* intense heat
ardoise [ardwaz] *nf* slate
ardu, -ue [ardy] *adj* arduous
are [ar] *nm (mesure)* ≃ 100 square metres
arène [arɛn] *nf (pour taureaux)* bullring; *(romaine)* arena; **arènes** bullring; *(romaines)* amphitheatre; *Fig* **a. politique** political arena
arête [arɛt] *nf (de poisson)* bone; *(de cube, dé)* edge; *(de montagne)* ridge
argent [arʒã] **1** *nm (métal)* silver; *(monnaie)* money; **a. liquide** cash; **a. de poche** pocket money
2 *adj (couleur)* silver ● **argenté, -ée** *adj (plaqué)* silver-plated; *(couleur)* silvery ● **argenterie** *nf* silverware
Argentine [arʒãtin] *nf* **l'A.** Argentina ● **argentin, -ine 1** *adj* Argentinian **2** *nmf* **A., Argentine** Argentinian
argile [arʒil] *nf* clay ● **argileux, -euse** *adj* clayey
argot [argo] *nm* slang ● **argotique** *adj (terme)* slang; *(texte)* of slang
arguer [argɥe] *vi Littéraire* **a. de qch** to put forward sth as an argument ● **argumentation** *nf* arguments, argumentation ● **argumenter** *vi* to argue
argument [argymã] *nm* argument
argus [argys] *nm* = guide to used car prices
aride [arid] *adj (terre)* arid, barren; *(sujet)* dry
aristocrate [aristɔkrat] *nmf* aristocrat ● **aristocratie** [-asi] *nf* aristocracy ● **aristocratique** *adj* aristocratic
arithmétique [aritmetik] **1** *adj* arithmetical
2 *nf* arithmetic
arlequin [arləkɛ̃] *nm* Harlequin
armateur [armatœr] *nm* shipowner
armature [armatyr] *nf (charpente)* framework; *(de lunettes, de tente)* frame
arme [arm] *nf* weapon; **prendre les armes** to take up arms; *Fig* **à armes égales** on equal terms; *Fig* **faire ses premières armes** to earn one's spurs; **a. à feu** firearm; **a. blanche** knife ● **armes** *nfpl (blason)* (coat of) arms
armée [arme] *nf* army; **être à l'a.** to be doing one's military service; **a. de l'air** air force; **a. de terre** army; **a. active/de métier** regular/professional army
armer [arme] **1** *vt (personne)* to arm (**de**

with); *(fusil)* to cock; *(appareil photo)* to set; *(navire)* to commission

2 s'armer *vpr* to arm oneself (**de** with); **s'a. de patience** to summon up one's patience ● **armements** [-əmɑ̃] *nmpl (armes)* armaments

armistice [armistis] *nm* armistice

armoire [armwar] *nf (penderie) Br* wardrobe, *Am* closet; **a. à pharmacie** medicine cabinet

armoiries [armwari] *nfpl* (coat of) arms

armure [armyr] *nf* armour

armurier [armyrje] *nm (vendeur)* gun dealer

arnaque [arnak] *nf Fam* rip-off ● **arnaquer** *vt Fam* to rip off; **se faire a.** to get ripped off

aromathérapie [arɔmaterapi] *nf* aromatherapy

arôme [arom] *nm (goût)* flavour; *(odeur)* aroma ● **aromate** *nm (herbe)* herbe; *(épice)* spice ● **aromatique** *adj* aromatic

arpenter [arpɑ̃te] *vt (mesurer)* to survey; *(parcourir)* to pace up and down ● **arpenteur** *nm* (land) surveyor

arqué, -ée [arke] *adj (sourcil)* arched; *(nez)* hooked; **jambes arquées** bow legs

arraché [araʃe] *nm* **gagner à l'a.** to snatch victory

arrache-pied [araʃpje] **d'arrache-pied** *adv* relentlessly

arracher [araʃe] *vt (plante, arbre)* to uproot; *(pommes de terre)* to lift; *(clou, dent, mauvaise herbe)* to pull out; *(page)* to tear out; *(vêtement, masque)* to tear off; **a. qch à qn** *(objet, enfant)* to snatch sth from sb; *(aveu, argent, promesse)* to force sth out of sb; **a. un bras à qn** *(obus)* to blow sb's arm off; **a. qn de son lit** to drag sb out of bed; **se faire a. une dent** to have a tooth out ● **arrachage** *nm (de plantes)* uprooting; *(de pommes de terre)* lifting; *(de clou, de dent)* pulling up

arraisonner [arɛzɔne] *vt (navire)* to board and examine

arranger [arɑ̃ʒe] **1** *vt (meuble, fleurs)* to arrange; *(maison)* to put in order; *(col)* to straighten; *(réparer)* to repair; *(organiser)* to arrange, to organize; *(différend)* to settle; *Fam* **a. qn** *(maltraiter)* to give sb a going over; **je vais a. ça** I'll fix that; **ça m'arrange** that suits me (fine)

2 s'arranger *vpr (se mettre d'accord)* to come to an agreement; *(finir bien)* to turn out fine; *(s'organiser)* to manage; **arrangez-vous pour être là** make sure you're there ● **arrangeant, -ante** *adj* accommodating ● **arrangement** *nm (dispo-*

sition) & *Mus* arrangement; *(accord)* agreement

arrestation [arɛstɑsjɔ̃] *nf* arrest

arrêt [arɛ] *nm (halte, endroit)* stop; *(action)* stopping; *Jur* judgement; **temps d'a.** pause; **à l'a.** stationary; **sans a.** continuously; **a. du cœur** cardiac arrest; *Sport* **a. de jeu** stoppage; **a. de mort** death sentence; **a. de travail** *(grève)* stoppage; *(congé)* sick leave ● **arrêt-maladie** *nm* sick leave

arrêté¹ [arete] *nm (décret)* order, decree

arrêté², -ée [arete] *adj (idées, projet)* fixed; *(volonté)* firm

arrêter [arete] **1** *vt (personne, animal, véhicule)* to stop; *(criminel)* to arrest; *(moteur)* to turn off; *(date)* to fix; *(études)* to give up

2 *vi* to stop; **a. de faire qch** to stop doing sth; **il n'arrête pas de critiquer** he's always criticizing

3 s'arrêter *vpr* to stop; **s'a. de faire qch** to stop doing sth

arrhes [ar] *nfpl (acompte)* deposit

arrière [arjɛr] **1** *nm (de maison)* back, rear; *(de bâteau)* stern; *Football* full back; **à l'a.** in/at the back

2 *adj inv (siège)* back, rear; **feu a.** rear light

3 *adv* **en a.** *(marcher, tomber)* backwards; *(rester)* behind; *(regarder)* back, behind; **en a. de qn/qch** behind sb/sth ● **arrière-boutique** *(pl* **arrière-boutiques)** *nm* back room ● **arrière-garde** *(pl* **arrière-gardes)** *nf* rearguard ● **arrière-goût** *(pl* **arrière-goûts)** *nm* aftertaste ● **arrière-grand-mère** *(pl* **arrière-grands-mères)** *nf* great-grandmother ● **arrière-grand-père** *(pl* **arrière-grands-pères)** *nm* great-grandfather ● **arrière-pays** *nm inv* hinterland ● **arrière-pensée** *(pl* **arrière-pensées)** *nf* ulterior motive ● **arrière-plan** *nm* background; **à l'a.** in the background ● **arrière-saison** *(pl* **arrière-saisons)** *nf Br* late autumn, *Am* late fall ● **arrière-train** *(pl* **arrière-trains)** *nm (d'animal)* hindquarters; *Fam (de personne)* rump

arriéré, -ée [arjere] **1** *adj (dans ses idées, dans son développement)* backward

2 *nm (dette)* arrears

arrimer [arime] *vt (fixer)* to rope down; *Naut* to stow

arriver [arive] **1** *(aux être) vi (venir)* to arrive; **a. à** *(lieu)* to reach; *(résultat)* to achieve; **l'eau m'arrive aux chevilles** the water comes up to my ankles; **a. à faire qch** to manage to do sth; **en a. à faire qch** to get to the point of doing sth

2 *v impersonnel (survenir)* to happen; **a. à qn** to happen to sb; **il m'arrive d'oublier** I sometimes forget; **qu'est-ce qu'il t'arrive?** what's wrong with you? ● **arrivage** *nm* consignment ● **arrivant, -ante** *nmf* new arrival ● **arrivée** *nf* arrival; *(ligne, poteau)* winning post ● **arriviste** *nmf* *Péj* social climber

arrogant, -ante [aʀɔgɑ̃, -ɑ̃t] *adj* arrogant ● **arrogance** *nf* arrogance

arroger [aʀɔʒe] **s'arroger** *vpr (droit)* to claim

arrondir [aʀɔ̃diʀ] *vt (somme, chiffre, angle, jupe)* to round off; **a. qch** to make sth round; **a. à l'euro supérieur/inférieur** to round up/down to the nearest euro; *Fam* **a. ses fins de mois** to supplement one's income ● **arrondi, -ie** *adj* round

arrondissement [aʀɔ̃dismɑ̃] *nm* = administrative subdivision of Paris, Lyons and Marseilles

arroser [aʀoze] *vt (terre, plante)* to water; *(pelouse)* to sprinkle; *(repas)* to wash down; *(succès)* to drink to ● **arrosage** *nm (de terre, de plante)* watering; *(de pelouse)* sprinkling ● **arrosoir** *nm* watering can

arsenal, -aux [aʀsənal, -o] *nm* *Mil* arsenal; *Fam (panoplie)* rgear

arsenic [aʀsənik] *nm* arsenic

art [aʀ] *nm* art; **film/critique d'a.** art film/critic; **arts martiaux** martial arts; **arts ménagers** home economics; **arts plastiques** fine arts

Arte [aʀte] *n* = French-German TV channel showing cultural programmes

artère [aʀtɛʀ] *nf (veine)* artery; *(rue)* main road

artichaut [aʀtiʃo] *nm* artichoke; **fond d'a.** artichoke heart

article [aʀtikl] *nm (de presse, de contrat, de traité) & Grammaire* article; *Com* item; **à l'a. de la mort** at death's door; **a. de fond** feature (article); **articles de toilette** toiletries; **articles de voyage** travel goods

articuler [aʀtikyle] **1** *vt (mot)* to articulate **2 s'articuler** *vpr (membre)* to articulate; *(idées)* to connect; **s'a. autour de qch** *(théorie)* to centre on ● **articulation** *nf (de membre)* joint; *(prononciation)* articulation

artifice [aʀtifis] *nm* trick

artificiel, -ielle [aʀtifisjɛl] *adj* artificial ● **artificiellement** *adv* artificially

artillerie [aʀtijʀi] *nf* artillery ● **artilleur** *nm* artilleryman

artisan [aʀtizɑ̃] *nm* craftsman, artisan ● **artisanal, -e, -aux, -ales** *adj* métier **a.** craft; **objet a.** object made by craftsmen;

bombe artisanale homemade bomb ● **artisanat** *nm* craft industry

artiste [aʀtist] *nmf* artist; *(acteur, musicien)* performer ● **artistique** *adj* artistic

as [ɑs] *nm (carte, champion)* ace; **a. du volant/de la mécanique** crack driver/mechanic; *Fam* **être plein aux as** to be rolling in it

ascendant [asɑ̃dɑ̃] **1** *adj* ascending; *(mouvement)* upward

2 *nm (influence)* influence; **ascendants** ancestors ● **ascendance** *nf (ancêtres)* ancestry

ascenseur [asɑ̃sœʀ] *nm Br* lift, *Am* elevator

ascension [asɑ̃sjɔ̃] *nf (escalade)* ascent; *Rel* **l'A.** Ascension Day

ascète [asɛt] *nmf* ascetic ● **ascétique** *adj* ascetic ● **ascétisme** *nm* asceticism

Asie [azi] *nf* **l'A.** Asia ● **asiatique 1** *adj* Asian **2** *nmf* **A.** Asian

asile [azil] *nm (abri)* refuge, shelter; *(pour vieillards)* home; *Péj* **a. (d'aliénés)** (lunatic) asylum; **a. politique** (political) asylum; **a. de paix** haven of peace

aspect [aspɛ] *nm (air)* appearance; *(angle)* point of view; *(perspective) & Grammaire* aspect

asperger [aspɛʀʒe] **1** *vt (par jeu ou accident)* to splash (**de** with); *(pour humecter)* to spray (**de** with); **se faire a.** to get splashed

2 s'asperger *vpr* **s'a. de parfum** to splash oneself with perfume

asperges [aspɛʀʒ] *nfpl* asparagus

aspérité [aspeʀite] *nf (de surface)* rough part

asphalte [asfalt] *nm* asphalt

asphyxie [asfiksi] *nf* asphyxiation ● **asphyxier 1** *vt* to asphyxiate **2 s'asphyxier** *vpr* to suffocate; *(volontairement)* to suffocate oneself

aspirant [aspiʀɑ̃] *nm (candidat)* candidate

aspirateur [aspiʀatœʀ] *nm* vacuum cleaner, *Br* Hoover®; **passer l'a. dans la maison** to vacuum the house

aspirer [aspiʀe] **1** *vt (liquide)* to suck up; *(air, parfum)* to breathe in, to inhale

2 *vi* **a. à qch** *(bonheur, gloire)* to aspire to sth ● **aspiration** *nf (inhalation)* inhalation; *(ambition)* aspiration (**à** for) ● **aspiré, -ée** *adj (son, lettre)* aspirate(d)

aspirine [aspiʀin] *nf* aspirin

assagir [asaʒiʀ] **s'assagir** *vpr* to settle down

assaillir [asajiʀ] *vt* to attack; **a. qn de questions** to bombard sb with questions ● **assaillant** *nm* attacker, assailant

assainir [asenir] *vt (purifier)* to clean up; *(marché, économie)* to stabilize

assaisonner [asezɔne] *vt* to season • **assaisonnement** *nm* seasoning

assassin [asasɛ̃] *nm* murderer; *(de politicien)* assassin • **assassinat** *nm* murder; *(de politicien)* assassination • **assassiner** *vt* to murder; *(politicien)* to assassinate

assaut [aso] *nm* attack, assault; *Mil* charge; **donner l'a. à** to storm; **prendre qch d'a.** *Mil* to take sth by storm; *Fig (buffet)* to make a run for sth

assécher [aseʃe] **1** *vt* to drain
2 s'assécher *vpr* to dry up

assemblée [asɑ̃ble] *nf (personnes réunies)* gathering; *(réunion)* meeting; **a. générale** *(de compagnie)* annual general meeting; **l'A. nationale** *Br* ≃ the House of Commons, *Am* ≃ the House of Representatives

assembler [asɑ̃ble] **1** *vt* to put together, to assemble
2 s'assembler *vpr* to gather • **assemblage** *nm (montage)* assembly; *(réunion d'objets)* collection

asséner [asene] *vt* **a. un coup à qn** to deliver a blow to sb

assentiment [asɑ̃timɑ̃] *nm* assent

asseoir* [aswar] **1** *vt (personne)* to seat (**sur** on); *Fig (autorité, réputation)* to establish
2 *vi* **faire a. qn** to ask sb to sit down
3 s'asseoir *vpr* to sit (down)

assermenté, -ée [asɛrmɑ̃te] *adj* sworn; *(témoin)* under oath

assertion [asɛrsjɔ̃] *nf* assertion

asservir [asɛrvir] *vt* to enslave • **asservissement** *nm* enslavement

assez [ase] *adv* (**a**) *(suffisament)* enough; **a. de pain/de gens** enough bread/people; **j'en ai a.** I've had enough (**de** of); **a. grand/intelligent** big/clever enough (**pour faire** to do) (**b**) *(plutôt)* quite, rather

assidu, -ue [asidy] *adj (toujours présent)* regular; *(appliqué)* diligent; **a. auprès de qn** attentive to sb • **assiduité** *nf (d'élève)* regularity; **poursuivre qn de ses assiduités** to force one's attention to sb • **assidûment** *adv (régulièrement)* regularly; *(avec application)* diligently assiduously

assiéger [asjeʒe] *vt (ville, magasin, guichet)* to besiege; *(personne)* to pester

assiette [asjɛt] *nf* (**a**) *(récipient)* plate; *Culin Br* **a. anglaise** *(assorted)* cold meats, *Am* cold cuts (**b**) *(à cheval)* seat; *Fam* **il n'est pas dans son a.** he's feeling out of sorts • **assiettée** *nf* plateful

assigner [asiɲe] *vt (attribuer)* to assign (**à** to); *(en justice)* to summon; **a. qn à résidence** to place sb under house arrest • **assignation** *nf Jur* summons

assimiler [asimile] **1** *vt (aliments, connaissances, immigrés)* to assimilate
2 s'assimiler *vpr (immigré)* to assimilate • **assimilation** *nf* assimilation

assis, -ise¹ [asi, -iz] *(pp de asseoir)* adj sitting (down), seated; *(situation)* secure; **rester a.** to remain seated; **place assise** seat

assise² [asiz] *nf (base)* foundation; **assises** *(d'un parti)* congress; *Jur* **les assises** the assizes

assistance [asistɑ̃s] *nf* (**a**) *(public)* audience (**b**) *(aide)* assistance; **être à l'A. publique** to be in care

assister [asiste] **1** *vt (aider)* to assist
2 *vi* **a. à** *(réunion, cours)* to attend; *(accident)* to witness • **assistant, -ante** *nmf* assistant; **assistante sociale** social worker; **assistante maternelle** *Br* child minder, *Am* baby-sitter • **assisté, -ée** *adj* **a. par ordinateur** computer-aided

association [asɔsjasjɔ̃] *nf* association; *Com* partnership; **a. de parents d'élèves** parent-teacher association; **a. sportive** sports club

associer [asɔsje] **1** *vt* to associate (**à** with); **a. qn à** *(travaux, affaire)* to involve sb in; *(profits)* to give sb a share in
2 s'associer *vpr* to join forces (**à** *ou* **avec** with); *Com* **s'a. avec qn** to enter into partnership with sb; **s'a. à un projet** to join in a project; **s'a. à la peine de qn** to share sb's grief • **associé, -ée 1** *nmf* partner, associate **2** *adj* **membre a.** associate member

assoiffé, -ée [aswafe] *adj* thirsty (**de** for)

assombrir [asɔ̃brir] **1** *vt (obscurcir)* to darken; *(attrister)* to cast a shadow over
2 s'assombrir *vpr (ciel, visage)* to cloud over; *(personne)* to become gloomy

assommer [asɔme] *vt* **a. qn** to knock sb unconscious; *Fig (ennuyer)* to bore sb to death • **assommant, -ante** *adj* very boring

Assomption [asɔ̃psjɔ̃] *nf Rel* **l'A.** the Assumption

assortir [asɔrtir] *vt (harmoniser)* to match; *Com (magasin)* to stock • **assorti, -ie** *adj (objet semblable)* matching; *(bonbons)* assorted; **époux bien assortis** well-matched couple; **bien a.** *(magasin)* well-stocked; **a. de** accompanied by • **assortiment** *nm* assortment

assoupir [asupir] **s'assoupir** *vpr* to doze off

assouplir [asuplir] **1** *vt (cuir, chaussure, muscles)* to make supple; *(corps)* to limber up; *Fig (réglementation)* to relax

2 s'**assouplir** *vpr (personne, chaussure, cuir)* to get supple ● **assouplissement** *nm* **exercices d'a.** limbering-up exercises

assourdir [asurdir] *vt (personne)* to deafen; *(son)* to muffle ● **assourdissant, -ante** *adj* deafening

assouvir [asuvir] *vt* to satisfy

assujettir [asyʒetir] *vt (soumettre)* to subject (à to); *(peuple)* to subjugate; *(objet)* to fix (à to); **être assujetti à l'impôt** to be liable for tax

assumer [asyme] **1** *vt (tâche, rôle, responsabilité)* to assume, to take on; *(risque, conséquences)* to take

2 *vi Fam* **tu vas devoir a.** you'll have to live with it

3 s'**assumer** *vpr* to come to terms with oneself

> ⚠ Il faut noter que le verbe anglais **to assume** est un faux ami. Il signifie le plus souvent **supposer**.

assurance [asyrãs] *nf (confiance)* (self-)assurance; *(promesse)* assurance; *(contrat)* insurance; **prendre une a.** to take out insurance; **a. au tiers/tous risques** third-party/comprehensive insurance; **a. maladie/vie** health/life insurance

assurer [asyre] **1** *vt (garantir) Br* to ensure, *Am* to insure; *(par un contrat)* to insure; *(fixer)* to secure; **a. qn de qch, a. qch à qn** to assure sb of sth; **a. à qn que...** to assure sb that...; **a. les fonctions de directeur** to be production manager; **un service régulier est assuré** there is a regular service

2 s'**assurer** *vpr (par un contrat)* to insure oneself; **s'a. l'aide de qn** to secure sb's help; **s'a. de qch/que...** to make sure of sth/that... ● **assuré, -ée 1** *adj (succès)* guaranteed; *(pas, voix)* firm; *(air, personne)* confident **2** *nmf* policyholder ● **assurément** *adv* certainly ● **assureur** *nm* insurer

astérisque [asterisk] *nm* asterisk

asthme [asm] *nm* asthma ● **asthmatique** *adj & nmf* asthmatic

asticot [astiko] *nm Br* maggot, *Am* worm

asticoter [astikɔte] *vt Fam* to bug

astiquer [astike] *vt* to polish

astre [astr] *nm* star

astreindre* [astrɛ̃dr] **1** *vt* **a. qn à faire qch** to compel sb to do sth

2 s'**astreindre** *vpr* **s'a. à un régime sévère** to strictly follow a diet **s'a. à faire qch** to force oneself to do sth ● **astreignant,**

-**ante** *adj* exacting ● **astreinte** *nf* constraint

astrologie [astrɔlɔʒi] *nf* astrology ● **astrologique** *adj* astrological ● **astrologue** *nm* astrologer

astronaute [astrɔnot] *nmf* astronaut ● **astronautique** *nf* space travel

astronomie [astrɔnɔmi] *nf* astronomy ● **astronome** *nm* astronomer ● **astronomique** *adj* astronomical

astuce [astys] *nf (truc)* trick; *(plaisanterie)* witticism; *(jeu de mots)* pun; *(finesse)* astuteness; **il y a une a.** there's a trick to it; **je ne saisis pas l'a.** I don't get it ● **astucieux, -ieuse** *adj* clever

atelier [atəlje] *nm (d'ouvrier)* workshop; *(de peintre)* studio; *(personnel)* workshop staff; *(groupe de travail)* work-group; **a. de carrosserie** bodyshop; **a. de montage** assembly shop; **a. de réparation** repair shop

atermoyer [atermwaje] *vi* to procrastinate

athée [ate] **1** *adj* atheistic

2 *nmf* atheist ● **athéisme** *nm* atheism

athénée [atene] *nm Belg Br* secondary school, *Am* high school

Athènes [atɛn] *nm ou f* Athens

athlète [atlɛt] *nmf* athlete ● **athlétique** *adj* athletic ● **athlétisme** *nm* athletics *(sing)*

atlantique [atlãtik] **1** *adj* Atlantic

2 *nm* **l'A.** the Atlantic

atlas [atlɑs] *nm* atlas

atmosphère [atmɔsfɛr] *nf* atmosphere ● **atmosphérique** *adj* atmospheric

atome [atom] *nm* atom; *Fig* **avoir des atomes crochus avec qn** to hit it off with sb ● **atomique** [atɔmik] *adj* atomic

atomiser [atɔmize] *vt (liquide)* to spray; *(région)* to destroy with nuclear weapons ● **atomiseur** *nm* spray

atone [atɔn] *adj (inerte)* lifeless; *(regard)* vacant

atours [atur] *nmpl Littéraire* finery; **paré de ses plus beaux a.** in all her finery

atout [atu] *nm* trump; *Fig (avantage)* asset; **a. cœur** hearts are trumps; *Fig* **avoir tous les atouts dans son jeu** to hold all the winning cards

âtre [ɑtr] *nm (foyer)* hearth

atroce [atrɔs] *adj* atrocious; *(douleur)* excruciating; *(rêve)* dreadful ● **atrocité** *nf (cruauté)* atrociousness; **les atrocités de la guerre** the atrocities committed in wartime

atrophie [atrɔfi] *nf* atrophy ● **atrophié, -iée** *adj* atrophied

attabler [atable] **s'attabler** *vpr* to sit down at a/the table •**attablé, -ée** *adj* (seated) at the table

attache [ataʃ] *nf (lien)* fastener; **attaches** *(amis)* links; **être sans attaches** to be unattached; **je n'avais plus aucune a. dans cette ville** there was nothing to keep me in this town

attaché-case [ataʃekɛz] (*pl* **attachés-cases**) *nm* attaché case

attachement [ataʃmɑ̃] *nm (affection)* attachment (à to)

attacher [ataʃe] **1** *vt* **a. qch à qch** to fasten sth to sth; *(avec de la ficelle)* to tie sth to sth; *(avec une chaîne)* to chain sth to sth; **a. ses lacets** to do one's shoelaces up; **a. de l'importance/de la valeur à qch** to attach great importance/value to sth **2** *vi (en cuisant)* to stick to the pan **3 s'attacher** *vpr (se fixer)* to be fastened; **s'a. à une tâche** to apply oneself to a task; **s'a. à qn** to get attached to sb; **je ne veux pas m'a.** *(sentimentalement)* I don't want to commit myself •**attachant, -ante** *adj* engaging •**attaché, -ée 1** *adj (fixé)* fastened; *(chien)* chained up; **être a. à qn** to be attached to sb; **les avantages attachés à une fonction** the benefits attached to a post **2** *nmf* attaché; **a. culturel/militaire** cultural/military attaché; **a. de presse** press officer

attaque [atak] *nf* attack; **passer à l'a.** to go on the offensive; *Fam* **d'a.** on top form; **a. aérienne** air raid; **a. à main armée** armed robbery

attaquer [atake] **1** *vt (physiquement, verbalement)* to attack; *(difficulté, sujet)* to tackle; *(morceau de musique)* to strike up; *Jur* **a. qn en justice** to bring an action against sb **2** *vi* to attack **3 s'attaquer** *vpr* **s'a. à** *(adversaire)* to attack; *(problème)* to tackle •**attaquant, -ante** *nmf* attacker

attarder [atarde] **s'attarder** *vpr* to linger; **s'a. à des détails** to dwell over details; **ne nous attardons pas sur ce point** let's not dwell on that point •**attardé, -ée** *adj (enfant)* mentally retarded; **il ne restait plus que quelques passants attardés** there were only a few people still about

atteindre* [atɛ̃dr] **1** *vt (parvenir à)* to reach; *(cible)* to hit; *(idéal)* to achieve; **être atteint d'une maladie** to be suffering from a disease; **le poumon est atteint** the lung is affected; *Fig* **rien ne l'atteint** nothing affects him/her; *Fam* **il est très atteint** *(fou)* he's completely cracked

2 *vi* **a. à la perfection** to be close to perfection

atteinte [atɛ̃t] *nf* attack (à on); **porter a. à** to undermine; **hors d'a.** *(objet, personne)* out of reach

atteler [atle] **1** *vt (bêtes)* to harness; **a. une voiture** to hitch up horses to a carriage **2 s'atteler** *vpr* **s'a. à une tâche** to apply oneself to a task •**attelage** *nm (bêtes)* team

attelle [atɛl] *nf* splint

attenant, -ante [atnɑ̃, -ɑ̃t] *adj* **a. (à)** adjoining

attendre [atɑ̃dr] **1** *vt (personne, train)* to wait for, **a. son tour** to wait one's turn; **elle attend un bébé** she's expecting a baby; **le bonheur qui nous attend** the happiness that awaits us; **a. que qn fasse qch** to wait for sb to do sth; **a. qch de qn** to expect sth from sb; **se faire a.** *(personne)* to keep people waiting; *(réponse, personne)* to be a long time coming **2** *vi* to wait; **faire a. qn** to keep sb waiting; *Fam* **attends voir!** let me see!; **en attendant** meanwhile; **en attendant que...** *(+ subjunctive)* until... **3 s'attendre** *vpr* **s'a. à qch/à faire qch** to expect sth/to do sth; **s'a. à ce que qn fasse qch** to expect sb to do sth; **je m'y attendais** I expected as much; **il fallait s'y a.** it was only to be expected •**attendu, -ue 1** *adj (prévu)* expected; *(avec joie)* eagerly-awaited **2** *prép Formel* considering; **a. que...** considering that...

attendrir [atɑ̃drir] **1** *vt (émouvoir)* to move; *(viande)* to tenderize **2 s'attendrir** *vpr* to be moved (**sur** by) •**attendri, -ie** *adj* compassionate •**attendrissant, -ante** *adj* moving

attentat [atɑ̃ta] *nm* attack; **a. à la bombe** bombing; **a. à la pudeur** indecent assault •**attenter** *vi* **a. à** to make an attempt on; **a. à ses jours** to attempt suicide

attente [atɑ̃t] *nf (fait d'attendre)* waiting; *(période)* wait; **une a. prolongée** a long wait; **en a.** *(au téléphone)* on hold; **être dans l'a. de** to be waiting for; **dans l'a. de vous rencontrer** *(dans une lettre)* I look forward to meeting you; **contre toute a.** against all expectations; **répondre aux attentes de qn** to live up to sb's expectations

attentif, -ive [atɑ̃tif, -iv] *adj* attentive; **a. à qch** to pay attention to sth; **écouter d'une oreille attentive** to listen attentively •**attentivement** *adv* attentively

attention [atɑ̃sjɔ̃] *nf (soin, amabilité)*

attention; **faire a. à qch** to pay attention to sth; **faire a. à sa santé** to look after one's health; **faire a. (à ce) que...** (+ subjunctive) to be careful that...; **a.!** watch out!; **a. à la voiture!** watch out for the car!; **à l'a. de qn** (sur lettre) for the attention of sb; **être plein d'attentions envers qn** to be very attentive towards sb • **attentionné, -ée** adj considerate

atténuer [atenɥe] **1** vt (effet, douleur) to reduce; (lumière) to dim

2 s'**atténuer** vpr (douleur) to ease; (lumière) to fade

atterrer [atere] vt to appal

atterrir [aterir] vi to land; **a. en catastrophe** to make an emergency landing; Fam **a. dans un bar** to land up in a bar • **atterrissage** nm landing; **a. forcé** forced landing

attester [ateste] vt to testify to; **a. que...** to testify that... • **attestation** nf (document) certificate

attifer [atife] vt Fam to dress (**de** in)

attirail [atiraj] nm equipment; Fam Péj gear

attirance [atirɑ̃s] nf attraction (**pour** for)

attirer [atire] **1** vt (sujet: aimant, planète, personne) to attract; (sujet: matière, pays) to appeal to; **a. l'attention de qn** to catch sb's attention; **a. l'attention de qn sur qch** to draw sb's attention to sth; **a. les regards** to catch the eye; **a. des ennuis à qn** to cause trouble for sb; **a. qn dans un coin** to take sb into a corner; **a. qn dans un piège** to lure sb into a trap

2 s'**attirer** vpr (mutuellement) to be attracted to each other; **s'a. des ennuis** to get oneself into trouble; **s'a. la colère de qn** to incur sb's anger • **attirant, -ante** adj attractive

attiser [atize] vt (feu) to poke; Fig (désir, colère) to stir up

attitré, -ée [atitre] adj (représentant) appointed; (marchand) regular

attitude [atityd] nf (conduite, position) attitude; (affectation) pose

attraction [atraksjɔ̃] nf (force, centre d'intérêt) attraction; **l'a. terrestre** the earth gravitational pull

attrait [atrɛ] nm attraction

attrape [atrap] nf (farce) trick • **attrape-nigaud** (pl **attrape-nigauds**) nm (ruse) trick

attraper [atrape] **1** vt (ballon, maladie, voleur, train) to catch; **a. froid** to catch cold; **se faire a.** to be caught; Fam (gronder) to get a good talking to; **se laisser a.** (duper) to get taken in

2 s'**attraper** vpr (maladie) to be caught

attrayant, -ante [atrɛjɑ̃, -ɑ̃t] adj attractive

attribuer [atribɥe] **1** vt (allouer) to assign (**à** to); (prix, bourse) to award (**à** to); (œuvre, crime) to attribute (**à** to); **a. de l'importance à qch** to attach importance to sth

2 s'**attribuer** vpr to claim • **attribuable** adj attributable (**à** to) • **attribution** nf (allocation) assigning (**à** to); (de prix) awarding (**à** to); (d'une œuvre, d'un crime) attribution (**à** to); **attributions** (fonctions) duties; **entrer dans les attributions de qn** to be part of sb's duties

attribut [atriby] nm (adjectif) predicate adjective; (caractéristique) attribute

attrister [atriste] vt to sadden

attrouper [atrupe] vt, s'**attrouper** vpr to gather • **attroupement** nm crowd

au [o] voir à

aubaine [obɛn] nf (bonne) a. godsend

aube [ob] nf dawn; **dès l'a.** at the crack of dawn

aubépine [obepin] nf hawthorn

auberge [obɛrʒ] nf inn; Fam **on n'est pas sorti de l'a.** we're not out of the woods yet; **a. de jeunesse** youth hostel • **aubergiste** nmf innkeeper

aubergine [obɛrʒin] nf Br aubergine, Am eggplant

aucun, -une [okœ̃, -yn] **1** adj no, not any; **il n'a a. talent** he has no talent; **a. professeur n'est venu** no teacher came

2 pron none; **il n'en a a.** he has none (at all); **a. d'entre nous** none of us; **a. des deux** neither of the two; Littéraire **d'aucuns** some (people) • **aucunement** adv not at all

audace [odas] nf (courage) daring, boldness; (impudence) audacity; **audaces** (de style) daring innovations; **avoir toutes les audaces** to do the most daring things • **audacieux, -ieuse** adj (courageux) daring, bold

au-dedans [odədɑ̃] adv inside

au-dehors [odəɔr] adv outside

au-delà [odəla] **1** adv beyond; **100 euros mais pas a.** 100 euros but no more

2 prép **a. de** beyond

3 nm **l'a.** the next world

au-dessous [odəsu] **1** adv (à l'étage inférieur) downstairs; (moins, dessous) below, under

2 prép **a. de** (dans l'espace) below, under, beneath; (âge, prix) under; (température) below; Fig **être a. de tout** to be beneath contempt

au-dessus [odəsy] **1** adv above; (à l'étage supérieur) upstairs

2 *prép* **a. de** above; *(âge, température, prix)* over; *(posé sur)* on top of; **vivre a. de ses moyens** to live beyond one's means

au-devant [odəvã] *prép* **aller a. de** *(personne)* to go to meet; *(danger)* to court; *(désirs de qn)* to anticipate

audible [odibl] *adj* audible

audience [odjãs] *nf (entretien)* audience; *(de tribunal)* hearing; *Jur* **l'a. est suspendue** the case is adjourned

audio [odjo] *adj inv (cassette)* audio ● **audiophone** *nm* hearing aid ● **audiovisuel, -elle 1** *adj (méthodes)* audiovisual; *(de la radio, de la télévision)* radio and television **2** *nm* **l'a.** radio and television

auditeur, -trice [oditœr, -tris] *nmf (de radio)* listener; *Univ* **a. libre** auditor *(student allowed to attend classes but not to sit examinations)*

audition [odisjõ] *nf (ouïe)* hearing; *(d'acteurs)* audition; **passer une a.** to have an audition; *Jur* **a. des témoins** examination of the witnesses ● **auditionner** *vti* to audition ● **auditoire** *nm* audience ● **auditorium** *nm* concert hall; *(studio)* recording studio

auge [oʒ] *nf* (feeding) trough

augmenter [ogmɑ̃te] **1** *vt* to increase (**de** by); **a. qn** to give sb a *Br* rise *or Am* raise **2** *vi* to increase (**de** by); *(prix, population)* to rise ● **augmentation** *nf* increase (**de** in, of); **a. de salaire** *Br* (pay) rise, *Am* raise; **être en a.** to be on the increase

augure [ogyr] *nm (présage)* omen; *(devin)* augur; **être de bon/mauvais a.** to be a good/bad omen ● **augurer** *vt* **a. bien/mal de qch** to augur well/ill for sth

aujourd'hui [oʒurdɥi] *adv* today; *(de nos jours)* nowadays, today; **a. en quinze** two weeks from today; **jusqu'à a.** to this very day; **les problèmes d'a.** today's problems

aumône [omon] *nf* alms; **faire l'a. à qn** to give alms to sb

aumônier [omonje] *nm* chaplain

auparavant [oparavã] *adv (avant)* before(-hand); *(d'abord)* first

auprès [oprɛ] **auprès de** *prép (assis, situé)* by, next to; *(en comparaison de)* compared to; **se renseigner a. de qn** to ask sb; **ambassadeur a. des Nations unies** ambassador to the United Nations

auquel [okɛl] *voir* **lequel**

aura, aurait [ora, orɛ] *voir* **avoir**

auréole [oreol] *nf (de saint)* halo; *(tache)* ring

auriculaire [orikylɛr] *nm* little finger

aurore [oror] *nf* dawn, daybreak; **à l'a.** at

dawn; *Fam* **aux aurores** at the crack of dawn

ausculter [oskylte] *vt (malade, cœur)* to listen to

auspices [ospis] *nmpl* **sous les a. de** under the auspices of

aussi [osi] **1** *adv* (**a**) *(comparaison)* as; **a. lourd que...** as heavy as... (**b**) *(également)* too, as well; **moi a.** so do/can/am I; **a. bien que...** as well as... (**c**) *(tellement)* so; **un repas a. délicieux** such a delicious meal (**d**) *(quelque)* **a. bizarre que cela paraisse** however odd this may seem **2** *conj (donc)* therefore

aussitôt [osito] *adv* immediately, straight away; **a. que...** as soon as...; **a. habillé, il partit** as soon as he was dressed, he left; **a. dit, a. fait** no sooner said than done

austère [ostɛr] *adj (vie, style)* austere; *(vêtement)* severe ● **austérité** *nf (de vie, de style)* austerity; *(de vêtement)* severity; **mesure d'a.** austerity measures

austral, -e, -als, -ales [ostral] *adj* southern

Australie [ostrali] *nf* **l'A.** Australia ● **australien, -ienne 1** *adj* Australian **2** *nmf* **A., Australienne** Australian

autant [otã] *adv* (**a**) **a. de... que** *(quantité)* as much... as; *(nombre)* as many... as; **il a a. d'argent/de pommes que vous** he has as much money/as many apples as you (**b**) **a. de** *(tant de)* so much; *(nombre)* so many; **je n'ai jamais vu a. d'argent/de pommes** I've never seen so much money/so many apples; **pourquoi manges-tu a.?** why are you eating so much? (**c**) **a. que** *(quantité)* as much as; *(nombre)* as many as; **il lit a. que vous/que possible** he reads as much as you/as possible; **il n'a jamais souffert a.** he's never suffered as *or* so much; **a. que je sache** as far as I know (**d**) *(expressions)* **d'a. (plus) que...** all the more (so) since...; **d'a. moins que...** even less since...; **a. dire que...** which amounts to saying...; **a. avouer** we/you might as well confess; **en faire a.** to do the same; **pour a.** *(malgré cela)* for all that; **j'aimerais a. aller au musée** I'd just as soon go to the museum

autel [otɛl] *nm* altar

auteur [otœr] *nm (de livre)* author, writer; *(de chanson)* composer; *(de tableau)* painter; *(de crime)* perpetrator; *(d'accident)* cause

authenticité [otɑ̃tisite] *nf* authenticity • **authentifier** *vt* to authenticate • **authentique** *adj* genuine, authentic

autiste [otist] *adj* autistic

autobiographie [otobjɔgrafi] *nf* autobiography • **autobiographique** *adj* autobiographical

autobus [otobys] *nm* bus

autocar [otokar] *nm* bus, *Br* coach

autochtone [otɔktɔn] *adj & nmf* native

autocollant, -ante [otokɔlɑ̃, -ɑ̃t] **1** *adj* self-adhesive; *(enveloppe, timbre)* self-seal **2** *nm* sticker

autocrate [otokrat] *nm* autocrat • **autocratique** *adj* autocratic

autocuiseur [otokɥizœr] *nm* pressure cooker

autodéfense [otodefɑ̃s] *nf* self-defence

autodestruction [otodɛstryksjɔ̃] *nf* self-destruction • **autodestructeur, -trice** *adj* self-destructive

autodidacte [otodidakt] *nmf* self-taught person

auto-école [otoekɔl] *(pl* **auto-écoles***) nf* driving school, *Br* school of motoring

autofinancer [otofinɑ̃se] **s'autofinancer** *vpr* to be self-financing

autogestion [otoʒɛstjɔ̃] *nf* self-management

autographe [otograf] *nm* autograph

automate [ɔtɔmat] *nm* automaton • **automation, automatisation** *nf* automation • **automatiser** *vt* to automate

automatique [ɔtɔmatik] *adj* automatic • **automatiquement** *adv* automatically

automatisme [otomatism] *nm (réflexe)* automatism; *(appareil)* automatic device; **agir par a.** to act automatically

automédication [otomedikasjɔ̃] *nf* self-medication

automitrailleuse [otomitrajøz] *nf Br* armoured *or Am* armored car

automne [otɔn] *nm* autumn, *Am* fall • **automnal, -e, -aux, -ales** *adj* autumnal

automobile [otomɔbil] **1** *adj (véhicule)* self-propelling **2** *nf* car, *Br* motorcar, *Am* automobile; **l'a.** *(industrie)* the car industry • **automobiliste** *nmf* motorist

autonettoyant, -ante [otonetwajɑ̃, -ɑ̃t] *adj* **four a.** self-cleaning oven

autonome [otonɔm] *adj (région)* autonomous, self-governing; *Fig (personne)* self-sufficient; *Ordinat* **calculateur a.** stand-alone (computer) • **autonomie** *nf (de région)* autonomy; *(de personne)* self-sufficiency; **a. de vol** *(d'avion)* range

autopsie [ɔtɔpsi] *nf* autopsy, post-mortem

autoradio [otoradjo] *nm* car radio

autorail [ɔtɔraj] *nm* railcar

autoriser [ɔtɔrize] *vt* **a. qn à faire qch** to authorize *or* permit sb to do sth; **ces découvertes nous autorisent à penser que...** these discoveries entitle us to believe that... • **autorisation** *nf (permission)* permission, authorization; *(document)* authorization; **demander à qn l'a. de faire qch** to ask sb permission to do sth; **donner à qn l'a. de faire qch** to give sb permission to do sth; *Admin* **a. de sortie du territoire** = parental authorization for a minor to travel abroad; *Av* **a. de vol** flight clearance • **autorisé, -ée** *adj (qualifié)* authoritative; *(permis)* permitted, allowed; **les milieux autorisés** official circles

autorité [ɔtɔrite] *nf (fermeté, domination, personne)* authority; **faire qch d'a.** to do sth on one's own authority; **faire a. en qch** *(personne)* to be an authority on; **ce livre fait a.** this book is the authoritative work; **les autorités** the authorities • **autoritaire** *adj* authoritarian

autoroute [otorut] *nf Br* motorway, *Am* highway, *Am* freeway; **a. à péage** *Br* toll motorway, *Am* turnpike (road); *Ordinat* **a. de l'information** information superhighway • **autoroutier** *adj* **réseau a.** *Br* motorway *or Am* freeway system

autosatisfaction [otosatisfaksjɔ̃] *nf* self-satisfaction

auto-stop [otostɔp] *nm* hitchhiking; **faire de l'a.** to hitchhike • **auto-stoppeur, -euse** *nmf* hitchhiker

autour [otur] **1** *adv* around; **tout a.** all around **2** *prép* **a. de** around, round; *(environ)* around, round about

autre [otr] *adj & pron* other; **un a. livre** another book; **un a.** another (one); **d'autres** others; **d'autres médecins/livres** other doctors/books; **as-tu d'autres questions?** have you any other *or* further questions?; **quelqu'un d'a.** somebody else; **personne/rien d'a.** no one/nothing else; **a. chose/part** something/somewhere else; **qui/quoi d'a.?** who/what else?; **l'un l'a., les uns les autres** each other; **l'un et l'a.** both (of them); **l'un ou l'a.** either (of them); **ni l'un ni l'a.** neither (of them); **les uns... les autres** some... others; **nous/vous autres Anglais** we/you English; **d'un moment à l'a.** any moment (now); **c'était un touriste**

comme un a. he was just an ordinary tourist

autrefois [otrəfwa] *adv* in the past, once

autrement [otrəmã] *adv (différemment)* differently; *(sinon)* otherwise; *(plus)* far more (**que** than); **pas a. satisfait** not particularly satisfied

Autriche [otriʃ] *nf* l'A. Austria •**autrichien, -ienne 1** *adj* Austrian **2** *nmf* **A., Autrichienne** Austrian

autruche [otryʃ] *nf* ostrich

autrui [otrɥi] *pron* others, other people

auvent [ovã] *nm (toit)* porch roof; *(de tente, magasin)* awning, canopy

aux [o] *voir* à

auxiliaire [ɔksiljɛr] **1** *adj (verbe, machine, troupes)* auxiliary
  2 *nm (verbe)* auxiliary
  3 *nmf (aide)* assistant; *(dans les hôpitaux)* auxiliary; *(dans l'administration)* temporary worker

auxquels, -elles [okɛl] *voir* lequel

av. *abrév* avenue

avachir [avaʃir] **s'avachir** *vpr (soulier, canapé)* to lose one's shape; *(personne) (physiquement)* to get flabby; **s'a. dans un fauteuil** to flop into an armchair

avait [avɛ] *voir* avoir

aval [aval] *nm* downstream section; **en a.** downstream (**de** from); *Fig* **donner l'a. à un projet** to give a project one's support

avalanche [avalãʃ] *nf* avalanche; *Fig (de lettres)* flood

avaler [avale] **1** *vt* to swallow; *Fig (livre)* to devour; **a. la fumée** to inhale; *Fig* **a. ses mots** to mumble; *Fig* **a. les kilomètres** to eat up the miles
  2 *vi* to swallow; **j'ai avalé de travers** it went down the wrong way

avance [avãs] *nf (progression, acompte)* advance; *(avantage)* lead; **faire une a. à qn** *(donner de l'argent)* to give sb an advance; **faire des avances à qn** *(chercher à séduire)* to make advances to sb; **avoir de l'a. sur qn** to be ahead of sb; **prendre de l'a. sur qn** to take the lead over sb; **à l'a., d'a., par a.** in advance; **en a.** *(arriver, partir)* early; *(avant l'horaire prévu)* ahead (of time); **être en a. pour son âge** to be advanced for one's age; **être en a. sur son temps** to be ahead of one's time; **avoir une heure d'a.** to be an hour early; **avoir un point d'a. sur qn** to be a point ahead of sb; *Scol* **avoir un an d'a.** to be a year ahead

avancé, -ée [avãse] *adj* advanced; **à un âge/stade a.** at an advanced age/stage; **à une heure avancée de la nuit** late in the

night; *Fig* **te voilà bien a.!** a lot of good that's done you!

avancée [avãse] *nf (saillie)* projection; *(progression, découverte)* advance

avancement [avãsmã] *nm (de personne)* promotion; *(de travail)* progress

avancer [avãse] **1** *vt (dans le temps)* to bring forward; *(dans l'espace)* to move forward; *(pion, thèse)* to advance; *(montre)* to put forward; **a. de l'argent à qn** to lend sb money; *Formel ou Hum* **l'automobile de Monsieur est avancée** Sir's carriage awaits
  2 *vi (aller de l'avant)* to move forward; *(armée)* to advance; *(faire des progrès)* to progress; *(faire saillie)* to jut out (**sur** over); **a. d'un pas** to take a step forward; **a. (de cinq minutes)** *(montre)* to be (five minutes) fast; **j'avance de 2 minutes** my watch is two minutes fast; **alors, ça avance?** how is it coming along?; **ça n'avance à rien de pleurer** it's no help crying; **faire a. les choses** to get things moving
  3 s'avancer *vpr* to move forward; **s'a. vers qch** to head towards sth

avant [avã] **1** *prép* before; **a. de faire qch** before doing sth; **je vous verrai a. de partir** I'll see you before I leave; **je vous verrai a. que vous (ne) partiez** I'll see you before you leave; **a. huit jours** within a week; **a. tout** above all; **a. toute chose** first and foremost; **la famille passe a. tout** family comes first
  2 *adv (auparavant)* before; *(d'abord)* beforehand; **a. j'avais les cheveux longs** I used to have long hair; **il vaut mieux téléphoner a.** it's better to phone first; **en a.** *(mouvement)* forward; *(en tête)* ahead; **faire un pas en a.** to take a step forward; **en a. de** in front of; **la nuit d'a.** the night before
  3 *nm (de navire, de voiture)* front; *Football (joueur)* forward; **à l'a.** in (the) front; **monter à l'a.** to go in (the) front; **aller de l'a.** to get on with it
  4 *adj inv (pneu, roue)* front •**avant-bras** *nm inv* forearm •**avant-centre** *(pl* **avants-centres)** *nm Football* centre-forward •**avant-coureur** *(pl* **avant-coureurs)** *adj m* precursory •**avant-dernier, -ière** *(mpl* **avant-derniers,** *fpl* **avant-dernières)** *adj & nmf* last but one •**avant-garde** *(pl* **avant-gardes)** *nf (d'armée)* advance guard; **d'a.** *(idée, film)* avant-garde •**avant-goût** *(pl* **avant-goûts)** *nm* foretaste (**de** of) •**avant-guerre** *nm ou f* pre-war period; **d'a.** pre-war •**avant-hier** [avãtjɛr] *adv*

the day before yesterday •**avant-poste** (*pl* **avant-postes**) *nm Mil* outpost •**avant-première** (*pl* **avant-premières**) *nf* preview •**avant-propos** *nm inv* foreword •**avant-veille** (*pl* **avant-veilles**) *nf* **l'a. (de)** two days before

avantage [avɑ̃taʒ] *nm* advantage; **être/tourner à l'a. de qn** to be/turn to sb's advantage; **tirer a. de qch** to turn sth to one's advantage; **prendre/conserver l'a.** *(dans une course)* to gain/retain the advantage; **tu aurais a. à être poli** you'd do well to be polite; **avantages en nature** benefits in kind; **avantages sociaux** social security benefits •**avantager** *vt* **a. qn** *(favoriser)* to give sb an advantage over; *(faire valoir)* to show sb off to advantage

avantageux, -euse [avɑ̃taʒø, -øz] *adj* *(offre)* attractive; *(prix)* reasonable; *(ton)* superior

avare [avar] **1** *adj* miserly; *Fig* **il n'est pas a. de compliments** he's generous with his compliments

2 *nmf* miser •**avarice** *nf* miserliness, avarice

avaries [avari] *nf* damage; **subir une a.** to be damaged •**avarié, -iée** *adj* *(aliment)* rotten

avatar [avatar] *nm* *(mésaventure)* misadventure

avec [avɛk] **1** *prép* with; **méchant/aimable a. qn** nasty/kind to sb; **a. enthousiasme** with enthusiasm, enthusiastically; **être bien/mal a. qn** *(s'entendre bien/mal)* to get on well/badly with sb; **diminuer a. l'âge** to decrease with age; **cela viendra a. le temps** it will come in time; *Fam* **et a. ça?** *(dans un magasin)* anything else?

2 *adv Fam* **il est venu a.** *(son parapluie, ses gants)* he came with it/them

avenant, -ante [avnɑ̃, -ɑ̃t] **1** *adj* *(personne, manières)* pleasing

2 *nm* **à l'a.** in keeping (**de** with)

avènement [avɛnmɑ̃] *nm* *(d'une ère)* advent; *(d'un roi)* accession

avenir [avnir] *nm* future; **à l'a.** *(désormais)* in future; **d'a.** *(métier)* with good prospects; **assurer l'a. de qn** to make provision for sb

aventure [avɑ̃tyr] *nf* adventure; *(en amour)* affair; **partir à l'a.** to set off in search of adventure; *(sans préparation)* to set out without making plans; **dire la bonne a. à qn** to tell sb's fortune •**s'aventurer** *vpr* to venture (**dans** into) •**aventureux, -euse** *adj* *(personne, vie)* adventurous; *(projet)* risky •**aventurier, -ière** *nmf* adventurer

avenue [avny] *nf* avenue

avérer [avere] **s'avérer** *vpr* *(se révéler)* to prove to be; **il s'avère que...** it turns out that... •**avéré, -ée** *adj* *(fait)* established

averse [avɛrs] *nf* shower

aversion [avɛrsjɔ̃] *nf* aversion (**pour** to)

avertir [avɛrtir] *vt* **a. qn de qch** *(informer)* to inform sb of sth; *(danger)* to warn sb of sth •**averti, -ie** *adj* *(public)* informed; **te voilà a.!** don't say I didn't warn you! •**avertissement** *nm* warning; *(de livre)* foreword •**avertisseur** *nm* *(klaxon®)* horn; **a. d'incendie** fire alarm

> ♫ Il faut noter que les termes anglais **to advertise** et **advertisement** sont des faux amis. Le premier ne signifie jamais **avertir** et le second se traduit par **publicité** ou **annonce**.

aveu, -x [avø] *nm* confession; **passer aux aveux** to make a confession; **de l'a. de tout le monde...** it is commonly acknowledged that...

aveugle [avœgl] **1** *adj* blind; **devenir a.** to go blind; **avoir une confiance a. en qn** to trust sb implicitly

2 *nmf* blind man, *f* blind woman; **les aveugles** the blind •**aveuglément** [-emɑ̃] *adv* blindly

aveugler [avœgle] *vt* *(éblouir)* & *Fig* to blind; **aveuglé par la colère** blind with rage •**aveuglement** [-əmɑ̃] *nm* *(moral, mental)* blindness

aveuglette [avœglɛt] **à l'aveuglette** *adv* blindly; **chercher qch à l'a.** to grope for sth

aviateur, -trice [avjatœr, -tris] *nmf* aviator •**aviation** *nf* *(secteur)* aviation; *(armée de l'air)* air force; **l'a.** *(activité)* flying

avide [avid] *adj* *(cupide)* greedy; *(passionné)* eager (**de** for); **a. de sang** bloodthirsty; **a. d'apprendre** eager to learn •**avidement** *adv* *(voracement)* greedily; *(avec passion)* eagerly •**avidité** *nf* *(voracité, cupidité)* greed; *(passion)* eagerness

avilir [avilir] *vt* to degrade

avion [avjɔ̃] *nm* plane, aircraft *inv, Br* aeroplane, *Am* airplane; **par a.** *(sur lettre)* airmail; **en a., par a.** *(voyager)* by plane, by air; **a. à réaction** jet; **a. de chasse** fighter (plane); **a. de ligne** airliner; **a. de tourisme** private plane

aviron [avirɔ̃] *nm* oar; **l'a.** *(sport)* rowing; **faire de l'a.** to row

avis [avi] *nm* opinion; *(communiqué)* notice; *(conseil)* advice; **à mon a.** in my opinion, to my mind; **être de l'a. de qn** to be of the same opinion as sb; **être d'a. de faire qch** to be of a mind to do sth;

changer d'a. to change one's mind; **sauf a. contraire** unless I/you/*etc* hear to the contrary

aviser [avize] **1** *vt* **a. qn de qch/que...** to inform sb of sth/that...

2 s'aviser *vpr* **s'a. de qch** to become aware of sth; **s'a. que...** to notice that...; **ne t'avise pas de recommencer!** don't you dare to start again! • **avisé, -ée** *adj* wise (**de faire** to do); **bien/mal a.** well-/ill-advised

aviver [avive] *vt (couleur)* to brighten up; *(douleur)* to sharpen; *(querelle)* to stir up

avocat¹, -ate [avɔka, -at] *nmf Jur* lawyer; *Fig* advocate; **a. général** assistant public prosecutor *(in a Court of Appeal)*

avocat² [avɔka] *nm (fruit)* avocado (pear)

avoine [avwan] *nf* oats

avoir* [avwar] **1** *v aux* to have; **je l'ai vu** I have *or* I've seen him; **je l'avais vu** I had *or* I'd seen him

2 *vt (posséder)* to have; *(obtenir)* to get; *(porter)* to wear; *Fam (tromper)* to take for a ride; **il a une fille** he has *or* he's got a daughter; **qu'est-ce que tu as?** what's the matter with you?; **j'ai à lui parler** I have to speak to her; **j'ai à faire** I have things to do; **il n'a qu'à essayer** he only has to try; **a. faim/chaud** to be *or* feel hungry/hot; **a. cinq ans** to be five (years old); **a. du diabète** to be diabetic; **j'en ai pour dix minutes** this will take me ten minutes; *(ne bougez pas)* I'll be with you in ten minutes; **en a. pour son argent** to get one's money's worth; **j'en ai eu pour dix euros** it cost me ten euros; **en a. après** *ou* **contre qn** to have a grudge against sb; *Fam* **se faire a.** to be conned

3 *v impersonnel* **il y a** there is, *pl* there are; **il y a six ans** six years ago; **il n'y a pas de quoi!** *(en réponse à 'merci')* don't mention it!; **qu'est-ce qu'il y a?** what's the matter?

4 *nm* assets, property; *(d'un compte)* credit

avoisiner [avwazine] *vt (dans l'espace)* to border on; *(en valeur)* to be close to • **avoisinant, -ante** *adj* neighbouring, nearby

avorter [avɔrte] *vi (subir une IVG)* to have an abortion; *(faire une fausse couche)* to miscarry; *Fig (projet)* to fall through; **(se faire) a.** *(femme)* to have an abortion • **avortement** [-əmã] *nm* abortion; *Fig (de projet)* failure

avouer [avwe] **1** *vt (crime)* to confess to; **il a fini par a.** he finally confessed; **il faut a. que...** it must be admitted that...

2 s'avouer *vpr* **s'a. vaincu** to acknowledge defeat • **avoué, -ée 1** *adj (auteur, partisan)* declared **2** *nm Br* ≃ solicitor, *Am* ≃ attorney

avril [avril] *nm* April

axe [aks] *nm (géométrique)* axis; *(essieu)* axle; **les grands axes** *(routes)* the main roads; *Fig* **les grands axes d'une politique** the main thrust of a policy • **axer** *vt* to centre (**sur** on)

axiome [aksjom] *nm* axiom

ayant [εjã], **ayez** [εje], **ayons** [εjɔ̃] *voir* avoir

azalée [azale] *nf* azalea

azimuts [azimyt] *nmpl Fam* **tous a.** *(guerre, publicité)* all-out

azote [azot] *nm* nitrogen

azur [azyr] *nm Littéraire (couleur)* azure; **l'a.** *(ciel)* the sky

azyme [azim] *adj* **pain a.** unleavened bread

B

B, b [be] *nm inv* B, b
baba¹ [baba] *n* **b. au rhum** rum baba
baba² [baba] *adj inv Fam* flabbergasted
baba cool [babakul] (*pl* **babas cool**) *nmf* hippie
babeurre [babœr] *nm* buttermilk
babillard [babijar] *nm Can* notice board
babiller [babije] *vi (enfant)* to babble • **babillage** *nm* babble
babines [babin] *nfpl (lèvres)* chops
babiole [babjɔl] *nf (objet)* knick-knack; *(futilité)* trifle
bâbord [bɑbɔr] *nm* port (side); **à b.** to port
babouin [babwɛ̃] *nm* baboon
baby-foot [babifut] *nm inv* table football
baby-sitting [babisitiŋ] *nm* baby-sitting; **faire du b.** to baby-sit • **baby-sitter** (*pl* **baby-sitters**) *n mf* baby-sitter
bac¹ [bak] *nm (bateau)* ferry(boat); *(cuve)* tank; **b. à glace** ice tray; **b. à légumes** salad drawer; **b. à sable** sandpit
bac² [bak] *(abrév* **baccalauréat**) *nm Fam* **passer le b.** to take *or Br* sit one's baccalauréat
baccalauréat [bakalɔrea] *nm* = secondary school examination qualifying for entry to university, *Br* ≃ A-levels, *Am* ≃ high school diploma
bâche [bɑʃ] *nf (de toile)* tarpaulin; *(de plastique)* plastic sheet • **bâcher** *vt* to cover *(with a tarpaulin or plastic sheet)*
bachelier, -ière [baʃəlje, -jɛr] *nmf* = student who has passed the baccalauréat
bachoter [baʃote] *vi Fam* to cram, *Br* to swot • **bachotage** *n Fam* cramming, *Br* swotting
bacille [basil] *nm* bacillus
bâcler [bɑkle] *vt Fam* to botch (up)
bactérie [bakteri] *nf* bacterium • **bactériologique** *adj* bacteriological; **la guerre b.** germ warfare
badaud, -aude [bado, -od] *nmf (promeneur)* stroller; *(curieux)* onlooker
badge [badʒ] *nm Br* badge, *Am* button
badigeonner [badiʒɔne] *vt (surface)* to daub (de with); *(mur)* to whitewash; *Culin* to brush (de with); *(plaie)* to paint (de with)

badin, -ine¹ [badɛ̃, -in] *adj* playful • **badinage** *nm* banter • **badiner** *vi* to jest; **il ne badine pas avec la ponctualité** he's very strict about punctuality
badine² [badin] *nf* switch
baffe [baf] *nf Fam* clout
baffle [bafl] *nm* speaker
bafouer [bafwe] *vt (person)* to jeer at; *(autorité)* to flout
bafouiller [bafuje] *vti* to stammer
bâfrer [bɑfre] *vi très Fam* to stuff oneself
bagage [bagaʒ] *nm Fig (connaissances)* knowledge (**en** of); **bagages** *(sacs, valises)* luggage, baggage; **faire ses bagages** to pack (one's bags); **plier bagages** to pack one's bags; **b. à main** piece of hand luggage • **bagagiste** *nm* baggage handler
bagarre [bagar] *nf* fight, brawl; **chercher la b.** to look for a fight; **des bagarres éclatèrent** fighting broke out • **se bagarrer** *vpr Fam* to fight • **bagarreur, -euse** *adj Fam (personne, caractère)* aggressive
bagatelle [bagatɛl] *nf* trifle; **pour la b. de 2000 euros** for a mere 2,000 euros
bagne [baɲ] *nm Hist (prison)* convict prison; *(peine)* penal servitude • **bagnard** *nm* convict
bagnole [baɲɔl] *nf Fam* car
bagou(t) [bagu] *nm Fam* glibness; **avoir du b.** to have the gift of the gab
bague [bag] *nf (anneau)* ring; *(de cigare)* band; **passer à qn la b. au doigt** to marry sb; **b. de fiançailles** engagement ring • **baguer** *vt (oiseau, arbre)* to ring
baguenauder [bagnode] *vi,* **se baguenauder** *vpr* to saunter around
baguette [bagɛt] *nf (canne)* stick; *(de chef d'orchestre)* baton; *(pain)* French stick; **baguettes** *(de tambour)* drumsticks; *(pour manger)* chopsticks; **mener qn à la b.** to rule sb with a rod of iron; **b. magique** magic wand
bahut [bay] *nm (coffre)* chest; *(buffet)* sideboard; *Fam (lycée)* school
baie¹ [bɛ] *nf Géog* bay
baie² [bɛ] *nf (fruit)* berry
baie³ [bɛ] *nf* **b. vitrée** picture window
baignade [bɛɲad] *nf (activité)* swim-

ming, *Br* bathing; *(endroit)* bathing place; **b. interdite** no swimming

baigner [beɲe] **1** *vt (pied, blessure)* to bathe; *(enfant) Br* to bath, *Am* to bathe; *(sujet: mer)* to wash; **être baigné de sueur/lumière** to be bathed in sweat/light; **un visage baigné de larmes** a face streaming with tears

2 *vi (tremper)* to soak (**dans** in); **les légumes baignent dans la sauce** the vegetables are swimming in the sauce; **il baignait dans son sang** he was lying in a pool of blood; *Fam* **tout baigne** everything's honky dory!

3 se baigner *vpr (nager)* to have a swim; *(se laver)* to have or take a bath ● **baigneur, -euse 1** *nmf* swimmer, *Br* bather **2** *nm (poupée)* baby doll ● **baignoire** *nf* bath (tub)

bail [baj] *(pl* **baux** [bo]) *nm* lease; *Fam* **ça fait un b. que je ne l'ai pas vu** I haven't seen him for ages ● **bailleur** *nm* **b. de fonds** financial backer

bâiller [baje] *vi* to yawn; *(col)* to gape; *(porte)* to be ajar; *Fam* **b. à se décrocher la mâchoire** to yawn one's head off ● **bâillement** *nm (de personne)* yawn

bâillon [bajɔ̃] *nm* gag; **mettre un b. à qn** to gag sb ● **bâillonner** *vt (victime, presse)* to gag

bain [bɛ̃] *nm* bath; *(de mer, de rivière)* swim, *Br* bathe; **prendre un b.** to have or take a bath; **prendre un b. de soleil** to sunbathe; *Fam* **être dans le b.** to be in the swing of things; **petit/grand b.** *(de piscine)* small/large pool; **b. de bouche** mouthwash; **b. moussant** bubble bath; *Fig* **b. de sang** bloodbath; **b. de vapeur** steam bath ● **bain-marie** *(pl* **bains-marie**) *nm* bain-marie *(cooking pan set over a second pan of boiling water)*

baïonnette [bajɔnɛt] *nf* bayonet

baisemain [bɛzmɛ̃] *nm* **faire un b. à qn** to kiss sb's hand

baiser¹ [beze] *nm* kiss; **bons baisers** *(dans une lettre)* (with) love

baiser² [beze] **1** *vt* (**a**) *Littéraire* **b. qn au front/sur la joue** to kiss sb on the forehead/cheek (**b**) *Vulg (duper)* to screw; *(coucher avec)* to fuck **2** *vi Vulg* to fuck

baisse [bes] *nf* fall, drop (**de** in); **en b.** *(température)* falling; *(popularité)* declining

baisser [bese] **1** *vt (rideau, vitre, prix)* to lower; *(radio, chauffage)* to turn down; **b. la tête** to lower one's head; **b. les yeux** to look down; **b. la voix** to lower one's voice; *Fig* **b. les bras** to give in

2 *vi (prix, niveau, température)* to fall; *(marée)* to ebb; *(malade)* to get weaker; *(vue, mémoire)* to fail; *(popularité, qualité)* to decline; **le jour baisse** night is falling

3 se baisser *vpr* to bend down; *(pour éviter qch)* to duck

baissier [besje] *adj m Fin* **marché b.** bear market

bajoues [baʒu] *nfpl (d'animal)* chops

bal [bal] *(pl* **bals**) *nm (élégant)* ball; *(populaire)* dance; **b. costumé**, **b. masqué** fancy dress ball; **b. musette** = dance to accordion music; **b. populaire** = dance, usually outdoors, open to the public

balade [balad] *nf Fam (à pied)* walk; *(en voiture)* drive; **faire une b.** *(à pied)* to go for a walk; *(en voiture)* to go for a drive ● **balader 1** *vt Fam (personne)* to take for a walk/drive; *(objet)* to drag around **2** *vi* **envoyer qn b.** to send sb packing **3 se balader** *vpr Fam (à pied)* to go for a walk; *(en voiture)* to go for a drive ● **baladeur** *nm* personal stereo ● **baladeuse** *nf* inspection lamp

baladin [baladɛ̃] *nm* strolling player

balafre [balafr] *nf (cicatrice)* scar; *(coupure)* gash ● **balafré** *nm* scarface ● **balafrer** *vt* to gash; **visage balafré** scarred face

balai [bale] *nm* broom; **donner un coup de b.** to give the floor a sweep; *Fam* **avoir quarante balais** to be forty; *Fam* **du b.!** clear off!; **b. mécanique** carpet sweeper ● **balai-brosse** *(pl* **balais-brosses**) *nm* = long-handled scrubbing brush

balaise [balɛz] *adj* = **balèze**

balance [balɑ̃s] *nf* (**a**) *(instrument)* (pair of) scales; *Écon* balance; *Fig* **ça pèse dans la b.** it carries some weight; **b. commerciale** balance of trade (**b**) **la B.** *(signe)* Libra; **être B.** to be a Libran (**c**) *Fam (mouchard)* squealer

balancer [balɑ̃se] **1** *vt (bras, jambe)* to swing; *(hanches)* to sway; *Fin (compte)* to balance; *Fam (lancer)* to chuck; *Fam (se débarrasser de)* to chuck out; *Fam (dénoncer)* to squeal on; *Fam* **elle a tout balancé** *(tout abandonné)* she's given it all up

2 se balancer *vpr (arbre, bateau)* to sway; *(sur une balançoire)* to swing; **se b. d'un pied sur l'autre** to rock from one foot to the other; *Fam* **je m'en balance!** I don't give a toss! ● **balancé, -ée** *adj Fam* **être bien b.** *(personne)* to have a good figure ● **balancement** *nm* swaying

balancier [balɑ̃sje] *nm (d'horloge)* pendulum; *(de funambule)* balancing pole

balançoire [balɑ̃swar] *nf (suspendue)* swing; *(bascule)* seesaw

balayer [baleje] *vt (pièce)* to sweep; *(feuilles, saletés)* to sweep up; *Fig (objections)* to brush aside; *(sujet: projecteurs)* to sweep; **le vent a balayé les nuages** the wind swept the clouds away; *Fig* **b. devant sa porte** to put one's own house in order ● **balayage** *nm (nettoyage)* sweeping; *(coiffure)* highlighting ● **balayette** *nf* small brush ● **balayeur, -euse¹** *nmf (personne)* road-sweeper ● **balayeuse²** *nf (véhicule)* road-sweeper

balbutier [balbysje] *vti* to stammer ● **balbutiement** *nm* **balbutiement(s)** stammering; **en être à ses premiers balbutiements** *(science)* to be in its infancy

balcon [balkɔ̃] *nm* balcony; *(de théâtre)* circle, *Am* mezzanine; **premier/deuxième b.** dress/upper circle

baldaquin [baldakɛ̃] *nm* canopy

Baléares [balear] *nfpl* **les B.** the Balearic Islands

baleine [balɛn] *nf (animal)* whale; *(de corset)* whalebone; *(de parapluie)* rib ● **baleinier** *nm (navire)* whaler ● **baleinière** *nf* whaleboat

balèze [balɛz] *adj Fam (grand et fort)* hefty; *(intelligent)* brainy; **b. en maths** brilliant at maths

balise [baliz] *nf Naut* beacon; *Av* light; *(de piste de ski)* marker; *Ordinat* tag; *Naut* **b. flottante** buoy ● **balisage** *nm (signaux) Naut* beacons; *Av* lights ● **baliser** *vt (chenal)* to beacon; *(aéroport)* to equip with lights; *(route)* to mark out with beacons; *(piste de ski)* to mark out

balistique [balistik] *adj* ballistic

balivernes [balivɛrn] *nfpl* twaddle

Balkans [balkɑ̃] *nmpl* **les B.** the Balkans

ballade [balad] *nf (légende, poème long)* ballad; *(musicale, poème court)* ballade

ballant, -ante [balɑ̃, -ɑ̃t] *adj (bras, jambes)* dangling

ballast [balast] *nm (de route, de voie ferrée)* ballast

balle¹ [bal] *nf (pour jouer)* ball; *(d'arme)* bullet; *Anciennement Fam* **balles** *(francs)* francs; **jouer à la b.** to play ball; *Tennis* **faire des balles** to knock the ball about; *Fig* **saisir la b. au bond** to seize the opportunity; *Fig* **se renvoyer la b.** to pass the buck; **b. de tennis** tennis ball; **b. de break/match** break/match point; **b. à blanc** blank; **b. perdue** stray bullet

balle² [bal] *nf (de coton, de laine)* bale

ballet [balɛ] *nm* ballet ● **ballerine** *nf (danseuse)* ballerina; *(chaussure)* pumps

ballon [balɔ̃] *nm (balle, dirigeable)* balloon; *(verre)* round glass wine; **jouer au b.** to play with a ball; **souffler dans le b.** *(pour l'Alcootest ®)* to blow into the bag; *Fig* **être un b. d'oxygène pour qn** to be a lifesaver for sb; **b. d'essai** pilot balloon; **b. de football** *Br* football, *Am* soccer ball

ballonné [balɔne] *adj m (ventre, personne)* bloated

ballot [balo] *nm (paquet)* bundle; *Fam (imbécile)* idiot

ballottage [balɔtaʒ] *nm Pol* **il y a b.** there will be a second ballot

ballotter [balɔte] *vti (bateau)* to toss about; *(passagers)* to shake about; *Fig* **un enfant ballotté entre son père et sa mère** a child passed backwards and forwards between its mother and father

balluchon [balyʃɔ̃] *nm Fam* **faire son b.** to pack one's bags

balnéaire [balneɛr] *adj* **station b.** *Br* seaside resort, *Am* beach resort

balourd, -ourde [balur, -urd] **1** *adj* oafish
  2 *nmf* clumsy oaf

balte [balt] *adj* **les États baltes** the Baltic states

Baltique [baltik] *nf* **la (mer) B.** the Baltic (Sea)

baluchon [balyʃɔ̃] *nm Fam* = **balluchon**

balustrade [balystrad] *nf (clôture)* railing

bambin [bɑ̃bɛ̃] *nm Fam* toddler

bambou [bɑ̃bu] *nm* bamboo; *Fam* **c'est le coup de b.!** it's a rip-off!

ban [bɑ̃] *nm (applaudissements)* round of applause; **bans** *(de mariage)* banns; **être au b. de la société** to be an outcast from society; **un b. pour…** three cheers for…

banal, -e, -als, -ales [banal] *adj (objet, gens)* ordinary; *(accident)* common; *(idée, remarque)* trite, banal; **pas b.** unusual ● **banalité** *nf (d'objet, de gens)* ordinariness; *(d'idée, de remarque)* triteness; *(d'accident)* commonness; **banalités** *(propos)* platitudes

banalisation [banalizajɔ̃] *nf* **la b. de qch** the way sth is becoming more common ● **banaliser** *vt (rendre commun)* to trivialize; **voiture banalisée** unmarked (police) car

banane [banan] *nf (fruit)* banana; *(petit sac) Br* bum bag, *Am* fanny pack; *(coiffure)* quiff ● **bananier** *nm (arbre)* banana tree

banc [bɑ̃] *nm (siège)* bench; *(établi)* work(-bench); *(de poissons)* shoal; **b. des accusés** dock; **b. d'église** pew; **b. d'essai** *Ind* test bed; *Comptr* benchtest; *Fig* test-

ing ground; *Can* **b. de neige** snowbank; **b. de sable** sandbank
bancaire [bɑ̃kɛr] *adj (opération)* banking; *(chèque, compte)* bank
bancal, -e, -als, -ales [bɑ̃kal] *adj (meuble)* wobbly; *Fig (raisonnement)* unsound
bandage [bɑ̃daʒ] *nm (pansement)* bandage
bandana [bɑ̃dana] *nm* bandana
bande [bɑ̃d] *nf* (**a**) *(de tissu, de papier, de terre)* strip; *(pansement)* bandage; *(motif)* stripe; *(pellicule)* film; *Radio* band; **b. (magnétique)** tape; *Aut* **b. d'arrêt d'urgence** *Br* hard shoulder, *Am* shoulder; *Fig* **par la b.** *(de façon détournée)* in a roundabout way; **b. dessinée** comic strip; *Aut* **b. médiane** central line; **b. originale** *(de film)* original soundtrack; **b. sonore** sound track (**b**) *(de personnes)* band, group; *(de voleurs)* gang; *(de loups)* pack; *(d'oiseaux)* flock; **une b. d'imbéciles** a bunch of idiots; **faire b. à part** *(agir seul)* to do one's own thing • **bande-annonce** *(pl* **bandes-annonces**) *nf* trailer (**de** for) • **bande-son** *(pl* **bandes-son**) *nf* soundtrack
bandeau, -x [bɑ̃do] *nm (pour les cheveux)* headband; *(pour les yeux)* blindfold
bander [bɑ̃de] *vt (blessure, main)* to bandage; *(ressort)* to tighten; *(arc)* to bend; **b. les yeux à qn** to blindfold sb
banderole [bɑ̃drɔl] *nf (de manifestants)* banner; *(publicitaire)* streamer
bandit [bɑ̃di] *nm (escroc)* crook; **b. de grand chemin** highwayman • **banditisme** *nm* crime; **le grand b.** organized crime
bandoulière [bɑ̃duljɛr] *nf (de sac)* shoulder strap; **en b.** slung across the shoulder
banjo [bɑ̃dʒo] *nm* banjo
banlieue [bɑ̃ljø] *nf* suburbs; **la b. parisienne** the suburbs of Paris; **la grande/proche b.** the outer/inner suburbs; **en b.** in the suburbs; **de b.** *(maison, magasin)* suburban; **train de b.** commuter train • **banlieusard, -arde** *nmf (habitant)* suburbanite; *(voyageur)* commuter
bannière [banjɛr] *nf* banner; **la b. étoilée** the Star-spangled Banner
bannir [banir] *vt (personne, idée)* to banish (**de** from) • **bannissement** *nm* banishment
banque [bɑ̃k] *nf (établissement)* bank; **la b.** *(activité)* banking; **employé de b.** bank clerk; **faire sauter la b.** *(au jeu)* to break the bank; *Ordinat* **b. de données** data bank; *Méd* **b. du sang** blood bank
banqueroute [bɑ̃krut] *nf Jur* bankruptcy; **faire b.** to go bankrupt

banquet [bɑ̃kɛ] *nm* banquet
banquette [bɑ̃kɛt] *nf (siège)* (bench) seat
banquier, -ière [bɑ̃kje, -jɛr] *nmf* banker
banquise [bɑ̃kiz] *nf* ice floe
baptême [batɛm] *nm Rel* christening, baptism; *Fig (de navire)* naming; **b. de l'air** first flight; **b. du feu** baptism of fire • **baptiser** *vt Rel* to christen, to baptize; *Fig (appeler)* to name
baquet [bakɛ] *nm (cuve)* tub
bar¹ [bar] *nm (café, comptoir)* bar
bar² [bar] *nm (poisson)* bass
baragouiner [baragwine] *Fam* **1** *vt (langue)* to speak badly; **qu'est-ce qu'il baragouine?** what's he jabbering about? **2** *vi* to jabber
baraque [barak] *nf (cabane)* hut, shack; *(de foire)* stall; *Fam (maison)* place • **baraqué, -ée** *adj Fam* hefty • **baraquement** *nm* shacks; *Mil* camp

> *Il faut noter que le nom anglais **barracks** est un faux ami. Il signifie **caserne**.*

baratin [baratɛ̃] *nm Fam (verbiage)* waffle; *(de séducteur)* sweet talk; *(de vendeur)* sales talk • **baratiner** *vt Fam (sujet: séducteur)* *Br* to chat up, *Am* to hit on
barbant, -ante [barbɑ̃, -ɑ̃t] *adj Fam* boring
barbare [barbar] **1** *adj (cruel, sauvage)* barbaric **2** *nmf* barbarian • **barbarie** *nf (cruauté)* barbarity • **barbarisme** *nm* barbarism
barbe [barb] *nf* beard; **b. de trois jours** stubble; **se faire la b.** to shave; *Fig* **à la b. de** right under sb's nose; **rire dans sa b.** to laugh up one's sleeve; *Fam* **quelle b.!** what a drag!; **b. à papa** *Br* candyfloss, *Am* cotton candy
barbecue [barbəkju] *nm* barbecue; **faire un b.** to have a barbecue
barbelé [barbəle] *adj m* **fil de fer b.** barbed wire • **barbelés** *nmpl* barbed wire
barber [barbe] **1** *vt Fam* **b. qn** to bore sb stiff **2 se barber** *vpr* to be bored stiff
barbiche [barbiʃ] *nf* goatee (beard)
barbiturique [barbityrik] *nm* barbiturate
barboter [barbɔte] **1** *vi* to splash about **2** *vt Fam (voler)* to pinch • **barboteuse** *nf* romper-suit
barbouiller [barbuje] *vt (salir)* to smear (**de** with); *(peindre)* to daub; *Fam* **avoir l'estomac barbouillé** to feel queasy
barbouze [barbuz] *nf Fam (agent secret)* secret agent

barbu, -ue [barby] **1** *adj* bearded
2 *nm* bearded man
barda [barda] *nm Fam* gear; *Mil* kit
barder¹ [barde] *vt Culin* to bard; *Fig*
bardé de décorations covered with decorations
barder² [barde] *v impersonnel Fam* **ça va
b.!** there's going to be trouble!
barème [barɛm] *nm (de notes, de salaires, de prix)* scale; *(pour calculer)* ready
reckoner
baril [baril] *nm (de pétrole, de vin)* barrel;
(de lessive) drum; **b. de poudre** powder keg
bariolé, -ée [barjɔle] *adj* multicoloured
barjo(t) [barʒo] *adj inv Fam (fou)* nutty
barman [barman] *(pl* **-men** [-men] *ou*
-mans) *nm Br* barman, *Am* bartender
baromètre [barɔmɛtr] *nm* barometer
baron [barɔ̃] *nm* baron; *Fig* **b. de la
finance** financial tycoon •**baronne** *nf*
baroness
baroque [barɔk] **1** *adj (édifice, style, musique)* baroque; *(idée)* bizarre
2 *nm Archit & Mus* **le b.** the baroque
baroud [barud] *nm* **b. d'honneur** last
stand •**baroudeur** *nm Fam (combattant)*
fighter; *(voyageur)* keen traveller
barouf(le) [baruf(l)] *nm Fam* din
barque [bark] *nf* (small) boat •**barquette**
nf (de fruit) punnet; *(de plat cuisiné)*
container
barrage [baraʒ] *nm (sur l'eau)* dam; **tir de
b.** barrage fire; **b. de police** police roadblock; **b. routier** roadblock
barre [bar] *nf (de fer, de bois)* bar; *(de
danse)* barre; *(trait)* line, stroke; *Naut
(volant de bateau)* helm; **b. de chocolat**
bar of chocolate; *Mus* **b. de mesure** bar
(line); *Jur* **b. des témoins** *Br* witness box,
Am witness stand; *Jur* **être appelé à la b.**
to be called to the witness box; **b. d'appui**
(de fenêtre) rail; **b. d'espacement** *(de clavier)* space bar; *Ordinat* **b. d'outils** tool
bar; *Ordinat* **b. de sélection** menu bar;
Sport **b. fixe** horizontal bar; *Sport* **barres
parallèles** parallel bars
barreau, -x [baro] *nm (de fenêtre, de
cage)* bar; *(d'échelle)* rung; *Jur* **le b.** the
bar; **être derrière les barreaux** *(en prison)*
to be behind bars
barrer [bare] **1** *vt (route, passage, chemin)*
to block off; *(porte, fenêtre)* to bar;
(chèque) to cross; *(mot, phrase)* to cross
out; *Naut (bateau)* to steer; **b. le passage
ou la route à qn** to bar sb's way; **'route
barrée'** 'road closed'; *Fam* **on est mal
barrés!** things don't look good!
2 se barrer *vpr Fam* to beat it

barrette [barɛt] *nf (pour les cheveux) Br*
(hair)slide, *Am* barrette
barreur [barœr] *nm Naut* helmsman; *(à
l'aviron)* cox
barricade [barikad] *nf* barricade •**barricader 1** *vt (rue, porte)* to barricade **2 se
barricader** *vpr* to barricade oneself (**dans**
in)
barrière [barjɛr] *nf (obstacle)* barrier; *(de
passage à niveau)* gate; *(clôture)* fence;
Com **barrières douanières** trade barriers
barrique [barik] *nf* (large) barrel
barrir [barir] *vi (éléphant)* to trumpet
baryton [baritɔ̃] *nm Mus* baritone
bas¹, basse¹ [ba, bas] **1** *adj (dans
l'espace, en quantité, en intensité) & Mus*
low; *(origine)* lowly; *Péj (acte)* mean, low;
(besogne) menial; **à b. prix** cheaply; **au b.
mot** at the very least; **enfant en b. âge**
young child; **avoir la vue basse** to be
short-sighted; *Péj* **le b. peuple** the hoi
polloi; *Boxe & Fig* **coup b.** blow below
the belt
2 *adv (dans l'espace)* low (down); *(dans
une hiérarchie)* low; *(dans un bâtiment)*
downstairs; *(parler)* quietly; **plus b.** further *or* lower down; **parle plus b.** lower
your voice, speak more quietly; **voir plus
b.** *(sur document)* see below; **en b.** at the
bottom; **en b. de** at the bottom of; **mettre
b.** *(sujet: animal)* to give birth; **à b. les
dictateurs!** down with dictators!; *Fam* **b.
les pattes!** hands off!
3 *nm (partie inférieure)* bottom; **l'étagère du b.** the bottom shelf; **au b. de** at
the bottom of; **de b. en haut** upwards
bas² [ba] *nm (chaussette)* stocking; **b. de
contention** elastic stockings; *Fig* **b. de
laine** *(économies)* nest egg
basané, -ée [bazane] *adj (bronzé)*
tanned
bas-côté [bakote] *(pl* **bas-côtés**) *nm (de
route)* verge; *(d'église)* (side)aisle
bascule [baskyl] *nf (balançoire)* seesaw;
(balance) weighing machine; **cheval/fauteuil à b.** rocking horse/chair •**basculer 1**
vt (chargement) to tip over; *(benne)* to tip
up **2** *vi (tomber)* to topple over; **faire b.**
(personne) to knock over; *(chargement)* to
tip over; **le pays a basculé dans l'anarchie**
the country tipped over into anarchy
base [baz] *nf (partie inférieure) & Chim
Math Mil* base; *(de parti politique)* rank
and file; *(principe)* basis; **jeter les bases
de qch** to lay the foundations for sth;
avoir de bonnes bases en anglais to have
a good grounding in English; **produit à b.
de lait** milk-based product; **de b.** basic;

militant de b. rank-and-file militant; **salaire de b.** basic pay; **b. de lancement** launch site; **b. de maquillage** foundation; *Ordinat* **b. de données** database • **baser 1** *vt* to base (**sur** on) **2 se baser** *vpr* **se b. sur** qch to base oneself on sth; **sur quoi te bases-tu pour dire cela?** what basis do you have for saying that?

bas-fond [bafɔ̃] (*pl* **bas-fonds**) *nm* (*de mer, de rivière*) shallow; *Péj* **les bas-fonds** (*de ville*) the rough areas

basic [bazik] *nm Ordinat* BASIC

basilic [bazilik] *nm* (*plante, aromate*) basil

basilique [bazilik] *nf* basilica

basket-ball [basketbol] *nm* basketball

baskets [basket] *nmpl ou nfpl* (*chaussures*) baseball boots; *Fam* **bien dans ses b.** *Br* sorted, *Am* very together

basque¹ [bask] **1** *adj* Basque
2 *nmf* **B.** Basque

basque² [bask] *nfpl* (*de veste*) tail; *Fig* **être toujours pendu aux basques de qn** to always be at sb's heels

basse² [bas] **1** *voir* **bas¹**
2 *nf Mus* (*contrebasse*) (double) bass; (*guitare*) bass (guitar)

basse-cour [baskur] (*pl* **basses-cours**) *nf* (*court*) *Br* farmyard, *Am* barnyard

bassement [basmɑ̃] *adv* basely; **être b. intéressé** to have one's own interests at heart

bassesse [bases] *nf* (*d'une action*) lowness; (*action*) low act

bassin [basɛ̃] *nm* (**a**) (*pièce d'eau*) ornamental lake; (*de fontaine*) basin; (*de port*) dock; (*récipient*) bowl, basin; **petit b.** (*de piscine*) children's pool; **grand b.** (*de piscine*) large pool (**b**) (*du corps*) pelvis (**c**) (*région*) basin; **b. houiller** coal basin; **le b. parisien** the Paris Basin • **bassine** *nf* (*en plastique*) bowl

bassiner [basine] *vt Fam* (*ennuyer*) to bore stiff

basson [basɔ̃] *nm* (*instrument*) bassoon; (*musicien*) bassoonist

basta [basta] *exclam Fam* that'll do it!

bastingage [bastɛ̃gaʒ] *nm Naut* rail

bastion [bastjɔ̃] *nm aussi Fig* bastion

baston [bastɔ̃] *nm ou f Fam* punch-up

bastringue [bastrɛ̃g] *nm Fam* (*affaires*) gear; **et tout le b.** and the whole caboodle

bas-ventre [bavɑ̃tr] *nm* lower abdomen

bat [ba] *voir* **battre**

bât [ba] *nm* packsaddle; *Fig* **c'est là que le b. blesse** there's the rub

bataclan [bataklɑ̃] *nm Fam* (*affaires*)

gear; *Fam* **et tout le b.** and the whole caboodle

bataille [bataj] *nf* (*lutte*) battle; (*jeu de cartes*) beggar-my-neighbour; **cheveux en b.** dishevelled hair • **batailler** *vi Fam* **b. pour faire qch** to fight to do sth • **batailleur, -euse** *adj* aggressive

bataillon [batajɔ̃] *nm Mil* batallion

bâtard, -arde [batar, -ard] **1** *adj* (*enfant*) illegitimate; *Péj* bastard; (*solution*) hybrid
2 *nmf* (*enfant*) illegitimate child; *Péj* bastard; (*chien*) mongrel; (*pain*) = small French stick

bateau, -x [bato] **1** *nm* (*embarcation*) boat; (*grand*) ship; **faire du b.** to go boating; **prendre le b.** to go/come by boat; *Fig* **mener qn en b.** to wind sb up; **b. à moteur** motorboat; **b. à voiles** *Br* sailing boat, *Am* sailboat; **b. de pêche** fishing boat; **b. de plaisance** pleasure boat
2 *adj inv Fam* (*question, sujet*) hackneyed; **col b.** boat neck • **bateau-mouche** (*pl* **bateaux-mouches**) *nm* river boat (*on the Seine*) • **batelier** *nm* boatman

batifoler [batifole] *vi Fam* to lark about

bâtiment [batimɑ̃] *nm* (*édifice*) building; (*navire*) vessel; **le b., l'industrie du b.** the building trade; **b. de guerre** warship

bâtir [batir] *vt* (*construire*) to build; *Couture* to tack; **terrain à b.** building site • **bâti, -ie 1** *adj* **bien b.** (*personne*) well-built **2** *nm* (*charpente*) frame; *Couture* tacking • **bâtisse** *nf Péj* ugly building • **bâtisseur, -euse** *nmf* builder (**de** of)

bâton [batɔ̃] *nm* (*canne*) stick; (*de maréchal*) baton; (*d'agent de police*) *Br* truncheon, *Am* nightstick; (*trait*) vertical line; **donner des coups de b. à qn** to beat sb (with a stick); *Fig* **parler à bâtons rompus** to talk about this and that; *Fig* **mener une vie de b. de chaise** to lead a wild life; *Fig* **mettre des bâtons dans les roues à qn** to put a spoke in sb's wheel; **b. de rouge à lèvres** lipstick; **bâtons de ski** ski sticks • **bâtonnet** *nm* stick

battage [bataʒ] *nm* (*du blé*) threshing; *Fam* (*publicité*) hype

battant¹ [batɑ̃] *nm* (**a**) (*de cloche*) tongue; (*de porte, de volet*) leaf; **porte à deux battants** double door (**b**) (*personne*) fighter

battant², -ante [batɑ̃, -ɑ̃t] *adj* **pluie b.** driving rain; **porte b.** *Br* swing door, *Am* swinging door; **le cœur b.** with a pounding heart

battement [batmɑ̃] *nm* (**a**) (*de tambour*) beat(ing); (*de porte*) banging; (*de paupiè-*

res) blink(ing); *(d'ailes)* flapping; **j'entendais les battements de son cœur** I could hear his/her heart beating (**b**) *(délai)* gap; **une heure de b.** an hour gap

batterie [batri] *nf (d'orchestre)* drums; *(ensemble)* & *Mil, Él* battery; *(de tests, de questions)* series; **être à la b.** *(sujet: musicien)* to be on drums; **élevage en b.** battery farming; **b. de cuisine** kitchen utensils

batteur [batœr] *nm (musicien)* drummer; *(de cuisine)* mixer

battre* [batr] **1** *vt (frapper, vaincre)* to beat; *(œufs)* to whisk; *(beurre)* to churn; *(blé)* to thresh; *(record)* to break; *(cartes)* to shuffle; **b. pavillon britannique** to fly the British flag; **b. le tambour** to beat the drum; *Mus* **b. la mesure** to beat time; **b. la campagne** to scour the countryside; **b. des œufs en neige** to whisk eggs stiffly

2 *vi (cœur)* to beat; *(porte, volet)* to bang; **b. des mains** to clap one's hands; **b. des cils** to flutter one's eyelashes; **b. des ailes** to flap its wings; **le vent fait b. la porte** the wind bangs the door; **j'ai le cœur qui bat** *(d'émotion)* my heart is pounding

3 se battre *vpr* to fight (**avec** with); **se b. au couteau** to fight with a knife; *très Fam* **je m'en bats l'œil** I dont give a toss

battu [baty] *adj (femme, enfant)* battered

battue [baty] *nf (à la chasse)* beat; *(pour retrouver qn)* serach

baudet [bodɛ] *nm* donkey

baudruche [bodryʃ] *nf* **ballon de b.** balloon

baume [bom] *nm aussi Fig* balm; *Fig* **mettre du b. au cœur de qn** to be a consolation for sb

baux [bo] *voir* **bail**

bavard, -arde [bavar, -ard] **1** *adj (qui parle beaucoup)* chatty; *(indiscret)* indiscreet

2 *nmf (qui parle beaucoup)* chatterbox; *(indiscret)* gossip • **bavardage** *nm (action)* chatting; *(commérage)* gossiping; **bavardages** *(paroles)* chats • **bavarder** *vi (parler)* to chat; *(commérer)* to gossip

bave [bav] *nf (de personne)* dribble; *(de chien)* slaver; *(de chien enragé)* froth; *(de limace)* slime • **baver** *vi (personne)* to dribble; *(chien)* to slaver; *(chien enragé)* to foam at the mouth; *(stylo)* to leak; *Fam* **en b. (des ronds de chapeaux)** to have a hard time of it

bavette [bavɛt] *nf (de bébé)* bib; *(de bœuf)* skirt (of beef); *Fam* **tailler une b.** to have a chat

baveux, -euse [bavø, -øz] *adj (bouche)* dribbling; *(omelette)* runny

bavoir [bavwar] *nm* bib

bavure [bavyr] *nf (tache)* smudge; *(erreur)* slip-up; **sans b.** faultess; **b. policière** case of police misconduct

bayer [baje] *vi* **b. aux corneilles** to stare into space

bazar [bazar] *nm (marché)* bazaar; *(magasin)* general store; *Fam (désordre)* shambles *(sing)*; *Fam (affaires)* gear; *Fam* **mettre du b. dans qch** to make a shambles of sth

bazarder [bazarde] *vt Fam (se débarrasser de)* to get shot of; *(jeter)* to chuck out

bazooka [bazuka] *nm* bazooka

BCBG [besebeʒe] *(abrév* **bon chic bon genre**) *adj inv Br* ≃ Sloany, *Am* ≃ preppy

BCG [beseʒe] *n Méd* BCG

BD [bede] *(abrév* **bande dessinée**) *nf* comic strip

bd *abrév* boulevard

béant, -ante [beã, -ãt] *adj (plaie)* gaping; *(gouffre)* yawning

béat, -e [bed, -at] *adj Hum (heureux)* blissful; *Péj (niais)* inane; **être b. d'admiration** to be open-mouthed in admiration • **béatement** *adv (sourire)* inanely • **béatitude** *nf Hum* bliss

béatifier [beatifje] *vt Rel* to beatify

beau, belle [bo, bɛl] *(pl* **beaux, belles**)

---

bel is used before masculine singular nouns beginning with a vowel or h mute.

---

1 *adj* (**a**) *(femme, enfant, fleur, histoire)* beautiful; *(homme)* handsome, goodlooking; *(spectacle, discours)* fine; *(maison, voyage, temps)* lovely; **une belle somme** a tidy sum; **avoir une belle situation** to have a good job; **se faire b.** to smarten oneself up; **ce n'est pas b. de mentir** it isn't nice to tell lies; **c'est trop b. pour être vrai** it's too good to be true; **c'est le plus b. jour de ma vie!** it's the best day of my life!; **j'ai eu une belle peur** I had an awful fright; **il en a fait de belles!** he got up to some real tricks; *très Fam* **un b. salaud** a real bastard

(**b**) *(expressions)* **au b. milieu de** right in the middle of; **de plus belle** with a vengeance; **bel et bien** *(complètement)* well and truly; **je me suis bel et bien trompé** I have indeed made a mistake

2 *adv* **il fait b.** it's fine; **j'ai b. crier...** it's no use (my) shouting...; **j'ai b. le lui expliquer...** no matter how many times I explain it to him...

3 *nm* **le b.** *(la beauté)* beauty; **faire le b.** *(chien)* to sit up and beg; **le plus b. de l'histoire, c'est que...** the best part of the story is that...; *Fam Ironic* **c'et du b.!** that's great!
4 *nf* **belle** *(aux cartes)* decider; *Hum (amie)* lady friend; *Fam* **se faire la b.** to run away; *(de prison)* to escape • **beau-fils** *(pl* **beaux-fils)** *nm (gendre)* son-in-law; *(après remariage)* stepson • **beau-frère** *(pl* **beaux-frères)** *nm* brother-in-law • **beau-père** *(pl* **beaux-pères)** *nm (père du conjoint)* father-in-law; *(après remariage)* stepfather • **beaux-arts** *nmpl* fine arts; **école des b., les B.** art school • **beaux-parents** *nmpl* parents-in-law

beaucoup [boku] *adv (intensément, en grande quantité)* a lot; **aimer b. qch** to like sth very much; **s'intéresser b. à qch** to be very interested in sth; **ça te plaît? – pas b.** do you like it? – not much; **il reste encore b. à faire** there's still a lot to do; **b. d'entre nous** many of us; **b. pensent que...** a lot of people think that...; **b. de** *(quantité)* a lot of; *(nombre)* many, a lot of; **pas b. d'argent** not much money; **pas b. de gens** not many people; **avec b. de soin** with great care; **j'en ai b.** *(quantité)* I have a lot; *(nombre)* I have lots; **b. plus/moins** much more/less, a lot more/less (**que** than); *(nombre)* many *or* a lot more/a lot fewer (**que** than); **b. trop** *(quantité)* much too much; *(nombre)* much too many; **beaucoup trop petit** much too small; **de b.** by far

beauf [bof] *nm Fam (beau-frère)* brother-in-law; *Péj* = stereotypical narrow-minded, average Frenchman

beauté [bote] *nf (qualité, femme)* beauty; **en b.** *(gagner, finir)* magnificently; **être en b.** to be looking magnificent; **de toute b.** magnificent; **se refaire une b.** to put one's face on

bébé [bebe] *nm* baby; **faire le b.** to behave like a baby; **b.-gazelle** baby gazelle • **bébé-éprouvette** *(pl* bébés-éprouvette) *nm* test-tube baby

bébête [bebɛt] *adj Fam* silly

bec [bɛk] *nm (d'oiseau)* beak, bill; *(de pot)* lip; *(de flûte)* mouthpiece; *Fam (bouche)* mouth; **coup de b.** peck; *Fam* **tomber sur un b.** to come up against a serious snag; *Fam* **clouer le b. à qn** to shut sb up; *Fam* **rester le b. dans l'eau** to be left high and dry; **b. de gaz** gas lamp; **b. verseur** spout • **bec-de-lièvre** *(pl* **becs-de-lièvre)** *nm* harelip

bécane [bekan] *nf Fam (vélo)* bike

bécarre [bekar] *nm Mus* natural

bécasse [bekas] *nf (oiseau)* woodcock; *Fam (idiote)* silly thing

bêche [bɛʃ] *nf* spade • **bêcher** [beʃe] *vt* to dig

bêcheur, -euse [beʃœr, -øz] *nmf Fam* stuck-up person

bécot [beko] *nm Fam* kiss • **bécoter** *vt*, **se bécoter** *vpr Fam* to snog

becquée [beke] *nf* beakful; **donner la b. à** *(oiseau)* to feed • **becqueter 1** *vt (sujet: oiseau)* to peck at **2** *vi très Fam (personne)* to eat

bedaine [bədɛn] *nf Fam* pot(-belly), paunch

bedeau, -x [bədo] *nm* verger

bedon [bədɔ̃] *nm Fam* pot(-belly), paunch • **bedonnant, -ante** *adj* pot-bellied, paunchy

bée [be] *adj f* **bouche b.** open-mouthed; **j'en suis resté bouche b.** I was speechless

beffroi [befrwa] *nm* belfry

bégayer [begeje] *vi* to stutter, to stammer • **bégaiement** *nm* stuttering, stammering

bégonia [begɔnja] *nm* begonia

bègue [bɛg] **1** *adj* **être b.** to stutter, to stammer
2 *nmf* stutterer, stammerer

bégueule [begœl] *adj* prudish

béguin [begɛ̃] *nm Fam Vieilli* **avoir le b. pour qn** to have taken a fancy to sb

beige [bɛʒ] *adj & nm* beige

beigne [bɛɲ] *nf Fam* clout

beignet [beɲɛ] *nm* fritter; **b. aux pommes** apple fritter

Beijing [beidʒiŋ] *nm ou f* Beijing

bel [bɛl] *voir* **beau**

bêler [bɛle] *vi* to bleat • **bêlement** *nm* bleat; **bêlements** bleating

belette [bəlɛt] *nf* weasel

Belgique [bɛlʒik] *nf* **la B.** Belgium • **belge 1** *adj* Belgian **2** *nmf* **B.** Belgian

bélier [belje] *nm (animal, machine)* ram; **le B.** *(signe)* Aries; **être B.** to be Aries

belle [bɛl] *voir* **beau** • **belle-famille** *(pl* **belles-familles)** *nf* in-laws • **belle-fille** *(pl* **belles-filles)** *nf (épouse du fils)* daughter-in-law; *(après remariage)* stepdaughter • **belle-mère** *(pl* **belles-mères)** *nf (mère du conjoint)* mother-in-law; *(après remariage)* stepmother • **belle-sœur** *(pl* **belles-sœurs)** *nf* sister-in-law

belligérant, -ante [beliʒerɑ̃, -ɑ̃t] **1** *adj* belligerent
2 *nm* **les belligérants** the warring nations

belliqueux, -euse [belikø, -øz] *adj (peuple, pays)* warlike; *(personne, ton)* aggressive

belote [bəlɔt] *nf* = card game
belvédère [belvedɛr] *nm (construction)* gazebo; *(sur site naturel)* viewpoint
bémol [bemɔl] *nm Mus* flat
ben [bɛ̃] *adv Fam* **b. oui!** well, yes!; **b. voilà, euh...** yeah, well, er...
bénédiction [benediksjɔ̃] *nf Rel & Fig* blessing
bénéfice [benefis] *nm (financier)* profit; *(avantage)* benefit; **accorder le b. du doute à qn** to give sb the benefit of the doubt; **au b. de** *(œuvre de charité)* in aid of
bénéficiaire [benefisjɛr] **1** *nmf (de chèque)* payee; *Jur* beneficiary
2 *adj (entreprise)* profit-making; *(compte)* in credit; **marge b.** profit margin
bénéficier [benefisje] *vi* **b. de qch** *(profiter de)* to benefit from sth; *(avoir)* to have sth; **b. de conditions idéales** to enjoy ideal conditions; **faire b. qn de son expérience** to give sb the benefit of one's experience
bénéfique [benefik] *adj* beneficial (à to)
Bénélux [benelyks] *nm* **le b.** the Benelux
benêt [bənɛ] **1** *adj m* simple
2 *nm* simpleton
bénévole [benevɔl] **1** *adj (travail, infirmière)* voluntary
2 *nmf* volunteer, voluntary worker • **bénévolat** *nm* voluntary work
bénin, -igne [benɛ̃, -iɲ] *adj (accident, opération)* minor; *(tumeur)* benign
bénir [benir] *vt* to bless; **(que) Dieu te bénisse!** (may) God bless you! • **bénit, -ite** *adj* **eau bénite** holy water; **pain b.** consecrated bread
bénitier [benitje] *nm Rel* holy-water stoup
benjamin, -ine [bɛ̃ʒamɛ̃, -in] *nmf* youngest child; *Sport* junior
benne [bɛn] *nf (de camion)* tipping body; *(de mine)* tub; *(de téléphérique)* cable car; **b. à ordures** bin lorry
béotien, -ienne [beɔsjɛ̃, -jɛn] *nmf Péj* philistine
BEP [beəpe] *(abrév* **brevet d'études professionnelles**) *nm Scol* = vocational diploma taken at 18
BEPC [beəpese] *(abrév* **brevet d'études du premier cycle**) *nm Scol* = school leaving certificate taken at 15
béquille [bekij] *nf (canne)* crutch; *(de moto)* stand; **marcher avec des béquilles** to be on crutches
bercail [bɛrkaj] *nm Hum* **rentrer au b.** to return to the fold
berceau, -x [bɛrso] *nm (de bébé)* cradle; *Fig (de civilisation)* birthplace

bercer [bɛrse] **1** *vt (bébé)* to rock; *Fig* **b. qn de promesses** to delude sb with promises
2 se bercer *vpr* **se b. d'illusions** to delude oneself • **berceuse** *nf* lullaby
béret [bere] *nm* beret
berge¹ [bɛrʒ] *nf (rive)* bank
berge² [bɛrʒ] *nf Fam* **avoir trente berges** to be thirty
berger [bɛrʒe] *nm* shepherd; **b. allemand** German shepherd, *Br* Alsatian • **bergère** *nf* shepherdess • **bergerie** *nf* sheepfold
berk [bɛrk] *exclam* yuck!
berline [bɛrlin] *nf (voiture) Br* (four-door) saloon, *Am* sedan
berlingot [bɛrlɛ̃go] *nm (bonbon) Br* boiled sweet, *Am* hard candy; *(de lait)* carton
berlue [bɛrly] *nf* **avoir la b.** to be seeing things
bermuda [bɛrmyda] *nm* Bermuda shorts
Bermudes [bɛrmyd] *nfpl* **les B.** Bermuda
berne [bɛrn] **en berne** *adv Naut Br* at half-mast, *Am* at half-staff; *Mil* furled
berner [bɛrne] *vt* to fool
besace [bəzas] *nf (de mendiant)* bag; **sac b.** = large, soft bag
bésef [bezɛf] *adv Fam* **voir bézef**
besogne [bəzɔɲ] *nf* job, task; *Fig & Péj* **aller vite en b.** to jump the gun • **besogneux, -euse** *adj Péj (travailleur)* plodding
besoin [bəzwɛ̃] *nm* need; **avoir b. de qn/ qch** to need sb/sth; **avoir b. de faire qch** to need to do sth; **éprouver le b. de faire qch** to feel the need to do sth; **au b., si b. est** if necessary, if need be; **en cas de b.** if need be; **être dans le b.** *(très pauvre)* to be in need; **faire ses besoins** *(personne)* to relieve oneself; *(animal)* to do its business
bestial, -e, -iaux, -iales [bɛstjal, -jo] *adj* bestial • **bestiaux** *nmpl* livestock
bestiole [bɛstjɔl] *nf (insecte) Br* creepy-crawly, *Am* creepy-crawler
bêta, -asse [bɛta, -as] *adj Fam* silly
bétail [betaj] *nm* livestock
bête¹ [bɛt] *adj* stupid, silly; *Fam* **être b. comme ses pieds** to be as thick as two short planks; **ce n'est pas b.** *(suggestion)* it's not a bad idea; **c'est b., on a loupé le film!** what a shame, we've missed the film!; **c'est b. comme chou!** it's as easy as pie • **bêtement** *adv* stupidly; **tout b.** quite simply • **bêtise** [betiz] *nf (manque d'intelligence)* stupidity; *(action, parole)* stupid thing; *(bagatelle)* mere trifle; **faire/dire une b.** to do/say something stupid; **dire des bêtises** to talk nonsense

bête² [bɛt] *nf* animal; *(insecte)* bug; *Fig* **chercher la petite b.** to nit-pick; **elle m'a regardé comme une b.** **curieuse** she looked at me as if I was from another planet; *Péj* **b. à concours** *Br* swot, *Am* grind; **b. à bon dieu** *Br* ladybird, *Am* ladybug; **b. de somme** beast of burden; **b. féroce** wild animal; **b. noire** *Br* pet hate, *Am* pet peeve

béton [betɔ̃] *nm* (**a**) *(matériau)* concrete; **mur en b.** concrete wall; **alibi en b.** cast-iron alibi; **b. armé** reinforced concrete (**b**) *Fam* **laisse b.!** drop it! • **bétonnière, bétonneuse** *nf* cement mixer

bette [bɛt] *nf* Swiss chard

betterave [betrav] *nf (plante)* *Br* beet-root, *Am* beet; **b. sucrière** sugar beet

beugler [bøgle] *vi (taureau)* to bellow; *(vache)* to moo; *Fig (radio)* to blare

beur [bœr] *nmf* = North African born in France of immigrant parents

beurre [bœr] *nm* butter; **au b.** *(pâtisserie)* made with butter; *Fig* **ça mettra du b. dans les épinards** that will make life a bit easier; *Fig* **il veut le b. et l'argent du b.** he wants to have his cake and eat it; *Fam* **ça compte pour du b.** that doesn't count; **b. d'anchois** anchovy paste • **beurré** *adj très Fam (ivre)* plastered • **beurrer** *vt* to butter • **beurrier** *nm* butter dish

beuverie [bøvri] *nf* drinking session

bévue [bevy] *nf* slip-up

bézef [bezɛf] *adv Fam* **il n'y en a pas b.** *(pain, confiture)* there isn't much of it; *(légumes, livres)* there aren't many of them

biais [bjɛ] *nm (de mur)* slant; *(moyen)* way; *(aspect)* angle; **regarder qn de b.** to look sideways at sb; **traverser en b.** to cross at an angle; **par le b. de** through

biaiser [bjeze] *vi (ruser)* to dodge the issue

bibelot [biblo] *nm* curio

biberon [bibrɔ̃] *nm* (feeding) bottle; **nourrir un bébé au b.** to bottle-feed a child

bibi [bibi] *pron Fam (moi)* yours truly

bibine [bibin] *nf Fam (boisson)* dishwater

bible [bibl] *nf* bible; **la B.** the Bible • **biblique** *adj* biblical

bibliobus [biblijɔbys] *nm* mobile library

bibliographie [biblijɔgrafi] *nf* bibliography

bibliothèque [biblijɔtɛk] *nf (bâtiment, salle)* library; *(meuble)* bookcase; **b. municipale** public library • **bibliothécaire** *nmf* librarian

Bic® [bik] *nm* ballpoint, *Br* biro®

bicarbonate [bikarbɔnat] *nm Chim* bicarbonate; **b. de soude** bicarbonate of soda

bicentenaire [bisɑ̃tnɛr] *nm Br* bicentenary, *Am* bicentennial

biceps [bisɛps] *nm* biceps

biche [biʃ] *nf (animal)* doe, hind; **ma b.** *(ma chérie)* darling

bichonner [biʃɔne] **1** *vt (préparer)* to doll up; *(soigner)* to pamper
2 se bichonner *vpr* to doll oneself up

bicolore [bikɔlɔr] *adj* two-coloured

bicoque [bikɔk] *nf Fam (maison)* house

bicyclette [bisiklɛt] *nf* bicycle; **la b.** *(sport)* cycling; **faire de la b.** to go cycling; **aller en ville à b.** to cycle to town; **je ne sais pas faire de la b.** I can't ride a bicycle

bidasse [bidas] *nm très Fam Br* squaddie, *Am* G.I.

bide [bid] *nm Fam (ventre)* belly; **faire un b.** *(film, roman)* to bomb, *Br* to flop

bidet [bidɛ] *nm (cuvette)* bidet

bidoche [bidɔʃ] *nf très Fam* meat

bidon [bidɔ̃] **1** *nm (d'essence, d'huile)* can; *(de lait)* churn; *Fam (ventre)* belly; *Fam* **c'est du b.** it's a load of tosh; **b. d'essence** petrol can, jerry can
2 *adj inv Fam (simulé)* phoney, fake

bidonner [bidɔne] **se bidonner** *vpr Fam* to laugh one's head off • **bidonnant, ante** *adj Fam* hilarious

bidonville [bidɔ̃vil] *nf* shantytown

bidule [bidyl] *nm Fam (chose)* whatsit; **B.** *(personne)* what's-his-name, *f* what's-her-name

bielle [bjɛl] *nf Aut* connecting rod

bien [bjɛ̃] **1** *adv* (**a**) *(convenablement)* well; **il joue b.** he plays well; **je vais b.** I'm fine *or* well; **écoutez-moi b.!** listen carefully; *Ironique* **ça commence b.!** that's a good start!
(**b**) *(moralement)* right; **b. se conduire** to behave (well); **vous avez b. fait** you did the right thing; **tu ferais b. de te méfier** you would be wise to behave
(**c**) *(très)* very; **vous arrivez b. tard** you're very late
(**d**) *(beaucoup)* a lot, a great deal; **b. plus/moins** much more/less; **b. des gens** a lot of people; **b. des fois** many times; **il faut b. du courage pour...** it takes a lot of courage to...; **tu as b. de la chance** you're really lucky!; **merci b.!** thanks very much!
(**e**) *(en intensif)* **regarder qn b. en face** to look sb right in the face; **je sais b.** I'm well aware of it; **je vous l'avais b. dit** I told you so!; **j'y suis b. obligé** I just have to; **nos**

verrons **b.!** we'll see!; **c'est b. fait pour lui** it serves him right; **c'est b. ce que je pensais** that's what I thought; **c'est b. cela** that's right; **c'est b. compris?** is that quite understood?; **c'est b. toi?** is it really you? (**f**) (locutions) **b. que...** (+ subjunctive) although, though; **b. entendu, b. sûr** of course; **b. sûr que non!** of course, not!; **b. sûr que je viendrai!** of course, I'll come!
2 adj inv (satisfaisant) good; (à l'aise) comfortable; (en forme) well; (moral) decent; (beau) attractive; **être b. avec qn** (en bons termes) to be on good terms with sb; **on est b. ici** it's nice here; **ce n'est pas b. de mentir** it's not nice to lie; **elle est b. sur cette photo** she looks good on this photo; Fam **nous voilà b.!** we're in a right mess!
3 exclam fine!, right!; **eh b.!** well!
4 nm Phil & Rel good; (chose, capital) possession; Jur asset; **le b. et le mal** good and evil; Jur **biens** property; **faire le b.** to do good; **ça te fera du b.** it will do you good; **dire du b. de qn** to speak well of sb; **c'est pour ton b.** it's for your own good; **grand b. te fasse!** much good may it do you!; **biens de consommation** consumer goods; **biens immobiliers** real estate or property • **bien-aimé, -ée** (mpl **bien-aimés**, fpl **bien-aimées**) adj & nmf beloved • **bien-être** nm well-being • **bien-fondé** nm validity • **bien-pensant, -ante** (mpl **bien-pensants**, fpl **bien-pensantes**) adj & nmf conformist

bienfaisance [bjɛ̃fəzɑ̃s] nf œuvre de b. charity

bienfaisant, -ante [bjɛ̃fəzɑ̃, -ɑ̃t] adj (remède) beneficial; (personne) charitable

bienfait [bjɛ̃fɛ] nm (acte) kindness; (avantage) benefit

bienfaiteur, -trice [bjɛ̃fɛtœr, -tris] nmf benefactor, f benefactress

bienheureux, -euse [bjɛ̃nœrø, -øz] adj blissful; Rel blessed

biennal, -e, -aux, -ales [bjenal, -o] adj biennial

bienséant, -ante [bjɛ̃seɑ̃, -ɑ̃t] adj proper • **bienséance** nf propriety

bientôt [bjɛ̃to] adv soon; **à b.!** see you soon!; **il est b. dix heures** it's nearly ten o'clock; Fam **tu n'as pas b. fini?** have you quite finished?

bienveillant, -ante [bjɛ̃vɛjɑ̃, -ɑ̃t] adj kind • **bienveillance** nf kindness; **avec b.** kindly

bienvenu, -ue [bjɛ̃vny] **1** adj (repos, explication) welcome
2 nmf **soyez le b.!** welcome!; **tu seras toujours le b. chez nous** you'll always be welcome here • **bienvenue** nf welcome; **souhaiter la b. à qn** to welcome sb

bière¹ [bjɛr] nf (boisson) beer; **b. blonde** lager; **b. brune** Br brown ale, Am dark beer; **b. pression** Br draught beer, Am draft beer

bière² [bjɛr] nf (cercueil) coffin

biffer [bife] vt to cross out

bifteck [biftɛk] nm steak; Fam **gagner son b.** to earn one's bread and butter; **b. haché** Br mince, Am mincemeat

bifurquer [bifyrke] vi (route, chemin) to fork; (automobiliste) to turn off • **bifurcation** nf fork

bigame [bigam] adj bigamous • **bigamie** nf bigamy

bigarré, -ée [bigare] adj (étoffe) multicoloured; (foule) motley

bigareau, -x [bigaro] nm = type of cherry

bigler [bigle] vi Fam (loucher) to have a squint; **b. sur qch** to have a good look at sth • **bigleux, -euse** adj Fam (qui louche) cross-eyed; (myope) short-sighted

bigorneau, -x [bigɔrno] nm winkle

bigot, -ote [bigo, -ɔt] Péj **1** adj sanctimonious
2 nmf (religious) bigot

> ⟡ Il faut noter que le terme anglais **bigot** est un faux ami. Il se rapporte au sectarisme religieux et non à une attitude excessivement dévote.

bigoudi [bigudi] nm (hair) curler or roller

bigrement [bigrəmɑ̃] adv Fam (très) awfully; (beaucoup) a heck of a lot

bihebdomadaire [biɛbdɔmadɛr] adj twice-weekly

bijou, -x [biʒu] nm jewel; Fig gem • **bijouterie** [-tri] nf (boutique) Br jeweller's shop, Am jewelry shop; (commerce, fabrication) jeweller's trade • **bijoutier, -ière** nmf Br jeweller, Am jeweler

bikini® [bikini] nm bikini

bilan [bilɑ̃] nm (de situation) assessment; (résultats) results; (d'un accident) toll; **faire le b. de la situation** to stock of the situation; Com **déposer son b.** to file one's petition for bankruptcy; **b. de santé** complete check-up; Fin **b. (comptable)** balance sheet

bilatéral, -e, -aux, -ales [bilateral, -o] adj bilateral

bilboquet [bilbɔkɛ] nm cup-and-ball

bile [bil] nf bile; Fam **se faire de la b. (pour qch)** to fret (about sth) • **se biler** vpr Fam to fret

bilingue [bilɛ̃g] *adj* bilingual
billard [bijar] *nm (jeu)* billiards; *(table)* billiard table; *Fam* **passer sur le b.** to go under the knife; **b. américain** pool; **b. électrique** pinball
bille [bij] *nf (de verre)* marble; *(de billard)* billiard ball; **jouer aux billes** to play marbles; *Fam* **reprendre ses billes** to pull out; *Fam* **toucher sa b. en qch** to know a thing or two about sth
billet [bijɛ] *nm* ticket; **b. (de banque)** *Br* (bank)note, *Am* bill; **b. d'avion/de train** plane/train ticket; **b. de première/seconde** first-class/second-class ticket; **b. simple** single ticket, *Am* one-way ticket; **b. aller retour** return ticket, *Am* round trip ticket; *Fam* **je te fiche mon b. que...** I bet my bottom dollar that...; **b. doux** love letter
billetterie [bijɛtri] *nf (lieu)* ticket office; **b. automatique** *(de billet de transport)* ticket machine
billion [biljɔ̃] *nm* trillion
billot [bijo] *nm* block
bimensuel, -elle [bimɑ̃sɥɛl] *adj* bimonthly, *Br* fortnightly
bimoteur [bimɔtœr] *adj* twin-engined
binaire [binɛr] *adj Math* binary
biner [bine] *vt* to hoe • **binette** *nf* hoe; *très Fam (visage)* mug
binocle [binɔkl] *nm* pince-nez
biochimie [bjoʃimi] *nf* biochemistry • **biochimique** *adj* biochemical
biodégradable [bjɔdegradabl] *adj* biodegradable
biodiversité [bjodivɛrsite] *nf* biodiversity
biographie [bjɔgrafi] *nf* biography • **biographe** *nmf* biographer • **biographique** *adj* biographical
bio-industrie [bjoɛ̃dystri] *(pl* **bio-industries***) nf* biotechnology industry
biologie [bjɔlɔʒi] *nf* biology • **biologique** *adj* biological; *(sans engrais chimiques)* organic • **biologiste** *nm* biologist
biotechnologie [bjotɛknɔlɔʒi] *nf* biotechnology
bip [bip] *nm (son)* beep; *(appareil)* beeper; **faire b.** to beep
bipède [bipɛd] *nm* biped
bique [bik] *nf Fam (chèvre)* nanny goat
biréacteur [bireaktœr] *nm* twin-engine jet
Birmanie [birmani] *nf* **la B.** Burma • **birman, -ane 1** *adj* Burmese **2** *nmf* **B., Birmane** Burmese
bis¹ [bis] *adv (au théâtre)* encore; *(en musique)* repeat; **4 bis** *(adresse)* ≃ 4A

bis², bise [bi, biz] *adj Br* greyish-brown, *Am* grayish-brown
bisbille [bisbij] *nf Fam* squabble; **en b. avec qn** at odds with sb
biscornu, -ue [biskɔrny] *adj (objet)* oddly shaped; *Fam (idée)* cranky
biscotte [biskɔt] *nf* rusk
biscuit [biskɥi] *nm (sucré)* *Br* biscuit, *Am* cookie; **biscuits salés** crackers
bise¹ [biz] *nf (vent)* north wind
bise² [biz] *nf Fam (baiser)* kiss; **faire la b. à qn** to give sb a kiss
biseau, -x [bizo] *nm (outil, bord)* bevel; **en b.** bevel-edged
bisexuel, -uelle [bisɛksɥɛl] *adj* bisexual
bison [bizɔ̃] *nm* bison
bisou [bizu] *nm Fam* kiss
bissextile [bisɛkstil] *adj f* **année b.** leap year
bistouri [bisturi] *nm* lancet
bistro(t) [bistro] *nm Fam* bar
bitume [bitym] *nm (revêtement)* asphalt
bivouac [bivwak] *nm* bivouac • **bivouaquer** *vi* to bivouac
bizarre [bizar] *adj* odd • **bizarrement** *adv* oddly • **bizarroïde** *adj Fam* weird
bizutage [bizytaʒ] *nm Fam* = practical jokes played on first-year students
blabla [blabla] *nm Fam* claptrap
blafard, -arde [blafar, -ard] *adj* pallid
blague [blag] *nf (plaisanterie)* joke; **faire une b. à qn** to play a joke on sb; **raconter des blagues** *(mensonges)* to lie; **sans b.?** no kidding? • **blaguer** *vi Fam* to joke • **blagueur, -euse** *nmf* joker
blair [blɛr] *nm très Fam (nez)* snout, *Br* conk
blaireau, -x [blɛro] *nm (animal)* badger; *(brosse)* shaving brush
blairer [blere] *vt Fam* **je ne peux pas le b.** I can't stick him
blâme [blɑm] *nm (reproche)* blame; *(sanction)* reprimand • **blâmer** *vt (désapprouver)* to blame; *(sanctionner)* to reprimand
blanc, blanche [blɑ̃, blɑ̃ʃ] **1** *adj* white; *(peau)* pale; *(page)* blank; **d'une voix blanche** in a toneless voice
 2 *nm (couleur)* white; *(espace, domino)* blank; *(vin)* white wine; **(article de) b.** *(linge)* linen; **en b.** *(chèque)* blank; **à b.** *(cartouche)* blank; **tirer à b.** to fire blanks; **chauffé à b.** white-hot; **regarder qn dans le b. de yeux** to look sb straight in the eye; **b. d'œuf** egg white; **b. de poulet** chicken breast; **b. cassé** off-white
 3 *nf (note de musique) Br* minim, *Am* half-note

4 *nmf* **B.** *(personne)* White man, *f* White woman; **les B.** the Whites • **blanchâtre** *adj* whitish • **blancheur** *nf* whiteness

blanchiment [blɑ̃ʃimɑ̃] *nm (d'argent)* laundering

blanchir [blɑ̃ʃir] **1** *vt* to whiten; *(mur)* to whitewash; *(linge)* to launder; *Culin* to blanch; *Fig (argent)* to launder; **b. qn** *(disculper)* to clear sb
2 *vi* to turn white • **blanchissage** *nm (de linge)* laundering • **blanchisserie** *nf (lieu)* laundry • **blanchisseur, -euse** *nmf* laundryman, *f* laundrywoman

blanquette [blɑ̃kɛt] *nf* **b. de veau** = veal stew in white sauce; **b. de Limoux** = sparkling white wine from Limoux

blasé, -ée [blɑze] *adj* blasé

blason [blazɔ̃] *nm* coat of arms

blasphème [blasfɛm] *nf* blasphemy • **blasphématoire** *adj* blasphemous • **blasphémer** *vi* to blaspheme

blatte [blat] *nf* cockroach

blazer [blazœr] *nm* blazer

bld *abrév* **boulevard**

blé [ble] *nm* wheat, *Br* corn; *Fam (argent)* bread

bled [blɛd] *nm Fam (lieu isolé)* dump; **dans un b. perdu** in the middle of nowhere

blême [blɛm] *adj* sickly pale; **b. de colère** livid with anger • **blêmir** *vi* to turn pale

> 📖 Il faut noter que le verbe anglais **to blemish** est un faux ami. Il ne signifie jamais **devenir pâle**.

blesser [blese] **1** *vt (dans un accident)* to injure, to hurt; *(par arme)* to wound; *(offenser)* to hurt
2 se blesser *vpr (par accident)* to hurt *or* injure oneself; *(avec une arme)* to wound oneself; **se b. au bras** to hurt one's arm • **blessant, -ante** *adj* hurtful • **blessé, -ée** *nmf (victime d'accident)* injured person; *(victime d'aggression)* wounded person; **les blessés** the injured/wounded • **blessure** *nf (dans un accident)* injury; *(par arme)* wound

blette [blɛt] *nf* = **bette**

bleu, -e [blø] *(mpl -s)* **1** *adj* blue; *(steak)* very rare
2 *n (couleur)* blue; *(ecchymose)* bruise; *(fromage)* blue cheese; *Fam (novice)* novice; **b. de travail** *Br* overalls, *Am* overall; **se faire un b. au genou** to bruise one's knee; **b. ciel** sky blue; **b. marine** navy blue; **b. roi** royal blue • **bleuâtre** *adj* bluish • **bleuté, -ée** *adj* bluish

bleuet [bløɛ] *nm (plante)* cornflower

blinder [blɛ̃de] *vt (véhicule)* to armour-plate • **blindé, -ée 1** *adj Mil* armoured, armour-plated; *(voiture)* bulletproof; **porte blindée** steel security door; *Fam* **je suis b.** I'm hardened to it **2** *nm Mil* armoured vehicle

bloc [blɔk] *nm (de pierre, de bois)* block; *(de papier)* pad; *(de maison)* & *Pol* bloc; *(masse compacte)* unit; **faire b. contre qn** to join forces against sb; **en b.** *(démissionner)* all together; **tout refuser en b.** to reject everything in its entirety; **à b.** *(visser, serrer)* as tightly as possible; *très Fam* **être au b.** *(en prison)* to be in the clink; **b. opératoire** operating theatre • **bloc-notes** *(pl* **blocs-notes**) *nm* notepad

blocage [blɔkaʒ] *nm (de mécanisme)* jamming; *(de freins, de roues)* locking; **b. des prix** price freeze; **faire un b. psychologique** to have a mental block

blocus [blɔkys] *nm* blockade; **lever le b.** to raise the blockade

blond, -onde [blɔ̃, -ɔ̃d] **1** *adj (cheveux, personne)* blond; *(sable)* golden
2 *nm (homme)* fair-haired man; *(couleur)* blond; **b. cendré** ash blond; **b. vénitien** strawberry blond
3 *nf (femme)* fair-haired woman, blonde • **blondeur** *nf* fairness, blondness

blondinet, -ette [blɔ̃dinɛ, -ɛt] *adj* fair-haired

bloquer [blɔke] **1** *vt (route, ballon, compte)* to block; *(porte, mécanisme)* to jam; *(roue)* to lock; *(salaires, prix, crédits)* to freeze; *(grouper)* to group together; **b. le passage à qn** to block sb's way; **bloqué par la neige** snowbound; *Fam* **je suis bloqué à l'hôpital** I'm stuck in hospital
2 se bloquer *vpr (machine)* to get stuck

blottir [blɔtir] **se blottir** *vpr* to snuggle up; **se b. contre qn** to snuggle up to sb; **blottis les uns contre les autres** huddled up together

blouse [bluz] *nf (tablier)* overall; *(corsage)* blouse; **b. blanche** *(de médecin, de biologiste)* white coat • **blouson** *nm (lumber-)*jacket; *(plus léger)* blouson; **b. en cuir** leather jacket; **b. d'aviateur** bomber jacket

blue-jean [bludʒin] *(pl* **blue-jeans** [-dʒinz]) *nm Vieilli* jeans

bluff [blœf] *nm* bluff • **bluffer** *vti (aux cartes)* & *Fam* to bluff

blush [blœʃ] *nm* blusher

boa [bɔa] *nm (serpent, tour de cou)* boa

bobard [bɔbar] *nm Fam* tall story

bobine [bɔbin] *nf (de ruban, de fil)* reel; *(de machine à coudre)* bobbin; *(de film, de* *papier)* roll; *(de machine à écrire)* spool; *Él* coil; *Fam (visage)* mug

bobo [bobo] *nm Langage enfantin (coupure)* cut; *(piqûre)* sting; **ça fait b.** it hurts

bocage [bɔkaʒ] *nm* bocage *(countryside with many hedges, trees and small fields)*

bocal, -aux [bɔkal, -o] *nm* jar; *(aquarium)* bowl

bock [bɔk] *nm* beer glass

bœuf [bœf] *(pl -fs* [bø]*)* **1** *nm (animal)* bullock; *(de trait)* ox *(pl* oxen); *(viande)* beef

2 *adj inv Fam* **avoir un succès b.** to be incredibly successful; **faire un effet b.** to make a really big impression

bof [bɔf] *exclam Fam* **ça te plaît? – b.!** pas tellement do you like it? – not really, no; **il est chouette, mon nouveau pull – b.** my new sweater's great – I suppose so

bogue [bɔg] *nm Ordinat* bug

bohème [bɔɛm] *adj & nmf* bohemian • **bohémien, -ienne** *adj & nmf* gypsy

boire* [bwar] **1** *vt (sujet: personne)* to drink; *(sujet: plante)* to soak up; *Fig* **b. les paroles de qn** to drink in sb's every words

2 *vi (sujet: personne)* to drink; *(sujet: plante)* to soak in; **b. comme un trou** to drink like a fish; *Fam* **b. un coup** to have a drink; **b. à la bouteille** to drink from the bottle; **b. à petits coups** to sip; **b. au succès de qn** to drink to sb's success; **donner à b. à qn** to give sb a drink; **faire b. les chevaux** to water the horses

3 se boire *vpr* to be drunk

4 *nm* **le b. et le manger** food and drink

bois [bwa] *nm (matériau, forêt)* wood; *(de raquette)* frame; **en** *ou* **de b.** wooden; **les b.** *(d'un cerf)* the antlers; *(d'un orchestre)* woodwind instruments; *Fig* **ils vont voir de quel b. je me chauffe!** I'll show them!; **petit b.** kindling; **b. de chauffage** firewood; **b. de construction** timber; **b. de lit** bed frame; **b. mort** dead wood • **boisé, -ée** *adj* wooded • **boiseries** *nfpl Br* panelling, *Am* paneling

boisson [bwasɔ̃] *nf* drink

boit [bwa] *voir* **boire**

boîte [bwat] *nf* (**a**) *(récipient)* box; **b. d'allumettes** *(pleine)* box of matches; *(vide)* matchbox; **des haricots en b.** canned *or Br* tinned beans; *Fam* **mettre qn en b.** to pull sb's leg; **b. à bijoux** jewel box; **b. à gants** glove compartment; **b. à** *ou* **aux lettres** *Br* postbox, *Am* mailbox; **b. à musique** music box; **b. à outils** toolbox; **b. de conserve** can, *Br* tin; *Aut* **b. de vitesse** gearbox; *Av* **b. noire** black box; **b. postale** Post Office Box; **b. vocale** voice

mail (**b**) *Fam (entreprise)* firm; *Péj* **b. à bac** crammer; **b. de jazz** jazz club; **b. de nuit** nightclub • **boîtier** *nm (de montre)* case

boiter [bwate] *vi* to limp • **boiteux, -euse** *adj (personne)* lame; *Fig (raisonnement)* shaky • **boitiller** *vi* to limp slightly

boive [bwav] *subjonctif de* **boire**

bol [bɔl] *nm (récipient, contenu)* bowl; **prendre un b. d'air** to get a good breath of fresh air; *Fam* **avoir du b.** to be lucky; *Fam* **coup de b.** stroke of luck

bolide [bɔlid] *nm (voiture)* racing car

Bolivie [bɔlivi] *nf* **la B.** Bolivia • **bolivien, -ienne 1** *adj* Bolivian **2** *nmf* **B., Bolivienne** Bolivian

bombance [bɔ̃bɑ̃s] *nf Fam* **faire b.** to feast

bombarder [bɔ̃barde] *vt (avec des bombes)* to bomb; *(avec des obus)* to shell; **b. de qn de questions** to bombard sb with letters • **bombardement** [-əmɑ̃] *nm (avec des bombes)* bombing; *(avec des obus)* shelling • **bombardier** *nm (avion)* bomber

bombe [bɔ̃b] *nf* (**a**) *(explosif)* bomb; *Fig* **faire l'effet d'une b.** to be a bombshell; *Fam* **faire la b.** to whoop it up; **b. à eau** water bomb; **b. à retardement** time bombe (**b**) *(atomiseur)* spray (can) (**c**) *(chapeau)* riding hat

bomber [bɔ̃be] **1** *vt* **b. le torse** to throw out one's chest

2 *vi (mur)* to bulge; *(planche)* to warp • **bombé, -ée** *adj* bulging

bon¹, bonne [bɔ̃, bɔn] **1** *adj* (**a**) *(satisfaisant)* good; **avoir de bons résultats** to get good results; **c'est b.** *(d'accord)* that's fine (**b**) *(agréable)* nice, good; **passer une bonne soirée** to spend a pleasant evening; **il fait b. se reposer** it's nice *or* good to rest; **b. anniversaire!** happy birthday!; **bonne année!** Happy New Year!

(**c**) *(charitable)* kind, good *(avec qn* to sb)

(**d**) *(correct)* right; **le b. choix/moment/ livre** the right choice/moment/book

(**e**) *(apte)* fit; **b. à manger** fit to eat; *Mil* **b. pour le service** fit for duty; **elle n'est b. à rien** she's useless

(**f**) *(prudent)* wise, good; **juger b. de partir** to think it wise to leave

(**g**) *(compétent)* good; **b. en français** good at French

(**h**) *(profitable) (investissement, conseil, idée)* good; **c'est b. à savoir** it's worth knowing

(**i**) *(valable)* valid; **ce billet est encore b.** this ticket is still valid; **le lait est-il encore b.?** is that milk still all right to drink?

(**j**) *(en intensif)* **un b. rhume** a bad cold;

dix bonnes minutes a good ten minutes; **j'ai mis un b. moment à comprendre** it took me a while to understand (**k**) *(locutions)* **à quoi b.?** what's the point?; **quand b. vous semble** whenever you like; **pour de b.** *(partir, revenir)* for good; **tenir b.** *(personne)* to hold out; **avoir qn à la bonne** to have a soft spot for sb; **elle est bien b.!** that's a good one! **2** *nm* **avoir du b.** to have some good points; **un b. à rien** a good-for-nothing; **les bons et les méchants** the goodies and the baddies

3 *adv* **sentir b.** to smell good; **il fait b.** it's nice and warm

4 *exclam* **b.! on y va?** right, shall we go?; **ah b., je ne le savais pas** really? I didn't know; **ah b.?** is that so?

bon² [bɔ̃] *nm (papier)* coupon, *Br* voucher; *Fin (titre)* bond; **b. d'achat** gift voucher; **b. de commande** order form; **b. de réduction** money-off coupon; *Fin* **b. du Trésor** treasury bond

bonasse [bɔnas] *adj* soft

bonbon [bɔ̃bɔ̃] *nm Br* sweet, *Am* candy; **b. à la menthe** mint •**bonbonnière** *nf Br* sweet box, *Am* candy box

bonbonne [bɔ̃bɔn] *nf (bouteille)* demi-john; *(de gaz)* cylinder

bond [bɔ̃] *nm* leap, jump; *(de balle)* bounce; **faire un b.** to leap up; *Fig (prix)* to shoot up; **se lever d'un b.** *(du lit)* to jump out of bed; *(d'une chaise)* to leap up; **faire faux b. à qn** to leave sb in the lurch

bonde [bɔ̃d] *nf (bouchon)* plug; *(trou)* plughole

bondé, -ée [bɔ̃de] *adj* packed, crammed

bondir [bɔ̃dir] *vi* to leap, to jump; **b. sur qn/qch** to pounce on sb/sth; *Fig* **ça me fait b.** it makes me hopping mad

bon enfant [bɔnɑ̃fɑ̃] *adj inv* easy-going

bonheur [bɔnœr] *nm (bien-être)* happiness; *(chance)* good fortune; **faire le b. de qn** to make sb happy; **porter b. à qn** to bring sb luck; **par b.** luckily; **au petit b.** at random

bonhomie [bɔnɔmi] *nf* good-naturedness

bonhomme [bɔnɔm] *(pl* **bonshommes** [bɔ̃zɔm]) *nm* fellow, guy; **aller son petit b. de chemin** to be jogging along nicely; **b. de neige** snowman

boniche [bɔniʃ] *nf Fam Péj* maid

boniment [bɔnimɑ̃] *nm (discours)* patter; *Fam (mensonge)* tall story

bonjour [bɔ̃ʒur] *nm & exclam (le matin)* good morning; *(l'après-midi)* good afternoon; **dire b. à qn** to say hello to sb; *Fam*

b. l'ambiance! there was one hell of an atmosphere

bonne¹ [bɔn] *voir* **bon¹**

bonne² [bɔn] *nf (domestique)* maid; **b. d'enfants** nanny

bonnement [bɔnmɑ̃] *adv* **tout b.** simply

bonnet [bɔnɛ] *nm (coiffure)* hat; *(de soutien-gorge)* cup; *Fig* **c'est b. blanc blanc b.** it's six of one and half a dozen of the other; *Fam* **gros b.** bigshot; **b. d'âne** *Br* dunce's cap, *Am* dunce cap; **b. de bain** bathing cap •**bonneterie** [-ɛtri] *nf (bas)* hosiery

bonniche [bɔniʃ] *nf =* **boniche**

bonsoir [bɔ̃swar] *nm & exclam (en rencontrant qn)* good evening; *(en quittant qn)* goodbye; *(au coucher)* goodnight

bonté [bɔ̃te] *nf* kindness, goodness; **avoir la b. de faire qch** to be so kind as to do sth

bonus [bɔnys] *nm (de salaire)* bonus; *(d'assurance)* no-claims bonus

bon vivant [bɔ̃vivɑ̃] *adj m* **être b.** to enjoy life

boom [bum] *nm (économique)* boom

bord [bɔr] *nm (limite)* edge; *(de chapeau)* brim; *(de verre)* rim; **le b. du trottoir** *Br* the kerb, *Am* the curb; **au b. de la route** at the side of the road; **au b. de la rivière** beside the river; **au b. de la mer** at the seaside; **au b. de la ruine** on the brink *or* verge of ruin; **au b. des larmes** on the verge of tears; **à bord d'un bateau/d'un avion** on board a boat/a plane; **monter à b.** to go on board; **être le seul maître à b.** to be the one in charge; **par-dessus b.** overboard

bordeaux [bɔrdo] **1** *nm (vin)* Bordeaux (wine); *(rouge)* claret

2 *adj inv* maroon

bordée [bɔrde] *nf Naut (salve)* broadside; *Fig (d'injures)* torrent

bordel [bɔrdɛl] *nm très Fam (lieu)* brothel; *(désordre)* mess; **mettre le b. dans qch** to make a mess of sth •**bordélique** *adj très Fam (organisation, pièce)* shambolic; **être b.** *(personne)* to be a slob

border [bɔrde] *vt (lit)* to tuck in; *(sujet: arbres)* to line; **b. qch de qch** to edge sth with sth; **b. qn dans son lit** to tuck sb in

bordereau, -x [bɔrdəro] *nm Fig & Com* note

bordure [bɔrdyr] *nf (bord)* edge; *(de vêtement)* border; **en b. de route** by the roadside

borgne [bɔrɲ] *adj (personne)* one-eyed; *(louche)* shady

borne [bɔrn] *nf (limite)* boundary marker; (pierre) boundary stone; Él terminal; Fam (kilomètre) kilometer; Fig sans bornes boundless; Fig dépasser les bornes to go too far; **b. kilométrique** ≃ milestone

borner [bɔrne] **1** vt (terrain) to mark out **2 se borner** vpr **se b. à qch/à** faire qch (personne) to restrict oneself to sth/to doing sth; **se b. à qch** (chose) to be limited to sth • **borné, -ée** adj (personne) narrow-minded; (esprit) narrow

Bosnie [bɔzni] nf **la B.** Bosnia

bosquet [bɔskɛ] nm grove

bosse [bɔs] nf (de bossu, de chameau) hump; (enflure) bump, lump; (de terrain) bump; **se faire une b.** to get a bump; Fam **avoir la b. du commerce** to have a good head for commerce; Fam **il a roulé sa b.** he's knocked about a bit

bosseler [bɔsle] vt (déformer) to dent

bosser [bɔse] vi Fam to work • **bosseur, -euse** nmf Fam hard-worker

bossu, -ue [bɔsy] **1** adj (personne) hunchbacked **2** nmf hunchback

bot [bo] adj m **pied b.** clubfoot

botanique [bɔtanik] **1** adj botanical **2** nf botany

botte [bɔt] nf (chaussure) boot; (de fleurs, de radis) bunch; Fig **b. secrète** secret weapon; Fam **en avoir plein les bottes** to be fed up to the back teeth; **bottes en caoutchouc** rubber boots • **botter** vt **botté de cuir** wearing leather boots; Fam **b. le derrière à qn** to boot sb up the backside; Fam **ça me botte** I dig it • **bottier** nm bootmaker • **bottillon** nm, **bottine** nf ankle boot

Bottin® [bɔtɛ̃] nm phone book

bouc [buk] nm (animal) billy goat; (barbe) goatee; **b. émissaire** scapegoat

boucan [bukɑ̃] nm Fam din, row; **faire du b.** to kick up a row

bouche [buʃ] nf mouth; **de b. à oreille** by word of mouth; Fig **faire la fine b.** to be fussy; **b. d'égout** manhole; **b. d'incendie** Br fire hydrant, Am fireplug; **b. de métro** métro entrance • **bouche-à-bouche** nm mouth-to-mouth resuscitation • **bouchée** nf mouthful; Fig **mettre les bouchées doubles** to really get a move on

boucher¹ [buʃe] **1** vt (fente, trou) to fill in; (conduite, fenêtre) to block up; (vue, rue, artère) to block; (bouteille) to cork; Fam **ça m'en a bouché un coin** it took the wind out of my sails **2 se boucher** vpr (conduite) to get blocked up; **se b. le nez** to hold one's nose • **bouché, -ée** adj (conduite) blocked;

(temps) overcast; Fam (personne) dense; **j'ai le nez b.** my nose is stuffed up • **bouche-trou** (pl **bouche-trous**) nm Fam stopgap

boucher², -ère [buʃe, -ɛr] nmf butcher • **boucherie** nf butcher's (shop); Fig (carnage) butchery

bouchon [buʃɔ̃] nm (a) (à vis) cap, top; (de tonneau) stopper; (de liège) cork; (de canne à pêche) float (b) (embouteillage) traffic jam • **bouchonner** vt Fam **ça bouchonne** (sur la route) there's congestion

boucle [bukl] nf (de ceinture) buckle; (de cheveu) curl; (méandre) loop; **écouter un disque en b.** to listen to a record over and over again; **b. d'oreille** earring

boucler [bukle] **1** vt (ceinture, valise) to buckle; (quartier) to seal off; (maison) to lock up; Fam (travail) to finish off; Fam (prisonnier) to bang up; **b. ses valises** (se préparer à partir) to pack one's bags; **b. la boucle** Av to loop the loop; Fig to come full circle; Fam **boucle-la!** belt up! **2** vi (cheveux) to be curly • **bouclé, -ée** adj (cheveux) curly

bouclier [buklije] nm shield

bouddhiste [budist] adj & nmf Buddhist

bouder [bude] **1** vi to sulk **2** vt (personne) to refuse to talk to; **b. une élection** to refuse to vote • **boudeur, -euse** adj sulky

boudin [budɛ̃] nm **b. noir** Br black pudding, Am blood sausage; **b. blanc** white pudding • **boudiné, -ée** adj (doigt) podgy

boue [bu] nf mud • **boueux, -euse 1** adj muddy **2** nm Fam Br dustman, Am garbage collector

bouée [bwe] nf Naut buoy; **b. de sauvetage** lifebelt; **b. (gonflable)** (d'enfant) (inflatable) rubber ring

bouffe [buf] nf Fam (nourriture) grub • **bouffer¹** vti Fam (manger) to eat

bouffée [bufe] nf (de fumée) puff; (de parfum) whiff; Fig (de colère) outburst; **une b. d'air pur** a breath of fresh air; Méd **b. de chaleur** Br hot flush, Am hot flash

bouffer² [bufe] vi (manche, jupe) to puff out • **bouffant, -ante** adj **manche bouffante** puff(ed) sleeve • **bouffi, -ie** adj (yeux, visage) puffy

bouffon, -onne [bufɔ̃, -ɔn] **1** adj farcical **2** nm buffoon • **bouffonneries** nfpl (actes) antics

bouge [buʒ] nm Péj (bar) dive; (taudis) hovel

bougeoir [buʒwar] nm candlestick

bougeotte [buʒɔt] nf Fam **avoir la b.** to be fidgety

bouger [buʒe] **1** *vti* to move; **rester sans b.** to keep still **2 se bouger** *vpr Fam (se déplacer)* to move; *(s'activer)* to get a move on

bougie [buʒi] *nf (en cire)* candle; *(de moteur)* spark plug

bougon, -onne [bugɔ̃, -ɔn] *adj Fam* grumpy ● **bougonner** *vi Fam* to grumble

bougre [bugr] *nm Fam* **le pauvre b.** the poor devil ● **bougrement** [-əmã] *adv Fam* damned; **il fait b. froid** it's damn cold

bouillabaisse [bujabɛs] *nf* = provençal fish soup

bouille [buj] *nf Fam (visage)* mug; **il a une bonne b.** he looks a good sort

bouillie [buji] *nf (pour bébé)* baby food; *(à base de céréales)* baby cereal; **réduire qch en b.** to mash sth

bouillir* [bujir] *vi* to boil; **faire b. qch** to boil sth; **b. de colère** to seethe with anger ● **bouillant, -ante** *adj (qui bout)* boiling; *(très chaud, fiévreux)* boiling hot ● **bouilli** *adj* boiled

bouilloire [bujwar] *nf* kettle

bouillon [bujɔ̃] *nm (aliment)* stock; *(bulles)* bubbles; **bouillir à gros bouillons** to boil hard; **b. de culture** culture medium ● **bouillonner** *vi* to bubble

bouillotte [bujɔt] *nf* hot-water bottle

boulanger, -ère [bulãʒe, -ɛr] *nmf* baker ● **boulangerie** *nf* baker's (shop)

boule [bul] *nf (sphère)* ball; **boules** *(jeu)* bowls; **se mettre en b.** *(chat)* to curl up into a ball; *Fam* **perdre la b.** to go off one's head; *Fam* **avoir la b. à zéro** to be a skinhead; *Fam* **avoir les boules** *(être énervé)* to be pissed off; *(avoir peur)* to be wetting oneself; **b. de neige** snowball; *Fig* **faire b. de neige** to snowball; **b. puante** stink bomb; **boules Quiès®** earplugs

bouleau, -x [bulo] *nm* (silver) birch; *(bois)* birch(wood)

bouledogue [buldɔg] *nm* bulldog

bouler [bule] *vi Fam* **envoyer qn b.** to send sb packing

boulet [bulɛ] *nm (de forçat)* ball and chain; **b. de canon** cannonball

boulette [bulɛt] *nf (de papier)* ball; *(de viande)* meatball; *Fam (gaffe) Br* boob, *Am* boo-boo

boulevard [bulvar] *nm* boulevard

bouleverser [bulvɛrse] *vt (émouvoir)* to move deeply; *(perturber)* to distress; *(projets, habitudes)* to disrupt; *(vie)* to turn upside down ● **bouleversant, -ante** *adj (émouvant)* deeply moving, *(perturbant)* distressing ● **bouleversement** [-əmã] *nm* *(de projets, d'habitudes)* disruption; *(de personne)* emotion; **bouleversements économiques** economic upheavals

boulimie [bulimi] *nf Méd* bulimia ● **boulimique** *adj* **être b.** to have bulimia

boulon [bulɔ̃] *nm* bolt

boulot¹ [bulo] *nm Fam (emploi)* job; *(travail)* work

boulot², -otte [bulo, -ɔt] *adj Fam* tubby

boum [bum] **1** *exclam & nm* bang **2** *nf Fam (fête)* party *(for young people)*

bouquet [bukɛ] *nm (fleurs)* bunch of flowers; *(d'arbres)* clump; *(de vin)* bouquet; *Fig* **c'est le b.!** that takes the *Br* biscuit *or Am* cake!; **b. final** *(de feu d'artifice)* grand finale

bouquin [bukɛ̃] *nm Fam* book ● **bouquiner** *vti Fam* to read ● **bouquiniste** *nmf* second-hand bookseller

bourbeux, -euse [burbø, -øz] *adj* muddy ● **bourbier** *nm (lieu, situation)* quagmire

bourde [burd] *nf Fam (gaffe)* blunder; **faire une b.** to put one's foot in it

bourdon [burdɔ̃] *nm (insecte)* bumblebee ● **bourdonnement** *nm (d'insecte)* buzz(ing); **avoir des bourdonnements d'oreilles** to have a buzzing in one's ears ● **bourdonner** *vi (insecte, oreilles)* to buzz

bourg [bur] *nm* market town ● **bourgade** *nf* village

bourge [burʒ] *adj Fam (bourgeois)* upper-class

bourgeois, -oise [burʒwa, -waz] **1** *adj* middle-class **2** *nmf* middle-class person ● **bourgeoisie** *nf* middle class

bourgeon [burʒɔ̃] *nm* bud ● **bourgeonner** *vi* to bud

bourgmestre [burgmɛstr] *nm (en Belgique, en Suisse)* burgmaster

bourgogne [burgɔɲ] *nm (vin)* Burgundy

bourlinguer [burlɛ̃ge] *vi Fam (voyager)* to knock about

bourrade [burad] *nf* shove

bourrage [buraʒ] *nm Fam* **b. de crâne** brainwashing

bourrasque [burask] *nf* squall, gust of wind; **souffler en bourrasques** to gust

bourratif, -ive [buratif, -iv] *adj Fam* stodgy

bourre [bur] *nf (pour rembourrer)* stuffing; *Fam* **à la b.** in a rush

bourreau, -x [buro] *nm* executioner; *Hum* **b. des curs** ladykiller; **b. d'enfants** child-beater; **b. de travail** workaholic

bourrelet [burlɛ] *nm (contre les courants*

d'air) weather strip; **b. de graisse** spare *Br* tyre *orAm* tire

bourrer [bure] **1** *vt (coussin)* to stuff (**de** with); *(sac)* to cram (**de** with); *(pipe)* to fill; **b. qn de qch** *(gaver)* to fill sb up with sth; **b. qn coups** to beat sb up; *Fam* **b. le crâne à qn** *(élève)* to stuff sb's head with facts

2 se bourrer *vpr* **se b. de qch** *(se gaver)* to stuff oneself up with; *très Fam* **se b. la gueule** to get plastered • **bourré, -ée** *adj* (**a**) *(plein)* **b. à craquer** full to bursting; *Fam* **être b. de complexes** to be a mass of complexes (**b**) *très Fam (ivre)* plastered

bourricot [buriko] *nm* small donkey

bourrique [burik] *nf* she-ass; *Fam* **faire tourner qn en b.** to drive sb crazy

bourru, -ue [bury] *adj* surly

bourse [burs] *nf (sac)* purse; **sans b. délier** without spending a penny; *Scol & Univ* **b. (d'étude)** grant; **la B.** the Stock Exchange • **boursier, -ière 1** *adj* **opération boursière** Stock Exchange transaction **2** *nmf (élève, étudiant)* grant holder

boursouflé, -ée [bursufle] *adj (visage, yeux)* puffy

bous [bu] *voir* **bouillir**

bousculer [buskyle] **1** *vt (pousser)* to jostle; *(presser)* to rush; *Fig (habitudes)* to disrupt

2 se bousculer *(foule)* to push and shove; **les idées se bousculaient dans sa tête** his/her head was buzzing with ideas • **bousculade** *nf (agitation)* pushing and shoving

bouse [buz] *nf* **de la b. de vache** cow dung

bousiller [buzije] *vt Fam* to wreck

boussole [busɔl] *nf* compass

boustifaille [bustifaj] *nf très Fam* grub

bout¹ [bu] *voir* **bouillir**

bout² [bu] *nm (extrémité)* end; *(de langue, de doigt)* tip; *(moceau)* bit; **un b. de temps** a little while; **faire un b. de chemin** to go part of the way; **d'un b. à l'autre** from one end to the other; **au b. de la rue** at the end of the street; **au b. d'un moment** after a while; *Fam* **au b. du fil** *(au téléphone)* on the other end; **jusqu'au b.** *(lire, rester)* (right) to the end; **à b. de forces** exhausted; **à b. de souffle** out of breath; **à b. de bras** at arm's length; **pousser qn à b.** to push sb too far; **venir à b. de** *(travail)* to get through; *(adversaire)* to get the better of; **à b. portant** point-blank; **à tout b. de champ** at every possible opportunity; *Fig* **voir le b. du tunnel** to see the light at the end of the tunnel; *Fam* **je n'en vois pas le**

b. I'm nowhere near the end of it; *Cin* **b. d'essai** screen test

boutade [butad] *nf (plaisanterie)* quip

boute-en-train [butɑ̃trɛ̃] *nm inv (personne)* live wire

bouteille [butɛj] *nf* bottle; *(de gaz)* cylinder

boutique [butik] *nf Br* shop, *Am* store; *(de couturier)* boutique; **fermer b.** to shut up shop • **boutiquier, -ière** *nmf Br* shopkeeper, *Am* storekeeper

boutoir [butwar] *nm* **coup de b.** staggering blow

bouton [butɔ̃] *nm (bourgeon)* bud; *(au visage)* spot; *(de vêtement)* button; *(de porte, de télévision)* knob; **b. de manchette** cufflink • **bouton-d'or** (*pl* **boutons-d'or**) *nm* buttercup • **bouton-pression** (*pl* **boutons-pression**) *nm Br* press-stud, *Am* snap fastener • **boutonner** *vt*, **se boutonner** *vpr (vêtement)* to button (up) • **boutonneux, -euse** *adj* spotty

boutonnière [butɔnjɛr] *nf* buttonhole

bouture [butyr] *nf* cutting

bouvreuil [buvrœj] *nm* bullfinch

bovin, -ine [bɔvɛ̃, -in] *adj* bovine • **bovins** *nmpl* cattle

bowling [bolin] *nm (jeu) Br* tenpin bowling, *Am* tenpins; *(lieu)* bowling alley

box [bɔks] (*pl* **boxes**) *nm (d'écurie)* stall; *(de dortoir)* cubicle; *(garage)* lock-up garage; *Jur* **b. des accusés** dock

boxe [bɔks] *nf* boxing; **b. française** kick boxing • **boxer** *vi* to box • **boxeur** *nm* boxer

boyau, -x [bwajo] *nm (intestin)* gut; *(corde)* catgut; *(de vélo)* tubular *Br* tyre *orAm* tire; *(de mine)* narrow gallery

boycotter [bɔjkɔte] *vt* to boycott • **boycottage** *nm* boycott

BP [bepe] (*abrév* **boîte postale**) *nf* PO Box

bracelet [brasle] *nm (bijou)* bracelet; *(rigide)* bangle; *(de montre) Br* strap, *Am* band • **bracelet-montre** (*pl* **bracelets-montres**) *nm* wristwatch

braconner [brakɔne] *vi* to poach • **braconnier** *nm* poacher

brader [brade] *vt* to sell off cheaply • **braderie** *nf* clearance sale

braguette [bragɛt] *nf (de pantalon)* fly, *Br* flies

braille [braj] *nm* Braille; **en b.** in Braille

brailler [braje] *vti* to yell

braire* [brɛr] *vi (âne)* to bray

braise(s) [brɛz] *nf(pl)* embers • **braiser** [breze] *vt Culin* to braise

brancard [brɑ̃kar] *nm (civière)* stretcher;

(de charrette) shaft • **brancardier** *nm* stretcher-bearer

branche [brɑ̃ʃ] *nf (d'arbre, d'une science)* branch; *(de compas)* leg; *(de lunettes)* side piece • **branchages** *nmpl (des arbres)* branches; *(coupés)* cut branches

branché, -ée [brɑ̃ʃe] *adj Fam (à la mode)* trendy

brancher [brɑ̃ʃe] **1** *vt (à une prise)* to plug in; *(à un réseau)* to connect
2 se brancher *vpr* **se b. sur** *(station de radio)* to tune in to • **branchement** *nm (assemblage de fils)* connection

brandade [brɑ̃dad] *nf Culin* = salt cod puréed with garlic, oil and cream

brandir [brɑ̃dir] *vt* to brandish

branle [brɑ̃l] *nm* **mettre qch en b.** to set sth in motion • **branlant, -ante** *adj (chaise, escalier)* rickety • **branle-bas** *nm inv* **b. (de combat)** commotion • **branler** *vi (chaise, escalier)* to be rickety

braquer [brake] **1** *vt (diriger)* to point (**sur** at); *(regard)* to fix (**sur** on); *Fam (banque)* to hold up; **b. qn contre qn/qch** to turn sb against sb/sth
2 *vi Aut* to turn the steering wheel • **braquage** *nm (de roues)* turning; *Fam (vol)* hold-up; **(angle de) b.** steering lock

braquet [brakɛ] *nm* gear ratio

bras [bra] *nm* arm; **donner le b. à qn** to give sb one's arm; **b. dessus b. dessous** arm in arm; **les b. croisés** with one's arms folded; **à b. ouverts** with open arms; **à tour de b.** with all one's might; **en b. de chemise** in one's shirtsleeves; *Fig* **avoir le b. long** to have a lot of influence; *Fig* **se retrouver avec qch sur les b.** to be left with sth on one's hands; *Fam* **faire un b. d'honneur à qn** ≃ to stick two fingers up at sb; **prendre qn à b.-le-corps** to seize sb round the waist; **b. de lecture** pickup arm; **b. de mer** arm of the sea; *Fig* **b. droit** *(assistant)* right-hand man

brasier [brazje] *nm* blaze, inferno

brassard [brasar] *nm* armband

brasse [bras] *nf (nage)* breaststroke; *(mouvement)* stoke; **b. papillon** butterfly stroke

brassée [brase] *nf* armful

brasser [brase] *vt (mélanger)* to mix; *(bière)* to brew • **brassage** *nm (mélange)* mixing; *(de la bière)* brewing • **brasserie** *nf (usine)* brewery; *(café)* brasserie

brassière [brasjɛr] *nf (de bébé) Br* vest, *Am* undershirt

bravade [bravad] *nf* **par b.** out of bravado

brave [brav] **1** *adj (courageux)* brave; *(bon)* good

2 *nm (héros)* brave man • **bravement** *adv (courageusement)* bravely

braver [brave] *vt (personne, lois)* to defy; *(danger, mort)* to brave

bravo [bravo] **1** *exclam* bravo!
2 *nm* **bravos** cheers

bravoure [bravur] *nf* bravery

break [brɛk] *nm (voiture) Br* estate car, *Am* station wagon

brebis [brəbi] *nf* ewe; *Fig* **b. galeuse** black sheep

brèche [brɛʃ] *nf* gap; *(dans la coque d'un bateau)* hole; **battre qch en b.** to demolish sth

bréchet [breʃɛ] *nm* breastbone

bredouille [brəduj] *adj* empty-handed

bredouiller [brəduje] *vti* to mumble

bref, brève [brɛf, brɛv] **1** *adj* brief, short
2 *adv* in short; **enfin b....** in a word…

breloque [brələk] *nf (de bracelet)* charm

Brésil [brezil] *nm* **le B.** Brazil • **brésilien, -ienne 1** *adj* Brazilian **2** *nmf* **B., Brésilienne** Brazilian

Bretagne [brətaɲ] *nf* **la B.** Brittany • **breton, -onne 1** *adj* Breton **2** *nmf* **B., Bretonne** Breton

bretelle [brətɛl] *nf* strap; **bretelles** *(de pantalon) Br* braces, *Am* suspenders; **b. (d'accès)** *(route)* access road

breuvage [brœvaʒ] *nm* potion

brève [brɛv] *voir* **bref**

brevet [brəvɛ] *nm (certificat)* certificate; *(diplôme)* diploma; *Scol* **b. des collèges** = general exam taken at 15; **b. de technicien supérieur** = advanced vocational training certificate; **b. (d'invention)** patent • **breveter** *vt* to patent

bréviaire [brevjɛr] *nm Rel* breviary

bribes [brib] *nfpl* **b. de conversation** snatches of conversation

bric-à-brac [brikabrak] *nm inv (vieux objets)* odds and ends

bric et de broc [brikedəbrɔk] **de bric et de broc** *adv* haphazardly

bricole [brikɔl] *nf (objet, futilité)* trifle; *Fam* **il va lui arriver des bricoles** he's/she's going to get into a pickle

bricoler [brikɔle] **1** *vt (construire)* to put together; *(réparer)* to tinker with
2 *vi* to do-it-yourself • **bricolage** *nm (travail)* DIY, do-it-yourself; **faire du b.** to do some DIY • **bricoleur, -euse 1** *adj* **être b.** to be good with one's hands **2** *nmf* handyman, *f* handywoman

bride [brid] *nf (de cheval)* bridle; **aller à b. abattue** to ride full tilt • **brider** *vt (cheval)* to bridle; *(personne, désir)* to curb; **avoir les yeux bridés** to have slanting eyes

bridge [bridʒ] *nm (jeu, prothèse)* bridge
brièvement [brijɛvmɑ̃] *adv* briefly • **brièveté** *nf* brevity
brigade [brigad] *nf (de gendarmerie)*
squad; *Mil* brigade; **b. antigang** organized crime squad • **brigadier** *nm (de police)* police sergeant; *Mil* corporal
brigand [brigɑ̃] *nm (bandit)* brigand;
(personne malhonnête) crook
briguer [brige] *vt (honneur, poste)* to
sollicit
brillant, -ante [brijɑ̃, -ɑ̃t] **1** *adj (luisant)*
shining; *(couleur)* bright; *(cheveux, cuir)*
shiny; *Fig (remarquable)* brilliant
  2 *nm* shine; *(diamant)* diamond; **b. à
lèvres** lip gloss • **brillamment** [-amɑ̃] *adv*
brilliantly
briller [brije] *vi* to shine; **faire b.** *(chaussures)* to polish; **b. de colère** to shine with
anger; **b. par son absence** to be conspicuous by one's absence; **b. de mille
feux** to sparkle brilliantly
brimer [brime] *vt* to bully • **brimade** *nf
(d'élèves)* bullying; *Fig (humiliation)* vexation
brin [brɛ̃] *nm (d'herbe)* blade; *(de persil)*
sprig; *(de muguet)* spray; *(de corde, de fil)*
strand; *Fig* **un b. de qch** a bit of sth; **faire
un b. de toilette** to have a quick wash
brindille [brɛ̃dij] *nf* twig
bringue¹ [brɛ̃g] *nf Fam* **faire la b.** to go on
a binge
bringue² [brɛ̃g] *nf Fam* **grande b.** *(fille)*
beanpole
bringuebaler [brɛ̃gbale] *vti Fam* to
shake about
brio [brijo] *nm* brilliance; **avec b.** brilliantly
brioche [brijɔʃ] *nf* brioche; *Fam (ventre)*
paunch • **brioché** *adj* **pain b.** = milk bread
brique [brik] *nf* (**a**) *(de construction)*
brick; **mur de briques** brick wall (**b**)
Anciennement Fam (10 000 francs) 10,000
francs
briquer [brike] *vt (nettoyer)* to scrub
down
briquet [brikɛ] *nm (cigarette)* lighter
bris [bri] *nm (de verre)* breaking; **b. de
glaces** broken windows
brise [briz] *nf* breeze
briser [brize] **1** *vt* to break; *(opposition,
résistance)* to crush; *(espoir, carrière)* to
wreck; *(fatiguer)* to exhaust; **la voix brisée par l'émotion** his/her voice choked
by emotion
  2 se briser *vpr* to break • **brisants** *nmpl*
reefs • **brise-glace** *nm inv (navire)* ice
breaker • **brise-lames** *nm inv* breakwater

britannique [britanik] **1** *adj* British
  2 *nmf* **B.** Briton; **les Britanniques** the
British
broc [bro] *nm* pitcher, jug
brocante [brɔkɑ̃t] *nf (commerce)* second-
hand trade • **brocanteur, -euse** *nmf*
secondhand dealer
broche [brɔʃ] *nf (pour rôtir)* spit; *(bijou)*
brooch; *(pour fracture)* pin; **faire cuire
qch à la b.** to spit-roast sth • **brochette** *nf
(tige)* skewer; *(plat)* kebab
broché, -ée [brɔʃe] *adj* **livre b.** paperback
brochet [brɔʃɛ] *nm* pike
brochure [brɔʃyr] *nf* brochure, pamphlet
brocolis [brɔkɔli] *nmpl* broccoli
broder [brɔde] *vt* to embroider (**de** with)
• **broderie** *nf (activité)* embroidery; **faire
de la b.** to embroider; **des broderies** embroidery
broncher [brɔ̃ʃe] *vi* **sans b.** without bat-
ting an eyelid; **il n'a pas bronché** he didn't
bat an eyelid
bronches [brɔ̃ʃ] *nfpl* bronchial tubes
• **bronchite** *nf* bronchitis; **avoir une b.** to
have bronchitis
bronze [brɔ̃z] *nm* bronze
bronzer [brɔ̃ze] *vi* to tan • **bronzage** *nm*
(sun)tan
brosse [brɔs] *nf* brush; **donner un coup
de b. à qch** to give sth a brush; **cheveux en
b.** crew cut; **b. à dents** toothbrush • **brosser 1** *vt (tapis, cheveux)* to brush; **b. un
tableau de qch** to give an outline of sth **2
se brosser** *vpr* **se b. les dents/les cheveux**
to brush one's teeth/one's hair
brouette [bruɛt] *nf* wheelbarrow
brouhaha [bruaa] *nm* hubbub
brouillard [brujar] *nm* fog; **il y a du b.** it's
foggy
brouille [bruj] *nf* disagreement, quarrel
brouiller [bruje] **1** *vt (idées)* to muddle
up; *(vue)* to blur; *(émission radio)* to jam;
les yeux brouillés de larmes eyes blurred
with tears; *Fig* **b. les pistes** to cover one's
tracks
  2 se brouiller *vpr (idées)* to get muddled
up; *(vue)* to get blurred; *(se disputer)* to fall
out (**avec** with); **le temps se brouille** it's
clouding over • **brouillé, -ée** *adj (teint)*
blotchy; **être b. avec qn** to have fallen
out with sb
brouillon, -onne [brujɔ̃, -ɔn] **1** *adj (mal
organisé)* disorganized; *(mal présenté)*
untidy
  2 *nm* rough draft; **(papier) b.** *Br* scrap
paper, *Am* scratch paper

broussailles [brusɑj] *nfpl* scrub
brousse [brus] *nf* **la b.** the bush
brouter [brute] *vti* to graze
broutille [brutij] *nf* trifle
broyer [brwaje] *vt* to grind; *(doigt, bras)* to crush; *Fig* **b. du noir** to be down in the dumps
bru [bry] *nf* daughter-in-law
brugnon [bryɲɔ̃] *nm* nectarine
bruine [brɥin] *nf* drizzle •**bruiner** *v impersonnel* to drizzle; **il bruine** it's drizzling
bruissement [brɥismɑ̃] *nm (de feuilles)* rustle, rustling
bruit [brɥi] *nm* noise, sound; *(nouvelle)* rumour; **faire du b.** to make a noise •**bruitage** *nm Cin* sound effects
brûlant, -ante [brylɑ̃, -ɑ̃t] *adj (objet, soupe)* burning hot; *(soleil)* scorching; *Fig (sujet)* burning
brûlé, -ée [bryle] *nm* **odeur de b.** burnt smell; **sentir le b.** to smell burnt
brûle-pourpoint [brylpurpwɛ̃] **à brûle-pourpoint** *adv* point-blank
brûler [bryle] **1** *vt (sujet: flamme, acide)* to burn; *(électricité, combustible)* to use; *(feu rouge)* to go through; **être brûlé vif** *(être supplicié)* to be burnt at the stake
  2 *vi* to burn; *Fig* **b. d'envie de faire qch** to be dying to do sth; *Fig* **b. de désir** to be burning with desire; **attention, ça brûle!** careful, it's hot!
  3 se brûler *vpr* to burn oneself; **se b. la langue** to burn one's tongue
brûlure [brylyr] *nf* burn; **brûlures d'estomac** heartburn
brume [brym] *nf* mist, haze •**brumeux, -euse** *adj* misty, hazy; *Fig (obscur)* hazy
brun, brune [brœ̃, bryn] **1** *adj (cheveux)* dark, brown; *(personne)* dark-haired; **être b. de peau** to be dark-skinned
  2 *nm (couleur)* brown
  3 *nmf* dark-haired man, *f* dark-haired woman •**brunette** *nf* brunette •**brunir** *vi (personne, peau)* to tan; *(cheveux)* to darken
brushing® [brœʃiŋ] *nm* blow-dry; **faire un b. à qn** to blow-dry sb's hair
brusque [brysk] *adj (personne)* •**brusquement** [-əmɑ̃] *adv* abruptly •**brusquer** *vt (décision)* to rush •**brusquerie** *nf* abruptness
brut, -e [bryt] *adj (pétrole)* crude; *(diamant)* rough; *(soie)* raw; *(poids, salaire)* gross; *(champagne)* extra-dry; **à l'état b.** in its raw state
brutal, -e, -aux, -ales [brytal, -o] *adj (personnes, manières, paroles)* brutal; *(choc)* violent; *(franchise, réponse)* crude, blunt; *(changement)* abrupt; **être b. avec**

qn to be rough with sb •**brutalement** *adv (violemment)* brutally; *(avec brusquerie)* roughly; *(soudainement)* abruptly •**brutaliser** *vt* to ill-treat •**brutalité** *nf (violence, acte)* brutality; *(soudaineté)* abruptness •**brute** *nf* brute
Bruxelles [brysɛl] *nm ou f* Brussels
bruyant, -ante [brɥijɑ̃, -ɑ̃t] *adj* noisy •**bruyamment** [-amɑ̃] *adv* noisily
bruyère [bryjɛr] *nf (plante)* heather; *(terrain)* heath
BTS [beteɛs] *abrév* **brevet de technicien supérieur**
bu, -e [by] *pp de* **boire**
buanderie [bɥɑ̃dri] *nf (lieu)* laundry
bûche [byʃ] *nf* log; *Fam* **prendre une b.** *Br* to come a cropper, *Am* to take a spill; **b. de Noël** Yule log •**bûcher¹** *nm (à bois)* woodshed; *(de supplice)* stake
bûcher² [byʃe] *Fam* **1** *vt (étudier)* to bone up on, *Br* to swot up
  2 *vi Br* to swot, *Am* to grind •**bûcheur, -euse** *nmf Br* swot, *Am* grind
bûcheron [byʃrɔ̃] *nm* woodcutter
budget [bydʒɛ] *nm* budget •**budgétaire** *adj* budgetary; *(année)* financial; **déficit b.** budget deficit
buée [bɥe] *nf (sur vitre)* condensation; *(sur miroir)* mist
buffet [byfɛ] *nm (meuble bas)* sideboard; *(meuble haut)* dresser; *(repas)* buffet
buffle [byfl] *nm* buffalo
buis [bɥi] *nm (arbre)* box; *(bois)* boxwood
buisson [bɥisɔ̃] *nm* bush
buissonnière [bɥisɔnjɛr] *adj f* **faire l'école b.** *Br* to play truant, *Am* to play hookey
bulbe [bylb] *nm* bulb
Bulgarie [bylgari] *nf* **la B.** Bulgaria •**bulgare 1** *adj* Bulgarian **2** *nmf* **B.** Bulgarian
bulldozer [byldozœr] *nm* bulldozer
bulle [byl] *nf (d'air, de savon)* bubble; *(de bande dessinée)* balloon; *(décret du pape)* bull; **faire des bulles** to blow bubbles
buller [byle] *vi Fam* to laze about
bulletin [byltɛ̃] *nm (communiqué, revue)* bulletin; *(météo)* report; **b. d'informations** news bulletin; **b. de paie** *ou* **de salaire** *Br* pay slip, *Am* pay stub; **b. de santé** medical bulletin; **b. de vote** ballot paper; **b. météo** weather report; **b. scolaire** *Br* school report, *Am* report card
buraliste [byralist] *nmf (à la poste)* clerk; *(au tabac)* tobacconist
bureau, -x [byro] *nm (table)* desk; *(lieu)* office; *(comité)* committee; **b. de change** bureau de change; **b. de poste** post of-

fice; **b. de tabac** *Br* tobacconist's (shop), *Am* tobacco store

bureaucrate [byrokrat] *nmf* bureaucrat • **bureaucratie** [-asi] *nf* bureaucracy • **bureaucratique** *adj* bureaucratic

Bureautique® [byrotik] *nf* office automation

burette [byrɛt] *nf (pour huile)* oilcan; *(de chimiste)* burette

burin [byrɛ̃] *nm (de graveur)* burin; *(pour découper)* (cold) chisel

buriné, -ée [byrine] *adj (visage)* seamed

burlesque [byrlɛsk] *adj (idée)* ludicrous; *(genre)* burlesque

bus¹ [bys] *nm* bus

bus² [by] *pt de* boire

busqué [byske] *adj m (nez)* hooked

buste [byst] *nm (torse)* chest; *(sculpture)* bust • **bustier** *nm (corsage)* bustier

but¹ [by(t)] *nm (objectif)* aim, goal; *(intention)* purpose; *Football* goal; *Fig* **aller droit au b.** to go straight to the point; **dire qch en blanc** to say sth straight out; **c'est le b. de l'opération** that's the point of the operation

but² [by] *pt de* boire

butane [bytan] *nm* butane

buter [byte] **1** *vt* (**a**) **b. qn** to put sb's back up (**b**) *très Fam (tuer)* to bump off

2 *vi* **b. contre qch** *(cogner)* to bump into sth; *(trébucher)* to stumble over sth; *Fig (difficulté)* to come up against sth

3 se buter *vpr (s'entêter)* to dig one's heels in • **buté, -ée** *adj* obstinate

butin [bytɛ̃] *nm (de voleur)* loot; *(de pillards)* spoils; *(d'armée)* booty

butiner [bytine] *vi (abeille)* to gather pollen and nectar

butoir [bytwar] *nm (pour train)* buffer; *(de porte)* stopper, *Br* stop

butte [byt] *nf* hillock; *Fig* **être en b. à qch** to be exposed to sth

buvable [byvabl] *adj* drinkable • **buveur, -euse** *nmf* drinker; **un grand b.** a heavy drinker

buvard [byvar] *adj & nm* **(papier) b.** blotting paper

buvette [byvɛt] *nf* refreshment bar

buviez [byvje] *voir* boire

C

C, c [se] *nm inv* C, c

c' [s] *voir* **ce¹**

ça [sa] (*abrév* **cela**) *pron démonstratif* (*pour désigner*) that; (*plus près*) this; (*sujet indéfini*) it, that; **qu'est-ce que c'est que ça?** what (on earth) is that/this?; **c'est qui/quoi ça?** who's/what's that?; **où/quand/comment ça?** where?/when?/how?; **ça dépend** it depends; **ça m'ennuie** it annoys me; **ça m'amuse** I find it amusing; **ça va?** how are things?; **ça va!** fine!, OK!; **ça alors!** my goodness!; **ça y est, j'ai fini** that's it, I'm finished; **c'est ça** that's right

çà [sa] **çà et là** *adv* here and there

caban [kabɑ̃] *nm* reefer

cabane [kaban] *nf* (*baraque*) hut; (*en rondin*) cabin; (*de jardin*) shed; **c. à outils** tool shed; **c. à lapins** rabbit hutch

cabaret [kabarɛ] *nm* cabaret

cabas [kabɑ] *nm* shopping bag

cabillaud [kabijo] *nm* (fresh) cod

cabine [kabin] *nf* (*de bateau*) cabin; (*de camion*) cab; (*d'ascenseur*) *Br* cage, *Am* car; **c. de bain** (*de plage*) *Br* beach hut, *Am* cabana; (*de piscine*) cubicle; **c. d'essayage** fitting room; **c. de pilotage** cockpit; (*d'un grand avion*) flight deck; **c. téléphonique** phone box

cabinet [kabinɛ] *nm* (*de médecin*) *Br* surgery, *Am* office; (*de ministre*) departmental staff; **c. de toilette** (small) bathroom; **c. de travail** study; *Fam* **les cabinets** *Br* the loo, *Am* the john; **c. dentaire** dental surgery; **c. juridique** law firm

câble [kɑbl] *nm* cable; *TV* **le c.** cable • **câblé** *adj Fam* (*à la page*) hip • **câbler** *vt TV* (*ville, quartier*) to install cable television in

caboche [kabɔʃ] *nf Fam* (*tête*) nut

cabosser [kabɔse] *vt* (*métal, voiture*) to bash up

caboteur [kabɔtœr] *nm* (*bateau*) coaster

cabotin, -ine [kabɔtɛ̃, -in] *nmf* (*acteur*) ham actor; (*actrice*) ham actress; (*vantard*) show-off

cabrer [kabre] **se cabrer** *vpr* (*cheval*) to rear (up); *Fig* (*personne*) to recoil

cabri [kabri] *nm* (*chevreau*) kid

cabriole [kabrijɔl] *nf* (*saut*) caper; **faire des cabrioles** to caper about

cabriolet [kabrijɔlɛ] *nm* (*auto*) convertible

caca [kaka] *nm Langage enfantin* number two, *Br* poo; **faire c.** to do a number two or *Br* a poo

cacah(o)uète [kakawɛt] *nf* peanut

cacao [kakao] *nm* (*boisson*) cocoa

cacatoès [kakatɔɛs] *nm* cockatoo

cachalot [kaʃalo] *nm* sperm whale

cache [kaʃ] *nf* hidding place; **c. d'armes** arms cache • **cache-cache** *nm inv* **jouer à c.** to play hide and seek • **cache-nez** *nm inv* scarf

cachemire [kaʃmir] *nm* (*laine*) cashmere

cacher [kaʃe] **1** *vt* to hide (**à** from); **c. la lumière à qn** to stand in sb's light; **il ne cache pas que...** he makes no secret of the fact that...; **je ne vous cache pas que j'ai été surpris** I won't pretend I wasn't surprised; **pour ne rien vous c.** to be completely open with you

2 se cacher *vpr* to hide; **sans se c.** openly; **je ne m'en cache pas** I make no secret of it

cachet [kaʃɛ] *nm* (*sceau*) seal; (*de fabrication*) stamp; (*comprimé*) tablet; (*d'acteur*) fee; (*originalité*) distinctive character; **c. de la poste** postmark • **cacheter** *vt* to seal

cachette [kaʃɛt] *nf* hiding place; **en c.** in secret; **en c. de qn** without sb knowing

cachot [kaʃo] *nm* dungeon

cachotteries [kaʃɔtri] *nfpl* **faire des cachotteries** to be secretive • **cachottier, -ière** *adj* secretive

cachou [kaʃu] *nm* = liquorice sweet

cacophonie [kakɔfɔni] *nf* cacophony

cactus [kaktys] *nm* cactus

c.-à-d. (*abrév* **c'est-à-dire**) i.e.

cadastre [kadastr] *nm* (*registre*) ≃ land register

cadavre [kadɑvr] *nm* corpse • **cadavérique** *adj* (*teint*) deathly pale

caddie® [kadi] *nm Br* trolley, *Am* cart

cadeau, -x [kado] *nm* present, gift; **faire un c. à qn** to give sb a present; **faire c. de qch à qn** to make sb a present of sth

cadenas [kadnɑ] *nm* padlock • **cadenasser** *vt* to padlock

cadence [kadɑ̃s] *nf (taux, vitesse)* rate; *(de chanson)* rhythm • **cadencé, -ée** *adj* rhythmical

cadet, -ette [kade, -ɛt] **1** *adj (de deux)* younger; *(de plus de deux)* youngest

2 *nmf (de deux)* younger (one); *(de plus de deux)* youngest (one); *Sport* junior; **c'est le c. de mes soucis!** that's the least of my worries

cadran [kadrɑ̃] *nm (de téléphone)* dial; *(de montre)* face; **faire le tour du c.** to sleep round the clock; **c. solaire** sundial

cadre [kadr] *nm* (**a**) *(de photo, de vélo)* frame; *(décor)* setting; *(d'imprimé)* box; **dans le c. de** within the framework of; **c. de vie** environment (**b**) *(d'entreprise)* executive, manager; **les cadres** the management; *Mil* the officers

cadrer [kadre] **1** *vt (photo)* to centre

2 *vi (correspondre)* to tally (**avec** with) • **cadreur** *nm* cameraman

caduc, -uque [kadyk] *adj (feuille)* deciduous; *Jur (accord)* lapsed; *(loi)* null and void

cafard, -arde [kafar, -ard] *nm (insecte)* cockroach; *Fam* **avoir le c.** to feel low

café [kafe] *nm (produit, boisson)* coffee; *(bar)* café; **c. au lait, c. crème** *Br* white coffee, *Am* coffee with milk; **c. noir** black coffee; **c. soluble** *ou* **instantané** instant coffee; **c. tabac** = café-cum-tobacconist's; **c.-théâtre** *Br* ≃ pub theatre • **caféine** *nf* caffeine • **cafétéria** *nf* cafeteria • **cafetier** *nm* café owner • **cafetière** *nf (récipient)* coffeepot; *(électrique)* coffee machine

cafouiller [kafuje] *vi Fam (personne)* to get into a muddle; *(moteur)* to misfire • **cafouillage** *nm Fam (confusion)* muddle

cage [kaʒ] *nf (d'oiseau, de zoo)* cage; *(d'ascenseur)* shaft; *Football* goal; **c. d'escalier** stairwell; *Anat* **c. thoracique** rib cage

cageot [kaʒo] *nm* crate

cagibi [kaʒibi] *nm Fam* storage room

cagneux [kaɲø] *adj* **avoir les genoux c.** to have knock-knees

cagnotte [kaɲɔt] *nf (caisse commune)* kitty; *(de jeux)* pool

cagoule [kagul] *nf (de bandit)* hood; *(d'enfant)* *Br* balaclava, *Am* ski mask

cahier [kaje] *nm* notebook; *(d'écolier)* exercise book; **c. de brouillon** *Br* rough book, *Am* ≃ scratch pad; *Scol* **c. d'appel** register

cahin-caha [kaɛ̃kaa] *adv Fam* **aller c.** *(se déplacer)* to struggle along

cahot [kao] *nm* jolt • **cahoté, -ée** *adj* **être**

c. to be jolted about • **cahoter** *vi* to jolt along • **cahoteux, -euse** *adj* bumpy

caïd [kaid] *nm Fam (chef de bande)* gang leader; **jouer les caïds** to act high and mighty

caille [kɑj] *nf (oiseau)* quail

cailler [kɑje] **1** *vi (lait)* to curdle; *Fam* **ça caille** it's freezing

2 se cailler *vpr Fam* **on se (les) caille** it's freezing • **caillot** *nm (de sang)* clot

caillou, -x [kaju] *nm* stone; *(sur la plage)* pebble; *Fam* **il n'a plus un poil sur le c.** he's as bald as a coot • **caillouteux, -euse** *adj (route)* stony

Caire [kɛr] *nm* **le C.** Cairo

caisse [kɛs] *nf* (**a**) *(boîte)* case; *(d'outils)* box; *(cageot)* crate; *(de véhicule)* body; *très Fam (voiture)* car; *Mus* **la grosse c.** the bass drum (**b**) *(coffre)* cash box; *(de magasin)* cash desk; *(de supermarché)* checkout; *(argent)* cash (in hand); **faire sa c.** to do the till; **c. d'épargne** savings bank; **c. de résonance** sound box; **c. de retraite** pension fund; **c. enregistreuse** cash register; **c. noire** slush fund

caissier, -ière [kesje, -jɛr] *nmf* cashier; *(de supermarché)* checkout operator

cajoler [kaʒɔle] *vt* to cuddle • **cajolerie** *nf* cuddle

cajou [kaʒu] *nm* **noix de c.** cashew nut

cake [kek] *nm* fruit cake

calamité [kalamite] *nf (fléau)* calamity; *(malheur)* great misfortune

calandre [kalɑ̃dr] *nf Aut* radiator grille

calcaire [kalkɛr] **1** *adj (eau)* hard; *(terrain)* chalky

2 *nm Géol* limestone; *(dépôt)* fur

calciné, -ée [kalsine] *adj* burnt to a cinder

calcium [kalsjɔm] *nm* calcium

calcul [kalkyl] *nm* (**a**) *(opérations, estimation)* calculation; *Scol* **le c.** arithmetic; **faire un c.** to make a calculation; *Fig* **faire un mauvais c.** to miscalculate; **c. mental** mental arithmetic (**b**) *Méd* stone; **c. rénal** kidney stone

calculateur [kalkylatœr] *nm Ordinat* calculator • **calculatrice** *nf* **c. (de poche)** (pocket) calculator

calculer [kalkyle] *vt (prix, superficie)* to calculate; *(chances, conséquences)* to weigh (up) • **calculé, -ée** *adj (risque)* calculated

calculette [kalkylɛt] *nf* (pocket) calculator

cale [kal] *nf* (**a**) *(de meuble, de porte)* wedge (**b**) *(de navire)* hold; **c. sèche** dry dock

calé, -ée [kale] *adj Fam (problème)* tough; **être c. en qch** to be well up in sth
calèche [kalɛʃ] *nf* barouche
caleçon [kalsɔ̃] *nm* boxer shorts; **c. long** long johns
calembour [kalɑ̃bur] *nm* pun, play on words
calendrier [kalɑ̃drije] *nm (mois et jours)* calendar; *(programme)* timetable
cale-pied [kalpje] *(pl* **cale-pieds**) *nm* toe clip
calepin [kalpɛ̃] *nm* notebook
caler [kale] **1** *vt (meuble, porte)* to wedge; *(chargement)* to secure; *Fam* **je suis calé** I'm full up
 2 *vi (moteur)* to stall; *Fam (abandonner)* to give up
 3 se caler *vpr (dans un fauteuil)* to settle oneself confortably
calfeutrer [kalføtre] **1** *vt (brèches)* to block up
 2 se calfeutrer *vpr* **se c. chez soi** to shut oneself away
calibre [kalibr] *nm (diamètre)* calibre; *(d'œuf, de fruit)* grade; *(outil)* gauge • **calibrer** *vt (œufs, fruits)* to grade
calice [kalis] *nm Rel* chalice
Californie [kalifɔrni] *nf* **la C.** California
califourchon [kalifurʃɔ̃] **à califourchon** *adv* astride; **se mettre à c. sur qch** to sit astride sth
câlin, -ine [kɑlɛ̃, -in] **1** *adj* affectionate
 2 *nm* cuddle; **faire un c. à qn** to give sb a cuddle • **câliner** *vt* to cuddle
calleux, -euse [kalø, -øz] *adj* callous
calligraphie [kaligrafi] *nf* calligraphy
calmant [kalmɑ̃] *nm (pour les nerfs)* sedative; *(la douleur)* painkiller
calmar [kalmar] *nm* squid
calme [kalm] **1** *adj (flegmatique)* calm, cool; *(tranquille)* quiet; *(mer)* calm
 2 *nm* calm(ness); **garder/perdre son c.** to keep/lose one's calm; **dans le c.** *(travailler, étudier)* in peace and quiet; **du c.!** *(taisez-vous)* keep quiet!; *(pas de panique)* keep calm!
calmer [kalme] **1** *vt (douleur)* to soothe; *(inquiétude)* to calm; *(fièvre)* to reduce; *(faim)* to appease; **c. qn** to calm sb down
 2 se calmer *vpr (personne)* to calm down; *(vent)* to die down; *(mer)* to become calm; *(douleur, fièvre)* to subside
calomnie [kalɔmni] *nf (en paroles)* slander; *(par écrit)* libel • **calomnier** *vt (en paroles)* to slander; *(par écrit)* to libel • **calomnieux, -euse** *adj (paroles)* slanderous; *(écrits)* libellous
calorie [kalɔri] *nf* calorie • **calorifique, calorique** *adj* calorific

calorifuge [kalɔrifyʒ] *adj* (heat-)insulating
calot [kalo] *nm (de soldat)* forage cap
calotte [kalɔt] *nf (chapeau rond)* skullcap; *Fam (gifle)* clout; *Géol* **c. glaciaire** ice cap
calque [kalk] *nm (copie)* tracing; *Fig (imitation)* exact copy; **(papier-)c.** tracing paper • **calquer** *vt (reproduire)* to trace; *Fig (imiter)* to copy; **il calque sa conduite sur celle de son frère** he models his behaviour on his brother's
calumet [kalymɛ] *nm* **c. de la paix** peace pipe
calvaire [kalvɛr] *nm Rel* calvary; *Fig* ordeal
calvitie [kalvisi] *nf* baldness
camarade [kamarad] *nmf* friend; *Pol* comrade; **c. de classe** classmate; **c. d'école** school friend; **c. de jeu** playmate • **camaraderie** *nf* camaraderie
Cambodge [kɑ̃bɔdʒ] *nm* **le C.** Cambodia
cambouis [kɑ̃bwi] *nm* dirty oil
cambrer [kɑ̃bre] **1** *vt* to arch; **c. les reins** to arch one's back
 2 se cambrer *vpr* to arch one's back • **cambrure** *nf (du pied, du dos)* arch
cambrioler [kɑ̃brijɔle] *vt Br* to burgle, *Am* to burglarize • **cambriolage** *nm* burglary • **cambrioleur, -euse** *nmf* burglar
cambrousse [kɑ̃brus] *nf Fam* country; **en pleine c.** in the middle of nowhere
came [kam] *nf Tech* cam
camée [kame] *nm* cameo
caméléon [kameleɔ̃] *nm* chameleon
camélia [kamelja] *nm* camellia
camelot [kamlo] *nm* street peddler *or Br* hawker, *Am* huckster • **camelote** *nf (pacotille)* junk; *(marchandise)* stuff
camembert [kamɑ̃ber] *nm (fromage)* Camembert (cheese)
camer [kame] **se camer** *vpr très Fam* to do drugs
caméra [kamera] *nf* camera • **cameraman** *(pl* **-mans** *ou* **-men**) *nm* cameraman
Caméscope® [kameskɔp] *nm* camcorder
camion [kamjɔ̃] *nm Br* lorry, *Am* truck; **c. de déménagement** *Br* removal van, *Am* moving van; **c. frigorifique** refrigerated lorry • **camion-benne** *(pl* **camions-bennes**) *nm* dumper truck • **camion-citerne** *(pl* **camions-citernes**) *nm Br* tanker, *Am* tank truck • **camionnage** *nm Br* (road) haulage, *Am* trucking • **camionnette** *nf* van • **camionneur** *nm (conducteur)* Br lorry driver, *Am* truck driver; *(entrepreneur)* Br haulier, *Am* trucker

camisole [kamizɔl] *nf* **c. de force** straitjacket

camomille [kamɔmij] *nf (plante)* camomile; *(tisane)* camomile tea

camoufler [kamufle] *vt Mil* to camouflage; *Fig (vérité)* to disguise ● **camouflage** *nm Mil* camouflage; *Fig (de vérité)* disguising

camp [kɑ̃] *nm (campement)* camp; *(de parti, de jeu)* side; **lever le c.** to strike camp; **c. de concentration** concentration camp; **c. de prisonniers** prison camp

campagne [kɑ̃paɲ] *nf* (a) *(par opposition à la ville)* country; *(paysage)* countryside; **à la c.** in the country; **en pleine c.** deep in the countryside; **en rase c.** in the open country (b) *Mil, Com & Pol* campaign; *Pol* **entrer en c.** to go on the campaign trail; **c. de presse/publicité** press/publicity campaign ● **campagnard, -arde** *adj* country

camper [kɑ̃pe] **1** *vi* to camp
2 *vt (chapeau)* to plant; **c. un personnage** *(sujet: acteur)* to play a part effectively
3 se camper *vpr* to plant oneself (**devant** in front of) ● **campement** *nm* camp; **établir un c.** to pitch camp ● **campeur, -euse** *nmf* camper

camphre [kɑ̃fr] *nm* camphor

camping [kɑ̃piŋ] *nm (activité)* camping; *(terrain)* camp(ing) site; **faire du c.** to go camping; **c. sauvage** unauthorized camping ● **camping-car** *(pl* **camping-cars)** *nm* camper

campus [kɑ̃pys] *nm* campus

camus, -use [kamy] *adj (nez)* flat

Canada [kanada] *nm* **le C.** Canada ● **canadien, -ienne 1** *adj* Canadian **2** *nmf* **C., Canadienne** Canadian ● **canadienne** *nf* fur-lined jacket

canaille [kanaj] **1** *nf* scoundrel
2 *adj (manière, accent)* vulgar

canal, -aux [kanal, -o] *nm (cours d'eau)* canal; *(conduite)* conduit; *Anat & Bot* duct; *Tel, Com & Fig* channel; *Fig* **par le c. de la poste** through the post

canaliser [kanalize] *vt (rivière, fleuve)* to canalize; *Fig (foule, énergie)* to channel ● **canalisation** *nf (conduite)* pipe

canapé [kanape] *nm* (a) *(siège)* sofa, couch (b) *(pour l'apéritif)* canapé ● **canapé-lit** *(pl* **canapés-lits)** *nm* sofa bed

canard [kanar] *nm* duck; *(mâle)* drake; *(fausse note)* false note; *Fam (journal)* rag

canarder [kanarde] *vt Fam* to snipe at

canari [kanari] *nm* canary

cancans [kɑ̃kɑ̃] *nmpl* gossip ● **cancaner** *vi* to gossip ● **cancanier, -ière** *adj* gossipy

cancer [kɑ̃sɛr] *nm (maladie)* cancer; **c. de l'estomac** stomach cancer; **avoir un c.** to have cancer; **le C.** *(signe)* Cancer; **être C.** to be Cancer ● **cancéreux, -euse 1** *adj* cancerous **2** *nmf* cancer patient ● **cancérigène** *adj* carcinogenic ● **cancérologue** *nmf* cancer specialist

cancre [kɑ̃kr] *nm Fam* dunce

cancrelat [kɑ̃krəla] *nm* cockroach

candélabre [kɑ̃delabr] *nm* candelabra

candeur [kɑ̃dœr] *nf* guilelessness ● **candide** *adj* guileless

> *⚬* Il faut noter que les termes anglais **candour** et **candid** sont des faux amis. Ils signifient respectivement **franchise** et **franc**.

candidat, -ate [kɑ̃dida, -at] *nmf (d'examen)* candidate (**à** for); *(de poste)* applicant (**à** for); **être c. aux élections** to stand for election ● **candidature** *nf (à un poste)* application (**à** for); *(aux élections)* candidature (**à** for); **poser sa c.** to apply (**à** for); **c. spontanée** unsolicited application

cane [kan] *nf (female)* duck ● **caneton** *nm* duckling

canette [kanɛt] *nf (bouteille)* bottle; *(boîte)* can; *(bobine)* spool

canevas [kanva] *nm (toile)* canvas; *(de film, de roman)* outline

caniche [kaniʃ] *nm* poodle

canicule [kanikyl] *nf* heatwave

canif [kanif] *nm* penknife

canine [kanin] **1** *adj f (espèce, race)* canine; **exposition c.** dog show
2 *nf (dent)* canine (tooth)

caniveau, -x [kanivo] *nm* gutter

cannabis [kanabis] *nm* cannabis

canne [kan] *nf (tige)* cane; *(pour marcher)* (walking) stick; **c. à pêche** fishing rod; **c. à sucre** sugar cane; **c. blanche** white stick

cannelle [kanɛl] *nf* cinnamon

cannelure [kanlyr] *nf* groove; *(de colonne)* fluting

cannette [kanɛt] *nf* = **canette**

cannibale [kanibal] **1** *nmf* cannibal
2 *adj (tribu)* cannibalistic ● **cannibalisme** *nm* cannibalism

canoë-kayak [kanɔekajak] *nm* canoeing

canon¹ [kanɔ̃] *nm (arme)* gun; *(ancien, à boulets)* cannon; *(de fusil)* barrel ● **canonnade** *nf* gunfire ● **canonnier** *nm* gunner

canon² [kanɔ̃] **1** *nm Rel & Fig (règle)* canon; *Fam (personne)* stunner
2 *adj inv Fam (beau)* stunning ● **canoniser** *vt Rel* to canonize

canot [kano] *nm* boat; **c. de sauvetage** lifeboat; **c. pneumatique** rubber dinghy

• **canotage** *nm* boating • **canoter** *vi* to go boating

cantate [kɑ̃tat] *nf Mus* cantata

cantatrice [kɑ̃tatris] *nf* opera singer

cantine [kɑ̃tin] *nf* (**a**) *(réfectoire)* canteen; *(d'école)* dining hall; **manger à la c.** *Br* to have school dinners, *Am* to have school lunch (**b**) *(coffre)* trunk

cantique [kɑ̃tik] *nm Rel* hymn

canton [kɑ̃tɔ̃] *nm* (en France) canton *(division of a department)*; *(en Suisse)* canton *(semi-autonomous region)*

cantonade [kɑ̃tɔnad] **à la cantonade** *adv* to everyone present

cantonner [kɑ̃tɔne] **1** *vt (troupes)* to quarter; **c. qn dans/à** to confine sb to **2 se cantonner** *vpr* **se c. dans/à** to confine oneself to • **cantonnement** *nm (lieu)* quarters

cantonnier [kɑ̃tɔnje] *nm* roadmender

canular [kanylar] *nm Fam* hoax

canyon [kajɔn] *nm* canyon

CAO [seao] *(abrév* **conception assistée par ordinateur**) *nf Ordinat* CAD

caoutchouc [kautʃu] *nm* rubber; *(élastique)* rubber band; *(plante)* rubber plant; **c. Mousse®** foam rubber • **caoutchouteux, -euse** *adj Péj* rubbery

CAP [seape] *(abrév* **certificat d'aptitude professionnelle**) *nm Scol* = vocational training certificate

cap [kap] *nm Géog* cape, headland; *Naut (direction)* course; **mettre le c. sur...** to set course for...; **changer de c.** to change course; **franchir** *ou* **doubler un c.** to round a cap; **franchir le c. de la trentaine** to turn thirty; **franchir le c. des mille employés** to pass the thousand-employee mark

capable [kapabl] *adj* capable, able; **c. de qch** capable of sth; **c. de faire qch** able to do sth, capable of doing sth; **elle est bien de les oublier!** she's quite capable of forgetting them! • **capacité** *nf* capacity; *(aptitude)* ability; **c. d'accueil** *(d'hôtel)* accommodation capacity; **c. de concentration** attention span

cape [kap] *nf* cape; *(grande)* cloak; **roman de c. et d'épée** swashbuckling novel

CAPES [kapɛs] *(abrév* **certificat d'aptitude professionnelle à l'enseignement secondaire**) *nm* = postgraduate teaching certificate

capillaire [kapilɛr] *adj* **huile/lotion c.** hair oil/lotion

capitaine [kapitɛn] *nm* captain

capital, -e, -aux, -ales [kapital, -o] **1** *adj (essentiel)* major

2 *adj f* **lettre capitale** capital letter

3 *nm Fin* capital • **capitale** *nf (lettre, ville)* capital

capitaliser [kapitalize] **1** *vt (intérêts)* to capitalize **2** *vi* to save

capitalisme [kapitalism] *nm* capitalism • **capitaliste** *adj & nmf* capitalist

capiteux, -euse [kapitø, -øz] *adj (vin, parfum)* heady

capitonné, -ée [kapitɔne] *adj* padded

capituler [kapityle] *vi* to surrender • **capitulation** *nf* surrender

caporal, -aux [kapɔral, -o] *nm Mil* corporal

capot [kapo] *nm Aut Br* bonnet, *Am* hood

capote [kapɔt] *nf Aut (de décapotable) Br* hood, *Am* top; *(manteau de soldat)* greatcoat; *Fam (préservatif)* condom, *Am* rubber

capoter [kapɔte] *vi (véhicule)* to overturn; *Fam (échouer)* to fall through

câpre [kɑpr] *nf* caper

caprice [kapris] *nm* whim; **faire un c.** to throw a tantrum • **capricieux, -euse** *adj (personne)* capricious; *(moteur)* temperamental

Capricorne [kaprikɔrn] *nm* **le C.** *(signe)* Capricorn; **être C.** to be Capricorne

capsule [kapsyl] *nf (spatiale, de médicament)* capsule; *(de bouteille)* cap

capter [kapte] *vt (signal, radio)* to pick up; *(attention)* to capture; *(eaux)* to harness

captif, -ive [kaptif, -iv] *adj & nmf* captive • **captivité** *nf* captivity; **en c.** in captivity

captiver [kaptive] *vt* to captivate • **captivant, -ante** *adj* captivating

capture [kaptyr] *nf* capture • **capturer** *vt* to capture

capuche [kapyʃ] *nf* hood • **capuchon** *nm (de manteau)* hood; *(de moine)* cowl; *(de stylo, de tube)* cap, top

capucine [kapysin] *nf* nasturtium

caquet [kakɛ] *nm (de poules)* cackle; *Fam* **rabattre le c. à qn** to shut sb up • **caqueter** *vi (poule)* to cackle

car¹ [kar] *conj* because, for

car² [kar] *nm* bus, *Br* coach; **c. de police** police van; **c. de ramassage scolaire** school bus

> *♪* Il faut noter que le nom anglais **car** est un faux ami. Il signifie **voiture**.

carabine [karabin] *nf* rifle; **c. à air comprimé** air gun

carabiné, -ée [karabine] *adj Fam (grippe)* violent; *(rhume)* stinking; *(punition, amende)* very stiff

caracoler [karakɔle] *vi (cheval)* to caracole

caractère¹ [karaktɛr] *nm (lettre)* character; **en petits caractères** in small print; **en caractères gras** in bold characters; **caractères d'imprimerie** block letters

caractère² [karaktɛr] *nm (tempérament, nature)* character, nature; *(attribut)* characteristic; **avoir bon c.** to be good-natured; **avoir mauvais c.** to be bad-tempered

caractériel, -ielle [karakterjɛl] **1** *adj (troubles)* emotional; **enfant c.** problem child
2 *nmf* emotionally disturbed person

caractériser [karakterize] **1** *vt* to characterize
2 se caractériser *vpr* **se c. par** to be characterized by

caractéristique [karakteristik] *adj & nf* characteristic

carafe [karaf] *nf (pour l'eau, le vin)* carafe; *(pour le whisky)* decanter

carambolage [karãbɔlaʒ] *nm* pile-up

caramel [karamɛl] *nm* caramel; **des caramels** *(mous)* fudge; *(durs) Br* toffee, *Am* taffy • **caraméliser** *vti* to caramelize

carapace [karapas] *nf (de tortue)* & *Fig* shell

carat [kara] *nm* carat; **or à 18 carats** 18-carat gold

caravane [karavan] *nf (pour camper) Br* caravan, *Am* trailer; *(dans le désert)* caravan • **caravaning, caravanage** *nm* caravanning; **faire du c.** to go caravanning

carbone [karbɔn] *nm* carbon; **(papier) c.** carbon (paper) • **carbonique** *adj* **gaz c.** carbon dioxide; **neige c.** dry ice

carbonisé, -ée [karbɔnize] *adj (nourriture)* burnt to a cinder; **mourir carbonisé** to burn to death

carburant [karbyrã] *nm* fuel • **carburateur** *nm Aut Br* carburettor, *Am* carburetor

carburer [karbyre] *vi* **mal c.** to be badly tuned; *Fam* **il carbure au café** coffee keeps him going

carcan [karkã] *nm* yoke

carcasse [karkas] *nf (os)* carcass; *(d'immeuble)* shell; *Fam (de personne)* body

carcéral, -e, -aux, -ales [karseral, -o] *adj* prison

cardiaque [kardjak] **1** *adj (arrêt, massage)* cardiac; **être c.** to have a heart condition
2 *nmf* heart patient

cardigan [kardigã] *nm* cardigan

cardinal, -e, -aux, -ales [kardinal, -o] **1** *adj (nombre, point, vertu)* cardinal
2 *nm Rel* cardinal

cardiologie [kardjɔlɔʒi] *nf* cardiology

carême [karɛm] *nm Rel* **le c.** Lent; **faire c.** to fast

carence [karãs] *nf (manque)* deficiency; **c. alimentaire** nutritional deficiency

carène [karɛn] *nf (de navire)* hull • **caréné, -ée** *adj (voiture, avion)* streamlined

caresse [karɛs] *nf* caress; **faire des caresses à** *(personne)* to caress; *(animal)* to stroke

caresser [karese] *vt (personne)* to caress; *(animal)* to stroke; *Fig (espoir)* to cherish • **caressant, -ante** *adj* affectionate

cargaison [kargɛzɔ̃] *nf* cargo • **cargo** *nm Naut* freighter

┌─────────────────────────────────────┐
│ ⌀ Il faut noter que le nom anglais **cargo** est un faux ami. Il signifie **cargaison**. │
└─────────────────────────────────────┘

caricature [karikatyr] *nf* caricature • **caricatural, -e, -aux, -ales** *adj* caricatured • **caricaturer** *vt* to caricature

carie [kari] *nf* **c. (dentaire)** tooth decay; **avoir une c.** to have a cavity • **cariée** *adj f* **dent c.** decayed tooth

carillon [karijɔ̃] *nm (sonnerie)* chimes; *(horloge)* chiming clock; *(de porte)* door chime • **carillonner** *vi (cloches)* to chime

caritatif, -ive [karitatif, -iv] *adj* charitable

carlingue [karlɛ̃g] *nf (d'avion)* cabin

carnage [karnaʒ] *nm* carnage

carnassier, -ière [karnasje, -jɛr] **1** *adj* flesh-eating
2 *nm* carnivore

carnaval, -als [karnaval] *nm* carnival

carnet [karnɛ] *nm* notebook; *(de timbres, chèques, adresses)* book; *(de tickets de métro)* = book of ten tickets; **c. d'adresses** address book; **c. de notes** *Br* school report, *Am* report card; **c. de route** logbook; **c. de santé** health record

carnivore [karnivɔr] **1** *adj* carnivorous
2 *nm* carnivore

carotte [karɔt] **1** *nf* carrot; *Fam* **les carottes sont cuites** we've/he's/*etc* had it
2 *adj inv* **roux c.** carroty

carotter [karɔte] *vt Fam (objet)* to pinch

carpe [karp] *nf* carp

carpette [karpɛt] *nf* rug; *Fam Péj* **c'est une vraie c.** he's a doormat

┌─────────────────────────────────────┐
│ ⌀ Il faut noter que le nom anglais **carpet** est un faux ami. Il signifie **moquette**. │
└─────────────────────────────────────┘

carquois [karkwa] *nm* quiver

carré, -ée [kare] **1** *adj* square; *(épaules)* square, broad; **être c. en affaires** to be straightforward in one's business dealings; **mètre c.** square metre

2 *nm Géom & Math* square; **avoir une coupe au c.** to have one's hair in a bob; *Culin* **c. d'agneau** rack of lamb; **c. de soie** silk scarf; *Cartes* **c. de valets** four jacks; *Naut* **c. des officiers** wardroom

carreau, -x [karo] *nm (motif)* square; *(sur tissu)* check; *(de céramique)* tile; *(vitre)* (window) pane; *Cartes (couleur)* diamonds; **tissu à carreaux** check(ed) material; *Fam* **se tenir à c.** to keep a low profile; *Fam* **rester sur le c.** to be killed; *(être blessé)* to be badly injured; *(être éliminé)* to be given the boot

carrefour [karfur] *nm* crossroads *(sing)*

carreler [karle] *vt* to tile • **carrelage** *nm (sol)* tiled floor; *(carreaux)* tiles

carrelet [karlɛ] *nm Br* plaice, *Am* flounder

carrément [karemã] *adv Fam (franchement)* straight out; *(très)* really

carrière [karjɛr] *nf* (a) *(lieu)* quarry (b) *(métier)* career; **faire c. dans** to make a career in

carriole [karjɔl] *nf* light cart

carrosse [karɔs] *nm Hist* (horse-drawn) carriage • **carrossable** *adj (chemin)* suitable for motor vehicles • **carrosserie** *nf (de véhicule)* bodywork

carrure [karyr] *nf (de personne)* build; *(de vêtement)* width across the shoulders

cartable [kartabl] *nm* school bag

carte [kart] *nf* (a) *(carton, document officiel, informatisé) & Ordinat* card; *(géographique)* map; *(marine, météo)* chart; *Fig* **avoir c. blanche** to have a free hand; **c. (à jouer)** (playing) card; **jouer aux cartes** to play cards; **c. à puce** smart card; **c. de crédit** credit card; **c. d'identité** identity card; **c. de séjour** residence permit; **c. de téléphone** phonecard; **c. de visite** *Br* visiting card, *Am* calling card; *(professionnelle)* business card; **c. de vœux** greetings card; *Aut* **c. grise** ≃ vehicle registration document; **C. Orange** = combined monthly season ticket for the Métro, bus and RER; **c. postale** postcard; **c. routière** road map

(b) *(de restaurant)* menu; **manger à la c.** to eat à la carte; **c. des vins** wine list

cartel [kartɛl] *nm Écon* cartel

carter [kartɛr] *nm (de moteur)* crankcase; *(de bicyclette)* chain guard

cartilage [kartilaʒ] *nm* cartilage

cartomancien, -ienne [kartɔmãsjɛ̃, -jɛn] *nmf* fortune-teller *(who uses cards)*

carton [kartɔ̃] *nm (matière)* cardboard;

(boîte) cardboard box; **faire un c.** *(au tir)* to have a shot; *Fam (à un examen)* to pass with flying colours; **c. à dessin** portfolio; *Football* **c. jaune/rouge** yellow/red card • **cartonner 1** *vt (livre)* to case; **livre cartonné** hardback **2** *vi Fam (à l'école)* to get excellent marks (**en** in)

cartouche [kartuʃ] *nf* cartridge; *(de cigarettes)* carton • **cartouchière** *nf* cartridge belt

cas [kɑ] *nm* case; **en tout c.** in any case; **en aucun c.** on no account; **en c. de besoin** if need be; **en c. d'accident** in the event of an accident; **en c. d'urgence** in an emergency; **au c. où elle tomberait** if she should fall; **pour le c. où il pleuvrait** in case it rains; **faire c. de/peu de c. de qn/qch** to set great/little store by sb/sth

casanier, -ière [kazanje, -jɛr] *adj* home-loving; *Péj* stay-at-home

casaque [kazak] *nf (de jockey)* blouse

cascade [kaskad] *nf* (a) *(d'eau)* waterfall; **en c.** in succession (b) *(de cinéma)* stunt • **cascadeur, -euse** *nmf* stunt man, *f* stunt woman

case [kɑz] *nf* (a) *(de tiroir)* compartment; *(d'échiquier)* square; *(de formulaire)* box; *Fam* **il a une c. de vide** he's got a screw loose (b) *(hutte)* hut

caser [kaze] **1** *vt (placer)* to fit in; *Fam* **c. qn** *(établir)* to fix sb up with a job; *(marier)* to marry sb off

2 se caser *vpr (se marier)* to get married and settle down

caserne [kazɛrn] *nf* barracks; **c. de pompiers** fire station

casier [kazje] *nm* compartment; *(pour le courrier)* pigeonhole; *(pour les vêtements)* locker; **c. à bouteilles** bottle/record rack; *Jur* **c. judiciaire** criminal *or* police record

casino [kazino] *nm* casino

casque [kask] *nm* helmet; *(de coiffeur)* hairdryer; **c. (à écouteurs)** headphones; **les Casques bleus** the Blue Berets • **casqué, -ée** *adj* helmeted

casquer [kaske] *vi Fam* to fork out

casquette [kaskɛt] *nf* cap

cassation [kasasjɔ̃] *nf Jur* annulment

casse¹ [kɑs] *nf* (a) *(objets cassés)* breakages; **aller à la c.** to go for scrap; *Fam* **il va y avoir de la c.** something will get broken (b) *(d'imprimerie)* case; **haut/bas de c.** upper/lower case

casse² [kɑs] *nm très Fam (cambriolage)* break-in

casser [kase] **1** *vt* (a) *(briser)* to break; *(noix)* to crack; *(voix)* to strain; *Fam* **c. les pieds à qn** *(agacer)* to get on sb's nerves;

Fam **c. les oreilles à qn** to deafen sb; *Fam* **c. la figure à qn** to smash sb's face in; *Fam* **c. sa pipe** to kick the bucket; *Fam* **ça ne casse des briques** it's nothing to write home about; *Fam* **ça vaut 50 euros à tout c.** it's worth 50 euros at the very most (**b**) *Jur (verdict)* to quash; *(mariage)* to annul **2** *vi* to break **3 se casser** *vpr* to break; *Fam (partir)* to clear off; **se c. la jambe** to break one's leg; *Fam* **se c. la figure** *(tomber)* to fall flat on one's face; *Fam* **se c. la tête** to rack one's brains; *Fam* **il ne s'est pas cassé** he didn't exhaust himself • **cassant, -ante** *adj (fragile)* brittle; *(brusque)* curt, abrupt • **casse-cou** *nmf inv (personne)* daredevil • **casse-croûte** *nm inv Fam* snack • **casse-gueule** *adj inv très Fam (lieu)* dangerous; *(entreprise)* risky • **casse-noisettes, casse-noix** *nm inv* nutcrackers • **casse-pieds** *nmf inv Fam (personne)* pain in the neck • **casse-tête** *nm inv (problème)* headache; *(jeu)* puzzle • **casseur** *nm (manifestant)* rioter
casserole [kasrɔl] *nf (sauce)* pan

> 📖 Il faut noter que le nom anglais **casserole** est un faux ami. Il signifie **ragoût** ou **cocotte** selon le contexte.

cassette [kasɛt] *nf (magnétique)* cassette, tape; **enregistrer qch sur c.** to tape sth; **c. video** video cassette
cassis [kasis] *nm (fruit)* blackcurrant; *(boisson)* blackcurrant liqueur
cassoulet [kasule] *nm* = stew of beans, pork and goose
cassure [kɑsyr] *nf* break; *Géol* fault
castagnettes [kastaɲɛt] *nfpl* castanets
caste [kast] *nf* caste
castor [kastɔr] *nm* beaver
castrer [kastre] *vt* to castrate; *(chat, chien)* to neuter
cataclysme [kataklism] *nm* cataclysm • **cataclysmique** *adj* cataclysmic
catacombes [katakɔ̃b] *nfpl* catacombs
catalogue [katalɔg] *nm Br* catalogue, *Am* catalog • **cataloguer** *vt Br* to catalogue, *Am* catalog; *Fig & Péj* to label
catalyseur [katalizœr] *nm Chim & Fig* catalyst
catalytique [katalitik] *adj Aut* **pot c.** catalytic converter
Cataphote® [katafɔt] *nm (de vélo)* reflector; *(sur la route)* cat's eye
cataplasme [kataplasm] *nm* poultice
catapulte [katapylt] *nf* catapult • **catapulter** *vt* to catapult
cataracte [katarakt] *nf (maladie, cascade)* cataract

catastrophe [katastrɔf] *nf* disaster, catastrophe; **en c.** *(à toute vitesse)* in a panic • **catastrophé, -ée** *adj Fam* stunned • **catastrophique** *adj* disastrous, catastrophic
catch [katʃ] *nm* wrestling • **catcheur, -euse** *nmf* wrestler
catéchisme [kateʃism] *nm Rel* catechism
catégorie [kategɔri] *nf* category; *(d'hôtel)* grade
catégorique [kategɔrik] *adj* categorical; **c'est lui, je suis c.** I'm positive it's him • **catégoriquement** *adv* categorically
cathédrale [katedral] *nf* cathedral
catholicisme [katɔlisism] *nm* Catholicism • **catholique** *adj & nmf* (Roman) Catholic; *Fam* **pas (très) c.** shady
catimini [katimini] **en catimini** *adv* on the sly
cauchemar [koʃmar] *nm aussi Fig* nightmare; **faire un c.** to have a nightmare
cause [koz] *nf (origine)* cause; *(procès, parti)* case; **à c. de qn/qch** because of sb/sth; **pour c. de décès** due to bereavement; **et pour c.!** for a very good reason!; **être en c.** *(sujet à cation)* to be in question; **mettre qn en c.** *(impliquer)* to implicate sb; **mettre qn hors de c.** to clear sb; **faire c. commune avec qn** to join forces with sb; **en tout état de c.** in any case
causer¹ [koze] *vt (provoquer)* to cause
causer² [koze] *vi (bavarder)* to chat (**de** about); *(cancaner)* to talk; *Ironique* **cause toujours (, tu m'intéresses!)** riveting! • **causant, -ante** *adj Fam* chatty • **causerie** *nf* talk • **causette** *nf Fam* **faire la c.** to have a little chat
caustique [kostik] *adj (substance, esprit)* caustic
cautériser [koterize] *vt Méd* to cauterize
caution [kosjɔ̃] *nf (d'appartement)* deposit; *Jur* bail; *(personne)* guarantor; *Fig (appui)* backing; *Jur* **sous c.** on bail; **sujet à c.** unconfirmed • **cautionner** *vt Fig (approuver)* to back

> 📖 Il faut noter que le nom anglais **caution** est un faux ami. Il signifie **prudence**.

cavalcade [kavalkad] *nf Fam* stampede; *(défilé)* cavalcade
cavale [kaval] *nf Fam* **en c.** on the run • **cavaler** *vi Fam (se démener)* to rush around; **c. après qn** to chase after sb
cavalerie [kavalri] *nf Mil* cavalry
cavalier, -ière [kavalje, -jɛr] **1** *nmf (à cheval)* rider; *Échecs* knight; *(de bal)* partner, escort; *Fig* **faire c. seul** to go it alone **2** *adj (manière, personne)* cavalier

cave¹ [kav] *nf* cellar • **caveau, -x** *nm (sépulture)* burial vault
cave² [kav] *adj (yeux)* sunken, hollow

> Il faut noter que le nom anglais **cave** est un faux ami. Il signifie **grotte**.

caverne [kavɛrn] *nf* cave, cavern; **homme des cavernes** caveman
caverneux, -euse [kavɛrnø, -øz] *adj (voix)* deep
caviar [kavjar] *nm* caviar
cavité [kavite] *nf* hollow, cavity
CCP [sesepe] *(abrév* **compte chèque postal***) nm Br* ≃ PO Giro account, *Am* ≃ Post Office checking account
CD [sede] *(abrév* **disque compact***) nm* CD • **CD-Rom** *nm inv Ordinat* CD-Rom
CDI [sedei] *(abrév* **centre de documentation et d'information***) nm inv* school library *(with special resources on how to find information)*
CE [səɑ] **1** *(abrév* **cours élémentaire***) nm Scol* **CE1** = second year of primary school; **CE2** = third year of primary school **2** *(abrév* **Communauté européenne***) nf* EC
ce¹ [sə]

> **ce** becomes **c'** before a vowel.

pron démonstratif (**a**) *(pour désigner, pour qualifier)* it, that; **c'est facile** it's easy; **c'est exact** that's right; **c'est mon père** that's my father; *(au téléphone)* it's my father; **c'est un médecin** he's a doctor; **ce sont eux qui...** they are the people who...; **qui est-ce?** *(en général)* who is it?; *(en désignant)* who is that?; **c'est à elle de jouer** it's her turn to play; **est-ce que tu viens?** are you coming?; **ce faisant** in so doing; **sur ce** thereupon (**b**) *(après une proposition)* **ce que..., ce qui...** what...; **je sais ce qui est bon/ce que tu veux** I know what is good/what you want; **elle est malade, ce qui est triste/ce que je ne savais pas** she's ill, which is sad/which I didn't know; **ce que c'est beau!** it's so beautiful!
ce², cette, ces [sə, sɛt, se]

> **cet** is used before a masculine singular adjective beginning with a vowel or mute h.

adj démonstratif this, that, *pl* these, those; **cet homme** this/that man; **cet homme-ci** this man; **cet homme-là** that man
ceci [səsi] *pron démonstratif* this; **c. étant dit** having said this
cécité [sesite] *nf* blindness

céder 1 [sede] *vt (donner)* to give up (**à** to); *(par testament)* to leave (**à** to); **c. sa place à qn** to give up one's seat to sb; **c. du terrain** to give ground; **'cédez le passage'** *Br* 'give way'; *Am* 'yield'; **'à céder'** 'for sale' **2** *vi (personne)* to give in (**à/devant** to); *(branche, chaise)* to give way
cédérom [sederɔm] *nm Ordinat* CD-ROM
cédille [sedij] *nf* cedilla
cèdre [sɛdr] *nm (arbre, bois)* cedar
CEE [seøø] *(abrév* **Communauté économique européenne***) nf* EEC
CEI [seøi] *(abrév* **Communauté d'États Indépendants***) nf* CIS
ceinture [sɛtyr] *nf (accessoire)* belt; *(taille)* waist; **la petite C.** = circular bus route around the centre of Paris; **c. de sécurité** *(de véhicule)* seatbelt
ceinturer [sɛtyre] *vt* to grab around the waist
cela [s(ə)la] *pron démonstratif (pour désigner)* that; *(sujet indéfini)* it, that; **c. m'attriste que...** it saddens me that...; **quand/comment c.?** when?/how?; **c'est c.** that is so
célèbre [selɛbr] *adj* famous • **célébrité** *nf* fame; *(personne)* celebrity
célébrer [selebre] *vt* to celebrate • **célébration** *nf* celebration (**de** of)
céleri [sɛlri] *nm* celery
céleste [selɛst] *adj* celestial, heavenly
célibat [seliba] *nm (de prêtre)* celibacy • **célibataire 1** *adj (non marié)* single, unmarried **2** *nmf* bachelor, *f* single woman

> Il faut noter que l'adjectif anglais **celibate** est un faux ami. Il signifie **chaste**.

celle *voir* **celui**
cellier [selje] *nm* storeroom
Cellophane® [selɔfan] *nf* cellophane®; **sous c.** cellophane-wrapped
cellule [selyl] *nf (de prison) & Biol* cell; **c. photoélectrique** photoelectric cell • **cellulaire** *adj Biol* cell; **téléphone c.** cellular phone
cellulite [selylit] *nf* cellulite
cellulose [selyloz] *nf* cellulose
celtique, celte [sɛltik, sɛlt] *adj* Celtic
celui, celle, ceux, celles [səlɥi, sɛl, sø, sɛl] *pron démonstratif* the one, *pl* those, the ones; **c. de Jean** John's (one); **ceux de Jean** John's (ones), those of John; **c. qui appartient à Jean** the one that belongs to John; **c.-ci** this one; *(le dernier)* the latter; **c.-là** that one; *(le premier)* the former; **elle alla voir son amie, mais celle-ci était absente** she went to see her friend but she was out

cendre [sãdr] *nf* ash •**cendrée** *nf (de stade)* cinder track
cendrier [sãdrije] *nm* ashtray
Cendrillon [sãdrijõ] *nf* Cinderella
censé, -ée [sãse] *adj* **être c. faire qch** to be supposed to do sth
censeur [sãsœr] *nm (de films, de journaux)* censor; *(de lycée) Br* deputy head, *Am* assistant principal •**censure** *nf (activité)* censorship; *(comité)* board of censors •**censurer** *vt (film)* to censor

> *Il faut noter que le verbe anglais* **to censure** *est un faux ami. Il signifie* **critiquer.**

cent [sã] *adj & nm* a hundred; **c. pages** a *or* one hundred pages; **deux cents pages** two hundred pages; **deux c. trois pages** two hundred and three pages; **cinq pour c.** five per cent •**centaine** *nf* **une c. (de)** about a hundred; **des centaines de** hundreds of; **plusieurs centaines de gens** several hundred people •**centenaire 1** *adj* hundred-year-old; **être c.** to be a hundred **2** *nmf* centenarian **3** *nm (anniversaire)* centenary •**centième** *adj & nmf* hundredth
centigrade [sãtigrad] *adj* centigrade
centime [sãtim] *nm* centime
centimètre [sãtimɛtr] *nm* centimetre; *(ruban)* tape measure
central, -e, -aux, -ales [sãtral, -o] **1** *adj* central
  2 *nm* **c. téléphonique** telephone exchange •**centrale** *nf* **c. électrique** *Br* power station, *Am* power plant; **c. nucléaire** nuclear *Br* power station *or Am* power plant; **d'achat** purchasing group •**centraliser** *vt* to centralize
centre [sãtr] *nm* centre; *Football (passe)* cross; **c. de loisirs** leisure centre; **c. de vacances** holiday centre; **c. aéré** outdoor activity centre; **c. commercial** shopping centre; **c. hospitalo-universitaire** ≃ teaching hospital •**centre-ville** *(pl centres-villes)* *nm* town centre; *(de grande ville) Br* city centre, *Am* downtown •**centrer** *vt* to centre
centrifuge [sãtrifyʒ] *adj* centrifugal •**centrifugeuse** *nf (pour fruits)* juice extractor
centuple [sãtypl] *nm* **x est le c. de y** x is a hundred times y; **au c.** a hundredfold
cep [sɛp] *nm* vine-stock •**cépage** *nm* vine
cependant [səpãdã] *conj* however, yet
céramique [seramik] *nf (matière)* ceramic; *(art)* ceramics *(sing)*; **de** *ou* **en c.** ceramic
cerceau, -x [sɛrso] *nm* hoop

cercle [sɛrkl] *nm (forme, groupe)* circle; **le c. polaire arctique** the Arctic Circle; **c. vicieux** vicious circle
cercueil [sɛrkœj] *nm* coffin
céréale [sereal] *nf* cereal
cérébral, -e, -aux, -ales [serebral, -o] *adj* cerebral
cérémonie [seremɔni] *nf* ceremony; **tenue de c.** ceremonial dress; **sans c.** *(inviter, manger)* informally; *Fam* **faire des cérémonies** to stand on ceremony •**cérémonial** *(pl* **-als)** *nm* ceremonial •**cérémonieux, -euse** *adj* ceremonious
cerf [sɛr] *nm* stag •**cerf-volant** *(pl cerfs-volants) nm (jeu)* kite
cerise [səriz] *nf* cherry •**cerisier** *nm* cherry tree
cerne [sɛrn] *nm* ring •**cerner** *vt* to surround; *(problème)* to define; **avoir les yeux cernés** to have rings under one's eyes
certain, -aine [sɛrtɛ̃, -ɛn] **1** *adj (sûr)* certain; **il est c. que tu réussiras** you're certain to succeed; **je suis c. de réussir** I'm certain I'll be successful *or* of being successful; **être c. de qch** to be certain of sth
  2 *adj indéfini (avant nom)* certain; **un c. temps** a while; **il a un c. charme** he has a certain charm
  3 *pron indéfini* **certains pensent que...** some people think that...; **certains d'entre nous** some of us •**certainement** *adv* most probably

> *Il faut noter que l'adverbe anglais* **certainly** *est un faux ami. Il signifie* **sans aucun doute.**

certes [sɛrt] *adv Littéraire* most certainly
certificat [sɛrtifika] *nm* certificate
certifier [sɛrtifje] *vt* to certify; **je vous certifie que...** I assure you that... •**certifié, -ée** *adj (professeur)* qualified
certitude [sɛrtityd] *nf* certainty; **avoir la c. que...** to be certain that...
cerveau, -x [sɛrvo] *nm (organe)* brain; *(intelligence)* mind, brain(s); *Fam (de projet)* mastermind
cervelas [sɛrvəla] *nm Br* saveloy
cervelle [sɛrvɛl] *nf (substance)* brain; *(plat)* brains; **se faire sauter le c.** to blow one's brains out
ces *voir* **ce²**
CES [seəes] *(abrév* **collège d'enseignement secondaire)** *nm Anciennement* = secondary school for pupils aged 12 to 15
César [sezar] *nm Cin* = French cinema awards
césarienne [sezarjɛn] *nf* Caesarean (section)

cessation [sesɑsjɔ̃] *nf* cessation; **c. de paiements** suspension of payments
cesse [ses] *nf* **sans c.** constantly; *Littéraire* **elle n'a (pas) eu de c. que je n'accepte** she had no rest until I accepted
cesser [sese] *vti* to stop; **faire c. qch** to put a stop to sth; **c. de faire qch** to stop doing sth; **il ne cesse de parler** he doesn't stop talking; **cela a cessé d'exister** that has ceased to exist • **cessez-le-feu** *nm inv* cease-fire
cession [sesjɔ̃] *nf Jur* transfer
c'est-à-dire [setadir] *conj* that is (to say)
cet, cette *voir* ce²
ceux *voir* celui
chacal, -als [ʃakal] *nm* jackal
chacun, -e [ʃakœ̃, -yn] *pron indéfini* each (one), every one; *(tous le monde)* everyone; **(à) c. son tour!** wait your turn!
chagrin [ʃagrɛ̃] **1** *nm* grief, sorrow; **avoir du c.** to be upset; **faire du c. à qn** to distress sb
　2 *adj Littéraire* woeful; **esprits chagrins** malcontents • **chagriner** *vt (peiner)* to grieve; *(contrarier)* to bother
chahut [ʃay] *nm Fam* racket • **chahuter** *Fam* **1** *vi* to make a racket **2** *vt (professeur)* to bait; **se faire c.** *(professeur)* to get baited
chai [ʃe] *nm* wine and spirits storehouse
chaîne [ʃen] *nf (attache, décoration, série)* chain; *(de montagnes)* chain, range; *(d'étoffe)* warp; **collision en c.** *(accident)* multiple collision; **réaction en c.** chain reaction; **travail à la c.** assembly line work; **travailler à la c.** to work on the assembly line; **faire la c.** to form a chain; *Aut* **chaînes** (snow) chains; **c. de montage** assembly line; **c. de télévision** television channel; **c. de vélo** bicycle chain; **c. alimentaire** food chain; **c. (hi-fi)** hi-fi (system) • **chaînette** *nf* (small) chain • **chaînon** *nm* link
chair [ʃer] *nf* flesh; **(couleur) c.** flesh-coloured; **en c. et en os** in the flesh; **bien en c.** plump; **avoir la c. de poule** to have *Br* goose pimples *or Am* goose bumps; **c. à saucisses** sausagemeat
chaire [ʃer] *nf (d'université)* chair; *(d'église)* pulpit
chaise [ʃez] *nf* chair; **c. longue** deckchair; **c. d'enfant,** high chair; **c. roulante** wheelchair
chaland [ʃalɑ̃] *nm* barge
châle [ʃal] *nm* shawl
chalet [ʃale] *nm* chalet
chaleur [ʃalœr] *nf* heat; *(de personne, de couleur, de voix)* warmth; **coup de c.**

heatstroke; **les grandes chaleurs** the hot season; **c. humaine** human warmth • **chaleureux, -euse** *adj* warm • **chaleureusement** *adv* warmly
challenge [ʃalɑ̃ʒ] *nm Sport* tournament; *(défi)* challenge
chaloupe [ʃalup] *nf* launch
chalumeau, -x [ʃalymo] *nm* blowtorch, *Br* blowlamp
chalut [ʃaly] *nm* trawl; **pêcher au c.** to trawl • **chalutier** *nm* trawler
chamade [ʃamad] *nf* **battre la c.** to beat wildly
chamailler [ʃamaje] **se chamailler** *vpr* to squabble • **chamailleries** *nfpl* squabbling
chamarré, -ée [ʃamare] *adj* richly coloured
chambarder [ʃɑ̃barde] *vt Fam* to turn upside down
chambouler [ʃɑ̃bule] *vt Fam* to turn upside down
chambre [ʃɑ̃br] *nf* bedroom; *(de tribunal)* division; **c. (d'hôtel)** (hotel) room; **garder la c.** to keep to one's room; **auriez-vous une c. libre?** do you have any vacancies?; **c. à coucher** *(pièce)* bedroom; *(mobilier)* bedroom suite; **c. d'ami** spare room; **c. d'hôte** ≃ guest house; *Jur* **c. d'accusation** Court of Criminal Appeal; **C. de commerce** Chamber of Commerce; *Pol* **C. des députés** = lower chamber of Parliament; **c. à air** inner tube; **c. à gaz** gaz chamber; **c. forte** strongroom; **c. froide** cold store; **c. noire** darkroom • **chambrée** *nf Mil* barrackroom • **chambrer** *vt (vin)* to bring to room temperature; *Fam* **c. qn** to pull sb's leg
chameau, -x [ʃamo] *nm* camel
chamois [ʃamwa] *nm (animal)* chamois; **peau de c.** chamois (leather)
champ [ʃɑ̃] *nm (étendue) & Él, Ordinat* field; *Fig (portée)* scope; **c. de blé** field of wheat, wheatfield; *Fig* **laisser le c. libre à qn** to leave the field free for sb; *Phot* **être dans le c.** to be in shot; **tombé au c. d'honneur** killed in action; **c. de bataille** battlefield; **c. de courses** *Br* racecourse, *Am* racetrack; **c. de foire** fairground; **c. de mines** minefield; **c. de tir** rifle range; **c. magnétique** magnetic field; **c. visuel** field of vision
champagne [ʃɑ̃paɲ] *nm* champagne
champêtre [ʃɑ̃petr] *adj* rustic
champignon [ʃɑ̃piɲɔ̃] *nm (végétal)* mushroom; *Méd* fungus; *Fam* **appuyer sur le c.** *Br* to put one's foot down, *Am* to step on the gas; **c. atomique** mushroom cloud; **c. de Paris** button mushroom; **c.**

vénéneux toadstool, poisonous mushroom

champion, -onne [ʃɑ̃pjɔ̃, -jɔn] **1** *nmf* champion

2 *adj* **l'équipe championne du monde** the world champions • **championnat** *nm* championship

chance [ʃɑ̃s] *nf (sort favorable)* luck; *(possibilité)* chance; **avoir de la c.** to be lucky; **ne pas avoir de c.** to be unlucky; **souhaiter bonne c. à qn** to wish sb luck; **tenter sa c.** to try one's luck; **avoir peu de chances de faire qch** to have little chance of doing sth; **il y a de fortes chances que...** there's every chance that...; **c'est une c. que je sois arrivé** it's lucky that I came; **avec un peu de c.** with a bit of luck; **quelle c.!** what a stroke of luck!; **par c.** luckily • **chanceux, -euse** *adj* lucky

chanceler [ʃɑ̃sle] *vi* to stagger; *Fig (courage, détermination)* to falter • **chancelant, -ante** *adj (pas)* unsteady; *(mémoire)* shaky; *(santé)* delicate

chancelier [ʃɑ̃səlje] *nm Pol* chancellor • **chancellerie** *nf (d'ambassade)* chancellery

chancre [ʃɑ̃kr] *nm Méd & Fig* canker

chandail [ʃɑ̃daj] *nm* sweater

Chandeleur [ʃɑ̃dlœr] *nf* **la C.** Candlemas

chandelier [ʃɑ̃dəlje] *nm (à une branche)* candlestick; *(à plusieurs branches)* candelabra

> *ℓ* Il faut noter que le nom anglais **chandelier** est un faux ami. Il signifie **lustre**.

chandelle [ʃɑ̃dɛl] *nf* candle; *Gym* shoulder stand; *Fig* **voir trente-six chandelles** to see stars

change [ʃɑ̃ʒ] *nm Fin* exchange; *Fig* **gagner au c.** to gain on the exchange; *Fig* **donner le c. à qn** to put sb off the scent

changer [ʃɑ̃ʒe] **1** *vt (modifier, remplacer, convertir)* to change; **c. un bébé** to change a baby; **c. qn/qch en qn/qch** to change sb/sth into sb/sth; **c. qch de place** to move sth; **ça lui changera les idées** that will take his mind off things; **ça va le c.!** it'll be a change for them!

2 *vi* to change; **c. de voiture/d'adresse** to change one's car/address; **c. de train/de côté** to change trains/sides; **c. de place avec qn** to change places avec qn; **c. de vitesse/de couleur** to change gear/colour; **c. de sujet** to change the subject; *Ironique* **pour c.** for a change

3 se changer *vpr* to change (one's clothes); **se c. les idées** to change one's ideas; **se c. en qch** to change into sth

• **changeant, -ante** *adj (temps)* unsettled; **d'humeur changeante** moody • **changement** *nm* change; *Aut* **c. de vitesse** *(levier)* *Br* gear lever, *Am* gear shift • **changeur** *nm* **c. de monnaie** change machine

chanoine [ʃanwan] *nm Rel* canon

chanson [ʃɑ̃sɔ̃] *nf* song • **chant** *nm (art)* singing; *(chanson)* song; **c. de Noël** Christmas carol

chanter [ʃɑ̃te] **1** *vt (chanson)* to sing; *(exploits)* to sing of; *Fam* **qu'est-ce que vous me chantez là?** what are you on about?

2 *vi (personne, oiseau)* to sing; *(coq)* to crow; **faire c. qn** to blackmail sb; *Fam* **si ça te chante** if you feel like it • **chantage** *nm* blackmail • **chantant, -ante** *adj (air, voix)* melodious • **chanteur, -euse** *nmf* singer

> *ℓ* Il faut noter que le verbe anglais **to chant** est un faux ami. Il signifie **scander**.

chantier [ʃɑ̃tje] *nm* (building) site; *(sur route)* roadworks; **mettre qch en c.** to get sth under way; *Fam* **quel c.!** *(désordre)* what a shambles!; **c. naval** shipyard

chantilly [ʃɑ̃tiji] *nf* whipped cream

chantonner [ʃɑ̃tɔne] *vti* to hum

chanvre [ʃɑ̃vr] *nm* hemp

chaos [kao] *nm* chaos • **chaotique** *adj* chaotic

chaparder [ʃaparde] *vt Fam* to pinch

chapeau, -x [ʃapo] *nm* hat; *(de champignon)* cap; *Fig* **tirer son c. à qn** to raise one's hat; **prendre un virage sur les chapeaux de roue** to take a corner at top speed; **c.!** well done!; **c. de paille** straw hat; **c. melon** bowler hat; **c. mou** *Br* trilby, *Am* fedora • **chapelier** *nm* hatter

chapeauter [ʃapote] *vt (contrôler)* to head

chapelet [ʃaplɛ] *nm* rosary; *Fig* **un c. d'injures** a stream of abuse

chapelle [ʃapɛl] *nf* chapel; **c. ardente** chapel of rest

chapelure [ʃaplyr] *nf* breadcrumbs

chaperon [ʃaprɔ̃] *nm* chaperon • **chaperonner** *vt* to chaperon

chapiteau, -x [ʃapito] *nm (de cirque)* big top; *(pour expositions)* tent, *Br* marquee; *Archit (de colonne)* capital

chapitre [ʃapitr] *nm (de livre) & Rel* chapter; *Fig* **sur le c. de** on the subject of; *Fig* **avoir voix au c.** to have a say in the matter

chaque [ʃak] *adj* each, every; **c. chose en son temps** all in good time

char [ʃar] *nm (romain)* chariot; *(de carnaval)* float; *Can Fam (voiture)* car; *Fam* **arrête ton c.!** come off it!; *Mil* **c. (d'assaut)** tank; **c. à voile** sand yacht

charabia [ʃarabja] *nm Fam* gibberish
charade [ʃarad] *nf* = charade that is described rather than acted out

> ℓ Il faut noter que le nom anglais **charade** est un faux ami.

charbon [ʃarbɔ̃] *nm* coal; *(pour dessiner)* & *Méd* charcoal; **c. de bois** charcoal; *Fig* **sur des charbons ardents** on tenterhooks • **charbonnages** *nmpl (houillères)* collieries • **charbonnier, -ière 1** *adj* **basin c.** coal basin; **industrie charbonnière** coal industry **2** *nm* coal merchant

charcuter [ʃarkyte] *vt Fam Péj (opérer)* to hack up

charcuterie [ʃarkytri] *nf (magasin)* pork butcher's shop; *(aliments)* cooked (pork) meats • **charcutier, -ière** *nmf* pork butcher

chardon [ʃardɔ̃] *nm (plante)* thistle

chardonneret [ʃardɔnrɛ] *nm* goldfinch

charge [ʃarʒ] *nf (poids)* load; *(responsabilité)* responsibility; *(d'une arme)* & *Él, Mil* charge; *(fonction)* office; **être en c. de qch** to be in charge of sth; **prendre qn/qch en c.** to take charge of sb/sth; **se prendre en c.** to be responsible for oneself; **être à la c. de qn** *(personne)* to be dependent on sb; *(frais)* to be payable by sb; **avoir un enfant à c.** a dependent child; *Fig* **revenir à la c.** to return to the attack; **charges (locatives)** maintenance charges; **charges sociales** *Br* national insurance contributions, *Am* Social Security contributions

charger [ʃarʒe] **1** *vt (véhicule, marchandises, arme)* & *Ordinat* to load; *(batterie)* & *Mil* to charge; **c. qn de qch** to entrust sb with; **c. qn de faire qch** to give sb the responsibility of doing sth
2 *vi Ordinat* to load up; *Mil* to charge
3 se charger *vpr (s'encombrer)* to weigh oneself down; **se c. de qn/qch** to take care of sb/sth; **se c. de faire qch** to undertake to do sth • **chargé, -ée 1** *adj (véhicule)* loaded (**de** with); *(arme)* loaded; *(journée, programme)* busy; **avoir la langue chargée** to have a furred tongue; **être c. de faire qch** to be responsible for doing sth; **être c. de famille** to have family responsibilities **2** *nmf Univ* **c. de cours** = part-time lecturer • **chargement** [-əmɑ̃] *nm (action)* loading; *(marchandises)* load; *(de bateau)* cargo • **chargeur** *nm (d'arme)* magazine; *Él* (battery) charger

chariot [ʃarjo] *nm (de supermarché) Br* trolley, *Am* cart; *(de ferme)* waggon; *(de machine à écrire)* carriage; **c. à bagages** luggage trolley

charisme [karism] *nm* charisma
charitable [ʃaritabl] *adj* charitable (**envers** towards)
charité [ʃarite] *nf (vertu)* charity; **faire la c.** to give to charity; **demander la c.** to ask for charity
charivari [ʃarivari] *nm Fam* hubbub, hullabaloo
charlatan [ʃarlatɑ̃] *nm Péj (escroc)* charlatan; *(médecin)* quack
charme¹ [ʃarm] *nm (attrait)* charm; *(magie)* spell; **avoir du c.** to have charm; **faire du c. à qn** to turn on the charm with sb; **être sous le c.** to be under the spell; *Fig* **se porter comme un c.** to be as fit as a fiddle
charme² [ʃarm] *nm (arbre)* hornbeam
charmer [ʃarme] *vt* to charm • **charmant, -ante** *adj* charming • **charmeur, -euse 1** *adj (sourire, air)* charming **2** *nmf* charmer; **c. de serpents** snake charmer
charnel, -elle [ʃarnɛl] *adj* carnal
charnier [ʃarnje] *nm* mass grave
charnière [ʃarnjɛr] *nf* hinge; *Fig* **à la c. de deux grandes époques** at the junction of two great eras; **époque c.** transitional period
charnu, -ue [ʃarny] *adj* fleshy
charogne [ʃarɔɲ] *nf* carrion
charpente [ʃarpɑ̃t] *nf* framework; *(de personne)* build • **charpenté, -ée** *adj* **bien c.** solidly built • **charpenterie** *nf* carpentry • **charpentier** *nm* carpenter
charpie [ʃarpi] *nf* **mettre qch en c.** to tear sth to shreds
charrette [ʃarɛt] *nf* cart • **charrier 1** *vt (transporter)* to cart; *(rivière)* to carry along; *Fam (taquiner)* to tease **2** *vi Fam* **faut pas c.!** come off it!
charrue [ʃary] *nf Br* plough, *Am* plow
charte [ʃart] *nf* charter
charter [ʃartɛr] *nm (vol)* charter (flight); *(avion)* charter plane
chas [ʃa] *nm* eye
chasse¹ [ʃas] *nf (activité)* hunting; *(événement)* hunt; *(poursuite)* chase; **aller à la c.** to go hunting; **faire la c. à** to hunt for; **donner la c. à qn/qch** to give chase to sb/sth; **c. à courre** hunting; **c. à l'homme** manhunt; **c. au trésor** treasure hunt; *Pol* **c. aux sorcières** witch hunt; **c. gardée** private hunting ground

> ℓ Il faut noter que le nom anglais **chase** est un faux ami. Il signifie **poursuite**.

chasse² [ʃas] *nf* **c. d'eau** flush; **tirer la c.** to flush the toilet
chassé-croisé [ʃasekrwaze] *(pl* **chassés-**

croisés) *nm (de personnes)* comings and goings

chasser [ʃase] **1** *vt (animal)* to hunt; *(faisan, perdrix)* to shoot; *(papillon)* to chase; **c. qn** *(expulser)* to chase sb away; *(employé)* to dismiss sb

2 *vi* to hunt; *Aut* to skid ● **chasse-neige** *nm inv Br* snowplough, *Am* snowplow ● **chasseur, -euse 1** *nmf* hunter; **c. de têtes** headhunter **2** *nm (d'hôtel) Br* pageboy, *Am* bellboy; *(avion)* fighter

> Il faut noter que le verbe anglais **to chase** est un faux ami. Il signifie **poursuivre**.

châssis [ʃɑsi] *nm* frame; *(d'automobile)* chassis

chaste [ʃast] *adj* chaste ● **chasteté** [-əte] *nf* chastity

chat [ʃa] *nm* cat; *Fig* **avoir un c. dans la gorge** to have a frog in one's throat; *Fig* **avoir d'autres chats à fouetter** to have other fish to fry; *Fig* **il n'y avait pas un c.** there wasn't a soul (around); **c. de gouttière** alley cat; **c. perché** *(jeu)* tag; **c. sauvage** wildcat

châtaigne [ʃatɛɲ] *nf* chestnut ● **châtaignier** *nm* chestnut tree ● **châtain** *adj (cheveux)* (chestnut) brown; *(personne)* brown-haired

château, -x [ʃato] *nm (forteresse)* castle; *(manoir)* mansion; *Fig* **bâtir des châteaux en Espagne** to build castles in the air; *Fig* **c. de cartes** house of cards; **c. d'eau** water tower; **c. fort** fortified castle

châtelain, -aine [ʃatlɛ̃, -ɛn] *nmf Hist* lord of the manor, *f* lady of the manor

châtiment [ʃatimɑ̃] *nm* punishment; **c. corporel** corporal punishment

chaton [ʃatɔ̃] *nm* **(a)** *(chat)* kitten **(b)** *(de bague)* bezel **(c)** *(d'arbre)* catkin

chatouilles [ʃatuj] *nfpl* **faire des c. à qn** to tickle sb ● **chatouiller** *vt* to tickle; *Fig (curiosité)* to arouse ● **chatouilleux, -euse** *adj* ticklish; *Fig (pointilleux)* sensitive (**sur** about)

chatoyer [ʃatwaje] *vi* to shimmer; *(pierre)* to sparkle

châtrer [ʃatre] *vt* to castrate

chatte [ʃat] *nf* (she)-cat; *Fam* **ma (petite) c.** my darling

chatterton [ʃatɛrtɔn] *nm Br* (adhesive) insulating tape, *Am* friction tape

chaud, -e [ʃo, ʃod] **1** *adj* **(a)** *(modérément)* warm; *(intensément)* hot **(b)** *Fig (couleur)* warm; *(voix)* sultry; *(discussion)* heated; *(partisan)* keen; **elle n'est pas chaude pour le projet** she's not keen on the plan

2 *adv* **j'aime manger c.** I like my food hot **3** *nm (modéré)* warmth; *(intense)* heat; **avoir c.** to be hot; *Fam (échapper de justesse)* to have a narrow escape; **garder qch au c.** to keep sth warm; **il fait c.** it's hot; *Fig* **ça ne me fait ni c. ni froid** it's all the same to me ● **chaudement** *adv (s'habiller, féliciter)* warmly

chaudière [ʃodjɛr] *nf* boiler

chauffage [ʃofaʒ] *nm* heating; *(de voiture)* heater

chauffard [ʃofar] *nm* reckless driver

chauffer [ʃofe] **1** *vt* to heat (up); *(moteur)* to warm up

2 *vi* to heat (up); *(s'échauffer) (moteur)* to overheat; **faire c. qch** to heat sth up; **ce radiateur chauffe bien** this radiator gives out a lot of heat; *Fam* **ça va c. s'il est en retard!** there'll be trouble if he's late!

3 se chauffer *vpr* to warm oneself; **se c. au mazout** to have oil-fired heating ● **chauffant, -ante** *adj* **couverture chauffante** electric blanket; **plaque chauffante** hot plate ● **chauffé, -ée** *adj (piscine)* heated; **la chambre n'est pas chauffée** there's no heating in the bedroom ● **chauffe-eau** *nm inv* water heater; **c. électrique** immersion heater ● **chauffe-plat** *(pl* **chauffe-plats***) nm* hotplate ● **chaufferie** *nf* boiler room

chauffeur [ʃofœr] *nm (de véhicule)* driver; *(employé)* chauffeur; **c. de taxi** taxi driver

chaume [ʃom] *nm (pour toits)* thatch; *(des céréales)* stubble; **toit de c.** thatched roof ● **chaumière** *nf (à toit de chaume)* thatched cottage; *(maison pauvre)* cottage

chaussée [ʃose] *nf* road(way)

chausser [ʃose] **1** *vt (chaussures, lunettes, skis)* to put on; *(aller à)* to fit; **c. qn** to put shoes on sb; **c. du 40** to take a size 40 shoe; **souliers qui chaussent bien** shoes that fit well

2 se chausser *vpr* to put one's shoes on ● **chausse-pied** *(pl* **chausse-pieds***) nm* shoehorn

chaussette [ʃosɛt] *nf* sock; **en chaussettes** in one's socks

chausson [ʃosɔ̃] *nm (pantoufle)* slipper; *(de danse)* ballet shoe; *(de bébé)* bootee; *Culin* **c. aux pommes** apple turnover

chaussure [ʃosyr] *nf* shoe; **(l'industrie de) la c.** the shoe industry; *Fig* **trouver c. à son pied** to find the right man/woman; **chaussures à lacets** lace-up shoes; **chaussures à semelles compensées** platform shoes; **chaussures à talons** high-heeled shoes; **chaussures de marches** walking boots; **chaussures de ski** ski boots; **chaussures de sport** sports shoes

chauve [ʃov] **1** *adj* bald

2 *nm* bald(-headed) man

chauve-souris [ʃovsuri] (*pl* **chauves-souris**) *nf* bat

chauvin, -ine [ʃovɛ̃, -in] **1** *adj* chauvinistic

2 *nmf* chauvinist • **chauvinisme** *nm* chauvinism

> ⚠ Il faut noter que le nom anglais **chauvinism** est un faux ami. Il signifie le plus souvent **phallocratie**.

chaux [ʃo] *nf* lime; **blanchir qch à la c.** to whitewash sth; **c. vive** quick lime

chavirer [ʃavire] *vti* (*bateau*) to capsize; **faire c. un bateau** to capsize a boat

chef [ʃɛf] *nm* (**a**) (*de parti, de bande*) leader; (*de tribu*) chief; *Fam* (*patron*) boss; **rédacteur en c.** editor in chief; **le c. du gouvernement** the head of government; *Fam* **se débrouiller comme un c.** to do really well; **c. d'atelier** (shop) foreman; **c. d'entreprise** company head; **c. d'équipe** foreman; **c. d'État** head of state; **c. d'état-major** chief of staff; **c. de famille** head of the family; **c. de file** leader; **c. de gare** stationmaster; **c. d'orchestre** conductor; **c. de service** departmental head (**b**) (*cuisinier*) chef (**c**) *Jur* **c. d'accusation** charge (**d**) **de son propre c.** on one's own authority

chef-d'œuvre [ʃedœvr] (*pl* **chefs-d'œuvre**) *nm* masterpiece

chef-lieu [ʃɛfljø] (*pl* **chefs-lieux**) *nm* = administrative centre of a *département*

cheik(h) [ʃɛk] *nm* sheik(h)

chlem [ʃlem] *nm Sport* **le grand c.** the grand slam

chemin [ʃəmɛ̃] *nm* (*route étroite*) path, track; (*itinéraire*) way (**de** to); *Fig* (*de la gloire*) road; **à mi-c.** half-way; **en c., c. faisant** on the way; **se mettre en c.** to set out; **avoir beaucoup de c. à faire** to have a long way to go; *Fig* **faire son c.** (*idée*) to gain ground; **suivre le droit c.** to stay on the straight and narrow; *Fig* **ne pas y aller par quatre chemins** to get straight to the point; **c. de grande randonnée** hiking trail; **c. de terre** track; **c. de traverse** path across the fields • **chemin de fer** (*pl* **chemins de fer**) *nm Br* railway, *Am* railroad

cheminée [ʃəmine] *nf* (*âtre*) fireplace; (*encadrement*) mantelpiece; (*sur le toit*) chimney; (*de navire*) funnel

cheminer [ʃəmine] *vi* (*personne*) to make one's way; *Fig* (*idée*) to gain ground • **cheminement** *nm* (*de personnes*) movement; *Fig* (*de pensée*) development

cheminot [ʃəmino] *nm Br* railwayman, *Am* railroader

chemise [ʃəmiz] *nf* (*vêtement*) shirt; (*classeur*) folder; *Fig* **changer de qch comme de c.** to change sth at the drop of a hat; **c. de nuit** (*de femme*) nightdress • **chemisette** *nf* short-sleeved shirt • **chemisier** *nm* (*corsage*) blouse

chenal, -aux [ʃənal, -o] *nm* channel

chenapan [ʃənapɑ̃] *nm Hum* scoundrel

chêne [ʃɛn] *nm* (*arbre, bois*) oak

chenet [ʃənɛ] *nm* firedog

chenil [ʃəni(l)] *nm Br* kennels, *Am* kennel

chenille [ʃənij] *nf* (*insecte*) caterpillar; (*de char*) caterpillar track

chenu, -e [ʃəny] *adj Littéraire* (*personne*) hoary; (*arbre*) leafless

cheptel [ʃɛptɛl] *nm* livestock

chèque [ʃɛk] *nm Br* cheque, *Am* check; **faire un c. à qn** to write sb a cheque; **payer qch par c.** to pay sth by cheque; *Fam* **c. en bois** rubber cheque; **c. sans provision** bad cheque; **c. de voyage** *Br* traveller's cheque, *Am* traveler's check • **chèque-repas** (*pl* **chèques-repas**), **chèque-restaurant** (*pl* **chèques-restaurants**) *nm Br* luncheon voucher, *Am* meal ticket • **chéquier** *nm Br* cheque book, *Am* checkbook

cher, chère¹ [ʃɛr] **1** *adj* (**a**) (*aimé*) dear (**à** to); **il a retrouvé son c. bureau** he's back in his beloved office; **C. Monsieur** (*dans une lettre*) Dear Mr X; (*officiel*) Dear Sir (**b**) (*coûteux*) expensive, dear; *Fam* **pas c.** cheap; **la vie chère** the high cost of living

2 *adv* **coûter c.** to be expensive; **payer qch c.** to pay a high price for sth; *Fig* **payer c. une erreur** to pay dearly for a mistake; *Fam* **je l'ai eu pour pas c.** I got it cheap; *Fig* **je donnerais c. pour savoir ce qu'il a dit** I'd give anything to know what he said to them

3 *nmf* **mon c., ma chère** my dear • **chère²** *nf Littéraire* **aimer la bonne c.** to be a lover of good food • **chèrement** *adv* (*à un prix élevé*) dearly; *Fig* **vendre c. sa peau** to sell one's life dearly

chercher [ʃɛrʃe] **1** *vt* to look for; (*secours, paix*) to seek; (*dans ses souvenirs*) to try to think of; (*dans un dictionnaire*) to look up; **c. qn du regard** to look around for sb; **c. ses mots** to search for words; **aller c. qn/qch** to (go and) fetch sb/sth; **venir c. qn/qch** to (come and) fetch sb/sth; **c. à faire**

qch to try to do sth; **tu l'as bien cherché!** you asked for it!; *Fam* **ça va a c. dans les 10 000 euros** you're talking about something like 10,000 euros; *Fam* **tu me cherches?** are you looking for a fight?

2 se chercher *vpr (chercher son identité)* to try to find oneself • **chercheur, -euse** *nmf (scientifique)* researcher; **c. d'or** gold digger

chérir [ʃerir] *vt* to cherish • **chéri, -ie 1** *adj* dear **2** *nmf* darling

chérot [ʃero] *adj inv Fam* pricey

cherté [ʃerte] *nf* high cost

chétif, -ive [ʃetif, -iv] *adj (personne)* puny

cheval, -aux [ʃəval, -o] *nm* horse; **à c.** on horseback; **faire du c.** *Br* to go horse riding, *Am* to go horseback riding; **être à à c. sur qch** to straddle sth; *Fig* **être à c. sur les principes** to be a stickler for principle; *Fig* **monter sur ses grands chevaux** to get on one's high horse; *Sport* **c. d'arçons** vaulting horse; **c. à bascule** rocking horse; **c. de bataille** hobby-horse; **chevaux de bois** merry-go-round; **c. de course** racehorse; **c. de trait** carthorse; *Aut* **c. (-vapeur)** horsepower

chevaleresque [ʃəvalrɛsk] *adj* chivalrous

chevalet [ʃəvalɛ] *nm (de peintre)* easel; *(de menuisier)* trestle

chevalier [ʃəvalje] *nm* knight

chevalière [ʃəvaljer] *nf* signet ring

chevaline [ʃəvalin] *adj f* **boucherie c.** horse butcher's (shop)

chevauchée [ʃəvoʃe] *nf* (horse) ride

chevaucher [ʃəvoʃe] **1** *vt* to straddle **2** *vi* **se chevaucher** *vpr* to overlap

chevelu, -ue [ʃəvly] *adj* long-haired • **chevelure** *nf* (head of) hair

chevet [ʃəvɛ] *nm* bedhead; **rester au c. de qn** to stay at sb's bedside

cheveu, -x [ʃəvø] *nm* **un c.** a hair; **cheveux** hair; **avoir les cheveux noirs** to have black hair; *Fig* **couper les cheveux en quatre** to split hairs; *Fig* **tiré par les cheveux** *(argument)* far-fetched

cheville [ʃəvij] *nf (partie du corps)* ankle; *(pour accrocher)* peg; *(pour boucher un trou)* plug; *Fam* **être en c. avec qn** to be in cahoots with sb; *Fig* **elle ne vous arrive pas à la c.** she can't hold a candle to you; *Fig* **c. ouvrière** mainspring

chèvre [ʃevr] **1** *nf* goat; *Fam* **rendre qn c.** to drive sb round the bend **2** *nm* goat's cheese • **chevreau, -x** *nm* kid

chèvrefeuille [ʃevrəfœj] *nm* honeysuckle

chevreuil [ʃəvrœj] *nm* roe deer; *(viande)* venison

chevron [ʃəvrɔ̃] *nm (poutre)* rafter; *Mil* stripe, chevron; **à chevrons** *(tissu, veste)* herringbone

chevronné, -ée [ʃəvrɔne] *adj* experienced

chevroter [ʃəvrɔte] *vi (voix)* to quaver

chez [ʃe] *prép* **c. qn** at sb's place; **il n'est pas c. lui** he isn't at home; **elle est rentrée c. elle** she's gone home; **faites comme c. vous** make yourself at home; **c. les Suisses/les jeunes** among the Swiss/the young; **c. Camus** in (the work of) Camus; **c. les mammifères** in mammals; **c'est devenu une habitude c. elle** it's become a habit with her; **c. Mme Dupont** *(adresse)* c/o Mme Dupont • **chez-soi** *nm inv* **son petit c.** one's own little home

chialer [ʃjale] *vi très Fam (pleurer)* to blubber

chiant, -ante [ʃjɑ̃, -ɑ̃t] *adj très Fam* damned annoying

chic [ʃik] **1** *adj inv* smart, stylish; *Fam (gentil)* decent **2** *nm (élégance)* style; **avoir le c. pour faire qch** to have the knack of doing sth

chicaner [ʃikane] *vi* **c. sur qch** to quibble over sth

chiche [ʃiʃ] *adj (repas)* scanty; *Fam* **tu n'es pas c. d'y aller!** I bet you don't go!; *Fam* **c.!** *(pour défier)* I dare you!; *(pour relever le défi)* you're on! • **chichement** *adv* meanly

chichis [ʃiʃi] *nmpl Fam* **faire des c.** *(compliquer les choses)* to make a lot of fuss

chicorée [ʃikɔre] *nf (en poudre)* chicory; **c. sauvage** chicory *inv*; **c. frisée** endive

chien, chienne [ʃjɛ̃, ʃjɛn] *nmf* dog, *f* bitch; *Fig* **se regarder en chiens de faïence** to stare at one another; *Fam* **quel temps de c.!** what foul weather!; *Fam* **une vie de c.** a dog's life; **entre c. et loup** at dusk; **c. d'arrêt** pointer; **c. d'aveugle** guide dog; **c. de berger** sheepdog; **c. de chasse** retriever; **c. de garde** guard dog; **c. policier** police dog; **c. de traîneau** husky • **chien-loup** *(pl* **chiens-loups***)* **nm** wolfhound

chiendent [ʃjɛ̃dɑ̃] *nm (plante)* couch grass; **brosse de c.** scrubbing brush

chiffe [ʃif] *nf Fam* **c'est une c. molle** he's a drip

chiffon [ʃifɔ̃] *nm* rag; **passer un coup de c. sur qch** to give sth a dust; **c. (de poussière)** *Br* duster, *Am* dustcloth • **chiffonner** *vt* to crumple; *Fig (ennuyer)* to bother • **chiffonnier** *nm* rag picker

chiffre [ʃifr] *nm (nombre)* figure, number; *(total)* total; **chiffres romains/arabes** Roman/Arabic numerals; **c. d'affaires** turnover • **chiffrer 1** *vt (montant)* to work out; *(réparations)* to assess; **message chiffré** coded message **2 se chiffrer** *vpr* **se c. à** to amount to

chignon [ʃiɲɔ̃] *nm* bun, chignon; **se faire un c.** to put one's hair in a bun

Chili [ʃili] *nm* **le C.** Chile • **chilien, -ienne 1** *adj* Chilean **2** *nmf* **C., Chilienne** Chilean

chimère [ʃimɛr] *nf Fig (rêve)* pipe dream

chimie [ʃimi] *nf* chemistry • **chimique** *adj* chemical • **chimiste** *nmf* (research) chemist

chimiothérapie [ʃimjɔterapi] *nf Méd* chemotherapy

chimpanzé [ʃɛ̃pɑ̃ze] *nm* chimpanzee

Chine [ʃin] *nf* **la C.** China • **chinois, -oise 1** *adj* Chinese **2** *nmf* **C., Chinoise** Chinese; **les C.** the Chinese **3** *nm (langue)* Chinese • **chinoiserie** *nf (objet)* Chinese curio; *Fam* **chinoiseries** *(complications)* pointless complications

chiner [ʃine] *vi* to hunt for bargains

chiot [ʃjo] *nm* puppy, pup

chiper [ʃipe] *vt Fam* to swipe, *Br* to pinch (**à** from)

chipie [ʃipi] *nf Fam* minx

chipoter [ʃipɔte] *vi (contester)* to quibble (**sur** about); *(picorer)* to pick at one's food

chips [ʃips] *nf Br* (potato) crisp, *Am* (potato) chip

> ⚠ Il faut noter que le nom anglais britannique **chips** est un faux ami. Il signifie **frites**.

chiqué [ʃike] *nm Fam* **faire du c.** to put on an act

chiquenaude [ʃiknod] *nf* flick (of the finger)

chiromancien, -ienne [kirɔmɑ̃sjɛ̃, -jɛn] *nmf* palmist

chirurgie [ʃiryrʒi] *nf* surgery; **c. esthétique** plastic surgery • **chirurgical, -e, -aux, -ales** *adj* surgical • **chirurgien, -e** surgeon • **chirurgien-dentiste** *(pl* **chirurgiens-dentistes***) nm* dental surgeon

chlinguer [ʃlɛ̃ge] *vi très Fam* to stink

chlore [klɔr] *nm* chlorine • **chlorer** *vt* to chlorinate

chloroforme [klɔrɔfɔrm] *nm* chloroform

choc [ʃɔk] **1** *nm (coup)* impact; *(forte émotion) Méd* shock; *(conflit)* clash; **faire un c. à** qn to give sb a shock; **être sous le c.** to be in shock; **troupes de c.** shock troops; *Méd* **c. opératoire** postoperative shock; **c. pétrolier** oil crisis **2** *adj* **image-c.** shocking image; **'prix-chocs'** 'drastic reductions'

chocolat [ʃɔkɔla] **1** *nm* chocolate; **gâteau au c.** chocolate cake; **c. à croquer** *Br* plain chocolate, *Am* bittersweet chocolate; **c. au lait** milk chocolate; **c. glacé** *Br* choc-ice, *Am* (chocolate) ice-cream bar **2** *adj inv* chocolate(-coloured); *Fam* **être c.** to have lost out • **chocolaté, -ée** *adj* chocolate

chœur [kœr] *nm Rel (chanteurs, nef)* choir; *(d'opéra) & Fig* chorus; **en c.** *(chanter)* (all) together

choir [ʃwar] *(aux* **être***) vi Littéraire (tomber)* to fall; *Fam* **laisser c.** qn to drop sb

choisir [ʃwazir] *vt* to choose, to pick; **c. de faire** qch to choose to do sth • **choisi, -ie** *adj (œuvres)* selected; *(termes, langage)* careful

choix [ʃwa] *nm* choice; *(assortiment)* selection; **avoir le c.** to have a choice; **faire son c.** to take one's pick; **laisser le c. à** qn to let sb choose; **viande ou poisson au c.** *(sur menu)* choice of meat or fish; **de premier/second c.** top-/second-grade

choléra [kɔlera] *nm Méd* cholera

cholestérol [kɔlɛsterɔl] *nm Méd* cholesterol; *Fam* **avoir du c.** to have a high cholesterol level

chômer [ʃome] *vi* **vous n'avez pas chômé!** you've not been idle!; **jour chômé** (public) holiday • **chômage** *nm* unemployment; **être au c.** to be unemployed; **être en c. technique** to have been laid off; **s'inscrire au c.** to sign on • **chômeur, -euse** *nmf* unemployed person; **les chômeurs** the unemployed

chope [ʃɔp] *nf (verre)* beer mug, *Br* tankard; *(contenu)* pint

choquer [ʃɔke] *vt (scandaliser)* to shock; **c. qn** *(commotionner)* to shake sb badly • **choquant, -ante** *adj* shocking

choral, -e, -aux *ou* **-als, -ales** [kɔral] *adj* choral • **chorale** *nf (club)* choral society; *(chanteurs)* choir • **choriste** *nmf* chorister

chorégraphe [kɔregraf] *nmf* choreographer • **chorégraphie** *nf* choreography

chose [ʃoz] **1** *nf* thing; **je vais te dire une c.** I'll tell you something; **dis bien des choses de ma part à...** remember me to...; **avant toute c.** first of all **2** *nm Fam* **monsieur C.** Mr What's-his-name **3** *adj inv Fam* **se sentir tout c.** to feel a bit funny

chou, -x [ʃu] *nm* cabbage; **choux de Bruxelles** Brussels sprouts; **mon petit c.!** my darling!; **c. à la crème** cream puff • **chou-fleur** *(pl* **choux-fleurs***) nm* cauliflower

chouchou, -oute [ʃuʃu, -ut] *nmf Fam (favori)* pet • **chouchouter** *vt Fam* to pamper

choucroute [ʃukrut] *nf* sauerkraut

chouette [ʃwɛt] **1** *nf (oiseau)* owl **2** *adj Fam (chic)* great **3** *exclam* great!

choyer [ʃwaje] *vt* to pamper

chrétien, -ienne [kretjɛ̃, -jɛn] *adj & nmf* Christian • **Christ** [krist] *nm* **le C.** Christ • **christianisme** *nm* Christianity

chrome [krom] *nm* chromium; chromes *(de voitures)* chrome • **chromé, -ée** *adj* chromium-plated

chromosome [krɔmozom] *nm* chromosome

chronique¹ [krɔnik] *adj (malade, chômage)* chronic

chronique² [krɔnik] *nf (de journal)* column; *(annales)* chronicle • **chroniqueur** *nm (historien)* chronicler; *(journaliste)* columnist

chronologie [krɔnɔlɔʒi] *nf* chronology • **chronologique** *adj* chronological

chronomètre [krɔnɔmɛtr] *nm* chronometer; *(pour le sport)* stopwatch • **chronométrer** *vt Sport* to time

chrysanthème [krizɑ̃tɛm] *nm* chrysanthemum

CHU [seaʃy] *(abrév* **centre hospitalo-universitaire***) nm inv* teaching hospital

chuchoter [ʃyʃɔte] *vti* to whisper • **chuchotement** *nm* whisper; **des chuchotements** whispering

chuinter [ʃwɛ̃te] *vi (siffler)* to hiss

chut [ʃyt] *exclam* sh!, shush!

chute [ʃyt] *nf* fall; *(d'histoire drôle)* punchline; *(de tissu)* scrap; **prévenir la c. des cheveux** to prevent hair loss; **c. d'eau** waterfall; **c. de neige** snowfall; **c. libre** free fall • **chuter** *vi (diminuer)* to fall, to drop; *Fam (tomber)* to fall

Chypre [ʃipr] *nm ou f* Cyprus • **chypriote 1** *adj* Cypriot **2** *nmf* **C.** Cypriot

ci [si] *pron dém* **comme ci comme ça** so so

-ci [si] *adv* **(a)** par-ci, par-là here and there **(b)** *voir* **ce², celui**

ci-après [siaprɛ] *adv* below; *Jur* hereinafter • **ci-contre** *adv* opposite • **ci-dessous** *adv* below • **ci-dessus** *adv* above • **ci-gît** *adv* here lies... *(on gravestones)* • **ci-joint, -jointe** *(mpl* **ci-joints***, fpl* **ci-jointes***)* **1** *adj* **le document c.** the enclosed document **2** *adv* **vous trouverez c. copie de...** please find enclosed a copy of…

cible [sibl] *nf* target • **ciblé, -ée** *adj* well-targeted

ciboulette [sibulet] *nf* chives

cicatrice [sikatris] *nf* scar

cicatriser [sikatrize] *vti*, **se cicatriser** *vpr* to heal • **cicatrisation** *nf* healing

cidre [sidr] *nm* cider

Cie *(abrév* **compagnie***)* Co

ciel [sjɛl] *nm* **(a)** *(pl* **ciels***)* sky; **à c. ouvert** open-air; **c. de lit** canopy **(b)** *(pl* **cieux** [sjø]*) (paradis)* heaven; **sous d'autres cieux** in other climes

cierge [sjɛrʒ] *nm Rel* candle

cigale [sigal] *nf* cicada

cigare [sigar] *nm* cigar • **cigarette** *nf* cigarette

cigogne [sigɔɲ] *nf* stork

cil [sil] *nm* eyelash

cime [sim] *nf (d'arbre)* top; *(de montagne)* peak

ciment [simɑ̃] *nm* cement • **cimenter** *vt* to cement

cimetière [simtjɛr] *nm* cemetery; *(d'église)* graveyard; **c. de voitures** scrapyard

ciné [sine] *nm Fam Br* pictures, *Am* movies • **cinéaste** *nm* film maker • **ciné-club** *(pl* **ciné-clubs***) nm* film club • **cinéphile** *nmf Br* film *or Am* movie enthusiast

cinéma [sinema] *nm (art, industrie) Br* cinema, *Am* movies; *(salle) Br* cinema, *Am* movie theater; **faire du c.** to be a film actor/actress; **aller au c.** to go to the *Br* cinema *or Am* movies; *Fam* **arrête ton c.!** stop making such a fuss!; **c. d'art et d'essai** art films; **c. muet** silent films • **CinémaScope**® *nm* CinemaScope® • **cinémathèque** *nf* film library • **cinématographique** *adj* film; **industrie c.** film indsutry

cinglé, -ée [sɛ̃gle] *adj Fam* crazy

cingler [sɛ̃gle] *vt* to lash • **cinglant, -ante** *adj (pluie)* lashing; *(vent, remarque)* cutting

cinoche [sinɔʃ] *nm Fam Br* cinema, *Am* movie theater

cinq [sɛ̃k] **1** *adj inv* five **2** *nm inv* five; **recevoir qn c. sur c.** to receive sb loud and clear • **cinquième** *adj & nmf* fifth; **un c.** a fifth

cinquante [sɛ̃kɑ̃t] *adj & nm inv* fifty • **cinquantaine** *nf* **une c. (de)** about fifty; **avoir la c.** to be about fifty • **cinquantenaire** *nm (anniversaire)* fiftieth anniversary • **cinquantième** *adj & nmf* fiftieth

cintre [sɛ̃tr] *nm* coathanger • **cintré, -ée** *adj (veste)* fitted

cirage [siraʒ] *nm (shoe)* polish; *Fam* **être dans le c.** to be feeling woozy

circoncis [sirkɔ̃si] *adj m* circumcised • **circoncision** *nf* circumcision

circonférence [sirkɔ̃ferɑ̃s] *nf* circumference

circonflexe [sirkɔ̃flɛks] *adj voir* accent

circonscription [sirkɔ̃skripsjɔ̃] *nf* division, district; **c. (électorale)** *Br* constituency, *Am* district

circonscrire* [sirkɔ̃skrir] *vt (encercler)* to encircle; *(incendie)* to contain

circonspect, -ecte [sirkɔ̃spɛ, -ɛkt] *adj* cautious, circumspect • **circonspection** *nf* caution

circonstance [sirkɔ̃stɑ̃s] *nf* circumstance; **pour/en la c.** for/on this occasion; **en pareilles circonstances** under such circumstances; **de c.** *(habit, parole)* appropriate; *Jur* **circonstances atténuantes** extenuating circumstances • **circonstancié, -ée** *adj* detailed • **circonstanciel, -ielle** *adj voir* **complément**

circuit [sirkɥi] *nm (électrique, sportif)* circuit; *(chemin)* way; **c. automobile** racing circuit; **c. de distribution** distribution network; **c. touristique** (organized) tour

circulaire [sirkylɛr] **1** *adj* circular **2** *nf (lettre)* circular

circulation [sirkylɑsjɔ̃] *nf (du sang, de l'information, de billets)* circulation; *(d'autos, d'avions)* traffic; **retirer un produit de la c.** to take a product off the market; **c. routière/aérienne** road/air traffic • **circuler** *vi (sang, air, rumeur, lettre)* to circulate; *(voyageur)* to travel; *(train, bus)* to run; **on circule très mal dans Paris** it's very difficult to drive about in Paris; **circulez!** keep moving!

cire [sir] *nf* wax; *(pour meubles)* polish • **ciré** *nm (vêtement)* oilskin(s) • **cirer** *vt* to polish; *très Fam* **il n'en a rien à c.** he doesn't give a damn! • **cireux, -euse** *adj* waxy

cirque [sirk] *nm (spectacle)* circus

cirrhose [siroz] *nf* **c. (du foie)** cirrhosis (of the liver)

cisaille(s) [sizɑj] *nf(pl)* (garden) shears • **ciseau, -x** *nm (de menuisier)* chisel; **(une paire de) ciseaux** (a pair of) scissors • **ciseler** *vt* to chisel; *(or, argent)* to chase

citadelle [sitadɛl] *nf* citadel • **citadin, -ine** **1** *adj* city; **vie citadine** city life **2** *nmf* city dweller

cité [site] *nf (ville)* city; *(immeubles) Br* housing estate, *Am* housing development; **c. universitaire** *Br* (students') halls of residence, *Am* university dormitory complex

citer [site] *vt (auteur, texte)* to quote; *(énumérer)* to name; *Jur* to summons;

(témoin) to subpoena; *Mil (soldat)* to mention; **c. qn en exemple** to quote sb as an example • **citation** *nf* quotation; *Jur* **c. à comparaître** *(d'accusé)* summons; *(de témoin)* subpoena

citerne [sitɛrn] *nf* tank

cithare [sitar] *nf (instrument moderne)* zither

citoyen, -enne [sitwajɛ̃, -ɛn] *nmf* citizen • **citoyenneté** *nf* citizenship

citron [sitrɔ̃] *nm* lemon; **c. pressé** = freshly squeezed lemon juice served with water and sugar; **c. vert** lime • **citronnade** *nf Br* lemon squash, *Am* lemonade

citrouille [sitruj] *nf* pumpkin

civet [sivɛ] *nm* stew; **c. de lièvre** ≃ jugged hare

civière [sivjɛr] *nf* stretcher

civil, -e [sivil] **1** *adj (guerre, mariage, droits)* civil; *(non militaire)* civilian; *(courtois)* civil; **année civile** calendar year **2** *nm* civilian; **dans le c.** in civilian life; **en c.** *(policier)* in plain clothes; *(soldat)* in civilian clothes • **civilement** *adv* **se marier c.** to have a civil wedding • **civilité** *nf* civility

civilisation [sivilizɑsjɔ̃] *nf* civilization • **civilisé, -ée** *adj* civilized

civique [sivik] *adj* civic; *Scol* **instruction c.** civics • **civisme** *nm* good citizenship

clair, -e [klɛr] **1** *adj (net, limpide, évident)* clear; *(éclairé, pâle)* light; *(soupe)* thin; **bleu/vert c.** light blue/green; **robe bleu/vert c.** light-blue/-green dress; **par temps c.** on a clear day **2** *adv (voir)* clearly; **il fait c.** it's light **3** *nm* **passer le plus c. de son temps à faire qch** to spend the better part of one's time doing sth; **tirer qch au c.** to clarify sth; **en c.** in plain laguage; **émission en c.** non-crypted broadcast; **c. de lune** moonlight • **clairement** *adv* clearly • **claire-voie** *nf* **à c.** open-work

clairière [klɛrjɛr] *nf* clearing

clairon [klɛrɔ̃] *nm* bugle; *(soldat)* bugler • **claironner** *vt (nouvelle)* to trumpet forth

clairsemé, -ée [klɛrsəme] *adj (cheveux, auditoire, population)* sparse

clairvoyant, -ante [klɛrvwajɑ̃, -ɑ̃t] *adj* perceptive

clamer [klame] *vt* to proclaim • **clameur** *nf* clamour

clan [klɑ̃] *nm (tribu)* clan; *Péj (groupe)* clique

clandestin, -ine [klɑ̃dɛstɛ̃, -in] *adj (rencontre)* clandestine; *(journal, mouvement)* underground; *(travailleur)* illegal;

passager c. stowaway • **clandestinité** *nf* **entrer dans la c.** to go underground
clapet [klapɛ] *nm (de pompe)* valve
clapier [klapje] *nm* (rabbit) hutch
clapoter [klapɔte] *vi (vagues)* to lap • **clapotement, clapotis** *nm* lapping
claque [klak] *nf* slap; **une paire de claques** a slap; *Fam* **j'en ai ma c.** I've had it up to here!
claquer [klake] **1** *vt (porte)* to slam; *Fam (dépenser)* to blow; **c. la langue** to click one's tongue
2 *vi (porte)* to slam; *(drapeau)* to flap; *(talons)* to click; *(coup de feu)* to ring out; *Fam (mourir)* to kick the bucket; **c. des doigts** to snap one's fingers; **c. des mains** to clap; **elle claque des dents** her teeth are chattering; **faire c. sa langue** to click one's tongue
3 se claquer *vpr* **se c. un muscle** to pull a muscle • **claquage** *nm (blessure)* pulled muscle; **se faire un c.** to pull a muscle • **claqué, -ée** *adj Fam (fatiguée) Br* shattered, *Am* bushed • **claquement** *nm (de porte)* slam(ming); *(de drapeau)* flap(ping)
claquettes [klakɛt] *nfpl* tap dancing; **faire des c.** to do tap dancing
clarifier [klarifje] *vt* to clarify • **clarification** *nf* clarification
clarinette [klarinɛt] *nf* clarinet
clarté [klarte] *nf (lumière)* light; *(transparence)* clearness; *Fig (d'explications)* clarity; **avec c.** clearly
classe [klɑs] **1** *nf (catégorie, qualité, leçon, élèves)* class; **en c. de sixième** *Br* in the first year, *Am* in fifth grade; **aller en c.** to go to school; *Mil* **faire ses classes** to undergo basic training; **avoir de la c.** *(personne)* to have class; **(salle de) c.** classroom; **c. de neige** = school study trip to the mountains; **de première c.** *(billet, compartiment)* first-class; **c. affaire/économique** business/economy class; **c. ouvrière/moyenne** working/middle class; **c. sociale** social class
2 *adj inv Fam* classy
classer [klɑse] **1** *vt (photos, spécimens)* to classify; *(papiers)* to file; *(étudiants)* to grade; **c. une affaire** to consider a matter closed
2 se classer *vpr* **se c. parmi les meilleurs** to rank among the best; *Sport* **se c. troisième** to be placed third • **classé, -ée** *adj (monument)* listed • **classement** *nm* classification; *(de papiers)* filing; *(rang)* place; *Football, Rugby* table • **classeur** *nm (meuble)* filing cabinet; *(portefeuille)* ring binder

classifier [klasifje] *vt* to classify • **classification** *nf* classification
classique [klasik] **1** *adj (période)* classical; *(typique, conventionnel)* classic
2 *nm (œuvre)* classic; *(auteur)* classical author • **classicisme** *nm* classicism
clause [kloz] *nf Jur* clause
claustrophobie [klostrɔfɔbi] *nf* claustrophobia • **claustrophobe** *adj* claustrophobic
clavecin [klavsɛ̃] *nm* harpsichord
clavicule [klavikyl] *nf* collarbone
clavier [klavje] *nm* keyboard
clé, clef [kle] **1** *nf (de porte)* key; *(outil) Br* spanner, *Am* wrench; **fermer qch à c.** to lock sth; **sous c.** under lock and key; **prix clés en main** *(de voiture)* on-the-road price; *(de maison)* all-inclusive price; **c. de contact** ignition key; *Mus* **c. de sol** trebble clef; *Fig* **c. de voûte** cornerstone
2 *adj* key; **poste/industrie c.** key post/industry
clément, -ente [klemɑ̃, -ɑ̃t] *adj (juge)* clement; *(temps)* mild • **clémence** *nf (de juge)* clemency; *(de temps)* mildness
clémentine [klemɑ̃tin] *nf* clementine
clerc [klɛr] *nm Rel* cleric; **c. de notaire** ≃ solicitor's clerk • **clergé** *nm* clergy • **clérical, -e, -aux, -ales** *adj* clerical
cliché [kliʃe] *nm (photo)* photo; *(negative)* negative; *(idée)* cliché
client, -ente [klijɑ̃, -ɑ̃t] *nmf (de magasin)* customer; *(d'avocat)* client; *(de médecin)* patient; *(d'hôtel)* guest; *(de taxi)* fare • **clientèle** *nf (de magasin)* customers; *(d'avocat, de médecin)* practice; **accorder sa c. à** to give one's custom to
cligner [kliɲe] *vi* **c. des yeux** to blink; **c. de l'œil** to wink
clignoter [kliɲɔte] *vi (lumière, voyant)* to flash; *(étoile)* to twinkle • **clignotant** *nm (de voiture) Br* indicator, *Am* flasher; **mettre son c.** to indicate
climat [klima] *nm (de région) & Fig* climate • **climatique** *adj* climatic
climatisation [klimatizasjɔ̃] *nf* air conditioning • **climatisé, -ée** *adj* air-conditioned • **climatiser** *vt* to air-condition
clin d'œil [klɛ̃dœj] *(pl* **clins d'œil**) *nm* wink; **faire un c. à qn** to wink at sb; **en un c. d'œil** in a flash
clinique [klinik] **1** *adj* clinical
2 *nf (hôpital)* clinic
clinquant, -ante [klɛ̃kɑ̃, -ɑ̃t] *adj* flashy
clip [klip] *nm (vidéo)* (music) video; *(bijou)* clip
clique [klik] *nf Fam (gang)* clique
cliquer [klike] *vi Ordinat* to click

cliqueter [klikte] *vi (monnaie, clefs)* to jingle; *(épées)* to clink; *(chaînes)* to rattle ● **cliquetis** *nm (de monnaie, de clefs)* jingling; *(d'épées)* clinking; *(de chaînes)* rattling
clivage [klivaʒ] *nm (dans la société)* divide; *(dans un parti)* split
cloaque [klɔak] *nm* cesspool
clochard, -arde [klɔʃar, -ard] *nmf* tramp ● **se clochardiser** *vpr* to turn into a tramp
cloche [klɔʃ] **1** *nf (d'église)* bell; *Fam (imbécile)* twit; **déménager à la c. de bois** to do a moonlight flit; **c. à fromage** covered cheese dish
   2 *adj Fam* stupid ● **clocher 1** *nm (d'église)* bell tower, steeple **2** *vi Fam* **il y a quelque chose qui cloche** there's something wrong somewhere ● **clochette** *nf (cloche)* small bell
cloche-pied [klɔʃpje] **à cloche-pied** *adv* **sauter à c.** to hop
cloison [klwazɔ̃] *nf (entre pièces)* partition ● **cloisonner** *vt (pièce)* to partition; *Fig (activités)* to compartmentalize
cloître [klwatr] *nm (partie de monastère)* cloister; *(bâtiment pour moines)* monastery; *(pour religieuses)* convent
clonage [klɔnaʒ] *nm Biol* cloning ● **clone** *nm Biol* clone
clope [klɔp] *nf Fam Br* fag, *Am* smoke
clopin-clopant [klɔpɛ̃klɔpɑ̃] *adv* **aller c.** to hobble along
clopinettes [klɔpinɛt] *nfpl Fam* **des c.** *Br* sweet FA, *Am* zilch
cloque [klɔk] *nf (au pied)* blister
clore* [klɔr] *vt (réunion, lettre)* to conclude; *(débat)* to close; *Ordinat* **c. une session** to log off ● **clos, -e 1** *adj (porte, volets)* closed; **l'incident est c.** the matter is closed; **espace c.** enclosed space **2** *nm* enclosure
clôture [klotyr] *nf (barrière)* fence; *(de réunion)* conclusion; *(de débat)* closing; *(de Bourse)* close ● **clôturer** *vt (terrain)* to enclose; *(session, débats)* to close
clou [klu] *nm (pointe)* nail; *(de spectacle)* main attraction; **les clous** *(passage) Br* the pedestrian crossing, *Am* the crosswalk; *Fam* **mettre qn au c.** *(en prison)* to lock sb up; *Fam* **des clous!** not a sausage!; **c. de girofle** clove ● **clouer** *vt (au mur)* to nail up; *(ensemble)* to nail together; *(caisse)* to nail down; **c. qn au sol** to pin sb down; **cloué au lit** confined to (one's) bed; **cloué sur place** rooted to the spot; *Fam* **c. le bec à qn** to shut sb up ● **clouté, -ée** *adj (chaussures)* studded
clown [klun] *nm* clown; **faire le c.** to clown around

club [klœb] *nm (association)* & *Golf* club
CM [seɛm] *(abrév* **cours moyen***) nm Scol* **CM1** = fourth year in primary school; **CM2** = fifth year of primary school
cm *(abrév* **centimètre***)* cm
coaguler [kɔagyle] *vti,* **se coaguler** *vpr (sang)* to clot
coaliser [kɔalize] **se coaliser** *vpr* to unite; *(partis)* to form a coalition ● **coalition** *nf* coalition
coasser [kɔase] *vi (grenouille)* to croak
cobaye [kɔbaj] *nm (animal)* & *Fig* guinea pig
cobra [kɔbra] *nm* cobra
cocaïne [kɔkain] *nf* cocaine
cocarde [kɔkard] *nf* rosette; *Hist (sur un chapeau)* cockade
cocasse [kɔkas] *adj Fam* comical
coccinelle [kɔksinɛl] *nf (insecte) Br* ladybird, *Am* ladybug; *(voiture)* beetle
coche [kɔʃ] *nm Fam* **louper le c.** to miss the boat
cocher¹ [kɔʃe] *vt Br* to tick (off), *Am* to check
cocher² [kɔʃe] *nm* coachman
cochon, -onne [kɔʃɔ̃, -ɔn] **1** *nm (animal)* pig; *(viande)* pork; **c. d'Inde** guinea pig
   2 *nmf (personne sale)* pig
   3 *adj (histoire, film)* dirty ● **cochonnerie** *nf (chose sans valeur)* trash, *Br* rubbish; *(obscénité)* smutty remark; *(mauvaise nourriture)* muck; **faire des cochonneries** to make a mess ● **cochonnet** *nm Boules* jack
cocktail [kɔktɛl] *nm (boisson)* cocktail; *(réunion)* cocktail party; **c. de fruits** fruit cocktail
coco [kɔko] *nm* (**a**) **noix de c.** coconut (**b**) *Fam* **un drôle de c.** a strange character ● **cocotier** *nm* coconut palm
cocon [kɔkɔ̃] *nm* cocoon
cocorico [kɔkɔriko] *exclam* & *nm* cock-a-doodle-doo; *Fam* **faire c.** to crow
cocotte [kɔkɔt] *nf (marmite)* casserole dish; **C. minute®** pressure cooker
cocu, -e [kɔky] **1** *adj* **il est c.** his wife's cheating on him
   2 *nm* cuckold
code [kɔd] *nm (symboles, lois)* & *Ordinat* code; **passer le c.** *(examen du permis de conduire)* to sit the written part of one's driving test; **codes** *Br* dipped headlights, *Am* low beams; **se mettre en c.** *Br* to dip one's headlights, *Am* to switch on one's low beams; **le C. de la route** *Br* the Highway Code, *Am* the traffic regulations; *Jur* **c. civil/pénal** civil/penal code; *Jur* **c. du travail** employment legislation;

c. confidentiel security code; *(de carte bancaire)* PIN; *Biol* **c. génétique** genetic code; **c. postal** *Br* postcode, *Am* zip code •**code-barres** (*pl* **codes-barres**) *nm* bar code •**coder** *vt* to code •**codifier** *vt* to codify

coefficient [kɔefisjɑ̃] *nm* coefficient

coéquipier, -ière [kɔekipje, -jɛr] *nmf* team-mate

cœur [kœr] *nm* heart; *Cartes (couleur)* hearts; **avoir mal au c.** to feel sick; **ça me soulève le c.** that turns my stomach; **avoir le c. gros** to have a heavy heart; **avoir bon c.** to be kind-hearted; **ça me tient à c.** that's close to my heart; **être opéré à c. ouvert** to have open-heart surgery; **au c. de la ville** in the heart of the town; **au c. de l'hiver** in the depths of winter; **par c.** (off) by heart; **de bon c.** *(volontiers)* willingly; *(rire)* heartily; **si le c. vous en dit** if you so desire; **c. d'artichaut** artichoke heart

coexister [kɔegziste] *vi* to coexist •**coexistence** *nf* coexistence

coffre [kɔr] *nm (meuble)* chest; *(pour objets de valeur)* safe; *(de voiture)* *Br* boot, *Am* trunk; **c. à bagages** *(d'avion)* baggage compartment; **c. à jouets** toy box •**coffre-fort** (*pl* **coffres-forts**) *nm* safe •**coffret** *nm (petit coffre)* box; **c. à bijoux** jewellery box

cogiter [kɔʒite] *vi Hum* to cogitate

cognac [kɔɲak] *nm* cognac

cogner [kɔɲe] **1** *vt (heurter)* to knock; *Fam* **c. qn** *(battre)* to knock about

2 *vi (buter)* to bang (**sur/contre** on); **c. à une porte** to bang on a door

3 se cogner *vpr* to bang oneself; **se c. la tête contre qch** to bang one's head on sth; **se c. à qch** to bang into sth

cohabiter [kɔabite] *vi* to live together; **c. avec qn** to live with sb •**cohabitation** *nf* living together; *Pol* cohabitation

cohérent, -ente [kɔerɑ̃, -ɑ̃t] *adj (discours)* coherent; *(attitude)* consistent •**cohérence** *nf (de discours)* coherence; *(d'attitude)* consistency •**cohésion** *nf* cohesion

cohorte [kɔɔrt] *nf (de gens)* horde

cohue [kɔy] *nf* crowd; **dans la c.** amidst the general pushing and shoving

coiffe [kwaf] *nf* headdress

coiffer [kwafe] **1** *vt Fig (surmonter)* to cap; *(service)* to head; **c. qn** to do sb's hair; **c. qn de qch** to put sth on sb's head; **elle est bien coiffée** her hair is lovely

2 se coiffer *vpr* to do one's hair; **se c. de qch** to put sth on •**coiffeur, coiffeuse**[1] *nmf* hairdresser •**coiffeuse**[2] *nf (meuble)* dressing table •**coiffure** *nf (chapeau)* headgear; *(coupe de cheveux)* hairstyle; *(métier)* hairdressing

coin [kwɛ̃] *nm (angle)* corner; *(endroit)* spot; *(parcelle)* patch; *(cale)* wedge; **faire le c.** to be on the corner; *Fig* **rester dans son c.** to keep to oneself; **du c.** *(magasin, gens)* local; **dans le c.** in the (local) area; **au c. du feu** by the fireside; *Fam* **le petit c.** *(toilettes)* the smallest room in the house •**coin-repas** (*pl* **coins-repas**) *nm* dining area

coincer [kwɛ̃se] **1** *vt (mécanisme, tiroir)* to jam; *(caler)* to wedge; *Fam* **c. qn** *(arrêter)* to nick sb

2 *vi (mécanisme, tiroir)* to jam

3 se coincer *vpr (mécanisme)* to jam; **se c. le doigt dans la porte** to catch one's finger in the door •**coincé, -ée** *adj (mécanisme, tiroir)* stuck, jammed; *Fam (inhibé)* hung up; *Fam* **être c.** *(dans un embouteillage)* to be stuck; *(être occupé)* to be tied up

coïncider [kɔɛ̃side] *vi* to coincide (**avec** with) •**coïncidence** *nf* coincidence

coin-coin [kwɛ̃kwɛ̃] **1** *exclam* quack! quack!

2 *nm inv (de canard)* quacking

coing [kwɛ̃] *nm* quince

coke [kɔk] *nm (combustible)* coke

col [kɔl] *nm (de chemise)* collar; *(de bouteille)* neck; *Géog* col; **c. en V** V-neck; **c. roulé** *Br* polo neck, *Am* turtleneck; *Anat* **c. de l'utérus** cervix

colère [kɔlɛr] *nf* anger; **être en c. (contre qn)** to be angry (with sb); **mettre qn en c.** to make sb angry; **se mettre en c.** to get angry (**contre** with); **elle est partie en c.** she left angrily; **faire une c.** *(enfant)* to throw a tantrum •**coléreux, -euse, colérique** *adj (personne)* quick-tempered

colibri [kɔlibri] *nm* humming-bird

colifichet [kɔlifiʃɛ] *nm* trinket

colimaçon [kɔlimasɔ̃] **en colimaçon** *adv* **escalier en c.** spiral staircase

colin [kɔlɛ̃] *nm (merlu)* hake; *(lieu noir)* coley

colique [kɔlik] *nf Br* diarrhoea, *Am* diarrhea; **coliques** *(douleur)* stomach pains; **c. néphrétique** renal colic

colis [kɔli] *nm* parcel

collaborer [kɔlabɔre] *vi* collaborate (**avec** with); **c. à qch** *(projet)* to take part in sth; *(journal)* to contribute to sth •**collaborateur, -trice** *nmf (aide)* assistant; *(de journal)* contributor •**collaboration** *nf (aide)* collaboration; *(à un journal)* contribution

collage [kɔlaʒ] *nm (œuvre, jeu)* collage
collant, -ante [kɔlɑ̃, -ɑ̃t] **1** *adj (papier)*
sticky; *(vêtement)* skin-tight; *Fam* **qu'est-
ce qu'il est c.!** you just can't shake him
off!
  2 *nm Br* tights, *Am* pantihose
collation [kɔlasjɔ̃] *nf (repas)* light meal
colle [kɔl] *nf (transparente)* glue; *(blanche)* paste; *Fam (question)* poser; *Fam
(interrogation)* oral test; *Fam (retenue)*
detention
collecte [kɔlɛkt] *nf* collection ● **collecter**
vt to collect
collectif, -ive [kɔlɛktif, -iv] *adj* collective; **billet c.** group ticket; **hystérie/dé-
mission collective** mass hysteria/
resignation ● **collectivement** *adv* collectively ● **collectivité** *nf (groupe)* community
collection [kɔlɛksjɔ̃] *nf (de timbres, de
vêtements)* collection; **faire la c. de qch** to
collect sth ● **collectionner** *vt* to collect
● **collectionneur, -euse** *nmf* collector
collège [kɔlɛʒ] *nm (école)* school; *Anciennement* **c. d'enseignement secondaire** = secondary school for pupils
aged 12 to 15 ● **collégien** *nm* schoolboy
● **collégienne** *nf* schoolgirl
collègue [kɔlɛg] *nmf* colleague
coller [kɔle] **1** *vt (timbre)* to stick; *(à la
colle transparente)* to glue; *(à la colle
blanche)* to paste; *(enveloppe)* to stick
(down); *(deux objets)* to stick together;
(affiche) to stick up; *(papier peint)* to
hang; **c. son oreille contre qch** to press
one's ear against sth; *Fam* **c. un élève** *(en
punition)* to keep a pupil in; *Fam* **être
collé** *(à un examen)* to fail
  2 *vi Fam (coïncider)* to tally (**avec** with);
ça colle! that's OK!
  3 se coller *vpr* **se c.** **contre un mur** to
flatten oneself against a wall ● **colleur,
-euse** *nmf* **c. d'affiches** billsticker
collet [kɔlɛ] *nm (piège)* snare; **prendre qn
au c.** to grab sb by the scruff of the neck;
être c. monté to be strait-laced
collier [kɔlje] *nm (bijou)* necklace; *(de
chien, de tuyau)* collar; **c. (de barbe)**
fringe of beard
colline [kɔlin] *nf* hill
collision [kɔlizjɔ̃] *nf (de véhicules)* collision; **entrer en c. avec qch** to collide with
sth
colloque [kɔlɔk] *nm (conférence)* seminar
collusion [kɔlyzjɔ̃] *nf* collusion
colmater [kɔlmate] *vt* to fill in
colombages [kɔlɔ̃baʃ] *nmpl* **maison à c.**
half-timbered house

colombe [kɔlɔ̃b] *nf* dove
Colombie [kɔlɔ̃bi] *nf* **la C.** Columbia ● **co-
lombien, -ienne 1** *adj* Columbian **2** *nmf* **C.,
Colombienne** Columbian
colon [kɔlɔ̃] *nm (pionnier)* settler, col-
onist; *(enfant)* child at camp
côlon [kɔlɔ̃] *nm Anat* colon
colonial, -e, -aux, -ales [kɔlɔnjal, -jo]
adj colonial ● **colonialisme** *nm* colonial-
ism
colonie [kɔlɔni] *nf* colony; **c. de vacances**
Br (children's) holiday camp, *Am* summer
camp
coloniser [kɔlɔnize] *vt* to colonize ● **colonisation** *nf* colonization
colonel [kɔlɔnɛl] *nm (d'infanterie)* colonel
colonne [kɔlɔn] *nf* column; **en c. par
deux** in columns of two; *Anat* **c. vertébrale** spine ● **colonnade** *nf* colonnade
colorer [kɔlɔre] *vt* to colour; **c. qch en
vert** to colour sth green ● **colorant, -ante 1**
adj colouring **2** *nm (pour teindre)* colorant; *(alimentaire)* colouring ● **coloration**
nf colouring ● **coloré, -ée** *adj* coloured;
(teint) ruddy; *Fig (style)* colourful ● **coloriage** *nm (action)* colouring; *(dessin)*
drawing; **album de coloriages** colouring
book ● **colorier** *vt (dessin)* to colour (in)
● **coloris** *nm (nuance)* shade
colosse [kɔlɔs] *nm* giant ● **colossal, -e,
-aux, -ales** *adj* colossal
colporter [kɔlpɔrte] *vt (marchandises)* to
hawk; *(rumeur)* to spread ● **colporteur** *nm*
hawker
coltiner [kɔltine] **se coltiner** *vpr Fam* **se c.
qn/qch** to get landed with sb/sth
colza [kɔlza] *nm* rape
coma [kɔma] *nm* coma; **être dans le c.** to
be in a coma
combat [kɔ̃ba] *nm (bataille)* & *Fig* fight;
(activité) combat; **c. de boxe** boxing
match ● **combatif, -ive** *adj* combative
● **combativité** *nf* combativeness
combattre* [kɔ̃batr] **1** *vt (personne, incendie)* to fight (against); *(maladie, inflation)* to fight
  2 *vi* to fight ● **combattant, -ante 1** *adj
(unité, troupe)* fighting **2** *nmf* combattant;
anciens combattants veterans
combien [kɔ̃bjɛ̃] **1** *adv* **(a)** *(en quantité)*
how much; *(en nombre)* how many; **c. de
money** how much money; **c. de temps**
how long; **c. de gens** how many people; **c.
y a-t-il d'ici à?** how far is it to? **(b)**
(comme) how; **tu verras c. il est bête**
you'll see how silly he is; **tu sais c. je
t'aime** you know how (much) I love you

2 *nm inv Fam* **le c. sommes-nous?** what's the date?; **tous les c.?** how often?

combinaison [kɔ̃binezɔ̃] *nf (assemblage)* combination; *(vêtement de travail)* Br boiler suit, *Am* coveralls; *(vêtement de femme)* catsuit; *(sous-vêtement)* slip; **c. de plongée/ski** wet/ski suit

combine [kɔ̃bin] *nf Fam* trick

combiner [kɔbine] **1** *vt (unir)* to combine; *Fam (plan)* to concoct

2 se combiner *vpr* to combine • **combiné** *nm (de téléphone)* receiver

comble [kɔ̃bl] **1** *adj (salle, bus)* packed; *Théâtre* **faire salle c.** to have a full house

2 *nm* **le c. du bonheur** the height of happiness; **au c. de la joie** overjoyed; **pour c. de malheur** to cap it all; **c'est un** *ou* **le c.!** that's the last straw! • **combles** *nmpl (mansarde)* attic; **sous les c.** in the attic

combler [kɔ̃ble] *vt (trou)* to fill in; *(perte)* to make good; *(découvert)* to pay off; *(lacune)* to fill; *(désir)* to satisfy; **c. son retard** to make up lost time; **c. qn de cadeaux** to shower sb with gifts; **c. qn de joie** to fill sb with joy; **je suis comblé** I have all I could wish for

combustible [kɔ̃bystibl] **1** *adj* combustible

2 *nm* fuel • **combustion** *nf* combustion

comédie [kɔmedi] *nf* comedy; **jouer la c.** to act; *Fig* to put on an act; **et pas de c.!** stop your nonsense; **c. musicale** musical • **comédien** *nm* actor • **comédienne** *nf* actress

> ∅ Il faut noter que le nom anglais **comedian** est un faux ami. Il signifie **comique**.

comestible [kɔmɛstibl] *adj* edible

comète [kɔmɛt] *nf* comet

comique [kɔmik] **1** *adj (amusant)* funny, comical; *(acteur, rôle)* comedy; **auteur c.** comedy writer

2 *nm (genre)* comedy; *(acteur)* comic actor; **c. de situation** situation comedy

comité [kɔmite] *nm* committee; **en petit c.** in a small group; **c. d'entreprise** works council

commandant [kɔmɑ̃dɑ̃] *nm (de navire)* captain; *(grade) (dans l'infanterie)* major; *(dans l'aviation)* squadron leader; *Av* **c. de bord** captain

commande [kɔmɑ̃d] *nf* **(a)** *(achat)* order; **sur c.** to order; **passer une c.** to place an order **(b)** *Tech (action, manette)* control; *Ordinat* command; **les commandes** *(d'avion)* the controls; **prendre les commandes** to take over the controls;

Fig (de compagnie) to take control; **c. à distance** remote control; **à c. vocale** voice-activated

commandement [kɔmɑ̃dmɑ̃] *nm (ordre, autorité)* command; *Rel* Commandment

commander [kɔmɑ̃de] **1** *vt (diriger, exiger)* to command; *(marchandises)* to order (**à** from); *(machine)* to control

2 *vi* **c. à qn de faire qch** to command sb to do sth; **qui est-ce qui commande ici?** who's in charge here?

commanditaire [kɔmɑ̃ditɛr] *nm (de société)* Br sleeping partner, *Am* silent partner

commando [kɔmɑ̃do] *nm* commando

comme [kɔm] **1** *adv* (**a**) *(devant nom, pronom)* like; **c. moi/elle** like me/her; **c. cela** like that; **qu'as-tu c. diplômes?** what do you have in the way of certificates?; **je l'ai c. professeur** he's my teacher; **les femmes c. les hommes** men and women alike; *Fam* **joli c. tout** very pretty, *Br* ever so pretty; *P* **c. pomme** p as in pomme; **c. par hasard** as if by chance; **c. quoi** *(disant que)* to the effect that; *(ce qui prouve que)* so, which goes to show that

(**b**) *(devant proposition)* as; **il écrit c. il parle** he writes as he speaks; **c. si** as if; **c. pour faire qch** as if to do sth

2 *adv (exclamatif)* **regarde c. il pleut!** look how it's raining!; **c. c'est petit!** isn't it small!

3 *conj (cause)* as, since; **c. tu es mon ami...** as *or* since you're my friend...; **c. elle entrait** (just) as she was coming in

commémorer [kɔmemɔre] *vt* to commemorate • **commémoratif, -ive** *adj* commemorative • **commémoration** *nf* commemoration

commencer [kɔmɑ̃se] *vti* to begin, to start (**à faire** to do, doing; **par qch** with sth; **par faire** by doing); **pour c.** to begin with • **commencement** *nm* beginning, start; **au c.** at the beginning *or* start

comment [kɔmɑ̃] *adv* how; **c. le sais-tu?** how do you know?; **c. t'appelles-tu?** what's your name?; **c. est-il?** what is he like?; **c. va-t-il?** how is he?; **c. faire?** what's to be done?; **c.?** *(pour faire répéter)* I beg your pardon?; **c.!** *(indignation)* what!; **et c.!** you bet!

commentaire [kɔmɑ̃tɛr] *nm (remarque)* comment; *(de radio, de télévision)* commentary • **commentateur, -trice** *nmf* commentator • **commenter** *vt* to comment (up)on

commérages [kɔmeraʒ] *nmpl* gossip

commerçant, -ante [kɔmɛrsɑ̃, -ɑ̃t] **1**

nmf trader; *(de magasin)* shopkeeper
2 *adj* **rue/quartier commerçant(e)** shopping street/area

commerce [kɔmɛrs] *nm (activité, secteur)* trade; *(affaires, magasin)* business; **faire du c.** **avec** to do business with; **ça se trouve dans le c.** you can buy it in the shops; **c. intérieur/extérieur** home/foreign trade; **c. de détail/gros** retail/wholesale trade; **c. de proximité** *Br* local shop, *Am* local store ● **commercial, -e, -iaux, -iales** *adj* commercial ● **commercialisation** *nf* marketing ● **commercialiser** *vt* to market

commère [kɔmɛr] *nf* gossip

commettre* [kɔmɛtr] *vt (délit)* to commit; *(erreur)* to make

commis [kɔmi] *nm (de magasin)* shop assistant; *(de bureau)* clerk

commissaire [kɔmisɛr]· *nm (de course)* steward; **c. (de police)** *Br* ≃ police superintendent, *Am* ≃ police captain; **c. aux comptes** government auditor ● **commissaire-priseur** *(pl* **commissaires-priseurs)** *nm* auctioneer ● **commissariat** *nm* **c. (de police)** (central) police station

commission [kɔmisjɔ̃] *nf (course)* errand; *(message)* message; *(comité)* commission, committee; *Com (pourcentage)* commission (**sur** on); **faire les commissions** to go shopping; **c. d'enquête** board of inquiry ● **commissionnaire** *nm* messenger; *(agent commercial)* agent

commode [kɔmɔd] **1** *adj (pratique)* handy; *(heure, lieu)* convenient; **pas c.** *(pas aimable)* awkward; *(difficile)* tricky
2 *nf* *Br* chest of drawers, *Am* dresser ● **commodément** *adv* comfortably ● **commodité** *nf* convenience; **pour plus de c.** for greater convenience

commotion [kɔmosjɔ̃] *nf* shock; *Méd* **c. cérébrale** concussion ● **commotionner** *vt* to shake up; *Méd* to concuss

commuer [kɔmɥe] *vt Jur (peine)* to commute (**en** to)

commun, -e [kɔmœ̃, -yn] **1** *adj (non exclusif, répandu, vulgaire)* common; *(frais, cuisine)* shared; *(démarche)* joint; **peu c.** uncommon; **ami c.** mutual friend; **en c.** in common; **mettre qch en c.** to share sth; **vivre/travailler en c.** to live/work together; **elle n'a rien de c. avec les autres** she has nothing in common with the others; **ils n'ont rien de c.** they have nothing in common
2 *nm* **le c. des mortels** ordinary mortals; **hors du c.** out of the ordinary ● **communs**

nmpl (bâtiments) outbuildings ● **communément** [kɔmynemɑ̃] *adv* commonly

communauté [kɔmynote] *nf (collectivité)* community; **la C. économique européenne** the European Economic Community; **la C. d'États indépendants** the Commonwealth of Independent States ● **communautaire** *adj (de la CEE)* Community; **vie c.** community life

commune [kɔmyn] *nf (municipalité)* commune ● **communal, -e, -aux, -ales** *adj Br* ≃ council, *Am* ≃ district; **école communale** ≃ local *Br* primary *or Am* grade school

communicatif, -ive [kɔmynikatif, -iv] *adj (personne)* communicative; *(rire)* infectious; **peu c.** uncommunicative

communication [kɔmynikɑsjɔ̃] *nf* communication; **c. téléphonique** telephone call; **je vous passe la c.** I'll put you through; **la c. est mauvaise** the line is bad

communier [kɔmynje] *vi Rel* to receive Communion ● **communion** *nf* communion; *Rel* (Holy) Communion

communiquer [kɔmynike] **1** *vt* to communicate (**à** to); *(maladie)* to pass on (**à** to)
2 *vi (personne, pièces)* to communicate (**avec** with)
3 se communiquer *vpr* to spread (**à** to) ● **communiqué** *nm (avis)* communiqué; **c. de presse** press release

communisme [kɔmynism] *nm* communism ● **communiste** *adj & nmf* communist

commutateur [kɔmytatœr] *nm (bouton)* switch

compact, -e [kɔ̃pakt] **1** *adj (foule, amas)* dense; *(appareil, véhicule)* compact
2 *nm (CD)* compact disc

compagne [kɔ̃paɲ] *nf (camarade)* companion; *(concubine)* partner

compagnie [kɔ̃paɲi] *nf (présence, société, soldats)* company; **tenir c. à qn** to keep sb company; **en c. de qn** in the company of sb

compagnon [kɔ̃paɲɔ̃] *nm* companion; *(concubin)* partner; **c. de jeu** playmate; **c. de route** travelling companion; **c. de travail** fellow worker, *Br* workmate

comparaître* [kɔ̃parɛtr] *vi (devant tribunal)* to appear (in court) (**devant** before)

comparer [kɔ̃pare] *vt* to compare (**à** to, with) ● **comparable** *adj* comparable (**à** to, with) ● **comparaison** *nf* comparison (**avec** with); *(métaphore)* simile; **en c. de...** in comparison with... ● **comparatif, -ive 1** *adj* comparative **2** *nm Grammaire* comparative • **comparé, -ée** adj (littérature, grammaire) comparative

comparse [kɔ̃pars] nmf Péj associate

compartiment [kɔ̃partimɑ̃] nm compartment; **c. à bagages** (de bus) luggage compartment; **c. fumeurs** smoking compartment; **c. non-fumeurs** nosmoking compartment • **compartimenter** vt (diviser) to partition

comparution [kɔ̃parysjɔ̃] nf Jur appearance

compas [kɔ̃pa] nm Math Br (pair of) compasses, Am compass; Naut compass

compassé, -ée [kɔ̃pase] adj (affecté) starchy, stiff

compassion [kɔ̃pasjɔ̃] nf compassion

compatible [kɔ̃patibl] adj compatible (avec with) • **compatibilité** nf compatibility

compatir [kɔ̃patir] vi to sympathize; **c. à la douleur de qn** to share in sb's grief • **compatissant, -ante** adj compassionate, sympathetic

compatriote [kɔ̃patrijɔt] nmf compatriot

compenser [kɔ̃pɑ̃se] 1 vt (perte, défaut) to make up for, to compensate for 2 vi to compensate; **pour c.** to make up for it, to compensate • **compensation** nf (de perte) compensation; **en c.** in compensation (de for)

compétent, -ente [kɔ̃petɑ̃, -ɑ̃t] adj competent • **compétence** nf competence; **compétences** (connaissances) skills, abilities

compétition [kɔ̃petisjɔ̃] nf (rivalité) competition; (épreuve sportive) event; **être en c. avec qn** to compete with sb; **sport de c.** competitive sport • **compétitif, -ive** adj competitive • **compétitivité** nf competitiveness

compiler [kɔ̃pile] vt to compile

complaire* [kɔ̃plɛr] **se complaire** vpr **se c. dans qch/à faire qch** to delight in sth/in doing sth

complaisant, -ante [kɔ̃plɛzɑ̃, -ɑ̃t] adj (bienveillant) kind, obliging; (satisfait) complacent • **complaisance** nf (bienveillance) kindness; (vanité) complacency

complément [kɔ̃plemɑ̃] nm (reste) rest; Grammaire complement; **un c. d'information** additional information; **c. circonstanciel** adverbial phrase; **c. d'agent** agent; **c. d'objet direct/indirect** direct/indirect object • **complémentaire** adj complementary; (détails) additional

complet, -ète [kɔ̃plɛ, -ɛt] 1 adj (entier, absolu) complete; (train, hôtel, théâtre) full; (pain) wholemeal

2 nm (costume) suit; **la famille au grand c.** the whole family • **complètement** adv completely

compléter [kɔ̃plete] 1 vt (collection, formation) to complete; (formulaire) to fill in; (somme) to make up 2 **se compléter** vpr to complement each other

complexe [kɔ̃plɛks] 1 adj complex 2 nm (sentiment, construction) complex; **avoir des complexes** to have a hang-up • **complexé, -ée** adj Fam hung up (par about) • **complexité** nf complexity

complication [kɔ̃plikasjɔ̃] nf (ennui) & Méd complication; (complexité) complexity

complice [kɔ̃plis] 1 nm accomplice 2 adj (regard) knowing; (silence) conniving; **être c. de qch** to be a party to sth • **complicité** nf complicity

compliment [kɔ̃plimɑ̃] nm compliment; **faire des compliments à qn** to pay sb compliments; **mes compliments!** congratulations! • **complimenter** vt to compliment (sur on)

compliquer [kɔ̃plike] 1 vt to complicate 2 **se compliquer** vpr (situation) to get complicated; **se c. la vie** to make life complicated for oneself • **compliqué, -ée** adj complicated

complot [kɔ̃plo] nm conspiracy (contre against) • **comploter** [kɔ̃plɔte] vti to plot (de faire to do)

comporter [kɔ̃pɔrte] 1 vt (contenir) to contain; (inconvénient) to involve; (être constitué de) to consist of 2 **se comporter** vpr (personne) to behave; (voiture) to handle • **comportement** [-əmɑ̃] nm behaviour

composer [kɔ̃poze] 1 vt (faire partie de) to make up; (musique, poème) to compose; (numéro de téléphone) to dial; Typ to set; **être composé de qch** to be made up or composed of sth 2 vi (étudiant) to take a test; **c. avec** (ennemi) to compromise with 3 **se composer** vpr **se c. de qch** to be made up or composed of sth • **composant** nm (chimique, électronique) component • **composante** nf (d'une idée, d'un ensemble) component • **composé, -ée** adj & nm compound

compositeur, -trice [kɔ̃pozitœr, -tris] nmf (musicien) composer; (typographe) typesetter

composition [kɔ̃pozisjɔ̃] nf (de musique, de poème) composing; Typ typesetting; (éléments) composition; (d'aliment) ingredients; *(examen)* test; **être de bonne c.** to be good-natured

composter [kɔ̃pɔste] *vt (billet)* to cancel

compote [kɔ̃pɔt] *nf Br* stewed fruit, *Am* sauce; **c. de pommes** *Br* stewed apples, *Am* applesauce • **compotier** *nm* fruit dish

compréhensible [kɔ̃preɑ̃sibl] *adj (justifié)* understandable; *(clair)* comprehensible • **compréhensif, -ive** *adj* understanding • **compréhension** *nf* understanding

⚠ Il faut noter que l'adjectif anglais **comprehensive** est un faux ami. Il signifie le plus souvent **complet**.

comprendre* [kɔ̃prɑ̃dr] **1** *vt (par l'esprit)* to understand; *(être composé de)* to consist of; *(comporter)* to include; **mal c. qch** to misunderstand sth; **je n'y comprends rien** I can't make head or tail of it; **se faire c.** to make oneself understood

2 se comprendre *vpr* **ça se comprend** that's understandable

compris, -ise [kɔ̃pri, -is] **1** *pp voir* **comprendre**

2 *adj (inclus)* included (**dans** in); **y c.** including; **c. entre** between

compresse [kɔ̃prɛs] *nf* compress

compresseur [kɔ̃prɛsœr] *adj* **rouleau c.** steamroller

comprimé [kɔ̃prime] *nm (médicament)* tablet

comprimer [kɔ̃prime] *vt (gaz, artère)* to compress; *(dépenses)* to reduce • **compression** *nf (de gaz)* compression; *(reduction)* reduction

compromettre* [kɔ̃prɔmɛtr] *vt (personne)* to compromise; *(sécurité)* to jeopardize • **compromis** *nm* compromise • **compromission** *nf Péj* compromise

comptabiliser [kɔ̃tabilize] *vt (compter)* to count

comptable [kɔ̃tabl] *nmf* accountant • **comptabilité** *nf (comptes)* accounts; *(science)* book-keeping, accounting; *(service)* accounts department

comptant [kɔ̃tɑ̃] **1** *adv* **payer c.** to pay (in) cash

2 *nm* **acheter au c.** to buy for cash

compte [kɔ̃t] *nm* (**a**) *(de banque, de commerçant)* account; *(calcul)* calculation; **avoir un c. en banque** to have a bank account; **faire ses comptes** to do one's accounts; **c. chèque** *Br* current account, *Am* checking account; **c. à rebours** countdown

(**b**) *(expressions)* **pour le c. de** on behalf

of; **en fin de c.** all things considered; **à bon c.** *(acheter)* cheap(ly); **s'en tirer à bon c.** to get off lightly; **demander des comptes à qn** to ask sb for an explanation; **avoir un c. à régler avec qn** to have a score to settle with sb; **tenir c. de qch** to take sth into account; **c. tenu de qch** considering sth; **entrer en ligne de c.** to be taken into account; **se rendre c. de qch** to realize sth; **rendre c. de qch** *(exposer)* to report on sth; *(justifier)* to account for sth; **travailler à son c.** to be self-employed; **s'installer à son c.** to start one's own business; *Fig* **être loin du c.** to be wide of the mark; *Fam* **avoir son c.** to have had enough • **compte-gouttes** *nm inv* dropper; *Fig* **au c.** in dribs and drabs

compter [kɔ̃te] **1** *vt (calculer)* to count; *(prévoir)* to allow; *(inclure)* to include; **c. faire qch** *(espérer)* to expect to do sth; *(avoir l'intention de)* to intend to do sth; **c. qch à qn** *(facturer)* to charge sb for sth; **il compte deux ans de service** he has two years' service; **ses jours sont comptés** his/her days are numbered; **sans c....** *(sans parler de)* not to mention...

2 *vi (calculer, être important)* to count; **c. sur qn/qch** to count *or* rely on sb/sth; **c. avec qn/qch** to reckon with sb/sth; **c. parmi les meilleurs** to rank among the best; **à c. de demain** as from tomorrow; **j'y compte bien!** I should hope so!

3 se compter *vpr* **ses membres se comptent par milliers** it has thousands of members • **compteur** *nm* meter; **c. de gaz** gas meter; **c. Geiger** Geiger counter; *Aut* **c. kilométrique** *Br* mileometer, *Am* odometer; *Aut* **c. de vitesse** speedometer

compte rendu [kɔ̃trɑ̃dy] *(pl* **comptes rendus**) *nm* report; *(de livre, de film)* review

comptoir [kɔ̃twar] *nm (de magasin)* counter; *(de café)* bar; *(dans un pays éloigné)* trading post; **c. de réception** reception desk

compulser [kɔ̃pylse] *vt (notes, archives)* to consult

comte [kɔ̃t] *nm (noble)* count; *(en Grande-Bretagne)* earl • **comté** *nm (subdivision administrative)* county • **comtesse** *nf* countess

con, conne [kɔ̃, kɔn] *très Fam* **1** *adj (idiot)* bloody stupid; **c'est pas c.!** that's pretty smart!

2 *nmf* stupid bastard

concave [kɔ̃kav] *adj* concave

concéder [kɔ̃sede] *vt (victoire, but)* to concede; **c. qch à qn** to grant sb sth

concentrer [kɔ̃sɑ̃tre] **1** *vt* to concentrate; *(attention, énergie)* to focus

2 se concentrer *vpr (réfléchir)* to concentrate • **concentration** *nf* concentration • **concentré, -ée 1** *adj (lait)* condensed; *(solution)* concentrated; *(attentif)* concentrating (hard) **2** *nm* **c. de tomates** tomato purée

concentrique [kɔ̃sɑ̃trik] *adj* concentric

concept [kɔ̃sɛpt] *nm* concept • **conception** *nf (d'idée)* conception; *(création)* design; **c. assistée par ordinateur** computer-aided design

concerner [kɔ̃sɛrne] *vt* to concern; **en ce qui me concerne** as far as I'm concerned • **concernant** *prép* concerning

concert [kɔ̃sɛr] *nm (de musique)* concert; *Fig (de protestations)* chorus; **de c.** *(agir)* together

concerter [kɔ̃sɛrte] **1** *vt (projet)* to devise together

2 se concerter *vpr* to consult together • **concertation** *nf* consultation • **concerté, -ée** *adj (action)* concerted

concerto [kɔ̃sɛrto] *nm Mus* concerto

concession [kɔ̃sesjɔ̃] *nf (compromis)* concession (à to); *(terrain)* plot • **concessionnaire** *nmf* dealer

concevoir* [kɔ̃səvwar] **1** *vt (enfant, plan, idée)* to conceive; *(produit)* to design; *(comprendre)* to understand

2 se concevoir *vpr* **ça se conçoit** that's understandable • **concevable** *adj* conceivable

concierge [kɔ̃sjɛrʒ] *nmf* caretaker, *Am* janitor

concile [kɔ̃sil] *nm Rel* council

concilier [kɔ̃silje] **1** *vt (choses)* to reconcile

2 se concilier *vpr* **se c. la faveur de qn** to win sb's goodwill • **conciliant, -ante** *adj* conciliatory • **conciliation** *nf* conciliation

concis, -ise [kɔ̃si, -is] *adj* concise • **concision** *nf* concision

concitoyen, -enne [kɔ̃sitwajɛ̃, -ɛn] *nmf* fellow citizen

conclure* [kɔ̃klyr] **1** *vt (terminer)* to conclude; *(accord)* to finalize; *(marché)* to clinch; **c. que...** *(déduire)* to conclude that...

2 *vi* **c. à la culpabilité de qn** to conclude that sb is guilty • **concluant, -ante** *adj* conclusive • **conclusion** *nf* conclusion; **tirer une c. de qch** to draw a conclusion from sth

concombre [kɔ̃kɔ̃br] *nm* cucumber

concordance [kɔ̃kɔrdɑ̃s] *nf (de preuves)* tallying; *Grammaire* **c. des temps** sequence of tenses

concorder [kɔ̃kɔrde] *vi (preuves, dates, témoignages)* to tally (**avec** with)

concourir* [kɔ̃kurir] *vi Sport* to compete (**pour** for); *(converger)* to converge; **c. à qch/faire qch** to contribute to sth/to do sth

concours [kɔ̃kur] *nm (examen)* competitive examination; *(jeu)* competition; *(aide)* assistance; **c. de beauté** beauty contest; **c. circonstances** combination of circumstances; **c. hippique** horse show

concret, -ète [kɔ̃krɛ, -ɛt] *adj* concrete • **concrétiser 1** *vt (rêve)* to realize; *(projet)* to carry out **2 se concrétiser** *vpr* to materialize

conçu, -ue [kɔ̃sy] **1** *pp de* **concevoir**

2 *adj* **c. pour faire qch** designed to do sth; **bien c.** well designed

concubine [kɔ̃kybin] *nf Jur* cohabitant • **concubinage** *nm* cohabitation; **vivre en c.** to cohabit

concurrent, -ente [kɔ̃kyrɑ̃, -ɑ̃t] *nmf* competitor • **concurrence** *nf* competition; **faire c. à** to compete with; **jusqu'à c. de 100 euros** up to the amount of 100 euros • **concurrencer** *vt* to compete with • **concurrentiel, -ielle** *adj* competitive

condamnation [kɔ̃danasjɔ̃] *nf Jur (jugement)* conviction (**pour** for); *(peine)* sentence (à to); *(critique)* condemnation; **c. à mort** death sentence

condamner [kɔ̃dane] *vt (blâmer)* to condemn; *Jur* to sentence (**à** to); *(porte)* to block up; *(pièce)* to seal up; **c. qn à une amende** to fine sb; **c. qn à qch** *(forcer à)* to force sb into sth • **condamné, -ée 1** *adj (malade)* terminally ill **2** *nmf* convicted person

condenser [kɔ̃dɑ̃se] *vt*, **se condenser** *vpr* to condense • **condensation** *nf* condensation

condescendre [kɔ̃desɑ̃dr] *vi* to condescend (**à faire** to do) • **condescendance** *nf* condescension • **condescendant, -ante** *adj* condescending

condiment [kɔ̃dimɑ̃] *nm* condiment

condisciple [kɔ̃disipl] *nm (écolier)* schoolmate; *(étudiant)* fellow student

condition [kɔ̃disjɔ̃] *nf (état, stipulation, sort)* condition; *(classe sociale)* station; **conditions** *(circonstances)* conditions; *(d'accord, de vente)* terms; **être en bonne c. physique** to be in good shape; **à c. de faire qch, à c. que l'on fasse qch** providing *or* provided (that) one does sth; **sans c.** *(capitulation)* unconditional; *(se rendre)* unconditionally • **conditionnel, -elle 1** *adj* conditional **2** *nm Grammaire* conditional

conditionner [kɔ̃disjɔne] *vt (être la condition de)* to govern; *(emballer)* to package; *(personne)* to condition • **conditionnement** *nm (emballage)* packaging; *(de personne)* conditioning

condoléances [kɔ̃dɔleɑ̃s] *nfpl* condolences; **présenter ses c. à qn** to offerone's condolences to sb

conducteur, -trice [kɔ̃dyktœr, -tris] **1** *nmf (de véhicule, de train)* driver **2** *adj & nm Él* **(corps) c.** conductor; **(fil) c.** lead (wire)

> 𝄃 Il faut noter que le nom anglais **conductor** est un faux ami. Il signifie **chef d'orchestre** ou **contrôleur** selon le contexte.

conduire* [kɔ̃dyir] **1** *vt (troupeau)* to lead; *(voiture)* to drive; *(moto)* to ride; *(eau)* to carry; *(électricité)* to conduct; **c. qn à** *(accompagner)* to take sb to; **c. qn au suicide** to drive sb to suicide **2** *vi (en voiture)* to drive; **c. à** *(lieu)* to lead to **3 se conduire** *vpr* to behave

conduit [kɔ̃dyi] *nm (tuyau)* pipe

conduite [kɔ̃dyit] *nf (de véhicule)* driving (**de** of); *(d'entreprise, d'opération)* management; *(tuyau)* pipe; *(comportement)* conduct, behaviour; **c. à gauche/droite** *(volant)* left-hand/right-hand drive; **sous la c. de qn** under the guidance of sb; **c. de gaz** gas main

cône [kon] *nm* cone

confection [kɔ̃fɛksjɔ̃] *nf (de vêtement, de repas)* making (**de** of); *(industrie)* clothing industry; **vêtements de c.** ready-to-wear clothes • **confectionner** *vt* to make

confédération [kɔ̃federɑsjɔ̃] *nf* confederation • **confédéré, -ée** *adj* confederate

conférence [kɔ̃ferɑ̃s] *nf (réunion)* conference; *(exposé)* lecture; **c. de presse** press conference • **conférencier, -ière** *nmf* lecturer

conférer [kɔ̃fere] *vt (titre)* to confer (**à** on)

confesser [kɔ̃fese] *Rel* **1** *vt* to confess **2 se confesser** *vpr* to confess (**à** to) • **confession** *nf* confession • **confessional, -aux** *nm Rel* confessional • **confessionnel, -elle** *adj (école)* denominational

confettis [kɔ̃feti] *nmpl* confetti

confiance [kɔ̃fjɑ̃s] *nf* confidence; **faire c. à qn, avoir c. en qn** to trust sb; **de c.** *(mission)* of trust; *(personne)* trustworthy; **en toute c.** *(acheter, dire)* quite confidently; **c. en soi** self-confidence; **avoir c. en soi** to be self-confident

• **confiant, -ante** *adj (qui fait confiance)* trusting; *(optimiste)* confident; *(qui a confiance en soi)* self-confident

confidence [kɔ̃fidɑ̃s] *nf* confidence; **faire une c. à qn** to confide in sb • **confident, -ente** *nmf* confidant, *f* confidante • **confidentiel, -ielle** *adj* confidential

confier [kɔ̃fje] **1** *vt* **c. qch à qn** *(laisser)* to entrust sb with sth; *(dire)* to confide sth to sb **2 se confier** *vpr* **se c. à qn** to confide in sb

configuration [kɔ̃figyrɑsjɔ̃] *nf (disposition)* layout; *Ordinat* configuration

confiner [kɔ̃fine] **1** *vt* to confine **2** *vi* **c. à** to border on **3 se confiner** *vpr* **se c. chez soi** to shut oneself up indoors • **confiné, -ée** *adj (atmosphère)* enclosed

confins [kɔ̃fɛ̃] *nmpl* confines; **aux c. de** on the edge of

confirmer [kɔ̃firme] **1** *vt* to confirm (**que** that); **c. qn dans son opinion** to confirm sb in his/her opinion **2 se confirmer** *vpr (nouvelle)* to be confirmed; *(tendance)* to continue • **confirmation** *nf* confirmation

confiserie [kɔ̃fizri] *nf (magasin) Br* sweetshop, *Am* candy store; **confiseries** *(bonbons) Br* sweets, *Am* candy • **confiseur, -euse** *nmf* confectioner

confisquer [kɔ̃fiske] *vt* to confiscate (**à qn** from sb) • **confiscation** *nf* confiscation

confit, -e [kɔ̃fi] **1** *adj (fruits)* candied **2** *nm* **c. d'oie** potted goose

confiture [kɔ̃fityr] *nf* jam; **c. de fraises** strawberry jam

conflit [kɔ̃fli] *nm* conflict; **conflits sociaux** industrial disputes • **conflictuel, -elle** *adj (intérêts)* conflicting; **situation conflictuelle** situation of potential conflict

confluent [kɔ̃flyɑ̃] *nm* confluence

confondre [kɔ̃fɔ̃dr] **1** *vt (choses, personnes)* to mix up, to confuse; *(consterner)* to astound; *(démasquer)* to confound; **c. qn/qch avec qn/qch** to mistake sb/sth for sb/sth **2 se confondre** *vpr (couleurs, intérêts)* to merge; **se c. en excuses** to apologize profusely

conforme [kɔ̃fɔrm] *adj* **c. à** in accordance with; *(modèle)* true to; **copie c. à l'original** exact copy • **conformément** *adv* **c. à** in accordance with

conformer [kɔ̃fɔrme] **1** *vt* to model **2 se conformer** *vpr* to conform (**à** to)

conformisme [kɔ̃fɔrmism] *nm* conformism • **conformiste** *adj & nmf* conformist

conformité [kɔ̃fɔrmite] *nf* conformity (à with)

confort [kɔ̃fɔr] *nm* comfort • **confortable** *adj* comfortable

confrère [kɔ̃frɛr] *nm (de profession)* colleague • **confrérie** *nf Rel* brotherhood

confronter [kɔ̃frɔ̃te] *vt (personnes)* to confront; *(expériences, résultats)* to compare; **confronté à** *(difficulté)* confronted with • **confrontation** *nf (face-à-face)* confrontation; *(comparaison)* comparison

confus, -use [kɔ̃fy, -yz] *adj (esprit, situation, explication)* confused; *(bruit)* indistinct; *(gêné)* embarrassed • **confusément** *adv* vaguely • **confusion** *nf (désordre, méprise)* confusion; *(gêne)* embarrassment

---

⚠ Il faut noter que l'adjectif anglais **confus** est un faux ami. Il signifie **désorienté**.

---

congé [kɔ̃ʒe] *nm (vacances) Br* holiday, *Am* vacation; *(arrêt de travail)* leave; *(avis de renvoi)* notice; **donner son c. à qn** *(employé, locataire)* to give notice to sb; **prendre c. de qn** to take one's leave of sb; **c. de maladie** sick leave; **c. de maternité** maternity leave; **c. de paternité** paternity leave; **congés payés** *Br* paid holidays, *Am* paid vacation

congédier [kɔ̃ʒedje] *vt* to dismiss

congeler [kɔ̃ʒle] *vt* to freeze • **congélateur** *nm* freezer • **congélation** *nf* freezing

congénital, -e, -aux, -ales [kɔ̃ʒenital, -o] *adj* congenital

congère [kɔ̃ʒɛr] *nf* snowdrift

congestion [kɔ̃ʒestjɔ̃] *nf* congestion; **c. cérébrale** stroke • **congestionné, -ée** *adj (visage)* flushed

Congo [kɔ̃go] *nm* **le C.** Congo • **congolais, -aise 1** *adj* Congolese **2** *nmf* **C., Congolaise** Congolese

congratuler [kɔ̃gratyle] *vt* to congratulate (**sur** on)

congrégation [kɔ̃gregɑsjɔ̃] *nf Rel* congregation

congrès [kɔ̃grɛ] *nm* conference; **le C.** *(aux États-Unis)* the Congress • **congressiste** *nmf* delegate

conifère [kɔnifɛr] *nm* conifer

conique [kɔnik] *adj* conical

conjecture [kɔ̃ʒɛktyr] *nf* conjecture • **conjecturer** *vt* to conjecture

conjoint, -ointe [kɔ̃ʒwɛ̃, -wɛ̃t] **1** *adj* joint

2 *nm* spouse; **conjoints** husband and wife • **conjointement** *adv* jointly

conjonction [kɔ̃ʒɔ̃ksjɔ̃] *nf (union)* union; *Grammaire* conjunction

conjonctivite [kɔ̃ʒɔ̃ktivit] *nf Méd* conjunctivitis

conjoncture [kɔ̃ʒɔ̃ktyr] *nf* circumstances; **la c. économique** the economic situation

conjugal, -e, -aux, -ales [kɔ̃ʒygal, -o] *adj (bonheur)* marital; *(vie)* married; *(devoir)* conjugal

conjuguer [kɔ̃ʒyge] **1** *vt (verbe)* to conjugate; *(efforts)* to combine

2 se conjuguer *vpr (verbe)* to be conjugated • **conjugaison** *nf Grammaire* conjugation

conjurer [kɔ̃ʒyre] *vt (danger)* to avert; *(mauvais sort)* to ward off; **c. qn de faire qch** to beg sb to do sth • **conjuration** *nf (complot)* conspiracy • **conjuré, -ée** *nmf* conspirator

connaissance [kɔnɛsɑ̃s] *nf (savoir)* knowledge; *(personne)* acquaintance; **à ma c.** to my knowledge; **en c. de cause** with full knowledge of the facts; **avoir c. de qch** to be aware of sth; **avoir des connaissances en histoire** to have a good knowledge of history; **faire la c. de qn** to make sb's acquaintance; **faire c. avec qn** to get to know sb; **prendre c. de qch** to acquaint oneself with sth; **perdre/reprendre c.** to lose/regain consciousness; **sans c.** unconscious • **connaisseur** *nm* connoisseur

connaître* [kɔnɛtr] **1** *vt (personne, endroit, faits, amour)* to know; *(rencontrer)* to meet; *(famine, guerre)* to experience; **faire c. qch** to make sth known; **faire c. qn** *(présenter)* to introduce sb; *(rendre célèbre)* to make sb known; **ne pas c. de limites** to know no bounds

2 se connaître *vpr* **nous nous connaissons déjà** we've met before; **s'y c. en qch** to know all about sth

connecter [kɔnɛkte] *vt (appareil électrique)* to connect; *Ordinat* **connecté** on line • **connexion** *nf* connection

connerie [kɔnri] *nf très Fam (bêtise)* (damn) stupidity; *(action)* (damn) stupid thing; **dire des conneries** to talk bullshit

connivence [kɔnivɑ̃s] *nf* connivance

connotation [kɔnɔtɑsjɔ̃] *nf* connotation

connu, -ue [kɔny] **1** *pp de* **connaître**

2 *adj (célèbre)* well-known

conquérir* [kɔ̃kerir] *vt (pays, sommet)* to conquer; *(marché)* to capture; **conquis par son charme** won over by his/her charm • **conquérant, -ante** *nmf* conqueror • **conquête** *nf* conquest; **faire la c. de** *(pays)* to conquer

consacrer [kɔ̃sakre] **1** *vt (temps, vie)* to

devote (**à** to); *(église)* to consecrate; *(entériner)* to establish

2 se consacrer *vpr* **se c. à** to devote oneself to

consciemment [kɔ̃sjamɑ̃] *adv* consciously

conscience [kɔ̃sjɑ̃s] *nf* (**a**) *(esprit)* consciousness; **avoir/prendre c. de qch** to be/become aware of sth; **perdre c.** to lose consciousness (**b**) *(morale)* conscience; **avoir bonne/mauvaise c.** to have a clear/guilty conscience; **c. professionnelle** professional integrity • **consciencieux, -euse** *adj* conscientious

conscient, -ente [kɔ̃sjɑ̃, -ɑ̃t] *adj (lucide)* conscious; **c. de qch** aware *or* conscious of sth

conscrit [kɔ̃skri] *nm* conscript • **conscription** *nf* conscription, *Am* draft

consécration [kɔ̃sekrɑsjɔ̃] *nf (d'église)* consecration; *(aboutissement)* crowning moment

consécutif, -ive [kɔ̃sekytif, -iv] *adj* consecutive; **c. à** following upon • **consécutivement** *adv* consecutively

conseil [kɔ̃sɛj] *nm* (**a**) **un c.** *(recommandation)* a piece of advice; **des conseils** advice (**b**) *(assemblée)* council, committee; **c. d'administration** board of directors; *Scol* **c. de classe** = staff meeting with participation of class representatives; *Pol* **c. des ministres** cabinet meeting

conseiller¹ [kɔ̃seje] *vt (guider)* to advise; **c. qch à qn** to recommend sth to sb; **c. à qn de faire qch** to advise sb to do sth

conseiller², -ère [kɔ̃seje, -jɛr] *nmf (expert)* consultant, adviser; **c. d'orientation** careers adviser

consentir* [kɔ̃sɑ̃tir] **1** *vi* **c. à qch/à faire qch** to consent to sth/to do sth

2 *vt (prêt)* to grant (**à** to) • **consentement** *nm* consent

conséquence [kɔ̃sekɑ̃s] *nf* consequence; **en c.** accordingly; **agir en c.** to take appropriate action; **sans c.** *(sans importance)* of no importance

conséquent, -ente [kɔ̃sekɑ̃, -ɑ̃t] *adj (cohérent)* consistent; *Fam (somme)* tidy; **par c.** consequently

conservateur, -trice [kɔ̃sɛrvatœr, -tris] **1** *adj & nmf Pol* Conservative

2 *nmf (de musée)* curator; *(de bibliothèque)* librarian

3 *nm (alimentaire)* preservative • **conservatisme** *nm* conservatism

conservation [kɔ̃sɛrvɑsjɔ̃] *nf (d'aliments)* preserving

conservatoire [kɔ̃sɛrvatwar] *nm* school, academy

conserve [kɔ̃sɛrv] *nf* **conserves** canned *or Br* tinned food; **en c.** canned, *Br* tinned; **mettre qch en c.** to can sth, *Br* to tin sth

conserver [kɔ̃sɛrve] **1** *vt* to keep; *(droits)* to retain; *(fruits, tradition)* to preserve; **c. son calme** to keep one's calm

2 se conserver *vpr (aliment)* to keep

considérable [kɔ̃siderabl] *adj* considerable • **considérablement** [-əmɑ̃] *adv* considerably

considérer [kɔ̃sidere] *vt* to consider (**que** that); **c. qn/qch comme...** to consider sb/sth as...; **tout bien considéré** all things considered • **considération** *nf (respect)* regard, esteem; **considérations** *(remarques)* observations; **prendre qch en c.** to take sth into consideration

consigne [kɔ̃siɲ] *nf (instructions)* orders; *Mil (punition)* confinement to barracks; *(de bouteille)* deposit; **c. (à bagages)** *Br* left-luggage office, *Am* checkroom; **c. automatique** lockers • **consigné, -ée** *adj (bouteille)* returnable • **consigner** *vt (bouteille)* to charge a deposit on; *(bagages) Br* to deposit in the left-luggage office, *Am* to check; *(écrire)* to record; *(punir)* *(élève)* to keep in; *(soldat)* to confine to barracks

consistant, -ante [kɔ̃sistɑ̃, -ɑ̃t] *adj (sauce, bouillie)* thick; *(repas)* substantial • **consistance** *nf (de corps)* consistency

> *Il faut noter que l'adjectif anglais **consistent** est un faux ami. Il signifie le plus souvent **cohérent**.

consister [kɔ̃siste] *vi* **c. en qch** to consist of sth; **c. à faire qch** to consist in doing sth

consœur [kɔ̃sœr] *nf* female colleague

console [kɔ̃sɔl] *nf (d'ordinateur, de jeux)* console

consoler [kɔ̃sɔle] **1** *vt* to comfort, to console

2 se consoler *vpr* **se c. de qch** to get over sth • **consolation** *nf* comfort, consolation

consolider [kɔ̃sɔlide] *vt (mur, position)* to strengthen • **consolidation** *nf* strengthening

consommateur, -trice [kɔ̃sɔmatœr, -tris] *nmf* consumer; *(au café)* customer • **consommation** *nf (de nourriture, d'électricité)* consumption; *(de voiture)* fuel consumption; *(boisson)* drink

consommé, -ée [kɔ̃sɔme] **1** *adj* consummate

2 *nm Culin* consommé

consommer [kɔ̃sɔme] **1** *vt (aliment, carburant)* to consume; *(mariage)* to consummate
2 *vi (au café)* to drink
consonance [kɔ̃sɔnɑ̃s] *nf Mus & Ling* consonance
consonne [kɔ̃sɔn] *nf* consonant
consortium [kɔ̃sɔrsjɔm] *nm (entreprises)* consortium
conspirer [kɔ̃spire] *vi (comploter)* to conspire (**contre** against); **c. à faire qch** *(concourir)* to conspire to do sth • **conspirateur, -trice** *nmf* conspirator • **conspiration** *nf* conspiracy
conspuer [kɔ̃spɥe] *vt* to boo
constant, -ante [kɔ̃stɑ̃, -ɑ̃t] **1** *adj* constant
2 *nf* **constante** *Math* constant • **constamment** [-amɑ̃] *adv* constantly • **constance** *nf (en amour)* constancy
constat [kɔ̃sta] *nm* (official) report; **faire un c. d'échec** to acknowledge failure
constater [kɔ̃state] **1** *vt (observer)* to note (**que** that); *Jur (enregistrer)* to record; *(décès)* to certify
2 *vi* **je ne fais que c.** I'm merely stating a fact • **constatation** *nf (remarque)* observation
constellation [kɔ̃stɛlasjɔ̃] *nf* constellation • **constellé, -ée** *adj* **c. d'étoiles** studded with stars
consterner [kɔ̃stɛrne] *vt* to dismay • **consternation** *nf* dismay
constiper [kɔ̃stipe] *vt* to constipate • **constipation** *nf* constipation • **constipé, -ée** *adj* constipated; *Fam (gêné)* ill at ease
constituer [kɔ̃stitɥe] **1** *vt (composer)* to make up; *(équivaloir à)* to constitute; *(former)* to form; **constitué de** made up of
2 **se constituer** *vpr* **se c. prisonnier** to give oneself up
constitutif, -ive [kɔ̃stitytif, -iv] *adj* constituent
constitution [kɔ̃stitysjɔ̃] *nf (santé, lois)* constitution; *(de gouvernement)* formation • **constitutionnel, -elle** *adj* constitutional
constructeur [kɔ̃stryktœr] *nm (bâtisseur)* builder; *(fabricant)* maker (**de** of); **c. automobile** car manufacturer • **constructif, -ive** *adj* constructive • **construction** *nf (de pont, de route, de maison)* building, construction (**de** of); *(de phrase)* structure; *(édifice)* building; **en c.** under construction
construire* [kɔ̃strɥir] *vt (maison, route)* to build; *(phrase)* to construct
consul [kɔ̃syl] *nm* consul • **consulaire** *adj* consular • **consulat** *nm* consulate

consulter [kɔ̃sylte] **1** *vt* to consult
2 *vi (médecin)* to see patients, *Br* to take surgery
3 **se consulter** *vpr* to consult each other • **consultatif, -ive** *adj* consultative • **consultation** *nf* consultation; **être en c.** *(médecin)* to be with a patient
consumer [kɔ̃syme] *vt (brûler)* to consume
contact [kɔ̃takt] *nm (relation, peronne, toucher) & Él, Aut* contact; **être en c. avec qn** to be in contact with sb; **entrer en c. avec qn** to come into contact with sb; **prendre c.** to get in touch (**avec** with); *Aut* **mettre/couper le c.** to switch on/off • **contacter** *vt* to contact
contagieux, -euse [kɔ̃taʒjø, -øz] *adj (maladie, personne)* contagious; *(enthousiasme)* infectious • **contagion** *nf Méd* contagion
contaminer [kɔ̃tamine] *vt* to contaminate • **contamination** *nf* contamination
conte [kɔ̃t] *nm* tale; **c. de fées** fairy tale
contempler [kɔ̃tɑ̃ple] *vt* to gaze at, to contemplate • **contemplation** *nf* contemplation; **être en c. devant qch** to gaze at sth
contemporain, -aine [kɔ̃tɑ̃pɔrɛ̃, -ɛn] *adj & nmf* contemporary
contenance [kɔ̃tnɑ̃s] *nf* (**a**) *(de récipient)* capacity (**b**) *(allure)* bearing; **perdre c.** to lose one's composure
contenir* [kɔ̃tnir] **1** *vt (renfermer)* to contain; *(contrôler)* to hold back, to contain; **le théâtre contient mille places** the theatre seats a thousand
2 **se contenir** *vpr* to contain oneself • **contenant** *nm* container • **conteneur** *nm* container
content, -ente [kɔ̃tɑ̃, -ɑ̃t] **1** *adj* pleased, happy (**de** with; **de faire** to do); **être c. de soi** to be pleased with oneself; **non c. de mentir...** not content with lying...
2 *nm* **avoir son c.** to have had one's fill (**de** of)
contenter [kɔ̃tɑ̃te] **1** *vt (satisfaire)* to satisfy; *(faire plaisir à)* to please
2 **se contenter** *vpr* **se c. de qch** to content oneself with sth • **contentement** *nm* contentment, satisfaction
contentieux [kɔ̃tɑ̃sjø] *nm (querelles)* dispute; *Jur* litigation; *(service)* legal department
contenu [kɔ̃tny] *nm (de paquet, de bouteille)* contents; *(de lettre, de film)* content
conter [kɔ̃te] *vt* to tell (**à** to) • **conteur, -euse** *nmf* storyteller
contestable [kɔ̃testabl] *adj* debatable

contestataire [kɔ̃testatɛr] **1** *adj Pol* anti-establishement; **étudiant c.** student protester

2 *nmf Pol* protester • **contestation** *nf* protest; **faire de la c.** to protest; **sans c. possible** beyond dispute

conteste [kɔ̃tɛst] **sans conteste** *adv* indisputably

contester [kɔ̃tɛste] **1** *vt* to dispute

2 *vi* **faire qch sans c.** to do sth without protest • **contesté, -ée** *adj (théorie, dirigeant)* controversial

contexte [kɔ̃tɛkst] *nm* context

contigu, -uë [kɔ̃tigy] *adj (maisons)* adjoining; **c. à qch** adjoining sth • **contiguïté** *nf* close proximity

continent [kɔ̃tinɑ̃] *nm* continent; *(opposé à une île)* mainland • **continental, -e, -aux, -ales** *adj (climat, plateau)* continental

contingent [kɔ̃tɛ̃ʒɑ̃] *nm Mil* contingent; *(quota)* quota • **contingences** *nfpl* contingencies

continu, -ue [kɔ̃tiny] *adj* continuous • **continuel, -elle** *adj (ininterrompu)* continuous; *(qui se répète)* continual • **continuellement** *adv (de façon ininterrompue)* continuously; *(de façon répétitive)* continually

continuer [kɔ̃tinɥe] **1** *vt (études, efforts, politique)* to continue, to carry on with; **c. à** *ou* **de faire qch** to continue *or* carry on doing sth

2 *vi* to continue, to go on • **continuation** *nf* continuation; *Fam* **bonne c.!** all the best • **continuité** *nf* continuity

contondant [kɔ̃tɔ̃dɑ̃] *adj m* blunt

contorsion [kɔ̃tɔrsjɔ̃] *nf* contortion • **se contorsionner** *vpr* to contort oneself • **contorsionniste** *nmf* contortionist

contour [kɔ̃tur] *nm* outline

contourner [kɔ̃turne] *vt* to go round; *Fig (difficulté, loi)* to get round

contraception [kɔ̃trasɛpsjɔ̃] *nf* contraception • **contraceptif, -ive** *adj & nm* contraceptive

contracter [kɔ̃trakte] **1** *vt (muscle, habitude, dette)* to contract

2 se contracter *vpr (muscle)* to contract; *(personne)* to tense up • **contraction** *nf* contraction

contractuel, -elle [kɔ̃traktɥɛl] **1** *adj (politique)* contractual

2 *nmf Br* ≃ traffic warden, *Am* ≃ traffic policeman, *f* traffic policewoman

contradiction [kɔ̃tradiksjɔ̃] *nf* contradiction; **être en c. avec qch** to contradict sth; **avoir l'esprit de c.** to be contrary

• **contradictoire** *adj* contradictory; **débat c.** debate

contraindre* [kɔ̃trɛ̃dr] **1** *vt* to compel, to force (**à faire** to do)

2 se contraindre *vpr* to compel *or* force oneself (**à faire** to do) • **contraignant, -ante** *adj* restricting • **contrainte** *nf (obligation, limitation)* constraint; **sous la c.** under duress; **obtenir qch par la c.** to obtain sth by force

contraire [kɔ̃trɛr] **1** *adj (opposé)* conflicting; **c. à qch** contrary to sth; **en sens c.** in the opposite direction; **vent c.** headwind; **le sort nous est c.** fate is against us

2 *nm* opposite; **(bien) au c.** on the contrary • **contrairement** *adv* **c. à** contrary to; **c. à qn** unlike sb

contrarier [kɔ̃trarje] *vt (projet, action)* to thwart; *(personne)* to annoy • **contrariant, -ante** *adj (situation)* annoying; *(personne)* contrary • **contrariété** *nf* annoyance

contraste [kɔ̃trast] *nm* contrast • **contraster** *vi* to contrast (**avec** with)

contrat [kɔ̃tra] *nm* contract; **passer un c.** to enter into an agreement; **c. emploi-solidarité** = short-term contract subsidized by the French government

contravention [kɔ̃travɑ̃sjɔ̃] *nf (amende)* fine; *(pour stationnement interdit)* (parking) ticket

contre [kɔ̃tr] **1** *prép* against; *(en échange de)* (in exchange) for; **échanger qch c. qch** to exchange sth for sth; **fâché c. qn** angry with sb; **six voix c. deux** six votes to two; **Nîmes c. Arras** *(match)* Nîmes versus *or* against Arras; **sirop c. la toux** cough mixture; **par c.** on the other hand

2 *nm Volley, Basket-ball* block • **contre-attaque** *nf* counter-attack • **contre-attaquer** *vt* to counter-attack

contrebalancer [kɔ̃trəbalɑ̃se] *vt* to counterbalance; *Fig (compenser)* to offset

contrebande [kɔ̃trəbɑ̃d] *nf (activité)* smuggling; *(marchandises)* contraband; **tabac de c.** smuggled tobacco; **faire de la c.** to smuggle goods; **faire entrer qch en c.** to smuggle in sth • **contrebandier, -ière** *nmf* smuggler

contrebas [kɔ̃trəbɑ] **en contrebas** *adv & prép* (down) below; **en c. de** below

contrebasse [kɔ̃trəbɑs] *nf (instrument)* double-bass

contrecarrer [kɔ̃trəkare] *vt* to thwart

contrecœur [kɔ̃trəkœr] **à contrecœur** *adv* reluctantly

contrecoup [kɔ̃trəku] *nm* repercussions

contre-courant [kɔ̃trəkurɑ̃] **à contre-courant** *adv (nager)* against the current

contredanse [kɔ̃trədɑ̃s] *nf Fam (amende)* parking fine

contredire* [kɔ̃trədir] **1** *vt* to contradict **2 se contredire** *vpr (soi-même)* to contradict oneself; *(l'un l'autre)* to contradict each other

contrée [kɔ̃tre] *nf Littéraire (region)* region; *(pays)* land

contre-espionnage [kɔ̃trɛspjɔnaʒ] *nm* counter-espionage

contrefaçon [kɔ̃trəfasɔ̃] *nf (pratique)* counterfeiting; *(produit)* fake • **contrefaire*** *vt (voix, écriture)* to disguise; *(pièce)* to counterfeit; *(signature)* to forge

contreforts [kɔ̃trəfɔr] *nmpl (montagnes)* foothills

contre-indication [kɔ̃trɛ̃dikasjɔ̃] *(pl* **contre-indications**) *nf* countraindication

contre-jour [kɔ̃trəʒur] **à contre-jour** *adv* against the light

contremaître [kɔ̃trəmɛtr] *nm* foreman

contre-offensive [kɔ̃trɔfɑ̃siv] *(pl* **contre-offensives**) *nf* counter-offensive

contrepartie [kɔ̃trəparti] *nf* compensation; **en c. (de)** in return (for)

contre-performance [kɔ̃trəpɛrfɔrmɑ̃s] *(pl* **contre-performances**) *nf* substandard performance

contre-pied [kɔ̃trəpje] *nm* **prendre le c. de qch** *(dire le contraire de)* to take the opposite view to sth; *Sport* **prendre son adversaire à c.** to wrongfoot one's opponent

contreplaqué [kɔ̃trəplake] *nm* plywood

contrepoids [kɔ̃trəpwa] *nm* counterbalance; **faire c. à qch** to counterbalance sth

contrepoison [kɔ̃trəpwazɔ̃] *nm* antidote

contrer [kɔ̃tre] *vt (personne, attaque)* to counter

contre-révolution [kɔ̃trərevɔlysjɔ̃] *(pl* **contre-révolutions**) *nf* counter-revolution

contresens [kɔ̃trəsɑ̃s] *nm* misinterpretation; *(en traduisant)* mistranslation; **à c.** *(en voiture)* the wrong way; **prendre une rue à c.** to go down/up a street the wrong way

contresigner [kɔ̃trəsiɲe] *vt* to countersign

contretemps [kɔ̃trətɑ̃] *nm* hitch, mishap; **à c.** *Mus* off the beat; *Fig (arriver, intervenir)* at the wrong moment

contrevenir* [kɔ̃trəvnir] *vi* **c. à** to contravene

contrevérité [kɔ̃trəverite] *nf* untruth

contribuer [kɔ̃tribɥe] *vi* to contribute (**à** to); **c. à faire qch** to help (to) do sth • **contribuable** *nmf* taxpayer • **contribution** *nf* contribution (**à** to); *(impôt)* tax; **contributions** *(administration)* tax office; **mettre qn à c.** to use sb's services

contrit, -e [kɔ̃tri, -it] *adj* contrite • **contrition** *nf* contrition

contrôle [kɔ̃trol] *nm (vérification)* checking (**de** of); *(surveillance)* monitoring; *(maîtrise)* control; *Scol* test; **avoir le c. de qch** to have control of sth; **perdre le c. de son véhicule** to lose control of one's vehicle; **le c. des naissances** birth control; **c. d'identité** identity check; **c. de soi** self-control; **c. fiscal** tax inspection

contrôler [kɔ̃trole] **1** *vt (vérifier)* to check; *(surveiller)* to monitor; *(maîtriser)* to control **2 se contrôler** *vpr* to control oneself • **contrôleur, -euse** *nmf (de train, de bus) Br* (ticket) inspector, *Am* conductor; **c. aérien** air-traffic controller

contrordre [kɔ̃trɔrdr] *nm* **il y a c.** the orders have been changed

controverse [kɔ̃trɔvɛrs] *nf* controversy • **controversé, -ée** *adj* controversial

contumace [kɔ̃tymas] **par contumace** *adv Jur* in absentia

contusion [kɔ̃tyzjɔ̃] *nf* bruise • **contusionné, -ée** *adj* bruised

convaincre* [kɔ̃vɛ̃kr] *vt* to convince (**de** of); **c. qn de faire qch** to persuade sb to do sth • **convaincant, -ante** *adj* convincing • **convaincu, -e** *adj* convinced (**de** of; **que** that); *(partisan)* committed; **être c. de meurtre** to be found guilty of murder

convalescent, -ente [kɔ̃valɛsɑ̃, -ɑ̃t] *adj & nmf* convalescent • **convalescence** *nf* convalescence; **être en c.** to be convalescing

convenable [kɔ̃vnabl] *adj (approprié)* suitable; *(acceptable, décent)* decent • **convenablement** [-əmɑ̃] *adv (s'habiller, être payé)* decently

convenance [kɔ̃vnɑ̃s] *nf* **faire qch à sa c.** to do sth at one's own convenience; **pour c. personnelle** for personal reasons; **les convenances** *(usages)* the proprieties

convenir* [kɔ̃vnir] **1** *vi* **c. à** *(être fait pour)* to be suitable for; *(plaire à, aller à)* to suit; **c. de qch** *(lieu, prix)* to agree upon sth; *(erreur)* to admit sth; **c. de faire qch** to agree to do sth; **c. que...** to admit that... **2** *v impersonnel* **il convient de...** it is advisable to...; *(selon les usages)* it is proper to...; **il fut convenu que...** *(décidé)* it was agreed that... • **convenu, -ue** *adj* (*décidé*) agreed; *Péj (peu original)* conventional; **comme c.** as agreed

convention [kɔ̃vɑ̃sjɔ̃] *nf (accord)* agreement; *(règle)* convention; *Pol (assemblée)* assembly; **c. collective** collective agreement; **de c.** *(sourire)* superficial

conventionné, -ée [kɔ̃vɑ̃sjɔne] *adj (médecin, clinique)* attached to the health system, *Br* ≃ NHS; **médecin non c.** private doctor

conventionnel, -elle [kɔ̃vɑ̃sjɔnɛl] *adj* conventional

convergent, -ente [kɔ̃vɛrʒɑ̃, -ɑ̃t] *adj* convergent • **convergence** *nf* convergence • **converger** *vi* to converge (**vers** on)

conversation [kɔ̃vɛrsasjɔ̃] *nf* conversation; **engager la c.** to start a conversation • **converser** *vi Formel* to converse (**avec** with)

conversion [kɔ̃vɛrsjɔ̃] *nf (changement)* conversion (**en** into); *(à une doctrine)* conversion (**à** to) • **converti, -ie** *nmf Rel* convert • **convertible 1** *adj* convertible (**en** into) **2** *nm* sofa bed • **convertir 1** *vt (changer)* to convert (**en** into); *(à une doctrine)* to convert (**à** to) **2 se convertir** *vpr (à une doctrine)* to be converted (**à** to) • **convertisseur** *nm Ordinat* **c. analogique numérique** digitizer

convexe [kɔ̃vɛks] *adj* convex

conviction [kɔ̃viksjɔ̃] *nf (certitude, croyance)* conviction; **avoir la c. que... à** be convinced that...

convier [kɔ̃vje] *vt Formel* to invite (**à** to; **à faire** to do)

convive [kɔ̃viv] *nmf* guest

convivial, -e, -aux, -ales [kɔ̃vivjal, -jo] *adj* convivial; *Ordinat* user-friendly

convoi [kɔ̃vwa] *nm (véhicules, personnes)* convoy; *(train)* train; **c. funèbre** funeral procession

convoiter [kɔ̃vwate] *vt (poste, richesses)* to covet • **convoitise** *nf* covetousness

convoler [kɔ̃vɔle] *vi Hum* **c. en justes noces** to marry

convoquer [kɔ̃vɔke] *vt (témoin)* to summon; *(employé, postulant)* to call in; *(assemblée)* to convene; **c. qn à un examen** to notify sb of an examination • **convocation** *nf (lettre)* notice to attend; *(d'assemblée)* convening; *Jur* summons; **c. à un examen** notification of an examination

convoyer [kɔ̃vwaje] *vt (troupes)* to convoy; *(fonds)* to transport under armed guard • **convoyeur** *nm* **c. de fonds** security guard

convulser [kɔ̃vylse] *vt* to convulse

• **convulsif, -ive** *adj* convulsive • **convulsion** *nf* convulsion

coopérer [kɔɔpere] *vi* to co-operate (**à** in, **avec** with) • **coopératif, -ive** *adj & nf* co-operative • **coopération** *nf* co-operation (**entre** between); *Pol* overseas development

coopter [kɔɔpte] *vt* to co-opt

coordonner [kɔɔrdɔne] *vt* to co-ordinate (**à** ou **avec** with) • **coordination** *nf* co-ordination • **coordonnées** *nfpl (adresse, téléphone)* address and phone number; *Math* co-ordinates

copain [kɔpɛ̃] *nm Fam (camarade)* pal; *(petit ami)* boyfriend; **être c. avec qn** to be pals with sb

copeau, -x [kɔpo] *nm (de bois)* shaving

copie [kɔpi] *nf (manuscrit, double)* copy; *Scol (devoir, examen)* paper; **c. double** double sheet of paper • **copier** *vt (texte, musique, document) & Scol (à un examen)* to copy (**sur** from) • **copieur, -euse 1** *nmf (élève)* copier **2** *nm (machine)* photocopier

copieux, -euse [kɔpjø, -øz] *adj (repas)* copious; *(portion)* generous

copilote [kɔpilɔt] *nm Av* co-pilot

copine [kɔpin] *nf Fam (camarade)* pal; *(petite amie)* girlfriend; **être c. avec qn** to be pals with sb

copropriété [kɔprɔprijete] *nf* joint ownership; **(immeuble en) c.** *Br* block of flats in joint ownership, *Am* condominium

copulation [kɔpylasjɔ̃] *nf* copulation

coq [kɔk] *nm* cock, *Am* rooster; **c. au vin** coq au vin *(chicken cooked in red wine)*; **passer du c. à l'âne** to jump from one subject to another

coque [kɔk] *nf (de noix)* shell; *(de navire)* hull; *(fruit de mer)* cockle

coquelet [kɔklɛ] *nm* cockerel

coquelicot [kɔkliko] *nm* poppy

coqueluche [kɔklyʃ] *nf (maladie)* whooping cough; **être la c. de** to be the darling of

coquet, -ette [kɔkɛ, -ɛt] *adj (intérieur)* charming; *Fam (somme)* tidy; **elle est coquette** she's very clothes-conscious • **coquetterie** *nf (vestimentaire)* consciousness of one's appearance; *Fam* **avoir une c. dans l'œil** to have a cast in one's eye

coquetier [kɔktje] *nm* egg-cup

coquille [kɔkij] *nf* shell; *(faute d'imprimerie)* misprint; *Culin* **c. Saint-Jacques** scallop • **coquillage** *nm (mollusque)* shellfish *inv*; *(coquille)* shell

coquin, -e [kɔkɛ̃, -in] **1** *adj (sourire, air)* mischievous; *(sous-vêtements)* naughty **2** *nmf* rascal

cor [kɔr] *nm (instrument)* horn; *(durillon)* corn; **réclamer qch à c. et à cri** to clamour for sth

corail, -aux [kɔraj, -o] *nm* coral

Coran [kɔrɑ̃] *nm* **le C.** the Koran

corbeau, -x [kɔrbo] *nm (oiseau)* crow

corbeille [kɔrbɛj] *nf* (**a**) *(panier)* basket; **c. à pain** breadbasket; **c. à papier** wastepaper basket (**b**) *(à la Bourse)* trading floor (**c**)*Théâtre* dress circle

corbillard [kɔrbijar] *nm* hearse

cordage [kɔrdaʒ] *nm (corde)* rope; *(de raquette)* stringing

corde [kɔrd] *nf (lien)* rope; *(de raquette, de violon)* string; **usé jusqu'à la c.** threadbare; **monter à la c.** to climb up a rope; **tenir la c.** *(coureur)* to be on the inside; *Fam* **ce n'est pas dans mes cordes** it's not in my line; **c. à linge** washing *or* clothes line; **c. à sauter** *Br* skipping rope, *Am* jump-rope; **c. raide** tightrope; **cordes vocales** vocal cords • **cordée** *nf* roped party • **cordelette** *nf* cord • **corder** *vt (raquette)* to string

cordial, -e, -aux, -ales [kɔrdjal, -jo] **1** *adj (accueil, personne)* cordial **2** *nm (remontant)* tonic • **cordialité** *nf* cordiality

cordon [kɔrdɔ̃] *nm (de tablier, de sac)* string; *(de rideau)* cord; *(de policiers)* cordon; *Anat* **c. ombilical** umbilical cord • **cordon-bleu** (*pl* **cordons-bleus**) *nm Fam* first-class cook

cordonnier [kɔrdɔnje] *nm* shoe repairer • **cordonnerie** *nf (métier)* shoe-repairing; *(boutique)* shoe repairer's shop

Corée [kɔre] *nf* **la C.** Korea • **coréen, -enne 1** *adj* Korean **2** *nmf* **C., Coréenne** Korean

coriace [kɔrjas] *adj (viande, personne)* tough

corne [kɔrn] *nf (d'animal, matière, instrument)* horn; *(au pied, à la main)* hard skin; **faire une c. à une page** to turn down the corner of a page; **c. de brume** foghorn

cornée [kɔrne] *nf Anat* cornea

corneille [kɔrnɛj] *nf* crow

cornemuse [kɔrnəmyz] *nf* bagpipes

corner¹ [kɔrne] *vt (page)* to turn down the corner of; *(abîmer)* to make dog-eared

corner² [kɔrner] *nm Football* corner; **tirer un c.** to take a corner

cornet [kɔrnɛ] *nm (glace)* cone, *Br* cornet; **c. (de papier)** (paper) cone; **c. (à pistons)** cornet

corniaud [kɔrnjo] *nm (chien)* mongrel; *Fam (imbécile)* twit

corniche [kɔrniʃ] *nf (de rocher)* ledge; *(route)* coast road; *(en haut d'un mur)* cornice

cornichon [kɔrniʃɔ̃] *nm* gherkin

cornu, -ue [kɔrny] *adj (diable, animal)* horned

corollaire [kɔrɔlɛr] *nm (suite)* consequence

corporation [kɔrpɔrasjɔ̃] *nf* corporate body

corporel, -elle [kɔrpɔrɛl] *adj (besoin)* bodily; *(hygiène)* personal

corps [kɔr] *nm (organisme, cadavre) & Chim* body; *(partie principale)* main part; **c. et âme** body and soul; **à son c. défendant** under protest; **lutter c. à c.** to fight hand to hand; **prendre c.** *(projet)* to take shape; **donner c. à** *(rumeur, idée)* to give substance to; *Naut* **perdu c. et biens** lost with all hands; **c. d'armée/diplomatique** army/diplomatic corps; **c. électoral** electorate; **c. enseignant** teaching profession; **c. gras** fat

corpulent, -ente [kɔrpylɑ̃, -ɑ̃t] *adj* stout, corpulent • **corpulence** *nf* stoutness, corpulence

corpus [kɔrpys] *nm Jur & Ling* corpus

correct, -e [kɔrɛkt] *adj (exact, courtois)* correct; *Fam (acceptable)* reasonable • **correctement** [-əmɑ̃] *adv (sans faire de fautes, décemment)* correctly; *Fam (de façon acceptable)* reasonably; **gagner c. sa vie** to make a reasonable living

correcteur, -trice [kɔrɛktœr, -tris] **1** *adj* **verres correcteurs** corrective lenses **2** *nmf (d'examen)* examiner; *(en typographie)* proofreader **3** *nm Ordinat* **c. d'orthographe** spellchecker

correction [kɔrɛksjɔ̃] *nf (rectification)* correction; *(punition)* beating; *(décence, courtoisie)* correctness; *Scol (de devoirs, d'examens)* marking

correctionnel, -elle [kɔrɛksjɔnɛl] **1** *adj* **tribunal c.** criminal court **2** *nf* **correctionnelle** criminal court; **passer en c.** to go before a criminal court

corrélation [kɔrelasjɔ̃] *nf* correlation

correspondance [kɔrɛspɔ̃dɑ̃s] *nf (relation, lettres)* correspondence; *(de train, d'autocar)* *Br* connection, *Am* transfer

correspondre [kɔrɛspɔ̃dr] *vi* **c. à qch** to correspond to sth; **c. avec qn** *(par lettres)* to correspond with sb • **correspondant, -ante 1** *adj* corresponding (**à** to) **2** *nmf (reporter)* correspondent; *(par lettres)* pen friend, pen pal; *(au téléphone)* caller; **c. de guerre** war correspondent

corrida [kɔrida] *nf* bullfight
corridor [kɔridɔr] *nm* corridor
corriger [kɔriʒe] **1** *vt (texte, erreur, myopie, injustice)* to correct; *(exercice, devoir)* to mark; **c. qn** to give sb a beating; **c. qn de qch** to cure sb of sth
  2 se corriger *vpr* to mend one's ways; **se c. de qch** to cure oneself of sth • **corrigé** *nm (d'exercice)* correct answers (**de** to)
corroborer [kɔrɔbɔre] *vt* to corroborate
corroder [kɔrɔde] *vt* to corrode • **corrosif, -ive** *adj* corrosive • **corrosion** *nf* corrosion
corrompre* [kɔrɔ̃pr] *vt (personne, goût)* to corrupt; *(soudoyer)* to bribe • **corrompu, -e** *adj* corrupt • **corruption** *nf (par l'argent)* bribery; *(vice)* corruption
corsage [kɔrsaʒ] *nm* blouse
corsaire [kɔrsɛr] *nm Hist (marin)* corsair
Corse [kɔrs] *nf* la C. Corsica • **corse 1** *adj* Corsican **2** *nmf* C. Corsican
corser [kɔrse] **1** *vt (plat)* to spice up; *Fig (récit)* to liven up
  2 se corser *vpr* ça se corse things getting complicated • **corsé, -ée** *adj (café)* full-flavoured; *(vin)* full-bodied; *Fig (histoire)* spicy
corset [kɔrsɛ] *nm* corset
cortège [kɔrtɛʒ] *nm (défilé)* procession; **c. funèbre** funeral cortège
corvée [kɔrve] *nf* chore; *Mil* fatigue duty
cosmétique [kɔsmetik] *adj & nm* cosmetic
cosmopolite [kɔsmɔpɔlit] *adj* cosmopolitan
cosmos [kɔsmɔs] *nm (univers)* cosmos; *(espace)* outer space • **cosmique** *adj* cosmic • **cosmonaute** *nmf* cosmonaut
cosse [kɔs] *nf (de pois)* pod
cossu, -e [kɔsy] *adj (personne)* well-to-do; *(maison, intérieur)* opulent
costaud [kɔsto] **1** *adj* sturdy
  2 *nm* sturdy man
costume [kɔstym] *nm (habit)* costume; *(complet)* suit
cotation [kɔtasjɔ̃] *nf* **c. (en Bourse)** quotation (on the Stock Exchange)
cote [kɔt] *nf (marque de classement)* classification mark; *(valeur)* quotation; *(liste)* share index; *(de cheval)* odds; *(altitude)* altitude; *Fam* **avoir la c.** to be popular; **c. d'alerte** danger level; **c. de popularité** popularity rating
côte [kot] *nf* (a) *(os)* rib; **à côtes** *(étoffe)* ribbed; **c. à c.** side by side; **se tenir les côtes** *(de rire)* to split one's sides (laughing); **c. d'agneau/de porc** lamb/pork chop; **c. de bœuf** rib of beef (b) *(de*

montagne) slope (c) *(littoral)* coast; **la C. d'Azur** the French Riviera
côté [kote] *nm* side; **de l'autre c.** on the other side (**de** of); *(direction)* the other way; **de ce c.** *(passer)* this way; **du c. de** *(près de)* near; **à c.** close by, nearby; *(pièce)* in the other room; *(maison)* next door; **la maison d'à c.** the house next door; **à c. de qn/qch** next to sb/sth; *(en comparaison de)* compared to sb/sth; **passer à c.** *(balle)* to fall wide (**de** of); **à mes côtés** by my side; **mettre qch de c.** to put sth aside; **venir de tous côtés** to come from all directions; **d'un c.... d'un autre c....** on the one hand... on the other hand...; **de mon c.** for my part; **le bon c. de qch** the bright side of sth; *Fam* **c. argent** moneywise
coteau, -x [kɔto] *nm* hill; *(versant)* hillside
côtelé, -ée [kotle] *adj* **velours c.** corduroy
côtelette [kotlɛt] *nf (d'agneau, de porc)* chop
coter [kɔte] *vt (prix, action)* to quote • **coté, -ée** *adj* **bien c.** highly rated; **c. en Bourse** quoted on the Stock Market
côtier, -ière [kotje, -jɛr] *adj* coastal; *(pêche)* inshore
cotiser [kɔtize] **1** *vi (à un cadeau, pour la retraite)* to contribute (**à** to; **pour** towards)
  2 se cotiser *vpr Br* to club together, *Am* to club in • **cotisation** *nf (de club)* dues, subscription; *(de retraite, de chômage)* contribution
coton [kɔtɔ̃] *nm* cotton; **c. hydrophile** *Br* cotton wool, *Am* absorbent cotton • **cotonnade** *nf* cotton fabric
côtoyer [kotwaje] *vt (personnes)* to mix with; *Fig (rivière, forêt)* to border on
cotte [kɔt] *nf* **c. de maille** coat of mail
cou [ku] *nm* neck; **sauter au c. de qn** to throw one's arms around sb; *Fam* **endetté jusqu'au c.** up to one's ears in debt
couchage [kuʃaʒ] *nm* **sac de s.** sleeping bag
couche [kuʃ] *nf* (a) *(épaisseur)* layer; *(de peinture)* coat; **couches sociales** levels of society; **la c. d'ozone** the ozone layer; *Fam* **il en tient une c.!** he's really stupid (b) *(linge de bébé)* *Br* nappy, *Am* diaper • **couche-culotte** *(pl* **couches-culottes***) nf Br* disposable nappy, *Am* disposable diaper
coucher [kuʃe] **1** *nm (moment)* bedtime; **l'heure du c.** bedtime; **au c.** at bedtime; **c. de soleil** sunset

2 *vt (allonger)* to lay down; **c. qn** to put sb to bed; **c. qn sur son testament** to mention sb in one's will

3 *vi* to sleep (**avec** with)

4 se coucher *vpr (personne)* to go to bed; *(s'allonger)* to lie down; *(soleil)* to set, to go down; **aller se c.** to go to bed • **couchant 1** *adj m* **soleil c.** setting sun **2** *nm* **le c.** *(ouest)* the west • **couché, -ée** *adj* **être c.** to be in bed; *(étendu)* to be lying (down)

couchette [kuʃɛt] *nf (de train)* couchette; *(de bateau)* bunk

couci-couça [kusikusa] *adv Fam* so-so

coucou [kuku] **1** *nm (oiseau)* cuckoo; *(pendule)* cuckoo clock; *(fleur)* cowslip **2** *exclam* peek-a-boo!

coude [kud] *nm* elbow; *(tournant)* bend; **donner un coup de c. à** to nudge sb; **pousser qn du c.** to nudge sb; **être au c. à c.** to be neck and neck; *Fig* **se serrer les coudes** to stick together

cou-de-pied [kudpje] *(pl* **cous-de-pied***)* *nm* instep

coudre* [kudr] *vti* to sew

couenne [kwan] *nf* rind

couette¹ [kwɛt] *nf (édredon)* duvet, *Br* continental quilt

couette² [kwɛt] *nf Fam (coiffure)* bunch; **se faire des couettes** to put one's hair in bunches

couffin [kufɛ̃] *nm (de bébé) Br* Moses basket, *Am* bassinet

couillon, -onne [kujɔ̃, -ɔn] *nmf très Fam* twat

couiner [kwine] *vi (animal)* to squeal; *(enfant)* to whine

coulée [kule] *nf* **c. de lave** lava flow; **c. de boue** mudslide

couler [kule] **1** *vt* (**a**) *(métal, statue)* to cast; *(liquide, ciment)* to pour; **c. des jours heureux** to lead a happy life (**b**) *(navire)* to sink; *Fig* **c. qn** to bring sb down

2 *vi* (**a**) *(eau, rivière)* to flow; *(nez, sueur)* to run; *(robinet)* to leak; *Fig* **faire c. un bain** to run a bath; **faire c. le sang** to cause bloodshed; *Fig* **c. de source** to be obvious (**b**) *(bateau, nageur)* to sink; **c. à pic** to sink to the bottom

3 se couler *vpr* **se c. dans** *(passer)* to slip into; *Fam* **se la c. douce** to take things easy • **coulant, -ante** *adj (fromage)* runny; *Fig (style)* flowing; *Fam (personne)* easy-going

couleur [kulœr] *nf (teinte) Br* colour, *Am* color; *(colorant)* paint; *(pour cheveux)* dye; *Cartes* suit; **couleurs** *(de drapeau, de club)* colours; **de quelle c. est...?** what colour is...?; **prendre des couleurs** to get some colour in one's cheeks; *Fam* **il nous en a fait voir de toutes les couleurs** he gave us a hard time; **homme de c.** coloured man; **boîte de couleurs** paintbox; **photo en couleurs** colour photo; **télévision c.** *ou* **en couleurs** colour television set

couleuvre [kulœvr] *nf* grass snake

coulis [kuli] *nm* **c. de tomates** tomato coulis

coulisse [kulis] *nf (de porte)* runner; **porte à c.** sliding door; *Théâtre* **les coulisses** the wings • **coulissant, -ante** *adj* sliding

couloir [kulwar] *nm (de maison, de train)* corridor; *(en natation, en athlétisme)* lane; **c. aérien** air corridor; **c. de bus** bus lane

coup [ku] *nm* (**a**) *(choc)* blow; *(essai)* attempt, go; *Échecs* move; **donner un c. à qn** to hit sb; **se donner un c. contre qch** to knock against sth; **donner un c. de bâton à qn** to hit sb with a stick; **donner un c. de couteau à qn** to knife sb; **c. de pied** kick; **donner un c. de pied à qn** to kick sb; **c. de poing** punch; **donner un c. de poing à qn** to punch sb; *Fig* **donner un c. de main à qn** to give sb a hand; **c. de tête** header; **mauvais c.** piece of mischief; *Fam* **sale c.** dirty trick; *Fam* **c. dur** nasty blow

(**b**) *(action soudaine, événement soudain)* **c. de vent** gust of wind; **donner un c. de frein** to brake; **prendre un c. de soleil** to get sunburned; *Fam* **avoir un c. de barre** to have munchies; *Fig* **ça a été le c. de foudre** it was love at first sight; **c. de chance** stroke of luck; **c. d'État** coup; *Fam* **c. de pub** publicity stunt; **c. de théâtre** coup de théâtre

(**c**) *(bruit)* **c. de feu** shot; **c. de fusil** shot; **c. de sifflet** whistle; **c. de sonnette** ring; **c. de tonnerre** clap of thunder; **sur le c. de midi** on the stroke of twelve; **l'horloge sonna deux coups** the clock struck two

(**d**) *(expressions)* **après c.** after the event; **sur le c.** *(alors)* at the time; **tué sur le c.** killed outright; **à c. sûr** for certain; **c. sur c.** one after the other; **tout à c., tout d'un c.** suddenly; **d'un seul c.** *(avaler)* in one go; *(soudain)* all of a sudden; **du premier c.** at the first attempt; *Fam* **du c.** and so; **sous le c. de la colère** in a fit of anger; **faire les quatre cents coups** to sow one's wild oats; **tenir le c.** to hold out; **tomber sous le c. de la loi** to be an offence; *Fam* **tenter le c.** to have a go; *Fam* **réussir son c.** to be a great success; *Fam* **il est dans le c.** he's in the know; *Football & Rugby* **c. d'envoi** kickoff;

c. de maître masterstroke; *Tennis* **c. droit** forehand; *Football* **c. franc** free kick; **c. monté** put-up job

coupable [kupabl] **1** *adj* guilty (**de** of); *(négligence)* culpable; **se sentir c.** to feel guilty

  2 *nmf* culprit

coupe¹ [kup] *nf (trophée)* cup; *(récipient)* bowl; **la C. du monde** the World Cup; **c. à champagne** champagne glass

coupe² [kup] *nf (de vêtement)* cut; *(plan)* section; *Fig* **être sous la c. de qn** to be under sb's thumb; **c. de cheveux** haircut • **coupe-faim** *nm inv* appetite suppressant • **coupe-gorge** *nm inv* cut-throat alley • **coupe-ongles** *nm inv* nail clippers • **coupe-papier** *nm inv* paper knife • **coupe-vent** *nm inv (blouson) Br* windcheater, *Am* Windbreaker ®

couper [kupe] **1** *vt (trancher, supprimer)* to cut; *(arbre)* to cut down; **c. le courant** *(pour réparation)* to switch off the current; *(pour non-paiement)* to cut off the power; **c. la parole à qn** to cut sb short; **c. l'appétit à qn** to spoil sb's appetite; *Fig* **c. les cheveux en quatre** to split hairs; **être coupé du monde** to be cut off from the outside world; **nous avons été coupés** *(au téléphone)* we were cut off; *Fam* **j'en donnerais ma main** *ou* **ma tête à c.** I'd stake my life on it

  2 *vi (être tranchant)* to be sharp; *(aux cartes)* to cut; *(prendre un raccourci)* to take a short cut; **c. à travers champs** to cut across country; **c. court à qn** to cut sth short; *Fam* **c. à qch** *(se dérober)* to get out of sth; **ne coupez pas!** *(au téléphone)* hold the line!

  3 se couper *vpr (routes)* to intersect; **se c. au doigt** to cut one's finger; **se c. les cheveux** to cut one's hair • **coupant, -ante** *adj* sharp • **coupé** *nm (voiture)* coupé

couperet [kupre] *nm (de boucher)* cleaver; *(de guillotine)* blade

couperosé, -ée [kuproze] *adj (visage)* blotchy

couple [kupl] *nm* couple

couplet [kuplε] *nm* verse

coupole [kupɔl] *nf* dome

coupon [kupɔ̃] *nm (tissu)* remnant; **c. de réduction** money-off coupon; **c.-réponse** reply coupon

coupure [kupyr] *nf (blessure)* cut; **50 000 euros en petites coupures** 50,000 euros in small notes; **c. d'électricité** *ou* **de courant** blackout, *Br* power cut; **c. de presse** newspaper cutting

cour [kur] *nf* **(a)** *(de maison, de ferme)*

yard; **c. de récréation** *Br* playground, *Am* schoolyard (**b**) *(de roi, tribunal)* court; **c. d'appel** court of appeal; **c. d'assises** court of assizes; **c. de cassation** ≃ Supreme Court of Appeal (**c**) **faire la c. à qn** to court sb

courage [kuraʒ] *nm* courage; **perdre c.** to lose heart; **s'armer de c.** to pluck up courage; **bon c.!** good luck! • **courageux, -euse** *adj (brave)* courageous; *(énergique)* spirited • **courageusement** *adv (bravely)* courageously

couramment [kuramɑ̃] *adv (parler)* fluently; *(généralement)* commonly

courant, -ante [kurɑ̃, -ɑ̃t] **1** *adj (commun)* common; *(en cours)* current; *Com* **le dix c.** the tenth of this month, *Br* the tenth inst.

  2 *nm (de rivière)* current; **dans le c. du mois** during the course of the month; **être au c. de qch** to know about sth; **mettre qn au c. de qch** to tell sb about sth; **c. d'air** *Br* draught, *Am* draft; **c. électrique** electric current

> ⚠ Il faut noter que l'adjectif anglais **current** est un faux ami. Il signifie **actuel**.

courbature [kurbatyr] *nf* ache; **avoir des courbatures** to be aching (all over) • **courbaturé, -ée** *adj* aching (all over)

courbe [kurb] **1** *adj* curved

  2 *nf* curve; **c. de niveau** contour line • **courber 1** *vti* to bend **2 se courber** *vpr (personne)* to bend down; **se c. en deux** to bend double

courge [kurʒ] *nf Br* marrow, *Am* squash • **courgette** *nf Br* courgette, *Am* zucchini

courir [kurir] **1** *vi* to run; *(à une course automobile)* to race; **c. après qn/qch** to run after sb/sth; **c. à sa perte** to be heading for disaster; **descendre une colline en courant** to run down a hill; *Fam* **faire qch en courant** to do sth in a rush; **faire c. un bruit** to spread a rumour; **le bruit court que…** rumour has it that…; **le voleur court toujours** the thief is still at large

  2 *vt* **c. un risque** to run a risk; **c. le 100 mètres** to run the 100 meters; **c. le monde** to roam the world; **c. les théâtres** to go to the theatre all the time; **c. les filles** to chase women • **coureur** *nm (sportif)* runner; *(cycliste)* cyclist; **c. automobile** racing driver; **c. de jupons** womanizer

couronne [kurɔn] *nf (de roi, de reine)* crown; *(pour enterrement)* wreath; *(de dent)* crown • **couronnement** [-əmɑ̃] *nm (de roi)* coronation; *Fig (réussite)* crowning achievement • **couronner** *vt (roi)* to crown; *(auteur, ouvrage)* to award a prize to; **leurs efforts furent couronnés de succès** their efforts were crowned with success; **et pour c. le tout...** and to crown it all...

courre [kur] *voir* **chasse**

courrier [kurje] *nm (lettres)* mail, *Br* post; **j'ai du c. à faire** I have (some) letters to write; **par retour du c.** *Br* by return of post, *Am* by return mail; *Journ* **c. du cœur** problem page; **c. électronique** electronic mail, e-mail

courroie [kurwa] *nf (attache)* strap; **c. de transmission** driving belt

courroux [kuru] *nm Littéraire* wrath

cours [kur] *nm* (**a**) *(de rivière, d'astre)* course; *(de monnaie)* currency; *Fin (d'action)* price; **suivre son c.** to run its course; **suivre le c. de ses pensées** to follow one's train of thoughts; **donner libre c. à qch** to give free rein to sth; **avoir c.** *(monnaie)* to be legal tender; *(pratique)* to be current; **en c.** *(travail)* in progress; *(année)* current; *(affaires)* outstanding; **en c. de route** on the way; **au c. de qch** in the course of sth; **c. d'eau** river, stream (**b**) *(leçon)* class; *(série de leçons)* course; *(conférence)* lecture; *(établissement)* school; **faire c.** to teach; **aller en c.** to go to school; **suivre un c.** to take a course; **c. magistral** lecture; **c. particulier** private lesson; **c. du soir** evening class; *Scol* **c. moyen** = fourth and fifth years of primary school; *Scol* **c. préparatoire** = first year of primary school (**c**) *(allée)* avenue

course¹ [kurs] *nf (action de courir)* running; *Sport (épreuve)* race; *(discipline)* racing; *(trajet en taxi)* journey; *(de projectile, de planète)* course; **les courses de chevaux** the races; **faire la c. avec qn** to race sb; *Fam* **il n'est plus dans la c.** he's out of touch; **c. automobile** motor race; **c. cycliste** cycle race

course² [kurs] *nf (commission)* errand; **courses** *(achats)* shopping; **faire une c.** to get something from the shops; **faire des courses** to go shopping; **faire les courses** to do the shopping

coursier, -ière [kursje, -jɛr] *nmf* messenger

court, -e [kur, kurt] **1** *adj* short; *Fam* **c'est un peu c.** that's not very much

2 *adv* short; **prendre qn de c.** *(en lui laissant peu de temps)* to give sb short notice; **pris de c.** caught unawares; **on l'appelle Charles tout c.** people just call

him Charles; **à c. d'argent** short of money

3 *nm* **c.** **(de tennis)** tennis court • **court-bouillon** *(pl* **courts-bouillons**) *nm* court-bouillon • **court-circuit** *(pl* **courts-circuits**) *nm* short-circuit

courtier, -ière [kurtje, -jɛr] *nmf* broker

courtisan [kurtizɑ̃] *nm Hist* courtier • **courtisane** *nf Littéraire* courtesan • **courtiser** *vt (femme)* to court

courtois, -oise [kurtwa, -waz] *adj* courteous • **courtoisie** *nf* courtesy

couru, -e [kury] *adj (spectacle, lieu)* popular; *Fam* **c'est c. d'avance** it's a sure thing

couscous [kuskus] *nm* couscous

cousin, -ine [kuzɛ̃, -in] **1** *nmf* cousin; **c. germain** first cousin

2 *nm (insecte)* mosquito

coussin [kusɛ̃] *nm* cushion; **c. d'air** air cushion

cousu, -e [kuzy] *adj* sewn; **c. main** hand-sewn

coût [ku] *nm* cost; **le c. de la vie** the cost of living • **coûter** *vti* to cost; **ça coûte combien?** how much is it?, how much does it cost?; *Fig* **ça coûte les yeux de la tête** that costs the earth; *Fig* **cette erreur va vous c. cher** that error will cost you dearly; **coûte que coûte** at all costs

couteau, -x [kuto] *nm* knife; *Fig* **être à couteaux tirés avec qn** to be at daggers drawn with sb; *Fig* **retourner le c. dans la plaie** to rub it in; **c. à pain** breadknife; **c.-scie** serrated knife

coûteux, -euse [kutø, -øz] *adj* costly, expensive

coutume [kutym] *nf (habitude, tradition)* custom; **avoir c. de faire qch** to be accustomed to doing sth; **comme de c.** as usual • **coutumier, -ière** *adj* customary

couture [kutyr] *nf (activité)* sewing, needlework; *(raccord)* seam; **faire de la c.** to sew • **couturier** *nm* fashion designer • **couturière** *nf* dressmaker

couvent [kuvɑ̃] *nm (de religieuses)* convent; *(de moines)* monastery; *(pensionnat)* convent school

couver [kuve] **1** *vt (œufs)* to sit on; *Fig (personne)* to mollycoddle; *(maladie)* to be coming down with

2 *vi (poule)* to brood; *(feu) Br* to smoulder, *Am* to smolder; *(mal, complot)* to be brewing • **couvée** *nf (petits oiseaux)* brood; *(œufs)* clutch • **couveuse** *nf (pour nouveaux-nés)* incubator

couvercle [kuvɛrkl] *nm* lid; *(vissé)* cap

couvert¹ [kuvɛr] *nm* (**a**) **mettre le c.** to set *or Br* lay the table; **table de cinq**

couverts table set *or Br* laid for five; **couverts** *(ustensiles)* cutlery (**b**) **sous le c. de** *(sous l'apparence de)* under cover of; **se mettre à c.** to take cover

couvert², -e [kuvɛr, -ɛrt] **1** *pp de* **couvrir 2** *adj* covered (**de** with *or* in); *(ciel)* overcast; **être bien c.** *(habillé chaudement)* to be warmly dressed

couverture [kuvɛrtyr] *nf (de lit)* blanket; *(de livre, de magazine)* cover; *(de bâtiment)* roofing; *Journ* coverage; **c. chauffante** electric blanket; **c. sociale** social security cover

couvrir* [kuvrir] **1** *vt* to cover (**de** with); *(bruit)* to drown; **c. qn de cadeaux** to shower sb with gifts
2 se couvrir *vpr (s'habiller)* to wrap up; *(se coiffer)* to cover one's head; *(ciel)* to cloud over; **se c. de ridicule** to cover oneself with ridicule • **couvre-chef** (*pl* **couvre-chefs**) *nm Hum* headgear • **couvre-feu** (*pl* **couvre-feux**) *nm* curfew • **couvre-lit** (*pl* **couvre-lits**) *nm* bedspread • **couvreur** *nm* roofer

covoiturage [kovwatyraʒ] *nm* carpooling

cow-boy [kɔbɔj] (*pl* **cow-boys**) *nm* cowboy

CP [sepe] *abrév* **cours préparatoire**

CPE [sepeə] (*abrév* **conseiller principal d'éducation**) *nm inv* school administrator

crabe [krab] *nm* crab

crac [krak] *exclam (objet qui casse)* snap!

crachat [kraʃa] *nm* gob of spit; **crachats** spit

cracher [kraʃe] **1** *vt* to spit out; **c. du sang** to spit blood
2 *vi (personne)* to spit; *(stylo)* to splutter; *(radio)* to crackle; *Fam* **c. dans la soupe** to bite the hand that feeds • **craché** *adj Fam* **c'est sa mère tout c.** he's the spitting image of his mother

crachin [kraʃɛ̃] *nm* (fine) drizzle

crack [krak] *nm Fam (champion)* ace

crade [krad], **cradingue** [kradɛ̃g] *adj Fam* filthy

craie [krɛ] *nf (matière)* chalk; *(bâton)* stick of chalk; **écrire qch à la c.** to write sth in chalk

craignos [krɛɲos] *adj Fam (louche)* dodgy

craindre* [krɛ̃dr] **1** *vt (redouter)* to be afraid of, to fear; *(chaleur, froid)* to be sensitive to; **c. de faire qch** to be afraid of doing sth; **je crains qu'elle ne soit partie** I'm afraid she's left; **ne craignez rien** *(n'ayez pas peur)* don't be afraid; *(ne vous inquiétez pas)* don't worry

2 *vi Fam* **ça craint!** *(c'est ennuyeux)* what a pain!; *(c'est louche)* it's dodgy

crainte [krɛ̃t] *nf* fear; **de c. de faire qch** for fear of doing sth; **de c. qu'on ne l'entende** for fear of being overheard • **craintif, -ive** *adj* timid

cramoisi, -ie [kramwazi] *adj* crimson

crampe [krãp] *nf* cramp

crampon [krãpɔ̃] *nm (de chaussure)* stud; *(pour l'alpinisme)* crampon

cramponner [krãpɔne] **se cramponner** *vpr* to hold on; **se c. à qn/qch** to hold on to sb/sth

cran [krã] *nm* (**a**) *(entaille)* notch; *(de ceinture)* hole; *Fig* **avancer d'un c.** to go up a notch; **c. d'arrêt** *ou* **de sûreté** safety catch (**b**) *(de cheveux)* wave (**c**) *Fam (courage)* guts; **avoir du c.** to have guts (**d**) *Fam* **être à c.** *(excédé)* to be wound up

crâne [krɑn] *nm* skull; *Fam* **mets-toi ça dans le c.!** get that into your head! • **crânien, -ienne** *adj Anat* cranial; **boîte crânienne** skull, cranium

crâner [krɑne] *vi Fam* to show off

crapaud [krapo] *nm* toad

crapule [krapyl] *nf* villain, scoundrel • **crapuleux, -euse** *adj (malhonnête)* villainous; **crime c.** crime committed for financial gain

> ⚠ Il faut noter que l'adjectif anglais **crapulous** est un faux ami. Il signifie **intempérant**.

craqueler [krakle] *vt*, **se craqueler** *vpr* to crack

craquer [krake] **1** *vt (allumette)* to strike
2 *vi (branche)* to crack; *(escalier)* to creak; *(se casser)* to snap; *(se déchirer)* to rip; *Fam (personne)* to crack up • **craquements** *nmpl* cracking/creaking

crasse [kras] **1** *nf* filth
2 *adj (ignorance)* crass • **crasseux, -euse** *adj* filthy

cratère [kratɛr] *nm* crater

cravache [kravaʃ] *nf* riding crop

cravate [kravat] *nf* tie

crawl [krol] *nm* crawl; **nager le c.** to do the crawl • **crawlé** *adj m* **dos c.** backstroke

crayeux, -euse [krɛjø, -jøz] *adj* chalky

crayon [krɛjɔ̃] *nm (en bois)* pencil; **c. de couleur** coloured pencil; *(en cire)* crayon; **c. à lèvres** lip pencil

créance [kreãs] *nf* debt • **créancier, -ière** *nmf* creditor

créateur, -trice [kreatœr, -tris] **1** *adj* creative
2 *nmf* creator • **créatif, -ive** *adj* creative

●**création** *nf* creation; **1000 créations d'emplois** 1,000 new jobs ● **créativité** *nf* creativity

créature [kreatyr] *nf (être vivant)* creature

crécelle [kresɛl] *nf* rattle

crèche [krɛʃ] *nf (de Noël)* manger, *Br* crib; *(garderie)* (day) nursery, *Br* crèche ● **crécher** *vi Fam* to live

crédible [kredibl] *adj* credible ● **crédibilité** *nf* credibility

crédit [kredi] *nm (prêt, influence)* credit; **crédits** *(somme d'argent)* funds; **à c.** on credit; **faire c. à qn** to give sb credit ● **créditer** *vt (compte)* to credit (**de** with); *Fig* **c. qn de qch** to give sb credit for sth ● **créditeur, -trice** *adj* **solde c.** credit balance; **être c.** to be in credit

crédule [kredyl] *adj* credulous ● **crédulité** *nf* credulity

créer [kree] *vt* to create

crémaillère [kremajɛr] *nf* **pendre la c.** to have a housewarming (party)

crématoire [krematwar] *adj* **four c.** crematorium

crématorium [krematɔrjɔm] *nm Br* crematorium, *Am* crematory

crème [krɛm] **1** *nf (de lait, dessert, cosmétique)* cream; **c. anglaise** custard; **c. Chantilly** whipped cream; **c. glacée** ice cream; **c. à raser** shaving cream
2 *adj inv* cream(-coloured)
3 *nm Fam* coffee with milk, *Br* white coffee ● **crémerie** *nf (magasin)* dairy ● **crémeux, -euse** *adj* creamy ● **crémier, -ière** *nmf* dairyman, *f* dairywoman

créneau, -x [kreno] *nm Com* niche; *TV, Radio* slot; **créneaux** *(de château) Br* crenellations, *Am* crenelations; **faire un c.** *(pour se garer)* to reverse into a parking space

créole [kreɔl] **1** *adj* creole
2 *nmf* Creole
3 *nm (langue)* Creole

crêpe [krɛp] **1** *nf* pancake
2 *nm (tissu)* crepe; *(caoutchouc)* crepe (rubber) ● **crêperie** *nf* pancake restaurant

crépi, -e [krepi] *adj & nm* roughcast

crépiter [krepite] *vi (feu)* to crackle ● **crépitement** *nm (du feu)* crackling

crépu, -e [krepy] *adj* frizzy

crépuscule [krepyskyl] *nm* twilight

crescendo [kreʃendo] *adv & nm* crescendo

cresson [kresɔ̃] *nm* watercress

Crète [krɛt] *nf* **la C.** Crete

crête [krɛt] *nf (de montagne, d'oiseau, de vague)* crest; **c. de coq** cockscomb

crétin, -e [kretɛ̃, -in] *nmf Fam* cretin

creuser [krøze] **1** *vt (trou, puits)* to dig; *(évider)* to hollow (out); *Fig (idée)* to look into; **c. la terre** to dig
2 *vi* to dig; *Fam* **ça creuse** it whets the appetite
3 se creuser *vpr (joues)* to become hollow; *Fig (abîme)* to form; *Fam* **se c. la tête** *ou* **la cervelle** to rack one's brains

creuset [krøzɛ] *nm (récipient)* crucible; *Fig (lieu)* melting pot

creux, -euse [krø, -øz] **1** *adj (tube, joues, arbre, paroles)* hollow; *(sans activité)* slack; **assiette creuse** soup plate; *Fam* **avoir le ventre c.** to be hungry
2 *nm* hollow; *(moment)* slack period; **le c. des reins** the small of the back; *Fig* **être au c. de la vague** to have hit rock bottom

crevaison [krəvɛzɔ̃] *nf (de pneu)* flat, *Br* puncture

crevasse [krəvas] *nf (trou)* crack; *(de glacier)* crevasse; **avoir des crevasses aux mains** to have chapped hands

crève [krɛv] *nf très Fam* **avoir la c.** to have a stinking cold

crever [krəve] **1** *vt (ballon, bulle)* to burst; *Fam (épuiser)* to wear out; **ça crève le cœur** it's heartbreaking; *Fam* **ça crève les yeux** it sticks out a mile; *très Fam* **c. la dalle** to be bloody starving
2 *vi (bulle, ballon, pneu)* to burst; **c. de jalousie** to be bursting with jealousy; *Fam* **c. d'ennui/de froid** to be bored/to freeze to death; *Fam* **c. de faim** to be starving; *Fam* **je crève de chaud** I'm boiling ● **crevant, -ante** *adj Fam (fatigant)* exhausting ● **crevé, -ée** *adj (ballon, pneu)* burst; *Fam (fatigué)* worn out, *Br* dead beat ● **crève-cœur** *nm inv* heartbreak

crevette [krəvɛt] *nf (grise)* shrimp; *(rose)* prawn

cri [kri] *nm (de personne)* cry, shout; *(perçant)* scream; *(d'animal)* cry; **c. de guerre** war cry ● **criard, -arde** *adj (son)* shrill; *(couleur)* loud

criant, -ante [krijɑ̃, -ɑ̃t] *adj (injustice, preuve)* glaring; **c. de vérité** *(témoignage)* obviously true

crible [kribl] *nm* sieve ● **criblé, -ée** *adj* **c. de balles/dettes** riddled with bullets/debts

cric [krik] *nm* jack

cricket [krikɛt] *nm* cricket

crier [krije] **1** *vt (injure, ordre)* to shout (**à** to); **c. vengeance** to cry out for vengeance; **c. son innocence** to protest one's innocence
2 *vi (personne)* to shout, to cry out; *(fort)*

to scream; *(parler très fort)* to shout; **c. au scandale** to protest; **c. au secours** to shout for help; *Fam* **c. après qn** to shout at sb

crime [krim] *nm* crime; *(assassinat)* murder; **crimes de guerre** war crimes • **criminalité** *nf* crime • **criminel, -elle 1** *adj* criminal **2** *nmf* criminal; *(assassin)* murderer

crin [krɛ̃] *nm* horsehair; *Fig* **à tous crins** out-and-out • **crinière** *nf* mane

crique [krik] *nf* creek

criquet [krike] *nm* locust

crise [kriz] *nf* crisis; *(de maladie)* attack; *Fam* **faire une c.** to throw a fit; *Fam* **la c.!** what a hoot!; **c. de colère** fit of anger; **c. de conscience** (moral) dilemma; **c. de nerfs** fit of hysteria

crisper [krispe] **1** *vt (poing)* to clench; *(muscle)* to tense; *Fam* **c. qn** to irritate sb **2 se crisper** *vpr (visage)* to tense; *(personne)* to get tense • **crispant, -ante** *adj Fam* irritating • **crispé, -ée** *adj (personne)* tense

crisser [krise] *vi (pneu, roue)* to squeal; *(neige)* to crunch

cristal, -aux [kristal, -o] *nm* crystal; **cristaux** *(objets)* crystal(ware); *(de sels)* crystals; *Tech* **cristaux liquides** liquid crystal • **cristallin, -e** *adj (eau, son)* crystal-clear • **cristalliser** *vti*, **se cristalliser** *vpr* to crystallize

critère [kritɛr] *nm* criterion

critérium [kriterjɔm] *nm (épreuve sportive)* heat

critique [kritik] **1** *adj (situation, phase)* critical **2** *nf (reproche)* criticism; *(de film, de livre)* review; **faire la c. de** *(film)* to review; **affronter la c.** to confront the critics **3** *nm* critic • **critiquer** *vt* to criticize

croasser [krɔase] *vi* to caw

Croatie [krɔasi] *nf* **la C.** Croatia

croc [kro] *nm (crochet)* hook; *(dent)* fang

croc-en-jambe [krɔkɑ̃ʒɑ̃b] *(pl* **crocs-en-jambe***) nm* trip; **faire un c. à qn** to trip sb up

croche [krɔʃ] *nf Mus Br* quaver, *Am* eighth (note)

croche-pied [krɔʃpje] *nm* trip; **faire un c. à qn** to trip sb up

crochet [krɔʃɛ] *nm (pour accrocher)* & *Boxe* hook; *(aiguille)* crochet hook; *(parenthèse)* square bracket; **faire du c.** to crochet; **faire un c.** *(détour)* to make a detour; *(route)* to make a sudden turn; *Fam* **vivre aux crochets de qn** to live off sb • **crocheter** *vt (serrure)* to pick

crochu, -e [krɔʃy] *adj (nez)* hooked; *(doigts)* claw-like

crocodile [krɔkɔdil] *nm* crocodile

crocus [krɔkys] *nm* crocus

croire* [krwar] **1** *vt* to believe; *(penser)* to think (**que** that); **j'ai cru la voir** I thought saw her; **je crois que oui** I think *or* believe so; **je n'en crois pas mes yeux** I can't believe my eyes; **à l'en c.** according to him/her **2** *vt (personne, talent, Dieu)* to believe (**à** *ou* **en** in) **3 se croire** *vpr* **il se croit malin** he thinks he's smart

croisé¹ [krwaze] *nm Hist* crusader • **croisade** *nf Hist* crusade

croiser [krwaze] **1** *vt (passer)* to pass; *(ligne)* to cross; *(espèce)* to crossbreed; **c. les jambes** to cross one's legs; **c. les bras** to fold one's arms; **c. le regard de qn** to meet sb's gaze; *Fig* **c. les doigts** to keep one's fingers crossed **2** *vi (navire)* to cruise **3 se croiser** *vpr (voitures)* to pass each other; *(lignes, routes)* to cross, to intersect; *(lettres)* to cross; *(regards)* to meet • **croisé², -ée** *adj (bras)* folded; *(veston)* double-breasted • **croisement** *nm (de routes)* crossroads *(sing)*, intersection; *(d'animaux)* crossing

croiseur [krwazœr] *nm Naut* cruiser

croisière [krwazjɛr] *nf* cruise; **faire une c.** to go on a cruise

croître* [krwatr] *vi (plante)* to grow; *(augmenter)* to grow, to increase (**de** by); *(lune)* to wax • **croissance** *nf* growth • **croissant, -ante 1** *adj (nombre)* growing **2** *nm* crescent; *(pâtisserie)* croissant

croix [krwa] *nf* cross; **la C.-Rouge** the Red Cross

croquer [krɔke] **1** *vt (manger)* to crunch; *(peindre)* to sketch; **joli à c.** pretty as a picture **2** *vi (fruit)* to be crunchy; **c. dans qch** to bite into sth • **croquant, -ante** *adj* crunchy • **croque-monsieur** *nm inv* = toasted cheese and ham sandwich • **croque-mort** *(pl* **croque-morts***) nm Fam* undertaker • **croquette** *nf Culin* croquette

croquis [krɔki] *nm* sketch; **faire un c. de qch** to make a sketch of sth

crosse [krɔs] *nf (de fusil)* butt; *(de hockey)* stick; *(d'évêque)* crook

crotte [krɔt] *nf (de mouton, de lapin)* droppings; **c. de chien** dog dirt • **crottin** *nm* dung

crotté, -ée [krɔte] *adj* muddy

crouler [krule] *vi (édifice)* to crumble; **c. sous le poids de qch** to give way under the weight of sth; **c. sous le travail** to be

snowed under with work • **croulant, -ante**
1 *adj (mur)* crumbling **2** *nm Fam* **vieux c.**
old wrinkly

croupe [krup] *nf* rump; **monter en c.** to
ride behind • **croupion** *nm (de poulet) Br*
parson's nose, *Am* pope's nose

croupier [krupje] *nm* croupier

croupir [krupir] *vi (eau)* to stagnate; **c. en**
prison to rot in prison

croustiller [krustije] *vi* to be crunchy;
(pain) to be crusty • **croustillant, -ante**
adj crunchy; *(pain)* crusty; *Fig (histoire)*
spicy

croûte [krut] *nf (de pain)* crust; *(de fro-*
mage) rind; *(de plaie)* scab; *Fam* **casser la**
c. to have a snack; *Fam* **gagner sa c.** to
earn one's bread and butter • **croûton** *nm*
(de pain) end; **croûtons** *(pour la soupe)*
croûtons

croyable [krwajabl] *adj* credible, believable; **pas c.** unbelievable, incredible
• **croyance** *nf* belief (**en in**) • **croyant,**
-ante 1 *adj* **être c.** to be a believer **2** *nmf*
believer

CRS [seeres] *(abrév* **compagnie républi-**
caine de sécurité) *nm* = French riot
policeman

cru¹, crue¹ [kry] *pp de* **croire**

cru², crue² [kry] **1** *adj (aliment)* raw; *(lait)*
unpasteurized; *(lumière)* garish; *(propos)*
crude; **monter à c.** to ride bareback
2 *nm (vignoble)* vineyard; **un grand c.**
(vin) a vintage wine; **vin du c.** local wine

cruauté [kryote] *nf* cruelty (**envers** to)

cruche [kryʃ] *nf* pitcher, jug

crucial, -e, -aux, -ales [krysjal, -jo] *adj*
crucial

crucifier [krysifje] *vt* to crucify • **crucifix**
[krysifi] *nm* crucifix • **crucifixion** *nf* crucifixion

crudité [krydite] *nf (grossièreté)* crudeness • **crudités** *nfpl (légumes)* assorted
raw vegetables

crue³ [kry] *nf (montée)* swelling; *(inonda-*
tion) flood; **en c.** *(rivière, fleuve)* in spate

cruel, -elle [kryɛl] *adj* cruel (**envers** *ou*
avec to) • **cruellement** *adv* cruelly; **faire c.**
défaut to be sadly lacking

crûment [krymɑ̃] *adv (sans détour)*
bluntly; *(grossièrement)* crudely

crustacés [krystase] *nmpl Culin* shellfish *inv*

crypte [kript] *nf* crypt

crypté, -ée [kripte] *adj (message)* & *TV*
coded

Cuba [kyba] *n* Cuba • **cubain, -aine 1** *adj*
Cuban **2** *nmf* **C., Cubaine** Cuban

cube [kyb] **1** *nm* cube; *(de jeu)* building
block

2 *adj* **mètre c.** cubic metre • **cubique** *adj*
cubic

cueillir* [kœjir] *vt* to pick, to gather; *Fam*
c. qn to pick sb up • **cueillette** *nf* picking,
gathering; *(fruits)* harvest

cuiller, cuillère [kɥijɛr] *nf* spoon; *(me-*
sure) spoonful; **c. à café, petite c.** teaspoon; **c. à soupe** tablespoon • **cuillerée**
nf spoonful; **c. à café** teaspoonful; **c. à**
soupe tablespoonful

cuir [kɥir] *nm* leather; *(d'éléphant)* hide;
pantalon en c. leather trousers; **c. che-**
velu scalp

cuirasse [kɥiras] *nf Hist* breastplate • **cui-**
rassé *nm Naut* battleship

cuire* [kɥir] **1** *vt (aliment, plat)* to cook; **c.**
qch à l'eau to boil sth; **c. qch au four** to
bake sth; *(viande)* to roast sth
2 *vi (aliment)* to cook; **faire c. qch** to
cook sth; **faire trop c. qch** to overcook
sth; *Fam* **on cuit!** it's baking hot

cuisant, -ante [kɥizɑ̃, -ɑ̃t] *adj (douleur)*
burning; *(affront, blessure)* stinging

cuisine [kɥizin] *nf (pièce)* kitchen; *(art)*
cookery, cooking; *Fam (intrigues)* scheming; **faire la c.** to do the cooking; **faire**
de la bonne c. to be a good cook • **cuisiner**
vti to cook; *Fam* **c. qn** *(interroger)* to grill
sb • **cuisinier, -ière** *nmf* cook • **cuisinière** *nf*
(appareil) stove, *Br* cooker

cuisse [kɥis] *nf* thigh; **c. de poulet**
chicken leg; **cuisses de grenouilles** frogs'
legs

cuisson [kɥisɔ̃] *nm (d'aliments)* cooking;
(de pain) baking

cuissot [kɥiso] *nm (de venaison)* haunch

cuit, -e [kɥi, kɥit] **1** *pp de* **cuire**
2 *adj* cooked; **bien c.** well done; **trop c.**
overcooked; **pas assez c.** undercooked;
Fam **nous sommes cuits** we're finished;
Fam **c'est cuit!** we've had it!

cuite [kɥit] *nf Fam* **prendre une c.** to get
plastered

cuivre [kɥivr] *nm (rouge)* copper; *(jaune)*
brass; *Mus* **les cuivres** the brass • **cuivré,**
-ée *adj* copper-coloured

cul [ky] *nm Fam (derrière)* backside; *(de*
bouteille, de verre) bottom; **rester sur le c.**
to be flabbergasted; **c'est à se taper le c.**
par terre it's an absolute scream; **avoir**
du c. to be jammy • **cul-de-jatte** *(pl* **culs-**
de-jatte) *nm* legless cripple • **cul-de-sac**
(pl **culs-de-sac)** *nm* dead end, *Br* cul-de-
sac

culasse [kylas] *nf (de moteur)* cylinder
head; *(de fusil)* breech

culbute [kylbyt] *nf (saut)* somersault;
(chute) tumble; **faire la c.** to tumble; *(acro-*

bate) to somersault ● **culbuter** *vi (personne)* to take a tumble

culinaire [kylinɛr] *adj* culinary

culminer [kylmine] *vi (tension, crise)* to peak; **la montagne culmine à 3000 mètres** the mountain is 3,000 metres at its highest point ● **culminant** *adj* point **c.** *(de montagne)* highest point

culot [kylo] *nm (d'ampoule, de lampe)* base; *Fam (audace)* nerve, *Br* cheek ● **culotté, -ée** *adj Fam Br* cheeky, *Am* sassy

culotte [kylɔt] *nf (de femme)* knickers, *Am* panties; *(d'enfant)* pants; **culottes courtes** *Br* short trousers, *Am* short pants; **c. de cheval** jodhpurs

culpabiliser [kylpabilize] **1** *vt* **c. qn** to make sb feel guilty

2 se culpabiliser *vpr* to feel guilty ● **culpabilité** *nf* guilt

culte [kylt] **1** *nm (de dieu)* worship; *(religion)* religion; *Fig* **vouer à qn un c.** to worship sb; **c. de la personnalité** personality cult

2 *adj* **film c.** cult film

cultiver [kyltive] **1** *vt (terre, amitié)* to cultivate; *(plantes)* to grow

2 se cultiver *vpr* to improve one's mind ● **cultivateur, -trice** *nmf* farmer ● **cultivé, -ée** *adj (terre)* cultivated; *(esprit, personne)* cultured, cultivated

culture [kyltyr] *nf* (**a**) *(action)* farming, cultivation; *(de plantes)* growing; **cultures** *(terres)* fields under cultivation; *(plantes)* crops (**b**) *(éducation, civilisation)* & *Biol* culture; **c. générale** general knowledge; **c. physique** physical training ● **culturel, -elle** *adj* cultural

culturisme [kyltyrism] *nm* body-building

cumin [kymɛ̃] *nm* cumin

cumul [kymyl] *nm* **c. des mandats** plurality of offices ● **cumulatif, -ive** *adj* cumulative ● **cumuler** *vt* **c. deux fonctions** to hold two offices

cupide [kypid] *adj* avaricious ● **cupidité** *nf* cupidity

curable [kyrabl] *adj* curable

cure [kyr] *nf* (**a**) *(traitement)* (course of) treatment; **faire une c. de repos** to go/be on a rest cure; **c. d'amaigrissement** slimming treatment; **c. thermale** spa cure (**b**) *(fonction)* office of a parish priest ● **curatif, -ive** *adj (traitement)* curative

curé [kyre] *nm* parish priest

curer [kyre] **1** *vt* to clean out

2 se curer *vpr* **se c. les dents** to clean one's teeth ● **cure-dents** *nm inv* toothpick

curieux, -euse [kyrjø, -jøz] **1** *adj (bizarre)* curious; *(indiscret)* inquisitive, curious (**de** about); **je serais c. de savoir** I'd be curious to know

2 *nmf* inquisitive person; *(badaud)* onlooker ● **curieusement** *adv* curiously ● **curiosité** *nf* curiosity; *(chose)* curio; **les curiosités d'une ville** the interesting sights of a town

curriculum vitae [kyrikylɔmvite] *nm inv Br* curriculum vitae, *Am* résumé

curseur [kyrsœr] *nm Ordinat* cursor

cutané, -ée [kytane] *adj* **maladie cutanée** skin condition ● **cuti** *nf* skin test

cuve [kyv] *nf (réservoir)* & *Photo* tank; *(de fermentation)* vat ● **cuvée** *nf (récolte)* vintage ● **cuver** *vt Fam* **c. son vin** to sleep it off ● **cuvette** *nf (récipient)* & *Géog* basin; *(des cabinets)* bowl

CV [seve] *(abrév* **curriculum vitae**) *nm Br* CV, *Am* résumé

cyanure [sjanyr] *nm* cyanide

cybercafé [sibɛrkafe] *nm* cybercafé

cybernétique [sibɛrnetik] *nf* cybernetics *(sing)*

cycle [sikl] *nm* (**a**) *(série, movement)* cycle (**b**) **premier/second c.** *Scol* = lower/upper classes in secondary school; *Univ* = first/last two years of a degree course (**c**) *(bicyclette)* cycle ● **cyclable** *adj* **piste c.** cycle path ● **cyclique** *adj* cyclical

cyclisme [siklism] *nm* cycling ● **cycliste 1** *nmf* cyclist **2** *adj* **course c.** cycle race; **champion c.** cycling champion; **coureur c.** racing cyclist

cyclomoteur [siklɔmotœr] *nm* moped

cyclone [siklon] *nm* cyclone

cyclotourisme [sikloturism] *nm* bicycle touring

cygne [siɲ] *nm* swan

cylindre [silɛ̃dr] *nm* cylinder; *(rouleau)* roller ● **cylindrée** *nf* (cubic) capacity ● **cylindrique** *adj* cylindrical

cymbale [sɛ̃bal] *nf* cymbal

cynique [sinik] **1** *adj* cynical

2 *nmf* cynic ● **cynisme** *nm* cynicism

cyprès [siprɛ] *nm* cypress

cypriote [siprijɔt] **1** *adj* Cypriot

2 *nmf* **C.** Cypriot

D, d [de] **1** nm inv D, d
2 (abrév **route départementale**) = designation of a secondary road
dactylo [daktilo] nf (personne) typist; (action) typing • **dactylographie** nf typing • **dactylographier** vt to type
dada [dada] nm Fam (manie) hobbyhorse
dadais [dade] nm Fam **grand d.** big oaf
dahlia [dalja] nm dahlia
daigner [deɲe] vt **d. faire qch** to deign to do sth
daim [dɛ̃] nm (animal) fallow deer; (mâle) buck; (cuir) suede
dais [dɛ] nm canopy
dalle [dal] nf (de pierre) paving stone; (de marbre) slab; Fam **que d.** (rien) damn all; Fam **crever la d.** to be starving • **dallage** nm (action, surface) paving • **daller** vt to pave
daltonien, -ienne [daltɔnjɛ̃, -jɛn] adj colour-blind • **daltonisme** nm colour blindness
dam [dam] nm **au grand d. de qn** to the great displeasure of sb
dame [dam] nf (femme) lady; Échecs & Cartes queen; (au jeu de dames) king; **dames** (jeu) Br draughts, Am checkers • **damer** vt Fam **d. le pion à qn** to put one over on sb • **damier** nm Br draughtboard, Am checkerboard
damner [dane] **1** vt to damn
2 se damner vpr to damn oneself • **damnation** nf damnation
dandiner [dɑ̃dine] **se dandiner** vpr to waddle
dandy [dɑ̃di] nm dandy
Danemark [danmark] nm **le D.** Denmark • **danois, -oise 1** adj Danish **2** nmf **D., Danoise** Dane **3** nm (langue) Danish
danger [dɑ̃ʒe] nm danger; **en d.** in danger; **mettre qn en d.** to endanger sb; **en d. de mort** in mortal danger; **'d. de mort'** (panneau) 'danger'; **hors de d.** out of danger; Fam **pas de d.!** no way! • **dangereusement** adv dangerously • **dangereux, -euse** adj dangerous (**pour** to)
dans [dɑ̃] prép (**a**) in; (changement de lieu) into; (à l'intérieur de) inside; **d. le**

jardin/journal in the garden/newspaper; **d. la boîte** in or inside the box; **d. Paris** in Paris (itself); **mettre qch d. qch** to put sth in(to) sth; **entrer d. une pièce** to go into a room; **d. un rayon de...** within (a radius of)...; **marcher d. les rues** to walk through or around the streets
(**b**) (provenance) from, out of; **boire d. un verre** to drink out of a glass
(**c**) (exprime la temporalité) in; **d. deux jours** in two days, in two days' time
(**d**) (exprime une approximation) **d. les dix euros** about ten euros
danse [dɑ̃s] nf (mouvement, musique) dance; **la d.** (art) dancing; **d. classique** ballet • **danser** vti to dance • **danseur, -euse** nmf dancer; **danseuse étoile** prima ballerina; **en danseuse** (cycliste) standing on the pedals
Danube [danyb] nm **le D.** the Danube
dard [dar] nm (d'insecte) sting • **darder** vt Littéraire **le soleil dardait ses rayons** the sun cast down its burning rays
dare-dare [dardar] adv Fam at the double
date [dat] nf date; **amitié de longue d.** long-standing friendship; **faire d.** to be a landmark; **en d. du** dated the; **d. de naissance** date of birth; **d. limite** deadline; **d. limite de vente** sell-by date • **datation** nf dating • **dater 1** vt (lettre) to date **2** vi **à d. du 15** as from the 15th; **ça commence à d.** it's beginning to date • **dateur** adj m **tampon d.** date stamp
datte [dat] nf date • **dattier** nm date palm
daube [dob] nf **bœuf en d.** braised beef stew
dauphin [dofɛ̃] nm (animal) dolphin
daurade [dorad] nf sea bream
davantage [davɑ̃taʒ] adv more; **d. de temps/d'argent** more time/money; **nous ne resterons pas d.** we won't stay any longer
de¹ [də]

de becomes **d'** before vowel and h mute; de + le = **du**, de + les = **des**.

prép (**a**) (complément d'un nom) of; **les rayons du soleil** the rays of the sun, the sun's rays; **le livre de Paul** Paul's book; **la ville de Paris** the town of Paris; **un livre de Flaubert** a book by Flaubert; **un pont de fer** an iron bridge; **le train de Londres** the London train; **une augmentation de salaire** an increase in salary

(**b**) *(complément d'un adjectif)* **digne de qn** worthy of sb; **content de qn/qch** pleased with sb/sth; **heureux de partir** happy to leave

(**c**) *(complément d'un verbe)* **parler de qn/qch** to speak of sb/sth; **se souvenir de qn/qch** to remember sb/sth; **décider de faire qch** to decide to do sth; **empêcher qn de faire qch** to stop sb from doing sth; **traiter qn de lâche** to call sb a coward

(**d**) *(indique la provenance)* from; **venir/dater de...** to come/date from...; **mes amis du village** my friends from the village, my village friends; **le train de Londres** the train from London; **sortir de qch** to come out of sth

(**e**) *(introduit agent)* **accompagné de qn** accompanied by sb; **entouré de qch** surrounded by *or* with sth

(**f**) *(introduit le moyen)* **armé de qch** armed with sth; **se nourrir de...** to live on...

(**g**) *(introduit la manière)* **d'une voix douce** in a gentle voice

(**h**) *(introduit la cause)* **puni de son impatience** punished for his/her impatience; **mourir de faim** to die of hunger; **sauter de joie** to jump for joy

(**i**) *(introduit le temps)* **travailler de nuit/de jour** to work by night/by day; **six heures du matin** six o'clock in the morning

(**j**) *(mesure)* **avoir six mètres de haut, être haut de six mètres** to be six metres high; **retarder qn/qch de deux heures** to delay sb/sth by two hours; **homme de trente ans** thirty-year-old man; **gagner vingt euros de l'heure** to earn twenty euros an hour

de² [də] *art partitif* some; **elle boit du vin** she drinks (some) wine; **il ne boit pas de vin** he doesn't drink (any) wine; **est-ce que vous buvez du vin?** do you drink (any) wine?; **elle achète des épinards** she buys (some) spinach; *Fam* **il y en a six de tués** there are six killed; **un(e) de trop** one too many

de³ [də] *art indéfini* **de, des** some; **des fleurs** (some) flowers; **de jolies fleurs** (some) pretty flowers; **d'agréables soirées** (some) pleasant evenings; **je n'ai plus de problème** I haven't got any problem any more

dé [de] *nm (à jouer)* dice; *(à coudre)* thimble; **jouer aux dés** to play dice; *Fig* **les dés sont jetés** the die is cast; **couper qch en dés** to dice sth

déambuler [deɑ̃byle] *vi* to stroll

débâcle [debɑkl] *nf (d'une armée)* rout; *(des glaces)* breaking up; *Fig (de monnaie)* collapse

déballer [debale] *vt* to unpack; *Fam (sentiments)* to pour out •**déballage** *nm* unpacking; *Fam (aveu)* outpouring

débandade [debɑ̃dad] *nf* rout

débaptiser [debatize] *vt (rue, chien)* to rename

débarbouiller [debarbuje] **1** *vt* **d. qn** to wash sb's face
2 se débarbouiller *vpr* to wash one's face

débarcadère [debarkadɛr] *nm* landing stage; *(pour marchandises)* wharf

débardeur [debardœr] *nm (personne)* docker, stevedore; *(vêtement)* vest

débarquer [debarke] **1** *vt (passagers)* to land; *(marchandises)* to unload
2 *vi (passagers)* to disembark; *Fam (être naïf)* to be not quite with it; *Fam* **d. chez qn** to turn up suddenly at sb's place •**débarquement** [-əmɑ̃] *nm (de passagers, de troupes)* landing; *(de marchandises)* unloading

débarras [debara] *nm Br* lumber room, *Am* storeroom; *Fam* **bon d.!** good riddance! •**débarrasser 1** *vt (chambre, table)* to clear (**de** of); **d. qn de qch** to relieve sb of sth **2 se débarrasser** *vpr* **se d. de qn/qch** to get rid of sb/sth

débat [deba] *nm* debate; *Pol* **débats (parlementaires)** (parliamentary) proceedings •**débattre*** **1** *vt* to discuss, to debate; **d. de qch** to discuss sth; **prix à d.** price negotiable **2 se débattre** *vpr* to struggle

débauche [deboʃ] *nf* debauchery; *Fig* **une d. de** a wealth *or* profusion of •**débauché, -ée 1** *adj* debauched **2** *nmf* debauchee

débaucher [deboʃe] *vt* **d. qn** *(licencier)* to lay sb off; *(inciter à la débauche)* to corrupt sb

débile [debil] **1** *adj (faible)* weak; *Fam* stupid **2** *nmf Fam (imbécile)* moron •**débilité** *nf (faiblesse)* debility; *Fam (niaiserie)* stupidity •**débiliter** *vt* to debilitate

débiner [debine] *Fam* **1** *vt* to run down
2 se débiner *vpr* to clear off

débit [debi] *nm Fin* debit; *(ventes)* turnover; *(de fleuve)* flow; *(d'orateur)* delivery; **d. de boissons** bar; **d. de tabac** *Br* tobacconist's (shop), *Am* tobacco store

débiter [debite] *vt (découper)* to cut up (**en** into); *(vendre)* to sell; *(fournir)* to produce; *(compte)* to debit; *Péj (dire)* to spout • **débiteur, -trice 1** *nmf* debtor **2** *adj* **solde d.** debit balance; **son compte est d.** his/her account is in debit

déblais [deblɛ] *nmpl (terre)* earth; *(décombres)* rubble • **déblayer** [debleje] *vt (terrain, décombres)* to clear

débloquer [deblɔke] **1** *vt (mécanisme)* to unjam; *(compte, prix)* to unfreeze; **d. des crédits** to release funds
    2 *vi Fam (dire n'importe quoi)* to talk nonsense

déboires [debwar] *nmpl (déceptions)* disappointments

déboiser [debwaze] *vt (terrain)* to clear of trees

déboîter [debwate] **1** *vt (tuyau)* to disconnect
    2 *vi (véhicule)* to pull out
    3 se déboîter *vpr* **se d. l'épaule** to dislocate one's shoulder • **déboîtement** *nm (d'articulation)* dislocation

débonnaire [debɔnɛr] *adj* good-natured, easy-going

déborder [debɔrde] **1** *vi (fleuve, liquide)* to overflow; *(en bouillant)* to boil over; *(en coloriant)* to go over the edge; **l'eau déborde du vase** the vase is overflowing; *Fig* **d. de joie** to be overflowing with joy; **d. de vie** to be bursting with vitality
    2 *vt (dépasser)* to go beyond; *(faire saillie)* to stick out from; *(dans une bataille)* to outflank; **débordé de travail** snowed under with work • **débordement** [-əmɑ̃] *nm* overflowing; *Fig (de joie)* outburst

débouché [debuʃe] *nm (carrière)* opening; *(marché pour produit)* outlet

déboucher [debuʃe] **1** *vt (bouteille)* to uncork; *(bouchon vissé)* to uncap; *(lavabo, tuyau)* to unblock
    2 *vi (surgir)* to emerge (**de** from); **d. sur** *(rue)* to lead out onto/into; *Fig (aboutir à)* to lead to

débouler [debule] *vi Fam (arriver)* to turn up

déboulonner [debulɔne] *vt* to unbolt; *Fam* **d. qn** *(renvoyer)* to kick sb out; *(critiquer)* to debunk sb

débourser [deburse] *vt (argent)* to lay out; **sans rien d.** without spending a penny

debout [dəbu] *adv (personne)* standing; *(objet)* upright; **mettre qch d.** to stand sth up; **se mettre d.** to stand up; **se tenir** *ou* **rester d.** to stand; **cent ans plus tard, la maison est encore d.** the house is still

standing a hundred years later; *Fig* **ça ne tient pas d.** *(théorie)* that doesn't make sense; **être d.** *(hors du lit)* to be up; **d.!** get up!

déboutonner [debutɔne] **1** *vt* to unbutton
    2 se déboutonner *vpr (personne)* to undo one's coat/jacket/*etc*

débraillé, -ée [debrɑje] *adj* slovenly

débrancher [debrɑ̃ʃe] *vt* to unplug

débrayer [debreje] *vi* (**a**) *Aut* to release the clutch (**b**) *(se mettre en grève)* to stop work • **débrayage** (**a**) *Aut* declutching (**b**) *(grève)* stoppage

débridé, -ée [debride] *adj (passion)* unbridled

débris [debri] *nmpl (de voiture, d'avion)* debris; *(de verre, de bois)* fragments

débrouiller [debruje] **1** *vt (fil, mystère)* to unravel
    2 se débrouiller *vpr Fam* to manage; *(en langues, en math)* to get by; **se d. pour faire qch** to manage (somehow) to do sth • **débrouillard, -arde** *adj Fam* resourceful • **débrouillardise** *nf Fam* resourcefulness

débroussailler [debrusaje] *vt (chemin)* to clear of undergrowth; *Fig (question)* to clarify

débusquer [debyske] *vt* to flush out

début [deby] *nm* beginning, start; **au d. (de)** at the beginning (of); **au tout d.** at the very beginning; **dès le d.** (right) from the start *or* beginning; *Théâtre* **faire ses débuts** to make one's debut

débuter [debyte] *vi* to start, to begin (**par** with); *(dans une carrière)* to start out; *Théâtre* to make one's debut • **débutant, -ante 1** *nmf* beginner **2** *adj* novice

deçà [dəsa] **en deçà 1** *adv* (on) this side
    2 *prép* **en d. de** (on) this side of; *Fig* **être en d. de la vérité** to be some way from the truth

décacheter [dekaʃte] *vt (lettre)* to unseal

décadent, -ente [dekadɑ̃, -ɑ̃t] *adj* decadent • **décadence** *nf (état)* decadence; *(processus)* decline

décaféiné, -ée [dekafeine] *adj* decaffeinated

décalcomanie [dekalkɔmani] *nf (image) Br* transfer, *Am* decal

décaler [dekale] **1** *vt (dans le temps)* to change the time of; *(dans l'espace)* to shift, to move
    2 se décaler *vpr* to move, to shift • **décalage** *nm (écart)* gap (**entre** between); *(entre des faits, des idées)* discrepancy; **d. horaire** time difference; **souffrir du d. horaire** to have jet lag

décalquer [dekalke] *vt* to trace
décamper [dekɑ̃pe] *vi Fam* to clear off
décanter [dekɑ̃te] **1** *vt (vin)* to decant
  2 se décanter *vpr (vin)* to settle; *Fig (situation)* to become clearer
décaper [dekape] *vt (avec un produit)* to strip; *(au papier de verre)* to sand (down); *(four)* to clean • **décapant** *nm (pour peinture)* paint stripper; *(pour four)* oven cleaner; *Fig (humour)* caustic
décapiter [dekapite] *vt (personne)* to decapitate
décapotable [dekapɔtabl] *adj & nf* convertible
décapsuler [dekapsyle] *vt* to take the top off • **décapsuleur** *nm* bottle opener
décarcasser [dekarkase] **se décarcasser** *vpr Fam* to sweat blood (**pour faire** to do)
décathlon [dekatlɔ̃] *nm Sport* decathlon
décéder [desede] *vi* to die • **décédé, -ée** *adj* deceased
déceler [desle] *vt (trouver)* to detect; *(indiquer)* to indicate
décembre [desɑ̃br] *nm* December
décence [desɑ̃s] *nf (de comportement)* propriety; *(d'habillement)* decency; **avoir la d. de faire qch** to have the decency to do sth • **décemment** [-samɑ̃] *adv (se comporter)* properly; *(s'habiller)* decently • **décent, -ente** *adj (comportement)* proper; *(vêtements)* decent
décennie [deseni] *nf* decade
décentraliser [desɑ̃tralize] *vt* to decentralize • **décentralisation** *nf* decentralization
déception [desɛpsjɔ̃] *nf* disappointment

> *Il faut noter que le nom anglais **deception** est un faux ami. Il signifie **tromperie**.*

décerner [deserne] *vt (prix)* to award (**à** to)
décès [desɛ] *nm* death
décevoir* [desəvwar] *vt* to disappoint • **décevant, -ante** *adj* disappointing

> *Il faut noter que le verbe anglais **to deceive** est un faux ami. Il signifie **tromper**.*

déchaîner [deʃene] **1** *vt (colère, violence)* to unleash; **d. l'hilarité** to provoke laughter
  2 se déchaîner *vpr (tempête, vent)* to rage; *(personne)* to fly into a rage (**contre** with) • **déchaîné, -ée** *adj (mer, vent)* raging; *(personne)* wild • **déchaînement** [-ɛnmɑ̃] *nm (des éléments)* fury; *(de passions)* outburst
déchanter [deʃɑ̃te] *vi Fam* to become disillusioned
décharge [deʃarʒ] *nf Jur (d'accusé)* acquittal; **d. (électrique)** (electric) shock; **d.**

(publique) *Br* (rubbish) dump, *Am* (garbage) dump; *Fig* **à la d. de qn** in sb's *Br* defence *or Am* defense
décharger [deʃarʒe] **1** *vt (camion, navire, cargaison)* to unload; **d. qn de qch** *(tâche, responsabilité)* to relieve sb of; *Jur (d'accusation)* to acquit sb of sth; **d. son arme sur qn** to fire one's weapon at sb
  2 se décharger *vpr (batterie)* to go flat; **se d. sur qn d'une tâche** to offload a task onto sb • **déchargement** [-əmɑ̃] *nm* unloading
décharné, -ée [deʃarne] *adj (visage, corps)* emaciated
déchausser [deʃose] **1** *vt* **d. qn** to take sb's shoes off
  2 se déchausser *vpr (personne)* to take one's shoes off; **avoir les dents qui se déchaussent** to have receding gums
dèche [dɛʃ] *nf Fam* **être dans la d.** to be stony broke
déchéance [deʃeɑ̃s] *nf (déclin)* decline
déchet [deʃɛ] *nm* **il y a du d.** there's some wastage; **déchets** scraps; **déchets radioactifs** radioactive waste
déchiffrer [deʃifre] *vt (message, écriture)* to decipher; *(signaux)* to interpret; *Mus* to sight-read
déchiqueter [deʃikte] *vt* to tear to shreds • **déchiqueté, -ée** *adj (tissu)* torn to shreds; *(côte)* jagged
déchirer [deʃire] **1** *vt (accidentellement)* to tear; *(volontairement)* to tear up; *(enveloppe)* to tear open; *Fig (pays, groupe)* to tear apart; **un cri déchira le silence** a loud cry pierced the silence; **bruit qui déchire le tympan** ear-splitting noise
  2 se déchirer *vpr (tissu, papier)* to tear; *Fig (couple)* to tear each other apart; **se d. un muscle** to tear a muscle • **déchirant, -ante** *adj (spectacle, dieux)* heartrending • **déchirement** *nm (peine)* heartbreak • **déchirure** *nf* tear; **d. musculaire** torn muscle
déchoir* [deʃwar] *vi (personne)* to demean oneself • **déchu, -ue** *adj* **ange d.** fallen angel; **être d. de qch** to be stripped of sth
décibel [desibɛl] *nm* decibel
décidé, -ée [deside] *adj (personne, air)* determined; *(fixé)* settled; **d'un ton d.** in a decisive tone; **être d. à faire qch** to be determined to do sth
décidément [desidemɑ̃] *adv* really

> *Il faut noter que l'adverbe anglais **decidedly** est un faux ami. Il signifie lè plus souvent **vraiment**.*

décider [deside] **1** *vt* d. quand/que... to decide when/that...; **d. qn à faire qch** to persuade sb to do sth

2 *vi* **d. de qch** to decide on sth; **d. de faire qch** to decide to do sth; **cet événement décida de sa carrière** the event determined his/her career

3 se décider *vpr* **se d. (à faire qch)** to make up one's mind (to do sth); **se d. pour qch** to decide on sth • **décideur, -euse** *nmf* decision-maker

décilitre [desilitr] *nm* decilitre

décimal, -e, -aux, -ales [desimal, -o] *adj* decimal • **décimale** *nf* decimal

décimer [desime] *vt* to decimate

décimètre [desimɛtr] *nm* decimetre; **double d.** ruler

décisif, -ive [desizif, -iv] *adj (bataille)* decisive; *(moment)* critical • **décision** *nf* decision (**de faire** to do); *(fermeté)* determination; **prendre une d.** to make a decision; **avec d.** decisively

déclamer [deklame] *vt* to declaim; *Péj* to spout • **déclamatoire** *adj Péj (style)* declamatory

déclaration [deklarasjɔ̃] *nf (annonce)* statement; *(de naissance, de décès)* registration; *(à la police)* report; **faire sa d.** to declare one's love to sb; **d. d'amour** declaration of love; **d. d'impôts** *ou* **de revenus** income tax return; **d. de guerre** declaration of war

déclarer [deklare] **1** *vt (annoncer)* to declare (**que** that); *(naissance, décès, vol)* to register; *Jur* **d. qn coupable** to find sb guilty (**de** of); **d. la guerre** to declare war (**à** on); *Sport* **d. forfait** to scratch; **rien à d.** *(en douane)* nothing to declare

2 se déclarer *vpr (incendie, maladie)* to break out; *(avouer son amour)* to declare one's love; **se d. pour/contre qch** to declare oneself in favour of/against sth; **se d. surpris** to declare oneself surprised

déclasser [deklase] *vt (livres)* to put out of order; *(hôtel)* to downgrade; *Sport* **d. qn** to relegate sb

déclencher [deklɑ̃ʃe] **1** *vt (appareil)* to start; *(mécanisme)* to activate; *(sonnerie)* to set off; *(révolte, grève, conflit)* to trigger off; *Mil (attaque)* to launch

2 se déclencher *vpr (alarme, sonnerie)* to go off; *(incendie)* to start • **déclenchement** *nm (d'appareil)* starting; *(de mécanisme)* activation; *(de sonnerie)* setting off

déclic [deklik] *nm (bruit)* click

déclin [deklɛ̃] *nm* decline; *(du jour)* close; *(de la lune)* wane; **être en d.** to be in decline

déclinaison [deklinezɔ̃] *nf Grammaire* declension

décliner [dekline] **1** *vi (forces)* to decline; *(jour)* to draw to a close

2 *vt Formel (refuser)* to decline; *(identité)* to state; **d. toute responsabilité** to accept no liability

décocher [dekɔʃe] *vt (flèche)* to shoot; *Fig (remarque)* to fire off (**à** at); *Fig (sourire)* to flash (**à** at)

décoder [dekɔde] *vt* to decode • **décodeur** *nm TV* decoder

décoiffer [dekwafe] **1** *vt* **d. qn** to mess up sb's hair; **tu es tout décoiffé** your hair's in a mess

2 se décoiffer *vpr (se dépeigner)* to mess up one's hair; *(ôter son chapeau)* to remove one's hat

décoincer [dekwɛ̃se] *vt*, **se décoincer** *vpr (tiroir, mécanisme)* to loosen; *Fam (personne)* to loosen up

décoller [dekɔle] **1** *vt (timbre)* to peel off

2 *vi (avion, économie)* to take off; *Fam* **je ne décollerai pas d'ici tant que...** I'm not budging until...

3 se décoller *vpr* to peel off • **décollage** *nm (d'avion)* takeoff

décolleté, -ée [dekɔlte] **1** *adj (robe)* low-cut

2 *nm (de robe)* low neckline; *(haut des seins)* cleavage

décoloniser [dekɔlɔnize] *vt* to decolonize • **décolonisation** *nf* decolonization

décolorer [dekɔlɔre] **1** *vt (tissu)* to fade; *(cheveux)* to bleach

2 se décolorer *vpr (tissu)* to fade; **se d. les cheveux** to bleach one's hair • **décolorant** *nm* bleaching agent • **décoloration** *nf (de tissu)* fading; *(de cheveux)* bleaching

décombres [dekɔ̃br] *nmpl* ruins, debris

décommander [dekɔmɑ̃de] **1** *vt (marchandises, invitation)* to cancel; *(invité)* to put off

2 se décommander *vpr* to cancel

décomposer [dekɔ̃poze] **1** *vt Chim* to decompose; *(phrase)* to break down (**en** into); **il est arrivé complètement décomposé** *(par l'émotion)* he arrived quite distraught

2 se décomposer *vpr (pourrir)* to decompose; *Fig (visage)* to become distorted • **décomposition** *nf* decomposition

décompresser [dekɔ̃prese] **1** *vt* to decompress

2 *vi Fam (se détendre)* to unwind • **décompression** *nf* decompression

décompte [dekɔ̃t] *nm (soustraction)* deduction; *(détail)* breakdown • **décompter** *vt* to deduct (**de** from)

déconcentrer [dekɔ̃sɑ̃tre] **se décon-centrer** *vpr* to lose concentration

déconcerter [dekɔ̃sɛrte] *vt* to disconcert

déconfit, -ite [dekɔ̃fi, -it] *adj (personne, mine)* crestfallen • **déconfiture** *nf Fam (échec)* defeat

décongeler [dekɔ̃ʒle] *vt* to thaw, to defrost

décongestionner [dekɔ̃ʒɛstjɔne] *vt (rue, poumons)* to relieve congestion in

déconnecter [dekɔnɛkte] *vt (appareil, fil)* to disconnect

déconner [dekɔne] *vi très Fam (mal fonctionner)* to play up; *(dire des bêtises)* to talk garbage; **faire qch pour d.** to do sth for a laugh; **sans d.!** *(réponse)* no kidding!

déconseiller [dekɔ̃seje] *vt* **d. qch à qn** to advise sb against sth; **d. à qn de faire qch** to advise sb against doing sth; **il est déconseillé de...** it is not advisable to...

déconsidérer [dekɔ̃sidere] *vt* to discredit

décontaminer [dekɔ̃tamine] *vt* to decontaminate

décontenancer [dekɔ̃tnɑ̃se] **1** *vt* to disconcert

2 se décontenancer *vpr* to become disconcerted

décontracter [dekɔ̃trakte] **1** *vt (muscle)* to relax

2 se décontracter *vpr* to relax • **décontracté, -ée** *adj (ambiance, personne)* relaxed; *(vêtement)* casual • **décontraction** *nf* relaxation

déconvenue [dekɔ̃vny] *nf Formel* disappointment

décor [dekɔr] *nm (de maison)* decor; *(paysage)* surroundings; **décors** *(de théâtre, de cinéma)* scenery, set; *Fam* **aller dans le d.** *(véhicule, automobiliste)* to go off the road

décorer [dekɔre] *vt (maison, soldat)* to decorate (**de** with) • **décorateur, -trice** *nmf* (interior) decorator; *Théâtre* stage designer; *Cin* set designer • **décoratif, -ive** *adj* decorative • **décoration** *nf (action, ornement, médaille)* decoration

décortiquer [dekɔrtike] *vt (riz, orge)* to hull; *(crevette, noisette)* to shell; *Fam (texte)* to dissect

découcher [dekuʃe] *vi* to stay out all night

découdre* [dekudr] **1** *vt (ourlet, vêtement)* to unstitch; *(bouton)* to take off

2 *vi Fam* **en d. (avec qn)** to fight it out (with sb)

3 se découdre *vpr (ourlet, vêtement)* to come unstitched; *(bouton)* to come off

découler [dekule] *vi* **d. de** to follow from; **il en découle que...** it follows that...

découper [dekupe] **1** *vt (viande)* to carve; *(gâteau, papier)* to cut up; **d. un article dans un journal** to cut an article out of a newspaper

2 se découper *vpr* **se d. sur qch** to stand out against sth • **découpage** *nm (de gâteau)* cutting up; *(de viande)* carving; *(image)* cutout • **découpé, -ée** *adj (irrégulier)* jagged

décourager [dekuraʒe] **1** *vt (dissuader)* to discourage (**de faire** from doing); *(démoraliser)* to dishearten, to discourage

2 se décourager *vpr* to get discouraged *or* disheartened • **découragement** *nm* discouragement

décousu, -ue [dekuzy] *adj (ourlet, vêtement)* unstitched; *Fig (propos)* disjointed

découvert, -erte [dekuvɛr, -ɛrt] **1** *adj (terrain)* open; *(tête, épaule)* bare

2 *nm (de compte)* overdraft; **à d.** unprotected; **agir à d.** to act openly

découverte [dekuvɛrt] *nf* discovery; **partir** *ou* **aller à la d. de qch** to go off to explore of sth; **faire une d.** to make a discovery

découvrir* [dekuvrir] **1** *vt (trouver, apprendre à connaître)* to discover; *(secret, vérité, statue)* to uncover; *(casserole)* to take the lid off; *(bras, épaule)* to bare; *(voir)* to have a view of; **d. que...** to discover that...; **faire d. qch à qn** to introduce sb to sth

2 se découvrir *vpr (dans son lit)* to push the bedcovers off; *(enlever son chapeau)* to take one's hat off; *(ciel)* to clear

décrasser [dekrase] *vt (nettoyer)* to clean; *Fam* **d. qn** to take the rough edges off sb

décrépit, -ite [dekrepi, -it] *adj (personne, maison)* decrepit • **décrépitude** *nf* decrepitude; *(décadence)* decay

décret [dekrɛ] *nm* decree • **décréter** *vt Jur* to decree

décrié, ée [dekrije] *adj* disparaged

décrire* [dekrir] *vt (représenter)* to describe

décrisper [dekrispe] **1** *vt (atmosphere)* to lighten; *(personne)* to relax

2 se décrisper *vpr* to relax

décrocher [dekrɔʃe] **1** *vt (détacher)* to unhook; *(tableau, rideau)* to take down; *Fam (prix, poste)* to land; **d. (le téléphone)** *(pour répondre)* to pick up the phone; *(pour ne pas être dérangé)* to take the phone off the hook

2 *vi Fam (ne plus se concentrer)* to switch off

3 se décrocher *vpr (tableau, rideau)* to come unhooked

décroître* [dekrwatr] *vi (forces, nombre, mortalité)* to decrease; *(eaux)* to subside; *(jours)* to get shorter; **aller en décroissant** to be decreasing

décrotter [dekrɔte] *vt (chaussures)* to clean the mud off

décrue [dekry] *nf (de rivière)* drop in level

décrypter [dekripte] *vt* to decipher

déçu, -ue [desy] **1** *pp de* **décevoir**
2 *adj* disappointed

déculotter [dekylɔte] **se déculotter** *vpr (enlever son pantalon)* to take off one's *Br* trousers *or Am* pants ● **déculottée** *nf Fam* thrashing

déculpabiliser [dekylpabilize] *vt* **d. qn** to stop sb feeling guilty

décupler [dekyple] *vti* to increase tenfold

dédaigner [dedeɲe] *vt (offre, richesse)* to scorn; *(conseil, injure)* to disregard ● **dédaigneux, -euse** *adj* scornful, disdainful (**de** of)

dédain [dedɛ̃] *nm* scorn, disdain (**pour/ de** for)

dédale [dedal] *nm* maze

dedans [dədɑ̃] **1** *adv* inside; **de d.** from (the) inside; **en d.** on the inside; **tomber d.** *(trou)* to fall in (it); *Fam* **tomber en plein d.** *(être dupé)* to fall right into the trap; *Fam* **je me suis fichu d.** I got it wrong; *Fam* **je me suis fait rentrer d.** *(par un automobiliste)* someone drove straight into me
2 *nm* **le d.** the inside

dédicace [dedikas] *nf* dedication ● **dédicacer** *vt (signer)* to sign (**à** for); *(chanson)* to dedicate (**à** to)

dédier [dedje] *vt* to dedicate (**à** to)

dédire* [dedir] **se dédire** *vpr* **se d. d'une promesse** to go back on one's words

dédommager [dedɔmaʒe] *vt* to compensate (**de** for) ● **dédommagement** *nm* compensation

dédouaner [dedwane] *vt (marchandises)* to clear through customs; *(personne)* to clear

dédoubler [deduble] **1** *vt (partager)* to split into two
2 **se déboubler** *vpr Hum* **je ne peux pas me d.** I can't be in two places at once ● **dédoublement** [-əmɑ̃] *nm* **d. de la personnalité** split personality

dédramatiser [dedramatize] *vt* **d. qch** to make sth less dramatic

déduire* [dedɥir] *vt (retirer)* to deduct (**de** from); *(conclure)* to deduce (**de** from) ● **déductible** *adj* deductible ● **déduction** *nf (raisonnement, décompte)* deduction

déesse [dees] *nf* goddess

défaillir* [defajir] *vi (s'évanouir)* to faint; *(forces, mémoire)* to fail ● **défaillance** *nf (évanouissement)* fainting fit; *(faiblesse)* weakness; *(panne)* failure; **avoir une d.** *(s'évanouir)* to faint; *(faiblir)* to feel weak; **d. cardiaque** heart failure ● **défaillant, -ante** *adj (forces, santé)* failing; *(cœur)* weak

défaire* [defɛr] **1** *vt (nœud)* to undo; *(valises)* to unpack; *(installation)* to take down; *(coiffure)* to mess up
2 **se défaire** *vpr (nœud)* to come undone; **se d. de qch** to get rid of sth ● **défait, -aite** *adj (lit)* unmade; *(cheveux)* dishevelled, untidy; *(visage)* haggard; *(armée)* defeated

défaite [defet] *nf* defeat ● **défaitisme** *nm* defeatism

défalquer [defalke] *vt* to deduct (**de** from)

défaut [defo] *nm (de personne)* fault, shortcoming; *(de machine)* defect; *(de diamant, de verre, de raisonnement)* flaw; *(désavantage)* drawback; **faire d.** to be lacking; *Jur* to default; **l'argent lui fait d.** he/she is short of money; **à d. de qch** for lack of sth; **ou, à d....** or, failing that...; **prendre qn en d.** to catch sb out; *Math* **total approché par d.** total rounded down; *Ordinat* **police/lecteur par d.** default font/drive; **d. de fabrication** manufacturing fault; **d. de prononciation** speech impediment

défaveur [defavœr] *nf* **être en d. auprès de qn** to be in disfavour with sb ● **défavorable** *adj* unfavourable (**à** to) ● **défavorisé, -ée** *adj (milieu)* underpriviledged ● **défavoriser** *vt* to put at a disadvantage

défection [defeksjɔ̃] *nf (de soldat, d'espion)* defection; **faire d.** *(ne pas venir)* to fail to turn up

défectueux, -ueuse [defektɥø, -ɥøz] *adj* faulty, defective

défendre [defɑ̃dr] **1** *vt (protéger, soutenir)* to defend (**contre** against); **d. à qn de faire qch** to forbid sb to do sth; **d. qch à qn** to forbid sb sth
2 **se défendre** *vpr* to defend oneself; **se d. de faire qch** to refrain from doing sth; *Fam* **je me défends en anglais** I can get by in English ● **défendable** *adj* defensible

défense¹ [defɑ̃s] *nf (protection) Br* defence, *Am* defense; **prendre la d. de qn** to come to sb's defence; *Jur* **assurer la d. de qn** to conduct the case for the defence; **en état de légitime d.** acting in self-defence; **sans d.** *Br* defenceless, *Am*

defenseless; **'d. de fumer'** 'no smoking'; **'d. (absolue) d'entrer'** '(strictly) no entry'
défense² [defɑ̃s] nf (d'éléphant) tusk
défenseur [defɑ̃sœr] nm defender; Jur counsel for the defence
défensif, -ive [defɑ̃sif, -iv] **1** adj defensive **2** nf **sur la défensive** on the defensive
déférence [deferɑ̃s] nf deference
déférer [defere] vtJur **d. qn à la justice** to hand sb over to the police
déferler [deferle] vi (vagues) to break; **les vacanciers déferlent sur les routes** holiday-makers are taking to the roads in droves
défi [defi] nm challenge (à to); **lancer un d. à qn** to challenge sb; **mettre qn au d. de faire qch** to defy sb to do sth; **relever un d.** to take up a challenge
défiance [defjɑ̃s] nf mistrust
déficient, -ente [defisjɑ̃, -ɑ̃t] adj deficient • **déficience** nf deficiency
déficit [defisit] nm deficit; **être en d.** to be in deficit; **d. commercial** trade deficit • **déficitaire** adj (budget) in deficit; (entreprise) loss-making; (compte) in debit
défier [defje] **1** vt (provoquer) to challenge; (danger, mort) to defy; **d. qn à la course** to challenge sb to a race; **d. qn de faire qch** to defy sb to do sth; **des prix qui défient toute concurrence** unbeatable prices
    2 se défier vpr **se d. de** to mistrust • **défiance** nf mistrust • **défiant, -ante** adj mistrustful (**l'égard de** of)
défigurer [defigyre] vt (personne, paysage) to disfigure; Fig (vérité) to distort • **défiguré, -ée** adj (personne) disfigured
défilé [defile] nm (cortège) procession; (de manifestants) march; (de visiteurs) stream; Mil parade; Géog pass; **d. de mode** fashion show
défiler¹ [defile] vi (chars de carnaval) to drive in procession; (manifestants) to march; (touristes) to stream; (paysage, jours) to pass by; (images) to flash by; Mil to parade; Ordinat **faire d. un document** to scroll through a document
défiler² [defile] **se défiler** vpr Fam (se dérober) to slope off
définir [definir] vt to define • **défini, -ie** adj definite • **définition** nf definition; (de mots croisés) clue
définitif, -ive [definitif, -iv] **1** adj (jugement, version) final; (séparation, fermeture) permanent
    2 nf **en définitive** in the final analysis • **définitivement** adv (partir, exclure) for good

déflagration [deflagrasjɔ̃] nf explosion
déflation [deflasjɔ̃] nf Écon deflation
déflorer [deflɔre] vt (personne) to deflower; Fig (sujet) to spoil
défoncer [defɔ̃se] **1** vt (porte, mur) to smash in; (trottoir, route) to break up
    2 se défoncer vpr Fam (faire un gros effort) to sweat blood (**pour faire qch** to do sth); (drogué) to get high (**à** on) • **défoncé, -ée** adj (route) bumpy; Fam (drogué) high
déformation [defɔrmasjɔ̃] nf (de membre) deformation; (de fait) distortion; **d. professionnelle** habits acquired through the type of work one does
déformer [defɔrme] **1** vt (membre) to deform; (vêtement, chaussures) to put out of shape; (faits, image) to distort; (propos) to twist
    2 se déformer vpr to lose its shape • **déformé, -ée** adj (objet) misshapen; (corps) deformed
défouler [defule] **se défouler** vpr Fam to let off steam; **se d. sur qn** to take it out on sb
défraîchi, -ie [defrɛʃi] adj (fleur, beauté) faded; (vêtement) shabby
défrayer [defreje] vt **d. la chronique** to be the talk of the town; **d. qn** to pay or defray sb's expenses
défricher [defriʃe] vt (terrain) to clear; Fig (sujet) to open up; Fig **d. le terrain** to prepare the ground
défriser [defrize] vt (cheveux) to straighten; Fam (personne) to bug
défroisser [defrwase] vt to smooth out
défroqué, -ée [defrɔke] adj (prêtre) defrocked
défunt, -unte [defœ̃, -œ̃t] **1** adj (mort) departed; **son d. mari** her late husband
    2 nmf **le d., la défunte** the deceased
dégager [degaʒe] **1** vt (passage, voie) to clear (**de** of); (odeur, chaleur) to emit; (crédit) to release; Fig (impression) to give off; **d. qn de** (décombres) to free sb from; (promesse) to release sb from; Football **d. le ballon en touche** to kick the ball into touch; Fam **dégage!** clear off!
    2 se dégager vpr (odeur, gaz) to be given off; (rue, ciel) to clear; **se d. de** (personne) to free oneself from • **dégagé, -ée** adj (ciel) clear; (allure, ton) casual; (vue) open • **dégagement** nm (action) clearing; (d'odeur, de chaleur) emission; Football clearance
dégaine [degɛn] nf Fam (apparence) strange appearance
dégainer [degene] vti to draw

dégarnir [degarnir] **1** *vt* to empty
2 se dégarnir *vpr (personne)* to go bald; *(salle)* to empty •**dégarni, -ie** *adj (personne)* balding; **avoir le front d.** to have a receding hairline

dégâts [dega] *nmpl* damage; *Fig* **limiter les d.** to limit the damage

dégel [deʒɛl] *nm* thaw •**dégeler 1** *vt* to thaw; *(surgelé)* to defrost; *(crédits)* to unfreeze **2** *vi* to thaw; **faire d. qch, mettre qch à d.** *(surgelé)* to defrost sth **3** *v impersonnel* to thaw; **il dégèle** it's thawing **4 se dégeler** *vpr Fig (atmosphère)* to become less chilly

dégénérer [deʒenere] *vi* to degenerate (**en** into) •**dégénéré, -ée** *adj & nmf (dépravé)* degenerate •**dégénérescence** *nf* degeneration

dégingandé, -ée [deʒɛ̃gɑ̃de] *adj* gangling, lanky

dégivrer [deʒivre] *vt (réfrigérateur)* to defrost; *(voiture, avion)* to de-ice

déglinguer [deglɛ̃ge] **se déglinguer** *vpr Fam* to fall to bits; *(appareil)* to go wrong

dégobiller [degɔbije] *vt très Fam* to puke

dégonfler [degɔ̃fle] **1** *vt (pneu)* to let the air out of
2 se dégonfler *vpr (pneu)* to go flat; *Fam (personne)* to chicken out •**dégonflé, -ée 1** *adj (pneu)* flat; *Fam (lâche)* chicken **2** *nmf Fam* chicken

dégorger [degɔrʒe] **1** *vt (évacuer)* to discharge; *(tuyau)* to unblock
2 *vi* **faire d. des concombres** = to remove water from cucumbers by sprinkling them with salt

dégot(t)er [degɔte] *vt Fam* to dig up

dégouliner [deguline] *vi* to trickle

dégourdir [degurdir] **1** *vt (doigts)* to take the numbness out of; *Fig* **d. qn** to teach sb a thing or two
2 se dégourdir *vpr* to learn a thing or two; **se d. les jambes** to stretch one's legs •**dégourdi, -ie** *adj (malin)* smart

dégoût [degu] *nm* disgust; **le d. de la vie** world-weariness; **éprouver du d. pour qch** to be disgusted by sth

dégoûter [degute] *vt (moralement)* to disgust; *(physiquement)* to turn sb's stomach; **d. qn de qch** to put sb off sth •**dégoûtant, -ante** *adj* disgusting •**dégoûté, -ée 1** *adj* disgusted; **être d. de qch** to be sick of sth; *Ironique* **il n'est pas d.!** he's not too fussy **2** *nm* **faire le d.** to turn up one's nose

dégradation [degradasjɔ̃] *nf (de monument)* defacement; *(de matériel)* damage

(**de** to); *Fig (de santé, de situation)* deterioration

dégrader [degrade] **1** *vt (monument)* to deface; *(matériel)* to damage; *Mil* to demote; *Fig (avilir)* to degrade
2 se dégrader *vpr (édifice, santé, situation)* to deteriorate; *(maison)* to fall into disrepair; *Fig (s'avilir)* to degrade onself •**dégradant, -ante** *adj* degrading •**dégradé** *nm (de couleurs)* gradation

dégrafer [degrafe] **1** *vt (vêtement, bracelet)* to undo
2 se dégrader *vpr (vêtement, bracelet)* to come undone

dégraisser [degrese] *vt (bœuf)* to take the fat off; *(bouillon)* to skim; *Fam (entreprise)* to down size

degré [dəgre] *nm (d'angle, de température)* degree; *(d'alcool)* proof; *(niveau)* stage; *(d'escalier)* step; *(d'échelle)* rung; **au plus haut d.** in the extreme

dégressif, -ive [degresif, -iv] *adj* **tarif d.** tapering rate

dégrèvement [degrɛvmɑ̃] *nm* **d. fiscal** tax relief

dégriffé [degrife] *nm* = reduced-price designer item with its label removed

dégringoler [degrɛ̃gɔle] *Fam* **1** *vt (escalier)* to rush down
2 *vi (personne)* to tumble (down); *(prix)* to slump •**dégringolade** *nf Fam (chute)* tumble; *(de prix)* slump (**de** in)

dégriser [degrize] *vt Fig* **d. qn** to sober sb up

dégrossir [degrosir] *vt (travail)* to rough out; *Fig* **d. qn** to knock the rough edges off sb

déguerpir [degɛrpir] *vi Fam* to clear off

dégueulasse [degœlas] *adj très Fam (crasseux)* filthy; *(mauvais, désagréable)* disgusting •**déguelasser** *vt très Fam* to mess up

dégueuler [degœle] *vi très Fam* to puke

déguiser [degize] **1** *vt (pour tromper)* to disguise; **d. qn en** *(costumer)* to dress sb up as
2 se déguiser *vpr (pour s'amuser)* to dress oneself up (**en** as); *(pour tromper)* to disguise oneself (**en** as) •**déguisement** *nm* disguise; *(de bal costumé)* fancy dress

déguster [degyste] **1** *vt (goûter)* to taste; *(savourer)* to savour
2 *vi Fam* **tu vas d.!** you're in for it! •**dégustation** *nf* tasting

déhancher [deɑ̃ʃe] **se déhancher** *vpr (femme)* to sway one's hips

dehors [dəɔr] **1** *adv* outside; *(pas chez soi)* out; *(en plein air)* out of doors; **en d.**

(s'ouvrir) outwards; **en d. de la maison** outside the house; **en d. de la ville** out of town; *Fig* **en d. de** *(excepté)* apart from; *Fam* **mettre qn d.** to throw sb out; *(employé)* to fire sb

2 *nm (extérieur)* outside; **au d.** on the outside; *(se pencher)* out; **sous des d. timides** beneath an outward appearance of shyness

déjà [deʒa] *adv* already; **est-il d. parti?** has he left yet *or* already?; **elle l'a d. vu** she's seen it before, she's already seen it; *Fam* **c'est d. pas mal** that's not bad at all; *Fam* **quand partez-vous, d.?** when did you say you're leaving?

déjanter [deʒɑ̃te] *vi très Fam (être fou)* to be off one's rocker

déjeuner [deʒœne] **1** *nm* lunch; **petit d.** breakfast; **prendre son d.** to have lunch/breakfast

2 *vi (à midi)* to have lunch; *(le matin)* to have breakfast

déjouer [deʒwe] *vt (intrigue, plans)* to foil

déjuger [deʒyʒe] **se déjuger** *vpr* to go back on one's decision

délabrer [delabre] **se délabrer** *vpr (édifice)* to fall into disrepair; *(santé)* to deteriorate ●**délabré, -ée** *adj (bâtiment)* dilapidated ●**délabrement** [-əmɑ̃] *nm (de bâtiment)* dilapidated state

délacer [delase] **1** *vt (chaussure)* to untie

2 **se délacer** *vpr (chaussure)* to come untied

délai [delɛ] *nm (laps de temps)* time allowed; *(sursis)* extension; **respecter les délais** to meet the deadline; **dans un d. de dix jours** within ten days; **sans d.** without delay; **dans les plus brefs délais** as soon as possible; **dernier d.** final date

> ⚠ Il faut noter que le nom anglais **delay** est un faux ami. Il signifie **retard**.

délaisser [delese] *vt (négliger)* to neglect; *(abandonner)* to abandon

délasser [delase] *vt*, **se délasser** *vpr* to relax ●**délassement** *nm* relaxation

délateur, -trice [delatœr, -tris] *nmf* informer

délavé, -ée [delave] *adj (tissu, jean)* faded; *(couleur, ciel)* watery

délayer [deleje] *vt (poudre)* to add water to; *(liquide)* to water down; *Fig (discours, texte)* to pad out

Delco® [delko] *nm Aut* distributor

délecter [delɛkte] **se délecter** *vpr* **se d. de qch/à faire qch** to take delight in sth/in doing sth ●**délectable** *adj* delectable

déléguer [delege] *vt* to delegate (**à** to) ●**délégation** *nf* delegation ●**délégué, -ée** *nmf* delegate; *Scol* **d. de classe** = class representative at class meetings

délestage [delɛstaʒ] *nm* **itinéraire de d.** alternative route *(to relieve congestion)*

délester [delɛste] *vt (navire, ballon)* to unballast; *Hum* **d. qn de qch** to relieve sb of sth

délibérer [delibere] *vi (discuter)* to deliberate (**de** about); *(réfléchir)* to deliberate (**sur** upon); *Jur (jury)* to consider its verdict ●**délibération** *nf* deliberation ●**délibéré, -ée** *adj (intentionnel)* deliberate; **de propos d.** deliberately ●**délibérément** *adv* deliberately

délicat, -ate [delika, -at] *adj (santé, travail)* delicate; *(question)* tricky, delicate; *(peau)* sensitive; *(geste)* tactful; *(exigeant)* fussy; **des procédés peu délicats** unscrupulous methods ●**délicatement** *adv (légèrement)* delicately; *(avec tact)* tactfully ●**délicatesse** *nf (de fleur, de couleur)* delicacy; *(tact)* tact

délice [delis] *nm* delight ●**délices** *nfpl Littéraire* delights ●**délicieux, -euse** *adj (mets, sensation)* delicious; *(endroit, parfum)* delightful

délié, -ée [delje] **1** *adj (taille)* slim; *(doigts)* nimble

2 *nm (de lettre)* thin stroke

délier [delje] **1** *vt* to untie; *Fig (langue)* to loosen; **d. qn de qch** to release sb from sth

2 **se délier** *vpr* **les langues se délient** people start talking

délimiter [delimite] *vt (terrain)* to mark off; *(sujet)* to define

délinquant, -ante [delɛ̃kɑ̃, -ɑ̃t] *adj & nmf* delinquent ●**délinquance** *nf* delinquency

délire [delir] *nm Méd* delirium; *(exaltation)* frenzy; *Fam* **c'est du d.** it's utter madness ●**délirant, -ante** *adj (malade)* delirious; *(joie)* frenzied; *(déraisonnable)* utterly absurd ●**délirer** *vi (patient)* to be delirious; *(dire n'importe quoi)* to rave

délit [deli] *nm Br* offence, *Am* offense; **d. d'initié** insider trading *or* dealing

délivrer [delivre] *vt* (**a**) *(captif)* to rescue; *(ville)* to liberate; *(peuple)* to set free; **d. qn de qch** to rid sb of sth (**b**) *(marchandises)* to deliver; *(passeport, billet)* to issue (**à** to) ●**délivrance** *nf (soulagement)* relief; *(de passeport)* issue

déloger [deloʒe] *vt (envahisseur)* to drive out (**de** from); *(locataire)* to evict

déloyal, -e, -aux, -ales [delwajal, -jo] *adj* disloyal; *(concurrence)* unfair

delta [delta] *nm (de fleuve)* delta
deltaplane [deltaplan] *nm* hang-glider; **faire du d.** to go hang-gliding
déluge [delyʒ] *nm* flood; *(de pluie)* downpour; *Fig (d'injures)* flood, deluge; *Fig (de coups)* shower
déluré, -ée [delyre] *adj (vif)* smart, sharp; *Péj (provocant)* forward
démagogie [demagɔʒi] *nf* demagogy • **démagogue** *nmf* demagogue
demain [dəmɛ̃] *adv* tomorrow; **d. soir** tomorrow evening; **à d.!** see you tomorrow!; *Fam* **ce n'est pas d. la veille** that won't happen for a long time yet
demande [dəmɑ̃d] *nf (requête)* request (**de** for); *Écon* demand; **faire une d. de qch** *(prêt, permis)* to apply for sth; **à la d. générale** by popular demand; **sur d.** on request; **d. en mariage** proposal of marriage; **faire sa d. (en mariage)** to propose; **demandes d'emploi** *(dans le journal)* jobs wanted, *Br* situations wanted

> ⚠ Il faut noter que le nom anglais **demand** est un faux ami. Il signifie le plus souvent **exigence**.

demander [dəmɑ̃de] **1** *vt* to ask for; *(prix, raison)* to ask; *(exiger)* to demand; *(nécessiter)* to require; **d. le chemin/l'heure** to ask the way/the time; **d. qch à qn** to ask sb for sth; **d. à qn de faire qch** to ask sb to do sth; **d. si/où...** to ask *or* inquire whether/where...; **ça demande du temps** it takes time; **je peux vous d. votre nom?** may I ask your name?; **d. qn en mariage** to propose (marriage) to sb; **elle est très demandée** she's in great demand; **on te demande!** you're wanted!
2 se demander *vpr* to wonder, to ask oneself (**pourquoi** why, **si** if) • **demandeur, -euse** *nmf* **d. d'emploi** job seeker

> ⚠ Il faut noter que le verbe anglais **to demand** est un faux ami. Il signifie **exiger**.

démanger [demɑ̃ʒe] *vti* to itch; **le bras me démange** my arm's itching; **ça me démange de lui dire** *(j'ai très envie de)* I'm itching to tell him/her • **démangeaison** *nf* itch; **avoir des démangeaisons** to be itching; **j'ai une d. au bras** my arm's itching
démanteler [demɑ̃tle] *vt* to break up
démantibuler [demɑ̃tibyle] *vt Fam (meuble)* to break up
démaquiller [demakije] **se démaquiller** *vpr* to remove one's make-up • **démaquillant** *nm* cleanser
démarcation [demarkɑsjɔ̃] *nf* demarcation

démarche [demarʃ] *nf (allure)* walk, gait; *(requête)* step; **faire les démarches nécessaires pour...** to take the necessary steps to...; **faire une d. auprès de qn** to approach sb; **d. intellectuelle** thought process
démarcheur, -euse [demarʃœr, -øz] *nmf (vendeur)* door-to-door salesman, *f* saleswoman
démarquer [demarke] **1** *vt (marchandises)* to mark down
2 se démarquer *vpr Sport* to lose one's marker; *Fig* **se d. de qn** to distinguish from sb
démarrer [demare] **1** *vi (moteur)* to start; *(voiture)* to move off; *Fig (entreprise)* to get off the ground
2 *vt Fam (commencer)* to start • **démarrage** *nm (de moteur)* starting; **au d.** when moving off; **d. en côte** hill start • **démarreur** *nm Aut* starter
démasquer [demaske] *vt* to unmask
démêler [demele] *vt* to untangle; *Fig* **d. le vrai du faux** to disentangle the truth from the lies • **démêlé** *nm (dispute)* disagreement; **avoir des démêlés avec la justice** to be in trouble with the law
démembrer [demɑ̃bre] *vt (empire)* to break up
déménager [demenaʒe] **1** *vi* to move; *Fam (musique)* to be mind-blowing
2 *vt (meubles)* to move • **déménagement** *nm* move • **déménageur** *nm Br* removal man, *Am* (furniture) mover
démener [demne] **se démener** *vpr (s'agiter)* to thrash about; **se d. pour faire qch** to spare no effort to do sth
dément, -ente [demɑ̃, -ɑ̃t] **1** *adj* insane; *Fam (formidable)* fantastic
2 *nmf* lunatic • **démence** *nf* insanity • **démentiel, -ielle** *adj* insane
démentir [demɑ̃tir] *vt (nouvelle, fait)* to deny; *(être en contradiction avec)* to belie • **démenti** *nm* denial; **opposer un d. à qch** to make a formal denial of sth
démerder [demerde] **se démerder** *vpr très Fam* to get by; **se d. pour faire qch** to manage to do sth
démesure [deməzyr] *nf* excess • **démesuré, -ée** *adj* excessive
démettre* [demɛtr] **1** *vt* **d. qn de ses fonctions** to remove sb from his/her post
2 se démettre *vpr* **se d. l'épaule** to dislocate one's shoulder; **se d. de ses fonctions** to resign from one's post
demeurant [dəmœrɑ̃] **au demeurant** *adv (malgré tout)* for all that; *(d'ailleurs)* after all

demeure [dəmœr] *nf (belle maison)* mansion; **à d.** permanently; **mettre qn en d. de faire qch** to instruct sb to do sth

demeuré, -ée *adj Fam Péj* halfwitted

demeurer [dəmœre] *vi* (**a**) *(aux être) (rester)* to remain; **en d. là** *(affaire)* to rest there (**b**) *(aux avoir) Formel (habiter)* to reside

demi, -ie [dəmi] **1** *adj* half; **une heure et demie** an hour and a half; *(à l'horloge)* half past one, one-thirty

2 *adv* (**à**) **d. plein** half-full; **à d. nu** half-naked; **dormir à d.** to be half asleep; **ouvrir qch à d.** to open sth halfway; **faire les choses à d.** to do things by halves

3 *nmf (moitié)* half

4 *nm* **un d.** *(bière)* a beer; *Football* midfielder; *Rugby* **d. de mêlée** scrum half

5 *nf* **à la demie** *(à l'horloge)* at half-past • **demi-cercle** *(pl* **demi-cercles***) nm* semicircle • **demi-douzaine** *(pl* **demi-douzaines***) nf* **une d. (de)** half a dozen • **demi-écrémé** *adj* semi-skimmed • **demi-finale** *(pl* **demi-finales***) nf Sport* semifinal • **demi-frère** *(pl* **demi-frères***) nm* half brother • **demi-heure** *(pl* **demi-heures***) nf* **une d.** half an hour • **demi-journée** *(pl* **demi-journées***) nf* half-day • **demi-mesure** *(pl* **demi-mesures***) nf* half-measure • **demi-mot** *mn* **comprendre à d.** to take the hint • **demi-pension** *nf Br* halfboard; *Am* breakfast and one meal • **demi-pensionnaire** *(pl* **demi-pensionnaires***) nmf Br* = pupil who has school dinners • **demi-saison** *(pl* **demi-saisons***) nf* **de d.** *(vêtement)* spring and autumn • **demi-sel** *adj inv (beurre)* slightly salted; **fromage d.** slightly salted cream cheese • **demi-sœur** *(pl* **demi-sœurs***) nf* half sister • **demi-tarif** *(pl* **demi-tarifs***) nm* halfprice • **demi-tour** *(pl* **demi-tours***) nm Br* about turn, *Am* about face; *(en voiture)* U-turn; **faire d.** *(à pied)* to turn back; *(en voiture)* to do a U-turn

déminéralisée [demineralize] *adj f* **eau d.** distilled water

démis, -ise [demi, -miz] *adj* **avoir l'épaule démise** to have a dislocated shoulder

démission [demisjɔ̃] *nf* resignation; **donner sa d.** to hand in one's resignation • **démissionner** *vi* to resign

démobiliser [demɔbilize] *vt* to demobilize • **démobilisation** *nf* demobilization

démocrate [demɔkrat] **1** *adj* democratic

2 *nmf* democrat • **démocratie** [-asi] *nf* democracy • **démocratique** *adj* democratic

démodé, -ée [demɔde] *adj* oldfashioned

démographie [demɔgrafi] *nf* demography

demoiselle [dəmwazɛl] *nf (jeune fille)* young lady; *(célibataire)* single woman; **d. d'honneur** *(de mariée)* bridesmaid

démolir [demɔlir] *vt (maison)* to pull down, to demolish; *(jouet)* to wreck; *Fig (théorie, adversaire)* to demolish; *Fam* **d. le portrait à qn** to smash sb's face in • **démolition** *nf* demolition; **en d.** being demolished

démon [demɔ̃] *nm* demon; **le d.** the Devil • **démoniaque** *adj* demonic

démonstratif, -ive [demɔ̃stratif, -iv] **1** *adj* demonstrative

2 *nm Grammaire* demonstrative

démonstration [demɔ̃strasjɔ̃] *nf* demonstration; *Math* **faire la d. de qch** to demonstrate sth; **être en d.** *(appareil)* to be a display model; **d. de force** show of force

démonter [demɔ̃te] **1** *vt (mécanisme, tente)* to dismantle; *(pneu)* to remove; *Fam (déconcerter)* to throw; **une mer démontée** a raging sea

2 se démonter *vpr (mécanisme)* to come apart; *Fam* **elle ne s'est pas démontée pour si peu** she wasn't so easily thrown

démontrer [demɔ̃tre] *vt* to demonstrate

démoraliser [demɔralize] **1** *vt* to demoralize

2 se démoraliser *vpr* to become demoralized • **démoralisation** *nf* demoralization

démordre [demɔrdr] *vi* **ne pas d. de qch** to stick to sth

démouler [demule] *vt (gâteau)* to turn out

démuni, -e [demyni] *adj* penniless

démunir [demynir] **1** *vt* **d. qn de qch** to deprive sb of sth

2 se démunir *vpr* **se d. de qch** to part with sth

démystifier [demistifje] *vt* to demystify

dénationaliser [denasjɔnalize] *vt* to denationalize

dénaturer [denatyre] *vt (propos, faits)* to distort; *(goût)* to alter • **dénaturé, -ée** *adj (parents, goût)* unnatural

dénégation [denegasjɔ̃] *nf* denial

déneiger [deneʒe] *vt* to clear the snow from

dénicher [deniʃe] *vt Fam (objet)* to unearth; *(personne)* to track down

dénier [denje] *vt (responsabilité, faute)* to deny; **d. qch à qn** to deny sb sth

dénigrer [denigre] *vt* to denigrate • **déni-grement** [-əmã] *nm* denigration

dénivellation [denivɛlasjɔ̃] *nf* difference in level; **dénivellations** *(relief)* bumps

dénombrer [denɔ̃bre] *vt* to count

dénominateur [denɔminatœr] *nm Math* denominator

dénommer [denɔme] *vt* to name • **déno-mination** *nf* designation • **dénommé, -ée** *nmf* **un d. Dupont** a man named Dupont

dénoncer [denɔ̃se] **1** *vt (injustice, abus, malfaiteur)* to denounce (**à** to); *(élève)* to tell on (**à** to)
2 se dénoncer *vpr (malfaiteur)* to give oneself up (**à** to); *(élève)* to own up (**à** to) • **dénonciation** *nf* denunciation

dénoter [denɔte] *vt* to denote

dénouement [denumã] *nm (de livre)* ending; *(de pièce de théâtre)* dénoue-ment; *(d'affaire)* outcome

dénouer [denwe] **1** *vt (nœud, corde)* to undo, to untie; *(cheveux)* to let down, to undo; *Fig (intrigue)* to unravel
2 se dénouer *vpr (nœud)* to come un-done; *(cheveux)* to come down

dénoyauter [denwajote] *vt Br* to stone, *Am* to pit

denrée [dãre] *nf* foodstuff; **denrées ali-mentaires** foodstuffs; **denrées périssa-bles** perishable goods

dense [dãs] *adj* dense • **densité** *nf* den-sity

dent [dã] *nf* tooth *(pl* teeth); *(de roue)* cog; *(de fourchette)* prong; *(de timbre-poste)* perforation; **d. de lait/sagesse** milk/wisdom tooth; **faire ses dents** *(en-fant)* to be teething; **coup de d.** bite; **n'avoir rien à se mettre sous la d.** to have nothing to eat; **manger du bout des dents** to pick at one's food; **être sur les dents** *(énervé)* to be on edge; *(surmené)* to be exhausted; *Fam* **avoir une d. contre qn** to have a grudge against sb; **en dents de scie** serrated; *Fig (résultats)* uneven • **dentaire** *adj* dental • **dentée** *adj f* **roue d.** cogwheel

dentelé, -ée [dãtle] *adj (côte, feuille)* jagged • **dentelure** *nf* jagged outline

dentelle [dãtɛl] *nf* lace

dentier [dãtje] *nm* (set of) false teeth, dentures

dentifrice [dãtifris] *nm* toothpaste

dentiste [dãtist] *nmf* dentist • **dentition** *nf (dents)* (set of) teeth • **denture** *nf* set of teeth

> 𝒍 Il faut noter que le nom anglais **dentures** est un faux ami. Il signifie **dentier**.

dénuder [denyde] *vt* to (lay) bare • **dé-nudé, -ée** *adj* bare

dénué, -ée [denɥe] *adj* **d. de sens/d'in-térêt** devoid of sense/interest

dénuement [denymã] *nm* destitution; **dans le d.** poverty-stricken

déodorant [deɔdɔrã] *nm* deodorant • **déodoriser** *vt* to deodorize

dépanner [depane] *vt (machine)* to re-pair; *Fam* **d. qn** to help sb out • **dépan-nage** *nm* (emergency) repairs; **voiture/ service de d.** breakdown vehicle/service • **dépanneur** *nm (de télévision)* repair-man; *(de voiture)* breakdown mechanic • **dépanneuse** *nf (voiture) Br* breakdown lorry, *Am* wrecker

dépareillé, -ée [depareje] *adj (chaus-sure)* odd; *(collection)* incomplete

départ [depar] *nm* departure; *(de course)* start; **les grands départs** the great holi-day exodus; **point/ligne de d.** starting point/post; **salaire de d.** starting salary; **au d.** at the outset; **dès le d.** (right) from the start; **au d. de Paris** *(excursion)* leaving from Paris; **à mon d. de Paris** when I left Paris

départager [departaʒe] *vt* to decide be-tween

département [departəmã] *nm* depart-ment *(division of local government)* • **dé-partemental, -e, -aux, -ales** *adj* departmental; **route départementale** secondary road, *Br* ≃ B road

départir* [departir] **se départir** *vpr* **il ne s'est jamais départi de son calme** his calm never deserted him

dépasser [depase] **1** *vt (véhicule) Br* to overtake, *Am* to pass; *(endroit)* to go past; *(prévisions, vitesse)* to exceed; **d. qn** *(en hauteur)* to be taller than sb; *(surclasser)* to be ahead of sb; *Fig* **ça me dépasse** that's (quite) beyond me
2 *vi (jupon, clou)* to stick out • **dépassé, -ée** *adj (démodé)* outdated; *(incapable)* unable to cope • **dépassement** *nm (en voiture) Br* overtaking, *Am* passing

dépayser [depeize] *vt Br* to disorientate, *Am* to disorient • **dépaysement** *nm* dis-orientation

dépecer [depəse] *vt (animal)* to cut up

dépêche [depɛʃ] *nf* dispatch • **dépêcher 1** *vt* to dispatch **2 se dépêcher** *vpr* to hurry (up); **se d. de faire qch** to hurry to do sth

dépeindre* [depɛ̃dr] *vt* to depict

dépenaillé, -ée [depənaje] *adj (rideau)* ragged; *(personne)* in tatters rags

dépendant, -ante [depãdã, -ãt] depend-ent (**de** on) • **dépendance** *nf* dependence;

sous la d. de qn under sb's domination • **dépendances** *nfpl (bâtiments)* outbuildings

dépendre [depãdr] *vi* to depend (**de** on, upon); **d. de** *(appartenir à)* to belong to; *(être soumis à)* to be dependent on; **ça dépend de toi** that's up to you

dépens [depã] *nmpl* **aux d. de** at the expense of; **apprendre qch à ses d.** to learn sth to one's cost

dépense [depãs] *nf (frais)* expense, expenditure; **faire des dépenses** to spend money; **d. physique** physical exertion • **dépenser 1** *vt (argent)* to spend; *(électricité)* to use; *(forces)* to exert **2 se dépenser** *vpr* to burn up energy

dépensier, -ière [depãsje, -jɛr] *adj* extravagant

déperdition [depɛrdisjõ] *nf (de chaleur)* loss

dépérir [deperir] *vi (personne)* to waste away; *(plante)* to wither

dépêtrer [depetre] **se dépêtrer** *vpr Fam* to extricate oneself (**de** from)

dépeupler [depœple] **1** *vt* to depopulate **2 se dépeupler** *vpr* to become depopulated • **dépeuplement** [-əmã] *nm* depopulation

dépilatoire [depilatwar] *nm* hairremover

dépister [depiste] *vt (criminel)* to track down; *(maladie)* to detect • **dépistage** *nm (de maladie)* screening

dépit [depi] *nm* spite; **par d.** out of spite; **en d. de** in spite of; **en d. du bon sens** *(mal)* atrociously

dépité, -ée [depite] *adj* annoyed

déplacement [deplasmã] *nm (voyage)* trip; *(d'ouragan, de troupes)* movement; **être en d.** *(homme d'affaires)* to be on a business trip; **frais de d.** *Br* travelling *or Am* traveling expenses

déplacer [deplase] **1** *vt (objet)* to move; *(fonctionnaire)* to transfer **2 se déplacer** *vpr (aiguille d'une montre)* to move; *(personne, animal)* to move (about); *(marcher)* to walk (around); *(voyager)* to travel • **déplacé, -ée** *adj (mal à propos)* out of place; **personne déplacée** *(réfugié)* displaced person

déplaire* [deplɛr] **1** *vi* **d. à qn** to displease sb; **ça me déplaît** I don't like it; *Ironique* **n'en déplaise à...** with all due respect to...
2 se déplaîre *vpr* **il se déplaît à Paris** he doesn't like it in Paris • **déplaisant, -ante** *adj* unpleasant • **déplaisir** *nm* displeasure

déplier [deplije] *vt* to open out, to unfold • **dépliant** *nm (prospectus)* leaflet

déplorer [deplɔre] *vt (regretter)* to deplore; **d. que...** *(+ subjunctive)* to deplore the fact that...; **d. la mort de qn** to mourn sb's death • **déplorable** *adj* deplorable

déployer [deplwaje] *vt (ailes)* to spread; *(journal, carte)* to unfold; *(troupes)* to deploy **2 se déployer** *vpr (drapeau)* to unfurl • **déploiement** *nm (démonstration)* display; *(d'une armée)* deployment

dépoli, -ie [depɔli] *adj* **verre d.** frosted glass

déplumé, -ée [deplyme] *adj* featherless

déporter [depɔrte] *vt* **d. qn** to send sb to a concentration camp • **déportation** *nf* internment • **déporté, -ée** *nmf* internee

déposer [depoze] **1** *vt (poser)* to put down; *(gerbe)* to lay; *(brevet)* to register; *(projet de loi)* to introduce; *(souverain)* to depose; **d. qn** *(en voiture)* to drop sb off; **d. une lettre à la poste** to mail a letter; **d. de l'argent sur un compte** to deposit money in an account; **d. les armes** to lay down one's arms; **d. une plainte contre qn** to lodge a complaint against sb
2 *vi Jur* to testify; *(liquide)* to leave a deposit
3 se déposer *vpr (poussière, lie)* to settle

dépositaire [depozitɛr] *nmf (vendeur)* agent; *(de secret)* custodian

déposition [depozisjõ] *nf Jur* statement; *(de souverain)* deposing

déposséder [deposede] *vt* to deprive, to dispossess (**de** of)

dépôt [depo] *nm (de vin)* deposit, sediment; *(argent)* deposit; *(entrepôt)* depot; *(prison)* jail; **d. calcaire** *(de bouilloire)* fur; **mettre qch en d.** to put sth in storage; **d. de munitions** munitions depot; **d. d'ordures** *Br* rubbish dump, *Am* garbage dump; **d.-vente** = secondhand clothes shop

dépotoir [depotwar] *nm* dump; *Fam (classe)* dumping ground

dépouille [depuj] *nf (d'animal)* hide, skin; **les dépouilles** *(butin)* the spoils; **d. (mortelle)** *(de défunt)* mortal remains

dépouiller [depuje] **1** *vt (animal)* to skin; *(analyser)* to go through; **d. qn de qch** to deprive sb of sth; **d. un scrutin** to count the votes
2 se dépouiller *vpr* **se d. de qch** to rid oneself of sth • **dépouillé, -ée** *adj (arbre)* bare; *(style)* austere • **dépouillement** *nm (de documents)* analysis; *(privation)* deprivation; *(sobriété)* austerity; **d. du scrutin** counting of the votes

dépourvu, -ue [depurvy] *adj* **d. de qch** devoid of sth; **prendre qn au d.** to catch sb off guard

dépoussiérer [depusjere] *vt* to dust

dépraver [deprave] *vt* to deprave • **dépravation** *nf* depravity • **dépravé, -ée** *adj* depraved

déprécier [depresje] **1** *vt* to undervalue **2 se déprécier** *vpr (valeurs, marchandises)* to depreciate • **dépréciation** *nf* depreciation

déprédation [depredɑsjɔ̃] *nf* depredation

dépression [depresjɔ̃] *nf (creux, maladie)* depression; **zone de d. atmosphérique** trough of low pressure; **d. économique** slump; **d. nerveuse** nervous breakdown; **faire de la d.** to be suffering from depression • **dépressif, -ive** *adj* depressive

déprime [deprim] *nf Fam* depression; **avoir un petit coup de d.** to feel a bit low • **déprimé, -ée** *adj* depressed • **déprimer 1** *vt* to depress **2** *vi Fam* to be feeling low

depuis [dəpɥi] **1** *prép* since; **d. lundi/1990** since Monday/1990; **j'habite ici d. un mois** I've been living here for a month; **d. quand êtes-vous là?, d. combien de temps êtes-vous là?** how long have you been here?; **d. peu/longtemps** for a short/long time; **je le connais d. toujours** I've known him all my life; *Fam* **d. des siècles** for ages; **d. le temps que je le connais!** I've known him for ages!; **d. Paris jusqu'à Londres** from Paris to London **2** *adv* since (then), ever since **3** *conj* **d. que** since; **d. qu'elle est partie** since she left

député [depyte] *nm Pol* deputy, *Br* ≃ MP, *Am* ≃ representative; **d. du Parlement européen** Member of the European Parliament

déraciner [derasine] *vt (arbre, personne)* to uproot

dérailler [deraje] *vi (train)* to leave the rails; *Fam (personne)* to talk drivel; **faire d. un train** to derail a train • **déraillement** *nm (de train)* derailment • **dérailleur** *nm (de bicyclette)* derailleur (gears)

déraisonnable [derɛzɔnabl] *adj* unreasonable • **déraisonner** *vi* to talk nonsense

déranger [derɑ̃ʒe] **1** *vt (affaires)* to disturb; *(projets)* to upset; *(vêtements)* to mess up; **je viendrai si ça ne te dérange pas** I'll come if that' all right with you; **ça vous dérange si je fume?** do you mind if I smoke?; **avoir l'estomac dérangé** to have an upset stomach; **il a l'esprit dérangé** he's deranged **2 se déranger** *vpr* to put oneself to a lot

of trouble (**pour faire** to do); *(se déplacer)* to move; **ne te dérange pas!** don't bother! • **dérangement** *nm (gêne)* trouble; **excusez-moi pour le d.** I'm sorry to trouble you; **en d.** *(téléphone)* out of order

déraper [derape] *vi (véhicule)* to skid; *Fam (personne)* to slip • **dérapage** *nm* skid; *Fig* **le d. des prix** spiralling prices

dératé [derate] *nm Fam* **courir comme un d.** to run like mad

dérégler [deregle] **1** *vt (mécanisme)* to cause to malfunction **2 se dérégler** *vpr (mécanisme)* to go wrong • **dérèglement** [-ɛɡləmɑ̃] *nm (de mécanisme)* malfunctioning

dérider [deride] *vt*, **se dérider** *vpr* to cheer up

> 🖉 Il faut noter que le verbe anglais **to deride** est un faux ami. Il signifie le plus souvent **ridiculiser**.

dérision [derizjɔ̃] *nf* derision; **tourner qch en d.** to deride sth; **par d.** derisively • **dérisoire** *adj (somme)* derisory

dérivatif [derivatif] *nm* distraction (**à** from)

dérive [deriv] *nf Naut* drift; **à la d.** adrift

dériver [derive] **1** *vt (cours d'eau)* to divert **2** *vi Naut* to drift; **d. de** *(mot)* to be derived from • **dérivation** *nf (de cours d'eau)* diversion • **dérivé** *nm (mot, substance)* derivative

dermatologie [dermatɔlɔʒi] *nf* dermatology

dernier, -ière [dernje, -jɛr] **1** *adj (ultime)* last; *(marquant la fin)* final; *(nouvelles, mode)* latest; *(étage)* top; *(degré)* highest; **le d. rang** the back *or* last row; **de d. ordre** third-rate; **ces derniers mois** these past few months; **les dix dernières minutes** the last ten minutes; **de la dernière importance** of (the) utmost importance; **en d.** last **2** *nmf* last; **ce d.** *(de deux)* the latter; *(de plusieurs)* the last-mentioned; **être le d. de la classe** to be (at the) bottom of the class; **le d. des derniers** the lowest of the low; **le d. de mes soucis** the least of my worries; **avoir le d. mot** to have the last word • **dernier-né, dernière-née** *(mpl* **derniers-nés,** *fpl* **dernières-nées)** *nmf* youngest (child) • **dernièrement** *adv* recently

dérobade [derɔbad] *nf (esquive)* evasion

dérober [derɔbe] **1** *vt (voler)* to steal (**à** from); *(cacher)* to hide (**à** from) **2 se dérober** *vpr (s'esquiver)* to slip away; *(éviter de répondre)* to dodge the issue; **se**

d. à la curiosité de qn to avoid sb's prying eyes; **se d. aux regards** to hide from view; **ses jambes se sont dérobées sous lui** his legs gave way beneath him • **dérobé, -ée** *adj (porte)* hidden; **à la dérobée** on the sly

dérogation [deʀɔgasjɔ̃] *nf* exemption (**à** from)

déroger [deʀɔʒe] *vi* **d. à une règle** to depart from a rule

dérouiller [deʀuje] *Fam* **1** *vt* **d. qn** *(battre)* to thrash sb

2 se dérouiller *vpr* **se d. les jambes** to stretch one's legs • **dérouillée** *nf Fam* belting

dérouler [deʀule] **1** *vt (tapis)* to unroll; *(fil)* to unwind

2 se dérouler *vpr (tapis)* to unroll; *(fil)* to unwind; *Fig (événement)* to take place • **déroulement** *nm (d'action)* unfolding

déroute [deʀut] *nf (d'armée)* rout

dérouter [deʀute] *vt (avion, navire)* to divert, to reroute; *(poursuivant)* to throw off the scent; *Fig (étonner)* to throw

derrière [deʀjɛʀ] **1** *prép & adv* behind; **d. moi** behind me; **assis d.** *(dans une voiture)* sitting in the back; **par d.** *(attaquer)* from behind, from the rear

2 *nm (de maison)* back, rear; *(fesses)* behind; **patte de d.** hind leg; **roue de d.** back *or* rear wheel

des [dɛ] *voir* **de, un**

dès [dɛ] *prép* from; **d. le début** (right) from the start; **d. maintenant** from now on; **d. son enfance** since *or* from childhood; **d. le VI siècle** as early as *or* as far back as the sixth century; **d. l'aube** at (the crack of) dawn; **d. lors** *(dans le temps)* from then on; *(en conséquence)* consequently; **d. leur arrivée** as soon as they arrive/arrived; **d. qu'elle viendra** as soon as she comes

désabusé, -ée [dezabyze] *adj* disillusioned

désaccord [dezakɔʀ] *nm* disagreement; **être en d. avec qn** to disagree with sb • **désaccordé, -ée** *adj (instrument)* out of tune

désaccoutumer [dezakutyme] **se désaccoutumer** *vpr* **se d. de qch** to get out of the habit of sth

désaffecté, -ée [dezafɛkte] *adj* disused

désaffection [dezafɛksjɔ̃] *nf* disaffection (**à l'égard de** with)

désagréable [dezagʀeabl] *adj* unpleasant

désagréger [dezagʀeʒe] *vt,* **se désagréger** *vpr* to disintegrate • **désagrégation** *nf* disintegration

désagrément [dezagʀemɑ̃] *nm (gêne)* trouble; *(souci, aspect négatif)* problem

désaltérer [dezalteʀe] **1** *vt* **d. qn** to quench sb's thirst

2 se désaltérer *vpr* to quench one's thirst • **désaltérant, -ante** *adj* thirst-quenching

désamorcer [dezamɔʀse] *vt (bombe, conflit)* to defuse

désappointer [dezapwɛte] *vt Littéraire* to disappoint

désapprouver [dezapʀuve] **1** *vt* to disapprove of

2 *vi* to disapprove • **désapprobateur, -trice** *adj* disapproving • **désapprobation** *nf* disapproval

désarçonner [dezaʀsɔne] *vt (jockey)* to throw, to unseat; *Fig (déconcerter)* to throw

désarmer [dezaʀme] **1** *vt (soldat, nation)* to disarm; *Fig* **d. qn** *(franchise, attitude)* to disarm sb

2 *vi (pays)* to disarm; **il ne désarme pas** he won't give up • **désarmant, -ante** *adj* disarming • **désarmé, -ée** *adj (sans défense)* unarmed; *Fig (sans défenses)* helpless • **désarmement** [-əmɑ̃] *nm (de nation)* disarmament

désarroi [dezaʀwa] *nm* confusion; **être en plein d.** to be in a state of utter confusion

désarticulé, -ée [dezaʀtikyle] *adj (pantin, clown)* double-jointed

désastre [dezastʀ] *nm* disaster • **désastreux, -euse** *adj* disastrous

désavantage [dezavɑ̃taʒ] *nm* disadvantage • **désavantager** *vt* to put at a disadvantage • **désavantageux, -euse** *adj* disadvantageous

désaveu, -x [dezavø] *nm (reniement)* disowning

désavouer [dezavwe] *vt (renier)* to disown

désaxé, -ée [dezakse] *nmf* unbalanced person

desceller [desele] **1** *vt (pierre)* to loosen

2 se desceller *vpr* to come loose

descendant, -ante [desɑ̃dɑ̃, -ɑ̃t] **1** *adj* descending

2 *nmf* descendant • **descendance** *nf (enfants)* descendants; *(origine)* descent

descendre [desɑ̃dʀ] **1** *(aux être)* *vi* to come/go down (**de** from); *(d'un train)* to get off (**de** from); *(d'un arbre)* to climb down (**de** from); *(nuit, thermomètre)* to fall; *(marée)* to go out; **d. de cheval** to dismount; **d. à l'hôtel** to put up at a hotel; **d. chez un ami** to stay with a friend; **d. de** *(être issu de)* to be descended from

2 *(aux* **avoir***)* *vt (escalier)* to come/go down; *(objet)* to bring/take down; *Fam* **d. qn** *(tuer)* to bump sb off

descente [desɑ̃t] *nf (d'avion)* descent; *(en parachute)* drop; *(pente)* slope; *(de police)* raid (**dans** upon); **il fut accueilli à sa d. d'avion** he was met as he got off the plane; **d. de lit** bedside rug

descriptif, -ive [deskriptif, -iv] *adj* descriptive • **description** *nf* description

désemparé, -ée [dezɑ̃pare] *adj (personne)* at a loss

désemplir [dezɑ̃plir] *vi* **ce magasin ne désemplit pas** this shop is always crowded

désenchanté, -ée [dezɑ̃ʃɑ̃te] *adj* disillusioned • **désenchantement** *nm* disenchantment

désencombrer [dezɑ̃kɔ̃bre] *vt (passage)* to clear

désenfler [dezɑ̃fle] *vi (genou, cheville)* to go down, to become less swollen

déséquilibre [dezekilibr] *nm* imbalance; **en d.** unsteady • **déséquilibré, -ée 1** *adj* unbalanced **2** *nmf* unbalanced person • **déséquilibrer** *vt* to throw off balance; *Fig (esprit, personne)* to unbalance

désert, -erte [dezɛr, -ɛrt] **1** *adj (lieu)* deserted; *(région)* uninhabited; **île déserte** desert island

2 *nm* desert • **désertique** *adj* **région d.** desert region

déserter [dezɛrte] *vti* to desert • **déserteur** *nm* deserter • **désertion** *nf* desertion

désespérer [dezɛspere] **1** *vt* to drive to despair

2 *vi* to despair (**de** of)

3 se désespérer *vpr* to despair • **désespérant, -ante** *adj (situation, personne)* hopeless • **désespéré, -ée 1** *adj (personne)* in despair; *(cas, situation, efforts)* desperate **2** *nmf* desparate person • **désespérément** *adv* desperately

désespoir [dezɛspwar] *nm* despair; **au d. in** despair; **en d. de cause** in desperation

déshabiller [dezabije] *vt,* **se déshabiller** *vpr* to undress

déshabituer [dezabitɥe] *vt* **d. qn de qch** to get sb out of the habit of sth

désherber [dezɛrbe] *vti* to weed • **désherbant** *nm* weedkiller

déshériter [dezerite] *vt* to disinherit • **déshérité, -ée** *adj (pauvre)* deprived

déshonneur [dezɔnœr] *nm* dishonour

déshonorer [dezɔnɔre] *vt* to disgrace • **déshonorant, -ante** *adj* dishonourable

déshydrater [dezidrate] **1** *vt* to dehydrate

2 se déshydrater *vpr* to become dehydrated

désigner [deziɲe] *vt (montrer)* to point to; *(choisir)* to choose; *(nommer)* to appoint; *(signifier)* to designate; **il est tout désigné pour ce travail** he's just the person for the job • **désignation** *nf* designation

désillusion [dezilyzjɔ̃] *nf* disillusion • **désillusionner** *vt* to disillusion

désinence [dezinɑ̃s] *nf Grammaire* ending

désinfecter [dezɛ̃fɛkte] *vt* to disinfect • **désinfectant, -ante** *nm & adj* disinfectant • **désinfection** *nf* disinfection

désinformation [dezɛ̃fɔrmasjɔ̃] *nf* disinformation

désintégrer [dezɛ̃tegre] **se désintégrer** *vpr* to disintegrate • **désintégration** *nf* disintegration

désintéresser [dezɛ̃terese] **se désintéresser** *vpr* **se d. de qch** to lose interest in sth • **désintéressé, -ée** *adj (altruiste)* disinterested • **désintérêt** *nm* lack of interest

désintoxiquer [dezɛ̃tɔksike] *vt (alcoolique, drogué)* to treat for alcoholism/drug abuse

désinvolte [dezɛ̃vɔlt] *adj (dégagé)* casual; *(insolent)* offhand • **désinvolture** *nf* casualness; *(insolence)* offhandedness

désir [dezir] *nm* desire; **prendre ses désirs pour des réalités** to indulge in wishful thinking • **désirable** *adj* desirable • **désirer** *vt* to wish; *(convoiter)* to desire; **je désire venir** I wish to come; **je désire que tu viennes** I want you to come; **ça laisse à d.** it leaves a lot to be desired

désireux, -euse [desirø, -øz] *adj* **d. de faire qch** anxious to do sth

désister [deziste] **se désister** *vpr* to withdraw • **désistement** [-əmɑ̃] *nm* withdrawal

désobéir [dezɔbeir] *vi* to disobey; **d. à qn** to disobey sb • **désobéissance** *nf* disobedience (**à** to) • **désobéissant, -ante** *adj* disobedient

désobligeant, -ante [dezɔbliʒɑ̃, -ɑ̃t] *adj* disagreeable

désodorisant [dezɔdɔrizɑ̃] *nm* air freshener

désœuvré, -ée [dezœvre] *adj* idle • **désœuvrement** [-əmɑ̃] *nm* idleness

désoler [dezɔle] **1** *vt* to upset

2 se désoler *vpr* to be upset (**de** at) • **désolant, -ante** *adj* upsetting • **désolation** *nf (peine)* distress • **désolé, -ée** *adj (région)* desolate; *(affligé)* upset; **être d. que...** *(+ subjunctive)* to be sorry that...; **je suis d. de vous déranger** I'm sorry to disturb you

désolidariser [desɔlidarize] **se désolidariser** *vpr* to dissociate oneself (**de** from)

désopilant, -ante [dezɔpilɑ̃, -ɑ̃t] *adj* hilarious

désordonné, -ée [dezɔrdɔne] *adj (personne, chambre)* untidy

désordre [dezɔrdr] *nm (manque d'ordre)* mess; *(manque d'organisation)* disorder; **en d.** untidy, messy; **de graves désordres** *(émeutes)* serious disturbances

désorganiser [dezɔrganize] *vt* to disorganize • **désorganisation** *nf* disorganization • **désorganisé, -ée** *adj* disorganized

désorienter [dezɔrjɑ̃te] *vt* **d. qn** to bewilder sb

désormais [dezɔrmɛ] *adv* from now on, in future

désosser [dezose] *vt (viande)* to bone

despote [despɔt] *nm* despot • **despotique** *adj* despotic

desquels, desquelles [dekɛl] *voir* lequel

dessaisir [desezir] **se dessaisir** *vpr* **se d. de qch** to relinquish sth

dessaler [desale] *vt (poisson)* to remove the salt from *(by soaking)*

dessécher [deseʃe] **1** *vt (peau)* to dry up; *(végétation)* to wither
   2 se dessécher *vpr (peau)* to dry up; *(végétation)* to wither

dessein [desɛ̃] *nm* intention; **dans le d. de faire qch** with the intention of doing sth; **à d.** intentionally

desserrer [desere] **1** *vt (ceinture)* to loosen; *(poing)* to unclench; *(frein)* to release; *Fig* **il n'a pas desserré les dents** he didn't open his mouth
   2 se desserrer *vpr (ceinture)* to come loose

dessert [desɛr] *nm* dessert, *Br* pudding

desserte [desɛrt] *nf* **assurer la d. de** *(village)* to provide a service to

desservir [desɛrvir] *vt (table)* to clear (away); **d. qn** to do sb a disservice; **le car dessert ce village** the bus stops at this village; **ce quartier est bien desservi** this district is well served by public transport

dessin [desɛ̃] *nm* drawing; *(rapide)* sketch; *(motif)* design, pattern; *(contour)* outline; **d. animé** cartoon; **d. humoristique** *(de journal)* cartoon

dessinateur, -trice [desinatœr, -tris] *nmf* drawer; **d. humoristique** cartoonist; **d. de modes** dress designer; **d. industriel** *Br* draughtsman, *Am* draftsman

dessiner [desine] **1** *vt* to draw; *(rapidement)* to sketch; *(meuble, robe)* to design;

(indiquer) to outline; **d. (bien) la taille** *(vêtement)* to show off the figure
   2 se dessiner *vpr (colline)* to stand out; *(projet)* to take shape

dessoûler [desule] *vti Fam* to sober up

dessous [dəsu] **1** *adv* underneath; **en d.** underneath; **en d. de** below; *Fam* **être en d. de tout** to be worse than useless
   2 *nm* underside; *(du pied)* bottom; **des d.** *(sous-vêtements)* underwear; **drap de d.** bottom sheet; **les gens du d.** the people downstairs *or* below; **avoir le d.** to get the worst of it • **dessous-de-plat** *nm inv* table mat • **dessous-de-table** *nm inv* bribe, *Br* backhander

dessus [dəsy] **1** *adv (marcher, écrire)* on it/them; *(monter)* on top (of it/them), on it/them; *(passer)* over it/them; **de d. la table** off *or* from the table
   2 *nm* top; *(de chaussure)* upper; **drap de d.** top sheet; **les gens du d.** the people upstairs *or* above; **avoir le d.** to have the upper hand; **reprendre le d.** *(se remettre)* to get over it • **dessus-de-lit** *nm inv* bedspread

déstabiliser [destabilize] *vt* to destabilize

destin [dɛstɛ̃] *nm* fate, destiny • **destinée** *nf* destiny

destinataire [dɛstinatɛr] *nmf* addressee

destination [dɛstinasjɔ̃] *nf (lieu)* destination; **trains à d. de...** trains to...; **arriver à d.** to reach one's destination

destiner [dɛstine] **1** *vt* **d. qch à qn** to intend sth for sb; **d. qn à** *(carrière, fonction)* to intend *or* destine sb for; **destiné à mourir** *(condamné)* destined *or* fated to die
   2 se destiner *vpr* **se d. à** *(carrière)* to intend to take up

destituer [dɛstitɥe] *vt (fonctionnaire)* to remove from office • **destitution** *nf* removal from office

destroy [dɛstrɔj] *adj Fam (musique)* = loud, fast and aggressive; **avoir une allure complètement d.** to look wasted

destructeur, -trice [dɛstryktœr, -tris] *adj* destructive

destruction [dɛstryksjɔ̃] *nf* destruction

désuet, -uète [desɥe, -ɥɛt] *adj* obsolete • **désuétude** *nf* **tomber en d.** *(expression)* to become obsolete

désunir [dezynir] *vt (famille, personnes)* to divide

détachant [detaʃɑ̃] *nm* stain remover

détachement [detaʃmɑ̃] *nm* (**a**) *(indifférence)* detachment (**b**) *(de fonctionnaire)* secondment; *(de troupes)* detachment

détacher¹ [detaʃe] **1** *vt (ceinture, vête-ment)* to undo; *(mains, personne)* to untie; *(ôter)* to take off; *(mots)* to pronounce clearly; **d. qn** *(libérer)* to untie sb; *(affec-ter)* to transfer sb (on assignment) (**à** to); **d. les yeux de qn/qch** to take one's eyes off sb/sth; **'détachez en suivant les poin-tillés'** 'tear off along the dotted line'
2 se détacher *vpr (chien, prisonnier)* to break loose; *(se dénouer)* to come undone; **se d. (de qch)** *(fragment)* to come off (sth); **se d. de ses amis** to break away from one's friends; **se d. (sur)** *(ressortir)* to stand out (against) •**détaché, -ée** *adj (nœud)* loose, undone; *(air, ton)* detached
détacher² [detaʃe] *vt (linge)* to remove the stains from
détail [detaj] *nm* detail; **en d.** in detail; **entrer dans les détails** to go into detail; **le d. de** *(dépenses)* a breakdown of; **maga-sin/prix de d.** retail store/price; **vendre au d.** to sell retail
détaillant [detajɑ̃] *nm* retailer
détailler [detaje] *vt (énumérer)* to detail •**détaillé, -ée** *adj (récit, description)* detailed; *(facture)* itemized
détaler [detale] *vi Fam* to take off
détartrer [detartre] *vt (chaudière, dents)* to scale
détaxer [detakse] *vt* to exempt from tax; **produit détaxé** duty-free article
détecter [detɛkte] *vt* to detect •**détec-teur** *nm (appareil)* detector; **d. de fumée** smoke detector •**détection** *nf* detection
détective [detɛktiv] *nm* **d. (privé)** (pri-vate) detective
déteindre* [detɛ̃dr] *vi (couleur, tissu)* to run; **ton tablier bleu a déteint sur ma chemise** the blue of your apron has come off on(to) my shirt; *Fig* **d. sur qn** *(influen-cer)* to leave one's mark on sb
dételer [detle] *vt (chevaux)* to unharness
détendre [detɑ̃dr] **1** *vt (corde)* to slaken; *(arc)* to unbend; **d. l'atmosphère** to make the atmosphere less tense; **d. qn** to relax sb
2 se détendre *vpr (corde)* to slaken; *(arc)* to unbend; *(atmosphère)* to become less tense; *(personne)* to relax •**détendu, -ue** *adj (visage, atmosphère)* relaxed; *(ressort, câble)* slack
détenir* [detənir] *vt (record, pouvoir, titre, prisonnier)* to hold; *(secret, objet volé)* to be in possession of •**détenteur, -trice** *nmf (de record)* holder •**détention** *nf (d'armes)* possession; *(captivité)* de-tention; **d. provisoire** detention pending trial •**détenu, -ue** *nmf* prisoner

détente [detɑ̃t] *nf* (**a**) *(repos)* relaxation; *(entre deux pays)* détente (**b**) *(saut)* spring (**c**) *(gâchette)* trigger
détergent [detɛrʒɑ̃] *nm* detergent
détériorer [deterjɔre] **1** *vt* to damage
2 se détériorer *vpr* to deteriorate •**dété-rioration** *nf* damage (**de** to); *(d'une sit-uation)* deterioration (**de** in)
détermination [determinɑsjɔ̃] *nf (fer-meté)* determination; *(de date, de lieu)* fixing
déterminer [detɛrmine] **1** *vt (préciser)* to determine; *(causer)* to bring about; **d. qn à faire qch** to induce sb to do sth
2 se déterminer *vpr* **se d. à faire qch** to make up one's mind to do sth •**détermi-nant, -ante 1** *adj* decisive **2** *nm Gram-maire* determiner •**déterminé, -ée** *adj (précis)* specific; *(résolu)* determined
déterrer [detere] *vt* to dig up
détester [detɛste] *vt* to hate, to detest; **d. faire qch** to hate doing *or* to do sth •**dé-testable** *adj* foul
détonateur [dnatœr] *nm* detonator •**dé-tonation** *nf* explosion; *(d'arme)* bang
détonner [detɔne] *vi (contraster)* to clash
détour [detur] *nm (crochet)* detour; *(de route)* bend, curve; **sans d.** *(parler)* with-out beating about the bush; **faire un d.** to make a detour; **faire des détours** *(route)* to wind
détourner [deturne] **1** *vt (dévier)* to di-vert; *(avion)* to hijack; *(conversation, sens)* to change; *(fonds)* to embezzle; *(coup)* to ward off; **d. la tête** to turn one's head away; **d. les yeux** to look away; **d. qn de** *(son devoir, ses amis)* to take sb away from; *(sa route)* to lead sb away from
2 se détourner *vpr* to turn away •**dé-tourné, -ée** *adj (chemin, moyen)* round-about, indirect •**détournement** [-əmɑ̃] *nm (de cours d'eau)* diversion; **d. d'avion** hijack(ing); **d. de fonds** embezzlement
détracteur, -trice [detraktœr, -tris] *nmf* detractor
détraquer [detrake] **1** *vt (mécanisme)* to put out of order
2 se détraquer *vpr (machine)* to go wrong; **se d. l'estomac** to upset one's stomach; **se d. la santé** to ruin one's health •**détraqué, -ée 1** *adj (appareil)* out of order; *(cerveau)* deranged **2** *nmf (obsédé)* sex maniac
détremper [detrɑ̃pe] *vt* to soak; **des terres détrempées** waterlogged ground
détresse [detrɛs] *nf* distress; **en d.** *(na-vire, âme)* in distress; **dans la d.** *(misère)* in (great) distress

détriment [detrimã] **au détriment de** *prép* to the detriment of

détritus [detritys] *nmpl Br* rubbish, *Am* garbage

détroit [detrwa] *nm* strait

détromper [detrɔ̃pe] **1** *vt* **d. qn** to put sb right

2 se détromper *vpr* **détrompez-vous!** don't you believe it!

détrôner [detrone] *vt (souverain)* to dethrone; *(supplanter)* to supersede

détrousser [detruse] *vt Hum* **d. qn** to relieve sb of one's valuables

détruire* [detrɥir] *vt (ravager)* to destroy; *(tuer)* to kill; *(santé)* to ruin, to wreck

dette [dɛt] *nf* debt; **avoir des dettes** to be in debt; **faire des dettes** to run into debt

DEUG [døg] *(abrév* **diplôme d'études universitaires générales)** *nm* = degree gained after two years' study at university

deuil [dœj] *nm (affliction, vêtements)* mourning; *(décès)* bereavement; **être en d., porter le d.** to be in mourning; **faire son d. de qch** to give sth up as lost

deux [dø] *adj inv & nm inv* two; **d. fois** twice; **mes d. sœurs** both my sisters, my two sisters; **tous (les) d.** both; *Fam* **en moins de d.** in no time (at all) •**deux-pièces** *nm inv (maillot de bain)* bikini; *(appartement)* two-roomed *Br* flat *or Am* apartment •**deux-points** *nm inv* colon •**deux-roues** *nm inv* two-wheeled vehicle •**deux-temps** *nm inv (moteur)* two-stroke *or Am* two-cycle (engine)

deuxième [døzjɛm] *adj & nmf* second •**deuxièmement** *adv* secondly

dévaler [devale] **1** *vt (escalier)* to hurtle down

2 *vi (personne, pièces)* to hurtle down; *(eau, lave)* to rush down

dévaliser [devalize] *vt (personne, banque)* to rob; *(maison)* to burgle

dévaloriser [devalɔrize] **1** *vt (monnaie, diplôme)* to devalue; *(personne, politique)* to discredit

2 se dévaloriser *vpr (monnaie)* to depreciate; *(personne)* to put oneself down •**dévalorisation** *nf (de diplôme)* loss of value

dévaluer [devalɥe] *vt (monnaie)* to devalue •**dévaluation** *nf Fin* devaluation

devancer [dəvɑ̃se] *vt (concurrent)* to be ahead of; *(question)* to anticipate; *(arriver avant)* to arrive before; *Mil* **d. l'appel** to enlist before call-up

devant [dəvɑ̃] **1** *prép & adv* in front (of); **d. l'hôtel** in front of the hotel; **passer d. (l'église)** to go past (the church); **marcher d. (qn)** to walk in front (of sb); **assis d.** *(dans une voiture)* sitting in the front; **par d.** from *or* at the front; **loin d.** a long way ahead *or* in front; **d. le danger** *(confronté à)* in the face of danger; **d. mes yeux/la loi** before my eyes/the law; **l'avenir est d. toi** the future is ahead of you

2 *nm* front; **roue/porte de d.** front wheel/door; **patte de d.** foreleg; **prendre les devants** *(action)* to take the initiative

devanture [dəvɑ̃tyr] *nf (vitrine)* window; *(façade)* front

dévaster [devaste] *vt* to devastate •**dévastation** *nf* devastation

déveine [devɛn] *nf Fam* bad luck

développer [devlɔpe] *vt,* **se développer** *vpr* to develop •**développement** *nm* development; *(de photo)* developing; **en plein d.** *(entreprise, pays)* growing fast

devenir* [dəvnir] *(aux* **être)** *vi* to become; **d. médecin** to become a doctor; **d. un papillon/un homme** to grow into a butterfly/a man; **d. vieux** to get *or* grow old; **d. tout rouge** to go all red; **qu'est-il devenu?** what has become of him/it?; *Fam* **qu'est-ce que tu deviens?** how are you getting on?

dévergonder [devergɔ̃de] **se dévergonder** *vpr* to get into bad ways •**dévergondé, -ée** *adj* shameless

déverser [devɛrse] **1** *vt (liquide)* to pour out; *(bombes, ordures)* to dump

2 se déverser *vpr (liquide, rivière)* to empty (**dans** into)

dévêtir [devɛtir] *vt,* **se dévêtir** *vpr* to undress

dévier [devje] **1** *vt (circulation)* to divert; *(coup, rayons)* to deflect

2 *vi (balle)* to deflect; *(véhicule)* to veer; **d. de sa route** to veer off course •**déviation** *nf (itinéraire provisoire) Br* diversion, *Am* detour; *(modification)* deviation

devin [dəvɛ̃] *nm* soothsayer; *Fam* **je ne suis pas d.** I can't predict what will happen

deviner [dəvine] *vt* to guess (**que** that); *(avenir)* to predict; *(pensée)* to read •**devinette** *nf* riddle

devis [dəvi] *nm* estimate; **faire faire un d. pour qch** to get an estimate for sth

dévisager [devizaʒe] *vt* **d. qn** to stare at sb

devise [dəviz] *nf (légende)* motto; *(monnaie)* currency; **devises étrangères** foreign currency

dévisser [devise] **1** *vt* to unscrew

2 *vi Alpinisme* to fall

3 se dévisser *vpr (bouchon)* to unscrew; *(par accident)* to come unscrewed

dévoiler [devwale] **1** *vt (statue)* to unveil; *Fig (secret)* to disclose
2 se dévoiler *vpr (mystère)* to come to light

devoir*¹ [dəvwar] *v aux* (**a**) *(indique la nécessité)* **je dois refuser** I must refuse, I have (got) to refuse; **j'ai dû refuser** I had to refuse
(**b**) *(indique une forte probabilité)* **il doit être tard** it must be late; **elle a dû oublier** she must have forgotten; **il ne doit pas être bête** he can't be stupid; **cela devait arriver** it had to happen
(**c**) *(indique l'obligation)* **tu dois apprendre tes leçons** you must learn your lessons; **vous devriez rester** you should stay, you ought to stay; **il aurait dû venir** he should have come, he ought to have come
(**d**) *(indique l'intention)* **elle doit venir** she's supposed to be coming, she's due to come; **le train devait arriver à midi** the train was due (to arrive) at noon; **je devais le voir** I was (due) to see him

devoir*² [dəvwar] **1** *vt* to owe; **d. qch à qn** to owe sb sth, to owe sth to sb; **l'argent qui m'est dû** the money due to *or* owing to me, the money owed (to) me
2 se devoir *vpr* **se d. à sa famille** to have to devote oneself to one's family; **comme il se doit** as is proper
3 *nm (obligation)* duty; **présenter ses devoirs à qn** to pay one's respects to sb; *Scol* **devoirs** homework; **faire ses devoirs** to do one's homework; **d. sur table** class examination

dévolu, -ue [devɔly] **1** *adj* **d. à qn** *(pouvoirs, tâche)* assigned to sb
2 *nm* **jeter son d. sur qn/qch** to set one's heart on sb/sth

dévorer [devɔre] *vt (manger)* to devour; *Fig (kilomètres)* to eat up; **d. qn/qch du regard** to devour sb/sth with one's eyes; **être dévoré par la jalousie** to be consumed by jealousy ● **dévorant, -ante** *adj (faim)* ravenous; *(passion)* devouring

dévot, -ote [devo, -ɔt] **1** *adj* devout
2 *nmf* devout person ● **dévotion** *nf (adoration)* devotion

dévouer [devwe] **se dévouer** *vpr (se sacrifier)* to volunteer; *(se consacrer)* to devote oneself (**à** to) ● **dévoué, -ée** *adj (ami, femme)* devoted (**à** to) ● **dévouement** [-umã] *nm* devotion; *(de héros)* devotion to duty

dévoyé, -ée [devwaje] *adj & nmf* delinquent

dextérité [dɛksterite] *nf* dexterity, skill

diabète [djabɛt] *nm Méd* diabetes; **avoir du d.** to have diabetes ● **diabétique** *adj & nmf* diabetic

diable [djɑbl] *nm* devil; **le d.** the Devil; **habiter au d.** to live miles from anywhere; **faire qch à la d.** to do something anyhow; **se débattre comme un beau d.** to struggle with all one's might; **tirer le d. par la queue** to live from hand to mouth; **c'est bien le d. si** I'll be damned if; **quel d., cet enfant!** what a little devil that child is!; **où/pourquoi d....?** where/why the devil...? ● **diabolique** *adj* diabolical

diadème [djadɛm] *nm* tiara

diagnostic [djagnɔstik] *nm* diagnosis ● **diagnostiquer** *vt* to diagnose

diagonal, -e, -aux, -ales [djagɔnal, -o] *adj* diagonal ● **diagonale** *nf* diagonal (line); **en d.** diagonally; *Fam* **lire qch en d.** to skim through sth

diagramme [djagram] *nm* diagram

dialecte [djalɛkt] *nm* dialect

dialogue [djalɔg] *nm Br* dialogue, *Am* dialog; *(conversation)* conversation ● **dialoguer** *vi* to communicate; *Ordinat* to interact

dialyse [djaliz] *nf Méd* dialysis

diamant [djamã] *nm* diamond

diamètre [djamɛtr] *nm* diameter ● **diamétralement** *adv* **d. opposés** diametrically opposed

diapason [djapazɔ̃] *nm Mus (appareil)* tuning fork; *Fig* **se mettre au d.** to fall in with the others

diaphane [djafan] *adj* diaphanous

diaphragme [djafragm] *nm* diaphragm

diapositive, *Fam* **diapo** [djapozitiv, djapo] *nf* slide

diarrhée [djare] *nf* diarrhoea; **avoir la d.** to have diarrhoea

diatribe [djatrib] *nf* diatribe

dictateur [diktatœr] *nm* dictator ● **dictatorial, -e, -aux, -ales** *adj* dictatorial ● **dictature** *nf* dictatorship

dicter [dikte] *vt* to dictate (**à** to) ● **dictée** *nf* dictation; **prendre qch sous la d. de qn** to take sth down at sb's dictation ● **Dictaphone**® *nm* dictaphone®

diction [diksjɔ̃] *nf* diction

dictionnaire [diksjɔnɛr] *nm* dictionary

dicton [diktɔ̃] *nm* saying

didactique [didaktik] *adj* didactic

dièse [djɛz] *adj & nm Mus* sharp

diesel [djezɛl] *adj & nm* **(moteur) d.** diesel (engine)

diète [djɛt] *nf (partielle)* diet; *(totale)* fast; **être à la d.** to be on a diet/to be fasting

diététicien, -ienne [djetetisjɛ̃, -jɛn] *nmf*

dietician • **diététique 1** *nf* dietetics *(sing)*
2 *adj* **aliment** *ou* **produit d.** health food;
magasin/restaurant d. health-food
shop/restaurant
dieu, -x [djø] *nm* god; **D.** God; **le bon D.**
God; **on lui donnerait le bon D. sans
confession** butter wouldn't melt in his
mouth; **D. seul le sait!** God only knows!;
D. merci! thank God!, thank goodness!;
Fam **laisse-moi tranquille, bon D.!** leave
me alone, for God's sake!
diffamation [difamɑsjɔ̃] *nf (en paroles)*
slander; *(par écrit)* libel; **procès en d.**
slander/libel trial • **diffamatoire** *adj (paroles)* slanderous; *(écrit)* libellous
différé [difere] *nm* **en d.** *(émission)* pre-
recorded
différence [diferɑ̃s] *nf* difference (**de** in);
à la d. de qn/qch unlike sb/sth; **faire la d.
entre** to make a distinction between
différencier [diferɑ̃sje] **1** *vt* to differentiate (**de** from)
　　2 se différencier *vpr* to differ (**de** from)
différend [diferɑ̃] *nm* difference of opinion
différent, -ente [diferɑ̃, -ɑ̃t] *adj* different; **différents** *(divers)* different, various;
d. de different from • **différemment**
[-amɑ̃] *adv* differently (**de** from)
différentiel, -ielle [diferɑ̃sjɛl] *adj* differ-
ential
différer [difere] **1** *vt (remettre)* to postpone; *(paiement)* to defer
　　2 *vi* to differ (**de** from)
difficile [difisil] *adj* difficult; *(exigeant)*
fussy; **c'est d. à faire** it's hard *or* difficult to
do; **il nous est d. d'accepter** it's hard *or*
difficult for us to accept • **difficilement**
adv with difficulty; **d. lisible** not easy to
read
difficulté [difikylte] *nf* difficulty (**à faire**
in doing); **en d.** in a difficult situation;
avoir de la d. à faire qch to have difficulty
(in) doing sth
difforme [difɔrm] *adj* deformed, misshapen • **difformité** *nf* deformity
diffus, -use [dify, -yz] *adj (lumière)* diffuse; *(impression)* vague
diffuser [difyze] *vt (émission)* to broadcast; *(nouvelle)* to spread; *(lumière, chaleur)* to diffuse; *(livre)* to distribute
• **diffusion** *nf (d'émission)* broadcasting;
(de lumière, de chaleur) diffusion; *(de
livre)* distribution
digérer [diʒere] **1** *vt* to digest; *Fam (endurer)* to stomach
　　2 *vi* to digest; **avoir du mal à d.** to have
trouble digesting • **digeste** *adj* easily digestible

digestif, -ive [diʒɛstif, -iv] **1** *adj (tube,
sucs)* digestive
　　2 *nmf* after-dinner liqueur
digestion [diʒɛstjɔ̃] *nf* digestion
Digicode® [diʒikɔd] *nm* door code *(for
entrance to building)*
digitale [diʒital] *adj f* **empreinte d.**
fingerprint
digne [diɲ] *adj (air, attitude)* dignified; **d.
de qn/qch** worthy of sb/sth; **d. d'admiration** worthy of *or* deserving of admiration; **d. de foi** reliable; **il n'est pas d.
d'exister** he's not fit to live • **dignement**
[-əmɑ̃] *adv* with dignity; **être d. récom-
pensé** to be justly rewarded
dignitaire [diɲitɛr] *nm* dignitary
dignité [diɲite] *nf* dignity
digression [digrɛsjɔ̃] *nf* digression
digue [dig] *nf* dike, dyke; *(en bord de mer)*
sea wall
dilapider [dilapide] *vt* to squander
dilater [dilate] *vt*, **se dilater** *vpr (pupille)*
to dilate • **dilatation** *nf (de pupille)* dilation
dilatoire [dilatwar] *adj* **manœuvre d.**
delaying tactic
dilemme [dilɛm] *nm* dilemma
dilettante [diletɑ̃t] *nmf* dilettante; **faire
qch en d.** to dabble in sth
diligence [diliʒɑ̃s] *nf (rapidité)* speedy
efficiency; *(véhicule)* stagecoach • **diligent, -ente** *adj (prompt)* speedy and efficient; *(soin)* diligent
diluer [dilɥe] *vt (liquide, substance)* to
dilute (**dans** in) • **dilution** *nf* dilution
diluvienne [dilyvjɛn] *adj f* **pluie d.** torrential rain
dimanche [dimɑ̃ʃ] *nm* Sunday
dimension [dimɑ̃sjɔ̃] *nf (mesure, aspect)*
dimension; *(taille)* size; **à deux dimensions** two-dimensional; **prendre les dimensions de qch** to take the
measurements of sth
diminuer [diminɥe] **1** *vt* to reduce, to
decrease; *(affaiblir)* to weaken; **d. qn**
(rabaisser) to belittle sb; **il est très dimi-
nué depuis l'accident** he has been far less
able-bodied since the accident
　　2 *vi (réserves, nombre)* to decrease, to
diminish; *(jours)* to get shorter; *(prix,
profits)* to decrease, to drop • **diminution**
nf reduction, decrease (**de** in)
diminutif, -ive [diminytif, -iv] *nm (nom)*
diminutive
dinde [dɛ̃d] *nf (volaille, viande)* turkey
• **dindon** *nm* turkey (cock); *Fig* **être le d.
de la farce** to be made a fool of
dîner [dine] **1** *nm (repas du soir)* dinner;

(repas de midi) lunch; *(soirée)* dinner party

2 *vi* to have dinner; *(au Canada, en Belgique)* to (have) lunch

dînette [dinɛt] *nf (jouet)* doll's teaset; **jouer à la d.** to have a doll's tea party

dingue [dɛ̃g] *Fam* **1** *adj* crazy, nuts; **être d. de qn/qch** to be crazy about sb/sth

2 *nmf* nutcase; **être un d. de moto** to be a motorbike nut

dinosaure [dinozɔr] *nm* dinosaur

diocèse [djɔsɛz] *nm Rel* diocese

diphtérie [difteri] *nf Méd* diphtheria

diphtongue [diftɔ̃g] *nf* diphthong

diplomate [diplɔmat] **1** *adj* diplomatic

2 *nmf* diplomat ● **diplomatie** [-asi] *nf (tact)* diplomacy; *(carrière)* diplomatic service ● **diplomatique** *adj* diplomatic

diplôme [diplom] *nm* diploma; *(d'université)* degree ● **diplômé, -ée 1** *adj* qualified; *Univ* **être d. (de)** to be a graduate (of) **2** *nmf* holder of a diploma; *Univ* graduate

dire* [dir] **1** *nm* **au d. de** according to; **selon ses dires** according to him/her

2 *vt (mot, avis)* to say; *(vérité, secret, heure)* to tell; **d. des bêtises** to talk nonsense; **d. qch à qn** to tell sb sth, to say sth to sb; **d. à qn que...** to tell sb that..., to say to sb that...; **elle dit que tu mens** she says (that) you're lying; **d. à qn de faire qch** to tell sb to do sth; **d. du mal/du bien de qn** to speak ill/well of sb; **on dirait un château** it looks like a castle; **on dirait du Mozart** it sounds like Mozart; **on dirait du cabillaud** it tastes like cod; **que diriez-vous d'un verre de vin?** what would you say to a glass of wine?; **qu'est-ce que tu en dis?** what do you think?; **on dirait que...** it would seem that...; **ça ne me dit rien de manger chinois** I don't really fancy Chinese food; **ce nom ne me dit rien** that name doesn't ring a bell; **ça ne me dit rien qui vaille** I don't like the look of it; **ça vous dit de rester?** do you feel like staying?; **ça va sans d.** that goes without saying; **c'est beaucoup d.** that's going too far; **dites donc!** look here!; **autrement dit** in other words; **ceci dit** having said this; **à vrai d.** to tell the truth; **à l'heure dite** at the agreed time

3 se dire *vpr* **il se dit malade** he says he's ill; **comment ça se dit en anglais?** how do you say that in English?

direct, -e [dirɛkt] **1** *adj* direct

2 *nm Radio & TV* live broadcasting; **en d. (de)** live (from); *Boxe* **d. du gauche** straight left ● **directement** [-əmɑ̃] *adv*

(sans intermédiaire) directly; *(sans détour)* straight

directeur, -trice [dirɛktœr, -tris] **1** *nmf* director; *(de magasin, de service)* manager; *(de journal)* editor; *(d'école)* *Br* headmaster, *f* headmistress, *Am* principal; **d. commercial** sales director

2 *adj (principe)* guiding; *(idées)* main; *(équipe)* management

direction [dirɛksjɔ̃] *nf* **(a)** *(sens)* direction; **train en d. de...** train to **(b)** *(de société, de club)* running, management; *(de parti)* leadership; *Aut* steering; **prendre la d. de** *(parti)* to take charge of; **sous la d. de** under the supervision of; *(orchestre)* conducted by; **la d.** *(l'équipe dirigeante)* the management; **un poste de d.** a management post; **d. du personnel** personnel department

directive [dirɛktiv] *nf* directive

dirigeable [diriʒabl] *adj & nm* **(ballon) d.** airship, dirigible

dirigeant, -ante [diriʒɑ̃, -ɑ̃t] **1** *adj (classe)* ruling

2 *nm (de pays)* leader; *(d'entreprise, de club)* manager

diriger [diriʒe] **1** *vt (entreprise, club)* to run, to manage; *(pays, parti, cheval)* to lead; *(séance, orchestre)* to conduct; *(travaux, études)* to supervise; *(acteur)* to direct; *(orienter)* to turn (**vers** to); *(arme, lumière)* to point (**sur** at); *(véhicule)* to steer

2 se diriger *vpr* **se d. vers** *(lieu, objet)* to head for; *(personne)* to go up to; *(dans une carrière)* to go into ● **dirigisme** *nm* state control

dis, disant [di, dizɑ̃] *voir* **dire**

discerner [disɛrne] *vt (voir)* to make out; *(différencier)* to distinguish (**de** from) ● **discernement** [-əmɑ̃] *nm* discernment; **sans d.** rashly

disciple [disipl] *nm* disciple

discipline [disiplin] *nf (règle, matière)* discipline ● **disciplinaire** *adj* disciplinary

discipliner [disipline] **1** *vt (enfant)* to control

2 se discipliner *vpr* to discipline oneself ● **discipliné, -ée** *adj* well-disciplined

discontinu, -ue [diskɔ̃tiny] *adj (ligne)* broken; *(bruit)* intermittent ● **discontinuer** *vi* **sans d.** without stopping

disconvenir* [diskɔ̃vnir] *vi Littéraire* **je n'en disconviens pas** I don't deny it

discorde [diskɔrd] *nf* discord ● **discordant, -ante** *adj (son)* discordant; *(témoignages)* conflicting; *(couleurs)* clashing

discothèque [diskɔtɛk] *nf (organisme)*

record library; *(club)* disco; **aller en d.** to go to a disco

discours [diskur] *nm* speech; *(écrit littéraire)* discourse; **faire un d.** to make a speech; **tenir de longs d. à qn sur qch** to go on and on to sb about sth

discrédit [diskredi] *nm* discredit; **jeter le d. sur qn** to bring discredit on sb

discréditer [diskredite] **1** *vt* to discredit **2 se discréditer** *vpr (personne)* to discredit oneself

discret, -ète [diskrɛ, -ɛt] *adj (personne, manière)* discreet; *(vêtement)* simple • **discrètement** *adv (avec retenue)* discreetly; *(sobrement)* simply

discrétion [diskresjɔ̃] *nf* discretion; **laisser qch à la d. de qn** to leave sth to sb's discretion; **vin à d.** unlimited

discrimination [diskriminasjɔ̃] *nf* discrimination • **discriminatoire** *adj* discriminatory

disculper [diskylpe] *vt* to exonerate (**de** from)

discussion [diskysjɔ̃] *nf* discussion; **avoir une d. (sur)** to have a discussion (about); **pas de d.!** no argument!

discutable [diskytabl] *adj* questionable

discuter [diskyte] **1** *vt* to discuss; *(contester)* to question **2** *vi* to discuss; *(protester)* to argue; **d. de qch avec qn** to discuss sth with sb **3 se discuter** *vpr* **ça se discute** that's debatable

dise, disent [diz] *voir* **dire**

disette [dizɛt] *nf* food shortage

diseuse [dizøz] *nf* **d. de bonne aventure** fortune-teller

disgrace [disgras] *nf* **tomber en d.** to fall into disfavour • **disgracier** *vt* to disgrace • **disgracieux, -ieuse** *adj* ungainly

> ⚠ Il faut noter que l'adjectif anglais **disgraceful** est un faux ami. Il signifie **honteux**.

disjoindre* [disʒwɛ̃dr] *vt* to separate • **disjoint, -ointe** *adj* separated

disjoncter [disʒɔ̃kte] *vi (circuit électrique)* to fuse; *Fam (s'effondrer)* to crack up • **disjoncteur** *nm* circuit breaker

dislocation [dislɔkasjɔ̃] *nf (de membre)* dislocation

disloquer [dislɔke] **1** *vt (membre)* to dislocate; *(empire)* to break up **2 se disloquer** *vpr (empire)* to break up; **se d. le bras** to dislocate one's arm

disons [dizɔ̃] *voir* **dire**

disparaître* [disparɛtr] *vi* to disappear; *(être porté manquant)* to go missing; *(mourir)* to die; *(coutume)* to die out; **d. en mer** to be lost at sea; **faire d. qch** to get rid of sth • **disparition** *nf* disappearance; *(mort)* death • **disparu, -ue** *adj (personne)* missing; **être porté d.** to be reported missing **2** *nmf (absent)* missing person; *(mort)* departed

disparate [disparat] *adj* ill-assorted

disparité [disparite] *nf* disparity (**entre, de** between)

dispensaire [dispãsɛr] *nm* community health centre

dispense [dispãs] **1** *nf (d'obligation)* exemption • **dispenser** *vt (soins, bienfaits)* to dispense; **d. qn de qch** to exempt sb from sth; **d. qn de faire qch** to exempt sb from doing sth; **je vous dispense de vos réflexions** you can keep your comments to yourselves **2** *vpr* **se d. de faire qch** to get out of sth; **se d. de faire qch** to get out of doing sth

disperser [dispɛrse] **1** *vt (papiers, foule)* to scatter; *(brouillard)* to disperse; *(collection)* to break up **2 se disperser** *vpr (foule)* to scatter, to disperse; **elle se disperse trop** she tries to do too many things at once • **dispersion** *nf (d'armée, de manifestants, de brouillard)* dispersal

disponible [dispɔnibl] *adj (article, place, personne)* available; **es-tu d. ce soir?** are you free tonight? • **disponibilité** *nf* availability; **disponibilités** *(fonds)* available funds; **être en d.** *(fonctionnaire)* to be on leave of absence

dispos [dispo] *adj m (personne)* fit and well; **frais et d.** hale and hearty

disposé, -ée [dispoze] *adj* **bien/mal d.** in a good/bad mood; **bien d. envers** *ou* à l'égard de qn well disposed towards sb; **d. à faire qch** disposed to do sth

disposer [dispoze] **1** *vt (objets)* to arrange; *(table)* to lay; **d. qn à (faire) qch** to dispose sb to (do) sth **2** *vi* **d. de qch** to have sth at one's disposal **3 se disposer** *vpr* **se d. à faire qch** to prepare to do sth

dispositif [dispozitif] *nm (mécanisme)* device; **d. policier** police presence

disposition [dispozisjɔ̃] *nf* arrangement; *(tendance)* tendency (**à** to); *(de maison, de page)* layout; *Jur (de loi)* clause; **être** *ou* **rester** *ou* **se tenir à la d. de qn** to be *or* remain at sb's disposal; **dispositions** *(aptitudes)* ability, aptitude (**pour** for); **prendre ses** *ou* **des dispositions** to make arrangements; *(pour l'avenir)* to make

provision; **dans de bonnes dispositions à l'égard de qn** well disposed towards sb
disproportion [dispʀɔpɔʀsjɔ̃] *nf* disproportion • **disproportionné, -ée** *adj* disproportionate
dispute [dispyt] *nf* quarrel • **disputer 1** *vt* (*match*) to play; (*rallye*) to compete in; (*combat de boxe*) to fight; (*droit*) to contest; **d. qch à qn** (*prix, première place*) to fight with sb for *or* over sth; *Fam* **d. qn** (*gronder*) to tell sb off **2 se disputer** *vpr* to quarrel (**avec** with); (*match*) to take place; **se d. qch** to fight over sth
disqualifier [diskalifje] *vt* (*équipe, athlète*) to disqualify • **disqualification** *nf* disqualification
disque [disk] *nm* (*de musique*) record; (*cercle*) *Br* disc, *Am* disk; *Ordinat* disk; *Sport* discus; **mettre un d.** to play a record; **d. compact** compact *Br* disc *or Am* disk; **d. dur** hard disk • **disquaire** *nmf* record dealer • **disquette** *nf* *Ordinat* floppy (disk), diskette
dissection [diseksjɔ̃] *nf* dissection
dissemblable [disɑ̃mblabl] *adj* dissimilar (**à** to)
disséminer [disemine] *vt* (*graines, mines*) to scatter • **dissémination** *nf* scattering
dissension [disɑ̃sjɔ̃] *nf* dissension
disséquer [diseke] *vt* to dissect
disserter [diserte] *vi* **d. sur qch** to discourse on sth; (*écrire*) to write about sth • **dissertation** *nf* essay
dissident, -ente [disidɑ̃, -ɑ̃t] *adj & nmf* dissident • **dissidence** *nf* dissidence
dissimuler [disimyle] **1** *vt* (*cacher*) to conceal (**à** from)
2 se dissimuler *vpr* to be hidden • **dissimulation** *nf* concealment; (*duplicité*) deceit
dissipation [disipasjɔ̃] *nf* (*de brouillard, de malentendu*) clearing; (*indiscipline*) misbehaviour; *Littéraire* (*débauche*) dissipation
dissiper [disipe] **1** *vt* (*nuages*) to disperse; (*brouillard*) to clear; (*malentendu*) to clear up; (*craintes*) to dispel; **d. qn** to lead sb astray
2 se dissiper *vpr* (*nuage*) to disperse; (*brume*) to clear; (*craintes*) to vanish; (*élève*) to misbehave • **dissipé, -ée** *adj* (*élève*) unruly
dissocier [disɔsje] *vt* to dissociate (**de** from)
dissolu, -ue [disɔly] *adj* (*vie*) dissolute
dissolution [disɔlysjɔ̃] *nf* dissolution
dissolvant, -ante [disɔlvɑ̃, -ɑ̃t] *adj & nm*

(*produit*) **d.** solvent; (*pour vernis à ongles*) nail polish remover
dissoudre* [disudʀ] *vt*, **se dissoudre** *vpr* to dissolve
dissuader [disɥade] *vt* to dissuade (**de qch** from sth; **de faire** from doing) • **dissuasif, -ive** *adj* deterrent; **avoir un effet d.** to be a deterrent • **dissuasion** *nf* dissuasion; *Mil* **force de d.** deterrent
distance [distɑ̃s] *nf* distance; **à deux mètres de d.** two metres apart; **à d.** at *or* from a distance; **garder ses distances** to keep one's distance (**vis-à-vis de** from); **tenir qn à d.** to keep sb at a distance; **commandé à d.** remote-controlled; **à quelle d. se trouve la poste?** how far is it to the post office?
distancer [distɑ̃se] *vt* to outstrip; **se laisser d.** to fall behind
distant, -ante [distɑ̃, -ɑ̃t] *adj* distant; (*personne*) aloof, distant; **d. de dix kilomètres** (*éloigné*) ten kilometres away; (*à intervalles*) ten kilometres apart
distendre [distɑ̃dʀ] *vt*, **se distendre** *vpr* to stretch
distiller [distile] *vt* to distil • **distillation** *nf* distillation • **distillerie** *nf* (*lieu*) distillery
distinct, -incte [distɛ̃, -ɛ̃kt] *adj* (*différent*) distinct, separate (**de** from); (*net*) clear, distinct • **distinctement** [-əmɑ̃] *adv* distinctly, clearly • **distinctif, -ive** *adj* distinctive • **distinction** *nf* (*différence, raffinement*) distinction
distinguer [distɛ̃ge] **1** *vt* (*différencier*) to distinguish; (*voir*) to make out; (*choisir*) to single out; **d. le bien du mal** to tell good from evil
2 se distinguer *vpr* (*s'illustrer*) to distinguish oneself; **se d. de qn/qch (par)** to be distinguishable from sb/sth (by); **se d. par sa beauté** to be conspicuous for one's beauty • **distingué, -ée** *adj* (*bien élevé, éminent*) distinguished
distorsion [distɔʀsjɔ̃] *nf* distortion
distraction [distʀaksjɔ̃] *nf* (*étourderie*) absent-mindedness; **ça manque de distractions** there's nothing to do • **distraire*** **1** *vt* (*divertir*) to entertain; **d. qn (de qch)** to distract sb (from sth) **2 se distraire** *vpr* to amuse oneself • **distrait, -aite** *adj* absent-minded • **distraitement** *adv* absent-mindedly • **distrayant, -ante** *adj* entertaining

> *Il faut noter que l'adjectif anglais **distracted** est un faux ami. Il signifie **préoccupé**.*

distribuer [distribɥe] *vt (donner) & Com* to distribute; *(courrier)* to deliver; *(cartes)* to deal; *(tâches)* to allocate; *(eau)* to supply

distributeur [distribytœr] *nm Com* distributor; **d. automatique** vending machine; **d. de billets** *(de train)* ticket machine; *(de billets de banque)* cash machine

distribution [distribysjɔ̃] *nf* distribution; *(du courrier)* delivery; *(de l'eau)* supply; *(acteurs de cinéma)* cast; **d. des prix** prizegiving

district [distrikt] *nm* district

dit¹, dite [di, dit] **1** *pp de* **dire**
2 *adj (convenu)* agreed; *(surnommé)* called

dit², dites [di, dit] *voir* **dire**

divaguer [divage] *vi (dérailler)* to rave •**divagations** *nfpl* ravings

divan [divɑ̃] *nm* divan, couch

divergent, -ente [diverʒɑ̃, -ɑ̃t] *adj (lignes)* divergent; *(opinions)* differing •**divergence** *nf (de lignes)* divergence; *(d'opinions)* difference •**diverger** *vi* to diverge (**de** from)

divers, -erse [diver, -ɛrs] *adj (varié)* varied; **divers(es)** *(plusieurs)* various •**diversement** [-əmɑ̃] *adv* in various ways

diversifier [diversifje] *vt*, **se diversifier** *vpr* to diversify

diversion [diversjɔ̃] *nf* diversion; **faire d.** to create a diversion

diversité [diversite] *nf* diversity

divertir [divertir] **1** *vt* to entertain
2 se divertir *vpr* to enjoy oneself •**divertissement** *nm* entertainment, amusement

dividende [dividɑ̃d] *nm Math & Fin* dividend

divin, -ine [divɛ̃, -in] *adj* divine •**divinité** *nf* divinity

diviser [divize] *vt*, **se diviser** *vpr* to divide (**en** into) •**divisible** *adj* divisible •**division** *nf* division

divorce [divɔrs] *nm* divorce •**divorcer** *vi* to get divorced; **d. d'avec qn** to divorce sb •**divorcé, -ée 1** *adj* divorced (**d'avec** from) **2** *nmf* divorcee

divulguer [divylge] *vt* to divulge •**divulgation** *nf* disclosure

dix [dis] ([di] *before consonant,* [diz] *before vowel)* *adj & nm* ten •**dixième** [dizjɛm] *adj & nmf* tenth; **un d.** a tenth •**dix-huit** *adj & nm* eighteen •**dix-huitième** *adj & nmf* eighteenth •**dix-neuf** [diznœf] *adj & nm* nineteen •**dix-neuvième** *adj & nmf* nineteenth •**dix-**

sept [disɛt] *adj & nm* seventeen •**dix-septième** *adj & nmf* seventeenth

dizaine [dizen] *nf* **une d. (de)** about ten

do [do] *nm inv (note)* C

docile [dɔsil] *adj* docile •**docilité** *nf* docility

dock [dɔk] *nm (bassin)* dock; *(magasin)* warehouse •**docker** [dɔkɛr] *nm* docker

docteur [dɔktœr] *nm (en médecine, d'université)* doctor (**ès, en** of) •**doctorat** *nm* doctorate, ≃ PhD (**ès/en** in)

doctrine [dɔktrin] *nf* doctrine

document [dɔkymɑ̃] *nm* document •**documentaire** *adj & nm* documentary •**documentaliste** *nmf* archivist; *(à l'école)* (school) librarian

documentation [dɔkymɑ̃tasjɔ̃] *nf (documents)* documentation, *(brochures)* literature •**documenté, -ée** *adj (personne)* well-informed; **un article solidement d.** a well-documented article •**se documenter** *vpr* to gather information *or* material (**sur** on)

dodeliner [dɔdline] *vi* **d. de la tête** to nod (one's head)

dodo [dodo] *nm Langage enfantin* **faire d.** to sleep; **aller au d.** to go beddy-byes

dodu, -ue [dɔdy] *adj* chubby, plump

dogme [dɔgm] *nm* dogma •**dogmatique** *adj* dogmatic •**dogmatisme** *nm* dogmatism

dogue [dɔg] *nm (chien)* mastiff

doigt [dwa] *nm* finger; **d. de pied** toe; **petit d.** little finger; *Am & Scot* pinkie; **un d. de vin** a drop of wine; **à deux doigts de** within an ace of; **montrer qn du d.** to point one's finger at sb; **savoir qch sur le bout du d.** to have sth at one's finger tips; **elle ne lèvera pas le petit d. pour vous aider** she won't lift a finger to help you; **c'est mon petit d. qui me l'a dit** a little birdie told me

doigté [dwate] *nm Mus* fingering; *(savoir-faire)* tact

dois, doit [dwa] *voir* **devoir¹,²**

doléances [dɔleɑ̃s] *nfpl (plaintes)* grievances

dollar [dɔlar] *nm* dollar

domaine [dɔmen] *nm (terres)* estate, domain; *(matière)* field, domain; **être du d. public** to be in the public domain

dôme [dom] *nm* dome

domestique [dɔmɛstik] **1** *adj (vie, marché, produit, querelle)* domestic; **travaux domestiques** housework; **à usage d.** for domestic use
2 *nmf* servant •**domestiquer** *vt* to domesticate

domicile [dɔmisil] *nm* home; *(demeure légale)* abode; **travailler à d.** to work from home; **livrer à d.** to deliver (to the house); **dernier d. connu** last known address; **sans d. fixe** of no fixed abode; *Jur* **d. conjugal** marital home ● **domicilié, -ée** *adj* resident (**à/chez** at)

dominateur, -trice [dɔminatœr, -tris] *adj* domineering ● **domination** *nf* domination

dominer [dɔmine] **1** *vt* to dominate; *(situation, sentiment)* to master; *(être supérieur à)* to surpass; **d. la situation** to keep the situation under control; **d. le monde** to rule the world

2 *vi (être le plus fort)* to be dominant; *(être le plus important)* to predominate

3 se dominer *vpr* to control oneself ● **dominant, -ante** *adj* dominant ● **dominante** *nf* dominant feature

dominicain, -aine [dɔminikɛ̃, -ɛn] **1** *adj* & *nmf Rel* Dominican

2 *adj Géog* Dominican; **la République dominicaine** the Dominican Republic

3 *nmf* **D., Dominicaine** Dominican

dominical, -e, -aux, -ales [dɔminikal, -o] *adj* **repos d.** Sunday rest

domino [dɔmino] *nm* domino; **dominos** *(jeu)* dominoes

dommage [dɔmaʒ] *nm (tort)* harm; **dommages** *(dégâts)* damage; **(c'est) d.!** it's a pity, it's a shame! **(que** that); **quel d.!** what a pity, what a shame!; **c'est (bien) d. qu'elle ne soit pas venue** it's a (great) pity *or* shame she didn't come; **dommages-intérêts** damages

dompter [dɔ̃te] *vt (animal)* to tame; *(passions, rebelles)* to subdue ● **dompteur, -euse** *nmf* tamer

DOM-TOM [dɔmtɔm] *(abrév* **départements et territoires d'outre-mer**) *nmpl* = French overseas departments and territories

don [dɔ̃] *nm (cadeau, aptitude)* gift; *(à un musée, à une œuvre)* donation; **faire d. de qch** to give sth; **avoir le d. de faire qch** to have the knack for doing sth; **d. du sang** blood donation

donateur, -trice [dɔnatœr, -tris] *nmf* donor ● **donation** *nf* donation

donc [dɔ̃(k)] *conj* so, then; *(par conséquent)* so, therefore; **asseyez-vous d.!** *(intensif)* do sit down!; **qui/quoi d.?** who?/what?; **allons d.!** come on!; *Fam* **dis d.!** excuse me!

donjon [dɔ̃ʒɔ̃] *nm* keep

donne [dɔn] *nf Cartes* deal

données [dɔne] *nfpl Ordinat* data; *(de*

problème) facts; **avoir toutes les données du problème** to have all the information on the problem

donner [dɔne] **1** *vt* to give; *(récolte, résultat)* to produce; *(sa place)* to give up; *(cartes)* to deal; *(pièce, film)* to put on; **pourriez-vous me d. l'heure?** could you tell me the time?; **d. un coup à qn** to hit sb; **d. le bonjour à qn** to say hello to sb; **d. qch à réparer** to take sth (in) to be repaired; **d. à manger à qn** *(animal, enfant)* to feed sb; **d. raison à qn** to say sb is right; **elle m'a donné de ses nouvelles** she told me how she was doing; **ça donne soif/faim** it makes you thirsty/hungry; **je lui donne trente ans** I'd say he/she was thirty; **ça n'a rien donné** *(efforts)* it hasn't got us anywhere; *Fam* **c'est donné** it's dirt cheap; **étant donné** *(la situation)* considering, in view of; **étant donné que...** seeing (that), considering (that)...; **à un moment donné** at some stage

2 *vi* **d. sur** *(fenêtre)* to overlook, to look out onto; *(porte)* to open onto; **d. dans** *(piège)* to fall into; *Fam* **ne plus savoir où d. de la tête** not to know which way to turn

3 se donner *vpr (se consacrer)* to devote oneself (**à** to); **se d. du mal** to go to a lot of trouble (**pour faire** to do); **s'en d. à cœur joie** to have a whale of a time

donneur, -euse [dɔnœr, -øz] *nmf (de sang, d'organe)* donor; *Cartes* dealer

dont [dɔ̃] (= **de qui, duquel, de quoi**) *pron relatif (personne)* of whom; *(chose)* of which; *(appartenance: personne)* whose, of whom; *(appartenance: chose)* of which, whose; **une mère d. le fils est malade** a mother whose son is ill; **la fille d. il est fier** the daughter he is proud of *or* of whom he is proud; **les outils d. j'ai besoin** the tools I need; **la façon d. elle joue** the way (in which) she plays; **cinq enfants d. deux filles** five children two of whom are daughters, five children including two daughters; **voici ce d. il s'agit** here's what it's about

doper [dɔpe] **1** *vt* to dope

2 se doper *vpr* to take drugs ● **dopage** *nm (action)* doping; *(de sportif)* drug-taking

dorénavant [dɔrenavɑ̃] *adv* from now on

dorer [dɔre] **1** *vt (objet)* to gild; *Fig* **d. la pilule à qn** to sweeten the pill for sb

2 *vi (à la cuisson)* to brown

3 se dorer *vpr* **se d. au soleil** to sunbathe ● **doré, -ée** *adj (objet)* gilt, gold; *(couleur)* golden ● **dorure** *nf* gilding

dorloter [dɔrlɔte] *vt* to pamper, to coddle

dormir* [dɔrmir] *vi* to sleep; *(être endormi)* to be asleep; *Fig (argent)* to lie idle; **avoir envie de d.** to feel sleepy; **dormez tranquille!** set your mind at rest!, rest easy!; **histoire à d.** debout tall story, cock-and-bull story; **eau dormante** stagnant water

dortoir [dɔrtwar] *nm* dormitory

dos [do] *nm (de personne, d'animal)* back; *(de livre)* spine; **'voir au d.'** *(verso)* 'see over'; **voir qn de d.** to have a back view of sb; *Fam* **mettre qch sur le d. de qn** *(accuser qn)* to pin sth on sb; *Fam* **avoir qn sur le d.** to have sb on one's back; *Fam* **j'en ai plein le d.** I'm sick of it

dose [doz] *nf* dose; *(dans un mélange)* proportion; *Fig* **forcer la d.** to overdo it • **doser** *vt (médicament, ingrédients)* to measure out • **dosage** *nm (de médicament)* dosage; *(d'ingrédients)* proportioning • **doseur** *nm* **bouchon d.** measuring cap

dossard [dosar] *nm (de sportif)* number *(worn by player/competitor)*

dossier [dosje] *nm (de siège)* back; *(documents)* file, dossier; *(classeur)* folder, file

dot [dɔt] *nf* dowry

doter [dɔte] *vt (équiper)* to equip (**de** with); **elle est dotée d'une grande intelligence** she's endowed with great intelligence • **dotation** *nf (d'hôpital)* endowment

douane [dwan] *nf* customs; **passer la d.** to go through customs • **douanier, -ière 1** *nm* customs officer **2** *adj* **union douanière** customs union

doublage [dublaʒ] *nm (de film)* dubbing

double [dubl] **1** *adj* double; *(rôle, avantage)* twofold, double; **en d. exemplaire** in duplicate; **enfermer qn à d. tour** to lock sb in; **fermer une porte à d. tour** to double-lock a door; **doubles rideaux** lined curtains; *Am* (thick) drapes
2 *adv* double
3 *nm (de personne)* double; *(copie)* copy, duplicate; *(de timbre)* swap, duplicate; **le d. (de)** *(quantité)* twice as much (as); **je l'ai en d.** I have two of them • **doublement** [-əmã] **1** *adv* doubly **2** *nm (de nombres, de lettres)* doubling

doubler [duble] **1** *vt (augmenter)* to double; *(vêtement)* to line; *(film)* to dub; *(acteur)* to dub the voice of; *(classe à l'école)* to repeat; *(cap) (en bateau)* to round
2 *vi (augmenter)* to double; **d. de volume** to double in volume

3 *vti (en voiture) Br* to overtake, *Am* to pass
4 se doubler *vpr* **se d. de** to be coupled with

doublure [dublyr] *nf (étoffe)* lining; *(au théâtre)* understudy; *(au cinéma)* stand-in

douce [dus] *voir* **doux** • **doucement** *adv (délicatement)* gently; *(bas)* softly; *(lentement)* slowly; *(sans bruit)* quietly; *Fam (assez bien)* so-so • **douceur** *nf (de miel)* sweetness; *(de peau)* softness; *(de temps)* mildness; *(de personne)* gentleness; **douceurs** *(sucreries) Br* sweets, *Am* candies; **la voiture a démarré en d.** the car started smoothly

douche [duʃ] *nf* shower; **prendre une d.** to have or take a shower; **être sous la d.** to be in the shower • **doucher 1** *vt* **d. qn** to give sb a shower **2 se doucher** *vpr* to have or take a shower

doué, -ée [dwe] *adj* gifted, talented (**en** at); **d. de raison** gifted with reason; **être d. pour qch** to have a gift for sth

douille [duj] *nf (d'ampoule)* socket; *(de cartouche)* case

douillet, -ette [duje, -ɛt] *adj (lit) Br* cosy, *Am* cozy; **tu es d.** *(délicat)* you're such a baby

douleur [dulœr] *nf (mal)* pain; *(chagrin)* sorrow, grief • **douloureux, -euse** *adj (maladie, membre, décision, perte)* painful

doute [dut] *nm* doubt; **sans d.** no doubt, probably; **sans aucun d.** without (any) doubt; **mettre qch en d.** to cast doubt on sth; **dans le d.** doubtful; **ça ne fait pas de d.** there is no doubt about it

douter [dute] **1** *vi* to doubt; *Fam* **ne d. de rien** to have lots of or *Br* bags of self-confidence
2 *vt* **je doute qu'il soit assez fort** I doubt whether he's strong enough
3 se douter *vpr* **se d. de qch** to suspect sth; **je m'en doutais bien** I suspect as much

douteux, -euse [dutø, -øz] *adj* doubtful; *(louche, médiocre)* dubious

douve [duv] *nf (de château)* moat

Douvres [duvr] *nm ou f* Dover

doux, douce [du, dus] *adj (miel, son)* sweet; *(peau, lumière, drogue)* soft; *(temps, climat)* mild; *(personne, pente)* gentle; *(émotion, souvenir)* pleasant; **d. comme un agneau** as gentle as a lamb; *Fam* **faire qch en douce** to do sth on the quiet

douze [duz] *adj & nm* twelve • **douzaine** *nf (douze)* dozen; *(environ)* about twelve;

une **d. d'œufs** a dozen eggs •**douzième** *adj & nmf* twelfth; **un d.** a twelfth

doyen, -enne [dwajɛ̃, -ɛn] *nmf (d'université, ecclésiastique)* dean; **d. (d'âge)** oldest person

draconien, -ienne [drakɔnjɛ̃, -jɛn] *adj (mesures)* drastic

dragée [draʒe] *nf* sugared almond; *Fig* **tenir la d. haute à qn** to stand up to sb

dragon [dragɔ̃] *nm (animal, personne acariâtre)* dragon; *Hist (soldat)* dragoon

draguer [drage] *vt (rivière)* to dredge; *Fam* **d. qn** *Br* to chat sb up, *Am* to hit on sb

drainer [drene] *vt* to drain

dramaturge [dramatyrʒ] *nmf* dramatist

drame [dram] *nm (genre littéraire)* drama; *(catastrophe)* tragedy •**dramatique 1** *adj* dramatic; **critique d.** drama critic; **auteur d.** playwright, dramatist **2** *nf* drama •**dramatiser** *vt* to dramatize

> ⚠ Il faut noter que le nom anglais **drama** est un faux ami. Il s'utilise uniquement dans un contexte théâtral.

drap [dra] *nm (de lit)* sheet; *(tissu)* cloth; **d.-housse** fitted sheet; **d. de bain** bath towel; *Fam* **être dans de beaux draps** to be in a fine mess

drapeau, -x [drapo] *nm* flag; **être sous les drapeaux** *(soldat)* to be doing one's military service

draper [drape] **1** *vt* to drape (**de** with) **2 se draper** *vpr Fig* **se d. dans sa dignité** to stand on one's dignity

dresser [drese] **1** *vt (échelle, statue)* to put up, to erect; *(liste)* to draw up; *(piège)* to set, to lay; *(animal)* to train; **d. les oreilles** to prick up one's ears **2 se dresser** *vpr (personne)* to stand up; *(statue, montagne)* to rise up •**dressage** *nm* training •**dresseur, -euse** *nmf* trainer

dribbler [drible] *vi Football* to dribble

drogue [drɔg] *nf (stupéfiant)* drug; *Péj (médicament)* medicine; **d. dure/douce** hard/soft drug •**drogué, -ée** *nmf* drug addict •**droguer 1** *vt (victime)* to drug; *(malade)* to dose up **2 se droguer** *vpr* to take drugs

droguerie [drɔgri] *nf* hardware *Br* shop or *Am* store •**droguiste** *nmf* hardware dealer

droit¹ [drwa] *nm (privilège)* right; *(d'inscription)* fee(s); **le d.** *(science juridique)* law; **à bon d.** rightly; **avoir d. à qch** to be entitled to sth; **avoir le d. de faire qch** to be entitled to do sth, to have the right to do sth; **d. d'entrée** entrance fee; **droits d'auteur** royalties; **droits de douane** (customs) duty; **droits de l'homme** human rights

droit², droite¹ [drwa, drwat] **1** *adj (route, ligne)* straight; *(angle)* right; *(veston)* single-breasted; *Fig (honnête)* upright **2** *adv* straight; **tout d.** straight or right ahead; **aller d. au but** to go straight to the point •**droite²** *nf (ligne)* straight line

droit³, droite³ [drwa, drwat] **1** *adj (côté, bras)* right **2** *nm Boxe (coup)* right •**droite⁴** *nf* **la d.** *(côté)* the right (side); *Pol* the right (wing); **à d.** *(tourner)* (to the) right; *(rouler, se tenir)* on the right, on the right (-hand) side; **de d.** *(fenêtre)* right-hand; *(candidat)* right-wing; **voter à d.** to vote right-wing; **à d. de** on or to the right of; **à d. et à gauche** *(voyager)* here, there and everywhere

droitier, -ière [drwatje, -jɛr] **1** *adj* right-handed **2** *nmf* right-handed person

droiture [drwatyr] *nf* rectitude

drôle [drol] *adj* funny; **d. d'air/de type** funny look/fellow; **faire une d. de tête** to pull a face •**drôlement** *adv* funnily; *Fam (extrêmement)* terribly, dreadfully

dromadaire [drɔmader] *nm* dromedary

dru, drue [dry] **1** *adj (herbe)* thick, dense **2** *adv* **tomber d.** *(pluie)* to pour down heavily; **pousser d.** to grow thick(ly)

du [dy] *voir* **de¹,²**

dû, due [dy] **1** *adj* **d. à qch** due to sth; **en bonne et due forme** in due form **2** *nm* due

dualité [dɥalite] *nf* duality

dubitatif, -ive [dybitatif, -iv] *adj* doubtful

duc [dyk] *nm* duke •**duché** *nm* duchy •**duchesse** *nf* duchess

duel [dɥɛl] *nm* duel

dûment [dymã] *adv* duly

dune [dyn] *nf (sand)* dune

duo [dɥo] *nm Mus* duet; **d. comique** comic duo

dupe [dyp] **1** *adj* **être d. de** to be taken in by; **il n'est pas d.** he's well aware of it **2** *nf* dupe •**duper** *vt* to fool, to dupe

duplex [dyplɛks] *nm Br* maisonnette, *Am* duplex; *TV* **(émission en) d.** link-up

duplicata [dyplikata] *nm inv* duplicate

duplicité [dyplisite] *nf* duplicity

duquel [dykɛl] *voir* **lequel**

dur, dure [dyr] **1** *adj (substance)* hard; *(difficile)* hard, tough; *(viande)* tough; *(hiver, ton)* harsh; *(personne)* hard, harsh; *(œuf)* hard-boiled; *(brosse, carton)* stiff; **d. d'oreille** hard of hearing; *Fam* **d. à cuire** hard-bitten, tough

2 *adv (travailler)* hard; **croire à qch d. comme fer** to have a cast-iron belief in sth

3 *nm Fam (personne)* tough guy • **durement** *adv* harshly • **dureté** *nf (de substance)* hardness; *(d'hiver, de ton)* harshness; *(de viande)* toughness

durable [dyrabl] *adj* lasting

durant [dyrã] *prép* during; **d. l'hiver** during the winter; **des heures d.** for hours and hours

durcir [dyrsir] *vti*, **se durcir** *vpr* to harden • **durcissement** *nm* hardening

durée [dyre] *nf (de film, d'événement)* length; *(période)* duration; *(de pile électrique)* life; **de longue d.** *(bonheur)* lasting; **chômage de longue d.** long-term unemployment; **disque de longue d.** long-playing record; **pile longue d.** long-life battery; **de courte d.** *(attente)* short; *(bonheur)* short-lived

durer [dyre] *vi* to last; **ça dure depuis...** it's been going on for...

durillon [dyrijɔ̃] *nm (de la main)* callus; *(du pied)* corn

DUT [deyte] *(abrév* **diplôme universitaire de technologie***) nm* = post-baccalauréat technical qualification awarded after two years

duvet [dyvɛ] *nm (d'oiseau, de visage)* down; *(sac)* sleeping bag • **duveteux, -euse** *adj* downy

dynamique [dinamik] **1** *adj* dynamic **2** *nf (force)* dynamic force, thrust • **dynamisme** *nm* dynamism

dynamite [dinamit] *nf* dynamite • **dynamiter** *vt* to dynamite

dynamo [dinamo] *nf* dynamo

dynastie [dinasti] *nf* dynasty

dysenterie [disãtri] *nf Méd* dysentery

dyslexique [dislɛksik] *adj* dyslexic

E, e [ə] *nm inv* E, e

EAO [əao] (*abrév* **enseignement assisté par ordinateur**) *nm inv* CAL

eau, -x [o] *nf* water; **grandes eaux** (*d'un parc*) ornamental fountains; **tout en e.** sweating; **prendre l'e.** to let in water; *Fam* **tomber à l'e.** (*projet*) to fall through; **il est tombé beaucoup d'e.** a lot of rain fell; *Fig* **apporter de l'e. au moulin de qn** to strengthen sb's case; **ça lui fait venir l'e. à la bouche** it makes his/her mouth water; **sports d'e.** vive white water sports; **e. de Cologne** eau de Cologne; **e. de toilette** toilet water; **e. du robinet** tap water; **e. douce** fresh water; **e. plate** still water; **e. salée** salt water • **eau-de-vie** (*pl* **eaux-de-vie**) *nf* brandy • **eau-forte** (*pl* **eaux-fortes**) *nf* (*gravure*) etching

ébahir [ebair] *vt* to astound

ébattre [ebatr] **s'ébattre** *vpr* to frolic • **ébats** *nmpl* frolicking

ébauche [ebo∫] *nf* (*esquisse*) rough sketch; (*de roman*) outline; (*début*) beginnings; **l'e. d'un sourire** the ghost of a smile • **ébaucher** *vt* (*tableau, roman*) to rough out; (*lettre*) to draft; **e. un sourire** to give a faint smile

ébène [ebɛn] *nf* ebony

ébéniste [ebenist] *nm* cabinet maker

éberlué, -uée [ebɛrlɥe] *adj Fam* dumbfounded

éblouir [ebluir] *vt* to dazzle • **éblouissement** *nm* (*aveuglement*) dazzle; (*malaise*) fit of dizziness

éborgner [ebɔrɲe] *vt* **é. qn** to put sb's eye out

éboueur [ebwœr] *nm Br* dustman, *Am* garbage collector

ébouillanter [ebujɑ̃te] **1** *vt* to scald **2 s'ébouillanter** *vpr* to scald oneself

ébouler [ebule] **s'ébouler** *vpr* (*falaise*) to collapse; (*tunnel*) to cave in • **éboulement** *nm* (*écroulement*) collapse; (*de mine*) cave-in • **éboulis** *nm* (mass of) fallen debris

ébouriffé, -ée [eburife] *adj* dishevelled

ébranler [ebrɑ̃le] **1** *vt* (*mur, confiance, personne*) to shake; (*santé*) to weaken **2 s'ébranler** *vpr* (*train, cortège*) to move off

ébrécher [ebre∫e] *vt* (*assiette*) to chip; (*lame*) to nick

ébriété [ebrijete] *nf* **en état d'é.** under the influence of drink

ébrouer [ebrue] **s'ébrouer** *vpr* (*chien*) to shake itself; (*cheval*) to snort

ébruiter [ebrɥite] *vt* (*nouvelle*) to spread

EBS [øbeɛs] (*abrév* **encéphalite bovine spongiforme**) *nf* BSE

ébullition [ebylisjɔ̃] *nf* boiling; **être en é.** (*eau*) to be boiling; *Fig* (*ville*) to be in turmoil; **porter qch à é.** to bring sth to the boil

écaille [ekɑj] *nf* (*de poisson*) scale; (*de tortue, d'huître*) shell • **écailler 1** *vt* (*poisson*) to scale; (*huître*) to shell **2 s'écailler** *vpr* (*peinture*) to peel (off)

écarlate [ekarlat] *adj* scarlet

écarquiller [ekarkije] *vt* **é. les yeux** to open one's eyes wide

écart [ekar] *nm* (*intervalle*) gap, distance; (*différence*) difference (**de** in; **entre** between); **faire le grand é.** to do the splits; **à l'é.** out of the way; **tenir qn à l'é.** to keep sb out of things; **à l'é. de** away from; **écarts de conduite** misbehaviour; **écarts de langage** bad language

écartelé, -ée [ekartəle] *adj* **é. entre** (*tiraillé*) torn between

écartement [ekartəmɑ̃] *nm* (*espace*) gap, distance (**de** between)

écarter [ekarte] **1** *vt* (*objets, personnes*) to move apart; (*jambes, doigts*) to spread; (*rideaux*) to draw (back); (*crainte, idée*) to brush aside; (*candidat, proposition*) to turn down; **é. qch de qch** to move sth away from sth

2 s'écarter *vpr* (**a**) (*se séparer*) (*personnes*) to move apart (**de** from); (*foule*) to part (**b**) (*piéton*) to move away (**de** from); (*voiture*) to swerve; **s'é. du sujet** to wander from the subject • **écarté, -ée** *adj* (*endroit*) remote; **les jambes écartées** with his/her legs (wide) apart

ecchymose [ekimoz] *nf* bruise

ecclésiastique [eklezjastik] **1** *adj* ecclesiastical

2 *nm* clergyman

écervelé, -ée [esɛrvəle] **1** *adj* scatter-brained
  2 *nmf* scatterbrain
échafaud [eʃafo] *nm* scaffold
échafaudage [eʃafodaʒ] *nm* scaffolding; **des échafaudages** scaffolding •**échafauder** *vt (empiler)* to pile up
échalas [eʃala] *nm Fam* **grand é.** beanpole
échalote [eʃalɔt] *nf* shallot
échancré, -ée [eʃɑ̃kre] *adj* low-cut •**échancrure** *nf* low neckline
échange [eʃɑ̃ʒ] *nm* exchange; **en é.** in exchange (**de** for) •**échanger** *vt* to exchange (**contre** for)
échangeur [eʃɑ̃ʒœr] *nm* interchange
échantillon [eʃɑ̃tijɔ̃] *nm* sample •**échantillonnage** *nm (collection)* range of samples
échappatoire [eʃapatwar] *nf* way out
échappement [eʃapmɑ̃] *nm (de véhicule)* **tuyau d'é.** exhaust pipe; **pot d'é.** exhaust
échapper [eʃape] **1** *vi* **é. à qn** to escape from sb; **é. à la mort/un danger** to escape death/danger; **son nom m'échappe** his/her name escapes me; **ça m'a échappé** *(je n'ai pas compris)* I didn't catch it; **ça lui a échappé (des mains)** it slipped out of his/her hands; **laisser é.** *(cri)* to let out; *(objet, occasion)* to let slip
  2 *vt* **il l'a échappé belle** he had a narrow escape
  3 **s'échapper** *vpr (personne, gaz, eau)* to escape (**de** from) •**échappée** *nf (de cyclistes)* breakaway; *(vue)* vista
écharde [eʃard] *nf* splinter
écharpe [eʃarp] *nf* scarf; *(de maire)* sash; **avoir le bras en é.** to have one's arm in a sling
écharper [eʃarpe] *vt Fam* **é. qn** to cut sb to bits
échasse [eʃas] *nf (bâton)* stilt •**échassier** *nm* wader
échaudé, -ée [eʃode] *adj Fig* **être é.** to get one's fingers burnt
échauffer [eʃofe] **1** *vt (moteur)* to overheat; **é. les esprits** to get people worked up
  2 **s'échauffer** *vpr (discussion, sportif)* to warm up •**échauffement** *nm (de moteur)* overheating; *(de sportif)* warm(ing)-up
échauffourée [eʃofure] *nf (bagarre)* clash, brawl, skirmish
échéance [eʃeɑ̃s] *nf (de facture, de dette)* date of payment; **à brève/longue é.** *(projet, emprunt)* short-/long-term; **faire face à ses échéances** to meet one's financial obligations

échéant [eʃeɑ̃] **le cas échéant** *adv* if need be
échec [eʃɛk] *nm (insuccès)* failure; **faire é. à qch** to hold sth in check; **les échecs** *(jeu)* chess; **é.!** check!; **é. et mat!** checkmate!
échelle [eʃɛl] *nf* (**a**) *(marches)* ladder; **faire la courte é. à qn** to give sb *Br* a leg up *or Am* a boost (**b**) *(de carte)* scale; **à l'é. nationale** on a national scale
échelon [eʃlɔ̃] *nm (d'échelle)* rung; *(de fonctionnaire)* grade; *(d'organisation)* echelon; **à l'é. régional/national** on a regional/national level
échelonner [eʃlɔne] **1** *vt (paiements)* to spread
  2 **s'échelonner** *vpr* to be spread out
écheveau, -x [eʃ(ə)vo] *nm (de laine)* skein; *Fig (d'une intrigue)* muddle, tangle
échevelé, -ée [eʃəv(ə)le] *adj (ébouriffé)* dishevelled; *Fig (course, danse)* wild
échine [eʃin] *nf Anat* backbone, spine; **courber l'é. devant qn** to submit to sb •**s'échiner** *vpr Fam* **s'é. à faire qch** to wear oneself out doing sth
échiquier [eʃikje] *nm (plateau)* chessboard
écho [eko] *nm (d'un son)* echo; **échos** *(dans la presse)* gossip column; **avoir des échos de qch** to hear some news about sth; **se faire l'é. de qch** to echo sth
échographie [ekografi] *nf* (ultrasound) scan; **passer une é.** to have a scan
échoir* [eʃwar] *vi* **é. à qn** to fall to sb
échouer [eʃwe] **1** *vi* to fail; **é. à** *(examen)* to fail; **faire é. un projet** to wreck a plan; **faire é. un complot** to foil a plot
  2 *vi,* **s'échouer** *vpr (navire)* to run aground
éclabousser [eklabuse] *vt* to splash, to spatter (**avec** with) •**éclaboussure** *nf* splash
éclair [eklɛr] **1** *nm* (**a**) *(lumière)* flash; *(d'orage)* flash of lightning; **un é. de génie** a flash of genius (**b**) *(gâteau)* éclair
  2 *adj inv* **visite/raid é.** lightning visit/raid
éclairage [eklɛraʒ] *nm* lighting
éclaircie [eklɛrsi] *nf* sunny spell
éclaircir [eklɛrsir] **1** *vt (couleur)* to lighten; *(teint)* to clear; *(mystère)* to clear up; *(sauce)* to thin out
  2 **s'éclaircir** *vpr (ciel)* to clear; *(mystère)* to be cleared up; *(cheveux)* to thin; **s'é. la voix** to clear one's throat •**éclaircissement** *nm (explication)* explanation; **demander des éclaircissements sur qch** to ask for an explanation of sth

éclairer [eklere] **1** *vt (pièce)* to light (up); **é. qn** *(avec une lampe)* to give sb some light; *(informer)* to enlighten s.o (**sur** about); **é. une situation d'un jour nouveau** to shed *or* throw new light on a situation
2 *vi (lampe)* to give light; **é. bien/mal** to give good/poor light
3 s'éclairer *vpr (visage)* to light up; **s'é. à la bougie** to use candlelight; **s'é. à l'électricité** to have electric lighting ▪ **éclairé, -ée** *adj (averti)* enlightened; **bien/mal é.** *(illuminé)* well-/badly lit
éclaireur, -euse [eklɛrœr, -øz] **1** *nmf* (boy) scout, (girl) guide
2 *nm (soldat)* scout
éclat [ekla] *nm* (**a**) *(de lumière)* brightness; *(de phare)* glare; *(de diamant)* flash; *(splendeur)* brilliance, radiance; *Fig* **l'é. de la jeunesse** the bloom of youth (**b**) *(de verre, de bois)* splinter; **é. d'obus** shrapnel; **é. de rire** burst of laughter; **éclats de voix** noisy outbursts, shouts
éclatant, -ante [eklatɑ̃, -ɑ̃t] *adj (lumière, couleur, succès)* brilliant; *(beauté, santé)* radiant; *(rire)* loud; **être é. de santé** to be glowing with health
éclater [eklate] *vi (pneu, obus)* to burst; *(bombe, pétard)* to go off, to explode; *(verre)* to shatter; *(guerre, incendie)* to break out; *(orage, scandale)* to break; *(parti)* to break up; **é. de rire** to burst out laughing; **é. en sanglots** to burst into tears ▪ **éclatement** *nm (de pneu)* bursting; *(de bombe)* explosion; *(de parti)* break-up
éclectique [eklɛktik] *adj* eclectic
éclipse [eklips] *nf (de soleil, de lune)* eclipse ▪ **éclipser 1** *vt* to eclipse **2 s'éclipser** *vpr (soleil)* to be eclipsed; *Fam (partir)* to slip away
éclopé, -ée [eklɔpe] **1** *adj* lame
2 *nmf* lame person
éclore* [eklɔr] *vi (œuf)* to hatch; *(fleur)* to open (out), to blossom ▪ **éclosion** *nf* hatching; *(de fleur)* opening, blossoming
écluse [eklyz] *nf (de canal)* lock
écobilan [ekɔbilɑ̃] *nm* life-cycle analysis
écœurer [ekœre] *vt* **é. qn** *(aliment)* to make sb feel sick; *(au moral)* to sicken sb ▪ **écœurant, -ante** *adj* disgusting, sickening ▪ **écœurement** *nm (nausée)* nausea; *(indignation)* disgust
école [ekɔl] *nf (local; militaire)* academy; **à l'é.** at school; **aller à l'é.** to go to school; **faire é.** to gain a following; **les grandes écoles** = university-level colleges specializing in professional training; **é. de danse/dessin** dancing/art school; **é. normale** *Br* teachers' training college, *Am* teachers' college; **é. privée** private school; **é. publique** *Br* state school, *Am* public school ▪ **écolier, -ière** *nmf* schoolboy, *f* schoolgirl
écologie [ekɔlɔʒi] *nf* ecology ▪ **écologique** *adj* ecological ▪ **écologiste** *adj & nmf* environmentalist
éconduire* [ekɔ̃dɥir] *vt Littéraire (repousser)* to reject
économe [ekɔnɔm] **1** *adj* thrifty, economical
2 *nmf (de collège)* bursar
économie [ekɔnɔmi] *nf (activité, vertu)* economy; **économies** *(argent)* savings; **une é. de** *(gain)* a saving of; **faire une é. de temps** to save time; **faire des économies** to save (up); **faire des économies d'énergie** to conserve *or* save energy; **é. de marché** market economy; **é. dirigée** planned economy; **é. libérale** open market economy ▪ **économique** *adj* (**a**) *(relatif à l'économie)* economic; **science é.** economics *(sing)* (**b**) *(avantageux)* economical ▪ **économiquement** *adv* economically
économiser [ekɔnɔmize] **1** *vt (forces, argent, énergie)* to save
2 *vi* to economize (**sur** on)
économiste [ekɔnɔmist] *nmf* economist
écoper [ekɔpe] **1** *vt (bateau)* to bail out, *Br* to bale out
2 *vi Fam* **é. de qch** *(punition, amende)* to get sth
écorce [ekɔrs] *nf (d'arbre)* bark; *(de fruit)* peel; **l'é. terrestre** the earth's crust
écorcher [ekɔrʃe] **1** *vt (érafler)* to graze; *(animal)* to flay; *Fig (nom)* to mispronounce; **é. les oreilles à qn** to grate on sb's ears
2 s'écorcher *vpr* to graze oneself; **s'é. le genou** to graze one's knee ▪ **écorchure** *nf* graze
Écosse [ekɔs] *nf* **l'É.** Scotland ▪ **écossais, -aise 1** *adj* Scottish; *(tissu)* tartan; *(whisky)* Scotch **2** *nmf* **É., Écossaise** Scot
écosser [ekɔse] *vt (pois)* to shell
écot [eko] *nm* **payer son é.** to pay one's share
écouler [ekule] **1** *vt (se débarrasser de)* to dispose of
2 s'écouler *vpr (eau)* to flow out, to run out; *(temps)* to pass ▪ **écoulé, -ée** *adj (années)* past ▪ **écoulement** *nm (de liquide)* flow; *(de temps)* passage; *(de marchandises)* sale
écourter [ekurte] *vt (séjour, discours)* to cut short; *(texte, tige)* to shorten
écoute [ekut] *nf* listening; **être à l'é.** to be

listening in (**de** to); **rester à l'é.** to keep listening; **être à l'é. de qn** to listen (sympathetically) to sb; **heure de grande é.** *Radio* peak listening time; *TV* peak viewing time; **écoutes téléphoniques** phone tapping

écouter [ekute] **1** *vt* to listen to; **faire é. qch à qn** *(disque)* to play sb sth **2 s'écouter** *vpr* **si je m'écoutais** if I did what I wanted; **il s'écoute parler** he likes the sound of his own voice ● **écouteur** *nm (de téléphone)* earpiece; **écouteurs** *(casque)* headphones

écrabouiller [ekrabuje] *vt Fam* to crush

écran [ekrɑ̃] *nm* screen; **à l'é.** on screen; **le petit é.** television; **é. publicitaire** commercial break; **é. total** sun block

écraser [ekraze] **1** *vt (broyer, vaincre)* to crush; *(fruit, insecte)* to squash; *(cigarette)* to put out; *(piéton)* to run over; **se faire é. par une voiture** to get run over by a car; *Fam* **se faire é.** to be clobbered **2 s'écraser** *vpr (avion)* to crash (**contre** into) ● **écrasant, -ante** *adj (victoire, chaleur)* overwhelming ● **écrasé** *adj m* **nez é.** snub nose

écrémer [ekreme] *vt (lait)* to skim; *Fig (choisir)* to cream off the best from

écrevisse [ekrəvis] *nf* crayfish *inv*

écrier [ekrije] **s'écrier** *vpr* to exclaim, to cry out (**que** that)

écrin [ekrɛ̃] *nm (jewel)* case

écrire* [ekrir] **1** *vt* to write; *(noter)* to write down; **é. à la machine** to type **2** *vi* to write **3 s'écrire** *vpr (mot)* to be spelt; **comment ça s'écrit?** how do you spell it? ● **écrit** *nm* written document; *(examen)* written examination; **écrits** *(œuvres)* writings; **par é.** in writing

écriteau, -x [ekrito] *nm* notice, sign

écriture [ekrityr] *nf (système)* writing; *(personnelle)* (hand)writing; *Com* **écritures** accounts; **les Écritures** *(la Bible)* the Scriptures

écrivain [ekrivɛ̃] *nm* writer

écrou [ekru] *nm (de boulon)* nut

écrouer [ekrue] *vt* to imprison

écrouler [ekrule] **s'écrouler** *vpr (édifice, blessé)* to collapse; **être écroulé de fatigue** to be dropping with exhaustion; *Fam* **être écroulé (de rire)** to be doubled up (with laughter) ● **écroulement** *nm* collapse

écru, -ue [ekry] *adj (beige)* écru; *(naturel)* unbleached

ÉCU [eky] *(abrév* **European Currency Unit***) nm* ECU

écueil [ekœj] *nm (rocher)* reef; *Fig (obstacle)* pitfall

écuelle [ekɥɛl] *nf* bowl

éculé, -ée [ekyle] *adj (chaussure)* down-at-heel; *Fig (plaisanterie)* hackneyed

écume [ekym] *nf (de mer, bave d'animal)* foam; *(de pot-au-feu)* scum ● **écumer 1** *vt (pot-au-feu)* to skim; *(piller)* to plunder **2** *vi* to foam (**de rage** with anger) ● **écumoire** *nf (ustensile)* skimmer

écureuil [ekyrœj] *nm* squirrel

écurie [ekyri] *nf* stable

écusson [ekysɔ̃] *nm (en étoffe)* badge

écuyer, -ère [ekɥije, -ɛr] *nmf (cavalier)* rider

eczéma [ɛgzema] *nm Méd* eczema

édenté, -ée [edɑ̃te] *adj* toothless

EDF [ədeɛf] (*abrév* **Électricité de France**) *nf =* French electricity company

édifice [edifis] *nm* edifice ● **édification** *nf (de monument)* construction; *(instruction morale)* edification ● **édifier** *vt (bâtiment)* to erect; *(théorie)* to construct; **é. qn** *(moralement)* to edify sb

Édimbourg [edɛ̃bur] *nm ou f* Edinburgh

édit [edi] *nm Hist* edict

éditer [edite] *vt (publier)* to publish; *(annoter)* & *Ordinat* to edit ● **éditeur, -trice** *nmf (dans l'édition)* publisher; *(commentateur)* editor ● **édition** *nf (livre, journal)* edition; *(métier, diffusion)* publishing

> ⚠ Il faut noter que le nom anglais **edition** est un faux ami. Il ne désigne jamais l'industrie du livre.

éditorial, -iaux [editɔrjal, -jo] *nm (article)* editorial, *Br* leader ● **éditorialiste** *nmf* editorial *or Br* leader writer

édredon [edrədɔ̃] *nm* eiderdown

éducateur, -trice [edykatœr, -tris] *nmf* educator

éducatif, -ive [edykatif, -iv] *adj* educational

éducation [edykasjɔ̃] *nf (enseignement)* education; *(par les parents)* upbringing; **avoir de l'é.** to have good manners; **l'É. nationale** ≃ the Department of Education; **é. physique** physical education *or* training; **é. sexuelle** sex education ● **éduquer** *vt (à l'école)* to educate; *(à la maison)* to bring up

EEE [əəə] (*abrév* **Espace économique européen**) *nm* EEA

effacé, -ée [efase] *adj (modeste)* self-effacing ● **effacement** *nm (modestie)* self-effacement

effacer [efase] **1** *vt (gommer)* to rub out, to erase; *(en lavant)* to wash out; *(avec un*

chiffon) to wipe away; *Fig (souvenir)* to blot out, to erase
2 s'effacer *vpr (souvenir, couleur)* to fade; *(se placer en retrait)* to step aside
effarer [efaʀe] *vt* to astound ● **effarant, -ante** *adj* astounding ● **effarement** *nm* astonishment
effaroucher [efaʀuʃe] **1** *vt* to scare away **2 s'effaroucher** *vpr* to take fright
effectif, -ive [efɛktif, -iv] **1** *adj (réel)* effective
2 *nm (de classe)* size; *(d'une armée)* (total) strength; *(employés)* staff ● **effectivement** *adv (en effet)* actually

> ⊘ Il faut noter que l'adverbe anglais **effectively** est un faux ami. Il signifie **efficacement**.

effectuer [efɛktɥe] *vt (expérience, geste difficile)* to carry out, to perform; *(paiement, trajet)* to make
efféminé, -ée [efemine] *adj* effeminate
effervescent, -ente [efɛʀvesɑ̃, -ɑ̃t] *adj (médicament)* effervescent ● **effervescence** *nf (exaltation)* excitement
effet [efɛ] *nm (résultat)* effect; *(impression)* impression (**sur** on); **en e.** indeed, in fact; **à cet e.** to this end, for this purpose; **sous l'e. de la colère** *(agir)* in anger, out of anger; **faire de l'e.** *(remède)* to be effective; *Tennis* **donner de l'e. à une balle** to put spin on a ball; **il me fait l'e. d'être fatigué** he seems to me to be tired; **ce n'est pas l'e. du hasard si** it is not simply a matter of chance if; **e. de commerce** bill of exchange; **e. de serre** greenhouse effect; **e. secondaire** side effect; *Cin* **effets spéciaux** special effects
effets [efɛ] *nmpl (vêtements)* clothes, things
efficace [efikas] *adj (mesure)* effective; *(personne)* efficient ● **efficacité** *nf (de mesure)* effectiveness; *(de personne)* efficiency
effigie [efiʒi] *nf* effigy; **à l'e. de qn** bearing the image of sb
effilé, -ée [efile] *adj (doigt, lame)* tapering
effilocher [efilɔʃe] **s'effilocher** *vpr* to fray
efflanqué, -ée [eflɑ̃ke] *adj* emaciated
effleurer [eflœʀe] *vt (frôler)* to touch lightly; *Fig (question)* to touch on; **e. qn** *(pensée)* to cross sb's mind
effondrer [efɔ̃dʀe] **s'effondrer** *vpr (édifice, Bourse)* to collapse; *(plan)* to fall through; *(personne)* to go to pieces; **avoir l'air effondré** to look completely dejected ● **effondrement** *nm (d'édifice, de la Bourse)* collapse; *(de personne)* dejection

efforcer [efɔʀse] **s'efforcer** *vpr* **s'e. de faire qch** to try hard to do sth
effort [efɔʀ] *nm* effort; **sans e.** *(réussir)* effortlessly; **faire des efforts** to make an effort; **allons! encore un petit e.!** come on, try again!
effraction [efʀaksjɔ̃] *nf* **entrer par e.** to break in; **vol avec e.** housebreaking
effranger [efʀɑ̃ʒe] **s'effranger** *vpr* to fray
effrayer [efʀeje] **1** *vt* to frighten, to scare **2 s'effrayer** *vpr* to be frightened *or* scared ● **effrayant, -ante** *adj* frightening, scary
effréné, -ée [efʀene] *adj* unrestrained; *(course)* frantic
effriter [efʀite] **s'effriter** *vpr* to crumble
effroi [efʀwa] *nm Littéraire* dread ● **effroyable** *adj* dreadful ● **effroyablement** [-əmɑ̃] *adv* dreadfully
effronté, -ée [efʀɔ̃te] *adj (personne)* impudent ● **effronterie** *nf* impudence
effusion [efyzjɔ̃] *nf (manifestation)* effusiveness; **avec e.** effusively; **e. de sang** bloodshed
égal, -e, -aux, -ales [egal, -o] **1** *adj* equal (**à** to); *(uniforme, régulier)* even; **ça m'est é.** it's all the same to me; **combattre à armes égales** to fight on equal terms; *Sport* **faire jeu é.** to be evenly matched; **se trouver à égale distance de** to be equidistant from
2 *nmf (personne)* equal; **traiter qn d'é. à é.** *ou* **en é.** to treat sb as an equal; **sans é.** without match ● **également** *adv (au même degré)* equally; *(aussi)* also, as well ● **égaler** *vt* to equal, to match (**en** in); **3 plus 4 égale(nt) 7** 3 plus 4 equals 7
égaliser [egalize] **1** *vt (salaire)* to equalize; *(terrain)* to level
2 *vi Sport* to equalize ● **égalisation** *nf Sport* equalization; *(de terrain)* levelling
égalité [egalite] *nf* equality; *(régularité)* evenness; *Tennis* deuce; *Sport* **à é. (de score)** even, equal (in points) ● **égalitaire** *adj* egalitarian
égard [egaʀ] *nm* **à l'é. de** *(envers)* towards; *(concernant)* with respect *or* regard to; **à cet é.** in this respect; **à certains égards** in some respects; **eu é. à** considering, in consideration of; **par é. pour qn** out of consideration for sb
égarement [egaʀmɑ̃] *nm (folie)* distraction; **égarements** *(actes immoraux)* wild behaviour
égarer [egaʀe] **1** *vt (objet)* to mislay; *(personne)* to mislead; *(soupçons)* to avert
2 s'égarer *vpr (personne, lettre)* to get

lost; *(objet)* to go astray; *(sortir du sujet)* to wander from the point

égayer [egeje] **1** *vt (pièce)* to brighten up; **é. qn** *(réconforter, amuser)* to cheer sb up **2 s'égayer** *vpr (s'animer)* to cheer up

égide [eʒid] *nf* **sous l'é. de** under the aegis of

églantier [eglɑ̃tje] *nm* wild rose •**églantine** *nf* wild rose

église [egliz] *nf* church

égocentrique [egɔsɑ̃trik] *adj* egocentric

égoïsme [egɔism] *nm* selfishness •**égoïste 1** *adj* selfish **2** *nmf* selfish person

égorger [egɔrʒe] *vt* to cut *or* slit the throat of

égosiller [egɔzije] **s'égosiller** *vpr* to scream one's head off, to bawl out

égotisme [egɔtism] *nm* egotism

égout [egu] *nm* sewer; **eaux d'é.** sewage

égoutter [egute] **1** *vt* to drain **2** *vi,* **s'égoutter** *vpr* to drain •**égouttoir** *nm (panier)* drainer

égratigner [egratiɲe] **1** *vt* to scratch **2 s'égratigner** *vpr* to scratch oneself •**égratignure** *nf* scratch

égrener [egrəne] *vt (raisins)* to pick the grapes off; *(maïs, pois)* to shell; *Rel* **é. son chapelet** to tell one's beads; **l'horloge égrène les heures** the clock slowly marks the hours

Égypte [eʒipt] *nf* **l'É.** Egypt •**égyptien, -ienne** [-sjɛ̃, -sjɛn] **1** *adj* Egyptian **2** *nmf* **É., Égyptienne** Egyptian

eh [e] *exclam* hey!; **eh bien!** well!

éhonté, -ée [eɔ̃te] *adj* shameless; **mensonge é.** barefaced lie

éjecter [eʒɛkte] *vt* to eject; *Fam* **se faire é.** to get thrown out •**éjectable** *adj* **siège é.** *(d'avion)* ejector seat •**éjection** *nf (de pilote)* ejection

élaborer [elabɔre] *vt (plan, idée)* to develop •**élaboration** *nf (de plan, d'idée)* development

élaguer [elage] *vt (arbre, texte)* to prune

élan¹ [elɑ̃] *nm (vitesse)* momentum; *(course)* run-up; *Fig (impulsion)* boost; **un é. de tendresse** a surge of affection; **prendre son é.** to take a run-up; **d'un seul é.** in one go

élan² [elɑ̃] *nm (animal)* elk

élancé, -ée [elɑ̃se] *adj (personne, taille)* slender

élancer [elɑ̃se] **1** *vi (abcès)* to give shooting pains **2 s'élancer** *vpr (bondir)* to rush forward; *Sport* to take a run-up •**élancement** *nm* shooting pain

élargir [elarʒir] **1** *vt (chemin)* to widen; *(vêtement)* to let out; *(esprit, débat)* to broaden **2 s'élargir** *vpr (sentier)* to widen out; *(vêtement)* to stretch

élastique [elastik] **1** *adj (objet, gaz, métal)* elastic; *(règlement, notion)* flexible, supple **2** *nm (lien)* rubber band, *Br* elastic band; *(pour la couture)* elastic •**élasticité** *nf* elasticity

élection [elɛksjɔ̃] *nf* election; **é. partielle** by-election •**électeur, -trice** *nmf* voter, elector •**électoral, -e, -aux, -ales** *adj* **campagne électorale** election campaign; **liste électorale** electoral roll •**électorat** *nm (électeurs)* electorate, voters

électricien [elɛktrisjɛ̃] *nm* electrician •**électricité** *nf* electricity •**électrifier** *vt (voie ferrée)* to electrify •**électrique** *adj (pendule, décharge)* & *Fig* electric; *(courant, fil)* electric(al) •**électriser** *vt Fig (animer)* to electrify

électrocardiogramme [elɛktrɔkardjɔgram] *nm* electrocardiogram

électrochoc [elɛktrɔʃɔk] *nm (traitement)* electric shock treatment

électrocuter [elɛktrɔkyte] *vt* to electrocute

électrode [elɛktrɔd] *nf El* electrode

électrogène [elɛktrɔʒɛn] *adj El* **groupe é.** generator

électroménager [elɛktrɔmenaʒe] **1** *adj m* **appareil é.** household electrical appliance **2** *nm* household appliances

électron [elɛktrɔ̃] *nm* electron •**électronicien, -ienne** *nmf* electronics engineer •**électronique 1** *adj* electronic; **microscope é.** electron microscope **2** *nf* electronics *(sing)*

électrophone [elɛktrɔfɔn] *nm* record player

élégant, -ante [elegɑ̃, -ɑ̃t] *adj (bien habillé)* smart, elegant; *(solution)* neat •**élégamment** [-amɑ̃] *adv* elegantly, smartly •**élégance** *nf* elegance; **avec é.** elegantly

élégie [eleʒi] *nf* elegy

élément [elemɑ̃] *nm (composante, personne)* & *Chim* element; *(de meuble)* unit; *Math* member; *Fig* **être dans son é.** to be in one's element

élémentaire [elemɑ̃tɛr] *adj* basic; *(cours, école)* elementary

éléphant [elefɑ̃] *nm* elephant •**éléphantesque** *adj Fam (énorme)* elephantine

élevage [elvaʒ] *nm (production)* breeding (**de** of); *(ferme)* cattle farm; **faire l'é. de** to breed

élévateur [elevatœr] *adj m* **chariot é.** forklift truck

élévation [elevɑsjɔ̃] *nf* raising; **é. de** *(hausse)* rise in

élevé, -ée [elve] *adj (haut)* high; *(noble)* noble; **bien/mal é.** well-/bad-mannered

élève [elɛv] *nmf (à l'école)* pupil

élever [elve] **1** *vt (prix, voix, objection)* to raise; *(enfant)* to bring up; *(animal)* to breed; *(âme)* to uplift

2 s'élever *vpr (prix, ton, montagne)* to rise; *(cerf-volant)* to rise into the sky; *(monument)* to stand; **un cri s'éleva dans la foule** a shout went up from the crowd; **s'é. à** *(prix)* to amount to; **s'é. contre** to rise up against

éleveur, -euse [elvœr, -øz] *nmf* breeder

éligible [eliʒibl] *adj* eligible (**à** for)

élimé, -ée [elime] *adj (tissu)* threadbare, worn thin

éliminer [elimine] *vt* to eliminate ● **élimination** *nf* elimination ● **éliminatoire** *adj* **épreuve é.** *Sport* qualifying round, heat; *Scol* qualifying exam; *Scol* **note é.** disqualifying mark ● **éliminatoires** *nfpl Sport* qualifying rounds

élire* [elir] *vt* to elect (**à** to)

élision [elizjɔ̃] *nf Ling* elision

élite [elit] *nf* elite (**de** of); **les élites** the elite; **troupes d'é.** crack *or* elite troops

elle [ɛl] *pron personnel* (**a**) *(sujet)* she; *(chose, animal)* it; **elles they; e. est** she is/it is; **elles sont** they are (**b**) *(complément)* her; *(chose, animal)* it; **elles** them; **pour e.** for her; **pour elles** for them; **plus grande qu'e./qu'elles** taller than her/them ● **elle-même** *pron* herself; *(chose, animal)* itself; **elles-mêmes** themselves

ellipse [elips] *nf* ellipse ● **elliptique** *adj* elliptical

élocution [elɔkysjɔ̃] *nf* diction

éloge [elɔʒ] *nm (compliment)* praise; *(panégyrique)* eulogy; **faire l'é. de** to praise; **é. funèbre** funeral oration ● **élogieux, -ieuse** *adj* laudatory

éloigné, -ée [elwaɲe] *adj (lieu)* far away, remote; *(date, parent)* distant; **é. de** *(village, maison)* far (away) from; *(très différent)* far removed from

éloignement [elwaɲəmɑ̃] *nm* remoteness, distance; *(absence)* separation (**de** from); **avec l'é.** *(avec le recul)* with time

éloigner [elwaɲe] **1** *vt (chose, personne)* to move away (**de** from); *(malade, moustiques)* to keep away; *(crainte, idée)* to

banish; **é. qn de** *(sujet, but)* to take sb away from

2 s'éloigner *vpr (partir)* to move away (**de** from); *(dans le passé)* to become (more) remote; **s'é. de** *(sujet, but)* to wander from

élongation [elɔ̃gɑsjɔ̃] *nf Méd* pulled muscle; **se faire une é.** to pull a muscle

éloquent, -ente [elɔkɑ̃, -ɑ̃t] *adj* eloquent ● **éloquence** *nf* eloquence

élu, -ue [ely] **1** *pp de* **élire**

2 *adj Rel* **le peuple é.** the chosen people

3 *nmf Pol* elected member *or* representative; *Rel* **les élus** the chosen ones; **l'heureux é./l'heureuse élue** *(futur mari, future femme)* the lucky man/woman

élucider [elyside] *vt* to elucidate

élucubrations [elykybrɑsjɔ̃] *nfpl Péj* flights of fancy

éluder [elyde] *vt* to evade

Élysée [elize] *nm* **(le palais de) l'É.** the Élysée palace *(French President's residence)*

émacié, -iée [emasje] *adj* emaciated

émail, -aux [emaj, -o] *nm* enamel; **casserole en é.** enamel saucepan ● **émaillé, -ée** *adj* **é. de fautes** peppered with errors

e-mail [imɛl] *nm* e-mail; **envoyer un e.** to send an e-mail

émanciper [emɑ̃sipe] **1** *vt (femmes)* to emancipate

2 s'émanciper *vpr* to become emancipated ● **émancipation** *nf* emancipation; **l'é. de la femme** the emancipation of women

émaner [emane] *vt* **é. de** to emanate from ● **émanation** *nf* **des émanations** *(odeurs)* smells; *(vapeurs)* fumes; **émanations toxiques** toxic fumes

émarger [emarʒe] **1** *vt (signer)* to sign

2 *vi (recevoir un salaire)* to draw one's salary

emballer [ɑ̃bale] **1** *vt* (**a**) *(dans une caisse)* to pack; *(dans du papier)* to wrap (up) (**b**) *(moteur)* to race; *Fam* **e. qn** *(passionner)* to grab sb

2 s'emballer *vpr Fam (personne)* to get carried away; *(cheval)* to bolt; *(moteur)* to race ● **emballage** *nm (action)* packing; *(dans du papier)* wrapping; *(caisse)* packaging; **papier d'e.** wrapping paper ● **emballé, -ée** *adj Fam* enthusiastic

embarcadère [ɑ̃barkadɛr] *nm* landing stage

embarcation [ɑ̃barkɑsjɔ̃] *nf* (small) boat

embardée [ɑ̃barde] *nf (de véhicule)* swerve; **faire une e.** to swerve

embargo [ɑ̃bargo] *nm* embargo; **imposer/lever un e.** to impose/lift an embargo

embarquer [ãbarke] **1** vt (passagers) to take on board; (marchandises) to load; Fam (voler) to walk off with; Fam **e. qn** (au commissariat) to cart sb off

2 vi, **s'embarquer** vpr to (go on) board; Fam **s'e. dans** (aventure) to embark on • **embarquement** [-əmã] nm (de passagers) boarding

embarras [ãbara] nm (gêne, malaise) embarrassment; (difficulté) difficulty, trouble; **dans l'e.** in an awkward situation; (financièrement) in financial difficulties; **n'avoir que l'e. du choix** to be spoilt for choice

embarrasser [ãbarase] **1** vt (encombrer) to clutter up; **e. qn** (empêcher le passage de) to be in sb's way; (gêner) to embarrass sb

2 s'embarrasser vpr s'e. de to burden oneself with; (se soucier) to bother oneself about • **embarrassant, -ante** adj (paquet) cumbersome; (question) embarrassing

embauche [ãboʃ] nf (action) hiring; (travail) work; **bureau d'e.** employment office • **embaucher** vt (ouvrier) to hire, to take on

embaumer [ãbome] **1** vt (parfumer) to give a sweet smell to; (cadavre) to embalm

2 vi to smell sweet

embellie [ãbɛli] nf bright spell; Naut calm spell

embellir [ãbɛlir] **1** vt (pièce, personne) to make more attractive; (texte, vérité) to embellish

2 vi (jeune fille) to grow more attractive • **embellissement** nm (de lieu) improvement; (de récit) embellishment

emberlificoter [ãbɛrlifikɔte] vt Fam (empêtrer) to tangle up; Fig **se laisser e. dans** (affaire) to get tangled up in

embêter [ãbete] Fam **1** vt (agacer) to annoy; (ennuyer) to bore

2 s'embêter vpr to get bored • **embêtant, -ante** adj Fam annoying • **embêtement** [-ɛtmã] nm Fam problem; **des embêtements** bother, trouble

emblée [ãble] **d'emblée** adv right away

emblème [ãblɛm] nm emblem

embobiner [ãbɔbine] vt Fam (tromper) to take in

emboîter [ãbwate] **1** vt to fit together; **e. le pas à qn** to follow close on sb's heels; Fig (imiter) to follow in sb's footsteps

2 s'emboîter vpr to fit together

embonpoint [ãbɔ̃pwɛ̃] nm stoutness

embouché, -ée [ãbuʃe] adj Fam **mal e.** foul-tempered

embouchure [ãbuʃyr] nf (de fleuve) mouth; (d'un instrument à vent) mouthpiece

embourber [ãburbe] **s'embourber** vpr (véhicule) & Fig to get bogged down

embourgeoiser [ãburʒwaze] **s'embourgeoiser** vpr to become middle-class

embout [ãbu] nm (de canne) tip; (de tuyau) nozzle

embouteillage [ãbutejaʒ] nm traffic jam • **embouteillé, -ée** [ãbuteje] adj (rue) congested; **route embouteillée sur 5 km** road with a 5-km-long traffic jam

emboutir [ãbutir] vt (voiture) to crash into; (métal) to stamp; **il a eu l'arrière embouti** someone crashed into the back of his car

embranchement [ãbrãʃmã] nm (de voie) junction

embraser [ãbraze] **1** vt to set ablaze

2 s'embraser vpr (prendre feu) to flare up

embrasser [ãbrase] **1** vt **e. qn** (donner un baiser à) to kiss sb; (serrer contre soi) to embrace or hug sb; **e. une croyance** to embrace a belief; **e. qch du regard** to take sth in at one glance

2 s'embrasser vpr to kiss (each other) • **embrassade** nf embrace, hug

> **𝄞** Il faut noter que le verbe anglais **to embrace** est un faux ami. Il ne signifie jamais **donner un baiser**.

embrasure [ãbrazyr] nf (de fenêtre, de porte) aperture; **dans l'e. de la porte** in the doorway

embrayer [ãbreje] vi Aut to engage the clutch • **embrayage** [-ɛjaʒ] nm (mécanisme, pédale) clutch

embrigader [ãbrigade] vt Péj to dragoon (**dans** into)

embrocher [ãbrɔʃe] vt (volaille) to put on a spit; Fam **e. qn** (avec une épée) to skewer sb

embrouiller [ãbruje] **1** vt (fils) to tangle (up); (papiers) to mix up, to muddle (up); **e. qn** to confuse sb, to get sb muddled; **tu vas m'e. les idées** you're going to get me confused

2 s'embrouiller vpr to get confused or muddled (**dans** in or with) • **embrouillamini** nm Fam muddle • **embrouille** nf Fam muddle; **un sac d'embrouilles** a muddle of the first order

embroussaillé, -ée [ãbrusaje] adj (barbe, chemin) bushy

embruns [ãbrœ̃] nmpl (sea) spray

embryon [ãbrijɔ̃] nm embryo • **embryonnaire** adj Méd & Fig embryonic

embûches [ãbyʃ] *nfpl (difficultés)* traps, pitfalls; **tendre des e. à qn** to set traps for sb; **semé d'e.** full of pitfalls

embuer [ãbɥe] *vt (vitre, yeux)* to mist up; **des yeux embués de larmes** eyes misted over with tears

embusquer [ãbyske] **s'embusquer** *vpr* to lie in ambush • **embuscade** *nf* ambush

éméché, -ée [emeʃe] *adj Fam (ivre)* tipsy

émeraude [emrod] *nf & adj inv* emerald

émerger [emɛrʒe] *vi* to emerge (**de** from)

émeri [emri] *nm* **toile/papier (d')é.** emery cloth/paper

émérite [emerit] *adj* **professeur é.** emeritus professor

émerveiller [emɛrveje] **1** *vt* to amaze, to fill with wonder

2 s'émerveiller *vpr* to marvel, to be filled with wonder (**de** at) • **émerveillement** *nm* wonder, amazement

émettre* [emɛtr] *vt (lumière, son)* to give out, to emit; *(message radio)* to broadcast; *(timbre, monnaie)* to issue; *(opinion, vœu)* to express; *(cri)* to utter; *(chèque)* to draw; *(emprunt)* to float • **émetteur** *adj & nm Radio* **(poste) é.** transmitter

émeute [emøt] *nf* riot • **émeutier, -ière** *nmf* rioter

émietter [emjete] *vt*, **s'émietter** *vpr (pain)* to crumble

émigrer [emigre] *vi (personne)* to emigrate • **émigrant, -ante** *nmf* emigrant • **émigration** *nf* emigration • **émigré, -ée 1** *nmf* exile, émigré **2** *adj* **travailleur é.** migrant worker

éminent, -ente [eminã, -ãt] *adj* eminent • **éminemment** [-amã] *adv* eminently • **éminence** *nf (colline)* hill; **son É. (le cardinal)** *(titre honorifique)* His Eminence (the Cardinal); *Fig* **une é. grise** *(conseiller)* an éminence grise

émir [emir] *nm* emir • **émirat** *nm* emirate

émissaire [emiser] *nm* emissary

émission [emisjõ] *nf (de radio)* programme; *(diffusion)* transmission; *(de timbre, monnaie)* issue; *(de lumière, de son)* emission (**de** of)

emmagasiner [ãmagazine] *vt* to store (up); *Fig* **e. de l'énergie/des souvenirs** to store energy/memories

emmanchure [ãmãʃyr] *nf* armhole

emmêler [ãmele] **1** *vt (fil, cheveux)* to tangle (up)

2 s'emmêler *vpr* to get tangled

emménager [ãmenaʒe] *vi (dans un logement)* to move in; **e. dans** to move into • **emménagement** *nm* moving in

emmener [ãmne] *vt* to take (**à** to); *(pri-*

sonnier) to take away; **e. qn faire une promenade** to take sb for a walk; **e. qn en voiture** to give sb a *Br* lift *or Am* ride

emmerder [ãmɛrde] *très Fam* **1** *vt* **e. qn** *(agacer)* to get on sb's nerves; *(ennuyer)* to bore sb stiff

2 s'emmerder *vpr* to get bored stiff • **emmerdement** [-əmã] *nm très Fam* bloody nuisance • **emmerdeur, -euse** *nmf très Fam (personne)* pain in the arse

emmitoufler [ãmitufle] **s'emmitoufler** *vpr* to wrap (oneself) up (**dans** in)

emmurer [ãmyre] *vt (personne)* to wall in

émoi [emwa] *nm* emotion; **en é.** in a flutter

émoluments [emɔlymã] *nmpl (de fonctionnaire)* remuneration

émotion [emosjõ] *nf (sentiment)* emotion; *(frayeur)* fright; **donner des émotions à qn** to give sb a real fright; **aimer les émotions fortes** to love thrills • **émotif, -ive** *adj* emotional • **émotionné, -ée** *adj Fam* upset

émousser [emuse] *vt (pointe)* to blunt; *Fig (sentiment)* to dull • **émoussé, -ée** *adj (pointe)* blunt; *Fig (sentiment)* dulled

émouvoir* [emuvwar] **1** *vt (affecter)* to move, to touch

2 s'émouvoir *vpr* to be moved *or* touched • **émouvant, -ante** *adj* moving, touching

empailler [ãpaje] *vt (animal)* to stuff

empaler [ãpale] *vt* to impale

empaqueter [ãpakte] *vt* to pack

emparer [ãpare] **s'emparer** *vpr* **s'e. de** *(lieu, personne, objet)* to seize; *(sujet: émotion)* to take hold of

empâter [ãpate] **s'empâter** *vpr* to become bloated • **empâté, -ée** *adj* fleshy, fat

empêcher [ãpeʃe] *vt* to prevent, to stop; **e. qn de faire qch** to prevent *or* stop sb from doing sth; **elle ne peut pas s'e. de rire** she can't help laughing; *Fig* **ça ne m'empêche pas de dormir** I don't lose any sleep over it; **e. l'accès d'un lieu** to prevent access to a place; *Fam* **n'empêche qu'elle a raison** all the same, she's right; *Fam* **n'empêche** all the same • **empêchement** [-ɛʃmã] *nm* hitch; **il a/j'ai eu un e.** something came up

empereur [ãprœr] *nm* emperor

empester [ãpeste] **1** *vt (tabac)* to stink of; *(pièce)* to stink out; **e. qn** to stink sb out

2 *vi* to stink

empêtrer [ãpetre] **s'empêtrer** *vpr* to get entangled (**dans** in)

emphase [ãfaz] *nf* pomposity • **emphatique** *adj* pompous

empiéter [ɑ̃pjete] *vi* **e. sur** to encroach (up)on • **empiétement** *nm* encroachment

empiffrer [ɑ̃pifre] **s'empiffrer** *vpr Fam* to stuff oneself (**de** with)

empiler [ɑ̃pile] **1** *vt* to pile up (**sur** on) **2 s'empiler** *vpr* to pile up (**sur** on); **s'e. dans** *(passagers)* to cram into

empire [ɑ̃pir] *nm (territoires)* empire; *(autorité)* hold, influence; **sous l'e. de la peur** in the grip of fear

empirer [ɑ̃pire] *vi* to worsen, to get worse

empirique [ɑ̃pirik] *adj* empirical • **empirisme** *nm* empiricism

emplacement [ɑ̃plasmɑ̃] *nm (de construction)* site, location; *(de stationnement)* place

emplâtre [ɑ̃plɑtr] *nm (pansement)* plaster

emplette [ɑ̃plɛt] *nf* purchase; **faire des emplettes** to do some shopping

emplir [ɑ̃plir] *vt*, **s'emplir** *vpr* to fill (**de** with)

emploi [ɑ̃plwa] *nm* (**a**) *(usage)* use; **e. du temps** timetable (**b**) *(travail)* job; **sans e.** unemployed; **la situation de l'e.** the employment situation

employer [ɑ̃plwaje] **1** *vt (utiliser)* to use; **e. qn** *(occuper)* to employ sb **2 s'employer** *vpr (expression)* to be used; **s'e. à faire qch** to devote oneself to doing sth • **employé, -ée** *nmf* employee; **e. de banque** bank clerk; **e. de bureau** office worker; **e. de maison** domestic employee; **e. des postes** postal worker • **employeur, -euse** *nmf* employer

empocher [ɑ̃pɔʃe] *vt* to pocket

empoigner [ɑ̃pwaɲe] **1** *vt (saisir)* to grab **2 s'empoigner** *vpr* to come to blows • **empoignade** *nf (querelle)* fight

empoisonner [ɑ̃pwazɔne] **1** *vt (personne, aliment, atmosphère)* to poison; *(empester)* to stink out; *Fam* **e. qn** to get on sb's nerves; *Fam* **e. la vie à qn** to make sb's life a misery **2 s'empoisonner** *vpr (par accident)* to be poisoned; *(volontairement)* to poison oneself; *Fam (s'ennuyer)* to get bored stiff • **empoisonnant, -ante** *adj Fam (embêtant)* irritating • **empoisonnement** *nm* poisoning; *Fam (ennui)* problem

emporter [ɑ̃pɔrte] **1** *vt (prendre)* to take (**avec soi** with one); *(transporter)* to take away; *(prix, trophée)* to carry off; *(décision)* to carry; *(entraîner)* to carry along or away; *(par le vent)* to blow off or away; *(par les vagues)* to sweep away; *(par la maladie)* to carry off; **pizza à e.** takeaway

pizza; **l'e. sur qn** to get the upper hand over sb; **il l'a emporté** he won; *Fig* **se laisser e.** to get carried away (**par** by); **elle ne l'emportera pas au paradis** she'll soon be smiling on the other side of her face **2 s'emporter** *vpr* to lose one's temper (**contre** with) • **emporté, -ée** *adj (caractère)* hot-tempered • **emportement** [-əmɑ̃] *nm* anger; **emportements** fits of anger

empoté, -ée [ɑ̃pɔte] *adj Fam* clumsy

empourprer [ɑ̃purpre] **s'empourprer** *vpr* to turn crimson

empreint, -einte [ɑ̃prɛ̃, -ɛ̃t] *adj Littéraire* **e. de bonté** full of kindness; **e. de danger** fraught with danger

empreinte [ɑ̃prɛ̃t] *nf (marque)* & *Fig* mark; **e. digitale** fingerprint; **e. de pas** footprint

empresser [ɑ̃prese] **s'empresser** *vpr* **s'e. de faire qch** to hasten to do sth; **s'e. auprès de qn** to be attentive to sb • **empressé, -ée** *adj* attentive • **empressement** [-ɛsmɑ̃] *nm (hâte)* eagerness; *(prévenance)* attentiveness

emprise [ɑ̃priz] *nf* hold (**sur** over)

emprisonner [ɑ̃prizɔne] *vt* to imprison • **emprisonnement** *nm* imprisonment

emprunt [ɑ̃prœ̃] *nm (argent)* loan; *Ling (mot)* borrowing; **faire un e.** *(auprès d'une banque)* to take out a loan; **d'e.** borrowed; **nom d'e.** assumed name • **emprunter** *vt (argent, objet)* to borrow (**à qn** from sb); *(route)* to take

emprunté, -ée [ɑ̃prœ̃te] *adj (gêné)* ill at ease

empuantir [ɑ̃pɥɑ̃tir] *vt* to stink out

ému, -ue [emy] **1** *pp de* **émouvoir** **2** *adj (attendri)* moved; *(attristé)* upset; *(apeuré)* nervous; **une voix émue** a voice charged with emotion

émulation [emylasjɔ̃] *nf (sentiment)* & *Ordinat* emulation

émule [emyl] *nmf* emulator

en¹ [ɑ̃] *prép* (**a**) *(indique le lieu)* in; *(indique la direction)* to; **être en ville/en France** to be in town/in France; **aller en ville/en France** to go (in)to town/to France (**b**) *(indique le temps)* in; **en février** in February; **en été** in summer; **d'heure en heure** from hour to hour (**c**) *(indique le moyen)* by; *(indique l'état)* in; **en avion** by plane; **en groupe** in a group; **en fleur** in flower; **en congé** on leave; **en mer** at sea; **en guerre** at war (**d**) *(indique la matière)* in; **en bois** made of wood, wooden; **chemise en Nylon**® nylon shirt; **c'est en or** it's (made of) gold (**e**) *(domaine)* **étudiant en lettres** humanities *or Br* arts student; **docteur en médecine** doctor of medicine (**f**) *(comme)* **en cadeau** as a present; **en ami** as a friend (**g**) *(+ participe présent)* **en mangeant/chantant** while eating/singing; **en apprenant que** on hearing that; **en souriant** smiling, with a smile; **en ne disant rien** by saying nothing; **sortir en courant** to run out (**h**) *(transformation)* into; **traduire en français** to translate into French

en² [ɑ̃] *pron* (**a**) *(indique la provenance)* from there; **j'en viens** I've just come from there (**b**) *(remplace les compléments introduits par 'de')* **il en est content** he's pleased with it/him/them; **en parler** to talk about it; **en mourir** to die of *or* from it; **elle m'en frappa** she struck me with it; **il s'en souviendra** he'll remember it (**c**) *(partitif)* some; **j'en ai** I have some; **en veux-tu?** do you want some?; **donne-lui-en** give some to him/her; **je t'en supplie** I beg you (to)

ENA [ena] *(abrév* **École nationale d'administration***) nf* = university-level college preparing students for senior positions in law and economics • **énarque** *nmf* = graduate from ENA

encablure [ɑ̃kablyr] *nf* **à quelques encablures du rivage** a short distance (away) from the shore

encadrer [ɑ̃kadre] *vt (tableau)* to frame; *(entourer d'un trait)* to circle; *(étudiants, troupes)* to supervise; *(personnel)* to manage; *(prisonnier, accusé)* to flank; *Fam* **je ne peux pas l'e.** I can't stand him/her • **encadrement** *nm (action)* framing; *(d'étudiants)* supervision; *(de personnel)* management; *(de porte, de photo)* frame; **personnel d'e.** training and supervisory staff

encaissé, -ée [ɑ̃kese] *adj (vallée)* deep

encaisser [ɑ̃kese] *vt (argent, loyer)* to collect; *(chèque)* to cash; *Fam (coup)* to take; *Fam* **je ne peux pas l'e.** I can't stand him/her • **encaissement** [-ɛsmɑ̃] *nm (de loyer)* collection; *(de chèque)* cashing

encart [ɑ̃kar] *nm (feuille)* insert; **e. publicitaire** publicity insert

en-cas [ɑ̃kɑ] *nm inv (repas)* snack

encastrer [ɑ̃kastre] *vt* to build in (**dans** to) • **encastré, -ée** *adj* built-in

encaustique [ɑ̃kostik] *nf* wax, polish

enceinte¹ [ɑ̃sɛ̃t] *adj f (femme)* pregnant; **e. de six mois** six months pregnant

enceinte² [ɑ̃sɛ̃t] *nf (muraille)* (surrounding) wall; *(espace)* enclosure; **dans l'e. de** within, inside; **e. (acoustique)** speakers

encens [ɑ̃sɑ̃] *nm* incense • **encensoir** *nm* censer

encercler [ɑ̃sɛrkle] *vt (lieu, ennemi)* to surround, to encircle; *(mot)* to circle

enchaîner [ɑ̃ʃene] **1** *vt (animal, prisonnier)* to chain up; *(idées)* to link (up) **2** *vi (continuer à parler)* to continue **3 s'enchaîner** *vpr (idées)* to be linked (up) • **enchaînement** [-ɛnmɑ̃] *nm (succession)* chain, series; *(liaison)* link(ing) (**de** between *or* of); *(en gymnastique, en danse)* enchaînement

enchanter [ɑ̃ʃɑ̃te] *vt (ravir)* to delight, to enchant; *(ensorceler)* to bewitch • **enchanté, -ée** *adj (ravi)* delighted (**de** with; **que** + *subjunctive* that); *(magique)* enchanted; **e. de faire votre connaissance!** pleased to meet you! • **enchantement** *nm (ravissement)* delight; *(sortilège)* magic spell; **comme par e.** as if by magic • **enchanteur, -eresse 1** *adj* delightful, enchanting **2** *nm (sorcier)* magician

enchâsser [ɑ̃ʃase] *vt (diamant)* to set

enchère [ɑ̃ʃɛr] *nf (offre)* bid; **vente aux enchères** auction; **mettre qch aux enchères** to put sth up for auction, to auction sth • **enchérir** *vi* to make a higher bid; **e. sur qn** to outbid sb

enchevêtrer [ɑ̃ʃvetre] **1** *vt* to (en)tangle **2 s'enchevêtrer** *vpr* to get entangled (**dans** in) • **enchevêtrement** [-ɛtrəmɑ̃] *nm* tangle, entanglement

enclave [ɑ̃klav] *nf* enclave

enclencher [ɑ̃klɑ̃ʃe] *vt Tech* to engage

enclin, -ine [ɑ̃klɛ̃, -in] *adj* **e.** à inclined to

enclos [ɑ̃klo] *nm (terrain, clôture)* enclosure • **enclore*** *vt (terrain)* to enclose

enclume [ɑ̃klym] *nf* anvil

encoche [ɑ̃kɔʃ] *nf* notch (**à** in)

encoignure [ɑ̃kwaɲyr] *nf* corner

encoller [ɑ̃kɔle] *vt (papier peint)* to paste

encolure [ɑ̃kɔlyr] *nf (de cheval, vêtement)* neck; *(tour du cou)* collar (size); **robe à e. carrée** square-neck(ed) dress

encombre [ɑ̃kɔ̃br] **sans encombre** *adv* without a hitch

encombrer [ɑ̃kɔ̃bre] **1** *vt (pièce, couloir)* to clutter up (**de** with); *(rue, passage)* to block; **e. qn** to hamper sb **2 s'encombrer** *vpr* **s'e. de** to load oneself down with • **encombrant, -ante** *adj (paquet)* bulky, cumbersome; *(présence)* awkward • **encombré, -ée** *adj (lignes téléphoniques, route)* jammed • **encombrement** [-əmɑ̃] *nm (d'objets)* clutter;

(embouteillage) traffic jam; *(volume)* bulk(iness)

encontre [ãkɔ̃trə] **à l'encontre de** *prép* against

encore [ãkɔr] *adv* (**a**) *(toujours)* still; **tu es e. là?** are you still here? (**b**) *(avec négation)* **pas e.** not yet; **je ne suis pas e. prêt** I'm not ready yet (**c**) *(de nouveau)* again; **essaie e.** try again (**d**) *(de plus, en plus)* **e. un café** another coffee, one more coffee; **e. une fois** (once) again, once more; **e. un** another (one), one more; **e. du pain** (some) more bread; **que veut-il e.?** what else *or* more does he want?; **e. quelque chose** something else; **qui/quoi e.?** who/what else? (**e**) *(avec comparatif)* even, still; **e. mieux** even better, better still (**f**) *(aussi)* **mais e.** but also (**g**) **si e.** *(si seulement)* if only; **et e.** *(à peine)* if that, only just (**h**) **e. que...** *(+ subjunctive)* although...

encourager [ãkuraʒe] *vt* to encourage (**à faire** to do) ●**encourageant, -ante** *adj* encouraging ●**encouragement** *nm* encouragement

encourir* [ãkurir] *vt* to incur

encrasser [ãkrase] **1** *vt* to clog up (with dirt) **2 s'encrasser** *vpr* to get clogged up

encre [ãkr] *nf* ink; **faire couler beaucoup d'e.** to be much written about; **e. de Chine** *Br* Indian *or Am* India ink; **e. sympathique** invisible ink ●**encrier** *nm* inkpot

encroûter [ãkrute] **s'encroûter** *vpr Péj* to get into a rut

encyclique [ãsiklik] *nf Rel* encyclical

encyclopédie [ãsiklɔpedi] *nf* encyclopedia ●**encyclopédique** *adj* encyclopedic

endémique [ãdemik] *adj* endemic

endetter [ãdete] **1** *vt* **e. qn** to get sb into debt **2 s'endetter** *vpr* to get into debt ●**endettement** *nm* debts

endeuiller [ãdœje] *vt (famille, nation)* to plunge into mourning

endiablé, -ée [ãdjable] *adj (rythme)* wild

endiguer [ãdige] *vt (fleuve)* to dyke (up); *Fig (réprimer)* to contain

endimanché, -ée [ãdimãʃe] *adj* in one's Sunday best

endive [ãdiv] *nf* chicory *inv,* endive

endoctriner [ãdɔktrine] *vt* to indoctrinate ●**endoctrinement** *nm* indoctrination

endolori, -ie [ãdɔlɔri] *adj* painful

endommager [ãdɔmaʒe] *vt* to damage

endormir* [ãdɔrmir] **1** *vt (enfant)* to put to sleep; *(ennuyer)* to send to sleep;

(soupçons) to lull; *(douleur)* to deaden **2 s'endormir** *vpr* to fall asleep, to go to sleep ●**endormi, -ie** *adj* asleep, sleeping; *Fam (indolent)* sluggish

endosser [ãdose] *vt (vêtement)* to put on; *(responsabilité)* to assume; *(chèque)* to endorse

endroit [ãdrwa] *nm* (**a**) *(lieu)* place, spot; **à cet e. du récit** at this point in the story; **par endroits** in places (**b**) *(de tissu)* right side; **à l'e.** *(vêtement)* the right way round

enduire* [ãdɥir] *vt* to smear, to coat (**de** with) ●**enduit** *nm* coating; *(de mur)* plaster

endurant, -ante [ãdyrã, -ãt] *adj* hardy, tough ●**endurance** *nf* stamina; **course d'e.** endurance race

endurcir [ãdyrsir] **1** *vt* **e. qn à** *(douleur)* to harden sb to **2 s'endurcir** *vpr (moralement)* to become hard; *(physiquement)* to toughen up ●**endurci, -ie** *adj (insensible)* hardened; **célibataire e.** confirmed bachelor

endurer [ãdyre] *vt* to endure, to bear

énergie [enɛrʒi] *nf* energy; **avec é.** *(protester)* forcefully ●**énergétique** *adj* **aliment é.** energy food; **ressources énergétiques** energy resources ●**énergique** *adj (dynamique)* energetic; *(remède)* powerful; *(mesure, ton)* forceful ●**énergiquement** *adv (protester)* energetically

énergumène [enɛrgymɛn] *nmf Péj* eccentric

énerver [enɛrve] **1** *vt* **é. qn** *(irriter)* to get on sb's nerves; *(rendre nerveux)* to make sb nervous **2 s'énerver** *vpr* to get worked up ●**énervé, -ée** *adj (agacé)* irritated; *(excité)* on edge, agitated ●**énervement** [-əmã] *nm (agacement)* irritation; *(excitation)* agitation

> 🖋 Il faut noter que le verbe anglais **to unnerve** est un faux ami. Il signifie **troubler**.

enfance [ãfãs] *nf* childhood; **petite e.** infancy, early childhood; *Fam* **c'est l'e. de l'art** it's child's play ●**enfanter** *vt* to give birth to ●**enfantillages** *nmpl* childish behaviour ●**enfantin, -ine** *adj (voix, joie)* childlike; *(langage)* children's; *(puéril)* childish; *(simple)* easy

enfant [ãfã] *nmf* child *(pl* children); **attendre un e.** to be expecting a baby; **c'est un e. de...** *(originaire)* he's a native of...; **c'est un jeu d'e.** it's child's play; **e. en bas âge** infant; *Rel* **e. de chœur** altar boy; **e. gâté** spoilt child; **e. prodige** child prodigy; **e. prodigue** prodigal son; **e. trouvé** foundling; **e. unique** only child

enfer [ãfɛr] *nm* hell; **d'e.** *(bruit, vision)* infernal; **à un train d'e.** at breakneck speed; *Fam* **un plan d'e.** a hell of a (good) plan

enfermer [ãfɛrme] **1** *vt (personne, chose)* to shut up; **e. qn/qch à clef** to lock sb/sth up

2 s'enfermer *upr* **s'e. dans** *(chambre)* to shut oneself (up) in; *Fig (attitude)* to maintain stubbornly; **s'e. à clef** to lock oneself in

enferrer [ãfere] **s'enferrer** *upr Fig* **s'e. dans** to get tangled up in

enfiévré, -ée [ãfjevre] *adj (front, imagination)* fevered

enfilade [ãfilad] *nf (série)* row, string; **des pièces en e.** a suite of rooms

enfiler [ãfile] *vt (aiguille)* to thread; *(perles)* to string; *Fam (vêtement)* to slip on

enfin [ãfɛ̃] *adv (à la fin)* finally, at last; *(en dernier lieu)* lastly; *(en somme)* in a word; *(de résignation)* well; *Fam* **e. bref...** *(en somme)* in a word...; **mais e.** but; **(mais) e.!** for heaven's sake!; **il est grand, e. pas trop petit** he's tall – well, not too short anyhow

enflammer [ãflame] **1** *vt* to set fire to; *(allumette)* to light; *(irriter)* to inflame; *(imagination)* to stir

2 s'enflammer *upr* to catch fire ● **enflammé, -ée** *adj (discours)* fiery

enfler [ãfle] **1** *vt (rivière, membre)* to swell

2 *vi (membre)* to swell (up) ● **enflure** *nf* swelling

enfoncer [ãfɔ̃se] **1** *vt (clou)* to bang in; *(pieu)* to drive in; *(porte, voiture)* to smash in; *(chapeau)* to push down; **e. dans qch** *(couteau, mains)* to plunge into sth

2 *vi (s'enliser)* to sink (**dans** into); *(couteau)* to go in

3 s'enfoncer *upr (s'enliser)* to sink (**dans** into); *(couteau)* to go in; **s'e. dans** *(pénétrer)* to disappear into ● **enfoncé, -ée** *adj (yeux)* sunken

enfouir [ãfwir] *vt* to bury

enfourcher [ãfurʃe] *vt (cheval)* to mount

enfourner [ãfurne] *vt* to put in the oven

enfreindre* [ãfrɛ̃dr] *vt* to infringe

enfuir* [ãfɥir] **s'enfuir** *upr* to run away (**de** from)

enfumer [ãfyme] *vt (pièce)* to fill with smoke; *(personne)* to smoke out

engager [ãɡaʒe] **1** *vt (discussion, combat)* to start; *(bijou)* to pawn; *(parole)* to pledge; *(clef)* to insert (**dans** into); **e. qn** *(embaucher)* to hire sb; *(lier)* to bind sb; **e.** **qn dans** *(affaire)* to involve sb in; **e. qn à faire qch** to urge sb to do sth; **e. la partie** to start the match

2 s'engager *upr (dans l'armée)* to enlist; *(prendre position)* to commit oneself; *(partie)* to start; **s'e. à faire qch** to undertake to do sth; **s'e. dans** *(voie)* to enter; *(affaire)* to get involved in; **s'e. dans une aventure** to get involved in an adventure ● **engagé, -ée** *adj (écrivain)* committed ● **engageant, -ante** *adj* engaging ● **engagement** *nm (promesse)* commitment; *(de soldats)* enlistment; *(commencement)* start; *Football* kick-off; **sans e. de votre part** without obligation (on your part); **prendre l'e. de faire qch** to undertake to do sth

> *Il faut noter que l'adjectif anglais **engaged** est un faux ami. Il ne s'utilise jamais dans un contexte politique.*

engelure [ãʒlyr] *nf* chilblain

engendrer [ãʒãdre] *vt (causer)* to generate, to engender; *(procréer)* to father

engin [ãʒɛ̃] *nm (machine)* machine; *(outil)* device; **e. explosif** explosive device; **e. spatial** spacecraft

> *Il faut noter que le nom anglais **engine** est un faux ami. Il signifie **moteur**.*

englober [ãɡlɔbe] *vt* to include

engloutir [ãɡlutir] *vt (nourriture)* to wolf down; *(bateau, village)* to submerge

engorger [ãɡɔrʒe] *vt* to block up, to clog

engouement [ãɡumã] *nm* craze (**pour** for)

engouffrer [ãɡufre] **1** *vt Fam (avaler)* to wolf down

2 s'engouffrer *upr* **s'e. dans** to rush into

engourdir [ãɡurdir] **1** *vt (membre)* to numb; *(esprit)* to dull

2 s'engourdir *upr (membre)* to go numb; *(esprit)* to become dull(ed) ● **engourdissement** *nm* numbness

engrais [ãɡrɛ] *nm* fertilizer

engraisser [ãɡrese] **1** *vt (animal, personne)* to fatten up

2 *vi Fam* to get fat

engrenage [ãɡrənaʒ] *nm Tech* gears; *Fig* chain; *Fig* **pris dans l'e.** caught in the system

engueuler [ãɡœle] *Fam* **1** **e. qn** to give sb an earbashing; **se faire e.** to get an earbashing

2 s'engueuler *upr* to have a row ● **engueulade** *nf Fam (réprimande)* earbashing; *(dispute)* row, *Br* slanging match

enhardir [ãardir] **1** *vt* to make bolder

2 s'enhardir *vpr* **s'e. à faire qch** to pluck up courage to do sth

énième [enjɛm] *adj Fam* umpteenth, nth

énigme [enigm] *nf (devinette)* riddle; *(mystère)* enigma • **énigmatique** *adj* enigmatic

enivrer [ɑ̃nivre] **1** *vt (soûler)* to intoxicate **2 s'enivrer** *vpr* to get drunk (**de** on)

enjamber [ɑ̃ʒɑ̃be] *vt* to step over; *(sujet: pont) (rivière)* to span • **enjambée** *nf* stride

enjeu, -x [ɑ̃ʒø] *nm (mise)* stake; *Fig (de guerre)* stakes

enjoindre* [ɑ̃ʒwɛ̃dr] *vt Littéraire* **e. à qn de faire qch** to enjoin sb to do sth

enjôler [ɑ̃ʒole] *vt* to coax

enjoliver [ɑ̃ʒɔlive] *vt* to embellish • **enjoliveur** *nm* hubcap

enjoué, -ée [ɑ̃ʒwe] *adj* playful • **enjouement** *nm* playfulness

enlacer [ɑ̃lase] *vt (mêler)* to entwine; *(embrasser)* to clasp

enlaidir [ɑ̃ledir] **1** *vt* to make ugly **2** *vi* to grow ugly

enlevé, -ée [ɑ̃lve] *adj (style, danse)* lively

enlever [ɑ̃l(ə)ve] **1** *vt* to remove; *(meubles)* to take away, to remove; *(vêtement, couvercle)* to take off, to remove; *(tapis)* to take up; *(rideau)* to take down; *(enfant)* to kidnap, to abduct; *(ordures)* to collect **2 s'enlever** *vpr (tache)* to come out; *(vernis)* to come off • **enlèvement** [-ɛvmɑ̃] *nm (d'enfant)* kidnapping, abduction; *(d'un objet)* removal; *(des ordures)* collection

enliser [ɑ̃lize] **s'enliser** *vpr (véhicule)* & *Fig* to get bogged down (**dans** in)

enneigé, -ée [ɑ̃neʒe] *adj* snow-covered • **enneigement** [-ɛʒmɑ̃] *nm* snow coverage; **bulletin d'e.** snow report

ennemi, -ie [enmi] **1** *nmf* enemy **2** *adj (personne)* hostile (**de** to); **pays/ soldat e.** enemy country/soldier

ennui [ɑ̃nɥi] *nm (lassitude)* boredom; *(souci)* problem; **avoir des ennuis** *(soucis)* to be worried; *(problèmes)* to have problems; **l'e., c'est que…** the annoying thing is that…

ennuyer [ɑ̃nɥije] **1** *vt (agacer)* to annoy; *(préoccuper)* to bother; *(lasser)* to bore; **si ça ne t'ennuie pas** if you don't mind **2 s'ennuyer** *vpr* to get bored • **ennuyé, -ée** *adj (air)* bored; **je suis très e.** *(confus)* I feel bad (about it) • **ennuyeux, -euse** *adj (contrariant)* annoying; *(lassant)* boring

énoncé [enɔ̃se] *nm (de question)* wording; *(de faits)* statement; *(de sentence)* pronouncement • **énoncer** *vt* to state

enorgueillir [ɑ̃nɔrgœjir] **s'enorgueillir** *vpr* **s'e. de qch** to pride oneself on sth

énorme [enɔrm] *adj* enormous, huge • **énormément** *adv (travailler, pleurer)* an awful lot; **je le regrette é.** I'm awfully sorry about it; **il n'a pas é. d'argent** he hasn't got a huge amount of money • **énormité** *nf (de demande, de crime, de somme)* enormity; *(de personne)* huge size; *(faute)* glaring mistake

enquérir* [ɑ̃kerir] **s'enquérir** *vpr* **s'e. de qch** to inquire about sth

enquête [ɑ̃kɛt] *nf (de policiers, de journalistes)* investigation; *(judiciaire, administrative)* inquiry; *(sondage)* survey • **enquêter** *vi (policier, journaliste)* to investigate; **e. sur qch** to investigate sth • **enquêteur, -euse** *nmf (policier)* investigator; *(sondeur)* researcher

enquiquiner [ɑ̃kikine] *vt Fam* to annoy

enraciner [ɑ̃rasine] **s'enraciner** *vpr* to take root; **enraciné dans** *(personne, souvenir)* rooted in; **bien enraciné** *(préjugé)* deep-rooted

enrager [ɑ̃raʒe] *vi* to be furious (**de faire** about doing); **faire e. qn** to get on sb's nerves • **enragé, -ée** *adj (chien)* rabid; *Fam (joueur)* fanatical (**de** about) • **enrageant, -ante** *adj* infuriating

enrayer [ɑ̃reje] **1** *vt (maladie)* to check **2 s'enrayer** *vpr (fusil)* to jam

enregistrer [ɑ̃r(ə)ʒistre] *vt (par écrit, sur bande)* to record; *(sur registre)* to register; *(constater)* to register; **(faire) e. ses bagages** *(à l'aéroport)* to check in, to check one's luggage in; **ça enregistre** it's recording • **enregistrement** [-əmɑ̃] *nm (d'un acte)* registration; *(sur bande)* recording; **l'e. des bagages** *(à l'aéroport)* (luggage) check-in; **se présenter à l'e.** to check in • **enregistreur, -euse** *adj* **appareil e.** recording apparatus; **caisse enregistreuse** cash register

enrhumer [ɑ̃ryme] **s'enrhumer** *vpr* to catch a cold; **être enrhumé** to have a cold

enrichir [ɑ̃riʃir] **1** *vt* to enrich (**de** with) **2 s'enrichir** *vpr (personne)* to get rich

enrober [ɑ̃rɔbe] *vt* to coat (**de** in); **enrobé de chocolat** chocolate-coated

enrôler [ɑ̃role] *vt*, **s'enrôler** *vpr* to enlist • **enrôlement** *nm* enlistment

enrouer [ɑ̃rwe] **s'enrouer** *vpr* to get hoarse • **enroué, -ée** *adj* hoarse

enrouler [ɑ̃rule] **1** *vt (fil)* to wind; *(tapis, cordage)* to roll up **2 s'enrouler** *vpr* **s'e. dans qch** *(couvertures)* to wrap oneself up in sth; **s'e. sur** *ou* **autour de qch** to wind round sth

ensabler [ãsable] *vt*, **s'ensabler** *vpr (port)* to silt up

ensanglanté, -ée [ãsãglãte] *adj* bloodstained

enseigne [ãsɛɲ] **1** *nf (de magasin)* sign; *Fig* **logés à la même e.** in the same boat; **e. lumineuse** neon sign **2** *nm* **e. de vaisseau** *Br* lieutenant, *Am* ensign

enseigner [ãseɲe] **1** *vt* to teach; **e. qch à qn** to teach sb sth **2** *vi* to teach •**enseignant, -ante** [-eɲã, -ãt] **1** *nmf* teacher **2** *adj* **corps e.** teaching profession •**enseignement** [-ɛɲəmã] *nm* education; *(action, métier)* teaching; **être dans l'e.** to be a teacher; **e. par correspondance** distance learning; **e. privé** private education; **e. public** *Br* state *or Am* public education

ensemble [ãsãbl] **1** *adv* together; **aller (bien) e.** *(couleurs)* to go together; *(personnes)* to be well-matched **2** *nm (d'objets)* group, set; *Math* set; *(vêtement)* outfit; *Mus* ensemble; *(harmonie)* unity; **l'e. du personnel** *(totalité)* the whole (of the) staff; **l'e. des enseignants** all (of) the teachers; **dans l'e.** on the whole; **vue d'e.** general view; **grand e.** *(quartier)* housing *Br* complex *or Am* development

ensemencer [ãsəmãse] *vt (terre)* to sow

ensevelir [ãsəvlir] *vt* to bury

ensoleillé, -ée [ãsɔleje] *adj (endroit, journée)* sunny

ensommeillé, -ée [ãsɔmeje] *adj* sleepy

ensorceler [ãsɔrsəle] *vt (envoûter, séduire)* to bewitch •**ensorcellement** [-ɛlmã] *nm (séduction)* spell

ensuite [ãsɥit] *adv (puis)* next, then; *(plus tard)* afterwards

ensuivre* [ãsɥivr] **s'ensuivre** *v impersonnel* **il s'ensuit que...** it follows that...; **et tout ce qui s'ensuit** and all the rest of it; **jusqu'à ce que mort s'ensuive** until death

entacher [ãtaʃe] *vt (honneur)* to sully

entaille [ãtaj] *nf (fente)* notch; *(blessure)* gash, slash •**entailler** *vt* to notch; *(blesser)* to gash, to slash

entame [ãtam] *nf* first slice

entamer [ãtame] *vt (pain, peau)* to cut into; *(bouteille, boîte)* to open; *(négociations)* to enter into; *(capital)* to eat *or* break into; *(métal, plastique)* to damage; *(résolution, réputation)* to shake

entartrer [ãtartre] *vt*, **s'entartrer** *vpr (chaudière) Br* to fur up, *Am* to scale

entasser [ãtase] *vt*, **s'entasser** *vpr (objets)* to pile up, to heap up •**entassement** *nm (tas)* pile, heap; *(de gens)* crowding

entendement [ãtãdmã] *nm (faculté)* understanding

entendre [ãtãdr] **1** *vt* to hear; *(comprendre)* to understand; *(vouloir)* to intend; **e. parler de qn/qch** to hear of sb/sth; **e. dire que...** to hear (it said) that...; **e. raison** to listen to reason; **laisser e. à qn que...** to give sb to understand that... **2** **s'entendre** *vpr (être entendu)* to be heard; *(être compris)* to be understood; **s'e. (sur)** *(être d'accord)* to agree (on); **(bien) s'e. avec qn** to get along *or Br* on with sb; **on ne s'entend plus!** *(à cause du bruit)* we can't hear ourselves speak!; **il s'y entend** *(est expert)* he knows all about that

entendu, -ue [ãtãdy] *adj (convenu)* agreed; *(compris)* understood; *(sourire, air)* knowing; **e.!** all right!; **bien e.** of course

entente [ãtãt] *nf (accord)* agreement, understanding; **(bonne) e.** *(amitié)* harmony

entériner [ãterine] *vt* to ratify

enterrer [ãtere] *vt (défunt)* to bury; *Fig (projet)* to scrap •**enterrement** [-ɛrmã] *nm* burial; *(funérailles)* funeral

en-tête [ãtɛt] *(pl* **en-têtes)** *nm (de papier)* heading; **papier à e.** *Br* headed paper, *Am* letterhead

entêter [ãtete] **s'entêter** *vpr* to persist (**à faire** in doing) •**entêté, -ée** *adj* stubborn •**entêtement** [ãtɛtmã] *nm* stubbornness; **e. à faire qch** persistence in doing sth

enthousiasme [ãtuzjasm] *nm* enthusiasm •**enthousiasmant, -ante** *adj* exciting •**enthousiasmer 1** *vt* to fill with enthusiasm **2** **s'enthousiasmer** *vpr* **s'e. pour qch** to get enthusiastic about sth •**enthousiaste** *adj* enthusiastic

enticher [ãtiʃe] **s'enticher** *vpr* **s'e. de qn/ qch** to become infatuated with sb/sth

entier, -ière [ãtje, -jɛr] **1** *adj (total)* whole, entire; *(intact)* intact; *(absolu)* absolute, complete; *(caractère, personne)* uncompromising; **payer place entière** to pay full price; **le pays tout e.** the whole *or* entire country **2** *nm (unité)* whole; **en e., dans son e.** in its entirety, completely •**entièrement** *adv* entirely

entité [ãtite] *nf* entity

entonner [ãtɔne] *vt (air)* to start singing

entonnoir [ãtɔnwar] *nm* funnel

entorse [ãtɔrs] *nf Méd* sprain; **se faire une e. à la cheville** to sprain one's ankle;

Fig **faire une e. au règlement** to stretch the rules

entortiller [ãtɔrtije] **1** *vt* to wrap (**dans** in); *Fam* **e. qn** to dupe sb

2 s'entortiller *vpr (lierre)* to coil (**autour de** round)

entourage [ãturaʒ] *nm (proches)* circle of family and friends

entourer [ãture] **1** *vt* to surround (**de** with); *(envelopper)* to wrap (**de** in); **entouré de** surrounded by; **e. qn de ses bras** to put one's arms round sb; **il est très entouré** *(soutenu)* he has lots of supportive people around him

2 s'entourer *vpr* **s'e. de** to surround oneself with

entourloupette [ãturlupɛt] *nf Fam* nasty trick

entracte [ãtrakt] *nm (de théâtre) Br* interval, *Am* intermission

entraide [ãtrɛd] *nf* mutual aid ● **s'entraider** [sãtrede] *vpr* to help each other

entrailles [ãtrɑj] *nfpl* entrails

entrain [ãtrɛ̃] *nm* get-up-and-go; **plein d'e.** lively; **sans e.** lifeless

entraînant, -ante [ãtrɛnã, -ãt] *adj (musique)* lively

entraîner [ãtrene] **1** *vt* (**a**) *(charrier)* to carry away; *(causer)* to bring about; *(dépenses, modifications)* to entail; *Tech (roue)* to drive; **e. qn** *(emmener)* to lead sb away; *(de force)* to drag sb away; *(attirer)* to lure sb; **e. qn à faire qch** to lead sb to do sth; **se laisser e.** to allow oneself to be led astray (**b**) *(athlète, cheval)* to train (**à** for)

2 s'entraîner *vpr* to train oneself (**à faire qch** to do sth); *Sport* to train ● **entraînement** [-ɛnmã] *nm Sport* training; *(élan)* impulse; *Tech* drive ● **entraîneur** [-ɛnœr] *nm (d'athlète)* coach; *(de cheval)* trainer

entrave [ãtrav] *nf Fig (obstacle)* hindrance (**à** to) ● **entraver** *vt* to hinder, to hamper

entre [ãtr] *prép* between; *(parmi)* among(st); **l'un d'e. vous** one of you; **(soit dit) e. nous** between you and me; **se dévorer e. eux** *(réciprocité)* to devour each other; **e. deux âges** middle-aged; **e. autres (choses)** among other things

entrebâiller [ãtrəbɑje] *vt (porte)* to open slightly ● **entrebâillement** *nm* **par l'e. de la porte** through the half-open door ● **entrebâilleur** *nm* **e. (de porte)** door chain

entrechoquer [ãtrəʃɔke] **s'entrechoquer** *vpr (bouteilles)* to knock against each other

entrecôte [ãtrəkot] *nf* rib steak

entrecouper [ãtrəkupe] *vt (entremêler)* to punctuate (**de** with)

entrecroiser [ãtrəkrwaze] *vt*, **s'entrecroiser** *vpr (fils)* to interlace; *(routes)* to intersect

entre-deux-guerres [ãtrədøgɛr] *nm inv* inter-war period

entrée [ãtre] *nf (action)* entry, entrance; *(porte)* entrance; *(vestibule)* entrance hall, entry; *(accès)* admission, entry (**de** to); *Ordinat* input; *(plat)* starter; **à son e.** as he/she came in; **faire son e.** to make one's entrance; **à l'e. de l'hiver** at the beginning of winter; **'e. interdite'** 'no entry', 'no admittance'; **'e. libre'** 'admission free'; **e. en matière** *(d'un discours)* opening, introduction; **e. en vigueur** *(d'une loi)* date of application; *Scol* **e. en sixième** *Br* ≃ entering the first form, *Am* ≃ entering the sixth grade; **e. de service** service *or Br* tradesmen's entrance; **e. des artistes** stage door

entrefaites [ãtrəfɛt] **sur ces entrefaites** *adv* at that moment

entrefilet [ãtrəfilɛ] *nm* short (news) item

entrejambe [ãtrəʒãb] *nm* crotch

entrelacer [ãtrəlase] *vt*, **s'entrelacer** *vpr* to intertwine

entremêler [ãtrəmele] *vt*, **s'entremêler** *vpr* to intermingle

entremets [ãtrəmɛ] *nm (plat)* dessert, *Br* sweet

entremetteur, -euse [ãtrəmɛtœr, -øz] *nmf* go-between

entremise [ãtrəmiz] *nf* intervention; **par l'e. de qn** through sb

entreposer [ãtrəpoze] *vt* to store ● **entrepôt** *nm* warehouse

entreprendre* [ãtrəprãdr] *vt (travail, voyage)* to undertake; **e. de faire qch** to undertake to do sth ● **entreprenant, -ante** [-ãnã] *adj* enterprising; *(galant)* forward

entrepreneur [ãtrəprənœr] *nm (en bâtiment)* contractor

entreprise [ãtrəpriz] *nf (firme)* company, firm; *(opération)* undertaking

entrer [ãtre] **1** *vi (aux être) (aller)* to go in, to enter; *(venir)* to come in, to enter; **e. dans** to go into; *(pièce)* to come/go into, to enter; *(club)* to join; *(carrière)* to enter, to go into; **e. dans un arbre** *(en voiture)* to crash into a tree; **e. à l'université** to start university; **e. en action** to go into action; **e. en ébullition** to start boiling; **e. dans les détails** to go into detail; **faire/laisser e. qn** to show/let sb in; **entrez!** come in!

2 *vt Ordinat* **e. des données** to enter data (**dans** into)

entresol [ɑ̃trəsɔl] *nm* mezzanine floor
entre-temps [ɑ̃trətɑ̃] *adv* meanwhile
entretenir* [ɑ̃trət(ə)nir] **1** *vt (voiture, maison, famille)* to maintain; *(relations, souvenir)* to keep; *(sentiment)* to entertain; **e. sa forme/sa santé** to keep fit/healthy; **e. qn de qch** to talk to sb about sth
2 s'entretenir *vpr* **s'e. de** to talk about (avec with) • **entretenu, -ue** *adj* **bien/mal e.** *(maison)* well-kept/badly kept; **femme entretenue** kept woman

> *Il faut noter que le verbe anglais **to entertain** est un faux ami. Il signifie le plus souvent **divertir**.*

entretien [ɑ̃trətjɛ̃] *nm (de route, de maison)* maintenance, upkeep; *(dialogue)* conversation; *(entrevue)* interview; **entretiens** *(négociations)* talks
entre-tuer [ɑ̃trətɥe] **s'entre-tuer** *vpr* to kill each other
entrevoir* [ɑ̃trəvwar] *vt (rapidement)* to catch a glimpse of; *(pressentir)* to foresee
entrevue [ɑ̃trəvy] *nf* interview
entrouvrir* [ɑ̃truvrir] *vt*, **s'entrouvrir** *vpr* to half-open • **entrouvert, -erte** *adj (porte, fenêtre)* half-open
énumérer [enymere] *vt* to list • **énumération** *nf* listing
envahir [ɑ̃vair] *vt (pays)* to invade; *(marché)* to flood; **e. qn** *(doute, peur)* to overcome sb • **envahissant, -ante** *adj (voisin)* intrusive • **envahissement** *nm* invasion • **envahisseur** *nm* invader
enveloppant, -ante [ɑ̃vlɔpɑ̃, -ɑ̃t] *adj (séduisant)* captivating
enveloppe [ɑ̃vlɔp] *nf (pour lettre)* envelope; *(de colis)* wrapping; *(de pneu)* casing; *Fig (apparence)* exterior; **mettre qch sous e.** to put sth into an envelope; **e. timbrée à votre adresse** *Br* stamped addressed envelope, *Am* stamped self-addressed envelope
envelopper [ɑ̃vlɔpe] **1** *vt* to wrap (up) (dans in); **e. la ville** *(brouillard)* to blanket *or* envelop the town; **enveloppé de mystère** shrouded in mystery
2 s'envelopper *vpr* to wrap oneself (up) (dans in)
envenimer [ɑ̃v(ə)nime] **1** *vt (plaie)* to make septic; *Fig (querelle)* to embitter
2 s'envenimer *vpr (plaie)* to turn septic; *Fig* to become acrimonious
envergure [ɑ̃vɛrgyr] *nf (d'avion, d'oiseau)* wingspan; *(de personne)* calibre; *(ampleur)* scope; **de grande e.** *(réforme)* far-reaching

envers [ɑ̃vɛr] **1** *prép Br* towards, *Am* toward(s), to; **e. et contre tous** in the face of all opposition
2 *nm (de tissu)* wrong side; *(de médaille)* reverse side; **à l'e.** *(chaussette)* inside out; *(pantalon)* back to front; *(la tête en bas)* upside down; *(à contresens)* the wrong way
envie [ɑ̃vi] *nf (jalousie)* envy; *(désir)* desire; *Fam (des ongles)* hangnail; **avoir e. de qch** to want sth; **j'ai e. de faire qch** I feel like doing sth; **elle meurt d'e. de faire qch** she's dying to do sth; **ça me fait e.** I really like that • **envier** *vt* to envy (**qch à qn** sb sth) • **envieux, -ieuse** *adj* envious; **faire des e.** to make people envious
environ [ɑ̃virɔ̃] *adv (à peu près)* about • **environs** *nmpl* outskirts, surroundings; **aux e. de** *(Paris, Noël, 10 euros)* around, in the vicinity of
environner [ɑ̃virɔne] *vt* to surround • **environnant, -ante** *adj* surrounding • **environnement** *nm* environment
envisager [ɑ̃vizaʒe] *vt (considérer)* to consider; *(projeter) Br* to envisage, *Am* to envision; **e. de faire qch** to consider doing sth • **envisageable** *adj* conceivable; **pas e.** unthinkable
envoi [ɑ̃vwa] *nm (action)* sending; *(paquet)* package; *(marchandises)* consignment
envol [ɑ̃vɔl] *nm (d'oiseau)* taking flight; *(d'avion)* take-off • **envolée** *nf Fig (élan)* flight • **s'envoler** *vpr (oiseau)* to fly away; *(avion)* to take off; *(chapeau)* to blow away; *Fig (espoir)* to vanish
envoûter [ɑ̃vute] *vt* to bewitch • **envoûtement** *nm* bewitchment
envoyer* [ɑ̃vwaje] **1** *vt* to send; *(lancer)* to throw; *Fam (gifle)* to give; **e. chercher qn** to send for sb; *Fam* **e. promener qn** to send sb packing
2 s'envoyer *vpr Fam (repas)* to put *or* stash away • **envoyé, -ée** *nmf* envoy; **e. spécial** *(reporter)* special correspondent • **envoyeur** *nm* sender; **'retour à l'e.'** 'return to sender'
épagneul, -eule [epaɲœl] *nmf* spaniel
épais, -aisse [epɛ, -ɛs] *adj* thick • **épaisseur** *nf* thickness; **avoir 1 m d'é.** to be 1 m thick • **épaissir** [epesir] **1** *vt* to thicken **2** *vi*, **s'épaissir** *vpr* to thicken; *(grossir)* to fill out; **le mystère s'épaissit** the mystery is deepening
épancher [epɑ̃ʃe] **1** *vt Fig (cœur)* to pour out
2 s'épancher *vpr* to pour out one's heart • **épanchement** *nm (aveu)* outpouring

épanouir [epanwir] **s'épanouir** *vpr (fleur)* to bloom; *Fig (personne)* to blossom; *(visage)* to beam • **épanoui, -ouie** *adj (fleur, personne)* in full bloom; *(visage)* beaming • **épanouissement** *nm (de fleur)* full bloom; *(de personne)* blossoming

épargne [eparɲ] *nf (action, vertu)* saving; *(sommes)* savings • **épargnant, -ante** *nmf* saver • **épargner** *vt (argent, provisions)* to save; *(ennemi)* to spare; **e. qch à qn** *(ennuis, chagrin)* to spare sb sth

éparpiller [eparpije] *vt,* **s'éparpiller** *vpr* to scatter; *(efforts)* to dissipate • **épars, -arse** *adj* scattered

épaté, -ée [epate] *adj (nez)* flat

épater [epate] *vt Fam* to astound • **épatant, -ante** *adj Fam* splendid

épaule [epol] *nf* shoulder • **épauler 1** *vt (fusil)* to raise (to one's shoulder); **é. qn** *(aider)* to back sb up **2** *vi* to take aim • **épaulette** *nf (de veste)* shoulder pad

épave [epav] *nf (bateau, personne)* wreck

épée [epe] *nf* sword

épeler [ep(ə)le] *vt* to spell

éperdu, -ue [eperdy] *adj (regard)* distraught; *(amour)* passionate • **éperdument** *adv (aimer)* madly; **elle s'en moque e.** she couldn't care less

éperon [eprɔ̃] *nm (de cavalier, de coq)* spur • **éperonner** *vt* to spur on

épervier [epɛrvje] *nm* sparrowhawk

éphémère [efemɛr] *adj* short-lived, ephemeral

épi [epi] *nm (de blé)* ear; *(de cheveux)* tuft of hair

épice [epis] *nf* spice • **épicé, -ée 1** *adj (plat, récit)* spicy **2** *adv* **manger é.** to eat spicy food • **épicer** *vt* to spice

épicier, -ière [episje, -jɛr] *nmf* grocer • **épicerie** *nf (magasin) Br* grocer's (shop), *Am* grocery (store); **é. fine** delicatessen

épidémie [epidemi] *nf* epidemic • **épidémique** *adj* epidemic

épiderme [epidɛrm] *nm* skin

épier [epje] *vt (observer)* to watch closely; *(occasion)* to watch out for; **é. qn** to spy on sb

épilepsie [epilɛpsi] *nf Méd* epilepsy • **épileptique** *adj & nmf* epileptic

épiler [epile] *vt (jambes)* to remove unwanted hair from; *(sourcils)* to pluck

épilogue [epilɔg] *nm* epilogue

épinard [epinar] *nm (plante)* spinach; **épinards** spinach

épine [epin] *nf (de plante)* thorn; *(d'animal)* spine, prickle; *Anat* **é. dorsale** spine • **épineux, -euse** *adj (tige, question)* thorny; *(poisson)* spiny

épingle [epɛ̃gl] *nf* pin; *Fig* tiré à quatre **épingles** immaculately turned out; **é. à cheveux** hairpin; **virage en é. à cheveux** hairpin bend; **é. de** *ou* **à nourrice, é. de sûreté** safety pin; **é. à linge** *Br* clothes peg, *Am* clothes pin • **épingler** *vt* to pin; *Fam* **é. qn** *(arrêter)* to nab sb

Épiphanie [epifani] *nf* **l'É.** Epiphany

épique [epik] *adj* epic

épiscopal, -e, -aux, -ales [episkɔpal, -o] *adj* episcopal

épisode [epizɔd] *nm* episode; **feuilleton en six épisodes** serial in six episodes, six-part serial • **épisodique** *adj (intermittent)* occasional; *(accessoire)* minor

épitaphe [epitaf] *nf* epitaph

épithète [epitɛt] *nf* epithet; *Grammaire* attribute

épître [epitr] *nf* epistle

éploré, -ée [eplɔre] *adj (veuve, air)* tearful

éplucher [eplyʃe] *vt (carotte, pomme)* to peel; *(salade)* to clean; *Fig (texte)* to dissect • **épluchure** *nf (accessoire)*

éponge [epɔ̃ʒ] *nf* sponge; *Fig* **jeter l'é.** to throw in the towel • **éponger 1** *vt (liquide)* to mop up; *(surface)* to sponge down; *(dette)* to absorb **2 s'éponger** *vpr* **s'é. le front** to mop one's brow

épopée [epɔpe] *nf* epic

époque [epɔk] *nf (date)* time, period; *(historique)* age; **meubles d'é.** period furniture; **à l'é.** at the *or* that time

épouse [epuz] *nf* wife

épouser [epuze] *vt* to marry; *Fig (cause)* to espouse; *Fig* **é. la forme de qch** to take on the exact shape of sth

épousseter [epuste] *vt* to dust

époustoufler [epustufle] *vt Fam* to astound • **époustouflant, -ante** *adj Fam* astounding

épouvantable [epuvɑ̃tabl] *adj* appalling

épouvantail [epuvɑ̃taj] *nm (de jardin)* scarecrow

épouvante [epuvɑ̃t] *nf* terror • **épouvanter** *vt* to terrify

époux [epu] *nm* husband; **les é.** the husband and wife

éprendre* [eprɑ̃dr] **s'éprendre** *vpr* **s'é. de qn** to fall in love with sb • **épris, -ise** *adj* in love (**de** with)

épreuve [eprœv] *nf (essai, examen)* test; *(sportive)* event; *(malheur)* ordeal, trial; *(photo)* print; *(texte imprimé)* proof; **mettre qn/qch à l'é.** to put sb/sth to the test; **à toute é.** *(patience)* unfailing; *(nerfs)* rock-solid; **à l'é. des balles/du feu** bulletproof/fireproof

éprouver [epruve] *vt (méthode, personne, courage)* to test; *(sentiment)* to feel; *(difficultés)* to meet with • **éprouvant, -ante** *adj (pénible)* trying • **éprouvé, -ée** *adj (remède)* well-tried; *(famille)* sorely tried; *(région)* hard-hit

éprouvette [epruvɛt] *nf* test tube

EPS [əpeɛs] *(abrév* **éducation physique et sportive**) *nf* PE

épuiser [epɥize] **1** *vt (personne, provisions, sujet)* to exhaust
2 s'épuiser *vpr (réserves, patience)* to run out; **s'é. à faire qch** to exhaust oneself doing sth • **épuisant, -ante** *adj* exhausting • **épuisé, -ée** *adj* exhausted; *(marchandise)* sold out; *(édition)* out of print • **épuisement** *nm* exhaustion

épuisette [epɥizɛt] *nf* landing net

épurer [epyre] *vt (eau, gaz)* to purify; *(minerai)* to refine • **épuration** *nf* purification; *(de minerai)* refining; **station d'é.** purification *Br* works *or Am* plant

équateur [ekwatœr] *nm* equator; **sous l'é.** at the equator • **équatorial, -e, -iaux, -iales** *adj* equatorial

équation [ekwɑsjɔ̃] *nf Math* equation

équerre [ekɛr] *nf* **é. (à dessin)** *Br* set square, *Am* triangle; **d'é.** straight, square

équestre [ekɛstr] *adj (statue, sports)* equestrian

équilibre [ekilibr] *nm* balance; **mettre qch en é.** to balance sth (**sur** on); **se tenir en é.** to (keep one's) balance; **garder/perdre l'é.** to keep/lose one's balance • **équilibriste** *nmf* tightrope walker

équilibrer [ekilibre] **1** *vt (charge, composition, budget)* to balance
2 s'équilibrer *vpr (équipes)* to balance each other out; *(comptes)* to balance

équinoxe [ekinɔks] *nm* equinox

équipage [ekipaʒ] *nm (de navire, d'avion)* crew

équipe [ekip] *nf* team; *(d'ouvriers)* gang; **faire é. avec qn** to team up with sb; **é. de nuit** night shift; **é. de secours** rescue team • **équipier, -ière** *nmf* team member

équipée [ekipe] *nf* escapade

équiper [ekipe] **1** *vt* to equip (**de** with)
2 s'équiper *vpr* to equip oneself (**de** with) • **équipement** *nm* equipment

équitation [ekitɑsjɔ̃] *nf Br* (horse) riding, *Am* (horseback) riding; **faire de l'é.** to go riding

équité [ekite] *nf* fairness • **équitable** *adj* fair, equitable • **équitablement** [-əmɑ̃] *adv* fairly

équivalent, -ente [ekivalɑ̃, -ɑ̃t] *adj & nm* equivalent • **équivalence** *nf* equivalence • **équivaloir*** *vi* **é. à qch** to be equivalent to sth

équivoque [ekivɔk] **1** *adj (ambigu)* equivocal; *(douteux)* dubious; **sans é.** *(déclaration)* unequivocal
2 *nf* ambiguity

érable [erabl] *nm (arbre, bois)* maple

érafler [erafle] *vt* to graze, to scratch • **éraflure** *nf* graze, scratch

éraillée [erɑje] *adj f* **voix e.** rasping voice

ère [ɛr] *nf* era; **avant notre è.** BC; **en l'an 800 de notre è.** in the year 800 AD

érection [erɛksjɔ̃] *nf* erection

éreinter [erɛ̃te] **1** *vt (fatiguer)* to exhaust; *(critiquer)* to tear to pieces
2 s'éreinter *vpr* **s'é. à faire qch** to wear oneself out doing sth

érémiste [eremist] *nm Fam* = person receiving the RMI benefit

ergot [ɛrgo] *nm (de coq)* spur

ergoter [ɛrgɔte] *vi* to quibble (**sur** about)

ériger [eriʒe] **1** *vt* to erect
2 s'ériger *vpr* **s'é. en qch** to set oneself up as sth

ermite [ɛrmit] *nm* hermit

érosion [erozjɔ̃] *nf* erosion • **éroder** *vt* to erode

érotique [erɔtik] *adj* erotic • **érotisme** *nm* eroticism

errer [ɛre] *vi* to wander • **errant, -ante** *adj* wandering; **chien/chat e.** stray dog/cat

erreur [ɛrœr] *nf (faute)* mistake, error; **par e.** by mistake; **dans l'e.** mistaken; **sauf e. de ma part** unless I'm mistaken; **faire e.** *(au téléphone)* to dial the wrong number; **e. de calcul** miscalculation; **e. judiciaire** miscarriage of justice • **erroné, -ée** *adj* erroneous

ersatz [ɛrzats] *nm* substitute

éructer [erykte] *vi* to belch

érudit, -ite [erydi, -it] **1** *adj* scholarly, erudite
2 *nmf* scholar • **érudition** *nf* scholarship, erudition

éruption [erypsjɔ̃] *nf (de volcan)* eruption; *(de boutons)* rash

es [ɛ] *voir* **être**

ès [ɛs] *prép* of; **licencié/docteur ès lettres** ≃ BA/PhD

escabeau, -x [ɛskabo] *nm (marchepied)* stepladder, *Br* (pair of) steps; *(tabouret)* stool

escadre [ɛskadr] *nf Naut* squadron • **escadrille** *nf Av (unité)* flight • **escadron** *nm* squadron

escalade [ɛskalad] *nf* climbing; *(de prix, de violence, de guerre)* escalation • **escalader** *vt* to climb, to scale

escale [ɛskal] *nf Av* stopover; *Naut (lieu)* port of call; **faire e. à** *(avion)* to stop (over) at; *(navire)* to put in at; **vol sans e.** nonstop flight; **e. technique** refuelling stop

escalier [ɛskalje] *nm (marches)* stairs; *(cage)* staircase; **l'é., les escaliers** the stairs; **e. mécanique** *ou* **roulant** escalator; **e. de secours** fire escape; **e. de service** service stairs

escalope [ɛskalɔp] *nf* escalope

escamoter [ɛskamɔte] *vt (faire disparaître)* to make vanish; *(esquiver)* to dodge
• **escamotable** *adj Tech* retractable

escampette [ɛskɑ̃pɛt] *nf Fam* **prendre la poudre d'e.** to make off

escapade [ɛskapad] *nf* jaunt; **faire une e.** to go on a jaunt

escargot [ɛskargo] *nm* snail

escarmouche [ɛskarmuʃ] *nf* skirmish

escarpé, -ée [ɛskarpe] *adj* steep • **escarpement** [-əmɑ̃] *nm (côte)* steep slope

escarpin [ɛskarpɛ̃] *nm (soulier)* pump, *Br* court shoe

escient [ɛsjɑ̃] *nm* **à bon e.** wisely

esclaffer [ɛsklafe] **s'esclaffer** *vpr* to roar with laughter

esclandre [ɛsklɑ̃dr] *nm* (noisy) scene; **causer un e.** to make a scene

esclave [ɛsklav] *nmf* slave; **être l'e. de qn/qch** to be a slave to sb/sth • **esclavage** *nm* slavery

escompte [ɛskɔ̃t] *nm* discount; **taux d'e.** bank discount rate • **escompter** *vt (espérer)* to anticipate (**faire** doing), to expect (**faire** to do)

escorte [ɛskɔrt] *nf* escort; **sous bonne e.** under escort • **escorter** *vt* to escort

escouade [ɛskwad] *nf Mil* squad

escrime [ɛskrim] *nf Sport* fencing; **faire de l'e.** to fence • **escrimeur, -euse** *nmf* fencer

escrimer [ɛskrime] **s'escrimer** *vpr* **s'e. à faire qch** to struggle to do sth

escroc [ɛskro] *nm* crook, swindler
• **escroquer** *vt* **e. qn** to swindle sb; **e. qch à qn** to swindle sb out of sth • **escroquerie** *nf (action)* swindling; *(résultat)* swindle; *Fam* **c'est de l'e.!** it's a rip-off!

espace [ɛspas] *nm* space; **e. aérien** air space; **e. vert** garden, park • **espacer 1** *vt* to space out; **espacés d'un mètre** one metre apart **2 s'espacer** *vpr (maisons, visites)* to become less frequent

espadon [ɛspadɔ̃] *nm* swordfish

espadrille [ɛspadrij] *nf* = rope-soled sandal

Espagne [ɛspaɲ] *nf* **l'E.** Spain • **espagnol, -ole 1** *adj* Spanish **2** *nmf* **E., Espagnole** Spaniard **3** *nm (langue)* Spanish

espèce [ɛspɛs] *nf (race)* species; *(genre)* kind, sort; *Fam* **un e. d'idiot/une e. d'idiote** a silly fool; *Fam* **e. d'idiot!** you silly fool! • **espèces** *nfpl (argent)* cash; **en e.** in cash

espérance [ɛsperɑ̃s] *nf* hope; **au-delà de nos espérances** beyond our expectations; **répondre aux espérances de qn** to live up to sb's expectations; **e. de vie** life expectancy

espérer [ɛspere] **1** *vt* to hope for; **e. que...** to hope that...; **e. faire qch** to hope to do sth **2** *vi* to hope; **e. en qn/qch** to trust in sb/sth; **j'espère (bien)!** I hope so!

espiègle [ɛspjɛgl] *adj* mischievous • **espièglerie** [-əri] *nf* mischievousness

espion, -ionne [ɛspjɔ̃, -jɔn] *nmf* spy • **espionnage** *nm* spying, espionage • **espionner 1** *vt* to spy on **2** *vi* to spy

esplanade [ɛsplanad] *nf* esplanade

espoir [ɛspwar] *nm* hope; **avoir l'e. de faire qch** to have hopes of doing sth; **il n'y a plus d'e.** *(il va mourir)* there's no hope for him; **sans e.** *(cas)* hopeless; **les espoirs de la danse** the young hopefuls of the dancing world

esprit [ɛspri] *nm (attitude, fantôme)* spirit; *(intellect)* mind; *(humour)* wit; **venir à l'e. de qn** to cross sb's mind; **avoir de l'e.** to be witty; **avoir l'e. large/étroit** to be broad-/narrow-minded; **perdre l'e.** to go out of one's mind

esquimau, -aude, -aux, -audes [ɛskimo, -od] **1** *adj* Eskimo, *Am* Inuit
2 *nmf* **E., Esquimaude** Eskimo, *Am* Inuit
3 *nm* **E.**® *(glace) Br* ≃ choc-ice *(on a stick)*, *Am* ≃ ice-cream bar

esquinter [ɛskɛ̃te] *Fam* **1** *vt (voiture)* to damage; *(blesser)* to hurt
2 s'esquinter *vpr* **s'e. la jambe** to hurt one's leg; **s'e. la santé** to damage one's health; **s'e. à faire qch** to wear oneself out doing sth

esquisse [ɛskis] *nf (croquis, plan)* sketch
• **esquisser** *vt* to sketch; **e. un geste** to make a (slight) gesture

esquiver [ɛskive] **1** *vt (coup, problème)* to dodge
2 s'esquiver *vpr* to slip away

essai [esɛ] *nm (test)* test, trial; *(tentative) & Rugby* try; *(ouvrage)* essay; **à l'e.** *(objet)* on a trial basis; **coup d'e.** first attempt

essaim [esɛ̃] *nm* swarm

essayer [eseje] *vt* to try (**de faire** to do); *(vêtement)* to try on; *(méthode, restaurant)* to try out; **s'e. à qch/à faire qch** to try one's hand at sth/at doing sth • **essayage** [-ɛjaʒ] *nm (de vêtement)* fitting

essence [esãs] *nf (carburant) Br* petrol, *Am* gas; *(extrait) & Phil* essence; **par e.** essentially; **e. sans plomb** unleaded; **e. ordinaire** *Br* two-star petrol, *Am* regular gas

essentiel, -ielle [esãsjɛl] **1** *adj* essential (**à/pour** for)
2 *nm* **l'e.** *(le plus important)* the main thing; *(le minimum)* the essentials; **l'e. de** the majority of •**essentiellement** *adv* essentially

essieu, -x [esjø] *nm* axle

essor [esɔr] *nm (d'oiseau)* flight; *(de pays, d'entreprise)* rapid growth; **en plein e.** booming; **prendre son e.** to take off

essorer [esɔre] *vt (linge)* to wring; *(dans une essoreuse)* to spin-dry; *(dans une machine à laver)* to spin •**essoreuse** *nf (à main)* wringer; *(électrique)* spin-dryer

essouffler [esufle] **1** *vt* to make out of breath
2 **s'essouffler** *vpr* to get out of breath

essuyer [esɥije] **1** *vt (objet, surface)* to wipe; *(liquide)* to wipe up; *(larmes)* to wipe away; *(défaite)* to suffer; *(refus)* to meet with; **e. la vaisselle** to dry the dishes
2 **s'essuyer** *vpr* to wipe oneself; **s'e. les yeux** to wipe one's eyes •**essuie-glace** *(pl essuie-glaces)* *nm Br* windscreen wiper, *Am* windshield wiper •**essuie-mains** *nm inv* hand towel

est¹ [ɛ] *voir* **être**

est² [ɛst] **1** *nm* east; **à l'e.** in the east; *(direction)* (to the) east (**de** of); **d'e.** *(vent)* east(erly); **de l'e.** eastern
2 *adj inv (côte)* east(ern)

estafilade [ɛstafilad] *nf* gash

estampe [ɛstãp] *nf* print

estampille [ɛstãpij] *nf (de produit)* mark; *(de document)* stamp

esthète [ɛstɛt] *nmf Br* aesthete, *Am* esthete

esthéticienne [ɛstetisjɛn] *nf* beautician

esthétique [ɛstetik] *adj Br* aesthetic, *Am* esthetic

estime [ɛstim] *nf* esteem, regard

estimer [ɛstime] **1** *vt (tableau)* to value (**à** at); *(prix, distance, poids)* to estimate; *(dommages, besoins)* to assess; *(juger)* to consider (**que** that); **e. dangereux de faire qch** to consider it dangerous to do sth; **e. qn** to esteem sb
2 **s'estimer** *vpr* **s'e. heureux** to consider oneself happy •**estimable** *adj* respectable •**estimation** *nf (de mobilier)* valuation; *(de prix, de distance, de poids)* estimation; *(de dommages, de besoins)* assessment

estival, -e, -aux, -ales [ɛstival, -o] *adj* **travail/température estival(e)** summer work/temperature •**estivant, -ante** *nmf Br* holidaymaker, *Am* vacationer

estomac [ɛstɔma] *nm* stomach

estomaquer [ɛstɔmake] *vt Fam* to flabbergast

estomper [ɛstɔpe] **1** *vt (rendre flou)* to blur
2 **s'estomper** *vpr* to become blurred

estrade [ɛstrad] *nf* platform

estragon [ɛstragɔ̃] *nm (plante, condiment)* tarragon

estropier [ɛstrɔpje] *vt* to cripple, to maim •**estropié, -iée** *nmf* cripple

estuaire [ɛstɥɛr] *nm* estuary

esturgeon [ɛstyrʒɔ̃] *nm* sturgeon

et [e] *conj* and; **vingt et un** twenty-one; **et moi?** what about me?

étable [etabl] *nf* cowshed

établi [etabli] *nm* workbench

établir [etablir] **1** *vt (paix, relations, principe)* to establish; *(agence)* to set up; *(liste)* to draw up; *(record)* to set; *(démontrer)* to establish, to prove
2 **s'établir** *vpr (pour habiter)* to settle; *(pour exercer un métier)* to set up in business •**établissement** *nm (de paix, de relations, de principe)* establishment; *(entreprise)* business, firm; **é. scolaire** school

étage [etaʒ] *nm (d'immeuble)* floor, *Br* storey, *Am* story; *(de fusée)* stage; **à l'é.** upstairs; **au premier é.** on the *Br* first or *Am* second floor; **maison à deux étages** *Br* two-storeyed *or Am* two-storied house •**s'étager** *vpr* to rise in tiers

étagère [etaʒɛr] *nf* shelf; *(meuble)* shelving unit

étai [etɛ] *nm Tech* prop

étain [etɛ̃] *nm (métal)* tin; *(de gobelet)* pewter

étais, était [etɛ] *voir* **être**

étal [etal] *(pl* **étals**) *nm (au marché)* stall

étalage [etalaʒ] *nm* display; *(vitrine)* display window; **faire é. de son savoir** to show off one's knowledge •**étalagiste** *nmf* window dresser

étaler [etale] **1** *vt (disposer)* to lay out; *(en vitrine)* to display; *(beurre)* to spread; *(vacances, paiements)* to stagger; *Fig (érudition)* to show off
2 **s'étaler** *vpr Fam (s'affaler)* to sprawl; **s'é. sur** *(congés, paiements)* to be spread over; *Fam* **s'é. de tout son long** to fall flat on one's face •**étalement** *nm (de vacances, de paiements)* staggering

étalon [etalɔ̃] *nm (cheval)* stallion; *(modèle)* standard; **é.-or** gold standard

étanche [etɑ̃ʃ] *adj* watertight; *(montre)* waterproof

étancher [etɑ̃ʃe] *vt (sang)* to stop the flow of; *(soif)* to quench

étang [etɑ̃] *nm* pond

étant [etɑ̃] *p prés de* **être**

étape [etap] *nf (de voyage)* stage; *(lieu)* stop(over); **faire é. à** to stop off *or* over at; **par (petites) étapes** in (easy) stages; *Fig* **brûler les étapes** *(dans sa carrière)* to shoot to the top

état [eta] *nm* (a) *(condition, manière d'être)* state; *(inventaire)* statement; **à l'é. brut** in a raw state; **à l'é. neuf** as new; **de son é.** *(métier)* by trade; **en bon é.** in good condition; **en é. de marche** in working order; **en é. de faire qch** in a position to do sth; **hors d'é. de faire qch** not in a position to do sth; **faire é. de qch** to mention sth; **(ne pas) être dans son é. normal** (not) to be one's usual self; **être dans un é. second** to be spaced out; *Fam* **être dans tous ses états** to be in a state; **mettre qn en é. d'arrestation** to put sb under arrest; **remettre qch en é.** to repair sth; **é. d'âme** mood; **é. d'esprit** state *or* frame of mind; **é. de choses** state of affairs; **é. de santé** state of health; **é. des lieux** inventory of fixtures; **é. civil** register office (b) *(autorité centrale)* **É.** *(nation)* State • **étatisé, -ée** *adj* state-controlled

état-major [etamaʒɔr] *(pl* **états-majors***) nm Mil* (general) staff; *(de parti)* senior staff

États-Unis [etazyni] *nmpl* **les É. (d'Amérique)** the United States (of America)

étau, -x [eto] *nm (instrument) Br* vice, *Am* vise

étayer [eteje] *vt (mur)* to shore up; *(théorie)* to support

été¹ [ete] *nm* summer

été² [ete] *pp de* **être**

éteindre* [etɛ̃dr] **1** *vt (feu, cigarette)* to put out, to extinguish; *(lampe)* to switch off; *(gaz)* to turn off **2** *vi* to switch off **3 s'éteindre** *vpr (feu)* to go out; *(personne)* to pass away; *(race)* to die out; *(amour)* to die • **éteint, -einte** *adj (feu, bougie)* out; *(lampe, lumière)* off; *(volcan, race, famille)* extinct; *(voix)* faint

étendard [etɑ̃dar] *nm (drapeau)* standard

étendre [etɑ̃dr] **1** *vt (linge)* to hang out; *(nappe)* to spread out; *(beurre)* to spread; *(agrandir)* to extend; **é. le bras** to stretch out one's arm; **é. qn** to stretch sb out **2 s'étendre** *vpr (personne)* to lie down; *(plaine)* to stretch; *(feu)* to spread; *(pouvoir)* to extend; **s'é. sur qch** *(sujet)* to dwell on sth • **étendu, -ue** *adj (forêt, vocabulaire)* extensive; *(personne)* lying • **étendue** *nf (importance)* extent; *(surface)* area; *(d'eau)* expanse

éternel, -elle [etɛrnɛl] *adj* eternal • **éternellement** *adv* eternally, for ever • **s'éterniser** *vpr (débat)* to drag on endlessly; *Fam (visiteur)* to stay for ever • **éternité** *nf* eternity

éternuer [etɛrnɥe] *vi* to sneeze • **éternuement** [-ymɑ̃] *nm* sneeze

êtes [ɛt] *voir* **être**

éther [etɛr] *nm* ether

Éthiopie [etjɔpi] *nf* **l'É.** Ethiopia • **éthiopien, -ienne** **1** *adj* Ethiopian **2** *nmf* **É., Éthiopienne** Ethiopian

éthique [etik] **1** *adj* ethical **2** *nf Phil* ethics *(sing)*; **l'é. puritaine** the Puritan ethic

ethnie [etni] *nf* ethnic group • **ethnique** *adj* ethnic

étinceler [etɛ̃s(ə)le] *vi* to sparkle • **étincelle** *nf* spark; *Fam* **ça va faire des étincelles** sparks will fly

étioler [etjɔle] **s'étioler** *vpr* to wilt

étiqueter [etikte] *vt* to label • **étiquette** *nf* **1** *(marque)* label **2** *(protocole)* (diplomatic *or* court) etiquette

étirer [etire] **1** *vt* to stretch **2 s'étirer** *vpr* to stretch (oneself)

étoffe [etɔf] *nf* material, fabric; **avoir l'é. d'un héros** to be the stuff heroes are made of

étoffer [etɔfe] **1** *vt* to fill out; *(texte)* to make more meaty **2 s'étoffer** *vpr (personne)* to fill out

étoile [etwal] *nf* star; **à la belle é.** in the open; **être né sous une bonne é.** to be born under a lucky star; **é. de mer** starfish; **é. filante** shooting star • **étoilé, -ée** *adj (ciel, nuit)* starry; *(vitre)* cracked *(star-shaped)*

étonner [etɔne] **1** *vt* to surprise **2 s'étonner** *vpr* to be surprised (**de qch** at sth; **que** + *subjunctive* that) • **étonnant, -ante** *adj (ahurissant)* surprising; *(remarquable)* amazing • **étonnement** *nm* surprise

étouffer [etufe] **1** *vt (tuer)* to suffocate; *(bruit)* to muffle; *(feu)* to smother; *Fig (révolte, sentiment)* to stifle; *Fig (scandale)* to hush up **2** *vi* to suffocate; **on étouffe!** it's stifling!; **é. de colère** to choke with anger **3 s'étouffer** *vpr (en mangeant)* to choke (avec on); *(mourir)* to suffocate •**étouffant, -ante** *adj (air)* stifling •**étouffement** *nm* suffocation

étourdi, -ie [eturdi] **1** *adj* scatterbrained **2** *nmf* scatterbrain •**étourderie** *nf* absent-mindedness; **une é.** a thoughtless blunder

étourdir [eturdir] *vt* to stun, to daze; *(sujet: vin, vitesse)* to make dizzy •**étourdissant, -ante** *adj (bruit)* deafening; *(beauté)* stunning •**étourdissement** *nm (malaise)* dizzy spell

étourneau, -x [eturno] *nm* starling

étrange [etrɑ̃ʒ] *adj* strange, odd •**étrangement** *adv* strangely, oddly •**étrangeté** *nf* strangeness, oddness

étranger, -ère [etrɑ̃ʒe, -ɛr] **1** *adj (d'un autre pays)* foreign; *(non familier)* strange (à to); **il m'est é.** he's unknown to me **2** *nmf (d'un autre pays)* foreigner; *(inconnu)* stranger; **à l'é.** abroad; **de l'é.** from abroad

étrangler [etrɑ̃gle] **1** *vt* **é. qn** *(tuer)* to strangle sb; *(col)* to choke sb **2** **s'étrangler** *vpr (de colère, en mangeant)* to choke •**étranglé, -ée** *adj (voix)* choking; *(passage)* constricted •**étranglement** [-əmɑ̃] *nm (de personne)* strangulation

être* [ɛtr] **1** *vi* to be; **il est tailleur** he's a tailor; **est-ce qu'elle vient?** is she coming?; **il vient, n'est-ce pas?** he's coming, isn't he?; **est-ce qu'il aime le thé?** does he like tea?; **nous sommes dix** there are ten of us; **nous sommes le dix** today is the tenth; **où en es-tu?** how far have you *Br* got *or Am* gotten?; **il a été à Paris** *(il y est allé)* he has been to Paris; **elle est de Paris** she's from Paris; **elle est de la famille** she's one of the family; **il est cinq heures** it's five (o'clock); **il était une fois...** once upon a time, there was...; **c'est à lire pour demain** *(obligation)* this has to be read for tomorrow; **c'est à voir absolument** *(exposition)* it's well worth seeing; **c'est à lui** it's his; **il n'est plus** *(il est mort)* he is dead; **si j'étais vous** if I were *or* was you; **cela étant** that being so **2** *v aux (avec 'venir', 'partir')* to have/to be; **elle est (déjà) arrivée** she has (already) arrived; **elle est née en 1980** she was born in 1980; **nous y sommes toujours bien reçus** *(passif)* we are always well received **3** *nm (personne)* being; **les êtres chers** the loved ones; **ê. humain** human being; **ê. vivant** living being

étreindre* [etrɛ̃dr] *vt* to grip; *(avec amour)* to embrace •**étreinte** *nf* grip; *(amoureuse)* embrace

étrenner [etrene] *vt* to use for the first time; *(vêtement)* to wear for the first time

étrennes [etrɛn] *nfpl* New Year gift; *(gratification)* ≃ Christmas tip *or Br* box

étrier [etrije] *nm* stirrup; **mettre le pied à l'é. à qn** to help sb get off to a good start

étriper [etripe] **s'étriper** *vpr Fam* to tear each other apart

étriqué, -ée [etrike] *adj (vêtement)* tight; *Fig (esprit, vie)* narrow

étroit, -oite [etrwa, -at] *adj* narrow; *(vêtement)* tight; *(lien, collaboration)* close; **être à l'é.** to be cramped •**étroitement** *adv (surveiller)* closely •**étroitesse** *nf* narrowness; *(de lien)* closeness; **é. d'esprit** narrow-mindedness

étude [etyd] *nf (action, ouvrage)* study; *(de notaire)* office; *Scol (pièce)* study room; *(période)* study period; **à l'é.** *(projet)* under consideration; **faire des études de français** to study French; **faire une é. de marché** to do market research; **é. de cas** case study

étudiant, -iante [etydjɑ̃, -jɑ̃t] **1** *nmf* student; **être é. en droit** to be a law student **2** *adj (vie)* student

étudier [etydje] *vti* to study

étui [etɥi] *nm (à lunettes, à cigarettes)* case; *(de revolver)* holster

étymologie [etimɔlɔʒi] *nf* etymology

eu, eue [y] *pp de* **avoir**

eucalyptus [økaliptys] *nm* eucalyptus

eucharistie [økaristi] *nf Rel* **l'e.** the Eucharist

eugénisme [øʒenism] *nm* eugenics *(sing)*

euh [ø] *exclam* hem!, er!, well!

euphémisme [øfemism] *nm* euphemism

euphorie [øfɔri] *nf* euphoria

eurent [yr] *voir* **avoir**

euro [øro] *nm (monnaie)* euro

euro- [øro] *préf* Euro-

eurocrate [ørɔkrat] *nmf* Eurocrat

eurodéputé [ørodepyte] *nm* Euro MP

eurodollar [ørɔdɔlar] *nm* Eurodollar

Europe [ørɔp] *nf* **l'E.** Europe; **l'E. (des douze)** the Twelve (countries of the Common Market); **l'E. verte** European Community agriculture •**européen, -éenne 1** *adj* European **2** *nmf* **E., Européenne** European

eurosceptique [ørosɛptik] *nmf* Eurosceptic

eut [y] *voir* **avoir**

euthanasie [øtanazi] *nf* euthanasia

eux [ø] *pron personnel (sujet)* they; *(complément)* them; *(réfléchi, emphase)* themselves •**eux-mêmes** *pron* themselves

évacuer [evakɥe] *vt* to evacuate; *(liquide)* to drain off •**évacuation** *nf* evacuation

évader [evade] **s'évader** *vpr* to escape (**de** from) •**évadé, -ée** *nmf* escaped prisoner

> ℓ Il faut noter que le verbe anglais **to evade** est un faux ami. Il signifie **éviter**.

évaluer [evalɥe] *vt (fortune)* to estimate; *(meuble)* to value •**évaluation** *nf* estimation; *(de meuble)* valuation

évangile [evãʒil] *nm* gospel; **l'É.** the Gospel; *Fig* **parole d'é.** gospel (truth) •**évangélique** *adj* evangelical

évanouir [evanwir] **s'évanouir** *vpr (personne)* to faint; *(espoir, crainte)* to vanish •**évanoui, -ouie** *adj* unconscious •**évanouissement** *nm (syncope)* fainting fit

évaporer [evapɔre] **s'évaporer** *vpr* to evaporate; *Fig (disparaître)* to vanish into thin air •**évaporation** *nf* evaporation

évasé, -ée [evaze] *adj (jupe)* flared

évasif, -ive [evazif, -iv] *adj* evasive

évasion [evazjɔ̃] *nf* escape (**de** from); *(hors de la réalité)* escapism; **é. de capitaux** flight of capital; **é. fiscale** tax evasion

> ℓ Il faut noter que le nom anglais **evasion** est un faux ami. Il signifie le plus souvent **dérobade**.

évêché [eveʃe] *nm (territoire)* bishopric, see

éveil [evɛj] *nm* awakening; **être en é.** to be alert; **donner l'é. à qn** to alert sb; *Scol* **activité d'é.** early-learning activity

éveiller [eveje] **1** *vt (susciter)* to arouse; **é. qn** to awaken sb
2 s'éveiller *vpr* to awaken (**à** to); *(intelligence)* to develop •**éveillé, -ée** *adj* awake; *(vif)* alert

événement [evɛnmã] *nm* event

éventail [evãtaj] *nm (instrument)* fan; *(choix)* range; **en é.** *(orteils)* spread out

éventer [evãte] **1** *vt (secret)* to discover; **é. qn** to fan sb
2 s'éventer *vpr (vin, parfum)* to turn stale; *(bière)* to go flat •**éventé, -ée** *adj (vin, parfum)* stale; *(bière)* flat

éventrer [evãtre] *vt (oreiller)* to rip open; *(animal)* to open up

éventuel, -uelle [evãtɥel] *adj* possible •**éventualité** *nf* possibility; **dans l'é. de** in

the event of; **parer à toute é.** to be prepared for all eventualities •**éventuellement** *adv* possibly

> ℓ Il faut noter que les termes anglais **eventual** et **eventually** sont des faux amis. Ils signifient respectivement **final** et **finalement**.

évêque [evɛk] *nm* bishop

évertuer [evɛrtɥe] **s'évertuer** *vpr* **s'é. à faire qch** to endeavour to do sth

éviction [eviksjɔ̃] *nf (de concurrent, de président)* ousting; *(de locataire)* eviction

évident, -ente [evidã, -ãt] *adj* obvious (**que** that); *Fam (facile)* easy •**évidemment** [-amã] *adv* obviously •**évidence** *nf* obviousness; **une é.** an obvious fact; **nier l'é.** to deny the obvious; **en é.** in a prominent position; **mettre qch en é.** to highlight sth; **se rendre à l'é.** to face the facts; **à l'é.** obviously

> ℓ Il faut noter que les termes anglais **evidently** et **evidence** sont des faux amis. Le premier signifie **manifestement**, et le second signifie le plus souvent **preuve**.

évider [evide] *vt* to hollow out

évier [evje] *nm* (kitchen) sink

évincer [evɛ̃se] *vt (concurrent, président)* to oust (**de** from)

> ℓ Il faut noter que le verbe anglais **to evince** est un faux ami. Il signifie **faire preuve de**.

éviter [evite] *vt* to avoid (**de faire** doing); **é. qch à qn** to spare *or* save sb sth; **je voulais é. que vous ne vous déplaciez pour rien** I wanted to save you coming for nothing

évoluer [evɔlɥe] *vi (changer)* to develop; *(société, idée, situation)* to evolve; *(se déplacer)* to move around; **é. dans un milieu artistique** to move in artistic circles •**évolué, -uée** *adj (pays)* advanced; *(personne)* enlightened •**évolution** *nf (changement)* development; *Biol* evolution; **évolutions** *(mouvements)* movements

évoquer [evɔke] *vt* to evoke •**évocateur, -trice** *adj* evocative •**évocation** *nf* evocation

ex [ɛks] *nmf Fam (mari, femme)* ex

ex- [ɛks] *préf* ex-; **ex-mari** ex-husband

exacerber [ɛgzasɛrbe] *vt (douleur)* to exacerbate

exact, -e [ɛgzakt] *adj (quantité, poids, nombre)* exact, precise; *(rapport, description)* exact, accurate; *(mot)* right, correct;

(ponctuel) punctual • **exactement** [-əmã] *adv* exactly • **exactitude** *nf (précision, fidélité)* exactness; *(justesse)* correctness; *(ponctualité)* punctuality

exactions [ɛgzaksjɔ̃] *nfpl* atrocities

ex æquo [ɛgzeko] **1** *adj inv Sport* être classés e. to tie, to be equally placed **2** *adv* être troisième e. to tie for third place

exagérer [ɛgzaʒere] **1** *vt* to exaggerate **2** *vi (parler)* to exaggerate; *(agir)* to go too far • **exagération** *nf* exaggeration • **exagéré, -ée** *adj* excessive • **exagérément** *adv* excessively

exalter [ɛgzalte] *vt (glorifier)* to exalt; *(passionner)* to stir • **exaltant, -ante** *adj* stirring • **exaltation** *nf (délire)* intense excitement • **exalté, -ée 1** *adj (sentiment)* impassioned **2** *nmf Péj* fanatic

examen [ɛgzamɛ̃] *nm* examination; **e. blanc** mock exam; **e. médical** medical examination; **e. de la vue** eye test • **examinateur, -trice** *nmf* examiner • **examiner** *vt (considérer, regarder)* to examine

exaspérer [ɛgzaspere] *vt (personne)* to exasperate; *Fig (douleur)* to aggravate • **exaspération** *nf* exasperation

exaucer [ɛgzose] *vt (désir)* to grant; **e. qn** to grant sb's wish

excavation [ɛkskavasjɔ̃] *nf (trou, action)* excavation

excéder [ɛksede] *vt (dépasser)* to exceed; **é. qn** *(énerver)* to exasperate sb • **excédent** *nm* surplus, excess; **e. de bagages** excess luggage *or Am* baggage • **excédentaire** *adj* **poids e.** excess weight

excellent, -ente [ɛkselã, -ãt] *adj* excellent • **excellence** *nf* excellence; **c'est le chercheur par e.** he's the researcher par excellence; **E.** *(titre)* Excellency • **exceller** *vi* to excel **(en** at)

excentrique [ɛksãtrik] *adj & nmf* eccentric • **excentricité** *nf* eccentricity

excepté¹ [ɛksɛpte] *prép* except • **excepté², -ée** *adj* except (for); **les femmes exceptées** except (for) the women • **excepter** *vt* to except

exception [ɛksɛpsjɔ̃] *nf* exception; **à l'e. de** except (for), with the exception of; **faire e.** to be an exception • **exceptionnel, -elle** *adj* exceptional • **exceptionnellement** *adv* exceptionally

excès [ɛksɛ] *nm* excess; **faire des e. (de table)** to overindulge; **e. de vitesse** speeding; **faire un e. de vitesse** to speed • **excessif, -ive** *adj* excessive • **excessivement** *adv* excessively

excitation [ɛksitasjɔ̃] *nf (agitation)* excitement; **e. à** *(haine)* incitement to

exciter [ɛksite] **1** *vt (faire naître)* to arouse; **e. qn** *(énerver)* to excite sb; **e. qn à la révolte** to incite sb to revolt **2** s'**exciter** *vpr (devenir nerveux)* to get excited • **excitable** *adj* excitable • **excitant, -ante 1** *adj Fam* exciting **2** *nm* stimulant • **excité, -ée** *adj* excited

exclamer [ɛksklame] s'**exclamer** *vpr* to exclaim • **exclamatif, -ive** *adj* exclamatory • **exclamation** *nf* exclamation

exclure* [ɛksklyr] *vt (écarter)* to exclude (**de** from); *(chasser)* to expel (**de** from); **e. qch** *(rendre impossible)* to preclude sth • **exclu, -ue** *adj (solution)* out of the question; *(avec une date)* exclusive

exclusif, -ive [ɛksklyzif, -iv] *adj (droit, modèle, préoccupation)* exclusive • **exclusivement** *adv* exclusively • **exclusivité** *nf Com* exclusive rights; *(dans la presse)* scoop; **en e.** *(film)* having an exclusive showing (**à** at)

exclusion [ɛksklyzjɔ̃] *nf* exclusion; **à l'e. de** with the exception of

excommunier [ɛkskɔmynje] *vt* to excommunicate • **excommunication** *nf* excommunication

excréments [ɛkskremã] *nmpl* excrement

excroissance [ɛkskrwasãs] *nf* excrescence

excursion [ɛkskyrsjɔ̃] *nf* trip, excursion; *(de plusieurs jours)* tour; **faire une e.** to go on a trip/tour

excuse [ɛkskyz] *nf (prétexte)* excuse; **excuses** *(regrets)* apology; **faire des excuses** to apologize (**à** to); **toutes mes excuses** (my) sincere apologies • **excuser 1** *vt (justifier, pardonner)* to excuse (**qn d'avoir fait/qn de faire** sb for doing) **2** s'**excuser** *vpr* to apologize (**de** for; **auprès de** to); **excusez-moi!, je m'excuse!** excuse me!

exécrer [ɛgzekre] *vt* to loathe • **exécrable** *adj* atrocious

exécuter [ɛgzekyte] **1** *vt (travail, projet, tâche)* to carry out; *(peinture)* to execute; *Mus (jouer)* to perform; *Ordinat* to run; **e. qn** to execute sb **2** s'**exécuter** *vpr* to comply • **exécutant, -ante** *nmf (musicien)* performer; *(ouvrier, employé)* subordinate • **exécution** *nf (de travail)* carrying out; *(de musique)* performance; *(de peinture, de condamné) & Ordinat* execution; **mettre qch à e.** to carry sth out

exécutif [ɛgzekytif] **1** *adj m* **pouvoir e.** executive power **2** *nm* **l'e.** the executive

exemplaire [ɛgzãplɛr] **1** *adj* exemplary **2** *nm (livre)* copy; **photocopier un docu-**

ment en double e. to make two photo-copies of a document

exemple [ɛgzãpl] *nm* example; **par e.** for example, for instance; **donner l'e.** to set an example (**à** to); **prendre e. sur qn** to follow sb's example; **faire un e.** to make an example (of someone); **c'est un e. de vertu** he's a model of virtue; *Fam* **(ça) par e.!** good heavens!

exempt, -empte [ɛgzã, -ãt] *adj* **e. de** *(dispensé de)* exempt from; *(sans)* free from •**exempter** [ɛgzãte] *vt* to exempt (**de** from) •**exemption** *nf* exemption

exercer [ɛgzɛrse] **1** *vt (voix, droits)* to exercise; *(autorité, influence)* to exert (**sur** on); *(profession) Br* to practise, *Am* to practice; **e. qn à qch** to train sb in sth; **e. qn à faire qch** to train sb to do sth **2** *vi (médecin) Br* to practise, *Am* to practice **3 s'exercer** *vpr (s'entraîner)* to train; **s'e. à qch** to *Br* practise *orAm* practice sth; **s'e. à faire qch** to *Br* practise *or Am* practice doing sth

exercice [ɛgzɛrsis] *nm (physique)* & *Scol* exercise; *Mil* drill; *(de métier)* practice; **l'e. de** *(pouvoir)* the exercise of; **en e.** *(fonctionnaire)* in office; *(médecin)* in practice; **dans l'e. de ses fonctions** in the exercise of one's duties; **faire de l'e., prendre de l'e.** to (take) exercise

exhaler [ɛgzale] *vt (odeur)* to give off

exhaustif, -ive [ɛgzostif, -iv] *adj* exhaustive

exhiber [ɛgzibe] *vt (documents, passe-port)* to produce; *Péj (savoir, richesses)* to show off, to flaunt •**exhibition** *nf Péj* flaunting •**exhibitionniste** *nmf* exhibitionist

⌐⌐⌐⌐⌐⌐⌐⌐⌐⌐⌐⌐⌐⌐⌐⌐⌐⌐⌐⌐⌐⌐⌐⌐⌐⌐⌐⌐⌐⌐
🔔 Il faut noter que le nom anglais **exhibition** est un faux ami. Il signifie le plus souvent **exposition**.
⌐⌐⌐⌐⌐⌐⌐⌐⌐⌐⌐⌐⌐⌐⌐⌐⌐⌐⌐⌐⌐⌐⌐⌐⌐⌐⌐⌐⌐⌐

exhorter [ɛgzɔrte] *vt* to exhort (**à faire** to do)

exhumer [ɛgzyme] *vt (corps)* to exhume; *(vestiges)* to dig up

exiger [ɛgziʒe] *vt (exiger)* to demand (**de** from); *(nécessiter)* to require; **e. que qch soit fait** to demand that sth be done •**exigeant, -ante** *adj* demanding, exacting •**exigence** *nf (caractère)* exacting nature; *(condition)* demand

exigu, -uë [ɛgzigy] *adj* cramped, tiny •**exiguïté** *nf* crampedness

exil [ɛgzil] *nm* exile •**exilé, -ée** *nmf (personne)* exile •**exiler 1** *vt* to exile **2 s'exiler** *vpr* to go into exile

existence [ɛgzistãs] *nf (fait d'exister)* existence; *(vie)* life; **moyen d'e.** means of existence •**existant, -ante** *adj* existing •**existentialisme** *nm* existentialism •**exister 1** *vi* to exist **2** *v impersonnel* **il existe** there is/there are

exode [ɛgzɔd] *nm* exodus; **e. rural** rural depopulation

exonérer [ɛgzɔnere] *vt* to exempt (**de** from); **exonéré d'impôts** exempt from tax •**exonération** *nf* exemption

exorbitant, -ante [ɛgzɔrbitã, -ãt] *adj* exorbitant

exorbité, -ée [ɛgzɔrbite] *adj* **yeux exorbités** bulging eyes

exorciser [ɛgzɔrsize] *vt* to exorcize •**exorcisme** *nm* exorcism

exotique [ɛgzɔtik] *adj* exotic •**exotisme** *nm* exoticism

expansif, -ive [ɛkspãsif, -iv] *adj* expansive

expansion [ɛkspãsjɔ̃] *nf (de commerce, de pays, de gaz)* expansion; **en (pleine) e.** *(fast or rapidly)* expanding

expatrier [ɛkspatrije] **s'expatrier** *vpr* to leave one's country •**expatrié, -iée** *adj* & *nmf* expatriate

expectative [ɛkspɛktativ] *nf* **être dans l'e.** to be waiting to see what happens

expédient [ɛkspedjã] *nm (moyen)* expedient

expédier [ɛkspedje] *vt (envoyer)* to send, to dispatch; *(affaires, client)* to deal promptly with •**expéditeur, -trice** *nmf* sender •**expéditif, -ive** *adj* hasty •**expédition** *nf (envoi)* dispatch; *(voyage)* expedition

expérience [ɛksperjãs] *nf (connaissance)* experience; *(scientifique)* experiment; **faire l'e. de qch** to experience sth; **avoir de l'e.** to have experience; **être sans e.** to have no experience; **un homme d'e.** a man of experience •**expérimental, -e, -aux, -ales** *adj* experimental •**expérimentation** *nf* experimentation

expérimenter [ɛksperimãte] *vt (remède, vaccin)* to try out •**expérimenté, -ée** *adj* experienced

expert, -erte [ɛkspɛr, -ɛrt] **1** *adj* expert, skilled (**en** in); **être e. en la matière** to be an expert on the subject **2** *nm* expert (**en** on *or* in); *(d'assurances)* valuer •**expert-comptable** *(pl* **experts-comptables***) nm Br* ≃ chartered account-ant, *Am* ≃ certified public accountant •**expertise** *nf (évaluation)* valuation; *(rapport)* expert's report; *(compétence)* expertise

expier [ɛkspje] *vt (péchés, crime)* to expiate, to atone for •**expiation** *nf* expiation (**de** of)

expirer [ɛkspire] **1** *vti* to breathe out **2** *vi (mourir)* to pass away; *(finir, cesser)* to expire •**expiration** *nf (respiration)* breathing out; *(échéance)* Br expiry, Am expiration; **arriver à e.** to expire

explication [ɛksplikɑsjɔ̃] *nf* explanation; *(mise au point)* discussion; *Scol* **e. de texte** textual analysis

explicite [ɛksplisit] *adj* explicit •**explicitement** *adv* explicitly

expliquer [ɛksplike] **1** *vt* to explain (**à** to; **que** that) **2 s'expliquer** *vpr* to explain oneself; *(discuter)* to talk things over (**avec** with); **s'e. qch** *(comprendre)* to understand sth; **ça s'explique** that is understandable •**explicable** *adj* understandable •**explicatif, -ive** *adj* explanatory

exploit [ɛksplwa] *nm* feat

exploiter [ɛksplwate] *vt (champs)* to farm; *(ferme, entreprise)* to run; *(mine)* to work; *Fig & Péj (personne, situation)* to exploit •**exploitant, -ante** *nmf* **e. agricole** farmer •**exploitation** *nf (de champs)* farming; *(de ferme)* running; *(de mine)* working; *Péj* exploitation; *Ordinat* **système d'e.** operating system; **e. agricole** farm; **e. minière** mine

explorer [ɛksplɔre] *vt* to explore •**explorateur, -trice** *nmf* explorer •**exploration** *nf* exploration

exploser [ɛksploze] *vi (gaz, bombe, personne)* to explode; **faire e. qch** to explode sth •**explosif, -ive** *adj & nm* explosive •**explosion** *nf* explosion; *(de colère, joie)* outburst

exporter [ɛkspɔrte] *vt* to export (**vers** to; **de** from) •**exportateur, -trice 1** *nmf* exporter **2** *adj* exporting •**exportation** *nf (produit)* export; *(action)* export(ation); *Ordinat (de fichier)* exporting

exposer [ɛkspoze] **1** *vt (tableau)* to exhibit; *(marchandises)* to display; *(raison, théorie)* to set out; *(vie, réputation)* to risk, to endanger; *Phot (film)* to expose; **e. qch à la lumière** to expose sth to the light; **e. qn à la critique** to expose sb to criticism; **je leur ai exposé ma situation** I explained my situation to them **2 s'exposer** *vpr* **s'e. au danger** to put oneself in danger; **s'e. à la critique** to lay oneself open to criticism; **ne t'expose pas trop longtemps** don't stay in the sun too long •**exposant, -ante** *nmf (artiste, commerçant)* exhibitor •**exposé, -ée 1** *adj*

e. au sud facing south **2** *nm (compte rendu)* account (**de** of); *(présentation)* talk; *Scol* paper

exposition [ɛkspozisjɔ̃] *nf (d'objets d'art)* exhibition; *(de marchandises)* display; *(au danger) & Phot* exposure (**à** to); *(de maison)* aspect

exprès¹ [ɛksprɛ] *adv* on purpose, intentionally; *(spécialement)* specially; **comme (par) un fait e.** almost as if it was meant to be

exprès², -esse [ɛksprɛs] *adj (ordre, condition)* express •**expressément** *adv* expressly

exprès³ [ɛksprɛs] *adj inv* **lettre/colis e.** special delivery letter/parcel

express [ɛksprɛs] *adj & nm inv (train)* express; *(café)* espresso

expressif, -ive [ɛkspresif, -iv] *adj* expressive •**expression** *nf (phrase, mine)* expression; *Fig* **réduire qch à sa plus simple e.** to reduce sth to its simplest form •**exprimer 1** *vt* to express **2 s'exprimer** *vpr* to express oneself

exproprier [ɛksprɔprije] *vt* to expropriate

expulser [ɛkspylse] *vt* to expel (**de** from); *(joueur)* to send off; *(locataire)* to evict •**expulsion** *nf* expulsion; *(de joueur)* sending off; *(de locataire)* eviction

expurger [ɛkspyrʒe] *vt* to expurgate

exquis, -ise [ɛkski, -iz] *adj (nourriture)* exquisite

exsangue [ɛksɑ̃g] *adj (visage)* bloodless

extase [ɛkstɑz] *nf* ecstasy; **tomber en e. devant qch** to be in raptures over sth •**s'extasier** *vpr* to be in raptures (**sur** over or about)

extensible [ɛkstɑ̃sibl] *adj (métal)* tensile; *(tissu)* stretch •**extension** *nf (de muscle)* stretching; *(de durée, de contrat)* extension; *(essor)* expansion; **par e.** by extension

exténuer [ɛkstenɥe] *vt (fatiguer)* to exhaust •**exténué, -uée** *adj* exhausted

> ℓ Il faut noter que le verbe anglais **to extenuate** est un faux ami. Il signifie **atténuer**.

extérieur, -ieure [ɛksterjœr] **1** *adj (monde)* outside; *(surface)* outer, external; *(signe)* outward, external; *(politique)* foreign; **e. à qch** external to sth; **signe e. de richesse** outward sign of wealth **2** *nm* outside, exterior; **à l'e. (de)** outside; **à l'e.** *(match)* away; **tourner un film en e.** to shoot a film on location •**exté-**

rieurement *adv* externally; *(en appa-rence)* outwardly ●**extérioriser** *vt* to ex-press

exterminer [ɛkstɛrmine] *vt* to extermin-ate ●**extermination** *nf* extermination

externat [ɛkstɛrna] *nm (école)* day school

externe [ɛkstɛrn] **1** *adj* external **2** *nmf (élève)* day pupil; *Méd* = non-resident hospital medical student, *Am* extern

extincteur [ɛkstɛ̃ktœr] *nm* fire extin-guisher ●**extinction** *nf (de feu)* extin-guishing; *(de race)* extinction; **e. de voix** loss of voice

extirper [ɛkstirpe] **1** *vt* to eradicate **2 s'extirper** *vpr* **s'e. de** *(endroit)* to ex-tricate oneself from

extorquer [ɛkstɔrke] *vt* to extort (**à** from) ●**extorsion** *nf* extortion; **e. de fonds** ex-tortion

extra [ɛkstra] **1** *adj inv Fam (très bon)* top-quality **2** *nm inv Culin (gâterie)* (extra-special) treat; *(serviteur)* extra hand

extra- [ɛkstra] *préf* extra- ●**extrafin, -ine** *adj* extra-fine ●**extrafort, -orte** *adj* extra-strong

extradition [ɛkstradisjɔ̃] *nf* extradition ●**extrader** *vt* to extradite

extraire* [ɛkstrɛr] *vt* to extract (**de** from); *(charbon)* to mine ●**extraction** *nf* extrac-tion ●**extrait** *nm* extract; **e. de naissance** birth certificate

extralucide [ɛkstralysid] *adj & nmf* clair-voyant

extraordinaire [ɛkstraɔrdinɛr] *adj* ex-traordinary; **si par e.** if by some remote chance ●**extraordinairement** *adv* excep-tionally; *(très, bizarrement)* extraordinar-ily

extraterrestre [ɛkstratɛrɛstr] *adj & nmf* extraterrestrial

extravagant, -ante [ɛkstravagɑ̃, -ɑ̃t] *adj (idée, comportement)* extravagant ●**ex-travagance** *nf (d'idée, de comportement)* extravagance

extraverti, -ie [ɛkstravɛrti] *nmf* extrovert

extrême [ɛkstrɛm] **1** *adj* extreme; *Pol* **l'e. droite/gauche** the far *or* extreme right/left **2** *nm* extreme; **pousser qch à l'e.** to take *or* carry sth to extremes ●**extrêmement** *adv* extremely ●**Extrême-Orient** *nm* **l'E.** the Far East ●**extrémiste** *adj & nmf* ex-tremist ●**extrémité** *nf (bout)* extremity, end; **extrémités** *(pieds et mains)* extrem-ities; **être à la dernière e.** to be on the point of death

exubérant, -ante [ɛgzyberɑ̃, -ɑ̃t] *adj* exuberant ●**exubérance** *nf* exuberance

exulter [ɛgzylte] *vi* to exult, to rejoice ●**exultation** *nf* exultation

exutoire [ɛgzytwar] *nm* outlet (**à** for)

F¹, f [ɛf] *nm inv* F, f
F² *abrév* franc(s)
fa [fɑ] *nm (note de musique)* F
fable [fɑbl] *nf* fable
fabricant, -ante [fabrikɑ̃, -ɑ̃t] *nmf* manufacturer • **fabrication** *nf* manufacture; **f. artisanale** production by craftsmen; **de f. artisanale** hand-made; **de f. française** of French make
fabrique [fabrik] *nf* factory

> ⓘ Il faut noter que le nom anglais **fabric** est un faux ami. Il signifie le plus souvent **tissu**.

fabriquer [fabrike] *vt (objet)* to make; *(en usine)* to manufacture; *Péj (récit)* to fabricate, to make up; *Fam* **qu'est-ce qu'il fabrique?** what's he up to?
fabuler [fabyle] *vi* to make up stories
fabuleux, -euse [fabylø, -øz] *adj (légendaire, incroyable)* fabulous
fac [fak] *nf Fam* university; **à la f.** *Br* at university, *Am* at school
façade [fasad] *nf* façade
face [fas] *nf (visage)* face; *(de cube, de montagne)* side; *(de pièce de monnaie)* head; **en f.** opposite; **en f. de** opposite, facing; *(en présence de)* in front of; **f. à** *(vis-à-vis)* facing; **f. à f.** face to face; **f. à un problème** faced with a problem; **faire f. à** *(situation)* to face up to; **regarder qn en f.** to look sb in the face; **sauver/perdre la f.** to save/lose face; *Fig* **se voiler la f.** to hide from reality; **photo de f.** full-face (photo) • **face-à-face** *nm inv* **f. télévisé** face-to-face TV encounter
facétie [fasesi] *nf* joke • **facétieux, -ieuse** [-esjø, -øz] *adj (personne)* facetious
facette [faset] *nf (de diamant, de problème)* facet
fâcher [fɑʃe] **1** *vt* to anger
2 se fâcher *vpr* to get angry (**contre** with); **se f. avec qn** to fall out with sb • **fâché, -ée** *adj (air)* angry; *(amis)* on bad terms; **f. avec** *ou* **contre qn** angry with sb; *Fam* **être f. avec l'orthographe** to be a hopeless speller; **f. de qch** sorry about sth • **fâcheux, -euse** *adj (nouvelle)* unfortunate
facho [faʃo] *adj & nmf Fam* fascist

facile [fasil] *adj* easy; *(caractère, humeur)* easy-going; *Péj (banal)* facile; **c'est f. à faire** it's easy to do; **il nous est f. de faire ça** it's easy for us to do that; **f. à vivre** easy to get along with • **facilement** *adv* easily • **facilité** *nf (simplicité)* easiness; *(aisance)* ease; *Com* **facilités de paiement** payment facilities; **avoir des facilités pour qch** to have an aptitude for sth • **faciliter** *vt* to make easier, to facilitate
façon [fasɔ̃] *nf* (**a**) *(manière)* way; **la f. dont elle parle** the way (in which) she talks; **de quelle f.?** how?; **façons** *(comportements)* manners; **une f. de parler** a manner of speaking; **à la f. de** in the fashion of; **de toute f.** anyway, anyhow; **d'une certaine f.** in some way; **de f. à** so as to; **de f. à ce qu'on vous comprenne** so as to be understood, so that you may be understood; **de f. générale** generally speaking; **d'une f. ou d'une autre** one way or another; **à ma f.** my way, (in) my own way; **faire des façons** to make a fuss; **accepter qch sans f.** to accept sth without fuss; **table f. chêne** imitation oak table; **f. cuir** imitation leather
(**b**) *(coupe de vêtement)* cut, style
façonner [fasɔne] *vt (travailler, former)* to shape; *(fabriquer)* to make
facteur [faktœr] *nm* (**a**) *(employé) Br* postman, *Am* mailman (**b**) *(élément)* factor • **factrice** *nf Fam Br* postwoman, *Am* mailwoman
factice [faktis] *adj* false; **diamant f.** imitation diamond
faction [faksjɔ̃] *nf (groupe)* faction; **de f.** *(soldat)* on guard duty
facture [faktyr] *nf Com* bill, invoice • **facturer** *vt* to bill, to invoice
facultatif, -ive [fakyltatif, -iv] *adj (travail)* optional; *Scol* **matière/épreuve facultative** optional subject/test paper
faculté [fakylte] *nf* (**a**) *(aptitude)* faculty; **une grande f. de travail** a great capacity for work; **facultés mentales** faculties (**b**) *(d'université)* faculty; **à la f.** *Br* at university, *Am* at school
fada [fada] *Fam* **1** *adj* nuts
2 *nm* nutcase

fadaises [fadɛz] *nfpl* nonsense

fade [fad] *adj* insipid • **fadasse** *adj Fam* wishy-washy

fagot [fago] *nm* bundle of firewood • **fagoter** *vt Péj* to dress

faible [fɛbl] **1** *adj* weak, feeble; *(bruit, voix)* faint; *(vent, chances)* slight; *(quantité, revenus)* small; **f. en anglais** poor at English

2 *nm* weakling; **les faibles** the weak; **f. d'esprit** feeble-minded person; **avoir un f. pour qn** to have a soft spot for sb • **faiblement** [-əmã] *adv (protester)* weakly; *(éclairer)* faintly • **faiblesse** *nf (physique, morale)* weakness; *(de vent)* lightness; *(de revenus)* smallness

faiblir [fɛblir] *vi (forces)* to weaken; *(courage, vue)* to fail; *(vent)* to drop

faïence [fajãs] *nf (matière)* earthenware; **faïences** *(objets)* earthenware

faille¹ [faj] *nf Géol* fault; *Fig* flaw

faille² [faj] *voir* **falloir**

faillible [fajibl] *adj* fallible

faillir* [fajir] *vi* **il a failli tomber** he almost *or* nearly fell; **f. à un devoir** to fail in a duty

faillite [fajit] *nf Com* bankruptcy; *Fig* failure; **faire f.** to go bankrupt

faim [fɛ̃] *nf* hunger; **avoir f.** to be hungry; **donner f. à qn** to make sb hungry; **manger à sa f.** to eat one's fill; **rester sur sa f.** to remain hungry; **mourir de f.** to die of starvation; *Fig (avoir très faim)* to be starving

fainéant, -éante [feneã, -eãt] **1** *adj* idle

2 *nmf* idler • **fainéanter** *vi* to idle • **fainéantise** *nf* idleness

faire* [fɛr] **1** *vt (bruit, faute, gâteau, voyage, repas)* to make; *(devoir, ménage, dégâts)* to do; *(rêve, chute)* to have; *(sourire)* to give; *(promenade, sieste)* to have, to take; *(guerre)* to wage, to make; **ça fait 10 m de large** it's 10 m wide; **ça fait 10 euros** it's *or* that's 10 euros; **2 et 2 font 4** 2 and 2 are 4; **qu'a-t-il fait de...?** what's he done with...?; **que f.?** what's to be done? **f. du tennis/du piano** to play tennis/the piano; **f. du droit/de la médecine** to study law/medicine; **f. du bien à qn** to do sb good; **f. du mal à qn** to hurt *or* harm sb; **f. l'idiot** to act *or* play the fool; **il fera un bon médecin** he'll be *or* make a good doctor; **ça ne fait rien** that doesn't matter; **comment as-tu fait pour...?** how did you manage to...?; **il ne fait que travailler** he does nothing but work; **je ne fais que d'arriver** I've just arrived; **'oui', fit-elle** 'yes', she said

2 *vi (agir)* to do; *(paraître)* to look; **f. comme chez soi** to make oneself at home; **faites donc!** please do!; **elle ferait bien de partir** she'd do well to leave; **il fait vieux** he looks old; **il fait (bien) son âge** he looks his age

3 *v impersonnel* **il fait beau/froid** it's fine/cold; **il fait du vent/soleil** it's windy/sunny; **quel temps fait-il?** what's the weather like?; **ça fait deux ans que je ne l'ai pas vu** I haven't seen him for two years, it's (been) two years since I saw him; **ça fait un an que je suis là** I've been here for a year

4 *v aux* (+ *infinitive*) **f. construire une maison** to have a house built (**à qn** for sb; **par qn** by sb); **f. crier/souffrir qn** to make sb shout/suffer

5 se faire *vpr (fabrication)* to be made; *(activité)* to be done; **se f. couper les cheveux** to have one's hair cut; **se f. tuer/renverser** to get killed/knocked down; **se f. des illusions** to have illusions; **se f. des amis** to make friends; **se f. vieux** to get old; **il se fait tard** it's getting late; **comment se fait-il que...?** how is it that...?; **ça se fait beaucoup** people do that a lot; **se f. à** to get used to; **ne t'en fais pas!** don't worry! • **faire-part** *nm inv* announcement

fais, fait [fɛ] *voir* **faire**

faisable [fəzabl] *adj* feasible

faisan [fəzã] *nm* pheasant • **faisandé, -ée** *adj (gibier)* high

faisceau, -x [feso] *nm (rayons)* beam; *Fig* **un f. de preuves** a body of proof; **f. lumineux** beam of light

fait, -e [fɛ, fɛt] **1** *pp de* **faire**

2 *adj (fromage)* ripe; *(yeux)* made up; *(ongles)* polished; *(homme)* grown; **tout f.** ready made; **bien f.** *(jambes, corps)* shapely; **c'est bien f. (pour toi)!** it serves you right!

3 *nm (événement)* event; *(donnée, réalité)* fact; **du f. de** on account of; **au f. (à propos)** by the way; **en f.** in fact; **en f. de** *(en guise de)* by way of; *(au lieu de)* instead of; **prendre qn sur le f.** to catch sb red-handed *or* in the act; **aller au f., en venir au f.** to get to the point; **faits et gestes** actions; **prendre f. et cause pour qn** to stand up for sb; **mettre qn devant un f. accompli** to present sb with a fait accompli; *Journ* **faits divers** ≃ news in brief

faîte [fɛt] *nm (haut)* top; *Fig (apogée)* height

faites [fɛt] *voir* **faire**

fait-tout [fɛtu] *nm inv* stewpot

falaise [falɛz] *nf* cliff

falloir* [falwar] **1** *v impersonnel* **il faut qn/qch** I/you/we/*etc* need sb/sth; **il lui faut un stylo** he/she needs a pen; **il faut partir** I/you/we/*etc* have to go; **il faut que je parte** I have to go; **il faudrait qu'elle reste** she ought to stay; **il faut un jour** it takes a day (**pour faire** to do); **comme il faut** proper(ly); **s'il le faut** if need be **2 s'en falloir** *vpr* **il s'en est fallu de peu qu'il ne pleure, peu s'en est fallu qu'il ne pleure** he almost cried; **tant s'en faut** far from it

falsifier [falsifje] *vt (texte)* to falsify • **falsification** *nf* falsification

famé [fame] **mal famé, -ée** *adj* of ill repute

famélique [famelik] *adj* half-starved

fameux, -euse [famø, -øz] *adj (célèbre)* famous; *Fam (excellent)* first-class; *Fam* **pas f.** not much good

familial, -e, -iaux, -iales [familjal, -jo] *adj (atmosphère, ennuis)* family; *(entreprise)* family-run

familier, -ière [familje, -jɛr] **1** *adj (connu)* familiar (**à** to); *(désinvolte)* informal (**avec** with); *(locution)* colloquial **2** *nm (de club)* regular visitor (**de** to) • **familiariser 1** *vt* to familiarize (**avec** with) **2 se familiariser** *vpr* to familiarize oneself (**avec** with) • **familiarité** *nf (désinvolture)* informality; *Péj* **familiarités** liberties

famille [famij] *nf* family; **en f.** with one's family

famine [famin] *nf* famine

fan [fan], **fana** [fana] *nmf Fam* fan; **être f. de** to be crazy about

fanal, -aux [fanal, -o] *nm* lantern

fanatique [fanatik] **1** *adj* fanatical **2** *nmf* fanatic • **fanatisme** *nm* fanaticism

faner [fane] **se faner** *vpr (fleur, beauté)* to fade • **fané, -ée** *adj* faded

fanfare [fɑ̃far] *nf (orchestre)* brass band; *Fam* **réveil en f.** brutal awakening

fanfaron, -onne [fɑ̃farɔ̃, -ɔn] **1** *adj* boastful **2** *nmf* braggart

fanfreluches [fɑ̃frəlyʃ] *nfpl Péj* frills

fange [fɑ̃ʒ] *nf Littéraire* mire

fanion [fanjɔ̃] *nm (de club)* pennant

fantaisie [fɑ̃tezi] *nf (caprice)* whim; *(imagination)* imagination; **bijoux f.** novelty *or* fancy jewellery • **fantaisiste** *adj (pas sérieux)* fanciful; *(excentrique)* unorthodox

> *Il faut noter que le nom anglais **fantasy** est un faux ami. Il signifie **rêve**.*

fantasme [fɑ̃tasm] *nm* fantasy • **fantasmer** *vi* to fantasize (**sur** about)

fantasque [fɑ̃task] *adj* whimsical

fantassin [fɑ̃tasɛ̃] *nm* infantryman

fantastique [fɑ̃tastik] *adj (imaginaire, excellent)* fantastic

fantoche [fɑ̃tɔʃ] *nm & adj* puppet

fantôme [fɑ̃tom] **1** *nm* ghost, phantom **2** *adj* **ville/train f.** ghost town/train; **firme f.** bogus company *or* firm

faon [fɑ̃] *nm* fawn

faramineux, -euse [faraminø, -øz] *adj Fam* fantastic

farce¹ [fars] *nf (tour)* practical joke, prank; *(pièce de théâtre)* farce; **magasin de farces et attrapes** joke shop; **faire une f. à qn** to play a practical joke *or* a prank on sb • **farceur, -euse** *nmf (blagueur)* practical joker

farce² [fars] *nf Culin* stuffing • **farcir** *vt (poulet)* to stuff; *Fam* **se f. qn** to put up with sb; **se f. qch** to get landed with sth

fard [far] *nm* make-up • **farder 1** *vt (maquiller)* to make up **2 se farder** *vpr (se maquiller)* to put on one's make-up; **se f. les yeux** to put eyeshadow on

fardeau, -x [fardo] *nm* burden, load

farfelu, -ue [farfəly] *Fam* **1** *adj* weird **2** *nmf* weirdo

farfouiller [farfuje] *vi Fam* to rummage (**dans** through)

fariboles [faribɔl] *nfpl Fam* nonsense

farine [farin] *nf (de blé)* flour; **f. d'avoine** oatmeal • **farineux, -euse** *adj* floury

farouche [faruʃ] *adj (personne)* shy; *(animal)* timid; *(haine, regard)* fierce • **farouchement** *adv* fiercely

fart [far(t)] *nm (ski)* wax • **farter** *vt* to wax

fascicule [fasikyl] *nm (de publication)* instalment; *(brochure)* brochure

fasciner [fasine] *vt* to fascinate • **fascination** *nf* fascination

fascisme [faʃism] *nm* fascism • **fasciste** *adj & nmf* fascist

fasse(s), fassent [fas] *voir* **faire**

faste [fast] **1** *nm* splendour **2** *adj* **jour/période f.** lucky day/period

fastidieux, -ieuse [fastidjø, -jøz] *adj* tedious

> *Il faut noter que l'adjectif anglais **fastidious** est un faux ami. Il signifie **pointilleux**.*

fatal, -e, -als, -ales [fatal] *adj (mortel)* fatal; *(inévitable)* inevitable; *(moment,* *ton)* fateful; **c'était f.!** it was bound to happen! • **fatalement** *adv* inevitably • **fataliste 1** *adj* fatalistic **2** *nmf* fatalist • **fatalité** *nf (destin)* fate • **fatidique** *adj (jour, date)* fateful

> ⚠ Il faut noter que les termes anglais **fatally** et **fatality** sont des faux amis. Ils signifient respectivement **mortellement** ou **irrémédiablement**, et **victime**.

fatigant, -ante [fatigɑ̃, -ɑ̃t] *adj (épuisant)* tiring; *(ennuyeux)* tiresome

fatigue [fatig] *nf* tiredness; **tomber de f.** to be dead tired

fatiguer [fatige] **1** *vt (épuiser)* to tire; *(yeux)* to strain; *(ennuyer)* to bore **2** *vi (personne)* to get tired; *(moteur)* to labour **3 se fatiguer** *vpr (s'épuiser, se lasser)* to get tired (**de** of); **se f. à faire qch** to tire oneself out doing sth; **se f. les yeux** to strain one's eyes • **fatigué, -ée** *adj* tired (**de** of)

fatras [fatra] *nm* jumble, muddle

faubourg [fobur] *nm* suburb

fauché, -ée [foʃe] *adj Fam (sans argent)* broke

faucher [foʃe] *vt (herbe)* to mow; *(blé)* to reap; *Fam (voler)* to snatch, *Br* to pinch; *Fig* **f. qn** *(faire tomber brutalement)* to mow sb down • **faucheuse** *nf (machine)* reaper

faucille [fosij] *nf* sickle

faucon [fokɔ̃] *nm* hawk, falcon

faudra, faudrait [fodra, fodrɛ] *voir* **falloir**

faufiler [fofile] **se faufiler** *vpr* to work one's way (**dans** through *or* into; **entre** between)

faune [fon] *nf* wildlife, fauna; *Péj (gens)* set

faussaire [fosɛr] *nm* forger

fausse [fos] *voir* **faux¹** • **faussement** *adv* falsely

fausser [fose] *vt (réalité)* to distort; *(clé)* to buckle; **f. compagnie à qn** to give sb the slip

fausseté [foste] *nf (de raisonnement)* falseness; *(hypocrisie)* duplicity

faut [fo] *voir* **falloir**

faute [fot] *nf (erreur)* mistake; *(responsabilité)* & *Tennis* fault; *Football* foul; *Fam* **c'est de ta f., c'est ta f.** it's your fault; **f. de temps** for lack of time; **f. de mieux** for want of anything better; **en f.** at fault; **sans f.** without fail; **faire une f.** to make a mistake; **f. d'impression** printing error

fauteuil [fotœj] *nm* armchair; *(de président)* chair; *Fam* **arriver dans un f.** to win

hands down; *Théâtre* **f. d'orchestre** seat in the *Br* stalls *or Am* orchestra; **f. pivotant** swivel chair; **f. roulant** wheelchair

fauteur [fotœr] *nm* **f. de troubles** troublemaker

fautif, -ive [fotif, -iv] *adj (personne)* at fault; *(erroné)* faulty

fauve [fov] **1** *nm* big cat; **chasse aux grands fauves** big game hunting **2** *adj & nm (couleur)* fawn

faux¹, fausse [fo, fos] **1** *adj (pas vrai)* false, untrue; *(inexact)* wrong; *(inauthentique)* false; *(monnaie)* forged; *(tableau)* fake; **faire fausse route** to take the wrong road; *Fig* to be on the wrong track; **faire un f. mouvement** to make a sudden (awkward) movement; **faire une fausse note** *(musicien)* to play a wrong note; **faire une fausse couche** to have a miscarriage; *Fam* **avoir tout f.** to get it all wrong; *Ling* **f. ami** false friend; **f. col** detachable collar; **f. départ** false start; **f. diamant** fake diamond; **f. nez** false nose **2** *adv (chanter)* out of tune **3** *nm (tableau)* fake; *(document)* forgery • **faux-filet** *(pl* **faux-filets**) *nm* sirloin • **faux-fuyant** *(pl* **faux-fuyants**) *nm* subterfuge • **faux-monnayeur** *(pl* **faux-monnayeurs**) *nm* counterfeiter

faux² [fo] *nf (instrument)* scythe

faveur [favœr] *nf* favour; **en f. de** *(au profit de)* in aid of; **être en f. de qch** to be in favour of sth; **de f.** *(billet)* complimentary; *(traitement, régime)* preferential • **favorable** *adj* favourable (**à** to) • **favori, -ite** *adj & nmf* favourite • **favoriser** *vt* to favour • **favoritisme** *nm* favouritism

favoris [favɔri] *nmpl* sideburns

fax [faks] *nm (appareil, message)* fax • **faxer** *vt (message)* to fax

fébrile [febril] *adj* feverish • **fébrilité** *nf* feverishness

fécond, -onde [fekɔ̃, -ɔ̃d] *adj (femme, idée)* fertile • **féconder** *vt* to fertilize • **fécondité** *nf* fertility

fécule [fekyl] *nf* starch • **féculents** *nmpl (aliments)* starchy food

fédéral, -e, -aux, -ales [federal, -o] *adj* federal • **fédération** *nf* federation • **fédérer** *vt* to federate

fée [fe] *nf* fairy • **féerique** *adj (personnage, monde)* fairy; *(vision)* enchanting

feindre* [fɛ̃dr] *vt* to feign; **f. de faire qch** to pretend to do sth • **feint, -e** *adj* feigned • **feinte** *nf (ruse)* ruse; *Football* & *Rugby* dummy run

fêler [fele] *vt,* **se fêler** *vpr* to crack • **fêlure** *nf* crack

féliciter [felisite] **1** *vt* to congratulate (**de** *ou* **sur** on)

2 se féliciter *vpr* **se f. de qch** to congratulate oneself on sth •**félicitations** *nfpl* congratulations (**pour** on)

félin, -ine [felɛ̃, -in] *adj & nm* feline

femelle [fəmɛl] *adj & nf* female

féminin, -ine [feminɛ̃, -in] *adj (prénom, hormone)* female; *(trait, intuition, pronom)* feminine; *(mode, revue, équipe)* women's •**féministe** *adj & nmf* feminist •**féminité** *nf* femininity

femme [fam] *nf* woman (*pl* women); *(épouse)* wife; **f. médecin** woman doctor; **f. d'affaires** businesswoman; **f. de chambre** (chamber)maid; **f. de ménage** cleaning lady, maid; **f. au foyer** housewife; **f.-objet** woman as a sex object; *Fam* **bonne f.** woman

fémur [femyr] *nm* thighbone, femur

fendiller [fɑ̃dije] **se fendiller** *vpr* to crack

fendre [fɑ̃dr] **1** *vt (bois)* to split; *(foule)* to force one's way through; *(air)* to cleave; *Fig (cœur)* to break; **jupe fendue** slit skirt

2 se fendre *vpr (se fissurer)* to crack; *Fam* **se f. de 50 euros** to fork out 50 euros; *Fam* **se f. la gueule** to laugh one's head off

fenêtre [fənɛtr] *nf* window

fenouil [fənuj] *nm* fennel

fente [fɑ̃t] *nf (de tirelire, palissade, jupe)* slit; *(de rocher)* split, crack

féodal, -e, -aux, -ales [feɔdal, -o] *adj* feudal

fer [fɛr] *nm* iron; *(partie métallique de qch)* metal (part); **barre de** *ou* **en f.** iron bar; **boîte en f.** can, *Br* tin; *Fig* **santé de f.** cast-iron constitution; *Fig* **main/volonté de f.** iron hand/will; **f. à cheval** horseshoe; **f. forgé** wrought iron **f. à friser** curling tongs; *Fig* **f. de lance** spearhead; **f. à repasser** iron •**fer-blanc** (*pl* **fersblancs**) *nm* tin(-plate)

fera, ferait *etc* [fəra, fərɛ] *voir* **faire**

férié [ferje] *adj m* **jour f.** (public) holiday

ferme¹ [fɛrm] *nf* farm; *(maison)* farm (house)

ferme² [fɛrm] **1** *adj (beurre, décision)* firm; *(pas, voix)* steady; *(pâte)* stiff; *(autoritaire)* firm (**avec** with)

2 *adv (discuter)* keenly; *(travailler, boire)* hard; **s'ennuyer f.** to be bored stiff •**fermement** [-əmɑ̃] *adv* firmly

ferment [fɛrmɑ̃] *nm* ferment •**fermentation** *nf* fermentation •**fermenter** *vi* to ferment

fermer [fɛrme] **1** *vt* to close, to shut; *(gaz, radio)* to turn *or* switch off; *(vêtement)* to do up; *(passage)* to block; **f. qch à clef** to lock sth; **f. un magasin** *(définitivement)* to close *or* shut (down) a shop; **f. la marche** to bring up the rear; *Fam* **ferme-la!, la ferme!** shut up!

2 *vi*, **se fermer** *vpr* to close, to shut •**fermé, -ée** *adj (porte, magasin)* closed, shut; *(route, circuit)* closed; *(gaz)* off

fermeté [fɛrməte] *nf* firmness; *(de geste, de voix)* steadiness

fermeture [fɛrmətyr] *nf* closing, closure; *(heure)* closing time; *(mécanisme)* catch; **f. annuelle** annual closure; **f. Éclair®** *Br* zip (fastener), *Am* zipper

fermier, -ière [fɛrmje, -jɛr] **1** *nmf* farmer **2** *adj* **poulet f.** farm chicken

fermoir [fɛrmwar] *nm* clasp

féroce [ferɔs] *adj* ferocious •**férocité** *nf* ferocity

feront [fərɔ̃] *voir* **faire**

ferraille [feraj] *nf* scrap iron; **mettre qch à la f.** to scrap sth •**ferrailleur** *nm* scrap metal dealer *or Br* merchant

ferré, -ée [fere] *adj (canne)* metal-tipped

ferrer [fere] *vt (cheval)* to shoe

ferronnerie [ferɔnri] *nf* ironwork

ferroviaire [ferɔvjɛr] *adj* **compagnie f.** *Br* railway company, *Am* railroad company; **catastrophe f.** rail disaster

ferry [fɛri] (*pl* **ferrys** *ou* **ferries**) *nm* ferry

fertile [fɛrtil] *adj (terre, imagination)* fertile; **f. en incidents** eventful •**fertiliser** *vt* to fertilize •**fertilité** *nf* fertility

fervent, -ente [fɛrvɑ̃, -ɑ̃t] **1** *adj* fervent **2** *nmf* devotee (**de** of) •**ferveur** *nf* fervour

fesse [fɛs] *nf* buttock; **fesses** *Br* bottom, *Am* butt •**fessée** *nf* spanking

festin [fɛstɛ̃] *nm* feast

festival, -als [fɛstival] *nm* festival; *Fig* **nous avons assisté à un vrai f.** we witnessed a dazzling performance

festivités [fɛstivite] *nfpl* festivities

festoyer [fɛstwaje] *vi* to feast

fête [fɛt] *nf (civile)* holiday; *(religieuse)* festival, feast; *(entre amis)* party; **jour de f.** (public) holiday; **air de f.** festive air; **les fêtes (de Noël et du nouvel an)** the Christmas holidays; **faire la f.** to have a good time; **c'est sa f.** it's his/her saint's day; *Fam* **ça va être ta f.!** you're in for it!; **f. de famille** family celebration; **la f. des Mères** Mother's Day; **la f. du Travail** Labour Day; **f. du village** village fair *or* fête; **f. nationale** national holiday •**fêter** *vt (événement)* to celebrate

fétiche [fetiʃ] *nm (objet de culte)* fetish; *Fig (mascotte)* mascot

fétide [fetid] *adj* fetid

feu¹, -x [fø] *nm* fire; *(de réchaud)* burner; *Aut, Naut & Av (lumière)* light; **tous feux éteints** *(rouler)* without lights; **en f.** on fire, ablaze; **mettre le f. à qch** to set fire to sth; **faire du f.** to light *or* make a fire; **prendre f.** to catch fire; **donner du f. à qn** to give sb a light; **avez-vous du f.?** have you got a light?; **faire cuire qch à f. doux** to cook sth on a low heat; *Fig* **dans le f. de la dispute** in the heat of the argument; *Fig* **mettre le f. aux poudres** to spark things off; *Fig* **donner le f. vert** to give the go-ahead (**à** to); *Fig* **ne pas faire long f.** not to last very long; **au f.!** (there's a) fire!; *Mil* **f.!** fire!; **feux de croisement** *Br* dipped headlights, *Am* low beams; **feux de détresse** (hazard) warning lights; **feux de position** parking lights; *Aut* **f. rouge** *(lumière)* red light; *(objet)* traffic lights; **feux tricolores** traffic lights

feu², -e [fø] *adj* late; **f. ma tante** my late aunt

feuille [fœj] *nf* leaf; *(de papier)* sheet; *(de température)* chart; *(de journal)* news-sheet; **f. d'impôt** tax form *or* return; **f. de maladie** = form given by doctor to patient for claiming reimbursement from Social Security; **f. de paie** *Br* pay slip, *Am* pay stub; *Scol* **f. de présence** attendance sheet •**feuillage** *nm* leaves, foliage •**feuillu, -ue** *adj* leafy

feuillet [fœjɛ] *nm (de livre)* leaf •**feuilleté** *nm* **f. au fromage** cheese pastry •**feuilleter** *vt (livre)* to flip through

feuilleton [fœjtɔ̃] *nm (roman, film)* serial; **f. télévisé** television serial

feutre [føtr] *nm* felt; *(chapeau)* felt hat; **(crayon) f.** felt-tip(ped) pen •**feutré, -ée** *adj (lainage)* matted; *(bruit)* muffled; **à pas feutrés** silently •**feutrine** *nf* light-weight felt

fève [fɛv] *nf* (broad) bean; *(de la galette des Rois)* charm

février [fevrije] *nm* February

fiable [fjabl] *adj* reliable •**fiabilité** *nf* reliability

fiacre [fjakr] *nm Hist* hackney carriage

fiancer [fjɑ̃se] **se fiancer** *vpr* to become engaged (**avec** to) •**fiançailles** *nfpl* engagement •**fiancé** *nm* fiancé; **fiancés** engaged couple •**fiancée** *nf* fiancée

fiasco [fjasko] *nm* fiasco

fibre [fibr] *nf* fibre; **f. de verre** fibreglass; **fibres optiques** optical fibres; **câble en fibres optiques** fibre-optic cable

ficelle [fisɛl] *nf (de corde)* string; *(pain)* = long thin loaf; **les ficelles du métier** the tricks of the trade •**ficeler** *vt* to tie up

fiche [fiʃ] *nf* (a) *(carte)* index card; *(papier)* form; **f. d'état civil** = administrative record of birth details and marital status; **f. de paie** *Br* pay slip, *Am* pay stub; **f. technique** data record (b) *Él (broche)* pin; *(prise)* plug •**fichier** *nm* card index, file; *Ordinat* file

fiche(r) [fiʃ(e)] *(pp fichu)* Fam **1** *vt (faire)* to do; *(donner)* to give; *(jeter)* to throw; *(mettre)* to put; **f. le camp** to shove off; **fiche-moi la paix!** leave me alone!

2 se ficher *vpr* **se f. de qn** to make fun of sb; **je m'en fiche!** I don't give a damn!; **je me suis fichu dedans** I goofed

ficher [fiʃe] *vt (enfoncer)* to drive in; *(mettre sur fiche)* to put on file

fichu¹, -ue [fiʃy] *adj Fam (mauvais)* lousy, rotten; *(capable)* able (**de faire** to do); **mal f.** *(malade)* not well; **c'est f.** *(abîmé)* it's had it; **il est f.** *(condamné)* he's had it, *Br* he's done for

fichu² [fiʃy] *nm (étoffe)* (head)scarf

fictif, -ive [fiktif, -iv] *adj* fictitious •**fiction** *nf* fiction

fidèle [fidɛl] **1** *adj* faithful (**à** to)

2 *nmf* faithful supporter; *(client)* regular (customer); **les fidèles** *(croyants)* the faithful; *(à l'église)* the congregation •**fidèlement** *adv* faithfully •**fidélité** *nf* fidelity, faithfulness

fief [fjɛf] *nm* domain

fieffé, -ée [fjefe] *adj* **un f. menteur** an out-and-out liar

fiel [fjɛl] *nm* gall

fier¹ [fje] **se fier** *vpr* **se f. à qn/qch** to trust sb/sth

fier², fière [fjɛr] *adj* proud (**de** of); **avoir fière allure** to cut a fine figure •**fièrement** *adv* proudly •**fierté** *nf* pride

fièvre [fjɛvr] *nf (maladie)* fever; *(agitation)* frenzy; **avoir de la f.** to have a temperature *or* a fever •**fiévreux, -euse** *adj* feverish

figer [fiʒe] **1** *vt (liquide)* to congeal; *Fig* **f. qn** to paralyse sb

2 se figer *vpr (liquide)* to congeal; *Fig (sourire, personne)* to freeze •**figé, -ée** *adj (locution)* set, fixed; *(regard)* frozen; *(société)* fossilized

fignoler [fiɲɔle] *vt Fam* to put the finishing touches to

figue [fig] *nf* fig •**figuier** *nm* fig tree

figurant, -ante [figyrɑ̃, -ɑ̃t] *nmf (de film)* extra

figure [figyr] *nf (visage)* face; *(personnage, illustration) & Math* figure; **faire f. de favori** to be considered the favourite; **f. de style** stylistic device; **figures impo-**

sées compulsory figures; **figures libres** freestyle • **figurine** *nf* statuette

figurer [figyʁe] **1** *vt* to represent **2** *vi* to appear **3** **se figurer** *vpr* to imagine; **figurez-vous que…?** would you believe that…? • **figuré, -ée 1** *adj (sens)* figurative **2** *nm* **au f.** figuratively

fil [fil] *nm* **1** (a) *(de coton, de pensée)* thread; *(lin)* linen; **de f. en aiguille** bit by bit; *Fig* **cousu de f. blanc** plain for all to see, as plain as day; *Fig* **donner du f. à retordre à qn** to give sb trouble; **f. dentaire** dental floss (b) *(métallique)* wire; **f. de fer** wire; **f. à plomb** plumbline (c) *(de couteau)* edge (d) *(expressions)* **au f. de l'eau/des jours** with the current/the passing of time; **au bout du f.** *(au téléphone)* on the line

filaire [filɛʁ] *nm* corded phone

filament [filamɑ̃] *nm Biol & Él* filament

filandreux, -euse [filɑ̃dʁø, -øz] *adj (viande)* stringy

filature [filatyʁ] *nf (usine)* textile mill; *(surveillance)* shadowing; **prendre qn en f.** to shadow sb

file [fil] *nf* line; *Aut (couloir)* lane; **f. d'attente** *Br* queue, *Am* line; **en f. indienne** in single file; **être en double f.** to be double-parked

filer [file] **1** *vt (coton)* to spin; **f. qn** to shadow sb; *Fam* **f. qch à qn** to give sb sth **2** *vi (partir)* to rush off; *(aller vite)* to speed along; *(temps)* to fly; *(bas, collant)* to run, *Br* to ladder; **f. entre les doigts à qn** to slip through sb's fingers; **f. doux** to be obedient; **filez!** beat it!, *Br* hop it!

filet [filɛ] *nm* (a) *(en maille)* net; **coup de f.** *(opération de police)* police haul; **f. à bagages** luggage rack; **f. à provisions** string bag (b) *(d'eau)* trickle (c) *(de poisson, de viande)* fillet

filial, -e, -iaux, -iales [filjal, -jo] *adj* filial • **filiale** *nf* subsidiary (company)

filiation [filjasjɔ̃] *nf (relation)* relationship

filière [filjɛʁ] *nf (voie obligée)* channels; *(domaine d'études)* field of study; *(organisation clandestine)* network; **suivre la f. normale** to go through the official channels; *(employé)* to work one's way up; *Scol* **suivre la f. scientifique** to study scientific subjects; **remonter la f.** *(police)* to go back through the network (to reach the person at the top)

filigrane [filigʁan] *nm (sur papier)* watermark

filin [filɛ̃] *nm Naut* rope

fille [fij] *nf (enfant)* girl; *(descendante)* daughter; **petite f.** (little *or* young) girl; **jeune f.** girl, young lady; *Péj* **vieille f.** old maid • **fillette** *nf* little girl

filleul [fijœl] *nm* godson • **filleule** *nf* goddaughter

film [film] *nm (œuvre)* film, movie; *(pour photo)* film; *Fig* **le f. des événements** the sequence of events; **f. d'aventures** adventure film; **f. muet/parlant** silent/talking film; **f. policier** thriller; **f. plastique** *Br* clingfilm, *Am* plastic wrap • **filmer** *vt (personne, scène)* to film

filon [filɔ̃] *nm Géol* seam; *Fam* **trouver le f.** to strike it lucky

filou [filu] *nm (escroc)* rogue

fils [fis] *nm* son; **f. à papa** daddy's boy

filtre [filtʁ] *nm* filter; **(à bout) f.** *(cigarette)* (filter-)tipped; **(bout) f.** filter tip • **filtrer 1** *vt* to filter; *(personne, nouvelles)* to screen **2** *vi (liquide)* to filter (through); *(nouvelle)* to leak out

fin¹ [fɛ̃] *nf* (a) *(conclusion)* end; **mettre f. à qch** to put an end to sth; **prendre f.** to come to an end; **tirer à sa f.** to draw to a close; **sans f.** endless; **à la f.** in the end; **arrêtez, à la f.!** stop, for heaven's sake!; **f. mai** at the end of May; **f. de semaine** weekend (b) *(but)* end, aim; **arriver à ses fins** to achieve one's ends; **à cette f.** to this end

fin², fine [fɛ̃, fin] **1** *adj (pointe, tissu)* fine; *(peu épais)* thin; *(plat)* delicate; *(esprit, oreille)* sharp; *(observation)* sharp, fine; *(intelligent)* clever; **au f. fond de** in the depths of; **jouer au plus f. avec qn** to try and be smarter than sb **2** *adv (couper, moudre)* finely; *(écrire)* small

final, -e, -aux *ou* **-als, -ales** [final, -o] *adj* final • **finale 1** *nf Sport* final **2** *nm Mus* finale • **finalement** *adv* finally • **finaliste** *nmf Sport* finalist

finance [finɑ̃s] *nf* finance • **financement** *nm* financing • **financer** *vt* to finance

financier, -ière [finɑ̃sje, -jɛʁ] **1** *adj* financial **2** *nm* financier • **financièrement** *adv* financially

fine [fin] *nf* liqueur brandy

finement [finmɑ̃] *adv (couper, broder)* finely; *(agir)* cleverly; **f. joué** nicely played

finesse [finɛs] *nf (de pointe)* fineness; *(de taille)* thinness; *(de plat)* delicacy; *(d'esprit, de goût)* finesse; **finesses** *(de langue)* niceties

finir [finiʁ] **1** *vt* to finish; *(discours, vie)* to end, to finish

2 *vi* to finish, to end; **f. bien/mal** to have a happy/an unhappy ending; **f. de faire qch** to finish doing sth; **f. par faire qch** to end up doing sth; **f. par qch** to finish (up) *or* end (up) with sth; **en f. avec qn/qch** to have done with sb/sth; **elle n'en finit pas de pleurer** there's nothing that can make her stop crying; **il finira tout seul** *(il mourra tout seul)* he'll come to a lonely end ●**fini, -ie 1** *adj (produit)* finished; *(univers) & Math* finite; **c'est f.** it's over *or* finished; **il est f.** *(trop vieux)* he's finished **2** *nm (d'objet manufacturé)* finish ●**finition** *nm inv Sport* finish; *Fam* **avoir qn au f.** *(à l'usure)* to get sb in the end ●**finition** *nf Tech (action)* finishing; *(résultat)* finish

Finlande [fɛ̃lɑ̃d] *nf* **la F.** Finland ●**finlandais, -aise 1** *adj* Finnish **2** *nmf* **F., Finlandaise** Finn ●**finnois, -oise 1** *adj* Finnish **2** *nmf* **F., Finnoise** Finn **3** *nm (langue)* Finnish

fiole [fjɔl] *nf* phial

firme [firm] *nf* firm

fisc [fisk] *nm Br* ≃ Inland Revenue, *Am* ≃ Internal Revenue ●**fiscal, -e, -aux, -ales** *adj* **droit f.** tax law; **charges fiscales** taxes; **fraude fiscale** tax fraud *or* evasion ●**fiscalité** *nf* tax system

fissure [fisyr] *nf* crack ●**se fissurer** *vpr* to crack

fiston [fistɔ̃] *nm Fam* son, lad

fixateur [fiksatœr] *nm Phot* fixer

fixation [fiksasjɔ̃] *nf (action)* fixing; *(dispositif)* fastening, binding; *(idée fixe)* fixation; **faire une f. sur qn/qch** to be fixated on sb/sth

fixe [fiks] **1** *adj* fixed; *(prix, heure)* set, fixed; **être au beau f.** *(temps)* to be set fair **2** *nm (paie)* fixed salary ●**fixement** [-əmɑ̃] *adv* **regarder qn/qch f.** to stare at sb/sth

fixer [fikse] **1** *vt (attacher)* to fix (**à** to); *(choix)* to settle; *(date, règle)* to decide, to fix; **f. qn/qch (du regard)** to stare at sb/sth; **être fixé** *(décidé)* to be decided; **comme ça, on est fixé!** *(renseigné)* we've got the picture! **2 se fixer** *vpr (regard)* to become fixed; *(s'établir)* to settle

flacon [flakɔ̃] *nm* small bottle

flageoler [flaʒɔle] *vi* to shake, to tremble

flageolet [flaʒɔlɛ] *nm (haricot)* flageolet bean

flagrant, -ante [flagrɑ̃, -ɑ̃t] *adj (injustice)* flagrant, blatant; **pris en f. délit** caught in the act *or* red-handed

flair [flɛr] *nm (d'un chien)* (sense of) smell, scent; *(clairvoyance)* intuition,

flair ●**flairer** *vt* to smell, to sniff at; *Fig (discerner)* to smell

flamand, -ande [flamɑ̃, -ɑ̃d] **1** *adj* Flemish **2** *nmf* **F., Flamande** Fleming **3** *nm (langue)* Flemish

flamant [flamɑ̃] *nm* **f. (rose)** flamingo

flambant [flɑ̃bɑ̃] *adv* **f. neuf** brand new

flambeau, -x [flɑ̃bo] *nm* torch

flambée [flɑ̃be] *nf* blaze; *Fig (de colère, des prix)* surge; *(de violence)* flare-up

flamber [flɑ̃be] **1** *vt Méd (aiguille)* to sterilize; *(poulet)* to singe; **bananes flambées** flambéed bananas **2** *vi* to blaze; *Fam (jouer)* to gamble for big money ●**flambeur** *nm Fam* big-time gambler

flamboyer [flɑ̃bwaje] *vi* to blaze

flamme [flam] *nf* flame; *Fig (ardeur)* fire; **en flammes** on fire ●**flammèche** *nf* spark

flan [flɑ̃] *nm* baked custard

flanc [flɑ̃] *nm* side; *(d'armée, d'animal)* flank; *Fam* **tirer au f.** to shirk

flancher [flɑ̃ʃe] *vi Fam* to give in

Flandre [flɑ̃dr] *nf* **la F., les Flandres** Flanders

flanelle [flanɛl] *nf* flannel

flâner [flɑne] *vi* to stroll

flanquer [flɑ̃ke] **1** *vt* to flank (**de** with); *Fam (jeter)* to chuck; *Fam (donner)* to give; *Fam* **f. qn à la porte** to kick sb out **2 se flanquer** *vpr* **se f. par terre** to go sprawling

flaque [flak] *nf (d'eau)* puddle; *(de sang)* pool

flash [flaʃ] *(pl* **flashes**) *nm Phot* flashlight; *Radio & TV* **f. d'informations** (news)flash ●**flasher** *vi Fam* **f. sur qn/qch** to fall for sb/sth in a big way

flasque [flask] *adj* flabby

flatter [flate] **1** *vt* to flatter **2 se flatter** *vpr* **se f. de faire qch** to flatter oneself on doing sth ●**flatté, -ée** *adj* flattered (**de qch** by sth; **de faire** to do; **que** that) ●**flatterie** *nf* flattery ●**flatteur, -euse 1** *adj* flattering **2** *nmf* flatterer

fléau, -x [fleo] *nm (catastrophe)* scourge; *Fig (personne)* pain; *Agr* flail

flèche [flɛʃ] *nf* arrow; *(d'église)* spire; **monter en f.** *(prix)* to shoot up ●**flécher** *vt* to signpost (with arrows) ●**fléchette** *nf* dart; **fléchettes** *(jeu)* darts

fléchir [fleʃir] **1** *vt (membre)* to bend; *Fig* **f. qn** to sway sb **2** *vi (membre)* to bend; *(poutre)* to sag; *(faiblir)* to give way; *(baisser)* to fall

flegme [flɛgm] *nm* composure ●**flegmatique** *adj* phlegmatic

flemme [flɛm] *nf Fam* laziness; **il a la f.** he can't be bothered •**flemmard, -arde** *Fam* **1** *adj* lazy **2** *nmf* lazybones

flétrir [fletrir] *vt*, **se flétrir** *vpr* to wither

fleur [flœr] *nf* flower; *(d'arbre, d'arbuste)* blossom; **en fleur(s)** in flower, in bloom; *(arbre)* in blossom; **à fleurs** *(tissu)* floral; **à ou dans la f. de l'âge** in the prime of life; **à f. d'eau** just above the water; **la fine f. de la marine française** the cream of the French navy; *Fam* **arriver comme une f.** to arrive innocent and unsuspecting; *Fam* **faire une f. à qn** to do sb a favour; **il a un côté f. bleue** he has a romantic side

fleurir [flœrir] **1** *vt (table)* to decorate with flowers; *(tombe)* to lay flowers on **2** *vi (plante)* to flower, to bloom; *(arbre)* to blossom; *Fig (art, commerce)* to flourish •**fleuri, -ie** *adj (fleur, jardin)* in bloom; *(tissu)* floral; *(style)* flowery, florid

fleuriste [flœrist] *nmf* florist

fleuve [flœv] *nm* river

flexible [flɛksibl] *adj* flexible •**flexibilité** *nf* flexibility

flexion [flɛksjɔ̃] *nf (fléchissement)* bending

flic [flik] *nm Fam* cop

flinguer [flɛ̃ge] *vt Fam* **f. qn** to gun sb down

flipper [flipœr] *nm (jeu)* pinball; *(appareil)* pinball machine

flocon [flɔkɔ̃] *nm* flake; **il neige à gros flocons** big flakes of snow are falling; **f. de neige** snowflake; **flocons d'avoine** porridge oats •**floconneux, -euse** *adj* fluffy

floraison [flɔrɛzɔ̃] *nf* flowering; **en pleine f.** in full bloom •**floral, -e, -aux, -ales** *adj* floral •**floralies** *nfpl* flower show

flore [flɔr] *nf* flora

florissant, -ante [flɔrisɑ̃, -ɑ̃t] *adj* flourishing

flot [flo] *nm (de souvenirs, de larmes)* flood, stream; **les flots** *(la mer)* the waves; **à f.** *(bateau, personne)* afloat; *Fig* **remettre qn à f.** to restore sb's fortunes; *Fig* **couler à flots** *(argent, vin)* to flow freely; **le soleil entrait à flots** the sun was streaming in

flotte [flɔt] *nf (de bateaux, d'avions)* fleet; *Fam (pluie)* rain; *Fam (eau)* water

flottement [flɔtmɑ̃] *nm (hésitation)* indecision

flotter [flɔte] *vi (bateau)* to float; *(drapeau)* to fly; *(cheveux)* to flow; *Fam (pleuvoir)* to rain •**flotteur** *nm* float

flou, -e [flu] **1** *adj (photo)* fuzzy, blurred; *(idée)* vague

2 *nm* fuzziness; *Fig* vagueness; *Phot* **f. artistique** soft focus (effect)

fluctuant, -uante [flyktɥɑ̃, -ɥɑ̃t] *adj (prix, opinions)* fluctuating •**fluctuations** *nfpl* fluctuation(s) (**de** in)

fluet, -uette [flye, -yɛt] *adj* thin, slender

fluide [flɥid] **1** *adj (liquide)* & *Fig* fluid **2** *nm (liquide)* fluid •**fluidité** *nf* fluidity

fluo [flyo] *adj inv Fam* fluorescent

fluorescent, -ente [flyɔresɑ̃, -ɑ̃t] *adj* fluorescent

flûte [flyt] **1** *nf (instrument)* flute; *(verre)* champagne glass

2 *exclam Fam* damn! •**flûtiste** *nmf Br* flautist, *Am* flutist

fluvial, -e, -iaux, -iales [flyvjal, -jo] *adj* **navigation fluviale** river navigation

flux [fly] *nm (abondance)* flow; **f. et reflux** ebb and flow

focal, -e, -aux, -ales [fɔkal, -o] *adj* focal •**focaliser** *vt* to focus (**sur** on)

fœtus [fetys] *nm Br* foetus, *Am* fetus

foi [fwa] *nf* faith; **sur la f. de** on the strength of; **être de bonne/mauvaise f.** to be sincere/insincere; **avoir la f.** to have faith; **ma f., oui!** yes, indeed!

foie [fwa] *nm* liver; **f. gras** foie gras; **crise de f.** bout of indigestion

foin [fwɛ̃] *nm* hay; *Fam* **faire du f.** *(scandale)* to kick up a fuss

foire [fwar] *nf* fair; *Fam* **faire la f.** to muck about

fois [fwa] *nf* time; **une f.** once; **deux f.** twice; **trois f.** three times; **deux f. trois** two times three; **payer qch en plusieurs f.** to pay for sth in several instalments; **chaque f. que...** whenever..., each time (that)...; **une f. qu'il sera arrivé** *(dès que)* once he has arrived; **une f. pour toutes** once and for all; **à la f.** at the same time, at once; **à la f. riche et heureux** both rich and happy; *Fam* **des f.** sometimes; *Fam* **non mais des f.!** really now!

foison [fwazɔ̃] *nf* **à f.** in abundance •**foisonnement** *nm* abundance •**foisonner** *vi* to abound (**de ou en** in)

fol [fɔl] *voir* **fou**

folâtre [fɔlɑtr] *adj* playful •**folâtrer** *vi* to romp, to frolic

folichon, -onne [fɔliʃɔ̃, -ɔn] *adj Fam* **pas f.** not much fun

folie [fɔli] *nf* madness; **faire une f.** to do a foolish thing; *(dépense)* to be very extravagant; **faire des folies pour qn** to do anything for sb; **aimer qn à la f.** to be madly in love with sb; **la f. des grandeurs** delusions of grandeur

folklore [fɔlklɔr] *nm* folklore •**folklo-**

rique adj (costume) traditional; (danse) folk; Fam (endroit, soirée) bizarre

folle [fɔl] voir **fou** • **follement** adv madly

fomenter [fɔmɑ̃te] vt to foment

foncé, -ée [fɔ̃se] adj dark

foncer [fɔ̃se] **1** vi (aller vite) to tear or charge along; Fam (s'y mettre) to get one's head down; **f. sur qn/qch** to swoop on sb/sth
2 vti (couleur) to darken • **fonceur, -euse** nmf Fam go-getter

foncier, -ière [fɔ̃sje, -jɛr] adj (fondamental) fundamental, basic; (impôt) land; **crédit f.** land loan • **foncièrement** adv fundamentally

fonction [fɔ̃ksjɔ̃] nf (rôle) & Math function; (emploi) office; **en f. de** according to; **faire f. de** (personne) to act as; (objet) to serve or act as; **prendre ses fonctions** to take up one's duties; **la f. publique** the civil service; Ordinat **f. recherche et remplacement** search and replace function; Ordinat **f. de sauvegarde** save function • **fonctionnaire** nmf civil servant; **haut f.** high-ranking civil servant • **fonctionnel, -elle** adj functional

fonctionner [fɔ̃ksjɔne] vi (machine) to work, to function; Ordinat to run; **faire f. qch** to operate sth • **fonctionnement** nm (de machine) working; **en état de f.** in working order; Ordinat **f. en réseau** networking

fond [fɔ̃] nm (de boîte, de jardin, de vallée) bottom; (de salle, d'armoire) back; (arrière-plan) background; **au f. de** (boîte, jardin) at the bottom of; (salle) at the back of; Fig **au f., dans le f.** basically; **à f.** (connaître) thoroughly; Fam **à f. la caisse** (très vite) hell for leather; **de f. en comble** from top to bottom; **course/coureur de f.** long-distance race/runner; **ski de f.** cross-country skiing; **bruits de f.** background noise; **toucher le f. (du désespoir)** to have hit rock-bottom; **user ses fonds de culotte sur les bancs d'une école** to spend a great deal of time at a school; **f. de bouteille** (contenu) dregs; **f. de teint** foundation (cream); **f. sonore** background music

fondamental, -e, -aux, -ales [fɔ̃damɑ̃tal, -o] adj fundamental, basic

fonder [fɔ̃de] **1** vt (ville) to found; (commerce) to set up; (famille) to start; **f. qch sur qch** to base sth on sth; **être fondé à croire** to be justified in thinking; **bien fondé** well-founded
2 se fonder vpr se **f. sur qch** (sujet: théorie, remarque) to be based on sth;

sur quoi se fonde-t-il pour...? what are his grounds for...? • **fondateur, -trice 1** nmf founder **2** adj **membre f.** founding member • **fondation** nf (création, œuvre) foundation (**de** of); **fondations** (de bâtiment) foundations • **fondement** nm foundation

fonderie [fɔ̃dri] nf foundry

fondre [fɔ̃dr] **1** vt (métal) to melt down; (neige) to melt; (cloche) to cast; Fig (couleurs) to blend (**avec** with); **faire f. qch** (sucre) to dissolve sth
2 vi (se liquéfier) to melt; (sucre) to dissolve; **f. en larmes** to burst into tears; **f. sur qch** to swoop on sth
3 se fondre vpr se **f. en eau** (glaçon) to melt away; **se f. dans qch** (brume) to merge into sth • **fondant, -ante** adj (fruit) which melts in the mouth • **fondu** nm Cin **f. enchaîné** dissolve

fonds [fɔ̃] **1** nm (organisme) fund; (de bibliothèque) collection; **f. de commerce** business; **F. monétaire international** International Monetary Fund
2 nmpl (argent) funds; **être en f.** to be in funds

fondue [fɔ̃dy] nf Culin fondue; **f. bourguignonne** beef fondue **f. savoyarde** cheese fondue

font [fɔ̃] voir **faire**

fontaine [fɔ̃tɛn] nf (construction) fountain; (source) spring

fonte [fɔ̃t] nf (**a**) (de neige) melting; (d'acier) smelting (**b**) (alliage) cast iron; **en f.** (poêle) cast-iron (**c**) Typ font

fonts [fɔ̃] nmpl Rel **f. baptismaux** font

football [futbol] nm Br football, Am soccer • **footballeur, -euse** nmf Br footballer, Am soccer player

footing [futiŋ] nm Sport jogging; **faire du f.** to go jogging

for [fɔr] nm Littéraire **en son f. intérieur** in one's heart of hearts

forage [fɔraʒ] nm drilling, boring

forain [fɔrɛ̃] nm fairground stallholder

forçat [fɔrsa] nm (prisonnier) convict

force [fɔrs] nf (violence) & Phys force; (vigueur) strength; **de toutes ses forces** with all one's strength; **de f.** by force, forcibly; **en f.** (attaquer, venir) in force; **à f. de volonté** through sheer willpower; **à f. de faire qch** through doing sth; Fam **à f., il va se mettre en colère** he'll end up losing his temper; **dans la f. de l'âge** in the prime of life; **par la f. des choses** through force of circumstance; **les forces armées** the armed forces; **les forces de l'ordre** the police; **f. de frappe** strike force

forcé, -ée [fɔrse] adj forced (**de faire** to

do); *Fam* **c'est f.** it's inevitable • **forcément** *adv* inevitably; **pas f.** not necessarily

forcené, -ée [fɔrsəne] **1** *adj* fanatical **2** *nmf* maniac

forceps [fɔrsɛps] *nm* forceps

forcer [fɔrse] **1** *vt (obliger)* to force; *(porte)* to force open; *(voix)* to strain; **f. qn à faire qch** to force sb to do sth; **f. la main à qn** to force sb's hand; *Fam* **f. la dose** to overdo it **2** *vi (appuyer, tirer)* to force it; *(se surmener)* to overdo it **3 se forcer** *vpr* to force oneself (**à faire** to do)

forcir [fɔrsir] *vi* to get bigger

forer [fɔre] *vt* to drill, to bore

forêt [fɔrɛ] *nf* forest; **f.-noire** *(gâteau)* Black Forest gateau; **f. vierge** virgin forest • **forestier, -ière 1** *adj* **chemin f.** forest road **2** *nm* forester

forfait [fɔrfɛ] *nm* (**a**) *(prix)* all-in price; *(de ski)* pass; **f. week-end** weekend package (**b**) *(crime)* heinous crime • **forfaitaire** *adj (indemnités)* basic; **prix f.** all-in price

forge [fɔrʒ] *nf* forge • **forger** *vt (métal, liens)* to forge; *Fig (caractère)* to form; *Fig (histoire)* to make up • **forgeron** [-ərɔ̃] *nm* (black)smith

formaliser [fɔrmalize] **se formaliser** *vpr* to take offence (**de** at)

formalité [fɔrmalite] *nf* formality

format [fɔrma] *nm* format; **f. de poche** pocket format

formater [fɔrmate] *vt* Ordinat to format • **formatage** *nm* Ordinat formatting

formation [fɔrmasjɔ̃] *nf (de roche, de mot)* formation; *(éducation)* education; **f. permanente** continuing education; **f. professionnelle** vocational training • **formateur, -trice 1** *adj* formative **2** *nmf* trainer

forme [fɔrm] *nf (contour)* shape, form; *(manière, bonne santé)* form; **formes** *(de femme)* figure; **en f. de qch** in the shape of sth; **en f. de poire** pear-shaped; **sous f. de qch** in the form of sth; **dans les formes** in the accepted way; **en bonne et due f.** in due form; **en (pleine) f.** *(en bonne santé)* on (top) form; **sans autre f. de procès** without further ado; **prendre f.** to take shape; **y mettre les formes** to do things tactfully

formel, -elle [fɔrmɛl] *adj (structure, logique)* formal; *(démenti)* flat; *(personne, preuve)* positive; *(interdiction)* strict • **formellement** *adv (interdire)* strictly

former [fɔrme] **1** *vt (groupe, caractère)* to form; *(apprenti)* to train

2 se former *vpr (apparaître)* to form; *(association, liens)* to be formed; *(apprendre son métier)* to train oneself

formidable [fɔrmidabl] *adj (fantastique)* great; *(gigantesque)* tremendous

> 🖉 Il faut noter que l'adjectif anglais **formidable** est un faux ami. Il signifie **redoutable**.

formulaire [fɔrmylɛr] *nm* form

formule [fɔrmyl] *nf Math* formula; *(phrase)* expression; *(solution)* method; **nouvelle f.** *(abonnement, menu)* new-style; **f. magique** magic formula; **f. de politesse** polite phrase • **formulation** *nf* formulation • **formuler** *vt* to formulate

fort¹, -e [fɔr, fɔrt] **1** *adj (vigoureux)* strong; *(gros, important)* large; *(pluie, mer, chute de neige)* heavy; *(voix)* loud; *(fièvre)* high; *(pente)* steep; **être f. en qch** *(doué)* to be good at sth; **il y a de fortes chances que ça réussisse** there's a good chance it will work; **c'est plus f. qu'elle** she can't help it; *Fam* **c'est un peu f.!** that's a bit much!

2 *adv* (**a**) *(frapper)* hard; *(pleuvoir)* hard, heavily; *(parler)* loud(ly); *(serrer)* tight; **sentir f.** to have a strong smell; **respirer f.** to breathe heavily; *Fam* **y aller f.** to overdo it; *Fam* **faire très f.** *(très bien)* to do really brilliantly

(**b**) *Littéraire (très)* very; *(beaucoup)* very much

3 *nm (spécialité)* strong point; **au plus f. de qch** *(hiver)* in the depths of sth; *(épidémie)* at the height of sth • **fortement** [-əmɑ̃] *adv (désirer, influencer)* strongly; *(tirer, pousser)* hard; *(impressionner)* greatly; **f. épicé** highly spiced

fort² [fɔr] *nm Hist & Mil* fort • **forteresse** *nf* fortress

fortifié, -iée [fɔrtifje] *adj (ville, camp)* fortified • **fortification** *nf* fortification

fortifier [fɔrtifje] *vt (mur, ville)* to fortify; *(corps)* to strengthen • **fortifiant** *nm* tonic

fortuit, -uite [fɔrtɥi, -ɥit] *adj* **rencontre fortuite** chance meeting

fortune [fɔrtyn] *nf (richesse, hasard)* fortune; **moyens de f.** makeshift means; **faire f.** to make one's fortune; **dîner à la f. du pot** to take pot luck; **faire contre mauvaise f. bon cœur** to make the best of it • **fortuné, -ée** *adj (riche)* wealthy

forum [fɔrɔm] *nm* forum

fosse [fos] *nf (trou)* pit; *(tombe)* grave; **f. d'aisances** cesspool; **f. d'orchestre** orchestra pit; **f. commune** mass grave

fossé [fose] *nm* ditch; *(de château)* moat; *Fig (désaccord)* gulf

fossette [fosɛt] *nf* dimple
fossile [fɔsil] *nm & adj* fossil
fossoyeur [foswajœr] *nm* gravedigger
fou, folle [fu, fɔl]

> fol is used before masculine singular nouns beginning with a vowel or h mute.

1 *adj (personne, projet)* mad, insane; *(succès, temps)* tremendous; *(envie)* wild, mad; *(espoir)* foolish; *(cheval, camion)* runaway; **f. à lier** raving mad; **f. de qch** *(musique, personne)* mad about sth; **f. de joie** beside oneself with joy; **f. rire** uncontrollable giggling; **avoir le f. rire** to have the giggles

　2 *nmf* madman, *f* madwoman
　3 *nm (bouffon)* jester; *Échecs* bishop; **faire le f.** to play the fool
foudre [fudr] *nf* **la f.** lightning • **foudroyant, -ante** *adj (succès, vitesse)* staggering; *(regard)* withering • **foudroyer** *vt* to strike; **f. qn du regard** to give sb a withering look
fouet [fwɛ] *nm* whip; *Culin* (egg-)whisk; **coup de f.** lash (with a whip); **de plein f.** head-on • **fouetter** *vt* to whip; *(œufs)* to whisk; *(sujet: pluie)* to lash (against); **crème fouettée** whipped cream
fougère [fuʒɛr] *nf* fern
fougue [fug] *nf* fire, spirit • **fougueux, -euse** *adj* fiery, ardent
fouille [fuj] **1** *nf (de personne, de bagages)* search
　2 *nfpl* **fouilles archéologiques** excavations, dig • **fouillé, -ée** *adj* detailed • **fouiller 1** *vt (personne, maison)* to search **2** *vi* **f. dans qch** *(tiroir)* to search through sth **3** *vti (creuser)* to dig
fouillis [fuji] *nm* jumble
fouine [fwin] *nf* stone marten
fouiner [fwine] *vi Fam* to nose about (**dans** in) • **fouineur, -euse** *Fam* **1** *adj* nosey **2** *nmf* nosey parker
foulard [fular] *nm* (head)scarf
foule [ful] *nf* crowd; **en f.** in mass; **une f. de** *(objets)* a mass of; **bain de f.** walkabout
foulée [fule] *nf (de coureur, de cheval)* stride; *Fam* **dans la f., j'ai vérifié les comptes** while I was at it, I checked the accounts
fouler [fule] **1** *vt (raisin)* to press; *(sol)* to tread; **f. qch aux pieds** to trample sth underfoot
　2 se fouler *vpr* **se f. la cheville** to sprain one's ankle; *Fam* **il ne se foule pas** he doesn't exactly exert himself • **foulure** *nf* sprain

four [fur] *nm (de cuisine)* oven; *(de potier)* kiln; *Fam (fiasco)* flop; **faire un f.** to flop; **petit f.** *(gâteau)* (small) fancy cake
fourbe [furb] **1** *adj* deceitful
　2 *nmf* cheat • **fourberie** *nf* deceit
fourbi [furbi] *nm Fam (désordre)* mess; *(choses)* stuff
fourbu, -ue [furby] *adj (fatigué)* exhausted
fourche [furʃ] *nf (outil, embranchement)* fork; **faire une f.** to fork • **fourcher** *vi (arbre)* to fork; **ma langue a fourché** I made a slip of the tongue • **fourchette** *nf (pour manger)* fork; *(de salaires)* bracket • **fourchu, -ue** *adj* forked; **avoir les cheveux fourchus** to have split ends
fourgon [furgɔ̃] *nm (camion)* van; **f. cellulaire** *Br* prison van, *Am* patrol wagon; **f. funéraire** hearse; **f. postal** *Br* postal van, *Am* mail car • **fourgonnette** *nf* (small) van
fourguer [furge] *vt Fam* **f. qch à qn** to unload sth onto sb
fourmi [furmi] *nf (insecte)* ant; **avoir des fourmis dans les jambes** to have pins and needles in one's legs • **fourmilière** *nf* anthill • **fourmiller** *vi* to teem, to swarm (**de** with)
fournaise [furnɛz] *nf* furnace
fourneau, -x [furno] *nm (de cuisine)* stove; *(de verrier)* furnace
fournée [furne] *nf (de pain, de gens)* batch
fournil [furni] *nm* bakehouse
fournir [furnir] **1** *vt (approvisionner)* to supply (**en** with); *(alibi, preuve, document)* to provide; *(effort)* to make; **f. qch à qn** to provide sb with sth; **pièces à f.** required documents
　2 se fournir *vpr* **se f. en qch** to get in supplies of sth; **se f. chez qn** to get one's supplies from sb • **fourni, -ie** *adj (barbe)* bushy; **bien f.** *(boutique)* well-stocked • **fournisseur** *nm (commerçant)* supplier; *Ordinat* **f. d'accès** access provider • **fourniture** *nf (action)* supply(ing) (**de** of); **fournitures de bureau** office supplies; **fournitures scolaires** educational stationery
fourrage [furaʒ] *nm* fodder
fourrager [furaʒe] *vi Fam* to rummage (**dans** in)
fourré, -ée [fure] **1** *adj (gant)* fur-lined; *(gâteau)* jam-/cream-filled; *Fam* **coup f.** *(traîtrise)* stab in the back
　2 *nm Bot* thicket
fourreau, -x [furo] *nm (gaine)* sheath
fourrer [fure] **1** *vt (gâteau, chou)* to fill;

(vêtement) to fur-line; *Fam (mettre)* to stick; *Fam* **f. son nez dans qch** to poke one's nose into sth

2 se fourrer *vpr Fam* to put oneself (**dans** in); **se f. dans une sale affaire** to get involved in a nasty business; **se f. le doigt dans l'œil** to kid oneself; **où est-il allé se f.?** where's he got to? • **fourre-tout** *nm inv (pièce)* junk room; *(sac) Br* holdall, *Am* carryall

fourrière [furjɛr] *nf (lieu)* pound; **mettre à la f.** *(voiture)* to impound; *(chien)* to put in the pound

fourrure [furyr] *nf* fur • **fourreur** *nm* furrier

fourvoyer [furvwaje] **se fourvoyer** *vpr Littéraire & Fig* to go astray

foutaises [futɛz] *nfpl Fam* crap

foutoir [futwar] *nm Fam* dump

foutre* [futr] *très Fam* **1** *vt (mettre)* to stick; *(faire)* to do; *(donner)* to give; **f. qch par terre** to chuck sth on the ground; **f. qn à la porte** to kick sb out; **f. qch en l'air** *(faire échouer)* to screw sth up; **f. le camp** to piss off; **ne rien f.** to do damn all; **je n'en ai rien à f.!** I couldn't give a damn!

2 se foutre *vpr* **se f. un coup** to bang oneself; **se f. du monde** to take the piss; **se f. de la gueule de qn** to take the piss out of sb; **je m'en fous** I don't give a damn • **foutu, -ue** *adj Fam (maudit)* damn; **être f.** *(en mauvais état)* to have had it; **être bien f.** *(beau)* to have a nice body; *(bien conçu)* to be well designed; **être mal f.** *(malade)* to be under the weather; **être f. de faire qch** to be quite likely to do sth

foyer [fwaje] *nm (maison)* home; *(d'étudiants)* residence; *(de travailleurs)* hostel; *(de théâtre)* foyer; *(de lunettes)* focus; *(de chaleur, d'infection)* source; *(d'incendie)* seat; *(âtre)* hearth; *(famille)* family; **fonder un f.** to start a family

fracas [fraka] *nm* crash • **fracassant, -ante** *adj (nouvelle, révélation)* shattering • **fracasser** *vt*, **se fracasser** *vpr* to smash

fraction [fraksjɔ̃] *nf* fraction; *(partie)* part • **fractionner** *vt*, **se fractionner** *vpr* to split (up)

fracture [fraktyr] *nf* fracture; *Fig* **f. sociale** social fracture • **fracturer 1** *vt (porte)* to break open; *(os)* to fracture **2 se fracturer** *vpr* **se f. la jambe** to fracture one's leg

fragile [fraʒil] *adj (objet, matériau)* fragile; *(santé, équilibre)* delicate; *(personne) (physiquement)* frail; *(mentalement)* sensitive • **fragilité** *nf (d'objet, de matériau)* fragility; *(de personne) (physique)* frailty; *(mentale)* sensitivity

fragment [fragmɑ̃] *nm* fragment • **fragmentaire** *adj* fragmentary • **fragmenter** *vt* to fragment

frais¹, fraîche [frɛ, frɛʃ] **1** *adj (aliment, fleurs, teint)* fresh; *(vent, air)* cool, fresh; *(nouvelles)* recent; *(peinture)* wet; **connaître qn de fraîche date** to have known sb for a short time

2 *adv* **servir f.** *(vin)* to serve chilled; **f. émoulu de** fresh out of

3 *nm* **prendre le f.** to get some fresh air; **mettre qch au f.** to put sth in a cool place; *(au réfrigérateur)* to refrigerate sth; **il fait f.** it's cool • **fraîchement** *adv (récemment)* newly; *(accueillir)* coolly • **fraîcheur** *nf (d'aliments, du teint)* freshness; *(de température, d'accueil)* coolness • **fraîchir** *vi (temps)* to freshen

frais² [frɛ] *nmpl* expenses; **à mes f.** at my (own) expense; **à grands f.** at great expense; **faire des f., se mettre en f.** to go to great expense; **faire les f.** to bear the cost (**de** of); **j'en ai été pour mes f.** I wasted my time and effort; **faux f.** incidental expenses; **f. d'inscription** *(d'université)* registration fees; *(de club)* enrolment fee(s); **f. de scolarité** school fees; **f. généraux** *Br* overheads, *Am* overhead

fraise [frɛz] *nf (fruit)* strawberry; *(de dentiste)* drill • **fraisier** *nm (plante)* strawberry plant; *(gâteau)* strawberry cream cake

framboise [frɑ̃bwaz] *nf* raspberry • **framboisier** *nm* raspberry bush

franc¹, franche [frɑ̃, frɑ̃ʃ] *adj* (**a**) *(sincère)* frank; *(visage)* open (**b**) *(net) (couleur)* pure; *(cassure)* clean (**c**) *(zone, ville, port)* free • **franchement** *adv (sincèrement)* frankly; *(vraiment)* really; *(sans ambiguïté)* clearly

franc² [frɑ̃] *nm (monnaie)* franc

France [frɑ̃s] *nf* la **F.** France • **français, -aise 1** *adj* French **2** *nmf* **F.** Frenchman; **Française** Frenchwoman; **les F.** the French **3** *nm (langue)* French

franchir [frɑ̃ʃir] *vt (obstacle, difficulté)* to get over; *(fossé)* to jump over; *(frontière, ligne d'arrivée)* to cross; *(porte)* to go through; *(distance)* to cover; *Fig (seuil, limite)* to exceed

franchise [frɑ̃ʃiz] *nf (sincérité)* frankness; *(exonération)* exemption; *Com* franchise; **en toute f.** quite frankly; **f. postale** ≃ postage paid

franc-maçon [frɑ̃masɔ̃] *(pl* **francs-maçons)** *nm* freemason • **franc-maçonnerie** *nf* freemasonry

franco [frɑ̃ko] *adv* **f. de port** post paid, *Br* carriage paid

franco- [frãko] *préf* Franco-
francophile [frãkɔfil] *adj & nmf* Francophile
francophone [frãkɔfɔn] **1** *adj* French-speaking **2** *nmf* French speaker • **francophonie** *nf* **la f.** the French-speaking world
franc-parler [frãparle] *nm* **avoir son f.** to speak one's mind
franc-tireur [frãtirœr] (*pl* **francs-tireurs**) *nm* irregular (soldier)
frange [frãʒ] *nf (de cheveux) Br* fringe, *Am* bangs; *(de vêtement)* fringe
frangin [frãʒɛ̃] *nm Fam* brother • **frangine** *nf Fam* sister
franquette [frãkɛt] **à la bonne franquette** *adv* without ceremony
frappe [frap] *nf (sur machine à écrire)* typing; *(sur ordinateur)* typing; *(de monnaie)* minting; *Football* kick; **faute de f.** typing error; *Mil* **force de f.** strike force
frapper [frape] **1** *vt (battre)* to strike, to hit; *(monnaie)* to mint; **f. qn** *(impressionner)* to strike sb; *(impôt, mesure)* to hit sb **2** *vi (donner un coup)* to strike, to hit; **f. du pied** to stamp (one's foot); **f. du poing sur la table** to bang (on) the table; **f. dans ses mains** to clap one's hands; **f. à une porte** to knock on a door; *Fig* **f. à toutes les portes** to try everywhere; **'entrez sans f.'** 'go straight in' **3 se frapper** *vpr Fam (s'inquiéter)* to get oneself worked up • **frappant, -ante** *adj* striking • **frappé, -ée** *adj (vin)* chilled; *Fam (fou)* crazy; **f. de stupeur** astounded, flabbergasted
frasques [frask] *nfpl* carryings-on
fraternel, -elle [fratɛrnɛl] *adj* fraternal, brotherly • **fraterniser** *vi* to fraternize (**avec** with) • **fraternité** *nf* fraternity, brotherhood
fraude [frod] *nf* fraud; **passer qch en f.** to smuggle sth in; **f. électorale** electoral fraud; **f. fiscale** tax evasion • **frauder 1** *vt* to defraud; **f. le fisc** to evade tax **2** *vi* to cheat (**sur** on) • **fraudeur, -euse** *nmf* defrauder • **frauduleux, -euse** *adj* fraudulent
frayer [freje] **1** *vi (poisson)* to spawn; *Fig* **f. avec qn** to mix with sb **2 se frayer** *vpr* **se f. un chemin** to clear a way (**à travers/dans** through)
frayeur [frejœr] *nf* fright
fredaines [frədɛn] *nfpl* pranks, escapades
fredonner [frədɔne] *vti* to hum
freezer [frizœr] *nm* freezer compartment
frégate [fregat] *nf (navire)* frigate

frein [frɛ̃] *nm* brake; **donner un coup de f.** to put on the brakes; *Fig* **mettre un f. à qch** to curb sth; **f. à main** handbrake • **freinage** *nm Aut* braking • **freiner 1** *vt (véhicule)* to slow down; *(chute)* to break; *Fig (inflation, production)* to curb **2** *vi* to brake
frelaté, -ée [frəlate] *adj (vin) & Fig* adulterated
frêle [frɛl] *adj* frail
frelon [frəlɔ̃] *nm* hornet
frémir [fremir] *vi (personne)* to tremble (**de** with); *(feuilles)* to rustle; *(eau chaude)* to simmer • **frémissement** *nm (de peur)* shudder; *(de plaisir)* thrill; *(de colère)* quiver; *(de feuilles)* rustle; *(d'eau chaude)* simmering
frêne [frɛn] *nm (arbre, bois)* ash
frénésie [frenezi] *nf* frenzy • **frénétique** *adj* frenzied
fréquent, -ente [frekã, -ãt] *adj* frequent • **fréquemment** [-amã] *adv* frequently • **fréquence** *nf* frequency
fréquenter [frekãte] **1** *vt (lieu)* to frequent; **f. qn** to see sb regularly **2 se fréquenter** *vpr (se voir régulièrement)* to see each other socially • **fréquentable** *adj* **peu f.** *(personne, endroit)* not very commendable • **fréquentation** *nf (de lieu)* frequenting; **fréquentations** *(relations)* company; **avoir de mauvaises fréquentations** to keep bad company • **fréquenté, -ée** *adj* **très f.** very busy; **mal f.** of ill repute; **bien f.** reputable, of good repute
frère [frɛr] *nm* brother
fresque [frɛsk] *nf* fresco
fret [frɛ] *nm* freight
frétiller [fretije] *vi (poisson, personne)* to wriggle; **f. d'impatience** to quiver with impatience; **f. de joie** to tingle with excitement
fretin [frətɛ̃] *nm* **menu f.** *(poissons, personnes)* small fry
friable [frijabl] *adj* crumbly
friand, -e [frijã, -ãd] **1** *adj* **f. de qch** fond of sth **2** *nm (salé)* = small savoury pastry • **friandise** *nf Br* titbit, *Am* tidbit
fric [frik] *nm Fam (argent)* dough
friche [friʃ] **en friche** *adv* fallow; **laisser une terre en f.** to let a piece of land lie fallow
friction [friksjɔ̃] *nf (massage)* rubdown; *(de cuir chevelu)* scalp massage; *(désaccord)* friction • **frictionner** *vt (partie du corps)* to rub; *(personne)* to rub down
Frigidaire® [friʒidɛr] *nm* fridge • **frigo**

nm Fam fridge • **frigorifié, -iée** *adj Fam (personne)* frozen stiff • **frigorifique** *adj voir* camion

frigide [friʒid] *adj* frigid • **frigidité** *nf* frigidity

frileux, -euse [frilø, -øz] *adj* **être f.** to feel the cold

frime [frim] *nf Fam* show • **frimer** *vi Fam* to show off

frimousse [frimus] *nf Fam* sweet little face

fringale [frɛ̃gal] *nf Fam* hunger; **avoir la f.** to be starving

fringant, -ante [frɛ̃gɑ̃, -ɑ̃t] *adj (personne, allure)* dashing

fringues [frɛ̃g] *nfpl Fam (vêtements)* gear • **se fringuer** *vpr Fam* to get dressed

friper [fripe] **1** *vt* to crumple
2 se friper *vpr* to get crumpled • **fripé, -ée** *adj* crumpled

fripier, -ière [fripje, -jɛr] *nmf* second-hand clothes dealer

fripon, -onne [fripɔ̃, -ɔn] *Fam* **1** *adj* mischievous
2 *nmf* rascal

fripouille [fripuj] *nf Fam* rogue

friqué, -ée [frike] *adj Fam (riche)* loaded

frire* [frir] **1** *vt* to fry
2 *vi* to fry; **faire f. qch** to fry sth

frise [friz] *nf* frieze

friser [frize] **1** *vt (cheveux)* to curl; *(effleurer)* to skim; **f. les cheveux à qn** to curl sb's hair; **f. la trentaine** to be close to thirty; **f. la catastrophe** to come within an inch of disaster
2 *vi (cheveux)* to curl; *(personne)* to have curly hair • **frisé, -ée** *adj (cheveux)* curly; *(personne)* curly-haired • **frisette** *nf* small curl

frisquet, -ette [friskɛ, -ɛt] *adj Fam* chilly; **il fait f.** it's chilly

frisson [frisɔ̃] *nm (de froid, de peur)* shiver; *(de plaisir)* thrill; **avoir des frissons** to shiver; **donner le f. à qn** to give sb the shivers • **frissonner** *vi (de froid, de peur)* to shiver

frit, -e [fri, -it] **1** *pp de* frire
2 *adj* fried • **frite** *nf Fam* **avoir la f.** to be on form • **frites** *nfpl Br* chips, *Am* French fries • **friteuse** *nf* (deep) frier, *Br* chip pan; **f. électrique** electric frier • **friture** *nf (mode de cuisson)* frying; *(corps gras)* frying fat; *(aliment)* fried food; *Radio & Tél (bruit)* crackling

frivole [frivɔl] *adj* frivolous • **frivolité** *nf* frivolity

froc [frɔk] *nm Fam (pantalon) Br* trousers, *Am* pants

froid, -e [frwa, frwad] **1** *adj* cold
2 *nm* cold; **avoir/prendre f.** to be/catch cold; **avoir f. aux mains** to have cold hands; **démarrer à f.** *(véhicule)* to start (from) cold; **être en f.** to be on bad terms (**avec qn** with sb); *Fig* **n'avoir pas f. aux yeux** to have plenty of nerve; *Fam* **jeter un f.** to cast a chill (**dans** over); **il fait f.** it's cold • **froidement** *adv (accueillir)* coldly; *(abattre)* cold-bloodedly; *(répondre)* coolly • **froideur** *nf* coldness

froisser [frwase] **1** *vt (tissu)* to crumple, to crease; *Fig* **f. qn** to offend sb
2 se froisser *vpr (tissu)* to crease, to crumple; *Fig* to take offence (**de** at); **se f. un muscle** to strain a muscle

frôler [frole] *vt (effleurer)* to brush against, to touch lightly; *Fig (la mort, la catastrophe)* to come close to

fromage [frɔmaʒ] *nm* cheese; **f. de chèvre** goat's cheese; **f. de tête** *Br* brawn, *Am* headcheese; **f. blanc** fromage frais; **f. frais** soft cheese • **fromager, -ère 1** *adj* **industrie fromagère** cheese industry **2** *nmf (fabricant)* cheesemaker; *(commerçant)* cheese seller • **fromagerie** *nf (magasin)* cheese shop

froment [frɔmɑ̃] *nm* wheat

fronce [frɔ̃s] *nf* gather • **froncement** *nm* **f. de sourcils** frown • **froncer** *vt (tissu)* to gather; **f. les sourcils** to frown

fronde [frɔ̃d] *nf (arme)* sling; *(sédition)* revolt

front [frɔ̃] *nm (du visage)* forehead; *(avant)*, *Mil & Pol* front; **de f.** *(heurter)* head-on; *(côte à côte)* abreast; *(à la fois)* (all) at once; **faire f. à qn/qch** to face up to sb/sth; **f. de mer** sea front • **frontal, -e, -aux, -ales** *adj (collision)* head-on

frontière [frɔ̃tjɛr] **1** *nf (entre pays)* border, frontier
2 *adj inv* **ville f.** border town • **frontalier, -ière** *adj* **ville frontalière** border *or* frontier town

fronton [frɔ̃tɔ̃] *nm (de monument)* pediment

frotter [frɔte] **1** *vt* to rub; *(plancher)* to scrub; *(allumette)* to strike
2 *vi* to rub (**contre** against)
3 se frotter *vpr* to rub oneself; **se f. le dos** to scrub one's back; *Fig* **se f. à qn** *(l'attaquer)* to meddle with sb • **frottement** *nm* rubbing; *Tech* friction

froufrou [frufru] *nm (bruit)* rustling; **froufrous** *(de vêtements)* frills

frousse [frus] *nf Fam* fear; **avoir la f.** to be scared • **froussard, -arde** *nmf Fam* chicken

fructifier [fryktifje] *vi (arbre, capital)* to bear fruit; **faire f. son capital** to make one's capital grow ● **fructueux, -ueuse** *adj* fruitful

frugal, -e, -aux, -ales [frygal, -o] *adj* frugal ● **frugalité** *nf* frugality

fruit [frɥi] *nm* fruit; **des fruits** fruit; **un f.** a piece of fruit; **porter ses fruits** *(placement)* to bear fruit; **fruits de mer** seafood; **fruits rouges** red berries and currants; **fruits secs** dried fruit ● **fruité, -ée** *adj* fruity ● **fruitier, -ière 1** *adj* **arbre f.** fruit tree **2** *nmf* fruit seller, *Br* fruiterer

frusques [frysk] *nfpl Fam* gear

fruste [fryst] *adj (personne)* rough

frustrer [frystre] *vt* **f. qn** to frustrate sb; **f. qn de qch** to deprive sb of sth ● **frustration** *nf* frustration ● **frustré, -ée** *adj* frustrated

fuel [fjul] *nm* fuel oil

fugace [fygas] *adj* fleeting

fugitif, -ive [fyʒitif, -iv] **1** *adj (passager)* fleeting
    2 *nmf* runaway, fugitive

fugue [fyg] *nf (œuvre musicale)* fugue; **faire une f.** *(enfant)* to run away ● **fuguer** *vi Fam* to run away

fuir* [fɥir] **1** *vt (pays)* to flee; *(personne)* to run away from; *(guerre)* to escape; *(responsabilités)* to shirk
    2 *vi (s'échapper)* to run away (**devant** from); *(gaz, robinet, stylo)* to leak; *Littéraire (temps)* to fly ● **fuite** *nf (évasion)* flight (**devant** from); *(de gaz)* leak; **en f.** on the run; **prendre la f.** to take flight; **f. des cerveaux** brain drain

fulgurant, -ante [fylgyrɑ̃, -ɑ̃t] *adj (progrès)* spectacular; *(vitesse)* lightning; *(douleur)* searing

fulminer [fylmine] *vi* to fulminate (**contre** against)

fumée [fyme] *nf* smoke; *(vapeur)* steam

fumer [fyme] **1** *vt (cigarette, poisson)* to smoke; **f. la pipe** to smoke a pipe
    2 *vi (fumeur, feu, moteur)* to smoke; *(liquide brûlant)* to steam ● **fumé, -ée** *adj (poisson, verre)* smoked ● **fume-cigare** *nm inv* cigar holder ● **fumeur, -euse** *nmf* smoker

> *Il faut noter que le verbe anglais **to fume** est un faux ami. Il signifie **fulminer**.*

fumet [fymɛ] *nm* aroma

fumeux, -euse [fymø, -øz] *adj Fig (idée)* hazy

fumier [fymje] *nm (engrais)* manure, dung

fumigation [fymigasjɔ̃] *nf* fumigation

fumiste [fymist] *nmf Fam (sur qui on ne peut compter)* clown ● **fumisterie** *nf Fam (farce)* con

funambule [fynɑ̃byl] *nmf* tightrope walker

funèbre [fynɛbr] *adj (lugubre)* gloomy; **service/marche f.** funeral service/march ● **funérailles** *nfpl* funeral ● **funéraire** *adj (frais)* funeral

funeste [fynɛst] *adj (désastreux)* disastrous

funiculaire [fynikylɛr] *nm* funicular

fur [fyr] **au fur et à mesure** *adv* as one goes along, progressively; **au f. et à mesure de vos besoins** as your needs dictate; **au f. et à mesure que...** as...

furent [fyr] *voir* être

furet [fyrɛ] *nm* ferret

fureter [fyr(ə)te] *vi Péj* to ferret about

fureur [fyrœr] *nf (colère)* fury, rage; *(passion)* passion (**de** for); **en f.** furious; *Fam* **faire f.** to be all the rage ● **furibond, -onde** *adj* furious ● **furie** *nf (colère)* fury; *Fig (femme)* shrew; **comme une f.** like a wild thing ● **furieux, -ieuse** *adj (en colère)* furious (**contre** with); *(vent)* raging; *Fig (envie)* tremendous

furoncle [fyrɔ̃kl] *nm* boil

furtif, -ive [fyrtif, -iv] *adj* furtive, stealthy

fusain [fyzɛ̃] *nm (crayon, dessin)* charcoal; **dessin au f.** charcoal drawing

fuseau, -x [fyzo] *nm (pantalon)* ski pants; *Tex* spindle; **f. horaire** time zone ● **fuselé, -ée** *adj* slender; *(voiture)* streamlined

fusée [fyze] *nf (projectile)* rocket; **f. de détresse** flare, distress signal; **f. éclairante** flare

fuselage [fyzlaʒ] *nm (d'avion)* fuselage

fuser [fyze] *vi (rires)* to burst forth

fusible [fyzibl] *nm* fuse

fusil [fyzi] *nm* rifle, gun; *(de chasse)* shotgun; **un bon f.** *(personne)* a good shot ● **fusillade** *nf (tirs)* gunfire ● **fusiller** *vt (exécuter)* to shoot; *Fam (abîmer)* to wreck; *Fam* **f. qn du regard** to look daggers at sb

fusion [fyzjɔ̃] *nf* **(a)** *(de métal)* melting; *Phys* fusion; **point de f.** melting point; **métal en f.** molten metal **(b)** *(de sociétés)* merger ● **fusionner** *vti (sociétés)* to merge

fustiger [fystiʒe] *vt (critiquer)* to castigate

fut [fy] *voir* être

fût [fy] *nm (tonneau)* barrel, cask; *(d'arbre)* bole ● **futaie** *nf* forest *(producing timber from full-grown trees)*

futal, -als [fytal], **fute** [fyt] *nm Fam Br* trousers, *Am* pants

futé, -ée [fyte] *adj* crafty

futile [fytil] *adj (personne)* frivolous; *(occupation, prétexte)* trivial •**futilité** *nf* triviality

futur, -ure [fytyr] **1** *adj* future; **future mère** mother-to-be

2 *nmf* **mon f./ma future** my intended

3 *nm (avenir)* future; *Grammaire* future (tense)

fuyant [fɥijã] *p prés de* **fuir** •**fuyant, -ante** *adj (front, ligne)* receding; *(personne)* evasive; *(yeux)* shifty •**fuyard** *nm* runaway

G, g [ʒe] *nm inv* G, g
gabardine [gabardin] *nf (tissu, imper-méable)* gabardine
gabarit [gabari] *nm (dimension)* size
gâcher [gaʃe] *vt (gâter)* to spoil; *(gaspiller)* to waste; *(plâtre)* to mix; **g. sa vie** to waste one's life • **gâchis** *nm* waste
gâchette [gaʃɛt] *nf* trigger; **appuyer sur la g.** to pull the trigger
gadget [gadʒɛt] *nm* gadget
gadoue [gadu] *nf* mud
gaffe [gaf] *nf Fam (bévue)* blunder; **faire une g.** to put one's foot in it; **faire g.** to pay attention • **gaffer** *vi Fam* to put one's foot in it • **gaffeur, -euse** *nmf Fam* blunderer
gag [gag] *nm* gag
gaga [gaga] *adj Fam* gaga
gage [gaʒ] *nm (garantie)* guarantee; *(au jeu)* forfeit; *(de prêteur sur gages)* pledge; *(preuve)* token; **mettre qch en g.** to pawn sth; **donner qch en g. de fidélité** to give sth as a token of one's fidelity • **gages** *nmpl Vieilli (salaire)* pay
gager [gaʒe] *vt Littéraire* **g. que...** to wager that... • **gageure** [gaʒyr] *nf Littéraire* wager
gagnant, -ante [gaɲɑ̃, -ɑ̃t] **1** *adj (billet, cheval)* winning
2 *nmf* winner
gagner [gaɲe] **1** *vt (par le travail)* to earn; *(par le jeu)* to win; *(obtenir)* to gain; *(atteindre)* to reach; *(sujet: feu, épidémie)* to spread to; **g. sa vie** to earn one's living; *Fam* **g. des mille et des cents** to earn a bundle *or Br* a packet; **g. une heure** to save an hour; **g. du temps** *(aller plus vite)* to save time; *(temporiser)* to gain time; **g. du terrain/du poids** to gain ground/weight; **g. de la place** to save space; **g. qn** *(sommeil, faim, panique)* to overcome sb; *Fam* **c'est toujours ça de gagné** that's something, anyway
2 *vi (être vainqueur)* to win; *(croître)* to increase; **g. à être connu** to improve with acquaintance; **g. sur tous les tableaux** to win on all counts • **gagne-pain** *nm inv* livelihood
gai, -e [gɛ] *adj* cheerful; *Fam* **être un peu g.** to be tipsy • **gaiement** *adv* cheerfully

• **gaieté** *nf* cheerfulness; **je ne le fais pas de g. de cœur** I don't enjoy doing it
gaillard, -arde [gajar, -ard] **1** *adj (fort)* vigorous; *(grivois)* bawdy
2 *nm (homme)* hearty type; **un grand g.** a strapping man
gain [gɛ̃] *nm (profit)* gain, profit; *(succès)* winning; **gains** *(à la Bourse)* profits; *(au jeu)* winnings; **un g. de temps** a saving of time; **obtenir g. de cause** to win one's case
gaine [gɛn] *nf (sous-vêtement)* girdle; *(étui)* sheath
gala [gala] *nm* gala
galant, -ante [galɑ̃, -ɑ̃t] *adj (homme)* gallant; *(rendez-vous)* romantic • **galanterie** *nf* gallantry
galaxie [galaksi] *nf* galaxy
galbe [galb] *nm* curve • **galbé, -ée** *adj (jambes)* shapely
gale [gal] *nf Méd* **la g.** scabies; *(de chien)* mange • **galeux, -euse** *adj (chien)* mangy
galère [galɛr] *nf Hist (navire)* galley • **galérer** *vi Fam* to have a hard time • **galérien** *nm Hist* galley slave
galerie [galri] *nf (passage, salle)* gallery; *(de taupe)* tunnel; *Théâtre* balcony; *Aut (porte-bagages)* roof rack; *Fam* **épater la g.** to show off; **g. d'art** art gallery; **g. marchande** (shopping) mall
galet [galɛ] *nm* pebble; **plage de galets** shingle beach
galette [galɛt] *nf (gâteau)* butter biscuit; *(crêpe)* buckwheat pancake; **g. des Rois** Twelfth Night cake
galimatias [galimatja] *nm* gibberish
galipette [galipɛt] *nf Fam* somersault
Galles [gal] *nfpl* **pays de G.** Wales • **gallois, -oise** **1** *adj* Welsh **2** *nmf* **G.** Welshman; **Galloise** Welshwoman **3** *nm (langue)* Welsh
gallicisme [galisism] *nm* Gallicism
galon [galɔ̃] *nm (ruban)* braid; *(de soldat)* stripe; *Fam* **prendre du g.** to get promoted
galop [galo] *nm* gallop; **aller au g.** to gallop; *Fig* **g. d'essai** trial run • **galopade** *nf (ruée)* stampede • **galoper** *vi (cheval)* to gallop; *(personne)* to rush; **inflation galopante** galloping inflation

galopin [galɔpɛ̃] *nm Fam* urchin
galvaniser [galvanize] *vt* to galvanize
galvauder [galvode] *vt (talent, avantage)* to misuse
gambade [gɑ̃bad] *nf* leap • **gambader** *vi* to leap *or* frisk about
gambas [gɑ̃bas] *nfpl* large prawns
Gambie [gɑ̃bi] *nf* **la G.** The Gambia
gamelle [gamɛl] *nf (de chien)* bowl; *(d'ouvrier)* billy(can); *(de soldat)* mess tin; *Fam* **se prendre une g.** *Br* to come a cropper, *Am* to take a spill
gamin, -ine [gamɛ̃, -in] **1** *nmf Fam (enfant)* kid
2 *adj (puéril)* childish • **gaminerie** *nf (comportement)* childishness; *(acte)* childish prank
gamme [gam] *nf Mus* scale; *(éventail)* range; **téléviseur haut/bas de g.** top-of-the-range/bottom-of-the-range television
gammée [game] *adj f* **croix g.** swastika
gang [gɑ̃g] *nm* gang • **gangster** *nm* gangster
Gange [gɑ̃ʒ] *nm* **le G.** the Ganges
gangrène [gɑ̃grɛn] *nf Méd* gangrene • **se gangrener** [səgɑ̃grəne] *vpr* to become gangrenous
gant [gɑ̃] *nm* glove; *Fig* **aller comme un g. à qn** *(vêtement)* to fit sb like a glove; *Fig* **jeter/relever le g.** to throw down/take up the gauntlet; **g. de boxe** boxing glove; **g. de toilette** ≃ facecloth • **ganté, -ée** *adj (main)* gloved; *(personne)* wearing gloves
garage [garaʒ] *nm (pour véhicules)* garage • **garagiste** *nmf (mécanicien)* garage mechanic; *(propriétaire)* garage owner
garant, -ante [garɑ̃, -ɑ̃t] *nmf Jur (personne)* guarantor; **se porter g. de qn** to stand guarantor for sb; **se porter g. de qch** to vouch for sth
garantie [garɑ̃ti] *nf* guarantee; *Fig (précaution)* safeguard; **être sous g.** to be under guarantee • **garantir** *vt* to guarantee; *(emprunt)* to secure; **g. à qn que...** to give sb the guarantee that...; **g. qch de qch** *(protéger)* to protect sth from sth; **je te le garantis** I can vouch for it
garce [gars] *nf Fam* bitch
garçon [garsɔ̃] *nm* boy; *(jeune homme)* young man; *(serveur)* waiter; **de g.** *(comportement)* boyish; **vieux g.** (old) bachelor; **g. de café** waiter; **g. d'honneur** best man; **g. manqué** tomboy • **garçonnet** *nm* little boy • **garçonnière** *nf* bachelor *Br* flat *or Am* apartment
garde [gard] **1** *nm (gardien)* guard; *(soldat)* guardsman; **g. champêtre** rural

policeman; **g. du corps** bodyguard; **g. des Sceaux** Justice Minister
2 *nf* (**a**) *(d'enfants, de bagages)* care, custody (**de** of); **avoir la g. de** to be in charge of; **faire bonne g.** to keep a close watch; **prendre g.** to pay attention (**à qch** to sth); **prendre g. de ne pas faire qch** to be careful not to do sth; **mettre qn en g.** to warn sb (**contre** against); **mise en g.** warning; **être de g.** to be on duty; *(soldat)* to be on guard duty; **médecin de g.** duty doctor; **monter la g.** to mount guard; **être sur ses gardes** to be on one's guard; **g. à vue** police custody
(**b**) *(escorte, soldats)* guard
3 *nmf* **g. d'enfants** child minder; **g. de nuit** *(de malade)* night nurse • **garde-à-vous** *nm inv Mil* (position of) attention; **se mettre au g.** to stand to attention • **garde-boue** *nm inv Br* mudguard, *Am* fender • **garde-chasse** *(pl* **gardes-chasses**) *nm* gamekeeper • **garde-chiourme** *(pl* **gardes-chiourmes**) *nm (surveillant sévère)* martinet • **garde-côte** *(pl* **garde-côtes**) *nm (bateau)* coastguard vessel • **garde-fou** *(pl* **garde-fous**) *nm (rambarde)* railings; *(mur)* parapet • **garde-malade** *(pl* **gardes-malades**) *nmf* nurse • **garde-manger** *nm inv (armoire)* food safe; *(pièce)* pantry, *Br* larder • **garde-robe** *(pl* **garde-robes**) *nf (habits, armoire)* wardrobe
garder [garde] **1** *vt (conserver)* to keep; *(vêtement)* to keep on; *(habitude)* to keep up; *(surveiller)* to look after; *(défendre)* to protect; **g. qn à dîner** to get sb to stay for dinner; **g. la chambre** to keep to one's room; **g. le lit** to stay in bed; **g. la tête** keep a cool head
2 **se garder** *vpr (aliment)* to keep; **se g. de qch** to beware of sth; **se g. de faire qch** to take care not to do sth
garderie [gardəri] *nf Br* (day) nursery, *Am* daycare center
gardien, -ienne [gardjɛ̃, -jɛn] *nmf (d'immeuble, d'hôtel)* caretaker, *Am* janitor; *(de prison)* (prison) guard, *Br* warder; *(de zoo, parc)* keeper; *(de musée) Br* attendant, *Am* guard; *Fig* **g. de** *(libertés)* guardian of; *Football* **g. de but** goalkeeper; **gardienne d'enfants** child minder, babysitter; **g. de nuit** night watchman; **g. de la paix** policeman
gardon [gardɔ̃] *nm* roach; *Fig* **frais comme un g.** fresh as a daisy
gare¹ [gar] *nf (pour trains)* station; **g. routière** bus *or Br* coach station
gare² [gar] *exclam* **g. à toi si on l'apprend** woe betide you if anyone finds out; **g. aux**

orties! mind the nettles!; **sans crier g.** without warning
garer [gare] **1** *vt (voiture)* to park
   2 se garer *vpr (automobiliste)* to park; **se g. de qch** *(se protéger)* to steer clear of sth
gargariser [gargarize] **se gargariser** *vpr* to gargle ● **gargarisme** *nm* gargle
gargote [gargɔt] *nf Péj* cheap restaurant
gargouiller [garguje] *vi (fontaine, eau)* to gurgle; *(ventre)* to rumble ● **gargouillis, gargouillement** *nm* gurgling; *(de ventre)* rumbling
garnement [garnəmɑ̃] *nm* rascal
garnir [garnir] *vt (équiper)* to fit out (**de** with); *(couvrir)* to cover; *(remplir)* to fill; *(magasin)* to stock (**de** with); *(tiroir)* to line; *(robe, chapeau)* to trim (**de** with); *Culin* to garnish ● **garni, -ie** *adj (plat)* served with vegetables; *Fig* **bien g.** *(portefeuille)* well-lined ● **garniture** *nf Culin* garnish; *Aut* **g. de frein** brake lining; **g. de lit** bedding
garnison [garnizɔ̃] *nf* garrison
garrot [garo] *nm (de cheval)* withers; *Méd (lien)* tourniquet
gars [gɑ] *nm Fam* fellow, guy
gas-oil [gɑzwal] *nm* diesel (oil)
gaspiller [gaspije] *vt* to waste ● **gaspillage** *nm* waste
gastrique [gastrik] *adj* gastric
gastronome [gastrɔnɔm] *nmf* gourmet ● **gastronomie** *nf* gastronomy
gâteau, -x [gɑto] *nm* cake; *Fam* **c'était du g.** *(facile)* it was a piece of cake; **g. de riz** rice pudding; **g. sec** *Br* biscuit, *Am* cookie
gâter [gɑte] **1** *vt* to spoil
   2 se gâter *vpr (aliment, dent)* to go bad; *(temps, situation)* to take a turn for the worst; *(relations)* to turn sour ● **gâté, -ée** *adj (dent, fruit)* bad ● **gâterie** *nf (cadeau, friandise)* treat
gâteux, -euse [gɑtø, -øz] *adj* senile
gauche¹ [goʃ] **1** *adj (côté, main)* left
   2 *nf* **la g.** *(côté)* the left (side); *Pol* the left (wing); **à g.** *(tourner)* (to the) left; *(marcher, se tenir)* on the left, on the left (-hand) side; **de g.** *(fenêtre)* left-hand; *(parti, politique)* left-wing; **à g. de** on *or* to the left of ● **gaucher, -ère 1** *adj* left-handed **2** *nmf* left-hander ● **gauchisant, -ante** *adj Pol* leftish ● **gauchiste** *adj & nmf Pol* (extreme) leftist
gauche² [goʃ] *adj (maladroit)* awkward ● **gauchement** *adv* awkwardly ● **gaucherie** *nf* awkwardness
gauchir [goʃir] *vti* to warp
gaufre [gofr] *nf* waffle ● **gaufrette** *nf* wafer (biscuit)

Gaule [gol] *nf Hist* **la G.** *(pays)* Gaul ● **gaulois, -oise 1** *adj* Gallic; *Fig (propos)* bawdy **2** *nmpl Hist* **les G.** the Gauls ● **gauloiserie** *nf (plaisanterie)* bawdy joke
gaule [gol] *nf* long pole; *Pêche* fishing rod
gausser [gose] **se gausser** *vpr Littéraire* to mock
gaver [gave] **1** *vt (animal)* to force-feed; *Fig (personne)* to stuff (**de** with)
   2 se gaver *vpr* to stuff oneself (**de** with)
gaz [gɑz] *nm inv* gas; **réchaud/masque à g.** gas stove/mask; **avoir des g.** to have wind; *Fam* **il y a de l'eau dans le g.** things aren't going too well; **g. carbonique** carbon dioxide; **g. d'échappement** exhaust fumes ● **gazeux, -euse** *adj (état)* gaseous; *(boisson, eau) Br* fizzy, carbonated ● **gazomètre** *nm Br* gasometer, gas storage tank
Gaza [gaza] *nf* Gaza; **la bande de G.** the Gaza Strip
gaze [gɑz] *nf* gauze
gazelle [gazɛl] *nf* gazelle
gazer [gɑze] **1** *vt (asphyxier)* to gas
   2 *vi Fam* **ça gaze!** everything's just fine!; **ça gaze?** how's everything?
gazette [gazɛt] *nf (journal)* newspaper
gazinière [gazinjɛr] *nf Br* gas cooker, *Am* gas stove
gazoduc [gazɔdyk] *nm* gas pipeline
gazole [gazɔl] *nm* diesel oil
gazon [gazɔ̃] *nm (herbe)* grass; *(surface)* lawn
gazouiller [gazuje] *vi (oiseau)* to chirp; *(bébé, ruisseau)* to babble ● **gazouillis, gazouillement** *nm (d'oiseau)* chirping; *(de bébé)* babbling
GDF [ʒedeɛf] *(abrév* **Gaz de France** *) nm =* French gas company
geai [ʒɛ] *nm* jay
géant, -e [ʒeɑ̃, -ɑ̃t] *adj & nmf* giant
Geiger [ʒeʒɛr] *nm* **compteur G.** Geiger counter
geindre* [ʒɛ̃dr] *vi (gémir)* to moan; *Fam (se plaindre)* to whine
gel [ʒɛl] *nm* (a) *(temps, glace)* frost; *Écon* **g. des salaires** wage freeze (b) *(pour cheveux)* gel ● **gelé, -ée** *adj* frozen; *Méd (doigts, mains, pieds)* frostbitten ● **gelée** *nf* (a) frost; **g. blanche** ground frost (b) *(de fruits, de viande)* jelly; *(de fruits, de viande)* jelly; **œufs en g.** jellied eggs ● **geler 1** *vt* to freeze **2** *vi* to freeze; **on gèle ici** it's freezing here **3** *v impersonnel* **il gèle** it's freezing
gélatine [ʒelatin] *nf* gelatine
gélule [ʒelyl] *nf* capsule
Gémeaux [ʒemo] *nmpl* **les G.** *(signe)* Gemini; **être G.** to be Gemini

gémir [ʒemir] *vi* to groan, to moan •**gémissement** *nm* groan, moan

gencive [ʒɑ̃siv] *nf* gum

gendarme [ʒɑ̃darm] *nm* gendarme, policeman; **g. couché** sleeping policeman •**gendarmerie** *nf (corps)* police force; *(local)* police headquarters

gendre [ʒɑ̃dr] *nm* son-in-law

gène [ʒɛn] *nm* gene

gêne [ʒɛn] *nf (trouble physique)* discomfort; *(confusion)* embarrassment; *(dérangement)* inconvenience; **dans la g.** *(à court d'argent)* in financial difficulties

généalogie [ʒenealɔʒi] *nf* genealogy •**généalogique** *adj* genealogical; **arbre g.** family tree

gêner [ʒene] **1** *vt (déranger, irriter)* to bother; *(troubler)* to embarrass; *(mouvement, action)* to hamper; *(circulation)* to hold up; **g. qn** *(vêtement)* to be uncomfortable on sb; *(par sa présence)* to be in sb's way; **ça ne me gêne pas** I don't mind (**si** if) **2 se gêner** *vpr (se déranger)* to put oneself out; **ne te gêne pas pour moi!** don't mind me! •**gênant, -ante** *adj (objet)* cumbersome; *(présence, situation)* awkward; *(bruit, personne)* annoying •**gêné, -ée** *adj (intimidé)* embarrassed; *(silence, sourire)* awkward; *(sans argent)* short of money

général, -e, -aux, -ales [ʒeneral, -o] **1** *adj* general; **en g.** in general **2** *nm Mil* general; **oui, mon g.!** yes, general! •**générale** *nf Théâtre* dress rehearsal •**généralement** *adv* generally; **g. parlant** broadly *or* generally speaking •**généralité** *nf* generality

généralisation [ʒeneralizasjɔ̃] *nf* generalization •**généraliser 1** *vti* to generalize **2 se généraliser** *vpr* to become widespread •**généraliste** *nmf (médecin)* general practitioner, GP

générateur [ʒeneratœr] *nm Él* generator

génération [ʒenerasjɔ̃] *nf* generation

génératrice [ʒeneratris] *nf Él* generator

générer [ʒenere] *vt* to generate

généreux, -euse [ʒenerø, -øz] *adj* generous (**de** with) •**généreusement** *adv* generously •**générosité** *nf* generosity

générique [ʒenerik] **1** *nm (de film)* credits **2** *adj* **produit g.** generic product

genèse [ʒənɛz] *nf* genesis

genêt [ʒənɛ] *nm* broom

génétique [ʒenetik] **1** *nf* genetics *(sing)* **2** *adj* genetic; **manipulation g.** genetic engineering •**génétiquement** *adv* **g. modifié** genetically modified

Genève [ʒənɛv] *nm ou f* Geneva

génial, -e, -iaux, -iales [ʒenjal, -jo] *adj (personne, invention)* brilliant; *Fam (formidable)* fantastic

> Ⓘ Il faut noter que l'adjectif anglais **genial** est un faux ami. Il signifie **cordial**.

génie [ʒeni] *nm* (**a**) *(aptitude, personne)* genius; **inventeur de g.** inventor of genius; **avoir le g. pour faire/de qch** to have a genius for doing/for sth (**b**) **g. civil** civil engineering; **g. génétique/informatique** genetic/computer engineering; **g. militaire** engineering corps (**c**) *(esprit)* genie, spirit; **bon/mauvais g.** good/evil genie

génisse [ʒenis] *nf* heifer

génital, -e, -aux, -ales [ʒenital, -o] *adj* genital; **organes génitaux** genitals

génocide [ʒenɔsid] *nm* genocide

genou, -x [ʒ(ə)nu] *nm* knee; **être à genoux** to be kneeling (down); **se mettre à genoux** to kneel (down); **prendre qn sur ses genoux** to take sb on one's lap *or* knee; **écrire sur ses genoux** to write on one's lap •**genouillère** *nf* kneepad

genre [ʒɑ̃r] *nm (espèce)* kind, sort; *(attitude)* manner; *Littérature & Cin* genre; *Grammaire* gender; **en tous genres** of all kinds; **ce n'est pas son g.** that's not like him; **le g. humain** mankind

gens [ʒɑ̃] *nmpl* people; **jeunes g.** young people; *(hommes)* young men; **de petites g.** people of humble means; **g. de maison** domestic servants

gentil, -ille [ʒɑ̃ti, -ij] *adj (aimable)* nice (**avec** to); *(sage)* good; **une gentille somme** a nice little sum •**gentillesse** *nf* kindness; **avoir la g. de faire qch** to be kind enough to do sth •**gentiment** *adv (aimablement)* kindly; *(sagement)* nicely

> Ⓘ Il faut noter que les termes anglais **genteel** et **gentle** sont des faux amis. Le premier signifie **respectable** ou **affecté**, le second signifie **doux**.

gentilhomme [ʒɑ̃tijɔm] (*pl* **gentilshommes** [ʒɑ̃tizɔm]) *nm Hist (noble)* gentleman

géographie [ʒeɔgrafi] *nf* geography •**géographique** *adj* geographical

geôlier, -ière [ʒolje, -jɛr] *nmf* jailer, *Br* gaoler

géologie [ʒeɔlɔʒi] *nf* geology •**géologique** *adj* geological •**géologue** *nmf* geologist

géomètre [ʒeɔmɛtr] *nm* surveyor

géométrie [ʒeɔmetri] *nf* geometry; *Fig* **à g. variable** ever-changing •**géométrique** *adj* geometric(al)

géostationnaire [ʒeostasjɔnɛr] *adj (satellite)* geostationary

géranium [ʒeranjɔm] *nm* geranium

gérant, -ante [ʒerɑ̃, -ɑ̃t] *nmf* manager, *f* manageress •**gérance** *nf (gestion)* management

gerbe [ʒɛrb] *nf (de blé)* sheaf; *(de fleurs)* bunch; *(d'eau)* spray; *(d'étincelles)* shower

gercer [ʒɛrse] *vi*, **se gercer** *vpr (peau, lèvres)* to chap; **avoir les lèvres gercées** to have chapped lips •**gerçure** *nf* chap, crack; **avoir des gerçures aux mains** to have chapped hands

gérer [ʒere] *vt* to manage

germain, -aine [ʒɛrmɛ̃, -ɛn] *adj voir* **cousin**

germanique [ʒɛrmanik] *adj* Germanic

germe [ʒɛrm] *nm (microbe)* germ; *(de plante)* shoot; *Fig (d'une idée)* seed, germ •**germer** *vi (graine)* to start to grow; *(pomme de terre)* to sprout; *Fig (idée)* to germinate

gérondif [ʒerɔ̃dif] *nm Grammaire* gerund

gésir [ʒezir] *vi Littéraire (être étendu)* to be lying; **il gît/gisait** he is/was lying; **ci-gît...** *(sur tombe)* here lies...

gestation [ʒɛstasjɔ̃] *nf* gestation

geste [ʒɛst] *nm* gesture; **ne pas faire un g.** *(ne pas bouger)* not to make a move; **faire un g. de la main** to wave one's hand; **faire un g.** *(bouger, agir)* to make a gesture •**gesticuler** *vi* to gesticulate

gestion [ʒɛstjɔ̃] *nf (action)* management; **g. du personnel/de patrimoine** personnel/property management •**gestionnaire** *nmf* administrator

geyser [ʒezɛr] *nm* geyser

Ghana [gana] *nm* **le G.** Ghana

ghetto [gɛto] *nm* ghetto

gibecière [ʒibɔsjɛr] *nf (de chasseur)* game bag

gibier [ʒibje] *nm* game; **le gros g.** big game; *Fig* **g. de potence** gallows bird

giboulée [ʒibule] *nf* sudden shower; **giboulées de mars** ≃ April showers

gicler [ʒikle] *vi (liquide)* to spurt out; *(boue)* to splash up •**giclée** *nf* spurt •**gicleur** *nm Aut* jet

gifle [ʒifl] *nf* slap in the face •**gifler** *vt* **g. qn** to slap sb in the face

gigantesque [ʒigɑ̃tɛsk] *adj* gigantic

gigogne [ʒigɔɲ] *adj* **tables gigognes** nest of tables

gigot [ʒigo] *nm* leg of mutton/lamb

gigoter [ʒigɔte] *vi Fam* to wriggle, to fidget

gilet [ʒilɛ] *nm (cardigan)* cardigan; *(de costume) Br* waistcoat, *Am* vest; **g. pare-balles** bulletproof vest; **g. de sauvetage** life jacket

gin [dʒin] *nm* gin

gingembre [ʒɛ̃ʒɑ̃br] *nm* ginger

girafe [ʒiraf] *nf* giraffe

giratoire [ʒiratwar] *adj Aut* **sens g.** *Br* roundabout, *Am* traffic circle

girofle [ʒirɔfl] *nm* **clou de g.** clove

giroflée [ʒirɔfle] *nf* wallflower

girouette [ʒirwɛt] *nf Br* weathercock, *Am* weathervane; *Fig (personne)* weathercock

gisait [ʒizɛ] *voir* **gésir**

gisement [ʒizmɑ̃] *nm (de minerai)* deposit; **g. de pétrole** oilfield

gît [ʒi] *voir* **gésir**

gitan, -ane [ʒitɑ̃, -an] *nmf* gipsy

gîte [ʒit] *nm (abri)* resting place; **donner le g. et le couvert à qn** to give sb room and board; **g. rural** gîte, = self-catering holiday cottage or apartment

gîter [ʒite] *vi Naut* to list

givre [ʒivr] *nm* frost •**givré, -ée** *adj* frost-covered; *Fam (fou)* nuts, crazy •**se givrer** *vpr (pare-brise)* to ice up, to frost up

glabre [glabr] *adj (visage)* smooth

glace [glas] *nf* (**a**) *(eau gelée)* ice; *(crème glacée)* ice cream (**b**) *(vitre)* window; *(miroir)* mirror; *Fig* **briser la g.** to break the ice; **il est resté de g.** he showed no emotion

glacer [glase] **1** *vt (durcir)* to freeze; *(gâteau)* to ice; *Fig (sang)* to chill; **à vous g. le sang** spine-chilling

2 se glacer *vpr* **mon sang s'est glacé dans mes veines** my blood ran cold •**glaçage** *nm (de gâteau)* icing •**glacé, -ée** *adj (eau, pièce)* ice-cold, icy; *(vent)* freezing, icy; *(thé, café)* iced; *(fruit)* candied; *(papier)* glazed; *Fig (accueil)* icy, chilly; **avoir les pieds glacés** to have icy or frozen feet

glacial, -e, -iaux, -iales [glasjal, -jo] *adj* icy

glacier [glasje] *nm* (**a**) *Géol* glacier (**b**) *(vendeur)* ice-cream seller

glacière [glasjɛr] *nf (boîte)* icebox

glaçon [glasɔ̃] *nm Culin* ice cube; *Géol* block of ice; *(sur toit)* icicle

glaïeul [glajœl] *nm* gladiolus

glaire [glɛr] *nf Méd* phlegm

glaise [glɛz] *nf* clay

gland [glɑ̃] *nm Bot* acorn; *(pompon)* tassel

glande [glɑ̃d] *nf* gland

glander [glɑ̃de] *vi très Fam* to loaf around •**glandeur, -euse** *nmf très Fam* layabout

glandouiller [glɑ̃duje] *vi très Fam* to loaf about

glaner [glane] *vt (blé, renseignement)* to glean

glapir [glapir] *vi (chien)* to yap

glas [glɑ] *nm (de cloche)* knell; **on sonne le g.** the bell is tolling

glauque [glok] *adj* sea-green; *Fam (sinistre)* creepy

glisse [glis] *nf* **(sports de) g.** = sports involving sliding and gliding motion, eg skiing, surfing etc

glisser [glise] **1** *vt (introduire)* to slip (**dans** into); *(murmurer)* to whisper

2 *vi (involontairement)* to slip; *(volontairement) (sur glace)* to slide; *(sur l'eau)* to glide; *Fig* **g. sur** *(sujet)* to gloss over; *Ordinat* **faire g.** *(pointeur)* to drag; **se laisser g. le long de la gouttière** to slide down the drainpipe; **ça glisse** it's slippery; **ça m'a glissé des mains** it slipped out of my hands

3 se glisser *vpr* **se g. dans/sous qch** to slip into/under sth • **glissade** *nf (involontaire)* slip; *(volontaire)* slide • **glissant, -ante** *adj* slippery • **glissement** *nm* **g. de terrain** landslide

glissière [glisjɛr] *nf Tech* runner, slide; **porte à g.** sliding door; *Aut* **g. de sécurité** crash barrier

global, -e, -aux, -ales [glɔbal, -o] *adj* total, global; **somme globale** lump sum; *Scol* **méthode globale** word recognition method • **globalement** *adv* overall

globe [glɔb] *nm* globe; **g. oculaire** eyeball; **g. terrestre** *(mappemonde)* globe

globule [glɔbyl] *nm* **globules blancs/rouges** white/red corpuscles

globuleux, -euse [glɔbylø, -øz] *adj* **yeux g.** protruding eyes

gloire [glwar] *nf (renom)* glory; *(personne célèbre)* celebrity; **tirer g. de qch** to glory in sth; **à la g. de qn** in praise of sb • **glorieux, -ieuse** *adj* glorious • **glorifier 1** *vt* to glorify **2 se glorifier** *vpr* **se g. de qch** to glory in sth

glossaire [glɔsɛr] *nm* glossary

glouglou [gluglu] *nm Fam (de liquide)* gurgle • **glouglouter** *vi Fam* to gurgle

glousser [gluse] *vi (poule)* to cluck; *(personne)* to chuckle • **gloussement** *nm* clucking; *(de personne)* chuckling

glouton, -onne [glutɔ̃, -ɔn] **1** *adj* greedy, gluttonous

2 *nmf* glutton • **gloutonnerie** *nf* gluttony

gluant, -e [glɥɑ̃, -ɑ̃t] *adj* sticky

glucose [glykoz] *nm* glucose

glycérine [gliserin] *nf* glycerine

glycine [glisin] *nf (plante)* wisteria

gnome [gnom] *nm* gnome

gnon [ɲɔ̃] *nm Fam* thump; **se prendre un g.** to get thumped

go [go] **tout de go** *adv* straight away

goal [gol] *nm Football* goalkeeper

gobelet [gɔblɛ] *nm* tumbler; *(de plastique, de papier)* cup

gober [gɔbe] *vt (œuf, mouche)* to gulp down; *Fam (croire)* to swallow

godasse [gɔdas] *nf Fam* shoe

godet [gɔde] *nm (récipient)* pot; *Fam (verre)* drink

godillot [gɔdijo] *nm Fam* clodhopper

goéland [gɔelɑ̃] *nm* (sea)gull

goélette [gɔelɛt] *nf* schooner

gogo¹ [gogo] *nm Fam (homme naïf)* sucker

gogo² [gogo] **à gogo** *adv Fam* **whisky à g.** whisky galore

goguenard, -arde [gɔgnar, -ard] *adj* mocking

goinfre [gwɛ̃fr] *nmf Fam (glouton)* pig • **se goinfrer** *vpr Fam* to pig oneself (**de** with)

golf [gɔlf] *nm Sport* golf; *(terrain)* golf course • **golfeur, -euse** *nmf* golfer

golfe [gɔlf] *nm* gulf, bay

gomme [gɔm] *nf (substance)* gum; *(à effacer)* eraser, *Br* rubber; *Fam* **mettre la g.** *(accélérer)* to get a move on; *(en voiture)* to step on it; *Fam* **à la g.** useless • **gommé, -ée** *adj (papier)* gummed • **gommer** *vt (effacer)* to rub out, to erase

gond [gɔ̃] *nm (de porte)* hinge; *Fig* **sortir de ses gonds** to lose one's temper

gondole [gɔ̃dɔl] *nf* gondola • **gondolier** *nm* gondolier

gondoler [gɔ̃dɔle] **1** *vi (planche)* to warp; *(papier)* to crinkle

2 se gondoler *vpr (planche)* to warp; *(papier)* to crinkle; *Fam (rire)* to fall about laughing

gonflable [gɔ̃flabl] *adj* inflatable

gonfler [gɔ̃fle] **1** *vt* to swell; *(pneu)* to inflate; *très Fam (énerver)* to get up sb's nose

2 *vi* to swell

3 se gonfler *vpr* to swell; **se g. de joie** to fill with joy • **gonflé, -ée** *adj* swollen; *Fam* **être g.** *(courageux)* to have plenty of pluck; *(insolent)* to have plenty of nerve • **gonflement** [-əmɑ̃] *nm* swelling

gong [gɔ̃g] *nm* gong

gorge [gɔrʒ] *nf* throat; *Littéraire (poitrine)* bosom; *Géog* gorge; **avoir la g. serrée** to have a lump in one's throat; **rire à g. déployée** to roar with laughter; *Fig* **faire des gorges chaudes de qch** to have a field day pouring scorn on sth

gorgé, -ée [gɔrʒe] *adj* **g. de** *(saturé)* gorged with

gorgée [gɔrʒe] *nf* mouthful; **petite g.** sip; **d'une seule g.** in one gulp

gorger [gɔrʒe] **1** *vt (remplir)* to stuff (**de** with)
2 se gorger *vpr* **se g. de** to gorge oneself with

gorille [gɔrij] *nm (animal)* gorilla; *Fam (garde du corps)* bodyguard

gosier [gozje] *nm* throat

gosse [gɔs] *nmf Fam (enfant)* kid

gothique [gɔtik] *adj & nm* Gothic

gouache [gwaʃ] *nf (peinture)* gouache

goudron [gudrɔ̃] *nm* tar • **goudronner** *vt* to tar

gouffre [gufr] *nm* abyss

goujat [guʒa] *nm* boor

goulot [gulo] *nm (de bouteille)* neck; **boire au g.** to drink from the bottle

goulu, -ue [guly] *adj* greedy • **goulûment** *adv* greedily

goupille [gupij] *nf (de grenade)* pin

goupiller [gupije] *Fam* **1** *vt (arranger)* to fix up
2 se goupiller *vpr* **ça s'est bien goupillé** it worked out (well); **ça s'est mal goupillé** it didn't work out

gourde [gurd] *nf (à eau)* water bottle, flask; *Fam Péj (femme niaise)* dope

gourdin [gurdɛ̃] *nm* club, cudgel

gourer [gure] **se gourer** *vpr Fam* to make a mistake

gourmand, -ande [gurmã, -ãd] **1** *adj* fond of eating; *Fig (intéressé)* greedy; **g. de qch** fond of sth
2 *nmf* hearty eater • **gourmandise** *nf* fondness for food; **gourmandises** *(mets)* delicacies

gourmet [gurmɛ] *nm* gourmet; **fin g.** gourmet

gourmette [gurmɛt] *nf (bracelet)* chain

gousse [gus] *nf* **g. d'ail** clove of garlic

goût [gu] *nm* taste; **de bon g.** in good taste; **sans g.** tasteless; **par g.** by choice; **avoir du g.** *(personne)* to have good taste; **avoir un g. de noisette** to taste of hazelnut; **prendre g. à qch** to take a liking to sth; *Fam* **quelque chose dans ce g.-là!** something of that order!

goûter [gute] **1** *vt (aliment)* to taste; *(apprécier)* to enjoy; **g. à qch** to taste (a little of) sth
2 *vi* to have an afternoon snack, *Br* to have tea
3 *nm* afternoon snack, *Br* tea

goutte [gut] *nf* **(a)** *(de liquide)* drop; **couler g. à g.** to drip **(b)** *Méd* gout

• **goutte-à-goutte** *nm inv Méd* drip • **gouttelette** *nf* droplet • **goutter** *vi* to drip

gouttière [gutjɛr] *nf (le long du toit)* gutter; *(le long du mur)* drainpipe

gouvernail [guvɛrnaj] *nm (pale)* rudder; *(barre)* helm

gouvernante [guvɛrnãt] *nf* governess

gouvernement [guvɛrnəmã] *nm* government • **gouvernemental, -e, -aux, -ales** *adj* **politique gouvernementale** government policy; **l'équipe gouvernementale** the government

gouverner [guvɛrne] *vti Pol & Fig* to govern, to rule • **gouvernants** *nmpl* rulers • **gouverneur** *nm* governor

grabuge [grabyʒ] *nm Fam* **il y a du g.** there's a rumpus

grâce [grɑs] **1** *nf (charme) & Rel* grace; *Littéraire (faveur)* favour; *(acquittement)* pardon; **de bonne/mauvaise g.** with good/bad grace; **crier g.** to beg for mercy; **donner le coup de g. à** to finish off; **faire g. de qch à qn** to spare sb sth; **être dans les bonnes grâces de qn** to be in favour with sb; **rendre g. à qn** to give thanks to sb; **délai de g.** period of grace; **g. présidentielle** presidential pardon
2 *prép* **g. à** thanks to

gracier [grasje] *vt (condamné)* to pardon

gracieux, -ieuse [grasjø, -jøz] *adj (élégant)* graceful; *(aimable)* gracious; *(gratuit)* gratuitous; **à titre g.** free (of charge) • **gracieusement** *adv* gracefully; *(aimablement)* graciously; *(gratuitement)* free (of charge)

gracile [grasil] *adj Littéraire* slender

gradation [gradɑsjɔ̃] *nf* gradation

grade [grad] *nm (militaire)* rank; **monter en g.** to be promoted • **gradé** *nm Mil* non-commissioned officer

gradins [gradɛ̃] *nmpl (d'amphithéâtre)* rows of seats; *(de stade) Br* terraces, *Am* bleachers

graduel, -uelle [gradɥɛl] *adj* gradual

graduer [gradɥe] *vt (règle)* to graduate; *(augmenter)* to increase gradually

graffiti [grafiti] *nmpl* graffiti

grain [grɛ̃] *nm* **(a)** *(de blé) & Fig* grain; *(de café)* bean; *(de poussière)* speck; *(de chapelet)* bead; **le g.** *(de cuir, de papier)* the grain; *Fam* **avoir un g.** to be not quite right in the head; *Fam* **mettre son g. de sel** to stick one's oar in; **g. de beauté** mole; *(sur le visage)* beauty spot; **g. de raisin** grape **(b)** *(averse)* shower

graine [grɛn] *nf* seed; **mauvaise g.** *(enfant)* rotten egg, *Br* bad lot; **en prendre de la g.** to learn from someone's example

graisse [grɛs] *nf* fat; *(lubrifiant)* grease
• **graissage** *nm (de véhicule)* lubrication
• **graisser** *vt* to grease • **graisseux, -euse**
adj (vêtement) greasy, oily; *(bourrelets,
tissu)* fatty

grammaire [gramɛr] *nf* grammar; **livre
de g.** grammar (book) • **grammatical, -e,
-aux, -ales** *adj* grammatical

gramme [gram] *nm* gram(me)

grand, -e [grɑ̃, grɑ̃d] **1** *adj* big, large; *(en
hauteur)* tall; *(chaleur, découverte, âge,
mérite, ami)* great; *(bruit)* loud; *(différence)* big, great; *(adulte, mûr, plus âgé)*
grown-up, big; *(âme)* noble; *(illustre)*
great; **g. frère** *(plus âgé)* big brother; **le
g. air** the open air; **il est g. temps que je
parte** it's high time that I left; **il n'y avait
pas g. monde** there were not many people

2 *adv* **g. ouvert** *(yeux, fenêtre)* wide
open; **ouvrir g.** to open wide; **en g.** on a
grand *or* large scale

3 *nmf (à l'école)* senior; *(adulte)* grown-
up • **grandement** *adv (beaucoup)* greatly;
(généreusement) grandly; **avoir g. de quoi
vivre** to have plenty to live on • **grand-
mère** *(pl* grands-mères*)* *nf* grandmother
• **grand-père** *(pl* grands-pères*)* *nm* grandfather • **grand-route** *(pl* grand-routes*)* *nf*
main road • **grands-parents** *nmpl* grandparents

grand-chose [grɑ̃ʃoz] *pron* **pas g.** not
much

Grande-Bretagne [grɑ̃dbrətaɲ] *nf* **la G.**
Great Britain

grandeur [grɑ̃dœr] *nf (importance,
gloire)* greatness; *(dimension)* size; *(majesté, splendeur)* grandeur; **avoir la folie
des grandeurs** to have delusions of grandeur; **g. d'âme** magnanimity; **g. nature**
life-size

grandiose [grɑ̃djoz] *adj* imposing

grandir [grɑ̃dir] **1** *vi (en taille)* to grow; *(en
âge)* to grow up; *(bruit)* to grow louder; **g.
de 2 cm** to grow 2 cm

2 *vt* **g. qn** *(faire paraître plus grand)* to
make sb look taller

grange [grɑ̃ʒ] *nf* barn

granit(e) [granit] *nm* granite

granule [granyl] *nm* granule

graphique [grafik] **1** *adj (signe, art)*
graphic

2 *nm* graph; *Ordinat* graphic

grappe [grap] *nf (de fruits)* cluster; **g. de
raisin** bunch of grapes

Il faut noter que le nom anglais **grape** *est
un faux ami. Il signifie* **grain de raisin**.

grappin [grapɛ̃] *nm Fam* **mettre le g. sur
qn/qch** to get one's hands on sb/sth

gras, grasse [grɑ, grɑs] **1** *adj (personne,
ventre)* fat; *(aliment)* fatty; *(graisseux)*
greasy, oily; *(plante, contour)* thick; *(rire)*
throaty; *(toux)* loose; **faire la grasse matinée** to have a lie-in

2 *nm (de viande)* fat • **grassement** *adv* **g.
payé** handsomely paid • **grassouillet,
-ette** *adj* plump

gratifier [gratifje] *vt* **g. qn de qch** to
present sb with sth • **gratification** *nf
(prime)* bonus

gratin [gratɛ̃] *nm (plat)* = baked dish with
a cheese topping; *Fam (élite)* upper crust;
chou-fleur au g. cauliflower cheese • **gra-
tiner** *vt* to brown

gratis [gratis] *adv* free (of charge)

gratitude [gratityd] *nf* gratitude

gratte-ciel [gratsjɛl] *nm inv* skyscraper

gratte-papier [gratpapje] *nm inv Péj
(employé)* pen-pusher

gratter [grate] **1** *vt (avec un outil)* to
scrape; *(avec les ongles, les griffes)* to
scratch; *(boue)* to scrape off; *(effacer)* to
scratch out; *Fam* **ça me gratte** it itches

2 *vi (à la porte)* to scratch; *(tissu)* to be
scratchy

3 se gratter *vpr* to scratch oneself
• **grattoir** *nm* scraper

gratuit, -uite [gratɥi, -ɥit] *adj (billet,
entrée)* free; *(hypothèse, acte)* gratuitous
• **gratuité** *nf* **la g. de l'enseignement** free
education • **gratuitement** *adv (sans
payer)* free (of charge); *(sans motif)* gra-
tuitously

Il faut noter que le nom anglais **gratuity**
est un faux ami. Il signifie **pourboire**.

gravats [grava] *nmpl* rubble, debris

grave [grav] *adj (maladie, faute)* serious;
(juge, visage) grave; *(voix)* deep, low; **ce
n'est pas g.!** it's not important! • **gravement** *adv (malade, menacé)* seriously;
(dignement) gravely

graver [grave] *vt (sur métal)* to engrave;
(sur bois) to carve; *(disque)* to cut; *(dans
sa mémoire)* to engrave • **graveur** *nm*
engraver

gravier [gravje] *nm* gravel • **gravillon** *nm*
piece of gravel; **gravillons** gravel, *Br*
(loose) chippings

gravir [gravir] *vt* to climb; *Fig* **g. les
échelons** to climb the ladder

gravité [gravite] *nf (de situation)* seriousness; *(solennité)* & *Phys* gravity; **accident
sans g.** minor accident; *Phys* **centre de g.**
centre of gravity

graviter [gravite] *vi* to revolve (**autour around**) • **gravitation** *nf* gravitation

gravure [gravyr] *nf (image)* print; *(action, art)* engraving; **g. sur bois** *(action)* woodcarving; *(objet)* woodcut

gré [gre] *nm* **à son g.** *(goût)* to his/her taste; *(désir)* as he/she pleases; **de son plein g.** of one's own free will; **de bon g.** willingly; **contre le g. de qn** against sb's will; **bon g. mal g.** whether we/you/*etc* like it or not; **de g. ou de force** one way or another; **au g. de** *(vent)* at the mercy of; *Formel* **savoir g. de qch à qn** to be thankful to sb for sth

Grèce [grɛs] *nf* **la G.** Greece • **grec, grecque 1** *adj* Greek **2** *nmf* **G., Grecque** Greek **3** *nm (langue)* Greek

greffe [grɛf] **1** *nf (de peau, d'arbre)* graft; *(d'organe)* transplant **2** *nm Jur* record office • **greffer** *vt (peau)* & *Bot* to graft (**à** on to); *(organe)* to transplant • **greffier** *nm Jur* clerk (of the court) • **greffon** *nm (de peau)* & *Bot* graft

grégaire [greger] *adj* gregarious

grêle¹ [grɛl] *nf* hail; *Fig* **g. de balles** hail of bullets • **grêlé, -ée** *adj (visage)* pockmarked • **grêler** *v impersonnel* to hail; **il grêle** it's hailing • **grêlon** *nm* hailstone

grêle² [grɛl] *adj (jambes)* skinny; *(tige)* slender; *(voix)* shrill

grelot [grəlo] *nm* (small) bell

grelotter [grəlɔte] *vi* to shiver (**de** with)

grenade [grənad] *nf (fruit)* pomegranate; *(projectile)* grenade • **grenadine** *nf* grenadine

grenat [grəna] *adj inv (couleur)* dark red

grenier [grənje] *nm (de maison)* attic; *(pour le fourrage)* granary

grenouille [grənuj] *nf* frog

grès [grɛ] *nm (roche)* sandstone; *(poterie)* stoneware

grésiller [grezije] *vi (huile)* to sizzle; *(feu, radio)* to crackle

grève¹ [grɛv] *nf (arrêt du travail)* strike; **se mettre en g.** to go out on strike; **faire g.** to be on strike; **g. de la faim** hunger strike; **g. perlée** *Br* go-slow, *Am* slow-down (strike); **g. sauvage/sur le tas** wildcat/sit-down strike; **g. tournante** staggered strike; **g. du zèle** *Br* work-to-rule, *Am* rule-book slow-down • **gréviste** *nmf* striker

grève² [grɛv] *nf (de mer)* shore; *(de rivière)* bank

gribouiller [gribuje] *vti* to scribble • **gribouillis** *nm* scribble

grief [grijɛf] *nm (plainte)* grievance; **faire g. de qch à qn** to hold sth against sb

> 🖉 Il faut noter que le nom anglais **grief** est un faux ami. Il signifie **chagrin**.

grièvement [grijɛvmɑ̃] *adv* seriously, badly

griffe [grif] *nf (ongle)* claw; *(de couturier)* (designer) label; *Fig (style)* stamp; *Fig* **arracher qn des griffes de qn** to snatch sb out of sb's clutches • **griffé, -ée** *adj* **vêtements griffés** designer clothes • **griffer** *vt* to scratch

griffonner [grifɔne] *vt* to scribble, to scrawl • **griffonnage** *nm* scribble, scrawl

grignoter [griɲɔte] *vti* to nibble

gril [gril] *nm (ustensile de cuisine) Br* grill, *Am* broiler • **grillade** [grijad] *nf (viande) Br* grilled meat, *Am* broiled meat • **grille-pain** *nm inv* toaster • **griller 1** *vt (viande) Br* to grill, *Am* to broil; *(pain)* to toast; *(café)* to roast; *(ampoule électrique)* to blow; *(brûler)* to scorch; *Fam (cigarette)* to smoke; *Fam* **g. un feu rouge** to jump the lights; *Fam* **il est grillé** his game's up **2** *vi (viande)* to grill; *(pain)* to toast; **mettre qch à g.** to put sth on the grill, *Am* to broil sth; **g. d'impatience** to be burning with impatience

grille [grij] *nf (clôture)* railings; *(porte)* gate; *(de fourneau, de foyer)* grate; *Aut (de radiateur)* grille; *Fig (des salaires)* scale; **g. des horaires** schedule; **g. de mots croisés** crossword puzzle grid • **grillage** *nm* wire mesh *or* netting

grillon [grijɔ̃] *nm* cricket

grimace [grimas] *nf (pour faire rire)* (funny) face; *(de douleur)* grimace; **faire la g.** to pull a face • **grimacer** *vi* to make a face; *(de douleur)* to wince (**de** with)

grimer [grime] **1** *vt* to make up **2 se grimer** *vpr* to put one's make-up on

grimper [grɛ̃pe] **1** *vi* to climb (**à qch** up sth); *Fam (prix)* to rocket **2** *vt (escalier)* to climb • **grimpant, -ante** *adj* **plante grimpante** climbing plant

grincer [grɛ̃se] *vi* to creak; **g. des dents** to grind one's teeth • **grincement** *nm* creaking; **grincements de dents** grinding of teeth

grincheux, -euse [grɛ̃ʃø, -øz] *adj* grumpy

gringalet [grɛ̃galɛ] *nm Péj* weakling

grippe [grip] *nf (maladie)* flu, influenza; **g. intestinale** gastric flu; **prendre qn/qch en g.** to take a strong dislike to sb/sth • **grippé, -ée** *adj* **être g.** to have (the) flu

gripper [gripe] **se gripper** *vpr (moteur)* to seize up

grippe-sou [gripsu] *nm inv* skinflint, miser

gris, -e [gri, griz] **1** *adj Br* grey, *Am* gray; *(temps)* dull, grey; *(ivre)* tipsy

2 *nm Br* grey, *Am* gray •**grisaille** *nf (caractère morne)* dreariness •**grisâtre** *adj Br* greyish, *Am* grayish

griser [grize] *vt (vin)* to make tipsy; *(air vif, succès)* to exhilarate

grisonner [grizɔne] *vi (cheveux, personne)* to go *Br* grey *or Am* gray •**grisonnant, -ante** *adj Br* greying, *Am* graying; **avoir les tempes grisonnantes** to be going grey at the temples

grisou [grizu] *nm* firedamp; **coup de g.** firedamp explosion

grive [griv] *nf* thrush

grivois, -oise [grivwa, -waz] *adj* bawdy •**grivoiserie** *nf (propos)* bawdy talk

grizzli [grizli] *nm* grizzly bear

Groenland [grɔɛnlɑ̃d] *nm* **le G.** Greenland

grog [grɔg] *nm* hot toddy

grogner [grɔɲe] *vi (personne)* to grumble (**contre** at); *(cochon)* to grunt •**grogne** *nf Fam* discontent •**grognement** [-əmɑ̃] *nm (de personne)* growl; *(de cochon)* grunt •**grognon, -onne** *adj* grumpy

groin [grwɛ̃] *nm* snout

grol(l)e [grɔl] *nf très Fam* shoe

grommeler [grɔm(ə)le] *vti* to mutter

gronder [grɔ̃de] **1** *vt (réprimander)* to scold, to tell off

2 *vi (chien)* to growl; *(tonnerre, camion)* to rumble •**grondement** *nm (de chien)* growl; *(de tonnerre)* rumble

groom [grum] *nm Br* page, *Am* bellboy

gros, grosse [gro, gros] **1** *adj (corpulent, important)* big; *(gras)* fat; *(épais)* thick; *(effort, progrès)* great; *(somme, fortune)* large; *(averse, rhume, mer)* heavy; *(faute)* serious, gross; *(bruit)* loud; *(traits, laine, fil)* coarse; **g. mot** swearword

2 *adv* **gagner g.** to earn big money; **risquer g.** to take a big risk; **écrire g.** to write big; **en g.** *(globalement)* roughly; *(écrire)* in big letters; *(vendre)* in bulk, wholesale; *Fig* **en avoir g. sur le cœur** to be bitter

3 *nmf (personne)* fat man, *f* fat woman

4 *nm* **le g. de** the bulk of; **commerce/prix de g.** wholesale trade/prices

groseille [grozɛj] *nf* redcurrant; **g. à maquereau** gooseberry

grossesse [grosɛs] *nf* pregnancy

grosseur [grosœr] *nf (volume)* size; *(tumeur)* lump

grossier, -ière [grosje, -jɛr] *adj (tissu, traits)* rough, coarse; *(personne, manières)* rude, coarse; *(erreur)* gross; *(idée,*

solution) rough, crude; *(ruse, instrument)* crude; **être g. envers qn** to be rude to sb •**grossièrement** *adv (calculer)* roughly; *(répondre)* coarsely, rudely; *(se tromper)* grossly •**grossièreté** *nf (incorrection, vulgarité)* coarseness; *(mot)* rude word

grossir [grosir] **1** *vt (sujet: verre, loupe)* to magnify; *Fig (exagérer)* to exaggerate

2 *vi (personne)* to put on weight; *(fleuve)* to swell; *(bosse, foule, nombre)* to get bigger; *(bruit)* to get louder •**grossissant, -ante** *adj* **verre g.** magnifying glass •**grossissement** *nm (augmentation de taille)* increase in size; *(de microscope)* magnification

grossiste [grosist] *nmf Com* wholesaler

grosso modo [grosomɔdo] *adv (en gros)* roughly

grotesque [grɔtɛsk] *adj* ludicrous

grotte [grɔt] *nf* cave

grouiller [gruje] **1** *vi (se presser)* to swarm around; **g. de** to swarm with

2 se grouiller *vpr Fam (se hâter)* to get a move on •**grouillant, -ante** *adj* swarming (**de** with)

groupe [grup] *nm* group; **g. sanguin** blood group; **g. scolaire** *(bâtiments)* school block; **g. témoin** focus group •**groupement** *nm (action)* grouping; *(groupe)* group •**grouper 1** *vt* to group (together) **2 se grouper** *vpr (en association)* to form a group; **restez groupés** keep together

groupie [grupi] *nf Fam* groupie

grue [gry] *nf (machine, oiseau)* crane

gruger [gryʒe] *vt* to swindle; **se faire g.** to get swindled

grumeau, -x [grymo] *nm (dans une sauce)* lump •**grumeleux, -euse** *adj* lumpy

gruyère [gryjɛr] *nm* Gruyère (cheese)

Guadeloupe [gwadlup] *nf* **la G.** Guadeloupe

Guatemala [gwatemala] *nm* **le G.** Guatemala

gué [ge] *nm* ford; **passer à g.** to ford

guenilles [gənij] *nfpl* rags (and tatters)

guenon [gənɔ̃] *nf* female monkey

guépard [gepar] *nm* cheetah

guêpe [gɛp] *nf* wasp •**guêpier** *nm (nid)* wasp's nest; *Fig (piège)* trap

guère [gɛr] *adv* **(ne...)** **g.** *(pas beaucoup)* not much; *(pas longtemps)* hardly, scarcely; **il n'a g. d'amis** he hasn't got many friends; **il ne sort g.** he hardly *or* scarcely goes out; **il n'y a g. plus de six ans** just over six years ago

guéridon [geridɔ̃] *nm* pedestal table

guérilla [gerija] *nf* guerrilla warfare • **guérillero** *nm* guerrilla

> *Ø* Il faut noter que le nom anglais **guerrilla** est un faux ami. Il signifie **guérillero**.

guérir [gerir] **1** *vt (personne, maladie)* to cure (**de** of); *(blessure)* to heal **2** *vi (personne)* to get better, to recover; *(blessure)* to heal; *(rhume)* to get better **3** **se guérir** *vpr* to get better • **guéri, -ie** *adj* cured; *Fig* **être g. de qn/qch** to have got over sb/sth • **guérison** *nf (rétablissement)* recovery • **guérisseur, -euse** *nmf* faith healer

guérite [gerit] *nf Mil* sentry box

Guernesey [gɛrn(ə)zɛ] *nf* Guernsey

guerre [gɛr] *nf* war; *(technique)* warfare; **en g.** at war (**avec** with); **faire la g.** to wage *or* make war (**à** on *or* against); *(soldat)* to fight; **crime/cri de g.** war crime/cry; *Fig* **de g. lasse** for the sake of peace and quiet; *Fig* **c'est de bonne g.** that's fair enough; **g. d'usure** war of attrition • **guerrier, -ière 1** *adj* **danse guerrière** war dance; **chant g.** battle song; **nation guerrière** warlike nation **2** *nmf* warrior • **guerroyer** *vi Littéraire* to wage war (**contre** on)

guet [gɛ] *nm* **faire le g.** to be on the lookout • **guetter** [gete] *vt (occasion)* to watch out for; *(gibier)* to lie in wait for

guet-apens [gɛtapɑ̃] (*pl* **guets-apens**) *nm* ambush

guêtre [gɛtr] *nf* gaiter

gueule [gœl] *nf (d'animal, de canon)* mouth; *Fam (de personne)* mouth; *Fam (visage)* face; *Fam* **avoir la g. de bois** to have a hangover; *Fam* **faire la g.** to sulk; *Fam* **faire une g. d'enterrement** to look really pissed off • **gueuler** *vti très Fam* to bawl • **gueuleton** *nm Fam (repas)* Br blowout, feast

gui [gi] *nm* mistletoe

guichet [giʃɛ] *nm (de gare, de banque)* window; *(de théâtre)* box office; *Théâtre* **on joue à guichets fermés** the performance is sold out; **g. automatique** *(de banque)* cash dispenser • **guichetier, -ière** *nmf (de banque)* Br counter clerk, *Am* teller; *(à la gare)* ticket clerk

guide [gid] **1** *nm (personne, livre)* guide; **g. touristique** tourist guide **2** *nf (éclaireuse)* (Girl) Guide • **guider** *vt* to guide • **guides** *nfpl (rênes)* reins

guidon [gidɔ̃] *nm* handlebars

guigne [giɲ] *nf Fam (malchance)* bad luck

guignol [giɲɔl] *nm (spectacle)* ≃ Punch and Judy show; *Fam* **faire le g.** to clown around

guillemets [gijmɛ] *nmpl Typ* inverted commas, quotation marks; **entre g.** in inverted commas, in quotation marks

guilleret, -ette [gijrɛ, -ɛt] *adj* lively, perky

guillotine [gijɔtin] *nf* guillotine • **guillotiner** *vt* to guillotine

guimauve [gimov] *nf (confiserie)* marshmallow

guimbarde [gɛ̃bard] *nf Fam (voiture)* Br old banger, *Am* (old) wreck

guindé, -ée [gɛ̃de] *adj (peu naturel)* stiff; *(style)* stilted

Guinée [gine] *nf* **la G.** Guinea

guingois [gɛ̃gwa] **de guingois** *adv Fam* askew

guirlande [girlɑ̃d] *nf* garland; **g. de Noël** piece of tinsel

guise [giz] *nf* **agir à sa g.** to do as one pleases; **n'en faire qu'à sa g.** to do just as one pleases; **en g. de** by way of

guitare [gitar] *nf* guitar • **guitariste** *nmf* guitarist

guttural, -e, -aux, -ales [gytyral, -o] *adj* guttural

Guyane [gɥijan] *nf* **la G.** Guiana

gymnase [ʒimnɑz] *nm* gymnasium • **gymnaste** *nmf* gymnast • **gymnastique** *nf* gymnastics *(sing)*

gynécologie [ʒinekɔlɔʒi] *nf Br* gynaecology, *Am* gynecology • **gynécologue** *nmf Br* gynaecologist, *Am* gynecologist

gyrophare [ʒirofar] *nm* flashing light

H, h [aʃ] *nm inv* H, h; **l'heure H** zero hour; **bombe H** H-bomb

ha ['a] *exclam* ah!, oh!; **ha, ha!** *(rire)* ha-ha!

habile [abil] *adj* skilful, *Am* skillful (**à qch** at sth; **à faire** at doing); **h. de ses mains** good with one's hands •**habilement** *adv* skilfully, *Am* skillfully •**habileté** *nf* skill

habilité, -ée [abilite] *adj* (legally) authorized (**à faire** to do)

habiller [abije] **1** *vt (vêtir)* to dress (**de** in); *(fournir en vêtements)* to clothe; *(garnir)* to cover (**de** with); **h. qn en soldat** to dress sb up as a soldier; **un rien l'habille** he/she looks good in anything

2 s'habiller *vpr* to dress, to get dressed; *(avec élégance)* to dress up; **s'h. chez Dior** to buy one's clothes from Dior •**habillé, -ée** *adj* dressed (**de** in; **en** as); *(costume, robe)* smart; **soirée habillée** formal occasion •**habillement** *nm (vêtements)* clothes

habit [abi] *nm (tenue de soirée)* evening dress, tails; **habits** *(vêtements)* clothes

habitable [abitabl] *adj* (in)habitable; *(maison)* fit to live in

habitat [abita] *nm (d'animal, de plante)* habitat; *(conditions)* housing conditions

habitation [abitasjɔ̃] *nf (lieu)* dwelling; *(fait de résider)* living

habiter [abite] **1** *vt (maison, région)* to live in; *(planète)* to inhabit

2 *vi* to live (**à/en** in) •**habitant, -ante** *nmf (de pays)* inhabitant; *(de maison)* occupant •**habité, -ée** *adj (région)* inhabited; *(maison)* occupied

habitude [abityd] *nf* habit; **avoir l'h. de qch** to be used to sth; **avoir l'h. de faire qch** to be used to doing sth; **prendre l'h. de faire qch** to get into the habit of doing sth; **prendre de bonnes habitudes** to take on some good habits; **prendre de mauvaises habitudes** to pick up (some) bad habits; **d'h.** usually; **comme d'h.** as usual

habituel, -uelle [abityɛl] *adj* usual, customary •**habituellement** *adv* usually

habituer [abitɥe] **1** *vt* **h. qn à qch** to accustom sb to sth; **être habitué à qch/à faire qch** to be used to sth/to doing sth

2 s'habituer *vpr* **s'h. à qn/qch** to get used to sb/sth •**habitué, -uée** *nmf* regular; *(de maison)* regular visitor

hache ['aʃ] *nf* axe, *Am* ax •**hachette** *nf* hatchet

hacher ['aʃe] *vt (au couteau)* to chop up; *(avec un appareil)* Br to mince, *Am* to grind •**haché, -ée** *adj (viande)* Br minced, *Am* ground; *(légumes)* chopped; *(style)* jerky •**hachis** *nm (viande)* Br mince, *Am* ground meat; **h. Parmentier** ≃ cottage pie •**hachoir** *nm (couteau)* chopper; *(appareil)* Br mincer, *Am* grinder

hachures ['aʃyr] *nfpl* hatching •**hachurer** *vt* to hatch

hagard, -arde ['agar, -ard] *adj (visage)* haggard; *(yeux)* wild

haie ['ɛ] *nf (clôture)* hedge; *(rangée)* row; *Athlétisme* hurdle; *Équitation* fence; **400 mètres haies** 400-metre hurdles; *Équitation* **course de haies** steeplechase; **h. d'honneur** guard of honour

haillons ['ajɔ̃] *nmpl* rags; **en h.** in rags

haine ['ɛn] *nf* hatred, hate; *Fam* **avoir la h.** *(être révolté)* to be full of rage •**haineux, -euse** *adj* full of hatred

---

🖉 Il faut noter que l'adjectif anglais **heinous** est un faux ami. Il signifie **atroce**.

---

haïr* ['air] *vt* to hate •**haïssable** *adj* hateful

hâle ['al] *nm* suntan •**hâlé, -ée** *adj* suntanned

haleine [alɛn] *nf* breath; **hors d'h.** out of breath; **perdre h.** to get out of breath; **reprendre h.** to get one's breath back; **tenir qn en h.** to keep sb in suspense; **travail de longue h.** long job

haler ['ale] *vt* to tow •**halage** *nm* towing; **chemin de h.** towpath

haleter ['al(ə)te] *vi* to pant, to gasp •**haletant, -ante** *adj* panting, gasping

hall ['ol] *nm (de maison)* entrance hall; *(d'hôtel)* lobby; *(d'aéroport)* lounge; **h. de gare** station concourse

halle ['al] *nf* (covered) market; **les halles** the central food market

hallucination [alysinɑsjɔ̃] *nf* hallucination • **hallucinant, -ante** *adj* extraordinary

halo ['alo] *nm* halo

halogène [alɔʒɛn] *nm (lampe)* halogen lamp

halte ['alt] **1** *nf (arrêt)* stop, *Mil* halt; *(lieu)* stopping place; *Mil* halting place; **faire h.** to stop

2 *exclam* stop!, *Mil* halt!

haltère [altɛr] *nm* dumbbell • **haltérophile** *nmf* weightlifter • **haltérophilie** *nf* weightlifting

hamac ['amak] *nm* hammock

hamburger ['ãbœrgœr] *nm* burger

hameau, -x ['amo] *nm* hamlet

hameçon [amsɔ̃] *nm* (fish-)hook; *Fig* **mordre à l'h.** to swallow the bait

hamster ['amstɛr] *nm* hamster

hanche ['ãʃ] *nf* hip

handball ['ãdbal] *nm Sport* handball

handicap ['ãdikap] *nm (physique, mental)* disability; *Fig* handicap • **handicapé, -ée 1** *adj* disabled **2** *nmf* disabled person; **h. moteur** person with motor impairment; **h. physique/mental** physically/mentally handicapped person • **handicaper** *vt (physiquement, mentalement)* to disable; *Fig* to handicap

hangar ['ãgar] *nm (entrepôt)* shed; *(pour avions)* hangar; *(de bus)* depot

hanneton ['an(ə)tɔ̃] *nm* cockchafer

hanter ['ãte] *vt (sujet: fantôme, souvenir)* to haunt; *Fig (bars)* to hang around • **hanté, -ée** *adj (maison)* haunted • **hantise** *nf* **avoir la h. de qch** to really dread sth

happer ['ape] *vt (saisir)* to snatch; *(par la gueule)* to snap up

haras ['ara] *nm* stud farm

harasser ['arase] *vt* to exhaust • **harassé, -ée** *adj* exhausted

> 🖉 Il faut noter que le verbe anglais **to harass** est un faux ami. Il signifie **harceler**.

harceler ['arsəle] *vt (importuner)* to harass; *(insister auprès de)* to pester; **h. qn de questions** to pester sb with questions • **harcèlement** *nm* harassment; **h. sexuel** sexual harassment

hardi, -ie ['ardi] *adj* bold • **hardiesse** *nf* boldness • **hardiment** *adv* boldly

harem ['arɛm] *nm* harem

hareng ['arã] *nm* herring; **h. saur** smoked herring

hargne ['arɲ] *nf* bad temper • **hargneux, -euse** *adj* bad-tempered

haricot ['ariko] *nm* bean; *Fam* **c'est la fin des haricots** it's all over; **h. blanc** haricot bean; *Culin* **h. de mouton** mutton stew; **h.**

rouge kidney bean; **h. vert** green bean, *Br* French bean

harmonica [armɔnika] *nm* harmonica, mouthorgan

harmonie [armɔni] *nf* harmony • **harmonieux, -ieuse** *adj* harmonious • **harmonique** *adj Mus* harmonic • **harmoniser** *vt*, **s'harmoniser** *vpr* to harmonize • **harmonium** *nm* harmonium

harnacher ['arnaʃe] *vt (cheval)* to harness • **harnais** *nm (de cheval, de bébé)* harness

harpe ['arp] *nf* harp • **harpiste** *nmf* harpist

harpon ['arpɔ̃] *nm* harpoon • **harponner** *vt (baleine)* to harpoon; *Fam* **h. qn** *(sujet: importun)* to corner sb

hasard ['azar] *nm* **le h.** chance; **un h. a** coincidence; **un heureux h.** a stroke of luck; **un malheureux h.** a rotten piece of luck; **par h.** by chance; **par le plus grand des hasards** by a (sheer) fluke; **au h.** *(choisir, répondre)* at random; *(marcher)* aimlessly; **à tout h.** *(par précaution)* just in case; *(pour voir)* on the off chance; **si par h.** if by any chance; **les hasards de la vie** the fortunes of life • **hasarder 1** *vt (remarque, démarche)* to venture **2 se hasarder** *vpr* **se h. dans** to venture into; **se h. à faire qch** to risk doing sth • **hasardeux, -euse** *adj* risky, hazardous

> 🖉 Il faut noter que le nom anglais **hazard** est un faux ami. Il signifie uniquement **danger**.

haschisch ['aʃiʃ] *nm* hashish

hâte ['ɑt] *nf* haste; **à la h.** hastily; **en (toute) h.** hurriedly; **avoir h. de faire qch** to be eager to do sth • **hâter 1** *vt (pas, départ)* to hasten **2 se hâter** *vpr* to hurry *(de faire* to do) • **hâtif, -ive** *adj (trop rapide)* hasty

hausse ['os] *nf* rise (**de** in); **en h.** rising • **hausser 1** *vt (prix, voix)* to raise; *(épaules)* to shrug **2 se hausser** *vpr* **se h. sur la pointe des pieds** to stand on tiptoe

haussier ['osje] *adj m voir* **marché**

haut, -e ['o, 'ot] **1** *adj* high; *(en taille)* tall; *(dans le temps)* early; **h. de 5 m** 5 m high *or* tall; **à haute voix, à voix haute** aloud; **en haute mer** out at sea; **la mer est haute** it's high tide; **la haute couture** high fashion; **la haute coiffure** haute coiffure; **la haute société** high society; **la haute bourgeoisie** the upper middle class; **un instrument de haute précision** a precision instrument; **un renseignement de la plus haute importance** news of the utmost importance; **avoir une haute opinion de qn** to have a high opinion of sb; **obtenir qch de haute lutte** to get sth after a hard struggle; **haute trahison** high treason

2 *adv (dans l'espace) & Mus* high; *(dans une hiérarchie)* highly; *(parler)* loud, loudly; **tout h.** *(lire, penser)* out loud; **h. placé** *(personne)* in a high position; **plus h.** *(dans un texte)* above; **gagner h. la main** to win hands down

3 *nm (partie haute)* top; **en h. de** at the top of; **en h.** *(loger)* upstairs; *(regarder)* up; *(mettre)* on (the) top; **d'en h.** *(de la partie haute, du ciel)* from high up, from up above; **avoir 5 m de h.** to be 5 m high *or* tall; *Fig* **des hauts et des bas** ups and downs • **haut-de-forme** *(pl* **hauts-de-forme)** *nm* top hat • **haut-fourneau** *(pl* **hauts-fourneaux)** *nm* blast-furnace • **haut-le-cœur** *nm inv* **avoir un h.** to retch • **haut-parleur** *(pl* **haut-parleurs)** *nm* loudspeaker

hautain, -aine ['otɛ̃, -ɛn] *adj* haughty

hautbois ['obwa] *nm* oboe

hautement ['otmɑ̃] *adv (très)* highly • **hauteur** *nf* height; *(colline)* hill; *Péj (orgueil)* haughtiness; *Mus* pitch; **à h. de 100 000 euros** for a sum of 100,000 euros; **à la h. de** *(objet)* level with; *(rue)* opposite; **arriver à la h. de qch** *(mesurer)* to reach (the level of) sth; **à la h. de la situation** up to *or* equal to the situation; **il n'est pas à la h.** he isn't up to it

hâve ['av] *adj* gaunt

havre ['avr] *nm Littéraire* haven; **h. de paix** haven of peace

Haye ['ɛ] *nf* **La H.** The Hague

hayon ['ajɔ̃] *nm (de voiture)* hatchback

hé ['e] *exclam (appel)* hey!; **hé! hé!** *(appréciation, moquerie)* well, well!

hebdomadaire [ɛbdɔmadɛr] *adj & nm* weekly

héberger [ebɛrʒe] *vt* to put up • **hébergement** [-əmɑ̃] *nm* putting up; **centre d'h.** shelter

hébété, -ée [ebete] *adj* dazed

hébreu, -x [ebrø] **1** *adj m* Hebrew

2 *nm (langue)* Hebrew • **hébraïque** *adj* Hebrew

Hébrides [ebrid] *nfpl* **les H.** the Hebrides

hécatombe [ekatɔ̃b] *nf* slaughter

hectare [ɛktar] *nm* hectare *(= 2.47 acres)*

hégémonie [eʒemɔni] *nf* hegemony

hein ['ɛ̃] *exclam Fam (surprise, interrogation)* eh?; **ne fais plus jamais ça, h.?** don't ever do that again, OK?

hélas ['elas] *exclam* unfortunately

héler ['ele] *vt (taxi)* to hail

hélice [elis] *nf (d'avion, de navire)* propeller

hélicoptère [elikɔptɛr] *nm* helicopter • **héliport** *nm* heliport

helvétique [ɛlvetik] *adj* Swiss

hémicycle [emisikl] *nm Pol* **l'h.** *(de l'Assemblée nationale)* the chamber

hémisphère [emisfɛr] *nm* hemisphere

hémophile [emɔfil] **1** *adj* haemophilic

2 *nm* haemophiliac • **hémophilie** *nf Méd* haemophilia

hémorragie [emɔraʒi] *nf Méd* haemorrhage; *Fig (de capitaux)* drain; **faire une h.** to haemorrhage; **h. cérébrale** stroke

hémorroïdes [emɔrɔid] *nfpl* piles, haemorrhoids

hennir ['enir] *vi (cheval)* to neigh • **hennissement** *nm* neigh; **hennissements** neighing

hépatite [epatit] *nf Méd* hepatitis

herbe [ɛrb] *nf* grass; *(pour soigner)* herb; **mauvaise h.** weed; *Culin* **fines herbes** herbs; **blé en h.** green wheat; *Fig* **poète en h.** budding poet; **couper l'h. sous le pied de qn** to cut the ground from under sb's feet; *Fam* **fumer de l'h.** to smoke grass • **herbage** *nm* pasture • **herbeux, -euse** *adj* grassy • **herbicide** *nm* weedkiller • **herbivore** *adj* herbivorous • **herbu, -ue** *adj* grassy

herculéen, -éenne [ɛrkyleɛ̃, -ɛn] *adj* Herculean

hérédité [eredite] *nf Biol* heredity • **héréditaire** *adj* hereditary

hérésie [erezi] *nf* heresy • **hérétique 1** *adj* heretical **2** *nmf* heretic

hérisser ['erise] **1** *vt (poils)* to bristle up; *Fig* **h. qn** *(irriter)* to get sb's back up

2 se hérisser *vpr (animal, personne)* to bristle; *(poils, cheveux)* to stand on end • **hérissé, -ée** *adj (cheveux)* bristly; *(cactus)* prickly; **h. de** bristling with

hérisson ['erisɔ̃] *nm* hedgehog

hériter [erite] **1** *vt* to inherit (**qch de qn** sth from sb)

2 *vi* **h. de qch** to inherit sth • **héritage** *nm (biens)* inheritance; *Fig (culturel, politique)* heritage; **faire un h.** to come into an inheritance • **héritier** *nm* heir (**de** to) • **héritière** *nf* heiress (**de** to)

hermétique [ɛrmetik] *adj* hermetically sealed; *Fig (obscur)* impenetrable • **hermétiquement** *adv* hermetically

hermine [ɛrmin] *nf (animal, fourrure)* ermine

hernie ['ɛrni] *nf Méd* hernia; **h. discale** slipped disc

héron ['erɔ̃] *nm* heron

héros ['ero] *nm* hero • **héroïne** [erɔin] *nf (femme)* heroine; *(drogue)* heroin • **héroïque** [erɔik] *adj* heroic • **héroïsme** [erɔism] *nm* heroism

hésiter [ezite] *vi* to hesitate (**sur** over *or* about; **entre** between; **à faire** to do) • **hésitant, -ante** *adj* hesitant • **hésitation** *nf* hesitation; **avec h.** hesitatingly

hétéroclite [eterɔklit] *adj* motley

hétérogène [eterɔʒɛn] *adj* mixed

hêtre ['ɛtr] *nm (arbre, bois)* beech

heu ['ø] *exclam (hésitation)* er

heure [œr] *nf (mesure)* hour; *(moment)* time; **quelle h. est-il?** what time is it?; **il est six heures** it's six (o'clock); **six heures moins cinq** five to six; **six heures cinq** *Br* five past six, *Am* five after six; **à l'h.** *(arriver)* on time; *(être payé)* by the hour; **10 km à l'h.** 10 km an hour; **ils devraient être arrivés à l'h.** they ought to have arrived by now; **de bonne h.** early; **nouvelle de dernière h.** latest *or* last-minute news; **tout à l'h.** *(futur)* in a few moments, later; *(passé)* a moment ago; **à tout à l'h.!** *(au revoir)* see you soon!; **à toute h.** *(continuellement)* at all hours; **24 heures sur 24** 24 hours a day; **d'h. en h.** hourly, hour by hour; **faire des heures supplémentaires** to work or do overtime; **heures d'affluence, heures de pointe** *(circulation)* rush hour; *(dans les magasins)* peak period; **heures creuses** off-peak *or* slack periods; **h. d'été** *Br* summer time, *Am* daylight-saving time

heureux, -euse [œrø, -øz] **1** *adj* happy (**de** with); *(chanceux)* lucky, fortunate; *(issue, changement)* successful; *(expression, choix)* apt; **h. de faire qch** happy to do sth; **je suis h. que vous puissiez venir** I'm happy you can come
2 *adv (vivre, mourir)* happily • **heureusement** *adv (par chance)* fortunately, luckily (**pour** for); *(avec succès)* successfully

heurt ['œr] *nm* collision; *Fig (d'opinions)* clash; **sans heurts** smoothly

heurter ['œrte] **1** *vt (cogner)* to hit (**contre** against); *(entrer en collision avec)* to collide with; **h. qn** *(choquer)* to offend sb
2 se heurter *vpr* to collide (**à** *ou* **contre** against); *Fig* **se h. à qch** to meet with sth • **heurtoir** *nm* (door) knocker

hexagone [ɛgzagɔn] *nm* hexagon; *Fig* **l'H.** France • **hexagonal, -e, -aux, -ales** *adj* hexagonal; *Fam (français)* French

hiatus [jatys] *nm Fig* hiatus, gap

hiberner [ibɛrne] *vi* to hibernate • **hibernation** *nf* hibernation

hibou, -x ['ibu] *nm* owl

hic ['ik] *nm Fam* **voilà le h.!** that's the snag!

hideux, -euse ['idø, -øz] *adj* hideous

hier [ijɛr] *adv* yesterday; **h. soir** yesterday evening; **ça ne date pas d'h.** that's nothing new; *Fig* **elle n'est pas née d'h.** she wasn't born yesterday

hiérarchie ['jerarʃi] *nf* hierarchy • **hiérarchique** *adj* hierarchical; **par la voie h.** through the official channels

hi-fi ['ifi] *adj inv & nf inv* hi-fi

hilare [ilar] *adj* grinning • **hilarant, -ante** *adj* hilarious • **hilarité** *nf* hilarity, mirth

hindou, -oue [ɛ̃du] *adj & nmf* Hindu

hippie ['ipi] *nmf* hippie

hippique [ipik] *adj* **concours h.** horse show • **hippodrome** *nm Br* racecourse, *Am* racetrack

hippopotame [ipɔpɔtam] *nm* hippopotamus

hirondelle [irɔ̃dɛl] *nf* swallow

hirsute [irsyt] *adj (personne, barbe)* shaggy

hispanique [ispanik] *adj* Hispanic

hisser ['ise] **1** *vt* to hoist up
2 se hisser *vpr* to heave oneself up

histoire [istwar] *nf (science, événements)* history; *(récit)* story; *Fam (affaire)* business, matter; *Fam* **des histoires** *(mensonges)* fibs, stories; *(chichis)* fuss; *Fam* **raconter des histoires** to tell fibs; *Fam* **faire des histoires à qn** to make trouble for sb; *Fam* **c'est toute une h. pour lui faire prendre son bain** it's quite a business getting him/her to have a bath; *Fam* **h. de rire** for a laugh; **sans histoires** *(voyage)* uneventful

historien, -ienne [istɔrjɛ̃, -jɛn] *nmf* historian

historique [istɔrik] **1** *adj (concernant l'histoire)* historical; *(important)* historic
2 *nm* historical account

hiver [ivɛr] *nm* winter • **hivernal, -e, -aux, -ales** *adj* winter; *(temps)* wintry

HLM ['aʃɛlɛm] (*abrév* **habitation à loyer modéré**) *nm ou f Br* ≃ council flats, *Am* ≃ low-rent apartment building

hocher ['ɔʃe] *vt* **h. la tête** *(pour dire oui)* to nod; *(pour dire non)* to shake one's head • **hochement** *nm* **h. de tête** *(affirmatif)* nod; *(négatif)* shake of the head

hochet ['ɔʃɛ] *nm* rattle

hockey ['ɔkɛ] *nm* hockey; **h. sur glace** ice hockey; **h. sur gazon** *Br* hockey, *Am* field hockey

holà ['ɔla] **1** *exclam* stop!
2 *nm inv* **mettre le h. à qch** to put a stop to sth

hold-up ['ɔldœp] *nm inv* hold-up
Hollande ['ɔlɑ̃d] *nf* **la H.** Holland •**hollandais, -aise** **1** *adj* Dutch **2** *nmf* **H.** Dutchman; **Hollandaise** Dutchwoman; **les H.** the Dutch **3** *nm (langue)* Dutch
holocauste [ɔlɔkost] *nm* holocaust
homard ['ɔmar] *nm* lobster
homélie [ɔmeli] *nf* homily
homéopathie [ɔmeɔpati] *nf* homoeopathy
homicide [ɔmisid] *nm* homicide; **h. involontaire** *ou* **par imprudence** manslaughter; **h. volontaire** murder
hommage [ɔmaʒ] *nm* homage (**à** to); **rendre h. à qn** to pay homage to sb; **faire qch en h. à qn** to do sth as a tribute to sb *or* in homage to sb; **présenter ses hommages à une femme** to pay one's respects to a lady
homme [ɔm] *nm* man (*pl* men); **l'h.** *(genre humain)* man(kind); **des vêtements d'h.** men's clothes; **d'h. à h.** man to man; *Fig* **l'h. de la rue** the man in the street; **il n'est pas h. à vous laisser tomber** he's not the sort of man to let you down; **h. d'affaires** businessman; **h. politique** politician •**homme-grenouille** (*pl* **hommes-grenouilles**) *nm* frogman
homogène [ɔmɔʒɛn] *adj* homogeneous •**homogénéité** *nf* homogeneity
homologue [ɔmɔlɔg] *nmf* counterpart, opposite number
homologuer [ɔmɔlɔge] *vt (décision, accord, record)* to ratify
homonyme [ɔmɔnim] **1** *nm (mot)* homonym
2 *nmf (personne)* namesake
homosexuel, -uelle [ɔmɔsɛksɥɛl] *adj & nmf* homosexual •**homosexualité** *nf* homosexuality
Hongrie ['ɔ̃gri] *nf* **la H.** Hungary •**hongrois, -oise** **1** *adj* Hungarian **2** *nmf* **H., Hongroise** Hungarian **3** *nm (langue)* Hungarian
honnête [ɔnɛt] *adj (intègre)* honest; *(vie, gens)* decent; *(prix)* fair •**honnêtement** *adv (avec intégrité)* honestly; *(raisonnablement)* decently; **h., qu'est-ce que tu en penses?** be honest, what do you think? •**honnêteté** *nf (intégrité)* honesty
honneur [ɔnœr] *nm* honour; **en l'h. de qn** in honour of sb; **faire h. à** *(sa famille)* to be a credit to; *(par sa présence)* to do honour to; *(promesse)* to honour; *Fam (repas)* to do justice to; **être à l'h.** to have the place of honour; **donner sa parole d'h.** to give one's word of honour; **mettre un point d'h. à faire qch** to make it a point of

honour to do sth; **invité d'h.** guest of honour; **membre d'h.** honorary member
honorable [ɔnɔrabl] *adj* honourable; *Fig (résultat, salaire)* respectable
honoraire [ɔnɔrɛr] *adj (membre)* honorary •**honoraires** *nmpl* fees
honorer [ɔnɔre] **1** *vt* to honour (**de** with); **h. qn** *(conduite)* to be a credit to sb; **h. qn de sa confiance** to put one's trust in sb
2 **s'honorer** *vpr* **s'h. d'avoir fait qch** to pride oneself on having done sth •**honorifique** *adj* honorary
honte ['ɔ̃t] *nf* shame; **avoir h.** to be *or* feel ashamed (**de qch/de faire** of sth/to do *or* of doing); **faire h. à qn** to put sb to shame; **sans h.** shamelessly •**honteusement** *adv* shamefully •**honteux, -euse** *adj (personne)* ashamed (**de** of); *(conduite, acte)* shameful
hop ['ɔp] *exclam* **allez h., saute!** go on, jump!; **allez h., tout le monde dehors!** come on, everybody out!
hôpital, -aux [ɔpital, -o] *nm* hospital; **à l'h.** *Br* in hospital, *Am* in the hospital
hoquet ['ɔkɛ] *nm* hiccup; **avoir le h.** to have the hiccups •**hoqueter** [-əte] *vi* to hiccup
horaire [ɔrɛr] **1** *adj (salaire)* hourly; *(vitesse)* per hour
2 *nm* timetable, schedule; **horaires de travail** working hours
horde ['ɔrd] *nf* horde
horizon [ɔrizɔ̃] *nm* horizon; *(vue, paysage)* view; **à l'h.** on the horizon •**horizontal, -e, -aux, -ales** *adj* horizontal •**horizontalement** *adv* horizontally
horloge [ɔrlɔʒ] *nf* clock •**horloger, -ère** *nmf* watchmaker •**horlogerie** *nf (magasin)* watchmaker's (shop); *(industrie)* watchmaking
hormis ['ɔrmi] *prép Littéraire* save, except (for)
hormone [ɔrmɔn] *nf* hormone •**hormonal, -e, -aux, -ales** *adj* **traitement h.** hormone treatment
horoscope [ɔrɔskɔp] *nm* horoscope
horreur [ɔrœr] *nf* horror; **des horreurs** *(propos)* horrible things; **faire h. à qn** to disgust sb; **avoir h. de qch** to hate *or* loathe sth; **quelle h.!** how horrible!
horrible [ɔribl] *adj (effrayant)* horrible; *(laid)* hideous •**horriblement** [-əmɑ̃] *adv (défiguré)* horribly; *(cher, froid)* terribly
horrifiant, -iante [ɔrifjɑ̃, -jɑ̃t] *adj* horrifying •**horrifié, -iée** *adj* horrified
horripiler [ɔripile] *vt* to exasperate
hors ['ɔr] *prép* **h. de** *(maison, boîte)* outside; *Fig (danger, haleine)* out of; **h. de**

doute beyond doubt; **h. de soi** *(furieux)* beside oneself; *Fig* **être h. concours** to be in a class of one's own; *Football* **être h. jeu** to be offside • **hors-bord** *nm inv* speedboat; **moteur h.** outboard motor • **hors-d'œuvre** *nm inv (plat)* hors-d'œuvre, starter • **hors-jeu** *nm inv Football* offside • **hors-la-loi** *nm inv* outlaw • **hors-piste** *nm inv Ski* off-piste skiing; **faire du h.** to ski off piste • **hors service** *adj inv (appareil)* out of order • **hors taxe** *adj inv (magasin, objet)* duty-free

hortensia [ɔrtɑ̃sja] *nm* hydrangea

horticulteur, -trice [ɔrtikyltœr, -tris] *nmf* horticulturist • **horticole** *adj* horticultural • **horticulture** *nf* horticulture

hospice [ɔspis] *nm (asile)* home

hospitalier, -ière [ɔspitalje, -jɛr] *adj (accueillant)* hospitable; **centre h.** hospital (complex); **personnel h.** hospital staff • **hospitaliser** *vt* to hospitalize • **hospitalité** *nf* hospitality

hostie [ɔsti] *nf Rel* host

hostile [ɔstil] *adj* hostile (**à** to *or* towards) • **hostilité** *nf* hostility (**envers** to *or* towards); *Mil* **hostilités** hostilities

hôte [ot] **1** *nm (qui reçoit)* host **2** *nmf (invité)* guest • **hôtesse** *nf* hostess; **h. de l'air** air hostess

hôtel [otɛl] *nm* hotel; **h. particulier** mansion, town house; **h. de ville** *Br* town hall, *Am* city hall; **h. des impôts** tax office; **h. des ventes** auction rooms • **hôtelier, -ière 1** *nmf* hotel-keeper, hotelier **2** *adj* **industrie hôtelière** hotel industry • **hôtellerie** *nf (auberge)* inn; *(métier)* hotel trade

hotte ['ɔt] *nf (panier)* basket *(carried on back)*; *(de cheminée)* hood; **la h. du père Noël** *Br* Father Christmas's sack, *Am* Santa's sack; **h. aspirante** extractor hood

houblon ['ublɔ̃] *nm* **le h.** hops

houille ['uj] *nf* coal; **h. blanche** hydroelectric power • **houiller, -ère 1** *adj* **bassin h.** coalfield **2** *nf* **houillère** coalmine, *Br* colliery

houle ['ul] *nf* swell • **houleux, -euse** *adj (mer)* rough; *Fig (réunion)* stormy

houlette [ulɛt] *nf Fig* **sous la h. de qn** under the leadership of sb

houppette ['upɛt] *nf (de poudrier)* powder puff

hourra ['ura] **1** *exclam* hurray! **2** *nm* hurray

houspiller ['uspije] *vt* to tell off

housse ['us] *nf (protective)* cover

houx ['u] *nm* holly

hublot ['yblo] *nm (de navire, d'avion)* porthole

huche ['yʃ] *nf* **h. à pain** bread bin

hue ['y] *exclam* gee up!

huer ['ɥe] *vt* to boo • **huées** *nfpl* boos

huile [ɥil] *nf* oil; *Fam (personne)* big shot; *Fig* **mer d'h.** glassy sea; *Fig* **jeter de l'h. sur le feu** to add fuel to the fire; *Fam* **h. de coude** elbow grease; **h. d'arachide/d'olive** groundnut/olive oil; **h. essentielle** essential oil; **h. solaire** suntan oil • **huiler** *vt* to oil • **huileux, -euse** *adj* oily

huis [ɥi] *nm* **à h. clos** behind closed doors; *Jur* in camera

huissier [ɥisje] *nm (portier)* usher; *Jur* bailiff

huit ['ɥit, 'ɥi *before consonant]* *adj & nm inv* eight; **h. jours** a week; **dimanche en h.** *Br* a week on Sunday, *Am* a week from Sunday • **huitaine** *nf* (about) eight; *(semaine)* week; **une h. (de)** about eight • **huitième** *adj, nm & nmf* eighth; **un h.** an eighth; *Sport* **h. de finale** last sixteen

huître [ɥitr] *nf* oyster

hululer ['ylyle] *vi* to hoot

humain, -aine [ymɛ̃, -ɛn] **1** *adj (relatif à l'homme)* human; *(compatissant)* humane **2** *nmpl* **les humains** humans • **humainement** *adv (relatif à l'homme)* humanly; *(avec bonté)* humanely; **h. possible** humanly possible • **humanitaire** *adj* humanitarian • **humanité** *nf (genre humain, sentiment)* humanity

humble [œ̃bl] *adj* humble • **humblement** [-əmɑ̃] *adv* humbly

humecter [ymɛkte] *vt* to moisten

humer ['yme] *vt (respirer)* to breathe in; *(sentir)* to smell

humeur [ymœr] *nf (disposition)* mood; *(caractère)* temper; *(mauvaise humeur)* bad mood; **être de bonne/mauvaise h.** to be in a good/bad mood; **mettre qn de bonne/mauvaise h.** to put sb in a good/bad mood; **être d'une h. massacrante** to be in a foul mood; **d'h. égale** even-tempered

humide [ymid] *adj (linge)* damp, wet; *(climat, temps)* humid; **les yeux humides de larmes** eyes moist with tears • **humidifier** *vt* to humidify • **humidité** *nf (de maison)* dampness; *(de climat)* humidity

humilier [ymilje] *vt* to humiliate • **humiliant, -iante** *adj* humiliating • **humiliation** *nf* humiliation • **humilité** *nf* humility

humour [ymur] *nm* humour; **avoir de l'h. ou le sens de l'h.** to have a sense of humour; **h. noir** black humour • **humoriste** *nmf* humorist • **humoristique** *adj (ton)* humorous

huppé, -ée ['ype] *adj Fam (riche)* posh
hurler ['yrle] **1** *vt (slogans, injures)* to yell
   2 *vi (loup, vent)* to howl; *(personne)* to
   scream; *Fig* **h. avec les loups** to follow the
   crowd ● **hurlement** [-əmã] *nm (de loup, de
   vent)* howl; *(de personne)* scream
hurluberlu [yrlybɛrly] *nm* oddball
hutte ['yt] *nf* hut
hybride [ibrid] *adj & nm* hybrid
hydrater [idrate] *vt (peau)* to moisturize;
   crème hydratante moisturizing cream
hydraulique [idrolik] *adj* hydraulic
hydravion [idravjõ] *nm* seaplane
hydrocarbure [idrokarbyr] *nm* hydrocarbon
hydroélectrique [idroelɛktrik] *adj* hydroelectric
hydrogène [idrɔʒɛn] *nm* hydrogen
hydrophile [idrɔfil] *adj* **coton h.** *Br* cotton wool, *Am* (absorbent) cotton
hyène [jɛn] *nf* hyena
Hygiaphone® [iʒjafɔn] *nm (de guichet)*
   grille
hygiène [iʒjɛn] *nf* hygiene ● **hygiénique**
   adj hygienic; *(serviette, conditions)* sanitary
hymne [imn] *nm* hymn; **h. national**
   national anthem
hyper- [ipɛr] *préf* hyper- ● **hypermarché**

nm hypermarket ● **hypermétrope** *adj*
   longsighted ● **hypertension** *nf* **h. artérielle** high blood pressure; **faire de l'h.** to
   have high blood pressure
hypnose [ipnoz] *nf* hypnosis ● **hypno-
   tique** *adj* hypnotic ● **hypnotiser** *vt* to hypnotize ● **hypnotiseur** *nm* hypnotist
   ● **hypnotisme** *nm* hypnotism
hypoallergénique [ipɔalɛrʒenik] *adj*
   hypoallergenic
hypocalorique [ipɔkalɔrik] *adj (régime,
   aliment)* low-calorie
hypocondriaque [ipɔkɔ̃drijak] *adj &
   nmf* hypochondriac
hypocrisie [ipɔkrizi] *nf* hypocrisy ● **hypocrite 1** *adj* hypocritical **2** *nmf* hypocrite
hypodermique [ipɔdɛrmik] *adj* hypodermic
hypokhâgne [ipɔkaɲ] *nf Scol* = first-year
   arts class preparing students for the entrance examination for the *École normale
   supérieure*
hypothèque [ipɔtɛk] *nf* mortgage ● **hypothéquer** *vt (maison)* to mortgage
hypothèse [ipɔtɛz] *nf* hypothesis; **dans
   l'h. où** supposing (that) ● **hypothétique**
   adj hypothetical
hystérie [isteri] *nf* hysteria ● **hystérique**
   adj hysterical

I

I, i [i] *nm inv* I, i
iceberg [isbɛrg, ajsbɛrg] *nm* iceberg
ici [isi] *adv* here; **par i.** *(passer)* this way; *(habiter)* around here; **jusqu'i.** *(temps)* up to now; *(lieu)* as far as this *or* here; **d'i. à mardi** by Tuesday; **d'i. à une semaine** within a week; **d'i. peu** before long; **i. Dupont!** *(au téléphone)* this is Dupont!; **je ne suis pas d'i.** I'm a stranger around here; **les gens d'i.** the people from around here, the locals •**ici-bas** *adv* on earth
icône [ikon] *nf Rel & Ordinat* icon
idéal, -e, -aux *ou* **-als, -ales** [ideal, -o] **1** *adj* ideal
2 *n* ideal; **l'i. serait de/que...** the ideal *or* best solution would be to/if... •**idéalement** *adv* ideally •**idéaliser** *vt* to idealize •**idéalisme** *nm* idealism •**idéaliste 1** *adj* idealistic **2** *nmf* idealist
idée [ide] *nf* idea (**de** of; **que** that); **i. fixe** obsession; **changer d'i.** to change one's mind; **il m'est venu à l'i. que...** it occurred to me that...; **se faire une i. de qch** to get an idea of sth; *Fam* **se faire des idées** to imagine things; **avoir dans l'i. de faire qch** to have it in mind to do sth; **avoir son i. sur qch** to have one's own opinions about sth; **avoir une i. derrière la tête** to have an idea at the back of one's mind; *Fam* **avoir des idées** to be full of good ideas; **i. fixe** obsession; **idées noires** black thoughts
idem [idɛm] *adv* ditto
identifier [idãtifje] *vt*, **s'identifier** *vpr* to identify (**à** *ou* **avec** with) •**identification** *nf* identification
identique [idãtik] *adj* identical (**à** to)
identité [idãtite] *nf* identity
idéologie [ideɔlɔʒi] *nf* ideology •**idéologique** *adj* ideological
idiome [idjom] *nm* idiom •**idiomatique** *adj* idiomatic
idiot, -iote [idjo, -jɔt] **1** *adj* silly, idiotic
2 *nmf* idiot •**idiotie** [-ɔsi] *nf (état)* idiocy; **une i.** *(parole, action)* a silly thing
idole [idɔl] *nf* idol; **i. des jeunes** teenage idol
idylle [idil] *nf (amourette)* romance
idyllique [idilik] *adj* idyllic

if [if] *nm* yew (tree)
IFOP [ifɔp] *(abrév* **Institut français d'opinion publique)** *nm* = French market and opinion research institute
igloo [iglu] *nm* igloo
ignare [iɲar] **1** *adj* ignorant
2 *nmf* ignoramus
ignifugé, -ée [iɲifyʒe] *adj* fireproof(ed)
ignoble [iɲɔbl] *adj* vile
ignorant, -ante [iɲɔrã, -ãt] *adj* ignorant (**de** of) •**ignorance** *nf* ignorance
ignorer [iɲɔre] *vt* not to know; **j'ignore si...** I don't know if...; **je n'ignore pas les difficultés** I am not unaware of the difficulties; **i. qn** *(mépriser)* to ignore sb •**ignoré, -ée** *adj (inconnu)* unknown
il [il] •*pron personnel (personne)* he; *(chose, animal, impersonnel)* it; **il est** he/it is; **il pleut** it's raining; **il est vrai que...** it's true that...; **il y a...** there is/are...; **il y a six ans** six years ago; **il y a une heure qu'il travaille** he has been working for an hour; **qu'est-ce qu'il y a?** what's the matter?, what's wrong?; **il n'y a pas de quoi!** don't mention it!
île [il] *nf* island; **les îles Anglo-Normandes** the Channel Islands; **les îles Britanniques** the British Isles
illégal, -e, -aux, -ales [il(l)egal, -o] *adj* illegal •**illégalité** *nf* illegality
illégitime [il(l)eʒitim] *adj (enfant, revendication)* illegitimate; *(demande)* unwarranted
illettré, -ée [il(l)etre] *adj & nmf* illiterate
illicite [il(l)isit] *adj* unlawful, illicit
illico [il(l)iko] *adv Fam* **i. (presto)** pronto
illimité, -ée [il(l)imite] *adj* unlimited
illisible [il(l)izibl] *adj (écriture)* illegible; *(livre)* & *Ordinat* unreadable
illogique [il(l)ɔʒik] *adj* illogical
illuminer [il(l)ymine] **1** *vt* to light up, to illuminate
2 **s'illuminer** *vpr (visage, ciel)* to light up •**illumination** *nf (action, lumière)* illumination •**illuminé, -ée** *adj (monument)* floodlit
illusion [il(l)yzjɔ̃] *nf* illusion (**sur** about); **se faire des illusions** to delude oneself (**sur** about); **i. d'optique** optical illusion

• **s'illusionner** *vpr* to delude oneself (**sur** about) • **illusionniste** *nmf* conjurer • **illusoire** *adj* illusory

illustre [il(l)ystr] *adj* illustrious

illustrer [il(l)ystre] **1** *vt* (*livre, récit*) to illustrate (**de** with)
2 **s'illustrer** *vpr* to distinguish oneself (**par** by) • **illustration** *nf* illustration • **illustré, -ée** *adj* (*livre, magazine*) illustrated

îlot [ilo] *nm* (*île*) small island; (*maisons*) block

ils [il] *pron personnel mpl* they; **i. sont ici** they are here

image [imaʒ] *nf* picture; (*ressemblance, symbole*) image; (*dans une glace*) reflection; **i. de marque** (*de produit*) brand image; (*firme*) (public) image; *Ordinat* **i. de synthèse** computer-generated image • **imagé, -ée** *adj* (*style*) colourful, full of imagery

imaginable [imaʒinabl] *adj* imaginable • **imaginaire** *adj* imaginary • **imaginatif, -ive** *adj* imaginative

imagination [imaʒinɑsjɔ̃] *nf* imagination; **avoir de l'i.** to be imaginative

imaginer [imaʒine] **1** *vt* (*se figurer*) to imagine; (*inventer*) to devise
2 **s'imaginer** *vpr* (*se figurer*) to imagine (**que** that); (*se voir*) to picture oneself

imbattable [ɛ̃batabl] *adj* unbeatable

imbécile [ɛ̃besil] **1** *adj* idiotic
2 *nmf* idiot, imbecile • **imbécillité** *nf* (*état*) imbecility; **une i.** (*action, parole*) an idiotic thing

imberbe [ɛ̃bɛrb] *adj* beardless

imbiber [ɛ̃bibe] **1** *vt* to soak (**de** with *or* in)
2 **s'imbiber** *vpr* to become soaked (**de** with)

imbriquer [ɛ̃brike] **s'imbriquer** *vpr* (*s'emboîter*) to overlap

imbroglio [ɛ̃brɔglijo] *nm* imbroglio

imbu, -ue [ɛ̃by] *adj* **i. de soi-même** full of oneself

imbuvable [ɛ̃byvabl] *adj* undrinkable; *Fam* (*personne*) insufferable

imiter [imite] *vt* to imitate; (*signature*) to forge; **i. qn** (*pour rire*) to mimic sb; (*faire comme*) to do the same as sb; (*imitateur professionnel*) to impersonate sb • **imitateur, -trice** *nmf* imitator; (*professionnel*) impersonator • **imitation** *nf* imitation

immaculé, -ée [imakyle] *adj* (*sans tache, sans péché*) immaculate

immangeable [ɛ̃mɑ̃ʒabl] *adj* inedible

immanquable [ɛ̃mɑ̃kabl] *adj* inevitable

immatriculer [imatrikyle] *vt* to register; **se faire i.** to register • **immatriculation** *nf* registration

immédiat, -iate [imedja, -jat] **1** *adj* immediate
2 *nm* **dans l'i.** for the time being • **immédiatement** *adv* immediately

immense [imɑ̃s] *adj* immense • **immensément** *adv* immensely • **immensité** *nf* immensity

immerger [imɛrʒe] *vt* to immerse • **immersion** *nf* immersion (**dans** in)

immettable [ɛ̃metabl] *adj* unwearable

immeuble [imœbl] *nm* building; (*appartements*) *Br* block of flats, *Am* apartment block

immigrer [imigre] *vi* to immigrate • **immigrant, -ante** *nmf* immigrant • **immigration** *nf* immigration • **immigré, -ée** *adj & nmf* immigrant; **travailleur i.** immigrant worker

imminent, -ente [iminɑ̃, -ɑ̃t] *adj* imminent • **imminence** *nf* imminence

immiscer [imise] **s'immiscer** *vpr* to interfere (**dans** in)

immobile [imɔbil] *adj* still, motionless • **immobiliser 1** *vt* (*blessé*) to immobilize; (*train*) to bring to a stop; (*voiture*) (*avec un sabot*) to clamp **2** **s'immobiliser** *vpr* to come to a stop • **immobilité** *nf* stillness; (*de visage*) immobility

immobilier, -ière [imɔbilje, -jɛr] **1** *adj* **marché i.** property market; **vente immobilière** sale of property
2 *nm* **l'i.** *Br* property, *Am* real estate

immodéré, -ée [i(m)mɔdere] *adj* immoderate

immoler [i(m)mɔle] *Littéraire* **1** *vt* (*sacrifier*) to sacrifice
2 **s'immoler** *vpr* **s'i. par le feu** to die by setting fire to oneself

immonde [i(m)mɔ̃d] *adj* (*sale*) foul; (*ignoble, laid*) vile • **immondices** *nfpl* refuse

immoral, -e, -aux, -ales [i(m)mɔral, -o] *adj* immoral • **immoralité** *nf* immorality

immortel, -elle [i(m)mɔrtɛl] *adj* immortal; **les Immortels** the members of the *Académie Française* • **immortaliser** *vt* to immortalize • **immortalité** *nf* immortality

immuable [i(m)mɥabl] *adj* immutable, unchanging

immuniser [i(m)mynize] *vt* to immunize (**contre** against) • **immunitaire** *adj* *Méd* (*déficience, système*) immune • **immunité** *nf* immunity; **i. parlementaire** parliamentary immunity

impact [ɛ̃pakt] *nm* impact (**sur** on)

impair, -aire [ɛ̃pɛr] 1 *adj (nombre)* odd, uneven
2 *nm (maladresse)* blunder

imparable [ɛ̃parabl] *adj (coup)* unavoidable

impardonnable [ɛ̃pardɔnabl] *adj* unforgivable

imparfait, -aite [ɛ̃parfɛ, -ɛt] 1 *adj (connaissance)* imperfect
2 *nm Grammaire (temps)* imperfect

impartial, -e, -iaux, -iales [ɛ̃parsjal, -jo] *adj* impartial, unbiased • **impartialité** *nf* impartiality

impartir [ɛ̃partir] *vt* to grant (à to); **dans le temps qui nous est imparti** within the allotted time

impasse [ɛ̃pas] *nf (rue)* dead end; *Fig (situation)* impasse; **être dans une i.** to be deadlocked; **faire une i.** *(en révisant)* = to miss out part of a subject when revising

impassible [ɛ̃pasibl] *adj* impassive • **impassibilité** *nf* impassiveness

impatient, -iente [ɛ̃pasjɑ̃, -jɑ̃t] *adj* impatient; **i. de faire qch** impatient to do sth • **impatiemment** [-amɑ̃] *adv* impatiently • **impatience** *nf* impatience • **impatienter** 1 *vt* to annoy 2 **s'impatienter** *vpr* to get impatient

impavide [ɛ̃pavid] *adj Littéraire* impassive

impayable [ɛ̃pɛjabl] *adj Fam (comique)* priceless

impayé, -ée [ɛ̃peje] *adj* unpaid

impeccable [ɛ̃pekabl] *adj* impeccable • **impeccablement** [-əmɑ̃] *adv* impeccably

impénétrable [ɛ̃penetrabl] *adj (forêt, mystère)* impenetrable

impénitent, -ente [ɛ̃penitɑ̃, -ɑ̃t] *adj* unrepentant

impensable [ɛ̃pɑ̃sabl] *adj* unthinkable

imper [ɛ̃pɛr] *nm Fam* raincoat, *Br* mac

impératif, -ive [ɛ̃peratif, -iv] 1 *adj (consigne, besoin)* imperative; *(ton)* imperious
2 *nm Grammaire* imperative

impératrice [ɛ̃peratris] *nf* empress

imperceptible [ɛ̃pɛrsɛptibl] *adj* imperceptible (à to)

imperfection [ɛ̃pɛrfɛksjɔ̃] *nf* imperfection

impérial, -e, -iaux, -iales [ɛ̃perjal, -jo] *adj* imperial • **impérialisme** *nm* imperialism

impériale [ɛ̃perjal] *nf (d'autobus)* top deck; **autobus à i.** double-decker (bus)

impérieux, -ieuse [ɛ̃perjø, -jøz] *adj (autoritaire)* imperious; *(besoin)* pressing

impérissable [ɛ̃perisabl] *adj (souvenir)* enduring

imperméable [ɛ̃pɛrmeabl] 1 *adj* impervious (à to); *(tissu, manteau)* waterproof
2 *nm* raincoat, *Br* mackintosh • **imperméabilisé, -ée** *adj* waterproof

impersonnel, -elle [ɛ̃pɛrsɔnɛl] *adj* impersonal

impertinent, -ente [ɛ̃pɛrtinɑ̃, -ɑ̃t] *adj* impertinent (envers to) • **impertinence** *nf* impertinence

imperturbable [ɛ̃pɛrtyrbabl] *adj (personne)* imperturbable

impétueux, -ueuse [ɛ̃petɥø, -ɥøz] *adj* impetuous • **impétuosité** *nf* impetuosity

impie [ɛ̃pi] *adj Littéraire* impious

impitoyable [ɛ̃pitwajabl] *adj* merciless

implacable [ɛ̃plakabl] *adj (personne, vengeance)* implacable; *(avancée)* relentless

implant [ɛ̃plɑ̃] *nm* implant; **faire des implants** *(cheveux)* to have hair grafts

implanter [ɛ̃plɑ̃te] 1 *vt (installer)* to establish; *(chirurgicalement)* to implant
2 **s'implanter** *vpr* to become established • **implantation** *nf* establishment

implicite [ɛ̃plisit] *adj* implicit • **implicitement** *adv* implicitly

impliquer [ɛ̃plike] *vt (entraîner)* to imply; **i. que...** to imply that...; **i. qn** to implicate sb (dans in) • **implication** *nf (conséquence)* implication; *(participation)* involvement

implorer [ɛ̃plɔre] *vt* to implore (qn de faire sb to do)

impoli, -ie [ɛ̃pɔli] *adj* rude, impolite • **impolitesse** *nf* impoliteness, rudeness; **une i.** *(acte)* impolite act

impondérable [ɛ̃pɔ̃derabl] *nm* imponderable

impopulaire [ɛ̃pɔpylɛr] *adj* unpopular

import [ɛ̃pɔr] *nm* import

important, -ante [ɛ̃pɔrtɑ̃, -ɑ̃t] 1 *adj (personnage, événement)* important; *(quantité, somme, ville)* large; *(dégâts, retard)* considerable
2 *nm* **l'i., c'est de** the important thing is to • **importance** *nf* importance; *(taille)* size; *(de dégâts)* extent; **attacher de l'i. à qch** to attach importance to sth; **ça n'a pas d'i.** it doesn't matter

importer¹ [ɛ̃pɔrte] 1 *vi* to matter (à to)
2 *v impersonnel* **il importe de faire qch** it's important to do sth; **il importe que vous y soyez** it is important that you're there; **peu importe, n'importe** it doesn't matter; **n'importe qui/quoi/où/quand/comment** anyone/anything/anywhere/

any time/anyhow; *Péj* **dire n'importe quoi** to talk nonsense

importer² [ɛ̃pɔrte] *vt (marchandises)* to import (**de** from) •**importateur, -trice 1** *adj* importing **2** *nmf* importer •**importation** *nf (objet)* import; *(action)* importing, importation; **d'i.** *(article)* imported

importun, -une [ɛ̃pɔrtœ̃, -yn] **1** *adj (personne, question)* importunate; *(arrivée)* ill-timed

2 *nmf* nuisance •**importuner** *vt Formel* to bother

imposer [ɛ̃poze] **1** *vt (condition)* to impose; *(taxer)* to tax; **i. qch à qn** to impose sth on sb; **i. le respect** to command respect

2 *vi* **en i. à qn** to impress sb

3 **s'imposer** *vpr (faire reconnaître sa valeur)* to assert oneself; *(gagner)* to win; *(être nécessaire)* to be essential; *Péj (chez qn)* to impose; **s'i. de faire qch** to make it a rule to do sth •**imposable** *adj Fin* taxable •**imposant, -ante** *adj* imposing •**imposition** *nf Fin* taxation

impossible [ɛ̃pɔsibl] **1** *adj* impossible (**à faire** to do); **il (nous) est i. de faire qch** it is impossible (for us) to do sth; **il est i. que...** (+ *subjunctive*) it is impossible that...; **ça m'est i.** I cannot possibly; **i. n'est pas français** there's no such thing as 'impossible'

2 *nm* **tenter l'i.** to attempt the impossible; **faire l'i. pour faire qch** to do everything possible to do sth •**impossibilité** *nf* impossibility

imposteur [ɛ̃pɔstœr] *nm* impostor •**imposture** *nf* deception

impôt [ɛ̃po] *nm* tax; **(service des) impôts** tax authorities; **payer 1000 euros d'impôts** to pay 1,000 euros in tax; **impôts locaux** local taxes; **i. sur le revenu** income tax

impotent, -ente [ɛ̃pɔtɑ̃, -ɑ̃t] *adj* disabled; *(de vieillesse)* infirm

> ⚠ Il faut noter que l'adjectif anglais **impotent** est un faux ami. Il signifie **impuissant**.

impraticable [ɛ̃pratikabl] *adj (chemin)* impassable; *(projet)* impracticable

imprécis, -ise [ɛ̃presi, -iz] *adj* imprecise •**imprécision** *nf* imprecision

imprégner [ɛ̃preɲe] **1** *vt* to impregnate (**de** with); *Fig* **être imprégné de qch** to be full of sth

2 **s'imprégner** *vpr* to become impregnated (**de** with)

imprenable [ɛ̃prənabl] *adj (forteresse)* impregnable; *(vue)* unobstructed

imprésario [ɛ̃presarjo] *nm* manager

impression [ɛ̃presjɔ̃] *nf* (**a**) *(sensation)* impression; **avoir l'i. que...** to have the impression that...; **il donne l'i. d'être fatigué** he gives the impression of being tired; **faire bonne i. à qn** to make a good impression on sb (**b**) *(de livre)* printing

impressionner [ɛ̃presjɔne] *vt (bouleverser)* to upset; *(frapper)* to impress •**impressionnable** *adj* easily upset •**impressionnant, -ante** *adj* impressive

> ⚠ Il faut noter que l'adjectif anglais **impressionable** est un faux ami. Il signifie **influençable**.

imprévisible [ɛ̃previzibl] *adj (temps, réaction, personne)* unpredictable; *(événement)* unforeseeable •**imprévoyance** *nf* lack of foresight •**imprévoyant, -ante** *adj* lacking in foresight •**imprévu, -ue 1** *adj* unexpected, unforeseen **2** *nm* **en cas d'i.** in case of anything unexpected

imprimer [ɛ̃prime] *vt (livre, tissu)* to print; *(cachet)* to stamp; *Ordinat* to print (out); *Tech* **un mouvement à** to impart motion to •**imprimante** *nf* printer •**imprimé** *nm (formulaire)* printed form; **imprimés** *(journaux, prospectus)* printed matter •**imprimerie** *nf (technique)* printing; *(lieu) Br* printing works, *Am* print shop •**imprimeur** *nm* printer

improbable [ɛ̃prɔbabl] *adj* improbable, unlikely

impromptu, -ue [ɛ̃prɔ̃pty] *adj & adv* impromptu

impropre [ɛ̃prɔpr] *adj* inappropriate; **i. à qch** unfit for sth; **i. à la consommation** unfit for human consumption

improviser [ɛ̃prɔvize] *vti* to improvise •**improvisation** *nf* improvisation

improviste [ɛ̃prɔvist] **à l'improviste** *adv* unexpectedly

imprudent, -ente [ɛ̃prydɑ̃, -ɑ̃t] *adj (personne, action)* rash; **il est i. de...** it is unwise to... •**imprudemment** [-amɑ̃] *adv* rashly •**imprudence** *nf* rashness; **commettre une i.** to do something foolish

impudent, -ente [ɛ̃pydɑ̃, -ɑ̃t] *adj* impudent •**impudence** *nf* impudence

impudique [ɛ̃pydik] *adj* shameless

impuissant, -ante [ɛ̃pɥisɑ̃, -ɑ̃t] *adj* powerless; *Méd* impotent •**impuissance** *nf* powerlessness; *Méd* impotence

impulsif, -ive [ɛ̃pylsif, -iv] *adj* impulsive •**impulsion** *nf* impulse; *Fig* **donner une i. à qch** to give an impetus to sth

impunément [ɛ̃pynemɑ̃] *adv* with impunity •**impuni, -ie** *adj* unpunished

impur, -ure [ɛ̃pyr] *adj* impure • **impureté** *nf* impurity

imputer [ɛ̃pyte] *vt* to attribute (à to); *(frais)* to charge (à to) • **imputable** *adj* attributable (à to)

inabordable [inabɔrdabl] *adj (prix)* prohibitive; *(lieu)* inaccessible; *(personne)* unapproachable

inacceptable [inaksɛptabl] *adj* unacceptable

inaccessible [inaksesibl] *adj (lieu)* inaccessible; *(personne)* unapproachable

inachevé, -ée [inaʃve] *adj* unfinished

inactif, -ive [inaktif, -iv] *adj (personne)* inactive; *(remède)* ineffective • **inaction** *nf* inaction • **inactivité** *nf* inactivity

inadapté, -ée [inadapte] **1** *adj (socialement)* maladjusted; *(physiquement, mentalement)* handicapped; *(matériel)* unsuitable (à for)
2 *nmf (socialement)* maladjusted person

inadmissible [inadmisibl] *adj* inadmissible

inadvertance [inadvɛrtɑ̃s] **par inadvertance** *adv* inadvertently

inaltérable [inalterabl] *adj (matière)* stable; *Fig (sentiment)* unchanging

inamical, -e, -aux, -ales [inamikal, -o] *adj* unfriendly

inanimé, -ée [inanime] *adj (mort)* lifeless; *(évanoui)* unconscious; *(matière)* inanimate

inanité [inanite] *nf (d'effort)* futility; *(de conversation)* inanity

inanition [inanisjɔ̃] *nf* **mourir d'i.** to die of starvation

inaperçu, -ue [inapɛrsy] *adj* **passer i.** to go unnoticed

inapplicable [inaplikabl] *adj (loi)* unenforceable; *(théorie)* inapplicable (à to)

inappréciable [inapresjabl] *adj* invaluable

inapte [inapt] *adj (intellectuellement)* unsuited; *(médicalement)* unfit; **être i. à qch** to be unsuited/unfit for sth • **inaptitude** *nf (intellectuelle)* inaptitude; *(médicale)* unfitness (à for)

inarticulé, -ée [inartikyle] *adj (son, cri)* inarticulate

inattaquable [inatakabl] *adj* unassailable

inattendu, -ue [inatɑ̃dy] *adj* unexpected

inattentif, -ive [inatɑ̃tif, -iv] *adj* inattentive; **i. à qch** *(indifférent)* heedless of sth • **inattention** *nf* lack of attention; **moment d'i.** lapse of concentration

inaudible [inodibl] *adj* inaudible

inaugurer [inogyre] *vt (édifice)* to inaugurate; *(statue)* to unveil; *(politique)* to implement • **inaugural, -e, -aux, -ales** *adj* inaugural • **inauguration** *nf (d'édifice)* inauguration; *(de statue)* unveiling

inavouable [inavwabl] *adj* shameful

incalculable [ɛ̃kalkylabl] *adj* incalculable

incandescent, -ente [ɛ̃kɑ̃dɛsɑ̃, -ɑ̃t] *adj* incandescent

incapable [ɛ̃kapabl] **1** *adj* incapable; **i. de faire qch** incapable of doing sth
2 *nmf (personne)* incompetent • **incapacité** *nf (impossibilité)* inability (**de faire** to do); *(invalidité)* disability; **être dans l'i. de faire qch** to be unable to do sth

incarcérer [ɛ̃karsere] *vt* to incarcerate • **incarcération** *nf* incarceration

incarné, -ée [ɛ̃karne] *adj (ongle)* ingrown; **être la gentillesse incarnée** to be the very embodiment of kindness

incarner [ɛ̃karne] *vt* to embody; *Cin* **i. le rôle de qn** to play the part of sb • **incarnation** *nf* incarnation

incartade [ɛ̃kartad] *nf* indiscretion

incassable [ɛ̃kɑsabl] *adj* unbreakable

incendie [ɛ̃sɑ̃di] *nm* fire; **i. criminel** arson; **i. de forêt** forest fire • **incendiaire 1** *adj (bombe)* incendiary; *Fig (paroles)* inflammatory **2** *nmf* arsonist • **incendier** *vt* to set on fire

incertain, -aine [ɛ̃sɛrtɛ̃, -ɛn] *adj (résultat)* uncertain; *(temps)* unsettled; *(entreprise)* chancy; *(contour)* indistinct; *(personne)* indecisive • **incertitude** *nf* uncertainty; **être dans l'i. quant à qch** to be uncertain about sth

incessamment [ɛ̃sesamɑ̃] *adv* very soon

incessant, -ante [ɛ̃sesɑ̃, -ɑ̃t] *adj* incessant

inceste [ɛ̃sɛst] *nm* incest • **incestueux, -ueuse** *adj* incestuous

inchangé, -ée [ɛ̃ʃɑ̃ʒe] *adj* unchanged

incidence [ɛ̃sidɑ̃s] *nf (influence)* impact (**sur** on); *Méd* incidence

incident [ɛ̃sidɑ̃] *nm* incident; *(accroc)* hitch; **i. diplomatique** diplomatic incident; **i. de parcours** minor setback; **i. technique** technical hitch

incinérer [ɛ̃sinere] *vt (ordures)* to incinerate; *(cadavre)* to cremate • **incinération** *nf (d'ordures)* incineration; *(de cadavre)* cremation

inciser [ɛ̃size] *vt (peau)* to make an incision in; *(abcès)* to lance • **incision** *nf (entaille)* incision

incisif, -ive¹ [ɛ̃sizif, -iv] *adj* incisive • **incisive²** *nf (dent)* incisor (tooth)

inciter [ɛ̃site] *vt* to encourage (**à faire** to do); **i. qn à la prudence** *(sujet: événement)* to incline sb to be cautious • **incitation** *nf* incitement (**à** to)

incliner [ɛ̃kline] **1** *vt (pencher)* to tilt; **i. la tête** *(approuver)* to nod; *(saluer)* to bow one's head; *Fig* **i. qn à faire qch** to incline sb to do sth; *Fig* **i. qn à la prudence** to incline sb to be cautious

2 s'incliner *vpr (se pencher)* to lean forward; *(pour saluer)* to bow; *(chemin)* to slope down; *(bateau)* to heel over; *(avion)* to bank; *Fig (se soumettre)* to give in (**devant** to) • **inclinaison** *nf* incline, slope • **inclination** *nf (tendance)* inclination; **i. de la tête** *(pour saluer)* nod

inclure* [ɛ̃klyr] *vt* to include; *(dans un courrier)* to enclose (**dans** with) • **inclus, -use** *adj* **du 4 au 10 i.** from the 4th to the 10th inclusive; **jusqu'à lundi i.** *Br* up to and including Monday, *Am* through Monday • **inclusion** *nf* inclusion

incognito [ɛ̃kɔɲito] **1** *adv* incognito

2 *nm* **garder l'i.** to remain incognito

incohérent, -ente [ɛ̃kɔerɑ̃, -ɑ̃t] *adj (propos)* incoherent; *(histoire)* inconsistent • **incohérence** *nf (de propos)* incoherence; *(d'histoire)* inconsistency

incollable [ɛ̃kɔlabl] *adj (riz)* non-stick; *Fam (personne)* unbeatable

incolore [ɛ̃kɔlɔr] *adj* colourless; *(vernis, verre)* clear

incomber [ɛ̃kɔ̃be] *vi* **i. à qn** *(devoir)* to fall to sb; **il lui incombe de faire qch** it falls to him/her to do sth

incommensurable [ɛ̃kɔmɑ̃syrabl] *adj* immeasurable

incommode [ɛ̃kɔmɔd] *adj (situation)* awkward

incommoder [ɛ̃kɔmɔde] *vt* to bother • **incommodant, -ante** *adj* annoying

incomparable [ɛ̃kɔ̃parabl] *adj* matchless

incompatible [ɛ̃kɔ̃patibl] *adj* incompatible (**avec** with) • **incompatibilité** *nf* incompatibility; **i. d'humeur** mutual incompatibility

incompétent, -ente [ɛ̃kɔ̃petɑ̃, -ɑ̃t] *adj* incompetent • **incompétence** *nf* incompetence

incomplet, -ète [ɛ̃kɔ̃plɛ, -ɛt] *adj* incomplete

incompréhensible [ɛ̃kɔ̃preɑ̃sibl] *adj* incomprehensible • **incompréhension** *nf* incomprehension

incompris, -ise [ɛ̃kɔ̃pri, -iz] **1** *adj* misunderstood

2 *nmf* **être un i.** to be misunderstood

inconcevable [ɛ̃kɔ̃səvabl] *adj* inconceivable

inconciliable [ɛ̃kɔ̃siljabl] *adj (théorie)* irreconcilable; *(activité)* incompatible

inconditionnel, -elle [ɛ̃kɔ̃disjɔnɛl] *adj* unconditional; *(supporter)* staunch

inconfort [ɛ̃kɔ̃fɔr] *nm (matériel)* discomfort • **inconfortable** *adj* uncomfortable

incongru, -ue [ɛ̃kɔ̃gry] *adj* inappropriate

inconnu, -ue [ɛ̃kɔny] **1** *adj* unknown (**de** to)

2 *nmf (étranger)* stranger; *(auteur)* unknown

3 *nm* **l'i.** the unknown

4 *nf Math* **inconnue** unknown (quantity)

inconscient, -iente [ɛ̃kɔ̃sjɑ̃, -jɑ̃t] **1** *adj (sans connaissance)* unconscious; *(imprudent)* reckless; **i. de qch** unaware of sth

2 *nm* **l'i.** the unconscious • **inconsciemment** [-amɑ̃] *adv (dans l'inconscient)* subconsciously • **inconscience** *nf (perte de connaissance)* unconsciousness; *(irréflexion)* recklessness

inconséquence [ɛ̃kɔ̃sekɑ̃s] *nf (manque de prudence)* recklessness; *(manque de cohérence)* inconsistency

inconsidéré, -ée [ɛ̃kɔ̃sidere] *adj* thoughtless

inconsistant, -ante [ɛ̃kɔ̃sistɑ̃, -ɑ̃t] *adj (personne)* weak; *(film, roman)* flimsy; *(sauce, crème)* thin

> ⚠ Il faut noter que l'adjectif anglais **inconsistent** est un faux ami. Il signifie **incohérent**.

inconsolable [ɛ̃kɔ̃sɔlabl] *adj* inconsolable

inconstant, -ante [ɛ̃kɔ̃stɑ̃, -ɑ̃t] *adj* fickle • **inconstance** *nf* fickleness

incontestable [ɛ̃kɔ̃tɛstabl] *adj* indisputable • **incontesté, -ée** *adj* undisputed

incontinent, -ente [ɛ̃kɔ̃tinɑ̃, -ɑ̃t] *adj Méd* incontinent

incontournable [ɛ̃kɔ̃turnabl] *adj Fig (film)* unmissable; *(auteur)* who cannot be ignored

incontrôlé, -ée [ɛ̃kɔ̃trole] *adj* unchecked • **incontrôlable** *adj (invérifiable)* unverifiable; *(indomptable)* uncontrollable

inconvenant, -ante [ɛ̃kɔ̃vnɑ̃, -ɑ̃t] *adj* improper • **inconvenance** *nf* impropriety

inconvénient [ɛ̃kɔ̃venjɑ̃] *nm (désavantage)* drawback; **je n'y vois pas d'i.** I have no objection; **l'i. c'est que...** the annoying thing is that...

incorporer [ɛ̃kɔrpɔre] *vt (insérer)* to in-

sert (**à** in); *(troupes)* to draft; **i. qch à qch** to blend sth into sth ●**incorporation** *nf (mélange)* blending (**de qch dans qch** of sth into sth); *Mil* conscription
incorrect, -ecte [ɛ̃kɔrɛkt] *adj (inexact)* incorrect; *(grossier)* impolite; *(inconvenant)* improper ●**incorrection** *nf (impolitesse)* impoliteness; *(propos)* impolite remark; *(faute de grammaire)* mistake
incorrigible [ɛ̃kɔriʒibl] *adj* incorrigible
incorruptible [ɛ̃kɔryptibl] *adj* incorruptible
incrédule [ɛ̃kredyl] *adj* incredulous ●**incrédulité** *nf* incredulity
increvable [ɛ̃krəvabl] *adj (pneu)* puncture-proof; *Fam (personne)* tireless
incriminer [ɛ̃krimine] *vt (personne)* to accuse
incroyable [ɛ̃krwajabl] *adj* incredible ●**incroyablement** [-əmɑ̃] *adv* incredibly ●**incroyant, -ante 1** *adj* unbelieving **2** *nmf* unbeliever
incrusté, -ée [ɛ̃kryste] *adj* **i. de** *(orné)* inlaid with ●**incrustation** *nf (ornement)* inlay; *(dépôt)* fur ●**s'incruster** *vpr Fam (chez qn)* to be difficult to get rid of
incubation [ɛ̃kybɑsjɔ̃] *nf* incubation
inculper [ɛ̃kylpe] *vt (accuser)* to charge (**de** with) ●**inculpation** *nf* charge, indictment ●**inculpé, -ée** *nmf* **l'i.** the accused
inculquer [ɛ̃kylke] *vt* to instil (**à qn** in sb)
inculte [ɛ̃kylt] *adj (terre, personne)* uncultivated
incurable [ɛ̃kyrabl] *adj* incurable
incursion [ɛ̃kyrsjɔ̃] *nf (invasion)* incursion; *Fig (entrée soudaine)* intrusion
incurvé, -ée [ɛ̃kyrve] *adj* curved
Inde [ɛ̃d] *nf* **l'I.** India
indécent, -ente [ɛ̃desɑ̃, -ɑ̃t] *adj* indecent ●**indécence** *nf* indecency
indéchiffrable [ɛ̃deʃifrabl] *adj (illisible)* undecipherable
indécis, -ise [ɛ̃desi, -iz] *adj (personne) (de caractère)* indecisive; *(ponctuellement)* undecided; *(bataille)* inconclusive; *(contour)* vague ●**indécision** *nf (de caractère)* indecisiveness; *(ponctuelle)* indecision
indéfendable [ɛ̃defɑ̃dabl] *adj* indefensible
indéfini, -ie [ɛ̃defini] *adj (illimité)* & *Grammaire* indefinite; *(imprécis)* undefined ●**indéfiniment** *adv* indefinitely ●**indéfinissable** *adj* indefinable
indéformable [ɛ̃defɔrmabl] *adj (vêtement)* which keeps its shape
indélébile [ɛ̃delebil] *adj* indelible
indélicat, -ate [ɛ̃delika, -at] *adj (grossier)* insensitive; *(malhonnête)* unscrupulous ●**indélicatesse** *nf (manque de tact)* tactlessness

indemne [ɛ̃dɛmn] *adj* unhurt, unscathed
indemniser [ɛ̃dɛmnize] *vt* to compensate (**de** for) ●**indemnisation** *nf* compensation ●**indemnité** *nf (dédommagement)* compensation; *(allocation)* allowance; **i. de licenciement** redundancy payment
indémodable [ɛ̃demɔdabl] *adj* perennially fashionable
indéniable [ɛ̃denjabl] *adj* undeniable
indépendant, -ante [ɛ̃depɑ̃dɑ̃, -ɑ̃t] *adj* independent (**de** of); *(chambre)* self-contained; *(travailleur)* self-employed; **i. de ma volonté** beyond my control ●**indépendamment** [-amɑ̃] *adv* independently; **i. de** apart from ●**indépendance** *nf* independence ●**indépendantiste** *nmf Pol (activiste)* freedom fighter
indescriptible [ɛ̃dɛskriptibl] *adj* indescribable
indésirable [ɛ̃dezirabl] *adj* & *nmf* undesirable
indestructible [ɛ̃dɛstryktibl] *adj* indestructible
indéterminé, -ée [ɛ̃detɛrmine] *adj (date, heure)* unspecified; *(raison)* unknown
index [ɛ̃dɛks] *nm (doigt)* forefinger, index finger; *(liste)* & *Ordinat* index
indexer [ɛ̃dɛkse] *vt Écon* to index-link (**sur** to); *(ajouter un index à)* to index
indicateur, -trice [ɛ̃dikatœr, -tris] **1** *nm Rail* timetable; *Tech* indicator, gauge; *Écon* indicator; *(espion)* informer **2** *adj* **poteau i.** signpost; **panneau i.** road sign
indicatif, -ive [ɛ̃dikatif, -iv] **1** *adj* indicative (**de** of); **à titre i.** for information **2** *nm Radio* theme tune; *Grammaire* indicative; **i. téléphonique** *Br* dialling code, *Am* area code
indication [ɛ̃dikɑsjɔ̃] *nf* indication (**de** of); *(renseignement)* (piece of) information; *(directive)* instruction; **indications:...** *(de médicament)* suitable for...
indice [ɛ̃dis] *nm (signe)* sign; *(d'enquête)* clue; *Radio & TV* **i. d'écoute** audience rating; **i. des prix** price index
indien, -ienne [ɛ̃djɛ̃, -jɛn] **1** *adj* Indian **2** *nmf* **I., Indienne** Indian
indifférent, -ente [ɛ̃difɛrɑ̃, -ɑ̃t] *adj* indifferent (**à** to); **ça m'est i.** it's all the same to me ●**indifféremment** [-amɑ̃] *adv* indifferently ●**indifférence** *nf* indifference (**à** to)

indigène [ɛ̃diʒɛn] *adj & nmf* native
indigent, -ente [ɛ̃diʒɑ̃, -ɑ̃t] *adj* destitute ● **indigence** *nf* destitution
indigeste [ɛ̃diʒɛst] *adj* indigestible ● **indigestion** *nf* **avoir une i.** to have a stomach upset
indigne [ɛ̃diɲ] *adj (personne)* unworthy; *(conduite)* shameful; **i. de qn/qch** unworthy of sb/sth ● **indignité** *nf (de personne)* unworthiness; *(de conduite)* shamefulness; *(action)* shameful act
indigner [ɛ̃diɲe] **1** *vt* **i. qn** to make sb indignant
2 s'indigner *vpr* to be indignant (**de** at) ● **indignation** *nf* indignation ● **indigné, -ée** *adj* indignant
indigo [ɛ̃digo] *nm & adj inv* indigo
indiquer [ɛ̃dike] *vt (sujet: personne)* to point out; *(sujet: panneau, étiquette)* to show, to indicate; *(sujet: compteur)* to read; *(donner) (date, adresse)* to give; *(recommander)* to recommend; **i. qch du doigt** to point to *or* at sth; **i. le chemin à qn** to tell sb the way ● **indiqué, -ée** *adj (conseillé)* advisable; **à l'heure indiquée** at the appointed time; **il est tout i. pour ce poste** he's the right person for the job
indirect, -ecte [ɛ̃dirɛkt] *adj* indirect ● **indirectement** [-ǝmɑ̃] *adv* indirectly
indiscipline [ɛ̃disiplin] *nf* indiscipline ● **indiscipliné, -ée** *adj* unruly
indiscret, -ète [ɛ̃diskrɛ, -ɛt] *adj* Péj *(curieux)* inquisitive; *(qui parle trop)* indiscreet; **à l'abri des regards indiscrets** safe from prying eyes ● **indiscrétion** *nf* indiscretion
indiscutable [ɛ̃diskytabl] *adj* indisputable
indispensable [ɛ̃dispɑ̃sabl] *adj* essential, indispensable (**à qch** for sth); **i. à qn** indispensable to sb
indisponible [ɛ̃disponibl] *adj* unavailable
indisposer [ɛ̃dispoze] *vt (contrarier)* to annoy; **i. qn** *(odeur, climat)* to make sb feel ill ● **indisposé, -ée** *adj (malade)* indisposed, unwell ● **indisposition** *nf* indisposition
indissoluble [ɛ̃disɔlybl] *adj (liens)* indissoluble
indistinct, -incte [ɛ̃distɛ̃(kt), -ɛ̃kt] *adj* indistinct ● **indistinctement** [-ɛ̃ktǝmɑ̃] *adv (voir, parler)* indistinctly; *(également)* equally
individu [ɛ̃dividy] *nm* individual; Péj individual, character
individualiser [ɛ̃dividɥalize] *vt (adapter)* to adapt to individual circumstances

individualiste [ɛ̃dividɥalist] **1** *adj* individualistic
2 *nmf* individualist
individualité [ɛ̃dividɥalite] *nf* individuality
individuel, -uelle [ɛ̃dividɥɛl] *adj* individual; *(maison)* detached ● **individuellement** *adv* individually
indivisible [ɛ̃divizibl] *adj* indivisible
Indochine [ɛ̃dɔʃin] *nf* **l'I.** Indo-China
indolent, -ente [ɛ̃dɔlɑ̃, -ɑ̃t] *adj* lazy ● **indolence** *nf* laziness
indolore [ɛ̃dɔlɔr] *adj* painless
indomptable [ɛ̃dɔ̃(p)tabl] *adj (animal)* untamable; Fig *(orgueil, volonté)* indomitable ● **indompté, -ée** *adj (animal)* untamed
Indonésie [ɛ̃dɔnezi] *nf* **l'I.** Indonesia
indubitable [ɛ̃dybitabl] *adj* indisputable; **c'est i.** there's no doubt about it ● **indubitablement** [-ɔmɑ̃] *adv* undoubtedly
indue [ɛ̃dy] *adj f* **à une heure i.** at an ungodly hour; **rentrer à des heures indues** to come home at all hours of the night
induire* [ɛ̃dɥir] *vt* **i. qn en erreur** to lead sb astray
indulgent, -ente [ɛ̃dylʒɑ̃, -ɑ̃t] *adj* indulgent ● **indulgence** *nf* indulgence
industrie [ɛ̃dystri] *nf* industry ● **industrialisé, -ée** *adj* industrialized ● **industriel, -ielle 1** *adj* industrial **2** *nm* industrialist
inébranlable [inebrɑ̃labl] *adj* Fig *(certitude, personne)* unshakeable
inédit, -ite [inedi, -it] *adj (texte)* unpublished; Fig *(nouveau)* original
ineffable [inefabl] *adj* ineffable
inefficace [inefikas] *adj (mesure)* ineffective; *(personne)* inefficient ● **inefficacité** *nf (de mesure)* ineffectiveness; *(de personne)* inefficiency
inégal, -e, -aux, -ales [inegal, -o] *adj (parts, lutte)* unequal; *(sol, humeur)* uneven; Fig *(travail)* inconsistent ● **inégalable** *adj* incomparable ● **inégalé, -ée** *adj* unequalled ● **inégalité** *nf (injustice)* inequality; *(physique)* disparity (**de** in); *(de sol)* unevenness
inélégant, -ante [inelegɑ̃, -ɑ̃t] *adj (mal habillé)* inelegant; *(discourtois)* discourteous
inéligible [ineliʒibl] *adj* ineligible
inéluctable [inelyktabl] *adj* inescapable
inénarrable [inenarabl] *adj (comique)* indescribably funny
inepte [inɛpt] *adj (remarque, histoire)* inane; *(personne)* inept ● **ineptie** [inɛpsi]

nf (de comportement, de film) inanity; *(remarque)* stupid remark

inépuisable [inepɥizabl] *adj* inexhaustible

inerte [inɛrt] *adj (matière)* inert; *(corps)* lifeless • **inertie** [inɛrsi] *nf Phys* inertia; *(manque d'énergie)* apathy

inespéré, -ée [inɛspere] *adj* unhoped-for

inestimable [inɛstimabl] *adj (objet d'art)* priceless; **d'une valeur i.** priceless

inévitable [inevitabl] *adj* inevitable, unavoidable

inexact, -acte [inɛgzakt] *adj (erroné)* inaccurate; *(calcul)* wrong • **inexactitude** *nf (caractère erroné, erreur)* inaccuracy; *(manque de ponctualité)* unpunctuality

inexcusable [inɛkskyzabl] *adj* inexcusable

inexistant, -ante [inɛgzistɑ̃, -ɑ̃t] *adj* non-existent

inexorable [inɛgzɔrabl] *adj* inexorable; *(volonté)* inflexible

inexpérience [inɛksperjɑ̃s] *nf* inexperience • **inexpérimenté, -ée** *adj* inexperienced

inexplicable [inɛksplikabl] *adj* inexplicable • **inexpliqué, -ée** *adj* unexplained

inexploré, -ée [inɛksplɔre] *adj* unexplored

inexpressif, -ive [inɛkspresif, -iv] *adj* expressionless

inexprimable [inɛksprimabl] *adj* inexpressible

in extremis [inɛkstremis] *adv* at the very last minute

inextricable [inɛkstrikabl] *adj* inextricable

infaillible [ɛ̃fajibl] *adj* infallible • **infaillibilité** *nf* infallibility

infaisable [ɛ̃fəzabl] *adj (travail)* impossible

infamant, -ante [ɛ̃famɑ̃, -ɑ̃t] *adj (accusation)* defamatory

infâme [ɛ̃fɑm] *adj (personne)* despicable; *(acte)* unspeakable; *(taudis)* squalid; *(aliment)* revolting • **infamie** *nf (caractère infâme)* infamy; *(remarque)* slanderous remark

infanterie [ɛ̃fɑ̃tri] *nf* infantry

infantile [ɛ̃fɑ̃til] *adj (maladie)* childhood; *Péj (comportement, personne)* infantile

infarctus [ɛ̃farktys] *nm Méd* heart attack

infatigable [ɛ̃fatigabl] *adj* tireless

infect, -ecte [ɛ̃fɛkt] *adj* foul

infecter [ɛ̃fɛkte] **1** *vt (atmosphère)* to contaminate; *Méd* to infect
2 s'infecter *vpr* to become infected • **in-**

fectieux, -ieuse *adj* infectious • **infection** *nf Méd* infection; *(odeur)* stench

inférieur, -ieure [ɛ̃ferjœr] **1** *adj (étagère, niveau)* bottom; *(étage, lèvre, membre)* lower; *(qualité, marchandises)* inferior; **i. à** *(qualité)* inferior to; *(quantité)* less than; **i. à la moyenne** below average; **à l'étage i.** on the floor below
2 *nmf* inferior • **infériorité** *nf* inferiority

infernal, -e, -aux, -ales [ɛ̃fernal, -o] *adj (de l'enfer)* & *Fig (chaleur, bruit)* infernal; **cet enfant est i.** this child's a little devil

infester [ɛ̃fɛste] *vt* to infest *(de* with) • **infesté, -ée** *adj* **i. de requins/de fourmis** shark-/ant-infested

infidèle [ɛ̃fidɛl] *adj* unfaithful *(à* to) • **fidélité** *nf* unfaithfulness; **une i.** *(acte)* an infidelity

infiltrer [ɛ̃filtre] **1** *vt (party)* to infiltrate
2 s'infiltrer *vpr (liquide)* to seep *(dans* into); *(lumière)* to filter in; *Fig* **s'i. dans** *(groupe, esprit)* to infiltrate • **infiltration** *nf (de liquide, d'espions)* infiltration

infime [ɛ̃fim] *adj* tiny

infini, -ie [ɛ̃fini] **1** *adj* infinite
2 *nm Math & Phot* infinity; *Phil* infinite; **à l'i.** *(discuter)* ad infinitum; *Math* to infinity • **infiniment** *adv* infinitely; **je regrette i.** I'm very sorry • **infinité** *nf* **une i. de** an infinite number of

infinitif [ɛ̃finitif] *nm Grammaire* infinitive

infirme [ɛ̃firm] **1** *adj* disabled
2 *nmf* disabled person • **infirmité** *nf* disability

infirmer [ɛ̃firme] *vt* to invalidate

infirmerie [ɛ̃firməri] *nf (d'école, de bateau)* sick room; *(de caserne, de prison)* infirmary • **infirmier** *nm* male nurse • **infirmière** *nf* nurse

inflammable [ɛ̃flamabl] *adj* (in)flammable

inflammation [ɛ̃flamɑsjɔ̃] *nf Méd* inflammation

inflation [ɛ̃flɑsjɔ̃] *nf Écon* inflation • **inflationniste** *adj Écon* inflationary

infléchir [ɛ̃fleʃir] *vt (courber)* to bend; *(politique)* to change the direction of • **inflexion** *nf (de courbe, de voix)* inflection; **i. de la tête** tilt of the head; *(pour saluer)* nod

inflexible [ɛ̃flɛksibl] *adj* inflexible

infliger [ɛ̃fliʒe] *vt* to inflict *(à* on); *(amende)* to impose *(à* on)

influence [ɛ̃flyɑ̃s] *nf* influence; **sous l'i. de la drogue** under the influence of drugs; **sous l'i. de la colère** in the grip of anger • **influençable** *adj* easily influenced •**influencer** *vt* to influence •**influent, -uente** *adj* influential •**influer** *vi* **i. sur qch** to influence sth

info [ɛ̃fo] *nf Fam* news item; **les infos** the news *(sing)*

informateur, -trice [ɛ̃fɔrmatœr, -tris] *nmf* informant

informaticien, -ienne [ɛ̃fɔrmatisjɛ̃, -jɛn] *nmf* computer scientist

information [ɛ̃fɔrmasjɔ̃] *nf* information; *(nouvelle)* piece of news; *Jur (enquête)* inquiry; *Ordinat* data, information; *Radio & TV* **les informations** the news *(sing)*

informatique [ɛ̃fɔrmatik] **1** *nf (science)* computer science; *(technique)* data processing
  2 *adj* **programme/matériel i.** computer program/hardware •**informatisation** *nf* computerization •**informatiser** *vt* to computerize

informe [ɛ̃fɔrm] *adj* shapeless

informer [ɛ̃fɔrme] **1** *vt* to inform (**de** of *or* about; **que** that)
  2 **s'informer** *vpr (se renseigner)* to inquire (**de** about; **si** if *or* whether)

inforoute [ɛ̃fɔrut] *nf* information superhighway

infortune [ɛ̃fɔrtyn] *nf* misfortune •**infortuné, -ée** *adj* unfortunate

infospectacle [ɛ̃fɔspɛktakl] *nf* infotainment

infoutu, -ue [ɛ̃futy] *adj Fam* downright incapable (**de** of)

infraction [ɛ̃fraksjɔ̃] *nf (à un règlement)* infringement; *(délit) Br* offence, *Am* offense; **être en i.** to be committing an offence

infranchissable [ɛ̃frɑ̃ʃisabl] *adj (mur, fleuve)* impassable; *Fig (difficulté)* insurmountable

infrarouge [ɛ̃fraruʒ] *adj* infrared

infrastructure [ɛ̃frastryktyr] *nf (de bâtiment)* substructure; *(équipements)* infrastructure

infroissable [ɛ̃frwasabl] *adj* crease-resistant

infructueux, -ueuse [ɛ̃fryktɥø, -ɥøz] *adj* fruitless

infuser [ɛ̃fyze] *vi (thé)* to brew; *(tisane)* to infuse; **laisser i. le thé** to leave the tea to brew •**infusion** *nf (tisane)* herb tea

ingénier [ɛ̃ʒenje] **s'ingénier** *vpr* to strive (**à faire** to do)

ingénieur [ɛ̃ʒenjœr] *nm* engineer •**ingénierie** [-iri] *nf* engineering; **i. mécanique** mechanical engineering

ingénieux, -ieuse [ɛ̃ʒenjø, -jøz] *adj* ingenious •**ingéniosité** *nf* ingenuity

ingénu, -ue [ɛ̃ʒeny] *adj* ingenuous

ingérer [ɛ̃ʒere] **s'ingérer** *vpr* to interfere (**dans** in) •**ingérence** *nf* interference (**dans** in)

ingrat, -ate [ɛ̃gra, -at] *adj (personne)* ungrateful (**envers** to); *(tâche)* thankless; *(sol)* barren; *(visage)* unattractive; **l'âge i.** the awkward age •**ingratitude** *nf* ingratitude

ingrédient [ɛ̃gredjɑ̃] *nm* ingredient

inguérissable [ɛ̃gerisabl] *adj* incurable

ingurgiter [ɛ̃gyrʒite] *vt* to gulp down

inhabitable [inabitabl] *adj* uninhabitable •**inhabité, -ée** *adj* uninhabited

> 🖉 Il faut noter que les adjectifs anglais **inhabitable** et **inhabited** sont des faux amis. Ils signifient respectivement **habitable** et **habité**.

inhabituel, -uelle [inabitɥɛl] *adj* unusual

inhalateur [inalatœr] *nm Méd* inhaler •**inhalation** *nf* inhalation; **faire des inhalations** to inhale

inhérent, -ente [inerɑ̃, -ɑ̃t] *adj* inherent (**à** in)

inhibé, -ée [inibe] *adj* inhibited •**inhibition** *nf* inhibition

inhospitalier, -ière [inɔspitalje, -jɛr] *adj* inhospitable

inhumain, -aine [inymɛ̃, -ɛn] *adj (cruel, terrible)* inhuman

inhumer [inyme] *vt* to bury •**inhumation** *nf* burial

inimaginable [inimaʒinabl] *adj* unimaginable

inimitable [inimitabl] *adj* inimitable

inimitié [inimitje] *nf* enmity

ininflammable [inɛ̃flamabl] *adj* non-flammable

inintelligent, -ente [inɛ̃teliʒɑ̃, -ɑ̃t] *adj* unintelligent

inintelligible [inɛ̃teliʒibl] *adj* unintelligible

inintéressant, -ante [inɛ̃teresɑ̃, -ɑ̃t] *adj* uninteresting

ininterrompu, -ue [inɛ̃terɔ̃py] *adj* continuous

inique [inik] *adj* iniquitous •**iniquité** *nf* iniquity

initial, -e, -iaux, -iales [inisjal, -jo] *adj* initial •**initiale** *nf* initial •**initialement** *adv* initially

initialiser [inisjalize] *vt Ordinat (disque)* to initialize; *(ordinateur)* to boot

initiative [inisjativ] *nf* initiative; **de ma propre i.** on my own initiative

initier [inisje] **1** *vt (former)* to introduce (**à** to); *(rituellement)* to initiate (**à** into)

2 s'initier *vpr* **s'i. à qch** to start learning sth • **initiation** *nf* initiation • **initié, -iée** *nmf* initiate; **les initiés** the initiated

injecter [ɛ̃ʒekte] *vt* to inject (**dans** into); **injecté de sang** bloodshot • **injection** *nf* injection

injoignable [ɛ̃ʒwaɲabl] *adj* **il est i.** he cannot be reached

injonction [ɛ̃ʒɔ̃ksjɔ̃] *nf* injunction

injure [ɛ̃ʒyr] *nf* insult; **injures** abuse, insults • **injurier** *vt* to insult, to abuse • **injurieux, -ieuse** *adj* abusive, insulting (**pour** to)

> ⚠ Il faut noter que les termes anglais **injury** et **to injure** sont des faux amis. Ils signifient le plus souvent **blessure** et **blesser**.

injuste [ɛ̃ʒyst] *adj (contraire à la justice)* unjust; *(non équitable)* unfair • **injustice** *nf* injustice

injustifiable [ɛ̃ʒystifjabl] *adj* unjustifiable • **injustifié, -iée** *adj* unjustified

inlassable [ɛ̃lɑsabl] *adj* untiring

inné, -ée [ine] *adj* innate, inborn

innocent, -ente [inɔsɑ̃, -ɑ̃t] **1** *adj* innocent (**de** of)

2 *nmf (non coupable)* innocent person; *(idiot)* simpleton • **innocemment** [-amɑ̃] *adv* innocently • **innocence** *nf* innocence; **en toute i.** in all innocence • **innocenter** *vt* **i. qn** to clear sb (**de** of)

innombrable [inɔ̃brabl] *adj* countless, innumerable; *(foule)* huge

innommable [inɔmabl] *adj (conduite, actes)* unspeakable; *(nourriture, odeur)* vile

innover [inɔve] *vi* to innovate • **innovateur, -trice 1** *adj* innovative **2** *nmf* innovator • **innovation** *nf* innovation

inoccupé, -ée [inɔkype] *adj* unoccupied

inoculer [inɔkyle] *vt* **i. qch à qn** to inoculate sb with sth; **i. qn contre qch** to inoculate sb against sth • **inoculation** *nf Méd* inoculation

inodore [inɔdɔr] *adj* odourless

inoffensif, -ive [inɔfɑ̃sif, -iv] *adj* harmless

inonder [inɔ̃de] *vt (lieu)* to flood; *Fig (marché)* to flood, to inundate (**de** with); **inondé de réclamations** inundated with complaints; **inondé de larmes** *(visage)* streaming with tears; **inondé de soleil** bathed in sunlight • **inondation** *nf* flood; *(action)* flooding

inopérable [inɔperabl] *adj* inoperable

inopérant, -ante [inɔperɑ̃, -ɑ̃t] *adj* ineffective

inopiné, -ée [inɔpine] *adj* unexpected

inopportun, -une [inɔpɔrtœ̃, -yn] *adj* inopportune

inoubliable [inublijabl] *adj* unforgettable

inouï, inouïe [inwi] *adj* incredible

Inox® [inɔks] *nm* stainless steel; **couteau en I.** stainless-steel knife • **inoxydable** *adj (couteau)* stainless-steel

inqualifiable [ɛ̃kalifjabl] *adj* unspeakable

inquiet, -iète [ɛ̃kjɛ, -jɛt] *adj* worried, anxious (**de** about)

inquiéter [ɛ̃kjete] **1** *vt (préoccuper)* to worry

2 s'inquiéter *vpr* to worry (**de** about); **s'i. pour qn** to worry about sb • **inquiétant, -ante** *adj* worrying

inquiétude [ɛ̃kjetyd] *nf* anxiety, worry; **avoir quelques inquiétudes** to feel a bit worried

inquisiteur, -trice [ɛ̃kizitœr, -tris] *adj (regard)* inquisitive

insaisissable [ɛ̃sezisabl] *adj* elusive

insalubre [ɛ̃salybr] *adj (climat, habitation)* insalubrious

insanités [ɛ̃sanite] *nfpl (idioties)* complete nonsense

insatiable [ɛ̃sasjabl] *adj* insatiable

insatisfait, -aite [ɛ̃satisfɛ, -ɛt] *adj (personne)* dissatisfied

inscription [ɛ̃skripsjɔ̃] *nf (action)* entering; *(immatriculation)* registration; *(sur écriteau, mur, tombe)* inscription

inscrire* [ɛ̃skrir] **1** *vt (renseignements, date)* to write down; *(dans un journal, sur un registre)* to enter; *(graver)* to inscribe; **i. qn à un club** to *Br* enrol *or Am* enroll sb in a club

2 s'inscrire *vpr* to put one's name down; *(à une activité) Br* to enrol, *Am* to enroll (**à** at); *(à l'université)* to register (**à** at); **s'i. à un club** to join a club; **s'i. à un examen** to register for an exam; **s'i. dans le cadre de** to come within the framework of; **s'i. en faux contre qch** to deny sth absolutely

insecte [ɛ̃sɛkt] *nm* insect • **insecticide** *nm & adj* insecticide

insécurité [ɛ̃sekyrite] *nf* insecurity

INSEE [inse] *(abrév* **Institut national de la statistique et des études économiques)** *nm* = French national institute of statistics and economic studies

insémination [ɛ̃seminasjɔ̃] *nf Méd* **i. artificielle** artificial insemination

insensé, -ée [ɛ̃sɑ̃se] *adj (projet, idée)* crazy; *(espoir)* wild

insensible [ɛ̃sɑ̃sibl] *adj (indifférent)* insensitive (**à** to); *(imperceptible)* imperceptible ●**insensibilité** *nf* insensitivity ●**insensiblement** [-əmɑ̃] *adv* imperceptibly

inséparable [ɛ̃separabl] *adj* inseparable (**de** from)

insérer [ɛ̃sere] *vt* to insert (**dans** in) ●**insertion** [ɛ̃sɛrsjɔ̃] *nf* insertion; **i. professionnelle** integration into the job market

insidieux, -ieuse [ɛ̃sidjø, -jøz] *adj* insidious

insigne [ɛ̃siɲ] *nm* badge; **les insignes de la royauté** the insignia of royalty

insignifiant, -iante [ɛ̃siɲifjɑ̃, -jɑ̃t] *adj* insignificant ●**insignifiance** *nf* insignificance

insinuer [ɛ̃sinɥe] **1** *vt Péj* to insinuate (**que** that)

2 s'insinuer *vpr (froid)* to creep (**dans** into); *(personne)* to worm one's way (**dans** into); **le doute qui s'insinue dans mon esprit** the doubt that is creeping into my mind ●**insinuation** *nf* insinuation

insipide [ɛ̃sipid] *adj* insipid

insister [ɛ̃siste] *vi* to insist (**pour faire** on doing); *Fam (persévérer)* to persevere; **i. sur qch** to stress sth; **i. pour que...** (+ *subjunctive*) to insist that...; **il a beaucoup insisté** he was very insistent ●**insistance** *nf* insistence ●**insistant, -ante** *adj* insistent

insolation [ɛ̃sɔlasjɔ̃] *nf Méd* sunstroke

insolent, -ente [ɛ̃sɔlɑ̃, -ɑ̃t] *adj (impoli)* insolent; *(luxe)* unashamed ●**insolence** *nf* insolence

insolite [ɛ̃sɔlit] *adj* unusual, strange

insoluble [ɛ̃sɔlybl] *adj* insoluble

insolvable [ɛ̃sɔlvabl] *adj Fin* insolvent

insomnie [ɛ̃sɔmni] *nf* insomnia; **avoir des insomnies** to have insomnia; **nuit d'i.** sleepless night ●**insomniaque** *nmf* insomniac

insondable [ɛ̃sɔ̃dabl] *adj* unfathomable

insonoriser [ɛ̃sɔnɔrize] *vt* to soundproof ●**insonorisation** *nf* soundproofing

insouciant, -iante [ɛ̃susjɑ̃, -jɑ̃t] *adj* carefree; **i. de** unconcerned about ●**insouciance** *nf* carefree attitude

insoumis, -ise [ɛ̃sumi, -iz] *adj (personne)* rebellious; *Mil* absentee

insoupçonnable [ɛ̃supsɔnabl] *adj* beyond suspicion ●**insoupçonné, -ée** *adj* unsuspected

insoutenable [ɛ̃sutnabl] *adj (spectacle, odeur)* unbearable; *(théorie)* untenable

inspecter [ɛ̃spɛkte] *vt* to inspect ●**inspecteur, -trice** *nmf* inspector ●**inspection** *nf* inspection

inspirer [ɛ̃spire] **1** *vt* to inspire; **i. qch à qn** to inspire sb with sth; **i. confiance à qn** to inspire confidence in sb

2 *vi* to breathe in

3 s'inspirer *vpr* **s'i. de qn/qch** to take one's inspiration from sb/sth ●**inspiration** *nf (pour créer, idée)* inspiration; *(d'air)* breathing in ●**inspiré, -ée** *adj* inspired; **être bien i. de faire qch** to have the good idea to do sth

instable [ɛ̃stabl] *adj* unstable; *(temps)* changeable ●**instabilité** *nf* instability; *(de temps)* changeability

installer [ɛ̃stale] **1** *vt (appareil, meuble)* to install, to put in; *(étagère)* to put up; *(cuisine)* to fit out; **i. qn** *(dans une fonction, dans un logement)* to install sb (**dans** in); **i. qn dans un fauteuil** to settle sb down in an armchair

2 s'installer *vpr (s'asseoir)* to settle down; *(dans un bureau)* to install oneself; *(médecin)* to set oneself up; **s'i. à la campagne** to settle in the country ●**installateur** *nm* fitter ●**installation** *nf (de machine)* installation; *(de cuisine)* fitting out; *(de rideaux)* putting in; *(emménagement)* move; **installations** *(appareils)* fittings; *(bâtiments)* facilities

instamment [ɛ̃stamɑ̃] *adv* earnestly

instance [ɛ̃stɑ̃s] *nf (insistance)* plea; *(autorité)* authority; *Jur* proceedings; **en i. de divorce** waiting for a divorce; **courrier en i.** mail waiting to go out

instant [ɛ̃stɑ̃] *nm* moment, instant; **à l'i.** a moment ago; **à l'i. (même) où...** just as...; **pour l'i.** for the moment; **dès l'i. que...** from the moment that...; *(puisque)* seeing that... ●**instantané, -ée 1** *adj* instantaneous; **café i.** instant coffee **2** *nm (photo)* snapshot

instar [ɛ̃star] *nm* **à l'i. de qn** after the fashion of sb

instaurer [ɛ̃stɔre] *vt* to establish

instigateur, -trice [ɛ̃stigatœr, -tris] *nmf* instigator ●**instigation** *nf* instigation

instinct [ɛ̃stɛ̃] *nm* instinct; **d'i.** by instinct ●**instinctif, -ive** *adj* instinctive

instituer [ɛ̃stitɥe] *vt* to establish

institut [ɛ̃stity] *nm* institute; **i. de beauté** beauty salon

instituteur, -trice [ɛ̃stitytœr, -tris] *nmf Br* primary *or Am* elementary school teacher

institution [ɛ̃stitysjɔ̃] *nf (création)* establishment; *(coutume)* institution; *(école)* private school; *Pol* **institutions** institutions ●**institutionnel, -elle** *adj* institutional

instructif, -ive [ɛ̃stryktif, -iv] *adj* in-

structive
instruction [ɛ̃stryksjɔ̃] *nf (éducation)*
education; *Mil* training; *Jur* preliminary
investigation; **instructions** instructions; **i.**
civique civics *(sing)* •**instructeur** *nm* instructor
instruire* [ɛ̃strɥir] **1** *vt* to teach, to educate; *Mil* to train; *Jur* to investigate; **i. qn**
de qch to inform sb of sth
2 s'instruire *vpr* to educate oneself; **s'i.**
de to find out about •**instruit, -uite** *adj*
educated
instrument [ɛ̃strymɑ̃] *nm* instrument; **i.**
à vent wind instrument; **instruments de**
bord *(d'avion)* instruments •**instrumen-**
tal, -e, -aux, -ales *adj Mus* instrumental
•**instrumentiste** *nmf Mus* instrumentalist
insu [ɛ̃sy] **à l'insu de** *prép* without the
knowledge of; **à mon/son i.** *(sans m'en/*
s'en apercevoir) without being aware of it
insuccès [ɛ̃syksɛ] *nm* failure
insuffisant, -ante [ɛ̃syfizɑ̃, -ɑ̃t] *adj (en*
quantité) insufficient; *(en qualité)* inadequate •**insuffisance** *nf (manque)* in-
sufficiency; *(de moyens)* inadequacy;
insuffisances *(faiblesses)* shortcomings
insulaire [ɛ̃sylɛr] **1** *adj* insular
2 *nmf* islander
insuline [ɛ̃sylin] *nf Méd* insulin
insulte [ɛ̃sylt] *nf* insult (**à** to) •**insulter** *vt*
to insult
insupportable [ɛ̃sypɔrtabl] *adj* unbearable
insurger [ɛ̃syrʒe] **s'insurger** *vpr* to rise
up (**contre** against) •**insurgé, -ée** *nmf &*
adj insurgent •**insurrection** *nf* insurrection, uprising
insurmontable [ɛ̃syrmɔ̃tabl] *adj* insurmountable
intact, -acte [ɛ̃takt] *adj* intact
intangible [ɛ̃tɑ̃ʒibl] *adj (loi, institution)*
sacred
intarissable [ɛ̃tarisabl] *adj* inexhaustible
intégral, -e, -aux, -ales [ɛ̃tegral, -o] *adj*
(paiement) full; *(édition)* unabridged;
casque i. full-face crash helmet; **version**
intégrale *(de film)* uncut version •**inté-**
gralement *adv* in full, fully •**intégralité** *nf*
whole (**de** of); **dans son i.** in full
intègre [ɛ̃tɛgr] *adj* upright, honest •**in-**
tégrité *nf* integrity
intégrer [ɛ̃tegre] **1** *vt* to integrate (**dans**
in); *(école)* to get into
2 s'intégrer *vpr* to become integrated
•**intégrante** *adj f* **faire partie i. de qch** to
be an integral part of sth •**intégration** *nf*
(au sein d'un groupe) integration
intégrisme [ɛ̃tegrism] *nm* fundamental-
ism

intellectuel, -uelle [ɛ̃telɛktɥɛl] *adj &*
nmf intellectual
intelligent, -ente [ɛ̃teliʒɑ̃, -ɑ̃t] *adj* intelligent, clever •**intelligemment** [-amɑ̃]
adv intelligently •**intelligence** *nf (faculté)*
intelligence; **avoir l'i. de faire qch** to have
the intelligence to do sth; **vivre en bonne**
i. avec qn to be on good terms with sb;
Ordinat **i. artificielle** artificial intelligence
intelligentsia [inteligɛntsja] *nf* intelligentsia
intelligible [ɛ̃teliʒibl] *adj* intelligible
•**intelligibilité** *nf* intelligibility
intempéries [ɛ̃tɑ̃peri] *nfpl* **les i.** the bad
weather
intempestif, -ive [ɛ̃tɑ̃pɛstif, -iv] *adj* untimely
intenable [ɛ̃tnabl] *adj (position)* untenable; *Fam (enfant)* uncontrollable
intendant, -ante [ɛ̃tɑ̃dɑ̃, -ɑ̃t] *nmf Scol*
bursar •**intendance** *nf Scol* bursary
intense [ɛ̃tɑ̃s] *adj* intense; *(circulation)*
heavy •**intensément** *adv* intensely •**in-**
tensif, -ive *adj* intensive •**intensité** *nf*
intensity
intensifier [ɛ̃tɑ̃sifje] *vt*, **s'intensifier** *vpr*
to intensify
intenter [ɛ̃tɑ̃te] *vt Jur* **i. un procès à qn** to
institute proceedings against sb
intention [ɛ̃tɑ̃sjɔ̃] *nf* intention; *Jur* intent; **avoir l'i. de faire qch** to intend to do
sth; **à l'i. de qn** for sb •**intentionné, -ée**
adj **bien i.** well-intentioned; **mal i.** ill-
intentioned •**intentionnel, -elle** *adj* intentional •**intentionnellement** *adv* intentionally
interactif, -ive [ɛ̃tɛraktif, -iv] *adj Ordi-*
nat interactive
interaction [ɛ̃tɛraksjɔ̃] *nf* interaction
intercalaire [ɛ̃tɛrkalɛr] *adj & nm* **(feuil-**
let) i. *(de classeur)* divider
intercaler [ɛ̃tɛrkale] *vt* to insert
intercéder [ɛ̃tɛrsede] *vt* to intercede (**au-**
près de with; **en faveur de** on behalf of)
intercepter [ɛ̃tɛrsɛpte] *vt* to intercept
•**interception** *nf* interception
interchangeable [ɛ̃tɛrʃɑ̃ʒabl] *adj* interchangeable
interclasse [ɛ̃tɛrklɑs] *nm Scol* = short
break between classes
intercontinental, -e, -aux, -ales
[ɛ̃tɛrkɔ̃tinɑ̃tal, -o] *adj* intercontinental
interdépendant, -ante [ɛ̃tɛrdepɑ̃dɑ̃,
-ɑ̃t] *adj* interdependent
interdire* [ɛ̃tɛrdir] *vt* to forbid (**qch à qn**
sb sth); *(film, meeting)* to ban; **i. à qn de**

faire qch *(médecin, père)* to forbid sb to do sth; *(santé)* to prevent sb from doing sth •**interdiction** *nf* ban (**de** on); '**i. de fumer**' 'no smoking' •**interdit, -ite** *adj* (**a**) forbidden; **il est i. de...** it is forbidden to...; '**stationnement i.**' 'no parking' (**b**) *(étonné)* disconcerted

intéresser [ɛ̃terese] **1** *vt (captiver)* to interest; *(concerner)* to concern **2** **s'intéresser** *vpr* **s'i.** **à qn/qch** to be interested in sb/sth •**intéressant, -ante 1** *adj (captivant)* interesting; *(prix)* attractive **2** *nmf Péj* **faire l'i.** to show off •**intéressé, -ée 1** *adj (avide)* self-interested; *(motif)* selfish; *(concerné)* concerned **2** *nmf* **l'i.** the person concerned

intérêt [ɛ̃terɛ] *nm* interest; *Fin* **intérêts** interest; **tu as i. à le faire** you'd do well to do it; **sans i.** *(personne, film)* uninteresting

interface [ɛ̃terfas] *nf Ordinat* interface

intérieur, -ieure [ɛ̃terjœr] **1** *adj (escalier, paroi)* interior; *(cour, vie)* inner; *(poche)* inside; *(partie)* internal; *(vol)* internal, domestic; *(mer)* inland **2** *nm (de boîte, de maison)* inside (**de** of); *(de pays)* interior; *(maison)* home; **à l'i.** (**de**) inside; **à l'i. de nos frontières** within the country; **d'i.** *(vêtement, jeux)* indoor; **femme d'i.** home-loving woman •**intérieurement** *adv* inwardly

intérim [ɛ̃terim] *nm (travail temporaire)* temporary work; **assurer l'i.** to stand in (**de** for); **président par i.** acting president •**intérimaire 1** *adj (fonction, employé)* temporary **2** *nmf (travailleur)* temporary worker; *(secrétaire)* temp

intérioriser [ɛ̃terjɔrize] *vt* to internalize

interligne [ɛ̃terliɲ] *nm* line spacing

interlocuteur, -trice [ɛ̃terlɔkytœr, -tris] *nmf (de conversation)* speaker; *(de négociation)* discussion partner; **mon i.** the person I am/was speaking to

interloqué, -ée [ɛ̃terlɔke] *adj* dumbfounded

interlude [ɛ̃terlyd] *nm* interlude

intermède [ɛ̃termɛd] *nm* interlude

intermédiaire [ɛ̃termedjɛr] **1** *adj* intermediate **2** *nmf* intermediary; *Com* middleman; **par l'i. de** through; **sans i.** directly

interminable [ɛ̃terminabl] *adj* interminable

intermittent, -ente [ɛ̃termitã, -ãt] *adj* intermittent •**intermittence** *nf* **par i.** intermittently

internat [ɛ̃terna] *nm (école)* boarding school; *(concours de médecine)* = entrance examination for *Br* a housemanship *or Am* an internship •**interne 1** *adj (douleur)* internal; *(oreille)* inner **2** *nmf (élève)* boarder; **i. des hôpitaux** *Br* house doctor, *Am* intern

international, -e, -aux, -ales [ɛ̃ternasjɔnal, -o] **1** *adj* international **2** *nm (joueur de football)* international

interner [ɛ̃terne] *vt (prisonnier)* to intern; *(aliéné)* to commit •**internement** [-əmã] *nm (emprisonnement)* internment; *(d'aliéné)* confinement

Internet [ɛ̃termɛt] *nm* Internet; **sur I.** on the Internet •**internaute** *nmf* Internet surfer

interpeller [ɛ̃terpəle] *vt (appeler)* to call out to; *(dans une réunion)* to question; **i. qn** *(police)* to take sb in for questioning; **ce roman m'a interpellé** I can really relate to that novel •**interpellation** *nf* sharp address; *(dans une réunion)* question; **la police a procédé à plusieurs interpellations** the police took several people in for questioning

Interphone® [ɛ̃terfɔn] *nm (de bureau)* intercom; *(d'immeuble)* Entryphone®

interplanétaire [ɛ̃terplanetɛr] *adj* interplanetary

interpoler [ɛ̃terpɔle] *vt* to interpolate

interposer [ɛ̃terpoze] **s'interposer** *vpr (intervenir)* to intervene (**dans** in); **par personne interposée** through an intermediary

interprète [ɛ̃terprɛt] *nmf (traducteur)* interpreter; *(chanteur)* singer; *(musicien, acteur)* performer; *(porte-parole)* spokesman, *f* spokeswoman •**interprétariat** *nm* interpreting •**interprétation** *nf (de texte, de rôle, de rêve)* interpretation; *(traduction)* interpreting •**interpréter** *vt (texte, rôle, musique, rêve)* to interpret; *(chanter)* to sing; **mal i. les paroles de qn** to misinterpret sb's words

interroger [ɛ̃terɔʒe] *vt* to question; *(élève)* to test; *Ordinat (banque de données)* to query •**interrogateur, -trice** *adj (air)* questioning •**interrogatif, -ive** *adj & nm Grammaire* interrogative •**interrogation** *nf (question)* question; *(de prisonnier)* questioning; *Scol* **i. écrite/orale** written/oral test•**interrogatoire** *nm* interrogation

interrompre* [ɛ̃terɔ̃pr] **1** *vt* to interrupt **2** **s'interrompre** *vpr* to break off •**interrupteur** *nm* switch •**interruption** *nf* interruption; *(de négociations)* breaking off; **sans i.** continuously; **i. volontaire de grossesse** termination of pregnancy

intersection [ɛ̃tersɛksjɔ̃] *nf* intersection

interstice [ɛ̃tɛrstis] *nm* crack, chink
intervalle [ɛ̃tɛrval] *nm (dans l'espace)*
gap, space; *(dans le temps)* interval; **dans
l'i.** *(entretemps)* in the meantime; **par intervalles** (every) now and then, at intervals
intervenir* [ɛ̃tɛrvənir] *vi (agir, prendre la
parole)* to intervene; *(survenir)* to occur; **i.
auprès de qn** to intercede with sb; **être
intervenu** *(accord)* to be reached ● **intervention** *nf* intervention; *(discours)*
speech; **i. chirurgicale** operation
intervertir [ɛ̃tɛrvɛrtir] *vt (l'ordre de qch)*
to invert; *(objets)* to switch round ● **interversion** *nf* inversion
interview [ɛ̃tɛrvju] *nm ou f* interview
● **interviewer** [-vjuve] *vt* to interview
intestin [ɛ̃tɛstɛ̃] *nm* intestine ● **intestinal,
-e, -aux, -ales** *adj* intestinal
intime [ɛ̃tim] **1** *adj* intimate; *(ami)* close;
(toilette) personal; *(cérémonie)* quiet
   2 *nmf* close friend ● **intimement** [-əmɑ̃]
adv intimately; **i. liés** *(problèmes)* closely
linked ● **intimité** *nf (familiarité)* intimacy;
(vie privée) privacy; **dans l'i.** in private
intimider [ɛ̃timide] *vt* to intimidate ● **intimidation** *nf* intimidation
intituler [ɛ̃tityle] **1** *vt* to give a title to
   2 s'intituler *vpr* to be entitled
intolérable [ɛ̃tɔlerabl] *adj* intolerable
● **intolérance** *nf* intolerance ● **intolérant,
-ante** *adj* intolerant
intonation [ɛ̃tɔnasjɔ̃] *nf Ling* intonation
intoxiquer [ɛ̃tɔksike] **1** *vt (empoisonner)*
to poison
   2 s'intoxiquer *vpr* to poison oneself ● **intoxication** *nf (empoisonnement)* poisoning; **i. alimentaire** food poisoning
intraduisible [ɛ̃tradɥizibl] *adj* untranslatable
intraitable [ɛ̃trɛtabl] *adj* uncompromising
intransigeant, -ante [ɛ̃trɑ̃ziʒɑ̃, -ɑ̃t] *adj*
intransigent ● **intransigeance** *nf* intransigence
intransitif, -ive [ɛ̃trɑ̃zitif, -iv] *adj & nm
Grammaire* intransitive
intraveineux, -euse [ɛ̃travɛnø, -øz]
Méd **1** *adj* intravenous
   2 *nf* **intraveineuse** intravenous injection
intrépide [ɛ̃trepid] *adj* fearless, intrepid
● **intrépidité** *nf* fearlessness
intrigue [ɛ̃trig] *nf* intrigue; *(de film, roman)* plot ● **intrigant, -ante** *nmf* schemer
● **intriguer 1** *vt* **i. qn** to intrigue sb **2** *vi* to
scheme
intrinsèque [ɛ̃trɛ̃sɛk] *adj* intrinsic
introduire* [ɛ̃trɔdɥir] **1** *vt (insérer)* to

insert (**dans** into); *(marchandises)* to
bring in; *(réforme, mode)* to introduce;
(visiteur) to show in; **Com i. sur le marché**
to launch onto the market
   2 s'introduire *vpr* **s'i. dans une maison** to
get into a house ● **introduction** *nf (texte,
action)* introduction
introspectif, -ive [ɛ̃trɔspɛktif, -iv] *adj*
introspective ● **introspection** *nf* introspection
introuvable [ɛ̃truvabl] *adj (produit)*
unobtainable; *(personne)* nowhere to be
found
introverti, -ie [ɛ̃trɔvɛrti] *nmf* introvert
intrus, -use [ɛ̃try, -yz] *nmf* intruder ● **intrusion** *nf* intrusion (**dans** into)
intuition [ɛ̃tɥisjɔ̃] *nf* intuition ● **intuitif,
-ive** *adj* intuitive
inuit [inɥit] **1** *adj inv* Inuit
   2 *nmf inv* **I.** Inuit
inusable [inyzabl] *adj* hard-wearing
inusité, -ée [inyzite] *adj (mot, forme)*
uncommon
inutile [inytil] *adj (qui ne sert à rien)*
useless; *(précaution, bagage)* unnecessary; **c'est i. de crier** it's pointless shouting; **i. de dire que...** needless to say that...
● **inutilement** *adv* needlessly ● **inutilité** *nf*
uselessness
inutilisable [inytilizabl] *adj* unusable
● **inutilisé, -ée** *adj* unused
invaincu, -ue [ɛ̃vɛ̃ky] *adj Sport* unbeaten
invalide [ɛ̃valid] **1** *adj* disabled
   2 *nmf* disabled person; **i. de guerre** disabled ex-serviceman
invalider [ɛ̃valide] *vt* to invalidate
invariable [ɛ̃varjabl] *adj* invariable ● **invariablement** [-əmɑ̃] *adv* invariably
invasion [ɛ̃vazjɔ̃] *nf* invasion
invective [ɛ̃vɛktiv] *nf* invective ● **invectiver** *vt* to hurl abuse at
invendable [ɛ̃vɑ̃dabl] *adj* unsellable
● **invendu, -ue 1** *adj* unsold **2** *nmpl* **inven-
dus** unsold articles; *(journaux)* unsold
copies
inventaire [ɛ̃vɑ̃tɛr] *nm Com (liste)* inventory; *Fig (étude)* survey; *Com* **faire l'i.** to
do the stocktaking (**de** of)
inventer [ɛ̃vɑ̃te] *vt (créer)* to invent;
(concept) to think up; *(histoire, excuse)* to
make up ● **inventeur, -trice** *nmf* inventor
● **inventif, -ive** *adj* inventive ● **invention** *nf*
invention
inverse [ɛ̃vɛrs] **1** *adj (sens)* opposite;
(ordre) reverse; *Math* inverse
   2 *nm* **l'i.** the reverse, the opposite ● **inversement** [-əmɑ̃] *adv* conversely ● **in-**

verser *vt (ordre)* to reverse • **inversion** *nf* inversion

investigation [ɛ̃vɛstigasjɔ̃] *nf* investigation • **investigateur, -trice** *nmf* investigator

investir [ɛ̃vɛstir] **1** *vt (capitaux)* to invest (**dans** in); *(édifice, ville)* to besiege; **i. qn d'une mission** to entrust sb with a mission **2** *vi* to invest (**dans** in) • **investissement** *nm Fin* investment • **investiture** *nf Pol* nomination

invétéré, -ée [ɛ̃vetere] *adj* inveterate

invincible [ɛ̃vɛ̃sibl] *adj* invincible

invisible [ɛ̃vizibl] *adj* invisible

inviter [ɛ̃vite] *vt* to invite; **i. qn à faire qch** *(prier)* to request sb to do sth; *(inciter)* to urge sb to do sth; **i. qn à dîner** to invite sb to dinner • **invitation** *nf* invitation • **invité, -ée** *nmf* guest

invivable [ɛ̃vivabl] *adj* unbearable; *Fam (personne)* insufferable

involontaire [ɛ̃vɔlɔ̃tɛr] *adj (geste)* involuntary; *(témoin)* unwilling • **involontairement** *adv* involuntarily

invoquer [ɛ̃vɔke] *vt (argument)* to put forward; *(loi, texte)* to refer to; *(divinité)* to invoke • **invocation** *nf* invocation (**à** to)

invraisemblable [ɛ̃vrɛsɑ̃blabl] *adj (extraordinaire)* incredible; *(alibi)* implausible • **invraisemblance** *nf (improbabilité)* unlikelihood; *(d'alibi)* implausibility; **invraisemblances** implausibilities

invulnérable [ɛ̃vylnerabl] *adj* invulnerable

iode [jɔd] *nm* **teinture d'i.** *(antiseptique)* iodine

ira, irait *etc* [ira, irɛ] *voir* **aller¹**

Irak [irak] *nm* **l'I.** Iraq • **irakien, -ienne 1** *adj* Iraqi **2** *nmf* **I., Irakienne** Iraqi

Iran [irɑ̃] *nm* **l'I.** Iran • **iranien, -ienne 1** *adj* Iranian **2** *nmf* **I., Iranienne** Iranian

irascible [irasibl] *adj* irascible

iris [iris] *nm (plante)* & *Anat* iris

Irlande [irlɑ̃d] *nf* **l'I.** Ireland; **l'I. du Nord** Northern Ireland • **irlandais, -aise 1** *adj* Irish **2** *nmf* **I.** Irishman; **Irlandaise** Irishwoman; **les I.** the Irish **3** *nm (langue)* Irish

ironie [irɔni] *nf* irony • **ironique** *adj* ironic(al)

iront [irɔ̃] *voir* **aller¹**

irradier [iradje] *vt* to irradiate

irraisonné, -ée [irɛzɔne] *adj* irrational

irrationnel, -elle [irasjɔnɛl] *adj* irrational

irrattrapable [iratrapabl] *adj (retard)* that cannot be made up

irréalisable [irealizabl] *adj (projet)* impracticable

irréaliste [irealist] *adj* unrealistic

irrecevable [irəsəvabl] *adj Jur (preuve)* inadmissible

irrécupérable [irekyperabl] *adj (objet)* beyond repair; *(personne)* irredeemable

irrécusable [irekyzabl] *adj (preuve)* indisputable; *Jur (témoignage)* unimpeachable

irréductible [iredyktibl] **1** *adj (ennemi)* implacable **2** *nm* die-hard

irréel, -éelle [ireɛl] *adj* unreal

irréfléchi, -ie [irefleʃi] *adj* rash

irréfutable [irefytabl] *adj* irrefutable

irrégulier, -ière [iregylje, -jɛr] *adj (rythme, respiration, verbe, procédure)* irregular; *(sol)* uneven; *(résultats)* inconsistent; **être en situation irrégulière** *(voyageur)* not to hold a valid ticket; *(étranger)* not to have one's residence papers in order • **irrégularité** *nf* irregularity; *(de sol)* unevenness

irrémédiable [iremedjabl] *adj* irreparable

irremplaçable [irɑ̃plasabl] *adj* irreplaceable

irréparable [ireparabl] *adj (véhicule)* beyond repair; *(tort, perte)* irreparable

irrépressible [irepresibl] *adj* irrepressible

irréprochable [ireprɔʃabl] *adj* irreproachable

irrésistible [irezistibl] *adj (personne, charme)* irresistible

irrésolu, -ue [irezɔly] *adj (personne)* indecisive; *(problème)* unresolved

irrespect [irɛspɛ] *nm* disrespect • **irrespectueux, -ueuse** *adj* disrespectful

irrespirable [irɛspirabl] *adj (air)* unbreathable; *Fig (atmosphère)* unbearable

irresponsable [irɛspɔ̃sabl] *adj (personne)* irresponsible

irrévérencieux, -ieuse [ireverɑ̃sjø, -jøz] *adj* irreverent

irréversible [irevɛrsibl] *adj* irreversible

irrévocable [irevɔkabl] *adj* irrevocable

irriguer [irige] *vt* to irrigate • **irrigation** *nf* irrigation

irriter [irite] **1** *vt* to irritate **2 s'irriter** *vpr (s'énerver)* to get irritated (**de/contre** with/at); *(s'enflammer)* to become irritated • **irritable** *adj* irritable • **irritant, -ante** *adj (personne, comportement)* irritating; *(produit)* irritant • **irritation** *nf (colère)* & *Méd* irritation

irruption [irypsjɔ̃] *nf* **faire i. dans** to burst into

Islam [islam] *nm* **l'I.** Islam • **islamique** *adj* Islamic

Islande [islɑ̃d] *nf* **l'I.** Iceland • **islandais, -aise 1** *adj* Icelandic **2** *nmf* **I., Islandaise**

Icelander
isocèle [izɔsɛl] *adj* **triangle i.** isosceles triangle
isoler [izɔle] **1** *vt* to isolate (**de** from); *(du froid) & Él* to insulate
    2 s'isoler *vpr* to isolate oneself • **isolant, -ante 1** *adj* insulating **2** *nm* insulating material • **isolation** *nf* insulation • **isolé, -ée** *adj (personne, endroit, maison)* isolated; *(du froid)* insulated; **i. de** cut off *or* isolated from • **isolement** *nm (de personne)* isolation; **i. thermique** thermal insulation • **isolément** *adv (agir)* in isolation; *(interroger des gens)* individually
isoloir [izɔlwar] *nm Br* polling *or Am* voting booth
Israël [israel] *nm* Israel • **israélien, -ienne 1** *adj* Israeli **2** *nmf* **I., Israélienne** Israeli • **israélite 1** *adj* Jewish **2** *nmf* Jew
issu, -ue [isy] *adj* **être i. de** to come from
issue [isy] *nf (sortie)* exit; *Fig (solution)* way out; *(résultat)* outcome; *Fig* **situation sans i.** dead end; **à l'i. de** at the end of; **i. de secours** emergency exit

> 🖉 Il faut noter que le nom anglais **issue** est un faux ami. Il signifie le plus souvent **problème** ou **question**.

isthme [ism] *nm* isthmus
Italie [itali] *nf* **l'I.** Italy • **italien, -ienne 1** *adj* Italian **2** *nmf* **I., Italienne** Italian **3** *nm (langue)* Italian
italique [italik] **1** *adj (lettre)* italic **2** *nm* italics; **en i.** in italics
itinéraire [itinerɛr] *nm* route, itinerary; **i. bis** = alternative route recommended when roads are highly congested
itinérant, -ante [itinerɑ̃, -ɑ̃t] *adj Br* travelling, *Am* traveling
IUFM [iyɛfɛm] (*abrév* **Institut universitaire de formation des maîtres**) *nm* ≃ teacher training college
IUT [iyte] (*abrév* **institut universitaire de technologie**) *nm* = vocational higher education college
IVG [iveʒe] (*abrév* **interruption volontaire de grossesse**) *nf* (voluntary) abortion
ivoire [ivwar] *nm* ivory; **statuette en i.** *ou* **d'i.** ivory statuette
ivre [ivr] *adj* drunk (**de** with); *Fig* **i. de joie** wild with joy; **i. de bonheur** wildly happy • **ivresse** *nf* drunkenness; **en état d'i.** under the influence of drink • **ivrogne** *nmf* drunk(ard)

J

J, j [ʒi] *nm inv* J, j; **le jour J.** D-day
j' [ʒ] *voir* **je**
jacasser [ʒakase] *vi (personne, pie)* to chatter
jachère [ʒaʃɛr] **en jachère** *adv (champ)* fallow; **être en j.** to lie fallow
jacinthe [ʒasɛ̃t] *nf* hyacinth
Jacuzzi® [ʒakuzi] *nm* Jacuzzi®
jade [ʒad] *nm (pierre)* jade
jadis [ʒadis] *adv Littéraire* in times past
jaguar [ʒagwar] *nm* jaguar
jaillir [ʒajir] *vi (liquide)* to gush out; *(étincelles)* to shoot out; *(lumière)* to flash; *(cri)* to burst out
jais [ʒɛ] *nm* **(noir) de j.** jet-black
jalon [ʒalɔ̃] *nm* ranging pole; *Fig* **poser les jalons** to prepare the way (**de** for) • **jalonner** *vt (marquer)* to mark out; *(border)* to line
jaloux, -ouse [ʒalu, -uz] *adj* jealous (**de** of) • **jalouser** *vt* to envy • **jalousie** *nf (sentiment)* jealousy; *(store)* Venetian blind
Jamaïque [ʒamaik] *nf* **la J.** Jamaica
jamais [ʒamɛ] *adv* (**a**) *(négatif)* never; **elle ne sort j.** she never goes out; **sans j. sortir** without ever going out; **j. de la vie!** (absolutely) never! (**b**) *(positif)* ever; **à (tout) j.** for ever; **si j.** if ever; **le film le plus drôle que j'aie j. vu** the funniest film I have ever seen
jambe [ʒɑ̃b] *nf* leg; **à toutes jambes** as fast as one can; *Fig* **prendre ses jambes à son cou** to take to one's heels; **être dans les jambes de qn** to be under sb's feet; *Fam* **faire qch par-dessus la j.** to do sth any old how; *Fam* **ça me fait une belle j.!** a fat lot of good that does me!
jambon [ʒɑ̃bɔ̃] *nm* ham • **jambonneau, -x** *nm* knuckle of ham
jante [ʒɑ̃t] *nf* rim
janvier [ʒɑ̃vje] *nm* January
Japon [ʒapɔ̃] *nm* **le J.** Japan • **japonais, -aise 1** *adj* Japanese **2** *nmf* **J., Japonaise** Japanese *inv*; **les J.** the Japanese **3** *nm (langue)* Japanese
japper [ʒape] *vi (chien)* to yap, to yelp
jaquette [ʒakɛt] *nf (d'homme)* morning coat; *(de livre)* jacket; *Fam* **se faire la j.** to buzz off, *Br* to skip off

jardin [ʒardɛ̃] *nm* garden; **j. d'enfants** kindergarten; **j. public** gardens • **jardinage** *nm* gardening • **jardiner** *vi* to do some gardening • **jardinerie** *nf* garden centre • **jardinier** *nm* gardener • **jardinière** *nf (caisse à fleurs)* window box; **j. de légumes** mixed vegetables
jargon [ʒargɔ̃] *nm* jargon
jarret [ʒarɛ] *nm* back of the knee
jarretelle [ʒartɛl] *nf Br* suspender, *Am* garter • **jarretière** *nf* garter
jaser [ʒaze] *vi (médire)* to gossip
jasmin [ʒasmɛ̃] *nm* jasmine; **thé au j.** jasmine tea
jatte [ʒat] *nf* bowl
jauge [ʒoʒ] *nf (instrument)* gauge; *Naut* tonnage • **jauger** *vt Fig (personne, situation)* to size up
jaune [ʒon] **1** *adj* yellow
 2 *nm (couleur)* yellow; *Péj (ouvrier)* yellowbelly; **j. d'œuf** (egg) yolk
 3 *adv* **rire j.** to give a forced laugh • **jaunâtre** *adj* yellowish • **jaunir** *vti* to turn yellow • **jaunisse** *nf Méd* jaundice
Javel [ʒavɛl] **eau de Javel** *nf* bleach
javelot [ʒavlo] *nm* javelin
jazz [dʒaz] *nm* jazz
je [ʒə]

---

j' is used before a word beginning with a vowel or h mute.

---

pron personnel I; **je suis ici** I'm here
jean [dʒin] *nm* (pair of) jeans; **veste en j.** denim jacket
Jeep® [dʒip] *nf* Jeep®
je-m'en-foutisme [ʒmɑ̃futism] *nm inv très Fam* couldn't-care-less attitude
jérémiades [ʒeremjad] *nfpl* whining
jerrican [(d)ʒerikan] *nm* jerry can
Jersey [ʒɛrzɛ] *nf* Jersey
jésuite [ʒezɥit] *nm* Jesuit
Jésus-Christ [ʒezykrist] *nm* Jesus Christ; **avant/après J.** BC/AD
jet [ʒɛ] *nm (de pierre)* throwing; *(de vapeur, de liquide)* jet; *(de lumière)* flash; **premier j.** *(ébauche)* first draft; **d'un seul j.** in one go; **j. d'eau** fountain
jetable [ʒətabl] *adj* disposable
jetée [ʒəte] *nf* pier, jetty

jeter [ʒəte] **1** *vt* to throw (**à** to; **dans** into); *(à la poubelle)* to throw away; *(ancre, sort, regard)* to cast; *(bases)* to lay; *(cri)* to utter; *(éclat, lueur)* to give out; *(noter)* to jot down; **j. qch à qn** to throw sth to sb, to throw sb sth; **j. un coup d'œil à qn/qch** to have a quick look at sb/sth; *Fig* **j. l'argent par les fenêtres** to throw money down the drain; *Fam* **se faire j. de** to get chucked out of; **ça a jeté un froid** it cast a chill; *Fam* **ça en jette!** that's really something!

2 se jeter *vpr (personne)* to throw oneself; **se j. sur qn** to throw oneself at sb; *Fig* to pounce on sb; **se j. sur** *(nourriture)* to pounce on; *(occasion)* to jump at; **se j. contre** *(véhicule)* to crash into; **se j. dans** *(fleuve)* to flow into; **se j. à l'eau** *(plonger)* to jump into the water; *Fig (se décider)* to take the plunge

jeton [ʒətɔ̃] *nm (pièce)* token; *(au jeu)* chip; *Fam* **avoir les jetons** to have the jitters

jeu, -x [ʒø] *nm* (**a**) *(amusement)* play; *(activité)* & *Tennis* game; *(d'acteur)* acting; *(de musicien)* playing; **le j.** *(au casino)* gambling; **maison de jeux** gambling club; **en j.** *(en cause)* at stake; *(forces)* at work; **entrer en j.** to come into play; **d'entrée de j.** from the outset; *Fig* **tirer son épingle du j.** to play one's game profitably; **elle a beau j. de critiquer** it's easy for her to criticize; **c'est un j. d'enfant!** it's child's play!; **j.-concours** competition; **j. électronique** computer game; **jeux de hasard** games of chance; **j. de mots** play on words, pun; **jeux de société** *(devinettes)* parlour games; *(jeu de l'oie, petits chevaux)* board games; **j. télévisé** television game show; *(avec questions)* television quiz show; **j. vidéo** video game (**b**) *(série complète)* set; *(de cartes)* deck, *Br* pack; *(cartes en main)* hand; **j. d'échecs** *(boîte, pièces)* chess set (**c**) *Tech (de ressort, verrou)* play

jeudi [ʒødi] *nm* Thursday

jeun [ʒœ̃] **à jeun 1** *adv* on an empty stomach **2** *adj* **être à j.** to have eaten no food

jeune [ʒœn] **1** *adj* young; *(apparence)* youthful; **jeunes gens** young people **2** *nmf* young person; **les jeunes** young people • **jeunesse** *nf* youth; *(apparence)* youthfulness; **la j.** *(les jeunes)* the young

jeûne [ʒøn] *nm (période)* fast; *(pratique)* fasting • **jeûner** *vi* to fast

joaillier, -ière [ʒɔaje, -jɛr] *nmf Br* jeweller, *Am* jeweler • **joaillerie** *nf (bijoux) Br*

jewellery, *Am* jewelry; *(magasin) Br* jewellery or *Am* jewelry shop

jockey [ʒɔke] *nm* jockey

jogging [dʒɔgiŋ] *nm Sport* jogging; *(survêtement)* jogging suit; **faire du j.** to jog, to go jogging

joie [ʒwa] *nf* joy, delight; **avec j.** with pleasure, gladly; **faire la j. de qn** to make sb happy

joindre* [ʒwɛ̃dr] **1** *vt (réunir)* to join; *(ajouter)* to add (**à** to); *(dans une enveloppe)* to enclose (**à** with); **j. qn** *(contacter)* to get in touch with sb; **j. les mains** to put one's hands together; *Fig* **j. les deux bouts** to make ends meet

2 se joindre *vpr* **se j. à qn** to join sb; **se j. à qch** to join in sth • **joint, -e** *adj* **à pieds joints** with feet together; **les mains jointes** with hands together; **pièces jointes** *(de lettre)* enclosures **2** *nm Tech (articulation)* joint; *(d'étanchéité)* seal; *(de robinet)* washer; **j. de culasse** gasket • **jointure** *nf (articulation)* joint

joker [ʒɔker] *nm Cartes* joker

joli, -ie [ʒɔli] *adj* pretty; *(somme)* nice • **joliment** *adv* nicely; *Fam (très, beaucoup)* awfully

🖉 Il faut noter que l'adjectif anglais **jolly** est un faux ami. Il signifie **joyeux**.

jonc [ʒɔ̃] *nm (plante)* rush

joncher [ʒɔ̃ʃe] *vt* to strew (**de** with); **jonché de** strewn with

jonction [ʒɔ̃ksjɔ̃] *nf* junction

jongler [ʒɔ̃gle] *vi* to juggle (**avec** with) • **jongleur, -euse** *nmf* juggler

jonquille [ʒɔ̃kij] *nf* daffodil

Jordanie [ʒɔrdani] *nf* **la J.** Jordan

joue [ʒu] *nf (du visage)* cheek; **mettre qn en j.** to take aim at sb; **en j.!** (take) aim!

jouer [ʒwe] **1** *vt (musique, tour, carte, rôle)* to play; *(pièce de théâtre)* to perform; *(film)* to show; *(parier)* to stake (**sur** on); *(cheval)* to bet on; **j. la finale** to play in the final; **j. les héros** to play the hero; *Fig* **j. son avenir** to risk one's future

2 *vi* to play; *(acteur)* to act; *(au tiercé)* to gamble; *(être important)* to count; **j. au tennis/aux cartes** to play tennis/cards; **j. du piano/du violon** to play the piano/violin; **j. aux courses** to bet on the horses; *Fig* **j. en faveur de qn** to work in sb's favour; **j. des coudes** to elbow one's way through; **faire j. un ressort** to release a spring; **à toi de j.!** it's your turn (to play)!

3 se jouer *vpr (film, pièce)* to be on; **se j. de qn** to trifle with sb; **se j. des difficultés** to make light of difficulties

jouet [ʒwɛ] *nm* toy; *Fig* **être le j. de qn** to be sb's plaything

joueur, joueuse [ʒwœr, ʒwøz] *nmf* player; *(au tiercé)* gambler; **beau j., bon j.** good loser

joufflu, -ue [ʒufly] *adj (visage)* chubby; *(enfant)* chubby-cheeked

joug [ʒu] *nm Agr & Fig* yoke

jouir [ʒwir] *vi (sexuellement)* to have an orgasm; **j. de qch** to enjoy sth; **j. d'une bonne santé** to enjoy good health ● **jouissance** *nf (plaisir)* enjoyment; *(sexuel)* orgasm; *Jur (usage)* use

joujou, -x [ʒuʒu] *nm Langage enfantin* toy

jour [ʒur] *nm (journée, date)* day; *(clarté)* daylight; *(éclairage)* light; *(ouverture)* gap; **il fait j.** it's (day)light; **de j. en j.** day by day; **du j. au lendemain** overnight; **au j. le j.** from day to day; **en plein j., au grand j.** in broad daylight; **de nos jours** nowadays, these days; *Fig* **sous un j. nouveau** in a different light; **les beaux jours** *(l'été)* summer; **mettre qch à j.** to bring sth up to date; **se faire j.** to come to light; **donner le j. à qn** to give birth to sb; **mettre fin à ses jours** to commit suicide; **quel j. sommes-nous?** what day is it?; **il y a dix ans j. pour j.** ten years ago to the day; *Fam* **elle et lui, c'est le j. et la nuit** she and he are as different as night and day *or Br* as chalk and cheese; **le j. de l'an** New Year's Day

journal, -aux [ʒurnal, -o] *nm* (news) paper; *(spécialisé)* journal; *(intime)* diary; *Radio* **j. parlé** (radio) news *(sing)*; **j. télévisé** (TV) news *(sing)*; *Naut* **j. de bord** logbook ● **journalisme** *nm* journalism ● **journaliste** *nmf* journalist ● **journalistique** *adj (style)* journalistic

journalier, -ière [ʒurnalje, -jɛr] *adj* daily

journée [ʒurne] *nf* day; **pendant la j.** during the day(time); **toute la j.** all day (long) ● **journellement** *adv* daily

> 💡 Il faut noter que le nom anglais **journey** est un faux ami. Il signifie **voyage** ou **trajet**.

jouxter [ʒukste] *vt* to adjoin

jovial, -e, -iaux, -iales [ʒɔvjal, -jo] *adj* jovial, jolly ● **jovialité** *nf* joviality

joyau, -x [ʒwajo] *nm* jewel

joyeux, -euse [ʒwajø, -øz] *adj* joyful; **j. anniversaire!** happy birthday!; **j. Noël!** merry *or Br* happy Christmas! ● **joyeusement** *adv* joyfully

jubilé [ʒybile] *nm* jubilee

jubiler [ʒybile] *vi* to be jubilant ● **jubilation** *nf* jubilation

jucher [ʒyʃe] *vt*, **se jucher** *vpr* to perch (**sur** on)

judaïsme [ʒydaism] *nm* Judaism

judas [ʒyda] *nm (de porte)* peephole

judiciaire [ʒydisjɛr] *adj* judicial; *(autorité)* legal

judicieux, -ieuse [ʒydisjø, -jøz] *adj* judicious

judo [ʒydo] *nm* judo

juge [ʒyʒ] *nm* judge; **j. d'instruction** examining magistrate; *Football* **j. de touche** linesman, assistant referee

jugé [ʒyʒe] **au jugé** *adv (calculer)* roughly

jugement [ʒyʒmɑ̃] *nm (opinion, discernement)* judgement; *Jur (verdict)* sentence; **porter un j. sur qch** to pass judgement on sth; *Jur* **passer en j.** to stand trial

jugeote [ʒyʒɔt] *nf Fam* common sense

juger [ʒyʒe] **1** *vt (personne, question)* to judge; *(au tribunal)* to try; *(estimer)* to consider (**que** that); **j. utile de faire qch** to consider it useful to do sth

2 *vi* **j. de** to judge; **jugez de ma surprise!** imagine my surprise!

juguler [ʒygyle] *vt (inflation, épidémie)* to check

juif, juive [ʒɥif, ʒɥiv] **1** *adj* Jewish **2** *nmf* **J.** Jew

juillet [ʒɥijɛ] *nm* July

juin [ʒɥɛ̃] *nm* June

jumeau, -elle, -x, -elles [ʒymo, -ɛl] **1** *adj* **frère j.** twin brother; **sœur jumelle** twin sister; **lits jumeaux** twin beds

2 *nmf* twin ● **jumelage** *nm* twinning ● **jumeler** *vt (villes)* to twin ● **jumelles** *nfpl (pour regarder)* binoculars; **j. de théâtre** opera glasses

jument [ʒymɑ̃] *nf* mare

jungle [ʒœ̃gl] *nf* jungle

junior [ʒynjɔr] *nm & adj inv Sport* junior

junte [ʒœ̃t] *nf* junta

jupe [ʒyp] *nf* skirt ● **jupon** *nm* petticoat

jurer [ʒyre] **1** *vt (promettre)* to swear (**que** that; **de faire** to do)

2 *vi (dire un gros mot)* to swear (**contre** at); *(contraster)* to clash (**avec** with); **j. de qch** to swear to sth ● **juré, -ée 1** *adj* **ennemi j.** sworn enemy **2** *nm Jur* juror

juridiction [ʒyridiksjɔ̃] *nf* jurisdiction

juridique [ʒyridik] *adj* legal ● **juriste** *nmf* legal expert

juron [ʒyrɔ̃] *nm* swearword

jury [ʒyri] *nm Jur* jury; *(d'examen)* board of examiners

jus [ʒy] *nm (de fruits)* juice; *(de viande)* gravy; *Fam (café)* coffee; *Fam* **prendre du j.** *(électricité)* to get a shock; **j. d'orange** orange juice

jusque [ʒysk] **1** *prép* **jusqu'à** *(espace)* as far as, (right) up to; *(temps)* until, (up) till, to; *(même)* even; **jusqu'à 10 euros** up to 10 euros; **jusqu'en mai** until May; **jusqu'où?** how far?; **jusqu'ici** as far as this; *(temps)* up till now; **jusqu'à présent** up till now; **jusqu'à un certain point** up to a point; **jusqu'à la limite de ses forces** to the point of exhaustion; **j. dans/sous** right into/under; **j. chez moi** as far as my place; *Fam* **en avoir j.-là** to be fed up **2** *conj* **jusqu'à ce qu'il vienne** until he comes

juste [ʒyst] **1** *adj (équitable)* fair, just; *(exact)* right, correct; *(étroit)* tight; *(raisonnement)* sound; **un peu j.** *(quantité, qualité)* barely enough; **très j.!** quite so *or* right! **2** *adv (deviner, compter)* correctly, right; *(chanter)* in tune; *(précisément, à peine)* just; **au j.** exactly; **à trois heures j.** on the stroke of three; **un peu j.** *(mesurer, compter)* a bit on the short side; **calculer trop j. (pour)** not to allow enough (for); **ils ont tout j. fini de manger** they've only just finished eating; *Fam* **comme de j.** as one would expect **3** *nm (homme)* just man •**justement** [-əmã] *adv (précisément)* exactly; *(avec justesse, avec justice)* justly; **j. j'allais t'appeler** I was just going to ring you

justesse [ʒystɛs] *nf (exactitude)* accuracy; **de j.** *(éviter, gagner)* just

justice [ʒystis] *nf (équité)* justice; **la j.** *(autorité)* the law; **rendre j. à qn** to do justice to sb; **se faire j.** *(se venger)* to take the law into one's own hands •**justicier, -ière** *nmf* righter of wrongs

justifier [ʒystifje] **1** *vt* to justify **2 se justifier** *vpr* to justify oneself (**de** of) •**justifiable** *adj* justifiable •**justificatif, -ive** *adj* **pièces justificatives** supporting documents •**justification** *nf (explication)* justification; *(preuve)* proof

jute [ʒyt] *nm (fibre)* jute

juteux, -euse [ʒytø, -øz] *adj* juicy

juvénile [ʒyvenil] *adj* youthful

juxtaposer [ʒykstapoze] *vt* to juxtapose •**juxtaposition** *nf* juxtaposition

K, k [ka] *nm inv* K, k
kaki [kaki] *adj inv & nm* khaki
kaléidoscope [kaleidɔskɔp] *nm* kaleidoscope
kangourou [kãguru] *nm* kangaroo
karaté [karate] *nm Sport* karate
kart [kart] *nm Sport* (go-)kart • **karting** [-iŋ] *nm Sport* karting
kasher [kaʃɛr] *adj inv Rel* kosher
kayak [kajak] *nm (bateau de sport)* canoe
Kenya [kenja] *nm* le K. Kenya
képi [kepi] *nm* kepi
kermesse [kɛrmɛs] *nf* charity fair *or Br* fête; *(en Belgique)* village fair
kérosène [kerozɛn] *nm* kerosine
kibboutz [kibuts] *nm inv* kibbutz
kidnapper [kidnape] *vt* to kidnap • **kidnappeur, -euse** *nmf* kidnapper
kilo [kilo] *nm* kilo • **kilogramme** *nm* kilogram(me)
kilomètre [kilɔmɛtr] *nm* kilometre • **kilométrage** *nm Aut* ≃ mileage • **kilométrique** *adj* borne k. ≃ milestone
kilo-octet [kilɔɔktɛ] *(pl* kilo-octets*) nm Ordinat* kilobyte

kilowatt [kilɔwat] *nm* kilowatt
kimono [kimɔno] *nm* kimono
kinésithérapie [kineziterapi] *nf* physiotherapy • **kinésithérapeute** *nmf* physiotherapist
kiosque [kjɔsk] *nm (à fleurs)* kiosk, *Br* stall; k. à journaux newsstand; k. à musique bandstand
kit [kit] *nm* (self-assembly) kit; en k. in kit form
kiwi [kiwi] *nm (oiseau, fruit)* kiwi
Klaxon® [klaksɔn] *nm* horn • **klaxonner** *vi* to sound one's horn
km *(abrév* kilomètre*)* km • **km/h** *(abrév* kilomètre-heure*)* kph, ≃ mph
k.-o. [kao] *adj inv Boxe* mettre qn k. to knock sb out
Koweït [kɔwɛjt] *nm* le K. Kuwait • **koweïtien, -ienne** 1 *adj* Kuwaiti 2 *nmf* K., Koweïtienne Kuwaiti
kyrielle [kirjɛl] *nf* une k. de *(reproches, fautes)* a long string of; *(vedettes)* a whole series of
kyste [kist] *nm Méd* cyst

L, l [ɛl] *nm inv* L, l

l', la¹ [l, la] *voir* **le**

la² [la] *nm inv (note)* A; *Mus* **donner le la** to give an A

là [la] **1** *adv (là-bas)* there; *(ici)* here; **je reste là** I'll stay here; **c'est là que...** *(lieu)* that's where...; **c'est là ton erreur** that's *or* there's your mistake; **c'est là que j'ai compris** that's when I understood; **là où il est** where he is; **à 5 m de là** 5 m away; **de là son échec** *(cause)* hence his/her failure; **jusque-là** *(lieu)* as far as that; *(temps)* up till then

2 *exclam* **oh là là!** oh dear!; **alors là!** well!

3 *voir* **ce²**, **celui**

là-bas [labɑ] *adv* over there

label [labɛl] *nm Com* quality label

labeur [labœr] *nm Littéraire* toil

labo [labo] *nm Fam* lab •**laboratoire** *nm* laboratory; **l. de langues** language laboratory

laborieux, -ieuse [labɔrjø, -jøz] *adj (pénible)* laborious; **les masses laborieuses** the toiling masses

labour [labur] *nm Br* ploughing, *Am* plowing •**labourer** *vt (terre) Br* to plough, *Am* to plow; *Fig (griffer)* to furrow •**laboureur** *nm Br* ploughman, *Am* plowman

labyrinthe [labirɛ̃t] *nm* maze, labyrinth

lac [lak] *nm* lake

lacer [lase] *vt* to lace (up) •**lacet** *nm (de chaussure)* lace; *(de route)* sharp bend; **faire ses lacets** to tie one's laces; **route en l.** winding road

lacérer [lasere] *vt (déchirer)* to tear to shreds; *(lacérer)* to lacerate

lâche [lɑʃ] **1** *adj (ressort, nœud)* loose, slack; *Péj (personne, acte)* cowardly

2 *nmf* coward •**lâchement** *adv* in a cowardly manner •**lâcheté** *nf* cowardice; **une l.** *(action)* a cowardly act

lâcher [lɑʃe] **1** *vt (ne plus tenir)* to let go of; *(bombe)* to drop; *(colombe)* to release; *(poursuivant)* to shake off; *(dans une course)* to leave behind; *Fam (ami)* to let down; *(juron, cri)* to let out; **l. prise** to let go; *Fam* **lâche-moi les baskets!** get off my back!

2 *vi (corde)* to break

3 *nm* release •**lâcheur, -euse** *nmf Fam* unreliable person

laconique [lakɔnik] *adj* laconic

lacrymogène [lakrimɔʒɛn] *adj* **gaz l.** tear gas

lacté, -ée [lakte] *adj* **régime l.** milk diet

lacune [lakyn] *nf* gap, deficiency

lad [lad] *nm* stable boy

là-dedans [ladədɑ̃] *adv (lieu)* in there, inside

là-dessous [ladəsu] *adv* underneath

là-dessus [ladəsy] *adv* on there; *(monter)* on top; *(alors)* thereupon

lagon [lagɔ̃] *nm* lagoon •**lagune** *nf* lagoon

là-haut [lao] *adv* up there; *(à l'étage)* upstairs

laid, -e [lɛ, lɛd] *adj (personne, visage, endroit)* ugly; *(ignoble)* not nice •**laideur** *nf* ugliness

laine [lɛn] *nf* wool; **de l., en l.** *Br* woollen, *Am* woolen; **l. de verre** glass wool •**lainage** *nm (vêtement)* jumper; *(étoffe)* woollen material; *Com* **lainages** woollens •**laineux, -euse** *adj* woolly

laïque [laik] **1** *adj (école)* non-denominational; *(vie)* secular; *(tribunal)* lay

2 *nmf (non-prêtre)* layman, *f* laywoman

laisse [lɛs] *nf* lead, leash; **tenir un chien en l.** to keep a dog on a lead

laisser [lese] **1** *vt* to leave; **l. qn partir/ entrer** *(permettre)* to let sb go/come in; **l. qch à qn** *(confier, donner)* to leave sth with sb; **laissez-moi le temps de le faire** give me *or* leave me time to do it; **l. qn seul** to leave sb alone; **je vous laisse** *(je pars)* I'm leaving now; **je vous le laisse pour 100 euros** I'll let you have it for 100 euros

2 *se laisser vpr* **se l. aller** to let oneself go; **se l. faire** to be pushed around; **se l. surprendre par l'orage** to get caught out by the storm •**laissé-pour-compte** *(pl* **laissés-pour-compte**) *nm (personne)* misfit, reject •**laisser-aller** *nm inv* carelessness •**laissez-passer** *nm inv (sauf-conduit)* pass

lait [lɛ] *nm* milk; **l. entier/demi-écrémé/ écrémé** whole/semi-skimmed/skimmed milk; **frère/sœur de l.** foster-brother/-sister • **laitage** *nm* milk product • **laiterie** *nf* dairy • **laiteux, -euse** *adj* milky • **laitier, -ière 1** *adj* **produit l.** dairy product **2** *nm (livreur)* milkman; *(vendeur)* dairyman **3** *nf* **laitière** *(femme)* dairywoman

laiton [lɛtɔ̃] *nm* brass

laitue [lɛty] *nf* lettuce

laïus [lajys] *nm Fam* speech

lama [lama] *nm (animal)* llama

lambeau, -x [lãbo] *nm* scrap; **mettre qch en lambeaux** to tear sth to shreds; **tomber en lambeaux** to fall to bits

lambin, -ine [lãbɛ̃, -in] *nmf Fam* dawdler • **lambiner** *vi Fam* to dawdle

lambris [lãbri] *nm* panelling • **lambrisser** *vt* to panel

lame [lam] *nf (de couteau, de rasoir)* blade; *(de métal)* strip, plate; *(vague)* wave; **l. de fond** groundswell; **l. de parquet** floorboard

lamelle [lamɛl] *nf* thin strip; **l. de verre** *(de microscope)* cover glass

lamenter [lamãte] **se lamenter** *vpr* to moan; **se l. sur qch** to bemoan sth • **lamentable** *adj (mauvais)* terrible, deplorable; *(voix, cri)* mournful; *(personne)* pathetic • **lamentations** *nfpl (cris, pleurs)* wailing

laminé, -ée [lamine] *adj (métal)* laminated

lampadaire [lãpadɛr] *nm Br* standard lamp, *Am* floor lamp; *(de rue)* street lamp

lampe [lãp] *nf* lamp; **l. de bureau** desk lamp; **l. de poche** *Br* torch, *Am* flashlight; **l. à pétrole** oil lamp

lampée [lãpe] *nf Fam* gulp

lampion [lãpjɔ̃] *nm* paper lantern

lance [lãs] *nf* spear; **l. d'incendie** fire hose • **lance-flammes** *nm inv* flamethrower • **lance-pierres** *nm inv* catapult

lancer [lãse] **1** *vt (jeter)* to throw (**à** to); *(fusée, produit, mode, navire)* to launch; *(appel, ultimatum)* to issue; *(cri)* to utter; *(bombe)* to drop; *(regard)* to cast (**à** at); **'au revoir!' nous lança-t-il gaiement** 'goodbye!' he called out cheerfully to us **2 se lancer** *vpr (se précipiter)* to rush; *(se faire connaître)* to make a name for oneself; **se l. dans** *(aventure, discussion)* to launch into; **se l. à la poursuite de qn** to rush off in pursuit of sb **3** *Sport* **l. du javelot** throwing the javelin, *Basket* **l. franc** free throw • **lancée** *nf* **continuer sur sa l.** to keep going • **lancement** *nm (de fusée, de produit)* launch(ing)

lancinant, -ante [lãsinã, -ãt] *adj (douleur)* shooting; *(obsédant)* haunting

landau, -s [lãdo] *nm Br* pram, *Am* baby carriage

lande [lãd] *nf* moor, heath

langage [lãgaʒ] *nm* language; **l. chiffré** code; *Ordinat* **l. machine/naturel** computer/natural language

lange [lãʒ] *nm (couche) Br* nappy, *Am* diaper • **langer** *vt (bébé)* to change

langouste [lãgust] *nf* crayfish • **langoustine** *nf* Dublin Bay prawn

langue [lãg] *nf Anat* tongue; *Ling* language; **de l. anglaise/française** English-/French-speaking; *Fam* **mauvaise l.** *(personne)* gossip; *Fig* **tenir sa l.** to keep a secret; *Fig* **donner sa l. au chat** to give up; *Fig* **avoir un cheveu sur la l.** to lisp; *Fig* **avoir la l. bien pendue** to have the gift of the gab; *Fig* **avoir un mot sur le bout de la l.** to have a word on the tip of one's tongue; **l. maternelle** mother tongue; **langues mortes** ancient languages; **langues vivantes** modern languages • **languette** *nf (patte)* tongue

langueur [lãgœr] *nf (mélancolie)* languor • **languir** *vi* to languish (**après** for *or* after); *(conversation)* to flag; **ne nous fais pas l.** don't keep us in suspense

lanière [lanjɛr] *nf* strap; *(d'étoffe)* strip

lanterne [lãtɛrn] *nf (lampe)* lantern; *Aut* **lanternes** parking lights, *Br* sidelights; *Fig* **éclairer la l. de qn** to enlighten sb

lanterner [lãtɛrne] *vi Fam* to dawdle

lapalissade [lapalisad] *nf* statement of the obvious

laper [lape] *vt* to lap up

lapider [lapide] *vt* to stone

lapin [lapɛ̃] *nm* rabbit; **mon (petit) l.** my dear; *Fam* **poser un l. à qn** to stand sb up

laps [laps] *nm* **un l. de temps** a period of time

lapsus [lapsys] *nm* slip of the tongue; **faire un l.** to make a slip

laquais [lakɛ] *nm Hist* footman; *Fig & Péj* lackey

laque [lak] *nf (vernis)* lacquer; *(pour cheveux)* hair spray; *(peinture)* gloss (paint) • **laquer** *vt (objet, cheveux)* to lacquer

laquelle [lakɛl] *voir* **lequel**

larbin [larbɛ̃] *nm Fam Péj* flunkey

larcin [larsɛ̃] *nm* petty theft

lard [lar] *nm (gras)* (pig's) fat; *(viande)* bacon • **lardon** *nm Culin* strip of bacon

> *Il faut noter que le nom anglais **lard** est un faux ami. Il signifie **saindoux**.*

large [larʒ] **1** *adj (route, porte, chaussure)* wide; *(vêtement)* loose-fitting; *(nez, geste)* broad; *(considérable)* large; *(géné-*

reux) generous; **l. de 6 m** 6 m wide; **l. d'esprit** broad-minded; **avoir les idées larges** to be broad-minded; **dans une l. mesure** to a large extent

2 *adv* **compter l.** to allow for more

3 *nm* **avoir 6 m de l.** to be 6 m wide; **le l.** *(mer)* the open sea; **au l. de Cherbourg** off Cherbourg; **être au l. dans** *(vêtement)* to have lots of room in •**largement** [-əmã] *adv (répandu, critiqué)* widely; *(ouvrir)* wide; *(récompenser, payer, servir)* generously; *(dépasser)* by a long way; **avoir l. le temps** to have plenty of time •**largesse** *nf (générosité)* generosity; **largesses** *(dons)* generous gifts •**largeur** *nf (dimension)* width, breadth; **en l., dans la l.** widthwise; **l. d'esprit** broadmindedness

> ⚲ Il faut noter que l'adverbe anglais **largely** est un faux ami. Il signifie **en grande partie**.

larguer [large] *vt (bombe, parachutiste)* to drop; *Naut* **l. les amarres** to cast off; *Fam* **l. qn** *(abandonner)* to chuck sb; *Fam* **je suis largué** *(perdu)* I'm all at sea

larme [larm] *nf* tear; *Fam (goutte)* drop; **avoir les larmes aux yeux** to have tears in one's eyes; **en larmes** in tears; **rire aux larmes** to laugh till one cries •**larmoyer** *vi (yeux)* to water

larve [larv] *nf (d'insecte)* grub

larvé, -ée [larve] *adj (guerre)* latent

larynx [larɛ̃ks] *nm Anat* larynx •**laryngite** *nf Méd* laryngitis

las, lasse [lɑ, lɑs] *adj* weary (**de** of) •**lassant, -ante** *adj* tiresome •**lasser 1** *vt* to tire

2 se lasser *vpr* **se l. de qch/de faire qch** to get tired of sth/of doing sth •**lassitude** *nf* weariness

lasagnes [lazaɲ] *nfpl* lasagne

lascar [laskar] *nm Fam* rascal

lascif, -ive [lasif, -iv] *adj* lascivious

laser [lazɛr] *nm* laser

lasso [laso] *nm* lasso; **prendre au l.** to lasso

latent, -ente [latã, -ãt] *adj* latent

latéral, -e, -aux, -ales [lateral, -o] *adj* side; **rue latérale** side street

latin, -ine [latɛ̃, -in] **1** *adj* Latin

2 *nmf* **L., Latine** Latin

3 *nm (langue)* Latin; *Fam* **j'y perds mon l.** I can't make head nor tail of it

latitude [latityd] *nf Géog & Fig* latitude

latrines [latrin] *nfpl* latrines

latte [lat] *nf* lath; *(de plancher)* board

lauréat, -éate [lɔrea, -eat] *nmf (prize)* winner

laurier [lɔrje] *nm (arbre)* laurel; *Culin* bay leaves; *Fig* **s'endormir sur ses lauriers** to rest on one's laurels

lavabo [lavabo] *nm* washbasin; **lavabos** *(toilettes) Br* toilet(s), *Am* washroom

lavande [lavãd] *nf* lavender

lave [lav] *nf* lava

laver [lave] **1** *vt* to wash; **l. qch à l'eau froide** to wash sth in cold water; *Fig* **l. qn d'une accusation** to clear sb of an accusation

2 se laver *vpr* to wash (oneself), *Am* to wash up; **se l. les mains** to wash one's hands; **se l. les dents** to clean one's teeth •**lavable** *adj* washable •**lavage** *nm* washing; **l. de cerveau** brainwashing •**lave-auto** *(pl* lave-autos*) nm Can* carwash •**lave-glace** *(pl* lave-glaces*) nm Br* windscreen *or Am* windshield washer •**lave-linge** *nm inv* washing machine •**laverie** *nf (automatique) Br* launderette, *Am* Laundromat® •**lavette** *nf* dishcloth; *Péj (homme)* drip •**laveur** *nm* **l. de carreaux** window *Br* cleaner *or Am* washer •**lave-vaisselle** *nm inv* dishwasher •**lavoir** *nm (bâtiment)* washhouse

laxatif, -ive [laksatif, -iv] *nm & adj* laxative

laxisme [laksism] *nm* laxness •**laxiste** *adj* lax

layette [lɛjɛt] *nf* baby clothes

le, la, les [lə, la, le]

> **l'** is used instead of **le** or **la** before a word beginning with a vowel or h mute.

1 *article défini* (**a**) *(pour définir le nom)* the; **le garçon** the boy; **la fille** the girl; **les petits/rouges** the little ones/red ones; **mon ami le plus proche** my closest friend; **venez, les enfants!** come, children!

(**b**) *(avec les généralités, les notions)* **la beauté/vie** beauty/life; **la France** France; **les Français** the French; **les hommes** men; **aimer le café** to like coffee

(**c**) *(avec les parties du corps)* **il ouvrit la bouche** he opened his mouth; **se blesser au pied** to hurt one's foot; **avoir les cheveux blonds** to have blond hair

(**d**) *(distributif)* **10 euros le kilo** 10 euros a kilo

(**e**) *(dans les compléments de temps)* **elle vient le lundi/le matin** she comes on Mondays/in the morning(s); **elle passe le soir** she comes over in the evening(s); **l'an prochain** next year; **une fois l'an** once a year

2 *pron (homme)* him; *(femme)* her; *(chose, animal)* it; **les** them; **je la vois** I see her/it; **je le vois** I see him/it; **je les vois** I see them; **es-tu fatigué? – je le suis** are you tired? – I am; **je le crois** I think so

leader [lidœr] *nm* leader
lécher [leʃe] **1** *vt* to lick
2 se lécher *vpr* **se l. les doigts** to lick one's fingers • **lèche-vitrines** *nm Fam* **faire du l.** to go window-shopping
leçon [ləsɔ̃] *nf* lesson; **faire la l. à qn** to lecture sb; **servir de l. à qn** to teach sb a lesson
lecteur, -trice [lɛktœr, -tris] *nmf* reader; *Univ* foreign language assistant; **l. de cassettes/de CD** cassette/CD player; *Ordinat* **l. de disques** *ou* **de disquettes** disk drive • **lecture** *nf* reading; **faire la l. à qn** to read to sb; **de la l.** some reading matter; **donner l. des résultats** to read out the results; **lectures** *(livres)* books; *Ordinat* **l. optique** optical reading

> 🖉 Il faut noter que le nom anglais **lecture** est un faux ami. Il signifie **conférence**.

légal, -e, -aux, -ales [legal, -o] *adj* legal • **légalement** *adv* legally • **légaliser** *vt* to legalize • **légalité** *nf* legality (**de** of); **agir en toute l.** to act within the law
légataire [legatɛr] *nmf* legatee; **l. universel** sole legatee
légende [leʒɑ̃d] *nf (histoire)* legend; *(de carte)* key; *(de photo)* caption; **entrer dans la l.** to become a legend • **légendaire** *adj* legendary
léger, -ère [leʒe, -ɛr] **1** *adj* light; *(bruit, blessure, fièvre, nuance)* slight; *(café, thé, argument)* weak; *(bière, tabac)* mild; *(frivole)* frivolous; *(irréfléchi)* thoughtless
2 *adv* **manger l.** to have a light meal
3 *nf* **agir à la légère** to act thoughtlessly; **prendre qch à la légère** to make light of sth • **légèrement** *adv* lightly; *(un peu)* slightly; *(avec désinvolture)* rashly • **légèreté** *nf (d'objet, de danseur)* lightness; *(de blessure)* slightness; *(désinvolture)* thoughtlessness
légiférer [leʒifere] *vi* to legislate (**sur** on)
légion [leʒjɔ̃] *nf Mil* legion; *Fig* huge number; **L. d'honneur** Legion of Honour • **légionnaire** *nm (de la Légion étrangère)* legionnaire
législatif, -ive [leʒislatif, -iv] *adj* legislative; *(élections)* parliamentary • **législation** *nf* legislation • **législature** *nf (période)* term of office
légitime [leʒitim] *adj (action, enfant)* legitimate; *(héritier)* rightful; *(colère)* justified; **être en état de l. défense** to be acting in *Br* self-defence *or Am* self-defense • **légitimité** *nf* legitimacy
legs [lɛg] *nm Jur* legacy, bequest; *Fig*

(héritage) legacy • **léguer** *vt* to bequeath (**à** to)
légume [legym] **1** *nm* vegetable
2 *nf Fam* **grosse l.** bigwig, big shot
lendemain [lɑ̃dmɛ̃] *nm* **le l.** the next day; **le l. de** the day after; **le l. matin** the next morning; **sans l.** *(succès)* short-lived; **au l. de la guerre** soon after the war
lent, -e [lɑ̃, lɑ̃t] *adj* slow • **lentement** *adv* slowly • **lenteur** *nf* slowness
lentille [lɑ̃tij] *nf (plante, graine)* lentil; *(verre)* lens; **lentilles de contact** contact lenses
léopard [leɔpar] *nm* leopard
LEP [ɛlɛpe, lɛp] *(abrév* **lycée d'enseignement professionnel)** *nm Scol Ancienne-ment* ≃ technical college
lèpre [lɛpr] *nf* leprosy • **lépreux, -euse 1** *adj* leprous **2** *nmf* leper
lequel, laquelle [ləkɛl, lakɛl] *(mpl* **lesquels,** *fpl* **lesquelles** [lekɛl])

> **lequel** and **lesquel(le)s** contract with **à** to form **auquel** and **auxquel(le)s**, and with **de** to form **duquel** and **desquel(le)s**.

1 *pron relatif (chose, animal)* which; *(personne)* who; *(indirect)* whom; **dans l.** in which; **parmi lesquels** *(choses, animaux)* among which; *(personnes)* among whom
2 *pron interrogatif* which (one); **l. préférez-vous?** which (one) do you prefer?
les [le] *voir* **le**
lesbienne [lɛsbjɛn] *nf* lesbian
léser [leze] *vt (personne)* to wrong
lésiner [lezine] *vi* to skimp (**sur** on)
lésion [lezjɔ̃] *nf* lesion
lessive [lɛsiv] *nf (produit)* washing powder; *(liquide)* liquid detergent; *(linge)* washing; **faire la l.** to do the washing • **lessivé, -ée** *adj Fam* washed out • **lessiver** *vt* to wash • **lessiveuse** *nf* (laundry) boiler
lest [lɛst] *nm* ballast; **lâcher du l.** to discharge ballast • **lester** *vt* to ballast; *Fam (remplir)* to stuff
leste [lɛst] *adj (agile)* nimble; *(grivois)* risqué
léthargie [letarʒi] *nf* lethargy • **léthargique** *adj* lethargic
lettre [lɛtr] *nf (missive, caractère)* letter; **en toutes lettres** in full; **obéir à qch à la l.** to obey sth to the letter; **les lettres** *(discipline)* arts, humanities; **homme de lettres** man of letters; *Fam* **c'est passé comme une l. à la poste** it went off without a hitch; **l. ouverte** open letter • **lettré, -ée** *adj* well-read

leucémie [løsemi] *nf Méd Br* leukaemia, *Am* leukemia

leur [lœr] **1** *adj possessif* their; **l. chat** their cat; **leurs voitures** their cars

2 *pron possessif* **le l., la l., les leurs** theirs **3** *pron personnel (indirect)* to them; **donne-l. ta carte** give them your card; **il l. est facile de** it's easy for them to

leurre [lœr] *nm (illusion)* illusion • **leurrer 1** *vt* to delude **2 se leurrer** *vpr* to delude oneself

lever [ləve] **1** *vt (objet)* to lift, to raise; *(blocus, interdiction, immunité parlementaire)* to lift; *(séance)* to close; *(impôts, armée)* to levy; **l. les yeux** to look up

2 *vi (pâte)* to rise; *(blé)* to shoot

3 se lever *vpr* to get up; *(soleil, rideau)* to rise; *(jour)* to break; *(brume)* to clear, to lift **4** *nm* **le l. du jour** daybreak; **le l. du soleil** sunrise; *Théâtre* **l. de rideau** curtain up • **levant, -ante 1** *adj (soleil)* rising **2** *nm* **le l.** the east • **levé, -ée** *adj* **être l.** *(debout)* to be up • **levée** *nf (d'interdiction)* lifting; *(du courrier)* collection; *(d'impôts)* levying; *Fig* **l. de boucliers** public outcry

levier [ləvje] *nm* lever; *Aut* **l. de vitesse** *Br* gear lever, *Am* gearshift

lèvre [lɛvr] *nf* lip; **accepter du bout des lèvres** to accept grudgingly

lévrier [levrije] *nm* greyhound

levure [ləvyr] *nf* yeast

lexique [lɛksik] *nm (glossaire)* glossary

lézard [lezar] *nm* lizard

lézarde [lezard] *nf* crack • **lézarder 1** *vt* to crack **2** *vi Fam* to bask in the sun **3 se lézarder** *vpr* to crack

liaison [ljezɔ̃] *nf (rapport)* connection; *(entre mots)* & *Mil* liaison; **en l. avec qn** in contact with sb; **assurer la l. entre deux services** to liaise between two departments; **l. aérienne/ferroviaire** air/rail link; **l. radio/téléphonique** radio/telephone link; **l. amoureuse** love affair

liane [ljan] *nf* creeper

liant, -e [ljã, -ãt] *adj* sociable

liasse [ljas] *nf* bundle

Liban [libã] *nm* **le L.** (the) Lebanon • **libanais, -aise 1** *adj* Lebanese **2** *nmf* **L., Libanaise** Lebanese

libeller [libele] *vt (contrat)* to word; *(chèque)* to make out • **libellé** *nm* wording

libellule [libelyl] *nf* dragonfly

libéral, -e, -aux, -ales [liberal, -o] *adj* & *nmf* liberal • **libéraliser** *vt* to liberalize • **libéralisme** *nm Pol* liberalism; *Écon* free-market economics • **libéralité** *nf Littéraire (générosité)* generosity; *(don)* generous gift

libérer [libere] **1** *vt (prisonnier)* to free, to release; *(élève)* to let go; *(pays)* to liberate *(de* from); *(chambre)* to vacate; **l. qn d'un souci** to take the weight off sb's mind

2 se libérer *vpr* to free oneself *(de* from); **je n'ai pas pu me l. plus tôt** I couldn't get away any earlier • **libérateur, -trice 1** *adj* liberating **2** *nmf* liberator • **libération** *nf (de prisonnier)* release; *(de pays)* liberation; *Jur* **l. conditionnelle** parole; *Hist* **la L.** the Liberation *(from the Germans in 1944-45)*

liberté [liberte] *nf* freedom, liberty; *Jur* **en l. provisoire** on bail; **rendre sa l. à qn** to let sb go; **mettre qn en l.** to set sb free; **mise en l.** release

libraire [librɛr] *nmf* bookseller • **librairie** *nf (magasin)* bookshop

⚠ Il faut noter que les termes anglais **librarian** et **library** sont des faux amis. Ils signifient respectivement **bibliothécaire** et **bibliothèque**.

libre [libr] *adj (personne, siège)* free *(de qch* from sth; **de faire** to do); *(voie)* clear; **être l. comme l'air** to be as free as a bird; **avoir les mains libres** to have one's hands free; *Fig* **la voie est l.** the coast is clear; **école l.** independent Catholic school; **radio l.** independent radio; **l. arbitre** free will • **libre-échange** *nm Écon* free trade • **librement** [-əmã] *adv* freely • **libre-penseur** *(pl* **libres-penseurs)** *nm* free-thinker • **libre-service** *(pl* **libres-services)** *nm (système, magasin)* self-service

Libye [libi] *nf* **la L.** Libya • **libyen, -enne 1** *adj* Libyan **2** *nmf* **L., Libyenne** Libyan

licence [lisãs] *nf Sport* permit; *Com Br* licence, *Am* license; *Univ* (bachelor's) degree; **l. ès lettres/sciences** arts/science degree; **l. poétique** poetic licence • **licencié, -iée** *adj* & *nmf* graduate; **l. ès lettres/sciences** arts/science graduate

licencier [lisãsje] *vt (employé)* to lay off, *Br* to make redundant • **licenciement** *nm* lay-off, *Br* redundancy; **l. économique** lay-off, *Br* redundancy

licorne [likɔrn] *nf* unicorn

lie [li] *nf* dregs

liège [ljɛʒ] *nm* cork

lien [ljɛ̃] *nm (rapport)* link, connection; *(attache)* bond; **les liens sacrés du mariage** the sacred bonds of marriage; **l. de parenté** family relationship; *Ordinat* **l. hypertexte** hypertext link

lier [lje] *vt (attacher)* to tie up; *(contrat)* to be binding on; *(personnes)* to bind together; *(événements, paragraphes)* to connect, to link; *Culin (sauce)* to thicken; **l. qn** *(unir, engager)* to bind sb; **avoir les mains liées** to have one's hands tied; **être très lié avec qn** to be great friends with sb **2 se lier** *vpr* **se l.** **(d'amitié)** to become friends

lierre [ljɛr] *nm* ivy

lieu¹, -x [ljø] *nm* place; **les lieux** *(locaux)* the premises; **sur les lieux du crime/de l'accident** at the scene of the crime/accident; **être sur les lieux** to be on the spot; **avoir l.** to take place; **donner l. à qch** to give rise to sth; **avoir l. de faire qch** to have good reason to do sth; **il n'y a pas l. de s'inquiéter** there's no need to worry; **tenir l. de qch** to serve as sth; **se plaindre en haut l.** to complain to people in high places; **au l. de** instead of; **au l. de te plaindre** instead of complaining; **en premier l.** in the first place, firstly; **en dernier l.** lastly; **s'il y a l.** if necessary; **l. commun** commonplace; **l. de naissance** place of birth; **l. public** public place; **l. de vacances** *Br* holiday *or Am* vacation destination • **lieu-dit** *(pl* lieux-dits) *nm* locality

lieu², -s [ljø] *nm (poisson)* **l. noir** coalfish

lieue [ljø] *nf Hist & Naut (mesure)* league

lieutenant [ljøtnɑ̃] *nm* lieutenant

lièvre [ljɛvr] *nm* hare

lifting [liftiŋ] *nm* face lift

ligament [ligamɑ̃] *nm* ligament

ligne [liɲ] *nf (trait, contour, de transport)* line; *(belle silhouette)* figure; *(rangée)* row, line; **les grandes lignes** *(de train)* the main lines; *Fig (les idées principales)* the broad outline; **aller à la l.** to begin a new paragraph; *Fig* **sur toute la l.** completely; **(se) mettre en l.** to line up; **être en l.** *(au téléphone)* to be through; **entrer en l. de compte** to be taken into account; *Fam* **garder la l.** to stay slim; **l. d'autobus** bus service; *(parcours)* bus route; **l. de chemin de fer** *Br* railway *or Am* railroad line; **l. de conduite** line of conduct; *Sport* **l. de touche** touchline

lignée [liɲe] *nf* descendants; *Fig* **dans la l. de** in the tradition of

ligoter [ligɔte] *vt* to tie up (à to)

ligue [lig] *nf* league • **se liguer** *vpr (États)* to form a league (**contre** against); *(personnes)* to gang up (**contre** against)

lilas [lila] *nm & adj inv* lilac

limace [limas] *nf* slug

limaille [limaj] *nf* filings

limande [limɑ̃d] *nf* dab

lime [lim] *nf (outil)* file; **l. à ongles** nail file • **limer** *vt* to file

limier [limje] *nm (chien)* bloodhound; **fin l.** *(policier)* supersleuth

limitatif, -ive [limitatif, -iv] *adj* restrictive • **limitation** *nf* limitation; **l. de vitesse** speed limit

limite [limit] **1** *nf* limit (à to); *(de propriété)* boundary; **sans l.** unlimited, limitless; **jusqu'à la l. de ses forces** to the point of exhaustion; **à la l.** if absolutely necessary; **dans la l. des stocks disponibles** while stocks last; **ma patience a des limites!** there are limits to my patience! **2** *adj (vitesse, âge)* maximum; **cas l.** borderline case; *Fam* **je suis un peu l.** financièrement I'm a bit short of cash

limiter [limite] **1** *vt (restreindre)* to limit, to restrict (à to); *(territoire)* to bound **2 se limiter** *vpr* **se l. à qch/à faire qch** to limit *or* restrict oneself to sth/to doing sth

limoger [limɔʒe] *vt* to dismiss

limonade [limɔnad] *nf (boisson gazeuse)* lemonade

limpide [lɛ̃pid] *adj (eau, explication)* clear, crystal-clear • **limpidité** *nf* clearness

lin [lɛ̃] *nm (plante)* flax; *(tissu)* linen; **huile de l.** linseed oil

linceul [lɛ̃sœl] *nm* shroud

linéaire [lineɛr] *adj* linear

linge [lɛ̃ʒ] *nm (vêtements)* linen; *(à laver)* washing; *(morceau de tissu)* cloth; **l. de corps** underwear; **l. de maison** household linen • **lingerie** *nf (de femmes)* underwear; *(pièce)* linen room

lingot [lɛ̃go] *nm* ingot; **l. d'or** gold bar

linguiste [lɛ̃ɡɥist] *nmf* linguist • **linguistique 1** *adj* linguistic **2** *nf* linguistics *(sing)*

lino [lino] *nm* lino • **linoléum** *nm* linoleum

linotte [linɔt] *nf Fig* **tête de l.** scatterbrain

lion [ljɔ̃] *nm* lion; **le L.** *(signe)* Leo; **être L.** to be Leo • **lionceau, -x** *nm* lion cub • **lionne** *nf* lioness

liquéfier [likefje] *vt,* **se liquéfier** *vpr* to liquefy

liqueur [likœr] *nf* liqueur

🖉 Il faut noter que le nom **liquor** utilisé en américain est un faux ami. Il signifie **alcool**.

liquide [likid] **1** *adj* liquid **2** *nm* liquid; *(argent)* cash; **payer en l.** to pay cash

liquider [likide] *vt (dette, stock)* to clear; *Jur (société)* to liquidate; *Fam (travail, restes)* to polish off; *Fam* **l. qn** *(tuer)* to liquidate sb • **liquidation** *nf (de dette, de stock)* clearing; *Jur (de société)* liquidation; *Com* **l. totale** stock clearance

lire¹* [lir] **1** *vt* to read; **l. qch à qn** to read sth to sb

2 *vi* to read

lire² [lir] *nf (monnaie)* lira

lis¹ [lis] *nm (plante, fleur)* lily

lis², lisant, lise(nt) *etc* [li, lizã, liz] *voir* **lire¹**

liseron [lizrɔ̃] *nm (plante)* convolvulus

lisible [lizibl] *adj (écriture)* legible; *(livre)* readable ● **lisiblement** [-əmɑ̃] *adv* legibly

lisière [lizjɛr] *nf* edge

lisse [lis] *adj* smooth ● **lisser** *vt* to smooth; *(plumes)* to preen

liste [list] *nf* list; **sur la l. rouge** *(du téléphone)* Br ex-directory, Am unlisted; **faire une l. de qch** to make (out) a list of sth; **l. d'attente** waiting list; **l. électorale** electoral roll; **l. de mariage** wedding list

lit¹ [li] *nm* bed; **se mettre au l.** to go to bed; **garder le l.** to stay in bed; **faire son l.** to make one's bed; **sortir de son l.** *(rivière)* to burst its banks; **l. de camp** Br camp bed, Am cot; **l. d'enfant** Br cot, Am crib; **lits superposés** bunk beds ● **literie** *nf* bedding

lit² [li] *voir* **lire¹**

litanie [litani] *nf* litany

litière [litjɛr] *nf (de chat, de cheval)* litter

litige [litiʒ] *nm (conflit)* dispute; *Jur* lawsuit ● **litigieux, -ieuse** *adj* contentious

litre [litr] *nm* Br litre, Am liter

littéraire [literɛr] *adj* literary ● **littérature** *nf* literature

littéral, -e, -aux, -ales [literal, -o] *adj* literal ● **littéralement** *adv* literally

littoral, -e, -aux, -ales [litɔral, -o] **1** *adj* coastal

2 *nm* coast(line)

liturgie [lityrʒi] *nf* liturgy ● **liturgique** *adj* liturgical

livide [livid] *adj (pâle)* pallid

livraison [livrɛzɔ̃] *nf* delivery

livre [livr] **1** *nm* book; **le l., l'industrie du l.** the book industry; *Naut* **l. de bord** logbook; **l. de cuisine** cookery book; **l. de poche** paperback (book)

2 *nf (monnaie, poids)* pound ● **livresque** [-ɛsk] *adj (savoir)* bookish

livrée [livre] *nf (de domestique)* livery

livrer [livre] **1** *vt (marchandises)* to deliver (**à** to); *(secret)* to reveal; **l. qn à la police** to hand sb over to the police; **l. bataille** to join battle

2 se livrer *vpr (se rendre)* to give oneself up (**à** to); *(se confier)* to confide (**à** in); **se l. à** *(habitude, excès)* to indulge in; *(activité)* to devote oneself to; *(désespoir, destin)* to abandon oneself to ● **livraison** *nf*

delivery ● **livreur, -euse** *nmf* delivery man, *f* delivery woman

livret [livrɛ] *nm (petit livre)* booklet; *Mus* libretto; **l. de caisse d'épargne** bankbook, Br passbook; **l. de famille** family record book *(registering births and deaths)*; **l. scolaire** school report book

lobe [lɔb] *nm* Anat lobe

local, -e, -aux, -ales [lɔkal, -o] **1** *adj* local

2 *nm (pièce)* room; **locaux** *(bâtiment)* premises ● **localement** *adv* locally ● **localiser** *vt (déterminer)* to locate; *(appel téléphonique)* to trace

localité [lɔkalite] *nf* locality

locataire [lɔkatɛr] *nmf* tenant; *(chez le propriétaire)* lodger, Am roomer

location [lɔkasjɔ̃] *nf (de maison) (par le locataire)* renting; *(par le propriétaire)* renting out, Br letting; *(de voiture)* renting, Br hiring; *(appartement, maison)* rented accommodation; *(loyer)* rent; *(de place de spectacle)* booking; **bureau de l.** booking office; **en l.** on hire; **voiture de l.** rented *or* Br hired car; **l.-vente** *(crédit-bail)* leasing with option to buy

---

> 🖉 Il faut noter que le nom anglais **location** est un faux ami. Il signifie **endroit**.

---

locomotion [lɔkɔmosjɔ̃] *nf* **moyen de l.** means of transport

locomotive [lɔkɔmotiv] *nf (de train)* engine

locuteur, -trice [lɔkytœr, -tris] *nmf* Ling speaker ● **locution** *nf* phrase

loge [lɔʒ] *nf (de concierge)* lodge; *(d'acteur)* dressing-room; *Théâtre (de spectateur)* box; *Fig* **être aux premières loges** to have a ringside seat

loger [lɔʒe] **1** *vt (recevoir, mettre)* to accommodate; *(héberger)* to put up; **être logé et nourri** to have board and lodging

2 *vi (temporairement)* to stay; *(en permanence)* to live

3 se loger *vpr* **(trouver à) se l.** to find somewhere to live; *(temporairement)* to find somewhere to stay; **la balle se logea dans le mur** the bullet lodged (itself) in the wall ● **logement** *nm (habitation)* accommodation, lodging; *(appartement)* Br flat, Am apartment; *(maison)* house; *(action)* housing; **le l.** housing ● **logeur, -euse** *nmf* landlord, *f* landlady

loggia [lɔdʒja] *nf (balcon)* loggia

logiciel [lɔʒisjɛl] *nm* Ordinat software *inv*

logique [lɔʒik] **1** *adj* logical

2 *nf* logic ● **logiquement** *adv* logically

logistique [lɔʒistik] *nf* logistics *(sing)*

logo [lɔgo] *nm* logo

loi [lwa] *nf* law; **faire la l.** to lay down the law (à to)

loin [lwɛ̃] *adv* far (away *or* off) (**de** from); **Boston est l. de Paris** Boston is a long way away from Paris; **plus l.** further, farther; *(ci-après)* further on; **aller l.** *(réussir)* to go far; **aller trop l.** *(exagérer)* to go too far; **au l.** in the distance, far away; **de l.** from a distance; *(de beaucoup)* by far; **de l. en l.** every so often; **c'est l.**, **tout ça** *(passé)* that was a long time ago; *Fig* **l. de là** far from it • **lointain, -aine 1** *adj* distant, far-off; *(ressemblance, rapport)* remote **2** *nm* **dans le l.** in the distance

loir [lwar] *nm* dormouse

loisir [lwazir] *nm* **avoir le l. de faire qch** to have the time to do sth; **(tout) à l.** *(en prenant tout son temps)* at leisure; *(autant qu'on le désire)* as much as one would like; **loisirs** *(temps libre)* spare time, leisure (time); *(distractions)* leisure *or* spare-time activities

Londres [lɔ̃dr] *nm ou f* London • **londonien, -ienne 1** *adj* London, of London **2** *nmf* **L.**, **Londonienne** Londoner

long, longue [lɔ̃, lɔ̃g] **1** *adj* long; **être l. (à faire qch)** to be a long time (in doing sth); **l. de 2 m** 2 m long

2 *nm* **avoir 2 m de l.** to be 2 m long; **(tout) le l. de** *(espace)* (all) along; **tout le l. de** *(temps)* throughout; **de l. en large** *(marcher)* up and down; **en l. et en large** thoroughly; **en l.** lengthwise; **tomber de tout son l.** to fall flat (on one's face)

3 *adv* **en savoir/en dire l. sur** to know/ say a lot about; **leur attitude en disait l.** their attitude spoke volumes • **long-courrier** *(pl* **long-courriers)** *nm (avion)* long-haul aircraft

longer [lɔ̃ʒe] *vt (sujet: personne, voiture)* to go along; *(mur, côte)* to hug; *(sujet: sentier, canal)* to run alongside

longévité [lɔ̃ʒevite] *nf* longevity

longiligne [lɔ̃ʒiliɲ] *adj* willowy

longitude [lɔ̃ʒityd] *nf* longitude

longtemps [lɔ̃tɑ̃] *adv* (for) a long time; **trop/avant l.** too/before long; **aussi l. que** as long as

longue [lɔ̃g] *voir* **long** • **longuement** *adv (expliquer)* at length; *(attendre, réfléchir)* for a long time • **longuet, -ette** *adj Fam* longish • **longueur** *nf* length; *Péj* **longueurs** *(de texte, de film)* drawn-out passages; **à l. de journée** all day long; *Radio* **l. d'onde** wavelength; *Fig* **être sur la même l. d'onde** to be on the same wavelength

• **longue-vue** *(pl* **longues-vues)** *nf* telescope

look [luk] *nm Fam* look; **avoir un l. d'enfer** to look out of this world

lopin [lɔpɛ̃] *nm* **l. de terre** plot *or* patch of land

loquace [lɔkas] *adj* talkative

loque [lɔk] *nf (vêtement)* rag; *Fig (personne)* wreck; **être en loques** to be in rags

loquet [lɔkɛ] *nm* latch

lorgner [lɔrɲe] *vt (avec indiscrétion)* to eye; *(avec concupiscence)* to eye up; *(convoiter)* to have one's eye on

lors [lɔr] *adv* **l. de** at the time of; **depuis l.**, **dès l.** from then on; **dès l. que** *(puisque)* since

lorsque [lɔrsk(ə)] *conj* when

losange [lɔzɑ̃ʒ] *nm (forme)* diamond

lot [lo] *nm (de marchandises)* batch; *(de loterie)* prize; **gros l.** jackpot • **loterie** *nf* lottery

loti, -ie [lɔti] *adj Fig* **bien/mal l.** well-off/ badly off

lotion [losjɔ̃] *nf* lotion

lotissement [lɔtismɑ̃] *nm (terrain)* building plot; *(habitations)* housing *Br* estate *or Am* development

loto [lɔto] *nm (jeu)* lotto; *(jeu national)* national lottery

louable [lwabl] *adj* praiseworthy, laudable

louange [lwɑ̃ʒ] *nf* praise

louche¹ [luʃ] *nf (cuillère)* ladle

louche² [luʃ] *adj (suspect)* dodgy

loucher [luʃe] *vi* to squint; *Fam* **l. sur qch** to eye sth

louer¹ [lwe] *vt (prendre en location) (maison, appartement)* to rent; *(voiture)* to rent, *Br* to hire; *(donner en location) (maison, appartement)* to rent out, *Br* to let; *(voiture)* to rent out, *Br* to hire out; *(réserver)* to book; **maison/chambre à l.** house/ room to rent *or Br* to let

louer² [lwe] **1** *vt (exalter)* to praise (**de** for)

2 se louer *vpr* **se l. de qch** to be highly satisfied with sth

loufoque [lufɔk] *adj Fam (fou)* crazy

loukoum [lukum] *nm* piece of Turkish delight

loup [lu] *nm* wolf; **avoir une faim de l.** to be ravenous • **loup-garou** *(pl* **loups-garous)** *nm* werewolf

loupe [lup] *nf* magnifying glass

louper [lupe] *vt Fam (train)* to miss; *(examen)* to flunk; *(travail)* to mess up

lourd, -e [lur, lurd] **1** *adj* heavy (**de** with); *(temps, chaleur)* close; *(faute)* gross; *(tâche)* arduous; *(esprit)* dull

2 *adv* peser l. *(malle)* to be heavy • **lour-daud, -aude 1** *adj* oafish **2** *nmf* oaf • **lour-dement** [-əmã] *adv* heavily; **se tromper l.** to be greatly mistaken • **lourdeur** *nf* heaviness; *(d'esprit)* dullness; **avoir des lourdeurs d'estomac** to feel bloated

lourdingue [lurdɛ̃g] *adj Fam (personne, plaisanterie)* unsubtle

loutre [lutr] *nf* otter

louve [luv] *nf* she-wolf • **louveteau, -x** *nm (animal)* wolf cub; *(scout)* Cub (Scout)

louvoyer [luvwaje] *vi Fig (tergiverser)* to hedge

loyal, -e, -aux, -ales [lwajal, -o] *adj (honnête)* fair (**envers** to); *(dévoué)* loyal (**envers** to) • **loyalement** *adv (honnête)* fairly; *(avec dévouement)* loyally • **loyauté** *nf (honnêteté)* fairness; *(dévouement)* loyalty (**envers** to)

loyer [lwaje] *nm* rent

lu [ly] *pp de* **lire¹**

lubie [lybi] *nf* whim

lubrifier [lybrifje] *vt* to lubricate • **lubrifiant** *nm* lubricant

lubrique [lybrik] *adj* lustful

lucarne [lykarn] *nf (fenêtre)* dormer window; *(de toit)* skylight

lucide [lysid] *adj* lucid • **lucidité** *nf* lucidity

lucratif, -ive [lykratif, -iv] *adj* lucrative

lueur [lɥœr] *nf (lumière) & Fig* glimmer

luge [lyʒ] *nf Br* sledge, *Am* sled, toboggan

lugubre [lygybr] *adj* gloomy

lui [lɥi] *pron personnel* (**a**) *(objet indirect)* (to) him; *(femme)* (to) her; *(chose, animal)* (to) it; **je le l. ai montré** I showed it to him/her; **il l. est facile de** it's easy for him/her to

(**b**) *(complément direct)* him; **elle n'aime que l.** she only loves him; **elle n'écoute ni l. ni personne** she doesn't listen to him or to anybody

(**c**) *(après une préposition)* him; **pour/avec l.** for/with him; **elle pense à l.** she thinks of him; **il ne pense qu'à lui** he only thinks of himself; **ce livre est à l.** this book is his

(**d**) *(dans les comparaisons)* **elle est plus grande que l.** she's taller than he is *or* than him

(**e**) *(sujet)* **l., il ne viendra pas** *(emphatique)* HE won't come; **c'est l. qui me l'a dit** he is the one who told me • **lui-même** *pron* himself; *(chose, animal)* itself

luire* [lɥir] *vi* to shine • **luisant, -ante** *adj (métal)* shiny

lumbago [lɔ̃bago] *nm* lumbago

lumière [lymjɛr] *nf* light; **à la l. de** by the light of; *Fig (grâce à)* in the light of; *Fig* **faire toute la l. sur** to clear up; *Fig* **mettre en l.** to bring to light; *Fam* **ce n'est pas une l.** he's/she's not very bright • **luminaire** *nm (appareil)* lighting appliance

lumineux, -euse [lyminø, -øz] *adj (idée, ciel)* bright, brilliant; *(cadran, corps)* luminous; **source lumineuse** light source • **luminosité** *nf* luminosity

lunaire [lynɛr] *adj* lunar; **clarté l.** light *or* brightness of the moon

lunatique [lynatik] *adj* quirky

> ⚠ Il faut noter que l'adjectif anglais **lunatic** est un faux ami. Il signifie **fou**.

lundi [lœ̃di] *nm* Monday

lune [lyn] *nf* moon; **être dans la l.** to have one's head in the clouds; **l. de miel** honeymoon • **luné, -ée** *adj Fam* **être bien/mal l.** to be in a good/bad mood

lunette [lynɛt] *nf (astronomique)* telescope; **lunettes** *(de vue)* glasses, spectacles; *(de protection, de plongée)* goggles; **l. arrière** *(de voiture)* rear window; **lunettes de soleil** sunglasses

lurette [lyrɛt] *nf Fam* **il y a belle l.** ages ago

luron [lyrɔ̃] *nm* **c'est un gai l.** he's a bit of a lad

lustre [lystr] *nm (lampe)* chandelier; *(éclat)* lustre • **lustré, -ée** *adj (par l'usure)* shiny • **lustres** *nmpl Fam* **depuis des l.** for ages and ages

luth [lyt] *nm* lute

lutin [lytɛ̃] *nm* elf, imp

lutte [lyt] *nf* fight, struggle; *Sport* wrestling; **l. des classes** class struggle • **lutter** *vi* to fight, to struggle; *Sport* to wrestle • **lutteur, -euse** *nmf Sport* wrestler

luxation [lyksasjɔ̃] *nf Méd* dislocation; **se faire une l. à l'épaule** to dislocate one's shoulder

luxe [lyks] *nm* luxury; **un l. de** a wealth of; **article de l.** luxury article; **modèle de l.** de luxe model • **luxueux, -ueuse** *adj* luxurious

Luxembourg [lyksɑ̃bur] *nm* **le L.** Luxembourg

luxure [lyksyr] *nf Littéraire* lust

> ⚠ Il faut noter que le nom anglais **luxury** est un faux ami. Il signifie **luxe**.

luxuriant, -iante [lyksyrjɑ̃, -jɑ̃t] *adj* luxuriant

luzerne [lyzɛrn] *nf (plante) Br* lucerne, *Am* alfalfa

lycée [lise] *nm Br* ≃ secondary school, *Am* ≃ high school; **l. technique** *ou* **pro-**

fessionnel vocational *or* technical school • **lycéen, -éenne** *nmf* pupil *(at a lycée)*

lymphatique [lɛ̃fatik] *adj Biol* lymphatic; *(apathique)* lethargic

lyncher [lɛ̃ʃe] *vt* to lynch • **lynchage** *nm* lynching

lynx [lɛ̃ks] *nm* lynx; *Fig* **avoir des yeux de l.** to have eyes like a hawk

lyophiliser [ljɔfilize] *vt (café)* to freeze-dry

lyre [lir] *nf* lyre

lyrique [lirik] *adj (poème)* lyric; *Fig (passionné)* lyrical; **artiste l.** opera singer • **lyrisme** *nm* lyricism

lys [lis] *nm (plante, fleur)* lily

M

M¹, m¹ [ɛm] *nm inv* M, m
M² (*abrév* **Monsieur**) Mr
m² (*abrév* **mètre(s)**) m
m' [m] *voir* **me**
ma [ma] *voir* **mon**
macabre [makɑbr] *adj* macabre, gruesome
macadam [makadam] *nm* (*goudron*) macadam
macaron [makarɔ̃] *nm* (*gâteau*) macaroon; (*insigne*) badge; (*autocollant*) sticker
macaronis [makarɔni] *nmpl* macaroni
macédoine [masedwan] *nf* **m. de légumes** mixed vegetables; **m. de fruits** fruit salad
macérer [masere] *vti* to steep **• macération** *nf* steeping
mâche [mɑʃ] *nf* lamb's lettuce
mâcher [mɑʃe] *vt* to chew; **m. le travail à qn** to make sb's task easy; **ne pas m. ses mots** not to mince one's words
machiavélique [makjavelik] *adj* Machiavellian
machin, -ine [maʃɛ̃, -ʃin] *Fam* **1** *nmf* (*personne*) **M.** what's-his-name; **Machine** what's-her-name
2 *nm* (*chose*) thingy
machinal, -e, -aux, -ales [maʃinal, -o] *adj* (*geste, travail*) mechanical; (*réaction*) automatic **• machinalement** *adv* (*agir*) mechanically; (*réagir*) automatically
machination [maʃinɑsjɔ̃] *nf* conspiracy
machine [maʃin] *nf* (*appareil*) machine; (*locomotive, moteur*) engine; *Naut* **salle des machines** engine room; **m. à calculer** calculator; **m. à coudre** sewing machine; **m. à écrire** typewriter; **m. à laver** washing machine; **m. à laver la vaisselle** dishwasher; **m. à** *ou* **de traitement de texte** word processor **• machiniste** *nm* (*conducteur*) driver; (*de théâtre*) stagehand
machisme [maʃism] *nm* machismo **• macho** [matʃo] *adj & nm Fam* macho
mâchoire [mɑʃwar] *nf* jaw
mâchonner [mɑʃɔne] *vt* to chew
maçon [masɔ̃] *nm* (*de briques*) bricklayer; (*de pierres*) mason **• maçonnerie** *nf* (*travaux*) building work; (*ouvrage de briques*)

brickwork; (*de pierres*) masonry, stonework
macrobiotique [makrobjɔtik] *adj* macrobiotic
macro-commande [makrokɔmɑ̃d] (*pl* **macro-commandes**) *nf Ordinat* macro
maculer [makyle] *vt* to stain (**de** with)
Madagascar [madagaskar] *nf* Madagascar
madame [madam] (*pl* **mesdames**) *nf* (*en apostrophe*) madam; **bonjour mesdames** good morning(, ladies); **M. Legras** Mrs Legras; **M.** (*dans une lettre*) Dear Madam
madeleine [madlɛn] *nf* (*gâteau*) madeleine
mademoiselle [madmwazɛl] (*pl* **mesdemoiselles**) *nf* (*suivi d'un nom*) Miss; **M. Legras** Miss Legras; **merci m.** thank you; **bonjour mesdemoiselles** good morning(, ladies); **M.** (*dans une lettre*) Dear Madam
Madère [madɛr] *nf* (*île*) Madeira
madère [madɛr] *nm* (*vin*) Madeira
madone [madɔn] *nf Rel* Madonna
madrier [madrije] *nm* beam
Maf(f)ia [mafja] *nf* **la M.** the Mafia
magasin [magazɛ̃] *nm Br* shop, *Am* store; (*entrepôt*) warehouse; (*d'arme*) & *Phot* magazine; **grand m.** department store; **en m.** in stock **• magasinier** *nm* warehouseman
magazine [magazin] *nm* (*revue*) magazine
magie [maʒi] *nf* magic **• magicien, -ienne** *nmf* magician **• magique** *adj* (*surnaturel*) magic; (*enchanteur*) magical
magistral, -e, -aux, -ales [maʒistral, -o] *adj* (*démonstration*) masterly; (*erreur*) colossal **• magistralement** *adv* magnificently
magistrat [maʒistra] *nm* magistrate **• magistrature** *nf* magistrature
magma [magma] *nm* (*roche*) magma; *Fig* (*mélange*) jumble
magnanime [maɲanim] *adj* magnanimous
magnat [magna] *nm* tycoon, magnate; **m. de la presse** presse baron
magner [maɲe] **se magner** *vpr Fam* to get a move on

magnésium [maɲezjɔm] *nm* magnesium
magnétique [maɲetik] *adj* magnetic •**magnétiser** *vt* to magnetize •**magnétisme** *nm* magnetism
magnétophone [maɲetɔfɔn] (*Fam* **magnéto**) *nm* tape recorder; **m. à cassettes** cassette recorder
magnétoscope [maɲetɔskɔp] *nm* video recorder
magnifique [maɲifik] *adj* magnificent •**magnificence** *nf* magnificence •**magnifiquement** *adv* magnificently
magnolia [maɲɔlja] *nm (arbre)* magnolia
magot [mago] *nm Fam* hoard
magouille [maguj] *nf Fam* scheming •**magouilleur, -euse** *nmf Fam* schemer
magret [magrɛ] *nm* **m. de canard** *Br* fillet *or Am* filet of duck
mai [mɛ] *nm* May
maigre [mɛgr] **1** *adj (personne, partie du corps)* thin; *(viande)* lean; *(fromage, yaourt)* low-fat; *(repas, salaire, espoir)* meagre
2 *adv* **faire m.** to abstain from meat •**maigreur** *nf (de personne)* thinness •**maigrichon, -onne** [meg-] *adj Fam* skinny •**maigrir** *vi* to get thinner
maille [maj] *nf (de tricot)* stitch; *(de filet)* mesh; **m. filée** *(de bas)* run, *Br* ladder; *Fig* **avoir m. à partir avec qn** to have a set-to with sb •**maillon** *nm* link
maillet [majɛ] *nm* mallet
maillot [majo] *nm (de sportif)* jersey, shirt; **m. de bain** *(de femme)* swimsuit; *(d'homme)* (swimming) trunks; **m. de corps** *Br* vest, *Am* undershirt; **m. jaune** *(du Tour de France)* yellow jersey
main [mɛ̃] **1** *nf* hand; **à la m.** *(faire, écrire)* by hand; **tenir qch à la m.** to hold sth in one's hand; **sous la m.** handy; **la m. dans la m.** hand in hand; **en mains propres** in person; **donner la m. à qn** to hold sb's hand; *Fig* **avoir la m. heureuse** to be lucky; **avoir le coup de m.** to have the knack; *Fig* **mettre la dernière m. à qch** to put the finishing touches to sth; **demander la m. d'une femme** to ask for a woman's hand (in marriage); **faire m. basse sur qch** to get one's hands on sth; **mettre la m. à la pâte** to do one's bit; **ne pas y aller de m. morte** not to pull punches; **en venir aux mains** to come to blows; *Fig* **j'y mettrais ma m. au feu** I'd stake my life on it; **haut les mains!** hands up!; **m. courante** handrail
2 *adj* **fait m.** hand-made •**main-d'œuvre** *(pl* **mains-d'œuvre**) *nf* labour •**mainmise** *nf* seizure (**de** of)

maint, mainte [mɛ̃, mɛ̃t] *adj Littéraire* many a; **maintes fois, à maintes reprises** many a time
maintenant [mɛ̃tnɑ̃] *adv* now; *(de nos jours)* nowadays; **m. que...** now that...; **dès m.** from now on
maintenir* [mɛ̃tnir] **1** *vt (conserver)* to keep, to maintain; *(retenir)* to hold in position; *(foule)* to hold back; *(affirmer)* to maintain (**que** that)
2 se maintenir *vpr (durer)* to remain; *(malade, vieillard)* to hold up •**maintien** *nm (action)* maintenance (**de** of); *(allure)* bearing
maire [mɛr] *nm* mayor •**mairie** *nf Br* town hall, *Am* city hall; *(administration) Br* town council, *Am* city hall
mais [mɛ] *conj* but; **m. oui, m. si** of course; **m. non** definitely not
maïs [mais] *nm Br* maize, *Am* corn
maison [mɛzɔ̃] **1** *nf (bâtiment, famille)* house; *(foyer)* home; *(entreprise)* company; **à la m.** at home; **aller à la m.** to go home; **rentrer à la m.** to go/come (back) home; **m. de la culture** arts centre; **m. d'édition** publishing house; **m. des jeunes et de la culture** = youth club and arts centre; **m. de repos** rest home; **m. de retraite** old people's home; **m. de santé** nursing home; **la M.-Blanche** the White House
2 *adj inv (artisanal)* home-made •**maisonnée** *nf* household •**maisonnette** *nf* small house
maître [mɛtr] *nm* master; **être m. de la situation** to be in control of the situation; **être m. de ses émotions** to have one's emotions under control; **se rendre m. de qch** *(incendie)* to bring sth under control; *(pays)* to conquer sth; **m. d'école** teacher; **m. d'hôtel** *(de restaurant)* head waiter; **m. de maison** host; **m. chanteur** blackmailer; **m. nageur (sauveteur)** swimming instructor (and lifeguard)
maîtresse [mɛtrɛs] **1** *nf* mistress; **être m. de la situation** to be in control of the situation; **m. d'école** teacher; **m. de maison** hostess
2 *adj f (idée, poutre)* main; *(carte)* master
maîtrise [mɛtriz] *nf (contrôle, connaissance)* mastery (**de** of); *(diplôme)* ≃ master's degree (**de** in); **m. de soi** self-control •**maîtriser 1** *vt (incendie, passion)* to control; *(peur)* to overcome; *(sujet)* to master; *(véhicule)* to have under control; **m. qn** to overpower sb **2 se maîtriser** *vpr* to control oneself

majesté [maʒɛste] *nf* majesty; **Votre M.** *(titre)* Your Majesty • **majestueux, -ueuse** *adj* majestic

majeur, -eure [maʒœr] **1** *adj (important)* & *Mus* major; *Jur* **être m.** to be of age; **la majeure partie de** most of; **en majeure partie** for the most part **2** *nm (doigt)* middle finger

majorer [maʒɔre] *vt* to increase • **majoration** *nf (hausse)* increase (**de** in)

majorette [maʒɔrɛt] *nf* (drum) majorette

majorité [maʒɔrite] *nf* majority (**de** of); *(gouvernement)* government, party in office; **en m.** *(pour la plupart)* in the main; **m. civile** majority, coming of age • **majoritaire** *adj* majority; **être m.** to be in the majority; **être m. aux élections** to win the elections

Majorque [maʒɔrk] *nf* Majorca

majuscule [maʒyskyl] **1** *adj* capital **2** *nf* capital letter

mal, maux [mal, mo] **1** *nm (douleur)* pain; *(préjudice)* harm; *(maladie)* illness; *(malheur)* misfortune; *Phil* **le m.** evil; **avoir m. à la tête/à la gorge** to have a headache/sore throat; **ça me fait m., j'ai m.** it hurts (me); **avoir le m. de mer** to be seasick; **faire du m. à qn** to harm sb; **dire du m. de qn** to speak ill of sb; **avoir du m. à faire qch** to have trouble doing sth; **se donner du m. pour faire qch** to take pains to do sth; **m. de dents** toothache; **m. de gorge** sore throat; **m. de tête** headache; **m. de ventre** stomach ache; **avoir le m. de l'air** to be airsick; **avoir le m. des transports** to be travelsick; **m. du pays** homesickness; **avoir le m. du pays** to be homesick **2** *adv (avec médiocrité)* badly; *(incorrectement)* wrongly; **aller m.** *(projet)* to be going badly; *(personne)* to be ill; **être m. en point** to be in a bad way; **prendre m.** to catch cold; **m. comprendre** to misunderstand; **m. renseigner qn** to misinform sb; **se trouver m.** to faint; *Fam* **pas m.** *(beaucoup)* quite a lot (**de** of); **c'est m. de mentir** it's wrong to lie; **de m. en pis** from bad to worse

malade [malad] **1** *adj* ill, sick; *(arbre, dent)* diseased; *(estomac, jambe)* bad; **être m. du foie/cœur** to have a bad liver/heart **2** *nmf* sick person; *(de médecin)* patient; **les malades** the sick • **maladie** *nf* illness, disease; **m. émergente** new disease • **maladif, -ive** *adj (personne)* sickly; *(curiosité)* morbid

maladroit, -oite [maladrwa, -wat] *adj (malhabile)* clumsy, awkward; *(indélicat)* tactless • **maladresse** *nf (manque d'habileté)* clumsiness, awkwardness; *(indélicatesse)* tactlessness; *(bévue)* blunder

malaise [malɛz] *nm (angoisse)* uneasiness, malaise; *(indisposition)* feeling of sickness; *(étourdissement)* dizzy spell; **avoir un m.** to feel faint

malaisé, -ée [malɛze] *adj* difficult

Malaisie [malɛzi] *nf* **la M.** Malaysia

malaria [malarja] *nf* malaria

malavisé, -ée [malavize] *adj* ill-advised (**de faire** to do)

malaxer [malakse] *vt* to knead

malbouffe [malbuf] *nf* junk food

malchance [malʃãs] *nf* bad luck; **jouer de m.** to have no luck at all • **malchanceux, -euse** *adj* unlucky

malcommode [malkɔmɔd] *adj* awkward

mâle [mal] **1** *adj (du sexe masculin)* male; *(viril)* manly **2** *nm* male

malédiction [malediksjɔ̃] *nf* curse

maléfice [malefis] *nm* evil spell • **maléfique** *adj* evil

malencontreux, -euse [malɑ̃kɔ̃trø, -øz] *adj* unfortunate

malentendant, -ante [malɑ̃tɑ̃dɑ̃, -ɑ̃t] *nmf* person who is hard of hearing

malentendu [malɑ̃tɑ̃dy] *nm* misunderstanding

malfaçon [malfasɔ̃] *nf* defect

malfaisant, -ante [malfəzɑ̃, -ɑ̃t] *adj* harmful

malfaiteur [malfɛtœr] *nm* criminal

malfamé, -ée [malfame] *adj* disreputable

malformation [malfɔrmasjɔ̃] *nf* malformation

malgré [malgre] *prép* in spite of; **m. tout** for all that, after all; **m. soi** *(à contrecœur)* reluctantly

malhabile [malabil] *adj* clumsy

malheur [malœr] *nm (drame)* misfortune; *(malchance)* bad luck; **par m.** unfortunately; **porter m. à qn** to bring sb bad luck; **faire un m.** to be a big hit • **malheureusement** *adv* unfortunately • **malheureux, -euse 1** *adj (triste)* unhappy, miserable; *(malchanceux)* unlucky; *(candidat)* unsuccessful **2** *nmf (infortuné)* poor wretch; *(indigent)* needy person

malhonnête [malɔnɛt] *adj* dishonest • **malhonnêteté** *nf* dishonesty

malice [malis] *nf* mischievousness • **malicieux, -ieuse** *adj* mischievous

*Il faut noter que les termes anglais **malice** et **malicious** sont des faux amis. Ils signifient respectivement **méchanceté** ou **préméditation** selon le contexte, et **méchant**.*

malin, -igne [malɛ̃, -iɲ] *adj (astucieux)* clever, smart; *Méd (tumeur)* malignant; **prendre un m. plaisir à faire qch** to take a malicious pleasure in doing sth; *Ironique* **c'est ma.!** that's clever!

malingre [malɛ̃gr] *adj* puny

malintentionné, -ée [malɛ̃tɑ̃sjɔne] *adj* ill-intentioned (**à l'égard de** towards)

malle [mal] *nf (coffre)* trunk; *(de véhicule) Br* boot, *Am* trunk; *Fam* **se faire la m.** to clear off ● **mallette** *nf* briefcase

malléable [maleabl] *adj* malleable

mal-logés [mallɔʒe] *nmpl* **les m.** = people living in inadequate housing conditions

malmener [malmǝne] *vt* to manhandle, to treat badly

malnutrition [malnytrisjɔ̃] *nf* malnutrition

malodorant, -ante [malɔdɔrɑ̃, -ɑ̃t] *adj* smelly

malotru, -ue [malɔtry] *nmf* boor, lout

malpoli, -ie [malpɔli] *adj Fam* rude

malpropre [malprɔpr] *adj (sale)* dirty

malsain, -aine [malsɛ̃, -ɛn] *adj* unhealthy

malséant, -éante [malseɑ̃, -eɑ̃t] *adj Littéraire* unseemly

malt [malt] *nm* malt

Malte [malt] *nf* Malta ● **maltais, -aise 1** *adj* Maltese **2** *nmf* **M., Maltaise** Maltese

maltraiter [maltrɛte] *vt* to ill-treat ● **maltraitance** *nf* ill-treatment

malveillant, -ante [malvɛjɑ̃, -ɑ̃t] *adj* malevolent ● **malveillance** *nf* malevolence

malvenu, -ue [malvǝny] *adj (déplacé)* uncalled-for

malversation [malvɛrsasjɔ̃] *nf* embezzlement

maman [mamɑ̃] *nf Br* mum, *Am* mom

mamelle [mamɛl] *nf (d'animal)* teat; *(de vache)* udder ● **mamelon** *nm (de femme)* nipple; *(colline)* hillock

mamie [mami] *nf* grandma, granny

mammifère [mamifɛr] *nm* mammal

Manche [mɑ̃ʃ] *nf* **la M.** the Channel

manche¹ [mɑ̃ʃ] *nf (de vêtement)* sleeve; *Sport & Cartes* round; *Fam* **faire la m.** to beg; *Fam* **c'est une autre paire de manches!** it's a different ball game ● **manchette** *nf (de chemise)* cuff; *(de journal)* headline ● **manchon** *nm (en fourrure)* muff

manche² [mɑ̃ʃ] *nm (d'outil)* handle; **m. à balai** broomstick; *(d'avion, d'ordinateur)* joystick

manchot¹, -ote [mɑ̃ʃo, -ɔt] **1** *adj* one-armed **2** *nmf* one-armed person

manchot² [mɑ̃ʃo] *nm (oiseau)* penguin

mandale [mɑ̃dal] *nf très Fam* clout

mandarin [mɑ̃darɛ̃] *nm Péj (personnage influent)* mandarin

mandarine [mɑ̃darin] *nf (fruit)* mandarin (orange)

mandat [mɑ̃da] *nm (de député)* mandate; *(de président)* term of office; *(procuration)* power of attorney; **m. d'amener** = summons; **m. d'arrêt** warrant (**contre qn** for sb's arrest); **m. de perquisition** search warrant; **m. postal** *Br* postal order, *Am* money order ● **mandataire** *nmf (délégué)* representative ● **mandater** *vt* to delegate; *(député)* to give a mandate to

manège [manɛʒ] *nm* (**a**) *(de foire)* merry-go-round, *Br* roundabout; *Équitation* riding school (**b**) *(intrigue)* game

manette [manɛt] *nf* lever

mangeoire [mɑ̃ʒwar] *nf (feeding)* trough

manger [mɑ̃ʒe] **1** *vt* to eat; *(corroder)* to eat into; *Fig (consommer, dépenser)* to get through **2** *vi* to eat; **donner à m. à qn** to give sb sth to eat; **m. à sa faim** to have enough to eat; **on mange bien ici** the food is good here **3** *nm (nourriture)* food ● **mangeable** *adj (médiocre)* eatable ● **mangeur, -euse** *nmf* **être un gros m.** to be a big eater

mangue [mɑ̃g] *nf* mango

manie [mani] *nf (habitude)* odd habit; *(idée fixe)* mania (**de** for) ● **maniaque 1** *adj* fussy **2** *nmf Br* fusspot, *Am* fussbudget; **un m. de la propreté** a maniac for cleanliness

manier [manje] *vt* to handle ● **maniabilité** *nf (de véhicule) Br* manoeuvrability, *Am* maneuverability ● **maniable** *adj (outil)* handy; *(véhicule)* easy to handle ● **maniement** *nm* handling

manière [manjɛr] *nf* way, manner; **la m. dont elle parle** the way (in which) she talks; **manières** *(politesse)* manners; **faire des manières** *(se faire prier)* to make a fuss; *(être affecté)* to put on airs; **de toute m.** anyway, anyhow; **de cette m.** (in) this way; **de m. à faire qch** so as to do sth; **à ma m.** my way; **à la m. de** in the style of; **d'une m. générale** generally speaking ● **maniéré, -ée** *adj* affected

manif [manif] (*abrév* **manifestation**) *nf*
Fam demo
manifeste [manifɛst] **1** *adj* manifest, obvious
2 *nm Pol* manifesto • **manifestement**
[-əmã] *adv* obviously, manifestly
manifester [manifɛste] **1** *vt (exprimer)* to
show
2 *vi (protester)* to demonstrate
3 se manifester *vpr (maladie, sentiment)*
to show *or* manifest itself; *(personne)* to
make oneself known • **manifestant, -ante**
nmf demonstrator • **manifestation** *nf (défilé)* demonstration; *(réunion, fête)* event;
(de sentiments) display
manigances [manigãs] *nfpl* scheming
• **manigancer** *vt* to scheme
manipuler [manipyle] *vt (appareils, produits)* to handle; *Péj (personnes)* to manipulate • **manipulation** *nf (d'appareils, de
produits)* handling; *Péj (de personnes)*
manipulation (**de** of); **manipulations gé-
nétiques** genetic engineering
manivelle [manivɛl] *nf* crank
mannequin [mankɛ̃] *nm (personne)*
model; *(statue)* dummy
manœuvre [manœvr] **1** *nm (ouvrier)* unskilled worker
2 *nf (opération)* & *Mil Br* manoeuvre, *Am*
maneuver; *(intrigue)* scheme • **manœuvrer 1** *vt (véhicule, personne) Br* to manoeuvre, *Am* to maneuver; *(machine)* to
operate **2** *vi Br* to manoeuvre, *Am* to
maneuver
manoir [manwar] *nm* manor house
manomètre [manɔmɛtr] *nm* pressure
gauge
manque [mãk] *nm (insuffisance)* lack
(**de** of); *(lacune)* gap; **par m. de qch**
through lack of sth; **être en m.** *(drogué)*
to have withdrawal symptoms; **m. à gagner** loss of earnings
manquer [mãke] **1** *vt (cible, train,
chance)* to miss; *(échouer)* to fail
2 *vi (faire défaut)* to be lacking; *(être
absent)* to be missing; *(échouer)* to fail;
m. de *(pain, argent)* to be short of; *(attention, cohérence)* to lack; **m. à son devoir**
to fail in one's duty; **m. à sa parole** to
break one's word; *Mil* **m. à l'appel** to miss
(the) roll call; **ça manque de sel** there isn't
enough salt; **tu me manques** I miss you;
le temps lui manque he's short of time; **le
cœur m'a manqué** my courage failed me;
ça n'a pas manqué, il est arrivé en retard
sure enough, he was late; **je ne manquerai pas de venir** I won't fail to come; **je n'y
manquerai pas** I certainly will; **elle a**

manqué de tomber she nearly fell; **ne m.
de rien** to have all one needs
3 *v impersonnel* **il manque/il nous
manque dix tasses** there are/we are ten
cups short; **il manque quelques pages**
there are a few pages missing; **il ne
manquait plus que ça!** that's all I/we/*etc*
needed! • **manquant, -ante** *adj* missing
• **manqué, -ée** *adj (occasion)* missed; *(tentative)* unsuccessful • **manquement** *nm*
breach (**à** of)
mansarde [mãsard] *nf* attic
mansuétude [mãsɥetyd] *nf Littéraire* indulgence
manteau, -x [mãto] *nm* coat; *Fig* **sous le
m.** secretly
manucure [manykyr] **1** *nmf (personne)*
manicurist
2 *nf (soin)* manicure
manuel, -uelle [manɥɛl] **1** *adj (travail)*
manual
2 *nm (livre)* handbook, manual; **m. scolaire** textbook
manufacture [manyfaktyr] *nf* factory
• **manufacturé, -ée** *adj (produit)* manu-
factured
manuscrit [manyskri] *nm* manuscript;
(tapé à la machine) typescript
manutention [manytãsjɔ̃] *nf* handling
• **manutentionnaire** *nmf* packer
mappemonde [mapmɔ̃d] *nf (carte)* map
of the world; *(sphère)* globe
maquereau, -x [makro] *nm (poisson)*
mackerel
maquette [makɛt] *nf (de bâtiment)*
(scale) model; *(jouet)* model
maquiller [makije] **1** *vt (personne, visage)* to make up; *(voiture)* to tamper
with; *(documents)* to forge
2 se maquiller *vpr* to put one's make-up
on • **maquillage** *nm (fard)* make-up; *(action)* making up
maquis [maki] *nm (végétation)* & *Hist*
maquis; **prendre le m.** to take to the hills
maraîcher, -ère [mareʃe, -eʃɛr] **1** *nmf Br*
market gardener, *Am* truck farmer
2 *adj* **culture maraîchère** *Br* market
gardening, *Am* truck farming
marais [marɛ] *nm* marsh; **m. salant**
saltern, saltworks
marasme [marasm] *nm* **m. économique/
politique** economic/political stagnation
marathon [maratɔ̃] *nm* marathon
maraudeur, -euse [marodœr, -øz] *nmf*
petty thief
marbre [marbr] *nm* marble; **en m.**
marble; **rester de m.** to remain impassive
• **marbré, -ée** *adj (surface)* marbled; **gâ-**

teau m. marble cake • **marbrier** nm (funé-raire) monumental mason

marc [mar] nm (eau-de-vie) marc (brandy); **m. de café** coffee grounds

marchand, -ande [marʃɑ̃, -ɑ̃d] **1** nmf Br shopkeeper, Am storekeeper; (de vins, de charbon) merchant; (de voitures, de meubles) dealer; **m. de journaux** (dans la rue) newsvendor; (dans un magasin) Br newsagent; Am newsdealer; **m. de légumes** Br greengrocer, Am produce dealer **2** adj prix m. trade price; **valeur marchande** market value

marchander [marʃɑ̃de] **1** vt (objet, prix) to haggle over **2** vi to haggle • **marchandage** nm haggling

marchandises [marʃɑ̃diz] nfpl goods, merchandise

marche [marʃ] nf (a) (d'escalier) step, stair (b) (action) walking; (promenade) walk; Mus march; (de train, de véhicule) movement; (d'événement) course; **un train/véhicule en m.** a moving train/vehicle; **la bonne m. de** (opération, machine) the smooth running of; **dans le sens de la m.** (dans un train) facing forward; **faire m. arrière** (en voiture) Br to reverse, Am to back up; Fig to backtrack; **fermer la m.** to bring up the rear; **m. à suivre** procedure

marché [marʃe] **1** nm (lieu) & Écon market; (contrat) deal; Fig **par-dessus le m.** into the bargain; **faire son** ou **le m.** to go shopping; **vendre qch au m. noir** to sell sth on the black market; **le m. du travail** the labour market; **le M. commun** the Common Market; **le M. unique européen** the Single European Market; **m. des changes** foreign exchange market; **m. baissier/haussier** bear/bull market **2** adj inv **être bon m.** to be cheap; **c'est meilleur m.** it's cheaper

marchepied [marʃəpje] nm (de train, de bus) step

marcher [marʃe] vi (à pied) to walk; (poser le pied) to step (**dans** in); (machine) to run; (plans) to work; (soldats) to march; **faire m. qch** to operate sth; Fam **faire m. qn** to pull sb's leg; Fam **ça marche?** how's it going?; Fam **elle va m.** (accepter) she'll go along (with it) • **marcheur, -euse** nmf walker

mardi [mardi] nm Tuesday; **M. gras** Shrove Tuesday

mare [mar] nf (étang) pond; (grande quantité) pool

marécage [mareka3] nm marsh • **marécageux, -euse** adj marshy

maréchal, -aux [mareʃal, -o] nm **m. (de France)** field marshal • **maréchal-ferrant** (pl **maréchaux-ferrants**) nm blacksmith

marée [mare] nf tide; (poissons) fresh seafood; **m. haute/basse** high/low tide; **m. noire** oil slick

marelle [marɛl] nf (jeu) hopscotch; **jouer à la m.** to play hopscotch

marémotrice [maremɔtris] adj f **usine m.** tidal power station

margarine [margarin] nf margarine

marge [mar3] nf (de page) margin; **en m. de** (en dehors de) on the fringes of; **avoir de la m.** to have some leeway; **m. de manœuvre** room for manoeuvre; **m. de sécurité** safety margin • **marginal, -e, -aux, -ales** **1** adj (secondaire) marginal; (personne) on the fringes of society **2** nmf dropout

marguerite [margərit] nf (fleur) daisy

mari [mari] nm husband

mariage [marja3] nm (union) marriage; (cérémonie) wedding; Fig (de couleurs) blend; **m. blanc** marriage in name only; **m. de raison** marriage of convenience

marier [marje] **1** vt (couleurs) to blend; **m. qn** (sujet: prêtre, maire) to marry sb; (sujet: père) to marry sb off **2 se marier** vpr to get married; **se m. avec qn** to get married to sb, to marry sb • **marié, -iée 1** adj married **2** nm (bride)groom; **les mariés** the bride and groom; **les jeunes mariés** the newly-weds • **mariée** nf bride

marijuana [mariрyana] nf marijuana

marin, -ine [marɛ̃, -in] **1** adj (flore) marine; (mille) nautical; **air/sel m.** sea air/salt; **costume m.** sailor suit **2** nm sailor, seaman; **m. pêcheur** (deep-sea) fisherman • **marine 1** nf **m. de guerre** navy; **m. marchande** merchant navy **2** adj & nm inv (**bleu**) **m.** (couleur) navy (blue)

marina [marina] nf marina

mariner [marine] vti Culin to marinate

marionnette [marjɔnɛt] nf puppet; (à fils) marionette

maritalement [maritalmɑ̃] adv **vivre m.** to cohabit

maritime [maritim] adj (droit, climat) maritime; **port m.** seaport; **gare m.** harbour station; Can **les Provinces maritimes** the Maritime Provinces

marjolaine [marʒɔlɛn] nf marjoram

mark [mark] nm (monnaie) mark

marmaille [marmaj] nf Fam Péj (enfants) kids

marmelade [marməlad] *nf Br* stewed fruit, *Am* fruit compote; *Fig* **en m.** reduced to a pulp

marmite [marmit] *nf* (cooking) pot

marmonner [marmɔne] *vti* to mutter

marmot [marmo] *nm Fam (enfant)* kid

marmotte [marmɔt] *nf* marmot; *Fig* **dormir comme une m.** to sleep like a log

marmotter [marmɔte] *vti* to mumble

Maroc [marɔk] *nm* **le M.** Morocco ● **marocain, -aine 1** *adj* Moroccan **2** *nmf* **M., Marocaine** Moroccan

maroquinerie [marɔkinri] *nf (magasin)* leather goods shop ● **maroquinier** *nm* leather goods dealer

marotte [marɔt] *nf Fam (passion)* craze

marque [mark] *nf (trace, signe)* mark; *(de confiance)* sign; *(de produit)* brand; *(de voiture)* make; *Sport (points)* score; **de m.** *(hôte, visiteur)* distinguished; *(produit)* of quality; **à vos marques! prêts? partez!** on your marks! get set! go!; **m. de fabrique** trademark; **m. déposée** (registered) trademark

marquer [marke] **1** *vt (par une marque)* to mark; *(écrire)* to note down; *(indiquer)* to show; *Sport (point, but)* to score; **m. les points** to keep (the) score; *Fam* **m. le coup** to mark the event **2** *vi (laisser une trace)* to leave a mark; *(date, événement)* to stand out; *Sport* to score ● **marquant, -ante** *adj (remarquable)* outstanding; *(épisode)* significant ● **marqué, -ée** *adj (différence, accent)* marked; *(visage)* lined ● **marqueur** *nm (stylo)* marker

marquis [marki] *nm* marquis ● **marquise** *nf* **(a)** *(personne)* marchioness **(b)** *(auvent)* canopy

marraine [marɛn] *nf* godmother

marre [mar] *adv Fam* **en avoir m.** to be fed up (**de** with)

marrer [mare] **se marrer** *vpr Fam* to have a good laugh ● **marrant, -ante 1** *adj Fam* funny, hilarious **2** *nmf Fam* **c'est un m.** he's a good laugh

marron¹ [marɔ̃] **1** *nm (fruit)* chestnut; *(couleur)* (chestnut) brown; *Fam (coup)* thump; **m. d'Inde** horse chestnut **2** *adj inv (couleur)* (chestnut) brown ● **marronnier** *nm (arbre)* chestnut tree

marron², -onne [marɔ̃, -ɔn] *adj (médecin)* quack

mars [mars] *nm* March

marsouin [marswɛ̃] *nm* porpoise

marteau, -x [marto] *nm* hammer; *(de porte)* (door)knocker; **m. piqueur** pneu-matic drill ● **martèlement** *nm* hammering ● **marteler** *vt* to hammer

martial, -e, -iaux, -iales [marsjal, -jo] *adj* martial; **cour martiale** court martial; **loi martiale** martial law

martien, -ienne [marsjɛ̃, -jɛn] *nmf & adj* Martian

martinet [martinɛ] *nm (fouet)* strap

Martinique [martinik] *nf* **la M.** Martinique ● **martiniquais, -aise 1** *adj* Martinican **2** *nmf* **M., Martiniquaise** Martinican

martin-pêcheur [martɛ̃peʃœr] *(pl* **martins-pêcheurs**) *nm* kingfisher

martyr, -yre¹ [martir] **1** *nmf (personne)* martyr **2** *adj* **enfant m.** battered child ● **martyre²** *nm (souffrance)* martyrdom; **souffrir le m.** to be in agony ● **martyriser** *vt* to torture; *(enfant)* to batter

marxisme [marksism] *nm* Marxism ● **marxiste** *adj & nmf* Marxist

mascara [maskara] *nm* mascara

mascarade [maskarad] *nf* masquerade

mascotte [maskɔt] *nf* mascot

masculin, -ine [maskylɛ̃, -in] **1** *adj (sexe, mode, métier)* male; *(trait de caractère, femme) & Grammaire* masculine; *(équipe)* men's **2** *nm Grammaire* masculine ● **masculinité** *nf* masculinity

masochisme [mazɔʃism] *nm* masochism ● **masochiste** *(Fam* **maso) 1** *adj* masochistic **2** *nmf* masochist

masque [mask] *nm* mask; **m. à gaz/oxygène** gas/oxygen mask ● **masquer** *vt (dissimuler)* to mask (**à** from); *(cacher à la vue)* to block off

massacre [masakr] *nm (tuerie)* massacre; **jeu de m.** *Br* = Aunty Sally; *Fig* **faire un m.** *(avoir du succès)* to be a runaway success ● **massacrer** *vt* to massacre; *Fam (abîmer)* to ruin

massage [masaʒ] *nm* massage

masse [mas] *nf* **(a)** *(volume)* mass; *(gros morceau, majorité)* bulk (**de** of); **de m.** *(culture, communication)* mass; **en m.** en masse; **une m. de** masses of; **les masses** *(peuple)* the masses; *Fam* **des masses de** masses of; *Fam* **pas des masses** *(quantité)* not that much; *(nombre)* not many; *Fam* **être à la m.** to be off one's head **(b)** *(outil)* sledgehammer **(c)** *Él Br* earth, *Am* ground

masser [mase] **1** *vt (rassembler)* to assemble; *(pétrir)* to massage **2** **se masser** *vpr (foule)* to form ● **masseur** *nm* masseur ● **masseuse** *nf* masseuse

massif, -ive [masif, -iv] **1** *adj* massive; *(or, chêne)* solid

2 *nm (d'arbres, de fleurs)* clump; *Géog* massif ● **massivement** *adv (voter, répondre)* en masse

massue [masy] *nf* club

mastic [mastik] **1** *nm (pour vitres)* putty; *(pour bois)* filler

2 *adj inv (beige)* putty-coloured

mastiquer¹ [mastike] *vt (vitre)* to putty; *(bois)* to fill

mastiquer² [mastike] *vt (mâcher)* to chew

mastoc [mastɔk] *adj inv Fam Péj* massive

mastodonte [mastɔdɔ̃t] *nm Péj (personne)* colossus; *(objet)* hulking great thing

masturber [mastyrbe] **se masturber** *vpr* to masturbate ● **masturbation** *nf* masturbation

masure [mazyr] *nf* hovel

mat¹, mate [mat] *adj (papier, couleur)* matt; *(son)* dull

mat² [mat] *adj m inv & nm Échecs* (check-)mate; **faire m.** to (check)mate; **mettre qn m.** to (check)mate sb

mât [mɑ] *nm (de navire)* mast; *(poteau)* pole

match [matʃ] *nm Sport Br* match, *Am* game; **m. nul** draw; **faire m. nul** to draw; **m. aller** first leg; **m. retour** return leg

matelas [matla] *nm* mattress; **m. pneumatique** air bed ● **matelassé, -ée** *adj (tissu)* quilted; *(enveloppe)* padded

matelot [matlo] *nm* sailor

mater¹ [mate] *vt (se rendre maître de)* to bring to heel

mater² [mate] *vt Fam (regarder)* to ogle

matérialiser [materjalize] *vt*, **se matérialiser** *vpr* to materialize ● **matérialisation** *nf* materialization

matérialisme [materjalism] *nm* materialism ● **matérialiste 1** *adj* materialistic **2** *nmf* materialist

matériau, -x [materjo] *nm* material; **matériaux** *(de construction)* building material(s); *Fig (de roman, d'enquête)* material

matériel, -ielle [materjɛl] **1** *adj (confort, dégâts, besoins)* material; *(organisation, problème)* practical

2 *nm (de camping)* equipment; *Ordinat* **m. informatique** computer hardware ● **matériellement** *adv* materially; **m. impossible** physically impossible

maternel, -elle [matɛrnɛl] **1** *adj (amour, femme)* maternal; *(langue)* native

2 *nf* **(école) maternelle** *Br* nursery school, *Am* kindergarten ● **materner** *vt* to mother ● **maternité** *nf (état)* motherhood; *(hôpital)* maternity hospital

mathématique [matematik] *adj* mathematical ● **mathématicien, -ienne** *nmf* mathematician ● **mathématiques** *nfpl* mathematics *(sing)* ● **maths** [mat] *nfpl Fam Br* maths, *Am* math; *Fam* **M. Sup/ Spé** = first-/second-year class preparing for the science-orientated *grandes écoles*

matière [matjɛr] *nf (à l'école)* subject; *(de livre)* subject matter; *(substance)* material; *Phys* **la m.** matter; **en m. de qch** as regards sth; **s'y connaître en m. de qch** to be experienced in sth; **en la m.** *(sur ce sujet)* on the subject; **m. plastique** plastic; **m. première** raw material; **matières grasses** fat

Matignon [matiɲɔ̃] *nm* **(l'hôtel) M.** = the French Prime Minister's offices

matin [matɛ̃] *nm* morning; **le m.** *(chaque matin)* in the morning(s); **tous les mardis matin(s)** every Tuesday morning; **le 8 au m.** on the morning of the 8th; **à sept heures du m.** at seven in the morning; **de bon m., au petit m., de grand m.** very early (in the morning); **du m. au soir** from morning till night; **médicament à prendre m., midi et soir** medicine to be taken three times a day ● **matinal, -e, -aux, -ales** *adj (heure)* early; **soleil m.** morning sun; **être m.** to be an early riser

matinée [matine] *nf* morning; *Théâtre & Cin* matinée; **dans la m.** in the course of the morning

matos [matos] *nm Fam* gear

matou [matu] *nm* tomcat

matraque [matrak] *nf* bludgeon; *(de policier) Br* truncheon, *Am* nightstick ● **matraquage** *nm* **m. publicitaire** hype ● **matraquer** *vt (frapper)* to club; *Fig (harceler)* to bombard

matrice [matris] *nf (moule)* & *Math* matrix ● **matricielle** *adj f Ordinat* **imprimante m.** dot matrix printer

matricule [matrikyl] **1** *nm* number

2 *adj* **numéro m.** registration number

matrimonial, -e, -iaux, -iales [matrimɔnjal, -jo] *adj* matrimonial

mâture [mɑtyr] *nf (de navire)* masts

maturité [matyrite] *nf* maturity; **arriver à m.** *(fromage, vin)* to mature; *(fruit)* to ripen

maudire* [modir] *vt* to curse ● **maudit, -ite** *adj (damné)* cursed; *(insupportable)* damned

maugréer [mogree] *vi* to growl, to grumble (**contre** at)

Maurice [mɔris] *nm* **l'île M.** Mauritius

mausolée [mozɔle] *nm* mausoleum

maussade [mosad] *adj (personne)* sullen; *(temps)* gloomy

mauvais, -aise [move, -εz] **1** adj bad; (santé, vue) poor; (méchant) nasty; (mal choisi) wrong; (mer) rough; **plus m. que...** worse than...; **le plus m.** the worst; **être m. en anglais** to be bad at English; **être en mauvaise santé** to be in bad or ill or poor health
2 adv **il fait m.** the weather's bad; **ça sent m.** it smells bad
3 nm **le bon et le m.** the good and the bad
mauve [mov] adj & nm (couleur) mauve
mauviette [movjεt] nf Fam (personne) weakling
maux [mo] pl de **mal**
maxime [maksim] nf maxim
maximum [maksimɔm] (pl **maxima** [-ma] ou **maximums**) **1** nm maximum; **faire le m.** to do one's very best; **au m.** at the most; Fam **un m. de gens** (le plus possible) as many people as possible; (énormément) loads of people
2 adj maximum • **maximal, -e, -aux, -ales** adj maximum
mayonnaise [majɔnεz] nf mayonnaise
mazout [mazut] nm (fuel) oil
me [mə]

| m' is used before a vowel or mute h. |

pron personnel (**a**) (complément direct) me; **il me voit** he sees me (**b**) (complément indirect) (to) me; **elle me parle** she speaks to me; **tu me l'as dit** you told me (**c**) (réfléchi) myself; **je me lave** I wash myself (**d**) (avec les pronominaux) **je me suis trompé** I made a mistake
méandres [meɑ̃dr] nmpl (de rivière) meanders
mec [mεk] nm Fam (individu) guy, Br bloke
mécanicien [mekanisjɛ̃] nm mechanic; (de train) Br train driver, Am engineer
mécanique [mekanik] **1** adj mechanical; **jouet m.** wind-up toy
2 nf (science) mechanics (sing); (mécanisme) mechanism • **mécanisme** nm mechanism

| ⚠ Il faut noter que le nom anglais **mechanic** est un faux ami. Il signifie **mécanicien**. |

mécanisation [mekanizasjɔ̃] nf mechanization
mécène [mesεn] nm patron (of the arts)
méchant, -ante [meʃɑ̃, -ɑ̃t] adj (personne, remarque, blessure) nasty; (enfant) naughty; (chien) vicious; **être de méchante humeur** to be in a foul mood; **'attention! chien m.'** 'beware of the dog'

• **méchamment** [-amɑ̃] adv (cruellement) nastily; Fam (très) terribly • **méchanceté** nf nastiness; **une m.** (parole) a nasty remark; (acte) a nasty action
mèche [mεʃ] nf (**a**) (de cheveux) lock; **se faire des mèches** to have highlights put in one's hair (**b**) (de bougie) wick; (de pétard) fuse; (de perceuse) bit; Fig **vendre la m.** to spill the beans (**c**) Fam **être de m. avec qn** to be in cahoots with sb
méconnaître* [mekɔnεtr] vt (fait) to fail to take into account; (talent, artiste) to fail to recognize • **méconnaissable** adj unrecognizable • **méconnu, -ue** adj unrecognized
mécontent, -ente [mekɔ̃tɑ̃, -ɑ̃t] adj (insatisfait) displeased (**de** with); (contrarié) annoyed • **mécontentement** nm (insatisfaction) displeasure; (contrariété) annoyance • **mécontenter** vt (ne pas satisfaire) to displease; (contrarier) to annoy
Mecque [mεk] nf **La M.** Mecca
médaille [medaj] nf (décoration, bijou) & Sport medal; (portant le nom) pendant (with name engraved on it); (de chien) name tag; Sport **être m. d'or/d'argent** to be a gold/silver medallist • **médaillé, -ée** nmf medal holder • **médaillon** nm (bijou) locket; (de viande) medallion
médecin [medsɛ̃] nm doctor, physician; **m. de famille** family doctor; **m. généraliste** general practitioner; **m. traitant** consulting physician • **médecine** nf medicine; **médecines alternatives** ou **douces** alternative medicine; **m. traditionnelle** traditional medicine; **étudiant en m.** medical student • **médical, -e, -aux, -ales** adj medical • **médicament** nm medicine • **médicinal, -e, -aux, -ales** adj medicinal • **médico-légal, -e** (mpl **médico-légaux**, fpl **médico-légales**) adj forensic
média [medja] nm medium; **les médias** the media • **médiatique** adj **campagne/ événement m.** media campaign/event • **médiatiser** vt to give media coverage to
médiateur, -trice [medjatœr, -tris] nmf mediator • **médiation** nf mediation
médiéval, -e, -aux, -ales [medjeval, -o] adj medieval
médiocre [medjɔkr] adj mediocre • **médiocrité** nf mediocrity
médire* [medir] vi **m. de qn** to speak ill of sb • **médisance** nf (action) gossiping; **médisances** (propos) gossip
méditer [medite] **1** vt (réfléchir profondément à) to contemplate; **m. de faire qch** to be contemplating doing sth

2 *vi* to meditate (**sur** on) • **méditatif, -ive** *adj* meditative • **méditation** *nf* meditation

Méditerranée [mediterane] *nf* **la M.** the Mediterranean • **méditerranéen, -éenne** *adj* Mediterranean

médium [medjɔm] *nmf (voyant)* medium

méduse [medyz] *nf* jellyfish • **méduser** *vt* to dumbfound

meeting [mitiŋ] *nm* meeting

méfait [mefɛ] *nm* misdemeanour; **les méfaits du temps** the ravages of time

méfier [mefje] **se méfier** *vpr* to be careful; **se m. de qn** not to trust sb; **se m. de qch** to watch out for sth; **méfie-toi!** watch out!, beware! • **méfiance** *nf* distrust, mistrust • **méfiant, -iante** *adj* suspicious, distrustful

mégalomane [megalɔman] (*Fam* **mégalo**) *nmf* megalomaniac • **mégalomanie** *nf* megalomania

mégaoctet [megaɔktɛ] *nm Ordinat* megabyte

mégaphone [megafɔn] *nm Br* megaphone, *Am* bullhorn

mégarde [megard] **par mégarde** *adv* inadvertently

mégère [meʒɛr] *nf (femme)* shrew

mégot [mego] *nm* cigarette butt *or* end

meilleur, -eure [mejœr] **1** *adj* better (**que** than); **le m. résultat/moment** the best result/moment

2 *nmf* **le m., la meilleure** the best (one); **pour le m. et pour le pire** for better or for worse

3 *adv* **il fait m.** it's warmer

mél [mel] *nm (courrier)* e-mail

mélancolie [melãkɔli] *nf* melancholy • **mélancolique** *adj* melancholy

mélange [melãʒ] *nm (résultat)* mixture; *(opération)* mixing • **mélanger 1** *vt (mêler)* to mix; *(brouiller)* to mix up **2 se mélanger** *vpr (s'incorporer)* to mix; *(idées)* to get mixed up • **mélangeur** *nm Br* mixer tap, *Am* mixing faucet

mélasse [melas] *nf Br* treacle, *Am* molasses; *Fam* **être dans la m.** to be in a mess

mêler [mele] **1** *vt* to mix (**à** with); *(odeurs, thèmes)* to combine; **m. qn à qch** *(affaire, conversation)* to involve sb in sth

2 se mêler *vpr* to combine (**à** with); **se m. à qch** *(foule)* to mingle with sth; *(conversation)* to join in sth; **se m. de qch** to get involved in sth; **mêle-toi de tes affaires!** mind your own business! • **mêlé, -ée** *adj* mixed (**de** with) • **mêlée** *nf (bataille)* fray; *Rugby* scrum(mage)

méli-mélo [melimelo] (*pl* **mélis-mélos**) *nm Fam* muddle

mélo [melo] *Fam* **1** *adj* melodramatic **2** *nm* melodrama

mélodie [melɔdi] *nf* melody • **mélodieux, -ieuse** *adj* melodious • **mélodique** *adj* melodic • **mélomane** *nmf* music lover

mélodrame [melɔdram] *nm* melodrama • **mélodramatique** *adj* melodramatic

melon [məlɔ̃] *nm (fruit)* melon; **(chapeau) m.** *Br* bowler (hat), *Am* derby

membrane [mãbran] *nf* membrane

membre [mãbr] *nm (bras, jambe)* limb; *(de groupe)* member

même [mɛm] **1** *adj (identique)* same; **en m. temps** at the same time (**que** as); **le m. jour** the same day; **le jour m.** *(exact)* the very day; **il est la bonté m.** he is kindness itself; **lui-m./vous-m.** himself/yourself

2 *pron* **le/la m.** the same (one); **j'ai les mêmes** I have the same (ones); **cela revient au m.** it amounts to the same thing

3 *adv (y compris, aussi)* even; **m. si...** even if...; **ici m.** in this very place; **tout de m.,** *Fam* **quand m.** all the same; **de m.** likewise; **de m. que...** just as...; **être à m. de faire qch** to be in a position to do sth; **dormir à m. le sol** to sleep on the ground; **boire à m. la bouteille** to drink (straight) from the bottle

mémento [memɛ̃to] *nm (aide-mémoire)* handbook; *(carnet)* diary

mémère [memɛr] *nf Fam Péj* **une grosse m.** a fat old bag

mémoire [memwar] **1** *nf* memory; **de m.** *(citer)* from memory; **de m. d'homme** in living memory; **à la m. de** in memory of; *Ordinat* **m. morte/vive** read-only/random-access memory

2 *nm (rapport)* report; *Univ* dissertation; **Mémoires** *(chronique)* memoirs • **mémorable** *adj* memorable

mémorandum [memɔrãdɔm] *nm (note)* memorandum

mémorial, -iaux [memɔrjal, -jo] *nm (monument)* memorial

menace [mənas] *nf* threat • **menaçant, -ante** *adj* threatening • **menacer** *vt* to threaten (**de faire** to do)

ménage [menaʒ] *nm (entretien)* housekeeping; *(couple)* couple, household; **faire le m.** to do the housework; **faire bon m. avec qn** to get on well with sb • **ménager¹, -ère 1** *adj (équipement)* household **2** *nf* **ménagère** *(femme)* housewife

ménager² [menaʒe] **1** *vt (argent)* to use sparingly; *(forces)* to save; *(entrevue)* to arrange; *(sortie)* to provide; **m. qn** to treat sb carefully; **ne pas m. sa peine** to put in a lot of effort

2 se ménager *vpr (prendre soin de soi)* to look after oneself; *(se réserver)* to set aside •**ménagement** *nm (soin)* care; **sans m.** *(brutalement)* brutally

ménagerie [menaʒri] *nf* menagerie

mendier [mɑ̃dje] **1** *vt* to beg for
   2 *vi* to beg •**mendiant, -iante** *nmf* beggar •**mendicité** *nf* begging

menées [məne] *nfpl* intrigues

mener [məne] **1** *vt (personne)* to take (**à** to); *(course, vie)* to lead; *(enquête, tâche)* to carry out; **m. une campagne** to wage a campaign; *Fig* **m. la vie dure à qn** to give sb a hard time; *Fig* **m. qch à bien** to carry sth through; **ça ne mène à rien** it won't get you/us anywhere
   2 *vi Sport* to lead; **m. à un lieu** to lead to a place; *Fam* **elle n'en menait pas large** her heart was in her mouth •**meneur, -euse** *nmf (de révolte)* ringleader

méninges [menɛ̃ʒ] *nfpl Fam* brains

méningite [menɛ̃ʒit] *nf* meningitis

ménopause [menɔpoz] *nf* menopause

menottes [mənɔt] *nfpl* handcuffs; **passer les m. à qn** to handcuff sb

mensonge [mɑ̃sɔ̃ʒ] *nm (propos)* lie; *(action)* lying •**mensonger, -ère** *adj (propos)* untrue; *(publicité)* misleading

menstruation [mɑ̃stryasjɔ̃] *nf* menstruation

mensuel, -uelle [mɑ̃sɥɛl] **1** *adj* monthly
   2 *nm (revue)* monthly •**mensualité** *nf* monthly payment •**mensuellement** *adv* monthly

mensurations [mɑ̃syrasjɔ̃] *nfpl* measurements

mental, -e, -aux, -ales [mɑ̃tal, -o] *adj* mental •**mentalité** *nf* mentality

menthe [mɑ̃t] *nf* mint

mention [mɑ̃sjɔ̃] *nf (fait de citer)* mention; *(à un examen)* ≃ distinction; *Scol* **m. passable/assez bien/bien/très bien** ≃ C/B/A; **faire m. de qch** to mention sth; **'rayez les mentions inutiles'** 'delete as appropriate' •**mentionner** *vt* to mention

mentir* [mɑ̃tir] *vi* to lie (**à** to) •**menteur, -euse** *1 adj* lying **2** *nmf* liar

menton [mɑ̃tɔ̃] *nm* chin

menu¹ [məny] *nm (de restaurant)* set menu; *Ordinat* menu; **par le m.** in detail

menu², -ue [məny] **1** *adj (petit)* tiny; *(mince)* slim; *(détail, monnaie)* small
   2 *adv (hacher)* small, finely

menuisier [mənɥizje] *nm* carpenter, joiner •**menuiserie** *nf (atelier)* joiner's workshop; *(ouvrage)* woodwork

méprendre [meprɑ̃dr] **se méprendre** *vpr*

Littéraire **se m. sur** to be mistaken about •**méprise** *nf* mistake

mépris [mepri] *nm* contempt (**pour** for), scorn (**pour** for); **au m. de qch** without regard to sth; **avoir du m.** pour qn to despise sb •**méprisable** *adj* despicable •**méprisant, -ante** *adj* contemptuous, scornful •**mépriser** *vt* to despise

mer [mɛr] *nf* sea; *(marée)* tide; **en (haute) m.** at sea; **par m.** by sea; **aller à la m.** to go to the seaside; **prendre la m.** to set sail; *Fam* **ce n'est pas la m. à boire** it's no big deal; **un homme à la m.!** man overboard!

mercantile [mɛrkɑ̃til] *adj Péj* mercenary

mercatique [mɛrkatik] *nf* marketing

mercenaire [mɛrsənɛr] *adj & nm* mercenary

mercerie [mɛrsəri] *nf (magasin) Br* haberdasher's, *Am* notions store •**mercier, -ière** *nmf Br* haberdasher, *Am* notions dealer *or* merchant

merci [mɛrsi] **1** *exclam* thank you, thanks (**de** *ou* **pour** for); **non m.** no thank you; **m. bien** thanks very much
   2 *nf* **à la m. de qn/qch** at the mercy of sb/sth; **tenir qn à sa m.** to have sb at one's mercy; **sans m.** merciless

mercredi [mɛrkrədi] *nm* Wednesday

mercure [mɛrkyr] *nm* mercury

merde [mɛrd] *Vulg* **1** *nf* shit; *(voiture, télé)* shitty; **de m.** shitty; **être dans la m.** to be in the shit
   2 *exclam* shit! •**merder** *vi très Fam (ne pas marcher)* to go down the pan; **j'ai merdé à l'examen** I really screwed up in the exam •**merdique** *adj très Fam* shitty

mère [mɛr] *nf* mother; *Fam* **la m. Dubois** old Mrs Dubois; *Com* **maison m.** parent company; **m. de famille** wife and mother; **m. célibataire** single mother; **m. porteuse** surrogate mother; **m. poule** mother hen

méridien [meridjɛ̃] *nm* meridian

méridional, -e, -aux, -ales [meridjɔnal, -o] **1** *adj* southern
   2 *nmf* southerner

meringue [mərɛ̃g] *nf* meringue

merisier [mərizje] *nm (bois)* cherry

mérite [merit] *nm* merit; *(honneur)* credit; **avoir du m. à faire qch** to deserve credit for doing sth; **homme de m.** *(valeur)* man of worth •**méritant, -ante** *adj* deserving •**mériter** *vt (être digne de)* to deserve; *(demander)* to be worth; **m. de réussir** to deserve to succeed; **m. réflexion** to be worth thinking about; **ce livre mérite d'être lu** this book is worth reading •**méritoire** *adj* commendable

merlan [mɛrlɑ̃] *nm (poisson)* whiting; *très Fam (coiffeur)* hairdresser

merle [mɛrl] *nm* blackbird
merlu [mɛrly] *nm* hake
merveille [mɛrvɛj] *nf* wonder, marvel; **à m.** wonderfully (well); *Fig* **faire des merveilles** to work wonders; **les Sept Merveilles du monde** the Seven Wonders of the World
merveilleux, -euse [mɛrvejø, -øz] **1** *adj* wonderful, *Br* marvellous, *Am* marvelous **2** *nm* **le m.** the supernatural • **merveilleusement** *adv* wonderfully
mes [me] *voir* **mon**
mésange [mezɑ̃ʒ] *nf* tit
mésaventure [mezavɑ̃tyr] *nf* misadventure
mesdames [medam] *pl de* **madame**
mesdemoiselles [medmwazɛl] *pl de* **mademoiselle**
mésentente [mezɑ̃tɑ̃t] *nf* disagreement
mésestimer [mezɛstime] *vt* to underestimate
mesquin, -ine [meskɛ̃, -in] *adj* mean, petty • **mesquinerie** *nf* meanness, pettiness; **une m.** an act of meanness
mess [mes] *nm inv Mil (salle)* mess
message [mesaʒ] *nm* message; **m. publicitaire** advertisement • **messager, -ère** *nmf* messenger • **messagerie** *nf* courier company; **m. électronique** electronic mail service; **m. vocale** voice mail
messe [mes] *nf (office, musique)* mass; **aller à la m.** to go to mass; *Fig* **faire des messes basses** to whisper
messeigneurs [mesɛɲœr] *pl de* **monseigneur**
Messie [mesi] *nm* **le M.** the Messiah
messieurs [mesjø] *pl de* **monsieur**
mesure [məzyr] *nf (dimension)* measurement; *(action)* measuring; *(moyen)* measure; *(retenue)* moderation; *Mus (temps)* time; *Mus (division)* bar; **sur m.** *(vêtement)* made to measure; **être en m. de faire qch** to be in a position to do sth; **dépasser la m.** to exceed the bounds; **être sans commune m. avec qch** to be out of proportion to sth; **prendre la m. de qch** *(problème)* to size sth up; **prendre les mesures de qn** to measure sb; **prendre des mesures** to take measures; **à m. que...** as...; **dans la m. où...** in so far as...; **dans une certaine m.** to a certain extent; **dans la m. du possible** as far as possible
mesurer [məzyre] **1** *vt (dimension, taille)* to measure; *(déterminer)* to assess; *(argent, temps)* to ration (out) **2** *vi* **m. 1 m 83** *(personne)* ≃ to be 6 ft tall; *(objet)* to measure 6 ft **3 se mesurer** *vpr Fig* **se m. à** *ou* **avec qn** to

pit oneself against sb • **mesuré, -ée** *adj (pas, ton)* measured; *(personne)* moderate
met [me] *voir* **mettre**
métal, -aux [metal, -o] *nm* metal • **métallique** *adj (éclat, reflet)* metallic; **pont m.** metal bridge • **métallisé, -ée** *adj* **bleu m.** metallic blue
métallo [metalo] *nm Fam* steelworker
métallurgie [metalyrʒi] *nf (industrie)* steel industry; *(science)* metallurgy • **métallurgique** *adj* **usine m.** steelworks • **métallurgiste** *nm* metalworker
métamorphose [metamɔrfoz] *nf* metamorphosis • **métamorphoser** *vt*, **se métamorphoser** *vpr* to transform (**en** into)
métaphore [metafɔr] *nf* metaphor • **métaphorique** *adj* metaphorical
métaphysique [metafizik] *adj* metaphysical
météo [meteo] *nf Fam (bulletin)* weather forecast
météore [meteɔr] *nm* meteor • **météorite** *nf* meteorite
météorologie [meteɔrɔlɔʒi] *nf (science)* meteorology; *(service)* weather bureau • **météorologique** *adj* meteorological; **bulletin/station m.** weather report/station
méthode [metɔd] *nf (manière, soin)* method; *(livre)* course • **méthodique** *adj* methodical
méticuleux, -euse [metikylø, -øz] *adj* meticulous
métier [metje] *nm (manuel, commercial)* trade; *(intellectuel)* profession; *(savoir-faire)* experience; **homme de m.** specialist; **tailleur de son m.** tailor by trade; **être du m.** to be in the business; **m. à tisser** loom
métis, -isse [metis] *adj & nmf* half-caste
métrage [metraʒ] *nm (action)* measuring; *(tissu)* length; *(de film)* footage; **long m.** feature film; **court m.** short film
mètre [mɛtr] *nm (mesure) Br* metre, *Am* meter; *(règle)* (metre) rule; **m. carré/cube** square/cubic metre; **m. à ruban** tape measure • **métreur** *nm* quantity surveyor • **métrique** *adj (système)* metric
métro [metro] *nm Br* underground, *Am* subway
métropole [metrɔpɔl] *nf (ville)* metropolis; *(pays)* mother country • **métropolitain, -aine** *adj* metropolitan
mets [me] *nm (aliment)* dish
mettable [metabl] *adj* wearable
metteur [metœr] *nm* **m. en scène** director
mettre* [mɛtr] **1** *vt* to put; *(vêtement,*

lunettes) to put on; *(chauffage, radio)* to switch on; *(réveil)* to set (**à** for); **m. dix heures à venir** to take ten hours to come; **j'ai mis une heure** it took me an hour; **m. 100 euros** to spend 100 euros (**pour une robe** on a dress); **m. qn en colère** to make sb angry; **m. qn à l'aise** to put sb at ease; **m. qn en liberté** to free sb; **m. qch en bouteilles** to bottle sth; **m. qch plus fort** to turn sth up; **m. de la musique** to put some music on; **m. du soin à faire qch** to take care to do sth; **mettons que...** *(+ subjunctive)* let's suppose that...

2 se mettre *vpr (se placer)* to put oneself; *(debout)* to stand; *(assis)* to sit; *(objet)* to go; **se m. en pyjama** to get into one's pyjamas; **se m. à table** to sit (down) at the table; **se m. à l'aise** to make oneself comfortable; **se m. à la cuisine/au salon** to go into the kitchen/dining room; **se m. au travail** to start work; **se m. à faire qch** to start doing sth; **le temps s'est mis au beau/à la pluie** the weather has turned fine/rainy; **se m. en rapport avec qn** to get in touch with sb; *Fam* **se m. le doigt dans l'œil** to be badly mistaken

meuble [mœbl] **1** *adj (terre)* soft

2 *nm* piece of furniture; **meubles** furniture • **meublé** *nm* furnished *Br* flat *or Am* apartment • **meubler** *vt* to furnish; *Fig (remplir)* to fill

meuf [mœf] *nf très Fam Br* bird, *Am* chick

meugler [møgle] *vi (vache)* to moo • **meuglement** [-əmɑ̃] *nm* moo; **meuglements** mooing

meule [møl] *nf (d'herbe)* stack; *(de moulin)* millstone; **m. de foin** haystack

meunier, -ière [mønje, -jɛr] *nmf* miller

meurt [mœr] *voir* **mourir**

meurtre [mœrtr] *nm* murder • **meurtrier, -ière 1** *nmf* murderer **2** *adj* murderous; *(épidémie)* deadly

meurtrir [mœrtrir] *vt* to bruise • **meurtrissure** *nf* bruise

meute [møt] *nf* pack

Mexique [mɛksik] *nm* **le M.** Mexico • **mexicain, -aine 1** *adj* Mexican **2** *nmf* **M., Mexicaine** Mexican

mezzanine [medzanin] *nf (de pièce)* mezzanine floor

mi [mi] *nm inv (note)* E

mi- [mi] *préf* **la mi-mars** mid March; **à mi-distance** midway; **cheveux mi-longs** shoulder-length hair

miaou [mjau] *exclam* miaow • **miaulement** *nm* miaowing • **miauler** [mjole] *vi (chat)* to miaow

mi-bas [mibɑ] *nm inv* knee sock

miche [miʃ] *nf (pain)* round loaf

mi-chemin [miʃmɛ̃] **à mi-chemin** *adv* halfway

mi-clos, -close [miklo, -kloz] *(mpl* **mi-clos,** *fpl* **mi-closes)** *adj* half-closed

micmac [mikmak] *nm Fam (manigance)* muddle

mi-corps [mikɔr] **à mi-corps** *adv* (up) to the waist

mi-côte [mikot] **à mi-côte** *adv* halfway up the hill

micro [mikro] *nm (microphone)* mike; *Ordinat* micro(computer) • **microphone** *nm* microphone

microbe [mikrɔb] *nm* germ, microbe

microcosme [mikrɔkɔsm] *nm* microcosm

microfiche [mikrofiʃ] *nf* microfiche

microfilm [mikrofilm] *nm* microfilm

micro-informatique [mikroɛ̃fɔrmatik] *nf* microcomputing

micro-ondes [mikrɔɔ̃d] *nm inv* microwave; **four à m.** microwave oven

micro-ordinateur [mikroɔrdinatœr] *(pl* **micro-ordinateurs)** *nm* microcomputer

microprocesseur [mikroprɔsɛsœr] *nm Ordinat* microprocessor

microscope [mikrɔskɔp] *nm* microscope • **microscopique** *adj* microscopic

midi [midi] *nm* (**a**) *(heure)* twelve o'clock, midday; *(heure du déjeuner)* lunchtime; **entre m. et deux heures** at lunchtime; *Fig* **chercher m. à quatorze heures** to make unnecessary complications for oneself (**b**) *(sud)* south; **le M.** the South of France

mie [mi] *nf (de pain)* soft part

miel [mjɛl] *nm* honey • **mielleux, -euse** *adj Fig (parole, personne)* smooth

mien, mienne [mjɛ̃, mjɛn] **1** *pron possessif* **le m., la mienne** mine, *Br* my one; **les miens, les miennes** mine, *Br* my ones; **les deux miens** my two

2 *nmpl* **les miens** *(ma famille)* my family

miette [mjɛt] *nf (de pain)* crumb; **réduire qch en miettes** to smash sth to pieces; *Fam* **ne pas perdre une m. de qch** *(conversation)* not to miss a word of sth

mieux [mjø] **1** *adv* better (**que** than); **aller m.** to be (feeling) better; **de m. en m.** better and better; **faire qch à qui m. m.** to try to outdo each other doing sth; **le/la/les m.** *(être)* the best; *(de deux)* the better; **le m. serait de...** the best thing would be to...; **le plus tôt sera le m.** the sooner the better

2 *adj inv* better; *(plus beau)* better-looking; **si tu n'as rien de m. à faire** if you've got nothing better to do

3 *nm (amélioration)* improvement; **faire de son m.** to do one's best; **faites au m.** do the best you can

mièvre [mjɛvr] *adj* insipid

mignon, -onne [miɲɔ̃, -ɔn] *adj (charmant)* cute; *(gentil)* nice

migraine [migrɛn] *nf* headache; *Méd* migraine

migration [migrasjɔ̃] *nf* migration • **migrant, -ante** *adj & nmf* migrant • **migrateur, -trice** *adj* migratory

mijoter [miʒɔte] **1** *vt (avec soin)* to cook (lovingly); *(lentement)* to simmer; *Fam (tramer)* to cook up
2 *vi* to simmer

mil [mil] *adj inv* **l'an deux m.** the year two thousand

milice [milis] *nf* militia • **milicien** *nm* militiaman

milieu, -x [miljø] *nm (centre)* middle; *(cadre, groupe social)* environment; *(entre extrêmes)* middle course; *Phys* medium; **milieux littéraires/militaires** literary/military circles; **au m. de** in the middle of; **au m. du danger** in the midst of danger; **le juste m.** the happy medium; **le m. (la pègre)** the underworld

militaire [militɛr] **1** *adj* military
2 *nm* serviceman; *(dans l'armée de terre)* soldier

militer [milite] *vi (personne)* to campaign (**pour** for; **contre** against) • **militant, -ante** *adj & nmf* militant

mille [mil] **1** *adj inv & nm inv* thousand; **m. hommes** a *or* one thousand men; **deux m.** two thousand; *Fig* **mettre dans le m.** to hit the bull's-eye; **je vous le donne en m.!** you'll never guess!
2 *nm* **m. (marin)** nautical mile • **millefeuille** *(pl* **mille-feuilles)** *nm Br* ≃ vanilla slice, *Am* ≃ napoleon • **mille-pattes** *nm inv* centipede • **millième** *adj, nm & nmf* thousandth; **un m.** a thousandth • **millier** *nm* thousand; **un m. (de)** a thousand or so; **par milliers** in their thousands

millénaire [milenɛr] *nm* millennium

millésime [milezim] *nm (de vin)* year; *(de pièce de monnaie)* date

millet [mijɛ] *nm* millet

milliard [miljar] *nm* billion • **milliardaire** *adj & nmf* billionaire

millimètre [milimɛtr] *nm* millimetre

million [miljɔ̃] *nm* million; **un m. d'euros** a million euros; **deux millions** two million; **par millions** in millions • **millionième** *adj, nm & nmf* millionth • **millionnaire** *nmf* millionaire

mime [mim] **1** *nm (art)* mime **2** *nmf (artiste)* mime • **mimer** *vti (exprimer)* to mime • **mimique** *nf (mine)* (funny) face

mimétisme [mimetism] *nm* mimicry; **agir par m.** to mimic *or* copy sb's attitudes

mimosa [mimoza] *nm (arbre, fleur)* mimosa

minable [minabl] *adj (lieu, personne)* shabby; *(médiocre)* pathetic

minaret [minarɛ] *nm* minaret

minauder [minode] *vi* to simper

mince [mɛ̃s] **1** *adj* thin; *(élancé)* slim; *(insuffisant)* slight
2 *exclam Fam* **m. (alors)!** *(de déception)* oh heck!, *Br* blast (it)!; *(de surprise)* well, blow me! • **minceur** *nf* thinness; *(sveltesse)* slimness • **mincir** *vi* to get slimmer

mine [min] *nf* (**a**) *(physionomie)* look; **avoir bonne/mauvaise m.** to look well/ ill; **faire m. de faire qch** to make as if to do sth; **faire grise m.** to look anything but pleased; *Fam* **m. de rien** *(discrètement)* quite casually (**b**) *(gisement) & Fig* mine; **m. de charbon** coalmine (**c**) *(de crayon)* lead (**d**) *(engin explosif)* mine

miner [mine] *vt (terrain)* to mine; *Fig (saper)* to undermine; **m. qn** *(chagrin, maladie)* to wear sb down

minerai [minrɛ] *nm* ore

minéral, -e, -aux, -ales [mineral, -o] *adj & nm* mineral

minéralogique [mineralɔʒik] *adj* **plaque m.** *(de véhicule) Br* number *or Am* license plate

minerve [minɛrv] *nf* surgical collar

minet, -ette [minɛ, -ɛt] *nmf Fam (chat)* puss; *(personne)* trendy

mineur, -eure [minœr] **1** *nm (ouvrier)* miner; **m. de fond** underground worker
2 *adj (secondaire) & Mus* minor; *(de moins de 18 ans)* underage
3 *nmf Jur* minor • **minier, -ière** *adj* **industrie minière** mining industry

miniature [minjatyr] **1** *nf* miniature
2 *adj* **train m.** miniature train

minibus [minibys] *nm* minibus

minichaîne [miniʃɛn] *nf* mini (hi-fi) system

minidisc [minidisk] *nm* MiniDisc®

minigolf [minigɔlf] *nm* crazy golf

minijupe [miniʒyp] *nf* miniskirt

minimal, -ale, -aux, -ales [minimal, -o] *adj* minimum

minime [minim] *adj* minimal • **minimiser** *vt* to minimize

minimum [minimɔm] *(pl* **minima** [-ma] *ou* **minimums**) **1** *nm* minimum; **le m. de** *(force)* the minimum (amount of); **faire le**

m. to do the bare minimum; **en un m. de temps** in as short a time as possible; **au (grand) m.** at the very least; **le m. vital** a minimum to live on; **les minima sociaux** = basic income support
2 *adj* minimum

ministère [ministɛr] *nm (département)* ministry; *(gouvernement)* government, cabinet; **m. des Affaires étrangères** *Br* ≃ Foreign Office, *Am* ≃ State Department; **m. de l'Intérieur** *Br* ≃ Home Office, *Am* ≃ Department of the Interior; *Jur* **le m. public** ≃ the Crown Prosecution Service • **ministériel, -ielle** *adj* ministerial; **remaniement m.** cabinet *or* government reshuffle

ministre [ministr] *nm Pol & Rel* secretary, *Br* minister; **m. des Affaires étrangères** *Br* ≃ Foreign Secretary, *Am* ≃ Secretary of State; **m. de l'Intérieur** *Br* ≃ Home Secretary, *Am* ≃ Secretary of the Interior; **m. de la Justice** *Br* ≃ Lord Chancellor, *Am* ≃ Attorney General; **m. de la Culture** ≃ Arts Minister; **m. d'État** ≃ secretary of state, *Br* ≃ cabinet minister

Minitel® [minitɛl] *nm* = consumer information network accessible via home computer terminal

minois [minwa] *nm* **joli/petit m.** pretty/little face

minorer [minɔre] *vt (faire baisser)* to reduce

minorité [minɔrite] *nf* minority; **en m.** in the minority • **minoritaire** *adj* **parti m.** minority party; **être m.** to be in the minority

Minorque [minɔrk] *nf* Minorca

minou [minu] *nm Fam (chat)* puss

minuit [minɥi] *nm* midnight, twelve o'clock

minus [minys] *nm Fam (incapable)* nohoper

minuscule [minyskyl] 1 *adj (petit)* tiny, minute
2 *adj & nf* **(lettre) m.** small letter

minute [minyt] 1 *nf* minute; **à la m.** *(tout de suite)* this (very) minute; **d'une m. à l'autre** any minute (now)
2 *adj inv* **plats m.** convenience food • **minuter** *vt* to time • **minuterie** *nf (d'éclairage)* time switch • **minuteur** *nm* timer

minutie [minysi] *nf* meticulousness • **minutieux, -ieuse** *adj* meticulous

mioche [mjɔʃ] *nmf Fam (enfant)* kid

mirabelle [mirabɛl] *nf* mirabelle plum

miracle [mirakl] *nm* miracle; **par m.** miraculously • **miraculeux, -euse** *adj* miraculous

mirador [miradɔr] *nm* watchtower

mirage [miraʒ] *nm* mirage

mire [mir] *nf* **point de m.** *(cible) & Fig* target

mirettes [mirɛt] *nfpl Fam* eyes

mirifique [mirifik] *adj Hum* fabulous

mirobolant, -ante [mirɔbɔlɑ̃, -ɑ̃t] *adj Fam* fantastic

miroir [mirwar] *nm* mirror • **miroiter** *vi* to shimmer

mis, mise¹ [mi, miz] 1 *pp de* mettre
2 *adj* **bien m.** *(vêtu)* well-dressed

misanthrope [mizɑ̃trɔp] *nmf* misanthropist

mise² [miz] *nf* (a) *(placement)* putting; **m. à feu** *(de fusée)* blast-off; **m. au point** *(de rapport)* finalization; *Phot* focusing; *(de moteur)* tuning; *(de technique)* perfecting; *Fig (clarification)* clarification; **m. en garde** warning; **m. en marche** starting up; **m. en page(s)** page make-up; *Ordinat* **m. en réseau** networking; **m. en service** putting into service; **m. en scène** *Théâtre* production; *Cin* direction (b) *(argent)* stake (c) *(tenue)* attire (d) **être de m.** to be acceptable

miser [mize] *vt (argent)* to stake (**sur** on); **m. sur qn/qch** *(parier)* to bet on sb/sth; *(compter sur)* to count on sb/sth; **m. sur tous les tableaux** to hedge one's bets

misère [mizɛr] *nf* extreme poverty; **être dans la m.** to be poverty-stricken; **gagner une m.** to earn a pittance; **payer qch une m.** to pay next to nothing for sth; **faire des misères à qn** to give sb a hard time • **misérable 1** *(pitoyable)* miserable; *(pauvre)* destitute; *(condition, existence)* wretched; *(logement, quartier)* seedy, slummy **2** *nmf (indigent)* poor wretch; *(scélérat)* scoundrel • **miséreux, -euse 1** *adj* destitute **2** *nmf* pauper

> *Ⅱ* faut noter que le nom anglais **misery** est un faux ami. Il signifie **malheur** ou **tristesse**.

miséricorde [mizerikɔrd] *nf* mercy • **miséricordieux, -ieuse** *adj* merciful

misogyne [mizɔʒin] *nmf* misogynist

missile [misil] *nm* missile

mission [misjɔ̃] *nf (tâche, vocation, organisation)* mission; *(employé)* task; **partir en m.** *(cadre)* to go away on business; *(diplomate)* to go off on a mission; **m. accomplie** mission accomplished; **m. scientifique** scientific expedition • **missionnaire** *nmf & adj* missionary

missive [misiv] *nf Littéraire (lettre)* missive

mistral, -als [mistral] *nm* **le m.** the mistral
mite [mit] *nf* moth •**mité, -ée** *adj* moth-eaten •**miteux, -euse** *adj* shabby
mi-temps [mitɑ̃] **1** *nf inv Sport (pause)* half-time; *(période)* half
2 *nm inv* part-time job; **travailler à m.** to work part-time; **prendre un m.** to take on a part-time job
mitigé, -ée [mitiʒe] *adj (accueil)* luke-warm; *(sentiments)* mixed
mitonner [mitɔne] *vt (cuire à petit feu)* to simmer gently
mitoyen, -enne [mitwajɛ̃, -jɛn] *adj* common, shared; **mur m.** party wall
mitrailler [mitraje] *vt* to machine-gun; *Fam (photographier)* to click or snap away at; **m. qn de questions** to bombard sb with questions •**mitraillette** *nf* subma-chine gun •**mitrailleur** *adj* **fusil m.** ma-chine gun •**mitrailleuse** *nf* machine gun
mi-voix [mivwa] **à mi-voix** *adv* in a low voice
mixer [mikse] *vt (ingrédients, film)* to mix; *(rendre liquide)* to blend
mixe(u)r [miksœr] *nm (pour mélanger)* (food) mixer; *(pour rendre liquide)* liqui-dizer
mixte [mikst] *adj* mixed; *(école)* co-educational, *Br* mixed; *(commission)* joint; *(cuisinière)* gas-and-electric
mixture [mikstyr] *nf* mixture
MJC [ɛmʒise] *(abrév* **maison des jeunes et de la culture)** *nf* = youth club and arts centre
MLF [ɛmɛlɛf] *(abrév* **Mouvement de libé-ration des femmes)** *nm* ≃ Women's Liber-ation Movement
Mlle *(abrév* **Mademoiselle)** Miss
MM *(abrév* **Messieurs)** Messrs
mm *(abrév* **millimètre(s))** mm
Mme *(abrév* **Madame)** Mrs
mobile [mɔbil] **1** *adj (pièce, cible)* mov-ing; *(panneau, fête)* movable; *(personne)* mobile; *(feuillets)* loose; **échelle m.** sli-ding scale
2 *nm (décoration)* mobile; *(motif)* motive (**de** for) •**mobilité** *nf* mobility
mobilier [mɔbilje] *nm* furniture
mobiliser [mɔbilize] *vt,* **se mobiliser** *vpr* to mobilize •**mobilisation** *nf* mobiliza-tion
Mobylette® [mɔbilɛt] *nf* moped
mocassin [mɔkasɛ̃] *nm* moccasin
moche [mɔʃ] *adj Fam (laid)* ugly; *(mal)* rotten
modalité [mɔdalite] *nf (manière)* mode (**de** of); *(de contrat)* clause; **modalités de paiement** conditions of payment

mode¹ [mɔd] *nf (tendance)* fashion; *(in-dustrie)* fashion trade; **à la m.** fashion-able; **à la m. de** in the manner of; **passé de m.** out of fashion
mode² [mɔd] *nm* (**a**) *(manière)* & *Ordinat* & *Mus* mode; **m. d'emploi** instructions; **m. de paiement** means of payment; **m. de transport** mode of transport; **m. de vie** way of life (**b**) *Grammaire* mood
modèle [mɔdɛl] **1** *nm (schéma, exemple, personne)* model; *Tricot* pattern; **grand/petit m.** *(de vêtement)* large/small size; **m. déposé** registered design; **m. réduit** small-scale model
2 *adj* **élève/petite fille m.** model pupil/girl •**modeler 1** *vt* to model (**sur** on) **2 se modeler** *vpr* **se m. sur qn** to model oneself on sb •**modéliste** *nmf* stylist, designer
modem [mɔdɛm] *nm Ordinat* modem
modéré, -ée [mɔdere] *adj* moderate •**modérément** *adv* moderately
modérer [mɔdere] **1** *vt (passions, désirs)* to moderate, to restrain; *(vitesse, tempé-rature)* to reduce
2 se modérer *vpr* to calm down •**modé-rateur, -trice 1** *adj* moderating **2** *nmf (per-sonne)* moderator •**modération** *nf (retenue)* moderation; *(réduction)* reduc-tion; **avec m.** in moderation; **à consom-mer avec m.** drink in moderation *(health warning on all products advertising alco-holic drinks)*
moderne [mɔdɛrn] **1** *adj* modern
2 *nm* **le m.** *(mobilier)* modern furniture •**modernisation** *nf* modernization •**mo-derniser** *vt,* **se moderniser** *vpr* to modern-ize •**modernisme** *nm* modernism •**mo-dernité** *nf* modernity
modeste [mɔdɛst] *adj* modest •**modes-tement** [-əmɑ̃] *adv* modestly •**modestie** *nf* modesty
modifier [mɔdifje] **1** *vt* to alter, to modify
2 se modifier *vpr* to alter •**modification** *nf* alteration, modification; **apporter une m. à qch** to make an alteration to sth
modique [mɔdik] *adj (prix, somme)* modest •**modicité** *nf* modesty
modiste [mɔdist] *nmf* milliner
module [mɔdyl] *nm (élément)* unit; *(de vaisseau spatial)* & *Scol* module
moduler [mɔdyle] *vt (son, amplitude)* to modulate; *(ajuster)* to adjust (**en fonction de** in relation to) •**modulation** *nf (de son, d'amplitude)* modulation; *Radio* **m. de fréquence** frequency modulation
moelle [mwal] *nf (d'os)* marrow; *Fig* **jus-qu'à la m.** to the core; **m. épinière** spinal cord; **m. osseuse** bone marrow

moelleux, -euse [mwalø, -øz] *adj (lit, tissu)* soft; *(voix, vin)* mellow

mœurs [mœr(s)] *nfpl (morale)* morals; *(habitudes)* customs; **entrer dans les m.** to become part of everyday life

mohair [mɔɛr] *nm* mohair

moi [mwa] **1** *pron personnel* (**a**) *(après une préposition)* me; **pour/avec m.** for/with me; *Fam* **un ami à m.** a friend of mine (**b**) *(complément direct)* me; **laissez-m.** leave me (**c**) *(complément indirect)* (to) me; **montrez-le-m.** show it to me; **montrez-le-m.** show it to me, show me it (**d**) *(sujet)* I; **c'est m. qui vous le dis!** I'm telling you!; **il est plus grand que m.** he's taller than I am *or* than me; **m., je veux bien** that's OK by me

2 *nm inv* self, ego • **moi-même** *pron* myself

moignon [mwaɲɔ̃] *nm* stump

moindre [mwɛ̃dr] *adj (comparatif)* lesser; *(prix)* lower; *(quantité)* smaller; *(vitesse)* slower; **le/la m.** *(superlatif)* the least; **la m. erreur** the slightest mistake; **le m. doute** the slightest *or* least doubt; **pas la m. idée** not the slightest idea; **dans les moindres détails** in the smallest detail; **c'est un m. mal** it's not as bad as it might have been; **c'est la m. des choses** it's the least I/we/*etc* can do

moine [mwan] *nm* monk

moineau, -x [mwano] *nm* sparrow

moins [mwɛ̃] **1** ([mwɛ̃z] *before vowel*) *adv (comparatif)* less (**que** than); **m. de** *(temps, travail)* less (**que** than); *(gens, livres)* fewer (**que** than); *(100 euros)* less than; **le/la/les m.** *(superlatif)* the least; **le m. grand, la m. grande, les m. grand(e)s** the smallest; **pas le m. du monde** not in the least; **de m. en m.** [dəmɛ̃zɑ̃mwɛ̃] less and less; **au m., du m.** at least; **qch de m., qch en m.** *(qui manque)* sth missing; **dix ans de m.** ten years less; **en m.** *(personne, objet)* less; *(personnes, objets)* fewer; **les m. de vingt ans** those under twenty, the under-twenties; **à m. que...** *(+ subjunctive)* unless...

2 *prép Math* minus; **deux heures m. cinq** five to two; **il fait m. 10 (degrés)** it's minus 10 (degrees); *Fam* **c'était m. une** it was a close shave

mois [mwa] *nm* month; **au m. de juin** in (the month of) June

moisir [mwazir] *vi* to go *Br* mouldy *or Am* moldy; *Fam (stagner)* to moulder away; *(attendre)* to hang about • **moisi, -ie 1** *adj Br* mouldy, *Am* moldy **2** *nm Br* mould, *Am* mold; *(sur un mur)* mildew; **sentir le m.** to smell musty • **moisissure** *nf Br* mould, *Am* mold

moisson [mwasɔ̃] *nf* harvest; **faire la m.** to harvest • **moissonner** *vt (céréales)* to harvest; *(champ)* to reap • **moissonneuse-batteuse** (*pl* **moissonneuses-batteuses**) *nf* combine harvester

moite [mwat] *adj* sticky • **moiteur** *nf* stickiness

moitié [mwatje] *nf* half; **la m. de la pomme** half (of) the apple; **à m.** *(remplir)* halfway; **à m. plein/vide** half-full/-empty; **à m. prix** (at) half-price; **réduire qch de m.** to reduce sth by half; *Fam* **m.-m.** fifty-fifty; *Fam* **faire m.-m.** to go halves; *Fam (époux, épouse)* **ma m.** my better half

moka [mɔka] *nm (café)* mocha; *(gâteau)* coffee cake

mol [mɔl] *voir* **mou**

molaire [mɔlɛr] *nf* molar

molécule [mɔlekyl] *nf* molecule

moleskine [mɔleskin] *nf* imitation leather

molester [mɔlɛste] *vt* to manhandle

> ⚠ Il faut noter que le verbe anglais **to molest** est un faux ami. Il signifie **faire subir des sévices sexuels à**.

molette [mɔlɛt] *nf* **clé à m.** adjustable wrench *or Br* spanner

mollasse [mɔlas] *adj Fam (flasque)* flabby • **mollasson, -onne** *Fam* **1** *adj* lethargic **2** *nmf* lazy lump

molle [mɔl] *voir* **mou** • **mollement** *adv (sans énergie)* feebly; *(avec lenteur)* gently • **mollesse** *nf (de matelas)* softness; *(de personne)* lethargy • **mollir** *vi (matière)* to soften; *(courage)* to flag

mollet¹ [mɔlɛ] *nm (de jambe)* calf

mollet² [mɔlɛ] *adj* **œuf m.** soft-boiled egg

molleton [mɔltɔ̃] *nm (tissu en coton)* flannelette; *(sous-nappe)* table felt • **molletonné, -ée** *adj* fleece-lined

mollo [mɔlo] *adv Fam* **y aller m.** to take it easy

mollusque [mɔlysk] *nm* mollusc

molosse [mɔlɔs] *nm* big dog

môme [mom] *nmf Fam (enfant)* kid

moment [mɔmɑ̃] *nm (instant, durée)* moment; **un petit m.** a little while; **en ce m.** at the moment; **pour le m.** for the moment, for the time being; **sur le m.** at the time; **à ce m.-là** *(à ce moment précis)* at that (very) moment, at that time; *(dans ce cas)* then; **à un m. donné** at one point; **le m. venu** *(dans le futur)* when the time comes; **d'un m. à l'autre** any moment; **dans ces moments-là** at times like that; **par moments** at times; **au m. de partir** when just about to leave; **au m. où...** just as...; **jusqu'au m. où...** until...; **du m.**

que... *(puisque)* seeing that...; **arriver au bon m.** to arrive just at the right time; **c'est le m. ou jamais** it's now or never •**momentané, -ée** *adj (temporaire)* momentary; *(bref)* brief •**momentanément** *adv (temporairement)* temporarily; *(brièvement)* briefly

momie [mɔmi] *nf* mummy

mon, ma, mes [mɔ̃, ma, me]

> **ma** becomes **mon** [mɔ̃n] before a vowel or mute h.

adj possessif my; **m. père** my father; **ma mère** my mother; **m. ami(e)** my friend; **mes parents** my parents

Monaco [mɔnako] *nm* Monaco

monarque [mɔnark] *nm* monarch •**monarchie** *nf* monarchy •**monarchique** *adj* monarchic

monastère [mɔnastɛr] *nm* monastery

monceau, -x [mɔ̃so] *nm* heap, pile

mondain, -aine [mɔ̃dɛ̃, -ɛn] *adj* **réunion mondaine** society gathering; *Péj* **être très m.** *(personne)* to be a great socialite •**mondanités** *nfpl (événements)* social life; *(conversations superficielles)* social chitchat

> Il faut noter que l'adjectif anglais **mundane** est un faux ami. Il signifie **terre-à-terre**.

monde [mɔ̃d] *nm* world; *(gens)* people; **dans le m. entier** worldwide, all over the world; **le (grand) m.** (high) society; **tout le m.** everybody; **il y a du m.** there are a lot of people; **un m. fou** a tremendous crowd; **mettre qn au m.** to give birth to sb; **venir au m.** to come into the world; *Fam* **se faire un m. de qch** to get worked up about sth; **pas le moins du m.!** not in the least *or* slightest!; **c'est le m. à l'envers!** the world's gone mad! •**mondial, -e, -iaux, -iales** *adj (crise, renommée)* worldwide; **guerre mondiale** world war •**mondialement** *adv* throughout the world •**mondialisation** *nf* globalization

monégasque [mɔnegask] **1** *adj* Monegasque

2 *nmf* **M.** Monegasque

monétaire [mɔnetɛr] *adj* monetary

mongolien, -ienne [mɔ̃gɔljɛ̃, -jɛn] *Méd* **1** *adj* **être m.** to have Down's syndrome

2 *nmf* person with Down's syndrome •**mongolisme** *nm* Down's syndrome

moniteur, -trice [mɔnitœr, -tris] **1** *nmf* instructor; *(de colonie de vacances) Br* assistant, *Am* camp counselor

2 *nm* **Ordinat** *(écran)* monitor

monnaie [mɔnɛ] *nf (argent)* money; *(d'un pays)* currency; *(pièces)* change; **petite m.** small change; **faire de la m.** to get change; **avoir la m. de 10 euros** to have change for 10 euros; *Fig* **c'est m. courante** it's very frequent; **m. électronique** plastic money; **m. unique** single currency •**monnayer** *vt (talent, information)* to cash in on; *(bien, titre)* to convert into cash

mono [mɔno] *adj inv (disque)* mono

monocle [mɔnɔkl] *nm* monocle

monocorde [mɔnɔkɔrd] *adj* monotonous

monogamie [mɔnɔgami] *nf* monogamy

monokini [mɔnokini] *nm* monokini; **faire du m.** to go topless

monologue [mɔnɔlɔg] *nm Br* monologue, *Am* monolog

mononucléose [mɔnonykleoz] *nf* glandular fever

monoparentale [mɔnoparɑ̃tal] *adj f* **famille m.** one-parent family

monoplace [mɔnoplas] *adj & nmf* single-seater

monopole [mɔnɔpɔl] *nm* monopoly; **avoir le m. de qch** to have a monopoly on sth •**monopoliser** *vt* to monopolize

monoski [mɔnoski] *nm* mono-ski; **faire du m.** to mono-ski

monosyllabe [mɔnosilab] *nm* monosyllable •**monosyllabique** *adj* monosyllabic

monothéisme [mɔnoteism] *nm* monotheism

monotone [mɔnotɔn] *adj* monotonous •**monotonie** *nf* monotony

monseigneur [mɔ̃seɲœr] *(pl* **messeigneurs***) nm (évêque)* His/Your Lordship; *(prince)* His/Your Highness

monsieur [məsjø] *(pl* **messieurs***) nm (homme quelconque)* gentleman; **M. Legras** Mr Legras; **oui m.** yes; *(avec déférence)* yes, sir; **oui messieurs** yes(, gentlemen); **bonsoir, messieurs-dames!** good evening!; **M.** *(dans une lettre)* Dear Sir; **m. tout-le-monde** the man in the street

monstre [mɔ̃str] **1** *nm* monster; **m. sacré** giant

2 *adj Fam (énorme)* colossal •**monstrueux, -ueuse** *adj (mal formé, scandaleux)* monstrous; *(énorme)* huge •**monstruosité** *nf* monstrosity

mont [mɔ̃] *nm* mount; **être toujours par monts et par vaux** to be forever on the move

montage [mɔ̃taʒ] *nm Tech* assembling; *Cin* editing; *(image truquée)* montage; **m. vidéo** video editing

montagne [mɔ̃taɲ] *nf* mountain; **la m.** *(zone)* the mountains; **à la m.** in the mountains; **en haute m.** high in the mountains; *Fig* **une m. de qch** *(grande quantité)* a mountain of sth; *Fig* **se faire une m. de qch** to make a great song and dance about sth; **montagnes russes** *(attraction foraine)* rollercoaster •**montagnard, -arde 1** *nmf* mountain dweller **2** *adj* **peuple m.** mountain people •**montagneux, -euse** *adj* mountainous

montant, -ante 1 *adj (marée)* rising; *(col)* stand-up; **chaussure montante** boot **2** *nm (somme)* amount; *(de barrière)* post; *(d'échelle)* upright; **montants compensatoires** subsidies

mont-de-piété [mɔ̃dpjete] *(pl* **monts-de-piété)** *nm* pawnshop

monte-charge [mɔ̃tʃarʒ] *(pl* **monte-charges)** *nm* service *Br* lift *or Am* elevator

montée [mɔ̃te] *nf (ascension)* climb, ascent; *(chemin)* slope; *(des prix, du fascisme)* rise; **la m. des eaux** the rise in the water level

monte-plats [mɔ̃tpla] *nm inv* dumb waiter

monter [mɔ̃te] **1** *(aux* **avoir)** *vt (côte)* to climb (up); *(objet)* to bring/take up; *(cheval)* to ride; *(son)* to turn up; *(tente)* to put up; *(machine)* to assemble; *(bijou, complot)* to mount; *(affaire)* to hatch; *(pièce de théâtre)* to stage; *(film)* to edit; **m. l'escalier** to go/come upstairs *or* up the stairs; **m. qn contre qn** to set sb against sb

2 *(aux* **être)** *vi (personne)* to go/come up; *(ballon)* to go up; *(prix)* to rise; *(marée)* to come in; *(avion)* to climb; **faire m. qn** to show sb up; **m. dans un véhicule** to get in(to) a vehicle; **m. dans un train** to get on(to) a train; **m. sur qch** to climb onto sth; **m. sur** *ou* **à une échelle** to climb up a ladder; **m. sur le trône** to become king/queen; **m. en courant** to run up; *Sport* **m. à cheval** to ride (a horse); **le vin me monte à la tête** wine goes to my head

3 se monter *vpr* **se m. à** *(s'élever à)* to amount to; *Fam* **se m. la tête** to get carried away with oneself •**monté, -ée** *adj (police)* mounted

monteur, -euse [mɔ̃tœr, -øz] *nmf Cin* editor

montre [mɔ̃tr] *nf* **(a)** *(instrument)* (wrist-)watch; *Sport & Fig* **course contre la m.** race against the clock **(b)** **faire m. de qch** to show sth •**montre-bracelet** *(pl* **montres-bracelets)** *nf* wristwatch

Montréal [mɔ̃real] *nm ou f* Montreal

montrer [mɔ̃tre] **1** *vt* to show (**à** to); **m. qn/qch du doigt** to point to sb/sth; **m. le chemin à qn** to show sb the way

2 se montrer *vpr* to show oneself; **se m. courageux** to be courageous

monture [mɔ̃tyr] *nf (de lunettes)* frame; *(de bijou)* setting; *(cheval)* mount

monument [mɔnymɑ̃] *nm* monument; **m. historique** ancient monument; **m. aux morts** war memorial •**monumental, -e, -aux, -ales** *adj (imposant, énorme)* monumental

moquer [mɔke] **se moquer** *vpr* **se m. de qn** to make fun of sb; **se m. de qch** *(rire de)* to make fun of sth; *(ne pas se soucier)* not to care about sth; *Fam* **il se moque du monde** who does he think he is? •**moquerie** *nf* mockery •**moqueur, -euse** *adj* mocking

moquette [mɔkɛt] *nf Br* fitted carpet, *Am* wall-to-wall carpeting

moral, -e, -aux, -ales [mɔral, -o] **1** *adj* moral

2 *nm* **avoir le m.** to be in good spirits; **avoir le m. à zéro** to feel really down; **remonter le m. à qn** to cheer sb up •**morale** *nf (d'histoire)* moral; *(principes)* morals; *(règles)* morality; **faire la m. à qn** to lecture sb •**moralement** *adv* morally •**moraliste** *nmf* moralist •**moralité** *nf (mœurs)* morality; *(de récit)* moral

moratoire [mɔratwar] *nm Jur* moratorium

morbide [mɔrbid] *adj* morbid

morceau, -x [mɔrso] *nm* piece, bit; *(de sucre)* lump; *(de viande)* cut; *(d'une œuvre littéraire)* extract; **tomber en morceaux** to fall to pieces •**morceler** *vt (terrain)* to divide up

mordicus [mɔrdikys] *adv Fam* stubbornly

mordiller [mɔrdije] *vt* to nibble

mordre [mɔrdr] **1** *vti* to bite; **m. qn au bras** to bite sb's arm; **ça mord?** *(poissons)* are the fish biting?

2 se mordre *vpr Fig* **se m. les doigts d'avoir fait qch** to kick oneself for doing sth •**mordant, -ante 1** *adj (esprit, remarque, froid)* biting; *(personne, ironie)* caustic **2** *nm (causticité)* bite

mordu, -ue [mɔrdy] **1** *pp de* **mordre**
2 *nmf Fam* **un m. de jazz** a jazz fan

morfondre [mɔrfɔ̃dr] **se morfondre** *vpr* to mope (about)

morgue [mɔrg] *nf (d'hôpital)* mortuary; *(pour corps non identifiés)* morgue

moribond, -onde [mɔribɔ̃, -ɔ̃d] **1** *adj* dying
2 *nmf* dying person

morne [mɔrn] *adj (temps)* dismal; *(silence)* gloomy; *(personne)* glum
morose [mɔroz] *adj* morose
morphine [mɔrfin] *nf* morphine
morphologie [mɔrfɔlɔʒi] *nf* morphology
mors [mɔr] *nm (de harnais)* bit; *Fig* **prendre le m. aux dents** to take the bit between one's teeth
morse [mɔrs] *nm (code)* Morse (code); *(animal)* walrus
morsure [mɔrsyr] *nf* bite
mort¹ [mɔr] *nf* death; **mettre qn à m.** to put sb to death; **se donner la m.** to take one's own life; **en vouloir à m. à qn** to be dead set against sb; **un silence de m.** a deathly silence; **la m. dans l'âme** *(accepter qch)* with a heavy heart • **mortalité** *nf* death rate, mortality • **mortel, -elle 1** *adj (hommes, ennemi, danger)* mortal; *(accident)* fatal; *Fam (ennuyeux)* deadly (dull); *(pâleur)* deathly **2** *nmf* mortal • **mortellement** *adv (blessé)* fatally; *(ennuyeux)* deadly
mort², morte [mɔr, mɔrt] **1** *adj (personne, plante, ville)* dead; **m. de fatigue** dead tired; **m. de froid** numb with cold; **m. de peur** frightened to death; **m. ou vif** dead or alive; **être ivre m.** to be dead drunk
   2 *nmf* dead man, *f* dead woman; **les morts** the dead; **de nombreux morts** *(victimes)* many deaths; **le jour** *ou* **la fête des Morts** All Souls' Day • **morte-saison** *(pl* **mortes-saisons)** *nf* off-season • **mort-né, -née** *(mpl* **mort-nés,** *fpl* **mort-nées)** *adj (enfant) & Fig* stillborn
mortier [mɔrtje] *nm* mortar
mortifier [mɔrtifje] *vt* to mortify
mortuaire [mɔrtɥɛr] *adj* **couronne m.** funeral wreath
morue [mɔry] *nf* cod
morve [mɔrv] *nf* snot • **morveux, -euse** *adj Fam Péj (enfant)* snotty(-nosed)
mosaïque [mɔzaik] *nf* mosaic
Moscou [mɔsku] *nm ou f* Moscow
mosquée [mɔske] *nf* mosque
mot [mo] *nm* word; **envoyer un m. à qn** to drop sb a line; **m. à** *ou* **pour m.** word for word; **un bon m.** a witticism; **avoir le dernier m.** to have the last word; **avoir son m. à dire** to have one's say; **mots croisés** crossword (puzzle); **m. d'ordre** watchword; **m. de passe** password
motard [mɔtar] *nm Fam* motorcyclist
motel [mɔtɛl] *nm* motel
moteur¹ [mɔtœr] *nm (de véhicule)* engine; *(électrique)* motor

moteur², -trice [mɔtœr, -tris] **1** *adj (nerf, muscle)* motor; **force motrice** driving force; **voiture à quatre roues motrices** four-wheel drive (car)
   2 *nf* **motrice** *(de train)* engine
motif [mɔtif] *nm (raison)* reason (**de** for); *(dessin)* pattern
motion [mɔsjɔ̃] *nf Pol* motion; **m. de censure** motion of censure
motiver [mɔtive] *vt (inciter, causer)* to motivate; *(justifier)* to justify • **motivation** *nf* motivation • **motivé, -ée** *adj* motivated
moto [mɔto] *nf* motorbike • **motocycliste** *nmf* motorcyclist
motorisé, -ée [mɔtɔrize] *adj* motorized
motte [mɔt] *nf (de terre)* lump, clod; *(de beurre)* block
mou, molle [mu, mɔl]

> **mol** is used before masculine singular nouns beginning with a vowel or h mute.

1 *adj* soft; *(sans énergie)* feeble
   2 *nm* **avoir du m.** *(cordage)* to be slack
mouchard, -arde [muʃar, -ard] *nmf Fam Br* grass, *Am* fink • **moucharder** *vt Fam* **m. qn** to squeal on sb
mouche [muʃ] *nf (insecte)* fly; **faire m.** to hit the bull's-eye; **prendre la m.** to fly off the handle; *Fam* **quelle m. l'a piqué?** what has *Br* got *or Am* gotten into him? • **moucheron** *nm* midge
moucher [muʃe] **1** *vt* **m. qn** to wipe sb's nose
   2 se moucher *vpr* to blow one's nose
moucheté, -ée [muʃte] *adj* speckled
mouchoir [muʃwar] *nm* handkerchief; **m. en papier** tissue
moudre* [mudr] *vt* to grind
moue [mu] *nf* pout; **faire la m.** to pout
mouette [mwɛt] *nf* (sea)gull
moufle [mufl] *nf* mitten, mitt
mouiller [muje] **1** *vt* to wet; **se faire m.** to get wet
   2 *vi Naut* to anchor
   3 se mouiller *vpr* to get wet; *Fam (prendre position)* to stick one's neck out • **mouillage** *nm Naut (action)* anchoring; *(lieu)* anchorage • **mouillé, -ée** *adj* wet (**de** with)
moule¹ [mul] *nm Br* mould, *Am* mold; **m. à gâteaux** cake tin • **moulage** *nm (action)* casting; *(objet)* cast • **moulant, -ante** *adj (vêtement)* tight-fitting • **mouler** *vt Br* to mould, *Am* to mold; *(statue)* to cast; **m. qn** *(vêtement)* to fit sb tightly • **moulure** *nf Archit Br* moulding, *Am* molding
moule² [mul] *nf (mollusque)* mussel

moulin [mulɛ̃] *nm* mill; **m. à café** coffee grinder; *Fam* **m. à paroles** chatterbox; **m. à vent** windmill

moulinet [mulinɛ] *nm (de canne à pêche)* reel; **faire des moulinets** *(avec un bâton)* to twirl one's stick

moulu, -ue [muly] **1** *pp de* **moudre**
2 *adj (café)* ground; *Fig (éreinté)* dead tired

mourir* [murir] **1** *(aux* **être)** *vi* to die (**de** of *or* from); **m. de froid** to die of exposure; *Fig* **m. de fatigue/d'ennui** to be dead tired/bored; *Fig* **m. de peur** to be frightened to death; *Fig* **m. de rire** to laugh oneself silly; *Fig* **s'ennuyer à m.** to be bored to death; *Fig* **je meurs de faim!** I'm starving!
2 se mourir *vpr Littéraire* to be dying • **mourant, -ante 1** *adj* dying; *(voix)* faint **2** *nmf* dying person

mousquetaire [muskətɛr] *nm* musketeer

mousse [mus] **1** *nf (plante)* moss; *(écume)* foam; *(de bière)* head; *(de savon)* lather; **m. à raser** shaving foam; *Culin* **m. au chocolat** chocolate mousse
2 *nm (marin)* ship's boy • **mousser** *vi (bière)* to froth; *(savon)* to lather; *Fam* **se faire m.** to show off • **mousseux, -euse 1** *adj (bière)* frothy; *(vin)* sparkling **2** *nm* sparkling wine • **moussu, -ue** *adj* mossy

mousseline [muslin] *nf (tissu)* muslin

mousson [musɔ̃] *nf* monsoon

moustache [mustaʃ] *nf (d'homme) Br* moustache, *Am* mustache; *(de chat)* whiskers • **moustachu, -ue** *adj* with a moustache

moustique [mustik] *nm* mosquito • **moustiquaire** *nf* mosquito net; *(en métal)* screen

moutard [mutar] *nm Fam (enfant)* kid

moutarde [mutard] *nf* mustard

mouton [mutɔ̃] *nm* sheep *inv; (viande)* mutton; **moutons** *(écume) Br* white horses, *Am* whitecaps; *(poussière)* fluff; **peau de m.** sheepskin

mouvement [muvmɑ̃] *nm (geste, groupe, déplacement)* & *Mus* movement; *(élan)* impulse; *(de gymnastique)* exercise; **en m.** in motion; **m. de colère** fit of anger; **mouvements sociaux** workers' protest movements • **mouvementé, -ée** *adj (vie, voyage)* eventful

mouvoir* [muvwar] *vi,* **se mouvoir** *vpr* to move; **mû par** *(mécanisme)* driven by • **mouvant, -ante** *adj (changeant)* changing

moyen¹, -enne [mwajɛ̃, -ɛn] **1** *adj*

average; *(format, entreprise)* medium (-sized)
2 *nf* **moyenne** average; **en moyenne** on average; **la moyenne d'âge** the average age; **avoir la moyenne** *(à un examen) Br* to get a pass mark, *Am* to get a pass; *(à un devoir)* to get 50 percent, *Br* to get half marks; **le M. Âge** the Middle Ages • **moyennement** *adv* fairly, moderately

moyen² [mwajɛ̃] *nm (procédé, façon)* means, way (**de faire** of doing *or* to do); **moyens** *(capacités mentales)* ability; *(argent, ressources)* means; **il n'y a pas m. de le faire** it's not possible to do it; **je n'ai pas les moyens** *(argent)* I can't afford it; **au m. de qch** by means of sth; **par mes propres moyens** under my own steam; **utiliser les grands moyens** to take extreme measures; **faire avec les moyens du bord** to make do with what one has

moyennant [mwajɛnɑ̃] *prép (pour)* (in return) for; **m. finance** for a fee

moyeu, -x [mwajø] *nm* hub

Mozambique [mɔzɑ̃bik] *nm* **le M.** Mozambique

MST [ɛmɛste] *(abrév* **maladie sexuellement transmissible)** *nf* STD

mue [my] *nf (d'animal) Br* moulting, *Am* molting; *(de voix)* breaking of the voice • **muer** [mɥe] **1** *vi (animal) Br* to moult, *Am* to molt; *(voix)* to break **2 se muer** *vpr* **se m. en qch** to change into sth

muet, muette [mɥe, mɥɛt] **1** *adj (infirme)* dumb; *(de surprise)* speechless; *(film)* silent; *(voyelle)* silent, mute
2 *nmf* mute

mufle [myfl] *nm (d'animal)* muzzle; *Fam (personne)* lout

mugir [myʒir] *vi (bœuf)* to bellow; *(vache)* to moo; *Fig (vent)* to howl • **mugissement** *nm* bellow; *(de vache)* moo; **mugissements** *(de bœuf)* bellowing; *(de vache)* mooing; *(de vent)* howling

muguet [mygɛ] *nm* lily of the valley

mule [myl] *nf (pantoufle, animal)* mule • **mulet** *nm (équidé)* mule; *(poisson)* mullet

multicolore [myltikɔlɔr] *adj* multicoloured

multimédia [myltimedja] *adj & nm* multimedia

multinationale [myltinasjɔnal] *nf* multinational

multiple [myltipl] **1** *adj (nombreux)* numerous; *(varié)* multiple; **à de multiples reprises** repeatedly
2 *nm Math* multiple • **multiplication** *nf (calcul)* multiplication; *(augmentation)*

increase •**multiplicité** *nf* multiplicity •**multiplier 1** *vt* to multiply **2 se multiplier** *vpr* to increase; *(se reproduire)* to multiply

multithérapie [myltiterapi] *nf Méd* combination therapy

multitude [myltityd] *nf* multitude

municipal, -e, -aux, -ales [mynisipal, -o] *adj* municipal •**municipalité** *nf (maires et conseillers)* local council; *(commune)* municipality

munir [mynir] **1** *vt* **m. de qch** *(personne)* to provide with sth
2 se munir *vpr* **se m. de qch** to take sth

munitions [mynisjɔ̃] *nfpl* ammunition

muqueuse [mykøz] *nf* mucous membrane

mur [myr] *nm* wall; *Fig* **au pied du m.** with one's back to the wall; **m. du son** sound barrier •**muraille** *nf* (high) wall •**mural, -e, -aux, -ales** *adj* **carte murale** wall map; **peinture murale** mural (painting) •**murer 1** *vt (porte)* to wall up; *(jardin)* to wall in **2 se murer** *vpr Fig* **se m. dans le silence** to retreat into silence

mûr, mûre¹ [myr] *adj (fruit)* ripe; *(personne)* mature; **d'âge m.** middle-aged •**mûrement** *adv* **m. réfléchi** *(décision)* carefully thought-out •**mûrir** *vti (fruit)* to ripen; *(personne)* to mature

mûre² [myr] *nf (baie)* blackberry

muret [myrɛ] *nm* low wall

murmure [myrmyr] *nm* murmur •**murmurer** *vti* to murmur

musc [mysk] *nm* musk

muscade [myskad] *nf* nutmeg

muscat [myska] *nm (raisin)* muscat (grape); *(vin)* muscatel (wine)

muscle [myskl] *nm* muscle •**musclé, -ée** *adj (bras)* muscular •**musculaire** *adj (force, douleur)* muscular •**musculature** *nf* muscles

museau, -x [myzo] *nm (de chien, de chat)* muzzle; *(de porc)* snout •**museler** *vt (animal, presse)* to muzzle •**muselière** *nf* muzzle

musée [myze] *nm* museum; **m. de peinture** art gallery •**muséum** *nm* natural history museum

musette [myzɛt] *nf (sac)* bag

music-hall [myzikol] *(pl* **music-halls***) nm (genre, salle)* music hall

musique [myzik] *nf* music •**musical, -e, -aux, -ales** *adj* musical •**musicien, -ienne 1** *nmf* musician **2** *adj* musical

musulman, -ane [myzylmã, -an] *adj & nmf* Muslim, Moslem

muter [myte] *vt* to transfer •**mutant, -ante** *adj & nmf* mutant •**mutation** *nf (d'employé)* transfer; *Biol* mutation; *Fig* **en pleine m.** undergoing profound change

mutiler [mytile] *vt* to mutilate, to maim; **être mutilé** to be disabled •**mutilation** *nf* mutilation •**mutilé, -ée** *nmf* **m. de guerre** disabled *Br* ex-serviceman *or Am* veteran

mutin¹, -ine [mytɛ̃, -in] *adj (espiègle)* mischievous

mutin² [mytɛ̃] *nm (rebelle)* mutineer •**se mutiner** *vpr* to mutiny •**mutinerie** *nf* mutiny

mutisme [mytism] *nm* silence

mutualité [mytɥalite] *nf* mutual insurance

mutuel, -uelle [mytɥɛl] **1** *adj (réciproque)* mutual
2 *nf* **mutuelle** mutual insurance company •**mutuellement** *adv* each other

myope [mjɔp] *adj* shortsighted •**myopie** *nf* shortsightedness

myosotis [mjozɔtis] *nm* forget-me-not

myrtille [mirtij] *nf (baie)* bilberry

mystère [mistɛr] *nm* mystery; **faire des mystères** to be mysterious; **faire m. de qch** to make a secret of sth •**mystérieux, -ieuse** *adj* mysterious

mystifier [mistifje] *vt* to take in •**mystification** *nf* hoax

mystique [mistik] **1** *adj* mystical
2 *nmf (personne)* mystic •**mysticisme** *nm* mysticism

mythe [mit] *nm* myth •**mythique** *adj* mythical •**mythologie** *nf* mythology •**mythologique** *adj* mythological

mythomane [mitɔman] *nmf* compulsive liar

myxomatose [miksɔmatoz] *nf* myxomatosis

N¹, n [ɛn] *nm inv* N, n
N² (*abrév* **route nationale**) = designation of major road
n' [n] *voir* **ne**
nabot [nabo] *nm Péj* midget
nacelle [nasɛl] *nf (de ballon)* basket; *(de landau)* carriage, *Br* carrycot
nacre [nakr] *nf* mother-of-pearl •**nacré, -ée** *adj* pearly
nage [naʒ] *nf* (swimming) stroke; **traverser une rivière à la n.** to swim across a river; *Fig* **en n.** sweating; **n. libre** freestyle
nageoire [naʒwar] *nf (de poisson)* fin; *(de dauphin)* flipper
nager [naʒe] **1** *vi* to swim; *Fig* **n. dans le bonheur** to be blissfully happy; *Fam* **je nage complètement** I'm all at sea
2 *vt (crawl)* to swim •**nageur, -euse** *nmf* swimmer
naguère [nagɛr] *adv Littéraire* not long ago
naïf, naïve [naif, naiv] **1** *adj* naïve
2 *nmf* fool •**naïveté** *nf* naïvety
nain, naine [nɛ̃, nɛn] *adj & nmf* dwarf
naissance [nɛsɑ̃s] *nf (de personne, d'animal)* birth; *(de cou)* base; **donner n. à** *(enfant)* to give birth to; *Fig (rumeur)* to give rise to; **de n.** from birth
naître* [nɛtr] *vi* to be born; *(sentiment, difficulté)* to arise (**de** from); *(idée)* to originate; **faire n.** *(soupçon, industrie)* to give rise to; *Littéraire* **n. à qch** to awaken to sth; *Fam* **il n'est pas né de la dernière pluie** he wasn't born yesterday •**naissant, -ante** *adj (jour)* dawning
nana [nana] *nf Fam* girl
nantir [nɑ̃tir] *vt* **n. qn de qch** to provide sb with sth •**nanti, -ie 1** *adj* well-to-do **2** *nmpl Péj* **les nantis** the well-to-do
naphtaline [naftalin] *nf* mothballs
nappe [nap] *nf (de table)* tablecloth; **n. de brouillard** fog patch; **n. d'eau** expanse of water; **n. de pétrole** layer of oil; *(de marée noire)* oil slick •**napperon** *nm* mat
napper [nape] *vt* to coat (**de** with)
narcotique [narkɔtik] *adj & nm* narcotic
narguer [narge] *vt* to taunt
narine [narin] *nf* nostril
narquois, -oise [narkwa, -waz] *adj* sneering

narration [narɑsjɔ̃] *nf (genre)* narration; *(récit)* narrative •**narrateur, -trice** *nmf* narrator
nasal, -e, -aux, -ales [nazal, -o] *adj* nasal
nase [naz] *adj Fam (personne)* shattered; *(machine)* kaput
naseau, -x [nazo] *nm* nostril
nasillard, -arde [nazijar, -ard] *adj (voix)* nasal
natal, -e, -als, -ales [natal] *adj* native
natalité [natalite] *nf* birth rate
natation [natɑsjɔ̃] *nf* swimming
natif, -ive [natif, -iv] *adj & nmf* native; **être n. de** to be a native of
nation [nasjɔ̃] *nf* nation; **les Nations unies** the United Nations •**national, -e, -aux, -ales** *adj* national •**nationale** *nf (route) Br* ≃ A road, *Am* ≃ highway •**nationaliser** *vt* to nationalize •**nationaliste 1** *adj* nationalistic **2** *nmf* nationalist •**nationalité** *nf* nationality
natte [nat] *nf (de cheveux) Br* plait, *Am* braid; *(de paille)* mat •**natter** *vt Br* to plait, *Am* to braid
naturaliser [natyralize] *vt* to naturalize •**naturalisation** *nf* naturalization
nature [natyr] **1** *nf (univers, caractère)* nature; *(campagne)* country; **plus grand que n.** larger than life; **contre n.** unnatural; **en pleine n.** in the middle of the country; **être de n. à faire qch** to be likely to do sth; **payer en n.** to pay in kind; **seconde n.** second nature; **n. morte** still life
2 *adj inv (omelette, yaourt)* plain; *(thé)* without milk •**naturaliste** *nmf* naturalist •**naturiste** *nmf* naturist
naturel, -elle [natyrɛl] **1** *adj* natural; **mort naturelle** death from natural causes
2 *nm (caractère)* nature; *(simplicité)* naturalness •**naturellement** *adv* naturally
naufrage [nofraʒ] *nm* (ship)wreck; **faire n.** *(bateau)* to be wrecked; *(marin)* to be shipwrecked •**naufragé, -ée** *nmf* shipwrecked person
nausée [noze] *nf* nausea, sickness; **avoir la n.** to feel sick •**nauséabond, -onde** *adj* nauseating, sickening
nautique [notik] *adj* nautical

naval, -e, -als, -ales [naval] *adj* naval;
constructions navales shipbuilding
navet [nave] *nm (légume)* turnip; *Fam*
c'est un n. it's a load of rubbish
navette [navɛt] *nf (véhicule)* shuttle; faire
la n. *(véhicule, personne)* to shuttle back
and forth (entre between); n. spatiale
space shuttle
navigable [navigabl] *adj (fleuve)* navigable • **navigabilité** *nf (de bateau)* seawor-
thiness; *(d'avion)* airworthiness
navigant, -ante [navigɑ̃, -ɑ̃t] *adj Av*
personnel n. flight crew
navigateur [navigatœr] *nm (marin)* navigator; *Ordinat* browser; n. solitaire lone
yachtsman • **navigation** *nf* navigation
naviguer [navige] *vi (bateau)* to sail; n.
sur Internet to surf the Net
navire [navir] *nm* ship
navrer [navrɛ] *vt* to appal • **navrant, -ante**
adj appalling • **navré, -ée** *adj (air)* dis-
tressed; je suis n. I'm terribly sorry
nazi, -ie [nazi] *adj & nmf Hist* Nazi
ne [nə]

---
n' before vowel or mute h; used to form
negative verb with **pas, jamais, personne, rien** etc.

---

adv ne... pas not; il ne boit pas he does
not *or* doesn't drink; elle n'ose (pas) she
doesn't dare; ne... que only; il n'a qu'une
sœur he only has one sister; je crains qu'il
ne parte I'm afraid he'll leave
né, née [ne] **1** *pp de* naître born; il est né
en 1945 he was born in 1945; née Dupont
née Dupont
2 *adj* born; c'est un poète-né he's a born
poet
néanmoins [neɑ̃mwɛ̃] *adv* nevertheless
néant [neɑ̃] *nm* nothingness; *(sur formulaire)* ≃ none
nébuleux, -euse [nebylø, -øz] *adj* hazy
nécessaire [neseser] **1** *adj* necessary
2 *nm* le n. the necessities; faire le n. to
do what's necessary; n. de couture sewing kit; n. de toilette toilet bag • **nécessai-
rement** *adv* necessarily
nécessité [nesesite] *nf* necessity • **nécessiter** *vt* to require, to necessitate
nécessiteux, -euse [nesesitø, -øz] *adj*
needy
nécrologie [nekrɔlɔʒi] *nf* obituary
nectarine [nektarin] *nf* nectarine
néerlandais, -aise [neerlɑ̃dɛ, -ɛz] **1** *adj*
Dutch
2 *nmf* N. Dutchman; **Néerlandaise**
Dutchwoman
3 *nm (langue)* Dutch

nef [nɛf] *nf (d'église)* nave
néfaste [nefast] *adj* harmful (à to)
négatif, -ive [negatif, -iv] **1** *adj* negative
2 *nm (de photo)* negative • **négation** *nf*
negation (de of); *Grammaire* negative
négligeable [negliʒabl] *adj* negligible;
non n. *(quantité)* significant
négligent, -ente [negliʒɑ̃, -ɑ̃t] *adj* careless, negligent • **négligence** *nf (défaut)*
carelessness, negligence; *(oubli)* oversight
négliger [negliʒe] **1** *vt (personne, travail,
conseil)* to neglect; n. de faire qch to
neglect to do sth
2 se négliger *vpr* to neglect oneself • **négligé, -ée 1** *adj (tenue)* untidy; *(travail)*
careless **2** *nm (vêtement)* négligée
négocier [negɔsje] *vti* to negotiate • **négociable** *adj* negotiable • **négociant,
-iante** *nmf* merchant, dealer • **négociateur, -trice** *nmf* negotiator • **négociation**
nf negotiation
nègre [nɛgr] **1** *adj (art, sculpture)* Negro
2 *nm (écrivain)* ghost writer
neige [nɛʒ] *nf* snow; aller à la n. to go
skiing; n. carbonique dry ice; n. fondue
sleet • **neiger** *v impersonnel* to snow; il
neige it's snowing • **neigeux, -euse** *adj*
snowy
nénuphar [nenyfar] *nm* water lily
néon [neɔ̃] *nm (gaz)* neon; *(enseigne)*
neon sign; éclairage au n. neon lighting
néophyte [neɔfit] *nmf* novice
néo-zélandais, -aise [neɔzelɑ̃dɛ, -ɛz]
(mpl néo-zélandais, *fpl* néo-zélandaises)
1 *adj* New Zealand
2 *nmf* **Néo-Zélandais, Néo-Zélandaise**
New Zealander
nerf [nɛr] *nm* nerve; *Fig* être sur les nerfs
to live on one's nerves; *Fig* être à bout de
nerfs to be at the end of one's tether; *Fam*
ça me tape sur les nerfs it gets on my
nerves; *Fam* du n.!, un peu de n.! buck
up! • **nerveux, -euse** *adj* nervous • **nervosité** *nf* nervousness
nervure [nɛrvyr] *nf (de feuille)* vein
n'est-ce pas [nɛspa] *adv* isn't he?/don't
you?/won't they?/etc; tu viendras, n.?
you'll come, won't you?; il fait beau, n.?
the weather's fine, isn't it?
Net [nɛt] *nm* le N. the Net • **netiquette** *nf*
Ordinat netiquette
net, nette [nɛt] **1** *adj (propre)* clean;
(image, refus) clear; *(écriture)* neat; *(prix,
salaire)* net; n. d'impôt net of tax; *Fig* je
veux en avoir le cœur n. I want to get to
the bottom of it once and for all
2 *adv (casser, couper)* clean; *(tuer)* out-

right; *(refuser)* flatly; **s'arrêter n.** to stop dead •**nettement** *adv (avec précision)* clearly; *(incontestablement)* definitely; **il va n. mieux** he's much better •**netteté** *nf (propreté, précision)* cleanness; *(de travail)* neatness

nettoyer [netwaje] **1** *vt* to clean; *Fam (sujet: cambrioleur)* to clean out
2 se nettoyer *vpr* **se n. les oreilles** to clean one's ears •**nettoiement** *nm* **service du n.** refuse *or Am* garbage collection service •**nettoyage** *nm* cleaning; **n. à sec** dry-cleaning

neuf¹, neuve [nœf, nœv] **1** *adj* new; **quoi de n.?** what's new?
2 *nm* **remettre qch à n.** to make sth as good as new; **il y a du n.** there's been a new development

neuf² [nœf, nœv *before* **heures** & **ans**] *adj & nm* nine •**neuvième** *adj & nmf* ninth

neurone [nøron] *nm* neuron

neutre [nøtr] **1** *adj (pays, personne)* neutral
2 *nm Él* neutral
3 *adj & nm Grammaire* neuter •**neutraliser** *vt* to neutralize •**neutralité** *nf* neutrality

neutron [nøtrɔ̃] *nm* neutron

neveu, -x [nəvø] *nm* nephew

névralgie [nevralʒi] *nf Méd* neuralgia •**névralgique** *adj Fig* **centre n.** nerve centre

névrose [nevroz] *nf* neurosis •**névrosé, -ée** *adj & nmf* neurotic

nez [ne] *nm* nose; **n. à n.** face to face (**avec** with); **rire au n. de qn** to laugh in sb's face; **parler du n.** to speak through one's nose; *Fig* **mener qn par le bout du n.** to lead sb by the nose; *Fam* **avoir qch sous le n.** to have sth under one's very nose; *Fam* **avoir un verre dans le n.** to have had one too many; *Fam* **mettre le n. dehors** to stick one's nose outside; *Fam* **ça se voit comme le n. au milieu de la figure** it's as plain as the nose on your face

ni [ni] *conj* **ni... ni...** neither... nor...; **ni Pierre ni Paul ne sont venus** neither Peter nor Paul came; **il n'a ni faim ni soif** he's neither hungry nor thirsty; **sans manger ni boire** without eating or drinking; **ni l'un(e) ni l'autre** neither (of them)

niais, niaise [njɛ, njɛz] **1** *adj* silly
2 *nmf* fool •**niaiserie** *nf* silliness; **niaiseries** *(paroles)* nonsense

Nicaragua [nikaragwa] *nm* **le N.** Nicaragua

niche [niʃ] *nf (de chien) Br* kennel, *Am* doghouse; *(cavité)* niche, recess; **n. écologique** ecological niche

nicher [niʃe] **1** *vi (oiseau)* to nest
2 se nicher *vpr (oiseau)* to nest; *Fam (se cacher)* to hide oneself •**nichée** *nf (chiens)* litter; *(oiseaux)* brood

nickel [nikel] **1** *nm (métal)* nickel
2 *adj inv Fam (propre)* spotlessly clean

nicotine [nikotin] *nf* nicotine

nid [ni] *nm* nest; **n.-de-poule** pothole

nièce [njɛs] *nf* niece

nier [nje] **1** *vt* to deny (**que** that)
2 *vi (accusé)* to deny the charge

nigaud, -aude [nigo, -od] *nmf* silly fool

Niger [niʒɛr] *nm* **le N.** *(pays)* Niger

Nigéria [niʒerja] *nm* **le N.** Nigeria

Nil [nil] *nm* **le N.** the Nile

n'importe [nɛ̃port] *voir* **importer¹**

nippon, -one *ou* **-onne** [nipɔ̃, -ɔn] *adj* Japanese

niveau, -x [nivo] *nm (hauteur, étage, degré)* level; *Scol* standard; **au n. de la mer** at sea level; **être au n.** *(élève)* to be up to standard; *Fig* **se mettre au n. de qn** to put oneself on sb's level; **n. à bulle d'air** spirit level; **n. de vie** standard of living •**niveler** *vt (surface)* to level; *(fortunes)* to even out

noble [nɔbl] **1** *adj* noble
2 *nmf* nobleman, *f* noblewoman •**noblement** [-əmã] *adv* nobly •**noblesse** *nf (caractère, classe)* nobility

noce [nɔs] *nf* wedding; *Fam* **faire la n.** to live it up; **noces d'argent/d'or** silver/golden wedding •**noceur, -euse** *nmf Fam* raver

nocif, -ive [nɔsif, -iv] *adj* harmful •**nocivité** *nf* harmfulness

noctambule [nɔktãbyl] *nmf* night owl

nocturne [nɔktyrn] **1** *adj (animal)* nocturnal
2 *nf (de magasin)* late-night opening; *Sport* **(match en) n.** evening match

Noël [nɔɛl] *nm* Christmas; **arbre de N.** Christmas tree; **le père N.** Father Christmas, Santa Claus

nœud [nø] *nm* (**a**) *(entrecroisement)* knot; *(ruban)* bow; *Fig* **le n. du problème** the crux of the problem; **n. coulant** slipknot; **n. papillon** bow tie (**b**) *Naut (vitesse)* knot

noir, noire [nwar] **1** *adj* black; *(sombre)* dark; *(idées)* gloomy; *(misère)* dire; *Fig* **rue noire de monde** street swarming with people; **il fait n.** it's dark; **roman n.** thriller; **film n.** film noir
2 *nm (couleur)* black; *(obscurité)* dark; **N.** *(homme)* Black (man); *Fam* **travailler au n.** to moonlight
3 *nf* **noire** *(note) Br* crotchet, *Am* quarter

note; **Noire** *(femme)* Black (woman) •**noirceur** *nf* blackness •**noircir 1** *vt* to blacken **2** *vi*, **se noircir** *vpr* to turn black

noisette [nwazɛt] *nf* hazelnut •**noisetier** *nm* hazel (tree)

noix [nwa] *nf (du noyer)* walnut; *Fam* **à la n.** trashy, awful; **n. de beurre** knob of butter; **n. de coco** coconut

nom [nɔ̃] *nm* name; *Grammaire* noun; **au n. de qn** on sb's behalf; **au n. de la loi** in the name of the law; **sans n.** *(anonyme)* nameless; *(vil)* vile; *Fam* **n. d'un chien!** hell!; **n. de famille** surname; **n. de jeune fille** maiden name

nomade [nɔmad] **1** *adj* nomadic **2** *nmf* nomad

nombre [nɔ̃br] *nm* number; **être au** *ou* **du n. de** to be among; **ils sont au n. de dix** there are ten of them; **le plus grand n. de** the majority of; **bon n. de** a good many; *Math* **n. premier** prime number

nombreux, -euse [nɔ̃brø, -øz] *adj (amis, livres)* numerous, many; *(famille, collection)* large; **peu n.** few; **venir n.** to come in large numbers

nombril [nɔ̃bri] *nm* navel

nominal, -e, -aux, -ales [nɔminal, -o] *adj* nominal

nomination [nɔminɑsjɔ̃] *nf (à un poste)* appointment; *(pour récompense)* nomination

nommer [nɔme] **1** *vt (appeler)* to name; **n. qn** *(désigner)* to appoint sb (**à un poste** to a post); **n. qn président** to appoint sb chairman **2 se nommer** *vpr (s'appeler)* to be called •**nommément** *adv* by name

non [nɔ̃] *adv* no; **tu viens ou n.?** are you coming or not?; **n. seulement** not only; **n. (pas) que...** *(+ subjunctive)* not that...; **n. sans regret** not without regret; **n. loin** not far; **je crois que n.** I don't think so; **(ni) moi n. plus** neither do/am/can/etc I; *Fam* **c'est bien, n.?** it's all right, isn't it?; *Fam* **(ah) ça n.!** definitely not (that)!

nonante [nɔnɑ̃t] *adj & nm (en Belgique, en Suisse)* ninety

nonchalant, -ante [nɔ̃ʃalɑ̃, -ɑ̃t] *adj* nonchalant •**nonchalance** *nf* nonchalance

non-conformiste [nɔ̃kɔ̃fɔrmist] *adj & nmf* nonconformist

non-fumeur, -euse [nɔ̃fymœr, -øz] **1** *adj* non-smoking **2** *nmf* non-smoker

non-lieu [nɔ̃ljø] *nmJur* **bénéficier d'un n.** to be discharged through lack of evidence

non-polluant, -uante [nɔ̃pɔlɥɑ̃, -ɥɑ̃t] *(mpl* **non-polluants,** *fpl* **non-polluantes)** *adj* environmentally friendly

non-retour [nɔ̃rətur] *nm* **point de n.** point of no return

non-sens [nɔ̃sɑ̃s] *nm inv* absurdity

non-violence [nɔ̃vjɔlɑ̃s] *nf* non-violence

non-voyants [nɔ̃vwajɑ̃] *nmpl* **les n.** the unsighted

nord [nɔr] **1** *nm* north; **au n.** in the north; *(direction)* (to the) north (**de** of); **du n.** *(vent, direction)* northerly; *(ville)* northern; *(gens)* from/in the north; **l'Afrique du N.** North Africa; **l'Europe du N.** Northern Europe; **le grand N.** the Frozen North **2** *adj inv (côte)* north; *(régions)* northern •**nord-africain, -aine** *(mpl* **nord-africains,** *fpl* **nord-africaines)** **1** *adj* North African **2** *nmf* **Nord-Africain, Nord-Africaine** North African •**nord-américain, -aine** *(mpl* **nord-américains,** *fpl* **nord-américaines)** **1** *adj* North American **2** *nmf* **Nord-Américain, Nord-Américaine** North American •**nord-est** *nm & adj inv* northeast •**nord-ouest** *nm & adj inv* northwest

nordique [nɔrdik] **1** *adj* Scandinavian **2** *nmf* **N.** Scandinavian; *Can* Northern Canadian

noria [nɔrja] *nf* noria

normal, -e, -aux, -ales [nɔrmal, -o] *adj* normal •**normale** *nf* norm; **au-dessus/au-dessous de la n.** above/below average; *Fam* **N. Sup** = university-level college preparing students for senior posts in teaching •**normalement** *adv* normally •**normaliser** *vt (uniformiser)* to standardize; *(relations)* to normalize

normand, -ande [nɔrmɑ̃, -ɑ̃d] **1** *adj* Norman **2** *nmf* **N., Normande** Norman •**Normandie** *nf* **la N.** Normandy

norme [nɔrm] *nf* norm; **normes de sécurité** safety standards

Norvège [nɔrvɛʒ] *nf* **la N.** Norway •**norvégien, -ienne 1** *adj* Norwegian **2** *nmf* **N., Norvégienne** Norwegian **3** *nm (langue)* Norwegian

nos [no] *voir* **notre**

nostalgie [nɔstalʒi] *nf* nostalgia •**nostalgique** *adj* nostalgic

notable [nɔtabl] *adj & nm* notable •**notablement** [-əmɑ̃] *adv* notably

notaire [nɔtɛr] *nm* lawyer, *Br* notary (public)

notamment [nɔtamɑ̃] *adv* notably

note [nɔt] *nf (annotation, communica-*

tion) & Mus note; *Scol Br* mark, *Am* grade; *(facture) Br* bill, *Am* check; **prendre n. de qch, prendre qch en n.** to make a note of sth; **prendre des notes** to take notes; **n. de frais** expenses

noter [nɔte] *vt (remarquer)* to note; *(écrire)* to note down; *(devoir) Br* to mark, *Am* to grade

notice [nɔtis] *nf (mode d'emploi)* instructions; *(de médicament)* directions

> 🖉 Il faut noter que le nom anglais **notice** est un faux ami. Il signifie le plus souvent **avertissement** ou **écriteau** selon le contexte.

notifier [nɔtifje] *vt* **n. qch à qn** to notify sb of sth

notion [nosjɔ̃] *nf* notion; **notions** *(éléments)* rudiments; **avoir des notions de qch** to know the basics of sth

notoire [nɔtwar] *adj (criminel, bêtise)* notorious; *(fait)* well-known • **notoriété** *nf (renom)* fame; **il est de n. publique que…** it's common knowledge that…

notre, nos [nɔtr, no] *adj possessif* our • **nôtre 1** *pron possessif* **le/la n., les nôtres** ours **2** *nmpl* **les nôtres** *(parents)* our family; **serez-vous des nôtres ce soir?** will you be joining us this evening?

nouba [nuba] *nf Fam* **faire la n.** to party

nouer [nwe] **1** *vt (lacets)* to tie; *(cravate)* to knot; *Fig (relation)* to establish; **avoir la gorge nouée** to have a lump in one's throat

2 se nouer *vpr (intrigue)* to take shape • **noueux, noueuse** *adj (bois)* knotty; *(doigts)* gnarled

nougat [nuga] *nm* nougat

nouille [nuj] *nf Fam (idiot)* dimwit

nouilles [nuj] *nfpl* noodles

nounours [nunurs] *nm Langage enfantin* teddy bear

nourrice [nuris] *nf (assistante maternelle)* (children's) nurse, *Br* child minder; *(qui allaite)* wet nurse; **mettre un enfant en n.** to put a child out to nurse

nourrir [nurir] **1** *vt (alimenter)* to feed; *Fig (espoir)* to cherish; **enfant nourri au sein** breastfed child

2 se nourrir *vpr* to eat; **se n. de qch** to feed on sth • **nourrissant, -ante** *adj* nourishing

nourrisson [nurisɔ̃] *nm* infant

nourriture [nurityr] *nf* food

nous [nu] *pron personnel* **(a)** *(sujet)* we; **n. sommes ici** we are here **(b)** *(complément direct)* us; **il n. connaît** he knows us **(c)** *(complément indirect)* (to) us; **il n. l'a**

donné he gave it to us, he gave us it **(d)** *(réfléchi)* ourselves; **n. n. lavons** we wash ourselves; **n. n. habillons** we get dressed **(e)** *(réciproque)* each other; **n. n. détestons** we hate each other • **nous-mêmes** *pron* ourselves

nouveau, -elle¹, -x, -elles [nuvo, nuvɛl]

> **nouvel** is used before masculine singular nouns beginning with a vowel or mute h.

1 *adj* new; *(mode)* latest; **on craint de nouvelles inondations** *(d'autres)* further flooding is feared

2 *nmf (à l'école)* new boy, *f* new girl

3 *nm* **du n.** something new

4 *adv* **de n., à n.** again • **nouveau-né, -née** *(mpl* **nouveau-nés,** *fpl* **nouveau-nées)* **1** *adj* newborn **2** *nmf* newborn baby

nouveauté [nuvote] *nf* novelty; **nouveautés** *(livres)* new books; *(disques)* new releases

nouvelle² [nuvɛl] *nf* **(a)** **une n.** *(annonce)* a piece of news; **la n. de sa mort** the news of his/her death; **les nouvelles** the news *(sing)*; **les nouvelles sont bonnes/mauvaises** the news is good/bad; **avoir des nouvelles de qn** *(directement)* to have heard from sb; **demander des nouvelles de qn** to inquire about sb **(b)** *(récit)* short story

Nouvelle-Calédonie [nuvɛlkaledɔni] *nf* **la N.** New Caledonia

Nouvelle-Zélande [nuvɛlzelɑ̃d] *nf* **la N.** New Zealand

novateur, -trice [nɔvatœr, -tris] **1** *adj* innovative

2 *nmf* innovator

novembre [nɔvɑ̃br] *nm* November

novice [nɔvis] *nmf* novice

noyade [nwajad] *nf* drowning

noyau, -x [nwajo] *nm (de fruit)* stone, *Am* pit; *(d'atome, de cellule)* nucleus; *(groupe)* group; **n. dur** *(de groupe)* hard core

noyauter [nwajote] *vt* to infiltrate

noyer¹ [nwaje] **1** *vt (personne)* to drown; *(terres)* to flood; **n. son chagrin dans le vin** to drown one's sorrows in wine; *Fig* **n. le poisson** to confuse the issue deliberately; *Fig* **être noyé** *(perdu)* to be out of one's depth; *Fig* **noyé dans la masse** lumped in with the rest

2 se noyer *vpr* to drown; *(se suicider)* to drown oneself; **se n. dans les détails** to get bogged down in details • **noyé, -ée** *nmf* drowned person

noyer² [nwaje] *nm (arbre)* walnut tree

nu, nue [ny] **1** *adj (personne, vérité)* naked; *(mains, chambre)* bare; **tout nu** (stark) naked, (in the) nude; **tête nue, nu-tête** bare-headed; **aller pieds nus** to go barefoot; **se mettre nu** to strip off
2 *nm Art* nude; **mettre qch à nu** to expose sth

nuage [nҁaჳ] *nm* cloud; *Fig* **un n. de lait** a drop of milk; *Fig* **être dans les nuages** to have one's head in the clouds • **nuageux, -euse** *adj (ciel)* cloudy

nuance [nҁãs] *nf (de couleur)* shade; *(de sens)* nuance; *(de regret)* tinge • **nuancé, -ée** *adj (jugement)* qualified • **nuancer** *vt (pensée)* to qualify

nucléaire [nyklɛɛr] **1** *adj* nuclear
2 *nm* nuclear energy

nudisme [nydism] *nm* nudism • **nudiste** *nmf* nudist • **nudité** *nf (de personne)* nudity, nakedness; *(de mur)* bareness

nuée [nҁe] *nf* **une n. de** *(foule)* a horde of; *(groupe compact)* a cloud of

nues [ny] *nfpl* **tomber des n.** to be astounded; **porter qn aux n.** to praise sb to the skies

nuire* [nҁir] *vi* **n. à qn/qch** to harm sb/sth • **nuisible** *adj* harmful (**à** to)

nuit [nҁi] *nf* night; *(obscurité)* dark(ness); **la n.** *(se promener)* at night; **cette n.** *(hier)* last night; *(aujourd'hui)* tonight; **avant la n.** before nightfall; **il fait n.** it's dark; **il fait n. noire** it's pitch-black; **bonne n.!** good night!; **n. d'hôtel** overnight stay in a hotel • **nuitée** *nf* overnight stay

nul, nulle [nyl] **1** *adj (médiocre)* hopeless, useless; *(risque)* non-existent, nil; *Jur (non valable)* null (and void); **être n. en qch** to be hopeless at sth
2 *adj indéfini Littéraire (aucun)* no; **sans n. doute** without any doubt
3 *pron indéfini m Littéraire (aucun)* no one • **nullard, -arde** *nmf très Fam* useless idiot • **nullement** *adv* not at all • **nulle part** *adv* nowhere; **n. ailleurs** nowhere else • **nullité** *nf (d'un élève)* uselessness; *(personne)* useless person

numéraire [nymerɛr] *nm* cash

numéral, -e, -aux, -ales [nymeral, -o] *adj & nm* numeral

numérique [nymerik] *adj* numerical; *(montre, clavier, données)* digital

numéro [nymero] *nm (chiffre)* number; *(de journal)* issue, number; *(au cirque)* act; *Tél* **n. vert** *Br* ≃ Freefone® number, *Am* ≃ toll-free number; *Fam* **quel n.!** *(personne)* what a character!; **n. gagnant** *(au jeu)* winning number; **n. de téléphone** telephone number • **numérotage** *nm* numbering • **numéroter** *vt (pages, sièges)* to number

nu-pieds [nypje] *nmpl* sandals

nuptial, -iale, -iaux, -iales [nypsjal, -jo] *adj (chambre)* bridal; **cérémonie nuptiale** wedding ceremony

nuque [nyk] *nf* back of the neck

nurse [nœrs] *nf Vieilli* nanny

nutritif, -ive [nytritif, -iv] *adj* nutritious • **nutrition** *nf* nutrition

Nylon® [nilɔ̃] *nm (fibre)* nylon; **chemise en N.** nylon shirt

nymphe [nɛ̃f] *nf* nymph • **nymphomane** *nf* nymphomaniac

O

O, o [o] *nm inv* O, o
oasis [ɔazis] *nf* oasis
obédience [ɔbedjɑ̃s] *nf (politique)* allegiance
obéir [ɔbeir] *vi* to obey; **o. à qn/qch** to obey sb/sth; **être obéi** to be obeyed; **o. à qn au doigt et à l'œil** to be at sb's beck and call • **obéissance** *nf* obedience (**à** to) • **obéissant, -ante** *adj* obedient
obélisque [ɔbelisk] *nm* obelisk
obèse [ɔbɛz] *adj* obese • **obésité** [ɔbe-] *nf* obesity
objecter [ɔbʒɛkte] *vt* **o. que...** to object that...; **n'avoir rien à o. à qch** to have no objection to sth; **on m'objecta mon jeune âge** my youth was held against me • **objecteur** *nm* **o. de conscience** conscientious objector • **objection** *nf* objection; **si vous n'y voyez pas d'o.** if you have no objection(s)
objectif, -ive [ɔbʒɛktif, -iv] **1** *adj* objective
2 *nm (but)* objective; *(d'appareil photo)* lens; *Com* **o. de vente** sales target • **objectivement** *adv* objectively • **objectivité** *nf* objectivity
objet [ɔbʒɛ] *nm (chose, sujet, but)* object; **faire l'o. de** *(étude, critiques)* to be the subject of; *(soins, surveillance)* to be given; **sans o.** *(inquiétude)* groundless; **o. d'art** object d'art; **o. volant non identifié** unidentified flying object; **objets trouvés** *(bureau) Br* lost property, *Am* lost and found
obligation [ɔbligasjɔ̃] *nf (contrainte)* obligation; *Fin* bond; **se trouver dans l'o. de faire qch** to be obliged to do sth; **sans o. d'achat** no purchase necessary • **obligatoire** *adj* compulsory, obligatory; *Fam (inévitable)* inevitable • **obligatoirement** *adv (fatalement)* inevitably; **tu dois o. le faire** you have to do it; **pas o.** not necessarily
obligeant, -ante [ɔbliʒɑ̃, -ɑ̃t] *adj* obliging, kind • **obligeamment** [-amɑ̃] *adv* obligingly • **obligeance** *nf Formel* **avoir l'o. de faire qch** to be so kind as to do sth
obliger [ɔbliʒe] **1** *vt* (**a**) *(contraindre)* to force (**à faire** to do); **être obligé de faire**

qch to be obliged to do sth (**b**) *(rendre service à)* to oblige
2 s'obliger *vpr* **s'o. à faire qch** to force oneself to do sth • **obligé, -ée** *adj (obligatoire)* necessary; *Fam (fatal)* inevitable
oblique [ɔblik] *adj* oblique; *(regard)* sidelong; **en o.** at an (oblique) angle • **obliquer** *vi (véhicule)* to turn off
oblitérer [ɔblitere] *vt (timbre)* to cancel; **timbre oblitéré** used stamp
oblong, -ongue [ɔblɔ̃, -ɔ̃g] *adj* oblong
obnubilé, -ée [ɔbnybile] *adj (obsédé)* obsessed (**par** with)
obole [ɔbɔl] *nf* small contribution
obscène [ɔpsɛn] *adj* obscene • **obscénité** *nf* obscenity
obscur, -ure [ɔpskyr] *adj (sombre)* dark; *(difficile à comprendre, inconnu)* obscure • **obscurcir 1** *vt (pièce)* to darken; *(rendre confus)* to obscure **2 s'obscurcir** *vpr (ciel)* to darken; *(vue)* to grow dim • **obscurément** *adv* obscurely • **obscurité** *nf (noirceur)* darkness; *(anonymat)* obscurity; **dans l'o.** in the dark
obséder [ɔpsede] *vt* to obsess • **obsédant, -ante** *adj* haunting; *(pensée)* obsessive • **obsédé, -ée** *nmf* maniac (**de** for); **o. sexuel** sex maniac
obsèques [ɔpsɛk] *nfpl* funeral; **faire des o. nationales à qn** to give sb a state funeral
obséquieux, -ieuse [ɔpsekjø, -jøz] *adj* obsequious
observateur, -trice [ɔpsɛrvatœr, -tris] **1** *adj* observant
2 *nmf* observer
observation [ɔpsɛrvasjɔ̃] *nf (étude, remarque)* observation; *(reproche)* remark; *(respect)* observance; **en o.** *(malade)* under observation
observatoire [ɔpsɛrvatwar] *nm* observatory; *Mil* observation post
observer [ɔpsɛrve] *vt (regarder, respecter)* to observe; *(remarquer)* to notice; **faire o. qch à qn** to point sth out to sb
obsession [ɔpsesjɔ̃] *nf* obsession • **obsessionnel, -elle** *adj* obsessional
obsolète [ɔpsɔlɛt] *adj* obsolete
obstacle [ɔpstakl] *nm* obstacle; **faire o. à qch** to stand in the way of sth

obstétricien, -ienne [ɔpstetrisjɛ̃, -jɛn] *nmf* obstetrician

obstiner [ɔpstine] **s'obstiner** *vpr* to persist (**à faire** in doing) • **obstination** *nf* stubbornness, obstinacy • **obstiné, -ée** *adj* stubborn, obstinate

obstruction [ɔpstryksjɔ̃] *nf* obstruction; *Pol* **faire de l'o.** to be obstructive • **obstruer** *vt* to obstruct

obtempérer [ɔptɑ̃pere] *vi* **o. à qch** to comply with sth

obtenir* [ɔptənir] *vt* to get, to obtain • **obtention** *nf* obtaining

obturateur [ɔptyratœr] *nm (d'appareil photo)* shutter

obtus, -use [ɔpty, -yz] *adj (angle, esprit)* obtuse

obus [ɔby] *nm (projectile)* shell

occasion [ɔkazjɔ̃] *nf* (**a**) *(chance)* chance, opportunity (**de faire** to do); *(moment)* occasion; **à l'o.** when the occasion arises; **à l'o. de qch** on the occasion of sth; **pour les grandes occasions** for special occasions (**b**) *(affaire)* bargain; *(objet non neuf)* second-hand item; **d'o.** second-hand

occasionner [ɔkazjɔne] *vt* to cause; **o. qch à qn** to cause sb sth

occident [ɔksidɑ̃] *nm Pol* **l'O.** the West • **occidental, -e, -aux, -ales 1** *adj Géog & Pol* western **2** *nmpl Pol* **les Occidentaux** Westerners • **occidentalisé, -ée** *adj Pol* westernized

occulte [ɔkylt] *adj* occult

occupant, -ante [ɔkypɑ̃, -ɑ̃t] **1** *adj (armée)* occupying **2** *nmf (habitant)* occupant **3** *nm Mil* **l'o.** the occupying forces

occupation [ɔkypasjɔ̃] *nf (activité, travail) & Mil* occupation; *Hist* **l'O.** the Occupation

occupé, -ée [ɔkype] *adj* busy (**à faire** doing); *(place, maison)* occupied; *(ligne téléphonique) Br* engaged, *Am* busy

occuper [ɔkype] **1** *vt (bâtiment, pays, temps)* to occupy; *(place)* to take up, to occupy; *(poste)* to hold; **o. qn** *(jeu, travail)* to keep sb busy *or* occupied; *(ouvrier)* to employ sb **2 s'occuper** *vpr* to keep oneself busy (**à faire** doing); **s'o. de** *(affaire, problème)* to deal with; *(politique)* to be engaged in; **s'o. de qn** *(malade)* to take care of sb; *(client)* to see to sb; **est-ce qu'on s'occupe de vous?** *(dans un magasin)* are you being served?; *Fam* **occupe-toi de tes affaires!** mind your own business!

occurrence [ɔkyrɑ̃s] *nf Ling* occurrence; **en l'o.** in this case

océan [ɔseɑ̃] *nm* ocean; *Fig* **un o. de fleurs** a sea of flowers; *Fig* **un o. de larmes** floods of tears; **l'o. Atlantique/Pacifique** the Atlantic/Pacific Ocean • **océanique** *adj* oceanic

ocre [ɔkr] *nm & adj inv* ochre

octane [ɔktan] *nm* octane

octante [ɔktɑ̃t] *adj & nm inv (en Belgique, en Suisse)* eighty

octave [ɔktav] *nf Mus* octave

octet [ɔktɛ] *nm Ordinat* byte; **milliard d'octets** gigabyte

octobre [ɔktɔbr] *nm* October

octogénaire [ɔktɔʒenɛr] *nmf* octogenarian

octogone [ɔktɔgɔn] *nm* octagon • **octogonal, -e, -aux, -ales** *adj* octagonal

octroyer [ɔktrwaje] *vt Littéraire* to grant (**à** to)

oculaire [ɔkylɛr] *adj* **témoin o.** eyewitness • **oculiste** *nmf* eye specialist

ode [ɔd] *nf* ode

odeur [ɔdœr] *nf* smell; *(de fleur)* scent; **une o. de brûlé** a smell of burning • **odorant, -ante** *adj* sweet-smelling • **odorat** *nm* sense of smell

odieux, -ieuse [ɔdjø, -jøz] *adj* odious

œcuménique [ekymenik] *adj Rel* ecumenical

œil [œj] *(pl* **yeux** [jø]) *nm* eye; **l'o. du cyclone** the eye of the storm *or* cyclone; **avoir les yeux verts** to have green eyes; **avoir de grands yeux** to have big eyes; **lever/baisser les yeux** to look up/down; *Fig* **fermer les yeux sur qch** to turn a blind eye to sth; **je n'ai pas fermé l'o. de la nuit** I didn't sleep a wink all night; **coup d'o.** *(regard)* look, glance; **jeter un coup d'o. sur qch** to have a look at sth; **à vue d'o.** visibly; **à mes yeux** in my eyes; *Fam* **à l'o.** *(gratuitement)* free; **avoir qch sous les yeux** to have sth before one's very eyes; **regarder qn dans les yeux** to look sb in the eye; **être les yeux dans les yeux** to be gazing into each other's eyes; **faire les gros yeux à qn** to scowl at sb; *Fam* **faire de l'o. à qn** to give sb the eye; **avoir qn à l'o.** *(surveiller)* to keep an eye on sb; **ne pas avoir les yeux dans sa poche** to be very observant; *Fig* **o. poché, o. au beurre noir** black eye; **ouvre l'o.!** keep your eyes open!; *Fam* **mon o.!** *(incrédulité)* my foot!; *Fam* **entre quat'z'yeux** [katzjø] *(en privé)* in private • **œil-de-bœuf** *(pl* **œils-de-bœuf)** *nm* bull's-eye window

œillade [œjad] *nf* wink

œillères [œjer] *nfpl (de cheval) Br* blinkers, *Am* blinders

œillet [œjɛ] *nm (fleur)* carnation; *(trou de ceinture)* eyelet

œnologie [enɔlɔʃi, œ-] *nf* oenology

œuf [œf] *(pl* **œufs** [ø]) *nm* egg; **œufs** *(de poissons)* (hard) roe; *Fig* **étouffer qch dans l'o.** to nip sth in the bud; **o. à la coque** boiled egg; **o. sur le plat** fried egg; **o. dur** hard-boiled egg; **œufs brouillés** scrambled eggs; **o. de Pâques** Easter egg

œuvre [œvr] *nf (travail, livre)* work; **être à l'o.** to be at work; **mettre qch en o.** *(loi, système)* to implement sth; **mettre tout en o.** to do everything possible (**pour faire** to do); **se mettre à l'o.** to set to work; **o. d'art** work of art; **o. de charité** *(organisation)* charity • **œuvrer** *vi* to work

offense [ɔfɑ̃s] *nf* insult; *Rel* transgression • **offensant, -ante** *adj* offensive • **offenser** 1 *vt* to offend 2 **s'offenser** *vpr* **s'o. de qch** to take *Br* offence *or Am* offense at sth

offensif, -ive [ɔfɑ̃sif, -iv] 1 *adj* offensive 2 *nf* **offensive** offensive; **passer à l'o.** to go on the offensive; **offensive du froid** sudden cold spell

offert, -erte [ɔfɛr, -ɛrt] *pp de* **offrir**

office [ɔfis] *nm* (**a**) *Rel* service (**b**) *(pièce)* pantry (**c**) *(établissement)* office, bureau; **o. du tourisme** tourist information centre (**d**) *(charge)* office; **d'o.** without having any say; **faire o. de qch** to serve as sth

officiel, -ielle [ɔfisjɛl] *adj & nm* official • **officiellement** *adv* officially

officier [ɔfisje] 1 *nm (dans l'armée)* officier 2 *vi Rel* to officiate

officieux, -ieuse [ɔfisjø, -jøz] *adj* unofficial

offre [ɔfr] *nf* offer; *(aux enchères)* bid; *Fin* tender; *Écon* **l'o. et la demande** supply and demand; *Fin* **appel d'offres** invitation to tender; *Fin* **o. publique d'achat** takeover bid; **offres d'emploi** *(de journal)* job vacancies, *Br* situations vacant • **offrande** *nf* offering

offrir* [ɔfrir] 1 *vt (donner en cadeau)* to give; *(proposer)* to offer; **o. qch à qn** *(donner)* to give sb sth, to give sth to sb; *(proposer)* to offer sb sth, to offer sth to sb; **o. de faire qch** to offer to do sth; **o. sa démission** to offer one's resignation 2 **s'offrir** *vpr (cadeau)* to treat oneself to; *(se proposer)* to offer oneself (**comme** as); **s'o. aux regards** *(spectacle)* to greet one's eyes • **offrant** *nm* **au plus o.** to the highest bidder

offusquer [ɔfyske] 1 *vt* to offend 2 **s'offusquer** *vpr* **s'o. de qch** to take *Br* offence *or Am* offense at sth

ogive [ɔʒiv] *nf (de fusée)* head; *(de roquette)* nose cone; *Archit* rib; **o. nucléaire** nuclear warhead

OGM [ɔʒeɛm] *(abrév* **organisme génétiquement modifié)** *nm* GMO

ogre [ɔgr] *nm* ogre

oh [o] *exclam* oh!; **oh! hisse!** heave-ho!

ohé [ɔe] *exclam* hey (there)!

oie [wa] *nf* goose *(pl* geese)

oignon [ɔɲɔ̃] *nm (légume)* onion; *(de fleur)* bulb; *Fam* **en rang d'oignons** in a neat row; *Fam* **occupe-toi de tes oignons!** mind your own business!

oiseau, -x [wazo] *nm* bird; *Hum* **l'o. rare** the ideal person; *Péj* **drôle d'o.** *Br* queer or odd fish, *Am* oddball; **'attention! le petit o. va sortir!'** 'watch the birdie!'; **o. de proie** bird of prey

oiseux, -euse [wazø, -øz] *adj (conversation)* idle; *(explication)* unsatisfactory

oisif, -ive [wazif, -iv] *adj* idle • **oisiveté** *nf* idleness

oisillon [wazijɔ̃] *nm* fledgling

oléoduc [ɔleɔdyk] *nm* pipeline

olfactif, -ive [ɔlfaktif, -iv] *adj* olfactory

oligoélément [ɔligoelemɑ̃] *nm* trace element

olive [ɔliv] 1 *nf* olive 2 *adj inv* **(vert) o.** olive (green) • **olivier** *nm (arbre)* olive tree

olympique [ɔlɛ̃pik] *adj* Olympic; **les jeux Olympiques** the Olympic games

ombilical, -e, -aux, -ales [ɔ̃bilikal, -o] *adj* umbilical

ombrage [ɔ̃braʒ] *nm (ombre)* shade; *Littéraire* **prendre o. de qch** to take umbrage at sth • **ombragé, -ée** *adj* shady • **ombrager** *vt* to give shade to • **ombrageux, -euse** *adj (caractère, personne)* touchy

ombre [ɔ̃br] *nf (forme)* shadow; *(zone sombre)* shade; **30° à l'o.** 30° in the shade; *Fig* **dans l'o.** *(comploter)* in secret; *Fig* **rester dans l'o.** to remain in the background; **sans l'o. d'un doute** without the shadow of a doubt; **pas l'o. d'un reproche/remords** not a trace of blame/remorse; *Fig* **il y a une o. au tableau** there's a fly in the ointment; **o. à paupières** eyeshadow

ombrelle [ɔ̃brɛl] *nf* sunshade, parasol

Il faut noter que le nom anglais **umbrella** *est un faux ami. Il signifie* **parapluie.**

---

omelette [ɔmlɛt] *nf* omelet(te); **o. au fromage** cheese omelet(te); **o. norvégienne** baked Alaska

omettre* [ɔmɛtr] *vt* to omit (**de faire** to do) • **omission** *nf* omission

omnibus [ɔmnibys] *adj & nm* (train) **o.** slow train *(stopping at all stations)*

omnipotent, -ente [ɔmnipɔtɑ̃, -ɑ̃t] *adj* omnipotent

omniprésent, -ente [ɔmniprezɑ̃, ɑ̃t] *adj* omnipresent

omnisports [ɔmnispɔr] *adj inv* **centre o.** sports centre

omnivore [ɔmnivɔr] *adj* omnivorous

omoplate [ɔmɔplat] *nf* shoulder blade

on [ɔ̃] *(sometimes l'on* [lɔ̃]*) pron indéfini (les gens)* they, people; *(nous)* we, one; *(vous)* you, one; **on frappe** someone's knocking; **on dit** they say, people say; **on m'a dit que...** I was told that...; **on me l'a donné** somebody gave it to me

once [ɔ̃s] *nf (mesure) & Fig* ounce

oncle [ɔ̃kl] *nm* uncle

onctueux, -ueuse [ɔ̃ktɥø, -ɥøz] *adj* smooth

onde [ɔ̃d] *nf (à la radio) & Phys* wave; **grandes ondes** long wave; **ondes courtes/moyennes** short/medium wave; **o. de choc** shock wave; **sur les ondes** *(à l'antenne)* on the radio

ondée [ɔ̃de] *nf* sudden downpour

on-dit [ɔ̃di] *nm inv* rumour, hearsay

ondoyer [ɔ̃dwaje] *vi* to undulate

ondulation [ɔ̃dylɑsjɔ̃] *nf* undulation; *(de cheveux)* wave • **ondulé, -ée** *adj* wavy • **onduler** *vi* to undulate; *(cheveux)* to be wavy

onéreux, -euse [ɔnerø, -øz] *adj* costly

🖋 Il faut noter que le nom anglais **onerous** est un faux ami. Il signifie **lourd, pénible**.

ONG [ɔɛnʒe] *(abrév* **organisation non gouvernementale)** *nf* NGO

ongle [ɔ̃gl] *nm* (finger)nail; **se faire les ongles** to do one's nails

onglet [ɔ̃glɛ] *nm (de canif)* (nail) groove; **à onglets** *(dictionnaire)* with a thumb index

ont [ɔ̃] *voir* **avoir**

ONU [ɔny] *(abrév* **Organisation des Nations unies)** *nf* UN

onyx [ɔniks] *nm* onyx

onze [ɔ̃z] *adj & nm* eleven • **onzième** *adj & nmf* eleventh

OPA [ɔpeɑ] *abrév* **offre publique d'achat**

opale [ɔpal] *nf* opal

opaque [ɔpak] *adj* opaque • **opacité** *nf* opacity

opéra [ɔpera] *nm (musique)* opera; *(édifice)* opera house; **o. rock** rock opera • **opéra-comique** *(pl* **opéras-comiques)** *nm* comic opera • **opérette** *nf* operetta

opérateur, -trice [ɔperatœr, -tris] *nmf* *(personne)* operator; *Cin* cameraman; **o. de saisie** keyboarder

opération [ɔperɑsjɔ̃] *nf (action) & Méd, Mil & Math* operation; *Fin* deal; **faire une o. portes ouvertes** to open one's doors to the public; **o. à cœur ouvert** open-heart surgery • **opérationnel, -elle** *adj* operational • **opératoire** *adj (méthode)* operating

opérer [ɔpere] **1** *vt (exécuter)* to carry out; *(choix)* to make; *(patient)* to operate on *(* **de** for*)*; **se faire o.** to have an operation

2 *vi (agir)* to work; *(procéder)* to proceed; *(chirurgien)* to operate

3 **s'opérer** *vpr (se produire)* to take place

ophtalmologue [ɔftalmɔlɔg] *nmf* ophthalmologist

opiner [ɔpine] *vi* **o.** *(de la tête)* to nod assent

opiniâtre [ɔpinjɑtr] *adj* stubborn • **opiniâtreté** [-trate] *nf* stubbornness

opinion [ɔpinjɔ̃] *nf* opinion *(* **sur** about *or* on*)*; **sans o.** *(de sondage)* don't know; **mon o. est faite** my mind is made up; **o. publique** public opinion

opium [ɔpjɔm] *nm* opium

opportun, -une [ɔpɔrtœ̃, -yn] *adj* opportune, timely • **opportunément** *adv* opportunely • **opportunisme** *nm* opportunism • **opportunité** *nf* timeliness

opposant, -ante [ɔpozɑ̃, -ɑ̃t] *nmf* opponent *(* **à** of*)*

opposé, -ée [ɔpoze] **1** *adj (direction)* opposite; *(intérêts)* conflicting; *(armées, équipe)* opposing; **être o. à qch** to be opposed to sth

2 *nm* **l'o.** the opposite *(* **de** of*)*; **à l'o.** *(côté)* on the opposite side *(* **de** to*)*; **à l'o. de** *(contrairement à)* contrary to

opposer [ɔpoze] **1** *vt (résistance, argument)* to put up *(* **à** against*)*; *(équipes)* to pit against each other; *(armées)* to bring into conflict; *(styles, conceptions)* to contrast; **o. qn à qn** to set sb against sb; **match qui oppose** match between

2 **s'opposer** *vpr (équipes)* to confront each other; *(styles, conceptions)* to contrast; **s'o. à qch** to be opposed to sth; **je m'y oppose** I'm opposed to it

opposition [ɔpozisjɔ̃] *nf* opposition *(* **à** to*)*; **faire o. à** to oppose; *(chèque)* to stop; **par o. à** as opposed to

oppresser [ɔprese] *vt (gêner)* to oppress • **oppressant, -ante** *adj* oppressive • **oppresseur** *nm* oppressor • **oppressif, -ive** *adj (loi)* oppressive • **oppression** *nf* oppression • **opprimer** *vt (peuple, nation)* to oppress • **opprimés** *nmpl* **les o.** the oppressed

opter [ɔpte] *vi* **o. pour qch** to opt for sth

opticien, -ienne [ɔptisjɛ̃, -jɛn] *nmf* opticien

optimiser [ɔptimize] *vt* to optimize

optimisme [ɔptimism] *nm* optimism • **optimiste 1** *adj* optimistic **2** *nmf* optimist

optimum [ɔptimɔm] *nm & adj* optimum • **optimal, -e, -aux, -ales** *adj* optimal

option [ɔpsjɔ̃] *nf (choix)* option; *(chose)* optional extra; *Scol Br* optional subject, *Am* elective (subject)

optique [ɔptik] **1** *adj (nerf)* optic; *(verre, fibres)* optical **2** *nf* optics *(sing)*; *Fig (aspect)* perspective; **d'o.** *(instrument, appareil)* optical; **dans cette o.** from this perspective

opulent, -ente [ɔpylɑ̃, -ɑ̃t] *adj* opulent • **opulence** *nf* opulence

or¹ [ɔr] *nm* gold; **montre/chaîne en or** gold watch/chain; **règle/âge/cheveux d'or** golden rule/age/hair; **cœur d'or** heart of gold; **mine d'or** gold mine; **affaire en or** bargain; **or noir** *(pétrole)* black gold

or² [ɔr] *conj (cependant)* now, well

oracle [ɔrakl] *nm* oracle

orage [ɔraʒ] *nm* (thunder)storm • **orageux, -euse** *adj* stormy

oraison [ɔrezɔ̃] *nf* prayer; **o. funèbre** funeral oration

oral, -e, -aux, -ales [ɔral, -o] **1** *adj* oral **2** *nm Scol & Univ* oral

orange [ɔrɑ̃ʒ] **1** *nf* orange; **o. pressée** (fresh) orange juice **2** *adj & nm inv (couleur)* orange • **orangé, -ée** *adj & nm (couleur)* orange • **orangeade** *nf* orangeade • **oranger** *nm* orange tree

orang-outan(g) [ɔrɑ̃utɑ̃] *(pl* **orangs-outan(g)s)** *nm* orang-utan

orateur [ɔratœr] *nm* speaker, orator

orbite [ɔrbit] *nf (d'astre) & Fig* orbit; *(d'œil)* socket; **mettre qch sur o.** *(fusée)* to put sth into orbit • **orbital, -e, -aux, -ales** *adj* **station orbitale** space station

orchestre [ɔrkɛstr] *nm (classique)* orchestra; *(de jazz)* band; *Théâtre (places) Br* stalls, *Am* orchestra • **orchestration** *nf* orchestration • **orchestrer** *vt (organiser) & Mus* to orchestrate

orchidée [ɔrkide] *nf* orchid

ordinaire [ɔrdinɛr] *adj (habituel, normal)* ordinary, *Am* regular; *(médiocre)* ordinary, average; **d'o., à l'o.** usually; **comme d'o., comme à l'o.** as usual • **ordinairement** *adv* usually

ordinal, -e, -aux, -ales [ɔrdinal, -o] *adj* ordinal

ordinateur [ɔrdinatœr] *nm* computer; **o.**

individuel personal computer; **o. portable** laptop

ordination [ɔrdinɑsjɔ̃] *nf Rel* ordination

ordonnance [ɔrdɔnɑ̃s] *nf (de médecin)* prescription; *(de juge)* order, ruling; *(disposition)* arrangement; *(soldat)* orderly

ordonner [ɔrdɔne] *vt* **(a)** *(commander)* to order (**que** + *subjunctive* that); **o. à qn de faire qch** to order sb to do sth **(b)** *(ranger)* to organize **(c)** *(prêtre)* to ordain; **il a été ordonné prêtre** he has been ordained (as) a priest • **ordonné, -ée** *adj (personne, maison)* tidy

ordre [ɔrdr] *nm (organisation, discipline, catégorie, commandement) & Fin* order; *(absence de désordre)* tidiness; **en o.** *(chambre)* tidy; **mettre de l'o. dans qch** to tidy sth up; **rentrer dans l'o.** to return to normal; **jusqu'à nouvel o.** until further notice; **de l'o. de** *(environ)* of the order of; **du même o.** of the same order; **donnez-moi un o. de grandeur** give me a rough estimate; **de premier o.** first-rate; **par o. d'âge** in order of age; **assurer le maintien de l'o.** to maintain order; *Rel* **entrer dans les ordres** to take holy orders; *Mil* **à vos ordres!** yes sir!; **o. du jour** agenda; **l'o. public** law and order

ordures [ɔrdyr] *nfpl (déchets) Br* rubbish, *Am* garbage; **mettre qch aux o.** to throw sth out (in the *Br* rubbish *or Am* garbage) • **ordurier, -ière** *adj* filthy

oreille [ɔrɛj] *nf* ear; **faire la sourde o.** to turn a deaf ear; **être tout oreilles** to be all ears; **écouter d'une o. distraite** to listen with half an ear; **dire qch à l'o. de qn** to whisper sth in sb's ear; **être dur d'o.** to be hard of hearing

oreiller [ɔrɛje] *nm* pillow

oreillons [ɔrɛjɔ̃] *nmpl (maladie)* mumps

ores et déjà [ɔrzedeʒa] **d'ores et déjà** *adv* already

orfèvre [ɔrfɛvr] *nm (d'or)* goldsmith; *(d'argent)* silversmith • **orfèvrerie** [-vrəri] *nf (magasin)* goldsmith's/silversmith's shop; *(objets)* gold/silver plate

organe [ɔrgan] *nm Anat & Fig* organ; *(porte-parole)* mouthpiece • **organique** *adj* organic • **organisme** *nm (corps)* body; *Biol* organism; *(bureaux)* organization

organisateur, -trice [ɔrganizatœr, -tris] *nmf* organizer

organisation [ɔrganizasjɔ̃] *nf (arrangement, association)* organization

organiser [ɔrganize] **1** *vt* to organize **2 s'organiser** *vpr* to get organized • **organisé, -ée** *adj* organized • **organiseur** *nm* **o. personnel** personal organizer

organiste [ɔrganist] *nmf* organist
orgasme [ɔrgasm] *nm* orgasm
orge [ɔrʒ] *nf* barley
orgie [ɔrʒi] *nf* orgy
orgue [ɔrg] **1** *nm* organ; **o. de Barbarie** barrel organ
2 *nfpl* **orgues** organ; **grandes orgues** great organ
orgueil [ɔrgœj] *nm* pride • **orgueilleux, -euse** *adj* proud
orient [ɔrjɑ̃] *nm* **l'O.** the Orient, the East; **en O.** in the East • **oriental, -e, -aux, -ales 1** *adj (côte, région)* eastern; *(langue)* oriental **2** *nmf* **O., Orientale** Oriental
orientable [ɔrjɑ̃tabl] *adj (lampe)* adjustable; *(bras de machine)* movable
orientation [ɔrjɑ̃tasjɔ̃] *nf (détermination de position)* orientation; *(de grue, d'antenne)* positioning; *(de maison)* aspect; *(de politique, de recherche)* direction; **avoir le sens de l'o.** to have a good sense of direction; **o. professionnelle** careers guidance
orienter [ɔrjɑ̃te] **1** *vt (bâtiment)* to orientate; *(canon, télescope)* to point (**vers** at); **o. ses recherches sur** to direct one's research on; **être mal orienté** *(élève)* to have been given bad careers advice
2 s'orienter *vpr* to get one's bearings; **s'o. vers** *(carrière)* to specialize in • **orienté, -ée** *adj (peu objectif)* slanted; **o. à l'ouest** *(appartement)* facing west
orifice [ɔrifis] *nm* opening
originaire [ɔriʒinɛr] *adj* **être o. de** *(natif)* to be a native of
original, -e, -aux, -ales [ɔriʒinal, -o] **1** *adj (idée, artiste, version)* original **2** *nm (texte, tableau)* original **3** *nmf (personne)* eccentric • **originalité** *nf* originality
origine [ɔriʒin] *nf* origin; **à l'o.** originally; **être à l'o. de qch** to be at the origin of sth; **d'o.** *(pneu)* original; **pays d'o.** country of origin; **être d'o. française** to be of French origin • **originel, -elle** *adj* original
orme [ɔrm] *nm (arbre, bois)* elm
ornement [ɔrnəmɑ̃] *nm* ornament • **ornemental, -e, -aux, -ales** *adj* ornamental
orner [ɔrne] *vt* to decorate (**de** with)
ornière [ɔrnjɛr] *nf* rut; *Fig* **sortir de l'o.** to get out of trouble
orphelin, -ine [ɔrfəlɛ̃, -in] *nmf* orphan • **orphelinat** *nm* orphanage
ORSEC [ɔrsɛk] *(abrév* **organisation des secours) plan O.** = disaster contingency plan
orteil [ɔrtɛj] *nm* toe; **gros o.** big toe

orthodoxe [ɔrtɔdɔks] *adj* orthodox • **orthodoxie** *nf* orthodoxy
orthographe [ɔrtɔgraf] *nf* spelling • **orthographier** *vt* to spell; **mal o. qch** to misspell sth • **orthographique** *adj* orthographic
orthopédie [ɔrtɔpedi] *nf* orthopaedics *(sing)*
ortie [ɔrti] *nf* nettle
os [ɔs, *pl* o *ou* ɔs] *nm* bone; **trempé jusqu'aux os** soaked to the skin; **on lui voit les os** he's all skin and bone; **il ne fera pas de vieux os** he won't make old bones; *Fam* **tomber sur un os** to hit a snag
oscar [ɔskar] *nm (récompense)* Oscar
osciller [ɔsile] *vi Tech* to oscillate; *(pendule)* to swing; *(aiguille, flamme)* to flicker; *(bateau)* to rock; *Fig (varier)* to fluctuate (**entre** between) • **oscillation** *nf Tech* oscillation; *Fig (de l'opinion)* fluctuation
oseille [ozɛj] *nf (plante)* sorrel; *Fam (argent)* dosh
oser [oze] *vt* to dare; **o. faire qch** to dare (to) do sth • **osé, -ée** *adj* daring
osier [ozje] *nm* wicker; **panier d'o.** wicker basket
ossature [ɔsatyr] *nf (du corps)* frame; *(de bâtiment)* & *Fig* framework • **osselets** *nmpl (jeu)* jacks, *Br* knucklebones • **ossements** *nmpl* bones
osseux, -euse [ɔsø, -øz] *adj (maigre)* bony; **tissu o.** bone tissue
ostensible [ɔstɑ̃sibl] *adj* open • **ostensiblement** [-əmɑ̃] *adv* openly

> Il faut noter que les termes anglais **ostensible** et **ostensibly** sont des faux amis. Ils signifient respectivement **apparent** et **en apparence**.

ostentation [ɔstɑ̃tasjɔ̃] *nf* ostentation • **ostentatoire** *adj* ostentatious
ostréiculteur, -trice [ɔstreikytœr, -tris] *nmf* oyster farmer
otage [ɔtaʒ] *nm* hostage; **prendre qn en o.** to take sb hostage
OTAN [ɔtɑ̃] *(abrév* **Organisation du traité de l'Atlantique Nord)** *nf* NATO
otarie [ɔtari] *nf* sea lion
ôter [ote] **1** *vt* to take away, to remove (**à qn** from sb); *(vêtement)* to take off; *(déduire)* to take (away)
2 s'ôter *vpr Fam* **ôte-toi de là!** move yourself!
otite [ɔtit] *nf* ear infection
oto-rhino [ɔtɔrino] *(pl* **oto-rhinos)** *nmf Fam (médecin)* ENT specialist
ou [u] *conj* or; **ou bien** or else; **ou elle ou**

moi either her or me; **pour ou contre nous** for or against us

où [u] *adv & pron relatif* where; **le jour où...** the day when...; **la table où...** the table on which...; **l'état où...** the condition in which...; **par où?** which way?; **d'où?** where from?; **d'où ma surprise** hence my surprise; **le pays d'où je viens** the country from which I come; **où qu'il soit** wherever he may be

ouate [wat] *nf (pour pansement) Br* cotton wool, *Am* absorbent cotton

oubli [ubli] *nm (trou de mémoire)* oversight; *(lacune)* omission; **tomber dans l'o.** to fall into oblivion

oublier [ublije] **1** *vt* to forget (**de faire** to do); *(omettre)* to leave out

2 s'oublier *vpr (traditions)* to be forgotten; *Fig (personne)* to forget oneself

oubliettes [ublijɛt] *nfpl (de château)* dungeons; **être tombé aux o.** *(personne, projet)* to be long forgotten

oublieux, -ieuse [ublijø, -jøz] *adj* forgetful (**de** of)

ouest [wɛst] **1** *nm* west; **à l'o.** in the west; *(direction)* (to the) west (**de** of); **d'o.** *(vent)* west(erly); **de l'o.** western

2 *adj inv (côte)* west; *(région)* western

ouf [uf] *exclam (soulagement)* phew!

Ouganda [ugɑ̃da] *nm* **l'O.** Uganda

oui [wi] **1** *adv* yes; **ah, ça o.!** oh yes (indeed!); **tu viens, o. ou non?** are you coming or aren't you?; **je crois que o.** I think so; **si o.** if so

2 *nm inv* **pour un o. pour un non** for the slightest thing

ouï-dire [widir] *nm* hearsay; **par o.** by hearsay

ouïe [wi] *nf* hearing; *Hum* **être tout o.** to be all ears

ouïes [wi] *nfpl (de poisson)* gills

ouille [uj] *exclam* ouch!

ouragan [uragɑ̃] *nm* hurricane

ourler [urle] *vt* to hem • **ourlet** [-ɛ] *nm* hem

ours [urs] *nm* bear; **o. blanc** polar bear; *Fig* **o. mal léché** boor; **o. en peluche** teddy bear • **ourse** *nf* she-bear; **la Grande O.** the Great Bear

oursin [ursɛ̃] *nm* sea urchin

ouste [ust] *exclam Fam* scram!

outil [uti] *nm* tool • **outillage** *nm* tools; *(d'une usine)* equipment • **outiller** *vt* to equip

outrage [utraʒ] *nm* insult (**à** to) *Jur* **o. à magistrat** contempt of court • **outrageant, -ante** *adj* insulting

outrance [utrɑ̃s] *nf (excès)* excess; **à o.** to excess • **outrancier, -ière** *adj* excessive

outre [utr] **1** *prép* besides; **o. mesure** unduly

2 *adv* **en o.** besides; **passer o.** to take no notice (**à** of) • **outre-Manche** *adv* across the Channel • **outre-mer** *adv* overseas; **d'o.** *(marché)* overseas; **territoires d'o.** overseas territories

outré, -ée [utre] *adj (révolté)* outraged; *(excessif)* exaggerated

outrepasser [utrəpase] *vt* to go beyond, to exceed

ouvert, -erte [uvɛr, -ɛrt] **1** *pp de* **ouvrir**

2 *adj* open; *(robinet, gaz)* on • **ouvertement** [-əmɑ̃] *adv* openly • **ouverture** *nf* opening; *(trou)* hole; *Mus* overture; *Phot (d'objectif)* aperture; **o. d'esprit** open-mindedness

ouvrable [uvrabl] *adj* **jour o.** working or *Am* work day

ouvrage [uvraʒ] *nm (travail, livre, objet)* work; *(couture)* (needle)work; **un o.** *(travail)* a piece of work • **ouvragé, -ée** *adj (bijou)* finely worked

ouvreuse [uvrøz] *nf* usherette

ouvrier, -ière [uvrije, -jɛr] **1** *nmf* worker; **o. qualifié/spécialisé** skilled/semi-skilled worker; **o. agricole** farm worker

2 *adj (législation)* industrial; *(quartier, origine)* working-class

ouvrir* [uvrir] **1** *vt* to open; *(gaz, radio)* to turn on; *(hostilités)* to begin; *(appétit)* to whet; *(procession)* to head

2 *vi* to open

3 s'ouvrir *vpr (porte, boîte, fleur)* to open; **s'o. la jambe** to cut one's leg open; *Fig* **s'o. à qn** *(perspectives)* to open up for sb • **ouvre-boîtes** *nm inv Br* tin opener, *Am* can opener • **ouvre-bouteilles** *nm inv* bottle opener

ovaire [ovɛr] *nm Anat* ovary

ovale [oval] *adj & nm* oval

ovation [ovasjɔ̃] *nf* (standing) ovation

overdose [ovœrdoz] *nf* overdose

ovni [ovni] *(abrév objet volant non identifié) nm* UFO

oxyde [oksid] *nm Chim* oxide; **o. de carbone** carbon monoxide • **oxyder** *vt*, **s'oxyder** *vpr* to oxidize

oxygène [oksiʒɛn] *nm* oxygen; **masque/tente à o.** oxygen mask/tent • **oxygéné, -ée** *adj* **eau oxygénée** (hydrogen) peroxide; **cheveux blonds oxygénés** peroxide blonde hair, bleached hair • **s'oxygéner** *vpr Fam* to get some fresh air

ozone [ozon] *nm Chim* ozone

P

P, p [pe] *nm inv* P, p
PAC [pak] (*abrév* **politique agricole commune**) *nf* CAP
pacifier [pasifje] *vt* to pacify • **pacification** *nf* pacification
pacifique [pasifik] **1** *adj (manifestation)* peaceful; *(personne, peuple)* peace-loving; *(côte)* Pacific
2 *nm* **le P.** the Pacific
pacifiste [pasifist] *adj & nmf* pacifist
pack [pak] *nm (de lait)* carton
pacotille [pakɔtij] *nf* junk; **de p.** *(marchandise)* shoddy; *(bijou)* paste
pacs [paks] (*abrév* **Pacte civil de solidarité**) *nm* civil solidarity pact *(bill introduced in 1998 extending the legal rights of married couples to unmarried heterosexual couples and to homosexual couples, particularly with regard to inheritance and taxation)*
pacte [pakt] *nm* pact • **pactiser** *vi* **p. avec qn** to make a pact with sb
pactole [paktɔl] *nm Fam* jackpot
paf [paf] **1** *exclam* bang!
2 *adj inv Fam (ivre)* plastered, *Br* sozzled
pagaie [page] *nf* paddle • **pagayer** *vi* to paddle
pagaïe, pagaille [pagaj] *nf Fam (désordre)* mess; **en p.** in a mess; **des livres en p.** loads of books; **semer la p.** to cause chaos
page¹ [paʒ] *nf (de livre)* page; *Fig* **à la p.** up-to-date; **perdre la p.** to lose one's place; *Fig* **tourner la p.** to make a fresh start; *Ordinat* **p. d'accueil** home page; **p. de garde** flyleaf; **les pages jaunes** *(de l'annuaire)* the Yellow Pages®; *Radio* **p. de publicité** commercial break; *Ordinat* **p. précédente/suivante** page up/down; • **page-écran** (*pl* **pages-écrans**) *nf Ordinat* screenful
page² [paʒ] *nm (à la cour)* page(boy)
paginer [paʒine] *vt* to paginate • **pagination** *nf* pagination
pagne [paɲ] *nm* loincloth
pagode [pagɔd] *nf* pagoda
paie [pɛ] *nf* pay, wages; *Fam* **ça fait une p. que je ne l'ai pas vu** I haven't seen him for ages

paiement [pemã] *nm* payment
païen, païenne [pajɛ̃, pajɛn] *adj & nmf* pagan, heathen
paillasse [pajas] *nf (matelas)* straw mattress; *(d'évier)* draining board
paillasson [pajasɔ̃] *nm* (door)mat
paille [pɑj] *nf* straw; *(pour boire)* (drinking) straw; *Fig* **homme de p.** figurehead; *Fig* **feu de p.** flash in the pan; **tirer à la courte p.** to draw lots; *Fig* **sur la p.** penniless
paillette [pajɛt] *nf (d'habit)* sequin; **paillettes** *(de savon, lessive)* flakes; *(d'or)* gold dust • **pailleté, -ée** *adj (robe)* sequined
pain [pɛ̃] *nm* bread; **un p.** a loaf (of bread); *Fig* **avoir du p. sur la planche** to have a lot on one's plate; **petit p.** roll; **p. au chocolat** = chocolate-filled pastry; **p. complet** wholemeal bread; **p. d'épices** ≃ gingerbread; **p. grillé** toast; **p. de mie** sandwich loaf; **p. de savon** bar of soap; **p. de seigle** rye bread; **p. de sucre** sugar loaf
pair, paire [pɛr] **1** *adj (numéro)* even
2 *nm (personne)* peer; **hors p.** unrivalled; **aller de p.** to go hand in hand (**avec** with); **au p.** *(étudiante)* au pair; **travailler au p.** to work as an au pair
paire [pɛr] *nf* pair (**de** of)
paisible [pɛzibl] *adj (vie, endroit)* peaceful; *(caractère, personne)* quiet • **paisiblement** [-əmã] *adv* peacefully
paître* [pɛtr] *vi* to graze; *Fam* **envoyer qn p.** to send sb packing
paix [pɛ] *nf* peace; **en p.** *(vivre, laisser)* in peace (**avec** with); **être en p. avec qn** to be at peace with sb; **signer la p. avec qn** to sign a peace treaty with sb; **avoir la p.** to have (some) peace and quiet
Pakistan [pakistã] *nm* **le P.** Pakistan • **pakistanais, -aise 1** *adj* Pakistani **2** *nmf* **P., Pakistanaise** Pakistani
palabres [palabr] *nfpl* endless discussions
palace [palas] *nm* luxury hotel

> Il faut noter que le nom anglais **palace** est un faux ami. Il signifie **palais**.

palais [palɛ] *nm (château)* palace; *Anat* palate; **P. de justice** law courts; **p. des sports** sports centre

palan [palɑ̃] *nm* hoist

pâle [pɑl] *adj* pale; **être p. comme un linge** to be as white as a sheet; *Fam* **se faire porter p.** to report sick

Palestine [palɛstin] *nf* **la P.** Palestine •**palestinien, -ienne 1** *adj* Palestinian **2** *nmf* **P., Palestinienne** Palestinian

palet [palɛ] *nm (de hockey)* puck

paletot [palto] *nm (manteau)* (short) overcoat; *Fam* **tomber sur le p. à qn** *(l'attaquer)* to jump on sb

palette [palɛt] *nf (de peintre)* palette; *(pour marchandises)* pallet

pâleur [pɑlœr] *nf (de lumière)* paleness; *(de personne)* pallor •**pâlir** *vi* to turn pale (**de** with)

palier [palje] *nm (niveau)* level; *(d'escalier)* landing; *(phase de stabilité)* plateau; **par paliers** in stages; **être voisins de p.** to live on the same floor

palissade [palisad] *nf* fence

pallier [palje] **1** *vt (difficultés)* to alleviate **2** *vi* **p. à qch** to compensate for sth •**palliatif** *nm* palliative

palmarès [palmarɛs] *nm* prize list; *(de chansons)* charts

palme [palm] *nf (de palmier)* palm (branch); *(de nageur)* flipper; *Fig (symbole)* palm •**palmier** *nm* palm (tree)

palmé, -ée [palme] *adj (patte, pied)* webbed

palombe [palɔ̃b] *nf* wood pigeon

pâlot, -otte [pɑlo, -ɔt] *adj Fam* pale

palourde [palurd] *nf* clam

palper [palpe] *vt* to feel •**palpable** *adj* palpable

palpiter [palpite] *vi (cœur)* to flutter; *(plus fort)* to throb •**palpitant, -ante** *adj (film)* thrilling •**palpitations** *nfpl* palpitations

pâmer [pame] **se pâmer** *vpr Fig & Hum* **se p. devant qn/qch** to swoon over sb/sth; **se p. d'aise** to be blissfully happy

pamphlet [pɑ̃flɛ] *nm* lampoon

pamplemousse [pɑ̃pləmus] *nm* grapefruit

pan¹ [pɑ̃] *nm (de chemise)* tail; *(de ciel)* patch; **p. de mur** section of wall

pan² [pɑ̃] *exclam* bang!

panacée [panase] *nf* panacea

panachage [panaʃaʒ] *nm* **p. électoral** = voting for candidates from more than one list

panache [panaʃ] *nm (plume)* plume; *(brio)* panache

panaché, -ée [panaʃe] **1** *adj* multicoloured; **p. de blanc** streaked with white **2** *nm* shandy

Panama [panama] *nm* **le P.** Panama

pan-bagnat [pɑ̃baɲa] *(pl* **pans-bagnats***)* *nm* = large round sandwich filled with *salade niçoise*

pancarte [pɑ̃kart] *nf* sign, notice; *(de manifestant)* placard

pancréas [pɑ̃kreas] *nm Anat* pancreas

panda [pɑ̃da] *nm* panda

pané, -ée [pane] *adj (poisson)* breaded

panier [panje] *nm (ustensile, contenu)* basket; **jeter qch au p.** to throw sth into the wastepaper basket; *Sport* **marquer un p.** to score a basket; **p. à linge** *Br* linen basket, *Am* (clothes) hamper; **p. à salade** *(ustensile)* salad basket; *Fam (voiture de police) Br* black Maria, *Am* paddy wagon •**panier-repas** *(pl* **paniers-repas***)* *nm Br* packed lunch, *Am* (brown-bag) lunch

panique [panik] **1** *nf* panic; **pris de p.** panic-stricken **2** *adj* **peur p.** panic •**paniqué, -ée** *adj Fam* in a panic •**paniquer** *vi Fam* to panic

panne [pan] *nf* breakdown; **tomber en p.** to break down; **être en p.** to have broken down; **tomber en p. sèche** to run out of *Br* petrol *or Am* gas; **trouver la p.** to locate the cause of the problem; **p. d'électricité** blackout, *Br* power cut

panneau, -x [pano] *nm (écriteau)* sign, notice, board; *(de porte)* panel; *Fam* **tomber dans le p.** to fall into the trap; **p. d'affichage** *Br* notice board, *Am* bulletin board; **p. de signalisation** road sign •**panonceau, -x** *nm (enseigne)* sign

panoplie [panɔpli] *nf (jouet)* outfit; *(gamme)* set

panorama [panɔrama] *nm* panorama •**panoramique** *adj* panoramic; *Cin* **écran p.** wide screen

panse [pɑ̃s] *nf Fam* belly •**pansu, -ue** *adj* potbellied

panser [pɑ̃se] *vt (main)* to bandage; *(plaie)* to dress; *(cheval)* to groom; **p. qn** to dress sb's wounds •**pansement** *nm* dressing; **faire un p. à qn** to put a dressing on sb; **refaire le p.** to change the dressing; **p. adhésif** *Br* sticking plaster, *Am* Band-aid®

pantalon [pɑ̃talɔ̃] *nm Br* trousers *or Am* pants; **deux pantalons** two pairs of *Br* trousers *or Am* pants

pantelant, -ante [pɑ̃tlɑ̃, -ɑ̃t] *adj* panting

panthère [pɑ̃tɛr] *nf* panther

pantin [pɑ̃tɛ̃] *nm (jouet)* jumping-jack; *Péj (personne)* puppet

pantois, -oise [pɑ̃twa, -waz] *adj* flabbergasted; **elle en est restée pantoise** she was flabbergasted

pantoufle [pɑ̃tufl] *nf* slipper •**pantouflard, -arde** *nmf Fam* stay-at-home, *Am* homebody

PAO [peɑo] (*abrév* **publication assistée par ordinateur**) *nf* DTP

paon [pɑ̃] *nm* peacock

papa [papa] *nm* dad(dy); *Fam Péj* **de p.** outdated

papaye [papaj] *nf* papaya

pape [pap] *nm* pope •**papauté** *nf* papacy

paperasse [papras] *nf Péj* papers •**paperasserie** *nf Péj* (official) papers; (*procédure*) red tape

papeterie [papɛtri] *nf* (*magasin*) stationer's shop; (*articles*) stationery; (*fabrique*) paper mill •**papetier, -ière** *nmf* stationer

papi [papi] *nm* grand(d)ad

papier [papje] *nm* (*matière*) paper; **un p.** (*feuille*) a piece of paper; (*formulaire*) a form; (*de journal*) an article; *Fam* **être dans les petits papiers de qn** to be in sb's good books; **p. hygiénique** toilet paper; **papiers d'identité** identity papers; **p. journal** newspaper; **p. à lettres** writing paper; **p. peint** wallpaper; **p. de verre** sandpaper

papillon [papijɔ̃] *nm* (*insecte*) butterfly; (*écrou*) *Br* butterfly nut, *Am* wing nut; *Fam* (*contravention*) (parking) ticket; **p. de nuit** moth

papoter [papɔte] *vi Fam* to chat

paprika [paprika] *nm* paprika

papy [papi] *nm* grand(d)ad

Pâque [pɑk] *nf Rel* **la P. juive, P.** Passover

paquebot [pakbo] *nm* liner

pâquerette [pakrɛt] *nf* daisy

Pâques [pɑk] *nm sing & nfpl* Easter

paquet [pakɛ] *nm* (*sac*) packet; (*de sucre*) bag; (*de cigarettes*) packet, *Am* pack; *Br* (*postal*) parcel, package; *Fam* **y mettre le p.** to pull out all the stops

par [par] *prép* (**a**) (*indique l'agent, la manière, le moyen*) by; **choisi/frappé p. qn** chosen/hit by sb; **p. mer** by sea; **p. le train** by train; **p. le travail/la force** by *or* through work/force; **apprendre p. un ami** to learn from *or* through a friend; **commencer p. qch** (*récit*) to begin with sth; **p. erreur** by mistake; **p. chance** by a stroke of luck; **p. malchance** as ill luck would have it

(**b**) (*à travers*) through; **p. la porte/le tunnel** through the door/tunnel; **jeter/regarder p. la fenêtre** to throw/look out (of) the window; **p. ici/là** (*aller*) this/that way; (*habiter*) around here/there; **p. les rues** through the streets

(**c**) (*à cause de*) out of, from; **p. pitié/respect** out of pity/respect

(**d**) (*pendant*) **p. un jour d'hiver** on a winter's day; **p. ce froid** in this cold; **p. le passé** in the past

(**e**) (*distributif*) **dix fois p. an/mois** ten times a *or* per year/month; **100 euros p. personne** 100 euros per person; **deux p. deux** two by two; **p. deux fois** twice

(**f**) (*avec 'trop'*) **p. trop aimable** far too kind

para [para] *nm Fam* para(trooper)

parabole [parabɔl] *nf* (*récit*) parable; *Math* parabola

parachever [paraʃve] *vt* to complete

parachute [paraʃyt] *nm* parachute; **p. ascensionnel** parascending •**parachuter** *vt* to parachute in; *Fam* (*nommer*) to draft in •**parachutisme** *nm* parachute jumping •**parachutiste** *nmf* parachutist; (*soldat*) paratrooper

parade [parad] *nf* (*défilé*) parade; (*étalage*) show; *Boxe & Escrime* parry; *Fig* (*riposte*) reply •**parader** *vi* to show off

paradis [paradi] *nm* heaven; *Fig* paradise •**paradisiaque** *adj Fig* (*endroit*) heavenly

paradoxe [paradɔks] *nm* paradox •**paradoxal, -e, -aux, -ales** *adj* paradoxical •**paradoxalement** *adv* paradoxically

parafe [paraf] *nm* initials •**parafer** *vt* to initial

paraffine [parafin] *nf* paraffin (wax)

parages [paraʒ] *nmpl Naut* waters; **dans les p. de** in the vicinity of; *Fam* **est-ce qu'elle est dans les p.?** is she around?

paragraphe [paragraf] *nm* paragraph

Paraguay [paragwe] *nm* **le P.** Paraguay

paraître* [parɛtr] **1** *vi* (*sembler*) to seem, to appear; (*apparaître*) to appear; (*livre*) to come out, to be published

2 *v impersonnel* **il paraît qu'il va partir** it appears *or* seems (that) he's leaving; **à ce qu'il paraît** apparently

parallèle [paralɛl] **1** *adj* parallel (**à** with *or* to); (*police, marché*) unofficial; **mener une vie p.** to lead a secret life

2 *nf* parallel (line)

3 *nm* (*comparaison*) & *Géog* parallel; **mettre qch en p. avec qch** to draw a parallel between sth and sth •**parallèlement** *adv* **p. à** parallel to; (*simultanément*) at the same time as

paralyser [paralize] *vt Br* to paralyse, *Am* to paralyze •**paralysie** *nf* paralysis •**paralytique** *adj & nmf* paralytic

paramédical, -e, -aux, -ales [parame-dikal, -o] *adj* paramedical
paramètre [parametr] *nm* parameter • **paramétrer** *vt Ordinat* to configure
paramilitaire [paramiliter] *adj* paramilitary
parano [parano] *adj Fam* paranoid
paranoïa [paranɔja] *nf* paranoia • **paranoïaque** *adj & nmf* paranoiac
parapente [parapɑ̃t] *nm (activité)* paragliding; **faire du p.** to go paragliding
parapet [parapɛ] *nm* parapet
paraphe [paraf] *nm* initials • **parapher** *vt* to initial
paraphrase [parafraz] *nf* paraphrase • **paraphraser** *vt* to paraphrase
parapluie [paraplɥi] *nm* umbrella
parapsychologie [parapsikɔlɔʒi] *nf* parapsychology
parasite [parazit] **1** *nm (organisme, personne)* parasite; **parasites** *(à la radio)* interference
  2 *adj* parasitic
parasol [parasɔl] *nm* sunshade, parasol; *(de plage)* beach umbrella
paratonnerre [paratɔnɛr] *nm* lightning *Br* conductor *or Am* rod
paravent [paravɑ̃] *nm* screen
parc [park] *nm (jardin)* park; *(de château)* grounds; *(de bébé)* playpen; **p. d'attractions** amusement park; **p. de stationnement** *Br* car park, *Am* parking lot; **p. à huîtres** oyster bed; **p. automobile** *(de pays)* number of vehicles on the road; **p. naturel** nature reserve
parcelle [parsɛl] *nf* small piece; *(terrain)* plot; *Fig (de vérité)* grain
parce que [parsəkə] *conj* because
parchemin [parʃəmɛ̃] *nm* parchment
parcimonie [parsimɔni] *nf* **avec p.** parsimoniously • **parcimonieux, -ieuse** *adj* parsimonious
par-ci, par-là [parsiparla] *adv* here, there and everywhere
parcmètre [parkmɛtr] *nm* (parking) meter
parcourir* [parkurir] *vt (lieu)* to walk round; *(pays)* to travel through; *(mer)* to sail; *(distance)* to cover; *(texte)* to glance through; **p. qch des yeux** *ou* **du regard** to glance at sth; **il reste 2 km à p.** there are 2 km to go • **parcours** *nm (itinéraire)* route; **p. de golf** *(terrain)* golf course
par-delà [pardəla] *prép & adv* beyond
par-derrière [parderjer] **1** *prép* behind
  2 *adv (attaquer)* from behind; *(se boutonner)* at the back; **passer p.** to go in the back door

par-dessous [pardəsu] *prép & adv* underneath
pardessus [pardəsy] *nm* overcoat
par-dessus [pardəsy] **1** *prép* over; **p. tout** above all; *Fam* **en avoir p. la tête** to be completely fed up
  2 *adv* over
par-devant [pardəvɑ̃] *adv (attaquer)* from the front; *(se boutonner)* at the front
pardon [pardɔ̃] *nm* forgiveness; **p.!** *(excusez-moi)* sorry!; **p.?** *(pour demander)* excuse me?, *Am* pardon me?; **demander p.** to apologize (**à** to) • **pardonnable** *adj* forgivable • **pardonner** *vt* to forgive; **p. qch à qn** to forgive sb for sth; **elle m'a pardonné d'avoir oublié** she forgave me for forgetting
pare-balles [parbal] *adj inv* **gilet p.** bulletproof *Br* jacket *or Am* vest
pare-brise [parbriz] *nm inv Br* windscreen, *Am* windshield
pare-chocs [parʃɔk] *nm inv* bumper
pare-feu [parfø] *nm inv (de cheminée)* fireguard
pareil, -eille [parɛj] **1** *adj* (**a**) *(identique)* the same; **p. à** the same as (**b**) *(tel)* such; **en p. cas** in such cases
  2 *adv Fam* the same
  3 *nmf (personne)* equal; **sans p.** unparalleled, unique; **il n'a pas son p.** he's second to none
  4 *nf* **rendre la pareille à qn** *(se venger)* to get one's own back on sb • **pareillement** *adv (de la même manière)* in the same way; *(aussi)* likewise
parement [parmɑ̃] *nm (de vêtement)* facing
parent, -ente [parɑ̃, -ɑ̃t] **1** *nmf (oncle, tante, cousin)* relative, relation
  2 *nmpl* **parents** *(père et mère)* parents
  3 *adj* related (**de** to) • **parental, -e, -aux, -ales** *adj* parental • **parenté** *nf* relationship; **avoir un lien de p.** to be related
parenthèse [parɑ̃tɛz] *nf (signe)* bracket, parenthesis; *Fig (digression)* digression; **entre parenthèses** in brackets
parer¹ [pare] **1** *vt (coup)* to parry
  2 *vi* **p. à toute éventualité** to prepare for any contingency; **p. au plus pressé** to attend to the most urgent things first
parer² [pare] *vt (orner)* to adorn (**de** with)
paresse [parɛs] *nf* laziness • **paresser** *vi* to laze about • **paresseux, -euse 1** *adj* lazy
  2 *nmf* lazy person
parfaire* [parfɛr] *vt* to finish off • **parfait, -aite** *adj* perfect • **parfaitement** *adv (sans fautes, complètement)* perfectly; *(certainement)* certainly

parfois [parfwa] *adv* sometimes

parfum [parfœ̃] *nm (essence)* perfume; *(senteur)* fragrance; *(de glace)* flavour; *Fam* **être au p.** to be in the know • **parfumé, -ée** *adj (savon, fleur, mouchoir)* scented; **p. au café** coffee-flavoured • **parfumer 1** *vt (embaumer)* to scent; *(glace)* to flavour (**à** with) **2 se parfumer** *vpr* to put perfume on • **parfumerie** *nf (magasin)* perfumery

pari [pari] *nm* bet; **faire un p.** to make a bet; **p. mutuel** *Br* ≃ tote, *Am* ≃ parimutuel • **parier** *vti* to bet (**sur** on; **que** that); **il y a fort à p. que** the odds are that • **parieur, -ieuse** *nmf* better

Paris [pari] *nm ou f* Paris • **parisien, -ienne 1** *adj* Parisian **2** *nmf* **P., Parisienne** Parisian

parité [parite] *nf* parity

parjure [paʀʒyr] **1** *nm* perjury **2** *nmf* perjurer • **se parjurer** *vpr* to perjure oneself

parka [parka] *nm ou f* parka

parking [parkiŋ] *nm Br* car park, *Am* parking lot; **'p. payant'** *Br* ≃ 'pay-and-display car park'

parlement [parləmɑ̃] *nm* **le P.** Parliament • **parlementaire 1** *adj* parliamentary **2** *nmf* member of parliament

parlementer [parləmɑ̃te] *vi* to negotiate (**avec** with)

parler [parle] **1** *vi* to talk, to speak (**de** about *or* of; **à** to); **sans p. de** not to mention; **p. par gestes** to use sign language; **n'en parlons plus!** let's forget it!; *Fam* **tu parles!** you bet!

2 *vt (langue)* to speak; **p. affaires** to talk business

3 se parler *vpr (langue)* to be spoken; *(l'un l'autre)* to talk to each other

4 *nm* speech; *(régional)* dialect • **parlant, -ante** *adj (film)* talking; *(regard)* eloquent • **parlé, -ée** *adj (langue)* spoken

parloir [parlwar] *nm* visiting room

parmi [parmi] *prép* among(st)

parodie [parɔdi] *nf* parody • **parodier** *vt* to parody

paroi [parwa] *nf* wall; *(de rocher)* (rock) face

paroisse [parwas] *nf* parish • **paroissial, -e, -iaux, -iales** *adj* **registre p.** parish register • **paroissien, -ienne** *nmf* parishioner

parole [parɔl] *nf (mot, promesse)* word; *(faculté, langage)* speech; **paroles** *(de chanson)* words, lyrics; **adresser la p. à qn** to speak to sb; **prendre la p.** to speak; **demander la p.** to ask to speak; **tenir p.** to

keep one's word; **je te crois sur p.** I take your word for it; *Jur* **libéré sur p.** free(d) on parole; **ma p.!** my word!

paroxysme [parɔksism] *nm* **atteindre son p.** to reach its peak

parpaing [parpɛ̃] *nm* breeze block

parquer [parke] *vt (bœufs)* to pen in; *Péj (gens)* to confine

parquet [parke] *nm (sol)* wooden floor; *Jur* public prosecutor's office

parrain [parɛ̃] *nm Rel* godfather; *(de sportif, de club)* sponsor • **parrainer** *vt (sportif, membre)* to sponsor

pars [par] *voir* **partir**

parsemer [parsəme] *vt* to scatter (**de** with)

part¹ [par] *voir* **partir**

part² [par] *nf (portion)* share, part; *(de gâteau)* slice; **prendre p. à** *(activité)* to take part in; *(la joie de qn)* to share; **faire p. de qch à qn** to inform sb of sth; **de toutes parts** on all sides; **de p. et d'autre** on both sides; **d'une p.... d'autre p....** on the one hand... on the other hand...; **d'autre p.** *(d'ailleurs)* moreover; **de p. en p.** right through; **de la p. de qn** from sb; **c'est de la p. de qui?** *(au téléphone)* who's calling?; **pour ma p.** as for me; **à p.** *(mettre)* aside; *(excepté)* apart from; *(personne)* different; **une place à p.** a special place; **prendre qn à p.** to take sb aside; **membre à p. entière** full member

partage [partaʒ] *nm (action)* dividing up; *(de gâteau, de responsabilités)* sharing out; **faire le p. de qch** to divide sth up; **recevoir qch en p.** to be left sth *(in a will)*

partager [partaʒe] **1** *vt (avoir en commun)* to share (**avec** with); *(répartir)* to divide (up); **p. qch en deux** to divide sth in two; **p. l'avis de qn** to share sb's opinion

2 se partager *vpr (bénéfices)* to share (between themselves); **se p. entre** to divide one's time between • **partagé, -ée** *adj (amour)* mutual; **être p.** to be torn; **les avis sont partagés** opinions are divided

partance [partɑ̃s] **en partance** *adv (train)* about to depart; **en p. pour...** for...

partant, -ante [partɑ̃, -ɑ̃t] **1** *nmf (coureur, cheval)* starter

2 *adj Fam* **je suis p.!** count me in!

partenaire [partənɛr] *nmf* partner; **partenaires sociaux** workers and managers • **partenariat** *nm* partnership

parterre [partɛr] *nm (de fleurs)* flower bed; *Théâtre Br* stalls, *Am* orchestra; *Fam (sol)* floor

parti [parti] *nm (camp)* side; **prendre le p. de qn** to take sb's side; **tirer p. de qch** to make good use of sth; **p. (politique)** (political) party; **p. pris** bias; **un beau p.** *(personne)* a good match

partial, -e, -iaux, -iales [parsjal, -jo] *adj* biased • **partialité** *nf* bias

participe [partisip] *nm Grammaire* participle

participer [partisipe] *vi* **p. à** *(jeu)* to take part in, to participate in; *(bénéfices, joie)* to share (in); *(financièrement)* to contribute to • **participant, -ante** *nmf* participant • **participation** *nf* participation; *(d'élection)* turnout; *Fin* interest; **p. aux frais** contribution towards costs; **p. aux bénéfices** profit-sharing

particularité [partikylarite] *nf* peculiarity

particule [partikyl] *nf* particle; **avoir un nom à p.** to have a handle to one's name

particulier, -ière [partikylje, -jɛr] **1** *adj* *(propre)* characteristic (**à** of); *(remarquable)* unusual; *(soin, intérêt)* particular; *(maison, voiture, leçon)* private; *Péj (bizarre)* peculiar; **en p.** *(surtout)* in particular; *(à part)* in private; **cas p.** special case

2 *nm* private individual; **vente de p. à p.** private sale • **particulièrement** *adv* particularly; **tout p.** especially

partie [parti] *nf (morceau)* part; *(jeu)* game; *(domaine)* field; *Jur* party; **une p. de cartes** a game of cards; **en p.** partly, in part; **en grande p.** mainly; **faire p. de** to be a part of; *(club)* to belong to; *(comité)* to be on; **ça n'a pas été une p. de plaisir** it was no picnic; **ce n'est que p. remise** we'll do it another time • **partiel, -ielle 1** *adj* partial **2** *nm Univ* end-of-term exam • **partiellement** *adv* partially

partir* [partir] *(aux être) vi (s'en aller)* to go, to leave; *(se mettre en route)* to set off; *(s'éloigner)* to go away; *(douleur)* to go, to disappear; *(coup de feu)* to go off; *(flèche)* to shoot off; *(tache)* to come out; *(bouton, peinture)* to come off; *(moteur)* to start; **p. en voiture** to go by car, to drive; **p. en courant** to run off; **p. de** *(lieu)* to leave from; *(commencer par)* to start (off) with; **p. de rien** to start with nothing; **à p. de** *(date, prix)* from; **à p. de maintenant** from now on; **je pars du principe que...** I'm working on the assumption that...; **ça partait d'un bon sentiment** it was with the best of intentions; **je pars!** I'm going!; **c'est parti!** off we go! • **parti, -ie** *adj* **bien p.** off to a good start

partisan [partizɑ̃] **1** *nm* supporter; *(combattant)* partisan

2 *adj (esprit)* partisan; **être p. de qch/de** **faire qch** to be in favour of sth/of doing sth

partition [partisjɔ̃] *nf Mus* score

partout [partu] *adv* everywhere; **p. où je vais** everywhere *or* wherever I go; **un peu p.** all over the place; *Football* **3 buts p.** 3 all; *Tennis* **15 p.** 15 all

paru, -ue [pary] *pp de* paraître • **parution** *nf* publication

parure [paryr] *nf (ensemble)* set

parvenir* [parvənir] *(aux être) vi* **p. à** *(lieu)* to reach; *(objectif)* to achieve; **p. à faire qch** to manage to do sth • **parvenu, -ue** *nmf Péj* upstart

parvis [parvi] *nm* square *(in front of church)*

pas¹ [pɑ] *adv (de négation)* **(ne...) p.** not; **je ne sais p.** I do not *or* don't know; **je n'ai p. compris** I didn't understand; **je voudrais ne p. sortir** I would like not to go out; **p. de pain/de café** no bread/coffee; **p. du tout** not at all; **elle chantera – p. moi!** she'll sing – not me!

pas² [pɑ] *nm* (**a**) *(enjambée)* step; *(allure)* pace; *(bruit)* footstep; *(trace)* footprint; **p. à p.** step by step; **à p. de loup** stealthily; **à deux p. (de)** close by; **aller au p.** to go at a walking pace; **rouler au p.** *(véhicule)* to crawl along; **marcher au p. (cadencé)** to march in step; **faire un faux p.** *(en marchant)* to trip; *Fig (faute)* to make a faux pas; *Fig* **faire le premier p.** to make the first move; **faire ses premiers p.** to take one's first steps; **faire les cent p.** to pace up and down; **revenir sur ses p.** to retrace one's steps; **marcher à grands p.** to stride along; **le p. de la porte** the doorstep (**b**) *(de vis)* pitch (**c**) **le p. de Calais** the Straits of Dover

pascal, -e, -als *ou* **-aux, -ales** [paskal, -o] *adj* **semaine pascale** Easter week

passable [pɑsabl] *adj* passable, fair • **passablement** [-əmɑ̃] *adv* fairly

passage [pɑsaʒ] *nm (chemin, extrait)* passage; *(ruelle)* alley(way); *(traversée)* crossing; **être de p. dans une ville** to be passing through a town; **p. clouté** *ou* **pour piétons** *Br* (pedestrian) crossing, *Am* crosswalk; **p. souterrain** *Br* subway, *Am* underpass; **p. à niveau** *Br* level crossing, *Am* grade crossing; **'p. interdit'** 'no through traffic'; **'cédez le p.'** *(au carrefour) Br* 'give way', *Am* 'yield'; **p. pluvieux** rainy spell

passager, -ère [pasaʒe, -ɛr] **1** *adj* momentary

2 *nmf* passenger; **p. clandestin** stowaway

passant, -ante [pɑsɑ̃, -ɑ̃t] **1** *adj (rue)* busy
2 *nmf* passer-by
3 *nm (de ceinture)* loop

passe [pɑs] *nf Football* pass; *Fig* **une mauvaise p.** a bad patch; *Fig* **être en p. de faire qch** to be on the way to doing sth

passé, -ée [pɑse] **1** *adj (temps)* past; *(couleur)* faded; **la semaine passée** last week; **il est dix heures passées** it's after *or Br* gone ten o'clock; **être p.** *(personne)* to have been (and gone); *(orage)* to be over; **avoir vingt ans passés** to be over twenty; **p. de mode** out of fashion
2 *nm (temps, vie passée)* past; *Grammaire* past (tense); **par le p.** in the past
3 *prép* after; **p. huit heures** after eight o'clock

passe-montagne [pɑsmɔ̃taɲ] (*pl* **passe-montagnes**) *nm Br* balaclava, *Am* ski mask

passe-partout [pɑspartu] **1** *nm inv* master key
2 *adj inv* all-purpose

passe-passe [pɑspɑs] *nm inv* **tour de p.** conjuring trick

passe-plat [pɑsplɑ] (*pl* **passe-plats**) *nm* serving hatch

passeport [pɑspɔr] *nm* passport

passer [pɑse] **1** *(aux* **avoir***) vt (pont, frontière)* to go over; *(porte, douane)* to go through; *(ballon)* to pass; *(vêtement)* to slip on; *(film)* to show; *(disque)* to play; *(vacances)* to spend; *(examen)* to take; *(thé)* to strain; *(café)* to filter; *(commande)* to place; *(accord)* to conclude; *(visite médicale)* to have; *(omettre)* to leave out; **p. qch à qn** *(prêter)* to pass sth to sb; *(caprice)* to grant sb sth; **p. un coup d'éponge sur qch** to give sth a sponge; **p. son tour** to miss a turn; *Aut* **p. la seconde** to change into second; **p. sa colère sur qn** to vent one's anger on sb; **p. son temps à faire qch** to spend one's time doing sth; **j'ai passé l'âge de faire ça** I'm too old to do that; **je vous le passe** *(au téléphone)* I'm putting you through to him
2 *(aux* **être***) vi (se déplacer)* to pass; *(disparaître)* to go; *(facteur, laitier)* to come; *(temps)* to pass (by), to go by; *(film, programme)* to be on; *(douleur, mode)* to pass; *(couleur)* to fade; *(courant)* to flow; *(loi)* to be passed; **laisser p. qn** to let sb through; **p. prendre qn** to pick sb up; **p. voir qn** to drop in on sb; **p. de qch à qch** to go from sth to sth; **p. devant qn/qch** to go past sb/sth; **p. par Paris** to pass through Paris; **p. chez le boulanger** to go round to the baker's; **p. à la radio** to be on the radio; **p. à l'ennemi** to go over to the enemy; **p. pour** *(riche)* to be taken for; **faire p. qn pour** to pass sb off as; **faire p. qch sous/dans qch** to slide/push sth under/into sth; **faire p. un réfugié** to smuggle a refugee (**en Suisse** into Switzerland); **p. sur** *(détail)* to pass over; *Scol* **p. dans la classe supérieure** to move up a class; *Aut* **p. en seconde** to change into second; **p. capitaine** to be promoted to captain; **dire qch en passant** to mention sth in passing
3 **se passer** *vpr (se produire)* to happen; **se p. de qn/qch** to do without sb/sth; **cela se passe de commentaires** it needs no comment; **ça s'est bien passé** it went off well

passerelle [pɑsrɛl] *nf (pont)* footbridge; **p. d'embarquement** *(de navire)* gangway; *(d'avion)* steps

passe-temps [pɑstɑ̃] *nm inv* pastime

passeur, -euse [pɑsœr, -øz] *nmf (batelier)* ferryman, *f* ferrywoman; *(contrebandier)* smuggler

passible [pɑsibl] *adj Jur* **p. de** liable to

passif, -ive [pasif, -iv] **1** *adj* passive
2 *nm* **(a)** *Grammaire* passive **(b)** *Fin* liabilities • **passivité** *nf* passiveness, passivity

passion [pɑsjɔ̃] *nf* passion; **avoir la p. des voitures** to have a passion for cars • **passionnel, -elle** *adj* **crime p.** crime of passion

passionner [pɑsjɔne] **1** *vt* to fascinate
2 **se passionner** *vpr* **se p. pour qch** to have a passion for sth • **passionnant, -ante** *adj* fascinating • **passionné, -ée 1** *adj* passionate; **p. de qch** passionately fond of sth **2** *nmf* fan (**de** of) • **passionnément** *adv* passionately

passoire [pɑswar] *nf (pour liquides)* sieve; *(à thé)* strainer; *(à légumes)* colander

pastel [pastɛl] *adj inv & nm* pastel

pastèque [pastɛk] *nf* watermelon

pasteur [pastœr] *nm Rel* pastor

pasteurisé, -ée [pastœrize] *adj* pasteurized

pastiche [pastiʃ] *nm* pastiche

pastille [pastij] *nf* pastille; *(médicament)* lozenge

pastis [pastis] *nm* pastis

pastoral, -e, -aux, -ales [pastɔral, -o] *adj* pastoral

patate [patat] *nf Fam* spud; *Fig (idiot)* clot

patatras [patatra] *exclam* crash!

pataud, -aude [pato, -od] *adj Fam* clumsy

patauger [patoʒe] *vi (s'embourber)* to squelch; *(barboter)* to splash about; *Fam (s'embrouiller)* to flounder •**pataugeoire** *nf* paddling pool

pâte [pɑt] *nf (pour tarte)* pastry; *(pour pain)* dough; *(pour gâteau)* mixture; **fromage à p. molle** soft cheese; **p. d'amandes** marzipan; **p. de fruits** fruit jelly; **p. à frire** batter; **p. à modeler** modelling clay; **p. brisée** shortcrust pastry; **p. feuilletée** puff pastry; **pâtes (alimentaires)** pasta

pâté [pɑte] *nm (charcuterie)* pâté; *(tache d'encre)* blot; **p. en croûte** meat pie; **p. de sable** sand castle; **p. de maisons** block of houses

pâtée [pɑte] *nf (pour chien)* dog food; *(pour chat)* cat food; *Fam* **prendre la p.** to get thrashed

patelin [patlɛ̃] *nm Fam* village

patent, -ente [patɑ̃, -ɑ̃t] *adj* patent

patère [patɛr] *nf* (coat) peg

paternel, -elle [patɛrnɛl] *adj* paternal •**paternalisme** *nm* paternalism •**paternité** *nf (état)* paternity, fatherhood; *(de livre)* authorship

pâteux, -euse [pɑtø, -øz] *adj* doughy; **avoir la langue pâteuse** to have a furry tongue

pathétique [patetik] *adj* moving

> ⚠ Il faut noter que l'adjectif anglais **pathetic** est un faux ami. Il signifie souvent **lamentable**.

pathologie [patɔlɔʒi] *nf* pathology •**pathologique** *adj* pathological

patibulaire [patibylɛr] *adj* **avoir une mine p.** to look sinister

patience [pasjɑ̃s] *nf* patience; **avoir de la p.** to be patient; **perdre p.** to lose patience; **faire une p.** *(jeu de cartes)* to play a game of patience

patient, -iente [pasjɑ̃, -jɑ̃t] **1** *adj* patient **2** *nmf (malade)* patient •**patiemment** [-amɑ̃] *adv* patiently •**patienter** *vi* to wait

patin [patɛ̃] *nm (de patineur)* skate; *(pour parquet)* cloth pad; **p. à glace** ice skate; **p. à roulettes** roller skate; **p. de frein** brake shoe

patine [patin] *nf* patina

patiner [patine] *vi Sport* to skate; *(véhicule)* to skid; *(roue)* to spin around; *(embrayage)* to slip •**patinage** *nm Sport* skating; **p. artistique** figure skating •**patineur, -euse** *nmf* skater •**patinoire** *nf* skating rink, ice rink

pâtir [pɑtir] *vi* **p. de** to suffer because of

pâtisserie [pɑtisri] *nf (gâteau)* pastry, cake; *(magasin)* cake shop; *(art)* pastry-making •**pâtissier, -ière 1** *nmf* pastry cook; *(commerçant)* confectioner **2** *adj* **crème pâtissière** confectioner's custard

patois [patwa] *nm* patois

patraque [patrak] *adj Fam* out of sorts

patriarche [patrijarʃ] *nm* patriarch

patrie [patri] *nf* homeland

patrimoine [patrimwan] *nm* heritage; *(biens)* property; *Biol* **p. génétique** genotype

patriote [patrijɔt] **1** *adj* patriotic **2** *nmf* patriot •**patriotique** *adj* patriotic •**patriotisme** *nm* patriotism

patron, -onne [patrɔ̃, -ɔn] **1** *nmf (chef)* boss; *(propriétaire)* owner (**de** of); *(gérant)* manager, *f* manageress; *(de bar)* landlord, *f* landlady; *Rel* patron saint **2** *nm Couture* pattern

> ⚠ Il faut noter que le nom anglais **patron** est un faux ami. Il signifie le plus souvent **client**.

patronage [patrɔnaʒ] *nm (protection)* patronage; *(centre)* youth club

patronat [patrɔna] *nm* employers •**patronal, -e, -aux, -ales** *adj* employers'

patronyme [patrɔnim] *nm* family name

patrouille [patruj] *nf* patrol •**patrouiller** *vi* to patrol

patte [pat] *nf* (**a**) *(membre)* leg; *(de chat, de chien)* paw; **marcher à quatre pattes** to walk on all fours (**b**) *(languette)* tab; *(de poche)* flap •**pattes** *nfpl (favoris)* sideburns

pâturage [pɑtyraʒ] *nm* pasture

pâture [pɑtyr] *nf Fig* **donner qn en p. à qn** to serve sb up to sb

paume [pom] *nf* palm

paumer [pome] *vt Fam* to lose •**paumé, -ée** *Fam* **1** *adj* lost **2** *nmf* loser

paupière [popjɛr] *nf* eyelid

paupiette [popjɛt] *nf* **p. de veau** veal olive

pause [poz] *nf (arrêt)* break; *(en parlant)* pause

pauvre [povr] **1** *adj (personne, sol, excuse)* poor; *(meubles)* shabby; **p. en** *(calories)* low in; *(ressources)* low on **2** *nmf* poor man, *f* poor woman; **les pauvres** the poor •**pauvrement** [-amɑ̃] *adv* poorly •**pauvreté** [-əte] *nf* poverty

pavaner [pavane] **se pavaner** *vpr* to strut about

paver [pave] *vt* to pave •**pavage** *nm (travail, revêtement)* paving •**pavé** *nm* **un p.** a paving stone; *Fig* **sur le p.** on the streets

pavillon [pavijɔ̃] *nm* (**a**) *(maison)* detached house; *(d'hôpital)* wing; *(d'exposi-*

tion) pavilion; **p. de chasse** hunting lodge (**b**) *(drapeau)* flag; **p. de complaisance** flag of convenience

pavoiser [pavwaze] *vi Fam* to gloat

pavot [pavo] *nm* poppy

payable [pejabl] *adj* payable

paye [pɛj] *nf* pay, wages • **payement** *nm* payment

payer [peje] **1** *vt (personne, somme)* to pay; *(service, objet)* to pay for; *(récompenser)* to repay; **se faire p.** to get paid; *Fam* **p. qch à qn** *(offrir en cadeau)* to treat sb to sth; *Fam* **tu me le paieras!** you'll pay for this!

2 *vi* to pay

3 se payer *vpr Fam* **se p. qch** to treat oneself to sth; *Fam* **se p. la tête de qn** to take the mickey out of sb • **payant, -ante** [pejɑ̃, -ɑ̃t] *adj (hôte, spectateur)* paying; **l'entrée est payante** there's a charge for admission

pays [pei] *nm* country; *(région)* region; **du p.** *(vin, gens)* local

paysage [peizaʒ] *nm* landscape, scenery • **paysagiste** *nmf (jardinier)* landscape gardener

paysan, -anne [peizɑ̃, -an] **1** *nmf* farmer; *Péj* peasant

2 *adj* **coutume paysanne** rural *or* country custom; **le monde p.** the farming community

Pays-Bas [peibɑ] *nmpl* **les P.** the Netherlands

PCV [peseve] *(abrév* **paiement contre vérification***) nm* **téléphoner en P.** *Br* to reverse the charges, *Am* to call collect

P-DG [pedeʒe] *abrév* **président-directeur général**

péage [peaʒ] *nm (droit)* toll; *(lieu)* tollbooth; **pont à p.** toll bridge; *TV* **chaîne à p.** pay channel

peau, -x [po] *nf* skin; *(de fruit)* peel, skin; *(cuir)* hide; *(fourrure)* pelt; *Fig* **faire p. neuve** to turn over a new leaf; *Fig* **se mettre dans la p. de qn** to put oneself in sb's shoes; *Fam* **avoir qn dans la p.** to be crazy about sb; *Fam* **être bien dans sa p.** to feel good about oneself; *Fam* **laisser sa p. dans** *(aventure)* to lose one's life in; *Fam* **j'aurai sa p.!** I'll get him! • **Peau-Rouge** *(pl* **Peaux-Rouges***) nmf* Red Indian

péché [peʃe] *nm* sin; **p. mignon** weakness • **pécher** *vi* to sin; **p. par orgueil** to be too proud • **pécheur, -eresse** *nmf* sinner

pêche¹ [pɛʃ] *nf (activité)* fishing; *(poissons)* catch; **p. à la ligne** angling; **aller à la p.** to go fishing • **pêcher¹ 1** *vt (attraper)* to catch; *(chercher à prendre)* to fish for; *Fam*

(dénicher) to dig up **2** *vi* to fish • **pêcheur** *nm* fisherman; *(à la ligne)* angler

pêche² [pɛʃ] *nf (fruit)* peach; **avoir une peau de p.** to have soft, velvety skin; *Fam* **avoir la p.** to feel on top of the world • **pêcher²** *nm (arbre)* peach tree

pectoraux [pektɔro] *nmpl* chest muscles

pécule [pekyl] *nm* savings

pécuniaire [pekynjɛr] *adj* financial

pédagogie [pedagɔʒi] *nf (discipline)* pedagogy • **pédagogique** *adj* educational • **pédagogue** *nmf* teacher

pédale [pedal] *nf* (**a**) *(de voiture, de piano)* pedal; *Fam* **mettre la p. douce** to go easy; *Fam* **perdre les pédales** to lose one's marbles; **p. de frein** brake pedal (**b**) *Fam Péj (homosexuel)* queer, = offensive term used to refer to a male homosexual • **pédaler** *vi* to pedal; *Fam* **p. dans la semoule** to be all at sea

Pédalo® [pedalo] *nm* pedal boat, pedalo

pédant, -ante [pedɑ̃, -ɑ̃t] **1** *adj* pedantic **2** *nmf* pedant

pédé [pede] *nm très Fam Péj (homosexuel)* queer, = offensive term used to refer to a male homosexual

pédestre [pedɛstr] *adj* **randonnée p.** hike

pédiatre [pedjatr] *nmf* paediatrician

pedibus [pedibys] *adv Fam* on foot

pédicure [pedikyr] *nmf Br* chiropodist, *Am* podiatrist

pedigree [pedigre] *nm* pedigree

pègre [pɛgr] *nf* **la p.** the underworld

peigne [pɛɲ] *nm* comb; **se donner un coup de p.** to give one's hair a comb; *Fig* **passer qch au p. fin** to go through sth with a fine-tooth comb • **peigner 1** *vt (cheveux)* to comb; **p. qn** to comb sb's hair **2 se peigner** *vpr* to comb one's hair

peignoir [pɛɲwar] *nm Br* dressing gown, *Am* bathrobe; **p. de bain** bathrobe

peinard, -arde [pɛnar, -ard] *adj Fam* quiet (and easy)

peindre* [pɛ̃dr] **1** *vt* to paint; *Fig (décrire)* to depict; **p. qch en bleu** to paint sth blue **2** *vi* to paint

peine [pɛn] *nf* (**a**) *(châtiment)* punishment; **p. de mort** death penalty; **p. de prison** prison sentence; **'défense d'entrer sous p. d'amende'** 'trespassers will be prosecuted'

(**b**) *(chagrin)* sorrow; **avoir de la p.** to be upset; **faire de la p. à qn** to upset sb

(**c**) *(effort)* trouble; *(difficulté)* difficulty; **se donner de la p.** *ou* **beaucoup de p.** to go to a lot of trouble (**pour faire** to do); **avec p.** with difficulty; **ça vaut la p. d'attendre** it's worth waiting; **ce n'est pas** *ou*

ça ne vaut pas la p. it's not worth it (**d**) **à p.** hardly, scarcely; **à p. arrivée, elle...** no sooner had she arrived than she... • **peiner 1** *vt* to upset **2** *vi* to labour

peintre [pɛ̃tr] *nm (artiste)* painter; **p. en bâtiment** painter and decorator • **peinture** *nf (tableau, activité)* painting; *(matière)* paint; **p. à l'huile** oil painting; '**p. fraîche**' 'wet paint' • **peinturlurer** *vt Fam* to daub with paint

péjoratif, -ive [peʒɔratif, -iv] *adj* pejorative

Pékin [pekɛ̃] *nm ou f* Peking, Beijing

pékinois [pekinwa] *nm (chien)* Pekin(g)ese

pelage [pəlaʒ] *nm* coat, fur

pelé, -ée [pəle] *adj* bare

pêle-mêle [pɛlmɛl] *adv* higgledy-piggledy

peler [pəle] **1** *vt* to peel **2** *vi (personne, peau)* to peel; *Fam* **je pèle de froid** I'm freezing cold

pèlerin [pɛlrɛ̃] *nm* pilgrim • **pèlerinage** *nm* pilgrimage

pélican [pelikɑ̃] *nm* pelican

pelisse [pəlis] *nf* fur-lined coat

pelle [pɛl] *nf* shovel; *(d'enfant)* spade; **p. à tarte** cake server; *Fam* **à la p.** by the bucketful; *Fam* **ramasser** *ou* **prendre une p.** to fall flat on one's face • **pelletée** *nf* shovelful • **pelleteuse** *nf* mechanical shovel

pellicule [pelikyl] *nf (pour photos)* film; *(couche)* thin layer; **pellicules** *(de cheveux)* dandruff

pelote [pəlɔt] *nf (de laine)* ball; *(à épingles)* pincushion; *Sport* **p. basque** pelota

peloter [pəlɔte] *vt Fam* to pet

peloton [p(ə)lɔtɔ̃] *nm (de ficelle)* ball; *(de cyclistes)* pack; *Mil* platoon; **le p. de tête** the leaders; **p. d'exécution** firing squad

pelotonner [pəlɔtɔne] **se pelotonner** *vpr* to curl up (into a ball)

pelouse [pəluz] *nf* lawn

peluche [pəlyʃ] *nf (tissu)* plush; **(jouet en) p.** soft toy; **chien en p.** furry dog; **peluches** *(de pull)* fluff, lint • **pelucher** *vi* to pill

pelure [pəlyr] *nf (de légumes)* peelings; *(de fruits)* peel

pénal, -e, -aux, -ales [penal, -o] *adj* penal • **pénaliser** *vt* to penalize • **pénalité** *nf* penalty

penalty [penalti] *nm Football* penalty

penaud, -aude [pəno, -od] *adj* sheepish

penchant [pɑ̃ʃɑ̃] *nm (préférence)* penchant (**pour** for); *(tendance)* propensity (**pour** for)

pencher [pɑ̃ʃe] **1** *vt (objet)* to tilt; *(tête)* to lean **2** *vi (arbre)* to lean over; *Fig* **p. pour qch** to incline towards sth **3 se pencher** *vpr* to lean over; **se p. par la fenêtre** to lean out of the window; **se p. sur qch** *(problème)* to examine sth • **penché, -ée** *adj* leaning

pendable [pɑ̃dabl] *adj* **faire un tour p.** to play a wicked trick (**à qn** on sb)

pendaison [pɑ̃dɛzɔ̃] *nf* hanging

pendant¹ [pɑ̃dɑ̃] *prép (au cours de)* during; **p. la nuit** during the night; **p. deux mois** for two months; **p. tout le trajet** for the whole journey; **p. que...** while...

pendentif [pɑ̃dɑ̃tif] *nm (collier)* pendant

penderie [pɑ̃dri] *nf Br* wardrobe, *Am* closet

pendre [pɑ̃dr] **1** *vti* to hang (**à** from); **p. qn** to hang sb **2 se pendre** *vpr (se suicider)* to hang oneself; *(se suspendre)* to hang (**à** from) • **pendant²**, **-ante 1** *adj* hanging; *(langue)* hanging out; *Fig (en attente)* pending **2** *nm* **p. (d'oreille)** drop earring; **le p. de** the companion piece to • **pendu, -ue** *adj (objet)* hanging (**à** from); *Fam* **être p. au téléphone** to be never off the phone

pendule [pɑ̃dyl] **1** *nf* clock **2** *nm (balancier)* pendulum • **pendulette** *nf* small clock

pénétrer [penetre] **1** *vi* **p. dans** to enter; *(profondément)* to penetrate (into) **2** *vt (sujet: pluie)* to penetrate **3 se pénétrer** *vpr* **se p. d'une idée** to become convinced of an idea • **pénétrant, -ante** *adj (vent, froid)* piercing; *(esprit)* penetrating • **pénétration** *nf* penetration

pénible [penibl] *adj (difficile)* difficult; *(douloureux)* painful, distressing; *(ennuyeux)* tiresome • **péniblement** [-əmɑ̃] *adv* with difficulty

péniche [peniʃ] *nf* barge

pénicilline [penisilin] *nf* penicillin

péninsule [penɛ̃syl] *nf* peninsula

pénis [penis] *nm Anat* penis

pénitence [penitɑ̃s] *nf (punition)* punishment; *Rel (peine)* penance; *(regret)* penitence; **faire p.** to repent • **pénitent, -ente** *nmf Rel* penitent

pénitencier [penitɑ̃sje] *nm* prison, *Am* penitentiary • **pénitentiaire** *adj* **régime p.** prison system

pénombre [penɔ̃br] *nf* half-light

pense-bête [pɑ̃sbɛt] *(pl* pense-bêtes*) nm Fam* reminder

pensée [pɑ̃se] *nf* (**a**) *(idée)* thought; **à la**

p. de faire qch at the thought of doing sth (**b**) *(fleur)* pansy

penser [pɑ̃se] **1** *vi (réfléchir)* to think (**à** of *or* about); **p. à qn/qch** to think of *or* about sb/sth; **p. à faire qch** *(ne pas oublier)* to remember to do sth; **p. à tout** to think of everything; **penses-tu!** what an idea!

2 *vt (estimer)* to think (**que** that); *(concevoir)* to think out; **je pensais rester** I was thinking of staying; **je pense réussir** I hope to succeed; **que pensez-vous de…?** what do you think of *or* about…?; **p. du bien de qn/qch** to think highly of sb/sth •**pensant, -ante** *adj* thinking; **bien p.** orthodox •**penseur** *nm* thinker •**pensif, -ive** *adj* thoughtful, pensive

pension [pɑ̃sjɔ̃] *nf* (**a**) *(école)* boarding school; **mettre un enfant en p.** to send a child to boarding school (**b**) *(hôtel)* **p. de famille** boarding house; **p. complète** *Br* full board, *Am* American plan (**c**) *(allocation)* pension; **p. alimentaire** maintenance, alimony •**pensionnaire** *nmf (élève, résident)* boarder •**pensionnat** *nm* boarding school •**pensionné, -ée** *nmf* pensioner

> *Ɵ* Il faut noter que le nom anglais **pensioner** est un faux ami. Il signifie le plus souvent **retraité**.

pentagone [pɛ̃tagɔn] *nm Am Mil* **le P.** the Pentagon

pente [pɑ̃t] *nf* slope; **être en p.** to be sloping; *Fig* **être sur une mauvaise p.** to be going downhill •**pentu, -ue** *adj* sloping

Pentecôte [pɑ̃tkot] *nf Rel Br* Whitsun, *Am* Pentecost

pénurie [penyri] *nf* shortage (**de** of)

pépé [pepe] *nm* grandpa

pépère [pepɛr] *Fam* **1** *nm* grandad

2 *adj (lieu)* quiet; *(emploi)* cushy

pépier [pepje] *vi* to cheep, to chirp

pépin [pepɛ̃] *nm (de fruit) Br* pip, *Am* seed, pit; *Fam (ennui)* hitch; *Fam (parapluie)* umbrella, *Br* brolly

pépinière [pepinjɛr] *nf (pour plantes)* nursery; *Fig (école)* training ground (**de** for)

pépite [pepit] *nf (d'or)* nugget; **p. de chocolat** chocolate chip

péquenaud, -aude [pekno, -od] *nmf Fam* peasant

perçant, -ante [pɛrsɑ̃, -ɑ̃t] *adj (cri, froid)* piercing; *(vue)* sharp

percée [pɛrse] *nf (ouverture)* opening; *Mil, Sport & Tech* breakthrough

perce-neige [pɛrsənɛʒ] *nm ou f inv* snowdrop

perce-oreille [pɛrsɔrɛj] (*pl* **perce-oreilles**) *nm* earwig

percepteur [pɛrsɛptœr] *nm* tax collector •**perceptible** *adj* perceptible (**à** to) •**perception** *nf* (**a**) *(bureau)* tax office; *(d'impôt)* collection (**b**) *(sensation)* perception

percer [pɛrse] **1** *vt (trouer)* to pierce; *(avec une perceuse)* to drill; *(trou, ouverture)* to make; *(abcès)* to lance; *(secret)* to uncover; *(mystère)* to solve; **p. une dent** *(bébé)* to cut a tooth; **p. qch à jour** to see through sth

2 *vi (soleil)* to break through; *(abcès)* to burst; *(acteur)* to make a name for oneself •**perceuse** *nf* drill

percevoir* [pɛrsəvwar] *vt* (**a**) *(sensation)* to perceive; *(son)* to hear (**b**) *(impôt)* to collect

perche [pɛrʃ] *nf* (**a**) *(bâton)* pole; *Fig* **tendre la p. à qn** to throw sb a line; *Fam* **une grande p.** *(personne)* a beanpole (**b**) *(poisson)* perch •**perchiste** *nmf* pole vaulter

percher [pɛrʃe] **1** *vi (oiseau)* to perch; *(volailles)* to roost

2 *vt Fam (placer)* to perch

3 se percher *vpr (oiseau, personne)* to perch •**perchoir** *nm* perch; *(de volailles)* roost; *Fam Pol* = seat of the president of the *Assemblée nationale*

percolateur [pɛrkɔlatœr] *nm* percolator

percussion [pɛrkysjɔ̃] *nf Mus* percussion

percutant, -ante [pɛrkytɑ̃, -ɑ̃t] *adj Fig* forceful

percuter [pɛrkyte] **1** *vt (véhicule)* to crash into

2 *vi* **p. contre** to crash into

3 se percuter *vpr* to crash into each other

perdant, -ante [pɛrdɑ̃, -ɑ̃t] **1** *adj* losing

2 *nmf* loser

perdition [pɛrdisjɔ̃] **en perdition** *adv (navire)* in distress

perdre [pɛrdr] **1** *vt* to lose; *(habitude)* to get out of; **p. qn/qch de vue** to lose sight of sb/sth; **il a perdu son père** he lost his father; **sa passion du jeu l'a perdu** his passion for gambling was his undoing

2 *vi* to lose; **j'y perds** I lose out

3 se perdre *vpr (s'égarer)* to get lost; *(disparaître)* to die out; **se p. dans les détails** to get lost in details; *Fig* **je m'y perds** I'm lost; *Fig* **nous nous sommes perdus de vue** we lost touch •**perdu, -ue** *adj (égaré)* lost; *(gaspillé)* wasted; *(malade)* finished; *(lieu)* out-of-the-way; **à ses moments perdus** in one's spare time; **c'est du temps p.** it's a waste of time

perdrix [pɛrdri] *nf* partridge • **perdreau, -x** *nm* young partridge

père [pɛr] *nm* father; **de p. en fils** from father to son; **Dupont p.** Dupont senior; *Fam* **le p. Jean** old John; *Rel* **le p. Martin** Father Martin; *Rel* **mon p.** father; **p. de famille** father

péremption [perɑ̃psjɔ̃] *nf* **date de p.** use-by date

péremptoire [perɑ̃ptwar] *adj* peremptory

perfection [pɛrfɛksjɔ̃] *nf* perfection; **à la p.** to perfection

perfectionner [pɛrfɛksjɔne] **1** *vt* to improve, to perfect

2 se perfectionner *vpr* **se p. en anglais** to improve one's English • **perfectionné, -ée** *adj* advanced • **perfectionnement** *nm* improvement (**de** in; **par rapport à** on); **cours de p.** proficiency course

perfectionniste [pɛrfɛksjɔnist] *nmf* perfectionist

perfide [pɛrfid] *adj* perfidious • **perfidie** *nf Littéraire (déloyauté)* perfidiousness

perforer [pɛrfɔre] *vt (pneu, intestin)* to perforate; *(billet)* to punch; **carte perforée** punch card • **perforation** *nf* perforation; *(trou)* punched hole • **perforatrice** *nf (pour papier)* (hole) punch • **perforeuse** *nf* (hole) punch

performance [pɛrfɔrmɑ̃s] *nf* performance; *Fig (exploit)* achievement • **performant, -ante** *adj* highly efficient

perfusion [pɛrfyzjɔ̃] *nf* drip; **être sous p.** to be on a drip

péricliter [periklite] *vi* to collapse

péridurale [peridyral] *adj f & nf* **(anesthésie) p.** epidural; **accoucher sous p.** to give birth under an epidural

péril [peril] *nm* danger, peril; **à tes risques et périls** at your own risk; **mettre qch en p.** to endanger sth • **périlleux, -euse** *adj* dangerous, perilous

périmer [perime] *vi*, **se périmer** *vpr* **laisser qch (se) p.** to allow sth to expire • **périmé, -ée** *adj (billet)* expired; *(nourriture)* past its sell-by date

périmètre [perimɛtr] *nm* perimeter

période [perjɔd] *nf* period; **p. d'essai** trial period • **périodique 1** *adj* periodic **2** *nm (revue)* periodical

péripétie [peripesi] *nf Littéraire* event

périphérie [periferi] *nf (limite)* periphery; *(banlieue)* outskirts

périphérique [periferik] **1** *adj* peripheral; **radio p.** = radio station broadcasting from outside France

2 *nm & adj* **(boulevard) p.** *Br* ring road,

Am beltway • **périphériques** *nmpl Ordinat* peripherals

périphrase [perifrɑz] *nf* circumlocution

périple [peripl] *nm* trip, tour

périr [perir] *vi* to perish • **périssable** *adj (denrée)* perishable

périscope [periskɔp] *nm* periscope

perle [pɛrl] *nf (bijou)* pearl; *(de bois, de verre)* bead; *Fig (personne)* gem; *Ironique (erreur)* howler • **perler** *vi (sueur)* to form in beads

permanent, -ente [pɛrmanɑ̃, -ɑ̃t] **1** *adj* permanent; *Cin (spectacle)* continuous; *(comité)* standing

2 *nf* **permanente** perm • **permanence** *nf* permanence; *(salle d'étude)* study room; *(service, bureau)* duty office; **être de p.** to be on duty; **en p.** permanently

perméable [pɛrmeabl] *adj* permeable (**à** to)

permettre* [pɛrmɛtr] **1** *vt* to allow, to permit; **p. à qn de faire qch** to allow sb to do sth; **permettez!** excuse me!; **vous permettez? may I?**

2 se permettre *vpr* **se p. de faire qch** to take the liberty of doing sth; **je ne peux pas me p.** I can't afford it

permis, -ise [pɛrmi, -iz] **1** *adj* allowed, permitted

2 *nm Br* licence, *Am* license, permit; **p. de conduire** *Br* driving licence, *Am* driver's license; **passer son p. de conduire** to take one's driving test; **p. de construire** planning permission; **p. de séjour** residence permit; **p. de travail** work permit

permission [pɛrmisjɔ̃] *nf* permission; *Mil* leave; **en p.** on leave; **demander la p.** to ask permission (**de faire** to do)

permuter [pɛrmyte] **1** *vt (lettres, chiffres)* to transpose

2 *vi* to exchange posts • **permutation** *nf (de lettres, de chiffres)* transposition

pernicieux, -ieuse [pɛrnisjø, -jøz] *adj* pernicious

pérorer [perɔre] *vi Péj* to hold forth

Pérou [peru] *nm* **le P.** Peru

perpendiculaire [pɛrpɑ̃dikylɛr] *adj & nf* perpendicular (**à** to)

perpétrer [pɛrpetre] *vt* to perpetrate

perpétuel, -uelle [pɛrpetɥɛl] *adj* perpetual; *(membre)* permanent • **perpétuellement** *adv* perpetually • **perpétuer** *vt* to perpetuate • **perpétuité** *adv* **à p.** in perpetuity; **condamnation à p.** life sentence

perplexe [pɛrplɛks] *adj* perplexed, puzzled • **perplexité** *nf* perplexity

perquisition [pɛrkizisjɔ̃] *nf* search • **perquisitionner** *vi* to make a search

perron [pɛrɔ̃] *nm* steps *(leading to a building)*

perroquet [pɛrɔkɛ] *nm* parrot

perruche [peryʃ] *nf Br* budgerigar, *Am* parakeet

perruque [peryk] *nf* wig

pers [pɛr] *adj m Littéraire* blue-green

persan, -ane [pɛrsɑ̃, -an] **1** *adj* Persian **2** *nm (langue)* Persian

persécuter [pɛrsekyte] *vt* to persecute • **persécution** *nf* persecution

persévérer [pɛrsevere] *vi* to persevere (**dans** in) • **persévérance** *nf* perseverance • **persévérant, -ante** *adj* persevering

persienne [pɛrsjɛn] *nf* shutter

persil [pɛrsi] *nm* parsley • **persillé, -ée** *adj (plat)* sprinkled with parsley

Persique [pɛrsik] *adj* **le golfe P.** the Persian Gulf

persister [pɛrsiste] *vi* to persist (**à faire** in doing; **dans qch** in sth) • **persistance** *nf* persistence • **persistant, -ante** *adj* persistent; **à feuilles persistantes** evergreen

personnage [pɛrsɔnaʒ] *nm (de fiction, individu)* character; *(personnalité)* important person; **p. célèbre** celebrity; **p. officiel** VIP

personnaliser [pɛrsɔnalize] *vt* to personalize; *(voiture)* to customize

personnalité [pɛrsɔnalite] *nf (caractère, personnage)* personality; **avoir de la p.** to have lots of personality

personne [pɛrsɔn] **1** *nf* person; **deux personnes** two people; **grande p.** grown-up, adult; **p. âgée** elderly person; **les personnes âgées** the elderly; **en p.** in person; **être bien de sa p.** to be good-looking; **être content de sa petite p.** to be pleased with oneself
2 *pron indéfini (de négation)* **(ne...) p.** nobody, no one; **je ne vois p.** I don't see anybody *or* anyone; **p. ne saura** nobody *or* no one will know; **mieux que p.** better than anybody *or* anyone

personnel, -elle [pɛrsɔnɛl] **1** *adj* personal; *(joueur, jeu)* individualistic
2 *nm (de firme, d'école)* staff; *(d'usine)* workforce; **manquer de p.** to be understaffed; **p. au sol** ground personnel • **personnellement** *adv* personally

personnifier [pɛrsɔnifje] *vt* to personify • **personnification** *nf* personification

perspective [pɛrspɛktiv] *nf (de dessin)* perspective; *(idée)* prospect (**de** of); *Fig (point de vue)* viewpoint; *Fig* **en p.** in prospect; *Fig* **à la p. de faire qch** at the prospect of doing sth; **perspectives d'avenir** future prospects

perspicace [pɛrspikas] *adj* shrewd • **perspicacité** *nf* shrewdness

persuader [pɛrsɥade] *vt* **p. qn (de qch)** to persuade sb (of sth); **p. qn de faire qch** to persuade sb to do sth; **être persuadé de qch/que...** to be convinced of sth/that... • **persuasif, -ive** *adj* persuasive • **persuasion** *nf* persuasion

perte [pɛrt] *nf* loss; *(destruction)* ruin; **une p. de temps** a waste of time; **à p. de vue** as far as the eye can see; **en pure p.** to no purpose; **vendre qch à p.** to sell sth at a loss; *Fig* **courir à sa p.** to be heading for disaster; **vouloir la p. de qn** to seek sb's destruction; **p. sèche** dead loss

pertinent, -ente [pɛrtinɑ̃, -ɑ̃t] *adj* relevant, pertinent • **pertinemment** [-amɑ̃] *adv* **savoir qch p.** to know sth for a fact • **pertinence** *nf* relevance, pertinence

perturber [pɛrtyrbe] *vt (trafic, cérémonie)* to disrupt; *(personne)* to disturb • **perturbateur, -trice** **1** *adj* disruptive **2** *nmf* troublemaker • **perturbation** *nf* disruption; **p. atmosphérique** atmospheric disturbance

péruvien, -ienne [peryvjɛ̃, -jɛn] **1** *adj* Peruvian **2** *nmf* **P., Péruvienne** Peruvian

pervenche [pɛrvɑ̃ʃ] *nf (plante)* periwinkle; *Fam (contractuelle) Br* (woman) traffic warden, *Am* meter maid

pervers, -erse [pɛrvɛr, -ɛrs] **1** *adj* perverse **2** *nmf* pervert • **perversion** *nf* perversion • **perversité** *nf* perversity • **pervertir** *vt* to pervert

pesage [pəzaʒ] *nm Sport (vérification)* weigh-in; *(lieu)* weighing room

pesant, -ante [pəzɑ̃, -ɑ̃t] **1** *adj* heavy, weighty **2** *nm* **valoir son p. d'or** to be worth one's weight in gold • **pesamment** [-amɑ̃] *adv* heavily • **pesanteur** *nf* heaviness; *Phys* gravity

pesée [pəze] *nf* weighing; *Boxe* weigh-in; *(pression)* force

peser [pəze] **1** *vt* to weigh; **p. le pour et le contre** to weigh up the pros and the cons; **p. ses mots** to weigh one's words; *Fig* **tout bien pesé** all things considered
2 *vi* to weigh; **p. 2 kilos** to weigh 2 kilos; **p. lourd** to be heavy; *Fig (argument)* to carry weight; **p. sur** *(appuyer)* to press on; *(influer)* to bear upon; **p. sur qn** *(menace)* to hang over sb; **p. sur l'estomac** to lie heavy on the stomach; *Fam* **elle pèse 20 millions** she's worth 20 million • **pèse-personne** *(pl* **pèse-personnes***) nm* (bathroom) scales

pessimisme [pesimism] *nm* pessimism •**pessimiste 1** *adj* pessimistic **2** *nmf* pessimist

peste [pɛst] *nf (maladie)* plague; *Fig (personne)* pest

> *!* Il faut noter que le nom anglais **pest** est un faux ami. Il ne désigne jamais une maladie.

pester [pɛste] *vi* **p. contre qn/qch** to curse sb/sth

pestilentiel, -ielle [pɛstilãsjɛl] *adj* stinking

pétale [petal] *nm* petal

pétanque [petãk] *nf (jeu)* ≃ bowls

pétarades [petarad] *nfpl (de véhicule)* backfiring •**pétarader** *vi (véhicule)* to backfire

pétard [petar] *nm (feu d'artifice)* firecracker, *Br* banger; *Fam (pistolet)* shooter

péter [pete] *Fam* **1** *vt (casser)* to bust; **p. la forme** to be full of beans; **p. les plombs** to blow one's top **2** *vi (exploser)* to blow up; *(casser)* to bust; *(personne)* to fart •**pétante** *adj f Fam* **à une heure p.** at one o'clock on the dot

pétiller [petije] *vi (yeux, vin)* to sparkle •**pétillant, -ante** *adj (eau, vin, yeux)* sparkling

petit, -ite [pəti, -it] **1** *adj* small, little; *(de taille, distance, séjour)* short; *(bruit, coup, rhume)* slight; *(somme)* small; *(accident)* minor; *(mesquin)* petty; **tout p.** tiny; **un p. Français** a French boy; **une bonne petite employée** a good little worker; **mon p. frère** my little brother; *Fam* **se faire tout p.** to want to find a corner to hide in; **c'est une petite nature** he's/she's a weak sort of person; *Scol* **les petites classes** the lower classes **2** *nmf (little)* boy, *f (little)* girl; *(personne)* small person; *Scol* junior; **petits** *(d'animal)* young; *(de chien)* pups; *(de chat)* kittens **3** *adv* **écrire p.** to write small; **p. à p.** little by little •**petit-beurre** *(pl* **petits-beurre**) *nm Br* butter biscuit, *Am* butter cookie •**petit-bourgeois, petite-bourgeoise** *(mpl* **petits-bourgeois,** *fpl* **petites-bourgeoises**) *adj Péj* lower middle-class •**petite-fille** *(pl* **petites-filles**) *nf* granddaughter •**petitesse** *nf (de taille)* smallness; *(mesquinerie)* pettiness •**petit-fils** *(pl* **petits-fils**) *nm* grandson •**petits-enfants** *nmpl* grandchildren •**petit-suisse** *(pl* **petits-suisses**) *nm* = small dessert of thick fromage frais

pétition [petisjɔ̃] *nf* petition

pétrifier [petrifje] *vt* to petrify

pétrin [petrɛ̃] *nm Fam* **être dans le p.** to be in a mess

pétrir [petrir] *vt* to knead

pétrole [petrɔl] *nm* oil, petroleum; **p. lampant** *Br* paraffin, *Am* kerosene •**pétrolier, -ière 1** *adj* **industrie pétrolière** oil industry **2** *nm* oil tanker •**pétrolifère** *adj* **gisement p.** oilfield

> *!* Il faut noter que le nom anglais **petrol** est un faux ami. Il signifie **essence**.

pétulant, -ante [petylã, -ãt] *adj* exuberant

> *!* Il faut noter que l'adjectif anglais **petulant** est un faux ami. Il signifie le plus souvent **irascible**.

pétunia [petynja] *nm* petunia

peu [pø] **1** *adv (avec un verbe)* not much; *(avec un adjectif, un adverbe)* not very; *(un petit nombre)* few; **elle mange p.** she doesn't eat much; **p. intéressant/souvent** not very interesting/often; **p. ont compris** few understood; **p. de sel/de temps** not much salt/time, little salt/time; **p. de gens/de livres** few people/books; **p. à p.** little by little, gradually; **à p. près** more or less; **p. après/avant** shortly after/before; **sous p.** shortly; **pour p. que...** *(+ subjunctive)* if by chance... **2** *nm* **un p.** a little, a bit; **un p. grand** a bit big; **un p. de fromage** a little cheese, a bit of cheese; **un p. de sucre** a bit of sugar, a little sugar; **un (tout) petit p.** a (tiny) little bit; **le p. de fromage que j'ai** the little cheese I have; **reste encore un p.** stay a little longer; **pour un p. je l'aurais jeté dehors** I very nearly threw him out

peuplade [pœplad] *nf* tribe

peuple [pœpl] *nm (nation, citoyens)* people; **les gens du p.** ordinary people

peupler [pœple] *vt (habiter)* to inhabit •**peuplé, -ée** *adj (région)* inhabited (**de** by); **très/peu p.** highly/sparsely populated; *Fig* **p. de qch** full of sth •**peuplement** [-əmã] *nm (action)* populating; **zone de p.** area of population

peuplier [pøplije] *nm (arbre, bois)* poplar

peur [pœr] *nf* fear; **avoir p.** to be afraid *or* frightened (**de qn/qch** of sb/sth; **de faire qch** to do sth *or* of doing sth); **faire p. à qn** to frighten *or* scare sb; **de p. qu'il ne parte** for fear that he would leave; **de p. de faire qch** for fear of doing sth •**peureux, -euse** *adj* easily fearful

peut [pø] *voir* **pouvoir 1**

peut-être [pøtetr] *adv* perhaps, maybe; **p. qu'il viendra, p. viendra-t-il** perhaps *or* maybe he'll come; **p. que oui** perhaps; **p. que non** perhaps not

peuvent, peux [pœv, pø] *voir* **pouvoir 1**

phallique [falik] *adj* phallic • **phallocrate** *nm Péj* male chauvinist (pig)

pharaon [faraɔ̃] *nm Hist* Pharaoh

phare [far] **1** *nm (pour bateaux)* lighthouse; *(de véhicule)* headlight; **faire un appel de phares** to flash one's lights
  2 *adj* **épreuve-p.** star event

pharmacie [farmasi] *nf (magasin) Br* chemist's shop, *Am* drugstore; *(science)* pharmacy; *(armoire)* medicine cabinet • **pharmaceutique** *adj* pharmaceutical • **pharmacien, -ienne** *nmf Br* chemist, pharmacist, *Am* druggist

pharynx [farɛ̃ks] *nm Anat* pharynx

phase [faz] *nf* phase; *Méd* **cancer en p. terminale** terminal cancer; *Fig* **être en p. to see eye to eye**

phénomène [fenɔmɛn] *nm* phenomenon; *Fam (personne)* character • **phénoménal, -e, -aux, -ales** *adj Fam* phenomenal

philanthrope [filɑ̃trɔp] *nmf* philanthropist • **philanthropique** *adj* philanthropic

philatélie [filateli] *nf* stamp collecting, philately • **philatéliste** *nmf* stamp collector, philatelist

philharmonique [filarmɔnik] *adj* philharmonic

Philippines [filipin] *nfpl* **les P.** the Philippines

philosophe [filozɔf] **1** *nmf* philosopher
  2 *adj* philosophical • **philosopher** *vi* to philosophize (**sur** about) • **philosophie** *nf* philosophy • **philosophique** *adj* philosophical

philtre [filtr] *nm* love potion

phobie [fɔbi] *nf* phobia; **avoir la p. de qch** to have a phobia about sth

phonétique [fɔnetik] **1** *adj* phonetic
  2 *nf* phonetics *(sing)*

phonographe [fɔnɔgraf] *nm Br* gramophone, *Am* phonograph

phoque [fɔk] *nm (animal)* seal

phosphate [fɔsfat] *nm Chim* phosphate

phosphore [fɔsfɔr] *nm Chim* phosphorus • **phosphorescent, -ente** *adj* phosphorescent

photo [fɔto] **1** *nf (cliché)* photo; *(art)* photography; **prendre une p. de qn/qch, prendre qn/qch en p.** to take a photo of sb/sth; *Fam* **il veut ma p.?** who does he think he's staring at?; **p. d'identité** ID photo; **p. de mode** fashion photo
  2 *adj inv* **appareil p.** camera • **photogénique** *adj* photogenic • **photographe** *nmf* photographer • **photographie** *nf (art)* photography; *(cliché)* photograph • **photographier** *vt* to photograph; **se faire p.** to have one's photo taken • **photographique** *adj* photographic

> *Ⓛ* Il faut noter que le nom anglais **photograph** est un faux ami. Il signifie **photographie, cliché**.

photocopie [fɔtɔkɔpi] *nf* photocopy • **photocopier** *vt* to photocopy • **photocopieur** *nm*, **photocopieuse** *nf* photocopier

Photomaton® [fɔtɔmatɔ̃] *nm* photo booth

phrase [fraz] *nf* sentence

physicien, -ienne [fizisjɛ̃, -jɛn] *nmf* physicist

> *Ⓛ* Il faut noter que le nom anglais **physician** est un faux ami. Il signifie **médecin**.

physiologie [fizjɔlɔʒi] *nf* physiology • **physiologique** *adj* physiological

physionomie [fizjɔnɔmi] *nf* face

physique [fizik] **1** *adj* physical
  2 *nm (de personne)* physique
  3 *nf (science)* physics *(sing)* • **physiquement** *adv* physically

phytothérapie [fitɔterapi] *nf* herbal medicine

piaffer [pjafe] *vi (cheval)* to paw the ground; *Fig* **p. d'impatience** to fidget impatiently

piailler [pjaje] *vi (oiseau)* to cheep; *Fam (enfant)* to squeal

piano [pjano] *nm* piano; **jouer du p.** to play the piano; **p. droit/à queue** upright/grand piano • **pianiste** *nmf* pianist • **pianoter** *vi* **p. sur qch** *(table)* to drum one's fingers on sth

piaule [pjol] *nf Fam (chambre)* pad

PIB [peibe] *(abrév* **produit intérieur brut**) *nm Écon* GDP

pic [pik] *nm (cime)* peak; *(outil)* pick (axe); *(oiseau)* woodpecker; **couler à p.** to sink like a stone; **tomber à p.** *(falaise)* to go straight down; *Fam* to come at the right moment; **p. à glace** ice pick

pichenette [piʃnɛt] *nf* flick

pichet [piʃɛ] *nm Br* jug, *Am* pitcher

pickpocket [pikpɔkɛt] *nm* pickpocket

picoler [pikɔle] *vi Fam* to booze

picorer [pikɔre] *vt* to peck

picoter [pikɔte] *vt* **j'ai la gorge qui (me) picote** I've got a tickle in my throat • **picotement** *nm (de gorge)* tickling

pie [pi] **1** *nf (oiseau)* magpie; *Fam (personne)* chatterbox
  2 *adj inv (cheval)* piebald

pièce [pjɛs] *nf (de maison)* room; *(morceau, objet)* piece; *(de pantalon)* patch; *(écrit de dossier)* document; **p. (de monnaie)** coin; **p. (de théâtre)** play; **5 euros (la) p.** 5 euros each; **travailler à la p.** to do piecework; **mettre qch en pièces** to tear sth to pieces; **p. à conviction** exhibit *(in criminal case)*; **p. d'eau** ornamental lake; *(petite)* ornamental pond; **p. d'identité** proof of identity; **p. montée** = large tiered wedding cake; **pièces détachées** *ou* **de rechange** spare parts; **pièces justificatives** supporting documents

pied [pje] *nm (de personne)* foot *(pl* feet); *(de lit, d'arbre, de colline)* foot; *(de meuble)* leg; *(de verre, de lampe)* base; *(d'appareil photo)* stand; *(de salade)* head; **à p.** on foot; **aller à p.** to walk, to go on foot; **au p. de** at the foot *or* bottom of; *Fig* **au p. de la lettre** literally; **sur p.** *(personne)* up and about; **sur un p. d'égalité** on an equal footing; **sur le p. de guerre** on a war footing; *Fam* **comme un p.** dreadfully; **avoir p.** to be within one's depth; **avoir le p. marin** to be a good sailor; **avoir bon p. bon œil** to be hale and hearty; **faire un p. de nez à qn** to thumb one's nose at sb; **mettre qch sur p.** to set sth up; **attendre qn de p. ferme** to be ready and waiting for sb; **être à p. d'œuvre** to be ready to get on with the job; **faire qch au p. levé** to do sth at a moment's notice; *Fam* **ça lui fera les pieds!** that will serve him/her right!; *Fam* **c'est le p.!** it's fantastic!; **de p. en cap** from head to toe • **pied-bot** *(pl* **pieds-bots)** *nm* club-footed person • **pied-de-biche** *(pl* **pieds-de-biche)** *nm (outil)* nail claw • **pied-noir** *(pl* **pieds-noirs)** *nmf Fam* = French settler in North Africa

piédestal, -aux [pjedɛstal, -o] *nm* pedestal

piège [pjɛʒ] *nm (pour animal) & Fig* trap • **piéger** *vt (animal)* to trap; *(voiture)* to booby-trap; **voiture/lettre piégée** car/letter bomb

pierre [pjɛr] *nf* stone; *(de bijou)* gem, stone; **maison en p.** stone house; **geler à p. fendre** to freeze hard; *Fig* **faire d'une p. deux coups** to kill two birds with one stone; **p. à briquet** flint *(for lighter)*; **p. d'achoppement** stumbling block; **p. précieuse** precious stone, gem • **pierreries** *nfpl* gems, precious stones • **pierreux, -euse** *adj* stony

piété [pjete] *nf* piety

piétiner [pjetine] **1** *vt* **p. qch** *(en trépignant)* to stamp on sth; *(en marchant)* to trample on sth

2 *vi (ne pas avancer)* to stand around; **p. d'impatience** to stamp one's feet impatiently

piéton [pjetɔ̃] *nm* pedestrian • **piétonne, piétonnière** *adj f* **rue p.** pedestrian(ized) street; **zone p.** pedestrian precinct

piètre [pjɛtr] *adj Littéraire (compagnon)* wretched; *(excuse)* paltry

pieu, -x [pjø] *nm (piquet)* post, stake; *Fam (lit)* bed; **aller au p.** to hit the sack

pieuvre [pjœvr] *nf* octopus

pieux, pieuse [pjø, pjøz] *adj* pious

pif [pif] *nm Fam (nez)* conk; **faire qch au p.** to do sth by guesswork • **pifomètre** *nm Fam* **faire qch au p.** to do sth by guesswork

pif(f)er [pife] *vt Fam* **je ne peux pas le p.** I can't stomach him

pigeon [piʒɔ̃] *nm* pigeon; *Fam (personne)* sucker; **p. voyageur** carrier pigeon

piger [piʒe] *Fam* **1** *vt* to get

2 *vi* to get it

pigment [pigmã] *nm* pigment • **pigmentation** *nf* pigmentation

pignon¹ [piɲɔ̃] *nm (de mur)* gable; *Fig* **avoir p. sur rue** to be of some standing

pignon² [piɲɔ̃] *nm (graine)* pine nut

pile [pil] **1** *nf* (a) **p. (électrique)** battery; **radio à piles** battery radio (b) *(tas)* pile; **en p.** in a pile (c) *(de pièce)* **p. (ou face)?** heads (or tails)?; **jouer à p. ou face** to toss up

2 *adv Fam* **s'arrêter p.** to stop dead; *Fam* **à deux heures p.** at two on the dot

piler [pile] **1** *vt (broyer)* to crush; *(amandes)* to grind

2 *vi Fam (en voiture)* to slam on the brakes • **pilonner** *vt (bombarder)* to bombard

pilier [pilje] *nm* pillar

piller [pije] *vt* to loot, to pillage • **pillage** *nm* looting, pillaging • **pillard, -arde** *nmf* looter

pilon [pilɔ̃] *nm (de poulet)* drumstick

pilori [piləri] *nm Fig* **mettre qn au p.** to pillory sb

pilote [pilɔt] **1** *nm (d'avion, de bateau)* pilot; *(de voiture)* driver; **p. automatique** automatic pilot; **p. de chasse** fighter pilot; **p. d'essai** test pilot; **p. de ligne** airline pilot

2 *adj* **usine(-)p.** pilot factory • **pilotage** *nm* piloting; **p. automatique** automatic piloting • **piloter** *vt (avion)* to fly, to pilot; *(bateau)* to pilot; *(voiture)* to drive; *Fig* **p. qn** to show sb around

pilotis [piləti] *nmpl* **construit sur p.** built on piles

pilule [pilyl] *nf* pill; **prendre la p.** to be on the pill; **arrêter la p.** to come off the pill; **p. abortive** abortion pill

piment [pimã] *nm* chilli; *Fig* spice • **pimenté, -ée** *adj (plat) & Fig* spicy

pimpant, -ante [pɛ̃pã, -ãt] *adj* smart

pin [pɛ̃] *nm (arbre, bois)* pine; **pomme de p.** pine cone; *(de sapin)* fir cone

pinacle [pinakl] *nm* **être au p.** to be at the top

pinailler [pinaje] *vi Fam* to nitpick (**sur** over)

pinard [pinar] *nm Fam (vin)* wine

pince [pɛ̃s] *nf (outil)* pliers; *(sur vêtement)* dart; *(de crustacé)* pincer; *Fam* **serrer la p. à qn** to shake sb's hand; *Fam* **à pinces** on foot; **p. à cheveux** hair clip; **p. à épiler** tweezers; **p. à linge** (clothes) *Br* peg or *Am* pin; **p. à sucre** sugar tongs; **p. à vélo** bicycle clip

pinceau, -x [pɛ̃so] *nm* (paint)brush; *Fam* **s'emmêler les pinceaux** to get all muddled up

pincer [pɛ̃se] **1** *vt* to pinch; *(cordes d'un instrument)* to pluck; *Fam* **p. qn** *(arrêter)* to catch sb; *Fam* **se faire p.** to get caught **2 se pincer** *vpr* **se p. le doigt** to get one's finger caught (**dans** in); **se p. le nez** to hold one's nose • **pincé, -ée** *adj (air)* stiff; *(sourire)* tight-lipped • **pincée** *nf* pinch (**de** of) • **pince-sans-rire** *nmf inv* person with a dry sense of humour • **pincettes** *nfpl (à feu)* (fire) tongs; *(d'horloger)* tweezers; *Fig* **il n'est pas à prendre avec des p.** he's like a bear with a sore head • **pinçon** *nm* pinch mark

pinède [pinɛd] *nf* pine forest

pingouin [pɛ̃gwɛ̃] *nm* auk; *(manchot)* penguin

ping-pong [piŋpɔ̃g] *nm* table tennis, Ping-Pong®

pingre [pɛ̃gr] *adj* stingy

pin's [pinz] *nm inv* badge

pinson [pɛ̃sɔ̃] *nm* chaffinch

pintade [pɛ̃tad] *nf* guinea fowl

pinter [pɛ̃te] **se pinter** *vpr très Fam* to get sozzled

pin-up [pinœp] *nf inv* pin-up

pioche [pjɔʃ] *nf (outil)* pick(axe); *Cartes* stock, pile • **piocher** *vt (creuser)* to dig *(with a pick)*; **p. une carte** to draw a card

pion [pjɔ̃] *nm (au jeu de dames)* piece; *Échecs & Fig* pawn; *Fam (surveillant)* supervisor *(paid to supervise pupils outside class hours)*

pionnier [pjɔnje] *nm* pioneer

pipe [pip] *nf (de fumeur)* pipe; **fumer la p.** to smoke a pipe

pipeau, -x [pipo] *nm (flûte)* pipe

pipelette [piplɛt] *nf Fam* gossip

piper [pipe] *vt* **ne pas p. mot** to keep mum

pipi [pipi] *nm Fam* **faire p.** to pee

pique [pik] **1** *nm Cartes (couleur)* spades **2** *nf (allusion)* cutting remark; *(arme)* pike

pique-assiette [pikasjɛt] *(pl pique-assiettes) nmf Fam* scrounger

pique-nique [piknik] *(pl pique-niques) nm* picnic • **pique-niquer** *vi* to picnic

piquer [pike] **1** *vt (percer)* to prick; *(langue, yeux)* to sting; *(sujet: moustique)* to bite; *(coudre)* to stitch; *Fam (voler)* to pinch; **p. qch dans** *(enfoncer)* to stick sth into; **la fumée me pique les yeux** the smoke is making my eyes sting; *Fam* **p. qn** *(faire une piqûre à)* to give sb an injection; **faire p. un chien** to have a dog put to sleep; *Fig* **p. qn au vif** to cut sb to the quick; **p. la curiosité de qn** to arouse sb's curiosity; *Fam* **p. une colère** to fly into a rage; *Fam* **p. une crise (de nerfs)** to throw a fit; *Fam* **p. une tête** to dive; *Fam* **p. un cent mètres** to sprint off
2 *vi (avion)* to dive; *(moutarde)* to be hot; *Fig* **p. du nez** *(s'assoupir)* to nod off
3 se piquer *vpr* to prick oneself; *Fam (se droguer)* to shoot up; **se p. au doigt** to prick one's finger; **se p. au jeu** to get into it; *Littéraire* **se p. de faire qch** to pride oneself on doing sth • **piquant, -ante 1** *adj (au goût)* spicy, hot; *(plante, barbe)* prickly; *(détail)* spicy **2** *nm (de plante)* prickle, thorn; *(d'animal)* spine • **piqué, -ée 1** *adj (meuble)* worm-eaten; *Fam (fou)* bonkers **2** *nm Av* **descente en p.** nosedive

piquet [pikɛ] *nm (pieu)* stake, post; *(de tente)* peg; **envoyer qn au p.** to send sb to stand in the corner; **p. de grève** picket

piquette [pikɛt] *nf Péj (vin)* cheap wine; *Fam* **prendre la p.** to get a hammering

piqûre [pikyr] *nf (d'abeille)* sting; *(de moustique)* bite; *(d'épingle)* prick; *(de tissu)* stitching; *(de rouille)* spot; *Méd* injection; **faire une p. à qn** to give sb an injection

pirate [pirat] **1** *nm (des mers)* pirate; **p. de l'air** hijacker; **p. informatique** hacker **2** *adj* **radio p.** pirate radio; **édition/CD p.** pirated edition/CD • **piratage** *nm* pirating • **pirater** *vt (enregistrement)* to pirate; *Ordinat* to hack • **piraterie** *nf (sur les mers)* piracy; **p. aérienne** hijacking

pire [pir] **1** *adj* worse (**que** than); **c'est de p. en p.** it's getting worse and worse **2** *nmf* **le/la p.** the worst (one); **le p. de**

tout the worst thing of all; **au p.** at (the very) worst; **s'attendre au p.** to expect the (very) worst

pirogue [piʀɔg] nf canoe, dugout

pis¹ [pi] nm (de vache) udder

pis² [pi] **1** adj Littéraire worse
2 adv **aller de mal en p.** to go from bad to worse
3 nm Littéraire **le p.** the worst • **pis-aller** nm inv stopgap (solution)

piscine [pisin] nf swimming pool

pissenlit [pisɑ̃li] nm dandelion

pisser [pise] vi Fam to have a pee

pistache [pistaʃ] nf (graine, parfum) pistachio

piste [pist] nf (traces) track, trail; (indices) lead; (de magnétophone) & Sport track; (de cirque) ring; (de ski) run, piste; (pour chevaux) Br racecourse, Am racetrack; **être sur la p. de qn** to be on sb's track; Sport **tour de p.** lap; **jeu de p.** treasure hunt; **p. d'atterrissage** runway; **p. cyclable** Br cycle path, Am bicycle path; **p. de danse** dance floor

pistolet [pistɔlɛ] nm gun, pistol; (de peintre) spray gun; **p. à eau** water pistol

piston [pistɔ̃] nm (de véhicule) piston; Fam **avoir du p.** to have connections • **pistonner** vt Fam (appuyer) to pull strings for

pitié [pitje] nf pity; **avoir de la p. pour qn** to pity sb; **il me fait p.** I feel sorry for him; **être sans p.** to be ruthless • **piteux, -euse** adj pitiful; **en p. état** in a sorry state • **pitoyable** adj pitiful

piton [pitɔ̃] nm (d'alpiniste) piton; **p. (rocheux)** (rocky) peak

pitre [pitʀ] nm clown • **pitreries** [-əʀi] nfpl clowning

pittoresque [pitɔʀɛsk] adj picturesque

pivert [pivɛʀ] nm green woodpecker

pivoine [pivwan] nf peony

pivot [pivo] nm (axe, d'argumentation) pivot • **pivoter** vi to pivot, to swivel; **faire p. qch** to swivel sth round

pixel [piksɛl] nm Ordinat pixel

pizza [pidza] nf pizza • **pizzeria** nf pizzeria

PJ [peʒi] **1** (abrév **police judiciaire**) nf Br ≃ CID, Am ≃ FBI
2 (abrév **pièces jointes**) enc, encl

placage [plakaʒ] nm (en bois) veneer; Rugby tackle

placard [plakaʀ] nm (armoire) Br cupboard, Am closet; **p. publicitaire** large display advertisement • **placarder** vt (affiche) to stick up

---

📝 Il faut noter que le nom anglais **placard** est un faux ami. Il signifie **pancarte**.

place [plas] nf (endroit, rang) & Sport place; (lieu public) square; (espace) room; (siège) seat; (emploi) job, post; **à la p.** instead (**de** of); **à votre p.** in your place; **se mettre à la p. de qn** to put oneself in sb's position; **sur p.** on the spot; Fin **sur la p. de Paris** on the Paris market; **en p.** in place; **mettre qch en p.** to put sth in place; **il ne tient pas en p.** he can't keep still; Fig **remettre qn à sa p.** to put sb in his/her place; **changer de p.** to change places; **faire de la p. (à qn)** to make room (for sb); **faire p. à qn/qch** to give way to sb/sth; **faire p. nette** to have a clearout; **prendre p.** to take a seat; **p. de parking** parking space; **p. de train/bus** train/bus fare; **p. assise** seat; **p. financière** financial market; **p. forte** fortress

placer [plase] **1** vt (mettre) to put, to place; (faire asseoir) to seat; (trouver un emploi à) to place; (argent) to invest (**dans** in); (vendre) to sell; **je n'ai pas pu p. un mot** I couldn't get a word in Br edgeways or Am edgewise
2 se placer vpr (debout) to stand; (s'asseoir) to sit; (objet) to be put or placed; (cheval, coureur) to be placed; Sport **se p. troisième** to come third • **placé, -ée** adj (objet) & Sport placed; **bien/mal p. pour faire qch** well/badly placed to do sth; **les gens haut placés** people in high places • **placement** nm (d'argent) investment; **bureau de p.** (d'école) placement office

placide [plasid] adj placid

plafond [plafɔ̃] nm ceiling • **plafonner** vi (prix) to peak; (salaires) to have reached a ceiling (**à** of) • **plafonnier** nm ceiling light

plage [plaʒ] nf (grève) beach; (surface) area; (de disque) track; **p. de sable** sand beach; **p. arrière** (de voiture) back shelf; **p. horaire** time slot

plagiat [plaʒja] nm plagiarism • **plagier** vt to plagiarize

plaid [plɛd] nm travelling rug

plaider [plede] vti Jur (défendre) to plead; **p. coupable** to plead guilty • **plaidoirie** nf Jur speech for the Br defence or Am defense • **plaidoyer** nm Jur speech for the Br defence or Am defense; Fig plea

plaie [plɛ] nf wound; Fig (fléau) affliction; (personne) nuisance

plaignant, -ante [plɛɲɑ̃, -ɑ̃t] nmf Jur plaintiff

plaindre* [plɛ̃dr] **1** *vt* to feel sorry for, to pity
2 se plaindre *vpr (protester)* to complain (**de** about; **que** that); **se p. de** *(douleur)* to complain of •**plainte** *nf* complaint; *(gémissement)* moan; **porter p. contre qn** to lodge a complaint against sb; **p. contre X** complaint against person or persons unknown

plaine [plɛn] *nf* plain

plain-pied [plɛ̃pje] **de plain-pied** *adv* on the same level (**avec** as); *(maison)* single-storey

plaintif, -ive [plɛ̃tif, -iv] *adj* plaintive

plaire* [plɛr] **1** *vi* **elle me plaît** I like her; **ça me plaît** I like it; **je fais ce qui me plaît** I do whatever I want
2 *v impersonnel* **il me plaît de le faire** I like doing it; **s'il vous/te plaît** please; **comme il vous plaira** as you like it
3 se plaire *vpr (l'un l'autre)* to like each other; **se p. à Paris** to like it in Paris

plaisance [plɛzɑ̃s] *nf* **navigation de p.** yachting •**plaisancier** *nm* yachtsman

plaisant, -ante [plɛzɑ̃, -ɑ̃t] **1** *adj (drôle)* amusing; *(agréable)* pleasing
2 *nm* **mauvais p.** joker •**plaisanter** *vi* to joke (**sur** about); **on ne plaisante pas avec la drogue** drugs are no joking matter; **tu plaisantes!** you're joking! •**plaisanterie** *nf* joke; **par p.** for a joke; **elle ne comprend pas la p.** she can't take a joke •**plaisantin** *nm* joker

plaisir [plɛzir] *nm* pleasure; **faire p. à qn** to please sb; **pour le p.** for the fun of it; **au p. (de vous revoir)** see you again sometime; **faites-moi le p. de** would you be good enough to

plan¹ [plɑ̃] **1** *nm (projet, dessin, organisation)* plan; *(de ville)* map; *Math* plane; **au premier p.** in the foreground; *Phot* **au second p.** in the background; *Fig* **passer au second p.** to be forced into the background; **sur le p. politique, au p. politique** from the political viewpoint; **sur le même p.** on the same level; **de premier p.** of importance, major; *Fam* **laisser qn en p.** to leave sb in the lurch; *Fam* **un bon p.** *(combine)* a good trick; *Phot & Cin* **gros p.** close-up; **p. d'eau** stretch of water; *Fin* **p. d'épargne** savings plan; **p. social** = corporate restructuring plan, usually involving job losses

plan², plane [plɑ̃, plan] *adj (plat)* even, flat

planche [plɑ̃ʃ] *nf (en bois)* plank; *(plus large)* board; *(illustration)* plate; **faire la p.** to float on one's back; **monter sur les planches** *(au théâtre)* to go on the stage; **p. à repasser/à dessin** ironing/drawing board; **p. à roulettes** skateboard; **faire de la p. à roulettes** to skateboard; **p. à voile** sailboard; **faire de la p. à voile** to go windsurfing; **p. de surf** surfboard

plancher¹ [plɑ̃ʃe] *nm* floor; **prix p.** minimum price

plancher² [plɑ̃ʃe] *vi Fam Scol* to have an exam

planer [plane] *vi (oiseau, planeur)* to glide; *Fam (se sentir bien)* to be floating on air; *Fig* **p. sur qn/qch** *(mystère, danger)* to hang over sb/sth •**planeur** *nm (avion)* glider

planète [planɛt] *nf* planet •**planétaire** *adj* planetary •**planétarium** *nm* planetarium

planifier [planifje] *vt Écon* to plan •**planification** *nf Écon* planning •**planning** *nm (emploi du temps)* schedule; **p. familial** family planning

planisphère [planisfɛr] *nm* planisphere

planque [plɑ̃k] *nf Fam (travail)* cushy job; *(lieu)* hideout •**planquer** *vt,* **se planquer** *vpr Fam* to hide

plant [plɑ̃] *nm (de plante)* seedling

plantation [plɑ̃tasjɔ̃] *nf (action)* planting; *(exploitation agricole)* plantation

plante [plɑ̃t] *nf Bot* plant; **jardin des plantes** botanical gardens; **p. du pied** sole (of the foot); **p. verte, p. d'appartement** house plant

planter [plɑ̃te] **1** *vt (fleur, arbre)* to plant; *(clou, couteau)* to drive in; *(tente, drapeau)* to put up; *(mettre)* to put (**sur** on; **contre** against); *Fam* **p. là qn** to dump sb
2 se planter *vpr Fam (tomber)* to come a cropper; *Fam (se tromper)* to get it wrong; **se p. devant qn/qch** to stand in front of sb/sth •**planté, -ée** *adj (debout)* standing; **bien p.** *(robuste)* sturdy

planteur [plɑ̃tœr] *nm* plantation owner

planton [plɑ̃tɔ̃] *nm Mil* orderly

plantureux, -euse [plɑ̃tyrø, -øz] *adj (femme)* buxom

plaque [plak] *nf* plate; *(de verre, de métal)* sheet, plate; *(de verglas)* sheet; *(de marbre)* slab; *(de chocolat)* bar; *(commémorative)* plaque; *(sur la peau)* blotch; *Fam* **à côté de la p.** wide of the mark; **p. chauffante** hotplate; **p. dentaire** (dental) plaque; *Aut* **p. minéralogique, p. d'immatriculation** *Br* number *or Am* license plate; *Fig* **p. tournante** centre

plaquer [plake] **1** *vt (métal, bijou)* to plate; *(bois)* to veneer; *(cheveux)* to plaster down; *Rugby* to tackle; *(aplatir)* to flatten (**contre** against); *Fam* **p. qn** to ditch sb; *Fam* **tout p.** to chuck it all in **2 se plaquer** *vpr* **se p. contre** to flatten oneself against ● **plaquage** *nm Rugby* tackle ● **plaqué, -ée 1** *adj (bijou)* plated; **p. or** gold-plated **2** *nm* **p. or** gold plate

plasma [plasma] *nm Biol* plasma

plastic [plastik] *nm* plastic explosive ● **plastiquer** *vt* to bomb

plastifier [plastifje] *vt* to laminate

plastique [plastik] *adj & nm* plastic; **en p.** plastic

plastron [plastrɔ̃] *nm* shirt front

plat, plate [pla, plat] **1** *adj* flat; *(mer)* calm, smooth; *(ennuyeux)* flat, dull; **à fond p.** flat-bottomed; **à p. ventre** flat on one's face; **à p.** *(pneu, batterie)* flat; *Fam (épuisé)* run down; **poser qch à p.** to lay sth (down) flat; *Fig* **tomber à p.** *(être un échec)* to fall flat; **faire à qn de plates excuses** to make a humble apology to sb; **assiette plate** dinner plate; **calme p.** dead calm

2 *nm* (**a**) *(de la main)* flat (**b**) *(récipient, nourriture)* dish; *(partie du repas)* course; *Fig* **mettre les petits plats dans les grands** to put on a marvellous spread; *Fam* **en faire tout un p.** to make a song and dance about it; **p. du jour** today's special; **p. cuisiné** ready meal; **p. de résistance** main course ● **plate-bande** (*pl* **plates-bandes**) *nf* flower bed; *Fam* **marcher sur les plates-bandes de qn** to tread on sb's toes ● **plate-forme** (*pl* **plates-formes**) *nf* platform; **p. pétrolière** oil rig

platane [platan] *nm* plane tree

plateau, -x [plato] *nm* tray; *(de balance)* pan; *(de tourne-disque)* turntable; *TV & Cin* set; *Géog* plateau; **p. à fromages** cheeseboard ● **plateau-repas** (*pl* **plateaux-repas**) *nm* meal on a tray

platine¹ [platin] **1** *nm (métal)* platinum **2** *adj inv* platinum; **blond p.** platinum blond ● **platiné, -ée** *adj (cheveux)* platinum-blond(e)

platine² [platin] *nf (d'électrophone, de magnétophone)* deck; **p. laser** CD player

platitude [platityd] *nf (propos)* platitude

plâtre [platr] *nm (matière)* plaster; **un p.** *(de jambe cassée)* a plaster cast; **dans le p.** *(jambe, bras)* in plaster; **les plâtres** *(de maison)* the plasterwork; *Fam* **essuyer les plâtres** to put up with the teething problems ● **plâtrer** *vt (mur)* to plaster; *(membre)* to put in plaster ● **plâtrier** *nm* plasterer

plausible [plozibl] *adj* plausible

play-back [plɛbak] *nm inv* **chanter en p.** to mime

plébiscite [plebisit] *nm* plebiscite

plein, pleine [plɛ̃, plɛn] **1** *adj (rempli, complet)* full; *(solide)* solid; **p. de** full of; **p. à craquer** full to bursting; **en pleine mer** out at sea, on the open sea; **en pleine figure** right in the face; **en pleine nuit** in the middle of the night; **en p. jour** in broad daylight; **en p. hiver** in the depths of winter; **en p. soleil** in the full heat of the sun; **en pleine campagne** in the heart of the country; **être en p. travail** to be hard at work; **à la pleine lune** at full moon; **travailler à p. temps** to work full-time; *Fam* **être p. aux as** to be rolling in it; **p. sud** due south; **p. tarif** full price; *(de transport)* full fare

2 *adv* **des billes p. les poches** pockets full of marbles; **du chocolat p. la figure** chocolate all over one's face; *Fam* **p. de lettres/d'argent** *(beaucoup de)* lots of letters/money; **à p.** *(travailler)* to full capacity

3 *nm Aut* **faire le p. (d'essence)** to fill up (the tank); **battre son p.** *(fête)* to be in full swing ● **pleinement** *adv* fully

pléonasme [pleɔnasm] *nm* pleonasm

pléthore [pletɔr] *nf* plethora

pleurer [plœre] **1** *vi* to cry, to weep (**sur** over); **p. de rire** to laugh till one cries **2** *vt (personne)* to mourn (for); **p. toutes les larmes de son corps** to cry one's eyes out ● **pleurnicher** *vi Fam* to whine ● **pleurs** *mpl* **en p.** in tears

pleurésie [plœrezi] *nf Méd* pleurisy

pleuvoir* [pløvwar] **1** *v impersonnel* to rain; **il pleut** it's raining; *Fig* **il pleut des cordes** it's raining cats and dogs **2** *vi (coups)* to rain down (**sur** on)

Plexiglas® [plɛksiglas] *nm Br* Perspex®, *Am* Plexiglas®

pli [pli] *nm* (**a**) *(de papier, de rideau, de la peau)* fold; *(de jupe, de robe)* pleat; *(de pantalon, de bouche)* crease; **(faux) p.** crease; **mise en plis** set *(hairstyle)*; *Fam* **ça n'a pas fait un p.** there was no doubt about it (**b**) *(enveloppe)* envelope; *(lettre)* letter; **sous p. séparé** under separate cover (**c**) *Cartes* trick; **faire un p.** to take a trick (**d**) *(habitude)* habit; **prendre le p. de faire qch** to get into the habit of doing sth

plier [plije] **1** *vt (draps, vêtements)* to fold; *(parapluie)* to fold up; *(courber)* to bend; **p. qn à** to submit sb to; **p. bagages** to pack one's bags (and leave); **être plié en deux** *(de douleur)* to be doubled up **2** *vi (branche)* to bend **3 se plier** *vpr (lit, chaise)* to fold up; **se p.**

à to submit to •**plíable** *adj* foldable
•**pliage** *nm (manière)* fold; *(action)* folding •**pliant, pliante 1** *adj (chaise)* folding **2** *nm* folding stool

plinthe [plɛ̃t] *nf (de mur) Br* skirting board, *Am* baseboard

plisser [plise] *vt (tissu, jupe)* to pleat; *(lèvres)* to pucker; *(front)* to wrinkle; *(yeux)* to screw up •**plissé, -ée** *adj (tissu, jupe)* pleated

plomb [plɔ̃] *nm (métal)* lead; *(fusible)* fuse; *(pour rideau)* lead weight; **plombs** *(de chasse)* lead shot; **tuyau de p.** *ou* **en p.** lead pipe; *Fig* **de p.** *(sommeil)* heavy; *(soleil)* blazing; *(ciel)* leaden; *Fig* **avoir du p. dans l'aile** to be in a bad way; *Fig* **ça lui mettra du p. dans la cervelle** that will knock some sense into him

plombe [plɔ̃b] *nf Fam* hour

plomber [plɔ̃be] *vt (dent)* to fill; *(mettre des plombs à)* to weigh with lead •**plombage** *nm (de dent)* filling

plombier [plɔ̃bje] *nm* plumber •**plomberie** *nf (métier, installations)* plumbing

plonger [plɔ̃ʒe] **1** *vi (personne)* to dive *(dans* into); *(oiseau, avion)* to dive *(sur* onto); *Fig (route)* to plunge
2 *vt (enfoncer)* to plunge *(dans* into)
3 se plonger *vpr* **se p. dans** *(lecture)* to immerse oneself in; **plongé dans ses pensées** deep in thought; **plongé dans l'obscurité** plunged in darkness •**plonge** *nf Fam* **faire la p.** to wash the dishes •**plongeant, -ante** *adj (décolleté)* plunging; **vue plongeante** bird's-eye view •**plongée** *nf* diving; *(de sous-marin)* dive; **p. sous-marine** skin *or* scuba diving •**plongeoir** *nm* diving board •**plongeon** *nm* dive; **faire un p.** to dive •**plongeur, -euse** *nmf (nageur)* diver; *Fam (de restaurant)* dishwasher

plouc [pluk] *Fam* **1** *adj* naff
2 *nm* yokel

plouf [pluf] *exclam* splash!

ployer [plwaje] *vi Littéraire* to bend

plu [ply] *pp de* **plaire, pleuvoir**

pluie [plɥi] *nf* rain; **sous la p.** in the rain; *Fig* **une p. de pierres/coups** a shower *or* deluge of stones/blows; *Fam* **parler de la p. et du beau temps** to talk of this and that; **p. fine** drizzle; **pluies acides** acid rain

plume [plym] *nf (d'oiseau)* feather; *Hist (pour écrire)* quill (pen); *(pointe de stylo)* nib; *Fam* **vivre de sa p.** to live by one's pen •**plumage** *nm* plumage •**plumeau, -x** *nm* feather duster •**plumer** *vt (volaille)* to pluck; *Fig* **p. qn** *(voler)* to fleece sb •**plumier** *nm* pencil box

plupart [plypar] **la plupart** *nf* most; **la p. des cas** most cases; **la p. du temps** most of the time; **la p. d'entre eux** most of them; **pour la p.** mostly

pluriel, -ielle [plyrjɛl] *Grammaire* **1** *adj* plural
2 *nm* plural; **au p.** in the plural

plus¹ [ply] ([plyz] *before vowel*, [plys] *in end position)* *adv* (**a**) *(comparatif)* more *(que* than); **p. d'un kilo/de dix** more than a kilo/ten; **p. de thé** more tea; **p. beau/ rapidement** more beautiful/rapidly *(que* than); **p. tard** later; **p. petit** smaller; **de p. en p.** more and more; **de p. en p. vite** quicker and quicker; **p. ou moins** more or less; **en p.** in addition *(de* to); **au p.** at most; **de p.** more *(que* than); *(en outre)* moreover; **les enfants de p. de dix ans** children over ten; **j'ai dix ans de p. qu'elle** I'm ten years older than she is; **il est p. de cinq heures** it's after five (o'clock); **p. il crie, p. il s'enroue** the more he shouts, the more hoarse he gets
(**b**) *(superlatif)* **le p.** (the) most; **le p. beau** the most beautiful *(de* in); *(de deux)* the more beautiful; **le p. grand** the biggest *(de* in); *(de deux)* the bigger; **j'ai le p. de livres** I have the (most) most books; **j'en ai le p.** I have the most

plus² [ply] *adv (négation)* (**ne…**) **p.** no more; **il n'a p. de pain** he has no more bread, he doesn't have any more bread; **il n'y a p. rien** there's nothing left; **tu n'es p. jeune** you're not young any more *or* any longer, you're no longer young; **elle ne le fait p.** she no longer does it, she doesn't do it any more *or* any longer; **je ne la reverrai p.** I won't see her again; **je ne voyagerai p. jamais** I'll never travel again

plus³ [plys] **1** *conj* plus; **deux p. deux font quatre** two plus two are four; **il fait p. 2 (degrés)** it's 2 degrees above freezing
2 *nm* **le signe p.** the plus sign

plusieurs [plyzjœr] *adj & pron* several

plus-que-parfait [plyskəparfɛ] *nm Grammaire* pluperfect

plus-value [plyvaly] *(pl* **plus-values**) *nf (bénéfice)* profit

plutonium [plytɔnjɔm] *nm* plutonium

plutôt [plyto] *adv* rather *(que* than)

pluvieux, -ieuse [plyvjø, -jøz] *adj* rainy, wet

PME [peɛmø] *(abrév* **petite et moyenne entreprise)** *nf* small company

PMU [peɛmy] *(abrév* **Pari mutuel urbain)** *nm* = state-run betting system

PNB [peɛnbe] *(abrév* **produit national brut)** *nm Écon* GNP

pneu [pnø] (*pl* **pneus**) *nm* (*de roue*) *Br* tyre, *Am* tire; **p. neige** snow tyre; **p. pluie** wet-weather tyre •**pneumatique** *adj* (*qui fonctionne à l'air*) pneumatic; (*gonflable*) inflatable

pneumonie [pnømɔni] *nf* pneumonia

poche [pɔʃ] *nf* (*de vêtement*) pocket; (*de kangourou*) pouch; (*sac*) bag; **poches** (*sous les yeux*) bags; **faire des poches** (*pantalon*) to be baggy; *Fam* **faire les poches à qn** to go through sb's pockets; **j'ai un euro en p.** I have one euro on me; **elle connaît Paris comme sa poche** she knows Paris like the back of her hand; *Fam* **c'est dans la p.** it's in the bag •**pochette** *nf* (*sac*) bag; (*d'allumettes*) book; (*de disque*) sleeve; (*sac à main*) (clutch) bag; (*mouchoir*) pocket handkerchief

pocher [pɔʃe] *vt* (*œufs*) to poach; *Fam* **p. l'œil à qn** to give sb a black eye

podium [pɔdjɔm] *nm* podium

poêle [pwal] **1** *nm* (*chauffage*) stove **2** *nf* **p. (à frire)** frying pan

poème [pɔɛm] *nm* poem •**poésie** *nf* (*art*) poetry; (*poème*) poem •**poète 1** *nm* poet **2** *adj* **femme p.** woman poet, poetess •**poétique** *adj* poetic

pognon [pɔɲɔ̃] *nm Fam* dough

poids [pwa] *nm* weight; *Sport* shot; **au p.** by weight; *Fig* **de p.** (*argument*) influential; **prendre/perdre du p.** to gain/lose weight; *Sport* **lancer le p.** to put the shot; *Fig* **faire deux poids deux mesures** to apply double standards; **p. lourd** (*camion*) *Br* lorry, *Am* truck; *Boxe* (*personne*) heavyweight; *Boxe* **p. plume** featherweight

poignant, -ante [pwaɲɑ̃, -ɑ̃t] *adj* poignant

poignard [pwaɲar] *nm* dagger; **coup de p.** stab •**poignarder** *vt* to stab

poigne [pwaɲ] *nf* grip; *Fig* **avoir de la p.** to be firm

poignée [pwaɲe] *nf* (*quantité*) handful (**de** of); (*de porte, de casserole*) handle; (*d'épée*) hilt; **p. de main** handshake

poignet [pwaɲɛ] *nm* wrist; (*de chemise*) cuff

poil [pwal] *nm* hair; (*pelage*) coat; **poils** (*de brosse*) bristles; (*de tapis*) pile; *Fam* **à p.** stark naked; *Fam* **à un p. près** very nearly; *Fam* **au p.** great; *Fam* **de bon/ mauvais p.** in a good/bad mood; *Fam* **de tout p.** of all kinds; **p. à gratter** itching powder •**poilu, -ue** *adj* hairy

poinçon [pwɛ̃sɔ̃] *nm* (*outil*) awl; (*marque*) hallmark •**poinçonner** *vt* (*billet*) to punch; (*bijou*) to hallmark •**poinçonneuse** *nf* (*machine*) punching machine

poindre* [pwɛ̃dr] *vi Littéraire* (*jour*) to dawn

poing [pwɛ̃] *nm* fist; **dormir à poings fermés** to sleep like a log

point[1] [pwɛ̃] *nm* (*lieu, score, question*) point; (*sur i, à l'horizon*) dot; (*tache*) spot; (*de notation*) mark; *Couture* stitch; **être sur le p. de faire qch** to be about to do sth; **à p. nommé** (*arriver*) at the right moment; **à p.** (*steak*) medium rare; **déprimé au p. que** depressed to such an extent that; **mettre au p.** (*appareil photo*) to focus; (*moteur*) to tune; (*technique*) to perfect; *Fig* (*éclaircir*) to clarify; **être au p.** to be up to scratch; **au p. où j'en suis...** at the stage I've reached...; **au plus haut p.** extremely; **au p. mort** *Aut* in neutral; *Fig* at a standstill; *Fig* **faire le p.** to take stock; *Fig* **mettre les points sur les i** to make oneself perfectly clear; **un p., c'est tout!** that's final!, *Am* period!; **p. de côté** stitch; **p. de départ** starting point; **p. de vente** point of sale; **p. de vue** (*opinion*) point of view, viewpoint; (*endroit*) viewing point; **p. du jour** daybreak; **p. d'exclamation** exclamation *Br* mark *ou Am* point; **p. d'interrogation** question mark; **points de suspension** suspension points; **p. chaud** hot spot; **p. faible/fort** weak/strong point; **p. final** *Br* full stop, *Am* period; **p. noir** (*comédon*) blackhead; (*embouteillage*) blackspot •**point-virgule** (*pl* **points-virgules**) *nm* semicolon

point[2] [pwɛ̃] *adv Littéraire* = **pas**[1]

pointe [pwɛ̃t] *nf* (*extrémité*) tip, point; (*clou*) nail; *Géog* headland; *Fig* (*maximum*) peak; **une p. d'humour** a touch of humour; **sur la p. des pieds** on tiptoe; **en p.** pointed; **de p.** (*technologie, industrie*) state-of-the-art; **vitesse de p.** top speed; *Fig* **à la p. de** (*progrès*) in *or* at the forefront of; **faire des pointes** (*danseuse*) to dance on points; **p. d'asperge** asparagus tip; **p. de vitesse** burst of speed

pointer [pwɛ̃te] **1** *vt* (*cocher*) *Br* to tick off, *Am* to check (off); (*braquer*) to point (**sur/ vers** at); **p. les oreilles** to prick up its ears **2** *vi* (*employé*) (*à l'arrivée*) to clock in; (*à la sortie*) to clock out; (*jour*) to dawn; **p. vers** to rise towards **3 se pointer** *vpr Fam* (*arriver*) to show up •**pointage** *nm* (*sur une liste*) ticking off; (*au travail*) (*à l'arrivée*) clocking in; (*à la sortie*) clocking out

pointillé [pwɛ̃tije] *nm* dotted line; **ligne en p.** dotted line

pointilleux, -euse [pwɛ̃tijø, -øz] *adj* fussy, particular

pointu, -ue [pwɛ̃ty] *adj (en pointe)* pointed; *(voix)* shrill; *Fig (spécialisé)* specialized

pointure [pwɛ̃tyr] *nf* size

poire [pwar] *nf (fruit)* pear; *Fam (figure)* mug; *Fam (personne)* sucker; *Fig* **couper la p. en deux** to meet each other halfway • **poirier** *nm* pear tree

poireau, -x [pwaro] *nm* leek

poireauter [pwarote] *vi Fam* to hang around

pois [pwa] *nm (légume)* pea; *(dessin)* (polka) dot; **à p.** *(vêtement)* polka-dot; **petits p.** *Br* (garden) peas, *Am* peas; **p. de senteur** sweet pea; **p. chiche** chickpea

poison [pwazɔ̃] *nm* poison

poisse [pwas] *nf Fam* bad luck

poisseux, -euse [pwasø, -øz] *adj* sticky

poisson [pwasɔ̃] *nm* fish; **les Poissons** *(signe)* Pisces; **être Poissons** to be Pisces; **p. d'avril** April fool; **p. rouge** goldfish • **poissonnerie** *nf* fish shop • **poissonnier, -ière** *nmf* fishmonger

poitrine [pwatrin] *nf* chest; *(seins)* bust; *Culin (de veau)* breast

poivre [pwavr] *nm* pepper • **poivré, -ée** *adj* peppery • **poivrer** *vt* to pepper • **poivrier** *nm (plante)* pepper plant; *(ustensile)* pepper pot • **poivrière** *nf* pepper pot

poivron [pwavrɔ̃] *nm* pepper, capsicum

poivrot, -ote [pwavro, -ɔt] *nmf Fam* drunk

poker [pɔkɛr] *nm Cartes* poker

polar [pɔlar] *nm Fam (roman)* whodunnit

polariser [pɔlarize] *vt* to polarize

pôle [pol] *nm Géog* pole; **p. Nord/Sud** North/South Pole; *Fig* **p. d'attraction** centre of attraction • **polaire** *adj* polar

polémique [pɔlemik] **1** *adj* polemical **2** *nf* heated debate

poli, -ie [pɔli] *adj (courtois)* polite (**avec** to *or* with); *(lisse)* polished • **poliment** *adv* politely

police [pɔlis] *nf* police; **faire la p.** to keep order (**dans** in); **p. d'assurance** insurance policy; *Typ & Ordinat* **p. de caractères** font; **p. judiciaire** police investigation department; **p. mondaine** vice squad; **p. secours** emergency services • **policier, -ière 1** *adj* **enquête policière** police inquiry; **roman p.** detective novel **2** *nm* policeman, detective

polichinelle [pɔliʃinɛl] *nm (marionnette)* Punch; *Péj (personne)* buffoon; **secret de P.** open secret

polio [pɔljo] *(abrév* **poliomyélite***) nf Méd* polio • **poliomyélite** *nf* poliomyelitis

polir [pɔlir] *vt* to polish

polisson, -onne [pɔlisɔ̃, -ɔn] **1** *adj* naughty **2** *nmf* rascal

politesse [pɔlitɛs] *nf* politeness; **par p.** out of politeness

politique [pɔlitik] **1** *adj* political **2** *nf (activité, science)* politics *(sing)*; *(mesure)* policy; **faire de la p.** to be in politics **3** *nmf* politician • **politicien, -ienne** *nmf Péj* politician • **politiser** *vt* to politicize

pollen [pɔlɛn] *nm* pollen

polluer [pɔlɥe] *vt* to pollute • **polluant** *nm* pollutant • **pollueur, -euse 1** *adj* polluting **2** *nmf* polluter • **pollution** *nf* pollution

polo [pɔlo] *nm (chemise)* polo shirt; *Sport* polo

polochon [pɔlɔʃɔ̃] *nm Fam* bolster

Pologne [pɔlɔɲ] *nf* **la P.** Poland • **polonais, -aise 1** *adj* Polish **2** *nmf* **P., Polonaise** Pole **3** *nm (langue)* Polish

poltron, -onne [pɔltrɔ̃, -ɔn] **1** *adj* cowardly **2** *nmf* coward

polycopier [pɔlikɔpje] *vt* to duplicate • **polycopié** *nm Univ* duplicated course material

polyester [pɔliɛstɛr] *nm* polyester; **chemise en p.** polyester shirt

polygame [pɔligam] *adj* polygamous

Polynésie [pɔlinezi] *nf* **la P.** Polynesia

polype [pɔlip] *nm* polyp

polytechnique [pɔliteknik] *adj & nf* **École p., P.** = *grande école* specializing in technology • **polytechnicien, -ienne** *nmf* = student or graduate of the *École polytechnique*

> *Il faut noter que le nom anglais **polytechnic** est un faux ami. Il désigne un établissement comparable à un IUT.*

polyvalent, -ente [pɔlivalɑ̃, -ɑ̃t] **1** *adj (salle)* multi-purpose; *(personne)* versatile **2** *adj & nf Can* **(école) polyvalente** *Br* = secondary school, *Am* = high school

pommade [pɔmad] *nf* ointment

pomme [pɔm] *nf* (**a**) *(fruit)* apple; *Anat* **p. d'Adam** Adam's apple; **p. de terre** potato; **pommes chips** potato *Br* crisps *or Am* chips; **pommes frites** *Br* chips, *Am* French fries; **pommes vapeur** steamed potatoes (**b**) *(d'arrosoir)* rose (**c**) *(locutions) Fam* **tomber dans les pommes** to faint; *Fam* **être haut comme trois pommes** to be knee-high to a grasshopper; *Fam* **ma p.** *(moi)* yours truly • **pommier** *nm* apple tree

pommeau, -x [pɔmv] *nm (de canne)* knob

pommette [pɔmɛt] *nf* cheekbone; **pommettes saillantes** high cheekbones

pompe¹ [pɔ̃p] **1** *nf (machine)* pump; *Fam (chaussure)* shoe; *Gymnastique Br* press-up, *Am* push-up; *Fam* **coup de p.** (sudden) feeling of exhaustion; *Fam* **il est à côté de ses pompes** he's not with it; **p. à essence** *Br* petrol *or Am* gas station; **p. à incendie** fire engine; **p. à vélo** bicycle pump **2** *nfpl* **pompes funèbres** undertaker's; **entrepreneur des pompes funèbres** *Br* undertaker, *Am* mortician

pompe² [pɔ̃p] *nf (splendeur)* pomp; **en grande p.** with great ceremony

pomper [pɔ̃pe] **1** *vt (eau, air)* to pump; *(faire monter)* to pump up; *(évacuer)* to pump out; *Fam (copier)* to crib (**sur** from); *Fam* **p. qn** *(épuiser)* to do sb in; *Fam* **tu me pompes (l'air)** you're getting on my nerves **2** *vi* to pump; *Fam (copier)* to crib (**sur** from)

pompeux, -euse [pɔ̃pø, -øz] *adj* pompous

pompier [pɔ̃pje] *nm* fireman; **voiture des pompiers** fire engine

pompiste [pɔ̃pist] *nmf Br* petrol *or Am* gas station attendant

pompon [pɔ̃pɔ̃] *nm* pompom

pomponner [pɔ̃pɔne] **se pomponner** *vpr* to doll oneself up

ponce [pɔ̃s] *nf* **pierre p.** pumice stone • **poncer** *vt (au papier de verre)* to sand (down) • **ponceuse** *nf (machine)* sander

ponctuation [pɔ̃ktɥasjɔ̃] *nf* punctuation • **ponctuer** *vt* to punctuate (**de** with)

ponctuel, -uelle [pɔ̃ktɥɛl] *adj (à l'heure)* punctual; *(unique) Br* one-off, *Am* one-of-a-kind • **ponctualité** *nf* punctuality

pondéré, -ée [pɔ̃dere] *adj (personne)* level-headed • **pondération** *nf (modération)* level-headedness

pondre [pɔ̃dr] *vt (œuf)* to lay; *Fam Péj (livre, discours)* to turn out

poney [pɔne] *nm* pony

pont [pɔ̃] *nm* bridge; *(de bateau)* deck; *Fig* **faire le p.** to make a long weekend of it; *Fig* **faire un p. d'or à qn** to give sb a golden hello; **p. aérien** airlift • **pont-levis** (*pl* **ponts-levis**) *nm* drawbridge

ponte [pɔ̃t] **1** *nf (d'œufs)* laying **2** *nm Fam (personne)* big shot

pontife [pɔ̃tif] *nm Rel* **(souverain) p.** the Supreme Pontiff • **pontifical, -e, -aux, -ales** *adj* papal

ponton [pɔ̃tɔ̃] *nm* pontoon

pop [pɔp] *nf & adj inv (musique)* pop

popote [pɔpɔt] *nf Fam (cuisine)* cooking

populace [pɔpylas] *nf Péj* rabble

populaire [pɔpylɛr] *adj (personne, gouvernement)* popular; *(quartier, milieu)* working-class; *(expression)* vernacular • **populariser** *vt* to popularize • **popularité** *nf* popularity (**auprès de** with)

population [pɔpylasjɔ̃] *nf* population • **populeux, -euse** *adj* crowded

porc [pɔr] *nm (animal)* pig; *(viande)* pork; *Péj (personne)* swine

porcelaine [pɔrsəlɛn] *nf* china, porcelain

porc-épic [pɔrkepik] (*pl* **porcs-épics**) *nm* porcupine

porche [pɔrʃ] *nm* porch

porcherie [pɔrʃəri] *nf Br* (pig)sty, *Am* pigpen

pore [pɔr] *nm* pore • **poreux, -euse** *adj* porous

pornographie [pɔrnɔgrafi] *nf* pornography • **pornographique** *adj* pornographic

port [pɔr] *nm* (**a**) *(pour bateaux)* port, harbour; *Ordinat* port; *Fig* **arriver à bon p.** to arrive safely (**b**) *(d'armes)* carrying; *(de barbe)* wearing; *(prix)* carriage, postage; *(attitude)* bearing

portable [pɔrtabl] **1** *adj (ordinateur)* portable; *(téléphone)* mobile **2** *nm (ordinateur)* laptop; *(téléphone)* mobile

portail [pɔrtaj] *nm (de jardin)* gate; *(de cathédrale)* portal

portant, -ante [pɔrtɑ̃, -ɑ̃t] *adj* **bien p. in** good health

portatif, -ive [pɔrtatif, -iv] *adj* portable

porte [pɔrt] *nf* door, *(de jardin, de ville, de slalom)* gate; **Alger, p. de** Algiers, gateway to; **trouver p. close** to find nobody in; **faire du p.-à-p.** to go from door to door selling/canvassing/*etc*; **mettre qn à la p.** *(jeter dehors)* to throw sb out; *(renvoyer)* to fire sb; **p. à tambour** revolving door; **p. d'embarquement** *(d'aéroport)* (departure) gate; **p. d'entrée** front door; **p. cochère** carriage entrance

porte-à-faux [pɔrtafo] *nm inv* **en p.** unstable

portée [pɔrte] *nf* (**a**) *(de fusil)* range; *Fig* scope; **à la p. de qn** within reach of sb; *Fig (richesse, plaisir)* within sb's grasp; **à p. de la main** within reach; **à p. de voix** within earshot; **hors de p.** out of reach (**b**) *(animaux)* litter (**c**) *(impact)* significance (**d**) *Mus* stave

portefeuille [pɔrtəfœj] *nm Br* wallet, *Am* billfold; *(de ministre, d'actions)* portfolio

portemanteau, -x [pɔrtmɑ̃to] *nm (sur pied)* coat stand; *(crochet)* coat rack

porter [pɔrte] **1** *vt* to carry; *(vêtement, lunettes)* to wear; *(moustache, barbe)* to have; *(trace, responsabilité, fruits)* to bear; *(regard)* to cast; *(coup)* to strike; *(sentiment)* to have (à for); *(inscrire)* to enter; **p. qch à qn** to take/bring sth to sb; **p. bonheur/malheur** to bring good/bad luck; **p. une attaque contre qn** to attack sb; **p. son attention sur qch** to turn one's attention to sth; **tout (me) porte à croire que...** everything leads me to believe that...; **se faire p. malade** to report sick

2 *vi (voix)* to carry; *(coup)* to strike home; **p. sur** *(concerner)* to be about; *(accent)* to fall on

3 se porter *vpr (vêtement)* to be worn; **se p. bien** to be well; **comment te portes-tu?** how are you?; **se p. candidat** *Br* to stand *or Am* to run as a candidate ●**portant, -ante** *adj* **bien p.** in good health ●**porté, -ée** *adj* **p. à croire** inclined to believe; **p. sur qch** fond of sth ●**porte-avions** *nm inv* aircraft carrier ●**porte-bagages** *nm inv* luggage rack ●**porte-bébé** (*pl* **porte-bébés**) *nm* baby carrier ●**porte-bonheur** *nm inv* (lucky) charm ●**porte-cartes** *nm inv* card-holder ●**porte-clefs** *nm inv* key ring ●**porte-documents** *nm inv* briefcase ●**porte-drapeau** (*pl* **porte-drapeaux**) *nm* standard bearer ●**porte-fenêtre** (*pl* **portes-fenêtres**) *nf Br* French window, *Am* French door ●**porte-jarretelles** *nm inv Br* suspender *or Am* garter belt ●**porte-monnaie** *nm inv* purse ●**porte-parapluies** *nm inv* umbrella stand ●**porte-parole** *nmf inv* spokesperson (**de** for) ●**porte-plume** *nm inv* penholder ●**porte-revues** *nm inv* newspaper rack ●**porte-savon** (*pl* **porte-savons**) *nm* soapdish ●**porte-serviettes** *nm inv Br* towel rail, *Am* towel rack ●**porte-voix** *nm inv* megaphone

porteur, -euse [pɔrtœr, -øz] **1** *nm (de bagages)* porter

2 *nmf (malade)* carrier; *(de nouvelles, de chèque)* bearer; *Méd* **p. sain** = carrier who doesn't have the symptoms of the disease

3 *adj* **marché p.** growth market

portier [pɔrtje] *nm* doorkeeper, porter ●**portière** *nf (de véhicule, de train)* door ●**portillon** *nm* gate

portion [pɔrsjɔ̃] *nf* portion

portique [pɔrtik] *nm Archit* portico; *(pour agrès)* crossbeam

porto [pɔrto] *nm (vin)* port

Porto Rico [pɔrtoriko] *nm ou f* Puerto Rico

portrait [pɔrtrɛ] *nm (peinture, dessin, photo)* portrait; *(description)* description; **faire le p. de qn** to do sb's portrait; *Fig* **c'est tout le p. de son père** he's the spitting image of his father ●**portrait-robot** (*pl* **portraits-robots**) *nm* identikit picture, Photofit®

portuaire [pɔrtɥɛr] *adj* **installations portuaires** port *or* harbour facilities

Portugal [pɔrtygal] *nm* **le P.** Portugal ●**portugais, -aise 1** *adj* Portuguese **2** *nmf* **P., Portugaise** Portuguese *inv;* **les P.** the Portuguese **3** *nm (langue)* Portuguese

pose [poz] *nf* (**a**) *(de rideau, de papier peint)* putting up; *(de moquette)* laying (**b**) *(pour photo, portrait)* pose; *Phot* exposure; **prendre la p.** to pose

posé, -ée [poze] *adj (calme)* composed, staid ●**posément** *adv* calmly

poser [poze] **1** *vt* to put down; *(papier peint, rideaux)* to put up; *(mine, moquette, fondations)* to lay; *(bombe)* to plant; *(conditions, principe)* to lay down; **p. qch sur qch** to put sth on sth; **p. une question à qn** to ask sb a question; **p. un problème à qn** to pose a problem for sb; **p. sa candidature** *(à une élection)* to put oneself forward as a candidate; *(à un emploi)* to apply (à for)

2 *vi (modèle)* to pose (**pour** for)

3 se poser *vpr (oiseau, avion)* to land; *(problème, question)* to arise; **se p. sur** *(sujet: regard)* to rest on; **se p. des questions** to ask oneself questions

positif, -ive [pozitif, -iv] *adj* positive ●**positivement** *adv* positively

position [pozisjɔ̃] *nf* position; *Fig* **prendre p.** to take a stand (**contre** against); *Fig* **rester sur ses positions** to stand one's ground

posologie [pozɔlɔʒi] *nf Méd* dosage

posséder [posede] *vt (biens, talent)* to possess; *(sujet)* to have a thorough knowledge of; *(langue)* to have mastered; *Fam (duper)* to take in ●**possesseur** *nm* possessor; owner ●**possessif, -ive** *adj & nm Grammaire* possessive ●**possession** *nf* possession; **en p. de qch** in possession of sth; **être en pleine p. de ses moyens** to be at the peak of one's powers; **prendre p. de qch** to take possession of sth

possibilité [posibilite] *nf* possibility; **avoir la p. de faire qch** to have the chance *or* opportunity of doing sth; **avoir de grandes possibilités** to have great potential

possible [posibl] **1** *adj* possible (**à faire** to do); **il (nous) est p. de le faire** it is possible (for us) to do it; **il est p. que...** (+ subjunctive) it is possible that...; **si p.** if possible; **le plus tôt p.** as soon as possible; **autant que p.** as far as possible; **le plus p.** as much/as many as possible; **le moins de détails p.** as few details as possible

2 *nm* **faire (tout) son p.** to do one's utmost (**pour faire** to do)

postal, -e, -aux, -ales [pɔstal, -o] *adj* postal; *(train)* mail

postdater [pɔstdate] *vt* to postdate

poste¹ [pɔst] *nf (service)* mail, *Br* post; *(bureau)* post office; **la P.** the postal services; **par la p.** by mail, *Br* by post; **mettre qch à la p.** to mail *or Br* post sth; **p. aérienne** airmail; **p. restante** *Br* poste restante, *Am* general delivery

poste² [pɔst] *nm* (a) *(lieu, emploi)* post; **être à son p.** to be at one's post; **p. d'aiguillage** *Br* signal box, *Am* signal tower; **p. d'essence** *Br* petrol *or Am* gas station; **p. d'incendie** fire point; **p. de pilotage** cockpit; **p. de police** police station; **p. de secours** first-aid post; *Ordinat* **p. de travail** workstation (b) **p. (de radio/télévision)** radio/television set (c) *(de standard)* extension

poster¹ [pɔste] *vt (lettre)* to mail, *Br* to post

poster² [pɔste] **1** *vt (sentinelle, troupes)* to post, to station

2 se poster *vpr* to take up a position

poster³ [pɔstɛr] *nm* poster

postérieur, -ieure [pɔsterjœr] **1** *adj (dans le temps)* later; *(de derrière)* back; **p. à** after

2 *nm Fam (derrière)* posterior

postérité [pɔsterite] *nf* posterity

posthume [pɔstym] *adj* posthumous; **à titre p.** posthumously

postiche [pɔstiʃ] **1** *adj* false

2 *nm* hairpiece

postier, -ière [pɔstje, -jɛr] *nmf* postal worker

postillonner [pɔstijɔne] *vi* to splutter • **postillons** *nmpl* **envoyer des p.** to splutter

post-scriptum [pɔstskriptɔm] *nm inv* postscript

postuler [pɔstyle] **1** *vt Math* to postulate

2 *vi* **p. à un emploi** to apply for a job • **postulant, -ante** *nmf* applicant (**à** for)

posture [pɔstyr] *nf* posture; **être en fâcheuse p.** to be in an awkward situation

pot [po] *nm* pot; *(en verre)* jar; *(en carton)* carton; *(de bébé)* potty; *Fam* **prendre un p.** to have a drink; *Fam* **avoir du p.** to be

lucky; **p. à eau** water jug; **p. de chambre** chamber pot; **p. de fleurs** *(récipient)* flowerpot; **p. d'échappement** *Br* exhaust pipe, *Am* tail pipe

potable [pɔtabl] *adj* drinkable; *Fam (passable)* tolerable; **eau p.** drinking water

potage [pɔtaʒ] *nm* soup

potager, -ère [pɔtaʒe, -ɛr] **1** *adj* **jardin p.** vegetable garden; **plante potagère** vegetable

2 *nm* vegetable garden

potasser [pɔtase] *vt Fam (examen)* to bone up for

potassium [pɔtasjɔm] *nm* potassium

pot-au-feu [pɔtofø] *nm inv* = boiled beef with vegetables

pot-de-vin [podvɛ̃] *(pl* **pots-de-vin**) *nm* bribe

pote [pɔt] *nm Fam (ami)* pal

poteau, -x [pɔto] *nm* post; **p. électrique** electricity pylon; **p. indicateur** signpost; **p. télégraphique** telegraph pole

potelé, -ée [pɔtle] *adj* plump, chubby

potence [pɔtɑ̃s] *nf (gibet)* gallows *(sing)*

potentiel, -ielle [pɔtɑ̃sjɛl] *adj & nm* potential

poterie [pɔtri] *nf (art, objets)* pottery; *(objet)* piece of pottery; **faire de la p.** to make pottery • **potier, -ière** *nmf* potter

potin [pɔtɛ̃] *nm Fam (bruit)* row; **faire du p.** to kick up a row • **potins** *nmpl (ragots)* gossip

potion [posjɔ̃] *nf* potion

potiron [pɔtirɔ̃] *nm* pumpkin

pot-pourri [popuri] *(pl* **pots-pourris**) *nm (chansons)* medley

pou, -x [pu] *nm* louse; **poux** lice

poubelle [pubɛl] *nf Br* dustbin, *Am* garbage can; **mettre qch à la p.** to throw sth out

pouce [pus] *nm (doigt)* thumb; *Fam* **coup de p.** helping hand; *Fam* **se tourner les pouces** to twiddle one's thumbs

poudre [pudr] *nf (poussière, explosif)* powder; **en p.** *(lait)* powdered; *(chocolat)* drinking; **p. à récurer** scouring powder • **poudrer 1** *vt* to powder **2 se poudrer** *vpr* to powder one's face • **poudreux, -euse 1** *adj* powdery **2** *nf* **poudreuse** *(neige)* powder snow • **poudrier** *nm* (powder) compact • **poudrière** *nf (entrepôt)* powder magazine; *Fig (région)* powder keg

pouf [puf] **1** *exclam* thump!

2 *nm (siège)* pouf

pouffer [pufe] *vi* **p. (de rire)** to burst out laughing

pouilleux, -euse [pujø, -øz] *adj (personne)* filthy; *(quartier)* squalid

poulailler [pulaje] *nm* hen house; *Fam Théâtre* **le p.** the gods

poulain [pulɛ̃] *nm* foal; *Fig* protégé

poule¹ [pul] *nf (animal)* hen; *Culin* fowl; *Péj (femme)* tart; *Am* broad; *Fam* **ma p.** darling; *Péj* **p. mouillée** wimp

poule² [pul] *nf (groupe)* group

poulet [pulɛ] *nm (animal)* chicken; *Fam (policier)* cop

pouliche [puliʃ] *nf* filly

poulie [puli] *nf* pulley

poulpe [pulp] *nm* octopus

pouls [pu] *nm Méd* pulse; **prendre le p. de qn** to take sb's pulse

poumon [pumɔ̃] *nm* lung; **à pleins poumons** *(respirer)* deeply; **p. d'acier** iron lung

poupe [pup] *nf Naut* stern, poop; *Fig* **avoir le vent en p.** to have the wind in one's sails

poupée [pupe] *nf* doll; **jouer à la p.** to play with dolls

poupin [pupɛ̃] *adj* **visage p.** baby face

poupon [pupɔ̃] *nm (bébé)* baby; *(poupée)* baby doll

pour [pur] **1** *prép* for; **p. toi/moi** for you/me; **faites-le p. lui** do it for him, do it for his sake; **partir p. Paris/l'Italie** to leave for Paris/Italy; **elle part p. cinq ans** she's leaving for five years; **elle est p.** she's all for it, she's in favour of it; **p. faire qch** (in order) to do sth; **p. que tu le voies** so (that) you may see it; **p. quoi faire?** what for?; **trop poli p. faire qch** too polite to do sth; **assez grand p. faire qch** big enough to do sth; **p. femme/base** as a wife/basis; **p. affaires** on business; **p. cela** for that reason; **p. ma part** as for me; **jour p. jour/ heure p. heure** to the day/hour; **dix p. cent** ten percent; **acheter p. 5 euros de bonbons** to buy 5 euros' worth of *Br* sweets *or Am* candies; **p. intelligent qu'il soit** however clever he may be; **je n'y suis p. rien!** it's got nothing to do with me!; *Fam* **c'est fait p.** that's what it's there for

2 *nm* **le p. et le contre** the pros and cons

pourboire [purbwar] *nm* tip

pourcentage [pursɑ̃taʒ] *nm* percentage

pourchasser [purʃase] *vt* to pursue

> ⚠ Il faut noter que le verbe anglais **to pur-chase** est un faux ami. Il signifie **acheter**.

pourparlers [purparle] *nmpl* negotiations, talks; **p. de paix** peace talks

pourpre [purpr] *adj & nm* crimson

pourquoi [purkwa] **1** *adv & conj* why; **p. pas?** why not?

2 *nm inv* reason (**de** for); **le p. et le comment** the whys and wherefores

pourra, pourrait [pura, purɛ] *voir* **pouvoir 1**

pourrir [purir] **1** *vt* to rot; *Fig* **p. qn** to spoil sb

2 *vi* to rot • **pourri, -ie** *adj (fruit, temps, personne)* rotten; *Fam* **être p. de fric** to be stinking rich • **pourriture** *nf* rot

poursuite [pursɥit] **1** *nf (chasse)* pursuit; *(continuation)* continuation; **se lancer à la p. de qn** to set off in pursuit of sb

2 *nfpl Jur* **poursuites (judiciaires)** legal proceedings (**contre** against); **engager des poursuites contre qn** to start proceedings against sb

poursuivre* [pursɥivr] **1** *vt (chercher à atteindre)* to pursue; *(sujet: idée, crainte)* to haunt; *(sujet: malchance)* to dog; *(harceler)* to pester; *(continuer)* to continue, to go on with; *Jur* **p. qn (en justice)** to bring proceedings against sb; *(au criminel)* to prosecute sb

2 se poursuivre *vpr* to continue, to go on • **poursuivant, -ante** *nmf* pursuer

pourtant [purtɑ̃] *adv* yet, nevertheless; **et p.** and yet

pourtour [purtur] *nm* perimeter

pourvoir* [purvwar] **1** *vt* to provide (**de** with); **être pourvu de** to be provided with

2 *vi* **p. à** *(besoins)* to provide for

3 se pourvoir *vpr Jur* **se p. en cassation** to take one's case to the Court of Appeal • **pourvoyeur, -euse** *nmf* supplier

pourvu [purvy] **pourvu que** *conj* (**a**) *(condition)* provided (that) (**b**) *(souhait)* **p. qu'elle soit là!** I just hope (that) she's there!

pousse [pus] *nf (croissance)* growth; *(bourgeon)* shoot, sprout; **pousses de bambou** bamboo shoots

poussée [puse] *nf (pression)* pressure; *(coup)* push; *(d'ennemi)* thrust, push; *(de fièvre)* outbreak; *(de l'inflation)* upsurge

pousser [puse] **1** *vt (presser)* to push; *(moteur)* to drive hard; **p. qn du coude** to nudge sb with one's elbow; **p. qn à qch** to drive sb to sth; **p. qn à faire qch** *(sujet: faim)* to drive sb to do sth; *(sujet: personne)* to urge sb to do sth; **poussé par la curiosité** prompted by curiosity; **p. un cri** to shout; **p. un soupir** to sigh

2 *vi (presser)* to push; *(croître)* to grow; **faire p. qch** *(plante)* to grow sth; **se laisser p. les cheveux** to let one's hair grow; **p. jusqu'à Paris** to push on as far as Paris

3 se pousser *vpr (pour faire de la place)* to move over • **poussé, -ée** *adj (travail, études)* thorough • **pousse-café** *nm inv* after-dinner liqueur

poussette [pusɛt] *nf Br* pushchair, *Am* stroller

poussière [pusjɛr] *nf* dust; **une p.** a speck of dust; *Fam* **10 euros et des poussières** a bit over 10 euros • **poussiéreux, -euse** *adj* dusty

poussif, -ive [pusif, -iv] *adj* wheezy

poussin [pusɛ̃] *nm (animal)* chick

poutre [putr] *nf (en bois)* beam; *(en acier)* girder • **poutrelle** *nf* girder

pouvoir* [puvwar] **1** *v aux (être capable de)* can, to be able to; *(avoir la permission)* can, may, to be allowed; **je peux deviner** I can guess, I'm able to guess; **tu peux entrer** you may *or* can come in; **il peut être sorti** he may *or* might be out; **elle pourrait/pouvait venir** she might/could come; **j'ai pu l'obtenir** I managed to get it; **j'aurais pu l'obtenir** I could have *Br* got *or Am* gotten it; **je n'en peux plus** *(de fatigue)* I'm utterly exhausted

2 *v impersonnel* **il peut neiger** it may snow; **il se peut qu'elle parte** she might leave

3 *nm (puissance, attributions)* power; **au p.** *(parti)* in power; **il n'est pas en mon p. de vous aider** it's not in my power to help you; **p. d'achat** purchasing power; **les pouvoirs publics** the authorities

poux [pu] *pl de* **pou**

pragmatique [pragmatik] *adj* pragmatic

praire [prɛr] *nf* clam

prairie [preri] *nf* meadow

praline [pralin] *nf* praline • **praliné, -ée** *adj (glace)* praline-flavoured

praticable [pratikabl] *adj (route)* passable; *(terrain)* playable

praticien, -ienne [pratisjɛ̃, -jɛn] *nmf* practitioner

pratique [pratik] **1** *adj (méthode, personne)* practical; *(outil)* handy; **avoir l'esprit p.** to have a practical turn of mind

2 *nf (application, procédé, coutume)* practice; *(expérience)* practical experience; **la p. de la natation/du golf** swimming/golfing; **mettre qch en p.** to put sth into practice; **dans la p.** *(en réalité)* in practice • **pratiquement** *adv (presque)* practically; *(en réalité)* in practice

pratiquer [pratike] **1** *vt (religion) Br* to practise, *Am* to practice; *(activité)* to take part in; *(langue)* to use; *(sport)* to play; *(ouverture)* to make; *(opération)* to carry out; **p. la natation** to go swimming

2 *vi (médecin, avocat) Br* to practise, *Am* to practice • **pratiquant, -ante 1** *adj* practising **2** *nmf* practising Christian/Jew/Muslim/*etc*

pré [pre] *nm* meadow

préalable [prealabl] **1** *adj* prior, previous; **p. à** prior to

2 *nm* precondition, prerequisite; **au p.** beforehand • **préalablement** [-əmɑ̃] *adv* beforehand

préambule [preɑ̃byl] *nm* preamble; *Fig* **sans p., elle annonça que...** without any warning, she announced that...

PréAO [preao] *(abrév* **présentation assistée par ordinateur**) *nf Ordinat* computer-assisted presentation

préau, -x [preo] *nm (de cour d'école)* covered area; *(salle)* hall

préavis [preavi] *nm* (advance) notice (**de** of); **p. de grève** strike notice; **p. de licenciement** notice of dismissal

précaire [preker] *adj* precarious; *(santé)* delicate • **précarité** *nf* precariousness; **p. de l'emploi** lack of job security

précaution [prekosjɔ̃] *nf (mesure)* precaution; *(prudence)* caution; **par p.** as a precaution; **pour plus de p.** to be on the safe side; **prendre des précautions** to take precautions • **précautionneux, -euse** *adj* careful

précédent, -ente [presedɑ̃, -ɑ̃t] **1** *adj* previous

2 *nmf* previous one

3 *nm* precedent; **sans p.** unprecedented • **précédemment** [-amɑ̃] *adv* previously • **précéder** *vti* to precede

précepte [presɛpt] *nm* precept

précepteur, -trice [preseptœr, -tris] *nmf* (private) tutor

prêcher [preʃe] *vti* to preach

précieux, -ieuse [presjø, -jøz] *adj* precious

précipice [presipis] *nm* chasm, abyss; *(de ravin)* precipice

précipiter [presipite] **1** *vt (hâter)* to hasten; *(jeter)* to hurl down; *Fig* to plunge (**dans** into)

2 **se précipiter** *upr (se jeter)* to rush (**vers/sur** towards/at); *(se hâter)* to rush; **les événements se sont précipités** things started happening quickly • **précipitamment** [-amɑ̃] *adv* hastily • **précipitation** *nf* haste; **précipitations** *(pluie)* precipitation • **précipité, -ée** *adj* hasty

précis, -ise [presi, -iz] **1** *adj* precise, exact; *(mécanisme)* accurate, precise; **à deux heures précises** at two o'clock sharp *or* precisely

2 *nm (résumé)* summary; *(manuel)* handbook • **précisément** *adv* precisely • **précision** *nf* precision; *(de mécanisme, d'information)* accuracy; *(détail)* detail;

donner des précisions sur qch to give precise details about sth; **demander des précisions sur qch** to ask for further information about sth
préciser [presize] **1** *vt* to specify (**que** that)
2 se préciser *vpr* to become clear(er)
précoce [prekɔs] *adj (fruit, été)* early; *(enfant)* precocious • **précocité** *nf* precociousness; *(de fruit)* earliness
préconçu, -ue [prekɔ̃sy] *adj* preconceived
préconiser [prekɔnize] *vt* to advocate (**que** that)
précurseur [prekyrsœr] **1** *nm* forerunner, precursor
2 *adj* **signe p.** forewarning
prédécesseur [predesesœr] *nm* predecessor
prédestiné, -ée [predestine] *adj* predestined (**à faire** to do)
prédicateur [predikatœr] *nm* preacher
prédilection [predilɛksjɔ̃] *nf* predilection; **de p.** favourite
prédire* [predir] *vt* to predict (**que** that) • **prédiction** *nf* prediction
prédisposer [predispoze] *vt* to predispose (**à qch** to sth; **à faire** to do) • **prédisposition** *nf* predisposition (**à** to)
prédominer [predɔmine] *vi* to predominate • **prédominance** *nf* predominance • **prédominant, -ante** *adj* predominant
préfabriqué, -ée [prefabrike] *adj* prefabricated
préface [prefas] *nf* preface (**de** to) • **préfacer** *vt* to preface
préfecture [prefektyr] *nf* prefecture; **la P. de police** police headquarters • **préfectoral, -e, -aux, -ales** *adj* = relating to a 'préfecture' or 'préfet'
préférable [preferabl] *adj* preferable (**à** to)
préférence [preferɑ̃s] *nf* preference (**pour** for); **de p.** preferably; **de p. à** in preference to • **préférentiel, -ielle** *adj* preferential
préférer [prefere] *vt* to prefer (**à** to); **p. faire qch** to prefer to do sth; **je préférerais rester** I would rather stay, I would prefer to stay • **préféré, -ée** *adj* & *nmf* favourite
préfet [prefɛ] *nm* prefect *(chief administrator in a 'département')*; **p. de police** = chief commissioner of police
préfigurer [prefigyre] *vt* to herald, to foreshadow
préfixe [prefiks] *nm* prefix
préhistoire [preistwar] *nf* prehistory • **préhistorique** *adj* prehistoric

préjudice [preʒydis] *nm (à une cause)* prejudice; *(à une personne)* harm; **porter p. à qn** to do sb harm • **préjudiciable** *adj* prejudicial (**à** to)

> *Ⓘ* Il faut noter que le nom anglais **prejudice** est un faux ami. Il signifie le plus souvent **préjugé**.

préjugé [preʒyʒe] *nm* prejudice; **avoir des préjugés** to be prejudiced (**contre** against)
prélasser [prelɑse] **se prélasser** *vpr* to lounge
prélat [prela] *nm Rel* prelate
prélever [prel(ə)ve] *vt (échantillon)* to take (**sur** from); *(somme)* to deduct (**sur** from) • **prélèvement** *nm (d'échantillon)* taking; *(de somme)* deduction; **p. automatique** *Br* direct debit, *Am* automatic deduction; **prélèvements obligatoires** = tax and social security contributions
préliminaire [preliminɛr] **1** *adj* preliminary
2 *nmpl* **préliminaires** preliminaries
prélude [prelyd] *nm* prelude (**à** to)
prématuré, -ée [prematyre] **1** *adj* premature
2 *nmf* premature baby • **prématurément** *adv* prematurely
préméditer [premedite] *vt* to premeditate • **préméditation** *nf* premeditation; **meurtre avec p.** premeditated murder
prémices [premis] *nfpl Littéraire* **les p. de** the (very) beginnings of
premier, -ière [prəmje, -jɛr] **1** *adj* first; *(enfance)* early; *(page de journal)* front; *(qualité)* prime; *(état)* original; *(notion, cause)* basic; *(danseuse, rôle)* leading; *(marche)* bottom; **le p. rang** the front row; **les trois premiers mois** the first three months; **à la première occasion** at the earliest opportunity; **en p.** firstly; **P. ministre** Prime Minister
2 *nm (étage) Br* first *or Am* second floor; **le p. juin** June the first; **le p. de l'an** New Year's Day
3 *nmf* first (one); **arriver le p.** *ou* **en p.** to arrive first; **être le p. de la classe** to be (at the) top of the class
4 *nf* **première** *(wagon, billet)* first class; *(vitesse)* first (gear); *(événement historique)* first; *(de chaussure)* insole; *Théâtre* opening night; *Cin* première; *Scol Br* ≃ lower sixth, *Am* ≃ eleventh grade • **premièrement** *adv* firstly
prémisse [premis] *nf* premise
prémonition [premɔnisjɔ̃] *nf* premonition • **prémonitoire** *adj* premonitory

prémunir [premynir] **se prémunir** *vpr Littéraire* **se p. contre qch** to guard against sth

prenant, -ante [prənɑ̃, -ɑ̃t] *adj (film)* engrossing; *(travail)* time-consuming

prénatal, -e, -als, -ales [prenatal] *adj Br* antenatal, *Am* prenatal

prendre* [prɑ̃dr] **1** *vt* to take (**à qn** from sb); *(attraper)* to catch; *(repas, boisson, douche)* to have; *(nouvelles)* to get; *(air)* to put on; *(accent)* to pick up; *(pensionnaire)* to take in; *(bonne, assistant)* to take on; **p. qch dans un tiroir** to take sth out of a drawer; **p. qn pour** to take sb for; **p. feu** to catch fire; **p. du temps/une heure** to take time/an hour; **p. de la place** to take up room; **p. du poids/de la vitesse** to put on weight/gather speed; **p. l'eau** *(bateau, chaussure)* to be leaking; **p. l'air** *(se promener)* to get some fresh air; **passer p. qn** to come and get sb; *Fam* **p. un coup de poing dans la figure** to get a punch in the face; **qu'est-ce qui te prend?** what's *Br* got *or Am* gotten into you?; **à tout p.** on the whole

2 *vi (feu)* to catch; *(ciment, gelée)* to set; *(greffe, vaccin, plante)* to take; *(mode)* to catch on; **p. sur soi** to restrain oneself

3 se prendre *vpr (médicament)* to be taken; *(s'accrocher)* to get caught; **se p. les pieds dans qch** to get one's feet caught in sth; **s'y p. bien avec qn** to know how to handle sb; **s'en p. à qn** to take it out on sb; *Fig* **je me suis pris au jeu** I got really caught up in it

preneur, -euse [prənœr, -øz] *nmf (acheteur)* taker, buyer; **p. d'otages** hostage taker

prénom [prenɔ̃] *nm* first name • **prénommer** *vt* to name; **il se prénomme Daniel** his first name is Daniel

préoccuper [preɔkype] **1** *vt (inquiéter)* to worry

2 se préoccuper *vpr* **se p. de qn/qch** to concern oneself with sb/sth • **préoccupant, -ante** *adj* worrying • **préoccupation** *nf* preoccupation, concern • **préoccupé, -ée** *adj* worried (**par** about)

prépa [prepa] *nf Fam Scol* = preparatory class *(for the entrance exam to the 'grandes écoles')*

préparatifs [preparatif] *nmpl* preparations (**de** for) • **préparation** *nf* preparation • **préparatoire** *adj* preparatory

préparer [prepare] **1** *vt* to prepare (**qch pour** sth for); *(examen)* to study for; **p. qch à qn** to prepare sth for sb; **p. qn à** *(examen)* to prepare *or* coach sb for; **plats tout préparés** ready-cooked meals

2 se préparer *vpr (être imminent)* to be in the offing; *(s'apprêter)* to prepare oneself (**à** *ou* **pour qch** for sth); **se p. à faire qch** to prepare to do sth; **se p. qch** *(boisson)* to make oneself sth

prépondérant, -ante [prepɔ̃derɑ̃, -ɑ̃t] *adj* predominant • **prépondérance** *nf* predominance

préposer [prepoze] *vt* **p. qn à qch** to appoint sb to sth • **préposé, -ée** *nmf* employee; *(facteur)* postman, *f* postwoman

préposition [prepozisjɔ̃] *nf Grammaire* preposition

préretraite [prerətrɛt] *nf* early retirement

prérogative [prerɔgativ] *nf* prerogative

près [prɛ] *adv* **p. de qn/qch** near sb/sth, close to sb/sth; **p. de deux ans** nearly two years; **p. de partir** about to leave; **tout p.** nearby (**de qn/qch** sb/sth), close by (**de qn/qch** sb /sth); **de p.** *(suivre, examiner)* closely; **à peu de chose p.** more or less; **à cela p.** except for that; **voici le chiffre à un euro p.** here is the figure, give or take a euro; **calculer à l'euro p.** to calculate to the nearest euro

présage [prezaʒ] *nm* omen, sign • **présager** *vt (annoncer)* to presage; **ça ne présage rien de bon** it doesn't bode well

presbyte [presbit] *adj* long-sighted • **presbytie** [-bisi] *nf* long-sightedness

presbytère [presbitɛr] *nm* presbytery

préscolaire [preskɔler] *adj* preschool

prescrire* [preskrir] *vt (médicament)* to prescribe • **prescription** *nf (ordonnance)* prescription

préséance [preseɑ̃s] *nf* precedence (**sur** over)

présence [prezɑ̃s] *nf* presence; *(à l'école)* attendance (**à** at); **en p. de** in the presence of; **faire acte de p.** to put in an appearance; **p. d'esprit** presence of mind

présent¹, -ente [prezɑ̃, -ɑ̃t] **1** *adj (non absent, actuel)* present

2 *nm (temps)* present; *Grammaire* present (tense); **à p.** at present, now; **dès à p.** as from now

présent² [prezɑ̃] *nm Littéraire (cadeau)* present; **faire p. de qch à qn** to present sth to sb

présenter [prezɑ̃te] **1** *vt (montrer)* to show, to present; *(facture)* to submit; *(arguments)* to present; **p. qn à qn** to introduce sb to sb

2 *vi Fam* **elle présente bien** she looks good

3 se présenter *vpr (dire son nom)* to

introduce oneself (**à** to); *(chez qn)* to show up; *(occasion)* to arise; **se p. à** *(examen)* to take, *Br* to sit for; *(élections)* to run in; *(emploi)* to apply for; *(autorités)* to report to; **ça se présente bien** it looks promising • **présentable** *adj* presentable • **présentateur, -trice** *nmf* presenter • **présentation** *nf* presentation; *(de personnes)* introduction; **faire les présentations** to make the introductions; **p. de mode** fashion show

présentoir [prezãtwar] *nm* display unit

préservatif [prezɛrvatif] *nm* condom

> ⚠ Il faut noter que le nom anglais **preservative** est un faux ami. Il signifie **agent de conservation**.

préserver [prezɛrve] *vt* to protect, to preserve (**de** from) • **préservation** *nf* protection, preservation

présidence [prezidãs] *nf (de nation)* presidency; *(de firme)* chairmanship • **président, -ente** *nmf (de nation)* president; *(de firme)* chairman, *f* chairwoman; **p.-directeur général** *Br* (chairman and) managing director, *Am* chief executive officer; **p. du jury** *(d'examen)* chief examiner; *(de tribunal)* foreman of the jury • **présidentiel, -ielle** *adj* presidential

présider [prezide] *vt (réunion)* to chair; *(conseil)* to preside over

présomption [prezɔ̃psjɔ̃] *nf* presumption

présomptueux, -ueuse [prezɔ̃ptɥø, -ɥøz] *adj* presumptuous

presque [prɛsk] *adv* almost, nearly; **p. jamais/rien** hardly ever/anything

presqu'île [prɛskil] *nf* peninsula

presse [prɛs] *nf Tech* press; *Typ* (printing) press; **la p.** *(journaux)* the press; **la p. à sensation** the tabloids; **conférence de p.** press conference

pressentir* [presãtir] *vt (deviner)* to sense (**que** that) • **pressentiment** *nm* presentiment; *(de malheur)* foreboding

presser [prese] **1** *vt (serrer)* to squeeze; *(raisin)* to press; *(sonnette, bouton)* to press, to push; **p. qn** to hurry sb; **p. qn de questions** to bombard sb with questions; **p. qn de faire qch** to urge sb to do sth; **p. le pas** to speed up

2 *vi* **le temps presse** there's not much time left; **rien ne presse** there's no hurry

3 se presser *vpr (se hâter)* to hurry (**de faire** to do); *(se serrer)* to squeeze (together); *(se grouper)* to crowd (**autour de** around) • **pressant, -ante** *adj* urgent, pressing • **pressé, -ée** *adj (personne)* in a

hurry; *(air)* hurried • **presse-citron** *nm inv* lemon squeezer • **presse-papiers** *nm inv* paperweight; *Ordinat* clipboard • **presse-purée** *nm inv* potato masher

pressing [presiŋ] *nm* dry cleaner's

pression [presjɔ̃] *nf Tech* pressure; *(bouton)* snap (fastener); *Fam (bière) Br* draught beer, *Am* draft beer; **faire p. sur qn** to put pressure on sb, to pressurize sb; **subir des pressions** to be under pressure

pressoir [preswar] *nm (instrument)* press

pressuriser [presyrize] *vt (avion)* to pressurize • **pressurisation** *nf* pressurization

prestance [prestãs] *nf* presence

prestataire [prestatɛr] *nmf* **p. de service** service provider; *Ordinat* **p. d'accès** access provider

prestation [prestasjɔ̃] *nf* **(a)** *(allocation)* benefit; **prestations** *(services)* services; **prestations sociales** *Br* social security benefits, *Am* welfare payments **(b)** *(de comédien)* performance

prestidigitateur, -trice [prestidiʒitatœr, -tris] *nmf* conjurer • **prestidigitation** *nf* **tour de p.** conjuring trick

prestige [prestiʒ] *nm* prestige • **prestigieux, -ieuse** *adj* prestigious

présumer [prezyme] *vt* to presume (**que** that); **p. de qch** to overestimate sth

présupposer [presypoze] *vt* to presuppose (**que** that)

prêt¹, prête [prɛ, prɛt] *adj (préparé)* ready (**à faire** to do; **à qch** for sth); **être fin p.** to be all set; **être p. à tout** to be prepared to do anything • **prêt-à-porter** [prɛtaporte] *nm* ready-to-wear clothes

prêt² [prɛ] *nm (somme)* loan

prétendre [pretãdr] **1** *vt (déclarer)* to claim (**que** that); *(vouloir)* to intend (**faire** to do); **à qu'il prétend** according to him; **on le prétend fou** they say he's mad

2 *vi* **p. à** *(titre)* to lay claim to

3 se prétendre *vpr* to claim to be • **prétendant** *nm (amoureux)* suitor • **prétendu, -ue** *adj (progrès)* so-called; *(coupable)* alleged • **prétendument** *adv* supposedly

> ⚠ Il faut noter que le verbe anglais **to pretend** est un faux ami. Il signifie le plus souvent **faire semblant**.

prétentieux, -ieuse [pretãsjø, -jøz] *adj* pretentious • **prétention** *nf (vanité)* pretension; *(revendication, ambition)* claim; **sans p.** *(film, robe)* unpretentious

prêter [prete] **1** *vt (argent, objet)* to lend (**à** to); *(aide)* to give (**à** to); *(propos, inten-*

tion) to attribute (**à** to); **p. attention** to pay attention (**à** to); **p. serment** to take an oath; **p. main-forte à qn** to lend sb a hand

2 *vi* **p. à confusion** to give rise to confusion

3 se prêter *vpr* **se p. à** *(consentir)* to agree to; *(convenir)* to lend itself to • **prêteur, -euse** [prɛtœr, -øz] *nmf* lender; **p. sur gages** pawnbroker

prétérit [preterit] *nm Grammaire* preterite (tense)

prétexte [pretɛkst] *nm* excuse, pretext; **sous p. de/que** on the pretext of/that; **sous aucun p.** under no circumstances • **prétexter** *vt* to plead (**que** that)

prêtre [prɛtr] *nm* priest

preuve [prœv] *nf* piece of evidence; **preuves** evidence; **faire p. de qch** to prove sth; **faire p. de courage** to show courage; **faire ses preuves** *(personne)* to prove oneself; *(méthode)* to be tried and tested; **p. d'amour** token of love

prévaloir* [prevalwar] *vi* to prevail (**sur** over)

prévenant, -ante [prevnɑ̃, -ɑ̃t] *adj* considerate

prévenir* [prevnir] *vt* (**a**) *(mettre en garde)* to warn; *(aviser)* to inform (**de** of or about) (**b**) *(maladie)* to prevent; *(accident)* to avert • **préventif, -ive** *adj* preventive; **détention préventive** custody • **prévention** *nf* prevention; **p. routière** road safety • **prévenu, -ue** *nmf Jur* defendant, accused

prévisible [previzibl] *adj* foreseeable

prévision [previzjɔ̃] *nf* forecast; **en p. de** in expectation of; **prévisions météorologiques** weather forecast

prévoir* [prevwar] *vt (météo)* to forecast; *(difficultés, retard, réaction)* to expect; *(organiser)* to plan; **un repas est prévu** a meal is provided; **la réunion est prévue pour demain** the meeting is scheduled for tomorrow; **comme prévu** as planned; **plus tôt que prévu** earlier than expected; **prévu pour** *(véhicule, appareil)* designed for

prévoyant, -ante [prevwajɑ̃, -ɑ̃t] *adj* far-sighted • **prévoyance** *nf* foresight

prier [prije] **1** *vi Rel* to pray

2 *vt (Dieu)* to pray to; *(supplier)* to beg; **p. qn de faire qch** to ask sb to do sth; **je vous en prie** *(faites-le)* please; *(en réponse à 'merci')* don't mention it; **sans se faire p.** without hesitation; **il ne s'est pas fait p.** he didn't need much persuading

prière [prijɛr] *nf Rel* prayer; *(demande)* request; **p. de répondre** please answer

primaire [primɛr] **1** *adj* primary; **école p.** *Br* primary school, *Am* elementary school

2 *nm Scol Br* primary *or Am* elementary education; **entrer en p.** to be at *Br* primary *or Am* elementary school

primauté [primote] *nf* primacy

prime [prim] **1** *nf (sur salaire)* bonus; *(d'État)* subsidy; **en p.** *(cadeau)* as a free gift; **p. (d'assurance)** *(insurance)* premium; **p. de fin d'année** ≃ Christmas bonus; **p. de licenciement** severance allowance; **p. de transport** transport allowance

2 *adj* **de p. abord** at the very first glance

primé, -ée [prime] *adj (film, animal)* prizewinning

primer [prime] *vi* to come first; **p. sur qch** to take precedence over sth

primeurs [primœr] *nfpl* early fruit and vegetables

primevère [primvɛr] *nf* primrose

primitif, -ive [primitif, -iv] *adj (société, art)* primitive; *(état, sens)* original

primo [primo] *adv* first(ly)

primordial, -e, -iaux, -iales [primɔrdjal, -jo] *adj* vital (**de faire** to do)

prince [prɛ̃s] *nm* prince • **princesse** *nf* princess • **princier, -ière** *adj* princely • **principauté** *nf* principality

principal, -e, -aux, -ales [prɛ̃sipal, -o] **1** *adj* main, principal; *(rôle)* leading

2 *nm (de collège)* principal, *Br* headmaster, *f* headmistress; **le p.** *(l'essentiel)* the main thing • **principalement** *adv* mainly

principe [prɛ̃sip] *nm* principle; **en p.** theoretically, in principle; **par p.** on principle

printemps [prɛ̃tɑ̃] *nm* spring; **au p.** in the spring • **printanier, -ière** *adj* **température printanière** spring-like temperature

priorité [prijɔrite] *nf* priority (**sur** over); *Aut* right of way; *Aut* **avoir la p.** to have (the) right of way; *Aut* **p. à droite** right of way to traffic coming from the right; **'cédez la p.'** *Br* 'give way', *Am* 'yield'; **en p.** as a matter of priority • **prioritaire** *adj* **secteur p.** priority sector; **être p.** to have priority; *Aut* to have (the) right of way

pris, prise¹ [pri, priz] **1** *pp de* **prendre**

2 *adj (place)* taken; **avoir le nez p.** to have a blocked nose; **être p.** *(occupé)* to be busy; *(candidat)* to be accepted; **p. de** *(peur)* seized with; **p. de panique** panic-stricken

prise² [priz] *nf (action)* taking; *(objet saisi)* catch; *(manière d'empoigner)* grip; *(de* *judo)* hold; *(de tabac)* pinch; **lâcher p.** to lose one's grip; *Fig* **être aux prises avec qn/qch** to be struggling with sb/sth; **p. de sang** blood test; **faire une p. de sang à qn** to take a blood sample from sb; *Él* **p. (de courant)** *(mâle)* plug; *(femelle)* socket; *Él* **p. multiple** adaptor; **p. de conscience** awareness; **p. de contact** first meeting; *Fig* **p. de position** stand; **p. d'otages** hostage-taking; *Cin & TV* **p. de son** sound recording; *Cin & Phot* **p. de vue** *(action)* shooting; *(de tournage)* take; *(cliché)* shot

priser¹ [prize] **1** *vt* **p. du tabac** to take snuff
2 *vi* to take snuff

priser² [prize] *vt Littéraire (estimer)* to prize

prisme [prism] *nm* prism

prison [prizɔ̃] *nf* prison, jail; *(peine)* imprisonment; **être en p.** to be in prison *or* in jail; **mettre qn en p.** to put sb in prison, to jail sb • **prisonnier, -ière** *nmf* prisoner; **faire qn p.** to take sb prisoner; **p. de guerre** prisoner of war

privation [privasjɔ̃] *nf* deprivation (**de** of); **privations** *(manque)* hardship

privatiser [privatize] *vt* to privatize • **privatisation** *nf* privatization

privé, -ée [prive] **1** *adj* private
2 *nm* **le p.** the private sector; *Scol* the private education system; **en p.** in private; **dans le p.** privately; *(travailler)* in the private sector

priver [prive] **1** *vt* to deprive (**de** of)
2 se priver *vpr* **se p. de** to do without, to deprive oneself of

privilège [privilɛʒ] *nm* privilege • **privilégié, -iée** *adj* privileged

prix [pri] *nm (coût)* price; *(récompense)* prize; **à tout p.** at all costs; **à aucun p.** on no account; **hors de p.** exorbitant; **attacher du p. à qch** to attach importance to sth; **faire un p. à qn** to give sb a special price; **p. de revient** cost price; **p. de vente** selling price

proactif, -ive [prɔaktif, -iv] *adj* proactive

probable [prɔbabl] *adj* likely, probable; **peu p.** unlikely • **probabilité** *nf* probability, likelihood; **selon toute p.** in all probability • **probablement** [-əmɑ̃] *adv* probably

probant, -ante [prɔbɑ̃, -ɑ̃t] *adj* conclusive

probité [prɔbite] *nf* integrity

problème [prɔblɛm] *nm* problem • **problématique** *adj* problematic

procédé [prɔsede] *nm (technique)* pro-cess; *(méthode)* method; **p. de fabrication** manufacturing process

procéder [prɔsede] *vi (agir)* to proceed; **p. à** *(enquête, arrestation)* to carry out; **p. par élimination** to follow a process of elimination • **procédure** *nf (méthode)* procedure; *(règles juridiques)* procedure; *(procès)* proceedings

procès [prɔsɛ] *nm (criminel)* trial; *(civil)* lawsuit; **faire un p. à qn** to take sb to court

processeur [prɔsesœr] *nm Ordinat* processor

procession [prɔsesjɔ̃] *nf* procession

processus [prɔsesys] *nm* process

procès-verbal [prɔsɛvɛrbal] (*pl* **procès-verbaux** [-o]) *nm (amende)* fine; *(constat)* report; *(de réunion)* minutes

prochain, -aine [prɔʃɛ̃, -ɛn] **1** *adj* next; *(mort, arrivée)* impending; *(mariage)* forthcoming; **un jour p.** one day soon
2 *nf Fam* **je descends à la prochaine** I'll get off at the next station; **à la prochaine!** see you soon!
3 *nm (semblable)* fellow (man) • **prochainement** *adv* shortly, soon

proche [prɔʃ] *adj (dans l'espace)* near, close; *(dans le temps)* near, imminent; *(parent, ami)* close; **p. de** near (to), close to; **de p. en p.** step by step; **le P.-Orient** the Middle East • **proches** *nmpl* close relations

proclamer [prɔklame] *vt* to proclaim (**que** that); **p. qn roi** to proclaim sb king • **proclamation** *nf* proclamation

procréer [prɔkree] *vi* to procreate • **procréation** *nf* procreation; **p. médicalement assistée** assisted conception

procuration [prɔkyrasjɔ̃] *nf* power of attorney; **par p.** by proxy

procurer [prɔkyre] **1** *vt* **p. qch à qn** *(sujet: personne)* to get sth for sb; *(sujet: chose)* to bring sb sth
2 se procurer *vpr* **se p. qch** to obtain sth

procureur [prɔkyrœr] *nm* **p. de la République** *Br* ≃ public prosecutor, *Am* ≃ district attorney

prodige [prɔdiʒ] *nm (miracle)* wonder; *(personne)* prodigy; **tenir du p.** to be extraordinary • **prodigieux, -ieuse** *adj* prodigious

prodigue [prɔdig] *adj (dépensier)* wasteful; *(généreux)* lavish (**de** with)

prodiguer [prɔdige] *vt* **p. qch à qn** to lavish sth on sb; **p. des conseils à qn** to pour out advice to sb

production [prɔdyksjɔ̃] *nf* production; *(produit)* product; *(d'usine)* output • **producteur, -trice 1** *nmf* producer **2** *adj* producing; **pays p. de pétrole** oil-producing country ●**productif, -ive** *adj* productive ●**productivité** *nf* productivity

produire* [prɔdɥir] **1** *vt (marchandise, émission, gaz)* to produce; *(effet, résultat)* to produce, to bring about

2 se produire *vpr (événement)* to happen, to occur; *(acteur)* to perform ●**produit** *nm (article)* product; *(de vente, de collecte)* proceeds; **produits agricoles** farm produce; **p. de beauté** cosmetic; **p. de consommation courante** basic consumer product; **p. chimique** chemical; *Écon* **p. national brut** gross national product; *Écon* **p. intérieur brut** gross domestic product; **produits ménagers** cleaning products

proéminent, -ente [prɔeminã, -ãt] *adj* prominent

prof [prɔf] *nm Fam* teacher

profane [prɔfan] **1** *adj* secular

2 *nmf* lay person

profaner [prɔfane] *vt* to desecrate ●**profanation** *nf* desecration

proférer [prɔfere] *vt* to utter

professer [prɔfese] *vt* to profess (**que** that)

professeur [prɔfɛsœr] *nm* teacher; *(à l'université)* professor; **p. principal** *Br* class or form teacher, *Am* homeroom teacher

profession [prɔfɛsjɔ̃] *nf* occupation, profession; *(manuelle)* trade; **sans p.** not gainfully employed; **de p.** *(chanteur)* professional; **p. libérale** profession; **p. de foi** *Rel* profession of faith; *Fig* declaration of principles ●**professionnel, -elle 1** *adj* professional; *(enseignement)* vocational **2** *nmf* professional

profil [prɔfil] *nm* profile; **de p.** (viewed) from the side; **p. de poste** job description ●**se profiler** *vpr* to be outlined (**sur** against)

profit [prɔfi] *nm* profit; **tirer p. de qch** to benefit from sth; **mettre qch à p.** to put sth to good use; **au p. des pauvres** in aid of the poor ●**profitable** *adj* profitable (**à** to) ●**profiter** *vi* **p. de** to take advantage of; **p. de la vie** to make the most of life; **p. à qn** to benefit sb, to be of benefit to sb ●**profiteur, -euse** *nmf Péj* profiteer

profond, -onde [prɔfɔ̃, -ɔ̃d] **1** *adj* deep; *(joie, erreur)* profound; *(cause)* underlying; **p. de 2 m** 2 m deep

2 *adv* deep

3 *nm* **au plus p. de la terre** in the depths of the earth ●**profondément** *adv* deeply; *(dormir)* soundly; *(triste, ému)* pro-

foundly; *(creuser)* deep ●**profondeur** *nf* depth; **faire 6 m de p.** to be 6 m deep; **à 6 m de p.** at a depth of 6 m; **en p.** *(étude)* in-depth

profusion [prɔfyzjɔ̃] *nf* profusion; **à p.** in profusion

progéniture [prɔʒenityr] *nf* offspring

progiciel [prɔʒisjɛl] *nm Ordinat* (software) package

programmable [prɔgramabl] *adj* programmable ●**programmation** *nf Radio & TV* programme planning; *Ordinat* programming

programmateur [prɔgramatœr] *nm Tech* automatic control (device)

programme [prɔgram] *nm Br* programme, *Am* program; *(de parti politique)* manifesto; *Scol* curriculum; *(d'un cours)* syllabus; *Ordinat* program ●**programmer** *vt Ordinat* to program; *Radio, TV & Cin* to schedule ●**programmeur, -euse** *nmf* (computer) programmer

progrès [prɔgrɛ] *nm & nmpl* progress; **faire des p.** to make (good) progress ●**progresser** *vi* to progress ●**progressif, -ive** *adj* progressive ●**progression** *nf* progression ●**progressiste** *adj & nmf* progressive ●**progressivement** *adv* progressively

prohiber [prɔibe] *vt* to prohibit, to forbid ●**prohibitif, -ive** *adj* prohibitive ●**prohibition** *nf* prohibition

proie [prwa] *nf* prey; *Fig* **être la p. de qn** to fall prey to sb; **être la p. des flammes** to be consumed by fire; *Fig* **en p. au doute** racked with doubt

projecteur [prɔʒɛktœr] *nm (de monument, de stade)* floodlight; *(de prison, d'armée)* searchlight; *Théâtre* spotlight; *Cin* projector

projectile [prɔʒɛktil] *nm* missile

projection [prɔʒɛksjɔ̃] *nf (d'objet, de film)* projection; *(séance)* screening

projet [prɔʒɛ] *nm (intention)* plan; *(étude)* project; **faire des projets d'avenir** to make plans for the future; **p. de loi** bill

projeter [prɔʒte] *vt (lancer)* to project; *(liquide, boue)* to splash; *(lumière)* to flash; *(film)* to show; *(ombre)* to cast; *(prévoir)* to plan; **p. de faire qch** to plan to do sth

prolétaire [prɔleter] *nmf* proletarian ●**prolétariat** *nm* proletariat ●**prolétarien, -ienne** *adj* proletarian

proliférer [prɔlifere] *vi* to proliferate ●**prolifération** *nf* proliferation

prolifique [prɔlifik] *adj* prolific

prolixe [prɔliks] *adj* verbose, wordy

prologue [prɔlɔg] *nm* prologue (**de** to)
prolonger [prɔlɔ̃ʒe] **1** *vt (vie, débat, séjour)* to prolong; *(mur, route)* to extend
2 se prolonger *vpr (séjour)* to be prolonged; *(réunion)* to go on; *(rue)* to continue • **prolongation** *nf (de séjour)* extension; *Football* **prolongations** extra time • **prolongement** *nm (de rue)* continuation; *(de mur)* extension; **prolongements** *(d'affaires)* repercussions
promenade [prɔmnad] *nf (à pied)* walk; *(courte)* stroll; *(avenue)* promenade; **faire une p.** to go for a walk; **faire une p. à cheval** to go for a ride
promener [prɔmne] **1** *vt (personne, chien)* to take for a walk; *(visiteur)* to show around; **p. qch sur qch** *(main, regard)* to run sth over sth
2 se promener *vpr (à pied)* to go for a walk • **promeneur, -euse** *nmf* stroller, walker
promesse [prɔmɛs] *nf* promise; **tenir sa p.** to keep one's promise
promettre* [prɔmɛtr] **1** *vt* to promise (**qch à qn** sb sth; **que** that); **p. de faire qch** to promise to do sth; **c'est promis** it's a promise
2 *vi Fig* to be promising
3 se promettre *vpr* **se p. qch** *(à soi-même)* to promise oneself sth; *(l'un l'autre)* to promise each other sth; **se p. de faire qch** *(à soi-même)* to resolve to do sth • **prometteur, -euse** *adj* promising
promontoire [prɔmɔ̃twar] *nm* headland
promoteur [prɔmɔtœr] *nm* **p. (immobilier)** property developer
promotion [prɔmosjɔ̃] *nf* **(a)** *(avancement)* & *Com* promotion; **en p.** *(produit)* on (special) offer; **p. sociale** upward mobility **(b)** *(d'une école) Br* year, *Am* class • **promouvoir*** *vt (personne, produit)* to promote; **être promu** *(employé)* to be promoted (**à** to)
prompt, prompte [prɔ̃, prɔ̃t] *adj* prompt; **p. à faire qch** quick to do sth • **promptitude** *nf* promptness
promulguer [prɔmylge] *vt* to promulgate
prôner [prone] *vt* to advocate
pronom [prɔnɔ̃] *nm Grammaire* pronoun • **pronominal, -e, -aux, -ales** *adj Grammaire* pronominal
prononcer [prɔnɔ̃se] **1** *vt (articuler)* to pronounce; *(dire)* to utter; *(discours)* to deliver; *(jugement)* to pronounce
2 se prononcer *vpr (mot)* to be pronounced; *(personne)* to give one's opinion (**sur** about *or* on); **se p. pour/contre**

qch to come out in favour of/against sth
• **prononcé, -ée** *adj* pronounced, marked
• **prononciation** *nf* pronunciation
pronostic [prɔnɔstik] *nm* forecast; *Méd* prognosis • **pronostiquer** *vt* to forecast
propagande [prɔpagɑ̃d] *nf* propaganda
propager [prɔpaʒe] *vt*, **se propager** *vpr* to spread • **propagation** *nf* spreading
propension [prɔpɑ̃sjɔ̃] *nf* propensity (**à qch** for sth; **à faire** to do)
prophète [prɔfɛt] *nm* prophet • **prophétie** [-fesi] *nf* prophecy • **prophétique** *adj* prophetic
propice [prɔpis] *adj* favourable (**à** to); **le moment p.** the right moment
proportion [prɔpɔrsjɔ̃] *nf* proportion; **respecter les proportions** to get the proportions right; **en p. de** in proportion to; **hors de p.** out of proportion (**avec** to); **l'affaire a pris des proportions considérables** the affair has blown up into a scandal • **proportionné, -ée** *adj* proportionate (**à** to); **bien p.** well-proportioned • **proportionnel, -elle 1** *adj* proportional (**à** to)
2 *nf* **proportionnelle** *(scrutin)* proportional representation
propos [prɔpo] *nm (sujet)* subject; *(intention)* purpose; **des p.** *(paroles)* talk, words; **à p. de qn/qch** about sb/sth; **à tout p.** constantly; **à p.** *(arriver)* at the right time; **à p.!** by the way!; **c'est à quel p.?** what is it about?; **juger à p. de faire qch** to consider it fit to do sth
proposer [prɔpoze] **1** *vt (suggérer)* to suggest, to propose (**qch à qn** sth to sb; **que** + *subjunctive* that); *(offrir)* to offer (**qch à qn** sb sth; **de faire** to do); **je te propose de rester** I suggest (that) you stay
2 se proposer *vpr* to offer one's services; **se p. pour faire qch** to offer to do sth; **se p. de faire qch** to propose to do sth • **proposition** *nf* suggestion, proposal; *(offre)* offer; *Grammaire* clause; **faire une p. à qn** to make a suggestion to sb
propre¹ [prɔpr] **1** *adj* clean; *(soigné)* neat; **p. comme un sou neuf** spick and span
2 *nm* **mettre qch au p.** to make a fair copy of sth; *Fam* **c'est du p.!** what a shocking way to behave! • **proprement¹** [-əmɑ̃] *adv (avec propreté)* cleanly; *(avec soin)* neatly • **propreté** [-əte] *nf* cleanliness; *(soin)* neatness
propre² [prɔpr] **1** *adj (à soi)* own; **mon p. argent** my own money; **ses propres mots** his/her very words; **être p. à qn/qch** *(particulier)* to be characteristic of sb/

sth; **être p. à qch** *(adapté)* to be suitable for sth; **au sens p.** literally **2** *nm* **le p. de** *(qualité)* the distinctive quality of; **au p.** *(au sens propre)* literally • **proprement²** [-əmã] *adv (strictement)* strictly; **à p. parler** strictly speaking; **le village p. dit** the village proper

> 🖉 Il faut noter que l'adjectif anglais **proper** est un faux ami. Il ne se rapporte jamais à la propreté.

propriétaire [prɔprijetɛr] *nmf* owner; *(de location)* landlord, *f* landlady; **p. foncier** landowner
propriété [prɔprijete] *nf (fait de posséder)* ownership; *(chose possédée)* property; *(caractéristique)* property; **p. privée** private property; **p. littéraire** copyright

> 🖉 Il faut noter que le nom anglais **propriety** est un faux ami. Il signifie **bienséance**.

propulser [prɔpylse] *vt* to propel • **propulsion** *nf* propulsion; **sous-marin à p. nucléaire** nuclear-powered submarine
prosaïque [prozaik] *adj* prosaic
proscrire* [prɔskrir] *vt* to proscribe, to ban • **proscrit, -ite** *nmf Littéraire (banni)* exile
prose [proz] *nf* prose
prospecter [prɔspɛkte] *vt (sol)* to prospect; *(clients)* to canvass • **prospecteur, -trice** *nmf* prospector • **prospection** *nf (de sol)* prospecting; *Com* canvassing
prospectus [prɔspɛktys] *nm* leaflet
prospère [prɔspɛr] *adj* prosperous; *(santé)* glowing • **prospérer** *vi* to prosper • **prospérité** *nf* prosperity
prostate [prɔstat] *nf Anat* prostate (gland)
prosterner [prɔstɛrne] **se prosterner** *vpr* to prostrate oneself (**devant** before)
prostituer [prɔstitɥe] **1** *vt* to prostitute **2 se prostituer** *vpr* to prostitute oneself • **prostituée** *nf* prostitute • **prostitution** *nf* prostitution
prostré, -ée [prɔstre] *adj* prostrate
protagoniste [prɔtagɔnist] *nmf* protagonist
protecteur, -trice [prɔtɛktœr, -tris] **1** *nmf* protector; *(mécène)* patron **2** *adj (geste, crème)* protective; *Péj (ton, air)* patronizing • **protection** *nf* protection; **de p.** *(écran)* protective; **assurer la p. de qn** to ensure sb's safety; **p. de l'environnement** protection of the environment; **p. sociale** social welfare system • **protectionnisme** *nm Écon* protectionism

protéger [prɔteʒe] **1** *vt* to protect (**de** from; **contre** against) **2 se protéger** *vpr* to protect oneself • **protégé** *nm* protégé • **protège-cahier** *(pl* **protège-cahiers)** *nm* exercise book cover • **protégée** *nf* protégée
protéine [prɔtein] *nf* protein
protestant, -ante [prɔtɛstã, -ãt] *adj & nmf* Protestant • **protestantisme** *nm* Protestantism
protester [prɔtɛste] *vi* to protest (**contre** against); **p. de son innocence** to protest one's innocence • **protestataire** *nmf* protester • **protestation** *nf* protest (**contre** against); **en signe de p.** as a protest; **protestations d'amitiés** protestations of friendship
prothèse [prɔtɛz] *nf* prosthesis; **p. auditive** hearing aid; **p. dentaire** false teeth
protocole [prɔtɔkɔl] *nm* protocol
prototype [prɔtɔtip] *nm* prototype
protubérance [prɔtyberãs] *nf* protuberance
proue [pru] *nf* bows, prow
prouesse [pruɛs] *nf* feat
prouver [pruve] *vt* to prove (**que** that)
Provence [prɔvãs] *nf* **la P.** Provence • **provençal, -e, -aux, -ales 1** *adj* Provençal **2** *nmf* **P., Provençale** Provençal
provenir* [prɔvənir] *vi* **p. de** to come from • **provenance** *nf* origin; **en p. de** from
proverbe [prɔvɛrb] *nm* proverb • **proverbial, -e, -iaux, -iales** *adj* proverbial
providence [prɔvidãs] *nf* providence • **providentiel, -ielle** *adj* providential
province [prɔvɛ̃s] *nf* province; **la p.** the provinces; **en p.** in the provinces; **de p.** *(ville)* provincial • **provincial, -e, -iaux, -iales** *adj & nmf* provincial
proviseur [prɔvizœr] *nm Br* headmaster, *f* headmistress, *Am* principal
provision [prɔvizjɔ̃] *nf* **(a)** *(réserve)* supply, stock; **provisions** *(nourriture)* shopping; **panier/sac à provisions** shopping basket/bag; **faire des provisions de qch** to stock up on sth **(b)** *(somme)* credit; *(acompte)* deposit
provisoire [prɔvizwar] *adj* temporary; **à titre p.** temporarily • **provisoirement** *adv* temporarily, provisionally
provoquer [prɔvɔke] *vt (incendie, mort)* to cause; *(réaction)* to provoke; *(colère, désir)* to arouse; **p. un accouchement** to induce labour • **provocant, -ante** *adj* provocative • **provocateur** *nm* troublemaker • **provocation** *nf* provocation
proxénète [prɔksenɛt] *nm* pimp
proximité [prɔksimite] *nf* closeness,

proximity; **à p.** close by; **à p. de** close to; **de p.** local

prude [pryd] **1** *adj* prudish **2** *nf* prude

prudent, -ente [prydã, -ãt] *adj (personne)* cautious, careful; *(décision)* sensible •**prudemment** [-amã] *adv* cautiously, carefully •**prudence** *nf* caution, care; **par p.** as a precaution

prune [pryn] *nf (fruit)* plum; *Fam* **pour des prunes** for nothing •**pruneau, -x** *nm* prune •**prunier** *nm* plum tree

> *⚠* Il faut noter que le nom anglais **prune** est un faux ami. Il signifie le plus souvent **pruneau**.

prunelle [prynɛl] *nf (de l'œil)* pupil; **il y tient comme à la p. de ses yeux** it's the apple of his eye

P.-S. [peɛs] *(abrév* **post-scriptum***)* PS

psaume [psom] *nm* psalm

pseudonyme [psødɔnim] *nm* pseudonym

psychanalyse [psikanaliz] *nf* psychoanalysis •**psychanalyste** *nmf* psychoanalyst

psychédélique [psikedelik] *adj* psychedelic

psychiatre [psikjatr] *nmf* psychiatrist •**psychiatrie** *nf* psychiatry •**psychiatrique** *adj* psychiatric

psychique [psiʃik] *adj* psychic

psychologie [psikɔlɔʒi] *nf* psychology •**psychologique** *adj* psychological •**psychologue** *nmf* psychologist; **p. scolaire** educational psychologist

psychose [psikoz] *nf* psychosis

PTT [petete] *(abrév* **Postes, Télécommunications et Télédiffusion***) nfpl Anciennement* ≃ Post Office and Telecommunications Service

pu [py] *pp de* **pouvoir 1**

puant, puante [pɥã, pɥãt] *adj* stinking •**puanteur** *nf* stink, stench

pub [pyb] *nf Fam (secteur)* advertising; *(annonce)* ad

puberté [pybɛrte] *nf* puberty

public, -ique [pyblik] **1** *adj* public; **dette publique** national debt **2** *nm (de spectacle)* audience; **le grand p.** the general public; **film grand p.** film suitable for the general public; **en p.** in public; *(émission)* before a live audience; *Écon* **le p.** the public sector •**publiquement** *adv* publicly

publication [pyblikasjɔ̃] *nf (action, livre)* publication •**publier** *vt* to publish

publicité [pyblisite] *nf (secteur)* advertising; *(annonce)* advertisement, advert; *Radio & TV* commercial; **agence de p.** advertising agency; **faire de la p. pour qch** to advertise sth •**publicitaire 1** *adj* **agence de p.** advertising agency; **film p.** promotional film **2** *nmf* advertising executive

puce [pys] *nf (insecte)* flea; *Ordinat* (micro-)chip; **le marché aux puces, les puces** the flea market; *Fig* **mettre la p. à l'oreille de qn** to make sb suspicious

puceron [pysrɔ̃] *nm* greenfly

pudeur [pydœr] *nf* modesty; **par p.** out of a sense of decency •**pudibond, -onde** *adj* prudish •**pudique** *adj* modest

puer [pɥe] **1** *vt* to stink of **2** *vi* to stink

puériculture [pɥerikyltyr] *nf* child care •**puéricultrice** *nf* nursery nurse

puéril, -ile [pɥeril] *adj* puerile •**puérilité** *nf* puerility

puis [pɥi] *adv* then; **et p.** *(ensuite)* and then; *(en plus)* and besides

puiser [pɥize] **1** *vt* to draw (**à/dans** from) **2** *vi* **p. dans qch** to dip into sth

puisque [pɥisk(ə)] *conj* since, as

puissant, -ante [pɥisã, -ãt] *adj* powerful •**puissamment** [-amã] *adv* powerfully •**puissance** *nf (force, nation) & Math* power; **les grandes puissances** the great powers; **en p.** *(meurtrier)* potential; *Math* **dix p. quatre** ten to the power of four

puisse(s), puissent [pɥis] *voir* **pouvoir 1**

puits [pɥi] *nm* well; *(de mine)* shaft; *Fig* **un p. de science** a fount of knowledge; **p. de pétrole** oil well

pull-over [pylɔver] *(pl* **pull-overs***)*, **pull** [pyl] *nm* sweater, *Br* jumper

pulluler [pylyle] *vi (abonder)* to swarm

pulmonaire [pylmɔnɛr] *adj* pulmonary

pulpe [pylp] *nf (de fruits)* pulp

pulsation [pylsasjɔ̃] *nf* (heart)beat

pulsion [pylsjɔ̃] *nf* impulse; **p. de mort** death wish

pulvériser [pylverize] *vt (vaporiser)* to spray; *(broyer) & Fig* to pulverize; *Fam Sport* **p. un record** to smash a record •**pulvérisateur** *nm* spray •**pulvérisation** *nf (de liquide)* spraying

puma [pyma] *nm* puma

punaise [pynɛz] *nf (insecte)* bug; *(clou) Br* drawing pin, *Am* thumbtack •**punaiser** *vt Fam* to pin up

punch *nm* (**a**) [pɔ̃ʃ] *(boisson)* punch (**b**) [pœnʃ] *Fam (énergie)* punch

punir [pynir] *vt* to punish; **p. qn de qch** *(bêtise, crime)* to punish sb for sth; **p. qn**

de mort to punish sb with death •**puni- tion** *nf* punishment

punk [pœnk] *adj inv* & *nmf* punk

pupille [pypij] **1** *nf (de l'œil)* pupil **2** *nmf (enfant)* ward; **p. de la Nation** war orphan

pupitre [pypitr] *nm (d'écolier)* desk; *(d'orateur)* lectern; *Ordinat* console; *Or- dinat* **p. de visualisation** visual display unit

pur, pure [pyr] *adj* pure; *(alcool)* neat, straight •**purement** *adv* purely; **p. et sim- plement** purely and simply •**pureté** *nf* purity

purée [pyre] *nf* purée; **p. (de pommes de terre)** mashed potatoes, *Br* mash

purgatoire [pyrgatwar] *nm* purgatory

purge [pyrʒ] *nf (à des fins médicales, politiques)* purge

purger [pyrʒe] *vt (patient)* to purge; *(ra- diateur)* to bleed; *(peine de prison)* to serve

purifier [pyrifje] *vt* to purify •**purifica- tion** *nf* purification; **p. ethnique** ethnic cleansing

purin [pyrɛ̃] *nm* liquid manure

puriste [pyrist] *nmf* purist

puritain, -aine [pyritɛ̃, -ɛn] *adj* & *nmf* puritan

pur-sang [pyrsɑ̃] *nm inv* thoroughbred

pus¹ [py] *nm (liquide)* pus, matter

pus², put [py] *voir* **pouvoir 1**

putain [pytɛ̃] *nf Vulg* whore

putois [pytwa] *nm* polecat

putréfier [pytrefje] *vt*, **se putréfier** *vpr* to putrefy •**putréfaction** *nf* putrefaction

puzzle [pœzl] *nm (jigsaw)* puzzle

P.-V. [peve] *(abrév* **procès-verbal**) *nm Fam* (parking) ticket

PVC [pevese] *nm (matière plastique)* PVC

pygmée [pigme] *nmf* pygmy

pyjama [piʒama] *nm Br* pyjamas, *Am* pajamas; **un p.** a pair of *Br* pyjamas *or Am* pajamas; **être en p.** to be in *Br* pyja- mas *orAm* pajamas

pylône [pilon] *nm* pylon

pyramide [piramid] *nf* pyramid

Pyrénées [pirene] *nfpl* **les P.** the Pyren- ees

Pyrex® [pirɛks] *nm* Pyrex®; **plat en P.** Pyrex® dish

pyromane [piroman] *nmf* arsonist

python [pitɔ̃] *nm* python

Q, q [ky] *nm inv* Q, q

QCM [kyseɛm] (*abrév* **questionnaire à choix multiple**) *nm* multiple-choice questionnaire

QI [kyi] (*abrév* **quotient intellectuel**) *nm inv* IQ

qu' [k] *voir* **que**

quadragénaire [kwadraʒenɛr] (*Fam* **quadra** [kwadra]) **1** *adj* être q. to be in one's forties **2** *nmf* person in his/her forties

quadrillage [kadrijaʒ] *nm* (*de carte*) grid

quadriller [kadrije] *vt* (*quartier, ville*) to put under tight surveillance; (*papier*) to mark into squares •**quadrillé, -ée** *adj* (*papier*) squared

quadrupède [k(w)adrypɛd] *adj & nm* quadruped

quadruple [k(w)adrypl] **1** *adj* fourfold **2** *nm* **le q. (de)** (*quantité*) four times as much (as); (*nombre*) four times as many (as) •**quadrupler** *vti* to quadruple •**quadruplés, -ées** *nmfpl* quadruplets

quai [kɛ] *nm* (*de port*) quay; (*de fleuve*) embankment; (*de gare, de métro*) platform

qualification [kalifikɑsjɔ̃] *nf* (*action, d'équipe, de sportif*) qualification; (*désignation*) description •**qualificatif 1** *adj* Grammaire qualifying **2** *nm* (*mot*) term

qualifier [kalifje] **1** *vt* (*équipe*) to qualify (**pour qch** for sth; **pour faire** to do); (*décrire*) to describe (**de** as) **2 se qualifier** *vpr* (*équipe*) to qualify (**pour** for) •**qualifié, -iée** *adj* (*équipe*) that has qualified; **q. pour faire qch** qualified to do sth

qualité [kalite] *nf* (*de personne, de produit*) quality; (*occupation*) occupation; **produit de q.** quality product; **de bonne q.** of good quality; **en q. de** in his/her/*etc* capacity as; **q. de vie** quality of life •**qualitatif, -ive** *adj* qualitative

quand [kɑ̃] *conj & adv* when; **q. je viendrai** when I come; **à q. le mariage?** when's the wedding?; **q. bien même vous le feriez** even if you did it; *Fam* **q. même** all the same

quant [kɑ̃] **quant à** *prép* as for

quantifier [kɑ̃tifje] *vt* to quantify •**quantitatif, -ive** *adj* quantitative

quantité [kɑ̃tite] *nf* quantity; **une q., des quantités** (*beaucoup*) a lot (**de** of); **en q.** in abundance

quarante [karɑ̃t] *adj & nm inv* forty; **un q.-cinq tours** (*disque*) a single •**quarantaine** *nf* (**a**) **une q. (de)** (*nombre*) (about) forty; **avoir la q.** (*âge*) to be about forty (**b**) *Méd* quarantine; **mettre qn en q.** to quarantine sb •**quarantième** *adj & nmf* fortieth

quart [kar] *nm* (**a**) (*fraction*) quarter; **q. de litre** quarter litre, quarter of a litre; **q. d'heure** quarter of an hour; **une heure et q.** an hour and a quarter; **il est une heure et q.** it's a quarter *Br* past *or Am* after one; **une heure moins le q.** quarter to one; *Fam* **passer un mauvais q. d'heure** to have a bad time of it; *Sport* **quarts de finale** quarter finals (**b**) *Naut* watch; **être de q.** to be on watch •**quart-monde** *nm* **le q.** the least developed countries

quarté [karte] *nm* = system of betting on four horses in the same race

quartette [kwartɛt] *nm* jazz quartet

quartier [kartje] *nm* (**a**) (*de ville*) district; **de q.** local; **les beaux quartiers** the fashionable district; **q. général** headquarters (**b**) (*de lune*) quarter; (*de pomme*) piece; (*d'orange*) segment (**c**) (*expressions*) **ne pas faire de q.** to give no quarter; **avoir q. libre** to be free

quartz [kwarts] *nm* quartz; **montre à q.** quartz watch

quasi [kazi] *adv* almost •**quasi-** *préf* **quasi-obscurité** near darkness; **la quasi-totalité des membres** almost all the members •**quasiment** *adv* almost

quatorze [katɔrz] *adj & nm inv* fourteen •**quatorzième** *adj & nmf* fourteenth

quatre [katr] *adj & nm inv* four; *Fig* **se mettre en q.** to bend over backwards (**pour faire** to do); *Fam* **manger comme q.** to eat like a horse; *Fam* **un de ces q.** some day soon; *Fam* **q. heures** (*goûter*) afternoon snack •**quatrième** *adj & nmf* fourth

quatre-vingt [katrəvɛ̃] *adj & nm* eighty;

quatre-vingts ans eighty years; **q.-un** eighty-one; **page q.** page eighty • **quatre-vingt-dix** adj & nm inv ninety

quatuor [kwatyɔr] nm quartet; **q. à cordes** string quartet

que [kə]

> que becomes **qu'** before a vowel or mute h.

1 conj (**a**) (complétif) that; **je pense qu'elle restera** I think (that) she'll stay; **qu'elle vienne ou non** whether she comes or not; **qu'il s'en aille!** let him leave!; **ça fait un an q. je suis là** I've been here for a year; **ça fait un an q. je suis parti** I left a year ago

(**b**) (de comparaison) than; (avec 'aussi', 'même', 'tel', 'autant') as; **plus/moins âgé q. lui** older/younger than him; **aussi sage/fatigué q. toi** as wise/tired as you; **le même q. Pauline** the same as Pauline (**c**) (**ne...**) que only; **tu n'as qu'un euro** you only have one euro

2 adv (**ce**) **qu'il est bête!** (comme) he's really stupid!; **q. de gens!** what a lot of people!

3 pron relatif (chose) that, which; (personne) that, whom; (temps) when; **le livre q. j'ai** the book (that or which) I have; **l'ami q. j'ai** the friend (that or whom) I have; **un jour qu'il faisait beau** one day when the weather was fine

4 pron interrogatif what; **q. fait-il?, qu'est-ce qu'il fait?** what is he doing?; **qu'est-ce qui est dans ta poche?** what's in your pocket?; **q. préférez-vous?** which do you prefer?

Québec [kebɛk] nm le Q. Quebec

quel, quelle [kɛl] **1** adj interrogatif (chose) what, which; (personne) which; **q. livre préférez-vous?** which or what book do you prefer?; **q. est cet homme?** who is that man?; **je sais q. est ton but I** know what your aim is; **je ne sais à q. employé m'adresser** I don't know which clerk to ask

2 pron interrogatif which (one); **q. est le meilleur?** which (one) is the best?

3 adj exclamatif **q. idiot!** what a fool!; **q. joli bébé!** what a pretty baby!

4 adj relatif **q. qu'il soit** (chose) whatever it may be; (personne) whoever it or he may be

quelconque [kɛlkɔ̃k] **1** adj indéfini any; **donne-moi un livre q.** give me any book; **sous un prétexte q.** on some pretext or other

2 adj (insignifiant) ordinary

quelque [kɛlk] **1** adj indéfini some; **quelques** some, a few; **les quelques amies qu'elle a** the few friends she has; **sous q. prétexte que ce soit** on whatever pretext; **q. numéro qu'elle choisisse** whichever number she chooses

2 adv (environ) about, some; **q. peu** somewhat; **q. grand qu'il soit** however tall he may be; Fam **100 euros et q.** 100 euros and a bit

quelque chose [kɛlkəʃoz] pron indéfini something; **q. d'autre** something else; **q. de grand** something big; **q. de plus pratique/de moins lourd** something more practical/less heavy; **ça m'a fait q.** it touched me

quelquefois [kɛlkəfwa] adv sometimes

quelque part [kɛlkəpar] adv somewhere; (dans les questions) anywhere

quelques-uns, -unes [kɛlkəzœ̃, -yn] pron some

quelqu'un [kɛlkœ̃] pron indéfini someone, somebody; (dans les questions) anyone, anybody; **q. d'intelligent** someone clever

quémander [kemɑ̃de] vt to beg for

qu'en-dira-t-on [kɑ̃diratɔ̃] nm le q. gossip

quenelle [kənɛl] nf Culin quenelle

querelle [kərɛl] nf quarrel; **chercher q. à qn** to try to pick a fight with sb • **se quereller** vpr to quarrel • **querelleur, -euse** adj quarrelsome

question [kɛstjɔ̃] nf (interrogation) question; (affaire) matter, question; **il est q. qu'ils déménagent** there's some talk about them moving; **il a été q. de vous** we/they talked about you; **il n'en est pas q.** it's out of the question; **en q.** in question; **hors de q.** out of the question; **remettre qch en q.** to call sth into question; **q. de confiance** vote of confidence • **questionnaire** nm questionnaire • **questionner** vt to question (**sur** about)

quête [kɛt] nf (**a**) (collecte) collection; **faire la q.** to collect money (**b**) (recherche) quest (**de** for); **en q. de** in quest or search of • **quêter** [kete] **1** vt to seek **2** vi to collect money

queue [kø] nf (**a**) (d'animal) tail; (de fleur, de fruit) stalk; (de poêle) handle; (de train, de cortège) rear; **être en q. de classement** to be bottom of the table; **faire une q. de poisson à qn** to cut in front of sb; **à la q. leu leu** in single file; **ça n'a ni q. ni tête** it just doesn't make sense; **q. de cheval** (coiffure) ponytail (**b**) (file) Br queue, Am line; **faire la q.** Br to queue up, Am to

stand in line (**c**) *(de billard)* cue •**queue-de-pie** *(pl* **queues-de-pie**) *nf Fam* tails
qui [ki] **1** *pron interrogatif (personne)* who; *(en complément)* whom; **q. (est-ce qui) est là?** who's there?; **q. désirez-vous voir?, q. est-ce que vous désirez voir?** who(m) do you want to see?; **à q. est ce livre?** whose book is this?; **q. encore?, q. d'autre?** who else?; **je demande q. a téléphoné** I'm asking who phoned
   2 *pron relatif* (**a**) *(sujet) (personne)* who, that; *(chose)* which, that; **l'homme q. est là** the man who's here *or* that's here; **la maison q. se trouve en face** the house which is *or* that's opposite
   (**b**) *(sans antécédent)* **q. que vous soyez** whoever you are; **amène q. tu veux** bring along anyone you like *or* whoever you like; **q. que ce soit** anyone
   (**c**) *(après une préposition)* **la femme de q. je parle** the woman I'm talking about; **l'ami sur l'aide de q. je compte** the friend on whose help I rely
quiche [kiʃ] *nf* quiche; **q. lorraine** quiche lorraine
quiconque [kikɔ̃k] *pron (sujet)* whoever; *(complément)* anyone
quiétude [kjetyd] *nf Littéraire* quiet; **en toute q.** *(sans souci)* with an easy mind
quignon [kiɲɔ̃] *nm* chunk
quille [kij] *nf (de navire)* keel; *(de jeu)* (bowling) pin, *Br* skittle; *Fam (jambe)* pin; **jouer aux quilles** to bowl, *Br* to play skittles
quincaillier, -ière [kɛ̃kaje, -jɛr] *nmf* hardware dealer, *Br* ironmonger •**quincaillerie** *nf (magasin)* hardware shop; *(objets)* hardware
quinine [kinin] *nf* quinine
quinquennal, -e, -aux, -ales [kɛ̃kenal, -o] *adj* **plan q.** five-year plan •**quinquennat** *nm Pol* five-year term (of office)
quinte [kɛ̃t] *nf* **q. (de toux)** coughing fit
quintessence [kɛ̃tesɑ̃s] *nf* quintessence
quintette [kɛ̃tɛt] *nm* quintet
quintuple [kɛ̃typl] **1** *adj* **q. de** fivefold
   2 *nm* **le q. (de)** *(quantité)* five times as much (as); *(nombre)* five times as many (as) •**quintupler** *vti* to increase fivefold

•**quintuplés, -ées** *nmfpl* quintuplets
quinze [kɛ̃z] *adj & nm inv* fifteen; **q. jours** two weeks, *Br* a fortnight; *Rugby* **le q. de France** the French fifteen •**quinzaine** *nf* **une q. (de)** (about) fifteen; **une q. (de jours)** two weeks, *Br* a fortnight •**quinzième** *adj & nmf* fifteenth
quiproquo [kiprɔko] *nm* mix-up
quittance [kitɑ̃s] *nf (reçu)* receipt; **q. de loyer** rent receipt
quitte [kit] *adj* quits (**envers** with); **q. à faire qch** even if it means doing sth; **en être q. pour qch** to get off with sth
quitter [kite] **1** *vt (personne, lieu, poste)* to leave; *(vêtement)* to take off; **q. la route** to go off the road; **ne pas q. qn des yeux** to keep one's eyes on sb
   2 *vi* **ne quittez pas!** *(au téléphone)* hold the line!
   3 se quitter *vpr* to part; **ils ne se quittent plus** they are inseparable
qui-vive [kiviv] **sur le qui-vive** *adv* on the alert
quoi [kwa] *pron* what; *(après une préposition)* which; **à q. penses-tu?** what are you thinking about?; **après q.** after which; **ce à q. je m'attendais** what I was expecting; **de q. manger** something to eat; *(assez)* enough to eat; **de q. écrire** something to write with; **q. que je dise** whatever I say; **q. qu'il advienne** whatever happens; **q. qu'il en soit** be that as it may; **il n'y a pas de q.!** *(en réponse à 'merci')* don't mention it!; **q.?** what?; *Fam* **c'est un idiot, q.!** he's a fool!; **et puis q. encore!** really, what next!
quoique [kwak] *conj* (al)though; **quoiqu'il soit pauvre** (al)though he's poor
quolibet [kɔlibɛ] *nm Littéraire* gibe
quorum [kwɔrɔm] *nm* quorum
quota [kwɔta] *nm* quota
quote-part [kɔtpar] *(pl* **quotes-parts**) *nf* share
quotidien, -ienne [kɔtidjɛ̃, -jɛn] **1** *adj* daily
   2 *nm* daily (paper) •**quotidiennement** *adv* daily
quotient [kɔsjɑ̃] *nm* quotient

R

R, r [er] *nm inv* R, r

rab [rab] *nm Fam (nourriture)* extra; **faire du r.** *(au travail)* to put in a bit of overtime

rabâcher [rabaʃe] **1** *vt* to repeat endlessly

2 *vi* to say the same thing over and over again

rabais [rabɛ] *nm* reduction, discount; **faire un r. à qn** to give sb a discount

rabaisser [rabese] **1** *vt (dénigrer)* to belittle

2 se rabaisser *vpr* to belittle oneself

rabat-joie [rabaʒwa] *nm inv* killjoy

rabattre* [rabatr] **1** *vt (col)* to turn down; *(couvercle)* to close; *(strapontin) (pour s'asseoir)* to fold down; *(en se levant)* to fold up; *(gibier)* to drive

2 se rabattre *vpr (se refermer)* to close; *(strapontin)* to fold down; *(véhicule)* to pull back in; *Fig* **se r. sur qch** to fall back on sth

rabbin [rabɛ̃] *nm* rabbi

rabibocher [rabibɔʃe] *Fam* **1** *vt* to patch things up between

2 se rabibocher *vpr* to patch things up (**avec** with)

rabiot [rabjo] *nm Fam* = rab

râblé, -ée [rable] *adj* stocky

rabot [rabo] *nm* plane • **raboter** *vt* to plane

raboteux, -euse [rabotø, -øz] *adj* uneven

rabougri, -ie [rabugri] *adj (personne, plante)* stunted

rabrouer [rabrue] *vt* to snub

racaille [rakaj] *nf* scum

raccommoder [rakɔmɔde] **1** *vt (linge)* to mend; *(chaussette)* to darn; *Fam (personnes)* to patch things up between

2 se raccommoder *vpr Fam* to patch things up (**avec** with) • **raccommodage** *nm (de linge)* mending; *(de chaussette)* darning

raccompagner [rakɔ̃paɲe] *vt* to take back

raccord [rakɔr] *nm (dispositif)* connection; *(de papier peint)* join; *(de peinture)* touch-up • **raccordement** [-əmɑ̃] *nm (action, lien)* connection • **raccorder** *vt,* **se raccorder** *vpr* to link up (**à** to)

raccourcir [rakursir] **1** *vt* to shorten

2 *vi* to get shorter • **raccourci** *nm* short cut; **en r.** in brief

raccrocher [rakrɔʃe] **1** *vt (objet tombé)* to hang back up; *(téléphone)* to put down

2 *vi (au téléphone)* to hang up; *Fam (sportif)* to retire

3 se raccrocher *vpr* **se r. à qch** to catch hold of sth; *Fig* to cling to sth

race [ras] *nf (ethnie)* race; *(animale)* breed; **chien de r.** pedigree dog • **racé, -ée** *adj (cheval)* thoroughbred; *(personne)* distinguished • **racial, -e, -iaux, -iales** *adj* racial • **racisme** *nm* racism • **raciste** *adj & nmf* racist

rachat [raʃa] *nm (de voiture, d'appartement)* repurchase; *(de firme)* buy-out; *Rel* atonement • **racheter** **1** *vt (acheter davantage)* to buy some more; *(remplacer)* to buy another; *(firme)* to buy out; *(péché)* to atone for; *(faute)* to make up for **2 se racheter** *vpr* to make amends, to redeem oneself

racine [rasin] *nf (de plante, de personne) & Math* root; **prendre r.** to take root

racket [raket] *nm Fam* racket

raclée [rakle] *nf Fam* thrashing; **prendre une r.** to get a thrashing

racler [rakle] **1** *vt* to scrape; *(peinture, boue)* to scrape off

2 se racler *vpr* **se r. la gorge** to clear one's throat • **raclette** *nf (outil)* scraper; *(plat)* raclette *(Swiss dish consisting of potatoes and melted cheese)* • **racloir** *nm* scraper

racoler [rakɔle] *vt (sujet: prostituée)* to solicit • **racolage** *nm (de prostituée)* soliciting • **racoleur, -euse** *adj (publicité)* eye-catching

raconter [rakɔ̃te] *vt (histoire, mensonge)* to tell; *(événement)* to tell about; **r. qch à qn** *(histoire)* to tell sb sth; *(événement)* to tell sb about sth; **r. à qn que...** to tell sb that...; *Fam* **qu'est-ce que tu racontes?** what are you talking about? • **racontars** *nmpl* gossip

racornir [rakɔrnir] *vt,* **se racornir** *vpr (durcir)* to harden; *(dessécher)* to shrivel

radar [radar] *nm* radar; **contrôle r.** radar

speed check; *Fam* **être au r.** to be on automatic pilot

rade [rad] *nf* harbour; *Fam* **laisser qn en r.** to leave sb in the lurch

radeau, -x [rado] *nm* raft

radiateur [radjatœr] *nm* radiator; **r. électrique** electric heater

radiation [radjɑsjɔ̃] *nf Phys* radiation; *(suppression)* removal (**de** from) • **radier** *vt* to strike off (**de** from)

radical, -e, -aux, -ales [radikal, -o] **1** *adj* radical
2 *nm (de mot)* stem

radieux, -ieuse [radjø, -jøz] *adj (personne, visage, soleil)* radiant; *(temps)* glorious

radin, -ine [radɛ̃, -in] *Fam* **1** *adj* stingy
2 *nmf* skinflint

radio [radjo] **1** *nf* (**a**) *(poste)* radio; *(station)* radio station; **à la r.** on the radio; **r. libre** = independent radio station (**b**) *Méd* X-ray; **passer une r.** to have an X-ray; **faire passer une r. à qn** to give sb an X-ray
2 *nm (opérateur)* radio operator • **radio-réveil** (*pl* **radios-réveils**) *nm* radio alarm clock

radioactif, -ive [radjoaktif, -iv] *adj* radioactive • **radioactivité** *nf* radioactivity

radiodiffuser [radjodifyse] *vt* to broadcast • **radiodiffusion** *nf* broadcasting

radiographie [radjografi] *nf (photo)* X-ray; *(technique)* radiography • **radiographier** *vt* to X-ray • **radiologie** *nf Méd* radiology • **radiologue** *nmf (technicien)* radiographer; *(médecin)* radiologist

radioguidé, -ée [radjogide] *adj* radio-controlled

radiophonique [radjofɔnik] *adj* **émission r.** radio broadcast • **radiotélévisé, -ée** *adj* broadcast on radio and television

radis [radi] *nm* radish; **r. noir** black radish; *Fam* **je n'ai plus un r.** I don't have a bean

radoter [radɔte] **1** *vt Fam* to go on and on about
2 *vi (rabâcher)* to go on and on; *(divaguer)* to ramble on • **radotage** *nm (divagations)* rambling

radoucir [radusir] **se radoucir** *vpr (personne)* to calm down; *(temps)* to become milder • **radoucissement** *nm (du temps)* milder spell

rafale [rafal] *nf (vent)* gust; *(de mitrailleuse)* burst; **par rafales** in gusts

raffermir [rafɛrmir] **1** *vt (autorité)* to strengthen; *(muscles)* to tone up

2 se raffermir *vpr (muscle)* to become stronger

raffiné, -ée [rafine] *adj* refined • **raffinement** *nm* refinement

raffiner [rafine] *vt* to refine • **raffinage** *nm* refining • **raffinerie** *nf* refinery

raffoler [rafɔle] *vi Fam* **r. de qch** to be mad about sth

raffut [rafy] *nm Fam* din; **faire du r.** to make a din

rafiot [rafjo] *nm Péj* old tub

rafistoler [rafistɔle] *vt Fam* to patch up

rafle [rɑfl] *nf* raid • **rafler** *vt Fam* to swipe

rafraîchir [rafreʃir] **1** *vt (rendre frais)* to chill; *(pièce)* to air; *(raviver)* to freshen up; *Fam* **r. la mémoire à qn** to refresh sb's memory
2 *vi* to cool down
3 se rafraîchir *vpr (temps)* to get cooler; *(se laver)* to freshen up; *Fam (boire)* to have a cold drink • **rafraîchissant, -ante** *adj* refreshing • **rafraîchissement** *nm (de température)* cooling; *(boisson)* cold drink

ragaillardir [ragajardir] *vt Fam* to buck up

rage [raʒ] *nf (colère)* rage; *(maladie)* rabies; **faire r.** *(incendie, tempête)* to rage; **r. de dents** violent toothache • **rageant, -ante** *adj Fam* infuriating • **rager** *vi Fam (personne)* to fume • **rageur, -euse** *adj (ton)* furious

ragots [rago] *nmpl Fam* gossip

ragoût [ragu] *nm Culin* stew

ragoûtant, -ante [ragutɑ̃, -ɑ̃t] *adj* **peu r.** *(plat)* unappetizing; *(personne)* unsavoury

rai [rɛ] *nm (de lumière)* ray

raid [rɛd] *nm* raid; **r. aérien** air raid

raide [rɛd] **1** *adj (rigide, guindé)* stiff; *(côte, escalier)* steep; *(cheveux)* straight; *(corde)* taut
2 *adv (grimper)* steeply; **tomber r.** to fall to the ground; **tomber r. mort** to drop dead • **raideur** *nf (rigidité)* stiffness; *(de côte)* steepness • **raidillon** *nm (chemin)* steep path; *(partie de route)* steep rise • **raidir 1** *vt (bras, jambe)* to brace; *(corde)* to tauten **2 se raidir** *vpr (membres)* to stiffen; *(corde)* to tauten; *(personne)* to tense up

raie¹ [rɛ] *nf (motif)* stripe; *(de cheveux) Br* parting, *Am* part

raie² [rɛ] *nf (poisson)* skate

rail [rɑj] *nm* rail; **le r.** *(chemins de fer)* rail; **r. de sécurité** crash barrier

railler [rɑje] *vt* to mock • **raillerie** *nf* gibe • **railleur, -euse** *adj* mocking

rainure [rɛnyr] *nf* groove
raisin [rɛzɛ̃] *nm* **raisin(s)** grapes; **r. sec** raisin

> 🖉 Il faut noter que le nom anglais **raisin** est un faux ami. Il signifie **raisin sec**.

raison [rɛzɔ̃] *nf* (**a**) *(faculté, motif)* reason; **la r. de mon absence** the reason for my absence; **la r. pour laquelle je** the reason (why) I; **pour raisons de famille/de santé** for family/health reasons; **en r. de** *(cause)* on account of; **à r. de** *(proportion)* at the rate of; **à plus forte r.** all the more so; **plus que de r.** *(boire)* much too much; **r. de plus** all the more reason (**pour faire** to do *or* for doing); **avoir r. de qn/qch** to get the better of sb/sth; **se faire une r.** to resign oneself (**b**) **avoir r.** to be right (**de faire** to do *or* in doing); **donner r. à qn** to agree with sb; *(événement)* to prove sb right; **avec r.** rightly
raisonnable [rɛzɔnabl] *adj* reasonable
• **raisonnablement** [-əmɑ̃] *adv* reasonably
raisonner [rɛzɔne] **1** *vt* **r. qn** to reason with sb
2 *vi (penser)* to reason; *(discuter)* to argue • **raisonné, -ée** *adj (choix)* reasoned • **raisonnement** *nm (faculté, activité)* reasoning; *(argumentation)* argument
rajeunir [raʒœnir] **1** *vt (moderniser)* to modernize; **r. qn** *(faire paraître plus jeune)* to make sb look younger; *(donner moins que son âge à)* to underestimate how old sb is
2 *vi* to look younger • **rajeunissement** *nm (après traitement)* rejuvenation; *(de population)* decrease in age
rajout [raʒu] *nm* addition • **rajouter** *vt* to add (**à** to); *Fig* **en r.** to exaggerate
rajuster [raʒyste] **1** *vt (vêtements, lunettes)* to straighten, to adjust
2 se rajuster *vpr* to tidy oneself up
râle [rɑl] *nm (de mourant)* death rattle • **râler** *vi (mourant)* to give a death rattle; *Fam (protester)* to moan • **râleur, -euse** *nmf Fam* moaner
ralentir [ralɑ̃tir] *vti* to slow down • **ralenti** *nm Cin & TV* slow motion; **au r.** in slow motion; *(travailler)* at a slower pace; **tourner au r.** *(moteur, usine) Br* to tick over, *Am* to turn over • **ralentissement** *nm* slowing down; *(embouteillage)* hold-up
rallier [ralje] **1** *vt (réunir)* to rally; *(regagner)* to return to; **r. qn à qch** *(convertir)* to win sb over to sth

2 se rallier *vpr* **se r. à** *(avis)* to come round to; *(cause)* to rally to
rallonge [ralɔ̃ʒ] *nf (de table)* extension; *(fil électrique)* extension (lead) • **rallonger** *vti* to lengthen
rallumer [ralyme] **1** *vt (feu, pipe)* to light again; *(lampe)* to switch on again; *(conflit, haine)* to rekindle
2 se rallumer *vpr (lumière)* to come back on; *(guerre, incendie)* to flare up again
rallye [rali] *nm (course automobile)* rally
ramage [ramaʒ] *nm (d'oiseaux)* song • **ramages** *nmpl (dessin)* foliage
ramassé, -ée [ramase] *adj (trapu)* stocky; *(concis)* compact
ramasser [ramase] **1** *vt (prendre par terre, réunir)* to pick up; *(ordures, copies)* to collect; *(fruits, coquillages)* to gather; *Fam (gifle, rhume, amende)* to get
2 se ramasser *vpr (se pelotonner)* to curl up; *(se relever)* to pick oneself up; *Fam (tomber)* to fall flat on one's face; *Fam (échouer)* to fail • **ramassage** *nm (d'ordures)* collection; *(de fruits)* gathering; **r. scolaire** school bus service
ramassis [ramasi] *nm Péj* **r. de** *(voyous, vieux livres)* bunch of
rambarde [rɑ̃bard] *nf* guardrail
rame [ram] *nf (aviron)* oar; *(de métro)* train; *(de papier)* ream • **ramer** *vi* to row; *Fam (peiner)* to sweat blood • **rameur, -euse** *nmf* rower
rameau, -x [ramo] *nm* branch; *Rel* **le dimanche des Rameaux, les Rameaux** Palm Sunday
ramener [ramne] **1** *vt (amener)* to bring back; *(raccompagner)* to take back; *(remettre en place)* to put back; *(paix, ordre, calme)* to restore; **r. qch à qch** to reduce sth to sth; **r. qn à la vie** to bring sb back to life; *Fam* **r. sa fraise** to show off
2 se ramener *vpr Fam (arriver)* to roll up; **se r. à qch** *(se réduire)* to boil down to sth
ramier [ramje] *nm* **(pigeon) r.** wood pigeon
ramification [ramifikasjɔ̃] *nf* ramification
ramollir [ramɔlir] *vt*, **se ramollir** *vpr* to soften • **ramolli, -ie** *adj* soft; *(personne)* soft-headed
ramoner [ramɔne] *vt (cheminée)* to sweep • **ramonage** *nm* (chimney) sweeping • **ramoneur** *nm* (chimney) sweep
rampe [rɑ̃p] *nf (d'escalier)* banister; *(pente)* slope; **être sous les feux de la r.** to be in the limelight; **r. d'accès** *(de pont)* access ramp; **r. de lancement** launching ramp

ramper [rɑ̃pe] *vi* to crawl; *Péj* **r. devant qn** to grovel to sb

rancard [rɑ̃kar] *nm Fam (rendez-vous)* meeting

rancart [rɑ̃kar] *nm Fam* **mettre qch au r.** to chuck sth out

rance [rɑ̃s] *adj* rancid • **rancir** *vi* to go rancid

ranch [rɑ̃tʃ] *nm* ranch

rancœur [rɑ̃kœr] *nf* rancour, resentment

rançon [rɑ̃sɔ̃] *nf* ransom; *Fig* **la r. de la gloire** the price of fame • **rançonner** *vt* to hold to ransom

rancune [rɑ̃kyn] *nf* spite; **garder r. à qn** to bear sb a grudge; **sans r.!** no hard feelings! • **rancunier, -ière** *adj* spiteful

randonnée [rɑ̃dɔne] *nf (à pied)* hike; *(en vélo)* ride

rang [rɑ̃] *nm (rangée)* row; *(classement, grade)* rank; **en r. d'oignons** in a neat row; **par r. de taille** in order of size; **de haut r.** high-ranking; **se mettre en r.** to line up (**par trois** in threes) • **rangée¹** *nf* row

ranger [rɑ̃ʒe] **1** *vt (papiers, vaisselle)* to put away; *(chambre)* to tidy (up); *(classer)* to rank (**parmi** among); **r. par ordre alphabétique** to arrange in alphabetical order

2 se ranger *vpr (se disposer)* to line up; *(s'écarter)* to stand aside; *(voiture)* to pull over; *Fam (s'assagir)* to settle down; **se r. à l'avis de qn** to come round to sb's opinion • **rangé, -ée²** *adj (chambre)* tidy; *(personne)* steady • **rangement** *nm* putting away; *(de chambre)* tidying (up); **rangements** *(placards)* storage space; **faire du r.** to do some tidying up

ranimer [ranime] *vt (personne) (après évanouissement)* to bring round; *(après arrêt cardiaque)* to resuscitate; *(feu)* to rekindle; *(souvenir)* to reawaken; *(débat)* to revive

rapace [rapas] **1** *nm (oiseau)* bird of prey **2** *adj (personne)* grasping

rapatrier [rapatrije] *vt* to repatriate • **rapatriement** *nm* repatriation

râpe [rɑp] *nf Culin* grater; *(lime)* rasp • **râpé, -ée 1** *adj (fromage, carottes)* grated; *(vêtement)* threadbare; *Fam* **c'est r.** we've had it **2** *nm* grated cheese • **râper** *vt (fromage)* to grate; *(bois)* to rasp

rapetisser [raptise] **1** *vt (rendre plus petit)* to make smaller; *(faire paraître plus petit)* to make look smaller **2** *vi (vêtement, personne)* to shrink

râpeux, -euse [rɑpø, -øz] *adj* rough

raphia [rafja] *nm* raffia

rapide [rapid] **1** *adj* fast; *(progrès)* rapid; *(esprit, lecture)* quick; *(pente)* steep **2** *nm (train)* express (train); *(de fleuve)* rapid • **rapidement** *adv* quickly, rapidly • **rapidité** *nf* speed

rapiécer [rapjese] *vt* to patch

rappel [rapɛl] *nm (de diplomate)* recall; *(d'événement, de promesse)* reminder; *(de salaire)* back pay; *(au théâtre)* curtain call; *(vaccin)* booster; *Alpinisme* **descendre en r.** to abseil down; **r. à l'ordre** call to order

rappeler [rap(ə)le] **1** *vt (pour faire revenir, au téléphone)* to call back; *(souvenir, diplomate)* to recall; **r. qch à qn** to remind sb of sth

2 *vi (au téléphone)* to call back

3 se rappeler *vpr* **se r. qn/qch** to remember sb/sth; **se r. que...** to remember that...

rappliquer [raplike] *vi Fam (arriver)* to roll up

rapport [rapɔr] *nm* (a) *(lien)* connection, link; **par r. à** compared with; **sous ce r.** in this respect; **se mettre en r. avec qn** to get in touch with sb; **ça n'a aucun r.!** it has nothing to do with it!; **rapports** *(entre personnes)* relations; **rapports (sexuels)** (sexual) intercourse (**b**) *(profit)* return, yield (**c**) *(compte rendu)* report

rapporter [rapɔrte] **1** *vt (rendre)* to bring back; *(remporter)* to take back; *(raconter)* to report; *(profit)* to yield; **r. de l'argent** to be profitable; **r. qch à qn** *(financièrement)* to bring sb in sth; *(moralement)* to bring sb sth; **on rapporte que...** it is reported that...

2 *vi (chien)* to retrieve; *Péj (moucharder)* to tell tales

3 se rapporter *vpr* **se r. à qch** to relate to sth; **s'en r. à qn/qch** to rely on sb/sth • **rapporteur, -euse 1** *nmf Péj (mouchard)* telltale **2** *nm (de commission)* reporter; *(instrument)* protractor

rapprocher [raprɔʃe] **1** *vt (objet)* to move closer (**de** to); *(réconcilier)* to bring together; *(réunir)* to join; *(comparer)* to compare (**de** to or with)

2 se rapprocher *vpr* to get closer (**de** to); *(se réconcilier)* to be reconciled; *(ressembler)* to be similar (**de** to) • **rapproché, -ée** *adj* close; *(yeux)* close-set • **rapprochement** *nm (réconciliation)* reconciliation; *(rapport)* connection

rapt [rapt] *nm* abduction

raquette [rakɛt] *nf (de tennis)* racket; *(de ping-pong)* bat; *(de neige)* snowshoe

rare [rar] *adj* rare; *(argent, main-d'œuvre)* scarce; *(barbe, végétation)* sparse; **c'est r.**

qu'il pleuve ici it rarely rains here • **se raréfier** *vpr (denrées)* to get scarce • **rarement** *adv* rarely, seldom • **rareté** *nf (objet rare)* rarity; *(de main-d'œuvre)* scarcity; *(de phénomène)* rareness

RAS [ɛraɛs] *(abrév* **rien à signaler***) Fam* nothing to report

ras, rase [rɑ, rɑz] **1** *adj (cheveux)* close-cropped; *(herbe, barbe)* short; *(mesure)* full; **à r. bord** to the brim; **pull (au) r. du cou** crew-neck sweater
2 *nm* **au r. de, à r. de** level with; **voler au r. du sol** to fly close to the ground
3 *adv (coupé)* short; *Fam* **en avoir r. le bol** to be fed up (**de** with)

raser [rɑze] **1** *vt (menton, personne)* to shave; *(barbe, moustache)* to shave off; *(démolir)* to raze to the ground; *(frôler)* to skim; *Fam (ennuyer)* to bore
2 se raser *vpr* to shave • **rasage** *nm* shaving • **rasé, -ée** *adj* **être bien r.** to be clean-shaven • **rase-mottes** *nm inv Fam* **voler en r., faire du r.** to hedgehop • **raseur, -euse** *nmf Fam* bore

rasoir [rɑzwar] **1** *nm* razor; *(électrique)* shaver
2 *adj inv Fam* boring

rassasier [rasazje] *vt (faim, curiosité)* to satisfy

rassembler [rasɑ̃ble] **1** *vt (gens, objets)* to gather (together); *(courage)* to muster; **r. ses esprits** to collect oneself
2 se rassembler *vpr* to gather, to assemble • **rassemblement** [-əmɑ̃] *nm (action, groupe)* gathering

rasseoir* [raswar] **se rasseoir** *vpr* to sit down again

rassis, -ise [rasi, -iz] *adj (pain)* stale • **rassir** *vi* to go stale

rassurer [rasyre] **1** *vt* to reassure
2 se rassurer *vpr* **rassure-toi** don't worry • **rassurant, -ante** *adj* reassuring

rat [ra] *nm* rat; *Fig* **r. de bibliothèque** bookworm; **petit r. de l'Opéra** ballet pupil

ratatiner [ratatine] **se ratatiner** *vpr* to shrivel up; *(vieillard)* to become wizened

ratatouille [ratatuj] *nf Culin* **r. (niçoise)** ratatouille

rate [rat] *nf Anat* spleen

râteau, -x [rɑto] *nm* rake

râtelier [rɑtəlje] *nm (pour outils, pour armes)* rack; *Fam (dentier)* set of false teeth

rater [rate] **1** *vt (bus, cible, occasion)* to miss; *(travail, gâteau)* to ruin; *(examen)* to fail; *(vie)* to waste; *Fam* **il n'en rate pas une** he's always putting his foot in it

2 *vi Fam* to fail; **ça n'a pas raté!** inevitably that happened! • **raté, -ée 1** *nmf* loser **2** *nmpl* **avoir des ratés** *(moteur)* to backfire

ratifier [ratifje] *vt* to ratify • **ratification** *nf* ratification

ration [rasjɔ̃] *nf* ration • **rationnement** *nm* rationing • **rationner** *vt* to ration

rationaliser [rasjɔnalize] *vt* to rationalize • **rationalisation** *nf* rationalization

rationnel, -elle [rasjɔnɛl] *adj* rational

ratisser [ratise] *vt (allée)* to rake; *(feuilles)* to rake up; *Fam (fouiller)* to comb; *Fam* **se faire r.** *(au jeu)* to be cleaned out

raton [ratɔ̃] *nm* **r. laveur** raccoon

RATP [ɛratepe] *(abrév* **Régie autonome des transports parisiens***) nf* ≃ Paris transport authority

rattacher [rataʃe] **1** *vt (lacets)* to tie up again; *(région)* to unite (**à** with); *(idée)* to link (**à** to)
2 se rattacher *vpr* **se r. à** to be linked to • **rattachement** *nm (de région)* uniting (**à** with)

rattraper [ratrape] **1** *vt* to catch; *(prisonnier)* to recapture; *(erreur)* to correct; **r. qn** *(rejoindre)* to catch up with sb; **r. le temps perdu** to make up for lost time
2 se rattraper *vpr (se retenir)* to catch oneself in time; *(après une faute)* to make up for it; **se r. à qch** to catch hold of sth • **rattrapage** *nm Scol* **cours de r.** remedial class

rature [ratyr] *nf* crossing-out, deletion • **raturer** *vt* to cross out, to delete

rauque [rok] *adj (voix)* hoarse

ravages [ravaʒ] *nmpl* devastation; *(du temps, de maladie)* ravages; **faire des r.** to wreak havoc; *(femme)* to break hearts • **ravager** *vt* to devastate

ravaler [ravale] *vt (façade)* to clean; *(sanglots, salive)* to swallow; *Fig (colère)* to stifle; *Littéraire (avilir)* to lower (**à** to) • **ravalement** *nm* cleaning

ravi, -ie [ravi] *adj* delighted (**de** with; **de faire** to do; **que** that)

ravier [ravje] *nm* hors d'œuvre dish

ravigoter [ravigɔte] *vt Fam* **r. qn** to put new life into sb

ravin [ravɛ̃] *nm* ravine

ravioli [ravjɔli] *nmpl* ravioli

ravir [ravir] *vt (emporter)* to snatch (**à** from); *(plaire à)* to delight; **chanter à r.** to sing delightfully • **ravissant, -ante** *adj* delightful • **ravissement** *nm (extase)* ecstasy • **ravisseur, -euse** *nmf* kidnapper

raviser [ravize] **se raviser** *vpr* to change one's mind

ravitailler [ravitaje] **1** *vt* (*personnes*) to supply; (*avion*) to refuel
2 se ravitailler *vpr* to get in supplies • **ravitaillement** *nm* (*action*) supplying; (*d'avion*) refuelling; (*denrées*) supplies
raviver [ravive] *vt* (*feu, sentiment*) to rekindle; (*douleur*) to revive; (*couleur*) to brighten up
rayer [rɛje] *vt* (*érafler*) to scratch; (*mot*) to cross out; **r. qn d'une liste** to cross sb off a list • **rayé, -ée** *adj* (*verre, disque*) scratched; (*tissu, pantalon*) striped • **rayure** *nf* (*éraflure*) scratch; (*motif*) stripe; **à rayures** striped
rayon [rɛjɔ̃] *nm* (**a**) (*de lumière*) ray; (*de cercle*) radius; (*de roue*) spoke; **dans un r. de** within a radius of; **r. X** X-ray; **r. d'action** range; **r. de soleil** sunbeam (**b**) (*d'étagère*) shelf; (*de magasin*) department; (*de ruche*) honeycomb (**c**) (*expressions*) *Fam* **elle en connaît un r.** she's well clued up about it • **rayonnage** *nm* shelving, shelves
rayonner [rɛjɔne] *vi* (*avenue, douleur*) to radiate; (*dans une région*) to travel around (*from a central base*); (*soleil*) to beam; *Fig* **r. de joie** to beam with joy • **rayonnant, -ante** *adj* (*soleil*) radiant; *Fig* (*visage*) beaming (**de** with) • **rayonnement** *nm* (*du soleil*) radiance; (*influence*) influence
raz de marée [rɑdmare] *nm inv* tidal wave; *Fig* (*bouleversement*) upheaval; **r. électoral** landslide
razzia [ra(d)zja] *nf Fam* **faire une r. sur qch** to raid sth
ré [re] *nm inv* (*note*) D
réacteur [reaktœr] *nm* (*d'avion*) jet engine; (*nucléaire*) reactor
réaction [reaksjɔ̃] *nf* reaction; **r. en chaîne** chain reaction; **moteur à r.** jet engine • **réactionnaire** *adj & nmf* reactionary
réadapter [readapte] *vt*, **se réadapter** *vpr* to readjust (**à** to) • **réadaptation** *nf* readjustment
réaffirmer [reafirme] *vt* to reaffirm
réagir [reaʒir] *vi* to react (**contre** against; **à** to); *Fig* (*se secouer*) to shake oneself out of it
réaliser [realize] **1** *vt* (*projet*) to realize; (*rêve, ambition*) to fulfil; (*bénéfices, économies*) to make; (*film*) to direct; (*se rendre compte*) to realize (**que** that)
2 se réaliser *vpr* (*vœu*) to come true; (*personne*) to fulfil oneself • **réalisable** *adj* (*plan*) workable; (*rêve*) attainable • **réalisateur, -trice** *nmf* (*de film*) director

• **réalisation** *nf* (*de projet*) realization; (*de rêve*) fulfilment; (*de film*) direction; (*œuvre*) achievement
réalisme [realism] *nm* realism • **réaliste 1** *adj* realistic **2** *nmf* realist
réalité [realite] *nf* reality; **en r.** in reality
réanimation [reanimasjɔ̃] *nf* resuscitation; (**service de**) **r.** intensive care unit • **réanimer** *vt* to resuscitate
réapparaître* [reaparɛtr] *vi* to reappear • **réapparition** *nf* reappearance
réarmer [rearme] **1** *vt* (*fusil*) to reload
2 *vi* (*pays*) to rearm • **réarmement** [-əmɑ̃] *nm* rearmament
rébarbatif, -ive [rebarbatif, -iv] *adj* forbidding, *Br* off-putting
rebâtir [rəbɑtir] *vt* to rebuild
rebattu, -ue [rəbaty] *adj* (*sujet*) hackneyed
rebelle [rəbɛl] **1** *adj* (*enfant, esprit*) rebellious; (*mèche*) unruly; (*fièvre*) stubborn; **être r. à** (*sujet: enfant*) to resist; (*sujet: organisme*) to be resistant to
2 *nmf* rebel • **se rebeller** *vpr* to rebel (**contre** against) • **rébellion** *nf* rebellion
rebiffer [rəbife] **se rebiffer** *vpr Fam* to hit back (**contre** at)
rebiquer [rəbike] *vi Fam* (*mèche, col*) to stick up
reboiser [rəbwaze] *vt* to reafforest
rebond [rəbɔ̃] *nm* bounce; (*par ricochet*) rebound; **faux r.** bad bounce • **rebondir** *vi* to bounce; (*par ricochet*) to rebound; *Fam* (*se remettre*) to recover; **faire r. qch** (*affaire, discussion*) to get sth going again • **rebondissement** *nm* new development (**de** in)
rebondi, -ie [rəbɔ̃di] *adj* chubby
rebord [rəbɔr] *nm* edge; (*de plat*) rim; (*de vêtement*) hem; **r. de fenêtre** windowsill
reboucher [rəbuʃe] *vt* (*flacon*) to put the top back on; (*trou*) to fill in again
rebours [rəbur] **à rebours** *adv* the wrong way
rebrousse-poil [rəbruspwal] **à rebrousse-poil** *adv Fig* **prendre qn à r.** to rub sb up the wrong way
rebrousser [rəbruse] *vt* **r. chemin** to turn back
rebuffade [rəbyfad] *nf* rebuff
rébus [rebys] *nm* rebus
rebut [rəby] *nm* **mettre qch au r.** to throw sth out; *Péj* **le r. de la société** the dregs of society
rebuter [rəbyte] *vt* (*décourager*) to put off; (*déplaire*) to disgust • **rebutant, -ante** *adj* off-putting

récalcitrant, -ante [rekalsitrã, -ãt] *adj* recalcitrant

recaler [rəkale] *vt Fam Scol* **r. qn** to fail sb; *Fam Scol* **être recalé, se faire r.** to fail

récapituler [rekapityle] *vti* to recapitulate • **récapitulation** *nf* recapitulation

recel [rəsɛl] *nm* receiving stolen goods • **receler, recéler** *vt (mystère, secret)* to conceal; *(objet volé)* to receive; *(criminel)* to harbour • **receleur, -euse, recéleur, -euse** *nmf* receiver *(of stolen goods)*

recenser [rəsãse] *vt (population)* to take a census of; *(objets)* to make an inventory of • **recensement** *nm (de population)* census; *(d'objets)* inventory

récent, -ente [resã, -ãt] *adj* recent • **récemment** [-amã] *adv* recently

récépissé [resepise] *nm (reçu)* receipt

récepteur [resɛptœr] *nm (téléphone)* receiver • **réceptif, -ive** *adj* receptive (**à** to) • **réception** *nf (accueil, soirée) & Radio* reception; *(de lettre)* receipt; *(d'hôtel)* reception (desk); **dès r. de** on receipt of; **avec accusé de r.** with acknowledgement of receipt • **réceptionniste** *nmf* receptionist

récession [resesjõ] *nf Écon* recession

recette [rəsɛt] *nf Culin & Fig* recipe (**de** for); *(argent, bénéfice)* takings; *(bureau)* tax office; **recettes** *(gains)* takings; *Fig* **faire r.** to be a success

recevoir* [rəsəvwar] **1** *vt (amis, lettre, proposition, coup de téléphone)* to receive; *(gifle, coup)* to get; *(client)* to see; *(candidat)* to admit; *(station de radio)* to pick up; **r. la visite de qn** to have a visit from sb; **être reçu à un examen** to pass an exam; **être reçu premier** to come first

2 *vi (faire une fête)* to have guests; *(médecin)* to see patients • **recevable** *adj (excuse)* admissible • **receveur, -euse** *nmf (de bus)* (bus) conductor; **r. des Postes** postmaster, *f* postmistress

rechange [rəʃãʒ] **de rechange** *adj (outil, pièce)* spare; *(solution)* alternative; **des vêtements de r.** a change of clothes

rechapé, -ée [rəʃape] *adj* **pneu r.** retread

réchapper [reʃape] *vi* **r. de qch** to survive sth

recharge [rəʃarʒ] *nf (de stylo)* refill • **rechargeable** *adj (briquet)* refillable; *(pile)* rechargeable • **recharger** *vt (fusil, appareil photo, camion)* to reload; *(briquet, stylo)* to refill; *(batterie, pile)* to recharge

réchaud [reʃo] *nm* (portable) stove

réchauffer [reʃofe] **1** *vt (personne, aliment)* to warm up

2 se réchauffer *vpr (personne)* to get warm; *(temps)* to get warmer • **réchauffement** *nm (de température)* rise (**de** in); **le r. de la planète** global warming

rêche [rɛʃ] *adj* rough

recherche [rəʃɛrʃ] *nf* (**a**) *(quête)* search (**de** for); *(du pouvoir)* quest (**de** for); **à la r. de** in search of; **se mettre à la r. de qn/qch** to go in search of sb/sth (**b**) *(scientifique)* research (**sur** into); **faire de la r.** to do research (**c**) **recherches** *(de police)* search, hunt; **faire des recherches** to make inquiries (**d**) *(raffinement)* elegance

rechercher [rəʃɛrʃe] *vt (personne, objet)* to search for; *(emploi)* to look for; *(honneurs, faveurs)* to seek; *Ordinat* to do a search for • **recherché, -ée** *adj* (**a**) *(très demandé)* in demand; *(rare)* sought-after; **r. pour meurtre** wanted for murder (**b**) *(élégant)* elegant

rechigner [rəʃiɲe] *vi Fam* **r. à qch** to balk at sth; **faire qch en rechignant** to do sth with a bad grace

rechute [rəʃyt] *nf* relapse; **faire une r.** to have a relapse • **rechuter** *vi* to have a relapse

récidive [residiv] *nf (de malfaiteur)* repeat *Br* offence *or Am* offense; *(de maladie)* recurrence (**de** of) • **récidiver** *vi (malfaiteur)* to reoffend; *(maladie)* to recur • **récidiviste** *nmf (malfaiteur)* repeat offender

récif [resif] *nm* reef

récipient [resipjã] *nm* container

> 🖉 Il faut noter que le nom anglais **recipient** est un faux ami. Il signifie **destinataire**.

réciproque [resiprɔk] *adj (sentiments)* mutual; *(concessions)* reciprocal • **réciproquement** *adv* mutually; **et r.** and vice versa

récit [resi] *nm (histoire)* story; *(compte rendu)* account; **faire le r. de qch** to give an account of sth

récital, -als [resital] *nm* recital

réciter [resite] *vt* to recite • **récitation** *nf* recitation

réclame [reklam] *nf (publicité)* advertising; *(annonce)* advertisement; **en r.** on special offer

réclamer [reklame] **1** *vt (demander)* to ask for; *(exiger)* to demand; *(droit, allocation)* to claim; *(nécessiter)* to require

2 *vi* to complain

3 se réclamer *vpr* **se r. de qn** *(se recommander)* to mention sb's name • **réclamation** *nf* complaint; **faire une r.** to make a complaint; **(bureau des) réclamations** complaints department

📖 Il faut noter que le verbe anglais **to reclaim** est un faux ami. Il signifie le plus souvent **récupérer**.

reclasser [rəklase] *vt (fiches)* to reclassify; *(chômeur)* to find a new job for

reclus, -use [rəkly, -yz] **1** *adj* cloistered; **vivre r.** to lead a cloistered life **2** *nmf* recluse

réclusion [reklyzjɔ̃] *nf* **r. (criminelle)** imprisonment; **r. (criminelle) à perpétuité** life imprisonment

recoiffer [rəkwafe] **se recoiffer** *vpr (se repeigner)* to redo one's hair

recoin [rəkwɛ̃] *nm (de lieu)* nook; *(de mémoire)* recess

recoller [rəkɔle] *vt (objet cassé)* to stick back together; *(enveloppe)* to stick back down

récolte [rekɔlt] *nf (action)* harvesting; *(produits)* harvest; *Fig (de documents)* crop; **faire la r.** to harvest the crops • **récolter** *vt* to harvest; *Fig (recueillir)* to collect

recommandable [rəkɔmɑ̃dabl] *adj* **peu r.** disreputable

recommandation [rəkɔmɑ̃dasjɔ̃] *nf (appui, conseil)* recommendation

recommander [rəkɔmɑ̃de] **1** *vt (appuyer)* to recommend (**à** to; **pour** for); **r. à qn de faire qch** to advise sb to do sth; **r. son âme à Dieu** to commend one's soul to God **2 se recommander** *vpr* **se r. de qn** to give sb's name as a reference • **recommandé, -ée 1** *adj (lettre)* registered **2** *nm* **en r.** registered

recommencer [rəkɔmɑ̃se] *vti* to start *or* begin again • **recommencement** *nm* renewal (**de** of)

récompense [rekɔ̃pɑ̃s] *nf* reward (**pour** *ou* **de** for); *(prix)* award; **en r. de qch** as a reward for sth • **récompenser** *vt* to reward (**de** *ou* **pour** for)

réconcilier [rekɔ̃silje] **1** *vt* to reconcile (**avec** with) **2 se réconcilier** *vpr* to become reconciled, *Br* to make it up (**avec** with) • **réconciliation** *nf* reconciliation

reconduire* [rəkɔ̃dɥir] *vt (contrat)* to renew; *(politique)* to continue; **r. qn (à la porte)** to show sb out; **r. qn à la frontière** to escort sb back to the border • **reconduction** *nf (de contrat)* renewal

réconfort [rekɔ̃fɔr] *nm* comfort • **réconfortant, -ante** *adj* comforting • **réconforter** *vt* to comfort

reconnaissable [rəkɔnɛsabl] *adj* recognizable (**à qch** by sth)

reconnaissant, -ante [rəkɔnɛsɑ̃, -ɑ̃t] *adj* grateful (**à qn de qch** to sb for sth) • **reconnaissance** *nf (gratitude)* gratitude (**pour** for); *(de droit, de gouvernement)* recognition; *Mil* reconnaissance; *Mil* **partir en r.** to go off on reconnaissance; **r. de dette** IOU; *Ordinat* **r. vocale** speech recognition

reconnaître* [rəkɔnɛtr] **1** *vt (identifier, admettre)* to recognize (**à qch** by sth); *(enfant, erreur)* to acknowledge; *(terrain)* to reconnoitre; **être reconnu coupable** to be found guilty **2 se reconnaître** *vpr (soi-même)* to recognize oneself; *(l'un l'autre)* to recognize each other; **se r. coupable** to acknowledge one's guilt • **reconnu, -ue** *adj* recognized

reconquérir* [rəkɔ̃kerir] *vt (territoire)* to reconquer; *(liberté)* to win back

reconsidérer [rəkɔ̃sidere] *vt* to reconsider

reconstituant, -uante [rəkɔ̃stitɥɑ̃, -ɥɑ̃t] *adj & nm* tonic

reconstituer [rəkɔ̃stitɥe] *vt (armée, parti)* to reconstitute; *(crime, quartier)* to reconstruct; *(faits)* to piece together; *(fortune)* to build up again • **reconstitution** *nf (de crime)* reconstruction; **r. historique** historical reconstruction

reconstruire* [rəkɔ̃strɥir] *vt* to rebuild • **reconstruction** *nf* rebuilding

reconvertir [rəkɔ̃vɛrtir] **1** *vt (entreprise)* to convert; *(personne)* to retrain **2 se reconvertir** *vpr (personne)* to retrain; **se r. dans qch** to retrain for a new career in sth • **reconversion** *nf (d'usine)* conversion; *(de personne)* retraining

recopier [rəkɔpje] *vt (mettre au propre)* to copy out; *(faire un double de)* to recopy

record [rəkɔr] *nm & adj inv* record

recoucher [rəkuʃe] **se recoucher** *vpr* to go back to bed

recoudre* [rəkudr] *vt (bouton)* to sew back on; *(vêtement, plaie)* to stitch up

recouper [rəkupe] **1** *vt (couper de nouveau)* to recut; *(confirmer)* to confirm **2 se recouper** *vpr (témoignages)* to tally • **recoupement** *nm* crosscheck; **par r.** by crosschecking

recourber [rəkurbe] *vt,* **se recourber** *vpr* to bend • **recourbé, -ée** *adj (bec)* curved; *(nez)* hooked

recours [rəkur] *nm* recourse; **avoir r. à** *(chose)* to resort to; *(personne)* to turn to; **en dernier r.** as a last resort; *Jur* **r. en cassation** appeal • **recourir*** *vi* **r. à** *(moyen, violence)* to resort to; *(personne)* to turn to

recouvrer [rəkuvre] *vt (santé, bien)* to recover; *(vue)* to regain

recouvrir* [rəkuvrir] *vt (revêtir, inclure)* to cover (**de** with); *(couvrir de nouveau)* to re-cover; *(enfant)* to cover up again

récréation [rekreɑsjɔ̃] *nf (détente)* recreation; *Scol Br* break, *Am* recess; *(pour les plus jeunes)* playtime

récrier [rekrije] **se récrier** *vpr Littéraire* to protest (**contre** about)

récriminer [rekrimine] *vi* to complain bitterly (**contre** about) ● **récriminations** *nfpl* recriminations

récrire* [rekrir] *vt (lettre)* to rewrite

recroqueviller [rəkrɔkvije] **se recroqueviller** *vpr (personne)* to huddle up

recrudescence [rəkrydesɑ̃s] *nf* renewed outbreak (**de** of)

recrue [rəkry] *nf* recruit ● **recrutement** *nm* recruitment ● **recruter** *vt* to recruit

rectangle [rɛktɑ̃gl] *nm* rectangle ● **rectangulaire** *adj* rectangular

rectifier [rɛktifje] *vt (calcul, erreur)* to correct; *(compte)* to adjust; *Fig* **r. le tir** to take a slightly different tack ● **rectificatif** *nm* correction ● **rectification** *nf (de calcul, d'erreur)* correction; **faire une r.** to make a correction

recto [rɛkto] *nm* front; **r. verso** on both sides

rectorat [rɛktɔra] *nm Br* ≃ local education authority, *Am* ≃ board of education

reçu, -ue [rəsy] **1** *pp de* **recevoir**
2 *adj (idée)* received; *(candidat)* successful
3 *nm (récépissé)* receipt

recueil [rəkœj] *nm (de poèmes, de chansons)* collection (**de** of)

recueillir* [rəkœjir] **1** *vt (argent, renseignements)* to collect; *(suffrages)* to win; *(personne, animal)* to take in
2 se recueillir *vpr* to meditate; *(devant un monument)* to stand in silence ● **recueillement** *nm* meditation ● **recueilli, -ie** *adj* meditative

recul [rəkyl] *nm (d'armée, de négociateur, de maladie)* retreat; *(de canon)* recoil; *(déclin)* decline; **avoir un mouvement de r.** to recoil; *Fig* **manquer de r.** to be too closely involved; *Fig* **prendre du r.** to stand back from things ● **reculade** *nf Fig & Péj* climbdown

reculer [rəkyle] **1** *vi (personne)* to move back; *(automobiliste)* to reverse, *Am* to back up; *(armée)* to retreat; *(épidémie)* to lose ground; *(glacier)* to recede; *(renoncer)* to back down, to retreat; *(diminuer)* to decline; **faire r. la foule** to move the crowd back; *Fig* **il ne recule devant rien** nothing daunts him
2 *vt (meuble)* to move back; *(paiement, décision)* to postpone ● **reculé, -ée** *adj (endroit, temps)* remote

reculons [rəkylɔ̃] **à reculons** *adv* backwards

récupérer [rekypere] **1** *vt (objet prêté)* to get back, to recover; *(bagages)* & *Ordinat* to retrieve; *(forces)* to recover; *(recycler)* to salvage; *Péj (détourner à son profit)* to exploit; **r. des heures supplémentaires** to take time off in lieu
2 *vi (reprendre des forces)* to recover ● **récupération** *nf (d'objet)* recovery; *(de déchets)* salvage; *Péj (d'idée)* exploitation

récurer [rekyre] *vt* to scour

récuser [rekyze] **1** *vt* to challenge
2 se récuser *vpr* to decline to give an opinion

recycler [rəsikle] **1** *vt (matériaux)* to recycle; *(personne)* to retrain
2 se recycler *vpr (personne)* to retrain ● **recyclage** *nm (de matériaux)* recycling; *(de personne)* retraining

rédacteur, -trice [redaktœr, -tris] *nmf* writer; *(de journal)* editor; **r. en chef** *(de journal)* editor (in chief) ● **rédaction** *nf (action)* writing; *(de contrat)* drawing up; *Scol (devoir de français)* essay, composition; *(journalistes)* editorial staff; *(bureaux)* editorial offices

reddition [redisjɔ̃] *nf* surrender

redécouvrir [rədekuvrir] *vt (auteur, ouvrage)* to rediscover

redemander [rədəmɑ̃de] *vt (pain)* to ask for more; **r. qch à qn** *(objet prêté)* to ask sb for sth back; **il faut que je le lui redemande** *(que je pose la question à nouveau)* I'll have to ask him/her again

redémarrer [rədemare] *vi (voiture)* to start again; **faire r. une voiture** to start a car again

rédemption [redɑ̃psjɔ̃] *nf Rel* redemption

redescendre [rədesɑ̃dr] **1** *(aux avoir)* *vt (objet)* to bring/take back down
2 *(aux être)* *vi* to come/go back down

redevable [rədəvabl] *adj* **être r. de qch à qn** to be indebted to sb for sth

redevance [rədəvɑ̃s] *nf (de télévision)* licence fee

redevenir* [rədəvənir] *(aux être)* *vi* to become again

rediffusion [rədifyzjɔ̃] *nf (de film)* repeat

rédiger [rediʒe] *vt* to write; *(contrat)* to draw up

redire* [rədir] **1** *vt* to repeat

2 *vi* **avoir** *ou* **trouver à r. à qch** to find fault with sth ● **redite** *nf* (pointless) repetition

redondant, -ante [rədɔ̃dɑ̃, -ɑ̃t] *adj* redundant

redonner [rədɔne] *vt* *(rendre)* to give back; *(donner plus)* to give more

redoubler [rəduble] **1** *vt* to increase; *Scol* **r. une classe** to repeat a year *or Am* a grade; **à coups redoublés** *(frapper)* harder and harder

2 *vi Scol* to repeat a year *or Am* a grade; *(colère)* to intensify; **r. de patience** to be much more patient ● **redoublant, -ante** *nmf* pupil repeating a year *ou Am* a grade ● **redoublement** *nm* [-əmɑ̃] increase (**de in**)

redouter [rədute] *vt* to dread (**de faire** doing) ● **redoutable** *adj* *(adversaire, arme)* formidable; *(maladie)* dreadful

redresser [rədrese] **1** *vt* *(objet tordu)* to straighten (out); *(économie, situation, tort)* to put right; **r. la tête** to hold up one's head

2 se redresser *vpr* *(personne)* to straighten up; *(pays, économie)* to recover ● **redressement** [-ɛsmɑ̃] *nm* *(essor)* recovery; **plan de r.** recovery plan; **r. fiscal** tax adjustment

réduction [redyksjɔ̃] *nf* reduction (**de in**); *(rabais)* discount

réduire* [redɥir] **1** *vt* to reduce (**à** to; **de** by); **r. qch en cendres** to reduce sth to ashes; **r. qn à qch** *(misère, désespoir)* to reduce sb to sth

2 *vi (sauce)* to reduce

3 se réduire *vpr* **se r. à** *(se ramener à)* to come down to; **se r. en cendres** to be reduced to ashes ● **réduit, -uite 1** *adj* *(prix, vitesse)* reduced; *(moyens)* limited **2** *nm (pièce)* small room

réécrire* [reekrir] *vt* to rewrite

rééduquer [reedyke] *vt* *(personne)* to rehabilitate; *(partie du corps)* to re-educate ● **rééducation** *nf* *(de personne)* rehabilitation; *(de membre)* re-education; **faire de la r.** to have physiotherapy

réel, réelle [reɛl] **1** *adj* real **2** *nm* **le r.** reality ● **réellement** *adv* really

réélire* [reelir] *vt* to re-elect

réévaluer [reevalɥe] *vt* *(monnaie)* to revalue; *(salaires)* to reassess ● **réévaluation** *nf* *(de monnaie)* revaluation; *(de salaires)* reassessment

réexpédier [reɛkspedje] *vt* *(faire suivre)* to forward; *(à l'envoyeur)* to return

refaire* [rəfɛr] **1** *vt* *(exercice, travail)* to do again, to redo; *(chambre)* to do up;

(erreur, voyage) to make again; *Fam (duper)* to take in; **r. sa vie** to make a new life for oneself; **r. du riz** to make some more rice; **r. le monde** to put the world to rights; **se faire r. le nez** to have one's nose reshaped

2 se refaire *vpr* **se r. une santé** to recover

réfection [refɛksjɔ̃] *nf* repair

réfectoire [refɛktwar] *nm* dining hall, refectory

référence [referɑ̃s] *nf* reference; **faire r. à qch** to refer to sth

référendum [referɑ̃dɔm] *nm* referendum

référer [refere] **1** *vi* **en r. à** to refer the matter to

2 se référer *vpr* **se r. à** to refer to

refermer [rəfɛrme] *vt*, **se refermer** *vpr* to close *or* shut again

refiler [rəfile] *vt Fam* **r. qch à qn** *(donner)* to palm sth off on sb; *(maladie)* to give sb sth

réfléchir [refleʃir] **1** *vt (image, lumière)* to reflect; **r. que...** to realize that...

2 *vi* to think (**à** *ou* **sur** about)

3 se réfléchir *vpr* to be reflected ● **réfléchi, -ie** *adj (personne)* thoughtful; *(action, décision)* carefully thought-out; *Grammaire (verbe, pronom)* reflexive; **c'est tout r.** my mind is made up; **tout bien r.** all things considered

reflet [rəflɛ] *nm (image)* & *Fig* reflection; *(lumière)* glint; **reflets** *(de cheveux)* highlights ● **refléter 1** *vt* to reflect **2 se refléter** *vpr* to be reflected

refleurir [rəflœrir] *vi* to flower again

réflexe [reflɛks] *nm* & *adj* reflex

réflexion [reflɛksjɔ̃] *nf (d'image, de lumière)* reflection; *(pensée)* thought, reflection; *(remarque)* remark; **faire une r. à qn** to make a remark to sb; **r. faite, à la r.** on second *Br* thoughts *or Am* thought

refluer [rəflɥe] *vi (eaux)* to flow back; *(marée)* to ebb; *(foule)* to surge back ● **reflux** *nm (de marée)* ebb; *(de foule)* backward surge

réforme [refɔrm] *nf* reform ● **réformateur, -trice** *nmf* reformer ● **réformer** *vt (loi)* to reform; *(soldat)* to discharge as unfit

refouler [rəfule] *vt (personnes)* to force *or* drive back; *(étrangers)* to turn away; *(sentiment)* to repress; *(larmes)* to hold back ● **refoulé, -ée** *adj* repressed

réfractaire [refrakter] *adj (rebelle)* insubordinate; *(prêtre)* non-juring

refrain [rəfrɛ̃] *nm (de chanson)* chorus, refrain; *Fam* **c'est toujours le même r.** it's always the same old story

refréner [refrene] *vt* to curb
réfrigérer [refriʒere] *vt* to refrigerate
• **réfrigérant, -ante** *adj Fam (accueil)* icy
• **réfrigérateur** *nm* refrigerator • **réfrigération** *nf* refrigeration
refroidir [rəfrwadir] **1** *vt* to cool (down);
Fig (ardeur) to cool; *très Fam (tuer)* to kill;
Fam **ça m'a refroidi** *(déçu)* it dampened
my enthusiasm
2 *vi (devenir froid)* to get cold; *(devenir
moins chaud)* to cool down
3 se refroidir *vpr (temps)* to get colder;
Fig (ardeur) to cool • **refroidissement** *nm*
(baisse de température) drop in temperature; *(de l'eau)* cooling; *(rhume)* chill
refuge [rəfyʒ] *nm* refuge; *(de montagne)*
(mountain) hut; *(pour piétons)* traffic
island • **réfugié, -iée** *nmf* refugee • **se
réfugier** *vpr* to take refuge
refus [rəfy] *nm* refusal; *Fam* **ce n'est pas
de r.** I won't say no • **refuser 1** *vt* to refuse
(**qch à qn** sb sth; **de faire** to do); *(offre,
invitation)* to turn down; *(proposition)* to
reject; *(candidat)* to fail; *(client)* to turn
away **2 se refuser** *vpr (plaisir)* to deny
oneself; **ne rien se r.** not to stint oneself;
se r. à l'évidence to shut one's eyes to the
facts; **se r. à faire qch** to refuse to do sth

> ℓ Il faut noter que le nom anglais **refuse**
> est un faux ami. Il signifie **ordures**.

réfuter [refyte] *vt* to refute
regagner [rəgaɲe] *vt (récupérer)* to regain, to get back; *(revenir à)* to get back
to; **r. le temps perdu** to make up for lost
time • **regain** *nm (renouveau)* renewal; **un
r. d'énergie** renewed energy
régal, -als [regal] *nm* treat • **régaler 1** *vt* to
treat to a delicious meal **2 se régaler** *vpr*
je me régale *(en mangeant)* I'm really
enjoying it; *(je m'amuse)* I'm having a
great time
regard [rəgar] *nm (coup d'œil, expression)* look; **jeter** *ou* **lancer un r. sur** to
glance at; **au r. de la loi** in the eyes of the
law; **en r.** *(en face)* opposite

> ℓ Il faut noter que le nom anglais **regard**
> est un faux ami. Il ne correspond jamais au
> français **regard**.

regarder [rəgarde] **1** *vt* to look at; *(émission, film)* to watch; *(considérer)* to consider, to regard (**comme** as); *(concerner)* to
concern; **r. qn fixement** to stare at sb; **r.
qn faire qch** to watch sb do sth; **ça ne te
regarde pas!** it's none of your business!
2 *vi (observer)* to look; **r. autour de soi** to
look round; **r. par la fenêtre** *(du dedans)*

to look out of the window; **r. à la dépense**
to be careful with one's money; **y r. à deux
fois avant de faire qch** to think twice
before doing sth
3 se regarder *vpr (soi-même)* to look at
oneself; *(l'un l'autre)* to look at each
other; **se r. dans les yeux** to look into
each other's eyes • **regardant, -ante** *adj
Fam (avare)* careful with money

> ℓ Il faut noter que le verbe anglais **to regard** est un faux ami. Il ne signifie jamais **regarder**.

régate [regat] *nf* regatta
régence [reʒãs] *nf* regency
régénérer [reʒenere] *vt* to regenerate
régenter [reʒãte] *vt* **vouloir tout r.** to
want to run the whole show
régie [reʒi] *nf (entreprise)* state-owned
company; *Théâtre* stage management;
TV (organisation) production management; *(lieu)* control room
regimber [rəʒɛ̃be] *vi* to balk (**contre** at)
régime [reʒim] *nm (politique)* (form of)
government; *(de moteur)* speed; *(de bananes)* bunch; **r. (alimentaire)** diet; **se
mettre au r.** to go on a diet; **suivre un r.**
to be on a diet; **chocolat de r.** diet chocolate; *Fig* **à ce r.** at this rate
régiment [reʒimã] *nm (de soldats)* regiment; *Fam* **un r. de** *(quantité)* a host of
région [reʒjɔ̃] *nf* region, area; **la r. parisienne** the Paris region • **régional, -e,
-aux, -ales** *adj* regional
régir [reʒir] *vt (déterminer)* to govern
régisseur [reʒisœr] *nm (de propriété)*
manager; *Théâtre* stage manager; *Cin &
TV* assistant production manager
registre [rəʒistr] *nm* register
réglable [reglabl] *adj* adjustable • **réglage** *nm (de siège, de machine)* adjustment; *(de moteur, de télévision)* tuning
règle [rɛgl] *nf* (**a**) *(principe)* rule; **en r.**
(papiers d'identité) in order; **en r. générale** as a (general) rule; **dans les règles de
l'art** according to the book (**b**) *(instrument)* ruler • **règles** *nfpl (de femme)*
(monthly) period
règlement [rɛgləmã] *nm* (**a**) *(règles)*
regulations; **contraire au r.** against the
Br rules *or Am* rule (**b**) *(de conflit)* settling;
(paiement) payment; *Fig* **r. de comptes**
settling of scores • **réglementaire** *adj* in
accordance with the regulations; *Mil* **tenue r.** regulation uniform • **réglementation** *nf (action)* regulation; *(règles)*
regulations • **réglementer** *vt* to regulate
régler [regle] **1** *vt (problème, conflit)* to

settle; *(mécanisme)* to adjust; *(moteur, télévision)* to tune; *(payer)* to pay; **r. qn** to settle up with sb; *Fig* **r. son compte à qn** to settle old scores with sb

2 *vi* to pay

3 se régler *vpr* **se r. sur qn** to model oneself on sb • **réglé, -ée** *adj (vie)* ordered; *(papier)* ruled

réglisse [reglis] *nf Br* liquorice, *Am* licorice

réglo [reglo] *adj inv Fam* on the level

règne [rɛɲ] *nm (de souverain)* reign; *(animal, minéral, végétal)* kingdom • **régner** *vi (roi, silence)* to reign (**sur** over); *(prédominer)* to prevail; **faire r. l'ordre** to maintain law and order

regorger [rəgɔrʒe] *vi* **r. de** to be overflowing with

régresser [regrese] *vi* to regress • **régression** *nf* regression; **en r.** on the decline

regret [rəgrɛ] *nm* regret; **à r.** with regret; **avoir le r.** *ou* **être au r. de faire qch** to be sorry to do sth • **regrettable** *adj* regrettable • **regretter** [rəgrete] *vt* to regret; **r. qn** to miss sb; **je regrette, je le regrette** I'm sorry; **r. que...** (+ *subjunctive*) to be sorry that...

regrouper [rəgrupe] *vt*, **se regrouper** *vpr* to gather together

régulariser [regylarize] *vt (situation)* to regularize

régulation [regylɑsjɔ̃] *nf* control

régulier, -ière [regylje, -jɛr] *adj (intervalles, traits du visage, clergé)* & *Grammaire* regular; *(constant)* steady; *(écriture)* even; *(légal)* legal; *Fam (honnête)* on the level • **régularité** *nf (exactitude)* regularity; *(constance)* steadiness; *(de décision)* legality • **régulièrement** *adv* *(à intervalles fixes)* regularly; *(avec constance)* steadily; *(selon la loi)* legitimately

réhabiliter [reabilite] *vt (délinquant)* to rehabilitate; *(accusé)* to clear

réhabituer [reabitɥe] **se réhabituer** *vpr* **se r. à qch/à faire qch** to get used to sth/to doing sth again

rehausser [rəose] *vt (mur)* to make higher; *(teint)* to set off

réimpression [reɛ̃presjɔ̃] *nf (action)* reprinting *(résultat)* reprint

rein [rɛ̃] *nm* kidney; **les reins** *(dos)* the lower back; **avoir mal aux reins** to have a pain in the small of one's back; *Méd* **r. artificiel** kidney machine

reine [rɛn] *nf* queen; **la r. mère** the queen mother; **la r. Élisabeth** Queen Elizabeth • **reine-claude** (*pl* **reines-claudes**) *nf* greengage

réinsertion [reɛ̃sɛrsjɔ̃] *nf* reintegration; **r. sociale** rehabilitation

réintégrer [reɛ̃tegre] *vt (fonctionnaire)* to reinstate; *(lieu)* to return to

réitérer [reitere] *vt* to repeat

rejaillir [rəʒajir] *vi* to spurt out; *Fig* **r. sur qn** to reflect on sb

rejet [rəʒɛ] *nm (refus)* & *Méd* rejection • **rejeter** *vt (relancer)* to throw back; *(offre, candidature, greffe, personne)* to reject; *(épave)* to cast up; *(blâme)* to shift (**on** to); *(vomir)* to bring up • **rejeton** *nm Fam (enfant)* kid

rejoindre* [rəʒwɛ̃dr] **1** *vt (personne)* to meet; *(fugitif)* to catch up with; *(rue, rivière)* to join; *(lieu)* to reach; *(régiment)* to return to; *(concorder avec)* to coincide with

2 se rejoindre *vpr (personnes)* to meet up; *(rues, rivières)* to join up

rejouer [rəʒwe] *vt (match)* to replay

réjouir [reʒwir] **1** *vt* to delight

2 se réjouir *vpr* to be delighted (**de** at; **de faire** to do) • **réjoui, -ie** *adj* joyful • **réjouissance** *nf* rejoicing; **réjouissances** festivities • **réjouissant, -ante** *adj* delightful

relâche [rəlɑʃ] *nf Théâtre* & *Cin* (temporary) closure; **faire r.** *Théâtre* & *Cin* to be closed; *Naut* to put in (**dans un port** at a port); **sans r.** without a break

relâcher [rəlɑʃe] **1** *vt (corde, étreinte)* to loosen; *(discipline)* to relax; *(efforts)* to let up; *(prisonnier)* to release

2 *vi Naut* to put into port

3 se relâcher *vpr (corde)* to slacken; *(discipline)* to become lax; *(employé)* to slack off • **relâché, -ée** *adj* lax • **relâchement** *nm (de corde)* slackening; *(de discipline)* relaxation

relais [rəlɛ] *nm (dispositif émetteur)* relay; *Sport* **(course de) r.** relay (race); **passer le r. à qn** to hand over to sb; **prendre le r.** to take over (**de** from); **r. routier** *Br* transport café, *Am* truck stop *(café)*

relance [rəlɑ̃s] *nf (reprise)* revival • **relancer** *vt (lancer à nouveau)* to throw again; *(rendre)* to throw back; *(production)* to boost; *(moteur, logiciel)* to restart; *(client)* to follow up

relater [rəlate] *vt Littéraire* to relate (**que** that)

relatif, -ive [rəlatif, -iv] *adj* relative (**à** to) • **relativement** *adv (assez)* relatively; **r. à** compared to

relation [rəlɑsjɔ̃] *nf (rapport)* relationship; *(ami)* acquaintance; **être en r. avec qn** to be in touch with sb; **avoir des relations** *(amis influents)* to have contacts; **r. de travail** colleague; **r.**

(amoureuse) (love) affair; **relations extérieures** foreign affairs; **relations internationales** international relations; **relations publiques** public relations; **relations sexuelles** intercourse

relax [rəlaks] *adj Fam* laid-back

relaxer [rəlakse] **se relaxer** *vpr* to relax • **relaxation** *nf* relaxation

relayer [rəleje] **1** *vt (personne)* to take over from; *(émission)* to relay

2 se relayer *vpr* to take turns (**pour faire** doing); *Sport* to take over from one another

reléguer [rəlege] *vt (objet)* to relegate (**à** to); *Fig* **r. qch au second plan** to push sth into the background

relent [rəlɑ̃] *nm* stench

relevé [rəlve] *nm* list; *(de compteur)* reading; **r. de compte** bank statement; *Scol* **r. de notes** list of *Br* marks *or Am* grades

relève [rələv] *nf* relief; **prendre la r.** to take over (**de** from)

relèvement [rələvmɑ̃] *nm (d'économie, de pays)* recovery; *(de salaires)* raising

relever [rəlve] **1** *vt (ramasser)* to pick up; *(personne)* to help back up; *(pays)* to revive; *(col)* to turn up; *(manches)* to roll up; *(copies)* to collect; *(faute)* to pick out; *(empreinte)* to find; *(défi)* to accept; *(sauce)* to spice up; *(copier)* to note down; *(compteur)* to read; *(relayer)* to relieve; *(rehausser)* to enhance; *(augmenter)* to raise; **r. la tête** to look up; **r. qn de ses fonctions** to relieve sb of his/her duties

2 *vi* **r. de** *(dépendre de)* to come under; *(maladie)* to be recovering from

3 se relever *vpr (après une chute)* to get up; **se r. de qch** to get over sth

relief [rəljef] *nm (de paysage)* relief; **en r.** in relief; *Fig* **mettre qch en r.** to highlight sth • **reliefs** *nmpl (de repas)* remains

relier [rəlje] *vt* to connect, to link (**à** to); *(idées, faits)* to link together; *(livre)* to bind

religion [rəliʒjɔ̃] *nf* religion • **religieux, -ieuse 1** *adj* religious; **mariage r.** church wedding **2** *nm (moine)* monk • **religieuse** *nf (femme)* nun; *(gâteau)* cream puff

reliquat [rəlika] *nm (de dette)* remainder

relique [rəlik] *nf* relic

relire* [rəlir] *vt* to reread

reliure [rəljyr] *nf (couverture)* binding; *(art)* bookbinding

relooker [rəluke] *vt Fam* to revamp

reluire* [rəlɥir] *vi* to shine, to gleam; **faire r. qch** to polish sth up • **reluisant, -ante** *adj* shiny; *Fig* **peu r.** far from brilliant

reluquer [rəlyke] *vt Fam* to eye up

remâcher [rəmɑʃe] *vt Fig (souvenirs)* to brood over

remanier [rəmanje] *vt (texte)* to revise; *(ministère)* to reshuffle • **remaniement** *nm (de texte)* revision; **r. ministériel** cabinet reshuffle

remarier [rəmarje] **se remarier** *vpr* to remarry • **remariage** *nm* remarriage

remarquable [rəmarkabl] *adj* remarkable (**par** for) • **remarquablement** [-əmɑ̃] *adv* remarkably

remarque [rəmark] *nf* remark; **faire une r.** to make a remark

remarquer [rəmarke] *vt (apercevoir)* to notice (**que** that); *(dire)* to remark (**que** that); **faire r. qch** to point sth out (**à** to); **se faire r.** to attract attention; *Fam* **remarque, il n'est pas le seul!** mind you, he's not the only one!

> 🖉 Il faut noter que le verbe anglais **to remark** est un faux ami. Il signifie uniquement **faire remarquer**.

remballer [rɑ̃bale] *vt* to repack; *Fam* **il s'est fait r.** he was sent packing

rembarrer [rɑ̃bare] *vt Fam* to snub

remblai [rɑ̃ble] *nm* embankment • **remblayer** *vt (route)* to bank up

rembobiner [rɑ̃bɔbine] *vt*, **se rembobiner** *vpr* to rewind

rembourrer [rɑ̃bure] *vt (fauteuil, matelas)* to stuff • **rembourrage** *nm (action, matière)* stuffing

rembourser [rɑ̃burse] *vt (personne)* to pay back; *(billet, frais)* to refund • **remboursement** [-əmɑ̃] *nm* repayment; *(de billet)* refund; **envoi contre r.** cash on delivery

remède [rəmɛd] *nm* cure, remedy (**contre** for) • **remédier** *vi* **r. à qch** to remedy sth

remémorer [rəmemɔre] **se remémorer** *vpr* to remember

remercier [rəmɛrsje] *vt* (**a**) *(dire merci à)* to thank (**de** *ou* **pour qch** for sth); **je vous remercie d'être venu** thank you for coming; **non, je vous remercie** no thank you (**b**) *Euph (congédier)* to ask to leave • **remerciements** *nmpl* thanks

remettre* [rəmɛtr] **1** *vt (replacer)* to put back; *(vêtement)* to put back on; *(télévision)* to turn on again; *(disque)* to put on again; *(différer)* to postpone (**à** until); *(ajouter)* to add (**dans** to); **r. qch à qn** *(lettre, télégramme)* to deliver sth to sb; *(rapport)* to submit sth to sb; *(démission)* to hand sth in to sb; **r. qn en liberté** to set sb free; **r. qch en question** *ou* **en cause** to call sth into question; **r. qch en état** to repair sth; **r. qch à jour** to bring sth up to date; **r. une montre à l'heure** to set a watch to the correct time; *Fig* **r. les pendules à l'heure** to clear things up; **je ne vous remets pas** I can't place you; *Fam* **r. ça** to start again

2 se remettre *vpr* **se r. en question** to question oneself; **se r. à qch** to start sth again; **se r. à faire qch** to start to do sth again; **se r. de qch** to recover from sth; **s'en r. à qn** to rely on sb

réminiscences [reminisãs] *nfpl* (vague) recollections

remise [rəmiz] *nf* (**a**) *(de lettre)* delivery; **r. à neuf** *(de machine)* reconditioning; **r. en cause** *ou* **question** questioning; **r. en état** *(de maison)* restoration; *Football* **r. en jeu** throw-in (**b**) *(rabais)* discount (**c**) *Jur* **r. de peine** reduction of sentence (**d**) *(local)* shed

remiser [rəmize] *vt* to put away

rémission [remisjõ] *nf (de péché, de maladie) & Jur* remission; **sans r.** *(travailler)* relentlessly

remmener [rãməne] *vt* to take back

remontée [rəmõte] *nf (de pente)* ascent; *(d'eau, de prix)* rising; **r. mécanique** ski lift

remonter [rəmõte] **1** *(aux* **être)** *vi* to come/go back up; *(niveau, prix)* to rise again, to go back up; *(dans le temps)* to go back (**à** to); **r. dans** *(voiture)* to get back in(to); *(bus, train)* to get back on(to); **r. sur** *(cheval, vélo)* to get back on(to); **r. à dix ans** to go back ten years

2 *(aux* **avoir)** *vt (escalier, pente)* to come/go back up; *(porter)* to bring/take back up; *(montre)* to wind up; *(relever)* to raise; *(col)* to turn up; *(objet démonté)* to put back together, to reassemble; *(garderobe)* to restock; **r. qn** *(ragaillardir)* to buck sb up; **r. le moral à qn** to cheer sb up; *Fig* **r. la pente** to get back on to one's feet *(after a hard struggle)*; *Fam* **être (très) remonté contre qn** to be really furious with *or* mad at sb; *Fam* **se faire r. les bretelles** to get rapped over the knuckles, to get a serious talking-to • **remontant** *nm* tonic • **remonte-pente** *(pl* **remonte-pentes)** *nm* ski lift

remontoir [rəmõtwar] *nm* winder

remontrance [rəmõtrãs] *nf* remonstrance; **faire des remontrances à qn** to remonstrate with sb

remontrer [rəmõtre] *vt* to show again; **en r. à qn** to prove one's superiority over sb

remords [rəmɔr] *nm* remorse; **avoir du** *ou* **des r.** to feel remorse

remorque [rəmɔrk] *nf (de voiture)* trailer; **prendre qch en r.** to take sth in tow; *Fig* **être à la r.** to lag behind • **remorquer** *vt (voiture, bateau)* to tow • **remorqueur** *nm* tug(boat)

remous [rəmu] *nm (de rivière)* eddy; *Fig* **faire des r.** to cause a stir

rempailler [rãpaje] *vt (chaise)* to reseat

rempart [rãpar] *nm* rampart; **remparts** walls

remplacer [rãplase] *vt* to replace (**par** with); *(professionnellement)* to stand in for • **remplaçant, -ante** *nmf (personne)* replacement; *(enseignant)* substitute teacher, *Br* supply teacher; *(joueur)* substitute • **remplacement** *nm* replacement; **en r. de** in place of

remplir [rãplir] **1** *vt* to fill (up) (**de** with); *(formulaire)* to fill out, *Br* to fill in; *(promesse)* to fulfil

2 se remplir *vpr* to fill (up) (**de** with) • **remplissage** *nm* filling (up); *Péj* **faire du r.** to pad

remporter [rãpɔrte] *vt (objet)* to take back; *(prix, victoire)* to win; *(succès)* to achieve

remuer [rəmɥe] **1** *vt (bouger)* to move; *(café)* to stir; *(salade)* to toss; *(terre)* to turn over; **r. qn** *(émouvoir)* to move sb

2 *vi* to move; *(gigoter)* to fidget

3 se remuer *vpr* to move; *Fam (se démener)* to have plenty of get-up-and-go • **remuant, -uante** *adj (enfant)* hyperactive • **remue-ménage** *nm inv* commotion

rémunérer [remynere] *vt (personne)* to pay; *(travail)* to pay for • **rémunérateur, -trice** *adj* remunerative • **rémunération** *nf* payment (**de** for)

renâcler [rənakle] *vi Fam* **r. à faire qch** to balk at doing sth

renaître* [rənɛtr] *vi (personne)* to be born again; *(espoir, industrie)* to revive; *Fig* **r. de ses cendres** to rise from its ashes • **renaissance** *nf* rebirth; *(des arts)* renaissance

renard [rənar] *nm* fox

renchérir [rãʃerir] *vi (dire plus)* to go one better (**sur** than)

rencontre [rãkõtr] *nf (de personnes)* meeting; *(match) Br* match, *Am* game; **amours de r.** casual love affairs; **aller à la r. de qn** to go to meet sb • **rencontrer 1** *vt (personne)* to meet; *(difficulté, obstacle)* to come up against, to encounter; *(trouver)* to come across **2 se rencontrer** *vpr* to meet

rendement [rãdmã] *nm (de champ)* yield; *(d'investissement)* return, yield; *(de personne, de machine)* output

rendez-vous [rãdevu] *nm inv (rencontre)* appointment; *(amoureux)* date; *(lieu)* meeting place; **donner r. à qn** to arrange to meet sb; **prendre r. avec qn** to make an appointment with sb; **recevoir sur r.** *(médecin)* to see patients by appointment

rendormir* [rãdɔrmir] **se rendormir** *vpr* to go back to sleep

rendre [rãdr] **1** *vt (restituer)* to give back, to return (**à** to); *(son)* to give; *(jugement)* to deliver; *(armes)* to surrender; *(invitation)* to return; *(santé)* to restore; *(rembourser)* to pay back; *(exprimer)* to render; *(vomir)* to bring up; **r. célèbre/plus grand** to make famous/bigger; **r. la monnaie à qn** to give sb his/her change; **r. sa liberté à qn** to set sb free; **r. la justice** to dispense justice; **r. l'âme** to pass away; **r. les armes** to surrender

2 *vi (vomir)* to vomit; *(arbre, terre)* to yield

3 se rendre *vpr (criminel)* to give oneself up (**à** to); *(soldats)* to surrender (**à** to); *(aller)* to go (**à** to); **se r. à l'évidence** *(être lucide)* to face facts; **se r. malade/utile** to make oneself ill/useful • **rendu, -ue** *adj* **être r.** *(arrivé)* to have arrived

renégat, -ate [rənega, -at] *nmf* renegade

rênes [rɛn] *nfpl* reins

renfermer [rãfɛrme] **1** *vt* to contain

2 se renfermer *vpr* to withdraw into oneself • **renfermé, -ée 1** *adj (personne)* withdrawn **2** *nm* **sentir le r.** to smell musty

renflé, -ée [rãfle] *adj* bulging • **renflement** [-əmã] *nm* bulge

renflouer [rãflue] *vt (navire)* to refloat; **r. les caisses de l'État** to replenish the State coffers

renfoncement [rãfɔ̃s(ə)mã] *nm* recess; **dans le r. d'une porte** in a doorway

renforcer [rãfɔrse] *vt* to strengthen, to reinforce • **renforcement** [-əmã] *nm* reinforcement, strengthening

renfort [rãfɔr] *nm* **des renforts** *(troupes)* reinforcements; *Fig (aide)* backup, additional help; *Fig* **à grand r. de** with (the help of) a great deal of

renfrogner [rãfrɔɲe] **se renfrogner** *vpr* to scowl • **renfrogné, -ée** *adj* scowling

rengaine [rãgɛn] *nf Fam Péj* **la même r.** the same old story

rengorger [rãgɔrʒe] **se rengorger** *vpr* to strut

renier [rənje] *vt (ami, pays)* to disown; *(foi)* to deny • **reniement** *nm (d'ami, de pays)* disowning; *(de foi)* denial

renifler [rənifle] *vti* to sniff • **reniflement** [-əmã] *nm (bruit)* sniff

renne [rɛn] *nm* reindeer

renom [rənɔ̃] *nm* renown; **de r.** *(ouvrage, artiste)* famous, renowned • **renommé, -ée** *adj* famous, renowned (**pour** for) • **renommée** *nf* fame, renown

renoncer [rənɔ̃se] *vi* **r. à qch** to give up, to abandon sth; **r. à faire qch** to give up doing sth • **renoncement** *nm*, **renonciation** *nf* renunciation (**à** of)

renouer [rənwe] **1** *vt (lacet)* to tie again; *(conversation)* to resume

2 *vi* **r. avec qch** *(tradition)* to revive sth; **r. avec qn** to take up with sb again

renouveau, -x [rənuvo] *nm* revival

renouveler [rənuvəle] **1** *vt* to renew; *(erreur, expérience)* to repeat

2 se renouveler *vpr (incident)* to happen again, to recur; *(cellules, sang)* to be renewed • **renouvelable** [-vlabl] *adj* renewable • **renouvellement** [-ɛlmã] *nm* renewal

rénover [renɔve] *vt (édifice, meuble)* to renovate; *(institution)* to reform • **rénovation** *nf (d'édifice, de meuble)* renovation; *(d'institution)* reform

renseigner [rãseɲe] **1** *vt* to give some information to (**sur** about)

2 se renseigner *vpr* to make inquiries (**sur** about) • **renseignement** [-ɛɲəmã] *nm* piece of information; **renseignements** information; **les renseignements (téléphoniques)** *Br* directory inquiries, *Am* information; **prendre** *ou* **demander des renseignements** to make inquiries

rentable [rãtabl] *adj* profitable • **rentabilité** *nf* profitability

rente [rãt] *nf* (private) income; *(pension)* pension; **avoir des rentes** to have private means • **rentier, -ière** *nmf* person of private means

rentrée [rãtre] *nf (retour)* return; **r. des classes** start of the new school year; **rentrées d'argent** (cash) receipts; **r. parlementaire** reopening of Parliament

rentrer [rãtre] **1** *(aux* **être***)* *vi (entrer)* to go/come in; *(entrer de nouveau)* to go/come back in; *(chez soi)* to go/come (back) home; *(argent)* to come in; **r. en France** to return to France; **r. de vacances** to come back from holiday; **en rentrant de l'école** on my/his/her/*etc* way home from school; **r. dans qch** *(pénétrer)* to get into sth; *(sujet: voiture)* to crash into sth; **r. dans une catégorie** to fall into a category; **r. en classe** to go back to school; **r. dans ses frais** to recover one's expenses;

Fam **je lui suis rentré dedans** I laid into him/her

2 *(aux* **avoir)** *vt (linge, troupeau)* to bring/take in; *(chemise)* to tuck in; *(larmes)* to stifle; *(griffes)* to retract ● **rentré, -ée** *adj (colère)* suppressed

renverse [rãvɛrs] **à la renverse** *adv (tomber)* backwards

renverser [rãvɛrse] **1** *vt (faire tomber)* to knock over; *(liquide)* to spill; *(piéton)* to run over; *(tendance, situation)* to reverse; *(gouvernement)* to overthrow; *(tête)* to tilt back

2 se renverser *vpr (récipient)* to fall over; *(véhicule)* to overturn ● **renversant, -ante** *adj Fam* astounding ● **renversement** [-əmã] *nm (de situation, de tendance)* reversal; *(de gouvernement)* overthrow

renvoi [rãvwa] *nm (de marchandise, de lettre)* return; *(d'employé)* dismissal; *(d'élève)* expulsion; *(ajournement)* postponement; *(de texte)* cross-reference; *(rot)* belch, burp ● **renvoyer*** *vt (lettre, cadeau)* to send back, to return; *(employé)* to dismiss; *(élève)* to expel; *(balle)* to throw back; *(lumière, image)* to reflect; *(ajourner)* to postpone (**à** until)

réorganiser [reɔrganize] *vt* to reorganize ● **réorganisation** *nf* reorganization

réouverture [reuvɛrtyr] *nf* reopening

repaire [rəpɛr] *nm* den

repaître* [rəpɛtr] **se repaître** *vpr Fig* **se r. de qch** to revel in sth

répandre [repãdr] **1** *vt (liquide)* to spill; *(nouvelle, joie)* to spread; *(odeur)* to give off; *(lumière, larmes, sang, chargement)* to shed; *(gravillons)* to scatter; *(dons, bienfaits)* to lavish

2 se répandre *vpr (nouvelle, peur)* to spread; *(liquide)* to spill; **se r. dans** *(fumée, odeur)* to spread through ● **répandu, -ue** *adj (opinion, usage)* widespread

reparaître* [rəparɛtr] *vi* to reappear

réparer [repare] *vt (objet, machine)* to repair, to mend; *(faute)* to make amends for; *(dommage)* to make good; **faire r. qch** to get sth repaired ● **réparable** *adj (machine)* repairable ● **réparateur, -trice 1** *nmf* repairer **2** *adj (sommeil)* refreshing ● **réparation** *nf (action)* repairing; *(résultat)* repair; *(dédommagement)* reparation; **en r.** under repair; **faire des réparations** to do some repairs

reparler [rəparle] *vi* **r. de qch** to talk about sth again

repartie [reparti] *nf* retort

repartir* [rəpartir] *(aux* **être)** *vi (continuer)* to set off again; *(s'en retourner)* to go back; *(machine)* to start again; **r. à** *ou* **de zéro** to go back to square one

répartir [repartir] *vt (poids, charge)* to distribute; *(tâches, vivres)* to share (out); *(classer)* to divide (up); *(étaler dans le temps)* to spread (out) *(sur* over) ● **répartition** *nf (de poids)* distribution; *(de tâches)* sharing; *(classement)* division

repas [rəpɑ] *nm* meal; **prendre un r.** to have a meal

repasser [rəpɑse] **1** *vi* to come/go back; **r. chez qn** to drop in on sb again

2 *vt (montagne, frontière)* to go across again; *(examen)* to take again, *Br* to resit; *(leçon)* to go over; *(film)* to show again; *(disque, cassette)* to play again; *(linge)* to iron ● **repassage** *nm* ironing

repêcher [rəpeʃe] *vt (objet)* to fish out; *Fam (candidat)* to let through

repeindre* [rəpɛdr] *vt* to repaint

repenser [rəpãse] *vt* to rethink

repentir* [rəpãtir] *nm* repentance ● **se repentir*** *vpr Rel* to repent (**de** of); **se r. de qch/d'avoir fait qch** *(regretter)* to regret sth/doing sth ● **repenti, -ie** *adj* repentant

répercuter [repɛrkyte] **1** *vt (son)* to reflect; *(augmentation)* to pass

2 se répercuter *vpr (son, lumière)* to be reflected; *Fig* **se r. sur** to have repercussions on ● **répercussion** *nf (conséquence)* repercussion

repère [rəpɛr] *nm* mark; **point de r.** *(espace, temps)* reference point ● **repérer 1** *vt (endroit)* to locate; *Fam (remarquer)* to spot **2 se repérer** *vpr* to get one's bearings

répertoire [repɛrtwar] *nm (liste)* index; *(carnet)* (indexed) notebook; *Théâtre* repertoire; *Ordinat (de fichiers)* directory ● **répertorier** *vt* to list

répéter [repete] **1** *vt* to repeat; *(pièce de théâtre, rôle, symphonie)* to rehearse; **r. à qn que...** to tell sb again that...; **je te l'ai répété cent fois** I've told you a hundred times

2 *vi (redire)* to repeat; *(acteur)* to rehearse

3 se répéter *vpr (radoter)* to repeat oneself; *(événement)* to happen again ● **répétitif, -ive** *adj* repetitive ● **répétition** *nf (redite)* repetition; *Théâtre* rehearsal; **r. générale** dress rehearsal

repiquer [rəpike] *vt (plante)* to plant out; *(disque)* to record

répit [repi] *nm* rest, respite; **sans r.** ceaselessly

replacer [rəplase] *vt* to replace, to put back

replanter [rǝplɑ̃te] *vt* to replant

replet, -ète [rǝplɛ, -ɛt] *adj (personne)* podgy

repli [rǝpli] *nm (de vêtement, de terrain)* fold; *(d'armée)* withdrawal; *(de monnaie)* fall

replier [rǝplije] **1** *vt (objet)* to fold up; *(couteau)* to fold away; *(ailes)* to fold; *(jambes)* to tuck up
2 se replier *vpr (objet)* to fold up; *(armée)* to withdraw; *Fig* **se r. sur soi-même** to withdraw into oneself

réplique [replik] *nf (réponse)* retort; *(d'acteur)* lines; *(copie)* replica; **sans r.** *(argument)* unanswerable • **répliquer 1** *vt* **r. que...** to reply that... **2** *vi* to reply; *(avec impertinence)* to answer back

répondre [repɔ̃dr] **1** *vi* to answer, to reply; *(avec impertinence)* to answer back; *(réagir)* to respond (**à** to); **r. à qn** to answer sb, to reply to sb; *(avec impertinence)* to answer sb back; **r. à** *(lettre, question, objection)* to answer, to reply to; *(besoin)* to meet; *(salut)* to return; *(correspondre à)* to correspond to; **r. au téléphone** to answer the phone; **r. de qn/qch** to answer for sb/sth
2 *vt (remarque)* to answer *or* reply with; **r. que...** to answer *or* reply that... • **répondant** *nm Fam* **avoir du r.** to have money behind one • **répondeur** *nm* **r. (téléphonique)** answering machine

réponse [repɔ̃s] *nf* answer, reply; *(réaction)* response (**à** to); **en r. à** in answer *or* reply to

report [rǝpɔr] *nm (transcription)* transfer; *(de somme)* carrying forward; *(de rendez-vous)* postponement

> *ℓ* Il faut noter que le nom anglais **report** est un faux ami. Il signifie **rapport**.

reportage [rǝpɔrtaʒ] *nm (article, émission)* report; *(métier)* reporting

reporter¹ [rǝpɔrte] **1** *vt (objet)* to take back; *(réunion)* to put off, to postpone (**à** until); *(transcrire)* to transfer (**sur** to); *(somme)* to carry forward (**sur** to)
2 se reporter *vpr* **se r. à** *(texte)* to refer to; **se r. sur** *(sujet: colère)* to be transferred to

> *ℓ* Il faut noter que le verbe anglais **to report** est un faux ami. Il ne signifie jamais **reporter**.

reporter² [rǝpɔrtɛr] *nm* reporter

repos [rǝpo] *nm (détente)* rest; *(tranquillité)* peace; *Mil* **r.!** at ease!; **jour de r.** day off; **de tout r.** *(situation)* safe

reposer [rǝpoze] **1** *vt (objet)* to put back down; *(problème, question)* to raise again; *(délasser)* to rest, to relax; **r. sa tête sur** *(appuyer)* to lean one's head on
2 *vi (être enterré)* to lie; **r. sur** *(bâtiment)* to be built on; *(théorie)* to be based on; **laisser r.** *(liquide)* to allow to settle
3 se reposer *vpr* to rest; **se r. sur qn** to rely on sb • **reposant, -ante** *adj* restful, relaxing • **reposé, -ée** *adj* rested

repousser [rǝpuse] **1** *vt (en arrière)* to push back; *(sur le côté)* to push away; *(attaque, ennemi)* to beat off; *(réunion)* to put off; *(offre)* to reject; *(dégoûter)* to repel
2 *vi (cheveux, feuilles)* to grow again • **repoussant, -ante** *adj* repulsive

répréhensible [repreɑ̃sibl] *adj* reprehensible

reprendre* [rǝprɑ̃dr] **1** *vt (objet)* to take back; *(évadé, ville)* to recapture; *(passer prendre)* to pick up again; *(activité)* to take up again; *(refrain)* to take up; *(vêtement)* to alter; *(corriger)* to correct; *(blâmer)* to admonish; *(pièce de théâtre)* to put on again; **r. de la viande/un œuf** to take some more meat/another egg; **r. sa place** *(retourner s'asseoir)* to return to one's seat; **r. ses esprits** to come round; **r. des forces** to get one's strength back; *Fam* **je jure qu'on ne m'y reprendra plus** I swear I won't be caught out doing that again
2 *vi (plante)* to take root again; *(recommencer)* to start again; *(affaires)* to pick up; *(en parlant)* to go on, to continue
3 se reprendre *vpr (se ressaisir)* to get a grip on oneself; *(se corriger)* to correct oneself; **s'y r. à deux/plusieurs fois** to have another go/several goes (at it)

représailles [rǝprezaj] *nfpl* reprisals, retaliation

représenter [rǝprezɑ̃te] **1** *vt* to represent; *(pièce de théâtre)* to perform
2 se représenter *vpr (s'imaginer)* to imagine • **représentant, -ante** *nmf* representative; **r. de commerce** sales representative • **représentatif, -ive** *adj* representative (**de** of) • **représentation** *nf* representation; *Théâtre* performance

répression [represjɔ̃] *nf (d'émeute)* suppression; *(mesures de contrôle)* repression • **répressif, -ive** *adj* repressive • **réprimer** *vt (sentiment, révolte)* to suppress

réprimande [reprimɑ̃d] *nf* reprimand • **réprimander** *vt* to reprimand

repris [rǝpri] *nm* **r. de justice** hardened criminal

reprise [rəpriz] *nf (recommencement)* resumption; *Théâtre* revival; *(de film, d'émission)* repeat; *Boxe* round; *(de l'économie)* recovery; *(de locataire)* = money for fixtures and fittings *(paid by outgoing tenant)*; *(de marchandise)* taking back; *(pour nouvel achat)* part exchange, trade-in; **faire une r. à qch** to mend sth; **à plusieurs reprises** on several occasions • **repriser** *vt (chaussette)* to mend

réprobation [reprobasjɔ̃] *nf* disapproval • **réprobateur, -trice** *adj* disapproving

reproche [rəprɔʃ] *nm* reproach; **faire des reproches à qn sur qch** to reproach sb for sth; **sans r.** beyond reproach • **reprocher** **1** *vt* **r. qch à qn** to blame *or* reproach sb for sth; **qu'as-tu à r. à ce livre?** what do you have against this book? **2 se reprocher** *vpr* **n'avoir rien à se r.** to have nothing to reproach *or* blame oneself for

reproduire* [rəprɔdɥir] **1** *vt (modèle, son)* to reproduce
2 se reproduire *vpr (animaux)* to reproduce; *(incident)* to happen again • **reproducteur, -trice** *adj* reproductive • **reproduction** *nf (d'animaux, de son)* reproduction; *(copie)* copy

réprouver [repruve] *vt* to condemn

reptile [rɛptil] *nm* reptile

repu, -ue [rəpy] *adj (rassasié)* satiated

république [repyblik] *nf* republic • **républicain, -aine** *adj & nmf* republican

répudier [repydje] *vt* to repudiate

répugnant, -ante [repyɲɑ̃, -ɑ̃t] *adj* repulsive • **répugnance** *nf* repugnance, loathing (**pour** for); *(manque d'enthousiasme)* reluctance • **répugner** *vi* **à qn** to be repugnant to sb; **r. à faire qch** to be loath to do sth

répulsion [repylsjɔ̃] *nf* repulsion

réputation [repytasjɔ̃] *nf* reputation; **avoir la r. d'être franc** to have a reputation for being frank *or* for frankness; **connaître qn de r.** to know sb by reputation • **réputé, -ée** *adj (célèbre)* renowned (**pour** for); **r. pour être très intelligent** reputed to be very intelligent

requérir [rəkerir] *vt (nécessiter)* to require; *(solliciter)* to request; *(peine de prison)* to call for • **requis, -ise** *adj* required, requisite

requête [rəkɛt] *nf* request; *(auprès d'un juge)* petition

requiem [rekɥijɛm] *nm inv* requiem

requin [rəkɛ̃] *nm (poisson) & Fig* shark

requinquer [rəkɛ̃ke] *vt Fam* to perk up

réquisition [rekizisjɔ̃] *nf* requisition

• **réquisitionner** *vt* to requisition, to commandeer

réquisitoire [rekizitwar] *nm Jur* prosecution address; *(critique)* indictment (**contre** of)

RER [ɛrøɛr] (*abrév* **Réseau express régional**) *nm* = express rail network serving Paris and its suburbs

rescapé, -ée [rɛskape] **1** *adj* surviving
2 *nmf* survivor

rescousse [rɛskus] **à la rescousse** *adv* to the rescue

réseau, -x [rezo] *nm* network; **r. d'espionnage** spy ring *or* network

réservation [rezɛrvasjɔ̃] *nf* reservation, booking; **faire une r.** to make a booking

réserve [rezɛrv] *nf (provision, discrétion)* reserve; *(entrepôt)* storeroom; *(de bibliothèque)* stacks; *(de chasse, de pêche)* preserve; *(restriction)* reservation; *Mil* **la r.** the reserve; **en r.** in reserve; **sans r.** *(admiration)* unqualified; **sous r. de** subject to; **sous toutes réserves** without guarantee; **r. indienne** (native American) reservation; **r. naturelle** nature reserve

réserver [rezɛrve] **1** *vt* to reserve; *(garder)* to save, to keep (**à** for); *(marchandises)* to put aside (**à** for); *(sort, surprise)* to hold in store (**à** for)
2 se réserver *vpr* **se r. pour qch** to save oneself for sth; **se r. de faire qch** to reserve the right to do sth • **réservé, -ée** *adj (personne, place, chambre)* reserved

réservoir [rezɛrvwar] *nm (lac)* reservoir; *(cuve)* tank; **r. d'essence** *Br* petrol *or Am* gas tank

résidence [rezidɑ̃s] *nf* residence; **r. secondaire** second home; **r. universitaire** *Br* hall of residence, *Am* dormitory • **résident, -ente** *nmf* resident; **un r. français en Irlande** a French national resident in Ireland • **résidentiel, -ielle** *adj (quartier)* residential • **résider** *vi* to reside; **r. dans** *(consister en)* to lie in

résidu [rezidy] *nm* residue

résigner [reziɲe] **se résigner** *vpr* to resign oneself (**à qch** to sth; **à faire** to doing) • **résignation** *nf* resignation

résilier [rezilje] *vt (contrat)* to terminate • **résiliation** *nf* termination

résille [rezij] *nf* hairnet

résine [rezin] *nf* resin

résistance [rezistɑ̃s] *nf* resistance (**à** to); *Hist* **la R.** the Resistance

résister [reziste] *vi* **r. à** *(attaque, agresseur, tentation)* to resist; *(chaleur, fatigue, souffrance)* to withstand; *(mauvais traitement)* to stand up to; **r. à l'analyse** to stand up to analysis •**résistant, -ante 1** *adj* tough; **r. à la chaleur** heat-resistant; **r. au choc** shockproof **2** *nmf Hist* Resistance fighter

résolu, -ue [rezɔly] **1** *pp de* **résoudre**
2 *adj* determined, resolute; **r. à faire qch** determined to do sth •**résolument** *adv* resolutely •**résolution** *nf (décision)* resolution; *(fermeté)* determination

résonance [rezɔnãs] *nf* resonance

résonner [rezɔne] *vi (cri)* to resound; *(salle, voix)* to echo (**de** with)

résorber [rezɔrbe] **1** *vt (excédent)* to absorb; *(chômage)* to reduce
2 se résorber *vpr (excédent)* to be absorbed; *(chômage)* to be reduced •**résorption** *nf (de surplus, de déficit)* absorption

résoudre* [rezudr] **1** *vt (problème)* to solve; *(difficulté)* to resolve; **r. de faire qch** to resolve to do sth
2 se résoudre *vpr* **se r. à faire qch** to resolve to do sth

respect [respɛ] *nm* respect (**pour/de** for); **mes respects à...** my regards *or* respects to...; **tenir qn en r.** to hold sb in check •**respectabilité** *nf* respectability •**respectable** *adj (honorable, important)* respectable •**respecter** *vt* to respect; **qui se respecte** self-respecting; **r. la loi** to abide by the law; **faire r. la loi** to enforce the law •**respectueux, -ueuse** *adj* respectful (**envers** to; **de** of)

respectif, -ive [respɛktif, -iv] *adj* respective •**respectivement** *adv* respectively

respirer [respire] **1** *vi* to breathe; *Fig (être soulagé)* to breathe again
2 *vt* to breathe (in); *Fig (exprimer)* to radiate •**respiration** *nf* breathing; *(haleine)* breath; *Méd* **r. artificielle** artificial respiration •**respiratoire** *adj* **troubles respiratoires** breathing difficulties

resplendir [resplãdir] *vi* to shine; *(visage)* to glow (**de** with) •**resplendissant, -ante** *adj (personne, visage)* radiant (**de** with)

responsable [respɔ̃sabl] **1** *adj* responsible (**de qch** for sth; **devant qn** to sb)
2 *nmf (chef)* person in charge; *(dans une organisation)* official; *(coupable)* person responsible (**de** for) •**responsabilité** *nf* responsibility; *(légale)* liability

resquiller [reskije] *vi (au cinéma)* to sneak in without paying; *(dans le métro)* to dodge paying one's fare

ressaisir [rəsezir] **se ressaisir** *vpr* to pull oneself together

ressasser [rəsase] *vt (ruminer)* to brood over; *(répéter)* to keep trotting out

ressemblance [rəsãblãs] *nf* likeness, resemblance (**avec** to) •**ressemblant, -ante** *adj* lifelike •**ressembler 1** *vi.* **à** to look like, to resemble; **cela ne lui ressemble pas** *(ce n'est pas son genre)* that's not like him/her **2 se ressembler** *vpr* to look alike

ressentiment [rəsãtimã] *nm* resentment

ressentir* [rəsãtir] **1** *vt* to feel
2 se ressentir *vpr* **se r. de qch** *(personne)* to feel the effects of sth; *(travail)* to show the effects of sth

resserre [rəsɛr] *nf* storeroom; *(remise)* shed

resserrer [rəsere] **1** *vt (nœud, boulon)* to tighten; *Fig (liens)* to strengthen
2 se resserrer *vpr (nœud)* to tighten; *(amitié)* to become closer; *(route)* to narrow

resservir* [rəsɛrvir] **1** *vi (outil)* to come in useful (again)
2 se resservir *vpr* **se r. de** *(plat)* to have another helping of

ressort [rəsɔr] *nm (objet)* spring; *(énergie)* spirit; **du r. de** within the competence of; **en dernier r.** *(décider)* as a last resort

ressortir* [rəsɔrtir] **1** *(aux être) vi (personne)* to go/come back out; *(film)* to be shown again; *(se voir)* to stand out; **faire r. qch** to bring sth out; **il ressort de...** *(résulte)* it emerges from...
2 *(aux avoir) vi (vêtement)* to get out again

ressortissant, -ante [rəsɔrtisã, -ãt] *nmf* national

ressource [rəsurs] **1** *nfpl* **ressources** *(moyens, argent)* resources; **être sans ressources** to be without means; **ressources humaines** human resources
2 *nf (possibilité)* possibility (**de faire** of doing); **avoir de la r.** to be resourceful; **en dernière r.** as a last resort

ressusciter [resysite] **1** *vi* to rise from the dead
2 *vt (mort)* to raise

> ⚠ Il faut noter que le verbe anglais **to resuscitate** est un faux ami. Il ne signifie jamais **ressusciter**.

restant, -ante [restã, -ãt] **1** *adj* remaining
2 *nm* **le r.** the rest, the remainder; **un r. de viande** some leftover meat

restaurant [restɔrã] *nm* restaurant

restaurer [restɔre] **1** *vt (réparer, rétablir)* to restore
2 se restaurer *vpr* to have something to eat •**restaurateur, -trice** *nmf (hôtelier, hô-*

telière) restaurant owner; *(de tableaux)* restorer •**restauration** *nf (hôtellerie)* catering; *(de tableau)* restoration

reste [rɛst] *nm* rest, remainder (**de** of); **restes** remains (**de** of); *(de repas)* leftovers; **un r. de fromage** some leftover cheese; **au r., du r.** moreover, besides; **avoir qch de r.** to have sth to spare; **il est parti sans demander son r.** he left without further ado

rester [rɛste] *(aux être) vi* to stay, to remain; *(calme, jeune)* to keep, to stay, to remain; *(subsister)* to be left, to remain; **il reste du pain** there's some bread left (over); **il me reste une minute** I have one minute left; **l'argent qui lui reste** the money he/she has left; **reste à savoir** it remains to be seen; **il me reste deux choses à faire** I still have two things to do; **il me reste à vous remercier** it remains for me to thank you; **il n'en reste pas moins que** the fact remains that; **en r. à** to stop at; **restons-en là** let's leave it at that; **r. sur sa faim** to remain hungry; **les oignons me sont restés sur l'estomac** the onions are lying heavy on my stomach; *Fam* **elle a failli y r.** that was very nearly the end of her

restituer [rɛstitɥe] *vt(rendre)* to return (**à** to); *(argent)* to repay; *(son)* to reproduce; *(passé)* to re-create •**restitution** *nf (d'objet)* return; *(de son)* reproduction; *(du passé)* re-creation

restreindre* [rɛstrɛ̃dr] **1** *vt* to restrict (**à** to) **2 se restreindre** *upr (domaine)* to become more restricted; *(faire des économies)* to cut down •**restreint, -einte** *adj* restricted (**à** to); *(espace)* limited •**restrictif, -ive** *adj* restrictive •**restriction** *nf* restriction; **sans r.** *(approuver)* unreservedly

résultat [rezylta] *nm* result; **avoir qch pour r.** to result in sth •**résulter 1** *vi* **r. de** to result from **2** *v impersonnel* **il en résulte que...** the result of this is that...

résumer [rezyme] **1** *vt (abréger)* to summarize; *(récapituler)* to sum up **2 se résumer** *upr (orateur)* to sum up; **se r. à qch** *(se réduire à)* to boil down to sth •**résumé** *nm* summary; **en r.** in short

📖 Il faut noter que le verbe anglais **to resume** est un faux ami. Il signifie **recommencer**.

résurgence [rezyrʒɑ̃s] *nf* resurgence (**de** in)

résurrection [rezyrɛksjɔ̃] *nf* resurrection

rétablir [retablir] **1** *vt (communications,*

ordre) to restore; *(vérité)* to re-establish; *(employé)* to reinstate **2 se rétablir** *upr (ordre)* to be restored; *(malade)* to recover •**rétablissement** *nm (d'ordre, de dynastie)* restoration; *(de vérité)* re-establishment; *(de malade)* recovery

retaper [rətape] *vt Fam (maison, voiture)* to do up; *(lit)* to straighten; *(malade)* to buck up

retard [rətar] *nm (de personne)* lateness; *(sur un programme)* delay; *(de région)* backwardness; **en r.** late; **en r. dans qch** behind in sth; **en r. sur qn/qch** behind sb/sth; **rattraper** *ou* **combler son r.** to catch up; **avoir du r.** to be late; *(sur un programme)* to be behind (schedule); *(montre)* to be slow; **avoir une heure de r.** to be an hour late; **prendre du r.** *(montre)* to lose (time); *(personne)* to fall behind; **sans r.** without delay; *Fam* **il a toujours un métro de r.** he's slow on the uptake •**retardataire** *nmf* latecomer

retarder [rətarde] **1** *vt (faire arriver en retard)* to delay; *(date, montre, départ)* to put back; **r. qn** *(dans une activité)* to put sb behind **2** *vi (montre)* to be slow; **r. de cinq minutes** to be five minutes slow; *Fig* **r. (sur son temps)** *(personne)* to be behind the times •**retardé, -ée** *adj (enfant)* backward

retenir* [rətənir] **1** *vt (personne)* to keep; *(eau, chaleur)* to retain; *(cotisation)* to deduct (**sur** from); *(suggestion)* to adopt; *(larmes, foule)* to hold back; *Math (chiffre)* to carry; *(se souvenir de)* to remember; *(réserver)* to reserve; **r. qn par le bras** to hold sb back by the arm; **r. qn prisonnier** to keep sb prisoner; **r. l'attention de qn** to catch sb's attention; **r. qn de faire qch** to stop sb (from) doing sth; **votre candidature n'a pas été retenue** your application was unsuccessful **2 se retenir** *upr (se contenir)* to restrain oneself; **se r. de faire qch** to stop oneself (from) doing sth; **se r. à qn/qch** to cling to sb/sth

rentantir [rɑ̃tɑ̃tir] *vi* to ring out (**de** with); *Fig* **r. sur qch** to have an impact on sth •**retentissant, -ante** *adj (succès, échec)* resounding; *(scandale)* major •**retentissement** *nm (effet)* impact; **avoir un grand r.** *(film)* to create a stir

retenue [rətəny] *nf (modération)* restraint; *(de salaire)* deduction; *Math (chiffre)* figure carried over; *Scol (punition)* detention; **en r.** in detention

réticent, -ente [retisã, -ãt] *adj* hesitant, unwilling •**réticence** *nf* hesitation, unwillingness

> ⚲ Il faut noter que l'adjectif anglais **reticent** est un faux ami. Il signifie **discret**.

rétine [retin] *nf* retina

retirer [rətire] **1** *vt* to withdraw; *(faire sortir)* to take out; *(ôter)* to take off; *(éloigner)* to take away; *(aller chercher)* to pick up; **r. qch à qn** *(permis)* to take sth away from sb; **r. qch de qch** *(gagner)* to derive sth from sth
  2 se retirer *vpr* to withdraw (**de** from); *(mer)* to ebb •**retiré, -ée** *adj (lieu, vie)* secluded

retomber [rətɔ̃be] *vi* to fall again; *(après un saut)* to land; *(intérêt)* to slacken; **r. dans** *(l'oubli, le chaos)* to sink back into; *(le péché)* to lapse into; **r. malade** to fall ill again; **r. sur qn** *(responsabilité, frais)* to fall on sb; *Fam (rencontrer)* to bump into sb again; *Fig* **r. sur ses pieds** to land on one's feet •**retombées** *nfpl (radioactives)* fallout; *Fig (conséquences)* repercussions

rétorquer [retɔrke] *vt* **r. que...** to retort that...

retors, -orse [rətɔr, -ɔrs] *adj* wily, crafty

rétorsion [retɔrsjɔ̃] *nf* retaliation; **mesure de r.** reprisal

retouche [rətuʃ] *nf (de vêtement)* alteration; *(de photo)* touching up •**retoucher** *vt (vêtement, texte)* to alter; *(photo, tableau)* to touch up

retour [rətur] *nm* return; *(trajet)* return journey; *(de fortune)* reversal; **être de r.** to be back (**de** from); **en r.** *(en échange)* in return; **par r. du courrier** *Br* by return (of post), *Am* by return mail; **à mon r.** when I get/got back (**de** from); **r. à l'envoyeur** return to sender; *Fig* **r. de flamme** backlash; **match r.** return *Br* match *or Am* game

retourner [rəturne] **1** *(aux avoir) vt (matelas, steak)* to turn over; *(terre)* to turn; *(vêtement, sac)* to turn inside out; *(tableau)* to turn round; *(compliment, lettre)* to return; *Fam (maison)* to turn upside down; **r. qch contre qn** *(argument)* to turn sth against sb; *(arme)* to turn sth on sb ; *Fam* **r. qn** *(bouleverser)* to upset sb; *Fam* **savoir de quoi il retourne** to know what it's all about
  2 *(aux être) vi* to go back, to return
  3 se retourner *vpr (pour regarder)* to turn round; *(sur le dos)* to turn over; *(dans son lit)* to toss and turn; *(voiture)* to overturn; **s'en r.** to go back; *Fig* **se r.**

contre to turn against •**retournement** [-əmã] *nm* **le r. de la situation** the dramatic turn of events

retracer [rətrase] *vt (événement)* to recount

rétracter [retrakte] *vt*, **se rétracter** *vpr* to retract •**rétractation** *nf* retraction

retrait [rətrɛ] *nm* withdrawal; *(de bagages, de billets)* collection; *(des eaux)* receding; **en r.** *(maison)* set back; **ligne en r.** indented line; **commencer un paragraphe en r.** to indent a paragraph; **rester en r.** to stay in the background

retraite [rətrɛt] *nf (d'employé)* retirement; *(pension)* (retirement) pension; *(refuge)* retreat, refuge; *(d'une armée)* retreat; **mettre qn à la r.** to pension sb off; **prendre sa r.** to retire; **être à la r.** to be retired; *Mil & Fig* **battre en r.** to beat a retreat; **r. aux flambeaux** torchlight procession; **r. anticipée** early retirement •**retraité, -ée 1** *adj* retired **2** *nmf* senior citizen, *Br* (old age) pensioner

retraitement [rətrɛtmã] *nm* reprocessing; **usine de r. (des déchets nucléaires)** (nuclear) reprocessing plant

retrancher [rətrãʃe] **1** *vt (passage, nom)* to remove (**de** from); *(argent, quantité)* to deduct (**de** from)
  2 se retrancher *vpr (soldats)* to dig in; *Fig* **se r. dans/derrière qch** to hide in/behind sth •**retranchement** *nm Fig* **pousser qn dans ses derniers retranchements** to drive sb to the wall

retransmettre* [rətrãsmɛtr] *vt* to broadcast •**retransmission** *nf* broadcast

rétrécir [retresir] **1** *vt (vêtement)* to take in
  2 *vi (au lavage)* to shrink
  3 se rétrécir *vpr (rue)* to narrow •**rétréci, -ie** *adj (route)* narrow

rétribuer [retribye] *vt (personne)* to pay; *(travail)* to pay for •**rétribution** *nf* payment, remuneration

> ⚲ Il faut noter que le nom anglais **retribution** est un faux ami. Il signifie **châtiment**.

rétro [retro] *adj inv (personne, idée)* retro

rétroactif, -ive [retroaktif, -iv] *adj* retroactive; **augmentation avec effet r.** retroactive (pay) increase

rétrograde [retrograd] *adj* retrograde •**rétrograder 1** *vt (fonctionnaire, officier)* to demote **2** *vi (automobiliste)* to change down

rétroprojecteur [retroprɔʒɛktœr] *nm* overhead projector

rétrospectif, -ive [retrospɛktif, -iv] **1** *adj* retrospective

2 *nf* **rétrospective** retrospective •**rétrospectivement** *adv* in retrospect

retrousser [rətruse] *vt (manches)* to roll up; *(jupe)* to tuck up •**retroussé, -ée** *adj (nez)* turned-up, snub

retrouver [rətruve] **1** *vt (objet)* to find again; *(personne)* to meet again; *(forces, santé)* to regain; *(se rappeler)* to recall; *(découvrir)* to rediscover

2 se retrouver *vpr (être)* to find oneself; *(trouver son chemin)* to find one's way (**dans** round); *(se rencontrer)* to meet; **se r. à la rue** to find oneself homeless; **je me suis retrouvé rue d'Assas** I ended up in rue d'Assas; **je ne m'y retrouve plus!** I'm completely lost! •**retrouvailles** *nfpl* reunion

rétroviseur [retrɔvizœr] *nm* rear-view mirror

Réunion [reynjɔ̃] *nf* **la R.** Réunion

réunion [reynjɔ̃] *nf (séance)* meeting; *(d'objets)* collection, gathering; *(jonction)* joining; **être en r.** to be in a meeting; **r. de famille** family gathering; *Scol* **r. de parents d'élèves** parents meeting

réunir [reynir] **1** *vt (objets)* to put together; *(documents)* to gather together; *(fonds)* to raise; *(amis, famille)* to get together; *(après une rupture)* to reunite; *(avantages, qualités)* to combine; **r. qch à qch** to join sth to sth

2 se réunir *vpr (personnes, routes)* to meet; **se r. autour de qn/qch** to gather round sb/sth

réussir [reysir] **1** *vt (bien faire)* to make a success of; *(examen)* to pass

2 *vi* to succeed, to be successful (**à faire** in doing); *(à un examen)* to pass; **r. à qn** to work out well for sb; *(aliment, climat)* to agree with sb; **r. à un examen** to pass an exam •**réussi, -ie** *adj* successful •**réussite** *nf* success; *Cartes* **faire des réussites** to play patience

revaloir [rəvalwar] *vt* **je vous le revaudrai** *(en bien ou en mal)* I'll pay you back

revaloriser [rəvalɔrize] *vt (monnaie)* to revalue; *(salaires, profession)* to upgrade •**revalorisation** *nf (de monnaie)* revaluation; *(de salaires, de profession)* upgrading

revanche [rəvɑ̃ʃ] *nf* revenge; *(de match)* return game; **prendre sa r. (sur qn)** to get one's revenge (on sb); **en r.** on the other hand

rêve [rɛv] *nm* dream; **faire un r.** to have a dream; **maison/voiture de r.** dream house/car •**rêvasser** *vi* to daydream

revêche [rəvɛʃ] *adj* bad-tempered

réveil [revɛj] *nm (de personnes)* waking; *Fig* awakening; *(pendule)* alarm (clock); **à son r.** on waking

réveiller [revɛje] **1** *vt (personne)* to wake (up); *Fig (douleur)* to revive; *Fig (sentiment, souvenir)* to revive

2 se réveiller *vpr (personne)* to wake (up); *(nature)* to reawaken; *Fig (douleur)* to come back •**réveillé, -ée** *adj* awake •**réveille-matin** *nm inv* alarm clock

réveillon [revɛjɔ̃] *nm (repas)* midnight supper; *(soirée)* midnight party *(on Christmas Eve or New Year's Eve)* •**réveillonner** *vi* to see in Christmas/the New Year

révéler [revele] **1** *vt* to reveal (**que** that)

2 se révéler *vpr (personne)* to reveal oneself; *(talent)* to be revealed; **se r. facile** to turn out to be easy •**révélateur, -trice** *adj* revealing; **r. de qch** indicative of sth •**révélation** *nf (action, découverte)* revelation; *(personne)* discovery; **faire des révélations** to disclose important information

revenant [rəvɑ̃nɑ̃] *nm* ghost; *Fam* **tiens! un r.!** hello, stranger!

revendiquer [rəvɑ̃dike] *vt* to claim; *(attentat)* to claim responsibility for •**revendicatif, -ive** *adj* **mouvement r.** protest movement •**revendication** *nf* claim

revendre [rəvɑ̃dr] *vt* to resell; *Fig* **avoir (de) qch à r.** to have sth to spare •**revendeur, -euse** *nmf* retailer; *(d'occasion)* second-hand dealer; **r. (de drogue)** drug pusher •**revente** *nf* resale

revenir* [rəvənir] *(aux* **être)** *vi (personne)* to come back, to return; *(mot)* to crop up; *(date)* to come round again; **r. à 100 euros** to come to 100 euros; **le dîner nous est revenu à 100 euros** the dinner cost us 100 euros; **r. cher** to work out expensive; **r. à** *(activité, sujet)* to go back to, to return to; *(se résumer à)* to boil down to; **r. à qn** *(forces, mémoire)* to come back to sb; *(honneur)* to fall to sb; **r. à soi** to come round *or* to; **r. de** *(surprise)* to get over; **r. sur** *(décision, promesse)* to go back on; *(passé, question)* to go back over; **r. sur ses pas** to retrace one's steps; **faire r. qch** *(aliment)* to brown sth; *Fam* **sa tête ne me revient pas** I don't like the look of him; *Fam* **je n'en reviens pas!** I can't get over it!; *Fig* **elle revient de loin** she's been at death's door

revenu [rəvəny] *nm* income (**de** from); *(d'un État)* revenue (**de** from)

rêver [reve] **1** *vt* to dream (**que** that)

2 *vi* to dream (**de** of; **de faire** of doing) •**rêvé, -ée** *adj* ideal

réverbération [reverberasjɔ̃] *nf (de lumière)* reflection; *(de son)* reverberation

réverbère [reverbɛr] *nm* street lamp

reverdir [rəverdir] *vi* to grow green again

révérence [reverɑ̃s] *nf (respect)* reverence; *(salut de femme)* curtsey; **faire une r.** to curtsey • **révérer** *vt* to revere

révérend, -ende [reverɑ̃, -ɑ̃d] *adj & nm Rel* reverend

rêverie [revri] *nf* daydream

revers [rəver] *nm (de veste)* lapel; *(de pantalon) Br* turn-up, *Am* cuff; *(d'étoffe)* wrong side; *(de pièce)* reverse; *(coup du sort)* setback; *Tennis* backhand; **d'un r. de la main** with the back of one's hand; *Fig* **le r. de la médaille** the other side of the coin

reverser [rəverse] *vt (café, vin)* to pour more; *Fig (argent)* to transfer (**sur un compte** into an account)

réversible [reversibl] *adj* reversible

revêtir* [rəvetir] *vt* to cover (**de** with); *(habit)* to don; *(route)* to surface; *(caractère, forme)* to assume; **r. qn** *(habiller)* to dress sb (**de** in); **r. un document de** *(signature)* to provide a document with • **revêtement** *nm (surface)* covering; *(de route)* surface

rêveur, -euse [revœr, -øz] **1** *adj* dreamy **2** *nmf* dreamer

revient [rəvjɛ̃] *nm* **prix de r.** *Br* cost price, *Am* wholesale price

revigorer [rəvigɔre] *vt (personne)* to revive

revirement [rəvirmɑ̃] *nm (changement) Br* about-turn, *Am* about-face; *(de situation, d'opinion, de politique)* reversal

réviser [revize] *vt (leçon)* to revise; *(machine, voiture)* to service; *(jugement, règlement)* to review • **révision** *nf (de leçon)* revision; *(de machine)* service; *(de jugement)* review

revisser [rəvise] *vt (bouchon)* to screw back again

revivre* [rəvivr] **1** *vt (incident)* to relive **2** *vi* to live again; **faire r. qch** to revive sth

révocation [revɔkasjɔ̃] *nf (de fonctionnaire)* dismissal; *(de contrat)* revocation

revoici [rəvwasi] *prép* **me r.** here I am again

revoilà [rəvwala] *prép* **la r.** there she is again

revoir* [rəvwar] *vt* to see (again); *(texte, leçon)* to revise; **au r.** goodbye

révolte [revɔlt] *nf* revolt • **révoltant, -ante** *adj (honteux)* revolting • **révolté, -ée** *nmf* rebel • **révolter 1** *vt* to appal **2 se révolter** *upr* to rebel, to revolt (**contre** against)

révolu, -ue [revɔly] *adj (époque)* past; **avoir trente ans révolus** to be over thirty

révolution [revɔlysjɔ̃] *nf (changement, rotation)* revolution • **révolutionnaire** *adj & nmf* revolutionary • **révolutionner** *vt (transformer)* to revolutionize

revolver [revɔlver] *nm* revolver

révoquer [revɔke] *vt (fonctionnaire)* to dismiss; *(contrat)* to revoke

revue [rəvy] *nf (magazine)* magazine; *(spécialisée)* journal; *(spectacle)* revue; *Mil* review; **passer qch en r.** to review sth

révulser [revylse] *vt* to repulse, to disgust • **révulsé, -ée** *adj (visage)* contorted; *(yeux)* rolled back

rez-de-chaussée [redəʃose] *nm inv Br* ground floor, *Am* first floor

rhabiller [rabije] **se rhabiller** *upr* to get dressed again

rhapsodie [rapsɔdi] *nf* rhapsody

Rhésus [rezys] *nm* **R. positif/négatif** Rhesus positive/negative

rhétorique [retɔrik] *nf* rhetoric

Rhin [rɛ̃] *nm* **le R.** the Rhine

rhinocéros [rinɔserɔs] *nm* rhinoceros

rhododendron [rɔdɔdɛ̃drɔ̃] *nm* rhododendron

Rhône [ron] *nm* **le R.** the Rhône

rhubarbe [rybarb] *nf* rhubarb

rhum [rɔm] *nm* rum

rhumatisme [rymatism] *nm* rheumatism; **avoir des rhumatismes** to have rheumatism • **rhumatisant, -ante** *adj & nmf* rheumatic • **rhumatismal, -e, -aux, -ales** *adj* rheumatic

rhume [rym] *nm* cold; **r. de cerveau** head cold; **r. des foins** hay fever

ri [ri] *pp de* **rire**

riant, riante [rjɑ̃, rjɑ̃t] **1** *p prés de* **rire** **2** *adj* cheerful, smiling

ribambelle [ribɑ̃bɛl] *nf* **une r. d'enfants** a string of children

ricaner [rikane] *vi (sarcastiquement) Br* to snigger, *Am* to snicker; *(bêtement)* to giggle

riche [riʃ] **1** *adj (personne, pays, aliment)* rich; **r. en** *(vitamines, minérai)* rich in **2** *nmf* rich person; **les riches** the rich • **richement** *adv (vêtu, illustré)* richly • **richesse** *nf (de personne, de pays)* wealth; *(d'étoffe, de sol, de vocabulaire)* richness; **richesses** *(trésor)* riches; *(ressources)* wealth

ricin [risɛ̃] *nm* **huile de r.** castor oil

ricocher [rikɔʃe] *vi* to rebound, to ricochet • **ricochet** *nm* rebound, ricochet; *Fig* **par r.** indirectly

rictus [riktys] *nm* grimace

ride [rid] *nf (de visage)* wrinkle; *(sur l'eau)* ripple •**ridé, -ée** *adj* wrinkled •**rider 1** *vt (visage, peau)* to wrinkle; *(eau)* to ripple **2 se rider** *vpr (visage, peau)* to wrinkle

rideau, -x [rido] *nm* curtain; *(métallique)* shutter; *Fig (écran)* screen (**de** of)

ridicule [ridikyl] **1** *adj* ridiculous, ludicrous

2 *nm (moquerie)* ridicule; *(absurdité)* ridiculousness; **tourner qn/qch en r.** to ridicule sb/sth •**ridiculiser 1** *vt* to ridicule **2 se ridiculiser** *vpr* to make a fool of oneself

rien [rjɛ̃] **1** *pron* nothing; **il ne sait r.** he knows nothing, he doesn't know anything; **r. du tout** nothing at all; **r. d'autre/de bon** nothing else/good; **r. de tel** nothing like it; **il n'y avait r. que des filles** there were only girls there; **de r.!** *(je vous en prie)* don't mention it!; **ça ne fait r.** it doesn't matter; **trois fois r.** next to nothing; **avoir qch pour r.** *(à bas prix)* to get sth for next to nothing; **pour r. au monde** never in a thousand years; **comme si de r. n'était** as if nothing had happened; **il n'en est r.** *(ce n'est pas vrai)* nothing of the kind; *Fam* **je n'en ai r. à faire** I couldn't care less

2 *nm (mere)* nothing, trifle; **un r. de** a little; **en un r. de temps** in no time; **un r. trop petit** just a bit too small; **pleurer pour un r.** to cry for the slightest thing

rieur, rieuse [rijœr, rijøz] *adj* cheerful

rigide [riʒid] *adj* rigid; *(carton)* stiff; *Fig (personne)* inflexible; *(éducation)* strict •**rigidité** *nf* rigidity; *(de carton)* stiffness; *(de personne)* inflexibility; *(d'éducation)* strictness

rigole [rigɔl] *nf (conduit)* channel; *(filet d'eau)* rivulet

rigoler [rigɔle] *vi Fam* to laugh; *(s'amuser)* to have a laugh; *(plaisanter)* to joke (**avec** about) •**rigolade** *nf Fam* fun; **prendre qch à la r.** to make a joke out of sth •**rigolo, -ote** *Fam* **1** *adj* funny **2** *nmf* scream

rigueur [rigœr] *nf (d'analyse)* rigour; *(de climat)* harshness; *(de personne)* strictness; **être de r.** to be the rule; **à la r.** if need be; *Fig* **tenir r. à qn de qch** to hold sth against sb •**rigoureux, -euse** *adj (analyse)* rigorous; *(climat, punition)* harsh; *(personne, morale, neutralité)* strict

rillettes [rijɛt] *nfpl* potted minced pork

rime [rim] *nf* rhyme •**rimer** *vi* to rhyme (**avec** with); **ça ne rime à rien** it makes no sense

Rimmel® [rimɛl] *nm* mascara

rincer [rɛ̃se] *vt* to rinse; *(verre)* to rinse

(out) •**rinçage** *nm* rinsing; *(pour les cheveux)* rinse •**rince-doigts** *nm inv* finger bowl

ring [riŋ] *nm* (boxing) ring

ringard, -arde [rɛ̃gar, -ard] *adj Fam (démodé)* unhip

ripaille [ripaj] *nf Fam* **faire r.** to have a blow-out

riposte [ripɔst] *nf (réponse)* retort; *(attaque)* counterattack •**riposter 1** *vt* **r. que...** to retort that... **2** *vi* to counterattack; **r. à** *(attaque)* to counter; *(insulte)* to reply to

riquiqui [rikiki] *adj inv Fam* tiny

rire* [rir] **1** *nm* laugh; **rires** laughter; **le fou r.** the giggles

2 *vi* to laugh (**de** at); *(s'amuser)* to have a good time; *(plaisanter)* to joke; **r. aux éclats** to roar with laughter; **faire qch pour r.** to do sth for a joke *or* laugh

3 se rire *vpr Littéraire* **se r. de qch** *(se jouer de)* to make light of sth

ris [ri] *nm Culin* **r. de veau** calf's sweetbread

risée [rize] *nf* mockery; **être la r. de** to be the laughing stock of

risible [rizibl] *adj* laughable

risque [risk] *nm* risk; **au r. de faire qch** at the risk of doing sth; **les risques du métier** occupational hazards; **à vos risques et périls** at your own risk; **assurance tous risques** comprehensive insurance

risquer [riske] **1** *vt* to risk; *(question)* to venture; **r. le tout pour le tout** to go for broke; **r. de faire qch** to stand a good chance of doing sth; **ça risque de durer longtemps** that may well last for a long time; **qu'est-ce que tu risques?** what have you got to lose?

2 se risquer *vpr* **se r. à faire qch** to dare to do sth; **se r. dans qch** to venture into sth •**risqué, -ée** *adj (dangereux)* risky; *(osé)* risqué

ristourne [risturn] *nf* discount

rite [rit] *nm* rite; *Fig (habitude)* ritual •**rituel, -uelle** *adj & nm* ritual

rivage [rivaʒ] *nm* shore

rival, -e, -aux, -ales [rival, -o] *adj & nmf* rival •**rivaliser** *vi* to compete (**avec** with; **de** in) •**rivalité** *nf* rivalry

rive [riv] *nf (de fleuve)* bank; *(de lac)* shore

rivé, -ée [rive] *adj Fig* **r. à qch** glued to sth; *Fig* **r. sur qn/qch** *(yeux, regard)* riveted on sb/sth •**rivet** *nm* rivet •**riveter** *vt* to rivet

riverain, -aine [rivərɛ̃, -ɛn] **1** *adj (de rivière)* riverside; *(de lac)* lakeside

2 *nmf (près d'une rivière)* riverside resident; *(près d'un lac)* lakeside resident; *(de rue)* resident

rivière [rivjɛr] *nf* river; **r. de diamants** diamond necklace

rixe [riks] *nf* brawl

riz [ri] *nm* rice; **r. blanc/complet** white/brown rice; **r. au lait** rice pudding • **rizière** *nf* paddy (field), rice-field

RMI [ɛrɛmi] *(abrév* **revenu minimum d'insertion)** *nm Br* ≃ income support, *Am* ≃ welfare • **RMiste** *nmf Br* ≃ person on income support, *Am* ≃ person on welfare

RN *abrév* **route nationale**

robe [rɔb] *nf (de femme)* dress; *(d'ecclésiastique, de juge)* robe; *(de professeur)* gown; *(pelage)* coat; **r. de soirée** *ou* **du soir** evening dress; **r. de grossesse/de mariée** maternity/wedding dress; **r. de chambre** *Br* dressing gown, *Am* bathrobe; **pomme de terre en r. des champs** jacket potato, baked potato

robinet [rɔbinɛ] *nm Br* tap, *Am* faucet

robot [rɔbo] *nm* robot; **r. ménager** food processor • **robotique** *nf* robotics *(sing)*

robuste [rɔbyst] *adj* robust • **robustesse** *nf* robustness

roc [rɔk] *nm* rock

rocade [rɔkad] *nf (route)* bypass

rocaille [rɔkaj] *nf (terrain)* rocky ground; *(de jardin)* rockery • **rocailleux, -euse** *adj* rocky, stony; *(voix)* harsh

rocambolesque [rɔkãbɔlɛsk] *adj* fantastic

roche [rɔʃ] *nf* rock

rocher [rɔʃe] *nm (bloc, substance)* rock • **rocheux, -euse** *adj* rocky

rock [rɔk] **1** *nm (musique)* rock

2 *adj inv* **chanteur/opéra r.** rock singer/opera • **rockeur, -euse** *nmf (musicien)* rock musician

rodéo [rɔdeo] *nm (de chevaux)* rodeo

roder [rɔde] *vt (moteur, voiture) Br* to run in, *Am* to break in; *Fig* **être rodé** *(personne)* to have *Br* got *or Am* gotten the hang of things • **rodage** *nm Br* running in, *Am* breaking in

rôder [rɔde] *vi* to be on the prowl • **rôdeur, -euse** *nmf* prowler

rogne [rɔɲ] *nf Fam* bad temper; **être en r.** to be cross; **se mettre en r.** to get mad

rogner [rɔɲe] **1** *vt (ongles)* to trim, to clip; *Fig (économies)* to eat away at; *Fig* **r. les ailes à qn** to clip sb's wings

2 *vi* **r. sur qch** *(réduire)* to cut down on sth • **rognures** *nfpl (de cuir, de métal)* trimmings

rognon [rɔɲɔ̃] *nm* kidney

roi [rwa] *nm* king; **fête des Rois** Twelfth Night

roitelet [rwatlɛ] *nm (oiseau)* wren

rôle [rol] *nm* role, part; *(de père)* job; **à tour de r.** in turn

romain, -aine [rɔmɛ̃, -ɛn] **1** *adj* Roman

2 *nmf* **R., Romaine** Roman

3 *nf* **romaine** *(laitue) Br* cos (lettuce), *Am* romaine

roman¹ [rɔmã] *nm* novel; *Fig (histoire)* story; **r. d'aventures/d'amour** adventure/love story; **r.-fleuve** saga; **r.-photo** photostory • **romancé, -ée** *adj (histoire)* fictional • **romancier, -ière** *nmf* novelist

roman², -ane [rɔmã, -an] *adj (langue)* Romance; *Archit* Romanesque

> 🖉 Il faut noter que l'adjectif anglais **Roman** est un faux ami. Il signifie **romain**.

romanesque [rɔmanɛsk] *adj* romantic; *(incroyable)* fantastic

romanichel, -elle [rɔmaniʃɛl] *nmf* gipsy

romantique [rɔmãtik] *adj* romantic • **romantisme** *nm* romanticism

romarin [rɔmarɛ̃] *nm* rosemary

rompre* [rɔ̃pr] **1** *vt* to break; *(pourparlers, relations)* to break off; *(digue)* to burst

2 *vi (casser)* to break; *(digue)* to burst; *(fiancés)* to break it off; **r. avec la tradition** to break with tradition

3 se rompre *vpr (corde)* to break; *(digue)* to burst • **rompu, -ue** *adj (fatigué)* exhausted; **r. à qch** *(expérimenté)* used to sth

romsteck [rɔmstɛk] *nm* rump steak

ronces [rɔ̃s] *nfpl (branches)* brambles

ronchonner [rɔ̃ʃɔne] *vi Fam* to grouse, to grumble

rond, ronde¹ [rɔ̃, rɔ̃d] **1** *adj* round; *(gras)* plump; *Fam (ivre)* plastered; **chiffre r.** whole number; **ouvrir des yeux ronds** to be wide-eyed with astonishment, to look astonished; *Fam* **r. comme une queue de pelle** rat-arsed

2 *adv* **10 euros tout r.** 10 euros exactly

3 *nm (cercle)* circle; *Fam* **ronds** *(argent)* money; **r. de serviette** napkin ring; **en r.** *(s'asseoir)* in a circle; *Fig* **tourner en r.** to go round and round • **rond-de-cuir** *(pl* **ronds-de-cuir)** *nm Péj* pen-pusher • **rondelet, -ette** *adj* chubby; *Fig (somme)* tidy • **rondement** *adv (efficacement)* briskly; *(franchement)* bluntly; **mener qch r.** to make short work of sth • **rond-point** *(pl* **ronds-points)** *nm Br* roundabout, *Am* traffic circle

ronde² [rɔ̃d] *nf (de soldat)* round; *(de policier)* beat; *(danse)* round (dance); *Mus Br* semibreve, *Am* whole note; **à la r.** around; **faire sa r.** *(gardien)* to do one's rounds

rondelle [rɔ̃dɛl] *nf (tranche)* slice; *Tech* washer

rondeur [rɔ̃dœr] *nf* roundness; *(du corps)* plumpness, **rondeurs** *(de femme)* curves; *(embonpoint)* plumpness

rondin [rɔ̃dɛ̃] *nm* log

ronéotyper [rɔneɔtipe] *vt* to roneo

ronflant, -ante [rɔ̃flɑ̃, -ɑ̃t] *adj Péj (langage)* high-flown

ronfler [rɔ̃fle] *vi (personne)* to snore; *(moteur)* to hum • **ronflement** [-əmɑ̃] *nm (de personne)* snore; *(de moteur)* hum; **ronflements** snoring; *(de moteur)* humming

ronger [rɔ̃ʒe] **1** *vt* to gnaw (at); *(ver, mer, rouille)* to eat into; **r. qn** *(maladie, chagrin)* to consume sb; *Fig* **r. son frein** to champ at the bit
2 se ronger *vpr* **se r. les ongles** to bite one's nails; *Fam* **se r. les sangs** to worry oneself sick • **rongeur** *nm* rodent

ronronnement [rɔ̃rɔnmɑ̃] *(Fam* **ronron**) *nm* purr • **ronronner** *vi* to purr

roquefort [rɔkfɔr] *nm* Roquefort

roquette [rɔkɛt] *nf Mil* rocket

rosace [rozas] *nf* rosette; *(d'église)* rose window

rosbif [rɔzbif] *nm* **du r.** *(rôti)* roast beef; *(à rôtir)* roasting beef; **un r.** a joint of roast/roasting beef

rose [roz] **1** *adj (couleur)* pink; *(situation, teint)* rosy
2 *nm (couleur)* pink; **vieux r.** soft pink; **r. bonbon** bright pink
3 *nf (fleur)* rose; *Fam* **envoyer qn sur les roses** to send sb packing; *Fam* **découvrir le pot aux roses** to find out what's been going on • **rosé, -ée 1** *adj* pinkish **2** *adj & nm (vin)* rosé • **roseraie** *nf* rose garden • **rosier** *nm* rose bush

roseau, -x [rozo] *nm* reed

rosée [roze] *nf* dew

rosette [rozɛt] *nf (d'un officier)* rosette; *(nœud)* bow

rosser [rɔse] *vt* **r. qn** to beat sb up

rossignol [rɔsiɲɔl] *nm (oiseau)* nightingale; *(crochet)* picklock

rot [ro] *nm Fam* burp, belch • **roter** *vi Fam* to burp, to belch

rotation [rɔtasjɔ̃] *nf* rotation; *(de stock)* turnover • **rotatif, -ive 1** *adj* rotary **2** *nf* **rotative** rotary press

rotin [rɔtɛ̃] *nm* rattan; **chaise en r.** rattan chair

rôtir [rotir] **1** *vti* to roast; **faire r. qch** to roast sth
2 se rôtir *vpr Fam* **se r. au soleil** to roast in the sun • **rôti** *nm* **du r.** roasting meat; *(cuit)* roast meat; **un r.** a joint; **r. de porc / de bœuf** (joint of) roast pork/beef • **rôtissoire** *nf* (roasting) spit

rotule [rɔtyl] *nf* kneecap; *Fam* **être sur les rotules** to be exhausted *or Br* dead beat

roturier, -ière [rɔtyrje, -jɛr] *nmf* commoner

rouage [rwaʒ] *nm (de montre)* (working) part; *Fig (d'organisation)* workings

roublard, -arde [rublar, -ard] *adj Fam* wily

rouble [rubl] *nm (monnaie)* rouble

roucouler [rukule] *vi* to coo

roue [ru] *nf* wheel; **r. dentée** cogwheel; **faire la r.** *(paon)* to spread its tail; **être en r. libre** to freewheel; **les deux roues** two-wheeled vehicles

rouer [rwe] *vt* **r. qn de coups** to beat sb black and blue

rouet [rwɛ] *nm* spinning wheel

rouge [ruʒ] **1** *adj* red; *(fer)* red-hot
2 *nm (couleur)* red; *Fam (vin)* red wine; **le feu est au r.** the (traffic) lights are at red; **r. à lèvres** lipstick; **r. à joues** rouge • **rougeâtre** *adj* reddish • **rougeaud, -aude** *adj* red-faced • **rouge-gorge** *(pl* **rouges-gorges**) *nm* robin

rougeole [ruʒɔl] *nf* measles *(sing)*

rougeoyer [ruʒwaje] *vi* to turn red

rouget [ruʒɛ] *nm* red mullet

rougeur [ruʒœr] *nf* redness; *(due à la honte)* blush; *(due à l'émotion)* flush; **rougeurs** *(irritation)* rash, red blotches

rougir [ruʒir] **1** *vt (visage)* to redden; *(ciel, feuilles)* to turn red
2 *vi (de honte)* to blush (**de** with); *(d'émotion)* to flush (**de** with)

rouille [ruj] **1** *nf* rust
2 *adj inv (couleur)* rust(-coloured) • **rouillé, -ée** *adj* rusty • **rouiller 1** *vi* to rust
2 se rouiller *vpr* to rust; *Fig (esprit, sportif)* to get rusty

roulade [rulad] *nf Culin* **r. de poisson** rolled fish; *Sport* **r. avant/arrière** forward/backward roll; **faire une r.** to do a roll

rouleau, -x [rulo] *nm (outil, vague)* roller; *(de papier, de pellicule)* roll; **r. à pâtisserie** rolling pin; **r. compresseur** steamroller

roulement [rulmɑ̃] *nm (bruit)* rumbling, rumble; *(de tambour, de tonnerre, d'yeux)* roll; *(ordre)* rotation; **par r.** in rotation; *Tech* **r. à billes** ball bearing

rouler [rule] **1** *vt* to roll; *(crêpe, ficelle, manches)* to roll up; *Fam* **r. qn** *(duper)* to cheat sb

2 *vi (balle)* to roll; *(train, voiture)* to go, to travel; *(conducteur)* to drive; **r. sur** *(conversation)* to turn on; *Fig* **r. sur l'or** to be rolling in it; *Fam* **ça roule!** everything's fine!

3 se rouler *upr* to roll; **se r. dans** *(couverture)* to roll oneself (up) in • **roulant, -ante** *adj (escalier, trottoir)* moving; *(meuble)* on wheels; *Fig* **un feu r. de questions** a barrage of questions • **roulé** *nm (gâteau)* Swiss roll

roulette [rulɛt] *nf (de meuble)* castor; *(de dentiste)* drill; *(jeu)* roulette

roulis [ruli] *nm (de navire)* roll

roulotte [rulɔt] *nf (de gitan)* caravan

Roumanie [rumani] *nf* **la R.** Romania • **roumain, -aine 1** *adj* Romanian **2** *nmf* **R., Roumaine** Romanian **3** *nm (langue)* Romanian

round [rawnd, rund] *nm Boxe* round

roupiller [rupije] *vi Fam* to sleep, *Br* to kip

rouquin, -ine [rukɛ̃, -in] *Fam* **1** *adj* red-haired

2 *nmf* redhead

rouspéter [ruspete] *vi Fam* to grumble • **rouspéteur, -euse** *nmf Fam* grumbler

rousse [rus] *voir* **roux**

rousseur [rusœr] *nf (de chevelure)* redness; **tache de r.** freckle • **roussi** *nm* **ça sent le r.** there's a smell of burning • **roussir 1** *vt (brûler)* to scorch, to singe **2** *vi (feuilles)* to turn brown

rouste [rust] *nf Fam* severe thrashing, good hiding

routard, -arde [rutar, -ard] *nmf Fam* backpacker

route [rut] *nf* road (**de** to); *(itinéraire)* way, route; *Fig (chemin)* path; **grand-r., grande r.** main road; **code de la r.** *Br* Highway Code, *Am* traffic regulations; **en r.** on the way, en route; **en r.!** let's go!; **par la r.** by road; *Fig* **sur la bonne r.** on the right track; *Fig* **faire fausse r.** to be on the wrong track; **mettre qch en r.** *(voiture)* to start sth (up); **se mettre en r.** to set out (**pour** for); **une heure de r.** *(en voiture)* an hour's drive; **faire r. vers Paris** to head for Paris; **faire de la r.** to do a lot of driving; **bonne r.!** have a good trip!; *Fig* **leurs routes se sont croisées** their paths crossed; **r. des vins** wine trail; **r. départementale** secondary road, *Br* B road; **r. nationale** *Br* main road, A-road, *Am* (state) highway

routier, -ière [rutje, -jɛr] **1** *adj* **carte/sécurité routière** road map/safety; **réseau r.** road network

2 *nm (camionneur)* (long-distance) *Br* lorry *or Am* truck driver; *(restaurant) Br* transport café, *Am* truck stop

routine [rutin] *nf* routine; **contrôle de r.** routine check • **routinier, -ière** *adj* **travail r.** routine work; **être r.** *(personne)* to be set in one's ways

rouvrir* [ruvrir] *vti,* **se rouvrir** *upr* to reopen

roux, rousse [ru, rus] **1** *adj (cheveux)* red, ginger; *(personne)* red-haired

2 *nmf* redhead

royal, -e, -aux, -ales [rwajal, -jo] *adj (famille, palais)* royal; *(cadeau, festin)* fit for a king; *(salaire)* princely • **royalement** *adv (traiter)* royally; *Fam* **je m'en fiche r.** I couldn't care less (about it) • **royaliste** *adj & nmf* royalist

royaume [rwajom] *nm* kingdom • **Royaume-Uni** *nm* **le R.** the United Kingdom

royauté [rwajote] *nf (monarchie)* monarchy

ruade [rɥad] *nf (d'âne, de cheval)* kick

ruban [rybɑ̃] *nm* ribbon; *(de chapeau)* band; **r. adhésif** sticky *or* adhesive tape

rubéole [rybeɔl] *nf* German measles *(sing)*, rubella

rubis [rybi] *nm (pierre)* ruby; *(de montre)* jewel

rubrique [rybrik] *nf (article de journal)* column; *(catégorie, titre)* heading

ruche [ryʃ] *nf* beehive

rude [ryd] *adj (pénible)* tough; *(hiver, voix)* harsh; *(rêche)* rough • **rudement** *adv (parler, traiter)* harshly; *(frapper, tomber)* hard; *Fam (très)* awfully • **rudesse** *nf* harshness

⚠ Il faut noter que l'adjectif anglais **rude** est un faux ami. Il signifie **grossier**.

rudiments [rydimɑ̃] *nmpl* rudiments • **rudimentaire** *adj* rudimentary

rudoyer [rydwaje] *vt* to treat harshly

rue [ry] *nf* street; **être à la r.** *(sans domicile)* to be on the streets • **ruelle** *nf* alley (way)

ruer [rɥe] **1** *vi (cheval)* to kick (out)

2 se ruer *upr (foncer)* to rush (**sur** at) • **ruée** *nf* rush; **la r. vers l'or** the gold rush

rugby [rygbi] *nm* rugby • **rugbyman** [rygbiman] *(pl* **-men** [-men]) *nm* rugby player

rugir [ryʒir] *vi* to roar • **rugissement** *nm* roar

rugueux, -euse [rygø, -øz] *adj* rough
• **rugosité** *nf* roughness; **rugosités** *(aspé-rités)* rough spots

ruine [rɥin] *nf (décombres, destruction, faillite)* ruin; **en r.** *(bâtiment)* in ruins; **tomber en r.** *(bâtiment)* to become a ruin; *(mur)* to crumble • **ruiner 1** *vt (personne, santé, pays)* to ruin **2 se ruiner** *vpr (perdre tout son argent)* to ruin oneself; *(dépenser beaucoup d'argent)* to spend a fortune • **ruineux, -euse** *adj (goûts, projet)* ruinously expensive; *(dépense)* ruinous; **ce n'est pas r.** it won't ruin me/you/*etc*

ruisseau, -x [rɥiso] *nm* stream; *(caniveau)* gutter • **ruisseler** *vi* to stream (**de** with)

rumeur [rymœr] *nf (murmure)* murmur; *(nouvelle)* rumour

ruminer [rymine] **1** *vt (herbe)* to chew; *Fig (méditer)* to mull over **2** *vi (vache)* to chew the cud; *Fig* to brood

rumsteck [rɔmstɛk] *nm* rump steak

rupture [ryptyr] *nf* breaking; *(de fiançailles, de relations)* breaking off; *(de pourparlers)* breakdown (**de** in); *(brouille)* break-up; *Méd* rupture; **être en r. de stock** to be out of stock; **r. de contrat** breach of contract

rural, -e, -aux, -ales [ryral, -o] *adj (population)* rural; **vie/école rurale** country life/school • **ruraux** *nmpl* country people

ruse [ryz] *nf (subterfuge)* trick; **la r.** *(habileté)* cunning; *(fourberie)* trickery • **rusé, -ée 1** *adj* cunning, crafty **2** *nmf* **c'est un r.** he's a cunning *or* crafty one • **ruser** *vi* to resort to trickery

Russie [rysi] *nf* **la R.** Russia • **russe 1** *adj* Russian **2** *nmf* **R.** Russian **3** *nm (langue)* Russian

rustique [rystik] *adj (meuble)* rustic

rustre [rystr] *nm* lout, churl

rut [ryt] **en rut** *nm (animal) Br* on heat, *Am* in heat

rutabaga [rytabaga] *nm Br* swede, *Am* rutabaga

rutilant, -ante [rytilã, -ãt] *adj* gleaming

RV *abrév* **rendez-vous**

rythme [ritm] *nm* rhythm; *(de travail)* rate; *(allure)* pace; **au r. de trois par jour** at the rate of three a day • **rythmé, -ée, rythmique** *adj* rhythmic(al)

S, s [ɛs] *nm inv* S, s
s' [s] *voir* **se, si**
SA (*abrév* **société anonyme**) *Com Br* plc,
Am Inc
sa [sa] *voir* **son²**
sabbat [saba] *nm* Sabbath
sabbatique [sabatik] *adj (repos, année)*
sabbatical; **prendre un congé s.** to take a
sabbatical
sable [sabl] *nm* sand; **sables mouvants**
quicksands • **sabler** *vt (route)* to sand;
Fam **s. le champagne** to celebrate with
champagne • **sableux, -euse** *adj* sandy
sablier [sablije] *nm* hourglass; *Culin* egg
timer • **sablière** *nf (carrière)* sandpit
sablonneux, -euse [sablɔnø, -øz] *adj*
sandy
sablé [sable] *nm* shortbread *Br* biscuit *or*
Am cookie • **sablée** *adj f* **pâte sablée**
shortcrust pastry
saborder [sabɔrde] *vt (navire)* to scuttle;
Fig (entreprise) to scupper
sabot [sabo] *nm (de cheval)* hoof; *(chaussure)* clog; **s. de Denver** wheel clamp
saboter [sabɔte] *vt (machine, projet)* to
sabotage • **sabotage** *nm* sabotage; **un
acte de s.** an act of sabotage • **saboteur,
-euse** *nmf* saboteur
sabre [sabr] *nm* sabre
sabrer [sabre] *vt Fam (critiquer)* to slate;
se faire à s. un examen to flunk
sac [sak] *nm* bag; *(grand, en toile)* sack;
s. à main handbag; **s. à dos** rucksack;
s. de voyage travelling bag; *Fig* **prendre
qn la main dans le s.** to catch sb red-
handed; *Fam* **je les mets dans le même s.**
in my opinion they're as bad as each
other; *Fam* **l'affaire est dans le s.!** it's in
the bag!; **mettre une ville à s.** to sack a
town
saccade [sakad] *nf* jerk, jolt; **par saccades**
in fits and starts • **saccadé, -ée** *adj* jerky
saccager [sakaʒe] *vt (détruire)* to wreck
havoc in; *(piller)* to sack
saccharine [sakarin] *nf* saccharin
sacerdoce [sasɛrdɔs] *nm Rel* priesthood;
Fig vocation
sachant, sache(s), sachent [saʃɑ̃, saʃ]
voir **savoir**

sachet [saʃɛ] *nm (small) bag; (de lavande)* sachet; **s. de thé** teabag
sacoche [sakɔʃ] *nf* bag; *(de vélo, de moto)*
saddlebag; *(d'écolier)* satchel
sacquer [sake] *vt Fam (renvoyer)* to sack;
(élève) to give a bad *Br* mark *or Am* grade
to; *Fam* **je ne peux pas le s.** I can't stand
him
sacre [sakr] *nm (de roi)* coronation;
(d'évêque) consecration • **sacrer** *vt (roi)*
to crown; *(évêque)* to consecrate
sacré, -ée [sakre] *adj (saint)* sacred; *Fam*
un s. menteur a damned liar • **sacrément**
adv Fam (très) damn(ed); *(beaucoup)* a
hell of a lot
sacrement [sakrəmɑ̃] *nm Rel* sacrament
sacrifice [sakrifis] *nm* sacrifice • **sacrifier**
1 *vt* to sacrifice (**à** to) **2** *vi* **s. à la mode** to
be a slave to fashion **3 se sacrifier** *vpr* to
sacrifice oneself (**pour** for)
sacrilège [sakrilɛʒ] **1** *adj* sacrilegious
2 *nm* sacrilege
sacristie [sakristi] *nf* vestry
sacro-saint, -sainte [sakrosɛ̃, -sɛ̃t] (*mpl*
sacro-saints, *fpl* **sacro-saintes**) *adj Ironique* sacrosanct
sadisme [sadism] *nm* sadism • **sadique 1**
adj sadistic **2** *nmf* sadist
safari [safari] *nm* safari; **faire un s.** to go
on safari; **s.-photo** photographic safari
safran [safrɑ̃] *nm* saffron
sagace [sagas] *adj* shrewd • **sagacité** *nf*
shrewdness
sage [saʒ] **1** *adj (avisé)* wise; *(calme)*
good; *(robe)* sober
2 *nm* wise man • **sage-femme** (*pl* **sages-
femmes**) *nf* midwife • **sagement** *adv (raisonnablement)* wisely; *(avec calme)*
quietly • **sagesse** *nf (philosophie)* wisdom; *(calme)* good behaviour
Sagittaire [saʒitɛr] *nm* **le S.** *(signe)* Sagittarius; **être S.** to be Sagittarius
Sahara [saara] *nm* **le S.** the Sahara (desert)
saigner [seɲe] **1** *vi* to bleed; **s. du nez** to
have a nosebleed
2 se saigner *vpr Fig* **se s. aux quatre
veines** to bleed oneself dry • **saignant,
-ante** [seɲɑ̃, -ɑ̃t] *adj (viande)* rare • **sai-**

gnée *nf Méd* blood-letting •**saignement** [sɛɲəmã] *nm* bleeding; **s. de nez** nosebleed

saillant, -ante [sajã, -ãt] *adj* projecting; *Fig (trait)* salient •**saillie** *nf (partie avant)* projection

sain, saine [sɛ̃, sɛn] *adj* healthy; *(jugement)* sound; *(nourriture)* wholesome, healthy; **s. et sauf** safe and sound •**sainement** *adv (vivre)* healthily; *(raisonner)* sanely

saint, sainte [sɛ̃, sɛ̃t] **1** *adj (lieu)* holy; *(personne)* saintly; **s. Jean** Saint John; **la Sainte Vierge** the Blessed Virgin
2 *nmf* saint •**saint-bernard** *nm inv (chien)* St Bernard •**Saint-Esprit** *nm* **le S.** the Holy Spirit •**saint-frusquin** *nm Fam* **tout le s.** the whole caboodle •**saint-honoré** *nm inv* Saint-Honoré *(choux pastry ring filled with confectioner's custard)* •**Saint-Siège** *nm* **le S.** the Holy See •**Saint-Sylvestre** *nf* **la S.** New Year's Eve

sainteté [sɛ̃təte] *nf (de lieu)* holiness; *(de personne)* saintliness; **Sa S.** *(le pape)* His Holiness

saint-glinglin [sɛ̃glɛ̃glɛ̃] **à la saint-glinglin** *adv Fam* never in a month of Sundays

sais [sɛ] *voir* **savoir**

saisie [sezi] *nf (de biens)* seizure; *Ordinat* **s. de données** data capture, keyboarding

saisir [sezir] **1** *vt* to take hold of; *(brusquement)* to grab; *(occasion)* to seize, to grasp; *(comprendre)* to grasp; *Jur* to seize; *(viande)* to seal; *Fig (frapper)* to strike
2 se saisir *vpr* **se s. de qn/qch** to take hold of sb/sth; *(brusquement)* to grab sb/sth •**saisissant, -ante** *adj (film)* gripping; *(contraste, ressemblance)* striking •**saisissement** *nm (émotion)* shock

saison [sɛzɔ̃] *nf* season; **en/hors s.** in/out of season; **en haute/basse s.** in the high/low season; **la s. des pluies** the rainy season •**saisonnier, -ière** *adj* seasonal

sait [sɛ] *voir* **savoir**

salade [salad] *nf (laitue)* lettuce; *Fam (désordre)* mess; **s. verte** green salad; **s. de fruits** fruit salad; **s. niçoise** salade niçoise *(lettuce, tomatoes, olives, anchovies, eggs)* •**salades** *nfpl Fam (mensonges)* whoppers •**saladier** *nm* salad bowl

salaire [salɛr] *nm (mensuel)* salary

salaison [salɛzɔ̃] *nf Culin* salting; **salaisons** *(denrées)* salted meats

salamandre [salamãdr] *nf* salamander

salami [salami] *nm* salami

salarial, -e, -iaux, -iales [salarjal, -jo] *adj* **accord s.** wage agreement •**salarié,**

-ée 1 *adj (payé mensuellement)* salaried **2** *nmf (payé mensuellement)* salaried employee; **salariés** *(de société)* employees

salaud [salo] *nm Vulg* bastard

sale [sal] *adj* dirty; *(dégoûtant)* filthy; *(mauvais)* nasty; *Fam* **s. coup** dirty trick; *Fam* **s. temps** filthy weather; *Fam* **avoir une s. gueule** to look rotten •**salement** *adv (se conduire, manger)* disgustingly •**saleté** *nf (manque de soin)* dirtiness; *(crasse)* dirt; *Fam (camelote)* junk; **saletés** *(détritus) Br* rubbish, *Am* garbage; *(obscénités)* filth; **faire des saletés** to make a mess

saler [sale] *vt* to salt •**salé, -ée** *adj (goût, plat)* salty; *(aliment)* salted; *Fig (grivois)* spicy; *Fam (excessif)* steep •**salière** *nf Br* saltcellar, *Am* saltshaker

salir [salir] **1** *vt* to (make) dirty; *Fig (réputation, mémoire)* to sully
2 se salir *vpr* to get dirty •**salissant, -ante** *adj (travail)* dirty, messy; *(étoffe)* that shows the dirt •**salissure** *nf* dirty mark

salive [saliv] *nf* saliva •**saliver** *vi* to salivate

salle [sal] *nf* room; *(très grande, publique)* hall; *(de cinéma) Br* cinema, *Am* movie theater; *(d'hôpital)* ward; *(public de théâtre)* audience, house; **s. à manger** dining room; **s. de bain(s)** bathroom; **s. de classe** classroom; **s. de concert** concert hall; **s. de jeux** *(pour enfants)* games room; *(de casino)* gaming room; **s. de spectacle** auditorium; **s. d'embarquement** *(d'aéroport)* departure lounge; *Com* **s. d'exposition** showroom; **s. d'opération** *(d'hôpital)* operating *Br* theatre *or Am* room; **s. des fêtes** community hall; **s. des professeurs** staff room; **s. des ventes** auction room

salon [salɔ̃] *nm* living room, *Br* lounge; *(exposition)* show; **s. de coiffure** hairdressing salon; **s. de thé** tea room

salope [salɔp] *nf Vulg (femme)* bitch •**saloper** *vt Fam (salir)* to mess up •**saloperie** [-pri] *nf Fam (action)* dirty trick; *(camelote)* junk; **dire des saloperies sur qn** to bitch about sb

salopette [salɔpɛt] *nf Br* dungarees, *Am* overalls

salsifis [salsifi] *nf* salsify

saltimbanque [saltɛ̃bãk] *nmf* (travelling) acrobat

salubre [salybr] *adj* healthy •**salubrité** *nf* healthiness; **s. publique** public health

saluer [salɥe] *vt* to greet; *(en partant)* to take one's leave of; *(de la main)* to wave to; *(de la tête)* to nod to; *Mil* to salute

salut [saly] **1** *nm* greeting; *(de la main)*

wave; *(de la tête)* nod; *Mil* salute; *(sauvegarde)* rescue; *Rel* salvation

2 *exclam Fam* hi!; *(au revoir)* bye! • **salutation** *nf* greeting

salutaire [salytɛr] *adj* salutary

salve [salv] *nf* salvo

samedi [samdi] *nm* Saturday

SAMU [samy] *(abrév* **service d'aide médicale d'urgence)** *nm* emergency medical service

sanatorium [sanatɔrjɔm] *nm* sanatorium

sanctifier [sɑ̃ktifje] *vt* to sanctify

sanction [sɑ̃ksjɔ̃] *nf (approbation, peine)* sanction • **sanctionner** *vt (approuver)* to sanction; *(punir)* to punish

sanctuaire [sɑ̃ktɥer] *nm* sanctuary

sandale [sɑ̃dal] *nf* sandal

sandwich [sɑ̃dwitʃ] *nm* sandwich; **s. au fromage** cheese sandwich

sang [sɑ̃] *nm* blood; **être en s.** to be covered in blood; *Fig* **avoir du s. bleu** to have blue blood; *Fig* **avoir le s. chaud** to be hot-tempered; *Fam* **se faire du mauvais s.** to worry; *Fig* **mon s. n'a fait qu'un tour** my heart missed a beat • **sang-froid** *nm* self-control; **garder son s.** to keep calm; **avec s.** calmly; **tuer qn de s.** to kill sb in cold blood • **sanglant, -ante** *adj* bloody

sangle [sɑ̃gl] *nf* strap

sanglier [sɑ̃glije] *nm* wild boar

sanglot [sɑ̃glo] *nm* sob • **sangloter** *vi* to sob

sangsue [sɑ̃sy] *nf* leech

sanguin, -ine [sɑ̃gɛ̃, -in] **1** *adj (tempérament)* full-blooded; **vaisseau s.** blood vessel

2 *nf* **sanguine** *(fruit)* blood orange

sanguinaire [sɑ̃ginɛr] *adj* blood-thirsty

sanitaire [sanitɛr] *adj (conditions)* sanitary; *(personnel)* medical; **installation s.** bathroom fittings; **règlement s.** health regulations

sans [sɑ̃] ([sɑ̃z] *before vowel and mute h)* *prép* without; **s. faire qch** without doing sth; **s. qu'il le sache** without him *or* his knowing; **s. cela, s. quoi** otherwise; **s. plus** (but) no more than that; **s. faute/exception** without fail/exception; **s. importance/travail** unimportant/unemployed; **s. argent/manches** penniless/sleeveless; **ça va s. dire** that goes without saying • **sans-abri** *nmf inv* homeless person; **les s.** the homeless • **sans-cœur** *nmf inv Fam* heartless person • **sans-faute** *nm inv Équitation* clear round; *Fig* **faire un s.** not to put a foot wrong • **sans-gêne 1** *adj*

inv ill-mannered **2** *nm inv* lack of manners • **sans-papiers** *nmf inv* illegal immigrant

santé [sɑ̃te] *nf* health; **en bonne/mauvaise s.** in good/bad health; **(à votre) s.!** *(en trinquant)* cheers!; **boire à la s. de qn** to drink to sb's (good) health; **la s. publique** public health

santiag [sɑ̃tjag] *nf Fam* cowboy boot

saoul [su] *adj & nm* = **soûl**

saper [sape] *vt* to undermine; **s. le moral à qn** to sap sb's morale

sapeur-pompier [sapœrpɔ̃pje] *(pl* **sapeurs-pompiers)** *nm* fireman

saphir [safir] *nm* sapphire

sapin [sapɛ̃] *nm (arbre, bois)* fir; **s. de Noël** Christmas tree

sarbacane [sarbakan] *nf (jouet)* peashooter

sarcasme [sarkasm] *nm* sarcasm; *(remarque)* sarcastic remark • **sarcastique** *adj* sarcastic

sarcler [sarkle] *vt (jardin)* to weed

Sardaigne [sardɛɲ] *nf* **la S.** Sardinia • **sarde 1** *adj* Sardinian **2** *nmf* **S.** Sardinian

sardine [sardin] *nf* sardine; **sardines à l'huile** sardines in oil; *Fam* **serrés comme des sardines** squashed like sardines

sardonique [sardɔnik] *adj* sardonic

SARL [ɛsɑɛrɛl] *(abrév* **société à responsabilité limitée)** *nf* limited liability company

sarment [sarmɑ̃] *nm* vine shoot

sarrasin [sarazɛ̃] *nm (plante)* buckwheat

sas [sɑs] *nm (de bateau, d'avion)* airlock; **s. de sécurité** security screen

Satan [satɑ̃] *nm* Satan • **satané, -ée** *adj Fam (maudit)* damned • **satanique** *adj* satanic

satellite [satelit] *nm* satellite; **télévision par s.** satellite television

satiété [sasjete] *nf* **à s.** *(boire, manger)* one's fill

satin [satɛ̃] *nm* satin • **satiné, -ée** *adj* satiny

satire [satir] *nf* satire **(contre** on) • **satirique** *adj* satirical

satisfaction [satisfaksjɔ̃] *nf* satisfaction; **donner s. à qn** to give sb (complete) satisfaction • **satisfaire* 1** *vt* to satisfy **2** *vi* **s. à qch** *(conditions)* to satisfy sth; *(obligation)* to fulfil sth, *Am* to fulfill sth • **satisfaisant, -ante** *adj (acceptable)* satisfactory • **satisfait, -faite** *adj* satisfied **(de** with)

saturer [satyre] *vt* to saturate **(de** with) • **saturation** *nf* saturation; **arriver à s.** to reach saturation point

satyre [satir] *nm Fam* sex maniac
sauce [sos] *nf* sauce; **s. tomate** tomato sauce • **saucière** *nf* sauce boat
saucisse [sosis] *nf* sausage; **s. de Francfort** frankfurter; **s. de Strasbourg** = type of beef sausage • **saucisson** *nm* (cold) sausage
sauf¹ [sof] *prép* except; **s. avis contraire** unless you hear otherwise; **s. erreur** if I'm not mistaken
sauf², sauve [sof, sov] *adj* **avoir la vie sauve** to be unharmed • **sauf-conduit** (*pl* **sauf-conduits**) *nm* safe-conduct
sauge [soʒ] *nf* sage
saugrenu, -ue [sogrəny] *adj* preposterous
saule [sol] *nm* willow; **s. pleureur** weeping willow
saumâtre [somɑtr] *adj (eau)* brackish
saumon [somɔ̃] **1** *nm* salmon
  2 *adj inv (couleur)* salmon (pink)
saumure [somyr] *nf* brine
sauna [sona] *nm* sauna
saupoudrer [sopudre] *vt* to sprinkle (**de** with)
saur [sɔr] *adj m* **hareng s.** smoked herring
saura, saurait [sora, sore] *voir* **savoir**
saut [so] *nm* jump, leap; **faire un s.** to jump, to leap; *Fam* **faire un s. chez qn** to drop in on sb; **au s. du lit** first thing in the morning; **s. à la corde** *Br* skipping, *Am* jumping rope; **s. à l'élastique** bungee jumping; **s. en hauteur** high jump; **s. en longueur** long jump; **s. en parachute** parachute jump; *(activité)* parachute jumping
sauté, -ée [sote] *adj & nm Culin* sauté
sauter [sote] **1** *vt (franchir)* to jump (over); *(mot, repas, classe, ligne)* to skip
  2 *vi (personne, animal)* to jump, to leap; *(bombe)* to go off, to explode; *(fusible)* to blow; *(bouton)* to come off; **faire s. qch** *(pont, mine)* to blow sth up; *(serrure)* to force sth; *Fig (gouvernement)* to bring sth down; *Culin* to sauté sth; **s. à la corde** *Br* to skip, *Am* to jump rope; **s. en parachute** to do a parachute jump; *Fig* **s. sur l'occasion** to jump at the opportunity; **ça saute aux yeux** it's obvious; *Fam* **elle m'a sauté dessus** she pounced on me • **saute-mouton** *nm inv* leapfrog
sauterelle [sotrɛl] *nf* grasshopper
sautes [sot] *nfpl (d'humeur, de température)* sudden changes (**de** in)
sautiller [sotije] *vi* to hop about
sautoir [sotwar] *nm (de stade)* jumping area
sauvage [sovaʒ] *adj (animal, plante)* wild; *(tribu, homme)* primitive; *(cruel)* savage; *(farouche)* unsociable; *(illégal)* unauthorized • **sauvagerie** *nf (insociabilité)* unsociability; *(cruauté)* savagery
sauve [sov] *adj voir* **sauf²**
sauvegarde [sovgard] *nf* safeguard (**contre** against); *Ordinat* backup • **sauvegarder** *vt* to safeguard; *Ordinat* to save
sauver [sove] **1** *vt (personne)* to save, to rescue (**de** from); *(matériel)* to salvage; **s. la vie à qn** to save sb's life
  2 se sauver *vpr (s'enfuir)* to run away; *(s'échapper)* to escape; *Fam (partir)* to go • **sauvetage** *nm (de personne)* rescue • **sauveteur** *nm* rescuer • **sauveur** *nm* saviour
sauvette [sovɛt] **à la sauvette** *adv (pour ne pas être vu)* on the sly; **vendre qch à la s.** to peddle illegally on the streets
savane [savan] *nf* savanna
savant, -ante [savɑ̃, -ɑ̃t] **1** *adj (érudit)* learned; *(habile)* clever
  2 *nm (scientifique)* scientist • **savamment** [-amɑ̃] *adv (avec érudition)* learnedly; *(avec habileté)* cleverly
savate [savat] *nf Fam (pantoufle)* slipper
saveur [savœr] *nf (goût)* flavour; *Fig (piment)* savour
Savoie [savwa] *nf* **la S.** Savoy
savoir* [savwar] **1** *vt* to know; *(nouvelle)* to have heard; **s. lire/nager** to know how to read/swim; **faire s. à qn que...** to inform sb that...; **à s.** *(c'est-à-dire)* that is, namely; **pas que je sache** not that I know of; **je n'en sais rien** I have no idea, I don't know; **en s. long sur qn/qch** to know a lot about sb/sth
  2 *nm (culture)* learning, knowledge • **savoir-faire** *nm inv* know-how • **savoir-vivre** *nm inv* good manners
savon [savɔ̃] *nm* soap; *Fam* **passer un s. à qn** to give sb a telling-off • **savonner** *vt* to wash with soap • **savonnette** *nf* bar of soap • **savonneux, -euse** *adj* soapy
savourer [savure] *vt* to savour • **savoureux, -euse** *adj* tasty; *Fig (histoire)* juicy
savoyard, -arde [savwajar, -ard] **1** *adj* Savoyard
  2 *nmf* **S., Savoyarde** Savoyard
saxophone [saksɔfɔn] *nm* saxophone
saynette [sɛnɛt] *nf* sketch
sbire [sbir] *nm Péj* henchman
scabreux, -euse [skabrø, -øz] *adj* obscene
scalp [skalp] *nm (chevelure)* scalp • **scalper** *vt* to scalp
scalpel [skalpɛl] *nm* scalpel
scandale [skɑ̃dal] *nm* scandal; **faire s.**

(sujet: livre, événement) to cause a scandal; **faire un s.** *(sujet: personne)* to make a scene • **scandaleux, -euse** *adj* scandalous • **scandaliser 1** *vt* to scandalize, to shock **2 se scandaliser** *vpr* to be shocked *or* scandalized (**de** by)

scander [skãde] *vt (vers)* to scan; *(slogan)* to chant

Scandinavie [skãdinavi] *nf* la **S.** Scandinavia • **scandinave 1** *adj* Scandinavian **2** *nmf* **S.** Scandinavian

scanner 1 [skanɛr] *nm* scanner **2** [skane] *vt* to scan

scaphandre [skafãdr] *nm (de plongeur)* diving suit; *(de cosmonaute)* spacesuit; **s. autonome** aqualung • **scaphandrier** *nm* diver

scarabée [skarabe] *nm* beetle

scarlatine [skarlatin] *nf* scarlet fever

scarole [skarɔl] *nf* endive

sceau, -x [so] *nm* seal • **sceller** *vt (document)* to seal; *Tech (fixer)* to embed • **scellés** *nmpl (cachets de cire)* seals; **mettre les s.** to put on the seals

scélérat, -ate [selera, -at] *nmf Littéraire* scoundrel

scénario [senarjo] *nm* script, screenplay • **scénariste** *nmf* scriptwriter

scène [sɛn] *nf* (**a**) *(de théâtre)* scene; *(plateau)* stage; *(action)* action; **mettre qch en s.** *(pièce)* to stage sth; *(film)* to direct sth; **entrer en s.** *(acteur)* to come on; *Fig* **sur la s. internationale** on the international scene (**b**) *(dispute)* scene; **faire une s.** to make a scene; **elle m'a fait une s.** she made a scene; **s. de ménage** domestic quarrel

scepticisme [septisism] *nm Br* scepticism, *Am* skepticism • **sceptique 1** *adj Br* sceptical, *Am* skeptical **2** *nmf Br* sceptic, *Am* skeptic

schéma [ʃema] *nm* diagram; *Fig* outline • **schématique** *adj* schematic; *Péj* oversimplified • **schématiser** *vt* to schematize; *Péj* to oversimplify

schizophrène [skizɔfrɛn] *adj & nmf* schizophrenic

sciatique [sjatik] *nf* sciatica

scie [si] *nf (outil)* saw; **s. électrique** power saw; **s. musicale** musical saw • **scier** *vt* to saw • **scierie** *nf* sawmill

sciemment [sjamã] *adv* knowingly

science [sjãs] *nf* science; *(savoir)* knowledge; **étudier les sciences** to study science; **sciences humaines** social sciences; **sciences naturelles** biology • **science-fiction** *nf* science fiction • **scientifique 1** *adj* scientific **2** *nmf* scientist

scinder [sɛ̃de] *vt,* **se scinder** *vpr* to split up (**en** into)

scintiller [sɛ̃tije] *vi* to sparkle; *(étoile)* to twinkle • **scintillement** *nm* sparkling; *(d'étoile)* twinkling

scission [sisjɔ̃] *nf (de parti)* split (**de** in); **s. de l'atome** splitting of the atom

sciure [sjyr] *nf* sawdust

sclérose [skleroz] *nf Méd* sclerosis; *Fig* ossification; **s. en plaques** multiple sclerosis • **sclérosé, -ée** *adj Fig (société)* ossified

scolaire [skɔlɛr] *adj* **année s.** school year; **enfant d'âge s.** child of school age; **progrès scolaires** academic progress • **scolariser** *vt (enfant)* to send to school • **scolarité** *nf* schooling; **certificat de s.** certificate of attendance *(at school or university)*; **pendant ma s.** during my school years

scoliose [skɔljoz] *nf Méd* curvature of the spine

scooter [skuter] *nm* (motor) scooter; **s. des mers** jet ski

scorbut [skɔrbyt] *nm* scurvy

score [skɔr] *nm* score

scories [skɔri] *nfpl (résidu)* slag

scorpion [skɔrpjɔ̃] *nm* scorpion; **le S.** *(signe)* Scorpio; **être S.** to be Scorpio

Scotch [skɔtʃ] *(ruban adhésif) Br* sellotape®, *Am* scotch tape® • **scotcher** *vt Br* to sellotape, *Am* to tape

scotch [skɔtʃ] *nm (boisson)* Scotch

scout, -e [skut] *adj & nm* scout • **scoutisme** *nm (activité)* scouting

script [skript] *nm (écriture)* printing; *Cin* script

scripte [skript] *nf Cin* continuity girl

scrupule [skrypyl] *nm* scruple; **sans scrupules** unscrupulous; *(agir)* unscrupulously • **scrupuleusement** *adv* scrupulously • **scrupuleux, -euse** *adj* scrupulous

scruter [skryte] *vt* to scrutinize

scrutin [skrytɛ̃] *nm (vote)* ballot; *(élection)* poll; *(système)* voting system; **premier tour de s.** first ballot *or* round; **s. majoritaire** first-past-the-post voting system

sculpter [skylte] *vt (statue, pierre)* to sculpt; *(bois)* to carve; **s. qch dans qch** to sculpt/carve sth out of sth • **sculpteur** *nm* sculptor • **sculptural, -e, -aux, -ales** *adj (beauté, femme)* statuesque • **sculpture** *nf (art, œuvre)* sculpture; **s. sur bois** woodcarving

SDF [ɛsdeef] *(abrév* **sans domicile fixe)** *nm* person of no fixed abode

se [sə]

se becomes **s'** before vowel or mute h.

pron personnel (**a**) *(complément direct)* himself; *(féminin)* herself; *(non humain)* itself; *(indéfini)* oneself, *pl* themselves; **il se lave** he washes himself; **ils** *ou* **elles se lavent** they wash themselves

(**b**) *(indirect)* to himself/herself/itself/ oneself; **se dire qch** to say sth to oneself; **il se lave les mains** he washes his hands; **elle se lave les mains** she washes her hands

(**c**) *(réciproque)* each other; *(indirect)* to each other; **ils s'aiment** they love each other; **ils** *ou* **elles se parlent** they speak to each other

(**d**) *(passif)* **ça se fait** that is done; **ça se vend bien** it sells well

séance [seɑ̃s] *nf (de cinéma)* showing, performance; *(d'assemblée, de travail)* session; **s. de pose** sitting; **s. tenante** at once

seau, -x [so] *nm* bucket; **s. à glace** ice bucket

sec, sèche [sɛk, sɛʃ] **1** *adj* dry; *(fruits, légumes)* dried; *(ton)* curt; *(maigre)* lean; *Fig (cœur)* hard; **frapper un coup s.** to knock sharply; **bruit s.** snap

2 *adv (boire) Br* neat, *Am* straight; *(frapper, pleuvoir)* hard

3 *nm* **à s.** dry; *Fam (sans argent)* broke; **au s.** in a dry place

sécateur [sekatœr] *nm* pruning shears, *Br* secateurs

sécession [sesesjɔ̃] *nf* secession; **faire s.** to secede

sèche [sɛʃ] *voir* sec

sécher [seʃe] **1** *vt* to dry; *Fam (cours)* to skip

2 *vi* to dry; *Fam (ne pas savoir)* to be stumped; *Fam (être absent)* to skip classes

3 se sécher *vpr* to dry oneself • **séchage** *nm* drying • **sèche-cheveux** *nm inv* hair dryer • **sèche-linge** *nm inv Br* tumble dryer, *Am* (clothes) dryer

sécheresse [seʃrɛs] *nf (d'air, de sol, de peau)* dryness; *(de ton)* curtness; *(manque de pluie)* drought

séchoir [seʃwar] *nm (appareil)* dryer; **s. à linge** clothes horse

second, -onde¹ [səgɔ̃, -ɔ̃d] **1** *adj & nmf* second

2 *nm (adjoint)* second in command; *(étage) Br* second floor, *Am* third floor

3 *nf* **seconde** *Rail* second class; *Scol Br* ≃ fifth form, *Am* ≃ tenth grade; *Aut (vitesse)* second (gear) • **secondaire** *adj* secondary; **école s.** *Br* secondary school, *Am* high school

seconde² [səgɔ̃d] *nf (instant)* second

seconder [səgɔ̃de] *vt* to assist

secouer [səkwe] **1** *vt* to shake; *(poussière)* to shake off; **s. qn** *(maladie, nouvelle)* to shake sb up; **s. qch de qch** *(enlever)* to shake sth out of sth; **s. la tête** *(réponse affirmative)* to nod (one's head); *(réponse négative)* to shake one's head

2 se secouer *vpr Fam (faire un effort)* to snap out of it

secourir [səkurir] *vt* to assist, to help • **secourable** *adj* helpful • **secourisme** *nm* first aid • **secouriste** *nmf* first-aid worker

secours [səkur] *nm* help; *(financier, matériel)* aid; *Mil* **les s.** *(renforts)* relief; **premiers s.** first aid; **au s.!** help!; **porter s. à qn** to give sb help; **roue de s.** spare wheel

secousse [səkus] *nf* jolt, jerk; *(de tremblement de terre)* tremor

secret, -ète [səkrɛ, -ɛt] **1** *adj* secret; *(cachottier)* secretive

2 *nm* secret; *(discrétion)* secrecy; **s. d'État** state secret; **en s.** in secret, secretly; **dans le s.** *(au courant)* in on the secret; **au s.** *(en prison)* in solitary confinement

secrétaire [səkretɛr] **1** *nmf* secretary; **s. médicale** medical secretary; **s. d'État** Secretary of State; **s. de mairie** town clerk; *Journ* **s. de rédaction** *Br* sub-editor, *Am* copyeditor

2 *nm (meuble)* writing desk • **secrétariat** *nm (bureau)* secretary's office; *(d'organisation internationale)* secretariat; *(métier)* secretarial work; **école/travail de s.** secretarial school/work

sécréter [sekrete] *vt Biol* to secrete • **sécrétion** *nf* secretion

secte [sɛkt] *nf* sect • **sectaire** *adj & nmf Péj* sectarian

secteur [sɛktœr] *nm (zone)* area; *Écon* sector; *Él* mains; **branché sur s.** plugged into the mains; *Écon* **s. primaire/secondaire/tertiaire** primary/secondary/tertiary sector

section [sɛksjɔ̃] *nf* section; *(de ligne d'autobus)* stage; *Mil* platoon • **sectionner** *vt (diviser)* to divide (into sections); *(couper)* to sever

séculaire [sekylɛr] *adj (tradition)* age-old

séculier, -ière [sekylje, -jɛr] *adj* secular

secundo [səgɔ̃do] *adv* secondly

sécurité [sekyrite] *nf (absence de danger)* safety; *(tranquillité)* security; **s. routière** road safety; **S. sociale** *Br* Social Security, *Am* Welfare; **s. de l'emploi** job security; **en s.** *(hors de danger)* safe; *(tranquille)* secure • **sécuriser** *vt* to reassure

sédatif [sedatif] *nm* sedative
sédentaire [sedɑ̃tɛr] *adj* sedentary
sédiment [sedimɑ̃] *nm* sediment
séditieux, -ieuse [sedisjø, -jøz] *adj* seditious • **sédition** *nf* sedition
séduire* [sedɥir] *vt* to charm; *(plaire à)* to appeal to; *(abuser de)* to seduce • **séduisant, -ante** *adj* attractive • **séducteur, -trice** 1 *adj* seductive 2 *nmf* seducer, *f* seductress • **séduction** *nf* attraction; **pouvoir de s.** power of attraction

🖉 Il faut noter que le verbe anglais **to seduce** est un faux ami. Il ne signifie jamais **charmer**.

segment [sɛgmɑ̃] *nm* segment • **segmenter** *vt* to segment
ségrégation [segregasjɔ̃] *nf* segregation
seiche [sɛʃ] *nf* cuttlefish
seigle [sɛgl] *nm* rye; **pain de s.** rye bread
seigneur [sɛɲœr] *nm Hist (noble, maître)* lord; *Rel* **le S.** the Lord
sein [sɛ̃] *nm* breast; *Littéraire* bosom; **bout de s.** nipple; **donner le s. à** *(enfant)* to breastfeed; **au s. de** within
Seine [sɛn] *nf* **la S.** the Seine
séisme [seism] *nm* earthquake
seize [sɛz] *adj & nm inv* sixteen • **seizième** *adj & nmf* sixteenth; *Sport* **les seizièmes de finale** the first round *(of a four-round knockout competition)*
séjour [seʒur] *nm* stay; **s. linguistique** language-learning trip; **(salle de) s.** living room • **séjourner** *vi* to stay
sel [sɛl] *nm* salt; *Fig (piquant)* spice; **sels** *(à respirer)* (smelling) salts; **s. de mer** sea salt; **sels de bain** bath salts
sélect, -e [selɛkt] *adj Fam* select
sélectif, -ive [selɛktif, -iv] *adj* selective • **sélection** *nf* selection • **sélectionner** *vt* to select • **sélectionneur** *nm* selector
self(-service) [sɛlf(sɛrvis)] *nm* self-service restaurant
selle [sɛl] *nf (de cheval, de vélo)* saddle • **seller** [sele] *vt* to saddle
selles [sɛl] *nfpl Méd* **les s.** stools, *Br* motions
sellette [selɛt] *nf Fam* **sur la s.** in the hot seat
selon [səlɔ̃] *prép* according to; **s. que...** depending on whether...; *Fam* **c'est s.** it (all) depends
semailles [səmaj] *nfpl (travail)* sowing; *(période)* seedtime
semaine [səmɛn] *nf* week; **en s.** in the week; **à la s.** by the week, weekly; *Fam* **vivre la petite s.** to live from day to day
sémantique [semɑ̃tik] 1 *adj* semantic 2 *nf* semantics

sémaphore [semafɔr] *nm (pour trains)* semaphore; *Naut* signal station
semblable [sɑ̃blabl] 1 *adj* similar *(à* to); **de semblables propos** such remarks 2 *nm* fellow creature; **toi et tes semblables** you and your kind
semblant [sɑ̃blɑ̃] *nm* **faire s.** to pretend *(de faire* to do); **un s. de** a semblance of
sembler [sɑ̃ble] 1 *vi* to seem *(à* to); **il (me) semble vieux** he seems *or* looks old *(to me)*; **s. faire qch** to seem to do sth 2 *v impersonnel* **il semble que...** it seems that...; **il me semble que...** it seems to me that...; **quand bon lui semble** when he/she sees fit
semelle [səmɛl] *nf (de chaussure)* sole; *(intérieure)* insole; *Fig* **ne pas quitter qn d'une s.** to be always at sb's heels
semer [səme] *vt (graines)* to sow; *Fig (répandre)* to spread; *(poursuivant)* to shake off; *Fig* **semé de** strewn with • **semence** *nf* seed
semestre [səmɛstr] *nm* half-year; *Univ* semester • **semestriel, -ielle** *adj* half-yearly
séminaire [seminɛr] *nm Univ* seminar; *Rel* seminary • **séminariste** *nm Rel* seminarist
semi-remorque [səmirəmɔrk] *(pl* **semi-remorques)** *nm (camion) Br* articulated lorry, *Am* semi(trailer), *Am* trailer truck
semis [səmi] *nm* sowing; *(terrain)* seedbed; *(plant)* seedling
sémite [semit] 1 *adj* Semitic 2 *nmf* **S.** Semite • **sémitique** *adj (langue)* Semitic
semonce [səmɔ̃s] *nf* reprimand; **coup de s.** warning shot
semoule [səmul] *nf* semolina
sempiternel, -elle [sɑ̃pitɛrnɛl] *adj* endless, ceaseless
sénat [sena] *nm* senate • **sénateur** *nm* senator
sénile [senil] *adj* senile • **sénilité** *nf* senility
senior [senjɔr] *nm & adj inv Sport* senior
sens [sɑ̃s] *nm* (**a**) *(faculté, raison, instinct)* sense; **avoir le s. de l'humour** to have a sense of humour; **avoir du bon s.** to be sensible; **cela tombe sous le s.** that's obvious; **à mon s.** to my mind; **s. commun, bon sens** common sense (**b**) *(signification)* meaning, sense; **ça n'a pas de s.** that doesn't make sense; **dans un certain s.** in a way (**c**) *(direction)* direction; *Aut* **s. giratoire** *Br* roundabout, *Am* traffic circle, *Am* rotary; **s. interdit** *ou* **unique** *(rue)* one-way street; **'s. interdit'** 'no entry'; **à s.**

unique *(rue)* one-way; **s. dessus dessous** [săd(ə)syd(ə)su] upside down; **dans le s. des aiguilles d'une montre** clockwise; **dans le s. inverse des aiguilles d'une montre** *Br* anticlockwise, *Am* counterclockwise
sensation [sãsɑsjɔ̃] *nf* feeling, sensation; **faire s.** to create a sensation; *Péj* **à s.** *(film, roman)* sensational • **sensationnel, -elle** *adj* sensational; *Fam (excellent)* fantastic
sensé, -ée [sãse] *adj* sensible
sensible [sãsibl] *adj* sensitive (**à** to); *(douloureux)* tender, sore; *(perceptible)* perceptible; *(progrès, différence)* noticeable • **sensiblement** [-əmã] *adv (notablement)* noticeably; *(à peu près)* more or less • **sensibiliser** *vt* **s. qn à qch** *(problème)* to make sb aware of sth • **sensibilité** *nf* sensitivity

> *⚠* Il faut noter que l'adjectif anglais **sensible** est un faux ami. Il signifie **sensé**.

sensoriel, -ielle [sãsɔrjɛl] *adj* sensory
sensuel, -elle [sãsɥɛl] *adj* sensual • **sensualité** *nf* sensuality
sentence [sãtãs] *nf Jur (jugement)* sentence; *(maxime)* maxim
senteur [sãtœr] *nf (odeur)* scent
sentier [sãtje] *nm* path
sentiment [sãtimã] *nm* feeling; **avoir le s. que...** to have a feeling that...; **faire du s.** to be sentimental; **meilleurs sentiments** *(sur une carte de visite)* best wishes • **sentimental, -e, -aux, -ales** *adj* sentimental; **vie sentimentale** love life • **sentimentalité** *nf* sentimentality
sentinelle [sãtinɛl] *nf* sentry
sentir* [sãtir] **1** *vt (douleur)* to feel; *(odeur)* to smell; *(danger)* to sense; **s. le moisi/le parfum** to smell musty/of perfume; **s. le poisson** to smell of fish; **se faire s.** *(effet)* to make itself felt; *Fam* **je ne peux pas le s.** I can't stand him
2 *vi* to smell; **s. bon/mauvais** to smell good/bad
3 se sentir *vpr* **se s. fatigué/humilié** to feel tired/humiliated • **senti, -ie** *adj* **bien s.** *(remarque)* hard-hitting
séparation [separɑsjɔ̃] *nf* separation; *(départ)* parting
séparer [separe] **1** *vt* to separate (**de** from); *(cheveux)* to part; **plus rien ne nous sépare de la victoire** nothing stands between us and victory
2 se séparer *vpr (couple)* to separate; *(assemblée, cortège)* to disperse, to break up; *(se détacher)* to split off; **se s. de** *(objet aimé, chien)* to part with • **séparé, -ée** *adj*

(distinct) separate; *(époux)* separated (**de** from) • **séparément** *adv* separately
sept [sɛt] *adj & nm inv* seven • **septième** *adj & nmf* seventh; **un s.** a seventh
septante [sɛptãt] *adj (en Belgique, en Suisse)* seventy
septembre [sɛptãbr] *nm* September
septennat [sɛptena] *nm Pol* seven-year term (of office)
septentrional, -e, -aux, -ales [sɛptãtrijɔnal, -o] *adj* northern
sépulcre [sepylkr] *nm (tombeau)* sepulchre
sépulture [sepyltyr] *nf* burial; *(lieu)* burial place
séquelles [sekɛl] *nfpl (de maladie)* aftereffects; *(de guerre)* aftermath
séquence [sekãs] *nf* sequence; *Cartes* run; **s. de film** film sequence
séquestrer [sekɛstre] *vt* **s. qn** to keep sb locked up
sera, serait [səra, sərɛ] *voir* être
Serbie [sɛrbi] *nf* **la S.** Serbia • **serbe 1** *adj* Serbian **2** *nmf* **S.** Serbian
serein, -eine [sərɛ̃, -ɛn] *adj* serene • **sérénité** *nf* serenity
sérénade [serenad] *nf* serenade
sergent [sɛrʒã] *nm Mil* sergeant
série [seri] *nf* series; *(ensemble)* set; *Fig* **s. noire** series of disasters; **de s.** *(article, voiture)* standard; **fin de s.** discontinued line; **fabrication en s.** mass production; **numéro hors s.** special issue
sérieux, -ieuse [serjø, -jøz] **1** *adj (personne, doute)* serious; *(de bonne foi)* genuine, serious; *(fiable)* reliable; *(bénéfices)* substantial; **de sérieuses chances de...** a good chance of...
2 *nm (application)* seriousness; *(fiabilité)* reliability; **prendre qn/qch au s.** to take sb/sth seriously; **garder son s.** to keep a straight face; **se prendre (trop) au s.** to take oneself (too) seriously • **sérieusement** *adv* seriously
serin [sərɛ̃] *nm* canary
seriner [sərine] *vt Fig* **s. qch à qn** to repeat sth to sb over and over again
seringue [sərɛ̃g] *nf* syringe
serment [sɛrmã] *nm (affirmation solennelle)* oath; *(promesse)* pledge; **prêter s.** to take an oath; **faire le s. de faire qch** to swear to do sth; *Jur* **sous s.** on *or* under oath
sermon [sɛrmɔ̃] *nm (de prêtre)* sermon; *Péj (discours)* lecture • **sermonner** *vt (faire la morale à)* to lecture
séropositif, -ive [seropozitif, -iv] *adj Méd* HIV positive • **séronégatif, -ive** *adj Méd* HIV negative

serpe [sɛrp] *nf* billhook
serpent [sɛrpɑ̃] *nm* snake; **s. à sonnette** rattlesnake
serpenter [sɛrpɑ̃te] *vi (sentier)* to meander
serpentin [sɛrpɑ̃tɛ̃] *nm (ruban)* streamer
serpillière [sɛrpijɛr] *nf* floor cloth
serpolet [sɛrpɔle] *nm* wild thyme
serre [sɛr] *nf* greenhouse •**serres** *nfpl (d'oiseau)* claws, talons
serrement [sɛrmɑ̃] *nm* **s. de cœur** heavy-hearted feeling
serrer [sere] *vt (tenir)* to grip; *(nœud, vis)* to tighten; *(poing)* to clench; *(taille)* to hug; *(frein)* to apply; *(rapprocher)* to close up; **s. la main à qn** to shake hands with sb; **s. les rangs** to close ranks; *Fig* **s. les dents** to grit one's teeth; **s. qn** *(embrasser)* to hug sb; *(sujet: vêtement)* to be too tight for sb; **s. qn de près** *(talonner)* to be close behind sb
2 *vi* **s. à droite** to keep (to the) right
3 se serrer *vpr (se rapprocher)* to squeeze up; **se s. contre** to squeeze up against •**serré, -ée** *adj (nœud, budget, vêtement)* tight; *(gens)* packed (together); *(lutte)* close; *(rangs)* serried; *(écriture)* cramped; *Fig* **avoir le cœur s.** to have a heavy heart •**serre-livres** *nm inv* book-end •**serre-tête** *nm inv* headband
serrure [seryr] *nf* lock •**serrurier** *nm* locksmith
sertir [sɛrtir] *vt (diamant)* to set
sérum [serɔm] *nm* serum
servante [sɛrvɑ̃t] *nf* (maid)servant
serveur, -euse [sɛrvœr, -øz] *nmf* waiter, waitress; *(de bar)* barman, barmaid; *Ordinat* server
serviable [sɛrvjabl] *adj* helpful, obliging •**serviabilité** *nf* helpfulness
service [sɛrvis] *nm* service; *(travail)* duty; *(pourboire)* service (charge); *(d'entreprise)* department; *Tennis* serve, service; **un s.** *(aide)* a favour; **rendre s.** to be of service (à qn to sb); **rendre un mauvais s. à qn** to do sb a disservice; **être de s.** to be on duty; *Tennis* **être au s.** to be serving; **faire son s. (militaire)** to do one's military service; **à votre s.!** at your service!; **s. à café/à thé** coffee/tea set; **s. (non) compris** service (not) included; **s. d'ordre** *(policiers)* police; **s. après-vente** after-sales service
serviette [sɛrvjɛt] *nf (pour s'essuyer)* towel; *(sac)* briefcase; **s. de bain/de toilette** bath/hand towel; **s. de table** napkin, *Br* serviette; **s. hygiénique** sanitary *Br* towel *or Am* napkin •**serviette-éponge** *(pl* **serviettes-éponges)** *nf* terry towel

servile [sɛrvil] *adj* servile; *(imitation)* slavish •**servilité** *nf* servility; slavishness
servir* [sɛrvir] **1** *vt* to serve (**qch à qn** sb with sth, sth to sb); *(convive)* to wait on
2 *vi* to serve; **s. à qch/à faire qch** to be used for sth/to do *or* for doing sth; **ça ne sert à rien** it's useless, it's no good *or* use (**de faire** doing); **à quoi ça sert de protester** what's the use *or* good of protesting; **s. de qch** to be used for sth, to serve as sth; **ça me sert à faire qch/de qch** I use it to do *or* for doing sth/as sth; **s. à qn de guide** to act as a guide to sb
3 se servir *vpr (à table)* to help oneself (**de** to); **se s. de qch** *(utiliser)* to use sth
serviteur [sɛrvitœr] *nm* servant •**servitude** *nf (esclavage)* servitude; *Fig (contrainte)* constraint
ses [se] *voir* **son²**
session [sesjɔ̃] *nf* session
set [sɛt] *nm Tennis* set; **s. de table** place mat
seuil [sœj] *nm (entrée)* doorway; *Fig (limite)* threshold; *Fig* **au s. de** on the threshold of
seul, seule [sœl] **1** *adj (sans compagnie)* alone; *(unique)* only; **tout s.** by oneself, on one's own, all alone; **se sentir s.** to feel lonely *or* alone; **la seule femme** the only woman; **un s. chat** only one cat; **une seule fois** only once; **pas un s. livre** not a single book; **seuls les garçons, les garçons seuls** only the boys
2 *adv* **(tout) s.** *(rentrer, vivre)* by oneself, alone, on one's own; *(parler)* to oneself; **s. à s.** *(parler)* in private
3 *nmf* **le s., la seule** the only one; **un s., une seule** only one, one only; **pas un s.** not (a single) one
seulement [sœlmɑ̃] *adv* only; **non s. mais encore** not only but (also); **pas s.** *(même)* not even
sève [sɛv] *nf (de plante)* & *Fig* sap
sévère [sever] *adj* severe; *(parents, professeur, juge)* strict •**sévèrement** *adv* severely; *(éduquer)* strictly •**sévérité** *nf* severity; *(de parents)* strictness
sévices [sevis] *nmpl* ill-treatment; **s. à enfant** child abuse
sévir [sevir] *vi Fig (fléau)* to rage; **s. contre qch** to deal severely with sth
sevrer [səvre] *vt (enfant)* to wean
sexe [sɛks] *nm (catégorie, sexualité)* sex; *(organes)* genitals •**sexiste** *adj & nmf* sexist •**sexualité** *nf* sexuality •**sexuel, -elle** *adj* sexual; **éducation/vie sexuelle** sex education/life
sextuor [sɛkstɥɔr] *nm* sextet

seyant, -ante [sejɑ̃, -ɑ̃t] *adj (vêtement)* becoming

shampooing [ʃɑ̃pwɛ̃] *nm* shampoo; **s. colorant** rinse; **faire un s. à qn** to shampoo sb's hair

shérif [ʃerif] *nm (aux États-Unis)* sheriff

shooter [ʃute] **1** *vti Football* to shoot

2 se shooter *upr Fam (drogué)* to shoot up

short [ʃɔrt] *nm* (pair of) shorts

si¹ [si]

---

si becomes **s'** [s] before **il, ils**.

---

1 *conj* if; **si je pouvais** if I could; **s'il vient** if he comes; **si j'étais roi** if I were *or* was king; **je me demande si...** I wonder whether *or* if...; **si on restait?** *(suggestion)* what if we stayed?; **si je dis ça, c'est que...** I say this because...; **si ce n'est que...** *(sauf que)* apart from the fact that...; **si oui** if so; **si non** if not; **si seulement** if only; **même si** even if

2 *adv* (**a**) *(tellement)* so; **pas si riche que toi/que tu crois** not as rich as you/as you think; **un si bon dîner** such a good dinner; **si grand qu'il soit** however big he may be; **si bien que...** so much so that...

(**b**) *(après négative)* yes; **tu ne viens pas? – si!** you're not coming? – yes (I am)!

si² [si] *nm inv (note)* B

siamois, -oise [sjamwa, -waz] *adj* Siamese; **frères s., sœurs siamoises** Siamese twins

Sicile [sisil] *nf* **la S.** Sicily

SIDA [sida] (*abrév* **syndrome immunodéficitaire acquis**) *nm* AIDS; **malade/virus du S.** AIDS victim/virus • **sidéen, -enne** *nmf* AIDS sufferer

sidérer [sidere] *vt Fam* to stagger

sidérurgie [sideryrʒi] *nf* iron and steel industry • **sidérurgique** *adj* **industrie s.** iron and steel industry

siècle [sjɛkl] *nm* century; *(époque)* age; *Fam* **depuis des siècles** for ages (and ages)

siège [sjɛʒ] *nm* (**a**) *(meuble, centre)* & *Pol* seat; *(d'autorité, de parti)* headquarters; **s. social** head office (**b**) *Mil* siege; **faire le s. de** to lay siege to • **siéger** *vi (assemblée)* to sit

sien, sienne [sjɛ̃, sjɛn] **1** *pron possessif* **le s., la sienne, les sien(ne)s** *(d'homme)* his; *(de femme)* hers; *(de chose)* its; **les deux siens** his/her two

2 *nmpl* **les siens** *(sa famille)* one's family

3 *nfpl* **faire des siennes** to be up to one's tricks again

sieste [sjɛst] *nf* siesta; **faire la s.** to have a nap

siffler [sifle] **1** *vi* to whistle; *(avec un sifflet)* to blow one's whistle; *(gaz, serpent)* to hiss

2 *vt (chanson)* to whistle; *(chien)* to whistle at; *Sport (faute, fin de match)* to blow one's whistle for; *(acteur, pièce)* to boo; *Fam (boisson)* to knock back; **se faire s.** *(acteur)* to be booed • **sifflement** [-əmɑ̃] *nm* whistling; *(de serpent, de gaz)* hissing

sifflet [siflɛ] *nm (instrument)* whistle; **sifflets** *(de spectateurs)* booing • **siffloter** *vti* to whistle

sigle [sigl] *nm (initiales)* abbreviation; *(acronyme)* acronym

signal, -aux [siɲal, -o] *nm* signal; **s. d'alarme** alarm signal; **s. lumineux** warning light; **s. sonore** warning sound

signalement [siɲalmɑ̃] *nm* description, particulars

signaler [siɲale] **1** *vt (faire remarquer)* to point out (**à qn** to sb; **que** that); *(avec un panneau)* to signpost; *(rapporter à la police)* to report (**à** to)

2 se signaler *upr* **se s. par qch** to distinguish oneself by sth

signalétique [siɲaletik] *adj* **fiche s.** personal details card

signalisation [siɲalizasjɔ̃] *nf (sur les routes)* signposting; *(pour les trains)* signals; *(pour les avions)* lights and marking; **s. routière** *(signaux)* road signs

signature [siɲatyr] *nf* signature; *(action)* signing • **signataire** *nmf* signatory • **signer 1** *vt* to sign **2 se signer** *upr* to cross oneself

signe [siɲ] *nm (indice)* sign, indication; **en s. de protestation** as a sign of protest; **faire s. à qn** *(geste)* to motion (to) sb (**de faire** to do); *(contacter)* to get in touch with sb; **faire s. que oui** to nod (one's head); **faire s. que non** to shake one's head; **faire le s. de croix** to make the sign of the cross; **ne pas donner s. de vie** to give no sign of life; **s. particulier/de ponctuation** distinguishing/punctuation mark; **s. astrologique** astrological sign

signet [siɲɛ] *nm* bookmark

signification [siɲifikasjɔ̃] *nf* meaning • **significatif, -ive** *adj* significant, meaningful; **s. de qch** indicative of sth

signifier [siɲifje] *vt* to mean (**que** that); **s. qch à qn** *(notifier)* to notify sb of sth

silence [silɑ̃s] *nm* silence; *Mus* rest; **en s.** in silence; **garder le s.** to keep quiet *or* silent (**sur** about) • **silencieux, -ieuse 1** *adj* silent **2** *nm (de voiture) Br* silencer, *Am* muffler; *(d'arme)* silencer • **silencieuse-ment** *adv* silently

silex [silɛks] *nm* flint

silhouette [silwɛt] *nf* outline; *(en noir)* silhouette; *(du corps)* figure

silicium [silisjɔm] *nm* silicon; **pastille de s.** silicon chip • **silicone** *nf* silicone

sillage [sijaʒ] *nm (de bateau)* wake; *Fig* **dans le s. de** in the wake of

sillon [sijɔ̃] *nm (de champ)* furrow; *(de disque)* groove

sillonner [sijɔne] *vt (parcourir)* to criss-cross

silo [silo] *nm* silo

simagrées [simagre] *nfpl* airs and graces; *(minauderies)* fuss

similaire [similɛr] *adj* similar • **similitude** *nf* similarity

similicuir [similikɥir] *nm* imitation leather

simple [sɛ̃pl] **1** *adj (facile, crédule, sans prétention)* simple; *(composé d'un élément)* single; *(employé, particulier)* ordinary; *Fam* **c'est s. comme bonjour** it's as easy as pie
2 *nmf* **s. d'esprit** simpleton
3 *nm Tennis* singles; **passer du s. au double** to double • **simplement** [-əmɑ̃] *adv* simply • **simplet, -ette** *adj (personne)* simple • **simplicité** *nf* simplicity

simplifier [sɛ̃plifje] *vt* to simplify • **simplification** *nf* simplification

simpliste [sɛ̃plist] *adj* simplistic

simulacre [simylakr] *nm* **ce fut un s. de procès** the trial was a farce

simuler [simyle] *vt (reproduire)* to simulate; *(feindre)* to feign • **simulateur, -trice 1** *nmf (hypocrite)* shammer; *(malade)* malingerer **2** *nm (appareil)* simulator • **simulation** *nf (de phénomène)* simulation; *(action)* feigning

simultané, -ée [simyltane] *adj* simultaneous • **simultanément** *adv* simultaneously

sincère [sɛ̃sɛr] *adj* sincere • **sincèrement** *adv* sincerely • **sincérité** *nf* sincerity; **en toute s.** quite sincerely

sinécure [sinekyr] *nf* sinecure; *Fam* **ce n'est pas une s.** it's no rest cure

Singapour [sɛ̃gapur] *nm* Singapore

singe [sɛ̃ʒ] *nm* monkey; **grand s.** ape • **singer** *vt (imiter)* to ape, to mimic • **singeries** *nfpl* antics; **faire des s.** to clown around

singulariser [sɛ̃gylarize] **se singulariser** *vpr* to draw attention to oneself

singulier, -ière [sɛ̃gylje, -jɛr] **1** *adj (peu ordinaire)* peculiar, odd; **combat s.** single combat

2 *adj & nm Grammaire* singular; **au s.** in the singular • **singularité** *nf* peculiarity • **singulièrement** *adv (notamment)* particularly; *(beaucoup)* extremely

sinistre [sinistr] **1** *adj (effrayant)* sinister; *(triste)* grim
2 *nm* disaster; *(incendie)* fire; *Jur (dommage)* damage • **sinistré, -ée 1** *adj (population, région)* disaster-stricken **2** *nmf* disaster victim

sinon [sinɔ̃] *conj (autrement)* otherwise, or else; *(sauf)* except (**que** that); *(si ce n'est)* if not

sinueux, -ueuse [sinɥø, -ɥøz] *adj* winding • **sinuosités** *nfpl* twists (and turns)

sinus [sinys] *nm inv Anat* sinus • **sinusite** *nf* sinusitis; **avoir une s.** to have sinusitis

siphon [sifɔ̃] *nm* siphon; *(d'évier)* trap, *Br* U-bend

siphonné, -ée [sifɔne] *adj Fam* round the bend, crazy

sirène [sirɛn] *nf (d'usine)* siren; *(femme)* mermaid

sirop [siro] *nm* syrup; *(à diluer)* (fruit) cordial; **s. contre la toux** cough mixture • **syrupeux, -euse** *adj* syrupy

siroter [sirɔte] *vt Fam* to sip

sismique [sismik] *adj* seismic; **secousse s.** earth tremor

site [sit] *nm (endroit)* site; *(pittoresque)* beauty spot; **s. touristique** place of interest; **s. classé** conservation area; *Ordinat* **s. Web** website

sitôt [sito] *adv* **s. que...** as soon as...; **s. levée, elle partit** as soon as she was up, she left; **s. après** immediately after; **pas de s.** not for some time

situation [sitɥasjɔ̃] *nf* situation, position; *(emploi)* position; **s. de famille** marital status • **situé, -ée** *adj (maison)* situated (**à** in) • **situer 1** *vt (placer)* to situate; *(trouver)* to locate; *(dans le temps)* to set **2 se situer** *vpr (se trouver)* to be situated

six [sis] ([si] *before consonant,* [siz] *before vowel)* *adj & nm inv* six • **sixième** [sizjɛm] **1** *adj & nmf* sixth; **un s.** a sixth **2** *nf Scol Br* ≃ first form, *Am* ≃ sixth grade

Skaï® [skaj] *nm* imitation leather

sketch [skɛtʃ] *(pl* **sketches** *) nm* sketch

ski [ski] *nm (objet)* ski; *(sport)* skiing; **faire du s.** to ski; **s. alpin** downhill skiing; **s. de fond** cross-country skiing; **s. nautique** water skiing • **skiable** *adj (piste)* skiable, fit for skiing • **skier** *vi* to ski • **skieur, -ieuse** *nmf* skier

slalom [slalɔm] *nm Sport* slalom; **faire du s.** to slalom

slave [slav] **1** *adj* Slav; *(langue)* Slavonic **2** *nmf* **S.** Slav

slip [slip] *nm (d'homme)* briefs, underpants; *(de femme)* panties, *Br* knickers; **s. de bain** (swimming) trunks; *(de bikini®)* briefs

> *Il faut noter que le nom anglais **slip** est un faux ami. Il ne signifie jamais **culotte**.*

slogan [slɔgã] *nm* slogan

Slovaquie [slɔvaki] *nf* **la S.** Slovakia

Slovénie [slɔveni] *nf* **la S.** Slovenia

slow [slo] *nm* slow dance

SME [ɛsɛmə] *(abrév* **Système monétaire européen**) *nm* EMS

SMIC [smik] *(abrév* **salaire minimum interprofessionnel de croissance**) *nm* guaranteed minimum wage ● **smicard, -arde** *nmf* minimum wage earner

smoking [smɔkiŋ] *nm (veston, costume)* dinner jacket, *Am* tuxedo

snack(-bar) [snak(bar)] *nm* snack bar

SNCF [ɛsɛnseɛf] *(abrév* **Société nationale des chemins de fer français**) *nf* = French national railway company

sniffer [snife] *vt Fam (colle)* to sniff

snob [snɔb] **1** *adj* snobbish **2** *nmf* snob ● **snober** *vt* **s. qn** to snub sb ● **snobisme** *nm* snobbery

sobre [sɔbr] *adj* sober ● **sobriété** *nf* sobriety

sobriquet [sɔbrikɛ] *nm* nickname

sociable [sɔsjabl] *adj* sociable ● **sociabilité** *nf* sociability

social, -e, -iaux, -iales [sɔsjal, -jo] *adj* social ● **socialisme** *nm* socialism ● **socialiste** *adj & nmf* socialist

société [sɔsjete] *nf (communauté)* society; *(compagnie)* company; **s. anonyme** *Br* (public) limited company, *Am* corporation ● **sociétaire** *nmf (membre)* member

sociologie [sɔsjɔlɔʒi] *nf* sociology ● **sociologique** *adj* sociological ● **sociologue** *nmf* sociologist

socle [sɔkl] *nm (de statue, de colonne)* plinth, pedestal; *(de lampe)* base

socquette [sɔkɛt] *nf* ankle sock

soda [sɔda] *nm Br* fizzy drink, *Am* soda (pop)

sœur [sœr] *nf* sister; *(religieuse)* sister, nun; *Fam* **bonne s.** nun; *Fam* **et ta s.!** get lost!

sofa [sɔfa] *nm* sofa, settee

soi [swa] *pron personnel* oneself; **chacun pour s.** every man for himself; **en s.** *(concept)* in itself; **chez s.** at home; **prendre sur s.** to get a grip on oneself; **cela va de soi** it's self-evident (**que** that) ● **soi-même** *pron* oneself

soi-disant [swadizã] **1** *adj inv* so-called **2** *adv* supposedly

soie [swa] *nf (tissu)* silk; *(de porc)* bristle ● **soierie** *nf (tissu)* silk

soient [swa] *voir* être

SOFRES [sɔfrɛs] *(abrév* **Société française d'enquêtes par sondages**) *nf* = French opinion poll company

soif [swaf] *nf* thirst (**de** for); **avoir s.** to be thirsty; *Fig* **avoir s. de liberté** to thirst for freedom; **donner s. à qn** to make sb thirsty

soigner [swaɲe] **1** *vt* to look after, to take care of; *(sujet: médecin) (malade, maladie)* to treat; *(présentation, travail)* to take care over; **se faire s.** to have (medical) treatment **2 se soigner** *vpr* to take care of oneself, to look after oneself ● **soigné, -ée** *adj (personne, vêtement)* neat, tidy; *(travail)* careful

soigneux, -euse [swaɲø, -øz] *adj (attentif)* careful (**de** with); *(propre)* neat, tidy ● **soigneusement** *adv* carefully

soin [swɛ̃] *nm (attention)* care; *Méd* **soins** treatment, care; **soins de beauté** beauty care *or* treatment; **les premiers soins** first aid; **avoir** *ou* **prendre s. de qch/de faire qch** to take care of sth/to do sth; **être aux petits soins avec qn** to wait hand and foot on sb; **aux bons soins de** *(sur lettre)* care of, c/o; **avec s.** carefully, with care

soir [swar] *nm* evening; **le s.** *(chaque soir)* in the evening(s); **à neuf heures du s.** at nine in the evening; **repas du s.** evening meal ● **soirée** *nf* evening; *(réunion)* party; **s. dansante** dance

sois, soit¹ [swa] *voir* être

soit² **1** [swa] *conj (à savoir)* that is (to say); **s. s.** either or; *Math* **s. une droite** given a straight line **2** [swat] *adv (oui)* very well

soixante [swasãt] *adj & nm inv* sixty ● **soixantaine** *nf* **une s. (de)** *(nombre)* (about) sixty; **avoir la s.** *(âge)* to be about sixty ● **soixantième** *adj & nmf* sixtieth

soixante-dix [swasãtdis] *adj & nm inv* seventy ● **soixante-dixième** *adj & nmf* seventieth

soja [sɔʒa] *nm (plante)* soya; **graines de s.** soya bean; **germes** *ou* **pousses de s.** beansprouts

sol¹ [sɔl] *nm* ground; *(plancher)* floor; *(territoire, terrain)* soil

sol² [sɔl] *nm inv (note)* G

solaire [sɔlɛr] *adj* solar; **crème/huile s.** sun(-tan) lotion/oil

solarium [sɔlarjɔm] *nm* solarium

soldat [sɔlda] *nm* soldier; **simple s.** private
solde [sɔld] **1** *nm* (de compte, à payer) balance; **en s.** (acheter) in the sales, Am on sale; **soldes** (marchandises) sale goods; (vente) (clearance) sale(s); **faire les soldes** to go round the sales
2 *nf* (de soldat) pay; Fig Péj **à la s. de qn** in sb's pay
solder [sɔlde] **1** *vt* (articles) to clear, to sell off; (compte) to pay the balance of
2 se solder *vpr* **se s. par un échec** to end in failure • **soldé, -ée** *adj* (article) reduced
sole [sɔl] *nf* (poisson) sole
soleil [sɔlɛj] *nm* sun; (chaleur, lumière) sunshine; (fleur) sunflower; **au s.** in the sun; **il fait s.** it's sunny
solennel, -elle [sɔlanɛl] *adj* solemn • **solennellement** *adv* solemnly • **solennité** [-anite] *nf* solemnity
Solex® [sɔlɛks] *nm* moped
solfège [sɔlfɛʒ] *nm* rudiments of music
solidaire [sɔlidɛr] *adj* **être s.** (ouvriers) to show solidarity (**de** with); (pièce de machine) to be interdependent (**de** with) • **solidairement** *adv* jointly • **se solidariser** *vpr* to show solidarity (**avec** with) • **solidarité** *nf* (entre personnes) solidarity
solide [sɔlid] **1** *adj* (mur, meuble, voiture, état) solid; (amitié) strong; (argument, nerfs) sound; (personne) sturdy
2 *nm* (corps) solid • **solidement** *adv* solidly • **se solidifier** *vpr* to solidify • **solidité** *nf* (d'objet) solidity; (d'argument) soundness
soliste [sɔlist] *nmf Mus* soloist
solitaire [sɔlitɛr] **1** *adj* (par choix) solitary; (involontairement) lonely
2 *nmf* loner; **en s.** on one's own • **solitude** *nf* solitude; **aimer la s.** to like being alone
solive [sɔliv] *nf* joist, beam
solliciter [sɔlisite] *vt* (audience) to request; (emploi) to apply for; **s. qn** (faire appel à) to appeal to sb (**de faire** to do); **être (très) sollicité** (personne) to be in (great) demand • **sollicitation** *nf* request
sollicitude [sɔlisityd] *nf* solicitude, concern
solo [sɔlo] *adj inv & nm Mus* solo
solstice [sɔlstis] *nm* solstice
soluble [sɔlybl] *adj* (substance, problème) soluble
solution [sɔlysjɔ̃] *nf* (de problème) solution (**de** to); (mélange chimique) solution
solvable [sɔlvabl] *adj Fin* solvent • **solvabilité** *nf Fin* solvency

> Il faut noter que l'adjectif anglais **solvable** est un faux ami. Il signifie **soluble**.

solvant [sɔlvɑ̃] *nm* solvent
Somalie [sɔmali] *nf* **la S.** Somalia
sombre [sɔ̃br] *adj* dark; (triste) sombre, gloomy; **il fait s.** it's dark
sombrer [sɔ̃bre] *vi* (bateau) to sink; Fig **s. dans** (folie, sommeil) to sink into
sommaire [sɔmɛr] **1** *adj* summary; (repas) basic
2 *nm* (table des matières) contents
sommation [sɔmasjɔ̃] *nf Jur* summons; (de policier) warning
somme [sɔm] **1** *nf* sum; **faire la s. de** to add up; **en s., s. toute** in short
2 *nm* (sommeil) nap; **faire un s.** to have a nap
sommeil [sɔmɛj] *nm* sleep; **avoir s.** to feel sleepy; **être en plein s.** to be fast asleep; Fig **laisser qch en s.** to put sth on hold • **sommeiller** *vi* to doze; Fig (faculté, qualité) to lie dormant
sommelier [sɔməlje] *nm* wine waiter
sommer [sɔme] *vt* **s. qn de faire qch** to summon sb to do sth
sommes [sɔm] *voir* **être**
sommet [sɔmɛ] *nm* top; (de montagne) summit, top; Fig (de la gloire) height, summit; **conférence au s.** summit (conference)
sommier [sɔmje] *nm* (de lit) base; **s. à ressorts** sprung base
sommité [sɔmite] *nf* leading light (**de** in)
somnambule [sɔmnɑ̃byl] *nmf* sleepwalker; **être s.** to sleepwalk • **somnambulisme** *nm* sleepwalking
somnifère [sɔmnifɛr] *nm* sleeping pill
somnolence [sɔmnɔlɑ̃s] *nf* drowsiness, sleepiness • **somnolent, -ente** *adj* drowsy, sleepy • **somnoler** *vi* to doze
somptuaire [sɔ̃ptɥɛr] *adj* extravagant
somptueux, -ueuse [sɔ̃ptɥø, -ɥøz] *adj* sumptuous • **somptuosité** *nf* sumptuousness
son¹ [sɔ̃] *nm* (bruit) sound
son² [sɔ̃] *nm* (de grains) bran
son³, sa, ses [sɔ̃, sa, se]

> **sa** becomes **son** [sɔn] before a vowel or mute h.

adj possessif (d'homme) his; (de femme) her; (de chose) its; (indéfini) one's; **s. père/sa mère** his/her/one's father/mother; **s. ami(e)** his/her/one's friend
sonate [sɔnat] *nf Mus* sonata
sondage [sɔ̃daʒ] *nm* (de terrain) drilling; **s. (d'opinion)** opinion poll
sonde [sɔ̃d] *nf Géol* drill; Naut sounding line; Méd probe; (pour l'alimentation) (feeding) tube; **s. spatiale** space probe

sonder [sɔ̃de] *vt (rivière)* to sound; *(terrain)* to drill; *Méd* to probe; *Fig (personne, l'opinion)* to sound out

songe [sɔ̃ʒ] *nm* dream

songer [sɔ̃ʒe] **1** *vi* **s. à qch/à faire qch** to think of sth/of doing sth

2 *vt* **s. que...** to think that... • **songeur, -euse** *adj* thoughtful, pensive

sonner [sɔne] **1** *vi* to ring; *(cor, cloches)* to sound; **on a sonné (à la porte)** someone has rung the (door)bell; **midi a sonné** it has struck twelve

2 *vt (cloche)* to ring; *(domestique)* to ring for; *(cor)* to sound; *(l'heure)* to strike; *Fam (assommer)* to knock out • **sonnant, -ante** *adj* **en espèces sonnantes et trébuchantes** in hard cash, in coin of the realm; **à cinq heures sonnantes** on the stroke of five • **sonné, -ée** *adj Fam (fou)* crazy; *(assommé)* dazed, groggy

sonnerie [sɔnri] *nf (son)* ring(ing); *(de cor)* sound; *(appareil)* bell; *(de téléphone) Br* ringing tone, *Am* ring

sonnette [sɔnɛt] *nf* bell; **coup de s.** ring; **s. d'alarme** alarm (bell)

sonnet [sɔnɛ] *nm (poème)* sonnet

sonore [sɔnɔr] *adj (rire)* loud; *(salle, voix)* resonant; **effet s.** sound effect • **sonorité** *nf (de salle)* acoustics; *(de violon)* tone

sonorisation [sɔnɔrizasjɔ̃] *nf (matériel)* sound equipment • **sonoriser** *vt (salle)* to wire for sound; *(film)* to add the soundtrack to

sont [sɔ̃] *voir* **être**

sophistiqué, -ée [sɔfistike] *adj* sophisticated

soporifique [sɔpɔrifik] *adj (médicament, discours)* soporific

soprano [sɔprano] *Mus* **1** *nmf (personne)* soprano

2 *nm (voix)* soprano

sorbet [sɔrbɛ] *nm* sorbet

sorcellerie [sɔrsɛlri] *nf* witchcraft, sorcery • **sorcier 1** *nm* sorcerer **2** *adj m Fam* **ce n'est pas s.!** it's dead easy! • **sorcière** *nf* witch

sordide [sɔrdid] *adj (acte, affaire)* sordid; *(maison)* squalid

sornettes [sɔrnɛt] *nfpl Péj (propos)* twaddle, nonsense

sort [sɔr] *nm (destin)* fate; *(condition)* lot; *(maléfice)* spell

sortable [sɔrtabl] *adj Fam* **tu n'es pas s.!** I really can't take you anywhere!

sortant, -ante [sɔrtɑ̃, -ɑ̃t] *adj (numéro)* winning; *(député)* outgoing

sorte [sɔrt] *nf* sort, kind (**de** of); **toutes sortes de** all sorts *or* kinds of; **en quelque s.** in a way, as it were; **de (telle) s. que tu apprennes** so that *or* in such a way that you may learn; **de la s.** *(de cette façon)* in that way; **faire en s. que...** *(+ subjunctive)* to see to it that...

sortie [sɔrti] *nf (porte)* exit, way out; *(action de sortir)* leaving, exit, departure; *(de scène)* exit; *(promenade à pied)* walk; *(en voiture)* drive; *(excursion)* outing, trip; *Ordinat* output; *(de film, de disque)* release; *(de livre, de modèle)* appearance; *(de devises)* export; **sorties** *(argent)* outgoings; **à la s. de l'école** when the children come out of school; **l'heure de la s. de qn** the time at which sb leaves; **être de s.** to be out; **s. de bain** bathrobe; **s. de secours** emergency exit

sortilège [sɔrtilɛʒ] *nm (magic)* spell

sortir* [sɔrtir] **1** *(aux être) vi* to go out, to leave; *(pour s'amuser)* to go out; *(film, modèle)* to come out; *(numéro gagnant)* to come up; **s. de** *(endroit)* to leave; *(université)* to be a graduate of; *(famille, milieu)* to come from; *(légalité, limites)* to go beyond; *(compétence)* to be outside; *(sujet)* to stray from; *(gonds, rails)* to come off; **s. de table** to leave the table; **s. de terre** *(plante, fondations)* to come up; **s. de l'ordinaire** *ou* **du commun** to be out of the ordinary; **s. indemne** to escape unhurt (**de** from)

2 *(aux avoir) vt* to take out (**de** of); *(film, modèle, livre)* to bring out; *Fam (dire)* to come out with; *Fam (expulser)* to throw out

3 se sortir *vpr* **s'en s.** *(malade)* to pull through

4 *nm* **au s. de l'hiver** at the end of winter; **au s. du lit** on getting out of bed

SOS [ɛsoɛs] *nm* SOS; **lancer un SOS** to send (out) an SOS

sosie [sozi] *nm* double

sot, sotte [so, sɔt] **1** *adj* foolish

2 *nmf* fool • **sottement** *adv* foolishly • **sottise** *nf* foolishness; *(action, parole)* foolish thing; **faire des sottises** to do stupid things

> 🖉 Il faut noter que l'adjectif anglais **sot** est un faux ami. Il signifie **ivrogne**.

sou [su] *nm Hist (monnaie)* sou; *Fam* **sous** *(argent)* money; **elle n'a pas un** *ou* **le s.** she doesn't have a penny; *Fig* **n'avoir pas un s. de bon sens** not to have an ounce of good sense; **dépenser jusqu'à son dernier s.** to spend one's last penny; **machine à sous** fruit machine, *Am* slot machine

soubresaut [subrəso] *nm (sudden)* start, jolt

souche [suʃ] *nf (d'arbre)* stump; *(de carnet)* stub, counterfoil; *(de famille)* founder; *(de virus)* strain

souci [susi] *nm (inquiétude)* worry, concern; *(préoccupation)* concern (**de** for); **se faire du s.** to worry, to be worried; **ça lui donne du s.** it worries him/her • **se soucier** *vpr* **se s. de** to be worried *or* concerned about; *Fam* **se s. de qch comme de l'an quarante** not to give a hoot about sth • **soucieux, -euse** *adj* worried, concerned (**de qch** about sth); **s. de plaire** anxious to please

soucoupe [sukup] *nf* saucer; **s. volante** flying saucer

soudain, -aine [sudɛ̃, -ɛn] **1** *adj* sudden **2** *adv* suddenly • **soudainement** *adv* suddenly • **soudaineté** *nf* suddenness

Soudan [sudɑ̃] *nm* **le S.** Sudan

soude [sud] *nf* soda; **s. cautique** caustic soda

souder [sude] **1** *vt (par alliage)* to solder; *(par soudure autogène)* to weld; *Fig (groupes)* to unite (closely); **lampe à s.** blowlamp
2 se souder *vpr (os)* to knit (together) • **soudure** *nf (par alliage)* soldering; *(autogène)* welding

soudoyer [sudwaje] *vt* to bribe

souffle [sufl] *nm (d'air, de vent)* breat, puff; *(respiration)* breathing; *(de bombe)* blast; *Fig (inspiration)* inspiration; **reprendre son s.** to get one's breath back • **souffler 1** *vi (vent)* to blow; *(haleter)* to puff; **laisser s. qn** *(se reposer)* to give sb time to catch his/her breath **2** *vt (bougie)* to blow out; *(fumée, poussière, verre)* to blow; *(par une explosion)* to blast; *(chuchoter)* to whisper; *Fam (étonner)* to stagger; **s. une réplique à qn** *(acteur)* to give sb a prompt; **ne pas s. mot** not to breathe a word • **soufflet** *nm (de forge)* bellows; *(de train, d'autobus)* concertina vestibule • **souffleur, -euse** *nmf (de théâtre)* prompter

soufflé [sufle] *nm Culin* soufflé

souffrance [sufrɑ̃s] *nf* suffering; **en s.** *(colis)* unclaimed; *(travail)* pending

souffreteux, -euse [sufrətø, -øz] *adj* sickly

souffrir* [sufrir] **1** *vi* to suffer; **s. de** to suffer from; **faire s. qn** *(physiquement)* to hurt sb; *(moralement)* to make sb suffer; **ta réputation en souffrira** your reputation will suffer
2 *vt (endurer)* to suffer; *(exception)* to admit of; *Fam* **je ne peux pas le s.** I can't bear him • **souffrant, -ante** *adj* unwell

soufre [sufr] *nm Br* sulphur, *Am* sulfur

souhait [swɛ] *nm* wish; **à vos souhaits!** *(après un éternuement)* bless you!; **à s.** perfectly • **souhaitable** *adj* desirable • **souhaiter** [swete] *vt (bonheur)* to wish for; **s. qch à qn** to wish sb sth; **s. faire qch** to hope to do sth; **s. que...** *(+ subjunctive)* to hope that...

souiller [suje] *vt* to soil, to dirty; *Fig (déshonorer)* to tarnish • **souillon** *nf* slut

soûl, soûle [su, sul] **1** *adj* drunk **2** *nm* **tout son s.** *(boire)* to one's heart's content • **soûler** *vt* **s. qn** to make sb drunk **3 se soûler** *vpr* to get drunk

soulager [sulaʒe] *vt* to relieve (**de** of) • **soulagement** *nm* relief

soulever [suləve] **1** *vt* to lift (up); *(poussière, question)* to raise; *(peuple)* to stir up; *(sentiment)* to arouse; **cela me soulève le cœur** it makes me feel sick
2 se soulever *vpr (personne)* to lift oneself (up); *(se révolter)* to rise up • **soulèvement** [-ɛvmɑ̃] *nm (révolte)* uprising

soulier [sulje] *nm* shoe; *Fam* **être dans ses petits souliers** to feel awkward

souligner [suliɲe] *vt (d'un trait)* to underline; *(faire remarquer)* to emphasize

soumettre* [sumetr] **1** *vt (pays, rebelles)* to subdue; *(rapport, demande)* to submit (**à** to); **s. qn à** *(assujettir)* to subject sb to
2 se soumettre *vpr* to submit (**à** to) • **soumis, -ise** *adj (docile)* submissive; **s. à** subject to • **soumission** *nf (à une autorité)* submission; *(docilité)* submissiveness

soupape [supap] *nf* valve; **s. de sécurité** safety valve

soupçon [supsɔ̃] *nm* suspicion; *Fig* **un s. de** *(quantité)* a hint *or* touch of; **au-dessus de tout s.** above suspicion • **soupçonner** *vt* to suspect (**de** of; **d'avoir fait** of doing) • **soupçonneux, -euse** *adj* suspicious

soupe [sup] *nf* soup; *Fam* **être s. au lait** to be hot-tempered; **s. populaire** soup kitchen • **soupière** *nf* (soup) tureen

soupente [supɑ̃t] *nf (sous un toit)* loft

souper [supe] **1** *nm* supper **2** *vi* to have supper

soupeser [supəze] *vt (objet dans la main)* to feel the weight of; *Fig (arguments)* to weigh up

soupir [supir] *nm* sigh • **soupirant** *nm Hum* suitor • **soupirer** *vi* to sigh

soupirail, -aux [supiraj, -o] *nm* basement window

souple [supl] *adj (corps, personne)* supple; *(branche)* flexible • **souplesse** *nf (de corps)* suppleness; *(de branche)* flexibility

source [surs] *nf* (**a**) *(point d'eau)* spring;

prendre sa s. *(rivière)* to rise (à at) (**b**) *(origine)* source; **s. d'énergie** source of energy; **tenir qch de s. sûre** to have sth on good authority

sourcil [sursi] *nm* eyebrow • **sourciller** *vi Fig* **ne pas s.** not to bat an eyelid

sourd, sourde [sur, surd] **1** *adj (personne)* deaf (à to); *(douleur)* dull; **bruit s.** thump; **lutte sourde** secret struggle; *Fam* **s. comme un pot** deaf as a post

2 *nmf* deaf person • **sourd-muet, sourde-muette** *(mpl* **sourds-muets,** *fpl* **sourdes-muettes) 1** *adj* deaf-and-dumb **2** *nmf* deaf mute

sourdine [surdin] *nf Mus (dispositif)* mute; *Fig* **en s.** quietly, secretly

souricière [surisjɛr] *nf* mousetrap; *Fig* trap

sourire* [surir] **1** *nm* smile; **faire un s. à qn** to give sb a smile

2 *vi* to smile (à at); **s. à qn** *(fortune)* to smile on sb

souris [suri] *nf (animal)* & *Ordinat* mouse *(pl* mice)

sournois, -oise [surnwa, -waz] *adj* sly, underhand • **sournoisement** *adv* slyly • **sournoiserie** *nf* slyness

sous [su] *prép (position)* under, underneath, beneath; *(rang)* under; **s. la pluie** in the rain; **nager s. l'eau** to swim underwater; **s. calmants** under sedation; **s. cet angle** from that point of view; **s. le nom de** under the name of; **s. Charles X** under Charles X; **s. peu** *(bientôt)* shortly

sous-alimenté, -ée [suzalimɑ̃te] *(mpl* **sous-alimentés,** *fpl* **sous-alimentées)** *adj* underfed, undernourished • **sous-alimentation** *nf* malnutrition, undernourishment

sous-bois [subwa] *nm* undergrowth

sous-chef [suʃɛf] *(pl* **sous-chefs)** *nmf* second-in-command

souscrire* [suskrir] *vi* **s. à** *(payer, approuver)* to subscribe to • **souscription** *nf* subscription

sous-développé, -ée [sudevlɔpe] *(mpl* **sous-développés,** *fpl* **sous-développées)** *adj (pays)* underdeveloped

sous-directeur, -trice [sudirɛktœr, -tris] *(pl* **sous-directeurs)** *nmf* assistant manager, *f* assistant manageress

sous-emploi [suzɑ̃plwa] *nm* underemployment

sous-entendre [suzɑ̃tɑ̃dr] *vt* to imply • **sous-entendu** *(pl* **sous-entendus)** *nm* insinuation

sous-estimer [suzɛstime] *vt* to underestimate

sous-jacent, -ente [suʒasɑ̃, -ɑ̃t] *(mpl* **sous-jacents,** *fpl* **sous-jacentes)** *adj* underlying

sous-louer [sulwe] *vt (sujet: locataire)* to sublet

sous-main [sumɛ̃] *nm inv* desk blotter; **en s.** secretly

sous-marin, -ine [sumarɛ̃, -in] *(mpl* **sous-marins,** *fpl* **sous-marines) 1** *adj* underwater

2 *nm* submarine

sous-officier [suzɔfisje] *(pl* **sous-officiers)** *nm* non-commissioned officer

sous-payer [supeje] *vt* to underpay

sous-préfet [suprefɛ] *(pl* **sous-préfets)** *nm* subprefect • **sous-préfecture** *nf* subprefecture

sous-produit [suprɔdɥi] *(pl* **sous-produits)** *nm* by-product

soussigné, -ée [susiɲe] *adj* & *nmf* undersigned; **je s. I** the undersigned

sous-sol [susɔl] *(pl* **sous-sols)** *nm (d'immeuble)* basement; *Géol* subsoil

sous-titre [sutitr] *(pl* **sous-titres)** *nm* subtitle • **sous-titrer** *vt (film)* to subtitle

soustraire* [sustrɛr] **1** *vt* to remove; *Math* to take away, to subtract (**de** from); **s. qn à** *(danger)* to shield *or* protect sb from

2 se soustraire *vpr* **se s. à** to escape from; *(devoir, obligation)* to avoid • **soustraction** *nf Math* subtraction

sous-traiter [sutrete] *vt* to subcontract • **sous-traitance** *nf* **travailler en s. avec qn** to work as a subcontractor with sb • **sous-traitant** *nm* subcontractor

sous-verre [suvɛr] *nm inv (encadrement)* (frameless) glass mount

sous-vêtement [suvɛtmɑ̃] *nm* undergarment; **sous-vêtements** underwear

soutane [sutan] *nf (de prêtre)* cassock

soute [sut] *nf (de bateau)* hold

soutenir* [sutənir] *vt* to support, to hold up; *(opinion)* to uphold, to maintain; *(candidat)* to back; *(effort)* to sustain; *(thèse)* to defend; *(regard)* to hold; **s. que...** to maintain that... • **soutenu, -ue** *adj (attention, effort)* sustained; *(style)* lofty

souterrain, -aine [sutɛrɛ̃, -ɛn] **1** *adj* underground

2 *nm* underground passage

soutien [sutjɛ̃] *nm* support; *(personne)* supporter; **s. de famille** breadwinner • **soutien-gorge** *(pl* **soutiens-gorge)** *nm* bra

soutirer [sutire] *vt* **s. qch à qn** to extract sth from sb

souvenir [suvnir] *nm* memory, recollection; *(objet)* memento; *(cadeau)* keepsake; *(pour touristes)* souvenir; **en s. de** in memory of ● **se souvenir*** *vpr* **se s. de qn/qch** to remember sb/sth; **se s. que...** to remember that...

souvent [suvã] *adv* often; **peu s.** seldom; **le plus s.** usually, more often than not

souverain, -aine [suvərɛ̃, -ɛn] **1** *adj (puissance, état, remède)* sovereign; *(bonheur, mépris)* supreme **2** *nmf* sovereign ● **souveraineté** *nf* sovereignty

soviétique [sɔvjetik] *Anciennement* **1** *adj* Soviet; **l'Union s.** the Soviet Union **2** *nmf* Soviet citizen

soyeux, -euse [swajø, -jøz] silky

soyons, soyez [swajɔ̃, swaje] *voir* être

SPA [ɛspea] *(abrév* **Société protectrice des animaux)** *nf Br* ≃ RSPCA, *Am* ≃ ASPCA

spacieux, -ieuse [spasjø, -jøz] *adj* spacious, roomy

spaghettis [spageti] *nmpl* spaghetti

sparadrap [sparadra] *nm (pour pansement) Br* sticking plaster, *Am* adhesive tape

spasme [spasm] *nm* spasm ● **spasmodique** *adj* spasmodic

spatial, -e, -iaux, -iales [spasjal, -jo] *adj* **station spatiale** space station; **engin s.** spaceship, spacecraft

spatule [spatyl] *nf* spatula

speaker [spikœr] *nm,* **speakerine** [spikrin] *nf (de télévision, de radio)* announcer

spécial, -e, -iaux, -iales [spesjal, -jo] *adj* special; *(bizarre)* peculiar ● **spécialement** *adv (exprès)* specially; *(en particulier)* especially, particularly; *Fam* **pas s.** not particularly, not especially

spécialiser [spesjalize] **se spécialiser** *vpr* to specialize (**dans** in) ● **spécialisation** *nf* specialization ● **spécialiste** *nmf* specialist ● **spécialité** *nf Br* speciality, *Am* specialty

spécifier [spesifje] *vt* to specify (**que** that)

spécifique [spesifik] *adj* specific

spécimen [spesimɛn] *nm* specimen; *(livre)* specimen copy

spectacle [spɛktakl] *nm* (**a**) *(vue)* sight, spectacle; *Péj* **se donner en s.** to make an exhibition of oneself (**b**) *(représentation)* show; **le s.** *(industrie)* show business ● **spectateur, -trice** *nmf* spectator; *(au théâtre, au cinéma)* member of the audience; *(témoin)* witness; **spectateurs** *(au théâtre, au cinéma)* audience

spectaculaire [spɛktakylɛr] *adj* spectacular

spectre [spɛktr] *nm (fantôme)* spectre, ghost; *Phys* spectrum

spéculer [spekyle] *vi* to speculate; *Fig* **s. sur** *(compter sur)* to bank or rely on ● **spéculateur, -trice** *nmf* speculator ● **spéculatif, -ive** *adj* speculative ● **spéculation** *nf* speculation

spéléologie [speleɔlɔʒi] *nf (activité) Br* potholing, caving, *Am* spelunking ● **spéléologue** *nmf Br* potholer, *Am* spelunker

sperme [spɛrm] *nm* sperm, semen

sphère [sfɛr] *nf (boule, domaine)* sphere ● **sphérique** *adj* spherical

sphinx [sfɛ̃ks] *nm* sphinx

spirale [spiral] *nf* spiral

spirite [spirit] *nmf* spiritualist ● **spiritisme** *nm* spiritualism

spirituel, -uelle [spiritɥɛl] *adj (amusant)* witty; *(pouvoir, vie)* spiritual

spiritueux [spiritɥø] *nmpl (boissons)* spirits

splendide [splãdid] *adj* splendid ● **splendeur** *nf* splendour

spongieux, -ieuse [spɔ̃ʒjø, -jøz] *adj* spongy

spontané, -ée [spɔ̃tane] *adj* spontaneous ● **spontanéité** *nf* spontaneity ● **spontanément** *adv* spontaneously

sporadique [spɔradik] *adj* sporadic

sport [spɔr] *nm* sport; **faire du s.** to play *Br* sport *or Am* sports; **(de) s.** *(chaussures, vêtements)* casual, sports; **voiture/terrain de s.** sports car/ground; **sports de combat** combat sports; **sports d'équipe** team sports; **sports d'hiver** winter sports; **aller aux sports d'hiver** to go skiing; **sports mécaniques** motor sports *(on land, in the air, on water)*; **sports nautiques** water sports; **sports de plein air** outdoor sports ● **sportif, -ive** **1** *adj (personne)* fond of *Br* sport *or Am* sports; *(attitude, esprit)* sporting; *(association, journal, résultats)* sports, sporting; *(allure)* athletic **2** *nmf* sportsman, *f* sportswoman ● **sportivité** *nf* sportsmanship

spot [spɔt] *nm (lampe)* spotlight, *Fam* spot; **s. publicitaire** commercial

sprint [sprint] *nm Sport* sprint ● **sprinter** **1** *vt* to sprint **2** [-œr] *nm* sprinter ● **sprinteuse** *nf* sprinter

square [skwar] *nm* public garden

squash [skwaʃ] *nm (jeu)* squash

squat [skwat] *nm* squat ● **squatteur, -euse** *nmf* squatter ● **squatter** **1** *vi* to squat **2** [-œr] *nm* squatter

squelette [skəlɛt] *nm* skeleton ● **squelettique** *adj (personne, maigreur)* skeleton-like; *(exposé)* sketchy

stable [stabl] *adj* stable •**stabilisateur** *nm* stabilizer •**stabiliser** *vt,* **se stabiliser** *vpr* to stabilize •**stabilité** *nf* stability

stade [stad] *nm Sport* stadium; *(phase)* stage

stage [staʒ] *nm (période)* training period; *(cours)* (training) course; **faire un s.** to undergo training; **être en s.** to be on a training course •**stagiaire** *adj & nmf* trainee

> *Ɵ* Il faut noter que le nom anglais **stage** est un faux ami.

stagner [stagne] *vi* to stagnate •**stagnant, -ante** *adj* stagnant •**stagnation** *nf* stagnation

stalle [stal] *nf (d'écurie, d'église)* stall

stand [stɑ̃d] *nm (d'exposition)* stand, stall; *Sport* **s. de ravitaillement** pit; **s. de tir** *(de foire)* shooting range; *(militaire)* firing range

standard [stɑ̃dar] **1** *nm (téléphonique)* switchboard
2 *adj inv (modèle)* standard •**standardiser** *vt* to standardize •**standardiste** *nmf* (switchboard) operator

standing [stɑ̃diŋ] *nm* standing, status; **immeuble de (grand) s.** *Br* luxury block of flats, *Am* luxury apartment building

starter [startɛr] *nm (de véhicule)* choke; *Sport* starter

station [stasjɔ̃] *nf (de métro, d'observation, de radio)* station; *(de ski)* resort; *(d'autobus)* stop; **s. de taxis** *Br* taxi rank, *Am* taxi stand; **s. debout** standing (position) •**station-service** *(pl* **stations-service)** *nf* service station, *Br* petrol *or Am* gas station

stationnaire [stasjɔnɛr] *adj* stationary

stationner [stasjɔne] *vi (être garé)* to be parked; *(se garer)* to park •**stationnement** *nm* parking

statique [statik] *adj* static

statistique [statistik] **1** *adj* statistical
2 *nf (donnée)* statistic; **la s.** *(science)* statistics *(sing)*

statue [staty] *nf* statue •**statuette** *nf* statuette

statuer [statɥe] *vi* **s. sur** *(juge)* to rule on

statu quo [statykwo] *nm inv* status quo

stature [statyr] *nf* stature

statut [staty] *nm (position)* status; **statuts** *(règles)* statutes •**statutaire** *adj* statutory

steak [stɛk] *nm* steak

stencil [stɛnsil] *nm* stencil

sténo [steno] *nf (personne)* stenographer; *(sténographie)* shorthand, steno-

graphy; **prendre qch en s.** to take sth down in shorthand •**sténodactylo** *nf Br* shorthand typist, *Am* stenographer •**sténographie** *nf* shorthand, stenography

stéréo [stereo] **1** *nf* stereo; **en s.** in stereo
2 *adj inv (disque)* stereo •**stéréophonique** *adj* stereophonic

stéréotype [stereɔtip] *nm* stereotype •**stéréotypé, -ée** *adj* stereotyped

stérile [steril] *adj* sterile; *(terre)* barren •**stérilisation** *nf* sterilization •**stériliser** *vt* to sterilize •**stérilité** *nf* sterility; *(de terre)* barrenness

stérilet [sterilɛ] *nm* IUD, coil

stéroïde [sterɔid] *nm* steroid

stéthoscope [stetɔskɔp] *nm* stethoscope

steward [stiwart] *nm (d'avion, de bateau)* steward

stigmate [stigmat] *nm Fig* mark, stigma (**de** of) •**stigmatiser** *vt (dénoncer)* to stigmatize

stimuler [stimyle] *vt* to stimulate •**stimulant** *nm Fig* stimulus; *(médicament)* stimulant •**stimulateur** *nm* **s. cardiaque** pacemaker •**stimulation** *nf* stimulation

stimulus [stimylys] *(pl* **stimuli** [-li]) *nm (physiologique)* stimulus

stipuler [stipyle] *vt* to stipulate (**que** that) •**stipulation** *nf* stipulation

stock [stɔk] *nm* stock (**de** of); **en s.** in stock •**stockage** *nm* stocking •**stocker** *vt (provisions)* to stock

stoïque [stɔik] *adj* stoical •**stoïcisme** *nm* stoicism

stop [stɔp] **1** *exclam* stop
2 *nm Aut (panneau)* stop sign; *(feu arrière de véhicule)* brake light, *Br* stoplight; *Fam* **faire du s.** to hitchhike; *Fam* **prendre qn en s.** to give sb a *Br* lift *or Am* ride •**stopper** *vti* to stop

store [stɔr] *nm Br* blind, *Am* (window) shade; *(de magasin)* awning

strabisme [strabism] *nm* squint

strapontin [strapɔ̃tɛ̃] *nm* tip-up *ou* folding seat

stratagème [strataʒɛm] *nm* stratagem, ploy

stratège [strateʒ] *nm* strategist •**stratégie** *nf* strategy •**stratégique** *adj* strategic

stress [strɛs] *nm inv* stress •**stressant, -ante** *adj* stressful •**stressé, -ée** *adj* under stress

strict, -e [strikt] *adj (principes, professeur)* strict; *(tenue, vérité)* plain; **le s. minimum** the bare minimum; **mon droit le plus s.** my basic right; **dans la plus stricte intimité** in the strictest privacy •**strictement** [-əmɑ̃] *adv* strictly; *(vêtu)* plainly

strident, -ente [stridã, -ãt] *adj* shrill, strident

strie [stri] *nf (sillon)* groove; *(de couleur)* streak • **strier** *vt* to streak

strip-tease [striptiz] *nm* striptease • **strip-teaseuse** *nf* stripper

strophe [strɔf] *nf* verse, stanza

structure [stryktyr] *nf* structure • **structural, -e, -aux, -ales** *adj* structural • **structurer** *vt* to structure

STS (*abrév* **section de technicien supérieur**) *nf* = two-year advanced vocational course, taken after the baccalauréat

stuc [styk] *nm* stucco

studieux, -ieuse [stydjø, -jøz] *adj* studious; *(vacances)* devoted to study

studio [stydjo] *nm (de cinéma, de télévision, de peintre)* studio; *(logement)* Br studio flat, Am studio apartment

stupéfait, -aite [stypefɛ, -ɛt] *adj* amazed, astounded (**de** at, by) • **stupéfaction** *nf* amazement

stupéfier [stypefje] *vt* to amaze, to astound • **stupéfiant, -ante 1** *adj* amazing, astounding **2** *nm* drug, narcotic

stupeur [stypœr] *nf (étonnement)* amazement; *(inertie)* stupor

stupide [stypid] *adj* stupid • **stupidement** *adv* stupidly • **stupidité** *nf* stupidity; *(action, parole)* stupid thing

style [stil] *nm* style; **meubles de s.** period furniture • **stylisé, -ée** *adj* stylized • **styliste** *nmf (de mode)* designer • **stylistique** *adj* stylistic

stylé, -ée [stile] *adj* well-trained

stylo [stilo] *nm* pen; **s. à bille** ballpoint (pen), Br biro®; **s. à encre, s.-plume** fountain pen

su, sue [sy] *pp de* **savoir**

suave [sɥav] *adj (odeur, voix)* sweet

subalterne [sybaltɛrn] *adj & nmf* subordinate

subconscient, -ente [sypkɔ̃sjã, -ãt] *adj & nm* subconscious

subdiviser [sybdivize] *vt* to subdivide (**en** into) • **subdivision** *nf* subdivision

subir [sybir] *vt* to undergo; *(conséquences, défaite, perte, tortures)* to suffer; *(influence)* to be under; **faire s. qch à qn** to subject sb to sth; *Fam* **s. qn** *(supporter)* to put up with sb

subit, -ite [sybi, -it] *adj* sudden • **subitement** *adv* suddenly

subjectif, -ive [sybʒɛktif, -iv] *adj* subjective • **subjectivement** *adv* subjectively • **subjectivité** *nf* subjectivity

subjonctif [sybʒɔ̃ktif] *nm Grammaire* subjunctive

subjuguer [sybʒyge] *vt* to subjugate, to subdue; *(envoûter)* to captivate

sublime [syblim] *adj & nm* sublime

sublimer [syblime] *vt (passion)* to sublimate

submerger [sybmɛrʒe] *vt* to submerge; *Fig (envahir)* to overwhelm; *Fig* **submergé de travail** snowed under with work; **submergé par** *(ennemi, foule)* swamped by • **submersible** *nm* submarine

subodorer [sybodore] *vt Fam* to scent

subordonner [sybɔrdɔne] *vt* to subordinate (**à** to) • **subordination** *nf* subordination • **subordonné, -ée 1** *adj* subordinate (**à** to); **être s. à** *(dépendre de)* to depend on **2** *nmf* subordinate

subreptice [sybrɛptis] *adj* surreptitious • **subrepticement** *adv* surreptitiously

subside [sypsid] *nm* grant, subsidy

subsidiaire [sybsidjɛr] *adj* subsidiary; **question s.** *(de concours)* deciding question

subsister [sybziste] **1** *vi (chose)* to remain; *(personne)* to subsist

2 *v impersonnel* to remain; **il subsiste un doute/une erreur** there remains some doubt/an error • **subsistance** *nf* subsistence

substance [sypstãs] *nf* substance; *Fig* **en s.** in essence • **substantiel, -ielle** *adj* substantial

substantif [sypstãtif] *nm Grammaire* noun

substituer [sypstitɥe] **1** *vt* to substitute (**à** for)

2 se substituer *vpr* **se s. à qn** to take the place of sb, to substitute for sb • **substitution** *nf* substitution; **produit de s.** substitute (product)

substitut [sypstity] *nm (produit)* substitute (**de** for); *(magistrat)* deputy public prosecutor

subterfuge [saptɛrfyʒ] *nm* subterfuge

subtil, -e [syptil] *adj* subtle • **subtilité** *nf* subtlety

subtiliser [syptilize] *vt Fam (dérober)* to make off with

subvenir* [sybvənir] *vi* **s. à** *(besoins, frais)* to meet

subvention [sybvãsjɔ̃] *nf* subsidy • **subventionner** *vt* to subsidize

subversif, -ive [sybvɛrsif, -iv] *adj* subversive • **subversion** *nf* subversion

suc [syk] *nm (gastrique, de fruit)* juice; *(de plante)* sap

succédané [syksedane] *nm* substitute (**de** for)

succéder [syksede] 1 *vi* s. à qn to succeed sb; s. à qch to follow sth, to come after sth 2 se succéder *vpr (choses, personnes)* to follow one another

succès [syksɛ] *nm* success; s. de librairie *(livre)* best-seller; avoir du s. to be successful; à s. *(auteur, film)* successful; avec s. successfully

successeur [syksɛsœr] *nm* successor •successif, -ive *adj* successive •successivement *adv* successively •succession *nf* succession (de of, à to); *(série)* sequence (de of); *(patrimoine)* inheritance, estate; prendre la s. de qn to succeed sb

succinct, -incte [syksɛ̃, -ɛ̃t] *adj* succinct, brief

succion [sy(k)sjɔ̃] *nf* suction

succomber [sykɔ̃be] *vi (mourir)* to die; s. à *(céder à)* to succumb to; s. à ses blessures to die of one's wounds

succulent, -ente [sykylɑ̃, -ɑ̃t] *adj* succulent

succursale [sykyrsal] *nf (de magasin)* branch; magasin à succursales multiples chain store, *Br* multiple store

sucer [syse] *vt* to suck •sucette *nf* lollipop; *(tétine) Br* dummy, comforter, *Am* pacifier

sucre [sykr] *nm* sugar; *(morceau)* sugar lump; s. cristallisé granulated sugar; s. en morceaux lump sugar; s. en poudre, s. semoule *Br* castor *or* caster sugar, *Am* finely ground sugar; s. d'orge barley sugar

sucrer [sykre] *vt* to sugar, to sweeten •sucré, -ée *adj* sweet, sugary; *(artificiellement)* sweetened; *Fig (doucereux)* sugary, syrupy

sucrerie [sykrəri] *nf (usine)* sugar refinery; sucreries *(bonbons) Br* sweets, *Am* candy

sucrier, -ière [sykrije, -jɛr] 1 *adj* industrie sucrière sugar industry 2 *nm (récipient)* sugar bowl

sud [syd] 1 *nm* south; au s. in the south; *(direction)* (to the) south (de of); du s. *(vent, direction)* southerly; *(ville)* southern; *(gens)* from *or* in the south; l'A. du Sud South Africa 2 *adj inv (côte)* south(ern) •sud-africain, -aine *(mpl* sud-africains, *fpl* sud-africaines) 1 *adj* South African 2 *nmf* S.-Africain, S.-Africaine South African •sud-américain, -aine *(mpl* sud-américains, *fpl* sud-américaines) 1 *adj* South American 2 *nmf* S.-Américain, S.-Américaine South American •sud-est *nm & adj inv* south-east •sud-ouest *nm & adj inv* south-west

Suède [sɥɛd] *nf* la S. Sweden •suédois, -oise 1 *adj* Swedish 2 *nmf* S., Suédoise Swede 3 *nm (langue)* Swedish

suer [sɥe] 1 *vi (personne, mur)* to sweat; *Fam* faire s. qn to get on sb's nerves; *Fam* se faire s. to be bored stiff 2 *vt Fig* s. sang et eau to sweat blood •sueur *nf* sweat; (tout) en s. sweating; *Fam* avoir des sueurs froides to break out in a cold sweat

suffire* [syfir] 1 *vi* to be enough (à for); ça suffit! that's enough! 2 *v impersonnel* il suffit de faire qch one only has to do sth; il suffit d'une goutte/d'une heure pour faire qch a drop/an hour is enough to do sth; il ne me suffit pas de faire qch I'm not satisfied with doing sth 3 se suffire *vpr* se s. à soi-même to be self-sufficient

suffisance [syfizɑ̃s] *nf (vanité)* conceit

suffisant, -ante [syfizɑ̃, -ɑ̃t] *adj (satisfaisant)* sufficient, adequate; *(vaniteux)* conceited •suffisamment [-amɑ̃] *adv* sufficiently; s. de enough, sufficient

suffixe [syfiks] *nm Grammaire* suffix

suffoquer [syfɔke] *vti* to choke, to suffocate; *Fig* s. qn *(étonner)* to astound sb, to stagger sb •suffocant, -ante *adj* stifling, suffocating •suffocation *nf* suffocation; *(sensation)* feeling of suffocation

suffrage [syfraʒ] *nm Pol (voix)* vote; s. universel universal suffrage; suffrages exprimés (valid) votes cast; *Fig* remporter tous les suffrages to win universal approval

suggérer [sygʒere] *vt (proposer)* to suggest (à to; de faire doing; que + *subjunctive* that); *(évoquer)* to suggest •suggestif, -ive *adj* suggestive •suggestion *nf* suggestion

suicide [sɥisid] *nm* suicide •suicidaire *adj* suicidal •suicidé, -ée *nmf* suicide (victim) •se suicider *vpr* to commit suicide

suie [sɥi] *nf* soot

suif [sɥif] *nm* tallow

suinter [sɥɛ̃te] *vi* to ooze •suintement *nm* oozing

suis [sɥi] *voir* être, suivre

Suisse [sɥis] *nf* la S. Switzerland; S. allemande/romande German-speaking/French-speaking Switzerland •suisse 1 *adj* Swiss 2 *nmf* S. Swiss; les Suisses the Swiss •Suissesse *nf* Swiss *inv*

suite [sɥit] *nf (reste)* rest; *(continuation)* continuation; *(de film, de roman)* sequel; *(série)* series, sequence; *(appartement,* *escorte) & Mus* suite; *(cohérence)* order; **suites** *(séquelles)* effects; *(résultats)* consequences; **faire s. (à)** to follow; **donner s. à** *(demande)* to follow up; **prendre la s. de qn** to take over from sb; **attendre la s.** to wait and see what happens next; **avoir de la s. dans les idées** to be single-minded (of purpose); **par la s.** afterwards; **par s. de** as a result of; **à la s.** one after another; **à la s. de** *(derrière)* behind; *(événement, maladie)* as a result of; **de s.** *(deux jours)* in a row

suivant¹, -ante [sɥivɑ̃, -ɑ̃t] **1** *adj* next, following; *(ci-après)* following

2 *nmf* next (one); **au s.!** next!, next person! • **suivant²** *prép (selon)* according to

suivi, -ie [sɥivi] *adj (régulier)* regular, steady; *(cohérent)* coherent; **peu/très s.** *(cours)* poorly/well attended

suivre* [sɥivr] **1** *vt* to follow; *(accompagner)* to go with, to accompany; *(cours)* to attend, to go to; *(malade)* to treat; **s. qn/ qch des yeux** *ou* **du regard** to watch sb/ sth; **s. l'exemple de qn** to follow sb's example; **s. le mouvement** to follow the crowd; **s. l'actualité** to follow events *or* the news

2 *vi* to follow; **faire s.** *(courrier, lettre)* to forward; **'à s.'** 'to be continued'; **comme suit** as follows

3 se suivre *vpr* to follow each other

sujet¹, -ette [syʒɛ, -ɛt] **1** *adj* **s. à** *(maladie)* subject to; **s. à caution** *(information, nouvelle)* unconfirmed

2 *nmf (personne)* subject

sujet² [syʒɛ] *nm* **(a)** *(question) & Grammaire* subject; *(d'examen)* question; **au s. de** about; **à quel s.?** about what? **(b)** *(raison)* cause; **sujet(s) de dispute** grounds for dispute **(c)** *(individu)* subject; **un brillant s.** a brilliant student

sulfurique [sylfyrik] *adj (acide) Br* sulphuric, *Am* sulfuric

sultan [syltɑ̃] *nm* sultan

summum [sɔmɔm] *nm Fig (comble)* height

super [sypɛr] **1** *adj inv Fam (bon)* great, super

2 *nm (supercarburant) Br* four-star (petrol), *Am* premium *ou* hi(gh)-test gas • **supercarburant** *nm* high-octane *Br* petrol *ou Am* gasoline • **supergrand** *nm Pol Fam* superpower

superbe [sypɛrb] *adj* superb

supercherie [sypɛrʃəri] *nf* deception

supérette [sypɛrɛt] *nf* convenience store

superficie [sypɛrfisi] *nf* surface; *(dimen-*

sions) area • **superficiel, -ielle** *adj* superficial • **superficiellement** *adv* superficially

superflu, -ue [sypɛrfly] *adj* superfluous

supérieur, -e [sypɛrjœr] **1** *adj (étages, partie)* upper; *(qualité, air, ton)* superior; **à l'étage s.** on the floor above; **s. à** *(meilleur que)* superior to, better than; *(plus grand que)* above, greater than; **s. à la moyenne** above average; **études supérieures** higher *ou* university studies

2 *nmf* superior • **supériorité** *nf* superiority

superlatif, -ive [sypɛrlatif, -iv] *adj & nm Grammaire* superlative

supermarché [sypɛrmarʃe] *nm* supermarket

superposer [sypɛrpoze] *vt (objets)* to put on top of each other; *(images)* to superimpose

superproduction [sypɛrprodyksjɔ̃] *nf (film)* blockbuster

superpuissance [sypɛrpɥisɑ̃s] *nf Pol* superpower

supersonique [sypɛrsonik] *adj* supersonic

superstar [sypɛrstar] *nf* superstar

superstitieux, -ieuse [sypɛrstisjø, -jøz] *adj* superstitious • **superstition** *nf* superstition

superviser [sypɛrvize] *vt* to supervise

supplanter [syplɑ̃te] *vt* to take the place of

suppléer [syplee] *vi* **s. à** *(compenser)* to make up for • **suppléant, -ante** *adj & nmf (personne)* substitute, replacement; **(professeur) s.** substitute *or Br* supply teacher

supplément [syplemɑ̃] *nm (argent)* extra charge, supplement; *(de revue, de livre)* supplement; **en s.** extra; **un s. de** *(information, de travail)* extra, additional; **payer un s.** to pay extra, to pay a supplement • **supplémentaire** *adj* extra, additional

supplication [syplikasjɔ̃] *nf* plea, entreaty

supplice [syplis] *nm* torture; *Fig* **au s.** in agony • **supplicier** *vt* to torture

supplier [syplije] *vt* **s. qn de faire qch** to beg *or* implore sb to do sth; **je vous en supplie!** I beg *or* implore you! • **suppliant, -ante** *adj (regard)* imploring

support [sypor] *nm* support; *(d'instrument)* stand; *Fig (moyen)* medium; **s. audio-visuel** audio-visual aid

supporter¹ [syporte] *vt (malheur, conséquences)* to bear, to endure; *(chaleur)* to

withstand; *(plafond)* to support; *(frais)* to bear; *(affront)* to suffer; **je ne peux pas la s.** I can't bear her •**supportable** *adj* bearable; *(excusable, passable)* tolerable
supporter² [sypɔrtɛr] *nm (de football)* supporter
supposer [sypoze] *vt* to suppose, to assume (**que** that); *(impliquer)* to imply (**que** that); **à s. ou en supposant que...** *(+ subjunctive)* supposing (that)... •**supposition** *nf* assumption, supposition
suppositoire [sypozitwar] *nm* suppository
supprimer [syprime] **1** *vt* to get rid of, to remove; *(mot, passage)* to cut out, to delete; *(train)* to cancel; *(tuer)* to do away with; **s. des emplois** to axe jobs; **s. qch à qn** to take sth away from sb
2 se supprimer *vpr (se suicider)* to do away with oneself •**suppression** *nf* removal; *(de mot)* deletion; *(de train)* cancellation; *(d'emplois)* axing

> ♫ Il faut noter que le verbe anglais **to suppress** est un faux ami. Il signifie **réprimer** ou **interdire**.

supputer [sypyte] *vt* to calculate
suprématie [sypremasi] *nf* supremacy
suprême [syprɛm] *adj* supreme
sur [syr] *prép* on, upon; *(par-dessus)* over; *(au sujet de)* on, about; **six s. dix** six out of ten; **un jour s. deux** every other day; **six mètres s. dix** six metres by ten; **coup s. coup** blow after or upon blow; **s. ce** after which, and then; *(maintenant)* and now; **s. votre gauche** to or on your left; **mettre/monter s. qch** to put/climb on (to) sth; **aller s. ses vingt ans** to be approaching twenty; **être s. le départ** to be about to leave
sûr, sûre [syr] *adj* sure, certain (**de** of; **que** that); *(digne de confiance)* reliable; *(lieu)* safe; *(avenir)* secure; *(goût)* discerning; *(jugement)* sound; *(main)* steady; **c'est s. que...** *(+ indicative)* it's certain that...; **s. de soi** self-assured; *Fam* **être s. de son coup** to be quite sure of oneself; **bien s.!** of course!
surabondant, -ante [syrabɔ̃dɑ̃, -ɑ̃t] *adj* overabundant
suranné, -ée [syrane] *adj* outmoded
surarmement [syrarməmɑ̃] *nm* excessive arms build-up
surcharge [syrʃarʒ] *nf* (a) *(poids)* excess weight; **s. de travail** extra work; **en s.** *(passagers)* extra (b) *(correction)* alteration *(à payer)* surcharge •**surcharger** *vt (voiture, personne)* to overload (**de** with)
surchauffer [syrʃofe] *vt* to overheat

surchoix [syrʃwa] *adj inv* top-quality
surclasser [syrklase] *vt* to outclass
surcroît [syrkrwa] *nm* increase (**de** in); **de s., par s.** in addition
surdité [syrdite] *nf* deafness
surdose [syrdoz] *nf (de drogue)* overdose
surdoué, -ée [syrdwe] *nmf* gifted child
surélever [syrelve] *vt* to raise
sûrement [syrmɑ̃] *adv* certainly; *(sans danger)* safely
surenchère [syrɑ̃ʃɛr] *nf (offre d'achat)* higher bid •**surenchérir** *vi* to bid higher (**sur** than)
surestimer [syrɛstime] *vt* to overestimate; *(tableau)* to overvalue
sûreté [syrte] *nf* safety; *(de l'État)* security; *(garantie)* surety; *(de geste)* sureness; *(de jugement)* soundness; **être en s.** to be safe; **mettre qn/qch en s.** to put sb/sth in a safe place; **pour plus de s.** to be on the safe side
surexcité, -ée [syrɛksite] *adj* overexcited
surf [sœrf] *nm Sport* surfing; **faire du s.** to surf, to go surfing •**surfer** *vi* **s. sur le Net** to surf the Net
surface [syrfas] *nf* surface; *(étendue)* (surface) area; **faire s.** *(sous-marin)* to surface; **(magasin à) grande s.** hypermarket; **de s.** *(politesse)* superficial
surfait, -aite [syrfɛ, -ɛt] *adj* overrated
surgelé, -ée [syrʒəle] *adj* frozen •**surgelés** *nmpl* frozen foods
surgir [syrʒir] *vi* to appear suddenly (**de** from); *(problème)* to crop up
surhomme [syrɔm] *nm* superman •**surhumain, -aine** *adj* superhuman
sur-le-champ [syrləʃɑ̃] *adv* immediately
surlendemain [syrlɑ̃dəmɛ̃] *nm* **le s.** two days later; **le s. de** two days after
surligner [syrliɲe] *vt* to highlight •**surligneur** *nm* highlighter (pen)
surmener [syrməne] *vt, se surmener* *vpr* to overwork •**surmenage** *nm* overwork
surmonter [syrmɔ̃te] *vt (être placé sur)* to surmount; *Fig (obstacle, peur)* to overcome
surnager [syrnaʒe] *vi* to float
surnaturel, -elle [syrnatyrɛl] *adj & nm* supernatural
surnom [syrnɔ̃] *nm* nickname •**surnommer** *vt* to nickname

> ♫ Il faut noter que le nom anglais **surname** est un faux ami. Il signifie **nom de famille**.

surnombre [syrnɔ̃br] *nm* **en s.** too many; **je suis en s.** I am one too many
surpasser [syrpase] **1** *vt* to surpass (**en** in) **2 se surpasser** *vpr* to surpass oneself

surpeuplé, -ée [syrpœple] *adj* over-populated
surplace [syrplas] *nm* **faire du s.** *(dans un embouteillage)* & *Fig* to be hardly moving
surplomb [syrplɔ̃] *nm* **en s.** overhanging • **surplomber** *vti* to overhang
surplus [syrply] *nm* surplus
surprendre* [syrprɑ̃dr] **1** *vt (étonner)* to surprise; *(prendre sur le fait)* to catch; *(secret)* to discover; *(conversation)* to overhear
2 se surprendre *vpr* **se s. à faire qch** to find oneself doing sth • **surprenant, -ante** *adj* surprising • **surpris, -ise** *adj* surprised (**de** at; **que** + *subjunctive* that); **je suis s. de te voir** I'm surprised to see you • **surprise** *nf* surprise; **prendre qn par s.** to catch sb unawares
surproduction [syrprɔdyksjɔ̃] *nf* over-production
surréaliste [syrrealist] *adj (poète, peintre)* surrealist; *Fam (bizarre)* surrealistic
sursaut [syrso] *nm* (sudden) start *ou* jump; **s. d'énergie** burst of energy; **se réveiller en s.** to wake up with a start • **sursauter** *vi* to jump, start
sursis [syrsi] *nm (à l'armée)* deferment; *Fig (répit)* reprieve; **un an (de prison) avec s.** a one-year suspended sentence
surtaxe [syrtaks] *nf* surcharge
surtout [syrtu] *adv* especially; *(avant tout)* above all; **s. pas** certainly not; *Fam* **s. que...** especially since *ou* as...
surveiller [syrveje] **1** *vt (garder)* to watch, to keep an eye on; *(contrôler)* to supervise; *(épier)* to watch; *Fig* **s. son langage/ sa santé** to watch one's language/health
2 se surveiller *vpr* to watch oneself • **surveillance** *nf* watch (**sur** over); *(de travaux, d'ouvriers)* supervision; *(de police)* surveillance • **surveillant, -ante** *nmf (de lycée)* supervisor (in charge of discipline); *(de prison)* (prison) guard, *Br* warder; *(de chantier)* supervisor; **s. de plage** lifeguard

> 🖉 Il faut noter que les termes anglais **surveyor** et **to survey** sont des faux amis. Le premier signifie **géomètre** et le second ne se traduit jamais par **surveiller**.

survenir* [syrvənir] *vi* to occur; *(personne)* to turn up
survêtement [syrvɛtmɑ̃] *nm* tracksuit
survie [syrvi] *nf* survival • **survivre*** *vi* to survive (**à qch** sth); **s. à qn** to outlive sb • **survivance** *nf (chose)* survival, relic • **survivant, -ante** *nmf* survivor
survol [syrvɔl] *nm* **le s. de** *(en avion)* flying over; *Fig (question)* the overview

of • **survoler** *vt* to fly over; *Fig (question)* to skim over
survolté, -ée [syrvɔlte] *adj (surexcité)* overexcited
sus [sys] **en sus** *adv Littéraire* in addition
susceptible [syseptibl] *adj (ombrageux)* touchy, sensitive; **s. de** *(interprétations)* open to; **s. de faire qch** likely *or* liable to do sth; *(capable)* able to do sth • **susceptibilité** *nf* touchiness, sensitivity
susciter [sysite] *vt (sentiment)* to arouse; *(ennuis, obstacles)* to create
suspect, -ecte [syspɛ, -ɛkt] **1** *adj* suspicious, suspect; **s. de qch** suspected of sth
2 *nmf* suspect • **suspecter** *vt (personne)* to suspect (**de qch** of sth; **de faire** of doing); *(sincérité)* to question, to suspect
suspendre [syspɑ̃dr] **1** *vt (accrocher)* to hang (up) (**à** on); *(destituer, interrompre, différer)* to suspend
2 se suspendre *vpr* **se s. à** to hang from • **suspendu, -ue** *adj* **s. à** hanging from; **pont s.** suspension bridge; *Fig* **être s. aux paroles de qn** to hang upon sb's every word • **suspension** *nf (d'hostilités, d'employé, de véhicule)* suspension
suspens [syspɑ̃] **en suspens** *adv (affaire, travail)* in abeyance; *(en l'air)* suspended
suspense [syspɛns] *nm* suspense
suspicion [syspisjɔ̃] *nf* suspicion
susurrer [sysyre] *vti* to murmur
suture [sytyr] *nf* suture; *Méd* **point de s.** stitch • **suturer** *vt* to stitch up
svelte [svɛlt] *adj* slender • **sveltesse** *nf* slenderness
SVP [ɛsvepe] *(abrév* **s'il vous plaît**) please
syllabe [silab] *nf* syllable
symbole [sɛ̃bɔl] *nm* symbol • **symbolique** *adj* symbolic; *(salaire, cotisation, loyer)* nominal; **geste s.** symbolic *or* token gesture • **symboliser** *vt* to symbolize • **symbolisme** *nm* symbolism
symétrie [simetri] *nf* symmetry • **symétrique** *adj* symmetrical
sympa [sɛ̃pa] *adj inv Fam* nice
sympathie [sɛ̃pati] *nf (affinité)* liking; *(condoléances)* sympathy; **avoir de la s. pour qn** to be fond of sb • **sympathique** *adj* nice; *(accueil)* friendly • **sympathisant, -ante** *nmf (de parti politique)* sympathizer • **sympathiser** *vi* to get along well, *Br* to get on well (**avec** with)

> 🖉 Il faut noter que les termes anglais **sympathy**, **sympathetic** et **to sympathize** sont des faux amis. Ils signifient respectivement **compassion**, **compréhensif** et **compatir**.

symphonie [sɛ̃fɔni] *nf* symphony • **symphonique** *adj* symphonic; **orchestre s.** symphony orchestra

symposium [sɛ̃pozjɔm] *nm* symposium

symptôme [sɛ̃ptom] *nm Méd & Fig* symptom • **symptomatique** *adj* symptomatic (**de** of)

synagogue [sinagɔg] *nf* synagogue

synchroniser [sɛ̃krɔnize] *vt* to synchronize

syncope [sɛ̃kɔp] *nf (évanouissement)* blackout; **tomber en s.** to black out

syndicat [sɛ̃dika] *nm (d'ouvriers)* (*Br* trade *or Am* labor) union; *(de patrons)* association; **s. d'initiative** tourist (information) office • **syndical, -e, -aux, -ales** *adj* **réunion syndicale** (*Br* trade *or Am* labor) union meeting • **syndicalisme** *nm Br* trade *or Am* labor unionism • **syndicaliste 1** *nmf Br* trade *or Am* labor unionist **2** *adj* **esprit/idéal s.** union spirit/ideal

syndiquer [sɛ̃dike] **1** *vt* to unionize
2 se syndiquer *vpr (adhérer)* to join a (*Br* trade *or Am* labor) union • **syndiqué, -ée** *nmf* (*Br* trade *or Am* labor) union member

syndrome [sɛ̃drom] *nm Méd & Fig* syndrome; **s. immunodéficitaire acquis** acquired immune deficiency syndrome

synode [sinɔd] *nm Rel* synod

synonyme [sinɔnim] **1** *adj* synonymous (**de** with)
2 *nm* synonym

syntaxe [sɛ̃taks] *nf (grammaire)* syntax

synthèse [sɛ̃tɛz] *nf* synthesis • **synthétique** *adj* synthetic

synthétiseur [sɛ̃tetizœr] *nm* synthesizer

syphilis [sifilis] *nf Méd* syphilis

Syrie [siri] *nf* **la S.** Syria • **syrien, -ienne 1** *adj* Syrian **2** *nmf* **S., Syrienne** Syrian

système [sistɛm] *nm (structure, réseau) & Anat* system; **le s. immunitaire** the immune system; **le s. nerveux** the nervous system; *Fam* **le s. D** resourcefulness; *Ordinat* **s. d'exploitation** operating system • **systématique** *adj* systematic • **systématiquement** *adv* systematically

T, t [te] *nm inv* T, t
t' [t] *voir* te
ta [ta] *voir* ton¹
tabac [taba] *nm* tobacco; *(magasin) Br* tobacconist's (shop), *Am* tobacco store; *Fam* **faire un t.** to be a big hit; *Fam* **passer qn à t.** to beat sb up; *Fam* **passage à t.** beating up; **t. à priser** snuff • **tabasser** *vt Fam* to beat up; **se faire t.** to get beaten up
tabatière [tabatjɛr] *nf (boîte)* snuffbox
table [tabl] *nf* (a) *(meuble)* table; *(d'école)* desk; **mettre/débarrasser la t.** to set *or Br* lay/clear the table; **être à t.** to be sitting at the table; **à t.!** food's ready!; *Fig* **faire t. rase** to make a clean sweep (**de** of); **mettre qn sur t. d'écoute** to tap sb's phone; **t. à repasser** ironing board; **t. de nuit/d'opération/de jeu** bedside/operating/card table; **t. basse** coffee table; **t. ronde** *(réunion)* (round-table) conference; **t. roulante** *Br* (tea) trolley, *Am* (serving) cart (**b**) *(liste)* table; **t. des matières** table of contents
tableau, -x [tablo] *nm* (a) *(peinture)* picture, painting; *(image, description)* picture; *(scène de théâtre)* scene; **t. de maître** *(peinture)* old master (**b**) *(panneau)* board; *(liste)* list; *(graphique)* chart; **t. (noir)** (black)board; **t. d'affichage** *Br* notice board, *Am* bulletin board; **t. de bord** *(de véhicule)* dashboard; *(d'avion)* instrument panel; **t. des départs/arrivées** *(de gare, d'aéroport)* departures/arrivals board; *Scol* **avoir le t. d'honneur** *Br* to get one's name on the merit list, *Am* to make the honor roll
tabler [table] *vi* **t. sur qch** to count *or* rely on sth
tablette [tablɛt] *nf (de chocolat)* bar, slab; *(de lavabo)* shelf; *(de cheminée)* mantelpiece
tableur [tablœr] *nm Ordinat* spreadsheet
tablier [tablije] *nm* (a) *(vêtement)* apron; *(d'écolier)* smock; *Fig* **rendre son t.** to hand in one's notice (**b**) *(de pont)* roadway
tabou [tabu] *adj & nm* taboo
taboulé [tabule] *nm (plat)* tabbouleh
tabouret [taburɛ] *nm* stool

tabulateur [tabylatœr] *nm (d'ordinateur, de machine à écrire)* tabulator
tac [tak] *nm* **répondre du t. au t.** to give tit for tat
tache [taʃ] *nf* mark; *(salissure)* stain; *Péj* **faire t.** *(détonner)* to jar, to stand out; *Fig* **faire t. d'huile** to spread • **tacher** *vt, se tacher* *vpr (tissu)* to stain
tâche [taʃ] *nf* task, job; **être à la t.** to be on piecework; *Fig* **se tuer à la t.** to work oneself to death; **tâches ménagères** housework
tâcher [taʃe] *vi* **t. de faire qch** to try *or* endeavour to do sth
tâcheron [taʃrɔ̃] *nm Péj* drudge
tacheté, -ée [taʃte] *adj* speckled (**de** with)
tacite [tasit] *adj* tacit • **tacitement** *adv* tacitly
taciturne [tasityrn] *adj* taciturn
tacot [tako] *nm Fam (voiture)* (old) wreck, *Br* banger
tact [takt] *nm* tact; **avoir du t.** to be tactful
tactile [taktil] *adj* tactile
tactique [taktik] **1** *adj* tactical
2 *nf* tactics *(sing)*; **une t.** a tactic
tag [tag] *nm* tag *(spray-painted graffiti)* • **tagueur, -euse** *nmf* graffiti artist, tagger
Tahiti [taiti] *nm* Tahiti • **tahitien, -ienne** [taisjɛ̃, -jɛn] **1** *adj* Tahitian **2** *nmf* **T., Tahitienne** Tahitian
taie [te] *nf* **t. d'oreiller** pillowcase, pillowslip
taillade [tajad] *nf* gash, slash • **taillader** *vt* to gash, slash
taille¹ [taj] *nf* (a) *(hauteur)* height; *(dimension, mesure)* size; **de haute t.** *(personne)* tall; **de petite t.** short; **de t. moyenne** medium-sized; *Fig* **être de t. à faire qch** to be capable of doing sth; *Fam* **de t.** *(erreur, objet)* enormous (**b**) *(ceinture)* waist; **tour de t.** waist measurement
taille² [taj] *nf* cutting; *(de haie)* trimming; *(d'arbre)* pruning • **taillé, -ée** *adj* **t. en athlète** built like an athlete; *Fig* **t. pour faire qch** cut out for doing sth • **tailler 1** *vt* to cut; *(haie, barbe)* to trim; *(arbre)* to prune; *(crayon)* to sharpen; *(vêtement)* to cut out **2 se tailler** *vpr* (**a**) **se t. la part du**

lion to take the lion's share (**b**) *Fam (partir)* to beat it

taille-crayon [tɑjkrɛjɔ̃] *nm inv* pencil-sharpener

tailleur [tɑjœr] *nm (personne)* tailor; *(costume)* suit

taillis [tɑji] *nm* copse, coppice

tain [tɛ̃] *nm (de glace)* silvering; **glace sans t.** two-way mirror

taire* [tɛr] **1** *vt* to say nothing about
2 *vi* **faire t. qn** to silence sb
3 se taire *vpr (ne rien dire)* to keep quiet (**sur qch** about sth); *(cesser de parler)* to stop talking, to fall silent; **tais-toi!** be quiet!

Taiwan [tajwan] *nm ou f* Taiwan

talc [talk] *nm* talcum powder

talé, -ée [tale] *adj (fruit)* bruised

talent [talɑ̃] *nm* talent; **avoir du t.** to be talented **•talentueux, -ueuse** *adj* talented

talion [taljɔ̃] *nm* **la loi du t.** an eye for an eye

talisman [talismɑ̃] *nm* talisman

talkie-walkie [talkiwalki] (*pl* **talkies-walkies**) *nm* walkie-talkie

taloche [talɔʃ] *nf Fam (gifle)* clout

talon [talɔ̃] *nm* (**a**) *(de chaussure)* heel; **tourner les talons** to walk away; **c'est son t. d'Achille** it's his Achilles' heel; **(chaussures à) talons hauts** high heels, high-heeled shoes; **talons aiguilles** stiletto heels (**b**) *(de chèque)* stub, counterfoil; *(bout de pain)* crust; *(de jambon)* heel **•talonnette** *nf (pour chaussure)* heel pad

talonner [talɔne] **1** *vt (fugitif)* to follow on the heels of
2 *vi Rugby* to heel

talus [taly] *nm* slope

tambour [tɑ̃bur] *nm (de machine, instrument de musique)* drum; *(personne)* drummer; **sans t. ni trompette** quietly, without fuss **•tambourin** *nm* tambourine **•tambouriner** *vi (avec les doigts)* to drum (**sur** on)

tamis [tami] *nm* sieve **•tamiser** *vt (farine)* to sift; *(lumière)* to filter

Tamise [tamiz] *nf* **la T.** the Thames

tampon [tɑ̃pɔ̃] *nm* (**a**) *(marque, instrument)* stamp; **t. encreur** ink pad; **lettre à renvoyer avant minuit le t. de la poste faisant foi** letter to be postmarked no later than midnight (**b**) *(bouchon)* plug, stopper; *(de coton)* wad, pad; *(pour pansement)* swab; **t. hygiénique** *ou* **périodique** tampon; **t. à récurer** scouring pad (**c**) *(de train)* & *Fig* buffer; **état t.** buffer state

tamponner [tɑ̃pɔne] **1** *vt (lettre, document)* to stamp; *(visage)* to dab; *(plaie)* to swab; *(train, voiture)* to crash into
2 se tamponner *vpr* to crash into each other **•tamponneuses** *adj fpl* **autos t.** Dodgems®

tam-tam [tamtam] (*pl* **tam-tams**) *nm (tambour)* tom-tom

tandem [tɑ̃dɛm] *nm (bicyclette)* tandem; *Fig (duo)* duo; **travailler en t.** to work in tandem

tandis [tɑ̃di] **tandis que** *conj (simultanéité)* while; *(contraste)* whereas, while

tangent, -ente [tɑ̃ʒɑ̃, -ɑ̃t] *adj* tangential (**à** to); *Fam (juste)* touch and go **•tangente** *nf* tangent

tangible [tɑ̃ʒibl] *adj* tangible

tango [tɑ̃go] *nm* tango

tanguer [tɑ̃ge] *vi (bateau, avion)* to pitch **•tangage** *nm (de bateau, d'avion)* pitching

tanière [tanjɛr] *nf* den, lair

tank [tɑ̃k] *nm* tank

tanker [tɑ̃kɛr] *nm (navire)* tanker

tanner [tane] *vt (cuir)* to tan **•tanné, -ée** *adj (visage)* weather-beaten

tant [tɑ̃] *adv (travailler)* so much (**que** that); **t. de** *(pain, temps)* so much (**que** that); *(gens, choses)* so many (**que** that); **t. de fois** so often, so many times; **t. que** *(autant que)* as much as; *(aussi fort que)* as hard as; *(aussi longtemps que)* as long as; **en t. que** *(considéré comme)* as; **t. bien que mal** more or less, somehow or other; **t. mieux!** so much the better!; **t. pis!** too bad!, pity!; **t. mieux pour toi!** good for you!; **t. pis pour toi!** that's too bad (for you)!; **t. soit peu** (even) remotely *or* slightly; **un t. soit peu** somewhat; **t. s'en faut** far from it

tante [tɑ̃t] *nf* aunt

tantinet [tɑ̃tinɛ] *nm & adv* **un t.** a tiny bit (**de** of)

tantôt [tɑ̃to] *adv* (**a**) **t....t....** sometimes... sometimes... (**b**) *(cet après-midi)* this afternoon

taon [tɑ̃] *nm* horsefly, gadfly

tapage [tapaʒ] *nm* din, uproar **•tapageur, -euse** *adj (bruyant)* rowdy; *(criard)* flashy

tape [tap] *nf* slap

tape-à-l'œil [tapalœj] *adj inv Fam* flashy, gaudy

taper [tape] **1** *vt (enfant, cuisse)* to slap; *(table)* to bang; **t. qch à la machine** to type sth; *Fam* **t. qn** *(emprunter de l'argent à)* to cadge money off sb
2 *vi (soleil)* to beat down; **t. du pied** to

stamp one's foot; **t. à la porte** to knock on the door; **t. à la machine** to type; **t. sur qch** to bang on sth; *Fam* **t. sur qn** *(critiquer)* to knock sb; *Fam* **t. sur les nerfs de qn** to get on sb's nerves; *Fam* **t. dans** *(provisions)* to dig into; *Fam* **t. dans l'œil à qn** to take sb's fancy

3 se taper *upr Fam (travail)* to get landed with; *Fam (repas, vin)* to have • **tapant, -ante** *adj* **à huit heures tapantes** at eight sharp

tapeur, -euse [tapœr, -øz] *nmf Fam* scrounger

tapioca [tapjɔka] *nm* tapioca

tapir [tapir] **se tapir** *upr* to crouch • **tapi, -ie** *adj* crouching, crouched

tapis [tapi] *nm* carpet; **envoyer qn au t.** *(abattre)* to floor sb; **mettre qch sur le t.** *(sujet)* to bring sth up for discussion; **dérouler le t. rouge** to put out the red carpet; **t. de bain** bath mat; **t. de sol** earth mat; **t. roulant** *(pour marchandises)* conveyor belt; *(pour personnes)* moving walkway • **tapis-brosse** *(pl* **tapis-brosses)** *nm* door-mat

tapisser [tapise] *vt (mur)* to (wall)paper; *(de tentures)* to hang with tapestry; *Fig (recouvrir)* to cover • **tapisserie** *nf (papier peint)* wallpaper; *(broderie)* tapestry; *Fig* **faire t.** *(jeune fille)* to be a wallflower • **tapissier, -ière** *nmf (qui pose des tissus)* upholsterer

tapoter [tapɔte] **1** *vt* to tap; *(joue)* to pat
2 *vi* **t. sur** to tap (on)

taquin, -ine [takɛ̃, -in] *adj* teasing • **taquiner** *vt* to tease • **taquineries** *nfpl* teasing

tarabiscoté, -ée [tarabiskɔte] *adj* over-elaborate

tarabuster [tarabyste] *vt (idée)* to trouble

tarauder [tarode] *vt* to gnaw at

tard [tar] *adv* late; **plus t.** later (on); **au plus t.** at the latest; **sur le t.** late in life

tarder [tarde] **1** *vi (lettre, saison)* to be a long time coming; **sans t.** without delay; **t. à faire qch** to take one's time doing sth; **elle ne va pas t.** she won't be long
2 *v impersonnel* **il me tarde de le faire** I long to do it

tardif, -ive [tardif, -iv] *adj* late; *(regrets)* belated • **tardivement** *adv* late

tare [tar] *nf (poids)* tare; *Fig (défaut)* defect • **taré, -ée** *adj (anormal)* retarded; *Fam (fou)* mad

tarentule [tarɑ̃tyl] *nf* tarantula

targette [tarʒɛt] *nf (flat)* door bolt

targuer [targe] **se targuer** *upr* **se t. de**

qch/de faire qch to pride oneself on sth/on doing sth

tarif [tarif] *nm (prix)* rate; *(de train)* fare; *(tableau)* price list, *Br* tariff; **plein t.** full price; *(de train, bus)* full fare • **tarification** *nf* pricing

tarir [tarir] *vti,* **se tarir** *upr (fleuve)* & *Fig* to dry up; *Fig* **ne pas t. d'éloges sur qn** to rave about sb

tarot [taro] *nm* tarot

tartare [tartar] *adj* **sauce t.** tartar sauce

tarte [tart] **1** *nf (open)* pie, tart; *Fam* **ce n'est pas de la t.!** it isn't easy!
2 *adj inv Fam (sot)* silly • **tartelette** [-əlɛt] *nf (small)* tart

tartine [tartin] *nf* slice of bread; **t. de beurre/de confiture** slice of bread and butter/jam • **tartiner** *vt (beurre)* to spread; **fromage à t.** cheese spread

tartre [tartr] *nm (de bouilloire)* scale, *Br* fur; *(de dents)* tartar

tas [tɑ] *nm* pile, heap; *Fam* **un** *ou* **des t. de** *(beaucoup)* lots of; **mettre qch en t.** to pile *or* heap sth up; *Fam* **apprendre sur le t.** to learn on the job

tasse [tas] *nf* cup; **t. à café** coffee cup; **t. à thé** teacup; *Fam* **boire la t.** to swallow a mouthful *(when swimming)*

tasser [tɑse] **1** *vt* to pack (**dans** into); *(terre)* to pack down; *Fam* **un café bien tassé** *(fort)* a strong coffee
2 se tasser *upr (se serrer)* to squeeze up; *(sol)* to sink, to collapse; *(se voûter)* to become bowed; *Fam* **ça va se t.** *(s'arranger)* things will settle down

tâter [tɑte] **1** *vt* to feel; *Fig* **t. le terrain** to see how the land lies
2 *vi* **t. de** *(prison, métier)* to have a taste of
3 se tâter *upr (hésiter)* to be in two minds

tatillon, -onne [tatijɔ̃, -ɔn] *adj Fam* finicky

tâtonner [tɑtɔne] *vi* to grope about • **tâtonnement** *nm* **par t.** *(procéder)* by trial and error • **tâtons** *adv* **avancer à t.** to feel one's way (along); **chercher qch à t.** to grope for sth

tatouer [tatwe] *vt (corps, dessin)* to tattoo; **se faire t.** to get a tatoo; **se faire t. un bateau sur le bras** to get a boat tatooed on one's arm • **tatouage** *nm (dessin)* tattoo; *(action)* tattooing

taudis [todi] *nm* slum

taule [tol] *nf Fam (prison) Br* nick, *Am* can

taupe [top] *nf (animal, espion)* mole • **taupinière** *nf* molehill

taureau, -x [tɔro] *nm* bull; **le T.** *(signe)* Taurus; **être T.** to be Taurus • **tauromachie** *nf* bull-fighting

taux [to] *nm* rate; **t. d'alcool/de cholestérol** alcohol/cholesterol level; **t. d'intérêt/de change** interest/exchange rate; **t. de natalité** birth rate

taverne [tavɛrn] *nf* tavern

taxe [taks] *nf (impôt)* tax; **t. à la valeur ajoutée** value-added tax •**taxation** *nf* taxation

taxer [takse] *vt (produit, personne, firme)* to tax; **t. qn de qch** to accuse sb of sth; *Fam* **t. qch à qn** *(voler)* to cadge sth off sb •**taxé, -ée** *adj (produit)* taxed

taxi [taksi] *nm* taxi

Taxiphone® [taksifɔn] *nm* pay phone

tchador [tʃadɔr] *nm (voile)* chador

Tchécoslovaquie [tʃekɔslɔvaki] *nf* Anciennement **la T.** Czechoslovakia •**tchèque 1** *adj* Czech; **la République t.** the Czech Republic **2** *nmf* **T.** Czech **3** *nm (langue)* Czech

TD [tede] *(abrév* **travaux dirigés**) *nm* tutorial

te [tə]

> **t'** is used before a word beginning with a vowel or h mute.

pron personnel (**a**) *(complément direct)* you; **je te vois** I see you (**b**) *(indirect)* (to) you; **il te parle** he speaks to you; **elle te l'a dit** she told you (**c**) *(réfléchi)* yourself; **tu te laves** you wash yourself

technicien, -ienne [tɛknisjɛ̃, -jɛn] *nmf* technician •**technique 1** *adj* technical **2** *nf* technique •**techniquement** *adv* technically •**technocrate** *nm* technocrat •**technologie** *nf* technology •**technologique** *adj* technological

teck [tɛk] *nm (bois)* teak

teckel [tekɛl] *nm* dachshund

tee-shirt [tiʃœrt] *nm* tee-shirt

teindre* [tɛ̃dr] **1** *vt* to dye; **t. qch en rouge** to dye sth red **2 se teindre** *vpr* **se t. (les cheveux)** to dye one's hair

teint [tɛ̃] *nm (de visage)* complexion; **bon ou grand t.** *(tissu)* colourfast; *Fig Hum* **bon t.** *(catholique)* staunch

teinte [tɛ̃t] *nf* shade, tint •**teinter 1** *vt* to tint; *(bois)* to stain **2 se teinter** *vpr Fig* **se t. de** *(remarque, ciel)* to be tinged with

teinture [tɛ̃tyr] *nf* dyeing; *(produit)* dye •**teinturerie** [-rri] *nf (boutique)* (dry) cleaner's •**teinturier, -ière** *nmf* dry cleaner

tel, telle [tɛl] *adj* such; **un t. livre/homme** such a book/man; **un t. intérêt** such interest; **de tels mots** such words; **t. que** such as, like; **t. que je l'ai laissé** just as I left it; **laissez-le t. quel** leave it just as it is; **en tant que t., comme t.** as such; **t. ou t.** such and such; **rien de t. que** *(there's)* nothing like; **rien de t.** nothing like it; **t. père t. fils** like father like son

télé [tele] *nf Fam* TV, *Br* telly; **à la t.** on TV, *Br* on the telly; **regarder la t.** to watch TV *or Br* the telly

télébenne [telebɛn] *nf,* **télécabine** [telekabin] *nf (cabine, système)* cable car

Télécarte® [telekart] *nf* phone card

télécommande [telekɔmɑ̃d] *nf* remote control •**télécommander** *vt* to operate by remote control

télécommunications [telekɔmynikasjɔ̃] *nfpl* telecommunications

télécopie [telekɔpi] *nf* fax •**télécopieur** *nm* fax (machine)

téléfilm [telefilm] *nm* TV film

télégramme [telegram] *nm* telegram

télégraphe [telegraf] *nm* telegraph •**télégraphie** *nf* telegraphy •**télégraphier** *vt (message)* to wire, to cable (**que** that) •**télégraphique** *adj* **poteau/fil t.** telegraph pole/wire; *Fig* **style t.** telegraphic style •**télégraphiste** *nm (messager)* telegraph boy

téléguider [telegide] *vt* to operate by remote control •**téléguidage** *nm* remote control

télématique [telematik] *nf* telematics *(sing)*

téléobjectif [teleɔbʒɛktif] *nm* telephoto lens

télépathie [telepati] *nf* telepathy

téléphérique [teleferik] *nm* cable car

téléphone [telefɔn] *nm* (tele)phone; **coup de t.** (phone) call; **passer un coup de t. à qn** to give sb a ring *or* a call; **au t.** on the (tele-)phone; **avoir le t.** to be on the (tele)phone; **t. portable** mobile phone; **t. sans fil** cordless phone; *Fig* **apprendre qch par le t. arabe** to hear about sth on the grapevine •**téléphoner 1** *vt (nouvelle)* to (tele)phone (**à** to) **2** *vi* to (tele)phone; **t. à qn** to (tele)phone sb, to call sb (up) •**téléphonique** *adj* **appel t.** telephone call •**téléphoniste** *nmf* operator, *Br* telephonist

téléprompteur [teleprɔ̃ptœr] *nm* teleprompter, *Br* autocue

télescope [telɛskɔp] *nm* telescope •**télescopique** *adj* telescopic

télescoper [telɛskɔpe] **1** *vt (voiture, train)* to smash into **2 se télescoper** *vpr (voiture, train)* to concertina

téléscripteur [telɛskriptœr] *nm Br* teleprinter, *Am* teletypewriter

télésiège [telesjɛʒ] *nm* chair lift
téléski [teleski] *nm* ski tow
téléspectateur, -trice [telespɛktatœr, -tris] *nmf* (television) viewer
télétravail [teletravaj] *nm* teleworking
téléviser [televize] *vt* to televise • **téléviseur** *nm* television (set) • **télévision** *nf* television; **à la t.** on (the) television; **regarder la t.** to watch (the) television; **programme de t.** television programme
télex [telɛks] *nm (service, message)* telex
telle [tɛl] *voir* tel • **tellement** *adv (si)* so; *(tant)* so much; **t. grand que...** so big that...; **crier t. que...** to shout so much that...; **t. de travail** so much work; **t. de soucis** so many worries; **tu aimes ça? – pas t.!** *(pas beaucoup)* do you like it? – not much *or* a lot!; **personne ne peut le supporter, t. il est bavard** nobody can stand him, he's so talkative
tellurique [telyrik] *adj* **secousse t.** earth tremor
téméraire [temerɛr] *adj* reckless • **témérité** *nf* recklessness
témoigner [temwaɲe] **1** *vt (gratitude)* to show (**à qn** (to) sb); **t. que...** *(attester)* to testify that...
2 *vi Jur* to give evidence, to testify (**contre** against); **t. de qch** *(personne, attitude)* to testify to sth • **témoignage** *nm Jur* evidence, testimony; *(récit)* account; **faux t.** *(délit)* perjury; *Fig (d'affection)* token, sign (**de** of); **en t. de qch** as a token of sth
témoin [temwɛ̃] **1** *nm* (**a**)*Jur* witness; **t. à charge** witness for the prosecution; **être t. de qch** to witness sth (**b**) *(de relais)* baton
2 *adj* **appartement t.** *Br* show flat, *Am* model apartment
tempe [tɑ̃p] *nf Anat* temple
tempérament [tɑ̃peramɑ̃] *nm (caractère)* temperament; **acheter qch à t.** to buy sth on *Br* hire purchase *or Am* on the installment plan
tempérance [tɑ̃perɑ̃s] *nf* temperance
température [tɑ̃peratyr] *nf* temperature; **avoir de la t.** to have a temperature
tempérer [tɑ̃pere] *vt (ardeurs)* to moderate • **tempéré, -ée** *adj (climat, zone)* temperate
tempête [tɑ̃pɛt] *nf* storm; **t. de neige** snowstorm, blizzard
tempêter [tɑ̃pete] *vi (crier)* to storm, to rage (**contre** against)
temple [tɑ̃pl] *nm (romain, grec)* temple; *(protestant)* church
tempo [tempo] *nm* tempo

temporaire [tɑ̃pɔrɛr] *adj* temporary • **temporairement** *adv* temporarily
temporel, -elle [tɑ̃pɔrɛl] *adj* temporal; *(terrestre)* wordly
temporiser [tɑ̃pɔrize] *vi* to play for time
temps¹ [tɑ̃] *nm (durée, période, moment)* time; *Grammaire* tense; *(étape)* stage; **en t. de guerre** in wartime, in time of war; **avoir/trouver le t.** to have/find (the) time (**de faire** to do); **il est t.** it is time (**de faire** to do); **il était t.!** it was about time (too)!; **il est (grand) t. que vous partiez** it's (high) time you left; **ces derniers t.** lately; **de t. en t.** [dətɑ̃zɑ̃tɑ̃], **de t. à autre** [dətɑ̃zaotr] from time to time, now and again; **en t. utile** [ɑ̃tɑ̃zytil] in due course; **en t. voulu** in due course; **en même t.** at the same time (**que** as); **à t.** *(arriver)* in time; **à plein t.** *(travailler)* full-time; **à t. partiel** *(travailler)* part-time; **dans le t.** *(autrefois)* in the old days; **avec le t.** *(à la longue)* in time; **tout le t.** all the time; **de mon t.** in my time; **pendant un t.** for a while *or* time; *Fam* **par les t. qui courent** at the present time; **moteur à quatre t.** four-stroke engine, *Am* four-cycle engine; **t. d'arrêt** pause, break; **t. libre** free time; *Fig* **t. mort** lull
temps² [tɑ̃] *nm (climat)* weather; **il fait beau/mauvais t.** the weather's fine/bad; **quel t. fait-il?** what's the weather like?
tenable [tənabl] *adj* bearable
tenace [tənas] *adj* stubborn, tenacious • **ténacité** *nf* stubbornness, tenacity
tenailler [tənaje] *vt (faim, remords)* to torture
tenailles [tənaj] *nfpl (outil)* pincers
tenancier, -ière [tənɑ̃sje, -jɛr] *nmf (d'hôtel)* manager, *f* manageress
tenant, -ante [tənɑ̃, -ɑ̃t] **1** *nmf* **le t. du titre** *(champion)* the title holder
2 *nm (partisan)* supporter (**de** of) • **tenants** *nmpl* **les t. et les aboutissants d'une question** the ins and outs of a question
tendance [tɑ̃dɑ̃s] *nf (penchant)* tendency; *(évolution)* trend (**à** towards); **avoir t. à faire qch** to tend to do sth, to have a tendency to do sth
tendancieux, -ieuse [tɑ̃dɑ̃sjø, -jøz] *adj Péj* tendentious
tendeur [tɑ̃dœr] *nm (à bagages)* elastic strap, *Am* bungee
tendon [tɑ̃dɔ̃] *nm Anat* tendon
tendre¹ [tɑ̃dr] **1** *vt* to stretch; *(main)* to hold out (**à qn** to sb); *(bras, jambe)* to stretch out; *(cou)* to strain, to crane; *(muscle)* to tense; *(arc)* to bend; *(piège)* to set, to lay; *(filet)* to spread; **t. qch à qn**

to hold out sth to sb; *Fig* **t. l'oreille** to prick up one's ears

2 *vi* **t. à qch/à faire qch** to tend towards sth/to do sth

3 se tendre *vpr (rapports)* to become strained • **tendu, -ue** *adj (corde)* tight, taut; *(personne, situation, muscle)* tense; *(rapports)* strained

tendre² [tãdr] *adj (personne)* affectionate (**avec** to); *(parole, regard)* tender, loving; *(viande)* tender; *(bois, couleur)* soft; **depuis ma plus t.** enfance since I've been a young child • **tendrement** [-əmã] *adv* tenderly, lovingly • **tendresse** *nf (affection)* affection, tenderness • **tendreté** [-əte] *nf (de viande)* tenderness

ténèbres [tenɛbr] *nfpl* **les t.** the darkness • **ténébreux, -euse** *adj* dark, gloomy; *(mystérieux)* mysterious

teneur [tənœr] *nf (de lettre)* content; **t. en alcool** alcohol content (**de** of)

tenir* [tənir] **1** *vt (à la main)* to hold; *(promesse, comptes, hôtel)* to keep; *(rôle)* to play; *(propos)* to utter; **t. sa droite** *(conducteur)* to keep to the right; **t. la route** *(véhicule)* to hold the road; *Fig* **t. sa langue** to hold one's tongue; **t. qch propre/chaud** to keep sth clean/hot; **je le tiens!** *(je l'ai attrapé)* I've got him!; **je te tiens de Louis** *(fait)* I got it from Louis; *(caractère héréditaire)* I get it from Louis

2 *vi (nœud)* to hold; *(neige, coiffure)* to last, to hold; *(résister)* to hold out; *(offre)* to stand; **t. à qn/qch** to be attached to sb/sth; **t. à la vie** to value life; **t. à faire qch** to be anxious to do sth; **t. dans qch** *(être contenu)* to fit into sth; **t. de qn** to take after sb; **tenez!** *(prenez)* here (you are)!; **tiens!** *(surprise)* well!, hey!; **ça tient à sa maladie** it's due to his/her illness

3 *v impersonnel* **il ne tient qu'à vous de le faire** it's up to you to do it

4 se tenir *vpr (avoir lieu)* to be held; *(rester)* to remain; **se t. debout** to stand (up); **se t. droit** to stand up/sit up straight; **se t. par la main** to hold hands; **se t. bien** to behave oneself; **se t. à qch** to hold on to sth; **s'en t. à qch** *(se limiter à)* to stick to sth; **savoir à quoi s'en t.** to know what's what; *Fig* **tout se tient** it all hangs together

tennis [tenis] **1** *nm* tennis; *(terrain)* (tennis) court; **t. de table** table tennis

2 *nmpl Br (chaussures)* tennis shoes

ténor [tenɔr] *nm Mus* tenor

tension [tãsjɔ̃] *nf* tension; **t. artérielle** blood pressure; **avoir de la t.** to have high blood pressure

tentacule [tãtakyl] *nm* tentacle

tente [tãt] *nf* tent

tenter¹ [tãte] *vt (essayer)* to try; **t. de faire qch** to try *or* attempt to do sth • **tentative** *nf* attempt; **t. de suicide** suicide attempt

tenter² [tãte] *vt (faire envie à)* to tempt; **tenté de faire qch** tempted to do sth • **tentant, -ante** *adj* tempting • **tentation** *nf* temptation

tenture [tãtyr] *nf* (wall) hanging; *(de porte)* drape, curtain

tenu, -ue [təny] **1** *pp de* **tenir**

2 *adj* **t. de faire qch** obliged to do sth; **bien/mal t.** *(maison)* well/badly kept

ténu, -ue [teny] *adj (fil)* fine; *(soupçon, différence)* tenuous; *(voix)* thin

tenue [təny] *nf* **(a)** *(vêtements)* clothes, outfit; **être en petite t.** to be scantily dressed; **t. de combat** *(uniforme)* battle-dress; **t. de soirée** evening dress **(b)** *(conduite)* (good) behaviour; *(maintien)* posture **(c)** *(de maison, d'hôtel)* running; *(de comptes)* keeping **(d)** **t. de route** *(de véhicule)* road-holding

ter [tɛr] *adj* **4 t.** ≃ 4B

térébenthine [terebãtin] *nf* turpentine

Tergal® [tɛrgal] *nm Br* Terylene®, *Am* Dacron®

tergiverser [tɛrʒivɛrse] *vi* to equivocate

terme [tɛrm] *nm* **(a)** *(mot)* term **(b)** *(date limite)* time (limit); *(fin)* end; **mettre un t. à qch** to put an end to sth; **à court/long t.** *(conséquences, projet)* short-/long-term; **être né avant/à t.** to be born prematurely/at (full) term **(c)** **moyen t.** *(solution)* middle course **(d)** **en bons/mauvais termes** on good/bad terms (**avec qn** with sb) **(e)** *(loyer)* rent; *(jour)* rent day; *(période)* rental period

terminal, -e, -aux, -ales [tɛrminal, -o] **1** *adj* final; *(phase de maladie)* terminal

2 *adj & nf Scol* **(classe) terminale** *Br* ≃ sixth form, *Am* ≃ twelfth grade

3 *nm (d'ordinateur, pétrolier)* terminal

terminer [tɛrmine] **1** *vt* to end; *(achever)* to finish, to complete

2 se terminer *vpr* to end (**par** with; **en** in) • **terminaison** *nf (de mot)* ending

terminologie [tɛrminɔlɔʒi] *nf* terminology

terminus [tɛrminys] *nm* terminus

termite [tɛrmit] *nm* termite

terne [tɛrn] *adj (couleur, journée)* dull, drab; *(personne)* dull • **ternir 1** *vt (métal, réputation)* to tarnish; *(meuble, miroir)* to dull **2 se ternir** *vpr (métal)* to tarnish

terrain [terɛ̃] *nm (sol) & Fig* ground; *(étendue)* land; *(à bâtir)* plot, site; *(pour* *opérations militaires) & Géol* terrain; **un t.** a piece of land; **céder/gagner/perdre du t.** *(armée) & Fig* to give/gain/lose ground; *Fig* **trouver un t. d'entente** to find a common ground; *Fig* **être sur son t.** to be on familiar ground; **t. de camping** campsite; **t. de football/rugby** football/ rugby pitch; **t. de golf** golf course; **t. de jeu(x)** *(pour enfants)* playground; *(stade) Br* playing field, *Am* athletic field; **t. de sport** *Br* sports ground, *Am* athletic field; **t. d'aviation** airfield; **t. vague** waste ground, *Am* vacant lot

terrasse [teras] *nf (balcon, plate-forme)* terrace; *(toit)* terrace (roof); *(de café) Br* pavement *or Am* sidewalk area; **à la t.** outside

terrassement [terasmɑ̃] *nm (travail)* excavation

terrasser [terase] *vt (adversaire)* to floor; *Fig (accabler)* to overcome

terrassier [terasje] *nm* labourer

terre [tɛr] *nf (matière, monde)* earth; *(sol)* ground; *(opposé à mer, étendue)* land; **terres** *(domaine)* land, estate; *Él Br* earth, *Am* ground; **la t.** *(le monde)* the earth; **la T.** *(planète)* Earth; **à** *ou* **par t.** *(tomber)* to the ground; *(poser)* on the ground; **par t.** *(assis, couché)* on the ground; **aller à t.** *(marin)* to go ashore; **sous t.** underground; **t. cuite** (baked) clay, earthenware; **poterie en t. cuite** earthenware pottery; **t. battue** *(de court de tennis)* clay •**terre-à-terre** *adj inv* down-to-earth •**terre-plein** *(pl* **terres-pleins)** *nm* (earth) platform; *(de route) Br* central reservation, *Am* median strip

terreau [tero] *nm* compost

terrer [tere] **se terrer** *vpr (fugitif, animal)* to go to earth

terrestre [terɛstr] *adj (vie, joies)* earthly; **animal/transport t.** land animal/transportation

terreur [tɛrœr] *nf* terror; **vivre dans la t. de l'armée** to live in terror of the army •**terrible** *adj* awful, terrible; *Fam (formidable)* terrific; *Fam* **pas t.** nothing special •**terriblement** [-əmɑ̃] *adv (extrêmement)* terribly

terreux, -euse [terø, -øz] *adj (goût)* earthy; *(couleur, teint)* muddy

terrien, -ienne [terjɛ̃, -jɛn] **1** *adj* landowning; **propriétaire t.** landowner

   2 *nmf (habitant de la terre)* earthling

terrier [terje] *nm (de lapin)* burrow; *(chien)* terrier

terrifier [terifje] *vt* to terrify •**terrifiant, -ante** *adj* terrifying

terrine [terin] *nf (récipient)* terrine; *(pâté)* pâté

territoire [teritwar] *nm* territory •**territorial, -e, -iaux, iales** *adj* territorial; **eaux territoriales** territorial waters

terroir [terwar] *nm (sol)* soil; *(région)* region; **accent du t.** rural accent

terroriser [terɔrize] *vt* to terrorize •**terrorisme** *nm* terrorism •**terroriste** *adj & nmf* terrorist

tertiaire [tersjer] *adj* tertiary

tertre [tɛrtr] *nm* hillock, mound

tes [te] *voir* **ton¹**

tesson [tesɔ̃] *nm* **t. de bouteille** piece of broken bottle

test [tɛst] *nm* test •**tester** *vt (élève, produit)* to test

testament [tɛstamɑ̃] *nm (document)* will; *Fig (œuvre)* testament; *Rel* **Ancien/Nouveau T.** Old/NewTestament

testicule [tɛstikyl] *nm Anat* testicle

tétanos [tetanos] *nm* tetanus

têtard [tetar] *nm* tadpole

tête [tɛt] *nf* head; *(visage)* face; *(cerveau)* brain; *(de lit, de clou, de cortège)* head; *(de page, de liste)* top, head; *Football* header; **à t. reposée** at one's leisure; **à la t. de** *(entreprise, parti)* at the head of; *(classe)* at the top of; **de la t. aux pieds** from head *or* top to toe; **t. nue** bareheaded; **en t.** *(d'une course)* in the lead; **tenir t. à qn** *(s'opposer à)* to stand up to sb; **faire la t.** *(bouder)* to sulk; *Football* **faire une t.** to head the ball; **avoir/faire une drôle de t.** to have/give a funny look; **tomber la t. la première** to fall headlong *or* head first; **calculer qch de t.** to work sth out in one's head; **se mettre dans la t. de faire qch** to get it into one's head to do sth; *Fig* **perdre la t.** to lose one's head; *Fam* **se payer la t. de qn** to make fun of sb; *Fam* **j'en ai par-dessus la t.** I've had enough of it; *Fam* **ça me prend la t.** it gets under my skin; *Fam* **tu n'as pas de t.!** you're a scatterbrain!; **t. nucléaire** nuclear warhead •**tête-à-queue** *nm inv* **faire un t.** *(en voiture)* to spin right round •**tête-à-tête** *nm inv* tête-à-tête; **en t.** in private •**tête-bêche** *adv* head to tail

téter [tete] *vt (lait, biberon)* to suck; **t. sa mère** to feed *or* suck at one's mother's breast; **donner à t. à qn** to feed sb •**tétée** *nf (de bébé)* feed •**tétine** *nf (de biberon) Br* teat, *Am* nipple; *(sucette) Br* dummy, *Am* pacifier •**téton** *nm Fam (de femme)* tit

têtu, -ue [tety] *adj* stubborn, obstinate

texte [tɛkst] *nm* text; *(de théâtre)* lines; *(de chanson)* words •**textuel, -elle** *adj*

(traduction) literal •**textuellement** *adv* word for word
textile [tɛkstil] *adj & nm* textile
texture [tɛkstyr] *nf* texture
TGV [teʒeve] *abrév* = train à grande vitesse
Thaïlande [tailɑ̃d] *nf* la T. Thailand •**thaïlandais, -aise** 1 *adj* Thai 2 *nmf* T., **Thaïlandaise** Thai
thé [te] *nm (boisson, réunion)* tea •**théière** *nf* teapot
théâtre [teɑtr] *nm (art, lieu)* theatre; *(œuvres)* drama; *Fig (d'un crime)* scene; *Mil* t. des opérations theatre of operations; faire du t. to act •**théâtral, -e, -aux, -ales** *adj* theatrical
thème [tɛm] *nm* theme; *Scol (traduction)* translation, *Br* prose (composition)
théologie [teɔlɔʒi] *nf* theology •**théologien** *nm* theologian •**théologique** *adj* theological
théorème [teɔrɛm] *nm* theorem
théorie [teɔri] *nf* theory; **en t.** in theory •**théoricien, -ienne** *nmf* theorist, theoretician •**théorique** *adj* theoretical •**théoriquement** *adv* theoretically
thérapeutique [terapøtik] 1 *adj* therapeutic
2 *nf (traitement)* therapy •**thérapie** *nf* therapy
thermal, -e, -aux, -ales [tɛrmal, -o] *adj* station thermale spa; eaux thermales hot *or* thermal springs
thermique [tɛrmik] *adj (énergie, unité)* thermal
thermomètre [tɛrmɔmɛtr] *nm* thermometer
thermonucléaire [tɛrmɔnykleɛr] *adj* thermonuclear
Thermos® [tɛrmɔs] *nm ou f* Thermos® (*Br* flask *or Am* bottle)
thermostat [tɛrmɔsta] *nm* thermostat
thèse [tɛz] *nf (proposition, ouvrage)* thesis
thon [tɔ̃] *nm* tuna (fish)
thorax [tɔraks] *nm Anat* thorax
thym [tɛ̃] *nm (plante, aromate)* thyme
thyroïde [tirɔid] *adj & nf Anat* thyroid
Tibet [tibɛ] *nm* le T. Tibet
tibia [tibja] *nm* shinbone, tibia
tic [tik] *nm (contraction)* twitch, tic; *Fig (manie)* mannerism
ticket [tikɛ] *nm* ticket; **t. de quai** *(de gare)* platform ticket; **t. modérateur** = portion of the cost of medical treatment paid by the patient
tic-tac [tiktak] *exclam & nm inv* tick-tock
tiède [tjɛd] *adj* lukewarm, tepid; *(vent,*

climat) mild; *(accueil, partisan)* half-hearted •**tiédeur** *nf* tepidness; *(de vent)* mildness; *(d'accueil)* half-heartedness •**tiédir** *vti (refroidir)* to cool down; *(réchauffer)* to warm up
tien, tienne [tjɛ̃, tjɛn] 1 *pron possessif* le t., la tienne, les tien(ne)s yours; les deux tiens your two
2 *nmpl* les tiens *(ta famille)* your family
tiens, tient [tjɛ̃] *voir* tenir
tiercé [tjɛrse] *nm (pari)* place betting *(on the horses);* jouer/gagner au t. = to bet/win on the horses
tiers, tierce [tjɛr, tjɛrs] 1 *adj* third
2 *nm (fraction)* third; *(personne)* third party; t. provisionnel interim tax payment *(one third of previous year's tax)* •**Tiers-Monde** *nm* le T. the Third World
tifs [tif] *nmpl Fam* hair
tige [tiʒ] *nf (de plante)* stem, stalk; *(barre)* rod
tignasse [tiɲas] *nf Fam* mop (of hair)
tigre [tigr] *nm* tiger •**tigresse** *nf* tigress
tigré, -ée [tigre] *adj (rayé)* striped
tilleul [tijœl] *nm (arbre)* lime tree; *(infusion)* lime blossom tea
timbale [tɛ̃bal] *nf* (a) *(gobelet)* (metal) tumbler; *Fam* **décrocher la t.** to hit the jackpot (b) *(instrument)* kettledrum
timbre [tɛ̃br] *nm* (a) *(vignette)* stamp; *(pour traitement médicale)* patch (b) *(sonnette)* bell (c) *(d'instrument, de voix)* tone (quality) •**timbré, -ée** *adj (lettre)* stamped; *Fam (fou)* crazy •**timbre-poste** (*pl* **timbres-poste**) *nm* (postage) stamp •**timbrer** *vt (lettre)* to put a stamp on; *(document)* to stamp
timide [timid] *adj (gêné)* shy; *(protestations)* timid •**timidement** *adv* shyly; *(protester)* timidly •**timidité** *nf* shyness
timoré, -ée [timɔre] *adj* timorous, fearful
tintamarre [tɛ̃tamar] *nm Fam* din, racket
tinter [tɛ̃te] *vi (cloche)* to tinkle; *(clefs, monnaie)* to jingle; *(verres)* to chink •**tintement** *nm (de cloche)* tinkling; *(de clefs)* jingling; *(de verres)* chinking
tique [tik] *nf* tick
tiquer [tike] *vi Fam (personne)* to wince
tir [tir] *nm (sport)* shooting; *(action)* firing, shooting; *Football* shot; t. (forain) shooting *or* rifle range; **t. à l'arc** archery
tirade [tirad] *nf (au théâtre) & Fig Br* monologue, *Am* monolog
tirage [tiraʒ] *nm* (a) *(de journal)* circulation; *(de livre)* print run; *Typ Phot (impression)* printing (b) *(de loterie)* draw; t. au sort drawing lots (c) *(de cheminée)* Br draught, *Am* draft

tirailler [tiʀaje] **1** *vt* to pull at; *Fig* **tiraillé entre** *(possibilités)* torn between

2 *vi* **j'ai la peau qui tiraille** my skin feels tight • **tiraillement** *nm (crampe)* cramp

tirant [tiʀɑ̃] *nm* **t. d'eau** *(de bateau) Br* draught, *Am* draft

tire [tiʀ] *nf* (**a**) **vol à la t.** pickpocketing (**b**) *Fam (voiture)* car

tirelire [tiʀliʀ] *nf Br* moneybox, *Am* coin bank

tirer [tiʀe] **1** *vt* to pull; *(langue)* to stick out; *(trait, rideaux, conclusion)* to draw; *(balle)* to fire; *(gibier)* to shoot; *(journal, épreuves de livre, photo)* to print; **t. qch de qch** to pull sth out of sth; *(nom, origine)* to derive sth from sth; *(produit)* to extract sth from sth; **t. qn de qch** *(danger, lit)* to get sb out of sth; *Fig* **je vous tire mon chapeau** I take my hat off to you

2 *vi* to pull (**sur** on, at); *(faire feu)* to shoot, to fire (**sur** at); *Football* to shoot; *(cheminée)* to draw; **t. au sort** to draw lots; **t. à sa fin** to draw to a close; **t. sur le vert** to verge on green; *Fig* **t. à boulets rouges sur qn** to go for sb hammer and tongs

3 se tirer *vpr Fam (partir)* to make tracks; **se t. de qch** *(travail, problème)* to cope with sth; *(danger, situation)* to get out of sth; **se t. d'affaire** to get out of trouble; *Fam* **s'en t.** *(de malade)* to pull through; *(financièrement)* to make it • **tiré, -ée** *adj (traits, visage)* drawn; *Fig* **t. par les cheveux** far-fetched • **tire-au-flanc** *nm inv Fam (paresseux)* shirker • **tire-bouchon** *(pl* **tire-bouchons**) *nm* corkscrew • **tire-d'aile** *adv* **à t.** swiftly • **tire-fesses** *nm inv Fam*T-bar

tiret [tiʀɛ] *nm (trait)* dash

tireur [tiʀœʀ] *nm* gunman; **un bon t.** a good shot; **t. d'élite** marksman; **t. isolé** sniper • **tireuse** *nf* **t. de cartes** fortune-teller

tiroir [tiʀwaʀ] *nm (de commode)* drawer • **tiroir-caisse** *(pl* **tiroirs-caisses**) *nm* till, cash register

tisane [tizan] *nf* herbal tea

tison [tizɔ̃] *nm* (fire)brand • **tisonner** *vt* to poke • **tisonnier** *nm* poker

tisser [tise] *vt* to weave • **tissage** *nm (action)* weaving • **tisserand, -ande** *nmf* weaver

tissu [tisy] *nm* material, cloth; *Biol* tissue; **du t.-éponge** *Br* (terry) towelling, *Am* toweling; *Fig* **un t. de mensonges** a web of lies; **le t. social** the social fabric

titre [titʀ] *nm (nom, qualité)* title; *Fin* security; *(diplôme)* qualification; **(gros) t.** *(de journal)* headline; **à quel t.?** *(pour quelle raison)* on what grounds?; **à ce t.** *(en cette qualité)* as such; *(pour cette raison)* therefore; **à aucun t.** on no account; **au même t.** in the same way (**que** as); **à t. d'exemple** as an example; **à t. exceptionnel** exceptionally; **à t. privé** in a private capacity; **à t. provisoire** temporarily; **à t. indicatif** for general information; **à juste t.** rightly; **t. de propriété** title deed; **t. de transport** ticket; **t. de noblesse** title (of nobility)

titrer [titʀe] *vt (film)* to title; *(journal)* to run as a headline • **titré, -ée** *adj (personne)* titled

tituber [titybe] *vi* to stagger

titulaire [titylɛʀ] **1** *adj (enseignant)* tenured; **être t. de** *(permis)* to be the holder of; *(poste)* to hold

2 *nmf (de permis, de poste)* holder (**de** of) • **titularisation** *nf* granting of tenure • **titulariser** *vt (fonctionnaire)* to give tenure to

toast [tost] *nm (pain grillé)* piece *or* slice of toast; *(allocution)* toast; **porter un t. à** to drink (a toast) to

toboggan [tɔbɔgɑ̃] *nm (d'enfant)* slide; *Can (traîneau)* toboggan; *(voie de circulation) Br* flyover, *Am* overpass

toc [tɔk] **1** *exclam* **t. t.!** knock knock!

2 *nm* **du t.** *(camelote)* trash; **bijou en t.** imitation jewel

tocard [tɔkaʀ] *nm Fam* dead loss

tocsin [tɔksɛ̃] *nm* alarm bell

tohu-bohu [tɔybɔy] *nm (bruit)* hubbub; *(confusion)* confusion

toi [twa] *pron personnel* (**a**) *(après une préposition)* you; **avec t.** with you (**b**) *(sujet)* you; **t., tu peux** you may; **c'est t. qui** it's you who (**c**) *(réfléchi)* **assieds-t.** sit (yourself) down; **dépêche-t.** hurry up • **toi-même** *pron* yourself

toile [twal] *nf* (**a**) *(étoffe)* cloth; *(à voile, sac)* canvas; *(à draps)* linen; **une t.** a piece of cloth *or* canvas; *Théâtre & Fig* **t. de fond** backdrop; **t. de jute** hessian; **t. cirée** oil cloth (**b**) *(tableau)* painting, canvas (**c**) **t. d'araignée** (spider's) web, cobweb (**d**) *Fam* **se faire une t.** to go and see a movie

toilette [twalɛt] *nf (action)* wash(ing); *(vêtements)* clothes, outfit; **faire sa t.** to wash (and dress); **les toilettes** *(W-C) Br* the toilet(s), *Am* the men's/ladies' room

toiser [twaze] *vt* to eye scornfully

toison [twazɔ̃] *nf (de mouton)* fleece

toit [twa] *nm* roof; **t. ouvrant** sunroof • **toiture** *nf* roof(ing)

tôle [tol] *nf* sheet metal; **une t.** a metal sheet; **t. ondulée** corrugated iron

tolérer [tɔlere] *vt* *(permettre)* to tolerate; *(à la douane)* to allow • **tolérable** *adj* tolerable • **tolérance** *nf* tolerance; *(à la douane)* allowance • **tolérant, -ante** *adj* tolerant (**à l'égard de** of)

tollé [tɔle] *nm* outcry

tomate [tɔmat] *nf* tomato

tombe [tɔ̃b] *nf* grave; *(avec monument)* tomb • **tombale** *adj f* **pierre t.** gravestone, tombstone • **tombeau, -x** *nm* tomb

tomber [tɔ̃be] *(aux* **être***) vi* to fall; *(température)* to drop, to fall; *(vent)* to drop (off); *(robe)* to hang down; **t. malade** to fall ill; **t. par terre** to fall (down); **faire t.** *(personne)* to knock over; *(gouvernement, prix)* to bring down; **laisser t.** *(objet)* to drop; *Fig* **laisser t. qn** to let sb down; **se laisser t. dans un fauteuil** to drop into an armchair; *Fig* **tu tombes bien/mal** you've come at the right/wrong time; **t. de sommeil** *ou* **de fatigue** to be ready to drop; **t. un lundi** to fall on a Monday; **t. sur qch** *(trouver)* to come across sth; *Fam* **t. de haut** to be bitterly disappointed • **tombée** *nf* **la t. de la nuit** nightfall

tombereau, -x [tɔ̃bro] *nm (charrette)* tip-cart

tombola [tɔ̃bɔla] *nf* raffle

tome [tɔm] *nm (livre)* volume

tomme [tɔm] *nf* = cheese made in Savoie

ton¹, ta, tes [tɔ̃, ta, te]

> ta becomes **ton** [tɔ̃n] before a vowel or mute h.

adj possessif your; **t. père** your father; **ta mère** your mother; **t. ami(e)** your friend

ton² [tɔ̃] *nm (de voix)* tone; *(de couleur)* shade, tone; *Mus (gamme)* key; *(hauteur de son) & Ling* pitch; **de bon t.** *(goût)* in good taste; *Fig* **donner le t.** to set the tone • **tonalité** *nf (timbre, impression)* tone; *(de téléphone) Br* dialling tone, *Am* dial tone

tondre [tɔ̃dr] *vt (mouton)* to shear; *(gazon)* to mow; *Fam* **t. qn** *(escroquer)* to fleece sb • **tondeuse** *nf* shears; *(à cheveux)* clippers; **t. (à gazon)** (lawn)mower

tonifier [tɔnifje] *vt (muscles, peau)* to tone up; *(personne)* to invigorate • **tonifiant, -ante** *adj (activité, climat)* invigorating

tonique [tɔnik] **1** *adj (froid, effet)* tonic, invigorating; *Ling (accent)* tonic
2 *nm (médicament)* tonic; *(cosmétique)* toner

tonitruant, -ante [tɔnitryɑ̃, -ɑ̃t] *adj Fam (voix)* booming

tonnage [tɔnaʒ] *nm (de navire)* tonnage

tonne [tɔn] *nf (poids)* metric ton, tonne; *Fam* **des tonnes de** *(beaucoup)* tons of

tonneau, -x [tɔno] *nm* **(a)** *(récipient)* barrel, cask **(b)** *(acrobatie)* roll; **faire un t.** to roll over **(c)** *Fam* **du même t.** of the same kind

tonnelle [tɔnɛl] *nf* arbour, bower

tonner [tɔne] **1** *vi (canons)* to thunder; *Fig (crier)* to thunder, to rage (**contre** against)
2 *v impersonnel* **il tonne** it's thundering • **tonnerre** *nm* thunder; *Fam* **du t.** *(excellent)* terrific

tonte [tɔ̃t] *nf (de moutons)* shearing; *(de gazon)* mowing

tonton [tɔ̃tɔ̃] *nm Fam* uncle

tonus [tɔnys] *nm (énergie)* energy, vitality

top [tɔp] *nm (signal sonore)* beep

topaze [tɔpaz] *nf* topaz

topinambour [tɔpinɑ̃bur] *nm* Jerusalem artichoke

topo [tɔpo] *nm Fam (exposé)* rundown

topographie [tɔpɔgrafi] *nf* topography

toquade [tɔkad] *nf Fam (pour un objet)* craze (**pour** for); *(pour une personne)* crush (**pour** with)

toque [tɔk] *nf (de fourrure)* fur hat; *(de jockey)* cap; *(de cuisinier)* hat

toquer [tɔke] **se toquer** *vpr Fam* **se t. de qn** to go crazy over sb • **toqué, -ée** *adj Fam (fou)* crazy

torche [tɔrʃ] *nf (flamme)* torch; **t. électrique** *Br* torch, *Am* flashlight

torcher [tɔrʃe] *vt Fam (enfant)* to wipe; *(travail)* to botch

torchon [tɔrʃɔ̃] *nm (à vaisselle) Br* tea towel, *Am* dish towel

tordre [tɔrdr] **1** *vt* to twist; *(linge, cou)* to wring; *(barre)* to bend
2 se tordre *vpr* to twist; *(barre)* to bend; **se t. de douleur** to be doubled up with pain; **se t. (de rire)** to split one's sides (laughing); **se t. la cheville** to twist *or* sprain one's ankle • **tordant, -ante** *adj Fam (drôle)* hilarious • **tordu, -ue** *adj* twisted; *(esprit)* warped

tornade [tɔrnad] *nf* tornado

torpeur [tɔrpœr] *nf* torpor

torpille [tɔrpij] *nf* torpedo • **torpiller** *vt (navire, projet)* to torpedo • **torpilleur** *nm* torpedo boat

torréfier [tɔrefje] *vt (café)* to roast • **torréfaction** *nf* roasting

torrent [tɔrɑ̃] *nm* torrent; *Fig* **un t. de larmes** a flood of tears; **il pleut à torrents** it's pouring (down) • **torrentiel, -ielle** *adj (pluie)* torrential

torride [tɔrid] *adj (chaleur)* torrid

torsade [tɔrsad] *nf (de cheveux)* twist, coil • **torsader** *vt* to twist

torse [tɔrs] *nm Anat* chest; *(statue)* torso; **t. nu** stripped to the waist

torsion [tɔrsjɔ̃] *nf* twisting

tort [tɔr] *nm (dommage)* wrong; *(défaut)* fault; **avoir t.** to be wrong (**de faire** to do, in doing); **tu as t. de fumer!** you shouldn't smoke!; **être dans son t.** *ou* **en t.** to be in the wrong; **donner t. à qn** *(accuser)* to blame sb; *(faits)* to prove sb wrong; **faire du t. à qn** to harm sb; **à t.** wrongly; **à t. ou à raison** rightly or wrongly; **parler à t. et à travers** to talk nonsense

torticolis [tɔrtikɔli] *nm* **avoir le t.** to have a stiff neck

tortillard [tɔrtijar] *nm Fam* local train

tortiller [tɔrtije] **1** *vt* to twist; *(moustache)* to twirl

2 *vi Fam* **il n'y a pas à t.** there's no two ways about it

3 se tortiller *vpr (ver, personne)* to wriggle

tortionnaire [tɔrsjɔnɛr] *nm* torturer

tortue [tɔrty] *nf Br* tortoise, *Am* turtle; *(de mer)* turtle; *Fam (personne) Br* slowcoach, *Am* slowpoke

tortueux, -ueuse [tɔrtɥø, -ɥøz] *adj* tortuous

torture [tɔrtyr] *nf* torture • **torturer** *vt* to torture; *Fam* **se t. les méninges** to rack one's brains

tôt [to] *adv* early; **au plus t.** at the earliest; **le plus t. possible** as soon as possible; **t. ou tard** sooner or later; **je n'étais pas plus t. sorti que** no sooner had I gone out than

total, -e, -aux, -ales [tɔtal, -o] *adj & nm* total; **au t.** all in all, in total; *(somme toute)* all in all • **totalement** *adv* totally, completely • **totaliser** *vt* to total • **totalité** *nf* entirety; **la t. de** all of; **en t.** *(détruit)* entirely; *(payé)* fully

totalitaire [tɔtalitɛr] *adj (État, régime)* totalitarian

toubib [tubib] *nm Fam (médecin)* doctor

touche [tuʃ] *nf (de clavier)* key; *(de téléphone)* (push-)button; *(de peintre)* touch; *Football & Rugby* throw-in; *Pêche* bite; **téléphone à touches** push-button phone; **une t. de** *(un peu de)* a touch *or* hint of

toucher [tuʃe] **1** *nm (sens)* touch; **au t.** to the touch

2 *vt* to touch; *(paie)* to draw; *(chèque)* to cash; *(cible)* to hit; *(émouvoir)* to touch, to move; *(concerner)* to affect; **t. le fond (du désespoir)** to hit rock bottom

3 *vi* **t. à** to touch; *(sujet)* to touch on; *(but, fin)* to approach

4 se toucher *vpr (lignes, mains)* to touch • **touchant, -ante** *adj (émouvant)* moving,

touching • **touche-à-tout** *nmf inv (qui a plusieurs occupations)* dabbler

touffe [tuf] *nf (de cheveux, d'herbe)* tuft • **touffu, -ue** *adj (barbe, haie)* thick, bushy; *Fig (livre)* dense

touiller [tuje] *vt Fam (salade)* to toss

toujours [tuʒur] *adv (exprime la continuité, la répétition)* always; *(encore)* still; **pour t.** for ever; **essaie t.!** *(quand même)* try anyhow!; **t. est-il que...** [tuʒurzetilkə] the fact remains that...

toupet [tupɛ] *nm Fam (audace)* nerve, *Br* cheek

toupie [tupi] *nf* (spinning) top

tour¹ [tur] *nf (bâtiment) & Ordinat* tower; *(immeuble)* tower block, high-rise; *Échecs* castle, rook

tour² [tur] *nm* (**a**) *(mouvement, ordre, tournure)* turn; *(de magie)* trick; *(excursion)* trip, outing; *(à pied)* stroll, walk; *(en voiture)* drive; **t. (de piste)** *(de course)* lap; **faire un t. d'honneur** *(sportif)* to do a lap of honour; **de dix mètres de t.** ten metres round; **faire le t. de** to go round; *(question, situation)* to review; **faire le t. du monde** to go round the world; **faire un t.** *(à pied)* to go for a stroll *or* walk; *(en voiture)* to go for a drive; **jouer** *ou* **faire un t. à qn** to play a trick on sb; *Fam* **avoir plus d'un t. dans son sac** to have more than one trick up one's sleeve; **c'est mon t.** it's my turn; **à qui le tour?** whose turn (is it)?; **à son t.** in (one's) turn; **à t. de rôle** in turn; **t. à t.** in turn, by turns; **t. de cartes** card trick; **t. d'horizon** survey; **t. de poitrine** chest size

(**b**) *Tech* lathe; *(de potier)* wheel

tourbe [turb] *nf* peat • **tourbière** *nf* peat bog

tourbillon [turbijɔ̃] *nm (de vent)* whirlwind; *(d'eau)* whirlpool; *(de sable)* swirl; *Fig (tournoiement)* whirl • **tourbillonner** *vi* to whirl

tourelle [turɛl] *nf* turret

tourisme [turism] *nm* tourism; **faire du t.** to do some touring; **agence de t.** tourist agency • **touriste** *nmf* tourist • **touristique** *adj* **guide/menu t.** tourist guide/ menu; **route t., circuit t.** scenic route

tourment [turmɑ̃] *nm* torment • **tourmenté, -ée** *adj (mer, vie)* turbulent; *(expression, visage)* anguished; *(paysage)* wild • **tourmenter 1** *vt* to torment **2 se tourmenter** *vpr* to worry

tourmente [turmɑ̃t] *nf (troubles)* turmoil

tournage [turnaʒ] *nm (de film)* shooting, filming

tourne-disque [turnədisk] *(pl* **tournedisques**) *nm* record player

tournedos [turnədo] *nm* tournedos

tournée [turne] *nf (de facteur, de boissons)* round; *(spectacle)* tour; **faire sa t.** to do one's rounds; **faire la t. de** *(magasins, musées)* to go to, *Br* to go round

tournemain [turnəmɛ̃] **en un tournemain** *adv Littéraire* in an instant

tourner [turne] **1** *vt* to turn; *(film)* to shoot, to make; *(difficulté)* to get round; **t. qn/qch en ridicule** to ridicule sb/sth; **t. le dos à qn** to turn one's back on sb

2 *vi* to turn; *(tête, toupie)* to spin; *(Terre)* to revolve, to turn; *(moteur, usine)* to run; *(lait)* to go off; **t. autour de** *(objet)* to go round; *(maison, personne)* to hang around; *(question)* to centre on; **t. bien/mal** *(évoluer)* to turn out well/badly; **t. au froid** *(temps)* to turn cold; **t. à l'aigre** *(ton, conversation)* to turn nasty; *Fig* **t. autour du pot** to beat around the bush; *Fam* **t. de l'œil** to faint; *Fam* **faire t. qn en bourrique** to drive sb crazy; **ça me fait t. la tête** *(vin)* it goes to my head; *(manège)* it makes my head spin; **silence! on tourne** quiet we're filming *or* shooting!

3 se tourner *vpr* to turn (**vers** to, towards) ● **tournant, -ante 1** *adj* **pont t.** swing bridge **2** *nm (de route)* bend; *Fig (moment)* turning point (**de** in)

tournesol [turnəsɔl] *nm* sunflower

tourneur [turnœr] *nm (ouvrier)* turner

tournevis [turnəvis] *nm* screwdriver

tourniquet [turnikɛ] *nm (barrière)* turnstile; *(pour arroser)* sprinkler

tournis [turni] *nm Fam* **avoir le t.** to feel giddy; **donner le t. à qn** to make sb giddy

tournoi [turnwa] *nm (de tennis)* & *Hist* tournament

tournoyer [turnwaje] *vi* to swirl (round)

tournure [turnyr] *nf (expression)* turn of phrase; **t. d'esprit** way of thinking; **t. des événements** turn of events; **prendre t.** to take shape

tourte [turt] *nf* pie

tourterelle [turtərɛl] *nf* turtledove

Toussaint [tusɛ̃] *nf* **la T.** All Saints' Day

tousser [tuse] *vi* to cough

tout, toute, tous, toutes [tu, tut, tu, tut] **1** *adj* all; **tous les livres** all the books; **t. l'argent/le temps/le village** all the money/time/village; **toute la nuit** all night, the whole (of the) night; **tous (les) deux** both; **tous (les) trois** all three; **t. un problème** quite a problem

2 *adj indéfini (chaque)* every, each; *(n'importe quel)* any; **tous les ans/jours** every *or* each year/day; **tous les deux mois** every two months, every second

month; **tous les cinq mètres** every five metres; **à toute heure** at any time; **t. homme** [tutɔm] every *ou* any man

3 *pron pl* **tous** [tus] all; **ils sont tous là, tous sont là** they're all there

4 *pron m sing* **tout** everything; **dépenser t.** to spend everything, to spend it all; **t. ce qui est là** everything that's here; **t. ce que je sais** everything that *or* all that I know; **en t.** *(au total)* in all

5 *adv (tout à fait)* quite; *(très)* very; **t. simplement** quite simply; **t. petit** very small; **t. neuf** brand new; **t. seul** all alone; **t. droit** straight ahead; **t. autour** all around, right round; **t. au début** right at the beginning; **le t. premier** the very first; **t. au plus/moins** at the very most/least; **t. en chantant** while singing; **t. rusé qu'il est** *ou* **soit** however sly he may be; **t. à coup** suddenly, all of a sudden; **t. à fait** completely, quite; **t. de même** all the same; **t. de même!** *(indignation)* really!; **t. de suite** at once

6 *nm* **le t.** everything, the lot; **un t.** a whole; **le t. est que...** *(l'important)* the main thing is that...; **pas du t.** not at all; **rien du t.** nothing at all; **du t. au t.** *(changer)* entirely, completely ● **tout-à-l'égout** *nm inv* mains drainage ● **tout-puissant, toute-puissante** *(mpl* **tout-puissants**, *fpl* **toutes-puissantes)** *adj* all-powerful ● **tout-terrain 1** *(pl* **tout-terrains)** *adj* **véhicule t.** off-road *or* all terrain vehicle; **vélo t.** mountain bike **2** *nm* **faire du t.** to do off-road racing

toutefois [tutfwa] *adv* nevertheless, however

toutou [tutu] *nm Fam (chien)* doggie

toux [tu] *nf* cough

toxicomane [tɔksikɔman] *nmf* drug addict ● **toxicomanie** *nf* drug addiction

toxine [tɔksin] *nf* toxin ● **toxique** *adj* poisonous, toxic

TP [tepe] *(abrév* **travaux pratiques)** *nmpl* practical work

trac [trak] *nm* **le t.** *(peur)* the jitters; *(de candidat)* exam nerves; *(d'acteur)* stage fright; **avoir le t.** to be nervous

tracas [traka] *nm* worry ● **tracasser** *vt*, **se tracasser** *vpr* to worry ● **tracasseries** *nfpl* annoyances

trace [tras] *nf (quantité, tache, vestige)* trace; *(marque)* mark; *(de fugitif)* trail; **traces** *(de bête, de pneus)* tracks; **traces de pas** footprints; **disparaître sans laisser de traces** to disappear without trace; *Fig* **suivre** *ou* **marcher sur les traces de qn** to follow in sb's footsteps

tracer [trase] *vt (dessiner)* to draw; *(écrire)* to trace; **t. une route** to mark out a route; *(frayer)* to open up a route •**tracé** *nm (plan)* layout; *(ligne)* line

trachée [traʃe] *nf Anat* windpipe

tract [trakt] *nm* leaflet

tractations [traktasjɔ̃] *nfpl* dealings

tracter [trakte] *vt* to tow •**tracteur** *nm* tractor

traction [traksjɔ̃] *nf Tech* traction; *Gymnastique* pull-up; **t. arrière/avant** *(voiture)* rear-/front-wheel drive

tradition [tradisjɔ̃] *nf* tradition •**traditionnel, -elle** *adj* traditional

traduire* [tradɥir] *vt* to translate (**de** from, **en** into); *Fig (exprimer)* to express; **t. qn en justice** to bring sb before the courts •**traducteur, -trice** *nmf* translator •**traduction** *nf* translation •**traduisible** *adj* translatable

trafic [trafik] *nm (automobile, ferroviaire)* traffic; *(de marchandises)* traffic, trade; **faire le t. de** to traffic in, trade in •**trafiquant, -ante** *nmf* trafficker, dealer; **t. d'armes/de drogue** arms/drug trafficker or dealer •**trafiquer** *vt Fam (produit)* to tamper with

tragédie [traʒedi] *nf (pièce de théâtre, événement)* tragedy •**tragique** *adj* tragic; **prendre qch au t.** *(remarque)* to take sth too much to heart •**tragiquement** *adv* tragically

trahir [trair] **1** *vt* to betray; *(secret)* to give away, to betray; *(sujet: forces)* to fail
2 se trahir *vpr* to give oneself away •**trahison** *nf* betrayal; *(crime)* treason; **haute t.** high treason

train [trɛ̃] *nm* (**a**) *(de voyageurs, de marchandises)* train; **t. à grande vitesse** high-speed train; **t. corail** express train; **t. couchettes** sleeper; **t. autocouchettes** car-sleeper; *Fig* **prendre le t. en marche** to climb on the bandwaggon (**b**) **en t.** *(en forme)* on form; **se mettre en t.** to get (oneself) into shape; **être en t. de faire qch** to be (busy) doing sth; **mettre qch en t.** to get sth going, to start sth off (**c**) *(allure)* pace; **t. de vie** life style (**d**) *(de pneus)* set; *(de péniches, de véhicules)* string (**e**) **t. d'atterrissage** *(d'avion)* undercarriage •**train-train** *nm inv Fam* **le t. quotidien** the daily grind

traînailler [trɛnaje] *vi Fam* = **traînasser** •**traînard, -arde** *nmf Br* slowcoach, *Am* slowpoke •**traînasser** *vi Fam* to dawdle; *(errer)* to hang around

traîne [trɛn] *nf (de robe)* train; *Fam* **à la t.** *(en arrière)* lagging behind

traîneau, -x [trɛno] *nm* sleigh, *Br* sledge, *Am* sled

traînée [trɛne] *nf (de peinture, dans le ciel)* streak; *Fam (prostituée)* tart; *Fig* **se répandre comme une t. de poudre** to spread like wildfire

traîner [trɛne] **1** *vt* to drag; *(wagon)* to pull; **faire t. qch en longueur** to drag sth out
2 *vi (jouets, papiers)* to lie around; *(s'attarder)* to lag behind, to dawdle; *(errer)* to hang around; *(subsister)* to linger on; **t. par terre** *(robe)* to trail (on the ground); **t. en longueur** to drag on
3 se traîner *vpr (avancer)* to drag oneself (along); *(par terre)* to crawl; *(durer)* to drag on •**traînant, -ante** *adj (voix)* drawling

traire* [trɛr] *vt (vache)* to milk

trait [trɛ] *nm* line; *(en dessinant)* stroke; *(caractéristique)* feature, trait; **traits** *(du visage)* features; **d'un t.** *(boire)* in one gulp, in one go; **avoir t. à qch** to relate to sth; **t. de génie/d'esprit** flash of genius/wit; **t. d'union** hyphen

traite [trɛt] *nf (de vache)* milking; *(lettre de change)* bill, draft; **d'une (seule) t.** *(sans interruption)* in one go; **t. des Noirs** slave trade; **t. des Blanches** white slave trade

traité [trete] *nm (accord)* treaty; *(ouvrage)* treatise (**sur** on); **t. de paix** peace treaty

traiter [trete] **1** *vt (se comporter envers, soigner)* to treat; *(problème, sujet)* to deal with; *(marché)* to negotiate; *(matériau, produit)* to treat, to process; **t. qn de lâche** to call sb a coward; **t. qn de tous le noms** to call sb all the names under the sun
2 *vi* to negotiate, to deal (**avec** with); **t. de** *(sujet)* to deal with •**traitement** [trɛtmã] *nm (de personne, de maladie)* treatment; *(de matériau)* processing; *(gains)* salary; **t. de données/de texte** data/word processing; **machine à t. de texte** word processor

traiteur [trɛtœr] *nm (fournisseur)* caterer; **chez le t.** at the delicatessen

traître [trɛtr] **1** *nm* traitor; **en t.** treacherously
2 *adj (dangereux)* treacherous; **être t. à une cause** to be a traitor to a cause •**traîtrise** *nf* treachery

trajectoire [traʒɛktwar] *nf* path, trajectory

trajet [traʒɛ] *nm* journey; *(distance)* distance; *(itinéraire)* route

trame [tram] *nf (de récit)* framework; *(de tissu)* weft; **usé jusqu'à la t.** threadbare

tramer [trame] **1** vt (évasion) to plot; (complot) to hatch ˙ **2 se tramer** vpr **il se trame quelque chose** something's afoot

trampoline [trãpɔlin] nm trampoline

tramway [tramwɛ] nm Br tram, Am streetcar

tranche [trãʃ] nf (morceau) slice; (bord) edge; (partie) portion; (de salaire, d'impôts) bracket; **t. d'âge** age bracket

tranchée [trãʃe] nf trench

trancher [trãʃe] **1** vt to cut; (difficulté, question) to settle **2** vi (décider) to decide; (contraster) to contrast (**sur** with) • **tranchant, -ante 1** adj (couteau) sharp; (ton) curt **2** nm (cutting) edge; Fig **à double t.** double-edged • **tranché, -ée** adj (couleurs) distinct; (opinion) clear-cut

tranquille [trãkil] adj quiet; (mer) calm, still; (esprit) easy; Fam (certain) confident; **avoir la conscience t.** to have a clear conscience; **je suis t.** (rassuré) my mind is at rest; **soyez t.** don't worry; **laisser qch/ qn t.** to leave sth/sb alone • **tranquillement** adv calmly

tranquilliser [trãkilize] vt to reassure; **tranquillisez-vous** set your mind at rest • **tranquillisant** nm tranquillizer

tranquillité [trãkilite] nf (peace and) quiet; (d'esprit) peace of mind

transaction [trãzaksjõ] nf (opération) transaction; Jur compromise

transatlantique [trãzatlãtik] **1** adj transatlantic **2** nm (paquebot) transatlantic liner; (chaise) deckchair • **transat** [trãzat] nm (chaise) deckchair

transcender [trãsãde] vt to transcend • **transcendant, -ante** adj transcendent

transcrire* [trãskrir] vt to transcribe • **transcription** nf transcription; (document) transcript

transe [trãs] nf **en t.** (mystique) in a trance; (excité) very excited; **entrer en t.** to go into a trance

transférer [trãsfere] vt to transfer (**à** to) • **transfert** nm transfer

transfigurer [trãsfigyre] vt to transfigure

transformer [trãsfɔrme] **1** vt to transform; (maison) & Rugby to convert; (matière première) to process; (robe) to alter; **t. qch en qch** to turn sth into sth **2 se transformer** vpr to change, to be transformed (**en** into) • **transformateur** nm Él transformer • **transformation** nf change, transformation; (de maison) alteration

transfuge [trãsfyʒ] nmf defector

transfusion [trãsfyzjõ] nf **t. (sanguine)** (blood) transfusion

transgresser [trãsgrese] vt (ordres) to disobey; (loi) to infringe • **transgression** nf (de loi) infringement; (d'ordres) disobeying

transi, -ie [trãzi] adj (personne) numb with cold; **t. de peur** Br paralysed or Am paralyzed with fear

transiger [trãziʒe] vi to compromise

transistor [trãzistɔr] nm transistor

transit [trãzit] nm transit; **en t.** in transit • **transiter 1** vt (marchandises) to transit **2** vi to pass in transit

transitif, -ive [trãzitif, -iv] adj & nm Grammaire transitive

transition [trãzisjõ] nf transition • **transitoire** adj (qui passe) transient; (provisoire) transitional

translucide [trãslysid] adj translucent

transmettre* [trãsmɛtr] **1** vt (message, héritage) to pass on (**à** to); Radio & TV (informations) to transmit; (émission) to broadcast **2 se transmettre** vpr (maladie, tradition) to be passed on • **transmetteur** nm (appareil) transmitter • **transmission** nf transmission

transparaître* [trãsparɛtr] vi to show (through)

transparent, -ente [trãsparã, -ãt] adj clear, transparent • **transparence** nf transparency; **voir qch par t.** to see sth showing through

transpercer [trãspɛrse] vt to pierce

transpirer [trãspire] vi (suer) to sweat, to perspire; Fig (information) to leak out • **transpiration** nf perspiration

transplanter [trãsplãte] vt (organe, plante) to transplant • **transplantation** nf transplantation; (greffe d'organe) transplant

transport [trãspɔr] nm (action) transport, transportation (**de** of); **transports** (moyens) transport; **transports en commun** public transport; **frais de t.** transport costs; **moyen de t.** means of transport

transporter [trãspɔrte] vt (passagers, troupes, marchandises) to transport, to carry; **t. qn d'urgence à l'hôpital** to rush sb Br to hospital or Am to the hospital • **transporteur** nm **t. (routier)** Br haulier, Am trucker

transposer [trãspoze] vt to transpose • **transposition** nf transposition

transvaser [trãsvaze] vt to pour; (vin) to decant

transversal, -e, -aux, -ales [trãsversal, -o] *adj* **rue transversale** cross street
trapèze [trapɛz] *nm (de cirque)* trapeze • **trapéziste** *nmf* trapeze artist
trappe [trap] *nf (de plancher)* trap door
trappeur [trapœr] *nm* trapper
trapu, -ue [trapy] *adj (personne)* stocky, thickset; *Fam (problème)* tough
traquenard [traknar] *nm* trap
traquer [trake] *vt* to hunt (down)
traumatiser [tromatize] *vt* to traumatize • **traumatisant, -ante** *adj* traumatic • **traumatisme** *nm (choc)* trauma; **t. crânien** severe head injury
travail, -aux [travaj, -o] *nm (activité, lieu)* work; *(à effectuer)* job, task; *(emploi)* job; *(façonnage)* working (**de** of); *(ouvrage, étude)* work, publication; *Écon & Méd* labour; **travaux** work; *(dans la rue)* *Br* roadworks, *Am* roadwork; *(aménagement)* alterations; *Scol Univ* **travaux pratiques** practical work; *Scol* **travaux dirigés** tutorial; *Scol* **travaux manuels** handicrafts; **travaux ménagers** housework; **travaux forcés** hard labour; **travaux publics** public works
travailler [travaje] **1** *vi (personne)* to work (**à qch** on sth); *(bois)* to warp **2** *vt (discipline, rôle, style)* to work on; *(façonner)* to work; *Fam (inquiéter)* to worry; **t. la terre** to work the land • **travaillé, -ée** *adj (style)* elaborate • **travailleur, -euse 1** *adj* hard-working **2** *nmf* worker
travailliste [travajist] *Pol* **1** *adj* Labour **2** *nmf* member of the Labour party
travelling [travliŋ] *nm (mouvement de la caméra)* tracking; **faire un t.** to do a tracking shot
travers [travɛr] **1** *prép & adv* **à t.** through; **en t. (de)** across **2** *adv* **de t.** *(chapeau, nez)* crooked; *Fig* **aller de t.** to go wrong; **comprendre de t.** to misunderstand; **regarder qn de t.** *(avec suspicion)* to look askance at sb; **j'ai avalé de t.** it went down the wrong way **3** *nm (défaut)* failing
traverse [travɛrs] *nf (de voie ferrée) Br* sleeper, *Am* tie
traverser [travɛrse] *vt* to cross; *(foule, période, mur)* to go through • **traversée** *nf (voyage)* crossing
traversin [travɛrsɛ̃] *nm* bolster
travesti [travɛsti] *nm (acteur)* female impersonator; *(homosexuel)* transvestite
travestir [travɛstir] *vt* to disguise; *(pensée, vérité)* to misrepresent • **travestissement** *nm* disguise

trébucher [trebyʃe] *vi* to stumble (**sur** over); **faire t. qn** to trip sb (up)
trèfle [trɛfl] *nm (plante)* clover; *Cartes (couleur)* clubs
treille [trɛj] *nf* climbing vine
treillis [trɛji] *nm* (**a**) *(treillage)* lattice (work); *(en métal)* wire mesh (**b**) *(tenue militaire)* combat uniform
treize [trɛz] *adj & nm inv* thirteen • **treizième** *adj & nmf* thirteenth
tréma [trema] *nm* diaeresis
trembler [trãble] *vi* to shake, to tremble; *(de froid, peur)* to tremble (**de** with); *(flamme, lumière)* to flicker; *(voix)* to tremble, to quaver; *(avoir peur)* to be afraid (**que** + *subjunctive*) that); **t. pour qn** to fear for sb; **t. de tout son corps** to shake all over, to tremble violently • **tremblement** [-əmã] *nm (action, frisson)* shaking, trembling; **t. de terre** earthquake • **trembloter** *vi* to quiver
trémolos [tremɔlo] *nmpl* **avec des t. dans la voix** with a tremor in one's voice
trémousser [tremuse] **se trémousser** *vpr* to wriggle (about)
trempe [trãp] *nf* **un homme de sa t.** a man of his calibre; *Fam* **mettre une t. à qn** to give sb a thrashing
tremper [trãpe] **1** *vt* to soak, to drench; *(plonger)* to dip (**dans** in); *(acier)* to temper **2** *vi* to soak; **faire t. qch** to soak sth; *Péj* **t. dans** *(participer)* to be mixed up in **3** **se tremper** *vpr Fam (se baigner)* to take a dip • **trempette** *nf Fam* **faire t.** to take a dip
tremplin [trãplɛ̃] *nm Natation & Fig* springboard
trente [trãt] *adj & nm inv* thirty; **un t.-trois tours** *(disque)* an LP; **se mettre sur son t. et un** to get all dressed up; *Fam* **être au t. sixième dessous** to be (feeling) really down • **trentaine** *nf* **une t. (de)** *(nombre)* (about) thirty; **avoir la t.** *(âge)* to be about thirty • **trentième** *adj & nmf* thirtieth
trépas [trepa] *nm Littéraire* death; **passer de vie à t.** to pass away, to depart this life
trépidant, -ante [trepidã, -ãt] *adj (vie)* hectic
trépied [trepje] *nm* tripod
trépigner [trepiɲe] *vi* to stamp (one's feet)
très [trɛ] (**[trɛz]** *before vowel or mute h*) *adv* very; **t. aimé/critiqué** *(with past participle)* much *or* greatly liked/criticized
trésor [trezɔr] *nm* treasure; **le T. (public)** *(service)* public revenue (department);

(finances) public funds; **des trésors de patience** boundless patience • **trésorerie** [-rri] *nf (bureaux d'un club)* accounts department; *(gestion)* accounting; *(capitaux)* funds • **trésorier, -ière** *nmf* treasurer

tressaillir* [tresajir] *vi (frémir)* to shake, to quiver; *(de joie, de peur)* to tremble (**de** with); *(sursauter)* to jump, to start • **tressaillement** *nm (frémissement)* quiver; *(de joie)* trembling; *(de surprise)* start

tressauter [tresote] *vi (sursauter)* to start, to jump

tresse [trɛs] *nf (cordon)* braid; *(cheveux) Br* plait, *Am* braid • **tresser** [trese] *vt* to braid; *Br (cheveux)* to plait, *Am* to braid

tréteau, -x [treto] *nm* trestle

treuil [trœj] *nm* winch, windlass

trêve [trɛv] *nf (de combat)* truce; *Fig (répit)* respite; **la T. des confiseurs** the Christmas and New Year political truce; **t. de plaisanteries!** joking apart!

tri [tri] *nm* sorting (out); **faire le t. de** to sort (out); **(centre de) t.** *(des postes)* sorting office • **triage** *nm* sorting (out)

triangle [trijɑ̃gl] *nm* triangle • **triangulaire** *adj* triangular

tribord [tribɔr] *nm (de bateau, d'avion)* starboard

tribu [triby] *nf* tribe • **tribal, -e, -aux, -ales** *adj* tribal

tribulations [tribylasjɔ̃] *nfpl* tribulations

tribunal, -aux [tribynal, -o] *nm Jur* court; *(militaire)* tribunal

tribune [tribyn] *nf (de salle publique)* gallery; *(de stade)* (grand)stand; *(d'orateur)* rostrum; **t. libre** *(de journal)* open forum

tribut [triby] *nm* tribute (**à** to)

tributaire [tribytɛr] *adj Fig* **t. de** dependent on

tricher [triʃe] *vi* to cheat • **tricherie** *nf* cheating, trickery; **une t.** a piece of trickery • **tricheur, -euse** *nmf* cheat, *Am* cheater

tricolore [trikɔlɔr] *adj (cocarde)* red, white and blue; **le drapeau/l'équipe t.** the French flag/team

tricot [triko] *nm (activité, ouvrage)* knitting; *(chandail)* sweater, *Br* jumper; *(ouvrage)* piece of knitting; **en t.** knitted; **t. de corps** *Br* vest, *Am* undershirt • **tricoter** *vti* to knit

tricycle [trisikl] *nm* tricycle

trier [trije] *vt (lettres)* to sort; *(vêtements)* to sort through

trifouiller [trifuje] *vi Fam* to rummage around

trilingue [trilɛ̃g] *adj* trilingual

trilogie [trilɔʒi] *nf* trilogy

trimbal(l)er [trɛ̃bale] *Fam* **1** *vt* to cart around

2 se trimbal(l)er *vpr* to trail around

trimer [trime] *vi Fam* to slave (away)

trimestre [trimɛstr] *nm* quarter; *Scol* term; *Scol* **premier/second/troisième t.** *Br* autumn *or Am* fall/winter/summer term • **trimestriel, -ielle** *adj (revue)* quarterly; **bulletin t.** end-of-term *Br* report *or Am* report card

tringle [trɛ̃gl] *nf* rod; **t. à rideaux** curtain rod

Trinité [trinite] *nf* **la T.** *(fête)* Trinity; *(dogme)* the Trinity

trinquer [trɛ̃ke] *vi* to chink glasses; **t. à la santé de qn** to drink to sb's health

trio [trijo] *nm (groupe)* & *Mus* trio

triomphe [trijɔ̃f] *nm* triumph (**sur** over); **porter qn en t.** to carry sb shoulder-high • **triomphal, -e, -aux, -ales** *adj* triumphal • **triomphant, -ante** *adj* triumphant • **triompher** *vi* to triumph (**de** over); *(jubiler)* to be jubilant

tripes [trip] *nfpl Culin* tripe; *Fam* guts • **tripier, -ière** *nmf* tripe butcher

triple [tripl] **1** *adj* treble, triple; *Sport* **t. saut** triple jump

2 *nm* **le t.** three times as much (**de** as) • **tripler** *vti* to treble, to triple • **triplés, -ées** *nmfpl* triplets

tripot [tripo] *nm* gambling den

tripoter [tripote] *vt Fam Br* to fiddle with, *Am* to mess around with

trique [trik] *nf* cudgel

triste [trist] *adj* sad; *(sinistre)* dreary; *(lamentable)* unfortunate • **tristement** [-əmɑ̃] *adv* sadly • **tristesse** *nf* sadness; *(du temps)* dreariness

triturer [trityre] *vt (broyer)* to grind; *Fam (manipuler)* to fiddle with

trivial, -e, -iaux, -iales [trivjal, -jo] *adj* coarse, vulgar • **trivialité** *nf* coarseness, vulgarity

> ⚠ Il faut noter que l'adjectif anglais **trivial** est un faux ami. Il signifie **insignifiant**.

troc [trɔk] *nm* exchange; *(système économique)* barter

troène [trɔɛn] *nm* privet

trognon [trɔɲɔ̃] *nm (de fruit)* core; *(de chou)* stump

trois [trwa] *adj* & *nm inv* three; **les t. quarts (de)** three-quarters (of) • **troisième 1** *adj* & *nmf* third; **le t. âge** *(vieillesse)* the retirement years; **personne du t. âge** senior citizen **2** *nf Scol Br* **la t.** ≃ fourth year, *Am* ≃ eighth grade; *Aut* *(vitesse)* third gear ● **troisièmement** *adv* thirdly ● **trois-pièces** *nm inv (appartement)* three room(ed) *Br* flat *or Am* apartment

trombe [trɔb] *nf* **trombe(s) d'eau** *(pluie)* rainstorm, downpour; *Fig* **entrer en t.** to burst in like a whirlwind

trombone [trɔbɔn] *nm (instrument)* trombone; *(agrafe)* paper clip

trompe [trɔp] *nf (d'éléphant)* trunk; *(d'insecte)* proboscis; *(instrument de musique)* horn

tromper [trɔpe] **1** *vt (abuser)* to fool (**sur** about); *(être infidèle à)* to be unfaithful to; *(échapper à)* to elude

2 se tromper *vpr* to be mistaken; **se t. de route/de train** to take the wrong road/train; **se t. de date/de jour** to get the date/day wrong; **c'est à s'y t.** you can't tell the difference ● **trompe-l'œil** *nm inv* trompe-l'œil; **en t.** trompe-l'œil ● **tromperie** [-pri] *nf* deceit, deception ● **trompeur, -euse** *adj (apparences)* deceptive, misleading; *(personne)* deceitful

trompette [trɔpet] *nf* trumpet ● **trompettiste** *nmf* trumpet player

tronc [trɔ̃] *nm (d'arbre)* & *Anat* trunk; *(boîte)* collection box

tronçon [trɔsɔ̃] *nm* section ● **tronçonner** *vt* to cut into sections ● **tronçonneuse** *nf* chain saw

trône [tron] *nm* throne ● **trôner** *vi Fig (vase, personne)* to occupy the place of honour

tronquer [trɔke] *vt (mot, texte)* to shorten

trop [tro] *adv (avec adjectif, adverbe)* too; *(avec verbe)* too much; **t. dur/loin** too hard/far; **t. fatigué pour jouer** too tired to play; **boire/lire t.** to drink/read too much; **t. de sel** too much salt; **t. de gens** too many people; **du fromage en t.** too much cheese; **des œufs en t.** too many eggs; **un euro/verre en t.** one euro/glass too many; **t. souvent** too often; **t. peu** not enough; *Fig* **se sentir de t.** to feel in the way; *Fam* **en faire t.** to overdo it ● **trop-plein** *(pl* **trop-pleins***) nm (excédent)* overflow; *(dispositif)* overflow pipe

trophée [trɔfe] *nm* trophy

tropique [trɔpik] *nm* tropic; **les tropiques** the tropics; **sous les tropiques** in the tropics ● **tropical, -e, -aux, -ales** *adj* tropical

troquer [trɔke] *vt* to exchange (**contre** for)

trot [tro] *nm* trot; **aller au t.** to trot; *Fam* **au t.** *(sans traîner)* at the double ● **trotter**

[trɔte] *vi (cheval)* to trot; *Fig (personne)* to trot about

trotteuse [trɔtøz] *nf (de montre)* second hand ● **trotteur, -euse** *nmf (cheval)* trotter

trottiner [trɔtine] *vi (personne)* to trot along

trottinette [trɔtinet] *nf (jouet)* scooter; *Fam (voiture)* little car

trottoir [trɔtwar] *nm Br* pavement, *Am* sidewalk; **t. roulant** moving walkway

trou [tru] *nm* hole; *(d'aiguille)* eye; *Fam Péj (village)* dump, hole; *Fig (manque)* gap (**dans** in); **t. d'homme** *(ouverture)* manhole; **t. de (la) serrure** keyhole; *Fig* **t. de mémoire** memory lapse

trouble [trubl] **1** *adj (liquide)* cloudy; *(image)* blurred; *(affaire)* shady

2 *adv* **voir t.** to see things blurred

3 *nm Littéraire (émoi, émotion)* agitation; *(désarroi)* distress; *(désordre)* confusion; **troubles** *(de santé)* trouble; *(révolte)* disturbances, troubles

troubler [truble] **1** *vt* to disturb; *(vue)* to blur; *(liquide)* to make cloudy; *(esprit)* to unsettle; *(projet)* to upset; *(inquiéter)* to trouble

2 se troubler *vpr (liquide)* to become cloudy; *(candidat)* to become flustered ● **troublant, -ante** *adj (détail)* disturbing, disquieting ● **trouble-fête** *nmf inv* killjoy, spoilsport

trouer [true] *vt* to make a hole/holes in; *(silence, ténèbres)* to cut through ● **trouée** *nf* gap; *(de ciel)* patch

trouille [truj] *nf Fam* **avoir la t.** to be scared stiff ● **trouillard, -arde** *adj Fam (poltron)* chicken

troupe [trup] *nf (de soldats)* troop; *(groupe)* group; *(de théâtre)* company, troupe; **la t., les troupes** *(armée)* the troops

troupeau, -x [trupo] *nm (de vaches)* & *Fig Péj* herd; *(de moutons)* flock

trousse [trus] *nf (étui)* case, kit; *(d'écolier)* pencil case; **t. à outils** toolkit; **t. à pharmacie** first-aid kit; **t. de toilette** toilet bag

trousseau, -x [truso] *nm (de mariée)* trousseau; **t. de clefs** bunch of keys

trousses [trus] *nfpl Fig* **aux t. de qn** on sb's heels

trouvaille [truvaj] *nf (lucky)* find

trouver [truve] **1** *vt* to find; **aller/venir t. qn** to go/come and see sb; **je trouve que...** I think that...; **comment la trouvez-vous?** what do you think of her?

2 se trouver *vpr* to be; *(être situé)* to be situated; **se t. dans une situation difficile**

to find oneself in a difficult situation; **se t. mal** *(s'évanouir)* to faint; **se t. petit** to consider oneself small

3 *v impersonnel* **il se trouve que...** it happens that...

truand [tryɑ̃] *nm* crook

> ⚠ Il faut noter que le nom anglais **truant** est un faux ami. Il désigne un élève qui fait l'école buissonnière.

truander [tryɑ̃de] *vi Fam (tricher)* to cheat

truc [tryk] *nm Fam (chose)* thing; *(astuce)* trick; *(moyen)* way; **avoir/trouver le t.** to have/get the knack (**pour faire** of doing) • **trucage** *nm* = **truquage**

truchement [tryʃmɑ̃] *nm* **par le t. de qn** through (the intermediary of) sb

truculent, -ente [trykylɑ̃, -ɑ̃t] *adj (langage, personnage)* colourful

> ⚠ Il faut noter que l'adjectif anglais **truculent** est un faux ami. Il signifie **agressif**.

truelle [tryɛl] *nf* trowel

truffe [tryf] *nf (champignon)* truffle; *(de chien)* nose

truffer [tryfe] *vt (remplir)* to stuff (**de** with) • **truffé, -ée** *adj (pâté)* (garnished) with truffles

truie [trɥi] *nf* sow

truite [trɥit] *nf* trout

truquer [tryke] *vt (photo)* to fake; *(élections, match)* to rig • **truquage** *nm (de cinéma)* (special) effect; *(action)* faking; *(d'élections)* rigging • **truqué, -ée** *adj (élections, match)* rigged; **photo truquée** fake photo; *Cin* **scène truquée** scene with special effects

trust [trœst] *nm Com (cartel)* trust

tsar [dzar] *nm* tsar, czar

TSF [teɛsɛf] (*abrév* **télégraphie sans fil**) *nf Vieilli (poste de radio)* wireless

tsigane [tsigan] **1** *adj* gipsy **2** *nmf* **T.** gipsy

TSVP [teɛsvepe] (*abrév* **tournez s'il vous plaît**) PTO

TTC [tetese] (*abrév* **toutes taxes comprises**) inclusive of tax

tu¹ [ty] *pron personnel* you *(familiar form of address)*

tu² [ty] *pp de* **taire**

tuba [tyba] *nm (instrument de musique)* tuba; *(de plongée)* snorkel

tube [tyb] *nm* tube; *Fam (chanson, disque)* hit; **t. à essai** test tube; *Fam* **marcher à pleins tubes** *(stéréo)* to be going full blast • **tubulaire** *adj* tubular

tuberculose [tybɛrkyloz] *nf* TB, tuberculosis • **tuberculeux, -euse** *adj* tubercular; **être t.** to have TB *or* tuberculosis

TUC [tyk] (*abrév* **travail d'utilité collective**) *nm* = community work project for unemployed young people

tuer [tɥe] **1** *vt* to kill; *Fam (épuiser)* to wear out

2 se tuer *vpr* to kill oneself; *(dans un accident)* to be killed; *Fig* **se t. à faire qch** to wear oneself out doing sth • **tuant, -ante** *adj Fam (fatigant)* exhausting • **tuerie** *nf* slaughter • **tueur, -euse** *nmf* killer

tue-tête [tytɛt] **à tue-tête** *adv* at the top of one's voice

tuile [tɥil] *nf* tile; *Fam (malchance)* (stroke of) bad luck

tulipe [tylip] *nf* tulip

tuméfié, -ée [tymefje] *adj* swollen

tumeur [tymœr] *nf* tumour

tumulte [tymylt] *nm (de la foule)* commotion; *(des passions)* turmoil • **tumultueux, -ueuse** *adj* turbulent

tunique [tynik] *nf* tunic

Tunisie [tynizi] *nf* **la T.** Tunisia • **tunisien, -ienne 1** *adj* Tunisian **2** *nmf* **T., Tunisienne** Tunisian

tunnel [tynɛl] *nm* tunnel; **le t. sous la Manche** the Channel Tunnel

turban [tyrbɑ̃] *nm* turban

turbine [tyrbin] *nf* turbine

turbulences [tyrbylɑ̃s] *nfpl (tourbillons)* turbulence

turbulent, -ente [tyrbylɑ̃, -ɑ̃t] *adj (enfant)* boisterous

turfiste [tyrfist] *nmf* racegoer, *Br* punter

turlupiner [tyrlypine] *vt Fam* **t. qn** to bother sb

Turquie [tyrki] *nf* **la T.** Turkey • **turc, turque 1** *adj* Turkish **2** *nmf* **T., Turque** Turk **3** *nm (langue)* Turkish

turquoise [tyrkwaz] *adj inv* turquoise

tuteur, -trice [tytœr, -tris] **1** *nmf (de mineur)* guardian

2 *nm (bâton)* stake, prop • **tutelle** *nf Jur* guardianship; *Fig* protection

tutoyer [tytwaje] *vt* **t. qn** to address sb using the familiar *tu* form • **tutoiement** *nm* = use of the familiar *tu (instead of the more formal vous)*

tutu [tyty] *nm* tutu

tuyau, -x [tɥijo] *nm* pipe; *Fam (renseignement)* tip; **t. d'arrosage** hose(pipe); **t. de cheminée** flue; **t. d'échappement** *(de véhicule)* exhaust (pipe) • **tuyauter** *vt Fam* **t. qn** *(conseiller)* to give sb a tip • **tuyauterie** [-tri] *nf (tuyaux)* piping

TVA [tevea] (*abrév* **taxe à la valeur ajoutée**) *nf* VAT

tympan [tɛ̃pɑ̃] *nm* eardrum
type [tip] **1** *nm (genre)* type; *Fam (individu)* fellow, guy, *Br* bloke; *Fig* **le t. même de** the very model of
   2 *adj inv* typical; **lettre t.** standard letter • **typique** *adj* typical (**de** of) • **typiquement** *adv* typically
typé, -ée [tipe] *adj* **il est très t.** *(il est italien)* he looks typically Italian
typhoïde [tifɔid] *nf* typhoid (fever)

typhon [tifɔ̃] *nm* typhoon
typographie [tipɔgrafi] *nf* typography, printing • **typographe** *nmf* typographer • **typographique** *adj* typographical
tyran [tirɑ̃] *nm* tyrant • **tyrannie** *nf* tyranny • **tyrannique** *adj* tyrannical • **tyranniser** *vt* to tyrannize
tzigane [tzigan] **1** *adj* gipsy
   2 *nmf* **T.** gipsy

U, u [y] *nm inv* U, u
UE [yø] (*abrév* **Union européenne**) *nf* EU
Ukraine [ykrɛn] *nf* **l'U.** the Ukraine
ulcère [ylsɛr] *nm* ulcer •**ulcérer** *vt Fig* **u. qn** (*irriter*) to make sb seethe
ULM [yɛlɛm] (*abrév* **ultraléger motorisé**) *nm inv Av* microlight
ultérieur, -e [ylterjœr] *adj* later, subsequent (**à** to) •**ultérieurement** *adv* later (on), subsequently
ultimatum [yltimatɔm] *nm* ultimatum; **lancer un u. à qn** to give sb *or* issue sb with an ultimatum
ultime [yltim] *adj* last; (*préparatifs*) final
ultramoderne [yltramɔdɛrn] *adj* hightech
ultrasensible [yltrasɑ̃sibl] *adj* ultrasensitive
ultrason [yltrasɔ̃] *nm* ultrasound
ultraviolet, -ette [yltravjɔlɛ, -ɛt] *adj & nm* ultraviolet
un, une [œ̃, yn] **1** *art indéfini* a; (*devant voyelle*) an; **une page** a page; **un ange** [œ̃nɑ̃ʒ] an angel
   2 *adj* one; **la page un** page one; **un kilo** one kilo; **un jour** one day; **un type (quelconque)** some *or* a fellow
   3 *pron & nmf* one; **l'un** one; **les uns** some; **le numéro un** number one; **j'en ai un** I have one; **l'un d'eux, l'une d'elles** one of them; *Journ* **la une** front page; *Fam* **j'ai eu une de ces peurs!** I was really scared!
unanime [ynanim] *adj* unanimous •**unanimité** *nf* unanimity; **à l'u.** unanimously
Unetelle [yntɛl] *nf voir* **Untel**
uni, -ie [yni] *adj* (*famille, couple*) close; (*surface*) smooth; (*couleur, étoffe*) plain
unième [ynjɛm] *adj* (*after a number*) (-)first; **trente et u.** thirty-first; **cent u.** hundred and first
unifier [ynifje] *vt* to unify •**unification** *nf* unification
uniforme [ynifɔrm] **1** *adj* (*expression*) uniform; (*sol*) even; (*mouvement*) regular
   2 *nm* uniform •**uniformément** *adv* uniformly •**uniformiser** *vt* to standardize •**uniformité** *nf* (*de couleurs*) uniformity; (*monotonie*) monotony

unijambiste [yniʒɑ̃bist] **1** *adj* one-legged
   2 *nmf* one-legged man/woman
unilatéral, -e, -aux, -ales [ynilateral, -o] *adj* (*décision*) unilateral; (*contrat*) one-sided; (*stationnement*) on one side of the road/street only
union [ynjɔ̃] *nf* (*de partis, de consommateurs*) union, association; (*entente*) unity; (*mariage*) marriage; **l'U. européenne** the European Union; **u. monétaire** monetary union; **u. libre** cohabitation
unique [ynik] *adj* (**a**) (*fille, fils*) only; (*espoir, souci*) only, sole; (*prix, parti, salaire, marché*) single; **son seul et u. souci** his/her one and only worry (**b**) (*exceptionnel*) unique; *Fam* (*drôle*) priceless; **u. en son genre** completely unique •**uniquement** *adv* only, just
unir [ynir] **1** *vt* (*personnes, territoires*) to unite; (*marier*) to join in marriage; (*efforts, qualités*) to combine (**à** with); **l'amitié qui nous unit** the friendship that unites us
   2 s'unir *vpr* (*s'associer*) to unite; (*se marier*) to be joined in marriage; **s'u. à qn** to join forces with sb
unisexe [ynisɛks] *adj* unisex
unisson [ynisɔ̃] **à l'unisson** *adv* in unison (**de** with)
unité [ynite] *nf* (*de mesure, élément, régiment*) unit; (*cohésion*) unity; **u. de longueur** unit of measurement; **u. de production** production unit; *Univ* **u. de valeur** credit; *Ordinat* **u. centrale** central processing unit •**unitaire** *adj* (*prix*) per unit
univers [ynivɛr] *nm* universe; *Fig* world •**universalité** *nf* universality •**universel, -elle** *adj* universal •**universellement** *adv* universally
université [yniversite] *nf* university; **à l'u.** *Br* at university, *Am* in college •**universitaire 1** *adj* **ville/restaurant u.** university town/refectory **2** *nmf* academic
Untel, Unetelle [œ̃tɛl, yntɛl] *nmf* what's-his-name, *f* what's-her-name
uranium [yranjɔm] *nm* uranium
urbain, -aine [yrbɛ̃, -ɛn] *adj* urban •**ur-**

baniser *vt* to urbanize • **urbanisme** *nm Br* town planning, *Am* city planning • **urbaniste** *nmf Br* town planner, *Am* city planner

urgent, -ente [yrʒɑ̃, -ɑ̃t] *adj* urgent • **urgence** *nf (de décision, de tâche)* urgency; *(cas d'hôpital)* emergency; **d'u.** urgently; **mesures d'u.** emergency measures; *Pol* **état d'u.** state of emergency; **(service des) urgences** *(d'hôpital) Br* casualty (department), *Am* emergency room; **il y a u.** it's a matter of urgency

urine [yrin] *nf* urine • **uriner** *vi* to urinate • **urinoir** *nm* (public) urinal

urne [yrn] *nf (vase)* urn; *(pour voter)* ballot box; **aller aux urnes** to go to the polls

URSS [yɛrɛsɛs, yrs] *(abrév* **Union des républiques socialistes soviétiques)** *nf Anciennement* **l'U.** the USSR

urticaire [yrtikɛr] *nf* nettle rash

Uruguay [yrygwe] *nm* **l'U.** Uruguay

us [ys] *nmpl* **les us et coutumes** the ways and customs

usage [yzaʒ] *nm (utilisation)* use; *(coutume)* custom; *(de mot)* usage; **faire u. de qch** to make use of sth; **faire bon u. de qch** to put sth to good use; **faire de l'u.** *(vêtement)* to wear well; **d'u.** *(habituel)* customary; **à l'u. de** for (the use of); **hors d'u.** out of order; **je n'en ai pas l'u.** I have no use for it • **usagé, -ée** *adj (vêtement)* worn; *(billet)* used • **usager** *nm* user

user [yze] **1** *vt (vêtement)* to wear out; *(personne)* to wear down; *(consommer)* to use (up)

2 *vi* **u. de qch** to use sth

3 s'user *vpr (tissu, machine)* to wear out; *(talons, personne)* to wear down • **usé, -ée** *adj (tissu)* worn out; *(sujet)* stale; *(personne)* worn out; **eaux usées** dirty *or* waste water

usine [yzin] *nf* factory; **u. à gaz** gasworks; **u. métallurgique** ironworks

usiner [yzine] *vt Tech* to machine

usité, -ée [yzite] *adj* in common use; **peu u.** little used

ustensile [ystɑ̃sil] *nm* implement, tool; **u. de cuisine** kitchen utensil

usuel, -elle [yzɥɛl] *adj* everyday • **usuels** *nmpl (de bibliothèque)* reference books

usufruit [yzyfrɥi] *nm Jur* usufruct

usure [yzyr] *nf (de pneu)* wear; *(de sol)* wearing away; *Fig* **avoir qn à l'u.** to wear sb down

usurier, -ière [yzyrje, -jɛr] *nmf* usurer

usurper [yzyrpe] *vt* to usurp • **usurpateur, -trice** *nmf* usurper

utérus [yterys] *nm Anat* womb, uterus

utile [ytil] *adj* useful (**à** to); **puis-je vous être u.?** what can I do for you? • **utilement** *adv* usefully

utiliser [ytilize] *vt* to use • **utilisable** *adj* usable • **utilisateur, -trice** *nmf* user • **utilisation** *nf* use • **utilité** *nf* usefulness; **d'une grande u.** very useful; **déclaré d'u. publique** state-approved

utilitaire [ytilitɛr] *adj* utilitarian; **véhicule u.** commercial vehicle

utopie [ytɔpi] *nf (idéal)* utopia; *(projet, idée)* utopian plan/idea • **utopique** *adj* utopian

UV [yve] *(abrév* **ultraviolet)** *nm inv* UV

V, v [ve] *nm inv* V, v
va [va] *voir* **aller¹**
vacances [vakɑ̃s] *nfpl Br* holiday(s), *Am* vacation; **en v.** *Br* on holiday, *Am* on vacation; **partir en v.** to go on *Br* holiday *or Am* vacation; **prendre des v.** to take a holiday; **les grandes v.** the summer *Br* holidays *or Am* vacation •**vacancier, -ière** *nmf Br* holidaymaker, *Am* vacationer
vacant, -ante [vakɑ̃, -ɑ̃t] *adj* vacant
vacarme [vakarm] *nm* din, uproar
vaccin [vaksɛ̃] *nm* vaccine; **faire un v. à qn** to vaccinate sb •**vaccination** *nf* vaccination •**vacciner** *vt* to vaccinate; **se faire v.** to get vaccinated (**contre** against); *Fam* **je suis vacciné** I've learnt my lesson
vache [vaʃ] **1** *nf* cow; **v. laitière** dairy cow; *Fam* **(peau de) v.** *(personne)* swine; **maladie de la v. folle** mad cow disease
   2 *adj Fam (méchant)* nasty •**vachement** *adv Fam (très) Br* dead, *Am* real; *(beaucoup)* a hell of a lot •**vacher** *nm* cowherd •**vacherie** *nf Fam (action)* nasty trick; *(parole)* nasty remark
vaciller [vasije] *vi* to sway; *(flamme, lumière)* to flicker; *(mémoire)* to fail •**vacillant, -ante** *adj (lumière)* flickering; *(démarche)* staggering; *(mémoire)* failing
vadrouille [vadruj] *nf Fam* **en v.** roaming about •**vadrouiller** *vi Fam* to roam about
va-et-vient [vaevjɛ̃] *nm inv (mouvement)* movement to and fro; *(de personnes)* comings and goings
vagabond, -onde [vagabɔ̃, -ɔ̃d] **1** *nmf (clochard)* vagrant, tramp
   2 *adj* wandering •**vagabondage** *nm* vagrancy •**vagabonder** *vi* to roam, to wander; *Fig (pensée)* to wander
vagin [vaʒɛ̃] *nm Anat* vagina
vagir [vaʒir] *vi (bébé)* to cry
vague¹ [vag] **1** *adj* vague; *(regard)* vacant; *(souvenir)* dim, vague
   2 *nm* vagueness; **regarder dans le v.** to gaze into space, to gaze vacantly; **rester dans le v.** to be vague; **avoir du v. à l'âme** to be melancholy •**vaguement** *adv* vaguely
vague² [vag] *nf (de mer) & Fig* wave; **v. de**

chaleur heat wave; **v. de froid** cold spell *or* snap; *Fig* **v. de fond** ground swell
vaillant, -ante [vajɑ̃, -ɑ̃t] *adj (courageux)* brave, valiant; *(vigoureux)* healthy •**vaillamment** [-amɑ̃] *adv* valiantly •**vaillance** *nf* bravery
vaille, vailles *voir* **valoir** •**vaille que vaille** *adv* somehow or other
vain, vaine [vɛ̃, vɛn] *adj (sans résultat)* futile; *(mots, promesse)* empty; *(vaniteux)* vain; **en v.** in vain •**vainement** *adv* in vain
vaincre* [vɛ̃kr] *vt (adversaire)* to defeat; *(en sport)* to beat; *Fig (maladie, difficulté)* to overcome •**vaincu, -ue** *nmf* defeated man/woman; *(de match)* loser •**vainqueur 1** *nm* victor; *(de match)* winner **2** *adj m* victorious
vais [ve] *voir* **aller¹**
vaisseau, -x [veso] *nm Anat* vessel; *(bateau)* ship, vessel; **v. spatial** spaceship
vaisselier [vesəlje] *nm (meuble) Br* dresser, *Am* hutch
vaisselle [vesɛl] *nf* crockery; **faire la v.** to do the washing up, to do the dishes
val [val] *(pl* **vals** *ou* **vaux** [vo]*) nm* valley
valable [valabl] *adj (billet, motif)* valid; *Fam (remarquable, rentable)* worthwhile
valet [valɛ] *nm Cartes* jack; **v. de chambre** valet; **v. de ferme** farmhand
valeur [valœr] *nf (prix, qualité)* value; *(mérite)* worth; *(poids)* weight; *Fin* **valeurs** securities; **la v. de** *(équivalent)* the equivalent of; **avoir de la v.** to be valuable; **prendre de la v.** to increase in value; **mettre qch en v.** *(faire ressortir)* to highlight sth; **personne de v.** person of merit; **objets de v.** valuables; **v. refuge** safe investment
valide [valid] *adj (personne)* fit, ablebodied; *(billet)* valid •**valider** *vt* to validate; *(titre de transport)* to stamp; *Ordinat (option)* to confirm •**validité** *nf* validity
valise [valiz] *nf* suitcase; **v. diplomatique** diplomatic *Br* bag *or Am* pouch; **faire ses valises** to pack (one's bags)
vallée [vale] *nf* valley •**vallon** *nm* small valley •**vallonné, -ée** *adj (région)* undulating
valoir* [valwar] **1** *vi (avoir pour valeur)* to

be worth; *(s'appliquer)* to apply (**pour** to); **v. mille euros/cher** to be worth a thousand euros/a lot; **un vélo vaut bien une auto** a bicycle is just as good as a car; **il vaut mieux rester** it's better to stay; **il vaut mieux que j'attende** I'd better wait; **ça ne vaut rien** it's no good; *Fam* **ça vaut la peine** *ou* **le coup** it's worth while (**de faire** doing); **faire v. qch** *(faire ressortir)* to highlight sth; *(argument)* to put sth forward; *(droit)* to assert sth; **se faire v.** to get oneself noticed

2 *vt* **v. qch à qn** *(ennuis)* to bring sb sth

3 **se valoir** *vpr (objets, personnes)* to be as good as each other; *Fam* **ça se vaut** it's all the same

valse [vals] *nf* waltz • **valser** *vi* to waltz • **valseur, -euse** *nmf* waltzer

valve [valv] *nf* valve

vampire [vãpir] *nm* vampire

vandale [vãdal] *nmf* vandal • **vandalisme** *nm* vandalism

vanille [vanij] *nf* vanilla; **glace à la v.** vanilla ice cream • **vanillé, -ée** *adj* vanilla-flavoured; **sucre v.** vanilla sugar

vanité [vanite] *nf (orgueil)* vanity; *Littéraire (futilité)* futility • **vaniteux, -euse** *adj* vain, conceited

vanne [van] *nf (d'écluse)* sluice gate, floodgate; *Fam (remarque)* dig, jibe; *Fam* **envoyer une v. à qn** to have a dig at sb

vanné, -ée [vane] *adj Fam (fatigué)* knocked out, *Br* dead beat

vannerie [vanri] *nf (fabrication)* basketry; *(objets)* basketwork

vanter [vãte] **1** *vt* to praise

2 **se vanter** *vpr* to boast, to brag (**de** about, of); *Fam* **il n'y a pas de quoi se v.** there's nothing to brag *or* boast about • **vantard, -arde 1** *adj* boastful **2** *nmf* boaster, braggart • **vantardise** *nf (caractère)* boastfulness; *(propos)* boast

va-nu-pieds [vanypje] *nmf inv* beggar, down-and-out, *Br* tramp

vapeur [vapœr] *nf (brume, émanation)* vapour; **v. (d'eau)** steam; **cuire qch à la v.** to steam sth; **bateau à v.** steamboat • **vaporeux, -euse** *adj (atmosphère)* steamy; *(tissu)* flimsy

vaporiser [vaporize] *vt* to spray • **vaporisateur** *nm (appareil)* spray

vaquer [vake] *vi* **v. à qch** to attend to sth; **v. à ses occupations** to go about one's business

varappe [varap] *nf* rock-climbing

vareuse [varøz] *nf (d'uniforme)* tunic

variable [varjabl] **1** *adj* variable; *(humeur, temps)* changeable

2 *nf* variable • **variante** *nf* variant • **variation** *nf* variation

varicelle [varisɛl] *nf* chickenpox

varices [varis] *nfpl* varicose veins

varier [varje] *vti* to vary (**de** from) • **varié, -ée** *adj (diversifié)* varied; *(vocabulaire)* wide

variété [varjete] *nf* variety; **spectacle de variétés** *(chansons)* variety show

variole [varjɔl] *nf* smallpox

vas [va] *voir* **aller**¹

vasculaire [vaskylɛr] *adj* vascular

vase¹ [vaz] *nm (récipient)* vase

vase² [vaz] *nf (boue)* mud, silt • **vaseux, -euse** *adj (boueux)* muddy, silty; *Fam (faible)* under the weather, *Br* off colour; *Fam (idées)* woolly

vaseline [vazlin] *nf* Vaseline®

vasistas [vazistas] *nm* fanlight

vasouillard, -arde [vazujar, -ard] *adj Fam* under the weather

vaste [vast] *adj* vast, huge

Vatican [vatikã] *nm* **le V.** the Vatican

va-tout [vatu] *nm inv* **jouer son v.** to stake one's all

vaudeville [vodvil] *nm Théâtre* light comedy

vau-l'eau [volo] **à vau-l'eau** *adv* **aller à v.** to go to rack and ruin

vaurien, -ienne [vorjɛ̃, -jɛn] *nmf* good-for-nothing

vaut [vo] *voir* **valoir**

vautour [votur] *nm* vulture

vautrer [votre] **se vautrer** *vpr (personne)* to sprawl; **se v. dans la boue/le vice** to wallow in the mud/in vice

va-vite [vavit] **à la va-vite** *adv Fam* in a rush

veau, -x [vo] *nm (animal)* calf; *(viande)* veal; *(cuir)* calfskin; *Fam (voiture)* really slow car

vécu, -ue [veky] **1** *pp de* **vivre**

2 *adj (histoire)* real-life

3 *nm* real-life experience

vedette [vədɛt] *nf* **(a)** *(acteur)* star; **avoir la v., être en v.** *(dans un spectacle)* to top the bill **(b)** *(bateau)* launch

végétal, -e, -aux, -ales [veʒetal, -o] **1** *adj* **huile végétale** vegetable oil; **règne v.** vegetable kingdom

2 *nm* plant • **végétalien, -ienne** *nmf* vegan • **végétarien, -ienne** *adj & nmf* vegetarian • **végétation** *nf* vegetation • **végétations** *nfpl Méd* adenoids

végéter [veʒete] *vi Péj (personne)* to vegetate

véhément, -ente [veemã, -ãt] *adj* vehement • **véhémence** *nf* vehemence

véhicule [veikyl] *nm* vehicle; **v. tout-terrain** off-road *or* all-terrain vehicle • **véhiculer** *vt* to convey

veille [vɛj] *nf* (**a**) *(jour précédent)* **la v. (de qch)** the day before (sth); **la v. de Noël** Christmas Eve; **à la v. de qch** *(événement)* on the eve of sth; *Fam* **ce n'est pas demain la v.** that's not going to happen for quite a while (**b**) *(état)* wakefulness; *Ordinat* standby mode

veillée [veje] *nf (soirée)* evening; *(de mort)* vigil; **v. d'armes** knightly vigil

veiller [veje] **1** *vi* to stay up *or* awake; *(sentinelle)* to keep watch; **v. à qch** to see to sth; **v. à ce que...** *(+ subjunctive)* to make sure that...; **v. sur qn** to watch over sb; *Fig* **v. au grain** to keep an eye open for trouble
2 *vt (malade)* to sit up with • **veilleur** *nm* **v. de nuit** night watchman • **veilleuse** *nf (de voiture) Br* sidelight, *Am* parking light; *(de cuisinière)* pilot light; *(lampe allumée la nuit)* night light; *Fam* **mets-la en v.!** put a sock in it!

veinard, -arde [vɛnar, -ard] *nmf Fam* lucky devil

veine [vɛn] *nf Anat, Bot & Géol* vein; *Fam (chance)* luck; *Fam* **avoir de la v.** to be lucky

vêler [vele] *vi* to calve

vélin [velɛ̃] *nm (papier, peau)* vellum

véliplanchiste [veliplɑ̃ʃist] *nmf* windsurfer

velléité [veleite] *nf* vague desire

vélo [velo] *nm* bike, bicycle; *(activité)* cycling; **faire du v.** to cycle, to go cycling; **v. tout-terrain** mountain bike • **vélodrome** *nm* velodrome • **vélomoteur** *nm* moped

velours [vəlur] *nm* velvet; **v. côtelé** corduroy • **velouté, -ée 1** *adj* velvety; *(au goût)* mellow, smooth **2** *nm (texture)* smoothness; **v. d'asperges** cream of asparagus soup

velu, -ue [vəly] *adj* hairy

venaison [vənɛzɔ̃] *nf* venison

vénal, -e, -aux, -ales [venal, -o] *adj* mercenary

vendange [vɑ̃dɑ̃ʒ] *nf (récolte)* grape harvest; *(raisin récolté)* grapes (harvested); **une bonne v.** a good vintage; **vendanges** *(période)* grape-harvesting time; **faire les vendanges** to harvest *or* pick the grapes • **vendanger** *vi* to pick the grapes • **vendangeur, -euse** *nmf* grape picker

vendetta [vɑ̃deta] *nf* vendetta

vendre [vɑ̃dr] **1** *vt* to sell; **v. qch à qn** to sell sb sth, to sell sth to sb; **v. qch 10 euros** to sell sth for 10 euros; **'à v.'** 'for sale'
2 se vendre *vpr* to be sold; **ça se vend bien** it sells well • **vendeur, -euse** *nmf (de magasin) Br* sales *or* shop assistant, *Am* sales clerk; *(non professionnel)* seller

vendredi [vɑ̃drədi] *nm* Friday; **V. saint** Good Friday

vénéneux, -euse [venenø, -øz] *adj* poisonous

vénérable [venerabl] *adj* venerable • **vénérer** *vt* to venerate

vénérien, -ienne [venerjɛ̃, -jɛn] *adj* venereal

venger [vɑ̃ʒe] **1** *vt* to avenge
2 se venger *vpr* to get one's revenge (**de qn** on sb; **de qch** for sth) • **vengeance** *nf* revenge, vengeance • **vengeur, -eresse 1** *adj* vengeful **2** *nmf* avenger

venin [vənɛ̃] *nm* poison, venom; *Fig* venom • **venimeux, -euse** *adj* poisonous, venomous; *Fig (haineux)* venomous

venir* [vənir] **1** *(aux être)* *vi* to come (**de** from); **v. faire qch** to come to do sth; **viens me voir** come and see me; **je viens/venais d'arriver** I've/I'd just arrived; **en v. à** *(conclusion)* to come to; **où veux-tu en v.?** what are you getting *or* driving at?; **les jours qui viennent** the coming days; **faire v. qn** to send for sb; **une idée m'est venue** an idea occurred to me; **d'où vient que?** how is it that?
2 *v impersonnel* **s'il venait à pleuvoir** if it happened to rain

vent [vɑ̃] *nm* wind; **il y a** *ou* **il fait du v.** it's windy; **avoir v. de qch** to get wind of sth; *Fam* **dans le v.** *(à la mode)* trendy, with it

vente [vɑ̃t] *nf* sale; **en v.** *(en magasin)* on sale; **mettre qch en v.** to put sth up for sale; **v. aux enchères** auction (sale); **v. de charité** charity sale; **v. par correspondance** mail order

ventilateur [vɑ̃tilatœr] *nm (électrique)* fan; *(de voiture)* blower • **ventilation** *nf* ventilation • **ventiler** *vt* to ventilate

ventouse [vɑ̃tuz] *nf (pour fixer)* suction grip; *(en verre)* cupping glass

ventre [vɑ̃tr] *nm* stomach, belly; *(utérus)* womb; *(de cruche)* bulge; **à plat v.** flat on one's face; **avoir/prendre du v.** to have/get a paunch; **avoir mal au v.** to have a sore stomach; *Fam* **il n'a rien dans le v.** he has no guts • **ventru, -ue** *adj (personne)* pot-bellied; *(objet)* bulging

ventriloque [vɑ̃trilɔk] *nmf* ventriloquist

venu, -ue [vəny] **1** *pp de* **venir**
2 *adj* **bien v.** *(à propos)* timely; **mal v.** untimely

3 *nmf* **nouveau v., nouvelle venue** newcomer; **le premier v.** anyone
4 *nf* **venue** *(de personne, de printemps)* coming; **dès sa venue au monde** since he/she came into the world

> *Il faut noter que le nom anglais **venue** est un faux ami. Il désigne un lieu de réunion.

vêpres [vɛpr] *nfpl Rel* vespers
ver [vɛr] *nm* worm; *(larve)* grub; *(de fruits, de fromage)* maggot; *Fig* **tirer les vers du nez à qn** to drag it out of sb; **v. luisant** glow-worm; **v. de terre** (earth)worm; **v. à soie** silkworm; **v. solitaire** tapeworm
véracité [verasite] *nf* truthfulness
véranda [verɑ̃da] *nf* veranda(h); *(en verre)* conservatory
verbaliser [vɛrbalize] *vi (policier)* to record the details of an offence
verbe [vɛrb] *nm* verb ● **verbal, -e, -aux, -ales** *adj (promesse, expression)* verbal
verbeux, -euse [vɛrbø, -øz] *adj Péj* verbose ● **verbiage** *nm Péj* verbiage
verdâtre [vɛrdɑtr] *adj* greenish
verdeur [vɛrdœr] *nf (de fruit, de vin)* tartness; *(de vieillard)* sprightliness; *(de langage)* crudeness
verdict [vɛrdikt] *nm* verdict
verdir [vɛrdir] *vti* to turn green ● **verdoyant, -ante** *adj* green ● **verdure** *nf (végétation)* greenery; **théâtre de v.** open-air theatre
véreux, -euse [verø, -øz] *adj (fruit)* wormy, maggoty; *Fig (malhonnête)* dubious, shady
verger [vɛrʒe] *nm* orchard
vergetures [vɛrʒətyr] *nfpl* stretch marks
verglas [vɛrgla] *nm Br* (black) ice, *Am* glaze ● **verglacé, -ée** *adj (route)* icy
vergogne [vɛrgɔɲ] **sans vergogne 1** *adj* shameless
2 *adv* shamelessly
véridique [veridik] *adj* truthful
vérifier [verifje] **1** *vt* to check, to verify; *(comptes)* to audit
2 se vérifier *vpr* to prove correct ● **vérifiable** *adj* verifiable ● **vérification** *nf* checking, verification; *(de comptes)* audit(ing)
vérité [verite] *nf (de déclaration)* truth; *(de personnage, de tableau)* trueness to life; *(sincérité)* sincerity; **en v.** in fact; **dire la v.** to tell the truth
véritable [veritabl] *adj (histoire, ami)* true, real; *(cuir, or, nom)* real, genuine; *(en intensif)* real ● **véritablement** [-əmɑ̃] *adv* really
verlan [vɛrlɑ̃] *nm* back slang

vermeil, -eille [vɛrmɛj] *adj* bright red; **carte vermeil** = senior citizen's rail pass
vermicelle [vɛrmisɛl] *nm* vermicelli
vermine [vɛrmin] *nf (insectes, racaille)* vermin
vermoulu, -ue [vɛrmuly] *adj* worm-eaten
vermouth [vɛrmut] *nm* vermouth
verni, -ie [vɛrni] *adj (meuble, parquet)* varnished; *Fam (chanceux)* lucky
vernir [vɛrnir] *vt (bois)* to varnish; *(céramique)* to glaze ● **vernis** *nm* varnish; *(pour céramique)* glaze; *Fig (apparence)* veneer; **v. à ongles** nail polish *or Br* varnish ● **vernissage** *nm (d'exposition)* opening
verra, verrait [vera, vere] *voir* **voir**
verre [vɛr] *nm (substance, récipient)* glass; **boire** *ou* **prendre un v.** to have a drink; **porter des verres** to wear glasses; **gravure sous v.** glass-mounted engraving; **v. de bière** glass of beer; **v. à bière/ à vin** beer/wine glass; **v. à dents** toothbrush glass; **v. de contact** contact lens ● **verrerie** *nf (objets)* glassware ● **verrière** *nf (toit)* glass roof
verrou [veru] *nm* bolt; **fermer qch au v.** to bolt sth; **sous les verrous** behind bars ● **verrouiller** *vt (porte)* to bolt; *(quartier)* to seal off
verrue [very] *nf* wart; **v. plantaire** verruca
vers¹ [vɛr] *prép (direction)* toward(s); *(approximation)* around, about
vers² [vɛr] *nm (de poème)* line; **des vers** *(poésie)* verse
versant [vɛrsɑ̃] *nm* slope, side
versatile [vɛrsatil] *adj* fickle

> *Il faut noter que l'adjectif anglais **versatile** est un faux ami. Il signifie **polyvalent**.

verse [vɛrs] **à verse** *adv* **pleuvoir à v.** to pour (down); **la pluie tombait à v.** the rain was coming down in torrents
versé, -ée [vɛrse] *adj Littéraire* **v. dans** well-versed in
Verseau [vɛrso] *nm (signe)* Aquarius; **être V.** to be Aquarius
verser [vɛrse] **1** *vt* to pour (out); *(larmes, sang)* to shed; *(argent)* to pay (**sur un compte** into an account)
2 *vi (véhicule)* to overturn ● **versement** [-əmɑ̃] *nm* payment ● **verseur** *adj* **bec v.** spout
verset [vɛrse] *nm* verse
version [vɛrsjɔ̃] *nf (de film, d'incident)* version; *Scol (traduction)* translation, *Br* unseen; *Cin* **en v. originale** in the original language; **en v. française** dubbed *(into French)*

verso [vɛrso] *nm* back (of the page); **'voir au v.'** 'see overleaf'

vert, verte [vɛr, vɛrt] **1** *adj* green; *(pas mûr)* unripe; *(vin)* too young; *Fig (vieillard)* sprightly; **aller en classe verte** to go on a school trip to the countryside; *Fig* **en dire des vertes et des pas mûres** to say some pretty shocking things

2 *nm* green; **se mettre au v.** to go to the country (to recuperate); *Pol* **les Verts** the Greens • **vert-de-gris** *nm inv* verdigris

vertèbre [vɛrtɛbr] *nf* vertebra

vertement [vɛrtəmã] *adv* sharply

vertical, -e, -aux, -ales [vɛrtikal, -o] *adj & nf* vertical; **à la verticale** vertically • **verticalement** *adv* vertically

vertige [vɛrtiʒ] *nm (étourdissement)* (feeling of) dizziness *or* giddiness; *(peur du vide)* vertigo; **vertiges** dizzy spells; **avoir le v.** to be *or* feel dizzy *or* giddy; **donner le v. à qn** to make sb (feel) dizzy *or* giddy • **vertigineux, -euse** *adj (hauteur)* giddy, dizzy; *Fig (très grand)* staggering

vertu [vɛrty] *nf* virtue; **en v. de** in accordance with • **vertueux, -euse** *adj* virtuous

verve [vɛrv] *nf (d'orateur)* verve

verveine [vɛrvɛn] *nf (plante)* verbena; *(tisane)* verbena tea

vésicule [vezikyl] *nf* **v. biliaire** gall bladder

vessie [vesi] *nf* bladder

veste [vɛst] *nf* jacket, coat

vestiaire [vɛstjɛr] *nm (de théâtre)* cloakroom; *(de piscine, de stade)* changing room, *Am* locker room

vestibule [vɛstibyl] *nm* (entrance) hall

vestiges [vɛstiʒ] *nmpl (ruines)* remains; *(traces)* relics

vestimentaire [vɛstimãtɛr] *adj* **dépense v.** clothing expenditure

veston [vɛstɔ̃] *nm* (suit) jacket

vêtement [vɛtmã] *nm* garment, article of clothing; **vêtements** clothes; **vêtements de sport** sportswear; **industrie du v.** clothing industry

vétéran [veterã] *nm* veteran

vétérinaire [veterinɛr] **1** *adj* veterinary

2 *nmf* vet, *Br* veterinary surgeon, *Am* veterinarian

vétille [vetij] *nf* trifle, triviality

vêtir* [vetir] *vt,* **se vêtir** *vpr* to dress • **vêtu, -ue** *adj* dressed (**de** in)

veto [veto] *nm inv* veto; **opposer son v. à qch** to veto sth

vétuste [vetyst] *adj* dilapidated

veuf, veuve [vœf, vœv] **1** *adj* widowed

2 *nm* widower

3 *nf* widow

veuille(s), veuillent [vœj] *voir* **vouloir**

veule [vøl] *adj Littéraire* effete • **veulerie** *nf Littéraire* effeteness

veut, veux [vø] *voir* **vouloir**

vexer [vɛkse] **1** *vt* to upset, to hurt

2 **se vexer** *vpr* to get upset (**de** at) • **vexant, -ante** *adj* upsetting, hurtful; *(contrariant)* annoying • **vexation** *nf* humiliation

VF [veɛf] *(abrév* **version française***) nf* **film en VF** film dubbed into French

viable [vjabl] *adj (entreprise, enfant)* viable • **viabilité** *nf* viability

viaduc [vjadyk] *nm* viaduct

viager, -ère [vjaʒe, -ɛr] **1** *adj* **rente viagère** life annuity

2 *nm* life annuity

viande [vjɑ̃d] *nf* meat

vibrer [vibre] *vi* to vibrate; *(être ému)* to be stirred (**de** with); **faire v. qn** to stir sb; **sa voix vibrait de colère** his/her voice was shaking with anger • **vibrant, -ante** *adj (hommage)* stirring • **vibration** *nf* vibration • **vibromasseur** *nm* vibrator

vicaire [vikɛr] *nm (anglican)* curate

vice [vis] *nm (perversité)* vice; *(défectuosité)* defect; *Jur* **v. de forme** legal flaw

vice versa [vis(e)vɛrsa] *adv* vice versa

vicié, -ée [visje] *adj (air, atmosphère)* polluted

vicieux, -ieuse [visjø, -jøz] *adj (pervers)* depraved; *(perfide)* underhand

---

ℓ Il faut noter que l'adjectif anglais **vicious** est un faux ami. Il signifie **méchant**.

---

vicinal, -e, -aux, -ales [visinal, -o] *adj* **chemin v.** byroad, minor road

vicissitudes [visisityd] *nfpl* vicissitudes

vicomte [vikɔ̃t] *nm* viscount • **vicomtesse** *nf* viscountess

victime [viktim] *nf* victim; *(d'accident)* casualty; **être v. de** *(accident, attentat)* to be the victim of

victoire [viktwar] *nf* victory; *(en sport)* win • **victorieux, -ieuse** *adj* victorious; *(équipe)* winning

victuailles [viktɥaj] *nfpl* provisions

vidange [vidɑ̃ʒ] *nf* emptying, draining; *(de véhicule)* oil change • **vidanger** *vt* to empty, to drain

vide [vid] **1** *adj* empty

2 *nm (espace)* empty space; *(d'emploi du temps)* gap; *Phys* vacuum; **regarder dans le v.** to stare into space; **emballé sous v.** vacuum-packed; **à v.** empty

vidéo [video] *adj inv & nf* video • **vidéocassette** *nf* video (cassette) • **vidéoclip** *nm* video

vidéodisque [videodisk] *nm* videodisk
vider [vide] **1** *vt* to empty; *(lieu)* to vacate; *(poisson, volaille)* to gut; *Fam* **v. qn** *(chasser)* to throw sb out; *(épuiser)* to tire sb out; *Fam* **j'ai vidé mon sac** I got it off my chest

2 se vider *vpr* to empty • **vidé, -ée** *adj Fam (fatigué)* exhausted • **vide-ordures** *nm inv Br* rubbish *or Am* garbage chute • **vide-poches** *nm inv (de véhicule)* glove compartment • **videur** *nm (de boîte de nuit)* bouncer

vie [vi] *nf* life; *(durée)* lifetime; **en v.** living; **à v., pour la v.** for life; **donner la v. à qn** to give birth to sb; *Fig* **avoir la v. dure** *(préjugés)* to die hard

vieil, vieille [vjɛj] *voir* **vieux**

vieillard [vjɛjar] *nm* old man; **les vieillards** old people • **vieillerie** *nf (objet)* old thing; *(idée)* old idea • **vieillesse** *nf* old age

vieillir [vjejir] **1** *vi* to grow old; *(changer)* to age; *(théorie, mot)* to become old-fashioned

2 *vt* **v. qn** *(vêtement)* to make sb look old(er) • **vieilli, -ie** *adj (démodé)* old-fashioned • **vieillissant, -ante** *adj* ageing • **vieillissement** *nm* ageing

vieillot, -otte [vjɛjo, -ɔt] *adj* old-fashioned

Vienne [vjɛn] *nm ou f* Vienna

viens, vient [vjɛ̃] *voir* **venir**

vierge [vjɛrʒ] **1** *adj (femme, neige)* virgin; *(feuille de papier, film)* blank; **être v.** *(femme, homme)* to be a virgin

2 *nf* virgin; **la V.** *(signe)* Virgo; **être V.** to be Virgo

Viêt Nam [vjɛtnam] *nm* **le V.** Vietnam • **vietnamien, -ienne 1** *adj* Vietnamese **2** *nmf* **V., Vietnamienne** Vietnamese

vieux, vieille, vieux, vieilles [vjø, vjɛj]

> **vieil** is used before masculine singular nouns beginning with a vowel or mute h.

1 *adj* old; **être v. jeu** *(adj inv)* to be old-fashioned; *Péj* **v. garçon** bachelor; *Péj* **vieille fille** old maid; **se faire v.** to get old
2 *nm* old man; **les vieux** old people; *Fam* **mon v.!** *(mon ami) Br* mate!, pal!
3 *nf* **vieille** old woman; *Fam* **ma vieille!** *(mon amie)* dear!

vif, vive [vif, viv] **1** *adj (personne)* lively; *(imagination)* vivid; *(intelligence, vent, douleur)* sharp; *(intérêt, satisfaction)* great; *(couleur, lumière)* bright; *(froid)* biting; *(pas, mouvement)* quick; **brûler qn v.** to burn sb alive

2 *nm* **entrer dans le v. du sujet** to get to the heart of the matter; **à v.** *(plaie)* open; **piqué au v.** *(vexé)* cut to the quick

vigie [viʒi] *nf (matelot)* lookout; *(poste)* lookout post

vigilant, -ante [viʒilɑ̃, -ɑ̃t] *adj* vigilant • **vigilance** *nf* vigilance

vigile [viʒil] *nm* watchman

> **ℓ** Il faut noter que le nom anglais **vigil** est un faux ami. Il ne signifie jamais **gardien**.

vigne [viɲ] *nf (plante)* vine; *(plantation)* vineyard; **pied de v.** vine (stock) • **vigneron, -onne** [-ərɔ̃, -ɔn] *nmf* wine grower • **vignoble** *nm* vineyard; *(région)* vineyards

vignette [viɲɛt] *nf (de véhicule)* road tax sticker, *Br* ≃ road tax disc; *(de médicament)* label *(for reimbursement by Social Security)*

vigueur [vigœr] *nf* vigour; **entrer/être en v.** *(loi)* to come into/be in force • **vigoureux, -euse** *adj (personne, style)* vigorous; *(bras)* sturdy

vilain, -aine [vilɛ̃, -ɛn] *adj (laid)* ugly; *(peu sage)* naughty; *(impoli)* rude

villa [vila] *nf* villa

village [vilaʒ] *nm* village • **villageois, -oise** *nmf* villager

ville [vil] *nf* town; *(grande)* city; **aller/être en v.** to go (in)to/be in town; **v. d'eaux** spa (town)

villégiature [vileʒjatyr] *nf* **lieu de v.** *Br* holiday resort, *Am* resort

vin [vɛ̃] *nm* wine; **v. ordinaire** *ou* **de table** table wine; **v. d'honneur** reception *(in honour of sb)* • **vinicole** *adj (région)* wine-growing

vinaigre [vinɛgr] *nm* vinegar • **vinaigrette** *nf (sauce)* vinaigrette, *Br* French dressing, *Am* Italian dressing

vindicatif, -ive [vɛ̃dikatif, -iv] *adj* vindictive

vingt [vɛ̃] ([vɛ̃t] *before vowel or mute h and in numbers 22-29)* *adj & nm inv* twenty; **v. et un** twenty-one • **vingtaine** *nf* **une v. (de)** *(nombre)* about twenty • **vingtième** *adj & nmf* twentieth

vinyle [vinil] *nm* vinyl

viol [vjɔl] *nm* rape; *(de lieu)* violation • **violation** *nf* violation • **violenter** *vt* to rape • **violer** *vt (femme)* to rape; *(tombe)* to desecrate; *(secret)* to divulge • **violeur** *nm* rapist

violent, -ente [vjɔlɑ̃, -ɑ̃t] *adj* violent; *(effort)* strenuous • **violemment** [-amɑ̃] *adv* violently • **violence** *nf* violence; **acte de v.** act of violence

violet, -ette [vjɔlɛ, -ɛt] **1** *adj & nm (couleur)* purple

2 *nf* **violette** *(fleur)* violet • **violacé, -ée** *adj* purplish-blue

violon [vjɔlɔ̃] *nm* violin; *Fig* **accordons nos violons** let's make sure we get our stories straight • **violoncelle** *nm* cello • **violoncelliste** *nmf* cellist • **violoniste** *nmf* violinist

vipère [vipɛr] *nf* adder, viper

virage [viraʒ] *nm (de route)* bend; *(de véhicule)* turn; *Fig (revirement)* change of course

virée [vire] *nf Fam (en voiture)* drive

virer [vire] **1** *vi* to turn; **v. au bleu** to turn blue

2 *vt Fin (somme)* to transfer (à to); *Fam* **v. qn** to chuck sb out • **virement** *nm Fin* transfer

virevolter [virvɔlte] *vi* to spin round

virginité [virʒinite] *nf* virginity

virgule [virgyl] *nf (ponctuation)* comma; *Math* (decimal) point; **2 v. 5** 2 point 5

viril, -e [viril] *adj* virile; *(force, attribut)* male • **virilité** *nf* virility

virtuel, -elle [virtɥɛl] *adj* potential; *(image)* virtual; **réalité virtuelle** virtual reality

virtuose [virtɥoz] *nmf* virtuoso • **virtuosité** *nf* virtuosity

virulent, -ente [virylɑ̃, -ɑ̃t] *adj* virulent • **virulence** *nf* virulence

virus [virys] *nm Méd & Ordinat* virus

vis¹ [vi] *voir* **vivre, voir**

vis² [vis] *nf* screw

visa [viza] *nm (de passeport)* visa; **v. de censure** *(de film)* certificate

visage [vizaʒ] *nm* face

vis-à-vis [vizavi] **1** *prép* **v. de** *(en face de)* opposite; *(envers)* towards; *(comparé à)* compared to

2 *nm inv (personne)* person opposite

viscères [visɛr] *nmpl* intestines • **viscéral, -e, -aux, -ales** *adj Fig (haine)* deep-seated

viscosité [viskozite] *nf* viscosity

viser [vize] **1** *vt (cible)* to aim at; *(concerner)* to be aimed at; *(document)* to stamp

2 *vi* to aim (à at); **v. à faire qch** to aim to do sth • **visées** *nfpl Fig (desseins)* aims; **avoir des visées sur qn/qch** to have designs on sb/sth • **viseur** *nm Phot* viewfinder; *(d'arme)* sight

visible [vizibl] *adj* visible; **v. à l'œil nu** visible to the naked eye • **visibilité** *nf* visibility • **visiblement** [-əmɑ̃] *adv* visibly

visière [vizjɛr] *nf (de casquette)* peak; *(en plastique)* eyeshade; *(de casque)* visor

vision [vizjɔ̃] *nf (conception, image)* vision; *(sens)* sight; *Fam* **avoir des visions** to be seeing things • **visionnaire** *adj & nmf* visionary • **visionner** *vt (film)* to view • **visionneuse** *nf (pour diapositives)* viewer

visite [vizit] *nf* visit; *(personne)* visitor; *(examen)* inspection; **rendre v. à qn** to visit sb; **avoir de la v.** to have a visitor/visitors; **heures de v.** visiting hours; **v. (à domicile)** *(de médecin)* (house) call; **v. médicale** medical examination; **v. guidée** guided tour • **visiter** *vt (lieu touristique, patient)* to visit; *(examiner)* to inspect • **visiteur, -euse** *nmf* visitor

vison [vizɔ̃] *nm* mink

visqueux, -euse [viskø, -øz] *adj* viscous; *(surface)* sticky

visser [vise] *vt* to screw on

visu [vizy] **de visu** *adv Littéraire* with one's own eyes

visuel, -elle [vizɥɛl] *adj* visual • **visualiser** *vt* to visualize; *Ordinat (afficher)* to display

vit [vi] *voir* **vivre, voir**

vital, -e, -aux, -ales [vital, -o] *adj* vital • **vitalité** *nf* vitality

vitamine [vitamin] *nf* vitamin • **vitaminé, -ée** *adj* vitamin-enriched

vite [vit] *adv (rapidement)* quickly, fast; *(sous peu)* soon; **v.!** quick(ly)! • **vitesse** *nf* speed; *(de moteur)* gear; **à toute v.** at top full speed; *Fam* **en v.** quickly

viticole [vitikɔl] *adj (région)* winegrowing • **viticulteur** *nm* wine grower • **viticulture** *nf* wine growing

vitre [vitr] *nf* (window)pane; *(de véhicule, de train)* window • **vitrage** *nm (vitres)* windows • **vitrail, -aux** *nm* stained-glass window • **vitré, -ée** *adj* **porte vitrée** glass door • **vitreux, -euse** *adj Fig (regard, yeux)* glassy • **vitrier** *nm* glazier

vitrine [vitrin] *nf (de magasin)* (shop) window; *(meuble)* display cabinet

vitriol [vitrijɔl] *nm* vitriol

vivable [vivabl] *adj Fam (personne)* easy to live with; *(endroit)* fit to live in

vivace [vivas] *adj (plante)* perennial; *Fig (souvenir)* vivid • **vivacité** *nf* liveliness; *(d'imagination)* vividness; *(d'intelligence)* sharpness; *(de couleur)* brightness; *(emportement)* petulance; **v. d'esprit** quickwittedness

vivant, -ante [vivɑ̃, -ɑ̃t] **1** *adj (en vie)* alive, living; *(récit, rue, enfant)* lively; *(être, matière, preuve)* living

2 *nm* **de son v.** in one's lifetime; **les vivants** the living

vivats [viva] *nmpl* cheers

vive¹ [viv] *voir* **vif**

vive² [viv] *exclam* **v. le roi!** long live the king!

vivement [vivmã] *adv* quickly; *(répliquer)* sharply; *(regretter)* deeply; **v. demain!** I can hardly wait for tomorrow!, *Br* roll on tomorrow!; **v. qu'il parte** I'll be glad when he's gone

vivier [vivje] *nm* fish pond

vivifier [vivifje] *vt* to invigorate

vivisection [vivisɛksjɔ̃] *nf* vivisection

vivoter [vivɔte] *vi Fam* to struggle to get by

vivre* [vivr] **1** *vi* to live; **elle vit encore** she's still alive *or* living; **faire v. qn** *(famille)* to support sb; **v. vieux** to live to be old; **facile/difficile à v.** easy/hard to get along with; **v. de** *(fruits)* to live on; *(travail)* to live by; **avoir de quoi v.** to have enough to live on

2 *vt (vie)* to live; *(aventure, époque)* to live through; *(éprouver)* to experience • **vivres** *nmpl* food, supplies

vlan [vlã] *exclam* bang!, wham!

VO [veo] *(abrév* **version originale***) nf* film en VO film in the original language

vocabulaire [vɔkabylɛr] *nm* vocabulary

vocal, -e, -aux, -ales [vɔkal, -o] *adj* vocal • **vocalises** *nfpl* **faire des v.** to do voice exercises

vocation [vɔkasjɔ̃] *nf* vocation, calling

vociférer [vɔsifere] *vti* to shout angrily • **vociférations** *nfpl* shouting

vodka [vɔdka] *nf* vodka

vœu, -x [vø] *nm (souhait)* wish; *(promesse)* vow; **faire un v.** to make a wish; **faire le v. de faire qch** to vow to do sth; **tous mes vœux!** best wishes!

vogue [vɔg] *nf* fashion, vogue; **en v.** in vogue • **voguer** *vi Littéraire* to sail

voici [vwasi] *prép* here is/are; **me v.** here I am; **me v. triste** I'm sad now; **v. dix ans** ten years ago; **v. dix ans que...** it's ten years since...

voie [vwa] *nf (route)* road; *(rails)* track, line; *(partie de route)* lane; *(chemin)* way; *(de gare)* platform; *(de communication)* line; *(moyen)* means, way; *(diplomatique)* channels; *Fig* **préparer la v.** to pave the way; *Fig* **sur la bonne v.** on the right track; **en v. de** in the process of; **pays en v. de développement** developing country; **v. sans issue** dead end; **v. publique** public highway; **v. navigable** waterway

voilà [vwala] *prép* there is/are; **les v.** there they are; **v., j'arrive!** all right, I'm coming!; **le v. parti** he has left now; **v. dix ans** ten years ago; **v. dix ans que...** it's ten years since...; **et v.!** there you go!

voile¹ [vwal] *nm (étoffe, coiffure)* & *Fig* veil • **voilage** *nm* net curtain • **voilé, -ée** *adj (femme, allusion)* veiled; *(photo, lumière)* hazy • **voiler¹ 1** *vt (visage, vérité)* to veil **2 se voiler** *vpr (personne)* to wear a veil; *(ciel, regard)* to cloud over

voile² [vwal] *nf (de bateau)* sail; *(sport)* sailing; **faire de la v.** to sail • **voilier** *nm* sailing boat; *(de plaisance)* yacht • **voilure** *nf* sails

voiler² [vwale] *vt,* **se voiler** *vpr (roue)* to buckle

voir* [vwar] **1** *vt* to see; **faire** *ou* **laisser v. qch** to show sth; **v. qn do/doing sth** to see sb do/doing sth; *Fam* **je ne peux pas la v.** *(la supporter)* I can't stand the sight of her; *Fam* **elle lui en a fait v. de toutes les couleurs** she made his/her life a misery

2 *vi* to see; **fais v.** let me see, show me; **voyons!** *(sois raisonnable)* come on!; **on verra bien** *(attendons)* we'll see; **ça n'a rien à v. avec ça** that's got nothing to do with that; **y v. clair** *(comprendre)* to see clearly

3 se voir *vpr (soi-même)* to see oneself; *(se fréquenter)* to see each other; *(objet, attitude)* to be seen; *(reprise, tache)* to show; **ça se voit** that's obvious

voire [vwar] *adv* indeed

voirie [vwari] *nf (service des ordures)* refuse collection; *(routes)* public highways

voisin, -ine [vwazɛ̃, -in] **1** *adj (pays, village)* neighbouring; *(maison, pièce)* next (**de** to); *(idée, état)* similar (**de** to)

2 *nmf* neighbour • **voisinage** *nm (quartier, voisins)* neighbourhood; *(proximité)* closeness, proximity • **voisiner** *vi* **v. avec** to be side by side with

voiture [vwatyr] *nf* car; *(de train)* carriage, *Br* coach, *Am* car; *(charrette)* cart; **en v.!** *(dans le train)* all aboard!; **v. de course/de tourisme** racing/private car; **v. d'enfant** *Br* pram, *Am* baby carriage

voix [vwa] *nf* voice; *(d'électeur)* vote; **à v. basse** in a whisper; **à haute v.** aloud; **à portée de v.** within earshot; *Fig* **avoir v. au chapitre** to have a say (in the matter); *Fig* **rester sans v.** to remain speechless

vol [vɔl] *nm* (a) *(d'avion, d'oiseau)* flight; *(groupe d'oiseaux)* flock, flight; **à v. d'oiseau** as the crow flies; **attraper qch au v.** to catch sth in the air; **v. libre** hanggliding; **v. à voile** gliding (b) *(délit)* theft; **v. à main armée** armed robbery; **v. à l'étalage** shoplifting; **c'est du v.!** *(trop cher)* it's daylight robbery! • **vol-au-vent** *nm inv Culin* vol-au-vent

volage [vɔlaʒ] *adj* flighty, fickle
volaille [vɔlɑj] *nf* **la v.** poultry; **une v.** a fowl
volatile [vɔlatil] *nm* winged creature
volatiliser [vɔlatilize] **se volatiliser** *vpr* to vanish into thin air
volcan [vɔlkɑ̃] *nm* volcano • **volcanique** *adj* volcanic
voler¹ [vɔle] *vi (oiseau, avion)* to fly; *Fig (courir)* to rush • **volant, -ante 1** *adj (tapis)* flying; **feuille volante** loose sheet **2** *nm (de véhicule)* (steering) wheel; *(de badminton)* shuttlecock; *(de jupe)* flounce • **volée** *nf (de flèches)* flight; *(groupe d'oiseaux)* flock, flight; *(de coups)* thrashing; *Tennis & Football* volley; **sonner à toute v.** to ring out
voler² [vɔle] **1** *vt (prendre)* to steal (**à** from); **v. qn** to rob sb; *Fam* **tu ne l'as pas volé!** it serves you right!
2 *vi (prendre)* to steal
volet [vɔlɛ] *nm (de fenêtre)* shutter; *(de programme)* section, part
voleter [vɔlte] *vi* to flutter
voleur, -euse [vɔlœr, -øz] **1** *nmf* thief; **au v.!** stop thief!
2 *adj* thieving
volière [vɔljɛr] *nf* aviary
volley-ball [vɔlebol] *nm* volleyball • **volleyeur, -euse** *nmf* volleyball player
volontaire [vɔlɔ̃tɛr] **1** *adj (geste, omission)* deliberate; *(travail)* voluntary; *(opiniâtre) Br* wilful, *Am* willful
2 *nmf* volunteer • **volontairement** *adv (spontanément)* voluntarily; *(exprès)* deliberately
volontariat [vɔlɔ̃tarja] *nm* voluntary work
volonté [vɔlɔ̃te] *nf (faculté, intention)* will; *(détermination)* willpower; *(souhait)* wish; **bonne v.** willingness; **mauvaise v.** unwillingness; **à v.** *(quantité)* as much as desired
volontiers [vɔlɔ̃tje] *adv* gladly, willingly; **v.!** *(oui)* I'd love to!
volt [vɔlt] *nm* volt • **voltage** *nm* voltage
volte-face [vɔltəfas] *nf inv Br* about turn, *Am* about face; *Fig (changement d'opinion)* U-turn; **faire v.** to turn round; *Fig* to do a U-turn
voltige [vɔltiʒ] *nf* acrobatics
voltiger [vɔltiʒe] *vi (feuilles)* to flutter
volubile [vɔlybil] *adj* voluble
volume [vɔlym] *nm (de boîte, de son, livre)* volume • **volumineux, -euse** *adj* bulky, voluminous
volupté [vɔlypte] *nf* sensual pleasure • **voluptueux, -ueuse** *adj* voluptuous

vomir [vɔmir] **1** *vt* to bring up, to vomit; *Fig (exécrer)* to loathe
2 *vi* to vomit, *Br* to be sick • **vomi** *nm Fam* vomit • **vomissements** *nmpl* **avoir des v.** to vomit • **vomitif, -ive** *adj* emetic
vont [vɔ̃] *voir* **aller¹**
vorace [vɔras] *adj* voracious
vos [vo] *voir* **votre**
vote [vɔt] *nm (action)* vote, voting; *(suffrage)* vote; *(de loi)* passing; *Br* **bureau de v.** polling station, *Am* polling place • **votant, -ante** *nmf* voter • **voter 1** *vt (loi)* to pass; *(crédits)* to vote **2** *vi* to vote
votre, vos [vɔtr, vo] *adj possessif* your • **vôtre 1** *pron possessif* **le** *ou* **la v.** yours; **à la v.!** cheers! **2** *nmpl* **les vôtres** *(votre famille)* your family
voudra, voudrait [vudra, vudrɛ] *voir* **vouloir**
vouer [vwe] **1** *vt (promettre)* to vow (**à** to); *(consacrer)* to dedicate (**à** to); *(condamner)* to doom (**à** to)
2 se vouer *vpr* **se v. à** to dedicate oneself to
vouloir* [vulwar] *vt* to want (**faire** to do); **je veux qu'il parte** I want him to go; **v. dire** to mean (**que** that); **je voudrais un pain** I'd like a loaf of bread; **je voudrais rester** I'd like to stay; **je veux bien attendre** I don't mind waiting; **veuillez attendre** kindly wait; **ça ne veut pas bouger** it won't move; **voulez-vous me suivre** will you follow me; **si tu veux** if you like *or* wish; **en v. à qn d'avoir fait qch** to be angry with sb for doing sth; **l'usage veut que…** *(+ subjunctive)* custom dictates that…; **v. du bien à qn** to wish sb well; **que voulez-vous!** *(résignation)* what can you expect!; **sans le v.** unintentionally; **ne pas v. de qn/qch** not to want sb/sth • **voulu, -ue** *adj (requis)* required; *(délibéré)* deliberate, intentional
vous [vu] *pron personnel* (**a**) *(sujet, complément direct)* you; **v. êtes ici** you are here; **il v. connaît** he knows you (**b**) *(complément indirect)* (to) you; **il v. l'a donné** he gave it to you, he gave you it (**c**) *(réfléchi)* yourself, *pl* yourselves; **v. v. lavez** you wash yourself/yourselves (**d**) *(réciproque)* each other; **v. v. aimez** you love each other • **vous-même** *pron* yourself • **vous-mêmes** *pron pl* yourselves
voûte [vut] *nf (arch)* vault; **v. d'ogive** vault • **voûté, -ée** *adj (personne)* bent, stooped
vouvoyer [vuvwaje] *vt* **v. qn** to address sb as *vous* • **vouvoiement** *nm* = use of the formal *vous* (instead of the more familiar *tu*)

voyage [vwajaʒ] *nm* trip, journey; *(par mer)* voyage; **aimer les voyages** to like *Br* travelling *or Am* traveling; **faire un v., partir en v.** to go on a trip; **être en v.** to be (away) travelling; **bon v.!** have a pleasant trip!; **v. de noces** honeymoon; **v. organisé** (package) tour • **voyager** *vi* to travel • **voyageur, -euse** *nmf Br* traveller, *Am* traveler; *(passager)* passenger; **v. de commerce** travelling salesman, *Br* commercial traveller • **voyagiste** *nm* tour operator

voyant, -ante¹ [vwajã, -ãt] **1** *adj (couleur)* gaudy, loud

2 *nm (signal)* (warning) light; *(d'appareil électrique)* pilot light

voyant, -ante² [vwajã, -ãt] *nmf* clairvoyant

voyelle [vwajɛl] *nf* vowel

voyeur, -euse [vwajœr, -øz] *nmf* voyeur, *f* voyeuse

voyou [vwaju] *nm* hooligan

vrac [vrak] **en vrac** *adv (en désordre)* in a muddle; *(au poids)* loose

vrai [vrɛ] **1** *adj* true; *(réel)* real; *(authentique)* genuine

2 *adv* **dire v.** to be right (in what one says)

3 *nm (vérité)* truth • **vraiment** *adv* really

vraisemblable [vrɛsãblabl] *adj (probable)* likely, probable; *(crédible)* credible • **vraisemblablement** [-əmã] *adv* prob-ably • **vraisemblance** *nf* likelihood; *(crédibilité)* credibility

vrille [vrij] *nf (outil)* gimlet; *(acrobatie)* (tail)spin; **descendre en v.** to spin down

vrombir [vrɔ̃bir] *vi* to hum • **vrombissement** *nm* hum(ming)

VRP [veɛrpe] *(abrév* **voyageur représentant placier**) *nm* sales rep

VTT [vetete] *(abrév* **vélo tout terrain**) *nm inv* mountain bike

vu, -ue [vy] **1** *pp de* **voir**

2 *adj* **bien vu** well thought of; **mal vu** frowned upon

3 *prép* in view of; **vu que...** seeing that...

vue [vy] *nf (sens)* (eye)sight; *(panorama, photo, idée)* view; **en v.** *(proche)* in sight; *(en évidence)* on view; *Fig (personne)* in the public eye; **avoir qn/qch en v.** to have sb/sth in mind; **à v.** *(tirer)* on sight; *(payable)* at sight; **à première v.** at first sight; **à v. d'œil** *(grandir)* visibly; *Fam* **à v. de nez** at a rough guess; **de v.** *(connaître)* by sight; **en v. de faire qch** with a view to doing sth; **v. d'ensemble** overall view

vulgaire [vylgɛr] *adj (grossier)* vulgar; *(ordinaire)* common • **vulgairement** *adv (grossièrement)* vulgarly; *(appeler)* commonly • **vulgariser** *vt* to popularize • **vulgarité** *nf* vulgarity

vulnérable [vylnerabl] *adj* vulnerable • **vulnérabilité** *nf* vulnerability

W, w [dubləve] *nm inv* W, w

wagon [vagɔ̃] *nm (de voyageurs)* carriage, *Br* coach, *Am* car; *(de marchandises) Br* wagon, *Am* freight car •**wagon-lit** (*pl* **wagons-lits**) *nm* sleeping car, sleeper •**wagon-restaurant** (*pl* **wagons-restaurants**) *nm* dining *or* restaurant car

Walkman® [wɔkman] *nm* Walkman®, personal stereo

wallon, -onne [walɔ̃, -ɔn] **1** *adj* Walloon **2** *nmf* **W., Wallonne** Walloon

water-polo [watɛrpɔlɔ] *nm* water polo

watt [wat] *nm Él* watt

w-c [(dublə)vese] *nmpl Br* toilet, *Am* men's/ladies' room

week-end [wikɛnd] (*pl* **week-ends**) *nm* weekend; **partir en w.** to go away for the weekend

western [wɛstɛrn] *nm* western

whisky [wiski] (*pl* **-ies** *ou* **-ys**) *nm Br* whisky, *Am* whiskey

wysiwyg [wiziwig] *adj & nm Ordinat* WYSIWYG

X, x [iks] *nm inv* (*lettre, personne ou nombre inconnus*) X, x; **x fois** umpteen times; **film classé X** adults-only film, *Br* '18' film, *Am* X-rated film

xénophobe [gsenɔfɔb] **1** *adj* xenophobic **2** *nmf* xenophobe • **xénophobie** *nf* xenophobia

xérès [gzerɛs] *nm* sherry

xylophone [gsilɔfɔn] *nm* xylophone

Y, y¹ [igrɛk] *nm inv* Y, y

y² [i] **1** *adv* there; *(dedans)* in it/them; *(dessus)* on it/them; **elle y vivra** she'll live there; **j'y entrai** I entered (it); **allons-y** let's go; **j'y suis!** *(je comprends)* now I get it!

 2 *pron* **j'y pense** I'm thinking about it; **je m'y attendais** I was expecting it; **ça y est!** that's it!; **je n'y suis pour rien** I have nothing to do with it

yacht [jɔt] *nm* yacht

yaourt [jaurt] *nm* yoghurt

Yémen [jemɛn] *nm* **le Y.** Yemen

yen [jɛn] *nm* yen

yeux [jø] *voir* **œil**

yiddish [jidiʃ] *nm & adj* Yiddish

yoga [jɔga] *nm* yoga; **faire du y.** to do yoga

yog(h)ourt [jɔgurt] *nm* = **yaourt**

Yo-Yo [jojo] *nm inv* yoyo

Z

Z, z [zɛd] *nm inv* Z, z

Zaïre [zair] *nm* **le Z.** Zaïre

zapper [zape] *vi Fam* to channel-hop
• **zapping** *nm Fam* **faire du z.** to channel-hop

zèbre [zɛbr] *nm* zebra • **zébré, -ée** [ze-] *adj* striped, streaked (**de** with) • **zébrures** [ze-] *nfpl* stripes

zèle [zɛl] *nm* zeal; **faire du z.** to overdo it • **zélé, -ée** *adj* zealous

zénith [zenit] *nm* zenith

zéro [zero] *nm (chiffre)* zero, *Br* nought; *(de numéro de téléphone)* 0 [əʊ]; *(température)* zero; *(rien)* nothing; *Fig (personne)* nonentity; *Football* **deux buts à z.** *Br* two nil, *Am* two zero

zeste [zɛst] *nm* **un z. de citron** a piece of lemon peel

zézayer [zezeje] *vi* to lisp

zibeline [ziblin] *nf* sable

zigzag [zigzag] *nm* zigzag; **en z.** *(route)* zigzag(ging) • **zigzaguer** *vi* to zigzag

Zimbabwe [zimbabwe] *nm* **le Z.** Zimbabwe

zinc [zɛ̃g] *nm (métal)* zinc; *Fam (comptoir)* bar; *Fam (avion)* plane

zinzin [zɛ̃zɛ̃] *Fam* **1** *adj inv (fou)* nuts **2** *nm (chose)* whatsit

zipper [zipe] *vt Ordinat* to zip

zizanie [zizani] *nf* discord; **semer la z.** to sow discord

zodiaque [zɔdjak] *nm* zodiac; **signe du z.** sign of the zodiac

zona [zona] *nm* shingles *(sing)*

zone [zon] *nf* zone; **de seconde z.** second-rate; *Fam* **la z.** *(bidonvilles)* the slums; **z. industrielle** industrial *Br* estate *or Am* park; **z. fumeurs/non-fumeurs** smoking/no-smoking area • **zonard** *nm Fam (marginal)* dropout • **zoner** *vi Fam* to hang about

zoo [zo(o)] *nm* zoo • **zoologie** [zɔɔ-] *nf* zoology • **zoologique** *adj* zoological; **parc z.** zoo

zoom [zum] *nm (objectif)* zoom lens

zozo [zɔzo] *nm Fam* nitwit

zozoter [zɔzɔte] *vi Fam* to lisp

zut [zyt] *exclam Fam* blast!

zyeuter [zjøte] *vt Fam (avec insistance)* to eye up